FEDERAL COURTS IN CONTEXT

ASPEN CASEBOOK SERIES

Federal Courts in Context

Erwin Chemerinsky
Dean and Jesse H. Choper Distinguished Professor of Law
University of California, Berkeley School of Law

Seth Davis
Professor of Law
University of California, Berkeley School of Law

Fred O. Smith, Jr.
Charles Howard Candler Professor of Law
Emory University School of Law

Norman W. Spaulding
Nelson Bowman Sweitzer and Marie B. Sweitzer
Professor of Law
Stanford Law School

ASPEN PUBLISHING

To contact Customer Service, e-mail customer.service@aspenpublishing.com, call 1-800-950-5259, or mail correspondence to:

Aspen Publishing
Attn: Order Department
1 Wall Street
Burlington, MA 01803

Printed in the United States of America.

1 2 3 4 5 6 7 8 9 0

ISBN 978-1-5438-5031-4

Library of Congress Cataloging-in-Publication Data

Names: Chemerinsky, Erwin, author. | Davis, Seth (R. Seth), author. |
　Smith, Fred O., Jr. author. | Spaulding, Norman W., 1971- author.
Title: Federal courts in context / Erwin Chemerinsky, Dean and Jesse H.
　Choper Distinguished Professor of Law, University of California,
　Berkeley School of Law; Seth Davis, Professor of Law, University of
　California, Berkeley School of Law; Fred O. Smith Jr.,
　Charles Howard Candler Professor of Law,
　Emory University School of Law; Norman W. Spaulding, Nelson Bowman
　Sweitzer and Marie B. Sweitzer Professor of Law, Stanford Law School.
Description: Frederick, MD : Aspen Publishing, 2023. | Series: Aspen
　casebook series | Includes index. | Summary: "Casebook for law school
　courses on federal courts"—Provided by publisher.
Identifiers: LCCN 2022045763 (print) | LCCN 2022045764 (ebook) | ISBN
　9781543850314 (hardcover) | ISBN 9781543850321 (epub)
Subjects: LCSH: Courts—United States. | Judicial power—United States. |
　Jurisdiction—United States. | Federal government—United States. |
　LCGFT: Casebooks (Law)
Classification: LCC KF8719 .C44 2023 (print) | LCC KF8719 (ebook) | DDC
　347.73/2—dc23/eng/20230403
LC record available at https://lccn.loc.gov/2022045763
LC ebook record available at https://lccn.loc.gov/2022045764

About Aspen Publishing

Aspen Publishing is a leading provider of educational content and digital learning solutions to law schools in the U.S. and around the world. Aspen provides best-in-class solutions for legal education through authoritative textbooks, written by renowned authors, and breakthrough products such as Connected eBooks, Connected Quizzing, and PracticePerfect.

The Aspen Casebook Series (famously known among law faculty and students as the "red and black" casebooks) encompasses hundreds of highly regarded textbooks in more than eighty disciplines, from large enrollment courses, such as Torts and Contracts, to emerging electives, such as Sustainability and the Law of Policing. Study aids such as the *Examples & Explanations* and the *Emanuel Law Outlines* series, both highly popular collections, help law students master complex subject matter.

Major products, programs, and initiatives include:

- **Connected eBooks** are enhanced digital textbooks and study aids that come with a suite of online content and learning tools designed to maximize student success. Designed in collaboration with hundreds of faculty and students, the Connected eBook is a significant leap forward in the legal education learning tools available to students.
- **Connected Quizzing** is an easy-to-use formative assessment tool that tests law students' understanding and provides timely feedback to improve learning outcomes. Delivered through CasebookConnect.com, the learning platform already used by students to access their Aspen casebooks, Connected Quizzing is simple to implement and integrates seamlessly with law school course curricula.
- **PracticePerfect** is a visually engaging, interactive study aid to explain commonly encountered legal doctrines through easy-to-understand animated videos, illustrative examples, and numerous practice questions. Developed by a team of experts, PracticePerfect is the ideal study companion for today's law students.
- The **Aspen Learning Library** enables law schools to provide their students with access to the most popular study aids on the market across all of their courses. Available through an annual subscription, the online library consists of study aids in e-book, audio, and video formats with full text search, note-taking, and highlighting capabilities.
- Aspen's **Digital Bookshelf** is an institutional-level online education bookshelf, consolidating everything students and professors need to ensure success. This program ensures that every student has access to affordable course materials from day one.
- **Leading Edge** is a community centered on thinking differently about legal education and putting those thoughts into actionable strategies. At the core of the program is the Leading Edge Conference, an annual gathering of legal education thought leaders looking to pool ideas and identify promising directions of exploration.

To our students and the work of establishing justice.

Summary of Contents

CONTENTS

Most people go to court either to create change in their lives or prevent something from changing. We have written this casebook with this basic fact about adjudication, and these people, in mind. "The life of the law," Oliver Wendell Holmes famously insisted, is human "experience." Understanding why people come to court and how adjudication affects them (the practical objectives they set, the obstacles they face, the suffering they endure or inflict) is essential to understanding the development of the rules and principles of jurisdiction, judicial review, federalism, and separation of powers – the architecture, if you will, of the rule of law in America.

Placing federal courts doctrine in context has advantages beyond enhancing understanding of the rules and principles that animate the subject. Firstly, the doctrines covered in this course are powerful – delimiting the boundaries not only of judicial review and the enforcement of rights, but also the powers of the other branches of the federal government, Native nations, the states, and their courts. Revealing the circumstances that have tested these boundaries and the consequences of observing or breaching them exposes the gravity of decisions made in court and competing positions on structural constitutional law. The social and moral costs of exertions of judicial power become visible and must be reckoned with. Most fundamentally, attending to context teaches us whether rights actually get enforced and what follows from enforcement or failure to enforce for the people involved.

Secondly, contextualizing the human experience of federal courts and the federal system of adjudication brings voices into the conversation about doctrine and first principles that have all too often been left out of traditional treatments of the subject. We are, for example, a nation of three sovereign governments, not two. States and the federal government share governance with Native nations, and doctrines such as sovereign immunity have emerged from contests among these three sovereigns, not just two. Federalism cannot, in the American context, be disaggregated from the protection of slavery, its role in the dismantling of Reconstruction and the rise of Jim Crow segregation, or modern resistance to the legal achievements of the Civil Rights Movement, a second reconstruction. The rise of regulation by agencies and adjudication in non-Article III courts, with all this entails for traditional understandings of separation of powers, is intimately connected with the nineteenth and twentieth century labor movement. Standing doctrine has been profoundly influenced by contests over reproductive rights, religious liberty, and anti-discrimination law. Modern habeas jurisdiction has developed in the context of an unprecedented expansion of the carceral state. And so on. Inclusive pedagogy and intellectually rigorous immersion in the course are served by ensuring that these voices are heard.

Thirdly, Federal Courts deservedly has the reputation of being a difficult course. The doctrines often are complex and rarely are intuitive. A wide body of research shows that deep learning is promoted by arranging cases and materials to spark multimodal intellectual engagement. We have therefore followed the principles of contextualization and accessibility in form as well as content. Chapters are organized around the practical questions that arise when people go to court, working from basic principles and canonical cases to their modern application and elaboration. Brief contextual introductions lead into and/or follow canonical cases. And rather than long, obtuse notes designed more for experts than students, or extended series of questions without answers, we endeavor to answer the concrete questions we pose and concisely summarize the principal take-aways from the cases. The book also dovetails with Erwin Chemerinsky's treatise, *Federal Jurisdiction*, to promote engagement with broader questions, clear analysis, and further inquiry.

Lastly, as we enter what appears to be a period of doctrinal innovation on the part of the Supreme Court,[1] being clear-eyed about the various settings in which judicial restraint and activism have emerged provides an important benchmark against which to measure the Court's new exercises of judicial power. Ultimately, this book challenges students to consider what the role of the federal courts in American society should be and whether the doctrines developed by the Court fulfill this mission.

---

1. See Mark Lemley, *The Imperial Supreme Court*, 136 HARV. L. REV. F. 97 (2022).

We are deeply grateful to the incredible team of research assistants without whom this book could not have been produced: Samuel Charles, Ana Cutts Dougherty, Natalie Leifer, Bojan Mishko Srbinovski, and Sergio Filipe Zanutta Valente. All along the way they provided essential support, an invaluable second set of eyes, and student perspective. We are also grateful for the diligence and unflagging support of the reference librarians at Stanford Law School in locating sources, and for the faculty support group of Stanford Law School, in particular the utterly indispensable administrative assistance provided by Ginny Smith. Lastly, we are grateful to Erwin Chemerinsky and Norman W. Spaulding for permission to use a few cases and descriptive content from Federal Jurisdiction (Eighth Edition) and Civil Procedure: Cases and Problems (Seventh Edition).

We gratefully acknowledge permission to reprint the following:

Cases from State Supreme Courts, OT 2005 — OT 2019 (graph), in "Empirical SCOTUS: The importance of state court cases before the Supreme Court." SCOTUSblog (Sep. 4, 2020), https://www.scotusblog.com/2020/09/empirical-scotus-the-importance-of-state-court-cases-before-scotus/. Reprinted with permission from Adam Feldman.

Habeas Corpus Petitions and State Prisoner Populations, 1941-1997 (graph), in Caseload Highlights: Examining the World of State Courts, Vol. 4, No. 2. (September 1998). Copyright © Court Statistics Project. Reprinted with permission.

Immigration Court Asylum Applications (graph). Copyright © Transactional Records Access Clearinghouse (TRAC) at Syracuse University. Reprinted with permission.

Number of Multistate Lawsuits vs. Federal Defendants, by Year (graph). Copyright © 2023 State Litigation and AG Activity Database. Reprinted with permission.

Trends in prisoner litigation (graph), in Margo Schlanger, "Trends in Prisoner Litigation, as the PLRA Enters Adulthood." UC Irvine Law Review, Vol. 5, Iss. 1 (April 2015). Reprinted with permission.

U.S. State and Federal Prison Population, 1925-2019 (graph). Copyright © 2023 The Sentencing Project. All Rights Reserved. Reprinted with permission.

CHAPTER 1

PLACING FEDERAL COURTS IN CONTEXT

A. THE STAKES OF THE ENTERPRISE

After touring the United States in 1831, the French aristocrat and political scientist Alexis de Tocqueville observed that "[s]carcely any political question arises in the United States that is not resolved, sooner or later, into a judicial question."[1] Some readers of *Democracy in America* have insisted that this was "an exaggeration in his own time," because many aspects of life in antebellum America never came before the courts.[2] Be that as it may, the most consequential issues certainly did. And no one contends that the role of the courts, especially the federal courts, has diminished since the nineteenth century. Whether for good or ill, the Supreme Court has become "an ultimate arbiter on issues that might earlier have had to find political resolution."[3] The work of the lower federal courts, which decide hundreds of thousands of cases each year, is no less consequential, and the state courts, which decide 98 percent of all civil cases in America and most criminal cases too, regularly adjudicate a vast array of federal questions.

One way to understand the work of this course is as an extended inquiry into the kinds of social problems that have been resolved into "judicial questions" and the sources of authority that render these problems subject to judicial resolution. These debates about structural constitutional law, individual rights, and federal jurisdiction play out in particular cases with high stakes during particular historical moments. The consequences for the parties and the context that brought the parties to court in the first place cannot be lost in abstractions of constitutional theory. As you read this book, we encourage you to reflect upon your position on separation of powers, federalism, democracy, equality, due process, and the allocation of jurisdiction. And we invite you to take note of how the specific substantive rights at stake in the cases we study (and who suffers when they are denied or upheld) bear upon your assessment of structural constitutional doctrine and jurisprudence.

The moral seriousness of our work as lawyers and the work of the courts is drawn into sharp relief by Robert Cover's observation that "[l]egal interpretation

---

1. DEMOCRACY IN AMERICA 261 (2003).

2. Phil C. Neal, *De Tocqueville and the Role of the Lawyer in Society*, 50 MARQ. L. REV. 607, 608 (1967).

3. *Id.* at 609.

takes place on a field of pain and death."[4] The "interpretive acts" of judicial review "signal and occasion the imposition of violence upon others."[5] This is crystal clear in the field of criminal law (e.g., in habeas petitions and emergency requests for stays of capital punishment, see Chapters 8 and 9), but Cover is quick to remind us that it applies to adjudication *writ large.* "A judge articulates her understanding of a text, and as a result, somebody loses" not only "his freedom [or] his life," but, depending on the case, "his property [or] his children."[6] And when authoritative legal interpreters "have finished their work," the effect is very often to authorize other forms of violence—not only those which have already occurred and have been the subject of judicial review (e.g., a police intervention) but also those which ensue from the enforcement of a court order.[7]

Interpretations of Article III, the Constitution's structure, and federal jurisdictional statutes thus have enormous significance for the parties involved, for the legitimacy of the enterprise of constitutionalism, and for the integrity of the rule of law. In a passage often neglected in favor of the proposition that it is "emphatically the province of the courts to say what the law is," Chief Justice Marshall insisted in *Marbury v. Madison* that

> [t]he very essence of civil liberty certainly consists in the right of every individual to claim the protection of the laws, whenever he receives an injury. One of the first duties of government is to afford that protection. In the third volume of his commentaries, Blackstone states . . . "it is a general rule that *where there is a legal right, there is also a legal remedy* by suit or action at law whenever that right is invaded." . . . The government of the United States has been emphatically termed a government of laws, and not of men. It will certainly cease to deserve this high appellation, if the laws furnish no remedy for the violation of a vested legal right.[8]

Notably, Chief Justice Marshall ties the rule of law to the right/remedy nexus on the way to *denying* both jurisdiction and therefore a remedy (recall that the Court holds that it has no power to grant the remedy of mandamus to ensure delivery of Marbury's commission). We will see lofty rhetoric on judicial review paired with the denial of relief in more than a few cases in this casebook. We will see Marshall's position on the relationship between rights and remedies forcefully challenged as well. But if the facts of the case seem distant from the concerns of Robert Cover on the power of legal interpretation, it is well to remember that Marbury's commission was to become a law enforcement officer, and that the case arose from a highly partisan and pitched clash between Federalists and Jeffersonian Republicans about federal judicial power and who would exercise it.

Indeed, in many cases beyond *Marbury,* we will see debates about federal jurisdiction embedded in controversies over social issues central to the very nature and legitimacy of the American constitutional project. These include slavery,

---

4. Robert Cover, *Violence and the Word,* 95 YALE L.J. 1601 (1986).
5. *Id.*
6. *Id.*
7. *Id.*
8. 5 U.S. 137, 163 (1803) (emphasis added).

emancipation, reconstruction, desegregation and the second civil rights movement; westward expansion, including the expropriation of the lands of Native nations and Indigenous Peoples and attempts to undermine their sovereignty; the U.S.'s acquisition of an overseas empire; expansion of the administrative state in response to the economic crisis of the Great Depression; labor rights; prison conditions; reproductive rights; the regulation of sexual identity; the Warren Court's criminal justice reform movement; the power of the executive branch to respond to exigent circumstances, including war and other national security threats; and more. The "legal world" constructed in and through adjudication of these controversies has required, we might say with Cover, "commitments that place bodies on the line."[9]

Simply put, political and economic power shapes federal adjudication. So too does the perceived legitimacy of government actors—that is, whether the public accepts their decisions as worth obeying. In turn, federal adjudication shapes political and economic power and the perceived legitimacy of the courts. In Federalist 78, Alexander Hamilton famously called the federal judiciary the "least dangerous branch," given that it lacks the executive's power of the sword or the legislature's power of the purse.[10] Scholarly accounts of *Marbury* make similar claims about the courts relative to the power and legitimacy of the other branches of government.[11] More recently, at the end of the twentieth century, courts and commentators debated the wisdom of structural injunctions issued by lower federal courts in civil rights cases in light of the relative democratic standing of the politically accountable actors regulated by this exercise of equity power.[12]

Macroeconomic conditions have also shaped public law, including the law of federal jurisdiction.[13] Questions like whether a person should be allowed to sue a

---

9. Cover, *supra* note 4, at 1605.

10. The FEDERALIST No. 78.

11. For a collection of works that posit this view, see Louise Weinberg, *Our Marbury*, 89 VA. L. REV. 1235, 1412 n.101 (2003), citing CHARLES F. HOBSON, THE GREAT CHIEF JUSTICE: JOHN MARSHALL AND THE RULE OF LAW 49 (1996) ("*Marbury* actually marked a strategic retreat by the judiciary. . . ."); Richard H. Fallon, Jr., *Marbury and the Constitutional Mind: A Bicentennial Essay on the Wages of Doctrinal Tension*, 91 CALIF. L. REV. 1, 18 (2003) (calling the opinion in *Marbury* a "prudent retreat"); John A. Ferejohn & Larry D. Kramer, *Independent Judges, Dependent Judiciary: Institutionalizing Judicial Restraint*, 77 N.Y.U. L. REV. 962, 995-96 (2002); Jed H. Shugerman, *Marbury and Judicial Deference: The Shadow of Whittington v. Polk and the Maryland Judiciary Battle*, 5 U. PA. J. CONST. L. 58, 107 (2002) (describing the decision to decline jurisdiction as "a wise survival strategy").

12. *Compare* Abram Chayes, *The Role of the Judge in Public Law Litigation*, 89 HARV. L. REV. 1281 (1976); Owen M. Fiss, *The Supreme Court 1978 Term—Foreword: The Forms of Justice*, 93 HARV. L. REV. 1 (1979); *with* Frank H. Easterbrook, *Justice and Contract in Consent Judgments*, 1987 U. CHI. LEGAL F. 19; William A. Fletcher, *The Discretionary Constitution: Institutional Remedies and Judicial Legitimacy*, 91 YALE L.J. 635 (1982); Michael W. McConnell, *Why Hold Elections? Using Consent Decrees to Insulate Policies from Political Change*, 1987 U. CHI. LEGAL F. 295; Robert F. Nagel, *Separation of Powers and the Scope of Federal Equitable Remedies*, 30 STAN. L. REV. 661 (1978).

13. *See, e.g.*, ALISON LACROIX, THE INTERBELLUM CONSTITUTION: UNION, COMMERCE, AND SLAVERY FROM THE LONG FOUNDING MOMENT TO THE CIVIL WAR (2023) (forthcoming); Ernest A. Young, *Its Hour Come Round at Last? State Sovereign Immunity and the Great State Debt Crisis of the Early Twenty-First Century*, 35 HARV. J.L. & PUB. POL'Y 593, 593-96 (2012).

state for money damages (central to the doctrine of sovereign immunity) may find a different audience when states face crippling debts than when they do not.[14]

Who wields political and legal power also shapes federal courts law. Historically, the composition of the federal bench has not reflected the diversity of our society.[15] Critically, women, people of color, and religious and other minorities were excluded from federal and state judgeships for most of the nation's history. Whether it be decisions about the power of Congress during Reconstruction to strip the federal courts of jurisdiction in cases like *United States v. Klein*,[16] or the proper role for courts in breaking apartheid in the railroad travel in cases like *Railroad Commission v. Pullman Co.*,[17] the courts making those decisions were themselves defined by exclusion and caste.

Unlike more arid treatments of the subject, then, where context is all too often absent or relegated to footnotes, this book endeavors to place federal courts cases on the stage of the fascinating, vexed moral, political, and historical commitments that gave them meaning in their time. We invite inquiry into the commitments that have endured, and in so doing we seek to draw the concrete stakes of the doctrines the cases announce into relief. Put simply, we believe that federal jurisdiction is about the principles that animate power. If you are reading this book in law school, you already know that this power is no philosophical abstraction. After all, you will exercise that power in the profession—affirmatively by invoking federal jurisdiction, negatively by seeking to avoid or limit it. And bodies will be on the line. Placing the cases we study in context and taking stock of the interaction of substantive rights, procedure, and constitutional structure (rather than abstracting away from them) not only makes the complexities of the doctrine easier to grasp, it highlights and invites reflection on the responsibilities and commitments that travel with judicial power.

Our work of reading federal courts in context begins in this Chapter's introduction to structural constitutional principles and judicial review. Section B provides a brief overview of the two structural constitutional principles that animate the doctrines we will cover in the course. We cross reference Chapters in which the principles arise in the context of specific doctrines to give you a snapshot of the coverage of the book. Having set out these principles, Section C offers a snapshot of the principles in action from the founding and the Court's decisions in *Marbury v. Madison* and *Fletcher v. Peck*. In Section D we briefly contextualize nineteenth and twentieth century developments in the theory and practice of judicial review. Our purpose is to dispel the notion that the founding era settled debate on structural constitutional law and judicial review, and to preview some of the concrete social problems that surface recurrently in canonical cases throughout the casebook. Section E turns to the formalities of judicial power: the text of Article III, the structure of the First Judiciary Act of 1789 that breathed life into the spare words of the text and created a three-tiered system of federal courts, the growth of

---

14. Ernest A. Young, *Its Hour Come Round at Last? State Sovereign Immunity and the Great State Debt Crisis of the Early Twenty-First Century*, 35 HARV. J.L. & PUB. POL'Y 593 (2012).

15. *See generally* ERWIN CHEMERINSKY, THE CASE AGAINST THE SUPREME COURT (2014).

16. 80 U.S. 128 (1871).

17. 312 U.S. 496 (1941).

specialized federal courts, and important amendments that have affected federal court structure and jurisdiction since 1789. The Chapter closes in Section F by linking the topic of federal jurisdiction with the question of the legitimacy of the exercise of judicial review, underscoring the importance of placing the cases of federal courts law within their contexts.

B. ANIMATING PRINCIPLES: SEPARATION OF POWERS AND FEDERALISM

In fashioning the doctrines determining authority to exercise federal jurisdiction, the Supreme Court repeatedly has focused on two major structural constitutional questions. First, what is the proper role of the federal courts relative to the other branches of the federal government in resolving legal disputes? Second, what is the proper role of the federal courts relative to the states and especially to the state courts? Answering the latter question often involves consideration of the meaning of the Supremacy Clause — which refers directly to state judges — as well as other provisions of the Constitution distributing power between the states and the federal government. Answering both questions requires interrogation of foundational assumptions about the adversary system and the protean language of Article III extending "judicial power" to "cases and controversies." Separation of powers and federalism issues thus underlie virtually every topic discussed in this course.

This Section offers a brief discussion of these structural constitutional principles.

1. Separation of Powers and Federal Jurisdiction

The drafters of the Constitution agreed on the necessity of establishing a Supreme Court, a tribunal that did not exist under the Articles of Confederation. But they could not agree on whether to have lower federal courts. That decision was left to Congress by Article III, along with the power to define the jurisdiction of the lower federal courts. This means that separation of powers issues are present in every congressional grant and restriction of judicial power. For example, deciding whether Congress can withdraw federal court jurisdiction to hear specific controversial issues or whether Congress can create courts where judges lack life tenure requires analysis of the proper role of the national legislature relative to the judiciary.

Consider your own beliefs about how rights should be defined, and by which institutions of government. How important is it to preserve the independent judgment of courts? What about the role of democratically elected representatives? Is congressional control of federal jurisdiction, as one commentator has insisted, "the rock upon which rests the legitimacy of the judicial work in a democracy"?[18] Or is the risk too great that Congress will abuse its authority, not only diminishing federal jurisdiction, but in so doing, undercutting federal rights, including

---

18. Charles Black, *The Presidency and Congress*, 32 WASH. & LEE L. REV. 841, 846 (1975).

constitutional rights? Surely congressional control over jurisdiction, however sweeping, cannot eliminate "the essential constitutional functions" of judicial review protected by Article III.[19] These issues are discussed in detail in Chapters 2 and 4, which examine congressional authority to control federal court jurisdiction, to establish concurrent jurisdiction of federal questions in state courts, and to create so-called "non-Article III" courts whose judges lack the life tenure and salary protections assured in Article III. They surface again in Chapter 8 where we cover congressional grants of and limits on habeas jurisdiction.

Separation of powers issues also arise when the judiciary declines to exercise the authority granted to it or assumes power not clearly provided by the Constitution. These issues are considered in Chapter 3, which examines the doctrines of standing, ripeness, mootness, political questions, and the prohibition on advisory opinions. At least one function of restrictive justiciability doctrines is to leave certain problems to the political branches of government. This is perhaps most controversial, however, when the purpose of the assertion of federal jurisdiction is to restrain and remedy unconstitutional acts by the legislature or executive branch, or when the party seeking access to court is politically disenfranchised or marginalized and therefore less able to protect its interests in the political process. Moreover, justiciability rules that are not applied in an even-handed manner by the Supreme Court can convert doctrines of judicial restraint into doctrines of judicial imperialism—allowing the Court to expand federal judicial review of favored constitutional rights while limiting jurisdiction with respect to disfavored constitutional rights. Chapter 10 also discusses judge-made limits on federal district court jurisdiction, including abstention doctrines that direct lower federal courts to defer to pending state adjudication and state administrative agency action.

Similar separation of powers issues arise when the federal courts formulate federal common law. Some contend that the legislature alone has the authority to adopt rules that have the force of law and govern behavior—judicially created rules of decision usurp congressional prerogatives on this account. But others argue that federal common law must be developed in some areas to serve an interstitial function until Congress legislates or to fill legislative gaps in an enforcement system. Also, in some areas federal common law may be essential to implement the U.S. Constitution, such as where federal courts have created monetary remedies for violations of the Constitution by federal officers. The topic of federal common law and this dispute over separation of powers is discussed in Chapter 5 and the question of damage relief against federal officers is considered in Chapter 7.

There are especially vexing separation of powers concerns when Congress or the executive branch imposes limits on access to the writ of habeas corpus, which is protected against unlawful suspension even during states of emergency by the Suspension Clause. During the abolition movement, the Civil War, World War II and most recently in counter-terrorism policy, the right of access to the writ has been tested. Fundamental civil liberties have been at stake. We take up the "Great Writ" and important debates about political control of access to it in Chapter 8.

---

19. Leonard G. Ratner, *Congressional Power Over the Appellate Jurisdiction of the Supreme Court*, 109 U. PA. L. REV. 157, 200-01 (1960).

Although the doctrines covered in these Chapters are diverse, the underlying questions concern the role of the federal courts within a system of separated and shared federal powers. What congressional or judicial actions improperly usurp the prerogatives reserved to other branches of government? Which branch or branches of government will best establish justice and secure the blessings of liberty given the rights at stake in any given controversy?

2. *Judicial Federalism*

The other major underlying structural constitutional principle is federalism, especially the proper relationship of federal and state courts.[20] A federalist system is one in which a territory is governed by both a central government and geographically defined political subdivisions. In the United States, the existence of a federalist system means that federal courts are often expressly attentive to the implications their doctrines have for that system. This federalist system is deeply informed by federal law's recognition of the sovereignty of the United States, the governments of the 50 states, and the governments of federally recognized Native nations.

Federalism influences a wide range of doctrines throughout this textbook. For example, federal courts have considered when they should interfere with illegal state judicial proceedings, when they should refrain from deciding federal constitutional questions out of deference to state courts, the proper role of federal courts in deciding questions of state law, the reach of the U.S. Supreme Court's decisions on federal constitutional questions beyond the parties in a case, the power of federal courts to disturb state court judgments, the duty of state courts to decide federal law questions, and the circumstances in which individuals should be permitted to sue state governments and state officers in federal court. As federal courts address these questions, they must not only contend with the federal structure as it was constructed at the Founding, but also the radical reconstruction of the federal-state relationship after the Civil War, as the balance of power between the federal and state governments was revised to bring the nation closer to becoming an egalitarian democracy.[21]

Even the most basic jurisdictional issues are bound up with federalism. The Supremacy Clause states that "The Constitution, and the laws of the United States which shall be made in pursuance thereof; and all treaties made, or which shall be made . . . shall be the supreme law of the land; and the judges in every state shall

---

20. In an important article, Professor Richard Fallon argues that there are two competing models of federal jurisdiction. Richard H. Fallon, *The Ideologies of Federal Common Law*, 74 VA. L. REV. 1141 (1988). One, which he terms the "federalist" model, emphasizes the protection of state sovereignty and the parity between federal and state courts in deciding constitutional claims. The alternative approach, labeled the "nationalist model," emphasizes the supremacy of the national government and particularly the special role of the federal government in safeguarding federal rights. The nationalist model stresses the importance of access to the federal courts and the general superiority of the federal judiciary in resolving constitutional claims.

21. *See* Norman W. Spaulding, *Constitution as Countermonument: Federalism, Reconstruction, and the Problem of Collective Memory*, 103 COLUM. L. REV. 1992 (2003).

be bound thereby, anything in the Constitution or laws of any State to the contrary notwithstanding." One might reasonably conclude that the supremacy of federal law is fully secured by providing that it "shall be the supreme law of the land" and that the clause stating that "the judges in every state shall be bound thereby," is unnecessary surplusage. Why name this specific branch of state governments and *explicitly* require their fidelity to federal law? The drafters were well aware of the possibility that federal issues would continue to arise in the state courts even after national courts were created. And that has proved true. As we will see in Chapter 2, even in fairly run-of-the-mill cases that arise under state law, federal law can bear upon the outcome. And Congress has provided for concurrent jurisdiction in the state courts over many classes of cases that arise under federal law. *Exclusive* federal court jurisdiction is and always has been the exception, not the rule.

This shared division of labor presents federalism questions of parity and comity. Parity is the issue of whether, overall, state courts are equal to federal courts in their ability and willingness to protect federal rights.[22] There is a long, disturbing history of state court resistance to federal law and the authority of the Supreme Court. Among the most important nineteenth century examples are the use of state courts to resist enforcement of the federal Fugitive Slave Acts before the Civil War, on the one hand, and to resist federal civil rights laws passed to enforce the Reconstruction Amendments after the Civil War, on the other. In the twentieth century many state courts refused to faithfully enforce federal law that provided remedies to blue collar workers injured on the job, disregarded federal constitutional standards for fair criminal trials, and defied federal legislation that protected the sovereignty and lands of Native nations. Faithful enforcement of these and other federal statutory and constitutional rights turned on the exercise of appellate jurisdiction by the Supreme Court to correct erroneous state judgments and federal statutes offering parties the option to protect their rights by filing in (or removing) suits to the lower federal courts. At the same time, state courts have faithfully adjudicated and enforced many other federal laws. And in light of the fact that state courts conduct fully *98 percent* of all litigation in the United States, it is hard to imagine effective enforcement of many federal rights in the absence of concurrent jurisdiction of federal questions in state courts. In many states, federal courts are remote as well. The costs of travel to file and appear in federal court can alone be prohibitive for middle- and low-income litigants.

There are also different institutional characteristics of the two judicial systems. For example, federal judges generally enjoy greater insulation from political pressure because they are constitutionally guaranteed by Article III life tenure and salaries that cannot be decreased. In 38 states, by contrast there is some form of judicial election and during the late twentieth and early twenty-first centuries a *massive* funding crisis hobbled state courts, forcing them to rely increasingly on fines and fees assessed from people caught up in litigation, rather than general state tax funds.[23]

---

22. *See, e.g.*, Burt Neuborne, *The Myth of Parity*, 90 Harv. L. Rev. 1105 (1977). For a review of the literature in the debate over parity, see Erwin Chemerinsky, *Parity Reconsidered: Defining a Role for the Federal Judiciary*, 36 UCLA L. Rev. 233 (1988).

23. *See* Nat'l Center for State Courts, Landscape of Civil Litigation of State Courts (2015); Yale Liman Center, Fines, Fees and the Funding of Public Services (2020).

In some jurisdictions local courts have become dependent for their operating budgets on fees and fines assessed against low-income residents and people of color whose minor infractions quickly snowball into substantial court debts.[24] Federal due process guarantees are often disregarded in the imposition and collection of these debts.[25]

Beyond solicitude for federal interests, are there other reasons to think that federal judges might be more faithful to federal law? Judges who regularly handle federal law might be expected to develop deeper expertise, and the circuit court structure of federal intermediate appellate courts provides greater uniformity. If so, why doesn't the Constitution require exclusive federal jurisdiction for *all* federal law claims? Why hasn't Congress? How relevant is the historical resistance to federal law of state courts to twenty-first century debates about allocation of jurisdiction to decide federal questions? Given the degree of variance among the state courts (and, to be sure, many federal district courts) in their disposition toward specific federal rights, perhaps the important question is not what forum a dispute is adjudicated in but what specific right is at stake.[26]

Looking briefly to the past half century, the Warren Court generally expanded federal court jurisdiction based on the assumption that federal courts are often necessary to assure adequate protection of constitutional rights. This dovetailed with the passage of landmark civil rights statutes during the civil rights movement creating new federal causes of action and remedies—a veritable Second Reconstruction. As the Burger Court's more deferential stance to state courts took shape, critics worried that the insistence on the parity of state courts was a mere "pretext for funneling federal constitutional decision making into state courts precisely because they are less likely to be receptive to vigorous enforcement of federal constitutional doctrine."[27] The Rehnquist and Roberts Courts have been

---

24. *See* U.S. COMM'N ON CIVIL RIGHTS, TARGETED FINES AND FEES AGAINST COMMUNITIES OF COLOR (2017); U.S. DEP'T OF JUSTICE, INVESTIGATION OF THE FERGUSON POLICE DEPARTMENT (2015) (identifying dysfunction and bias in operation of municipal court and its enforcement of fines and fees for minor infractions); Norman W. Spaulding, *The Ideal and the Actual in Procedural Due Process*, 48 CONST. L.Q. 261 (2021).

25. ABA STANDING COMM. ON ETHICS AND PROFESSIONAL RESPONSIBILITY, FORMAL OPINION 490, ETHICAL OBLIGATIONS OF JUDGES IN COLLECTING LEGAL FINANCIAL OBLIGATIONS AND OTHER DEBTS (2020) (gathering cases on violation of due process standards set out in *Bearden v. Georgia*, 461 U.S. 660 (1983)).

26. *See, e.g.*, William Rubenstein, *The Myth of Superiority*, 16 CONST. COMMENT. 599 (1999) (arguing that state courts have been more receptive than federal courts to litigants seeking to establish and vindicate civil rights for gay and lesbian Americans); Burt Neuborne, *Parity Revisited: The Uses of a Judicial Forum of Excellence*, 44 DEPAUL L. REV. 797 (1995); Michael Wells, *Behind the Parity Debate: The Decline of the Legal Process Tradition in the Law of Federal Courts*, 71 B.U. L. REV. 609 (1991); Akhil Reed Amar, *Parity as a Constitutional Question*, 71 B.U. L. REV. 645 (1991); Susan N. Herman, *Why Parity Matters*, 71 B.U. L. REV. 651 (1991).

27. Neuborne, *supra* note 22, at 1105-06. *See also* Neuborne, *supra* note 26, at 799 (arguing that despite changes in recent decades "a relative institutional advantage for the plaintiff exists in federal court; an advantage resulting from a mix of political insulation, tradition, better resources and professional competence").

even more direct about state court parity—explicitly narrowing federal court jurisdiction based on the assertion that state courts are equally trustworthy in deciding constitutional claims. State courts, the modern Court has emphasized "have inherent authority, and are presumptively competent, to adjudicate claims arising under the laws of the United States."[28] The modern Court's confidence in state courts is reflected in its restrictions on federal habeas corpus relief from state criminal convictions,[29] limitations on §1983 suits against state officers,[30] expansion of states' Eleventh Amendment immunity from suit in federal court,[31] expansion of the abstention doctrines,[32] and expansion of the preclusive effect of state court decisions on the federal courts.[33]

A related issue to the perceived adequacy and fidelity of state courts to federal law is comity—the respect federal courts owe to courts of another sovereign, including state courts.[34] Comity requires that federal courts minimize friction with state courts and avoid any doctrines or practices premised on distrust of state courts.[35] Whether expressly invoked or operating as a background principle, many decisions of the modern Court rely on comity as a justification for restricting federal court jurisdiction. The principle can also affect standards of review when federal courts take up the decisions of state courts. In the context of federal habeas review of state criminal convictions, for instance, one commentator has

---

28. Tafflin v. Levitt, 493 U.S. 455, 458 (1990).

29. *See, e.g.*, McCleskey v. Zant, 499 U.S. 467 (1991) (limiting successive habeas corpus petitions); Teague v. Lane, 489 U.S. 288 (1989) (habeas petitions cannot seek recognition of new constitutional rights unless they are rights that would have retroactive application); Wainwright v. Sykes, 433 U.S. 72 (1977) (prisoners may not raise issues on habeas corpus that were not raised at trial unless they can demonstrate cause and prejudice for their procedural default); see Chapter 15 for a discussion of these issues concerning habeas corpus.

30. *See, e.g.*, Parratt v. Taylor, 451 U.S. 527 (1981) (§1983 does not create a remedy when the plaintiff seeks only a postdeprivation remedy for loss of property and the state provides an adequate postdeprivation remedy). See Chapter 8 for a discussion of issues concerning §1983.

31. *See, e.g.*, Seminole Tribe v. Florida, 517 U.S. 44 (1996) (denying jurisdiction of federal court to consider state's refusal to comply with federal statute regulating tribal and state compacts for gaming).

32. *See, e.g.*, Younger v. Harris, 401 U.S. 37 (1971) (federal courts may not enjoin pending state court proceedings); see Chapter 13 for a discussion of federal court abstention when there are pending state court proceedings.

33. *See, e.g.*, Allen v. McCurry, 449 U.S. 90 (1980) (state court decisions have preclusive effect on federal courts deciding claims under §1983).

34. *See* PAUL FINKELMAN, AN IMPERFECT UNION: SLAVERY, FEDERALISM, AND COMITY 4 (1981) (defining comity as "the courtesy or consideration that one jurisdiction gives by enforcing the laws of another, granted out of respect and deference rather than obligation").

35. *See, e.g.*, Younger v. Harris, 401 U.S. 37 (1971) (holding that because of comity federal courts may not enjoin pending state court proceedings); Railroad Comm'n of Texas v. Pullman Co., 312 U.S. 496 (1941) (holding that federal courts should abstain when state court clarification of unclear state law might make a federal court ruling unnecessary, in part, to avoid friction with state courts); *see also* Michael Wells, *The Role of Comity in the Law of Federal Courts*, 60 N.C. L. REV. 59 (1981).

insisted that "nothing [is] more subversive of a judge's sense of responsibility, of inner subjective conscientiousness which is so essential a part of the difficult and subtle art of judging well, than an indiscriminate acceptance of the notion that all the shots will always be called by someone else."[36] The fidelity of state judges to federal law isn't improved on this view by subjecting their decisions to the review of lower federal court judges. Against this view is the Supremacy Clause argument that federal courts should safeguard constitutional rights irrespective of the friction or insult that might be created. We will explore these issues in Chapter 3 in cases involving the standing of a federal court to grant injunctive relief against state officers where the state courts are also open to the claims, in Chapter 10 in the context of abstention doctrines, and in Chapter 8 in the context of federal habeas review of state criminal convictions.

3. Democracy and Individual Rights

In addition to the fundamental structural values of separation of powers and federalism, federal courts consider norms of democracy and individual rights in crafting the doctrines of federal jurisdiction. They may weigh and balance these values, which sometimes conflict with each other and with structural principles.

Article III judges are unelected. In a democratic society, there must be limits to their power. While few would disagree with this principle in the abstract, debates abound about what those limits should be. For example, while courts are called on to say what the law is, scholars have long debated how certain federal judges should be of a law's unconstitutionality before declaring it unconstitutional.[37] Active debate also surrounds the degree to which a federal judgment should have binding effect beyond the specific parties in a case, as occurs when a single plaintiff hand-picks a district court judge based on perceived political affiliation in order to obtain an injunction that suspends implementation of federal policy across the nation. Jurisdiction, appellate review, and doctrines of equity are all implicated in such cases. Justiciability doctrines like standing are also said to protect democratic self-government by circumscribing the judicial role, even as standing doctrines are sometimes used to restrict causes of action created by Congress.[38]

At the other end of the spectrum, democratic self-government does not always require limits on the judicial role. To the contrary, the Court has relied on democratic legitimacy as a reason for the exercise of federal jurisdiction, including judicial review. As an initial matter, for federal courts to refuse to exercise jurisdiction that Congress conferred arguably itself usurps Congress's role.[39]

---

36. Paul M. Bator, *Finality in Criminal Law and Federal Habeas Corpus for State Prisoners*, 76 HARV. L. REV. 441, 451 (1963).

37. Vicki C. Jackson, *Thayer, Holmes, Brandeis: Conceptions of Judicial Review, Factfinding, and Proportionality*, 130 HARV. L. REV. 2348 (2017).

38. Heather Elliott, *The Functions of Standing*, 61 STAN. L. REV. 459, 508 (2008).

39. Martin H. Redish, *Abstention, Separation of Powers, and the Limits of the Judicial Function*, 94 YALE L.J. 71, 114 (1984); Fred O. Smith, Jr., *Undemocratic Restraint*, 70 VAND. L. REV. 845, 915 (2017).

Moreover, politically accountable branches can "clog" or corrupt "the channels of political change" by restricting the right to vote, speak, or protest.[40] In some contexts, then, the federal courts are in a unique position to protect democracy by enforcing constitutional law that protects the rights of self-government.

Federal courts also appeal to norms of equality when shaping the judicial role. A basic axiom of procedural law is that parties play by the same rules. The indigent can sue the wealthy. The citizen can sue the government officials. And, to an extent, these parties are on equal footing in the view of the judicial system. In certain settings, however, the Court exhibits extraordinary deference to government officials, ostensibly to prevent undue interference by Article III judges with core Article II branch powers. In addition, judicial actors sometimes make appeals to anti-caste or anti-subordination principles when defining their role. On this view, an important role for courts is to correct instances in which political majorities irrationally target politically unpopular minorities for harm and subjugation.[41] Structural constitutional values like inter-branch deference, comity and state sovereignty are sometimes in tension with this role.[42] Courts thus face the delicate task of balancing competing constitutional principles.

Another recurring constitutional theme in the law of federal courts is due process. First, even as courts protect structural constitutional values, they also emphasize the importance of ensuring access to courts when federal rights are at stake. This informs debates about the extent to which federal forums should or must be available to entertain federal constitutional claims and provide a remedy when no other remedy is available. Second, courts work to ensure that when life, liberty, and property are at stake, there are fundamentally fair procedures in place—as one commentator succinctly put it, "some kind of a hearing" to test the factual and legal predicate for government intervention.[43] Third, and more broadly, federal jurisdictional doctrines also cite substantive notions of fairness (i.e., fair play and substantial justice) when determining the proper role for federal courts.

---

40. *See* John Hart Ely, Democracy and Distrust: A Theory of Judicial Review (1980).

41. Catharine A. MacKinnon, *Difference and Dominance: On Sex Discrimination, in* Feminism Unmodified 32 (1987) (advocating for anti-dominance framework for gender equality); Cass R. Sunstein, *The Anticaste Principle*, 92 Mich. L. Rev. 2410, 2411 (1994) (identifying the role that undoing caste has played in equality jurisprudence); Laurence H. Tribe, American Constitutional Law at 1515 (2d ed. 1988) (advocating for anti-subjugation framework); Darren Lenard Hutchinson, *"Unexplainable on Grounds Other Than Race": The Inversion of Privilege and Subordination in Equal Protection Jurisprudence*, 2003 U. Ill. L. Rev. 615, 700 (2003) (advocating for an anti-dominance approach to racial equality).

42. Norman W. Spaulding, *Constitution as Countermonument: Federalism, Reconstruction, and the Problem of Collective Memory*, 103 Colum. L. Rev. 1992 (2003). Malcolm Feeley & Edward Rubin, Federalism: Political Identity and Tragic Compromise (2011).

43. Henry Friendly, *Some Kind of a Hearing*, 123 U. Pa. L. Rev. 1267 (1975); *cf.* Norman W. Spaulding, *The Ideal and the Actual in Procedural Due Process*, 48 Hastings Const. L. Q. 261 (2021).

C.   THE EMERGENCE OF JUDICIAL REVIEW

Marbury v. Madison is said to be the single most important decision in American constitutional law and in defining the role of the federal courts.[44] It arose in the heat of sharp political clashes between Jeffersonian Republicans and Federalists over control of the federal government and the federal judiciary. The presidential election of 1800 was fiercely contested among four candidates: the incumbent, John Adams, Thomas Jefferson, Aaron Burr, and Charles Pinckney. Jefferson received a majority of the popular vote but tied in the electoral vote with Burr. The House of Representatives resolved the tie in favor of Jefferson and he took office on March 4, 1801.

In January 1801, Adams's Secretary of State, John Marshall, was named to serve as the third Chief Justice of the U.S. Supreme Court. In the waning months of Adams's presidency, Marshall served as both Secretary of State and Chief Justice. Adams was a Federalist, and the Federalists in Congress were determined to exercise their influence before the Republican, Jefferson, took office. On February 13, 1801, Congress enacted the Circuit Court Act, which reduced the number of Supreme Court justices from six to five, decreasing the opportunity for Republican control of the Court.[45] The Act also eliminated the Supreme Court justices' duty to serve as circuit court judges and created 16 new judgeships on the circuit courts. However, this change was short-lived; in 1802, Congress repealed this statute, restoring the practice of circuit riding by Supreme Court justices and eliminating the newly created circuit court judgeships. The constitutionality of congressional abolition of judgeships was not tested in the courts.

On February 27, 1801, less than a week before the end of Adams's term, Congress adopted the Organic Act of the District of Columbia, which authorized the President to appoint 42 justices of the peace. Adams announced his nominations on March 2, and on March 3, the day before Jefferson's inauguration, the Senate confirmed the nominees. Immediately, Secretary of State (and Chief Justice) John Marshall signed the commissions of these individuals and dispatched his brother, James Marshall, to deliver the commissions. A few commissions, including one for William Marbury, were not delivered before Jefferson's inauguration. President Jefferson instructed his secretary of state, James Madison, to withhold the commissions.

Marbury filed suit in the U.S. Supreme Court seeking a writ of mandamus to compel Madison, as Secretary of State, to deliver the commission. Marbury claimed that the Judiciary Act of 1789 authorized the Supreme Court to grant mandamus in a proceeding filed originally in the Supreme Court. Although Marbury's petition

---

44. For excellent reviews of the factual background and of the Supreme Court's decision, see BURT NEUBORNE, MADISON'S MUSIC 146-94 (2015); *Marbury and Its Legacy: A Symposium to Mark the 200th Anniversary of Marbury v. Madison*, 72 GEO. WASH. L. REV. 1 (2003); Marbury v. Madison: *A Bicentennial Symposium*, 89 VA. L. REV. 1105 (2003); Symposium, *Judging Judicial Review: Marbury in the Modern Era*, 101 MICH. L. REV. 2557 (2003); William W. Van Alstyne, *A Critical Guide to Marbury v. Madison*, 1969 DUKE L.J. 1.

45. Circuit Court Act, ch. 4, 2 Stat. 89 (1801). *See* Kathryn Turner, *The Midnight Judges*, 109 U. PA. L. REV. 494 (1961).

was filed in December 1801, the Supreme Court did not hear the case until 1803 because Congress, by statute, abolished the June and December 1802 Terms of the Supreme Court.

The Supreme Court ruled against Marbury on the ground that it had no power to hear the case as a matter of original jurisdiction. Although the Judiciary Act of 1789 authorized such jurisdiction, the statute was unconstitutional and hence void.

Marbury v. Madison

5 U.S. 137 (1803)

Mr. Chief Justice MARSHALL delivered the opinion of the Court.

At the last term, on the affidavits then read and filed with the clerk, a rule was granted in this case requiring the Secretary of State to show cause why a mandamus should not issue directing him to deliver to William Marbury his commission as a justice of the peace for the county of Washington, in the District of Columbia.

No cause has been shown, and the present motion is for a mandamus. The peculiar delicacy of this case, the novelty of some of its circumstances, and the real difficulty attending the points which occur in it require a complete exposition of the principles on which the opinion to be given by the Court is founded.

These principles have been, on the side of the applicant, very ably argued at the bar. In rendering the opinion of the Court, there will be some departure in form, though not in substance, from the points stated in that argument.

In the order in which the Court has viewed this subject, the following questions have been considered and decided.

1. Has the applicant a right to the commission he demands?
2. If he has a right, and that right has been violated, do the laws of his country afford him a remedy?
3. If they do afford him a remedy, is it a mandamus issuing from this court?

The first object of inquiry is:

1. Has the applicant a right to the commission he demands?

. . . To grant a commission to a person appointed might perhaps be deemed a duty enjoined by the Constitution. "He shall," says that instrument, "commission all the officers of the United States."

The acts of appointing to office and commissioning the person appointed can scarcely be considered as one and the same, since the power to perform them is given in two separate and distinct sections of the Constitution. The distinction between the appointment and the commission will be rendered more apparent by adverting to that provision in the second section of the second article of the Constitution which authorises Congress "to vest by law the appointment of such inferior officers as they think proper in the President alone, in the Courts of law, or in the heads of departments;" thus contemplating cases where the law may direct the President to commission an officer appointed by the Courts or by the heads of departments. In such a case, to issue a commission would be apparently a duty distinct from the appointment, the performance of which perhaps could not legally be refused.

Although that clause of the Constitution which requires the President to commission all the officers of the United States may never have been applied to officers appointed otherwise than by himself, yet it would be difficult to deny the legislative power to apply it to such cases. Of consequence, the constitutional distinction between the appointment to an office and the commission of an officer who has been appointed remains the same as if in practice the President had commissioned officers appointed by an authority other than his own.

It follows too from the existence of this distinction that, if an appointment was to be evidenced by any public act other than the commission, the performance of such public act would create the officer, and if he was not removable at the will of the President, would either give him a right to his commission or enable him to perform the duties without it.

These observations are premised solely for the purpose of rendering more intelligible those which apply more directly to the particular case under consideration. This is an appointment made by the President, by and with the advice and consent of the Senate, and is evidenced by no act but the commission itself. In such a case, therefore, the commission and the appointment seem inseparable, it being almost impossible to show an appointment otherwise than by proving the existence of a commission; still, the commission is not necessarily the appointment; though conclusive evidence of it.

But at what stage does it amount to this conclusive evidence?

The answer to this question seems an obvious one. . . .

Some point of time must be taken when the power of the Executive over an officer, not removable at his will, must cease. That point of time must be when the constitutional power of appointment has been exercised. And this power has been exercised when the last act required from the person possessing the power has been performed. This last act is the signature of the commission. This idea seems to have prevailed with the Legislature when the act passed converting the Department of Foreign Affairs into the Department of State. By that act, it is enacted that the Secretary of State shall keep the seal of the United States,

> and shall make out and record, and shall affix the said seal to all civil commissions to officers of the United States, to be appointed by the President: provided that the said seal shall not be affixed to any commission before the same shall have been signed by the President of the United States, nor to any other instrument or act without the special warrant of the President therefor.

The signature is a warrant for affixing the great seal to the commission, and the great seal is only to be affixed to an instrument which is complete. . . . The commission being signed, the subsequent duty of the Secretary of State is prescribed by law, and not to be guided by the will of the President. He is to affix the seal of the United States to the commission, and is to record it. . . .

He acts, in this respect, as has been very properly stated at the bar, under the authority of law, and not by the instructions of the President. It is a ministerial act which the law enjoins on a particular officer for a particular purpose.

No other solemnity is required by law; no other act is to be performed on the part of government. All that the Executive can do to invest the person with his office is done . . .

It has also occurred as possible, and barely possible, that the transmission of the commission and the acceptance thereof might be deemed necessary to complete the right of the plaintiff.

The transmission of the commission is a practice directed by convenience, but not by law. It cannot therefore be necessary to constitute the appointment, which must precede it and which is the mere act of the President. . . .

If the transmission of a commission be not considered as necessary to give validity to an appointment, still less is its acceptance. The appointment is the sole act of the President; the acceptance is the sole act of the officer, and is, in plain common sense, posterior to the appointment. As he may resign, so may he refuse to accept; but neither the one nor the other is capable of rendering the appointment a nonentity. . . .

Where an officer is removable at the will of the Executive, the circumstance which completes his appointment is of no concern, because the act is at any time revocable, and the commission may be arrested if still in the office. But when the officer is not removable at the will of the Executive, the appointment is not revocable, and cannot be annulled. It has conferred legal rights which cannot be resumed.

The discretion of the Executive is to be exercised until the appointment has been made. But having once made the appointment, his power over the office is terminated in all cases, where by law the officer is not removable by him. The right to the office is then in the person appointed, and he has the absolute, unconditional power of accepting or rejecting it.

Mr. Marbury, then, since his commission was signed by the President and sealed by the Secretary of State, was appointed, and as the law creating the office gave the officer a right to hold for five years independent of the Executive, the appointment was not revocable, but vested in the officer legal rights which are protected by the laws of his country.

To withhold the commission, therefore, is an act deemed by the Court not warranted by law, but violative of a vested legal right.

This brings us to the second inquiry, which is:

2. If he has a right, and that right has been violated, do the laws of his country afford him a remedy?

The very essence of civil liberty certainly consists in the right of every individual to claim the protection of the laws whenever he receives an injury. One of the first duties of government is to afford that protection. In Great Britain, the King himself is sued in the respectful form of a petition, and he never fails to comply with the judgment of his court.

In the third volume of his Commentaries . . . Blackstone states two cases in which a remedy is afforded by mere operation of law.

"In all other cases," he says, "it is a general and indisputable rule that where there is a legal right, there is also a legal remedy by suit or action at law whenever that right is invaded."

And afterwards . . . he says,

I am next to consider such injuries as are cognizable by the Courts of common law. And herein I shall for the present only remark that all possible injuries whatsoever that did not fall within the exclusive cognizance of either the ecclesiastical, military, or maritime tribunals are, for that very reason, within the cognizance of the common law courts of justice, for it is a settled and invariable principle in the laws of England that every right, when withheld, must have a remedy, and every injury its proper redress.

The Government of the United States has been emphatically termed a government of laws, and not of men. It will certainly cease to deserve this high appellation if the laws furnish no remedy for the violation of a vested legal right.

If this obloquy is to be cast on the jurisprudence of our country, it must arise from the peculiar character of the case.

It behooves us, then, to inquire whether there be in its composition any ingredient which shall exempt from legal investigation or exclude the injured party from legal redress. In pursuing this inquiry, the first question which presents itself is whether this can be arranged with that class of cases which come under the description of *damnum absque injuria*—a loss without an injury.

This description of cases never has been considered, and, it is believed, never can be considered, as comprehending offices of trust, of honour or of profit. The office of justice of peace in the District of Columbia is such an office; it is therefore worthy of the attention and guardianship of the laws. It has received that attention and guardianship. It has been created by special act of Congress, and has been secured, so far as the laws can give security to the person appointed to fill it, for five years. It is not then on account of the worthlessness of the thing pursued that the injured party can be alleged to be without remedy.

Is it in the nature of the transaction? Is the act of delivering or withholding a commission to be considered as a mere political act belonging to the Executive department alone, for the performance of which entire confidence is placed by our Constitution in the Supreme Executive, and for any misconduct respecting which the injured individual has no remedy?

That there may be such cases is not to be questioned, but that every act of duty to be performed in any of the great departments of government constitutes such a case is not to be admitted.

By the act concerning invalids, passed in June, 1794, the Secretary at War is ordered to place on the pension list all persons whose names are contained in a report previously made by him to Congress. If he should refuse to do so, would the wounded veteran be without remedy? Is it to be contended that where the law, in precise terms, directs the performance of an act in which an individual is interested, the law is incapable of securing obedience to its mandate? Is it on account of the character of the person against whom the complaint is made? Is it to be contended that the heads of departments are not amenable to the laws of their country?

Whatever the practice on particular occasions may be, the theory of this principle will certainly never be maintained. No act of the Legislature confers so extraordinary a privilege, nor can it derive countenance from the doctrines of the common law. After stating that personal injury from the King to a subject is presumed to be impossible, Blackstone says,

> but injuries to the rights of property can scarcely be committed by the Crown without the intervention of its officers, for whom, the law, in matters of right, entertains no respect or delicacy, but furnishes various

methods of detecting the errors and misconduct of those agents by whom the King has been deceived and induced to do a temporary injustice.

By the act passed in 1796, authorizing the sale of the lands above the mouth of Kentucky river, the purchaser, on paying his purchase money, becomes completely entitled to the property purchased, and, on producing to the Secretary of State the receipt of the treasurer upon a certificate required by the law, the President of the United States is authorized to grant him a patent. It is further enacted that all patents shall be countersigned by the Secretary of State, and recorded in his office. If the Secretary of State should choose to withhold this patent, or, the patent being lost, should refuse a copy of it, can it be imagined that the law furnishes to the injured person no remedy?

It is not believed that any person whatever would attempt to maintain such a proposition.

It follows, then, that the question whether the legality of an act of the head of a department be examinable in a court of justice or not must always depend on the nature of that act.

If some acts be examinable and others not, there must be some rule of law to guide the Court in the exercise of its jurisdiction.

In some instances, there may be difficulty in applying the rule to particular cases; but there cannot, it is believed, be much difficulty in laying down the rule.

By the Constitution of the United States, the President is invested with certain important political powers, in the exercise of which he is to use his own discretion, and is accountable only to his country in his political character and to his own conscience. To aid him in the performance of these duties, he is authorized to appoint certain officers, who act by his authority and in conformity with his orders.

In such cases, their acts are his acts; and whatever opinion may be entertained of the manner in which executive discretion may be used, still there exists, and can exist, no power to control that discretion. The subjects are political. They respect the nation, not individual rights, and, being entrusted to the Executive, the decision of the Executive is conclusive. The application of this remark will be perceived by adverting to the act of Congress for establishing the Department of Foreign Affairs. This officer, as his duties were prescribed by that act, is to conform precisely to the will of the President. He is the mere organ by whom that will is communicated. The acts of such an officer, as an officer, can never be examinable by the Courts.

But when the Legislature proceeds to impose on that officer other duties; when he is directed peremptorily to perform certain acts; when the rights of individuals are dependent on the performance of those acts; he is so far the officer of the law, is amenable to the laws for his conduct, and cannot at his discretion, sport away the vested rights of others.

The conclusion from this reasoning is that, where the heads of departments are the political or confidential agents of the Executive, merely to execute the will of the President, or rather to act in cases in which the Executive possesses a constitutional or legal discretion, nothing can be more perfectly clear than that their acts are only politically examinable. But where a specific duty is assigned by law, and individual rights depend upon the performance of that duty, it seems equally clear that the individual who considers himself injured has a right to resort to the laws of his country for a remedy.

If this be the rule, let us inquire how it applies to the case under the consideration of the Court. The power of nominating to the Senate, and the power of appointing the person nominated, are political powers, to be exercised by the President according to his own discretion. When he has made an appointment, he has exercised his whole power, and his discretion has been completely applied to the case. If, by law, the officer be removable at the will of the President, then a new appointment may be immediately made, and the rights of the officer are terminated. But as a fact which has existed cannot be made never to have existed, the appointment cannot be annihilated, and consequently, if the officer is by law not removable at the will of the President, the rights he has acquired are protected by the law, and are not resumable by the President. . . .

The question whether a right has vested or not is, in its nature, judicial, and must be tried by the judicial authority. If, for example, Mr. Marbury had taken the oaths of a magistrate and proceeded to act as one, in consequence of which a suit had been instituted against him in which his defence had depended on his being a magistrate; the validity of his appointment must have been determined by judicial authority.

So, if he conceives that, by virtue of his appointment, he has a legal right either to the commission which has been made out for him or to a copy of that commission, it is equally a question examinable in a court. . . .

It remains to be inquired whether,
3. He is entitled to the remedy for which he applies. This depends on:
1. The nature of the writ applied for, and
2. The power of this court.

1. The nature of the writ.

Blackstone, in the third volume of his Commentaries . . . defines a mandamus to be

> a command issuing in the King's name from the Court of King's Bench, and directed to any person, corporation, or inferior court of judicature within the King's dominions requiring them to do some particular thing therein specified which appertains to their office and duty, and which the Court of King's Bench has previously determined, or at least supposes, to be consonant to right and justice.

Lord Mansfield, in 3d Burrows, 1266, in the case of *The King v. Baker et al.*, states with much precision and explicitness the cases in which this writ may be used. "Whenever," says that very able judge, "there is a right to execute an office, perform a service, or exercise a franchise (more especially if it be in a matter of public concern or attended with profit), and a person is kept out of possession, or dispossessed of such right, and has no other specific legal remedy, this court ought to assist by mandamus, upon reasons of justice, as the writ expresses, and upon reasons of public policy, to preserve peace, order and good government."

In the same case, he says, "this writ ought to be used upon all occasions where the law has established no specific remedy, and where in justice and good government there ought to be one."

This writ, if awarded, would be directed to an officer of government, and its mandate to him would be, to use the words of Blackstone,

> to do a particular thing therein specified, which appertains to his office and duty and which the Court has previously determined or at least supposes to be consonant to right and justice.

Or, in the words of Lord Mansfield, the applicant, in this case, has a right to execute an office of public concern, and is kept out of possession of that right.

These circumstances certainly concur in this case.

Still, to render the mandamus a proper remedy, the officer to whom it is to be directed must be one to whom, on legal principles, such writ may be directed, and the person applying for it must be without any other specific and legal remedy.

1. With respect to the officer to whom it would be directed. The intimate political relation, subsisting between the President of the United States and the heads of departments, necessarily renders any legal investigation of the acts of one of those high officers peculiarly irksome, as well as delicate, and excites some hesitation with respect to the propriety of entering into such investigation. . . .

But . . . if so far from being an intrusion into the secrets of the cabinet . . . what is there in the exalted station of the officer which shall bar a citizen from asserting in a court of justice his legal rights, or shall forbid a court to listen to the claim or to issue a mandamus directing the performance of a duty not depending on Executive discretion, but on particular acts of Congress and the general principles of law?

If one of the heads of departments commits any illegal act under colour of his office by which an individual sustains an injury, it cannot be pretended that his office alone exempts him from being sued in the ordinary mode of proceeding, and being compelled to obey the judgment of the law. How then can his office exempt him from this particular mode of deciding on the legality of his conduct if the case be such a case as would, were any other individual the party complained of, authorize the process? . . . [I]t is not perceived on what ground the Courts of the country are further excused from the duty of giving judgment that right to be done to an injured individual than if the same services were to be performed by a person not the head of a department.

It must be well recollected that, in 1792, an act passed, directing the secretary at war to place on the pension list such disabled officers and soldiers as should be reported to him by the Circuit Courts, which act, so far as the duty was imposed on the Courts, was deemed unconstitutional; but some of the judges, thinking that the law might be executed by them in the character of commissioners, proceeded to act and to report in that character.

This law being deemed unconstitutional at the circuits, was repealed, and a different system was established; but the question whether those persons who had been reported by the judges, as commissioners, were entitled, in consequence of that report, to be placed on the pension list was a legal question, properly determinable in the Courts, although the act of placing such persons on the list was to be performed by the head of a department.

That this question might be properly settled, Congress passed an act in February, 1793, making it the duty of the Secretary of War, in conjunction with the Attorney General, to take such measures as might be necessary to obtain an adjudication of the Supreme Court of the United States on the validity of any such rights, claimed under the act aforesaid.

After the passage of this act, a mandamus was moved for, to be directed to the Secretary of War, commanding him to place on the pension list a person stating himself to be on the report of the judges.

There is, therefore, much reason to believe that this mode of trying the legal right of the complainant was deemed by the head of a department, and by the highest law officer of the United States, the most proper which could be selected for the purpose.

When the subject was brought before the Court, the decision was not that a mandamus would not lie to the head of a department directing him to perform an act enjoined by law, in the performance of which an individual had a vested interest, but that a mandamus ought not to issue in that case — the decision necessarily to be made if the report of the commissioners did not confer on the applicant a legal right.

The judgment in that case is understood to have decided the merits of all claims of that description, and the persons, on the report of the commissioners, found it necessary to pursue the mode prescribed by the law subsequent to that which had been deemed unconstitutional in order to place themselves on the pension list.

The doctrine, therefore, now advanced is by no means a novel one. . . .

It was at first doubted whether the action of detinue was not a specific legal remedy for the commission which has been withheld from Mr. Marbury, in which case a mandamus would be improper. But this doubt has yielded to the consideration that the judgment in detinue is for the thing itself, or its value. The value of a public office not to be sold is incapable of being ascertained, and the applicant has a right to the office itself, or to nothing. He will obtain the office by obtaining the commission or a copy of it from the record.

This, then, is a plain case of a mandamus, either to deliver the commission or a copy of it from the record, and it only remains to be inquired:

Whether it can issue from this Court.

The act to establish the judicial courts of the United States authorizes the Supreme Court

> "to issue writs of mandamus, in cases warranted by the principles and usages of law, to any courts appointed, or persons holding office, under the authority of the United States."

The Secretary of State, being a person, holding an office under the authority of the United States, is precisely within the letter of the description, and if this Court is not authorized to issue a writ of mandamus to such an officer, it must be because the law is unconstitutional, and therefore absolutely incapable of conferring the authority and assigning the duties which its words purport to confer and assign.

The Constitution vests the whole judicial power of the United States in one Supreme Court, and such inferior courts as Congress shall, from time to time, ordain and establish. This power is expressly extended to all cases arising under the laws of the United States; and consequently, in some form, may be exercised over the present case, because the right claimed is given by a law of the United States.

In the distribution of this power, it is declared that

The Supreme Court shall have original jurisdiction in all cases affecting ambassadors, other public ministers and consuls, and those in which a state shall be a party. In all other cases, the Supreme Court shall have appellate jurisdiction.

It has been insisted at the bar, that, as the original grant of jurisdiction to the Supreme and inferior courts is general, and the clause assigning original jurisdiction to the Supreme Court contains no negative or restrictive words, the power remains to the Legislature to assign original jurisdiction to that Court in other cases than those specified in the article which has been recited, provided those cases belong to the judicial power of the United States.

If it had been intended to leave it in the discretion of the Legislature to apportion the judicial power between the Supreme and inferior courts according to the will of that body, it would certainly have been useless to have proceeded further than to have defined the judicial power and the tribunals in which it should be vested. The subsequent part of the section is mere surplusage—is entirely without meaning—if such is to be the construction. If Congress remains at liberty to give this court appellate jurisdiction where the Constitution has declared their jurisdiction shall be original, and original jurisdiction where the Constitution has declared it shall be appellate, the distribution of jurisdiction made in the Constitution, is form without substance.

Affirmative words are often, in their operation, negative of other objects than those affirmed, and, in this case, a negative or exclusive sense must be given to them or they have no operation at all. . . .

When an instrument organizing fundamentally a judicial system divides it into one Supreme and so many inferior courts as the Legislature may ordain and establish, then enumerates its powers, and proceeds so far to distribute them as to define the jurisdiction of the Supreme Court by declaring the cases in which it shall take original jurisdiction, and that in others it shall take appellate jurisdiction, the plain import of the words seems to be that, in one class of cases, its jurisdiction is original, and not appellate; in the other, it is appellate, and not original. If any other construction would render the clause inoperative, that is an additional reason for rejecting such other construction, and for adhering to the obvious meaning.

To enable this court then to issue a mandamus, it must be shown to be an exercise of appellate jurisdiction, or to be necessary to enable them to exercise appellate jurisdiction.

It has been stated at the bar that the appellate jurisdiction may be exercised in a variety of forms, and that, if it be the will of the Legislature that a mandamus should be used for that purpose, that will must be obeyed. This is true; yet the jurisdiction must be appellate, not original.

It is the essential criterion of appellate jurisdiction that it revises and corrects the proceedings in a cause already instituted, and does not create that case. Although, therefore, a mandamus may be directed to courts, yet to issue such a writ to an officer for the delivery of a paper is, in effect, the same as to sustain an original action for that paper, and therefore seems not to belong to appellate, but to original jurisdiction. Neither is it necessary in such a case as this to enable the Court to exercise its appellate jurisdiction.

The authority, therefore, given to the Supreme Court by the act establishing the judicial courts of the United States to issue writs of mandamus to public officers appears not to be warranted by the Constitution, and it becomes necessary to inquire whether a jurisdiction so conferred can be exercised.

The question whether an act repugnant to the Constitution can become the law of the land is a question deeply interesting to the United States, but, happily, not of an intricacy proportioned to its interest. It seems only necessary to recognise certain principles, supposed to have been long and well established, to decide it.

That the people have an original right to establish for their future government such principles as, in their opinion, shall most conduce to their own happiness is the basis on which the whole American fabric has been erected. The exercise of this original right is a very great exertion; nor can it nor ought it to be frequently repeated. The principles, therefore, so established are deemed fundamental. And as the authority from which they proceed, is supreme, and can seldom act, they are designed to be permanent.

This original and supreme will organizes the government and assigns to different departments their respective powers. It may either stop here or establish certain limits not to be transcended by those departments.

The Government of the United States is of the latter description. The powers of the Legislature are defined and limited; and that those limits may not be mistaken or forgotten, the Constitution is written. To what purpose are powers limited, and to what purpose is that limitation committed to writing, if these limits may at any time be passed by those intended to be restrained? The distinction between a government with limited and unlimited powers is abolished if those limits do not confine the persons on whom they are imposed, and if acts prohibited and acts allowed are of equal obligation. It is a proposition too plain to be contested that the Constitution controls any legislative act repugnant to it, or that the Legislature may alter the Constitution by an ordinary act.

Between these alternatives there is no middle ground. The Constitution is either a superior, paramount law, unchangeable by ordinary means, or it is on a level with ordinary legislative acts, and, like other acts, is alterable when the legislature shall please to alter it.

If the former part of the alternative be true, then a legislative act contrary to the Constitution is not law; if the latter part be true, then written Constitutions are absurd attempts on the part of the people to limit a power in its own nature illimitable.

Certainly all those who have framed written Constitutions contemplate them as forming the fundamental and paramount law of the nation, and consequently the theory of every such government must be that an act of the Legislature repugnant to the Constitution is void.

This theory is essentially attached to a written Constitution, and is consequently to be considered by this Court as one of the fundamental principles of our society. It is not, therefore, to be lost sight of in the further consideration of this subject.

If an act of the Legislature repugnant to the Constitution is void, does it, notwithstanding its invalidity, bind the Courts and oblige them to give it effect? Or, in other words, though it be not law, does it constitute a rule as operative as if it was a law? This would be to overthrow in fact what was established in theory, and would seem, at first view, an absurdity too gross to be insisted on. It shall, however, receive a more attentive consideration.

It is emphatically the province and duty of the Judicial Department to say what the law is. Those who apply the rule to particular cases must, of necessity, expound and interpret that rule. If two laws conflict with each other, the Courts must decide on the operation of each.

So, if a law be in opposition to the Constitution, if both the law and the Constitution apply to a particular case, so that the Court must either decide that case conformably to the law, disregarding the Constitution, or conformably to the Constitution, disregarding the law, the Court must determine which of these conflicting rules governs the case. This is of the very essence of judicial duty.

If, then, the Courts are to regard the Constitution, and the Constitution is superior to any ordinary act of the Legislature, the Constitution, and not such ordinary act, must govern the case to which they both apply.

Those, then, who controvert the principle that the Constitution is to be considered in court as a paramount law are reduced to the necessity of maintaining that courts must close their eyes on the Constitution, and see only the law.

This doctrine would subvert the very foundation of all written Constitutions. It would declare that an act which, according to the principles and theory of our government, is entirely void, is yet, in practice, completely obligatory. It would declare that, if the Legislature shall do what is expressly forbidden, such act, notwithstanding the express prohibition, is in reality effectual. It would be giving to the Legislature a practical and real omnipotence with the same breath which professes to restrict their powers within narrow limits. It is prescribing limits, and declaring that those limits may be passed at pleasure.

That it thus reduces to nothing what we have deemed the greatest improvement on political institutions — a written Constitution, would of itself be sufficient, in America where written Constitutions have been viewed with so much reverence, for rejecting the construction. But the peculiar expressions of the Constitution of the United States furnish additional arguments in favour of its rejection.

The judicial power of the United States is extended to all cases arising under the Constitution. Could it be the intention of those who gave this power to say that, in using it, the Constitution should not be looked into? That a case arising under the Constitution should be decided without examining the instrument under which it arises?

This is too extravagant to be maintained.

In some cases then, the Constitution must be looked into by the judges. And if they can open it at all, what part of it are they forbidden to read or to obey?

There are many other parts of the Constitution which serve to illustrate this subject.

It is declared that "no tax or duty shall be laid on articles exported from any State." Suppose a duty on the export of cotton, of tobacco, or of flour, and a suit instituted to recover it. Ought judgment to be rendered in such a case? Ought the judges to close their eyes on the Constitution, and only see the law?

The Constitution declares that "no bill of attainder or *ex post facto* law shall be passed."

If, however, such a bill should be passed and a person should be prosecuted under it, must the Court condemn to death those victims whom the Constitution endeavours to preserve?

"No person," says the Constitution, "shall be convicted of treason unless on the testimony of two witnesses to the same overt act, or on confession in open court."

Here. the language of the Constitution is addressed especially to the Courts. It prescribes, directly for them, a rule of evidence not to be departed from. If the Legislature should change that rule, and declare one witness, or a confession out of court, sufficient for conviction, must the constitutional principle yield to the legislative act?

From these and many other selections which might be made, it is apparent that the framers of the Constitution contemplated that instrument as a rule for the government of courts, as well as of the Legislature.

Why otherwise does it direct the judges to take an oath to support it? This oath certainly applies in an especial manner to their conduct in their official character. How immoral to impose it on them if they were to be used as the instruments, and the knowing instruments, for violating what they swear to support! . . .

If such be the real state of things, this is worse than solemn mockery. To prescribe or to take this oath becomes equally a crime.

It is also not entirely unworthy of observation that, in declaring what shall be the supreme law of the land, the Constitution itself is first mentioned, and not the laws of the United States generally, but those only which shall be made in pursuance of the Constitution, have that rank.

Thus, the particular phraseology of the Constitution of the United States confirms and strengthens the principle, supposed to be essential to all written Constitutions, that a law repugnant to the Constitution is void, and that courts, as well as other departments, are bound by that instrument.

The rule must be discharged.

* * *

Politically, Marshall had little choice but to deny Marbury relief. The Jefferson administration surely would have refused to obey a writ of mandamus, which would have undermined the Court's authority at the outset of its exercise of judicial review. In addition, there was a real possibility that Jefferson might seek the impeachment of Federalist justices in an attempt to gain Republican control of the judiciary. One judge, albeit a clearly incompetent jurist, already had been impeached, and not long after his removal, the House of Representatives impeached Supreme Court Justice Samuel Chase on the grounds that he had made electioneering statements from the bench and had criticized the repeal of the 1801 Circuit Court Act.[46] Yet Marshall did more than simply rule in favor of the Jefferson administration; he used the occasion of deciding *Marbury v. Madison* to establish the power of the judiciary and a role for the federal courts that survives to this day.

An important additional element of the politics of the case is that Marshall's interests were not just centered on defending judicial review. He was the Secretary

---

46. *See* WILLIAM H. REHNQUIST, GRAND INQUESTS: THE HISTORIC IMPEACHMENTS OF JUSTICE SAMUEL CHASE AND PRESIDENT ANDREW JOHNSON (1992).

of State who had completed but failed to deliver the commissions before Jefferson took office and refused to do so—thus his own actions were at issue in the case. Whether the commissions existed and had been completed were hotly contested facts before the Supreme Court. But as a Justice sitting on the Court, he could not testify. Suspiciously, Marshall's brother ends up providing the crucial testimony regarding the commissions through an affidavit that one historian has suggested was "most likely a total fabrication."[47] How does this bear on the case's defense of judicial review? Can it be dismissed as a mere curio? At a minimum, one might legitimately wonder whether Marshall should have recused himself. And perhaps it shows the mistake of believing that the framers of the Constitution were above partisanship, or that partisanship quickly gave way to consensus on constitutional principles. There was a profound "gulf in assumptions between Federalists and Antifederalists" that was not resolved by the Constitution during or after its ratification.[48] Put differently, looking to the history of the founding era raises uncomfortable questions, not just easy answers.

In the heat of this deeply partisan conflict, Marshall nevertheless produced a brilliant, enduring defense of judicial review. The Court held that the judiciary could, assuming proper jurisdiction, issue a writ of mandamus to the executive. Are *all* actions of the executive branch therefore subject to judicial review? The power of the federal courts to review presidential actions defended in *Marbury* is responsible for many important Supreme Court decisions throughout American history. To take but one notable example, in *U.S. v. Nixon*, the Court's holding—that the President had to comply with a subpoena to provide tapes of conversations for use in a criminal trial—led to the resignation of President Richard Nixon.[49]

But there are limits. Foremost among those discussed by Marshall is the category of issues, termed "political questions," that are not reviewable by the federal courts. Indeed, *Marbury v. Madison* can be credited with originating the political question doctrine; a principle that certain matters are not judicially reviewable because they are committed to the other branches of government. The political question doctrine is discussed in detail in Chapter 3. For now, note its foundation in the distinction Marshall draws between discretionary and non-discretionary executive functions.

Marbury also establishes that Article III limits the Supreme Court's original jurisdiction: Congress has no power to expand jurisdiction beyond the heads of jurisdiction set out in Article III. The Supreme Court read §13 of the Judiciary Act of 1789 as authorizing mandamus as part of the Court's original jurisdiction. Was this a necessary conclusion? Section 13 stated, in part:

> The Supreme Court shall also have appellate jurisdiction from the circuit courts and the courts of the several states, in the cases herein after specially provided for; and shall have power to issue writs of prohibition to the district courts, when proceeding as courts of admiralty and maritime

---

47. Joel Richard Paul, Without Precedent: Chief Justice John Marshall and His Times (2018).

48. Gordon Wood, The Creation of the American Republic, 1766-1787, at 543 (1969) (discussing debate about the need for a bill of rights).

49. 418 U.S. 683 (1974).

jurisdiction, and writs of mandamus, in cases warranted by the principles and usages of law, to any courts appointed, or persons holding offices, under the authority of the United States.[50]

Alternative readings seem more plausible.[51] For example, the statute might be read as pertaining only to the Court's appellate jurisdiction because that is the only type of jurisdiction mentioned. Alternatively, the statute might simply be understood as granting the Court authority to issue mandamus, where appropriate, in cases otherwise within its jurisdiction. By this reading, the statute does not create original jurisdiction, but simply grants the Court remedial powers when it already has jurisdiction. Under either of these approaches, Marbury still would have lost, but the Court would have avoided the question as to whether the statute was constitutional. That of course wold have deprived the court of the opportunity to announce its power to declare statutes unconstitutional. Here is another signal, perhaps, that Marshall was seizing the case for purposes other than application of the law necessary to resolve it.

Returning to the more fundamental question taken up by the Court, why would it contravene the text of Article III to expand the Court's original jurisdiction? Article III can be read as simply setting a constitutional floor — providing that Congress cannot *withhold* original jurisdiction for the enumerated heads. This is a path not taken. To this day, *Marbury*'s holding that Congress cannot enlarge the Court's original jurisdiction is good law. However, the Court's statement that the categories of original and appellate jurisdiction are mutually exclusive has not been followed. The Supreme Court has long held that Congress may grant the district courts concurrent jurisdiction over matters within the Court's original jurisdiction.[52]

More generally, by viewing Article III as the ceiling of federal jurisdiction, *Marbury* helped establish the principle that federal courts may not hear matters unless there is constitutional authority, and Congress may not expand the jurisdiction granted in Article III of the Constitution. The federal courts are thus courts of *limited* subject matter jurisdiction.

The most commonly studied aspect of *Marbury* is its recognition of the power of the federal courts to declare federal statutes unconstitutional. Chief Justice Marshall's opinion concluded that the grant of original jurisdiction to issue mandamus was inconsistent with the Constitution. "An act, repugnant to the constitution" cannot "become the law of the land," and the federal courts may declare that an act is repugnant to the Constitution. What reasons does he give for this power? Is the power especially justified when the act at issue concerns the courts, as Section 13 of the First Judiciary Act did? The need to ensure that Congress does not enlarge federal judicial power beyond what Article III allows is arguably quite different from the courts operating as general censors of, for example, ordinary legislation concerning primary social action. The proposition that the courts cannot be forced to act unconstitutionally is not the same as

---

50. Judiciary Act of 1789 §13, 1 Stat. 73, 81.
51. *See* Van Alstyne, *supra* note 44, at 14-16.
52. *See, e.g.*, Ames v. Kansas *ex rel.* Johnston, 111 U.S. 449 (1884).

the proposition that the courts may (let alone must) generally supervise the constitutional compliance of other branches of government or the states.

Finally, *Marbury* states a claim that the Court is the authoritative interpreter of the Constitution. Perhaps the most frequently quoted part of the decision is the declaration: "It is emphatically the province and duty of the judicial department to say what the law is." This statement is read as establishing not only that the Court gets a voice in evaluating the constitutionality of statutes but also that it has the decisive say. In many of the ensuing chapters we will be concerned not with the abstract proposition that the Court is an authoritative interpreter, but rather the tools at the disposal of the Court and the lower federal courts to create effective remedies for their interpretative work.

The next case is the first exercise of judicial review by the Supreme Court to strike down a state law. The case arose out of Georgia's attempt to sell lands on the State's western border — lands of the Cherokee Nation, the Chickasaw Nation, the Choctaw Nation, and the Creek Nation. It is important to recognize the extent to which "[r]elations with Indians consumed much day-to-day federal governance under both the Articles and the new Constitution, and provoked some of the nation's earliest constitutional crises" touching foreign relations, removal, and the "fraught issues of western land, territory and statehood."[53] The Yazoo land case — so-called because the lands in question were referred to as the "Yazoo" territory — is an important example. In order to secure passage of a 1795 law transferring 35 million acres in what is now Alabama and Mississippi belonging to four land speculation companies for the bargain price of 1.5 cents per acre, senior Georgia Federalists bribed nearly every Georgia state legislator, other state officials, newspaper editors, and other elites in the state.

What followed was a dizzying set of political maneuvers by opponents and proponents of the land sale, one that pitted Federalists and Republicans against one another. In 1796, the Georgia Mississippi Land Company, which had bought 11 million acres, sold its interests to the New England Mississippi Land Company. On the same day, the Georgia Legislature, now controlled by Republicans who opposed the Yazoo land sale as corrupt, enacted a law rescinding the sale. Two years later, a constitutional amendment incorporated the statute's principles into Georgia's Constitution.

The controversy ended up in the U.S. Congress. In part to defeat any claims of title by land speculators based upon the 1795 law, Georgia later sold the lands to the federal government on the assurance that any remaining land claims of Native nations would be extinguished. Litigation ensued. Land speculators turned to lobbyists, with the New England Mississippi Land Company hiring future Justice Joseph Story, among others, to try to convince Congress to confirm their claims to lands that, it is worth stressing again, were territories of Native nations. Story and his fellow lobbyists failed to convince Congress to act.

In a collusive action designed to get the matter into federal court, Robert Fletcher, a shareholder in the New England Mississippi Land Company, sued John Peck, another shareholder, alleging that Peck had made false representations in a

---

53. Gregory Ablavsky, *The Savage Constitution*, 63 Duke L.J. 999, 1004-05 (2014).

deed conveying roughly 15,000 acres of Yazoo lands. In particular, Fletcher alleged that Peck had falsely represented that he had good title tracing back to the 1795 state land grant. The jury found for Peck. The Supreme Court was asked to decide whether Georgia's act of rescission was an unconstitutional impairment of the contracts of sale made in 1795.[54]

Fletcher v. Peck

10 U.S. 87 (1810)

Mr. Chief Justice MARSHALL delivered the opinion of the Court.

. . . The suit was instituted on several covenants contained in a deed made by John Peck, the defendant in error, conveying to Robert Fletcher, the plaintiff in error, certain lands which were part of a large purchase made by James Gunn and others, in the year 1795, from the State of Georgia, the contract for which was made in the form of a bill passed by the Legislature of that State. . . .

The second count assigns, in substance, as a breach . . . that the original grantees from the State of Georgia promised and assured divers members of the Legislature, then sitting in General Assembly that if the said members would assent to, and vote for, the passing of the Act, and if the said bill should pass, such members should have a share of, and be interested in, all the lands purchased from the said State by virtue of such law. And that divers of the said members to whom the said promises were made were unduly influenced thereby, and, under such influence, did vote for the passing of the said bill, by reason whereof the said law was a nullity, &c., and so the title of the State of Georgia did not pass to the said Peck, &c.

The plea to this count, after protesting that the promises it alleges were not made, avers that, until after the purchase made from the original grantees by James Greenleaf, under whom the said Peck claims, neither the said James Greenleaf nor the said Peck, nor any of the mesne vendors between the said Greenleaf and Peck, had any notice or knowledge that any such promises or assurances were made by the said original grantees, or either of them, to any of the members of the Legislature of the State of Georgia. To this plea the plaintiff demurred generally, and the defendant joined in the demurrer.

That corruption should find its way into the governments of our infant republics and contaminate the very source of legislation, or that impure motives should contribute to the passage of a law or the formation of a legislative contract are circumstances most deeply to be deplored. How far a court of justice would, in any case, be competent, on proceedings instituted by the State itself to vacate a contract thus formed, and to annul rights required under that contract by third persons having no notice of the improper means by which it was obtained is a question which the court would approach with much circumspection. . . .

---

54. For discussions of the case's history, see CHARLES F. HOBSON, THE GREAT YAZOO LANDS SALE: THE CASE OF *FLETCHER V. PECK* (2016); LINDSAY G. ROBERTSON, CONQUEST BY LAW: HOW THE DISCOVERY OF AMERICA DISPOSSESSED INDIGENOUS PEOPLES OF THEIR LANDS 30-31 (2005); C. PETER MAGRATH, YAZOO: LAW & POLITICS IN THE NEW REPUBLIC (1966).

If the majority of the Legislature be corrupted, it may well be doubted whether it be within the Province of the judiciary to control their conduct, and if less than a majority act from impure motives, the principle by which judicial interference would be regulated is not clearly discerned.

Whatever difficulties this subject might present when viewed under aspects of which it may be susceptible, this Court can perceive none in the particular pleadings now under consideration.

The case, as made out in the pleadings, is simply this. One individual who holds lands in the State of Georgia, under a deed covenanting that the title of Georgia was in the grantor, brings an action of covenant upon this deed, and assigns, as a breach that some of the members of the Legislature were induced to vote in favour of the law, which constituted the contract, by being promised an interest in it, and that therefore the act is a mere nullity.

This solemn question cannot be brought thus collaterally and incidentally before the court. It would be indecent in the extreme, upon a private contract, between two individuals, to enter into an inquiry respecting the corruption of the sovereign power of a State. If the title be plainly deduced from a legislative act, which the Legislature might constitutionally pass, if the act be clothed with all the requisite forms of a law, a court, sitting as a court of law cannot sustain a suit brought by one individual against another founded on the allegation that the act is a nullity in consequence of the impure motives which influenced certain members of the Legislature which passed the law.

The Circuit Court, therefore, did right in overruling this demurrer.

The fourth covenant in the deed is that the title to the premises has been in no way constitutionally or legally impaired by virtue of any subsequent act of any subsequent Legislature of the State of Georgia. . . . The count proceeds to recite at large, this rescinding act, and concludes with averring that, by reason of this act, the title of the said Peck in the premises was constitutionally and legally impaired and rendered null and void.

After protesting, as before, that no such promises were made as stated in this count, the defendant again pleads that himself and the first purchaser under the original grantees, and all intermediate holders of the property, were purchasers without notice. To this plea there is a demurrer and joinder.

The importance and the difficulty of the questions, presented by these pleadings are deeply felt by the Court. The lands in controversy vested absolutely in James Gunn and others, the original grantees, by the conveyance of the Governor, made in pursuance of an act of assembly to which the Legislature was fully competent. Being thus in full possession of the legal estate, they, for a valuable consideration, conveyed portions of the land to those who were willing to purchase. If the original transaction was infected with fraud, these purchasers did not participate in it, and had no notice of it. They were innocent. Yet the Legislature of Georgia has involved them in the fate of the first parties to the transaction, and, if the act be valid, has annihilated their rights also.

The Legislature of Georgia was a party to this transaction, and for a party to pronounce its own deed invalid, whatever cause may be assigned for its invalidity, must be considered as a mere act of power which must find its vindication in a train of reasoning not often heard in courts of justice. . . .

If the Legislature be its own judge in its own case, it would seem equitable that its decision should be regulated by those rules which would have regulated the decision of a judicial tribunal. The question was, in its nature, a question of title, and the tribunal which decided it was either acting in the character of a court of justice, and performing a duty usually assigned to a court, or it was exerting a mere act of power in which it was controlled only by its own will.

If a suit be brought to set aside a conveyance obtained by fraud, and the fraud be clearly proved, the conveyance will be set aside as between the parties, but the rights of third persons who are purchasers without notice, for a valuable consideration, cannot be disregarded. Titles, which, according to every legal test, are perfect are acquired with that confidence which is inspired by the opinion that the purchaser is safe. If there be any concealed defect, arising from the conduct of those who had held the property long before he acquired it, of which he had no notice, that concealed defect cannot be set up against him. He has paid his money for a title good at law; he is innocent, whatever may be the guilt of others, and equity will not subject him to the penalties attached to that guilt. All titles would be insecure, and the intercourse between man and man would be very seriously obstructed if this principle be overturned.

A court of chancery, therefore, had a bill been brought to set aside the conveyance made to James Gunn and others as being obtained by improper practices with the Legislature, whatever might have been its decision as respected the original grantees, would have been bound, by its own rules and by the clearest principles of equity, to leave unmolested those who were purchasers without notice for a valuable consideration.

If the Legislature felt itself absolved from those rules of property which are common to all the citizens of the United States, and from those principles of equity which are acknowledged in all our courts, its act is to be supported by its power alone, and the same power may devest any other individual of his lands if it shall be the will of the Legislature so to exert it.

It is not intended to speak with disrespect of the Legislature of Georgia, or of its acts. Far from it. The question is a general question, and is treated as one. For although such powerful objections to a legislative grant as are alleged against this may not again exist, yet the principle on which alone this rescinding act is to be supported may be applied to every case to which it shall be the will of any legislature to apply it. The principle is this: that a legislature may, by its own act, devest the vested estate of any man whatever, for reasons which shall, by itself, be deemed sufficient. . . .

Is the power of the Legislature competent to the annihilation of such title, and to a resumption of the property thus held?

The principle asserted is that one legislature is competent to repeal any act which a former legislature was competent to pass, and that one legislature cannot abridge the powers of a succeeding legislature.

The correctness of this principle, so far as respects general legislation, can never be controverted. But if an act be done under a law, a succeeding legislature cannot undo it. The past cannot be recalled by the most absolute power. Conveyances have been made, those conveyances have vested legal estate, and, if those estates may be seized by the sovereign authority, still that they originally vested is a fact, and cannot cease to be a fact.

When, then, a law is in its nature a contract, when absolute rights have vested under that contract, a repeal of the law cannot devest those rights; and the act of annulling them, if legitimate, is rendered so by a power applicable to the case of every individual in the community.

. . . Georgia cannot be viewed as a single, unconnected, sovereign power, on whose legislature no other restrictions are imposed than may be found in its own Constitution. She is a part of a large empire; she is a member of the American Union; and that Union has a Constitution the supremacy of which all acknowledge, and which imposes limits to the legislatures of the several States which none claim a right to pass. The Constitution of the United States declares that no State shall pass any bill of attainder, *ex post facto* law, or law impairing the obligation of contracts.

Does the case now under consideration come within this prohibitory section of the Constitution?

In considering this very interesting question, we immediately ask ourselves what is a contract? Is a grant a contract?

A contract is a compact between two or more parties, and is either executory or executed. An executory contract is one in which a party binds himself to do, or not to do, a particular thing; such was the law under which the conveyance was made by the Governor. A contract executed is one in which the object of contract is performed, and this, says Blackstone, differs in nothing from a grant. The contract between Georgia and the purchasers was executed by the grant. A contract executed, as well as one which is executory, contains obligations binding on the parties. A grant, in its own nature, amounts to an extinguishment of the right of the grantor, and implies a contract not to reassert that right. A party is therefore always estopped by his own grant.

Since, then, in fact, a grant is a contract executed, the obligation of which still continues, and since the Constitution uses the general term "contract" without distinguishing between those which are executory and those which are executed, it must be construed to comprehend the latter as well as the former. A law annulling conveyances between individuals, and declaring that the grantors should stand seised of their former estates, notwithstanding those grants, would be as repugnant to the Constitution as a law discharging the vendors of property from the obligation of executing their contracts by conveyances. It would be strange if a contract to convey was secured by the Constitution, while an absolute conveyance remained unprotected. . . .

Whatever respect might have been felt for the State sovereignties, it is not to be disguised that the framers of the Constitution viewed with some apprehension the violent acts which might grow out of the feelings of the moment, and that the people of the United States, in adopting that instrument, have manifested a determination to shield themselves and their property from the effects of those sudden and strong passions to which men are exposed. The restrictions on the legislative power of the States are obviously founded in this sentiment, and the Constitution of the United States contains what may be deemed a bill of rights for the people of each State.

. . . What motive, then, for implying, in words which import a general prohibition to impair the obligation of contracts, an exception in favour of the right to impair the obligation of those contracts into which the State may enter?

The State legislatures can pass no *ex post facto* law. An *ex post facto* law is one which renders an act punishable in a manner in which it was not punishable when it was committed. Such a law may inflict penalties on the person, or may inflict pecuniary penalties which swell the public treasury. The legislature is then prohibited from passing a law by which a man's estate, or any part of it, shall be seized for a crime which was not declared by some previous law to render him liable to that punishment. Why, then, should violence be done to the natural meaning of words for the purpose of leaving to the legislature the power of seizing for public use the estate of an individual in the form of a law annulling the title by which he holds that estate? The Court can perceive no sufficient grounds for making this distinction. This rescinding act would have the effect of an *ex post facto* law. It forfeits the estate of Fletcher for a crime not committed by himself, but by those from whom he purchased.

This cannot be effected in the form of an *ex post facto* law or bill of attainder; why, then, is it allowable in the form of a law annulling the original grant? . . .

It is, then, the unanimous opinion of the Court that, in this case, the estate having passed into the hands of a purchaser for a valuable consideration, without notice, the State of Georgia was restrained, either by general principles which are common to our free institutions or by the particular provisions of the Constitution of the United States, from passing a law whereby the estate of the plaintiff in the premises so purchased could be constitutionally and legally impaired and rendered null and void. . . .

The first covenant in the deed is that the State of Georgia, at the time of the act of the Legislature thereof entitled as aforesaid, was legally seised in fee of the soil thereof subject only to the extinguishment of part of the Indian title thereon.

The fourth count assigns, as a breach of this covenant that the right to the soil was in the United States, and not in Georgia. . . .

The reservation for the use of the Indians appears to be a temporary arrangement suspending for a time the settlement of the country reserved, and the powers of the royal Governor within the territory reserved, but is not conceived to amount to an alteration of the boundaries of the colony. If the language of the proclamation be in itself doubtful, the commissions subsequent thereto which were given to the Governors of Georgia entirely remove the doubt.

The question whether the vacant lands within the United States became a joint property or belonged to the separate States was a momentous question which at one time threatened to shake the American Confederacy to its foundation. This important and dangerous contest has been compromised, and the compromise is not now to be disturbed.

It is the opinion of the Court that the particular land stated in the declaration appears, from this special verdict, to lie within the State of Georgia, and that the State of Georgia had power to grant it.

Some difficulty was produced by the language of the covenant and of the pleadings. It was doubted whether a State can be seised in fee of lands subject to the Indian title, and whether a decision that they were seised in fee might not be construed to amount to a decision that their grantee might maintain an ejectment for them notwithstanding that title.

The majority of the Court is of opinion that the nature of the Indian title, which is certainly to be respected by all Courts until it be legitimately extinguished, is not such as to be absolutely repugnant to seisin in fee on the part of the State.

[The dissenting opinion of Justice JOHNSON is omitted.]

* * *

Until 1934, the Court's decision in *Fletcher v. Peck* limited state economic regulation of business corporations. *See Home Building & Loan v. Blaisdell* (1934) (upholding a state's two-year moratorium on foreclosure of farm mortgages as not violating the contracts clause). Chief Justice Marshall treats a legislative grant of land as a contract and government contracts as functionally comparable to the kinds of private contracts interference with which by the government it was the purpose of the contracts clause to prevent. How relevant do you think it is to this analysis that the "contract" involved land claimed as private property? Perhaps the contracts clause analysis is shadowed here by concerns about taking private property. One difficulty with this reading is that the first taking was from the tribes by the state of Georgia, not the revocation of a government grant of land to speculators. Another is that the case arose in the exercise of diversity jurisdiction. At the time, pre-*Erie*, this meant that the Court "could draw upon general principles of federal law as well as the Constitution for its sources."[55] This is arguably a more sweeping exercise of judicial review than in *Marbury*—state legislation regulating primary social action is struck down, and the Court relies on principles of general law to inform its constitutional analysis.

In 1823, the Court confronted head on the question of the land rights of Native nations in *Johnson v. M'Intosh*. The narrow question in the case was who had a better claim to title over lands within the traditional territories of several Native nations. One party traced their chain of title back to a purported transfer of land rights from the Piankawshaws and the Kaskaskia, Peoria, and Cahokia bands directly. These transfers, which occurred in 1773 and 1775, were clearly illegal under the Proclamation of 1763, by which the English Crown prohibited private parties from buying Native lands. The other party's claim rested upon a transfer of title from the United States, which had acquired its rights by treaty agreement with the tribes. Neither party was Native, and, indeed, neither the Illinois Nation nor the Piankashaw Nation were involved in the litigation, which may well have been collusively structured by land speculators as a test case.[56]

Johnson had broad implications for the U.S. property system and westward settlement. Many U.S. legal and political elites were land speculators themselves or had family members who were. John Marshall was one of them. And it was Marshall, sitting as Chief Justice, who wrote the Court's opinion in *Johnson*. As Marshall often did, he wrote an opinion that said more than was necessary to decide the dispute before him. The Court held that the winning party was the one who claimed title by way of transfer from the United States. Chief Justice Marshall further concluded that the doctrine of discovery is part of U.S. law—a foundational rule of the U.S. property system. This doctrine held that the first European Christians who discovered Indigenous lands held "ultimate title" to those lands, with Indigenous Peoples retaining aboriginal or "Indian" title. This meant that Native nations could not—as a matter of U.S. law, *not* their own laws—validly transfer title to their lands without the involvement of the U.S. government.

---

55. G. Edward White, The Marshall Court and Cultural Change 1815-1835, at 606 (1991).

56. For discussions of the history of *Johnson, see* Stuart Banner, How the Indians Lost Their Land: Law and Power on the Frontier 178-88 (2005); Robertson, *supra* note 54.

Among the most telling passages in the opinion is one that bears upon how we understand judicial review in historical perspective, which is the topic of the next section. "Courts of the conqueror," Chief Justice Marshall wrote, cannot question the chains of title upon which the conqueror's property law is based. Even if the doctrine "may be opposed to natural right, and to the usages of civilized nations, yet, if it be indispensable to that system under which the country has been settled, and be adapted to the actual condition of the two people, it may, perhaps, be supported by reason, and certainly cannot be rejected by Courts of justice."

Chief Justice Marshall did not explain why "Courts of justice" could not question the system under which the U.S. government claimed "ultimate title" to the lands of Native nations. Perhaps Marshall meant to preserve the public legitimacy of the courts. Or perhaps he was wary of questioning U.S. sovereignty. As you read the next section on the politics of judicial review in historical perspective, keep in mind the question that *Johnson* poses: What, in the end, are the federal "Courts of justice" for?

D.   THE POLITICS OF JUDICIAL REVIEW

1.   The Early Republic

Marbury and other Marshall Court cases such as *Fletcher* did not resolve concerns about judicial review and its democratic deficits. Indeed, the power of judicial review has remained hotly contested. In this section we trace a few of the most dominant and recurrent themes, tying them to Chapters in which relevant doctrine will be covered.

Much like the Whig-Federalist lawyers and judges he interviewed when he visited the United States and wrote *Democracy in America*, de Tocqueville was a strong proponent of judicial review. Adjudication conducted by elite lawyers and judges, he and Whig-Federalists believed, would have a leavening effect on popular democratic passions, provide a running civics lesson in deliberative democracy and the rule of law, and check majoritarian excesses of the political branches. Justice Story famously asserted that lawyers and judges serve as "public sentinels" on the ramparts of Republican constitutional government. Judicial review on the terms he and Marshall established on the Court was foundational to this enterprise. It also enabled them to promote the growth of a vibrant, truly national economy.[57]

---

57. *See* WHITE, *supra* note 55, *passim.* On the concept of the lawyer as "public sentinel" see Joseph Story, Discourse Pronounced upon the Inauguration of the Author as Dane Professor of Law in Harvard University (Aug. 25, 1829) ("The lawyer is placed, as it were, upon the outpost of defence, as a public sentinel, to watch the approach of danger, and to sound the alarm, when oppression is at hand. . . . It is then, that . . . the advocate stands alone, to maintain the supremacy of the law against power and numbers, and public applause, and private wealth."), reprinted in PERRY MILLER, ED., THE LEGAL MIND IN AMERICA: FROM INDEPENDENCE TO THE CIVIL WAR 176 (1962).

Jeffersonian-Jacksonian Democrats, by contrast, tended to view litigation as costly, time consuming, unduly complex, and controlled by a monopoly of elites who were unaccountable to the people through democratic channels of governance. Legislatures and local governments represented the voice of the people—the only voice, in their view, that should be controlling in any democracy worthy of the name.

As we will see in Chapter 2, the Supreme Court's authority to review state court judgments was rejected by dozens of states prior to the Civil War and Congress did not give the lower courts general federal question jurisdiction until 1875, so most federal law was adjudicated by state courts in the first instance. Early nineteenth century legislatures also sought to alter the adversary system and the power of legal elites by eliminating judge-controlled standards for entry to the bar (for White men), making state judicial office elective, legislating codes of substantive law to supplant common law doctrine and simplify rules of decision, and legislating sweeping procedural reforms to eliminate the writ system and make the courts more accessible to ordinary people. Democratically enacted codes of substantive law and procedure were designed to make law and the administration of justice reflect the will of the people and constrain judicial review.[58] By the end of the nineteenth century, as the *Lochner* Court repeatedly struck down progressive labor legislation that set wage and hour limits, protected the right to organize and strike, and regulated child labor, progressives again became sharply critical of the Court and federal judicial review of legislation.

Notice two implications of this conflict over judicial review. The first is political: for much of the nation's history progressives viewed the courts, and at times the federal courts in particular, as relatively unfriendly forums for the vindication of their interests. Indeed, many were skeptical of the adversary system as a whole, not just the power of courts to decide the validity of legislation. In the early and mid-twentieth century some of the most vocal defenders of workers' rights and the New Deal on the Court were therefore *proponents* of federalism and legislative power. This is the version of federalism endorsed by Justice Brandeis in *Erie*, eliminating the power of federal judges to substitute their own common law rules of decision in place of state common law when sitting in diversity. See Chapter 5. *Swift v. Tyson* (1842), the case reversed in *Erie*, was authored by Joseph Story and embodied the Whig-Federalist project of developing a nationally uniform body of commercial law through the adjudication of diversity disputes. Justice Brandeis also famously dissented from the Taft Court's decision in *Truax v. Corrigan* (1921) striking down an Arizona statute that prohibited the state's courts from interfering with the First Amendment rights of labor protesters. He wrote separately in *Crowell v. Benson* (1932) as well to insist that there is no structural constitutional barrier in Article III to Congress setting up administrative courts without the guarantees of tenure of office and salary protection for federal judges. *Truax*, the New Deal case reversing it (*Lauf v. Skinner* (1938)), and *Crowell* are examined in Chapter 4.

If federalism appears in the early twenty-first century to serve different political interests, e.g., limiting federal power to protect civil rights, one lesson is that the doctrines of structural constitutional law we study in this course have no fixed or necessary ideological valence.

---

58. Norman W. Spaulding, *The Luxury of the Law: The Codification Movement and the Right to Counsel,* 73 Fordham L. Rev. 983 (2004).

The second implication is jurisprudential: although there is much insight to be gained by looking to the founding era, the text of Article III and the nation's history complicate any claim that the founding era settled debate about the place of judicial review in the federal system. Begin with the text of Article III. On the one hand, it confirms a certain mistrust of states and their courts—diversity jurisdiction is grounded in concern that state courts may be biased against out-of-state litigants; original Supreme Court jurisdiction derives in part from concern that states cannot resolve their mutual disputes without an independent arbiter; and arising under jurisdiction in lower federal courts recognizes that a federal forum may be needed to interpret and enforce federal law. On the other hand, the Madisonian Compromise leaves the scope of lower federal court original jurisdiction and Supreme Court appellate jurisdiction largely to Congress to define.

Beyond the text, history shows that disagreement over whether judicial review is consistent with democratic accountability in rights definition has been amplified and distorted by white supremacy and the institutions of slavery, segregation, and Indian removal which it served. American structural constitutional law cannot be understood if we blink at this or the suffering it has caused. During the antebellum period, slavery, the extension of slavery into the territories in the wake of Indian removal, and the Supreme Court's intervention in the constitutional crises these actions caused, repeatedly embarrassed both Whig-Federalist defenses of judicial review and Jeffersonian-Jacksonian theories of judicial restraint.

The Supreme Court's decision in *Worcester v. Georgia* illustrates these themes. In *Worcester*, the Supreme Court was confronted with a criminal appeal in which the defendant challenged the constitutionality of a Georgia law that prohibited White Americans from entering the territory of the Cherokee Nation without a license from the state.[59] This criminal statute was accompanied by another Georgia law that purported to nullify all laws "made, passed or enacted, by the Cherokee Indians" and to deny any "Indian or descendant of any Indian" the right to testify in Georgia state court in suits in which "a white person may be a party, except such white person resides within the said nation."[60]

Before *Worcester*, the Cherokee Nation had challenged these intrusions upon its sovereignty in federal court in *Cherokee Nation v. Georgia*.[61] The Supreme Court had rejected that suit on the grounds that it lacked jurisdiction under Article III of the Constitution, because it was not a "foreign state." Instead, Chief Justice Marshall opined, Native nations were "domestic dependent nations." Professor Maggie Blackhawk has observed, "Holding to the contrary would have meant that the Supreme Court would become the front line in disputes between Native nations and states. Chief Justice

---

59. "[A]ll white persons residing within the limits of the Cherokee nation, on the 1st day of March next, or at any time thereafter, without a license or permit from his excellency the governor, or from such agent as his excellency the governor shall authorise to grant such permit or license, and who shall not have taken the oath hereinafter required, shall be guilty of a high misdemeanour, and, upon conviction thereof, shall be punished by confinement to the penitentiary at hard labour for a term not less than four years." Worcester v. State of Ga., 31 U.S. 515, 523 (1832).

60. *Id.* at 526.

61. 30 U.S. 1 (1831).

Marshall was willing to position the Court as having some power within Indian affairs to review the conduct of state and national governments, but he approached the power cautiously. It was soon revealed that this caution was warranted."[62]

It was against this backdrop that the Court decided *Worcester*. A White criminal defendant, Samuel Worcester, was arrested for violating the criminal statute banning White persons from being present on Cherokee territory without a Georgia license; he had been on Cherokee territory ministering Christianity without obtaining permission from the state of Georgia. The Supreme Court held that the Georgia law was unconstitutional. Federal law recognized the inherent tribal sovereignty of the Cherokee Nation. The Georgia law violated the Cherokee Nation's sovereignty and thus federal law, as the Supreme Court held.

The Supreme Court's decision in *Worcester* was met with truculent defiance by Georgia officials and by the President of the United States, Andrew Jackson. Georgia officials publicly disavowed the ruling, promising to disregard it.[63] And the year after the decision, President Jackson allowed the state of Georgia to implement a land lottery, in which White settlers could take title to tracks of Cherokee territory for $4.00.[64] Six years later, "federal soldiers and state militiamen forced the Cherokee people down the Trail of Tears to the Oklahoma Territory pursuant to the controversial Treaty of New Echota—a treaty signed not by Cherokee Nation leadership, but by a few individual Cherokee citizens."[65] The dispossession of Native nations from their lands, the assertion of sovereignty by Tribes, and contests over jurisdiction between Tribes, states, and the federal government surface in many federal court doctrines we will cover, most prominently in cases involving justiciability (Chapter 3) and government immunity (Chapter 6).

Andrew Jackson's presidency also had a lasting influence on federal courts law through Chief Justice Roger Taney, who served on the Court from his appointment by President Jackson in 1836 until 1864. He is conventionally lauded for "judicial self-restraint"—for "restrict[ing] the area of judicial discretion in constitutional decision" in order to "leave the maximum of freedom to those agencies of government whose actions he is called upon to weigh."[66] The Taney Court's expansion of political question doctrine as a limitation on federal jurisdiction and its vigorous defense of state police powers are illustrative. They have been described as "potentially healthy checks on the abuse of judicial power, the police-power idea stressing the regulatory power of the legislature and the political-question doctrine serving as a reminder to judges that power, law and order derive ultimately from the people and depend for their legitimacy on the people's consent."[67] The appearance of restraint was, however, aided by the fact that,

---

62. Maggie Blackhawk, *Federal Indian Law as Paradigm Within Public Law*, 132 Harv. L. Rev. 1787, 1821 (2019).

63. Joseph C. Burke, *The Cherokee Cases: A Study in Law, Politics, and Morality*, 21 Stan. L. Rev. 500, 520 (1969).

64. Blackhawk, *supra* note 62, at 1821.

65. *Id.*

66. Bernard Schwartz, A History of the Supreme Court 94 (1993) (quoting Dean Acheson).

67. Harold Hyman & William Wiecek, Equal Justice Under Law: Constitutional Development 1835-1875, at 84 (1982).

[f]or Taney, unlike Marshall, government was more often than not in the hands of political friends. And during the period of Democratic ascendancy from 1829 to 1861, the national government continued to operate within a very narrow functional range, offering little challenge to constitutional limitations. Thus the fact that the Taney Court waited twenty years before declaring an act of Congress unconstitutional must be attributed to lack of provocation rather than to judicial self-restraint. (The Chief Justice would reveal the extent to which he was a judicial activist when control of the federal government passed into hostile Republican hands in 1861.)[68]

Well before that moment, Taney's "intens[e] . . . devotion to the welfare of slavery"[69] and the Court's "consistent disposition to meet the issue head-on" in cases involving the federal Fugitive Slave Acts of 1793 and 1850, and most notoriously in cases concerning the status of slavery in territories seeking admission as states, belied the narrative of self-restraint.[70] At least on issues concerning slavery, Taney showed little self-restraint.[71] The precise role of *Dred Scott* in accelerating sectional conflict is contested among historians, but the range of disagreement concerns only how much the "constitutional cancer" of slavery metastasized as a result of the Supreme Court's intervention and how much the decision diminished the authority of the Court, not whether it did so.[72] In *Dred Scott*, as you may recall from your work in Constitutional Law, the Court struck down the Missouri Compromise, which had declared certain western territories taken from Native nations to be free. The Court also held that enslaved Black persons and their descendants were mere "property," not citizens entitled to the protection of the Privileges and Immunities Clause of the federal constitution. Travel to a free state could not alter this in the Court's view. This conclusion rejected the "*Somerset* principle" according to which "a slave who escaped into a free state might automatically become free because there was no free state law authorizing his continued enslavement."[73]

The sprawling opinion inserted the Court into the center of an already heated sectional conflict, feeding rather than tempering it. And in so doing the Court for the first time struck down a substantive federal statute, no less, a statute that concerned an issue long assumed to lie within the power of Congress (to permit or forbid slavery in the territories). The opinion thus demonstrated "that the Court was firmly committed to the defense of slavery" and was met by a "firestorm of criticism, protest, and resistance."[74] The Court also "undercut" its merits discussion by holding that the Court was without jurisdiction over Scott's appeal.[75] Absent jurisdiction, there was no justification for taking up the sweeping questions about

---

68. DON E. FEHRENBACHER, SLAVERY, LAW, AND POLITICS: THE DRED SCOTT CASE IN HISTORICAL PERSPECTIVE 117 (1981).

69. Hyman & Wiecek, *supra* note 67, at 85.

70. FEHRENBACHER, *supra* note 68, at 119; Hyman & Wiecek, *supra* note 67, at 100.

71. *Id.*

72. FEHRENBACHER, *supra* note 68, at 289-94; Hymand & Wiecek, *supra* note 67, at 13.

73. ETHAN GREENBERG, DRED SCOTT AND THE DANGERS OF A POLITICAL COURT 2 (2009).

74. *Id.* at 2.

75. *Id.* at 109.

the status of slavery in the territories in the first place. The decision left Scott, his wife Harriet and their four children, enslaved to Sandford, a relative of the slaveholder who had brought them to free territory.

2.   *The Civil War and Reconstruction*

Thus far we have offered two different lenses to supplement conventional accounts of Article III that focus primarily on its drafting, ratification, and early Marshall Court decisions. The first draws into relief the broader landscape of professional and popular sentiment about the adversary system and political efforts to limit its role in rights definition and enforcement. Restrictions on federal jurisdiction were but one of a range of checks on the courts. The second foregrounds certain contradictions in the exercise of judicial review elicited by sectional conflict over slavery and conflict among the states, the federal government, and Native nations.

A third lens involves the constitutional status and consequences of the Civil War and Reconstruction. Partly because the Civil War was so bloody, involving greater loss of life than all of America's other wars from the Revolution through World War II and the Korean War combined,[76] partly because many people involved in the Civil War believed they were fighting to "save the Union," not to alter it,[77] and partly because it remains difficult for many Americans to concede that slavery caused such a spectacular rupture in this society and its constitutional project,[78] the relationship between judicial review and the doctrines of federalism and separation of powers

---

76. Drew Gilpin Faust, The Republic of Suffering: Death and the American Civil War xi (2009).

77. Norman W. Spaulding, *Paradoxes of Constitutional Faith: Federalism, Emancipation, and the Original Thirteenth Amendment*, 3 Critical Analysis of Law 306 (2016).

78. "Lost cause" ideology—the foundation of which is the claim that southern states seceded from the Union not to defend slavery but merely to "vindicate state rights"—surged after the Civil War, powerfully influencing not only popular opinion in the South, but in the North. Many Whites were eager to put the war, sectional conflict, and conflict over Reconstruction behind them. Lawyers and judges were influenced by similar sentiments, as well as the work of professional historians who served as apologists for secession. As James McPherson summarizes:

> To concede that the Confederacy had broken up the United States and launched a war that killed 620,000 Americans in a vain attempt to keep four million people in slavery would not confer honor on their lost cause. But in 1861, when slavery flourished and was considered by most Southern whites to be divinely ordained, they had spoken differently. Then, Jefferson Davis, a large slaveholder himself, had justified secession as an act of self-defense against the new Republican administration of Abraham Lincoln, whose policy of excluding slavery from the territories would make "property in slaves so insecure as to be comparatively worthless . . . thereby annihilating in effect property worth thousands of millions of dollars."

To this day, McPherson emphasizes, Civil War Battlefield interpretive staff face visitors who believe that slavery and the war were separate problems and it remains difficult for some Americans "to admit that the noble cause for which their ancestors fought might have included the defense of slavery." James McPherson, *The Heart of the Matter*, N.Y. Rev., Oct. 23, 1997; James Oliver Horton, *Confronting Slavery and Revealing the Lost Cause*, National Park Service, March 10, 2017.

is all too often presented as if the Civil War and the Reconstruction Amendments did not significantly affect structural constitutional law. This can be seen in several conventional interpretive stances.

First, in some instances, both the Court and commentators simply disregard the Civil War, the Reconstruction Amendments, and the retreat from Reconstruction to Jim Crow segregation altogether, skipping over the period as if antebellum constitutional principles extend continuously from the founding to today. As we will see in Chapter 6, this is a standard feature of cases involving the Eleventh Amendment and state sovereign immunity. In *Younger* abstention doctrine, which we will study in Chapter 10, the modern Court refers reverentially to "Our Federalism" as "born in the early struggling days of our Union of States," and as "occupy[ing] a highly important place in our Nation's history and its future"[79] without so much as pausing its reverie to acknowledge that conflict over federalism and its protection of slavery prolonged the institution and caused more than 600,000 deaths in fratricidal warfare, or that federalism doctrine was central to the retreat from Reconstruction and the erection and enforcement of Jim Crow segregation.

Second, when the constitutional crisis of the war and Reconstruction are acknowledged, this all too often occurs on terms that minimize its significance, usually by pointing to the speeches and writings of contemporaries who themselves sought to minimize its significance even as the actions necessary to "save" the Union changed what was saved. Even the many federal jurisdiction cases that arise directly from the constitutional crises of the period tend to be cited and discussed in ways that discourage a full reckoning with the surrounding context. The consensus of modern historians, however, is that the Civil War and Reconstruction Amendments constituted nothing short of a "second revolution."[80] In Chapter 4 we will study *Ex parte McCardle*, the canonical case on congressional power to strip the appellate jurisdiction of the Supreme Court. Although it involves the constitutionality of the Military Reconstruction Act of 1867, the case is all too often presented without grappling with the fact that this statute was essential to the ratification of the Fourteenth Amendment and required breaking up unreconstructed Southern states into military districts subject to federal martial law fully two years after the South's surrender at Appomattox. The case thus implicated the constitutionality of Reconstruction and whether Southern states, which had enacted

---

79. Younger v. Harris, 401 U.S. 37, 44 (1971).

80. ERIC FONER, THE SECOND FOUNDING: HOW THE CIVIL WAR AND RECONSTRUCTION REMADE THE CONSTITUTION (2019); ANDRE M. FLESCHE, THE REVOLUTION OF 1861: THE AMERICAN CIVIL WAR IN THE AGE OF NATIONALIST CONFLICT 6 (2012) ("The American Revolution of 1776 did not create an organic nation. It never decisively answered the question of the compatibility of slavery with republican institutions, or determined what citizenship rights landless laborers should enjoy. Instead, it left a conglomeration of states, each with individual institutions, interests, rights, responsibilities, and approaches regarding race and labor. Nineteenth century Americans recognized as much. The federal constitution of 1787 had strived to create a 'more perfect Union' . . . [but] white southern revolutionaries offered an entirely different answer to the question of American national viability."); JAMES McPHERSON, ABRAHAM LINCOLN AND THE SECOND AMERICAN REVOLUTION (1992); Charles & Mary Beard, *The Second American Revolution*, in THE RISE OF AMERICAN CIVILIZATION 360 (1927).

"Black Codes" to resubordinate newly emancipated Black people, would be allowed back into the Union despite their defiance of the Thirteenth Amendment and the 1866 Civil Rights Act. Ratification of the Fourteenth Amendment was a condition imposed on the readmission of Southern states while they were subject to federal military governance. To read the case as more or less exclusively about congressional power to strip the Supreme Court of its appellate jurisdiction is to obscure one of the most consequential repudiations of antebellum understandings of federalism and separation of powers. Other canonical cases from the period were equally consequential.

Finally, cases from the period are sometimes dismissed as mere curios, or the bitter fruit of exigent circumstances having little relevance to "ordinary" structural constitutional analysis. Even commentators deeply sensitive to the contradictions of slavery revealed in theories of judicial review have been inclined to ask "whether the modern lawyer and scholar must forsake all the slavery cases as too infused with a substantive issue to be of any use in an understanding of our federal system."[81]

We think this is the wrong question. Substance, structure, and procedure are, as we suggested earlier, mutually constitutive. Thus, just as the doctrines of state and federal sovereignty cannot be understood without taking account of tribal sovereignty and incursions upon it by states and the federal government, we believe that federalism and separation of powers cannot be understood if the angle of approach invites cognitive dissonance regarding the Civil War, emancipation, the Reconstruction Amendments, and the retreat from Reconstruction to a near century of Jim Crow segregation. A hermeneutics of avoidance in the study of structural constitutional law regarding our second revolution evacuates the doctrine of both its hardest and most interesting questions, but also its moral weight. The point is *not* that the doctrines of constitutional structure are the mere playthings of substantive law, procedure and circumstance, but rather that any meaningful effort to define and follow first principles of federal judicial power requires awareness of and engagement with these forces.

3.   The Territorial Expansion of the United States and the Plenary Power Doctrine

The territorial expansion of the United States westward and overseas also shaped the role of the federal courts. As it did in the antebellum period, the Supreme Court once again faced constitutional controversies stemming from the settlement of Native lands by non-Natives. With respect to overseas empire, the Court self-consciously and expressly positioned itself in support of "American empire" through a series of cases known as the *Insular Cases*.[82] In both the domestic

---

81. ROBERT COVER, JUSTICE ACCUSED 166 n.* (1975).

82. Downes v. Bidwell, 182 U.S. 244, 279 (1901) (Brown, J., announcing judgment of Court) ("We are also of opinion that the power to acquire territory by treaty implies not only the power to govern such territory, but to prescribe upon what terms the United States will receive its inhabitants, and what their *status* shall be in what Chief Justice Marshall termed the 'American Empire.'").

and overseas cases, the Court adopted plenary power doctrines limiting the role of judicial review and affording Congress freedom to enact laws that otherwise would have violated well-established constitutional rights.

The Supreme Court facilitated the United States' parceling out of Native lands to Western settlers by deferring to Congress's allotment policy. In 1871, the U.S. ended the practice of making formal treaties with Native nations after the House of Representatives, eager to exert more of a role in Indian affairs, attached a rider to an appropriations bill that purported to deny the President the authority to enter into Indian treaties with the advice and consent of the Senate. Beginning in the 1880s, Congress enacted a series of statutes, most prominently the General Allotment Act, that provided for a system of converting the lands of Native nations into individual parcels to be owned in fee simple. The aim was to force assimilation of Native peoples by ending collective land ownership and to distribute so-called "surplus lands" to non-Native settlers. In many cases, the allotment policy conflicted with treaty promises that the United States had made to respect and protect the lands of particular Native nations.

In one such case, *Lone Wolf v. Hitchcock* (1903), the Supreme Court held that Congress had the authority to break treaty promises by providing for the allotment of lands of Native nations. The United States had by treaty promised the Kiowa, Comanche, and Apache Nations that it would recognize and protect their reservation of lands in exchange for, among other things, the transfer of some of their ancestral lands to the U.S. The allotment policy broke that promise by appropriating these lands for individual owners. A group of Tribal leaders and members sued for an injunction against the allotment of their lands, arguing that it violated the Fifth Amendment. The Court denied their request for relief, reasoning that "[p]lenary authority over the tribal relations of the Indians has been exercised by Congress from the beginning, and the power has always been deemed a political one, not subject to be controlled by the judicial department of the government." As we will see in Chapter 6, Congress continues to have broad powers and responsibilities in Indian affairs, as revealed by the Court's treatment of federal-state-Tribal relations and sovereign immunity.

Similarly, in the *Insular Cases* the Court adopted a plenary power doctrine that permitted the U.S. to acquire overseas territories and allowed Congress to legislate for them in ways that would otherwise have violated constitutional law. There is no one *Insular Case*, but rather a series of them involving several different overseas territories of the United States. Among these were Puerto Rico and the Philippines, which the U.S. had acquired through the peace treaty with Spain following the Spanish American War. These cases, which are discussed in detail in Chapters 3 and 4, repudiated the Taney Court's statement in *Dred Scott v. Sandford* that the U.S. government could not hold territories as colonial possessions in perpetuity. Another principle of the *Insular Cases*—that not all U.S. constitutional rights apply in unincorporated territories that are not on the path to statehood—reappears in cases involving federal jurisdiction and the War on Terror, as discussed in Chapter 8.

4. Twentieth and Twenty-First Century Developments

In the twentieth century federal jurisdiction was affected most profoundly not only by *Erie* in the domain of diversity jurisdiction and *Crowell* in the domain of non–Article III adjudication and the massive expansion of administrative agency adjudication it opened (see Chapter 4), but also by the civil rights movement. *Brown v. Board of Education* and the effort to dismantle Jim Crow segregation in institutions beyond public schools had ramifications for:

- lower federal court equity jurisdiction (most prominently the development of the structural reform injunction, see Chapters 2-4),
- appellate jurisdiction over state court judgments that avoided or violated federal law (especially adequate and independent state ground doctrine, see Chapters 2 and 11),
- lower federal court habeas jurisdiction over state court criminal convictions (including rules for procedural default, the retroactivity of new rules of constitutional criminal procedure, and the standards of review, see Chapter 9),
- the remedial power of Reconstruction era civil rights enforcement statutes such as 42 U.S.C. §1983 that had fallen into desuetude for decades (see Chapter 7), and
- private rights of action to enforce federal statutes and the constitution (see Chapter 2).

The persistence of Native nations, and their continuing exercise of sovereignty, have given rise to questions about the authority and legitimacy of the federal courts and their relationship to Tribal governments and Tribal courts, including in the areas of implied private rights of action and sovereign immunity (see Chapter 6). The rise of new constitutional rights claims, such as those at stake in the litigation for marriage equality, have also shaped debates about the proper role of the federal courts.

In the late twentieth and early twenty-first centuries the "second" reconstruction and the recognition of new civil rights claims has been disrupted and in some instances dismantled by a second retreat. To date, the Supreme Court's retreat from enforcement of the Reconstruction Amendments has been achieved for the most part through the use of jurisdictional and procedural rules, rather than outright reversal of landmark New Deal and Warren Court decisions on substantive constitutional rights. In some areas the Supreme Court has acted alone, relying on standing, political question doctrine, expansive government and officer immunity doctrines, strict retroactivity rules in habeas, and above all, a revived emphasis on deference to states and their courts visible in abstention and many other doctrines. In other areas, Congress has used its power over federal jurisdiction to join in, adopting strict constraints on federal jurisdiction and remedial power in the areas of prison conditions, immigration, and habeas litigation (see Chapter 4). While the Court has generally been solicitous of such jurisdiction-limiting legislation, it has repeatedly struck down legislation creating new causes of action designed to enforce the Reconstruction Amendments, to abrogate state sovereign immunity and hold state governments accountable for violations of federal law, and to compliment the enforcement authority of federal agencies with so-called "citizen suits" (see Chapters 3 and 7).

There has not only been a retreat from the second reconstruction but from the legal achievements of the second wave feminist movement that secured reproductive rights alongside other civil rights designed to protect women from discrimination in the workplace and society at large (e.g., Titles VII and IX of the Civil Rights Act and the extension of *Batson v. Kentucky* to gender). Even before the reversal of *Roe v. Wade* by *Dobbs v. Jackson Women's Health Org.* (2022), state legislation in Texas established a private right of action for damages against any doctor in the state who performed an abortion after six weeks of pregnancy—far earlier than the "viability" line drawn by *Roe* for state regulation. *See Whole Woman's Health v. Jackson* (2021). Although the statute plainly violated *Roe*, it was designed to avoid pre-enforcement review in federal court. We take up this case along with the structure of pre-enforcement constitutional challenges to state and federal law in Chapter 6. Reproductive rights cases have been important to the development of modern justiciability doctrine which we examine in Chapter 3.

Heightened partisanship has reduced the frequency of congressional legislation and with it the role of Congress in supervising the federal courts. There have been no new federal judgeships created since the turn of the century, leaving district and circuit courts with a thinner bench to respond to rising dockets. A severe, decades-long funding crisis in state courts has diminished their resources to respond to heavier caseloads. At both the state and federal level this has led to endorsement of alternatives to adjudication in court. The Supreme Court, to give but one example, has dramatically expanded enforcement of the Federal Arbitration Act of 1925—a statute sponsored by both the New York Chamber of Commerce, which sought to promote a more efficient method of dispute resolution for merchants, and early twentieth century progressive lawyers who endorsed alternatives to standard adversary adjudication.[83] The FAA now applies to a vast array of employment and consumer disputes, not just disputes between merchants, displacing not only individual litigation in court but class actions as well. In addition to expanding alternatives to adjudication even when at least one party wants to be in court, both state and federal courts have expanded the power of judges to take cases away from juries for cases that remain in court, reducing the role of a form of popular participation in the administration of justice the founders believed was central to its legitimacy.

State and federal courts are also increasingly experimenting with legal technology grounded in big data, predictive analytics and artificial intelligence to inform and in some instances displace human judgment about everything from bail, parole, and sentencing to civil discovery and, with the adoption of online dispute resolution, the dispositive adjudication of legal claims.[84] Concerns about these innovations include algorithmic bias resulting from bias in the data they rely upon, lack of transparency in how the technology works, and the privatization of the administration of justice as technology entrepreneurs accountable to no standards of due process or judicial ethics increasingly compete with court systems for control of dispute resolution. On the other hand, properly designed systems have the potential to realize Jeffersonian-Jacksonian ambitions of rendering the administration of justice less expensive and complex for ordinary people to navigate.

Counter-terrorism measures adopted by the executive branch following the attacks of September 11, 2001, have drawn the federal courts into a series of disputes over civil liberties, national security policy, and congressional power to foreclose litigation. Precedents established during the Civil War on federal habeas jurisdiction

---

83. Amalia D. Kessler, *Arbitration and Americanization: The Paternalism of Progressive Procedural Reform*, 124 YALE L.J. 2940 (2015).

84. Norman W. Spaulding, *Online Dispute Resolution and the End of Adversarial Justice?*, in LEGAL TECH AND THE FUTURE OF CIVIL JUSTICE (Davud Freeman Engstrom ed., forthcoming 2023).

and the power to suspend the writ of habeas corpus have become newly relevant, as have cases involving Japanese internment and trial by military commission of German spies in World War II. The separation of powers questions raised by cases involving government surveillance, torture, indefinite detention, and religious discrimination against Muslims include the forms of national security enforcement that are properly considered immune from judicial review, the competence of judges to assess the legality of fast-changing national security decisions, the circumstances justifying suspension of the writ of habeas corpus, whether the writ applies to extra-territorial military sites and non-citizens detained at them, and what alternatives to judicial review exist to ensure that ordinary rule of law principles are not indefinitely suspended in a constitutional republic. These cases are taken up in Chapter 9.

In sum, Chief Justice Marshall's admonition that for violations of right there must be a remedy remains as relevant in this century as when he made it to defend the legitimacy of judicial review in 1801. But there is no escaping the fact that the twenty-first century will transform what it means to see justice done. As we turn in the next Section to cases and materials on the modern mechanics of judicial review, think about how you would reconcile the limitations of judicial review explored in the cases with the principle that violations of right require a remedy.

E. ARTICLE III OF THE U.S. CONSTITUTION AND STATUTORY GRANTS OF JURISDICTION

Article III of the U.S. Constitution creates the federal judiciary and defines its powers. Many contemporary issues of federal jurisdiction are debated and decided as questions of how to interpret the text of this Article. In this Section we provide an overview of the basic principles derived from the text. We then turn to the implementation of these principles in the First Judiciary Act of 1789 and describe the development of a three-tiered federal court system.

Article III was a substantial departure from the Articles of Confederation. The Confederation Congress had very limited authority to create courts. The only national court established under the Articles of Confederation was the Court of Appeals in Cases of Capture. This court existed for admiralty cases, specifically for instances in which American ships seized vessels, termed *prizes*, belonging to enemy countries.[85] The Confederation Congress also had the authority to establish courts to punish piracies, but this power was immediately delegated to the states and never exercised at the national level.[86]

The Constitutional Convention recognized the need for a federal judiciary and, in fact, unanimously approved Edmund Randolph's resolution "that a

---

85. John P. Frank, *Historical Bases of the Federal Judicial System*, 13 LAW & CONTEMP. PROBS. 3, 8 (1948).

86. *Id.* Ad hoc tribunals were also created to resolve border disputes between the states. RICHARD H. FALLON, JR., JOHN F. MANNING, DANIEL J. MELTZER & DAVID L. SHAPIRO, HART & WECHSLER'S THE FEDERAL COURTS AND THE FEDERAL SYSTEM 6 n.34 (7th ed. 2015). For example, a court was created by joint consent to resolve a border dispute between Connecticut and Pennsylvania. *Id.*

National Judiciary be established."[87] Article III, as proposed by the Convention and ratified by the states, covers a number of important topics concerning the design and authority of the federal judiciary.

1.   A Mandatory Supreme Court and Congressional Power to Create Lower Courts

First, the initial words of Article III—"the judicial Power of the United States shall be vested"—create a federal judicial system. Although there was substantial disagreement about the appropriate structure and authority of the federal courts, there was a consensus that there should be a national judiciary. As Farrand remarked in his authoritative history of the proceedings of the Constitutional Convention, "[t]hat there should be a national judiciary was readily accepted by all."[88] In large part, federal courts were desired to effectively implement the powers of the national government; there was fear that state courts might not fully enforce and implement federal policies, especially where there was a conflict between federal and state interests.[89] At a minimum, a federal judiciary could help provide the uniform interpretation of the Constitution and laws of the United States. Additionally, federal courts were viewed by some, such as James Madison, as necessary to assure the protection of individual liberties.[90] Finally, there was agreement that a national tribunal was essential to resolve disputes between the states. A peaceful way to settle disagreements over matters such as borders was imperative, and state courts were obviously too parochial to perform this function.

Second, Article III vests the judicial power of the United States "in one supreme Court and in such inferior courts as Congress may from time to time ordain and establish." A major dispute at the Constitutional Convention was whether lower federal courts should exist. The Committee of the Whole, echoing resolutions offered by Randolph, proposed that there should be both a Supreme Court and inferior courts.[91] This proposal drew strong opposition from those who thought it was unnecessary and undesirable to create lower federal courts. Opponents of lower federal courts argued that they were unnecessary because state courts, subject to review by the Supreme Court, were sufficient to protect the interests of the national government. Furthermore, lower federal courts were perceived as an unnecessary expense and a likely intrusion on the sovereignty of the state governments. Farrand explains: "[Inferior courts] were regarded as an encroachment upon the rights of the individual states. It was claimed that the state courts were perfectly competent for the work required, and that it would be quite sufficient to grant an appeal from them to the national supreme court."[92]

---

87. MAX FARRAND, THE RECORDS OF THE FEDERAL CONVENTION 20-23 (1911).

88. MAX FARRAND, THE FRAMING OF THE CONSTITUTION OF THE UNITED STATES 79 (1913).

89. FALLON ET AL., *supra* note 86, at 6 n.30.

90. *Id.*

91. FARRAND, *supra* note 87, at 104-05.

92. FARRAND, *supra* note 88, at 79-80. For example, John Rutledge stated at the Convention, "[T]he State Tribunals might and ought to be left in all cases to decide in the first instance the right of appeal to the supreme national tribunal being sufficient to secure the national rights [and] uniformity of judgments." FARRAND, *supra* note 87, at 124.

But others expressed distrust in the ability and willingness of state courts to uphold federal law. James Madison stated, "Confidence cannot be put in the State Tribunals as guardians of the National authority and interests."[93] Madison argued that state judges were likely to be biased against federal law and could not be trusted, especially in instances where there were conflicting state and federal interests.[94] Appeal to the Supreme Court was claimed to be inadequate to protect federal interests because the number of such appeals would exceed the Court's limited capacity to hear and decide cases.

Thus, the question of whether state courts are equal to federal courts in their willingness and ability to uphold federal law—an issue that continues to be debated and that influences a great many aspects of the law of federal jurisdiction[95]—has its origins in the earliest discussions of the federal judicial power. The proposal to create lower federal courts was initially defeated five votes to four, with two states divided.[96]

Madison and James Wilson then proposed a compromise. They suggested that the Constitution mandate the existence of the Supreme Court but leave it up to Congress whether to create inferior federal courts. They said that "there was a distinction between establishing such tribunals absolutely, and giving a discretion to the Legislature to establish or not establish them."[97] Their proposal was adopted by a vote of eight states to two, with one state divided.[98] Congress, in its first judiciary act, established lower federal courts, and they have existed ever since.[99]

2.   *Judicial Independence: Tenure of Office and Protection Against Diminution of Salary*

Article III assures the independence of the federal judiciary by according all federal judges life tenure, "during good Behaviour," and salaries that cannot be decreased during their time in office. A federal judge must therefore be impeached to be replaced. In the American colonies, judges were appointed by the king of

---

93. FARRAND, *supra* note 88, at 27.

94. *Id.*

95. This question of whether federal courts are equal to state courts in their ability and willingness to protect federal rights is often referred to as the question of the "parity" between federal and state courts. *See* Burt Neuborne, *The Myth of Parity*, 90 HARV. L. REV. 1105 (1977).

96. FARRAND, *supra* note 87, at 125.

97. *Id.*

98. *Id.*

99. There are revisionist views of Article III that argue that the Convention intended for lower federal courts to exist. *See* JULIUS GOEBEL, HISTORY OF THE SUPREME COURT: ANTECEDENTS AND BEGINNINGS TO 1801, at 247 (1971) (arguing that change in wording done by the Committee of Style is responsible for the language that appears to accord Congress discretion to decide whether to create lower federal courts); *see also* Robert N. Clinton, *A Mandatory View of Federal Court Jurisdiction: A Guided Quest for the Original Understanding of Article III*, 132 U. PA. L. REV. 741 (1984). Whether lower federal courts must exist, and under what circumstances, is discussed in Chapter 4.

England and served at his pleasure.[100] There was great dissatisfaction with a court system beholden to the king and unresponsive to the needs of the colonists. The enumeration of grievances in the Declaration of Independence stated that the king "made judges dependent upon his will alone for the tenure of their offices and payment of their salaries."

Important contemporary issues exist with regard to Article III's assurance of life tenure and salary protection.[101] For example, under what circumstances may Congress create tribunals, often termed "legislative courts," in which the judges do not have life tenure and guaranteed salary during their terms of office? This question is vitally important as the federal courts decide just a fraction of the federal issues adjudicated every day by administrative judges who do not have tenure or salary protection. We address this in Chapter 4. Also, may Congress provide methods for disciplining judges short of impeachment? In 1980, Congress adopted a statute that allows federal judicial councils, composed of district and appeals court judges within a circuit, to discipline federal judges by private censure, public censure, temporary suspension of caseloads, and recommendation of impeachment.[102] The constitutionality of this act is uncertain and depends on whether impeachment will be regarded as the exclusive means for disciplining federal judges.[103] On the one hand, there is concern with preserving judicial independence, but on the other, there is a perceived need for a method to discipline judges short of impeachment, which is rarely used, as well as a process to deal with judges who become unfit (e.g., for health reasons). Moreover, proposals have been made in recent years to impose term limits, especially on Supreme Court justices, such as 18-year, non-renewable terms.

3. *Textual Limits on Judicial Power*

Article III defines the federal judicial power in terms of nine categories of "cases" and "controversies." These nine categories listed in section 2 of Article III

---

100. JEROME R. CORSI, JUDICIAL POLITICS: AN INTRODUCTION 104 (1984).

101. Additionally, there is an ongoing debate over the meaning of judicial independence. *See, e.g.*, CHARLES G. GEYH, WHEN COURTS AND CONGRESS COLLIDE: THE STRUGGLE FOR CONTROL OF AMERICA'S JUDICIAL SYSTEM (2006).

102. Judicial Councils Reform and Judicial Conduct and Disability Act of 1980, Pub. L. No. 96-458, 94 Stat. 2035 (1980).

103. *See, e.g.*, Hastings v. Judicial Conference of the United States, 593 F. Supp. 1371 (D.D.C. 1984) (holding the act constitutional), *rev'd*, 770 F.2d 1093 (D.C. Cir. 1985) (holding case was not ripe for adjudication), *cert. denied*, 477 U.S. 904 (1986); In the Matter of Certain Complaints Under Investigation by an Investigating Comm. of the Judicial Council of the Eleventh Circuit, 783 F.2d 1488 (11th Cir. 1986), *cert. denied*, 477 U.S. 904 (1986) (upholding the act as constitutional); Hastings v. Judicial Conference of the United States, 829 F.2d 91 (D.C. Cir. 1987) (holding that the act and recommendation of impeachment by judicial council are constitutional); *see also* Lynn A. Baker, *Note, Unnecessary and Improper: The Judicial Councils Reform and Judicial Conduct and Disability Act of 1980*, 94 YALE L.J. 1117 (1985); Edward Domenic Re, *Judicial Independence and Accountability: The Judicial Councils Reform and Judicial Conduct and Disability Act of 1980*, 8 N. KY. L. REV. 221 (1981).

fall into two major types of provisions.[104] One set of clauses authorizes the federal courts to vindicate and enforce the powers of the federal government. For example, the federal courts have the authority to decide all cases arising under the Constitution, treaties, and laws of the United States. Additionally, the federal courts have the ability to hear all cases in which the United States is a party. The federal government's powers in the area of foreign policy are protected by according the federal courts the authority to hear all cases affecting ambassadors, other public ministers, and consuls; to hear all cases of admiralty and maritime jurisdiction; and to hear cases between a state, or its citizens, and a foreign country or its citizens.

A second set of provisions authorizes the federal courts to serve an interstate umpiring function, resolving disputes between states and their citizens. Thus, Article III gives the federal courts the authority to decide controversies between two or more states, between a state and citizens of another state,[105] between citizens of different states, and between citizens of the same state claiming land in other states.

The Supreme Court has interpreted the terms "cases" and "controversies" as creating important limits on federal judicial power. These restrictions, often grouped under the label *justiciability*, are discussed in Chapter 2. Also, a central question concerning these provisions is whether they create the minimum or the maximum of federal court jurisdiction. Can Congress restrict the jurisdiction of the federal courts to hear controversial matters falling within Article III's enumeration of authority? Alternatively, may Congress expand the federal courts' authority to hear matters that previously were heard in state courts and are not mentioned in Article III? These questions are addressed in Chapter 3, which considers the ability of Congress to control the jurisdiction of the federal courts.

4. *Division of Labor Among the Courts and Other Provisions of Article III*

Article III allocates judicial power between the Supreme Court and the lower federal courts. Article III states that the Supreme Court has original jurisdiction over cases affecting ambassadors, other public ministers and consuls, and those in which a state shall be a party. In all other cases, the Supreme Court is granted appellate jurisdiction, both as to law and fact, subject to "such Exceptions and under such regulations as Congress shall make."

The Supreme Court has held that Congress can give the lower federal courts concurrent jurisdiction even over those matters where the Constitution specifies

---

104. Professor John P. Frank divides the nine categories into three types of provisions: those relating to an effective national government, to international affairs, and to property and trade. Frank, *supra* note 85, at 12-14. Hart and Wechsler divide these nine categories into four types of provisions: vindication of federal authority, foreign affairs, interstate umpiring, and controversies between citizens of different states. FALLON ET AL., *supra* note 86, at 13-18. For a discussion of the purposes behind each provision, see *id.; see also* Frank, *supra* note 85, at 12-28.

105. Some of these provisions were modified by the Eleventh Amendment, which provides that the judicial power of the United States does not extend to cases between a state and citizens of a different state or citizens of foreign nations. The Eleventh Amendment and the issue of sovereign immunity are discussed in detail in Chapter 7.

that the Supreme Court has original jurisdiction.[106] Under contemporary practice, the Supreme Court's original jurisdiction is limited to disputes between two or more states. An unresolved controversial issue is whether Congress may use its power to create exceptions to the Supreme Court's appellate jurisdiction to prevent Supreme Court review in particular areas, such as over state laws regulating abortion or permitting school prayer. This question is discussed in Chapter 4.

Also, Article III prescribes that the trial of all crimes, except in cases of impeachment, shall be by jury. Furthermore, it requires that the trial shall occur in the state where the crime was committed.

Finally, Article III provides that treason shall consist only in "levying war" against the United States or giving aid or comfort to the enemy and that no person shall be convicted of treason except on testimony of two witnesses or on confession in open court. Article III concludes by stating that Congress has the power to prescribe the punishments for treason, but that "no Attainder of Treason shall work corruption of blood, or Forfeiture except during the Life of the Person attained." In other words, the traitor's heirs and descendants may be punished only for their own wrongdoing.

Having surveyed what is included in Article III, it is useful to note what the Framers chose not to adopt. Article III does not expressly accord federal courts the power to declare federal and state laws unconstitutional. There were proposals at the Constitutional Convention to create a Council of Revision, composed of the President and members of the national judiciary. The Council of Revision would have reviewed "every act of the National Legislature before it [went into effect]."[107] The proposal for a Council of Revision was defended as a check on legislative powers and as a vehicle to improve the legislative process,[108] but the proposal was defeated every time it was raised. Opponents successfully argued that it was undesirable to involve the judiciary directly in the lawmaking process.[109]

There have been over two centuries of debate as to whether the rejection of the Council of Revision also was an implicit rejection of the power of the federal courts to declare statutes unconstitutional.[110] It is, however, "increasingly doubtful that any conclusive case can be made one way or the other."[111] Indeed, after

---

106. *See, e.g.,* Ames v. Kansas *ex rel.* Johnston, 111 U.S. 449, 464 (1884) (allowing concurrent jurisdiction over suits by ambassadors).

107. FARRAND, *supra* note 87, at 21 (for a discussion of the proposed Council of Revision, see *id.* at 97-110).

108. FALLON ET AL., *supra* note 86, at 12.

109. FARRAND, *supra* note 88, at 328-329.

110. For arguments that judicial review was intended by the Framers, see, e.g., RAOUL BERGER, CONGRESS V. THE SUPREME COURT (1969); GORDON S. WOOD, THE CREATION OF THE AMERICAN REPUBLIC (1969); Saikrishna B. Prakash & John C. Yoo, *The Origins of Judicial Review,* 70 U. CHI. L. REV. 887 (2003). For arguments that judicial review was not intended by the Framers, see, e.g., WILLIAM WINSLOW CROSSKEY, POLITICS AND THE CONSTITUTION 1008-46 (1953); LOUIS BOUDIANOFF BOUDIN, GOVERNMENT BY JUDICIARY (1932). For a contemporary argument against judicial review, see JAMES MACGREGOR BURNS, PACKING THE COURT: THE RISE OF JUDICIAL POWER AND THE COMING CRISIS OF THE SUPREME COURT 253 (2009).

111. Henry Paul Monaghan, *The Constitution Goes to Harvard,* 13 HARV. C.R.-C.L. L. REV. 117, 125 (1978).

more than 200 years of constitutional judicial review, it no longer is useful to argue whether the Framers intended the federal courts to exercise this authority. The power of the federal courts, and especially of the U.S. Supreme Court, to invalidate unconstitutional laws is an established and integral part of American government.

Also, Article III does not specify the relationship between the jurisdiction of the federal and state courts. The Constitution is unclear whether federal jurisdiction was meant to be exclusive of the states or concurrent with state courts. As discussed in Chapter 2, the practice since 1789 has been to allow state courts to exercise concurrent jurisdiction with federal courts except in instances where Congress specifies that federal courts are to exercise exclusive jurisdiction.

During the ratification process, Article III attracted some opposition, but it was not one of the major targets for attack.[112] Critics focused on the absence of a provision requiring jury trials in civil cases, on the Supreme Court's authority to review on appeal matters of fact as well as issues of law, and especially on the authority for diversity jurisdiction.[113] In the *Federalist Papers*, written to persuade New York to ratify the Constitution, James Madison and Alexander Hamilton wrote a series of essays dealing explicitly with the federal courts, including Hamilton's famous declaration that the courts are the "least dangerous branch" of government.[114] How the federal courts would function and compete with state courts was thus a concern during ratification.

5.   *The Judiciary Act of 1789 and the Structure of the Federal Courts*

The first session of Congress adopted a statute creating lower federal courts and defining the jurisdiction of the federal judiciary. The Judiciary Act of 1789 was crucial in determining the nature of the federal courts.[115] Many decisions made by Congress in adopting this statute have been followed throughout American history. For example, lower federal courts have existed since 1789, although the Constitution leaves their creation up to Congress. Also, by vesting the federal courts with less than the full jurisdiction authorized in Article III, the Judiciary Act established that federal courts may hear a case only if there is both constitutional and statutory authority.[116]

Several provisions of the Judiciary Act have never been changed significantly. For example, the Rules of Decision Act, adopted as §34 of the 1789 law, provides that the "laws of the several states, except where the constitution or treaties of

---

112. Frank, *supra* note 85, at 3 ("the judiciary clauses were almost immune from strenuous criticism or discussion").

113. *Id.*, at 3 n.1.

114. THE FEDERALIST No. 78 (Alexander Hamilton), at 465.

115. Judiciary Act of 1789, ch. 20, 1 Stat. 73, 92. For a particularly important and thorough history of the act, see Charles Warren, *New Light on the History of the Federal Judiciary Act of 1789*, 37 HARV. L. REV. 49 (1923). *See also* FELIX FRANKFURTER & JAMES M. LANDIS, THE BUSINESS OF THE SUPREME COURT (1927).

116. The ability of Congress to control federal court jurisdiction is discussed in Chapter 4. The doctrines concerning federal subject matter jurisdiction are discussed in Chapter 2.

the United States or Acts of Congress shall otherwise require or decide, shall be regarded as rules of decision in civil actions in the courts of the United States."[117] Although the Supreme Court's interpretation of this law has changed markedly over time, this provision is the key reason federal courts apply state law in diversity cases.[118]

Additionally, the Judiciary Act is especially important in understanding the federal court system because of the identity of its drafters. The Supreme Court observed that the act "was passed by the first Congress assembled under the Constitution, many members of which had taken part in framing that instrument, and is contemporaneous and weighty evidence of its true meaning."[119] The primary drafter of the statute was Oliver Ellsworth, previously an important delegate at the Constitutional Convention and later the third chief justice of the United States.

a. Structure of the Judiciary

The Judiciary Act reflected important choices as to both the structure of the federal court system and the appropriate content of its caseload. Structurally, the act created three levels of federal courts. The lowest tier was composed of the federal district courts. At least one such court was created for each state—a practice that continues to this day. The federal district courts had original jurisdiction of admiralty cases, minor civil matters, and civil cases brought by the United States that exceeded more than $100.[120]

The middle level of the federal judiciary was termed the circuit courts. These tribunals were not assigned permanent judges. Rather, the courts were to hold two sessions a year, which were to be staffed by two Supreme Court justices and one district court judge. Soon after its adoption, the act was amended in 1793 to permit circuit courts to be staffed by one Supreme Court justice and one district court judge.[121] The practice of making the Supreme Court justices "ride circuit" (i.e., travel) rather than appointing permanent judges to the courts of appeals continued for more than 100 years. Without a doubt, from the time of its passage, the most criticized aspect of the Judiciary Act of 1789 was the requirement that Supreme Court justices travel around the country serving as circuit court judges.

Three such circuit courts were created for the entire country, encompassing all of the states except Kentucky and Maine, which were considered remote and were the subject of special arrangements.[122] The circuit courts had both original and appellate jurisdiction. These tribunals had original jurisdiction over most federal crimes and over diversity cases worth more than $500. Also, the circuit courts had original jurisdiction for suits brought by the United States with an amount in controversy greater than $500. The circuit courts had appellate

---

117. 28 U.S.C. §1652 (1982). The one change in the Rules of Decision Act since 1789 has been the substitution of the words "civil action" for "trial at common law."

118. See Chapter 5 (discussing the law applied by the federal courts in diversity cases).

119. Wisconsin v. Pelican Ins. Co., 127 U.S. 265, 297 (1888).

120. 1 Stat. 73, §9.

121. Act of Mar. 2, 1793, ch. 22, 1 Stat. 333.

122. *Id.* §§3, 4.

jurisdiction from the district courts in civil cases where more than $50 was at stake, and in admiralty and maritime cases worth more than $300. As these and other amounts in controversy requirements show, from the very beginning, the jurisdiction of the federal courts was restricted to using dollar figures as a proxy for the significance of cases and this meant that even case types otherwise appropriate for federal jurisdiction were decided by state courts if they fell below the amount in controversy.

The Act additionally specified that there would be six Supreme Court justices. The Act granted the Court the original jurisdiction provided by the Constitution and authorized the Supreme Court to hear appeals from the circuit courts in civil cases worth more than $2,000. No authority was granted for the Supreme Court to review criminal convictions. Additionally, in the famous §25, the Act provided for judicial review of the final decisions of the highest state courts that ruled against a federal claimant. Specifically, the Supreme Court had the authority to review final judgments of a state court that ruled a federal treaty or statute invalid, upheld a state law against a claim that it violated federal law, or ruled against any right or privilege claimed under federal law.[123]

In other words, under the Judiciary Act of 1789, federal court review of state court decisions ruling in favor of a person raising a federal law issue was not permitted.

Another precedent-setting practice was the authorization for removal jurisdiction — the ability of the parties to remove certain cases from state to federal court. The Constitution does not speak of removal jurisdiction. Nonetheless, the Judiciary Act of 1789 allowed removal from state to federal courts of cases worth more than $500 involving an alien defendant and of cases where a plaintiff sues in his or her home state court against an out-of-state defendant.[124] Removal jurisdiction has existed ever since.[125]

The most notable omission from the Judiciary Act of 1789 was authority for the federal courts to hear cases arising under the Constitution, treaties, and laws of the United States. No provision created general federal question jurisdiction until 1875. However, congressional statutes on particular topics authorized judicial review of cases arising under those specific enactments.

Although much has changed in the structure of the federal judiciary since 1789, much has remained the same. The framework devised over 200 years ago has been remarkably resilient.

The jurisdiction of the Supreme Court is discussed in detail in Chapters 2 and 11.[126] In the following brief sketch of the evolution of the Supreme Court since 1789, we emphasize a few significant features.

---

123. 1 Stat. 73, §25.

124. *Id.* §12.

125. Removal jurisdiction is currently provided for in 28 U.S.C. §§1441-46 and is discussed in Chapter 2 *infra*.

126. *See also* PAUL ABRAHAM FREUND, THE SUPREME COURT OF THE UNITED STATES (1961); FELIX FRANKFURTER & JAMES LANDIS, THE BUSINESS OF THE SUPREME COURT (1927); CHARLES WARREN, THE SUPREME COURT IN UNITED STATES HISTORY (1922).

b. Changes in Supreme Court Size

The number of Supreme Court justices fluctuated for the first 70 years of American history, but has remained constant at nine since 1869. Initially, six justices were the Supreme Court. This number increased each time a new circuit court was added until ten justices were on the Court in 1864.[127] In 1866, in an effort to prevent beleaguered President Andrew Johnson from making appointments to the Court, the number of justices was reduced to seven.[128] In 1869, after Johnson left office, the number was increased to nine, where it has remained ever since.[129]

The only serious proposal for a change in size since Reconstruction came during the mid-1930s, when President Franklin Roosevelt advocated his famous "court-packing plan."[130] Angry over the Supreme Court's invalidation of New Deal legislation in the midst of the Depression, Roosevelt proposed adding one new justice to the Court for each justice over the age of 70, to a maximum of 15 justices.[131] The effect would have been to allow Roosevelt immediately to appoint a majority of the Court, thus securing approval of his legislative programs. He offered the plan in February 1937, and promoted it during one of his regular radio broadcasts (or "Fireside Chats") on March 9 of that year.[132] However, the plan became unnecessary when, in a decision issued on March 29, 1937, Justice Owen Roberts changed his position and voted to sustain important New Deal legislation.[133] Whether his shift was in response to the pressure of the court-packing plan always will be in dispute; nonetheless, his change of mind will forever be known as "the 'switch in time' that 'saved the nine.'"[134] Despite Roosevelt's immense popularity at the time, the court-packing plan was severely criticized and ultimately even renounced by a Democrat-controlled Senate Judiciary Committee in June 1937.[135] Soon thereafter many vacancies occurred on the Court, allowing Roosevelt to appoint seven new justices between 1937 and 1941, assuring a pro–New Deal majority.

---

127. *See* Act of Mar. 3, 1863, ch. 100, 12 Stat. 784 (adding tenth justice to the Supreme Court).

128. Act of July 23, 1866, ch. 210, 14 Stat. 209.

129. Act of Apr. 10, 1869, ch. 22, 16 Stat. 44.

130. For a discussion of the events surrounding the court-packing plan, see JEFF SHESOL, SUPREME POWER: FRANKLIN ROOSEVELT VS. THE SUPREME COURT (2010).

131. The plan is described, and Roosevelt's speech proposing it excerpted, in GERALD GUNTHER, CONSTITUTIONAL LAW 128-130 (11th ed. 1985).

132. Presidential Comm. on the Sup. Ct. of the U.S., Final Report 54 (2021).

133. West Coast Hotel Co. v. Parrish, 300 U.S. 379 (1937).

134. *See* GUNTHER, *supra* note 131, at 130 n.2 (describing evidence that Justice Roberts actually decided to change positions prior to Roosevelt's announcement of his court-packing plan).

135. SEN. JUD. COMM., 75TH CONG, S. 711, at 13-14 (1st Sess. 1937). The proposal met its final demise in July 1937, following the death of the Senate Majority Leader, a strong proponent of the court-expansion plan. SHESOL, *supra* note 130, at 481-89, 497-500.

In the last few years, there again has been talk, especially among some progressives, about expanding the size of the Supreme Court.[136] In April 2021, President Joseph Biden issued Executive Order 14023, which established The Presidential Commission on the Supreme Court of the United States.[137] According to a contemporaneous White House statement, the Commission's purpose was "to provide an analysis of the principal arguments in the contemporary public debate for and against Supreme Court reform," including on the topics of "the length of service and turnover of justices on the Court" and "the membership and size of the Court."[138] In turn, the Commission canvassed arguments in favor of and against expanding the size of the Court. These arguments included appeals to judicial independence, the need to respond to recently broken norms in the judicial nomination process, judicial independence, and judicial legitimacy.[139] The report did not take a position on whether a court-expansion proposal should be adopted.

c.　Increases in Supreme Court Control Over Its Docket

There has been a trend over the course of American history toward granting the Supreme Court discretion to determine what cases to hear and decide. Initially review was available in the Supreme Court by writ of error, and the Court was obligated to hear all such cases. In 1891, the Court was given discretion to decide whether to review diversity, admiralty, patent, and revenue cases.[140] The statute adopted in 1891 provided that review in such cases was to be by a writ of certiorari, rather than the obligatory writ of error. In other cases, the Court initially had jurisdiction only over state cases in which a federal right had been *denied*, not where the state court had upheld the federal right. In 1914, Congress eliminated this restriction.

In 1925, Congress went further in giving the Supreme Court control over its own docket.[141] In an act known as the "Judges' Bill," Congress divided most of the Court's docket into two categories: appeal and certiorari jurisdiction. Appeals were cases that the Court is obligated to take and decide. In 1988, Congress eliminated virtually all instances of Supreme Court review by appeal.[142] Now almost all cases come to the

---

136. According to the Presidential Commission on the Supreme Court of the United States, "[i]n 2020, more than 400 articles appeared in the New York Times, Wall Street Journal, Washington Post, and USA Today invoking the term "Court packing" in the context of the Supreme Court, in contrast to approximately 100 articles in 2019." Final Report, *supra* note 132, at 76.

137. Exec. Order No. 14023, 86 F.R. 19569.

138. *President Biden to Sign Executive Order Creating the Presidential Commission on the Supreme Court of the United States*, Presidential Statement (Apr. 9, 2021), https://www.whitehouse.gov/briefing-room/statements-releases/2021/04/09/president-biden-to-sign-executive-order-creating-the-presidential-commission-on-the-supreme-court-of-the-united-states/.

139. Final Report, *supra* note 132, at 74-84.

140. Act of Mar. 3, 1891, ch. 517, 26 Stat. 826 (known as the Evarts Act).

141. Act of Feb. 13, 1925, 43 Stat. 940. For a critical examination of the Judges' Act's enactment, see Edward A. Hartnett, *Questioning Certiorari: Some Reflections Seventy-Five Years After the Judges' Bill*, 100 Colum. L. Rev. 1643 (2000).

142. Pub. L. No. 100-352, 102 Stat. 662.

Supreme Court by certiorari, meaning that review is completely discretionary with the Court. This culminated the trend of giving the Supreme Court increasing control over its docket.

d. Enlargement of the Supreme Court's Jurisdiction and the End of Circuit Riding

Another change has been an enlargement of the Supreme Court's jurisdiction. Most notably, under the Judiciary Act of 1789, the Supreme Court could review state court judgments only when there was a final judgment ruling against a claim of a federal right. But in 1914, the Supreme Court was granted authority to hear, by writ of certiorari, cases in which the state court ruled in favor of a claim of a federal right, such as when it ruled a state law unconstitutional or upheld a federal statute.[143]

Finally, and perhaps most important, the responsibility for Supreme Court justices to sit as judges on the circuit courts was eliminated in 1891.[144] Without a doubt, the obligation for Supreme Court justices to "ride circuit" imposed an onerous burden, especially in an age when transportation was often quite difficult.

e. The U.S. Courts of Appeals

Undoubtedly, the most significant change in the structure of the federal courts during the past 200 years has involved the evolution of the courts of appeals. Initially, tribunals known as the circuit courts were created to occupy a place between the district courts and the Supreme Court. Under the Judiciary Act of 1789, the circuit courts exercised both appellate jurisdiction, reviewing decisions of the district courts, and original jurisdiction for most criminal cases and for certain civil cases where the amount in controversy was more than $500.[145] There were no permanent circuit court judges; rather, two Supreme Court justices and one district court judge staffed the circuit courts.

In 1793, the composition of the circuit courts was modified so that a court consisted of one Supreme Court justice and one district court judge.[146] The obvious problem was unresolved disagreements between the two judges. As the country grew, the number of circuits increased, but it was not until 1869 that the first permanent circuit judges were authorized.[147] Under the Act of 1869, one circuit judge was appointed for each circuit. This proved inadequate to deal with the workload, however, and the Supreme Court justices were still required to ride circuit.

In 1891, in the Evarts Act, Congress created new courts of appeals, establishing nine U.S. Courts of Appeals.[148] Each court was assigned two permanent judges, and the third judge in each case was to be either a district court judge or a Supreme Court justice. Also, for the first time, district court judges were prohibited from reviewing their own decisions when serving as appeals court judges. It should be

---

143. Act of Dec. 23, 1914, ch. 2, 38 Stat. 790.
144. The Evarts Act, 26 Stat. 826, 827, §3.
145. Act of Sept. 24, 1789, ch. 20, 1 Stat. 73, 78, §11.
146. Act of Mar. 2, 1793, ch. 22, 1 Stat. 333.
147. Act of Apr. 10, 1869, ch. 22, 16 Stat. 44.
148. The Evarts Act, 26 Stat. 826.

noted that the Evarts Act did not abolish the circuit courts; it transferred their appellate jurisdiction to the courts of appeals, but retained the circuit courts for cases for which they had original jurisdiction. In 1911, the circuit courts were eliminated, and their original jurisdictions were transferred to the district courts.[149]

The structure for the courts of appeals has remained essentially the same since they were established in 1891. Today, there are thirteen circuits. Eleven, numbered the first through the eleventh, cover specific geographic areas, each including district courts in more than one state. The U.S. Court of Appeals for the District of Columbia Circuit hears appeals from the U.S. District Court for the District of Columbia and is assigned, by statute, the responsibility of reviewing the decisions of many administrative agencies.[150] Finally, in 1982, Congress created the U.S. Court of Appeals for the Federal Circuit.[151] This court assumed the appellate jurisdiction previously assigned to the Court of Customs and Patent Appeals and the Court of Claims.[152] Additionally, the Federal Circuit has exclusive jurisdiction to hear appeals in patent, trademark, and plant variety cases.[153] The Federal Circuit also decides a variety of other matters, including reviewing decisions of the U.S. Court of International Trade, decisions on matters of law made by the secretary of commerce under the Tariff Schedules, decisions of the Merit Systems Protection Board, and decisions of an agency board of contract appeals.[154]

At times there have been proposals to divide the Ninth Circuit into two circuits,[155] as was done when the Fifth Circuit was split into the current Fifth and Eleventh Circuits. Although the Ninth Circuit is the largest in terms of number of judges and covers a vast geographic area, dividing the circuit is politically controversial as there is disagreement over whether the large size presents a significant problem and how the circuit could be best split.

The courts of appeals have obligatory jurisdiction to hear appeals from all final decisions of the district courts of the United States.[156] Although in limited instances the Supreme Court can review directly decisions of a district court, the usual practice is for appellate review to occur in the U.S. courts of appeals.

---

149. Act of Mar. 3, 1911, ch. 1, 36 Stat. 1087.

150. *See* 28 U.S.C. §§41, 43 (1982).

151. Federal Courts Improvement Act of 1982, Pub. L. No. 97-164, 96 Stat. 25.

152. 28 U.S.C. §1295 (1982).

153. *Id.*

154. 28 U.S.C. §1295(a)(6), (7), (9), (10) (1982).

155. In 1998, a Commission on Structural Alternatives for the Federal Courts of Appeals was considering the issue of splitting the Ninth Circuit. Created by federal law and with its members appointed by Chief Justice Rehnquist, the commission issued its report in 1998. The commission, chaired by former Supreme Court Justice Byron White, proposed retention of the Ninth Circuit's current size and boundaries, but proposed dividing the circuit into three regional divisions, with each having between seven and eleven judges. COMM. ON STRUCTURAL ALTERNATIVES FOR THE FED. CT. OF APPEALS, FINAL REPORT (1998). For criticisms of this proposal, see Carl Tobias, *The Unkindest Cut: The White Commission Proposal to Restructure the Ninth Circuit,* 73 S. CAL. L. REV. 377 (2000); Proctor Hug, *The Commission on Structural Alternatives for the Federal Court of Appeals' Report: An Analysis of the Commission's Recommendations for the Ninth Circuit,* 32 U.C. DAVIS L. REV. 887 (1999).

156. 28 U.S.C. §1291 (1982).

f. The U.S. District Courts

Federal district courts are the primary courts of original jurisdiction in the federal system. Cases are filed initially in the district courts, except for limited instances in which the Supreme Court has original jurisdiction and in which the courts of appeals directly review the decisions of federal administrative agencies.[157] There are 94 federal district courts.[158] Every state has at least one federal district court; larger states are divided into several districts. The territorial authority of federal district courts does not cross state lines.[159]

There have been two major changes in the federal district courts over time. First, there have been revisions in their subject matter jurisdiction. For example, the amount in controversy requirement in diversity cases has been increased, most recently in excess of $75,000.[160] This change was in response to proposals to increase the amount in light of the substantial inflation that has occurred over the past 30 years.[161] More important, in 1875, federal district courts were given subject matter jurisdiction to hear cases arising under the Constitution, laws, and treaties of the United States.[162] The general federal question jurisdiction is widely regarded as the most important aspect of federal court authority. Until 1980 federal question cases also had an amount in controversy requirement. The subject matter jurisdiction of the federal district courts is discussed in detail in Chapter 5.

A second major modification in the federal district courts was the use of three-judge courts, especially in instances in which injunctions were sought to halt allegedly unconstitutional government practices. Three-judge district courts were first authorized by the Expediting Act of 1903, which provided for these courts to be convened for antitrust suits brought by the U.S. government, litigation under acts regulating commerce, and instances where the U.S. attorney general deemed such courts to be appropriate.[163] A major expansion in the use of three-judge courts occurred in 1910, when Congress mandated their use in suits seeking to enjoin state officers from enforcing allegedly unconstitutional laws.[164] In 1937, the use of three-judge courts was expanded to include suits seeking injunctions to halt actions by federal officers enforcing allegedly unconstitutional federal laws.[165] The decisions of three-judge courts were reviewable, by appeal, to the U.S. Supreme Court.

---

157. For a discussion of the original jurisdiction of the U.S. Supreme Court, see Chapter 9 *infra.*

158. 28 U.S.C. §133 (1982).

159. The only exception to this is the district court for Wyoming, which has jurisdiction over the parts of Yellowstone National Park that are in Montana and Idaho. *See* CHARLES ALAN WRIGHT, LAW OF FEDERAL COURTS 8 n.3 (4th ed. 1983).

160. Federal Courts Improvement Act of 1996, Pub. L. No. 104-317, §205, 110 Stat. 3847.

161. *See, e.g.,* RICHARD A. POSNER, THE FEDERAL COURTS: CHALLENGE AND REFORM 131-33 (1996).

162. Act of Mar. 3, 1875, ch. 137, 18 Stat. 470.

163. Act of Feb. 11, 1903, ch. 544, 32 Stat. 823. Soon after the enactment of this law, three-judge courts were authorized for review of decisions of the Interstate Commerce Commission. Act of June 29, 1906, ch. 3591, 34 Stat. 584.

164. Act of June 18, 1910, ch. 309, 36 Stat. 539, 557, §17.

165. Act of Aug. 24, 1937, ch. 754, 50 Stat. 751.

In 1976, in response to many proposals to eliminate the multi-judge format, Congress repealed the statutes providing for three-judge courts in constitutional cases.[166] There remain, however, a few statutes directing the use of three-judge courts in specific circumstances. Federal laws require three-judge courts when there is a challenge to the apportionment of congressional districts or any statewide legislative body.[167] Also, the Civil Rights Act of 1964 provides for a three-judge court upon application of the attorney general of the United States.[168] The Voting Rights Act of 1965 provides for three-judge courts for several types of legal challenges to state and local election arrangements.[169] The Regional Rail Reorganization Act,[170] the Bipartisan Campaign Finance Reform Act of 2002, and the Prison Litigation Reform Act also have provisions authorizing the use of three-judge courts.[171] Decisions of these three-judge courts may be directly appealed to the U.S. Supreme Court.[172] There have been calls for restoration of the three-judge system in litigation seeking to enjoin federal agency action in the wake of a dramatic expansion of suits brought by state attorneys general of one party against the federal government when the White House is held by another party. These so-called "nationwide injunctions" are often filed in district courts selected by the plaintiffs on partisan grounds. In recent years, challenges to more liberal policies of Democratic presidents have often been filed in districts in Texas and suits seeking injunctions against the policies of President Trump were often filed in federal district courts in California,[173] with critics raising the charge of forum-shopping by state attorneys general.

The major proposal for change in the district courts is the repeatedly advanced suggestion to eliminate diversity jurisdiction. Diversity jurisdiction, and the arguments for and against retaining it, are discussed in Chapter 2.

g.   Specialized Federal Courts

Many federal courts are authorized to adjudicate only specific matters, such as bankruptcy or tax cases. Additionally, independent regulatory agencies and administrative bodies often are empowered to adjudicate questions arising under federal law. Frequently, these judges or administrative officials are not accorded life tenure or the protection against decreases in salary guaranteed judges under Article III. These tribunals are termed "non-Article III courts" or "legislative courts." Chapter 4 focuses on the situations in which it is permissible to establish such courts.

Four types of legislative courts exist. Each is briefly described here and discussed in detail in Chapter 4. First, legislative courts long have been used for federal territories

---

166. Act of Aug. 12, 1976, Pub. L. No. 94-381, 90 Stat. 1119.

167. 28 U.S.C. §2284 (1985).

168. 42 U.S.C. §2000a-5 (1985).

169. *See, e.g.,* 42 U.S.C. §1971(g) (1982).

170. 45 U.S.C. §701 (1982).

171. Pub. L. No. 107-155, 116 Stat. 181 (2002).

172. 28 U.S.C. §1253 (1982) provides for direct appeal from three-judge courts. Also, many of the specific statutes providing for three-judge courts also provide for appeal to the U.S. Supreme Court.

173. *See* Multistate Litigation Database, https://attorneysgeneral.org/multistate-lawsuits-vs-the-federal-government/list-of-lawsuits-1980-present/.

and the District of Columbia.[174] For example, there are federal courts in which the judges lack life tenure in the Canal Zone, Guam, the Northern Mariana Islands, and the Virgin Islands.[175] In addition, the District of Columbia Superior Court and the District of Columbia Court of Appeals are courts created by Congress to handle matters arising in the District of Columbia that typically would be raised in state courts.[176]

Second, there are specialized courts for the military in which judges lack life tenure. Such courts have existed since early in America's history.

Third, there are legislative courts for civil disputes between the government and private citizens. For example, a Court of Claims has long existed to hear monetary claims, other than for torts, against the United States.[177] After some uncertainty, the Supreme Court decided that the Court of Claims was an Article III court because its judges were accorded life tenure and salary protections.[178] The Federal Courts Improvement Act of 1982 divided the Court of Claims jurisdiction, giving its appellate jurisdiction to the new U.S. Court of Appeals for the Federal Circuit and according its trial jurisdiction to a new Claims Court, which is a legislative court.[179]

Another specialized court that exists to resolve civil disputes between the federal government and private citizens is the Court of International Trade, which exists to resolve disputes arising from import transactions.[180] The U.S. Tax Court is a legislative court whose judges sit for 15-year terms.[181] The Tax Court has jurisdiction to decide taxpayer challenges to deficiency determinations made by the Internal Revenue Service.

Fourth and finally, there are courts that exist as adjuncts to the federal district courts and resolve private civil disputes and even some criminal matters. For example, bankruptcy courts and federal magistrates decide a wide variety of federal law matters even though the bankruptcy judges and magistrates do not have life tenure, but instead sit for 14- and 8-year terms, respectively. The permissible scope of jurisdiction for these courts is discussed in detail in Chapter 4.

Numerically, agency and legislative courts handle vastly more federal litigation than the Article III courts. Practically speaking, it is not clear how the business of the federal government could be conducted or the needs of federal right holders and regulation met without reliance on these courts, especially since the federal courts' workload problem is already acute. In the setting of bankruptcy alone, efficiently processing millions of bankruptcy claims by consumers is essential to economic recovery and the fresh start bankruptcy law holds out. Even if every district court judge in the country dedicated all their energies to these cases, they could not make even a fractional contribution to the overall bankruptcy docket given how many cases

---

174. *See, e.g.*, American Ins. Co. v. Canter, 26 U.S. 511 (1828); see Chapter 2, *infra*.

175. 48 U.S.C. §§1406, 1424, 1694.

176. District of Columbia Reform and Criminal Procedure Act of 1970, Pub. L. No. 91-358, 84 Stat. 473.

177. 28 U.S.C. §§171-175 (1982).

178. *See* Glidden Co. v. Zdanok, 370 U.S. 530 (1962). The earlier decision holding that the Court of Claims was a legislative court was Williams v. United States, 289 U.S. 553 (1933).

179. Pub. L. No. 97-164, 96 Stat. 25.

180. 28 U.S.C. §§1581-1585 (1985).

181. 26 U.S.C. §§6213, 7441-7487 (1986).

are filed every year. Thus, a case can be made to significantly expand the number and type of bankruptcy and other specialized courts.[182] But the loss of generalist judges, and the danger in some areas of having judges likely drawn from the industry most affected by their decisions, raises the specter of special interest capture.[183] The modern Supreme Court has also demanded that specialized courts handle only the narrow subject matter unique to their specialized jurisdiction. In areas such as bankruptcy, this poses real problems because a bankrupt estate can involve many common law issues such as contracts, property, trusts and estates, tort claims, etc. The Court has also struggled to develop a coherent constitutional framework for testing congressional power to create non-Article III courts, leaving Congress uncertain of the value of their judgments.

F.   CONCLUSION: FEDERAL COURTS AND BATTLES OVER THE LEGITIMACY OF JUDICIAL REVIEW

If nothing else, the history of federal courts makes clear that debates about federal jurisdiction are also debates about the proper role of courts in a democratic society. These debates are not simply about the meaning of the "Judicial Power" in Article III. Indeed, calling them "debates" wrongly suggests that they take place only in courtrooms or lecture halls. To the contrary, political battles over the legitimacy of judicial review are sometimes fought far from 1 First Street, where the Supreme Court has sat since 1935. To understand the law of federal jurisdiction, then, it is not enough to consult the text of the Constitution. It is necessary to consider the federal courts in the contexts of the always political, and often politicized, contests over the legitimacy of judicial review.

There is no better illustration than the battles over the best known of the Supreme Court's decisions: *Brown v. Board of Education* (1954). In the following case, the Court addressed overt defiance of its holding in *Brown* by the executive and legislative branches of the state of Arkansas and a local school board seeking to further delay implementation of lower federal court injunctions requiring desegregation. The controversy boiled over when nine Black high school students—Ernest Green, Elizabeth Eckford, Jefferson Thomas, Terrence Roberts, Carlotta Walls LaNier, Minnijean Brown, Gloria Ray Karlmark, Thelma Mothershed, and Melba Pattillo Beals—sought to enroll in and integrate the then

---

182. *See* Ellen R. Jordan, *Specialized Courts: A Choice?*, 76 Nw. U. L. Rev. 745 (1981). The Federal Courts Study Committee proposed creating an Article I court for disability claims and the creation of an Article III appellate division of the U.S. Tax Court with exclusive jurisdiction over appeals in federal income, estate, and gift taxation claims. Report of the Federal Courts Study Committee 55-60, 69-72 (1990).

183. For a careful analysis of when specialized courts seem particularly useful and especially undesirable, see Richard L. Revesz, *Specialized Courts and the Administrative Lawmaking System*, 138 U. Pa. L. Rev. 1111 (1990). For an excellent criticism of the growth of Article I courts, see Judith Resnik, *Trial as Error, Jurisdiction as Injury: Transforming the Meaning of Article III*, 113 Harv. L. Rev. 924 (2000).

all-White Little Rock Central High School. Seeking to prevent their attendance, the Governor called out the national guard and ordered them to physically block the students from entering. White supremacists gathered at the school and spat on the students as they attempted to enter. President Eisenhower countermanded that order, invoking the Insurrection Act of 1807 to federalize the national guard and ordering them to support integration. Even after the national guard helped ensure the students could attend, they were subject to regular verbal and physical abuse by their White peers (acid was thrown in the face of Melba Patillo Beals and White girls in a school restroom threw burning paper at her hair). *See* Beals, *Warriors Don't Cry* (1994). Controversy over the so-called "Little Rock Nine" prompted the school board to seek a 30-month delay of the broader desegregation order until 1961. In the meantime, the school district explored ways to privatize in order to avoid desegregation altogether. The intervention of the national guard received continuous national media coverage, and the Court undoubtedly was well aware of the depth of resistance to *Brown* in Arkansas when the case came up on appeal.

Cooper v. Aaron

358 U.S. 1 (1958)

Opinion of the Court by THE CHIEF JUSTICE.

As this case reaches us it raises questions of the highest importance to the maintenance of our federal system of government. It necessarily involves a claim by the Governor and Legislature of a State that there is no duty on state officials to obey federal court orders resting on this Court's considered interpretation of the United States Constitution. Specifically it involves actions by the Governor and Legislature of Arkansas upon the premise that they are not bound by our holding in *Brown v. Board of Education*, (1954). That holding was that the Fourteenth Amendment forbids States to use their governmental powers to bar children on racial grounds from attending schools where there is state participation through any arrangement, management, funds or property. We are urged to uphold a suspension of the Little Rock School Board's plan to do away with segregated public schools in Little Rock until state laws and efforts to upset and nullify our holding in *Brown v. Board of Education* have been further challenged and tested in the courts. We reject these contentions.

On February 20, 1958, the School Board and the Superintendent of Schools filed a petition in the District Court seeking a postponement of their program for desegregation. Their position in essence was that because of extreme public hostility, which they stated had been engendered largely by the official attitudes and actions of the Governor and the Legislature, the maintenance of a sound educational program at Central High School, with the Negro students in attendance, would be impossible. The Board therefore proposed that the Negro students already admitted to the school be withdrawn and sent to segregated schools, and that all further steps to carry out the Board's desegregation program be postponed for a period later suggested by the Board to be two and one-half years.

After a hearing the District Court granted the relief requested by the Board. Among other things the court found that the past year at Central High School had been attended by conditions of "chaos, bedlam and turmoil;" that there were "repeated incidents of more or less serious violence directed against the Negro students and their property;" that there was "tension and unrest among the school administrators, the class-room teachers, the pupils, and the latters' parents, which inevitably had an adverse effect upon the educational program;" that a school official was threatened with violence; that a "serious financial burden" had been cast on the School District; that the education of the students had suffered "and under existing conditions will continue to suffer;" that the Board would continue to need "military assistance or its equivalent;" that the local police department would not be able "to detail enough men to afford the necessary protection;" and that the situation was "intolerable."

The Negro respondents appealed to the Court of Appeals for the Eighth Circuit. The Court of Appeals . . . , after convening in special session on August 4 and hearing the appeal, reversed the District Court.

We have accepted the findings of the District Court as to the conditions at Central High School during the 1957-1958 school year, and also the findings that the educational progress of all the students, white and colored, of that school has suffered and will continue to suffer if the conditions which prevailed last year are permitted to continue. The significance of these findings, however, is to be considered in light of the fact, indisputably revealed by the record before us, that the conditions they depict are directly traceable to the actions of legislators and executive officials of the State of Arkansas, taken in their official capacities, which reflect their own determination to resist this Court's decision in the *Brown* case and which have brought about violent resistance to that decision in Arkansas.

The constitutional rights of respondents are not to be sacrificed or yielded to the violence and disorder which have followed upon the actions of the Governor and Legislature. Thus law and order are not here to be preserved by depriving the Negro children of their constitutional rights. The record before us clearly establishes that the growth of the Board's difficulties to a magnitude beyond its unaided power to control is the product of state action. Those difficulties, as counsel for the Board forthrightly conceded on the oral argument in this Court, can also be brought under control by state action.

The controlling legal principles are plain. The command of the Fourteenth Amendment is that no "State" shall deny to any person within its jurisdiction the equal protection of the laws.

> A State acts by its legislative, its executive, or its judicial authorities. It can act in no other way. The constitutional provision, therefore, must mean that no agency of the State, or of the officers or agents by whom its powers are exerted, shall deny to any person within its jurisdiction the equal protection of the laws. Whoever, by virtue of public position under a State government, * * * denies or takes away the equal protection of the laws, violates the constitutional inhibition; and as he acts in the name and for the State, and is clothed with the State's power, his act is that of the State. This must be so, or the constitutional prohibition has no meaning.

Ex parte Virginia (1879). In short, the constitutional rights of children not to be discriminated against in school admission on grounds of race or color declared by this Court in the *Brown* case can neither be nullified openly and directly by state legislators or state executive or judicial officers, nor nullified indirectly by them through evasive schemes for segregation whether attempted "ingeniously or ingenuously."

What has been said, in the light of the facts developed, is enough to dispose of the case. However, we should answer the premise of the actions of the Governor and Legislature that they are not bound by our holding in the *Brown* case. It is necessary only to recall some basic constitutional propositions which are settled doctrine.

Article VI of the Constitution makes the Constitution the "supreme Law of the Land." In 1803, Chief Justice Marshall, speaking for a unanimous Court, referring to the Constitution as "the fundamental and paramount law of the nation," declared in the notable case of *Marbury v. Madison* (1803), that "It is emphatically the province and duty of the judicial department to say what the law is." This decision declared the basic principle that the federal judiciary is supreme in the exposition of the law of the Constitution, and that principle has ever since been respected by this Court and the Country as a permanent and indispensable feature of our constitutional system. It follows that the interpretation of the Fourteenth Amendment enunciated by this Court in the *Brown* case is the supreme law of the land, and Art. VI of the Constitution makes it of binding effect on the States "any Thing in the Constitution or Laws of any State to the Contrary notwithstanding." Every state legislator and executive and judicial officer is solemnly committed by oath taken pursuant to Art. VI, ¶3 "to support this Constitution." Chief Justice Taney, speaking for a unanimous Court in 1859, said that this requirement reflected the framers' "anxiety to preserve it [the Constitution] in full force, in all its powers, and to guard against resistance to or evasion of its authority, on the part of a State." *Ableman v. Booth* (1859). No state legislator or executive or judicial officer can war against the Constitution without violating his undertaking to support it.

It is, of course, quite true that the responsibility for public education is primarily the concern of the States, but it is equally true that such responsibilities, like all other state activity, must be exercised consistently with federal constitutional requirements as they apply to state action. The Constitution created a government dedicated to equal justice under law. The Fourteenth Amendment embodied and emphasized that ideal. Since the first *Brown* opinion three new Justices have come to the Court. They are at one with the Justices still on the Court who participated in that basic decision as to its correctness, and that decision is now unanimously reaffirmed. The principles announced in that decision and the obedience of the States to them, according to the command of the Constitution, are indispensable for the protection of the freedoms guaranteed by our fundamental charter for all of us. Our constitutional ideal of equal justice under law is thus made a living truth.

* * *

Ultimately, the law of federal jurisdiction is about what role the federal courts should play in the American system of government. That inevitably turns on what we want our government to be and to do. The doctrines you will learn in this course thus are not sealed off from the underlying merits of disputes that raise questions about federal jurisdiction. They raise profound questions about what justice is and how to achieve it—questions that we can see clearly when we read the cases in their contexts.

CHAPTER 2

INVOKING THE AUTHORITY OF THE FEDERAL COURTS

Article III vests the "judicial Power of the United States" in the Supreme Court and in lower federal courts that "Congress may from time to time ordain and establish." Sections 2 and 3 of Article III make clear that *all* federal courts are courts of limited subject matter jurisdiction, "carefully restricted to those causes which are manifestly proper for the cognizance of the national judicature."[1] For instance, the jurisdiction of the lower federal courts is limited to the specific heads of subject matter jurisdiction recognized in Section 2 and Congress must legislate not only to "ordain and establish" these courts, but also to confer the judicial power Article III makes available. The heads of jurisdiction recognized in Section 2 are:

- all cases, in law and equity, arising under this Constitution, the laws of the United States, and treaties made, or which shall be made, under their authority;
- all cases affecting ambassadors, other public ministers and consuls;
- all cases of admiralty and maritime jurisdiction;
- controversies to which the United States shall be a party;
- controversies between two or more states; between a state and citizens of another state; between citizens of different states; between citizens of the same state claiming lands under grants of different states; and between a state, or the citizens thereof, and foreign states, citizens, or subjects.

Is there a consistent thread to these various heads of jurisdiction? At least some in the founding generation thought that federal jurisdiction was important in those cases and controversies where states might be biased or otherwise incapable of fairly administering federal law. As Alexander Hamilton put it, concern about "the prevalency of a local spirit" might "disqualify" state courts or make them "improper channels of the judicial authority of the Union" in the eyes of Congress or litigants.[2] Justice Story was quite blunt about the risk of bias in state courts: "The constitution," he admonished, "has presumed (whether rightly or wrongly we do not inquire) that state attachments, state prejudices, state jealousies, and

---

1. THE FEDERALIST No. 81 (Alexander Hamilton).
2. *Id.*

state interests, might sometimes obstruct, or control, or be supposed to obstruct or control, the regular administration of justice."[3]

Diversity jurisdiction, for instance, was established to mitigate the risk of local prejudice in state courts against citizens of other states; alienage jurisdiction to deal with the concern that "foreigners cannot get justice done them" in state courts due to parochial bias.[4] Jurisdiction over federal questions is also grounded in concern about whether state courts will faithfully apply, or resist and otherwise undermine, federal law. Alexander Hamilton observed:

> The States, by the plan of the convention, are prohibited from doing a variety of things, some of which are incompatible with the interests of the Union, and others with the principles of good government. . . . No man of sense will believe, that such prohibitions would be scrupulously regarded, without some effectual power in the government to retrain or correct the infractions of them. This power must . . . be . . . an authority in the federal courts to overrule such as might be in manifest contravention of the articles of Union. . . . The mere necessity of uniformity in the interpretation of the national laws decides the question. Thirteen independent courts of final jurisdiction over the same causes, arising upon the same laws, is a hydra in government, from which nothing but contradiction and confusion can proceed.[5]

In Section A of this Chapter, we start with a few of the most commonly invoked heads of federal district court jurisdiction: cases that "arise under" federal law, *see* 28 U.S.C. §1331; diversity jurisdiction ("controversies between citizens of different states"), *see* 28 U.S.C. §1332(a)(1); and alienage jurisdiction, *see* 28 U.S.C. §1332(a)(2) & (3). We then turn to related topics such as the power of a federal court to exercise "supplemental" jurisdiction over state law claims if it already has proper jurisdiction over a case, *see* 28 U.S.C. §1367, the power to remove a case from state to federal court, focusing on federal officer removal, *see* 28 U.S.C. §1441 and §1442, and the strong presumption that state courts have concurrent jurisdiction of federal questions rather than such jurisdiction being exclusive to the federal courts.

In Section B of this Chapter, we turn to the statutory limits on taking appeals to the federal Circuit Courts, focusing on the final judgment rule, *see* 28 U.S.C. §1291, and exceptions such as the collateral order doctrine that allow appeals of interlocutory rulings of the district courts.

The Supreme Court's original jurisdiction is conferred directly by Article III and extends to "cases affecting ambassadors, other public ministers and consuls, and those in which a state shall be party." Article III, Section 3. It has appellate jurisdiction as to "all the other cases before mentioned" in Section 2, but Congress is given authority to set "exceptions" and "regulations," and so the power of the Supreme Court to review cases decided by state courts and the lower federal courts may

---

3. Martin v. Hunter's Lessee, 14 U.S. 304 (1816).

4. JONATHAN ELLIOTT, THE DEBATES IN THE SEVERAL STATE CONVENTIONS ON THE ADOPTION OF THE FEDERAL CONSTITUTION 583 (1836).

5. THE FEDERALIST No. 80.

be (and since the First Judiciary Act of 1789, always has been) limited by Congress.[6] The jurisdictional statutes and internal limits the Supreme Court has developed for its appellate jurisdiction are covered in Chapter 9. We mention them here simply to highlight the parallel between congressional control of the Supreme Court's appellate jurisdiction and congressional control of lower federal court jurisdiction.

The jurisdiction of *all* federal courts is further limited by the "case or controversy" requirement of Article III, Section I. A range of judicially developed doctrines known as "justiciability" rules enforce this limitation: the prohibition on advisory opinions, standing, ripeness, mootness, and political question doctrine. These are discussed in Chapter 3. Whether Congress may withdraw or "strip" jurisdiction previously conferred is taken up in Chapter 4. The limited circumstances in which federal courts may develop their own "common law" rules of decision are examined in Chapter 5.

As we proceed, it is important to remember that subject matter jurisdiction is just one of the essential prerequisites that must be met for a federal right holder or other interested party to sue in federal court. Generally, Congress must not only create jurisdiction but also create a cause of action, designating a private suit as one of the permissible modes of enforcement of the federal right. Not every federal right travels with a private right of action. Congress might, for instance, prefer that a federal agency have *exclusive* authority to design and manage enforcement or that federal agency enforcement be complimented by *state* causes of action that incorporate federal regulatory standards. Whether a statute, or the Constitution itself, requires a cause of action for individually effective redress in a judicial forum for the violation of a federal right *when Congress is silent on the matter* presents fundamental questions about the nature of the federal right and the role of the courts. The modern Supreme Court has not only narrowly construed Congress's power to create express federal rights of action, it has declined to "imply" federal causes of action from either legislation or the Constitution itself, and imposed limits on the power of federal district courts to hear state causes of action that raise necessary and substantial federal issues. These principles operate in the background of cases we cover in this Chapter, especially *Grable & Sons v. Darue Eng'g & Mfg.* (2005), in Section A.1. Express and implied rights of action are covered in greater detail in Chapter 5.

Notice, too, the sweeping implications of the rules for invoking federal judicial power. First, Congress has broad control over the forum of litigation (e.g., state courts, state courts with a right of removal, federal courts, concurrent jurisdiction in state and federal courts, interlocutory appeal from the court of first instance, and appeal to the Supreme Court). Second, Congress also has discretion to choose from a range of enforcement mechanisms (e.g., private rights of action, agency rulemaking, agency enforcement, and both private and agency enforcement) and

---

6. Section 25 of the First Judiciary Act limited appellate jurisdiction to state court decisions of federal law "against their validity" and state court decisions "in favor of [the] validity" of state law where a party challenged it as "repugnant to the constitution, treaties, or laws of the United States." The effect was to preclude appellate jurisdiction where the state courts upheld the federal right or the federal challenge to state law until amendments in 1914 expanded the Court's appellate jurisdiction to cover state decisions upholding federal rights.

remedies (e.g., at law, equity, declaratory relief, etc.). Third, even when Congress, as the Court in *Grable* puts it, "lays out the welcome mat" for federal litigation, there must be a justiciable case or controversy and the Supreme Court, not Congress, defines justiciability rules. Animating the cases and statutes we will examine are profound debates about federalism, especially state court fidelity to the supremacy of federal law, the deference federal courts owe on separation of powers grounds to congressional judgments and Article II agency decisions about enforcement of federal rights, and the connection between federal rights, judicial review, and individually effective remedies for federal right holders.

A.   THE SUBJECT MATTER JURISDICTION OF THE FEDERAL DISTRICT COURTS

1.   Federal Question Jurisdiction

The first clause of Section 2 of Article III provides that "judicial Power shall extend to all Cases, in Law and equity, arising under this Constitution, the Laws of the United States, and Treaties made, or which shall be made, under their Authority." This language raises at least two questions regarding subject matter jurisdiction over federal question cases. First, what does it mean for a case to "arise under" federal law? Second, has Congress extended to the district courts some or all of the constitutionally available judicial power for suits arising under federal law?

It may be helpful to imagine a spectrum, on one end of which are cases that *only* concern federal law—*pure federal law* cases in which there is no state law. On the other end, imagine cases that rest *entirely* on state law—*pure state law* cases involving no federal questions of any kind. In the middle are "mixed" cases resting on, for example, a state cause of action involving federal law relevant to the plaintiff's claim (e.g. a state malpractice claim regarding a lawyer's handling of a federal civil rights or copyright case), a federal defense to a state law cause of action (e.g., a state breach of contract claim where the defendant argues the contract is void under a federal statute), a federal cause of action to which a state claim is joined, or a federal cause of action as to which some aspect of state law is incorporated in or necessary to decide the case.

A suit that rests purely on state law obviously cannot "arise under" federal law within the meaning of Article III. A suit that rests entirely on federal law, by contrast, obviously "arises under" federal law, but it may be adjudicated by the lower federal courts only if Congress has legislated to permit the lower federal courts to exercise this judicial power. Notably, Congress did not legislate 28 U.S.C. §1331—the general federal question statute—until Reconstruction in 1875. Congress also separately recognized jurisdiction in the federal district courts during Reconstruction for certain civil rights suits in 28 U.S.C. §1343. Prior to these statutes, federal questions other than those as to which Congress provided for exclusive federal jurisdiction had to be litigated in the state courts.

Although arising under jurisdiction is conventionally presented outside its historical context and great emphasis is laid on the fact that there was no general federal question jurisdiction before 1875, the Reconstruction context of the jurisdictional grant is important. The Constitution was fundamentally revised by the Reconstruction Amendments in an effort to secure equal treatment for Black people and prevent the kinds of systematic state defiance of federal law that led to the Civil War—a bloodletting in which more Americans died than in all other military conflicts of the eighteenth century to the Korean War *combined*. The expansion of lower federal court jurisdiction was central to the efforts of the Reconstruction Congress to enforce the Reconstruction Amendments and restore the rule of law as Southern states and their courts refused to accept the outcome of the war and the civil rights of Black people. As one commentator summarized the jurisdictional achievements of the Reconstruction Congress:

> In no comparable period of our nation's history have the federal courts, lower and Supreme, enjoyed as great an expansion of their jurisdiction as they did in the years of Reconstruction, 1863 to 1876. The jurisdiction was enlarged in five ways. . . .
>
> First, Congress permitted many cases that had begun in state courts to be taken out of them and tried in federal courts. This procedure, known as "removal," first gave the federal courts new responsibilities for protecting the rights of Negroes and federal officials in the South. It was later used by corporations seeking to evade the hostility of Granger juries in state courts by resorting to the more sympathetic purlieus of the federal courts. Second, Congress extended the habeas corpus powers of the federal courts and transformed the nature of the Great Writ itself. Third, Congress organized a new federal court, the United States Court of Claims, to handle claims against the federal government, and allowed appeals to go from it to the United States Supreme Court. Fourth, Congress enacted a bankruptcy law which transferred much of the individual corporate insolvency business from the state courts to the federal courts. By creating a claims court and making federal district judges bankruptcy arbiters, Congress gave the federal courts wide powers to regulate the national economy. Finally, Congress redefined the limits of federal jurisdiction over "federal questions"—broadly speaking, questions arising under the laws, Constitution, or treaties of the United States. . . . The result by 1876 was clear: Congress had determined to expand the power of the federal courts, sometimes at its own expense, more often at the states', to make them partners in implementing national policy.[7]

Granting federal courts the power to hear all cases "arising under" federal law was particularly significant because it included not just pure federal law cases but "mixed" cases, giving the federal courts jurisdiction to protect federal interests and federal right holders even when the cause of action in a case was not federal. Wiecek's reference to "Granger juries" hints at a remarkable Jim Crow era drift in the exercise of this jurisdiction away from protecting the civil rights of Black people toward the use of the Fourteenth Amendment as a federal anvil upon which state regulation of corporations would be drawn. Everything from rate regulation

---

7. William Wiecek, *The Reconstruction of Federal Judicial Power, 1863-1876*, 13 AM. J. LEGAL HIST., 333-34 (1969).

of railroads to progressive state laws protecting wages, hours, and other workers' rights in the emerging mass industrial economy would be swept into federal court in this way.

Mixed cases thus draw into sharp relief the federalism consequences of the definition of "arising under" jurisdiction and Congress's extension of this judicial power to the lower federal courts. The broader the definition of what it means for a case to "arise under" Article III and §1331, the more *state* law can be pulled into federal courts. The narrower the definition, the more *federal* law will be adjudicated in the first instance in the state courts, subject to the rules for supplemental jurisdiction and removal we discuss in Sections 3 and 4 below, and (where litigation instead proceeds in state court) the appellate jurisdiction of the Supreme Court.

We begin with the basics. For a federal court to hear a case, there must be *both* constitutional and statutory authority. The definition of "arising under" jurisdiction in Article III is given by the Court in *Osborn v. Bank of the United States.* We then turn to what it means for a case to "arise under" federal law within the meaning of the statutory grant of subject matter jurisdiction in §1331. As we will see, Congress has never given all of the constitutionally available judicial power over federal questions to the federal district courts, but they nevertheless have jurisdiction over many mixed cases.

Osborn grew out of an extended, hotly contested dispute over the constitutionality of the Bank of the United States in the early nineteenth century and, more immediately, an economic downturn that caused state governments to attempt to use taxation of the Bank to support state bank lending to state residents.[8] The Bank obtained an injunction to prevent the Auditor of the State of Ohio from levying a state tax against the Bank under a state law that also permitted seizure of Bank assets to satisfy the tax. Having been duly served with the injunction, agents of Osborn nevertheless "proceeded by violence to the office of the Bank at Chilicothe, and took therefrom 100,000 dollars, in specie and bank notes, belonging to, or in deposit with [the Bank]" and delivered it to the state Treasurer. Upon learning of this, the Bank added the state Treasurer as a defendant and the district court amended the injunction to require the money seized be restored to the Bank.

---

8. The legal historian James Willard Hurst described the First and Second Bank of the United States as enjoying "great leverage on state banks and on the general economy by their charter authority to receive deposits of moneys paid to the federal government and to pay out federal funds. In this role the banks became the largest recipients and disbursers of money in the country. They also thus achieved a strategic position vis à vis the state banks, for the quantity of state bank notes taken in payments to the United States gave the national institutions the means of exerting pressure by demanding redemption of the notes in specie. [Branches of the Bank could also] effect[] throughout the country such monetary policies as its central management might adopt." A LEGAL HISTORY OF MONEY IN THE UNITED STATES, 1774-1970, at 160 (2001). Together with its decision in *McCulloch v. Maryland* (1819), the Supreme Court in *Osborn* "unreservedly acknowledged that Congress had constitutional warrant to take affirmative leadership in monetary policy, free of state interference." *Id.* at 174.

Osborn v. Bank of the United States

22 U.S. 738 (1824)

Chief Justice MARSHALL delivered the opinion of the Court, and, after stating the case, proceeded as follows:

At the close of the argument, a point was suggested [regarding] the right of the Bank to sue in the courts of the United States.

The appellants contest the jurisdiction of the Court on two grounds:

1st. That the act of Congress has not given it.

2d. That, under the Constitution, Congress cannot give it.

1. The first part of the objection depends entirely on the language of the act. The words are that the Bank shall be "made able and capable in law," "to sue and be sued, plead and be impleaded, answer and be answered, defend and be defended, in all state courts having competent jurisdiction, and in any circuit court of the United States."

These words seem to the Court to admit of but one interpretation. They cannot be made plainer by explanation. They give, expressly, the right "to sue and be sued," "in every circuit court of the United States," and it would be difficult to substitute other terms which would be more direct and appropriate for the purpose. The argument of the appellants is founded on the opinion of this Court in *Bank of the United States v. Deveaux* (1809). In that case, it was decided that the former Bank of the United States was not enabled, by the act which incorporated it, to sue in the federal courts. The words of the third section of that act are that the Bank may "sue and be sued," &c. "in courts of record, or any other place whatsoever." The Court was of opinion that these general words, which are usual in all acts of incorporation, gave only a general capacity to sue, not a particular privilege to sue in the courts of the United States, and this opinion was strengthened by the circumstance that the ninth rule of the seventh section of the same act subjects the directors, in case of excess in contracting debt, to be sued in their private capacity, "in any court of record of the United States, or either of them." The express grant of jurisdiction to the federal courts, in this case, was considered as having some influence on the construction of the general words of the third section, which does not mention those courts. Whether this decision be right or wrong, it amounts only to a declaration that a general capacity in the Bank to sue, without mentioning the courts of the Union, may not give a right to sue in those courts. To infer from this that words expressly conferring a right to sue in those courts, do not give the right, is surely a conclusion which the premises do not warrant.

The act of incorporation, then, confers jurisdiction on the circuit courts of the United States, if Congress can confer it.

2. We will now consider the constitutionality of the clause in the act of incorporation, which authorizes the Bank to sue in the federal courts.

In support of this clause, it is said that the legislative, executive, and judicial powers, of every well constructed government, are coextensive with each other; that is, they are potentially coextensive. The executive department may constitutionally execute every law which the legislature may constitutionally make, and the judicial department may receive from the legislature the power of construing every such law. All governments which are not extremely defective in their organization must possess within themselves the means of expounding, as well as enforcing, their own laws. If we examine the Constitution of the United States, we find that its framers kept this great political principle in view. The second article vests the whole executive power in the President; and the third article declares:

> that the judicial power shall extend to all cases in law and equity arising under this Constitution, the laws of the United States, and treaties made, or which shall be made, under their authority.

This clause enables the judicial department to receive jurisdiction to the full extent of the Constitution, laws, and treaties of the United States, when any question respecting them shall assume such a form that the judicial power is capable of acting on it. That power is capable of acting only when the subject is submitted to it by a party who asserts his rights in the form prescribed by law. It then becomes a case, and the Constitution declares that the judicial power shall extend to all cases arising under the Constitution, laws, and treaties of the United States.

The suit of *Bank of the United States v. Osborn* and others, is a case, and the question is whether it arises under a law of the United States?

The appellants contend that it does not, because several questions may arise in it which depend on the general principles of the law, not on any act of Congress.

If this were sufficient to withdraw a case from the jurisdiction of the federal courts, almost every case, although involving the construction of a law, would be withdrawn, and a clause in the Constitution, relating to a subject of vital importance to the government, and expressed in the most comprehensive terms, would be construed to mean almost nothing. There is scarcely any case every part of which depends on the Constitution, laws, or treaties of the United States. The questions whether the fact alleged as the foundation of the action be real or fictitious; whether the conduct of the plaintiff has been such as to entitle him to maintain his action, whether his right is barred, whether he has received satisfaction or has in any manner released his claims, are questions some or all of which may occur in almost every case, and if their existence be sufficient to arrest the jurisdiction of the Court, words which seem intended to be as extensive as the Constitution, laws, and treaties of the Union, which seem designed to give the courts of the government the construction of all its acts, so far as they affect the rights of individuals, would be reduced to almost nothing.

In those cases in which original jurisdiction is given to the Supreme Court, the judicial power of the United States cannot be exercised in its appellate form. In every other case, the power is to be exercised in its original or appellate form, or both, as the wisdom of Congress may direct. With the exception of these cases, in which original jurisdiction is given to this Court, there is none to which the judicial power extends from which the original jurisdiction of the inferior courts is excluded by the Constitution. Original jurisdiction, so far as the Constitution gives a rule, is coextensive with the judicial power. We find, in the Constitution, no prohibition to its exercise, in every case in which the judicial power can be exercised. It would be a very bold construction to say that this power could be applied in its appellate form only, to the most important class of cases to which it is applicable.

The Constitution establishes the Supreme Court, and defines its jurisdiction. It enumerates cases in which its jurisdiction is original and exclusive; and then defines that which is appellate, but does not insinuate that in any such case, the power cannot be exercised in its original form by courts of original jurisdiction. . . .

We perceive, then, no ground on which the proposition can be maintained that Congress is incapable of giving the circuit courts original jurisdiction in any case to which the appellate jurisdiction extends.

We ask, then, if it can be sufficient to exclude this jurisdiction that the case involves questions depending on general principles? A cause may depend on several questions of fact and law. Some of these may depend on the construction of a law of the United States; others on principles unconnected with that law. If it be a sufficient foundation for jurisdiction that the title or right set up by the party may be defeated by one construction of the Constitution or law of the United States, and sustained by the opposite construction, provided the facts necessary to support the action be made out, then all the other questions must be decided as incidental to this, which gives that jurisdiction. Those other questions cannot arrest the proceedings. Under this construction, the judicial power of the Union extends effectively and beneficially to that most important class of cases which depend on the character of the cause. On the opposite construction, the judicial power never can be extended to a whole case, as expressed by the Constitution, but to those parts of cases only which present the particular question involving the construction of the Constitution or the law. We say it never can be extended to the whole case because, if the circumstance that other points are involved in it shall disable Congress from authorizing the courts of the Union to take jurisdiction of the original cause, it equally disables Congress from authorizing those courts to take jurisdiction of the whole cause on an appeal, and thus will be restricted to a single question in that cause, and words obviously intended to secure to those who claim rights under the Constitution, laws, or treaties of the United States, a trial in the federal courts, will be restricted to the insecure remedy of an appeal upon an insulated point, after it has received that shape which may be given to it by another tribunal into which he is forced against his will.

We think, then that when a question to which the judicial power of the Union is extended by the Constitution forms an ingredient of the original cause, it is in the power of Congress to give the circuit courts jurisdiction of that cause, although other questions of fact or of law may be involved in it.

The case of the Bank is, we think, a very strong case of this description. The charter of incorporation not only creates it, but gives it every faculty which it possesses. The power to acquire rights of any description, to transact business of any description, to make contracts of any description, to sue on those contracts, is given and measured by its charter, and that charter is a law of the United States. This being can acquire no right, make no contract, bring no suit, which is not authorized by a law of the United States. It is not only itself the mere creature of a law, but all its actions and all its rights are dependant on the same law. Can a being thus constituted have a case which does not arise literally, as well as substantially, under the law?

Take the case of a contract, which is put as the strongest against the Bank.

When a Bank sues, the first question which presents itself, and which lies at the foundation of the cause, is has this legal entity a right to sue? Has it a right to come, not into this Court particularly, but into any court? This depends on a law of the United States. The next question is, has this being a right to make this particular contract? If this question be decided in the negative, the cause is determined against the plaintiff; and this question, too, depends entirely on a law of the United States. These are important questions, and they exist in every possible case. The right to sue, if decided once, is decided forever; but the power of Congress was exercised antecedently to the first decision on that right, and if it was constitutional then, it cannot cease to be so because the particular question is decided. It may be revived at the will of the party, and most probably would be renewed were the tribunal to be changed. But the question respecting the right to make a particular contract, or to acquire a particular property, or to sue on account of a particular injury, belongs to every particular case, and may be renewed in every case. The question forms an original ingredient in every cause. Whether it be in fact relied on or not in the defence, it is still a part of the cause, and may be relied on. The right of the plaintiff to sue cannot depend on the defence which the defendant may choose to set up. His right to sue is anterior to that defence, and must depend on the state of things when the action is brought. The questions which the case involves, then, must determine its character, whether those questions be made in the cause or not.

The appellants say that the case arises on the contract, but the validity of the contract depends on a law of the United States, and the plaintiff is compelled in every case to show its validity. The case arises emphatically under the law. The act of Congress is its foundation. The contract could never have been made but under the authority of that act. The act itself is the first ingredient in the case, is its origin, is that from which every other part arises. That other questions may also arise as the execution of the contract or its performance cannot change the case, or give it any other origin than the charter of incorporation. The action still originates in, and is sustained by, that charter.

The clause giving the Bank a right to sue in the circuit courts of the United States stands on the same principle with the acts authorizing officers of the United States who sue in their own names, to sue in the courts of the United States. The Postmaster General, for example, cannot sue under that part of the Constitution which gives jurisdiction to the federal courts in consequence of the character of the party, nor is he authorized to sue by the Judiciary Act. He comes into the courts of the Union under the authority of an act of Congress the constitutionality of which can only be sustained by the admission that his suit is a case arising under a law of the United States. If it be said that it is such a case because a law of the United States authorizes the contract, and authorizes the suit, the same reasons exist with respect to a suit brought by the Bank. That, too, is such a case, because that suit, too, is itself authorized, and is brought on a contract authorized by a law of the United States. It depends absolutely on that law, and cannot exist a moment without its authority.

If it be said that a suit brought by the Bank may depend in fact altogether on questions unconnected with any law of the United States, it is equally true with respect to suits brought by the Postmaster General. The plea in bar may be payment, if the suit be brought on a bond, or nonassumpsit, if it be brought on an open account, and no other question may arise than what respects the complete discharge of the demand. Yet the constitutionality of the act authorizing the Postmaster General to sue in the courts of the United States has never been drawn into question. It is sustained singly by an act of Congress, standing on that construction of the

Constitution which asserts the right of the legislature to give original jurisdiction to the circuit courts in cases arising under a law of the United States.

The clause in the patent law authorizing suits in the circuit courts stands, we think, on the same principle. Such a suit is a case arising under a law of the United States. Yet the defendant may not, at the trial, question the validity of the patent, or make any point which requires the construction of an act of Congress. He may rest his defence exclusively on the fact that he has not violated the right of the plaintiff. That this fact becomes the sole question made in the cause cannot oust the jurisdiction of the Court, or establish the position that the case does not arise under a law of the United States.

It is said that a clear distinction exists between the party and the cause; that the party may originate under a law with which the cause has no connexion; and that Congress may, with the same propriety, give a naturalized citizen, who is the mere creature of a law, a right to sue in the courts of the United States as give that right to the Bank.

This distinction is not denied; and, if the act of Congress was a simple act of incorporation, and contained nothing more, it might be entitled to great consideration. But the act does not stop with incorporating the Bank. It proceeds to bestow upon the being it has made all the faculties and capacities which that being possesses. Every act of the Bank grows out of this law and is tested by it. To use the language of the Constitution, every act of the Bank arises out of this law.

A naturalized citizen is indeed made a citizen under an act of Congress, but the act does not proceed to give, to regulate, or to prescribe his capacities. He becomes a member of the society, possessing all the rights of a native citizen, and standing, in the view of the Constitution, on the footing of a native. The Constitution does not authorize Congress to enlarge or abridge those rights. The simple power of the national legislature is to prescribe a uniform rule of naturalization, and the exercise of this power exhausts it so far as respects the individual. The Constitution then takes him up, and, among other rights, extends to him the capacity of suing in the courts of the United States precisely under the same circumstances under which a native might sue. He is distinguishable in nothing from a native citizen except so far as the Constitution makes the distinction. The law makes none.

There is, then, no resemblance between the act incorporating the Bank and the general naturalization law.

Upon the best consideration we have been able to bestow on this subject, we are of opinion that the clause in the act of incorporation, enabling the Bank to sue in the courts of the United States is consistent with the Constitution, and to be obeyed in all courts.

We will now proceed to consider the merits of the cause. . . .

We think, then that there is no error in the decree of the circuit court for the district of Ohio, so far as it directs restitution of the specific sum of ninety-eight thousand dollars, which was taken out of the Bank unlawfully, and was in the possession of the defendant Samuel Sullivan when the injunction was awarded in September, 1820, to restrain him from paying it away or in any manner using it; and so far as it directs the payment of the remaining sum of two thousand dollars by the defendants, Ralph Osborne and John L. Harper. . . . The decree of the circuit court for the district of Ohio is affirmed as to the said sums of ninety-eight thousand dollars and two thousand dollars, and reversed, as to the residue.

Mr. Justice JOHNSON [dissenting].

The argument in this cause presents three questions: 1. Has Congress granted to the Bank of the United States, an unlimited right of suing in the courts of the United States? 2. Could Congress constitutionally grant such a right? and 3. Has the power of the court been legally and constitutionally exercised in this suit?

. . . The Bank of the United States is now identified with the administration of the national government. It is an immense machine, economically and beneficially applied to the fiscal transactions of the nation. Attempts have been made to dispense with it, and they have failed; serious and very weighty doubts have been entertained of its constitutionality, but they have been abandoned; and it is now become the functionary that collects, the depository that holds, the vehicle that transports, the guard that protects, and the agent that distributes and pays away, the millions that pass annually through the national Treasury; and all this not only without expense to the government, but after paying a large bonus, and sustaining actual annual losses to a large amount; furnishing the only possible means of embodying the most ample security for so immense a charge. . . .

In the present instance, I cannot persuade myself that the Constitution sanctions the vesting of the right of action in this Bank . . . merely on the ground that a question might possibly be raised in it involving the Constitution or constitutionality of a law of the United States. . . .

[A]s was justly insisted in argument, there is not a tract of land in the United States, acquired under laws of the United States, whatever be the number of mesne transfers that it may have undergone, over which the jurisdiction of the courts of the United States might not be extended by Congress upon the very principle on which the right of suit in this Bank is here maintained. Nor is the case of the alien, put in argument, at all inapplicable. The one acquires its character of individual property, as the other does his political existence, under a law of the United States; and there is not a suit which may be instituted to recover the one, nor an action of ejectment to be brought by the other, in which a right acquired under a law of the United States does not lie as essentially at the basis of the right of action, as in the suits brought by this Bank. . . .

My own conclusion is . . . that the Bank may, by its corporate name and metaphysical existence, bring suit, or personate the natural man, in the courts specified, as though it were in fact a natural person; that is, in those cases in which, according to existing laws, suits may be brought in the courts specified respectively.

I next proceed to consider more distinctly the constitutional question on the right to vest the jurisdiction to the extent here contended for. . . .

Efforts have been made to fix the precise sense of the Constitution when it vests jurisdiction in the general government in "cases arising under the laws of the United States." To me, the question appears susceptible of a very simple solution—that all depends upon the identity of the case supposed—according to which idea, a case may be such in its very existence, or it may become such in its progress. An action may "live, move, and have its being," in a law of the United States; such is that given for the violation of a patent right, and four or five different actions given by this act of incorporation, particularly that against the President and Directors for over-issuing, in all of which cases the plaintiff must count upon the law itself as the ground of his action. And of the other description, would have been an action of trespass, in this case, had remedy been sought for an actual levy of the tax imposed. Such was the case of the former Bank against Deveaux, and many others that have occurred in this Court, in which the suit, in its form, was such as occur in ordinary cases, but *in which the pleadings or evidence raised the question on the law or Constitution of the United States.* In this class of cases, the occurrence of a question makes the case, and transfers it . . . to the jurisdiction of the United States. And this appears to me to present the only sound and practical construction of the Constitution on this subject, for no other cases does it regard as necessary to place under the control of the general government. It is only when the case exhibits one or the other of these characteristics that it is acted upon by the Constitution. Where no question is raised, there can be no contrariety of construction; and what else had the Constitution to guard against? . . . [U]ntil the plaintiff can control the defendant in his pleadings, I see no practical mode of determining when the case does occur otherwise than by permitting the cause to advance until the case for which the Constitution provides shall actually arise. . . .

But, dismissing the question of possibility, which, I must think, would embrace every other case as well as those to which this Bank is a party, in what sense can it be predicated of this case that it is one arising under a law of the United States? It cannot be denied that jurisdiction of this suit in equity could not be entertained unless the court could have had jurisdiction of the action of trespass, which this injunction was intended to anticipate. And, in fact, there is no question that the Bank here maintains that the right to sue extends to common trespass, as well as to contracts or any other cause of action. But suppose trespass in the common form instituted; the declaration is general, and the defendant pleads not guilty, and goes to trial. Where is the feature in such a cause that can give the court jurisdiction? What question arises under a law of the United States? or what question that must not be decided exclusively upon the *lex loci,* upon State laws? Take also the case of a contract, and in what sense can it be correctly predicated of that, that in common with every other act of the Bank, it arises out of the law that incorporates it? . . . Its contracts arise under its own acts, and not under a law of the United States; so far from it, indeed that their effect, their construction, their limitation, their concoction, are all the creatures of the respective State laws in which they originate. . . .

Various instances have been cited and relied on in which this right of suit in the courts of the United States has been given to particular officers of the United States. But . . . no such instance is in point until it be shown that Congress has authorized such officers to bring their private contracts and private controversies into the courts of the United States. In all the cases cited, the individual is acting distinctly as the organ of government. . . . The distinction is a clear one between all these cases and the Bank. The latter is a mere agent or attorney, in some instances; in others, and especially in the cases now before the court, it is a private person, acting on its own account, not clothed with an official character at all. But the acts of public officers are the acts of government, and emphatically so in suits by the Postmaster General; the money to be recovered being the property of the United States. . . .

Upon the whole, I feel compelled to dissent from the court, on the point of jurisdiction, and this renders it unnecessary for me to express my sentiments on the residue of the points in the cause.

* * *

Osborn is a case involving remarkable state defiance of federal law. Notwithstanding an injunction against collecting state taxes against the Bank of the United States, officers of the state of Ohio broke into a branch of the Bank of the United States and seized $100,000. Even if the state was convinced that the Bank was not constitutionally created by Congress, this was a violent, extralegal response to a federal statute creating a federal instrumentality, backed by a federal injunction. We will examine other examples of antebellum defiance of federal authority in this Chapter and others, including the resistance of state courts to the appellate jurisdiction of the Supreme Court, abolitionist resistance to the federal Fugitive Slave Acts, and federal judgments enforcing these statutes against emancipated Black people and people who came to their aid. Most immediately, however, recall that there was no general federal question jurisdiction at the time *Osborn* was decided. That is why the Court focuses on the meaning of the "sue and be sued" language of the statute creating the Bank. In the absence of §1331, this language was the only ground for arguing that a lower federal court had jurisdiction to entertain the Bank's request for an injunction against collection of the state tax. Assumptions about the treatment of the Bank of the United States if suit could only be brought in Ohio state court surely loomed in the background of the Court's conclusion that this language was jurisdiction-conferring.

Osborn stands for the proposition that a case arises under federal law for purposes of Article III judicial power if there is a federal law "ingredient" in the case. This arguably takes arising under jurisdiction out to the very limit of mixed cases, precluding federal court jurisdiction only where the case has *no* federal law component—a pure state law case. What are the federal ingredients in *Osborn*? Is it enough that the Bank of the United States was a federal instrumentality? *See Pacific Railroad Removal Cases* (1885) (holding that personal injury suits by passengers and others against private corporations originally formed by an act of Congress are "suits arising under the laws of the United States" for purposes of statute allowing removal to federal court). The Court in *Osborn* lays emphasis not just on the status of the Bank as a federal instrumentality, but on the possibility that important questions of federal law *might* arise regarding the federal law creating the Bank. *See Verlinden B.V. v. Central Bank* (1983) (noting that *Osborn* "reflects a broad conception of 'arising under' jurisdiction, according to which Congress may confer on the federal courts jurisdiction over any case or controversy *that might call for the application of federal law*"). This reading comports with Chief Justice Marshall's insistence that the original jurisdiction of the lower federal courts may be given "in any case to which the appellate jurisdiction extends." On the other hand, it raises the problem that a case could "arise under" federal law when, in fact, as the litigation develops, the possible federal issues never surface. Not all cases that could raise federal issues actually end up involving litigation of these issues. Much depends on the incentives and tactical maneuvers of the parties.

Perhaps this explains why Congress has never granted the full judicial power recognized as constitutionally available in *Osborn* over federal law to the district courts. Instead, the Court has interpreted 28 U.S.C. §1331 to require that the federal question appear on the face of the "well-pleaded" complaint. *Mottley* is the case that established this limitation on federal court power, holding that a state common law suit does not "arise under" federal law within the meaning of §1331 just because there is an anticipated federal defense.

Louisville & Nashville R.R. Co. v. Mottley

211 U.S. 149 (1908)

Statement by Justice MOODY.

The appellees (husband and wife), being residents and citizens of Kentucky, brought this suit in equity in the circuit court of the United States for the western district of Kentucky against the appellant, a railroad company and a citizen of the same state. The object of the suit was to compel the specific performance of the following contract:

> Louisville, Ky., Oct. 2d, 1871. The Louisville & Nashville Railroad Company, in consideration that E. L. Mottley and wife, Annie E. Mottley, have this day released company from all damages or claims for damages for injuries received by them on the 7th of September, 1871, in consequence of a collision of trains on the railroad of said company at Randolph's Station, Jefferson County, Kentucky, hereby agrees to issue free passes on said railroad and branches now existing or to exist, to said E. L. & Annie E. Mottley for the remainder of the present year, and thereafter to renew said passes annually during the lives of said Mottley and wife or either of them.

The bill alleged that in September, 1871, plaintiffs, while passengers upon the defendant railroad, were injured by the defendant's negligence, and released their respective claims for damages in consideration of the agreement for transportation during their lives, expressed in the contract. It is alleged that the contract was performed by the defendant up to January 1, 1907, when the defendant declined to renew the passes. The bill then alleges that the refusal to comply with the contract was based solely upon that part of the act of Congress of June 29, 1906, which forbids the giving of free passes or free transportation. The bill further alleges: First, that the act of Congress referred to does not prohibit the giving of passes under the circumstances of this case; and, second, that, if the law is to be construed as prohibiting such passes, it is in conflict with the 5th Amendment of the Constitution, because it deprives the plaintiffs of their property without due process of law. The defendant demurred to the bill. The judge of the circuit court overruled the demurrer, entered a decree for the relief prayed for, and the defendant appealed directly to this court. . . .

Justice MOODY, after making the foregoing statement, delivered the opinion of the court:

Two questions of law were raised by the demurrer to the bill, were brought here by appeal, and have been argued before us. They are, first, whether that part of the act of Congress of June 29, 1906, which forbids the giving of free passes or the collection of any different compensation for transportation of passengers than that specified in the tariff filed, makes it unlawful to perform a contract for transportation of persons who, in good faith, before the passage of the act, had accepted such contract in satisfaction of a valid cause of action against the railroad; and, second, whether the statute, if it should be construed to render such a contract unlawful, is in violation of the 5th Amendment of the Constitution of the United States. We do not deem it necessary, however, to consider either of these questions, because, in our opinion, the court below was without jurisdiction of the cause. Neither party has questioned that jurisdiction, but it is the duty of this court to see to it that the jurisdiction of the circuit court, which is defined and limited by statute, is not exceeded. This duty we have frequently performed of our own motion.

There was no diversity of citizenship, and it is not and cannot be suggested that there was any ground of jurisdiction, except that the case was a "suit . . . arising under the Constitution or laws of the United States." 25 Stat. at L. 434, chap. 866. It is the settled interpretation of these words, as used in this statute, conferring jurisdiction, that a suit arises under the Constitution and laws of the United States only when the plaintiff's statement of his own cause of action shows that it is based upon those laws or that Constitution. It is not enough that the plaintiff alleges some anticipated defense to his cause of action, and asserts that the defense is invalidated by some provision of the Constitution of the United States. Although such allegations show that very likely, in the course of the litigation, a question under the Constitution would arise, they do not show that the suit, that is, the plaintiff's original cause of action, arises under the Constitution. . . .

It is ordered that the judgment be reversed and the case remitted to the circuit court with instructions to dismiss the suit for want of jurisdiction.

* * *

The Mottleys were forced to turn to state court to pursue their breach of contract claim. Predictably, the railroad defended by invoking the authority of the federal statute for its actions and the case again reached the U.S. Supreme Court, this time through its exercise of appellate jurisdiction over decisions on important issues of federal law decided by the state courts. The Court upheld the right of the railroad to rescind the passes under the federal statute. *Louisville & Nashville R.R. Co. v. Mottley* (1911). *See also Holmes Group, Inc. v. Vornado Air Circulation Syst., Inc.* (2002) (holding that a federal patent infringement claim asserted as a counterclaim does not create federal subject matter jurisdiction because the well-pleaded complaint, not the counterclaim, determines whether a civil action "arises under" federal patent law).

If a necessary and substantial federal issue must appear on the face of the plaintiff's well-pleaded complaint, how should that rule apply to cases in which state courts have relied on federal regulatory standards in defining a state cause of action? With the dramatic expansion of federal regulation during and after the New Deal, this is a common occurrence because state consumer protection and tort law often incorporates federal standards. In *Merrell Dow Pharmaceutical v. Thompson* (1986), the U.S. Supreme Court addressed this question in the context of a state tort claim filed by parents against a pharmaceutical company alleging that their children's birth deformities were caused by the drug Bendectin. Under Ohio state tort law, misbranding of a drug in violation of the Federal Food, Drug, and Cosmetic Act creates a presumption of negligence and proximate cause. On its face, this was a classic "mixed" case in which state law provided the cause of action but federal law directly affected the standard of liability and thus would have to be adjudicated for the plaintiff to prevail. But granting §1331 jurisdiction in such cases would sweep into federal court *many* cases in which state law provides the cause of action and is the core of the case. On the other hand, relegating mixed cases of this kind to the state courts by denying §1331 jurisdiction would mean that important aspects of a federal regulatory standard would receive disuniform application in state courts.

Merrell Dow concluded that this kind of mixed case does not "arise under" federal law, relying heavily on the absence of either an express or implied federal right of action for the misbranding of drugs that injured the plaintiff. The Court reasoned:

> We . . . conclude that the congressional determination that there should be no federal remedy for the violation of this federal statute is tantamount to a congressional conclusion that the presence of a claimed violation of the statute as an element of a state cause of action is insufficiently "substantial" to confer federal-question jurisdiction. . . . Petitioner's concern about the uniformity of interpretation, moreover, is considerably mitigated by the fact that, even if there is no original district court jurisdiction for these kinds of action, this Court retains power to review the decision of a federal issue in a state cause of action. . . .

Some lower federal courts read the decision as strictly limiting federal question jurisdiction to cases in which Congress has created a private right of action in federal court. The language quoted above supports this reading. However, other lower courts tried to square the case with long-standing Supreme Court precedents not overturned in *Merrell Dow* and recognizing federal question jurisdiction in mixed cases despite the absence of a private right of action.

The following case clarified that a private federal right of action is *not* needed to establish arising under jurisdiction for a state cause of action that presents a necessary and substantial federal issue. *Grable* began as a suit to "quiet title" to land in Michigan that had been seized and resold by the IRS to satisfy back taxes. Like the tort law claims in *Merrell Dow*, a suit to resolve a dispute regarding title to land generally rests on state common law property doctrine. The federal issue concerned the validity of the IRS's method of giving notice of its seizure process.

Grable & Sons Metal Products, Inc. v. Darue Engineering & Mfg.

545 U.S. 308 (2005)

Justice SOUTER delivered the opinion of the Court.

The question is whether want of a federal cause of action to try claims of title to land obtained at a federal tax sale precludes removal to federal court of a state action with nondiverse parties raising a disputed issue of federal title law. We answer no, and hold that the national interest in providing a federal forum for federal tax litigation is sufficiently substantial to support the exercise of federal question jurisdiction over the disputed issue on removal, which would not distort any division of labor between the state and federal courts, provided or assumed by Congress.

I

In 1994, the Internal Revenue Service seized Michigan real property belonging to petitioner Grable & Sons Metal Products, Inc., to satisfy Grable's federal tax delinquency. Title 26 U.S.C. §6335 required the IRS to give notice of the seizure, and there is no dispute that Grable received actual notice by certified mail before the IRS sold the property to respondent Darue Engineering & Manufacturing. Although Grable also received notice of the sale itself, it did not exercise its statutory right to redeem the property within 180 days of the sale, §6337(b)(1), and after that period had passed, the Government gave Darue a quitclaim deed. §6339.

Five years later, Grable brought a quiet title action in state court, claiming that Darue's record title was invalid because the IRS had failed to notify Grable of its seizure of the property in the exact manner required by §6335(a), which provides that written notice must be "given by the Secretary to the owner of the property [or] left at his usual place of abode or business." Grable said that the statute required personal service, not service by certified mail.

Darue removed the case to Federal District Court as presenting a federal question, because the claim of title depended on the interpretation of the notice statute in the federal tax law. The District Court declined to remand the case at Grable's behest after finding that the "claim does pose a significant question of federal law," and ruling that Grable's lack of a federal right of action to enforce its claim against Darue did not bar the exercise of federal jurisdiction. . . .

The Court of Appeals for the Sixth Circuit affirmed. On the jurisdictional question, the panel thought it sufficed that the title claim raised an issue of federal law that had to be resolved, and implicated a substantial federal interest (in construing federal tax law). The court went on to affirm the District Court's judgment on the merits. We granted certiorari on the jurisdictional question alone, to resolve a split within the Courts of Appeals on whether *Merrell Dow Pharmaceuticals Inc. v. Thompson* (1986), always requires a federal cause of action as a condition for exercising federal-question jurisdiction. We now affirm.

II

Darue was entitled to remove the quiet title action if Grable could have brought it in federal district court originally, 28 U.S.C. §1441(a), as a civil action "arising under the Constitution, laws, or treaties of the United States," §1331. This provision for federal-question jurisdiction is invoked by and large by plaintiffs pleading a cause of action created by federal law (e.g., claims under 42 U.S.C. §1983). There is, however, another longstanding, if less frequently encountered, variety of federal "arising under" jurisdiction, this Court having recognized for nearly 100 years that in certain cases federal question jurisdiction will lie over state-law claims that implicate significant federal issues. The doctrine captures the commonsense notion that a federal court ought to be able to hear claims recognized under state law that nonetheless turn on substantial questions of federal law, and thus justify resort to the experience, solicitude, and hope of uniformity that a federal forum offers on federal issues.

The classic example is *Smith v. Kansas City Title & Trust Co.* (1921), a suit by a shareholder claiming that the defendant corporation could not lawfully buy certain bonds of the National Government because their issuance was unconstitutional. Although Missouri law provided the cause of action, the Court recognized federal-question jurisdiction because the principal issue in the case was the federal constitutionality of the bond issue. *Smith* thus held, in a somewhat generous statement of the scope of the doctrine, that a state-law claim could give rise to federal-question jurisdiction so long as it "appears from the [complaint] that the right to relief depends upon the construction or application of [federal law]."

The *Smith* statement has been subject to some trimming to fit earlier and later cases recognizing the vitality of the basic doctrine, but shying away from the expansive view that mere need to apply federal law in a state-law claim will suffice to open the "arising under" door. As early as 1912, this Court had confined federal-question jurisdiction over state-law claims to those that "really and substantially involv[e] a dispute or controversy respecting the validity, construction or effect of [federal] law." *Shulthis v. McDougal* (1912). This limitation was the ancestor of Justice Cardozo's later explanation that a request to exercise federal-question jurisdiction over a state action calls for a "common-sense accommodation of judgment to [the] kaleidoscopic situations" that present a federal issue, in "a selective process which picks the substantial causes out of the web and lays the other ones aside." *Gully v. First Nat. Bank in Meridian* (1936). It has in fact become a constant refrain in such cases that federal jurisdiction demands not only a contested federal issue, but a substantial one, indicating a serious federal interest in claiming the advantages thought to be inherent in a federal forum. *E.g., Chicago v. Int. Coll. of Surgeons* (1997); *Merrell Dow; Franchise Tax Bd. of Cal. v. Constr. Laborers Vacation Tr. for Southern Cal.* (1983).

But even when the state action discloses a contested and substantial federal question, the exercise of federal jurisdiction is subject to a possible veto. For the federal issue will ultimately qualify for a federal forum only if federal jurisdiction is consistent with congressional judgment about the sound division of labor between state and federal courts governing the application of §1331. Thus, *Franchise Tax Bd.* explained that the appropriateness of a federal forum to hear an embedded issue could be evaluated only after considering the "welter of issues regarding the interrelation of federal and state authority and the proper management of the federal judicial system." Because arising-under jurisdiction to hear a state-law claim always raises the possibility of upsetting the state-federal line drawn (or at least assumed) by Congress, the presence of a disputed federal issue and the ostensible importance of a federal forum are never necessarily dispositive; there must always be an assessment of any disruptive portent in exercising federal jurisdiction.

These considerations have kept us from stating a "single, precise, all-embracing" test for jurisdiction over federal issues embedded in state-law claims between nondiverse parties. *Christianson v. Colt Indus. Operating Corp.* (1988). We have not kept them out simply because they appeared in state raiment, as Justice Holmes would have done, but neither have we treated "federal issue" as a password opening federal courts to any state action embracing a point of federal law. Instead, the question is, does a state-law claim necessarily raise a stated federal issue, actually disputed and substantial, which a federal forum may entertain without disturbing any congressionally approved balance of federal and state judicial responsibilities.

III

A

This case warrants federal jurisdiction. Grable's state complaint must specify "the facts establishing the superiority of [its] claim," Mich. Ct. Rule 3.411(B)(2)(c)

(2005), and Grable has premised its superior title claim on a failure by the IRS to give it adequate notice, as defined by federal law. Whether Grable was given notice within the meaning of the federal statute is thus an essential element of its quiet title claim, and the meaning of the federal statute is actually in dispute; it appears to be the only legal or factual issue contested in the case. The meaning of the federal tax provision is an important issue of federal law that sensibly belongs in a federal court. The Government has a strong interest in the "prompt and certain collection of delinquent taxes," *U.S. v. Rodgers* (1983), and the ability of the IRS to satisfy its claims from the property of delinquents requires clear terms of notice to allow buyers like Darue to satisfy themselves that the Service has touched the bases necessary for good title. The Government thus has a direct interest in the availability of a federal forum to vindicate its own administrative action, and buyers (as well as tax delinquents) may find it valuable to come before judges used to federal tax matters. Finally, because it will be the rare state title case that raises a contested matter of federal law, federal jurisdiction to resolve genuine disagreement over federal tax title provisions will portend only a microscopic effect on the federal-state division of labor.

This conclusion puts us in venerable company, quiet title actions having been the subject of some of the earliest exercises of federal-question jurisdiction over state-law claims. . . .[3]

B

Merrell Dow Pharmaceuticals Inc. v. Thompson (1986), on which Grable rests its position, is not to the contrary. *Merrell Dow* considered a state tort claim resting in part on the allegation that the defendant drug company had violated a federal misbranding prohibition, and was thus presumptively negligent under Ohio law. The Court assumed that federal law would have to be applied to resolve the claim, but after closely examining the strength of the federal interest at stake and the implications of opening the federal forum, held federal jurisdiction unavailable. Congress had not provided a private federal cause of action for violation of the federal branding requirement, and the Court found "it would . . . flout, or at least undermine, congressional intent to conclude that federal courts might nevertheless exercise federal-question jurisdiction and provide remedies for violations of that federal statute solely because the violation . . . is said to be a . . . 'proximate cause' under state law."

---

3. The quiet title cases also show the limiting effect of the requirement that the federal issue in a state-law claim must actually be in dispute to justify federal-question jurisdiction. In *Shulthis v. McDougal* (1912), this Court found that there was no federal question jurisdiction to hear a plaintiff's quiet title claim in part because the federal statutes on which title depended were not subject to "any controversy respecting their validity, construction, or effect." *Id.*, at 570. As the Court put it, the requirement of an actual dispute about federal law was "especially" important in "suit[s] involving rights to land acquired under a law of the United States," because otherwise "every suit to establish title to land in the central and western states would so arise [under federal law], as all titles in those States are traceable back to those laws." *Id.*, at 569-570.

Because federal law provides for no quiet title action that could be brought against Darue, Grable argues that there can be no federal jurisdiction here, stressing some broad language in *Merrell Dow* (including the passage just quoted) that on its face supports Grable's position. But an opinion is to be read as a whole, and *Merrell Dow* cannot be read whole as overturning decades of precedent, as it would have done by effectively adopting the Holmes dissent in *Smith*, and converting a federal cause of action from a sufficient condition for federal-question jurisdiction into a necessary one.

In the first place, *Merrell Dow* disclaimed the adoption of any bright-line rule, as when the Court reiterated that "in exploring the outer reaches of §1331, determinations about federal jurisdiction require sensitive judgments about congressional intent, judicial power, and the federal system." The opinion included a lengthy footnote explaining that questions of jurisdiction over state-law claims require "careful judgments," about the "nature of the federal interest at stake." And as a final indication that it did not mean to make a federal right of action mandatory, it expressly approved the exercise of jurisdiction sustained in *Smith*, despite the want of any federal cause of action available to *Smith*'s shareholder plaintiff. *Merrell Dow* then, did not toss out, but specifically retained the contextual enquiry that had been *Smith*'s hallmark for over 60 years. At the end of *Merrell Dow*, Justice Holmes was still dissenting.

Accordingly, *Merrell Dow* should be read in its entirety as treating the absence of a federal private right of action as evidence relevant to, but not dispositive of, the "sensitive judgments about congressional intent" that §1331 requires. The absence of any federal cause of action affected *Merrell Dow*'s result two ways. The Court saw the fact as worth some consideration in the assessment of substantiality. But its primary importance emerged when the Court treated the combination of no federal cause of action and no preemption of state remedies for misbranding as an important clue to Congress's conception of the scope of jurisdiction to be exercised under §1331. The Court saw the missing cause of action not as a missing federal door key, always required, but as a missing welcome mat, required in the circumstances, when exercising federal jurisdiction over a state misbranding action would have attracted a horde of original filings and removal cases raising other state claims with embedded federal issues. For if the federal labeling standard without a federal cause of action could get a state claim into federal court, so could any other federal standard without a federal cause of action. And that would have meant a tremendous number of cases.

One only needed to consider the treatment of federal violations generally in garden variety state tort law. "The violation of federal statutes and regulations is commonly given negligence per se effect in state tort proceedings." Restatement (Third) of Torts §14, Comment *a. See also* W. Keeton, D. Dobbs, R. Keeton, & D. Owen, Prosser and Keeton on Torts, §36 (1984) ("[T]he breach of a federal statute may support a negligence per se claim as a matter of state law" (collecting authority)). A general rule of exercising federal jurisdiction over state claims resting on federal mislabeling and other statutory violations would thus have heralded a potentially enormous shift of traditionally state cases into federal courts. Expressing concern over the "increased volume of federal litigation," and noting the importance of adhering to "legislative intent," *Merrell Dow* thought it improbable that the Congress, having made no provision for a federal cause of action, would have meant to welcome any state-law tort case implicating federal law "solely because the violation of the federal statute is said to [create] a rebuttable presumption [of negligence] . . . under state law." In this situation, no welcome mat meant keep out. *Merrell Dow*'s analysis thus fits within the framework of examining the importance of having a federal forum for the issue, and the consistency of such a forum with Congress's intended division of labor between state and federal courts.

As already indicated, however, a comparable analysis yields a different jurisdictional conclusion in this case. Although Congress also indicated ambivalence in this case by providing no private right of action to Grable, it is the rare state quiet title action that involves contested issues of federal law. Consequently, jurisdiction over actions like Grable's would not materially affect, or threaten to affect, the normal currents of litigation. Given the absence of threatening structural consequences and the clear interest the Government, its buyers, and its delinquents have in the availability of a federal forum, there is no good reason to shirk from federal jurisdiction over the dispositive and contested federal issue at the heart of the state-law title claim.

IV

The judgment of the Court of Appeals, upholding federal jurisdiction over Grable's quiet title action, is affirmed.

It is so ordered.

[The concurring opinion of Justice THOMAS is omitted.]

* * *

Grable holds that while the presence of a private cause of action is sufficient to establish federal question jurisdiction, it is not necessary. Instead, the Court emphasizes the importance of nationally uniform standards for federal tax enforcement and endorses the long-standing "contextual enquiry" focusing on whether allowing cases into federal court will upset "the sound division of labor between state and federal courts," or, more precisely, the "congressionally approved balance of federal and state judicial responsibilities." Recognizing jurisdiction in *Grable* presented no threat to the federal/state balance, at least in part, the Court reasoned, because state title cases involving disputed issues of federal law are rare (unlike state tort cases involving violations of federal standards like *Merrell Dow*, which are quite common and would therefore overwhelm the federal courts). Does that mean there is a presumption against federal question jurisdiction whenever a federal issue involved in state law claims arises frequently? Shouldn't cases that frequently present important, contested issues of federal law be heard in federal court?

Because *Grable* doesn't overrule *Merrell Dow*, it is still important to ask whether an express or implied private cause of action is provided in the federal law invoked as part of a state law claim. When the federal statute expressly creates a cause of action, this is easy work—the statute says private individuals can sue to enforce the rights it protects. Express and implied rights of action are discussed in Chapter 5.

Since *Grable*, the Court has continued to take a dim view of assertions of federal question jurisdiction where Congress has not explicitly "set out the welcome mat." In *Empire Healthchoice Assurance, Inc. v. McVeigh* (2006), a 5-4 majority of the Court rejected federal question jurisdiction over an action to recover health care payments made to an injured federal employee after the employee prevailed in a tort action against the individuals responsible for his injuries. Although the plaintiff was a private insurer and the cause of action for reimbursement a standard state law claim, the company provided health benefits to federal employees under a federally regulated contract, the action for reimbursement against the federal employee was authorized by that contract, and the contract required that any reimbursements obtained be returned to the Federal Employees Health Benefits Fund, against which private insurance carriers draw to pay for benefits of enrolled federal employees.

While conceding that "distinctly federal interests are involved," the majority placed great weight on the fact that "Congress has not expressly created a federal right of action enabling insurance carriers like Empire to sue health-care beneficiaries in federal court to enforce reimbursement rights. . . ." Indeed, the Court drew a further inference against federal question jurisdiction for reimbursement actions from the fact that the statute creating the program expressly recognized a right for beneficiaries to sue in federal court if carriers denied benefits. "Had Congress found it necessary or proper to extend federal jurisdiction further, in particular, to encompass contract-derived reimbursement claims between carriers and insured workers, it would have been easy enough for Congress to say so." Even the statute's broad federal preemption provision (which states that the contract provisions the government negotiates with private carriers "shall supersede and preempt any State or local law" on questions relating to "the nature or extent of coverage or benefits") was insufficient to convince the Court that Congress intended reimbursement claims to be adjudicated in federal court. The Court found the case "poles apart from *Grable*," because plaintiff's reimbursement claim was fact-bound, would not aid the resolution of future cases, and "was triggered, not by the action of any federal department, agency, or service, but by the settlement of a personal-injury action launched in state court. . . ."

Justice Breyer, in dissent, emphasized the incongruity of denying federal question jurisdiction where:

> the statute is federal, the program it creates is federal, the program's beneficiaries are federal employees working throughout the country, the Federal Government pays all relevant costs, and the Federal Government receives all relevant payments. The private carrier's only role in this scheme is to administer the health benefits plan for the federal agency in exchange for a fixed service charge.

But the majority flatly rejected the view that a case arises under federal law simply because the dispute concerns the application of terms in a federal contract. "[U]niform federal law need not be applied to all questions in federal government litigation, even in cases involving government contracts. The prudent course, we have recognized, is often to adopt the readymade body of state law as the federal rule of decision until Congress strikes a different accommodation." Absent evidence of a "significant conflict . . . between an identifiable federal policy or interest and the operation of state law . . . there is no cause to displace state law, much less to lodge this case in federal court." As in *Merrell Dow*, the central inquiry for the majority is whether Congress has expressly created a federal right of action. Why should it make a difference, in distinguishing *Grable*, that this case involves adjudication of facts, whereas *Grable* presented a fairly pure question of law? Does the majority give adequate weight to the interest in uniformity in the law that governs the health benefits of federal employees?

In its 2013 decision in *Gunn v. Minton*, the Supreme Court again applied *Grable* to require dismissal of a state law cause of action with a necessary federal issue. Minton, a software programmer, lost a federal patent infringement lawsuit over a computer program and network he designed to facilitate securities trading. The court determined that Minton's patent was invalid because he marketed the patent more than a year before applying for a federal patent—the so-called "on sale" bar to patentability.

Minton blamed the law firm that represented him for the loss and sued the firm for malpractice in Texas state court. The state trial court granted summary judgment to the law firm, concluding that even if the firm had raised a possible exception to the "on-sale" bar in a timely fashion, Minton still would have lost the infringement suit. On appeal, Minton argued, for the first time, that the Texas state courts (which he had chosen) did not have subject matter jurisdiction because the malpractice lawsuit involved questions of federal patent law and federal courts have exclusive jurisdiction over "any civil action arising under any Act of Congress relating to patents." 28 U.S.C. §1338(a). He moved to have the trial court decision vacated and the suit dismissed so that he could start over in federal court.

The Texas appellate court refused to dismiss the case and the Texas Supreme Court reversed. In a unanimous decision, the U.S. Supreme Court applied the *Grable* framework for assessing mixed cases and reinstated the appellate court's decision that there is no federal question jurisdiction.

First, with respect to necessity, the Court emphasized that in Minton's malpractice case a federal patent question was raised on the face of the plaintiff's well-pleaded complaint, and it was "actually disputed." The following issues must therefore be resolved for plaintiff to prevail:

> Under Texas law, a plaintiff alleging legal malpractice must establish four elements: (1) that the defendant attorney owed the plaintiff a duty; (2) that the attorney breached that duty; (3) that the breach was the proximate cause of the plaintiff's injury; and (4) that damages occurred. *See Alexander v. Turtur & Associates, Inc.* (Tex. 2004). In cases like this one, in which the attorney's alleged error came in failing to make a particular argument, the causation element requires a "case within a case" analysis of whether, had the argument been made, the outcome of the earlier litigation would have been different. To prevail on his legal malpractice claim, therefore, Minton must show that he would have prevailed in his federal patent infringement case if only petitioners had timely made an [argument for an exception to the "on-sale" bar]. That will necessarily require application of patent law to the facts of Minton's case.

With respect to substantiality, the Court emphasized that the question is not whether the federal issue matters a lot to the parties in the case, but whether it is the kind of issue that implicates the distinctive purposes of federal court jurisdiction:

As our past cases show, however, it is not enough that the federal issue be significant to the particular parties in the immediate suit; that will *always* be true when the state claim "necessarily raise[s]" a disputed federal issue, as *Grable* separately requires. The substantiality inquiry under *Grable* looks instead to the importance of the issue to the federal system as a whole.

In *Grable* itself, for example, [we] emphasized the Government's "strong interest" in being able to recover delinquent taxes through seizure and sale of property, which in turn "require[d] clear terms of notice to allow buyers . . . to satisfy themselves that the Service has touched the bases necessary for good title."

A second illustration of the sort of substantiality we require comes from *Smith v. Kansas City Title & Tr. Co.* (1921), which *Grable* described as "[t]he classic example" of a state claim arising under federal law. . . . [T]he relevant point was not the importance of the question to the parties alone but rather the importance more generally of a determination that the Government "securities were issued under an unconstitutional law, and hence of no validity."

Here, the federal issue carries no such significance. Because of the backward-looking nature of a legal malpractice claim, the question is posed in a merely hypothetical sense: *If* Minton's lawyers had raised a timely [exception to the "on-sale" bar], would the result in the patent infringement proceeding have been different? No matter how the state courts resolve that hypothetical "case within a case," it will not change the real-world result of the prior federal patent litigation. Minton's patent will remain invalid.

Nor will allowing state courts to resolve these cases undermine "the development of a uniform body of [patent] law." *Bonito Boats, Inc. v. Thunder Craft Boats, Inc.* (1989). Congress ensured such uniformity by vesting exclusive jurisdiction over actual patent cases in the federal district courts and exclusive appellate jurisdiction in the Federal Circuit. *See* 28 U.S.C. §§1338(a), 1295(a)(1). In resolving the non-hypothetical patent questions those cases present, the federal courts are of course not bound by state court case-within-a-case patent rulings. *See Tafflin v. Levitt* (1990). In any event, the state court case-within-a-case inquiry asks what would have happened in the prior federal proceeding if a particular argument had been made. In answering that question, state courts can be expected to hew closely to the pertinent federal precedents. It is those precedents, after all, that would have applied had the argument been made.

As for more novel questions of patent law that may arise for the first time in a state court "case within a case," they will at some point be decided by a federal court in the context of an actual patent case, with review in the Federal Circuit. If the question arises frequently, it will soon be resolved within the federal system, laying to rest any contrary state court precedent; if it does not arise frequently, it is unlikely to implicate substantial federal interests. The present case is "poles apart from *Grable*," in which a state court's resolution of the federal question "would be controlling in numerous other cases." *Empire Healthchoice Assurance, Inc.* (2006).

Minton also suggests that state courts' answers to hypothetical patent questions can sometimes have real-world effect on other patents through issue preclusion. Minton, for example, has filed what is known as a "continuation patent" application related to his original patent. *See* 35 U.S.C. §120. He argues that, in evaluating this separate application, the patent examiner could be bound by the Texas trial court's interpretation of the scope of Minton's original patent. . . . Minton has not identified any case finding such preclusive effect based on a state court decision. But even assuming that a state court's case-within-a-case adjudication may be preclusive under some circumstances, the result would be limited to the parties and patents that had been before the state court. Such "fact-bound and situation-specific" effects are not sufficient to establish federal arising under jurisdiction. *Empire Healthchoice Assurance, Inc.* (2006).

Nor can we accept the suggestion that the federal courts' greater familiarity with patent law means that legal malpractice cases like this one belong in federal court. It is true that a similar interest was among those we considered in *Grable.* But the possibility that a state court will incorrectly resolve a state claim is not, by itself, enough to trigger the federal courts' exclusive patent jurisdiction, even if the potential error finds its root in a misunderstanding of patent law.

It follows from the foregoing that *Grable*'s fourth requirement is also not met. That requirement is concerned with the appropriate "balance of federal and state judicial responsibilities." We have already explained the absence of a substantial federal issue within the meaning of *Grable.* The States, on the other hand, have "a special responsibility for maintaining standards among members of the licensed professions." *Ohralik v. Ohio State Bar Assn.* (1978). Their "interest . . . in regulating lawyers is especially great since lawyers are essential to the primary governmental function of administering justice, and have historically been officers of the courts." *Goldfarb v. Va. State Bar* (1975). We have no reason to suppose that Congress—in establishing exclusive federal jurisdiction over patent cases—meant to bar from state courts state legal malpractice claims simply because they require resolution of a hypothetical patent issue.

2. *Diversity and Alienage Jurisdiction*

Unlike federal question jurisdiction, which Congress did not broadly recognize until 1875, diversity jurisdiction was established in the First Judiciary Act of 1789. The purpose of opening a federal judicial forum for such disputes is to mitigate the risk of local bias in state court. Similar concerns animate alienage jurisdiction. As Chief Justice Marshall delicately put it in an 1809 case:

> However true the fact may be, that the tribunals of the states will administer justice as impartially as those of the nation, to parties of every description, it is not less true that the Constitution itself either entertains

apprehensions on this subject, or views with such indulgence the possible fears and apprehensions of suitors, that it has established national tribunals for the decision of controversies between aliens and a citizen, or between citizens of different states.

Bank of U.S. v. Deveaux (1809) (holding that a corporation may invoke diversity jurisdiction, but that it is a "citizen" of all the states in which its shareholders are domiciled); cf. *Hertz Corp v. Friend* (2010) (stating the modern test according to which a corporation is a citizen of the state in which it is incorporated and its "nerve center," where its principal officers "direct, control, and coordinate" the company's activities).

Although the text of Article III requires neither complete diversity of citizenship nor an amount in controversy, Congress has always required *both* in 28 U.S.C. §1332. Complete diversity means that no party on one side of a dispute may share state citizenship (or alienage) with any party on the other side. In *Strawbridge v. Curtiss* (1806), a suit by citizens of the state of Massachusetts against Massachusetts and Vermont defendants, Chief Justice Marshall held that Congress's statutory grant of diversity jurisdiction required *complete* diversity:

> The words of the act of Congress are "where an alien is a party or the suit is between a citizen of a state where the suit is brought and a citizen of another state." The Court understands these expressions to mean that each distinct interest should be represented by persons all of whom are entitled to sue or may be sued in the federal courts. That is, that where the interest is joint, each of the persons concerned in that interest must be competent to sue or liable to be sued in those courts.

The rule in *Strawbridge* has been adhered to for two centuries.

Generally, the joinder of parties whose presence defeats diversity of citizenship is a defect that must be corrected at the trial court level by dismissing the nondiverse parties. If this has not occurred, then an appellate court's hands traditionally were tied according to the rule established in *New Orleans* v. *Winter* (1816). That case was an action in ejectment brought by two plaintiffs claiming as joint heirs. One was a citizen of Kentucky; the other, Gabriel Winter, was a citizen of the territory of Mississippi. Winter could not have sued alone under the rule then in effect that citizens of territories could not claim diversity jurisdiction. Writing for the Court, the Chief Justice noted that the parties initially could have elected to sue severally rather than jointly. Had they done so, Winter simply could have been dismissed as a proper but not indispensable party and diversity would have been preserved. But he then went on to state: "However this may be, having elected to sue jointly, the court is incapable of distinguishing their case, so far as respects jurisdiction, from one in which they were compelled to unite." Thus, the jurisdictional defect was fatal to the action.

In 1989, the Supreme Court qualified *Winter*, holding in *Newman-Green, Inc. v. Alfonzo-Larrain*, that a court of appeals has the power to grant a motion to dismiss a dispensable nondiverse party whose presence destroys statutory diversity jurisdiction rather than dismiss the entire suit as in *Winter*. The Court cautioned the courts of appeals to use this power sparingly and only in cases in which the dismissal of a nondiverse party would not prejudice other parties to the action.

In *C.L. Ritter Lumber Co.* v. *Consolidation Coal Co.* (4th Cir. 2002), the Fourth Circuit relied on *Newman-Green* in holding that the district court had the power to rescue subject matter jurisdiction after judgment on a jury verdict had been entered by splitting a suit into separate cases, with one embracing the claims asserted by the Texas plaintiffs and the other embracing the claims against the Texas defendants. Since none of the Texas plaintiffs asserted claims against any of the Texas defendants, the district court was not limited to dismissing the case for lack of complete diversity. The court of appeals reasoned that if the plaintiffs had filed separate complaints *ab initio*, there would have been no jurisdictional obstacle to joining the cases at trial, since the consolidation of proceedings does not merge separate cases into a single unit or make the parties in one case parties in the other. The court found that amending the judgment had the effect of retroactively creating two separate cases properly joined pursuant to Rule 21. The district court's remedy thus resulted in a trial unit over which the court validly could exercise jurisdiction. Given its unusual facts, *Ritter Lumber* may not be a case of general applicability.

The Class Action Fairness Act of 2005 significantly expanded the subject matter jurisdiction of the federal courts for class actions by deviating from the complete diversity requirement of ordinary §1332 diversity litigation. Previously, no member of the class could share state citizenship with any defendant. Under CAFA, if money damages are sought by 100 or more people, *at least one plaintiff class member is diverse from any defendant*, and the amount in controversy exceeds $5 million, the case may be brought in or removed to federal court. *See* 28 U.S.C. §§1332, 1453. The statute also allows aggregation of plaintiffs' claims: "[T]he claims of the individual class members shall be aggregated to determine whether the matter in controversy exceeds the sum or value of $5,000,000, exclusive of interest and costs." 28 U.S.C. §1332(d)(6). CAFA does not apply, however, where a state sues on behalf of injured consumers. *See Miss. ex. rel. Hood v. AU Optronics Corp.* (2014).

The most important exception to the new grant of jurisdiction is for class actions in which there is a substantial connection to a single state. For instance, if more than two-thirds of the class members are all citizens of the state in which the action is originally filed, a key defendant is a citizen of that state, and the principal injuries underlying the claim occurred there, federal courts cannot exercise jurisdiction. *See* 28 U.S.C. §1332(d)(4). Moreover, district courts have discretion to decline jurisdiction over class actions in which the primary defendants and between one-third and two-thirds of the plaintiff class members are citizens of the same state. *See* 28 U.S.C. §1332(d)(3); *In re Sprint Nextel Corp.* (7th Cir. 2010) (class action limited to residents of Kansas alleging Sprint conspired with other wireless companies to inflate text messaging rates; rejecting Sprint's claim that the denominator in the two-thirds number should be all possible plaintiffs in a nationwide class, rather than all members of the class in Kansas).

The net effect of CAFA is to place large-stakes, national class actions within the original jurisdiction of the federal courts. The statute passed with a groundswell of support from legislators who were generally oppposed to class actions and concerned about abuse of the procedure in state courts. As you might imagine, plaintiffs have a strong incentive to plead damages below $5 million if they want to remain in state court. If the complaint demands monetary relief of a specific sum in good faith, that sum is "deemed to be the amount in controversy." 28 U.S.C. §1446(c)(2).

Ordinarily, an *individual* plaintiff can enter a stipulation regarding the amount in controversy in order to avoid removal to federal court — that means making a binding promise not to seek more than a specific amount in damages. In *Standard Fire Ins. Co. v. Knowles* (2013), the Supreme Court addressed the question whether a named plaintiff in a class action may do this to avoid removal under CAFA. Greg Knowles filed a class action suit against Standard Fire Insurance for failing to include certain fees in its payments to insured homeowners for losses suffered. The complaint stated that the class would seek "to recover total aggregate damages of less than $5 million." Knowles also attached an affidavit to the complaint stipulating that he would "not at any time during this case . . . seek damages for the class . . . in excess of $5,000,000 in the aggregate." Defendants removed the case to federal court. In a hearing on Knowles' motion to remand, the defendant offered evidence that damages would likely just exceed $5 million. However, the district court remanded, pointing to the stipulation. The Eighth Circuit declined to hear the defendants' appeal and the Supreme Court reversed. The Court reasoned that for a stipulation to be effective it must be binding, and that Knowles could not speak for unnamed class members whom he hopes to represent if the class is certified.

> Because his precertification stipulation does not bind anyone but himself, Knowles has not reduced the value of the putative class members'. claims. For jurisdictional purposes, our inquiry is limited to examining the case "as of the time it was filed in state court," *Wis. Dept. of Corr. v. Schacht* (1998). At that point, Knowles lacked the authority to concede the amount-in-controversy issue for the absent class members.

With respect to the standard district courts must use in determining the amount in controversy, the Court held that, when the complaint alleges damages falling below the jurisdictional minimum, district courts must "look beyond the four corners of the complaint" and "add[] up the value of the claim of each person who falls within the definition of [the] proposed class."

A 2008 study by the Federal Judicial Center found that CAFA's enactment has led to an increase in the number of class actions filed in or removed to the federal courts based on diversity jurisdiction; however, in "the last months of the study period, diversity removals were at levels similar to those in the pre-CAFA period."[9] The observed increase was primarily associated with consumer class actions. The study also found that much of the increase in diversity class actions has been driven by an increase in original filings in federal courts, suggesting (contrary to the expectations of many) that plaintiffs' attorneys are choosing the federal forum, rather than leaving it to defense counsel to remove cases to federal court.

Congress also used minimum (rather than complete) diversity requirements to expand the subject matter jurisdiction of the lower federal courts to deal with complex litigation in The Multiparty, Multiforum Trial Jurisdiction Act (MMTJA) of 2002. The statute was passed following the terrorist attacks on September 11, 2001, as a means of centralizing litigation arising from large-scale accidents and disasters involving significant loss of life. *See* 28 U.S.C. §1369. The statute grants federal district courts original and removal jurisdiction over "any civil action *involving minimal diversity* between adverse parties that arises from a single accident, where

---

9. Emery G. Lee & Thomas E. Willing, *The Impact of the Class Action Fairness Act on the Federal Courts*, 156 U. Pa. L. Rev. 1723, 1754 (2008).

at least 75 natural persons have died in the accident at a discrete location," and where more than one state is involved because the accident took place in multiple locations, or because of the defendants' place of residence. §1369(a). Abstention is required if the claims are primarily local (i.e., where the "substantial majority" of the plaintiffs are citizens of a single state "of which the primary defendants are also citizens") and where "the claims asserted will be primarily governed by the laws of that State." §1369(b).

Congress's goal was to streamline multidistrict disaster litigation. As the House Conference Report on the MMTJA stated:

> It is common after a serious accident to have many lawsuits filed in several states, in both state and federal courts, with many different sets of plaintiffs' lawyers and several different defendants. Despite this multiplicity of suits, the principal issue that must be resolved first in each suit is virtually identical: Is one or more of the defendants liable? . . . The waste of judicial resources—and the costs to both plaintiffs and defendants—of litigating the same liability question several times over in separate lawsuits can be extreme.

The Class Action Fairness Act and the MMTJA suggest that Congress sees value in deviating from the complete diversity rule in certain forms of complex litigation. The expansion of jurisdiction does not, however, mean Congress favors these cases. The jurisdictional grants dovetail with the Supreme Court's imposition of significant new limitations on the certification of federal class actions, elevated pleading standards, and increased authority for district court judges to take cases away from juries.

As the *Winter* case above suggests, distinctive problems arise in dealing with litigation involving people who are not citizens of a state. *Winters* denied diversity jurisdiction in the federal district court of Louisiana over a dispute between a citizen of Kentucky and Winter, a citizen of the Mississippi territory. In *Hepburn v. Ellzey* (1805), the Supreme Court held that citizens of the District of Columbia are not citizens of any state for purposes of invoking diversity jurisdiction under the First Judiciary Act. *Id.* (denying diversity jurisdiction in Virginia federal court to a D.C. citizen). In the next case, Congress enacted legislation expressly authorizing diversity jurisdiction over litigation involving D.C. citizens and citizens of the territories.

National Mut. Ins. Co. v. Tidewater Transfer Co., Inc.

337 U.S. 582 (1949)

Mr. Justice JACKSON announced the judgment of the Court and an opinion in which Mr. Justice BLACK and Mr. Justice BURTON join.

This case calls up for review a holding that it is unconstitutional for Congress to open federal courts in the several states to action by a citizen of the District of Columbia against a citizen of one of the states. The petitioner, as plaintiff, commenced in the United States District Court for Maryland an action for money judgment on a claim arising out of an insurance contract. No cause of action under the laws or Constitution of the United States was pleaded, jurisdiction being predicated only upon an allegation of diverse citizenship. The diversity set forth was that plaintiff is a corporation created by District of Columbia law, while the defendant is a corporation chartered by Virginia, amenable to suit in Maryland by virtue of a license to do business there. The learned District Judge concluded that, while this diversity met jurisdictional requirements under the Act of Congress, it did not comply with diversity requirements of the Constitution as to federal jurisdiction, and so dismissed. The Court of Appeals, by a divided court, affirmed. . . . The controversy obviously was an appropriate one for review here, and writ of certiorari issued in the case.

The history of the controversy begins with that of the Republic. . . . In 1804, the Supreme Court, through Chief Justice Marshall, held that a citizen of the District of Columbia was not a citizen of a State within the meaning and intendment of this Act. [*Hepburn*] This decision closed federal courts in the states to citizens of the District of Columbia in diversity cases, and, for 136 years, they remained closed. In 1940, Congress enacted the statute challenged here. It confers on such courts jurisdiction if the action:

> is between citizens of different States, or citizens of the District of Columbia, the Territory of Hawaii, or Alaska, and any State or Territory.

The issue here depends upon the validity of this Act . . .

Before concentrating on detail, it may be well to place the general issue in a larger perspective. This constitutional issue affects only the mechanics of administering justice in our federation. It does not involve an extension or a denial of any fundamental right or immunity which goes to make up our freedoms. Those rights and freedoms do not include immunity from suit by a citizen of Columbia or exemption from process of the federal courts. Defendant concedes that it can presently be sued in some court of law, if not this one, and it grants that Congress may make it suable at plaintiff's complaint in some, if not this, federal court. Defendant's contention only amounts to this—that it cannot be made to answer this plaintiff in the particular court which Congress has decided is the just and convenient forum. . . .

In mere mechanics of government and administration, we should, so far as the language of the great Charter fairly will permit, give Congress freedom to adapt its machinery to the needs of changing times.

Our first inquiry is whether, under the third, or Judiciary, Article of the Constitution, extending the judicial power of the United States to cases or controversies "between citizens of different States," a citizen of the District of Columbia has the standing of a citizen of one of the states of the Union. This is the question which the opinion of Chief Justice Marshall answered in the negative, by way of dicta if not of actual decision. *Hepburn v. Ellzey* (1805). To be sure, nothing was before that Court except interpretation of a statute which conferred jurisdiction substantially in the words of the Constitution with nothing in the text or context to show that Congress intended to regard the District as a state. But Marshall resolved the statutory question by invoking the analogy of the constitutional provisions of the same tenor, and reasoned that the District was not a state for purposes of the Constitution, and, hence, was not for purposes of the Act. The opinion summarily disposed of arguments to the contrary, including the one repeated here, that other provisions of the Constitution indicate that "the term state is sometimes used in its more enlarged sense." . . . Nor did he underestimate the equitable claims which his decision denied to residents of the District, for he said that:

> It is true that, as citizens of the United States and of that particular district which is subject to the jurisdiction of congress, it is extraordinary that the courts of the United States, which are open to aliens and to the citizens of every state in the union, should be closed upon them. But this is a subject for legislative, not for judicial, consideration.

. . . [T]he opinion as a whole leaves no doubt that the Court did not then regard the District as a state for diversity purposes.

To now overrule this early decision of the Court on this point, and hold that the District of Columbia is a state, would, as that opinion pointed out, give to the word "state" a meaning in the Article which sets up the judicial establishment quite different from that which it carries in those Articles which set up the political departments and in other Articles of the instrument. . . .

In referring to the "States" in the fateful instrument which amalgamated them into the "United States," the Founders . . . obviously did not contemplate unorganized and dependent spaces as states. The District of Columbia being nonexistent in any form, much less as a state at the time of the compact, certainly was not taken into the Union of states by it, nor has it since been admitted as a new state is required to be admitted.

We therefore decline to overrule the opinion of Chief Justice Marshall, and we hold that the District of Columbia is not a state within Article III of the Constitution. . . .

This conclusion does not, however, determine that Congress lacks power under other provisions of the Constitution to enact this legislation. Congress, by the Act in question, sought not to challenge or disagree with the decision of Chief Justice Marshall that the District of Columbia is not a state for such purposes. It was careful to avoid conflict with that decision by basing the new legislation on powers that had not been relied upon by the First Congress in passing the Act of 1789.

The Judiciary Committee of the House of Representatives recommended the Act of April 20, 1940, as:

> a reasonable exercise of the constitutional power of Congress to legislate for the District of Columbia and for the Territories.

This power the Constitution confers in broad terms. By Art. I, Congress is empowered "to exercise exclusive Legislation in all Cases whatsoever, over such District." And, of course, it was also authorized "to make all Laws which shall be necessary and proper for carrying into Execution" such powers. These provisions were not relevant in Chief Justice Marshall's interpretation of the Act of 1789, because it did not refer in terms to the District, but only to states. It is therefore significant that, having decided that District citizens' cases were not brought within federal jurisdiction by Art. III and the statute enacted pursuant to it, the Chief Justice added . . . that the matter is a subject for "legislative, not for judicial, consideration." Even if it be considered speculation to say that this was an expression by the Chief Justice that Congress had the requisite power under Art. I, it would be in the teeth of his language to say that it is a denial of such power.

The Congress had acted on the belief that it possesses that power. We believe their conclusion is well founded.

It is elementary that the exclusive responsibility of Congress for the welfare of the District includes both power and duty to provide its inhabitants and citizens with courts adequate to adjudge not only controversies among themselves, but also their claims against, as well as suits brought by, citizens of the various states. It long has been held that Congress may clothe District of Columbia courts not only with the jurisdiction and powers of federal courts in the several states, but with such authority as a state may confer on her courts. *Kendall v. United States* (1838). . . .

However, it is contended that Congress may not combine this function, under Art. I, with those under Art. III, in district courts of the United States. Two objections are urged to this. One is that no jurisdiction other than specified in Art. III can be imposed on courts that exercise the judicial power of the United States thereunder. The other is that Art. I powers over the District of Columbia must be exercised solely within that geographic area. . . .

It is too late to hold that judicial functions incidental to Art. I powers of Congress cannot be conferred on courts existing under Art. III, for it has been done with this Court's approval. *O'Donoghue v. United States* (1933). In that case, it was held that, although District of Columbia courts are Art. III courts, they can also exercise judicial power conferred by Congress pursuant to Art. I. The fact that District of Columbia courts, as local courts, can also be given administrative or legislative functions which other Art. III courts cannot exercise does but emphasize the fact that, although the latter are limited to the exercise of judicial power, it may constitutionally be received from either Art. III, or Art. I, and that congressional power over the District, flowing from Art. I, is plenary in every respect.

It is likewise too late to say that we should reach this result by overruling Chief Justice Marshall's view, unless we are prepared also to overrule much more, including some of our own very recent utterances. Many powers of Congress other than its power to govern Columbia require for their intelligent and discriminating exercise determination of controversies of a justiciable character. In no instance has this Court yet held that jurisdiction of such cases could not be placed in the regular federal courts that Congress has been authorized to ordain and establish. We turn to some analogous situations in which we have approved the very course that Congress has taken here.

Congress is given power by Art. I to pay debts of the United States. That involves as an incident the determination of disputed claims. We have held unanimously that congressional authority under Art. I, not the Art. III jurisdiction over suits to which the United States is a party, is the sole source of power to establish the Court of Claims and of the judicial power which that court exercises. *Williams v. United States* (1933). In that decision, we also noted that it is this same Art. I power that is conferred on district courts by the Tucker Act, which authorizes them to hear and determine such claims in limited amounts. Since a legislative court such as the Court of Claims is "incapable of receiving" Art. III judicial power, *American Insurance Co. v. Canter* (1828), it is clear that the power thus exercised by that court and concurrently by the district courts flows from Art. I, not Art. III. Indeed, more recently, and again unanimously, this Court has said that, by the Tucker Act, the Congress authorized the district courts to sit as a court of claims, exercising the same, but no more, judicial power. *United States v. Sherwood* (1941). And, but a few terms ago, in considering an Act by which Congress directed rehearing of a rejected claim and its redetermination in conformity with directions given in the Act, Chief Justice Stone, with the concurrence of all sitting colleagues, reasoned that "The problem presented here is no different than if Congress had given a like direction to any district court to be followed as in other Tucker Act . . . cases." *Pope v. United States* (1944). Congress has taken us at our word, and recently conferred on the district courts exclusive jurisdiction of tort claims cognizable under the Federal Tort Claims Act, 60 Stat. 842, 843, also enacted pursuant to Art. I powers.

Congress also is given power in Art. I to make uniform laws on the subject of bankruptcies. That this, and not the judicial power under Art. III, is the source of our system of reorganizations and bankruptcy is obvious., *Continental Illinois Nat. Bank & Trust Co. v. Chicago Rock Island & Pacific R. Co.* (1935) But not only may the district courts be required to handle these proceedings, but Congress may add to their jurisdiction cases between the trustee and others that, but for the bankruptcy powers, would be beyond their jurisdiction because of lack of diversity required under Art. III. *Schumacher v. Beeler* (1934).

Consequently, we can deny validity to this present Act of Congress only by saying that the power over the District given by Art. I is somehow less ample than that over bankruptcy given by the same Article. If Congress could require this district court to decide this very case if it were brought by a trustee, it is hard to see why it may not require its decision for a solvent claimant when done in pursuance of other Art. I powers.

We conclude that, where Congress, in the exercise of its powers under Art. I, finds it necessary to provide those on whom its power is exerted with access to some kind of court or tribunal for determination of controversies that are within the traditional concept of the justiciable, it may open the regular federal courts to them regardless of lack of diversity of citizenship. The basis of the holdings we have discussed is that, when Congress deems that, for such purposes, it owes a forum to claimants and trustees, it may execute its power in this manner. The Congress, with equal justification apparently considers that it also owes such a forum to the residents of the District of Columbia in execution of its power and duty under the same Article. We do not see how the one could be sustained and the other denied.

We therefore hold that Congress may exert its power to govern the District of Columbia by imposing the judicial function of adjudicating justiciable controversies on the regular federal courts which, under the Constitution, it has the power to ordain and establish, and which it may invest with jurisdiction, and from which it may withhold jurisdiction "in the exact degrees and character which to Congress may seem proper for the public good." *Lockerty v. Phillips* (1943).

The judgment is

Reversed.

[Justice RUTLEDGE, joined by Justice MURPHY concurred in the judgment but rejected Justice JACKSON's reasoning that Congress could expand diversity jurisdiction without overruling *Hepburn*: "Although I agree with the Court's judgment, I think it overrules the *Hepburn* decision in all practical effect. With that I am in accord. But I am not in accord with the proposed extension of 'legislative' jurisdiction under Article I for the first time to the federal district courts outside the District of Columbia organized pursuant to Article III, and the consequent impairment of the latter Article's limitations upon judicial power, and I would dissent from such a holding even more strongly than I would from a decision today reaffirming the *Hepburn* ruling."]

Chief Justice VINSON, joined by Justice DOUGLAS, dissenting.

. . . The theory that §2 of Art. III is merely a supplement to the powers specifically granted Congress by the Constitution is not . . . accepted at face value even by those who urge it. For they still would require that a case or controversy be presented. . . .

When it became established [at the Convention] that inferior federal courts were to be authorized by the Constitution, the limits of their jurisdiction immediately became an issue of paramount importance. The outline of federal jurisdiction was established only after much give and take, proposal and counterproposal, and—in the end—compromise. . . . The judicial power was thus jealously guarded by the states and unwillingly granted to the national judiciary. Only when it could be demonstrated that a particular head of jurisdiction was acutely needed for the purposes of uniformity and national harmony was it granted. In every state convention for ratification of the Constitution, advocates and opponents of ratification considered in detail the kinds of cases and controversies to which the national judicial power was to extend. Each had to be justified. Far from assuming that the judicial power could be, by any means short of constitutional amendment, extended beyond those cases expressly provided for in Art. III, that Article was subjected to severe attacks on the ground that those powers specifically given would destroy the state courts. A delegate to the Virginia Convention, for example, stated that:

My next objection *to the federal judiciary* is that it is not expressed in a definite manner. The jurisdiction of all cases arising under the Constitution and the laws of the Union is of stupendous magnitude.

If, in addition to justifying every particle of power given to federal courts by the Constitution, its defenders had been obliged to justify the competence of Congress—itself suspect by those who opposed ratification—to extend that jurisdiction whenever it was thought necessary to effectuate one of the powers expressly given that body, their task would have been insuperable.

What has been said does not mean, of course, that legislative courts cannot exercise jurisdiction over questions of the same nature as those enumerated in Art. III, §2. It was clearly contemplated by the framers that state courts should have federal question jurisdiction concurrent with that exercised by inferior federal courts, yet they are not constitutional courts, nor do they exercise the judicial power of Art. III. The legislative courts created by Congress also can and do decide questions arising under the Constitution and laws of the United States (and, in the case of territorial courts, other types of jurisdiction enumerated in Art. III, §2 as well), but that jurisdiction is not, and cannot be, "a part of that judicial power which is defined in the 3d article of the Constitution." These courts are "incapable of receiving it." *American Insurance Co. v. Canter.*

The appellate jurisdiction of this Court is, in fact, dependent upon the fact that the case reviewed is of a kind within the Art. III enumeration. . . . We can no more review a legislative court's decision of a case which is not among those enumerated in Art. III than we can hear a case from a state court involving purely state law questions. But a question under the Constitution and laws of the United States, whether arising in a constitutional court, a state court, or a legislative court may, under the Constitution, be a subject of this Court's appellate jurisdiction. . . .

There is a certain surface appeal to the argument that, if Congress may create statutory courts to hear these cases, they should be able to adopt the less expensive and more practical expedient of vesting that jurisdiction in the existing and functioning federal courts throughout the country. No doubt a similar argument was pressed upon the judges in *Hayburn's Case*. Unless expediency is to be the test of jurisdiction of the federal courts, however, the argument falls of its own weight. The framers unquestionably intended that the jurisdiction of inferior federal courts be limited to those cases and controversies enumerated in Art. III. I would not sacrifice that principle on the altar of expediency.

Mr. Justice FRANKFURTER, joined by Justice REED, dissenting.

No provisions of the Constitution, barring only those that draw on arithmetic, as in prescribing the qualifying age for a President and members of a Congress or the length of their tenure of office, are more explicit and specific than those pertaining to courts established under Article III. "The judicial Power" which is "vested" in these tribunals and the safeguards under which their judges function are enumerated with particularity. Their tenure and compensation, the controversies which may be brought before them, and the distribution of original and appellate jurisdiction among these tribunals are defined and circumscribed, not left at large by vague and elastic phrasing. The precision which characterizes these portions of Article III is in striking contrast to the imprecision of so many other provisions of the Constitution dealing with other very vital aspects of government. . . . [W]hen the Constitution, in turn, gives strict definition of power or specific limitations upon it, we cannot extend the definition or remove the translation. . . .

There was deep distrust of a federal judicial system, as against the State judiciaries, in the Constitutional Convention. This distrust was reflected in the evolution of Article III. . . . [S]ince the judges of the courts for which Article III made provision not only had the last word (apart from amending the Constitution), but also enjoyed life tenure, it was an essential safeguard against control by the judiciary of its own jurisdiction to define the jurisdiction of those courts with particularity.

[I]t is conceded that the claim for which access is sought in the District Court for Maryland, one of the courts established under Article III, is not included among the "cases" to which the judicial power can be made to extend. But if the precise enumeration of cases as to which Article III authorized Congress to grant jurisdiction to the United States District Courts does not preclude Congress from vesting these courts with authority which Article III disallows, by what rule of reason is Congress to be precluded from bringing to its aid the advisory opinions of this Court or of the Courts of Appeals? In the exercise of its constitutional power to regulate commerce, to establish uniform rules of naturalization, to raise and support armies, or to execute any of the other powers of Congress that are no less vital than its power to legislate for the District of Columbia, the Congress may be greatly in need of informed and disinterested legal advice.

We are here concerned with the power of the federal courts to adjudicate merely because of the citizenship of the parties. Power to adjudicate between citizens of different states, merely because they are citizens of different states, has no relation to any substantive rights created by Congress. When the sole source of the right to be enforced is the law of a State, the right to resort to a federal court is restricted to "citizens of different States." The right to enforce such State-created obligations derives its sole strength from Article III. No other provision of the Constitution lends support. But for Article III, the judicial enforcement of rights which only a State, not the United States, creates would be confined to State courts. It is Article III, and nothing outside it, that authorizes Congress to treat federal courts as "only another court of the State," *Guaranty Trust Co. v. York* (1945), and Article III allows it to do so only when the parties are citizens of different "States." If Congress, in its lawmaking power over the District of Columbia, created some right for the inhabitants of the District, it could choose to provide for the enforcement of that right in any court of the United States, because the case would be one arising under "the Laws of the United States." But here, the controversy is one arising not under the laws of the United States, but under the laws of Maryland. By the command of the Constitution, this Maryland-created right can be enforced in a federal court only if the controversy is between "citizens of different States" in relation to the State in which the federal court is sitting.

The diversity jurisdiction of the federal courts was probably the most tenuously founded and most unwillingly granted of all the heads of federal jurisdiction which Congress was empowered by Article III to confer. It is a matter of common knowledge that the jurisdiction of the federal courts based merely on diversity of citizenship has been more continuously under fire than any other. Inertia largely accounts for its retention. By withdrawing the meretricious advantages which diversity jurisdiction afforded one of the parties in some types of litigation, *Erie R. Co. v. Tompkins* (1938), has happily eliminated some practical but indefensible reasons for its retention. . . .

But, in any event, the dislocation of the Constitutional scheme for the establishment of the federal judiciary and the distribution of jurisdiction among its tribunals so carefully formulated in Article III is too heavy a price to pay for whatever advantage there may be to a citizen of the District, natural or artificial, to go to a federal court in a particular State instead of to the State court in suing a citizen of that State. Nor is it merely a dislocation for the purpose of accomplishing a result of trivial importance in the practical affairs of life. The process of reasoning by which this result is reached invites a use of the federal courts which breaks with the whole history of the federal judiciary and disregards the wise policy behind that history. It was because Article III defines and confines the limits of jurisdiction of the courts which are established under Article III that the first Court of Claims Act fell, Gordon v. United States (1864). And it was in observance of these Constitutional limits that this Court had to decline appellate powers sought to be conferred by the Congress in an exercise of its legislative power over the District. *Keller v. Potomac Electric Power Co.* (1923).

. . . The other alternative—to expand "the judicial Power" of Article III to include a controversy between a citizen of the District of Columbia and a citizen of one of the States by virtue of the provision extending "the judicial Power" to controversies "between citizens of different States"—would disregard an explicit limitation of Article III. For a hundred and fifty years, "States," as there used, meant "States"—the political organizations that form the Union, and alone have power to amend the Constitution. The word did not cover the district which was to become "the Seat of the Government of the United States," nor the "Territory" belonging to the United States, both of which the Constitution dealt with in differentiation from the States. . . .

It is suggested that other provisions of the Constitution relating to "States" apply to the District. If the mere repetition of an inaccuracy begets truth, then that statement is true; not otherwise. Decisions concerned with the District involving trial by jury in criminal and civil cases, full faith and credit for its proceedings, and the power to tax residents, rest on provisions in the Constitution not limited to "States." There may be a decision in which the source of rights or obligations affecting the District of Columbia derives from a legal right relating solely to "States" or a duty to which only "States" must be obedient. I know of no such case.

. . . Congress need not establish inferior courts; Congress need not grant the full scope of jurisdiction which it is empowered to vest in them; Congress need not give this Court any appellate power; it may withdraw appellate jurisdiction once conferred, and it may do so even while a case is *sub judice. Ex parte McCardle* (1868). But when the Constitution defined the ultimate limits of judicial power exercisable by courts which derive their sole authority from Article III, it is beyond the power of Congress to extend those limits. If there is one subject as to which this Court ought not to feel inhibited in passing on the validity of legislation by doubts of its own competence to judge what Congress has done, it is legislation affecting the jurisdiction of the federal courts. When Congress, on a rare occasion, through inadvertence or generosity, exceeds those limitations, this Court should not good naturedly ignore such a transgression of congressional powers.

A substantial majority of the Court agrees that each of the two grounds urged in support of the attempt by Congress to extend diversity jurisdiction to cases involving citizens of the District of Columbia must be rejected—but not the same majority. And so, conflicting minorities in combination bring to pass a result—paradoxical as it may appear—which differing majorities of the Court find insupportable.

* * *

The plurality opinion by Justice Jackson has been described as coming "close to outright jurisdictional apostasy" for concluding that Article III does not set the outer limits of the jurisdiction that Congress can confer on Article III courts.[10] Certainly, the problem the Court was concerned with in the *Tidewater* case is no more abstract than the one that animates all diversity cases—if D.C. citizens are left to state court on state law claims, they may face bias there. Still, the force of Justice Frankfurter's dissent has left the decision, and other theories of federal jurisdiction addressed to the problem of bias in state court beyond the heads of jurisdiction recognized in Article III, "under something of a cloud."[11]

3. *Supplemental Jurisdiction*

It is common that multiple causes of action can be asserted for injuries arising from the same facts. Even a relatively simple tort case can create claims

---

10. James Pfander, *The Tidewater Problem: Article III and Constitutional Change*, 75 Notre Dame L. Rev. 1925, 1926 (2004).

11. *Id.* at 1927.

under state tort, property and contracts law, in addition to related federal claims. When only one of the causes of action meets the statutory requirements for subject matter jurisdiction in a federal court, the court must determine whether it has "supplemental" jurisdiction over the others claims. In 1990, Congress passed 28 U.S.C. §1367 to codify the best of the common law and to give the federal courts supplemental jurisdiction over some state law claims.

The central case of the common law period was *United Mine Workers v. Gibbs* (1966). The Supreme Court set out a test for adding claims and explained why there is power in a district court to adjudicate claims that wouldn't, standing alone, be a ground of jurisdiction in a federal court:

> Pendent jurisdiction, in the sense of judicial power, exists whenever there is a claim "arising under [the] Constitution, the Laws of the United States, and Treaties made or which shall be made, under their Authority . . . ," U.S. Const., Art. III, §2, and the relationship between that claim and the state claim permits the conclusion that the entire action before the court comprises but one constitutional "case." The federal claim must have substance sufficient to confer subject matter jurisdiction on the court. The state and federal claims must derive from a common nucleus of operative fact. But if, considered without regard to their federal or state character, a plaintiff's claims are such that he would ordinarily be expected to try them all in one judicial proceeding, then, assuming substantiality of the federal issues, there is power in federal courts to hear the whole.
>
> That power need not be exercised in every case in which it is found to exist. It has consistently been recognized that pendent jurisdiction is a doctrine of discretion, not of plaintiff's right. Its jurisdiction lies in considerations of judicial economy, convenience and fairness to litigants; if these are not present a federal court should hesitate to exercise jurisdiction over state claims, even though bound to apply state law to them.

In operation, the *Gibbs* test concentrated on factual relatedness and whether the claims would ordinarily be tried together. This included "ancillary jurisdiction" over counterclaims arising from the same transaction or occurrence as the plaintiff's claim even if they did not satisfy 28 U.S.C. §1331 or §1332. A party could even implead a third-party defendant (*see* Fed. R. Civ. P. 14) and assert a factually related cross-claim (*see* Fed. R. Civ. P. 13) against a codefendant without concern for the statutory jurisdiction demands of §1331 or §1332. In all of these cases, the party seeking to add the claim was in a defensive posture, and the claim grew out of the original dispute against her.

The outer boundaries of these rules were emphasized in a series of cases in which the Supreme Court refused to extend ancillary or pendent jurisdiction principles to claims that involved the addition of a new *pendent party*, notwithstanding the factual relatedness of these claims. *See Owen Equip. Co. v. Kroger* (1978) (no jurisdiction for a plaintiff's claim against a third-party defendant that was factually related to the underlying cause of action against the original defendant.); *Aldinger v. Howard* (1976) (denying jurisdiction over state law claims against a new nondiverse defendant despite factual relatedness to federal claims against original defendants); *Finley v. United States* (1989) (denying jurisdiction for factually related state law claim against one defendant even though claim against another defendant could only be filed in federal court, meaning the plaintiff would have to file two suits, one in state and one in federal court regarding the same event).

A year after *Finley* was decided, Congress passed the modern federal supplemental jurisdiction statute. The statute makes a broad grant of supplemental jurisdiction authority where the federal court has arising under jurisdiction, *see* §1367(a), and then a more limited grant with respect to diversity cases in §1367(b). Section 1367(b) instructs courts not to exercise supplemental jurisdiction in diversity cases over claims by plaintiffs against persons made parties under Rule 14 (impleader), 19 (compulsory joinder), 20 (permissive joinder) or 24 (intervention), or over claims by persons proposed to be joined as plaintiffs under Rule 19, or seeking to intervene as plaintiffs under Rule 24, where exercising such jurisdiction would be inconsistent with the jurisdictional requirements of §1332 (e.g., complete diversity).

Interpreting and applying §1367 has proven particularly challenging in the class action context. Courts and commentators have differed considerably over whether §1367(b), by omitting class actions under Rule 23 from the list of exceptions to §1367(a)'s broad grant of supplemental jurisdiction, was meant to overrule *Zahn v. Int'l Paper Co.* (1973). *Zahn* prohibited the exercise of supplemental jurisdiction in diversity cases over claims of unnamed class members for less than the jurisdictional amount.

Prompted by a sharp split in the circuit courts, the Supreme Court addressed the issue in the following decision. Unfortunately, as you will see, the Court itself was badly divided (5-4), so we cannot be certain that its reading of §1367 will endure. Notice too that the case consolidates two appeals from the circuit courts, one a class action in which the claims of some class members did not meet the amount-in-controversy requirement, another a standard multi-plaintiff personal injury case in which only one plaintiff met the amount-in-controversy requirement.

Exxon Mobil Corp. v. Allapattah Services, Inc.

545 U.S. 546 (2005)

Justice KENNEDY delivered the opinion of the Court.

These consolidated cases present the question whether a federal court in a diversity action may exercise supplemental jurisdiction over additional plaintiffs whose claims do not satisfy the minimum amount-in-controversy requirement, provided the claims are part of the same case or controversy as the claims of plaintiffs who do allege a sufficient amount in controversy. Our decision turns on the correct interpretation of 28 U.S.C. §1367. The question has divided the Courts of Appeals, and we granted certiorari to resolve the conflict.

We hold that, where the other elements of jurisdiction are present and at least one named plaintiff in the action satisfies the amount-in-controversy requirement, §1367 does authorize supplemental jurisdiction over the claims of other plaintiffs in the same Article III case or controversy, even if those claims are for less than the jurisdictional amount specified in the statute setting forth the requirements for diversity jurisdiction. We affirm the judgment of the Court of Appeals for the Eleventh Circuit in *[Allapattah]*, and we reverse the judgment of the Court of Appeals for the First Circuit in *[Star-Kist]*.

I

In 1991, about 10,000 Exxon dealers filed a class-action suit against the Exxon Corporation in the United States District Court for the Northern District of Florida. The dealers alleged an intentional and systematic scheme by Exxon under which they were overcharged for fuel purchased from Exxon. The plaintiffs invoked the District Court's §1332(a) diversity jurisdiction. After a unanimous jury verdict in favor of the plaintiffs, the District Court certified the case for interlocutory review, asking whether it had properly exercised §1367 supplemental jurisdiction over the claims of class members who did not meet the jurisdictional minimum amount in controversy.

The Court of Appeals for the Eleventh Circuit upheld the District Court's extension of supplemental jurisdiction to these class members. This decision accords with the views of the Courts of Appeals for the Fourth, Sixth, and Seventh Circuits. The Courts of Appeals for the Fifth and Ninth Circuits, adopting a similar analysis of the statute, have held that in a diversity class action the unnamed class members need not meet the amount-in-controversy requirement, provided the named class members do. These decisions, however, are unclear on whether all the named plaintiffs must satisfy this requirement.

In the other case now before us the Court of Appeals for the First Circuit took a different position on the meaning of §1367(a). In that case, a 9-year-old girl sued Star-Kist in a diversity action in the United States District Court for the District of Puerto Rico, seeking damages for unusually severe injuries she received when she sliced her finger on a tuna can. Her family joined in the suit, seeking damages for emotional distress and certain medical expenses. The District Court granted summary judgment to Star-Kist, finding that none of the plaintiffs met the minimum amount-in-controversy requirement. The Court of Appeals for the First Circuit, however, ruled that the injured girl, but not her family members, had made allegations of damages in the requisite amount.

The Court of Appeals then addressed whether, in light of the fact that one plaintiff met the requirements for original jurisdiction, supplemental jurisdiction over the remaining plaintiffs' claims was proper under §1367. The court held that §1367 authorizes supplemental jurisdiction only when the district court has original jurisdiction over the action, and that in a diversity case original jurisdiction is lacking if one plaintiff fails to satisfy the amount-in-controversy requirement. Although the Court of Appeals claimed to "express no view" on whether the result would be the same in a class action, its analysis is inconsistent with that of the Court of Appeals for the Eleventh Circuit. The Court of Appeals for the First Circuit's view of §1367 is, however, shared by the Courts of Appeal for the Third, Eighth, and Tenth Circuits, and the latter two Courts of Appeals have expressly applied this rule to class actions.

II

A

The district courts of the United States, as we have said many times, are "courts of limited jurisdiction. They possess only that power authorized by Constitution and statute." *Kokkonen v. Guardian Life Ins. Co. of America* (1994).

In order to provide a federal forum for plaintiffs who seek to vindicate federal rights, Congress has conferred on the district courts original jurisdiction in federal-question cases — civil actions that arise under the Constitution, laws, or treaties of the United States. 28 U.S.C. §1331. In order to provide a neutral forum for what have come to be known as diversity cases, Congress also has granted district courts original jurisdiction in civil actions between citizens of different States, between U.S. citizens and foreign citizens, or by foreign states against U.S. citizens. §1332. To ensure that diversity jurisdiction does not flood the federal courts with minor disputes, §1332(a) requires that the matter in controversy in a diversity case exceed a specified amount, currently $75,000.

Although the district courts may not exercise jurisdiction absent a statutory basis, it is well established — in certain classes of cases — that, once a court has original jurisdiction over some claims in the action, it may exercise supplemental jurisdiction over additional claims that are part of the same case or controversy. The leading modern case for this principle is *Mine Workers v. Gibbs* (1966). In *Gibbs*, the plaintiff alleged the defendant's conduct violated both federal and state law. The District Court, *Gibbs* held, had original jurisdiction over the action based on the federal claims. *Gibbs* confirmed that the District Court had the additional power (though not the obligation) to exercise supplemental jurisdiction over related state claims that arose from the same Article III case or controversy. *Id.* ("The federal claim must have substance sufficient to confer subject matter jurisdiction on the court. . . . [A]ssuming substantiality of the federal issues, there is *power* in federal courts to hear the whole.").

As we later noted, the decision allowing jurisdiction over pendent state claims in *Gibbs* did not mention, let alone come to grips with, the text of the jurisdictional statutes and the bedrock principle that federal courts have no jurisdiction without statutory authorization. *Finley v. United States* (1989). In *Finley*, we nonetheless reaffirmed and rationalized *Gibbs* and its progeny by inferring from it the interpretive principle that, in cases involving supplemental jurisdiction over additional claims between parties properly in federal court, the jurisdictional statutes should be read broadly, on the assumption that in this context Congress intended to authorize courts to exercise their full Article III power to dispose of an "'entire action before the court [which] comprises but one constitutional case.'"

We have not, however, applied *Gibbs*' expansive interpretive approach to other aspects of the jurisdictional statutes. For instance, we have consistently interpreted §1332 as requiring complete diversity: In a case with multiple plaintiffs and multiple defendants, the presence in the action of a single plaintiff from the same State as a single defendant deprives the district court of original diversity jurisdiction over the entire action. *Strawbridge v. Curtiss* (1806). The complete diversity requirement is not mandated by the Constitution, *State Farm Fire & Casualty Co. v. Tashire* (1967), or by the plain text of §1332(a). The Court, nonetheless, has adhered to the complete diversity rule in light of the purpose of the diversity requirement, which is to provide a federal forum for important disputes where state courts might favor, or be perceived as favoring, home-state litigants. The presence of parties from the same State on both sides of a case dispels this concern, eliminating a principal reason for conferring §1332 jurisdiction over any of the claims in the action. The specific purpose of the complete diversity rule explains both why we have not adopted *Gibbs*' expansive interpretive approach to this aspect of the jurisdictional statute and why *Gibbs* does not undermine the complete diversity rule. In order for a federal court to invoke supplemental jurisdiction under *Gibbs*, it must first have original jurisdiction over at least one claim in the action. Incomplete diversity destroys original jurisdiction with respect to all claims, so there is nothing to which supplemental jurisdiction can adhere.

In contrast to the diversity requirement, most of the other statutory prerequisites for federal jurisdiction, including the federal-question and amount-in-controversy requirements, can be analyzed claim by claim. True, it does not follow by necessity from this that a district court has authority to exercise supplemental jurisdiction over all claims provided there is original jurisdiction over just one. Before the enactment of §1367, the Court declined in contexts other than the pendent-claim instance to follow *Gibbs'* expansive approach to interpretation of the jurisdictional statutes. The Court took a more restrictive view of the proper interpretation of these statutes in so-called pendent-party cases involving supplemental jurisdiction over claims involving additional parties—plaintiffs or defendants—where the district courts would lack original jurisdiction over claims by each of the parties standing alone.

Thus, with respect to plaintiff-specific jurisdictional requirements, the Court held in *Clark v. Paul Gray, Inc.* (1939), that every plaintiff must separately satisfy the amount-in-controversy requirement. Though *Clark* was a federal-question case, at that time federal-question jurisdiction had an amount-in-controversy requirement analogous to the amount-in-controversy requirement for diversity cases. "Proper practice," *Clark* held, "requires that where each of several plaintiffs is bound to establish the jurisdictional amount with respect to his own claim, the suit should be dismissed as to those who fail to show that the requisite amount is involved." The Court reaffirmed this rule, in the context of a class action brought invoking §1332(a) diversity jurisdiction, in *Zahn v. International Paper Co.* (1973). It follows "inescapably" from *Clark*, the Court held in *Zahn*, that "any plaintiff without the jurisdictional amount must be dismissed from the case, even though others allege jurisdictionally sufficient claims."

The Court took a similar approach with respect to supplemental jurisdiction over claims against additional defendants that fall outside the district courts' original jurisdiction. In *Aldinger v. Howard*, (1976), the plaintiff brought a 42 U.S.C. §1983 action against county officials in district court pursuant to the statutory grant of jurisdiction in 28 U.S.C. §1343(3). The plaintiff further alleged the court had supplemental jurisdiction over her related state-law claims against the county, even though the county was not suable under §1983 and so was not subject to §1343(3)'s original jurisdiction. The Court held that supplemental jurisdiction could not be exercised because Congress, in enacting §1343(3), had declined (albeit implicitly) to extend federal jurisdiction over any party who could not be sued under the federal civil rights statutes. "Before it can be concluded that [supplemental] jurisdiction [over additional parties] exists," *Aldinger* held, "a federal court must satisfy itself not only that Art[icle] III permits it, but that Congress in the statutes conferring jurisdiction has not expressly or by implication negated its existence."

In *Finley v. United States* (1989), we confronted a similar issue in a different statutory context. The plaintiff in *Finley* brought a Federal Tort Claims Act negligence suit against the Federal Aviation Administration in District Court, which had original jurisdiction under §1346(b). The plaintiff tried to add related claims against other defendants, invoking the District Court's supplemental jurisdiction over so-called pendent parties. We held that the District Court lacked a sufficient statutory basis for exercising supplemental jurisdiction over these claims. Relying primarily on *Zahn*, *Aldinger*, and *Kroger*, we held in *Finley* that "a grant of jurisdiction over claims involving particular parties does not itself confer jurisdiction over additional claims by or against different parties." While *Finley* did not "limit or impair" *Gibbs'* liberal approach to interpreting the jurisdictional statutes in the context of supplemental jurisdiction over additional claims involving the same parties, *Finley* nevertheless declined to extend that interpretive assumption to claims involving additional parties. *Finley* held that in the context of parties, in contrast to claims, "we will not assume that the full constitutional power has been congressionally authorized, and will not read jurisdictional statutes broadly."

As the jurisdictional statutes existed in 1989, then, here is how matters stood: First, the diversity requirement in §1332(a) required complete diversity; absent complete diversity, the district court lacked original jurisdiction over all of the claims in the action. *Strawbridge.* Second, if the district court had original jurisdiction over at least one claim, the jurisdictional statutes implicitly authorized supplemental jurisdiction over all other claims between the same parties arising out of the same Article III case or controversy. *Gibbs.* Third, even when the district court had original jurisdiction over one or more claims between particular parties, the jurisdictional statutes did not authorize supplemental jurisdiction over additional claims involving other parties. *Clark.*

B

In *Finley* we emphasized that "[w]hatever we say regarding the scope of jurisdiction conferred by a particular statute can of course be changed by Congress." In 1990, Congress accepted the invitation. It passed the Judicial Improvements Act, which enacted §1367, the provision which controls these cases.

Section 1367 provides, in relevant part:

> (a) Except as provided in subsections (b) and (c) or as expressly provided otherwise by Federal statute, in any civil action of which the district courts have original jurisdiction, the district courts shall have supplemental jurisdiction over all other claims that are so related to claims in the action within such original jurisdiction that they form part of the same case or controversy under Article III of the United States Constitution. Such supplemental jurisdiction shall include claims that involve the joinder or intervention of additional parties.
>
> (b) In any civil action of which the district courts have original jurisdiction founded solely on section 1332 of this title, the district courts shall not have supplemental jurisdiction under subsection (a) over claims by plaintiffs against persons made parties under Rule 14, 19, 20, or 24 of the Federal Rules of Civil Procedure, or over claims by persons proposed to be joined as plaintiffs under Rule 19 of such rules, or seeking to intervene as plaintiffs under Rule 24 of such rules, when exercising supplemental jurisdiction over such claims would be inconsistent with the jurisdictional requirements of section 1332.

All parties to this litigation and all courts to consider the question agree that §1367 overturned the result in *Finley*. There is no warrant, however, for assuming that §1367 did no more than to overrule *Finley* and otherwise to codify the existing state of the law of supplemental jurisdiction. We must not give jurisdictional statutes a more expansive interpretation than their text warrants; but it is just as important not to adopt an artificial construction that is narrower than what the text provides. No sound canon of interpretation requires Congress to speak with extraordinary clarity in order to modify the rules of federal jurisdiction within appropriate constitutional bounds. Ordinary principles of statutory construction apply. In order to determine the scope of supplemental jurisdiction authorized by §1367, then, we must examine the statute's text in light of context, structure, and related statutory provisions.

Section 1367(a) is a broad grant of supplemental jurisdiction over other claims within the same case or controversy, as long as the action is one in which the district courts would have original jurisdiction. The last sentence of §1367(a) makes it clear that the grant of supplemental jurisdiction extends to claims involving joinder or intervention of additional parties. The single question before us, therefore, is whether a diversity case in which the claims of some plaintiffs satisfy the amount-in-controversy requirement, but the claims of others plaintiffs do not, presents a "civil action of which the district courts have original jurisdiction."

We now conclude the answer must be yes. When the well-pleaded complaint contains at least one claim that satisfies the amount-in-controversy requirement, and there are no other relevant jurisdictional defects, the district court, beyond all question, has original jurisdiction over that claim. The presence of other claims in the complaint, over which the district court may lack original jurisdiction, is of no moment. If the court has original jurisdiction over a single claim in the complaint, it has original jurisdiction over a "civil action" within the meaning of §1367(a), even if the civil action over which it has jurisdiction comprises fewer claims than were included in the complaint. Once the court determines it has original jurisdiction over the civil action, it can turn to the question whether it has a constitutional and statutory basis for exercising supplemental jurisdiction over the other claims in the action.

Section 1367(a) commences with the direction that §§1367(b) and (c), or other relevant statutes, may provide specific exceptions, but otherwise §1367(a) is a broad jurisdictional grant, with no distinction drawn between pendent-claim and pendent-party cases. In fact, the last sentence of §1367(a) makes clear that the provision grants supplemental jurisdiction over claims involving joinder or intervention of additional parties. The terms of §1367 do not acknowledge any distinction between pendent jurisdiction and the doctrine of so-called ancillary jurisdiction. Though the doctrines of pendent and ancillary jurisdiction developed separately as a historical matter, the Court has recognized that the doctrines are "two species of the same generic problem," *Kroger*. Nothing in §1367 indicates a congressional intent to recognize, preserve, or create some meaningful, substantive distinction between the jurisdictional categories we have historically labeled pendent and ancillary.

If §1367(a) were the sum total of the relevant statutory language, our holding would rest on that language alone. The statute, of course, instructs us to examine §1367(b) to determine if any of its exceptions apply, so we proceed to that section. While §1367(b) qualifies the broad rule of §1367(a), it does not withdraw supplemental jurisdiction over the claims of the additional parties at issue here. The specific exceptions to §1367(a) contained in §1367(b), moreover, provide additional support for our conclusion that §1367(a) confers supplemental jurisdiction over these claims. Section 1367(b), which applies only to diversity cases, withholds supplemental jurisdiction over the claims of plaintiffs proposed to be joined as indispensable parties under Federal Rule of Civil Procedure 19, or who seek to intervene pursuant to Rule 24. Nothing in the text of §1367(b), however, withholds supplemental jurisdiction over the claims of plaintiffs permissively joined under Rule 20 or certified as class-action members pursuant to Rule 23. The natural, indeed the necessary, inference is that §1367 confers supplemental jurisdiction over claims by Rule 20 and Rule 23 plaintiffs. This inference, at least with respect to Rule 20 plaintiffs, is strengthened by the fact that §1367(b) explicitly excludes supplemental jurisdiction over claims against defendants joined under Rule 20.

We cannot accept the view, urged by some of the parties, commentators, and Courts of Appeals, that a district court lacks original jurisdiction over a civil action unless the court has original jurisdiction over every claim in the complaint. As we understand this position, it requires assuming either that all claims in the complaint must stand or fall as a single, indivisible "civil action" as a matter of definitional necessity—what we will refer to as the "indivisibility theory"—or else that the inclusion of a claim or party falling outside the district court's original jurisdiction somehow contaminates every other claim in the complaint, depriving the court of original jurisdiction over any of these claims—what we will refer to as the "contamination theory."

The indivisibility theory is easily dismissed, as it is inconsistent with the whole notion of supplemental jurisdiction. If a district court must have original jurisdiction over every claim in the complaint in order to have "original jurisdiction" over a "civil action," then in *Gibbs* there was no civil action of which the district court could assume original jurisdiction under §1331, and so no basis for exercising supplemental jurisdiction over any of the claims. The indivisibility theory is further belied by our practice—in both federal-question and diversity cases—of allowing federal courts to cure jurisdictional defects by dismissing the offending parties rather than dismissing the entire action. . . .

The contamination theory, as we have noted, can make some sense in the special context of the complete diversity requirement because the presence of nondiverse parties on both sides of a lawsuit eliminates the justification for providing a federal forum. The theory, however, makes little sense with respect to the amount-in-controversy requirement, which is meant to ensure that a dispute is sufficiently important to warrant federal-court attention. The presence of a single nondiverse party may eliminate the fear of bias with respect to all claims, but the presence of a claim that falls short of the minimum amount in controversy does nothing to reduce the importance of the claims that do meet this requirement.

It is fallacious to suppose, simply from the proposition that §1332 imposes both the diversity requirement and the amount-in-controversy requirement, that the contamination theory germane to the former is also relevant to the latter. There is no inherent logical connection between the amount-in-controversy requirement and §1332 diversity jurisdiction. After all, federal-question jurisdiction once had an amount-in-controversy requirement as well. If such a requirement were revived under §1331, it is clear beyond peradventure that §1367(a) provides supplemental jurisdiction over federal-question cases where some, but not all, of the federal-law claims involve a sufficient amount in controversy. In other words, §1367(a) unambiguously overrules the holding and the result in *Clark*. If that is so, however, it would be quite extraordinary to say that §1367 did not also overrule *Zahn*, a case that was premised in substantial part on the holding in *Clark*.

In addition to the theoretical difficulties with the argument that a district court has original jurisdiction over a civil action only if it has original jurisdiction over each individual claim in the complaint, we have already considered and rejected a virtually identical argument in the closely analogous context of removal jurisdiction. In *Chicago v. International College of Surgeons* (1997), the plaintiff brought federal- and state-law claims in state court. The defendant removed to federal court. The plaintiff objected to removal, citing the text of the removal statute, 1441(a). That statutory provision, which bears a striking similarity to the relevant portion of §1367, authorizes removal of "any civil action . . . of which the district courts of the United States have original jurisdiction." The *College of Surgeons* plaintiff urged that, because its state-law claims were not within the District Court's original jurisdiction, §1441(a) did not authorize removal. We disagreed. The federal law claims, we held, "suffice to make the actions 'civil actions' within the 'original jurisdiction' of the district courts. . . . Nothing in the jurisdictional statutes suggests that the presence of related state law claims somehow alters the fact that [the plaintiff's] complaints, by virtue of their federal claims, were 'civil actions' within the federal courts' 'original jurisdiction.'" Once the case was removed, the District Court had original jurisdiction over the federal law claims and supplemental jurisdiction under §1367(a) over the state-law claims.

. . . More importantly for present purposes, *College of Surgeons* stressed that a district court has original jurisdiction of a civil action for purposes of §1441(a) as long as it has original jurisdiction over a subset of the claims constituting the action. Even the *College of Surgeons* dissent, which took issue with the Court's interpretation of §1367, did not appear to contest this view of §1441(a).

Although *College of Surgeons* involved additional claims between the same parties, its interpretation of §1441(a) applies equally to cases involving additional parties whose claims fall short of the jurisdictional amount. If we were to adopt the contrary view that the presence of additional parties means there is no "civil action . . . of which the district courts . . . have original jurisdiction," those cases simply would not be removable. To our knowledge, no court has issued a reasoned opinion adopting this view of the removal statute. It is settled, of course, that absent complete diversity a case is not removable because the district court would lack original jurisdiction. *Caterpillar Inc. v. Lewis* (1996). This, however, is altogether consistent with our view of §1441(a). A failure of complete diversity, unlike the failure of some claims to meet the requisite amount in controversy, contaminates every claim in the action.

We also reject the argument, similar to the attempted distinction of *College of Surgeons* discussed above, that while the presence of additional claims over which the district court lacks jurisdiction does not mean the civil action is outside the purview of §1367(a), the presence of additional parties does. The basis for this distinction is not altogether clear, and it is in considerable tension with statutory text. Section 1367(a) applies by its terms to any civil action of which the district courts have original jurisdiction, and the last sentence of §1367(a) expressly contemplates that the court may have supplemental jurisdiction over additional parties. So it cannot be the case that the presence of those parties destroys the court's original jurisdiction, within the meaning of §1367(a), over a civil action otherwise properly before it.

Also, §1367(b) expressly withholds supplemental jurisdiction in diversity cases over claims by plaintiffs joined as indispensable parties under Rule 19. If joinder of such parties were sufficient to deprive the district court of original jurisdiction over the civil action within the meaning of §1367(a), this specific limitation on supplemental jurisdiction in §1367(b) would be superfluous.

Finally, it is suggested that our interpretation of §1367(a) creates an anomaly regarding the exceptions listed in §1367(b): It is not immediately obvious why Congress would withhold supplemental jurisdiction over plaintiffs joined as parties "needed for just adjudication" under Rule 19 but would allow supplemental jurisdiction over plaintiffs permissively joined under Rule 20. The omission of Rule 20 plaintiffs from the list of exceptions in §1367(b) may have been an "unintentional drafting gap" *Meritcare Inc. v. St. Paul Mercury Ins. Co.* (3d Cir. 1998). If that is the case, it is up to Congress rather than the courts to fix it. The omission may seem odd, but it is not absurd. An alternative explanation for the different treatment of Rule 19 and Rule 20 is that Congress was concerned that extending supplemental jurisdiction to Rule 19 plaintiffs would allow circumvention of the complete diversity rule: A nondiverse plaintiff might be omitted intentionally from the original action, but joined later under Rule 19 as a necessary party. *See Stromberg Metal Works, Inc. v. Press Mechanical, Inc.* (7th. Cir. 1996). The contamination theory described above, if applicable, means this ruse would fail, but Congress may have wanted to make assurance double sure. More generally, Congress may have concluded that federal jurisdiction is only appropriate if the district court would have original jurisdiction over the claims of all those plaintiffs who are so essential to the action that they could be joined under Rule 19.

And so we circle back to the original question. When the well-pleaded complaint in district court includes multiple claims, all part of the same case or controversy, and some, but not all, of the claims are within the court's original jurisdiction, does the court have before it "any civil action of which the district courts have original jurisdiction"? It does. Under §1367, the court has original jurisdiction over the civil action comprising the claims for which there is no jurisdictional defect. No other reading of §1367 is plausible in light of the text and structure of the jurisdictional statute. Though the special nature and purpose of the diversity requirement mean that a single nondiverse party can contaminate every other claim in the lawsuit, the contamination does not occur with respect to jurisdictional defects that go only to the substantive importance of individual claims.

It follows from this conclusion that the threshold requirement of §1367(a) is satisfied in cases, like those now before us, where some, but not all, of the plaintiffs in a diversity action allege a sufficient amount in controversy. We hold that §1367 by its plain text overruled *Clark* and *Zahn* and authorized supplemental jurisdiction over all claims by diverse parties arising out of the same Article III case or controversy, subject only to enumerated exceptions not applicable in the cases now before us.

C

The proponents of the alternative view of §1367 insist that the statute is at least ambiguous and that we should look to other interpretive tools, including the legislative history of §1367, which supposedly demonstrate Congress did not intend §1367 to overrule *Zahn*.

Those who urge that the legislative history refutes our interpretation rely primarily on the House Judiciary Committee Report on the Judicial Improvements Act. H.R. Rep. (1990) (House Report or Report). This Report explained that §1367 would "authorize jurisdiction in a case like *Finley,* as well as essentially restore the pre-*Finley* understandings of the authorization for and limits on other forms of supplemental jurisdiction." . . . The Report then remarked that §1367(b) "is not intended to affect the jurisdictional requirements of [§1332] in diversity-only class actions, as those requirements were interpreted prior to *Finley.*"

As we have repeatedly held, the authoritative statement is the statutory text, not the legislative history or any other extrinsic material. . . . Judicial investigation of legislative history has a tendency to become, to borrow Judge Leventhal's memorable phrase, an exercise in "'looking over a crowd and picking out your friends.'" Second, judicial reliance on legislative materials like committee reports, which are not themselves subject to the requirements of Article I, may give unrepresentative committee members—or, worse yet, unelected staffers and lobbyists—both the power and the incentive to attempt strategic manipulations of legislative history to secure results they were unable to achieve through the statutory text.

[E]ven if we believed resort to legislative history were appropriate in these cases—a point we do not concede—we would not give significant weight to the House Report. The distinguished jurists who drafted the Subcommittee Working Paper, along with three of the participants in the drafting of §1367, agree that this provision, on its face, overrules *Zahn.* This accords with the best reading of the statute's text, and nothing in the legislative history indicates directly and explicitly that Congress understood the phrase "civil action of which the district courts have original jurisdiction" to exclude cases in which some but not all of the diversity plaintiffs meet the amount in controversy requirement.

D

Finally, we note that the Class Action Fairness Act (CAFA), enacted this year, has no bearing on our analysis of these cases. Subject to certain limitations, the CAFA confers federal diversity jurisdiction over class actions where the aggregate amount in controversy exceeds $5 million. It abrogates the rule against aggregating claims, a rule this Court recognized in *Ben-Hur* and reaffirmed in *Zahn.* The CAFA, however, is not retroactive, and the views of the 2005 Congress are not relevant to our interpretation of a text enacted by Congress in 1990. The CAFA, moreover, does not moot the significance of our interpretation of §1367, as many proposed exercises of supplemental jurisdiction, even in the class-action context, might not fall within the CAFA's ambit. The CAFA, then, has no impact, one way or the other, on our interpretation of §1367.

* * *

The judgment of the Court of Appeals for the Eleventh Circuit is affirmed. The judgment of the Court of Appeals for the First Circuit is reversed, and the case is remanded for proceedings consistent with this opinion.

It is so ordered.

Justice GINSBURG, with whom Justice STEVENS, Justice O'CONNOR, and Justice BREYER join, dissenting.

. . . Section 1367, all agree, was designed to overturn this Court's decision in *Finley v. United States*, (1989). *Finley* concerned not diversity-of-citizenship jurisdiction (28 U.S.C. §1332), but original federal-court jurisdiction in cases arising under federal law (28 U.S.C. §1331).

What more §1367 wrought is an issue on which courts of appeals have sharply divided. . . .

The Court adopts a plausibly broad reading of §1367, a measure that is hardly a model of the careful drafter's art. There is another plausible reading, however, one less disruptive of our jurisprudence regarding supplemental jurisdiction. If one reads §1367(a) to instruct, as the statute's text suggests, that the district court must first have "original jurisdiction" over a "civil action" before supplemental jurisdiction can attach, then *Clark* and *Zahn* are preserved, and supplemental jurisdiction does not open the way for joinder of plaintiffs, or inclusion of class members, who do not independently meet the amount-in-controversy requirement. For the reasons that follow, I conclude that this narrower construction is the better reading of §1367.

. . .

II

A

. . . This Court has long held that, in determining whether the amount-in-controversy requirement has been satisfied, a single plaintiff may aggregate two or more claims against a single defendant, even if the claims are unrelated. But in multiparty cases, including class actions, we have unyieldingly adhered to the nonaggregation rule stated in *Troy Bank*. *See Clark* (reaffirming the "familiar rule that when several plaintiffs assert separate and distinct demands in a single suit, the amount involved in each separate controversy must be of the requisite amount to be within the jurisdiction of the district court, and that those amounts cannot be added together to satisfy jurisdictional requirements"); *Snyder v. Harris* (1969) (abandonment of the nonaggregation rule in class actions would undercut the congressional "purpose . . . to check, to some degree, the rising caseload of the federal courts").

B

§1367(a) addresses "civil action[s] of which the district courts have original jurisdiction," a formulation that, in diversity cases, is sensibly read to incorporate the rules on joinder and aggregation tightly tied to §1332 at the time of §1367's enactment. On this reading, a complaint must first meet that "original jurisdiction" measurement. If it does not, no supplemental jurisdiction is authorized. If it does, §1367(a) authorizes "supplemental jurisdiction" over related claims. In other words, §1367(a) would preserve undiminished, as part and parcel of §1332 "original jurisdiction" determinations, both the "complete diversity" rule and the decisions restricting aggregation to arrive at the amount in controversy. Section 1367(b)'s office, then, would be "to prevent the erosion of the complete diversity [and amount-in-controversy] requirement[s] that might otherwise result from an expansive application of what was once termed the doctrine of ancillary jurisdiction." *See* Pfander, *Supplemental Jurisdiction and Section 1367: The Case for a Sympathetic Textualism*, 148 U. Pa. L. Rev. 109, 114 (1999). In contrast to the Court's construction of §1367, which draws a sharp line between the diversity and amount-in-controversy components of §1332, see ante, the interpretation presented here does not sever the two jurisdictional requirements.

The more restrained reading of §1367 just outlined would yield affirmance of the First Circuit's judgment in *Ortega*, and reversal of the Eleventh Circuit's judgment in *Exxon*. It would not discard entirely, as the Court does, the judicially developed doctrines of pendent and ancillary jurisdiction as they existed when *Finley* was decided. Instead, it would recognize §1367 essentially as a codification of those doctrines, placing them under a single heading, but largely retaining their substance, with overriding *Finley* the only basic change: Supplemental jurisdiction, once the district court has original jurisdiction, would now include "claims that involve the joinder or intervention of additional parties." §1367(a).

Not only would the reading I find persuasive "alig[n] statutory supplemental jurisdiction with the judicially developed doctrines of pendent and ancillary jurisdiction," *id.*, it would also synchronize 1367 with the removal statute, 28 U.S.C. §1441. As the First Circuit carefully explained:

> Section 1441, like §1367, applies only if the "civil action" in question is one "of which the district courts . . . have original jurisdiction." §1441(a). Relying on that language, the Supreme Court has interpreted §1441 to prohibit removal unless the entire action, as it stands at the time of removal, could have been filed in federal court in the first instance. Section 1441 has thus been held to incorporate the well-pleaded complaint rule, *see City of Chicago v. Int'l College of Surgeons* (1997) . . . ; the complete diversity rule, *see Caterpillar, Inc. v. Lewis* (1996); and rules for calculating the amount in controversy, *see St. Paul Mercury Indem. Co. v. Red Cab Co.* (1938). *Ortega*.

The less disruptive view I take of §1367 also accounts for the omission of Rule 20 plaintiffs and Rule 23 class actions in §1367(b)'s text. If one reads §1367(a) as a plenary grant of supplemental jurisdiction to federal courts sitting in diversity, one would indeed look for exceptions in §1367(b). Finding none for permissive joinder of parties or class actions, one would conclude that Congress effectively, even if unintentionally, overruled *Clark* and *Zahn*. But if one recognizes that the nonaggregation rule delineated in *Clark* and *Zahn* forms part of the determination whether "original jurisdiction" exists in a diversity case, then plaintiffs who do not meet the amount-in-controversy requirement would fail at the §1367(a) threshold. Congress would have no reason to resort to a §1367(b) exception to turn such plaintiffs away from federal court, given that their claims, from the start, would fall outside the court's §1332 jurisdiction.

What is the utility of §1367(b) under my reading of §1367(a)? Section 1367(a) allows parties other than the plaintiff to assert *reactive* claims once entertained under the heading ancillary jurisdiction. See supra, at 2633 (listing claims, including compulsory counterclaims and impleader claims, over which federal courts routinely exercised ancillary jurisdiction). As earlier observed, §1367(b) stops plaintiffs from circumventing §1332's jurisdictional requirements by using another's claim as a hook to add a claim that the plaintiff could not have brought in the first instance. *Kroger* is the paradigm case. See, supra, at 2633. There, the Court held that ancillary jurisdiction did not extend to a plaintiff's claim against a nondiverse party who had been impleaded by the defendant under Rule 14. Section 1367(b), then, is corroborative of §1367(a)'s coverage of claims formerly called ancillary, but provides exceptions to assure that accommodation of added claims would not fundamentally alter "the jurisdictional requirements of section 1332."

While §1367's enigmatic text defies flawless interpretation, . . . the precedent-preservative reading, I am persuaded, better accords with the historical and legal context of Congress' enactment of the supplemental jurisdiction statute, . . . and the established limits on pendent and ancillary jurisdiction. . . . It does not attribute to Congress a jurisdictional enlargement broader than the one to which the legislators adverted, and it follows the sound counsel that "close questions of [statutory] construction should be resolved in favor of continuity and against change." Shapiro, *Continuity and Change in Statutory Interpretation*, 67 N.Y.U. L. Rev. 921, 925 (1992).

[A separate dissenting opinion of Justice STEVENS, joined by Justice BREYER, is omitted.]

* * *

Even if supplemental jurisdiction is available, a court may nonetheless decline to exercise it. Section 1367(c) describes the grounds for declining to exercise supplemental jurisdiction. The U.S. Supreme Court construed §1367(c)'s relationship to *United Mine Workers of America v. Gibbs* (1966), and to abstention doctrine, in *City of Chicago v. Int'l College of Surgeons* (1997). The Court described these relationships as follows:

> [T]o say that the terms of §1367(a) authorize the district courts to exercise supplemental jurisdiction over state law claims . . . does not mean that the jurisdiction *must* be exercised in all cases. Our decisions have established that pendent jurisdiction is a doctrine of discretion, not of plaintiff's right, *Gibbs*, and that district courts can decline to exercise jurisdiction over pendent claims for a number of valid reasons, *id*. . . . Accordingly, we have indicated that district courts [should] deal with cases involving pendent claims in the manner that best serves the principles of economy, convenience, fairness, and comity which underlie the pendent jurisdiction doctrine. *Carnegie-Mellon Univ. v. Cohill* (1988).

The supplemental jurisdiction statute codifies these principles. After establishing that supplemental jurisdiction encompasses other claims, in the same case or controversy as a claim within the district court original jurisdiction, §1367(a), the statute confirms the discretionary nature of supplemental jurisdiction by enumerating the circumstances in which district courts can refuse its exercise:

(c) The district courts may decline to exercise supplemental jurisdiction over a claim under subsection (a) if

(1) the claim raises a novel or complex issue of State law,

(2) the claim substantially predominates over the claim or claims over which the district court has original jurisdiction

(3) the district court has dismissed all claims over which it has original jurisdiction, or

(4) in exceptional circumstances, there are other compelling reasons for declining jurisdiction. 28 U.S.C. §1367(c).

Depending on a host of factors, then — including the circumstances of the particular case, the nature of the state law claims, the character of the governing state law, and the relationship between the state and federal claims — district courts may decline to exercise jurisdiction over supplemental state law claims. The statute thereby reflects the understanding that, when deciding whether to exercise supplemental jurisdiction, "a federal court should consider and weigh in each case, and at every stage of the litigation, the values of judicial economy, convenience, fairness, and comity." *Cohill.* In this case, the District Court decided that those interests would be best served by exercising jurisdiction over ICS state law claims.

In addition to their discretion under §1367(c), district courts may be obligated not to decide state law claims (or to stay their adjudication) where one of the abstention doctrines articulated by this Court applies. Those doctrines embody the general notion that federal courts may decline to exercise their jurisdiction, in otherwise exceptional circumstances, where denying a federal forum would clearly serve an important countervailing interest, for example where abstention is warranted by considerations of proper constitutional adjudication, regard for federal-state relations, or wise judicial administration. *Quackenbush v. Allstate Ins. Co.* (1996).

4. Removal Jurisdiction

When an action that is filed in state court could have been brought in federal court, the defendant may remove the action from state court to federal court if the requirements of the federal removal statute (28 U.S.C. §1441) are met. The federal court to which the case must be removed is generally the court whose jurisdiction covers the jurisdiction of the state court in which the case was first filed. Thus, for example, if an action is filed in a state court located in Seattle, Washington, removal would be to the nearest federal district court, the U.S. District Court for the Western District of Washington, which sits in Seattle.

Congress, the Court has held, "is constitutionally free to establish the conditions under which civil or criminal proceedings involving federal issues may be removed from one court to another." *City of Greenwood v. Peacock* (1966). The power has also been long recognized for cases resting on diversity of citizenship. *See Railway Co. v. Whitton* (1871). One constitutional limit on the power to provide for removal is the Seventh Amendment. *See Justices v. Murray* (1870) ("so much of the [removal statute] as provides for the removal of a judgment in a State court, and in which the cause was tried by a jury, to the Circuit Court of the United States for a retrial on the facts and law, is not in pursuance of the Constitution, and is void").

The most important of the requirements of §1441 are as follows:

(a) The action could originally have been brought in federal court. Removal jurisdiction is no greater than original jurisdiction.

(b) All defendants must join in the petition for removal, unless the narrow requirements of §1441(c) are satisfied.

(c) The defendant cannot remove if the basis for federal court jurisdiction is diversity and the defendant is a citizen of the state in which the original action was filed. This rule is based on the notion that a resident defendant has no reason to fear bias by her own home courts. The rule applies only to diversity-based removal. *See Lincoln Prop. Co. v. Roche* (2005) (holding that a removing defendant is not obliged to inform federal court of local affiliates who are potential defendants and whose presence, if joined, would defeat removal).

(d) The defendant must remove before taking substantial steps to defend the action in the state court. An untimely petition will be denied.

After a case has been removed to federal court, the judge may remand the case only under the conditions set forth in the removal statutes. Construing these statutes, the U.S. Supreme Court held in *Thermtron Products, Inc. v. Hermansdorfer* (1976), that a judge could not remand a case merely because of a crowded federal court docket. Since the removal statutes do not list "overcrowded docket" as a basis for remanding a case, the court lacked power to remand on this basis.

Despite *Thermtron*, the Court in *Carnegie-Mellon University v. Cohill* (1988), held that a federal court could remand a case when, after removal, the federal claims in the case were dismissed and only the supplemental state law claims remained. Three Justices dissented on the ground that because the removal statutes did not expressly provide for remand in such circumstances, they should be construed to disallow remand of residual pendent state law claims. The majority position seems correct, however, especially in light of the federal judiciary's longstanding practice, now codified in the supplemental jurisdiction statute, of declining jurisdiction over pendent state law claims once the anchoring federal claims have been dismissed. 28 U.S.C. §1367(c)(3); *see also* 28 U.S.C. §1447(c).

As you might imagine, motions to remove and to remand are subject to elaborate strategic considerations regarding what the litigants perceive to be the costs and benefits of adjudicating in the state or federal forum. In high stakes cases, detailed research is conducted on average jury verdicts, differences in standards for pre-trial motion practice, and the composition of the judiciary in state and federal courts.

Generally speaking, there is no effective appeal from an order granting a remand to state court, no matter how clearly wrong the decision may be. *See, e.g., Cook v. Wikler* (3d Cir. 2003) (refusing to review remand order under 28 U.S.C. §1447(d); district court remanded case on ground that removal by third party defendant is improper). There are a few exceptions to the blanket rule against appeals, such as certain civil rights cases, and exercises of discretion under the supplemental jurisdiction statute, 28 U.S.C. §1367(c), as well as certain class action lawsuits falling under the recently enacted Class Action Fairness Act. *See* 28 U.S.C. §1453(c)(1).

Our next case interprets 28 U.S.C. §1442, the federal officer removal statute. It provides a broad right to seek removal to the

United States or any agency thereof or any officer (or any person acting under that officer) of the United States or of any agency thereof, in an official or individual capacity, for or relating to any act under color of such office or on account of any right, title or authority claimed under any Act of Congress for the apprehension or punishment of criminals or the collection of the revenue.

Davis, a deputy collector of internal revenue, was indicted for murder in state court following a shoot-out that took place when he attempted to seize an illegal alcohol distillery. His petition for removal stated that he acted in self-defense, returning fire only when fired upon, "while so attempting to enforce the revenue laws of the United States." Although the removal statute at the time was narrower, it covered revenue officers such as Davis.

Tennessee v. Davis

100 U.S. 259 (1879)

Mr. Justice STRONG delivered the opinion of the court.

The first of the questions certified is one of great importance, bringing as it does into consideration the relation of the general government to the government of the states, and bringing also into view not merely the construction of an act of Congress, but its constitutionality. That in this case the defendant's petition for removal of the cause was in the form prescribed by the act of Congress admits of no doubt. It represented that he had been indicted for murder in the Circuit Court of Grundy County and that the indictment and criminal prosecution were still pending. It represented further that no murder was committed, but that, on the other hand, the killing was committed in the petitioner's own necessary self-defense, to save his own life; that at the time when the alleged act for which he was indicted was committed, he was and still is an officer of the United States, . . . that what he did was done under and by right of his office, to-wit, as deputy collector of internal revenue; that it was his duty to seize illicit distilleries and the apparatus that is used for the illicit and unlawful distillation of spirits; and that while so attempting to enforce the revenue laws of the United States as deputy collector as aforesaid, he was assaulted and fired upon by a number of armed men, and that in defense of his life he returned the fire. The petition was verified by oath, and the certificate required by the act of Congress to be given by the petitioner's legal counsel was appended thereto. . . . Now certainly the petition for the removal represented that the act for which the defendant was indicted was done not merely under color of his office as a revenue collector, or under color of the revenue laws, not merely while he was engaged in performing his duties as a revenue officer, but that it was done under and by right of his office, and while he was resisted by an armed force in his attempts to discharge his official duty.

That the act of Congress does provide for the removal of criminal prosecutions for offenses against the state laws when there arises in them the claim of the federal right or authority is too plain to admit of denial. Such is its positive language, and it is not to be argued away by presenting the supposed incongruity of administering state criminal laws by other courts than those established by the state. It has been strenuously urged that murder within a state is not made a crime by any act of Congress, and that it is an offense against the peace and dignity of the state alone. Hence it is inferred that its trial and punishment can be conducted only in state tribunals, and it is argued that the act of Congress cannot mean what it says, but that it must intend only such prosecutions in state courts as are for offenses against the United States—offenses against the revenue laws. But there can be no criminal prosecution initiated in any state court for that which is merely an offense against the general government. If, therefore, the statute is to be allowed any meaning when it speaks of criminal prosecutions in state courts, it must intend those that are instituted for alleged violations of state laws in which defenses are set up or claimed under United States laws or authority.

We come, then, to the inquiry, most discussed during the argument, whether sec. 643 is a constitutional exercise of the power vested in Congress. Has the Constitution conferred upon Congress the power to authorize the removal, from a state court to a federal court, of an indictment against a revenue officer for an alleged crime against the state, and to order its removal before trial, when it appears that a federal question or a claim to a federal right is raised in the case and must be decided therein? A more important question can hardly be imagined. Upon its answer may depend the possibility of the general government's preserving its own existence. As was said in *Martin v. Hunter* (1816), "The general government must cease to exist whenever it loses the power of protecting itself in the exercise of its constitutional powers." It can act only through its officers and agents, and they must act within the states. If, when thus acting and within the scope of their authority, those officers can be arrested and brought to trial in a state court for an alleged offense against the law of the state, yet warranted by the federal authority they possess, and if the general government is powerless to interfere at once for their protection—if their protection must be left to the action of the state court—the operations of the general government may at any time be arrested at the will of one of its members. The legislation of a state may be unfriendly. It may affix penalties to acts done under the immediate direction of the national government and in obedience to its laws. It may deny the authority conferred by those laws. The state court may administer not only the laws of the state, but equally federal law, in such a manner as to paralyze the operations of the government. And even if, after trial and final judgment in the state court, the case can be brought into the United States court for review, the officer is withdrawn from the discharge of his duty during the pendency of the prosecution and the exercise of acknowledged federal power arrested.

We do not think such an element of weakness is to be found in the Constitution. The United States is a government with authority extending over the whole territory of the Union, acting upon the states and upon the people of the states. While it is limited in the number of its powers, so far as its sovereignty extends, it is supreme. No state government can exclude it from the exercise of any authority conferred upon it by the Constitution, obstruct its authorized officers against its will, or withhold from it for a moment the cognizance of any subject which that instrument has committed to it.

. . . Congress is invested with power to make all laws necessary and proper for carrying into execution not only all the powers previously specified, but also all other powers vested by the Constitution in the government of the United States or in any department or officer thereof. Among these is the judicial power of the government. That is declared by the second section of the third article to

> extend to all cases in law and equity arising under the Constitution, the laws of the United States, and treaties made, or which shall be made, under their authority. . . .

This provision embraces alike civil and criminal cases arising under the Constitution and laws. *Cohens v. Virginia* (1821). Both are equally within the domain of the judicial powers of the United States, and there is nothing in the grant to justify an assertion that whatever power may be exerted over a civil case may not be exerted as fully over a criminal one.

The constitutional right of Congress to authorize the removal before trial of civil cases arising under the laws of the United States has long since passed beyond doubt. It was exercised almost contemporaneously with the adoption of the Constitution, and the power has been in constant use ever since. The Judiciary Act of Sept. 24, 1789, was passed by the first Congress, many members of which had assisted in framing the Constitution, and though some doubts were soon after suggested whether cases could be removed from state courts before trial, those doubts soon disappeared. Whether removal from a state to a federal court is an exercise of appellate jurisdiction, as laid down in Story's Commentaries on the Constitution, sec. 1745, or an indirect mode of exercising original jurisdiction, as intimated in *Railway Company v. Whitton* (1871), we need not now inquire. . . . The judicial power is declared to extend to all cases of the character described, making no distinction between civil and criminal, and the reasons for conferring upon the courts of the national government superior jurisdiction over cases involving authority and rights under the laws of the United States are equally applicable to both. As we have already said, such a jurisdiction is necessary for the preservation of the acknowledged powers of the government. It is essential also to a uniform and consistent administration of national laws. It is required for the preservation of that supremacy which the Constitution gives to the general government . . .

The argument so much pressed upon us that it is an invasion of the sovereignty of a state to withdraw from its courts into the courts of the general government the trial of prosecutions for alleged offenses against the criminal laws of a state, even though the defense presents a case arising out of an act of Congress, ignores entirely the dual character of our government. It assumes that the states are completely and in all respects sovereign. But when the national government was formed, some of the attributes of state sovereignty were partially, and others wholly, surrendered and vested in the United States. . . . The removal of cases arising under those laws from state into federal courts is therefore no invasion of state domain. On the contrary, a denial of the right of the general government to remove them, to take charge of and try any case arising under the Constitution or laws of the United States, is a denial of the conceded sovereignty of that government over a subject expressly committed to it.

. . . It follows that the first question certified to us from the circuit court of Tennessee must be answered in the affirmative. . . .

[The dissenting opinion of Justice CLIFFORD, joined by Justice FIELD, is omitted].

* * *

The fact that the party seeking removal is a federal officer is a necessary but not sufficient ground for removal under §1442. Can you see the jurisdictional problem that would arise if the officer's federal status alone were sufficient? In what sense would the case "arise under" federal law if there were no federal defense? In *Mesa v. California* (1989), the Court denied federal officer removal where two postal workers were prosecuted in state court for misdemeanor manslaughter for, in one case, striking a cyclist and speeding, and, in the other, striking a police car, with their postal trucks. The Court emphasized that "[a]lthough we have not always spoken with the same clarity that [our] early decisions evince, we have not departed from the requirement that federal officer removal must be predicated on the allegation of a colorable federal defense." What is the federal defense in *Davis*? *See Mesa* ("[T]he successful legal defense of 'self-defense' depends on the truth of two distinct elements: that the act committed was, in a legal sense, an act of self-defense, and that the act was justified, that is, warranted under the circumstances.") In Davis's case, "the truth of the first element depended on a question of federal law: Was it Davis' duty under federal law to seize the distillery? If Davis had merely been a thief attempting to steal his assailants' property, returning their fire would simply not have been an act of self-defense, pretermitting any question of justification. Proof that Davis was not a thief depended on the federal revenue laws, and provided the necessary predicate for removal." *Mesa.*

By allowing removal based on a federal defense, §1442 deviates from the ordinary limitations on original federal question jurisdiction established by Congress, which, as we saw in *Mottley*, denies jurisdiction on the basis of an anticipated federal defense. This makes §1442 a broader ground of removal than §1441. Federal officer removal applies to both civil and criminal cases.

Note that the text of §1442 extends federal officer removal not only to any officer but to "any person acting under that officer." This means that agents, including private contractors of the federal government, can seek removal. The following case applies the principal Supreme Court precedent on agent removal to a cooperative federalism system for water quality regulation and state litigation over the Flint, Michigan water crisis. It is well established that consumption of lead even at low levels is associated with grave health effects:

> serious, irreversible damage to the developing brains and nervous systems of babies and young children. . . . In pregnant women, lead crosses the placental barrier of the womb and can harm the fetus [and even] low-level exposures . . . have been found to affect behavior and intelligence. . . . Even in otherwise healthy adults, lead exposure can cause adverse cardiovascular and kidney effects, cognitive dysfunction, and elevated blood pressure.

Natural Resources Defense Counsel, *What's in Your Water? Flint and Beyond: Analysis of EPA.* "The majority of Flint's residents are African American, and about 40 percent live below the poverty line. The median household income is $25,000 (about half the national level)." Contaminated water supply is not a problem isolated to Flint. "[E]xperts have estimated that 6 to 10 million lead service lines are being used in the United States, serving 15 to 22 million Americans. . . . National restrictions on lead pipes and lead-containing plumbing fixtures were introduced in 1986 . . . [but] were fairly weak until a law allowing no more than .25 percent lead content was enacted and made effective in 2014." *Id.* EPA data show "widespread violations" of the laws on lead content in water "across the country . . . 5,363 active community water systems . . . serv[ing] 18, 164,558 people." *Id.* A Virginia Tech study found that "children had elevated blood lead as a result of water lead exposure" in a number of cities that "publicly claimed their water was safe according to federal standards" only by "gam[ing] the system to avoid reporting results with high lead levels." *Id.* In 2015, more than 1,000 community water systems in 2015 serving 4 million people "exceeded the lead action level" set by the EPA to prevent adverse health effects. *Id.* A subsequent study of EPA data on lead and other hazardous contaminants in drinking water found over 12,000 health-based violations of the Safe Water Drinking Act in community water systems affecting more than 27 million people. Formal enforcement by regulators was taken in just a fraction of these cases.[12]

Race, ethnicity, low-income and areas with more non-native English speakers, are among the strongest factors determining whether one has access to clean water.[13] With respect to race in particular the study found that "[d]rinking water systems that consistently violate the law for years were 40 percent more likely to occur in places with higher percentages of residents who were people of color, according to EPA data from 2016-2019. . . . Even when actions were taken to compel systems to fix their violations, it took longer for water systems in communities of color to come back into compliance."[14]

Mays v. City of Flint

871 F.3d 437 (6th Cir. 2017)

Ronald Lee GILMAN, Circuit Judge.

This case arises out of the drinking-water crisis in Flint, Michigan. The Plaintiffs are residents of the City of Flint who represent themselves and seek to represent a class of similarly situated individuals. They allege that they have been harmed since April 2014 by the toxic condition of the Flint water supply. The Plaintiffs filed suit against several City and State officials in the Genesee County Circuit Court, asserting various state-law tort claims.

Complete diversity of citizenship is lacking, and no federal question is presented on the face of the complaint. Nevertheless, four of the State officials who are present or former employees of the Michigan Department of Environmental Quality (the MDEQ Defendants) removed the action from the state court to federal court on two grounds. They first invoked the "federal-officer removal" provision under 28 U.S.C. §1442(a)(1), contending that all of their conduct in question was performed under the supervision and direction of the United States Environmental Protection Agency (the EPA). Second, the MDEQ Defendants contend that the Plaintiffs' claims necessarily implicate a substantial federal issue that merits federal-question jurisdiction under 28 U.S.C. §1441.

---

12. *See* Kristi Pullen Fedinick & Erik D. Olson, Natural Resources Defense Council Report, *Threats on Tap: Widespread Violations Highlight Need for Investment in Water Infrastructure and Protections* 4 (2017).

13. *Id.*

14. *Id.*

The Plaintiffs objected to removal. They filed a motion seeking to have the district court remand the case back to the state court, which the district court granted. On appeal, the MDEQ Defendants ask us to reverse the remand order. For the reasons set forth below, we instead *affirm* the judgment of the district court.

I. BACKGROUND
a. Factual Background

Prior to April 2014, Flint had obtained its drinking water under contract with the City of Detroit. That month Flint switched its source of drinking water to the Flint River in order to save money.

In January 2016, several of the Plaintiffs filed a class-action lawsuit in the Genesee County Circuit Court. The complaint alleged state-law claims of gross negligence, fraud, assault and battery, and intentional infliction of emotional distress. According to the complaint, the MDEQ Defendants committed these tortious actions by allowing Flint to switch its water supply without using an anti-corrosive agent, despite knowledge that the water was "highly corrosive and unsafe." This knowledge allegedly came from a 2011 report commissioned by the City of Flint, which concluded that the Flint River water could not be safely used for drinking unless it was treated with an anti-corrosive agent. Such an agent would be necessary to prevent lead and other chemicals from leaching into the water. The MDEQ received a copy of this report in 2013. But the MDEQ Defendants nevertheless allegedly failed to introduce corrosion-control treatments in a timely manner.

Just days after the switch in the water supply, the Plaintiffs allege that the City of Flint began receiving complaints "that the water was cloudy and discolored in appearance and foul in taste and odor." Water users also began reporting physical symptoms that included hair loss, rashes, and vomiting within weeks of the switch. Similar complaints were continually made to both the City of Flint and MDEQ officials for the next eight months. Numerous children in Flint were found to have elevated blood-lead levels by late 2014, and the MDEQ Defendants allegedly knew of this problem by early 2015. But the MDEQ Defendants, according to the Plaintiffs, did not reveal this problem to the public until after an August 2015 report was publicly disclosed.

The complaint further contends that the MDEQ Defendants deliberately ignored evidence that the water was unsafe and "falsely reassure[d] [the public] and insist[ed] that the water was safe even though they knew that the foul taste, odor and appearance was attributable to the highly corrosive Flint River water, untreated with the proper anti-corrosive agents." It also alleges, among other things, that the MDEQ Defendants refused an opportunity to reconnect with Detroit's safe drinking-water supply, falsely told the EPA in February 2015 that the Flint River water was receiving corrosion-control treatments, failed to maintain proper records needed to identify which water users had lead pipes, and failed to carry out proper water-quality tests.

b. Procedural Background

In April 2016, the MDEQ Defendants filed a notice of removal in the United States District Court for the Eastern District of Michigan. The MDEQ Defendants sought removal under two statutory provisions: (1) 28 U.S.C. §1442, the federal-officer removal statute, and (2) 28 U.S.C. §1441, which allows removal for state-law causes of action that raise substantial federal questions.

According to the notice of removal, federal-officer removal is appropriate because the MDEQ Defendants are being sued for actions that they took while acting under the direction of the EPA. The MDEQ Defendants assert that they were acting under the EPA because the EPA delegated primary enforcement authority to the MDEQ to implement the federal Safe Drinking Water Act (SDWA) in Michigan. Among the SDWA's requirements is the submission to the EPA of quarterly and annual reports detailing the MDEQ's compliance with the EPA's Lead and Copper Rule (LCR). *See* 40 C.F.R. §142.15. Under this primary enforcement scheme, the MDEQ Defendants contend that the EPA retains "tremendous oversight authority" over the MDEQ, including the ability to intervene or to withdraw primary enforcement authority in the event that the State fails to meet regulatory requirements.

The MDEQ Defendants also assert that they are being sued for actions that were "guided by repeated written and verbal dialogue with a number of EPA officers who advised and oversaw" the MDEQ's regulation of the Flint water system. According to the notice of removal, the fact that the MDEQ Defendants were "acting under" the EPA "is most clearly demonstrated by" an emergency order that the EPA issued on January 21, 2016. The emergency order stated that the MDEQ and the City of Flint had failed to adequately respond to the drinking-water crisis, and it directed the MDEQ to take certain actions deemed necessary by the EPA. In addition, the EPA announced that it would begin conducting its own water-quality tests in the City of Flint and publishing the results on its website.

II. ANALYSIS
a. Standard of Review

We review de novo the district court's determination that it lacked subject-matter jurisdiction and its consequent decision to issue a remand order. As the party seeking removal, the MDEQ Defendants bear the burden of establishing federal court jurisdiction. Where, as here, the district court treats the motion to remand as a facial attack on the court's jurisdiction, we look only to the pleadings—the complaint and the notice of removal—for the relevant facts. This includes the consideration of exhibits attached to the pleadings "so long as they are referred to in the [pleadings] and central to the claims contained therein." *Rondigo, L.L.C. v. Twp. of Richmond* (6th Cir. 2011). As this court has previously stated, removal statutes are to be strictly construed, and "all doubts should be resolved against removal." *Harnden v. Jayco, Inc.* (6th Cir. 2007).

B. Removal by the MDEQ Defendants Under the Federal-Officer Removal Statute was Properly Denied.

The federal-officer removal statute allows removal of actions against "[t]he United States or any agency thereof or any officer (or any person acting under that officer) of the United States or of any agency thereof, in an official or individual capacity, for or relating to any act under color of such office." 28 U.S.C. §1442(a)(1). Persons like the MDEQ Defendants, who are not federal officers, must satisfy three requirements in order to invoke the federal-officer removal statute: (1) the defendants must establish that they acted under a federal officer, (2) those actions must have been performed under color of federal office, and (3) the defendants must raise a colorable federal defense.

The Supreme Court discussed the federal-officer removal statute most recently in *Watson v. Philip Morris Cos.* (2007). . . . The Court noted that Congress enacted the original federal-officer removal statute during the War of 1812. That war was especially unpopular in New England, where many state court actions had been filed against federal customs officials whose duties included enforcing a trade embargo on England. The Court explained that the "initial removal statute was 'obviously . . . an attempt to protect federal officers from interference by hostile state courts.'"

Originally, the federal-officer removal statute covered only federal customs officials and "any other person aiding or assisting" those officials. *Id.*

Over time, Congress gradually expanded the scope of the statute, first to include persons assisting federal revenue officials, and later to include all federal officials and persons acting under them. *Id.* But as the Court noted in *Watson*, these changes simply provided that more types of federal officials could take advantage of removal, with no indication that Congress intended to expand the scope of the words "acting under."

The *Watson* Court explained that these early cases "illustrate that the removal statute's 'basic' purpose is to protect the Federal Government from the interference with its 'operations'" that would occur if a federal officer could be tried in state court for a state offense related to the operation. Concerns about "'local prejudice' against unpopular federal laws or federal officials" thus underlie the federal-officer removal statute. As the Court explained, states that were antagonistic toward federal government operations might use state court proceedings to thwart the enforcement of federal law.

Watson involved a cigarette manufacturer, Philip Morris, which filed a notice of removal based on the federal-officer removal statute. The plaintiff-smokers in *Watson* alleged that Philip Morris had engaged in deceptive business practices by using testing methods for its cigarettes that underreported the levels of tar and nicotine contained in the cigarettes. Concluding that the complaint challenged Philip Morris's use of the federal government's method for testing cigarettes, the district court held that the federal-officer removal statute applied, and the Eighth Circuit affirmed that decision. The Supreme Court reversed, holding that "the fact that a federal regulatory agency directs, supervises, and monitors a company's activities in considerable detail" was not enough to establish that Philip Morris was "acting under" an officer of the federal government.

Watson . . . set forth several considerations that are helpful in analyzing the present case. After reviewing the history of the federal-officer removal statute, as discussed above, the Court concluded that "the word 'under' must refer to what has been described as a relationship that involves 'acting in a certain capacity, considered in relation to one holding a superior position or office.'" The acting-under relationship "typically involves 'subjection, guidance, or control.'" In addition, the Court explained that a private entity must be assisting the federal government in carrying out the government's own tasks in order to invoke federal-officer removal. Simply complying with a regulation is insufficient, even if the regulatory scheme is "highly detailed" and the defendant's "activities are highly supervised and monitored."

In the present case, the MDEQ Defendants emphasize that the EPA would have to enforce the SDWA in Michigan if the MDEQ did not have primary enforcement authority to do so. *Watson* indicates that this is a factor supporting removal. If this were the only factor for us to consider, then the MDEQ Defendants might well be entitled to remove the case under the federal-officer removal statute.

But we read *Watson* as requiring more. Specifically, *Watson* interprets "acting under" to mean that the defendant seeking removal must be in a relationship with the federal government where the government is functioning as the defendant's superior. The Court went on to explain that the federal-officer removal statute was inapplicable to the facts in *Watson* because there was "no evidence of any delegation of legal authority from the FTC to the industry association to undertake testing on the Government agency's behalf. Nor is there evidence of any contract, any payment, any employer/employee relationship, or any principal/agent arrangement."

In the present case, the MDEQ Defendants argue that they were acting under the EPA because the EPA delegated to the MDEQ primary enforcement authority over the SDWA in Michigan. The district court disagreed, concluding that there is no contract, no employer/employee relationship, nor any other indication of a principal/agent arrangement between the MDEQ and the EPA.

We acknowledge at the outset that the MDEQ does receive funds from the EPA. But we conclude that the receipt of federal funding alone cannot establish a delegation of legal authority because finding such a delegation on that basis is way beyond the reasoning of *Watson* and would allow myriad state agencies to invoke federal-officer removal.

We now turn to the question of whether the EPA's delegation to the MDEQ of primary enforcement authority warrants federal-officer removal under *Watson*. Our research has revealed no caselaw from the Supreme Court, this court, or our sister circuits addressing the issue of whether state officers working in a joint federal-state regulatory system can invoke the federal-officer removal statute. As the *Watson* Court noted, federal-officer removal has been found to be applicable to certain government contractors. The Court suggested that contracts could delegate legal authority as required for federal-officer removal where a government contractor is helping to fulfill the federal government's tasks.

We further note that a government contractor entitled to removal would presumably be contractually required to follow the federal government's specifications in making products or providing services. *See Isaacson v. Dow Chem. Co.* (2d Cir. 2008) (holding that a government contractor that manufactured Agent Orange for the government was entitled to federal-officer removal in a state-law tort action for injuries caused by the product, noting that the government had contractually required that the product be made to meet certain specifications). And a government contractor would not ordinarily have any authority to take actions beyond those specified in the contract. In these cases, the federal government can properly be viewed as acting in a superior relationship to the private entity.

The MDEQ Defendants insist that the government-contractor cases apply here. They heavily rely on a few such district court cases to support their argument, but these cases are distinguishable. In *Clio Convalescent Center v. Michigan Dep't of Consumer & Industry Servs.* (E.D. Mich. 1999), for example, the district court allowed a state agency to invoke the federal-officer removal statute because the agency had entered into an agreement with the Secretary of Health and Human Services to ensure compliance with Medicaid's nursing-home certification requirements. That agreement explicitly provided that the state agency would act on the Secretary's behalf. *Id.* The district court found that the Secretary was the real party in interest and that the state agency was acting as the Secretary's agent, evidenced in part by the fact that the Secretary moved to intervene in the case. *Id.* at 877. A similar outcome was reached in *Thompson v. Cmty. Ins. Co.* (S.D. Ohio 1999), because that case involved a contractual agreement with an insurance company to act as a "fiscal intermediary" of the federal government in administering a Medicare program.

In the present case, there is no comparable contract or other delegation of legal authority to the MDEQ to act as the EPA's agent or on the EPA's behalf. Furthermore, this court has recently indicated, albeit in an unpublished opinion, that the absence of language allowing a private entity to act on the federal government's behalf weighs against allowing federal-officer removal. *See Ohio State Chiropractic Ass'n v. Humana Health Plan Inc.* (6th Cir. 2016) (explaining that a Medicare Advantage Organization could not invoke the federal-officer removal statute because the relevant regulations did not permit the organization to act on the federal government's behalf, the organization had the freedom to use some innovative private-market techniques, the government was not controlling the entity's daily operations, and the government would not have to perform the exact same tasks as the organization in the absence of the contractual arrangement).

Another case relied on by the MDEQ Defendants is *City of St. Louis v. Velsicol Chemical Corp.* (E.D. Mich. 2010). In that case, the district court allowed federal officer removal by a defendant trust that had been created pursuant to a settlement under a federal environmental statute. *Id.* The trust's objective was to resolve claims for cleanup costs and to manage the money allocated for the cleanup. *Id.* As in *Clio*, the federal government intervened in the action, arguing that removal was proper on the basis of the EPA's control of the trusts. *Id.* We conclude that *Velsicol* is distinguishable from the present case because it involved a trust—a relationship that required the defendant trustee to act "solely in a fiduciary capacity consistent with, and in furtherance of, the purposes" of the trust and the settlement agreements. *Id.* (quoting trust agreements). As previously explained, there is no comparable legal relationship here.

Instead, in order for the MDEQ to obtain primary enforcement authority, the state of Michigan chose to enact its own state safe-drinking-water laws. *See* 42 U.S.C. §300g-2(a)(1) (providing that a state can obtain primary enforcement responsibility if, among other things, it "has adopted drinking water regulations that are no less stringent than the national primary drinking water regulations"). Although Michigan's laws had to comply with the standards set forth in the SDWA and its accompanying regulations in order for the MDEQ to obtain primary enforcement authority, Michigan was free to enact more stringent requirements for the protection of its residents. *See id.* That Michigan decided to enact a regulatory scheme that essentially mirrors the federal one does not mean that Michigan was required to do so.

Once the MDEQ received primary enforcement authority, it had to periodically submit reports to the EPA detailing compliance with regulations that had been adopted into state law. *See* 40 C.F.R. §142.15. The MDEQ points to these reports as evidence of the EPA's control over it, but *Watson* indicates that compliance reporting, even if detailed, is insufficient by itself to merit federal-officer removal.

Similarly, the MDEQ Defendants vaguely allege that they were guided by "repeated written and verbal dialogue" with the EPA in taking the actions (and inactions) that are challenged in this case. We note, however, that counsel for the MDEQ Defendants conceded at oral argument that the EPA was not involved in the key action underlying the Plaintiff's complaint—approval of the decision to switch Flint's water supply to the Flint River. And the notice of removal does not identify any specific actions or inactions alleged in the complaint that the EPA required the MDEQ Defendants to take or refrain from taking. Nor do the MDEQ Defendants explain how the SDWA required any of their actions or inactions, and they fail to identify any specific EPA officials who allegedly directed their conduct.

The MDEQ Defendants cite several communications with the EPA in their brief. But because the MDEQ Defendants did not cite these exhibits in the notice of removal, the communications are not among the pleadings that we can review on an appeal of the district court's determination that it facially lacked jurisdiction. And even if we could review these communications, they simply suggest that the EPA and the MDEQ discussed issues related to the Flint water crisis, but not that the EPA ordered the MDEQ to take any specific action.

We also find telling the MDEQ Defendants' statement in their notice of removal that the clearest indicator that they were acting under the EPA is the emergency order issued on January 21, 2016. That order, however, was issued two days after January 19, 2016, the date on which the Plaintiffs filed their complaint. So any actions that the MDEQ Defendants took pursuant to that order were obviously unrelated to the actions that the Plaintiffs challenge. True enough, the EPA retains the ability to intervene when a state with primary enforcement authority fails to meet the requirements to maintain such authority. *See* 40 C.F.R. §142.17(a)(2). But we disagree with the MDEQ Defendants' argument that this ability to intervene supports their invocation of federal-officer removal. The fact that the EPA can intervene if a state fails to properly exercise its primary enforcement authority suggests that, absent any such failure by the state, the state retains the freedom to enforce its own safe drinking-water laws and regulations. Michigan was so governing itself when the alleged actions and inactions giving rise to the Plaintiffs' claims occurred.

. . . We agree with the Plaintiffs that the MDEQ-EPA relationship is a model of cooperative federalism, not an agency relationship. *See* Philip J. Weiser, *Towards a Constitutional Architecture for Cooperative Federalism,* 79 N.C. L. REV. 663, 671 (2001) (discussing the popularity of cooperative federalism, of which the environmental regulations of the 1960s and 1970s are a notable example, and explaining that "the real authority under such regimes often rest with the states which ultimately exercise considerable discretion," even if the federal government sets forth the regulatory standards). The facts that the MDEQ Defendants allege—such as communications with the EPA and the MDEQ's attempts to follow guidance documents issued by the EPA—suggest that a joint relationship exists, not that the MDEQ is controlled by the EPA.

. . . The MDEQ Defendants might have been guided by the SDWA and its accompanying regulations in the present case, but they were ultimately enforcing Michigan law, which was designed to mirror federal regulations.

More importantly, any bias that the MDEQ Defendants will face in state court differs from the historic biases that the federal-officer removal statute was designed to protect against. . . . We acknowledge that the MDEQ Defendants are likely to be unpopular figures in Genesee County. But any bias that the MDEQ Defendants might face in state court would almost certainly come from the perception that their actions and inactions created the Flint water crisis by failing to guarantee that the Flint River water was safe to drink. We do not see how the MDEQ's relationship with the EPA or the relationship between Michigan's safe-drinking-water laws and the SDWA could be viewed as a source of bias.

Finally, we acknowledge the *Watson* Court's statement that "[t]he words 'acting under' are broad." But the Court also went on to explain that "[b]road language is not limitless. And a liberal construction can nonetheless find limits in a text's language, context, history, and purposes." . . . All three of the cases cited by *Watson* for the point that the statute's scope is broad involve situations where the undisputed facts showed that the defendant was a federal officer or an employee of a federal officer. In *Arizona v. Manypenny* (1981), for example, the defendant was a border-patrol agent employed by the Immigration and Naturalization Service who was indicted in state court for assault with a deadly weapon after shooting a man fleeing toward the border after the defendant told him to stop. There was no dispute that the defendant had satisfied the acting-under requirement. The Court noted that the statute was to be construed broadly in the context of discussing the fact that Arizona law would be applied in the federal proceeding.

Similarly, in *Willingham v. Morgan* (1969), the defendants were federal-prison employees who were sued under state tort law. The court remarked on the federal-officer removal statute's broad scope in the context of concluding that its "color of office" language covered acts taken while the defendants were allegedly "on a frolic of their own" instead of being engaged in official duties. And *Colorado v. Symes* (1932), involved the classic case of a prohibition agent who faced a murder prosecution in state court, which arose out of an encounter with a suspect who was openly drinking wine at a restaurant. Removal in these cases thus clearly served the historical purpose of the federal-officer removal statute. The present case is markedly different because the MDEQ Defendants are state officers who have been sued for actions and inactions related to their enforcement of state law.

We therefore conclude that the MDEQ Defendants were not "acting under" the EPA and thus are not eligible for federal-officer removal. Because we conclude that the acting-under requirement is not satisfied, we need not decide whether the MDEQ Defendants are being sued for actions taken under color of federal law or whether the MDEQ Defendants have raised a colorable federal defense.

c. This Case Does not Present a Substantial Federal Question That Merits Removal Under 28 U.S.C. §1441.

. . . In the present case, the Plaintiffs have alleged state-law claims of gross negligence, fraud, assault and battery, and intentional infliction of emotional distress. . . .

The MDEQ Defendants have vaguely alleged that the Plaintiffs' gross-negligence claims are inextricably related to the interpretation of the LCR because those regulations are "ambiguous and susceptible to multiple interpretations as applied to Flint." But the Supreme Court has held that, when a plaintiff's complaint raises garden-variety tort claims, "the presence of a claimed violation of [a federal] statute as an element of a state cause of action is insufficiently 'substantial' to confer federal-question jurisdiction." *Merrell Dow Pharm. Inc. v. Thompson* (1986) (concluding that a negligence per se claim based on alleged violations of a federal statute did not warrant federal jurisdiction). . . . And there is no private right of action for damages arising from a violation of the SDWA or the LCR.

We therefore conclude that removal under 28 U.S.C. §1441 is inappropriate in the present case.

* * *

5. *Concurrent and Exclusive Jurisdiction*

When Congress creates new rights, remedies, and causes of action, it has choices to make about where it wants litigation to occur. It can provide for exclusive federal court jurisdiction, concurrent jurisdiction (litigants can choose either state or federal court), concurrent jurisdiction with a right to remove, or exclusive state court jurisdiction (the status quo prior to the enactment of §1331 in 1875). What might motivate Congress to choose one of these enforcement systems over another?

As the next case teaches, there is a strong presumption of concurrent jurisdiction of state courts over federal questions. If Congress wants to overcome this presumption it must make a clear statement. As you read the case consider what justifies the presumption.

Tafflin v. Levitt

493 U.S. 455 (1990)

Justice O'CONNOR delivered the opinion of the Court.

This case requires us to decide whether state courts have concurrent jurisdiction over civil actions brought under the Racketeer Influenced and Corrupt Organizations Act (RICO), 18 U.S.C. §§1961-1968.

I

The underlying litigation arises from the failure of Old Court Savings & Loan, Inc. (Old Court), a Maryland savings and loan association, and the attendant collapse of the Maryland Savings-Share Insurance Corp. (MSSIC), a state-chartered nonprofit corporation created to insure accounts in Maryland savings and loan associations that were not federally insured. Petitioners are nonresidents of Maryland who hold unpaid certificates of deposit issued by Old Court. Respondents are the former officers and directors of Old Court, the former officers and directors of MSSIC, the law firm of Old Court and MSSIC, the accounting firm of Old Court, and the State of Maryland Deposit Insurance Fund Corp., the state-created successor to MSSIC. Petitioners allege various state law causes of action as well as claims under the Securities Exchange Act of 1934 (Exchange Act) and RICO.

The District Court granted respondents' motions to dismiss, concluding that petitioners had failed to state a claim under the Exchange Act and that, because state courts have concurrent jurisdiction over civil RICO claims, federal abstention was appropriate for the other causes of action because they had been raised in pending litigation in state court. The Court of Appeals for the Fourth Circuit affirmed. The Court of Appeals agreed with the district Court that "a RICO action could be instituted in a state court and that Maryland's 'comprehensive scheme for the rehabilitation and liquidation of insolvent state-chartered savings and loan associations,' provided a proper basis for the district court to abstain under the authority of *Burford v. Sun Oil Co.* (1943)."

To resolve a conflict among the federal appellate courts and state supreme courts we granted certiorari limited to the question whether state courts have concurrent jurisdiction over civil RICO claims. We hold that they do, and accordingly affirm the judgment of the Court of Appeals.

II

We begin with the axiom that, under our federal system, the States possess sovereignty concurrent with that of the Federal Government, subject only to limitations imposed by the Supremacy Clause. Under this system of dual sovereignty, we have consistently held that state courts have inherent authority, and are thus presumptively competent, to adjudicate claims arising under the laws of the United States. As we noted in *Claflin v. Houseman* (1876),

> if exclusive jurisdiction be neither express nor implied, the State courts have concurrent jurisdiction whenever, by their own constitution, they are competent to take it.

This deeply rooted presumption in favor of concurrent state court jurisdiction is, of course, rebutted if Congress affirmatively ousts the state courts of jurisdiction over a particular federal claim. *See, e.g., Claflin* ("Congress may, if it see[s] fit, give to the Federal courts exclusive jurisdiction"). As we stated in *Gulf Offshore Co. v. Mobil Oil Corp.* (1981):

> In considering the propriety of state court jurisdiction over any particular federal claim, the Court begins with the presumption that state courts enjoy concurrent jurisdiction. Congress, however, may confine jurisdiction to the federal courts either explicitly or implicitly. Thus, the presumption of concurrent jurisdiction can be rebutted by an explicit statutory directive, by unmistakable implication from legislative history, or by a clear incompatibility between state court jurisdiction and federal interests.

III

The precise question presented, therefore, is whether state courts have been divested of jurisdiction to hear civil RICO claims

> by an explicit statutory directive, by unmistakable implication from legislative history, or by a clear incompatibility between state court jurisdiction and federal interests.

Gulf Offshore. Because we find none of these factors present with respect to civil claims arising under RICO, we hold that state courts retain their presumptive authority to adjudicate such claims.

At the outset, petitioners concede that there is nothing in the language of RICO — much less an "explicit statutory directive" — to suggest that Congress has, by affirmative enactment, divested the state courts of jurisdiction to hear civil RICO claims. The statutory provision authorizing civil RICO claims provides in full:

> Any person injured in his business or property by reason of a violation of section 1962 of this chapter *may* sue therefor in any appropriate United States district court and shall recover threefold the damages he sustains and the cost of the suit, including a reasonable attorney's fee.

This grant of federal jurisdiction is plainly permissive, not mandatory, for "[t]he statute does not state nor even suggest that such jurisdiction shall be exclusive. It provides that suits of the kind described 'may' be brought in the federal district courts, not that they must be." *Charles Dowd Box Co. v. Courtney* (1962). Indeed, "[i]t is black letter law . . . that the mere grant of jurisdiction to a federal court does not operate to oust a state court from concurrent jurisdiction over the cause of action." *Gulf Offshore.*

Petitioners thus rely solely on the second and third factors suggested in *Gulf Offshore,* arguing that exclusive federal jurisdiction over civil RICO actions is established "by unmistakable implication from legislative history, or by a clear incompatibility between state-court jurisdiction and federal interests."

Our review of the legislative history, however, reveals no evidence that Congress even considered the question of concurrent state court jurisdiction over RICO claims, much less any suggestion that Congress affirmatively intended to confer exclusive jurisdiction over such claims on the federal courts. As the Courts of Appeals that have considered the question have concluded,

> [t]he legislative history contains no indication that Congress ever expressly considered the question of concurrent jurisdiction; indeed, as the principal draftsman of RICO has remarked, 'no one even thought of the issue.

Brandenburg v. Seidel (4th Cir. 1988). . . . Petitioners nonetheless insist that, if Congress had considered the issue, it would have granted federal courts exclusive jurisdiction over civil RICO claims. This argument, however, is misplaced, for even if we could reliably discern what Congress' intent might have been had it considered the question, we are not at liberty to so speculate; the fact that Congress did not even consider the issue readily disposes of any argument that Congress unmistakably intended to divest state courts of concurrent jurisdiction.

Sensing this void in the legislative history, petitioners rely, in the alternative, on our decisions in *Sedima, S.P.R.L. v. Imrex Co.* (1985), and *Agency Holding Corp. v. Malley-Duff & Assocs.* (1987), in which we noted that Congress modeled §1964(c) after §4 of the Clayton Act, 15 U.S.C. §15(a). Petitioners assert that, because we have interpreted §4 of the Clayton Act to confer exclusive jurisdiction on the federal courts, *see, e.g., General Investment Co. v. Lake Shore & M.S.R. Co.* (1922), and because Congress may be presumed to have been aware of and incorporated those interpretations when it used similar language in RICO, Congress intended, by implication, to grant exclusive federal jurisdiction over claims arising under §1964(c).

This argument is also flawed. To rebut the presumption of concurrent jurisdiction, the question is not whether any intent at all may be divined from legislative silence on the issue, but whether Congress in its deliberations may be said to have affirmatively or unmistakably intended jurisdiction to be exclusively federal. In the instant case, the lack of any indication in RICO's legislative history that Congress either considered or assumed that the importing of remedial language from the Clayton Act into RICO had any jurisdictional implications is dispositive. The "mere borrowing of statutory language does not imply that Congress also intended to incorporate all of the baggage that may be attached to the borrowed language." *Lou v. Belzberg* (9th Cir. 1987). Indeed, to the extent we impute to Congress knowledge of our Clayton Act precedents, it makes no less sense to impute to Congress knowledge of *Claflin* and *Dowd Box*, under which Congress, had it sought to confer exclusive jurisdiction over civil RICO claims, would have had every incentive to do so expressly.

Sedima and *Agency Holding* are not to the contrary. . . . [I]n both *Sedima* and *Agency Holding* we looked to the Clayton Act in interpreting RICO without the benefit of a background juridical presumption of the type present in this case. Thus, to whatever extent the Clayton Act analogy may be relevant to our interpretation of RICO generally, it has no place in our inquiry into the jurisdiction of state courts.

Petitioners finally urge that state court jurisdiction over civil RICO claims would be clearly incompatible with federal interests. We noted in *Gulf Offshore* that factors indicating clear incompatibility "include the desirability of uniform interpretation, the expertise of federal judges in federal law, and the assumed greater hospitality of federal courts to peculiarly federal claims."

Petitioners' primary contention is that concurrent jurisdiction is clearly incompatible with the federal interest in uniform interpretation of federal criminal laws, *see* 18 U.S.C. §3231, because state courts would be required to construe the federal crimes that constitute predicate acts defined as "racketeering activity," *see* 18 U.S.C. §§1961(1)(B), (C), and (D). Petitioners predict that if state courts are permitted to interpret federal criminal statutes, they will create a body of precedent relating to those statutes and that the federal courts will consequently lose control over the orderly and uniform development of federal criminal law.

We perceive no "clear incompatibility" between state court jurisdiction over civil RICO actions and federal interests. As a preliminary matter, concurrent jurisdiction over §1964(c) suits is clearly not incompatible with §3231 itself, for civil RICO claims are not "offenses against the laws of the United States," §3231, and do not result in the imposition of criminal sanctions — uniform or otherwise. *See Shearson/American Express Inc. v. McMahon* (1987) (civil RICO intended to be primarily remedial rather than punitive).

More to the point, . . . [a]lthough petitioners' concern with the need for uniformity and consistency of federal criminal law is well-taken, for they would not be bound by state court interpretations of the federal offenses constituting RICO's predicate acts state courts adjudicating civil RICO claims will, in addition, be guided by federal court interpretations of the relevant federal criminal statutes, just as federal courts sitting in diversity are guided by state court interpretations of state law. State court judgments misinterpreting federal criminal law would, of course, also be subject to direct review by this Court.

Moreover, contrary to petitioners' fears, we have full faith in the ability of state courts to handle the complexities of civil RICO actions, particularly since many RICO cases involve asserted violations of state law, such as state fraud claims, over which state courts presumably have greater expertise. *See* 18 U.S.C. §1961(1)(A) (listing state law offenses constituting predicate acts); *Gulf Offshore* ("State judges have greater expertise in applying" laws "whose governing rules are borrowed from state law"); *see also Sedima* (RICO "has become a tool for everyday fraud cases"); BNA, Civil RICO Report (Apr. 14, 1987) (54.9% of all RICO cases after *Sedima* involved "common law fraud" and another 18.0% involved either "nonsecurities fraud" or "theft or conversion"). To hold otherwise would not only denigrate the respect accorded co-equal sovereigns, but would also ignore our "consistent history of hospitable acceptance of concurrent jurisdiction." *Dowd Box.* Indeed, it would seem anomalous to rule that state courts are incompetent to adjudicate civil RICO suits when we have recently found no inconsistency in subjecting civil RICO claims to adjudication by arbitration. *See McMahon* (rejecting argument that "RICO claims are too complex to be subject to arbitration" and that "there is an irreconcilable conflict between arbitration and RICO's underlying purposes").

Petitioners further note, as evidence of incompatibility, that RICO's procedural mechanisms include extended venue and service-of-process provisions that are applicable only in federal court, *see* 18 U.S.C. §1965. We think it sufficient, however, to observe that we have previously found concurrent state court jurisdiction even where federal law provided for special procedural mechanisms similar to those found in RICO. *See, e.g., Dowd Box* (finding concurrent jurisdiction over Labor Management Relations Act §301(a) suits, despite federal enforcement and venue provisions); *Maine v. Thiboutot* (1980) (finding concurrent jurisdiction over 42 U.S.C. §1983 suits, despite federal procedural provisions in §1988); *cf. Hathorn v. Lovorn* (1982) (finding concurrent jurisdiction over disputes regarding the applicability of §5 of the Voting Rights Act of 1965, 42 U.S.C. §1973c, despite provision for a three-judge panel). Although congressional specification of procedural mechanisms applicable only in federal court may tend to suggest that Congress intended exclusive federal jurisdiction, it does not by itself suffice to create a "clear incompatibility" with federal interests.

Finally, we note that, far from disabling or frustrating federal interests, "[p]ermitting state courts to entertain federal causes of action facilitates the enforcement of federal rights." *Gulf Offshore; see also Dowd Box* (conflicts deriving from concurrent jurisdiction are "not necessarily unhealthy").

For all of the above reasons, we hold that state courts have concurrent jurisdiction to consider civil claims arising under RICO. Nothing in the language, structure, legislative history, or underlying policies of RICO suggests that Congress intended otherwise. The judgment of the Court of Appeals is accordingly affirmed.

[The concurring opinion of Justice WHITE is omitted.]

Justice SCALIA, with whom Justice KENNEDY joins, concurring.

I join the opinion of the Court, addressing the issues before us on the basis argued by the parties, which has included acceptance of the dictum in *Gulf Offshore Co. v. Mobil Oil Corp.* (1981), that "'the presumption of concurrent jurisdiction can be rebutted by an explicit statutory directive, by unmistakable implication from legislative history, or by a clear incompatibility between state court jurisdiction and federal interests.'"

Such dicta, when repeatedly used as the point of departure for analysis, have a regrettable tendency to acquire the practical status of legal rules. I write separately, before this one has become too entrenched, to note my view that, in one respect, it is not a correct statement of the law, and, in another respect, it may not be.

State courts have jurisdiction over federal causes of action not because it is "conferred" upon them by the Congress, nor even because their inherent powers permit them to entertain transitory causes of action arising under the laws of foreign sovereigns, but because "[t]he laws of the United States are laws in the several States, and just as much binding on the citizens and courts thereof as the State laws are. . . . The two together form one system of jurisprudence, which constitutes the law of the land for the State; and the courts of the two jurisdictions are not foreign to each other. . . ." *Claflin v. Houseman* (1876).

It therefore takes an affirmative act of power under the Supremacy Clause to oust the States of jurisdiction—an exercise of what one of our earliest cases referred to as "the power of congress to *withdraw*" federal claims from state court jurisdiction. *Houston v. Moore* (1820). *See also Minneapolis & St. Louis R. Co. v. Bombolis* (1916) (concurrent jurisdiction exists "unless excepted by express constitutional limitation or by valid legislation"); *Missouri ex rel. St. Louis, B. & M.R. Co. v. Taylor* (1924) ("As [Congress] made no provision concerning the remedy, the federal and the state courts have concurrent jurisdiction"). As an original proposition, it would be eminently arguable that depriving state courts of their sovereign authority to adjudicate the law of the land must be done, if not with the utmost clarity, *cf. Atascadero State Hospital v. Scanlon* (1985) (state sovereign immunity can be eliminated only by "clear statement"), at least expressly. That was the view of Alexander Hamilton: "When . . . we consider the State governments and the national governments, as they truly are, in the light of kindred systems, and as parts of ONE WHOLE, the inference seems to be conclusive that the State courts would have a concurrent jurisdiction in all cases arising under the laws of the Union, where it was not expressly prohibited." The Federalist No. 82, p. 132 (E. Bourne ed. 1947).

Although as early as *Claflin* and as late as *Gulf Offshore*, we have said that the exclusion of concurrent state jurisdiction could be achieved by implication, the only cases in which to my knowledge we have acted upon such a principle are those relating to the Sherman Act and the Clayton Act—where the full extent of our analysis was the less than compelling statement that provisions giving the right to sue in United States District Court "show that [the right] is to be exercised *only* in a court of the United States.'" *General Investment Co. v. Lake Shore & Michigan Southern R. Co.* (1922) (emphasis added). In the standard fields of exclusive federal jurisdiction, the governing statutes specifically recite that suit may be brought "only" in federal court, Investment Company Act of 1940, as amended, 84 Stat. 1429, 15 U.S.C. §80a-35(b)(5);

that the jurisdiction of the federal courts shall be "exclusive," Securities Exchange Act of 1934, as amended, 48 Stat. 902, 15 U.S.C. §78aa; Natural Gas Act of 1938, 52 Stat. 833, 15 U.S.C. §717u; Employee Retirement Income Security Act of 1974, 88 Stat. 892, 29 U.S.C. §1132(e)(1); or indeed even that the jurisdiction of the federal courts shall be "exclusive of the courts of the States," 18 U.S.C. §3231 (criminal cases); 28 U.S.C. §§1333 (admiralty, maritime, and prize cases), 1334 (bankruptcy cases), 1338 (patent, plant variety protection, and copyright cases), 1351 (actions against consuls or vice consuls of foreign states), 1355 (actions for recovery or enforcement of fine, penalty, or forfeiture incurred under Act of Congress), 1356 (seizures on land or water not within admiralty and maritime jurisdiction).

Assuming, however, that exclusion by implication is possible, surely what is required is implication in the text of the statute, and not merely, as the second part of the *Gulf Offshore* dictum would permit, through "unmistakable implication from legislative history." We have never found state jurisdiction excluded by "unmistakable implication" from legislative history. . . .

[I]t is simply wrong in principle to assert that Congress can effect this affirmative legislative act by simply talking about it with unmistakable clarity. What is needed to oust the States of jurisdiction is congressional *action* (*i.e.*, a provision of law), not merely congressional discussion.

It is perhaps also true that implied preclusion can be established by the fact that a statute expressly mentions only federal courts, plus the fact that state court jurisdiction would plainly disrupt the statutory scheme. That is conceivably what was meant by the third part of the *Gulf Offshore* dictum, "clear incompatibility between state court jurisdiction and federal interests." If the phrase is interpreted more broadly than that, however—if it is taken to assert some power on the part of this Court to exclude state court jurisdiction when systemic federal interests make it undesirable—it has absolutely no foundation in our precedent.

In sum: As the Court holds, the RICO cause of action meets none of the three tests for exclusion of state court jurisdiction recited in *Gulf Offshore*. Since that is so, the proposition that meeting any one of the tests would have sufficed is dictum here, as it was there. In my view, meeting the second test is assuredly not enough, and meeting the third may not be.

* * *

Although passed as Title IX of the Organized Crime Control Act of 1970, and motivated by the problem of organized crime syndicates, RICO included a provision that it should be liberally construed due to the protean nature of this criminal activity and its use expanded dramatically in the late twentieth century. It became "the darling of zealous prosecutors"[15] because of the breadth of conduct it criminalized, attracting criticism for, among other things, "federalizing 'garden variety' fraud and contract actions,"[16] drawing federal prosecutors into prosecution of local

---

15. Michael P. Kenny, *Rico and Federalism: A Case for Concurrent Jurisdiction*, 31 B.C. L. Rev. 239, 258 (1990).

16. *Id.*

gangs whose connections to interstate commerce were doubtful,[17] and, as *Tafflin* suggests, for providing a private right of action with a treble damage remedy, over and above the statute's criminal penalties.

In *Tafflin*, the target was financial institutions involved in the savings and loan crisis. Between 1985 and 1995 approximately one-third of the nation's savings and loan associations in the United States failed, causing the Federal Savings and Loan Insurance Corporation, which backed these small community banks with taxpayer money, to go insolvent. This ultimately cost taxpayers billions and contributed to a national recession in 1990. Deregulation in the banking sector in the early 1980s allowed these banks to make more unsecured loans and other risky investments knowing the FSLIC, not the bank's owners, would carry losses. In some cases, insiders were responsible for blatantly fraudulent self-dealing. The failure of the Old Court Savings and Loan in Maryland in 1985 was "the largest white-collar crime in Maryland history, affecting 35,000 depositors."[18] The bank's owner at the time, Jeffrey Levitt, pleaded guilty to stealing $14.5 million from the bank. "Before his arrest, Levitt lived the high life—his golf cart had a mock Rolls Royce front. He had 18 vehicles, homes in Maryland and Florida, and an $18,000 backyard putting green."[19] He served seven and a half years of a 30-year prison term before being released on parole. The bank's Maryland depositors recouped their savings deposits four years after the bank failed. Nonresident depositors brought the RICO suit.

Notice the broad list of defendants—not just the bank but its professional service providers. The misconduct at Old Court and the attendant economic fallout draw the broad remedial powers of the statute into relief—combining criminal prosecution with the possibility of civil suit for treble damages. Given the identity of the parties—especially the plaintiffs' status as nonresidents of Maryland—can you see why the defendants insisted on concurrent jurisdiction and state court litigation of this RICO claim?

In the same term that *Tafflin* was decided, a unanimous Court emphasized that the first prong of the *Gulf Offshore* test for exclusive jurisdiction is almost always dispositive. *See Yellow Freight Sys. v. Donnelly* (1990) ("Unlike a number of statutes in which Congress unequivocally stated that the jurisdiction of the federal courts is exclusive, Title VII contains no language that expressly confines jurisdiction to federal courts or ousts state courts of their presumptive jurisdiction. The omission of any such provision is strong, and arguably sufficient evidence that Congress had no such intent."); *id.* (finding no "incompatibility between the procedures provided in Title VII and state court jurisdiction over these claims"; "We have no reason to question the presumption that state courts are just as able as federal courts to adjudicate Title VII claims").

---

17. *Compare, e.g.*, Waucaush v. United States, 380 F.3d 251 (6th Cir. 2004) ("street gang" not involved in economic "enterprise" could not be convicted of RICO crimes absent "substantial" effect on interstate commerce), *with* United States v. Nascimento, 491 F.3d 25 (1st Cir. 2007) (*de minimis* effect on interstate commerce is sufficient).

18. *30 Years Ago, Old Court Savings and Loan Scandal Stunned Depositors*, Baltimore Sun, April 23, 2015.

19. *Id.*

Justice Scalia's concurring opinion in *Tafflin* accurately states examples of language that will satisfy the clear statement rule for explicitly creating exclusive jurisdiction. Making direct reference to federal courts without discussing state court jurisdiction is not adequate. Congress must say that "only" federal courts shall have jurisdiction.

6.   *State Law in Federal Court*

The Rules of Decision Act, today found at 28 U.S.C. §1652, reads as follows:

> The laws of the several states, except where the Constitution or treaties of the United States or Acts of Congress otherwise require or provide, shall be regarded as rules of decision in civil actions in the courts of the United States in cases where they apply.

The key interpretive issue in this clause is: What are "the laws of the several states"? Do they include both substantive and procedural rules? Both statutory and decisional law?

The modern answer, which dates from the famous case of *Erie R.R. Co. v. Tompkins* (1938), is that in federal court the Federal Rules govern procedural matters while state law (statutory and decisional) provides the rule of decision for substantive issues. Federal district courts look to the choice of law rules of the state in which they sit to determine which state's substantive law is controlling. *Klaxon Co. v. Stentor Elec.* (1941). As you learned in Civil Procedure, divisions within the Court persist to this day regarding how to determine whether a specific rule of decision is procedural or substantive. Underneath the formalism of the distinction is an important debate about how much deference federal courts owe to state law. This question arises not only in diversity and supplemental jurisdiction cases, but whenever state law arises in a federal case and when a federal court must devise a rule of decision (such as a statute of limitations) because Congress has not done so in the statute creating the cause of action. In the latter scenario, one option is to look to analogous state law claims for a rule of decision to borrow; another is to generate federal common law. *Erie* and its progeny are presented in Chapter 5.

B.   *FEDERAL COURT OF APPEALS JURISDICTION*

1.   *Final Judgments*

An appellate court ordinarily has jurisdiction only over decisions that resolve the merits and result in the entry of judgment. This is the final judgment rule and it has been in place since the First Judiciary Act of 1789. Its purpose is to protect the integrity of the trial process from the disruption of interlocutory appeals. In the following case, we see implementation of the final judgment rule to prevent interlocutory appeals from military condemnations of property during World War II. Property owners, the Court concludes, can appeal only after the government takes title to the land and after litigation regarding the value of the property seized is concluded.

Catlin v. United States

324 U.S. 229 (1945)

Justice RUTLEDGE delivered the opinion of the Court.

The proceeding is for the condemnation of land in Madison County, Illinois, under the War Purposes Act of 1917.[1] The question for review is whether orders entered in the course of the proceedings are appealable as "final decisions" within the meaning of §128 of the Judicial Code, as amended, 28 U.S.C. §225(a) [granting appellate jurisdiction over "final decisions"].

The petition for condemnation was filed in the District Court March 31, 1942. The same day, an order for immediate possession was entered *ex parte*. On November 12, 1942, pursuant to the Declaration of Taking Act of February 26, 1931, the Secretary of War filed a declaration and deposited in court $43,579.00 as the estimated compensation for Tract ED-7, to which petitioners assert ownership as trustees. The court thereupon entered "judgment," likewise *ex parte*, decreeing that title had vested in the United States upon the filing of the declaration and making of the deposit, also declaring the right of just compensation "now vested in the persons entitled thereto," and holding the cause open for further "orders, judgments and decrees."

Thereafter, on August 2, 1943, an order for service of process by publication was entered, and, in October following, petitioners moved to vacate the "judgment" and to dismiss the petition as to Tract ED-7 [arguing that condemning the tract for use as an engineering depot was outside the military purposes authorized by the statute]. After this . . . the court denied [the motion]. . . . The Circuit Court of Appeals held the orders not final decisions within §128 and dismissed the appeal. We granted certiorari in order to resolve conflict upon this question among several Circuit Courts of Appeals.

We think the judgment was right. Petitioners' motions raised issues grounded in contentions that the taking was not for a purpose authorized by the War Purposes Act.

Accordingly, they urged that neither petition stated a cause of action, the court acquired no jurisdiction of the cause or to enter the order relating to title, and it was error to deny the motion to vacate and to dismiss. Since the issue here is whether the orders are final, for purposes of appeal, we assume, though we do not decide, that the substantive issues have sufficient merit to warrant determination upon review. Even so, we think petitioners have mistaken their remedy.

Their right to appeal rests upon §128 of the Judicial Code. This limits review to "final decisions" in the District Court. A "final decision" generally is one which ends the litigation on the merits and leaves nothing for the court to do

---

1. The statute permits the Secretary of War to condemn property and convert it to use for specific military purposes relating to fortifications and weapons manufacturing. It further provides that "[w]hen such property is acquired in time of war, or the imminence thereof, upon the filing of the petition for the condemnation of any land, temporary use thereof, or other interest therein or right pertaining thereto to be acquired for any of the purposes aforesaid, *immediate possession thereof may be taken* to the extent of the interest to be acquired and the *lands may be occupied and used for military purposes.*"

but execute the judgment. *St. Louis I.M. & S.R. Co. v. Southern Express Co.* (1883). Hence, ordinarily in condemnation proceedings, appellate review may be had only upon an order or judgment disposing of the whole case, and adjudicating all rights, including ownership and just compensation, as well as the right to take the property. This has been the repeated holding of decisions here. The rule applies to review by this Court of judgments of state courts, in advance of determination of just compensation, although by local statute "judgments of condemnation," *i.e.*, of the right to condemn particular property, are reviewable before compensation is found and awarded. The foundation of this policy is not in merely technical conceptions of "finality." It is one against piecemeal litigation. "The case is not to be sent up in fragments. . . ." *Luxton v. North River Bridge Co.* (1893). Reasons other than conservation of judicial energy sustain the limitation. One is elimination of delays caused by interlocutory appeals.

The rule applies to proceedings under the War Purposes Act of 1917.[9] That act does not purport to change or depart from the generally prevailing rule concerning appeals in condemnation proceedings. . . . The 1917 act purports to authorize no judgment except one "for the acquirement by condemnation of any land," etc., for the purposes specified or, necessarily, one finally denying this. The provision for the proceedings "to be prosecuted in accordance with the laws relating to suits for the condemnation of property of the States wherein the proceedings may be instituted . . ." had no purpose to make the right of appeal in such proceedings depend upon and vary with the local procedure in this respect, or to incorporate local ideas of "finality" in the application of §128 to such suits. The language may be applied in other ways without introducing so much lack of uniformity into the application of §128, if indeed the quoted provision has not been largely nullified by the Federal Rules of Civil Procedure in all respects concerning appeals.[11]

Furthermore, the 1917 act contemplated emergency action to the extent that, upon the filing of the petition immediate possession might be taken and the lands occupied "for military purposes" during war "or the imminence thereof." This purpose, it seems clear, would be largely defeated if entry must be deferred until specific challenges to jurisdiction and the sufficiency of the petition are determined *seriatim*, not only by ruling of the trial court, but by separate appeals from each ruling which, if sustained, would end the litigation, but, if lacking in merit, could only prolong it. We find neither in the language nor in the purposes of the 1917 act an intent to authorize departure from the general course of applying §128 in condemnation proceedings.

---

9. No case has been found in which appeal was taken, or attempted to be taken, under the 1890 and 1917 acts from an order other than the final judgment disposing of all issues raised in the proceeding, including compensation. The uniform practice under those acts appears to have been, therefore, to confine appeals to such orders. Only three cases appear to have sought to raise, in appeals from final judgments, the question of the right to condemn. *See Forbes v. United States* (5th Cir. 1920); *Chappell v. United States* (4th Cir. 1897); *Henry v. United States* (3d Cir. 1931). Numerous other cases involved appeals on questions affecting compensation without raising question concerning title or authority to condemn.

11. "In proceedings for condemnation of property under the power of eminent domain, these rules govern appeals, but are not otherwise applicable." Rule 81(a)(7).

Indeed, we do not understand petitioners to urge that the 1917 act, without more, accomplishes the departure. They say, rather, that it does so when used in conjunction with the Declaration of Taking Act of 1931. It is the "judgment" upon "a declaration of taking" and the subsequent order denying their motion to vacate this "judgment" and to dismiss the proceedings which they contend are "final decisions" within §128, and therefore appealable. . . . But denial of a motion to dismiss, even when the motion is based upon jurisdictional grounds, is not immediately reviewable. Certainly this is true whenever the question may be saved for disposition upon review of final judgment disposing of all issues involved in the litigation or in some other adequate manner. As will appear, we think such a remedy is available in this case.

The "judgment" and the order denying the motion to vacate it stand no better. The [Declaratory Taking Act of 1931], like that of 1917, contains no language purporting to change the general rule relating to appeals in condemnation proceedings.

§1, which is the basis section, makes no express reference to appeals.[13] §2 implies the contrary effect. It provides:

> No appeal in any such cause nor any bond or undertaking given therein shall operate to prevent or delay the vesting of title to such lands in the United States.

While the section does not in terms deny the right of appeal contended for, neither does it confer that right. The possibility of delaying or preventing the vesting of title by appeals was explicitly in the mind of Congress when it included this section.

[Section 4] makes the right to take possession and title "in advance of final judgment" additional to other rights, powers or authority conferred by federal or local law, and expressly states that this right "shall not be construed as abrogating, limiting, or modifying any such right, power, or authority." One of the rights of

---

13. ". . . *Upon the filing said declaration of taking and of the deposit in the court,* to the use of the persons entitled thereto, *of the amount of the estimated compensation* stated in said declaration, *title to the said lands* in fee simple absolute, or such less estate or interest therein as is specified in said declaration, *shall vest in the United States of America, and said lands shall be deemed to be condemned* and taken for the use of the United States, *and the right to just compensation for the same shall vest in the persons entitled thereto,* and said compensation shall be ascertained and awarded in said proceeding and established by judgment therein, and the said judgment shall include, as part of the just compensation awarded, interest at the rate of 6 percentum per annum on the amount finally awarded as the value of the property as of the date of taking, from said date to the date of payment; but interest shall not be allowed on so much thereof as shall have been paid into the court. No sum so paid into the court shall be charged with commissions or poundage."

"Upon the application of the parties in interest, the court may order that the money deposited in the court, or any part thereof, be paid forthwith for or on account of the just compensation to be awarded in said proceeding. If the compensation finally awarded in respect of said lands, or any parcel thereof, shall exceed the amount of the money so received by any person entitled, the court shall enter judgment against the United States for the amount of the deficiency."

the Government under preexisting federal law was the right not to have the proceeding, or the taking of possession, delayed by separate appeals over issues of title or taking. Its right was rather to have these issues determined with others in the final judgment dispositive of the whole cause.

While the language and the wording of the act are not wholly free from doubt, we see no necessary inconsistency between the provisions for transfer of title upon filing of the declaration and making of the deposit and at the same time preserving the owner's preexisting right to question the validity of the taking as not being for a purpose authorized by the statute under which the main proceeding is brought. . . . The alternative construction, that title passes irrevocably, leaving the owner no opportunity to question the taking's validity or one for which the only remedy would be to accept the compensation which would be just if the taking were valid, would raise serious question concerning the statute's validity. In any event, we think it would run counter to what reasonable construction requires.

From the fact that the Government may become irrevocably committed to pay, it does not follow that the owner is irrevocably committed to submit to the taking, since the statute's terms are not *in pari materia* in this respect. Neither §3 nor §5 purports to bind the owner irrevocably. On the contrary, §5 deals only with authority to expend appropriated funds for demolition of existing structures and construction of new ones, and the concluding proviso, requiring the opinion of the Attorney General that "title has been vested in the United States or all persons having an interest therein have been made parties to such proceeding and will be bound *by the final judgment therein*" (emphasis added) before the funds are expended, seems clearly to contemplate that title is not indefeasibly vested in the United States merely by following the administrative procedure. Final judgment in "such proceeding," that is, the main condemnation suit, is necessary for that purpose. The operation of §§3 and 5 is to cut off the Government's right to abandon the proceedings. It is not to compel the owner to submit to unauthorized takings.

Accordingly, in our opinion, the right of the owner to challenge the validity of the taking for nonconformity with the prescribed statutory purposes was not destroyed by the 1931 act.

The judgment is

Affirmed.

Justice ROBERTS and Justice DOUGLAS concur in the result.

* * *

Can you imagine the Court reaching this conclusion regarding infringement of property rights protected by the Fifth Amendment outside the context of emergency war powers? Is the effect of the final judgment rule here to leave a dispossessed property owner no remedy other than ex post compensation?

The final judgment rule is now codified at 28 U.S.C. §1291. It provides:

The courts of appeals (other than the United States Court of Appeals for the Federal Circuit) shall have jurisdiction of appeals from all final decisions of the district courts of the United States, the United States

District Court for the District of the Canal Zone, the District Court of Guam, and the District Court of the Virgin Islands, except where a direct review may be had in the Supreme Court. The jurisdiction of the United States Court of Appeals for the Federal Circuit shall be limited to the jurisdiction described in sections 1292(c) and (d) and 1295 of this title.

If a final judgment under *Catlin* is a decision that "ends the litigation on the merits and leaves nothing for the court to do but execute the judgment," can a party appeal when there is outstanding litigation over attorney's fees? On the face of this language, the answer would seem to be no. Litigating attorney's fees is not execution of the judgment. In *Budinich v. Becton Dickinson & Co.* (1988), the Court held that a decision on the merits of a case is a final decision under §1291 even if there is outstanding litigation over prevailing party attorney's fees. In *Ray Haluch Gravel Co. v. Central Pension Fund* (2014), the Court extended the rule in *Budinich* to cover any outstanding attorney's fees litigation whether the right to the fees arises from a statute providing for prevailing party fees, a contract between the parties, or both. In either case, "the pendency of a ruling on an award for fees and costs does not prevent, as a general rule, the merits judgment from becoming final for purposes of appeal." Id. Attorney's fees, the Court reasoned, "do not remedy the injury giving rise to the action, are often available to the party defending the action, and were regarded at common law as an element of 'costs' awarded to a prevailing party, which are generally not treated as part of the merits judgment." In *Haluch Gravel*, the defendant employer was sued under ERISA for failing to pay its employees certain benefits due under a collective bargaining agreement. After a bench trial, the district court entered an order ruling that plaintiffs were entitled to the unpaid benefit contributions and a judgment in favor of plaintiffs was entered the same day. Five weeks later, the district court awarded more than $34,000 in attorney's fees and costs. Plaintiffs appealed three weeks after the fee and costs award, well beyond the 30-day time period to file a notice of appeal if the merits order and entry of judgment were "final decisions" under §1291. *See* Fed. R. App. Proc. 4 ("In a civil case, except as provided in Rules 4(a)(1)(B), 4(a)(4), and 4(c), the notice of appeal required by Rule 3 must be filed with the district clerk within 30 days after entry of the judgment or order appealed from.").

On appeal, plaintiffs argued that *Budinich* was distinguishable because, in contrast to statutory attorney's fees provisions, contractual provisions for fees and costs "are liquidated damages provisions intended to remedy the injury giving rise to the action." The fee award thus runs to the merits. The Court flatly rejected this argument, emphasizing that in *Budinich* itself, the Court held that attorney's fees are collateral orders for finality purposes irrespective of whether "law authorizing a particular fee claim treat[s] the fees as part of the merits." Leaving the time to appeal contingent on "the merits or nonmerits status of each attorney's fee provision," the Court emphasized, would amplify uncertainty about the deadline to file a notice of appeal.

2.   *Collateral Orders*

Although "final decisions" are usually orders entering judgment in the case, the Court has long recognized that some orders "collateral" to the merits are sufficiently conclusive regarding the issues they address to be subject to interlocutory appeal under §1291.

Cohen v. Beneficial Indus. Loan Corp. (1949) involved a derivative suit by a minority shareholder against a corporation and officers and directors accused of enriching themselves at the expense of the corporation in the midst of the Great Depression. Two years into the litigation, New Jersey enacted a law providing that in derivative suits a minority shareholder plaintiff is liable for attorney's fees of the defendants and all expenses if the suit fails. To proceed in the litigation, the plaintiff must post a bond of indemnification. Cohen's suit was in federal court, sitting in diversity, but the defendants moved to require a $125,000 bond. This presented the question whether *Erie* required the district court to adhere to the state rule of decision, and if so, whether the state law was unconstitutional as a denial of access to court leaving the plaintiff unable to sustain the litigation given the cost of the bond. The district court refused to enforce the state law bond requirement and the defendants sought immediate interlocutory appeal of that decision. The Supreme Court upheld appellate jurisdiction despite the final judgment rule on the following grounds:

> At the threshold, we are met with the question whether the District Court's order refusing to apply the statute was an appealable one. Title 28 U.S.C. §1291, provides, as did its predecessors, for appeal only "from all final decisions of the district courts," except when direct appeal to this Court is provided. Section 1292 allows appeals also from certain interlocutory orders, decrees and judgments, not material to this case except as they indicate the purpose to allow appeals from orders other than final judgments when they have a final and irreparable effect on the rights of the parties. It is obvious that, if Congress had allowed appeals only from those final judgments which terminate an action, this order would not be appealable.
>
> The effect of the statute is to disallow appeal from any decision which is tentative, informal or incomplete. Appeal gives the upper court a power of review, not one of intervention. So long as the matter remains open, unfinished or inconclusive, there may be no intrusion by appeal. But the District Court's action upon this application was concluded and closed, and its decision final in that sense, before the appeal was taken.
>
> Nor does the statute permit appeals, even from fully consummated decisions, where they are but steps towards final judgment in which they will merge. The purpose is to combine in one review all stages of the proceeding that effectively may be reviewed and corrected if and when final judgment results. But this order of the District Court did not make any step toward final disposition of the merits of the case, and will not be merged in final judgment. When that time comes, it will be too late effectively to review the present order, and the rights conferred by the statute, if it is applicable, will have been lost, probably irreparably. We conclude that the matters embraced in the decision appealed from are not of such an interlocutory nature as to affect, or to be affected by, decision of the merits of this case.

This decision appears to fall in that small class which finally determine claims of right separable from, and collateral to, rights asserted in the action, too important to be denied review and too independent of the cause itself to require that appellate consideration be deferred until the whole case is adjudicated. The Court has long given this provision of the statute this practical, rather than a technical, construction. *Bank of Columbia v. Sweeney* (1828).

We hold this order appealable because it is a final disposition of a claimed right which is not an ingredient of the cause of action and does not require consideration with it. But we do not mean that every order fixing security is subject to appeal. Here, it is the right to security that presents a serious and unsettled question. If the right were admitted or clear and the order involved only an exercise of discretion as to the amount of security, a matter the statute makes subject to reconsideration from time to time, appealability would present a different question.

On the merits, the Court upheld the statute, finding that the state has "plenary power over this type of litigation" and may create rules to restrict abuse of derivative litigation even if their effect is to close courthouse doors entirely. On the *Erie* question, the Court held that the statute is substantive because "it creates a new liability where none existed before, for it makes a stockholder who institutes a derivative action liable for the expense to which he puts the corporation and other defendants if he does not make good his claims. Such liability is not usual, and it goes beyond payment of what we know as 'costs.'" That the statute achieves this through a procedure for indemnification via a bond before the merits are decided does not alter the substantive nature of the indemnification.

In the next case, dealing with interlocutory appeal of a decision ordering disclosure of information over a claim of attorney-client privilege, the Court distinguished *Cohen.*

Mohawk Indus., Inc. v. Carpenter

558 U.S. 100 (2009)

Justice SOTOMAYOR delivered the opinion of the Court.

Section 1291 of the Judicial Code confers on federal courts of appeals jurisdiction to review "final decisions of the district courts." 28 U.S.C. §1291. Although "final decisions" typically are ones that trigger the entry of judgment, they also include a small set of prejudgment orders that are "collateral to" the merits of an action and "too important" to be denied immediate review. *Cohen v. Beneficial Industrial Loan Corp.* (1949). In this case, petitioner Mohawk Industries, Inc., attempted to bring a collateral order appeal after the District Court ordered it to disclose certain confidential materials on the ground that Mohawk had waived the attorney-client privilege. The Court of Appeals dismissed the appeal for want of jurisdiction.

The question before us is whether disclosure orders adverse to the attorney-client privilege qualify for immediate appeal under the collateral order doctrine. Agreeing with the Court of Appeals, we hold that they do not. Postjudgment appeals, together with other review mechanisms, suffice to protect the rights of litigants and preserve the vitality of the attorney-client privilege.

I

In 2007, respondent Norman Carpenter, a former shift supervisor at a Mohawk manufacturing facility, filed suit in the United States District Court for the Northern District of Georgia, alleging that Mohawk had terminated him in violation of 42 U.S.C. §1985(2) and various Georgia laws. According to Carpenter's complaint, his termination came after he informed a member of Mohawk's human resources department in an e-mail that the company was employing undocumented immigrants. At the time, unbeknownst to Carpenter, Mohawk stood accused in a pending class-action lawsuit of conspiring to drive down the wages of its legal employees by knowingly hiring undocumented workers in violation of federal and state racketeering laws. *See Williams v. Mohawk Indus., Inc.* (2004). Company officials directed Carpenter to meet with the company's retained counsel in the *Williams* case, and counsel allegedly pressured Carpenter to recant his statements. When he refused, Carpenter alleges, Mohawk fired him under false pretenses.

After learning of Carpenter's complaint, the plaintiffs in the *Williams* case sought an evidentiary hearing to explore Carpenter's allegations. In its response to their motion, Mohawk described Carpenter's accusations as "pure fantasy" and recounted the "true facts" of Carpenter's dismissal. According to Mohawk, Carpenter himself had "engaged in blatant and illegal misconduct" by attempting to have Mohawk hire an undocumented worker. The company "commenced an immediate investigation," during which retained counsel interviewed Carpenter. Because Carpenter's "efforts to cause Mohawk to circumvent federal immigration law" "blatantly violated Mohawk policy," the company terminated him.

As these events were unfolding in the *Williams* case, discovery was underway in Carpenter's case. Carpenter filed a motion to compel Mohawk to produce information concerning his meeting with retained counsel and the company's termination decision. Mohawk maintained that the requested information was protected by the attorney-client privilege.

The District Court agreed that the privilege applied to the requested information, but it granted Carpenter's motion to compel disclosure after concluding that Mohawk had implicitly waived the privilege through its representations in the *Williams* case. The court declined to certify its order for interlocutory appeal under 28 U.S.C. §1292(b). But, recognizing "the seriousness of its [waiver] finding," it stayed its ruling to allow Mohawk to explore other potential "avenues to appeal . . . , such as a petition for mandamus or appealing this Order under the collateral order doctrine."

Mohawk filed a notice of appeal and a petition for a writ of mandamus to the Eleventh Circuit. The Court of Appeals dismissed the appeal for lack of jurisdiction under 28 U.S.C. §1291, holding that the District Court's ruling did not qualify as an immediately appealable collateral order within the meaning of *Cohen*. "Under *Cohen*," the Court of Appeals explained, "an order is appealable if it (1) conclusively determines the disputed question; (2) resolves an important issue completely separate from the merits of the action; and (3) is effectively unreviewable on appeal from a final judgment." According to the court, the District Court's waiver ruling satisfied the first two of these requirements but not the third, because "a discovery order that implicates the attorney-client privilege" can be adequately reviewed "on appeal from a final judgment." The Court of Appeals also rejected Mohawk's mandamus petition, finding no "clear usurpation of power or abuse of discretion" by the District Court. We granted certiorari to resolve a conflict among the Circuits concerning the availability of collateral appeals in the attorney-client privilege context.

II
A

By statute, Courts of Appeals "have jurisdiction of appeals from all final decisions of the district courts of the United States, . . . except where a direct review may be had in the Supreme Court." 28 U.S.C. §1291. A "final decisio[n]" is typically one "by which a district court disassociates itself from a case." *Swint v. Chambers County Comm'n* (1995). This Court, however, "has long given" §1291 a "practical rather than a technical construction." *Cohen.* As we held in *Cohen,* the statute encompasses not only judgments that "terminate an action," but also a "small class" of collateral rulings that, although they do not end the litigation, are appropriately deemed "final." *Id.* "That small category includes only decisions that are conclusive, that resolve important questions separate from the merits, and that are effectively unreviewable on appeal from the final judgment in the underlying action." *Swint.*

In applying *Cohen*'s collateral order doctrine, we have stressed that it must "never be allowed to swallow the general rule that a party is entitled to a single appeal, to be deferred until final judgment has been entered." *Digital Equipment Corp. v. Desktop Direct, Inc.* (1994). Our admonition reflects a healthy respect for the virtues of the final-judgment rule. Permitting piecemeal, prejudgment appeals, we have recognized, undermines "efficient judicial administration" and encroaches upon the prerogatives of district court judges, who play a "special role" in managing ongoing litigation. *Firestone Tire & Rubber Co. v. Risjord* (1981); *see also Richardson-Merrell Inc. v. Koller* (1985) ("[T]he district judge can better exercise [his or her] responsibility [to police the prejudgment tactics of litigants] if the appellate courts do not repeatedly intervene to second-guess prejudgment rulings").

The justification for immediate appeal must therefore be sufficiently strong to overcome the usual benefits of deferring appeal until litigation concludes. This requirement finds expression in two of the three traditional *Cohen* conditions. The second condition insists upon "*important* questions separate from the merits." *Swint.* More significantly, "the third *Cohen* question, whether a right is 'adequately vindicable' or 'effectively reviewable,' simply cannot be answered without a judgment about the value of the interests that would be lost through rigorous application of a final judgment requirement." *Digital Equipment.* That a ruling "may burden litigants in ways that are only imperfectly reparable by appellate reversal of a final district court judgment . . . has never sufficed." *Id.* Instead, the decisive consideration is whether delaying review until the entry of final judgment "would imperil a substantial public interest" or "some particular value of a high order." *Will v. Hallock* (2006).

In making this determination, we do not engage in an "individualized jurisdictional inquiry." *Coopers & Lybrand v. Livesay* (1978). Rather, our focus is on "the entire category to which a claim belongs." *Digital Equipment.* As long as the class of claims, taken as a whole, can be adequately vindicated by other means, "the chance that the litigation at hand might be speeded, or a 'particular injustic[e]' averted," does not provide a basis for jurisdiction under §1291. *Ibid.*

B

In the present case, the Court of Appeals concluded that the District Court's privilege-waiver order satisfied the first two conditions of the collateral order doctrine — conclusiveness and separateness — but not the third — effective unreviewability. Because we agree with the Court of Appeals that collateral order appeals are not necessary to ensure effective review of orders adverse to the attorney-client privilege, we do not decide whether the other *Cohen* requirements are met.

Mohawk does not dispute that "we have generally denied review of pretrial discovery orders." *Firestone; see also* Wright & Miller ("[T]he rule remains settled that most discovery rulings are not final"). Mohawk contends, however, that rulings implicating the attorney-client privilege differ in kind from run-of-the-mill discovery orders because of the important institutional interests at stake. According to Mohawk, the right to maintain attorney-client confidences — the *sine qua non* of a meaningful attorney-client relationship — is "irreparably destroyed absent immediate appeal" of adverse privilege rulings.

We readily acknowledge the importance of the attorney-client privilege, which "is one of the oldest recognized privileges for confidential communications." *Swidler & Berlin v. United States* (1998). By assuring confidentiality, the privilege encourages clients to make "full and frank" disclosures to their attorneys, who are then better able to provide candid advice and effective representation. *Upjohn Co. v. United States* (1981). This, in turn, serves "broader public interests in the observance of law and administration of justice." *Ibid.*

The crucial question, however, is not whether an interest is important in the abstract; it is whether deferring review until final judgment so imperils the interest as to justify the cost of allowing immediate appeal of the entire class of relevant orders. We routinely require litigants to wait until after final judgment to vindicate valuable rights, including rights central to our adversarial system. *See, e.g., Richardson-Merrell* (holding an order disqualifying counsel in a civil case did not qualify for immediate appeal under the collateral order doctrine); *Flanagan v. United States* (1984) (reaching the same result in a criminal case, notwithstanding the Sixth Amendment rights at stake). In *Digital Equipment,* we rejected an assertion that collateral order review was necessary to promote "the public policy favoring voluntary resolution of disputes." "It defies common sense," we explained, "to maintain that parties' readiness to settle will be significantly dampened (or the corresponding public interest impaired) by a rule that a district court's decision to let allegedly barred litigation go forward may be challenged as a matter of right only on appeal from a judgment for the plaintiff's favor."

We reach a similar conclusion here. In our estimation, postjudgment appeals generally suffice to protect the rights of litigants and assure the vitality of the attorney-client privilege. Appellate courts can remedy the improper disclosure of privileged material in the same way they remedy a host of other erroneous evidentiary rulings: by vacating an adverse judgment and remanding for a new trial in which the protected material and its fruits are excluded from evidence.

Dismissing such relief as inadequate, Mohawk emphasizes that the attorney-client privilege does not merely "prohibi[t] use of protected information at trial"; it provides a "right not to disclose the privileged information in the first place." Mohawk is undoubtedly correct that an order to disclose privileged information intrudes on the confidentiality of attorney-client communications. But deferring review until final judgment does not meaningfully reduce the *ex ante* incentives for full and frank consultations between clients and counsel.

One reason for the lack of a discernible chill is that, in deciding how freely to speak, clients and counsel are unlikely to focus on the remote prospect of an erroneous disclosure order, let alone on the timing of a possible appeal. Whether or not immediate collateral order appeals are available, clients and counsel must account for the possibility that they will later be required by law to disclose their communications for a variety of reasons—for example, because they misjudged the scope of the privilege, because they waived the privilege, or because their communications fell within the privilege's crime-fraud exception. Most district court rulings on these matters involve the routine application of settled legal principles. They are unlikely to be reversed on appeal, particularly when they rest on factual determinations for which appellate deference is the norm. *See, e.g., Richardson-Merrell* ("Most pretrial orders of district judges are ultimately affirmed by appellate courts."); *Reise v. Board of Regents* (7th Cir. 1992) (noting that "almost all interlocutory appeals from discovery orders would end in affirmance" because "the district court possesses discretion, and review is deferential"). The breadth of the privilege and the narrowness of its exceptions will thus tend to exert a much greater influence on the conduct of clients and counsel than the small risk that the law will be misapplied.[2]

Moreover, were attorneys and clients to reflect upon their appellate options, they would find that litigants confronted with a particularly injurious or novel privilege ruling have several potential avenues of review apart from collateral order appeal. First, a party may ask the district court to certify, and the court of appeals to accept, an interlocutory appeal pursuant to 28 U.S.C. §1292(b). The preconditions for §1292(b) review—"a controlling question of law," the prompt resolution of which "may materially advance the ultimate termination of the litigation"—are most likely to be satisfied when a privilege ruling involves a new legal question or is of special consequence, and district courts should not hesitate to certify an interlocutory appeal in such cases. Second, in extraordinary circumstances—*i.e.,* when a disclosure order "amount[s] to a judicial usurpation of power or a clear abuse of discretion," or otherwise works a manifest injustice—a party may petition the court of appeals for a writ of mandamus. *Cheney v. United States Dist. Ct. for D.C.* (2004). While these discretionary review mechanisms do not provide relief in every case, they serve as useful "safety valve[s]" for promptly correcting serious errors. *Digital Equipment.*

Another long-recognized option is for a party to defy a disclosure order and incur court-imposed sanctions. District courts have a range of sanctions from which

---

2. Perhaps the situation would be different if district courts were systematically underenforcing the privilege, but we have no indication that this is the case.

to choose, including "directing that the matters embraced in the order or other designated facts be taken as established for purposes of the action," "prohibiting the disobedient party from supporting or opposing designated claims or defenses," or "striking pleadings in whole or in part." Fed. Rule Civ. Proc. 37(b)(2)(i)–(iii). Such sanctions allow a party to obtain postjudgment review without having to reveal its privileged information. Alternatively, when the circumstances warrant it, a district court may hold a noncomplying party in contempt. The party can then appeal directly from that ruling, at least when the contempt citation can be characterized as a criminal punishment. *See, e.g., Church of Scientology of Cal. v. United States* (1992).

These established mechanisms for appellate review not only provide assurances to clients and counsel about the security of their confidential communications; they also go a long way toward addressing Mohawk's concern that, absent collateral order appeals of adverse attorney-client privilege rulings, some litigants may experience severe hardship. . . . Moreover, protective orders are available to limit the spillover effects of disclosing sensitive information.

Permitting parties to undertake successive, piecemeal appeals of all adverse attorney-client rulings would unduly delay the resolution of district court litigation and needlessly burden the Courts of Appeals. *See* Wright & Miller ("Routine appeal from disputed discovery orders would disrupt the orderly progress of the litigation, swamp the courts of appeals, and substantially reduce the district court's ability to control the discovery process."); *cf. Cunningham* v. *Hamilton County* (1999) (expressing concern that allowing immediate appeal as of right from orders fining attorneys for discovery violations would result in "the very sorts of piecemeal appeals and concomitant delays that the final judgment rule was designed to prevent").

C

Congress in 1990 amended the Rules Enabling Act, 28 U.S.C. §2071 *et seq.*, to authorize this Court to adopt rules "defin[ing] when a ruling of a district court is final for the purposes of appeal under section 1291." §2072(c). Shortly thereafter, and along similar lines, Congress empowered this Court to "prescribe rules, in accordance with [§2072], to provide for an appeal of an interlocutory decision to the courts of appeals that is not otherwise provided for under [§1292]." §1292(e).

Any further avenue for immediate appeal of such rulings should be furnished, if at all, through rulemaking, with the opportunity for full airing it provides.

* * *

In sum, we conclude that the collateral order doctrine does not extend to disclosure orders adverse to the attorney-client privilege. Effective appellate review can be had by other means. Accordingly, we affirm the judgment of the Court of Appeals for the Eleventh Circuit.

It is so ordered.

* * *

The Court suggests that denying interlocutory review under §1291 will not affect the incentives of a client to be full and frank with her lawyer because the prospect of forced disclosure in discovery is too remote. That claim is hard to square with the facts of *Carpenter* itself, where the challenged communication occurred in the midst of an employment dispute that was the subject of the litigation while a class action lawsuit regarding the company conduct Carpenter challenged was pending.

The Supreme Court has long held that the concern about post hoc disclosure inhibiting full and frank communication between attorney and client justifies protecting the privilege even after the client has died. *See Swidler & Berlin v. United States* (1995) ("Knowing that communications will remain confidential even after death encourages the client to communicate fully and frankly with counsel. While the fear of disclosure, and the consequent withholding of information from counsel, may be reduced if disclosure is limited to posthumous disclosure in a criminal context, it seems unreasonable to assume that it vanishes altogether. Clients may be concerned about reputation, civil liability, or possible harm to friends or family. Posthumous disclosure of such communications may be as feared as disclosure during the client's lifetime.")

There is tension, of course, between emphasizing that collateral order review under §1291 of privilege decisions will invite piecemeal review and "disrupt the orderly progress of litigation," on the one hand, and recognizing the many other pathways for interlocutory review (mandamus, contempt, §1292(b), etc.) on the other.

3.   *Supplemental Appellate Jurisdiction*

Swint v. Chambers County Comm'n

514 U.S. 35 (1995)

Justice GINSBURG delivered the opinion of the Court.

In the wake of successive police raids on a nightclub in Chambers County, Alabama, two of the club's owners joined by an employee and a patron (petitioners here) sued the Chambers County Commission (respondent here), the city of Wadley, and three individual police officers. Petitioners sought damages and other relief, pursuant to 42 U.S.C. §1983, for alleged civil rights violations. We granted certiorari to review the decision of the United States Court of Appeals for the Eleventh Circuit, which held that the Chambers County Commission qualified for summary judgment because the sheriff who authorized the raids was a state executive officer and not an agent of the county commission. We do not reach that issue, however, because we conclude that the Eleventh Circuit lacked jurisdiction to rule on the county commission's liability at this interlocutory stage of the litigation.

The Eleventh Circuit unquestionably had jurisdiction to review the denial of the individual police officer defendants' motions for summary judgment based on their alleged qualified immunity from suit. But the Circuit Court did not thereby gain authority to review the denial of the Chambers County Commission's motion for summary judgment. The Commission's appeal, we hold, does not fit within the "collateral order" doctrine, nor is there "pendent party" appellate authority to take up the Commission's case. We therefore vacate the relevant portion of the Eleventh Circuit's judgment and remand for proceedings consistent with this opinion.

I

On December 14, 1990, and again on March 29, 1991, law enforcement officers from Chambers County and the City of Wadley, Alabama, raided the Capri Club in Chambers County as part of a narcotics operation. The raids were conducted without a search warrant or an arrest warrant. Petitioners filed suit, alleging, among other claims for relief, violations of their federal civil rights. Petitioners named as defendants the County Commission; the City of Wadley; and three individual defendants, Chambers County Sheriff James C. Morgan, Wadley Police Chief Freddie Morgan, and Wadley Police Officer Gregory Dendinger.

The five defendants moved for summary judgment on varying grounds. The three individual defendants asserted qualified immunity from suit on petitioners' federal claims. *See Anderson v. Creighton* (1987) (governmental officials are immune from suit for civil damages unless their conduct is unreasonable in light of clearly established law). Without addressing the question whether Wadley Police Chief Freddie Morgan, who participated in the raids, was a policymaker for the municipality, the City argued that a *respondeat superior* theory could not be used to hold it liable under §1983. *See Monell v. New York City Dept. of Soc Servs.* (1978) (a local government may not be sued under §1983 for injury inflicted solely by its nonpolicymaking employees or agents). The Chambers County Commission argued that County Sheriff James C. Morgan, who authorized the raids, was not a policymaker for the County.

The United States District Court for the Middle District of Alabama denied the motions for summary judgment. . . . The District Court later denied the defendants' motions for reconsideration, but indicated its intent to revisit, before jury deliberations, the question whether Sheriff Morgan was a policymaker for the County:

> The Chambers County Defendants correctly point out that whether Sheriff James Morgan was the final policy maker is a question of law that this Court can decide. What th[is] Court decided in its [prior order] was that the Plaintiffs had come forward with sufficient evidence to persuade this Court that Sheriff Morgan may be the final policy maker for the County. The parties will have an opportunity to convince this Court that Sheriff Morgan was or was not the final policy maker for the County, and the Court will make a ruling as a matter of law on that issue before the case goes to the jury.

Invoking the rule that an order denying qualified immunity is appealable before trial, *Mitchell v. Forsyth* (1985), the individual defendants immediately appealed. The City of Wadley and the Chambers County Commission also appealed, arguing, first, that the denial of their summary judgment motions–like the denial of the individual defendants' summary judgment motions–was immediately appealable as a collateral order satisfying the test announced in *Cohen v. Beneficial Industrial Loan Corp.* (1949) (decisions that are conclusive, that resolve important questions apart from the merits of the underlying action, and that are effectively unreviewable on appeal from final judgment may be appealed immediately). Alternatively, the City and County Commission urged the Eleventh Circuit Court of Appeals to exercise "pendent appellate jurisdiction," a power that court had asserted in earlier cases. Stressing the Eleventh Circuit's undisputed jurisdiction over the individual defendants' qualified immunity pleas, the City and County Commission maintained that, in the interest of judicial economy, the court should resolve, simultaneously, the City's and Commission's appeals.

The Eleventh Circuit affirmed in part and reversed in part the District Court's order denying summary judgment for the individual defendants. Next, the Eleventh Circuit held that the District Court's rejections of the County Commission's and City's summary judgment motions were not immediately appealable as collateral orders. Nevertheless, the Circuit Court decided to exercise pendent appellate jurisdiction over the County Commission's appeal. Holding that Sheriff James C. Morgan was not a policymaker for the County in the area of law enforcement, the Eleventh Circuit reversed the District Court's order denying the County Commission's motion for summary judgment. The Eleventh Circuit declined to exercise pendent appellate jurisdiction over the City's appeal because the District Court had not yet decided whether Wadley Police Chief Freddie Morgan was a policymaker for the City.

We granted certiorari to review the Court of Appeals' decision that Sheriff Morgan is not a policymaker for Chambers County. We then instructed the parties to file supplemental briefs addressing this question: Given the Eleventh Circuit's jurisdiction to review immediately the District Court's refusal to grant summary judgment for the individual defendants in response to their pleas of qualified immunity, did the Circuit Court also have jurisdiction to review at once the denial of the County Commission's summary judgment motion? We now hold that the Eleventh Circuit should have dismissed the County Commission's appeal for want of jurisdiction.

II

We inquire first whether the denial of the County Commission's summary judgment motion was appealable as a collateral order. The answer, as the Court of Appeals recognized, is a firm "No."

By statute, federal courts of appeals have "jurisdiction of appeals from all final decisions of the district courts," except where direct review may be had in this Court. 28 U.S.C. §1291. "The collateral order doctrine is best understood not as an exception to the 'final decision' rule laid down by Congress in §1291, but as a 'practical construction' of it." *Digital Equipment Corp. v. Desktop Direct, Inc.* (1994). In *Cohen*, we held that §1291 permits appeals not only from a final decision by which a district court disassociates itself from a case, but also from a small category of decisions that, although they do not end the litigation, must nonetheless be considered "final." That small category includes only decisions that are conclusive, that resolve important questions separate from the merits, and that are effectively unreviewable on appeal from the final judgment in the underlying action.

The District Court planned to reconsider its ruling on the County Commission's summary judgment motion before the case went to the jury. That court had initially determined only that "Sheriff Morgan *may have been* the final policy maker for the County." The ruling thus fails the *Cohen* test, which "disallow[s] appeal from any decision which is tentative, informal or incomplete." *Cohen; see Coopers & Lybrand v. Livesay* (1978) (order denying class certification held not appealable under collateral order doctrine, in part because such an order is "subject to revision in the District Court").

Moreover, the order denying the County Commission's summary judgment motion does not satisfy *Cohen*'s requirement that the decision be effectively unreviewable after final judgment. When we placed within the collateral order doctrine decisions denying pleas of government officials for qualified immunity, we stressed that an official's qualified immunity is "an *immunity from suit* rather than a mere defense to liability; and like an absolute immunity, it is effectively lost if a case is erroneously permitted to go to trial." *Mitchell.*

The County Commission invokes our decision in *Monell*, which held that municipalities are liable under §1983 only for violations of federal law that occur pursuant to official governmental policy or custom. *Monell*, the Commission contends, should be read to accord local governments a qualified right to be free from the burdens of trial. Accordingly, the Commission maintains, the Commission should be able to appeal immediately the District Court's denial of its summary judgment motion. This argument undervalues a core point we reiterated last Term: "§1291 requires courts of appeals to view claims of a 'right not to be tried' with skepticism, if not a jaundiced eye," *Digital Equipment*, for "virtually every right that could be enforced appropriately by pretrial dismissal might loosely be described as conferring a 'right not to stand trial.'" *Id.*; *cf. United States v. MacDonald* (1978) (denial of pretrial motion to dismiss an indictment on speedy trial grounds held not appealable under collateral order doctrine).

The Commission's assertion that Sheriff Morgan is not its policymaker does not rank, under our decisions, as an immunity from suit. Instead, the plea ranks as a "mere defense to liability." *Mitchell.* An erroneous ruling on liability may be reviewed effectively on appeal from final judgment. Therefore, the order denying the County Commission's summary judgment motion was not an appealable collateral order.

Although the Court of Appeals recognized that the District Court's order denying the County Commission's summary judgment motion was not appealable as a collateral order, the Circuit Court reviewed that ruling by assuming jurisdiction pendent to its undisputed jurisdiction to review the denial of the individual defendants' summary judgment motions. Describing this "pendent appellate jurisdiction" as discretionary, the Eleventh Circuit concluded that judicial economy warranted its exercise in the instant case: "If the County Commission is correct about the merits in its appeal," the court explained, "reviewing the district court's order would put an end to the entire case against the County. . . ."

Petitioners join respondent Chambers County Commission in urging that the Eleventh Circuit had pendent appellate jurisdiction to review the District Court's order denying the Commission's summary judgment motion. Both sides emphasize that §1291's final decision requirement is designed to prevent parties from interrupting litigation by pursuing piecemeal appeals. Once litigation has already been interrupted by an authorized pretrial appeal, petitioners and the County Commission reason, there is no cause to resist the economy that pendent appellate jurisdiction promotes. . . .

These arguments drift away from the statutory instructions Congress has given to control the timing of appellate proceedings. The main rule on review of "final decisions," 28 U.S.C. §1291 is followed by prescriptions for appeals from "interlocutory decisions," 28 U.S.C. §1292. Section 1292(a) lists three categories of immediately appealable interlocutory decisions. Of prime significance to the jurisdictional issue before us, Congress, in 1958, augmented the §1292 catalogue of immediately appealable orders; Congress added a provision, §1292(b), according the district courts circumscribed authority to certify for immediate appeal interlocutory orders deemed pivotal and debatable. Section 1292(b) provides:

> When a district judge, in making in a civil action an order not otherwise appealable under this section, shall be of the opinion that such order involves a controlling question of law as to which there is substantial ground for difference of opinion and that an immediate appeal from the order may materially advance the ultimate termination of the litigation, he shall so state in writing in such order. The Court of Appeals which would have jurisdiction of an appeal of such action may thereupon, in its discretion, permit an appeal to be taken from such order, if application is made to it within ten days after the entry of the order: *Provided, however,* That application for an appeal hereunder shall not stay proceedings in the district court unless the district judge or the Court of Appeals or a judge thereof shall so order.

Congress thus chose to confer on district courts first line discretion to allow interlocutory appeals. If courts of appeals had discretion to append to a *Cohen* authorized appeal from a collateral order further rulings of a kind neither independently appealable nor certified by the district court, then the two tiered arrangement §1292(b) mandates would be severely undermined.

Congress [also] has empowered this Court to clarify when a decision qualifies as "final" for appellate review purposes, and to expand the list of orders appealable on an interlocutory basis. The procedure Congress ordered for such changes, however, is not expansion by court decision, but by rulemaking under §2072.

Two decisions of this Court securely support the conclusion that the Eleventh Circuit lacked jurisdiction instantly to review the denial of the County Commission's summary judgment motion: *Abney v. United States* (1977) and *United States* v. *Stanley* (1987). In *Abney*, we permitted appeal before trial of an order denying a motion to dismiss an indictment on double jeopardy grounds. Immediate appeal of that ruling, we held, fit within the *Cohen* collateral order doctrine. But we further held that the Court of Appeals lacked authority to review simultaneously the trial court's rejection of the defendant's challenge to the sufficiency of the indictment. We explained:

> Our conclusion that a defendant may seek immediate appellate review of a district court's rejection of his double jeopardy claim is based on the special considerations permeating claims of that nature which justify a departure from the normal rule of finality. Quite obviously, such considerations do not extend beyond the claim of formal jeopardy and encompass other claims presented to, and rejected by, the district court in passing on the accused's motion to dismiss. Rather, such claims are appealable if, and only if, they too fall within *Cohen*'s collateral order exception to the final judgment rule. Any other rule would encourage

criminal defendants to seek review of, or assert, frivolous double jeopardy claims in order to bring more serious, but otherwise nonappealable questions to the attention of the courts of appeals prior to conviction and sentence.

[T]he concern expressed in *Abney*—that a rule loosely allowing pendent appellate jurisdiction would encourage parties to parlay *Cohen* type collateral orders into multi issue interlocutory appeal tickets—bears on civil cases as well.

In *Stanley*, we similarly refused to allow expansion of the scope of an interlocutory appeal. That civil case involved an order certified by the trial court, and accepted by the appellate court, for immediate review pursuant to §1292(b). Immediate appellate review, we held, was limited to the certified order; issues presented by other, noncertified orders could not be considered simultaneously.

The parties are correct that we have not universally required courts of appeals to confine review to the precise decision independently subject to appeal. *See, e.g., Thornburgh v. American College of Obstetricians and Gynecologists* (1986) (court of appeals reviewing district court's ruling on preliminary injunction request properly reviewed merits as well); *Eisen v. Carlisle & Jacquelin* (1974) (court of appeals reviewing district court's order allocating costs of class notification also had jurisdiction to review ruling on methods of notification); *Chicago, R.I. & P.R. Co. v. Stude* (1954) (court of appeals reviewing order granting motion to dismiss properly reviewed order denying opposing party's motion to remand); *Deckert v. Independence Shares Corp.* (1940) (court of appeals reviewing order granting preliminary injunction also had jurisdiction to review order denying motions to dismiss). *Cf. Schlagenhauf v. Holder* (1964) (court of appeals exercising mandamus power should have reviewed not only whether district court had authority to order mental and physical examinations of defendant in personal injury case, but also whether there was good cause for the ordered examinations).

We need not definitively or preemptively settle here whether or when it may be proper for a court of appeals with jurisdiction over one ruling to review, conjunctively, related rulings that are not themselves independently appealable. . . . The parties do not contend that the District Court's decision to deny the Chambers County Commission's summary judgment motion was inextricably intertwined with that court's decision to deny the individual defendants' qualified immunity motions, or that review of the former decision was necessary to ensure meaningful review of the latter. *Cf.* Kanji, The Proper Scope of Pendent Appellate Jurisdiction in the Collateral Order Context (1990) ("Only where essential to the resolution of properly appealed collateral orders should courts extend their *Cohen* jurisdiction to rulings that would not otherwise qualify for expedited consideration."). Nor could the parties so argue. The individual defendants' qualified immunity turns on whether they violated clearly established federal law; the County Commission's liability turns on the allocation of law enforcement power in Alabama.

. . .

We therefore vacate the relevant portion of the Eleventh Circuit's judgment, and remand for proceedings consistent with this opinion.

It is so ordered.

* * *

In *Ashcroft v. Iqbal* (2009), the Supreme Court enforced its new plausibility pleading rule to a claim brought against high-level national security officials for their role in violation of the constitutional rights of post-9/11 immigration detainees. The defendants were accused of directing federal agents to detain and mistreat Arab and Muslim detainees on the basis of their race, nationality and religion, in violation of the First and Fifth Amendments. The plaintiffs alleged that during their detention they were isolated 23 hours a day, beaten, denied medical care, subjected to strip searches and body cavity searches, denied prayer materials, and subject to other unconstitutional conditions without evidence they had any connection to the 9/11 attacks.

The defendants' motions to dismiss were grounded in the defense of qualified immunity, and, as *Swint* recognizes, denials of qualified immunity are collateral orders subject to interlocutory review. The plaintiffs challenged appellate jurisdiction, arguing that the question in a 12(b)(6) motion is the factual sufficiency of the pleadings, not just the legal issues applicable to the defense of qualified immunity. Thus, while the Second Circuit had jurisdiction to decide the discrete legal question of the clarity of the law at the time of the detentions, it had no power to review and decide the full merits of the 12(b)(6) motion.

The Court rejected this argument, concluding that its collateral order doctrine opinions are "not so strictly confined":

> In *Hartman v. Moore* (2006), the Court reviewed an interlocutory decision denying qualified immunity. The legal issue decided in *Hartman* concerned the elements a plaintiff "must plead and prove in order to win" a First Amendment retaliation claim. Similarly, two Terms ago in *Wilkie v. Robbins* (2007), the Court considered another interlocutory order denying qualified immunity. The legal issue there was whether a *Bivens* action can be employed to challenge interference with property rights. These cases cannot be squared with respondent's argument that the collateral-order doctrine restricts appellate jurisdiction to the "ultimate issu[e]" whether the legal wrong asserted was a violation of clearly established law while excluding the question whether the facts pleaded establish such a violation. Indeed, the latter question is even more clearly within the category of appealable decisions than the questions presented in *Hartman* and *Wilkie,* since whether a particular complaint sufficiently alleges a clearly established violation of law cannot be decided in isolation from the facts pleaded. In that sense the sufficiency of respondent's pleadings is both "inextricably intertwined with," *Swint v. Chambers County Comm'n* (1995), and "directly implicated by," *Hartman,* the qualified immunity defense.
>
> Respondent counters that our holding in *Johnson v. Jones* (1995), confirms the want of subject-matter jurisdiction here. That is incorrect. The allegation in *Johnson* was that five defendants, all of them police officers, unlawfully beat the plaintiff. *Johnson* considered "the appealability of a portion of" the District Court's summary judgment order that, "though entered in a 'qualified immunity' case, determine[d] only" that there was a genuine issue of material fact that three of the defendants participated in the beating.
>
> In finding that order not a "final decision" for purposes of §1291, the *Johnson* Court cited *Mitchell* for the proposition that only decisions

turning "'*on an issue of law*'" are subject to immediate appeal. Though determining whether there is a genuine issue of material fact at summary judgment is a question of law, it is a legal question that sits near the law-fact divide. Or as we said in *Johnson*, it is a "fact-related" legal inquiry. To conduct it, a court of appeals may be required to consult a "vast pretrial record, with numerous conflicting affidavits, depositions, and other discovery materials." That process generally involves matters more within a district court's ken and may replicate inefficiently questions that will arise on appeal following final judgment. *Ibid.* Finding those concerns predominant, *Johnson* held that the collateral orders that are "final" under *Mitchell* turn on "abstract," rather than "fact-based," issues of law.

The concerns that animated the decision in *Johnson* are absent when an appellate court considers the disposition of a motion to dismiss a complaint for insufficient pleadings. True, the categories of "fact-based" and "abstract" legal questions used to guide the Court's decision in *Johnson* are not well defined. Here, however, the order denying petitioners' motion to dismiss falls well within the latter class. Reviewing that order, the Court of Appeals considered only the allegations contained within the four corners of respondent's complaint; resort to a "vast pretrial record" on petitioners' motion to dismiss was unnecessary. *Johnson.* And determining whether respondent's complaint has the "heft" to state a claim is a task well within an appellate court's core competency. *Bell Atl. Corp v. Twombly* (2007). Evaluating the sufficiency of a complaint is not a "fact-based" question of law, so the problem the Court sought to avoid in *Johnson* is not implicated here. The District Court's order denying petitioners' motion to dismiss is a final decision under the collateral-order doctrine over which the Court of Appeals had, and this Court has, jurisdiction. We proceed to consider the merits of petitioners' appeal.

The Court went on to hold in *Iqbal* that the complaint failed to state a plausible claim for unconstitutional discrimination and remanded so the plaintiff could seek leave to amend.

4. Injunctions

Under 28 U.S.C. §1292(a)(1), the courts of appeal are given jurisdiction over interlocutory appeals for decisions "granting, continuing, modifying, refusing or dissolving injunctions, or refusing to dissolve or modify injunctions, except where a direct review may be had in the Supreme Court." The rule is not triggered by the "mere presence of words of restraint or direction in an order that is only a step an action" and is "unrelated to the substantive issues in the action, while awaiting trial." *Weight Watchers of Phil. v. Weight Watchers Intern., Inc.* (2d Cir. 1972). But it does apply preliminary injunctions that maintain the status quo during litigation, not just permanent injunctions. What matters is whether the practical effect of the district court's order is injunctive. As the Supreme Court has said:

> the label attached to an order is not dispositive. We have previously made clear that where an order has the "practical effect" of granting or denying an injunction, it should be treated as such for purposes of

appellate jurisdiction. *Carson v. American Brands, Inc.* (1981). We applied this test in *Carson*, holding that an order that declined to enter a consent decree prohibiting certain conduct could be appealed under §1292(a)(1) because it was the practical equivalent of an order denying an injunction and threatened serious and perhaps irreparable harm if not immediately reviewed.

This "practical effect" rule serves a valuable purpose. If an interlocutory injunction is improperly granted or denied, much harm can occur before the final decision in the district court. Lawful and important conduct may be barred, and unlawful and harmful conduct may be allowed to continue. Recognizing this, Congress authorized interlocutory appellate review of such orders. But if the availability of interlocutory review depended on the district court's use of the term "injunction" or some other particular language, Congress's scheme could be frustrated. The harms that Congress wanted to avoid could occur so long as the district court was careful about its terminology. The "practical effect" inquiry prevents such manipulation.

In analogous contexts, we have not allowed district courts to "shield [their] orders from appellate review" by avoiding the label "injunction." *Sampson v. Murray* (1974). For instance, in *Sampson*, we held that an order labeled a temporary restraining order (which is not appealable under §1292(a)(1)) should be treated as a "preliminary injunction" (which is appealable) since the order had the same practical effect as a preliminary injunction.

Abbott v. Perez (2018). Why is interlocutory review of injunctive relief warranted as compared to the many other forms of relief a court may order?

5. *Certification*

Congress has also created an exception to the final judgment rule where a district court certifies that an order it has issued "involves a controlling question of law as to which there is substantial ground for difference of opinion and that an immediate appeal from the order may materially advance the ultimate termination of the litigation, he shall so state in writing in such order." 28 U.S.C. §1292(b). The court of appeal may then, "in its discretion, permit an appeal to be taken from such order." This process has been characterized by one court as "a steep and thorny route" to interlocutory review. *Weir v. Propst* (7th Cir. 1990). One reason for this is that the first step involves convincing the district court that it may have erred. Even after a litigant succeeds in doing so, there remains the task of convincing the court of appeal to clear docket space for the appeal. The Supreme Court has held that the court of appeal "may deny the appeal for any reason, including docket congestion." *Coopers & Lybrand v. Livesay* (1978).

The statutory criteria require that the legal question be controlling, in the sense that it affects the outcome of the case or the subject matter jurisdiction of the district court; the question is legal, not factual; there is some division of authority, not a settled question of law; and resolution of the question will accelerate resolution of the dispute.

6. *Rulemaking*

Beyond the exceptions to the final judgment rule made by Congress in 28 U.S.C. §1292, the Advisory Committee for Civil Rules has from time to time provided explicitly for interlocutory review. Two of the most important are: (1) Rule 54(b), to deal with cases involving multiple claims at least one of which the district court has conclusively resolved, and (2) Rule 23(f), to deal with class action certification decisions. We discuss both briefly below.

Rule 54(b) makes interlocutory appeal possible where there are multiple claims for relief and the district court exercises its discretion to direct entry of judgment as to one or more but not all claims. The Supreme Court has described the standard for evaluating interlocutory appeals from Rule 54(b) judgments in the following terms:

> Nearly a quarter of a century ago, in *Sears, Roebuck & Co. v. Mackey* (1956), this Court outlined the steps to be followed in making determinations under Rule 54(b). A district court must first determine that it is dealing with a "final judgment." It must be a "judgment" in the sense that it is a decision upon a cognizable claim for relief, and it must be "final" in the sense that it is "an ultimate disposition of an individual claim entered in the course of a multiple claims action."
>
> Once having found finality, the district court must go on to determine whether there is any just reason for delay. Not all final judgments on individual claims should be immediately appealable, even if they are in some sense separate from the remaining unresolved claims. The function of the district court under the Rule is to act as a "dispatcher." *Id.* It is left to the sound judicial discretion of the district court to determine the "appropriate time" when each final decision in a multiple claims action is ready for appeal. This discretion is to be exercised "in the interest of sound judicial administration."
>
> Thus, in deciding whether there are no just reasons to delay the appeal of individual final judgments in a setting such as this, a district court must take into account judicial administrative interests, as well as the equities involved. Consideration of the former is necessary to assure that application of the Rule effectively "preserves the historic federal policy against piecemeal appeals." *Id.* It was therefore proper for the District Judge here to consider such factors as whether the claims under review were separable from the others remaining to be adjudicated and whether the nature of the claims already determined was such that no appellate court would have to decide the same issues more than once, even if there were subsequent appeals. . . .
>
> In *Sears*, the Court stated that the decision to certify was, with good reason, left to the sound judicial discretion of the district court. At the same time, the Court noted that, "[w]ith equally good reason, any *abuse* of that discretion remains reviewable by the Court of Appeals." The Court indicated that the standard against which a district court's exercise of discretion is to be judged is the "interest of sound judicial administration." Admittedly this presents issues not always easily resolved, but the proper role of the court of appeals is not to reweigh the equities or reassess the

facts, but to make sure that the conclusions derived from those weighings and assessments are juridically sound and supported by the record.

There are thus two aspects to the proper function of a reviewing court in Rule 54(b) cases. The court of appeals must, of course, scrutinize the district court's evaluation of such factors as the interrelationship of the claims so as to prevent piecemeal appeals in cases which should be reviewed only as single units. But once such juridical concerns have been met, the discretionary judgment of the district court should be given substantial deference, for that court is "the one most likely to be familiar with the case and with any justifiable reasons for delay." *Sears*. The reviewing court should disturb the trial court's assessment of the equities only if it can say that the judge's conclusion was clearly unreasonable.

Plainly, sound judicial administration does not require that Rule 54(b) requests be granted routinely. That is implicit in commending them to the sound discretion of a district court. Because this discretion "is, with good reason, vested by the rule primarily" in the district courts, *Sears*, and because the number of possible situations is large, we are reluctant either to fix or sanction narrow guidelines for the district courts to follow.

Curtiss-Wright Corp. v. General Elec. Co. (1980) (rejecting Advisory Committee Notes suggestion that Rule 54(b) interlocutory review was a remedy only for "the infrequent harsh case").

At the turn of the century, the Advisory Committee provided for interlocutory appeal of class certification decisions by amending Rule 23. Rule 23(f) provides:

> A court of appeals may permit an appeal from an order granting or denying class-action certification under this rule, but not from an order under Rule 23(e)(1). A party must file a petition for permission to appeal with the circuit clerk within 14 days after the order is entered or within 45 days after the order is entered if any party is the United States, a United States agency, or a United States officer or employee sued for an act or omission occurring in connection with duties performed on the United States' behalf. An appeal does not stay proceedings in the district court unless the district judge or the court of appeals so orders.

The rule was a response to concerns, on the one hand, about denials of class certification "sounding the death knell of the litigation" because without aggregation of claims many plaintiffs are likely abandon litigation altogether. *Newton v. Merrill Lynch* (3d Cir. 2001). And, on the other hand, concerns about grants of class certification that create an "undue and unnecessary risk of a monumental industry-busting error in entrusting the determination of potential multi-billion dollar liabilities to a single jury." *In re Rhone-Poulenc Rorer* (7th Cir. 1995).

Recent empirical work finds "significant variation over time in appeal outcomes post-Rule 23(f)," with defendants far more successful than plaintiffs prior to *Wal-Mart* and *Comcast*, and relative parity after.[20]

---

20. Stephen B. Burbank and Sean Farhang, *Class Certification in the U.S. Courts of Appeals: A Longitudinal Study*, 84 L. CONTEMP. PROBS. 73, 77 (2021).

JUSTICIABILITY: CONSTITUTIONAL AND PRUDENTIAL LIMITS ON FEDERAL JUDICIAL POWER

Article III provides that the judicial power shall extend to "all cases" that arise under federal law, and to certain "controversies" defined by party status. In Chapter 2, we examined what it meant for a case to arise under federal law and how to go about determining party status within the meaning of the constitutional grant of jurisdiction. We also examined the power of Congress to set limits on the actual jurisdiction of the lower federal courts within that grant. In this Chapter, we address justiciability rules, another set of limiting rules developed by the Court. Constitutional limits on justiciability are concerned with whether a dispute is a true "case" or "controversy." Prudential limits are not constitutional, but rather are based upon the Court's own sense of the proper role and practical limits on federal judicial power.

The case or controversy requirement in Article III relies upon traditional understandings of the adversary system. Recall, for example, Chief Justice Marshall's discussion of the doctrine of *damnum absque injuria* in *Marbury v. Madison* in Chapter 1. As you may have studied in Torts, *damnum absque injuria* means damage without legal injury. In *Marbury*, Marshall insisted that before the Court took up the question of the withholding of Marbury's commission, it had to "inquire whether there be in [the dispute] any ingredient which shall exempt from legal investigation or exclude the injured party from legal redress." And "[i]n pursuing this inquiry, the first question which presents itself is whether [the dispute] can be arranged with that class of cases which come under the description of *damnum absque injuria*—a loss without injury." If the failure to deliver the commission were not a legally cognizable harm, then there would be no judicial remedy for Marbury's loss and the Supreme Court would not have authority to adjudicate the dispute. There was a remedy, Marshall reasoned, because the office of justice of the peace had been created by Congress with a five-year term and was a position of "trust, of honor, or of profit"—a position of tangible value the deprivation of which merited the "attention and guardianship" of the laws.

Marshall went on to distinguish two types of suits. On the one hand, a suit against a high government officer such as the Secretary of State regarding a discretionary act or pure policy judgment might be a political question, as we learned in Chapter 1, for which a high government officer is answerable only to the President and the voters. On the other hand, a suit such as Marbury's, which demands that an official perform a non-discretionary legal obligation, is a justiciable case or controversy.

Standing, the requirement that the plaintiff have suffered legally cognizable harm a court can remedy, and the political question doctrine, are just two of the justiciability rules the Supreme Court has developed. The general purpose of these rules is to distinguish disputes proper to federal courts from those which belong in the political process. This means that the case or controversy requirement performs a separation of powers function, withholding judicial power from the courts where the problem the parties raise is better suited to resolution by politically accountable decision makers. Although conventionally described as a limit on judicial power, it is the Court that sets this limit. As we shall see, the Court has increasingly used justiciability rules to limit congressional power. It has limited Congress's power to shape the jurisdiction of the lower federal courts, to create new rights and remedies, and to empower individuals whose rights have been violated to sue for relief themselves rather than wait for enforcement by the executive branch. In short, justiciability rules have become enormously consequential.

We begin in Section A with the prohibition on advisory opinions and the requirement that a dispute be sufficiently adverse for judicial resolution. Generally, the federal courts can only decide a dispute that is truly contested by both sides and will result in a judgment binding on the parties appearing before it. These qualities of a "case or controversy" ensure a discrete, detailed factual record to focus and constrain judicial review. In Section B, we turn to the sprawling body of rules governing standing to sue—the requirement that a dispute involve a concrete, legally cognizable injury to the plaintiff, fairly traceable to the conduct of the defendant, which a federal court can remedy. In Section C, we take up ripeness doctrine—the rule that federal courts only decide cases that involve harm that has either already occurred, or is sufficiently imminent to justify judicial intervention. In Section D, we study mootness, the requirement that a case or controversy be a "live" dispute not just when it is filed but through all the stages of judicial review. For reasons similar to the prohibition on advisory opinions, the federal courts will not continue to exercise judicial review over legal questions where intervening circumstances eliminate the personal stakes the parties have in the dispute. Finally, in Section E, we take up modern political question doctrine, exploring the constitutional questions the Court has decided belong exclusively to the other branches of government to resolve.

A.   ADVISORY OPINIONS AND THE ADVERSENESS REQUIREMENT

Since the Founding, Article III has been read to prohibit the federal courts from issuing advisory opinions. In many states, state courts are authorized to provide opinions about the constitutionality of pending legislation or on constitutional questions referred to them by other branches of government.[1] Such advisory opinions are in many ways beneficial. By providing guidance to the legislature, these rulings can prevent the enactment of unconstitutional laws. Also, an advisory opinion can spare a legislature the effort of passing statutes soon to be invalidated by the courts and can save time by allowing the legislature to correct constitutional infirmities during drafting. Among other common-law countries, the Federal Supreme Court of India has discretion to issue advisory opinions on constitutional matters, especially whether pending legislation is constitutional. Canada permits provincial government executive branch officials to submit "references" of legal questions to provincial courts which can be appealed to the Supreme Court of Canada. And in English law the advisory opinion is "virtually unknown," but a committee of the House of Commons "is able to ask the Judicial committee of the Privy Council to give an Opinion."[2] In civil law countries that have constitutional courts — courts whose subject matter jurisdiction is limited to constitutional law — advisory opinions regarding the constitutionality of legislation and treaties are more common. Some international courts, such as the International Court of Justice, the European Court of Human Rights, and the International Tribunal for the Law of the Sea, have discretion to issue advisory opinions.[3]

Despite these benefits and the breadth of the practice in state courts and in the courts of other countries, it is firmly established that U.S. federal courts *cannot* issue advisory opinions. There are several reasons. First, separation of powers is maintained by keeping the courts out of the legislative process. The judicial role is limited to deciding actual disputes; it does not include giving advice to Congress or the President.

Second, judicial resources are conserved because advisory opinions might be requested in many instances in which a proposed bill ultimately would not be enacted into law by the legislature. The federal courts can decide the matter if it turns into an actual dispute; otherwise, judicial review is unnecessary, and a waste of precious docket space and capital.

Third, the prohibition against advisory opinions helps ensure that cases will be presented to the Court in terms of specific disputes, rather than as merely hypothetical legal questions. As the Court explained in *Flast v. Cohen* (1968):

> [T]he implicit policies embodied in Article III, and not history alone, impose the rule against advisory opinions. [The rule] implements the separation of powers [and] also recognizes that such suits often are not pressed before the Court with that clear concreteness provided when a question emerges precisely framed and necessary for decision from a clash of adversary argument exploring every aspect of a multifaceted situation embracing conflicting and demanding interests.

---

1. For an excellent discussion of advisory opinions in state courts, see Helen Hershkoff, *State Courts and the "Passive Virtues": Rethinking the Judicial Function*, 114 Harv. L. Rev. 1833 (2001).

2. Anthony Aust, *Advisory Opinions*, 1 J. Intl. Disp. Settlement 123, 124 (2010).

3. *Id.* at 126-27.

For a case to be justiciable and not an advisory opinion, two criteria must be met.[4] First, there must be an actual dispute between adverse litigants. This requirement dates back to the earliest days of the nation. During the administration of President George Washington, then Secretary of State Thomas Jefferson asked the Supreme Court for its answers to a long list of questions, 29 in all, concerning American neutrality in the war between France and England. In his letter to the Justices, Jefferson explained that the war between these countries had raised a number of important legal questions concerning the meaning of United States' treaties and laws. Jefferson's letter said that "[t]he President therefore would be much relieved if he found himself free to refer questions of this description to the opinions of the judges of the [Court], whose knowledge of the subject would secure us against errors dangerous to the peace of the United States." For example, Jefferson asked the Justices, "May we, within our own ports, sell ships to both parties, prepared merely for merchandise? May they be pierced for guns?"

The Justices responded:

> Sir
>
> We have considered the previous Question stated in a Letter written to us by your Direction, by the Secretary of State, on the 18th of last month.
>
> The Lines of Separation drawn by the Constitution between the three Departments of Government—their being in certain Respects checks on each other—and our being Judges of a court in the last Resort—are Considerations which afford strong arguments against the Propriety of our extrajudicially deciding the questions alluded to; especially as the Power given by the Constitution to the President of calling on the Heads of Departments for opinions, seems to have been purposely as well as expressly limited to executive Departments.
>
> We exceedingly regret every Event that may cause Embarrassment to your administration; but we derive Consolation from the Reflection, that your Judgment will discern what is Right, and that your usual Prudence, Decision and Firmness will surmount every obstacle to the Preservation of the Rights, Peace, and Dignity of the United States. We have the Honor to be, with perfect Respect, Sir, your most obedient and most h'ble servants.

Another example of the Court's insistence on an actual dispute between adverse litigants is *Muskrat v. United States* (1911). This case arose from the United States government's attempts to undermine the sovereignty of American Indian nations. Beginning in the late nineteenth century, with the end of formal treatymaking in 1871, the government adopted a policy that aimed to assimilate Indians and to acquire their lands and resources. Allotment was the centerpiece of this policy. In 1887, Congress enacted the General Allotment Act, which created

---

4. For a debate over whether this is a constitutional requirement, see James Pfander & Daniel Birk, *Article III Power, the Adverse-Party Requirement, and Non-Contentious Jurisdiction*, 124 YALE L.J. 1326 (2015); Ann Woolander, *Adverse Interests and Article III*, 111 Nw. U. L. Rev. 1025 (2017); James Pfander & Daniel Birk, *Adverse Interests and Article III: A Reply*, 111 Nw. U. L. Rev. 1067 (2017).

a system under which tribally owned lands would be allotted into parcels and distributed among individual Indians or sold to non-Indians as so-called "surplus" lands. In 1903, with *Lone Wolf v. Hitchcock*, the Supreme Court held that Congress had authority to order the allotment of Indian lands even when it would violate treaties between Native nations and the United States. The allotment policy was disastrous for Indians, with tribes losing over a hundred million acres of their lands as a result.

Various statutes during this period provided for the allotment of the lands of particular Native nations. In 1902, for example, Congress authorized the allotment of the lands of several tribes, including the lands of the Cherokee Nation. Four years later, Congress altered the allotment scheme by expanding the class of persons entitled to claim lands and money. To facilitate resolution of constitutional questions about the 1906 law, Congress subsequently adopted a statute permitting the filing of two lawsuits in the Court of Claims to determine the validity of the earlier law. Pursuant to this statutory authorization, a suit was initiated, but the Supreme Court ruled that it was not justiciable.

Muskrat v. United States

219 U.S. 346 (1911)

Justice DAY delivered the opinion of the court:

These cases arise under an act of Congress undertaking to confer jurisdiction upon the court of claims, and upon this court, on appeal, to determine the validity of certain acts of Congress hereinafter referred to.

Case No. 330 was brought by David Muskrat and J. Henry Dick, in their own behalf, and in behalf of others in a like situation, to determine the constitutional validity of the act of Congress of April 26, 1906 and to have the same declared invalid in so far as the same undertook to increase the number of persons entitled to share in the final distribution of lands and funds of the Cherokees beyond those enrolled on September 1, 1902, in accordance with the act of Congress passed July 1, 1902. The acts subsequent to that of July 1, 1902, have the effect to increase the number of persons entitled to participate in the division of the Cherokee lands and funds, by permitting the enrolment of children who were minors, living on March 4, 1906, whose parents had theretofore been enrolled as members of the Cherokee tribe, or had applications pending for that purpose.

Case No. 331 was brought by Brown and Gritts on their own behalf and on behalf of other Cherokee citizens having a like interest in the property allotted under the act of July 1, 1902. Under this act, Brown and Gritts received allotments. The subsequent act of March 11, 1904, empowered the Secretary of the Interior to grant rights of way for pipe lines over lands allotted to Indians under certain regulations. Another act, that of April 26, 1906, purported to extend to a period of twenty-five years the time within which full-blooded Indians of the Cherokee, Choctaw, Chickasaw, Creek, and Seminole tribes were forbidden to alienate, sell, dispose of, or encumber certain of their lands.

The object of the petition of Brown and Gritts was to have the subsequent legislation of 1904 and 1906 declared to be unconstitutional and void, and to have the lands allotted to them under the original act of July 1, 1902, adjudged to be theirs free from restraints upon the rights to sell and convey the same. From this statement it is apparent that the purpose of the proceedings instituted in the court of claims, and now appealed to this court, is to restrain the enforcement of such legislation subsequent to the act of July 1, 1902, upon the ground that the same is unconstitutional and void. The court of claims sustained the validity of the acts and dismissed the petitions.

These proceedings were begun under the supposed authority of an act of Congress passed March 1, 1907. As that legislation is important in this connection, so much of the act as authorized the beginning of these suits is here inserted in full:

> That William Brown and Levi B. Gritts, on their own behalf and on behalf of all other Cherokee citizens, having like interests in the property allotted under the act of July first, nineteen hundred and two, entitled, "An Act to Provide for the Allotment of Lands of the Cherokee Nation, for the Disposition of Town Sites Therein, and for Other Purposes," and David Muskrat and J. Henry Dick, on their own behalf, and on behalf of all Cherokee citizens enrolled as such for allotment as of September first, nineteen hundred and two, be, and they are hereby, authorized and empowered to institute their suits in the court of claims to determine the validity of any acts of Congress passed since the said act of July first, nineteen hundred and two, in so far as said acts, or any of them, attempt to increase or extend the restrictions upon alienation, encumbrance, or the right to lease the allotments of lands of Cherokee citizens, or to increase the number of persons entitled to share in the final distribution of lands and funds of the Cherokees beyond those enrolled for allotment as of September first, nineteen hundred and two, and provided for in the said act of July first, nineteen hundred and two.

> And jurisdiction is hereby conferred upon the court of claims, with the right of appeal, by either party, to the Supreme Court of the United States, to hear, determine, and adjudicate each of said suits.

> The suits brought hereunder shall be brought on or before September first, nineteen hundred and seven, against the United States as a party defendant, and, for the speedy disposition of the questions involved, preference shall be given to the same by courts, and by the Attorney General, who is hereby charged with the defense of said suits.

> Upon the rendition of final judgment by the court of claims or the Supreme Court of the United States, denying the validity of any portion of the said acts authorized to be brought into question, in either or both of said cases, the court of claims shall determine the amount to be paid the attorneys employed by the above-named parties in the prosecution thereof for services and expenses, and shall render judgment therefor, which shall be paid out of the funds in the United States Treasury belonging to the beneficiaries, under the said act of July first, nineteen hundred and two.

This act is the authority for the maintenance of these two suits.

The first question in these cases, as in others, involves the jurisdiction of the court to entertain the proceeding, and that depends upon whether the jurisdiction conferred is within the power of Congress, having in view the limitations of the judicial power, as established by the Constitution of the United States.

It will serve to elucidate the nature and extent of the judicial power thus conferred by the Constitution to note certain instances in which this court has had occasion to examine and define the same.

It therefore becomes necessary to inquire what is meant by the judicial power thus conferred by the Constitution upon this court, and, with the aid of appropriate legislation, upon the inferior courts of the United States. "Judicial power," says Mr. Justice Miller, in his work on the Constitution, "is the power of a court to decide and pronounce a judgment and carry it into effect between persons and parties who bring a case before it for decision." As we have already seen, by the express terms of the Constitution, the exercise of the judicial power is limited to "cases" and "controversies." Beyond this it does not extend, and unless it is asserted in a case or controversy within the meaning of the Constitution, the power to exercise it is nowhere conferred.

What, then, does the Constitution mean in conferring this judicial power with the right to determine "cases" and "controversies." By cases and controversies are intended the claims of litigants brought before the courts for determination by such regular proceedings as are established by law or custom for the protection or enforcement of rights, or the prevention, redress, or punishment of wrongs. Whenever the claim of a party under the Constitution, laws, or treaties of the United States takes such a form that the judicial power is capable of acting upon it, then it has become a case. The term implies the existence of present or possible adverse parties, whose contentions are submitted to the court for adjudication.

The power being thus limited to require an application of the judicial power to cases and controversies, is the act which undertook to authorize the present suits to determine the constitutional validity of certain legislation within the constitutional authority of the court? . . .

This attempt to obtain a judicial declaration of the validity of the act of Congress is not presented in a "case" or "controversy," to which, under the Constitution of the United States, the judicial power alone extends. It is true the United States is made a defendant to this action, but it has no interest adverse to the claimants. The object is not to assert a property right as against the government, or to demand compensation for alleged wrongs because of action upon its part. The whole purpose of the law is to determine the constitutional validity of this class of legislation, in a suit not arising between parties concerning a property right necessarily involved in the decision in question, but in a proceeding against the government in its sovereign capacity, and concerning which the only judgment required is to settle the doubtful character of the legislation in question. Such judgment will not conclude private parties, when actual litigation brings to the court the question of the constitutionality of such legislation. In a legal sense the judgment could not be executed, and amounts in fact to no more than an expression of opinion upon the validity of the acts in question.

Confining the jurisdiction of this court within the limitations conferred by the Constitution, which the court has hitherto been careful to observe, and whose boundaries it has refused to transcend, we think the Congress, in the act of March 1, 1907, exceeded the limitations of legislative authority, so far as it required of this court action not judicial in its nature within the meaning of the Constitution.

The questions involved in this proceeding as to the validity of the legislation may arise in suits between individuals, and when they do and are properly brought before this court for consideration they, of course, must be determined in the exercise of its judicial functions. For the reasons we have stated, we are constrained to hold that these actions present no justiciable controversy within the authority of the court, acting within the limitations of the Constitution under which it was created.

* * *

The issue of what is sufficient to create a dispute between adverse litigants arose in when the Obama administration refused to defend the provision of the federal Defense of Marriage Act (DOMA) that provided that for purposes of federal law, marriage had to be between a man and a woman. DOMA excluded same-sex marriages—a policy with broad consequences including eligibility for federal tax benefits that apply exclusively to spouses. Edith Windsor challenged the Act as a violation of the Fifth Amendment's Due Process Clause. Typically, the Department of Justice (DOJ) defends federal statutes against constitutional challenges in federal courts. In this instance, the DOJ decided not to do so in light of the Administration's conclusion that DOMA was unconstitutional. In a letter to Congress, the Administration explained that DOMA reflected "precisely the kind of stereotyped-based thinking and animus" that violates the equal protection component of Fifth Amendment due process. That stance was ultimately vindicated a few years later in 2015 when the Court held in *Obergefell v. Hodges* that same-sex couples have a fundamental right to marry under the Equal Protection and Due Process Clauses. In *United States v. Windsor* (2013), which was decided before *Obergefell*, the Court considered whether the Administration's decision not to defend DOMA deprived the Court of jurisdiction.

United States v. Windsor

570 U.S. 744 (2013)

Justice KENNEDY delivered the opinion of the Court.

Two women then resident in New York were married in a lawful ceremony in Ontario, Canada, in 2007. Edith Windsor and Thea Spyer returned to their home in New York City. When Spyer died in 2009, she left her entire estate to Windsor. Windsor sought to claim the estate tax exemption for surviving spouses. She was barred from doing so, however, by a federal law, the Defense of Marriage Act, which excludes a same-sex partner from the definition of "spouse" as that term is used in federal statutes. Windsor paid the taxes but filed suit to challenge the constitutionality of this provision. The United States District Court and the Court of Appeals ruled that this portion of the statute is unconstitutional and ordered the United States to pay Windsor a refund. This Court granted certiorari and now affirms the judgment in Windsor's favor.

In 1996, as some States were beginning to consider the concept of same-sex marriage, and before any State had acted to permit it, Congress enacted the Defense of Marriage Act (DOMA). DOMA contains two operative sections:

Section 2, which has not been challenged here, allows States to refuse to recognize same-sex marriages performed under the laws of other States.

Section 3 is at issue here. It amends the Dictionary Act in to provide a federal definition of "marriage" and "spouse." Section 3 of DOMA provides as follows: "In determining the meaning of any Act of Congress, or of any ruling, regulation, or interpretation of the various administrative bureaus and agencies of the United States, the word 'marriage' means only a legal union between one man and one woman as husband and wife, and the word 'spouse' refers only to a person of the opposite sex who is a husband or a wife."

The definitional provision does not by its terms forbid States from enacting laws permitting same-sex marriages or civil unions or providing state benefits to residents in that status. The enactment's comprehensive definition of marriage for purposes of all federal statutes and other regulations or directives covered by its terms, however, does control over 1,000 federal laws in which marital or spousal status is addressed as a matter of federal law.

While the tax refund suit was pending, the Attorney General of the United States notified the Speaker of the House of Representatives that the Department of Justice would no longer defend the constitutionality of DOMA's §3. Noting that "the Department has previously defended DOMA against . . . challenges involving legally married same-sex couples," the Attorney General informed Congress that "the President has concluded that given a number of factors, including a documented history of discrimination, classifications based on sexual orientation should be subject to a heightened standard of scrutiny."

Although "the President . . . instructed the Department not to defend the statute in *Windsor*," he also decided "that Section 3 will continue to be enforced by the Executive Branch" and that the United States had an "interest in providing Congress a full and fair opportunity to participate in the litigation of those cases." The stated rationale for this dual-track procedure (determination of unconstitutionality coupled with ongoing enforcement) was to "recogniz[e] the judiciary as the final arbiter of the constitutional claims raised."

In response to the notice from the Attorney General, the Bipartisan Legal Advisory Group (BLAG) of the House of Representatives voted to intervene in the litigation to defend the constitutionality of §3 of DOMA. The Department of Justice did not oppose limited intervention by BLAG . . . [and the District Court granted] intervention by BLAG as an interested party. *See* Fed. Rule Civ. Proc. 24(a)(2).

It is appropriate to begin by addressing whether either the Government or BLAG, or both of them, were entitled to appeal to the Court of Appeals and later to seek certiorari and appear as parties here.

There is no dispute that when this case was in the District Court it presented a concrete disagreement between opposing parties, a dispute suitable for judicial resolution. "[A] taxpayer has standing to challenge the collection of a specific tax assessment as unconstitutional; being forced to pay such a tax causes a real and immediate economic injury to the individual taxpayer."

Windsor suffered a redressable injury when she was required to pay estate taxes from which, in her view, she was exempt but for the alleged invalidity of §3 of DOMA.

The decision of the Executive not to defend the constitutionality of §3 in court while continuing to deny refunds and to assess deficiencies does introduce a complication. Even though the Executive's current position was announced before the District Court entered its judgment, the Government's agreement with

Windsor's position would not have deprived the District Court of jurisdiction to entertain and resolve the refund suit; for her injury (failure to obtain a refund allegedly required by law) was concrete, persisting, and unredressed. The Government's position—agreeing with Windsor's legal contention but refusing to give it effect—meant that there was a justiciable controversy between the parties, despite what the claimant would find to be an inconsistency in that stance. Windsor, the Government, BLAG, and the *amicus* appear to agree upon that point. The disagreement is over the standing of the parties, or aspiring parties, to take an appeal in the Court of Appeals and to appear as parties in further proceedings in this Court.

In this case the United States retains a stake sufficient to support Article III jurisdiction on appeal and in proceedings before this Court. The judgment in question orders the United States to pay Windsor the refund she seeks. An order directing the Treasury to pay money is "a real and immediate economic injury," indeed as real and immediate as an order directing an individual to pay a tax. That the Executive may welcome this order to pay the refund if it is accompanied by the constitutional ruling it wants does not eliminate the injury to the national Treasury if payment is made, or to the taxpayer if it is not. The judgment orders the United States to pay money that it would not disburse but for the court's order. The Government of the United States has a valid legal argument that it is injured even if the Executive disagrees with §3 of DOMA, which results in Windsor's liability for the tax. Windsor's ongoing claim for funds that the United States refuses to pay thus establishes a controversy sufficient for Article III jurisdiction. It would be a different case if the Executive had taken the further step of paying Windsor the refund to which she was entitled under the District Court's ruling.

While these principles suffice to show that this case presents a justiciable controversy under Article III, the prudential problems inherent in the Executive's unusual position require some further discussion. The Executive's agreement with Windsor's legal argument raises the risk that instead of a "'real, earnest and vital controversy,'" the Court faces a "friendly, non-adversary, proceeding . . . [in which] 'a party beaten in the legislature [seeks to] transfer to the courts an inquiry as to the constitutionality of the legislative act.'" Even when Article III permits the exercise of federal jurisdiction, prudential considerations demand that the Court insist upon "that concrete adverseness which sharpens the presentation of issues upon which the court so largely depends for illumination of difficult constitutional questions."

There are, of course, reasons to hear a case and issue a ruling even when one party is reluctant to prevail in its position. Unlike Article III requirements—which must be satisfied by the parties before judicial consideration is appropriate—the relevant prudential factors that counsel against hearing this case are subject to "countervailing considerations [that] may outweigh the concerns underlying the usual reluctance to exert judicial power." One consideration is the extent to which adversarial presentation of the issues is assured by the participation of *amici curiae* prepared to defend with vigor the constitutionality of the legislative act.

In the case now before the Court the attorneys for BLAG present a substantial argument for the constitutionality of §3 of DOMA. BLAG's sharp adversarial presentation of the issues satisfies the prudential concerns that otherwise might counsel against hearing an appeal from a decision with which the principal parties agree. Were this Court to hold that prudential rules require it to dismiss the case, and, in consequence, that the Court of Appeals erred in failing to dismiss it as well, extensive litigation would ensue. The district courts in 94 districts throughout the Nation would be without precedential guidance not only in tax refund suits but also in cases involving the whole of DOMA's sweep involving over 1,000 federal statutes and a myriad of federal regulations. For instance, the opinion of the Court of Appeals for the First Circuit, addressing the validity of DOMA in a case involving regulations of the Department of Health and Human Services, likely would be vacated with instructions to dismiss, its ruling and guidance also then erased. Rights and privileges of hundreds of thousands of persons would be adversely affected, pending a case in which all prudential concerns about justiciability are absent. That numerical prediction may not be certain, but it is certain that the cost in judicial resources and expense of litigation for all persons adversely affected would be immense. True, the very extent of DOMA's mandate means that at some point a case likely would arise without the prudential concerns raised here; but the costs, uncertainties, and alleged harm and injuries likely would continue for a time measured in years before the issue is resolved. In these unusual and urgent circumstances, the very term "prudential" counsels that it is a proper exercise of the Court's responsibility to take jurisdiction. For these reasons, the prudential and Article III requirements are met here.

[The Court went on to declare Section 3 of DOMA unconstitutional as denying equal protection to married same-sex couples.]

Justice SCALIA, with whom Justice THOMAS and with whom THE CHIEF JUSTICE joins as to Part I, dissenting.

This case is about power in several respects. It is about the power of our people to govern themselves, and the power of this Court to pronounce the law. Today's opinion aggrandizes the latter, with the predictable consequence of diminishing the former. We have no power to decide this case. And even if we did, we have no power under the Constitution to invalidate this democratically adopted legislation. The Court's errors on both points spring forth from the same diseased root: an exalted conception of the role of this institution in America.

The Court is eager — *hungry* — to tell everyone its view of the legal question at the heart of this case. Standing in the way is an obstacle, a technicality of little interest to anyone but the people of We the People, who created it as a barrier against judges' intrusion into their lives. They gave judges, in Article III, only the "judicial Power," a power to decide not abstract questions but real, concrete "Cases" and "Controversies." Yet the plaintiff and the Government agree entirely on what should happen in this lawsuit. They agree that the court below got it right; and they agreed in the court below that the court below that one got it right as well. What, then, are we *doing* here?

The answer lies at the heart of the jurisdictional portion of today's opinion, where a single sentence lays bare the majority's vision of our role. The Court says that we have the power to decide this case because if we did not, then our "primary role in determining the constitutionality of a law" (at least one that "has inflicted real injury on a plaintiff") would "become only secondary to the President's." But wait, the reader wonders — Windsor won below, and so *cured* her injury, and the President was glad to see it. True, says the majority, but judicial review must march on regardless, lest we "undermine the clear dictate of the separation-of-powers principle that when an Act of Congress is alleged to conflict with the Constitution, it is emphatically the province and duty of the judicial department to say what the law is."

That is jaw-dropping. It is an assertion of judicial supremacy over the people's Representatives in Congress and the Executive. It envisions a Supreme Court standing (or rather enthroned) at the apex of government, empowered to decide all constitutional questions, always and everywhere "primary" in its role.

This image of the Court would have been unrecognizable to those who wrote and ratified our national charter. They knew well the dangers of "primary" power, and so created branches of government that would be "perfectly coordinate by the terms of their common commission," none of which branches could "pretend to an exclusive or superior right of settling the boundaries between their respective powers." The Federalist, No. 49, p. 314 (C. Rossiter ed. 1961) (J. Madison). The people did this to protect themselves. They did it to guard their right to self-rule against the black-robed supremacy that today's majority finds so attractive. So it was that Madison could confidently state, with no fear of contradiction, that there was nothing of "greater intrinsic value" or "stamped with the authority of more enlightened patrons of liberty" than a government of separate and coordinate powers.

For this reason we are quite forbidden to say what the law is whenever (as today's opinion asserts) "'an Act of Congress is alleged to conflict with the Constitution.'" We can do so only when that allegation will determine the outcome of a lawsuit, and is contradicted by the other party. The judicial power as Americans have understood it (and their English ancestors before them) is the power to adjudicate, with conclusive effect, disputed government claims (civil or criminal) against private persons, and disputed claims by private persons against the government or other private persons.

In other words, declaring the compatibility of state or federal laws with the Constitution is not only not the "primary role" of this Court, it is not a separate, free-standing role *at all*. We perform that role incidentally — by accident, as it were — when that is necessary to resolve the dispute before us. Then, and only then, does it become "'the province and duty of the judicial department to say what the law is.'" That is why, in 1793, we politely declined the Washington Administration's request to "say what the law is" on a particular treaty matter that was not the subject of a concrete legal controversy. And that is why, as our opinions have said, some questions of law will *never* be presented to this Court, because there will never be anyone with standing to bring a lawsuit. Our authority begins and ends with the need to adjudge the rights of an injured party who stands before us seeking redress.

That is completely absent here. . . . What the petitioner United States asks us to do in the case before us is exactly what the respondent Windsor asks us to do: not to provide relief from the judgment below but to say that that judgment was correct.

We have never before agreed to speak — to "say what the law is" — where there is no controversy before us.

It may be argued that if what we say is true some Presidential determinations that statutes are unconstitutional will not be subject to our review. That is as it should be, when both the President and the plaintiff agree that the statute is unconstitutional. Where the Executive is enforcing an unconstitutional law, suit will of course lie; but if, in that suit, the Executive admits the unconstitutionality of the law, the litigation should end in an order or a consent decree enjoining enforcement. This suit saw the light of day only because the President enforced the Act (and thus gave Windsor standing to sue) even though he believed it unconstitutional. He could have equally chosen (more appropriately, some would say) neither to enforce nor to defend the statute he believed to be unconstitutional, in which event Windsor would not have been injured, the District Court could not have refereed this friendly scrimmage, and the Executive's determination of unconstitutionality would have escaped this Court's desire to blurt out its view of the law. The matter would have been left, as so many matters ought to be left, to a tug of war between the President and the Congress, which has innumerable means (up to and including impeachment) of compelling the President to enforce the laws it has written. Or the President could have evaded presentation of the constitutional issue to this Court simply by declining to appeal the District Court and Court of Appeals dispositions he agreed with. Be sure of this much: If a President wants to insulate his judgment of unconstitutionality from our review, he can. What the views urged in this dissent produce is not insulation from judicial review but insulation from Executive contrivance.

[Justice Scalia went on to argue that Section 3 of DOMA is constitutional.]

* * *

The second element of the prohibition on advisory opinions is that there must be a substantial likelihood that a federal court decision in favor of a claimant will bring about some change or have some effect. This requirement also dates back to the Supreme Court's earliest days. In *Hayburn's Case* (1792), the Court considered whether federal courts could express nonbinding opinions on the amounts of benefits owed to Revolutionary War veterans.

Congress adopted a law permitting these veterans to file pension claims in the U.S. Circuit Courts. The judges of these courts were to inform the Secretary of War of the nature of the claimant's disability and the amount of benefits to be paid. The Secretary could refuse to follow the court's recommendation.

Although the Supreme Court never explicitly ruled the statute unconstitutional, five of the six Supreme Court Justices, while serving as circuit court judges, found the assignment of these tasks to be unconstitutional. The Justices explained that the duty of making recommendations regarding pensions was "not of a judicial nature." They said that it would violate separation of powers because the judicial actions might be "revised and controuled by the legislature, and by an officer in the executive department. Such revision and controul we deemed radically inconsistent with the independence of that judicial power which is vested in the courts." The principle that unilateral revision of a decision of an Article III court by an officer of the executive branch renders the work of the court impermissibly advisory has endured.

Although these two principles are well established, there are and always have been ex parte proceedings in federal court where a litigant does not name an opponent in seeking relief. These "non-contentious" matters include naturalization proceedings, prize and salvage cases, trademark seizure orders, some elements of bankruptcy proceedings, warrant applications (most prominently in the context of counter-terrorism enforcement, FISA warrants), default judgments, consent decrees, and plea bargains.[5] The Court in *Windsor*, and *a fortiori* Justice Scalia's sharp dissent, "took no notice of the many instances in which the federal judiciary, without first consulting constitutional limitations or prudential considerations, proceeds in the absence of party adverseness," usually, as in the case of many of the examples listed above, with the explicit blessing of Congress.[6] Justice Scalia relied on English practice without observing that English courts regularly took jurisdiction of "non-adverse matters." How might this long history of "non-contentious" adjudication be squared with the prohibition on advisory opinions? Does the problem lie in Article III itself, or in the Court's assumptions about the connection between the degree of adversity in any given case and the judicial power Article III confers? One answer might be that when Congress permits non-contentious adjudication, nothing in the prohibition on advisory opinions should stand in the way as long as the principle against revision of the courts' decisions by another branch is not violated.

B.   STANDING

The doctrine of standing includes both constitutional and prudential limits on federal judicial power. It addresses whether a litigant is a proper party to bring an issue before the court. A litigant without standing is not entitled to have the court decide a dispute. To have standing, a litigant must meet several requirements. Plaintiffs must plead and prove these requirements in order to have standing throughout the litigation.

The Court has held that Article III and the separation of powers impose three constitutional standing requirements. First, the plaintiff must have suffered an injury in fact or face an imminent injury. Second, the plaintiff's injury must be fairly traceable to the defendant's conduct. Third, a favorable federal court decision must be likely to redress the plaintiff's injury.

In addition, plaintiffs must have prudential standing to sue. The prudential standing requirements are not based on the Constitution, but rather on the Supreme Court's ideas of restraint in the exercise of judicial power. Therefore, Congress may enact statutory law directing federal courts to ignore them, as it has done for particular types of cases.

The first prudential requirement is the limitation on third-party standing. Generally, litigants must assert their own rights and cannot litigate the claims of third parties not before the court. In cases from the 1970s and 1980s, the Court announced two other prudential requirements for standing. The "zone of interests" test required a litigant to raise a claim within the zone of interests

---

5. James E. Pfander & Daniel D. Birk, *Article III Judicial Power, the Adverse-Party Requirement, and Non-Contentious Jurisdiction*, 124 YALE L.J. 1346 (2015).

6. *Id.* at 1350.

protected by the law that the litigant seeks to enforce. The Court has recently explained that this test is mischaracterized as a prudential limit on standing rather than as a question about the scope of a cause of action — the proper question is not whether the plaintiff falls within the "zone of interests" but rather whether "a legislatively conferred cause of action encompasses the plaintiff's claim." *Lexmark v. Static Control* (2014). The *Lexmark* Court emphasized more broadly that prudential standing is "in some tension with our recent reaffirmation of the principle that 'a federal court's "obligation" to hear and decide' cases within its jurisdiction 'is virtually unflagging.' " The third prudential requirement is a bar on the litigation of generalized grievances. For example, the Court has held that a plaintiff may not sue as a taxpayer who shares a grievance in common with all other taxpayers. The Court has increasingly emphasized the constitutional dimensions of the prohibition on generalized grievances, holding that Congress is without power to authorize a citizen who has not suffered an injury in fact to sue in order to vindicate a widely shared public interest.

As this sketch of standing law suggests, the doctrine introduces complicated questions into the threshold justiciability analysis. Indeed, both judges and commentators have argued that the doctrine has become unnecessarily complicated and even incoherent insofar as it invites assessment of the merits before the facts are known and imposes requirements completely absent at the Founding and in nineteenth century doctrine. In recent decisions, such as *TransUnion v. Ramirez* (2021), which we will study below, various Justices have tried to reimagine the standing doctrine to make it more coherent. Some scholars, analyzing standing outcomes quantitatively, have concluded that judges manipulate the doctrine to reach outcomes they prefer on ideological and political grounds.[7]

Critics of standing doctrine have also argued that it protects the interests of individuals and groups who are already socially and politically powerful by imposing limits on structural reform litigation. In *Allen v. Wright* (1985), a canonical case in the materials that follow, the Court denied standing to plaintiffs who sought to challenge an Internal Revenue Service (IRS) policy that allegedly undermined efforts to implement the school desegregation mandate of *Brown v. Board of Education.* And in *Lyons v. City of Los Angeles* (1983), also below, the Court's standing decision made it more difficult for a Black plaintiff to obtain injunctive relief against racially discriminatory use of force policies in policing.

Defenders of standing doctrine argue that it serves several important values and is consistent with the federal courts' historically limited role in the federal system. The Court has concluded that Article III and the separation of powers require standing doctrine. The doctrine confines federal courts to the adjudication of "Cases" and "Controversies" properly before them. As the Court put it in *Allen v. Wright,* standing "is built on a single basic idea — the idea of separation of powers." By minimizing judicial review, standing doctrine ensures that federal courts do not encroach upon the authority of the political branches. In some cases, individual Justices have added a separation of powers rationale for standing based upon Article II: Standing, it is said, preserves the President's authority over the

---

7. *See, e.g.,* Richard J. Pierce, Jr., *Is Standing Law or Politics?,* 77 N.C. L. REV. 1741 (1999).

enforcement of federal law. During the New Deal standing doctrine was significantly expanded with a view to insulating new progressive agencies from constitutional challenge in the federal courts.[8]

Standing also arguably improves the quality of adjudication and preserves judicial resources. In theory, the doctrine sorts between litigants that have a personal stake and those who have only an ideological stake in the outcome. Ideological plaintiffs, the Court has suggested, are unlikely to be effective litigants. At the same time, they are likely to flood the courts with claims. By precluding ideological plaintiffs from suing, standing aims to limit federal courts to adjudicating cases where the litigants are likely to litigate the merits issues effectively. Closing the courthouse doors to ideological plaintiffs may also channel their energies into the political process where engagement based on ideology is more appropriate.

Finally, the doctrine may preclude litigants from interfering with the concerns of others who are not before the court. Its constitutional and prudential limits, particularly the limitation on third-party standing, deny standing to the so-called officious intermeddler who aims to vindicate the rights of someone else. As a proper party requirement, standing thus ensures that courts treat individuals fairly and do not issue judicial remedies when the rights-holders do not want judicial protection.

In short, standing presents questions about the meaning of the separation of powers and what the role of the federal courts should be. As you read the cases, consider how the Court approaches these questions and debates the history of the federal courts, the meaning of Article III, and the relationship between federal judicial power and politics. Consider also the relationship between justiciability and the merits in light of the social and political contexts within which the Court has considered standing questions.

1. *Injury*

Injury in fact is the first constitutional standing requirement. To have standing, plaintiffs must first plead and prove that they have sustained an injury in fact or are in imminent danger of suffering an injury in fact. As the Court put it in *Valley Forge Christian College v. Americans United for Separation of Church and State* (1982), this requirement of "some actual or threatened injury" is the "irreducible minimum" of Article III's limit of federal judicial power to the adjudication of "Cases" or "Controversies."

What, precisely, is an "injury in fact"? The term implies a distinction between factual injuries and injuries defined by law. This distinction is consistent with the Court's admonition that standing is not a merits question. Yet, as the cases below

---

8. Daniel E. Ho & Erica L. Ross, *Did Liberal Justices Invent the Standing Doctrine,* 62 STAN. L. REV. 591, 592 (2010) (empirical study finding "compelling evidence" that, at least prior to 1940, "progressive justices disproportionately denied standing to plaintiffs in cases that largely involve challenges to administrative agencies;" noting that standing played a role in the early twentieth century before the New Deal and that after 1940 "the political valence of the standing doctrine reverses").

show, the Court has struggled to draw a clear distinction between factual injuries and legal injuries.

An injury in fact, the Court has explained, must be concrete, particularized, and actual or imminent. An injury is "concrete" if it is "real, and not abstract." *Spokeo, Inc. v. Robins* (2016). To be "particularized," an injury "must affect the plaintiff in a personal and individual way." *Id.* And an injury is "actual" if it has already occurred, or there is a substantial risk of a threatened injury. In the national security context, where separation of powers demands special deference to the executive branch, an even higher threshold must be met: "threatened injury must be *certainly impending* to constitute injury in fact." *Clapper v. Amnesty Int'l* (2013).

The Court has identified different types of injuries that qualify as injuries in fact under these principles. Injuries to interests traditionally protected by the common law—such as property damage, economic harm flowing from a breach of contract, and personal injury from intentional torts or negligent conduct—suffice for standing. Injuries to constitutional rights also may suffice under the Court's precedent, although, as we shall see, standing jurisprudence has limited the enforcement of constitutional rights as well as statutory rights that do not connect to traditionally recognized forms of harm.

In the following case, *Lujan v. Defenders of Wildlife* (1992), the Supreme Court considered a challenge to an administrative agency action that did not threaten a traditional common law interest, but instead new interests protected by a federal statute. The Secretary of the Interior had promulgated a rule limiting the application of the Endangered Species Act's requirement that federal agencies consult with the Secretary concerning actions that might threaten endangered species. In particular, the rule provided that this obligation did not extend to federal agency activities outside the United States or on the high seas. Conservation and environmental organizations sued, claiming that the rule would increase the rate of extinction of endangered and threatened species. The Court held that they had not shown an injury in fact. It accepted that the "desire to use or observe an animal species, even for purely aesthetic purposes, is undeniably a cognizable interest for purpose of standing." Standing, in other words, was not limited to injuries to traditional common law interests.

At the same time, the Court questioned whether Congress may "convert the undifferentiated public interest in executive officers' compliance with the law into an 'individual' right vindicable in the courts," thus leaving in doubt the extent to which Congress may recognize injuries and authorize enforcement of rights to protect against them. In a prior case, *Warth v. Seldin* (1975), the Court had stated that "Congress may create a statutory right or entitlement the alleged deprivation of which can confer standing to sue even where the plaintiff would have suffered no judicially cognizable injury in the absence of statute." For example, in *Trafficante v. Metropolitan Life Ins. Co.* (1972), the Court held that the Civil Rights Act of 1968, which created a right to be free from the harms of racial discrimination in access to housing, supported standing for two White residents of an apartment complex that alleged that the owner's discrimination against Black applicants deprived them of the right to live in an integrated community. As you read *Lujan*, consider the Court's discussion of Congress's authority to recognize and protect rights against this backdrop.

Lujan v. Defenders of Wildlife

504 U.S. 555 (1992)

Justice SCALIA delivered the opinion of the Court with respect to Parts I, II, III-A, and IV, and an opinion with respect to Part III-B, in which THE CHIEF JUSTICE, Justice WHITE, and Justice THOMAS joined.

This case involves a challenge to a rule promulgated by the Secretary of the Interior interpreting §7 of the Endangered Species Act of 1973 (ESA), in such fashion as to render it applicable only to actions within the United States or on the high seas. The preliminary issue, and the only one we reach, is whether respondents here, plaintiffs below, have standing to seek judicial review of the rule.

I

The ESA, 87 Stat. 884, as amended, 16 U.S.C. §1531 *et seq.*, seeks to protect species of animals against threats to their continuing existence caused by man. The ESA instructs the Secretary of the Interior to promulgate by regulation a list of those species which are either endangered or threatened under enumerated criteria, and to define the critical habitat of these species. Section 7(a)(2) of the Act then provides, in pertinent part:

> Each Federal agency shall, in consultation with and with the assistance of the Secretary [of the Interior], insure that any action authorized, funded, or carried out by such agency . . . is not likely to jeopardize the continued existence of any endangered species or threatened species or result in the destruction or adverse modification of habitat of such species which is determined by the Secretary, after consultation as appropriate with affected States, to be critical. 16 U.S.C. §1536(a)(2).

In 1978, the Fish and Wildlife Service (FWS) and the National Marine Fisheries Service (NMFS), on behalf of the Secretary of the Interior and the Secretary of Commerce respectively, promulgated a joint regulation stating that the obligations imposed by §7(a)(2) extend to actions taken in foreign nations. The next year, however, the Interior Department began to reexamine its position. A revised joint regulation, reinterpreting §7(a)(2) to require consultation only for actions taken in the United States or on the high seas, was proposed in 1983, and promulgated in 1986.

Shortly thereafter, respondents, organizations dedicated to wildlife conservation and other environmental causes, filed this action against the Secretary of the Interior, seeking a declaratory judgment that the new regulation is in error as to the geographic scope of §7(a)(2) and an injunction requiring the Secretary to promulgate a new regulation restoring the initial interpretation.

II

While the Constitution of the United States divides all power conferred upon the Federal Government into "legislative Powers," Art. I, §1, "[t]he executive Power," Art. II, §1, and "[t]he judicial Power," Art. III, §1, it does not attempt to define those terms. To be sure, it limits the jurisdiction of federal courts to "Cases" and "Controversies," but an executive inquiry can bear the name "case" (the Hoffa case) and a legislative dispute can bear the name "controversy" (the Smoot-Hawley controversy). Obviously, then, the Constitution's central mechanism of separation of powers depends largely upon common understanding of what activities are appropriate to legislatures, to executives, and to courts. In The Federalist No. 48, Madison expressed the view that "[i]t is not infrequently a question of real nicety in legislative bodies whether the operation of a particular measure will, or will not, extend beyond the legislative sphere," whereas "the executive power [is] restrained within a narrower compass and . . . more simple in its nature," and "the judiciary [is] described by landmarks still less uncertain." One of those landmarks, setting apart the "Cases" and "Controversies" that are of the justiciable sort referred to in Article III — "serv[ing] to identify those disputes which are appropriately resolved through the judicial process," *Whitmore v. Arkansas* (1990) — is the doctrine of standing. Though some of its elements express merely prudential considerations that are part of judicial self-government, the core component of standing is an essential and unchanging part of the case-or-controversy requirement of Article III.

Over the years, our cases have established that the irreducible constitutional minimum of standing contains three elements. First, the plaintiff must have suffered an "injury in fact" — an invasion of a legally protected interest which is (a) concrete and particularized; and (b) "actual or imminent, not 'conjectural' or 'hypothetical,'" *Whitmore* (quoting *Los Angeles v. Lyons* (1983)). Second, there must be a causal connection between the injury and the conduct complained of — the injury has to be "fairly . . . trace[able] to the challenged action of the defendant, and not . . . th[e] result [of] the independent action of some third party not before the court." *Simon v. Eastern Ky. Welfare Rights Org.* (1976). Third, it must be "likely," as opposed to merely "speculative," that the injury will be "redressed by a favorable decision."

The party invoking federal jurisdiction bears the burden of establishing these elements. Since they are not mere pleading requirements but rather an indispensable part of the plaintiff's case, each element must be supported in the same way as any other matter on which the plaintiff bears the burden of proof, *i.e.*, with the manner and degree of evidence required at the successive stages of the litigation. When the suit is one challenging the legality of government action or inaction, the nature and extent of facts that must be averred (at the summary judgment stage) or proved (at the trial stage) in order to establish standing depends considerably upon whether the plaintiff is himself an object of the action (or forgone action) at issue. If he is, there is ordinarily little question that the action or inaction has caused him injury, and that a judgment preventing or requiring the action will redress it. When, however, as in this case, a plaintiff's asserted injury arises from the government's allegedly unlawful regulation (or lack of regulation) of *someone else*, much more is needed. In that circumstance, causation and redressability ordinarily hinge on the response of the regulated (or regulable) third party to the government action or inaction — and perhaps on the response of others as well. The existence of one or more of the essential elements of standing "depends on the unfettered choices made by independent actors not before the courts and whose exercise of broad and legitimate discretion the courts cannot presume either to control or to predict," *ASARCO Inc. v. Kadish* (1989) (opinion of Kennedy, J.); and it becomes the burden of the plaintiff to adduce facts showing that those choices have been or will be made in such manner as to produce causation and permit redressability of injury. Thus, when the plaintiff is not himself the object of the government action or inaction he challenges, standing is not precluded, but it is ordinarily "substantially more difficult" to establish. *Allen v. Wright* (1984).

III

We think the Court of Appeals failed to apply the foregoing principles in denying the Secretary's motion for summary judgment. Respondents had not made the requisite demonstration of (at least) injury and redressability.

A

Respondents' claim to injury is that the lack of consultation with respect to certain funded activities abroad "increas[es] the rate of extinction of endangered and threatened species." Of course, the desire to use or observe an animal species, even for purely esthetic purposes, is undeniably a cognizable interest for purpose of standing. "But the 'injury in fact' test requires more than an injury to a cognizable interest. It requires that the party seeking review be himself among the injured." *Sierra Club v. Morton* (1972). To survive the Secretary's summary judgment motion, respondents had to submit affidavits or other evidence showing, through specific facts, not only that listed species were in fact being threatened by funded activities abroad, but also that one or more of respondents' members would thereby be "directly" affected apart from their "'special interest' in th[e] subject."

With respect to this aspect of the case, the Court of Appeals focused on the affidavits of two Defenders' members — Joyce Kelly and Amy Skilbred. Ms. Kelly stated that she traveled to Egypt in 1986 and "observed the traditional habitat of the endangered nile crocodile there and intend[s] to do so again, and hope[s] to observe the crocodile directly," and that she "will suffer harm in fact as the result of [the] American . . . role . . . in overseeing the rehabilitation of the Aswan High Dam on the Nile . . . and [in] develop[ing] . . . Egypt's . . . Master Water Plan." Ms. Skilbred averred that she traveled to Sri Lanka in 1981 and "observed th[e] habitat" of "endangered species such as the Asian elephant and the leopard" at what is now the site of the Mahaweli project funded by the Agency for International Development (AID), although she "was unable to see any of the endangered species"; "this development project," she continued, "will seriously reduce endangered, threatened, and endemic species habitat including areas that I visited . . . [, which] may severely shorten the future of these species"; that threat, she concluded, harmed her because she "intend[s] to return to Sri Lanka in the future and hope[s] to be more fortunate in spotting at least the endangered elephant and leopard." When Ms. Skilbred was asked at a subsequent deposition if and when she had any plans to return to Sri Lanka, she reiterated that "I intend to go back to Sri Lanka," but confessed that she had no current plans: "I don't know [when]. There is a civil war going on right now. I don't know. Not next year, I will say. In the future."

We shall assume for the sake of argument that these affidavits contain facts showing that certain agency-funded projects threaten listed species — though that is questionable. They plainly contain no facts, however, showing how damage to the species will produce "imminent" injury to Mses. Kelly and Skilbred. That the women "had visited" the areas of the projects before the projects commenced proves nothing. As we have said in a related context, "'Past exposure to illegal conduct does not in itself show a present case or controversy regarding injunctive relief . . . if unaccompanied by any continuing, present adverse effects.'" *Los Angeles v. Lyons* (1983). And the affiants' profession of an "inten[t]" to return to the places they had visited before—where they will presumably, this time, be deprived of the opportunity to observe animals of the endangered species—is simply not enough. Such "some day" intentions—without any description of concrete plans, or indeed even any specification of *when* the some day will be—do not support a finding of the "actual or imminent" injury that our cases require.

Besides relying upon the Kelly and Skilbred affidavits, respondents propose a series of novel standing theories. The first, inelegantly styled "ecosystem nexus," proposes that any person who uses *any part* of a "contiguous ecosystem" adversely affected by a funded activity has standing even if the activity is located a great distance away. This approach, as the Court of Appeals correctly observed, is inconsistent with our opinion in *Lujan v. National Wildlife Federation* (1990), which held that a plaintiff claiming injury from environmental damage must use the area affected by the challenged activity and not an area roughly "in the vicinity" of it.

Respondents' other theories are called, alas, the "animal nexus" approach, whereby anyone who has an interest in studying or seeing the endangered animals anywhere on the globe has standing; and the "vocational nexus" approach, under which anyone with a professional interest in such animals can sue. Under these theories, anyone who goes to see Asian elephants in the Bronx Zoo, and anyone who is a keeper of Asian elephants in the Bronx Zoo, has standing to sue because the Director of the Agency for International Development (AID) did not consult with the Secretary regarding the AID-funded project in Sri Lanka. This is beyond all reason. Standing is not "an ingenious academic exercise in the conceivable," *United States v. SCRAP* (1973), but as we have said requires, at the summary judgment stage, a factual showing of perceptible harm. It is clear that the person who observes or works with a particular animal threatened by a federal decision is facing perceptible harm, since the very subject of his interest will no longer exist. It is even plausible—though it goes to the outermost limit of plausibility—to think that a person who observes or works with animals of a particular species in the very area of the world where that species is threatened by a federal decision is facing such harm, since some animals that might have been the subject of his interest will no longer exist. It goes beyond the limit, however, and into pure speculation and fantasy, to say that anyone who observes or works with an endangered species, anywhere in the world, is appreciably harmed by a single project affecting some portion of that species with which he has no more specific connection.

B

Besides failing to show injury, respondents failed to demonstrate redressability. Instead of attacking the separate decisions to fund particular projects allegedly causing them harm, respondents chose to challenge a more generalized level of Government action (rules regarding consultation), the invalidation of which would affect all overseas projects. This programmatic approach has obvious practical advantages, but also obvious difficulties insofar as proof of causation or redressability is concerned.

IV

The Court of Appeals found that respondents had standing for an additional reason: because they had suffered a "procedural injury." The so-called "citizen-suit" provision of the ESA provides, in pertinent part, that "any person may commence a civil suit on his own behalf (A) to enjoin any person, including the United States and any other governmental instrumentality or agency . . . who is alleged to be in violation of any provision of this chapter." The court held that, because §7(a)(2) requires interagency consultation, the citizen-suit provision creates a "procedural righ[t]" to consultation in all "persons" — so that *anyone* can file suit in federal court to challenge the Secretary's (or presumably any other official's) failure to follow the assertedly correct consultative procedure, notwithstanding his or her inability to allege any discrete injury flowing from that failure. To understand the remarkable nature of this holding one must be clear about what it does *not* rest upon: This is not a case where plaintiffs are seeking to enforce a procedural requirement the disregard of which could impair a separate concrete interest of theirs (e.g., the procedural requirement for a hearing prior to denial of their license application, or the procedural requirement for an environmental impact statement before a federal facility is constructed next door to them). Nor is it simply a case where concrete injury has been suffered by many persons, as in mass fraud or mass tort situations. Nor, finally, is it the unusual case in which Congress has created a concrete private interest in the outcome of a suit against a private party for the Government's benefit, by providing a cash bounty for the victorious plaintiff. Rather, the court held that the injury-in-fact requirement had been satisfied by congressional conferral upon *all* persons of an abstract, self contained, noninstrumental "right" to have the Executive observe the procedures required by law. We reject this view.

We have consistently held that a plaintiff raising only a generally available grievance about government — claiming only harm to his and every citizen's interest in proper application of the Constitution and laws, and seeking relief that no more directly and tangibly benefits him than it does the public at large — does not state an Article III case or controversy.

To be sure, our generalized-grievance cases have typically involved Government violation of procedures assertedly ordained by the Constitution rather than the Congress. But there is absolutely no basis for making the Article III inquiry turn on the source of the asserted right. Whether the courts were to act on their own, or at the invitation of Congress, in ignoring the concrete injury requirement described in our cases, they would be discarding a principle fundamental to the separate and distinct constitutional role of the Third Branch — one of the essential elements that identifies those "Cases" and "Controversies" that are the business of the courts rather than of the political branches. "The province of the court," as Chief Justice Marshall said in *Marbury v. Madison* (1803), "is, solely, to decide on the rights of individuals." Vindicating the *public* interest (including the public interest in Government observance of the Constitution and laws) is the function of Congress and the Chief Executive. The question presented here is whether the public interest in proper administration of the laws (specifically, in agencies' observance of a particular, statutorily prescribed procedure) can be converted into an individual right by a statute that denominates it as such, and that permits all citizens (or, for that matter, a subclass of citizens who suffer no distinctive concrete harm) to sue. If the concrete injury requirement has the separation-of-powers significance we have always said, the answer must be obvious: To permit Congress to convert the undifferentiated public interest in executive officers' compliance with the law into an "individual right" vindicable in the courts is to permit Congress to transfer from the President to the courts the Chief Executive's most important constitutional duty, to "take Care that the Laws be faithfully executed," Art. II, §3.

Nothing in this contradicts the principle that "[t]he . . . injury required by Art. III may exist solely by virtue of 'statutes creating legal rights, the invasion of which creates standing.'" *Warth v. Seldin* (1975) (quoting *Linda R.S. v. Richard D.* (1973)). Both of the cases used by *Linda R.S.* as an illustration of that principle involved Congress' elevating to the status of legally cognizable injuries concrete, *de facto* injuries that were previously inadequate in law (namely, injury to an individual's personal interest in living in a racially integrated community, and injury to a company's interest in marketing its product free from competition). As we said in *Sierra Club*, "[Statutory] broadening [of] the categories of injury that may be alleged in support of standing is a different matter from abandoning the requirement that the party seeking review must himself have suffered an injury."

We hold that respondents lack standing to bring this action and that the Court of Appeals erred in denying the summary judgment motion filed by the United States. The opinion of the Court of Appeals is hereby reversed, and the cause is remanded for proceedings consistent with this opinion.

Justice KENNEDY, with whom Justice SOUTER joins, concurring in part and concurring in the judgment

Although I agree with the essential parts of the Court's analysis, I write separately to make several observations.

I agree with the Court's conclusion in Part III-A that, on the record before us, respondents have failed to demonstrate that they themselves are "among the injured." *Sierra Club v. Morton* (1972). While it may seem trivial to require that Mses. Kelly and Skilbred acquire airline tickets to the project sites or announce a date certain upon which they will return, this is not a case where it is reasonable to assume that the affiants will be using the sites on a regular basis, nor do the affiants claim to have visited the sites since the projects commenced.

In light of the conclusion that respondents have not demonstrated a concrete injury here sufficient to support standing under our precedents, I would not reach the issue of redressability that is discussed by the plurality in Part III-B.

I also join Part IV of the Court's opinion with the following observations. As Government programs and policies become more complex and far reaching, we must be sensitive to the articulation of new rights of action that do not have clear analogs in our common-law tradition. Modern litigation has progressed far from the paradigm of Marbury suing Madison to get his commission, *Marbury v. Madison* (1803), or Ogden seeking an injunction to halt Gibbons' steamboat operations, *Gibbons v. Ogden* (1824). In my view, Congress has the power to define injuries and articulate chains of causation that will give rise to a case or controversy where none existed before, and I do not read the Court's opinion to suggest a contrary view. In exercising this power, however, Congress must at the very least identify the injury it seeks to vindicate and relate the injury to the class of persons entitled to bring suit. The citizen-suit provision of the Endangered Species Act does not meet these minimal requirements, because while the statute purports to confer a right on "any person . . . to enjoin . . . the United States and any other governmental instrumentality or agency . . . who is alleged to be in violation of any provision of this chapter," it does not of its own force establish that there is an injury in "any person" by virtue of any "violation."

The Court's holding that there is an outer limit to the power of Congress to confer rights of action is a direct and necessary consequence of the case and controversy limitations found in Article III. I agree that it would exceed those limitations if, at the behest of Congress and in the absence of any showing of concrete injury, we were to entertain citizen suits to vindicate the public's nonconcrete interest in the proper administration of the laws. While it does not matter how many persons have been injured by the challenged action, the party bringing suit must show that the action injures him in a concrete and personal way. This requirement is not just an empty formality. It preserves the vitality of the adversarial process by assuring both that the parties before the court have an actual, as opposed to professed, stake in the outcome, and that "the legal questions presented . . . will be resolved, not in the rarified atmosphere of a debating society, but in a concrete factual context conducive to a realistic appreciation of the consequences of judicial action." *Valley Forge Christian College v. Americans United for Separation of Church and State, Inc.* (1982).

Justice STEVENS' concurrence in the judgment is omitted.

Justice BLACKMUN, with whom Justice O'CONNOR joins, dissenting.

I part company with the Court in this case in two respects. First, I believe that respondents have raised genuine issues of fact sufficient to survive summary judgment—both as to injury and as to redressability. Second, I question the Court's breadth of language in rejecting standing for "procedural" injuries. I fear the Court seeks to impose fresh limitations on the constitutional authority of Congress to allow citizen suits in the federal courts for injuries deemed "procedural" in nature.

I

I think a reasonable finder of fact could conclude from the information in the affidavits and deposition testimony that either Kelly or Skilbred will soon return to the project sites, thereby satisfying the "actual or imminent" injury standard. A reasonable finder of fact could conclude, based not only upon their statements of intent to return, but upon their past visits to the project sites, as well as their professional backgrounds, that it was likely that Kelly and Skilbred would make a return trip to the project areas. . . . Many environmental injuries, however, cause harm distant from the area immediately affected by the challenged action. Environmental destruction may affect animals traveling over vast geographical ranges, or rivers running long geographical courses. It cannot seriously be contended that a litigant's failure to use the precise or exact site where animals are slaughtered or where toxic waste is dumped into a river means he or she cannot show injury. . . .

I have difficulty imagining this Court applying its rigid principles of geographic formalism anywhere outside the context of environmental claims.

II

Most governmental conduct can be classified as "procedural." Many injuries caused by governmental conduct, therefore, are categorizable at some level of generality as "procedural" injuries. Yet, these injuries are not categorically beyond the pale of redress by the federal courts.

The Court expresses concern that allowing judicial enforcement of "agencies' observance of a particular, statutorily prescribed procedure" would "transfer from the President to the courts the Chief Executive's most important constitutional duty, to 'take Care that the Laws be faithfully executed,' Art. II, §3." In fact, the principal effect of foreclosing judicial enforcement of such procedures is to transfer power into the hands of the Executive at the expense—not of the courts—but of Congress, from which that power originates and emanates.

In short, determining "injury" for Article III standing purposes is a fact-specific inquiry. There may be factual circumstances in which a congressionally imposed procedural requirement is so insubstantially connected to the prevention of a substantive harm that it cannot be said to work any conceivable injury to an individual litigant. But, as a general matter, the courts owe substantial deference to Congress' substantive purpose in imposing a certain procedural requirement.

III

In conclusion, I cannot join the Court on what amounts to a slash-and-burn expedition through the law of environmental standing. In my view, "[t]he very essence of civil liberty certainly consists in the right of every individual to claim the protection of the laws, whenever he receives an injury." *Marbury v. Madison* (1803).

* * *

As *Lujan* suggests, the rise of the modern administrative state has shaped federal courts law, including the debate about Article III standing doctrine's injury-in-fact requirement. In *Data Processing Serv. Orgs. v. Camp* (1970), data processing service businesses sued the Comptroller of the Currency, a federal agency official, seeking to challenge an administrative ruling that would have harmed their competitive position in the market. The Court held that the businesses had standing to sue. It began by stating, "[g]eneralizations about standing to sue are largely worthless as such." Then, it fatefully went on, "[t]he first question is whether the plaintiff alleges that the challenged action has caused him injury in fact, economic or otherwise." The businesses had adequately alleged an injury to their economic interests and therefore had standing.

The standing question, the *Data Processing* Court continued, "is different" from the "'legal interest' test," which "goes to the merits." To have standing, the Court reasoned, a plaintiff does not need to show that the defendant injured a legal right of the plaintiff. In drawing this distinction between injuries in fact and injuries in law, the Court apparently intended to expand the availability of judicial review of administrative action. It said, "[w]here statutes are concerned, the trend is toward enlargement of the class of people who may protest administrative action." The Administrative Procedure Act, a statute enacted in 1946 following the New Deal's expansion of the administrative state, authorizes a "person 'aggrieved by agency action'" to sue the agency. In *Data Processing*, the Court concluded that so long as plaintiffs have an injury in fact and show that their interests are "arguably within the zone of interests to be protected or regulated by the statute or constitutional guarantee in question," they have standing to sue an agency.

By the 1990s, however, a pattern began to emerge in which the Court became increasingly skeptical of suits by plaintiffs seeking to enforce statutes that *benefitted* but did not *regulate* them. Such regulatory beneficiary suits were common in environmental law and consumer protection law. In *Data Processing*, a regulatory beneficiary who was also a marketplace competitor sought to challenge an agency action that would have harmed their economic interests. While the federal courts had long allowed such suits, *see* FCC v. Sanders Brothers Radio (1940) ("one likely to be financially injured by the issue of a license would be the only person having a sufficient interest to [raise] errors of law in the action of the Commission. . . . It is within the power of Congress to confer such standing"), they began to question the standing of regulatory beneficiaries who were not market competitors, such as the conservation and environmental organizations that were plaintiffs in *Lujan*.

Following *Lujan*, narrow liberal majorities of the Court held in two cases that Congress still had authority to recognize injuries and create statutory rights that are the basis for Article III standing:

Federal Election Comm'n v. Akins (1998): Like *Data Processing* and *Lujan*, this case was a challenge to federal agency action. Voters sued to challenge a decision of the Federal Election Commission (FEC) that the American Israel Public Affairs Committee was not a "political committee" that had to comply with the reporting requirements of the Federal Election Campaign Act of 1971. They claimed a statutory right to information about political committees and argued that Congress had authorized them to enforce this right with a citizen-suit provision that permitted suit by any person "aggrieved" by a decision of the FEC. The Court held that the plaintiffs had standing to sue because "the informational injury at issue . . . directly related to voting, is sufficiently concrete and specific such that the fact that it is widely shared does not deprive Congress of constitutional power to authorize its vindication in the federal courts." Drawing an analogy to mass torts, the Court emphsized that harm can be both widely shared and concrete for purposes of standing.

Friends of the Earth, Inc. v. Laidlaw Env't Servs., Inc. (2000): This case also involved a citizen suit by beneficiaries of federal regulation. Several environmental organizations sued the owner of a hazardous waste incinerator and wastewater treatment plant under the citizen-suit provision of the Clean Water Act (CWA). They argued that the plant was discharging mercury at levels into a river that violated its permit under the CWA. The Court held that the plaintiffs had standing to sue because Congress had authorized citizens to sue and because they alleged that the discharges had "directly affected" their ability to use the river and the area around it for recreational purposes. Avoiding the river was a reasonable response to the probability of harm, in the Court's view, given the "undisputed" allegations of "continuous and pervasive illegal discharges of pollutants" at the time of the filing of the complaint.

The Court's opinions in *Akins* and *Laidlaw* thus held that violations of rights created by statute were sufficient for standing purposes. In a series of subsequent cases, the Court retreated from these holdings.

In *Spokeo v. Robins* (2016), the Court dealt with private enforcement of the Fair Credit Reporting Act of 1970 (FCRA). The plaintiff alleged that the defendant, a consumer reporting agency marketing a website to prospective employers and "prospective romantic partners" seeking personal information about someone, had posted incorrect information about his marital status, whether he had children, his age, his employment history, his wealth, and his level of education. The Ninth Circuit held that the plaintiff had established standing at the motion to dismiss stage by alleging that the defendant had violated "*his* statutory rights" and harmed his "personal interests in the handling of his credit information." These allegations established that the injury was particularized. The Supreme Court reversed and remanded because it concluded that the court of appeals had conflated the particularization component of the injury-in-fact requirement with the concreteness component. These are distinct components, the Court held, and an injury may be particularized without being concrete. An injury is "particularized" if it "affect[s] the plaintiff in a personal and individual way." An injury is concrete if it "real, and not abstract." The Court explained that Congress may identify particularized injuries that nevertheless are not concrete and therefore cannot establish standing: "Congress' role in identifying and elevating intangible harms does not mean that a plaintiff automatically satisfies the injury-in-fact requirement whenever a statute grants a person a statutory right and purports to authorize that person to sue to vindicate that right." On remand, the Court instructed, attention should focus on whether the "procedural violations" of the FCRA alleged "entail a degree of risk sufficient to meet the concreteness requirement."

In *TransUnion LLC v. Ramirez* (2021), which is below, the Court further refined the injury-in-fact requirement, holding that an injury must have "a close historical or common-law analogue" to be an injury in fact. Injuries to statutory rights that have no historical or common law analogue are not, under *TransUnion*, injuries in fact. Violation of these statutory rights can be enforced by federal agencies, but not by citizen suits.

The potential consequences of this aspect of the holding in *TransUnion* opinion are significant because in many areas of federal law Congress has authorized private individuals to sue to deal with problems that do not always fit comfortably into traditional common law forms of action. There are not only consumer protection laws such as the statute at issue in *TransUnion*, which authorizes litigation to prevent tangible economic harm to consumers before it occurs, but also civil rights laws, environmental laws, and laws prohibiting child labor. In these and other areas, citizen suits play a major role in the enforcement of modern federal law.

As you read *TransUnion*, consider what the implications of its holding are for other enforcement systems that rely on citizen suits. Consider as well whether Justice Kavanaugh or Justice Thomas has the better argument about the separation of powers.

TransUnion, LLC v. Ramirez

141 S. Ct. 2190 (2021)

Justice KAVANAUGH delivered the opinion of the Court.

To have Article III standing to sue in federal court, plaintiffs must demonstrate, among other things, that they suffered a concrete harm. No concrete harm, no standing. Central to assessing concreteness is whether the asserted harm has a "close relationship" to a harm traditionally recognized as providing a basis for a lawsuit in American courts — such as physical harm, monetary harm, or various intangible harms including (as relevant here) reputational harm.

In this case, a class of 8,185 individuals sued TransUnion, a credit reporting agency, in federal court under the Fair Credit Reporting Act. The plaintiffs claimed that TransUnion failed to use reasonable procedures to ensure the accuracy of their credit files, as maintained internally by TransUnion. For 1,853 of the class members, TransUnion provided misleading credit reports to third-party businesses. We conclude that those 1,853 class members have demonstrated concrete reputational harm and thus have Article III standing to sue on the reasonable-procedures claim. The internal credit files of the other 6,332 class members were *not* provided to third-party businesses during the relevant time period. We conclude that those 6,332 class members have not demonstrated concrete harm and thus lack Article III standing to sue on the reasonable-procedures claim.

In two other claims, all 8,185 class members complained about formatting defects in certain mailings sent to them by TransUnion. But the class members other than the named plaintiff Sergio Ramirez have not demonstrated that the alleged formatting errors caused them any concrete harm. Therefore, except for Ramirez, the class members do not have standing as to those two claims.

I

In 1970, Congress passed and President Nixon signed the Fair Credit Reporting Act. The Act seeks to promote "fair and accurate credit reporting" and to protect consumer privacy. To achieve those goals, the Act regulates the consumer reporting agencies that compile and disseminate personal information about consumers.

Three of the Act's requirements are relevant to this case. First, the Act requires consumer reporting agencies to "follow reasonable procedures to assure maximum possible accuracy" in consumer reports. Second, the Act provides that consumer reporting agencies must, upon request, disclose to the consumer "[a]ll information in the consumer's file at the time of the request." Third, the Act compels consumer reporting agencies to "provide to a consumer, with each written disclosure by the agency to the consumer," a "summary of rights" prepared by the Consumer Financial Protection Bureau.

The Act creates a cause of action for consumers to sue and recover damages for certain violations. The Act provides: "Any person who willfully fails to comply with any requirement imposed under this subchapter with respect to any consumer is liable to that consumer" for actual damages or for statutory damages not less than $100 and not more than $1,000, as well as for punitive damages and attorney's fees.

TransUnion is one of the "Big Three" credit reporting agencies, along with Equifax and Experian. As a credit reporting agency, TransUnion compiles personal and financial information about individual consumers to create consumer reports. TransUnion then sells those consumer reports for use by entities such as banks, landlords, and car dealerships that request information about the creditworthiness of individual consumers.

Beginning in 2002, TransUnion introduced an add-on product called OFAC Name Screen Alert. OFAC is the U.S. Treasury Department's Office of Foreign Assets Control. OFAC maintains a list of "specially designated nationals" who threaten America's national security. Individuals on the OFAC list are terrorists, drug traffickers, or other serious criminals. It is generally unlawful to transact business with any person on the list. TransUnion created the OFAC Name Screen Alert to help businesses avoid transacting with individuals on OFAC's list.

When this litigation arose[,] TransUnion would conduct its ordinary credit check of the consumer, and it would also use third-party software to compare the consumer's name against the OFAC list. If the consumer's first and last name matched the first and last name of an individual on OFAC's list, then TransUnion would place an alert on the credit report indicating that the consumer's name was a "potential match" to a name on the OFAC list. TransUnion did not compare any data other than first and last names. Unsurprisingly, TransUnion's Name Screen product generated many false positives. Thousands of law-abiding Americans happen to share a first and last name with one of the terrorists, drug traffickers, or serious criminals on OFAC's list of specially designated nationals.

Sergio Ramirez learned the hard way that he is one such individual. On February 27, 2011, Ramirez visited a Nissan dealership in Dublin, California, seeking to buy a Nissan Maxima. Ramirez was accompanied by his wife and his father-in-law. After Ramirez and his wife selected a color and negotiated a price, the dealership ran a credit check on both Ramirez and his wife. Ramirez's credit report, produced by TransUnion, contained the following alert: "***OFAC ADVISOR ALERT — INPUT NAME MATCHES NAME ON THE OFAC DATABASE." A Nissan salesman told Ramirez that Nissan would not sell the car to him because his name was on a "'terrorist list.'" Ramirez's wife had to purchase the car in her own name.

The next day, Ramirez called TransUnion and requested a copy of his credit file. TransUnion sent Ramirez a mailing that same day that included his credit file and the statutorily required summary of rights prepared by the CFPB. The mailing did not mention the OFAC alert in Ramirez's file. The following day, TransUnion sent Ramirez a second mailing — a letter alerting him that his name was considered a potential match to names on the OFAC list. The second mailing did not include an additional copy of the summary of rights. Concerned about the mailings, Ramirez consulted a lawyer and ultimately canceled a planned trip to Mexico. TransUnion eventually removed the OFAC alert from Ramirez's file.

In February 2012, Ramirez sued TransUnion and alleged three violations of the Fair Credit Reporting Act. First, he alleged that TransUnion, by using the Name Screen product, failed to follow reasonable procedures to ensure the accuracy of information in his credit file. Second, he claimed that TransUnion failed to provide him with all the information in his credit file upon his request. In particular, TransUnion's first mailing did not include the fact that Ramirez's name was a potential match for a name on the OFAC list. Third, Ramirez asserted that TransUnion violated its obligation to provide him with a summary of his rights "with each written disclosure," because TransUnion's second mailing did not contain a summary of Ramirez's rights. Ramirez requested statutory and punitive damages [and] also sought to certify a class of all people in the United States to whom TransUnion sent a mailing during the period from January 1, 2011, to July 26, 2011, that was similar in form to the second mailing that Ramirez received. TransUnion opposed certification. The U.S. District Court for the Northern District of California rejected TransUnion's argument and certified the class.

Before trial, the parties stipulated that the class contained 8,185 members, including Ramirez. The parties also stipulated that only 1,853 members of the class (including Ramirez) had their credit reports disseminated by TransUnion to potential creditors during the period from January 1, 2011, to July 26, 2011. The District Court ruled that all 8,185 class members had Article III standing.

After six days of trial, the jury returned a verdict for the plaintiffs. The jury awarded each class member $984.22 in statutory damages and $6,353.08 in punitive damages for a total award of more than $60 million.

II

Article III confines the federal judicial power to the resolution of "Cases" and "Controversies." For there to be a case or controversy under Article III, the plaintiff must have a "'personal stake'" in the case — in other words, standing. Raines v. Byrd (1997). To demonstrate their personal stake, plaintiffs must be able to sufficiently answer the question: "'What's it to you?'" Scalia, The Doctrine of Standing as an Essential Element of the Separation of Powers, 17 Suffolk U.L. Rev. 881, 882 (1983).

To answer that question in a way sufficient to establish standing, a plaintiff must show (i) that he suffered an injury in fact that is concrete, particularized, and actual or imminent; (ii) that the injury was likely caused by the defendant; and (iii) that the injury would likely be redressed by judicial relief.

The question in this case focuses on the Article III requirement that the plaintiff's injury in fact be "concrete" — that is, "real, and not abstract." *Spokeo, Inc. v. Robins* (2016). What makes a harm concrete for purposes of Article III? As a general matter, the Court has explained that "history and tradition offer a meaningful guide to the types of cases that Article III empowers federal courts to consider." *Sprint Communications Co. v. APCC Services, Inc.* (2008).

And with respect to the concrete-harm requirement in particular, this Court's opinion in *Spokeo* indicated that courts should assess whether the alleged injury to the plaintiff has a "close relationship" to a harm "traditionally" recognized as providing a basis for a lawsuit in American courts. That inquiry asks whether plaintiffs have identified a close historical or common-law analogue for their asserted injury. *Spokeo* does not require an exact duplicate in American history and tradition. But *Spokeo* is not an open-ended invitation for federal courts to loosen Article III based on contemporary, evolving beliefs about what kinds of suits should be heard in federal courts.

As *Spokeo* explained, certain harms readily qualify as concrete injuries under Article III. The most obvious are traditional tangible harms, such as physical harms and monetary harms. If a defendant has caused physical or monetary injury to the plaintiff, the plaintiff has suffered a concrete injury in fact under Article III.

Various intangible harms can also be concrete. Chief among them are injuries with a close relationship to harms traditionally recognized as providing a basis for lawsuits in American courts. Those include, for example, reputational harms, disclosure of private information, and intrusion upon seclusion. And those traditional harms may also include harms specified by the Constitution itself.

In determining whether a harm is sufficiently concrete to qualify as an injury in fact, the Court in *Spokeo* said that Congress's views may be "instructive." Courts must afford due respect to Congress's decision to impose a statutory prohibition or obligation on a defendant, and to grant a plaintiff a cause of action to sue over the defendant's violation of that statutory prohibition or obligation. In that way, Congress may "elevate to the status of legally cognizable injuries concrete, *de facto* injuries that were previously inadequate in law."

Importantly, this Court has rejected the proposition that "a plaintiff automatically satisfies the injury-in-fact requirement whenever a statute grants a person a statutory right and purports to authorize that person to sue to vindicate that right." As the Court emphasized in *Spokeo*, "Article III standing requires a concrete injury even in the context of a statutory violation."

Congress's creation of a statutory prohibition or obligation and a cause of action does not relieve courts of their responsibility to independently decide whether a plaintiff has suffered a concrete harm under Article III any more than, for example, Congress's enactment of a law regulating speech relieves courts of their responsibility to independently decide whether the law violates the First Amendment.

For standing purposes, therefore, an important difference exists between (i) a plaintiff's statutory cause of action to sue a defendant over the defendant's violation of federal law, and (ii) a plaintiff's suffering concrete harm because of the defendant's violation of federal law. Congress may enact legal prohibitions and obligations. And Congress may create causes of action for plaintiffs to sue defendants who violate those legal prohibitions or obligations. But under Article III, an injury in law is not an injury in fact. Only those plaintiffs who have been *concretely harmed* by a defendant's statutory violation may sue that private defendant over that violation in federal court.

To appreciate how the Article III "concrete harm" principle operates in practice, consider two different hypothetical plaintiffs. Suppose first that a Maine citizen's land is polluted by a nearby factory. She sues the company, alleging that it violated a federal environmental law and damaged her property. Suppose also that a second plaintiff in Hawaii files a federal lawsuit alleging that the same company in Maine violated that same environmental law by polluting land in Maine. The violation did not personally harm the plaintiff in Hawaii.

Even if Congress affords both hypothetical plaintiffs a cause of action (with statutory damages available) to sue over the defendant's legal violation, Article III standing doctrine sharply distinguishes between those two scenarios. The first lawsuit may of course proceed in federal court because the plaintiff has suffered concrete harm to her property. But the second lawsuit may not proceed because that plaintiff has not suffered any physical, monetary, or cognizable intangible harm traditionally recognized as providing a basis for a lawsuit in American courts. An uninjured plaintiff who sues in those circumstances is, by definition, not seeking to remedy any harm to herself but instead is merely seeking to ensure a defendant's "compliance with regulatory law" (and, of course, to obtain some money via the statutory damages). *Spokeo* (Thomas, J., concurring). Those are not grounds for Article III standing.[1]

A regime where Congress could freely authorize *unharmed* plaintiffs to sue defendants who violate federal law not only would violate Article III but also would infringe on the Executive Branch's Article II authority. We accept the "displacement of the democratically elected branches when necessary to decide an actual case." [Roberts, *Article III Limits on Statutory Standing*, 42 Duke L.J. 1219, 1230 (1993).] But otherwise, the choice of how to prioritize and how aggressively to pursue legal actions against defendants who violate the law falls within the discretion of the Executive Branch, not within the purview of private plaintiffs (and their attorneys). Private plaintiffs are not accountable to the people and are not charged with pursuing the public interest in enforcing a defendant's general compliance with regulatory law.

In sum, the concrete-harm requirement is essential to the Constitution's separation of powers. To be sure, the concrete-harm requirement can be difficult to apply in some cases. Some advocate that the concrete-harm requirement be ditched altogether, on the theory that it would be more efficient or convenient to simply say that a statutory violation and a cause of action suffice to afford a plaintiff standing. But as the Court has often stated, "the fact that a given law or procedure is efficient, convenient, and useful in facilitating functions of government, standing alone, will not save it if it is contrary to the Constitution." *INS v. Chadha* (1983). So it is here.

III

We now apply those fundamental standing principles to this lawsuit. We must determine whether the 8,185 class members have standing to sue TransUnion for its alleged violations of the Fair Credit Reporting Act. The plaintiffs argue that TransUnion failed to comply with statutory obligations (i) to follow reasonable procedures to ensure the accuracy of credit files so that the files would not include OFAC alerts labeling the plaintiffs as potential terrorists; and (ii) to provide a consumer, upon request, with his or her complete credit file, including a summary of rights.

Some preliminaries: As the party invoking federal jurisdiction, the plaintiffs bear the burden of demonstrating that they have standing. Every class member must have Article III standing in order to recover individual damages. Plaintiffs must maintain their personal interest in the dispute at all stages of litigation.

---

1. The lead dissent notes that the terminology of injury in fact became prevalent only in the latter half of the 20th century. That is unsurprising because until the 20th century, Congress did not often afford federal "citizen suit"-style causes of action to private plaintiffs who did not suffer concrete harms. *See* Magill, *Standing for the Public*, 95 Va. L. Rev. 1131 (2009). All told, until the 20th century, this Court had little reason to emphasize the injury-in-fact requirement because, until the 20th century, there were relatively few instances where litigants without concrete injuries had a cause of action to sue in federal court.

A

We first address the plaintiffs' claim that TransUnion failed to "follow reasonable procedures to assure maximum possible accuracy" of the plaintiffs' credit files maintained by TransUnion. In particular, the plaintiffs argue that TransUnion did not do enough to ensure that OFAC alerts labeling them as potential terrorists were not included in their credit files.

Assuming that the plaintiffs are correct that TransUnion violated its obligations under the Fair Credit Reporting Act to use reasonable procedures in internally maintaining the credit files, we must determine whether the 8,185 class members suffered concrete harm from TransUnion's failure to employ reasonable procedures.

1

Start with the 1,853 class members (including the named plaintiff Ramirez) whose reports were disseminated to third-party businesses. The plaintiffs argue that the publication to a third party of a credit report bearing a misleading OFAC alert injures the subject of the report. The plaintiffs contend that this injury bears a "close relationship" to a harm traditionally recognized as providing a basis for a lawsuit in American courts—namely, the reputational harm associated with the tort of defamation.

We agree with the plaintiffs. Under longstanding American law, a person is injured when a defamatory statement "that would subject him to hatred, contempt, or ridicule" is published to a third party. *Milkovich v. Lorain Journal Co.* (1990). TransUnion provided third parties with credit reports containing OFAC alerts that labeled the class members as potential terrorists, drug traffickers, or serious criminals. The 1,853 class members therefore suffered a harm with a "close relationship" to the harm associated with the tort of defamation. We have no trouble concluding that the 1,853 class members suffered a concrete harm that qualifies as an injury in fact.

TransUnion counters that those 1,853 class members did not suffer a harm with a "close relationship" to defamation because the OFAC alerts on the disseminated credit reports were only misleading and not literally false. TransUnion points out that the reports merely identified a consumer as a "potential match" to an individual on the OFAC list—a fact that TransUnion says is not technically false.

In looking to whether a plaintiff's asserted harm has a "close relationship" to a harm traditionally recognized as providing a basis for a lawsuit in American courts, we do not require an exact duplicate. The harm from being labeled a "potential terrorist" bears a close relationship to the harm from being labeled a "terrorist." In other words, the harm from a misleading statement of this kind bears a sufficiently close relationship to the harm from a false and defamatory statement.

In short, the 1,853 class members whose reports were disseminated to third parties suffered a concrete injury in fact under Article III.

2

The remaining 6,332 class members are a different story. To be sure, their credit files, which were maintained by TransUnion, contained misleading OFAC alerts. But the parties stipulated that TransUnion did not provide those plaintiffs' credit information to any potential creditors during the class period from January 2011 to July 2011. Given the absence of dissemination, we must determine whether the 6,332 class members suffered some other concrete harm for purposes of Article III.

The initial question is whether the mere existence of a misleading OFAC alert in a consumer's internal credit file at TransUnion constitutes a concrete injury. As Judge Tatel phrased it in a similar context, "if inaccurate information falls into" a consumer's credit file, "does it make a sound?" *Owner-Operator Ind. Drivers Ass'n v. U.S. Dep't of Transp.* (CADC 2018).

Writing the opinion for the D.C. Circuit in *Owner-Operator*, Judge Tatel answered no. Publication is "essential to liability" in a suit for defamation. Restatement of Torts §577, Comment *a*, at 192. And there is "no historical or common-law analog where the mere existence of inaccurate information, absent dissemination, amounts to concrete injury." *Owner-Operator.*

The standing inquiry in this case thus distinguishes between (i) credit files that consumer reporting agencies maintain internally and (ii) the consumer credit reports that consumer reporting agencies disseminate to third-party creditors. The mere presence of an inaccuracy in an internal credit file, if it is not disclosed to a third party, causes no concrete harm. In cases such as these where allegedly inaccurate or misleading information sits in a company database, the plaintiffs' harm is roughly the same, legally speaking, as if someone wrote a defamatory letter and then stored it in her desk drawer. A letter that is not sent does not harm anyone, no matter how insulting the letter is. So too here.

TransUnion advances a persuasive argument that in a suit for damages, the mere risk of future harm, standing alone, cannot qualify as a concrete harm—at least unless the exposure to the risk of future harm itself causes a separate concrete harm. TransUnion contends that if an individual is exposed to a risk of future harm, time will eventually reveal whether the risk materializes in the form of actual harm. If the risk of future harm materializes and the individual suffers a concrete harm, then the harm itself, and not the pre-existing risk, will constitute a basis for the person's injury and for damages. If the risk of future harm does not materialize, then the individual cannot establish a concrete harm sufficient for standing, according to TransUnion.

Consider an example. Suppose that a woman drives home from work a quarter mile ahead of a reckless driver who is dangerously swerving across lanes. The reckless driver has exposed the woman to a risk of future harm, but the risk does not materialize and the woman makes it home safely. As counsel for TransUnion stated, that would ordinarily be cause for celebration, not a lawsuit. But if the reckless driver crashes into the woman's car, the situation would be different, and (assuming a cause of action) the woman could sue the driver for damages.

Here, the 6,332 plaintiffs did not demonstrate that the risk of future harm materialized—that is, that the inaccurate OFAC alerts in their internal TransUnion credit files were ever provided to third parties or caused a denial of credit. Nor did those plaintiffs present evidence that the class members were independently harmed by their exposure to the risk itself—that is, that they suffered some other injury (such as an emotional injury) from the mere risk that their credit reports would be provided to third-party businesses. Therefore, the 6,332 plaintiffs' argument for standing for their damages claims based on an asserted risk of future harm is unavailing.

Moreover, the plaintiffs did not present any evidence that the 6,332 class members even knew that there were OFAC alerts in their internal TransUnion credit files. If those plaintiffs prevailed in this case, many of them would first learn that they were "injured" when they received a check compensating them for their supposed "injury." It is difficult to see how a risk of future harm could supply the basis for a plaintiff's standing when the plaintiff did not even know that there was a risk of future harm.

B

We next address the plaintiffs' standing to recover damages for two other claims in the complaint: the disclosure claim and the summary-of-rights claim. Those two claims are intertwined.

In the disclosure claim, the plaintiffs alleged that TransUnion breached its obligation to provide them with their complete credit files upon request. According to the plaintiffs, TransUnion sent the plaintiffs copies of their credit files that omitted the OFAC information, and then in a second mailing sent the OFAC information. In the summary-of-rights claim, the plaintiffs further asserted that TransUnion should have included another summary of rights in that second mailing — the mailing that included the OFAC information. As the plaintiffs note, the disclosure and summary-of-rights requirements are designed to protect consumers' interests in learning of any inaccuracies in their credit files so that they can promptly correct the files before they are disseminated to third parties.

In support of standing, the plaintiffs thus contend that the TransUnion mailings were formatted incorrectly and deprived them of their right to receive information in the format required by statute. But the plaintiffs have not demonstrated that the format of TransUnion's mailings caused them a harm with a close relationship to a harm traditionally recognized as providing a basis for a lawsuit in American courts. In fact, they do not demonstrate that they suffered any harm at all from the formatting violations. The plaintiffs presented no evidence that, other than Ramirez, "a single other class member so much as opened the dual mailings," "nor that they were confused, distressed, or relied on the information in any way." . . .

The plaintiffs separately argue that TransUnion's formatting violations created a risk of future harm. . . . As noted above, the risk of future harm on its own does not support Article III standing. . . .

No concrete harm, no standing. . . . We reverse the judgment of the U.S. Court of Appeals for the Ninth Circuit and remand the case for further proceedings consistent with this opinion. In light of our conclusion about Article III standing, we need not decide whether Ramirez's claims were typical of the claims of the class under Rule 23. On remand, the Ninth Circuit may consider in the first instance whether class certification is appropriate in light of our conclusion about standing.

Justice THOMAS, with whom Justice BREYER, Justice SOTOMAYOR, and Justice KAGAN join, dissenting.

Article III vests "[t]he judicial Power of the United States" in this Court "and in such inferior Courts as the Congress may from time to time ordain and establish." §1. This power "shall extend to *all* Cases, in Law and Equity, arising under this Constitution, the Laws of the United States, and Treaties made, or which shall be made, under their Authority." §2 (emphasis added). When a federal court has jurisdiction over a case or controversy, it has a "virtually unflagging obligation" to exercise it. *Colorado River Water Conservation Dist. v. United States* (1976).

Key to the scope of the judicial power . . . is whether an individual asserts his or her own rights. At the time of the founding, whether a court possessed judicial power over an action with no showing of actual damages depended on whether the plaintiff sought to enforce a right held privately by an individual or a duty owed broadly to the community. Where an individual sought to sue someone for a violation of his private rights, such as trespass on his land, the plaintiff needed only to allege the violation. Courts typically did not require any showing of actual damage. But where an individual sued based on the violation of a duty owed broadly to the whole community, such as the overgrazing of public lands, courts required "not only *injuria* [legal injury] but also *damnum* [damage]." *Spokeo v. Robins* (Thomas, J., concurring).

The principle that the violation of an individual right gives rise to an actionable harm was widespread at the founding, in early American history, and in many modern cases. And this understanding accords proper respect for the power of Congress and other legislatures to define legal rights. No one could seriously dispute, for example, that a violation of property rights is actionable, but as a general matter, "[p]roperty rights are created by the State." *Palazzolo v. Rhode Island* (2001). In light of this history, tradition, and common practice, our test should be clear: So long as a "statute fixes a minimum of recovery . . . , there would seem to be no doubt of the right of one who establishes a technical ground of action to recover this minimum sum without any specific showing of loss." T. Cooley, Law of Torts *271. While the Court today discusses the supposed failure to show "injury in fact," courts for centuries held that injury in law to a private right was enough to create a case or controversy.

Here, each class member established a violation of his or her private rights. The jury found that TransUnion violated three separate duties created by statute. All three of those duties are owed to individuals, not to the community writ large. Take §1681e(b), which requires a consumer reporting agency to "follow reasonable procedures to assure maximum possible accuracy of the information concerning the individual about whom the report relates." This statute creates a duty: to use reasonable procedures to assure maximum possible accuracy. And that duty is particularized to an individual: the subject of the report. Section 1681g does the same. It requires an agency to "clearly and accurately disclose" to a consumer, upon his request, "[a]ll information in the consumer's file at the time of the request" and to include a written "summary of rights" with that "written disclosure." Those directives likewise create duties: provide all information in the consumer's file and accompany the disclosure with a summary of rights. And these too are owed to a single person: the consumer who requests the information.

Were there any doubt that consumer reporting agencies owe these duties to specific individuals—and not to the larger community—Congress created a cause of action providing that "[a]ny person who willfully fails to comply" with an FCRA requirement "with respect to any *consumer* is liable to *that consumer.*" If a consumer reporting agency breaches any FCRA duty owed to a specific consumer, then that individual (not all consumers) may sue the agency. No one disputes that each class member possesses this cause of action. And no one disputes that the jury found that TransUnion violated each class member's individual rights. The plaintiffs thus have a sufficient injury to sue in federal court.

The Court chooses a different approach. Rejecting this history, the majority holds that the mere violation of a personal legal right is *not*—and never can be—an injury sufficient to establish standing. What matters for the Court is only that the "injury in fact be 'concrete.'" "No concrete harm, no standing."

That may be a pithy catchphrase, but it is worth pausing to ask why "concrete" injury in fact should be the sole inquiry. After all, it was not until 1970—"180 years after the ratification of Article III"—that this Court even introduced the "injury in fact" (as opposed to injury in law) concept of standing. *Sierra v. Hallandale Beach* (CA11 2021) (Newsom, J., concurring). And the concept then was not even about constitutional standing; it concerned a *statutory* cause of action under the Administrative Procedure Act. *See Association of Data Processing Service Organizations, Inc. v. Camp* (1970).

The Court later took this statutory requirement and began to graft it onto its constitutional standing analysis. So the introduction of an injury-in-fact requirement, in effect, "represented a substantial broadening of access to the federal courts." *Simon v. Eastern Ky. Welfare Rights Organization* (1976). A plaintiff could now invoke a federal court's judicial power by establishing injury by virtue of a violated legal right *or* by alleging some *other* type of "personal interest."

In the context of public rights, the Court continued to require more than just a legal violation. In *Lujan v. Defenders of Wildlife* (1992), for example, the Court concluded that several environmental organizations lacked standing to challenge a regulation about interagency communications, even though the organizations invoked a citizen-suit provision allowing "'any person [to] commence a civil suit . . . to enjoin any person . . . who is alleged to be in violation of'" the law. Echoing the historical distinction between duties owed to individuals and those owed to the community, the Court explained that a plaintiff must do more than raise "a generally available grievance about government—claiming only harm to his and every citizen's interest in proper application of the Constitution and laws." "Vindicating the *public* interest (including the public interest in Government observance of the Constitution and laws) is the function of Congress and the Chief Executive." "'The province of the court,'" in contrast, "'is, solely, to decide on the rights of individuals.'" *Lujan* (quoting *Marbury v. Madison* (1803)).

The same public-rights analysis prevailed in *Summers v. Earth Island Institute* (2009). There, a group of organizations sought to prevent the United States Forest Service from enforcing regulations that exempt certain projects from notice and comment. The Court, again, found that the mere violation of the law "without some concrete interest that is affected by the deprivation—a procedural right *in vacuo*—is insufficient to create Article III standing." But again, this was rooted in the context of public rights: "'It would exceed Article III's limitations if, at the behest of Congress and in the absence of any showing of concrete injury, we were to entertain citizen suits to vindicate the *public's* nonconcrete interest in the proper administration of the laws.'"

In *Spokeo*, the Court built on this approach. Based on a few sentences from *Lujan* and *Summers*, the Court concluded that a plaintiff does not automatically "satisf[y] the injury-in-fact requirement whenever a statute grants a person a statutory right and purports to authorize that person to sue to vindicate that right." But the Court made clear that "Congress is well positioned to identify intangible harms that meet minimum Article III requirements" and explained that "the violation of a procedural right granted by statute *can be* sufficient in some circumstances to constitute injury in fact."

Reconciling these statements has proved to be a challenge. But "[t]he historical restrictions on standing" offer considerable guidance. *Thole v. U.S. Bank* (2020) (Thomas, J., concurring). A statute that creates a public right plus a citizen-suit cause of action is insufficient by itself to establish standing. A statute that creates a private right and a cause of action, however, *does* give plaintiffs an adequate interest in vindicating their private rights in federal court.

The majority today, however, takes the road less traveled: "[U]nder Article III, an injury in law is not an injury in fact." No matter if the right is personal or if the legislature deems the right worthy of legal protection, legislatures are constitutionally unable to offer the protection of the federal courts for anything other than money, bodily integrity, and anything else that this Court thinks looks close enough to rights existing at common law. The 1970s injury-in-fact theory has now displaced the traditional gateway into federal courts.

This approach is remarkable in both its novelty and effects. Never before has this Court declared that legal injury is *inherently* insufficient to support standing. And never before has this Court declared that legislatures are constitutionally precluded from creating legal rights enforceable in federal court if those rights deviate too far from their common-law roots. According to the majority, courts alone have the power to sift and weigh harms to decide whether they merit the Federal Judiciary's attention. In the name of protecting the separation of powers, this Court has relieved the legislature of its power to create and define rights.

III

Even assuming that this Court should be in the business of second-guessing private rights, this is a rather odd case to say that Congress went too far. TransUnion's misconduct here is exactly the sort of thing that has long merited legal redress.

As an initial matter, this Court has recognized that the unlawful withholding of requested information causes "a sufficiently distinct injury to provide standing to sue." Here, TransUnion unlawfully withheld from each class member the OFAC version of his or her credit report that the class member requested. And TransUnion unlawfully failed to send a summary of rights. The majority's response is to contend that the plaintiffs actually did not allege that they failed to receive any required information; they alleged only that they received it in the "*wrong format.*"

Were there any doubt about the facts below, we have the helpful benefit of a jury verdict. The jury found that "Defendant TransUnion, LLC willfully fail[ed] to clearly and accurately disclose OFAC information in the written disclosures it sent to members of the class." And the jury found that "Defendant TransUnion, LLC willfully fail[ed] to provide class members a summary of their FCRA rights with each written disclosure made to them." I would not be so quick as to recharacterize these jury findings as mere "formatting" errors. *See also* U.S. Const., Amdt. 7 ("no fact tried by a jury, shall be otherwise re-examined in any Court of the United States, than according to the rules of the common law").

Moreover, to the extent this Court privileges concrete, *financial* injury for standing purposes, recall that TransUnion charged its clients extra to receive credit reports with the OFAC designation. According to TransUnion, these special

OFAC credit reports are valuable. Even the majority must admit that withholding something of value from another person—that is, "monetary harm"—falls in the heartland of tangible injury in fact. Recognizing as much, TransUnion admits that its clients would have standing to sue if they, like the class members, did not receive the OFAC credit reports they had requested.

And then there is the standalone harm caused by the rather extreme errors in the credit reports. The majority (rightly) decides that having one's identity falsely and publicly associated with terrorism and drug trafficking is itself a concrete harm. For good reason. This case is a particularly grave example of the harm this Court identified as central to the FCRA: "curb[ing] the dissemination of false information." *Spokeo v. Robins* (2016). And it aligns closely with a "harm that has traditionally been regarded as providing a basis for a lawsuit." *Id.* Historically, "[o]ne who falsely, and without a privilege to do so, publishes matter defamatory to another in such a manner as to make the publication a libel is liable to the other," even though "no special harm or loss of reputation results therefrom." Restatement of Torts §569, p. 165 (1938).

The question this Court has identified as key, then, is whether a plaintiff established "a degree of risk" that is "sufficient to meet the concreteness requirement." *Spokeo.* Here, in a 7-month period, it is undisputed that nearly 25 percent of the class had false OFAC-flags sent to potential creditors. Twenty-five percent over just a 7-month period seems, to me, "a degree of risk sufficient to meet the concreteness requirement." If 25 percent is insufficient, then, pray tell, what percentage is?

The majority deflects this line of analysis by all but eliminating the risk-of-harm analysis. According to the majority, an elevated risk of harm simply shows that a concrete harm is *imminent* and thus may support only a claim for injunctive relief. But this reworking of *Spokeo* fails for two reasons. First, it ignores what *Spokeo* said: "[Our opinion] does not mean . . . that the risk of real harm cannot satisfy the requirement of concreteness." Second, it ignores what *Spokeo* did. The Court in *Spokeo* remanded the respondent's claims for statutory damages to the Ninth Circuit to consider "whether the . . . violations alleged in this case entail a degree of risk sufficient to meet the concreteness requirement." The theory that risk of harm matters only for injunctive relief is thus squarely foreclosed by *Spokeo* itself.

But even if risk of harm is out, the Ninth Circuit indicated that every class member may have had an OFAC alert disclosed. According to the court below, TransUnion not only published this information to creditors for a quarter of the class but also "communicated about the database information and OFAC matches" with a third party. Respondent adds to this by pointing out that TransUnion published this information to vendors that printed and sent the mailings. In the historical context of libel, publication to even a single other party could be enough to give rise to suit. This was true, even where the third party was a telegraph company, an attorney, or a stenographer who merely writes the information down. Surely with a harm so closely paralleling a common-law harm, this is an instance where a plaintiff "need not allege any additional harm beyond the one Congress has identified." *Spokeo.*

But even setting aside everything already mentioned—the Constitution's text, history, precedent, financial harm, libel, the risk of publication, and actual disclosure to a third party—one need only tap into common sense to know that receiving a letter identifying you as a potential drug trafficker or terrorist is harmful. All the more so when the information comes in the context of a credit report, the entire purpose of which is to demonstrate that a person can be trusted.

And if this sort of confusing and frustrating communication is insufficient to establish a real injury, one wonders what could rise to that level. If, instead of falsely identifying Ramirez as a potential drug trafficker or terrorist, TransUnion had flagged him as a "potential" child molester, would that alone still be insufficient to open the courthouse doors? What about falsely labeling a person a racist? Including a slur on the report? Or what about openly reducing a person's credit score by several points because of his race? If none of these constitutes an injury in fact, how can that possibly square with our past cases indicating that the inability to "observe an animal species, even for purely esthetic purposes, . . . undeniably" is? *Lujan v. Defenders of Wildlife* (1992). Had the class members claimed an aesthetic interest in viewing an accurate report, would this case have come out differently?

And if some of these examples do cause sufficiently "concrete" and "real" — though "intangible" — harms, how do *we* go about picking and choosing which ones do and which do not? I see no way to engage in this "inescapably value-laden" inquiry without it "devolv[ing] into [pure] policy judgment." Weighing the harms caused by specific facts and choosing remedies seems to me like a much better fit for legislatures and juries than for this Court.

Ultimately, the majority seems to pose to the reader a single rhetorical question: Who could possibly think that a person is harmed when he requests and is sent an incomplete credit report, or is sent a suspicious notice informing him that he may be a designated drug trafficker or terrorist, or is *not* sent anything informing him of how to remove this inaccurate red flag? The answer is, of course, legion: Congress, the President, the jury, the District Court, the Ninth Circuit, and four Members of this Court.

Justice KAGAN, with whom Justice BREYER and Justice SOTOMAYOR join, dissenting.

The Court here transforms standing law from a doctrine of judicial modesty into a tool of judicial aggrandizement. It holds, for the first time, that a specific class of plaintiffs whom Congress allowed to bring a lawsuit cannot do so under Article III. I join Justice Thomas's dissent, which explains why the majority's decision is so mistaken. . . .

I differ with Justice Thomas on just one matter, unlikely to make much difference in practice. In his view, any "violation of an individual right" created by Congress gives rise to Article III standing. But in *Spokeo*, this Court held that "Article III requires a concrete injury even in the context of a statutory violation." I continue to adhere to that view, but think it should lead to the same result as Justice Thomas's approach in all but highly unusual cases. As *Spokeo* recognized, "Congress is well positioned to identify [both tangible and] intangible harms" meeting Article III standards. Article III requires for concreteness only a "real harm" (that is, a harm that "actually exist[s]") or a "risk of real harm." And as today's decision definitively proves, Congress is better suited than courts to determine when something causes a harm or risk of harm in the real world. For that reason, courts should give deference to those congressional judgments. Overriding an authorization to sue is appropriate when but only when Congress could not reasonably have thought that a suit will contribute to compensating or preventing the harm at issue. Subject to that qualification, I join Justice Thomas's dissent in full.

* * *

In *TransUnion*, Justice Thomas reminds the majority that the injury-in-fact concept is a relative latecomer to the jurisprudential scene. For most of U.S. history, he argues, an injury in law sufficed for standing purposes. Standing, as we know it, is a twentieth century innovation. The majority rejects that approach and holds that a federal court lacks jurisdiction to hear a claim if the plaintiff has not suffered an injury in fact even if the plaintiff has suffered an injury in law—that is, even if the plaintiff has a statutory right and right of action and the defendant has plainly violated the plaintiff's statutory right.

Judges and scholars continue to debate whether the history of the federal courts supports the modern injury-in-fact requirement. Justice Kavanaugh's *TransUnion* opinion concludes that history does support this requirement because, even if the federal courts did not speak in terms of an injury in fact prior to 1970, their decisions were consistent with such a requirement. Justice Thomas argues that the most important historical distinction was not between injuries in fact and injuries in law, but rather between private rights and public rights. In his view, Congress may create private rights and private rights of action and thus afford plaintiffs standing to sue in federal court. The injury-in-fact requirement applies only where Congress creates a *public* right—that is, a public interest in seeing that the law is enforced—and a citizen-suit right of action.[8] Justice Kagan, who basically agrees with Justice Thomas, takes the slightly different position that courts should defer to Congress unless it unreasonably concluded that a statutory right of action would prevent a real-world harm.

This debate raises a deeper question about the role that history should play in federal courts jurisprudence. The role of the federal courts has changed significantly since Article III's words were written and the Constitution was ratified. Beginning with Reconstruction and continuing to the present day, for example, Congress created various civil rights and rights of action and thus opened the doors of the federal courts to suits against discrimination and domination by majority interests. During and after the New Deal, the Court expanded standing doctrine to insulate the work of new regulatory agencies from judicial review. These cases have been used by the modern Supreme Court to limit civil rights enforcement.

One of the most important applications of the injury-in-fact requirement is to limit jurisdiction over suits seeking to prevent future harm. The key case is *City of Los Angeles v. Lyons* (1983), which arose from allegations of police violence and racial discrimination against African Americans in Los Angeles.

Although the case involved a single incident, police in Los Angeles had long been criticized for racial profiling and other forms of police misconduct. During the

---

8. For a historically grounded book supporting this view, see JAMES PFANDER, CASES WITHOUT CONTROVERSIES (2021).

Great Depression, the Los Angeles Police Department sent more than 100 officers to California's borders with orders to exclude economic migrants from other states (such as Oklahoma). This so-called "Bum Blockade" threatened migrants with 180-day sentences to hard labor.[9] Roughly a decade later, "hundreds of U.S. military personnel went on a two-week rampage in Los Angeles, California, attacking scores of Mexican American youth who wore the Zoot Suit style of dress."[10] The Police Department not only failed to stop the violence, it arrested Mexican Americans for disturbing the peace.[11] By the 1950s, "the nation's law enforcement community revered the Los Angeles Police Department (LAPD) for introducing the concept of 'hard-nosed' police professionalism."[12] In 1965, the so-called "Watts Riots," five days of civil unrest and protest against police misconduct in a then-predominantly working class African-American neighborhood became national news. A subsequent investigation identified a deep seated "schism" between the Black community and the police.[13]

The LAPD's use of force policies was challenged in *Lyons*. Between 1975 and 1982, sixteen people died from LAPD chokeholds. Twelve of the victims were Black men. Adolph Lyons, a 24-year-old Black man, survived an LAPD chokehold after officers stopped him for driving with a burnt-out taillight. In a 5-4 decision, the Court held that Lyons did not have standing to seek injunctive relief against the use of force policy simply because he had been subjected to an allegedly illegal chokehold himself. The prior incident provided no basis, the Court reasoned, for concluding that he was at a substantial risk of again being stopped and suffering a violation of his Fourth Amendment right against excessive use of force. The Court also held, for the first time, that standing analysis is remedy-specific — the fact that Lyons had standing for monetary relief did not bear on the question of standing to seek an injunction against the use of force policy to prevent future harm.

City of Los Angeles v. Lyons

461 U.S. 95 (1983)

Justice WHITE delivered the opinion of the Court.

The issue here is whether respondent Lyons satisfied the prerequisites for seeking injunctive relief in the Federal District Court.

I

This case began on February 7, 1977, when respondent, Adolph Lyons, filed a complaint for damages, injunction, and declaratory relief in the United States

---

9. Cecelia Rasmussen, *LAPD Blocked Dust Bowl Migrants at State Borders*, L.A. TIMES, Mar. 9, 2003.

10. Richard Griswold del Castillo, *The Los Angeles "Zoot Suit Riots" Revisited: Mexican and Latin American Perspectives*, 16 MEXICAN STUDIES/ESTUDIOS MEXICANOS 367, 367 (2000).

11. *Id.*

12. James R. Lasley & Michael K. Hooper, *On Racism and the LAPD: Was the Christopher Commission Wrong?*, 79 SOC. SCI. Q. 378, 378 (1998).

13. GOVERNOR'S COMM'N ON THE L.A. RIOTS, VIOLENCE IN THE CITY — AN END OR A BEGINNING? 19 (1965).

District Court for the Central District of California. The defendants were the City of Los Angeles and four of its police officers. The complaint alleged that on October 6, 1976, at 2 a.m., Lyons was stopped by the defendant officers for a traffic or vehicle code violation and that although Lyons offered no resistance or threat whatsoever, the officers, without provocation or justification, seized Lyons and applied a "chokehold"—either the "bar arm control" hold or the "carotid-artery control" hold or both—rendering him unconscious and causing damage to his larynx. Counts I through IV of the complaint sought damages against the officers and the City. Count V, with which we are principally concerned here, sought a preliminary and permanent injunction against the City barring the use of the control holds. That count alleged that the City's police officers, "pursuant to the authorization, instruction and encouragement of Defendant City of Los Angeles, regularly and routinely apply these choke holds in innumerable situations where they are not threatened by the use of any deadly force whatsoever," that numerous persons have been injured as the result of the application of the chokeholds, that Lyons and others similarly situated are threatened with irreparable injury in the form of bodily injury and loss of life, and that Lyons "justifiably fears that any contact he has with Los Angeles Police officers may result in his being choked and strangled to death without provocation, justification or other legal excuse." Lyons alleged the threatened impairment of rights protected by the First, Fourth, Eighth, and Fourteenth Amendments. Injunctive relief was sought against the use of the control holds "except in situations where the proposed victim of said control reasonably appears to be threatening the immediate use of deadly force." Count VI sought declaratory relief against the City, *i.e.*, a judgment that use of the chokeholds absent the threat of immediate use of deadly force is a *per se* violation of various constitutional rights.

[In Part II of its opinion, the Court concluded that the case was not mooted by the city's suspension of its use of force policy.]

III

It goes without saying that those who seek to invoke the jurisdiction of the federal courts must satisfy the threshold requirement imposed by Art. III of the Constitution by alleging an actual case or controversy. Plaintiffs must demonstrate a "personal stake in the outcome" in order to "assure that concrete adverseness which sharpens the presentation of issues" necessary for the proper resolution of constitutional questions. *Baker v. Carr* (1962) Abstract injury is not enough. The plaintiff must show that he "has sustained or is immediately in danger of sustaining some direct injury" as the result of the challenged official conduct and the injury or threat of injury must be both "real and immediate," not "conjectural" or "hypothetical." *Golden v. Zwickler* (1969).

In *O'Shea v. Littleton* (1974), we dealt with a case brought by a class of plaintiffs claiming that they had been subjected to discriminatory enforcement of the criminal law. Among other things, a county magistrate and judge were accused of discriminatory conduct in various respects, such as sentencing members of plaintiff's class more harshly than other defendants.

Although it was claimed in that case that particular members of the plaintiff class had actually suffered from the alleged unconstitutional practices, we observed that "[p]ast exposure to illegal conduct does not in itself show a present case or controversy regarding injunctive relief . . . if unaccompanied by any continuing, present adverse effects." Past wrongs were evidence bearing on "whether there is a real and immediate threat of repeated injury." But the prospect of future injury rested "on the likelihood that [plaintiffs] will again be arrested for and charged with violations of the criminal law and will again be subjected to bond proceedings, trial, or sentencing before petitioners." The most that could be said for plaintiffs' standing was "that *if* [plaintiffs] proceed to violate an unchallenged law and *if* they are charged, held to answer, and tried in any proceedings before petitioners, they will be subjected to the discriminatory practices that petitioners are alleged to have followed." We could not find a case or controversy in those circumstances.

We further observed that case-or-controversy considerations "obviously shade into those determining whether the complaint states a sound basis for equitable relief," and went on to hold that even if the complaint presented an existing case or controversy, an adequate basis for equitable relief against petitioners had not been demonstrated. Another relevant decision for present purposes is *Rizzo v. Goode* (1976), a case in which plaintiffs alleged widespread illegal and unconstitutional police conduct aimed at minority citizens and against city residents in general. The Court reiterated the holding in *O'Shea* that past wrongs do not in themselves amount to that real and immediate threat of injury necessary to make out a case or controversy.

Golden v. Zwickler (1969), a case arising in an analogous situation, is directly apposite. Zwickler sought a declaratory judgment that a New York statute prohibiting anonymous handbills directly pertaining to election campaigns was unconstitutional. Although Zwickler had once been convicted under the statute, his sole concern related to a Congressman who had left the House of Representatives for a place on the Supreme Court of New York and who would not likely be a candidate again. A unanimous Court held that because it was "most unlikely" that Zwickler would again be subject to the statute, no case or controversy of "'sufficient immediacy and reality'" was present to allow a declaratory judgment. Just as Zwickler's assertion that the former Congressman could be a candidate for Congress again was "hardly a substitute for evidence that this is a prospect of 'immediacy and reality,'" Lyons' assertion that he may again be subject to an illegal chokehold does not create the actual controversy that must exist for a declaratory judgment to be entered.

IV

No extension of *O'Shea* and *Rizzo* is necessary to hold that respondent Lyons has failed to demonstrate a case or controversy with the City that would justify the equitable relief sought. Lyons' standing to seek the injunction requested depended on whether he was likely to suffer future injury from the use of the chokeholds by police officers. Count V of the complaint alleged the traffic stop and choking incident five months before. That Lyons may have been illegally choked by the police, while presumably affording Lyons standing to claim damages against the individual officers and perhaps against the City, does nothing to establish a real and immediate threat that he would again be stopped for a traffic violation, or for any other offense, by an officer or officers who would illegally choke him into unconsciousness without any provocation or resistance on his part. The additional allegation in the complaint that the police in Los Angeles routinely apply chokeholds in situations where they are not threatened by the use of deadly force falls far short of the allegations that would be necessary to establish a case or controversy between these parties.

In order to establish an actual controversy in this case, Lyons would have had not only to allege that he would have another encounter with the police but also to make the incredible assertion either (1) that *all* police officers in Los Angeles *always* choke any citizen with whom they happen to have an encounter, whether for the purpose of arrest, issuing a citation, or for questioning, or (2) that the City ordered or authorized police officers to act in such manner. Although Count V alleged that the City authorized the use of the control holds in situations where deadly force was not threatened, it did not indicate why Lyons might be realistically threatened by police officers who acted within the strictures of the City's policy.

Under *O'Shea* and *Rizzo*, these allegations were an insufficient basis to provide a federal court with jurisdiction to entertain Count V of the complaint.

V

Lyons fares no better if it be assumed that his pending damages suit affords him Art. III standing to seek an injunction as a remedy for the claim arising out of the October 1976 events. The equitable remedy is unavailable absent a showing of irreparable injury, a requirement that cannot be met where there is no showing of any real or immediate threat that the plaintiff will be wronged again — a "likelihood of substantial and immediate irreparable injury." *O'Shea v. Littleton* (1974). The speculative nature of Lyons' claim of future injury requires a finding that this prerequisite of equitable relief has not been fulfilled.

Nor will the injury that Lyons allegedly suffered in 1976 go unrecompensed; for that injury, he has an adequate remedy at law. Contrary to the view of the Court of Appeals, it is not at all "difficult" under our holding "to see how anyone can ever challenge police or similar administrative practices." The legality of the violence to which Lyons claims he was once subjected is at issue in his suit for damages and can be determined there.

Absent a sufficient likelihood that he will again be wronged in a similar way, Lyons is no more entitled to an injunction than any other citizen of Los Angeles; and a federal court may not entertain a claim by any or all citizens who no more than assert that certain practices of law enforcement officers are unconstitutional. This is not to suggest that such undifferentiated claims should not be taken seriously by local authorities. Indeed, the interest of an alert and interested citizen is an essential element of an effective and fair government, whether on the local, state, or national level. A federal court, however, is not the proper forum to press such claims unless the requirements for entry and the prerequisites for injunctive relief are satisfied.

We decline the invitation to slight the preconditions for equitable relief; for as we have held, recognition of the need for a proper balance between state and federal authority counsels restraint in the issuance of injunctions against state officers engaged in the administration of the States' criminal laws in the absence of irreparable injury which is both great and immediate. In exercising their equitable powers federal courts must recognize "[t]he special delicacy of the adjustment to be preserved between federal equitable power and State administration of its own law." *Stefanelli v. Minard* (1951). The Court of Appeals failed to apply these factors properly and therefore erred in finding that the District Court had not abused its discretion in entering an injunction in this case.

Justice MARSHALL, with whom Justice BRENNAN, Justice BLACKMUN, and Justice STEVENS join, dissenting.

The District Court found that the city of Los Angeles authorizes its police officers to apply life-threatening chokeholds to citizens who pose no threat of violence, and that respondent, Adolph Lyons, was subjected to such a chokehold. The Court today holds that a federal court is without power to enjoin the enforcement of the city's policy, no matter how flagrantly unconstitutional it may be. Since no one can show that he will be choked in the future, no one — not even a person who, like Lyons, has almost been choked to death — has standing to challenge the continuation of the policy. The city is free to continue the policy indefinitely as long as it is willing to pay damages for the injuries and deaths that result. I dissent from this unprecedented and unwarranted approach to standing.

There is plainly a "case or controversy" concerning the constitutionality of the city's chokehold policy. The constitutionality of that policy is directly implicated by Lyons' claim for damages against the city. The complaint clearly alleges that the officer who choked Lyons was carrying out an official policy, and a municipality is liable under 42 U.S.C. §1983 for the conduct of its employees only if they acted pursuant to such a policy. Lyons therefore has standing to challenge the city's chokehold policy and to obtain whatever relief a court may ultimately deem appropriate. Standing has always depended on whether a plaintiff has a "personal stake in the outcome of the controversy," *Baker v. Carr* (1962), not on the "precise nature of the relief sought." *Jenkins v. McKeithen* (1969) (Marshall, J., joined by Warren, C.J., and Brennan, J.).

I

Respondent Adolph Lyons is a 24-year-old Negro male who resides in Los Angeles. According to the uncontradicted evidence in the record, at about 2 a.m. on October 6, 1976, Lyons was pulled over to the curb by two officers of the Los Angeles Police Department (LAPD) for a traffic infraction because one of his taillights was burned out. The officers greeted him with drawn revolvers as he exited from his car. Lyons was told to face his car and spread his legs. He did so. He was then ordered to clasp his hands and put them on top of his head. He again complied. After one of the officers completed a patdown search, Lyons dropped his hands, but was ordered to place them back above his head, and one of the officers grabbed Lyons' hands and slammed them onto his head. Lyons complained about the pain caused by the ring of keys he was holding in his hand. Within 5 to 10 seconds, the officer began to choke Lyons by applying a forearm against his throat. As Lyons struggled for air, the officer handcuffed him, but continued to apply the chokehold until he blacked out. When Lyons regained consciousness, he was lying face down on the ground, choking, gasping for air, and spitting up blood and dirt. He had urinated and defecated. He was issued a traffic citation and released.

Although the city instructs its officers that use of a chokehold does not constitute deadly force, since 1975 no less than 16 persons have died following the use of a chokehold by an LAPD police officer. Twelve have been Negro males. The evidence submitted to the District Court established that for many years it has been the official policy of the city to permit police officers to employ chokeholds in a variety of situations where they face no threat of violence. In reported "altercations" between LAPD officers and citizens the chokeholds are used more frequently than any other means of physical restraint. Between February 1975 and July 1980, LAPD officers applied chokeholds on at least 975 occasions, which represented more than three-quarters of the reported altercations.

It is undisputed that chokeholds pose a high and unpredictable risk of serious injury or death. Chokeholds are intended to bring a subject under control by causing pain and rendering him unconscious. Depending on the position of the officer's arm and the force applied, the victim's voluntary or involuntary reaction, and his state of health, an officer may inadvertently crush the victim's larynx, trachea, or hyoid. The result may be death caused by either cardiac arrest or asphyxiation. An LAPD officer described the reaction of a person to being choked as "do[ing] the chicken," in reference apparently to the reactions of a chicken when its neck is wrung. The victim experiences extreme pain. His face turns blue as he is deprived of oxygen, he goes into spasmodic convulsions, his eyes roll back, his body wriggles, his feet kick up and down, and his arms move about wildly.

Although there has been no occasion to determine the precise contours of the city's chokehold policy, the evidence submitted to the District Court provides some indications. LAPD Training Officer Terry Speer testified that an officer is authorized to deploy a chokehold whenever he "*feels* that there's about to be a bodily attack made on him." A training bulletin states that "[c]ontrol holds . . . allow officers to subdue *any* resistance by the suspects." In the proceedings below the city characterized its own policy as authorizing the use of chokeholds "'to gain control of a suspect who is violently resisting the officer *or trying to escape*,'" to "subdue *any* resistance by the suspects," and to permit an officer, "where . . . resisted, but *not necessarily threatened with serious bodily harm or death,* . . . to subdue a suspect who forcibly resists an officer."

The training given LAPD officers provides additional revealing evidence of the city's chokehold policy. Officer Speer testified that in instructing officers concerning the use of force, the LAPD does not distinguish between felony and misdemeanor suspects. Moreover, the officers are taught to maintain the chokehold until the suspect goes limp, despite substantial evidence that the application of a chokehold invariably induces a "flight or flee" syndrome, producing an *involuntary* struggle by the victim which can easily be misinterpreted by the officer as willful resistance that must be overcome by prolonging the chokehold and increasing the force applied. In addition, officers are instructed that the chokeholds can be safely deployed for up to three or four minutes. Robert Jarvis, the city's expert who has taught at the Los Angeles Police Academy for the past 12 years, admitted that officers are never told that the bar-arm control can cause death if applied for just two seconds. Of the nine deaths for which evidence was submitted to the District Court, the average duration of the choke where specified was approximately 40 seconds.

II

. . . An indispensable prerequisite of municipal liability under 42 U.S.C. §1983 is proof that the conduct complained of is attributable to an unconstitutional official policy or custom. It is not enough for a §1983 plaintiff to show that the employees or agents of a municipality have violated or will violate the Constitution, for a municipality will not be held liable solely on a theory of *respondeat superior.*

The Court errs in suggesting that Lyons' prayer for injunctive relief in Count V of his first amended complaint concerns a policy that was not responsible for his injuries and that therefore could not support an award of damages. Paragraph 8 of the complaint alleges that Lyons was choked "without provocation, legal justification or excuse." Paragraph 13 expressly alleges that "[t]he Defendant Officers were carrying out *the official policies, customs and practices* of the Los Angeles Police Department and the City of Los Angeles," and that "*by virtue thereof,* defendant City is liable for the actions" of the officers.

The Court apparently finds Lyons' complaint wanting because, although it alleges that he was choked without provocation and that the officers acted pursuant to an official policy, it fails to allege *in haec verba* that the city's policy authorizes the choking of suspects without provocation. I am aware of no case decided since the abolition of the old common-law forms of action, and the Court cites none, that in any way supports this crabbed construction of the complaint. A federal court is capable of concluding for itself that two plus two equals four.

In sum, it is absolutely clear that Lyons' requests for damages and for injunctive relief call into question the constitutionality of the city's policy concerning the use of chokeholds. If he does not show that that policy is unconstitutional, he will be no more entitled to damages than to an injunction.

III

. . . [B]y fragmenting a single claim into multiple claims for particular types of relief and requiring a separate showing of standing for each form of relief, the decision today departs from this Court's traditional conception of standing and of the remedial powers of the federal courts.

. . . In contrast to this case *O'Shea* and *Rizzo* involved disputes focusing solely on the threat of future injury which the plaintiffs in those cases alleged they faced. In *O'Shea* the plaintiffs did not allege past injury and did not seek compensatory relief. In *Rizzo,* the plaintiffs sought only declaratory and injunctive relief and alleged past instances of police misconduct only in an attempt to establish the substantiality of the threat of future injury. There was similarly no claim for damages based on past injuries in *Golden v. Zwickler* (1969), on which the Court also relies.

By contrast, Lyons' request for prospective relief is coupled with his claim for damages based on past injury. In addition to the risk that he will be subjected to a chokehold in the future, Lyons has suffered past injury. Because he has a live claim for damages, he need not rely solely on the threat of future injury to establish his personal stake in the outcome of the controversy. In the cases relied on by the majority, the Court simply had no occasion to decide whether a plaintiff who has standing to litigate a dispute must clear a separate standing hurdle with respect to each form of relief sought. . . .

No doubt the requests for injunctive relief may raise additional questions. But these questions involve familiar issues relating to the appropriateness of particular forms of relief, and have never been thought to implicate a litigant's standing to sue. The denial of standing separately to seek injunctive relief therefore cannot be justified by the basic concern underlying the Art. III standing requirement. . . .

We have never required more than that a plaintiff have standing to litigate a claim. Whether he will be entitled to obtain particular forms of relief should be prevail has never been understood to be an issue of standing. . . .

V

Apparently because it is unwilling to rely solely on its unprecedented rule of standing, the Court goes on to conclude that, even if Lyons has standing, "[t]he equitable remedy is unavailable." The Court's reliance on this alternative ground is puzzling for two reasons.

If, as the Court says, Lyons lacks standing under Art. III, the federal courts have no power to decide his entitlement to equitable relief on the merits. Under the Court's own view of Art. III, the Court's discussion in Part V is purely an advisory opinion. . . .

Even if the issue had been properly raised, I could not agree with the Court's disposition of it. Courts of equity have much greater latitude in granting injunctive relief "in furtherance of the public interest than . . . when only private interests are involved." *Virginian R. Co. v. Railway Employees* (1937). In this case we know that the District Court would have been amply justified in considering the risk to the public, for after the preliminary injunction was stayed, five additional deaths occurred prior to the adoption of a moratorium. Under these circumstances, I do not believe that the District Court abused its discretion.

VI

The Court's decision removes an entire class of constitutional violations from the equitable powers of a federal court. It immunizes from prospective equitable relief any policy that authorizes persistent deprivations of constitutional rights as long as no individual can establish with substantial certainty that he will be injured, or injured again, in the future. The Chief Justice asked in *Bivens v. Six Unknown Fed. Narcotics Agents* (1971) (dissenting opinion), "what would be the judicial response to a police order authorizing 'shoot to kill' with respect to every fugitive"? His answer was that it would be "easy to predict our collective wrath and outrage." We now learn that wrath and outrage cannot be translated into an order to cease the unconstitutional practice, but only an award of damages to those who are victimized by the practice and live to sue and to the survivors of those who are not so fortunate. Under the view expressed by the majority today, if the police adopt a policy of "shoot to kill," or a policy of shooting 1 out of 10 suspects, the federal courts will be powerless to enjoin its continuation. *Cf. Linda R.S. v. Richard D.* (1973) (White, J., dissenting). The federal judicial power is now limited to levying a toll for such a systematic constitutional violation.

* * *

NOTES ON STANDING AND THE RISK OF FUTURE INJURIES

The Court has repeatedly reaffirmed the rule that standing analysis is remedy-specific — standing for purposes of one remedy does not confer standing for other remedies the plaintiff seeks. When a lower federal court is asked to grant an injunction, it must, as a part of the traditional standard for equitable relief, inquire whether the remedy at law is adequate. If the remedy at law is adequate, it must deny equitable relief. There is, therefore, already a phase of litigation that takes care to distinguish remedies, and limits access to forward-looking equitable relief where retrospective monetary damages are sufficient to place the plaintiff in the rightful position. Why has the Court drawn this fact-intensive inquiry and its limitation on access to equitable relief into the factually dark phase of early pre-trial litigation over standing?

Police stops such as the one Lyons experienced remain common not only in Los Angeles, but as social media posts graphically detail, in many cities nationwide. As the African-American scholar Henry Gates, once put it, "'[t]here's a moving violation that many African-Americans know as D.W.B.: Driving While Black.'"[14] How might Lyons have repleaded his case to link his Fourth and Fourteenth Amendment claims more closely? Would this have made it easier to establish a substantial risk of recurrence of excessive use of force?

How likely must future constitutional injury be to create standing for injunctive relief to prevent it? "One does not have to await the consummation of threatened injury to obtain preventive relief," *Penn. v. West Virginia* (1923), but the Court has given various formulations of how close the threat must be. In *Clapper v. Amnesty International USA* (2013), a case involving a challenge to domestic digital surveillance of American's communications in violation of the Foreign Intelligence Surveillance Act, the Court said the harm must be "certainly impending," drawing on language from *Penn. v. West Virginia* saying that when harm is "certainly impending, that is enough." The Court in *Clapper* emphasized that the harm *must* be certainly impending in the national security setting given distinctive separation of powers concerns surrounding judicial review of sensitive policies implemented by the executive branch.

In the broader context of pre-enforcement challenges to legislation, the Court has held that the injury-in-fact requirement is met where the complaint alleges an intention on the part of the plaintiff "to engage in a course of conduct arguably affected with a constitutional interest, but proscribed by statute, and there exists a credible threat of prosecution. . . . [I]t is not necessary that [the plaintiff] first expose himself to actual arrest or prosecution to be entitled to challenge [the] statute that he claims deters the exercise of his constitutional rights." *Babbit v. Farm Workers* (1979).

In *Babbit*, farmworkers and their union sought a federal court injunction against an Arizona statute designed to prevent farmworkers from forming unions. The plaintiffs argued that the law violated their First Amendment rights. The record showed that they had engaged in public advocacy supporting and organizing

---

14. Washington v. Lambert, 98 F.3d 1181, 1188 (9th Cir. 1996) (quoting Henry L. Gates, Jr., *Thirteen Ways of Looking at a Black Man*, NEW YORKER, Oct. 23, 1995, at 59)).

boycotts of growers who abused labor rights. The statute carried criminal penalties for "dishonest, untruthful and deceptive publicity" which would expose plaintiffs to prosecution even for "inaccuracies *inadvertently* uttered in the course of consumer appeals." To avoid prosecution, plaintiffs alleged, they would have to curtail their consumer appeals "and thus forgo full exercise of what they insist[ed were] their First Amendment rights." Although no arrests or indictments had issued, the state had not "disavowed any intention of invoking the criminal penalty provision." The Court thus held that plaintiffs' fear of prosecution was "not imaginary or wholly speculative."

The Court held that the plaintiffs' challenge to other provisions of the law, including a compulsory arbitration provision and a rule stating that employers had no obligation to provide "information, time or facilities" to labor organizers to communicate with employees, were not justiciable. It was "impossible to know" whether employers would deny access to unions seeking to contact their employees and whether in the event of a strike an injunction would be sought, triggering the arbitration provision, or some other response would be preferred by employers. In sum, "[a] plaintiff who challenges a statute must demonstrate a realistic danger of sustaining a direct injury as a result of the statute's operation or enforcement."

In *Susan B. Anthony List (SBAL) v. Driehaus* (2014), an anti-abortion group challenged an Ohio election law that criminalized false statements regarding the voting record of a candidate or public official during the course of a political campaign, arguing the state law violated the First Amendment. During the 2010 election cycle, SBAL issued a press release stating that a congressman's vote in favor of the Affordable Care Act (ACA) was a vote in favor of "taxpayer funded abortion." The congressman, Steve Driehaus, filed a complaint with the Ohio Elections Commission, which found probable cause to believe the statute had been violated by SBAL and initiated discovery. When Driehaus lost the election, he withdrew his complaint from the Commission. SBAL persisted in its suit for declaratory and injunctive relief in federal court after the congressman lost his re-election bid. Standing was challenged on the ground that Driehaus' loss and withdrawal of the state election law complaint removed the threat of enforcement of the state law against SBAL.

The Court held that "an allegation of future injury may suffice if the injury is certainly impending, or there is a substantial risk that the harm will occur." SBAL had standing because the organization pled "specific statements they intend[ed] to make in future election cycles" regarding representatives in Congress who voted for the ACA, not just former congressman Driehaus. This conduct is "arguably proscribed by the statute they wish to challenge," and "a Commission panel here already found probable cause to believe that SBAL violated the statute [with the Driehaus press release] — the same sort of statement petitioners plan to disseminate in the future." For these reasons, and unlike the *Zwickler* case cited in *Lyons*, it didn't matter whether Driehaus would run again. The threat of future enforcement, the Court emphasized, is "substantial. Most obviously, there is a history of past enforcement here . . . [and] past enforcement against the same conduct is good evidence that the threat of enforcement is not chimerical. . . . Indeed, future complainants may well invoke the prior probable cause finding to prove that SBAL *knowingly* lied." Moreover, unlike ordinary criminal statutes, where prosecutors are "constrained by explicit guidelines or ethical obligations, there is a real risk of complaints from, for example, political opponents" because any person with knowledge of a purported violation can file a complaint with the Commission. Lastly, the Court noted that complaints to the Commission are not rare, the Commission "has not disavowed enforcement if petitioners make similar statements in the future," and the Commission's administrative sanctions such as cease-and-desist orders are "backed by the additional threat of criminal prosecution."

Why was the past administrative investigation before the Ohio election commission relevant to the risk of future harm in *Driehaus* when the chokehold Lyons suffered did not bear on the risk of future police violence in his case?

2. *Causation and Redressability*

The following two cases, *Linda R.S. v. Richard D.* and *Allen v. Wright,* concern the meaning of the causation and redressability requirements for constitutional standing. Both must be met for a plaintiff to have standing. To meet them, plaintiffs must allege and prove that the defendant caused their harm, and that it is likely that a favorable court decision will remedy their injury. In reading these cases, you may notice features they share — both involve claims of discriminatory treatment under law and requests for relief that would have required changes in how agencies regulated third parties. In both cases, the Court recognized that the plaintiffs had suffered an injury, but held that the plaintiffs in neither case had standing to sue. Together, these two cases show how the characterization of injury in fact shapes what plaintiffs must allege and prove to make out causation and redressability. They also raise questions about whether the Court's standing decisions trace a principled line between plaintiffs that have standing and those who do not.

Linda R.S. addressed whether a plaintiff has standing to challenge the government's decision not to enforce a criminal law against a third party. The Texas law in question required an absent parent to pay child support. The plaintiff was the mother of a child born out of wedlock and sued for an injunction to force the district attorney to prosecute the child's father for not paying child support. *Linda R.S.* was decided the same year as *Roe v. Wade* (1973), during a time of "continuing stigma of unwed motherhood," as *Roe* recognized.[15] More broadly, across all income levels today, single mothers disproportionately bear the costs of noncustodial parents' failure to make consistent financial contributions to child support. As late as 2020 U.S. Census data shows that 82 percent of single-parent households are headed by mothers. Collection and enforcement of child support can be an extraordinary burden for single mothers with low to modest incomes, consuming valuable time and resources to secure support necessary to pay for groceries, the "utility bill, or to make up a shortfall on housing costs."[16]

---

15. *See generally* Melissa Murray, *What's So New About the New Illegitimacy?*, 20 AM. U. J. GENDER SOC. POL'Y & L. 387, 413 (2012) (tracing the history of stigma against unwed child-rearing and arguing that "the stigma of illegitimacy remains as pronounced as ever").

16. Leslie Silva, *The Socio-Economic Division Among Women in Child Support Proceedings,* A.B.A.: PRACTICE POINTS (June 18, 2021), https://www.americanbar.org/groups /litigation/committees/woman-advocate/practice/2021/the-socio-economic-division -among-women-in-child-support-proceedings.

The Texas statute at issue in *Linda R.S.* empowered district attorneys to prosecute non-support, but prosecutors declined to enforce it against parents of children born out of wedlock. In a 5-4 decision, the Court held that the plaintiff lacked standing to bring her claim that the State had violated the Equal Protection Clause of the Fourteenth Amendment by enforcing the child support statute for only the parents of children born during marriage.

Linda R.S. v. Richard D.

410 U.S. 614 (1973)

Justice MARSHALL delivered the opinion of the Court.

Appellant, the mother of an illegitimate child, brought this action in United States District Court on behalf of herself, her child, and others similarly situated to enjoin the "discriminatory application" of Art. 602 of the Texas Penal Code. A three-judge court was convened pursuant to 28 U.S.C. §2281, but that court dismissed the action for want of standing. We postponed consideration of jurisdiction until argument on the merits, and now affirm the judgment below.

Article 602, in relevant part, provides: "any parent who shall willfully desert, neglect or refuse to provide for the support and maintenance of his or her child or children under eighteen years of age, shall be guilty of a misdemeanor, and upon conviction, shall be punished by confinement in the County Jail for not more than two years." The Texas courts have consistently construed this statute to apply solely to the parents of legitimate children and to impose no duty of support on the parents of illegitimate children. In her complaint, appellant alleges that one Richard D. is the father of her child, that Richard D. has refused to provide support for the child, and that although appellant made application to the local district attorney for enforcement of Art. 602 against Richard D., the district attorney refused to take action for the express reason that, in his view, the fathers of illegitimate children were not within the scope of Art. 602.

Appellant argues that this interpretation of Art. 602 discriminates between legitimate and illegitimate children without rational foundation and therefore violates the Equal Protection Clause of the Fourteenth Amendment. Although her complaint is not entirely clear on this point, she apparently seeks an injunction running against the district attorney forbidding him from declining prosecution on the ground that the unsupported child is illegitimate.

Before we can consider the merits of appellant's claim or the propriety of the relief requested, however, appellant must first demonstrate that she is entitled to invoke the judicial process. She must, in other words, show that the facts alleged present the court with a "case or controversy" in the constitutional sense and that she is a proper plaintiff to raise the issues sought to be litigated. The threshold question which must be answered is whether the appellant has "alleged such a personal stake in the outcome of the controversy as to assure that concrete adverseness which sharpens the presentation of issues upon which the court so largely depends for illumination of difficult constitutional questions." *Baker v. Carr* (1962).

Although the law of standing has been greatly changed in the last 10 years, we have steadfastly adhered to the requirement that, at least in the absence of a statute expressly conferring standing, federal plaintiffs must allege some threatened or actual injury resulting from the putatively illegal action before a federal court may assume jurisdiction.

Applying this test to the facts of this case, we hold that, in the unique context of a challenge to a criminal statute, appellant has failed to allege a sufficient nexus between her injury and the government action which she attacks to justify judicial intervention. To be sure, appellant no doubt suffered an injury stemming from the failure of her child's father to contribute support payments. But the bare existence of an abstract injury meets only the first half of the standing requirement.

Here, appellant has made no showing that her failure to secure support payments results from the nonenforcement, as to her child's father, of Art. 602. Although the Texas statute appears to create a continuing duty, it does not follow the civil contempt model whereby the defendant "keeps the keys to the jail in his own pocket" and may be released whenever he complies with his legal obligations. On the contrary, the statute creates a completed offense with a fixed penalty as soon as a parent fails to support his child. Thus, if appellant were granted the requested relief, it would result only in the jailing of the child's father. The prospect that prosecution will, at least in the future, result in payment of support can, at best, be termed only speculative. Certainly the "direct" relationship between the alleged injury and the claim sought to be adjudicated, which previous decisions of this Court suggest is a prerequisite of standing, is absent in this case.

In American jurisprudence at least, a private citizen lacks a judicially cognizable interest in the prosecution or nonprosecution of another. Appellant does have an interest in the support of her child. But given the special status of criminal prosecutions in our system, we hold that appellant has made an insufficient showing of a direct nexus between the vindication of her interest and the enforcement of the State's criminal laws. The District Court was therefore correct in dismissing the action for want of standing, and its judgment must be affirmed.

Justice WHITE, with whom Justice DOUGLAS joins, dissenting.

Obviously, there are serious difficulties with appellant's complaint insofar as it may be construed as seeking to require the official appellees to prosecute Richard D. or others, or to obtain what amounts to a federal child-support order. But those difficulties go to the question of what relief the court may ultimately grant appellant. They do not affect her right to bring this class action. The Court notes, as it must, that the father of a legitimate child, if prosecuted under Art. 602, could properly raise the statute's underinclusiveness as an affirmative defense. Presumably, that same father would have standing to affirmatively seek to enjoin enforcement of the statute against him. The question then becomes simply: why should only an actual or potential criminal defendant have a recognizable interest in attacking this allegedly discriminatory statute and not appellant and her class? They are not, after all, in the position of members of the public at large who wish merely to force an enlargement of state criminal laws. Appellant, her daughter, and the children born out of wedlock whom she is attempting to represent have all allegedly been excluded intentionally from the class of persons protected by a particular criminal law. They do not get the protection of the laws that other women and children get. Under Art. 602, they are rendered nonpersons; a father may ignore them with full knowledge that he will be subjected to no penal sanctions. The Court states that the actual coercive effect of those sanctions on Richard D. or others "can, at best, be termed only speculative." This is a very odd statement. I had always thought our civilization has assumed that the threat of penal sanctions had something more than a "speculative" effect on a person's conduct. This Court has long acted on that assumption in demanding that criminal laws be plainly and explicitly worded so that people will know what they mean and be in a position to conform their conduct to the mandates of law. Certainly Texas does not share the Court's surprisingly novel view. It assumes that criminal sanctions are useful in coercing fathers to fulfill their support obligations to their legitimate children.

Unquestionably, Texas prosecutes fathers of legitimate children on the complaint of the mother asserting non-support and refuses to entertain like complaints from a mother of an illegitimate child. I see no basis for saying that the latter mother has no standing to demand that the discrimination be ended, one way or the other.

If a State were to pass a law that made only the murder of a white person a crime, I would think that Negroes as a class would have sufficient interest to seek a declaration that that law invidiously discriminated against them. Appellant and her class have no less interest in challenging their exclusion from what their own State perceives as being the beneficial protections that flow from the existence and enforcement of a criminal child-support law.

* * *

Allen v. Wright, decided in 1984, is an important case in the law of standing that concerns school desegregation. In *Brown v. Board of Education* (1954), the Supreme Court held that de jure school segregation was unconstitutional. Many school districts tried to evade the Court's desegregation mandate. As table 1 shows,[17] the Supreme Court decided *Allen* at a time when the United States had approached the highest rate of school integration in its history, which was in no small measure a result of federal court school desegregation orders. In implementing *Brown,* federal courts provided broad structural relief, including orders mandating busing of students to integrate schools. In so doing, they followed the lead of the Warren Court, which emphasized the breadth of lower federal court authority to fashion equitable relief. There was significant backlash to these busing orders. As the table below depicts, in the 1980s, limitations on the remedial authority of the lower federal courts to order such structural relief developed by the Burger Court began to affect patterns of school desegregation.

---

17. Table 1 is based on data presented in Erica Frankenberg et al., Harming Our Common Future: America's Segregated Schools 65 Years after *Brown*, The Civil Rights Project (2019), at https://www.civilrightsproject.ucla.edu/research/k-12 -education/integration-and-diversity/harming-our-common-future-americas-segregated -schools-65-years-after-brown/Brown-65-050919v4-final.pdf.

Percentage of black students in the South who attend schools that are at least 50 percent white

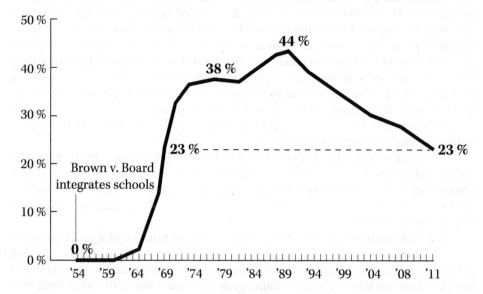

Data from the National Center for Education Statistics, via UCLA's Civil Rights Project

Allen presented a related question about federal court equity power in the context of federal tax policy. The Internal Revenue Service's policy of treating racially discriminatory private schools as tax exempt supported a central tactic for maintaining racial segregation in schooling. In *Bob Jones Univ. v. United States* (1983), the Supreme Court held that the IRS had authority to deny tax-exempt status to private schools with racially discriminatory admissions standards. In *Allen*, decided the next year, the Court held that Black families lacked standing to challenge the IRS's policy of affording tax-exempt status based upon a school's certification that it did not discriminate. The Court reasoned that the families' request for equitable relief against the federal agency presented separation-of-powers problems that standing doctrine was designed to solve.

Allen v. Wright

468 U.S. 737 (1984)

Justice O'CONNOR delivered the opinion of the Court.

Parents of black public school children allege in this nation-wide class action that the Internal Revenue Service (IRS) has not adopted sufficient standards and procedures to fulfill its obligation to deny tax-exempt status to racially discriminatory private schools. They assert that the IRS thereby harms them directly and interferes with the ability of their children to receive an education in desegregated public schools. The issue before is whether plaintiffs have standing to bring this suit. We hold that they do not.

I

The IRS denies tax-exempt status under the Internal Revenue Code, and hence eligibility to receive charitable contributions deductible from income taxes to racially discriminatory private schools. The IRS policy requires that a school applying for tax-exempt status show that it "admits the students of any race to all the rights, privileges, programs, and activities generally accorded or made available to students at that school and that the school does not discriminate on the basis of race in administration of its educational policies, admissions policies, scholarship and loan programs, and athletic and other-school administered programs." To carry out this policy, the IRS has established guidelines and procedures for determining whether a particular school is in fact racially nondiscriminatory. Failure to comply with the guidelines "will ordinarily result in the proposed revocation" of tax-exempt status.

In 1976 respondents challenged these guidelines and procedures in a suit filed in Federal District Court against the Secretary of the Treasury and the Commissioner of Internal Revenue. The plaintiffs named in the complaint are parents of black children who, at the time the complaint was filed, were attending public schools in seven States in school districts undergoing desegregation. They brought this nationwide class action "on behalf of themselves and their children, and . . . on behalf of all other parents of black children attending public school systems undergoing, or which may in the future undergo, desegregation pursuant to court order [or] HEW regulations and guidelines, under state law, or voluntarily." They estimated that the class they seek to represent includes several million persons.

Respondents allege in their complaint that many racially segregated private schools were created or expanded in their communities at the time the public schools were undergoing desegregation. According to the complaint, many such private schools, including 17 schools or school systems identified by name in the complaint (perhaps some 30 schools in all), receive tax exemptions either directly or through the tax-exempt status of "umbrella" organizations that operate or support the schools. Respondents allege that, despite the IRS policy of denying tax-exempt status to racially discriminatory private schools and despite the IRS guidelines and procedures for implementing that policy, some of the tax-exempt racially segregated private schools created or expanded in desegregating districts in fact have racially discriminatory policies. Respondents allege that the IRS grant of tax exemptions to such racially discriminatory schools is unlawful.

Respondents allege that the challenged Government conduct harms them in two ways. The challenged conduct

> (a) constitutes tangible federal financial aid and other support for racially segregated educational institutions, and
> (b) fosters and encourages the organization, operation and expansion of institutions providing racially segregated educational opportunities for white children avoiding attendance in desegregating public school districts and thereby interferes with the efforts of federal courts, HEW and local school authorities to desegregate public school districts which have been operating racially dual school systems.

Thus, respondents do not allege that their children have been the victims of discriminatory exclusion from the schools whose tax exemptions they challenge as unlawful. Indeed, they have not alleged at any stage of this litigation that their children have ever applied or would ever apply to any private school. Rather, respondents claim a direct injury from the mere fact of the challenged Government conduct and, as indicated by the restriction of the plaintiff class to parents of children in desegregating school districts, injury to their children's opportunity to receive a desegregated education. The latter injury is traceable to the IRS grant of tax exemptions to racially discriminatory schools, respondents allege, chiefly because contributions to such schools are deductible from income taxes under §§170(a)(1) and (c)(2) of the Internal Revenue Code and the "deductions facilitate the raising of funds to organize new schools and expand existing schools in order to accommodate white students avoiding attendance in desegregating public school districts."

Respondents request only prospective relief. They ask for a declaratory judgment that the challenged IRS tax-exemption practices are unlawful. They also ask for an injunction requiring the IRS to deny tax exemptions to a considerably broader class of private schools than the class of racially discriminatory private schools. Under the requested injunction, the IRS would have to deny tax-exempt status to all private schools

> which have insubstantial or nonexistent minority enrollments, which are located in or serve desegregating public school districts, and which either—
> (1) were established or expanded at or about the time the public school districts in which they are located or which they serve were desegregating;
> (2) have been determined in adversary judicial or administrative proceedings to be racially segregated; or
> (3) cannot demonstrate that they do not provide racially segregated educational opportunities for white children avoiding attendance in desegregating public school systems. . . .

Finally, respondents ask for an order directing the IRS to replace its 1975 guidelines with standards consistent with the requested injunction.

[Following the filing of the lawsuit,] the IRS reviewed its challenged policies and proposed new Revenue Procedures to tighten requirements for eligibility for tax-exempt status for private schools. In 1979, however, Congress blocked any strengthening of the IRS guidelines at least until October 1980. The District Court thereupon considered and granted the defendants' motion to dismiss the complaint, concluding that respondents lack standing, that the judicial task proposed by respondents is inappropriately intrusive for a federal court, and that awarding the requested relief would be contrary to the will of Congress expressed in the 1979 ban on strengthening IRS guidelines.

The United States Court of Appeals for the District of Columbia Circuit reversed, concluding that respondents have standing to maintain this lawsuit.

II

A

Article III of the Constitution confines the federal courts to adjudicating actual "cases" and "controversies." As the Court explained in *Valley Forge Christian College v. Americans United for Separation of Church and State, Inc.* (1982), the "case or controversy" requirement defines with respect to the Judicial Branch the idea of separation of powers on which the Federal Government is founded. The several doctrines that have grown up to elaborate that requirement are "founded in concern about the proper—and properly limited—role of the courts in a democratic society." *Warth v. Seldin* (1975). The case-or-controversy doctrines state fundamental limits on federal judicial power in our system of government.

The Art. III doctrine that requires a litigant to have "standing" to invoke the power of a federal court is perhaps the most important of these doctrines. "In essence the question of standing is whether the litigant is entitled to have the court decide the merits of the dispute or of particular issues." *Warth v. Seldin* (1975). Standing doctrine embraces several judicially self-imposed limits on the exercise of federal jurisdiction, such as the general prohibition on a litigant's raising another person's legal rights, the rule barring adjudication of generalized grievances more appropriately addressed in the representative branches, and the requirement that a plaintiff's complaint fall within the zone of interests protected by the law invoked. The requirement of standing, however, has a core component derived directly from the Constitution. A plaintiff must allege personal injury fairly traceable to the defendant's allegedly unlawful conduct and likely to be redressed by the requested relief.

Like the prudential component, the constitutional component of standing doctrine incorporates concepts concededly not susceptible of precise definition. The injury alleged must be, for example, "'distinct and palpable,'" *Gladstone, Realtors v. Village of Belwood* (1979) (quoting *Warth v. Seldin* (1975)), and not "abstract" or "conjectural" or "hypothetical," *Los Angeles v. Lyons* (1983). The injury must be "fairly" traceable to the challenged action, and relief from the injury must be "likely" to follow from a favorable decision. *See Simon v. Eastern Kentucky Welfare Rights Org.* (1976). These terms cannot be defined so as to make application of the constitutional standing requirement a mechanical exercise.

In many cases the standing question can be answered chiefly by comparing the allegations of the particular complaint to those made in prior standing cases. More important, the law of Art. III standing is built on a single basic idea—the idea of separation of powers. It is this fact which makes possible the gradual clarification of the law through judicial application.

The standing inquiry requires careful judicial examination of a complaint's allegations to ascertain whether the particular plaintiff is entitled to an adjudication of the particular claims asserted. Is the injury too abstract, or otherwise not appropriate, to be considered judicially cognizable? Is the line of causation between the illegal conduct and injury too attenuated? Is the prospect of obtaining relief from the injury as a result of a favorable ruling too speculative? These questions and any others relevant to the standing inquiry must be answered by reference to the Art. III notion that federal courts may exercise power only "in the last resort, and as a necessity," *Chicago & Grant Trunk R. Co. v. Wellman* (1892), and only when adjudication is "consistent with a system of separated powers and [the dispute is one] traditionally thought to be capable of resolution through the judicial process," *Flast v. Cohen* (1968).

B

Respondents allege two injuries in their complaint to support their standing to bring this lawsuit. First, they say that they are harmed directly by the mere fact of Government financial aid to discriminatory private schools. Second, they say that the federal tax exemptions to racially discriminatory private schools in their communities impair their ability to have their public schools desegregated.

We conclude that neither suffices to support respondents' standing. The first fails under clear precedents of this Court because it does not constitute judicially cognizable injury. The second fails because the alleged injury is not fairly traceable to the assertedly unlawful conduct of the IRS.[19]

1

Respondents' first claim of injury can be interpreted in two ways. It might be a claim simply to have the Government avoid the violation of law alleged in respondents' complaint. Alternatively, it might be a claim of stigmatic injury, or denigration, suffered by all members of a racial group when the Government discriminates on the basis of race. Under neither interpretation is this claim of injury judicially cognizable.

This Court has repeatedly held that an asserted right to have the Government act in accordance with law is not sufficient, standing alone, to confer jurisdiction on a federal court. In *Schlesinger v. Reservists Comm.* (1974), for example, the Court rejected a claim of citizen standing to challenge Armed Forces Reserve commissions held by Members of Congress as violating the Incompatibility Clause of Art. I, §6, of the Constitution. As citizens, the Court held, plaintiffs alleged nothing but "the abstract injury in nondisclosure of the Constitution. . . ." Respondents here have no standing to complain simply that their Government is violating the law.

Neither do they have standing to litigate their claims based on the stigmatizing injury often caused by racial discrimination. There can be no doubt that this sort of noneconomic injury is one of the most serious consequences of discriminatory government action and is sufficient in some circumstances to support standing. Our cases make clear, however, that such injury accords a basis for standing only to "those persons who are personally denied equal treatment" by the challenged discriminatory conduct. *Heckler v. Matthews* (1984).

The consequences of recognizing respondents' standing on the basis of their first claim of injury illustrate why our cases plainly hold that such injury is not judicially cognizable. If the abstract stigmatic injury were cognizable, standing would extend nationwide to all members of the particular racial groups against which the Government was alleged to be discriminating by its grant of a tax exemption to a racially discriminatory school, regardless of the location of that

---

19. To the extent there is a difference [between the causation and redressability requirements], it is that the former examines the causal connection between the assertedly unlawful conduct and the alleged injury, whereas the latter examines the causal connection between the alleged injury and the judicial relief requested. Cases such as this, in which the relief requested goes well beyond the violation of law alleged, illustrate why it is important to keep the inquiries separate if the "redressability" component is to focus on the requested relief. Even if the relief respondents request might have a substantial effect on the desegregation of public schools, whatever deficiencies exist in the opportunities for desegregated education for respondents' children might not be traceable to IRS violations of law—grants of tax exemptions to racially discriminatory schools in respondents' communities.

school. All such persons could claim the same sort of abstract stigmatic injury respondents assert in their first claim of injury. A black person in Hawaii could challenge the grant of a tax exemption to a racially discriminatory school in Maine. Recognition of standing in such circumstances would transform the federal courts into "no more than a vehicle for the vindication of the value interests of concerned bystanders." *United States v. SCRAP* (1973). Constitutional limits on the role of the federal courts preclude such a transformation.

2

It is in their complaint's second claim of injury that respondents allege harm to a concrete, personal interest that can support standing in some circumstances. The injury they identify — their children's diminished ability to receive an education in a racially integrated school — is, beyond any doubt, not only judicially cognizable but, as shown by cases from *Brown v. Board of Education* (1954) to *Bob Jones University v. United States* (1983), one of the most serious injuries recognized in our legal system. Despite the constitutional importance of curing the injury alleged by respondents, however, the federal judiciary may not redress it unless standing requirements are met. In this case, respondents' second claim of injury cannot support standing because the injury alleged is not fairly traceable to the Government conduct respondents challenge as unlawful.

The illegal conduct challenged by respondents is the IRS's grant of tax exemptions to some racially discriminatory schools. The line of causation between that conduct and desegregation of respondents' schools is attenuated at best. From the perspective of the IRS, the injury to respondents is highly indirect and "results from the independent action of some third party not before the court." *Simon v. Eastern Kentucky Welfare Rights Org.* (1976).

The diminished ability of respondents' children to receive a desegregated education would be fairly traceable to unlawful IRS grants of tax exemptions only if there were enough racially discriminatory private schools receiving tax exemptions in respondents' communities for withdrawal of those exemptions to make an appreciable difference in public school integration. Respondents have made no such allegation. It is, first, uncertain how many racially discriminatory private schools are in fact receiving tax exemptions. Moreover, it is entirely speculative, as respondents themselves conceded in the Court of Appeals, whether withdrawal of a tax exemption from any particular school would lead the school to change its policies. It is just as speculative whether any given parent of a child attending such a private school would decide to transfer the child to public school as a result of any changes in educational or financial policy made by the private school once it was threatened with loss of tax-exempt status. It is also pure speculation whether, in a particular community, a large enough number of the numerous relevant school officials and parents would reach decisions that collectively would have a significant impact on the racial composition of the public schools.

The links in the chain of causation between the challenged Government conduct and the asserted injury are far too weak for the chain as a whole to sustain respondents' standing. In *Simon v. Eastern Kentucky Welfare Rights Org.*, the Court held that standing to challenge a Government grant of a tax exemption to hospitals could not be founded on the asserted connection between the grant of tax-exempt status and the hospitals' policy concerning the provision of medical services to indigents. The causal connection depended on the decisions hospitals would make in response to withdrawal of tax-exempt status, and those decisions were sufficiently uncertain to break the chain of causation between the plaintiffs' injury and the challenged Government action. The chain of causation is even weaker in this case. It involves numerous third parties (officials of racially discriminatory schools receiving tax exemptions and the parents of children attending such schools) who may not even exist in respondents' communities and whose independent decisions may not collectively have a significant effect on the ability of public school students to receive a desegregated education.

The idea of separation of powers that underlies standing doctrine explains why our cases preclude the conclusion that respondents' alleged injury "fairly can be traced to the challenged action" of the IRS. *Simon v. Eastern Kentucky Welfare Rights Org.* (1976). That conclusion would pave the way generally for suits challenging, not specifically identifiable Government violations of law, but the particular programs agencies establish to carry out their legal obligations. Such suits, even when premised on allegations of several instances of violations of law, are rarely if ever appropriate for federal-court adjudication.

When transported into the Art. III context, that principle, grounded as it is in the idea of separation of powers, counsels against recognizing standing in a case brought, not to enforce specific legal obligations whose violation works a direct harm, but to seek a restructuring of the apparatus established by the Executive Branch to fulfill its legal duties. The Constitution, after all, assigns to the Executive Branch, and not to the Judicial Branch, the duty to "take Care that the Laws be faithfully executed." U.S. Const., Art. II, §3. We could not recognize respondents' standing in this case without running afoul of that structural principle.

C

The Court of Appeals relied for its contrary conclusion on *Gilmore v. City of Montgomery* (1974), on *Norwood v. Harrison* (1973), and on *Coit v. Green* (1971). None of the cases, however, requires that we find standing in this lawsuit.

In *Gilmore v. City of Montgomery*, the plaintiffs asserted a constitutional right, recognized in an outstanding injunction, to use the city's public parks on a nondiscriminatory basis. They alleged that the city was violating that equal protection right by permitting racially discriminatory private schools and other groups to use the public parks. The Court recognized plaintiffs' standing to challenge this city policy insofar as the policy permitted the exclusive use of the parks by racially discriminatory private schools: the plaintiffs had alleged direct cognizable injury to their right to nondiscriminatory access to the public parks.

Standing in *Gilmore* thus rested on an allegation of direct deprivation of a right to equal use of the parks. Like the plaintiff in *Heckler v. Mathews*—indeed, like the plaintiffs having standing in virtually any equal protection case—the plaintiffs in *Gilmore* alleged that they were personally being denied equal treatment. The *Gilmore* Court did not rest its finding of standing on an abstract denigration injury, and no problem of attenuated causation attended the plaintiffs' claim of injury.

In *Norwood v. Harrison*, parents of public school children in Tunica County, Miss., filed a statewide class action challenging the State's provision of textbooks to students attending racially discriminatory private schools in the State. The Court held the State's practice unconstitutional because it breached "the State's acknowledged duty to establish a unitary school system." The Court did not expressly address the basis for the plaintiffs' standing.

In *Gilmore,* however, the Court identified the basis for standing in *Norwood:*

> The plaintiffs in *Norwood* were parties to a school desegregation order, and the relief they sought was directly related to the concrete injury they suffered.

Through the school desegregation decree, the plaintiffs had acquired a right to have the State "steer clear" of any perpetuation of the racially dual school system that it had once sponsored. The interest acquired was judicially cognizable because it was a personal interest, created by law, in having the State refrain from taking specific actions. The plaintiffs' complaint alleged that the State directly injured that interest by aiding racially discriminatory private schools. Respondents in this lawsuit, of course, have no injunctive rights against the IRS that are allegedly being harmed by the challenged IRS action.

Unlike *Gilmore* and *Norwood, Coit v. Green* cannot easily be seen to have based standing on an injury different in kind from any asserted by respondents here. The plaintiffs in *Coit,* parents of black schoolchildren in Mississippi, sued to enjoin the IRS grant of tax exemptions to racially discriminatory private schools in the State. Nevertheless, *Coit* in no way mandates the conclusion that respondents have standing.

First, the decision has little weight as a precedent on the law of standing. This Court's decision in *Coit* was merely a summary affirmance; for that reason alone, it could hardly establish principles contrary to those set out in opinions issued after full briefing and argument. . . . Moreover, the District Court found, based on extensive evidence before it as well as on the findings in *Coffey v. State Educational Finance Comm'n* (S.D. Miss. 1969), that large numbers of segregated private schools had been established in the State for the purpose of avoiding a unitary public school system; that the tax exemptions were critically important to the ability of such schools to succeed; and that the connection between the grant of tax exemptions to discriminatory schools and desegregation of the public schools in the particular State was close enough to warrant the conclusion that irreparable injury to the interest in desegregated education was threatened if the tax exemptions continued.[29] What made possible those findings was the fact that, when the Mississippi plaintiffs filed their suit, the IRS had a policy of granting tax exemptions to racially discriminatory private schools; thus, the suit was initially brought, not simply to reform Executive Branch enforcement procedures, but to

---

29. In *Norwood v. Harrison,* (1973), this Court described the experience of one county in Mississippi:

> all white children were withdrawn from public schools and placed in a private academy housed in local church facilities and staffed by the principal and 17 high school teachers of the county system, who resigned in mid-year to accept jobs at the new academy.

The Court observed that similar histories in various other localities in Mississippi were recited by the plaintiffs without challenge.

challenge a fundamental IRS policy decision, which affected numerous identifiable schools in the State of Mississippi.

The limited setting, the history of school desegregation in Mississippi at the time of the *Coit* litigation, the nature of the IRS conduct challenged at the outset of the litigation, and the District Court's particular findings, which were never challenged as clearly erroneous, amply distinguish the *Coit* case from respondents' lawsuit. Thus, we need not consider whether standing was properly found to exist in *Coit*. Whatever the answer to that question, respondents' complaint, which aims at nationwide relief and does not challenge particular identified unlawful IRS actions, alleges no connection between the asserted desegregation injury and the challenged IRS conduct direct enough to overcome the substantial separation of powers barriers to a suit seeking an injunction to reform administrative procedures.

Justice MARSHALL took no part in the decision of these cases.

Justice BRENNAN, dissenting.

The Court's attempt to obscure the standing question must be seen . . . as no more than a cover for its failure to recognize the nature of the specific claims raised by the respondents in these cases. By relying on generalities concerning our tripartite system of government, the Court is able to conclude that the respondents lack standing to maintain this action without acknowledging the precise nature of the injuries they have alleged. In so doing, the Court displays a startling insensitivity to the historical role played by the federal courts in eradicating race discrimination from our Nation's schools—a role that has played a prominent part in this Court's decisions from *Brown v. Board of Education* (1954), through *Bob Jones University v. United States* (1983).

More than one commentator has noted that the causation component of the Court's standing inquiry is no more than a poor disguise for the Court's view of the merits of the underlying claims. The Court today does nothing to avoid that criticism. What is most disturbing about today's decision, therefore, is not the standing analysis applied, but the indifference evidenced by the Court to the detrimental effects that racially segregated schools, supported by tax-exempt status from the Federal Government, have on the respondents' attempt to obtain an education in a racially integrated school system. I cannot join such indifference, and would give the respondents a chance to prove their case on the merits.

Justice STEVENS, with whom Justice BLACKMUN joins, dissenting.

Three propositions are clear to me: (1) respondents have adequately alleged "injury in fact"; (2) their injury is fairly traceable to the conduct that they claim to be unlawful; and (3) the "separation of powers" principle does not create a jurisdictional obstacle to the consideration of the merits of their claim.

In final analysis, the wrong respondents allege that the Government has committed is to subsidize the exodus of white children from schools that would otherwise be racially integrated. The critical question in these cases, therefore, is whether respondents have alleged that the Government has created that kind of subsidy.

In answering that question, we must of course assume that respondents can prove what they have alleged. Furthermore, at this stage of the litigation we must put to one side all questions about the appropriateness of a nationwide class action. The controlling issue is whether the causal connection between the injury and the wrong has been adequately alleged.

We have held that when a subsidy makes a given activity more or less expensive, injury can be fairly traced to the subsidy for purposes of standing analysis because of the resulting increase or decrease in the ability to engage in the activity. Indeed, we have employed exactly this causation analysis in the same context at issue here—subsidies given private schools that practice racial discrimination.

This causation analysis is nothing more than a restatement of elementary economics: when something becomes more expensive, less of it will be purchased. Sections 170 and 501(c)(3) are premised on that recognition. If racially discriminatory private schools lose the "cash grants" that flow from the operation of the statutes, the education they provide will become more expensive and hence less of their services will be purchased. Conversely, maintenance of these tax benefits makes an education in segregated private schools relatively more attractive, by decreasing its cost. Accordingly, without tax-exempt status, private schools will either not be competitive in terms of cost, or have to change their admissions policies, hence reducing their competitiveness for parents seeking "a racially segregated alternative" to public schools, which is what respondents have alleged many white parents in desegregating school districts seek.

The Court could mean one of three things by its invocation of the separation of powers. First, it could simply be expressing the idea that if the plaintiff lacks Art. III standing to bring a lawsuit, then there is no "case or controversy" within the meaning of Art. III and hence the matter is not within the area of responsibility assigned to the Judiciary by the Constitution. While there can be no quarrel with this proposition, in itself it provides no guidance for determining if the injury respondents have alleged is fairly traceable to the conduct they have challenged.

Second, the Court could be saying that it will require a more direct causal connection when it is troubled by the separation of powers implications of the case before it. That approach confuses the standing doctrine with the justiciability of the issues that respondents seek to raise. The purpose of the standing inquiry is to measure the plaintiff's stake in the outcome, not whether a court has the authority to provide it with the outcome it seeks. Imposing an undefined but clearly more rigorous standard for redressability for reasons unrelated to the causal nexus between the injury and the challenged conduct can only encourage undisciplined, ad hoc litigation, a result that would be avoided if the Court straightforwardly considered the justiciability of the issues respondents seek to raise, rather than using those issues to obfuscate standing analysis.

Third, the Court could be saying that it will not treat as legally cognizable injuries that stem from an administrative decision concerning how enforcement resources will be allocated. This surely is an important point. Respondents do seek to restructure the IRS's mechanisms for enforcing the legal requirement that discriminatory institutions not receive tax-exempt status. Such restructuring would dramatically affect the way in which the IRS exercises its prosecutorial discretion. The Executive requires latitude to decide how best to enforce the law, and in general the Court may well be correct that the exercise of that discretion, especially in the tax context, is unchallengeable.

However, as the Court also recognizes, this principle does not apply when suit is brought "to enforce specific legal obligations whose violation works a direct harm." For example, despite the fact that they were challenging the methods used by the Executive to enforce the law, citizens were accorded standing to challenge a pattern of police misconduct that violated the constitutional constraints on law enforcement activities in *Allee v. Medrano* (1974). Here, respondents contend that the IRS is violating a specific constitutional limitation on its enforcement discretion. There is a solid basis for that contention. In *Norwood v. Harrison* (1973), we wrote:

> A State's constitutional obligation requires it to steer clear, not only of operating the old dual system of racially segregated schools, but also of giving significant aid to institutions that practice racial or other invidious discrimination.

It has been clear since *Marbury v. Madison* (1803), that "[i]t is emphatically the province and duty of the judicial department to say what the law is." Deciding whether the Treasury has violated a specific legal limitation on its enforcement discretion does not intrude upon the prerogatives of the Executive, for in so deciding we are merely saying "what the law is."

* * *

NOTES ON CAUSATION AND REDRESSABILITY

In both *Linda R.S.* and *Allen*, the Court was troubled by litigation seeking to force an executive actor to enforce the law against a third party. The Court's focus in *Linda R.S.* was on the "special status of criminal prosecutions," which might be thought to threaten individual liberty. And in *Allen*, the Court suggested that lawsuits challenging "the particular programs agencies establish to carry out their legal obligations . . . are rarely if ever appropriate for federal-court adjudication." Both decisions question whether private parties have an interest in law enforcement policies and have been criticized for implying that there is not a causal relationship between nonenforcement of the law and the behavior of regulated parties.

A crucial feature of the Court's opinion in *Allen* is its premise that constitutional standing doctrine is "built on a single basic idea — the idea of separation of powers." The Court's concern about causation and redressability might connect with the separation of powers in several ways. These requirements might implement the rule against issuing an advisory opinion. If a judicial remedy will not redress the plaintiff's injury, then the federal court decision would be merely advisory. The *Allen* Court also was concerned about encroaching upon the enforcement policies of the Executive Branch, which the Court notes, has the constitutional duty to "take Care that the Laws be faithfully executed." U.S. Const., Art. II, §3. The Court may also have given weight to the apparent view of Congress, which blocked IRS's decision in 1979 to strengthen its guidelines.

Critics of the causation and redressability requirements have argued that standing is a threshold determination ill-suited to answering fundamental separation-of-powers questions. Whether judicial intervention is warranted to rectify or prevent unconstitutional government acts is a question better addressed at the remedies phase when the nature and scope of the constitutional violation has been established on a full fact record, not pre-trial. Redressability is often a deeply factual question as well: How likely is it that a judicial remedy will affect the plaintiff's injury? It is arguably inappropriate to resolve this factual question on the pleadings at the threshold of litigation.

Critics have also argued that the causation and redressability inquiries are manipulable and depend upon how the court defines the injury in fact. In *Allen*, for example, the Court might have found causation and redressability if it had characterized the plaintiffs' injury "as the deprivation of an opportunity to undergo desegregation in school systems unaffected by unlawful tax deductions."[19] As Justice Brennan put it in his *Allen* dissent, the underlying worry is that standing analysis becomes "no more than a poor disguise for the Court's view of the merits of the underlying claims."

For example, one criticism is that the Court's decisions in *Linda R.S.* and *Allen* are inconsistent with its recognition of standing in other cases, such as *Regents of the University of California v. Bakke* (1978), that also involved claims for equal treatment under law. In *Bakke*, the Court held the White plaintiff had standing to challenge the denial of an equal chance to compete for a slot even though he could not show that in the absence of the university's affirmative action plan to increase enrollment of students of color, he would have been admitted. *Bakke* is part of a line of cases in which the Court has taken this more generous approach to causation contrasting sharply with its approach in cases such as *Allen*. Here is how the Court explained this line of authority on the relationship between injury and causation in *Northeastern Florida Ass'n General Contractors v. Jacksonville* (1993), a case challenging the city's adoption of a minority set-aside program to diversify the contractors with which it did business:

> The Court of Appeals held that petitioner could not establish standing because it failed to allege that one or more of its members would have been awarded a contract but for the challenged ordinance. Under these circumstances, the Court of Appeals concluded, there is no "injury." This holding cannot be reconciled with our precedents.
>
> In *Turner v. Fouche* (1970), a Georgia law limiting school board membership to property owners was challenged on equal protection grounds. We held that a plaintiff who did not own property had standing to challenge the law, and although we did not say so explicitly, our holding did not depend upon an allegation that he would have been appointed to the board but for the property requirement. All that was necessary was that the plaintiff wished to be considered for the position.
>
> We confronted a similar issue in *Clements v. Fashing* (1982). There, a number of officeholders claimed that their equal protection rights were violated by the "automatic resignation" provision of the Texas Constitution, which requires the immediate resignation of some (but not all) state officeholders upon their announcement of a candidacy for

---

19. Cass R. Sunstein, *Standing and the Privatization of Public Law*, 88 COLUM. L. REV. 1432, 1465-66 (1988).

another office. Noting that the plaintiffs had alleged that they would have announced their candidacy were it not for the consequences of doing so, we rejected the claim that the dispute was "merely hypothetical," and that the allegations were insufficient to create an "actual case or controversy." Citing *Turner v. Fouche*, we emphasized that the plaintiffs' injury was the "obstacle to [their] *candidacy*;" we did not require any allegation that the plaintiffs would actually have been elected but for the prohibition.

The decision that is most closely analogous to this case, however, is *Regents of Univ. of Gal. v. Bakke* (1978), where a twice-rejected white male applicant claimed that a medical school's admissions program, which reserved 16 of the 100 places in the entering class for minority applicants, was inconsistent with the Equal Protection Clause. Addressing the argument that the applicant lacked standing to challenge the program, Justice Powell concluded that the "constitutional requirements of Art. III" had been satisfied, because the requisite "injury" was the medical school's "decision not to permit Bakke to *compete* for all 100 places in the class, simply because of his race." Thus, "even if Bakke had been unable to prove that he would have been *admitted* in the absence of the special program, it would not follow that he lacked standing." This portion of Justice Powell's opinion was joined by four other Justices.

Singly and collectively, these cases stand for the following proposition: When the government erects a barrier that makes it more difficult for members of one group to obtain a benefit than it is for members of another group, a member of the former group seeking to challenge the barrier need not allege that he would have obtained the benefit but for the barrier in order to establish standing. The "injury in fact" in an equal protection case of this variety is the denial of equal treatment resulting from the imposition of the barrier, not the ultimate inability to obtain the benefit. *See, e.g., Turner v. Fouche* ("We may assume that the [plaintiffs] have no right to be appointed to the . . . board of education. But [they] do have a federal constitutional right to be *considered* for public service without the burden of invidiously discriminatory disqualifications"). And in the context of a challenge to a set-aside program, the "injury in fact" is the inability to compete on an equal footing in the bidding process, not the loss of a contract.

In other anti-affirmative action cases, the Court has upheld standing on the same grounds. *See, e.g., Gutter v. Bollinger* (2003) (standing to challenge Michigan Law School admissions policy that allegedly gave "certain minority groups 'a significantly greater chance of admission than students with similar credentials from disfavored racial groups'"). And in the context of sex discrimination, the Court has also upheld standing on the same grounds. Perhaps the clearest example is *Heckler v. Mathews*, 465 U.S. 728 (1984). The plaintiff was a male retired postal worker who challenged a federal law that provided greater pension benefits for female retirees than for male retirees in some cases. He alleged that this distinction violated the equal protection component of the Fifth Amendment Due Process Clause. Standing was challenged because Congress had included a severability clause in the federal law providing that the benefits for female retirees would be *lowered* to the level of male retirees if the law was declared unconstitutional. The plaintiff therefore would receive no additional pension benefit even if he prevailed on the merits. The Court held that he had standing to challenge "discrimination itself," which "can cause serious noneconomic injuries to those persons denied equal treatment solely because of their membership in a disfavored group." The Court reasoned that the severability clause would not prevent it from affording relief that mandated equal treatment between male and female retirees.

Contrast this approach to the Court's holding in *Warth v. Seldin* (1975). The plaintiffs were individuals who wanted to move to Penfield, New York as well as an association of home builders that wanted to build low-income housing there. They alleged that the Town's zoning ordinance excluded low- and middle-income people. The ordinance, for example, allocated only 0.3 percent of the land available for residential construction to multifamily uses such as apartments. This exclusionary zoning precluded most members of minority racial and ethnic groups from residing in Penfield. The plaintiffs raised claims under the First, Ninth, and Fourteenth Amendments. The Court held that "a plaintiff who seeks to challenge exclusionary zoning practices must allege specific, concrete facts demonstrating that the challenged practices harm *him,* and that he personally would benefit in a tangible way from the court's intervention." None of the plaintiffs had standing under this test. The individual plaintiffs failed to show that they would be able to afford to live in Penfield even if the Court afforded them relief. In particular, their ability to do so depended upon whether third parties would build affordable housing in Penfield. The home builders might decide to do so, but they might not even if the plaintiffs prevailed.

Similarly, in *Simon v. Eastern Kentucky Welfare Rights Org.* (1976), plaintiffs challenged an Internal Revenue Service decision that changed the requirements for tax-exempt hospitals. The IRS had required tax-exempt hospitals to provide free care for indigent individuals generally, but then revised its policy to require only free emergency care. Plaintiffs alleged that they had been denied care as a result of this policy change. The Supreme Court held that they did not have standing to sue on causation and redressability grounds. As to causation, it was "purely speculative" whether the IRS's policy change caused the hospitals to deny the plaintiffs medical care. And as to redressability, "the complaint suggest[ed] no substantial likelihood that victory in this suit would result in respondents' receiving the hospital treatment they desire."

In at least one case outside the context of discrimination, the Court has relaxed causation. *Duke Power Co. v. Carolina Env't Study Grp., Inc.* (1978) was a lawsuit filed by an environmental organization, labor union, and individuals who lived near nuclear power plants that were under construction. They challenged the constitutionality of the Price-Anderson Act, which encouraged the construction of nuclear power plants by capping damages for nuclear accidents at $560 million. In their view, the cap violated due process because it was not rationally related to the amount of damage that a nuclear accident could potentially cause. The Court held that the plaintiffs had standing, given the "immediate" adverse effects of construction of the plants. Moreover, the plaintiffs established a "but for" causal connection between the Act and the plants' construction.

Is there a unifying thread to these cases?

3.   The Limitation on Third-Party Standing

A litigant who has pled and proven injury in fact, causation, and redressability has satisfied the constitutional requirements for Article III standing. In addition, a litigant must satisfy prudential requirements for standing unless Congress has enacted a statute waiving those requirements. These judge-made requirements serve some of the same values as the constitutional standing limitations. The prudential limitation on third-party standing, for example, is said to improve judicial decision-making and to protect the rights of people who would be most affected by a judicial decision.

The third-party standing limitation generally prevents a plaintiff with constitutional standing from asserting the rights or interests of third parties. It might seem surprising that a litigant could satisfy the constitutional standing requirements while seeking to litigate based upon someone else's rights. But in a wide range of cases, many of them involving civil rights, third-party standing issues have arisen. For instance, such issues may arise from market transactions where the law seeks to prevent two parties from contracting. In *Barrows v. Jackson* (1953), for example, a White homeowner in Los Angeles was sued after she conveyed property in violation of a racially restrictive covenant that prohibited occupancy "by persons not wholly of the white or Caucasian race." The homeowner's defense was that the racially restrictive covenant could not be enforced by a court. *Shelley v. Kraemer* (1948) had held that equitable enforcement of a racially restrictive covenant would violate Black individuals' right to equal protection under the Fourteenth Amendment. In *Barrows*, the Supreme Court held that a White litigant had third-party standing to raise a Black individual's equal protection right as a defense to enforcement of a racially restrictive covenant through a damages remedy. The Court concluded that its prudential "rule of self-restraint" did not bar standing where the rights-holders were not parties to the covenant and not before the court to challenge it.

Barrows stands for one of several exceptions to the prudential limitation on third-party standing. In particular, it held that a litigant may assert a third party's rights when there are substantial obstacles to the third party asserting their rights and there is reason to believe that the litigant will effectively represent the third party's interests. A second exception exists where there is an identity of interests between the litigant and the third party whose rights the suit would vindicate. The third and final exception is the overbreadth doctrine, which allows a litigant to challenge a statute as violating the constitutional rights of a third party even though the law may constitutionally be applied to the litigant. This doctrine has been repeatedly applied in First Amendment cases, where the Court has been especially concerned about the risk that an unconstitutional speech restriction will chill constitutionally protected speech and evade review.

The following cases illustrate the limitation on third-party standing and the first two exceptions. They concern the constitutional right of a woman to decide whether to terminate a pregnancy—a right described by feminist legal scholars as "crucial to women's control over their own destiny" in view of the "enormous physical, psychological, and socioeconomic consequences of an unwanted child."[20]

---

20. DEBORAH L. RHODE, JUSTICE AND GENDER 208 (1989).

Restrictions on access to health care for pregnancy and abortion affect other people profoundly as well. Health experts estimate that up to 30 percent of transgender men experience unplanned pregnancies and report that transgender individuals face stigma, other forms of discrimination, and ignorance regarding their needs in reproductive health care.[21]

At common law, and in American statues enacted in the 1820s-1840s, abortion was "prohibited only post-quickening" (movement in the uterus, usually around 16 to 20 weeks) and courts "placed high burdens of proof on prosecutors," diminishing enforcement even post-quickening.[22] As Deborah Rhode explained, "[v]arious cultural trends that began in the mid-nineteenth century contributed to a more stringent regulatory climate," including:

> fear[] that any separation of sex from procreation would result in increased venereal disease, psychological "derange[ment]," and social instability. The decline in fertility among the "better" classes [as contraception and abortion medicine developed] coupled with substantial population growth among immigrants, prompted fears of "race suicide." . . . In addition to concerns about the decline of their own class, leaders of the organzied medical profession . . . mobiliz[ed] against abortion [and their efforts] coincided with those of other moral reformers interested in restricting all forms of birth control and obscene materials. In 1873 Congress passed the Comstock Law, which prohibited dissemination of information about abortion or contraception. Over the next several decades, all but one state made abortion a felony, and such statutes remained largely unchanged until the 1960s.

Rhode went on to note that "[t]hese developments were ironic in several respects." Doctors "often justified their campaign in terms of protecting maternal health . . . just as medical advances had reduced the risks of abortion, making it substantially safer than childbirth." She adds that "religious leaders were relatively uninterested in the crusade." Nor, she emphasizes, "did the feminist movement actively support abortion reform despite the obvious significance of the issue for women's independence. To some movement leaders, reproductive issues were 'too narrow . . . and too sordid." For others, they were too threatening. . . . For the vast majority of late-nineteenth century and early-twentieth-century women, marriage and motherhood were the best sources of economic security and social status. Any threat to the family was not worth provoking, particularly if the major gain was to license sexual activity that many women had experienced as duty rather

---

21. *Pregnant Transgender Men at Risk for Depression and Lack of Care, Rutgers Study Finds*, AMERICAN ASSOCIATION FOR THE ADVANCEMENT OF SCIENCE, RUTGER'S TODAY, Aug. 15, 2019 (noting as well that developments in medical technology may soon make it possible for transgender women to bear children with transplanted uteruses), at www.rutgers.edu/news/pregnant-transgender-men-risk-depression-and-lack-care-rutgers-study-finds. *See also* Junoa Obedin-Meyer & Harvey Makadon, *Transgender Men and Pregnancy*, 9 OBSTETRIC MEDICINE 4 (2016) (describing a "gaping chasm between what is taught in health professional schools and postgraduate training programs and the transgender individual's needs").

22. RHODE, *supra* note 20, at 201.

than pleasure." There was commitment to "'voluntary motherhood,'" but "they wished to ensure it through abstinence." By the 1960s, however, with "increase[s] in the number of unwanted pregnancies," shifts in the priorities of the feminist movement, and improvements in medical technology "the rigidity of existing statutes became more apparent."[23]

In 1973, the Supreme Court held in *Roe v. Wade* that bans on abortion infringe on the constitutionally protected right of privacy. In reaching the merits, the Court reasoned that a plaintiff who is no longer pregnant may still maintain a claim because the issue is one "'capable of repetition yet evading review'" and thus not moot. (It ordinarily takes nine months to carry a pregnancy to term, so litigation over the right of access to abortion which takes years would almost always be mooted without the capable of repetition yet evading review exception to mootness.)

Singleton v. Wulff (1976), decided three years after *Roe*, presented a different justiciability question in a case involving the same right. In *Singleton*, physicians rather than patients sued to challenge a state law denying Medicaid coverage for abortions that were not "medically indicated." After *Roe*, and even more so after it was overturned by *Dobbs v. Jackson Womens' Health Org.* (2022), many states sought to limit abortion access through various methods. One of the common pre-*Dobbs* policies was to deny publicly funded healthcare benefits through Medicaid, a federal program administered jointly by the federal government and the states that provides funding for healthcare services for people with low incomes. For many individuals, and disproportionally for low income women and women of color, the denial of public benefits amounted to a denial of the opportunity to exercise their constitutionally-protected right to choose.[24] Physicians who brought suit to enjoin the implementation of state laws denying Medicaid benefits had an obvious financial interest in addition to professional duties of care for their patients. Rather than argue that the right recognized in *Roe* protected their interests directly, they argued that their suits were necessary to ensure that their patients could exercise their constitutionally protected right under *Roe*.

Singleton v. Wulff

428 U.S. 106 (1976)

Justice BLACKMUN delivered the opinion of the Court (Parts I, II-A, and III) together with an opinion (Part II-B), in which Justice BRENNAN, Justice WHITE, and Justice MARSHALL joined.

---

23. *Id.* at 203-07.

24. *See* Dorothy E. Roberts, *The Future of Reproductive Choice for Poor Women and Women of Color,* 14 WOMEN'S RTS. L. REP. 305, 312 (1992) ("[T]he reality for poor women is that these decisions do deny them the choice to terminate their pregnancy."); Christine Dehlendorf et al., *Disparities in Abortion Rates: A Public Health Approach,* 103 AM. J. PUB. HEALTH 1772 (2013); James Trussell et al., *The Impact of Restricting Medicaid Financing for Abortion,* 12 FAM. PLAN. PERSP. 120 (1980).

Like its companions, this case involves a claim of a State's unconstitutional interference with the decision to terminate pregnancy. The particular object of the challenge is a Missouri statute excluding abortions that are not "medically indicated" from the purposes for which Medicaid benefits are available to needy persons. In its present posture, however, the case presents [an] issue[] not going to the merits of this dispute[:] whether the plaintiff-appellees, as physicians who perform nonmedically indicated abortions, have standing to maintain the suit, to which we answer that they do.

I

Missouri participates in the so-called Medicaid program, under which the Federal Government partially underwrites qualifying state plans for medical assistance to the needy. Missouri's plan, which is set out in Mo. Rev. Stat. §§208.151-208.158 (Supp. 1975), includes, in §208.152, a list of 12 categories of medical services that are eligible for Medicaid funding. The last is:

> (12) Family planning services as defined by federal rules and regulations; provided, however, that such family planning services shall not include abortions unless such abortions are medically indicated.

This provision is the subject of the litigation before us.

The suit was filed in the United States District Court for the Eastern District of Missouri by two Missouri licensed physicians. Each plaintiff avers, in an affidavit filed in opposition to a motion to dismiss, that he "has provided, and anticipates providing abortions to welfare patients who are eligible for Medicaid payments." The plaintiffs further allege in their affidavits that all Medicaid applications filed in connection with abortions performed by them have been refused by the defendant, who is the responsible state official, in reliance on the challenged §208.152(12).

The complaint sought a declaration of the statute's invalidity and an injunction against its enforcement. A number of grounds were stated, among them that the statute, "on its face and as applied," is unconstitutionally vague, "[d]eprives plaintiffs of their right to practice medicine according to the highest standards of medical practice"; "[d]eprives plaintiffs' patients of the fundamental right of a woman to determine for herself whether to bear children"; "[i]nfringes upon plaintiffs' right to render and their patients' right to receive safe and adequate medical advice and treatment"; and "[d]eprives plaintiffs and their patients, each in their own classification, of the equal protection of the laws."

II

Although we are not certain that they have been clearly separated in the District Court's and Court of Appeals' opinions, two distinct standing questions are presented. We have distinguished them in prior cases, and they are these: First, whether the plaintiff-respondents allege "injury in fact," that is, a sufficiently concrete interest in the outcome of their suit to make it a case or controversy subject to a federal court's Art. III jurisdiction, and, second, whether, as a prudential matter, the plaintiff-respondents are proper proponents of the particular legal rights on which they base their suit.

A

The first of these questions needs little comment, for there is no doubt now that the respondent-physicians suffer concrete injury from the operation of the challenged statute. Their complaint and affidavits allege that they have performed and will continue to perform operations for which they would be reimbursed under the Medicaid program, were it not for the limitation of reimbursable abortions to those that are "medically indicated." If the physicians prevail in their suit to remove this limitation, they will benefit, for they will then receive payment for the abortions. The State (and Federal Government) will be out of pocket by the amount of the payments. The relationship between the parties is classically adverse, and there clearly exists between them a case or controversy in the constitutional sense.

B

The question of what rights the doctors may assert in seeking to resolve that controversy is more difficult. The Court of Appeals adverted to what it perceived to be the doctor's own "constitutional rights to practice medicine." We have no occasion to decide whether such rights exist. Assuming that they do, the doctors, of course, can assert them. It appears, however, that the Court of Appeals also accorded the doctors standing to assert, and indeed granted them relief based partly upon, the rights of their patients. We must decide whether this assertion of *jus tertii* was a proper one.

Federal courts must hesitate before resolving a controversy, even one within their constitutional power to resolve, on the basis of the rights of third persons not parties to the litigation. The reasons are two. First, the courts should not adjudicate such rights unnecessarily, and it may be that in fact the holders of those rights either do not wish to assert them, or will be able to enjoy them regardless of whether the in-court litigant is successful or not. *See Ashwander v. TVA* (1936) (Brandeis, J., concurring). Second, third parties themselves usually will be the best proponents of their own rights. The courts depend on effective advocacy, and therefore should prefer to construe legal rights only when the most effective advocates of those rights are before them. The holders of the rights may have a like preference, to the extent they will be bound by the courts' decisions under the doctrine of *stare decisis.* These two considerations underlie the Court's general rule: "Ordinarily, one may not claim standing in this Court to vindicate the constitutional rights of some third party." *Barrows v. Jackson* (1953).

Like any general rule, however, this one should not be applied where its underlying justifications are absent. With this in mind, the Court has looked primarily to two factual elements to determine whether the rule should apply in a particular case. The first is the relationship of the litigant to the person whose right he seeks to assert. If the enjoyment of the right is inextricably bound up with the activity the litigant wishes to pursue, the court at least can be sure that its construction of the right is not unnecessary in the sense that the right's enjoyment will be unaffected by the outcome of the suit. Furthermore, the relationship between the litigant and the third party may be such that the former is fully, or very nearly, as effective a proponent of the right as the latter. Thus in *Griswold v. Connecticut* (1965), where two persons had been convicted of giving advice on contraception, the Court permitted the defendants, one of whom was a licensed physician, to assert the privacy rights of the married persons whom they advised. The Court pointed to the "confidential" nature of the relationship between the defendants and the married persons, and reasoned that the rights of the latter were "likely to be diluted or adversely affected" if they could not be asserted in such a case. *Id.*, at 481. *See also Eisenstadt v. Baird* (1972) (stressing "advocate" relationship and "impact of the litigation on the third-party interests"); *Barrows v. Jackson* (1953) (owner of real estate subject to racial covenant granted standing to challenge such covenant in part because she was "the one in whose charge and keeping repose[d] the power to continue to use her property to discriminate or to discontinue such use"). A doctor-patient relationship similar to that in *Griswold* existed in *Doe v. Bolton* (1973), where the Court also permitted physicians to assert the rights of their patients. Indeed, since that right was the right to an abortion, *Doe* would flatly control the instant case were it not for the fact that there the physicians were seeking protection from possible criminal prosecution.

The other factual element to which the Court has looked is the ability of the third party to assert his own right. Even where the relationship is close, the reasons for requiring persons to assert their own rights will generally still apply. If there is some genuine obstacle to such assertion, however, the third party's absence from court loses its tendency to suggest that his right is not truly at stake, or truly important to him, and the party who is in court becomes by default the right's best available proponent. Thus, in *NAACP v. Alabama* (1958), the Court held that the National Association for the Advancement of Colored People, in resisting a court order that it divulge the names of its members, could assert the First and Fourteenth Amendments rights of those members to remain anonymous. The Court reasoned that "[t]o require that [the right] be claimed by the members themselves would result in nullification of the right at the very moment of its assertion."

Application of these principles to the present case quickly yields its proper result. The closeness of the relationship is patent, as it was in *Griswold* and in *Doe*. A woman cannot safely secure an abortion without the aid of a physician, and an impecunious woman cannot easily secure an abortion without the physician's being paid by the State. The woman's exercise of her right to an abortion, whatever its dimension, is therefore necessarily at stake here. Moreover, the constitutionally protected abortion decision is one in which the physician is intimately involved. Aside from the woman herself, therefore, the physician is uniquely qualified to litigate the constitutionality of the State's interference with, or discrimination against, that decision.

As to the woman's assertion of her own rights, there are several obstacles. For one thing, she may be chilled from such assertion by a desire to protect the very privacy of her decision from the publicity of a court suit. A second obstacle is the imminent mootness, at least in the technical sense, of any individual woman's claim. Only a few months, at the most, after the maturing of the decision to undergo an abortion, her right thereto will have been irrevocably lost, assuming, as it seems fair to assume, that unless the impecunious woman can establish Medicaid eligibility she must forgo abortion. It is true that these obstacles are not insurmountable. Suit may be brought under a pseudonym, as so frequently has been done. A woman who is no longer pregnant may nonetheless retain the right to litigate the point because it is "'capable of repetition yet evading review.'" *Roe v. Wade* (1973). And it may be that a class could be assembled, whose fluid membership always included some women with live claims. But if the assertion of the right is to be "representative" to such an extent anyway, there seems little loss in terms of effective advocacy from allowing its assertion by a physician.

For these reasons, we conclude that it generally is appropriate to allow a physician to assert the rights of women patients as against governmental interference with the abortion decision, and we decline to restrict our holding to that effect in *Doe* to its purely criminal context.

Justice STEVENS, concurring in part.

In this case (1) the plaintiff-physicians have a financial stake in the outcome of the litigation, and (2) they claim that the statute impairs their own constitutional rights. They therefore clearly have standing to bring this action.

Because these two facts are present, I agree that the analysis in Part II-B of MR. JUSTICE BLACKMUN's opinion provides an adequate basis for considering the arguments based on the effect of the statute on the constitutional rights of their patients. Because I am not sure whether the analysis in Part II-B would, or should, sustain the doctors' standing, apart from those two facts, I join only Parts I, II-A, and III of the Court's opinion.

Justice POWELL, with whom THE CHIEF JUSTICE, Justice STEWART, and Justice REHNQUIST join, concurring in part and dissenting in part.

The Court holds that the respondents have standing to bring this suit and to assert their own constitutional rights, if any, in an attack on Mo. Rev. Stat. §208.152(12) (Supp. 1975). The Court also holds that the Court of Appeals erred in proceeding to the merits of respondents' challenge. I agree with both of these holdings and therefore concur in Parts I, II-A, and III of Justice Blackmun's opinion, as well as in the first four sentences of Part II-B.

The Court further holds that after remand to the District Court the respondents may assert, in addition to their own rights, the constitutional rights of their patients who would be eligible for Medicaid assistance in obtaining elective abortions but for the exclusion of such abortions in §208.152(12). I dissent from this holding.

I

As the Court notes, respondents by complaint and affidavit established their Art. III standing to invoke the judicial power of the District Court. They have performed abortions for which Missouri's Medicaid system would compensate them directly if the challenged statutory section did not preclude it. Respondents allege an intention to continue to perform such abortions, and that the statute deprives them of compensation. These arguments, if proved, would give respondents a personal stake in the controversy over the statute's constitutionality.

II

[The prudential standing] inquiry is a matter of "judicial self-governance." *Warth v. Selding* (1975). The usual—and wise—stance of the federal courts when policing their own exercise of power in this manner is one of cautious reserve. *See generally Ashwander v. TVA* (1936) (Brandeis, J., concurring).

The plurality acknowledges this general rule, but identifies "two factual elements"—thought to be derived from prior cases—that justify the adjudication of the asserted third-party rights: (i) obstacles to the assertion by the third party of her own rights, and (ii) the existence of some "relationship" such as the one between physician and patient. In my view these factors do not justify allowing these physicians to assert their patients' rights.

A

Our prior decisions are enlightening. . . .

The plurality purports to derive from these cases the principle that a party may assert another's rights if there is "some genuine obstacle" to the third party's own litigation. But this understates the teaching of those cases: On their facts they indicate that such an assertion is proper, not when there is merely some "obstacle" to the rightholder's own litigation, but when such litigation is in all practicable terms impossible. Thus, in its framing of this principle, the plurality has gone far beyond our major precedents.

Moreover, on the plurality's own statement of this principle and on its own discussion of the facts, the litigation of third-party rights cannot be justified in this case. The plurality virtually concedes, as it must, that the two alleged "obstacles" to the women's assertion of their rights are chimerical. Our docket regularly contains cases in which women, using pseudonyms, challenge statutes that allegedly infringe their right to exercise the abortion decision. Nor is there basis for the "obstacle" of incipient mootness when the plurality itself quotes from the portion of *Roe v. Wade* (1973), that shows no such obstacle exists. . . . Rather than being a logical descendant of *Barrows, NAACP,* and *Eisenstadt,* this case is much closer to *Warth v. Seldin,* in which taxpayers were refused leave to assert the constitutional rights of low-income persons in part because there was no obstacle to those low-income persons' asserting their own rights in a proper case.

B

The plurality places primary reliance on a second element, the existence of a "confidential relationship" between the rightholder and the party seeking to assert her rights.

With all respect, I do not read the[] cases [cited by the plurality] as merging the physician and his patient for constitutional purposes. The principle they support turns not upon the confidential nature of a physician-patient relationship but upon the nature of the State's impact upon that relationship. In each instance the State directly interdicted the normal functioning of the physician-patient relationship by criminalizing certain procedures. In the circumstances of direct interference, I agree that one party to the relationship should be permitted to assert the constitutional rights of the other, for a judicial rule of self-restraint should not preclude an attack on a State's proscription of constitutionally protected activity. But Missouri has not directly interfered with the abortion decision—neither the physicians nor their patients are forbidden to engage in the procedure. The only impact of §208.152(12) is that, because of the way Missouri chose to structure its Medicaid payments, it causes these doctors financial detriment. This affords them Art. III standing because they aver injury in fact, but it does not justify abandonment of the salutary rule against assertion of third-party rights.

C

The physicians have offered no special reason for allowing them to assert their patients' rights in an attack on this welfare statute, and I can think of none. Moreover, there are persuasive reasons not to permit them to do so. It seems wholly inappropriate, as a matter of judicial self-governance, for a court to reach unnecessarily to decide a difficult constitutional issue in a case in which nothing more is at stake than remuneration for professional services. And second, this case may well set a precedent that will prove difficult to cabin. No reason immediately comes to mind, after today's holding, why any provider of services should be denied standing to assert his client's or customer's constitutional rights, if any, in an attack on a welfare statute that excludes from coverage his particular transaction.

Putting it differently, the Court's holding invites litigation by those who perhaps have the least legitimate ground for seeking to assert the rights of third parties. Before today I certainly would not have thought that an interest in being compensated for professional services, without more, would be deemed a sufficiently compelling reason to justify departing from a rule of restraint that well serves society and our judicial system. The Court quite recently stated, with respect to the rule against assertion of third-party rights as well as certain other doctrines of judicial self-restraint, that "[t]hese principles rest on more than the fussiness of judges. They reflect the conviction that under our constitutional system courts are not roving commissions assigned to pass judgment on the validity of the Nation's laws. . . . Constitutional judgments . . . are justified only out of the necessity of adjudicating rights in particular cases between the litigants brought before the Court." *Broadrick v. Oklahoma* (1973). Today's holding threatens to make just such "roving commissions" of the federal courts.

* * *

As *Singleton* shows, physicians may have third-party standing to raise the rights of their patients based upon an identity of interests between them. There are many such cases involving contraceptive and abortion access.

The next case, *June Medical Services, LLC v. Russo* (2020), presented a challenge to these precedents. States began to enact abortion laws with the purported aim of protecting women's health. One example was legislation requiring abortion providers to have active admitting privileges at a hospital within a particular distance of their offices. In some states, the effect of this legislation was to significantly restrict, or even eliminate, individuals' access to abortion providers. In Louisiana, the state whose admitting privileges law was challenged in *June Medical Services*, the effect was to cut the number of available providers in half. The effect was particularly acute on women with low or no incomes and thus no means to travel out of state for abortions. States claimed that admitting privileges requirements would protect women, while physicians, drawing on the standard set out in *Planned Parenthood v. Casey* (1992), sought to challenge them as "unduly burdening" the constitutional right to choose to terminate a pregnancy. States argued that physicians could not invoke their patients' rights under *Casey* to challenge admitting privileges requirements because the physicians' interests in limiting their compliance obligations conflicted with their patients' interests in their own health. As you read the decision, consider the interaction between the justices' analysis of the justiciability issue and their different senses of the merits of the constitutional right at stake, mindful that two years later the Court would reverse its holdings in *Roe* and *Casey* in *Dobbs v. Jackson Women's Health Org.* (2022).

June Medical Services, LLC v. Russo

140 S. Ct. 2103 (2020)

Justice BREYER announced the judgment of the Court and delivered an opinion, in which Justice GINSBURG, Justice SOTOMAYOR, and Justice KAGAN joined.

In *Whole Woman's Health v. Hellerstedt* (2016), we held that "'[u]nnecessary health regulations that have the purpose or effect of presenting a substantial obstacle to a woman seeking an abortion impose an undue burden on the right'" and are therefore "constitutionally invalid." We explained that this standard requires courts independently to review the legislative findings upon which an abortion-related statute rests and to weigh the law's "asserted benefits against the burdens" it imposes on abortion access.

The Texas statute at issue in *Whole Woman's Health* required abortion providers to hold "'active admitting privileges at a hospital'" within 30 miles of the place where they perform abortions. In this case, we consider the constitutionality of a Louisiana statute, Act 620, that is almost word-for-word identical to Texas' admitting-privileges law. As in *Whole Woman's Health*, the District Court found that the statute offers no significant health benefit. It found that conditions on admitting privileges common to hospitals throughout the State have made and will continue to make it impossible for abortion providers to obtain conforming privileges for reasons that have nothing to do with the State's asserted interests in promoting women's health and safety. And it found that this inability places a substantial obstacle in the path of women seeking an abortion. As in *Whole Woman's Health*, the substantial obstacle the Act imposes, and the absence of any health-related benefit, led the District Court to conclude that the law imposes an undue burden and is therefore unconstitutional.

The Court of Appeals agreed with the District Court's interpretation of the standards we have said apply to regulations on abortion. It thought, however, that the District Court was mistaken on the facts. We disagree. We have examined the extensive record carefully and conclude that it supports the District Court's findings of fact. Those findings mirror those made in *Whole Woman's Health* in every relevant respect and require the same result. We consequently hold that the Louisiana statute is unconstitutional.

We initially consider a procedural argument that the State raised for the first time in its cross-petition for certiorari. The plaintiff abortion providers and clinics in this case have challenged Act 620 on the ground that it infringes their patients' rights to access an abortion. The State contends that the proper parties to assert these rights are the patients themselves. We think that the State has waived that argument.

The State's argument rests on the rule that a party cannot ordinarily "'rest his claim to relief on the legal rights or interests of third parties.'" *Kowalski v. Tesmer*

(2004) (quoting *Warth v. Seldin* (1975)). This rule is "prudential." It does not involve the Constitution's "case-or-controversy requirement." And so, we have explained, it can be forfeited or waived.

The State's memorandum opposing the plaintiffs' TRO request urged the District Court to proceed swiftly to the merits of the plaintiffs' undue-burden claim. It argued that there was "no question that the physicians had standing to contest" Act 620. And it told the District Court that the Fifth Circuit had found that doctors challenging Texas' "identical" law "had third-party standing to assert their patients' rights." Noting that the Texas law had "already been upheld," the State asserted that it had "a keen interest in removing any cloud upon the validity of its law." It insisted that this suit was "the proper vehicle to do so." The State did not mention its current objection until it filed its cross-petition—more than five years after it argued that the plaintiffs' standing was beyond question.

The State's unmistakable concession of standing as part of its effort to obtain a quick decision from the District Court on the merits of the plaintiffs' undue-burden claims bars our consideration of it here.

The State refers to the Fifth Circuit's finding of standing in *Whole Woman's Health* as an excuse for its concession. But the standing argument the State makes here rests on reasons that it tells us are specific to abortion providers *in Louisiana*. We are not persuaded that the State could have thought it was precluded from making those arguments by a decision with respect to *Texas* doctors.

And even if the State had merely forfeited its objection by failing to raise it at any point over the last five years, we would not now undo all that has come before on that basis. What we said some 45 years ago in *Craig v. Boren* (1976) applies equally today: "[A] decision by us to forgo consideration of the constitutional merits"—after "the parties have sought or at least have never resisted an authoritative constitutional determination" in the courts below—"in order to await the initiation of a new challenge to the statute by injured third parties would be impermissibly to foster repetitive and time-consuming litigation under the guise of caution and prudence."

In any event, the rule the State invokes is hardly absolute. We have long permitted abortion providers to invoke the rights of their actual or potential patients in challenges to abortion-related regulations. And we have generally permitted plaintiffs to assert third-party rights in cases where the "'enforcement of the challenged restriction *against the litigant* would result indirectly in the violation of third parties' rights.'" *Kowalski v. Tesmer* (2004). In such cases, we have explained, "the obvious claimant" and "the least awkward challenger" is the party upon whom the challenged statute imposes "legal duties and disabilities." *Craig v. Boren* (1976).

The case before us lies at the intersection of these two lines of precedent. The plaintiffs are abortion providers challenging a law that regulates their conduct. The "threatened imposition of governmental sanctions" for noncompliance eliminates any risk that their claims are abstract or hypothetical. *Craig v. Boren* (1976). That threat also assures us that the plaintiffs have every incentive to "resist efforts at restricting their operations by acting as advocates of the rights of third parties who seek access to their market or function." *Id.* And, as the parties who must actually go through the process of applying for and maintaining admitting privileges, they are far better positioned than their patients to address the burdens of compliance.

Our dissenting colleagues suggest that this case is different because the plaintiffs have challenged a law ostensibly enacted to protect the women whose rights they are asserting. But that is a common feature of cases in which we have found third-party standing. The restriction on sales of 3.2% beer to young men challenged by a drive-through convenience store in *Craig* was defended on "public health and safety grounds," including the premise that young men were particularly susceptible to driving while intoxicated.

Nor is this the first abortion case to address provider standing to challenge regulations said to protect women. Both the hospitalization requirement in *City of Akron v. Akron Center for Reproductive Health* (1983), and the hospital-accreditation requirement in *Doe v. Bolton* (1973), were defended as health and safety regulations. And the ban on saline amniocentesis in *Planned Parenthood of Central Missouri v. Danforth* (1976) was based on the legislative finding "that the technique is deleterious to maternal health."

In short, the State's strategic waiver and a long line of well-established precedents foreclose its belated challenge to the plaintiffs' standing. We consequently proceed to consider the merits of the plaintiffs' claims.

[On the merits, the Court held that] the District Court's significant factual findings—both as to burdens and as to benefits—have ample evidentiary support. None is "clearly erroneous." Given the facts found, we must also uphold the District Court's related factual and legal determinations. These include its determination that Louisiana's law poses a "substantial obstacle" to women seeking an abortion; its determination that the law offers no significant health-related benefits; and its determination that the law consequently imposes an "undue burden" on a woman's constitutional right to choose to have an abortion. We also agree with its ultimate legal conclusion that, in light of these findings and our precedents, Act 620 violates the Constitution.

Chief Justice ROBERTS, concurring in the judgment.

I joined the dissent in *Whole Woman's Health* and continue to believe that the case was wrongly decided. The question today however is not whether *Whole Woman's Health* was right or wrong, but whether to adhere to it in deciding the present case.

The legal doctrine of *stare decisis* requires us, absent special circumstances, to treat like cases alike. The Louisiana law imposes a burden on access to abortion just as severe as that imposed by the Texas law, for the same reasons. Therefore Louisiana's law cannot stand under our precedents.

Justice THOMAS, dissenting.

Today a majority of the Court perpetuates its ill-founded abortion jurisprudence by enjoining a perfectly legitimate state law and doing so without jurisdiction. As is often the case with legal challenges to abortion regulations, this suit was brought by abortionists and abortion clinics. Their sole claim before this Court is that Louisiana's law violates the purported substantive due process right of a woman to abort her unborn child. But they concede that this right does not belong to them, and they seek to vindicate no private rights of their own. Under a proper understanding of Article III, these plaintiffs lack standing to invoke our jurisdiction.

The plurality and the Chief Justice ultimately cast aside this jurisdictional barrier to conclude that Louisiana's law is unconstitutional under our precedents. But those decisions created the right to abortion out of whole cloth, without a shred of support from the Constitution's text. Our abortion precedents are grievously wrong and should be overruled. Because we have neither jurisdiction nor constitutional authority to declare Louisiana's duly enacted law unconstitutional, I respectfully dissent.

I

For most of its history, this Court maintained that private parties could not bring suit to vindicate the constitutional rights of individuals who are not before the Court. But in the 20th century, the Court began to deviate from this traditional rule against third-party standing. From these deviations emerged our prudential third-party standing doctrine, which allows litigants to vicariously assert the constitutional rights of others when "the party asserting the right has a 'close' relationship with the person who possesses the right" and "there is a 'hindrance' to the possessor's ability to protect his own interests." *Kowalski v. Tesmer* (2004).

The plurality feints toward this doctrine, claiming that third-party standing for abortionists is well settled by our precedents. But, ultimately, it dodges the question, claiming that Louisiana's standing challenge was waived below. Both assertions are erroneous.

A

As an initial matter, this Court has never provided a coherent explanation for why the rule against third-party standing is properly characterized as prudential. Many cases reciting this claim rely on the Court's decision in *Barrows v. Jackson* (1953), which stated that the rule against third-party standing is a "rule of self-restraint" "[a]part from the jurisdictional requirement" of Article III. But *Barrows* provides no reasoning to support that distinction and even admits that the rule against third-party standing is "not always clearly distinguished from the constitutional limitation[s]" on standing.

It is especially puzzling that a majority of the Court insists on continuing to treat the rule against third-party standing as prudential when our recent decision in *Lexmark Int'l, Inc. v. Static Control Components, Inc.* (2014), questioned the validity of our prudential standing doctrine more generally. In that case, we acknowledged that requiring a litigant who has Article III standing to also demonstrate "prudential standing" is inconsistent "with our recent reaffirmation of the principle that 'a federal court's "obligation" to hear and decide' cases within its jurisdiction 'is "virtually unflagging."'" The Court therefore suggested that the "prudential" label for these doctrines was "inapt." As an example, it noted that the Court previously considered the rule against generalized grievances to be "prudential" but now recognizes that rule to be a part of Article III's case-or-controversy requirement. The Court specifically questioned the prudential label for the rule against third-party standing, but because *Lexmark* did not involve any questions of third-party standing, the Court stated that "consideration of that doctrine's proper place in the standing firmament [could] await another day."

The Court's previous statements on the rule against third-party standing have long suggested that the "proper place" for that rule is in Article III's case-or-controversy requirement.

And most recently, in *Spokeo, Inc. v. Robins* (2016), the Court appeared to incorporate the rule against third-party standing into its understanding of Article III's injury-in-fact requirement. There, the Court stated that to establish an injury-in-fact a plaintiff must "show that he or she suffered 'an invasion of a legally protected interest' that is 'concrete and particularized' and 'actual or imminent, not conjectural or hypothetical.'" The Court further explained that whether a plaintiff "alleges that [the defendant] violated *his* statutory rights" rather than "the statutory rights of other people" was a question of "particularization" for an Article III injury. It is hard to reconcile this language in *Spokeo* with the plurality's assertion that third-party standing is permitted under Article III.

B

A brief historical examination of Article III's case-or-controversy requirement confirms what our recent decisions suggest.

The limitations imposed on suits at common law varied based on the type of right the plaintiff sought to vindicate. The rights adjudicated by common-law courts generally fell into one of two categories: public or private. Public rights are those "owed 'to the whole community . . . in its social aggregate capacity.'" *Spokeo* (Thomas, J., concurring) (quoting 4 W. Blackstone, Commentaries *5). Private rights, on the other hand, are those "'belonging to individuals, considered as individuals.'" *Id.* (quoting 3 Blackstone, Commentaries *2).

When a plaintiff sought to vindicate a private right, "courts historically presumed that the plaintiff suffered a *de facto* injury merely from having his personal, legal rights invaded." *Spokeo* (Thomas, J., concurring). But a plaintiff generally "need[ed] to have a private interest of his or her own to litigate; otherwise, no sufficient interest [was] at stake on the plaintiff's side, and the clash of interests necessary for a 'Case' or 'Controversy' [did] not exist." Thus, 19th-century judges uniformly refused to "listen to an objection made to the constitutionality of an act by a party whose rights" were not at issue. *Clark v. Kansas City* (1900).

Moreover, it was not enough for a plaintiff to allege *damnum*—i.e., real-world damages or practical injury—if the law he was challenging did not violate a legally protected interest of his own. At common law, this sort of "factual harm without a legal injury was *damnum absque injuria* and provided no basis for relief." Hessick, Standing, Injury in Fact, and Private Rights, 93 Cornell L. Rev. 275, 280-281 (2008). In the 18th century, many common-law courts ceased requiring *damnum* in suits alleging violations of private rights. But they continued to require legal injury, adhering to the "obvious" and "ancient maxim" that one's real-world damages alone cannot "lay the foundation of an action." *Parker v. Griswold* (1846). Thus, a plaintiff had to assert "[a]n injury, [which,] legally speaking, consists of a wrong done to a person, or, in other words, a violation of his right."

This brief historical review demonstrates that third-party standing is inconsistent with the case-or-controversy requirement of Article III. When a private plaintiff seeks to vindicate someone else's legal injury, he has no private right of his own genuinely at stake in the litigation. Even if the plaintiff has suffered damages as a result of another's legal injury, he has no standing to challenge a law that does not violate his own private rights.

C

Applying these principles to the case at hand, plaintiffs lack standing under Article III and we, in turn, lack jurisdiction to decide these cases.

1

Contrary to the plurality's assertion otherwise, abortionists' standing to assert the putative rights of their clients has not been settled by our precedents. . . . The first—and only—time the Court squarely addressed this question with a reasoned decision was in *Singleton v. Wulff* (1976). In that case, a fractured Court concluded that two abortionists had standing to challenge a State's refusal to provide Medicaid reimbursements for abortions. . . . Because Justice Stevens' opinion "concurred in the judgmen[t] on the narrowest grounds," it is the controlling opinion regarding abortionists' third-party standing. *Marks v. United States* (1977).

To the extent Justice Stevens' opinion could be read as concluding that abortionists have standing to vicariously assert their clients' rights so long as the abortionists establish standing on their own legal claims, his position has been abrogated by this Court's more recent decisions, which have "confirm[ed] that a plaintiff must demonstrate standing for each claim he seeks to press." *DaimlerChrysler Corp. v. Cuno* (2006). But more importantly, Justice Stevens' opinion does not support the abortionists in these cases, because his opinion rested on case-specific facts not implicated here—namely, the fact that the abortionists would directly receive Medicaid payments from the defendant agency if they prevailed and that they asserted violations of *their own* constitutional rights. In these cases, there is no dispute that the abortionists' sole claim before this Court is that Louisiana's law violates the purported substantive due process rights *of their clients*.

2

Under a proper understanding of Article III, plaintiffs lack standing. [The] purported substantive due process right to abort an unborn child . . . is an individual right that is inherently personal. Because this right belongs to the woman making that choice, not to those who provide abortions, plaintiffs cannot establish a personal legal injury by asserting that this right has been violated.

The only injury asserted by plaintiffs in this suit is the possibility of facing criminal sanctions if the abortionists conduct abortions without admitting privileges in violation of the law. But plaintiffs do not claim any right to provide abortions, nor do they contest that the State has authority to regulate such procedures. They have therefore demonstrated only real-world damages (or more accurately, the *possibility* of real-world damages), but no legal injury, or "invasion of a legally protected interest," that belongs to them. *Spokeo v. Robins* (2016). Thus, under a proper understanding of Article III, plaintiffs lack standing and, consequently, this Court lacks jurisdiction.

Justice ALITO, with whom Justice GORSUCH joins, with whom Justice THOMAS joins except as to Parts III-C and IV-F, and with whom Justice KAVANAUGH joins as to Parts I, II, and III, dissenting.

The plurality holds that Louisiana waived any objection to June Medical's third-party standing, but that is a misreading of the record. The plurality relies on a passing statement in a brief filed by the State in District Court in connection with the plaintiffs' request for a temporary restraining order, but the statement is simply an accurate statement of circuit precedent on the standing of abortion providers. It does not constitute a waiver.

It is true that Louisiana did not affirmatively make the third-party standing argument until it filed its cross-petition for certiorari, but "[w]e may make exceptions to our general approach to claims not raised below." *Polar Tankers, Inc. v. City of Valdez* (2009).

In this case, no one disputes that the Fifth Circuit passed on the issue of third-party standing in Louisiana's appeal from the District Court's entry of a preliminary injunction. And when we granted the State's cross-petition, we took up this question and received briefing and argument on it.

We have a strong reason to decide the question of third-party standing because it implicates the integrity of future proceedings that should occur in this case. This case should be remanded for a new trial, and we should not allow that to occur without a proper plaintiff.

This case features a blatant conflict of interest between an abortion provider and its patients. Like any other regulated entity, an abortion provider has a financial interest in avoiding burdensome regulations such as Act 620's admitting privileges requirement. Applying for privileges takes time and energy, and maintaining privileges may impose additional burdens. Women seeking abortions, on the other hand, have an interest in the preservation of regulations that protect their health. The conflict inherent in such a situation is glaring.

Some may not see the conflict in this case because they are convinced that the admitting privileges requirement does nothing to promote safety and is really just a ploy. But an abortion provider's ability to assert the rights of women when it challenges ostensible safety regulations should not turn on the merits of its claim.

The problem with the rule that the majority embraces is highlighted if we consider challenges to other safety regulations. Suppose, for example, that a clinic in a State that allows certified non-physicians to perform abortions claims that the State's certification requirements are too onerous and that they imperil the clinic's continued operation. Should the clinic be able to assert the rights of women in attacking this regulation, which the state lawmakers thought was important to protect women's health?

When an abortion regulation is enacted for the asserted purpose of protecting the health of women, an abortion provider seeking to strike down that law should not be able to rely on the constitutional rights of women. Like any other party unhappy with burdensome regulation, the provider should be limited to its own rights.

This rule is supported by precedent and follows from general principles regarding conflicts of interest. We have already held that third-party standing is not appropriate where there is a potential conflict of interest between the plaintiff and the third party. In *Elk Grove Unified School District v. Newdow* (2004), a potential conflict of interest between the plaintiff and his daughter arose on appeal. The father had asserted that his daughter had a constitutional right not to hear others recite the words "'under God'" when the pledge of allegiance was recited at her public school, but the child's mother maintained that her daughter had "no objection either to reciting or hearing" the full pledge. The Court held that the father lacked prudential standing, because "the interests of this parent and this child are not parallel and, indeed, are potentially in conflict."

The conflict of interest inherent in a case like this is reason enough to reject third-party standing, and our standard rules on third-party standing provide a second, independent reason. As a general rule, a plaintiff "must assert his own legal rights and interests, and cannot rest his claim to relief on the legal rights or interests of third parties." *Warth v. Seldin* (1975). We have recognized a "limited" exception to this rule, but in order to qualify, a litigant must demonstrate (1) closeness to the third party and (2) a hindrance to the third party's ability to bring suit.

The record shows that abortion providers cannot satisfy either prong of this test. First, a woman who obtains an abortion typically does not develop a close relationship with the doctor who performs the procedure. On the contrary, their relationship is generally brief and very limited. For these reasons, the first prong of the third-party standing rule cannot be met.

Nor can the second, which requires that there be a hindrance to the ability of the third party to bring suit. The plurality opinion in *Singleton v. Wulff* (1976), found that women seeking abortions were hindered from bringing suit, but the reasoning in that opinion is hard to defend. The opinion identified two purported obstacles to suits by women wishing to obtain abortions — the women's desire to protect their privacy and the prospect of mootness. But as Justice Powell said at the time, these "alleged 'obstacles' . . . are chimerical."

First, a woman who challenges an abortion restriction can sue under a pseudonym, and many have done so. Other precautions may be taken during the course of litigation to avoid revealing their identities. And there is little reason to think that a woman who challenges an abortion restriction will have to pay for counsel.

Second, if a woman seeking an abortion brings suit, her claim will survive the end of her pregnancy under the capable-of-repetition-yet-evading-review exception to mootness. To be sure, when the pregnancy terminates, an individual plaintiff's immediate interest in prosecuting the case may diminish. But this is generally true whenever the capable-of-repetition-yet-evading-review exception applies.

The *Singleton* plurality opinion is the only opinion in which any Members of this Court have ever attempted to justify third-party standing for abortion providers, and judged on its own merits, the opinion is thoroughly unconvincing.

As The Chief Justice points out, *stare decisis* generally counsels adherence to precedent, and in deciding whether to overrule a prior decision, we consider factors beyond the strength of the precedent's reasoning. But here, such factors weigh in favor of overruling.

Reexamination of a precedent may be appropriate when it is an "outlier" and its reasoning cannot be reconciled with other established precedents, and that is true of the rule allowing abortion providers to assert their patients' rights. The parties have not brought to our attention any other situation in which a party is allowed to invoke the right of a third party with blatantly adverse interests. The rule that the majority applies here is an abortion-only rule.

* * *

Was *June Medical Services* a true third-party standing case? The state law at issue *directly* regulated the doctors who were plaintiffs in the case, not the patients whom they serve. The criminal penalties the statute imposed (prison time and fines) applied to doctors who performed abortions without the required admitting privileges. The statutory penalties also included license revocation, fines, and civil liability for offending clinics. When a state imposes penalties on someone for helping others exercise their constitutional rights, the person who faces prosecution and other penalties surely has standing in relation to the injury those penalties could cause.[25] How important is the asserted conflict of interest the law creates between doctors and women seeking abortion access? How closely must the interests of the constitutional right holder and the plaintiff align?

NOTES ON OVERBREADTH DOCTRINE

In *Singleton* and *June Medical,* the Justices disagreed about the scope and application of the first two exceptions to the limitation on third-party standing. The third exception was not at issue. The overbreadth doctrine, which the Supreme Court has applied in First Amendment cases, permits a litigant with Article III standing to challenge a statute on constitutional grounds even when the government may constitutionally apply the statute to that litigant. As the Court has summarized the doctrine, "[g]iven a case or controversy, a litigant whose own activities are unprotected may nevertheless challenge a statute by showing that it substantially abridges the First Amendment rights of other parties not before the court." *Village of Schaumburg v. Citizens for a Better Environment* (1980). The following cases illustrate this doctrine and its limitations.

In *Broadrick v. Oklahoma* (1973), the plaintiffs were three employees of an Oklahoma state commission who argued that the state had unconstitutionally regulated the political speech of state employees. The challenged law prohibited some state employees from "directly or indirectly, solicit[ing], receiv[ing], or in any manner be[ing] concerned in soliciting or receiving any assessment . . . or contribution for any political organization, candidacy or other political purpose." In addition, the law prohibited the covered employees from being "a member of any national, state or local committee of a political party, or an officer or member of a committee of a partisan political club, or candidate for nomination or election to any paid public office." Finally, the law prohibited covered employees from "tak[ing] part in the management or affairs of any political party or in any political campaign," but did not prohibit employees from voting or expressing their opinions about an election. The plaintiffs argued that these provisions were unconstitutionally vague and overbroad, arguing that the law reached clearly protected conduct such as displaying bumper stickers on one's car. But that is not what the plaintiffs themselves had done. The State Personnel Board had alleged that they lobbied their coworkers and solicited money for their boss's campaign for re-election to a position on a state agency. The Court held that the plaintiffs could not invoke the overbreadth doctrine to have the state law struck down

---

25. *See* Henry Paul Monaghan, *Third Party Standing,* 84 COLUM. L. REV. 227 (1984).

on its face. Applying this doctrine in a facial challenge is, the Court reasoned, "manifestly strong medicine." This medicine should typically be limited where "the otherwise unprotected behavior that it forbids the State to sanction moves from 'pure speech' toward conduct." Moreover, the Court held, "particularly where conduct and not merely speech is involved, . . . the overbreadth of a statute must not only be real, but substantial as well, judged in relation to the statute's plainly legitimate sweep." Thus, the Court recognized that the challenged overbreadth must be "substantial." It concluded that the challenged Oklahoma law was not substantially overbroad because it was "even-handed and neutral" in its aims, had a wide range of constitutional applications, and at most reached some instances of "arguably protected conduct."

In *Village of Schaumburg v. Citizens for a Better Environment* (1980), the plaintiff charity challenged a municipal ordinance prohibiting charities from soliciting contributions door-to-door or on public streets if the charities did not use at least 75 percent of their receipts for charitable purposes. The Court concluded that the First Amendment protects charitable solicitations within residential neighborhoods. The overbreadth doctrine does not apply to commercial speech, but this case involved charitable speech. The Village argued that it could validly apply its ordinance to the plaintiff organization, which allegedly spent more than 75 percent of its receipts "for the benefit of its employees," rather than for charitable purposes. The Court applied the overbreadth doctrine, holding that it could strike down the ordinance on its face if it prohibited "canvassing by a substantial category of charities to which the 75-percent limitation could not be [constitutionally] applied . . . , even if there was no demonstration that the CBE itself was one of those organizations." The ordinance was substantially overbroad because it prohibited solicitations by a "class of charitable organizations as to which the 75-percent rule could not be constitutionally applied," such as "organizations whose primary purpose is . . . to gather and disseminate information and advocate positions on matters of public concern."

Virginia v. Hicks (2003) involved a challenge to the trespass policy of the Richmond Redevelopment and Housing Authority (RRHA), a state agency that owned and operated a housing development for individuals with low incomes. Hicks, who did not reside at the housing development, had been convicted of trespassing in violation of the RRHA's policy. He did not argue that the First Amendment protected his conduct. Instead, he invoked the overbreadth doctrine to argue that the state had closed off a public forum and prohibited constitutionally-protected speech and conduct there. The Virginia Supreme Court had held that the policy violated the First Amendment, presenting a merits question that the U.S. Supreme Court could reach even though federal standing rules do not limit state courts. The U.S. Supreme Court explained that the overbreadth doctrine is an exception to its normal practice for facial challenges, one that stems from "concern that the threat of enforcement of an overbroad law may deter or 'chill' constitutionally protected speech—especially when the overbroad statute imposes criminal sanctions." Though the case involved criminal sanctions, the Court cited *Broadrick v. Oklahoma* (1973) in support of its concern that "there are substantial social costs *created* by the overbreadth doctrine when it blocks application of a law to constitutionally unprotected speech." There was no substantial overbreadth, the Court reasoned, because the policy applied to "strollers, loiterers, drug dealers, roller skaters, bird watchers, soccer players, and others not engaged in constitutionally protected conduct—a group that would seemingly far outnumber First Amendment speakers." Protected speakers could, the Court reasoned, obtain remedies in as-applied challenges, "but the Virginia Supreme Court should not have used the 'strong medicine' of overbreadth to invalidate the entire RRHA trespass policy."

4. The Prohibition Against Generalized Grievances

The Supreme Court once characterized its prohibition against generalized grievances as a "prudential principle," but in more recent cases has identified that prohibition as a constitutional principle intertwined with the injury-in-fact requirement. The prohibition against generalized grievances denies standing "when the asserted harm is a generalized grievance shared in a substantially equal measure by all or a large class of citizens." *Warth v. Seldin* (1975). Thus stated, the principle seems to imply that there is no standing to challenge clearly unconstitutional laws that harm every member of the public. But the Court has never so held. To the contrary, it has held that a litigant who has suffered an injury in fact may sue to redress a "widely shared" harm. *Federal Election Commission v. Akins* (1998).

Consider, for example, a mass torts case in which a single product purchased by millions of people causes physical injury, or a class action asserting that a widely purchased product doesn't work and was sold using fraudulently deceptive marketing and sales contracts. Millions of people may be harmed, but in both cases their injuries are concrete (physical injuries in the mass torts example and financial losses in the consumer fraud example). Neither presents a generalized grievance. Thus, breadth of harm is not, on its own, the measure of a generalized grievance.

There are two classes of cases, however, in which the Court has applied the prohibition against generalized grievances to limit standing to redress widely shared harms. First, plaintiffs do not have standing to sue solely based upon their interest as citizens in seeing that the government follows the law. Citizen standing, in other words, is generally not a basis for suing in federal court. We saw this principle operating in *Lujan, TransUnion,* and *Allen.* Second, a plaintiff generally does not have taxpayer standing to sue as a taxpayer seeking to enjoin allegedly unlawful government expenditures.

The following case, *Hein v. Freedom from Religion Foundation* (2007), is now the Supreme Court's leading decision on taxpayer standing. Although there is no majority opinion, the case makes clear that taxpayer standing is exceedingly limited under current law.

As you read the multiple opinions, pay careful attention to the debate about the prior case law, including *Flast v. Cohen* (1968). In that case, the Warren Court expanded taxpayer standing. It held that a plaintiff has standing to argue that Congress's expenditure of federal money would violate a particular constitutional provision such as the First Amendment's prohibition against government establishment of religion. The Court explained that a taxpayer must satisfy two factors to sue as a taxpayer. First, "the taxpayer must establish a logical link between [their taxpayer] status and the type of legislative enactment attacked." Second, the "taxpayer must establish a nexus between that status and the precise nature of the constitutional infringement alleged." Applying this test, the Court distinguished precedent such as *Frothingham v. Mellon* (1921), which denied taxpayer standing to raise a Tenth Amendment claim, from a case in which a taxpayer sues to enforce a constitutional provision such as the Establishment Clause that limits Congress's taxing and spending authority.

Following *Flast*, the Burger Court steadily cut back on taxpayer and citizen standing. In *Valley Forge Christian College v. Americans United for Separation of Church and State, Inc.* (1982), the Supreme Court held that a taxpayer lacked standing to challenge a decision by an executive agency to transfer a parcel of federal property to a religious college. By the time that the Roberts Court decided *Hein*, *Flast* was ripe to be overruled. But Justice Alito's plurality opinion distinguished *Flast*, prompting sharp disagreement from both the concurring and dissenting Justices.

Hein v. Freedom from Religion Foundation

551 U.S. 587 (2007)

Justice ALITO announced the judgment of the Court and delivered an opinion, in which THE CHIEF JUSTICE and Justice KENNEDY join.

This is a lawsuit in which it was claimed that conferences held as part of the President's Faith-Based and Community Initiatives program violated the Establishment Clause of the First Amendment because, among other things, President Bush and former Secretary of Education Paige gave speeches that used "religious imagery" and praised the efficacy of faith-based programs in delivering social services. The plaintiffs contend that they meet the standing requirements of Article III of the Constitution because they pay federal taxes.

It has long been established, however, that the payment of taxes is generally not enough to establish standing to challenge an action taken by the Federal Government. In light of the size of the federal budget, it is a complete fiction to argue that an unconstitutional federal expenditure causes an individual federal taxpayer any measurable economic harm. And if every federal taxpayer could sue to challenge any Government expenditure, the federal courts would cease to function as courts of law and would be cast in the role of general complaint bureaus.

In *Flast v. Cohen* (1968), we recognized a narrow exception to the general rule against federal taxpayer standing. Under *Flast*, a plaintiff asserting an Establishment Clause claim has standing to challenge a law authorizing the use of federal funds in a way that allegedly violates the Establishment Clause. In the present case, Congress did not specifically authorize the use of federal funds to pay for the conferences or speeches that the plaintiffs challenged. Instead, the conferences and speeches were paid for out of general Executive Branch appropriations. The Court of Appeals, however, held that the plaintiffs have standing as taxpayers because the conferences were paid for with money appropriated by Congress.

The question that is presented here is whether this broad reading of *Flast* is correct. We hold that it is not. We therefore reverse the decision of the Court of Appeals.

I

A

In 2001, the President issued an executive order creating the White House Office of Faith-Based and Community Initiatives within the Executive Office of the President. The purpose of this new office was to ensure that "private and charitable community groups, including religious ones . . . have the fullest opportunity permitted by law to compete on a level playing field, so long as they achieve valid public purposes" and adhere to "the bedrock principles of pluralism, nondiscrimination, evenhandedness, and neutrality." The office was specifically charged with the task of eliminating unnecessary bureaucratic, legislative, and regulatory barriers that could impede such organizations' effectiveness and ability to compete equally for federal assistance.

By separate executive orders, the President also created Executive Department Centers for Faith-Based and Community Initiatives within several federal agencies and departments. These centers were given the job of ensuring that faith-based community groups would be eligible to compete for federal financial support without impairing their independence or autonomy, as long as they did "not use direct Federal financial assistance to support any inherently religious activities, such as worship, religious instruction, or proselytization." To this end, the President directed that "[n]o organization should be discriminated against on the basis of religion or religious belief in the administration or distribution of Federal financial assistance under social service programs," and that "[a]ll organizations that receive Federal financial assistance under social services programs should be prohibited from discriminating against beneficiaries or potential beneficiaries of the social services programs on the basis of religion or religious belief." Petitioners, who have been sued in their official capacities, are the directors of the White House Office and various Executive Department Centers.

No congressional legislation specifically authorized the creation of the White House Office or the Executive Department Centers. Nor has Congress enacted any law specifically appropriating money for these entities' activities. Instead, their activities are funded through general Executive Branch appropriations.

B

The respondents are Freedom From Religion Foundation, Inc., a nonstock corporation "opposed to government endorsement of religion," and three of its members. Respondents brought suit in the United States District Court for the Western District of Wisconsin, alleging that petitioners violated the Establishment Clause by organizing conferences at which faith-based organizations allegedly "are singled out as being particularly worthy of federal funding . . . , and the belief in God is extolled as distinguishing the claimed effectiveness of faith-based social services." Respondents further alleged that the content of these conferences sent a message to religious believers "that they are insiders and favored members of the political community" and that the conferences sent the message to nonbelievers "that they are outsiders" and "not full members of the political community." In short, respondents alleged that the conferences were designed to promote, and had the effect of promoting, religious community groups over secular ones.

The only asserted basis for standing was that the individual respondents are federal taxpayers who are "opposed to the use of Congressional taxpayer appropriations to advance and promote religion." In their capacity as federal taxpayers, respondents sought to challenge Executive Branch expenditures for these conferences, which, they contended, violated the Establishment Clause.

II

A

Article III of the Constitution limits the judicial power of the United States to the resolution of "Cases" and "Controversies," and "'Article III standing . . . enforces the Constitution's case-or-controversy requirement.'" *DaimlerChrysler Corp. v. Cuno* (2006).

The requisite elements of Article III standing are well established: "A plaintiff must allege personal injury fairly traceable to the defendant's allegedly unlawful conduct and likely to be redressed by the requested relief." *Allen v. Wright* (1984).

The constitutionally mandated standing inquiry is especially important in a case like this one, in which taxpayers seek "to challenge laws of general application where their own injury is not distinct from that suffered in general by other taxpayers or citizens." *ASARCO v. Kadish* (1989) (opinion of Kennedy, J.) This is because "[t]he judicial power of the United States defined by Art. III is not an unconditioned authority to determine the constitutionality of legislative or executive acts." *Valley Forge Christian College v. Americans United for Separation of Church and State, Inc.* (1982). The federal courts are not empowered to seek out and strike down any governmental act that they deem to be repugnant to the Constitution. Rather, federal courts sit "solely, to decide on the rights of individuals." *Marbury v. Madison* (1803). As we held over 80 years ago, in another case involving the question of taxpayer standing:

> We have no power *per se* to review and annul acts of Congress on the ground that they are unconstitutional. That question may be considered only when the justification for some direct injury suffered or threatened, presenting a justiciable issue, is made to rest upon such an act. . . . The party who invokes the power must be able to show not only that the statute is invalid but that he has sustained or is immediately in danger of sustaining some direct injury as the result of its enforcement, and not merely that he suffers in some indefinite way in common with people generally. *Frothingham v. Mellon* (1923).

B

As a general matter, the interest of a federal taxpayer in seeing that Treasury funds are spent in accordance with the Constitution does not give rise to the kind of redressable "personal injury" required for Article III standing. Of course, a taxpayer has standing to challenge the *collection* of a specific tax assessment as unconstitutional; being forced to pay such a tax causes a real and immediate economic injury to the individual taxpayer. But that is not the interest on which respondents assert standing here. Rather, their claim is that, having paid lawfully collected taxes into the Federal Treasury at some point, they have a continuing, legally cognizable interest in ensuring that those funds are not *used* by the Government in a way that violates the Constitution.

We have consistently held that this type of interest is too generalized and attenuated to support Article III standing. In *Frothingham*, a federal taxpayer sought to challenge federal appropriations for mothers' and children's health, arguing that federal involvement in this area intruded on the rights reserved to the States under the Tenth Amendment and would "increase the burden of future taxation and thereby take [the plaintiff's] property without due process of law." We concluded that the plaintiff lacked the kind of particularized injury required for Article III standing. Because the interests of the taxpayer are, in essence, the interests of the public at large, deciding a constitutional claim based solely on taxpayer standing "would be[,] not to decide a judicial controversy, but to assume a position of authority over the governmental acts of another and co-equal department, an authority which plainly we do not possess."

In *Doremus v. Board of Education of Hawthorne* (1952), we reaffirmed this principle, explaining that "the interests of a taxpayer in the moneys of the federal treasury are too indeterminable, remote, uncertain and indirect to furnish a basis for an appeal to the preventive powers of the Court over their manner of expenditure." We therefore rejected a state taxpayer's claim of standing to challenge a state law authorizing public school teachers to read from the Bible because "the grievance which [the plaintiff] sought to litigate . . . is not a direct dollars-and-cents injury but is a religious difference." In so doing, we gave effect to the basic constitutional principle that

> a plaintiff raising only a generally available grievance about government — claiming only harm to his and every citizen's interest in proper application of the Constitution and laws, and seeking relief that no more directly and tangibly benefits him than it does the public at large — does not state an Article III case or controversy. *Lujan v. Defenders of Wildlife* (1992).

C

In *Flast*, the Court carved out a narrow exception to the general constitutional prohibition against taxpayer standing. The taxpayer-plaintiffs in that case challenged the distribution of federal funds to religious schools under the Elementary and Secondary Education Act of 1965, alleging that such aid violated the Establishment Clause. The Court set out a two-part test for determining whether a federal taxpayer has standing to challenge an allegedly unconstitutional expenditure:

> First, the taxpayer must establish a logical link between that status and the type of legislative enactment attacked. Thus, a taxpayer will be a proper party to allege the unconstitutionality only of exercises of congressional power under the taxing and spending clause of Art. I, §8, of the Constitution. It will not be sufficient to allege an incidental expenditure of tax funds in the administration of an essentially regulatory statute. . . . Secondly, the taxpayer must establish a nexus between that status and the precise nature of the constitutional infringement alleged. Under this requirement,

the taxpayer must show that the challenged enactment exceeds specific constitutional limitations imposed upon the exercise of the congressional taxing and spending power and not simply that the enactment is generally beyond the powers delegated to Congress by Art. I, §8.

The Court held that the taxpayer-plaintiffs in *Flast* had satisfied both prongs of this test: The plaintiff's "constitutional challenge [was] made to an exercise by Congress of its power under Art. I, §8, to spend for the general welfare," and she alleged a violation of the Establishment Clause, which "operates as a specific constitutional limitation upon the exercise by Congress of the taxing and spending power conferred by Art. I, §8."

III
A

Respondents argue that this case falls within the *Flast* exception, which they read to cover any "expenditure of government funds in violation of the Establishment Clause."

The expenditures challenged in *Flast* were funded by a specific congressional appropriation and were disbursed to private schools (including religiously affiliated schools) pursuant to a direct and unambiguous congressional mandate. Indeed, the *Flast* taxpayer-plaintiffs' constitutional claim was premised on the contention that if the Government's actions were "'within the authority and intent of the Act, the Act is to that extent unconstitutional and void.'"

Given that the alleged Establishment Clause violation in *Flast* was funded by a specific congressional appropriation and was undertaken pursuant to an express congressional mandate, the Court concluded that the taxpayer-plaintiffs had established the requisite "logical link between [their taxpayer] status and the type of legislative enactment attacked."

B

The link between congressional action and constitutional violation that supported taxpayer standing in *Flast* is missing here. Respondents do not challenge any specific congressional action or appropriation; nor do they ask the Court to invalidate any congressional enactment or legislatively created program as unconstitutional. That is because the expenditures at issue here were not made pursuant to any Act of Congress. Rather, Congress provided general appropriations to the Executive Branch to fund its day-to-day activities. These appropriations did not expressly authorize, direct, or even mention the expenditures of which respondents complain. Those expenditures resulted from executive discretion, not congressional action.

We have never found taxpayer standing under such circumstances. In *Valley Forge*, we held that a taxpayer lacked standing to challenge "a decision by [the federal Department of Health, Education and Welfare] to transfer a parcel of federal property" to a religious college because this transfer was "not a congressional action."

Similarly, in *Schlesinger v. Reservists Comm. to Stop the War* (1974), the taxpayer-plaintiffs contended that the Incompatibility Clause of Article I prohibited

Members of Congress from holding commissions in the Armed Forces Reserve. We held that these plaintiffs lacked standing under *Flast* because they "did not challenge an enactment under Art. I, §8, but rather the action of the Executive Branch in permitting Members of Congress to maintain their Reserve status."

In short, this case falls outside "the narrow exception" that *Flast* "created to the general rule against taxpayer standing established in *Frothingham*." *Bowen v. Kendrick* (1988). Because the expenditures that respondents challenge were not expressly authorized or mandated by any specific congressional enactment, respondents' lawsuit is not directed at an exercise of congressional power, and thus lacks the requisite "logical nexus" between taxpayer status "and the type of legislative enactment attacked." *Flast v. Cohen* (1968).

IV

A

1

Respondents argue that it is "arbitrary" to distinguish between money spent pursuant to congressional mandate and expenditures made in the course of executive discretion, because "the injury to taxpayers in both situations is the very injury targeted by the Establishment Clause and *Flast*—the expenditure for the support of religion of funds exacted from taxpayers."

But *Flast* focused on congressional action, and we must decline this invitation to extend its holding to encompass discretionary Executive Branch expenditures. It is significant that, in the four decades since its creation, the *Flast* exception has largely been confined to its facts. We have declined to lower the taxpayer standing bar in suits alleging violations of any constitutional provision apart from the Establishment Clause. We have similarly refused to extend *Flast* to permit taxpayer standing for Establishment Clause challenges that do not implicate Congress' taxing and spending power.

2

While respondents argue that Executive Branch expenditures in support of religion are no different from legislative extractions, *Flast* itself rejected this equivalence: "It will not be sufficient to allege an incidental expenditure of tax funds in the administration of an essentially regulatory statute."

Because almost all Executive Branch activity is ultimately funded by some congressional appropriation, extending the *Flast* exception to purely executive expenditures would effectively subject every federal action—be it a conference, proclamation, or speech—to Establishment Clause challenge by any taxpayer in federal court. To see the wide swathe of activity that respondents' proposed rule would cover, one need look no further than the amended complaint in this action, which focuses largely on speeches and presentations made by Executive Branch officials. Such a broad reading would ignore the first prong of *Flast*'s standing test, which requires "a logical link between [taxpayer] status and the type of legislative enactment attacked."

It would also raise serious separation-of-powers concerns. As we have recognized, *Flast* itself gave too little weight to these concerns. By framing the standing question solely in terms of whether the dispute would be presented in an adversary context and in a form traditionally viewed as capable of judicial resolution, *Flast* "failed to recognize that this doctrine has a separation-of-powers component, which keeps courts within certain traditional bounds vis-à-vis the other branches, concrete adverseness or not." *Lewis v. Casey* (1996). Respondents' position, if adopted, would repeat and compound this mistake.

B

Respondents set out a parade of horribles that they claim could occur if *Flast* is not extended to discretionary Executive Branch expenditures. For example, they say, a federal agency could use its discretionary funds to build a house of worship or to hire clergy of one denomination and send them out to spread their faith. Or an agency could use its funds to make bulk purchases of Stars of David, crucifixes, or depictions of the star and crescent for use in its offices or for distribution to the employees or the general public. Of course, none of these things has happened, even though *Flast* has not previously been expanded in the way that respondents urge. In the unlikely event that any of these executive actions did take place, Congress could quickly step in. And respondents make no effort to show that these improbable abuses could not be challenged in federal court by plaintiffs who would possess standing based on grounds other than taxpayer standing.

C

Over the years, *Flast* has been defended by some and criticized by others. But the present case does not require us to reconsider that precedent. The Court of Appeals did not apply *Flast;* it extended *Flast*. It is a necessary concomitant of the doctrine of *stare decisis* that a precedent is not always expanded to the limit of its logic. We do not extend *Flast,* but we also do not overrule it. We leave *Flast* as we found it.

We need go no further to decide this case. Relying on the provision of the Constitution that limits our role to resolving the "Cases" and "Controversies" before us, we decide only the case at hand.

[Justice KENNEDY's concurring opinion is omitted].

Justice SCALIA, with whom Justice THOMAS joins, concurring in the judgment.

Today's opinion is, in one significant respect, entirely consistent with our previous cases addressing taxpayer standing to raise Establishment Clause challenges to government expenditures. Unfortunately, the consistency lies in the creation of utterly meaningless distinctions which separate the case at hand from the precedents that have come out differently, but which cannot possibly be (in any sane world) the reason it comes out differently. If this Court is to decide cases by rule of law rather than show of hands, we must surrender to logic and choose sides: Either *Flast v. Cohen* (1968) should be applied to (at a minimum) *all* challenges to the governmental expenditure of general tax revenues in a manner alleged to violate a constitutional provision specifically limiting the taxing and spending power, or *Flast* should be repudiated. For me, the choice is easy. *Flast* is wholly irreconcilable with the Article III restrictions on federal-court jurisdiction that this Court has repeatedly confirmed are embodied in the doctrine of standing.

We have alternately relied on two entirely distinct conceptions of injury in fact, which for convenience I will call "Wallet Injury" and "Psychic Injury."

Wallet Injury is the type of concrete and particularized injury one would expect to be asserted in a *taxpayer* suit, namely, a claim that the plaintiff's tax liability is higher than it would be, but for the allegedly unlawful government action. The stumbling block for suits challenging government expenditures based on this conventional type of injury is quite predictable. The plaintiff cannot satisfy the traceability and redressability prongs of standing. It is uncertain what the plaintiff's tax bill would have been had the allegedly forbidden expenditure not been made, and it is even more speculative whether the government will, in response to an adverse court decision, lower taxes rather than spend the funds in some other manner.

Psychic Injury, on the other hand, has nothing to do with the plaintiff's tax liability. Instead, the injury consists of the taxpayer's *mental displeasure* that money extracted from him is being spent in an unlawful manner. This shift in focus eliminates traceability and redressability problems. Psychic Injury is directly traceable to the improper *use* of taxpayer funds, and it is redressed when the improper use is enjoined, regardless of whether that injunction affects the taxpayer's purse. *Flast* and the cases following its teaching have invoked a peculiarly restricted version of Psychic Injury, permitting taxpayer displeasure over unconstitutional spending to support standing *only if* the constitutional provision allegedly violated is a specific limitation on the taxing and spending power. Restricted or not, this conceptualizing of injury in fact in purely mental terms conflicts squarely with the familiar proposition that a plaintiff lacks a concrete and particularized injury when his only complaint is the generalized grievance that the law is being violated.

We initially denied taxpayer standing based on Wallet Injury, but then found standing in some later cases based on the limited version of Psychic Injury described above. The basic logical flaw in our cases is thus twofold: We have never explained why Psychic Injury was insufficient in the cases in which standing was denied, and we have never explained why Psychic Injury, however limited, is cognizable under Article III.

Two pre-*Flast* cases are of critical importance. In *Frothingham v. Mellon* (1923), decided with *Massachusetts v. Mellon* (1923), the taxpayer challenged the constitutionality of the Maternity Act of 1921, alleging in part that the federal funding provided by the Act was not authorized by any provision of the Constitution. The Court held that the taxpayer lacked standing. The Court [described] the traceability and redressability problems with Wallet Injury, and rejecting Psychic Injury as a generalized grievance rather than concrete and particularized harm.

The second significant pre-*Flast* case is *Doremus v. Board of Education of Hawthorne* (1952). There the taxpayers challenged under the Establishment Clause a state law requiring public-school teachers to read the Bible at the beginning of each schoolday. Relying extensively on *Frothingham*, the Court denied standing. In addition to reiterating *Frothingham*'s description of the unavoidable obstacles to recovery under a taxpayer theory of Wallet Injury, *Doremus* rejected Psychic Injury in unmistakable terms. The opinion's deprecation of a mere "religious difference," in contrast to a real "dollars-and-cents injury," can only be understood as a flat denial of standing supported only by taxpayer disapproval of the unconstitutional use of tax funds.

Sixteen years after *Doremus,* the Court took a pivotal turn. In *Flast v. Cohen* (1968), taxpayers challenged the Elementary and Secondary Education Act of 1965, alleging that funds expended pursuant to the Act were being used to support parochial schools. They argued that either the Act itself proscribed such expenditures or that the Act violated the Establishment Clause. The Court held that the taxpayers had standing. *Flast* held that the taxpayers had standing.

Wallet Injury could not possibly have been the basis for this conclusion, since the taxpayers in *Flast* were no more able to prove that success on the merits would reduce their tax burden than was the taxpayer in *Frothingham.* Thus, *Flast* relied on Psychic Injury to support standing, describing the "injury" as the taxpayer's allegation that "his tax money is being extracted and spent in violation of specific constitutional protections against such abuses of legislative power."

But that created a problem: If the taxpayers in *Flast* had standing based on Psychic Injury, and without regard to the effect of the litigation on their ultimate tax liability, why did not the taxpayers in *Doremus* and *Frothingham* have standing on a similar basis?

The plurality is unwilling to acknowledge that the logic of *Flast* (its Psychic Injury rationale) is simply wrong, and *for that reason* should not be extended to other cases. Why pick a distinguishing fact that may breathe life into *Flast* in future cases, preserving the disreputable disarray of our Establishment Clause standing jurisprudence? Why not hold that only taxpayers raising Establishment Clause challenges to expenditures pursuant to the Elementary and Secondary Education Act of 1965 have standing? That, I suppose, would be too obvious a repudiation of *Flast,* and thus an impediment to the plurality's pose of minimalism.

Ultimately, the arguments by the parties in this case and the opinions of my colleagues serve only to confirm that *Flast*'s adoption of Psychic Injury has to be addressed head-on. Minimalism is an admirable judicial trait, but not when it comes at the cost of meaningless and disingenuous distinctions that hold the sure promise of engendering further meaningless and disingenuous distinctions in the future. The rule of law is ill served by forcing lawyers and judges to make arguments that deaden the soul of the law, which is logic and reason. Either *Flast* was correct, and must be accorded the wide application that it logically dictates, or it was not, and must be abandoned in its entirety. I turn, finally, to that question.

Is a taxpayer's purely psychological displeasure that his funds are being spent in an allegedly unlawful manner ever sufficiently concrete and particularized to support Article III standing? The answer is plainly no.

Flast is damaged goods, not only because its fanciful two-pronged "nexus" test has been demonstrated to be irrelevant to the test's supposed objective, but also because its cavalier treatment of the standing requirement rested upon a fundamental underestimation of that requirement's importance. *Flast* was explicitly and erroneously premised on the idea that Article III standing does not perform a crucial separation-of-powers function:

> The question whether a particular person is a proper party to maintain the action does not, by its own force, raise separation of powers problems related to improper judicial interference in areas committed to other branches of the Federal Government. Such problems arise, if at all, only from the substantive issues the individual seeks to have adjudicated. Thus, in terms of Article III limitations on federal court jurisdiction, the

question of standing is related only to whether the dispute sought to be adjudicated will be presented in an adversary context and in a form historically viewed as capable of judicial resolution.

Flast's crabbed (and judge-empowering) understanding of the role Article III standing plays in preserving our system of separated powers has been repudiated. We twice have noted explicitly that *Flast* failed to recognize the vital separation-of-powers aspect of Article III standing. *See Spencer v. Kemna* (1998); *Lewis v. Casey* (1996). And once a proper understanding of the relationship of standing to the separation of powers is brought to bear, Psychic Injury, even as limited in *Flast*, is revealed for what it is: a contradiction of the basic propositions that the function of the judicial power "is, solely, to decide on the rights of individuals," *Marbury v. Madison* (1803), and that generalized grievances affecting the public at large have their remedy in the political process.

I can think of few cases less warranting of *stare decisis* respect. It is time — it is past time — to call an end. *Flast* should be overruled.

Justice SOUTER, with whom Justice STEVENS, Justice GINSBURG, and Justice BREYER join, dissenting.

Flast v. Cohen (1968) held that plaintiffs with an Establishment Clause claim could "demonstrate the necessary stake as taxpayers in the outcome of the litigation to satisfy Article III requirements." Here, the controlling, plurality opinion declares that *Flast* does not apply, but a search of that opinion for a suggestion that these taxpayers have any less stake in the outcome than the taxpayers in *Flast* will come up empty: the plurality makes no such finding, nor could it. Instead, the controlling opinion closes the door on these taxpayers because the Executive Branch, and not the Legislative Branch, caused their injury. I see no basis for this distinction in either logic or precedent, and respectfully dissent.

I

We held in *Flast*, and repeated just last Term, that the "'injury' alleged in Establishment Clause challenges to federal spending" is "the very 'extract[ion] and spen[ding]' of 'tax money' in aid of religion." *DaimlerChrysler Corp. v. Cuno* (2006). As the Court said in *Flast*, the importance of that type of injury has deep historical roots going back to the ideal of religious liberty in James Madison's Memorial and Remonstrance Against Religious Assessments, that the government in a free society may not "force a citizen to contribute three pence only of his property for the support of any one establishment" of religion.

The right of conscience and the expenditure of an identifiable three pence raised by taxes for the support of a religious cause are therefore not to be split off from one another. The three pence implicates the conscience, and the injury from Government expenditures on religion is not accurately classified with the "Psychic Injury" that results whenever a congressional appropriation or executive expenditure raises hackles of disagreement with the policy supported.

Here, there is no dispute that taxpayer money in identifiable amounts is funding conferences, and these are alleged to have the purpose of promoting religion. The taxpayers therefore seek not to "extend" *Flast*, but merely to apply it. When executive agencies spend identifiable sums of tax money for religious purposes, no less than when Congress authorizes the same thing, taxpayers suffer injury. And once we recognize the injury as sufficient for Article III, there can be no serious question about the other elements of the standing enquiry: the injury is indisputably "traceable" to the spending, and "likely to be redressed by" an injunction prohibiting it.

The plurality points to the separation of powers to explain its distinction between legislative and executive spending decisions, but there is no difference on that point of view between a Judicial Branch review of an executive decision and a judicial evaluation of a congressional one. We owe respect to each of the other branches, no more to the former than to the latter, and no one has suggested that the Establishment Clause lacks applicability to executive uses of money. It would surely violate the Establishment Clause for the Department of Health and Human Services to draw on a general appropriation to build a chapel for weekly church services (no less than if a statute required it), and for good reason: if the Executive could accomplish through the exercise of discretion exactly what Congress cannot do through legislation, Establishment Clause protection would melt away.

II

While *Flast* standing to assert the right of conscience is in a class by itself, it would be a mistake to think that case is unique in recognizing standing in a plaintiff without injury to flesh or purse.

In the case of economic or physical harms, of course, the "injury in fact" question is straightforward. But once one strays from these obvious cases, the enquiry can turn subtle. Are esthetic harms sufficient for Article III standing? What about being forced to compete on an uneven playing field based on race (without showing that an economic loss resulted), or living in a racially gerrymandered electoral district? These injuries are no more concrete than seeing one's tax dollars spent on religion, but we have recognized each one as enough for standing.

Thus, *Flast* speaks for this Court's recognition (shared by a majority of the Court today) that when the Government spends money for religious purposes a taxpayer's injury is serious and concrete enough to be "judicially cognizable." *Allen v. Wright* (1984).

Because the taxpayers in this case have alleged the type of injury this Court has seen as sufficient for standing, I would affirm.

* * *

5.   *Governmental Standing*

Beginning in the 2010s, if not earlier, there has been a trend towards increased intergovernmental litigation. Many high-profile public law cases involving constitutional questions have been litigated in suits between the federal government and the states. As then Texas Attorney General Greg Abbott famously described his job, "I go to the office, I sue the federal government, and I go home."[26]

---

26. Ross Ramsey, *Law, Like Politics, Makes Strange Bedfellows*, TEX. TRIB., Sept. 14, 2014.

Number of Multistate Lawsuits vs. Federal Defendants, by Year

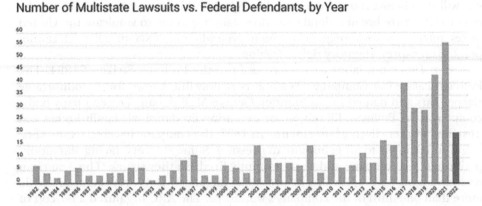

https://attorneysgeneral.org/multistate-lawsuits-vs-the-federal-government/statistics-and-visualizations-multistate-litigation-vs-the-federal-government/

In part, this trend is due to Supreme Court precedents holding that governmental standing to vindicate public interests is broader than private standing to do so. The Court has tied more relaxed standing requirements to the distinctive power of sovereign governments to represent the interests of their people.

a. The Standing of the Federal Government

The United States government, acting through the federal Executive Branch, generally has standing to enforce federal law. There is no question, for instance, that the U.S. Department of Justice (DOJ) may bring a civil or criminal enforcement proceeding to enforce a federal statute that provides for such penalties. In such a case, the federal courts have never required the DOJ to plead and prove a specific injury in fact to the federal government. Federal statutes that can be traced to the founding of the Department of Justice during Reconstruction in 1870 explicitly authorize the Attorney General to represent the United States and to coordinate all litigation to which the United States, an agency, or a federal officer is a party. *See* 28 U.S.C. §§516, 519, and 5 U.S.C. §3106. The founding of the Department of Justice arose in no small part from the need to centralize and coordinate Reconstruction litigation, bringing field United States Attorneys under the supervision of the Attorney General and to bring "a unity of decision, a unity of jurisprudence in the executive law of the United States."[27]

In concert with these statutory grants, the federal government's sovereign interest in enforcing federal law justifies its standing in litigation. The federal government also clearly has standing to sue to vindicate its interests as a property owner and a party to contracts.

Harder cases arise when the federal government sues without express statutory authorization and without a proprietary interest clearly at stake. *In re Debs*, which

---

27. Cong. Globe, 41st Cong. 2d Sess. 3055-39, 3065-66 (1870). *See also* Norman W. Spaulding, *Professional Independence in the Office of the Attorney General*, 60 Stan. L. Rev. 1931 (2010).

you will read below, is one such case. Though not without controversy, *Debs* can be read to recognize broad federal executive standing to sue to vindicate the United States' interests as a sovereign government even when the Executive Branch cannot point to an express statutory right of action.

In re Debs was a labor case. It arose from the Pullman Strike of 1894. The Pullman Palace Car Company was a luxury railway line known for its comfortable sleeper cars and named for its founder, George M. Pullman. The company had a company town, Pullman, Illinois, where executives lived in single-family homes and unskilled workers lived in tenements. In 1893, the company lowered its workers' wages in response to an economic depression. Some workers, facing starvation, petitioned the company and were promptly fired. So they struck. The American Railway Union (ARU), lead by its president Eugene V. Debs, represented a little more than one-third of the company's workforce. The ARU organized a boycott of the Pullman Company.

The U.S. Attorney General got involved by filing a bill for an injunction against the ARU leadership. The government argued that the ARU was violating the Sherman Antitrust Act and the Interstate Commerce Act. It adverted as well to the United States' interest in protecting the U.S. mail, which had been harmed when workers derailed a locomotive that was attached to a train carrying the mail. Once the injunction had issued, President Grover Cleveland ordered troops to prevent the striking workers and their allies from disrupting the U.S. mail. The troops' presence fueled rather than prevented violence. On July 7, 1894, a crowd attacked the national guard, which in turn fired upon the crowd, killing at least four people. That same day, the federal government arrested Debs, who had tried to discourage violence. He was convicted of contempt of court on the theory that his actions violated the injunction against the ARU's activities.

The federal government's actions were controversial. In 1896, the Democratic Party's platform addressed the use of labor injunctions: "[G]overnment by injunction," the platform stated, is "a new and highly dangerous form of oppression by which Federal Judges, in contempt of the laws of the States and rights of citizens, become at once legislators, judges, and executioners."[28] As the Supreme Court's opinion *In re Debs* reveals, Congress had not expressly authorized the federal Executive to seek a labor injunction. Even so, the criminal contempt conviction of Debs was lawful, the government argued, because the United States had standing to seek an injunction and the relief it obtained was lawful. In making this argument, the Executive appealed to the United States' sovereign interest in regulating interstate commerce and its proprietary interest in the U.S. mail as the bases for standing. As you read the case, consider the shift in the disposition of the Court toward federal equity power in the twentieth century civil rights standing cases involving structural injunctive relief (e.g., *Lyons* and *Allen*). Is the status of the government as the party invoking that power the most important distinction?

---

28. 1896 Democratic Party Platform, AM. PRESIDENCY PROJECT, www.presidency.ucsb. edu/documents/1896-democratic-party-platform. *See* Aditya Bamzai & Samuel L. Bray, Debs *and the Federal Equity Jurisdiction*, 98 NOTRE DAME L. REV. 699, 701 (2022).

In re Debs

158 U.S. 564 (1895)

Justice BREWER delivered the opinion of the Court.

The case presented by the bill is this: The United States, finding that the interstate transportation of persons and property, as well as the carriage of the mails, is forcibly obstructed, and that a combination and conspiracy exists to subject the control of such transportation to the will of the conspirators, applied to one of their courts, sitting as a court of equity, for an injunction to restrain such obstruction and prevent carrying into effect such conspiracy. Two questions of importance are presented: First. Are the relations of the general government to interstate commerce and the transportation of the mails such as authorize a direct interference to prevent a forcible obstruction thereof? Second. If authority exists, as authority in governmental affairs implies both power and duty, has a court of equity jurisdiction to issue an injunction in aid of the performance of such duty.

First. Among the powers expressly given to the national government are the control of interstate commerce and the creation and management of a post office system for the nation. Article I, section 8, of the Constitution provides that "the Congress shall have power. . . . Third, to regulate commerce with foreign nations and among the several States, and with the Indian tribes. . . . Seventh, to establish post offices and post roads."

As, under the Constitution, power over interstate commerce and the transportation of the mails is vested in the national government, and Congress by virtue of such grant has assumed actual and direct control, it follows that the national government may prevent any unlawful and forcible interference therewith. But how shall this be accomplished? Doubtless, it is within the competency of Congress to prescribe by legislation that any interference with these matters shall be offences against the United States, and prosecuted and punished by indictment in the proper courts. But is that the only remedy? Have the vast interests of the nation in interstate commerce, and in the transportation of the mails, no other protection than lies in the possible punishment of those who interfere with it? To ask the question is to answer it. By article 3, section 2, clause 3, of the Federal Constitution it is provided: "The trial of all crimes except in cases of impeachment shall be by jury; and such trial shall be held in the State where the said crime shall have been committed." If all the inhabitants of a State, or even a great body of them, should combine to obstruct interstate commerce or the transportation of the mails, prosecutions for such offences had in such a community would be doomed in advance to failure. And if the certainty of such failure was known, and the national government had no other way to enforce the freedom of interstate commerce and the transportation of the mails than by prosecution and punishment for interference therewith, the whole interests of the nation in these respects would be at the absolute mercy of a portion of the inhabitants of that single State.

But there is no such impotency in the national government. The entire strength of the nation may be used to enforce in any part of the land the full and free exercise of all national powers and the security of all rights entrusted by the Constitution to its care. The strong arm of the national government may be put forth to brush away all obstructions to the freedom of interstate commerce or the transportation of the mails. If the emergency arises, the army of the Nation, and all its militia, are at the service of the Nation to compel obedience to its laws.

But passing to the second question, is there no other alternative than the use of force on the part of the executive authorities whenever obstructions arise to the freedom of interstate commerce or the transportation of the mails? Is the army the only instrument by which rights of the public can be enforced and the peace of the nation preserved? Grant that any public nuisance may be forcibly abated either at the instance of the authorities, or by any individual suffering private damage therefrom, the existence of this right of forcible abatement is not inconsistent with nor does it destroy the right of appeal in an orderly way to the courts for a judicial determination, and an exercise of their powers by writ of injunction and otherwise to accomplish the same result.

Neither can it be doubted that the government has such an interest in the subject-matter as enables it to appear as party plaintiff in this suit. It is said that equity only interferes for the protection of property, and that the government has no property interest. A sufficient reply is that the United States have a property in the mails, the protection of which was one of the purposes of this bill.

We do not care to place our decision upon this ground alone. Every government, entrusted, by the very terms of its being, with powers and duties to be exercised and discharged for the general welfare, has a right to apply to its own courts for any proper assistance in the exercise of the one and the discharge of the other, and it is no sufficient answer to its appeal to one of those courts that it has no pecuniary interest in the matter. The obligations which it is under to promote the interest of all, and to prevent the wrongdoing of one resulting in injury to the general welfare, is often of itself sufficient to give it a standing in court.

It is obvious from these decisions that while it is not the province of the government to interfere in any mere matter of private controversy between individuals, or to use its great powers to enforce the rights of one against another, yet, whenever the wrongs complained of are such as affect the public at large, and are in respect of matters which by the Constitution are entrusted to the care of the Nation, and concerning which the Nation owes the duty to all the citizens of securing to them their common rights, then the mere fact that the government has no pecuniary interest in the controversy is not sufficient to exclude it from the courts, or prevent it from taking measures therein to fully discharge those constitutional duties.

The national government, given by the Constitution power to regulate interstate commerce, has by express statute assumed jurisdiction over such commerce when carried upon railroads. It is charged, therefore, with the duty of keeping those highways of interstate commerce free from obstruction, for it has always been recognized as one of the powers and duties of a government to remove obstructions from the highways under its control.

A most earnest and eloquent appeal was made to us in eulogy of the heroic spirit of those who threw up their employment, and gave up their means of earning a livelihood, not in defence of their own rights, but in sympathy for and to assist others whom they believed to be wronged. We yield to none in our admiration of any act of heroism or self-sacrifice, but we may be permitted to add that it is a lesson which cannot be learned too soon or too thoroughly that under this government of and by the people the means of redress of all wrongs are through the courts and at the ballot-box, and that no wrong, real or fancied, carries with it legal warrant to invite as a means of redress the coöperation of a mob, with its accompanying acts of violence.

We have given to this case the most careful and anxious attention, for we realize that it touches closely questions of supreme importance to the people of this country. Summing up our conclusions, we hold that the government of the United States is one having jurisdiction over every foot of soil within its territory, and acting directly upon each citizen; that while it is a government of enumerated powers, it has within the limits of those powers all the attributes of sovereignty; that to it is committed power over interstate commerce and the transmission of the mail; that the powers thus conferred upon the national government are not dormant, but have been assumed and put into practical exercise by the legislation of Congress; that in the exercise of those powers it is competent for the nation to remove all obstructions upon highways, natural or artificial, to the passage of interstate commerce or the carrying of the mail; that while it may be competent for the government (through the executive branch and in the use of the entire executive power of the nation) to forcibly remove all such obstructions, it is equally within its competency to appeal to the civil courts for an inquiry and determination as to the existence and character of any alleged obstructions, and if such are found to exist, or threaten to occur, to invoke the powers of those courts to remove or restrain such obstructions; that the jurisdiction of courts to interfere in such matters by injunction is one recognized from ancient times and by indubitable authority; that such jurisdiction is not ousted by the fact that the obstructions are accompanied by or consist of acts in themselves violations of the criminal law; that the proceeding by injunction is of a civil character, and may be enforced by proceedings in contempt; that such proceedings are not in execution of the criminal laws of the land; that the penalty for a violation of injunction is no substitute for and no defence to a prosecution for any criminal offences committed in the course of such violation; that the complaint filed in this case clearly showed an existing obstruction of artificial highways for the passage of interstate commerce and the transmission of the mail—an obstruction not only temporarily existing, but threatening to continue; that under such complaint the Circuit Court had power to issue its process of injunction; that it having been issued and served on these defendants, the Circuit Court had authority to inquire whether its orders had been disobeyed, and when it found that they had been, then to proceed under section 725, Revised Statutes, which grants power "to punish, by fine or imprisonment, . . . disobedience, . . . by any party . . . or other person, to any lawful writ, process, order, rule, decree or command," and enter the order of punishment complained of; and, finally, that, the Circuit Court, having full jurisdiction in the premises, its finding of the fact of disobedience is not open to review on habeas corpus in this or any other court.

* * *

The United States has invoked *Debs* in support of standing to vindicate constitutional rights in the absence of express statutory authorization. During the 1960s, for instance, the federal courts held that the federal Executive could sue to enjoin violations of the civil rights of Black people by local governments in the South. More recently, in *United States v. Texas* (2021), the United States cited *Debs* in support of its suit to enjoin S.B. 8, the State of Texas's "fetal heartbeat" law, which banned abortions as soon as a fetal heartbeat could be detected. This law clearly violated *Roe v. Wade* (1973) and *Planned Parenthood v. Casey* (1992), both of which were the law of the land when S.B. 8 was enacted. In the typical course, a private litigant, such as a patient or healthcare provider, would be able to challenge such a law by suing the state officials responsible for implementing it without violating state sovereign immunity, as was the case in *Ex parte Young* (1908), discussed in detail in Chapter 6. But Texas's S.B. 8 did not vest enforcement authority in any state official or office. Instead, it created a private right of action empowering private parties to sue in Texas state court anyone who aided or abetted, or intended to aid and abet, a prohibited abortion. According to the U.S. government, *Debs* supported its standing to seek an injunction against implementation of a law that would violate the constitutional rights of individuals yet evade any attempt by those individuals to seek judicial relief from a federal court. A federal district court agreed and issued a preliminary injunction, which the Fifth Circuit Court of Appeals stayed. The Supreme Court granted the petition for a writ of certiorari but ultimately dismissed the petition as improvidently granted, instead addressing the merits issues in a related lawsuit brought by private litigants. Thus, the precise scope of federal government standing under *Debs* remains unsettled.

b.   State Standing

The standing of the United States within its own judicial system presents one governmental standing question. The standing of states to sue in federal court presents another. One aspect of this question concerns the original jurisdiction of the Supreme Court, which includes cases "in which a state shall be party." U.S. Const. art. III, §2, cl. 2. A second aspect concerns the types of interests that may support state standing in a federal court.

The Court has addressed the state standing question when states have invoked the Court's original jurisdiction. For example, in *Georgia v. Pennsylvania R.R. Co.* (1945), the Court held that the State of Georgia could bring an original action in the Supreme Court against railroad companies for alleged antitrust violations in a *parens patriae* capacity to protect the state's economy. In a *parens patriae* suit, a state must allege that its citizens have suffered harm of the sort that the state would likely address through its lawmaking process. The doctrine suggests that the scope of *parens patriae* standing may be quite broad.

There are, however, reasons for the Court to limit state standing. One reason is that the Court's original jurisdiction is a scarce resource. In *Pennsylvania R.R. Co.*, the Court described its original jurisdiction as "one of the mighty instruments which the framers of the Constitution provided so that adequate machinery might be available for the peaceful settlement of disputes" involving states, "as an alternative" to the "traditional methods available to a sovereign for the settlement of such disputes"—namely, "diplomacy and war." Not every case involving a state presents such high stakes. Concern about preserving the Court's original jurisdiction for high stakes cases involving states may explain some of the Court's pronouncements on state standing. In *Pennsylvania v. New Jersey* (1976), for instance, the Court raised concerns about a potential flood of original jurisdiction cases when it held that a state lacks standing to litigate based solely upon "the personal claims of its citizens."

States increasingly, however, have sued the federal government in United States District Courts in public law cases seeking injunctive relief against the implementation of federal laws and regulations. The merits questions are often politically controversial, with states attorney general from one of the two major political parties suing federal agencies when the sitting President is from the other major party in district courts selected for judges likely to enjoin the agency action. In these cases, the Supreme Court has sought to distinguish among the various types of interests that a state may seek to protect through federal litigation.[29] To understand the modern framework for *parens patriae* standing, we begin with *Alfred L. Snapp & Son, Inc. v. Puerto Rico ex rel. Barez* (1982) and then turn to *Massachusetts v. EPA* (2007).

The plaintiff in *Snapp* was not a state, but rather a U.S. territory. In that case, Puerto Rico sued apple growers in Virginia for allegedly discriminating against Puerto Rican workers in violation of federal law. Invoking *parens patriae* standing, Puerto Rico argued that the apple growers had harmed not only Puerto Rican workers, but also Puerto Rico's economy.

Puerto Rico's territorial history provides a necessary backdrop to understanding the case. By the late nineteenth century, the United States began to assert itself as an expansionary power in competition with European imperial powers. In 1898, the United States acquired Puerto Rico from Spain as part of the settlement of the Spanish-American War. The Division of Customs and Insular Affairs, a bureau within the Office of the Secretary of War that eventually became the Bureau of Insular Affairs, was tasked with civil administration of the territory. In a series of decisions known as the *Insular Cases*, the U.S. Supreme Court developed the doctrine of unincorporated territories. This doctrine distinguishes between incorporated territories on the path to statehood and unincorporated territories that are subject to the plenary power of Congress and are not on the path to statehood unless and until Congress decides otherwise. The Constitution does not apply fully to unincorporated territories. Rather, the Court said in the *Insular Cases*, only "fundamental" constitutional rights apply in unincorporated territories.

Puerto Rico is an unincorporated territory. Since the Jones Act of 1917, the residents of Puerto Rico have been U.S. citizens, but they do not enjoy all the political rights that other U.S. citizens enjoy. Residents of the territory do not have a right to vote in presidential elections and do not have voting representation in Congress. In 1952, the citizens of Puerto Rico adopted a constitution for the Estado Libre Asociado de Puerto Rico, or "Free Associated State of Puerto Rico," typically called the "Commonwealth of Puerto Rico" in English. According to the Supreme Court in *Puerto Rico v. Sanchez Valle* (2016), however, the "ultimate source" of Puerto Rico's sovereignty remains the U.S. Congress. Many decades of wealth extraction from Puerto Rico have left its economy dependent upon transfers and aid from the federal government. There is persistently high unemployment in Puerto Rico, which has led many Puerto Ricans to move to the mainland United States permanently or seasonally for work.

The *Snapp* case arose from this pattern of labor migration. Puerto Rico alleged that the defendant apple growers had failed to comply with their obligation under federal law to give Puerto Rican workers preference over non-U.S. citizen migrant workers. The defendants argued that Puerto Rico lacked standing to litigate based upon the rights of Puerto Rican migrant workers. The Court held, however, that

---

29. *See* Seth Davis, *The New Public Standing*, 71 Stan. L. Rev. 1229 (2019).

Puerto Rico had *parens patriae* standing to bring its suit. In reaching this holding, the Court treated Puerto Rico as a state for standing purposes and distinguished among the various interests that may give a state standing to sue in federal court.

As you read the case, notice the Court's reliance on the history of discrimination against Puerto Ricans and the problems of unemployment in Puerto Rico in its analysis of the relationship between *parens patriae* standing and sovereignty.[30]

Alfred L. Snapp & Son, Inc. v. Puerto Rico ex rel. Barez

458 U.S. 592 (1982)

Justice WHITE delivered the opinion of the Court.

In this case, the Commonwealth of Puerto Rico seeks to bring suit in its capacity as *parens patriae* against petitioners for their alleged violations of federal law. Puerto Rico contends that those violations discriminated against Puerto Ricans and injured the Puerto Rican economy. The question presented here is whether Puerto Rico has standing to maintain this suit.

I

A

The factual background of this case involves the interaction of two federal statutes, the Wagner-Peyser Act, 48 Stat. 113, 29 U.S.C. §49 *et seq.*, and the Immigration and Nationality Act of 1952, 66 Stat. 163, as amended, 8 U.S.C. §1101 *et seq.* The Wagner-Peyser Act was passed in 1933 in order to deal with the massive problem of unemployment resulting from the Depression. Federal regulations issued pursuant to that authority have established an interstate clearance system to provide employers a means of recruiting nonlocal workers, when the supply of local workers is inadequate. If local workers are not available, a "clearance order" is sent through the Employment and Training Administration of the Department of Labor to other state agencies in order to give them an opportunity to meet the request.

Some of petitioners' obligations under the employment system established by the Wagner-Peyser Act stem from the Immigration and Nationality Act of 1952, insofar as it regulates the admission of nonimmigrant aliens into the United States. The latter Act authorizes the admission of temporary foreign workers into the United States only "if unemployed persons capable of performing such service or labor cannot be found in this country." To [ensure compliance with this Act], the Secretary of Labor relies upon the employment referral system established under the Wagner-Peyser Act.

Any employer who wants to employ temporary foreign agricultural laborers must first seek domestic laborers for the openings through use of the interstate clearance system.

The obvious point of this somewhat complicated statutory and regulatory framework is to provide two assurances to United States workers, including the citizens of Puerto Rico. First, these workers are given a preference over foreign

---

30. *See* Seth Davis, *State Standing for Equality,* 79 LA. L. REV. 147 (2018).

workers for jobs that become available within this country. Second, to the extent that foreign workers are brought in, the working conditions of domestic employees are not to be adversely affected, nor are United States workers to be discriminated against in favor of foreign workers.

B

The particular facts of this case involve the 1978 apple harvest on the east coast. That was apparently a good year for apples, resulting in a substantial need for temporary farm laborers to pick the crop. To meet this need the apple growers filed clearance orders with their state employment agencies. Through the system described above, a total of 2,318 job openings were transmitted to Puerto Rico on August 2, 1978. As of August 14, which marked the end of the 60-day "availability" period, the Commonwealth Department of Labor had recruited 1,094 Puerto Rican workers. Puerto Rican workers for the remaining openings were subsequently recruited. As stated in Puerto Rico's complaint:

> Of this total number of 2,318 Puerto Rican workers, only 992 actually arrived on the mainland. The remainder never left Puerto Rico because of oral advice from the United States Department of Labor requesting cancellation of remaining flights because many of the defendant growers had refused to employ Puerto Rican workers who had already arrived. Of the 992 workers who arrived at the orchards, 420 came to Virginia orchards. Of these 420 workers, fewer than 30 had employment three weeks later, the growers having refused to employ most of these workers and having dismissed most of the rest within a brief time for alleged unproductivity.

[Puerto Rico's] complaint alleged that the defendants had violated the Wagner-Peyser Act, the Immigration and Nationality Act of 1952, and various federal regulations implementing those statutes, by failing to provide employment for qualified Puerto Rican migrant farmworkers, by subjecting those Puerto Rican workers that were employed to working conditions more burdensome than those established for temporary foreign workers,[5] and by improperly terminating employment of Puerto Rican workers.

---

5. The theory of the complaint was that the apple growers were discriminating against the Puerto Ricans in favor of Jamaican workers. In August 1978, apple growers in several States, including Virginia, filed suit in Federal District Court seeking an injunction against the United States Secretary of Labor, the Commissioner of the Immigration and Naturalization Service, and their subordinates, to permit the recruitment and employment of foreign workers. Puerto Rico was allowed to intervene in this suit to represent the interests of its residents in these work opportunities. The growers complained that the federal employment service had not produced sufficient laborers to assure that the harvest, which was about to begin, could be successfully accomplished with sufficient speed. The District Court issued a preliminary injunction ordering that a certain number of foreign workers be allowed to enter this country to pick apples. The Jamaicans secured entry under this order. Prior to issuing this injunction, however, the court was assured by the apple growers that they recognized their obligation to give priority to Puerto Rican workers, notwithstanding the court order. Puerto Rico's complaint was founded on the charge that the apple growers failed to meet this commitment and, thus, failed to meet their obligations under federal law.

We granted certiorari to determine whether Puerto Rico could maintain a *parens patriae* action here, despite the small number of individuals directly involved.

II

Parens patriae means literally "parent of the country." The *parens patriae* action has its roots in the common-law concept of the "royal prerogative." The royal prerogative included the right or responsibility to take care of persons who "are legally unable, on account of mental incapacity, whether it proceed from 1st. nonage: 2. idiocy: or 3. lunacy: to take proper care of themselves and their property."

This common-law approach, however, has relatively little to do with the concept of *parens patriae* standing that has developed in American law. That concept does not involve the State's stepping in to represent the interests of particular citizens who, for whatever reason, cannot represent themselves. In fact, if nothing more than this is involved — *i.e.*, if the State is only a nominal party without a real interest of its own — then it will not have standing under the *parens patriae* doctrine. Rather, to have such standing the State must assert an injury to what has been characterized as a "quasi-sovereign" interest, which is a judicial construct that does not lend itself to a simple or exact definition. Its nature is perhaps best understood by comparing it to other kinds of interests that a State may pursue and then by examining those interests that have historically been found to fall within this category.

Two sovereign interests are easily identified: First, the exercise of sovereign power over individuals and entities within the relevant jurisdiction — this involves the power to create and enforce a legal code, both civil and criminal; second, the demand for recognition from other sovereigns — most frequently this involves the maintenance and recognition of borders. The former is regularly at issue in constitutional litigation. The latter is also a frequent subject of litigation, particularly in this Court:

> The original jurisdiction of this Court is one of the mighty instruments which the framers of the Constitution provided so that adequate machinery might be available for the peaceful settlement of disputes between States and between a State and citizens of another State. . . . The traditional methods available to a sovereign for the settlement of such disputes were diplomacy and war. Suit in this Court was provided as an alternative. *Georgia v. Pennsylvania R. Co.* (1945).

Not all that a State does, however, is based on its sovereign character. Two kinds of nonsovereign interests are to be distinguished. First, like other associations and private parties, a State is bound to have a variety of proprietary interests. A State may, for example, own land or participate in a business venture. As a proprietor, it is likely to have the same interests as other similarly situated proprietors. And like other such proprietors it may at times need to pursue those interests in court. Second, a State may, for a variety of reasons, attempt to pursue the interests of a private party, and pursue those interests only for the sake of the real party in interest. Interests of private parties are obviously not in themselves sovereign interests, and they do not become such simply by virtue of the State's aiding in their achievement. In such situations, the State is no more than a nominal party.

Quasi-sovereign interests stand apart from all three of the above: They are not sovereign interests, proprietary interests, or private interests pursued by the State as a nominal party. They consist of a set of interests that the State has in the well-being of its populace. Formulated so broadly, the concept risks being too vague to survive the standing requirements of Art. III: A quasi-sovereign interest must be sufficiently concrete to create an actual controversy between the State and the defendant. The vagueness of this concept can only be filled in by turning to individual cases.

In *Missouri v. Illinois* (1901), Missouri sought to enjoin the defendants from discharging sewage in such a way as to pollute the Mississippi River in Missouri. The Court relied upon an analogy to independent countries in order to delineate those interests that a State could pursue in federal court as *parens patriae*, apart from its sovereign and proprietary interests:

> If Missouri were an independent and sovereign State all must admit that she could seek a remedy by negotiation, and, that failing, by force. Diplomatic powers and the right to make war having been surrendered to the general government, it was to be expected that upon the latter would be devolved the duty of providing a remedy and that remedy, we think, is found in the constitutional provisions we are considering.

This analogy to an independent country was also articulated in *Georgia v. Tennessee Copper Co.* (1907), a case involving air pollution in Georgia caused by the discharge of noxious gasses from the defendant's plant in Tennessee. Justice Holmes, writing for the Court, described the State's interest under these circumstances as follows:

> [T]he State has an interest independent of and behind the titles of its citizens, in all the earth and air within its domain. It has the last word as to whether its mountains shall be stripped of their forests and its inhabitants shall breathe pure air. It might have to pay individuals before it could utter that word, but with it remains the final power. . . .
>
> . . . When the States by their union made the forcible abatement of outside nuisances impossible to each, they did not thereby agree to submit to whatever might be done. They did not renounce the possibility of making reasonable demands on the ground of their still remaining *quasi-*sovereign interests.

Both the Missouri case and the Georgia case involved the State's interest in the abatement of public nuisances, instances in which the injury to the public health and comfort was graphic and direct. Although there are numerous examples of such *parens patriae* suits, *parens patriae* interests extend well beyond the prevention of such traditional public nuisances.

In *Pennsylvania v. West Virginia* (1923), for example, Pennsylvania was recognized as a proper party to represent the interests of its residents in maintaining access to natural gas produced in West Virginia. The public nuisance and economic well-being lines of cases were specifically brought together in *Georgia v. Pennsylvania R. Co.* (1945), in which Georgia alleged that some 20 railroads had conspired to fix freight rates in a manner that discriminated against Georgia shippers in violation of the federal antitrust laws:

> If the allegations of the bill are taken as true, the economy of Georgia and the welfare of her citizens have seriously suffered as the result of this alleged conspiracy. . . . [Trade barriers] may cause a blight no less serious than the spread of noxious gas over the land or the deposit of sewage in the streams. They may affect the prosperity and welfare of a State as profoundly as any diversion of waters from the rivers. . . . Georgia as a representative of the public is complaining of a wrong which, if proven, limits the opportunities of her people, shackles her industries, retards her development, and relegates her to an inferior economic position among her sister States. These are matters of grave public concern in which Georgia has an interest apart from that of particular individuals who may be affected.

This summary of the case law involving *parens patriae* actions leads to the following conclusions. In order to maintain such an action, the State must articulate an interest apart from the interests of particular private parties, *i.e.*, the State must be more than a nominal party. The State must express a quasi-sovereign interest. Although the articulation of such interests is a matter for case-by-case development—neither an exhaustive formal definition nor a definitive list of qualifying interests can be presented in the abstract—certain characteristics of such interests are so far evident. These characteristics fall into two general categories. First, a State has a quasi-sovereign interest in the health and well-being—both physical and economic—of its residents in general. Second, a State has a quasi-sovereign interest in not being discriminatorily denied its rightful status within the federal system.

The Court has not attempted to draw any definitive limits on the proportion of the population of the State that must be adversely affected by the challenged behavior. Although more must be alleged than injury to an identifiable group of individual residents, the indirect effects of the injury must be considered as well in determining whether the State has alleged injury to a sufficiently substantial segment of its population. One helpful indication in determining whether an alleged injury to the health and welfare of its citizens suffices to give the State standing to sue as *parens patriae* is whether the injury is one that the State, if it could, would likely attempt to address through its sovereign lawmaking powers.

Distinct from but related to the general well-being of its residents, the State has an interest in securing observance of the terms under which it participates in the federal system. In the context of *parens patriae* actions, this means ensuring that the State and its residents are not excluded from the benefits that are to flow from participation in the federal system. Thus, the State need not wait for the Federal Government to vindicate the State's interest in the removal of barriers to the participation by its residents in the free flow of interstate commerce. Similarly, federal statutes creating benefits or alleviating hardships create interests that a State will obviously wish to have accrue to its residents. Once again, we caution that the State must be more than a nominal party. But a State does have an interest, independent of the benefits that might accrue to any particular individual, in assuring that the benefits of the federal system are not denied to its general population.

We turn now to the allegations of the complaint to determine whether they satisfy either or both of these criteria.[15]

III

The complaint presents two fundamental contentions. First, it alleges that the petitioners discriminated against Puerto Ricans in favor of foreign laborers. Second, it alleges that Puerto Ricans were denied the benefits of access to domestic work opportunities that the Wagner-Peyser Act and the Immigration and Nationality Act of 1952 were designed to secure for United States workers. We find each of these allegations to fall within the Commonwealth's quasi-sovereign interests and, therefore, each will support a *parens patriae* action.

Petitioners contend that at most there were only 787 job opportunities at stake in Virginia and that this number of temporary jobs could not have a substantial direct or indirect effect on the Puerto Rican economy. We believe that this is too narrow a view of the interests at stake here. Just as we have long recognized that a State's interests in the health and well-being of its residents extend beyond mere physical interests to economic and commercial interests, we recognize a similar state interest in securing residents from the harmful effects of discrimination. This Court has had too much experience with the political, social, and moral damage of discrimination not to recognize that a State has a substantial interest in assuring its residents that it will act to protect them from these evils. This interest is peculiarly strong in the case of Puerto Rico simply because of the unfortunate fact that invidious discrimination frequently occurs along ethnic lines. Puerto Rico's situation differs somewhat from the States in this regard—not in theory but in fact—simply because this country has for the most part been spared the evil of invidious discrimination based on state lines. Were this to come to pass, however, we have no doubt that a State could seek, in the federal courts, to protect its residents from such discrimination to the extent that it violates federal law. Puerto Rico claims that it faces this problem now. Regardless of the possibly limited effect of the alleged financial loss at issue here, we agree with the Court of Appeals that "[d]eliberate efforts to stigmatize the labor force as inferior carry a universal sting."

Alternatively, we find that Puerto Rico does have *parens patriae* standing to pursue the interests of its residents in the Commonwealth's full and equal participation in the federal employment service scheme established pursuant to the Wagner-Peyser Act and the Immigration and Nationality Act of 1952. Unemployment among Puerto Rican residents is surely a legitimate object of the Commonwealth's concern. Just as it may address that problem through its own legislation, it may also seek to assure its residents that they will have the full benefit of federal laws designed to address this problem. The Commonwealth's position in this respect is not distinguishable from that of Georgia when it sought

---

15. Although we have spoken throughout of a "State's" standing as *parens patriae*, we agree with the lower courts and the parties that the Commonwealth of Puerto Rico is similarly situated to a State in this respect: It has a claim to represent its quasi-sovereign interests in federal court at least as strong as that of any State.

the protection of the federal antitrust laws in order to eliminate freight rates that discriminated against Georgia shippers. Indeed, the fact that the Commonwealth participates directly in the operation of the federal employment scheme makes even more compelling its *parens patriae* interest in assuring that the scheme operates to the full benefit of its residents.[16]

Justice POWELL took no part in the decision of this case.

Justice BRENNAN, with whom Justice MARSHALL, Justice BLACKMUN, and Justice STEVENS join, concurring.

As the Court notes, the question whether a State can bring a *parens patriae* action within the original jurisdiction of this Court may well turn on considerations quite different from those implicated where the State seeks to press a *parens patriae* claim in the district courts. The Framers, in establishing original jurisdiction in this Court for suits "in which a State shall be a Party," Art. III, §2, cl. 2, and Congress, in implementing the grant of original jurisdiction with respect to suits between States, 28 U.S.C. §1251(a) (1976 ed., Supp. IV), may well have conceived of a somewhat narrower category of cases as presenting issues appropriate for initial determination in this Court than the full range of cases to which a State may have an interest cognizable by a federal court. The institutional limits on the Court's ability to accommodate such suits accentuates the need for more restrictive access to the original docket. In addition, because the judicial power of the United States does not extend to suits "commenced or prosecuted against one of the United States by Citizens of another State," U.S. Const., Amdt. 11, where one State brings a suit *parens patriae* against another *State*, a more circumspect inquiry may be required in order to ensure that the provisions of the Eleventh Amendment are not being too easily circumvented by the device of the State's bringing suit on behalf of some private party. Of course, none of the concerns that might counsel for a restrictive approach to the question of *parens patriae* standing is present in this case.

In cases such as the present one, I can discern no basis either in the Constitution or in policy for denying a State the opportunity to vindicate the federal rights of its citizens. At the *very* least, the prerogative of a State to bring suits in federal court should be commensurate with the ability of private organizations. A private organization may bring suit to vindicate its own concrete interest in performing those activities for which it was formed.

More significantly, a State is no ordinary litigant. As a sovereign entity, a State is entitled to assess its needs, and decide which concerns of its citizens warrant its protection and intervention. I know of nothing — except the Constitution

---

16. A State does not have standing as *parens patriae* to bring an action against the Federal Government. *Massachusetts v. Mellon* (1923) ("While the State, under some circumstances, may sue in that capacity for the protection of its citizens, it is no part of its duty or power to enforce their rights in respect of their relations with the Federal Government. In that field it is the United States, and not the State, which represents them as *parens patriae*"). Here, however, the Commonwealth is seeking to secure the federally created interests of its residents against private defendants. Indeed, the Secretary of Labor has represented that he has no objection to Puerto Rico's standing as *parens patriae* under these circumstances.

or overriding federal law—that might lead a federal court to superimpose its judgment for that of a State with respect to the substantiality or legitimacy of a State's assertion of sovereign interest.

* * *

Justice Brennan's concurring opinion in *Snapp* stated that "a State is no ordinary litigant." In what way does a state differ from private litigants for standing purposes? The Court addressed that question in Massachusetts v. EPA (2007), when it opined that a state is due "special solicitude" when it comes to standing.

Massachusetts v. EPA

549 U.S. 247 (2007)

Justice STEVENS delivered the opinion of the Court.

A well-documented rise in global temperatures has coincided with a significant increase in the concentration of carbon dioxide in the atmosphere. Respected scientists believe the two trends are related. For when carbon dioxide is released into the atmosphere, it acts like the ceiling of a greenhouse, trapping solar energy and retarding the escape of reflected heat. It is therefore a species—the most important species—of a "greenhouse gas."

Calling global warming "the most pressing environmental challenge of our time," a group of States, local governments, and private organizations, alleged in a petition for certiorari that the Environmental Protection Agency (EPA) has abdicated its responsibility under the Clean Air Act to regulate the emissions of four greenhouse gases, including carbon dioxide. Specifically, petitioners asked us to answer two questions concerning the meaning of §202(a)(1) of the Act: whether EPA has the statutory authority to regulate greenhouse gas emissions from new motor vehicles; and if so, whether its stated reasons for refusing to do so are consistent with the statute.

In response, EPA, supported by 10 intervening States and six trade associations, correctly argued that we may not address those two questions unless at least one petitioner has standing to invoke our jurisdiction under Article III of the Constitution.

Article III of the Constitution limits federal-court jurisdiction to "Cases" and "Controversies." Those two words confine "the business of federal courts to questions presented in an adversary context and in a form historically viewed as capable of resolution through the judicial process." *Flast v. Cohen* (1968). It is therefore familiar learning that no justiciable "controversy" exists when parties seek adjudication of a political question, when they ask for an advisory opinion, or when the question sought to be adjudicated has been mooted by subsequent developments. This case suffers from none of these defects.

The parties' dispute turns on the proper construction of a congressional statute, a question eminently suitable to resolution in federal court. Congress has moreover authorized this type of challenge to EPA action. *See* 42 U.S.C. §7607(b)(1). That authorization is of critical importance to the standing inquiry:

"Congress has the power to define injuries and articulate chains of causation that will give rise to a case or controversy where none existed before." *Lujan v. Defenders of Wildlife* (1992) (Kennedy, J., concurring in part and concurring in judgment). "In exercising this power, however, Congress must at the very least identify the injury it seeks to vindicate and relate the injury to the class of persons entitled to bring suit." We will not, therefore, "entertain citizen suits to vindicate the public's non-concrete interest in the proper administration of the laws."

EPA maintains that because greenhouse gas emissions inflict widespread harm, the doctrine of standing presents an insuperable jurisdictional obstacle. We do not agree. At bottom, "the gist of the question of standing" is whether petitioners have "such a personal stake in the outcome of the controversy as to assure that concrete adverseness which sharpens the presentation of issues upon which the court so largely depends for illumination." *Baker v. Carr* (1962).

To ensure the proper adversarial presentation, *Lujan v. Defenders of Wildlife* (1992), holds that a litigant must demonstrate that it has suffered a concrete and particularized injury that is either actual or imminent, that the injury is fairly traceable to the defendant, and that it is likely that a favorable decision will redress that injury. However, a litigant to whom Congress has "accorded a procedural right to protect his concrete interests," — here, the right to challenge agency action unlawfully withheld, §7607(b)(1) — "can assert that right without meeting all the normal standards for redressability and immediacy." When a litigant is vested with a procedural right, that litigant has standing if there is some possibility that the requested relief will prompt the injury-causing party to reconsider the decision that allegedly harmed the litigant.

Only one of the petitioners needs to have standing to permit us to consider the petition for review. We stress here the special position and interest of Massachusetts. It is of considerable relevance that the party seeking review here is a sovereign State and not, as it was in *Lujan*, a private individual.

Well before the creation of the modern administrative state, we recognized that States are not normal litigants for the purposes of invoking federal jurisdiction. As Justice Holmes explained in *Georgia v. Tennessee Copper Co.* (1907), a case in which Georgia sought to protect its citizens from air pollution originating outside its borders:

> The case has been argued largely as if it were one between two private parties; but it is not. . . . This is a suit by a State for an injury to it in its capacity of *quasi*-sovereign. In that capacity the State has an interest independent of and behind the titles of its citizens, in all the earth and air within its domain. It has the last word as to whether its mountains shall be stripped of their forests and its inhabitants shall breathe pure air.

Just as Georgia's independent interest "in all the earth and air within its domain" supported federal jurisdiction a century ago, so too does Massachusetts' well-founded desire to preserve its sovereign territory today. That Massachusetts does in fact own a great deal of the "territory alleged to be affected" only reinforces the conclusion that its stake in the outcome of this case is sufficiently concrete to warrant the exercise of federal judicial power.

When a State enters the Union, it surrenders certain sovereign prerogatives. Massachusetts cannot invade Rhode Island to force reductions in greenhouse gas emissions, it cannot negotiate an emissions treaty with China or India, and in some circumstances the exercise of its police powers to reduce in-state motor-vehicle emissions might well be pre-empted.

These sovereign prerogatives are now lodged in the Federal Government, and Congress has ordered EPA to protect Massachusetts (among others) by prescribing standards applicable to the "emission of any air pollutant from any class or classes of new motor vehicle engines, which in [the Administrator's] judgment cause, or contribute to, air pollution which may reasonably be anticipated to endanger public health or welfare." 42 U.S.C. §7521(a)(1). Congress has moreover recognized a concomitant procedural right to challenge the rejection of its rulemaking petition as arbitrary and capricious. §7607(b)(1). Given that procedural right and Massachusetts' stake in protecting its quasi-sovereign interests, the Commonwealth is entitled to special solicitude in our standing analysis.

With that in mind, it is clear that petitioners' submissions as they pertain to Massachusetts have satisfied the most demanding standards of the adversarial process. EPA's steadfast refusal to regulate greenhouse gas emissions presents a risk of harm to Massachusetts that is both "actual" and "imminent." There is, moreover, a "substantial likelihood that the judicial relief requested" will prompt EPA to take steps to reduce that risk. *Duke Power Co. v. Carolina Env'tl Study Grp., Inc.* (1978).

THE INJURY

The harms associated with climate change are serious and well recognized. Indeed, the NRC Report itself — which EPA regards as an "objective and independent assessment of the relevant science" — identifies a number of environmental changes that have already inflicted significant harms, including "the global retreat of mountain glaciers, reduction in snow-cover extent, the earlier spring melting of ice on rivers and lakes, [and] the accelerated rate of rise of sea levels during the 20th century relative to the past few thousand years. . . ."

Petitioners allege that this only hints at the environmental damage yet to come. According to the climate scientist Michael MacCracken, "qualified scientific experts involved in climate change research" have reached a "strong consensus" that global warming threatens (among other things) a precipitate rise in sea levels by the end of the century, "severe and irreversible changes to natural ecosystems," a "significant reduction in water storage in winter snowpack in mountainous regions with direct and important economic consequences," and an increase in the spread of disease. He also observes that rising ocean temperatures may contribute to the ferocity of hurricanes.

That these climate-change risks are "widely shared" does not minimize Massachusetts' interest in the outcome of this litigation. *See FEC v. Akins* (1998) ("[W]here a harm is concrete, though widely shared, the Court has found 'injury in fact'"). According to petitioners' unchallenged affidavits, global sea levels rose somewhere between 10 and 20 centimeters over the 20th century as a result of global warming. These rising seas have already begun to swallow Massachusetts' coastal land. Because the Commonwealth "owns a substantial portion of the state's coastal property," it has alleged a particularized injury in its capacity as a landowner. The severity of that injury will only increase over the course of the next century: If sea levels continue to rise as predicted, one Massachusetts official believes that a significant fraction of coastal property will be "either permanently lost through inundation or temporarily lost through periodic storm surge and flooding events." Remediation costs alone, petitioners allege, could run well into the hundreds of millions of dollars.

CAUSATION

EPA does not dispute the existence of a causal connection between manmade greenhouse gas emissions and global warming. At a minimum, therefore, EPA's refusal to regulate such emissions "contributes" to Massachusetts' injuries.

EPA nevertheless maintains that its decision not to regulate greenhouse gas emissions from new motor vehicles contributes so insignificantly to petitioners' injuries that the Agency cannot be haled into federal court to answer for them. For the same reason, EPA does not believe that any realistic possibility exists that the relief petitioners seek would mitigate global climate change and remedy their injuries. That is especially so because predicted increases in greenhouse gas emissions from developing nations, particularly China and India, are likely to offset any marginal domestic decrease.

But EPA overstates its case. Its argument rests on the erroneous assumption that a small incremental step, because it is incremental, can never be attacked in a federal judicial forum. Yet accepting that premise would doom most challenges to regulatory action. Agencies, like legislatures, do not generally resolve massive problems in one fell regulatory swoop. They instead whittle away at them over time, refining their preferred approach as circumstances change and as they develop a more nuanced understanding of how best to proceed. That a first step might be tentative does not by itself support the notion that federal courts lack jurisdiction to determine whether that step conforms to law.

And reducing domestic automobile emissions is hardly a tentative step. Even leaving aside the other greenhouse gases, the United States transportation sector emits an enormous quantity of carbon dioxide into the atmosphere—according to the MacCracken affidavit, more than 1.7 billion metric tons in 1999 alone. That accounts for more than 6% of worldwide carbon dioxide emissions. To put this in perspective: Considering just emissions from the transportation sector, which represent less than one-third of this country's total carbon dioxide emissions, the United States would still rank as the third-largest emitter of carbon dioxide in the world, outpaced only by the European Union and China. Judged by any standard, U.S. motor-vehicle emissions make a meaningful contribution to greenhouse gas concentrations and hence, according to petitioners, to global warming.

THE REMEDY

While it may be true that regulating motor-vehicle emissions will not by itself *reverse* global warming, it by no means follows that we lack jurisdiction to decide whether EPA has a duty to take steps to *slow* or *reduce* it. Because of the enormity of the potential consequences associated with manmade climate change, the fact that the effectiveness of a remedy might be delayed during the (relatively short) time it takes for a new motor-vehicle fleet to replace an older one is essentially irrelevant. Nor is it dispositive that developing countries such as China and India are poised to increase greenhouse gas emissions substantially over the next century: A reduction in domestic emissions would slow the pace of global emissions increases, no matter what happens elsewhere.

In sum—at least according to petitioners' uncontested affidavits—the rise in sea levels associated with global warming has already harmed and will continue to harm Massachusetts. The risk of catastrophic harm, though remote, is nevertheless real. That risk would be reduced to some extent if petitioners received the relief they seek. We therefore hold that petitioners have standing to challenge EPA's denial of their rulemaking petition.

[The Court went on to hold that the EPA had statutory authority to promulgate regulations addressing global climate change and either had to do so or justify not doing so.]

Chief Justice ROBERTS, with whom Justice SCALIA, Justice THOMAS, and Justice ALITO join, dissenting.

Global warming may be a "crisis," even "the most pressing environmental problem of our time." Indeed, it may ultimately affect nearly everyone on the planet in some potentially adverse way, and it may be that governments have done too little to address it. It is not a problem, however, that has escaped the attention of policymakers in the Executive and Legislative Branches of our Government, who continue to consider regulatory, legislative, and treaty-based means of addressing global climate change.

Apparently dissatisfied with the pace of progress on this issue in the elected branches, petitioners have come to the courts claiming broad-ranging injury, and attempting to tie that injury to the Government's alleged failure to comply with a rather narrow statutory provision. I would reject these challenges as nonjusticiable. Such a conclusion involves no judgment on whether global warming exists, what causes it, or the extent of the problem. Nor does it render petitioners without recourse. This Court's standing jurisprudence simply recognizes that redress of grievances of the sort at issue here "is the function of Congress and the Chief Executive," not the federal courts. *Lujan v. Defenders of Wildlife* (1992).

I

Our modern framework for addressing standing is familiar: "A plaintiff must allege personal injury fairly traceable to the defendant's allegedly unlawful conduct and likely to be redressed by the requested relief." *DaimlerChrysler Corp. v. Cuno* (2006). Applying that standard here, petitioners bear the burden of alleging an injury that is fairly traceable to the Environmental Protection Agency's failure to promulgate new motor vehicle greenhouse gas emission standards, and that is likely to be redressed by the prospective issuance of such standards.

Before determining whether petitioners can meet this familiar test, however, the Court changes the rules. It asserts that "States are not normal litigants for the purposes of invoking federal jurisdiction," and that given "Massachusetts' stake in protecting its quasi-sovereign interests, the Commonwealth is entitled to *special solicitude* in our standing analysis."

Relaxing Article III standing requirements because asserted injuries are pressed by a State, however, has no basis in our jurisprudence, and support for any such "special solicitude" is conspicuously absent from the Court's opinion. The general judicial review provision cited by the Court, 42 U.S.C. §7607(b)(1), affords States no special rights or status. Congress knows how to do that when it wants to, *see, e.g.,* §7426(b) (affording States the right to petition EPA to directly regulate certain sources of pollution), but it has done nothing of the sort here. Under the law on which petitioners rely, Congress treated public and private litigants exactly the same.

Nor does the case law cited by the Court provide any support for the notion that Article III somehow implicitly treats public and private litigants differently. The Court has to go back a full century in an attempt to justify its novel standing rule, but even there it comes up short. The Court's analysis hinges on *Georgia v. Tennessee Copper Co.* (1907) — a case that did indeed draw a distinction between a State and private litigants, but solely with respect to available remedies. The case had nothing to do with Article III standing.

In *Tennessee Copper*, the State of Georgia sought to enjoin copper companies in neighboring Tennessee from discharging pollutants that were inflicting "a wholesale destruction of forests, orchards and crops" in bordering Georgia counties. Although the State owned very little of the territory allegedly affected, the Court reasoned that Georgia — in its capacity as a "*quasi*-sovereign" — "has an interest independent of and behind the titles of its citizens, in all the earth and air within its domain." The Court explained that while "[t]he very elements that would be relied upon in a suit between fellow-citizens as a ground for equitable relief [were] wanting," a State "is not lightly to be required to give up *quasi*-sovereign rights for pay." Thus while a complaining private litigant would have to make do with a *legal* remedy — one "for pay" — the State was entitled to *equitable* relief.

In contrast to the present case, there was no question in *Tennessee Copper* about Article III injury. There was certainly no suggestion that the State could show standing where the private parties could not; there was no dispute, after all, that the private landowners had "an action at law." *Tennessee Copper* has since stood for nothing more than a State's right, in an original jurisdiction action, to sue in a representative capacity as *parens patriae*. Nothing about a State's ability to sue in that capacity dilutes the bedrock requirement of showing injury, causation, and redressability to satisfy Article III.

A claim of *parens patriae* standing is distinct from an allegation of direct injury. Far from being a substitute for Article III injury, *parens patriae* actions raise an additional hurdle for a state litigant: the articulation of a "quasi-sovereign interest" "*apart* from the interests of particular private parties." *Alfred L. Snapp & Son, Inc. v. Puerto Rico ex rel. Barez* (1982). Just as an association suing on behalf of its members must show not only that it represents the members but that at least one satisfies Article III requirements, so too a State asserting quasi-sovereign interests as *parens patriae* must still show that its citizens satisfy Article III. Focusing on Massachusetts's interests as quasi-sovereign makes the required showing here harder, not easier. The Court, in effect, takes what has always been regarded as a *necessary* condition for *parens patriae* standing — a quasi-sovereign interest — and converts it into a *sufficient* showing for purposes of Article III.

On top of everything else, the Court overlooks the fact that our cases cast significant doubt on a State's standing to assert a quasi-sovereign interest — as opposed to a direct injury — against the Federal Government. As a general rule, we have held that while a State might assert a quasi-sovereign right as *parens patriae* "for the protection of its citizens, it is no part of its duty or power to enforce their rights in respect of their relations with the Federal Government. In that field it is the United States, and not the State, which represents them." *Massachusetts v. Mellon* (1923).

II

It is not at all clear how the Court's "special solicitude" for Massachusetts plays out in the standing analysis, except as an implicit concession that petitioners cannot establish standing on traditional terms. But the status of Massachusetts as a State cannot compensate for petitioners' failure to demonstrate injury in fact, causation, and redressability.

If petitioners rely on loss of land as the Article III injury, however, they must ground the rest of the standing analysis in that specific injury. That alleged injury must be "concrete and particularized," and "distinct and palpable." Central to this concept of "particularized" injury is the requirement that a plaintiff be affected in a "personal and individual way," and seek relief that "directly and tangibly benefits him" in a manner distinct from its impact on "the public at large."

The very concept of global warming seems inconsistent with this particularization requirement. Global warming is a phenomenon "harmful to humanity at large," and the redress petitioners seek is focused no more on them than on the public generally—it is literally to change the atmosphere around the world.

If petitioners' particularized injury is loss of coastal land, it is also that injury that must be "actual or imminent, not conjectural or hypothetical," "real and immediate," and "certainly impending."

As to "actual" injury, the Court observes that "global sea levels rose somewhere between 10 and 20 centimeters over the 20th century as a result of global warming" and that "[t]hese rising seas have already begun to swallow Massachusetts' coastal land." But none of petitioners' declarations supports that connection. One declaration states that "a rise in sea level due to climate change is occurring on the coast of Massachusetts, in the metropolitan Boston area," but there is no elaboration. And the declarant goes on to identify a "significan[t]" *non*-global warming cause of Boston's rising sea level: land subsidence. Thus, aside from a single conclusory statement, there is nothing in petitioners' 43 standing declarations and accompanying exhibits to support an inference of actual loss of Massachusetts coastal land from 20th-century global sea level increases. It is pure conjecture.

The Court's attempts to identify "imminent" or "certainly impending" loss of Massachusetts coastal land fares no better. One of petitioners' declarants predicts global warming will cause sea level to rise by 20 to 70 centimeters *by the year 2100*. [A]ccepting a century-long time horizon and a series of compounded estimates renders requirements of imminence and immediacy utterly toothless.

* * *

Taken together, *Snapp* and *Massachusetts v. EPA* set forth a framework that distinguishes among the various interests that a state might seek to vindicate through litigation. A state may sue based upon a proprietary interest much as a private litigant may sue to protect property and contract rights. A state may sue, for example, to prevent a trespass upon property that it owns. Conversely, it may sue in a uniquely public capacity as a sovereign government. It may sue, for example, to vindicate an interest in its authority to make and enforce law. A state's quasi-sovereign interests are different from both proprietary and sovereign interests. Quasi-sovereign interests include a state's interest in the "health and well-being — both physical and economic — of its residents in general" and its interest in ensuring that it "and its residents are not excluded from the benefits that are to flow from participation in the federal system." These quasi-sovereign interests, the Court held in *Snapp*, support a state's *parens patriae* standing to sue to protect its residents.

The distinctions among these types of interests are not always clear. In *Massachusetts v. EPA*, for example, the Court seemed to lump proprietary, sovereign, and quasi-sovereign interests together in the standing analysis. It pointed to Massachusetts' ownership of its coastline, a proprietary interest. It referred to the "sovereign prerogatives" of states to exercise their police powers, without clearly distinguishing that sovereign interest from "Massachusetts' stake in protecting its quasi-sovereign interests" in protecting its residents.

Yet these distinctions matter for various doctrinal purposes. Importantly, the Court has said that states may not bring *parens patriae* suits against the federal government. In *Massachusetts v. Mellon* (1923), the Court stated that "[i]t cannot be conceded that a State, as *parens patriae*, may institute judicial proceedings to protect the citizens of the United States from the operation of the statutes thereof." Yet states may bring proprietary suits against the federal government. And in some cases, states have sued the federal government to vindicate sovereign interests. For example, in *New York v. United States* (1992), a state successfully vindicated its sovereign interest under the Tenth Amendment against commandeering by the federal government. And notwithstanding the limit on state *parens patriae* suits against the federal government, *Massachusetts v. EPA* permitted a state to sue a federal agency to vindicate "quasi-sovereign interests" alongside proprietary and sovereign interests.

It is also unclear when a federal court should afford states "special solicitude" in the standing analysis. The lower courts have treated states with special solicitude in a variety of cases, ranging from Texas's suit to enjoin implementation of the Obama Administration's immigration policies to California and New Mexico's challenge to the Trump Administration's construction of a wall along the Mexico/U.S. border. Since *Massachusetts v. EPA*, however, the Supreme Court has not invoked special solicitude in a state standing decision, although individual Justices continue to refer to the doctrine.

Judges and scholars continue to debate special solicitude for states. Defenders of the doctrine argue that states should be treated more favorably than private parties in standing analysis because state officials are more politically accountable than private litigants. They also argue that state litigation is necessary to hold the federal government accountable and enforce federal law. On the other hand, there is concern that state suits against the federal government bring too many politically charged controversies before the federal courts without sufficient facts to allow for a sensible judicial resolution. Some such cases are litigated soon after the enactment of statute, before a federal agency has time to implement it, and involve requests for preliminary injunctive relief, often on a nationwide scale. The concern, in other words, is that state standing "empower[s] state attorneys general to manipulate the presentation of public law issues in the lower federal courts" and "to meddle in national matters that should not be their concern."[31]

6. Representational Standing: Organizational Standing and Legislative Standing

Parens patriae suits by governments are one example of a standing problem common to several areas of standing law. The problem is when a litigant has standing to sue as a representative of another's interests. This problem arises in third-party standing cases. It also arises when organizations and legislators sue.

a. Organizational Standing

Organizational standing is an important mechanism of representational litigation across a wide variety of issue areas, including civil rights, constitutional law, and environmental law. Organizations may sue to vindicate their own interests as entities. They may also sue on behalf of their members.

As an entity, an organization may have standing to protect its proprietary interests, its ability to attract members or raise revenue, or its capacity to vindicate its organizational purposes. The last category of cases presents the most difficult standing questions. Under current doctrine, an organization must allege "far more than simply a setback to the organization's abstract social interests." Rather, as the Court held in *Havens Realty Corp. v. Coleman* (1982), an organization must show that it has suffered a concrete injury to its ability to accomplish its purposes. In *Coleman*, an organization sued a realty company, alleging that it discriminated on the basis of race in providing information about housing. The plaintiff organization's purpose was to secure open housing. Taking that purpose into account, the Court held that the organization had standing because the realty company's discriminatory practices had caused it to spend resources investigating and responding to complaints of housing discrimination.

Civil rights and other membership organizations may also have standing to sue on behalf of their members. For example, during the mid-twentieth century as Southern states violently resisted *Brown v. Bd. of Education* (1954) and other desegregation efforts, the Court was confronted with the question whether a civil rights organization could protect its members' anonymity while asserting their constitutional rights. Many states have laws requiring business and nonprofit corporations from outside the state to qualify to do business within the state by making various disclosures. In 1956, the Attorney General of the State of Alabama sought to enforce this type of statute against the NAACP as a way of shutting down its activities in the state. That same year, the NAACP had supported the Montgomery bus boycott as a protest against racial segregation in public transit

---

31. Davis, *supra* note 29, at 1278-79.

in Montgomery, Alabama. During the litigation, the Alabama courts ordered the NAACP to disclose its membership lists. In *NAACP v. Alabama* (1958), the Court held that the NAACP had standing to challenge this order on the grounds that it violated the associational and free speech rights of NAACP members.

Following *NAACP v. Alabama*, the Court developed a three-part test for an organization's standing to sue as a representative of its members in *Hunt v. Washington State Apple Advertising Comm'n* (1977). The organization in *Hunt* was a state agency that represented the apple growers and dealers of the State of Washington. The organization sued North Carolina state officials to enjoin implementation of a law that had the effect of prohibiting Washington apple growers from displaying Washington State apple grades on their containers shipped to North Carolina. The Washington apple grading system was a key marketing strategy for Washington apple growers. The Court held that the organization could bring a dormant commerce clause claim on behalf of its members. Its three-part test requires an organization to show that: "(1) its members would otherwise have standing to sue in their own right; (2) the interests it seeks to protect are germane to the organization's purpose; and (3) neither the claim asserted nor the relief requested requires the participation in the lawsuit of the individual members." The Court held that the organization's "status as a state agency, rather than a traditional voluntary membership organization," did not preclude it from suing when all three requirements were met.

The Court's decision in *TransUnion v. Ramirez*, discussed above in Section B, may lead to a narrowing of this line of organizational standing cases. In *TransUnion*, the Court stated that a plaintiff has standing to enforce federal law if the plaintiff claims an injury for which there is "a close historical or common-law analogue." Thus, if under the first prong of the *Hunt* test members do not have standing in the absence of a close historical or common-law analogue, their organization would not have standing. The rights at issue in *Coleman*, for example, were not traditional common law rights. They involved interference with the organization's advocacy efforts. It is not clear, therefore, that the organizational plaintiff in *Coleman* would have standing under *TransUnion*'s test.[32]

b.   Legislative Standing

Questions of representational standing also arise when legislative representatives sue. As with organizations, legislators may sue for injuries they personally suffer. For example, in 1967, the House of Representatives refused to seat Representative Adam Clayton Powell, Jr., the first African American elected to Congress from New York, after his reelection in 1966. Representative Powell had been accused of misappropriating congressional funds. The House Select

---

32. There were also individual plaintiffs in *Coleman*: "testers"—that is, "individuals who, without an intent to rent or purchase a home or apartment, pose as renters or purchasers for the purpose of collective evidence of unlawful steering practices." The Court held that individual testers had standing because Congress had created a statutory right for all "persons" to obtain truthful, nondiscriminatory information about housing opportunities. This standing decision also may be in doubt after *TransUnion*.

Committee that investigated the accusations did not recommend exclusion, but rather a fine. Nevertheless, the House voted to exclude him. In *Powell v. McCormack* (1969), the Court held that Representative Powell, who by that time had been seated, could sue for back pay to redress a personal injury.

In *Raines v. Byrd* (1997), the Court addressed a different question: May legislators sue based upon an injury to their capacity to act as representatives of their constituents? As the Court explained, the weight of authority holds that legislators have only limited standing to sue based upon allegations that their effectiveness as representatives has been diminished. The Court held that members of Congress lacked an injury in fact when they sued to challenge the constitutionality of the Line Item Veto Act. This statute permitted the President to cancel particular spending and tax measures *after* they had become law. Members of Congress sued under the Act, which provided a right of action and a path to expedited review in the Supreme Court. They argued that the Line Item Veto Act diminished the effectiveness of their votes. The Court held, however, that the members lacked standing because they could not show that their votes had been "stripped of [their] validity" or "denied [their] full validity in relation to the votes of their colleagues." The upshot is that legislators lack standing unless they have been singled out for discriminatory treatment, denied the opportunity to vote, or had their vote completely nullified. See the discussion in Section A of the efforts of members of Congress to appear in *Windsor* to defend the Defense of Marriage Act.

C. RIPENESS

Standing is not the only justiciability doctrine not spelled out in the Constitution but which, according to the Court, follows from Article III and the separation of powers. While standing limits the proper parties to litigate an issue, ripeness (and its close cousin, mootness, discussed below in Section D) concern the timing of litigation. Sometimes litigation is initiated too soon, before the issues are adequately developed for judicial review. Sometimes litigation is pressed too late, after the justification for judicial intervention has lapsed. Ripeness is about litigation that comes too soon.

The Court has said that ripeness turns upon two considerations. First, would the parties suffer a hardship if the court withholds consideration of the dispute? Second, are the issues fit for judicial decision? These questions, the Court has explained, reflect both the constitutional case or controversy requirement and prudential considerations about the quality of the record.

The distinction between standing and ripeness is sometimes difficult to draw. The Court has not always been consistent in how it has distinguished the two concepts. In particular, it sometimes has used "ripeness" to ask whether the plaintiff has suffered or imminently will suffer an injury in fact. This question dovetails with standing requirements, and in *Susan B. Anthony List v. Driehaus* (2014), discussed in the note after *Lyons* in our analysis of standing in Section B, the Court indicated that prudential ripeness is not a ground for denying jurisdiction as long as the threat of future harm constitutes injury in fact for purposes of Article III standing. Recall that the case involved a challenge to an Ohio election law prohibiting false statements regarding candidates or office holders. The petitioner, Susan B. Anthony List, wanted to continue accusing representatives who voted for the Affordable Care Act of supporting "taxpayer funded abortions." The Court found injury in fact in the "substantial" threat of administrative and criminal enforcement of the state law. The Court then addressed the question whether a case could be unripe if there is standing:

> In concluding that petitioners' claims were not justiciable, the Sixth Circuit separately considered two other factors: whether the factual record was sufficiently developed, and whether hardship to the parties would result if judicial relief is denied at this stage in the proceedings. Respondents contend that these "prudential ripeness" factors confirm that the claims at issue are nonjusticiable. But we have already concluded that petitioners have alleged a sufficient Article III injury. To the extent respondents would have us deem petitioners' claims nonjusticiable "on grounds that are 'prudential,' rather than constitutional," "[t]hat request is in some tension with our recent reaffirmation of the principle that 'a federal court's obligation to hear and decide' cases within its jurisdiction 'is virtually unflagging.'" *Lexmark Int'l, Inc. v. Static Control Components, Inc.* (2014).

The Court noted that, on the facts, the record and hardship factors were "easily" met. But the vitality of the ripeness doctrine we cover in what follows must be considered with the Court's admonition in *Driehaus* in mind.

The constitutional dimension of ripeness doctrine is addressed in *O'Shea v. Littleton* (1974), which, as you may recall, was cited and discussed in *Lyons.* O'Shea arose out of civil rights protests in Cairo, Illinois, a city with a long history of racial discrimination against African Americans, including a 1909 lynching attended by 10,000 people, later investigated by the famous journalist and civil rights leader Ida B. Wells. During the 1960s, continuing police violence, boycotts, and protests roiled the city. Nineteen citizens of Cairo filed a class action alleging systemic racial discrimination by state and local officials, including a county magistrate and a judge, who allegedly were setting higher bail and sentences for African Americans than for Whites in an effort to hamstring the civil rights protesters. The Court held that the case was nonjusticiable. Note as you read the overlap with injury-in-fact analysis for standing.

O'Shea v. Littleton

414 U.S. 488 (1974)

Justice WHITE delivered the opinion of the Court.

The respondents are 19 named individuals who commenced this civil rights action, individually and on behalf of a class of citizens of the city of Cairo, Illinois, against the State's Attorney for Alexander County, Illinois, his investigator, the Police Commissioner of Cairo, and the petitioners here, Michael O'Shea and Dorothy Spomer, Magistrate and Associate Judge of the Alexander County Circuit Court, respectively, alleging that they have intentionally engaged in, and are continuing to engage in, various patterns and practices of conduct in the administration of the criminal justice system in Alexander County that deprive respondents of rights secured by the First, Sixth, Eighth, Thirteenth, and Fourteenth Amendments, and by 42 U.S.C. §§1981, 1982, 1983, and 1985. The complaint, as amended, alleges that since the early 1960's, black citizens of Cairo, together with a small number of white persons on their behalf, have been actively, peaceably and lawfully seeking equality of opportunity and treatment in employment, housing, education, participation in governmental decisionmaking and in ordinary day-to-day relations with white citizens and officials of Cairo, and have, as an important part of their protest, participated in, and encouraged others to participate in, an economic boycott of city merchants who respondents consider have engaged in racial discrimination. Allegedly, there had resulted a great deal of tension and antagonism among the white citizens and officials of Cairo.

The individual respondents are 17 black and two white residents of Cairo. The class, or classes, which they purport to represent are alleged to include "all those who, on account of their race or creed and because of their exercise of First Amendment rights, have [been] in the past and continue to be subjected to the unconstitutional and selectively discriminatory enforcement and administration of criminal justice in Alexander County," as well as financially poor persons "who, on account of their poverty, are unable to afford bail, or are unable to afford counsel and jury trials in city ordinance violation cases." The complaint charges the State's Attorney, his investigator, and the Police Commissioner with a pattern and practice of intentional racial discrimination in the performance of their duties, by which the state criminal laws and procedures are deliberately applied more harshly to black residents of Cairo and inadequately applied to white persons who victimize blacks, to deter respondents from engaging in their lawful attempt to achieve equality. Specific supporting examples of such conduct involving some of the individual respondents are detailed in the complaint as to the State's Attorney and his investigator.

With respect to the petitioners, the county magistrate and judge, a continuing pattern and practice of conduct, under color of law, is alleged to have denied and to continue to deny the constitutional rights of respondents and members of their class in three respects: (1) petitioners set bond in criminal cases according to an unofficial bond schedule without regard to the facts of a case or circumstances of an individual defendant in violation of the Eighth and Fourteenth Amendments; (2) "on information and belief" they set sentences higher and impose harsher conditions for respondents and members of their class than for white persons; and (3) they require respondents and members of their class when charged with violations of city ordinances which carry fines and possible jail penalties if the fine cannot be paid, to pay for a trial by jury in violation of the Sixth, Eighth, and Fourteenth Amendments. Each of these continuing practices is alleged to have been carried out intentionally to deprive respondents and their class of the protections of the county criminal justice system and to deter them from engaging in their boycott and similar activities. The complaint further alleges that there is no adequate remedy at law and requests that the practices be enjoined. No damages were sought against the petitioners in this case, nor were any specific instances involving the individually named respondents set forth in the claim against these judicial officers.

We reverse the judgment of the Court of Appeals [for the respondents]. The complaint failed to satisfy the threshold requirement imposed by Art. III of the Constitution that those who seek to invoke the power of federal courts must allege an actual case or controversy. Plaintiffs in the federal courts "must allege some threatened or actual injury resulting from the putatively illegal action before a federal court may assume jurisdiction." *Linda R.S. v. Richard D.* (1973). There must be a "personal stake in the outcome" such as to "assure that concrete adverseness which sharpens the presentation of issues upon which the court so largely depends for illumination of difficult constitutional questions." *Baker v. Carr* (1962). Nor is the principle different where statutory issues are raised. Abstract injury is not enough. It must be alleged that the plaintiff "has sustained or is immediately in danger of sustaining some direct injury" as the result of the challenged statute or official conduct. The injury or threat of injury must be both "real and immediate," not "conjectural" or "hypothetical." Moreover, if none of the named plaintiffs purporting to represent a class establishes the requisite of a case or controversy with the defendants, none may seek relief on behalf of himself or any other member of the class.

In the complaint that began this action, the sole allegations of injury are that petitioners "have engaged in and continue to engage in, a pattern and practice of conduct . . . all of which has deprived and continues to deprive plaintiffs and members of their class of their" constitutional rights and, again, that petitioners "have denied and continue to deny to plaintiffs and members of their class their constitutional rights" by illegal bondsetting, sentencing, and jury-fee practices. None of the named plaintiffs is identified as himself having suffered any injury in the manner specified. In sharp contrast to the claim for relief against the State's Attorney where specific instances of misconduct with respect to particular individuals are alleged, the claim against petitioners alleges injury in only the most general terms. At oral argument, respondents' counsel stated that some of the named plaintiffs-respondents, who could be identified by name if necessary, had actually been defendants in proceedings before petitioners and had suffered from the alleged unconstitutional practices. Past exposure to illegal conduct does not in itself show a present case or controversy regarding injunctive relief, however, if unaccompanied by any continuing, present adverse effects. Neither the complaint nor respondents' counsel suggested that any of the named plaintiffs at the time the complaint was filed were themselves serving an allegedly illegal sentence or were on trial or awaiting trial before petitioners. Indeed, if any of the respondents were then serving an assertedly unlawful sentence, the complaint would inappropriately be seeking relief from or modification of current, existing custody. Furthermore, if any were then on trial or awaiting trial in state proceedings, the complaint would be seeking injunctive relief that a federal court should not provide. *Younger v. Harris* (1971). We thus do not strain to read inappropriate meaning into the conclusory allegations of this complaint.

Of course, past wrongs are evidence bearing on whether there is a real and immediate threat of repeated injury. But here the prospect of future injury rests on the likelihood that respondents will again be arrested for and charged with violations of the criminal law and will again be subjected to bond proceedings, trial, or sentencing before petitioners. Important to this assessment is the absence of allegations that any relevant criminal statute of the State of Illinois is unconstitutional on its face or as applied or that respondents have been or will be improperly charged with violating criminal law. If the statutes that might possibly be enforced against respondents are valid laws, and if charges under these statutes are not improvidently made or pressed, the question becomes whether any perceived threat to respondents is sufficiently real and immediate to show an existing controversy simply because they anticipate violating lawful criminal statutes and being tried for their offenses, in which event they may appear before petitioners and, if they do, will be affected by the allegedly illegal conduct charged. Apparently, the proposition is that *if* respondents proceed to violate an unchallenged law and *if* they are charged, held to answer, and tried in any proceedings before petitioners, they will be subjected to the discriminatory practices that petitioners are alleged to have followed. But it seems to us that attempting to anticipate whether and when these respondents will be charged with crime and will be made to appear before either petitioner takes us into the area of speculation and conjecture. The nature of respondents' activities is not described in detail and no specific threats are alleged to have been made against them. Accepting that they are deeply involved in a program to eliminate racial discrimination in Cairo and that tensions are high, we are nonetheless unable to conclude that the case-or-controversy requirement is satisfied by general assertions or inferences that in the course of their activities respondents will be prosecuted for violating valid criminal laws. We assume that respondents will conduct their activities within the law and so avoid prosecution and conviction as well as exposure to the challenged course of conduct said to be followed by petitioners.

As in *Golden v. Zwickler* (1969), we doubt that there is "'sufficient immediacy and reality'" to respondents' allegations of future injury to warrant invocation of the jurisdiction of the District Court. There, "it was wholly conjectural that another occasion might arise when Zwickler might be prosecuted for distributing the handbills referred to in the complaint." Here we can only speculate whether respondents will be arrested, either again or for the first time, for violating a municipal ordinance or a state statute, particularly in the absence of any allegations that unconstitutional criminal statutes are being employed to deter constitutionally protected conduct. Even though Zwickler attacked a specific statute under which he had previously been prosecuted, the threat of a new prosecution was not sufficiently imminent to satisfy the jurisdictional requirements of the federal courts. Similarly, respondents here have not pointed to any imminent prosecutions contemplated against any of their number and they naturally do not suggest that any one of them expects to violate valid criminal laws. Yet their vulnerability to the alleged threatened injury from which relief is sought is necessarily contingent upon the bringing of prosecutions against one or more of them. Under these circumstances, where respondents do not claim any constitutional right to engage in conduct proscribed by therefore presumably permissible state laws, or indicate that it is otherwise their intention to so conduct themselves, the threat of injury from the alleged course of conduct they attack is simply too remote to satisfy the case-or-controversy requirement and permit adjudication by a federal court.

[Opinion of Justice BLACKMUN, concurring in part, omitted.]

Justice DOUGLAS, with whom Justice BRENNAN and Justice MARSHALL concur, dissenting.

The respondents in this case are black and indigent citizens of Cairo, Illinois. Suing in federal court, they alleged that since the early 1960's black citizens of Cairo have been actively seeking equal opportunity and treatment in employment, housing, education, and ordinary day-to-day relations with the white citizens and officials of Cairo. In this quest, blacks have engaged in a boycott of local merchants deemed to have engaged in racial discrimination.

This Court now decides for the first time in the course of this litigation that the complaint is deficient because it does not state a "case or controversy" within the meaning of Art. III.

The fact that no party has raised that issue in this closely contested case is no barrier, of course, to our consideration of it. But the reasoning and result reached by the Court are to say the least a *tour de force* and quite inconsistent with the allegations in the complaint, which are within constitutional requirements.

We know from the record and oral argument that Cairo, Illinois, is boiling with racial conflicts. This class action brought under 42 U.S.C. §§1981, 1982, 1983, and 1985 is to remedy vast invasions of civil rights. The Court, however, says that it is not a "case or controversy" because none of the named plaintiffs has alleged infringement of his rights and the fact that other members of the class may have been injured is not enough.

[T]he amended complaint is sufficiently specific to warrant a trial.

As respects O'Shea, the Magistrate, and Spomer, the Circuit Judge, the charges concerning *named plaintiffs* are as follows:

> (1) that excessive bonds have been required in violation of the Eighth and Fourteenth Amendments because petitioners follow an unofficial bond schedule without regard to the facts of individual cases;
>
> (2) on information and belief, that petitioners set higher sentences and impose harsher conditions for respondents and members of their class than for white persons;
>
> (3) that, where the named plaintiffs have been fined and at times sentenced to jail and cannot pay the fines, these judges have required them to pay for a trial by jury.

Moreover, the amended complaint alleges that O'Shea and Spomer "continue to engage in a pattern and practice" which "has deprived and continues to deprive" the named plaintiffs and members of their class of their constitutional rights. Moreover, it is alleged that since early in the 1960's the blacks of Cairo and some whites have been actively and peaceably seeking to end discrimination in Cairo and that those activities have generated and continue to generate tension and antagonism in Cairo.

It is also alleged that the police commissioner in Cairo has denied and continues to deny to plaintiffs and members of their class their constitutional rights in the following ways:

> (a) Defendant has made or caused to be made or cooperated in the making of arrests and the filing of charges against plaintiffs and members of their class where such charges are not warranted and are merely for the purpose of harassment and to discourage and prevent plaintiffs and their class from exercising their constitutional rights.
>
> (b) Defendant has made or caused to be made or cooperated in the making of arrests and the filing of charges against plaintiffs and members of their class where there may be some colorable basis to the arrest or charge, but the crime defined in the charge is much harsher than is warranted by the facts and is far more severe than like charges would be against a white person.

These allegations support the likelihood that the named plaintiffs as well as members of their class will be arrested in the future and therefore will be brought before O'Shea and Spomer and be subjected to the alleged discriminatory practices in the administration of justice.

These allegations of past and continuing wrongdoings clearly state a case or controversy in the Art. III sense.

What has been alleged here is not only wrongs done to named plaintiffs, but a recurring pattern of wrongs which establishes, if proved, that the legal regime under control of the whites in Cairo, Illinois, is used over and over again to keep the blacks from exercising First Amendment rights, to discriminate against them, to keep from the blacks the protection of the law in their lawful activities, to weight the scales of justice repeatedly on the side of white prejudices and against black protests, fears, and suffering. This is a more pervasive scheme for suppression of blacks and their civil rights than I have ever seen. It may not survive a trial. But if this case does not present a "case or controversy" involving the named plaintiffs, then that concept has been so watered down as to be no longer recognizable. This will please the white superstructure, but it does violence to the conception of evenhanded justice envisioned by the Constitution.

* * *

The Court's decision in *O'Shea* could be characterized as a standing holding—i.e., there was no concrete injury and no imminent threat of one—and it was relied on in standing cases as we saw in *Lyons*. The Court cites it in pre-enforcement standing cases such as *Babbitt* as well (discussed in the note after *Lyons*). But it could be characterized in ripeness terms to the extent that it is concerned with the appropriateness of judicial intervention when injury has not yet occurred. This perhaps explains the Court's statement in *Driehaus* that the concerns that animate ripeness may not be relevant if the threat of future injury is substantial enough to meet the requirements for standing.

Consider whether there is a meaningful distinction in *Poe v. Ullman* (1961), a case in which the Court uses ripeness doctrine to avoid deciding whether there is a constitutional right to distribute or use contraception. *Poe* involved married women whose physical and mental health were threatened by pregnancy. Along with their doctors, they challenged a state law preventing the distribution or use of contraceptives. The Court held that the suit was not justiciable because there had been only one prosecution under the law in over eight decades.

The case stands for the proposition that hardship is a prerequisite for ripeness—where there is minimal harm from denying review, the case may be dismissed on ripeness grounds. Yet, as the dissenting opinions explained, the threat of prosecution under the state law limited the availability of contraceptives and led to the closing of all women's health clinics in the state, which explains why the plaintiffs filed in the first place. Indeed, four years later, after the state prosecuted a Planned Parenthood clinic, the Supreme Court held in *Griswold v. Connecticut* (1965) that the state law was unconstitutional. As you read, consider the weight given to prosecutorial discretion in enforcement of the law, especially compared to its role in other justiciability cases we have covered (most prominently *Linda R.S.*, *O'Shea*, and *Driehaus*).

Poe v. Ullman

367 U.S. 497 (1961)

Mr. Justice FRANKFURTER announced the judgment of the Court and an opinion in which THE CHIEF JUSTICE, Mr. Justice CLARK and Mr. Justice WHITTAKER join.

These appeals challenge the constitutionality, under the Fourteenth Amendment, of Connecticut statutes which, as authoritatively construed by the Connecticut Supreme Court of Errors, prohibit the use of contraceptive devices and the giving of medical advice in the use of such devices. In proceedings seeking declarations of law, not on review of convictions for violation of the statutes, that court has ruled that these statutes would be applicable in the case of married couples and even under claim that conception would constitute a serious threat to the health or life of the female spouse.

No. 60 combines two actions brought in a Connecticut Superior Court for declaratory relief. The complaint in the first alleges that the plaintiffs, Paul and Pauline Poe, are a husband and wife, thirty and twenty-six years old respectively, who live together and have no children. Mrs. Poe has had three consecutive pregnancies terminating in infants with multiple congenital abnormalities from which each died shortly after birth. Plaintiffs have consulted Dr. Buxton, an obstetrician and gynecologist of eminence, and it is Dr. Buxton's opinion that the cause of the infants' abnormalities is genetic, although the underlying "mechanism" is unclear. In view of the great emotional stress already suffered by plaintiffs, the probable consequence of another pregnancy is psychological strain extremely disturbing to the physical and mental health of both husband and wife. Plaintiffs know that it is Dr. Buxton's opinion that the best and safest medical treatment which could be prescribed for their situation is advice in methods of preventing conception. Dr. Buxton knows of drugs, medicinal articles and instruments which can be safely used to effect contraception. Medically, the use of these devices is indicated as the best and safest preventive measure necessary for the protection of plaintiffs' health. Plaintiffs, however, have been unable to obtain this information for the sole reason that its delivery and use may or will be claimed by the defendant State's Attorney (appellee in this Court) to constitute offenses against Connecticut law. The State's Attorney intends to prosecute offenses against the State's laws, and claims that the giving of contraceptive advice and the use of contraceptive devices would be offenses forbidden by [Connecticut law]. Alleging irreparable injury and a substantial uncertainty of legal relations (a local procedural requisite for a declaration), plaintiffs ask a declaratory judgment that [the challenged Connecticut statutes] are unconstitutional, in that they deprive the plaintiffs of life and liberty without due process of law.

The second action in No. 60 is brought by Jane Doe, a twenty-five-year-old housewife. Mrs. Doe, it is alleged, lives with her husband, they have no children; Mrs. Doe recently underwent a pregnancy which induced in her a critical physical illness — two weeks' unconsciousness and a total of nine weeks' acute sickness which left her with partial paralysis, marked impairment of speech, and emotional instability. Another pregnancy would be exceedingly perilous to her life. She, too, has consulted Dr. Buxton, who believes that the best and safest treatment for her is contraceptive advice. The remaining allegations of Mrs. Doe's complaint, and the relief sought, are similar to those in the case of Mr. and Mrs. Poe.

In No. 61, also a declaratory judgment action, Dr. Buxton is the plaintiff. Setting forth facts identical to those alleged by Jane Doe, he asks that the Connecticut statutes prohibiting his giving of contraceptive advice to Mrs. Doe be adjudged unconstitutional, as depriving him of liberty and property without due process.

Appellants' complaints in these declaratory judgment proceedings do not clearly, and certainly do not in terms, allege that appellee Ullman threatens to prosecute them for use of, or for giving advice concerning, contraceptive devices. The allegations are merely that, in the course of his public duty, he intends to prosecute any offenses against Connecticut law, and that he claims that use of and advice concerning contraceptives would constitute offenses. The lack of immediacy of the threat described by these allegations might alone raise serious questions of non-justiciability of appellants' claims. But even were we to read the allegations to convey a clear threat of imminent prosecutions, we are not bound to accept as true all that is alleged on the face of the complaint and admitted, technically, by demurrer, any more than the Court is bound by stipulation of the parties. Formal agreement between parties that collides with plausibility is too fragile a foundation for indulging in constitutional adjudication.

The Connecticut law prohibiting the use of contraceptives has been on the State's books since 1879. During the more than three-quarters of a century since its enactment, a prosecution for its violation seems never to have been initiated, save in *State v. Nelson* (Conn. 1940). The circumstances of that case, decided in 1940, only prove the abstract character of what is before us. There, a test case was brought to determine the constitutionality of the Act as applied against two doctors and a nurse who had allegedly disseminated contraceptive information. After the Supreme Court of Errors sustained the legislation on appeal from a demurrer to the information, the State moved to dismiss the information. Neither counsel nor our own researches have discovered any other attempt to enforce the prohibition of distribution or use of contraceptive devices by criminal process. The unreality of these law suits is illumined by another circumstance. We were advised by counsel for appellants that contraceptives are commonly and notoriously sold in Connecticut drug stores. Yet no prosecutions are recorded; and certainly such ubiquitous, open, public sales would more quickly invite the attention of enforcement officials than the conduct in which the present appellants wish to engage — the giving of private medical advice by a doctor to his individual patients, and their private use of the devices prescribed. The undeviating policy of nullification by Connecticut of its anti-contraceptive laws throughout all the long years that they have been on the statute books bespeaks more than prosecutorial paralysis.

The restriction of our jurisdiction to cases and controversies within the meaning of Article III of the Constitution, *see Muskrat v. United States* (1911), is not the sole limitation on the exercise of our appellate powers, especially in cases raising constitutional questions. The policy reflected in numerous cases and over a long period was thus summarized in the oft-quoted statement of Mr. Justice Brandeis: "The Court [has] developed, for its own governance in the cases confessedly within its jurisdiction, a series of rules under which it has avoided passing upon a large part of all the constitutional questions pressed upon it for decision." *Ashwander v. Tennessee Valley Authority* (1936). In part the rules summarized in the *Ashwander* opinion have derived from the historically defined, limited nature and function of courts and from the recognition that, within the framework of our adversary system, the adjudicatory process is most securely founded when it is exercised under the impact of a lively conflict between antagonistic demands, actively pressed, which make resolution of the controverted issue a practical necessity. In part they derive from the fundamental federal and tripartite character of our National Government and from the role—restricted by its very responsibility—of the federal courts, and particularly this Court, within that structure.

These considerations press with special urgency in cases challenging legislative action or state judicial action as repugnant to the Constitution. "The best teaching of this Court's experience admonishes us not to entertain constitutional questions in advance of the strictest necessity." *Parker v. County of Los Angeles* (1949). The various doctrines of "standing," "ripeness," and "mootness," which this Court has evolved with particular, though not exclusive, reference to such cases are but several manifestations—each having its own "varied application"—of the primary conception that federal judicial power is to be exercised to strike down legislation, whether state or federal, only at the instance of one who is himself immediately harmed, or immediately threatened with harm, by the challenged action.

[J]ust as the declaratory judgment device does not "purport to alter the character of the controversies which are the subject of the judicial power under the Constitution," *United States v. West Virginia* (1935), it does not permit litigants to invoke the power of this Court to obtain constitutional rulings in advance of necessity. The Court has been on the alert against use of the declaratory judgment device for avoiding the rigorous insistence on exigent adversity as a condition for evoking Court adjudication. This is as true of state court suits for declaratory judgments as of federal. By exercising their jurisdiction, state courts cannot determine the jurisdiction to be exercised by this Court. Although we have held that a state declaratory-judgment suit may constitute a case or controversy within our appellate jurisdiction, it is to be reviewed here only "so long as the case retains the essentials of an adversary proceeding, involving a real, not a hypothetical, controversy, which is finally determined by the judgment below." *Nashville, C. & St. L. Ry. Co. v. Wallace* (1933).

It is clear that the mere existence of a state penal statute would constitute insufficient grounds to support a federal court's adjudication of its constitutionality in proceedings brought against the State's prosecuting officials if real threat of enforcement is wanting. If the prosecutor expressly agrees not to prosecute, a suit against him for declaratory and injunctive relief is not such an adversary case as will be reviewed here. Eighty years of Connecticut history demonstrate a similar, albeit tacit agreement. The fact that Connecticut has not chosen to press the enforcement of this statute deprives these controversies of the immediacy which is an indispensable condition of constitutional adjudication. This Court cannot be umpire to debates concerning harmless, empty shadows. To find it necessary to pass on these statutes now, in order to protect appellants from the hazards of prosecution. would be to close our eyes to reality.

Nor does the allegation by the Poes and Doe that they are unable to obtain information concerning contraceptive devices from Dr. Buxton, "for the sole reason that the delivery and use of such information and advice may or will be claimed by the defendant State's Attorney to constitute offenses," disclose a necessity for present constitutional decision. It is true that this Court has several times passed upon criminal statutes challenged by persons who claimed that the effects of the statutes were to deter others from maintaining profitable or advantageous relations with the complainants. But in these cases the deterrent effect complained of was one which was grounded in a realistic fear of prosecution. We cannot agree that if Dr. Buxton's compliance with these statutes is uncoerced by the risk of their enforcement, his patients are entitled to a declaratory judgment concerning the statutes' validity. And, with due regard to Dr. Buxton's standing as a physician and to his personal sensitiveness, we cannot accept, as the basis of constitutional adjudication, other than as chimerical the fear of enforcement of provisions that have during so many years gone uniformly and without exception unenforced.

Justiciability is of course not a legal concept with a fixed content or susceptible of scientific verification. Its utilization is the resultant of many subtle pressures, including the appropriateness of the issues for decision by this Court and the actual hardship to the litigants of denying them the relief sought. Both these factors justify withholding adjudication of the constitutional issue raised under the circumstances and in the manner in which they are now before the Court.

Mr. Justice BRENNAN, concurring in the judgment.

I agree that this appeal must be dismissed for failure to present a real and substantial controversy which unequivocally calls for adjudication of the rights claimed in advance of any attempt by the State to curtail them by criminal prosecution. I am not convinced, on this skimpy record, that these appellants as individuals are truly caught in an inescapable dilemma. The true controversy in this case is over the opening of birth-control clinics on a large scale; it is that which the State has prevented in the past, not the use of contraceptives by isolated and individual married couples. It will be time enough to decide the constitutional questions urged upon us when, if ever, that real controversy flares up again. Until it does, or until the State makes a definite and concrete threat to enforce these laws against individual married couples — a threat which it has never made in the past except under the provocation of litigation — this Court may not be compelled to exercise its most delicate power of constitutional adjudication.

Mr. Justice DOUGLAS, dissenting.

These cases are dismissed because a majority of the members of this Court conclude, for varying reasons, that this controversy does not present a justiciable question. That conclusion is too transparent to require an extended reply. The device of the declaratory judgment is an honored one. Its use in the federal system is restricted to "cases" or "controversies" within the meaning of Article III. The question must be "appropriate for judicial determination," not hypothetical, abstract, academic or moot. *Aetna Life Ins. Co. v. Haworth* (1937). It must touch "the legal relations of parties having adverse legal interests." It must be "real and substantial" and admit of "specific relief through a decree of a conclusive character." The fact that damages are not awarded or an injunction does not issue, the fact that there are no allegations of irreparable injury are irrelevant. This is hornbook law. The need for this remedy in the federal field was summarized in a Senate Report as follows: ". . . it is often necessary, in the absence of the declaratory judgment procedure, to violate or purport to violate a statute in order to obtain a judicial determination of its meaning or validity."

If there is a case where the need for this remedy in the shadow of a criminal prosecution is shown, it is this one. Plaintiffs in No. 60 are two sets of husband and wife. One wife is pathetically ill, having delivered a stillborn fetus. If she becomes pregnant again, her life will be gravely jeopardized. This couple have been unable to get medical advice concerning the "best and safest" means to avoid pregnancy from their physician, plaintiff in No. 61, because if he gave it he would commit a crime. The use of contraceptive devices would also constitute a crime. And it is alleged—and admitted by the State—that the State's Attorney intends to enforce the law by prosecuting offenses under the laws.

A public clinic dispensing birth-control information has indeed been closed by the State. Doctors and a nurse working in that clinic were arrested by the police and charged with advising married women on the use of contraceptives. That litigation produced *State v. Nelson* (Conn. 1940), which upheld these statutes. That same police raid on the clinic resulted in the seizure of a quantity of the clinic's contraception literature and medical equipment and supplies.

The Court refers to the *Nelson* prosecution as a "test case" and implies that it had little impact. Yet its impact was described differently by a contemporary observer who concluded his comment with this sentence: "This serious setback to the birth control movement [the *Nelson* case] led to the closing of all the clinics in the state, just as they had been previously closed in the state of Massachusetts." At oral argument, counsel for appellants confirmed that the clinics are still closed. In response to a question from the bench, he affirmed that "no public or private clinic" has dared give birth-control advice since the decision in the *Nelson* case.

These, then, are the circumstances in which the Court feels that it can, contrary to every principle of American or English common law, go outside the record to conclude that there exists a "tacit agreement" that these statutes will not be enforced. No lawyer, I think, would advise his clients to rely on that "tacit agreement." No police official, I think, would feel himself bound by that "tacit agreement." After our national experience during the prohibition era, it would be absurd to pretend that all criminal statutes are adequately enforced. But that does not mean that bootlegging was the less a crime. In fact, an arbitrary administrative pattern of non-enforcement may increase the hardships of those subject to the law.

What are these people—doctor and patients—to do? Flout the law and go to prison? Violate the law surreptitiously and hope they will not get caught? By today's decision we leave them no other alternatives. It is not the choice they need have under the regime of the declaratory judgment and our constitutional system. It is not the choice worthy of a civilized society. A sick wife, a concerned husband, a conscientious doctor seek a dignified, discrete, orderly answer to the critical problem confronting them. We should not turn them away and make them flout the law and get arrested to have their constitutional rights determined. They are entitled to an answer to their predicament here and now.

Mr. Justice HARLAN, dissenting.

I do not think these appeals may be dismissed for want of "ripeness" as that concept has been understood in its "varied applications." Certainly the appellants have stated in their pleadings fully and unequivocally what it is that they intend to do; no clarifying or resolving contingency stands in their way before they may embark on that conduct. Thus there is no circumstance besides that of detection or prosecution to make remote the particular controversy. And it is clear beyond cavil that the mere fact that a controversy such as this is rendered still more unavoidable by an actual prosecution, is not alone sufficient to make the case too remote, not ideally enough "ripe" for adjudication, at the prior stage of anticipatory relief.

I cannot see what further elaboration is required to enable us to decide the appellants' claims, and indeed neither the plurality opinion nor the concurring opinion — notwithstanding the latter's characterization of this record as "skimpy" — suggests what more grist is needed before the judicial mill could turn.

As far as the record is concerned, I think it is pure conjecture, and indeed conjecture which to me seems contrary to realities, that an open violation of the statute by a doctor (or more obviously still by a birth-control clinic) would not result in a substantial threat of prosecution.

In short, I fear that the Court has indulged in a bit of sleight of hand to be rid of this case. It has treated the significance of the absence of prosecutions during the twenty years since *Nelson* as identical with that of the absence of prosecutions during the years before *Nelson*. It has ignored the fact that the very purpose of the *Nelson* prosecution was to change defiance into compliance. It has ignored the very possibility that this purpose may have been successful. The result is to postulate a security from prosecution for open defiance of the statute which I do not believe the record supports.

Here is the core of my disagreement with the present disposition. . . . [T]he most substantial claim which these married persons press is their right to enjoy the privacy of their marital relations free of the enquiry of the criminal law, whether it be in a prosecution of them or of a doctor whom they have consulted. And I cannot agree that their enjoyment of this privacy is not substantially impinged upon, when they are told that if they use contraceptives, indeed whether they do so or not, the only thing which stands between them and being forced to render criminal account of their marital privacy is the whim of the prosecutor.

* * *

The massive growth of the administrative state in the twentieth century led to refinements in ripeness doctrine as it applies to challenges to pending agency actions. The next two cases illustrate the modern doctrine. *Abbott Laboratories* is foundational modern case, while *Trump v. New York* provides a recent statement of the basic principle that litigation may be filed too soon, before a concrete dispute has arisen.

Abbott Laboratories v. Gardner

387 U.S. 136 (1967)

Justice HARLAN delivered the opinion of the Court.

In 1962 Congress amended the Federal Food, Drug, and Cosmetic Act, to require manufacturers of prescription drugs to print the "established name" of the drug "prominently and in type at least half as large as that used thereon for any proprietary name or designation for such drug," on labels and other printed material. The "established name" is one designated by the Secretary of Health, Education, and Welfare pursuant to §502(e)(2) of the Act; the "proprietary name" is usually a trade name under which a particular drug is marketed. The underlying purpose of the 1962 amendment was to bring to the attention of doctors and patients the fact that many of the drugs sold under familiar trade names are actually identical to drugs sold under their "established" or less familiar trade names at significantly lower prices. The Commissioner of Food and Drugs, exercising authority delegated to him by the Secretary, published proposed regulations designed to implement the statute. After inviting and considering comments submitted by interested parties the Commissioner promulgated the following regulation for the "efficient enforcement" of the Act:

> If the label or labeling of a prescription drug bears a proprietary name or designation for the drug or any ingredient thereof, the established name, if such there be, corresponding to such proprietary name or designation, shall accompany each appearance of such proprietary name or designation. 21 CFR §1.104(g)(1).

A similar rule was made applicable to advertisements for prescription drugs, 21 CFR §1.105(b)(1).

The present action was brought by a group of 37 individual drug manufacturers and by the Pharmaceutical Manufacturers Association, of which all the petitioner companies are members, and which includes manufacturers of more than 90% of the Nation's supply of prescription drugs. They challenged the regulations on the ground that the Commissioner exceeded his authority under the statute by promulgating an order requiring labels, advertisements, and other printed matter relating to prescription drugs to designate the established name of the particular drug involved every time its trade name is used anywhere in such material

I

The first question we consider is whether Congress by the Federal Food. Drug, and Cosmetic Act intended to forbid pre-enforcement review of this sort of regulation promulgated by the Commissioner. [J]udicial review of a final agency action by an aggrieved person will not be cut off unless there is persuasive reason to believe that such was the purpose of Congress. Early cases in which this type of judicial review was entertained, have been reinforced by the enactment of the Administrative Procedure Act, which embodies the basic presumption of judicial review to one "suffering legal wrong because of agency action, or adversely affected or aggrieved by agency action within the meaning of a relevant statute," 5 U.S.C. §702, so long as no statute precludes such relief or the action is not one committed by law to agency discretion, 5 U.S.C. §701(a).

The Government relies on no explicit statutory authority for its argument that pre-enforcement review is unavailable, but insists instead that because the statute includes a specific procedure for such review of certain enumerated kinds of regulations, not encompassing those of the kind involved here, other types were necessarily meant to be excluded from any pre-enforcement review. The issue, however, is not so readily resolved; we must go further and inquire whether in the context of the entire legislative scheme the existence of that circumscribed remedy evinces a congressional purpose to bar agency action not within its purview from judicial review.

In this case the Government has not demonstrated such a purpose; indeed, a study of the legislative history shows rather conclusively that the specific review provisions were designed to give an additional remedy and not to cut down more traditional channels of review. At the time the Food, Drug, and Cosmetic Act was under consideration, in the late 1930's, the Administrative Procedure Act had not yet been enacted, the Declaratory Judgment Act was in its infancy, and the scope of judicial review of administrative decisions under the equity power was unclear. It was these factors that led to the form the statute ultimately took. There is no evidence at all that members of Congress meant to preclude traditional avenues of judicial relief.

[W]e think it quite apparent that the special-review procedures provided in §701(f), applying to regulations embodying technical factual determinations, were simply intended to assure adequate judicial review of such agency decisions, and that their enactment does not manifest a congressional purpose to eliminate judicial review of other kinds of agency action.

II

A further inquiry must, however, be made. The injunctive and declaratory judgment remedies are discretionary, and courts traditionally have been reluctant to apply them to administrative determinations unless these arise in the context of a controversy "ripe" for judicial resolution. Without undertaking to survey the intricacies of the ripeness doctrine it is fair to say that its basic rationale is to prevent the courts, through avoidance of premature adjudication, from entangling themselves in abstract disagreements over administrative policies, and also to protect the agencies from judicial interference until an administrative decision has been formalized and its effects felt in a concrete way by the challenging parties. The problem is best seen in a twofold aspect, requiring us to evaluate both the fitness of the issues for judicial decision and the hardship to the parties of withholding court consideration.

As to the former factor, we believe the issues presented are appropriate for judicial resolution at this time. First, all parties agree that the issue tendered is a purely legal one: whether the statute was properly construed by the Commissioner to require the established name of the drug to be used *every time* the proprietary name is employed. Both sides moved for summary judgment in the District Court, and no claim is made here that further administrative proceedings are contemplated. It is suggested that the justification for this rule might vary with different circumstances, and that the expertise of the Commissioner is relevant to passing upon the validity of the regulation. This of course is true, but the suggestion overlooks the fact that both sides have approached this case as one purely of congressional intent, and that the Government made no effort to justify the regulation in factual terms.

Second, the regulations in issue we find to be "final agency action" within the meaning of §10 of the Administrative Procedure Act, 5 U.S.C. §704, as construed in judicial decisions. An "agency action" includes any "rule," defined by the Act as "an agency statement of general or particular applicability and future effect designed to implement, interpret, or prescribe law or policy," §§2(c), 2(g), 5 U.S.C. §§551(4), 551(13).

The regulation challenged here, promulgated in a formal manner after announcement in the Federal Register and consideration of comments by interested parties is quite clearly definitive. There is no hint that this regulation is informal, or only the ruling of a subordinate official, or tentative. It was made effective upon publication, and the Assistant General Counsel for Food and Drugs stated in the District Court that compliance was expected.

The Government argues, however, that the present case can be distinguished from [prior cases finding that an agency action was final] on the ground that in those instances the agency involved could implement its policy directly, while here the Attorney General must authorize criminal and seizure actions for violations of the statute. In the context of this case, we do not find this argument persuasive. These regulations are not meant to advise the Attorney General, but purport to be directly authorized by the statute. Thus, if within the Commissioner's authority, they have the status of law and violations of them carry heavy criminal and civil sanctions. Also, there is no representation that the Attorney General and the Commissioner disagree in this area; the Justice Department is defending this very suit. It would be adherence to a mere technicality to give any credence to this contention. Moreover the agency does have direct authority to enforce this regulation in the context of passing upon applications for clearance of new drugs, or certification of certain antibiotics.

This is also a case in which the impact of the regulations upon the petitioners is sufficiently direct and immediate as to render the issue appropriate for judicial review at this stage. These regulations purport to give an authoritative interpretation of a statutory provision that has a direct effect on the day-to-day business of all prescription drug companies; its promulgation puts petitioners in a dilemma that it was the very purpose of the Declaratory Judgment Act to ameliorate. As the District Court found on the basis of uncontested allegations, "Either they must comply with the every time requirement and incur the costs of changing over their promotional material and labeling or they must follow their present course and risk prosecution." The regulations are clear-cut, and were made effective immediately upon publication; as noted earlier the agency's counsel represented to the District Court that immediate compliance with their terms was expected. If petitioners wish to comply they must change all their labels, advertisements, and promotional materials; they must destroy stocks of printed matter; and they must invest heavily in new printing type and new supplies. The alternative to compliance—continued use of material which they believe in good faith meets the statutory requirements, but which clearly does not meet the regulation of the Commissioner—may be even more costly. That course would risk serious criminal and civil penalties for the unlawful distribution of "misbranded" drugs.

It is relevant at this juncture to recognize that petitioners deal in a sensitive industry, in which public confidence in their drug products is especially important. To require them to challenge these regulations only as a defense to an action brought by the Government might harm them severely and unnecessarily. Where the legal issue presented is fit for judicial resolution, and where a regulation requires an immediate and significant change in the plaintiffs' conduct of their affairs with serious penalties attached to noncompliance, access to the courts under the Administrative Procedure Act and the Declaratory Judgment Act must be permitted, absent a statutory bar or some other unusual circumstance, neither of which appears here.

Trump v. New York

141 S. Ct. 530 (2020)

Per Curiam.

Every ten years, the Nation undertakes an "Enumeration" of its population "in such Manner" as Congress "shall by Law direct." U.S. Const., Art. I, §2, cl. 3. This census plays a critical role in apportioning Members of the House of Representatives among the States, allocating federal funds to the States, providing information for intrastate redistricting, and supplying data for numerous initiatives conducted by governmental entities, businesses, and academic researchers.

Congress has given both the Secretary of Commerce and the President functions to perform in the enumeration and apportionment process. The Secretary must "take a decennial census of population . . . in such form and content as he may determine," and then must report to the President "[t]he tabulation of total population by States" under the census "as required for the apportionment." The President in turn must transmit to Congress a "statement showing the whole number of persons in each State, excluding Indians not taxed, as ascertained" under the census. In that statement, the President must apply a mathematical formula called the "method of equal proportions" to the population counts in order to calculate the number of House seats for each State.

This past July, the President issued a memorandum to the Secretary respecting the apportionment following the 2020 census. The memorandum announced a policy of excluding "from the apportionment base aliens who are not in a lawful immigration status." To facilitate implementation "to the maximum extent feasible and consistent with the discretion delegated to the executive branch," the President ordered the Secretary, in preparing his report, "to provide information permitting the President, to the extent practicable, to exercise the President's discretion to carry out the policy." The President directed the Secretary to include such information in addition to a tabulation of population according to the criteria promulgated by the Census Bureau for counting each State's residents.

This case arises from one of several challenges to the memorandum brought by various States, local governments, organizations, and individuals.

A foundational principle of Article III is that "an actual controversy must exist not only at the time the complaint is filed, but through all stages of the litigation." *Already, LLC v. Nike, Inc.* (2013). As the plaintiffs concede, any chilling effect from the memorandum dissipated upon the conclusion of the census response period. The plaintiffs now seek to substitute an alternative theory of a "legally cognizable injury" premised on the threatened impact of an unlawful apportionment on congressional representation and federal funding. As the case comes to us, however, we conclude that it does not—at this time—present a dispute "appropriately resolved through the judicial process." *Susan B. Anthony List v. Driehaus* (2014).

Two related doctrines of justiciability—each originating in the case-or-controversy requirement of Article III—underlie this determination. First, a plaintiff must demonstrate standing, including "an injury that is concrete, particularized, and imminent rather than conjectural or hypothetical." Second, the case must be "ripe"—not dependent on "contingent future events that may not occur as anticipated, or indeed may not occur at all."

At present, this case is riddled with contingencies and speculation that impede judicial review. The President, to be sure, has made clear his desire to exclude aliens without lawful status from the apportionment base. But the President qualified his directive by providing that the Secretary should gather information "to the extent practicable" and that aliens should be excluded "to the extent feasible." Any prediction how the Executive Branch might eventually implement this general statement of policy is "no more than conjecture" at this time.

To begin with, the policy may not prove feasible to implement in any manner whatsoever, let alone in a manner substantially likely to harm any of the plaintiffs here. Pre-apportionment litigation always "presents a moving target" because the Secretary may make (and the President may direct) changes to the census up until the President transmits his statement to the House. *Franklin v. Massachusetts* (1992). And as the Government recognizes, any such changes must comply with the constitutional requirement of an "actual Enumeration" of the persons in each State, as opposed to a conjectural estimate. Here the record is silent on which (and how many) aliens have administrative records that would allow the Secretary to avoid impermissible estimation, and whether the Census Bureau can even match the records in its possession to census data in a timely manner. Uncertainty likewise pervades which (and how many) aliens the President will exclude from the census if the Secretary manages to gather and match suitable administrative records. We simply do not know whether and to what extent the President might direct the Secretary to "reform the census" to implement his general policy with respect to apportionment.

While the plaintiffs agree that the dispute will take a more concrete shape once the Secretary delivers his report, they insist that the record already establishes a "substantial risk" of reduced representation and federal resources, *Clapper v. Amnesty Int'l USA* (2013). That conclusion, however, involves a significant degree of guesswork. Unlike other pre-apportionment challenges, the Secretary has not altered census operations in a concrete manner that will predictably change the count. The count here is complete; the present dispute involves the apportionment process, which remains at a preliminary stage. The Government's eventual action will reflect both legal and practical constraints, making any prediction about future injury just that—a prediction.

Everyone agrees by now that the Government cannot feasibly implement the memorandum by excluding the estimated 10.5 million aliens without lawful status. Yet the only evidence speaking to the predicted change in apportionment unrealistically assumes that the President will exclude the entire undocumented population. Nothing in the record addresses the consequences of a partial implementation of the memorandum, much less supports the dissent's speculation that excluding aliens in ICE detention will impact interstate apportionment.

The impact on funding is no more certain. According to the Government, federal funds are tied to data derived from the census, but not necessarily to the apportionment counts addressed by the memorandum. Under that view, changes to the Secretary's report or to the President's statement will not inexorably have the direct effect on downstream access to funds or other resources predicted by the dissent. How that question will be addressed by the Secretary and the President is yet another fundamental uncertainty impeding proper judicial consideration at this time.

At the end of the day, the standing and ripeness inquiries both lead to the conclusion that judicial resolution of this dispute is premature. Consistent with our determination that standing has not been shown and that the case is not ripe, we express no view on the merits of the constitutional and related statutory claims presented. We hold only that they are not suitable for adjudication at this time.

Justice BREYER, with whom Justice SOTOMAYOR and Justice KAGAN join, dissenting.

Under a straightforward application of our precedents, the plaintiffs have standing to sue. The question is ripe for resolution. And, in my view, the plaintiffs should also prevail on the merits.

Begin with the threatened injury. The plaintiffs allege two forms of future injury: a loss of representation in the apportionment count and decreased federal funding tied to the census totals.

Here, inquiry into the threatened injury is unusually straightforward. The harm is clear on the face of the policy. The title of the Presidential memorandum reads: "Excluding Illegal Aliens From the Apportionment Base Following the 2020 Census." That memorandum announces "the policy of the United States [shall be] to exclude from the apportionment base aliens who are not in a lawful immigration status . . . to the maximum extent feasible and consistent with the discretion delegated to the executive branch." The memorandum also announces the reason for this policy: to diminish the "political influence" and "congressional representation" of States "home to" unauthorized immigrants. It notes that "one State"—now known to be California—is "home to more than 2.2 million illegal aliens," and excluding such individuals from apportionment "could result in the allocation of two or three [fewer] congressional seats than would otherwise be allocated." Other consequences will flow from this attempt to alter apportionment. We have previously noted that "the States use the results in drawing intrastate political districts," and "[t]he Federal Government [also] considers census data in dispensing funds through federal programs to the States."

Given the clarity of the Presidential memorandum, it is unsurprising the Government does not contest that plaintiffs have alleged a threatened injury. Rather, it contends that both the alleged representational and funding injuries remain "too speculative" to satisfy Article III's ripeness requirement prior to the President's actual enumeration. That is because—although the Secretary's report to the President is due in just two weeks—the Bureau's plan to implement the memorandum remains uncertain and "depends on various unknowable contingencies about the data," and until "later in December or January, the Bureau cannot predict or even estimate the results." At root, the Government contends that "ripeness principles support deferring judicial review of the Memorandum until it is implemented."

Whether viewed as a question of standing or ripeness, the Government's arguments are insufficient. Looking to the facts here, the memorandum presents the "substantial risk" that our precedents require.

The Government's current plans suggest it will be able to exclude a significant number of people under its policy. To start, even a few weeks out, the Government still does not disclaim its intent to carry out the policy to the full extent it can do so. Indeed, the Bureau is committed to excluding as many people as possible even if it must act beyond the December 31 statutory deadline to do so. And there is a "substantial risk" that it will be able to do so to the point that it causes significant harm. Both here and in related litigation below, the Government has said that as of early December, it was already feasible to exclude aliens without lawful status housed in ICE detention centers on census day, a "category [that] is likely in the tens of thousands, spread out over multiple States." Beyond these detainees, appellees note that the Government has also identified at least several million more aliens without lawful status that it can "individually identify" and seek to exclude from the tabulation. We have been told the Bureau is "working very hard to try to report on" (and exclude from the apportionment tabulation) a large number of aliens without lawful status, including "almost 200,000 persons who are subject to final orders of removal," "700,000 DACA recipients," and about "3.2 million non-detained individuals in removal proceedings." All told, the Bureau already possesses the administrative records necessary to exclude at least four to five million aliens. Those figures are certainly large enough to affect apportionment.

Of equal importance, plaintiffs argue that aside from apportionment itself, the exclusion of aliens without lawful status from the apportionment count will also negatively affect federal funding that is based on per-State proportional decennial population totals. The Government counters that appellees have not identified any reason why the individuals unlawfully removed from the tabulation could not be *added back in* for purposes of applying funding statutes. But there is no indication that the Secretary could or would do any such thing — unless of course a court holds that the removal was unlawful. And the possibility of adding back those who have otherwise been unlawfully removed from the count does not undercut a plaintiff's standing to pursue a claim of unlawfulness in the first instance.

Presumably, waiting to resolve this issue until after the President submits his tabulation will cause further hardship by delaying redistricting further. States will begin to consider the consequences of reapportionment soon. It is of course possible that the Bureau will be unable to find a significant number of matches between the millions of records it has and the census data it is producing in time for the President to exclude them from his tabulation submitted to Congress. But even if the Secretary were to limit severely his compliance with the President's memorandum—say, by choosing to "report" only those 50,000 aliens that are estimated to be in ICE detention centers and omitting them from his census "tabulation"—that omission alone presents a "substantial risk" of affecting the census calculation for purposes of apportionment and funding. That is the very kind of injury of which plaintiffs complain. Taken together, these considerations demonstrate that now is the appropriate time to resolve this case. *Cf. Abbott Laboratories v. Gardner* (1967) (explaining that the timing of judicial review turns on "the fitness of the issues for judicial decision and the hardship to the parties of withholding court consideration")....

Where, as here, the Government acknowledges it is working to achieve an allegedly illegal goal, this Court should not decline to resolve the case simply because the Government speculates that it might not fully succeed.

* * *

D.   MOOTNESS

As you have learned, federal courts are obligated to decide only "cases or controversies"; to confine themselves to exercising "the judicial power"; and to refrain from issuing advisory opinions. Alongside the doctrine of standing, ripeness, and the prohibition on advisory opinions, these obligations also sustain the related doctrine of mootness. A case or controversy must exist throughout the life of a federal case. When a case is resolved without the need for federal judicial intervention, a case should be dismissed as moot. Professor Henry Monaghan once described mootness as "standing set in a time frame: The requisite personal interest that must exist at the commencement of the litigation (standing) must continue throughout its existence (mootness)."[33] This is a useful heuristic, but it is important to note that the analogy to standing is not perfect. As the Court has put it,

> Standing doctrine functions to ensure, among other things, that the scarce resources of the federal courts are devoted to those disputes in which the parties have a concrete stake. In contrast, by the time mootness is an issue, the case has been brought and litigated, often . . . for years. To abandon the case at an advanced stage may prove more wasteful than frugal. This argument from sunk costs does not license courts to retain jurisdiction over cases in which one or both of the parties plainly lacks a continuing interest, as when the parties have settled. . . . But the argument "surely highlights an important difference between the two doctrines.

Friends of the Earth v. Laidlaw (2000).

Mootness is thus a flexible, highly fact-intensive inquiry, and one that depends substantially upon the type of relief the litigant is seeking. Some factual circumstances might render the need for prospective relief moot, without affecting one's claims for damages. Damages relief, after all, tends to ameliorate injuries that have happened in the past. Prospective relief, by contrast, depends on a showing that the defendant will cause the plaintiff harm in the future. Suppose, for example, that a plaintiff challenges a law that prevents individuals under the age of 21 from exercising a constitutional right. Our hypothetical plaintiff seeks damages for the harm the law has caused her in the past, and contemporaneously seeks an injunction prohibiting enforcement of the law in the future. If, during the litigation, the plaintiff turns 21, the plaintiff's need for such an injunction may have dissipated, even though damages for the past harm may be warranted. By contrast, there are other circumstances that can cause both damages relief and prospective relief to become moot, such as settlement or, depending on laws governing a claim's survivability, the death of a party.

1.   When Does a Case Become Moot?

There are innumerable circumstances in which cases or controversies disappear before judicial resolution. Yet, a case will not be dismissed for mootness "[a]s long as the parties have a concrete interest, however small, in the outcome of the litigation." *Ellis v. Railway Clerks* (1984). For illustrative purposes, included here are two cases in which the Supreme Court confronted the question of mootness. In the first case, the Court considered whether a child custody dispute had become moot when, consistent with a federal court order, a parent moved the child abroad. In the second case, the Court considered whether a case became moot when a

---

33. Henry Monaghan, *Constitutional Adjudication: The Who and the When*, 82 Yale L.J. 1363, 1384 (1973) (citation omitted).

defendant made an unaccepted, untendered settlement offer, a strategy that has sometimes been used as a means of mooting class actions before they have been certified.[34]

Chafin v. Chafin

568 U.S. 165 (2013)

Chief Justice ROBERTS delivered the opinion of the Court.

The Hague Convention on the Civil Aspects of International Child Abduction generally requires courts in the United States to order children returned to their countries of habitual residence, if the courts find that the children have been wrongfully removed to or retained in the United States. The question is whether, after a child is returned pursuant to such an order, any appeal of the order is moot.

I

A

The Hague Conference on Private International Law adopted the Hague Convention on the Civil Aspects of International Child Abduction in 1980. T.I.A.S. No. 11670, S. Treaty Doc. No. 99–11. In 1988, the United States ratified the treaty and passed implementing legislation, known as the International Child Abduction Remedies Act (ICARA), 102 Stat. 437, 42 U.S.C. §11601 et seq. *See generally Abbott v. Abbott* (2010).

The Convention seeks "to secure the prompt return of children wrongfully removed to or retained in any Contracting State" and "to ensure that rights of custody and of access under the law of one Contracting State are effectively respected in the other Contracting States." Art. 1, S. Treaty Doc. No. 99–11, at 7. Article 3 of the Convention provides that the "removal or the retention of a child is to be considered wrongful" when "it is in breach of rights of custody attributed to a person, an institution or any other body, either jointly or alone, under the law of the State in which the child was habitually resident immediately before the removal or retention" and "at the time of removal or retention those rights were actually exercised, either jointly or alone, or would have been so exercised but for the removal or retention."

Article 12 then states:

> Where a child has been wrongfully removed or retained in terms of Article 3 and, at the date of the commencement of the proceedings before the judicial or administrative authority of the Contracting State where the child is, a period of less than one year has elapsed from the date of the wrongful removal or retention, the authority concerned shall order the return of the child forthwith.

---

34. David Hill Koysza, Note, *Preventing Defendants from Mooting Class Actions by Picking off Named Plaintiffs*, 53 DUKE L.J. 781 (2003).

Congress established procedures for implementing the Convention in ICARA. *See* 42 U.S.C. §11601(b)(1). The Act grants federal and state courts concurrent jurisdiction over actions arising under the Convention, §11603(a), and directs them to "decide the case in accordance with the Convention," §11603(d). If those courts find children to have been wrongfully removed or retained, the children "are to be promptly returned." §11601(a)(4). ICARA also provides that courts ordering children returned generally must require defendants to pay various expenses incurred by plaintiffs, including court costs, legal fees, and transportation costs associated with the return of the children. §11607(b)(3). Eighty-nine nations are party to the Convention as of this writing.

B

Petitioner Jeffrey Lee Chafin is a citizen of the United States and a sergeant first class in the U.S. Army. While stationed in Germany in 2006, he married respondent Lynne Hales Chafin, a citizen of the United Kingdom. Their daughter E.C. was born the following year.

Later in 2007, Mr. Chafin was deployed to Afghanistan, and Ms. Chafin took E.C. to Scotland. Mr. Chafin was eventually transferred to Huntsville, Alabama, and in February 2010, Ms. Chafin traveled to Alabama with E.C. Soon thereafter, however, Mr. Chafin filed for divorce and for child custody in Alabama state court. Towards the end of the year, Ms. Chafin was arrested for domestic violence, an incident that alerted U.S. Citizenship and Immigration Services to the fact that she had overstayed her visa. She was deported in February 2011, and E.C. remained in Mr. Chafin's care for several more months.

In May 2011, Ms. Chafin initiated this case in the U.S. District Court for the Northern District of Alabama. She filed a petition under the Convention and ICARA seeking an order for E.C.'s return to Scotland. On October 11 and 12, 2011, the District Court held a bench trial. Upon the close of arguments, the court ruled in favor of Ms. Chafin, concluding that E.C.'s country of habitual residence was Scotland and granting the petition for return. Mr. Chafin immediately moved for a stay pending appeal, but the court denied his request. Within hours, Ms. Chafin left the country with E.C., headed for Scotland. By December 2011, she had initiated custody proceedings there. The Scottish court soon granted her interim custody and a preliminary injunction, prohibiting Mr. Chafin from removing E.C. from Scotland. In the meantime, Mr. Chafin had appealed the District Court order to the Court of Appeals for the Eleventh Circuit.

In February 2012, the Eleventh Circuit dismissed Mr. Chafin's appeal as moot because the court "became powerless" to grant relief. In accordance with *Bekier*[, a circuit precedent,] the Court of Appeals remanded this case to the District Court with instructions to dismiss the suit as moot and vacate its order.

On remand, the District Court did so, and also ordered Mr. Chafin to pay Ms. Chafin over $94,000 in court costs, attorney's fees, and travel expenses. Meanwhile, the Alabama state court had dismissed the child custody proceeding initiated by Mr. Chafin for lack of jurisdiction. The Alabama Court of Civil Appeals affirmed, relying in part on the U.S. District Court's finding that the child's habitual residence was not Alabama, but Scotland.

We granted certiorari to review the judgment of the Court of Appeals for the Eleventh Circuit.

II

The "case-or-controversy requirement subsists through all stages of federal judicial proceedings, trial and appellate." "[I]t is not enough that a dispute was very much alive when suit was filed"; the parties must "continue to have a 'personal stake'" in the ultimate disposition of the lawsuit.

There is thus no case or controversy, and a suit becomes moot, "when the issues presented are no longer 'live' or the parties lack a legally cognizable interest in the outcome." But a case "becomes moot only when it is impossible for a court to grant any effectual relief whatever to the prevailing party." "As long as the parties have a concrete interest, however small, in the outcome of the litigation, the case is not moot."

III

This dispute is still very much alive. Mr. Chafin continues to contend that his daughter's country of habitual residence is the United States, while Ms. Chafin maintains that E.C.'s home is in Scotland. Mr. Chafin also argues that even if E.C.'s habitual residence was Scotland, she should not have been returned because the Convention's defenses to return apply. Mr. Chafin seeks custody of E.C., and wants to pursue that relief in the United States, while Ms. Chafin is pursuing that right for herself in Scotland. And Mr. Chafin wants the orders that he pay Ms. Chafin over $94,000 vacated, while Ms. Chafin asserts the money is rightfully owed.

On many levels, the Chafins continue to vigorously contest the question of where their daughter will be raised. This is not a case where a decision would address "a hypothetical state of facts." And there is not the slightest doubt that there continues to exist between the parties "that concrete adverseness which sharpens the presentation of issues."

A

At this point in the ongoing dispute, Mr. Chafin seeks reversal of the District Court determination that E.C.'s habitual residence was Scotland and, if that determination is reversed, an order that E.C. be returned to the United States (or "re-return," as the parties have put it). In short, Mr. Chafin is asking for typical appellate relief: that the Court of Appeals reverse the District Court and that the District Court undo what it has done. The question is whether such relief would be effectual in this case.

Ms. Chafin argues that this case is moot because the District Court lacks the authority to issue a re-return order either under the Convention or pursuant to its inherent equitable powers. But that argument—which goes to the meaning of the Convention and the legal availability of a certain kind of relief—confuses mootness with the merits. In *Powell v. McCormack* (1969), this Court held that a claim for backpay saved the case from mootness, even though the defendants argued that the backpay claim had been brought in the wrong court and therefore could not result in relief. As the Court explained, "this argument . . . confuses mootness with whether [the plaintiff] has established a right to recover . . . , a question which it is inappropriate to treat at this stage of the litigation." Mr. Chafin's claim for re-return—under the Convention itself or according to general equitable principles—cannot be dismissed as so implausible that it is insufficient to preserve jurisdiction, and his prospects of success are therefore not pertinent to the mootness inquiry.

As to the effectiveness of any relief, Ms. Chafin asserts that even if the habitual residence ruling were reversed and the District Court were to issue a re-return order, that relief would be ineffectual because Scotland would simply ignore it. But even if Scotland were to ignore a U.S. re-return order, or decline to assist in enforcing it, this case would not be moot. The U.S. courts continue to have personal jurisdiction over Ms. Chafin, may command her to take action even outside the United States, and may back up any such command with sanctions. No law of physics prevents E.C.'s return from Scotland, and Ms. Chafin might decide to comply with an order against her and return E.C. to the United States. After all, the consequence of compliance presumably would not be relinquishment of custody rights, but simply custody proceedings in a different forum.

Enforcement of the order may be uncertain if Ms. Chafin chooses to defy it, but such uncertainty does not typically render cases moot. Courts often adjudicate disputes where the practical impact of any decision is not assured. For example, courts issue default judgments against defendants who failed to appear or participate in the proceedings and therefore seem less likely to comply. *See* Fed. R. Civ. P. 55. Similarly, the fact that a defendant is insolvent does not moot a claim for damages. Courts also decide cases against foreign nations, whose choices to respect final rulings are not guaranteed.

So too here. A re-return order may not result in the return of E.C. to the United States, just as an order that an insolvent defendant pay $100 million may not make the plaintiff rich. But it cannot be said that the parties here have no "concrete interest" in whether Mr. Chafin secures a re-return order. "[H]owever small" that concrete interest may be due to potential difficulties in enforcement, it is not simply a matter of academic debate, and is enough to save this case from mootness.

B

Mr. Chafin also seeks, if he prevails, vacatur of the District Court's expense orders. The District Court ordered Mr. Chafin to pay Ms. Chafin over $94,000 in court costs, attorney's fees, and travel expenses. That award was predicated on the District Court's earlier judgment allowing Ms. Chafin to return with her daughter to Scotland. Thus, in conjunction with reversal of the judgment, Mr. Chafin desires vacatur of the award. That too is common relief on appeal.

At oral argument, Ms. Chafin contended that such relief was "gone in this case," and that the case was therefore moot, because Mr. Chafin had failed to pursue an appeal of the expense orders, which had been entered as separate judgments. But this is another argument on the merits. Mr. Chafin's requested relief is not so implausible that it may be disregarded on the question of jurisdiction; there is authority for the proposition that failure to appeal such judgments separately does not preclude relief. It is thus for lower courts at later stages of the litigation to decide whether Mr. Chafin is in fact entitled to the relief he seeks—vacatur of the expense orders.

Such relief would of course not be "'fully satisfactory,'" but with respect to the case as a whole, "even the availability of a 'partial remedy' is 'sufficient to prevent [a] case from being moot.'"

IV

Ms. Chafin is correct to emphasize that both the Hague Convention and ICARA stress the importance of the prompt return of children wrongfully removed or retained. We are also sympathetic to the concern that shuttling children back and forth between parents and across international borders may be detrimental to those children. But courts can achieve the ends of the Convention and ICARA—and protect the well-being of the affected children—through the familiar judicial tools of expediting proceedings and granting stays where appropriate. There is no need to manipulate constitutional doctrine and hold these cases moot. Indeed, doing so may very well undermine the goals of the treaty and harm the children it is meant to protect.

. . .

The Hague Convention mandates the prompt return of children to their countries of habitual residence. But such return does not render this case moot; there is a live dispute between the parties over where their child will be raised, and there is a possibility of effectual relief for the prevailing parent. The courts below therefore continue to have jurisdiction to adjudicate the merits of the parties' respective claims.

The judgment of the United States Court of Appeals for the Eleventh Circuit is vacated, and the case is remanded for further proceedings consistent with this opinion.

[The concurring opinion emphasizing the need for prompt resolution of child abduction cases is omitted.]

* * *

In *Chafin*, the Court emphasized that so long as a federal judicial remedy will ameliorate a plaintiff's injury, the case is not moot. The Court recently reaffirmed that principle in *Uzuegbunam v. Preczewski* (2021). In that case, religious students on the campus of a public college challenged a policy that prohibited them from distributing religious literature. The college changed its policy, resulting in dismissal of the claims for prospective relief. The Supreme Court held, however, that the plaintiff's quest for nominal damages was not moot. Assuming that nominal damages—or $1—would not fully vindicate the plaintiff's interests, the award would at least partially redress the harm caused by the government's actions. As the Court emphasized, "[b]ecause every violation [of a right] imports damage, nominal damages can redress [a plaintiff's] injury even if he cannot or chooses not to quantify that harm in economic terms."

On the other hand, in *Genesis Healthcare Corp. v. Symczyk* (2013), the Supreme Court confronted a case in which, prior to certification of a class, a defendant made a settlement offer to the plaintiff that would have satisfied the individual relief she sought in her complaint. The Court held that, assuming the settlement mooted the lead plaintiff's case, the entire case became moot as well. In the following case, *Campbell-Ewald Co. v. Gomez*, the Court expressly addressed the issue that *Symczyk* assumed without deciding: Does an unaccepted, untendered offer of settlement moot a case?

Campbell-Ewald Co. v. Gomez

577 U.S. 153 (2016)

Justice GINSBURG delivered the opinion of the Court.

Is an unaccepted offer to satisfy the named plaintiff's individual claim sufficient to render a case moot when the complaint seeks relief on behalf of the plaintiff and a class of persons similarly situated? We hold today, in accord with Rule 68 of the Federal Rules of Civil Procedure, that an unaccepted settlement offer has no force. Like other unaccepted contract offers, it creates no lasting right or obligation. With the offer off the table, and the defendant's continuing denial of liability, adversity between the parties persists.

I

The Telephone Consumer Protection Act (TCPA or Act) prohibits any person, absent the prior express consent of a telephone-call recipient, from "mak[ing] any call . . . using any automatic telephone dialing system . . . to any telephone number assigned to a paging service [or] cellular telephone service." A text message to a cellular telephone, it is undisputed, qualifies as a "call" within the compass of §227(b)(1)(A)(iii). For damages occasioned by conduct violating the TCPA, §227(b)(3) authorizes a private right of action. A plaintiff successful in such an action may recover her "actual monetary loss" or $500 for each violation, "whichever is greater." Damages may be trebled if "the defendant willfully or knowingly violated" the Act.

Petitioner Campbell-Ewald Company (Campbell) is a nationwide advertising and marketing communications agency. Beginning in 2000, the United States Navy engaged Campbell to develop and execute a multimedia recruiting campaign. In 2005 and 2006, Campbell proposed to the Navy a campaign involving text messages sent to young adults, the Navy's target audience, encouraging them to learn more about the Navy. The Navy approved Campbell's proposal, conditioned on sending the messages only to individuals who had "opted in" to receipt of marketing solicitations on topics that included service in the Navy.

Campbell then contracted with Mindmatics LLC, which generated a list of cellular phone numbers geared to the Navy's target audience—namely, cellular phone users between the ages of 18 and 24 who had consented to receiving solicitations by text message. In May 2006, Mindmatics transmitted the Navy's message to over 100,000 recipients.

Respondent Jose Gomez was a recipient of the Navy's recruiting message. Alleging that he had never consented to receiving the message, that his age was nearly 40, and that Campbell had violated the TCPA by sending the message (and perhaps others like it), Gomez filed a class-action complaint in the District Court for the Central District of California in 2010. On behalf of a nationwide class of individuals who had received, but had not consented to receipt of, the text message, Gomez sought treble statutory damages, costs, and attorney's fees, also an injunction against Campbell's involvement in unsolicited messaging.

Prior to the agreed-upon deadline for Gomez to file a motion for class certification, Campbell proposed to settle Gomez's individual claim and filed an offer of judgment pursuant to Federal Rule of Civil Procedure 68. Campbell offered to pay Gomez his costs, excluding attorney's fees, and $1,503 per message for the May 2006 text message and any other text message Gomez could show he had received, thereby satisfying his personal treble-damages claim. Campbell also proposed a stipulated injunction in which it agreed to be barred from sending text messages in violation of the TCPA. The proposed injunction, however, denied liability and the allegations made in the complaint, and disclaimed the existence of grounds for the imposition of an injunction. The settlement offer did not include attorney's fees, Campbell observed, because the TCPA does not provide for an attorney's-fee award. Gomez did not accept the settlement offer and allowed Campbell's Rule 68 submission to lapse after the time, 14 days, specified in the Rule.

Campbell thereafter moved to dismiss the case pursuant to Federal Rule of Civil Procedure 12(b)(1) for lack of subject-matter jurisdiction. No Article III case or controversy remained, Campbell urged, because its offer mooted Gomez's individual claim by providing him with complete relief. Gomez had not moved for class certification before his claim became moot, Campbell added, so the putative class claims also became moot. The District Court denied Campbell's motion. Gomez was not dilatory in filing his certification request, the District Court determined; consequently, the court noted, the class claims would "relat[e] back" to the date Gomez filed the complaint.

The Court of Appeals for the Ninth Circuit agreed that Gomez's case remained live. We granted certiorari to resolve a disagreement among the Courts of Appeals over whether an unaccepted offer can moot a plaintiff's claim, thereby depriving federal courts of Article III jurisdiction.

II

Article III of the Constitution limits federal-court jurisdiction to "cases" and "controversies." U.S. Const., Art. III, §2. We have interpreted this requirement to demand that "an actual controversy . . . be extant at all stages of review, not merely at the time the complaint is filed." "If an intervening circumstance deprives the plaintiff of a 'personal stake in the outcome of the lawsuit,' at any point during litigation, the action can no longer proceed and must be dismissed as moot." A case becomes moot, however, "only when it is impossible for a court to grant any effectual relief whatever to the prevailing party." "As long as the parties have a concrete interest, however small, in the outcome of the litigation, the case is not moot."

We hold that Gomez's complaint was not effaced by Campbell's unaccepted offer to satisfy his individual claim. As earlier recounted, Gomez commenced an action against Campbell for violation of the TCPA, suing on behalf of himself and others similarly situated. Gomez sought treble statutory damages and an injunction on behalf of a nationwide class, but Campbell's settlement offer proposed relief for Gomez alone, and it did not admit liability. Gomez rejected Campbell's settlement terms and the offer of judgment.

Under basic principles of contract law, Campbell's settlement bid and Rule 68 offer of judgment, once rejected, had no continuing efficacy. Absent Gomez's acceptance, Campbell's settlement offer remained only a proposal, binding neither Campbell nor Gomez. Having rejected Campbell's settlement bid, and given

Campbell's continuing denial of liability, Gomez gained no entitlement to the relief Campbell previously offered. In short, with no settlement offer still operative, the parties remained adverse; both retained the same stake in the litigation they had at the outset.

The Federal Rule in point, Rule 68, hardly supports the argument that an unaccepted settlement offer can moot a complaint. An offer of judgment, the Rule provides, "is considered withdrawn" if not accepted within 14 days of its service. Fed. R. Civ. P. 68(a), (b). The sole built-in sanction: "If the [ultimate] judgment . . . is not more favorable than the unaccepted offer, the offeree must pay the costs incurred after the offer was made." Rule 68(d).

When the settlement offer Campbell extended to Gomez expired, Gomez remained emptyhanded; his TCPA complaint, which Campbell opposed on the merits, stood wholly unsatisfied. Because Gomez's individual claim was not made moot by the expired settlement offer, that claim would retain vitality during the time involved in determining whether the case could proceed on behalf of a class.

The Chief Justice's dissent asserts that our decision transfers authority from the federal courts and "hands it to the plaintiff." Quite the contrary. The dissent's approach would place the defendant in the driver's seat.

In sum, an unaccepted settlement offer or offer of judgment does not moot a plaintiff's case, so the District Court retained jurisdiction to adjudicate Gomez's complaint. That ruling suffices to decide this case. We need not, and do not, now decide whether the result would be different if a defendant deposits the full amount of the plaintiff's individual claim in an account payable to the plaintiff, and the court then enters judgment for the plaintiff in that amount. That question is appropriately reserved for a case in which it is not hypothetical.

Justice Thomas, concurring in the judgment.

The Court correctly concludes that an offer of complete relief on a claim does not render that claim moot. But, in my view, the Court does not advance a sound basis for this conclusion. The Court rests its conclusion on modern contract law principles and a recent dissent concerning Federal Rule of Civil Procedure 68. I would rest instead on the common-law history of tenders. That history—which led to Rule 68—demonstrates that a mere offer of the sum owed is insufficient to eliminate a court's jurisdiction to decide the case to which the offer related. I therefore concur only in the judgment.

Chief Justice Roberts, with whom Justice Scalia and Justice Alito join, dissenting.

[I]t is clear that the lawsuit is moot. All agree that at the time Gomez filed suit, he had a personal stake in the litigation. In his complaint, Gomez alleged that he suffered an injury in fact when he received unauthorized text messages from Campbell. To remedy that injury, he requested $1500 in statutory damages for each unauthorized text message. (It was later determined that he received only one text message.)

What happened next, however, is critical: After Gomez's initial legal volley, Campbell did not return fire. Instead, Campbell responded to the complaint with a freestanding offer to pay Gomez the maximum amount that he could recover under the statute: $1500 per unauthorized text message, plus court costs. Campbell also made an offer of judgment on the same terms under Rule 68 of the Federal Rules of Civil Procedure, which permits a defendant to recover certain attorney's fees if the Rule 68 offer is unaccepted and the plaintiff later recovers no more than the amount of the offer. Crucially, the District Court found that the "parties do not dispute" that Campbell's Rule 68 offer — reflecting the same terms as the freestanding offer — "would have fully satisfied the individual claims asserted, or that could have been asserted," by Gomez.

When a plaintiff files suit seeking redress for an alleged injury, and the defendant agrees to fully redress that injury, there is no longer a case or controversy for purposes of Article III. After all, if the defendant is willing to remedy the plaintiff's injury without forcing him to litigate, the plaintiff cannot demonstrate an injury in need of redress by the court, and the defendant's interests are not adverse to the plaintiff. At that point, there is no longer any "necessity" to "expound and interpret" the law, *Marbury*, and the federal courts lack authority to hear the case. That is exactly what happened here: Once Campbell offered to fully remedy Gomez's injury, there was no longer any "necessity" for the District Court to hear the merits of his case, rendering the lawsuit moot.

It is true that although Campbell has offered Gomez full relief, Campbell has not yet paid up. That does not affect the mootness inquiry under the facts of this case. Campbell is a multimillion dollar company, and the settlement offer here is for a few thousand dollars. The settlement offer promises "prompt payment," and it would be mere pettifoggery to argue that Campbell might not make good on that promise. In any event, to the extent there is a question whether Campbell is willing and able to pay, there is an easy answer: have the firm deposit a certified check with the trial court.

The case or controversy requirement serves an essential purpose: It ensures that the federal courts expound the law "only in the last resort, and as a necessity." It is the necessity of resolving a live dispute that reconciles the exercise of profound power by unelected judges with the principles of self-governance, ensuring adherence to "the proper — and properly limited — role of the courts in a democratic society." There is no such necessity here.

The good news is that this case is limited to its facts. The majority holds that an offer of complete relief is insufficient to moot a case. The majority does not say that payment of complete relief leads to the same result. For aught that appears, the majority's analysis may have come out differently if Campbell had deposited the offered funds with the District Court. This Court leaves that question for another day — assuming there are other plaintiffs out there who, like Gomez, won't take "yes" for an answer.

Justice ALITO, dissenting.

I join the Chief Justice's dissent. I agree that a defendant may extinguish a plaintiff's personal stake in pursuing a claim by offering complete relief on the claim, even if the plaintiff spurns the offer. Our Article III precedents make clear that, for mootness purposes, there is nothing talismanic about the plaintiff's acceptance. I write separately to emphasize what I see as the linchpin for finding mootness in this case: There is no real dispute that Campbell would "make good on [its] promise" to pay Gomez the money it offered him if the case were dismissed. Absent this fact, I would be compelled to find that the case is not moot.

* * *

2. What Should Happen to Underlying Relief?

As *Chafin v. Chafin* suggests, there are circumstances in which a case becomes moot after a lower court has already issued relief. When this occurs, what should the Supreme Court or Court of Appeals do with the underlying relief? This question is most acute with respect to prospective relief. Sometimes, after a federal court has enjoined unconstitutional actions or policies, events take place during the appeal that make it unlikely that the plaintiff will experience a redressable injury again in the future. Appellate courts must then confront whether to vacate the lower courts' injunctions or declaratory judgments.

There are two important principles that govern this circumstance. The first is when a federal civil case becomes moot while on appeal, the established practice is generally "to reverse or vacate the judgment below and remand with a direction to dismiss." *United States v. Munsingwear, Inc.* (1950). Second, however, when the losing party's conduct causes the case to become moot, the appellate court should *not* vacate the underlying relief. *U.S. Bancorp Mortg. Co. v. Bonner Mall P'ship* (1994). The following case describes these principles, and their rationale.

U.S. Bancorp Mortg. Co. v. Bonner Mall P'ship
513 U.S. 18 (1994)

Justice SCALIA delivered the opinion of the Court.

The question in this case is whether appellate courts in the federal system should vacate civil judgments of subordinate courts in cases that are settled after appeal is filed or certiorari sought.

I

In 1984 and 1985, Northtown Investments built the Bonner Mall in Bonner County, Idaho, with financing from a bank in that State. In 1986, respondent Bonner Mall Partnership (Bonner) acquired the mall, while petitioner U.S. Bancorp Mortgage Co. (Bancorp) acquired the loan and mortgage from the Idaho bank. In 1990, Bonner defaulted on its real-estate taxes and Bancorp scheduled a foreclosure sale.

The day before the sale, Bonner filed a petition under Chapter 11 of the Bankruptcy Code, 11 U.S.C. §1101 et seq., in the United States Bankruptcy Court for the District of Idaho. It filed a reorganization plan that depended on the "new value exception" to the absolute priority rule. Bancorp moved to suspend the automatic stay of its foreclosure imposed by 11 U.S.C. §362(a), arguing that Bonner's plan was unconfirmable as a matter of law for a number of reasons, including unavailability of the new value exception. The Bankruptcy Court eventually granted the motion, concluding that the new value exception had not survived enactment of the Bankruptcy Code. The court stayed its order pending an appeal by Bonner.

The United States District Court for the District of Idaho reversed; Bancorp took an appeal in turn, but the Court of Appeals for the Ninth Circuit affirmed.

Bancorp then petitioned for a writ of certiorari. After we granted the petition, and received briefing on the merits, Bancorp and Bonner stipulated to a consensual plan of reorganization, which received the approval of the Bankruptcy Court. The parties agreed that confirmation of the plan constituted a settlement that mooted the case. Bancorp, however, also requested that we exercise our power under 28 U.S.C. §2106 to vacate the judgment of the Court of Appeals. Bonner opposed the motion. We set the vacatur question for briefing and argument.

II

Respondent questions our power to entertain petitioner's motion to vacate, suggesting that the limitations on the judicial power conferred by Article III, *see* U.S. Const., Art. III, §1, "may, at least in some cases, prohibit an act of vacatur when no live dispute exists due to a settlement that has rendered a case moot."

The statute that supplies the power of vacatur provides:

> "The Supreme Court or any other court of appellate jurisdiction may affirm, modify, vacate, set aside or reverse any judgment, decree, or order of a court lawfully brought before it for review, and may remand the cause and direct the entry of such appropriate judgment, decree, or order, or require such further proceedings to be had as may be just under the circumstances." 28 U.S.C. §2106.

Of course, no statute could authorize a federal court to decide the merits of a legal question not posed in an Article III case or controversy. For that purpose, a case must exist at all the stages of appellate review. But reason and authority refute the quite different notion that a federal appellate court may not take any action with regard to a piece of litigation once it has been determined that the requirements of Article III no longer are (or indeed never were) met. That proposition is contradicted whenever an appellate court holds that a district court lacked Article III jurisdiction in the first instance, vacates the decision, and remands with directions to dismiss. In cases that become moot while awaiting review, respondent's logic would hold the Court powerless to award costs, or even to enter an order of dismissal.

Article III does not prescribe such paralysis. "If a judgment has become moot [while awaiting review], this Court may not consider its merits, but may make such disposition of the whole case as justice may require." As with other matters of judicial administration and practice "reasonably ancillary to the primary, dispute-deciding function" of the federal courts, Congress may authorize us to enter orders necessary and appropriate to the final disposition of a suit that is before us for review.

III

The leading case on vacatur is *United States v. Munsingwear*, Inc. (1950), in which the United States sought injunctive and monetary relief for violation of a price control regulation. The damages claim was held in abeyance pending a decision on the injunction. The District Court held that the respondent's prices complied with the regulations and dismissed the complaint. While the United States' appeal was pending, the commodity at issue was decontrolled; at the respondent's request, the case was dismissed as moot, a disposition in which the United States acquiesced.

The respondent then obtained dismissal of the damages action on the ground of res judicata, and we took the case to review that ruling. The United States protested the unfairness of according preclusive effect to a decision that it had tried to appeal but could not. We saw no such unfairness, reasoning that the United States should have asked the Court of Appeals to vacate the District Court's decision before the appeal was dismissed. We stated that "[t]he established practice of the Court in dealing with a civil case from a court in the federal system which has become moot while on its way here or pending our decision on the merits is to reverse or vacate the judgment below and remand with a direction to dismiss." We explained that vacatur "clears the path for future relitigation of the issues between the parties and eliminates a judgment, review of which was prevented through happenstance." Finding that the United States had "slept on its rights," we affirmed.

The parties in the present case agree that vacatur must be decreed for those judgments whose review is, in the words of *Munsingwear*, "'prevented through happenstance'"—that is to say, where a controversy presented for review has "become moot due to circumstances unattributable to any of the parties." They also agree that vacatur must be granted where mootness results from the unilateral action of the party who prevailed in the lower court. The contested question is whether courts should vacate where mootness results from a settlement. The centerpiece of petitioner's argument is that the *Munsingwear* procedure has already been held to apply in such cases. *Munsingwear*'s description of the "established practice" (the argument runs) drew no distinctions between categories of moot cases; opinions in later cases granting vacatur have reiterated the breadth of the rule; and at least some of those cases specifically involved mootness by reason of settlement.

But *Munsingwear*, and the post-*Munsingwear* practice, cannot bear the weight of the present case. To begin with, the portion of Justice Douglas' opinion in *Munsingwear* describing the "established practice" for vacatur was dictum; all that was needful for the decision was (at most) the proposition that vacatur should have been sought, not that it necessarily would have been granted. Moreover, as *Munsingwear* itself acknowledged, the "established practice" (in addition to being unconsidered) was not entirely uniform, at least three cases having been dismissed for mootness without vacatur within the four Terms preceding *Munsingwear*. Nor has the post-Munsingwear practice been as uniform as petitioner claims. Of course all of those decisions, both granting vacatur and denying it, were per curiam, with the single exception of *Karcher v. May* (1987), in which we declined to vacate. This seems to us a prime occasion for invoking our customary refusal to be bound by dicta, and our customary skepticism toward per curiam dispositions that lack the reasoned consideration of a full opinion. Today we examine vacatur once more in the light shed by adversary presentation.

The principles that have always been implicit in our treatment of moot cases counsel against extending *Munsingwear* to settlement. From the beginning we have disposed of moot cases in the manner "'most consonant to justice' . . . in view of the nature and character of the conditions which have caused the case to become moot." The principal condition to which we have looked is whether the party seeking relief from the judgment below caused the mootness by voluntary action.

The reference to "happenstance" in *Munsingwear* must be understood as an allusion to this equitable tradition of vacatur. A party who seeks review of the merits of an adverse ruling, but is frustrated by the vagaries of circumstance, ought not in fairness be forced to acquiesce in the judgment. The same is true when mootness results from unilateral action of the party who prevailed below. Where mootness results from settlement, however, the losing party has voluntarily forfeited his legal remedy by the ordinary processes of appeal or certiorari, thereby surrendering his claim to the equitable remedy of vacatur. The judgment is not unreviewable, but simply unreviewed by his own choice. The denial of vacatur is merely one application of the principle that "[a] suitor's conduct in relation to the matter at hand may disentitle him to the relief he seeks."

In these respects the case stands no differently than it would if jurisdiction were lacking because the losing party failed to appeal at all. In *Karcher v. May*, two state legislators, acting in their capacities as presiding officers of the legislature, appealed from a federal judgment that invalidated a state statute on constitutional grounds. After the jurisdictional statement was filed the legislators lost their posts, and their successors in office withdrew the appeal. Holding that we lacked jurisdiction for want of a proper appellant, we dismissed. The legislators then argued that the judgments should be vacated under *Munsingwear*. But we denied the request, noting that "[t]his controversy did not become moot due to circumstances unattributable to any of the parties. The controversy ended when the losing party—the [State] Legislature—declined to pursue its appeal. Accordingly, the *Munsingwear* procedure is inapplicable to this case." So, too, here.

It is true, of course, that respondent agreed to the settlement that caused the mootness. Petitioner argues that vacatur is therefore fair to respondent, and seeks to distinguish our prior cases on that ground. But that misconceives the emphasis on fault in our decisions. That the parties are jointly responsible for settling may in some sense put them on even footing, but petitioner's case needs more than that. Respondent won below. It is petitioner's burden, as the party seeking relief from the status quo of the appellate judgment, to demonstrate not merely equivalent responsibility for the mootness, but equitable entitlement to the extraordinary remedy of vacatur. Petitioner's voluntary forfeiture of review constitutes a failure of equity that makes the burden decisive, whatever respondent's share in the mooting of the case might have been.

As always when federal courts contemplate equitable relief, our holding must also take account of the public interest. "Judicial precedents are presumptively correct and valuable to the legal community as a whole. They are not merely the property of private litigants and should stand unless a court concludes that the public interest would be served by a vacatur." Congress has prescribed a primary route, by appeal as of right and certiorari, through which parties may seek relief from the legal consequences of judicial judgments. To allow a party who steps off the statutory path to employ the secondary remedy of vacatur as a refined form of collateral attack on the judgment would—quite apart from any considerations of fairness to the parties—disturb the orderly operation of the federal judicial system. *Munsingwear* establishes that the public interest is best served by granting relief when the demands of "orderly procedure," cannot be honored; we think conversely that the public interest requires those demands to be honored when they can.

We hold that mootness by reason of settlement does not justify vacatur of a judgment under review. This is not to say that vacatur can never be granted when mootness is produced in that fashion. As we have described, the determination is an equitable one, and exceptional circumstances may conceivably counsel in favor of such a course. It should be clear from our discussion, however, that those exceptional circumstances do not include the mere fact that the settlement agreement provides for vacatur—which neither diminishes the voluntariness of the abandonment of review nor alters any of the policy considerations we have discussed. Of course even in the absence of, or before considering the existence of, extraordinary circumstances, a court of appeals presented with a request for vacatur of a district-court judgment may remand the case with instructions that the district court consider the request, which it may do pursuant to Federal Rule of Civil Procedure 60(b).

* * *

3. Exceptions to Mootness

There are important exceptions to mootness doctrine. First, a case should not be dismissed as moot when the plaintiff will continue to experience collateral consequences as a result of the defendant's purportedly illegal actions. Second, a case should not be dismissed as moot when it is capable of repetition and evades review. This exception applies when (a) there is a claim that, by its nature, will generally dissipate before a lawsuit can be resolved; and (b) the plaintiff may experience the harm again in the future. Third, under the "voluntary cessation" exception, a defendant's promise to stop breaking the law will not be sufficient to moot a case unless there is no reasonable expectation that the wrong will be repeated. Fourth, there is a class action exception. When a federal court has properly certified a case, that case should not be dismissed as moot so long as someone in the class has a case or controversy. It is of no moment that the lead plaintiff's case or controversy has disappeared.

a.   Collateral Consequences

A "criminal case is moot only if it is shown that there is no possibility that any collateral legal consequences will be imposed on the basis of the challenged conviction." *Sibron v. New York* (1968). The Court has explained, "the obvious fact of life that most criminal convictions do in fact entail adverse collateral legal consequences. The mere 'possibility' that this will be the case is enough to preserve a criminal case from ending 'ignominiously in the limbo of mootness.'" In reaching this conclusion, the Court recognized that the enforcement of low-level crimes, through governmental conduct like stop and frisks, colors some individuals' relationship to their government. Because punishment for resultant convictions may often be shorter than the life of the appellate process, an intolerable gap in constitutional enforcement would occur were the rule otherwise. In *Sibron*, the Court explained:

Many deep and abiding constitutional problems are encountered primarily at a level of "low visibility" in the criminal process—in the context of prosecutions for "minor" offenses which carry only short sentences. We do not believe that the Constitution contemplates that people deprived of constitutional rights at this level should be left utterly remediless and defenseless against repetitions of unconstitutional conduct.[35]

Those convicted of crimes, then, may generally continue to appeal their convictions even after the conclusion of their sentence.

Relatedly, the government may appeal or seek certiorari to obtain a longer sentence, even after the defendant has finished serving the initial sentence. The Court reasoned in *Pennsylvania v. Mimms*:

> If the prospect of the State's visiting such collateral consequences on a criminal defendant who has served his sentence is a sufficient burden as to enable him to seek reversal of a decision affirming his conviction, the prospect of the State's inability to impose such a burden following a reversal of the conviction of a criminal defendant in its own courts must likewise be sufficient to enable the State to obtain review of its claims on the merits here.

At the same time, a defendant may not typically challenge a *sentence* that has already been completed, because generally there are not collateral consequences that flow from the length of one's sentence (as opposed to the fact of one's conviction). As the Court observed in *North Carolina v. Rice*, while "[n]ullification of a conviction may have important benefits for a defendant," "the correction of a sentence already served is another matter."

Beyond the criminal context, civil cases can implicate this exception as well. If a litigant seeks multiple forms of relief, and the primary relief that the plaintiff seeks becomes moot, the plaintiff may continue to pursue the less consequential forms of relief, as long as there is harm that those remedies would continue to redress. *See Havens Realty Corp. v. Coleman* (1982). A plaintiff seeking reinstatement and backpay, for example, may continue to pursue backpay, even if reinstatement is no longer a tenable opinion. *See Firefighter's Local 1784 v. Stotts* (1984).

---

35. For additional evidence of the democratic and social costs of low-level crime control, see, e.g., Issa Kohler-Hausmann, Misdemeanorland: Criminal Courts and Social Control in an Age of Broken Windows Policing (2018); Amy E. Lerman & Vesla M. Weaver, Arresting Citizenship: The Democratic Consequences of American Crime Control (2014) (describing the diminished political participation that is correlated with arrests); Charles R. Epp et al., Pulled Over: How Police Stops Define Race and Citizenship (2014) (documenting the disproportionately invasive traffic stops endured by Black Americans, and ways that impacted individuals' perspectives on citizenship); Monica C. Bell, *Police Reform and the Dismantling of Legal Estrangement*, 126 Yale L.J. 2054, 2067 (2017) ("[A]t both an interactional and structural level, current regimes can operate to effectively banish whole communities from the body politic.").

b. Capable of Repetition Yet Evading Review

The capable-of-repetition exception applies when two circumstances are both present. First, there is a reasonable expectation that the same litigant will experience the same illegal conduct again. Second, the challenged conduct is inherently too short in its duration to be fully litigated before the facts fundamentally change. Election cases, for example, are sometimes "capable of repetition" because an unconstitutionally burdensome law will sometimes affect political parties or voters in similar ways across multiple election cycles. Yet, these cases often "evade review" because of the limited duration of an election cycle. An election will often take place before the case is fully litigated.

Likewise, there is often a reasonable likelihood that government-imposed burdens obstructing reproductive autonomy will affect the same person more than once. An oft-cited case for this proposition is *Roe v. Wade* (1973), in which the Supreme Court famously held that when a pregnancy is in its early stages, the government generally may not force a person to carry a fetus to term and give birth. Because of the decision, individuals across the country had a constitutional right to access to abortion care for almost 50 years. When considering the threshold question of justiciability, the *Roe* Court observed that the plaintiff who initially brought the action was no longer pregnant, which was in tension with "the usual rule in federal cases is that an actual controversy must exist at stages of appellate or certiorari review, and not simply at the date the action is initiated." The Court explained, however, that:

> [W]hen, as here, pregnancy is a significant fact in the litigation, the normal 266-day human gestation period is so short that the pregnancy will come to term before the usual appellate process is complete. If that termination makes a case moot, pregnancy litigation seldom will survive much beyond the trial stage, and appellate review will be effectively denied. Our law should not be that rigid. Pregnancy often comes more than once to the same woman, and in the general population, if man is to survive, it will always be with us. Pregnancy provides a classic justification for a conclusion of nonmootness. It truly could be "capable of repetition, yet evading review."

Roe v. Wade (1973). Both requirements were met, then. First, the facts giving rise to the dispute, by their nature, would not last as long as many federal lawsuits. Second, the same plaintiff could reasonably experience the injury again the future.

In a more recent opinion, *Dobbs v. Jackson Women's Health Org.*, 597 U.S. ___ (2022), the Supreme Court overruled *Roe*'s core constitutional holding as to the scope of the right to privacy. State governments may now compel Americans to remain pregnant and give birth without running afoul of the Constitution's right to privacy. Consistent with that ruling, major restrictions on reproductive decisions have become law in many states, ending safe, legal abortion care in large parts of the country. But while *Roe*'s core holding concerning the scope of the right to privacy has been overturned, the case remains, to date, an axiomatic example of the "capable or repetition but evading review" exception to mootness.

In addition to cases about elections and reproductive autonomy, other types of cases also give rise to this exception. For example, the exception is often raised in time-sensitive First Amendment cases, such as cases about time-sensitive protests or prior restraint of speech.[36] *See Nebraska Press Ass'n v. Stuart* (1982). The exception is also often raised in cases about matters like labor disputes, which often have a temporal shelf-life that is much shorter than the timespan of federal cases.[37]

The following cases are illustrative: *Weinstein v. Bradford* (1975) and *Honig v. Doe* (1988). *Weinstein* presented the question of mootness in an area where it arises frequently—litigation concerning the administration of corrections.[38] The question is whether and to what extent the mootness doctrine will shield aspects of corrections administration from review. In *Weinstein*, this question arose when a former inmate, who was no longer subject to corrections management, challenged the procedures used to decide his application for parole. *Honig* also involved a question implicating the coercive authority of the state, one arising within schools rather than the carceral system. The question in that case was whether the San Francisco Unified School District could expel students on the grounds that they were dangerously violent and emotionally disturbed. The Court addressed this question against the backdrop of a federal statute that protected the right of disabled children to receive public education and, among other things, limited the discretion of school officials to expel students. Congress enacted this statute in response to a common problem of public schools failing to accommodate and even expelling students with disabilities.

In reading these cases, note that the Court looks to ensure both requirements are satisfied before applying this exception. Also consider debates among the Justices in *Honig* as to whether the doctrine of mootness actually inheres in the Constitution.

Weinstein v. Bradford

423 U.S. 147 (1975)

PER CURIAM.

Respondent Bradford sued petitioner members of the North Carolina Board of Parole in the United States District Court for the Eastern District of North Carolina, claiming that petitioners were obligated under the Fourteenth Amendment of the United States Constitution to accord him certain procedural rights in considering his eligibility for parole. [T]he District Court . . . dismissed the complaint. On respondent's appeal to the Court of Appeals for the Fourth Circuit, that court sustained his claim that he was constitutionally entitled to procedural rights in connection with petitioners' consideration of his application for parole. [W]e granted certiorari.

Respondent has now filed a suggestion of mootness with this Court. It is undisputed that respondent was temporarily paroled on December 18, 1974, and that this status ripened into a complete release from supervision on March 25, 1975. From that date forward it is plain that respondent can have no interest whatever in the procedures followed by petitioners in granting parole.

---

36. *See also* ERWIN CHEMERINSKY, FEDERAL JURISDICTION §2.5.3 (8th ed. 2021).

37. *See* Burlington N. R.R. v. Bhd. of Maint. of Way Emps. (1987); Brock v. Roadway Express, Inc. (1987); Super Tire Eng'g Co. v. McCorkle (1974).

38. *See generally* Steven B. Dow, *Navigating Through the Problem of Mootness in Corrections Litigation*, 43 CAP. U. L. REV. 651 (2015).

Conceding this fact, petitioners urge that this is an issue which is "capable of repetition, yet evading review" as that term has been used in our cases dealing with mootness. Petitioners rely on *Super Tire Engineering Co. v. McCorkle* (1974), to support their contention that the case is not moot. But there the posture of the parties was quite different. Petitioner employer was engaged in cyclically recurring bargaining with the union representing its employees, and respondent state official was continuously following a policy of paying unemployment compensation benefits to strikers. Even though the particular strike which had been the occasion for the filing of the lawsuit was terminated, the Court held that it was enough that the petitioner employer showed "the existence of an immediate and definite governmental action or policy that has adversely affected and continues to affect a present interest," and noted that "the great majority of economic strikes do not last long enough for complete judicial review of the controversies they engender." But in the instant case, respondent, who challenged the "governmental action or policy" in question, no longer has any present interest affected by that policy.

In *Sosna v. Iowa* (1975), we reviewed in some detail the historical developments of the mootness doctrine in this Court. *Southern Pacific Terminal Co. v. ICC* (1911), was the first case to enunciate the "capable of repetition, yet evading review" branch of the law of mootness. There it was held that because of the short duration of the Interstate Commerce Commission order challenged, it was virtually impossible to litigate the validity of the order prior to its expiration. Because of this fact, and the additional fact that the same party would in all probability be subject to the same kind of order in the future, review was allowed even though the order in question had expired by its own terms.

Sosna decided that in the absence of a class action, the "capable of repetition, yet evading review" doctrine was limited to the situation where two elements combined: (1) the challenged action was in its duration too short to be fully litigated prior to its cessation or expiration, and (2) there was a reasonable expectation that the same complaining party would be subjected to the same action again. The instant case, not a class action, clearly does not satisfy the latter element. While petitioners will continue to administer the North Carolina parole system with respect to those who at any given moment are subject to their jurisdiction, there is no demonstrated probability that respondent will again be among that number. *O'Shea v. Littleton* (1974).

It appearing, therefore, that the case is moot, the judgment of the Court of Appeals is vacated, and the case is remanded to the District Court with instructions to dismiss the complaint. *United States v. Munsingwear, Inc.* (1950).

* * *

Honig v. Doe

484 U.S. 305 (1988)

Justice BRENNAN delivered the opinion of the Court.

As a condition of federal financial assistance, the Education of the Handicapped Act requires States to ensure a "free appropriate public education" for all disabled children within their jurisdictions. In aid of this goal, the Act establishes a comprehensive system of procedural safeguards designed to ensure parental participation in decisions concerning the education of their disabled children and to provide administrative and judicial review of any decisions with which those parents disagree.

I

In the Education of the Handicapped Act (EHA or the Act), Congress sought "to assure that all handicapped children have available to them . . . a free appropriate public education which emphasizes special education and related services designed to meet their unique needs, [and] to assure that the rights of handicapped children and their parents or guardians are protected." §1400(c). When the law was passed in 1975, Congress had before it ample evidence that such legislative assurances were sorely needed: 21 years after this Court declared education to be "perhaps the most important function of state and local governments," *Brown v. Board of Education* (1954), congressional studies revealed that better than half of the Nation's 8 million disabled children were not receiving appropriate educational services. §1400(b)(3). Indeed, one out of every eight of these children was excluded from the public school system altogether, §1400(b)(4); many others were simply "warehoused" in special classes or were neglectfully shepherded through the system until they were old enough to drop out.

[T]he EHA confers upon disabled students an enforceable substantive right to public education in participating States, and conditions federal financial assistance upon a State's compliance with the substantive and procedural goals of the Act. The primary vehicle for implementing these congressional goals is the "individualized educational program" (IEP), which the EHA mandates for each disabled child. Prepared at meetings between a representative of the local school district, the child's teacher, the parents or guardians, and, whenever appropriate, the disabled child, the IEP sets out the child's present educational performance, establishes annual and short-term objectives for improvements in that performance, and describes the specially designed instruction and services that will enable the child to meet those objectives.

The present dispute grows out of the efforts of certain officials of the San Francisco Unified School District (SFUSD) to expel two emotionally disturbed children from school indefinitely for violent and disruptive conduct related to their disabilities. [Both students—John Doe and Jack Smith—brought suit against state and local officials alleging that their expulsions violated their IEP and, in turn, federal law.] The District Court subsequently entered summary judgment in favor of respondents on their EHA claims and issued a permanent injunction. On appeal, the Court of Appeals for the Ninth Circuit affirmed the orders with slight modifications. We granted certiorari.

II

At the outset, we address the suggestion that this case is moot. Under Article III of the Constitution this Court may only adjudicate actual, ongoing controversies. That the dispute between the parties was very much alive when suit was filed, or at the time the Court of Appeals rendered its judgment, cannot substitute for the actual case or controversy that an exercise of this Court's jurisdiction requires. *Roe v. Wade* (1973). In the present case, we have jurisdiction if there is a reasonable likelihood that respondents will again suffer the deprivation of EHA-mandated rights that gave rise to this suit. We believe that, at least with respect to respondent Smith, such a possibility does in fact exist and that the case therefore remains justiciable.

Respondent John Doe is now 24 years old and, accordingly, is no longer entitled to the protections and benefits of the EHA, which limits eligibility to disabled children between the ages of 3 and 21. *See* 20 U.S.C. §1412(2)(B). It is clear, therefore, that whatever rights to state educational services he may yet have as a ward of the State, the Act would not govern the State's provision of those services, and thus the case is moot as to him.

Respondent Jack Smith, however, is currently 20 and has not yet completed high school. Although at present he is not faced with any proposed expulsion or suspension proceedings, and indeed no longer even resides within the SFUSD, he remains a resident of California and is entitled to a "free appropriate public education" within that State. His claims under the EHA, therefore, are not moot if the conduct he originally complained of is "'capable of repetition, yet evading review.'" Given Smith's continued eligibility for educational services under the EHA, the nature of his disability, and petitioner's insistence that all local school districts retain residual authority to exclude disabled children for dangerous conduct, we have little difficulty concluding that there is a "reasonable expectation," that Smith would once again be subjected to a unilateral "change in placement" for conduct growing out of his disabilities were it not for the statewide injunctive relief issued below.

Our cases reveal that, for purposes of assessing the likelihood that state authorities will reinflict a given injury, we generally have been unwilling to assume that the party seeking relief will repeat the type of misconduct that would once again place him or her at risk of that injury. No such reluctance, however, is warranted here. It is respondent Smith's very inability to conform his conduct to socially acceptable norms that renders him "handicapped" within the meaning of the EHA.

We think it equally probable that, should he do so, respondent will again be subjected to the same unilateral school action for which he initially sought relief. In this regard, it matters not that Smith no longer resides within the SFUSD. While the actions of SFUSD officials first gave rise to this litigation, the District Judge expressly found that the lack of a state policy governing local school responses to disability-related misconduct had led to, and would continue to result in, EHA violations, and she therefore enjoined the state defendant from authorizing, among other things, unilateral placement changes. Only petitioner, the State Superintendent of Public Instruction, has invoked our jurisdiction, and he now urges us to hold that local school districts retain unilateral authority under the EHA to suspend or otherwise remove disabled children for dangerous conduct.

Chief Justice Rehnquist, concurring.

I write separately on the mootness issue in this case to explain why I have joined Part II of the Court's opinion, and why I think reconsideration of our mootness jurisprudence may be in order when dealing with cases decided by this Court.

The present rule in federal cases is that an actual controversy must exist at all stages of appellate review, not merely at the time the complaint is filed. All agree that this case was "very much alive," when the action was filed in the District Court, and very probably when the Court of Appeals decided the case. It is supervening events since the decision of the Court of Appeals which have caused the dispute between the majority and the dissent over whether this case is moot. Therefore, all that the Court actually holds is that these supervening events do not deprive this Court of the authority to hear the case. I agree with that holding, and would go still further in the direction of relaxing the test of mootness where the events giving rise to the claim of mootness have occurred after our decision to grant certiorari or to note probable jurisdiction.

The Court implies in its opinion, and the dissent expressly states, that the mootness doctrine is based upon Art. III of the Constitution. If it were indeed Art. III which — by reason of its requirement of a case or controversy for the exercise of federal judicial power — underlies the mootness doctrine, the "capable of repetition, yet evading review" exception relied upon by the Court in this case would be incomprehensible. Article III extends the judicial power of the United States only to cases and controversies; it does not except from this requirement other lawsuits which are "capable of repetition, yet evading review." If our mootness doctrine were forced upon us by the case or controversy requirement of Art. III itself, we would have no more power to decide lawsuits which are "moot" but which also raise questions which are capable of repetition but evading review than we would to decide cases which are "moot" but raise no such questions.

The logical conclusion to be drawn from [precedent], and from the historical development of the principle of mootness, is that while an unwillingness to decide moot cases may be connected to the case or controversy requirement of Art. III, it is an attenuated connection that may be overridden where there are strong reasons to override it. The "capable of repetition, yet evading review" exception is an example.

I believe that we should adopt an additional exception to our present mootness doctrine for those cases where the events which render the case moot have supervened since our grant of certiorari or noting of probable jurisdiction in the case. Dissents from denial of certiorari in this Court illustrate the proposition that the roughly 150 or 160 cases which we decide each year on the merits are less than the number of cases warranting review by us if we are to remain, as Chief Justice Taft said many years ago, "the last word on every important issue under the Constitution and the statutes of the United States." But these unique resources — the time spent preparing to decide the case by reading briefs, hearing oral argument, and conferring — are squandered in every case in which it becomes apparent after the decisional process is underway that we may not reach the question presented.

Justice SCALIA, with whom Justice O'CONNOR joins, dissenting.

Without expressing any views on the merits of this case, I respectfully dissent because in my opinion we have no authority to decide it. I think the controversy is moot.

I

The Court correctly acknowledges that we have no power under Art. III of the Constitution to adjudicate a case that no longer presents an actual, ongoing dispute between the named parties. Here, there is obviously no present controversy between the parties, since both respondents are no longer in school and therefore no longer subject to a unilateral "change in placement." The Court concedes mootness with respect to respondent John Doe, who is now too old to receive the benefits of the Education of the Handicapped Act (EHA). It concludes, however, that the case is not moot as to respondent Jack Smith, who has two more years of eligibility but is no longer in the public schools, because the controversy is "capable of repetition, yet evading review."

Jurisdiction on the basis that a dispute is "capable of repetition, yet evading review" is limited to the "exceptional situatio[n]," where the following two circumstances simultaneously occur: "'(1) the challenged action [is] in its duration too short to be fully litigated prior to its cessation or expiration, and (2) there [is] a reasonable expectation that the same complaining party would be subjected to the same action again.'" *Murphy v. Hunt* (1982). The second of these requirements is not met in this case.

For there to be a "reasonable expectation" that Smith will be subjected to the same action again, that event must be a "demonstrated probability." I am surprised by the Court's contention, fraught with potential for future mischief, that "reasonable expectation" is satisfied by something less than "demonstrated probability." No one expects that to happen which he does not think probable; and his expectation cannot be shown to be reasonable unless the probability is demonstrated.

If our established mode of analysis were followed, the conclusion that a live controversy exists in the present case would require a demonstrated probability that all of the following events will occur: (1) Smith will return to public school; (2) he will be placed in an educational setting that is unable to tolerate his dangerous behavior; (3) he will again engage in dangerous behavior; and (4) local school officials will again attempt unilaterally to change his placement and the state defendants will fail to prevent such action. The Court spends considerable time establishing that the last two of these events are likely to recur, but relegates to a footnote its discussion of the first event, upon which all others depend, and only briefly alludes to the second. Neither the facts in the record, nor even the extrarecord assurances of counsel, establish a demonstrated probability of either of them.

The conclusion that the case is moot is reinforced, moreover, when one considers that, even if Smith does return to public school, the controversy will still not recur unless he is again placed in an educational setting that is unable to tolerate his behavior. It seems to me not only not demonstrably probable, but indeed quite unlikely, given what is now known about Smith's behavioral problems, that local school authorities would again place him in an educational setting that could not control his dangerous conduct, causing a suspension that would replicate the legal issues in this suit.

III

The Chief Justice joins the majority opinion on the ground, not that this case is not moot, but that where the events giving rise to the mootness have occurred after we have granted certiorari we may disregard them, since mootness is only a prudential doctrine and not part of the "case or controversy" requirement of Art. III.

I do not see how that can be. There is no more reason to intuit that mootness is merely a prudential doctrine than to intuit that initial standing is. Both doctrines have equivalently deep roots in the common-law understanding, and hence the constitutional understanding, of what makes a matter appropriate for judicial disposition. *See Flast v. Cohen* (1968) (describing mootness and standing as various illustrations of the requirement of "justiciability" in Art. III).

It is assuredly frustrating to find that a jurisdictional impediment prevents us from reaching the important merits issues that were the reason for our agreeing to hear this case. But we cannot ignore such impediments for purposes of our appellate review without simultaneously affecting the principles that govern district courts in their assertion or retention of original jurisdiction. We thus do substantial harm to a governmental structure designed to restrict the courts to matters that actually affect the litigants before them.

* * *

c. Voluntary Cessation

In *United States v. W.T. Grant Co.* (1953), the Supreme Court established the general principle that a defendant's "voluntary cessation of allegedly illegal conduct . . . does not make the case moot." Were the rule otherwise, the defendant could "return to his old ways. This together with a public interest in having the legality of the practices settled, militates against a mootness conclusion." For example, a defendant's mere promise to stop violating the law is an insufficient ground to hold that a case is moot. As the Court explained in *Quern v. Mandley* (1978), such a representation may "not operate to deprive the successful plaintiffs, and indeed the public, of a final and binding determination of the legality of the old practice."

There is, however, an exception to the principle that voluntary cessation does not moot a case: The defendant's decision to stop violating the law renders a case "moot if subsequent events made it absolutely clear that the allegedly wrongful behavior could not reasonably be expected to recur." *Friends of the Earth v. Laidlaw Env't Servs. (TOC), Inc.* (2000). Formally adopted changes in legislative or written policies, for example, have sometimes resulted in dismissals for mootness when there is no realistic probability that the defendant will reenact the offending policy. For example, in *Lewis v. Continental Bank Corp.* (1990), a case was dismissed as moot because Congress amended the disputed statute. In *Princeton University v. Schmid* (1982), a formally adopted change in a university's policy was sufficient. Even compliance with a judicial decree has sometimes mooted cases, but only when there was no realistic probability that the illegal conduct will resume. *See County of Los Angeles v. Davis* (1979).

On the other hand, legislative changes should not result in dismissal when a defendant has not met the burden of proving that there is no realistic probability that the offending law or policy will be reenacted. In *City of Mesquite v. Aladdin's Castle* (1982), even though a city repealed a disputed ordinance, the repeal did not result in dismissal because the city had also announced its plans to reinstate the contested ordinance if it prevailed in the suit. The Court reasoned, "[i]n this case the City's repeal of the objectionable language would not preclude it from reenacting precisely the same provision" if the action were deemed moot.

In the following case, *DeFunis v. Odegaard* (1974), the Court dismissed a case as moot, despite the plaintiff's contention that the defendant's voluntary compliance with a court order had caused the mootness. The Court also rejected the plaintiff's contention that this was a case that was "capable of repetition yet evading review," demonstrating that multiple mootness exceptions are sometimes raised and considered in the same cases.

DeFunis presented an early challenge to affirmative action programs in higher education. In particular, Marco DeFunis challenged the University of Washington Law School's admissions process, arguing that it discriminated against White applicants in violation of equal protection. At the time, the Association of American Law Schools reported that the majority of law schools had affirmative action processes that aimed to increase access to legal education for racial and ethnic minorities.[39] The American Bar Association filed an amicus brief arguing that such programs were necessary to address longstanding discrimination.[40] Indeed, the case was an instance of a now-common practice of voluminous amicus briefing: "Thirty briefs were filed in the Supreme Court, vigorously arguing one side or the other of the complex constitutional issues involved."[41] The Court did not reach the merits of those constitutional issues, which continue to arise in the federal courts.[42]

DeFunis v. Odegaard

416 U.S. 312 (1974)

PER CURIAM.

In 1971 the petitioner Marco DeFunis, Jr., applied for admission as a first-year student at the University of Washington Law School, a state-operated institution. The size of the incoming first-year class was to be limited to 150 persons, and the Law School received some 1,600 applications for these 150 places. DeFunis was eventually notified that he had been denied admission. He thereupon commenced this suit in a Washington trial court, contending that the procedures and criteria employed by the Law School Admissions Committee invidiously discriminated against him on account of his race in violation of the Equal Protection Clause of the Fourteenth Amendment to the United States Constitution.

---

39. ASSOCIATION OF AMERICAN LAW SCHOOLS & THE LAW SCHOOL ADMISSION COUNCIL, 1973-74 PREWLAW HANDBOOK — OFFICIAL LAW SCHOOL GUIDE (1973).

40. Br. of the Am. Bar Ass'n as Amicus Curiae in support of Respondents, at 7, DeFunis v. Odegaard, 416 U.S. 312 (1974).

41. Martin H. Redish, *Preferential Law School Admissions and the Equal Protection Clause: An Analysis of the Competing Arguments*, 22 UCLA L. REV. 343, 344 (1974).

42. When this book went to press, the Supreme Court had not yet decided two pending cases presenting the question whether the Court should overrule its precedent permitting institutions of higher education to use racial identity as a factor in admissions decisions. Those cases are *Students for Fair Admissions v. President & Fellows of Harvard College* (No. 20-1199) and *Students for Fair Admissions v. University of North Carolina* (No. 21-707).

DeFunis brought the suit on behalf of himself alone, and not as the representative of any class, against the various respondents, who are officers, faculty members, and members of the Board of Regents of the University of Washington. He asked the trial court to issue a mandatory injunction commanding the respondents to admit him as a member of the first-year class entering in September 1971, on the ground that the Law School admissions policy had resulted in the unconstitutional denial of his application for admission. The trial court agreed with his claim and granted the requested relief. DeFunis was, accordingly, admitted to the Law School and began his legal studies there in the fall of 1971. On appeal, the Washington Supreme Court reversed the judgment of the trial court and held that the Law School admissions policy did not violate the Constitution. By this time DeFunis was in his second year at the Law School.

He then petitioned this Court for a writ of certiorari, and Mr. Justice Douglas, as Circuit Justice, stayed the judgment of the Washington Supreme Court pending the "final disposition of the case by this Court." By virtue of this stay, DeFunis has remained in law school, and was in the first term of his third and final year when this Court first considered his certiorari petition in the fall of 1973. In response to questions raised from the bench during the oral argument, counsel for the petitioner has informed the Court that DeFunis has now registered "for his final quarter in law school." In light of DeFunis' recent registration for the last quarter of his final law school year, and the Law School's assurance that his registration is fully effective, the insistent question again arises whether this case is not moot, and to that question we now turn.

The starting point for analysis is the familiar proposition that "federal courts are without power to decide questions that cannot affect the rights of litigants in the case before them." The inability of the federal judiciary "to review moot cases derives from the requirement of Art. III of the Constitution under which the exercise of judicial power depends upon the existence of a case or controversy." Although as a matter of Washington state law it appears that this case would be saved from mootness by "the great public interest in the continuing issues raised by this appeal," the fact remains that under Art. III "(e)ven in cases arising in the state courts, the question of mootness is a federal one which a federal court must resolve before it assumes jurisdiction."

The respondents have represented that, without regard to the ultimate resolution of the issues in this case, DeFunis will remain a student in the Law School for the duration of any term in which he has already enrolled. Since he has now registered for his final term, it is evident that he will be given an opportunity to complete all academic and other requirements for graduation, and, if he does so, will receive his diploma regardless of any decision this Court might reach on the merits of this case. In short, all parties agree that DeFunis is now entitled to complete his legal studies at the University of Washington and to receive his degree from that institution. A determination by this Court of the legal issues tendered by the parties is no longer necessary to compel that result, and could not serve to prevent it. DeFunis did not cast his suit as a class action, and the only remedy he requested was an injunction commanding his admission to the Law School. He was not only accorded that remedy, but he now has also been irrevocably admitted to the final term of the final year of the Law School course. The controversy between the parties has thus clearly ceased to be "definite and concrete" and no longer "touch(es) the legal relations of parties having adverse legal interests."

It matters not that these circumstances partially stem from a policy decision on the part of the respondent Law School authorities. The respondents, through their counsel, the Attorney General of the State, have professionally represented that in no event will the status of DeFunis now be affected by any view this Court might express on the merits of this controversy. And it has been the settled practice of the Court, in contexts no less significant, fully to accept representations such as these as parameters for decision.

There is a line of decisions in this Court standing for the proposition that the "voluntary cessation of allegedly illegal conduct does not deprive the tribunal of power to hear and determine the case, i.e., does not make the case moot." *United States v. W. T. Grant Co.* (1953). These decisions and the doctrine they reflect would be quite relevant if the question of mootness here had arisen by reason of a unilateral change in the admissions procedures of the Law School. For it was the admissions procedures that were the target of this litigation, and a voluntary cessation of the admissions practices complained of could make this case moot only if it could be said with assurance that there is no reasonable expectation that the wrong will be repeated. Otherwise, the defendant is free to return to his old ways, and this fact would be enough to prevent mootness because of the public interest in having the legality of the practices settled. But mootness in the present case depends not at all upon a "voluntary cessation" of the admissions practices that were the subject of this litigation. It depends, instead, upon the simple fact that DeFunis is now in the final quarter of the final year of his course of study, and the settled and unchallenged policy of the Law School to permit him to complete the term for which he is now enrolled.

It might also be suggested that this case presents a question that is "capable of repetition, yet evading review," and is thus amenable to federal adjudication even though it might otherwise be considered moot. But DeFunis will never again be required to run the gantlet of the Law School's admission process, and so the question is certainly not "capable of repetition" so far as he is concerned. Moreover, just because this particular case did not reach the Court until the eve of the petitioner's graduation from Law School, it hardly follows that the issue he raises will in the future evade review. If the admissions procedures of the Law School remain unchanged, there is no reason to suppose that a subsequent case attacking those procedures will not come with relative speed to this Court, now that the Supreme Court of Washington has spoken.

Because the petitioner will complete his law school studies at the end of the term for which he has now registered regardless of any decision this Court might reach on the merits of this litigation, we conclude that the Court cannot, consistently with the limitations of Art. III of the Constitution, consider the substantive constitutional issues tendered by the parties. Accordingly, the judgment of the Supreme Court of Washington is vacated, and the cause is remanded for such proceedings as by that court may be deemed appropriate.

Mr. Justice DOUGLAS, dissenting.

I agree with Mr. Justice BRENNAN that this case is not moot, and because of the significance of the issues raised I think it is important to reach the merits.

[Merits discussion omitted.]

Mr. Justice BRENNAN, with whom Mr. Justice DOUGLAS, Mr. Justice WHITE, and Mr. Justice MARSHALL concur, dissenting.

I respectfully dissent. Many weeks of the school term remain, and petitioner may not receive his degree despite respondents' assurances that petitioner will be allowed to complete this term's schooling regardless of our decision. Any number of unexpected events—illness, economic necessity, even academic failure—might prevent his graduation at the end of the term. Were that misfortune to befall, and were petitioner required to register for yet another term, the prospect that he would again face the hurdle of the admissions policy is real, not fanciful; for respondents warn that "Mr. DeFunis would have to take some appropriate action to request continued admission for the remainder of his law school education, and some discretionary action by the University on such request would have to be taken." Thus, respondents' assurances have not dissipated the possibility that petitioner might once again have to run the gantlet of the University's allegedly unlawful admissions policy.

The Court therefore proceeds on an erroneous premise in resting its mootness holding on a supposed inability to render any judgment that may affect one way or the other petitioner's completion of his law studies. For surely if we were to reverse the Washington Supreme Court, we could insure that, if for some reason petitioner did not graduate this spring, he would be entitled to re-enrollment at a later time on the same basis as others who have not faced the hurdle of the University's allegedly unlawful admissions policy.

In these circumstances, and because the University's position implies no concession that its admissions policy is unlawful, this controversy falls squarely within the Court's long line of decisions holding that the "(m)ere voluntary cessation of allegedly illegal conduct does not moot a case." Since respondents' voluntary representation to this Court is only that they will permit petitioner to complete this term's studies, respondents have not borne the "heavy burden," of demonstrating that there was not even a "mere possibility" that petitioner would once again be subject to the challenged admissions policy. On the contrary, respondents have positioned themselves so as to be "free to return to (their) old ways."

I can thus find no justification for the Court's straining to rid itself of this dispute. While we must be vigilant to require that litigants maintain a personal stake in the outcome of a controversy to assure that "the questions will be framed with the necessary specificity, that the issues will be contested with the necessity adverseness and that the litigation will be pursued with the necessary vigor to assure that the constitutional challenge will be made in a form traditionally thought to be capable of judicial resolution," *Flast v. Cohen* (1968), there is no want of an adversary contest in this case. Indeed, the Court concedes that, if petitioner has lost his stake in this controversy, he did so only when he registered for the spring term. But appellant took that action only after the case had been fully litigated in the state courts, briefs had been filed in this Court, and oral argument had been heard. The case is thus ripe for decision on a fully developed factual record with sharply defined and fully canvassed legal issues.

Moreover, in endeavoring to dispose of this case as moot, the Court clearly disserves the public interest. The constitutional issues which are avoided today concern vast numbers of people, organizations, and colleges and universities, as evidenced by the filing of twenty-six amicus curiae briefs. Few constitutional questions in recent history have stirred as much debate, and they will not disappear. They must inevitably return to the federal courts and ultimately again to this Court. Because avoidance of repetitious litigation serves the public interest, that inevitability counsels against mootness determinations, as here, not compelled by the record. Although the Court should, of course, avoid unnecessary decisions of constitutional questions, we should not transform principles of avoidance of constitutional decisions into devices for sidestepping resolution of difficult cases.

On what appears in this case, I would find that there is an extant controversy and decide the merits of the very important constitutional questions presented.

* * *

4. Class Action

Another important exception to mootness is a properly certified class action. When a named plaintiff's case becomes moot, a properly certified class action should not be dismissed so long as a member of the class continues to have a case or controversy. In the leading case, *Sosna v. Iowa* (1975), the Court explained that "the class of unnamed persons described in the certification acquired a legal status separate from the interest asserted by the plaintiff."

This exception has sustained several important cases. In *Zablocki v. Redhail* (1978), a case in which the Supreme Court recognized Americans' fundamental right to marry, a plaintiff challenged a Wisconsin law that generally prohibited individuals who owed arrears in child support from marrying. The lead plaintiff had gotten married in another state during the litigation. Nonetheless, the Court reached the merits because, among other things, "the dispute over the statute's constitutionality remain[ed] live with respect to members of the class appellee represent[ed]." Likewise, in *Gerstein v. Pugh* (1975), the Supreme Court held that a Florida policy and practice that allowed the individuals to be detained without timely probable cause determinations violated the Fourth Amendment. Although the lead plaintiffs' pretrial detentions had come to an end, the Court reaffirmed that the "termination of a class representative's claim does not moot the claims of the unnamed members of the class." The same rule applied in *Gratz v. Bollinger* (2003), a case that overturned the University of Michigan's undergraduate affirmative action policy. The case survived, even after the lead plaintiff graduated.

When must a class action be certified to fall within this exception? Suppose, for example, that a trial court denies a class certification motion erroneously, and the lead plaintiff's case becomes moot while that denial is appealed? The Court extended the class exception to this circumstance in *United States Parole Comm'n v. Geraghty* (1980). There, the Court held that "when a District Court erroneously denies a procedural motion, which, if correctly decided, would have prevented the action from becoming moot, an appeal lies from the denial and the corrected ruling 'relates back' to the date of the original denial."

A similar "relates-back" approach has sometimes applied when a federal court has not acted on a class certification motion before a case has become moot, especially when the facts giving rise to the suit are of an inherently limited duration. *See Gerstein* (1991). In *City of Riverside v. McLaughlin* (1991), for example, a group of plaintiffs contended that they had been denied prompt probable cause determinations in violation of the Fourth Amendment. The lead plaintiffs filed a class certification motion, which was granted after those plaintiffs' pre-trial detention had terminated. In holding that the class action exception to mootness applied, the Court explained:

> It is true, of course, that the claims of the named plaintiffs have since been rendered moot; eventually, they either received probable cause determinations or were released. Our cases leave no doubt, however, that by obtaining class certification, plaintiffs preserved the merits of the controversy for our review. In factually similar cases we have held that "the termination of a class representative's claim does not moot the claims of the unnamed members of the class." That the class was not certified until after the named plaintiffs' claims had become moot does not deprive us of jurisdiction. We recognized in *Gerstein* that "[s]ome claims are so inherently transitory that the trial court will not have even enough time to rule on a motion for class certification before the proposed representative's individual interest expires." *United States Parole Comm'n v. Geraghty* (1980). In such cases, the "relation back" doctrine is properly invoked to preserve the merits of the case for judicial resolution.

Like most rules discussed in this book, it is important to recall that these nuances of Article III doctrines like mootness only describe the lay of the land in federal court. State courts sometimes have more expansive doctrines that permit its courts to entertain a wider range of claims.[43] As the Court observed in *DeFunis*, the State of Washington allows appeals on matters in which the resolution was important for the broader public interest, especially where the allegedly unconstitutional harm will inevitably befall others. Many other states have also adopted this exception. In Illinois, for example, state courts may entertain cases that have otherwise become moot if: "(1) the question at issue is of a substantial public nature; (2) an authoritative determination is needed for future guidance [of public officers]; and (3) the circumstances are likely to recur." *Felzak v. Hruby* (Ill. 2007). Indeed, in Justice Brennan's dissent in *DeFunis*, he charged that the majority's refusal to entertain the merits "disserve[d] the public interest."

---

43. *See generally* Helen Hershkoff, *State Courts and the "Passive Virtues": Rethinking the Judicial Function*, 114 Harv. L. Rev. 1833 (2001).

The Supreme Court has not adopted this public interest exception to the mootness doctrine. The class action exception is limited to circumstances in which a litigant seeks, and was entitled to receive, class certification. For example, in *United States v. Sanchez-Gomez* (2018), the Court rejected the Ninth Circuit's recognition of a "functional class action" exception to mootness. In that case, federal criminal defendants alleged that being shackled during their proceedings violated their due process rights. Their criminal cases were resolved, however, before the Ninth Circuit reached the merits. Because the resolution of the claims would provide relief to other similarly situated persons, the Ninth Circuit held that the case was functionally a class action, and therefore should not be dismissed as moot. The Supreme Court disagreed, explaining:

> The certification of a suit as a class action has important consequences for the unnamed members of the class. Those class members may be "bound by the judgment" and are considered parties to the litigation in many important respects. A certified class thus "acquires a legal status separate from the interest asserted by the named plaintiff."
>
> . . .
>
> The court below designated respondents' case a "functional class action" because respondents were pursuing relief "not merely for themselves, but for all in-custody defendants in the district." But, the "mere presence of . . . allegations" that might, if resolved in respondents' favor, benefit other similarly situated individuals cannot "save [respondents'] suit from mootness once the[ir] individual claim[s]" have dissipated.

E.   POLITICAL QUESTION DOCTRINE

While standing is about the proper party to bring a claim, and ripeness and mootness are about the timing of the litigation, the political question doctrine is about whether a particular subject matter is proper for judicial review. The Supreme Court has held that some constitutional claims present political questions that federal courts may not address. Instead, these questions are for the President and Congress to decide. Examples include questions involving the electoral process and the constitutional guarantee of a "republican form of government," foreign policy and national security, the internal processes of Congress, impeachment and removal of a government official, and the process of ratifying constitutional amendments.

The political question doctrine has changed over time. The Supreme Court referred to the concept of a political question in *Marbury v. Madison* (1803), when Chief Justice Marshall wrote that certain "subjects are political" and "entrusted to the executive." On these subjects, Marshall wrote, "the decision of the executive is conclusive." Such "[q]uestions, in their nature political, or which are by the constitution and laws, submitted to the executive can never be made in this court."

Early political question cases treated the doctrine as a narrow one that required courts to defer to the political branches' determinations of certain factual questions committed to them.[44] For example, the federal courts would defer to the federal Executive's recognition of foreign countries as sovereign states or the political branches' recognition of American Indian Tribal governments. But the Supreme Court did not hold that constitutional claims involving individual rights were political questions beyond judicial review. To the contrary, in *Marbury* Chief Justice Marshall explained that individual rights claims did not present political questions.

The Court's 1849 decision in *Luther v. Borden* is now understood as a turning point in the history of the political question doctrine. This case arose out of Dorr's Rebellion, a contest for political power in Rhode Island. Rhode Island's government was based upon a 1663 charter from King Charles II, not upon a state constitution. Under the charter, only male landowners could vote and representation in the legislature heavily favored rural voters. The state legislature consistently rejected attempts to reform the charter even as the rest of the country eliminated property ownership as a requirement for voting. In 1841, Thomas Dorr led a People's Convention, which ratified a new constitution enfranchising all White men who had resided in Rhode Island for one year and addressing the malapportionment of the legislature. The existing government had criminalized participation in elections under the People's Constitution. Nevertheless, some Rhode Islanders voted in those elections and a majority elected Dorr as governor. His tenure lasted two days.

The litigation arose in 1842 after Sheriff Luther Borden broke into the home of Martin Luther looking for evidence that Luther had participated in the illegal election. Luther brought a common law trespass action against Borden, whose defense was that he acted lawfully as an officer of Rhode Island's charter government. Luther responded that the charter government violated Article IV, Section 4 of the U.S. Constitution, the so-called Guarantee Clause, which provides that "[t]he United States shall guarantee to every State in this Union a Republican form of government." Therefore, Luther argued, Borden committed a trespass because he was acting on behalf of an unconstitutional government.

In an ambiguous opinion, the Supreme Court held that it could not decline to recognize Rhode Island's charter government as a legitimate government. Some scholars have argued the Court's opinion applied the narrow political question doctrine under which federal courts deferred to the political branches in matters of recognition of other governments. The Court stated that under the Guarantee Clause "it rests with Congress to decide what government is the established one in a State." The Court, however, also more generally opined that the Constitution "had treated the subject as political in its nature, and placed the power in the hands of that department."

As *Luther* might suggest, contestation over political power is a thread that runs throughout many of the political question cases. Indeed, during the nineteenth and early twentieth centuries, some of the most high-profile contests over political power prompted Supreme Court Justices to cite the political question concept. Not only Dorr's Rebellion, but also the conflict over territorial sovereignty between Georgia and the Cherokee Nation in the 1830s, as well as Georgia's resistance to

---

44. *See* Tara Leigh Grove, *The Last History of the Political Question Doctrine*, 90 N.Y.U. L. REV 1908 (2015).

Reconstruction after the Civil War, prompted discussion of the justiciability of political questions.[45] For example, in *Georgia v. Stanton* (1867), the Court dismissed Georgia's bill to enjoin the U.S. Secretary of State and two U.S. Army generals from implementing the Reconstruction Acts, reasoning that a court may not pass "judgment . . . upon political questions."

Following Reconstruction, the federal courts also refrained from intervening to stop Southern states from discriminating against Black voters, with the Court announcing in *Giles v. Harris* (1903), that its equitable jurisdiction did not extend to the enforcement of "political rights." That same year, the Court decided *Lone Wolf v. Hitchcock*, a case holding that "Congress possessed full power" to break the United States' treaty promises by authorizing the taking of Indian lands, treating it as a political question notwithstanding the Fifth Amendment's protections for property rights. In *Lone Wolf*, the Court cited its 1889 decision in *Chae Chan Ping*, also known as the *Chinese Exclusion Case*, which similarly treated Congress' decision to break an international treaty as beyond the "domain" of the courts.

Today, *Luther* is understood as the foundation of a political question doctrine that treats some subject matter as nonjusticiable even where there is an allegation that the Constitution has been violated. In the key modern case, *Baker v. Carr* (1962), the Court held that redistricting is a justiciable question under the Fourteenth Amendment. The Court thus rejected prior cases holding that voting rights were nonjusticiable political rights and that the drawing of electoral boundaries presented political questions. In holding that the design of legislative districts was justiciable, the Court tried to make sense of the doctrine:

> Prominent on the surface of any case held to involve a political question is found a textually demonstrable commitment of the issue to a coordinate political department; or a lack of judicially discoverable and manageable standards for resolving it; or the impossibility of deciding without an initial policy determination of a kind clearly for nonjudicial discretion; or the impossibility of a court's undertaking independent resolution without expressing lack of the respect due coordinate branches of government; or an unusual need for unquestioning adherence to a political decision already made; or the potentiality of embarrassment from multifarious pronouncements by various departments on one question.

Unfortunately, the Court's doctrinal restatement made matters only more confusing. Courts recite the *Baker* factors, but their political question analyses do not always seem to turn upon them. Much more useful, and something you should keep in mind as you read the cases, is to identify the categories of questions that courts have deemed to be political.

The Court has identified various types of political questions, as the cases below reveal. Cases involving congressional self-governance, as well as impeachment and removal from office, are paradigmatic political question cases. *Nixon v. United States* (1993), which presented a challenge to the Senate's impeachment rules, is one such case. Another type of political question case, illustrated below by *Goldwater v. Carter* (1979) and *Zivotofsky v. Clinton* (2012), involves matters of foreign policy

---

45. Seth Davis, *Empire in Equity*, 97 Notre Dame L. Rev. 1985, 2006-12 (2022).

that the Court has concluded are within the exclusive competence of the political branches. The structure of government and electoral processes are other instances where the Court has found some questions to be nonjusticiable, as in the case of *Rucho v. Common Cause* (2019), which involved the controversial and practically important problem of political gerrymandering.

1.   *Congressional Self-Governance and Impeachment and Removal from Office*

One area where the Court has held that cases are nonjusticiable political questions is challenges to the impeachment and removal process.

Nixon v. United States

506 U.S. 224 (1993)

Chief Justice REHNQUIST delivered the opinion of the Court.

Petitioner Walter L. Nixon, Jr., asks this Court to decide whether Senate Rule XI, which allows a committee of Senators to hear evidence against an individual who has been impeached and to report that evidence to the full Senate, violates the Impeachment Trial Clause, Art. I, §3, cl. 6. That Clause provides that the "Senate shall have the sole Power to try all Impeachments." But before we reach the merits of such a claim, we must decide whether it is "justiciable," that is, whether it is a claim that may be resolved by the courts. We conclude that it is not.

Nixon, a former Chief Judge of the United States District Court for the Southern District of Mississippi, was convicted by a jury of two counts of making false statements before a federal grand jury and sentenced to prison. The grand jury investigation stemmed from reports that Nixon had accepted a gratuity from a Mississippi businessman in exchange for asking a local district attorney to halt the prosecution of the businessman's son. Because Nixon refused to resign from his office as a United States District Judge, he continued to collect his judicial salary while serving out his prison sentence.

On May 10, 1989, the House of Representatives adopted three articles of impeachment for high crimes and misdemeanors. The first two articles charged Nixon with giving false testimony before the grand jury and the third article charged him with bringing disrepute on the Federal Judiciary.

After the House presented the articles to the Senate, the Senate voted to invoke its own Impeachment Rule XI, under which the presiding officer appoints a committee of Senators to "receive evidence and take testimony." The Senate committee held four days of hearings, during which 10 witnesses, including Nixon, testified. Pursuant to Rule XI, the committee presented the full Senate with a complete transcript of the proceeding and a Report stating the uncontested facts and summarizing the evidence on the contested facts. Nixon and the House impeachment managers submitted extensive final briefs to the full Senate and delivered arguments from the Senate floor during the three hours set aside for oral argument in front of that body. Nixon himself gave a personal appeal, and several

Senators posed questions directly to both parties. The Senate voted by more than the constitutionally required two-thirds majority to convict Nixon on the first two articles. The presiding officer then entered judgment removing Nixon from his office as United States District Judge.

Nixon thereafter commenced the present suit, arguing that Senate Rule XI violates the constitutional grant of authority to the Senate to "try" all impeachments because it prohibits the whole Senate from taking part in the evidentiary hearings. *See* Art. I, §3, cl. 6. Nixon sought a declaratory judgment that his impeachment conviction was void and that his judicial salary and privileges should be reinstated. The District Court held that his claim was nonjusticiable, and the Court of Appeals for the District of Columbia Circuit agreed. We granted certiorari.

A controversy is nonjusticiable — *i.e.*, involves a political question — where there is "a textually demonstrable constitutional commitment of the issue to a coordinate political department; or a lack of judicially discoverable and manageable standards for resolving it. . . ." *Baker v. Carr* (1962). But the courts must, in the first instance, interpret the text in question and determine whether and to what extent the issue is textually committed. As the discussion that follows makes clear, the concept of a textual commitment to a coordinate political department is not completely separate from the concept of a lack of judicially discoverable and manageable standards for resolving it; the lack of judicially manageable standards may strengthen the conclusion that there is a textually demonstrable commitment to a coordinate branch.

In this case, we must examine Art. I, §3, cl. 6, to determine the scope of authority conferred upon the Senate by the Framers regarding impeachment. It provides:

> The Senate shall have the sole Power to try all Impeachments. When sitting for that Purpose, they shall be on Oath or Affirmation. When the President of the United States is tried, the Chief Justice shall preside: And no Person shall be convicted without the Concurrence of two thirds of the Members present.

The language and structure of this Clause are revealing. The first sentence is a grant of authority to the Senate, and the word "sole" indicates that this authority is reposed in the Senate and nowhere else. The next two sentences specify requirements to which the Senate proceedings shall conform: The Senate shall be on oath or affirmation, a two-thirds vote is required to convict, and when the President is tried the Chief Justice shall preside.

Petitioner argues that the word "try" in the first sentence imposes by implication an additional requirement on the Senate in that the proceedings must be in the nature of a judicial trial. From there petitioner goes on to argue that this limitation precludes the Senate from delegating to a select committee the task of hearing the testimony of witnesses, as was done pursuant to Senate Rule XI. Petitioner concludes from this that courts may review whether or not the Senate "tried" him before convicting him.

There are several difficulties with this position which lead us ultimately to reject it. The word "try" both in 1787 and later, has considerably broader meanings than those to which petitioner would limit it. Older dictionaries define try as "[t]o examine" or "[t]o examine as a judge." In more modern usage the term has various meanings. For example, try can mean "to examine or investigate judicially," "to conduct the trial of," or "to put to the test by experiment, investigation, or trial." Based on the variety of definitions, we cannot say that the Framers used the word "try" as an implied limitation on the method by which the Senate might proceed in trying impeachments.

The conclusion that the use of the word "try" in the first sentence of the Impeachment Trial Clause lacks sufficient precision to afford any judicially manageable standard of review of the Senate's actions is fortified by the existence of the three very specific requirements that the Constitution does impose on the Senate when trying impeachments: The Members must be under oath, a two-thirds vote is required to convict, and the Chief Justice presides when the President is tried. These limitations are quite precise, and their nature suggests that the Framers did not intend to impose additional limitations on the form of the Senate proceedings by the use of the word "try" in the first sentence.

Petitioner devotes only two pages in his brief to negating the significance of the word "sole" in the first sentence of Clause 6. As noted above, that sentence provides that "[t]he Senate shall have the sole Power to try all Impeachments." We think that the word "sole" is of considerable significance. Indeed, the word "sole" appears only one other time in the Constitution—with respect to the House of Representatives' "*sole* Power of Impeachment." Art. I, §2, cl. 5 (emphasis added). The commonsense meaning of the word "sole" is that the Senate alone shall have authority to determine whether an individual should be acquitted or convicted.

Nixon asserts that the word "sole" has no substantive meaning. To support this contention, he argues that the word is nothing more than a mere "cosmetic edit" added by the Committee of Style after the delegates had approved the substance of the Impeachment Trial Clause. There are two difficulties with this argument. First, accepting as we must the proposition that the Committee of Style had no authority from the Convention to alter the meaning of the Clause, we must presume that the Committee's reorganization or rephrasing accurately captured what the Framers meant in their unadorned language. This presumption is buttressed by the fact that the Constitutional Convention voted on, and accepted, the Committee of Style's linguistic version. Second, carrying Nixon's argument to its logical conclusion would constrain us to say that the *second to last draft* would govern in every instance where the Committee of Style added an arguably substantive word. Such a result is at odds with the fact that the Convention passed the Committee's version, and with the well-established rule that the plain language of the enacted text is the best indicator of intent.

Petitioner also contends that the word "sole" should not bear on the question of justiciability because Art. II, §2, cl. 1, of the Constitution grants the President pardon authority "except in Cases of Impeachment." He argues that such a limitation on the President's pardon power would not have been necessary if the Framers thought that the Senate alone had authority to deal with such questions. But the granting of a pardon is in no sense an overturning of a judgment of conviction by some other tribunal; it is "[a]n executive action that mitigates or sets aside *punishment* for a crime." Black's Law Dictionary 1113 (6th ed. 1990) (emphasis added). Authority in the Senate to determine procedures for trying an impeached official, unreviewable by the courts, is therefore not at all inconsistent with authority in the President to grant a pardon to the convicted official. The exception from the President's pardon authority of cases of impeachment was a separate determination by the Framers that executive clemency should not be available in such cases.

Petitioner finally argues that even if significance be attributed to the word "sole" in the first sentence of the Clause, the authority granted is to the Senate, and this means that "the Senate — not the courts, not a lay jury, not a Senate Committee — shall try impeachments." It would be possible to read the first sentence of the Clause this way, but it is not a natural reading. Petitioner's interpretation would bring into judicial purview not merely the sort of claim made by petitioner, but other similar claims based on the conclusion that the word "Senate" has imposed by implication limitations on procedures which the Senate might adopt. Such limitations would be inconsistent with the construction of the Clause as a whole, which, as we have noted, sets out three express limitations in separate sentences.

The history and contemporary understanding of the impeachment provisions support our reading of the constitutional language. The parties do not offer evidence of a single word in the history of the Constitutional Convention or in contemporary commentary that even alludes to the possibility of judicial review in the context of the impeachment powers.

The Framers labored over the question of where the impeachment power should lie. Significantly, in at least two considered scenarios the power was placed with the Federal Judiciary. Indeed, James Madison and the Committee of Detail proposed that the Supreme Court should have the power to determine impeachments. Despite these proposals, the Convention ultimately decided that the Senate would have "the sole Power to try all Impeachments." Art. I, §3, cl. 6. According to Alexander Hamilton, the Senate was the "most fit depositary of this important trust" because its Members are representatives of the people. *See* The Federalist No. 65 (J. Cooke ed. 1961). The Supreme Court was not the proper body because the Framers "doubted whether the members of that tribunal would, at all times, be endowed with so eminent a portion of fortitude as would be called for in the execution of so difficult a task" or whether the Court "would possess the degree of credit and authority" to carry out its judgment if it conflicted with the accusation brought by the Legislature — the people's representative. In addition, the Framers believed the Court was too small in number: "The awful discretion, which a court of impeachments must necessarily have, to doom to honor or to infamy the most confidential and the most distinguished characters of the community, forbids the commitment of the trust to a small number of persons."

There are two additional reasons why the Judiciary, and the Supreme Court in particular, were not chosen to have any role in impeachments. First, the Framers recognized that most likely there would be two sets of proceedings for individuals who commit impeachable offenses — the impeachment trial and a separate criminal trial. In fact, the Constitution explicitly provides for two separate proceedings. *See* Art. I, §3, cl. 7. The Framers deliberately separated the two forums to avoid raising the specter of bias and to ensure independent judgments. Certainly judicial review of the Senate's "trial" would introduce the same risk of bias as would participation in the trial itself.

Second, judicial review would be inconsistent with the Framers' insistence that our system be one of checks and balances. In our constitutional system, impeachment was designed to be the *only* check on the Judicial Branch by the Legislature. On the topic of judicial accountability, Hamilton wrote:

The precautions for their responsibility are comprised in the article respecting impeachments. They are liable to be impeached for mal-conduct by the house of representatives, and tried by the senate, and if convicted, may be dismissed from office and disqualified for holding any other. *This is the only provision on the point, which is consistent with the necessary independence of the judicial character, and is the only one which we find in our own constitution in respect to our own judges.*

Judicial involvement in impeachment proceedings, even if only for purposes of judicial review, is counterintuitive because it would eviscerate the "important constitutional check" placed on the Judiciary by the Framers. Nixon's argument would place final reviewing authority with respect to impeachments in the hands of the same body that the impeachment process is meant to regulate.

Nevertheless, Nixon argues that judicial review is necessary in order to place a check on the Legislature. Nixon fears that if the Senate is given unreviewable authority to interpret the Impeachment Trial Clause, there is a grave risk that the Senate will usurp judicial power. The Framers anticipated this objection and created two constitutional safeguards to keep the Senate in check. The first safeguard is that the whole of the impeachment power is divided between the two legislative bodies, with the House given the right to accuse and the Senate given the right to judge. The second safeguard is the two-thirds supermajority vote requirement.

In addition to the textual commitment argument, we are persuaded that the lack of finality and the difficulty of fashioning relief counsel against justiciability. We agree with the Court of Appeals that opening the door of judicial review to the procedures used by the Senate in trying impeachments would "expose the political life of the country to months, or perhaps years, of chaos." This lack of finality would manifest itself most dramatically if the President were impeached. The legitimacy of any successor, and hence his effectiveness, would be impaired severely, not merely while the judicial process was running its course, but during any retrial that a differently constituted Senate might conduct if its first judgment of conviction were invalidated. Equally uncertain is the question of what relief a court may give other than simply setting aside the judgment of conviction. Could it order the reinstatement of a convicted federal judge, or order Congress to create an additional judgeship if the seat had been filled in the interim?

[Concurring opinion of Justice STEVENS omitted.]

Justice WHITE, with whom Justice BLACKMUN joins, concurring in the judgment.

Petitioner contends that the method by which the Senate convicted him on two articles of impeachment violates Art. I, §3, cl. 6, of the Constitution, which mandates that the Senate "try" impeachments. The Court is of the view that the Constitution forbids us even to consider his contention. I find no such prohibition and would therefore reach the merits of the claim. I concur in the judgment because the Senate fulfilled its constitutional obligation to "try" petitioner.

It should be said at the outset that, as a practical matter, it will likely make little difference whether the Court's or my view controls this case. This is so because the Senate has very wide discretion in specifying impeachment trial procedures and because it is extremely unlikely that the Senate would abuse its discretion and insist on a procedure that could not be deemed a trial by reasonable judges. Even taking a wholly practical approach, I would prefer not to announce an unreviewable discretion in the Senate to ignore completely the constitutional direction to "try" impeachment cases. When asked at oral argument whether that direction would be satisfied if, after a House vote to impeach, the Senate, without any procedure whatsoever, unanimously found the accused guilty of being "a bad guy," counsel for the United States answered that the Government's theory "leads me to answer that question yes." Especially in light of this advice from the Solicitor General, I would not issue an invitation to the Senate to find an excuse, in the name of other pressing business, to be dismissive of its critical role in the impeachment process.

Practicalities aside, however, since the meaning of a constitutional provision is at issue, my disagreement with the Court should be stated.

The majority finds a clear textual commitment in the Constitution's use of the word "sole" in the phrase "[t]he Senate shall have the sole Power to try all Impeachments." Art. I, §3, cl. 6.

The significance of the Constitution's use of the term "sole" lies not in the infrequency with which the term appears, but in the fact that it appears exactly twice, in parallel provisions concerning impeachment. That the word "sole" is found only in the House and Senate Impeachment Clauses demonstrates that its purpose is to emphasize the distinct role of each in the impeachment process. As the majority notes, the Framers, following English practice, were very much concerned to separate the prosecutorial from the adjudicative aspects of impeachment. Giving each House "sole" power with respect to its role in impeachments effected this division of labor. While the majority is thus right to interpret the term "sole" to indicate that the Senate ought to "'functio[n] independently and without assistance or interference,'" it wrongly identifies the Judiciary, rather than the House, as the source of potential interference with which the Framers were concerned when they employed the term "sole."

The majority also claims support in the history and early interpretations of the Impeachment Clauses, noting the various arguments in support of the current system made at the Constitutional Convention and expressed powerfully by Hamilton in The Federalist Nos. 65 and 66.

What the relevant history mainly reveals is deep ambivalence among many of the Framers over the very institution of impeachment, which, by its nature, is not easily reconciled with our system of checks and balances. As they clearly recognized, the branch of the Federal Government which is possessed of the authority to try impeachments, by having final say over the membership of each branch, holds a potentially unanswerable power over the others. In addition, that branch, insofar as it is called upon to try not only members of other branches, but also its own, will have the advantage of being the judge of its own members' causes.

The historical evidence reveals above all else that the Framers were deeply concerned about placing in any branch the "awful discretion, which a court of impeachments must necessarily have." The Federalist No. 65. Viewed against this history, the discord between the majority's position and the basic principles of checks and balances underlying the Constitution's separation of powers is clear. In essence, the majority suggests that the Framers conferred upon Congress a potential tool of legislative dominance yet at the same time rendered Congress' exercise of that power one of the very few areas of legislative authority immune from any judicial review. While the majority rejects petitioner's justiciability argument as espousing a view "inconsistent with the Framers' insistence that our system be one of checks and balances," it is the Court's finding of nonjusticiability that truly upsets the Framers' careful design. In a truly balanced system, impeachments tried by the Senate would serve as a means of controlling the largely unaccountable Judiciary, even as judicial review would ensure that the Senate adhered to a minimal set of procedural standards in conducting impeachment trials.

The majority's conclusion that "try" is incapable of meaningful judicial construction is not without irony. One might think that if any class of concepts would fall within the definitional abilities of the Judiciary, it would be that class having to do with procedural justice.

Petitioner has not asked the Court to conduct his impeachment trial; he has asked instead that it determine whether his impeachment was tried by the Senate. The majority refuses to reach this determination out of a laudable desire to respect the authority of the Legislature. Regrettably, this concern is manifested in a manner that does needless violence to the Constitution. The deference that is owed can be found in the Constitution itself, which provides the Senate ample discretion to determine how best to try impeachments.

Justice SOUTER, concurring in the judgment.

I agree with the Court that this case presents a nonjusticiable political question. Because my analysis differs somewhat from the Court's, however, I concur in its judgment by this separate opinion.

As we cautioned in *Baker v. Carr* (1962), "the 'political question' label" tends "to obscure the need for case-by-case inquiry." The need for such close examination is nevertheless clear from our precedents, which demonstrate that the functional nature of the political question doctrine requires analysis of "the precise facts and posture of the particular case," and precludes "resolution by any semantic cataloguing."

It seems fair to conclude that the [Impeachment Trial] Clause contemplates that the Senate may determine, within broad boundaries, such subsidiary issues as the procedures for receipt and consideration of evidence necessary to satisfy its duty to "try" impeachments. Other significant considerations confirm a conclusion that this case presents a nonjusticiable political question: the "unusual need for unquestioning adherence to a political decision already made," as well as "the potentiality of embarrassment from multifarious pronouncements by various departments on one question." *Baker*. As the Court observes, judicial review of an impeachment trial would under the best of circumstances entail significant disruption of government.

One can, nevertheless, envision different and unusual circumstances that might justify a more searching review of impeachment proceedings. If the Senate were to act in a manner seriously threatening the integrity of its results, convicting, say, upon a coin toss, or upon a summary determination that an officer of the United States was simply "'a bad guy,'" judicial interference might well be appropriate. In such circumstances, the Senate's action might be so far beyond the scope of its constitutional authority, and the consequent impact on the Republic so great, as to merit a judicial response despite the prudential concerns that would ordinarily counsel silence. "The political question doctrine, a tool for maintenance of governmental order, will not be so applied as to promote only disorder." *Baker*.

* * *

2. *Foreign Policy*

Nixon v. United States illustrated that matters of congressional self-governance and impeachment proceedings to remove federal officials may present nonjusticiable political questions. A second type of political question involves the conduct of foreign policy. The Court has held, for example, that the recognition of foreign governments presents a political question, as do many issues concerning the ratification and interpretation of treaties.

Goldwater v. Carter (1979), the first case below, presented a nonjusticiable foreign policy question. This case arose when Senator Barry Goldwater argued that President Jimmy Carter lacked constitutional authority to rescind a U.S. treaty with Taiwan without approval of two-thirds of the U.S. Senate. President Carter did so as part of an effort to establish diplomatic relations with the People's Republic of China. A plurality of the Court concluded that Senator Goldwater's suit presented a political dispute between coequal branches, not a justiciable case that could be resolved by reference to the text of the Constitution, which is silent on the recission of treaties.

Not all foreign policy disputes—even those implicating recognition of foreign state sovereignty—present nonjusticiable political questions. In the second case below, *Zivotofsky v. Clinton* (2012), the Supreme Court held that the federal courts could rule on the constitutionality of a federal law that afforded American parents who have a child born in Jerusalem the right to request that the child's passport list Israel as the country of birth. President George W. Bush signed the bill into law in 2002 with a signing statement that concluded the law would unconstitutionally encroach upon presidential power. Since 1948, U.S. Presidents had taken a neutral position regarding which sovereign had authority over Jerusalem, a policy that President Donald Trump changed in 2017. In *Zivotofsky*, the Court held that the constitutionality of the 2002 law could be determined by reference to "textual, structural, and historical evidence" and thus was justiciable.

Goldwater v. Carter

444 U.S. 996 (1979)

ORDER

The petition for a writ of certiorari is granted. The judgment of the Court of Appeals is vacated and the case is remanded to the District Court with directions to dismiss the complaint.

Mr. Justice REHNQUIST, with whom THE CHIEF JUSTICE, Mr. Justice STEWART, and Mr. Justice STEVENS join, concurring in the judgment.

I am of the view that the basic question presented by the petitioners in this case is "political" and therefore nonjusticiable because it involves the authority of the President in the conduct of our country's foreign relations and the extent to which the Senate or the Congress is authorized to negate the action of the President. In *Coleman v. Miller* (1939), a case in which members of the Kansas Legislature brought an action attacking a vote of the State Senate in favor of the ratification of the Child Labor Amendment, Mr. Chief Justice Hughes wrote in what is referred to as the "Opinion of the Court":

> We think that . . . the question of the efficacy of ratifications by state legislatures, in the light of previous rejection or attempted withdrawal, should be regarded as a political question pertaining to the political departments, with the ultimate authority in the Congress in the exercise of its control over the promulgation of the adoption of the Amendment.
>
> The precise question as now raised is whether, when the legislature of the State, as we have found, has actually ratified the proposed amendment, the Court should restrain the state officers from certifying the ratification to the Secretary of State, because of an earlier rejection, and thus prevent the question from coming before the political departments. We find no basis in either Constitution or statute for such judicial action. Article V, speaking solely of ratification, contains no provision as to rejection. . . .

Thus, Mr. Chief Justice Hughes' opinion concluded that "Congress in controlling the promulgation of the adoption of a constitutional amendment has the final determination of the question whether by lapse of time its proposal of the amendment had lost its vitality prior to the required ratifications."

I believe it follows *a fortiori* from *Coleman* that the controversy in the instant case is a nonjusticiable political dispute that should be left for resolution by the Executive and Legislative Branches of the Government. Here, while the Constitution is express as to the manner in which the Senate shall participate in the ratification of a treaty, it is silent as to that body's participation in the abrogation of a treaty. In this respect the case is directly analogous to *Coleman*.

I think that the justifications for concluding that the question here is political in nature are even more compelling than in *Coleman* because it involves foreign relations—specifically a treaty commitment to use military force in the defense of a foreign government if attacked.

Having decided that the question presented in this action is nonjusticiable, I believe that the appropriate disposition is for this Court to vacate the decision of the Court of Appeals and remand with instructions for the District Court to dismiss the complaint. This procedure derives support from our practice in disposing of moot actions in federal courts. For more than 30 years, we have instructed lower courts to vacate any decision on the merits of an action that has become moot prior to a resolution of the case in this Court. *United States v. Munsingwear, Inc.* (1950). The Court has required such decisions to be vacated in order to "prevent a judgment, unreviewable because of mootness, from spawning any legal consequences." It is even more imperative that this Court invoke this procedure to ensure that resolution of a "political question," which should not have been decided by a lower court, does not "spawn any legal consequences." An Art. III court's resolution of a question that is "political" in character can create far more disruption among the three coequal branches of Government than the resolution of a question presented in a moot controversy. Since the political nature of the questions presented should have precluded the lower courts from considering or deciding the merits of the controversy, the prior proceedings in the federal courts must be vacated, and the complaint dismissed.

Mr. Justice BRENNAN, dissenting.

In stating that this case presents a nonjusticiable "political question," Mr. Justice Rehnquist, in my view, profoundly misapprehends the political-question principle as it applies to matters of foreign relations. Properly understood, the political-question doctrine restrains courts from reviewing an exercise of foreign policy judgment by the coordinate political branch to which authority to make that judgment has been "constitutional[ly] commit[ted]." *Baker v. Carr* (1962). But the doctrine does not pertain when a court is faced with the antecedent question whether a particular branch has been constitutionally designated as the repository of political decisionmaking power. The issue of decisionmaking authority must be resolved as a matter of constitutional law, not political discretion; accordingly, it falls within the competence of the courts.

The constitutional question raised here is prudently answered in narrow terms. Abrogation of the defense treaty with Taiwan was a necessary incident to Executive recognition of the Peking Government, because the defense treaty was predicated upon the now-abandoned view that the Taiwan Government was the only legitimate political authority in China. Our cases firmly establish that the Constitution commits to the President alone the power to recognize, and withdraw recognition from, foreign regimes. That mandate being clear, our judicial inquiry into the treaty rupture can go no further.

* * *

Zivotofsky v. Clinton

566 U.S. 189 (2012)

Chief Justice ROBERTS delivered the opinion of the Court.

Congress enacted a statute providing that Americans born in Jerusalem may elect to have "Israel" listed as the place of birth on their passports. The State Department declined to follow that law, citing its longstanding policy of not taking a position on the political status of Jerusalem. When sued by an American who invoked the statute, the Secretary of State argued that the courts lacked authority to decide the case because it presented a political question. The Court of Appeals so held.

We disagree. The courts are fully capable of determining whether this statute may be given effect, or instead must be struck down in light of authority conferred on the Executive by the Constitution.

I

A

In 2002, Congress enacted the Foreign Relations Authorization Act. Section 214 of the Act is entitled "United States Policy with Respect to Jerusalem as the Capital of Israel." The first two subsections express Congress's "commitment" to relocating the United States Embassy in Israel to Jerusalem. The third bars funding for the publication of official Government documents that do not list Jerusalem as the capital of Israel. The fourth and final provision, §214(d), is the only one at stake in this case. Entitled "Record of Place of Birth as Israel for Passport Purposes," it provides that "[f]or purposes of the registration of birth, certification of nationality, or issuance of a passport of a United States citizen born in the city of Jerusalem, the Secretary shall, upon the request of the citizen or the citizen's legal guardian, record the place of birth as Israel."

The State Department's Foreign Affairs Manual states that "[w]here the birthplace of the applicant is located in territory disputed by another country, the city or area of birth may be written in the passport." The manual specifically directs that passport officials should enter "JERUSALEM" and should "not write Israel or Jordan" when recording the birthplace of a person born in Jerusalem on a passport.

Section 214(d) sought to override this instruction by allowing citizens born in Jerusalem to have "Israel" recorded on their passports if they wish. In signing the Foreign Relations Authorization Act into law, President George W. Bush stated his belief that §214 "impermissibly interferes with the President's constitutional authority to conduct the Nation's foreign affairs and to supervise the unitary executive branch." He added that if the section is "construed as mandatory," then it would "interfere with the President's constitutional authority to formulate the position of the United States, speak for the Nation in international affairs, and determine the terms on which recognition is given to foreign states." He concluded by emphasizing that "U.S. policy regarding Jerusalem has not changed." The President made no specific reference to the passport mandate in §214(d).

B

Petitioner Menachem Binyamin Zivotofsky was born in Jerusalem on October 17, 2002, shortly after §214(d) was enacted. Zivotofsky's parents were American citizens and he accordingly was as well, by virtue of congressional enactment. Zivotofsky's mother filed an application for a consular report of birth abroad and a United States passport. She requested that his place of birth be listed as "Jerusalem, Israel," on both documents. U.S. officials informed Zivotofsky's mother that State Department policy prohibits recording "Israel" as Zivotofsky's place of birth. Pursuant to that policy, Zivotofsky was issued a passport and consular report of birth abroad listing only "Jerusalem."

Zivotofsky's parents filed a complaint on his behalf against the Secretary of State. Zivotofsky sought a declaratory judgment and a permanent injunction ordering the Secretary to identify his place of birth as "Jerusalem, Israel," in the official documents.

II

The lower courts concluded that Zivotofsky's claim presents a political question and therefore cannot be adjudicated. We disagree.

In general, the Judiciary has a responsibility to decide cases properly before it, even those it "would gladly avoid." *Cohens v. Virginia* (1821). Our precedents have identified a narrow exception to that rule, known as the "political question" doctrine. We have explained that a controversy "involves a political question . . . where there is 'a textually demonstrable constitutional commitment of the issue to a coordinate political department; or a lack of judicially discoverable and manageable standards for resolving it.'" *Nixon v. United States* (1993) (quoting *Baker v. Carr* (1962)). In such a case, we have held that a court lacks the authority to decide the dispute before it.

The lower courts ruled that this case involves a political question because deciding Zivotofsky's claim would force the Judicial Branch to interfere with the President's exercise of constitutional power committed to him alone. The District Court understood Zivotofsky to ask the courts to "decide the political status of Jerusalem." This misunderstands the issue presented. Zivotofsky does not ask the courts to determine whether Jerusalem is the capital of Israel. He instead seeks to determine whether he may vindicate his statutory right, under §214(d), to choose to have Israel recorded on his passport as his place of birth.

The existence of a statutory right is certainly relevant to the Judiciary's power to decide Zivotofsky's claim. The federal courts are not being asked to supplant a foreign policy decision of the political branches with the courts' own unmoored determination of what United States policy toward Jerusalem should be. Instead, Zivotofsky requests that the courts enforce a specific statutory right. To resolve his claim, the Judiciary must decide if Zivotofsky's interpretation of the statute is correct, and whether the statute is constitutional. This is a familiar judicial exercise.

Moreover, because the parties do not dispute the interpretation of §214(d), the only real question for the courts is whether the statute is constitutional. At least since *Marbury v. Madison* (1803), we have recognized that when an Act of Congress is alleged to conflict with the Constitution, "[i]t is emphatically the province and duty of the judicial department to say what the law is." That duty will sometimes involve the "[r]esolution of litigation challenging the constitutional authority of one of the three branches," but courts cannot avoid their responsibility merely "because the issues have political implications." *INS v. Chadha* (1983).

In this case, determining the constitutionality of §214(d) involves deciding whether the statute impermissibly intrudes upon Presidential powers under the Constitution. If so, the law must be invalidated and Zivotofsky's case should be dismissed for failure to state a claim. If, on the other hand, the statute does not trench on the President's powers, then the Secretary must be ordered to issue Zivotofsky a passport that complies with §214(d). Either way, the political question doctrine is not implicated.

The Secretary contends that "there is 'a textually demonstrable constitutional commitment'" to the President of the sole power to recognize foreign sovereigns and, as a corollary, to determine whether an American born in Jerusalem may choose to have Israel listed as his place of birth on his passport. Perhaps. But there is, of course, no exclusive commitment to the Executive of the power to determine the constitutionality of a statute. The Judicial Branch appropriately exercises that authority, including in a case such as this, where the question is whether Congress or the Executive is "aggrandizing its power at the expense of another branch." *Freytag v. Commissioner* (1991).

Our precedents have also found the political question doctrine implicated when there is "'a lack of judicially discoverable and manageable standards for resolving'" the question before the court. Framing the issue as the lower courts did, in terms of whether the Judiciary may decide the political status of Jerusalem, certainly raises those concerns. They dissipate, however, when the issue is recognized to be the more focused one of the constitutionality of §214(d). Indeed, both sides offer detailed legal arguments regarding whether §214(d) is constitutional in light of powers committed to the Executive, and whether Congress's own powers with respect to passports must be weighed in analyzing this question.

For example, the Secretary reprises on the merits her argument on the political question issue, claiming that the Constitution gives the Executive the exclusive power to formulate recognition policy. She roots her claim in the Constitution's declaration that the President shall "receive Ambassadors and other public Ministers." U.S. Const., Art. II, §3. According to the Secretary, "[c]enturies-long Executive Branch practice, congressional acquiescence, and decisions by this Court" confirm that the "receive Ambassadors" clause confers upon the Executive the exclusive power of recognition.

The Secretary further contends that §214(d) constitutes an impermissible exercise of the recognition power because "the decision as to how to describe the place of birth . . . operates as an official statement of whether the United States recognizes a state's sovereignty over a territorial area." The Secretary will not "list[] as a place of birth a country whose sovereignty over the relevant territory the United States does not recognize." Therefore, she claims, "listing 'Israel' as the place of birth would constitute an official decision by the United States to begin to treat Jerusalem as a city located within Israel."

For his part, Zivotofsky argues that, far from being an exercise of the recognition power, §214(d) is instead a "legitimate and permissible" exercise of Congress's "authority to legislate on the form and content of a passport." Zivotofsky suggests that Congress's authority to enact §214(d) derives specifically from its powers over naturalization, U.S. Const., Art. I, §8, cl. 4, and foreign commerce, §8, cl. 3. According to Zivotofsky, Congress has used these powers to pass laws regulating the content and issuance of passports since 1856.

Zivotofsky contends that §214(d) fits squarely within this tradition. Moreover, Zivotofsky argues, the "place of birth" entry cannot be taken as a means for recognizing foreign sovereigns, because the State Department authorizes recording unrecognized territories—such as the Gaza Strip and the West Bank—as places of birth.

Further, Zivotofsky claims that even if §214(d) does implicate the recognition power, that is not a power the Constitution commits exclusively to the Executive. Zivotofsky argues that the Secretary is overreading the authority granted to the President in the "receive Ambassadors" clause. Zivotofsky also points to other clauses in the Constitution, such as Congress's power to declare war, that suggest some congressional role in recognition. Finally, Zivotofsky contends that even if the "receive Ambassadors" clause confers some exclusive recognition power on the President, simply allowing a choice as to the "place of birth" entry on a passport does not significantly intrude on that power.

Recitation of these arguments—which sound in familiar principles of constitutional interpretation—is enough to establish that this case does not "turn on standards that defy judicial application." Resolution of Zivotofsky's claim demands careful examination of the textual, structural, and historical evidence put forward by the parties regarding the nature of the statute and of the passport and recognition powers. This is what courts do. The political question doctrine poses no bar to judicial review of this case.

III

To say that Zivotofsky's claim presents issues the Judiciary is competent to resolve is not to say that reaching a decision in this case is simple. Because the

District Court and the D.C. Circuit believed that review was barred by the political question doctrine, we are without the benefit of thorough lower court opinions to guide our analysis of the merits. Ours is "a court of final review and not first view." *Adarand Constructors, Inc. v. Mineta* (2001). Ordinarily, "we do not decide in the first instance issues not decided below." *NCAA v. Smith* (1999). In particular, when we reverse on a threshold question, we typically remand for resolution of any claims the lower courts' error prevented them from addressing. We see no reason to depart from this approach in this case. Having determined that this case is justiciable, we leave it to the lower courts to consider the merits in the first instance.

Justice SOTOMAYOR, with whom Justice BREYER joins, concurring in part and concurring in the judgment.

As this case illustrates, the proper application of *Baker*'s six factors has generated substantial confusion in the lower courts. I concur in the Court's conclusion that this case does not present a political question. I write separately, however, because I understand the inquiry required by the political question doctrine to be more demanding than that suggested by the Court.

I

The political question doctrine speaks to an amalgam of circumstances in which courts properly examine whether a particular suit is justiciable — that is, whether the dispute is appropriate for resolution by courts. The doctrine is "essentially a function of the separation of powers," *Baker v. Carr* (1962), which recognizes the limits that Article III imposes upon courts and accords appropriate respect to the other branches' exercise of their own constitutional powers.

In my view, the *Baker* factors reflect three distinct justifications for withholding judgment on the merits of a dispute. When a case would require a court to decide an issue whose resolution is textually committed to a coordinate political department, as envisioned by *Baker*'s first factor, abstention is warranted because the court lacks authority to resolve that issue. In such cases, the Constitution itself requires that another branch resolve the question presented.

The second and third *Baker* factors reflect circumstances in which a dispute calls for decisionmaking beyond courts' competence. "'The judicial Power' created by Article III, §1, of the Constitution is not *whatever* judges choose to do," but rather the power "to act in the manner traditional for English and American courts." *Vieth v. Jubelirer* (2004) (plurality opinion). That traditional role involves the application of some manageable and cognizable standard within the competence of the Judiciary to ascertain and employ to the facts of a concrete case. When a court is given no standard by which to adjudicate a dispute, or cannot resolve a dispute in the absence of a yet-unmade policy determination charged to a political branch, resolution of the suit is beyond the judicial role envisioned by Article III. This is not to say, of course, that courts are incapable of interpreting or applying somewhat ambiguous standards using familiar tools of statutory or constitutional interpretation. But where an issue leaves courts truly rudderless, there can be "no doubt of [the] validity" of a court's decision to abstain from judgment. *Vieth.*

The final three *Baker* factors address circumstances in which prudence may counsel against a court's resolution of an issue presented. Courts should be particularly cautious before forgoing adjudication of a dispute on the basis that judicial intervention risks "embarrassment from multifarious pronouncements by various departments on one question," would express a "lack of the respect due coordinate branches of government," or because there exists an "unusual need for unquestioning adherence to a political decision already made." We have repeatedly rejected the view that these thresholds are met whenever a court is called upon to resolve the constitutionality or propriety of the act of another branch of Government. A court may not refuse to adjudicate a dispute merely because a decision "may have significant political overtones" or affect "the conduct of this Nation's foreign relations." *Japan Whaling Ass'n v. American Cetacean Soc.* (1986). Nor may courts decline to resolve a controversy within their traditional competence and proper jurisdiction simply because the question is difficult, the consequences weighty, or the potential real for conflict with the policy preferences of the political branches.

Rare occasions implicating *Baker*'s final factors, however, may present an "'unusual case'" unfit for judicial disposition. Because of the respect due to a coequal and independent department, for instance, courts properly resist calls to question the good faith with which another branch attests to the authenticity of its internal acts. Likewise, we have long acknowledged that courts are particularly ill suited to intervening in exigent disputes necessitating unusual need for "attributing finality to the action of the political departments," *Coleman v. Miller* (1939), or creating acute "risk [of] embarrassment of our government abroad, or grave disturbance at home." Finally, it may be appropriate for courts to stay their hand in cases implicating delicate questions concerning the distribution of political authority between coordinate branches until a dispute is ripe, intractable, and incapable of resolution by the political process. Abstention merely reflects that judicial intervention in such cases is "legitimate only in the last resort," *Chi. & Grand Trunk Ry. Co. v. Wellman* (1892), and is disfavored relative to the prospect of accommodation between the political branches.

When such unusual cases arise, abstention accommodates considerations inherent in the separation of powers and the limitations envisioned by Article III, which conferred authority to federal courts against a common-law backdrop that recognized the propriety of abstention in exceptional cases. The political questions envisioned by *Baker*'s final categories find common ground, therefore, with many longstanding doctrines under which considerations of justiciability or comity lead courts to abstain from deciding questions whose initial resolution is better suited to another time.

To be sure, it will be the rare case in which *Baker*'s final factors alone render a case nonjusticiable. But our long historical tradition recognizes that such exceptional cases arise, and due regard for the separation of powers and the judicial role envisioned by Article III confirms that abstention may be an appropriate response.

II

The court below held that this case presented a political question because it thought petitioner's suit asked the court to decide an issue "textually committed" to a coordinate branch—namely, "to review a policy of the State Department implementing the President's decision" to keep the United States out of the debate over the status of Jerusalem. Largely for the reasons set out by the Court, I agree that the Court of Appeals misapprehended the nature of its task. In two respects, however, my understanding of the political question doctrine might require a court to engage in further analysis beyond that relied upon by the Court.

First, the Court appropriately recognizes that petitioner's claim to a statutory right is "relevant" to the justiciability inquiry required in this case. In order to evaluate whether a case presents a political question, a court must first identify with precision the issue it is being asked to decide. Here, petitioner's suit claims that a federal statute provides him with a right to have "Israel" listed as his place of birth on his passport and other related documents. To decide that question, a court must determine whether the statute is constitutional, and therefore mandates the Secretary of State to issue petitioner's desired passport, or unconstitutional, in which case his suit is at an end. Resolution of that issue is not one "textually committed" to another branch; to the contrary, it is committed to this one. In no fashion does the question require a court to review the wisdom of the President's policy toward Jerusalem or any other decision committed to the discretion of a coordinate department. For that reason, I agree that the decision below should be reversed.

That is not to say, however, that no statute could give rise to a political question. It is not impossible to imagine a case involving the application or even the constitutionality of an enactment that would present a nonjusticiable issue. Indeed, this Court refused to determine whether an Ohio state constitutional provision offended the Republican Guarantee Clause, Art. IV, §4, holding that "the question of whether that guarantee of the Constitution has been disregarded presents no justiciable controversy." *Ohio* ex rel. *Davis v. Hildebrant* (1916). A similar result would follow if Congress passed a statute, for instance, purporting to award financial relief to those improperly "tried" of impeachment offenses. To adjudicate claims under such a statute would require a court to resolve the very same issue we found nonjusticiable in *Nixon*. Such examples are atypical, but they suffice to show that the foreclosure altogether of political question analysis in statutory cases is unwarranted.

Second, the Court suggests that this case does not implicate the political question doctrine's concern with issues exhibiting "'a lack of judicially discoverable and manageable standards,'" because the parties' arguments rely on textual, structural, and historical evidence of the kind that courts routinely consider. But that was equally true in *Nixon*, a case in which we found that "the use of the word 'try' in the first sentence of the Impeachment Trial Clause lacks sufficient precision to afford any judicially manageable standard of review of the Senate's actions." We reached that conclusion even though the parties' briefs focused upon the text of the Impeachment Trial Clause, "the Constitution's drafting history," "contemporaneous commentary," "the unbroken practice of the Senate for 150 years," contemporary dictionary meanings, "Hamilton's Federalist essays," and the practice in the House of Lords prior to ratification. Such evidence was no more or less unfamiliar to courts than that on which the parties rely here.

In my view, it is not whether the evidence upon which litigants rely is common to judicial consideration that determines whether a case lacks judicially discoverable and manageable standards. Rather, it is whether that evidence in fact provides a court a basis to adjudicate meaningfully the issue with which it is presented. The answer will almost always be yes, but if the parties' textual, structural, and historical evidence is inapposite or wholly unilluminating, rendering judicial decision no more than guesswork, a case relying on the ordinary kinds of arguments offered to courts might well still present justiciability concerns.

In this case, however, the Court of Appeals majority found a political question solely on the basis that this case required resolution of an issue "textually committed" to the Executive Branch. Because there was no such textual commitment, I respectfully concur in the Court's decision to reverse the Court of Appeals.

[The opinion of Justice ALITO, concurring in the judgment, is omitted.]

Justice BREYER, dissenting.

I join Part I of Justice Sotomayor's opinion. But in my view we nonetheless have before us . . . a case [presenting a political question]. Four sets of prudential considerations, *taken together*, lead me to that conclusion.

First, the issue before us arises in the field of foreign affairs. Decisionmaking in this area typically is highly political. It often rests upon information readily available to the Executive Branch and to the intelligence committees of Congress, but not readily available to the courts. At the same time, where foreign affairs is at issue, the practical need for the United States to speak "with one voice and ac[t] as one" is particularly important. *See United States v. Pink* (1942) (Frankfurter, J., concurring).

Second, if the courts must answer the constitutional question before us, they may well have to evaluate the foreign policy implications of foreign policy decisions. Were the statutory provision undisputedly concerned only with purely administrative matters (or were its enforcement undisputedly to involve only major foreign policy matters), judicial efforts to answer the constitutional question might not involve judges in trying to answer questions of foreign policy. But in the Middle East, administrative matters can have implications that extend far beyond the purely administrative. Political reactions in that region can prove uncertain. And in that context it may well turn out that resolution of the constitutional argument will require a court to decide how far the statute, in practice, reaches beyond the purely administrative, determining not only whether but also the extent to which enforcement will interfere with the President's ability to make significant recognition-related foreign policy decisions.

Third, the countervailing interests in obtaining judicial resolution of the constitutional determination are not particularly strong ones. Zivotofsky does not assert the kind of interest, *e.g.*, an interest in property or bodily integrity, which courts have traditionally sought to protect. Nor, importantly, does he assert an interest in vindicating a basic right of the kind that the Constitution grants to individuals and that courts traditionally have protected from invasion by the other branches of Government. And I emphasize this fact because the need for judicial action in such cases can trump the foreign policy concerns that I have mentioned.

The interest that Zivotofsky asserts, however, is akin to an ideological interest. And insofar as an individual suffers an injury that is purely ideological, courts have often refused to consider the matter, leaving the injured party to look to the political branches for protection. This is not to say that Zivotofsky's claim is unimportant or that the injury is not serious or even that it is purely ideological. It is to point out that those suffering somewhat similar harms have sometimes had to look to the political branches for resolution of relevant legal issues.

Fourth, insofar as the controversy reflects different foreign policy views among the political branches of Government, those branches have nonjudicial methods of working out their differences. The Executive and Legislative Branches frequently work out disagreements through ongoing contacts and relationships, involving, for example, budget authorizations, confirmation of personnel, committee hearings, and a host of more informal contacts, which, taken together, ensure that, in practice, Members of Congress as well as the President play an important role in the shaping of foreign policy. Indeed, both the Legislative Branch and the Executive Branch typically understand the need to work each with the other in order to create effective foreign policy. In that understanding, those related contacts, and the continuous foreign policy-related relationship lies the possibility of working out the kind of disagreement we see before us.

The upshot is that this case is unusual both in its minimal need for judicial intervention and in its more serious risk that intervention will bring about "embarrassment," show lack of "respect" for the other branches, and potentially disrupt sound foreign policy decisionmaking. For these prudential reasons, I would hold that the political-question doctrine bars further judicial consideration of this case.

* * *

3. The Structure of Government and Electoral Processes

Partisan gerrymandering is where the political party that controls the legislature draws election districts to maximize safe seats for that party. Partisan gerrymandering is nothing new; it takes its name from a former Governor of Massachusetts and former Vice President, Elbridge Gerry. But because of sophisticated computer programs, partisan gerrymandering can be done much more effectively than ever before. The issue in *Rucho v. Common Cause* was whether federal courts may hear challenges to gerrymandering or whether such cases are a non-justiciable political question.

Rucho v. Common Cause

139 S. Ct. 2484 (2019)

Chief Justice ROBERTS delivered the opinion of the Court.

Voters and other plaintiffs in North Carolina and Maryland challenged their States' congressional districting maps as unconstitutional partisan gerrymanders. The North Carolina plaintiffs complained that the State's districting plan discriminated against Democrats; the Maryland plaintiffs complained that their State's plan discriminated against Republicans. The plaintiffs alleged that the gerrymandering violated the First Amendment, the Equal Protection Clause of the Fourteenth Amendment, the Elections Clause, and Article I, §2, of the Constitution. The District Courts in both cases ruled in favor of the plaintiffs, and the defendants appealed directly to this Court.

These cases require us to consider once again whether claims of excessive partisanship in districting are "justiciable"—that is, properly suited for resolution by the federal courts. This Court has not previously struck down a districting plan as an unconstitutional partisan gerrymander, and has struggled without success over the past several decades to discern judicially manageable standards for deciding such claims. The districting plans at issue here are highly partisan, by any measure. The question is whether the courts below appropriately exercised judicial power when they found them unconstitutional as well.

I

A

The first case involves a challenge to the congressional redistricting plan enacted by the Republican-controlled North Carolina General Assembly in 2016. The Republican legislators leading the redistricting effort instructed their mapmaker to use political data to draw a map that would produce a congressional delegation of ten Republicans and three Democrats. As one of the two Republicans chairing the redistricting committee stated, "I think electing Republicans is better than electing Democrats. So I drew this map to help foster what I think is better for the country." He further explained that the map was drawn with the aim of electing ten Republicans and three Democrats because he did "not believe it [would be] possible to draw a map with 11 Republicans and 2 Democrats." One Democratic state senator objected that entrenching the 10-3 advantage for Republicans was not "fair, reasonable, [or] balanced" because, as recently as 2012, "Democratic congressional candidates had received more votes on a statewide basis than Republican candidates." The General Assembly was not swayed by that objection and approved the 2016 Plan by a party-line vote.

In November 2016, North Carolina conducted congressional elections using the 2016 Plan, and Republican candidates won 10 of the 13 congressional districts. In the 2018 elections, Republican candidates won nine congressional districts, while Democratic candidates won three. The Republican candidate narrowly prevailed in the remaining district, but the State Board of Elections called a new election after allegations of fraud.

This litigation began in August 2016, when the North Carolina Democratic Party, Common Cause (a nonprofit organization), and 14 individual North Carolina voters sued the two lawmakers who had led the redistricting effort and other state defendants in Federal District Court. Shortly thereafter, the League of Women Voters of North Carolina and a dozen additional North Carolina voters filed a similar complaint. The two cases were consolidated.

After a four-day trial, the three-judge District Court unanimously concluded that the 2016 Plan violated the Equal Protection Clause and Article I of the Constitution. The court further held, with Judge Osteen dissenting, that the Plan violated the First Amendment. The defendants appealed directly to this Court under 28 U.S.C. §1253.

After deciding *Gill v. Whitford* (2018), we remanded the present case for further consideration by the District Court. On remand, the District Court again struck down the 2016 Plan. On the merits, the court found that "the General Assembly's predominant intent was to discriminate against voters who supported or were likely to support non-Republican candidates," and to "entrench Republican candidates" through widespread cracking and packing of Democratic voters. In the end, the District Court held that 12 of the 13 districts constituted partisan gerrymanders that violated the Equal Protection Clause.

B

The second case before us is *Lamone v. Benisek*. In 2011, the Maryland Legislature — dominated by Democrats — undertook to redraw the lines of that State's eight congressional districts. The Governor at the time, Democrat Martin O'Malley, led the process. He appointed a redistricting committee to help redraw the map, and asked Congressman Steny Hoyer, who has described himself as a "serial gerrymanderer," to advise the committee. The Governor later testified that his aim was to "use the redistricting process to change the overall composition of Maryland's congressional delegation to 7 Democrats and 1 Republican by flipping" one district. "[A] decision was made to go for the Sixth," which had been held by a Republican for nearly two decades. The map was adopted by a party-line vote. It was used in the 2012 election and succeeded in flipping the Sixth District. A Democrat has·held the seat ever since.

In November 2013, three Maryland voters filed this lawsuit. They alleged that the 2011 Plan violated the First Amendment, the Elections Clause, and Article I, §2, of the Constitution. After considerable procedural skirmishing and litigation over preliminary relief, the District Court entered summary judgment for the plaintiffs. The District Court permanently enjoined the State from using the 2011 Plan and ordered it to promptly adopt a new plan for the 2020 election. The defendants appealed directly to this Court under 28 U.S.C. §1253.

II
A

Article III of the Constitution limits federal courts to deciding "Cases" and "Controversies." We have understood that limitation to mean that federal courts can address only questions "historically viewed as capable of resolution through the judicial process." *Flast v. Cohen* (1968).

Chief Justice Marshall famously wrote that it is "the province and duty of the judicial department to say what the law is." *Marbury v. Madison* (1803). Sometimes, however, "the law is that the judicial department has no business entertaining the claim of unlawfulness — because the question is entrusted to one of the political branches or involves no judicially enforceable rights." *Vieth v. Jubelirer* (2004). In such a case the claim is said to present a "political question" and to be nonjusticiable — outside the courts' competence and therefore beyond the courts' jurisdiction. *Baker v. Carr* (1962). Among the political question cases the Court has identified are those that lack "judicially discoverable and manageable standards for resolving [them]."

B

Partisan gerrymandering is nothing new. Nor is frustration with it. The practice was known in the Colonies prior to Independence, and the Framers were familiar with it at the time of the drafting and ratification of the Constitution.

During the very first congressional elections, George Washington and his Federalist allies accused Patrick Henry of trying to gerrymander Virginia's districts against their candidates—in particular James Madison, who ultimately prevailed over fellow future President James Monroe.

In 1812, Governor of Massachusetts and future Vice President Elbridge Gerry notoriously approved congressional districts that the legislature had drawn to aid the Democratic-Republican Party. The moniker "gerrymander" was born when an outraged Federalist newspaper observed that one of the misshapen districts resembled a salamander.

The Framers addressed the election of Representatives to Congress in the Elections Clause. Art. I, §4, cl. 1. That provision assigns to state legislatures the power to prescribe the "Times, Places and Manner of holding Elections" for Members of Congress, while giving Congress the power to "make or alter" any such regulations.

Congress has regularly exercised its Elections Clause power, including to address partisan gerrymandering. The Apportionment Act of 1842, which required single-member districts for the first time, specified that those districts be "composed of contiguous territory," in "an attempt to forbid the practice of the gerrymander." E. Griffith, The Rise and Development of the Gerrymander 12 (1907). Later statutes added requirements of compactness and equality of population. Congress also used its Elections Clause power in 1870, enacting the first comprehensive federal statute dealing with elections as a way to enforce the Fifteenth Amendment. Starting in the 1950s, Congress enacted a series of laws to protect the right to vote through measures such as the suspension of literacy tests and the prohibition of English-only elections.

Appellants suggest that, through the Elections Clause, the Framers set aside electoral issues such as the one before us as questions that only Congress can resolve. We do not agree. In two areas—one-person, one-vote and racial gerrymandering—our cases have held that there is a role for the courts with respect to at least some issues that could arise from a State's drawing of congressional districts.

But the history is not irrelevant. The Framers were aware of electoral districting problems and considered what to do about them. They settled on a characteristic approach, assigning the issue to the state legislatures, expressly checked and balanced by the Federal Congress. At no point was there a suggestion that the federal courts had a role to play. Nor was there any indication that the Framers had ever heard of courts doing such a thing.

C

Courts have nevertheless been called upon to resolve a variety of questions surrounding districting. Early on, doubts were raised about the competence of the federal courts to resolve those questions.

In the leading case of *Baker v. Carr*, voters in Tennessee complained that the State's districting plan for state representatives "debase[d]" their votes, because the plan was predicated on a 60-year-old census that no longer reflected the distribution of population in the State. This Court . . . identified various considerations relevant to determining whether a claim is a nonjusticiable political question, including whether there is "a lack of judicially discoverable and manageable standards for resolving it." The Court concluded that the claim of population inequality among districts did not fall into that category, because such a claim could be decided under basic equal protection principles.

Another line of challenges to districting plans has focused on race. Laws that explicitly discriminate on the basis of race, as well as those that are race neutral on their face but are unexplainable on grounds other than race, are of course presumptively invalid.

Partisan gerrymandering claims have proved far more difficult to adjudicate. The basic reason is that, while it is illegal for a jurisdiction to depart from the one-person, one-vote rule, or to engage in racial discrimination in districting, "a jurisdiction may engage in constitutional political gerrymandering." *Hunt v. Cromartie* (1999).

To hold that legislators cannot take partisan interests into account when drawing district lines would essentially countermand the Framers' decision to entrust districting to political entities. The "central problem" is not determining whether a jurisdiction has engaged in partisan gerrymandering. It is "determining when political gerrymandering has gone too far." *Vieth v. Jubelirer* (2004).

III
A

In considering whether partisan gerrymandering claims are justiciable, we are mindful of Justice Kennedy's counsel in *Vieth*: Any standard for resolving such claims must be grounded in a "limited and precise rationale" and be "clear, manageable, and politically neutral." As noted, the question is one of degree: How to "provid[e] a standard for deciding how much partisan dominance is too much." *LULAC v. Perry* (2006) (opinion of Kennedy, J.). And it is vital in such circumstances that the Court act only in accord with especially clear standards: "With uncertain limits, intervening courts—even when proceeding with best intentions—would risk assuming political, not legal, responsibility for a process that often produces ill will and distrust." *Vieth* (opinion of Kennedy, J.).

B

Partisan gerrymandering claims rest on an instinct that groups with a certain level of political support should enjoy a commensurate level of political power and influence. Explicitly or implicitly, a districting map is alleged to be unconstitutional because it makes it too difficult for one party to translate statewide support into seats in the legislature. But such a claim is based on a "norm that does not exist" in our electoral system—"statewide elections for representatives along party lines." *Bandemer v. Davis* (1986) (opinion of O'Connor, J.).

Partisan gerrymandering claims invariably sound in a desire for proportional representation. As Justice O'Connor put it [in *Bandemer*], such claims are based on "a conviction that the greater the departure from proportionality, the more suspect an apportionment plan becomes." "Our cases, however, clearly foreclose any claim that the Constitution requires proportional representation or that legislatures in reapportioning must draw district lines to come as near as possible to allocating seats to the contending parties in proportion to what their anticipated statewide vote will be." *Id.* (plurality opinion).

The Founders certainly did not think proportional representation was required. For more than 50 years after ratification of the Constitution, many States elected their congressional representatives through at-large or "general ticket" elections. That meant that a party could garner nearly half of the vote statewide and wind up without any seats in the congressional delegation.

Unable to claim that the Constitution requires proportional representation out-right, plaintiffs inevitably ask the courts to make their own political judgment about how much representation particular political parties *deserve*—based on the votes of their supporters—and to rearrange the challenged districts to achieve that end. But federal courts are not equipped to apportion political power as a matter of fairness, nor is there any basis for concluding that they were authorized to do so.

There are no legal standards discernible in the Constitution for making such judgments, let alone limited and precise standards that are clear, manageable, and politically neutral. Any judicial decision on what is "fair" in this context would be an "unmoored determination" of the sort characteristic of a political question beyond the competence of the federal courts. *Zivotofsky v. Clinton* (2012).

And it is only after determining how to define fairness that you can even begin to answer the determinative question: "How much is too much?" At what point does permissible partisanship become unconstitutional? If compliance with traditional districting criteria is the fairness touchstone, for example, how much deviation from those criteria is constitutionally acceptable and how should mapdrawers prioritize competing criteria? Should a court "reverse gerrymander" other parts of a State to counteract "natural" gerrymandering caused, for example, by the urban concentration of one party? If a districting plan protected half of the incumbents but redistricted the rest into head to head races, would that be constitutional? A court would have to rank the relative importance of those traditional criteria and weigh how much deviation from each to allow.

Appellees contend that if we can adjudicate one-person, one-vote claims, we can also assess partisan gerrymandering claims. But the one-person, one-vote rule is relatively easy to administer as a matter of math. The same cannot be said of partisan gerrymandering claims, because the Constitution supplies no objective measure for assessing whether a districting map treats a political party fairly. It hardly follows from the principle that each person must have an equal say in the election of representatives that a person is entitled to have his political party achieve representation in some way commensurate to its share of statewide support.

More fundamentally, "vote dilution" in the one-person, one-vote cases refers to the idea that each vote must carry equal weight. In other words, each representative must be accountable to (approximately) the same number of constituents. That requirement does not extend to political parties. It does not mean that each party must be influential in proportion to its number of supporters.

Nor do our racial gerrymandering cases provide an appropriate standard for assessing partisan gerrymandering. Unlike partisan gerrymandering claims, a racial gerrymandering claim does not ask for a fair share of political power and influence, with all the justiciability conundrums that entails. It asks instead for the elimination of a racial classification. A partisan gerrymandering claim cannot ask for the elimination of partisanship.

IV

Appellees and the dissent propose a number of "tests" for evaluating partisan gerrymandering claims, but none meets the need for a limited and precise standard that is judicially discernible and manageable. And none provides a solid grounding for judges to take the extraordinary step of reallocating power and influence between political parties.

V

Excessive partisanship in districting leads to results that reasonably seem unjust. But the fact that such gerrymandering is "incompatible with democratic principles," *Ariz. State Legis. v. Ariz. Ind. Redistricting Comm'n* (2015), does not mean that the solution lies with the federal judiciary. We conclude that partisan gerrymandering claims present political questions beyond the reach of the federal courts. Federal judges have no license to reallocate political power between the two major political parties, with no plausible grant of authority in the Constitution, and no legal standards to limit and direct their decisions. "[J]udicial action must be governed by *standard*, by *rule*," and must be "principled, rational, and based upon reasoned distinctions" found in the Constitution or laws. *Vieth* (plurality opinion). Judicial review of partisan gerrymandering does not meet those basic requirements.

What the appellees and dissent seek is an unprecedented expansion of judicial power. We have never struck down a partisan gerrymander as unconstitutional—despite various requests over the past 45 years. The expansion of judicial authority would not be into just any area of controversy, but into one of the most intensely partisan aspects of American political life. That intervention would be unlimited in scope and duration—it would recur over and over again around the country with each new round of districting, for state as well as federal representatives. Consideration of the impact of today's ruling on democratic principles cannot ignore the effect of the unelected and politically unaccountable branch of the Federal Government assuming such an extraordinary and unprecedented role.

Our conclusion does not condone excessive partisan gerrymandering. Nor does our conclusion condemn complaints about districting to echo into a void. The States, for example, are actively addressing the issue on a number of fronts. In 2015, the Supreme Court of Florida struck down that State's congressional districting plan as a violation of the Fair Districts Amendment to the Florida Constitution. The dissent wonders why we can't do the same. The answer is that there is no "Fair Districts Amendment" to the Federal Constitution. Provisions in state statutes and state constitutions can provide standards and guidance for state courts to apply. Indeed, numerous other States are restricting partisan considerations in districting through legislation. One way they are doing so is by placing power to draw electoral districts in the hands of independent commissions. For example, in November 2018, voters in Colorado and Michigan approved constitutional amendments creating multimember commissions that will be responsible in whole or in part for creating and approving district maps for congressional and state legislative districts. Missouri is trying a different tack. Voters there overwhelmingly approved the creation of a new position—state demographer—to draw state legislative district lines.

As noted, the Framers gave Congress the power to do something about partisan gerrymandering in the Elections Clause. The first bill introduced in the 116th Congress would require States to create 15-member independent commissions to draw congressional districts and would establish certain redistricting criteria, including protection for communities of interest, and ban partisan gerrymandering.

Dozens of other bills have been introduced to limit reliance on political considerations in redistricting. In 2010, H.R. 6250 would have required States to follow standards of compactness, contiguity, and respect for political subdivisions in redistricting. It also would have prohibited the establishment of congressional districts "with the major purpose of diluting the voting strength of any person, or group, including any political party," except when necessary to comply with the Voting Rights Act of 1965.

Another example is the Fairness and Independence in Redistricting Act, which was introduced in 2005 and has been reintroduced in every Congress since. That bill would require every State to establish an independent commission to adopt redistricting plans. The bill also set forth criteria for the independent commissions to use, such as compactness, contiguity, and population equality. It would prohibit consideration of voting history, political party affiliation, or incumbent Representative's residence.

We express no view on any of these pending proposals. We simply note that the avenue for reform established by the Framers, and used by Congress in the past, remains open.

No one can accuse this Court of having a crabbed view of the reach of its competence. But we have no commission to allocate political power and influence in the absence of a constitutional directive or legal standards to guide us in the exercise of such authority. "It is emphatically the province and duty of the judicial department to say what the law is." *Marbury v. Madison* (1803). In this rare circumstance, that means our duty is to say "this is not law."

Justice KAGAN, with whom Justice GINSBURG, Justice BREYER, and Justice SOTOMAYOR joins, dissenting.

For the first time ever, this Court refuses to remedy a constitutional violation because it thinks the task beyond judicial capabilities.

And not just any constitutional violation. The partisan gerrymanders in these cases deprived citizens of the most fundamental of their constitutional rights: the rights to participate equally in the political process, to join with others to advance political beliefs, and to choose their political representatives. In so doing, the partisan gerrymanders here debased and dishonored our democracy, turning upside-down the core American idea that all governmental power derives from the people. These gerrymanders enabled politicians to entrench themselves in office as against voters' preferences. They promoted partisanship above respect for the popular will. They encouraged a politics of polarization and dysfunction. If left unchecked, gerrymanders like the ones here may irreparably damage our system of government.

And checking them is *not* beyond the courts. The majority's abdication comes just when courts across the country, including those below, have coalesced around manageable judicial standards to resolve partisan gerrymandering claims. Those standards satisfy the majority's own benchmarks. They do not require—indeed, they do not permit—courts to rely on their own ideas of electoral fairness, whether proportional representation or any other. And they limit courts to correcting only egregious gerrymanders, so judges do not become omnipresent players in the political process. But yes, the standards used here do allow—as well they should—judicial intervention in the worst-of-the-worst cases of democratic subversion, causing blatant constitutional harms. In other words, they allow courts to undo partisan gerrymanders of the kind we face today from North Carolina and Maryland. In giving such gerrymanders a pass from judicial review, the majority goes tragically wrong.

I

Maybe the majority errs in these cases because it pays so little attention to the constitutional harms at their core. After dutifully reciting each case's facts, the majority leaves them forever behind, instead immersing itself in everything that could conceivably go amiss if courts became involved. So it is necessary to fill in the gaps. To recount exactly what politicians in North Carolina and Maryland did to entrench their parties in political office, whatever the electorate might think. And to elaborate on the constitutional injury those politicians wreaked, to our democratic system and to individuals' rights. All that will help in considering whether courts confronting partisan gerrymandering claims are really so hamstrung—so unable to carry out their constitutional duties—as the majority thinks.

The plaintiffs here challenge two congressional districting plans—one adopted by Republicans in North Carolina and the other by Democrats in Maryland—as unconstitutional partisan gerrymanders. As I relate what happened in those two States, ask yourself: Is this how American democracy is supposed to work?

Start with North Carolina. After the 2010 census, the North Carolina General Assembly, with Republican majorities in both its House and its Senate, enacted a new congressional districting plan. That plan governed the two next national elections. In 2012, Republican candidates won 9 of the State's 13 seats in the U.S. House of Representatives, although they received only 49% of the statewide vote. In 2014, Republican candidates increased their total to 10 of the 13 seats, this time based on 55% of the vote. Soon afterward, a District Court struck down two districts in the plan as unconstitutional racial gerrymanders. The General Assembly, with both chambers still controlled by Republicans, went back to the drawing board to craft the needed remedial state map. And here is how the process unfolded:

- The Republican co-chairs of the Assembly's redistricting committee, Rep. David Lewis and Sen. Robert Rucho, instructed Dr. Thomas Hofeller, a Republican districting specialist, to create a new map that would maintain the 10-3 composition of the State's congressional delegation come what might. Using sophisticated technological tools and precinct-level election results selected to predict voting behavior, Hofeller drew district lines to minimize Democrats' voting strength and ensure the election of 10 Republican Congressmen.

- Lewis then presented for the redistricting committee's (retroactive) approval a list of the criteria Hofeller had employed—including one labeled "Partisan Advantage." That criterion, endorsed by a party-line vote, stated that the committee would make all "reasonable efforts to construct districts" to "maintain the current [10-3] partisan makeup" of the State's congressional delegation.

- Lewis explained the Partisan Advantage criterion to legislators as follows: We are "draw[ing] the maps to give a partisan advantage to 10 Republicans and 3 Democrats because [I] d[o] not believe it['s] possible to draw a map with 11 Republicans and 2 Democrats."
- The committee and the General Assembly later enacted, again on a party-line vote, the map Hofeller had drawn.
- Lewis announced: "I think electing Republicans is better than electing Democrats. So I drew this map to help foster what I think is better for the country."
- You might think that judgment best left to the American people. But give Lewis credit for this much: The map has worked just as he planned and predicted. In 2016, Republican congressional candidates won 10 of North Carolina's 13 seats, with 53% of the statewide vote. Two years later, Republican candidates won 9 of 12 seats though they received only 50% of the vote. (The 13th seat has not yet been filled because fraud tainted the initial election.)
- Events in Maryland make for a similarly grisly tale. For 50 years, Maryland's 8-person congressional delegation typically consisted of 2 or 3 Republicans and 5 or 6 Democrats. After the 2000 districting, for example, the First and Sixth Districts reliably elected Republicans, and the other districts as reliably elected Democrats. But in the 2010 districting cycle, the State's Democratic leaders, who controlled the governorship and both houses of the General Assembly, decided to press their advantage.
- Governor Martin O'Malley, who oversaw the process, decided (in his own later words) "to create a map that was more favorable for Democrats over the next ten years." Because flipping the First District was geographically next-to-impossible, "a decision was made to go for the Sixth."
- O'Malley appointed an advisory committee as the public face of his effort, while asking Congressman Steny Hoyer, a self-described "serial gerrymanderer," to hire and direct a mapmaker. Hoyer retained Eric Hawkins, an analyst at a political consulting firm providing services to Democrats.
- Hawkins received only two instructions: to ensure that the new map produced 7 reliable Democratic seats, and to protect all Democratic incumbents.
- Using similar technologies and election data as Hofeller, Hawkins produced a map to those specifications. Although new census figures required removing only 10,000 residents from the Sixth District, Hawkins proposed a large-scale population transfer. The map moved about 360,000 voters out of the district and another 350,000 in. That swap decreased the number of registered Republicans in the district by over 66,000 and increased the number of registered Democrats by about 24,000, all to produce a safe Democratic district.
- After the advisory committee adopted the map on a party-line vote, State Senate President Thomas Miller briefed the General Assembly's Democratic

caucuses about the new map's aims. Miller told his colleagues that the map would give "Democrats a real opportunity to pick up a seventh seat in the delegation" and that "[i]n the face of Republican gains in redistricting in other states[,] we have a serious obligation to create this opportunity."

• The General Assembly adopted the plan on a party-line vote.

Maryland's Democrats proved no less successful than North Carolina's Republicans in devising a voter-proof map. In the four elections that followed (from 2012 through 2018), Democrats have never received more than 65% of the statewide congressional vote. Yet in each of those elections, Democrats have won (you guessed it) 7 of 8 House seats—including the once-reliably-Republican Sixth District.

B

Now back to the question I asked before: Is that how American democracy is supposed to work? I have yet to meet the person who thinks so.

"Governments," the Declaration of Independence states, "deriv[e] their just Powers from the Consent of the Governed." The Constitution begins: "We the People of the United States." The Gettysburg Address (almost) ends: "[G]overnment of the people, by the people, for the people." If there is a single idea that made our Nation (and that our Nation commended to the world), it is this one: The people are sovereign. The "power," James Madison wrote, "is in the people over the Government, and not in the Government over the people." 4 Annals of Cong. 934 (1794).

Free and fair and periodic elections are the key to that vision. The people get to choose their representatives. And then they get to decide, at regular intervals, whether to keep them. Election day—next year, and two years later, and two years after that—is what links the people to their representatives, and gives the people their sovereign power. That day is the foundation of democratic governance.

And partisan gerrymandering can make it meaningless. At its most extreme—as in North Carolina and Maryland—the practice amounts to "rigging elections." *Vieth v. Jubelirer* (2004) (Kennedy, J., concurring in judgment). By drawing districts to maximize the power of some voters and minimize the power of others, a party in office at the right time can entrench itself there for a decade or more, no matter what the voters would prefer. Just ask the people of North Carolina and Maryland. The "core principle of republican government," this Court has recognized, is "that the voters should choose their representatives, not the other way around." *Ariz. State Legis. v. Ariz. Ind. Redistricting Comm'n* (2015). Partisan gerrymandering turns it the other way around. By that mechanism, politicians can cherry-pick voters to ensure their reelection. And the power becomes, as Madison put it, "in the Government over the people."

The majority disputes none of this. I think it important to underscore that fact: The majority disputes none of what I have said (or will say) about how gerrymanders undermine democracy. Indeed, the majority concedes (really, how could it not?) that gerrymandering is "incompatible with democratic principles." And therefore what? That recognition would seem to demand a response. The majority offers two ideas that might qualify as such. One is that the political process can deal with the problem—a proposition so dubious on its face that I feel secure in delaying my answer for some time. The other is that political gerrymanders have always been with us. To its credit, the majority does not frame that point as an originalist constitutional argument. After all (as the majority rightly notes), racial and residential gerrymanders were also once with us, but the Court has done something about that fact. The majority's idea instead seems to be that if we have lived with partisan gerrymanders so long, we will survive.

That complacency has no cause. Yes, partisan gerrymandering goes back to the Republic's earliest days. (As does vociferous opposition to it.) But big data and modern technology—of just the kind that the mapmakers in North Carolina and Maryland used—make today's gerrymandering altogether different from the crude linedrawing of the past. Old-time efforts, based on little more than guesses, sometimes led to so-called dummymanders—gerrymanders that went spectacularly wrong. Not likely in today's world. Mapmakers now have access to more granular data about party preference and voting behavior than ever before. County-level voting data has given way to precinct-level or city-block-level data; and increasingly, mapmakers avail themselves of data sets providing wide-ranging information about even individual voters. Just as important, advancements in computing technology have enabled mapmakers to put that information to use with unprecedented efficiency and precision. While bygone mapmakers may have drafted three or four alternative districting plans, today's mapmakers can generate thousands of possibilities at the touch of a key—and then choose the one giving their party maximum advantage (usually while still meeting traditional districting requirements). The effect is to make gerrymanders far more effective and durable than before, insulating politicians against all but the most titanic shifts in the political tides. These are not your grandfather's—let alone the Framers'—gerrymanders.

The proof is in the 2010 pudding. That redistricting cycle produced some of the most extreme partisan gerrymanders in this country's history. I've already recounted the results from North Carolina and Maryland, and you'll hear even more about those. And gerrymanders will only get worse (or depending on your perspective, better) as time goes on—as data becomes ever more fine-grained and data analysis techniques continue to improve. What was possible with paper and pen—or even with Windows 95—doesn't hold a candle (or an LED bulb?) to what will become possible with developments like machine learning. And someplace along this road, "we the people" become sovereign no longer.

C

Partisan gerrymandering of the kind before us not only subverts democracy (as if that weren't bad enough). It violates individuals' constitutional rights as well. That statement is not the lonesome cry of a dissenting Justice. This Court has recognized extreme partisan gerrymandering as such a violation for many years.

Partisan gerrymandering operates through vote dilution—the devaluation of one citizen's vote as compared to others. A mapmaker draws district lines to "pack" and "crack" voters likely to support the disfavored party. He packs supermajorities of those voters into a relatively few districts, in numbers far greater than needed for their preferred candidates to prevail. Then he cracks the rest across many more districts, spreading them so thin that their candidates will not be able to win. Whether the person is packed or cracked, his vote carries less weight—has less consequence—than it would under a neutrally drawn (non-partisan) map. In short, the mapmaker has made some votes count for less, because they are likely to go for the other party.

That practice implicates the Fourteenth Amendment's Equal Protection Clause. The Fourteenth Amendment, we long ago recognized, "guarantees the opportunity for equal participation by all voters in the election" of legislators. *Reynolds v. Sims* (1964). And that opportunity "can be denied by a debasement or dilution of the weight of a citizen's vote just as effectively as by wholly prohibiting the free exercise of the franchise." Based on that principle, this Court in its one-person-one-vote decisions prohibited creating districts with significantly different populations. A State could not, we explained, thus "dilut[e] the weight of votes because of place of residence." The constitutional injury in a partisan gerrymandering case is much the same, except that the dilution is based on party affiliation.

And partisan gerrymandering implicates the First Amendment too. That Amendment gives its greatest protection to political beliefs, speech, and association. Yet partisan gerrymanders subject certain voters to "disfavored treatment"—again, counting their votes for less—precisely because of "their voting history [and] their expression of political views." And added to that strictly personal harm is an associational one. By diluting the votes of certain citizens, the State frustrates their efforts to translate [political] affiliations into political effectiveness.

Though different Justices have described the constitutional harm in diverse ways, nearly all have agreed on this much: Extreme partisan gerrymandering (as happened in North Carolina and Maryland) violates the Constitution. Once again, the majority never disagrees; it appears to accept the "principle that each person must have an equal say in the election of representatives." And indeed, without this settled and shared understanding that cases like these inflict constitutional injury, the question of whether there are judicially manageable standards for resolving them would never come up.

II

So the only way to understand the majority's opinion is as follows: In the face of grievous harm to democratic governance and flagrant infringements on individuals' rights—in the face of escalating partisan manipulation whose compatibility with this Nation's values and law no one defends—the majority declines to provide any remedy. For the first time in this Nation's history, the majority declares that it can do nothing about an acknowledged constitutional violation because it has searched high and low and cannot find a workable legal standard to apply.

The majority gives two reasons for thinking that the adjudication of partisan gerrymandering claims is beyond judicial capabilities. First and foremost, the majority says, it cannot find a neutral baseline—one not based on contestable notions of political fairness—from which to measure injury.

I'll give the majority this one—and important—thing: It identifies some dangers everyone should want to avoid. Judges should not be apportioning political power based on their own vision of electoral fairness, whether proportional representation or any other. And judges should not be striking down maps left, right, and center, on the view that every smidgen of politics is a smidgen too much.

Respect for state legislative processes—and restraint in the exercise of judicial authority—counsels intervention in only egregious cases.

But in throwing up its hands, the majority misses something under its nose: What it says can't be done *has* been done. Over the past several years, federal courts across the country—including, but not exclusively, in the decisions below—have largely converged on a standard for adjudicating partisan gerrymandering claims (striking down both Democratic and Republican districting plans in the process). And that standard does what the majority says is impossible. The standard does not use any judge-made conception of electoral fairness—either proportional representation or any other; instead, it takes as its baseline a State's *own* criteria of fairness, apart from partisan gain. And by requiring plaintiffs to make difficult showings relating to both purpose and effects, the standard invalidates the most extreme, but only the most extreme, partisan gerrymanders.

Start with the standard the lower courts used. The majority disaggregates the opinions below, distinguishing the one from the other and then chopping up each into "a number of 'tests.'" But in doing so, it fails to convey the decisions' most significant—and common—features. Both courts focused on the harm of vote dilution, though the North Carolina court mostly grounded its analysis in the Fourteenth Amendment and the Maryland court in the First. And both courts (like others around the country) used basically the same three-part test to decide whether the plaintiffs had made out a vote dilution claim. As many legal standards do, that test has three parts: (1) intent; (2) effects; and (3) causation. First, the plaintiffs challenging a districting plan must prove that state officials' "predominant purpose" in drawing a district's lines was to "entrench [their party] in power" by diluting the votes of citizens favoring its rival. Second, the plaintiffs must establish that the lines drawn in fact have the intended effect by "substantially" diluting their votes. And third, if the plaintiffs make those showings, the State must come up with a legitimate, non-partisan justification to save its map. If you are a lawyer, you know that this test looks utterly ordinary. It is the sort of thing courts work with every day.

Turn now to the test's application. First, did the North Carolina and Maryland districters have the predominant purpose of entrenching their own party in power? Here, the two District Courts catalogued the overwhelming direct evidence that they did. To remind you of some highlights: North Carolina's redistricting committee used "Partisan Advantage" as an official criterion for drawing district lines. And from the first to the last, that committee's chair (along with his mapmaker) acted to ensure a 10-3 partisan split, whatever the statewide vote, because he thought that "electing Republicans is better than electing Democrats." For their part, Maryland's Democrats—the Governor, senior Congressman, and State Senate President alike—openly admitted to a single driving purpose: flip the Sixth District from Republican to Democratic. They did not blanch from moving some 700,000 voters into new districts (when one-person-one-vote rules required relocating just 10,000) for that reason and that reason alone.

The majority's response to the District Courts' purpose analysis is discomfiting. The majority does not contest the lower courts' findings; how could it? Instead, the majority says that state officials' intent to entrench their party in power is perfectly "permissible," even when it is the predominant factor in drawing district lines. But that is wrong. True enough, that the intent to inject "political considerations" into districting may not raise any constitutional concerns. In *Gaffney v. Cummings* (1973), for example, we thought it non-problematic when state officials used political data to ensure rough proportional representation between the two parties. And true enough that even the naked purpose to gain partisan advantage may not rise to the level of constitutional notice when it is not the driving force in mapmaking or when the intended gain is slight. But when political actors have a specific and predominant intent to entrench themselves in power by manipulating district lines, that goes too far.

On to the second step of the analysis, where the plaintiffs must prove that the districting plan substantially dilutes their votes. The majority fails to discuss most of the evidence the District Courts relied on to find that the plaintiffs had done so. But that evidence—particularly from North Carolina—is the key to understanding both the problem these cases present and the solution to it they offer. The evidence reveals just how bad the two gerrymanders were (in case you had any doubts). And it shows how the same technologies and data that today facilitate extreme partisan gerrymanders also enable courts to discover them, by exposing just how much they dilute votes.

The majority claims all these findings are mere "prognostications" about the future, in which no one "can have any confidence." But the courts below did not gaze into crystal balls, as the majority tries to suggest. Their findings about these gerrymanders' effects on voters—both in the past and predictably in the future—were evidence-based, data-based, statistics-based. Knowledge-based, one might say. The courts did what anyone would want a decisionmaker to do when so much hangs in the balance. They looked hard at the facts, and they went where the facts led them. They availed themselves of all the information that mapmakers (like Hofeller and Hawkins) and politicians (like Lewis and O'Malley) work so hard to amass and then use to make every districting decision. They refused to content themselves with unsupported and out-of-date musings about the unpredictability of the American voter. They did not bet America's future—as today the majority does—on the idea that maps constructed with so much expertise and care to make electoral outcomes impervious to voting would somehow or other come apart. They looked at the evidence—at the facts about how these districts operated—and they could reach only one conclusion. By substantially diluting the votes of citizens favoring their rivals, the politicians of one party had succeeded in entrenching themselves in office. They had beat democracy.

B

The majority's broadest claim, as I've noted, is that this is a price we must pay because judicial oversight of partisan gerrymandering cannot be "politically neutral" or "manageable." Courts, the majority argues, will have to choose among contested notions of electoral fairness. (Should they take as the ideal mode of districting proportional representation, many competitive seats, adherence to traditional districting criteria, or so forth?) And even once courts have chosen, the majority continues, they will have to decide "[h]ow much is too much?"—that is, how much deviation from the chosen "touchstone" to allow? In answering that question, the majority surmises, they will likely go far too far. So the whole thing is impossible, the majority concludes. [But] [t]hat kind of oversight is not only possible; it's been done.

Consider neutrality first. Contrary to the majority's suggestion, the District Courts did not have to—and in fact did not—choose among competing visions of electoral fairness. That is because they did not try to compare the State's actual map to an "ideally fair" one (whether based on proportional representation or some other criterion). Instead, they looked at the difference between what the State did and what the State would have done if politicians hadn't been intent on partisan gain. Or put differently, the comparator (or baseline or touchstone) is the result not of a judge's philosophizing but of the State's own characteristics and judgments. Still more, the courts' analyses used the State's own criteria for electoral fairness—except for naked partisan gain. Under their approach, in other words, the State selected its own fairness baseline in the form of its other districting criteria. All the courts did was determine how far the State had gone off that track because of its politicians' effort to entrench themselves in office.

The majority's sole response misses the point. According to the majority, "it does not make sense to use" a State's own (non-partisan) districting criteria as the baseline from which to measure partisan gerrymandering because those criteria "will vary from State to State and year to year." But that is a virtue, not a vice—a feature, not a bug. Using the criteria the State itself has chosen at the relevant time prevents any judicial predilections from affecting the analysis—exactly what the majority claims it wants. At the same time, using those criteria enables a court to measure just what it should: the extent to which the pursuit of partisan advantage—by these legislators at this moment—has distorted the State's districting decisions.

And the combined inquiry used in these cases set the bar high, so that courts could intervene in the worst partisan gerrymanders, but no others. Or to say the same thing, so that courts could intervene in the kind of extreme gerrymanders that nearly every Justice for decades has thought to violate the Constitution. Illicit purpose was simple to show here only because politicians and mapmakers thought their actions could not be attacked in court. They therefore felt free to openly proclaim their intent to entrench their party in office. But if the Court today had declared that behavior justiciable, such smoking guns would all but disappear. Even assuming some officials continued to try implementing extreme partisan gerrymanders, they would not brag about their efforts. So plaintiffs would have to prove the intent to entrench through circumstantial evidence—essentially showing that no other explanation (no geographic feature or non-partisan districting objective) could explain the districting plan's vote dilutive effects. And that would be impossible unless those effects were even more than substantial—unless mapmakers had packed and cracked with abandon in unprecedented ways. As again, they did here. That the two courts below found constitutional violations does not mean their tests were unrigorous; it means that the conduct they confronted was constitutionally appalling—by even the strictest measure, inordinately partisan.

The majority, in the end, fails to understand both the plaintiffs' claims and the decisions below. Everything in today's opinion assumes that these cases grew out of a "desire for proportional representation" or, more generally phrased, a "fair share of political power." And everything in it assumes that the courts below had to (and did) decide what that fair share would be. But that is not so. The plaintiffs objected to one specific practice—the extreme manipulation of district lines for partisan gain. Elimination of that practice could have led to proportional representation. Or it could have led to nothing close. What was left after the practice's removal could have been fair, or could have been unfair, by any number of measures. That was not the crux of this suit. The plaintiffs asked only that the courts bar politicians from entrenching themselves in power by diluting the votes of their rivals' supporters. And the courts, using neutral and manageable—and eminently legal—standards, provided that (and only that) relief. This Court should have cheered, not overturned, that restoration of the people's power to vote.

III

This Court has long understood that it has a special responsibility to remedy violations of constitutional rights resulting from politicians' districting decisions. Over 50 years ago, we committed to providing judicial review in that sphere, recognizing as we established the one-person-one-vote rule that "our oath and our office require no less." *Reynolds v. Sims.* Of course, our oath and our office require us to vindicate all constitutional rights. But the need for judicial review is at its most urgent in cases like these. [P]oliticians want to stay in office. No one can look to them for effective relief.

The majority disagrees, concluding its opinion with a paean to congressional bills limiting partisan gerrymanders. "Dozens of [those] bills have been introduced," the majority says. One was "introduced in 2005 and has been reintroduced in every Congress since." And might be reintroduced until the end of time. Because what all these *bills* have in common is that they are not *laws.* The politicians who benefit from partisan gerrymandering are unlikely to change partisan gerrymandering. And because those politicians maintain themselves in office through partisan gerrymandering, the chances for legislative reform are slight.

No worries, the majority says; it has another idea. The majority notes that voters themselves have recently approved ballot initiatives to put power over districting in the hands of independent commissions or other non-partisan actors. Some Members of the majority, of course, once thought such initiatives unconstitutional. *See Ariz. State Legis.* (Roberts, C.J., dissenting). But put that aside. Fewer than half the States offer voters an opportunity to put initiatives to direct vote; in all the rest (including North Carolina and Maryland), voters are dependent on legislators to make electoral changes (which for all the reasons already given, they are unlikely to do). And even when voters have a mechanism they can work themselves, legislators often fight their efforts tooth and nail. Look at Missouri. There, the majority touts a voter approved proposal to turn districting over to a state demographer. But before the demographer had drawn a single line, Members of the state legislature had introduced a bill to start undoing the change. I'd put better odds on that bill's passage than on all the congressional proposals the majority cites.

The majority's most perplexing "solution" is to look to state courts. "[O]ur conclusion," the majority states, does not "condemn complaints about districting to echo into a void": Just a few years back, "the Supreme Court of Florida struck down that State's congressional districting plan as a violation" of the State Constitution. And indeed, the majority might have added, the Supreme Court of Pennsylvania last year did the same thing. But what do those courts know that this Court does not? If they can develop and apply neutral and manageable standards to identify unconstitutional gerrymanders, why couldn't we?

We could have, and we should have. The gerrymanders here — and they are typical of many — violated the constitutional rights of many hundreds of thousands of American citizens. Those voters (Republicans in the one case, Democrats in the other) did not have an equal opportunity to participate in the political process. Their votes counted for far less than they should have because of their partisan affiliation. When faced with such constitutional wrongs, courts must intervene: "It is emphatically the province and duty of the judicial department to say what the law is." *Marbury v. Madison* (1803). That is what the courts below did. Their decisions are worth a read. They (and others that have recently remedied similar violations) are detailed, thorough, painstaking. They evaluated with immense care the factual evidence and legal arguments the parties presented. They used neutral and manageable and strict standards. They had not a shred of politics about them. Contra the majority, this *was* law.

Of all times to abandon the Court's duty to declare the law, this was not the one. The practices challenged in these cases imperil our system of government. Part of the Court's role in that system is to defend its foundations. None is more important than free and fair elections. With respect but deep sadness, I dissent.

* * *

Now that you have read the cases, it is worth considering whether there should be a political question doctrine. *Baker v. Carr*'s grab bag of political question factors reflects the multiple and not always congruent justifications for the doctrine. As you consider these common justifications, reflect upon the cases you have read. Not every political question case implicates every justification for the doctrine. First, as Alexander Bickel famously argued, the federal courts should not decide cases when a merits determination would lead to a backlash against the court. The court's legitimacy is fragile, Bickel worried, and its role should therefore be limited in controversial constitutional cases. "[I]n a mature democracy," as he put it, "an institution which is electorally irresponsible and has no earth to draw strength from" should be cautious in answering controversial constitutional questions.[46] But others disagree and believe that it is the Court's role to enforce the Constitution; it should not dismiss cases because the decisions might be controversial.

Second, supporters of the political question doctrine argue that the political branches have greater expertise than the judiciary when it comes to political questions, such as those involved in foreign affairs. Others, though, say that the expertise of other branches of government justifies deference on the merits, but not the abdication of the political question doctrine.

Third, some argue that the Court should treat questions as nonjusticiable when its institutional self-interest would call its impartiality into question. The Court, for example, has a stake in the constitutional amendment process because amendments can overturn the Court's constitutional decisions. Others say that this calls for judicial restraint and deference, not dismissing cases.

---

46. ALEXANDER BICKEL, THE LEAST DANGEROUS BRANCH 184 (1962).

Fourth, the Court should not answer a constitutional question when doing so would require judicial micromanagement of the political branches. This remedial concern might arise, for example, when plaintiffs request structural injunctive relief that requires ongoing judicial involvement in the daily operations of executive or legislative officials. But, on the other side, it is argued that courts can and must provide remedies for constitutional violations.

Critics of the political question doctrine have made several arguments. First, some critics have argued that history does not support the modern political question doctrine. Traditionally, they argue, the doctrine was much narrower than it is today and did not apply when a court adjudicated individual constitutional rights. Second, critics argue that the political question doctrine is inconsistent with the separation of powers. Under the constitutional system of government, the courts' role is to enforce the Constitution's restraints upon the political branches, not to defer to the political branches in constitutional enforcement. These critics do not deny that it may be appropriate for the courts to defer to the political branches on particular issues that may arise in litigation. Indeed, traditionally the courts did so, as for instance, when they deferred to the political branches on the recognition of foreign nations and Native nations. But the political question doctrine today is a doctrine of abdication on matters of constitutional interpretation, not a doctrine of deference. Third, critics question whether the federal courts' sociological legitimacy is fragile and argue that abdicating from adjudication of particular constitutional questions *undermines* rather than reinforces the courts' legitimacy.

CHAPTER 4
CONGRESSIONAL CONTROL OF FEDERAL AND STATE ADJUDICATION

The text of Article III grants Congress authority over federal courts in several important respects. The first sentence of Section 1 provides that the Supreme Court is the only constitutionally mandatory federal court. It states that "[t]he judicial power of the United States, *shall be vested* in one Supreme Court, and in such inferior courts *as the Congress may from time to time ordain and establish.*" All other inferior federal courts must therefore be created by congressional legislation, and presumably can be eliminated by Congress as well. Even with respect to the Supreme Court, there is no textual requirement for the number of justices or the number of votes needed to support an outcome.

According to the second paragraph of Section 2, the Supreme Court's constitutionally mandatory "original" jurisdiction extends to "all cases affecting ambassadors, other public ministers and consuls, and those in which a state shall be a party." Its appellate jurisdiction, however, is limited by "*such exceptions, and under such regulations as the Congress shall make.*" Although this clause might be read to give Congress authority over only the outer limits of the Supreme Court's appellate jurisdiction—to make "exceptions" and "regulations"—the Court has treated congressional power over its appellate jurisdiction as plenary. As we will see in Section A of this Chapter, the power to *create* the lower federal courts has also long been considered to include plenary congressional authority over the jurisdiction, remedies, and rules of practice and procedure of the lower federal courts. Access to the Article III courts is therefore politically contingent, dependent in important respects upon the will of Congress. This is true despite the mandatory language of Article III, Section 2 stating that federal judicial power "*shall extend* to *all cases*, in law and equity, arising under" federal law, and "*all cases* of admiralty and maritime jurisdiction."

The combined power of Congress over the appellate jurisdiction of the Supreme Court and the existence and jurisdiction of the lower federal courts raises profound questions. These include whether Congress can, consistent with the Supremacy Clause, eliminate both appellate jurisdiction of the Supreme Court and the jurisdiction of the lower federal courts as to certain classes of cases, and whether the power over jurisdiction includes power to create rules of decision that dictate the results of federal adjudication and/or alter final judgments. We will also encounter potential constitutional limits on congressional power over the Article III courts, such as the Suspension Clause, due process, executive power, and equal protection.

The question of how far Congress may legally go in restricting access to Article III tribunals is one that is often associated with the origins of the field we now call federal courts. Its complexities were famously explored in the 1950s by one of the founders of the field, Henry M. Hart, in *The Power of Congress to Limit the Jurisdiction of Federal Courts: An Exercise in Dialectic*, 66 HARV. L. REV. 1362 (1953). Over the ensuing generations, the question has not faded from importance, as members of Congress have sometimes proposed restrictions on federal courts' ability to hear cases on issues that include racial segregation, religious liberty, abortion, gay rights, and property rights.[1] While these efforts have generally failed, some legislative restrictions have been successfully enacted. These include restrictions on the writ of habeas corpus for individuals detained by the military, people incarcerated in state prisons, and immigrants. Congress has also successfully enacted sweeping limitations on the power of federal courts to address unconstitutional prison conditions. If you find that some of the issues associated with jurisdiction defy conclusive answers, this is also, Justice Breyer has noted, "the most fascinating and difficult question in . . . the course federal courts."[2]

In Section B of this Chapter, we ask when and under what circumstances Congress might use its Article I legislative power to make an end-run around Article III courts by creating forums for adjudication of federal rights without meeting the requirements of the tenure of office clause of Article III, Section 1. That clause requires that justices of the Supreme Court and judges of inferior federal courts "shall hold their offices during good behavior, and shall, at stated times, receive for their services, a compensation, which shall not be diminished during their continuance in office." Full Article III judges cannot be removed except by impeachment, nor can their salary be diminished just because the political branches are displeased with a decision or decisions. The purpose of the clause is to support the exercise of independent judgment by Article III judges in the cases and controversies they decide.

The Court has struggled to elaborate coherent doctrine in this area. On the one hand, since the founding of the republic it has never been true that adjudication of federal rights occurs exclusively in Article III courts—agencies, military courts, territorial courts, immigration proceedings, etc., have regularly decided cases within their purview and the judges who sit on these courts do not enjoy the protections of the tenure of office clause. Immigration judges, for example, are appointed by and serve under the supervision of the Attorney General. That means these judges can be fired for failing to meet performance standards set in accordance with executive branch immigration enforcement priorities, such as the number of cases they decide per year.[3] There are over a million immigration cases

---

1. *See generally* Tara Leigh Grove, *The Structural Safeguards of Federal Jurisdiction*, 124 HARV. L. REV. 869, 914 (2011) (describing many of these attempts, and offering an explanatory account of why they failed).

2. Transcript of Oral Argument, 16-498 Patchak v. Zinke, 53:12, Nov. 7, 2017.

3. *See* Liz Robbins, *In Immigration Court It Is Judges vs. Justice Department*, N.Y. TIMES, Sept. 7, 2018 (describing new quota of 700 cases per year and risk of negative performance reviews if 15 percent of their decisions are overturned on appeal).

pending every year, so handing these cases over to federal district court judges would swamp their dockets. Or consider the bankruptcy courts, which handle well over two times the total number of civil filings in the U.S. District Courts every year. As these examples suggest, the work of the federal government would grind to a halt if every federal question had to be submitted in the first instance to an Article III judge. On the other hand, there are circumstances in which it would be unconstitutional to leave the interpretation and enforcement of federal law entirely to adjudicators who lack the guarantees of independent judgment Article III provides. In Sections B and D, we explore this tension and the Court's effort to mediate it through a system in which Article III courts exercise a form of appellate supervision over non–Article III courts.

Lastly, recall that state courts regularly decide federal questions in the exercise of concurrent jurisdiction. Indeed, during the drafting of the Constitution there was debate over whether already existing state courts should continue to handle adjudication of most federal rights or whether national courts were necessary—and if necessary, whether their existence and jurisdiction should be mandated by the Constitution or left to the political branches to define. Madison suggested the balance described above: constitutionally mandating the existence of the Supreme Court but leaving the creation and jurisdiction of inferior courts politically contingent on the will of Congress. This is the "Madisonian Compromise." However compelling you find the conventional account emphasizing the Madisonian Compromise, alternative readings of Article III are available and were forcefully advocated by prominent early American jurists. Justice Story famously argued that the "shall be vested" language of Article III, Section 1, meant that Congress was constitutionally obliged to "vest the *whole judicial power*" in the Supreme Court and in such inferior federal courts as would be needed to ensure full vesting of jurisdiction in federal fora. *Martin v. Hunter's Lessee* (1816). Justice Story emphasized that "[i]f Congress may lawfully omit to establish inferior Courts, it might follow that, in some of the enumerated cases, the judicial power could nowhere exist." This would violate Article III and jeopardize federal rights.

Notice, in view of this, the importance to the Madisonian Compromise of the background assumption that state courts are open, reliable, and faithful adjudicators of federal rights. For proponents of expansive congressional authority over federal courts, the political contingency of these courts is not a concern because state courts can be trusted to faithfully exercise concurrent jurisdiction. No federal right holder will ultimately be deprived of a judicial forum even if Congress limits (or even eliminates) federal courts as long as Congress does not simultaneously eliminate concurrent jurisdiction of the state courts, the state courts treat federal right-holders fairly, and the Supreme Court has the capacity and commitment to supervise state courts' adjudication of federal rights.

Slavery, nullification, secession, resistance to Reconstruction, assertions of tribal sovereignty, efforts to limit reproductive rights, and the labor movement have all repeatedly tested these premises, drawing into vivid and sometimes tragic relief the resistance of state courts to federal constitutional rights and national sovereignty. The fidelity, *vel non*, of the state courts to federal rights and federal right holders thus permeates the caselaw covered in this chapter. In Section C, we take the issue up directly, examining the concurrent jurisdiction of state courts over federal questions. The Supreme Court has enforced a strong presumption that when Congress creates federal rights of action, state courts shall have concurrent jurisdiction over those claims if the plaintiff files in state court. (As you may recall from civil procedure, there are very few areas of *exclusive* federal jurisdiction and Congress must be explicit when it wants adjudication of a federal question to occur exclusively in the federal courts. Concurrent jurisdiction is the norm.)

Under what circumstances might a state court refuse to hear a case in an area where Congress has provided for concurrent jurisdiction? When might a state close its courts to a class or classes of federal questions without running afoul of the Supremacy Clause? Consider, for instance, a state that feels its courts are deluged with federal civil rights prison conditions claims by state prisoners. Could the state legislature impose unique barriers to filing such cases in state courts as long as the federal courts are open to such plaintiffs? The Court has consistently held, as we will see, that state courts are obliged to entertain federal questions as long as the federal claim is comparable to state law claims which the state court is jurisdictionally competent to decide.

Taking the three sections together, this Chapter concerns the relationship between federal rights and the forum in which an alleged violation of those rights is redressed: Article III courts, agencies and legislative courts, the state courts, tribal courts, territorial courts, and/or the political process. As a general matter, when Congress creates new rights it makes sense that it should be able to decide what kind of enforcement regime should be used to secure those rights. Weighing against this is Chief Justice Marshall's admonition in *Marbury*, relying on Blackstone, that

> "where there is a legal right, there is also a legal remedy by suit or action at law whenever that right is invaded." . . . The Government of the United States has been emphatically termed a government of laws, and not of men. It will certainly cease to deserve this high appellation if the laws furnish no remedy for the violation of a vested legal right.

Marbury v. Madison (1803) (quoting Blackstone). Some federal rights are of constitutional provenance, not mere creatures of congressional legislation. Among the most important are those whose function it is to protect minorities from the excesses of the political branches of the federal government and the states. A central question in this Chapter is therefore whether there are certain rights for which an Article III court, with the guarantees of the Tenure of Office Clause, *must* provide the remedy.

A.   CONGRESSIONAL CONTROL OF FEDERAL COURT JURISDICTION

1.   Lower Federal Court Jurisdiction

a.   Congressional Restriction on the Jurisdiction of Lower Federal Courts and Statutory Limitations on Federal Remedies

We begin with the power of Congress over the jurisdiction of the lower federal courts. Article III leaves the existence of the lower federal courts to Congress. The Court has long interpreted the power to create lower federal courts to include the power to control their jurisdiction, remedies, and rules of procedure and practice. Among the clearest and most forceful statements of this principle is the one given in the following case.

Sheldon v. Sill

49 U.S. 441 (1850)

Mr. Justice GRIER delivered the opinion of the court.

The only question which it will be necessary to notice in this case is, whether the Circuit Court had jurisdiction.

Sill, the complainant below, a citizen of New York, filed his bill in the Circuit Court of the United States for Michigan, against Sheldon, claiming to recover the amount of a bond and mortgage, which had been assigned to [Sill] by Hastings, the President of the Bank of Michigan.

[Sheldon's answer pled that there is no diversity jurisdiction because Hastings and Sheldon are both citizens of Michigan and Congress provided in Section 11 of the Judiciary Act that an assignment of a debt cannot create diversity. Sill argued that Section 11 conflicted with Article III, Section 2, which contains no limits on diversity jurisdiction tied to assignments of debts.]

It must be admitted, that if the Constitution had ordained and established the inferior courts, and distributed to them their respective powers, they could not be restricted or divested by Congress. But as it has made no such distribution, one of two consequences must result, — either that each inferior court created by Congress must exercise all the judicial powers not given to the Supreme Court, or that Congress, having the power to establish the courts, must define their respective jurisdictions. The first of these inferences has never been asserted, and could not be defended with any show of reason, and if not, the latter would seem to follow as a necessary consequence. And it would seem to follow, also, that, having a right to prescribe, Congress may withhold from any court of its creation jurisdiction of any of the enumerated controversies. Courts created by statute can have no jurisdiction but such as the statute confers. No one of them can assert a just claim to jurisdiction exclusively conferred on another, or withheld from all.

The Constitution has defined the limits of the judicial power of the United States, but has not prescribed how much of it shall be exercised by the Circuit Court; consequently, the statute which does prescribe the limits of their jurisdiction, cannot be in conflict with the Constitution, unless it confers powers not enumerated therein.

Such has been the doctrine held by this court since its first establishment. To enumerate all the cases in which it has been either directly advanced or tacitly assumed would be tedious and unnecessary.

In the case of *Turner v. Bank of North America* (1799), the Court said, — "The political truth is, that the disposal of the judicial power (except in a few specified instances) belongs to Congress; and Congress is not bound to enlarge the jurisdiction of the Federal courts to every subject, in every form which the Constitution might warrant."

[I]t is now here ordered and decreed by this court, that this cause be . . . reversed, for the want of jurisdiction in that court, and that this cause be . . . remanded to the said Circuit Court, with directions to dismiss the bill of complaint for the want of jurisdiction.

* * *

If *Sheldon* stands for the principle that the authority of Congress over the *jurisdiction* of the lower federal courts is *plenary*, is it relevant that the state courts remain open to entertain the litigation? Can Congress can deny a judicial forum to a federal right holder altogether? Can it do so even if the right is constitutional rather than merely statutory? The Court confronted these questions in the following case involving the discharge of a CIA employee because he was gay. Anti-gay government policies and political rhetoric were pervasive in the late twentieth century. For example, a high-level White House officer in the Reagan Administration claimed that AIDS was "nature's revenge on gay men"; the Department of Defense announced in 1982 that being gay was "incompatible" with military service, leading to the discharge of 17,000 gay soldiers in the 1980s;[4] and the Supreme Court upheld state anti-sodomy laws used to criminalize same-sex sexual acts in *Bowers v. Hardwick* (1986) (reversed after the turn of the century in *Lawrence v. Texas* (2003)).[5] The Court took up the CIA employee's discrimination claim against this backdrop.

Webster v. Doe

486 U.S. 592 (1988)

Chief Justice Rehnquist delivered the opinion of the Court.
Section 102(c) of the National Security Act of 1947 provides that:

[T]he Director of Central Intelligence may, in his discretion, terminate the employment of any officer or employee of the Agency whenever he shall deem such termination necessary or advisable in the interests of the United States. . . .

50 U.S.C. §403(c). In this case we decide whether, and to what extent, the termination decisions of the Director under §102(c) are judicially reviewable.

I

Respondent John Doe was first employed by the Central Intelligence Agency (CIA or Agency) in 1973 as a clerk typist. He received periodic fitness reports that

---

4. History of the Anti-Gay Movement since 1977, S. Poverty L. Ctr.: Intel. Rep. (Apr. 28, 2005), https://www.splcenter.org/fighting-hate/intelligence-report/2005/history-anti-gay-movement-1977.

5. *See* Janet E. Halley, *Reasoning About Sodomy: Act and Identity In and After* Bowers v. Hardwick, 79 Va. L. Rev. 1721 (1993) (characterizing the definitional "instability" of sodomy in *Hardwick* as "crucial to the subordination of homosexuality and the superordination of heterosexual identity").

consistently rated him as an excellent or outstanding employee. By 1977, respondent had been promoted to a position as a covert electronics technician.

In January, 1982, respondent voluntarily informed a CIA security officer that he was a homosexual. Almost immediately, the Agency placed respondent on paid administrative leave pending an investigation of his sexual orientation and conduct. On February 12 and again on February 17, respondent was extensively questioned by a polygraph officer concerning his homosexuality and possible security violations. Respondent denied having sexual relations with any foreign nationals, and maintained that he had not disclosed classified information to any of his sexual partners. After these interviews, the officer told respondent that the polygraph tests indicated that he had truthfully answered all questions.

On April 14, 1982, a CIA security agent informed respondent that the Agency's Office of Security had determined that respondent's homosexuality posed a threat to security, but declined to explain the nature of the danger. Respondent was then asked to resign. When he refused to do so, the Office of Security recommended to the CIA Director (petitioner's predecessor) that respondent be dismissed. After reviewing respondent's records and the evaluations of his subordinates, the Director

> deemed it necessary and advisable in the interests of the United States to terminate [respondent's] employment with this Agency pursuant to section 102(c) of the National Security Act. . . . Respondent was also advised that, while the CIA would give him a positive recommendation in any future job search, if he applied for a job requiring a security clearance, the Agency would inform the prospective employer that it had concluded that respondent's homosexuality presented a security threat.

Respondent then filed an action against petitioner in the United States District Court for the District of Columbia.

Respondent's amended complaint asserted a variety of statutory and constitutional claims against the Director. Respondent alleged that the Director's decision to terminate his employment violated the Administrative Procedure Act (APA), 5 U.S.C. §706, because it was arbitrary and capricious, represented an abuse of discretion, and was reached without observing the procedures required by law and CIA regulations.[3] He also complained that the Director's termination of his employment deprived him of constitutionally protected rights to property, liberty, and privacy in violation of the First, Fourth, Fifth, and Ninth Amendments. Finally,

---

3. Title 5 U.S.C. §706 provides in pertinent part:

Scope of review

To the extent necessary to decision and when presented, the reviewing court shall decide all relevant questions of law, interpret constitutional and statutory provisions, and determine the meaning or applicability of the terms of an agency action. The reviewing court shall—

(1) compel agency action unlawfully withheld or unreasonably delayed; and
(2) hold unlawful and set aside agency action, findings, and conclusions found to be—
    (A) arbitrary, capricious, an abuse of discretion, or otherwise not in accordance with law;
    (B) contrary to constitutional right, power, privilege, or immunity;
    (C) in excess of statutory jurisdiction, authority, or limitations, or short of statutory right;
    (D) without observance of procedure required by law.

he asserted that his dismissal transgressed the procedural due process and equal protection of the laws guaranteed by the Fifth Amendment. Respondent requested a declaratory judgment that the Director had violated the APA and the Constitution, and asked the District Court for an injunction ordering petitioner to reinstate him to the position he held with the CIA prior to his dismissal. As an alternative remedy, he suggested that he be returned to paid administrative leave and that petitioner be ordered to reevaluate respondent's employment termination and provide a statement of the reasons for any adverse final determination. Respondent sought no monetary damages in his amended complaint.

Petitioner moved to dismiss respondent's amended complaint on the ground that §102(c) of the National Security Act (NSA) precludes judicial review of the Director's termination decisions under the provisions of the APA set forth in 5 U.S.C. §§701, 702, and 706.

> Section 702 provides judicial review to any:

> person suffering legal wrong because of agency action, or adversely affected or aggrieved by agency action within the meaning of a relevant statute.

The section further instructs that:

> [a]n action in a court of the United States seeking relief other than money damages and stating a claim that an agency or an officer or employee thereof acted or failed to act in an official capacity or under color of legal authority shall not be dismissed nor relief therein be denied on the ground that it is against the United States or that the United States is an indispensable party.

The scope of judicial review under §702, however, is circumscribed by §706, and its availability at all is predicated on satisfying the requirements of §701, which provide:

> (a) This chapter applies, according to the provisions thereof, except to the extent that—
> > (1) statutes preclude judicial review; or
> > (2) agency action is committed to agency discretion by law.

The District Court denied petitioner's motion to dismiss, and granted respondent's motion for partial summary judgment. The court determined that the APA provided judicial review of petitioner's termination decisions made under §102(c) of the NSA, and found that respondent had been unlawfully discharged because the CIA had not followed the procedures described in its own regulations. The District Court declined, however, to address respondent's constitutional claims.

A divided panel of the Court of Appeals for the District of Columbia Circuit vacated the District Court's judgment [holding] that, while an agency must normally follow its own regulations . . . with respect to terminations pursuant to §102(c), the Director need not follow standard discharge procedures, but may direct that an employee "be separated immediately and without regard to any suggested procedural steps." . . . We granted certiorari to decide the question whether the Director's decision to discharge a CIA employee under §102(c) of the NSA is judicially reviewable under the APA.

II

Passed shortly after the close of the Second World War, the NSA created the CIA and gave its Director the responsibility "for protecting intelligence sources and methods from unauthorized disclosure." *See* 50 U.S.C. §403(d)(3). Section 102(c) is an integral part of that statute, because the Agency's efficacy, and the Nation's security, depend in large measure on the reliability and trustworthiness of the Agency's employees. As we recognized in *Snepp v. United States* (1980), employment with the CIA entails a high degree of trust that is perhaps unmatched in Government service.

This overriding need for ensuring integrity in the Agency led us to uphold the Director's use of §102(d)(3) of the NSA to withhold the identities of protected intelligence sources in *CIA v. Sims* (1985). . . . Section 102(c), that portion of the NSA under consideration in the present case, is part and parcel of the entire Act, and likewise exhibits the Act's extraordinary deference to the Director in his decision to terminate individual employees.

We thus find that the language and structure of §102(c) indicate that Congress meant to commit individual employee discharges to the Director's discretion, and that §701(a)(2) accordingly precludes judicial review of these decisions under the APA. We reverse the Court of Appeals to the extent that it found such terminations reviewable by the courts.

III

Petitioner maintains that, no matter what the nature of respondent's constitutional claim, judicial review is precluded by the language and intent of §102(c). In petitioner's view, all Agency employment termination decisions, even those based on policies normally repugnant to the Constitution, are given over to the absolute discretion of the Director, and are hence unreviewable under the APA. We do not think §102(c) may be read to exclude review of constitutional claims. We emphasized in *Johnson v. Robison* (1974), that, where Congress intends to preclude judicial review of constitutional claims, its intent to do so must be clear. In *Weinberger v. Salfi* (1975), we reaffirmed that view. We require this heightened showing in part to avoid the "serious constitutional question" that would arise if a federal statute were construed to deny any judicial forum for a colorable constitutional claim. *See Bowen v. Mich. Acad. of Phys.* (1986).

Our review of §102(c) convinces us that it cannot bear the preclusive weight petitioner would have it support. . . . Subsections (a)(1) and (a)(2) of §701 . . . remove from judicial review only those determinations specifically identified by Congress or "committed to agency discretion by law." Nothing in §102(c) persuades us that Congress meant to preclude consideration of colorable constitutional claims arising out of the actions of the Director pursuant to that section; we believe that a constitutional claim based on an individual discharge may be reviewed by the District Court.[8] We agree with the Court of Appeals that there must be further proceedings in the District Court on this issue.

---

8. Petitioner asserts that respondent fails to present a colorable constitutional claim when he asserts that there is a general CIA policy against employing homosexuals. Petitioner relies on our decision in *Bowers v. Hardwick* (1986), to support this view. This question was not presented in the petition for certiorari, and we decline to consider it at this stage of the litigation.

Petitioner complains that judicial review even of constitutional claims will entail extensive "rummaging around" in the Agency's affairs to the detriment of national security. But petitioner acknowledges that Title VII claims attacking the hiring and promotion policies of the Agency are routinely entertained in federal court, and the inquiry and discovery associated with those proceedings would seem to involve some of the same sort of rummaging. Furthermore, the District Court has the latitude to control any discovery process which may be instituted so as to balance respondent's need for access to proof which would support a colorable constitutional claim against the extraordinary needs of the CIA for confidentiality and the protection of its methods, sources, and mission.

Petitioner also contends that, even if respondent has raised a colorable constitutional claim arising out of his discharge, Congress in the interest of national security may deny the courts the authority to decide the claim, and to order respondent's reinstatement if the claim is upheld. For the reasons previously stated, we do not think Congress meant to impose such restrictions when it enacted §102(c) of the NSA. Even without such prohibitory legislation from Congress, of course, traditional equitable principles requiring the balancing of public and private interests control the grant of declaratory or injunctive relief in the federal courts. On remand, the District Court should thus address respondent's constitutional claims and the propriety of the equitable remedies sought.

The judgment of the Court of Appeals is affirmed in part, reversed in part, and the case is remanded for further proceedings consistent with this opinion.

Justice KENNEDY took no part in the consideration or decision of this case.

[Justice O'CONNOR concurred in the conclusion that termination decisions are committed to agency discretion and therefore unreviewable. She dissented from the Court's conclusion that the district court had jurisdiction to consider constitutional claims. "Whatever may be the exact scope of Congress' power to close the lower federal courts to constitutional claims in other contexts, I have no doubt about its authority to do so here. The functions performed by the Central Intelligence Agency . . . lie at the core of the very delicate, plenary and exclusive power of the President as the sole organ of the federal government in the field of international relations. . . . Congress may surely provide that the inferior federal courts are not used to infringe on the President's constitutional authority. Section 102(c) plainly indicates that Congress has done exactly that. . . ."]

Justice SCALIA, dissenting.

II

Before taking the reader through the terrain of the Court's holding that respondent may assert constitutional claims in this suit, I would like to try to clear some of the underbrush, consisting primarily of the Court's ominous warning that

> [a] "serious constitutional question" . . . would arise if a federal statute were construed to deny any judicial forum for a colorable constitutional claim.

The first response to the Court's grave doubt about the constitutionality of denying all judicial review to a "colorable constitutional claim" is that the denial of all judicial review is not at issue here, but merely the denial of review in United States district courts. As to that, the law is, and has long been, clear. Article III, §2, of the Constitution extends the judicial power to "all Cases . . . arising under this Constitution." But Article III, §1, provides that the judicial power shall be vested "in one supreme Court, *and in such inferior Courts as the Congress may from time to time ordain and establish.*" We long ago held that the power not to create any lower federal courts at all includes the power to invest them with less than all of the judicial power. *Sheldon v. Sill* (1850). Thus, if there is any truth to the proposition that judicial cognizance of constitutional claims cannot be eliminated, it is, at most, that they cannot be eliminated from state courts, and from this Court's appellate jurisdiction over cases from state courts (or eases from federal courts, should there be any) involving such claims. Narrowly viewed, therefore, there is no shadow of a constitutional doubt that we are free to hold that the present suit, whether based on constitutional grounds or not, will not lie.

It can fairly be argued, however, that our interpretation of §701(a)(2) indirectly implicates the constitutional question whether state courts can be deprived of jurisdiction, because if they cannot, then interpreting §701(a)(2) to exclude relief here would impute to Congress the peculiar intent to let state courts review Federal Government action that it is unwilling to let federal district courts review—or, alternatively, the peculiar intent to let federal district courts review, upon removal from state courts pursuant to 28 U.S.C. §1442(a)(1), claims that it is unwilling to let federal district courts review in original actions. I turn, then, to the substance of the Court's warning that judicial review of all "colorable constitutional claims" arising out of the respondent's dismissal may well be constitutionally required. What could possibly be the basis for this fear? Surely not some general principle that all constitutional violations must be remediable in the courts. The very text of the Constitution refutes that principle, since it provides that "[e]ach House shall be the Judge of the Elections, Returns and Qualifications of its own Members," Art. I, §5, and that "for any Speech or Debate in either House, [the Senators and Representatives] shall not be questioned in any other Place," Art. I, §6. Claims concerning constitutional violations committed in these contexts—for example, the rather grave constitutional claim that an election has been stolen—cannot be addressed to the courts. Even apart from the strict text of the Constitution, we have found some constitutional claims to be beyond judicial review because they involve "political questions." The doctrine of sovereign immunity—not repealed by the Constitution, but to the contrary at least partly reaffirmed as to the States by the Eleventh Amendment—is a monument to the principle that some constitutional claims can go unheard. No one would suggest that, if Congress had not passed the Tucker Act, 28 U.S.C. §1491(a)(1), the courts would be able to order disbursements from the Treasury to pay for property taken under lawful authority (and subsequently destroyed) without just compensation. And finally, the doctrine of equitable discretion, which permits a court to refuse relief, even where no relief at law is available, when that would unduly impair the public interest, does not stand aside simply because the basis for the relief is a constitutional claim. In sum, it is simply untenable that there must be a judicial remedy for every constitutional violation.

Members of Congress and the supervising officers of the Executive Branch take the same oath to uphold the Constitution that we do, and sometimes they are left to perform that oath unreviewed, as we always are.

Perhaps, then, the Court means to appeal to a more limited principle that, although there may be areas where judicial review of a constitutional claim will be denied, the scope of those areas is fixed by the Constitution and judicial tradition, and cannot be affected by *Congress* through the enactment of a statute such as §102(c). That would be a rather counterintuitive principle, especially since Congress has in reality been the principal determiner of the scope of review, for constitutional claims as well as all other claims, through its waiver of the preexisting doctrine of sovereign immunity. On the merits of the point, however: It seems to me clear that courts would not entertain, for example, an action for backpay by a dismissed Secretary of State claiming that the reason he lost his Government job was that the President did not like his religious views—surely a colorable violation of the First Amendment. I am confident we would hold that the President's choice of his Secretary of State is a "political question." But what about a similar suit by the Deputy Secretary of State? Or one of the Under Secretaries? Or an Assistant Secretary? Or the head of the European Desk? Is there really a constitutional line that falls at some immutable point between one and another of these offices at which the principle of unreviewability cuts in, and which cannot be altered by congressional prescription? I think not. I think Congress can prescribe, at least within broad limits, that, for certain jobs, the dismissal decision will be unreviewable—that is, will be "committed to agency discretion by law."

Once it is acknowledged, as I think it must be, (1) that not all constitutional claims require a judicial remedy, and (2) that the identification of those that do not can, even if only within narrow limits, be determined by Congress, then it is clear that the "serious constitutional question" feared by the Court is an illusion. Indeed, it seems to me that, if one is in a mood to worry about serious constitutional questions, the one to worry about is not whether Congress can, by enacting §102(c), give the President, through his Director of Central Intelligence, unreviewable discretion in firing the agents that he employs to gather military and foreign affairs intelligence, but rather whether Congress could constitutionally permit the courts to review all such decisions if it wanted to. . . . We have . . . recognized that the "authority to classify and control access to information bearing on national security and to determine whether an individual is sufficiently trustworthy to occupy a position in the Executive Branch that will give that person access to such information flows primarily from [a] constitutional investment of power in the President [over national security], *and exists quite apart from any explicit congressional grant." Department of Navy v. Egan* (1988).

I think it entirely beyond doubt that, if Congress intended, by the APA in 5 U.S.C. §701(a)(2), to exclude judicial review of the President's decision (through the Director of Central Intelligence) to dismiss an officer of the Central Intelligence Agency, that disposition would be constitutionally permissible.

III

I turn, then, to whether that executive action is, within the meaning of §701(a)(2), "committed to agency discretion by law." . . . Given this statutory text, and given (as discussed above) that the area to which the text pertains is one of predominant executive authority and of traditional judicial abstention, it is difficult to conceive of a statutory scheme that more clearly reflects that "commit[ment] to agency discretion by law" to which §701(a)(2) refers.

If the §102(c) assessment is really "the Director's alone," the only conceivable basis for review of respondent's dismissal (which is what this case is about) would be that the dismissal was not *really* the result of a §102(c) assessment by the Director. But respondent has never contended that, nor could he. . . . Even if the basis for the Director's assessment was the respondent's homosexuality, and even if the connection between that and the interests of the United States is an irrational, and hence an unconstitutional one, if that assessment is really "the Director's alone," there is nothing more to litigate about.

Perhaps, then, [in the eyes of the majority] a constitutional right is by its nature so much more important to the claimant than a statutory right that a statute which plainly excludes the latter should not be read to exclude the former unless it says so. That principle has never been announced — and with good reason, because its premise is not true. An individual's contention that the government has reneged upon a $100,000 debt owing under a contract is much more important to him — both financially and, I suspect, in the sense of injustice that he feels — than the same individual's claim that a particular federal licensing provision requiring a $100 license denies him equal protection of the laws, or that a particular state tax violates the Commerce Clause. A citizen would much rather have his statutory entitlement correctly acknowledged after a constitutionally inadequate hearing than have it incorrectly denied after a proceeding that fulfills all the requirements of the Due Process Clause. The *only* respect in which a constitutional claim is necessarily more significant than any other kind of claim is that, regardless of how trivial its real-life importance may be in the case at hand, it can be asserted against the action of the legislature itself, whereas a nonconstitutional claim (no matter how significant) cannot. That is an important distinction, and one relevant to the constitutional analysis that I conducted above. But it has no relevance to the question whether, as between executive violations of statute and executive violations of the Constitution — both of which are equally unlawful, and neither of which can be said, *a priori*, to be more harmful or more unfair to the plaintiff — one or the other category should be favored by a presumption against exclusion of judicial review.

Even if we were to assume, however, contrary to all reason, that every constitutional claim is *ipso facto* more worthy, and every statutory claim less worthy, of judicial review, there would be no basis for writing that preference into a statute that makes no distinction between the two. . . . Neither of the two decisions cited by the Court to sustain its power to read in a limitation for constitutional claims remotely supports that proposition. In *Johnson v. Robison* (1974), we considered a statute precluding judicial review of "the decisions of the Administrator on any question of law or fact under any law administered by the Veterans' Administration." We concluded that this statute did not bar judicial review of a challenge to the constitutionality of the statute itself, since that was a challenge not to a decision of the Administrator, but to a decision of Congress. Our holding was based upon the text, and not upon some judicial power to read in a "constitutional claims" exception. And in *Weinberger v. Salfi* (1975), we held that 42 U.S.C. §405(h), a statute depriving district courts of federal question jurisdiction over "any claim arising under" Title II of the

Social Security Act, did embrace even constitutional challenges, since its language was "quite different" from that at issue in *Johnson*, and "extend[ed] to any 'action' seeking 'to recover on any [Social Security] claim'—irrespective of whether resort to judicial processes is necessitated by . . . allegedly unconstitutional statutory restrictions." *Salfi*. In *Salfi*, to be sure, another statutory provision was available that would enable judicial review of the constitutional claim, but . . . that distinction does not justify drawing a line that has no basis in the statute.

The Court seeks to downplay the harm produced by today's decision by observing that

> petitioner acknowledges that Title VII claims attacking the hiring and promotion policies of the Agency are routinely entertained in federal court.

Assuming that those suits are statutorily authorized . . . it is obvious that, if the Director thinks that a particular hiring or promotion suit is genuinely contrary to the interests of the United States, he can simply make the hiring or grant the promotion, and then dismiss the prospective litigant under §102(c).

The harm done by today's decision is that, contrary to what Congress knows is preferable, it brings a significant decisionmaking process of our intelligence services into a forum where it does not belong. Neither the Constitution, nor our laws, nor common sense gives an individual a right to come into court to litigate the reasons for his dismissal as an intelligence agent. It is of course not just *valid* constitutional claims that today's decision makes the basis for judicial review of the Director's action, but all *colorable* constitutional claims, whether meritorious or not. And in determining whether what is colorable is in fact meritorious, a court will necessarily have to review the entire decision. . . . I would, in any event, not like to be the agent who has to explain to the intelligence services of other nations, with which we sometimes cooperate, that they need have no worry that the secret information they give us will be subjected to the notoriously broad discovery powers of our courts, because, although we have to litigate the dismissal of our spies, we have available a protection of somewhat uncertain scope known as executive privilege, which the President can invoke if he is willing to take the political damage that it often entails.

If constitutional claims can be raised in this highly sensitive context, it is hard to imagine where they cannot. The assumption that there are any executive decisions that cannot be hauled into the courts may no longer be valid.

I respectfully dissent.

* * *

The majority in *Webster* relies on three earlier cases for the proposition that, absent a clear statement, jurisdiction stripping legislation will not be read to foreclose judicial review of a constitutional claim: *Johnson v. Robison* (1974), *Weinberger v. Salfi* (1975), and *Bowen v. Academy of Family Physicians* (1986).

In *Johnson*, veterans' educational benefits were denied to a conscientious objector who performed required alternative civilian service in a hospital during the Vietnam War. He brought a class action for a declaratory judgment that denial of veterans' benefits to the class violated the First Amendment guarantee of free exercise of religion and the equal protection clause (as incorporated against the federal government by the Fifth Amendment). Under 38 U.S.C. §211(a), decisions of the Veterans' Administrator "on any question of fact or law under any law administered by the Veterans' Administration providing benefits for veterans and their dependents or survivors shall be final and conclusive and no other official or any court of the United States shall have power or jurisdiction to review any such decision by an action in the nature of mandamus or otherwise." As the legislative history showed, the restriction was imposed by Congress because federal court litigation would be time consuming, costly, and

> "medical, legal, and other technical questions constantly arise . . . which are not readily susceptible of judicial standardization. Among other questions to be determined in the adjudication of such claims are those involving the length and character of service, origin of disabilities, complex rating schedules, and the application of established norms to the peculiarities of the particular case. These matters have . . . been regarded as apt subjects for the purely administrative procedure. Due to the nature and complexity of the determinations to be made, it is inevitable that the decisions of the courts in such matters would lack uniformity."

But "nothing whatever" in the legislative record, the Court reasoned, "suggests any congressional intent to preclude judicial cognizance of constitutional challenges to veterans' benefits legislation. Such challenges obviously do not contravene the purposes of the no-review clause, for they cannot be expected to burden the courts by their volume, nor do they involve technical considerations of Veterans' Administration policy." A limit on access to judicial review of a constitutional question would require "clear and convincing evidence of congressional intent." *Id.* (denying constitutional claims on the merits).

In *Salfi*, social security survivors' benefits were denied to a widow and her daughter on the ground that the statutory definitions of an eligible "widow" and "child" exclude surviving wives and stepchildren if the wage earner dies less than nine months after the marriage. Congress' purpose was to prevent the use of "sham marriages to secure Social Security payments." Salfi sued on behalf of a class of similarly situated survivors seeking declaratory, injunctive relief, and damages in the amount of past due benefits. Under 42 U.S.C. §405(h) there is no §1331 arising under jurisdiction in federal court "against the United States, the Secretary [of Health and Human Services], or any officer or employee thereof . . . to recover on any claim arising under [Title II of the Social Security Act]" which includes the provisions of the Social Security Act covering survivors' benefits.

The Court began by noting that, unlike the statute in *Johnson*, which could not be read to apply to constitutional claims, the statute here is more sweeping, extending "to any 'action' . . . irrespective of whether resort to judicial process is necessitated by discretionary decisions of the Secretary or by his non-discretionary application of allegedly unconstitutional statutory restrictions." On the other hand, the Court emphasized, at least with respect to "final" decisions of the Secretary, the statute expressly provides an alternative pathway for judicial review. The restrictions on judicial review in §405(h) therefore "do not preclude constitutional challenges. They simply require that they be brought under jurisdictional grants contained in the Act, and thus in conformity with the same standards which are applicable to nonconstitutional claims," rather than through §1331's broader grant of arising under jurisdiction. The combined practical effect of §405(g) & (h), then, is simply to force full administrative exhaustion, foreclosing judicial review until that has occurred. On the merits, the Court concluded that given the "administrative difficulties of individual eligibility determinations . . . Congress may . . . rely on rules which sweep more broadly than the evils with which they seek to deal. . . . It is an expression of Congress' policy choice that the Social Security system . . . would be best served by a prophylactic rule which . . . is . . . objective and easily administered. The constitution does not preclude such policy choices. . . ."

In *Bowen*, doctors challenged Medicare Part B payments authorized in different amounts for similar services they provided. The Court emphasized that the statute restricted judicial review only as to "amount determinations . . . those 'quite minor matters,' remitted finally and exclusively to adjudication by private insurance carriers in a 'fair hearing.'" Any "matters which Congress did not delegate to private carriers," however, "such as challenges to the validity of the Secretary's instructions and regulations, are cognizable in courts of law." The Court squarely rejected the government's claim that the statute contemplated no judicial review of "substantial statutory and constitutional challenges to the Secretary's administration of part B of the Medicare program" as "extreme"—a position "we would be most reluctant to adopt without a showing of clear and convincing evidence to overcome the strong presumption that Congress did not mean to prohibit all judicial review of executive action. We ordinarily presume that Congress intends the executive to obey its statutory commands and, accordingly, that it expects the courts to grant relief when an executive agency violates such a command." The Court affirmed the appellate court's finding of jurisdiction and remanded for adjudication on the merits.

Sheldon and *Webster* concern the authority of Congress to grant or withhold access to a judicial forum. The next case establishes that congressional authority over the lower federal courts extends beyond subject matter jurisdiction to the *remedies* a lower court can issue. Labor rights were a centerpiece of progressive activism in the late nineteenth and early twentieth centuries. For much of that period both federal and state courts were staffed by judges who had spent their careers in law practice representing large corporations before rising to the bench. During the "*Lochner* Era" as it came to be known, these judges regularly struck down pro-labor legislation designed to protect worker safety, eliminate child labor, set wage and hour standards, etc., in the name of the free contract rights of corporations and individual workers. *See* Morton J. Horowitz, *The Transformation of American Law, 1870-1960: The Crisis of Legal Orthodoxy* (1992). They also regularly issued so-called "anti-strike" injunctions designed to disable strikes before they gained momentum despite the clear First Amendment rights of workers.

In 1932, Congress passed the Norris-LaGuardia Act. Its most significant provisions reversed *Hitchman Coal & Coke Co. v. Mitchell*, which had held that "yellow-dog" contracts (used by employers to secure pledges from employees not to join a union) were enforceable in federal court, and *strictly* limited the authority of federal courts to issue injunctions in labor disputes. The latter provisions essentially stripped the lower federal courts of their equity power in this domain. The New Deal Court's deference to Congress' power to limit lower court remedial power is on full display in *Lauf v. E.G. Skinner & Co.* (1938). Despite clear evidence that an "outside" union sought to pressure an employer to have its employees abandon their own pre-existing organization in favor of the outside union, the Court finds the Norris-LaGuardia Act controlling and concludes that the lower court was without power to grant an injunction.

The case represents a decisive break from *Truax v. Corrigan* (1921), in which the Court had struck down a state anti-injunction statute as fundamentally inconsistent with the employer's Fifth Amendment property rights and the Due Process Clause of the Fourteenth Amendment. The Court in *Truax* had emphasized that depriving a person of all remedies for a violation of constitutional rights is itself unconstitutional. *See id.* ("no one has a vested right in any particular rule of common law, but . . . a purely arbitrary or capricious exercise of [legislative] power whereby a [property] owner [is] stripped of all real remedy is wholly at variance with th[e] principles [of due process of law").

Lauf v. E.G. Shinner & Co.

303 U.S. 323 (1938)

Mr. Justice ROBERTS delivered the opinion of the Court.

This is a suit to restrain the petitioners from picketing the respondent's place of business, from coercing the respondent to discharge any of its employees who do not belong to the petitioning union, or to compel them to become members of the union and to accept it as their bargaining agent and representative, and from advertising that the respondent is unfair to organized labor or molesting customers or prospective customers or persuading them to cease patronizing it. After a hearing, and upon findings of fact and conclusions of law, the District Court granted a preliminary injunction. The Circuit Court of Appeals affirmed.

The District Court found the following facts: the respondent is a Delaware corporation maintaining five meat markets in Milwaukee, Wisconsin. The petitioners are, respectively, an unincorporated labor union and its business manager, citizens and residents of Wisconsin. The respondent's employees number about thirty-five; none of them are members of the petitioning union. The petitioners made demand upon the respondent to require its employees, as a condition of their continued employment, to become members of the union. The respondent notified the employees that they were free to do this, and that it was willing to permit them to join, but they declined, and refused to join. The union had not been chosen by the employees to represent them in any matter connected with the respondent. For the purpose of coercing the respondent to require its employees to join the union and to accept it as their bargaining agent and representative, as a condition of continued employment, and for the purpose of injuring and destroying the business if the respondent refused to yield to such coercion, the petitioners conspired to do the following things, and did them: they caused false and misleading signs to be placed before the respondent's markets; caused persons who were not respondent's employees to parade and picket before the markets; falsely accused respondent of being unfair to organized labor in its dealings with employees, and, by molestation, annoyance, threats, and intimidation, prevented patrons and prospective patrons of respondent from patronizing its markets; respondent suffered and will suffer irreparable injury from the continuance of the practice, and customers will be intimidated and restrained from patronizing the stores as a consequence of petitioners' acts.

The District Court held that no labor dispute, as defined by federal or state law, exists between the respondent and the petitioners, or either of them; that the respondent is bound to permit its employees free agency in the matter of choice of union organization or representation, and that the respondent had no adequate remedy at law. It entered a final decree enjoining the petitioners from seeking to coerce the respondent to discharge any of its employees for refusal to join the union or to coerce the respondent to compel employees to become members of the organization, from advertising that the respondent is unfair to organized labor, and from annoying or molesting patrons or persuading or soliciting customers, present or prospective, not to patronize the respondent's markets.

The institution of the suit in the federal court is justified by the findings as to diversity of citizenship and the amount in controversy. As the acts complained of occurred in Wisconsin, the law of that state governs the substantive rights of the parties. But the power of the court to grant the relief prayed depends upon the jurisdiction conferred upon it by the statutes of the United States.

First. The District Court erred in holding that no labor dispute, as defined by the law of Wisconsin, existed between the parties. . . . The District Court was bound by the construction of the section by the Supreme Court of the state, which has held a controversy indistinguishable from that here disclosed to be a labor dispute within the meaning of the statute.

Second. The District Court erred in not applying the provisions of section 103.5 of the Wisconsin Labor Code, which declares certain conduct lawful in labor disputes; *inter alia*, "giving publicity to . . . the existence of, or the facts involved in, any dispute . . . by . . . patrolling any public street . . . without intimidation or coercion, or by any other method not involving fraud, violence, breach of the peace, or threat thereof;" advising, urging, or inducing, without fraud, violence, or threat thereof, others to cease to patronize any person; peaceful picketing or patrolling, whether singly or in numbers. A Wisconsin court could not enjoin acts declared by the statute to be lawful, and the District Court has no greater power to do so. The error into which the court fell as to the existence of a labor dispute led it into the further error of issuing an order so sweeping as to enjoin acts made lawful by the state statute. The decree forbade all picketing, all advertising that the respondent was unfair to organized labor, and all persuasion and solicitation of customers or prospective customers not to trade with respondent.

Third. The District Court erred in granting an injunction in the absence of findings which the Norris-La Guardia Act makes prerequisites to the exercise of jurisdiction.

Section 13(c) of the act is:

> The term "labor dispute" includes any controversy concerning terms or conditions of employment, or concerning the association or representation of the persons in negotiating, fixing, maintaining, changing, or seeking to arrange terms or conditions of employment, regardless of whether or not the disputants stand in the proximate relation of employer and employee.

This definition does not differ materially from that above quoted from the Wisconsin Labor Code, and the facts of the instant case bring it within both. Section 7 declares that:

> no court of the United States shall have jurisdiction to issue a temporary or permanent injunction in any case involving or growing out of a labor dispute, as herein defined,

except after a hearing of a described character,

> and except after findings of fact by the court, to the effect (a) that unlawful acts have been threatened and will be committed unless restrained or have been committed and will be continued unless restrained,

and that no injunction

> shall be issued on account of any threat or unlawful act excepting against the person or persons, association, or organization making the threat or committing the unlawful act or actually authorizing or ratifying the same.

By subsections (b) to (e), it is provided that relief shall not be granted unless the court finds that substantial and irreparable injury to complainants' property will follow; that, as to each item of relief granted, greater injury will be inflicted upon the complainant by denying the relief than will be inflicted upon defendants by granting it; that complainant has no adequate remedy at law, and that the public officers charged with the duty to protect complainants' property are unable or unwilling to provide adequate protection.

There can be no question of the power of Congress thus to define and limit the jurisdiction of the inferior courts of the United States.[11] The District Court made none of the required findings, save as to irreparable injury and lack of remedy at law. It follows that, in issuing the injunction, it exceeded its jurisdiction.

The judgment is reversed, and the cause remanded to the District Court for further proceedings in conformity with this opinion.

Mr. Justice CARDOZO and Mr. Justice REED took no part in the consideration or decision of this case.

Mr. Justice BUTLER, dissenting.

In every legal sense, the union is a stranger both to respondent and its employees. Shortly before petitioners conspired to destroy respondent's business, one Joyce, of the American Federation of Labor, called by telephone respondent's vice-president, Russell, at his Chicago office. The latter's uncontradicted narration of the conversation follows:

> Mr. Joyce . . . said "We are in Milwaukee and want you fellows to join our Union up there. They tell me up there you are the man I must see, to get a contract signed for Shinner & Company with the Butchers Union up there." I told him I could not sign any contract with him, that our men had their own association and were perfectly well satisfied, and didn't want to belong to any other union. He said "Well, I am going there tonight and if you don't join, I will declare war on you." I said, "There is nothing I can do about it." He said "All right, the war is on, and may the best man win," and he hung up.

---

11. *Kline v. Burke Construction Co.* (1922).

Then followed *a demand by the union that respondent compel its employees, on pain of dismissal from their employment, to join the union and constitute it their bargaining representative and agent.* Respondent rightly declined to undertake any such interference with the liberty of its employees, but informed them that they were free to do as they saw fit. It left them wholly free to join or not to join the union; the union was left free to invite, urge, persuade, or induce them to join.

1. Respondent's business constitutes a property right, and the free opportunity of respondent and its customers to deal with one another in that business is an incident inseparable therefrom. It is hard to imagine a case which more clearly calls for equitable relief, and the court below rightly granted an injunction. *Truax v. Corrigan* (1921), and cases cited.

To say that a "labor dispute" is created by the mere refusal of respondent to comply with the demand that it compel its employees to designate the union as their representative unmistakably subverts this policy, and consequently puts a construction upon the words contrary to the manifest congressional intent.

Moreover, the immediately preceding section of the act, 29 U.S.C. §101, provides that no restraining order or injunction in a case involving or growing out of a labor dispute shall issue "contrary to the public policy declared in this chapter." Sections 101 and 102, taken together, constitute nothing less than an expression of the legislative will that the court shall enforce the public policy set forth in §102 and shall have regard thereto in reaching a determination as to whether it has jurisdiction to issue an injunction in any particular case. Since the whole aim of the injury here inflicted and threatened to be inflicted by the union was to compel respondent to influence and coerce its employees in the designation of their representatives, the acts of the union were in plain defiance of the declared policy of Congress, and find no support in its substantive provisions.

2. But, putting aside the congressional declaration of policy as an indication of meaning and considering the phrase entirely apart, the facts of this case plainly do not constitute a "labor dispute" as defined by the act. Undoubtedly "dispute" is used in its primary sense, as meaning a verbal controversy involving an expression of opposing views or claims. The act itself, 29 U.S.C. §113(c), so regards it: "*The term* labor dispute' includes any controversy concerning terms or conditions of employment," etc. In this case, there was no interchange or consideration of conflicting views in respect of the settlement of a controversial problem. There was simply an overbearing demand by the union that respondent should do an unlawful thing and a natural refusal on its part to comply. If a demand by a labor union that an employer compel its employees to submit to the will of the union, and the employer's refusal, constitute a labor controversy, the highwayman's demand for the money of his victim and the latter's refusal to stand and deliver constitute a financial controversy.

There being an utter lack of connection between the petitioners and respondent or its employees, the union was an intruder into the affairs of the employer and its employees. The union had the right to try to persuade the employees to join its organization, but, persuasive methods failing, its right under the law in any manner to intermeddle came to an end. . . . Clearly the union could not be authorized by statute to resort to coercive measures directly against the employees to compel submission to its wishes, for that would be to give one group of workmen autocratic power of control in respect of the liberties of another group, in contravention of the Fifth Amendment as well as of the policy of Congress expressly declared in this act. And that being true, the attempt to coerce submission through constrained interference of the employer was equally unlawful.

So far as concerns the question here involved, the phrase "labor dispute" is the basic element of the act. For, unless there was such a dispute — that is to say, a "controversy" — the act does not even purport to limit the District Court's jurisdiction in equity. The phrase must receive a sensible construction in harmony with the congressional intent and policy. There can be no dispute without disputants.

The case is a simple one. Respondent's employees had no connection with the union, and were unwilling to have any. The union, being unable to persuade the employees to assent to its wishes in that regard, undertook to subjugate them to its will by coercing an unlawful interference with their freedom of action on the part of the employer. If that is a "labor dispute," destructive of the historical power of equity to intervene, then the Norris-La Guardia Act attempts to legalize an arbitrary and alien state of affairs wholly at variance with those principles of constitutional liberty by which the exercise of despotic power hitherto has been curbed. And nothing is plainer under our decisions than that, if the act does that, its effect will be to deprive the respondent of its property and business without due process of law, in contravention of the Fifth Amendment. *Truax.*

* * *

Felix Frankfurter was a principal drafter of the Norris-LaGuardia Act. As a legal scholar he had been one of the leading critics of the use of equity power to interfere with the First Amendment rights of labor organizers and co-authored an entire book on the subject. FRANKFURTER & GREEN, THE LABOR INJUNCTION (1930). His objection was that there were almost always adequate remedies at law in labor cases and the exercise of equity power aggregated all the powers of government into the judiciary — a judge wrote the law (the injunction), initiated prosecution of the defendant for contempt (through the order to show cause), and adjudicated the question (with both civil and criminal penalties available upon finding the defendant in contempt). Here is how he put it:

> The history of the labor injunction in action puts some matters beyond question. In larger part, dissatisfaction and resentment are caused, first, by the refusal of courts to recognize that breaches of the peace may be redressed though criminal prosecution and civil action for damages, and, second, by the expansion of a simple, judicial devise to an enveloping code of prohibited conduct, absorbing, *en masse*, executive and police functions and affecting the livelihood, and even lives of multitudes. Especially those zealous for the unimpaired prestige of our courts have observed how the administration of law by decrees which through vast and vague phrases surmount law, undermines the esteem of courts. . . . Not government, but "government by injunction," characterized by the consequences of a criminal prosecution without its safeguards, has been challenged.

If these are the vices of equity power, what are its virtues?

Among the most significant, recent limitations on lower federal court equity power is the Prison Litigation Reform Act of 1996. The legislation passed on a congressional record saturated with references to the number of prison civil rights suits filed in federal courts and allegations that prisoners were clogging the courts with frivolous claims. The purpose of the statute was to "reduce the quantity and improve the quality of prisoner suits." *Porter v. Nussle* (2002). Notably, almost all prisoner §1983 cases fail, giving them the lowest success rate of federal case types other than habeas petitions. One reason for the low success rate is that 90 percent of prisoner suits are filed *pro se*.[6] Other reasons include the strict legal standards that apply to prison conditions suits and, as the statute's proponents emphasized, abuse of legal process.

For most of the nation's history, suits challenging conditions in both federal and state prisons were not heard at all in court under the so-called "hands off" doctrine:

> The doctrine states that "courts are without power to supervise prison administration or to interfere with the ordinary prison rules or regulations." Courts have justified the doctrine procedurally by citing the separation of powers of the judicial and executive branches. In cases involving state prisoners in federal courts the decisions have rested on considerations of federalism as well.

Barry M. Fox, *The First Amendment Rights of Prisoners*, 63 J. Crim. L. 162, 162 (1972). Considerations such as "the lack of judicial expertise in penology or in the administration of prisons" and the "apprehension that judicial efforts to review prison officials' treatment of prisoners might open a 'Pandora's Box' leading to judicial supervision of every aspect of prison life" weighed heavily against the use of equity power in particular.

The most odious formulation of the doctrine developed during and after Reconstruction as Southern states increasingly turned to criminal law as a means of resubordinating newly liberated Black people. Black prisoners, often arrested on vague charges such as vagrancy and imprisoned for failure to pay associated fines and costs, were leased out to private corporations for forced labor in squalid, life threatening conditions without adequate food or medical treatment. "Leasing prisoners to private individuals or companies provided revenue and eliminated the need to build prisons." Douglas A. Blackmon, *From Alabama's Past, Capitalism Teamed With Racism to Create a Cruel Partnership*, Wall Street Journal, July 16, 2001. Courts refused to intervene not just on the ground that judicial review of challenges to the system would draw them into matters of prison administration, but on the ground that prisoners, having forfeited their legal rights upon conviction, were "*civiliter mortus*." As the Virginia Court of Appeals held in an 1871 case involving a prisoner alleged to have killed a private guard after having been leased out to work on the Chesapeake and Ohio Railroad, the prisoner had no right to challenge the process by which he was convicted and sentenced to be hung because:

> [t]he bill of rights is a declaration of general principles to govern a society of freemen, and not of convicted felons and men civilly dead. Such men have some rights it is true, such as the law in its benignity accords to them, but not the rights of freemen. They are slaves of the State undergoing punishment. . . . While in this state of penal servitude, they must be subject to the regulations of the institution of which they are inmates, and the laws of the State to whom their service is due in expiation of their crimes.

Ruffin v. Commonwealth of Virginia (Va. 1871) (affirming capital sentence).

---

6. Tables B & D, https://incarcerationlaw.com/resources/data-update/.

The hands-off doctrine endured until 1964 when the Supreme Court held that Muslim prisoners could state a claim for religious discrimination under §1983 for being refused access to religious materials. *Cooper v. Pate* (1964).[7] Over the next 30 years, the Court recognized the constitutional right of prisoners not only to free exercise of religion, but also to protection against cruel and unusual punishment under the Eighth Amendment, procedurally fair disciplinary rules and access to courts under the Due Process Clause, access to minimally adequate medical treatment under the Eighth Amendment, and other basic constitutional rights. Prisoner civil rights cases increased significantly in the same period.

Table A: Incarcerated Population and Prison/Jail Civil Rights Filings, FY1970–FY2021

	Incarcerated Population				Prisoner Civil Rights Filings in Fed. District Court			
Fiscal Year	Total Incar. Pop.	State Prison Pop.	Federal Prison Pop.	Local Jail Pop.	Total Filings	Non-federal Def'ts	Federal Def'ts	Filings / 1,000 Incar. Pop.
1970	359,419	178,654	20,038	160,727	2,244	2,091	153	6.2
1971	353,740	177,113	20,948	155,679	3,179	2,969	210	9.0
1972	352,326	174,379	21,713	156,234	3,635	3,393	242	10.3
1973	360,999	181,396	22,815	156,788	4,665	4,257	408	12.9
1974	387,063	207,360	22,361	157,342	5,574	5,186	388	14.4
1975	411,712	229,685	24,131	157,896	6,527	6,020	507	15.9
1976	436,451	248,883	29,117	158,451	7,095	6,701	394	16.3
1977	448,568	258,643	30,920	159,005	8,348	7,843	505	18.6
1978	456,877	269,765	26,285	160,827	10,087	9,520	567	22.1
1979	477,154	281,233	23,356	172,565	11,713	11,149	564	24.5
1980	506,082	295,819	23,779	186,484	13,079	12,496	583	25.8
1981	560,431	333,251	26,778	200,402	16,333	15,544	789	29.1
1982	617,235	375,603	27,311	214,321	16,809	16,075	734	27.2
1983	652,725	394,953	28,945	228,827	17,517	16,793	724	26.8
1984	691,538	417,389	30,875	243,274	18,340	17,471	869	26.5
1985	746,870	451,812	35,781	259,277	18,489	17,662	827	24.8
1986	818,383	496,834	39,781	281,768	20,366	19,657	709	24.9
1987	867,040	520,336	42,478	304,226	22,073	21,415	658	25.5
1988	948,971	562,605	44,205	342,161	22,657	21,879	778	23.9
1989	1,070,824	629,995	53,387	387,442	23,736	22,803	933	22.2
1990	1,154,265	684,544	58,838	410,883	24,051	23,028	1,023	20.8
1991	1,220,168	728,605	63,930	427,633	24,355	23,570	785	20.0
1992	1,300,736	778,495	72,071	450,170	28,544	27,723	821	21.9

---

7. *See also* United States v. Muniz (1963) (allowing federal inmates to state claims for injuries in federal custody under the Federal Tort Claims Act).

| | Incarcerated Population | | | Prisoner Civil Rights Filings in Fed. District Court | | | |
Fiscal Year	Total Incar. Pop.	State Prison Pop.	Federal Prison Pop.	Local Jail Pop.	Total Filings	Non-federal Def'ts	Federal Def'ts	Filings / 1,000 Incar. Pop.
1993	1,382,523	828,566	80,815	473,142	31,692	30,841	851	22.9
1994	1,478,242	904,647	85,500	488,095	36,596	35,551	1,045	24.8
1995	1,597,044	989,004	89,538	518,502	39,053	38,022	1,031	24.5
1996	1,654,574	1,032,676	95,088	526,810	38,262	37,126	1,136	23.1
1997	1,740,897	1,074,809	101,755	564,333	26,095	25,226	869	15.0
1998	1,816,310	1,111,927	110,793	593,590	24,221	23,313	908	13.3
1999	1,894,857	1,155,878	125,682	613,297	23,512	22,645	867	12.4
2000	1,946,822	1,177,240	140,064	629,518	23,357	22,399	958	12.0
2001	1,971,139	1,179,954	149,852	641,333	22,132	21,225	907	11.2
2002	2,032,723	1,209,145	158,216	665,362	21,989	21,045	944	10.8
2003	2,088,155	1,225,971	168,144	694,040	22,062	20,915	1,147	10.6
2004	2,141,694	1,244,216	177,600	719,878	21,554	20,338	1,216	10.1
2005	2,184,175	1,261,071	186,364	736,740	22,484	21,317	1,167	10.3
2006	2,250,203	1,297,536	190,844	761,823	22,464	21,438	1,026	10.0
2007	2,283,402	1,316,105	197,285	770,012	21,966	20,814	1,152	9.6
2008	2,301,154	1,324,539	198,414	778,201	23,547	22,387	1,160	10.2
2009	2,297,547	1,319,563	205,087	772,897	22,656	21,510	1,146	9.9
2010	2,280,045	1,314,445	206,968	758,632	22,651	21,548	1,103	9.9
2011	2,254,980	1,290,212	214,774	749,994	23,292	22,011	1,281	10.3
2012	2,232,015	1,262,102	216,915	752,998	22,636	21,627	1,009	10.1
2013	2,244,289	1,269,828	214,989	759,472	23,989	22,535	1,454	10.7
2014	2,232,842	1,260,159	209,561	763,122	25,270	24,082	1,188	11.3
2015	2,172,112	1,243,520	195,622	732,970	23,443	22,547	896	10.8
2016	2,150,260	1,228,822	188,311	733,127	24,444	23,604	840	11.4
2017	2,133,606	1,210,947	182,147	740,512	26,550	25,611	939	12.4
2018	2,107,681	1,191,342	179,213	737,126	25,533	24,428	1,105	12.1
2019	2,081,078	1,164,737	174,391	741,950	26,241	25,244	997	12.6
2020	1,789,244	978,988	152,156	658,100	26,217	25,080	1,137	14.7
2021	N/A	N/A	155,826	N/A	24,372	23,326	1,046	N/A

Consistent state underfunding meant that prison conditions in many states remained shockingly inadequate in the late twentieth century. As the Supreme Court admonished in an important case upholding broad lower court equity power: "The routine conditions that the ordinary Arkansas convict had to endure [constituted] a dark and alien world completely alien to the free world." *Hutto v. Finney (1978)*. Inmates were lashed with a wooden-handled leather strap five feet long and four inches wide . . . for minor offenses until their skin was bloody and bruised. . . . [A] hand cranked device was used to administer electrical shocks to various sensitive parts of an inmate's body. . . . [M]ost guards were simply inmates who had been issued guns. . . . [Mattresses were shared despite the fact that some prisoners were known to suffer from infectious disease. . . . prisoners] in isolation received fewer than 1,000 calories a day [in] 4-inch squares of "grue," a substance created by mashing [food] into a paste and baking the mixture in a pan.

The Court upheld a comprehensive remedial order, including strict limits on the length of solitary confinement, in light of the scope of the violation of prisoners' constitutional rights, "the interdependence of the conditions producing the violation," and the failure of the state to devise other means of coming into compliance. By the mid 1980s over 40 percent of the prison population of the states, and 50 percent of the states' jail population, were subject to some form of injunctive order.[8] This kind of continuing court supervision became quite common, extending in some cases for decades. As Justice Breyer once noted regarding an injunction in the First Circuit, the "very pervasiveness and seriousness of the conditions . . . made those conditions difficult to cure quickly. *Miller v. French* (2000) (Breyer, J., dissenting). Over the next decade, the District Court entered further orders embodied in 15 published opinions, affecting 21 prison institutions. . . . Their implementation involved the services of two monitors, two assistants, and a special master. Along the way, the court documented a degree of 'administrative chaos' in the prison system, and entered findings of contempt . . . followed by the assessment and collection of more than $74 million in fines."

The Prison Litigation Reform Act passed against the backdrop of these long-standing forms of equitable supervision, state non-compliance, and an acceleration in mass incarceration. Since the mid-1970s there has been a 500 percent increase in incarceration. The U.S. has 4 percent of the world's population but incarcerates 22 percent of the world's prison population, more than any other country, including numerous authoritarian regimes.

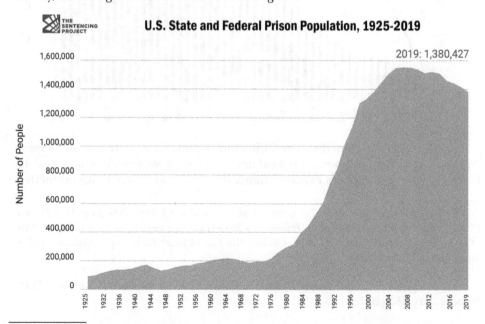

8. Margo Schlanger, *Civil Rights Injunctions Over Time: A Case Study*, 81 N.Y.U. L. Rev. 550, 578 (2006) (Table 2).

There is also a significant racial disparity in American prisons—Black Americans are five times as likely to be incarcerated as White people and empirical studies confirm that White defendants are statistically more likely to receive lenient sentences or diversion for similar offenses.[9] Since 1980 there also has been a 775 percent increase in the number of women incarcerated in U.S. prisons.[10]

The PLRA imposes strict procedural limits on the filing of prison lawsuits: prisoners must exhaust the prison's administrative grievance system before filing in federal court, 42 U.S.C. §1997e(a); courts are obliged to dismiss *sua sponte* if the court is "satisfied that the action is frivolous, malicious, fails to state a claim upon which relief can be granted, or seeks monetary relief from a defendant who is immune from such relief," 28 U.S.C. §1915(e)(2); prisoners have to pay a filing fee of $350 even if they would otherwise qualify for filing in forma pauperis, 28 U.S.C. §1915(b); prisoners are barred from refiling after filing three or more suits dismissed as frivolous, malicious, or failing to state a claim, 28 U.S.C. §1915(g); and remote appearance is required whenever practicable rather than live hearings 28 U.S.C. §1915(f).

As the table below depicts, the effect on filing rates in prison cases has been significant.[11]

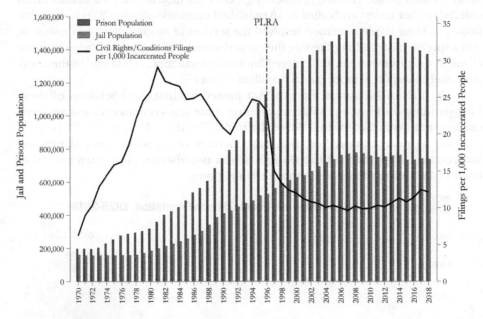

With respect to remedies, the PLRA limits prevailing party attorney's fees, 28 U.S.C. §1915(d); imposes a physical injury rule on compensatory damages, 42 U.S.C. §1997e(e); imposes exacting limits on issuing and sustaining injunctive

---

9. The Sentencing Project, *The Color of Justice: Racial and Ethnic Disparity in State Prisons* (2021); Bureau of Justice Statistics, *Prisoners in 2018* (noting a decline in prison population of 15 percent between 2008 and 2018, but that the rate of Black male imprisonment was 5.8 times that of White males).

10. *Id.*

11. Margo Schlanger, *Trends in Prisoner Litigation, as the PLRA Enters Adulthood*, 5 U.C. IRVINE L. REV. 153 (2015).

relief against a prison and its officers, and applies the same standards for injunctions reached by settlement, known as "consent decrees." 42 U.S.C. §3626(a) & (b). As we will see below, the latter provisions limiting injunctive relief have resulted in the termination of longstanding court orders that empowered federal courts to supervise state prisons and use contempt and other tools to induce compliance with the federal constitutional rights of prisoners.

In the following case, the Court wrestled with provisions of the statute that limit the equity power of federal courts to issue injunctive relief in prison conditions cases. As you read the case, note how long the lower courts' supervision of the state system endured without improvement of the underlying conditions. Think about what interventions, if any, might have improved matters, how the courts attempted to work with state executive branch officials responsible for the prison, and pay close attention to how the majority justifies upholding a prison release order. Consider as well the similarities and differences to the limitations on equity power in the Norris-LaGuardia Act. Does the nature of the substantive right at issue in labor disputes and prison conditions cases bear upon the power of Congress to limit remedies?

Brown v. Plata

563 U.S. 493 (2011)

Justice KENNEDY delivered the opinion of the Court.

The authority to order release of prisoners as a remedy to cure a systemic violation of the Eighth Amendment is a power reserved to a three-judge district court, not a single-judge district court. 18 U.S.C. §3626(a).

The appeal presents the question whether the remedial order issued by the three-judge court is consistent with requirements and procedures set forth in a congressional statute, the Prison Litigation Reform Act of 1995 (PLRA). 18 U.S.C. §3626. The order leaves the choice of means to reduce overcrowding to the discretion of state officials. But absent compliance through new construction, out-of-state transfers, or other means—or modification of the order upon a further showing by the State—the State will be required to release some number of prisoners before their full sentences have been served. High recidivism rates must serve as a warning that mistaken or premature release of even one prisoner can cause injury and harm. The release of prisoners in large numbers—assuming the State finds no other way to comply with the order—is a matter of undoubted, grave concern.

At the time of trial, California's correctional facilities held some 156,000 persons. This is nearly double the number that California's prisons were designed to hold, and California has been ordered to reduce its prison population to 137.5% of design capacity. By the three-judge court's own estimate, the required population reduction could be as high as 46,000 persons. Although the State has reduced the population by at least 9,000 persons during the pendency of this appeal, this means a further reduction of 37,000 persons could be required. . . . The State may employ measures, including good-time credits and diversion of low-risk offenders and technical parole violators to community-based programs, that will mitigate the order's impact. The population reduction potentially required is nevertheless of unprecedented sweep and extent.

Yet so too is the continuing injury and harm resulting from these serious constitutional violations. For years the medical and mental health care provided by California's prisons has fallen short of minimum constitutional requirements and has failed to meet prisoners' basic health needs. Needless suffering and death have been the well-documented result. Over the whole course of years during which this litigation has been pending, no other remedies have been found to be sufficient. Efforts to remedy the violation have been frustrated by severe overcrowding in California's prison system. . . .

The overcrowding is the "primary cause of the violation of a Federal right," 18 U.S.C. §3626(a)(3)(E)(i), specifically the severe and unlawful mistreatment of prisoners through grossly inadequate provision of medical and mental health care.

This Court now holds that the PLRA does authorize the relief afforded in this case and that the court-mandated population limit is necessary to remedy the violation of prisoners' constitutional rights. The order of the three-judge court, subject to the right of the State to seek its modification in appropriate circumstances, must be affirmed.

I

A

The degree of overcrowding in California's prisons is exceptional. California's prisons are designed to house a population just under 80,000, but at the time of the three-judge court's decision the population was almost double that. The State's prisons had operated at around 200% of design capacity for at least 11 years. Prisoners are crammed into spaces neither designed nor intended to house inmates. As many as 200 prisoners may live in a gymnasium, monitored by as few as two or three correctional officers. As many as 54 prisoners may share a single toilet.

The Corrections Independent Review Panel, a body appointed by the Governor and composed of correctional consultants and representatives from state agencies, concluded that California's prisons are "severely overcrowded, imperiling the safety of both correctional employees and inmates."[1] In 2006, then-Governor

---

1. A similar conclusion was reached by the Little Hoover Commission, a bipartisan and independent state body, which stated that "[o]vercrowded conditions inside the prison walls are unsafe for inmates and staff," Solving California's Corrections Crisis: Time is Running Out 17 (Jan. 2007), and that "California's correctional system is in a tailspin."

At trial, current and former California prison officials also testified to the degree of overcrowding. Jeanne Woodford, who recently administered California's prison system, stated that "[o]vercrowding in the [California Department of Corrections and Rehabilitation (CDCR)] is extreme, its effects are pervasive and it is preventing the Department from providing adequate mental and medical health care to prisoners." Matthew Cate, the head of the California prison system, stated that "overpopulation makes everything we do more difficult." And Robin Dezember, chief deputy secretary of Correctional Healthcare Services, stated that "we are terribly overcrowded in our prison system" and "overcrowding has negative effects on everybody in the prison system."

Experts from outside California offered similar assessments. Doyle Wayne Scott, the former head of corrections in Texas, described conditions in California's prisons as "appalling," "inhumane," and "unacceptable" and stated that "[i]n more than 35 years of prison work experience, I have never seen anything like it." Joseph Lehman, the former head of correctional systems in Washington, Maine, and Pennsylvania, concluded that "[t]here is no question that California's prisons are overcrowded" and that "this is an emergency situation; it calls for drastic and immediate action."

Schwarzenegger declared a state of emergency in the prisons, as "immediate action is necessary to prevent death and harm caused by California's severe prison over-crowding." The consequences of overcrowding identified by the Governor include "increased, substantial risk for transmission of infectious illness" and a suicide rate "approaching an average of one per week."

Prisoners in California with serious mental illness do not receive minimal, ade-quate care. Because of a shortage of treatment beds, suicidal inmates may be held for prolonged periods in telephone-booth sized cages without toilets. A psychiatric expert reported observing an inmate who had been held in such a cage for nearly 24 hours, standing in a pool of his own urine, unresponsive and nearly catatonic. Prison officials explained they had "no place to put him." Other inmates await-ing care may be held for months in administrative segregation, where they endure harsh and isolated conditions and receive only limited mental health services. Wait times for mental health care range as high as 12 months. In 2006, the suicide rate in California's prisons was nearly 80% higher than the national average for prison populations; and a court-appointed Special Master found that 72.1% of suicides involved "some measure of inadequate assessment, treatment, or intervention, and were therefore most probably foreseeable and/or preventable."[2]

Prisoners suffering from physical illness also receive severely deficient care. California's prisons were designed to meet the medical needs of a population at 100% of design capacity and so have only half the clinical space needed to treat the current population. A correctional officer testified that, in one prison, up to 50 sick inmates may be held together in a 12- by 20-foot cage for up to five hours awaiting treatment. The number of staff is inadequate, and prisoners face significant delays in access to care. A prisoner with severe abdominal pain died after a 5-week delay in referral to a specialist; a prisoner with "constant and extreme" chest pain died after an 8-hour delay in evaluation by a doctor; and a prisoner died of testicular cancer after a "failure of MDs to work up for cancer in a young man with 17 months of testicular pain."[3] Doctor Ronald Shansky, former medical director of the Illinois state prison system, surveyed death reviews for California prisoners. He concluded

---

2. At the time of the three-judge court's decision, 2006 was the most recent year for which the Special Master had conducted a detailed study of suicides in the California pris-ons. The Special Master later issued an analysis for the year 2007. This report concluded that the 2007 suicide rate was "a continuation of the CDCR's pattern of exceeding the national prison suicide rate." The report found that the rate of suicides involving inadequate assess-ment, treatment, or intervention had risen to 82% and concluded that "[t]hese numbers clearly indicate no improvement in this area during the past several years, and possibly sig-nal a trend of ongoing deterioration." No detailed study has been filed since then, but in September 2010 the Special Master filed a report stating that "the data for 2010 so far is not showing improvement in suicide prevention."

3. Because plaintiffs do not base their case on deficiencies in care provided on any one occasion, this Court has no occasion to consider whether these instances of delay—or any other particular deficiency in medical care complained of by the plaintiffs—would violate the Constitution under *Estelle v. Gamble* (1976), if considered in isolation. Plaintiffs rely on systemwide deficiencies in the provision of medical and mental health care that, taken as a whole, subject sick and mentally ill prisoners in California to "substantial risk of serious harm" and cause the delivery of care in the prisons to fall below the evolving standards of decency that mark the progress of a maturing society. *Farmer v. Brennan* (1994).

that extreme departures from the standard of care were "widespread," and that the proportion of "possibly preventable or preventable" deaths was "extremely high."[4] Many more prisoners, suffering from severe but not life-threatening conditions, experience prolonged illness and unnecessary pain.

B

These conditions are the subject of two federal cases. The first to commence, *Coleman* v. *Brown,* was filed in 1990. *Coleman* involves the class of seriously mentally ill persons in California prisons. Over 15 years ago, in 1995, after a 39-day trial, the *Coleman* District Court found "overwhelming evidence of the systematic failure to deliver necessary care to mentally ill inmates" in California prisons. 1995. The prisons were "seriously and chronically understaffed," and had "no effective method for ensuring . . . the competence of their staff." The prisons had failed to implement necessary suicide-prevention procedures, "due in large measure to the severe understaffing." Mentally ill inmates "languished for months, or even years, without access to necessary care." "They suffer from severe hallucinations, [and] they decompensate into catatonic states." The court appointed a Special Master to oversee development and implementation of a remedial plan of action.

In 2007, 12 years after his appointment, the Special Master in *Coleman* filed a report stating that, after years of slow improvement, the state of mental health care in California's prisons was deteriorating. The Special Master ascribed this change to increased overcrowding. The rise in population had led to greater demand for care, and existing programming space and staffing levels were inadequate to keep pace. . . . The Special Master concluded that many early "achievements have succumbed to the inexorably rising tide of population, leaving behind growing frustration and despair."

C

The second action, *Plata v. Brown,* involves the class of state prisoners with serious medical conditions. After this action commenced in 2001, the State conceded that deficiencies in prison medical care violated prisoners' Eighth Amendment rights. The State stipulated to a remedial injunction. The State failed to comply with that injunction, and in 2005 the court appointed a Receiver to oversee remedial efforts. The court found that "the California prison medical care system is broken beyond repair," resulting in an "unconscionable degree of suffering and death." The court found: "[I]t is an uncontested fact that, on average, an inmate in one of California's prisons needlessly dies every six to seven days due to constitutional

---

4. [D]uring 2006 and 2007, a preventable or possibly preventable death occurred once every five to six days. Both preventable and possibly preventable deaths involve major lapses in medical care and are a serious cause for concern. In one typical case classified as a possibly preventable death, an analysis revealed the following lapses: "16 month delay in evaluating abnormal liver mass; 8 month delay in receiving regular chemotherapy . . . ; multiple providers fail to respond to jaundice and abnormal liver function tests causing 17 month delay in diagnosis." California Prison Health Care Receivership Corp., K. Imai, Analysis of Year 2009 Inmate Death Reviews—California Prison Health Care System 12 (Sept. 2010).

deficiencies in the [California prisons'] medical delivery system." And the court made findings regarding specific instances of neglect, including the following:

> [A] San Quentin prisoner with hypertension, diabetes and renal failure was prescribed two different medications that actually served to exacerbate his renal failure. An optometrist noted the patient's retinal bleeding due to very high blood pressure and referred him for immediate evaluation, but this evaluation never took place. It was not until a year later that the patient's renal failure was recognized, at which point he was referred to a nephrologist on an urgent basis; he should have been seen by the specialist within 14 days but the consultation never happened and the patient died three months later.

Prisons were unable to retain sufficient numbers of competent medical staff, and would "hire any doctor who had 'a license, a pulse and a pair of shoes.'" Medical facilities lacked "necessary medical equipment" and did "not meet basic sanitation standards." "Exam tables and counter tops, where prisoners with . . . communicable diseases are treated, [were] not routinely disinfected."

In 2008, three years after the District Court's decision, the Receiver described continuing deficiencies in the health care provided by California prisons:

> . . . Adequate housing for the disabled and aged does not exist. The medical facilities, when they exist at all, are in an abysmal state of disrepair. Basic medical equipment is often not available or used. Medications and other treatment options are too often not available when needed. . . . Indeed, it is a misnomer to call the existing chaos a "medical delivery system"—it is more an act of desperation than a system.

A report by the Receiver detailed the impact of overcrowding on efforts to remedy the violation. . . . Overcrowding had increased the incidence of infectious disease, and had led to rising prison violence and greater reliance by custodial staff on lockdowns, which "inhibit the delivery of medical care and increase the staffing necessary for such care." "Every day," the Receiver reported, "California prison wardens and health care managers make the difficult decision as to which of the class actions, *Coleman* . . . or *Plata* they will fail to comply with because of staff shortages and patient loads."

D

The *Coleman* and *Plata* plaintiffs, believing that a remedy for unconstitutional medical and mental health care could not be achieved without reducing overcrowding, moved their respective District Courts to convene a three-judge court empowered under the PLRA to order reductions in the prison population. . . .

The three-judge court heard 14 days of testimony and issued a 184-page opinion, making extensive findings of fact. . . . Because it appears all but certain that the State cannot complete sufficient construction to comply fully with the order, the prison population will have to be reduced to at least some extent. The court did not order the State to achieve this reduction in any particular manner. Instead, the court ordered the State to formulate a plan for compliance and submit its plan for approval by the court.

The State appealed to this Court pursuant to 28 U.S.C. §1253. . . .

II

As a consequence of their own actions, prisoners may be deprived of rights that are fundamental to liberty. Yet the law and the Constitution demand recognition of certain other rights. Prisoners retain the essence of human dignity inherent in all persons. Respect for that dignity animates the Eighth Amendment prohibition against cruel and unusual punishment. "'The basic concept underlying the Eighth Amendment is nothing less than the dignity of man.'" *Atkins v. Virginia* (2002).

To incarcerate, society takes from prisoners the means to provide for their own needs. Prisoners are dependent on the State for food, clothing, and necessary medical care. A prison's failure to provide sustenance for inmates "may actually produce physical 'torture or a lingering death.'" *Estelle v. Gamble* (1976). Just as a prisoner may starve if not fed, he or she may suffer or die if not provided adequate medical care. A prison that deprives prisoners of basic sustenance, including adequate medical care, is incompatible with the concept of human dignity and has no place in civilized society.

If government fails to fulfill this obligation, the courts have a responsibility to remedy the resulting Eighth Amendment violation. *See Hutto v. Finney* (1978). Courts must be sensitive to the State's interest in punishment, deterrence, and rehabilitation, as well as the need for deference to experienced and expert prison administrators faced with the difficult and dangerous task of housing large numbers of convicted criminals. *See Bell v. Wolfish* (1979). Courts nevertheless must not shrink from their obligation to "enforce the constitutional rights of all 'persons,' including prisoners." *Cruz v. Beto* (1972). Courts may not allow constitutional violations to continue simply because a remedy would involve intrusion into the realm of prison administration.

Courts faced with the sensitive task of remedying unconstitutional prison conditions must consider a range of available options, including appointment of special masters or receivers and the possibility of consent decrees. When necessary to ensure compliance with a constitutional mandate, courts may enter orders placing limits on a prison's population. By its terms, the PLRA restricts the circumstances in which a court may enter an order "that has the purpose or effect of reducing or limiting the prison population." 18 U.S.C. §3626(g)(4). The order in this case does not necessarily require the State to release any prisoners. The State may comply by raising the design capacity of its prisons or by transferring prisoners to county facilities or facilities in other States. Because the order limits the prison population as a percentage of design capacity, it nonetheless has the "effect of reducing or limiting the prison population."

Under the PLRA, only a three-judge court may enter an order limiting a prison population. §3626(a)(3)(B). Before a three-judge court may be convened, a district court first must have entered an order for less intrusive relief that failed to remedy the constitutional violation and must have given the defendant a reasonable time to comply with its prior orders. §3626(a)(3)(A). The party requesting a three-judge court must then submit "materials sufficient to demonstrate that [these requirements] have been met." §3626(a)(3)(C). If the district court concludes that the materials are, in fact, sufficient, a three-judge court may be convened.

The three-judge court must then find by clear and convincing evidence that "crowding is the primary cause of the violation of a Federal right" and that "no other relief will remedy the violation of the Federal right." 18 U.S.C. §3626(a)(3)(E). As with any award of prospective relief under the PLRA, the relief "shall extend no further than necessary to correct the violation of the Federal right of a particular plaintiff or plaintiffs." §3626(a)(1)(A). The three-judge court must therefore find that the relief is "narrowly drawn, extends no further than necessary . . . , and is the least intrusive means necessary to correct the violation of the Federal right." In making this determination, the three-judge court must give "substantial weight to any adverse impact on public safety or the operation of a criminal justice system caused by the relief."

This Court's review of the three-judge court's legal determinations is *de novo*, but factual findings are reviewed for clear error.

A

The State contends that it was error to convene the three-judge court without affording it more time to comply with the prior orders in *Coleman* and *Plata*.

2

Having engaged in remedial efforts for 5 years in *Plata* and 12 in *Coleman*, the District Courts were not required to wait to see whether their more recent efforts would yield equal disappointment. . . . A contrary reading of the reasonable time requirement would in effect require district courts to impose a moratorium on new remedial orders before issuing a population limit. This unnecessary period of inaction would delay an eventual remedy and would prolong the courts' involvement, serving neither the State nor the prisoners. Congress did not require this unreasonable result when it used the term "reasonable."

B

Once a three-judge court has been convened, the court must find additional requirements satisfied before it may impose a population limit. The first of these requirements is that "crowding is the primary cause of the violation of a Federal right." 18 U.S.C. §3626(a)(3)(E)(i).

1

" . . . Because the "district court is 'better positioned' . . . to decide the issue," our review of the three-judge court's primary cause determination is deferential.

The record documents the severe impact of burgeoning demand on the provision of care. At the time of trial, vacancy rates for medical and mental health staff ranged as high as 20% for surgeons, 25% for physicians, 39% for nurse practitioners, and 54.1% for psychiatrists. These percentages are based on the number of positions budgeted by the State. Dr. Ronald Shansky, former medical director of the Illinois prison system, concluded that these numbers understate the severity of the crisis because the State has not budgeted sufficient staff to meet demand. According to Dr. Shansky, "even if the prisons were able to fill all of their vacant health care positions, which they have not been able to do to date, . . . the prisons would still be unable to handle the level of need given the current overcrowding." Dr. Craig Haney, a professor of psychology, reported that mental health staff are "managing far larger caseloads than is appropriate or effective." A prison psychiatrist told Dr. Haney that "we are doing about 50% of what we should be doing." In the context of physical care Dr. Shansky agreed that "demand for care, particularly for the high priority cases, continues to overwhelm the resources available."

Even on the assumption that vacant positions could be filled, the evidence suggested there would be insufficient space for the necessary additional staff to perform their jobs. The *Plata* Receiver, in his report on overcrowding, concluded that even the "newest and most modern prisons" had been "designed with clinic space which is only one-half that necessary for the real-life capacity of the prisons." Dr. Haney reported that "[e]ach one of the facilities I toured was short of significant amounts of space needed to perform otherwise critical tasks and responsibilities."

This shortfall of resources relative to demand contributes to significant delays in treatment. Mentally ill prisoners are housed in administrative segregation while awaiting transfer to scarce mental health treatment beds for appropriate care. One correctional officer indicated that he had kept mentally ill prisoners in segregation for "6 months or more." Other prisoners awaiting care are held in tiny, phone-booth sized cages. The record documents instances of prisoners committing suicide while awaiting treatment.

Delays are no less severe in the context of physical care. Prisons have backlogs of up to 700 prisoners waiting to see a doctor. A review of referrals for urgent specialty care at one prison revealed that only 105 of 316 pending referrals had a scheduled appointment, and only 2 had an appointment scheduled to occur within 14 days. Urgent specialty referrals at one prison had been pending for six months to a year.

Crowding also creates unsafe and unsanitary living conditions that hamper effective delivery of medical and mental health care. A medical expert described living quarters in converted gymnasiums or dayrooms, where large numbers of prisoners may share just a few toilets and showers, as "breeding grounds for disease."[7] Cramped conditions promote unrest and violence, making it difficult for prison officials to monitor and control the prison population. On any given day, prisoners in the general prison population may become ill, thus entering the plaintiff class; and overcrowding may prevent immediate medical attention necessary to avoid suffering, death, or spread of disease. . . . Living in crowded, unsafe, and unsanitary conditions can cause prisoners with latent mental illnesses to worsen and develop overt symptoms. Crowding may also impede efforts to improve delivery of care. Two prisoners committed suicide by hanging after being placed in cells that had been identified as requiring a simple fix to remove attachment points that could support a noose. The repair was not made because doing so would involve removing prisoners from the cells, and there was no place to put them. More generally, Jeanne Woodford, the former acting secretary of California's prisons, testified that there "'are simply too many issues that arise from such a large number of prisoners,'" and that, as a result, "'management spends virtually all of its time fighting fires instead

---

7. Correctional officials at trial described several outbreaks of disease. One officer testified that antibiotic-resistant staph infections spread widely among the prison population and described prisoners "bleeding, oozing with pus that is soaking through their clothes when they come in to get the wound covered and treated."

of engaging in thoughtful decision-making and planning'" of the sort needed to fashion an effective remedy for these constitutional violations.

Increased violence also requires increased reliance on lockdowns to keep order, and lockdowns further impede the effective delivery of care. In 2006, prison officials instituted 449 lockdowns. The average lockdown lasted 12 days, and 20 lockdowns lasted 60 days or longer. During lockdowns, staff must either escort prisoners to medical facilities or bring medical staff to the prisoners. . . .

Numerous experts testified that crowding is the primary cause of the constitutional violations. . . . [T]he current secretary of the Pennsylvania Department of Corrections testified that "'the biggest inhibiting factor right now in California being able to deliver appropriate mental health and medical care is the severe overcrowding.'" . . .

3

The three-judge court acknowledged that the violations were caused by factors in addition to overcrowding and that reducing crowding in the prisons would not entirely cure the violations. This is consistent with the reports of the *Coleman* Special Master and *Plata* Receiver, both of whom concluded that even a significant reduction in the prison population would not remedy the violations absent continued efforts to train staff, improve facilities, and reform procedures.[8] The three-judge court nevertheless found that overcrowding was the primary cause in the sense of being the foremost cause of the violation.

This understanding of the primary cause requirement is consistent with the text of the PLRA. The State in fact concedes that it proposed this very definition of primary cause to the three-judge court. . . . Overcrowding need only be the foremost, chief, or principal cause of the violation. If Congress had intended to require that crowding be the only cause, it would have said so, assuming in its judgment that definition would be consistent with constitutional limitations.

In addition to overcrowding the failure of California's prisons to provide adequate medical and mental health care may be ascribed to chronic and worsening budget shortfalls, a lack of political will in favor of reform, inadequate facilities, and systemic administrative failures. The *Plata* District Judge, in his order appointing the Receiver, compared the problem to "'a spider web, in which the tension of the various strands is determined by the relationship among all the parts of the web, so that if one pulls on a single strand, the tension of the entire web is redistributed in a new and complex pattern.'" Fletcher, The Discretionary Constitution: Institutional Remedies and Judicial Legitimacy, 91 YALE L.J. 635, 645 (1982)). . . . Only a multifaceted approach aimed at many causes, including overcrowding, will yield a solution.

---

8. The Plata Receiver concluded that those who believed a population reduction would be a panacea were "simply wrong." . . . The Coleman Special Master likewise found that a large release of prisoners, without other relief, would leave the violation "largely unmitigated" even though deficiencies in care "are unquestionably exacerbated by overcrowding" and "defendants' ability to provide required mental health services would be enhanced considerably by a reduction in the overall census" of the prisons.

The PLRA should not be interpreted to place undue restrictions on the authority of federal courts to fashion practical remedies when confronted with complex and intractable constitutional violations. Congress limited the availability of limits on prison populations, but it did not forbid these measures altogether. . . . A reading of the PLRA that would render population limits unavailable in practice would raise serious constitutional concerns. A finding that overcrowding is the "primary cause" of a violation is therefore permissible, despite the fact that additional steps will be required to remedy the violation.

C

The three-judge court was also required to find by clear and convincing evidence that "no other relief will remedy the violation of the Federal right." §3626(a)(3)(E)(ii).

Even if out-of-state transfers could be regarded as a less restrictive alternative, the three-judge court found no evidence of plans for transfers in numbers sufficient to relieve overcrowding.

Construction of new facilities, in theory, could alleviate overcrowding, but the three-judge court found no realistic possibility that California would be able to build itself out of this crisis. . . . Particularly in light of California's ongoing fiscal crisis, the three-judge court deemed "chimerical" any "remedy that requires significant additional spending by the state."

The three-judge court also rejected additional hiring as a realistic means to achieve a remedy. The State for years had been unable to fill positions necessary for the adequate provision of medical and mental health care, and the three-judge court found no reason to expect a change.

D

The PLRA states that no prospective relief shall issue with respect to prison conditions unless it is narrowly drawn, extends no further than necessary to correct the violation of a federal right, and is the least intrusive means necessary to correct the violation. 18 U.S.C. §3626(a). When determining whether these requirements are met, courts must "give substantial weight to any adverse impact on public safety or the operation of a criminal justice system."

1

The three-judge court acknowledged that its order "is likely to affect inmates without medical conditions or serious mental illness." This is because reducing California's prison population will require reducing the number of prisoners outside the class through steps such as parole reform, sentencing reform, use of good-time credits, or other means to be determined by the State. Reducing overcrowding will also have positive effects beyond facilitating timely and adequate access to medical care, including reducing the incidence of prison violence and ameliorating unsafe living conditions. According to the State, these collateral consequences are evidence that the order sweeps more broadly than necessary.

The population limit imposed by the three-judge court does not fail narrow tailoring simply because it will have positive effects beyond the plaintiff class. Narrow tailoring requires a "fit between the [remedy's] ends and the means chosen to accomplish those ends." *Board of Trustees of State Univ. of N.Y. v. Fox* (1989). The scope of the remedy must be proportional to the scope of the violation, and the order must extend no further than necessary to remedy the violation. This Court has rejected remedial orders that unnecessarily reach out to improve prison conditions other than those that violate the Constitution. *Lewis v. Casey* (1996). But the precedents do not suggest that a narrow and otherwise proper remedy for a constitutional violation is invalid simply because it will have collateral effects.

Nor does anything in the text of the PLRA require that result. The PLRA states that a remedy shall extend no further than necessary to remedy the violation of the rights of a "particular plaintiff or plaintiffs." 18 U.S.C. §3626(a)(1)(A). This means only that the scope of the order must be determined with reference to the constitutional violations established by the specific plaintiffs before the court.

This case is unlike cases where courts have impermissibly reached out to control the treatment of persons or institutions beyond the scope of the violation. Even prisoners with no present physical or mental illness may become afflicted, and all prisoners in California are at risk so long as the State continues to provide inadequate care. Prisoners in the general population will become sick, and will become members of the plaintiff classes, with routine frequency; and overcrowding may prevent the timely diagnosis and care necessary to provide effective treatment and to prevent further spread of disease. Relief targeted only at present members of the plaintiff classes may therefore fail to adequately protect future class members who will develop serious physical or mental illness. Prisoners who are not sick or mentally ill do not yet have a claim that they have been subjected to care that violates the Eighth Amendment, but in no sense are they remote bystanders in California's medical care system. They are that system's next potential victims.

A release order limited to prisoners within the plaintiff classes would, if anything, unduly limit the ability of State officials to determine which prisoners should be released. As the State acknowledges in its brief, "release of seriously mentally ill inmates [would be] likely to create special dangers because of their recidivism rates."

The order also is not overbroad because it encompasses the entire prison system, rather than separately assessing the need for a population limit at every institution. The *Coleman* court found a systemwide violation when it first afforded relief, and in *Plata* the State stipulated to systemwide relief when it conceded the existence of a violation. Both the *Coleman* Special Master and the *Plata* Receiver have filed numerous reports detailing systemwide deficiencies in medical and mental health care. California's medical care program is run at a systemwide level, and resources are shared among the correctional facilities.

Although the three-judge court's order addresses the entire California prison system, it affords the State flexibility to accommodate differences between institutions. There is no requirement that every facility comply with the 137.5% limit. . . . The alternative—a series of institution-specific population limits—would require federal judges to make these choices. Leaving this discretion to state officials does not make the order overbroad.

While the order does in some respects shape or control the State's authority in the realm of prison administration, it does so in a manner that leaves much to the State's discretion. The State may choose how to allocate prisoners between institutions; it may choose whether to increase the prisons' capacity through construction or reduce the population; and, if it does reduce the population, it may decide what steps to take to achieve the necessary reduction. The order's limited scope is necessary to remedy a constitutional violation.

The State's desire to avoid a population limit, justified as according respect to state authority, creates a certain and unacceptable risk of continuing violations of the rights of sick and mentally ill prisoners, with the result that many more will die or needlessly suffer. The Constitution does not permit this wrong.

2

In reaching its decision, the three-judge court gave "substantial weight" to any potential adverse impact on public safety from its order. The court devoted nearly 10 days of trial to the issue of public safety, and it gave the question extensive attention in its opinion. Ultimately, the court concluded that it would be possible to reduce the prison population "in a manner that preserves public safety and the operation of the criminal justice system."

The PLRA's requirement that a court give "substantial weight" to public safety does not require the court to certify that its order has no possible adverse impact on the public. A contrary reading would depart from the statute's text by replacing the word "substantial" with "conclusive."

This inquiry necessarily involves difficult predictive judgments regarding the likely effects of court orders. Although these judgments are normally made by state officials, they necessarily must be made by courts when those courts fashion injunctive relief to remedy serious constitutional violations in the prisons. These questions are difficult and sensitive, but they are factual questions and should be treated as such. Courts can, and should, rely on relevant and informed expert testimony when making factual findings. It was proper for the three-judge court to rely on the testimony of prison officials from California and other States. Those experts testified on the basis of empirical evidence and extensive experience in the field of prison administration.

Some evidence indicated that reducing overcrowding in California's prisons could even improve public safety. Then-Governor Schwarzenegger, in his emergency proclamation on overcrowding, acknowledged that "overcrowding causes harm to people and property, leads to inmate unrest and misconduct, . . . and increases recidivism as shown within this state and in others." The former warden of San Quentin and acting secretary of the California prison system testified that she "absolutely believe[s] that we make people worse, and that we are not meeting public safety by the way we treat people."[10]

---

10. The former head of correctional systems in Washington, Maine, and Pennsylvania, likewise referred to California's prisons as "'criminogenic.'" The Yolo County chief probation officer testified that "'it seems like [the prisons] produce additional criminal behavior.'" A former professor of sociology at George Washington University, reported that California's present recidivism rate is among the highest in the Nation. And the three-judge court noted the report of California's Little Hoover Commission, which stated that "'[e]ach year, California communities are burdened with absorbing 123,000 offenders returning from prison, often more dangerous than when they left.'"

Expert witnesses produced statistical evidence that prison populations had been lowered without adversely affecting public safety in a number of jurisdictions, including certain counties in California, as well as Wisconsin, Illinois, Texas, Colorado, Montana, Michigan, Florida, and Canada. . . . In light of this evidence, the three-judge court concluded that any negative impact on public safety would be "substantially offset, and perhaps entirely eliminated, by the public safety benefits" of a reduction in overcrowding.

The court found that various available methods of reducing overcrowding would have little or no impact on public safety. Expansion of good-time credits would allow the State to give early release to only those prisoners who pose the least risk of reoffending. Diverting low-risk offenders to community programs such as drug treatment, day reporting centers, and electronic monitoring would likewise lower the prison population without releasing violent convicts. The State now sends large numbers of persons to prison for violating a technical term or condition of their parole, and it could reduce the prison population by punishing technical parole violations through community-based programs. This last measure would be particularly beneficial as it would reduce crowding in the reception centers, which are especially hard hit by overcrowding. The court's order took account of public safety concerns by giving the State substantial flexibility to select among these and other means of reducing overcrowding.

III

Establishing the population at which the State could begin to provide constitutionally adequate medical and mental health care, and the appropriate time frame within which to achieve the necessary reduction, requires a degree of judgment. The inquiry involves uncertain predictions regarding the effects of population reductions, as well as difficult determinations regarding the capacity of prison officials to provide adequate care at various population levels. Courts have substantial flexibility when making these judgments. "Once invoked, the scope of a district court's equitable powers . . . is broad, for breadth and flexibility are inherent in equitable remedies." *Hutto* (quoting *Milliken v. Bradley* (1977), in turn quoting *Swann v. Charlotte-Mecklenburg Bd. of Ed.* (1971)).

Nevertheless, the PLRA requires a court to adopt a remedy that is "narrowly tailored" to the constitutional violation and that gives "substantial weight" to public safety. 18 U.S.C. §3626(a). When a court is imposing a population limit, this means the court must set the limit at the highest population consistent with an efficacious remedy. The court must also order the population reduction achieved in the shortest period of time reasonably consistent with public safety.

A

The three-judge court concluded that the population of California's prisons should be capped at 137.5% of design capacity. This conclusion is supported by the record. Indeed, some evidence supported a limit as low as 100% of design capacity.

The three-judge court made the most precise determination it could in light of the record before it. The PLRA's narrow tailoring requirement is satisfied so long as these equitable, remedial judgments are made with the objective of releasing the fewest possible prisoners consistent with an efficacious remedy. In light of substantial evidence supporting an even more drastic remedy, the three-judge court complied with the requirement of the PLRA in this case.

. . . .

The relief ordered by the three-judge court is required by the Constitution and was authorized by Congress in the PLRA. The State shall implement the order without further delay.

Justice SCALIA, with whom Justice THOMAS joins, dissenting.

Today the Court affirms what is perhaps the most radical injunction issued by a court in our Nation's history: an order requiring California to release the staggering number of 46,000 convicted criminals.

There comes before us, now and then, a case whose proper outcome is so clearly indicated by tradition and common sense, that its decision ought to shape the law, rather than vice versa. One would think that, before allowing the decree of a federal district court to release 46,000 convicted felons, this Court would bend every effort to read the law in such a way as to avoid that outrageous result. Today, quite to the contrary, the Court disregards stringently drawn provisions of the governing statute, and traditional constitutional limitations upon the power of a federal judge, in order to uphold the absurd.

The proceedings that led to this result were a judicial travesty. I dissent because the institutional reform the District Court has undertaken violates the terms of the governing statute, ignores bedrock limitations on the power of Article III judges, and takes federal courts wildly beyond their institutional capacity.

I

A

What has been alleged here, and what the injunction issued by the Court is tailored (narrowly or not) to remedy is the running of a prison system with inadequate medical facilities. That may result in the denial of needed medical treatment to "a particular [prisoner] or [prisoners]," thereby violating (according to our cases) his or their Eighth Amendment rights. But the mere existence of the inadequate system does not subject to cruel and unusual punishment the entire prison population in need of medical care, including those who receive it.

The Court acknowledges that the plaintiffs "do not base their case on deficiencies in care provided on any one occasion;" rather, "[p]laintiffs rely on system-wide deficiencies in the provision of medical and mental health care that, taken as a whole, subject sick and mentally ill prisoners in California to 'substantial risk of serious harm' and cause the delivery of care in the prisons to fall below the evolving standards of decency that mark the progress of a maturing society." But our judge-empowering "evolving standards of decency" jurisprudence (with which, by the way, I heartily disagree), *see, e.g., Roper v. Simmons* (2005) (Scalia, J., dissenting) does not prescribe (or at least has not until today prescribed) rules for the "decent" running of schools, prisons, and other government institutions. It forbids "indecent" treatment of individuals — in the context of this case, the *denial of medical care* to those who need it. And the persons who have a constitutional claim for denial of medical care are those who are denied medical care—not all who face a "substantial risk" (whatever that is) of being denied medical care.

The *Coleman* litigation involves "the class of seriously mentally ill persons in California prisons," and the *Plata* litigation involves "the class of state prisoners with serious medical conditions." The plaintiffs do not appear to claim—and it would absurd to suggest—that every single one of those prisoners has personally experienced "torture or a lingering death," as a consequence of that bad medical system. Indeed, it is inconceivable that anything more than a small proportion of prisoners in the plaintiff classes have personally received sufficiently atrocious treatment that their Eighth Amendment right was violated—which, as the Court recognizes, is why the plaintiffs do not premise their claim on "deficiencies in care provided on any one occasion." Rather, the plaintiffs' claim is that they are all part of a medical system so defective that some number of prisoners will inevitably be injured by incompetent medical care, and that this number is sufficiently high so as to render the system, as a whole, unconstitutional.

But what procedural principle justifies certifying a class of plaintiffs so they may assert a claim of systemic unconstitutionality? I can think of two possibilities, both of which are untenable. The first is that although some or most plaintiffs in the class do not *individually* have viable Eighth Amendment claims, the class as a whole has collectively suffered an Eighth Amendment violation. That theory is .contrary to the bedrock rule that the sole purpose of classwide adjudication is to aggregate claims that are individually viable. "A class action, no less than traditional joinder (of which it is a species), merely enables a federal court to adjudicate claims of multiple parties at once, instead of in separate suits. And like traditional joinder, it leaves the parties' legal rights and duties intact and the rules of decision unchanged." *Shady Grove Orthopedic Associates, P.A. v. Allstate Ins. Co.* (2010).

The second possibility is that every member of the plaintiff class *has* suffered an Eighth Amendment violation merely by virtue of being a patient in a poorly-run prison system, and the purpose of the class is merely to aggregate all those individually viable claims. This theory has the virtue of being consistent with procedural principles, but at the cost of a gross substantive departure from our case law. Under this theory, each and every prisoner who happens to be a patient in a system that has systemic weaknesses—such as "hir[ing] any doctor who had a license, a pulse and a pair of shoes"—has suffered cruel or unusual punishment, even if that person cannot make an individualized showing of mistreatment. Such a theory of the Eighth Amendment is preposterous. And we have said as much in the past: "If . . . a healthy inmate who had suffered no deprivation of needed medical treatment were able to claim violation of his constitutional right to medical care . . . simply on the ground that the prison medical facilities were inadequate, the essential distinction between judge and executive would have disappeared: it would have become the function of the courts to assure adequate medical care in prisons." *Lewis v. Casey* (1996).

If (as is the case) the only viable constitutional claims consist of individual instances of mistreatment, then a remedy reforming the system as a whole goes far beyond what the statute allows.

It is also worth noting the peculiarity that the vast majority of inmates most generously rewarded by the release order—the 46,000 whose incarceration will be ended—do not form part of any aggrieved class even under the Court's expansive notion of constitutional violation. Most of them will not be prisoners with medical conditions or severe mental illness; and many will undoubtedly be fine physical specimens who have developed intimidating muscles pumping iron in the prison gym.

B

Even if I accepted the implausible premise that the plaintiffs have established a systemwide violation of the Eighth Amendment, I would dissent from the Court's endorsement of a decrowding order. That order is an example of what has become known as a "structural injunction." As I have previously explained, structural injunctions are radically different from the injunctions traditionally issued by courts of equity, and presumably part of "the judicial Power" conferred on federal courts by Article III:

> The mandatory injunctions issued upon termination of litigation usually required "a single simple act." H. McClintock, Principles of Equity. Indeed, there was a "historical prejudice of the court of chancery against rendering decrees which called for more than a single affirmative act." *Id.* And where specific performance of contracts was sought, it was the categorical rule that no decree would issue that required ongoing supervision. . . . Compliance with these "single act" mandates could, in addition to being simple, be quick; and once it was achieved the contemnor's relationship with the court came to an end, at least insofar as the subject of the order was concerned. Once the document was turned over or the land conveyed, the litigant's obligation to the court, and the court's coercive power over the litigant, ceased. . . . The court did not engage in any ongoing supervision of the litigant's conduct, nor did its order continue to regulate its behavior.

Mine Workers v. Bagwell (1994) (Scalia, J., concurring).

Structural injunctions depart from that historical practice, turning judges into long-term administrators of complex social institutions such as schools, prisons, and police departments. Indeed, they require judges to play a role essentially indistinguishable from the role ordinarily played by executive officials. Today's decision not only affirms the structural injunction but vastly expands its use, by holding that an entire system is unconstitutional because it *may produce* constitutional violations.

The drawbacks of structural injunctions have been described at great length elsewhere. This case illustrates one of their most pernicious aspects: that they force judges to engage in a form of factfinding-as-policymaking that is outside the traditional judicial role. The factfinding judges traditionally engage in involves the determination of past or present facts based (except for a limited set of materials of which courts may take "judicial notice") exclusively upon a closed trial record. That is one reason why a district judge's factual findings are entitled to plain-error review: because having viewed the trial first hand he is in a better position to evaluate the evidence than a judge reviewing a cold record. In a very limited category of cases, judges have also traditionally been called upon to make some predictive judgments: which custody will best serve the interests of the child, for example, or whether a particular one-shot injunction will remedy the plaintiff's grievance. When a judge manages a structural injunction, however, he will inevitably be required to make very broad empirical predictions necessarily based in large part upon policy views—the sort of predictions regularly made by legislators and executive officials, but inappropriate for the Third Branch.

This feature of structural injunctions is superbly illustrated by the District Court's proceeding concerning the decrowding order's effect on public safety . . . making the "factual finding" that "the state has available methods by which it could readily reduce the prison population to 137.5% design capacity or less without an adverse impact on public safety or the operation of the criminal justice system." . . . It found that "the diversion of offenders to community correctional programs has significant beneficial effects on public safety."

The District Court cast these predictions (and the Court today accepts them) as "factual findings," made in reliance on the procession of expert witnesses that testified at trial. Because these "findings" have support in the record, it is difficult to reverse them under a plain-error standard of review. And given that the District Court devoted nearly 10 days of trial and 70 pages of its opinion to this issue, it is difficult to dispute that the District Court has discharged its statutory obligation to give "substantial weight to any adverse impact on public safety."

But the idea that the three District Judges in this case relied solely on the credibility of the testifying expert witnesses is fanciful. *Of course* they were relying largely on their own beliefs about penology and recidivism. And *of course* different district judges, of different policy views, would have "found" that rehabilitation would not work and that releasing prisoners would increase the crime rate. I am not saying that the District Judges rendered their factual findings in bad faith. I am saying that it is impossible for judges to make "factual findings" without inserting their own policy judgments, when the factual findings *are* policy judgments. . . .

Three years of law school and familiarity with pertinent Supreme Court precedents give no insight whatsoever into the management of social institutions. Thus, in the proceeding below the District Court determined that constitutionally adequate medical services could be provided if the prison population was 137.5% of design capacity. This was an empirical finding it was utterly unqualified to make. . . . [T]he ability of judges to spit back or even average-out numbers spoon-fed to them by expert witnesses does not render them competent decisionmakers in areas in which they are otherwise unqualified.

C

My general concerns associated with judges' running social institutions are magnified when they run prison systems, and doubly magnified when they force prison officials to release convicted criminals. As we have previously recognized:

> [C]ourts are ill equipped to deal with the increasingly urgent problems of prison administration and reform. . . . [T]he problems of prisons in America are complex and intractable, and, more to the point, they are not readily susceptible of resolution by decree. . . . Running a prison is an inordinately difficult undertaking that requires expertise, planning, and the commitment of resources, all of which are peculiarly within the province of the legislative and executive branches of government. Prison is, moreover, a task that has been committed to the responsibility of those branches, and

separation of powers concerns counsel a policy of judicial restraint. Where a state penal system is involved, federal courts have . . . additional reason to accord deference to the appropriate prison authorities.

Turner v. Safley (1987).

These principles apply doubly to a prisoner-release order. . . . Recognizing that habeas relief must be granted sparingly, we have reversed the Ninth Circuit's erroneous grant of habeas relief to individual California prisoners four times this Term alone. And yet here, the Court affirms an order granting the functional equivalent of 46,000 writs of habeas corpus, based on its paean to courts' "substantial flexibility when making these judgments." It seems that the Court's respect for state sovereignty has vanished in the case where it most matters. . . .

The District Court's order that California release 46,000 prisoners extends "further than necessary to correct the violation of the Federal right of a particular plaintiff or plaintiffs" who have been denied needed medical care. 18 U.S.C. §3626(a)(1)(A). It is accordingly forbidden by the PLRA — besides defying all sound conception of the proper role of judges.

[Justice ALITO, joined by The CHIEF JUSTICE, dissented, contending that "[t]he three-judge court ordered the premature release of approximately 46,000 criminals — the equivalent of three Army divisions" and that the court gave inadequate weight to the impact of its decree on public safety.]

* * *

The majority went to great lengths to show how the dire circumstances in California's prisons met the specific standards the PLRA sets out for an overcrowding order that will result in the release of prisoners. But in addition to these requirements, §3626(a) limits all forms of injunctive relief in prisons cases to orders that extend no further than necessary to correct the violation of the constitutional right, are the least restrictive means, and are narrowly tailored. Congress' intent is crystal clear: no relief can be granted unless it is strictly necessary to correct the violation of the constitutional right. Isn't an order that will result in the release of healthy prisoners by definition overbroad under §3626(a)? Is it enough that prior more modest efforts to address the systemic problems in health care had failed? That the state played a role in designing the prior reforms?

Congress can restrict equity power of the lower federal courts. Can it do so even if the effect would be to deny a remedy for violation of a constitutional right? Perhaps this explains the majority's interpretation of §3626(a).

Another area in which Congress has limited lower federal court equity power includes the Tax Injunction Act of 1937, which provides that the federal "district courts shall not enjoin, suspend or restrain the assessment, levy or collection of any tax under State law where a plain, speedy and efficient remedy may be had in the courts of such State." 28 U.S.C. §1341. Is it appropriate that even non-resident taxpayers will have to litigate in state court and accept the resolution of their federal constitutional rights regarding the state tax as final absent certiorari in the U.S. Supreme Court?

Is it sufficient to defend the constitutionality of the Norris-LaGuardia Act to point to the availability of state law remedies in state court which the statute does not disturb? Note that in the collection of *federal* taxes there is an even more sweeping jurisdictional bar. The Tax Anti-Injunction Act of 1867 provides that "no suit for the purpose of restraining the assessment or collection of any tax shall be maintained *in any court by any person. . . .*" 26 U.S.C. §7421. A taxpayer's only recourse is to pay the taxes assessed by the IRS, file a formal administrative claim for a refund with the IRS, and then sue in federal court if the administrative claim is denied. *See* 26 U.S.C. §7422; 28 U.S.C. §1346(a)(1); *Flora v. United States* (1960).

Note that Congress also imposes limits on remedies other than injunctions. Title VII of the Civil Rights Act, for instance, caps money damages for employment discrimination according to the size of the employer. Liability for compensatory damages against an employer with 100 or fewer employees is limited to $50,000; the cap is $300,000 for an employer with more than 500 employees. 42 U.S.C. 1981a(b)(3)(A) & (D). Backpay is excluded. 42 U.S.C. §1981a(b)(1). And a specific standard of "malice or . . . reckless indifference to the federally protected rights of an aggrieved individual" is set out for punitive damages. 42 U.S.C. §1981a(b)(1).

2. Congressional Control of the Jurisdiction of the U.S. Supreme Court

In addition to the control of lower federal court jurisdiction conferred on Congress by the "inferior courts" clause of Article III, the "exceptions clause" confers on Congress the power to make "exceptions" to the appellate jurisdiction of the Supreme Court. Article III, Section 2 states that in all cases not within the Court's original jurisdiction, "the Supreme Court shall have appellate jurisdiction, both as to law and fact, with such exceptions, and under such regulations as the Congress may have directed."

The question whether there are any limits to Congress' control of the Court's appellate jurisdiction is taken up in the following cases. The canonical case, *Ex parte McCardle*, was decided in the throws of Reconstruction. Historians generally divide Reconstruction into three phases. The first, Military Reconstruction, begins with the self-emancipation of African Americans during the war and the ensuing decision of the Lincoln Administration to issue the Emancipation Proclamation in 1863. Emancipation raises the question of how the Union will recognize the freedom, status, and rights of Black people escaping from slavery. As the Union Army defeats Confederate opposition and comes into possession and control of land south of the Mason-Dixon line, the question how and on what terms to reconstruct Southern governments becomes unavoidable.

The second phase, Presidential Reconstruction, begins with the assassination of Lincoln in 1865, the ratification of the Thirteenth Amendment, and the constitutional crisis provoked by Andrew Johnson's commitment to undermine Reconstruction and move directly to reconciliation. There were no treason trials of Confederate officials. Instead, Johnson granted thousands of pardons to unreconstructed white supremacist former Confederate officials and ordered the immediate readmission of Southern states run by these officials back into the Union even as they were legislating and enforcing "Black Codes" to resubordinate African Americans. Drawn on the model of Slave Codes of the antebellum era, these new legal codes deemed Black people to be "vagrants" if they did not have work and "unlawfully assembl[ed] together." Mississippi Black Code, Section 2 (1865). In this way Black people were made subject to arrest, fines, and "hiring out" for terms of labor if the fines could not be paid. Section 5. Failure to pay a state tax by a

Black person was grounds for impressing the person into labor. Section 7. The law required local law enforcement officers to track down and impress Black minor children into "apprentice" labor with a "preference" granted to "the former owner[s]." Section 1. Corporal punishment was expressly authorized, and criminal punishment "as provided for by law for desertion" was authorized if a minor abandoned the work. Section 2. Adult Black people were treated as criminal fugitives if they "deserted" their "legal employer," subject not only to criminal punishment but remand back to the employer by law enforcement officers. Section 7. Quitting employment forfeited all wages earned for the year to that point. Section 6.

The Republican-controlled Congress responded by passing the 1866 Civil Rights Act and, in order to ensure ratification of the Fourteenth Amendment, the 1867 Military Reconstruction Act. That statute, passed over Johnson's veto, opened the third phase of Reconstruction in which Republican majorities in Congress seized the reins of Reconstruction policy from the President—so-called Congressional Reconstruction. The Military Reconstruction Act dissolved the Southern states into five military districts subject to federal martial law, charged the military with suppressing insurrection, disorder and violence, and punished crimes and disruptions of the peace using either local tribunals or military commissions. It disenfranchised Southerners who had participated in the rebellion against the republic, enfranchised all other men "of whatever race, color, or previous condition," and then conditioned formal readmission to the Union of these states upon their ratification of the Fourteenth Amendment.[12]

Alongside the Military Reconstruction Act, Congress also passed a new Habeas Corpus Act in 1867 to ensure the availability of a federal forum to challenge deprivations of liberty arising from the Black Codes and other efforts in the Southern states to interfere with Reconstruction. The new Habeas Corpus Act provided that the lower federal courts "should have power to grant writs of habeas corpus in all cases where any person may be restrained of his or her liberty in violation of the Constitution, or of any treaty or law of the United States." *Ex parte McCardle* (1868). The statute also extended appellate jurisdiction to the Supreme Court from any judgment of the circuit courts granting or denying the writ.

Although written with a view to protecting Black people and proponents of Reconstruction held in state custody, the statute by its terms provided jurisdiction over people held in federal custody as well. William McCardle was a staunch Southern opponent of Reconstruction and newspaper editor for the Vicksburg Times. He was arrested by the federal military on charges of disturbing the peace, inciting to insurrection and disorder, libel and impeding Reconstruction, "solely on the basis of several vituperative, anti-reconstructionist editorials. . . ."[13] One editorial urged Whites to boycott an "election to authorize a state constitutional convention" that would ratify the Fourteenth Amendment and "offered to pay one dollar for the name of any white known to have voted and promised to publish the names in the Times."[14] He unsuccessfully sought habeas relief from the local federal circuit court in Mississippi, and appealed to the Supreme Court. The essence of McCardle's appeal was that his arrest and trial by military commission were unconstitutional abridgments of his right to be tried by an Article III court under *Ex parte Milligan* (1867), and that

---

12. Harold Hyman and William Wiecek, *Equal Justice Under Law: Constitutional Development 1835-1875* (1982).

13. William Van Alstyne, *A Critical Guide to* Ex parte McCardle, 15 Ariz. L. Rev. 229 (1973).

14. *Id.* at 236 n.42.

the Military Reconstruction Act's suspension of trial by ordinary criminal courts was unconstitutional. In this way, the Habeas Corpus Act of 1867, "intended by its sponsors to establish habeas jurisdiction principally to enable the Supreme Court to review *state* laws impeding reconstruction and subordinating federal rights, was about to be used with the immediate prospect that a *federal* statute deemed vital to reconstruction might be held unconstitutional."[15] The constitutionality of the very centerpiece of congressional reconstruction—a massive assertion of national sovereignty against states still in active resistance two years after Appomattox—was suddenly before the Court on terms that might result in the entire project being held unconstitutional.

Republicans in Congress sensed the danger. Three months after the Court heard oral argument on the case Congress attached the following rider to a tax appeals bill:

> And be it further enacted, That so much of the act approved February [5, 1867], entitled "An act to establish the judicial courts of the United States, approved September [24, 1789]," as authorizes an appeal from the judgment of the circuit court to the Supreme Court of the United States, or the exercise of any such jurisdiction by said Supreme Court on appeals which have been or may hereafter be taken, be, and the same is, hereby repealed.

Act of March 27, 1868, Ch. 34, §2. Johnson vetoed the bill, arguing that the essence of habeas jurisdiction is to "'secure the blessings of liberty'" and that the bill "'establishes a precedent which, if followed, may eventually sweep away every check on arbitrary and unconstitutional legislation.'"[16] Congress overrode the veto, its opponents taking pains to insist that Republicans were altering jurisdictional rules to suit their purposes: "We all know, the whole world knows," Sen. Doolittle of Wisconsin insisted in response to supporters' claim that the bill was "of very little importance," that "this case of McCardle is pending in the Supreme Court."[17] As you read the case, pay close attention to the principles of statutory construction used to justify dismissal of McCardle's appeal even as jurisdiction is expressly reserved despite the clear language of the 1868 Repealer Act and the clear in intention of Congress to preclude the Court from addressing the constitutionality of the Military Reconstruction Act on petitions for habeas corpus.

Ex parte McCardle

74 U.S. 506 (1868)

THE CHIEF JUSTICE delivered the opinion of the court.

The first question necessarily is that of jurisdiction, for if the act of March, 1868, takes away the jurisdiction defined by the act of February, 1867, it is useless, if not improper, to enter into any discussion of other questions.

It is quite true, as was argued by the counsel for the petitioner, that the appellate jurisdiction of this court is not derived from acts of Congress. It is, strictly speaking, conferred by the Constitution. But it is conferred "with such exceptions and under such regulations as Congress shall make."

---

15. *Id.* at 238.

16. *Id.* at 240 (quoting President Johnson).

17. *Id.* at 241 n.53 (quoting Sen. Doolittle).

It is unnecessary to consider whether, if Congress had made no exceptions and no regulations, this court might not have exercised general appellate jurisdiction under rules prescribed by itself. For among the earliest acts of the first Congress, at its first session, was the act of September 24th, 1789, to establish the judicial courts of the United States. That act provided for the organization of this court, and prescribed regulations for the exercise of its jurisdiction.

The source of that jurisdiction, and the limitations of it by the Constitution and by statute, have been on several occasions subjects of consideration here. In the case of *Durousseau v. United States* (1810), particularly, the whole matter was carefully examined, and the court held that, while "the appellate powers of this court are not given by the judicial act, but are given by the Constitution," they are, nevertheless, "limited and regulated by that act, and by such other acts as have been passed on the subject." The court said further that the judicial act was an exercise of the power given by the Constitution to Congress "of making exceptions to the appellate jurisdiction of the Supreme Court." "They have described affirmatively," said the court, "its jurisdiction, and this affirmative description has been understood to imply a negation of the exercise of such appellate power as is not comprehended within it."

The principle that the affirmation of appellate jurisdiction implies the negation of all such jurisdiction not affirmed having been thus established, it was an almost necessary consequence that acts of Congress, providing for the exercise of jurisdiction, should come to be spoken of as acts granting jurisdiction, and not as acts making exceptions to the constitutional grant of it.

The exception to appellate jurisdiction in the case before us, however, is not an inference from the affirmation of other appellate jurisdiction. It is made in terms. The provision of the act of 1867 affirming the appellate jurisdiction of this court in cases of habeas corpus is expressly repealed. It is hardly possible to imagine a plainer instance of positive exception.

We are not at liberty to inquire into the motives of the legislature. We can only examine into its power under the Constitution, and the power to make exceptions to the appellate jurisdiction of this court is given by express words.

What, then, is the effect of the repealing act upon the case before us? We cannot doubt as to this. Without jurisdiction, the court cannot proceed at all in any cause. Jurisdiction is power to declare the law, and, when it ceases to exist, the only function remaining to the court is that of announcing the fact and dismissing the cause. And this is not less clear upon authority than upon principle.

The subject was fully considered in *Norris v. Crocker* (1851), and more recently in *Insurance Company v. Ritchie* (1866). In both of these cases, it was held that no judgment could be rendered in a suit after the repeal of the act under which it was brought and prosecuted.

It is quite clear, therefore, that this court cannot proceed to pronounce judgment in this case, for it has no longer jurisdiction of the appeal, and judicial duty is not less fitly performed by declining ungranted jurisdiction than in exercising firmly that which the Constitution and the laws confer.

Counsel seem to have supposed, if effect be given to the repealing act in question, that the whole appellate power of the court, in cases of habeas corpus, is denied. But this is an error. The act of 1868 does not except from that jurisdiction any cases but appeals from Circuit Courts under the act of 1867. It does not affect the jurisdiction which was previously exercised.[8]

The appeal of the petitioner in this case must be *dismissed for want of jurisdiction.*

* * *

The Repealer Act was not the only instance of congressional action to limit the powers of the Supreme Court in the period. In 1866, it cut the size of the Court from ten to seven members. And it was working on a bill to require a supermajority vote of the justices of the Court to overturn an act of Congress.[18] Do these strike you as more or less controversial than stripping the Court of its appellate jurisdiction in a pending case?

The Court was presented with another habeas petition involving the constitutionality of the Military Reconstruction Act's provision for trial by military commission in the following case. Yerger, like McCardle, was a Southern loyalist and newspaper editor. He was charged with the murder of Colonel Joseph Crane—a U.S. Army officer functioning as mayor of the City of Jackson, Mississippi to enforce Reconstruction laws. In an "act of rage and vengeance" that "epitomized the violent recalcitrance of the . . . South" and stoked debate about the feasibility of "military occupation of the former Confederate states," Yerger stabbed Colonel Crane to death on a public street in a drunken fury, ostensibly for having a piano of Yerger's seized to satisfy his substantial public debts.[19] He sought relief from trial by military commission in the Fifth Circuit. That petition was denied and, following the path marked by the Supreme Court in the concluding paragraphs of its opinion in *McCardle*, he appealed. As in *McCardle*, pay close attention to the canons of statutory construction the Court uses to interpret Congress' exercise of its exceptions clause power.

Ex parte Yerger

75 U.S. 85 (1868)

. . . The great writ of habeas corpus has been for centuries esteemed the best and only sufficient defense of personal freedom.

In England, after a long struggle, it was firmly guaranteed by the famous Habeas Corpus Act of May 27, 1679, "for the better securing of the liberty of the subject," which, as Blackstone says, "is frequently considered as another Magna Charta."

It was brought to America by the colonists and claimed as among the immemorial rights descended to them from their ancestors.

---

8. *Ex parte McCardle* (1867). [The Court's earlier decision in *McCardle* recognized that "the exercise of appellate jurisdiction was not unknown to the practice of this Court before the act of 1867" under Section 14 of the First Judiciary Act of 1789, an independent head of habeas jurisdiction.]

18. Van Alstyne, *supra* note 13, at 248 n.72.

19. TED OWNBY, ET AL., THE MISSISSIPPI ENCYCLOPEDIA 408 (2017).

Naturally, therefore, when the confederated colonies became united States and the formation of a common government engaged their deliberations in convention, this great writ found prominent sanction in the Constitution. That sanction is in these words:

> The privilege of the writ of habeas corpus shall not be suspended unless when in cases of rebellion or invasion the public safety may require it.

The terms of this provision necessarily imply judicial action. In England, all the higher courts where open to applicants for the writ, and it is hardly supposable that, under the new government founded on more liberal ideas and principles, any court would be intentionally closed to them.

We find accordingly that the first Congress under the Constitution, after defining, by various sections of the Act of September 24, 1789, the jurisdiction of the district courts, the circuit courts, and the Supreme Court in other cases, proceeded in the 14th section to enact,

> That all the beforementioned courts of the United States shall have power to issue writs of *scire facias*, habeas corpus, and all other writs, not specially provided by statute, which may be necessary for the exercise of their respective jurisdictions and agreeable to the principles and usages of law.

In the same section, it was further provided

> that either of the Justices of the Supreme Court, as well as Judges of the district courts, shall have power to grant writs of habeas corpus for the purpose of an inquiry into the cause of commitment, provided that writs of habeas corpus shall in no case extend to prisoners in jail unless they are in custody under or by color of the authority of the United States or are committed for trial before some court of the same or are necessary to be brought into court to testify.

That this Court is one of the courts to which the power to issue writs of habeas corpus is expressly given by the terms of this section has never been questioned. It would have been, indeed, a remarkable anomaly if this Court, ordained by the Constitution for the exercise in the United States of the most important powers in civil cases of all the highest courts of England, had been denied, under a constitution which absolutely prohibits the suspension of the writ except under extraordinary exigencies, that power in cases of alleged unlawful restraint which the Habeas Corpus Act of Charles II expressly declares those courts to possess.

But the power vested in this Court is, in an important particular, unlike that possessed by the English courts. The jurisdiction of this Court is conferred by the Constitution, and is appellate, whereas that of the English courts, though declared and defined by statutes, is derived from the common law and is original. . . . If the question were new one, it would perhaps deserve inquiry whether Congress might not, under the power to make exceptions from this appellate jurisdiction, extend the original jurisdiction to other cases than those expressly enumerated in the Constitution, and especially, in view of the constitutional guaranty of the writ of habeas corpus, to cases arising upon petition for that writ.

But in the case of *Marbury v. Madison* it was determined upon full consideration that the power to issue writs of mandamus given to this Court by the 13th section of the Judiciary Act is, under the Constitution, an appellate jurisdiction, to be exercised only in the revision of judicial decisions. And this judgment has ever since been accepted as fixing the construction of this part of the Constitution.

It was pronounced in 1803. In 1807, the same construction was given to the provision of the 14th section relating to the writ of habeas corpus, in the case of [*Ex parte*] *Bollman and Swartwout* (1807).

In the case of *Bollman and Swartwout*, . . . the nature of the jurisdiction was carefully examined, and it was declared to be appellate. The question then determined has not since been drawn into controversy.

The doctrine of the Constitution and of the cases thus far may be summed up in these propositions:

(1) The original jurisdiction of this Court cannot be extended by Congress to any other cases than those expressly defined by the Constitution.

(2) The appellate jurisdiction of this Court, conferred by the Constitution, extends to all other cases within the judicial power of the United States.

(3) This appellate jurisdiction is subject to such exceptions and must be exercised under such regulations as Congress, in the exercise of its discretion, has made or may see fit to make.

(4) Congress not only has not excepted writs of habeas corpus and mandamus from this appellate jurisdiction, but has expressly provided for the exercise of this jurisdiction by means of these writs.

We come, then, to consider the first great question made in the case now before us. We shall assume upon the authority of the decisions referred to what we should hold were the question now for the first time presented to us, that in a proper case this Court, under the Act of 1789, and under all the subsequent acts, giving jurisdiction in cases of habeas corpus may, in the exercise of its appellate power, revise the decisions of inferior courts of the United States and relieve from unlawful imprisonment authorized by them except in cases within some limitations of the jurisdiction by Congress.

It remains to inquire whether the case before us is a proper one for such interposition. Is it within any such limitation? In other words, can this Court inquire into the lawfulness of detention, and relieve from it if found unlawful, when the detention complained of is not by civil authority under a commitment made by an inferior court, but by military officers, for trial before a military tribunal, after an examination into the cause of detention by the inferior court, resulting in an order remanding the prisoner to custody?

It was insisted in argument that

to bring a case within the appellate jurisdiction of this Court in the sense requisite to enable it to award the writ of habeas corpus under the Judiciary Act, it is necessary that the commitment should appear to have been by a tribunal whose decisions are subject to revision by this Court.

The great and leading intent of the Constitution and the law . . . in respect to the writ of habeas corpus, is . . . that every citizen may be protected by judicial action from unlawful imprisonment. To this end, the Act of 1789 provided that every court of the United States should have power to issue the writ. The jurisdiction thus given in law to the circuit and district courts is original; that given by the Constitution and the law to this Court is appellate. Given in general terms, it must necessarily extend to all cases to which the judicial power of the United States extends other than those expressly excepted from it.

As limited by the Act of 1789, it did not extend to cases of imprisonment after conviction under sentences of competent tribunals, nor to prisoners in jail unless in custody under or by color of the authority of the United States or committed for trial before some court of the United States or required to be brought into court to testify. But this limitation has been gradually narrowed, and the benefits of the writ have been extended, first in 1833[19] to prisoners confined under any authority, whether state of national, for any act done or omitted in pursuance of a law of the United States or of any order, process, or decree of any judge of court of the United States; then in 1842[20] to prisoners being subjects or citizens of foreign states, in custody under national or state authority for acts done or omitted by or under color of foreign authority and alleged to be valid under the law of nations, and finally, in 1867, to all cases where any person may be restrained of liberty in violation of the Constitution or of any treaty or law of the United States.

This brief statement shows how the general spirit and genius of our institutions has tended to the widening and enlarging of the habeas corpus jurisdiction of the courts and judges of the United States, and this tendency, except in one recent instance, has been constant and uniform, and it is in the light of it that we must determine the true meaning of the Constitution and the law in respect to the appellate jurisdiction of this Court. We are not at liberty to except from it any cases not plainly excepted by law, and we think it sufficiently appears from what has been said that no exception to this jurisdiction embraces such a case as that now before the Court. On the contrary, the case is one of those expressly declared not to be excepted from the general grant of jurisdiction. For it is a case of imprisonment alleged to be unlawful and to be under color of authority of the United States.

It seems to be a necessary consequence that if the appellate jurisdiction of habeas corpus extends to any case, it extends to this. It is unimportant in what custody the prisoner may be if it is a custody to which he has been remanded by the order of an inferior court of the United States. It is proper to add that we are not aware of anything in any act of Congress, except the Act of 1868, which indicates any intention to withhold appellate jurisdiction in habeas corpus cases from this Court or to abridge the jurisdiction derived from the Constitution and defined by the Act of 1789. We agree that it is given subject to exception and regulation by Congress, but it is too plain for argument that the denial to this Court of appellate jurisdiction in this class of cases must greatly weaken the efficacy of the writ, deprive the citizen in many cases of its benefits, and seriously hinder the establishment of that uniformity in deciding upon questions of personal rights which can only be attained through appellate jurisdiction, exercised upon the decisions of courts of original jurisdiction.

In the particular class of cases of which that before the court is an example, when the custody to which the prisoner is remanded is that of some authority other than that of the remanding court, it is evident that the imprisoned citizen, however unlawful his imprisonment may be in fact, is wholly without remedy unless it be found in the appellate jurisdiction of this Court.

These considerations forbid any construction giving to doubtful words the effect of withholding or abridging this jurisdiction. They would strongly persuade against the denial of the jurisdiction even were the reasons for affirming it less cogent than they are.

---

19. Act of March 2, 1833.
20. Act of August 29, 1842.

We are obliged to hold, therefore, that in all cases where a circuit court of the United States has, in the exercise of its original jurisdiction, caused a prisoner to be brought before it and has, after inquiring into the cause of detention, remanded him to the custody from which he was taken, this Court, in the exercise of its appellate jurisdiction, may, by the writ of habeas corpus, aided by the writ of certiorari, revise the decision of the circuit court, and if it be found unwarranted by law, relieve the prisoner from the unlawful restraint to which he has been remanded.

This conclusion brings us to the inquiry whether the 2d section of the Act of March 27, 1868, takes away or affects the appellate jurisdiction of this Court under the Constitution and the acts of Congress prior to 1867.

In *McCardle's Case* (1868), we expressed the opinion that it does not, and we have now reexamined the grounds of that opinion.

The circumstances under which the Act of 1868 was passed were peculiar. . . . The effect of the act was to oust the Court of its jurisdiction of the particular case then before it on appeal, and it is not to be doubted that such was the effect intended. Nor will it be questioned that legislation of this character is unusual and hardly to be justified except upon some imperious public exigency.

It was doubtless within the constitutional discretion of Congress to determine whether such an exigency existed, but it is not to be presumed that an act, passed under such circumstances, was intended to have any further effect than that plainly apparent from its terms.

It is quite clear that the words of the act reach not only all appeals pending, but all future appeals to this Court under the Act of 1867, but they appear to be limited to appeals taken under that act.

The words of the repealing section are . . . not of doubtful interpretation. They repeal only so much of the Act of 1867 as authorized appeals or the exercise of appellate jurisdiction by this Court.

It has been suggested, however, that the Act of 1789, so far as it provided for the issuing of writs of habeas corpus by this Court, was already repealed by the Act of 1867. We have already observed that there are no repealing words in the Act of 1867. If it repealed the Act of 1789, it did so by implication, and any implication which would give to it this effect upon the Act of 1789 would give it the same effect upon the Acts of 1833 and 1842. If one was repealed, all were repealed.

Repeals by implication are not favored.

Our conclusion is that none of the acts prior to 1867 authorizing this Court to exercise appellate jurisdiction by means of the writ of habeas corpus was repealed by the act of that year, and that the repealing section of the Act of 1868 is limited in terms, and must be limited in effect to the appellate jurisdiction authorized by the Act of 1867.

We could come to no other conclusion without holding that the whole appellate jurisdiction of this Court, in cases of habeas corpus, conferred by the Constitution, recognized by law, and exercised from the foundation of the government hitherto, has been taken away, without the expression of such intent and by mere implication, through the operation of the Acts of 1867 and 1868.

* * *

After the Court upheld its jurisdiction over Yerger's petition, the Grant Administration, more serious about enforcing Reconstruction than Andrew Johnson, mooted the appeal by remanding Yerger out of federal military custody to state authorities in Mississippi. No longer in federal custody, the writ could provide no relief. Yerger fled to Maryland and escaped all legal accountability for the murder.

In a series of modern cases, the Supreme Court has applied the same canons of statutory construction to congressional efforts to strip its appellate jurisdiction, especially the grant of habeas jurisdiction contained in the First Judiciary Act. *Felker v. Turpin* (1996) relies on *Yerger* and examines new limits on review of "successive" post-conviction habeas petitions filed by a defendant convicted of murder and multiple sexual assaults.

Felker v. Turpin

518 U.S. 651 (1996)

Chief Justice REHNQUIST delivered the opinion of the Court.

Title I of the Antiterrorism and Effective Death Penalty Act of 1996 (Act) works substantial changes to chapter 153 of Title 28 of the United States Code, which authorizes federal courts to grant the writ of habeas corpus. We hold that the Act does not preclude this Court from entertaining an application for habeas corpus relief, although it does affect the standards governing the granting of such relief. We also conclude that the availability of such relief in this Court obviates any claim by petitioner under the Exceptions Clause of Article III, §2, of the Constitution, and that the operative provisions of the Act do not violate the Suspension Clause of the Constitution, Art. I, §9.

I

On a night in 1976, petitioner approached Jane W. in his car as she got out of hers. Claiming to be lost and looking for a party nearby, he used a series of deceptions to induce Jane to accompany him to his trailer home in town. Petitioner forcibly subdued her, raped her, and sodomized her. Jane pleaded with petitioner to let her go, but he said he could not because she would notify the police. She escaped later, when petitioner fell asleep. Jane notified the police, and petitioner was eventually convicted of aggravated sodomy and sentenced to 12 years' imprisonment.

Petitioner was paroled four years later. On November 23, 1981, he met Joy Ludlam, a cocktail waitress, at the lounge where she worked. She was interested in changing jobs, and petitioner used a series of deceptions involving offering her a job at "The Leather Shoppe," a business he owned, to induce her to visit him the next day. The last time Joy was seen alive was the evening of the next day. Her dead body was discovered two weeks later in a creek. Forensic analysis established that she had been beaten, raped, and sodomized, and that she had been strangled to death before being left in the creek. Investigators discovered hair resembling petitioner's on Joy's body and clothes, hair resembling Joy's in petitioner's bedroom, and clothing fibers like those in Joy's coat in the hatchback of petitioner's car. One of petitioner's neighbors reported seeing Joy's car at petitioner's house the day she disappeared.

A jury convicted petitioner of murder, rape, aggravated sodomy, and false imprisonment. Petitioner was sentenced to death on the murder charge. The Georgia Supreme Court affirmed petitioner's conviction and death sentence, and we denied certiorari. A state trial court denied collateral relief, the Georgia Supreme Court declined to issue a certificate of probable cause to appeal the denial, and we again denied certiorari.

Petitioner then filed a petition for a writ of habeas corpus in the United States District Court for the Middle District of Georgia, alleging that (1) the State's evidence was insufficient to convict him; (2) the State withheld exculpatory evidence, in violation of *Brady v. Maryland* (1963); (3) petitioner's counsel rendered ineffective assistance at sentencing; (4) the State improperly used hypnosis to refresh a witness' memory; and (5) the State violated double jeopardy and collateral estoppel principles by using petitioner's crime against Jane W. as evidence at petitioner's trial for crimes against Joy Ludlam. The District Court denied the petition. The United States Court of Appeals for the Eleventh Circuit affirmed . . . and we denied certiorari.

The State scheduled petitioner's execution for the period May 2-9, 1996. On April 29, 1996, petitioner filed a second petition for state collateral relief. The state trial court denied this petition on May 1, and the Georgia Supreme Court denied certiorari on May 2.

On April 24, 1996, the President signed the Act into law. Title I of this Act contained a series of amendments to existing federal habeas corpus law. The provisions of the Act pertinent to this case concern second or successive habeas corpus applications by state prisoners. Section 106(b) specifies the conditions under which claims in second or successive applications must be dismissed, amending 28 U.S.C. §2244(b) to read:

(1) A claim presented in a second or successive habeas corpus application under section 2254 that was presented in a prior application shall be dismissed.

(2) A claim presented in a second or successive habeas corpus application under section 2254 that was not presented in a prior application shall be dismissed unless —

(A) the applicant shows that the claim relies on a new rule of constitutional law, made retroactive to cases on collateral review by the Supreme Court, that was previously unavailable; or

(B)(i) the factual predicate for the claim could not have been discovered previously through the exercise of due diligence; and

(ii) the facts underlying the claim, if proven and viewed in light of the evidence as a whole, would be sufficient to establish by clear and convincing evidence that, but for constitutional error, no reasonable factfinder would have found the applicant guilty of the underlying offense.

28 U.S.C. §2244(b)(3) creates a "gatekeeping" mechanism for the consideration of second or successive applications in district court. The prospective applicant must file in the court of appeals a motion for leave to file a second or successive habeas application in the district court. §2244(b)(3)(A). A three-judge panel has 30 days to determine whether "the application makes a prima facie showing that the application satisfies the requirements of" §2244(b); 2244(b)(3)(C); *see* §§2244(b)(3)(B), (D). Section 2244(b)(3)(E) specifies that "[t]he grant or denial of an authorization by a court of appeals to file a second or successive application shall not be appealable and shall not be the subject of a petition for rehearing or for a writ of certiorari."

On May 2, 1996, petitioner filed in the United States Court of Appeals for the Eleventh Circuit a motion for stay of execution and a motion for leave to file a second or successive federal habeas corpus petition under §2254. Petitioner sought to raise two claims in his second petition, the first being that the state trial court violated due process by equating guilt "beyond a reasonable doubt" with "moral certainty" of guilt in *voir dire* and jury instructions. He also alleged that qualified experts, reviewing the forensic evidence after his conviction, had established that Joy must have died during a period when petitioner was under police surveillance for Joy's disappearance and thus had a valid alibi. He claimed that the testimony of the State's forensic expert at trial was suspect because he is not a licensed physician, and that the new expert testimony so discredited the State's testimony at trial that petitioner had a colorable claim of factual innocence.

The Court of Appeals denied both motions the day they were filed. . . . Petitioner filed in this Court a pleading styled a "Petition for Writ of Habeas Corpus, for Appellate or Certiorari Review of the Decision of the United States Circuit Court for the Eleventh Circuit, and for Stay of Execution." On May 3, we granted petitioner's stay application and petition for certiorari.

II

We first consider to what extent the provisions of Title I of the Act apply to petitions for habeas corpus filed as original matters in this Court pursuant to 28 U.S.C. §§2241 and 2254. We conclude that although the Act does impose new conditions on our authority to grant relief, it does not deprive this Court of jurisdiction to entertain original habeas petitions.

A

Section 2244(b)(3)(E) prevents this Court from reviewing a court of appeals order denying leave to file a second habeas petition by appeal or by writ of certiorari. More than a century ago, we considered whether a statute barring review by appeal of the judgment of a circuit court in a habeas case also deprived this Court of power to entertain an original habeas petition. *Ex parte Yerger* (1869). We consider the same question here with respect to §2244(b)(3)(E).

Yerger's holding is best understood in the light of the availability of habeas corpus review at that time. Section 14 of the Judiciary Act of 1789 authorized all federal courts, including this Court, to grant the writ of habeas corpus when prisoners were "in custody, under or by colour of the authority of the United States, or [were] committed for trial before some court of the same." Act of Sept. 24, 1789, ch. 20, §14.[1] Congress greatly expanded the scope of federal habeas corpus in 1867, authorizing federal courts to grant the writ, "in addition to the authority already conferred by law," "in all cases where any person may be restrained of his or her liberty in violation of the constitution, or of any treaty or law of the United States." Act of Feb. 5, 1867, ch. 28.[2]

---

1. Section 14 is the direct ancestor of 28 U.S.C. §2241, subsection (a) of which now states in pertinent part: "Writs of habeas corpus may be granted by the Supreme Court, any justice thereof, the district courts and any circuit judge within their respective jurisdictions."

2. This language from the 1867 Act is the direct ancestor of §2241(c)(3), which states: "The writ of habeas corpus shall not extend to a prisoner unless . . . [h]e is in custody in violation of the Constitution or laws or treaties of the United States."

. . .

In *Yerger*, we considered whether the Act of 1868 deprived us not only of power to hear an appeal from an inferior court's decision on a habeas petition, but also of power to entertain a habeas petition to this Court under §14 of the Act of 1789. We concluded that the 1868 Act did not affect our power to entertain such habeas petitions. We explained that the 1868 Act's text addressed only jurisdiction over appeals conferred under the Act of 1867, not habeas jurisdiction conferred under the Acts of 1789 and 1867. We rejected the suggestion that the Act of 1867 had repealed our habeas power by implication.

Turning to the present case, we conclude that Title I of the Act has not repealed our authority to entertain original habeas petitions, for reasons similar to those stated in *Yerger*. No provision of Title I mentions our authority to entertain original habeas petitions; in contrast, §103 amends the Federal Rules of Appellate Procedure to bar consideration of original habeas petitions in the courts of appeals. Although §2244(b)(3)(E) precludes us from reviewing, by appeal or petition for certiorari, a judgment on an application for leave to file a second habeas petition in district court, it makes no mention of our authority to hear habeas petitions filed as original matters in this Court. As we declined to find a repeal of §14 of the Judiciary Act of 1789 as applied to this Court by implication then, we decline to find a similar repeal of §2241 of Title 28—its descendant by implication now.

This conclusion obviates one of the constitutional challenges raised. . . . The Act does remove our authority to entertain an appeal or a petition for a writ of certiorari to review a decision of a court of appeals exercising its "gatekeeping" function over a second petition. But since it does not repeal our authority to entertain a petition for habeas corpus, there can be no plausible argument that the Act has deprived this Court of appellate jurisdiction in violation of Article III, §2. . . .

III

Next, we consider whether the Act suspends the writ of habeas corpus in violation of Article I, §9, clause 2, of the Constitution. This Clause provides that "[t]he Privilege of the Writ of Habeas Corpus shall not be suspended, unless when in Cases of Rebellion or Invasion the public Safety may require it." . . . The Act requires a habeas petitioner to obtain leave from the court of appeals before filing a second habeas petition in the district court. But this requirement simply transfers from the district court to the court of appeals a screening function which would previously have been performed by the district court as required by 28 U.S.C. §2254 Rule 9(b). The Act also codifies some of the pre-existing limits on successive petitions, and further restricts the availability of relief to habeas petitioners. But we have long recognized that "the power to award the writ by any of the courts of the United States, must be given by written law," *Ex parte Bollman* (1807), and we have likewise recognized that judgments about the proper scope of the writ are "normally for Congress to make." *Lonchar v. Thomas* (1996).

The new restrictions on successive petitions constitute a modified res judicata rule, a restraint on what is called in habeas corpus practice "abuse of the writ." In *McCleskey v. Zant* (1991), we said that "the doctrine of abuse of the writ refers to a complex and evolving body of equitable principles informed and controlled by historical usage, statutory developments, and judicial decisions." The added restrictions which the Act places on second habeas petitions are well within the compass of this evolutionary process, and we hold that they do not amount to a "suspension" of the writ contrary to Article I, §9.

IV

We have answered the questions presented by the petition for certiorari in this case, and we now dispose of the petition for an original writ of habeas corpus. Our Rule 20.4(a) delineates the standards under which we grant such writs:

". . . To justify the granting of a writ of habeas corpus, the petitioner must show exceptional circumstances warranting the exercise of the Court's discretionary powers and must show that adequate relief cannot be obtained in any other form or from any other court. These writs are rarely granted."

Reviewing petitioner's claims here, they do not materially differ from numerous other claims made by successive habeas petitioners which we have had occasion to review on stay applications to this Court. Neither of them satisfies the requirements of the relevant provisions of the Act, let alone the requirement that there be "exceptional circumstances" justifying the issuance of the writ.

* * *

The Court has protected its appellate jurisdiction in other modern cases such as *Hamdan v. Rumsfeld* (2006), involving the habeas petition of a Guantanamo detainee charged with conspiracy to commit offenses triable by military commission. Hamdan challenged the proceedings in a habeas petition asserting that: (a) Congress had not authorized the government to try him by military commission for conspiracy because that is not a violation of the law of war; and (b) the procedures for the military commission denied him basic rights such as the right to see and hear evidence against him. Hamdan prevailed in the district court and while the appeal of his petition was pending before the Supreme Court on writ of certiorari, Congress enacted a law providing that "no court, justice, or judge shall have jurisdiction to hear or consider— (1) an application for writ of habeas corpus filed by or on behalf of an alien detained by the Department of Defense at Guantanamo Bay, Cuba." 28 U.S.C §2241(e). The Court emphasized that while other provisions of the statute limiting jurisdiction declared that they applied to pending cases, Congress "omitted paragraph (1) from" that directive, and it did so "after having rejected earlier proposed versions of the statute that would have included what is now paragraph (1) within the scope of that directive."

Is it relevant that if a Guantanamo detainee were not brought to trial in an Article III court or before a military commission that there would be no judicial forum whatsoever in which to challenge their indefinite detention? Put in general terms, can Congress close *all* judicial forums? Consider two examples, one from the context of immigration enforcement and the second from the post 9/11 detention of suspected enemy combatants at Guantanamo Bay.

In *I.N.S. v. St. Cyr* (2001), the Court interpreted jurisdiction stripping provisions of 1996 legislation (AEDPA and IRRIRA) for immigration litigation, including 8 U.S.C. §1252(a)(2)(c), which provides: "Notwithstanding any other provision of law, no court shall have jurisdiction to review any final order of removal against an alien who is removable by reason of having committed [one or more enumerated] criminal offense[s]."

The Court held 5-4 that:

a serious Suspension Clause issue would arise if we were to accept the INS'
submission that the 1996 statutes have withdrawn that power from federal
judges and provided no adequate substitute for its exercise. The necessity of resolving such a serious and difficult constitutional issue—and the
desirability of avoiding that necessity—simply reinforce the reasons for
requiring a clear and unambiguous statement of congressional intent.
Moreover, to conclude that the writ is no longer available in this context
would represent a departure from historical practice in immigration law.
The writ of habeas corpus has always been available to review the legality of executive detention. . . . Before and after the enactment in 1875
of the first statute regulating immigration, that jurisdiction was regularly
invoked on behalf of noncitizens, particularly in the immigration context.

Turning to the statutes, the Court concluded:

Neither the title nor the text of [AEDPA] makes any mention of 28 U.S.C.
§2241. . . . [Repeal of other grants of habeas jurisdiction in immigration
cases] cannot be sufficient to eliminate what [those statutes] did not originally grant, namely, habeas jurisdiction pursuant to 28 U.S.C. §2241. *See
Ex parte Yerger* (1868). . . . At no point . . . does IIRIRA make express reference to §2241. Given the historic use of §2241 jurisdiction as a means
of reviewing deportation and exclusion orders, Congress' failure to refer
specifically to §2241 is particularly significant.

Dissenting, Justice Scalia argued that the majority

finds ambiguity in the utterly clear language of a statute that forbids the
district court (and all other courts) to entertain the claim of aliens such
as respondent St. Cyr, who have been found deportable by reason of their
criminal acts. It fabricates a superclear statement, "magic words" requirement for the congressional expression of such an intent, unjustified in
law. . . . And as the fruit of its labors, it brings for a version of the statute
that affords *criminal* aliens *more* opportunities for delay-inducing judicial
review than are afforded to non-criminal aliens [despite Congress' clear]
design[] to *expedite* their removal.

In *Boumediene v. Bush* (2008), as described in greater detail in Chapter 8, the
Court considered a statute enacted after *Hamdan* that again sought to completely
eliminate habeas jurisdiction for any non-citizen who has been "determined by the
United States to have been properly detained as an enemy combatant or is awaiting such determination." These statutes provided, as a substitute to habeas, limited
review in the D.C. Circuit of decisions on a detainee's status as an enemy combatant by the Department of Defense's Combatant Status Review Tribunals. The Court
struck down the elimination of habeas jurisdiction, concluding that the Suspension Clause applies to non-citizens detained overseas. The Court reasoned that the
United States exercised functional control over Guantanamo Bay; the petitioners
contested their status as "enemy combatants"; and there were few practical difficulties associated with providing petitioners with access to federal court. Accordingly,
in the absence of a suspension of the writ, Congress' effort to deny the detainess

access to federal district court constituted an inadequate substitute for the writ of habeas corpus. Relying on historical evidence, the Court concluded that the Suspension Clause "not only protects against arbitrary suspensions of the writ but also guarantees an affirmative right to judicial inquiry into the causes of detention."

If Congress has power over the appellate jurisdiction of the Supreme Court and federal courts should on separation of powers grounds defer to Congress' decisions about when judicial power exists, why is the Court working so hard to reserve some portion of its appellate jurisdiction even when Congress seeks to oust it? If the federal courts are courts of limited subject matter jurisdiction under Article III, why does the Supreme Court apply strict rules of construction to statutes limiting jurisdiction? Why are the central cases involving reservation of jurisdiction habeas cases?

3.   *Dictating Rules of Decision in Pending Cases: The* Klein *Principle*

Congress regularly legislates procedural rules of decision that have effects on the outcomes of cases. The rules of procedure contained in Title 28 and the Federal Rules of Civil Procedure, along with the Federal Rules of Evidence, are straightforward examples. Congress also legislates substantive rules of decision that have outcome determinative effects. Such legislation generally applies to pending litigation. But what if Congress goes beyond merely providing a rule of decision and purports to dictate the outcome in a case? In *United States v. Klein* (1871), the Court considered this question. In a series of statutes passed between 1861 and 1863, Congress enacted that all property used in aiding, abetting, or promoting the insurrection of the confederate states could be subject to seizure and forfeiture, and that anyone engaging in or aiding the rebellion shall forfeit their property. A cause of action would lie in the Court of Claims for two years after the suppression of the rebellion to recoup the proceeds of any property mistakenly seized and sold upon proof "that he has never given any aid or comfort to the present rebellion."

This confiscation policy served multiple goals that changed over the course of the war. The policy siphoned off sources of the Confederacy's financing and encouraged those living in the South to support the Union. The policy also provided resources for the Department of War and the Bureau of Refugees, Freedmen, and Abandoned Lands (the "Freedmen's Bureau") to assist refugees and formerly enslaved persons to secure full citizenship and meaningful economic opportunities. These latter plans were obstructed, however, by President Andrew Johnson who favored prompt sectional reconciliation over Reconstruction. Upon coming to power, Johnson sought "to have the seceded States return back to their former condition as quickly as possible,"[20] and, as described in Section A.2 of this Chapter, he freely granted pardons to Southerners to achieve that goal. President Johnson also directly interfered with efforts to distribute land to formerly enslaved Black

---

20. Steven F. Miller, Susan E. O'Donovan, John C. Rodrigue & Leslie S. Rowland, *Between Emancipation and Enfranchisement: Law and the Political Mobilization of Black Southerners during Presidential Reconstruction, 1865–1867–Freedom: Political,* 70 CHI.-KENT L. REV. 1059, 1060 (1995).

Americans, ordering a termination of policies like Gerneral Sherman's famed attempt to redistribute "forty acres and a mule" to them. President Johnson's efforts helped restore the antebellum White aristocratic powerbase in the South built on economic exploitation, violent terror, and legal apartheid.[21]

Klein, the administrator of the estate of a Southerner who had been pardoned by President Lincoln, sued in the Court of Claims to recover the proceeds of the sale of cotton seized by federal treasury agents. Klein recovered $125,300 for the estate, relying heavily on the fact that the owner of the cotton had received a presidential pardon before his death. While Klein's case was on appeal, the Supreme Court held in a separate case that a presidential pardon made a claimant "as innocent in law as though he had never participated." Within three months of the Supreme Court's decision in that case, and while the government's appeal in *Klein* was still pending, Congress passed a law providing that

> no pardon or amnesty granted by the President . . . shall be admissible in evidence on the part of any claimant in the Court of Claims as evidence in support of any claim against the United States . . . nor shall any such pardon . . . be used or considered by the appellate court on appeal from said court, in deciding upon the claim of said claimant, or any appeal therefrom, as any part of the proof to sustain the claim of the claimant. . . . And in all cases where judgment shall have been heretofore rendered in the Court of Claims in favor of any claimant . . . the Supreme Court shall, on appeal, have no further jurisdiction of the cause, and shall dismiss the same for want of jurisdiction.

The statute went on to require that a presidential pardon shall be treated as "conclusive evidence that" the recipient "did take part in, and give aid and comfort to, the late rebellion . . . and the court shall forthwith dismiss the suit of such claimant."

The Supreme Court held the statute unconstitutional. The defect was not, the Court insisted, that Congress had modified the operation of the Court of Claims or appeals therefrom. "Undoubtedly," the Court conceded, "the legislature has complete control over the organization and existence of that court, and may confer or withhold the right of appeal from its decisions. And if this act did nothing more . . . there could be no doubt that it must be regarded as an exercise of the power of Congress to make 'such exceptions from the appellate jurisdiction' as should seem to it expedient." The problem, the Court continued, is that

> the language of the proviso shows plainly that it does not intend to withhold appellate jurisdiction except as a means to an end. Its great and controlling purpose is to deny to pardons granted by the President the effect which this court had adjudged them to have. . . . [T]he denial of jurisdiction to this court, as well as to the Court of Claims, is founded solely on the application of a rule of decision, in causes pending, prescribed by Congress. The court has jurisdiction of the cause to a given point, but when it ascertains that a certain state of things exists, its jurisdiction is to cease and it is required to dismiss the cause for want of jurisdiction. . . . What is this but to prescribe a rule for the decision of a cause in a particular way? . . . In the case before us, no new circumstances have been created

---

21. Helen Hershkoff & Fred Smith, *Reconstructing* Klein, 90 U. Chi. L. Rev. __ (2023).

by legislation. But the court is forbidden to give the effect to evidence which, in its own judgment, such evidence should have, and is directed to give it an effect precisely contrary. We must think that Congress has inadvertently passed the limit which separates the legislative from the judicial power. . . . The rule prescribed is also liable to just exception as impairing the effect of a pardon, and thus infringing the constitutional power of the Executive. . . . This court is required to disregard pardons granted . . . and to deny them their legal effect. This certainly impairs the executive authority, and directs the court to be instrumental to that end.

Consider how to define the holding of *Klein*. Is it simply that Congress cannot redefine the meaning of a pardon because that power belongs to the Executive branch? Is it that Congress cannot require the courts to redefine the meaning of a pardon because that power belongs to the Executive branch? How might Congress' power to waive the sovereign immunity of the federal government in suits against it bear on the question whether the President's pardon power is being altered when Congress decides who shall be permitted to compensation for property seized and forfeited during the Civil War? And how should the answers to these questions be informed by the case's racialized context? The case bolstered the effects of President Johnson's aggressive use of the pardon power—pardons that obstructed Congressional efforts to break an oligarchic caste system in the former Confederacy.[22]

Whatever one makes of the reading of *Klein* as protecting the President's pardon power, the case uses broader language, suggesting that Congress cannot "prescribe a rule of decision" to the federal courts that strictly circumscribes judicial review and requires dismissal of pending cases. The language resonates with the common sense intuition that deciding cases, the exercise of "judicial power" in the language of Article III, is a form of judgment, not a mechanical, robotic automation of the will of Congress. On the other hand, it is difficult to reconcile the broader language in *Klein* with the fact that Congress alters rules of decision all the time, federal courts apply those new rules in pending cases, and the result is to determine the outcomes of these cases.

In a series of modern cases the Court has declined to enforce *Klein* when Congress targets pending litigation and legislates an outcome determinative rule of decision. As you read the next case, consider what harms attend legislative alterations to rules of decision that apply to a specific case or category of cases.

Bank Markazi v. Peterson

578 U.S. 212 (2016)

Justice GINSBURG delivered the opinion of the Court.

A provision of the Iran Threat Reduction and Syria Human Rights Act of 2012, 22 U.S.C. §8772, makes available for postjudgment execution a set of assets held at a New York bank for Bank Markazi, the Central Bank of Iran. The assets would partially satisfy judgments gained in separate actions by over 1,000 victims of terrorist

---

22. Henry P. Monaghan, *Jurisdiction Stripping Circa 2020: What The Dialogue (Still) Has to Teach Us*, 69 DUKE L.J. 1, 18-19 (2019).

acts sponsored by Iran. The judgments remain unpaid. Section 8772 is an unusual statute: It designates a particular set of assets and renders them available to satisfy the liability and damages judgments underlying a consolidated enforcement proceeding that the statute identifies by the District Court's docket number. The question raised by petitioner Bank Markazi: Does §8772 violate the separation of powers by purporting to change the law for, and directing a particular result in, a single pending case?

Section 8772, we hold . . . covers a category of postjudgment execution claims filed by numerous plaintiffs who, in multiple civil actions, obtained evidence-based judgments against Iran together amounting to billions of dollars. Section 8772 subjects the designated assets to execution "to satisfy *any* judgment" against Iran for damages caused by specified acts of terrorism. §8772(a)(1). Congress, our decisions make clear, may amend the law and make the change applicable to pending cases, even when the amendment is outcome determinative.

Adding weight to our decision, Congress passed, and the President signed, §8772 in furtherance of their stance on a matter of foreign policy. Action in that realm warrants respectful review by courts. The Executive has historically made case-specific sovereign-immunity determinations to which courts have deferred. . . . [W]e perceive in §8772 no violation of separation-of-powers principles, and no threat to the independence of the Judiciary.

I

A

We set out here statutory provisions relevant to this case. American nationals may file suit against state sponsors of terrorism in the courts of the United States. *See* 28 U.S.C. §1605A. Specifically, they may seek "money damages . . . against a foreign state for personal injury or death that was caused by" acts of terrorism, including "torture, extrajudicial killing, aircraft sabotage, hostage taking, or the provision of material support" to terrorist activities. §1605A(a)(1). This authorization—known as the "terrorism exception"—is among enumerated exceptions prescribed in the Foreign Sovereign Immunities Act of 1976 (FSIA) to the general rule of sovereign immunity.

. . . After gaining a judgment, however, plaintiffs proceeding under the terrorism exception "have often faced practical and legal difficulties" at the enforcement stage. Subject to stated exceptions, the FSIA shields foreign-state property from execution. §1609. When the terrorism exception was adopted, only foreign-state property located in the United States and "used for a commercial activity" was available for the satisfaction of judgments. §1610(a)(7), (b)(3). Further limiting judgment-enforcement prospects, the FSIA shields from execution property "of a foreign central bank or monetary authority held for its own account." §1611(b)(1).

To lessen these enforcement difficulties, Congress enacted the Terrorism Risk Insurance Act of 2002 (TRIA), which authorizes execution of judgments obtained under the FSIA's terrorism exception against "the blocked assets of [a] terrorist party (including the blocked assets of any agency or instrumentality of that terrorist party)." §201(a).

A "blocked asset" is any asset seized by the Executive Branch pursuant to either the Trading with the Enemy Act (TWEA), or the International Emergency Economic Powers Act (IEEPA). *See* TRIA §201(d)(2). Both measures, TWEA and IEEPA, authorize the President to freeze the assets of "foreign enemy state[s]" and their agencies and instrumentalities. These blocking regimes "put control of foreign assets in the hands of the President so that he may dispose of them in the manner that best furthers the United States' foreign-relations and national-security interests."

Invoking his authority under the IEEPA, the President, in February 2012, issued an Executive Order blocking "[a]ll property and interests in property of any Iranian financial institution, including the Central Bank of Iran, that are in the United States." Exec. Order No. 13599. The availability of these assets for execution, however, was contested.

To place beyond dispute the availability of some of the Executive Order No. 13599-blocked assets for satisfaction of judgments rendered in terrorism cases, Congress passed the statute at issue here: §502 of the Iran Threat Reduction and Syria Human Rights Act of 2012, 22 U.S.C. §8772. Enacted as a freestanding measure, not as an amendment to the FSIA or the TRIA, §8772 provides that, if a court makes specified findings, "a financial asset . . . shall be subject to execution . . . in order to satisfy any judgment to the extent of any compensatory damages awarded against Iran for damages for personal injury or death caused by" the acts of terrorism enumerated in the FSIA's terrorism exception. §8772(a)(1). Section 8772(b) defines as available for execution by holders of terrorism judgments against Iran "the financial assets that are identified in and the subject of proceedings in the United States District Court for the Southern District of New York in *Peterson v. Islamic Republic of Iran* (2013), that were restrained by restraining notices and levies secured by the plaintiffs in those proceedings."

Before allowing execution against an asset described in §8772(b), a court must determine that the asset is:

> (A) held in the United States for a foreign securities intermediary doing business in the United States;
> (B) a blocked asset (whether or not subsequently unblocked) . . . ; and
> (C) equal in value to a financial asset of Iran, including an asset of the central bank or monetary authority of the Government of Iran. . . .

§8772(a)(1).

In addition, the court in which execution is sought must determine "whether Iran holds equitable title to, or the beneficial interest in, the assets . . . and that no other person possesses a constitutionally protected interest in the assets . . . under the Fifth Amendment to the Constitution of the United States." §8772(a)(2).

B

Respondents are victims of Iran-sponsored acts of terrorism, their estate representatives, and surviving family members. Numbering more than 1,000, respondents rank within 16 discrete groups, each of which brought a lawsuit against Iran pursuant to the FSIA's terrorism exception. All of the suits were filed in United States District Court for the District of Columbia. Upon finding a clear evidentiary basis for Iran's liability to each suitor, the court entered judgments by default. The majority of respondents sought redress for injuries suffered in connection with the 1983 bombing of the U.S. Marine barracks in Beirut, Lebanon. "Together, [respondents] have obtained billions of dollars in judgments against Iran, the vast majority of which remain unpaid." The validity of those judgments is not in dispute.

To enforce their judgments, the 16 groups of respondents first registered them in the United States District Court for the Southern District of New York. *See*

28 U.S.C. §1963 ("A judgment . . . may be registered . . . in any other district. . . . A judgment so registered shall have the same effect as a judgment of the district court of the district where registered and may be enforced in like manner."). They then moved under Federal Rule of Civil Procedure 69 for turnover of about $1.75 billion in bond assets held in a New York bank account — assets that, respondents alleged, were owned by Bank Markazi. . . . It is this consolidated judgment-enforcement proceeding and assets restrained in that proceeding that §8772 addresses.

. . . Making the findings necessary under §8772, the District Court ordered the requested turnover.

In reaching its decision, the court reviewed the financial history of the assets and other record evidence showing that Bank Markazi owned the assets. Since at least early 2008, the court recounted, the bond assets have been held in a New York account at Citibank directly controlled by Clearstream Banking, S.A. (Clearstream), a Luxembourg-based company that serves "as an intermediary between financial institutions worldwide."

Resisting turnover of the bond assets, Bank Markazi and Clearstream . . . conceded that Iran held the requisite "equitable title to, or beneficial interest in, the assets," §8772(a)(2)(A), but maintained that §8772 could not withstand inspection under the separation-of-powers doctrine.

"[I]n passing §8772," Bank Markazi argued, "Congress effectively dictated specific factual findings in connection with a specific litigation — invading the province of the courts." The District Court disagreed. The ownership determinations §8772 required, the court said, "[were] not mere fig leaves," for "it [was] quite possible that the [c]ourt could have found that defendants raised a triable issue as to whether the [b]locked [a]ssets were owned by Iran, or that Clearstream and/or UBAE ha[d] some form of beneficial or equitable interest." . . . Further, the court reminded, "Iran's liability and its required payment of damages was . . . established years prior to the [enactment of §8772]"; "[a]t issue [here] is merely execution [of judgments] on assets present in this district."

The Court of Appeals for the Second Circuit unanimously affirmed.

II

Article III of the Constitution establishes an independent Judiciary, a Third Branch of Government with the "province and duty . . . to say what the law is" in particular cases and controversies. *Marbury v. Madison* (1803). Necessarily, that endowment of authority blocks Congress from "requir[ing] federal courts to exercise the judicial power in a manner that Article III forbids." *Plaut v. Spendthrift Farm, Inc.* (1995). Congress, no doubt, "may not usurp a court's power to interpret and apply the law to the [circumstances] before it," Brief for Former Senior Officials of the Office of Legal Counsel as *Amici Curiae* for "[t]hose who apply [a] rule to particular cases, must of necessity expound and interpret that rule," *Marbury*.[18] And our

---

18. Consistent with this limitation, respondents rightly acknowledged at oral argument that Congress could not enact a statute directing that, in "Smith v. Jones," "Smith wins." Such a statute would create no new substantive law; it would instead direct the court how pre-existing law applies to particular circumstances. The Chief Justice challenges this distinction, but it is solidly grounded in our precedent. *See Robertson v. Seattle Audubon Soc.* (1992) (A statute is invalid if it "fail[s] to supply new law, but direct[s] results under old law.") . . .

decisions place off limits to Congress "vest[ing] review of the decisions of Article III courts in officials of the Executive Branch." *Plaut* (citing *Hayburn's Case* (1792)). Congress, we have also held, may not "retroactively comman[d] the federal courts to reopen final judgments." *Plaut.*

A

Citing *United States v. Klein* (1872), Bank Markazi urges a further limitation. Congress treads impermissibly on judicial turf, the Bank maintains, when it "prescribe[s] rules of decision to the Judicial Department . . .in [pending] cases." *Klein.* According to the Bank, §8772 fits that description. *Klein* has been called "a deeply puzzling decision," Meltzer, *Congress, Courts, and Constitutional Remedies,* 86 Geo. L.J. 2537 (1998). More recent decisions, however, have made it clear that *Klein* does not inhibit Congress from "amend[ing] applicable law." *Robertson v. Seattle Audubon Soc.* (1992); *see Plaut* (*Klein*'s "prohibition does not take hold when Congress 'amend[s] applicable law.'"). Section 8772, we hold, did just that.

Klein involved Civil War legislation providing that persons whose property had been seized and sold in wartime could recover the proceeds of the sale in the Court of Claims upon proof that they had "never given any aid or comfort to the present rebellion." Ch. 120, §3. In 1863, President Lincoln pardoned "persons who . . . participated in the . . . rebellion" if they swore an oath of loyalty to the United States. Presidential Proclamation No. 11. One of the persons so pardoned was a southerner named Wilson, whose cotton had been seized and sold by Government agents. Klein was the administrator of Wilson's estate. *Klein.* In *United States v. Padelford* (1870), this Court held that the recipient of a Presidential pardon must be treated as loyal, *i.e.*, the pardon operated as "a complete substitute for proof that [the recipient] gave no aid or comfort to the rebellion." Thereafter, Klein prevailed in an action in the Court of Claims, yielding an award of $125,300 for Wilson's cotton. *Klein.*

During the pendency of an appeal to this Court from the Court of Claims judgment in *Klein*, Congress enacted a statute providing that no pardon should be admissible as proof of loyalty. Moreover, acceptance of a pardon without disclaiming participation in the rebellion would serve as conclusive evidence of disloyalty. The statute directed the Court of Claims and the Supreme Court to dismiss for want of jurisdiction any claim based on a pardon. . . . Affirming the judgment of the Court of Claims, this Court held that Congress had no authority to "impai[r] the effect of a pardon," for the Constitution entrusted the pardon power "[t]o the executive alone." The Legislature, the Court stated, "cannot change the effect of . . . a pardon any more than the executive can change a law." Lacking authority to impair the pardon power of the Executive, Congress could not "direc[t] [a] court to be instrumental to that end." In other words, the statute in *Klein* infringed the judicial power, not because it left too little for courts to do, but because it attempted to direct the result without altering the legal standards governing the effect of a pardon—standards Congress was powerless to prescribe. *See Klein*; *Robertson* (Congress may not "compe[l] . . . findings or results under old law").

The Bank points to a statement in the *Klein* opinion questioning whether "the legislature may prescribe rules of decision to the Judicial Department . . . in cases pending before it." One cannot take this language from *Klein* "at face value," however, "for congressional power to make valid statutes retroactively applicable to pending cases has often been recognized." Hart and Wechsler. *See, e.g., United States v. Schooner Peggy* (1801). As we explained in *Landgraf v. USI Film Products* (1994), the restrictions that the Constitution places on retroactive legislation "are of limited scope":

> The *Ex Post Facto* Clause flatly prohibits retroactive application of penal legislation. Article I, §10, cl. 1, prohibits States from passing . . . laws "impairing the Obligation of Contracts." The Fifth Amendment's Takings Clause prevents the Legislature (and other government actors) from depriving private persons of vested property rights except for a "public use" and upon payment of "just compensation." The prohibitions on "Bills of Attainder" in Art. I, §§9-10, prohibit legislatures from singling out disfavored persons and meting out summary punishment for past conduct. The Due Process Clause also protects the interests in fair notice and repose that may be compromised by retroactive legislation; a justification sufficient to validate a statute's prospective application under the Clause 'may not suffice' to warrant its retroactive application.

"Absent a violation of one of those specific provisions," when a new law makes clear that it is retroactive, the arguable "unfairness of retroactive civil legislation is not a sufficient reason for a court to fail to give [that law] its intended scope." So yes, we have affirmed, Congress may indeed direct courts to apply newly enacted, outcome-altering legislation in pending civil cases.

Bank Markazi argues most strenuously that §8772 did not simply amend pre-existing law. Because the judicial findings contemplated by §8772 were "foregone conclusions," the Bank urges, the statute "effectively" directed certain factfindings and specified the outcome under the amended law. Recall that the District Court, closely monitoring the case, disagreed. [The District Court stated that the] "determinations [required by §8772] [were] not mere fig leaves," for "it [was] quite possible that the [c]ourt could have found that defendants raised a triable issue as to whether the [b]locked [a]ssets were owned by Iran, or that Clearstream and/or UBAE ha[d] some form of beneficial or equitable interest."

In any event, a statute does not impinge on judicial power when it directs courts to apply a new legal standard to undisputed facts. "When a plaintiff brings suit to enforce a legal obligation it is not any less a case or controversy upon which a court possessing the federal judicial power may rightly give judgment, because the plaintiff's claim is uncontested or incontestable." *Pope v. United States* (1944). In *Schooner Peggy* (1801), for example, this Court applied a newly ratified treaty that, by requiring the return of captured property, effectively permitted only one possible outcome. And in *Robertson*, a statute replaced governing environmental-law restraints on timber harvesting with new legislation that permitted harvesting in all but certain designated areas. Without inquiring whether the new statute's application in pending cases was a "foregone conclusio[n]," we upheld the legislation because it left for judicial determination whether any particular actions violated the new prescription. In short, §8772 changed the law by establishing new substantive standards, entrusting to the District Court application of those standards to the facts (contested or uncontested) found by the court.

Resisting this conclusion, The Chief Justice compares §8772 to a hypothetical "law directing judgment for Smith if the court finds that Jones was duly served with notice of the proceedings." Of course, the hypothesized law would be invalid—as would a law directing judgment for Smith, for instance, if the court finds that the sun rises in the east. For one thing, a law so cast may well be irrational and, therefore, unconstitutional for reasons distinct from the separation-of-powers issues considered here. For another, the law imagined by the dissent does what *Robertson* says Congress cannot do: Like a statute that directs, in "Smith v. Jones," "Smith wins," it "compel[s] . . . findings or results under old law," for it fails to supply any new legal standard effectuating the lawmakers' reasonable policy judgment. By contrast, §8772 provides a new standard clarifying that, if Iran owns certain assets, the victims of Iran-sponsored terrorist attacks will be permitted to execute against those assets. Applying laws implementing Congress' policy judgments, with fidelity to those judgments, is commonplace for the Judiciary.

B

Section 8772 remains "unprecedented," Bank Markazi charges, because it "prescribes a rule for a single pending case—identified by caption and docket number." The amended law in *Robertson*, however, also applied to cases identified by caption and docket number, and was nonetheless upheld. Moreover, §8772, as already described, facilitates execution of judgments in 16 suits, together encompassing more than 1,000 victims of Iran-sponsored terrorist attacks. Although consolidated for administrative purposes at the execution stage, the judgment-execution claims brought pursuant to Federal Rule of Civil Procedure 69 were not independent of the original actions for damages and each claim retained its separate character. *See Mackey v. Lanier Collection Agency & Service, Inc.* (1988) (postjudgment garnishment action brought under Rule 69 is part of the "process to enforce a judgment," not a new suit).

The Bank's argument is further flawed, for it rests on the assumption that legislation must be generally applicable, that "there is something wrong with particularized legislative action." *Plaut.* We have found that assumption suspect:

> While legislatures usually act through laws of general applicability, that is by no means their only legitimate mode of action. Private bills in Congress are still common, and were even more so in the days before establishment of the Claims Court. Even laws that impose a duty or liability upon a single individual or firm are not on that account invalid—or else we would not have the extensive jurisprudence that we do concerning the Bill of Attainder Clause, including cases which say that [the Clause] requires not merely "singling out" but also *punishment, see, e.g., United States* v. *Lovett* (1946), [or] a case [holding] that Congress may legislate "a legitimate class of one," *Nixon v. Administrator of General Services* (1977).[28]

This Court and lower courts have upheld as a valid exercise of Congress' legislative power diverse laws that governed one or a very small number of specific subjects. *E.g., Regional Rail Reorganization Act Cases* (1974) (upholding Act that applied

---

28. Laws narrow in scope, including "class of one" legislation, may violate the Equal Protection Clause if arbitrary or inadequately justified. *Village of Willowbrook v. Olech* (2000).

to specific railroads in a single region); *Pope* (upholding special Act giving a contractor the right to recover additional compensation from the Government); *The Clinton Bridge* (1870) (upholding Act governing a single bridge); *Pennsylvania v. Wheeling & Belmont Bridge Co.* (1856) (similar).

C

Particularly pertinent, the Executive, prior to the enactment of the FSIA, regularly made case-specific determinations whether sovereign immunity should be recognized, and courts accepted those determinations as binding. As this Court explained in *Republic of Mexico v. Hoffman* (1945), it is "not for the courts to deny an immunity which our government has seen fit to allow, or to allow an immunity on new grounds which the government has not seen fit to recognize." This practice, too, was never perceived as an encroachment on the federal courts' jurisdiction. *See Dames & Moore* ("[P]rior to the enactment of the FSIA [courts would not have] reject[ed] as an encroachment on their jurisdiction the President's determination of a foreign state's sovereign immunity.").

Enacting the FSIA in 1976, Congress transferred from the Executive to the courts the principal responsibility for determining a foreign state's amenability to suit. *See Verlinden B.V. v. Central Bank of Nigeria* (1983). But it remains Congress' prerogative to alter a foreign state's immunity and to render the alteration dispositive of judicial proceedings in progress. By altering the law governing the attachment of particular property belonging to Iran, Congress acted comfortably within the political branches' authority over foreign sovereign immunity and foreign-state assets.

Chief Justice ROBERTS, with whom Justice SOTOMAYOR joins, dissenting.

Imagine your neighbor sues you, claiming that your fence is on his property. His evidence is a letter from the previous owner of your home, accepting your neighbor's version of the facts. Your defense is an official county map, which under state law establishes the boundaries of your land. The map shows the fence on your side of the property line. You also argue that your neighbor's claim is six months outside the statute of limitations.

Now imagine that while the lawsuit is pending, your neighbor persuades the legislature to enact a new statute. The new statute provides that for your case, and your case alone, a letter from one neighbor to another is conclusive of property boundaries, and the statute of limitations is one year longer. Your neighbor wins. Who would you say decided your case: the legislature, which targeted your specific case and eliminated your specific defenses so as to ensure your neighbor's victory, or the court, which presided over the *fait accompli*?

That question lies at the root of the case the Court confronts today. Article III of the Constitution commits the power to decide cases to the Judiciary alone. *See Stern v. Marshall* (2011). Yet, in this case, Congress arrogated that power to itself. Since 2008, respondents have sought $1.75 billion in assets owned by Bank Markazi, Iran's central bank, in order to satisfy judgments against Iran for acts of terrorism. The Bank has vigorously opposed those efforts, asserting numerous legal defenses. So, in 2012, four years into the litigation, respondents persuaded Congress to enact a statute, 22 U.S.C. §8772, that for this case alone eliminates each of the defenses standing in respondents' way. Then, having gotten Congress to resolve all outstanding issues in their favor, respondents returned to court . . . and won.

Contrary to the majority, I would hold that §8772 violates the separation of powers.

I

. . . "The Framers of our Constitution lived among the ruins of a system of intermingled legislative and judicial powers." *Plaut v. Spendthrift Farm, Inc.* (1995). . . .

The Revolution-era "crescendo of legislative interference with private judgments of the courts," however, soon prompted a "sense of a sharp necessity to separate the legislative from the judicial power." *Plaut.*

The States' experiences ultimately shaped the Federal Constitution, figuring prominently in the Framers' decision to devise a system for securing liberty through the division of power:

> "Before and during the debates on ratification, Madison, Jefferson, and
> Hamilton each wrote of the factional disorders and disarray that the sys-
> tem of legislative equity had produced in the years before the framing;
> and each thought that the separation of the legislative from the judicial
> power in the new Constitution would cure them." *Plaut.*

As Professor Manning has concluded, "Article III, in large measure, reflects a reaction against the practice" of legislative interference with state courts. Manning, Response, Deriving Rules of Statutory Interpretation from the Constitution. . . .

The Framers saw that if the "power of judging . . . were joined to legislative power, the power over the life and liberty of the citizens would be arbitrary." Montesquieu, The Spirit of the Laws. They accordingly resolved to take the unprecedented step of establishing a "truly distinct" judiciary. The Federalist No. 78 (A. Hamilton). To help ensure the "complete independence of the courts of justice," they provided life tenure for judges and protection against diminution of their compensation. But such safeguards against indirect interference would have been meaningless if Congress could simply exercise the judicial power directly.

II
A

Mindful of this history, our decisions have recognized three kinds of "unconstitutional restriction[s] upon the exercise of judicial power." *Plaut.* Two concern the effect of judgments once they have been rendered: "Congress cannot vest review of the decisions of Article III courts in officials of the Executive Branch," for to do so would make a court's judgment merely "an advisory opinion in its most obnoxious form," *Chicago & Southern Air Lines, Inc. v. Waterman S.S. Corp.* (1948). And Congress cannot "retroactively command[ ] the federal courts to reopen final judgments," because Article III "gives the Federal Judiciary the power, not merely to rule on cases, but to *decide* them, subject to review only by superior courts in the Article III hierarchy." *Plaut.* Neither of these rules is directly implicated here.

This case is about the third type of unconstitutional interference with the judicial function, whereby Congress assumes the role of judge and decides a particular pending case in the first instance. Section 8772 does precisely that, changing the law—for these proceedings alone—simply to guarantee that respondents win. The law serves no other purpose—a point, indeed, that is hardly in dispute. As the majority acknowledges, the statute "'sweeps away . . . any . . . federal or state law impediments that might otherwise exist'" to bar respondents from obtaining Bank Markazi's assets. In the District Court, Bank Markazi had invoked sovereign immunity under the Foreign Sovereign Immunities Act of 1976, 28 U.S.C. §1611(b)(1). Section 8772(a)(1) eliminates that immunity. Bank Markazi had argued that its status as a separate juridical entity under federal common law and international law freed it from liability for Iran's debts. Section 8772(d)(3) ensures that the Bank is liable. Bank Markazi had argued that New York law did not allow respondents to execute their judgments against the Bank's assets. *See* N.Y.U.C.C. Law Ann. §8-112(c). Section 8772(a)(1) makes those assets subject to execution.

Section 8772 authorized attachment, moreover, only for the

> "financial assets that are identified in and the subject of proceedings in the United States District Court for the Southern District of New York in *Peterson v. Islamic Republic of Iran*, Case No. 10 Civ. 4518, that were restrained by restraining notices and levies secured by the plaintiffs in those proceedings. . . ." §8772(b).

And lest there be any doubt that Congress's sole concern was deciding this particular case, rather than establishing any generally applicable rules, §8772 provided that nothing in the statute "shall be construed . . . to affect the availability, or lack thereof, of a right to satisfy a judgment in any other action against a terrorist party in any proceedings other than" these. §8772(c).

B

There has never been anything like §8772 before. Neither the majority nor respondents have identified another statute that changed the law for a pending case in an outcome-determinative way and explicitly limited its effect to particular judicial proceedings. . . . Congress's "prolonged reticence would be amazing if such interference were not understood to be constitutionally proscribed." *Plaut.*

Section 8772 violates the bedrock rule of Article III that the judicial power is vested in the Judicial Branch alone. We first enforced that rule against an Act of Congress during the Reconstruction era in *United States v. Klein* (1872).

The majority characterizes *Klein* as a delphic, puzzling decision whose central holding—that Congress may not prescribe the result in pending cases—cannot be taken at face value.[2] It is true that *Klein* can be read too broadly, in a way that would

---

2. The majority instead seeks to recast *Klein* as being primarily about congressional impairment of the President's pardon power, despite *Klein's* unmistakable indication that the impairment of the pardon power was an *alternative* ground for its holding, secondary to its Article III concerns. *Klein* ("The rule prescribed is *also* liable to just exception as impairing the effect of a pardon, and thus infringing the constitutional power of the Executive."). The majority then suggests that *Klein* stands simply for the proposition that Congress may not require courts to act unconstitutionally. That is without doubt a good rule, recognized by this Court since *Marbury v. Madison* (1803). But it is hard to reconstruct *Klein* along these lines, given its focus on the threat to the separation of powers from allowing Congress to manipulate jurisdictional rules to dictate judicial results. *See* Hart, *The Power of Congress To Limit the Jurisdiction of Federal Courts: An Exercise in Dialectic* (1953) ("[I]f Congress directs an Article III court to decide a case, I can easily read into Article III a limitation on the power of Congress to tell the court *how* to decide it . . . as the Court itself made clear long ago in *United States v. Klein.*").

swallow the rule that courts generally must apply a retroactively applicable statute to pending cases. *See United States v. Schooner Peggy* (1801). But *Schooner Peggy* can be read too broadly, too. Applying a retroactive law that says "Smith wins" to the pending case of *Smith v. Jones* implicates profound issues of separation of powers, issues not adequately answered by a citation to *Schooner Peggy*. And just because *Klein* did not set forth clear rules defining the limits on Congress's authority to legislate with respect to a pending case does not mean—as the majority seems to think—that Article III itself imposes no such limits.

"Smith wins" is a new law, tailored to one case in the same way as §8772 and having the same effect. . . . The cause for concern is that though the statutes are indistinguishable, it is plain that the majority recognizes no limit under the separation of powers beyond the prohibition on statutes as brazen as "Smith wins." . . .

It is true that some of the precedents cited by the majority have allowed Congress to approach the boundary between legislative and judicial power. None, however, involved statutes comparable to §8772. In *Robertson* v. *Seattle Audubon Soc.* (1992), for example, the statute at issue referenced particular cases only as a shorthand for describing certain environmental law requirements, not to limit the statute's effect to those cases alone. . . .[3]

I readily concede, without embarrassment, that it can sometimes be difficult to draw the line between legislative and judicial power. . . . But however difficult it may be to discern the line between the Legislative and Judicial Branches, the entire constitutional enterprise depends on there *being* such a line.

C

Finally, the majority suggests that §8772 is analogous to the Executive's historical power to recognize foreign state sovereign immunity on a case-by-case basis. As discussed above, however, §8772 does considerably more than withdraw the Bank's sovereign immunity. It strips the Bank of any protection that federal common law, international law, or New York State law might have offered against respondents' claims. That is without analogue or precedent. In any event, the practice of applying case-specific Executive submissions on sovereign immunity was not judicial acquiescence in an intrusion on the Judiciary's role. It was instead the result of substantive sovereign immunity law, developed and applied by the courts, which treated such a submission as a dispositive fact.

Hereafter, with this Court's seal of approval, Congress can unabashedly pick the winners and losers in particular pending cases. Today's decision will indeed become a "blueprint for extensive expansion of the legislative power" at the Judiciary's expense, *Metropolitan Washington Airports Authority v. Citizens for Abatement of Aircraft Noise, Inc.* (1991), feeding Congress's tendency to "extend[ ] the sphere of its activity and draw[ ] all power into its impetuous vortex," The Federalist No. 48 (J. Madison).

I respectfully dissent.

* * *

---

3. We have also upheld Congress's long practice of settling individual claims involving public rights, such as claims against the Government, through private bills. *See generally Pope v. United States* (1944). But the Court points to no example of a private bill that retroactively changed the law for a single case involving private rights.

The Court again refused to apply *Klein* in *Patchak v. Zinke* (2018). David Patchak sued the Secretary of the Interior challenging the Secretary's authority to take into trust land in support of the Match-E-Be-Nash-She-Wish Band of Pottawatomi Indians' plan to build a casino. Patchak was a nearby landowner concerned about potential changes to the rural nature of the area. The Supreme Court had earlier held that the Secretary could not assert the defense of sovereign immunity from the suit and remanded for further proceedings. Congress responded to this turn of events by enacting a statute that expressly "reaffirmed as trust land" the specific piece of property. The statute further provided that "an action . . . relating to [the specific land] shall not be filed or maintained in a Federal court and shall be promptly dismissed." The district court dismissed the suit and the circuit court affirmed.

The Court upheld the legislation. In a plurality opinion, Justice Thomas emphasized that the statute simply "changes the law" by stripping the federal courts of jurisdiction. He stated that Congress cannot "compel findings or results under old law," but it "does not violate Article III when it changes the law," including by changing jurisdictional rules. Relying on *McCardle*, Justice Thomas wrote that:

> Congress generally does not violate Article III when it strips federal jurisdiction over a class of cases. . . . Jurisdiction-stripping cases can violate other provisions of the Constitution. And, under our precedents, jurisdiction-stripping statutes can violate Article III if they "attempt to direct the result" by effectively altering legal standards that Congress is "powerless to prescribe." . . . This Court has reaffirmed these principles on many occasions. Congress generally does not infringe the judicial power when it strips jurisdiction because, with limited exceptions, a congressional grant of jurisdiction is a prerequisite to the exercise of judicial power.

Id. (quoting *Bank Markazi*).

Justice Thomas then distinguished *Klein*, concluding that "a statute does not violate Article III merely because it uses mandatory language. Instead of directing outcomes, the mandatory language . . . simply imposes the consequences of a court's determination that it lacks jurisdiction because a suit relates [to the specific property the Secretary took into land for the casino]." Relying on *Bank Markazi*, the plurality noted that unlike *Klein*, the statute here "does not attempt to exercise a power that the Constitution vests in another branch. And unlike the selective jurisdiction stripping statute in *Klein*, [the statute] strips jurisdiction over every suit relating to the [land]."

Justice Breyer concurred on the ground that in regulating relations with Indian tribes and their lands, Congress has authority to "retroactively ratify Government action that was unauthorized when taken. . . . The jurisdictional part of the statute . . . [simply] eliminate[s] the cost of litigating a lawsuit that will inevitably uphold the land's trust status." For that reason, the case is also unlike *Klein* where Congress sought to reach through the courts a result "that it could not constitutionally reach directly."

Justices Ginsburg and Sotomayor concurred on the ground that "consent of the United States to suit may be withdrawn at any time. . . . Retraction of consent to be sued (effectively restoration of immunity) is just what Congress achieved" by this legislation, displacing the APA's waiver.

Chief Justice Roberts, joined by Justices Kennedy and Gorsuch, dissented, contending that "Congress . . . has never gone so far as to target a single party for adverse treatment and direct the precise disposition of his pending case. . . . Even . . . the Court in *Bank Markazi* did not have before it anything like [this statute], which prevents the court from applying any new legal standards and explicitly dictates dismissal of a pending proceeding. . . . [Here] Congress, in crafting a law tailored to Patchak's suit, has pronounced the equivalent of 'Smith wins.'"

> Contrary to the plurality, I would hold that Congress exercises the judicial power when it manipulates jurisdictional rules to decide the outcome of a particular pending case. Because the Legislature has no authority to direct entry of judgment for a party, it cannot achieve the same result by stripping jurisdiction over a particular proceeding. Does the plurality really believe that there is a material difference between a law stating "The court lacks jurisdiction over Jones's pending suit against Smith" and one stating "In the case of Smith v. Jones, Smith wins"? In both instances, Congress has resolved the specific case in Smith's favor.
>
> Over and over, the plurality intones that §2(b) does not impinge on the judicial power because the provision "changes the law." But all that §2(b) does is deprive the court of jurisdiction in a single proceeding. If that is sufficient to change the law, the plurality's rule "provides no limiting principle" on Congress's ability to assume the role of judge and decide the outcome of pending cases. *Northern Pipeline Constr. Co. v. Marathon Pipe Line Co.* (1982).
>
> In my view, the concept of "changing the law" must imply some measure of generality or preservation of an adjudicative role for the courts.

With respect to the plurality's reliance on *McCardle*, the dissent suggested the decision may deserve less weight than *Klein*.

> The Court's decision in *McCardle* has been alternatively described as "caving to the political dominance" of the Radical Republicans or "acceding to Congress's effort to silence the Court." Meltzer, *The Story of Ex parte McCardle*, in FEDERAL COURTS STORIES. Read for all it is worth, the decision is also inconsistent with the approach the Court took just three years later in *Klein*, where Chief Justice Chase (a dominant character in this drama) stressed that "[i]t is of vital importance" that the legislative and judicial powers "be kept distinct."
>
> The facts of *McCardle*, however, can support a more limited understanding of Congress's power to divest the courts of jurisdiction. For starters, the repealer provision covered more than a single pending dispute; it applied to a class of cases, barring anyone from invoking the Supreme Court's appellate jurisdiction in habeas cases for the next two decades. In addition, the Court's decision did not foreclose all avenues for judicial review of McCardle's complaint. As Chase made clear in the penultimate paragraph of the opinion—and confirmed later that year in his opinion for the Court in *Ex parte Yerger* (1869)—the statute did not deny "the whole appellate power of the Court." McCardle, by taking a different procedural route and filing an original habeas action, could have had his case heard on the merits.

[The statute here], on the other hand, has neither saving grace. It ends Patchak's suit for good. His federal case is dismissed, and he has no alternative means of review anywhere else. . . .

The Framers saw this case coming. They knew that if Congress exercised the judicial power, it would be impossible "to guard the Constitution and the rights of individuals from . . . serious oppressions." The Federalist No. 78 (A. Hamilton). Patchak thought his rights were violated, and went to court. He expected to have his case decided by judges whose independence from political pressure was ensured by the safeguards of Article III—life tenure and salary protection. It was instead decided by Congress, in favor of the litigant it preferred, under a law adopted just for the occasion.

Bank Markazi and *Patchak* indicate that the Court remains divided about the separation of powers principles for which *Klein* stands. All at least agree that it would violate separation of powers for Congress to prescribe a rule of decision that interferes with the pardon power or a comparable power of a coordinate branch. And there appears to be a majority of Justices who believe that Congress is free to legislate rules of decision that target and control the disposition of specific cases, as long as there remains some form of application of law to fact for the courts, however perfunctory that may be. Further, recall that whatever the import of *Klein*, Congress has the power to modify sub-constitutional law in ways that effectively reverse a decision of the Court after it has issued. In *Lyng v. Northwest Indian Cemetery Protective Ass'n* (1988), the Court reversed an injunction granted by lower federal courts to prevent clearcutting and construction of a road by the Forest Service through territory on the California-Oregon border commonly used for spiritual purposes by the Yurok, Karuk, and Tolowa tribes. The Court held that the project could not be suspended to protect the free exercise rights of the plaintiffs. Their rights do not confer a "veto over public programs that do not prohibit the free exercise of religion" and "do not divest the Government of its right to use what is, after all, *its* land." Two years later, Congress prevented the Forest Service from constructing the road and protected the surrounding mountain region sacred to the tribes from development through the Smith River National Recreation Area Act of 1990. In precisely what ways is it more controversial for Congress to prescribe a rule of decision in pending litigation? The next section considers limits on the power of Congress to interfere with final judgments.

4. *Interference with Final Decisions*

Hayburn's Case, discussed in Chapter 3 and in *Bank Markazi*, stands for the proposition that final judgments of the federal courts are not subject to legislative review or revision. Congress could not, consistent with the separation of powers, set up a system for determining veterans' benefits that allowed executive branch officers to review and reverse determinations of eligibility made by Article III judges. In this section, we address the broader question of when and under what circumstances Congress can reopen the final judgments of federal courts to further litigation *within the courts.* The first case deals with final judgments resulting in equitable relief and stands for the proposition that when a judgment contemplates continuing supervision by the court for compliance, the court must be sensitive to changes in the law supporting the judgment. As the law and facts change, so too may the judgment. The second case deals with final money judgments, an area in which the Court has held that separation of powers protects the integrity of a court's judgment from being unilaterally reopened by Congress.

Pennsylvania v. Wheeling & Belmont Bridge Co.

59 U.S. 421 (1855)

Mr. Justice NELSON delivered the opinion of the Court.

The motion in this case is founded upon a bill filed to carry into execution a decree of the court, rendered against the defendants at the adjourned term in May, 1852, which decree declared the bridge erected by them across the Ohio River, between Wheeling and Zane's Island, to be an obstruction of the free navigation of the said river, and thereby occasioned a special damage to the plaintiff for which there was not an adequate remedy at law, and directed that the obstruction be removed either by elevating the bridge to a height designated or by abatement.

Since the rendition of this decree, and on the 31st August, 1852, an act of Congress has been passed as follows:

> That the bridges across the Ohio River at Wheeling, in the State of Virginia, and at Bridgeport, in the State of Ohio, abutting on Zane's Island in said river are hereby declared to be lawful structures in their present positions and elevations, and shall be so held and taken to be anything in the law or laws of the United States to the contrary notwithstanding

And further:

> That the said bridges be declared to be and are established post roads for the passage of the mails of the United States, and that the Wheeling & Belmont Bridge Company are authorized to have and maintain their bridges at their present site and elevation, and the officers and crews of all vessels and boats navigating said river are required to regulate the use of their said vessels, and of any pipes or chimneys belonging thereto, so as not to interfere with the elevation and construction of said bridges.

The defendants rely upon this act of Congress as furnishing authority for the continuance of the bridge as constructed, and as superseding the effect and operation of the decree of the Court previously rendered declaring it an obstruction to the navigation.

On the part of the plaintiff it is insisted that the act is unconstitutional and void, which raises the principal question in the case.

In order to a proper understanding of this question, it is material to recur to the ground and principles upon which the majority of the Court proceeded in rendering the decree now sought to be enforced.

The bridge had been constructed under an act of the Legislature of the State of Virginia, and it was admitted that act conferred full authority upon the defendants for the erection, subject only to the power of Congress in the regulation of commerce. It was claimed, however, that Congress had acted upon the subject and had regulated the navigation of the Ohio River, and had thereby secured to the public, by virtue of its authority, the free and unobstructed use of the same, and that the erection of the bridge, so far as it interfered with the enjoyment of this use, was inconsistent with and in violation of the acts of Congress.

This being the view of the case taken by a majority of the Court, they found no difficulty . . . in applying the appropriate remedy in behalf of the plaintiff. *Wheeling Bridge I* (1851).

Since, however, the rendition of this decree, the acts of Congress, already referred to have been passed by which the bridge is made a post road for the passage of the mails of the United States and the defendants are authorized to have and maintain it at its present site and elevation, and requiring all persons navigating the river to regulate such navigation so as not to interfere with it.

So far, therefore, as this bridge created an obstruction to the free navigation of the river, in view of the previous acts of Congress, they are to be regarded as modified by this subsequent legislation, and although it still may be an obstruction in fact, is not so in the contemplation of law. We have already said, and the principle is undoubted, that the act of the Legislature of Virginia conferred full authority to erect and maintain the bridge, subject to the exercise of the power of Congress to regulate the navigation of the river. That body having in the exercise of this power regulated the navigation consistent with its preservation and continuation, the authority to maintain it would seem to be complete.

But it is urged that the act of Congress cannot have the effect and operation to annul the judgment of the Court already rendered or the rights determined thereby in favor of the plaintiff. This, as a general proposition, is certainly not to be denied, especially as it respects adjudication upon the private rights of parties. When they have passed into judgment, the right becomes absolute, and it is the duty of the Court to enforce it.

The case before us, however, is distinguishable from this class of cases so far as it respects that portion of the decree directing the abatement of the bridge. Its interference with the free navigation of the river constituted an obstruction of a public right secured by acts of Congress.

Now we agree, if the remedy in this case had been an action at law and a judgment rendered in favor of the plaintiff for damages, the right to these would have passed beyond the reach of the power of Congress. It would have depended not upon the public right of the free navigation of the river, but upon the judgment of the Court. The decree before us, so far as it respect the costs adjudged, stands upon the same principles and is unaffected by the subsequent law. But that part of the decree directing the abatement of the obstruction is executory, a continuing decree, which requires not only the removal of the bridge but enjoins the defendants against any reconstruction or continuance. Now whether it is a future existing or continuing obstruction depends upon the question whether or not it interferes with the right of navigation. If, in the meantime, since the decree, this right has been modified by the competent authority so that the bridge is no longer an unlawful obstruction, it is quite plain the decree of the Court cannot be enforced. There is no longer any interference with the enjoyment of the public right inconsistent with law, no more than there would be where the plaintiff himself had consented to it after the rendition of the decree. Suppose the decree had been executed, and after that the passage of the law in question, can it be doubted but that the defendants would have had a right to reconstruct it? And is it not equally clear that the right to maintain it, if not abated, existed from the moment of the enactment?. . . .

Upon the whole, without pursuing the examination further, our conclusion is that, so far as respects that portion of the decree which directs the alteration or abatement of the bridge, it cannot be carried into execution, since the act of Congress which regulates the navigation of the Ohio River, consistent with the existence and continuance of the bridge, and that this part of the motion in behalf of the plaintiff must be denied. But that so far as respects that portion of the decree which directs the costs to be paid by the defendants, the motion must be granted.

The motion for the attachment is denied, and the injunction dissolved.

Mr. Justice McLEAN, dissenting.

The decree in the *Wheeling Bridge I* case was the result of a judicial investigation, founded upon facts ascertained in the course of the hearing. It was strictly a judicial question. The complaint was an obstruction of commerce, by the bridge, to the injury of the complainant, and the Court found the fact to be as alleged in the bill. It was said by Chief Justice Marshall, many years ago, that Congress could do many things, but that it could not alter a fact. This it has attempted to do in the above act. An obstruction to the navigation of the river was, technically, a nuisance, and, in their decree, this Court so pronounced.

Congress could not undertake to hear the complaint of Pennsylvania in this case, take testimony or cause it to be taken, examine the surveys and reports of engineers, decide the questions of law which arise on the admission of the testimony, and give the proper and legal effect to the evidence in the final decree. To do this is the appropriate duty of the judicial power. And this is what was done by this Court before the above act of Congress was passed. The Court held that the bridge obstructed the navigation of the Ohio River and that consequently it was a nuisance. The act declared the bridge to be a legal structure, and consequently that it was not a nuisance. Now is this a legislative or a judicial act? Whether it be a nuisance or not depends upon the fact of obstruction, and this would seem to be strictly a judicial question, to be decided on evidence produced by the parties in a case.

We do not speak of a public commercial right, but of an obstruction to it by which an individual wrong is done that at law is irremediable.

. . . [Is there even] a power in Congress to legalize a bridge over a navigable water within the jurisdiction of any state or states? It has the power to regulate commerce among the several states, requiring two or more states to authorize the regulation. But this does not necessarily include the power to construct bridges which may obstruct commerce, but can never increase its facilities on a navigable water.

Mr. Justice WAYNE, dissenting in part [on the same grounds as Justice McLean].

* * *

A court sitting in equity has authority to modify or even dissolve or vacate an injunction, most obviously when the party bound has fully complied with it, or when compliance becomes factually impossible. *Wheeling Bridge I & II* stand for the proposition that injunctions and other continuing decrees may be terminated or otherwise affected by changes in the law supporting the injunction. Legal change includes the exercise of legislative powers conferred upon Congress which alter the legal status of the parties or their conduct. In the next case, the Court takes up the question whether a judgment at law can be reopened by Congress.

Plaut v. Spendthrift Farm

514 U.S. 211 (1995)

Justice SCALIA delivered the opinion of the Court.

The question presented in this case is whether §27A(b) of the Securities Exchange Act of 1934, to the extent that it requires federal courts to reopen final judgments in private civil actions under §10(b) of the Act, contravenes the Constitution's separation of powers or the Due Process Clause of the Fifth Amendment.

I

In 1987, petitioners brought a civil action against respondents in the United States District Court for the Eastern District of Kentucky. The complaint alleged that in 1983 and 1984 respondents had committed fraud and deceit in the sale of stock in violation of §10(b) of the Securities Exchange Act of 1934 and Rule 10b-5 of the Securities and Exchange Commission. The case was mired in pretrial proceedings in the District Court until June 20, 1991, when we decided *Lampf v. Gilbertson. Lampf* held that "[l]itigation instituted pursuant to §10(b) and Rule 10b-5 . . . must be commenced within one year after the discovery of the facts constituting the violation and within three years after such violation." We applied that holding to the plaintiff-respondents in *Lampf* itself, found their suit untimely, and reinstated a summary judgment previously entered in favor of the defendant-petitioners. On the same day we decided *James B. Beam Distilling Co. v. Georgia* (1991), in which a majority of the Court held, albeit in different opinions, that a new rule of federal law that is applied to the parties in the case announcing the rule must be applied as well to all cases pending on direct review. The joint effect of *Lampf* and *Beam* was to mandate application of the 1-year/3-year limitations period to petitioners' suit. The District Court, finding that petitioners' claims were untimely under the *Lampf* rule, dismissed their action with prejudice on August 13, 1991. Petitioners filed no appeal; the judgment accordingly became final 30 days later. *See* 28 U.S.C. §2107(a).

On December 19, 1991, the President signed the Federal Deposit Insurance Corporation Improvement Act of 1991. Section 476 of the Act—a section that had nothing to do with FDIC improvements—became §27A of the Securities Exchange Act of 1934, and was later codified as 15 U.S.C. §78aa-1. It provides:

> (a) Effect on pending causes of action
>
> The limitation period for any private civil action implied under section 78j(b) of this title [§10(b) of the Securities Exchange Act of 1934] that was commenced on or before June 19, 1991, shall be the limitation period

provided by the laws applicable in the jurisdiction, including principles of retroactivity, as such laws existed on June 19, 1991.

(b) Effect on dismissed causes of action

Any private civil action implied under section 78j(b) of this title that was commenced on or before June 19, 1991 —

(1) which was dismissed as time barred subsequent to June 19, 1991, and

(2) which would have been timely filed under the limitation period provided by the laws applicable in the jurisdiction, including principles of retroactivity, as such laws existed on June 19, 1991, shall be reinstated on motion by the plaintiff not later than 60 days after December 19, 1991.

On February 11, 1992, petitioners returned to the District Court and filed a motion to reinstate the action previously dismissed with prejudice. The District Court found that the conditions set out in §§27A(b)(1) and (2) were met, so that petitioners' motion was required to be granted by the terms of the statute. It nonetheless denied the motion, agreeing with respondents that §27A(b) is unconstitutional. The United States Court of Appeals for the Sixth Circuit affirmed.

II

. . . [T]here is no reasonable construction on which §27A(b) does not require federal courts to reopen final judgments in suits dismissed with prejudice by virtue of *Lampf.*

III

Respondents submit that §27A(b) violates both the separation of powers and the Due Process Clause of the Fifth Amendment. Because the latter submission, if correct, might dictate a similar result in a challenge to state legislation under the Fourteenth Amendment, the former is the narrower ground for adjudication of the constitutional questions in the case, and we therefore consider it first. *Ashwander v. TVA* (1936). We conclude that in §27A(b) Congress has exceeded its authority by requiring the federal courts to exercise "[t]he judicial Power of the United States," U.S. Const., Art. III, §1, in a manner repugnant to the text, structure, and traditions of Article III.

Our decisions to date have identified two types of legislation that require federal courts to exercise the judicial power in a manner that Article III forbids. The first appears in *United States v. Klein* (1872), where we refused to give effect to a statute that was said "[to] prescribe rules of decision to the Judicial Department of the government in cases pending before it." Whatever the precise scope of *Klein*, however, later decisions have made clear that its prohibition does not take hold when Congress "amend[s] applicable law." *Robertson v. Seattle Audubon Soc.* (1992). Section 27A(b) indisputably does set out substantive legal standards for the Judiciary to apply, and in that sense changes the law (even if solely retroactively). The second type of unconstitutional restriction upon the exercise of judicial power identified by past cases is exemplified by *Hayburn's Case* (1792), which stands for the principle that Congress cannot vest review of the decisions of Article III courts in officials of the Executive Branch. Yet under any application of §27A(b) only courts are involved; no officials of other departments sit in direct review of their decisions. Section 27A(b) therefore offends neither of these previously established prohibitions.

We think, however, that §27A(b) offends a postulate of Article III just as deeply rooted in our law as those we have mentioned. Article III establishes a "judicial department" with the "province and duty . . . to say what the law is" in particular cases and controversies. *Marbury v. Madison* (1803). The record of history shows that the Framers crafted this charter of the judicial department with an expressed understanding that it gives the Federal Judiciary the power, not merely to rule on cases, but to *decide* them, subject to review only by superior courts in the Article III hierarchy—with an understanding, in short, that "a judgment conclusively resolves the case" because "a 'judicial Power' is one to render dispositive judgments." Easterbrook, Presidential Review. By retroactively commanding the federal courts to reopen final judgments, Congress has violated this fundamental principle.

A

The Framers of our Constitution lived among the ruins of a system of intermingled legislative and judicial powers, which had been prevalent in the colonies long before the Revolution, and which after the Revolution had produced factional strife and partisan oppression. In the 17th and 18th centuries colonial assemblies and legislatures functioned as courts of equity of last resort, hearing original actions or providing appellate review of judicial judgments. G. WOOD, THE CREATION OF THE AMERICAN REPUBLIC 1776-1787. Often, however, they chose to correct the judicial process through special bills or other enacted legislation. It was common for such legislation not to prescribe a resolution of the dispute, but rather simply to set aside the judgment and order a new trial or appeal. M. CLARKE, PARLIAMENTARY PRIVILEGE IN THE AMERICAN COLONIES. Thus, as described in our discussion of *Hayburn's Case,* such legislation bears not on the problem of interbranch review but on the problem of finality of judicial judgments.

The vigorous, indeed often radical, populism of the revolutionary legislatures and assemblies increased the frequency of legislative correction of judgments. WOOD, *supra. See also INS v. Chadha* (1983) (Powell, J., concurring). "The period 1780-1787 . . . was a period of 'constitutional reaction'" to these developments, "which . . . leaped suddenly to its climax in the Philadelphia Convention." Voices from many quarters, official as well as private, decried the increasing legislative interference with the private-law judgments of the courts. In 1786, the Vermont Council of Censors issued an "Address of the Council of Censors to the Freemen of the State of Vermont" . . . A principal method of usurpation identified by the censors was "[t]he instances . . . of judgments being vacated by legislative acts." The council delivered an opinion "that . . . it is an imposition on the suitor, to give him the trouble of obtaining, after several expensive trials, a final judgment agreeably to the known established laws of the land; if the Legislature, by a sovereign act, can interfere, reverse the judgment, and decree in such manner, as they, unfettered by rules, shall think proper."

So too, the famous report of the Pennsylvania Council of Censors in 1784 detailed the abuses of legislative interference with the courts at the behest of private interests and factions. As the General Assembly had (they wrote) made a custom of "extending their deliberations to the cases of individuals," the people had "been taught to consider an application to the legislature, as a shorter and more certain mode of obtaining relief from hardships and losses, than the usual process of law." The censors noted that because "favour and partiality have, from the nature of public bodies of men, predominated in the distribution of this relief . . . [t]hese dangerous procedures have been too often recurred to, since the revolution."

This sense of a sharp necessity to separate the legislative from the judicial power, prompted by the crescendo of legislative interference with private judgments of the courts, triumphed among the Framers of the new Federal Constitution. . . . Before and during the debates on ratification, Madison, Jefferson, and Hamilton each wrote of the factional disorders and disarray that the system of legislative equity had produced in the years before the framing; and each thought that the separation of the legislative from the judicial power in the new Constitution would cure them. Madison's Federalist No. 48, the famous description of the process by which "[t]he legislative department is every where extending the sphere of its activity, and drawing all power into its impetuous vortex," referred to the report of the Pennsylvania Council of Censors to show that in that State "cases belonging to the judiciary department [had been] frequently drawn within legislative cognizance and determination." Madison relied as well on Jefferson's Notes on the State of Virginia, which mentioned, as one example of the dangerous concentration of governmental powers into the hands of the legislature, that "the Legislature . . . in many instances decided rights which should have been left to judiciary controversy." The Federalist No. 48.

If the need for separation of legislative from judicial power was plain, the principal effect to be accomplished by that separation was even plainer. As Hamilton wrote in his exegesis of Article III, §1, in The Federalist No. 81:

> It is not true . . . that the parliament of Great Britain, or the legislatures of the particular states, can rectify the exceptionable decisions of their respective courts, in any other sense than might be done by a future legislature of the United States. The theory neither of the British, nor the state constitutions, authorises the revisal of a judicial sentence, by a legislative act. . . . A legislature without exceeding its province cannot reverse a determination once made, in a particular case; though it may prescribe a new rule for future cases.

The essential balance created by this allocation of authority was a simple one. The Legislature would be possessed of power to "prescrib[e] the rules by which the duties and rights of every citizen are to be regulated," but the power of "[t]he interpretation of the laws" would be "the proper and peculiar province of the courts." Federalist Paper No. 78. The Judiciary would be, "from the nature of its functions, . . . the [department] least dangerous to the political rights of the constitution," not because its acts were subject to legislative correction, but because the binding effect of its acts was limited to particular cases and controversies. Thus, "though individual oppression may now and then proceed from the courts of justice, the general liberty of the people can never be endangered from that quarter: . . . so long as the judiciary remains truly distinct from both the legislative and executive." *Id.*

Judicial decisions in the period immediately after ratification of the Constitution confirm the understanding that it forbade interference with the final judgments of courts. In *Calder v. Bull* (1798), the Legislature of Connecticut had enacted a statute that set aside the final judgment of a state court in a civil case. Although the issue before this Court was the construction of the *Ex Post Facto* Clause, Art. I, §10, Justice Iredell (a leading Federalist who had guided the Constitution to ratification in North Carolina) noted that:

> the Legislature of [Connecticut] has been in the uniform, uninterrupted, habit of exercising a general superintending power over its courts of law, by granting new trials. It may, indeed, appear strange to some of us, that in any form, there should exist a power to grant, with respect to suits depending or adjudged, new rights of trial, new privileges of proceeding, not previously recognized and regulated by positive institutions. . . . The power . . . is judicial in its nature; and whenever it is exercised, as in the present instance, it is an exercise of judicial, not of legislative, authority.

The state courts of the era showed a similar understanding of the separation of powers, in decisions that drew little distinction between the federal and state constitutions. . . . *[See] Merrill v. Sherburne* (N.H. 1818) (legislature may not vacate a final judgment and grant a new trial); *Lewis v. Webb* (Me. 1825) (same).

B

Section 27A(b) effects a clear violation of the separation of powers principle we have just discussed. It is, of course, retroactive legislation, that is, legislation that prescribes what the law *was* at an earlier time, when the act whose effect is controlled by the legislation occurred—in this case, the filing of the initial Rule 10b-5 action in the District Court. When retroactive legislation requires its own application in a case already finally adjudicated, it does no more and no less than "reverse a determination once made, in a particular case." The Federalist No. 81. . . .

It is true, as petitioners contend, that Congress can always revise the judgments of Article III courts in one sense: When a new law makes clear that it is retroactive, an appellate court must apply that law in reviewing judgments still on appeal that were rendered before the law was enacted, and must alter the outcome accordingly. *See United States v. Schooner Peggy* (1801). Since that is so, petitioners argue, federal courts must apply the "new" law created by §27A(b) in finally adjudicated cases as well; for the line that separates lower court judgments that are pending on appeal (or may still be appealed), from lower court judgments that are final, is determined by statute, *see, e.g.,* 28 U.S.C. §2107(a) (30-day time limit for appeal to federal court of appeals), and so cannot possibly be a *constitutional* line. But a distinction between judgments from which all appeals have been forgone or completed, and judgments that remain on appeal (or subject to being appealed), is implicit in what Article III creates: not a batch of unconnected courts, but a judicial *department* composed of "inferior Courts" and "one supreme Court." Within that hierarchy, the decision of an inferior court is not (unless the time for appeal has expired) the final word of the department as a whole. It is the obligation of the last court in the hierarchy that rules on the case to give effect to Congress's latest enactment, even when that has the effect of overturning the judgment of an inferior court, since each court, at every level, must "decide according to existing laws." *Schooner Peggy*. Having achieved finality, however, a judicial decision becomes the last word of the judicial department with regard to a particular case or controversy, and Congress may not declare by retroactive legislation that the law applicable *to that very case* was something other than what the courts said it was. Finality of a legal judgment is determined by statute, just as entitlement to a government benefit is a statutory creation; but that no more deprives the former of its constitutional significance for separation of powers analysis than it deprives the latter of its significance for due process purposes.

C

Apart from the statute we review today, we know of no instance in which Congress has attempted to set aside the final judgment of an Article III court by retroactive legislation. That prolonged reticence would be amazing if such interference were not understood to be constitutionally proscribed. The closest analogue that the Government has been able to put forward is the statute at issue in *United States v. Sioux Nation* (1980). That law required the Court of Claims, "'[n]otwithstanding any other provision of law . . . [to] review on the merits, without regard to the defense of res judicata or collateral estoppel,'" a Sioux claim for just compensation from the United States even though the Court of Claims had previously heard and rejected that very claim. We considered and rejected separation-of-powers objections to the statute based upon *Hayburn's Case* and *United States v. Klein*. The basis for our rejection was a line of precedent (starting with *Cherokee Nation v. United States* (1926)) that stood, we said, for the proposition that "Congress has the power to waive the res judicata effect of a prior judgment entered in the Government's favor on a claim against the United States." And our holding was as narrow as the precedent on which we had relied: "In sum, . . . Congress' mere waiver of the res judicata effect of a prior judicial decision rejecting the validity of a legal claim against the United States does not violate the doctrine of separation of powers."

The Solicitor General suggests that even if *Sioux Nation* is read in accord with its holding, it nonetheless establishes that Congress may require Article III courts to reopen their final judgments, since "if res judicata were compelled by Article III to safeguard the structural independence of the courts, the doctrine would not be subject to waiver by any party litigant." But the proposition that legal defenses based upon doctrines central to the courts' structural independence can never be waived simply does not accord with our cases. Certainly one such doctrine consists of the "judicial Power" to disregard an unconstitutional statute, *see Marbury*; yet none would suggest that a litigant may never waive the defense that a statute is unconstitutional. *See, e.g., G.D. Searle & Co. v. Cohn* (1982).

Petitioners also rely on a miscellany of decisions upholding legislation that altered rights fixed by the final judgments of non-Article III courts, *see, e.g., Sampeyreac v. United States* (1833), or administrative agencies, *Paramino Lumber Co. v. Marshall* (1940), or that altered the prospective effect of injunctions entered by Article III courts, *Wheeling & Belmont Bridge Co.* These cases distinguish themselves; nothing in our holding today calls them into question. Petitioners rely on general statements from some of these cases that legislative annulment of final judgments is not an exercise of judicial power. But even if it were our practice to decide cases by weight of prior dicta, we would find the many dicta that reject congressional power to revise the judgments of Article III courts to be the more instructive authority.

Finally, petitioners liken §27A(b) to Federal Rule of Civil Procedure 60(b), which authorizes courts to relieve parties from a final judgment for grounds such as excusable neglect, newly discovered evidence, fraud, or "any other reason justifying relief. . . ." We see little resemblance. Rule 60(b), which authorizes discretionary judicial revision of judgments in the listed situations and in other "'extraordinary circumstances,'" *Liljeberg v. Health Services Acquisition Corp.* (1988), does not impose any legislative mandate to reopen upon the courts, but merely reflects and confirms the courts' own inherent and discretionary power, "firmly established in English practice long before the foundation of our Republic," to set aside a judgment whose enforcement would work inequity. *Hazel-Atlas Glass Co. v. Hartford-Empire Co.* (1944).

. . . If the law then applicable says that the judgment may be reopened for certain reasons, that limitation is built into the judgment itself, and its finality is so conditioned. The present case, however, involves a judgment that Congress subjected to a reopening requirement which did not exist when the judgment was pronounced. The dissent provides not a single clear prior instance of such congressional action.

The same is true of another of the dissent's examples, 28 U.S.C. §2255, which provides federal prisoners a statutory motion to vacate a federal sentence. This procedure "'restates, clarifies and simplifies the procedure in the nature of the ancient writ of error coram nobis.'" *United States v. Hayman* (1952). It is meaningless to speak of these statutes as applying "retroactively," since they simply codified judicial practice that pre-existed.

The dissent sets forth a number of hypothetical horribles flowing from our assertedly "rigid holding"—for example, the inability to set aside a civil judgment that has become final during a period when a natural disaster prevented the timely filing of a certiorari petition. That is horrible not because of our holding, but because the underlying statute *itself* enacts a "rigid" jurisdictional bar to entertaining untimely civil petitions. Congress could undoubtedly enact *prospective* legislation permitting, or indeed requiring, this Court to make equitable exceptions to an otherwise applicable rule of finality, just as district courts do pursuant to Rule 60(b). It is no indication whatever of the invalidity of the constitutional rule which we announce, that it produces unhappy consequences when a legislature lacks foresight, and acts belatedly to remedy a deficiency in the law. That is a routine result of constitutional rules. *See, e.g., Collins v. Youngblood* (1990) *(Ex Post Facto* Clause precludes postoffense statutory extension of a criminal sentence); *United States Trust Co. of N.Y. v. New Jersey* (1977) (Contract Clause prevents retroactive alteration of contract with state bondholders).

To be sure, the class of actions identified by §27A(b) could have been more expansive (*e.g.,* all actions that were *or could have been* filed *pre-Lampf*) and the provision could have been written to have prospective as well as retroactive effect (*e.g.,* "all *post-Lampf* dismissed actions, plus all future actions under Rule 10b-5, shall be timely if brought within 30 years of the injury"). But it escapes us how this could in any way cause the statute to be any less an infringement upon the judicial power.

The nub of that infringement consists *not* of the Legislature's acting in a particularized and hence (according to the concurrence) nonlegislative fashion;[9] but rather of the Legislature's nullifying prior, authoritative judicial action. It makes no difference whatever to that separation-of-powers violation that it is in gross rather than particularized (*e.g.*, "we hereby set aside *all* hitherto entered judicial orders"), or that it is not accompanied by an "almost" violation of the Bill of Attainder Clause, or an "almost" violation of any other constitutional provision.

We know of no previous instance in which Congress has enacted retroactive legislation requiring an Article III court to set aside a final judgment, and for good reason. The Constitution's separation of legislative and judicial powers denies it the authority to do so. Section 27A(b) is unconstitutional to the extent that it requires federal courts to reopen final judgments entered before its enactment.

[Justice BREYER concurred in the judgment, writing separately to insist that legislative reopening of judgments might not be unconstitutional if Congress does not "single out" a small group of litigants or an individual.]

[Justice STEVENS, joined by Justice GINSBURG, dissented, noting that "we have never held that the Constitution requires that the three branches of Government operate with absolute independence," distinguishing the founding era examples as dealing principally with special legislation addressed to individual cases, not a group of cases, and relying on *Sampeyreac, Freeborn, Sioux Nation,* Rule 60(b), 28 U.S.C. §2255, and other laws for the proposition that Congress can and frequently has "specif[ied] new grounds for the reopening of final judgments."]

* * *

Neither *Plaut* nor *Wheeling Bridge* dealt with constitutional rights outside the power of Congress to alter by legislation. In the next case, prisoners challenged provisions of the Prison Litigation Reform Act that reopened, stayed, and required termination of a permanent injunction that had been in place since 1975 to correct unconstitutional prison conditions. As you read the case consider how to reconcile the automatic stay provision of the PLRA with the Court's interpretation in *Plata* of the limitations on prison injunctions imposed by the PLRA discussed earlier in this Chapter.

---

9. The premise that there is something wrong with particularized legislative action is of course questionable. While legislatures usually act through laws of general applicability, that is by no means their only legitimate mode of action. Private bills in Congress are still common, and were even more so in the days before establishment of the Claims Court. Even laws that impose a duty or liability upon a single individual or firm are not on that account invalid—or else we would not have the extensive jurisprudence that we do concerning the Bill of Attainder Clause, including cases which say that it requires not merely "singling out" but also *punishment, see, e.g., United States v. Lovett* (1946), and a case which says that Congress may legislate "a legitimate class of one," *Nixon v. Administrator of General Services* (1977).

Miller v. French

530 U.S. 327 (2000)

Justice O'CONNOR delivered the opinion of the Court.

The Prison Litigation Reform Act (PLRA) establishes standards for the entry and termination of prospective relief in civil actions challenging prison conditions. If prospective relief under an existing injunction does not satisfy these standards, a defendant or intervenor is entitled to "immediate termination" of that relief. 18 U.S.C. §3626(b)(2). And under the PLRA's "automatic stay" provision, a motion to terminate prospective relief "shall operate as a stay" of that relief during the period beginning 30 days after the filing of the motion (extendable to up to 90 days for "good cause") and ending when the court rules on the motion. §§3626(e)(2), (3). The superintendent of Indiana's Pendleton Correctional Facility, which is currently operating under an ongoing injunction to remedy violations of the Eighth Amendment regarding conditions of confinement, filed a motion to terminate prospective relief under the PLRA. Respondent prisoners moved to enjoin the operation of the automatic stay provision of §3626(e)(2), arguing that it is unconstitutional. The District Court enjoined the stay, and the Court of Appeals for the Seventh Circuit affirmed. We must decide whether a district court may enjoin the operation of the PLRA's automatic stay provision and, if not, whether that provision violates separation of powers principles.

I

A

This litigation began in 1975, when four inmates at what is now the Pendleton Correctional Facility brought a class action under 42 U.S.C. §1983, on behalf of all persons who were, or would be, confined at the facility against the predecessors in office of petitioners (hereinafter State). After a trial, the District Court found that living conditions at the prison violated . . . federal law, including the Eighth Amendment's prohibition against cruel and unusual punishment, and the court issued an injunction to correct those violations.

The Court of Appeals affirmed the . . . remedial order as to those aspects governing overcrowding and double celling, the use of mechanical restraints, staffing, and the quality of food and medical services, but it vacated those portions pertaining to exercise and recreation, protective custody, and fire and occupational safety standards. This ongoing injunctive relief has remained in effect ever since, with the last modification occurring in October 1988, when the parties resolved by joint stipulation the remaining issues related to fire and occupational safety standards.

B

In 1996, Congress enacted the PLRA. As relevant here, the PLRA establishes standards for the entry and termination of prospective relief in civil actions challenging conditions at prison facilities. . . . In particular, §3626(b)(2) provides:

> In any civil action with respect to prison conditions, a defendant or intervener shall be entitled to the immediate termination of any prospective relief if the relief was approved or granted in the absence of a finding by

the court that the relief is narrowly drawn, extends no further than necessary to correct the violation of the Federal right, and is the least intrusive means necessary to correct the violation of the Federal right.

A court may not terminate prospective relief, however, if it "makes written findings based on the record that prospective relief remains necessary to correct a current and ongoing violation of the Federal right, extends no further than necessary to correct the violation of the Federal right, and that the prospective relief is narrowly drawn and the least intrusive means necessary to correct the violation." §3626(b)(3). The PLRA also requires courts to rule "promptly" on motions to terminate prospective relief, with mandamus available to remedy a court's failure to do so. §3626(e)(1).

Finally, the provision at issue here, §3626(e)(2), dictates that, in certain circumstances, prospective relief shall be stayed pending resolution of a motion to terminate. Specifically, subsection (e)(2), entitled "Automatic Stay," states:

> Any motion to modify or terminate prospective relief made under subsection (b) shall operate as a stay during the period—
> (A)(i) beginning on the 30th day after such motion is filed, in the case of a motion made under paragraph (1) or (2) of subsection (b); . . .
> (ii) . . . and "(B) ending on the date the court enters a final order ruling on the motion.

As one of several 1997 amendments to the PLRA, Congress permitted courts to postpone the entry of the automatic stay for not more than 60 days for "good cause," which cannot include general congestion of the court's docket. 18 U.S.C. §3626(e)(3).

C

On June 5, 1997, the State filed a motion under §3626(b) to terminate the prospective relief governing the conditions of confinement at the Pendleton Correctional Facility. In response, the prisoner class moved for a temporary restraining order or preliminary injunction to enjoin the operation of the automatic stay, arguing that §3626(e)(2) is unconstitutional as both a violation of the Due Process Clause of the Fifth Amendment and separation of powers principles. The District Court granted the prisoners' motion, enjoining the automatic stay. The State appealed, and the United States intervened pursuant to 28 U.S.C. §2403(a) to defend the constitutionality of §3626(e)(2).

The Court of Appeals for the Seventh Circuit affirmed the District Court's order, concluding that although §3626(e)(2) precluded courts from exercising their equitable powers to enjoin operation of the automatic stay, the statute, so construed, was unconstitutional on separation of powers grounds. . . . [T]he court characterized §3626(e)(2) as "a self-executing legislative determination that a specific decree of a federal court . . . must be set aside at least for a period of time." As such, it concluded that §3626(e)(2) directly suspends a court order in violation of the separation of powers doctrine under *Plaut v. Spendthrift Farm, Inc.* (1995), and mandates a particular rule of decision, at least during the pendency of the §3626(b)(2) termination motion, contrary to *United States v. Klein* (1872).

We granted certiorari to resolve a conflict among the Courts of Appeals.

II

We address the statutory question first. Both the State and the prisoner class agree, as did the majority and dissenting judges below, that §3626(e)(2) precludes a district court from exercising its equitable powers to enjoin the automatic stay. The Government argues, however, that §3626(e)(2) should be construed to leave intact the federal courts' traditional equitable discretion to "stay the stay," invoking two canons of statutory construction. . . . Section 3626(e)(2) states that a motion to terminate prospective relief *"shall operate* as a stay *during"* the specified time period from 30 (or 90) days after the filing of the §3626(b) motion *until* the court rules on that motion. Thus, not only does the statute employ the mandatory term "shall," but it also specifies the points at which the operation of the stay is to begin and end. . . . To allow courts to exercise their equitable discretion to prevent the stay from "operating" during this statutorily prescribed period would be to contradict §3626(e)(2)'s plain terms. It would mean that the motion to terminate merely *may* operate as a stay, despite the statute's command that it "shall" have such effect. . . .

Thus, although we should not construe a statute to displace courts' traditional equitable authority absent the "clearest command," *Califano v. Yamasaki* (1979), or an "inescapable inference" to the contrary, *Porter v. Warner Holding Co.* (1946), we are convinced that Congress' intent to remove such discretion is unmistakable in §3626(e)(2). And while this construction raises constitutional questions, the canon of constitutional doubt permits us to avoid such questions only where the saving construction is not "plainly contrary to the intent of Congress." *Edward J. DeBartolo Corp. v. Florida Gulf Coast Building & Constr. Trades Council* (1988). "We cannot press statutory construction 'to the point of disingenuous evasion' even to avoid a constitutional question." *United States v. Locke* (1985). . . . [Therefore,] we must confront the constitutional issue.

III

. . . Respondent prisoners contend that §3626(e)(2) encroaches on the central prerogatives of the Judiciary and thereby violates the separation of powers doctrine. It does this, the prisoners assert, by legislatively suspending a final judgment of an Article III court in violation of *Plaut* and *Hayburn's Case* (1792). According to the prisoners, the remedial order governing living conditions at the Pendleton Correctional Facility is a final judgment of an Article III court, and §3626(e)(2) constitutes an impermissible usurpation of judicial power because it commands the district court to suspend prospective relief under that order, albeit temporarily. An analysis of the principles underlying *Hayburn's Case* and *Plaut*, as well as an examination of §3626(e)(2)'s interaction with the other provisions of §3626, makes clear that §3626(e)(2) does not offend these separation of powers principles.

Although this Court did not reach the constitutional issue in *Hayburn's Case*, the statements of five Justices, acting as circuit judges, were reported, and we have since recognized that the case "stands for the principle that Congress cannot vest review of the decisions of Article III courts in officials of the Executive Branch." *Plaut, see also Morrison v. Olson* (1988). As we recognized in *Plaut*, such an effort by a coequal branch to "annul a final judgment" is "'an assumption of Judicial power' and therefore forbidden."

Unlike the situation in *Hayburn's Case*, §3626(e)(2) does not involve the direct review of a judicial decision by officials of the Legislative or Executive Branches. Nonetheless, the prisoners suggest that §3626(e)(2) falls within *Hayburn's* prohibition against an indirect legislative "suspension" or reopening of a final judgment, such as that addressed in *Plaut. See Plaut* (quoting *Hayburn's Case* (opinion of Iredell, J., and Sitgreaves, D.J.) ("'[N]o decision of any court of the United States can, under any circumstances, . . . be liable to a revision, or even suspension, by the [l]egislature itself, in whom no judicial power of any kind appears to be vested'")). In *Plaut*, we held that a federal statute that required federal courts to reopen final judgments that had been entered before the statute's enactment was unconstitutional on separation of powers grounds.

Plaut, however, was careful to distinguish the situation before the Court in that case—legislation that attempted to reopen the dismissal of a suit seeking money damages—from legislation that "altered the prospective effect of injunctions entered by Article III courts." We emphasized that "nothing in our holding today calls . . . into question" Congress' authority to alter the prospective effect of previously entered injunctions. Prospective relief under a continuing, executory decree remains subject to alteration due to changes in the underlying law. *Cf. Landgraf v. USI Film Products* (1994) ("When the intervening statute authorizes or affects the propriety of prospective relief, application of the new provision is not retroactive"). This conclusion follows from our decisions in *Pennsylvania v. Wheeling & Belmont Bridge Co.* (1851) (*Wheeling Bridge* 1), and *Pennsylvania v. Wheeling & Belmont Bridge Co.* (1855) (*Wheeling Bridge II*).

Applied here, the principles of *Wheeling Bridge II* demonstrate that the automatic stay of §3626(e)(2) does not unconstitutionally "suspend" or reopen a judgment of an Article III court. Section 3626(e)(2) does not by itself "tell judges when, how, or what to do." Instead, §3626(e)(2) merely reflects the change implemented by §3626(b), which does the "heavy lifting" in the statutory scheme by establishing new standards for prospective relief. . . . Accordingly, if prospective relief under an existing decree had been granted or approved absent such findings, then that prospective relief must cease, *see* §3626(b)(2), unless and until the court makes findings on the record that such relief remains necessary to correct an ongoing violation and is narrowly tailored, *see* §3626(b)(3). The PLRA's automatic stay provision assists in the enforcement of §§3626(b)(2) and (3) by requiring the court to stay any prospective relief that, due to the change in the underlying standard, is no longer enforceable, *i.e.*, prospective relief that is not supported by the findings specified in §§3626(b)(2) and (3).

By establishing new standards for the enforcement of prospective relief in §3626(b), Congress has altered the relevant underlying law. The PLRA has restricted courts' authority to issue and enforce prospective relief concerning prison conditions, requiring that such relief be supported by findings and precisely tailored to what is needed to remedy the violation of a federal right. We note that the constitutionality of §3626(b) is not challenged here; we assume, without deciding, that the new standards it pronounces are effective. As *Plaut* and *Wheeling Bridge II* instruct, when Congress changes the law underlying a judgment awarding prospective relief, that relief is no longer enforceable to the extent it is inconsistent with the new law. Although the remedial injunction here is a "final judgment" for purposes of appeal, it is not the "last word of the judicial department." *Plaut*. The provision of prospective relief is subject to the continuing supervisory jurisdiction of the court, and therefore may be altered according to subsequent changes in the law. Prospective relief must be "modified if, as it later turns out, one or more of the obligations placed upon the parties has become impermissible under federal law." *Rufo v. Inmates of Suffolk County Jail* (1992); *see also Railway Employees v. Wright* (1961) (a court has the authority to alter the prospective effect of an injunction to reflect a change in circumstances, whether of law or fact, that has occurred since the injunction was entered); *Lauf v. E.G. Skinner & Co.* (1938) (applying the Norris-LaGuardia Act's prohibition on a district court's entry of injunctive relief in the absence of findings).

The entry of the automatic stay under §3626(e)(2) . . . merely reflects the changed legal circumstances-that prospective relief under the existing decree is no longer enforceable, and remains unenforceable unless and until the court makes the findings required by §3626(b)(3).

For the same reasons, §3626(e)(2) does not violate the separation of powers principle articulated in *United States v. Klein* (1872). . . . As we noted in *Plaut* . . . "[w]hatever the precise scope of *Klein*, . . . later decisions have made clear that its prohibition does not take hold when Congress 'amends] applicable law.'" *Plaut* (quoting *Robertson v. Seattle Audubon Soc.* (1992)). The prisoners concede this point but contend that, because §3626(e)(2) does not itself amend the legal standard, *Klein* is still applicable. As we have explained, however, §3626(e)(2) must be read not in isolation, but in the context of §3626 as a whole. Section 3626(e)(2) operates in conjunction with the new standards for the continuation of prospective relief; if the new standards of §3626(b)(2) are not met, then the stay "shall operate" unless and until the court makes the findings required by §3626(b)(3). Rather than prescribing a rule of decision, §3626(e)(2) simply imposes the consequences of the court's application of the new legal standard.

Finally, the prisoners assert that, even if §3626(e)(2) does not fall within the recognized prohibitions of *Hayburn's Case, Plaut,* or *Klein*, it still offends the principles of separation of powers because it places a deadline on judicial decisionmaking, thereby interfering with core judicial functions. . . . But whether the time is so short that it deprives litigants of a meaningful opportunity to be heard is a due process question, an issue that is not before us. We leave open, therefore, the question whether this time limit, particularly in a complex case, may implicate due process concerns.

The PLRA does not deprive courts of their adjudicatory role, but merely provides a new legal standard for relief and encourages courts to apply that standard promptly.

Accordingly, the judgment of the Court of Appeals for the Seventh Circuit is reversed, and the action is remanded for further proceedings consistent with this opinion.

[Justice SOUTER, joined by Justice GINSBURG, concurred in part and dissented in part on the ground that the short timeframe allowed to make the findings required by §3626(b) may violate due process and that the case should be remanded for resolution of that issue.]

Justice BREYER, with whom Justice STEVENS joins, dissenting.

. . . The majority interprets the words "shall operate as a stay" to mean [that a permanent] injunction must become ineffective after the 90th day, *no matter what.*

The Solicitor General, however, believes that the view adopted by the majority interpretation is too rigid and calls into doubt the constitutionality of the provision.

I

At the outset, one must understand why a more flexible interpretation of the statute might be needed. To do so, one must keep in mind the extreme circumstances that at least some prison litigation originally sought to correct, the complexity of the resulting judicial decrees, and the potential difficulties arising out of the subsequent need to review those decrees in order to make certain they follow Congress' PLRA directives. A hypothetical example based on actual circumstances may help.

In January 1979, a Federal District Court made 81 factual findings describing extremely poor-indeed "barbaric and shocking"-prison conditions in the Commonwealth of Puerto Rico. *Morales Feliciano v. Romero Barcelo* (P.R. 1979). These conditions included prisons typically operating with twice the number of prisoners they were designed to hold; inmates living in 16 square feet of space (*i.e.*, only 4 feet by 4 feet); inmates without medical care, without psychiatric care, without beds, without mattresses, without hot water, without soap or towels or toothbrushes or underwear; food prepared on a budget of $1.50 per day and "tons of food . . . destroyed because of . . . rats, vermin, worms, and spoilage"; "no working toilets or showers," "urinals [that] flush into the sinks," "plumbing systems . . . in a state of collapse," and a "stench" that was "omnipresent"; "exposed wiring . . . no fire extinguisher, . . . [and] poor ventilation"; "calabozos," or dungeons, "like cages with bars on the top" or with two slits in a steel door opening onto a central corridor, the floors of which were "covered with raw sewage" and which contained prisoners with severe mental illnesses, "caged like wild animals," sometimes for months; areas of a prison where mentally ill inmates were "kept in cells naked, without beds, without mattresses, without any private possessions, and most of them without toilets that work and without drinking water." These conditions had led to epidemics of communicable diseases, untreated mental illness, suicides, and murders.

The District Court held that these conditions amounted to constitutionally forbidden "cruel and unusual punishment." It entered 30 specific orders designed to produce constitutionally mandated improvement by requiring the prison system to, for example, screen food handlers for communicable diseases, close the "calabozos," move mentally ill patients to hospitals, fix broken plumbing, and provide at least 35 square feet (*i.e.*, 5 feet by 7 feet) of living space to each prisoner.

The very pervasiveness and seriousness of the conditions described in the court's opinion made those conditions difficult to cure quickly. Over the next decade, the District Court entered further orders embodied in 15 published opinions, affecting 21 prison institutions. These orders concerned, *inter alia*, overcrowding, security, disciplinary proceedings, prisoner classification, rehabilitation, parole, and drug addiction treatment. Not surprisingly, the related proceedings involved extensive evidence and argument consuming thousands of pages of transcript. Their implementation involved the services of two monitors, two assistants, and a Special Master. Along the way, the court documented a degree of "administrative chaos" in the prison system and entered findings of contempt of court against the Commonwealth, followed by the assessment and collection of more than $74 million in fines.

Prison conditions subsequently have improved in some respects. I express no opinion as to whether, or which of, the earlier orders are still needed. But my brief summary of the litigation should illustrate the potential difficulties involved in making the determination of continuing necessity required by the PLRA. Where prison litigation is as complex as the litigation I have just described, it may prove difficult for a district court to reach a fair and accurate decision about which orders remain necessary, and are the "least intrusive means" available, to prevent or correct a continuing violation of federal law. The orders, which were needed to resolve serious constitutional problems and may still be needed where compliance has not yet been assured, are complex, interrelated, and applicable to many different institutions. Ninety days might not provide sufficient time to ascertain the views of several different parties, including monitors, to allow them to present evidence, and to permit each to respond to the arguments and evidence of the others.

It is at least possible, then, that the statute, as the majority reads it, would sometimes terminate a complex system of orders entered over a period of years by a court familiar with the local problem—perhaps only to reinstate those orders later, when the termination motion can be decided. Such an automatic termination could leave constitutionally prohibited conditions unremedied, at least temporarily. Alternatively, the threat of termination could lead a district court to abbreviate proceedings that fairness would otherwise demand. At a minimum, the mandatory automatic stay would provide a recipe for uncertainty, as complex judicial orders that have long governed the administration of particular prison systems suddenly turn off, then (perhaps selectively) back on. So read, the statute directly interferes with a court's exercise of its traditional equitable authority, rendering temporarily ineffective pre-existing remedies aimed at correcting past, and perhaps ongoing, violations of the Constitution. That interpretation, as the majority itself concedes, might give rise to serious constitutional problems.

II

The Solicitor General's more flexible reading of the statute avoids all these problems. He notes that the relevant language says that the motion to modify or terminate prospective relief "shall operate as a stay" after a period of 30 days, extendable for "good cause" to 90 days. 18 U.S.C. §3626(e)(2). The language says nothing, however, about the district court's power to modify or suspend the operation of the "stay." In the Solicitor General's view, the "stay" would determine the legal status quo; but the district court would retain its traditional equitable power to change that status quo once the party seeking the modification or suspension of the operation of the stay demonstrates that the stay "would cause irreparable injury, that the termination motion is likely to be defeated, and that the merits of the motion cannot be resolved before the automatic stay takes effect." Where this is shown, the "court has discretion to suspend the automatic stay and require prison officials to comply with outstanding court orders until the court resolves the termination motion on the merits," subject to immediate appellate review, 18 U.S.C. §3626(e)(4).

Finally, the more flexible interpretation is consistent with Congress' purposes as revealed in the statute. Those purposes include the avoidance of new judicial relief that is overly broad or no longer necessary and the reassessment of pre-existing relief to bring it into conformity with these standards. But Congress has simultaneously expressed its intent to maintain relief that is narrowly drawn and necessary to end unconstitutional practices. *See* 18 U.S.C. §§3626(a)(1), (a)(2), (b)(3).

* * *

After the passage of the PLRA, defendant prison administrators all around the country moved to terminate under §3626(b). Quite apart from the effect of the automatic stay provisions, it is almost impossible to deny a motion to terminate under §3626(b) because the prison's failure to comply with the Constitution must be "continuing and ongoing." Thus, a prison that has episodically complied but is at or below the line of non-compliance with the Eighth Amendment when a motion to terminate is filed may still prevail. Even if the violation is continuing and ongoing, a remedy that is no longer narrowly tailored, the least restrictive means or extends further than necessary to correct the violation, must be terminated. By 2005, statewide injunctions existed for only five state's prisons and only two state's jails. Margo Schlanger, *Trends in Prisoner Litigation as the PLRA Approaches*, 5 U.C. IRVINE L. REV. 153, 169 (2005).

Is it relevant to assessing the constitutionality of the automatic stay provisions or the termination provisions of the PLRA that Congress has no power to alter the meaning of the Eighth Amendment?

B. CONGRESSIONAL POWER TO CREATE LEGISLATIVE COURTS AND TO AUTHORIZE ADMINISTRATIVE ADJUDICATION

Though we have generally focused upon the business of Article III courts, there is a vast system of federal adjudication outside of the Article III judiciary. The most well-known example is agency adjudication within the modern administrative state. Administrative agencies handle hundreds of thousands of adjudications, if not more, in any given year. For example, judges at the Board of Veterans Appeals, which decides military veterans' appeals from denials of applications for benefits, must work at a punishing pace of 25 to 30 decisions per week if they do not want to add to a multi-year backlog of cases at the Board.[23] The Social Security Administration employs more than 1,500 administrative law judges (ALJs), spread across 10 regional offices and more than 160 hearing offices.[24] These ALJs decide more than 650,000 appeals each year.[25] There are, in other words, more ALJs in the Social Security Administration than there are authorized Article III judgeships. (In 2022, there were 870 sitting Article III judges.) And those ALJs decide more cases than are filed within the U.S. district courts in a given year.[26]

There is, to be sure, an apples and oranges problem in this rough comparison. But it is illustrative of the crucial point—the business of the Article III courts must be understood in the context of a larger system of federal adjudication. Administrative adjudication within federal agencies is but one example of congressionally

---

23. David Ames et al., *Due Process and Mass Adjudication: Crisis and Reform*, 72 STAN. L. REV. 1, 4 (2020).

24. *Information About SSA's Hearings and Appeals Operations*, SOC. SEC. ADMIN., https://www.ssa.gov/appeals/about_us.html.

25. *Id.*

26. *Federal Judicial Caseload Statistics 2022*, U.S. CTS., https://www.uscourts.gov/statistics-reports/federal-judicial-caseload-statistics-2022.

authorized adjudication outside of Article III. Congress has created various "legislative courts" to decide matters that might, at least in theory, be committed to Article III judges. For example, decisions of the Board of Veterans Appeals may be appealed to the U.S. Court of Veterans Appeals, a legislative court independent of the Veterans Administration and the entire executive branch. Appeals are then heard by the Federal Circuit. *See* 38 U.S. §7292. The U.S. Tax Court is also an Article I court. Its decisions may be appealed to a U.S. Court of Appeal. *See* 26 U.S.C. §7441; U.S. Tax Court Rule 190.

The question naturally arises: How much discretion does Congress have to structure this vast adjudicatory system of which Article III courts are a part? What is the source (or sources) of Congress' authority to create legislative courts? What, if any, are the limits on Congress' authority to assign disputes to legislative courts rather than to Article III courts? As this Section discusses, these questions cannot be answered wholesale, but instead turn upon the particular contexts and rights at stake in a given dispute or class or disputes. The relevant contexts include legislative courts for the territories and the District of Columbia; military courts and military tribunals; and so-called "public rights" matters involving the government, as contrasted with matters of "private right" arising in civil disputes.

1. Legislative Courts for the Territories and the District of Columbia

a. Territorial Courts, Constitutional Rights, and the Doctrine of Unincorporated Territories

Today, the conventional map of the United States does not include its overseas territories. That was not always the case, however. In the early twentieth century, American mapmakers printed maps of the "Greater United States," which included U.S. territories such as Puerto Rico, the Philippines, and Guantanamo Bay—not to mention Alaska and Hawai'i, which were not yet states of the Union.[27]

Indeed, the idea of "legislative courts" owes its origins to territorial possessions. From the Founding, the U.S. government has faced the question of what to do about judicial proceedings in its territories. The Northwest Ordinance of 1787 contemplated territorial courts with jurisdiction to resolve local disputes, but not to act as federal courts. After the ratification of the Constitution, the U.S. Supreme Court, in an opinion written by Chief Justice Marshall, held that Congress could create a "legislative court[]" for the territory of Florida. The case was *American Ins. Co. v. Canter* (1828). It presented the question whether Congress could authorize a territorial court, whose judges did not have life tenure, to decide an admiralty matter involving cargo salvaged off Florida's coast. The Court held that Congress could, reasoning that the Florida territorial court was not a "constitutional Court[]," but instead a "legislative Court[], created in virtue of that general right of sovereignty which exists in the government, or in virtue of the clause which enables Congress to make all needful rules and regulations, respecting the territory belonging to the United States."

---

27. Daniel Immerwahr, How to Hide an Empire: A History of the Greater United States (2019).

There are still legislative courts in some territories today. These include the district courts for Guam, the U.S. Virgin Islands, and the Northern Mariana Islands. By contrast, the federal District Court for the District of Puerto Rico is an Article III court, and its decisions are appealable to the First Circuit Court of Appeals.

The traditional justification for legislative courts in the territories was based upon the assumption that territories would become states of the Union. The creation of Article III courts for the territories would pose a logistical problem upon statehood. Why? Territorial courts decided both local matters and those involving national — that is, federal — law. Given their broad jurisdiction, territorial courts needed multiple federal judges, more than would be necessary once the territory had become a state with its own judiciary.

This justification does not explain the persistence of legislative courts in overseas territories that Congress has not put on the path to statehood. The U.S. continues to claim authority over these so-called "unincorporated territories" under a doctrine established by the *Insular Cases*. The *Insular Cases* were a series of U.S. Supreme Court decisions from the first few decades of the twentieth century. The key cases concerned overseas territories such as Puerto Rico and the Philippines that the U.S. possessed by virtue of the treaty ending the Spanish-American War. During this period, the U.S. was aggressively asserting its global position alongside European empires, a fact made clear by the case below, *Dorr v. United States* (1904), which concerned the question whether a territorial court in the Philippines had to afford an accused the right to trial by jury.

The *Dorr* Court held that the jury trial right was not a fundamental right guaranteed in the unincorporated territories. In so holding, the Court drew upon a distinction first drawn by Justice White in a concurring opinion in *Downes v. Bidwell* (1901). That case presented the question whether Puerto Rico was part of the United States for purposes of the Uniformity Clause, which requires that "all duties, imposts, and excises shall be uniform throughout the United States." The Court held that Puerto Rico was not part of the U.S. within the meaning of the Clause. In so holding, the Court blessed Congress' aim to hold some territories indefinitely without incorporating them into the Union as states. Justice White's concurring opinion, relying upon a law review article,[28] distinguished between incorporated territories, such as Florida had once been, which were on the path to statehood, and unincorporated territories, which Congress could hold as territories for as long as it wanted. Subsequent cases held that not all constitutional rights applied in the unincorporated territories. Instead, only certain "fundamental rights" constrained Congress as it constituted territorial governments.

The doctrine of unincorporated territories made new law. In *Scott v. Sanford* (1856), by contrast, Chief Justice Taney had reasoned that "[t]here is certainly no power given by the Constitution to the Federal Government to establish or maintain colonies bordering on the United States or at a distance, to be ruled and governed at its own pleasure; nor to enlarge its territorial limits in any way, except by the admission of new States." This reasoning was one of the bases for Taney's conclusion that Congress could not outlaw slavery in the northern part of the Louisiana Purchase. That anti-imperialists of the early twentieth century would cite

---

28. Abbott Lawrence Lowell, *The Status of Our New Possessions — A Third View*, 13 HARV. L. REV. 155 (1899).

the *Dred Scott* case is but one of the strange features of the constitutional debate concerning the unincorporated territories.

The racialized justification for the doctrine of unincorporated territories is another feature that is apparent from *Dorr*. This case arose from a prosecution for libel involving an English-language newspaper that printed an article alleging that a Filipino member of the Insular Government was a "traitor, seducer, and perjurer." The Supreme Court held that the Constitution did not require Congress to provide for a trial by jury. As you read this case, consider the Court's apparent understanding of its role in facilitating overseas imperialism and the justifications it offers for concluding that a jury trial was not a fundamental right.

Dorr v. United States

195 U.S. 138 (1904)

Justice DAY delivered the opinion of the court.

This case presents the question whether, in the absence of a statute of Congress expressly conferring the right, trial by jury is a necessary incident of judicial procedure in the Philippine Islands, where demand for trial by that method has been made by the accused and denied by the courts established in the islands.

The recent consideration by this court and the full discussion had in the opinions delivered in the so-called "Insular cases," renders superfluous any attempt to reconsider the constitutional relation of the powers of the government to territory acquired by a treaty cession to the United States. In the still more recent case of *Hawaii v. Mankichi* (1903), the right to a jury trial in outlying territory of the United States was under consideration.

The convention which framed the Constitution of the United States, in view of the territory already possessed and the possibility of acquiring more, inserted article IV, section 3, a grant of express power to Congress "to dispose of and make all needful rules and regulations respecting the territory or other property belonging to the United States" [*see Sere v. Pitot* (1810) and *Am. Ins. Co. v. Canter* (1828)].

In every case where Congress undertakes to legislate in the exercise of the power conferred by the Constitution, the question may arise as to how far the exercise of the power is limited by the "prohibitions" of that instrument. The limitations which are to be applied in any given case involving territorial government must depend upon the relation of the particular territory to the United States, concerning which Congress is exercising the power conferred by the Constitution. That the United States may have territory, which is not incorporated into the United States as a body politic, we think was recognized by the framers of the Constitution in enacting the article already considered, giving power over the territories, and is sanctioned by the opinions of the justices concurring in the judgment in *Downes v. Bidwell* (1901).

Until Congress shall see fit to incorporate territory ceded by treaty into the United States, we regard it as settled by that decision that the territory is to be governed under the power existing in Congress to make laws for such territories and subject to such constitutional restrictions upon the powers of that body as are applicable to the situation.

For this case, the practical question is, must Congress, in establishing a system for trial of crimes and offenses committed in the Philippine Islands, carry to their people by proper affirmative legislation a system of trial by jury?

If the treaty-making power could incorporate territory into the United States without Congressional action, it is apparent that the treaty with Spain, ceding the Philippines to the United States, carefully refrained from so doing; for it is expressly provided that (Article IX) "the civil rights and political status of the native inhabitants of the territories hereby ceded to the United States shall be determined by the Congress." In this language it is clear that it was the intention of the framers of the treaty to reserve to Congress, so far as it could be constitutionally done, a free hand in dealing with these newly-acquired possessions.

The legislation upon the subject shows that not only has Congress hitherto refrained from incorporating the Philippines into the United States, but in the act of 1902, providing for temporary civil government, there is express provision that section 1891 of the Revised Statutes of 1878 shall not apply to the Philippine Islands. This is the section giving force and effect to the Constitution and laws of the United States, not locally inapplicable, within all the organized territories, and every territory thereafter organized, as elsewhere within the United States.

The requirements of the Constitution as to a jury are found in article III, section 2: "The trial of all crimes, except in cases of impeachment, shall be by jury; and such trial shall be held in the States where such crimes shall have been committed; but when not committed within any State, the trial shall be at such place or places as the Congress may by law have directed."

And in article six of the amendments to the Constitution: "In all criminal prosecutions the accused shall enjoy the right to a speedy and public trial, by an impartial jury, of the State and district wherein the crime shall have been committed, which district shall have been previously ascertained by law, and to be informed of the nature and cause of the accusation; to be confronted with the witnesses against him; to have compulsory process for obtaining witnesses in his favor, and to have the assistance of counsel for his defence."

It was said in the *Mankichi* case, that when the territory had not been incorporated into the United States these requirements were not limitations upon the power of Congress in providing a government for territory in execution of the powers conferred upon Congress. In the same case Mr. Justice Brown, in the course of his opinion, said:

> We would even go farther, and say that most, if not all, the privileges and immunities contained in the bill of rights of the Constitution were intended to apply from the moment of annexation; but we place our decision of this case upon the ground that the two rights alleged to be violated in this case [right to trial by jury and presentment by grand jury] are not fundamental in their nature, but concern merely a method of procedure which sixty years of practice had shown to be suited to the conditions of the islands, and well calculated to conserve the rights of their citizens to their lives, their property and their well being.

[T]he President, in his instructions to the Philippine Commission, while impressing the necessity of carrying into the new government the guarantees of the Bill of Rights securing those safeguards to life and liberty which are deemed essential to our government, was careful to reserve the right to trial by jury, which was doubtless due to the fact that the civilized portion of the islands had a system of jurisprudence founded upon the civil law, and the uncivilized parts of the archipelago were wholly unfitted to exercise the right of trial by jury. The Spanish system, in force in the Philippines, gave the right to the accused to be tried before judges, who acted in effect as a court of inquiry and whose judgments were not final until passed in review before the audiencia or Supreme Court, with right of final review and power to grant a new trial for errors of law in the Supreme Court at Madrid. To this system the Philippine Commission, in executing the power conferred by the orders of the President and sanctioned by act of Congress, has added a guaranty of the right of the accused to be heard by himself and counsel, to demand the nature and cause of the accusation against him, to have a speedy and public trial, to meet the witnesses against him face to face, and to have compulsory process to compel the attendance of witnesses in his behalf. And, further, that no person shall be held to answer for a criminal offense without due process of law, nor be put twice in jeopardy of punishment for the same offense, nor be compelled in any criminal case to be a witness against himself. [T]he accused is given the right of appeal from the judgment of the court of first instance to the Supreme Court, and, in capital cases, the case goes to the latter court without appeal. It cannot be successfully maintained that this system does not give an adequate and efficient method of protecting the rights of the accused as well as executing the criminal law by judicial proceedings, which give full opportunity to be heard by competent tribunals before judgment can be pronounced.

If the right to trial by jury were a fundamental right which goes wherever the jurisdiction of the United States extends, or if Congress, in framing laws for outlying territory belonging to the United States, was obliged to establish that system by affirmative legislation, it would follow that, no matter what the needs or capacities of the people, trial by jury, and in no other way, must be forthwith established, although the result may be to work injustice and provoke disturbance rather than to aid the orderly administration of justice. If the United States, impelled by its duty or advantage, shall acquire territory peopled by savages, and of which it may dispose or not hold for ultimate admission to Statehood, if this doctrine is sound, it must establish there the trial by jury. To state such a proposition demonstrates the impossibility for carrying it into practice. Again, if the United States shall acquire by treaty the cession of territory having an established system of jurisprudence, where jury trials are unknown, but a method of fair and orderly trial prevails under an acceptable and long-established code, the preference of the people must be disregarded, their established customs ignored and they themselves coerced to accept, in advance of incorporation into the United States, a system of trial unknown to them and unsuited to their needs. We do not think it was intended, in giving power to Congress to make regulations for the territories, to hamper its exercise with this condition.

We conclude that the power to govern territory, implied in the right to acquire it, and given to Congress in the Constitution in Article IV, §3, to whatever other limitations it may be subject, the extent of which must be decided as questions arise, does not require that body to enact for ceded territory, not made a part of the United States by Congressional action, a system of laws which shall include the right of trial by jury, and that the Constitution does not, without legislation and of its own force, carry such right to territory so situated.

Mr. Justice HARLAN, dissenting:

In my opinion, guaranties for the protection of life, liberty and property, as embodied in the Constitution, are for the benefit of all, of whatever race or nativity, in the States composing the Union, or in any territory, however acquired, over the inhabitants of which the Government of the United States may exercise the powers conferred upon it by the Constitution.

The Constitution declares that it "shall be the supreme law of the land." But the court in effect adjudges that the Philippine Islands are not part of the "land," within the meaning of the Constitution, although they are governed by the sovereign authority of the United States, and although their inhabitants are subject in all respects to its jurisdiction — as much so as are the people in the District of Columbia or in the several States of the Union. No power exists in the judiciary to suspend the operation of the Constitution in any territory governed, as to its affairs and people, by authority of the United States. As a Filipino committing the crime of murder in the Philippine Islands may be hung by the sovereign authority of the United States, and as the Philippine Islands are under a civil, not military, government, the suggestion that he may not, of right, appeal for his protection to the jury provisions of the Constitution, which constitutes the only source of the power that the Government may exercise at any time or at any place, is utterly revolting to my mind, and can never receive my sanction. . . . There are many thousands of American soldiers in the Philippines. [If one, in] discharge of his duty to his country, goes into what some call our "outlying dependencies," he is, it seems, "outside of the Constitution," in respect of a right which this court has said . . . was from very early times insisted on by our ancestors in the parent country "as the great bulwark of their civil and political liberties."

* * *

b.   District of Columbia Courts

Like the territories, the District of Columbia has presented questions of Congress' authority to constitute non-Article III courts. For much of its history, D.C.'s courts performed various tasks, including adjudication of questions of state and federal law as well as administrative matters. In 1930, the U.S. Supreme Court held that the D.C. Court of Appeals was an Article I court that Congress could vest with nonjudicial authority. But after Congress reduced the salaries of Article I judges in 1932, the Supreme Court swiftly reversed course in *O'Donoghue v. United States* (1933), and held that the D.C. Court of Appeals was an Article III court, thus protecting the salaries of its judges. The Court also held that Congress' plenary authority with respect to D.C. permitted it to vest the D.C. Court of Appeals with administrative authority that Article III judges do not typically possess.

Subsequent reforms of the D.C. court system raised the question whether Congress may vest a legislative court with jurisdiction over federal criminal law cases. Congress enacted a statute reassigning strictly local matters from the U.S. District Court for the District of Columbia and the U.S. Court of Appeals for the D.C. Circuit to the newly created D.C. Superior Court, with review in a D.C. Court of Appeals. The statute expressly stated that the D.C. Superior Court was "established pursuant to article I" and its judges lacked life tenure. A criminal defendant being prosecuted under federal law challenged the D.C. Superior Court's jurisdiction. The Court held that there was no constitutional requirement of criminal prosecution in an Article III court for a felony committed in D.C. It stressed the unique situation of D.C., which was subject to Congress' "plenary" authority "to legislate with respect to specialized areas having particularized needs and warranting distinctive treatment." *Palmore v. United States* (1973) ("[N]either this Court nor Congress has read the Constitution as requiring every federal question, or even every [federal] criminal prosecution, to be tried in an Article III court."). Thus, just as Congress might exercise its Article IV authority to regulate the territories by constituting territorial courts, so too Congress might exercise its Article I authority to govern the U.S. capital by constituting D.C. courts and vesting them with criminal jurisdiction for prosecutions of violations of statutes applying to only D.C.

2.   Legislative Courts for the Military

Territorial courts are not the only example of legislative courts that do not have many of the features and rights protections of Article III courts. Military courts—that is, tribunals that may imprison or even sentence military personnel to death—do not have life tenure for judges, grand jury indictments, or a constitutional right to trial by jury. Decisions of the Court of Appeals for the Armed Forces are, however, subject to review by the Supreme Court.

Their jurisdiction is limited to individuals who are currently serving in the military, who may be prosecuted for both service-related and non-service-related crimes. The foundational precedent is *Reid v. Covert* (1957), which held that Congress could not subject the dependents of service personnel to prosecution in military courts for capital crimes. Congress' authority to constitute military courts, the Court held, stemmed from its enumerated power to regulate the "land and naval Forces" of the United States. Subsequent cases extended *Reid*'s principle to non-capital crimes and also held that military courts could not try civilian employees working for the armed services abroad.

The constitutional argument for a distinct system of military courts turns, as with many constitutional arguments concerning the armed forces, upon the need for discipline. According to this argument, Congress must have authority to create legislative courts in order to meet the uniquely pressing need for order among the ranks of the armed services. For example, military discipline may not function if military courts must respect all the procedural rights afforded civilians in Article III courts. Some critics argue that the jurisdiction of military courts sweeps too broadly when it subjects personnel to prosecution without grand jury indictment or jury trial for non-service-related crimes. Others more generally argue that the purported need for unique procedures does not explain why military judges lack life tenure or salary protections that would guarantee their independence.

The use of military tribunals to try individuals detained as enemy combatants and accused of crimes associated with terrorism have also raised constitutional issues, which are discussed in Chapter 8.

3.   *Non-Article III Adjudication of "Public Rights" Cases*

Much of the business of non-Article III adjudication involves civil disputes between the federal government and private parties. These disputes may be adjudicated, at least in the first instance, by legislative courts or administrative agencies. The Tax Court, staffed with Article I judges, is one example of a legislative court that adjudicates disputes between the government and citizens. There is no shortage of examples of administrative agency adjudication of such disputes. They range from cases in which the government seeks to impose penalties upon regulated parties that violate the law to those in which the government decides whether to afford benefits under entitlement programs.

The foundational case is *Murray's Lessee v. Hoboken Land & Improvement Co.* (1856), which you will read below. It involved a distress warrant, a non-judicial mechanism of property seizure that allowed the federal government to seize an employee's property to satisfy a debt. Congress had authorized the Treasury Department to issue such warrants. The Department did so in order to recover over $1 million in customs fees that Samuel Swartout, the Collector of the Port of New York, had embezzled. Then, more so than today, the collection of customs was a vital source of revenue for the U.S. government. In issuing the distress warrants, the Treasury Department voided the sale of lands that Swartout had purchased using the embezzled funds. Because it involved a dispute over the right to possess real property, the suit arose as an action of ejectment between two parties that both claimed title.

As you read *Murray's Lessee*, consider the Court's use of history in its discussion of the meaning of due process, and ask whether there is a principled reason for affording Congress the discretion to assign public-rights matters to non-Article III adjudicators.

Murray's Lessee v. Hoboken Land & Improvement Co.

59 U.S. 272 (1856)

Justice CURTIS delivered the opinion of the Court.

This case comes before us on a certificate of division of opinion of the judges of the circuit court of the United States for the district of New Jersey. It is an action of ejectment, in which both parties claim title under Samuel Swartwout by virtue of what is denominated a distress warrant, issued by the solicitor of the treasury under the act of congress of May 15, 1820. This act having provided, by its first section, that a lien for the amount due should exist on the lands of the debtor from the time of the levy and record thereof in the office of the district court of the United States for the proper district, and the date of that levy in this case being prior to the date of the judgment under which the plaintiffs' title was made, the question occurred [whether the distress warrant was consistent with due process of law]. Upon this question, the judges being of opposite opinions, it was certified to this court, and has been argued by counsel.

No objection has been taken to the warrant on account of any defect or irregularity in the proceedings which preceded its issue. It is not denied that they were in conformity with the requirements of the act of congress. The special verdict finds that Swartwout was collector of the customs for the port of New York for eight years before the 29th of March, 1838: that, on the 10th of November, 1838, his account, as such collector, was audited by the first auditor, and certified by the first comptroller of the treasury; and for the balance thus found, amounting to the sum of $1,374,119 65/100, the warrant in question was issued by the solicitor of the treasury. Its validity is denied by the plaintiffs, upon the ground that so much of the act of congress as authorized it is in conflict with the constitution of the United States.

It must be admitted that, if the auditing of this account, and the ascertainment of its balance, and the issuing of this process, was an exercise of the judicial power of the United States, the proceeding was void; for the officers who performed these acts could exercise no part of that judicial power. They neither constituted a court of the United States, nor were they, or either of them, so connected with any such court as to perform even any of the ministerial duties which arise out of judicial proceedings.

The question, whether these acts were an exercise of the judicial power of the United States, can best be considered under another inquiry, raised by the further objection of the plaintiff, that the effect of the proceedings authorized by the act in question is to deprive the party, against whom the warrant issues, of his liberty and property, "without due process of law"; and, therefore, is in conflict with the fifth article of the amendments of the constitution.

Taking these two objections together, they raise the questions, whether, under the constitution of the United States, a collector of the customs, from whom a balance of account has been found to be due by accounting officers of the treasury, designated for that purpose by law, can be deprived of his liberty, or property, in order to enforce payment of that balance, without the exercise of the judicial power of the United States, and yet by due process of law, within the meaning of those terms in the constitution; and if so, then, secondly, whether the warrant in question was such due process of law?

That the warrant now in question is legal process, is not denied. It was issued in conformity with an act of Congress. But is it "due process of law"? The constitution contains no description of those processes which it was intended to allow or forbid. It does not even declare what principles are to be applied to ascertain whether it be due process. It is manifest that it was not left to the legislative power to enact any process which might be devised. The article is a restraint on the legislative as well as on the executive and judicial powers of the government, and cannot be so construed as to leave congress free to make any process "due process of law," by its mere will. To what principles, then, are we to resort to ascertain whether this process, enacted by congress, is due process? To this the answer must be two-fold. We must examine the constitution itself, to see whether this process be in conflict with any of its provisions. If not found to be so, we must look to those settled usages and modes of proceeding existing in the common and statue law of England, before the emigration of our ancestors, and which are shown not to have been unsuited to their civil and political condition by having been acted on by them after the settlement of this country. We apprehend there has been no period, since the establishment of the English monarchy, when there has not been, by the law of the land, a summary method for the recovery of debts due to the crown, and especially those due from receivers of the revenues.

Tested by the common and statute law of England prior to the emigration of our ancestors, and by the laws of many of the States at the time of the adoption of this amendment, the proceedings authorized by the act of 1820 cannot be denied to be due process of law, when applied to the ascertainment and recovery of balances due to the government from a collector of customs, unless there exists in the constitution some other provision which restrains congress from authorizing such proceedings. For, though "due process of law" generally implies and includes actor, reus, judex, regular allegations, opportunity to answer, and a trial according to some settled course of judicial proceedings, yet, this is not universally true. There may be, and we have seen that there are cases, under the law of England after Magna Charta, and as it was brought to this country and acted on here, in which process, in its nature final, issues against the body, lands, and goods of certain public debtors without any such trial; and this brings us to the question, whether those provisions of the constitution which relate to the judicial power are incompatible with these proceedings?

That the auditing of the accounts of a receiver of public moneys may be, in an enlarged sense, a judicial act, must be admitted. So are all those administrative duties the performance of which involves an inquiry into the existence of facts and the application to them of rules of law. In this sense the act of the President in calling out the militia under the act of 1795, or of a commissioner who makes a certificate for the extradition of a criminal, under a treaty, is judicial. But it is not sufficient to bring such matters under the judicial power, that they involve the exercise of judgment upon law and fact. It is necessary to go further, and show not only that the adjustment of the balances due from accounting officers may be, but from their nature must be, controversies to which the United States is a party, within the meaning of the second section of the third article of the constitution. We do not doubt the power of congress to provide by law that such a question shall form the subject-matter of a suit in which the judicial power can be exerted. The act of 1820 makes such a provision for reviewing the decision of the accounting officers of the treasury. But, until reviewed, it is final and binding; and the question is, whether its subject-matter is necessarily, and without regard to the consent of congress, a judicial controversy. And we are of opinion it is not.

The power to collect and disburse revenue, and to make all laws which shall be necessary and proper for carrying that power into effect, includes all known and appropriate means of effectually collecting and disbursing that revenue, unless some such means should be forbidden in some other part of the constitution. The power has not been exhausted by the receipt of the money by the collector. Its purpose is to raise money and use it in payment of the debts of the government; and, whoever may have possession of the public money, until it is actually disbursed, the power to use those known and appropriate means to secure its due application continues.

The means provided by the act of 1820 do not differ in principle from those employed in England from remote antiquity — and in many of the States, so far as we know without objection — for this purpose, at the time the constitution was formed. It may be added, that probably there are few governments which do or can permit their claims for public taxes, either on the citizen or the officer employed for their collection or disbursement, to become subjects of judicial controversy, according to the course of the law of the land. Imperative necessity has forced a distinction between such claims and all others, which has sometimes been carried out by summary methods of proceeding, and sometimes by systems of fines and penalties, but always in some way observed and yielded to.

Though, generally, both public and private wrongs are redressed through judicial action, there are more summary extrajudicial remedies for both. An instance of extrajudicial redress of a private wrong is, the recapture of goods by their lawful owner; of a public wrong, by a private person, is the abatement of a public nuisance; and the recovery of public dues by a summary process of distress, issued by some public officer authorized by law, is an instance of redress of a particular kind of public wrong, by the act of the public through its authorized agents. There is, however, an important distinction between these. Though a private person may retake his property, or abate a nuisance, he is directly responsible for his acts to the proper judicial tribunals. His authority to do these acts depends not merely on the law, but upon the existence of such facts as are, in point of law, sufficient to constitute that authority; and he may be required, by an action at law, to prove those facts; but a public agent, who acts pursuant to the command of a legal precept, can justify his act by the production of such precept. He cannot be made responsible in a judicial tribunal for obeying the lawful command of the government; and the government itself, which gave the command, cannot be sued without its own consent.

At the same time there can be no doubt that the mere question, whether a collector of the customs is indebted to the United States, may be one of judicial cognizance. It is competent for the United States to sue any of its debtors in a court of law. It is equally clear that the United States may consent to be sued, and may yield this consent upon such terms and under such restrictions as it may think just. Though both the marshal and the government are exempt from suit, for anything done by the former in obedience to legal process, still, congress may provide by law, that both, or either, shall, in a particular class of cases, and under such restrictions as they may think proper to impose, come into a court of law or equity and abide by its determination. The United States may thus place the government upon the same ground which is occupied by private persons who proceed to take extrajudicial remedies for their wrongs, and they may do so to such extent, and with such restrictions, as may be thought fit.

When, therefore, the act of 1820 enacts, that after the levy of the distress warrant has been begun, the collector may bring before a district court the question, whether he is indebted as recited in the warrant, it simply waives a privilege which belongs to the government, and consents to make the legality of its future proceedings dependent on the judgment of the court; as we have already stated in case of a private person, every fact upon which the legality of the extrajudicial remedy depends may be drawn in question by a suit against him. The United States consents that this fact of indebtedness may be drawn in question by a suit against them. Though they might have withheld their consent, we think that, by granting it, nothing which may not be a subject of judicial cognizance is brought before the court.

To avoid misconstruction upon so grave a subject, we think it proper to state that we do not consider congress can either withdraw from judicial cognizance any matter which, from its nature, is the subject of a suit at the common law, or in equity, or admiralty; nor, on the other hand, can it bring under the judicial power a matter which, from its nature, is not a subject for judicial determination. At the same time there are matters, involving public rights, which may be presented in such form that the judicial power is capable of acting on them, and which are susceptible of judicial determination, but which congress may or may not bring within the cognizance of the courts of the United States, as it may deem proper. Equitable claims to land by the inhabitants of ceded territories form a striking instance of such a class of cases; and as it depends upon the will of congress whether a remedy in the courts shall be allowed at all, in such cases, they may regulate it and prescribe such rules of determination as they may think just and needful.

It is true, also, that even in a suit between private persons to try a question of private right, the action of the executive power, upon a matter committed to its determination by the constitution and laws, is conclusive.

To apply these principles to the case before us, we say that, though a suit may be brought against the marshal for seizing property under such a warrant of distress, and he may be put to show his justification; yet the action of the executive power in issuing the warrant, pursuant to the act of 1820, passed under the powers to collect and disburse the revenue granted by the constitution, is conclusive evidence of the facts recited in it, and of the authority to make the levy; that though no suit can be brought against the United States without the consent of congress, yet congress may consent to have a suit brought, to try the question whether the collector be indebted, that being a subject capable of judicial determination, and may empower a court to act on that determination, and restrain the levy of the warrant of distress within the limits of the debt judicially found to exist.

* * *

The Court's opinion in *Murray's Lessee* has come to stand for a public-rights exception to Article III. Congress may assign the adjudication of a public-rights dispute between private parties and the federal government. To understand this case, it is necessary to understand the common law distinction between private rights and public rights. Private rights involved personal rights, including, for example, a landowner's right to possess their property, a party's right under a contract, or a person's right to bodily security. Today, we would think of these examples in terms of property, contract, and tort law. But private rights were not necessarily limited to these three common law fields, or even to the common law generally. Just as today, there are private rights that are protected by constitutional and statutory law. Public rights, by contrast, involved duties that someone owed to the public at large, or what Blackstone called "the whole community, considered as a community, in its social aggregate capacity."[29] Disputes arising between a private party and the government might involve public rights. In *Murray's Lessee*, notice that the underlying dispute is between the government and one of its own employees regarding money belonging to the government. Here, the interests of the "whole community" or the sovereign are particularly strong in establishing a forum for adjudication that provides prompt relief. Another example involves public franchises granted by the government.

---

29. 4 WILLIAM BLACKSTONE, COMMENTARIES *5.

The Supreme Court returned to the public rights-exception in a series of other cases. The first, *Ex parte Bakelite Corp.* (1929), upheld the creation of the U.S. Court of Customs Appeals. This court adjudicated appeals from decisions of the Board of General Appraisers concerning the duties imposed upon products. The Court held that the Court of Customs Appeals was not an Article III court but did not need to be. Rather, its exercise of jurisdiction was constitutional because it did not decide anything "which inherently or necessarily requires judicial determination, but only matters the determination of which may be, and at times has been, committed exclusively to executive officers." In the second case, *Williams v. United States* (1933), the Supreme Court held that the Court of Claims was not an Article III court. Congress could, therefore, reduce the salaries of judges on the Court of Claims. This court adjudicated private parties' claims for monetary relief from the federal government. According to the Court, demands for monetary relief from the federal government are a legislative, not a judicial matter, because Congress had the discretion to determine whether to permit such claims. Under the doctrine of sovereign immunity, the government could categorically refuse to pay such claims.

The third case, *Glidden Co. v. Zdanok* (1962), held that Congress could assign public rights matters to either Article III courts or legislative courts. Congress had enacted a statute identifying the Court of Customs and Patent Appeals and the Court of Claims—the courts at issue in *Bakelite* and *Williams*—and declaring them to "be established under Article III of the Constitution." The Court confronted the question whether judges appointed to these courts prior to Congress' declaration were Article III judges. It held that they were and, therefore, that these judges could sit by designation on other Article III courts. In reaching its holding, the Court concluded that Congress "may create tribunals under Article III for the sole purpose of adjudicating matters that it might have reserved for legislative or executive decision."

The Supreme Court has also held that Congress may use legislative courts for private law and criminal matters if the Article III courts remain involved in the ultimate resolution of the matter. However, the doctrine in this area has shifted with the dramatic expansion of the administrative state and administrative adjudication in the twentieth century. Indeed, by the end the century, as we will see in the cases that follow, the Court blurred the public/private rights distinction.

A common thread is that if Congress commits a private law or criminal matter to a non-Article III tribunal, it must subject that body's decisions to review by an Article III court.[30] For example, when government agencies have been granted authority to adjudicate in the first instance, they have traditionally been designed as "adjuncts" of Article III courts. This is achieved by limiting enforcement authority to the Article III courts and setting a standard of review of agency adjudications. The canonical case is *Crowell v. Benson* (1932), presented below, holding that an Article III court must have authority to review *de novo* both questions of law and questions of fact that form the basis of a claim of a constitutional violation; ordinary agency factfinding, however, is entitled to finality.

---

30. *See* Thomas W. Merrill, *Article III, Agency Adjudication, and the Origins of the Appellate Review Model of Administrative Law*, 111 COLUM. L. REV. 939 (2011).

Two interpretive approaches have developed as the New Deal administrative state expanded in the second half of the twentieth century. One is relatively categorical, upholding non-Article III adjudication of private rights cases where the adjunct model vesting enforcement in an Article III court is used. This approach has roots in the public/private rights distinction drawn by nineteenth century courts, including *Murray's Lessee*. The other is more functionalist, concentrating less on the fact that a private right is at issue and more on the costs and benefits of assigning a matter to a non-Article III court in light of the broader regulatory scheme established by Congress. As you might imagine, the latter approach is more agency-enabling, deferring to the power of Congress to establish comprehensive regulatory systems and to delegate to agencies the power to adjudicate claims that touch and concern the system. But it blurs the line between traditional public and private rights cases, drawing more common law disputes between private parties into non-Article III courts. The former is more concerned with separation of powers and preserving a default presumption of access to federal court in cases involving private rights.

After *Crowell* we present two bankruptcy cases to illustrate the divergent interpretive approaches. It is no accident that bankruptcy law has produced some of the sharpest clashes over non-Article III adjudication. The core right is federal, and the enactment of the first federal bankruptcy laws were transformative exercises of federal power to revise notoriously punitive debtor-creditor laws in the nineteenth century.[31] At the same time, this exercise of federal authority necessarily implicates state law because the adjudication of many bankruptcy claims by definition involves assets, debts, and liabilities that are defined by and enforced through private rights in the form of state common law claims. The plurality opinion in *Northern Pipeline Constr. Co. v. Marathon Pipe Line Co.* (1982) represents the formalist approach. Justice Scalia's concurring opinion in *Stern v. Marshall* (2011) also takes this approach. Chief Justice Robert's majority opinion attempts to harmonize the two approaches.

The functionalist approach is advocated by Justice Breyer's dissent in *Stern*. Note as you read that he relies on cases decided after *Northern Pipeline* in which a majority of the Court emphasized functional considerations. We close with another case at the border of public and private rights: inter partes review of the validity of patents before the Patent Trial and Appeal Board.

Crowell v. Benson

285 U.S. 22 (1932)

Chief Justice HUGHES delivered the opinion of the Court.

This suit was brought in the District Court to enjoin the enforcement of an award made by petitioner Crowell, as deputy commissioner of the United States Employees' Compensation Commission, in favor of the petitioner Knudsen and against the respondent Benson. The award was made under the Longshoremen's

---

31. *See* BRUCE MANN, REPUBLIC OF DEBTORS: BANKRUPTCY IN THE AGE OF AMERICAN INDEPENDENCE (2002) (describing use of debtors' prisons to punish debtors).

and Harbor Workers' Compensation Act and rested upon the finding of the deputy commissioner that Knudsen was injured while in the employ of Benson and performing service upon the navigable waters of the United States. The complainant alleged that the award was contrary to law for the reason that Knudsen was not at the time of his injury an employee of the complainant and his claim was not "within the jurisdiction" of the deputy commissioner. An amended complaint charged that the Act was unconstitutional upon the grounds that it violated the due process clause of the Fifth Amendment, the provision of the Seventh Amendment as to trial by jury, that of the Fourth Amendment as to unreasonable search and seizure, and the provisions of Article III with respect to the judicial power of the United States. The District Judge denied motions to dismiss and granted a hearing *de novo* upon the facts and the law, expressing the opinion that the Act would be invalid if not construed to permit such a hearing. The case was transferred to the admiralty docket, answers were filed presenting the issue as to the fact of employment, and the evidence of both parties having been heard, the District Court decided that Knudsen was not in the employ of the petitioner and restrained the enforcement of the award. The decree was affirmed by the Circuit Court of Appeals, and this Court granted writs of certiorari.

First. The Act has two limitations that are fundamental. It deals exclusively with compensation in respect of disability or death resulting "from an injury occurring upon the navigable waters of the United States" if recovery "through workmen's compensation proceedings may not validly be provided by State law," and it applies only when the relation of master and servant exists. "Injury," within the statute, "means accidental injury or death arising out of and in the course of employment," and the term "employer" means one "any of whose employees are employed in maritime employment, in whole or in part," upon such navigable waters. Employers are made liable for the payment to their employees of prescribed compensation "irrespective of fault as a cause for the injury." Employers must secure the payment of compensation by procuring insurance or by becoming self-insurers in the manner stipulated. Failure to provide such security is a misdemeanor.

As the Act relates solely to injuries occurring upon the navigable waters of the United States the general authority of the Congress to alter or revise the maritime law which shall prevail throughout the country is beyond dispute. In limiting the application of the Act to cases where recovery "through workmen's compensation proceedings may not validly be provided by State law," the Congress evidently had in view the decisions of this Court with respect to the scope of the exclusive authority of the national legislature.

As the claims which are subject to the provisions of the Act are governed by the maritime law as established by the Congress and are within the admiralty jurisdiction, the objection raised by the respondent's pleading as to the right to a trial by jury under the Seventh Amendment is unavailing; and that under the Fourth Amendment is neither explained nor urged. The other objections as to procedure invoke the due process clause and the provision as to the judicial power of the United States.

(1) The contention under the due process clause of the Fifth Amendment relates to the determination of questions of fact. Rulings of the deputy commissioner upon questions of law are without finality. So far as the latter are concerned,

full opportunity is afforded for their determination by the Federal courts through proceedings to suspend or to set aside a compensation order, by the requirement that judgment is to be entered on a supplementary order declaring default only in case the order follows the law, and by the provision that the issue of injunction or other process in a proceeding by a beneficiary to compel obedience to a compensation order is dependent upon a determination by the court that the order was lawfully made and served. Moreover, the statute contains no express limitation attempting to preclude the court, in proceedings to set aside an order as not in accordance with law, from making its own examination and determination of facts whenever that is deemed to be necessary to enforce a constitutional right properly asserted. As the statute is to be construed so as to support rather than to defeat it, no such limitation is to be implied.

Apart from cases involving constitutional rights to be appropriately enforced by proceedings in court, there can be no doubt that the Act contemplates that, as to questions of fact arising with respect to injuries to employees within the purview of the Act, the findings of the deputy commissioner, supported by evidence and within the scope of his authority, shall be final. To hold otherwise would be to defeat the obvious purpose of the legislation to furnish a prompt, continuous, expert and inexpensive method for dealing with a class of questions of fact which are peculiarly suited to examination and determination by an administrative agency specially assigned to that task. The object is to secure . . . an immediate investigation and a sound practical judgment, and the efficacy of the plan depends upon the finality of the determinations of fact with respect to the employee's injuries and the amount of compensation that should be awarded. The use of the administrative method for these purposes, assuming due notice, proper opportunity to be heard, and that findings are based upon evidence, falls easily within the principle of the decisions sustaining similar procedure against objections under the due process clauses of the Fifth and Fourteenth Amendments.

(2) The contention based upon the judicial power of the United States, as extended "to all cases of admiralty and maritime jurisdiction" (Const. Art. III), presents a distinct question. In *Murray's Lessee v. Hoboken Land & Improvement Co.* (1855), this Court, speaking through Mr. Justice Curtis, said: "To avoid misconstruction upon so grave a subject, we think it proper to state that we do not consider congress can either withdraw from judicial cognizance any matter which, from its nature, is the subject of a suit at the common law, or in equity, or admiralty; nor, on the other hand, can it bring under the judicial power a matter which, from its nature, is not a subject for judicial determination."

The question in the instant case, in this aspect, can be deemed to relate only to determinations of fact. The reservation of legal questions is to the same court that has jurisdiction in admiralty, and the mere fact that the court is not described as such is unimportant. Nor is the provision for injunction proceedings open to objection. The Congress was at liberty to draw upon another system of procedure to equip the court with suitable and adequate means for enforcing the standards of the maritime law as defined by the Act. By statute and rules, courts of admiralty may be empowered to grant injunctions, as in the case of limitation of liability proceedings. The Congress did not attempt to define questions of law, and the generality of the description leaves no doubt of the intention to reserve to the Federal court full authority to pass upon all matters which this Court had held to fall within that category. There is thus no attempt to interfere with, but rather provision is made to facilitate, the exercise by the court of its jurisdiction to deny effect to any administrative finding which is without evidence, or "contrary to the indisputable character of the evidence" or where the hearing is "inadequate," or "unfair," or arbitrary in any respect.

As to determinations of fact, the distinction is at once apparent between cases of private right and those which arise between the Government and persons subject to its authority in connection with the performance of the constitutional functions of the executive or legislative departments. The Court referred to this distinction in *Murray's Lessee* pointing out that "there are matters, involving public rights, which may be presented in such form that the judicial power is capable of acting on them, and which are susceptible of judicial determination, but which Congress may or may not bring within the cognizance of the courts of the United States, as it may deem proper." Thus the Congress, in exercising the powers confided to it, may establish "legislative" courts (as distinguished from "constitutional courts in which the judicial power conferred by the Constitution can be deposited") which are to form part of the government of territories or of the District of Columbia, or to serve as special tribunals "to examine and determine various matters, arising between the government and others, which from their nature do not require judicial determination and yet are susceptible of it." But "the mode of determining matters of this class is completely within congressional control. Congress may reserve to itself the power to decide, may delegate that power to executive officers, or may commit it to judicial tribunals." *Ex parte Bakelite Corp.* (1929). Familiar illustrations of administrative agencies created for the determination of such matters are found in connection with the exercise of the congressional power as to interstate and foreign commerce, taxation, immigration, the public lands, public health, the facilities of the post office, pensions and payments to veterans.

The present case does not fall within the categories just described but is one of private right, that is, of the liability of one individual to another under the law as defined. But in cases of that sort, there is no requirement that, in order to maintain the essential attributes of the judicial power, all determinations of fact in constitutional courts shall be made by judges. On the common law side of the Federal courts, the aid of juries is not only deemed appropriate but is required by the Constitution itself. In cases of equity and admiralty, it is historic practice to call to the assistance of the courts, without the consent of the parties, masters and commissioners or assessors, to pass upon certain classes of questions, as, for example, to take and state an account or to find the amount of damages. While the reports of masters and commissioners in such cases are essentially of an advisory nature, it has not been the practice to disturb their findings when they are properly based upon evidence, in the absence of errors of law, and the parties have no right to demand that the court shall redetermine the facts thus found.

In deciding whether the Congress, in enacting the statute under review, has exceeded the limits of its authority to prescribe procedure in cases of injury upon navigable waters, regard must be had, as in other cases where constitutional limits are invoked, not to mere matters of form but to the substance of what is required. The statute has a limited application, being confined to the relation of master and servant, and the method of determining the questions of fact, which arise in the routine of making compensation awards to employees under the Act, is necessary to its effective enforcement. The Act itself, where it applies, establishes the measure of the employer's liability, thus leaving open for determination the questions of fact as to the circumstances, nature, extent and consequences of the injuries sustained by the employee for which compensation is to be made in accordance with the prescribed standards. Findings of fact by the deputy commissioner upon such questions are closely analogous to the findings of the amount of damages that are made, according to familiar practice, by commissioners or assessors; and the reservation of full authority to the court to deal with matters of law provides for the appropriate exercise of the judicial function in this class of cases. For the purposes stated, we are unable to find any constitutional obstacle to the action of the Congress in availing itself of a method shown by experience to be essential in order to apply its standards to the thousands of cases involved, thus relieving the courts of a most serious burden while preserving their complete authority to insure the proper application of the law.

(3) What has been said thus far relates to the determination of claims of employees within the purview of the Act. A different question is presented where the determinations of fact are fundamental or "jurisdictional,"[17] in the sense that their existence is a condition precedent to the operation of the statutory scheme. These fundamental requirements are that the injury occur upon the navigable waters of the United States and that the relation of master and servant exist. These conditions are indispensable to the application of the statute, not only because the Congress has so provided explicitly, but also because the power of the Congress to enact the legislation turns upon the existence of these conditions.

In amending and revising the maritime law, the Congress cannot reach beyond the constitutional limits which are inherent in the admiralty and maritime jurisdiction. Unless the injuries to which the Act relates occur upon the navigable waters of the United States, they fall outside that jurisdiction. In the present instance, the Congress has imposed liability without fault only where the relation of master and servant exists in maritime employment and, while we hold that the Congress could do this, the fact of that relation is the pivot of the statute and, in the absence of any other justification, underlies the constitutionality of this enactment. If the person injured was not an employee of the person sought to be held, or if the injury did not occur upon the navigable waters of the United States, there is no ground for an assertion that the person against whom the proceeding was directed could constitutionally be subjected, in the absence of fault upon his part, to the liability which the statute creates.

In relation to these basic facts, the question is not the ordinary one as to the propriety of provision for administrative determinations. The recognition of the utility and convenience of administrative agencies for the investigation and finding of facts within their proper province, and the support of their authorized action, does not require the conclusion that there is no limitation of their use, and that the Congress could completely oust the courts of all determinations of fact by vesting

---

17. The term "jurisdictional," although frequently used, suggests analogies which are not complete when the reference is to administrative officials or bodies. In relation to administrative agencies, the question in a given case is whether it falls within the scope of the authority validly conferred.

the authority to make them with finality in its own instrumentalities or in the Executive Department. That would be to sap the judicial power as it exists under the Federal Constitution, and to establish a government of a bureaucratic character alien to our system, wherever fundamental rights depend, as not infrequently they do depend, upon the facts, and finality as to facts becomes in effect finality in law.

In cases brought to enforce constitutional rights, the judicial power of the United States necessarily extends to the independent determination of all questions, both of fact and law, necessary to the performance of that supreme function. Jurisdiction in the Executive to order deportation exists only if the person arrested is an alien, and while, if there were jurisdiction, the findings of fact of the Executive Department would be conclusive, the claim of citizenship "is a denial of an essential jurisdictional fact" both in the statutory and the constitutional sense, and a writ of *habeas corpus* will issue "to determine the status." Persons claiming to be citizens of the United States "are entitled to a judicial determination of their claims," said this Court in *Ng Fung Ho. v. White* (1922), and in that case the cause was remanded to the Federal District Court "for trial in that court of the question of citizenship."

Assuming that the Federal court may determine for itself the existence of these fundamental or jurisdictional facts, we come to the question, — Upon what record is the determination to be made? There is no provision of the statute which seeks to confine the court in such a case to the record before the deputy commissioner or to the evidence which he has taken. The remedy which the statute makes available is not by an appeal or by a writ of certiorari for a review of his determination upon the record before him. The remedy is "through injunction proceedings, mandatory or otherwise." The question in the instant case is not whether the deputy commissioner has acted improperly or arbitrarily as shown by the record of his proceedings in the course of administration in cases contemplated by the statute, but whether he has acted in a case to which the statute is inapplicable. By providing for injunction proceedings, the Congress evidently contemplated a suit as in equity, and in such a suit the complainant would have full opportunity to plead and prove either that the injury did not occur upon the navigable waters of the United States or that the relation of master and servant did not exist, and hence that the case lay outside the purview of the statute. As the question is one of the constitutional authority of the deputy commissioner as an administrative agency, the court is under no obligation to give weight to his proceedings pending the determination of that question. If the court finds that the facts existed which gave the deputy commissioner jurisdiction to pass upon the claim for compensation, the injunction will be denied in so far as these fundamental questions are concerned; if, on the contrary, the court is satisfied that the deputy commissioner had no jurisdiction of the proceedings before him, that determination will deprive them of their effectiveness for any purpose. We think that the essential independence of the exercise of the judicial power of the United States in the enforcement of constitutional rights requires that the Federal court should determine such an issue upon its own record and the facts elicited before it.

Justice BRANDEIS, dissenting.

To hold that Congress conferred the right to a trial *de novo* on the issue of the employer-employee relation seems to me a remaking of the statute and not a construction of it.

Trial *de novo* of the issue of the existence of the employer-employee relation is not required by the due process clause. That clause ordinarily does not even require that parties shall be permitted to have a judicial tribunal pass upon the weight of the evidence introduced before the administrative body. The findings of fact of the deputy commissioner, the Court now decides, are conclusive as to most issues, if supported by evidence. Yet as to the issue of employment the Court holds not only that such findings may not be declared final, but that it would create a serious constitutional doubt to construe the Act as committing to the deputy commissioner the simple function of collecting the evidence upon which the court will ultimately decide the issue.

It is suggested that this exception is required as to issues of fact involving claims of constitutional right. For reasons which I shall later discuss, I cannot believe that the issue of employment is one of constitutional right. But even assuming it to be so, the conclusion does not follow that the trial of the issue must therefore be upon a record made in the district court. That the function of collecting evidence may be committed to an administrative tribunal is settled by a host of cases, and supported by persuasive analogies, none of which justify a distinction between issues of constitutional right and any others. Resort to administrative remedies may be made a condition precedent to a judicial hearing. This is so even though a party is asserting deprivation of rights secured by the Federal Constitution.

Even if the constitutional power of Congress to provide compensation is limited to cases in which the employer-employee relation exists, I see no basis for a contention that the denial of the right to a trial *de novo* upon the issue of employment is in any manner subversive of the independence of the federal judicial power. Nothing in the Constitution, or in any prior decision of this Court to which attention has been called, lends support to the doctrine that a judicial finding of any fact involved in any civil proceeding to enforce a pecuniary liability may not be made upon evidence introduced before a properly constituted administrative tribunal, or that a determination so made may not be deemed an independent judicial determination. Congress has repeatedly exercised authority to confer upon the tribunals which it creates, be they administrative bodies or courts of limited jurisdiction, the power to receive evidence concerning the facts upon which the exercise of federal power must be predicated, and to determine whether those facts exist. The power of Congress to provide by legislation for liability under certain circumstances subsumes the power to provide for the determination of the existence of those circumstances. It does not depend upon the absolute existence in reality of any fact.

It is true that, so far as Knudsen is concerned, proof of the existence of the employer-employee relation is essential to recovery under the Act. But that fact is not jurisdictional. It is *quasi*-jurisdictional. The existence of a relation of employment is a question going to the applicability of the substantive law, not to the jurisdiction of the tribunal. Jurisdiction is the power to adjudicate between the parties concerning the subject-matter.

The "judicial power" of Article III of the Constitution is the power of the federal government, and not of any inferior tribunal. There is in that Article nothing which requires any controversy to be determined as of first instance in the federal district courts. The jurisdiction of those courts is subject to the control of Congress. Matters which may be placed within their jurisdiction may instead be committed to the state courts. If there be any controversy to which the judicial power extends that may not be subjected to the conclusive determination of administrative bodies or federal legislative courts, it is not because of any prohibition against the diminution of the jurisdiction of the federal district courts as such, but because, under certain circumstances, the constitutional requirement of due process is a requirement of judicial process. I do not conceive that Article III has properly any bearing upon the question presented in this case.

* * *

Northern Pipeline Constr. Co. v. Marathon Pipe Line Co.

458 U.S. 50 (1982)

Justice BRENNAN announced the judgment of the Court and delivered an opinion, in which Justice MARSHALL, Justice BLACKMUN, and Justice STEVENS joined.

The question presented is whether the assignment by Congress to bankruptcy judges of the jurisdiction granted in 28 U.S.C. §1471 (1976 ed., Supp. IV) by §241(a) of the Bankruptcy Act of 1978 violates Art. III of the Constitution.

I

A

In 1978, after almost 10 years of study and investigation, Congress enacted a comprehensive revision of the bankruptcy laws. The Bankruptcy Act of 1978 (Act) made significant changes in both the substantive and procedural law of bankruptcy. It is the changes in the latter that are at issue in this case.

Before the Act, federal district courts served as bankruptcy courts and employed a "referee" system. Bankruptcy proceedings were generally conducted before referees, except in those instances in which the district court elected to withdraw a case from a referee. The referee's final order was appealable to the district court. The bankruptcy courts were vested with "summary jurisdiction"—that is, with jurisdiction over controversies involving property in the actual or constructive possession of the court. And, with consent, the bankruptcy court also had jurisdiction over some "plenary" matters—such as disputes involving property in the possession of a third person.

The Act eliminates the referee system and establishes "in each judicial district, as an adjunct to the district court for such district, a bankruptcy court which shall be a court of record known as the United States Bankruptcy Court for the district." The judges of these courts are appointed to office for 14-year terms by the President, with the advice and consent of the Senate. They are subject to removal by the "judicial council of the circuit" on account of "incompetency, misconduct, neglect of duty or physical or mental disability." In addition, the salaries of the bankruptcy judges are set by statute and are subject to adjustment under the Federal Salary Act.

The jurisdiction of the bankruptcy courts created by the Act is much broader than that exercised under the former referee system. Eliminating the distinction between "summary" and "plenary" jurisdiction, the Act grants the new courts jurisdiction over all "civil proceedings arising under title 11 [the Bankruptcy title] or arising in or related to cases under title 11." This jurisdictional grant empowers bankruptcy courts to entertain a wide variety of cases involving claims that may affect the property of the estate once a petition has been filed under Title 11. Included within the bankruptcy courts' jurisdiction are suits to recover accounts, controversies involving exempt property, actions to avoid transfers and payments as preferences or fraudulent conveyances, and causes of action owned by the debtor at the time of the petition for bankruptcy. The bankruptcy courts can hear claims based on state law as well as those based on federal law.

The judges of the bankruptcy courts are vested with all of the "powers of a court of equity, law, and admiralty," except that they "may not enjoin another court or punish a criminal contempt not committed in the presence of the judge of the court or warranting a punishment of imprisonment." In addition to this broad grant of power, Congress has allowed bankruptcy judges the power to hold jury trials; to issue declaratory judgments; to issue writs of habeas corpus under certain circumstances; to issue all writs necessary in aid of the bankruptcy court's expanded jurisdiction; and to issue any order, process or judgment that is necessary or appropriate to carry out the provisions of Title 11.

The Act also establishes a special procedure for appeals from orders of bankruptcy courts. The circuit council is empowered to direct the chief judge of the circuit to designate panels of three bankruptcy judges to hear appeals. These panels have jurisdiction of all appeals from final judgments, orders, and decrees of bankruptcy courts, and, with leave of the panel, of interlocutory appeals. If no such appeals panel is designated, the district court is empowered to exercise appellate jurisdiction. The court of appeals is given jurisdiction over appeals from the appellate panels or from the district court. If the parties agree, a direct appeal to the court of appeals may be taken from a final judgment of a bankruptcy court.

The Act provides for a transition period before the new provisions take full effect in April 1984. During the transition period, previously existing bankruptcy courts continue in existence. Incumbent bankruptcy referees, who served 6-year terms for compensation subject to adjustment by Congress, are to serve as bankruptcy judges until March 31, 1984, or until their successors take office. During this period they are empowered to exercise essentially all of the jurisdiction and powers discussed above. The procedure for taking appeals is similar to that provided after the transition period.

B

This case arises out of proceedings initiated in the United States Bankruptcy Court for the District of Minnesota after appellant Northern Pipeline Construction Co. (Northern) filed a petition for reorganization in January 1980. In March 1980 Northern, pursuant to the Act, filed in that court a suit against appellee Marathon Pipe Line Co. (Marathon). Appellant sought damages for alleged breaches of contract and warranty, as well as for alleged misrepresentation, coercion, and duress. Marathon sought dismissal of the suit, on the ground that the Act unconstitutionally conferred Art. III judicial power upon judges who lacked life tenure and protection against salary diminution. The United States intervened to defend the validity of the statute.

II

A

As an inseparable element of the constitutional system of checks and balances, and as a guarantee of judicial impartiality, Art. III both defines the power and protects the independence of the Judicial Branch. It provides that "The judicial Power of the United States, shall be vested in one supreme Court, and in such inferior Courts as the Congress may from time to time ordain and establish." Art. III, §1. The inexorable command of this provision is clear and definite: The judicial power of the United States must be exercised by courts having the attributes prescribed in Art. III. Those attributes are also clearly set forth: "The Judges, both of the supreme and inferior Courts, shall hold their Offices during good Behaviour, and shall, at stated Times, receive for their Services, a Compensation, which shall not be diminished during their Continuance in Office." Art. III, §1.

The "good Behaviour" Clause guarantees that Art. III judges shall enjoy life tenure, subject only to removal by impeachment. The Compensation Clause guarantees Art. III judges a fixed and irreducible compensation for their services. Both of these provisions were incorporated into the Constitution to ensure the independence of the Judiciary from the control of the Executive and Legislative Branches of government.[10] [T]he guarantees eventually included in Art. III were clearly foreshadowed in the Declaration of Independence, "which, among the injuries and usurpations recited against the King of Great Britain, declared that he had 'made judges dependent on his will alone, for the tenure of their offices, and the amount and payment of their salaries.'" *O'Donoghue v. United States* (1933). The Framers thus recognized:

> Next to permanency in office, nothing can contribute more to the independence of the judges than a fixed provision for their support. . . . In the general course of human nature, *a power over a man's subsistence amounts to a power over his will.*" The Federalist No. 79, p. 491 (H. Lodge ed. 1888) (A. Hamilton) (emphasis in original).[11]

In sum, our Constitution unambiguously enunciates a fundamental principle — that the "judicial Power of the United States" must be reposed in an independent Judiciary. It commands that the independence of the Judiciary be jealously guarded, and it provides clear institutional protections for that independence.

----

10. These provisions serve other institutional values as well. The independence from political forces that they guarantee helps to promote public confidence in judicial determinations. The security that they provide to members of the Judicial Branch helps to attract well-qualified persons to the federal bench. The guarantee of life tenure insulates the individual judge from improper influences not only by other branches but by colleagues as well, and thus promotes judicial individualism.

11. Further evidence of the Framers' concern for assuring the independence of the Judicial Branch may be found in the fact that the Constitutional Convention soundly defeated a proposal to allow the removal of judges by the Executive and Legislative Branches.

B

It is undisputed that the bankruptcy judges whose offices were created by the Bankruptcy Act of 1978 do not enjoy the protections constitutionally afforded to Art. III judges. The bankruptcy judges do not serve for life subject to their continued "good Behaviour." Rather, they are appointed for 14-year terms, and can be removed by the judicial council of the circuit in which they serve on grounds of "incompetency, misconduct, neglect of duty, or physical or mental disability." Second, the salaries of the bankruptcy judges are not immune from diminution by Congress. In short, there is no doubt that the bankruptcy judges created by the Act are not Art. III judges.

III

Congress did not constitute the bankruptcy courts as legislative courts. Appellants contend, however, that the bankruptcy courts could have been so constituted, and that as a result the "adjunct" system in fact chosen by Congress does not impermissibly encroach upon the judicial power. In advancing this argument, appellants rely upon cases in which we have identified certain matters that "congress may or may not bring within the cognizance of [Art. III courts], as it may deem proper." *Murray's Lessee v. Hoboken Land & Improvement Co.* (1856). But when properly understood, these precedents represent no broad departure from the constitutional command that the judicial power of the United States must be vested in Art. III courts.[15] Rather, they reduce to three narrow situations not subject to that command, each recognizing a circumstance in which the grant of power to the Legislative and Executive Branches was historically and constitutionally so exceptional that the congressional assertion of a power to create legislative courts was consistent with, rather than threatening to, the constitutional mandate of separation of powers. These precedents simply acknowledge that the literal command of Art. III, assigning the judicial power of the United States to courts insulated from Legislative or Executive interference, must be interpreted in light of the historical context in which the Constitution was written, and of the structural imperatives of the Constitution as a whole.

Appellants first rely upon a series of cases in which this Court has upheld the creation by Congress of non-Art. III "territorial courts." This exception from the general prescription of Art. III dates from the earliest days of the Republic, when it was perceived that the Framers intended that as to certain geographical areas, in which no State operated as sovereign, Congress was to exercise the general powers of government. For example, in *American Ins. Co. v. Canter* (1828), the Court

---

15. Justice White's dissent finds particular significance in the fact that Congress could have assigned all bankruptcy matters to the state courts. But, of course, virtually all matters that might be heard in Art. III courts could also be left by Congress to state courts. This fact is simply irrelevant to the question before us. Congress has no control over state-court judges; accordingly the principle of separation of powers is not threatened by leaving the adjudication of federal disputes to such judges. The Framers chose to leave to Congress the precise role to be played by the lower federal courts in the administration of justice. But the Framers did not leave it to Congress to define the character of those courts—they were to be independent of the political branches and presided over by judges with guaranteed salary and life tenure.

observed that Art. IV bestowed upon Congress alone a complete power of government over territories not within the States that constituted the United States. The
Court then acknowledged Congress' authority to create courts for those territories
that were not in conformity with Art. III. The Court followed the same reasoning
when it reviewed Congress' creation of non-Art. III courts in the District of Columbia.
It noted that there was in the District

> no division of powers between the general and state governments. Con-
> gress has the entire control over the district for every purpose of gov-
> ernment; and it is reasonable to suppose, that in organizing a judicial
> department here, all judicial power necessary for the purposes of gov-
> ernment would be vested in the courts of justice. *Kendall v. United States*
> (1838).

Appellants next advert to a second class of cases — those in which this Court
has sustained the exercise by Congress and the Executive of the power to establish
and administer courts-martial. The situation in these cases strongly resembles the
situation with respect to territorial courts: It too involves a constitutional grant of
power that has been historically understood as giving the political Branches of Government extraordinary control over the precise subject matter at issue. Article I, §8,
cls. 13, 14, confer upon Congress the power "[t]o provide and maintain a Navy,"
and "[t]o make Rules for the Government and Regulation of the land and naval
Forces." The Fifth Amendment, which requires a presentment or indictment of a
grand jury before a person may be held to answer for a capital or otherwise infamous crime, contains an express exception for "cases arising in the land or naval
forces." And Art. II, §2, cl. 1, provides that "The President shall be Commander in
Chief of the Army and Navy of the United States, and of the Militia of the several
States, when called into the actual Service of the United States." Noting these constitutional directives, the Court in *Dynes v. Hoover* (1857), explained:

> These provisions show that Congress has the power to provide for the trial
> and punishment of military and naval offences in the manner then and
> now practiced by civilized nations; and that the power to do so is given
> without any connection between it and the 3d article of the Constitution
> defining the judicial power of the United States; indeed, that the two pow-
> ers are entirely independent of each other.

Finally, appellants rely on a third group of cases, in which this Court has
upheld the constitutionality of legislative courts and administrative agencies created by Congress to adjudicate cases involving "public rights."[18] The "public rights"
doctrine was first set forth in *Murray's Lessee v. Hoboken Land & Improvement Co.*
(1856). This doctrine may be explained in part by reference to the traditional principle of sovereign immunity, which recognizes that the Government may attach
conditions to its consent to be sued. But the public-rights doctrine also draws upon

---

18. Congress' power to create legislative courts to adjudicate public rights carries with it
the lesser power to create administrative agencies for the same purpose, and to provide for
review of those agency decisions in Art. III courts. *See, e.g., Atlas Roofing Co. v. Occupational
Safety and Health Review Comm'n* (1977).

the principle of separation of powers, and a historical understanding that certain prerogatives were reserved to the political Branches of Government. The doctrine extends only to matters arising "between the Government and persons subject to its authority in connection with the performance of the constitutional functions of the executive or legislative departments," *Crowell v. Benson* (1932), and only to matters that historically could have been determined exclusively by those departments. The understanding of these cases is that the Framers expected that Congress would be free to commit such matters completely to nonjudicial executive determination, and that as a result there can be no constitutional objection to Congress' employing the less drastic expedient of committing their determination to a legislative court or an administrative agency.

The public-rights doctrine is grounded in a historically recognized distinction between matters that could be conclusively determined by the Executive and Legislative Branches and matters that are "inherently . . . judicial." *Ex parte Bakelite Corp.* (1929). For example, the Court in *Murray's Lessee* looked to the law of England and the States at the time the Constitution was adopted, in order to determine whether the issue presented was customarily cognizable in the courts. Concluding that the matter had not traditionally been one for judicial determination, the Court perceived no bar to Congress' establishment of summary procedures, outside of Art. III courts, to collect a debt due to the Government from one of its customs agents.[20] The distinction between public rights and private rights has not been definitively explained in our precedents. Nor is it necessary to do so in the present cases, for it suffices to observe that a matter of public rights must at a minimum arise "between the government and others." *Ex parte Bakelite Corp.*[23] In contrast, "the liability of one individual to another under the law as defined," *Crowell*, is a matter of private rights. Our precedents clearly establish that only controversies in the former category may be removed from Art. III courts and delegated to legislative courts or administrative agencies for their determination. Private-rights disputes, on the other hand, lie at the core of the historically recognized judicial power.

In sum, this Court has identified three situations in which Art. III does not bar the creation of legislative courts. In each of these situations, the Court has recognized certain exceptional powers bestowed upon Congress by the Constitution or by historical consensus. Only in the face of such an exceptional grant of power has

---

20. Doubtless it could be argued that the need for independent judicial determination is greatest in cases arising between the Government and an individual. But the rationale for the public-rights line of cases lies not in political theory, but rather in Congress' and this Court's understanding of what power was reserved to the Judiciary by the Constitution as a matter of historical fact.

23. Congress cannot "withdraw from [Art. III] judicial cognizance any matter which, from its nature, is the subject of a suit at the common law, or in equity, or admiralty." *Murray's Lessee*. It is thus clear that the presence of the United States as a proper party to the proceeding is a necessary but not sufficient means of distinguishing "private rights" from "public rights." And it is also clear that even with respect to matters that arguably fall within the scope of the "public rights" doctrine, the presumption is in favor of Art. III courts. Moreover, when Congress assigns these matters to administrative agencies, or to legislative courts, it has generally provided, and we have suggested that it may be required to provide, for Art. III judicial review.

the Court declined to hold the authority of Congress subject to the general prescriptions of Art. III.[25]

We discern no such exceptional grant of power applicable in the cases before us. The courts created by the Bankruptcy Act of 1978 do not lie exclusively outside the States of the Federal Union, like those in the District of Columbia and the Territories. Nor do the bankruptcy courts bear any resemblance to courts-martial, which are founded upon the Constitution's grant of plenary authority over the Nation's military forces to the Legislative and Executive Branches. Finally, the substantive legal rights at issue in the present action cannot be deemed "public rights." Appellants argue that a discharge in bankruptcy is indeed a "public right," similar to such congressionally created benefits as "radio station licenses, pilot licenses, or certificates for common carriers" granted by administrative agencies. But the restructuring of debtor-creditor relations, which is at the core of the federal bankruptcy power, must be distinguished from the adjudication of state-created private rights, such as the right to recover contract damages that is at issue in this case. The former may well be a "public right," but the latter obviously is not. Appellant Northern's right to recover contract damages to augment its estate is "one of private right, that is, of the liability of one individual to another under the law as defined." *Crowell.*

Recognizing that the present cases may not fall within the scope of any of our prior cases permitting the establishment of legislative courts, appellants argue that we should recognize an additional situation beyond the command of Art. III, sufficiently broad to sustain the Act. Appellants contend that Congress' constitutional authority to establish "uniform Laws on the subject of Bankruptcies throughout the United States," Art. I, §8, cl. 4, carries with it an inherent power to establish legislative courts capable of adjudicating "bankruptcy-related controversies."

Appellants' contention, in essence, is that pursuant to any of its Art. I powers, Congress may create courts free of Art. III's requirements whenever it finds that course expedient.

The flaw in appellants' analysis is that it provides no limiting principle. It thus threatens to supplant completely our system of adjudication in independent Art. III tribunals and replace it with a system of "specialized" legislative courts. The potential for encroachment upon powers reserved to the Judicial Branch through the device of "specialized" legislative courts is dramatically evidenced in the jurisdiction granted to the courts created by the Act before us. The broad range of questions that can be brought into a bankruptcy court because they are "related to cases under title 11," 28 U.S.C. §1471(b) (1976 ed., Supp. IV), is the clearest proof that even when Congress acts through a "specialized" court, and pursuant to only one of its many Art. I powers, appellants' analysis fails to provide any real protection against the erosion of Art. III jurisdiction by the unilateral action of the political Branches.

---

25. What clearly remains subject to Art. III are all private adjudications in federal courts within the States—matters from their nature subject to "a suit at common law or in equity or admiralty"—and all criminal matters, with the narrow exception of military crimes. There is no doubt that when the Framers assigned the "judicial Power" to an independent Art. III Branch, these matters lay at what they perceived to be the protected core of that power.

In sum, Art. III bars Congress from establishing legislative courts to exercise jurisdiction over all matters related to those arising under the bankruptcy laws. The establishment of such courts does not fall within any of the historically recognized situations in which the general principle of independent adjudication commanded by Art. III does not apply. Nor can we discern any persuasive reason, in logic, history, or the Constitution, why the bankruptcy courts here established lie beyond the reach of Art. III.

IV

Appellants advance a second argument for upholding the constitutionality of the Act: that "viewed within the entire judicial framework set up by Congress," the bankruptcy court is merely an "adjunct" to the district court, and that the delegation of certain adjudicative functions to the bankruptcy court is accordingly consistent with the principle that the judicial power of the United States must be vested in Art. III courts. The question to which we turn, therefore, is whether the Act has retained "the essential attributes of the judicial power," *Crowell*, in Art. III tribunals.

It is, of course, true that while the power to adjudicate "private rights" must be vested in an Art. III court, "this Court has accepted factfinding by an administrative agency, . . . as an adjunct to the Art. III court, analogizing the agency to a jury or a special master and permitting it in admiralty cases to perform the function of the special master." *Atlas Roofing Co. v. OSH Rev. Comm'n* (1977).

The use of administrative agencies as adjuncts was first upheld in *Crowell*. *Crowell* involved the adjudication of congressionally created rights. But this Court has sustained the use of adjunct factfinders even in the adjudication of constitutional rights—so long as those adjuncts were subject to sufficient control by an Art. III district court. In *United States v. Raddatz* (1980), the Court upheld the 1978 Federal Magistrates Act, which permitted district court judges to refer certain pretrial motions, including suppression motions based on alleged violations of constitutional rights, to a magistrate for initial determination. The Court observed that the magistrate's proposed findings and recommendations were subject to *de novo* review by the district court, which was free to rehear the evidence or to call for additional evidence. Moreover, it was noted that the magistrate considered motions only upon reference from the district court, and that the magistrates were appointed, and subject to removal, by the district court. In short, the ultimate decisionmaking authority respecting all pretrial motions clearly remained with the district court. Under these circumstances, the Court held that the Act did not violate the constraints of Art. III.

Together these cases establish two principles that aid us in determining the extent to which Congress may constitutionally vest traditionally judicial functions in non-Art. III officers. First, it is clear that when Congress creates a substantive federal right, it possesses substantial discretion to prescribe the manner in which that right may be adjudicated—including the assignment to an adjunct of some functions historically performed by judges. Thus *Crowell* recognized that Art. III does not require "all determinations of fact [to] be made by judges"; with respect to congressionally created rights, some factual determinations may be made by a specialized factfinding tribunal designed by Congress, without constitutional bar. Second, the functions of the adjunct must be limited in such a way that "the essential attributes" of judicial power are retained in the Art. III court. Thus in upholding the adjunct scheme challenged in *Crowell*, the Court emphasized that "the reservation of full authority to the court to deal with matters of law provides for the appropriate exercise of the judicial function in this class of cases." And in refusing to invalidate the Magistrates Act at issue in *Raddatz*, the Court stressed that under the congressional scheme "'[t]he authority—and the responsibility—to make an informed, final determination . . . remains with the judge'"; the statute's delegation of power was therefore permissible, since "the ultimate decision is made by the district court."

These two principles assist us in evaluating the "adjunct" scheme presented in these cases. Appellants assume that Congress' power to create "adjuncts" to consider all cases related to those arising under Title 11 is as great as it was in the circumstances of *Crowell*. But while *Crowell* certainly endorsed the proposition that Congress possesses broad discretion to assign factfinding functions to an adjunct created to aid in the adjudication of congressionally created statutory rights, *Crowell* does not support the further proposition necessary to appellants' argument—that Congress possesses the same degree of discretion in assigning traditionally judicial power to adjuncts engaged in the adjudication of rights not created by Congress.[34]

Although *Crowell* and *Raddatz* do not explicitly distinguish between rights created by Congress and other rights, such a distinction underlies in part *Crowell's* and *Raddatz's* recognition of a critical difference between rights created by federal statute and rights recognized by the Constitution. Moreover, such a distinction seems to us to be necessary in light of the delicate accommodations required by the principle of separation of powers reflected in Art. III. The constitutional system of checks and balances is designed to guard against "encroachment or aggrandizement" by Congress at the expense of the other branches of government. *Buckley v. Valeo* (1976). But when Congress creates a statutory right, it clearly has the discretion, in defining that right, to create presumptions, or assign burdens of proof, or prescribe remedies; it may also provide that persons seeking to vindicate that right must do so before particularized tribunals created to perform the specialized adjudicative tasks related to that right. Such provisions do, in a sense, affect the exercise of judicial power, but they are also incidental to Congress' power to define the right that it has created. No comparable justification exists, however, when the right being adjudicated is not of congressional creation. In such a situation, substantial inroads into functions that have traditionally been performed by the Judiciary cannot be characterized merely as incidental extensions of Congress' power to define rights that it has created. Rather, such inroads suggest unwarranted encroachments upon the judicial power of the United States, which our Constitution reserves for Art. III courts.

We hold that the Bankruptcy Act of 1978 carries the possibility of such an unwarranted encroachment. Many of the rights subject to adjudication by the Act's bankruptcy courts, like the rights implicated in *Raddatz*, are not of Congress' creation. Indeed, the cases before us, which center upon appellant Northern's claim

---

34. *Crowell's* precise holding with respect to "jurisdictional" and "constitutional" facts that arise within ordinary administrative proceedings has been undermined by later cases. *See St. Joseph Stock Yards v. U.S.* (1936) [agency factfinding "will not be disturbed save as they are *plainly* shown to be overborne"].

for damages for breach of contract and misrepresentation, involve a right created by *state* law, a right independent of and antecedent to the reorganization petition that conferred jurisdiction upon the Bankruptcy Court. Accordingly, Congress' authority to control the manner in which that right is adjudicated, through assignment of historically judicial functions to a non-Art. III "adjunct," plainly must be deemed at a minimum. Yet it is equally plain that Congress has vested the "adjunct" bankruptcy judges with powers over Northern's state-created right that far exceed the powers that it has vested in administrative agencies that adjudicate only rights of Congress' own creation.

Unlike the administrative scheme that we reviewed in *Crowell*, the Act vests all "essential attributes" of the judicial power of the United States in the "adjunct" bankruptcy court. First, the agency in *Crowell* made only specialized, narrowly confined factual determinations regarding a particularized area of law. In contrast, the subject-matter jurisdiction of the bankruptcy courts encompasses not only traditional matters of bankruptcy, but also "all civil proceedings arising under title 11 or arising in or *related to* cases under title 11." Second, while the agency in *Crowell* engaged in statutorily channeled factfinding functions, the bankruptcy courts exercise "*all* of the jurisdiction" conferred by the Act on the district courts. Third, the agency in *Crowell* possessed only a limited power to issue compensation orders pursuant to specialized procedures, and its orders could be enforced only by order of the district court. By contrast, the bankruptcy courts exercise all ordinary powers of district courts, including the power to preside over jury trials, the power to issue declaratory judgments, the power to issue writs of habeas corpus, and the power to issue any order, process, or judgment appropriate for the enforcement of the provisions of Title 11. Fourth, while orders issued by the agency in *Crowell* were to be set aside if "not supported by the evidence," the judgments of the bankruptcy courts are apparently subject to review only under the more deferential "clearly erroneous" standard. Finally, the agency in *Crowell* was required by law to seek enforcement of its compensation orders in the district court. In contrast, the bankruptcy courts issue final judgments, which are binding and enforceable even in the absence of an appeal. In short, the "adjunct" bankruptcy courts created by the Act exercise jurisdiction behind the facade of a grant to the district courts, and are exercising powers far greater than those lodged in the adjuncts approved in either *Crowell* or *Raddatz*.

We conclude that 28 U.S.C. §1471 (1976 ed., Supp. IV), as added by §241(a) of the Bankruptcy Act of 1978, has impermissibly removed most, if not all, of "the essential attributes of the judicial power" from the Art. III district court, and has vested those attributes in a non-Art. III adjunct. Such a grant of jurisdiction cannot be sustained as an exercise of Congress' power to create adjuncts to Art. III courts.

Justice REHNQUIST, with whom Justice O'CONNOR joins, concurring in the judgment.

The cases dealing with the authority of Congress to create courts other than by use of its power under Art. III do not admit of easy synthesis. I need not decide whether these cases in fact support a general proposition and three tidy exceptions, as the plurality believes, or whether instead they are but landmarks on a judicial "darkling plain" where ignorant armies have clashed by night, as JUSTICE WHITE apparently believes them to be. None of the cases has gone so far as to sanction the type of adjudication to which Marathon will be subjected against its will under the provisions of the 1978 Act. To whatever extent different powers granted under that Act might be sustained under the "public rights" doctrine of *Murray's Lessee v. Hoboken Land & Improvement Co.* (1856), and succeeding cases, I am satisfied that the adjudication of Northern's lawsuit cannot be so sustained.

I am likewise of the opinion that the extent of review by Art. III courts provided on appeal from a decision of the bankruptcy court in a case such as Northern's does not save the grant of authority to the latter under the rule espoused in *Crowell v. Benson* (1932). All matters of fact and law in whatever domains of the law to which the parties' dispute may lead are to be resolved by the bankruptcy court in the first instance, with only traditional appellate review by Art. III courts apparently contemplated. Acting in this manner the bankruptcy court is not an "adjunct" of either the district court or the court of appeals.

I would, therefore, hold so much of the Bankruptcy Act of 1978 as enables a Bankruptcy Court to entertain and decide Northern's lawsuit over Marathon's objection to be violative of Art. III of the United States Constitution. Because I agree with the plurality that this grant of authority is not readily severable from the remaining grant of authority to bankruptcy courts under §1471, I concur in the judgment.

Chief Justice BURGER, dissenting.

I join JUSTICE WHITE's dissenting opinion, but I write separately to emphasize that the Court's holding is limited to the proposition stated by JUSTICE REHNQUIST in his concurrence in the judgment—that a "traditional" state common-law action, not made subject to a federal rule of decision, and related only peripherally to an adjudication of bankruptcy under federal law, must, absent the consent of the litigants, be heard by an "Art. III court" if it is to be heard by any court or agency of the United States.

It will not be necessary for Congress, in order to meet the requirements of the Court's holding, to undertake a radical restructuring of the present system of bankruptcy adjudication. The problems arising from today's judgment can be resolved simply by providing that ancillary common-law actions, such as the one involved in these cases, be routed to the United States district court of which the bankruptcy court is an adjunct.

Justice WHITE, with whom THE CHIEF JUSTICE and Justice POWELL join, dissenting.

I

First . . . [e]ven if the Court is correct that [the] state-law claim [against Marathon] cannot be heard by a bankruptcy judge, there is no basis for doing more than declaring the section unconstitutional as applied to the claim against Marathon, leaving the section otherwise intact. In that event, cases such as these would have to be heard by Art. III judges or by state courts—unless the defendant consents to suit before the bankruptcy judge—just as they were before the 1978 Act was adopted. But this would remove from the jurisdiction of the bankruptcy judge only a tiny fraction of the cases he is now empowered to adjudicate and would not otherwise limit his jurisdiction.

Second, the distinction between claims based on state law and those based on federal law disregards the real character of bankruptcy proceedings. The routine in ordinary bankruptcy cases now, as it was before 1978, is to stay actions against the bankrupt, collect the bankrupt's assets, require creditors to file claims or be forever barred, allow or disallow claims that are filed, adjudicate preferences and fraudulent transfers, and make pro rata distributions to creditors, who will be barred by the discharge from taking further actions against the bankrupt. The crucial point to be made is that in the ordinary bankruptcy proceeding the great bulk of creditor claims are claims that have accrued under state law prior to bankruptcy—claims for goods sold, wages, rent, utilities, and the like. Hence, the bankruptcy judge is constantly enmeshed in state-law issues.

The new aspect of the Bankruptcy Act of 1978, in this regard, therefore, is not the extension of federal jurisdiction to state-law claims, but its extension to particular kinds of state-law claims, such as contract cases against third parties or disputes involving property in the possession of a third person. Prior to 1978, a claim of a bankrupt against a third party, such as the claim against Marathon in this case, was not within the jurisdiction of the bankruptcy judge. The old limits were based, of course, on the restrictions implicit within the concept of *in rem* jurisdiction; the new extension is based on the concept of *in personam* jurisdiction. The difference between the new and old Acts, therefore, is not to be found in a distinction between state-law and federal-law matters; rather, it is in a distinction between *in rem* and *in personam* jurisdiction. The majority at no place explains why this distinction should have constitutional implications.

There is very little reason to strike down §1471 on its face on the ground that it extends, in a comparatively minimal way, the referees' authority to deal with state-law questions. To do so is to lose all sense of proportion.

II

Judicial review of the orders of bankruptcy judges is more stringent than that of many modern administrative agencies. Generally courts are not free to set aside the findings of administrative agencies, if supported by substantial evidence. But more importantly, courts are also admonished to give substantial deference to the agency's interpretation of the statute it is enforcing. No such deference is required with respect to decisions on the law made by bankruptcy judges.

Finally, the plurality suggests that, unlike the agency considered in *Crowell*, the orders of a post-1978 bankruptcy judge are final and binding even though not appealed. To attribute any constitutional significance to this, unless the plurality intends to throw into question a large body of administrative law, is strange. More directly, this simply does not represent any change in bankruptcy practice.

Even if there are specific powers now vested in bankruptcy judges that should be performed by Art. III judges, the great bulk of their functions are unexceptionable and should be left intact.

IV

There is no difference in principle between the work that Congress may assign to an Art. I court and that which the Constitution assigns to Art. III courts. Unless we want to overrule a large number of our precedents upholding a variety of Art. I courts—not to speak of those Art. I courts that go by the contemporary name of "administrative agencies"—this conclusion is inevitable. It is too late to go back that far; too late to return to the simplicity of the principle pronounced in Art. III and defended so vigorously and persuasively by Hamilton in The Federalist Nos. 78-82.

Crowell suggests that the presence of appellate review by an Art. III court will go a long way toward insuring a proper separation of powers. Appellate review of the decisions of legislative courts, like appellate review of state-court decisions, provides a firm check on the ability of the political institutions of government to ignore or transgress constitutional limits on their own authority. Obviously, therefore, a scheme of Art. I courts that provides for appellate review by Art. III courts should be substantially less controversial than a legislative attempt entirely to avoid judicial review in a constitutional court.

V

I believe that the new bankruptcy courts established by the Bankruptcy Act of 1978 satisfy this standard.

First, ample provision is made for appellate review by Art. III courts. Appeals may in some circumstances be brought directly to the district courts. Decisions of the district courts are further appealable to the court of appeals. In other circumstances, appeals go first to a panel of bankruptcy judges, and then to the court of appeals. In still other circumstances—when the parties agree—appeals may go directly to the court of appeals. In sum, there is in every instance a right of appeal to at least one Art. III court. Had Congress decided to assign all bankruptcy matters to the state courts, a power it clearly possesses, no greater review in an Art. III court would exist.

Second, no one seriously argues that the Bankruptcy Act of 1978 represents an attempt by the political branches of government to aggrandize themselves at the expense of the third branch or an attempt to undermine the authority of constitutional courts in general. . . .

Finally, . . . [t]he stresses placed upon the old bankruptcy system by the tremendous increase in bankruptcy cases were well documented and were clearly a matter to which Congress could respond. There is no question that the existence of several hundred bankruptcy judges with life tenure would have severely limited Congress' future options. Furthermore, the number of bankruptcies may fluctuate, producing a substantially reduced need for bankruptcy judges.

For all of these reasons, I would defer to the congressional judgment. Accordingly, I dissent.

* * *

Congress went back to the drawing board in 1984 and legislated a new framework for bankruptcy adjudication. That framework was challenged as inconsistent with Article III in *Stern v. Marshall* (2011), reprinted below.

In the intervening years, however, a series of other cases came to the Supreme Court challenging non-Article III adjudication. In the first two the Court's approach was functionalist, much like the balancing test advocated by Justice White in his *Northern Pipeline* dissent. In the first case, *Thomas v. Union Carbide Agricultural Products Co.* (1985), the Court held that Congress could assign a dispute among private parties to arbitrators as part of a regulatory scheme administered by a federal agency. Under the relevant scheme, the manufacturers of pesticides had to submit data about the safety of their products to the Environmental Protection Agency (EPA) in order to register (and, of course, to market) those products. In some cases, one manufacturer would piggyback on another's data—that is, one company making a similar product would rely on another's safety data, rather than generate their own. In those cases, the piggybacking company was required to pay compensation to the manufacturer that had done the research and submitted the data. Rather than burden the EPA, Congress tasked arbitrators with determining disputes about the amount of compensation owed. Article III courts were authorized to review the arbitrators' decisions, *inter alia,* for "fraud, misrepresentation, or other misconduct."

Thirteen pesticide manufacturers challenged the constitutionality of the scheme on several grounds, including Article III. They argued that Congress had violated Article III by assigning a private law matter—a dispute between private companies about what one owed the other—to a non-Article III tribunal.

The Court held that the arbitration system did not violate Article III. Justice O'Connor's opinion for the Court stressed that the arbitration of private disputes between pesticide manufacturers was integrally related to a regulatory scheme. Justice O'Connor wrote that "Congress, acting for a valid legislative purpose pursuant to its constitutional powers under Article I, may create a seemingly 'private' right that is so closely integrated into a public regulatory scheme as to be a matter appropriate for agency resolution." This scheme did not encroach upon Article III courts as it did not substitute for a traditional common law action. Article III courts, moreover, had a role to play in reviewing the arbitrators' decisions.

As in *Thomas*, the Court in *Commodity Futures Trading Comm'n v. Schor* (1986) employed a functional test to hold that Congress could assign resolution of a private rights matter to a non-Article III tribunal. In *Schor*, the question concerned the jurisdiction of the Commodity Futures Tradition Commission (CFTC) over state law matters. The CFTC had statutory authority to order brokers to provide reparations when their transactions injured consumers through fraud or unlawful manipulation. Under the agency's regulations, it could address counterclaims arising out of the same transactions. The Court addressed two questions about this adjudicatory scheme. First, it held that the CTFC's authority to order reparations was constitutional because the agency served as an adjunct to an Article III court. The agency had no authority to enforce its reparative orders, but instead had to seek enforcement in an Article III court. Second, the Court held that the CFTC could adjudicate state law counterclaims. The Court balanced the benefits of permitting the CFTC authority over these private rights disputes against the "purposes underlying the requirements of Article III." Those purposes were maintaining the Article III courts' role in the separation of powers and ensuring fairness to litigants. Applying this test, the Court reasoned that any encroachment upon the Article III courts' role was at most *de minimis* because the CFTC was exercising an adjudicatory authority similar to that long exercised by administrative agencies. The Court also emphasized that there was no unfairness to the defendant because the defendant had consented to the administrative proceedings.

In *Granfinanciera v. Nordberg* (1989), the Court returned to bankruptcy, this time holding that the Seventh Amendment applies to a bankruptcy trustee's action to recover a fraudulent conveyance from a third party who had not submitted a claim against the bankruptcy estate. Writing for the Court, Justice Brennan began by emphasizing that a fraudulent conveyance cause of action is an action long recognized at common law to which the Seventh Amendment applies. It is also properly classified as a private right, the Court concluded, so Congress cannot require its adjudication in a tribunal that does not use a jury as a factfinder:

> In *Atlas Roofing Co. v. OSHRC* (1977), we noted that,
>
>> when Congress creates new statutory "public rights," it may assign their adjudication to an administrative agency with which a jury trial would be incompatible, without violating the Seventh Amendment's injunction that jury trial is to be "preserved" in "suits at common law."
>
> We emphasized, however, that Congress' power to block application of the Seventh Amendment to a cause of action has limits. Congress may only deny trials by jury in actions at law, we said, in cases where "public rights" are litigated:
>
>> Our prior cases support administrative factfinding in only those situations involving "public rights," *e.g.*, where the Government is involved in its sovereign capacity under an otherwise valid statute creating enforceable public rights. Wholly private tort, contract, and property cases, as well as a vast range of other cases, are not at all implicated.
>
> *Id.* We adhere to that general teaching.

As *Thomas, Schor* and *Granfinanciera* show, the Court has been oscillating between the categorical and functional approach to the constitutionality of non-Article III courts. Notice too, the drift in *Thomas* and *Schor* towards treating a public rights case merely as one involving a statutorily created right connected to a "public regulatory scheme," rather than, as in *Murray's Lessee* and other early cases, requiring the presence of the government as a party. As the next cases show, the Court's oscillation continues.

Stern v. Marshall

564 U.S. 462 (2011)

Chief Justice ROBERTS delivered the opinion of the Court.

This "suit has, in course of time, become so complicated, that . . . no two . . . lawyers can talk about it for five minutes, without coming to a total disagreement as to all the premises. Innumerable children have been born into the cause: innumerable young people have married into it"; and, sadly, the original parties "have died out of it." A "long procession of [judges] has come in and gone out" during that time, and still the suit "drags its weary length before the Court."

Those words were not written about this case, *see* C. Dickens, *Bleak House* (1891), but they could have been. This is the second time we have had occasion to weigh in on this long-running dispute between Vickie Lynn Marshall and E. Pierce Marshall over the fortune of J. Howard Marshall II, a man believed to have been one of the richest people in Texas. The Marshalls' litigation has worked its way through state and federal courts in Louisiana, Texas, and California, and two of those courts—a Texas state probate court and the Bankruptcy Court for the Central District of California—have reached contrary decisions on its merits. The Court of Appeals below held that the Texas state decision controlled, after concluding that the Bankruptcy Court lacked the authority to enter final judgment on a counterclaim that Vickie brought against Pierce in her bankruptcy proceeding. To determine whether the Court of Appeals was correct in that regard, we must resolve two issues: (1) whether the Bankruptcy Court had the statutory authority under 28 U.S.C. §157(b) to issue a final judgment on Vickie's counterclaim; and (2) if so, whether conferring that authority on the Bankruptcy Court is constitutional.

Although the history of this litigation is complicated, its resolution ultimately turns on very basic principles. The Bankruptcy Court in this case exercised the judicial power of the United States by entering final judgment on a common law tort claim, even though the judges of such courts enjoy neither tenure during good behavior nor salary protection. We conclude that, although the Bankruptcy Court had the statutory authority to enter judgment on Vickie's counterclaim, it lacked the constitutional authority to do so.

I

Known to the public as Anna Nicole Smith, Vickie was J. Howard's third wife and married him about a year before his death. Although J. Howard bestowed on Vickie many monetary and other gifts during their courtship and marriage, he did not include her in his will. Before J. Howard passed away, Vickie filed suit in Texas state probate court, asserting that Pierce—J. Howard's younger son—fraudulently induced J. Howard to sign a living trust that did not include her, even though J. Howard meant to give her half his property. Pierce denied any fraudulent activity and defended the validity of J. Howard's trust and, eventually, his will.

After J. Howard's death, Vickie filed a petition for bankruptcy in the Central District of California. Pierce filed a complaint in that bankruptcy proceeding, contending that Vickie had defamed him by inducing her lawyers to tell members of the press that he had engaged in fraud to gain control of his father's assets. The complaint sought a declaration that Pierce's defamation claim was not dischargeable in the bankruptcy proceedings. Pierce subsequently filed a proof of claim for the defamation action, meaning that he sought to recover damages for it from Vickie's bankruptcy estate. Vickie responded to Pierce's initial complaint by asserting truth as a defense to the alleged defamation and by filing a counterclaim for tortious interference with the gift she expected from J. Howard. As she had in state court, Vickie alleged that Pierce had wrongfully prevented J. Howard from taking the legal steps necessary to provide her with half his property.

On November 5, 1999, the Bankruptcy Court issued an order granting Vickie summary judgment on Pierce's claim for defamation. On September 27, 2000, after a bench trial, the Bankruptcy Court issued a judgment on Vickie's counterclaim in her favor. The court later awarded Vickie over $400 million in compensatory damages and $25 million in punitive damages.

In post-trial proceedings, Pierce argued that the Bankruptcy Court lacked jurisdiction over Vickie's counterclaim. In particular, Pierce renewed a claim he had made earlier in the litigation, asserting that the Bankruptcy Court's authority over the counterclaim was limited because Vickie's counterclaim was not a "core proceeding" under 28 U.S.C. §157(b)(2)(C). As explained below, bankruptcy courts may hear and enter final judgments in "core proceedings" in a bankruptcy case. In noncore proceedings, the bankruptcy courts instead submit proposed findings of fact and conclusions of law to the district court, for that court's review and issuance of final judgment. The Bankruptcy Court in this case concluded that Vickie's counterclaim was "a core proceeding" under §157(b)(2)(C), and the court therefore had the "power to enter judgment" on the counterclaim under §157(b)(1).

II

A

With certain exceptions not relevant here, the district courts of the United States have "original and exclusive jurisdiction of all cases under title 11." Congress has divided bankruptcy proceedings into three categories: those that "aris[e] under title 11;" those that "aris[e] in" a Title 11 case; and those that are "related to a case under title 11." §157(a). District courts may refer any or all such proceedings to the bankruptcy judges of their district, which is how the Bankruptcy Court in this case came to preside over Vickie's bankruptcy proceedings. District courts also may withdraw a case or proceeding referred to the bankruptcy court "for cause shown." §157(d). Since Congress enacted the Bankruptcy Amendments and Federal Judgeship Act of 1984 (1984 Act), bankruptcy judges for each district have been appointed to 14-year terms by the courts of appeals for the circuits in which their district is located. §152(a)(1).

The manner in which a bankruptcy judge may act on a referred matter depends on the type of proceeding involved. Bankruptcy judges may hear and enter final judgments in "all core proceedings arising under title 11, or arising in a case under title 11." §157(b)(1). "Core proceedings include, but are not limited to" 16 different types of matters, including "counterclaims by [a debtor's] estate against persons filing claims against the estate." §157(b)(2)(C). Parties may appeal final judgments of a bankruptcy court in core proceedings to the district court, which reviews them under traditional appellate standards. See §158(a).

When a bankruptcy judge determines that a referred "proceeding . . . is not a core proceeding but . . . is otherwise related to a case under title 11," the judge may only "submit proposed findings of fact and conclusions of law to the district court." §157(c)(1). It is the district court that enters final judgment in such cases after reviewing de novo any matter to which a party objects. . . .

III

Although we conclude that §157(b)(2)(C) permits the Bankruptcy Court to enter final judgment on Vickie's counterclaim, Article III of the Constitution does not.

A

As its text and our precedent confirm, Article III is "an inseparable element of the constitutional system of checks and balances" that "both defines the power and protects the independence of the Judicial Branch." *Northern Pipeline Constr. Co. v. Marathon Pipe Line Co.* (1982) (plurality opinion). Under "the basic concept of separation of powers . . . that flow[s] from the scheme of a tripartite government" adopted in the Constitution, "the 'judicial Power of the United States' . . . can no more be shared" with another branch than "the Chief Executive, for example, can share with the Judiciary the veto power, or the Congress share with the Judiciary the power to override a Presidential veto." *United States v. Nixon* (1974) (quoting U.S. Const., Art. III, §1).

In establishing the system of divided power in the Constitution, the Framers considered it essential that "the judiciary remain[ ] truly distinct from both the legislature and the executive." The Federalist No. 78. As Hamilton put it, quoting Montesquieu, "'there is no liberty if the power of judging be not separated from the legislative and executive powers.'"

We have recognized that the three branches are not hermetically sealed from one another, but it remains true that Article III imposes some basic limitations that the other branches may not transgress. Those limitations serve two related purposes. "Separation-of-powers principles are intended, in part, to protect each branch of government from incursion by the others. Yet the dynamic between and among the branches is not the only object of the Constitution's concern. The structural principles secured by the separation of powers protect the individual as well." *Bond v. United States* (2011).

Article III protects liberty not only through its role in implementing the separation of powers, but also by specifying the defining characteristics of Article III judges. The colonists had been subjected to judicial abuses at the hand of the Crown, and the Framers knew the main reasons why: because the King of Great Britain "made Judges dependent on his Will alone, for the tenure of their offices, and the amount and payment of their salaries." The Declaration of Independence ¶ 11. The Framers undertook in Article III to protect citizens subject to the judicial power of the new Federal Government from a repeat of those abuses.

Article III could neither serve its purpose in the system of checks and balances nor preserve the integrity of judicial decisionmaking if the other branches of the Federal Government could confer the Government's "judicial Power" on entities outside Article III. That is why we have long recognized that, in general, Congress may not "withdraw from judicial cognizance any matter which, from its nature, is the subject of a suit at the common law, or in equity, or admiralty." *Murray's Lessee v. Hoboken Land & Improvement Co.* (1856). When a suit is made of "the stuff of the traditional actions at common law tried by the courts at Westminster in 1789," *Northern Pipeline* (Rehnquist, J., concurring in judgment), and is brought within the bounds of federal jurisdiction, the responsibility for deciding that suit rests with Article III judges in Article III courts.

B

This is not the first time we have faced an Article III challenge to a bankruptcy court's resolution of a debtor's suit. In *Northern Pipeline*, we considered whether bankruptcy judges serving under the Bankruptcy Act of 1978—appointed by the President and confirmed by the Senate, but lacking the tenure and salary guarantees of Article III—could "constitutionally be vested with jurisdiction to decide [a] state-law contract claim" against an entity that was not otherwise part of the bankruptcy proceedings. The Court concluded that assignment of such state law claims for resolution by those judges "violates Art. III of the Constitution." *Id.* (plurality opinion).

The plurality in *Northern Pipeline* recognized that there was a category of cases involving "public rights" that Congress could constitutionally assign to "legislative" courts for resolution. That opinion concluded that this "public rights" exception extended "only to matters arising between" individuals and the Government "in connection with the performance of the constitutional functions of the executive or legislative departments . . . that historically could have been determined exclusively by those" branches. A full majority of the Court, while not agreeing on the scope of the exception, concluded that the doctrine did not encompass adjudication of the state law claim at issue in that case.

A full majority of Justices in *Northern Pipeline* also rejected the debtor's argument that the bankruptcy court's exercise of jurisdiction was constitutional because the bankruptcy judge was acting merely as an adjunct of the district court or court of appeals.

After our decision in *Northern Pipeline*, Congress revised the statutes governing bankruptcy jurisdiction and bankruptcy judges. In the 1984 Act, Congress provided that the judges of the new bankruptcy courts would be appointed by the courts of appeals for the circuits in which their districts are located. And, as we have explained, Congress permitted the newly constituted bankruptcy courts to enter final judgments only in "core" proceedings.

With respect to such "core" matters, however, the bankruptcy courts under the 1984 Act exercise the same powers they wielded under the Bankruptcy Act of 1978 (1978 Act). As in *Northern Pipeline*, for example, the newly constituted bankruptcy courts are charged under §157(b)(2)(C) with resolving "[a]ll matters of fact and law in whatever domains of the law to which" a counterclaim may lead. As in *Northern Pipeline*, the new courts in core proceedings "issue final judgments, which are binding and enforceable even in the absence of an appeal." And, as in *Northern Pipeline*, the district courts review the judgments of the bankruptcy courts in core proceedings only under the usual limited appellate standards. That requires marked deference to, among other things, the bankruptcy judges' findings of fact.

C

Vickie and the dissent argue that the Bankruptcy Court's entry of final judgment on her state common law counterclaim was constitutional, despite the similarities between the bankruptcy courts under the 1978 Act and those exercising core jurisdiction under the 1984 Act. We disagree. It is clear that the Bankruptcy Court in this case exercised the "judicial Power of the United States" in purporting to resolve and enter final judgment on a state common law claim, just as the court did in *Northern Pipeline*. No "public right" exception excuses the failure to comply with Article III in doing so, any more than in *Northern Pipeline*. Vickie argues that this case is different because the defendant is a creditor in the bankruptcy. But the debtors' claims in the cases on which she relies were themselves federal claims under bankruptcy law, which would be completely resolved in the bankruptcy process of allowing or disallowing claims. Here Vickie's claim is a state law action independent of the federal bankruptcy law and not necessarily resolvable by a ruling on the creditor's proof of claim in bankruptcy. *Northern Pipeline* and our subsequent decision in *Granfinanciera v. Nordberg* (1989), rejected the application of the "public rights" exception in such cases.

Nor can the bankruptcy courts under the 1984 Act be dismissed as mere adjuncts of Article III courts, any more than could the bankruptcy courts under the 1978 Act. The judicial powers the courts exercise in cases such as this remain the same, and a court exercising such broad powers is no mere adjunct of anyone.

1

Vickie's counterclaim cannot be deemed a matter of "public right" that can be decided outside the Judicial Branch. As explained above, in *Northern Pipeline* we rejected the argument that the public rights doctrine permitted a bankruptcy court to adjudicate a state law suit brought by a debtor against a company that had not filed a claim against the estate. Although our discussion of the public rights exception since that time has not been entirely consistent, and the exception has been the subject of some debate, this case does not fall within any of the various formulations of the concept that appear in this Court's opinions. We first recognized the category of public rights in *Murray's Lessee* (1856). The challenge to the Treasury Department's sale of the customs collector's land fell within the "public rights" category because it could only be brought if the Government chose to allow it by waiving sovereign immunity. Subsequent decisions contrasted cases that were instead matters of "private right, that is, of one individual to another." *Crowell*.[6]

Shortly after *Northern Pipeline*, the Court rejected the limitation of the public rights exception to actions involving the Government as a party. The Court has continued, however, to limit the exception to cases in which the claim at issue derives from a federal regulatory scheme, or in which resolution of the claim by an expert Government agency is deemed essential to a limited regulatory objective within the agency's authority. In other words, it is still the case that what makes a right "public" rather than private is that the right is integrally related to particular Federal Government action.

---

6. The Court in *Crowell* [permitted non-Article III adjudication of a private rights case] only after observing that the administrative adjudicator had only limited authority to make specialized, narrowly confined factual determinations regarding a particularized area of law and to issue orders that could be enforced only by action of the District Court. In other words, the agency in *Crowell* functioned as a true "adjunct." That is not the case here.

Our decision in *Thomas v. Union Carbide Agricultural Products Co.* (1985), for example, involved a data-sharing arrangement between companies under a federal statute providing that disputes about compensation between the companies would be decided by binding arbitration. This Court held that the scheme did not violate Article III, explaining that "[a]ny right to compensation . . . results from [the statute] and does not depend on or replace a right to such compensation under state law."

Commodity Futures Trading Comm'n v. Schor (1986) concerned a statutory scheme that created a procedure for customers injured by a broker's violation of the federal commodities law to seek reparations from the broker before the Commodity Futures Trading Commission (CFTC). A customer filed such a claim to recover a debit balance in his account, while the broker filed a lawsuit in Federal District Court to recover the same amount as lawfully due from the customer. The broker later submitted its claim to the CFTC, but after that agency ruled against the customer, the customer argued that agency jurisdiction over the broker's counterclaim violated Article III. This Court disagreed, but only after observing that (1) the claim and the counterclaim concerned a "single dispute" — the same account balance; (2) the CFTC's assertion of authority involved only "a narrow class of common law claims" in a "'particularized area of law'"; (3) the area of law in question was governed by "a specific and limited federal regulatory scheme" as to which the agency had "obvious expertise"; (4) the parties had freely elected to resolve their differences before the CFTC; and (5) CFTC orders were "enforceable only by order of the district court." Most significantly, given that the customer's reparations claim before the agency and the broker's counterclaim were competing claims to the same amount, the Court repeatedly emphasized that it was "necessary" to allow the agency to exercise jurisdiction over the broker's claim, or else "the reparations procedure would have been confounded."

The most recent case in which we considered application of the public rights exception — and the only case in which we have considered that doctrine in the bankruptcy context since *Northern Pipeline*—is *Granfinanciera v. Nordberg* (1989). In *Granfinanciera* we rejected a bankruptcy trustee's argument that a fraudulent conveyance action filed on behalf of a bankruptcy estate against a noncreditor in a bankruptcy proceeding fell within the "public rights" exception. We explained that, "[i]f a statutory right is not closely intertwined with a federal regulatory program Congress has power to enact, and if that right neither belongs to nor exists against the Federal Government, then it must be adjudicated by an Article III court." We reasoned that fraudulent conveyance suits were "quintessentially suits at common law that more nearly resemble state law contract claims brought by a bankrupt corporation to augment the bankruptcy estate than they do creditors' hierarchically ordered claims to a pro rata share of the bankruptcy res." As a consequence, we concluded that fraudulent conveyance actions were "more accurately characterized as a private rather than a public right as we have used those terms in our Article III decisions."

Vickie's counterclaim — like the fraudulent conveyance claim at issue in *Granfinanciera*—does not fall within any of the varied formulations of the public rights exception in this Court's cases. It is not a matter that can be pursued only by grace of the other branches, as in *Murray's Lessee*, or one that "historically could have been determined exclusively by" those branches, *Northern Pipeline*. The claim is instead one under state common law between two private parties. It does not "depend[ ] upon the will of congress," *Murray's Lessee*; Congress has nothing to do with it.

In addition, Vickie's claimed right to relief does not flow from a federal statutory scheme, as in *Thomas*, or *Atlas Roofing*. It is not "completely dependent upon" adjudication of a claim created by federal law, as in *Schor*. And in contrast to the objecting party in *Schor*, Pierce did not truly consent to resolution of Vickie's claim in the bankruptcy court proceedings. He had nowhere else to go if he wished to recover from Vickie's estate.

Furthermore, the asserted authority to decide Vickie's claim is not limited to a "particularized area of the law," as in *Crowell*, *Thomas*, and *Schor*. We deal here not with an agency but with a court, with substantive jurisdiction reaching any area of the *corpus juris*. This is not a situation in which Congress devised an "expert and inexpensive method for dealing with a class of questions of fact which are particularly suited to examination and determination by an administrative agency specially assigned to that task." The "experts" in the federal system at resolving common law counterclaims such as Vickie's are the Article III courts, and it is with those courts that her claim must stay.

The dissent reads our cases differently, and in particular contends that more recent cases view *Northern Pipeline* as "'establish[ing] only that Congress may not vest in a non-Article III court the power to adjudicate, render final judgment, and issue binding orders in a traditional contract action arising under state law, without consent of the litigants, and subject only to ordinary appellate review.'" Just so: Substitute "tort" for "contract," and that statement directly covers this case.

We recognize that there may be instances in which the distinction between public and private rights—at least as framed by some of our recent cases—fails to provide concrete guidance as to whether, for example, a particular agency can adjudicate legal issues under a substantive regulatory scheme. Given the extent to which this case is so markedly distinct from the agency cases discussing the public rights exception in the context of such a regime, however, we do not in this opinion express any view on how the doctrine might apply in that different context.

What is plain here is that this case involves the most prototypical exercise of judicial power: the entry of a final, binding judgment by a court with broad substantive jurisdiction, on a common law cause of action, when the action neither derives from nor depends upon any agency regulatory regime. If such an exercise of judicial power may nonetheless be taken from the Article III Judiciary simply by deeming it part of some amorphous "public right," then Article III would be transformed from the guardian of individual liberty and separation of powers we have long recognized into mere wishful thinking.

2

Vickie and the dissent next attempt to distinguish *Northern Pipeline* and *Granfinanciera* on the ground that Pierce, unlike the defendants in those cases, had filed a proof of claim in the bankruptcy proceedings.

We do not agree. Pierce's claim for defamation in no way affects the nature of Vickie's counterclaim for tortious interference as one at common law that simply attempts to augment the bankruptcy estate—the very type of claim that we held in *Northern Pipeline* and *Granfinanciera* must be decided by an Article III court.

3

Vickie additionally argues that the Bankruptcy Court's final judgment was constitutional because bankruptcy courts under the 1984 Act are properly deemed "adjuncts" of the district courts. We rejected a similar argument in *Northern Pipeline*, and our reasoning there holds true today.

To begin, as explained above, it is still the bankruptcy court itself that exercises the essential attributes of judicial power over a matter such as Vickie's counterclaim. The new bankruptcy courts, like the old, do not "ma[k]e only specialized, narrowly confined factual determinations regarding a particularized area of law" or engage in "statutorily channeled factfinding functions." *Northern Pipeline*. Instead, bankruptcy courts under the 1984 Act resolve "[a]ll matters of fact and law in whatever domains of the law to which" the parties' counterclaims might lead.

In addition, whereas the adjunct agency in *Crowell v. Benson* "possessed only a limited power to issue compensation orders . . . [that] could be enforced only by order of the district court," *Northern Pipeline*, a bankruptcy court resolving a counterclaim under 28 U.S.C. §157(b)(2)(C) has the power to enter "appropriate orders and judgments"—including final judgments—subject to review only if a party chooses to appeal, *see* §§157(b)(1), 158(a)-(b). It is thus no less the case here than it was in *Northern Pipeline* that "[t]he authority—and the responsibility—to make an informed, final determination . . . remains with" the bankruptcy judge, not the district court. Given that authority, a bankruptcy court can no more be deemed a mere "adjunct" of the district court than a district court can be deemed such an "adjunct" of the court of appeals.

It does not affect our analysis that, as Vickie notes, bankruptcy judges under the current Act are appointed by the Article III courts, rather than the President. The constitutional bar remains.

D

Finally, Vickie and her amici predict as a practical matter that restrictions on a bankruptcy court's ability to hear and finally resolve compulsory counterclaims will create significant delays and impose additional costs on the bankruptcy process. It goes without saying that "the fact that a given law or procedure is efficient, convenient, and useful in facilitating functions of government, standing alone, will not save it if it is contrary to the Constitution." *INS v. Chadha* (1983).

In addition, we are not convinced that the practical consequences of such limitations on the authority of bankruptcy courts to enter final judgments are as significant as Vickie and the dissent suggest. We do not think the removal of counterclaims such as Vickie's from core bankruptcy jurisdiction meaningfully changes the division of labor in the current statute; we agree with the United States that the question presented here is a "narrow" one.

If our decision today does not change all that much, then why the fuss? Is there really a threat to the separation of powers where Congress has conferred the judicial power outside Article III only over certain counterclaims in bankruptcy? The short but emphatic answer is yes. A statute may no more lawfully chip away at the authority of the Judicial Branch than it may eliminate it entirely. "Slight encroachments create new boundaries from which legions of power can seek new territory to capture." *Reid v. Covert* (1957) (plurality opinion). Although "[i]t may be that it is the obnoxious thing in its mildest and least repulsive form," we cannot overlook the intrusion: "illegitimate and unconstitutional practices get their first footing in that way, namely, by silent approaches and slight deviations from legal modes of procedure." *Boyd v. United States* (1886). We cannot compromise the integrity of the system of separated powers and the role of the Judiciary in that system, even with respect to challenges that may seem innocuous at first blush.

The Bankruptcy Court below lacked the constitutional authority to enter a final judgment on a state law counterclaim that is not resolved in the process of ruling on a creditor's proof of claim.

Justice SCALIA, concurring.

I agree with the Court's interpretation of our Article III precedents, and I accordingly join its opinion. I adhere to my view, however, that — our contrary precedents notwithstanding — "a matter of public rights . . . must at a minimum arise between the government and others," *Granfinanciera v. Nordberg* (1989) (Scalia, J., concurring in part and concurring in judgment).

The sheer surfeit of factors that the Court was required to consider in this case should arouse the suspicion that something is seriously amiss with our jurisprudence in this area. I count at least seven different reasons given in the Court's opinion for concluding that an Article III judge was required to adjudicate this lawsuit: that it was one "under state common law" which was "not a matter that can be pursued only by grace of the other branches," that it was "not 'completely dependent upon' adjudication of a claim created by federal law," that "Pierce did not truly consent to resolution of Vickie's claim in the bankruptcy court proceedings," that "the asserted authority to decide Vickie's claim is not limited to a 'particularized area of the law,'" that "there was never any reason to believe that the process of adjudicating Pierce's proof of claim would necessarily resolve Vickie's counterclaim," that the trustee was not "asserting a right of recovery created by federal bankruptcy law," and that the Bankruptcy Judge "ha[d] the power to enter 'appropriate orders and judgments' — including final judgments — subject to review only if a party chooses to appeal."

Apart from their sheer numerosity, the more fundamental flaw in the many tests suggested by our jurisprudence is that they have nothing to do with the text or tradition of Article III. For example, Article III gives no indication that state-law claims have preferential entitlement to an Article III judge; nor does it make pertinent the extent to which the area of the law is "particularized." The multifactors relied upon today seem to have entered our jurisprudence almost randomly.

Leaving aside certain adjudications by federal administrative agencies, which are governed (for better or worse) by our landmark decision in *Crowell v. Benson* (1932), in my view an Article III judge is required in all federal adjudications, unless there is a firmly established historical practice to the contrary. For that reason — and not because of some intuitive balancing of benefits and harms — I agree that Article III judges are not required in the context of territorial courts, courts-martial, or true "public rights" cases. But Vickie points to no historical practice that authorizes a non-Article III judge to adjudicate a counterclaim of the sort at issue here.

Justice BREYER, with whom Justice GINSBURG, Justice SOTOMAYOR, and Justice KAGAN join, dissenting.

I agree with the Court that the bankruptcy statute, §157(b)(2)(C), authorizes a bankruptcy court to adjudicate the counterclaim. But I do not agree with the majority about the statute's constitutionality. I believe the statute is consistent with the Constitution's delegation of the "judicial Power of the United States" to the Judicial Branch of Government. Art. III, §1. Consequently, it is constitutional.

I

My disagreement with the majority's conclusion stems in part from my disagreement about the way in which it interprets, or at least emphasizes, certain precedents. In my view, the majority overstates the current relevance of statements this Court made in an 1856 case, *Murray's Lessee v. Hoboken Land & Improvement Co.*, and it overstates the importance of an analysis that did not command a Court majority in *Northern Pipeline Constr. Co. v. Marathon Pipe Line Co.* (1982), and that was subsequently disavowed. At the same time, I fear the Court understates the importance of a watershed opinion widely thought to demonstrate the constitutional basis for the current authority of administrative agencies to adjudicate private disputes, namely, *Crowell v. Benson* (1932). And it fails to follow the analysis that this Court more recently has held applicable to the evaluation of claims of a kind before us here, namely, claims that a congressional delegation of adjudicatory authority violates separation-of-powers principles derived from Article III.

I shall describe these cases in some detail in order to explain why I believe we should put less weight than does the majority upon the statement in *Murray's Lessee* and the analysis followed by the *Northern Pipeline* plurality and instead should apply the approach this Court has applied in *Crowell, Thomas*, and *Schor*.

II
A

This case law requires us to determine pragmatically whether a congressional delegation of adjudicatory authority to a non-Article III judge violates the separation-of-powers principles inherent in Article III. That is to say, we must determine through an examination of certain relevant factors whether that delegation constitutes a significant encroachment by the Legislative or Executive Branches of Government upon the realm of authority that Article III reserves for exercise by the Judicial Branch of Government. Those factors include (1) the nature of the claim to be adjudicated; (2) the nature of the non-Article III tribunal; (3) the extent to which Article III courts exercise control over the proceeding; (4) the presence or absence of the parties' consent; and (5) the nature and importance of the legislative purpose served by the grant of adjudicatory authority to a tribunal with judges who lack Article III's tenure and compensation protections. *CFTC v. Schor* (1986). The presence of "private rights" does not automatically determine the outcome of the question but requires a more "searching" examination of the relevant factors.

Insofar as the majority would apply more formal standards, it simply disregards recent, controlling precedent. *Thomas* ("[P]ractical attention to substance rather than doctrinaire reliance on formal categories should inform application of Article III"); *Schor* ("[T]he Court has declined to adopt formalistic and unbending rules" for deciding Article III cases).

B

Applying *Schor's* approach here, I conclude that the delegation of adjudicatory authority before us is constitutional. A grant of authority to a bankruptcy court to adjudicate compulsory counterclaims does not violate any constitutional separation-of-powers principle related to Article III.

First, I concede that *the nature of the claim to be adjudicated* argues against my conclusion. Vickie Marshall's counterclaim—a kind of tort suit—resembles "a suit at the common law." Although not determinative of the question, delegation of authority to a non-Article III judge to adjudicate a claim of that kind poses a heightened risk of encroachment on the Federal Judiciary.

At the same time the significance of this factor is mitigated here by the fact that bankruptcy courts often decide claims that similarly resemble various common-law actions. Suppose, for example, that ownership of 40 acres of land in the bankruptcy debtor's possession is disputed by a creditor. If that creditor brings a claim in the bankruptcy court, resolution of that dispute requires the bankruptcy court to apply the same state property law that would govern in a state-court proceeding. This kind of dispute arises with regularity in bankruptcy proceedings.

Of course, in this instance the state-law question is embedded in a debtor's counterclaim, not a creditor's claim. But the counterclaim is "compulsory." It "arises out of the transaction or occurrence that is the subject matter of the opposing party's claim." FRCP 13(a); FRBP 7013. Thus, resolution of the counterclaim will often turn on facts identical to, or at least related to, those at issue in a creditor's claim that is undisputedly proper for the bankruptcy court to decide.

Second, *the nature of the non-Article III tribunal* argues in favor of constitutionality. That is because the tribunal is made up of judges who enjoy considerable protection from improper political influence. Unlike the 1978 Act which provided for the appointment of bankruptcy judges by the President with the advice and consent of the Senate, current law provides that the federal courts of appeals appoint federal bankruptcy judges. Bankruptcy judges are removable by the circuit judicial council (made up of federal court of appeals and district court judges) and only for cause. Their salaries are pegged to those of federal district court judges, and the cost of their courthouses and other work-related expenses are paid by the Judiciary. Thus, although Congress technically exercised its Article I power when it created bankruptcy courts, functionally, bankruptcy judges can be compared to magistrate judges, law clerks, and the Judiciary's administrative officials, whose lack of Article III tenure and compensation protections do not endanger the independence of the Judicial Branch.

Third, *the control exercised by Article III judges over bankruptcy proceedings* argues in favor of constitutionality. Article III judges control and supervise the bankruptcy court's determinations—at least to the same degree that Article III judges supervised the agency's determinations in *Crowell*, if not more so. Any party may appeal those determinations to the federal district court, where the federal judge will review all determinations of fact for clear error and will review all determinations of law *de novo*. But for the here-irrelevant matter of what *Crowell* considered to be special "constitutional" facts, the standard of review for factual findings here ("clearly erroneous") is more stringent than the standard at issue in *Crowell* (whether the agency's factfinding was "supported by evidence in the record"). And, as *Crowell* noted, "there is no requirement that, in order to maintain the essential attributes of the judicial power, all determinations of fact in constitutional courts shall be made by judges."

Moreover, in one important respect Article III judges maintain greater control over the bankruptcy court proceedings at issue here than they did over the relevant proceedings in any of the previous cases in which this Court has upheld a delegation of adjudicatory power. The District Court here may "withdraw, in whole or in part, any case or proceeding referred [to the Bankruptcy Court] . . . on its own motion or on timely motion of any party, for cause shown." 28 U.S.C. §157(d).

Fourth, the fact that *the parties have consented* to Bankruptcy Court jurisdiction argues in favor of constitutionality, and strongly so. Pierce Marshall, the counter-claim defendant, is not a stranger to the litigation, forced to appear in Bankruptcy Court against his will. Rather, he appeared voluntarily in Bankruptcy Court as one of Vickie Marshall's creditors, seeking a favorable resolution of his claim against Vickie Marshall to the detriment of her other creditors. He need not have filed a claim, perhaps not even at the cost of bringing it in the future, for he says his claim is "nondischargeable," in which case he could have litigated it in a state or federal court after distribution. Thus, Pierce Marshall likely had "an alternative forum to the bankruptcy court in which to pursue [his] clai[m]."

The majority argues that Pierce Marshall "did not truly consent" to bankruptcy jurisdiction, but filing a proof of claim was sufficient in *Langenkamp* and *Granfinanciera*, and there is no relevant distinction between the claims filed in those cases and the claim filed here.

Fifth, *the nature and importance of the legislative purpose served* by the grant of adjudicatory authority to bankruptcy tribunals argues strongly in favor of constitutionality. Congress' delegation of adjudicatory powers over counterclaims asserted against bankruptcy claimants constitutes an important means of securing a constitutionally authorized end. Article I, §8, of the Constitution explicitly grants Congress the "Power To . . . establish . . . uniform Laws on the subject of Bankruptcies throughout the United States."

Congress established the first Bankruptcy Act in 1800. From the beginning, the "core" of federal bankruptcy proceedings has been "the restructuring of debtor-creditor relations." *No. Pipeline*. And, to be effective, a single tribunal must have broad authority to restructure those relations, "having jurisdiction of the parties to controversies brought before them," "decid[ing] all matters in dispute," and "decree[ing] complete relief." *Katchen*.

Considering these factors together, I conclude that, as in *Schor*, "the magnitude of any intrusion on the Judicial Branch can only be termed *de minimis*." I would similarly find the statute before us constitutional.

III

The majority predicts that as a "practical matter" today's decision "does not change all that much." But I doubt that is so. Consider a typical case: A tenant files for bankruptcy. The landlord files a claim for unpaid rent. The tenant asserts a counterclaim for damages suffered by the landlord's (1) failing to fulfill his obligations as lessor, and (2) improperly recovering possession of the premises by misrepresenting the facts in housing court. This state-law counterclaim does not "ste[m] from the bankruptcy itself," it would not "necessarily be resolved in the claims allowance process," and it would require the debtor to prove damages suffered by the lessor's failures, the extent to which the landlord's representations to the housing court were untrue, and damages suffered by improper recovery of possession of the premises. Thus, under the majority's holding, the federal district judge, not the bankruptcy judge, would have to hear and resolve the counterclaim.

Why is that a problem? Because these types of disputes arise in bankruptcy court with some frequency. Because the volume of bankruptcy cases is staggering, involving almost 1.6 million filings last year, compared to a federal district court docket of around 280,000 civil cases and 78,000 criminal cases. Because unlike the "related" noncore state-law claims that bankruptcy courts must abstain from hearing, compulsory counterclaims involve the same factual disputes as the claims that may be finally adjudicated by the bankruptcy courts. Because under these circumstances, a constitutionally required game of jurisdictional ping-pong between courts would lead to inefficiency, increased cost, delay, and needless additional suffering among those faced with bankruptcy.

For these reasons, with respect, I dissent.

* * *

Stern v. Marshall left open the question whether the parties' consent could solve the constitutional problem it identified. As a practical matter, the Court's decision in *Stern* is not disruptive if parties may consent to bankruptcy jurisdiction over state law claims.

The Court answered this open question in *Wellness Int'l Network Ltd. v. Sharif* (2015). It held "that Article III is not violated when the parties knowingly and voluntarily consent to adjudication by a bankruptcy judge." This decision is important not only for its holding, which minimized the practical impact of *Stern* on the bankruptcy system, but also for the methodology the Court employed. Writing for the Court, Justice Sotomayor identified *Commodity Futures Trading Commission v. Schor* (1986), which employed a functionalist methodology, as the "foundational case in the modern era." Employing that methodology, Justice Sotomayor stated that "the entitlement to an Article III adjudicator is 'a personal right' and thus ordinarily 'subject to waiver.'" This personal right could be waived explicitly, of course, but also, the Court held, by implication, that is, by "'actions rather than words.'" The remaining question under *Schor* balancing was whether allowing parties to waive this personal right would threaten the Article III courts' "'constitutionally assigned role.'" The Court held that there was no threat because bankruptcy judges deciding state law questions "are subject to control by the Article III courts." Chief Justice

Roberts, joined by Justices Scalia and Thomas, dissented, putting his objection to the Court's methodology thus: "The Court justifies its decision largely on pragmatic grounds. I would not yield so fully to functionalism."

The next case, *Oil States Energy Servs. v. Greene's Energy Group* (2018), is the Court's most recent statement concerning the private rights/public rights distinction. As this case makes clear, a simple statement of the distinction risks papering over inconsistency and indeterminacy in the doctrine. The *Stern* Court recognized that the public-rights doctrine has "not been entirely consistent." As you read *Oil States Energy*, consider the role that history and the public-rights exception play in determining contemporary debates about Congress' authority to assign disputes to non-Article III tribunals, and why the distinction remains so hotly contested.

Oil States Energy Servs. v. Greene's Energy Group, LLC

138 S. Ct. 1365 (2018)

Justice THOMAS delivered the opinion of the Court.

The Leahy-Smith America Invents Act establishes a process called "inter partes review." Under that process, the United States Patent and Trademark Office (PTO) is authorized to reconsider and to cancel an issued patent claim in limited circumstances. In this case, we address whether inter partes review violates Article III or the Seventh Amendment of the Constitution. We hold that it violates neither.

I
A

Under the Patent Act, the PTO is "responsible for the granting and issuing of patents." When an inventor applies for a patent, an examiner reviews the proposed claims and the prior art to determine if the claims meet the statutory requirements. Those requirements include utility, novelty, and nonobviousness based on the prior art. The Director of the PTO then approves or rejects the application. An applicant can seek judicial review of a final rejection.

B

Over the last several decades, Congress has created administrative processes that authorize the PTO to reconsider and cancel patent claims that were wrongly issued. In 1980, Congress established "ex parte reexamination," which still exists today. Ex parte reexamination permits "[a]ny person at any time" to "file a request for reexamination." If the Director determines that there is "a substantial new question of patentability" for "any claim of the patent," the PTO can reexamine the patent. The reexamination process follows the same procedures as the initial examination.

C

The America Invents Act [authorized] inter partes review, the procedure at issue here. Any person other than the patent owner can file a petition for inter partes review. The petition can request cancellation of "1 or more claims of a patent" on the grounds that the claim fails the novelty or nonobviousness standards for patentability. The challenges must be made "only on the basis of prior art consisting of patents or printed publications." If a petition is filed, the patent owner has the right to file a preliminary response explaining why inter partes review should not be instituted.

Before he can institute inter partes review, the Director must determine "that there is a reasonable likelihood that the petitioner would prevail with respect to at least 1 of the claims challenged." The decision whether to institute inter partes review is committed to the Director's discretion. The Director's decision is "final and nonappealable."

Once inter partes review is instituted, the Patent Trial and Appeal Board—an adjudicatory body within the PTO created to conduct inter partes review—examines the patent's validity. The Board sits in three-member panels of administrative patent judges. During the inter partes review, the petitioner and the patent owner are entitled to certain discovery; to file affidavits, declarations, and written memoranda; and to receive an oral hearing before the Board. The petitioner has the burden of proving unpatentability by a preponderance of the evidence. The owner can file a motion to amend the patent by voluntarily canceling a claim or by "propos[ing] a reasonable number of substitute claims." The owner can also settle with the petitioner by filing a written agreement prior to the Board's final decision, which terminates the proceedings with respect to that petitioner. If the settlement results in no petitioner remaining in the inter partes review, the Board can terminate the proceeding or issue a final written decision.

If the proceeding does not terminate, the Board must issue a final written decision no later than a year after it notices the institution of inter partes review, but that deadline can be extended up to six months for good cause. If the Board's decision becomes final, the Director must "issue and publish a certificate." The certificate cancels patent claims "finally determined to be unpatentable," confirms patent claims "determined to be patentable," and incorporates into the patent "any new or amended claim determined to be patentable."

A party dissatisfied with the Board's decision can seek judicial review in the Court of Appeals for the Federal Circuit. Any party to the inter partes review can be a party in the Federal Circuit. The Director can intervene to defend the Board's decision, even if no party does. When reviewing the Board's decision, the Federal Circuit assesses "the Board's compliance with governing legal standards de novo and its underlying factual determinations for substantial evidence."

II

Petitioner Oil States Energy Services, LLC, and respondent Greene's Energy Group, LLC, are both oilfield services companies. In 2001, Oil States obtained a patent relating to an apparatus and method for protecting wellhead equipment used in hydraulic fracturing. In 2012, Oil States sued Greene's Energy in Federal District Court for infringing that patent. Greene's Energy responded by challenging the patent's validity. Near the close of discovery, Greene's Energy also petitioned the Board to institute inter partes review. It argued that two of the patent's claims were unpatentable because they were anticipated by prior art not mentioned by Oil States in its original patent application. Oil States filed a response opposing review.

The Board found that Greene's Energy had established a reasonable likelihood that the two claims were unpatentable and, thus, instituted inter partes review.

The proceedings before the District Court and the Board progressed in parallel. In June 2014, the District Court issued a claim-construction order. The order construed the challenged claims in a way that foreclosed Greene's Energy's arguments about the prior art. But a few months later, the Board issued a final written decision concluding that the claims were unpatentable. The Board acknowledged the District Court's contrary decision, but nonetheless concluded that the claims were anticipated by the prior art.

The Federal Circuit summarily affirmed the Board's decision in this case.

III

Article III vests the judicial power of the United States "in one supreme Court, and in such inferior Courts as the Congress may from time to time ordain and establish." §1. Consequently, Congress cannot "confer the Government's 'judicial Power' on entities outside Article III." *Stern v. Marshall* (2011). When determining whether a proceeding involves an exercise of Article III judicial power, this Court's precedents have distinguished between "public rights" and "private rights." Those precedents have given Congress significant latitude to assign adjudication of public rights to entities other than Article III courts.

This Court has not "definitively explained" the distinction between public and private rights, *Northern Pipeline Constr. Co. v. Marathon Pipe Line Co.* (1982), and its precedents applying the public-rights doctrine have "not been entirely consistent." *Stern.* But this case does not require us to add to the "various formulations" of the public-rights doctrine. Our precedents have recognized that the doctrine covers matters "which arise between the Government and persons subject to its authority in connection with the performance of the constitutional functions of the executive or legislative departments." *Crowell v. Benson* (1932). In other words, the public-rights doctrine applies to matters arising between the government and others, which from their nature do not require judicial determination and yet are susceptible of it. Inter partes review involves one such matter: reconsideration of the Government's decision to grant a public franchise.

A

Inter partes review falls squarely within the public-rights doctrine. This Court has recognized, and the parties do not dispute, that the decision to grant a patent is a matter involving public rights—specifically, the grant of a public franchise. Inter partes review is simply a reconsideration of that grant, and Congress has permissibly reserved the PTO's authority to conduct that reconsideration. Thus, the PTO can do so without violating Article III.

1

This Court has long recognized that the grant of a patent is a "'matte[r] involving public rights.'" *United States v. Duell* (1899) (quoting *Murray's Lessee v. Hoboken Land & Improvement Co.* (1856)). It has the key features to fall within this Court's longstanding formulation of the public-rights doctrine.

Ab initio, the grant of a patent involves a matter "arising between the government and others." *Ex parte Bakelite Corp.* (1929). By "issuing patents," the PTO "take[s] from the public rights of immense value, and bestow[s] them upon the patentee." *United States v. American Bell Telephone Co.* (1888). Specifically, patents are "public franchises" that the Government grants "to the inventors of new and useful improvements." *Seymour v. Osborne* (1871).

The franchise gives the patent owner "the right to exclude others from making, using, offering for sale, or selling the invention throughout the United States." 35 U.S.C. §154(a)(1). That right "did not exist at common law." *Gayler v. Wilder* (1851). Rather, it is a "creature of statute law." *Crown Die & Tool Co. v. Nye Tool & Machine Works* (1923).

Additionally, granting patents is one of "the constitutional functions" that can be carried out by "the executive or legislative departments" without "'judicial determination.'" *Crowell.* Article I gives Congress the power "[t]o promote the Progress of Science and useful Arts, by securing for limited Times to Authors and Inventors the exclusive Right to their respective Writings and Discoveries." §8, cl. 8. Congress can grant patents itself by statute. And, from the founding to today, Congress has authorized the Executive Branch to grant patents that meet the statutory requirements for patentability. When the PTO "adjudicate[s] the patentability of inventions," it is "exercising the executive power." *Freytag v. Commissioner* (1991) (Scalia, J., concurring in part and concurring in judgment).

Accordingly, the determination to grant a patent is a "matte[r] involving public rights." It need not be adjudicated in Article III court.

2

Inter partes review involves the same basic matter as the grant of a patent. So it, too, falls on the public-rights side of the line.

Inter partes review is "a second look at an earlier administrative grant of a patent." The Board considers the same statutory requirements that the PTO considered when granting the patent. Those statutory requirements prevent the "issuance of patents whose effects are to remove existent knowledge from the public domain." *Graham v. John Deere Co. of Kansas City* (1966). Thus, inter partes review involves the same interests as the determination to grant a patent in the first instance.

The primary distinction between inter partes review and the initial grant of a patent is that inter partes review occurs after the patent has issued. But that distinction does not make a difference here. Patent claims are granted subject to the qualification that the PTO has "the authority to reexamine — and perhaps cancel — a patent claim" in an inter partes review.

This Court has recognized that franchises can be qualified in this manner. For example, Congress can grant a franchise that permits a company to erect a toll bridge, but qualify the grant by reserving its authority to revoke or amend the franchise. Even after the bridge is built, the Government can exercise its reserved authority through legislation or an administrative proceeding. The same is true for franchises that permit companies to build railroads or telegraph lines.

Thus, the public-rights doctrine covers the matter resolved in inter partes review. The Constitution does not prohibit the Board from resolving it outside of an Article III court.

B

Oil States challenges this conclusion, citing three decisions that recognize patent rights as the "private property of the patentee." But those cases do not contradict our conclusion.

Patents convey only a specific form of property right—a public franchise. And patents are "entitled to protection as any other property, consisting of a franchise." As a public franchise, a patent can confer only the rights that "the statute prescribes."

The Patent Act provides that, "[s]ubject to the provisions of this title, patents shall have the attributes of personal property." This provision qualifies any property rights that a patent owner has in an issued patent, subjecting them to the express provisions of the Patent Act. Those provisions include inter partes review.

C

Oil States and the dissent contend that inter partes review violates the "general" principle that "Congress may not 'withdraw from judicial cognizance any matter which, from its nature, is the subject of a suit at the common law, or in equity, or admiralty.'" *Stern* (quoting *Murray's Lessee*). They argue that this is so because patent validity was often decided in English courts of law in the 18th century. For example, if a patent owner brought an infringement action, the defendant could challenge the validity of the patent as an affirmative defense. Or, an individual could challenge the validity of a patent by filing a writ of scire facias in the Court of Chancery, which would sit as a law court when adjudicating the writ.

But this history does not establish that patent validity is a matter that, "from its nature," must be decided by a court. The aforementioned proceedings were between private parties. But there was another means of canceling a patent in 18th-century England, which more closely resembles inter partes review: a petition to the Privy Council to vacate a patent. The Privy Council was composed of the Crown's advisers. From the 17th through the 20th centuries, English patents had a standard revocation clause that permitted six or more Privy Counsellors to declare a patent void if they determined the invention was contrary to law, "prejudicial" or "inconvenient," not new, or not invented by the patent owner. Individuals could petition the Council to revoke a patent, and the petition was referred to the Attorney General. The Attorney General examined the petition, considered affidavits from the petitioner and patent owner, and heard from counsel. Depending on the Attorney General's conclusion, the Council would either void the patent or dismiss the petition.

The Privy Council was a prominent feature of the English system. It had exclusive authority to revoke patents until 1753, and after that, it had concurrent jurisdiction with the courts. The Privy Council continued to consider revocation claims and to revoke patents throughout the 18th century. Its last revocation was in 1779. It considered, but did not act on, revocation claims in 1782, 1794, and 1810.

The Patent Clause in our Constitution "was written against the backdrop" of the English system. Based on the practice of the Privy Council, it was well understood at the founding that a patent system could include a practice of granting patents subject to potential cancellation in the executive proceeding of the Privy Council.

For similar reasons, we disagree with the dissent's assumption that, because courts have traditionally adjudicated patent validity in this country, courts must forever continue to do so. Historical practice is not decisive here because matters governed by the public-rights doctrine "from their nature" can be resolved in multiple ways: Congress can "reserve to itself the power to decide," "delegate that power to executive officers," or "commit it to judicial tribunals." *Ex parte Bakelite Corp.* That Congress chose the courts in the past does not foreclose its choice of the PTO today.

IV

In addition to Article III, Oil States challenges inter partes review under the Seventh Amendment. This Court's precedents establish that, when Congress properly assigns a matter to adjudication in a non-Article III tribunal, "the Seventh Amendment poses no independent bar to the adjudication of that action by a non-jury factfinder." *Granfinanciera, S.A. v. Nordberg* (1989). Thus, our rejection of Oil States' Article III challenge also resolves its Seventh Amendment challenge.

Justice BREYER, with whom Justice GINSBURG and Justice SOTOMAYOR join, concurring.

I join the Court's opinion in full. The conclusion that inter partes review is a matter involving public rights is sufficient to show that it violates neither Article III nor the Seventh Amendment. But the Court's opinion should not be read to say that matters involving private rights may never be adjudicated other than by Article III courts, say, sometimes by agencies.

Justice GORSUCH, with whom THE CHIEF JUSTICE joins, dissenting.

After much hard work and no little investment you devise something you think truly novel. Then you endure the further cost and effort of applying for a patent, devoting maybe $30,000 and two years to that process alone. At the end of it all, the Patent Office agrees your invention is novel and issues a patent. The patent affords you exclusive rights to the fruits of your labor for two decades. But what happens if someone later emerges from the woodwork, arguing that it was all a mistake and your patent should be canceled? Can a political appointee and his administrative agents, instead of an independent judge, resolve the dispute? The Court says yes. Respectfully, I disagree.

We sometimes take it for granted today that independent judges will hear our cases and controversies. But it wasn't always so. Before the Revolution, colonial judges depended on the crown for their tenure and salary and often enough their decisions followed their interests. The problem was so serious that the founders cited it in their Declaration of Independence. Once free, the framers went to great lengths to guarantee a degree of judicial independence for future generations that they themselves had not experienced. Under the Constitution, judges "hold their Offices during good Behaviour" and their "Compensation . . . shall not be diminished during the[ir] Continuance in Office." The framers knew that "a fixed provision" for judges' financial support would help secure "the independence of the judges," because "a power over a man's subsistence amounts to a power over his will." The Federalist No. 79 (A. Hamilton). They were convinced, too, that "[p]eriodical appointments, however regulated, or by whomsoever made, would, in some way or other, be fatal to [the courts'] necessary independence." The Federalist No. 78 (A. Hamilton).

Today, the government invites us to retreat from the promise of judicial independence. Until recently, most everyone considered an issued patent a personal right—no less than a home or farm—that the federal government could revoke only with the concurrence of independent judges. But in the statute before us Congress has tapped an executive agency, the Patent Trial and Appeal Board, for the job. Supporters say this is a good thing because the Patent Office issues too many low quality patents; allowing a subdivision of that office to clean up problems after the fact, they assure us, promises an efficient solution. And, no doubt, dispensing with constitutionally prescribed procedures is often expedient. Whether it is the guarantee of a warrant before a search, a jury trial before a conviction—or, yes, a judicial hearing before a property interest is stripped away—the Constitution's constraints can slow things down. But economy supplies no license for ignoring these—often vitally inefficient—protections. The Constitution "reflects a judgment by the American people that the benefits of its restrictions on the Government outweigh the costs," and it is not our place to replace that judgment with our own. *United States v. Stevens* (2010).

Of course, all this invites the question: how do we know which cases independent judges must hear? The Constitution's original public meaning supplies the key, for the Constitution cannot secure the people's liberty any less today than it did the day it was ratified. The relevant constitutional provision, Article III, explains that the federal "judicial Power" is vested in independent judges. As originally understood, the judicial power extended to "suit[s] at the common law, or in equity, or admiralty." *Murray's Lessee v. Hoboken Land & Improvement Co.* (1856). From this and as we've recently explained, it follows that, "[w]hen a suit is made of the stuff of the traditional actions at common law tried by the courts at Westminster in 1789 . . . and is brought within the bounds of federal jurisdiction, the responsibility for deciding that suit rests with" Article III judges endowed with the protections for their independence the framers thought so important. *Stern v. Marshall* (2011).

As I read the historical record presented to us, only courts could hear patent challenges in England at the time of the founding. If facts were in dispute, the matter first had to proceed in the law courts. If successful there, a challenger then had to obtain a writ of scire facias in the law side of the Court of Chancery.

The last time an executive body (the King's Privy Council) invalidated an invention patent on an ordinary application was in 1746[,] and the last time the Privy Council even considered doing so was in 1753.

This shift to courts paralleled a shift in thinking. Patents began as little more than feudal favors. The crown both issued and revoked them. And they often permitted the lucky recipient the exclusive right to do very ordinary things, like operate a toll bridge or run a tavern. But by the 18th century, inventors were busy in Britain and invention patents came to be seen in a different light. They came to be viewed not as endowing accidental and anticompetitive monopolies on the fortunate few but as a procompetitive means to secure to individuals the fruits of their labor and ingenuity; encourage others to emulate them; and promote public access to new technologies that would not otherwise exist. The Constitution itself reflects this new thinking, authorizing the issuance of patents precisely because of their contribution to the "Progress of Science and useful Arts." "In essence, there was a change in perception—from viewing a patent as a contract between the crown and the patentee to viewing it as a 'social contract' between the patentee and society." WALTERSHEID, THE EARLY EVOLUTION OF THE UNITED STATES PATENT LAW: ANTECEDENTS (Part 3) (1995). And as invention patents came to be seen so differently, it is no surprise courts came to treat them more solicitously.

Today's decision may not represent a rout but it at least signals a retreat from Article III's guarantees. Ceding to the political branches ground they wish to take in the name of efficient government may seem like an act of judicial restraint. But enforcing Article III isn't about protecting judicial authority for its own sake. It's about ensuring the people today and tomorrow enjoy no fewer rights against governmental intrusion than those who came before. And the loss of the right to an independent judge is never a small thing.

* * *

There are several typical justifications for the public-rights exception to Article III. As *Oil States Energy* shows, one important justification is historical. The Court has said that there is a historical distinction between inherently judicial matters, which Congress may not assign to non-Article III adjudicators, and matters that a non-Article institution may decide. Public rights disputes are not inherently judicial. What about private rights disputes? In *Oil States Energy*, Justice Breyer took pains in his concurring opinion to say that private rights matters are not inherently judicial. But the Court has sometimes suggested otherwise.

As we saw in *Murray's Lessee*, sovereign immunity is another rationale for the public-rights exception. A private party may not sue the United States unless Congress waives the U.S.'s sovereign immunity or the Executive Branch does so pursuant to congressional authorization. Congress' authority to deny public-rights claims against the United States might imply that Congress has discretion to condition the litigation of a public-rights claim upon a private party bringing the claim in a non-Article III forum.

Do you find these rationales persuasive? One criticism is that the history is indeterminate. For instance, as the Court itself has acknowledged, the distinction between public rights and private rights is not always clear. A second criticism of the historical rationale is that the public-rights exception does not track the Constitution's purpose in vesting the "judicial Power" in independent judges. On this view, Article III judges have life tenure and salary protection to reduce the risk that they will act arbitrarily and to ensure that they will check the political branches. Public rights cases—which pit private parties against the government—are just the sort of cases in which one might think judicial independence is most needed. The main criticism of the sovereign immunity rationale is different. Congress may withhold the U.S.'s consent to suit, to be sure. But when Congress does authorize a public rights claim to proceed, can it also preclude all Article III jurisdiction over that claim and set up a court that may be structured to favor the government's interests? To assign jurisdiction over a public rights claim to a court (or agency) lacking structural guarantees of independence and impartiality is arguably to impose an unconstitutional condition on the exercise of a federal right. Is it sufficient to satisfy any constitutional concerns that an Article III court exercises some form of appellate review over the decisions of non-Article III courts?

A final rationale is practical. There simply is not enough capacity in the Article III courts to adjudicate the vast number of public rights cases. Congress can create new Article III judgeships, to be sure, but it has been unwilling or unable to do so since 1990. This approach would also deprive Congress of the power to adapt the number and type of judges and courts to changing circumstances since Article III judges can only be removed by impeachment.

C. CONGRESSIONAL POWER TO HAVE STATE COURTS DECIDE FEDERAL LAW MATTERS

When Congress creates a statute, it may grant exclusive jurisdiction to federal courts to resolve those issues. This phenomenon is described in more detail in Chapter 2. Outside of those contexts, however, federal and state courts have concurrent jurisdiction over federal claims. This outcome is, in some respects, an outgrowth of constitutional design. As Alexander Hamilton described in Federalist No. 82, state tribunals generally retain their "pre-existing" authority to hear cases grounded in federal law. This role for state courts is an important feature in the development of federal law. The Constitution has never been read to require that Congress bestow inferior federal courts with every head of jurisdicition enumerated in Article III. Indeed, for most of the nineteenth century, until the Judiciary Act of 1875, federal inferior courts were not authorized to entertain most suits grounded in federal questions. Before that Act, then, state courts were the primary site of most suits rooted in federal questions. Moreover, shortly after federal courts were granted federal question jurisdiction, the Supreme Court expressly affirmed that state courts would also continue to have the authority to entertain federal claims. *Claflin v. Houseman* (1876). As late as 1953, the year before *Brown v. Board of Education* (1954), Professor Henry Hart called state courts the "primary guarantors of constitutional rights."[32]

While state courts *can* hear most federal questions, a related question is whether they *must*. For a period in the 1800s, the answer was "no," as exemplified by the case of *Prigg v. Pennsylvania* (1842). That case involved a Black woman named Margeret Morgan, who lived with her family in Pennsylvania in the 1830s. In 1837, three men entered her home and kidnapped her and her children, taking them to Maryland to be enslaved; the men claimed that Morgan was legally owned by a White family in that state. And while Pennsylvania had created a procedure that allowed individuals to obtain warrants for legally sanctioned kidnappings of enslaved persons, the men who seized Morgan had no such warrant. A magistrate had refused to issue one on the ground that Morgan and her kids were legally free.

The kidnappers were subsequently convicted under an 1826 Pennsylvania statute that prohibited the forcible removal of Blacks from the state with the intention of selling or enslaving them. But in *Prigg*—which one noted commentator has called arguably "the worst Supreme Court decision ever issued"[33]—the

---

32. Henry M. Hart, Jr., *The Power of Congress to Limit the Jurisdiction of Federal Courts: An Exercise in Dialectic*, 66 HARV. L. REV. 1362, 1401 (1953).

33. Jamal Greene, *The Anticanon*, 125 HARV. L. REV. 379 (2011). For another excellent description and analysis of *Prigg*, see Paul Finkelman, *Story Telling on the Supreme Court: Prigg v. Pennsylvania and Justice Joseph Story's Judicial Nationalism*, 1994 SUP. CT. REV. 247 (1994).

Court reversed the conviction, finding that the Pennsylvania kidnapping statute was unconstitutional. The Court held that the Pennsylvania law conflicted with the Fugitive Slave Clause of Article IV and Fugitive Slave Act of 1793. Those two federal mandates facilitated the forced return of enslaved persons from free states to slave states.

In reaching this tragic conclusion, the Court relied in part on the view that state courts had no obligation to enforce federal law.[34] Pennsylvania's argument before the Court had showcased its state judicial procedures, which allowed magistrates to issue warrants to enslavers to legally capture Black Americans. According to Pennsylvania, this demonstrated that Pennsylvania law was consistent with the federal law. The Court rejected Pennsylvania's defense, however, on the ground that Pennyslvania's warrant process could not be relied upon to protect federal law. Since "every state is perfectly competent, and has the exclusive right, . . . to deny jurisdiction over cases, which its own policy and its own institutions either prohibit or discountenance, there was no guarantee that state judicial officials could be relied on to exercise any of the authority that Congress might properly choose to give them." *Prigg*. "[T]he States cannot . . . be compelled to enforce" federal law. *Id.* Thus, Pennsylvania's promises of state judicial cooperation were unenforceable.

The view that state courts may decline to entertain federal law, however, faded from Supremacy Clause doctrine following the Civil War. Under prevailing jurisprudence today, the Supremacy Clause imposes at least two limits upon states' power to refuse to hear such claims.[35]

First, state courts may not discriminate against federal claims. *See Mondou v. New York, N.H. & H.R. Co.* (1912) ("We conclude that rights arising under the act in question may be enforced, as of right, in the courts of the states when their jurisdiction, as prescribed by local laws, is adequate to the occasion."); *McKnett v. St. Louis & S.F. Ry. Co.* (1934) ("[T]he Federal Constitution prohibits state courts of general jurisdiction from refusing to [exercise jurisdiction] solely because the suit is brought under a federal law.). Both *Mondou* and *McKnett* involved refusals by state courts to hear cases brought under the Federal Employers' Liability Act. Passed in 1908, that law creates a cause of action for railroad workers to sue when injured on the job when the railroad's negligence (or partial negligence) caused the injury. In both cases, the Supreme Court held that state courts could not discrimate against federal claims if those same courts entertain analogous state law suits.

Second, a state law "rule cannot be used as a device to undermine federal law, no matter how evenhanded it may appear." *Haywood v. Drown* (2009). This principle originally developed in cases in which state courts applied procedural rules that also applied to state law claims. *See Howlett v. Rose* (1990) (finding that a statute granting sovereign immunity to all state officials unduly interfered with federal constitutional Section 1983 suits against state officials); *Felder v. Casey* (1988) (finding that a 120-day notice-of-claim rule for suits against state officials unduly

---

34. Michael G. Collins, *Article III Cases, State Court Duties, and the Madisonian Compromise*, 1995 Wis. L. Rev. 39, 147 (1995) (analyzing this aspect of the Court's reasoning in *Prigg* and concluding that it was "extreme").

35. *See* Martin H. Redish & John E. Muench, *Adjudication of Federal Causes of Action in State Court*, 75 Mich. L. Rev. 311 (1976).

obstructed federal constitutional Section 1983 litigation against state officials). *Dice v. Akron, Canton & Youngstown R. Co.* (1952) (a release of FELA liability is void if induced by "deliberately false statements of the railroad's representatives made to deceive the employee"; even if validity of releases of liability is a question of equity under Ohio law, and therefore subject to a bench trial, in a FELA case, the plaintiff has the right to a jury trial; that right is "too substantial a part of the rights accorded by [FELA] to permit it to be classified as a mere "local rule of procedure for denial in [this] manner"); *Bailey v. Central Vt. Ry., Inc.* (1943) (the right to trial by jury is "part and parcel of the remedy afforded railroad workers under" FELA; reversing directed verdict for defendant). In *Haywood*, the Court struck down a state statute that divested New York's courts of general jurisdiction from entertaining civil rights suits against corrections officers. The Court explained, "[a]lthough §1983, a Reconstruction-era statute, was passed to interpose the federal courts between the States and the people, as guardians of the people's federal rights, state courts as well as federal courts are entrusted with providing a forum for the vindication of federal rights violated by state or local officials acting under color of state law."

Both of these principles are explored in greater detail below.

1.   Discrimination Against Federal Claims

The leading case for the proposition that states have a general duty to entertain federal law claims is *Testa v. Katt* (1947). "*Testa* stands for the proposition that state courts cannot refuse to apply federal law—a conclusion mandated by the terms of the Supremacy Clause." *Printz v. United States* (1997). At issue in *Testa* was a New Deal-era statute called the Emergency Price Control Act of 1942, which created temporary limits on the costs of certain goods and services as a means of controlling and mitigating inflation to support the economy in the midst of World War II. The Act allowed for treble damages for prevailing plaintiffs who demonstrated that sellers violated these limits. But the Rhode Island Supreme Court refused to enforce the Act, declining to exercise jurisdiction over a federal "penal" law. In the opinion that follows, the U.S. Supreme Court reversed.

Testa v. Katt

330 U.S. 386 (1947)

Mr. Justice BLACK delivered the opinion of the Court.

Section 205(e) of the Emergency Price Control Act provides that a buyer of goods above the prescribed ceiling price may sue the seller "in any court of competent jurisdiction" for not more than three times the amount of the overcharge plus costs and a reasonable attorney's fee. Section 205(c) provides that federal district courts shall have jurisdiction of such suits "concurrently with State and Territorial courts." Such a suit under §205(e) must be brought "in the district or county in which the defendant resides or has a place of business * * *."

The respondent was in the automobile business in Providence, Providence County, Rhode Island. In 1944 he sold an automobile to petitioner Testa, who also resides in Providence, for $1100, $210 above the ceiling price. The petitioner later filed this suit against respondent in the State District Court in Providence. Recovery was sought under §205(e). The court awarded a judgment of treble damages and costs to petitioner. On appeal to the State Superior Court, where the trial was de novo, the petitioner was again awarded judgment, but only for the amount of the overcharge plus attorney's fees. Pending appeal from this judgment, the Price Administrator was allowed to intervene. On appeal, the State Supreme Court reversed. It interpreted §205(e) to be "a penal statute in the international sense." It held that an action for violation of §205(e) could not be maintained in the courts of that State. Whether state courts may decline to enforce federal laws on these grounds is a question of great importance. For this reason, and because the Rhode Island Supreme Court's holding was alleged to conflict with this Court's previous holding in *Mondou v. New York, N.H. & H.R. Co.*, 223 U.S. 1 (1912), we granted certiorari.

For the purposes of this case, we assume, without deciding, that §205(e) is a penal statute in the "public international," "private international," or any other sense. So far as the question of whether the Rhode Island courts properly declined to try this action, it makes no difference into which of these categories the Rhode Island court chose to place the statute which Congress has passed. For we cannot accept the basic premise on which the Rhode Island Supreme Court held that it has no more obligation to enforce a valid penal law of the United States than it has to enforce a penal law of another state or a foreign country. Such a broad assumption flies in the face of the fact that the States of the Union constitute a nation. It disregards the purpose and effect of Article VI, §2 of the Constitution which provides: "This Constitution, and the Laws of the United States which shall be made in Pursuance thereof; and all Treaties made, or which shall be made, under the Authority of the United States, shall be the supreme Law of the Land; and the Judges in every State shall be bound thereby, any Thing in the Constitution or Laws of any State to the Contrary notwithstanding."

It cannot be assumed, the supremacy clause considered, that the responsibilities of a state to enforce the laws of a sister state are identical with its responsibilities to enforce federal laws. Such an assumption represents an erroneous evaluation of the statutes of Congress and the prior decisions of this Court in their historic setting. Those decisions establish that state courts do not bear the same relation to the United States that they do to foreign countries. The first Congress that convened after the Constitution was adopted conferred jurisdiction upon the state courts to enforce important federal civil laws,[4] and succeeding Congresses conferred on the states jurisdiction over federal crimes and actions for penalties and forfeitures.

Enforcement of federal laws by state courts did not go unchallenged. Violent public controversies existed throughout the first part of the Nineteenth Century until the 1860's concerning the extent of the constitutional supremacy of the Federal Government. During that period there were instances in which this Court and state courts broadly questioned the power and duty of state courts to exercise their jurisdiction to enforce United States civil and penal statutes or the power of the

---

4. Judiciary Act of 1789, 1 Stat. 73, 77 (suits by aliens for torts committed in violation of federal laws and treaties; suits by the United States).

Federal Government to require them to do so. But after the fundamental issues over the extent of federal supremacy had been resolved by war, this Court took occasion in 1876 to review the phase of the controversy concerning the relationship of state courts to the Federal Government. *Claflin v. Houseman* (1876). The opinion of a unanimous court in that case was strongly buttressed by historic references and persuasive reasoning. It repudiated the assumption that federal laws can be considered by the states as though they were laws emanating from a foreign sovereign. Its teaching is that the Constitution and the laws passed pursuant to it are the supreme laws of the land, binding alike upon states, courts, and the people, "anything in the Constitution or Laws of any State to the contrary notwithstanding." It asserted that the obligation of states to enforce these federal laws is not lessened by reason of the form in which they are cast or the remedy which they provide. And the Court stated that "If an act of Congress gives a penalty to a party aggrieved, without specifying a remedy for its enforcement, there is no reason why it should not be enforced, if not provided otherwise by some act of Congress, by a proper action in a state court."

The *Claflin* opinion thus answered most of the arguments theretofore advanced against the power and duty of state courts to enforce federal penal laws. And since that decision, the remaining areas of doubt have been steadily narrowed. There have been statements in cases concerned with the obligation of states to give full faith and credit to the proceedings of sister states which suggested a theory contrary to that pronounced in the *Claflin* opinion. But when in *Mondou v. New York, N.H. & H.R. Co.* (1912), this Court was presented with a case testing the power and duty of states to enforce federal laws, it found the solution in the broad principles announced in the *Claflin* opinion.

The precise question in the *Mondou* case was whether rights arising under the Federal Employers' Liability Act could "be enforced, as of right, in the courts of the states when their jurisdiction, as prescribed by local laws, is adequate to the occasion. . . ." The Supreme Court of Connecticut had decided that they could not. Except for the penalty feature, the factors it considered and its reasoning were strikingly similar to that on which the Rhode Island Supreme Court declined to enforce the federal law here involved [*e.g.*, that FELA departed from common law rules such as the fellow-servant rule, contributory negligence, and assumption of risk]. But this Court held that the Connecticut court could not decline to entertain the action. The contention that enforcement of the congressionally created right was contrary to Connecticut policy was answered as follows:

> The suggestion that the act of Congress is not in harmony with the policy of the State, and therefore that the courts of the state are free to decline jurisdiction, is quite inadmissible, because it presupposes what in legal contemplation does not exist. When Congress, in the exertion of the power confided to it by the Constitution, adopted that act, it spoke for all the people and all the states, and thereby established a policy for all. That policy is as much the policy of Connecticut as if the act had emanated from its own legislature, and should be respected accordingly in the courts of the state.

Mondou v. New York, N.H. & H.R. Co. (1912).

So here, the fact that Rhode Island has an established policy against enforcement by its courts of statutes of other states and the United States which it deems penal, cannot be accepted as a "valid excuse." *Cf. Douglas v. N.Y.N.H.R.* (1929). For the policy of the federal Act is the prevailing policy in every state. Thus, in a case which chiefly relied upon the *Claflin* and *Mondou* precedents, this Court stated that a state court cannot "refuse to enforce the right arising from the law of the United States because of conceptions of impolicy or want of wisdom on the part of Congress in having called into play its lawful powers." *Minneapolis & St. L. R. Co. v. Bombolis* (1916).

Our question concerns only the right of a state to deny enforcement to claims growing out of a valid federal law.

It is conceded that this same type of claim arising under Rhode Island law would be enforced by that State's courts. Its courts have enforced claims for double damages growing out of the Fair Labor Standards Act. Thus the Rhode Island courts have jurisdiction adequate and appropriate under established local law to adjudicate this action. Under these circumstances the State courts are not free to refuse enforcement of petitioners' claim. *See McKnett v. St. Louis & S.F. R. Co.* (1934) *and compare Herb v. Pitcairn* (1995). The case is reversed and the cause is remanded for proceedings not inconsistent with this opinion.

* * *

Although *Testa* involves the Emergency Price Contol Act, the two most common areas in which the Supreme Court has addressed the duty of state courts sitting in concurrent jurisdiction over federal claims are the Federal Employees Liability Act and §1983 civil rights suits. FELA provides a federal cause of action to injured railroad workers. Passed in 1908, it was designed to displace state common law tort doctrine that had, for decades in the late nineteenth and early twentieth centuries, been used by state courts to deny relief to railroad workers—often by judges who were themselves former corporate railroad lawyers. The core purpose of the statute was to create more plaintiff-favorable substantive law to ensure proper compensation of workers for their injuries sustained in workplace accidents. Thus, for example, it eliminated the fellow-servant rule, contributory negligence and assumption of risk, all doctrines which were prevalent in state tort law, and it relaxed the standard of causation. Concurrent jurisdiction was an important feature of FELA as well, making local state courts available instead of forcing injured plaintiffs to file and appear in often distant federal courthouses. State judges and legislatures, however, remained keen to see state tort law prevail. Hence a series of cases reached the Court raising the question whether and on what circumstances a State could deny jurisdiction of FELA claims or otherwise deviate from its plaintiff-favorable provisions in exercising jurisdiction.

Notice, as example, that the principal case relied upon by the Court in *Testa* is *Mondou*—a FELA case in which the courts of Connecticut read the federal statute as "not in harmony" with the policies of its common law. Several other principal cases relied upon in *Testa* are also FELA cases. *See McKnett* (reversing Alabama state court's dismissal of FELA claim for want of jurisdiction; Alabama law provided subject matter jurisdiction in its courts over causes of action against a foreign corporation for a tort arising in another state but Alabama courts refused to entertain FELA cases of this kind: "While Congress has not attempted to compel the states to provide courts for the enforcement of FELA, the Federal Constitution prohibits state courts of general jurisdiction from refusing to do so because the suit is brought under federal law. The denial of jurisdiction by the Alabama court is based solely upon the source of law sought to be enforced. . . . A state may not discriminate against rights arising under federal laws"); *Herb* ("It would not be open for us to say that the state in setting up a [city] court could not limit its jurisdiction to actions arising within the city for which it is established."); *Bombolis* (distinguishing *Mondou* and holding that state's non-unanimity rule allowing party to prevail by 5/6ths vote of jury if, after twelve hours jury cannot reach a unanimous verdict, may be applied to FELA claim; Seventh Amendment, which requires unanimity, applies only in federal courts).

The second major category of cases in which concurrent jurisdiction has been resisted by state courts is §1983 litigation. The next case discusses earlier precedent in the context of a New York statute drafted to limit civil rights damages suits by state prisoners. Although the rate of imprisonment in New York began to fall in the first decade of the twenty-first century after an increase paralleling the trend of mass incarceration across the country in the late twentieth century, the state's per capita incarceration rate in 2021 still exceeded that of every industrialized nation other than the United States.[36] Prison condition litigation increased with the increase in the prison population. Believing many suits against corrections officers to be frivolous, the state legislature imposed procedural and remedial limitations on them. A distinguishing feature of the statute, relative to *Testa* as well as earlier §1983 and FELA cases, is that it imposed these limitations not only on federal §1983 claims, but on their state analogue, to avoid the charge that the law discriminated against a federal cause of action. As you read the case, pay close attention to how the majority deals with this aspect of the statute.

Haywood v. Drown

556 U.S. 729 (2009)

Justice STEVENS delivered the opinion of the Court.

In our federal system of government, state as well as federal courts have jurisdiction over suits brought pursuant to 42 U.S.C. §1983, the statute that creates a remedy for violations of federal rights committed by persons acting under color of state law. While that rule is generally applicable to New York's supreme courts — the State's trial courts of general jurisdiction — New York's Correction Law §24 divests those courts of jurisdiction over §1983 suits that seek money damages from correction officers. New York thus prohibits the trial courts that generally exercise jurisdiction over §1983 suits brought against other state officials from hearing virtually all such suits brought against state correction officers. The question presented is whether that exceptional treatment of a limited category of §1983 claims is consistent with the Supremacy Clause of the United States Constitution.

---

36. *New York Profile*, PRISON POLICY INITIATIVE, https://www.prisonpolicy.org/profiles/NY.html.

I

Petitioner, an inmate in New York's Attica Correctional Facility, commenced two §1983 actions against several correction employees alleging that they violated his civil rights in connection with three prisoner disciplinary proceedings and an altercation. Proceeding *pro se*, petitioner filed his claims in State Supreme Court and sought punitive damages and attorney's fees. The trial court dismissed the actions on the ground that, under N.Y. Correct. Law Ann. §24 (West 1987) (hereinafter Correction Law §24), it lacked jurisdiction to entertain any suit arising under state or federal law seeking money damages from correction officers for actions taken in the scope of their employment. The intermediate appellate court summarily affirmed the trial court.

The New York Court of Appeals, by a 4-to-3 vote, also affirmed the dismissal of petitioner's damages action. The Court of Appeals rejected petitioner's argument that Correction Law §24's jurisdictional limitation interfered with §1983 and therefore ran afoul of the Supremacy Clause of the United States Constitution. The majority reasoned that, because Correction Law §24 treats state and federal damages actions against correction officers equally (that is, neither can be brought in New York courts), the statute should be properly characterized as a "neutral state rule regarding the administration of the courts" and therefore a "valid excuse" for the State's refusal to entertain the federal cause of action. The majority understood our Supremacy Clause precedents to set forth the general rule that so long as a State does not refuse to hear a federal claim for the "sole reason that the cause of action arises under federal law," its withdrawal of jurisdiction will be deemed constitutional. So read, discrimination *vel non* is the focal point of Supremacy Clause analysis.

In dissent, Judge Jones argued that Correction Law §24 is not a neutral rule of judicial administration. Noting that the State's trial courts handle all other §1983 damages actions he concluded that the State had created courts of competent jurisdiction to entertain §1983 suits. In his view, "once a state opens its courts to hear section 1983 actions, it may not selectively exclude section 1983 actions by denominating state policies as jurisdictional."

Recognizing the importance of the question decided by the New York Court of Appeals, we granted certiorari. We now reverse.

II

Motivated by the belief that damages suits filed by prisoners against state correction officers were by and large frivolous and vexatious, New York passed Correction Law §24. The statute employs a two-step process to strip its courts of jurisdiction over such damages claims and to replace those claims with the State's preferred alternative. The provision states in full:

> 1. No civil action shall be brought in any court of the state, except by the attorney general on behalf of the state, against any officer or employee of the department, in his personal capacity, for damages arising out of any act done or the failure to perform any act within the scope of employment and in the discharge of the duties by such officer or employee.

2. Any claim for damages arising out of any act done or the failure to perform any act within the scope of employment and in the discharge of the duties of any officer or employee of the department shall be brought and maintained in the court of claims as a claim against the state.

Thus, under this scheme, a prisoner seeking damages from a correction officer will have his claim dismissed for want of jurisdiction and will be left, instead, to pursue a claim for damages against an entirely different party (the State) in the Court of Claims—a court of limited jurisdiction.[4]

For prisoners seeking redress, pursuing the Court of Claims alternative comes with strict conditions. In addition to facing a different defendant, plaintiffs in that court are not provided with the same relief, or the same procedural protections, made available in §1983 actions brought in state courts of general jurisdiction. Specifically, under New York law, plaintiffs in the Court of Claims must comply with a 90-day notice requirement, Court of Claims Act §9; are not entitled to a jury trial, §12; have no right to attorney's fees, §27; and may not seek punitive damages or injunctive relief.

We must decide whether Correction Law §24, as applied to §1983 claims, violates the Supremacy Clause.

III

This Court has long made clear that federal law is as much the law of the several States as are the laws passed by their legislatures. Federal and state law "together form one system of jurisprudence, which constitutes the law of the land for the State; and the courts of the two jurisdictions are not foreign to each other, nor to be treated by each other as such, but as courts of the same country, having jurisdiction partly different and partly concurrent." *Claflin v. Houseman* (1876); *Minneapolis & St. Louis R. Co. v. Bombolis* (1916); The Federalist No. 82, p. 132 (E. Bourne ed. 1947, Book II) (A. Hamilton) ("[T]he inference seems to be conclusive, that the State courts would have a concurrent jurisdiction in all cases arising under the laws of the Union, where it was not expressly prohibited"). Although §1983, a Reconstruction-era statute, was passed "to interpose the federal courts between the States and the people, as guardians of the people's federal rights," *Mitchum v. Foster* (1972), state courts as well as federal courts are entrusted with providing a forum for the vindication of federal rights violated by state or local officials acting under color of state law.

So strong is the presumption of concurrency that it is defeated only in two narrowly defined circumstances: first, when Congress expressly ousts state courts of jurisdiction; and second, "[w]hen a state court refuses jurisdiction because of a neutral state rule regarding the administration of the courts," *Howlett v. Rose* (1990). Focusing on the latter circumstance, we have emphasized that only a neutral jurisdictional rule will be deemed a "valid excuse" for departing from the default assumption that "state courts have inherent authority, and are thus presumptively

---

4. Although the State has waived its sovereign immunity from liability by allowing itself to be sued in the Court of Claims, a plaintiff seeking damages against the State in that court cannot use §1983 as a vehicle for redress because a State is not a "person" under §1983. *See Will v. Michigan Dept. of State Police*, 491 U.S. 58, 66 (1989).

competent, to adjudicate claims arising under the laws of the United States." *Tafflin* v. *Levitt* (1990).

In determining whether a state law qualifies as a neutral rule of judicial administration, our cases have established that a State cannot employ a jurisdictional rule "to dissociate [itself] from federal law because of disagreement with its content or a refusal to recognize the superior authority of its source." *Howlett*. In other words, although States retain substantial leeway to establish the contours of their judicial systems, they lack authority to nullify a federal right or cause of action they believe is inconsistent with their local policies. "The suggestion that [an] act of Congress is not in harmony with the policy of the State, and therefore that the courts of the State are free to decline jurisdiction, is quite inadmissible, because it presupposes what in legal contemplation does not exist." *Second Employers' Liability Cases* (1912).

It is principally on this basis that Correction Law §24 violates the Supremacy Clause. In passing Correction Law §24, New York made the judgment that correction officers should not be burdened with suits for damages arising out of conduct performed in the scope of their employment. Because it regards these suits as too numerous or too frivolous (or both), the State's longstanding policy has been to shield this narrow class of defendants from liability when sued for damages.[5]

The State's policy, whatever its merits, is contrary to Congress' judgment that *all* persons who violate federal rights while acting under color of state law shall be held liable for damages. As we have unanimously recognized, "[a] State may not . . . relieve congestion in its courts by declaring a whole category of federal claims to be frivolous. Until it has been proved that the claim has no merit, that judgment is not up to the States to make." *Howlett*, 496 U.S., at 380. That New York strongly favors a rule shielding correction officers from personal damages liability and substituting the State as the party responsible for compensating individual victims is irrelevant. The State cannot condition its enforcement of federal law on the demand that those individuals whose conduct federal law seeks to regulate must nevertheless escape liability.

---

5. In many respects, Correction Law §24 operates more as an immunity-from-damages provision than as a jurisdictional rule. Indeed, the original version of the statute gave correction officers qualified immunity, providing that no officer would be "liable for damages if he shall have acted in good faith, with reasonable care and upon probable cause." N. Y. Correct. Law. §6-b (McKinney Supp. 1947). And, more recently, a state legislative proposal seeking to extend Correction Law §24's scheme to other state employees explained that its purpose was to grant "the same immunity from civil damage actions as all other State employees who work in the prisons." In *Howlett v. Rose* (1990), we considered the question whether a Florida school board could assert a state-law immunity defense in a §1983 action brought in state court when the defense would not have been available if the action had been brought in federal court. We unanimously held that the State's decision to extend immunity "over and above [that which is] already provided in §1983 . . . directly violates federal law," and explained that the "elements of, and the defenses to, a federal cause of action are defined by federal law." Thus, if Correction Law §24 were understood as offering an immunity defense, *Howlett* would compel the conclusion that it violates the Supremacy Clause.

IV

While our cases have uniformly applied the principle that a State cannot simply refuse to entertain a federal claim based on a policy disagreement, we have yet to confront a statute like New York's that registers its dissent by divesting its courts of jurisdiction over a disfavored federal claim in addition to an identical state claim. The New York Court of Appeals' holding was based on the misunderstanding that this equal treatment of federal and state claims rendered Correction Law §24 constitutional. To the extent our cases have created this misperception, we now make clear that equality of treatment does not ensure that a state law will be deemed a neutral rule of judicial administration and therefore a valid excuse for refusing to entertain a federal cause of action.

Respondents correctly observe that, in the handful of cases in which this Court has found a valid excuse, the state rule at issue treated state and federal claims equally. In *Douglas v. New York, N.H. & H.R. Co.* (1929), we upheld a state law that granted state courts discretion to decline jurisdiction over state and federal claims alike when neither party was a resident of the State. Later, in *Herb v. Pitcairn* (1945), a city court dismissed an action brought under the Federal Employers' Liability Act (FELA), for want of jurisdiction because the cause of action arose outside the court's territorial jurisdiction. We upheld the dismissal on the ground that the State's venue laws were not being applied in a way that discriminated against the federal claim. In a third case, *Missouri ex rel. Southern R. Co. v. Mayfield* (1950), we held that a State's application of the *forum non conveniens* doctrine to bar adjudication of a FELA case brought by nonresidents was constitutionally sound as long as the policy was enforced impartially. And our most recent decision finding a valid excuse, *Johnson v. Fankell* (1997), rested largely on the fact that Idaho's rule limiting interlocutory jurisdiction did not discriminate against §1983 actions.

Although the absence of discrimination is necessary to our finding a state law neutral, it is not sufficient. A jurisdictional rule cannot be used as a device to undermine federal law, no matter how evenhanded it may appear. As we made clear in *Howlett*, "[t]he fact that a rule is denominated jurisdictional does not provide a court an excuse to avoid the obligation to enforce federal law if the rule does not reflect the concerns of power over the person and competence over the subject matter that jurisdictional rules are designed to protect." Ensuring equality of treatment is thus the beginning, not the end, of the Supremacy Clause analysis.

In addition to giving too much weight to equality of treatment, respondents mistakenly treat this case as implicating the "great latitude [States enjoy] to establish the structure and jurisdiction of their own courts." Although Correction Law §24 denies state courts authority to entertain damages actions against correction officers, this case does not require us to decide whether Congress may compel a State to offer a forum, otherwise unavailable under state law, to hear suits brought pursuant to §1983. The State of New York has made this inquiry unnecessary by creating courts of general jurisdiction that routinely sit to hear analogous §1983 actions. New York's constitution vests the state supreme courts with general original jurisdiction, N.Y. Const., Art. VI, §7(a), and the "inviolate authority to hear and resolve all causes in law and equity." For instance, if petitioner had attempted to sue a police officer for damages under §1983, the suit would be properly adjudicated by a state supreme court. Similarly, if petitioner had sought declaratory or injunctive relief against a correction officer, that suit would be heard in a state supreme court. It is only a particular species of suits—those seeking damages relief against correction officers—that the State deems inappropriate for its trial courts.[6]

We therefore hold that, having made the decision to create courts of general jurisdiction that regularly sit to entertain analogous suits, New York is not at liberty to shut the courthouse door to federal claims that it considers at odds with its local policy. A State's authority to organize its courts, while considerable, remains subject to the strictures of the Constitution. *See, e.g., McKnett v. St. Louis & San Francisco R. Co.* (1934). We have never treated a State's invocation of "jurisdiction" as a trump that ends the Supremacy Clause inquiry, *see Howlett,* and we decline to do so in this case. Because New York's supreme courts generally have personal jurisdiction over the parties in §1983 suits brought by prisoners against correction officers and because they hear the lion's share of all other §1983 actions, we find little concerning "power over the person and competence over the subject matter" in Correction Law §24.

V

The judgment of the New York Court of Appeals is reversed, and the case is remanded to that court for further proceedings not inconsistent with this opinion.

Justice THOMAS, with whom THE CHIEF JUSTICE, Justice SCALIA, and Justice ALITO join as to Part III, dissenting.

Because neither the Constitution nor our precedent requires New York to open its courts to §1983 federal actions, I respectfully dissent.

I

Although the majority decides this case on the basis of the Supremacy Clause, the proper starting point is Article III of the Constitution. The history of the drafting and ratification of this Article establishes that it leaves untouched the States' plenary authority to decide whether their local courts will have subject-matter jurisdiction over federal causes of action.

The text of Article III reflects the Framers' agreement that the National Government needed a Supreme Court. There was sharp disagreement at the Philadelphia Convention, however, over the need for lower federal courts. Several of the Framers, most notably James Madison, favored a strong central government that included

---

6. While we have looked to a State's "common-law tort analogues" in deciding whether a state procedural rule is neutral, *see Felder v. Casey* (1988), we have never equated "analogous claims" with "identical claims." Instead, we have searched for a similar claim under state law to determine whether a State has established courts of adequate and appropriate jurisdiction capable of hearing a §1983 suit. *See Testa v. Katt* (1947); *Martinez v. California* (1980) ("[W]here the same type of claim, if arising under state law, would be enforced in the state courts, the state courts are generally not free to refuse enforcement of the federal claim"). Section 1983 damages claims against other state officials and equitable claims against correction officers are both sufficiently analogous to petitioner's §1983 claims.

lower federal tribunals. Under the Virginia Plan, the Constitution would have established a "National Judiciary . . . to consist of one or more supreme tribunals, and of inferior tribunals to be chosen by the National Legislature." 1 Records of the Federal Convention of 1787, p. 21 (M. Farrand ed. 1911). A revised version of the proposal, which stated that the National Judiciary would "'consist of One supreme tribunal, and of one or more inferior tribunals,'" was approved on June 4, 1787.

The following day, however, John Rutledge raised an objection to "establishing any national tribunal except a single supreme one." He proposed striking the language providing for the creation of lower federal courts because state courts were "most proper" for deciding "all cases in the first instance." According to Rutledge, "the right of appeal to the supreme national tribunal [was] sufficient to secure the national rights [and] uniformity of Judgm[en]ts," and the lower federal courts were thus an "unnecessary encroachment" on the sovereign prerogative of the States to adjudicate federal claims. Madison nonetheless defended the Virginia Plan. He countered that "inferior [federal] tribunals . . . dispersed throughout the Republic" were necessary to meet the needs of the newly formed government: "An effective Judiciary establishment commensurate to the legislative authority [is] essential. A Government without a proper Executive [and] Judiciary would be the mere trunk of a body without arms or legs to act or move." But despite Madison's objections, Rutledge's motion prevailed.

Madison and James Wilson soon thereafter proposed alternative language that "'empowered [Congress] to institute inferior tribunals.'" This version moderated the original Virginia Plan because of the "distinction between establishing such tribunals absolutely, and giving a discretion to the Legislature to establish or not establish [inferior federal courts]." Over continued objections that such courts were an unnecessary expense and an affront to the States, the scaled-back version of the Virginia Plan passed.

On June 15, 1787, however, the New Jersey Plan was introduced. Although it did not directly challenge the decision to permit Congress to "institute" inferior federal courts, the plan, among other things, required state courts to adjudicate federal claims. . . .

The introduction of the New Jersey Plan reignited the debate over the need for lower federal courts. In light of the plan's provision for mandatory state-court jurisdiction over federal claims, Pierce Butler "could see no necessity for such tribunals." Luther Martin added that lower federal courts would "create jealousies [and] oppositions in the State tribunals, with the jurisdiction of which they will interfere." But Nathaniel Ghorum responded that inferior federal tribunals were "essential to render the authority of the Nat[ional] Legislature effectual." Edmund Randolph bluntly argued that "the Courts of the States can not be trusted with the administration of the National laws." George Mason suggested that, at the very least, "many circumstances might arise not now to be foreseen, which might render such a power absolutely necessary." Roger Sherman also "was willing to give the power to the Legislature," even though he "wished them to make use of the State Tribunals whenever it could be done . . . with safety to the general interest."

At the conclusion of this debate, the New Jersey Plan, including its component requiring state-court consideration of federal claims, was defeated and the Madison-Wilson proposal was . . . amended . . . to its current form in Article III, which gives Congress the power to "ordain and establish" inferior federal courts.

. . . The assumption that state courts would continue to exercise concurrent jurisdiction over federal claims was essential to this compromise. *See* The Federalist No. 82, pp. 130, 132 (E. Bourne ed. 1947) (A. Hamilton) ("[T]he inference seems to be conclusive, that the State courts would have a concurrent jurisdiction in all cases arising under the laws of the Union, where it was not expressly prohibited"). In light of that historical understanding, this Court has held that, absent an Act of Congress providing for exclusive jurisdiction in the lower federal courts, the "state courts have inherent authority, and are thus presumptively competent, to adjudicate claims arising under the laws of the United States." *Tafflin v. Levitt* (1990).

The Constitution's implicit preservation of state authority to entertain federal claims, however, did not impose a duty on state courts to do so. . . .

The earliest decisions addressing this question, written by then-serving and future Supreme Court Justices, confirm that state courts remain "tribunals over which the government of the Union has no adequate control, and which may be closed to any claim asserted under a law of the United States." *Osborn v. Bank of United States* (1824); *see also Stearns v. United States* (DC Vt. 1835) (Thompson, J.) (Article III does not give Congress authority to "compel a state court to entertain jurisdiction in any case; they are not inferior courts in the sense of the constitution; they are not ordained by congress. State courts are left to consult their own duty from their own state authority and organization"). "The states, in providing their own judicial tribunals, have a right to limit, control, and restrict their judicial functions, and jurisdiction, according to their own mere pleasure." *Mitchell v. Great Works Milling & Mfg. Co.* (CCD Me. 1843) (Story, J.). In short, there was "a very clear intimation given by the judges of the Supreme Court, that the state courts were not bound in consequence of any act of congress, to assume and exercise jurisdiction in such cases. It was merely permitted to them to do so as far, as was compatible with their state obligations."

Under our federal system, therefore, the States have unfettered authority to determine whether their local courts may entertain a federal cause of action. Once a State exercises its sovereign prerogative to deprive its courts of subject-matter jurisdiction over a federal cause of action, it is the end of the matter as far as the Constitution is concerned.

The present case can be resolved under this principle alone. . . . Because New York's decision to withdraw jurisdiction over §1983 damages actions — or indeed, over any claims — does not offend the Constitution, the judgment below should be affirmed.

II

The Court has evaded Article III's limitations by finding that the Supremacy Clause constrains the States' authority to define the subject-matter jurisdiction of their own courts. . . . There is no textual or historical support for the Court's incorporation of this antidiscrimination principle into the Supremacy Clause.

A

1

The Supremacy Clause provides that . . . a valid federal law is substantively superior to a state law; "if a state measure conflicts with a federal requirement, the state provision must give way." *Swift & Co. v. Wickham* (1965). As a textual matter, however, the Supremacy Clause does not address whether a state court must entertain a federal cause of action; it provides only a rule of decision that the state court must follow if it adjudicates the claim. *See* R. BERGER, CONGRESS V. THE SUPREME COURT 245 (1969) (The Supremacy Clause only "'enacts what the law shall be'. . . . [I]t defines the governing 'supreme law,' and *if* a State court *has* jurisdiction, it commands that that law shall govern").

The Supremacy Clause's path to adoption at the Convention confirms this focus. Its precursor was introduced as part of the New Jersey Plan. . . .

After the adoption of the Madisonian Compromise and the defeat of the New Jersey Plan, the Framers returned to the question of federal supremacy. A proposal was introduced granting Congress the power to "'negative all laws passed by the several States (contravening in the opinion of [Congress] the articles of Union, or any treaties subsisting under the authority of [Congress]).'" James Madison believed the proposal "essential to the efficacy [and] security of the [federal] Gov[ernmen]t." But others at the Convention, including Roger Sherman, "thought it unnecessary, as the Courts of the States would not consider as valid any law contravening the Authority of the Union, and which the legislature would wish to be negatived." In the end, Madison's proposal was defeated. But as a substitute for that rejected proposal, Luther Martin resurrected the Supremacy Clause provision from the New Jersey Plan and it was unanimously approved.

This historical record makes clear that the Supremacy Clause's exclusive function is to disable state laws that are substantively inconsistent with federal law—not to require state courts to hear federal claims over which the courts lack jurisdiction. This was necessarily the case when the clause was first introduced as part of the New Jersey Plan, as it included a separate provision to confront the jurisdictional question. Had that plan prevailed and been ratified by the States, construing the Supremacy Clause to address state-court jurisdiction would have rendered the separate jurisdictional component of the New Jersey Plan mere surplusage.

The Supremacy Clause's exclusive focus on substantive state law is also evident from the context in which it was revived. First, the Clause was not adopted until after the New Jersey Plan's rejection, as part of the entirely separate debate over Madison's proposal to grant Congress the power to "negative" the laws of the States. By then, the Framers had already adopted Article III, thereby ending the fight over state-court jurisdiction. The question before the Convention thus was not which courts (state or federal) were best suited to adjudicate federal claims, but which branch of government (Congress or the courts) would be most effective in vindicating the substantive superiority of federal law. The Supremacy Clause was directly responsive to that question.

Second, the timing of the Clause's adoption suggests that the Framers viewed it as achieving the same end as Madison's congressional "negative" proposal. Although Madison believed that Congress could most effectively countermand inconsistent state laws, the Framers decided that the Judiciary could adequately perform that function. There is no evidence that the Framers envisioned the Supremacy Clause as having a substantively broader sweep than the proposal it replaced. The Supremacy Clause does not require state courts to entertain federal causes of action. Rather, it only requires that in reaching the merits of such claims, state courts must decide the legal question in favor of the "law of the Land." Art. VI, cl. 2.

The supremacy of federal law, therefore, is not impugned by a State's decision to strip its local courts of subject-matter jurisdiction to hear certain federal claims. Subject-matter jurisdiction determines only whether a court has the power to entertain a particular claim—a condition precedent to reaching the merits of a legal dispute. . . . "The federal law in any field within which Congress is empowered to legislate is the supreme law of the land in the sense that it may supplant state legislation in that field, but not in the sense that it may supplant the existing rules of litigation in state courts. Congress has full power to provide its own courts for litigating federal rights. The state courts belong to the States." *Brown v. Gerdes* (1944) (Frankfurter, J., concurring).

2

The Court was originally faithful to this conception of federal supremacy. In *Claflin*, the Court was careful to also explain that the Constitution did not impose an obligation on the States to accept jurisdiction over such claims. *See Claflin* (explaining that there "is no reason why the State courts should not be open for the prosecution of rights growing out of the laws of the United States, to which their jurisdiction is competent, and not denied"). The Constitution instead left the States with the choice—but not the obligation—to entertain federal actions. . . .

It was not until five years after *Douglas* that the Court used the Supremacy Clause to strike down a state jurisdictional statute for its failure to permit state-court adjudication of federal claims. *See McKnett.*

For all the reasons identified above, *McKnett* cannot be reconciled with the decisions of this Court that preceded it. . . .

In *Testa*, the Court struck down the Rhode Island Supreme Court's refusal to entertain a claim under the federal Emergency Price Control Act. There was no dispute that "the Rhode Island courts [had] jurisdiction adequate and appropriate under established local law to adjudicate this action." . . .

Testa thus represents a routine application of the rule of law set forth in *Second Employers'*: As long as jurisdiction over a federal claim exists as a matter of state law, state-court judges cannot *sua sponte* refuse to enforce federal law because they disagree with Congress' decision to allow for adjudication of certain federal claims in state court.

In *Howlett*, the Court likewise correctly struck down a Florida Supreme Court decision affirming the dismissal of a §1983 suit on state-law sovereign immunity grounds. The Florida court had interpreted the State's statutory "waiver of sovereign immunity" not to extend to federal claims brought in state court. According to the state court, absent a statutory waiver, Florida's pre-existing common-law sovereign immunity rule provided a "blanket immunity on [state] governmental entities from federal civil rights actions under §1983" brought in Florida courts. Based on this rule, the Florida Supreme Court affirmed the dismissal with prejudice of the §1983 suit against the state officials. *See also Howlett v. Rose* (1989) (concluding that Florida's "common law immunity" rule barred "the use of its courts for suits against the state in those state courts").

Second, Florida's sovereign immunity rule violated the Supremacy Clause by operating as a state-law defense to a federal law. *See Martinez v. California* (1980) ("'[P]ermitt[ing] a state immunity defense to have controlling effect'" over a federal claim violates the Supremacy Clause). Resolving a federal claim with preclusive effect based on a state-law defense is far different from simply closing the door of the state courthouse to that federal claim. The first changes federal law by denying relief on the merits; the second merely dictates the forum in which the federal claim will be heard.

. . . To read the Supremacy Clause to include an anti-discrimination principle undermines the compromise that shaped Article III and contradicts the original understanding of Constitution. There is no justification for preserving such a principle.

B

NYCLA §24 does not conflict with §1983. . . . Moreover, Congress has created inferior federal courts that have the power to adjudicate all §1983 actions. And this Court has expressly determined that §1983 plaintiffs do not have to exhaust state-court remedies before proceeding in federal court.

Therefore, even if every state court closed its doors to §1983 plaintiffs, the plaintiffs could proceed with their claims in the federal forum. And because the dismissal of §1983 claims from state court pursuant to NYCLA §24 is for lack of subject-matter jurisdiction, it has no preclusive effect on claims refiled in federal court, *see Allen v. McCurry* (1980) (requiring "a final judgment on the merits" before a §1983 would be barred in federal court under the doctrine of claim preclusion), and thus does not alter the substance of the federal claim.

I cannot agree with the approach employed in *Felder* "that pre-empts state laws merely because they 'stand as an obstacle to the accomplishment and execution of the full purposes and objectives' of federal law . . . as perceived by this Court."

III

Even accepting the entirety of the Court's precedent in this area of the law, however, I still could not join the majority's resolution of this case as it mischaracterizes and broadens this Court's decisions.

The majority's assertion that jurisdictional neutrality is not the touchstone because "[a] jurisdictional rule cannot be used as a device to undermine federal law, no matter how even-handed it may appear," reflects a misunderstanding of the law. A jurisdictional statute simply deprives the relevant court of the power to decide the case altogether. *See* 10A C. WRIGHT, A. MILLER, & M. KANE, FEDERAL PRACTICE AND PROCEDURE §2713, p. 239 (3d ed. 1998) ("If the court has no jurisdiction, it has no power to enter a judgment on the merits and must dismiss the action"); Restatement (Second) of Judgments §11, p. 108 (1980) (defining subject-matter jurisdiction as a court's "authority to adjudicate the type of controversy involved in the action"). Such a statute necessarily operates without prejudice to the adjudication of the matter in a competent forum. Jurisdictional statutes therefore by definition are incapable of undermining federal law. NYCLA §24 no more undermines §1983 than the amount-in-controversy requirement for federal diversity jurisdiction undermines state law. The relevant law (state or federal) remains fully operative in both circumstances. The sole consequence of the jurisdictional barrier is that the law cannot be enforced in one particular judicial forum.

The States "remain independent and autonomous within their proper sphere of authority." *Printz v. United States* (1997). New York has the organic authority, therefore, to tailor the jurisdiction of state courts to meet its policy goals.

Unlike the Florida immunity rule in *Howlett*, NYCLA §24 is not a defense to a federal claim and the dismissal it authorizes is without prejudice. For this reason, NYCLA §24 is not merely "denominated" as jurisdictional — it actually is jurisdictional.

The Supremacy Clause does not fossilize the jurisdiction of state courts in their original form. Under this Court's precedent, States remain free to alter the structure of their judicial system even if that means certain federal causes of action will no longer be heard in state court, so long as States do so on nondiscriminatory terms. *See Printz* (explaining that "the States obviously regulate the 'ordinary jurisdiction' of their courts"); *Johnson v. Fankell* (1997) ("We have made it quite clear that it is a matter for each State to decide how to structure its judicial system"). Today's decision thus represents a dramatic and unwarranted expansion of this Court's precedent.

* * *

In *Testa* and *Mondou*, the state courts' hostility to federal law is clear. In *Haywood*, by contrast, the state targeted not only Section 1983 claims for money damages against corrections officers, but also the state law analogue cause of action. Consider what a state would have to do, after *Haywood*, to make a jurisdiction-limiting rule that the Court would deem neutral and uphold.

In a series of cases the Court has held that the federal government cannot "commandeer" state governments. *See, e.g., Printz v. United States* (1997) (Congress cannot require state and local law enforcement officers to conduct background checks for handgun purchases); *New York v. United States* (1992) (Congress cannot require states to take title of radioactive waste if they fail to timely dispose of it). Is the obligation on state courts to decide federal claims different?

Testa and *Haywood* address the question whether there are circumstances when the Constitution *requires* a state court to extend jurisdiction to and faithfully adjudicate federal rights. Are there circumstances when the Constitution *ousts* the state courts of jurisdiction — circumstances, that is, where the exercise of state court jurisdiction to interpret federal law or the actions of federal officers is so inconsistent with the Constitution's allocation of powers to the national government that state court jurisdiction cannot be tolerated? In the next case the Court prohibited state courts from exercising habeas jurisdiction over the U.S. Army's detention of an enlistee during Reconstruction — a power that state courts "routinely" exercised prior to the Civil War in cases involving federal executive detention.[37]

Tarble's Case

80 U.S. (13 Wall.) 397 (1871)

This was a proceeding on *habeas corpus* for the discharge of one Edward Tarble, held in the custody of a recruiting officer of the United States as an enlisted soldier, on the alleged ground that he was a minor, under the age of eighteen years at the time of his enlistment, and that he enlisted without the consent of his father.

The writ was issued on the 10th of August, 1869, by a court commissioner of Dane County, Wisconsin, an officer authorized by the laws of that State to issue the writ of *habeas corpus*. It was issued in this case upon the petition of the father of Tarble, in which he alleged that his son, who had enlisted under the name of Frank Brown, was confined and restrained of his liberty by Lieutenant Stone, of the United States army, in Madison, Wisconsin; that the cause of his confinement and restraint was that he had, on the 20th of the preceding July, enlisted, and been mustered into the military service of the United States; that he was under the age of eighteen years at the time of such enlistment; that the same was made without the knowledge, consent, or approval of the petitioner, and was therefore, as the petitioner was advised and believed, illegal, and that the petitioner was lawfully entitled to the custody, care, and services of his son.

The officer thereupon produced Tarble before the commissioner and made a return in writing to the writ protesting that the commissioner had no jurisdiction in the premises and stating that he, the officer, was a first lieutenant in the Army of the United States, and by due authority was detailed as a recruiting officer and had the custody and command of all soldiers recruited for the army; that the prisoner was regularly enlisted as a soldier in the Army of the United States for the period of five years unless sooner discharged by proper authority; that he then duly took the oath in which he declared that he was of the age of twenty-one years, and mustered into the service of the United States; that subsequently he deserted the service, and being retaken, was then in custody and confinement under charges of desertion, awaiting trial by the proper military authorities.

To this return the petitioner filed a reply alleging that [the prisoner] was enticed into the enlistment, which was without the knowledge, consent, or approval of the petitioner; that the only oath taken by the prisoner at the time of his enlistment was an oath of allegiance; and that the prisoner was not, and never had been, a deserter from the military service of the United States.

---

37. Todd E. Pettys, *State Habeas Relief for Federal Extrajudicial Detainees*, 92 MINN. L. REV. 265, 268 (2007) (noting that "[w]hen suffering restraints at the hands of federal authorities, citizens often turned not to the courts of the new and unfamiliar sovereign—a sovereign that many feared would abuse its power in oppressive ways—but rather to the courts of the sovereign that had already earned the people's confidence and loyalty"; gathering antebellum state cases).

On the 12th of August, to which day the hearing of the petition was adjourned, the commissioner proceeded to take the testimony of different witnesses [and] held that the prisoner was illegally imprisoned and detained by Lieutenant Stone, and commanded that officer forthwith to discharge him from custody.

[The Wisconsin Supreme Court affirmed and the United States filed a writ of error in the U.S. Supreme Court.]

Justice FIELD, delivered the opinion of Court.

The question presented may be more generally stated thus: whether any judicial officer of a State has jurisdiction to issue a writ of *habeas corpus* or to continue proceedings under the writ when issued for the discharge of a person held under the authority, or claim and color of the authority, of the United States by an officer of that government. For it is evident, if it may be exercised with reference to soldiers detained in the military service of the United States whose enlistment is alleged to have been illegally made, it may be exercised with reference to persons employed in any other department of the public service when their illegal detention is asserted. It may be exercised in all cases where parties are held under the authority of the United States, whenever the invalidity of the exercise of that authority is affirmed. The jurisdiction, if it exist at all, can only be limited in its application by the legislative power of the State. It may even reach to parties imprisoned under sentence of the national courts, after regular indictment, trial, and conviction, for offenses against the laws of the United States. As we read the opinion of the Supreme Court of Wisconsin in this case, this is the claim of authority asserted by that tribunal for itself and for the judicial officers of that State. It does indeed disclaim any right of either to interfere with parties in custody, under judicial sentence, when the national court pronouncing sentence had jurisdiction to try and punish the offenders, but it asserts at the same time, for itself and for each of those officers, the right to determine upon *habeas corpus* in all cases whether that court ever had such jurisdiction. In the case of [*Ableman v. Booth* (1859)], which subsequently came before this Court, it not only sustained the action of one of its justices in discharging a prisoner held in custody by a marshal of the United States under a warrant of commitment for an offense against the laws of the United States issued by a commissioner of the United States, but it discharged the same prisoner when subsequently confined under sentence of the district court of the United States for the same offense, after indictment, trial, and conviction, on the ground that in its judgment the act of Congress creating the offense was unconstitutional, and in order that its decision in that respect should be final and conclusive, directed its clerk to refuse obedience to the writ of error issued by this Court, under the act of Congress, to being up the decision for review.

It is evident, as said by this Court when the case of *Booth* was finally brought before it, if the power asserted by that State court existed, no offense against the laws of the United States could be punished by their own tribunals without the permission and according to the judgment of the courts of the State in which the parties happen to be imprisoned; that if that power existed in that State court, it belonged equally to every other State court in the Union where a prisoner was within its territorial limits; and, as the different State courts could not always agree, it would often happen that an act, which was admitted to be an offense and justly punishable in one State, would be regarded as innocent and even praiseworthy in another, and no one could suppose that a government, which had hitherto lasted for seventy years,

> enforcing its laws by its own tribunals and preserving the union of the States could have lasted a single year, or fulfilled the trusts committed to it, if offenses against its laws could not have been punished without the consent of the State in which the culprit was found.

The decision of this Court in the two cases which grew out of the arrest of Booth, that of *Ableman v. Booth* and that of *United States v. Booth*, disposes alike of the claim of jurisdiction by a State court or by a State judge to interfere with the authority of the United States, whether that authority be exercised by a federal officer or be exercised by a federal tribunal. In the first of these cases, Booth had been arrested and committed to the custody of a marshal of the United States by a commissioner appointed by the district court of the United States upon a charge of having aided and abetted the escape of a fugitive slave. Whilst thus in custody, a justice of the Supreme Court of Wisconsin issued a writ of *habeas corpus* directed to the marshal, requiring him to produce the body of Booth with the cause of his imprisonment. The justice held his detention illegal, and ordered his discharge. The marshal thereupon applied for and obtained a certiorari and had the proceedings removed to the supreme court of the state, where, after argument, the order of the justice discharging the prisoner from custody was affirmed. The decision proceeded upon the ground that the act of Congress respecting fugitive slaves was unconstitutional and void.

In the second case, Booth had been indicted for the [federal] offense with which he was charged before the commissioner, and from which the State judge had discharged him, and had been tried and convicted in the District Court of the United States for the District of Wisconsin, and been sentenced to pay a fine of $1,000 and to be imprisoned for one month. Whilst in imprisonment in execution of this sentence, application was made by Booth to the supreme court of the state for a writ of *habeas corpus*, alleging in his application that his imprisonment was illegal by reason of the unconstitutionality of the fugitive slave law, and that the district court had no jurisdiction to try or punish him for the matter charged against him. The court granted the application and adjudged the imprisonment of Booth to be illegal and ordered him to be discharged from custody, and he was accordingly set at liberty.

For a review in this Court of the judgments in both of these cases, writs of error were prosecuted. And in answer to this assumption of judicial power by the judges and by the Supreme Court of Wisconsin thus made, the Chief Justice said as follows: if they

> possess the jurisdiction they claim, they must derive it either from the United States or the state. It certainly has not been conferred on them by the United States, and it is equally clear it was not in the power of the state to confer it, even if it had attempted to do so, for no state can authorize one of its judges or courts to exercise judicial power, by *habeas corpus* or otherwise, within the jurisdiction of another and independent government. And although the State of Wisconsin is sovereign within its territorial limits to a certain extent, yet that sovereignty is limited and restricted by the Constitution of the United States. And the powers of the general government

and of the state, although both exist and are exercised within the same territorial limits, are yet separate and distinct sovereignties, acting separately and independently of each other within their respective spheres. And the sphere of action appropriated to the United States is as far beyond the reach of the judicial process issued by a state judge or a state court as if the line of division was traced by landmarks and monuments visible to the eye. And the State of Wisconsin had no more power to authorize these proceedings of its judges and courts than it would have had if the prisoner had been confined in Michigan, or in any other state of the Union, for an offense against the laws of the state in which he was imprisoned.

It is in the consideration of this distinct and independent character of the government of the United States from that of the government of the several States that the solution of the question presented in this case and in similar cases must be found. There are within the territorial limits of each State two governments, restricted in their spheres of action but independent of each other and supreme within their respective spheres. Each has its separate departments, each has its distinct laws, and each has its own tribunals for their enforcement. Neither government can intrude within the jurisdiction, or authorize any interference therein by its judicial officers with the action of the other. The two governments in each State stand in their respective spheres of action in the same independent relation to each other, except in one particular, that they would if their authority embraced distinct territories. That particular consists in the supremacy of the authority of the United States when any conflict arises between the two governments. The Constitution and the laws passed in pursuance of it are declared by the Constitution itself to be the supreme law of the land, and the judges of every State are bound thereby, "anything in the constitution or laws of any State to the contrary notwithstanding."

Whenever, therefore, any conflict arises between the enactments of the two sovereignties or in the enforcement of their asserted authorities, those of the national government must have supremacy until the validity of the different enactments and authorities can be finally determined by the tribunals of the United States. This temporary supremacy until judicial decision by the national tribunals, and the ultimate determination of the conflict by such decision, are essential to the preservation of order and peace, and the avoidance of forcible collision between the two governments.

Such being the distinct and independent character of the two governments within their respective spheres of action, it follows that neither can intrude with its judicial process into the domain of the other except so far as such intrusion may be necessary on the part of the national government to preserve its rightful supremacy in cases of conflict of authority. In their laws and mode of enforcement, neither is responsible to the other. How their respective laws shall be enacted, how they shall be carried into execution, and in what tribunals, or by what officers, and how much discretion, or whether any at all shall be vested in their officers are matters subject to their own control, and in the regulation of which neither can interfere with the other.

Now among the powers assigned to the national government is the power "to raise and support armies," and the power "to provide for the government and regulation of the land and naval forces." The execution of these powers falls within the line of its duties, and its control over the subject is plenary and exclusive. It can determine, without question from any State authority, how the armies shall be raised, whether by voluntary enlistment or forced draft, the age at which the soldier shall be received, and the period for which he shall be taken, the compensation he shall be allowed, and the service to which he shall be assigned. And it can provide the rules for the government and regulation of the forces after they are raised, define what shall constitute military offenses, and prescribe their punishment. No interference with the execution of this power of the national government in the formation, organization, and government of its armies by any State officials could be permitted without greatly impairing the efficiency, if it did not utterly destroy, this branch of the public service. Probably in every county and city in the several States there are one or more officers authorized by law to issue writs of *habeas corpus* on behalf of persons alleged to be illegally restrained of their liberty, and if soldiers could be taken from the Army of the United States and the validity of their enlistment inquired into by any one of these officers, such proceeding could be taken by all of them, and no movement could be made by the national troops without their commanders' being subjected to constant annoyance and embarrassment from this source. The experience of the late rebellion has shown us that in times of great popular excitement there may be found in every State large numbers ready and anxious to embarrass the operations of the government, and easily persuaded to believe every step taken for the enforcement of its authority illegal and void. Power to issue writs of *habeas corpus* for the discharge of soldiers in the military service, in the hands of parties thus disposed, might be used, and often would be used, to the great detriment of the public service. In many exigencies, the measures of the national government might in this way be entirely bereft of their efficacy and value. An appeal in such cases to this Court to correct the erroneous action of these officers would afford no adequate remedy. Proceedings on *habeas corpus* are summary, and the delay incident to bringing the decision of a State officer, through the highest tribunal of the State, to this Court for review would necessarily occupy years, and in the meantime, where the soldier was discharged, the mischief would be accomplished. It is manifest that the powers of the national government could not be exercised with energy and efficiency at all times if its acts could be interfered with and controlled for any period by officers or tribunals of another sovereignty.

It is true similar embarrassment might sometimes be occasioned, though in a less degree, by the exercise of the authority to issue the writ possessed by judicial officers of the United States, but the ability to provide a speedy remedy for any inconvenience following from this source would always exist with the national legislature.

This right to inquire by process of *habeas corpus*, and the duty of the officer to make a return, "grow necessarily," says Mr. Chief Justice Taney,

> out of the complex character of our government and the existence of two distinct and separate sovereignties within the same territorial space, each of them restricted in its power and each within its sphere of action prescribed by the Constitution of the United States, independent of the other. But after the return is made and the State judge or court judicially apprised that the party is in custody under the authority of the United States, they can proceed no further. They then know that the prisoner is within the dominion and jurisdiction of another government, and that neither the writ of *habeas corpus* nor any other process issued under State authority can pass over the line of division between the two sovereignties.

He is then within the dominion and exclusive jurisdiction of the United States. If he has committed an offense against their laws, their tribunals alone can punish him. If he is wrongfully imprisoned, their judicial tribunals can release him and afford him redress.

If a party thus held be illegally imprisoned, it is for the courts or judicial officers of the United States, and those courts or officers alone, to grant him release.

This limitation upon the power of State tribunals and State officers furnishes no just ground to apprehend that the liberty of the citizen will thereby be endangered. The United States are as much interested in protecting the citizen from illegal restraint under their authority as the several States are to protect him from the like restraint under their authority, and are no more likely to tolerate any oppression. Their courts and judicial officers are clothed with the power to issue the writ of *habeas corpus* in all cases where a party is illegally restrained of his liberty by an officer of the United States, whether such illegality consist in the character of the process, the authority of the officer, or the invalidity of the law under which he is held. And there is no just reason to believe that they will exhibit any hesitation to exert their power when it is properly invoked. Certainly there can be no ground for supposing that their action will be less prompt and effect in such cases than would be that of State tribunals and State officers.

It follows from the views we have expressed that the Court Commissioner of Dane County was without jurisdiction to issue the writ of *habeas corpus* for the discharge of the prisoner in this case. The commissioner was, both by the application for the writ and the return to it, apprised that the prisoner was within the dominion and jurisdiction of another government and that no writ of *habeas corpus* issued by him could pass over the line which divided the two sovereignties.

Judgment reversed.

THE CHIEF JUSTICE, dissenting.

I cannot concur in the opinion just read. I have no doubt of the right of a State court to inquire into the jurisdiction of a federal court upon *habeas corpus* and to discharge when satisfied that the petitioner for the writ is restrained of liberty by the sentence of a court without jurisdiction. If it errs in deciding the question of jurisdiction, the error must be corrected in the mode prescribed by the 25th section of the Judiciary Act, not by denial of the right to make inquiry.

I have still less doubt, if possible, that a writ of *habeas corpus* may issue from a State court to inquire into the validity of imprisonment or detention, without the sentence of any court whatever, by an officer of the United States. The state court may err, and if it does, the error may be corrected here. The mode has been prescribed, and should be followed.

To deny the right of State courts to issue the writ, or, what amounts to the same thing, to concede the right to issue and to deny the right to adjudicate, is to deny the right to protect the citizen by *habeas corpus* against arbitrary imprisonment in a large class of cases, and, I am thoroughly persuaded, was never within the contemplation of the Convention which framed, or the people who adopted, the Constitution. That instrument expressly declares that "the privilege of the writ of *habeas corpus* shall not be suspended, unless when, in case of rebellion or invasion, the public safety may require it."

* * *

Even if state habeas jurisdiction over detention at the hands of federal officers was common before the Civil War,[23] note that the Court does not acknowledge this in the case. It relies instead almost exclusively on *Ableman*. By 1871, the Supreme Court surely would have been concerned about recognizing such jurisdiction given its experience with state court resistance to the Fugitive Slave Act before the war, and open state defiance of the authority of federal officers in the South during Reconstruction.

Are any other remedies available in state court against federal officers? In *McClung v. Silliman* (1821), the Court held that, given the exceptional nature of the mandamus remedy, a state court could not use mandamus to compel the federal land office to recognize a conveyance of federal land. "It is not easy to conceive on what legal ground a State tribunal can, in any instance, exercise the power of issuing a mandamus to the register of the land office. The United States have not thought proper to delegate that power to their own Courts. . . . The question in this case, as to the power of the State Courts, over the officers of the general Government, employed in disposing of land, under the laws passed for that purpose. [W]hatever doubts have from time to time been suggested, as to the supremacy of the United States no one has ever contested its supreme right to dispose of its own property in its own way." The Court went on to emphasize that while mandamus was certainly improper from a state court if federal courts had no such authority from Congress, other remedies less intrusive than mandamus might nevertheless be appropriate:

> [W]hen we find withholding from its own Courts, the exercise of this controlling power over its ministerial officers, employed in the appropriation of its lands, the inference clear is, that all violations of private right, resulting from the acts of such officers, should be the subject of actions for damages, or to recover the specific property, (according to circumstances) in Courts of competent jurisdiction. That is, that parties should be referred to the ordinary mode of obtaining justice, instead of resorting to the extraordinary and unprecedented mode of trying such questions on a motion for a mandamus. *McClung v. Silliman* (1821).

Suits seeking common law remedies in state court against federal officers have been recognized by the Court since the early 1900s. The canonical Marshall Court case is *Slocum v. Mayberry* (1817), a case in which a federal customs officer seized a ship at port in Rhode Island. The owners of the cargo in the ship brought an action for replevin in the state courts of Rhode Island. Although the federal courts had exclusive jurisdiction of all seizures of vessels made by federal agents on land or water pursuant to federal law, and federal courts could order the officer to justify the forfeiture and order the vessel returned if justification was wanting, the federal statute did not cover the cargo of the vessel. This being so, the Court reasoned,

> the owner has the same right to his cargo that he has to any other property. . . . He may consequently demand it from the officer in whose

---

23. Todd E. Pettys, *State Habeas Relief for Federal Extrajudicial Detainees*, 92 MINN. L. REV. 265, 269 (2007) (prior to *Ableman* and *Tarble's Case*, "state courts frequently granted habeas relief to individuals being held by federal officials without judicial process").

possession it is that officer having no legal right to withhold it from him, and if it be withheld, he has a consequent right to appeal to the laws . . . for relief. . . . The courts of the United States have no jurisdiction in the case [with the possible exception of a suit in admiralty for] restitution of the property unlawfully detained. But the act of Congress neither expressly nor by implication forbids the state courts to take cognizance of suits instituted for property in possession of an officer of the United States not detained under some law of the United States; consequently their jurisdiction remains. Had this action been brought for the vessel instead of the cargo, the case would have been essentially different. The detention would have been by virtue of an act of Congress, and the jurisdiction of a state court could not have been sustained. But the action having been brought for the cargo, to detain which the law gave no authority, it was triable in the state court.

Note that the federal officer removal statute, discussed earlier in this Chapter, generally allows the federal officer to remove such litigation to federal court. We discuss suits against federal officers and the federal government in detail in Chapter 7.

D.   CONGRESSIONAL POWER TO SEPARATE CHALLENGES TO THE VALIDITY OF REGULATIONS FROM THE COURT IN WHICH THEY ARE ENFORCED

Typically, a court with proper subject matter jurisdiction decides the entire dispute before it. There are, however, circumstances in which a court may adjudicate only part of a dispute, or in which a court may rely on determinations made in earlier proceedings rather than relitigating them. The most obvious example flows from preclusion doctrine—issue preclusion may require a subsequent court to accept an earlier court's resolution of an issue; res judicata may preclude a court from entertaining a claim that could have been raised in an earlier proceeding. A second example we have seen in our study of non-Article III courts in Section B of this Chapter—agency determinations of fact are not usually relitigated in Article III courts. Even agency legal conclusions are entitled to deference. A third example arises when a criminal court relies on an earlier proceeding to determine culpability or the proper sentence. The stakes are particularly high in this setting, not only because of the infringement on liberty caused by criminal conviction, incarceration, and other penalties, but because of the heightened constitutional requirements of procedural integrity in criminal cases. Generally, due process rights are at their peak when the government brings an enforcement proceeding, especially one that works a deprivation of liberty. The Sixth Amendment imposes other requirements.

In the final case of this Chapter, the procedural integrity of a prior agency determination is challenged in a subsequent criminal enforcement court. As you read the case, consider the power of Congress to set up specialized courts whose findings are made immune from collateral attack in Article III courts charged with enforcing laws that depend upon the earlier findings.

United States v. Mendoza-Lopez

481 U.S. 828 (1987)

Justice MARSHALL delivered the opinion of the Court.

In this case, we must determine whether an alien who is prosecuted under 8 U.S.C. §1326 for illegal entry following deportation may assert in that criminal proceeding the invalidity of the underlying deportation order.

I

Respondents, Jose Mendoza-Lopez and Angel Landeros-Quinones, were arrested at separate locations in Lincoln, Nebraska, on October 23, 1984, by agents of the Immigration and Naturalization Service. On October 30, 1984, they were transported to Denver, Colorado, where a group deportation hearing was held for respondents along with 11 other persons, all of whom were, like respondents, Mexican nationals. After the hearing, respondents were ordered deported and were bused to El Paso, Texas. They were deported from El Paso on November 1, 1984. Each received, at the time of his deportation, a copy of Form I-294, which advised, in both Spanish and English, that a return to the United States without permission following deportation would constitute a felony.

On December 12, 1984, both respondents were once again separately arrested in Lincoln, Nebraska. They were subsequently indicted by a grand jury in the District of Nebraska on charges of violating 8 U.S.C. §1326, which provides:

> Any alien who (1) has been arrested and deported or excluded and deported, and thereafter (2) enters, attempts to enter, or is at any time found in the United States . . . shall be guilty of a felony, and upon conviction thereof, be punished by imprisonment of not more than two years, or by a fine of not more than $1,000, or both.

Respondents moved in the District Court to dismiss their indictments on the ground that they were denied fundamentally fair deportation hearings. The District Court . . . rejected their claims that they were not adequately informed of their right to counsel. It found, however, that respondents had apparently failed to understand the Immigration Judge's explanation of suspension of deportation.[4] The District Court concluded that [it was] "inconceivable that they would so lightly waive their rights to appeal, and thus to the relief they now claim entitlement, if

---

4. The District Court found that the Immigration Judge did not answer a question from one of the respondents regarding application for suspension of deportation; that the Immigration Judge addressed the wrong respondent while discussing eligibility for the remedy; that the Immigration Judge did not make clear how much time he would allow respondents to apply for suspension; and that Landeros-Quinones asked a question which demonstrated that he did not understand the concept of suspension of deportation, but that the Immigration Judge failed to explain further. The District Court contrasted this cursory and confusing treatment of the issue of suspension of deportation with the extensive inquiry that took place when two of the other aliens sought voluntary departure in lieu of deportation, one of whom was ultimately granted voluntary departure.

they had been fully apprised of the ramifications of such a choice." Holding that the "failure to overcome these defendants' lack of understanding about the proceedings . . . totally undermined the reliability of the proceedings," the District Court dismissed the indictments in both cases.

The Court of Appeals for the Eighth Circuit affirmed [noting] that a material element of the offense prohibited by §1326 was a "lawful" deportation. It went on to state that principles of fundamental fairness required a pretrial review of the underlying deportation to examine whether the alien received due process of law.

We affirm.

II

In *United States v. Spector* (1952), we left open whether the validity of an underlying order of deportation may be challenged in a criminal prosecution in which that prior deportation is an element of the crime.[7] Today, we squarely confront this question in the context of §1326 . . . The issue before us is whether a federal court must *always* accept as conclusive the fact of the deportation order, even if the deportation proceeding was not conducted in conformity with due process.

The first question we must address is whether the statute itself provides for a challenge to the validity of the deportation order in a proceeding under §1326. . . .

Congress . . . had available to it in at least one of the predecessor sections—§180(a)—express language that would have permitted collateral challenges to the validity of deportation proceedings in a criminal prosecution for reentry after deportation. It nonetheless failed to include in §1326 the "in pursuance of law" language of §180(a). . . .

> The Immigration and Nationality Act does include sections that limit judicial review of deportation orders. . . . The enumerated exceptions . . . are not directly applicable to this case. . . . Congress considered and addressed some of the various circumstances in which challenges to deportation orders might arise and did not mention §1326.

The text and background of §1326 thus indicate no congressional intent to sanction challenges to deportation orders in proceedings under §1326.

---

7. The Court noted the argument that the statute was unconstitutional because it afforded no opportunity for the court trying the criminal charge to pass on the validity of the order of deportation, but declined to address the issue because it "was neither raised by the appellee nor briefed nor argued here." . . . Justice Jackson, with whom Justice Frankfurter joined, dissented on the ground that the statute at issue impermissibly allowed the use of an administrative determination as conclusive evidence of a fact in a criminal prosecution:

> Having thus dispensed with important constitutional safeguards in obtaining an administrative adjudication that the alien is guilty of conduct making him deportable on the ground it is only a civil proceeding, the Government seeks to turn around and use the result as a conclusive determination of that fact in a criminal proceeding. We think it cannot make that use of such an order.

III

A

That Congress did not intend the validity of the deportation order to be contestable in a §1326 prosecution does not end our inquiry. If the statute envisions that a court may impose a criminal penalty for reentry after any deportation, regardless of how violative of the rights of the alien the deportation proceeding may have been, the statute does not comport with the constitutional requirement of due process.[14]

Our cases establish that where a determination made in an administrative proceeding is to play a critical role in the subsequent imposition of a criminal sanction, there must be *some* meaningful review of the administrative proceeding. *See Estep v. United States* (1946) [defendant in criminal prosecution under Selective Training and Service Act of 1940 for "willful" failure to report for induction allowed to challenge jurisdiction of local induction board in Article III criminal court after having exhausted administrative remedies]; *Yakus v. United States* (1944); *cf. McKart v. United States* (1969) [defendant in criminal prosecution for failure to report for induction permitted to challenge induction board's failure to grant "sole surviving son" exemption even though defendant failed to exhaust available administrative remedies because the board's finding of eligibility for induction had "no basis in fact"].[15] This principle means, at the very least, that, where the defects in an administrative proceeding foreclose judicial review of that proceeding, an alternative means of obtaining judicial review must be made available before the administrative order may be used to establish conclusively an element of a criminal offense. The result of those proceedings may subsequently be used to convert the misdemeanor of unlawful entry into the felony of unlawful entry after a deportation. Depriving an alien of the right to have the disposition in a deportation hearing reviewed in a judicial forum requires, at a minimum, that review be made available in any subsequent proceeding in which the result of the deportation proceeding is used to establish an element of a criminal offense.

---

14. The Government stated at oral argument that it was the position of the United States that there were "absolutely no due process limitations to the enforcement of Section 1326."

15. Even with this safeguard, the use of the result of an administrative proceeding to establish an element of a criminal offense is troubling. *See United States v. Spector* (1952) (Jackson, J., dissenting). While the Court has permitted criminal conviction for violation of an administrative regulation [promulgated under the Emergency Price Control Act of 1942] where the validity of the regulation could not be challenged in the criminal proceeding, *Yakus v. United States* (1944), the decision in that case was motivated by the exigencies of wartime, dealt with the propriety of regulations, rather than the legitimacy of an adjudicative procedure, and, most significantly, turned on the fact that adequate judicial review of the validity of the regulation was available in another forum. Under different circumstances, the propriety of using an administrative ruling in such a way remains open to question. We do not reach this issue here, however, holding that, at a minimum, the result of an administrative proceeding may not be used as a conclusive element of a criminal offense where the judicial review that legitimated such a practice in the first instance has effectively been denied.

B

Having established that a collateral challenge to the use of a deportation proceeding as an element of a criminal offense must be permitted where the deportation proceeding effectively eliminates the right of the alien to obtain judicial review, the question remains whether that occurred in this case. The United States did not seek this Court's review of the determination of the courts below that respondents' rights to due process were violated. . . . We consequently accept the legal conclusions of the court below that the deportation hearing violated due process. If the violation of respondents' rights that took place in this case amounted to a complete deprivation of judicial review of the determination, that determination may not be used to enhance the penalty for an unlawful entry under §1326. We think that it did.

C

The United States asserts that our decision in *Lewis v. United States* (1980), answered any constitutional objections to the scheme employed in §1326. In *Lewis*, the Court held that a state court conviction, even though it was uncounseled and therefore obtained in violation of the Sixth and Fourteenth Amendment rights of the defendant under *Gideon v. Wainwright* (1963), could be used as a predicate for a subsequent conviction under §1202(a)(1) of Title VII of the Omnibus Crime Control and Safe Streets Act of 1968, which forbade any person convicted of a felony from receiving, possessing, or transporting a firearm. We do not consider *Lewis* to control the issues raised by this case. The question in *Lewis* was whether Congress could define that "class of persons who should be disabled from dealing in or possessing firearms," by reference to prior state felony convictions, even if those convictions had resulted from procedures, such as the denial of counsel, subsequently condemned as unconstitutional.[18] The Court there rejected Lewis' statutory challenge, holding that Congress had manifested no intent to permit collateral attacks upon the prior state convictions in federal criminal proceedings, and further held that this use of uncounseled prior convictions did not violate the equal protection component of the Due Process Clause of the Fifth Amendment. In rejecting the notion that the statute permitted, or the Constitution required, this "new form of collateral attack" on prior convictions, the Court pointed to the availability of alternative means to secure judicial review of the conviction:

> [I]t is important to note that a convicted felon may challenge the validity of a prior conviction, or otherwise remove his disability, before obtaining a firearm.

_____

18. *Cf. Burgett v. Texas* (1967); *see also Baldasar v. Illinois* (1980) (Marshall, J., concurring) (court may not constitutionally use prior uncounseled misdemeanor conviction collaterally to enhance a subsequent misdemeanor to a felony with an increased term of imprisonment); *United States v. Tucker* (1972) (court may not consider constitutionally invalid prior convictions in imposing sentence on unrelated offense).

It is precisely the unavailability of effective judicial review of the administrative determination at issue here that sets this case apart from *Lewis*. The fundamental procedural defects of the deportation hearing in this case rendered direct review of the Immigration Judge's determination unavailable to respondents. What was assumed in *Lewis*, namely the opportunity to challenge the predicate conviction in a judicial forum, was precisely that which was denied to respondents here. Persons charged with crime are entitled to have the factual and legal determinations upon which convictions are based subjected to the scrutiny of an impartial judicial officer.

Lewis does not reject that basic principle, and our decision today merely reaffirms it.

Because respondents were deprived of their rights to appeal, and of any basis to appeal, since the only relief for which they would have been eligible was not adequately explained to them, the deportation proceeding in which these events occurred may not be used to support a criminal conviction, and the dismissal of the indictments against them was therefore proper. The judgment of the Court of Appeals is

Affirmed.

Chief Justice REHNQUIST, with whom Justice WHITE and Justice O'CONNOR join, dissenting.

I agree with the view that there may be exceptional circumstances where the Due Process Clause prohibits the Government from using an alien's prior deportation as a basis for imposing criminal liability under §1326. In my view, however, respondents have fallen far short of establishing such exceptional circumstances here. The Court, in reaching a contrary conclusion, misreads the decision of the District Court.

Respondents did not claim that the judge failed to explain adequately their rights to appeal, or that their waivers of these rights were, as we are told today, "not considered or intelligent." It is true that the District Court, *sua sponte*, raised the issue whether respondents knowingly waived their rights to appeal the deportation orders. The court, however, treated the issue as subsidiary to its determination that the Immigration Judge did not fully apprise respondents of their rights to apply for suspension of deportation.

Given that suspension of deportation is provided only as a matter of legislative grace and entrusted to the broad discretion of the Attorney General, the Immigration Judge's failure to undertake further efforts to make certain that respondents were fully knowledgeable of this privilege hardly compares to the procedural defects this Court has previously identified as fundamentally unfair. *See Rose v. Clark* (1986) (use of a coerced confession, adjudication by a biased judge). The judge's failure to engage respondents in an extended colloquy concerning suspension of their deportations neither "aborted the basic trial process" nor rendered it presumptively prejudicial. *Id.*

In fact, several factual findings by the District Court below, not mentioned by the Court, suggest that the Immigration Judge expended considerable effort to ensure the fairness of the hearing. For example, the District Court noted that the Immigration Judge commenced the hearing by instructing respondents "that, if any of them did not understand any of the proceedings, to raise their hands and their misunderstandings would be addressed so as to eliminate any confusion." Respondents indicated their understanding of this arrangement. Moreover, the Immigration Judge informed respondents that they were entitled to be represented by counsel, and made certain that they received a list of the free legal services available to them. . . . Under these circumstances, I cannot say that respondents' deportation proceedings violated the dictates of the Due Process Clause.

Justice SCALIA, dissenting.

I think it clear that Congress may constitutionally make it a felony for deportees—irrespective of the legality of their deportations—to reenter the United States illegally. *See Lewis v. United States* (1980) (Congress may constitutionally make it a felony for convicted felons—irrespective of the legality of their convictions—to deal in or possess firearms). The sole ground upon which the Court attempts to distinguish *Lewis* is that, in this case, respondents were completely foreclosed from obtaining "effective judicial review" of their deportations, while in *Lewis*, the felons could have obtained collateral review of their convictions before obtaining firearms. It is true that the Court in *Lewis* relied on the availability of collateral review. But, contrary to the Court's implication, neither *Lewis* nor any of the other cases relied upon by the Court squarely holds that the Due Process Clause invariably forbids reliance upon the outcome of unreviewable administrative determinations in subsequent criminal proceedings.

The Court's apparent adoption of that conclusion today seems to me wrong. To illustrate that point by one out of many possible examples, imagine that a State establishes an administrative agency that (after investigation and full judicial-type administrative hearings) periodically publishes a list of unethical businesses. Further imagine that the State, having discovered that a number of previously listed businesses are bribing the agency's investigators to avoid future listing, passes a law making it a felony for a business that has been listed to bribe agency investigators. It cannot be that the Due Process Clause forbids the State to punish violations of that law unless it either makes the agency's listing decisions judicially reviewable or permits those charged with violating the law to defend themselves on the ground that the original listing decisions were in some way unlawful.

Even if I believed the availability of "effective judicial review" to be relevant, I would still dissent, because review was available here. It is true, as the Court notes, that the District Court found that respondents' waivers of any appeal from the Immigration Judge's deportation order were "not the result of considered judgments," because they were affected by the Immigration Judge's failure adequately to explain to respondents that they could apply for suspension of deportation. There is a world of difference, however, between denial of a right to appeal and failure to assure that parties understand the available grounds for appeal, and forgo them in a "considered" fashion. Since, to my knowledge, administrative agencies rarely undertake such assurance, the Court's unbounded and unexplained conception of "effective" denial of a right of appeal, apparently leads to the peculiar conclusion that administrative proceedings are almost always without judicial review. I reject this conclusion. . . .

For these reasons, I think that, if respondents' reentry into the United States was unlawful, respondents may constitutionally be punished for violating §1326. I would reverse the contrary judgment of the Court of Appeals.

* * *

The majority is at pains to distinguish *Yakus* in footnote 15. Yakus was criminally prosecuted for violating the Emergency Price Control Act, a statute enacted to control inflation during World War II. The statute set up a new agency and empowered its price administrator to set ceilings on prices. It also provided that challenges to the validity of price regulations and other agency orders had to be made before the administrator, and had to be filed 60 days after the price regulations issued. Jurisdiction over appeals rested *exclusively* with a new Article III court composed of circuit and district court judges (the Emergency Court of Appeals). *See Lockerty v. Phillips* (1943) (holding that only the ECA could entertain a request to enjoin enforcement of price regulations; "By this statute, Congress has seen fit to confer on the Emergency Court equity jurisdiction to restrain the enforcement of price orders. At the same time, it has withdrawn that jurisdiction from every other federal and state court. There is nothing in the Constitution which requires Congress to confer equity jurisdiction on any particular inferior federal court. [Thus] it is plain that Congress has power to provide that the equity jurisdiction to restrain enforcement of the Act of regulations promulgated under it be restricted to the [ECA]"). The statute gave the Supreme Court appellate jurisdiction over the ECA.

Federal district courts were granted jurisdiction to entertain requests for injunctive relief by the administrator to secure compliance with price regulations as well as jurisdiction over criminal prosecution of noncompliance with price regulations. As we saw in *Testa*, in the previous Section of this Chapter, state and federal courts had concurrent jurisdiction over private civil claims for treble damages against regulated entities that violated the price regulations.

The question in *Yakus* was whether due process and the Sixth Amendment required that the defendant facing criminal charges be allowed to challenge the price regulation that formed the basis of his prosecution. The Court held that, having failed to challenge the price regulation before the price administrator, the defendant could not raise this defense in the criminal prosecution:

> Congress, through its power to define the jurisdiction of inferior federal courts and to create such courts for the exercise of the judicial power, could, subject to other constitutional limitations, create the Emergency Court of Appeals, give to it exclusive equity jurisdiction to determine the validity of price regulations prescribed by the Administrator, and foreclose any further or other consideration of the validity of a regulation as a defense to a prosecution for its violation.
>
> Unlike most penal statutes and regulations, whose validity can be determined only by running the risk of violation, the present statute provides a mode of testing the validity of a regulation by an independent administrative proceeding. There is no constitutional requirement that that test be made in one tribunal, rather than in another, so long as there is an opportunity to be heard and for judicial review which satisfies the

demands of due process, as is the case here. This has never been doubted by this Court. And we are pointed to no principle of law or provision of the Constitution which precludes Congress from making criminal the violation of an administrative regulation, by one who has failed to avail himself of an adequate separate procedure for the adjudication of its validity, or which precludes the practice, in many ways desirable, of splitting the trial for violations of an administrative regulation by committing the determination of the issue of its validity to the agency which created it, and the issue of violation to a court which is given jurisdiction to punish violations. Such a requirement presents no novel constitutional issue.

No procedural principle is more familiar to this Court than that a constitutional right may be forfeited in criminal, as well as civil, cases by the failure to make timely assertion of the right before a tribunal having jurisdiction to determine it. For more than fifty years, it has been a penal offense for shippers and interstate rail carriers to fail to observe the duly filed tariffs fixing freight rates—including, since 1906, rates prescribed by the Commission—even though the validity of those rates is open to attack only in a separate administrative proceeding before the Interstate Commerce Commission.

Two justices dissented, emphasizing that the case involved more than the ordinary principle of exhaustion of administrative remedies.

It is one thing for Congress to withhold jurisdiction. It is entirely another to confer it and direct that it be exercised in a manner inconsistent with constitutional requirements, or, what in some instances may be the same thing, without regard to them. The problem therefore is not solely one of individual right or due process of law. It is equally one of the separation and independence of the powers of government and of the constitutional integrity of the judicial process, more especially in criminal trials.

Whatever may be the limitations on judicial review in criminal proceedings under other administrative enforcement patterns, no one of these arrangements goes as far as the combination presented by this Act. It restricts the individual's right to review to the protest procedure and appeal through the Emergency Court of Appeals. Both are short-cut proceedings, trimmed almost to the bone of due process, even for wholly civil purposes, and pared down further by a short statute of limitations. Protest must be filed within the sixty-day period. The only *right* is to submit written evidence and argument to the administrator. There is none to present additional evidence to the [ECA]. Necessarily, there is none of cross-examination. No court can suspend the order unless or until a judgment of the Emergency Court invalidating it becomes final. The penalties, civil and criminal, attach at once on violation and, it would seem, until the contrary is decided, with finality.

It places the affected individual just where the Court, speaking through Mr. Justice Lamar in *Wadley Southern Ry. Co. v. Georgia* said he could not be put: "He must either obey what may finally be held to be a void order or disobey what may ultimately be held to be a lawful order." Yet the Court holds this special proceeding "adequate," and therefore effective to foreclose all opportunity for defense in a criminal prosecution on the ground the regulation is void.

This is no answer. A procedure so summary, imposing such risks, does not meet the requirements heretofore considered essential to the determination or foreclosure of issues material to guilt in criminal causes.

To say that this does not operate unconstitutionally on the accused because he has the choice of refraining from violation or of testing the constitutional questions in a civil proceeding beforehand entirely misses the point. The fact is that, if he violates the regulation, he must be convicted, in a trial in which either an earlier and summary civil determination or the complete absence of a determination forecloses him on a crucial constitutional question. In short, his trial for the crime is either in two parts in two courts or on only a portion of the issues material to guilt in one court. This may be all very well for some civil proceedings. But, so far as I know, criminal proceedings of this character never before have received the sanction of Congress or of this Court.

From what has been said, it seems clear that Congress cannot forbid the enforcing court, exercising the criminal jurisdiction, to consider the constitutional validity of an order invalid on its face. Any other view would permit Congress to compel the courts to enforce unconstitutional laws. Nor, in my opinion, can Congress forbid consideration of validity in all cases, if it can in any, where the invalidity appears only from proof of facts extrinsic to the regulation.

Is *Yakus* good law after *Mendoza-Lopez?* Two years after passing the EPCA Congress passed amendments eliminating the 60 day statute of limitations for challenges to validity of price regulations before the price administrator and allowing regulated entities to seek a stay of enforcement pending the adjudication of challenges to validity of price regulations. 50 U.S.C.A. §901 et seq. Do these amendments resolve the constitutional concerns raised by the *Yakus* dissent? *Mendoza-Lopez* suggests congressional authority to split challenges to validity from criminal enforcement is context sensitive, emphasizing the exigent circumstances of sustaining the national economy during World War II. The amendments eliminating a statute of limitations and providing for a stay of enforcement suits are significant in that they reduce the risk that a regulated entity loses the opportunity to challenge validity before the price administrator and ECA merely by virtue of failing to vigilantly monitor the issuance of new regulations.

The ECA no longer exists. But *Mendoza-Lopez* shows that adjudications outside the Article III courts can bear on Article III adjudication in many other ways.

Note, finally, that Congress has from time to time set up other specialized Article III courts whose jurisdiction is strictly circumscribed. A prominent modern example is the Foreign Intelligence Surveillance Court, established in 1978 when Congress passed the Foreign Intelligence Surveillance Act, 50 U.S.C. §§1801-1885. The Court sits in Washington, D.C., and is composed of eleven federal district court judges selected by the Chief Justice of the United States to serve seven year terms. The FISA court entertains applications submitted by the federal government for approval of electronic surveillance and other foreign intelligence investigative activity. In order to protect classified national security information the court generally conducts its work *ex parte* and in secret.[38] The grant rate of government applications is, like Title III wiretap requests, almost 100 percent. Of the 33,900 *ex parte* requests to the FISC submitted by the government between 1979 and 2012, only eleven were denied.[39] The government takes steps to prevent submitting applications that are likely to be denied, but this is still a remarkable grant rate. Although some FISC applications involve targets who could be criminally prosecuted, criminal prosecution is not the highest national security priority driving surveillance programs.

---

38. https://www.fisc.uscourts.gov/sites/default/files/Leahy.pdf

39. Conor Clarke, *Is the FISC Really a Rubber Stamp? Ex Parte Proceedings and the FISC Win Rate*, 66 Stan. L. Rev. 125 (2014).

CHAPTER 5

FEDERAL
COMMON LAW

You may be familiar with the famous phrase from *Erie R.R. Co. v. Tompkins* (1938), that "[t]here is no federal general common law." If so, you may be wondering why this casebook contains a chapter on "federal common law." Recall, however, that *Erie*'s dramatic statement about federal *general* common law was made in the context of overturning the power of federal courts under *Swift v. Tyson* (1842), to create their own substantive rules of decision when sitting in diversity jurisdiction. Outside this context, there is, and has always been, federal common law. It exists to protect federal interests and to achieve the purposes of congressional grants of federal jurisdiction when a controlling rule of decision does not appear in the constitution or statute before the court. As Professor Martha Field puts it, "'federal common law' . . . refer[s] to any rule of federal law created by a court . . . when the substance of that rule is not clearly suggested by federal enactments—constitutional or congressional."[1] The scope of this doctrine is drawn into relief when we consider how much "unwritten" law is relied upon in federal litigation. As another scholar notes,

> what we currently call "federal common law" might include (1) traditional principles of common law, admiralty, or equity jurisprudence; (2) rules that reflect customary practices of other sorts; (3) rules that reflect common themes in the written laws of the fifty states; (4) rules that the federal courts have developed in light of the purposes behind specific federal statutes; and (5) rules that federal judges simply make up out of whole cloth.[2]

The scope of federal common law is limited in two ways. First, federal common law does not exist in the criminal law area; there is no federal common law of crimes. Second, there is a strong presumption against the federal courts fashioning common law to decide civil cases. There are separation of powers and federalism justifications for this presumption. The development of federal common law raises separation of powers issues to the extent federal courts encroach upon the lawmaking authority of Congress or the President's authority to execute the laws. Some scholars have argued, for example, that the Rules of Decision Act, discussed below,

---

1. Martha A. Field, *Sources of Law: The Scope of Federal Common Law*, 99 HARV. L. REV. 881, 890 (1986).
2. Caleb Nelson, *The Legitimacy of (Some) Federal Common Law*, 101 VA. L. REV. 1, 63 (2015).

precludes federal common lawmaking, though the federal courts have fashioned such law during the two centuries since Congress enacted the Act. Federal common law also raises federalism issues by displacing state law. At the same time, a decision not to fashion federal common law and instead to apply state law may frustrate federal interests expressed in the Constitution or federal statutes, thereby undermining the supremacy of federal law.

The cases in this Chapter illustrate the doctrinal debates about federal common law in a variety of historical contexts. They raise difficult questions to which there are not always clear answers. For example, the presumption against federal common law does not apply where federal courts are simply interpreting and applying the U.S. Constitution or a federal statute. Drawing the line between constitutional or statutory interpretation on the one hand, and federal common law on the other, therefore becomes important. But it is often difficult to separate interpretation and common law rulemaking. And while the values of the separation of powers and federalism are integral to the development of federal common law, neither provides conclusive guidance as to when federal courts may or may not create law to protect federal interests or effectuate federal enactments.

As you read the cases in this Chapter, it is important to remain mindful of the contexts in which they arise. As Professor Stewart Jay has explained, the "matter [of federal common law] has a great deal to do with the balance of political forces in the society, the degree of attention that courts wish to devote to certain areas, and a range of other elements that form the judicial personalities of an era."[3] Federal common law has developed in an ad hoc fashion in a number of different areas. Consider for example, the development of federal common law concerning the relationships between Native Nations and the United States. While the Court, especially in the modern era, has often applied a presumption against federal common law, in the field of Indian affairs the Court, including in the modern era, has developed federal common law without even mentioning this presumption. In doing so, the Court has assumed significant power over the lives of Native peoples, power that it has elsewhere disclaimed. Here, and in other settings we will examine, tension between first principles, power, and practicalities is vividly apparent.

A.   THE SCOPE OF FEDERAL COMMON LAW

Federal common law, the Supreme Court has stated, is limited to a "few and restricted" instances.[4] Federal courts do not have the common law powers of their state counterparts. While state courts may be courts of general jurisdiction that can develop common law by creating their own rules of decision, federal courts, by contrast, are courts of limited jurisdiction. Federal common law is therefore the exception, not the rule.

Two cases are foundational to this conception of federal common law. Early in American history, the Supreme Court refused requests to create a federal common

---

3. Stewart Jay, *Origins of Federal Common Law: Part One*, 133 U. PA. L. REV. 1003, 1009 (1985).

4. City of Milwaukee v. Illinois, 451 U.S. 304, 314 (1981).

law of crimes. In *United States v. Hudson & Goodwin* (1812), the Court held that federal trial courts lack the authority to create and punish common law crimes against the United States. This case was the culmination of a clash between Federalists and Jeffersonian Republicans, ideologically distinct political factions fighting bitterly over control of the national government. The second case, *Erie R.R. Co. v. Tompkins* (1938), was also decided at a pivotal moment in the history of the federal courts. Corporations were using diversity jurisdiction in order to take advantage of favorable general federal common law in suits brought by injured consumers and employees. The Supreme Court was in the throws of its transition from striking down to upholding New Deal legislation, and the procedural rules of decision of the Supreme Court underwent a dramatic transformation with the enactment of the Rules Enabling Act in 1934 and the culmination of the civil rules drafting process it created with the Federal Rules of Civil Procedure the same year *Erie* was decided.

1. *The Prohibition of Federal Common Law Crimes*

The prohibition of federal common law crimes established in *Hudson & Goodwin* involved indictments of several members of the Federalist Party in 1806 and 1807. The defendants included a state judge and Federalist newspaper editors; they were charged with seditious libel. According to the indictment, the defendants had libeled Thomas Jefferson, a founder of the Republican Party and President when the indictments were made. Hudson and Goodwin were editors of a newspaper that had stated "that Jefferson had conspired to grant Napoleon two million dollars."[5] The grand jury was "picked by a Republican marshall" and charged by a "Republican federal district judge."[6] Given that "Republicans had spent a great deal of political effort in the prior ten years denying the existence of federal common-law crimes," this prosecution had "more than a small appearance of hypocrisy."[7] Prior to the 1798 enactment of the Alien and Sedition Acts, federal criminal laws that were the basis of egregious prosecutions of critics of President John Adams's Administration, the "Federalists had been bringing seditious prosecutions at common law . . . against well-known Republican [newspaper] editors."[8] Republicans had criticized these prosecutions as unlawful, but by 1806 they were willing to turn the tables on their political foes.

The historical record is unclear on Jefferson's view of these prosecutions of Federalists for allegedly libeling him. There is evidence that he may have sought to stop them because he was concerned that one of the defendants could prevail by showing that he had spoken truthfully about Jefferson's extramarital dalliances. The Court ultimately held that the indictments must be dismissed because there were no federal common law crimes. This principle, Justice William Johnson wrote for the Court, had "been long since settled in public opinion." The statement was

---

5. Jay, *supra* note 3, at 1013-14.

6. *Id.* at 1013.

7. *Id.*

8. *Id.* at 1075.

contradicted by "the virtually unanimous opinion of federal judges . . . that indictments could be sustained in federal court under the common law for crimes against the United States."[9] In rejecting this view, Justice Johnson's opinion reflected the Republicans' "preference for legislative authority over the other branches of government"[10]—a preference that, as it happened, Jefferson followed fitfully during his Presidency.[11]

United States v. Hudson and Goodwin

11 U.S. (7 Cranch) 32 (1812)

The Court, having taken time to consider, the following opinion was delivered (on the last day of the term, all the judges being present) by JOHNSON, J.

The only question which this case presents is, whether the Circuit Courts of the United States can exercise a common law jurisdiction in criminal cases. We state it thus broadly because a decision on a case of libel will apply to every case in which jurisdiction is not vested in those Courts by statute.

Although this question is brought up now for the first time to be decided by this Court, we consider it as having been long since settled in public opinion. In no other case for many years has this jurisdiction been asserted; and the general acquiescence of legal men shews the prevalence of opinion in favor of the negative of the proposition.

The course of reasoning which leads to this conclusion is simple, obvious, and admits of but little illustration. The powers of the general Government are made up of concessions from the several states—whatever is not expressly given to the former, the latter expressly reserve. The judicial power of the United States is a constituent part of those concessions—that power is to be exercised by Courts organized for the purpose, and brought into existence by an effort of the legislative power of the Union. Of all the Courts which the United States may, under their general powers, constitute, one only, the Supreme Court, possesses jurisdiction derived immediately from the constitution, and of which the legislative power cannot deprive it. All other Courts created by the general Government possess no jurisdiction but what is given them by the power that creates them, and can be vested with none but what the power ceded to the general Government will authorize them to confer.

It is not necessary to inquire whether the general Government, in any and what extent, possesses the power of conferring on its Courts a jurisdiction in cases similar to the present; it is enough that such jurisdiction has not been conferred by any legislative act, if it does not result to those Courts as a consequence of their creation.

And such is the opinion of the majority of this Court: For, the power which congress possess to create Courts of inferior jurisdiction, necessarily implies the

---

9. *Id.* at 1016.

10. *Id.* at 1022.

11. John Yoo, *Jefferson and Executive Power,* 88 B.U. L. REV. 421, 422 (2008) ("Jefferson said one thing about presidential power, but did another.").

power to limit the jurisdiction of those Courts to particular objects, and when a Court is created, and its operations confined to certain specific objects, with what propriety can it assume to itself a jurisdiction — much more extended — in its nature very indefinite — applicable to a great variety of subjects — varying in every state in the Union — and with regard to which there exists no definite criterion of distribution between the district and Circuit Courts of the same district?

The only ground on which it has ever been contended that this jurisdiction could be maintained is, that, upon the formation of any political body, an implied power to preserve its own existence and promote the end and object of its creation, necessarily results to it. But, without examining how far this consideration is applicable to the peculiar character of our constitution, it may be remarked that it is a principle by no means peculiar to the common law. It is coeval, probably, with the first formation of a limited Government; belongs to a system of universal law, and may as well support the assumption of many other powers as those more peculiarly acknowledged by the common law of England.

But if admitted as applicable to the state of things in this country, the consequence would not result from it which is here contended for. If it may communicate certain implied powers to the general Government, it would not follow that the Courts of that Government are vested with jurisdiction over any particular act done by an individual in supposed violation of the peace and dignity of the sovereign power. The legislative authority of the Union must first make an act a crime, affix a punishment to it, and declare the Court that shall have jurisdiction of the offence.

Certain implied powers must necessarily result to our Courts of justice from the nature of their institution. But jurisdiction of crimes against the state is not among those powers. To fine for contempt — imprison for contumacy — inforce the observance of order, &c. are powers which cannot be dispensed with in a Court, because they are necessary to the exercise of all others and so far our Courts no doubt possess powers not immediately derived from statute, but all exercise of criminal jurisdiction in common law cases we are of opinion is not within their implied powers.

* * *

Hudson & Goodwin (1812) is still good law: no federal common law creates criminal offenses against the United States. Today, the controversial question is whether and to what extent the principles announced in *Hudson & Goodwin* extend to the development of federal common law in civil actions. The existence of federal question jurisdiction does not by itself authorize the creation of federal common law crimes. Is the same true for civil actions? According to the Court, the answer is yes: "[t]he vesting of jurisdiction in the federal courts does not in and of itself give rise to authority to formulate federal common law." *Texas Indus., Inc. v. Radcliffe Materials, Inc.* (1981). More broadly, *Hudson & Goodwin* has sometimes been cited for the proposition that there is no federal common law.

It is not obvious what to make of *Hudson & Goodwin*'s holding in light of the case's historical context. The common law indictments of Federalists for statements about Thomas Jefferson smacked of hypocrisy given that Jefferson's Republican allies had criticized Federalist prosecutions of Republicans under the common law.

These sort of "institutional flip-flops" are not uncommon in the history of constitutional law.[12] Even if the Jeffersonian Republicans contradicted themselves on the question of federal common law crimes, that does not mean that the Court erred in concluding that federal courts lack jurisdiction to punish them.

But the Court's reasoning in *Hudson & Goodwin* invites close examination based upon the history of the partisan contest that preceded it. Notice that Justice Johnson's opinion for the Court did not discuss specific constitutional or statutory text in detail. Rather, Justice Johnson pointed first and foremost to "public opinion" and to a purported history of "general acquiescence of legal men," claiming that "[i]n no other case for many years has this jurisdiction been asserted." Perhaps Justice Johnson meant to suggest that a prosecutorial practice (or lack thereof) had "liquidated" the meaning of Article III. To the extent that Justice Johnson mischaracterized the history of "public opinion," the Court's holding in *Hudson & Goodwin* is open to criticism on its own terms, and invites us to question to what extent its "broad and seemingly universal pronouncements" were "an artifact of short-term judgments about substance."[13] In this regard, consider that "without acknowledging it, the *Hudson* Court disapproved at least eight circuit court cases, brushed off the views of all but one Justice who sat on the Court prior to 1804, and departed from what was arguably the original understanding of those who framed the Constitution and penned the Judiciary Act."[14]

Hudson & Goodwin's holding might be justified upon individual rights grounds that the opinion did not discuss. The Court has many times offered some variation on the theme that "the constitutional structure of our Government . . . protects individual liberty." *Bond v. United States*, 564 U.S. 211, 233 (2011). By denying the existence of federal common law crimes, the Court has required the actions of all three branches before someone may be convicted of a federal crime. As the Court put it in *Hudson & Goodwin*, "[t]he legislative authority of the Union must first make an act a crime, affix a punishment to it, and declare the Court that shall have jurisdiction of the offence." To the extent that individual liberty concerns with criminal punishment by federal common law explain the prohibition, *Hudson & Goodwin* may not be very relevant to the debate about federal common law in civil actions.

Lastly, note that despite *Hudson & Goodwin*'s holding, there is some judge-made federal criminal law, albeit quite narrow in scope. In *Hudson & Goodwin*, the Court stated that "[c]ertain implied powers must necessarily result to our Courts of justice from the nature of their institutions." The Court included the power to punish contempt of court among these implied powers. In subsequent cases, the Court has confirmed this inherent judicial authority. *See Young v. United States ex rel. Vuitton et Fils S.A.* (1987). What distinguishes criminal punishment for contempt of court from a federal common law of crimes?

---

12. Eric A. Posner & Cass R. Sunstein, *Institutional Flip-Flops*, 94 Tex. L. Rev. 486 (2016).
13. *Id.* at 488.
14. Gary D. Rowe, *Note, The Sound of Silence:* United States v. Hudson & Goodwin, *The Jeffersonian Ascendancy, and the Abolition of Federal Common Law Crimes*, 101 Yale L.J. 919, 920-21 (1992).

2. The Erie *Doctrine and the Development of Federal Common Law in Civil Actions*

Under modern doctrine, there is a strong presumption against the federal courts fashioning common law to decide civil cases. The Rules of Decision Act, which was part of the Judiciary Act of 1789 and remains largely unchanged to this day, states that "the laws of the several states, except where the Constitution or treaties of the United States or Acts of Congress otherwise require or provide, shall be regarded as rules of decisions in civil actions in the courts of the United States, in cases where they apply."[15] This law, by its very terms, seems to deny the existence of federal common law; the Rules of Decision Act commands that in the absence of positive federal law, federal courts must apply state law. Nevertheless, the Supreme Court held in *Swift v. Tyson* (1842), that federal courts could develop a body of substantive federal common law to address matters of "general"—as opposed to local—concern that arose in diversity suits. So-called general federal common law governed the substantive law in diversity cases whenever no positive state law on point existed (statutory or constitutional) and the case did not concern truly "local" unwritten law (such as common law land claims). On the other hand, the federal district courts (lacking general procedural rules of their own) used the procedural rules of the state's decisions in which they were located, except in matters arising in equity. This doctrine persisted for nearly a century until the Court held in *Erie R.R. Co. v. Tompkins* (1938), that there was no general federal common law upon which federal courts could draw for substantive rules decision and mandated that state law applies in diversity suits. The same rule applies when a federal court has supplemental jurisdiction over a state law claim. The Federal Rules of Civil Procedure (FRCP), which took effect in 1938, provided federal rules of decision for procedure.

However, *Erie* does not mean that there is no federal common law in civil actions. To the contrary, both before and after *Erie*, federal common law has developed in some areas of civil litigation out of necessity. Most obviously, there are often gaps in *federal* law claims. Where federal statutory rules do not exist for all aspects of a federal claim, federal courts must elaborate rules of decision to resolve them. Before we turn to this doctrine, we revisit the principles of judicial federalism that the Court relied upon in *Erie* and briefly examine the cases enforcing judicial federalism through the substance/procedure distinction.

Scholars and judges have debated how to place *Erie* within its historical context. In 1941, three years after the Court decided *Erie*, proponents of the decision were keen to insist that it "was not impelled by 'supervening economic events,' nor was it a part of the program of any political party."[16] Yet studies of its effects during the time it was decided make clear that it expressed well-settled progressive sentiment about the pro-corporate bias of *Swift*. Corporations, unlike individuals, could

---

15. 28 U.S.C. §1652. As originally enacted in the Judiciary Act of 1789, the Rules of Decision Act was identical, except the words "in trials at common law" were used instead of the current phrase "civil actions." 1 Stat. 92 (1789).

16. ROBERT H. JACKSON, THE STRUGGLE FOR JUDICIAL SUPREMACY: A STUDY OF A CRISIS IN AMERICAN POWER POLITICS 273 (1941).

change their state citizenship to take advantage of diversity jurisdiction and favorable general federal common law with the stroke of a pen.[17] Other progressive concerns about the fairness of *Swift* included a "growing arbitrariness—the fact that the value of a case could be determined largely by the tactical possibilities open to the parties, not by its merits. . . . The arbitrariness no longer related merely to the basic questions of whether plaintiff lived in a town that was distant from the nearest federal court," although this was often a determinative factor in cases where an injured plaintiff simply could not afford to travel.[18] Arbitrariness extended to cases in which state "and federal common law conflicted," cases where the federal court "had a particularly heavy backlog," and as opposition to the New Deal grew in corporations facing new regulations, cases where a company "shopped across the country for the judges and circuits that were most willing to block government agencies . . . cleverly employ[ing] shareholder derivative suits to obtain injunctions prohibiting company compliance with the laws. The latter tactic allowed suspiciously 'friendly' suits with minimal opposition on agreed-upon facts, and it often prevented the government from even participating in the defense of the challenged laws or administrative actions."[19]

Lastly, *Erie* was a 6-3 decision to overturn *Swift* that hinged on two new liberal appointments by President Roosevelt joining the Court and two Justices switching their positions from an earlier case, *Black & White Taxicab & Transfer Co. v. Brown & Yellow Taxicab & Transfer Co.* (1928). Case selection by the new liberal majority (in *Erie* it is the injured plaintiff who seeks the benefit of general federal common law; the railroad prefers the state common law rule) thinly masked the political project of *Erie* grounded in early twentieth century progressives' commitment to federalism. Ironically, though, it came at the same time that the progressives on the Court triumphed in rejecting federalism as a limit on congressional power, which had been used for the first third of the twentieth century to strike down progressive federal legislation. Judicial federalism thus diverged from federalism as limit on congressional power.

Erie R.R. Co. v. Tompkins

304 U.S. 64 (1938)

Justice BRANDEIS delivered the opinion of the Court.

The question for decision is whether the oft-challenged doctrine of *Swift v. Tyson* (1842), shall now be disapproved.

Tompkins, a citizen of Pennsylvania, was injured on a dark night by a passing freight train of the Erie Railroad Company while walking along its right of way at Hughestown in that State. He claimed that the accident occurred through negligence in the operation, or maintenance, of the train; that he was rightfully on the premises as licensee because on a commonly used beaten footpath which ran for a short distance alongside the tracks; and that he was struck by something which

---

17. EDWARD A. PURCELL, JR., BRANDEIS AND THE PROGRESSIVE CONSTITUTION (2000).

18. EDWARD A. PURCELL JR., LITIGATION AND INEQUALITY: FEDERAL DIVERSITY JURISDICTION IN INDUSTRIAL AMERICA 1870-1958, 226-30 (1992).

19. *Id.*

looked like a door projecting from one of the moving cars. To enforce that claim
he brought an action in the federal court for southern New York, which had jurisdiction because the company is a corporation of that State. It denied liability; and
the case was tried by a jury.

The Erie insisted that its duty to Tompkins was no greater than that owed to a
trespasser. It contended, among other things, that its duty to Tompkins, and hence
its liability, should be determined in accordance with the Pennsylvania law; that
under the law of Pennsylvania, as declared by its highest court, persons who use
pathways along the railroad right of way—that is a longitudinal pathway as distinguished from a crossing—are to be deemed trespassers; and that the railroad is not
liable for injuries to undiscovered trespassers resulting from its negligence, unless
it be wanton or willful. Tompkins denied that any such rule had been established
by the decisions of the Pennsylvania courts; and contended that, since there was
no statute of the State on the subject, the railroad's duty and liability is to be determined in federal courts as a matter of general law.

The trial judge refused to rule that the applicable law precluded recovery.
The jury brought in a verdict of $30,000; and the judgment entered thereon was
affirmed by the Circuit Court of Appeals, which held that it was unnecessary to consider whether the law of Pennsylvania was as contended, because the question was
one not of local, but of general, law and that

> upon questions of general law the federal courts are free, in absence of a
> local statute, to exercise their independent judgment as to what the law is;
> and it is well settled that the question of the responsibility of a railroad for
> injuries caused by its servants is one of general law. . . . Where the public
> has made open and notorious use of a railroad right of way for a long
> period of time and without objection, the company owes to persons on
> such permissive pathway a duty of care in the operation of its trains. . . . It
> is likewise generally recognized law that a jury may find that negligence
> exists toward a pedestrian using a permissive path on the railroad right of
> way if he is hit by some object projecting from the side of the train.

The Erie had contended that application of the Pennsylvania rule was
required, among other things, by §34 of the Federal Judiciary Act of September
24, 1789, which provides: "The laws of the several States, except where the Constitution, treaties, or statutes of the United States otherwise require or provide, shall
be regarded as rules of decision in trials at common law, in the courts of the United
States, in cases where they apply."

Because of the importance of the question whether the federal court was
free to disregard the alleged rule of the Pennsylvania common law, we granted
certiorari.

First. *Swift v. Tyson* (1842) held that federal courts exercising jurisdiction on
the ground of diversity of citizenship need not, in matters of general jurisprudence,
apply the unwritten law of the State as declared by its highest court; that they are
free to exercise an independent judgment as to what the common law of the State
is—or should be; and that, as there stated by Mr. Justice Story:

> [T]he true interpretation of the thirty-fourth section limited its application
> to State laws strictly local, that is to say, to the positive statutes of the state,

and the construction thereof adopted by the local tribunals, and to rights and titles to things having a permanent locality, such as the rights and titles to real estate, and other matters immovable and intraterritorial in their nature and character. It never has been supposed by us, that the section did apply, or was designed to apply, to questions of more general nature, not at all dependent upon local statutes or local usages of a fixed and permanent operation, as, for example, to the construction of ordinary contracts or other written instruments, and especially to questions of general commercial law, where the State tribunals are called upon to perform the like functions as ourselves, that is, to ascertain upon general reasoning and legal analogies, what is the true exposition of the contract or instrument, or what is the just rule furnished by the principles of commercial law to govern the case.

The Court in applying the rule of §34 to equity cases, in *Mason v. United States* (1923), said: "The statute, however, is merely declarative of the rule which would exist in the absence of the statute." The federal courts assumed, in the broad field of "general law," the power to declare rules of decision which Congress was confessedly without power to enact as statutes. Doubt was repeatedly expressed as to the correctness of the construction given §34, and as to the soundness of the rule which it introduced. But it was the more recent research of a competent scholar, who examined the original document, which established that the construction given to it by the Court was erroneous; and that the purpose of the section was merely to make certain that, in all matters except those in which some federal law is controlling, the federal courts exercising jurisdiction in diversity of citizenship cases would apply as their rules of decision the law of the State, unwritten as well as written.[5]

Criticism of the doctrine became widespread after the decision of *Black & White Taxicab & Transfer Co. v. Brown & Yellow Taxicab & Transfer Co.* (1928). There, Brown and Yellow, a Kentucky corporation owned by Kentuckians, and the Louisville and Nashville Railroad, also a Kentucky corporation, wished that the former should have the exclusive privilege of soliciting passenger and baggage transportation at the Bowling Green, Kentucky, railroad station; and that the Black and White, a competing Kentucky corporation, should be prevented from interfering with that privilege. Knowing that such a contract would be void under the common law of Kentucky, it was arranged that the Brown and Yellow reincorporate under the law of Tennessee, and that the contract with the railroad should be executed there. The suit was then brought by the Tennessee corporation in the federal court for western Kentucky to enjoin competition by the Black and White; an injunction issued by the district court was sustained by the Court of Appeals; and this court, citing many decisions in which the doctrine of *Swift v. Tyson* (1842) had been applied, affirmed the decree.

Second. Experience in applying the doctrine of *Swift v. Tyson* (1842) had revealed its defects, political and social; and the benefits expected to flow from the rule did not accrue. Persistence of state courts in their own opinions on questions

---

5. Charles Warren, *New Light on the History of the Federal Judiciary Act of 1789*, 37 HARV. L. REV. 49, 51-52, 81-88, 108 (1923).

of common law prevented uniformity; and the impossibility of discovering a satis-factory line of demarcation between the province of general law and that of local law developed a new well of uncertainties.

On the other hand, the mischievous results of the doctrine had become apparent. Diversity of citizenship jurisdiction was conferred in order to prevent apprehended discrimination in state courts against those not citizens of the State. *Swift v. Tyson* introduced grave discrimination by noncitizens against citizens. It made rights enjoyed under the unwritten "general law" vary according to whether enforcement was sought in the state or in the federal court; and the privilege of selecting the court in which the right should be determined was conferred upon the noncitizen. Thus, the doctrine rendered impossible equal protection of the law. In attempting to promote uniformity of law throughout the United States, the doctrine had prevented uniformity in the administration of the law of the State.

The discrimination resulting became in practice far-reaching. This resulted in part from the broad province accorded to the so-called "general law" as to which federal courts exercised an independent judgment. In addition to questions of purely commercial law, "general law" was held to include the obligations under contracts entered into and to be performed within the State, the extent to which a carrier operating within a State may stipulate for exemption from liability for his own negligence or that of his employee; the liability for torts committed within the State upon persons resident or property located there, even where the question of liability depended upon the scope of a property right conferred by the State; and the right to exemplary or punitive damages. Furthermore, state decisions construing local deeds, mineral conveyances, and even devises of real estate were disregarded.

In part the discrimination resulted from the wide range of persons held enti-tled to avail themselves of the federal rule by resort to the diversity of citizenship jurisdiction. Through this jurisdiction, individual citizens willing to remove from their own State and become citizens of another might avail themselves of the fed-eral rule. And, without even change of residence, a corporate citizen of the State could avail itself of the federal rule by reincorporating under the laws of another state, as was done in the *Taxicab* case.

·The injustice and confusion incident to the doctrine of *Swift v. Tyson* have been repeatedly urged as reasons for abolishing or limiting diversity of citizenship jurisdiction. Other legislative relief has been proposed. If only a question of statu-tory construction were involved, we should not be prepared to abandon a doctrine so widely applied throughout nearly a century. But the unconstitutionality of the course pursued has now been made clear and compels us to do so.

Third. Except in matters governed by the Federal Constitution or by Acts of Congress, the law to be applied in any case is the law of the State. And whether the law of the State shall be declared by its Legislature in a statute or by its highest court in a decision is not a matter of federal concern. There is no federal general common law. Congress has no power to declare substantive rules of common law applicable in a State whether they be local in their nature or "general," be they commercial law or a part of the law of torts. And no clause in the Constitution pur-ports to confer such a power upon the federal courts.

The fallacy underlying the rule declared in *Swift v. Tyson* is made clear by Mr. Justice Holmes [in *Black & White Taxicab*]. The doctrine rests upon the assumption that there is "a transcendental body of law outside of any particular State but obligatory within it unless and until changed by statute," that federal courts have the power to use their judgment as to what the rules of common law are; and that in the federal courts "the parties are entitled to an independent judgment on matters of general law":

> [B]ut law in the sense in which courts speak of it today does not exist without some definite authority behind it. The common law so far as it is enforced in a State, whether called common law or not, is not the common law generally but the law of that State existing by the authority of that State without regard to what it may have been in England or anywhere else. . . . The authority and only authority is the state, and if that be so, the voice adopted by the State as its own [whether it be of its Legislature or of its Supreme Court] should utter the last word.

Thus the doctrine of *Swift v. Tyson* is, as Mr. Justice Holmes said, "an unconstitutional assumption of power by courts of the United States which no lapse of time or respectable array of opinion should make us hesitate to correct." In disapproving that doctrine we do not hold unconstitutional §34 of the Federal Judiciary Act of 1789, or any other Act of Congress. We merely declare that in applying the doctrine this Court and the lower courts have invaded rights which in our opinion are reserved by the Constitution to the several States. . . .

* * *

In *Erie*, the Court held that the federal courts must apply state law in diversity suits because there was no general federal common law for them to draw upon in making substantive decisions. In general, determining state law involves two steps. First, the federal court must look to the conflict of law rules of the state in which it sits to determine which states substantive law will provide the rules of decision for the merits of the case. *See Klaxon v. Stentor Elecrtric Mfg. Co.* (1941). Second, once the federal court knows which state's substantive rules of decision control, the court looks to that state's supreme court decisions. In the absence of controlling supreme court decisions, the federal court may consider opinions of state intermediate appellate courts, scholarly articles, the Restatement of Law, and treatises. *See generally Bernhardt v. Polygraphic Co. of Am.* (1956); *Comm'r v. Estate of Bosch* (1967).

An enduring puzzle is whether the holding of *Erie* was constitutionally required, as Justice Brandeis suggested, or if this was merely a statutory requirement. After all, the Constitution gives Congress the power to establish federal courts and to afford those courts power to hear actions arising between citizens of different states. Why, some commentators have asked, does the congressional power to establish those courts not include the power to create courts that may determine both the procedure and the substance of diversity actions? Regardless of whether the Constitution requires it, however, the Court has interpreted the applicable congressional acts to mean that federal courts in diversity cases must apply state substantive law. The relevant statutes are the Rules of Decision Act, 28 U.S.C. §1652, and the Rules Enabling Act, 28 U.S.C. §§2072-2077.

The Rules Enabling Act, the current version of which is found at 28 U.S.C. §2072, provides that the "Supreme Court shall have the power to prescribe general rules of practice and procedure and rules of evidence for cases in the United States district courts" and that "these rules shall not abridge, enlarge, or modify any substantive right." Taken together and grossly simplified, the two acts mean that federal courts apply their own procedure and state substantive law in diversity suits.

Less than a decade after *Erie*, the Court decided *Guaranty Trust Co. v. York* (1945), which set the highwater mark for the Court's federalism-based deference to state rules of decision. In *Guaranty Trust*, the Court reasoned that the *Erie* doctrine expressed a fundamental "policy" concerning the relationship between the federal courts and the state courts:

> *Erie R.R. Co. v. Tompkins* was not an endeavor to formulate scientific legal terminology. It expressed a policy that touches vitally the proper distribution of judicial power between State and federal courts. In essence, the intent of that decision was to insure that, in all cases where a federal court is exercising jurisdiction solely because of the diversity of citizenship of the parties, the outcome of the litigation in the federal court should be substantially the same, so far as legal rules determine the outcome of a litigation, as it would be if tried in a State court. The nub of the policy that underlies *Erie R.R. Co. v. Tompkins* is that for the same transaction the accident of a suit by a nonresident litigant in a federal court instead of in a State court a block away should not lead to a substantially different result.

The Court retreated from *York* in *Byrd v. Blue Ridge Rural Elec. Coop., Inc.* (1958), and identified "affirmative countervailing considerations" that cut against the "policy" of the *Erie* doctrine, including the federal interest in providing an "independent system for administering justice to litigants who properly invoke its jurisdiction." As the Court emphasized, "[a]n essential characteristic of that system is the manner in which, in civil common-law actions, it distributes trial functions between judge and jury and, under the influence—if not the command—of the Seventh Amendment, assigns the decisions of disputed questions of fact to the jury. [*Erie*'s] policy of uniform enforcement of state created rights and obligations," the Court concluded, "cannot in every case exact compliance with a state rule—not bound up with rights and obligations—which disrupts the federal system of allocating functions between judge and jury." Thus, at least where the federal Seventh Amendment right to a jury trial was at stake in the choice between the federal and state procedural rule of decision, state law would not control.

The Court in *Byrd* thus rejected a rigid application of *York*'s outcome-determinative test, instead calling on courts to balance competing state and federal policies, particularly where, as in *Byrd*, any difference in outcome was purely speculative and the constitutional right to a jury trial was at stake.

The Court further limited *York*'s outcome-determinative test and clarified the *Erie* doctrine in *Hanna v. Plumer* (1965), holding that congressionally authorized federal procedural rules of decision are generally controlling in federal court. The plaintiff filed a personal injury claim arising from an automobile accident in Massachusetts federal court. Service of process was made in compliance with Rule 4, which permits leaving a copy of the complaint and summons with a person of suitable age at the defendant's dwelling or place of abode. State law required personal service upon the defendant. The defendant sought to dismiss the case because the plaintiff failed to comply with the state service of process rule. The Court rejected the defendant's argument that *Erie* required application of the state service of process rule even though the rule could be construed as outcome determinative under *York*. The Court emphasized that *Erie* itself did not involve a legislatively prescribed rule of procedure and was therefore simply not controlling where Congress had set out such a rule.

> *Erie* and its offspring cast no doubt on the long-recognized power of Congress to prescribe housekeeping rules for federal courts even though some of those rules will inevitably differ from comparable state rules. "When, because the plaintiff happens to be a non-resident, such a right is enforceable in a federal as well as in a State court, the forms and mode of enforcing the right may at times, naturally enough, vary because the two judicial systems are not identical." *Guaranty Trust Co. v. York*. Thus, though a court, in measuring a Federal Rule against the standards contained in the Enabling Act and the Constitution, need not wholly blind itself to the degree to which the Rule makes the character and result of the federal litigation stray from the course it would follow in state courts, *Sibbach v. Wilson & Co.* (1941), it cannot be forgotten that the *Erie* rule, and the guidelines suggested in *York*, were created to serve another purpose altogether. To hold that a Federal Rule of Civil Procedure must cease to function whenever it alters the mode of enforcing state-created rights would be to disembowel either the Constitution's grant of power over federal procedure or Congress' attempt to exercise that power in the Enabling Act. Rule 4(d)(1) is valid and controls the instant case.

Hanna clarified that when a federal procedural rule of decision has been created by Congress, it is generally controlling by virtue of the Supremacy Clause — the federalism interests underlying *Erie* give way here to the authority of Congress to set rules of decision for courts of its own creation under Article III. Since *Hanna*, the modern Court has oscillated in its commitment to the judicial federalism principles of *Erie* and the supremacy clause and congressional authority principles of *Hanna*.

In *Gasperini v. Center for Humanities, Inc.* (1986), for example, the Court considered a New York state law that provided a standard for reviewing jury verdicts for excessiveness. That standard granted judges more discretion to reverse arguably excessive verdicts than the applicable federal procedural rule. The federal rule reflected constraints imposed by the Seventh Amendment on federal judicial review of jury verdicts. By a 5-4 vote, the Court distinguished *Byrd* and held that federal trial courts sitting in diversity must apply the broader state standard for determining excessiveness. Looking to the "twin aims of *Erie*," the majority reasoned that application of the federal standard would encourage forum shopping because there would be both a perceived and a real difference in the size of recoveries on jury verdicts. Moreover, New York citizens would be subjected to unchecked damages in the federal courts when they would be protected in their own courts. This would constitute inequitable administration of the laws. In a dissenting opinion, Justice Scalia accused the majority of committing "the classic *Erie* mistake of regarding whatever changes the outcome as substantive," and reminded the majority of the admonition in *Hanna* that outcome determination "was never intended to serve as a talisman." He argued that Rule 59 of the Federal Rules, which sets the standard for granting a new trial in federal court, is controlling under *Hanna*. Rule 59 is the product of "Congress's 'power to regulate matters which, though falling within the uncertain area between substance and procedure, are rationally capable of classification as either.'"

In *Semtek Int'l Inc. v. Lockheed Martin Corp.* (2001), the Court continued to interpret potential federal-state procedural conflicts in a manner that accommodates state procedural practices. The Court unanimously held that the claim-preclusive effect of a federal judgment dismissing a diversity action on statute-of-limitations grounds is determined by the law of the state in which the federal court sits. The Court relied in part upon an 1875 case, *Dupasseur v. Rochereau*, which held that the *res judicata* effect of a federal diversity judgment "is such as would belong to judgments of state courts rendered under similar circumstances." The respondent argued that *Dupasseur* was not controlling because it was decided in an era in which federal courts were required by the Conformity Act of 1872 to apply the *procedural* law of the forum state in *non-equity* cases. Moreover, the respondent maintained that Rule 41(b) was controlling, because the order of dismissal did not "otherwise specify[]" that the dismissal would "operate[] as an adjudication upon the merits."

The Court disagreed, concluding that Rule 41(b)'s phrase "on the merits" did not necessarily mean "entitled to claim preclusive effect." Indeed, such an operation of the rule might violate the Rules Enabling Act, insofar as it might "abridge, enlarge or modify [a] substantive right." 28 U.S.C. §2072(b). "[T]he traditional rule is that expiration of the applicable statute of limitations merely bars the remedy and does not extinguish the substantive right, so that dismissal on that ground does not have claim-preclusive effect in other jurisdictions with longer, unexpired limitations periods." If federal court dismissals on statute-of-limitations grounds would bar suit everywhere, this could lead to forum shopping: "[o]ut-of-state defendants sued on stale claims . . . in . . . States adhering to this traditional rule would systematically remove state-law suits brought against them to federal court. . . ."

Given that Rule 41(b) did not determine the outcome, and given these competing federalism principles, the Court concluded that federal common law should incorporate state law regarding the claim-preclusive effect of dismissals, *except* "in situations in which the state law is incompatible with federal interests." Finding no such incompatibility in *Semtek*, the Court held that the state law of preclusion should control.

Whatever factors prompted the Court to speak with one voice in *Semtek* disappeared a decade later when the Court took up the following case. As you will see, Justice Scalia cobbles together a majority for the proposition that Fed. R. Civ. P. 23 is controlling, but he has only a plurality for the rest of his analysis. That means the Court still has not settled on a method for distinguishing substantive and procedural rules of decision or a method for determining whether state and federal rules of decision conflict. As you read the case, consider how the Justices views on the viability and legitimacy of class actions may inform their positions on the judicial federalism principles of *Erie*. By the time *Shady Grove* is decided in 2010, two decades of Supreme Court precedent making it more difficult to certify a federal class action had become a formidable barrier to this form of aggregate litigation, although there is some evidence that at the turn of the century both federal and state courts were equally unlikely to certify a class action.[20] A year later the Court would fundamentally alter certification standards in Rule 23(b)(3) class actions in *Walmart v. Dukes* (2011) by tightening the commonality requirement. This amplified incentives for plaintiffs either to file class actions in state court and resist removal, or to focus on regional rather than nationwide class actions.

Shady Grove Orthopedic Assocs. P.A. v. Allstate Ins. Co.

559 U.S. 393 (2010)

Justice SCALIA announced the judgment of the Court and delivered the opinion of the Court with respect to Parts I and II-A, an opinion with respect to Parts II-B and II-D, in which THE CHIEF JUSTICE, Justice THOMAS, and Justice SOTOMAYOR join, and an opinion with respect to Part II-C, in which THE CHIEF JUSTICE and Justice THOMAS join.

New York law prohibits class actions in suits seeking penalties or statutory minimum damages.[1] We consider whether this precludes a federal district court sitting in diversity from entertaining a class action under Federal Rule of Civil Procedure 23.

I

The petitioner's complaint alleged the following: Shady Grove Orthopedic Associates, P.A., provided medical care to Sonia E. Galvez for injuries she suffered in an automobile accident. As partial payment for that care, Galvez assigned to Shady Grove her rights to insurance benefits under a policy issued in New York by Allstate Insurance Co. Shady Grove tendered a claim for the assigned benefits to Allstate, which under New York law had 30 days to pay the claim or deny it. . . . Allstate apparently paid, but not on time, and it refused to pay the statutory interest that accrued on the overdue benefits (at two percent per month).

Shady Grove filed this diversity suit in the Eastern District of New York to recover the unpaid statutory interest. Alleging that Allstate routinely refuses to pay interest on overdue benefits, Shady Grove sought relief on behalf of itself and a class of all others to whom Allstate owes interest. The District Court dismissed

---

20. THOMAS E. WILLGING & SHANNON R. WEATMAN, FEDERAL JUDICIAL CENTER, AN EMPIRICAL EXAMINATION OF ATTORNEYS' CHOICE OF FORUM IN CLASS ACTION LITIGATION (2005).

1. N.Y. Civ. Prac. Law Ann. §901 (2006) provides:

(a) One or more members of a class may sue or be sued as representative parties on behalf of all if: 1. the class is so numerous that joinder of all members, whether otherwise required or permitted, is impracticable; 2. there are questions of law or fact common to the class which predominate over any questions affecting only individual members; 3. the claims or defenses of the representative parties are typical of the claims or defenses of the class; 4. the representative parties will fairly and adequately protect the interests of the class; and 5. a class action is superior to other available methods for the fair and efficient adjudication of the controversy.

(b) Unless a statute creating or imposing a penalty, or a minimum measure of recovery specifically authorizes the recovery thereof in a class action, an action to recover a penalty, or minimum measure of recovery created or imposed by statute may not be maintained as a class action.

the suit for lack of jurisdiction. It reasoned that N.Y. Civ. Prac. Law Ann. §901(b), which precludes a suit to recover a "penalty" from proceeding as a class action, applies in diversity suits in federal court, despite Federal Rule of Civil Procedure 23. Concluding that statutory interest is a "penalty" under New York law, it held that §901(b) prohibited the proposed class action. And, since Shady Grove conceded that its individual claim (worth roughly $500) fell far short of the amount-in-controversy requirement for individual suits under 28 U.S.C. §1332(a), the suit did not belong in federal court.[3]

The Second Circuit affirmed.

II

The framework for our decision is familiar. We must first determine whether Rule 23 answers the question in dispute. *Burlington Northern R. Co. v. Woods* (1987). If it does, it governs — New York's law notwithstanding — unless it exceeds statutory authorization or Congress's rulemaking power. *See Hanna v. Plumer* (1965). We do not wade into *Erie*'s murky waters unless the federal rule is inapplicable or invalid.

A

The question in dispute is whether Shady Grove's suit may proceed as a class action. Rule 23 provides an answer. It states that "[a] class action may be maintained" if two conditions are met: The suit must satisfy the criteria set forth in subdivision (a) (i.e., numerosity, commonality, typicality, and adequacy of representation), and it also must fit into one of the three categories described in subdivision (b). By its terms this creates a categorical rule entitling a plaintiff whose suit meets the specified criteria to pursue his claim as a class action. (The Federal Rules regularly use "may" to confer categorical permission, as do federal statutes that establish procedural entitlements.) Thus, Rule 23 provides a one-size-fits-all formula for deciding the class-action question. Because §901(b) attempts to answer the same question — i.e., it states that Shady Grove's suit "may *not* be maintained as a class action" because of the relief it seeks — it cannot apply in diversity suits unless Rule 23 is *ultra vires*.

The Second Circuit believed that §901(b) and Rule 23 do not conflict because they address different issues. Rule 23, it said, concerns only the criteria for determining whether a given class can and should be certified; section 901(b), on the other hand, addresses an antecedent question: whether the particular type of claim is eligible for class treatment in the first place — a question on which Rule 23 is silent. Allstate embraces this analysis.

We disagree. To begin with, the line between eligibility and certifiability is entirely artificial. Both are preconditions for maintaining a class action. Allstate suggests that eligibility must depend on the "particular cause of action" asserted, instead of some other attribute of the suit. But that is not so. Congress could, for example, provide that only claims involving more than a certain number of

---

3. Shady Grove had asserted jurisdiction under 28 U.S.C. §1332(d)(2), which relaxes, for class actions seeking at least $5 million, the rule against aggregating separate claims for calculation of the amount in controversy. *See Exxon Mobil Corp. v. Allapattah Services, Inc.* (2005).

plaintiffs are "eligible" for class treatment in federal court. In other words, rela-
beling Rule 23(a)'s prerequisites "eligibility criteria" would obviate Allstate's objection—a sure sign that its eligibility-certifiability distinction is made-to-order.

Allstate points out that Congress has carved out some federal claims from
Rule 23's reach, *see, e.g.,* 8 U.S.C. §1252(e)(1)(B)—which shows, Allstate contends,
that Rule 23 does not authorize class actions for all claims, but rather leaves room
for laws like §901(b). But Congress, unlike New York, has ultimate authority over
the Federal Rules of Civil Procedure; it can create exceptions to an individual rule
as it sees fit—either by directly amending the rule or by enacting a separate statute
overriding it in certain instances. The fact that Congress has created specific exceptions to Rule 23 hardly proves that the Rule does not apply generally. In fact, it
proves the opposite. If Rule 23 did *not* authorize class actions across the board, the
statutory exceptions would be unnecessary.

Allstate next suggests that the structure of §901 shows that Rule 23 addresses
only certifiability. Section 901(a), it notes, establishes class certification criteria
roughly analogous to those in Rule 23 (wherefore it agrees *that* subsection is pre-
empted). But §901(b)'s rule barring class actions for certain claims is set off as its
own subsection, and where it applies §901(a) does not. Rule 23 permits all class
actions that meet its requirements, and a State cannot limit that permission by
structuring one part of its statute to track Rule 23 and enacting another part that
imposes additional requirements. Both of §901's subsections undeniably answer
the same question as Rule 23: whether a class action may proceed for a given suit.

The dissent argues that §901(b) has nothing to do with whether Shady Grove
may maintain its suit as a class action, but affects only the *remedy* it may obtain if
it wins. Whereas "Rule 23 governs procedural aspects of class litigation" by "prescrib[ing] the considerations relevant to class certification and postcertification
proceedings," §901(b) addresses only "the size of a monetary award a class plaintiff
may pursue." Accordingly, the dissent says, Rule 23 and New York's law may coexist
in peace.

Unlike a law that sets a ceiling on damages (or puts other remedies out of
reach) in properly filed class actions, §901(b) says nothing about what remedies a
court may award; it prevents the class actions it covers from coming into existence
at all. Consequently, a court bound by §901(b) could not certify a class action seeking both statutory penalties and other remedies even if it announces in advance
that it will refuse to award the penalties in the event the plaintiffs prevail; to do so
would violate the statute's clear prohibition on "maintain[ing]" such suits as class
actions.

The evidence of the New York Legislature's purpose is pretty sparse. But even
accepting the dissent's account of the Legislature's objective at face value, it cannot
override the statute's clear text. Even if its aim is to restrict the remedy a plaintiff
can obtain, §901(b) achieves that end by limiting a plaintiff's power to maintain a
class action. The manner in which the law "could have been written," has no bearing; what matters is the law the Legislature *did* enact. We cannot rewrite that to
reflect our perception of legislative purpose.

But while the dissent does indeed artificially narrow the scope of §901(b) by
finding that it pursues only substantive policies, that is not the central difficulty of
the dissent's position. The central difficulty is that even artificial narrowing cannot render §901(b) compatible with Rule 23. *Whatever* the policies they pursue,
they flatly contradict each other. Allstate asserts (and the dissent implies) that we

can (and must) *interpret* Rule 23 in a manner that avoids overstepping its authorizing statute. If the Rule were susceptible of two meanings—one that would violate §2072(b) and another that would not—we would agree. But it is not. Rule 23 unambiguously authorizes *any* plaintiff, in *any* federal civil proceeding, to maintain a class action if the Rule's prerequisites are met. We cannot contort its text, even to avert a collision with state law that might render it invalid. What the dissent's approach achieves is not the avoiding of a "conflict between Rule 23 and §901(b)," but rather the invalidation of Rule 23 (pursuant to §2072(b) of the Rules Enabling Act) to the extent that it conflicts with the substantive policies of §901. There is no other way to reach the dissent's destination. We must therefore confront head-on whether Rule 23 falls within the statutory authorization.

B

    Erie involved the constitutional power of federal courts to supplant state law with judge-made rules. In that context, it made no difference whether the rule was technically one of substance or procedure; the touchstone was whether it "significantly affect[s] the result of a litigation." *Guaranty Trust Co. v. York* (1945). That is not the test for either the constitutionality or the statutory validity of a Federal Rule of Procedure. Congress has undoubted power to supplant state law, and undoubted power to prescribe rules for the courts it has created, so long as those rules regulate matters "rationally capable of classification" as procedure. *Hanna.* In the Rules Enabling Act, Congress authorized this Court to promulgate rules of procedure subject to its review, 28 U.S.C. §2072(a), but with the limitation that those rules "shall not abridge, enlarge or modify any substantive right," §2072(b).

    We have long held that this limitation means that the Rule must "really regulat[e] procedure, the judicial process for enforcing rights and duties recognized by substantive law and for justly administering remedy and redress for disregard or infraction of them." *Sibbach v. Wilson & Co.* (1941). The test is not whether the rule affects a litigant's substantive rights; most procedural rules do. *Mississippi Publishing Corp. v. Murphree* (1946). What matters is what the rule itself regulates: If it governs only "the manner and the means" by which the litigants' rights are "enforced," it is valid; if it alters "the rules of decision by which [the] court will adjudicate [those] rights," it is not.

    Applying that test, we have rejected every statutory challenge to a Federal Rule that has come before us. We have found to be in compliance with §2072(b) rules prescribing methods for serving process, and requiring litigants whose mental or physical condition is in dispute to submit to examinations. Likewise, we have upheld rules authorizing imposition of sanctions upon those who file frivolous appeals, or who sign court papers without a reasonable inquiry into the facts asserted. Each of these rules had some practical effect on the parties' rights, but each undeniably regulated only the process for enforcing those rights; none altered the rights themselves, the available remedies, or the rules of decision by which the court adjudicated either.

    Applying that criterion, we think it obvious that rules allowing multiple claims (and claims by or against multiple parties) to be litigated together are also valid. *See, e.g.,* Fed. Rules Civ. Proc. 18 (joinder of claims), 20 (joinder of parties), 42(a) (consolidation of actions). Such rules neither change plaintiffs' separate entitlements to relief nor abridge defendants' rights; they alter only how the claims are processed. For the same reason, Rule 23—at least insofar as it allows willing plaintiffs to join their separate claims against the same defendants in a class action—falls within §2072(b)'s authorization. A class action, no less than traditional joinder (of which it is a species), merely enables a federal court to adjudicate claims of multiple parties at once, instead of in separate suits. And like traditional joinder, it leaves the parties' legal rights and duties intact and the rules of decision unchanged.

Allstate contends that the authorization of class actions is not substantively neutral: Allowing Shady Grove to sue on behalf of a class "transform[s] [the] dispute over a five *hundred* dollar penalty into a dispute over a five *million* dollar penalty." Allstate's aggregate liability, however, does not depend on whether the suit proceeds as a class action. Each of the 1,000-plus members of the putative class could (as Allstate acknowledges) bring a freestanding suit asserting his individual claim. It is undoubtedly true that some plaintiffs who would not bring individual suits for the relatively small sums involved will choose to join a class action. That has no bearing, however, on Allstate's or the plaintiffs' legal rights. The likelihood that some (even many) plaintiffs will be induced to sue by the availability of a class action is just the sort of "incidental effec[t]" we have long held does not violate §2072(b), *Mississippi Publishing* (1946).

Allstate argues that Rule 23 violates §2072(b) because the state law it displaces, §901(b), creates a right that the Federal Rule abridges—namely, a "substantive right . . . not to be subjected to aggregated class-action liability" in a single suit. To begin with, we doubt that that is so. Nothing in the text of §901(b) (which is to be found in New York's procedural code) confines it to claims under New York law; and of course New York has no power to alter substantive rights and duties created by other sovereigns. As we have said, the *consequence* of excluding certain class actions may be to cap the damages a defendant can face in a single suit, but the law itself alters only procedure. In that respect, §901(b) is no different from a state law forbidding simple joinder. As a fallback argument, Allstate argues that even if §901(b) is a procedural provision, it was enacted "for *substantive* reasons." Its end was not to improve "the conduct of the litigation process itself" but to alter "the outcome of that process."

The fundamental difficulty with both these arguments is that the substantive nature of New York's law, or its substantive purpose, *makes no difference.* A Federal Rule of Procedure is not valid in some jurisdictions and invalid in others—or valid in some cases and invalid in others—depending upon whether its effect is to frustrate a state substantive law (or a state procedural law enacted for substantive purposes). *Hanna* unmistakably expressed the same understanding that compliance of a Federal Rule with the Enabling Act is to be assessed by consulting the Rule itself, and not its effects in individual applications.

In sum, it is not the substantive or procedural nature or purpose of the affected state law that matters, but the substantive or procedural nature of the Federal Rule. We have held since *Sibbach,* and reaffirmed repeatedly, that the validity of a Federal Rule depends entirely upon whether it regulates procedure. If it does, it is authorized by §2072 and is valid in all jurisdictions, with respect to all claims, regardless of its incidental effect upon state-created rights.

C

The concurrence would decide this case on the basis, not that Rule 23 is procedural, but that the state law it displaces is procedural, in the sense that it does not "function as a part of the State's definition of substantive rights and remedies." A state procedural rule is not preempted, according to the concurrence, so long as it is "so bound up with," or "sufficiently intertwined with," a substantive state-law right or remedy "that it defines the scope of that substantive right or remedy."

This analysis squarely conflicts with *Sibbach*, which established the rule we apply.

D

We must acknowledge the reality that keeping the federal-court door open to class actions that cannot proceed in state court will produce forum shopping. That is unacceptable when it comes as the consequence of judge-made rules created to fill supposed "gaps" in positive federal law. For where neither the Constitution, a treaty, nor a statute provides the rule of decision or authorizes a federal court to supply one, "state law must govern because there can be no other law." *Hanna.* But divergence from state law, with the attendant consequence of forum shopping, is the inevitable (indeed, one might say the intended) result of a uniform system of federal procedure. Congress itself has created the possibility that the same case may follow a different course if filed in federal instead of state court. . . . The short of the matter is that a Federal Rule governing procedure is valid whether or not it alters the outcome of the case in a way that induces forum shopping. To hold otherwise would be to "disembowel either the Constitution's grant of power over federal procedure" or Congress's exercise of it. *Hanna.*

Justice STEVENS, concurring in part and concurring in the judgment.
. . . Justice SCALIA believes that the sole Enabling Act question is whether the federal rule "really regulates procedure," which means, apparently, whether it regulates "the manner and the means by which the litigants' rights are enforced." I respectfully disagree.[7] This interpretation of the Enabling Act is consonant with the Act's first limitation to "general rules of practice and procedure," §2072(a). But it ignores the second limitation that such rules also "not abridge, enlarge or modify any substantive right," §2072(b) (emphasis added), and in so doing ignores the balance that Congress struck between uniform rules of federal procedure and respect for a State's construction of its own rights and remedies. It also ignores the separation-of-powers presumption, and federalism presumption, that counsel against judicially created rules displacing state substantive law.

Accordingly, I concur in part and concur in the judgment.

---

7. This understanding of the Enabling Act has been the subject of substantial academic criticism, and rightfully so. *See, e.g.,* CHARLES A. WRIGHT ET AL., 19 FEDERAL PRACTICE AND PROCEDURE §4509, at 264, 269-70, 272 (3d. ed. 2002); John Hart Ely, *The Irrepressible Myth of Erie,* 87 HARV. L. REV. 693, 719 (1974) (hereinafter Ely); *see also* RICHARD H. FALLON, J. ET AL., HART AND WECHSLER'S THE FEDERAL COURTS AND THE FEDERAL SYSTEM 593, n.6 (6th ed. 2009) (discussing Ely).

Justice GINSBURG, with whom Justice KENNEDY, Justice BREYER, and Justice ALITO join, dissenting.

The Court today approves Shady Grove's attempt to transform a $500 case into a $5,000,000 award, although the State creating the right to recover has proscribed this alchemy. If Shady Grove had filed suit in New York state court, the 2% interest payment authorized by New York Ins. Law Ann. §5106(a), as a penalty for overdue benefits would, by Shady Grove's own measure, amount to no more than $500. By instead filing in federal court based on the parties' diverse citizenship and requesting class certification, Shady Grove hopes to recover, for the class, statutory damages of more than $5,000,000. The New York Legislature has barred this remedy. . . .

The Court reads Rule 23 relentlessly to override New York's restriction on the availability of statutory damages. Our decisions, however, caution us to ask, before undermining state legislation: Is this conflict really necessary?

I

. . .

B

In our prior decisions in point, many of them not mentioned in the Court's opinion, we have avoided immoderate interpretations of the Federal Rules that would trench on state prerogatives without serving any countervailing federal interest. "Application of the *Hanna* analysis," we have said, "is premised on a 'direct collision' between the Federal Rule and the state law." *Walker v. Armco Steel Corp.* (1980). To displace state law, a Federal Rule, "when fairly construed," must be "'sufficiently broad'" so as "to 'control the issue' before the court, thereby leaving no room for the operation of that law." *Burlington Northern R. Co. v. Woods* (1987).

In pre-*Hanna* decisions, the Court vigilantly read the Federal Rules to avoid conflict with state laws.

In all of these cases, the Court stated in *Hanna*, "the scope of the Federal Rule was not as broad as the losing party urged, and therefore, there being no Federal Rule which covered the point in dispute, *Erie* commanded the enforcement of state law." In *Hanna* itself, the Court found the clash "unavoidable;" the petitioner had effected service of process as prescribed by Federal Rule 4(d)(1), but that "how-to" method did not satisfy the special Massachusetts law applicable to service on an executor or administrator. . . .

Following *Hanna*, we continued to "interpre[t] the federal rules to avoid conflict with important state regulatory policies."

Most recently, in *Semtek*, we addressed the claim-preclusive effect of a federal-court judgment dismissing a diversity action on the basis of a California statute of limitations. The case came to us after the same plaintiff renewed the same fray against the same defendant in a Maryland state court. (Plaintiff chose Maryland because that State's limitations period had not yet run.) We held that Federal Rule 41(b), which provided that an involuntary dismissal "operate[d] as an adjudication on the merits," did not bar maintenance of the renewed action in Maryland. To hold that Rule 41(b) precluded the Maryland courts from entertaining the case, we said, "would arguably violate the jurisdictional limitation of the Rules Enabling Act," and "would in many cases violate [*Erie*'s] federalism principle."

In sum, both before and after *Hanna*, the above-described decisions show, federal courts have been cautioned by this Court to "interpre[t] the Federal Rules . . . with sensitivity to important state interests," *Gasperini v. Center for Humanities, Inc.* (1996), and a will "to avoid conflict with important state regulatory policies." The Court veers away from that approach—and conspicuously, its most recent reiteration in *Gasperini*, in favor of a mechanical reading of Federal Rules, insensitive to state interests and productive of discord.

C

. . . The limitation [of §901(b)] was not designed with the fair conduct or efficiency of litigation in mind. Indeed, suits seeking statutory damages are arguably best suited to the class device because individual proof of actual damages is unnecessary. New York's decision instead to block class-action proceedings for statutory damages therefore makes scant sense, except as a means to a manifestly substantive end: Limiting a defendant's liability in a single lawsuit in order to prevent the exorbitant inflation of penalties—remedies the New York Legislature created with individual suits in mind.

D

As the Second Circuit well understood, Rule 23 prescribes the considerations relevant to class certification and post-certification proceedings—but it does not command that a particular remedy be available when a party sues in a representative capacity. Section 901(b), in contrast, trains on that latter issue. Sensibly read, Rule 23 governs procedural aspects of class litigation, but allows state law to control the size of a monetary award a class plaintiff may pursue.

In other words, Rule 23 describes a method of enforcing a claim for relief, while §901(b) defines the dimensions of the claim itself. In this regard, it is immaterial that §901(b) bars statutory penalties in wholesale, rather than retail, fashion. The New York Legislature could have embedded the limitation in every provision creating a cause of action for which a penalty is authorized; §901(b) operates as shorthand to the same effect. It is as much a part of the delineation of the claim for relief as it would be were it included claim by claim in the New York Code. . . .

The fair and efficient *conduct* of class litigation is the legitimate concern of Rule 23; the *remedy* for an infraction of state law, however, is the legitimate concern of the State's lawmakers and not of the federal rulemakers. *Cf.* Ely, *The Irrepressible Myth of* Erie, 87 Harv. L. Rev. 693, 722 (1974) (It is relevant "whether the state provision embodies a substantive policy or represents only a procedural disagreement with the federal rulemakers respecting the fairest and most efficient way of conducting litigation.").

The absence of an inevitable collision between Rule 23 and §901(b) becomes evident once it is comprehended that a federal court sitting in diversity can accord due respect to both state and federal prescriptions. Plaintiffs seeking to vindicate claims for which the State has provided a statutory penalty may pursue relief through a class action if they forgo statutory damages and instead seek actual damages or injunctive or declaratory relief; any putative class member who objects can opt out and pursue actual damages, if available, and the statutory penalty in an individual action. In this manner, the Second Circuit explained, "Rule 23's procedural requirements for class actions can be applied along with the substantive requirement of CPLR 901(b)." In sum, while phrased as responsive to the question whether certain class actions may begin, §901(b) is unmistakably aimed at controlling how those actions must end. On that remedial issue, Rule 23 is silent.

Any doubt whether Rule 23 leaves §901(b) in control of the remedial issue at the core of this case should be dispelled by our *Erie* jurisprudence, including *Hanna*, which counsels us to read Federal Rules moderately and cautions against stretching a rule to cover every situation it could conceivably reach. The Court states that "[t]here is no reason . . . to read Rule 23 as addressing only whether claims made eligible for class treatment by some other law should be certified as class actions." To the contrary, *Palmer, Ragan, Cohen, Walker, Gasperini,* and *Semtek* provide good reason to look to the law that creates the right to recover. That is plainly so on a more accurate statement of what is at stake: Is there any reason to read Rule 23 as authorizing a claim for relief when the State that created the remedy disallows its pursuit on behalf of a class? None at all is the answer our federal system should give.

By finding a conflict without considering whether Rule 23 rationally should be read to avoid any collision, the Court unwisely and unnecessarily retreats from the federalism principles undergirding *Erie*.

II

Because I perceive no unavoidable conflict between Rule 23 and §901(b), I would decide this case by inquiring "whether application of the [state] rule would have so important an effect upon the fortunes of one or both of the litigants that failure to [apply] it would be likely to cause a plaintiff to choose the federal court." *Hanna.*

. . . [S]tatutes qualify as "substantive" for *Erie* purposes even when they have "procedural" thrusts as well. They supply "substantive" law in diversity suits, *see York*, 326 U.S. at 109-112, even though, as Shady Grove acknowledges, state courts often apply the forum's limitations period as a "procedural" bar to claims arising under the law of another State. Similarly, federal courts sitting in diversity give effect to state laws governing the burden of proving contributory negligence, yet state courts adjudicating foreign causes of action often apply their own local law to this issue.

In short, Shady Grove's effort to characterize §901(b) as simply "procedural" cannot successfully elide this fundamental norm: When no federal law or rule is dispositive of an issue, and a state statute is outcome affective in the sense our cases on *Erie* (pre- and post-*Hanna*) develop, the Rules of Decision Act commands application of the State's law in diversity suits. *Gasperini.* As this case starkly demonstrates, if federal courts exercising diversity jurisdiction are compelled by Rule 23 to award statutory penalties in class actions while New York courts are bound by §901(b)'s proscription, "substantial variations between state and federal [money judgments] may be expected." The "variation" here is indeed "substantial." Shady Grove seeks class relief that is *ten thousand times* greater than the individual remedy available to it in state court. As the plurality acknowledges, forum shopping will undoubtedly result if a plaintiff need only file in federal instead of state court to seek a massive monetary award explicitly barred by state law. *See id.* ("*Erie* precludes a recovery in federal court significantly larger than the recovery that would have been tolerated in state court."). The "accident of diversity of citizenship," *Klaxon Co. v. Stentor Elec. Mfg. Co.*, (1941), should not subject a defendant to such augmented liability. *See Hanna* ("The *Erie* rule is rooted in part in a realization that it would be unfair for the character or result of a litigation materially to differ because the suit had been brought in a federal court."). . . .

Gasperini's observations apply with full force in this case. By barring the recovery of statutory damages in a class action, §901(b) controls a defendant's maximum liability in a suit seeking such a remedy. The remedial provision could have been written as an explicit cap: "In any class action seeking statutory damages, relief is limited to the amount the named plaintiff would have recovered in an individual suit." That New York's Legislature used other words to express the very same meaning should be inconsequential.

We have long recognized the impropriety of displacing, in a diversity action, state-law limitations on state-created remedies. *See Woods* (in a diversity case, a plaintiff "barred from recovery in the state court . . . should likewise be barred in the federal court"); *York* (federal court sitting in diversity "cannot afford recovery if the right to recover is made unavailable by the State nor can it substantively affect the enforcement of the right as given by the State"). Just as *Erie* precludes a federal court from entering a deficiency judgment when a State has "authoritatively announced that [such] judgments cannot be secured within its borders," *Angel v. Bullington* (1947), so too *Erie* should prevent a federal court from awarding statutory penalties aggregated through a class action when New York prohibits this recovery.

III

The Court's erosion of *Erie*'s federalism grounding impels me to point out the large irony in today's judgment. Shady Grove is able to pursue its claim in federal court only by virtue of the recent enactment of the Class Action Fairness Act of 2005 (CAFA), 28 U.S.C. §1332(d). In CAFA, Congress opened federal-court doors to state-law-based class actions so long as there is minimal diversity, at least 100 class members, and at least $5,000,000 in controversy. By providing a federal forum, Congress sought to check what it considered to be the over-readiness of some state courts to certify class actions. *See, e.g.,* S. Rep. No. 109-114 (2005) (CAFA prevents lawyers from "gam[ing] the procedural rules [to] keep nationwide or multi-state class actions in state courts whose judges have reputations for readily certifying classes."); *id.* (disapproving "the 'I never met a class action I didn't like' approach to class certification" that "is prevalent in state courts in some localities"). In other words, Congress envisioned fewer — not more — class actions overall. Congress surely never anticipated that CAFA would make federal courts a mecca for suits of the kind Shady Grove has launched: class actions seeking state-created penalties for claims arising under state law-claims that would be barred from class treatment in the State's own courts.

I would continue to approach *Erie* questions in a manner mindful of the purposes underlying the Rules of Decision Act and the Rules Enabling Act, faithful to precedent, and respectful of important state interests. I would therefore hold that the New York Legislature's limitation on the recovery of statutory damages applies in this case, and would affirm the Second Circuit's judgment.

* * *

Note that very few attorneys would be interested in representing an individual client with a claim for statutory damages of just $500. The contingency fee would barely cover the costs of filing the suit. So even if thousands of people suffered comparable injury as a result of an insurer's refusal to pay interest on overdue benefits, the insurer is unlikely to be held liable unless a class action can be filed. Aggregating the claims not only creates an attractive contingency fee, it establishes a remedy for injuries that would otherwise go uncompensated.

The central issue in *Shady Grove* is whether creating a procedure leading to a remedy is the same thing as creating substantive liability. In Justice Scalia's view, if Allstate owes the penalty on the interest to each member of the class, its substantive liability has not been expanded by virtue of Rule 23. All Rule 23 does is make recovery on that liability more feasible. In Justice Ginsburg's view, the procedural device allowing for class litigation in federal court expands Allstate's substantive liability in contravention of New York state law. Both are reasonable conclusions, aren't they?

Justices Scalia and Ginsburg take very different routes to determining whether there is a conflict between state and federal rules of decision. Justice Scalia begins with congressional power over the jurisdiction and thus procedural rules of decision for federal courts. Justice Ginsburg begins with the *Erie/York* framework of deference to state law. The latter approach is clearly more likely to result in a finding of conflict.

B. THE DEVELOPMENT OF FEDERAL COMMON LAW TO PROTECT FEDERAL INTERESTS

The strong presumption against federal common law does not entirely preclude the development of federal common law in civil actions. In fact, federal courts have created common law to protect federal interests as they arise in various categories of cases. These categories include federal common law to protect the federal government's proprietary interests, federal common law concerning international relations, and federal common law to resolve disputes among sovereigns within the U.S. federal system.

1. Federal Common Law to Protect Proprietary Interests

Federal common law has been created to protect the federal government's interests. The Supreme Court has articulated a two-part inquiry in deciding whether to create federal law to safeguard federal interests.[21] First, the Court

---

21. The separation of the inquiry into two parts was first articulated in Henry J. Friendly, *In Praise of* Erie — *and of the New Federal Common Law*, 39 N.Y.U. L. Rev. 383, 410 (1964). Professor Martha Field has phrased the two-part inquiry as follows: "[F]irst, a court should ask whether the issue before it is properly subject to the exercise of federal power; if it is, the court should go on to determine whether, in light of the competing state and federal interests involved, it is wise as a matter of policy to adopt a federal substantive rule to govern the issue." Field, *supra* note 1, at 886.

considers whether the matter justifies creating federal law. Second, if federal law is to be developed, the Court decides its content; specifically, the Court determines whether to copy existing state law principles or to formulate new rules.

A classic example of the first inquiry—whether a matter warrants the creation of federal law—is found in *Clearfield Trust Co. v. United States* (1943), where the Supreme Court held that federal common law should be created for transactions involving banking and the rights of the United States with regard to commercial paper.

Clearfield Trust Co. v. United States

318 U.S. 363 (1943)

Justice DOUGLAS delivered the opinion of the Court.

On April 28, 1936, a check was drawn on the Treasurer of the United States through the Federal Reserve Bank of Philadelphia to the order of Clair A. Barner in the amount of $24.20. It was dated at Harrisburg, Pennsylvania and was drawn for services rendered by Barner to the Works Progress Administration. The check was placed in the mail addressed to Barner at his address in Mackeyville, Pa. Barner never received the check. Some unknown person obtained it in a mysterious manner and presented it to the J. C. Penney Co. store in Clearfield, Pa., representing that he was the payee and identifying himself to the satisfaction of the employees of J. C. Penney Co. He endorsed the check in the name of Barner and transferred it to J. C. Penney Co. in exchange for cash and merchandise. Barner never authorized the endorsement nor participated in the proceeds of the check. J. C. Penney Co. endorsed the check over to the Clearfield Trust Co. which accepted it as agent for the purpose of collection and endorsed it as follows: 'Pay to the order of Federal Reserve Bank of Philadelphia, Prior Endorsements Guaranteed.' Clearfield Trust Co. collected the check from the United States through the Federal Reserve Bank of Philadelphia and paid the full amount thereof to J. C. Penney Co. Neither the Clearfield Trust Co. nor J. C. Penney Co. had any knowledge or suspicion of the forgery. Each acted in good faith. On or before May 10, 1936, Barner advised the timekeeper and the foreman of the W.P.A. project on which he was employed that he had not received the check in question. This information was duly communicated to other agents of the United States and on November 30, 1936, Barner executed an affidavit alleging that the endorsement of his name on the check was a forgery. No notice was given the Clearfield Trust Co. or J. C. Penney Co. of the forgery until January 12, 1937, at which time the Clearfield Trust Co. was notified. The first notice received by Clearfield Trust Co. that the United States was asking reimbursement was on August 31, 1937.

This suit was instituted in 1939 by the United States against the Clearfield Trust Co., the jurisdiction of the federal District Court being invoked. The cause of action was based on the express guaranty of prior endorsements made by the Clearfield Trust Co. J. C. Penney Co. intervened as a defendant. The case was heard on complaint, answer and stipulation of facts. The District Court held that the rights of the parties were to be determined by the law of Pennsylvania and that since the

United States unreasonably delayed in giving notice of the forgery to the Clearfield Trust Co., it was barred from recovery. It accordingly dismissed the complaint. On appeal the Circuit Court of Appeals reversed.

We agree with the Circuit Court of Appeals that the rule of *Erie R.R. Co. v. Tompkins* (1938) does not apply to this action. The rights and duties of the United States on commercial paper which it issues are governed by federal rather than local law. When the United States disburses its funds or pays its debts, it is exercising a constitutional function or power. This check was issued for services performed under the Federal Emergency Relief Act of 1935. The authority to issue the check had its origin in the Constitution and the statutes of the United States and was in no way dependent on the laws of Pennsylvania or of any other state. The duties imposed upon the United States and the rights acquired by it as a result of the issuance find their roots in the same federal sources. In absence of an applicable Act of Congress it is for the federal courts to fashion the governing rule of law according to their own standards.

In our choice of the applicable federal rule we have occasionally selected state law. But reasons which may make state law at times the appropriate federal rule are singularly inappropriate here. The issuance of commercial paper by the United States is on a vast scale and transactions in that paper from issuance to payment will commonly occur in several states. The application of state law, even without the conflict of laws rules of the forum, would subject the rights and duties of the United States to exceptional uncertainty. It would lead to great diversity in results by making identical transactions subject to the vagaries of the laws of the several states. The desirability of a uniform rule is plain.

* * *

This proposition has been extended beyond matters involving commercial paper. For example, it is firmly established that federal common law is to be fashioned to protect the federal government's interest in real property. In *United States v. Little Lake Misere Land Co.* (1973), the Supreme Court held that state law may not be used to abrogate federal government contracts that acquire land for public uses. The United States brought a suit to quiet title on two parcels of land that it had obtained pursuant to a federal statute. A provision in a state law seemingly invalidated some of the terms in the land acquisition agreement. The Supreme Court, however, held that federal law, not the state's, governed the matter.

The Court engaged in the two-step inquiry described above. First, the Court concluded that the matter was one that should be governed by federal common law. The Court explained that "[t]here will often be no specific federal legislation governing a particular transaction to which the United States is a party. . . . But silence on that score in federal legislation is no reason for limiting the reach of federal law. . . . To the contrary, the inevitable incompleteness presented by all legislation means that interstitial federal lawmaking is a basic responsibility of the federal courts." The Court held that federal common law was needed to protect the interests of the United States and in order to effectuate Congress's purpose in enacting the statute authorizing the acquisition of the land in question.

The Court then considered the second part of the analysis and concluded that the federal common law principles should not be borrowed from state law. The Court reasoned that the specific state provisions run counter to the interests of the federal government under the statute and thus should not be applied. The Court quoted, with approval, Professor Paul Mishkin's statement that when the United States is a party to a contract and "the issue's outcome bears some relationship to a federal program, no rule may be applied which would not be wholly in accord with that program."[22]

In analyzing the second step in the inquiry, the Court has articulated a balancing test for deciding whether to incorporate state law as the federal rule of decision or whether to create federal law. In *United States v. Kimbell Foods, Inc.*, the Court described the relevant considerations.

United States v. Kimbell Foods, Inc.

440 U.S. 715 (1979)

Justice MARSHALL delivered the opinion of the Court.

We granted certiorari in these cases to determine whether contractual liens arising from certain federal loan programs take precedence over private liens, in the absence of a federal statute setting priorities. To resolve this question, we must decide first whether federal or state law governs the controversies; and second, if federal law applies, whether this Court should fashion a uniform priority rule or incorporate state commercial law. We conclude that the source of law is federal, but that a national rule is unnecessary to protect the federal interests underlying the loan programs. Accordingly, we adopt state law as the appropriate federal rule for establishing the relative priority of these competing federal and private liens.

I

In 1968, O.K. Super Markets borrowed $27,000 from Kimbell Foods, Inc. (Kimbell), a grocery wholesaler. Two security agreements identified the supermarket's equipment and merchandise as collateral. The agreements also contained a standard "dragnet" clause providing that this collateral would secure future advances from Kimbell to O.K. Super Markets. Kimbell properly perfected its security interests by filing financing statements with the Texas Secretary of State according to Texas law.

In February 1969, O.K. Super Markets obtained a $300,000 loan from Republic National Bank of Dallas (Republic). The bank accepted as security the same property specified in Kimbell's 1968 agreements, and filed a financing statement with the Texas Secretary of State to perfect its security interest. The SBA guaranteed 90% of this loan under the Small Business Act, which authorizes such assistance but, with one exception, does not specify priority rules to govern the SBA's security interests.

O.K. Super Markets used the Republic loan proceeds to satisfy the remainder of the 1968 obligation and to discharge an indebtedness for inventory purchased

---

22. Paul J. Mishkin, *The Variousness of "Federal Law": Competence and Discretion in teh Choice of National and State Rules for Decision*, 105 U. PA. L. REV. 797, 799 (1957).

from Kimbell on open account. Kimbell continued credit sales to O.K. Super Markets until the balance due reached $18,258.57 on January 15, 1971. Thereupon, Kimbell initiated state proceedings against O.K. Super Markets to recover this inventory debt.

Shortly before Kimbell filed suit, O.K. Super Markets had defaulted on the SBA-guaranteed loan. Republic assigned its security interest to the SBA in late December 1970, and recorded the assignment with Texas authorities on January 21, 1971. The United States then honored its guarantee and paid Republic $252,331.93 (90% of the outstanding indebtedness) on February 3, 1971. That same day, O.K. Super Markets, with the approval of its creditors, sold its equipment and inventory and placed the proceeds in escrow pending resolution of the competing claims to the funds. Approximately one year later, the state court entered judgment against O.K. Super Markets, and awarded Kimbell $24,445.37, representing the inventory debt, plus interest and attorney's fees.

Kimbell thereafter brought the instant action to foreclose on its lien, claiming that its security interest in the escrow fund was superior to the SBA's. The District Court held for the Government. On determining that federal law controlled the controversy, the court applied principles developed by this Court to afford federal statutory tax liens special priority over state and private liens where the governing statute does not specify priorities. Under these rules, the lien "first in time" is "first in right." However, to be considered first in time, the nonfederal lien must be "choate," that is, sufficiently specific, when the federal lien arises. A state-created lien is not choate until the "identity of the lienor, the property subject to the lien, and the amount of the lien are established." Failure to meet any one of these conditions forecloses priority over the federal lien, even if under state law the nonfederal lien was enforceable for all purposes when the federal lien arose.

Because Kimbell did not reduce its lien to judgment until February 1972, and the federal lien had been created either in 1969, when Republic filed its financing statement, or in 1971, when Republic recorded its assignment, the District Court concluded that respondent's lien was inchoate when the federal lien arose. Alternatively, the court held that even under state law, the SBA lien was superior to Kimbell's claim because the future advance clauses in the 1968 agreements were not intended to secure the debts arising from O.K. Super Market's subsequent inventory purchases.

The Court of Appeals reversed. It agreed that federal law governs the rights of the United States under its SBA loan program, and that the "first in time, first in right" priority principle should control the competing claims. However, the court refused to extend the choateness rule to situations in which the Federal Government was not an involuntary creditor of tax delinquents, but rather a voluntary commercial lender. Instead, it fashioned a new federal rule for determining which lien was first in time, and concluded that "in the context of competing state security interests arising under the U. C. C.," the first to meet UCC perfection requirements achieved priority.

II

This Court has consistently held that federal law governs questions involving the rights of the United States arising under nationwide federal programs. *Clearfield*

Trust Co. v. United States. Guided by these principles, we think it clear that the priority of liens stemming from federal lending programs must be determined with reference to federal law. The SBA and FHA unquestionably perform federal functions within the meaning of *Clearfield.* Since the agencies derive their authority to effectuate loan transactions from specific Acts of Congress passed in the exercise of a "constitutional function or power," their rights, as well, should derive from a federal source. When Government activities "aris[e] from and bea[r] heavily upon a federal . . . program," the Constitution and Acts of Congress "'require' otherwise than that state law govern of its own force." In such contexts, federal interests are sufficiently implicated to warrant the protection of federal law.

That the statutes authorizing these federal lending programs do not specify the appropriate rule of decision in no way limits the reach of federal law. It is precisely when Congress has not spoken "'in an area comprising issues substantially related to an established program of government operation,'" that *Clearfield* directs federal courts to fill the interstices of federal legislation "according to their own standards."

Federal law therefore controls the Government's priority rights. The more difficult task, to which we turn, is giving content to this federal rule.

III

Controversies directly affecting the operations of federal programs, although governed by federal law, do not inevitably require resort to uniform federal rules. Whether to adopt state law or to fashion a nationwide federal rule is a matter of judicial policy "dependent upon a variety of considerations always relevant to the nature of the specific governmental interests and to the effects upon them of applying state law."

Undoubtedly, federal programs that "by their nature are and must be uniform in character throughout the Nation" necessitate formulation of controlling federal rules Conversely, when there is little need for a nationally uniform body of law, state law may be incorporated as the federal rule of decision. Apart from considerations of uniformity, we must also determine whether application of state law would frustrate specific objectives of the federal programs. If so, we must fashion special rules solicitous of those federal interests. Finally, our choice-of-law inquiry must consider the extent to which application of a federal rule would disrupt commercial relationships predicated on state law.

The Government argues that effective administration of its lending programs requires uniform federal rules of priority. It contends further that resort to any rules other than first in time, first in right and choateness would conflict with protectionist fiscal policies underlying the programs. We are unpersuaded that, in the circumstances presented here, nationwide standards favoring claims of the United States are necessary to ease program administration or to safeguard the Federal Treasury from defaulting debtors. Because the state commercial codes "furnish convenient solutions in no way inconsistent with adequate protection of the federal interest[s]," we decline to override intricate state laws of general applicability on which private creditors base their daily commercial transactions.

Incorporating state law to determine the rights of the United States as against private creditors would in no way hinder administration of the SBA and FHA loan programs. [T]he agencies' own operating practices belie their assertion that a federal rule of priority is needed to avoid the administrative burdens created by disparate state commercial rules. The programs already conform to each State's commercial standards. By using local lending offices and employees who are familiar with the law of their respective localities, the agencies function effectively without uniform procedures and legal rules.

Because the ultimate consequences of altering settled commercial practices are so difficult to foresee, we hesitate to create new uncertainties, in the absence of careful legislative deliberation. Of course, formulating special rules to govern the priority of the federal consensual liens in issue here would be justified if necessary to vindicate important national interests. But neither the Government nor the Court of Appeals advanced any concrete reasons for rejecting well-established commercial rules which have proven workable over time. Thus, the prudent course is to adopt the readymade body of state law as the federal rule of decision until Congress strikes a different accommodation.

Accordingly, we hold that, absent a congressional directive, the relative priority of private liens and consensual liens arising from these Government lending programs is to be determined under nondiscriminatory state laws.

2. *Federal Common Law to Protect Federal Interests in International Relations*

In some instances, the Court has developed federal common law in questions involving international relations. Federal common law is created because of the uniquely federal interest in foreign affairs and because the application of state law would frustrate the uniformity needed in the United States' relations with other countries. The most important example of the development of federal common law to protect federal interests in international relations is *Banco Nacional de Cuba v. Sabbatino.*

Banco Nacional de Cuba v. Sabbatino

376 U.S. 398 (1964)

Justice HARLAN delivered the opinion of the Court.

The question which brought this case here, and is now found to be the dispositive issue, is whether the so-called act of state doctrine serves to sustain petitioner's claims in this litigation. Such claims are ultimately founded on a decree of the Government of Cuba expropriating certain property, the right to the proceeds of which is here in controversy. The act of state doctrine in its traditional formulation precludes the courts of this country from inquiring into the validity of the public acts a recognized foreign sovereign power committed within its own territory.

In February and July of 1960, respondent Farr, Whitlock & Co., an American commodity broker, contracted to purchase Cuban sugar, free alongside the steamer, from a wholly owned subsidiary of Compania Azucarera Vertientes-Camaguey de Cuba (C. A. V.), a corporation organized under Cuban law whose capital stock was owned principally by United States residents. Farr, Whitlock agreed to pay for the sugar in New York upon presentation of the shipping documents and a sight draft.

On July 6, 1960, the Congress of the United States amended the Sugar Act of 1948 to permit a presidentially directed reduction of the sugar quota for Cuba. On the same day President Eisenhower exercised the granted power. The day of the congressional enactment, the Cuban Council of Ministers adopted "Law No. 851," which characterized this reduction in the Cuban sugar quota as an act of "aggression, for political purposes" on the part of the United States, justifying the taking of countermeasures by Cuba. The law gave the Cuban President and Prime Minister discretionary power to nationalize by forced expropriation property or enterprises in which American nationals had an interest. Although a system of compensation was formally provided, the possibility of payment under it may well be deemed illusory. Our State Department has described the Cuban law as "manifestly in violation of those principles of international law which have long been accepted by the free countries of the West. It is in its essence discriminatory, arbitrary and confiscatory."

Between August 6 and August 9, 1960, the sugar covered by the contract between Farr, Whitlock and C.A.V. was loaded, destined for Morocco, onto the S.S. *Hornfels*, which was standing offshore at the Cuban port of Jucaro (Santa Maria). On the day loading commenced, the Cuban President and Prime Minister, acting pursuant to Law No. 851, issued Executive Power Resolution No. 1. It provided for the compulsory expropriation of all property and enterprises, and of rights and interests arising therefrom, of certain listed companies, including C.A.V., wholly or principally owned by American nationals. The preamble reiterated the alleged injustice of the American reduction of the Cuban sugar quota and emphasized the importance of Cuba's serving as an example for other countries to follow "in their struggle to free themselves from the brutal claws of Imperialism." In consequence of the resolution, the consent of the Cuban Government was necessary before a ship carrying sugar of a named company could leave Cuban waters. In order to obtain this consent, Farr, Whitlock, on August 11, entered into contracts, identical to those it had made with C.A.V., with the Banco Para el Comercio Exterior de Cuba, an instrumentality of the Cuban Government. The S.S. *Hornfels* sailed for Morocco on August 12.

Banco Exterior assigned the bills of lading to petitioner, also an instrumentality of the Cuban Government, which instructed its agent in New York, Societe Generale, to deliver the bills and a sight draft in the sum of $175,250.69 to Farr, Whitlock in return for payment. Societe Generale's initial tender of the documents was refused by Farr, Whitlock, which on the same day was notified of C.A.V.'s claim that as rightful owner of the sugar it was entitled to the proceeds. In return for a promise not to turn the funds over to petitioner or its agent, C.A.V. agreed to indemnify Farr, Whitlock for any loss. Farr, Whitlock subsequently accepted the shipping documents, negotiated the bills of lading to its customer, and received payment for the sugar. It refused, however, to hand over the proceeds to Societe Generale. Shortly thereafter, Farr, Whitlock was served with an order of the New York Supreme Court, which had appointed Sabbatino as Temporary Receiver of C.A.V.'s New York assets, enjoining it from taking any action in regard to the money claimed by C.A.V. that might result in its removal from the State. Following this, Farr, Whitlock, pursuant to court order, transferred the funds to Sabbatino, to abide the event of a judicial determination as to their ownership.

Petitioner then instituted this action in the Federal District Court for the Southern District of New York. Alleging conversion of the bills of lading it sought to recover the proceeds thereof from Farr, Whitlock and to enjoin the receiver from exercising any dominion over such proceeds.

Preliminarily, we discuss the foundations on which we deem the act of state doctrine to rest, and more particularly the question of whether state or federal law governs its application in a federal diversity case.

We do not believe that this doctrine is compelled either by the inherent nature of sovereign authority, as some of the earlier decision seem to imply, or by some principle of international law. If a transaction takes place in one jurisdiction and the forum is in another, the forum does not by dismissing an action or by applying its own law purport to divest the first jurisdiction of its territorial sovereignty; it merely declines to adjudicate or makes applicable its own law to parties or property before it. The refusal of one country to enforce the penal laws of another is a typical example of an instance when a court will not entertain a cause of action arising in another jurisdiction. While historic notions of sovereign authority do bear upon the wisdom or employing the act of state doctrine, they do not dictate its existence.

That international law does not require application of the doctrine is evidenced by the practice of nations. Most of the countries rendering decisions on the subject to follow the rule rigidly. No international arbitral or judicial decision discovered suggests that international law prescribes recognition of sovereign acts of foreign governments, and apparently no claim has ever been raised before an international tribunal that failure to apply the act of state doctrine constitutes a breach of international obligation. If international law does not prescribe use of the doctrine, neither does it forbid application of the rule even if it is claimed that the act of state in question violated international law. The traditional view of international law is that it establishes substantive principles for determining whether one country has wronged another. Because of its peculiar nation-to-nation character the usual method for an individual to seek relief is to exhaust local remedies and then repair to the executive authorities of his own state to persuade them to champion his claim in diplomacy or before an international tribunal. Although it is, of course, true that United States courts apply international law as a part of our own in appropriate circumstances, the public law of nations can hardly dictate to a country which is in theory wronged how to treat that wrong within its domestic borders.

The act of state doctrine does, however, have "constitutional" underpinnings. It arises out of the basic relationships between branches of government in a system of separation of powers. It concerns the competency of dissimilar institutions to make and implement particular kinds of decisions in the area of international relations. The doctrine as formulated in past decisions expresses the strong sense of the Judicial Branch that its engagement in the task of passing on the validity of foreign acts of state may hinder rather than further this country's pursuit of goals both for itself and for the community of nations as a whole in the international sphere. Whatever considerations are thought to predominate, it is plain that the problems involved are uniquely federal in nature. If federal authority, in this instance this Court, orders the field of judicial competence in this area for the federal courts, and the state courts are left free to formulate their own rules, the purposes behind the doctrine could be as effectively undermined as if there had been no federal pronouncement on the subject.

[W]e are constrained to make it clear that an issue concerned with a basic choice regarding the competence and function of the Judiciary and the National Executive in ordering our relationships with other members of the international community must be treated exclusively as an aspect of federal law. It seems fair to assume that the Court did not have rules like the act of state doctrine in mind when it decided *Erie R.R. Co. v. Tompkins.*

3. Federal Common Law to Resolve Disputes Among Sovereigns

a. Federal Common Law and Interstate Controversies

The development of federal common law is particularly important in resolving disputes between state governments. A crucial function of the federal courts, and particularly the U.S. Supreme Court, is to provide a forum for the peaceful resolution of disputes between the states. Obviously, in a conflict between two states, neither state's laws can be applied to resolve the dispute. Therefore, in the absence of a pertinent federal statute, federal common law must be created to protect the federal government's interest in interstate harmony.

The Supreme Court has expressly recognized its authority to create federal common law to resolve such disputes. In *Kansas v. Colorado* (1907), the Court explained that when two states conflict, "[the] court is called upon to settle that dispute in such a way as will recognize the equal rights of both and at the same time establish justice between them." The Court said that through its "successive . . . decisions this court is practically building up what may not improperly be called interstate common law."

For example, the Court has developed federal common law to resolve disputes between states concerning interstate waters. In *Hinderlider v. La Plata River & Cherry Creek Ditch Co.* (1938), the Supreme Court held that federal common law should be created to apportion water from an interstate stream between two states. In *Hinderlider*, decided the same day as *Erie R.R. v. Tompkins*, the Court declared: "For whether the water of an interstate stream must be apportioned between two States is a question of 'federal common law' upon which neither the statutes nor the decisions of either State can be conclusive."

Another decision concerning the use of federal common law to resolve a dispute concerning interstate waters is *Illinois v. City of Milwaukee* (1972).

Illinois v. City of Milwaukee

406 U.S. 91 (1972)

Justice DOUGLAS announced the opinion of the Court.

This is a motion by Illinois to file a bill of complaint under our original jurisdiction against four cities of Wisconsin, the Sewerage Commission of the City of

Milwaukee, and the Metropolitan Sewerage Commission of the County of Milwaukee. The cause of action alleged is pollution by the defendants of Lake Michigan, a body of interstate water. According to plaintiff, some 200 million gallons of raw or inadequately treated sewage and other waste materials are discharged daily into the lake in the Milwaukee area alone. Plaintiff alleges that it and its subdivisions prohibit and prevent such discharges, but that the defendants do not take such actions. Plaintiff asks that we abate this public nuisance.

Congress has enacted numerous laws touching interstate waters. In 1899 it established some surveillance by the Army Corps of Engineers over industrial pollution, not including sewage, Rivers and Harbors Act of March 3, 1899. The 1899 Act has been reinforced and broadened by a complex of laws recently enacted. The Federal Water Pollution Control Act tightens control over discharges into navigable waters so as not to lower applicable water quality standards. By the National Environmental Policy Act of 1969, Congress "authorizes and directs" that "the policies, regulations, and public laws of the United States shall be interpreted and administered in accordance with the policies set forth in this Act" and that "all agencies of the Federal Government shall . . . identify and develop methods and procedures . . . which will insure that presently unquantified environmental amenities and values may be given appropriate consideration in decisionmaking along with economic and technical considerations." Congress has evinced increasing concern with the quality of the aquatic environment as it affects the conservation and safeguarding of fish and wildlife resources.

The remedy sought by Illinois is not within the precise scope of remedies prescribed by Congress. Yet the remedies which Congress provides are not necessarily the only federal remedies available. "It is not uncommon for federal courts to fashion federal law where federal rights are concerned." When we deal with air and water in their ambient or interstate aspects, there is a federal common law. The application of federal common law to abate a public nuisance in interstate or navigable waters is not inconsistent with the Water Pollution Control Act. Congress provided in §10(b) of that Act that, save as a court may decree otherwise in an enforcement action, "(s)tate and interstate action to abate pollution of interstate or navigable waters shall be encouraged and shall not . . . be displaced by Federal enforcement action."

Our decisions concerning interstate waters contain the same theme. Rights in interstate streams, like questions of boundaries, "have been recognized as presenting federal questions." The question of apportionment of interstate waters is a question of "federal common law" upon which state statutes or decisions are not conclusive.

It may happen that new federal laws and new federal regulations may in time pre-empt the field of federal common law of nuisance. But until that comes to pass, federal courts will be empowered to appraise the equities of the suits alleging creation of a public nuisance by water pollution. While federal law governs, consideration of state standards may be relevant. Thus, a State with high water-quality standards may well ask that its strict standards be honored and that it not be compelled to lower itself to the more degrading standards of a neighbor. There are no fixed rules that govern; these will be equity suits in which the informed judgment of the chancellor will largely govern.

* * *

Subsequently, the Supreme Court held that the 1972 Amendments to the Water Pollution Control Act prevented a federal common law action for nuisance as a result of pollution of interstate waters.

City of Milwaukee v. Illinois

451 U.S. 304 (1981)

Justice REHNQUIST delivered the decision of the Court.

When this litigation was first before us, we recognized the existence of a federal "common law" which could give rise to a claim for abatement of a nuisance caused by interstate water pollution. *Illinois v. City of Milwaukee* (1972). Subsequent to our decision, Congress enacted the Federal Water Pollution Control Act Amendments of 1972. We granted certiorari to consider the effect of this legislation on the previously recognized cause of action.

Federal courts, unlike state courts, are not general common-law courts and do not possess a general power to develop and apply their own rules of decision. *Erie R.R. Co. v. Tompkins* (1938); *United States v. Hudson & Goodwin* (1812). The enactment of a federal rule in an area of national concern, and the decision whether to displace state law in doing so, is generally made not by the federal judiciary, purposefully insulated from democratic pressures, but by the people through their elected representatives in Congress. *Erie* recognized as much in ruling that a federal court could not generally apply a federal rule of decision, despite the existence of jurisdiction, in the absence of an applicable Act of Congress.

When Congress has not spoken to a particular issue, however, and when there exists a "significant conflict between some federal policy or interest and the use of state law," the Court has found it necessary, in a "few and restricted" instances, to develop federal common law. Nothing in this process suggests that courts are better suited to develop national policy in areas governed by federal common law than they are in other areas, or that the usual and important concerns of an appropriate division of functions between the Congress and the federal judiciary are inapplicable. We have always recognized that federal common law is "subject to the paramount authority of Congress."

Contrary to the suggestions of respondents, the appropriate analysis in determining if federal statutory law governs a question previously the subject of federal common law is not the same as that employed in deciding if federal law pre-empts state law. In considering the latter question "'we start with the assumption that the historic police powers of the States were not to be superseded by the Federal Act unless that was the clear and manifest purpose of Congress.'" Such concerns are not implicated in the same fashion when the question is whether federal statutory or federal common law governs, and accordingly the same sort of evidence of a clear and manifest purpose is not required. Indeed, as noted, in cases such as the present "we start with the assumption" that it is for Congress, not federal courts, to articulate the appropriate standards to be applied as a matter of federal law.

We conclude that, at least so far as concerns the claims of respondents, Congress has not left the formulation of appropriate federal standards to the courts through application of often vague and indeterminate nuisance concepts and maxims of equity jurisprudence, but rather has occupied the field through the establishment of a comprehensive regulatory program supervised by an expert administrative agency. The 1972 Amendments to the Federal Water Pollution Control Act were not merely another law "touching interstate waters" of the sort surveyed in and found inadequate to supplant federal common law. Rather, the Amendments were viewed by Congress as a "total restructuring" and "complete rewriting" of the existing water pollution legislation considered in that case. Congress' intent in enacting the Amendments was clearly to establish an all-encompassing program of water pollution regulation. *Every* point source discharge is prohibited unless covered by a permit, which directly subjects the discharger to the administrative apparatus established by Congress to achieve its goals. The "major purpose" of the Amendments was "to establish a *comprehensive* long-range policy for the elimination of water pollution." The establishment of such a self-consciously comprehensive program by Congress, which certainly did not exist when *Illinois v. Milwaukee* (1972) was decided, strongly suggests that there is no room for courts to attempt to improve on that program with federal common law.

Turning to the particular claims involved in this case, the action of Congress in supplanting the federal common law is perhaps clearest when the question of effluent limitations for discharges from the two treatment plants is considered. There is thus no question that the problem of effluent limitations has been thoroughly addressed through the administrative scheme established by Congress, as contemplated by Congress. This being so there is no basis for a federal court to impose more stringent limitations than those imposed under the regulatory regime by reference to federal common law, as the District Court did in this case.

Federal courts lack authority to impose more stringent effluent limitations under federal common law than those imposed by the agency charged by Congress with administering this comprehensive scheme.

We therefore conclude that no federal common-law remedy was available to respondents in this case.

Justice BLACKMUN, with whom Justice MARSHALL and Justice STEVENS join, dissenting.

Nine years ago, in *Illinois v. Milwaukee* (1972), this Court unanimously determined that Illinois could bring a federal common-law action against the city of Milwaukee, three other Wisconsin cities, and two sewerage commissions. Today, the Court decides that this 9-year judicial exercise has been just a meaningless charade, inasmuch as, it says, the federal common-law remedy approved in *Illinois v. Milwaukee* was implicitly extinguished by Congress just six months after the 1972 decision. Because I believe that Congress intended no such extinction, and surely did not contemplate the result reached by the Court today, I respectfully dissent.

The Court's analysis of federal common-law displacement rests, I am convinced, on a faulty assumption. In contrasting congressional displacement of the common law with federal pre-emption of state law, the Court assumes that as soon as Congress "addresses a question previously governed" by federal common law, "the need for such an unusual exercise of lawmaking by federal courts disappears." This "automatic displacement" approach is inadequate in two respects. It fails to reflect the unique role federal common law plays in resolving disputes between one State and the citizens or government of another. In addition, it ignores this Court's frequent recognition that federal common law may complement congressional action in the fulfillment of federal policies.

It is well settled that a body of federal common law has survived the decision in *Erie.* The Court, however, did not there upset, nor has it since disturbed, a deeply rooted, more specialized federal common law that has arisen to effectuate federal interests embodied either in the Constitution or an Act of Congress. Chief among the federal interests served by this common law are the resolution of interstate disputes and the implementation of national statutory or regulatory policies.

Both before and after *Erie,* the Court has fashioned federal law where the interstate nature of a controversy renders inappropriate the law of either State. Thus, quite contrary to the statements and intimations of the Court today, *Illinois v. Milwaukee* did not create the federal common law of nuisance. Well before this Court and Congress acted in 1972, there was ample recognition of and foundation for a federal common law of nuisance applicable to Illinois' situation. Congress cannot be presumed to have been unaware of the relevant common-law history, any more than it can be deemed to have been oblivious to the decision in *Illinois v. Milwaukee,* announced six months prior to the passage of the Federal Water Pollution Control Act Amendments of 1972. The central question is whether, given its presumed awareness, Congress, in passing these Amendments, intended to prevent recourse to the federal common law of nuisance.

The answer to this question, it seems to me, requires a more thorough exploration of congressional intent than is offered by the Court. The fact that Congress in 1972 once again addressed the complicated and difficult problem of purifying our Nation's waters should not be taken as presumptive evidence, let alone conclusive proof, that Congress meant to foreclose pre-existing approaches to controlling interstate water pollution. Where the possible extinction of federal common law is at issue, a reviewing court is obligated to look not only to the magnitude of the legislative action but also with some care to the evidence of specific congressional intent.

In my view, the language and structure of the Clean Water Act leaves no doubt that Congress intended to preserve the federal common law of nuisance. Section 505(e) of the Act reads: "Nothing in this section shall restrict any right which *any person* (or class of persons) may have under *any statute or common law* to seek enforcement of any effluent standard or limitation *or to seek any other relief* (including relief against the Administrator or a State agency)." The Act specifically defines "person" to include States, and thus embraces respondents Illinois and Michigan. §502(5). It preserves their right to bring an action against the governmental entities who are charged with enforcing the statute.

This deliberate preservation of all remedies previously available at common law makes no distinction between the common law of individual States and federal common law. Indeed, the legislative debates indicate that Congress was specifically aware of the presence of federal common law and intended that it would survive passage of the 1972 Amendments.

b.   Federal Common Law and Indian Affairs

Though the modern Supreme Court has stated that the areas for federal common law are "'few and restricted,'" *O'Melveny & Myers v. FDIC* (1994), there are fields within which the Court has made common law rules without discussing this presumption against federal common law. Indian affairs is one such field. Even though the Court has said that Congress possesses plenary power to legislate with respect to the United States' relationship with Native Nations, the Court has developed federal common law rules of decision to address fundamental questions of law and policy in Indian affairs, including Tribal sovereignty and Tribal land rights and the availability of remedies to enforce federal Indian law. This body of federal common law reflects the Court's longstanding sense, stretching back to *Worcester v. Georgia* (1832), a case discussed in Chapter 1, that the federal government, not the states, has authority over Indian affairs. As the next case illustrates, the development of federal common law in Indian affairs has sparked intense debates about the role of the courts versus Congress and the availability of judicial relief to redress longstanding violations of federal law.

County of Oneida, N.Y. v. Oneida Nation of N.Y. State

470 U.S. 226 (1985)

Justice POWELL delivered the opinion of the Court.

These cases present the question whether three Tribes of the Oneida Indians may bring a suit for damages for the occupation and use of tribal land allegedly conveyed unlawfully in 1795.

I

The Oneida Indian Nation of New York, the Oneida Indian Nation of Wisconsin, and the Oneida of the Thames Band Council (the Oneidas) instituted this suit in 1970 against the Counties of Oneida and Madison, New York. The Oneidas alleged that their ancestors conveyed 100,000 acres to the State of New York under a 1795 agreement that violated the Trade and Intercourse Act of 1793 (Nonintercourse Act), and thus that the transaction was void. The Oneidas' complaint sought damages representing the fair rental value of that part of the land presently owned and occupied by the Counties of Oneida and Madison, for the period January 1, 1968, through December 31, 1969.

The United States District Court for the Northern District of New York initially dismissed the action on the ground that the complaint failed to state a claim arising under the laws of the United States. The United States Court of Appeals for the Second Circuit affirmed. We held unanimously that, at least for jurisdictional purposes, the Oneidas stated a claim for possession under federal law. The case was remanded for trial.

On remand, the District Court trifurcated trial of the issues. In the first phase, the court found the counties liable to the Oneidas for wrongful possession of their lands. In the second phase, it awarded the Oneidas damages in the amount of $16,694, plus interest, representing the fair rental value of the land in question for the 2-year period specified in the complaint. Finally, the District Court held that the State of New York, a third-party defendant brought into the case by the counties, must indemnify the counties for the damages owed to the Oneidas. The Court of Appeals affirmed the trial court's rulings with respect to liability and indemnification. It remanded, however, for further proceedings on the amount of damages. The counties and the State petitioned for review of these rulings. Recognizing the importance of the Court of Appeals' decision not only for the Oneidas, but potentially for many eastern Indian land claims, we granted certiorari, to determine whether an Indian tribe may have a live cause of action for a violation of its possessory rights that occurred 175 years ago. We hold that the Court of Appeals correctly so ruled.

II

The respondents in these cases are the direct descendants of members of the Oneida Indian Nation, one of the six nations of the Iroquois, the most powerful Indian Tribe in the Northeast at the time of the American Revolution. *See* B. Graymont, The Iroquois in the American Revolution (1972) (hereinafter Graymont). From time immemorial to shortly after the Revolution, the Oneidas inhabited what is now central New York State. Their aboriginal land was approximately six million acres, extending from the Pennsylvania border to the St. Lawrence River, from the shores of Lake Ontario to the western foothills of the Adirondack Mountains.

Although most of the Iroquois sided with the British, the Oneidas actively supported the colonists in the Revolution. *See also* Graymont, *supra*. This assistance prevented the Iroquois from asserting a united effort against the colonists, and thus the Oneidas' support was of considerable aid. After the War, the United States recognized the importance of the Oneidas' role, and in the Treaty of Fort Stanwix, the National Government promised that the Oneidas would be secure "in the possession of the lands on which they are settled." Within a short period of time, the United States twice reaffirmed this promise, in the Treaties of Fort Harmar, and of Canandaigua.

During this period, the State of New York came under increasingly heavy pressure to open the Oneidas' land for settlement. Consequently, in 1788, the State entered into a "treaty" with the Indians, in which it purchased the vast majority of the Oneidas' land. The Oneidas retained a reservation of about 300,000 acres, an area that, the parties stipulated below, included the land involved in this suit.

In 1790, at the urging of President Washington and Secretary of War Knox, Congress passed the first Indian Trade and Intercourse Act. The Act prohibited the conveyance of Indian land except where such conveyances were entered pursuant to the treaty power of the United States. In 1793, Congress passed a stronger, more detailed version of the Act, providing that "no purchase or grant of lands, or of any title or claim thereto, from any Indians or nation or tribe of Indians, within the bounds of the United States, shall be of any validity in law or equity, unless the same be made by a treaty or convention entered into pursuant to the constitution . . . [and] in the presence, and with the approbation of the commissioner or commissioners of the United States" appointed to supervise such transactions. Unlike the 1790 version, the new statute included criminal penalties for violation of its terms.

Despite Congress' clear policy that no person or entity should purchase Indian land without the acquiescence of the Federal Government, in 1795 the State of New York began negotiations to buy the remainder of the Oneidas' land. When this fact came to the attention of Secretary of War Pickering, he warned Governor Clinton, and later Governor Jay, that New York was required by the Nonintercourse Act to request the appointment of federal commissioners to supervise any land transaction with the Oneidas. The State ignored these warnings, and in the summer of 1795 entered into an agreement with the Oneidas whereby they conveyed virtually all of their remaining land to the State for annual cash payments. It is this transaction that is the basis of the Oneidas' complaint in this case.

III

At the outset, we are faced with petitioner counties' contention that the Oneidas have no right of action for the violation of the 1793 Act. Both the District Court and the Court of Appeals rejected this claim, finding that the Oneidas had the right to sue on two theories: first, a common-law right of action for unlawful possession; and second, an implied statutory cause of action under the Nonintercourse Act of 1793. We need not reach the latter question as we think the Indians' common-law right to sue is firmly established.

A
Federal Common Law

By the time of the Revolutionary War, several well-defined principles had been established governing the nature of a tribe's interest in its property and how those interests could be conveyed. It was accepted that Indian nations held "aboriginal title" to lands they had inhabited from time immemorial. The "doctrine of discovery" provided, however, that discovering nations held fee title to these lands, subject to the Indians' right of occupancy and use. As a consequence, no one could purchase Indian land or otherwise terminate aboriginal title without the consent of the sovereign.

With the adoption of the Constitution, Indian relations became the exclusive province of federal law. Thus, "the possessory right claimed [by the Oneidas] is a *federal* right to the lands at issue in this case." Numerous decisions of this Court prior to *Oneida I* recognized at least implicitly that Indians have a federal common-law right to sue to enforce their aboriginal land rights. In keeping with these well-established principles, we hold that the Oneidas can maintain this action for violation of their possessory rights based on federal common law.

B
Pre-emption

Petitioners argue that the Nonintercourse Acts pre-empted whatever right of action the Oneidas may have had at common law, relying on our decisions in We find this view to be unpersuasive. In determining whether a federal statute pre-empts common-law causes of action, the relevant inquiry is whether the statute "[speaks] *directly* to [the] question" otherwise answered by federal common law. The Nonintercourse Act of 1793 does not speak directly to the question of remedies for unlawful conveyances of Indian land. A comparison of the 1793 Act and the statute at issue in *Milwaukee II* is instructive.

Milwaukee II raised the question whether a common-law action for the abatement of a nuisance caused by the pollution of interstate waterways survived the passage of the 1972 amendments to the Federal Water Pollution Control Act. FWPCA established an elaborate system for dealing with the problem of interstate water pollution, providing for enforcement of its terms by agency action and citizens suits. It also made available civil penalties for violations of the Act. The legislative history indicated that Congress intended FWPCA to provide a comprehensive solution to the problem of interstate water pollution.

In contrast, the Nonintercourse Act of 1793 did not establish a comprehensive remedial plan for dealing with violations of Indian property rights. There is no indication in the legislative history that Congress intended to pre-empt common-law remedies. [T]he Nonintercourse Act does not address directly the problem of restoring unlawfully conveyed land to the Indians, in contrast to the specific remedial provisions contained in FWPCA.

One would have thought that claims dating back for more than a century and a half would have been barred long ago. As our opinion indicates, however, neither petitioners nor we have found any applicable statute of limitations or other relevant legal basis for holding that the Oneidas' claims are barred or otherwise have been satisfied.

Justice STEVENS, with whom THE CHIEF JUSTICE, Justice WHITE, and Justice REHNQUIST join, dissenting.

In 1790, the President of the United States notified Cornplanter, the Chief of the Senecas, that federal law would securely protect Seneca lands from acquisition by any State or person:

> If . . . you have any just cause of complaint against [a purchaser] and can make satisfactory proof thereof, the federal courts will be open to you for redress, as to all other persons.

The elders of the Oneida Indian Nation received comparable notice of their capacity to maintain the federal claim that is at issue in this litigation. They made no attempt to assert the claim, and their successors in interest waited 175 years before bringing suit to avoid a 1795 conveyance that the Tribe freely made, for a valuable consideration. The absence of any evidence of deception, concealment, or interference with the Tribe's right to assert a claim, together with the societal interests that always underlie statutes of repose — particularly when title to real property is at stake — convince me that this claim is barred by the extraordinary passage of time. It is worthy of emphasis that this claim arose when George Washington was the President of the United States.

The Framers recognized that no one ought be condemned for his forefathers' misdeeds — even when the crime is a most grave offense against the Republic. The Court today ignores that principle in fashioning a common-law remedy for the Oneida Nation that allows the Tribe to avoid its 1795 conveyance 175 years after it was made. This decision upsets long-settled expectations in the ownership of real property in the Counties of Oneida and Madison, New York, and the disruption it is sure to cause will confirm the common-law wisdom that ancient claims are best left in repose. The Court, no doubt, believes that it is undoing a grave historical injustice, but in doing so it has caused another, which only Congress may now rectify.

* * *

In *County of Oneida*, the Court fashioned a federal common law remedy to allow the Oneida Indian Nation to seek redress for the unlawful transfer of their lands. Subsequent cases have cut back on the scope of availability of this judge-made remedy, as the federal courts recognized defenses to relief that echo Justice Stevens's argument that the passage of time may preclude judicial relief. Interestingly, Justice Stevens dissented in one of these subsequent cases, *City of Sherrill v. Oneida Indian Nation* (2005), in which the Court's majority held that laches barred the Oneida Indian Nation from seeking equitable relief to assert its federally protected immunity from state and local taxation on reservation lands that the Tribe had repurchased on the open market. According to Justice Stevens, in recognizing a laches defense, "the Court ha[d] ventured into legal territory that belongs to Congress."

Native Nations have argued that the Court has encroached upon Congress' authority in a series of cases recognizing federal common law limits on the exercise of Tribal jurisdiction over individuals who are not Tribal members. In *Montana v. United States* (1981), for example, the Court held that Native Nations have been implicitly divested of some civil jurisdiction over the activities of nonmembers on non-Indian lands owned in fee simple on Indian reservations. The Court's decision rested in part upon its prior holding in *Oliphant v. Suquamish Indian Tribe* (1978) that Tribes have been implicitly divested of criminal jurisdiction over non-Indians. These cases are examples of federal common law that restricts the rights of Native Nations to exercise their sovereignty and thus are a counterpoint to the Court's recognition of Tribal rights in cases such as *County of Oneida*.

C.   THE DEVELOPMENT OF FEDERAL COMMON LAW TO EFFECTUATE CONGRESSIONAL INTENT

The second major area of federal common law rules is where the federal courts develop rules of decision to effectuate congressional intent. Some cases involving common law to protect federal interests implicate federal statutes, as several of the cases in section 5.B of this Chapter underscore. When a federal statute is implicated, the question arises whether to characterize judicial rulemaking as mere statutory interpretation or instead as creating federal common law. This question matters because of the strong presumption against federal courts fashioning common law to decide cases and the Court's repeated statements that the areas for federal common law are "few and restricted." *O'Melveny & Myers v. FDIC* (1994).

This section discusses several problems in drawing the line between rule making that can be characterized as statutory interpretation and federal common law-making without the blessing of Congress. One problem involves instances where Congress has authorized federal courts to apply federal common law to issues that a federal statute does not expressly address unless there is a valid, applicable state rule of decision to follow. This problem is illustrated by *Robertson v. Wegmann* (1978), our next case discussed below.

Another problem arises when Congress has created a statutory right but no express statutory cause of action. In some cases, the Court has inferred a private right of action under federal statutes in order to fulfill Congress' purpose, though in recent years the Court has adopted an approach that rejects implied rights of action by requiring textual evidence that Congress intended to create them. This problem of implied private rights of action under federal statutes is illustrated by *Touche Ross & Co. v. Redington* (1979), and the Court's rejection of the practice of implying rights of action in *Alexander v. Sandoval* (2000), also below.

This section concludes by considering a third problem: preemption of state law by federal statutes. A finding of preemption turns upon congressional intent. In principle, at least, state law is not preempted unless a court concludes that Congress intended to preempt state law. Therefore, according to the Court's theory, federal courts are not engaging in common lawmaking when they conclude that a statute preempts state law. In practice, however, the line between statutory interpretation and common lawmaking to effectuate congressional intent is sometimes difficult to draw when it comes to federal preemption. That is particularly true in those cases where the Court has held that a federal statute impliedly preempts state law. These themes are illustrated below by *PLIVA, Inc. v. Mensing* (2011) and *Arizona v. United States* (2012).

1. The Application of Federal Common Law versus State Law to Answer Questions That a Federal Statute Does Not Expressly Address

Sometimes, Congress directly incorporates state law into a federal statute. The Federal Tort Claims Act,[23] for example, creates a federal cause of action against federal officials who violate *state* tort law. Other times, Congress takes a different approach, leaving it to federal courts to apply and construct their own common law rules of decision. This can include authority to borrow state law if the federal courts believe state law provides an appropriate rule of decision. But unlike the FTCA, looking to state law is not required in these settings. Such is the case for key components of the Taft-Hartley Act, an important labor law statute, as described in the famous case *Textile Workers Union of Am. v. Lincoln Mills of Ala.* (1957):

> [W]hat is the substantive law to be applied in suits under §301(a) [of the Taft-Hartley Act when resolving labor-management disputes in sectors that affect interstate commerce]? We conclude that the substantive law to apply in suits under §301(a) is federal law, which the courts must fashion from the policy of our national labor laws. The Labor Management Relations Act expressly furnishes some substantive law. It points out what the parties may or may not do in certain situations. Other problems will lie in the penumbra of express statutory mandates. Some will lack express statutory sanction but will be solved by looking at the policy of the legislation and fashioning a remedy that will effectuate that policy. The range of judicial inventiveness will be determined by the nature of the problem. Federal interpretation of the federal law will govern, not state law. But state law, if compatible with the purpose of §301, may be resorted to in order to find the rule that will best effectuate the federal policy. Any state

---

23. 28 U.S.C. §1346.

law applied, however, will be absorbed as federal law and will not be an independent source of private rights.

It is not uncommon for federal courts to fashion federal law where federal rights are concerned. Congress has indicated by §301(a) the purpose to follow that course here. There is no constitutional difficulty. Article III, §2, extends the judicial power to cases "arising under * * * the Laws of the United States * * *." The power of Congress to regulate these labor-management controversies under the Commerce Clause is plain. A case or controversy arising under §301(a) is, therefore, one within the purview of judicial power as defined in Article III.

In other instances, Congress has enacted a hybrid approach, instructing federal courts to apply to federal common law issues that a federal statute does not expressly address *unless* there is a valid state law in the jurisdiction that governs the issue. This is the approach that controls in civil rights actions under §1983 on questions such as the proper statute of limitations, or whether the suit survives the death of a party. This hybrid approach is exemplified by the following case. Although the facts are somewhat unusual (involving an alleged conspiracy to assassinate President Kennedy), the use of a §1983 suit for money damages following wrongful conviction is not unusual.[24]

Robertson v. Wegmann

436 U.S. 584 (1978)

Justice MARSHALL delivered the opinion of the Court.

In early 1970, Clay L. Shaw filed a civil rights action under 42 U.S.C. §1983 in the United States District Court for the Eastern District of Louisiana. Four years later, before trial had commenced, Shaw died. The question presented is whether the District Court was required to adopt as federal law a Louisiana survivorship statute, which would have caused this action to abate, or was free instead to create a federal common-law rule allowing the action to survive. Resolution of this question turns on whether the state statute is "inconsistent with the Constitution and laws of the United States." 42 U.S.C. §1988.[1]

---

24. Martin Schwartz, *Wrongful Conviction Claims Under Section 1983*, 27 TOURO L. REV. 221 (2011).

1. Title 42 U.S.C. §1988 provides in pertinent part:

"The jurisdiction in civil and criminal matters conferred on the district courts by the provisions of this chapter and Title 18, for the protection of all persons in the United States in their civil rights, and for their vindication, shall be exercised and enforced in conformity with the laws of the United States, so far as such laws are suitable to carry the same into effect; but in all cases where they are not adapted to the object, or are deficient in the provisions necessary to furnish suitable remedies and punish offenses against law, the common law, as modified and changed by the constitution and statutes of the State wherein the court having jurisdiction of such civil or criminal cause is held, so far as the same is not inconsistent with the Constitution and laws of the United States, shall be extended to and govern the said courts in the trial and disposition of the cause, and, if it is of a criminal nature, in the infliction of punishment on the party found guilty."

In 1969, Shaw was tried in a Louisiana state court on charges of having participated in a conspiracy to assassinate President John F. Kennedy. He was acquitted by a jury but within days was arrested on charges of having committed perjury in his testimony at the conspiracy trial. Alleging that these prosecutions were undertaken in bad faith Shaw filed this action against the district attorney and others government officials. [When] Shaw died, [t]he executor of his estate, respondent Edward F. Wegmann, moved to be substituted as plaintiff, and the District Court granted the motion. Petitioner and other defendants then moved to dismiss the action on the ground that it had abated on Shaw's death.

[T]he applicable survivorship rule is governed by 42 U.S.C. §1988. This statute recognizes that in certain areas "federal law is unsuited or insufficient 'to furnish suitable remedies'"; federal law simply does not "cover every issue that may arise in the context of a federal civil rights action." When federal law is thus "deficient," §1988 instructs us to turn to "the common law, as modified and changed by the constitution and statutes of the [forum] State," as long as these are "not inconsistent with the Constitution and laws of the United States." Regardless of the source of the law applied in a particular case, however, it is clear that the ultimate rule adopted under §1988 "is a federal rule responsive to the need whenever a federal right is impaired. . . ."

[O]ne specific area not covered by federal law is that relating to "the survival of civil rights actions under §1983 upon the death of either the plaintiff or defendant." State statutes governing the survival of state actions do exist, however. These statutes, which vary widely with regard to both the types of claims that survive and the parties as to whom survivorship is allowed, were intended to modify the simple, if harsh, 19th-century common-law rule: "[An] injured party's personal claim was [always] extinguished . . . upon the death of either the injured party himself or the alleged wrongdoer." Under §1988, this state statutory law, modifying the common law, provides the principal reference point in determining survival of civil rights actions, subject to the important proviso that state law may not be applied when it is "inconsistent with the Constitution and laws of the United States." Because of this proviso, the courts below refused to adopt as federal law the Louisiana survivorship statute and, in its place, created a federal common-law rule.

In resolving questions of inconsistency between state and federal law raised under §1988, courts must look not only at particular federal statutes and constitutional provisions, but also at "the policies expressed in [them]." Of particular importance is whether application of state law "would be inconsistent with the federal policy underlying the cause of action under consideration." The instant cause of action arises under 42 U.S.C. §1983, one of the "Reconstruction civil rights statutes" that this Court has accorded "a sweep as broad as [their] language."

Despite the broad sweep of §1983, we can find nothing in the statute or its underlying policies to indicate that a state law causing abatement of a particular action should invariably be ignored in favor of a rule of absolute survivorship. The policies underlying §1983 include compensation of persons injured by deprivation of federal rights and prevention of abuses of power by those acting under color of state law. No claim is made here that Louisiana's survivorship laws are in general inconsistent with these policies, and indeed most Louisiana actions survive the plaintiff's death. Moreover, certain types of actions that would abate automatically on the plaintiff's death in many States—for example, actions for defamation and malicious prosecution—would apparently survive in Louisiana. In actions other than those for damage to property, however, Louisiana does not allow the deceased's personal representative to be substituted as plaintiff; rather, the action survives only in favor of a spouse, children, parents, or siblings. [N]o contention is made here that Louisiana's decision to restrict certain survivorship rights in this manner is an unreasonable one.

It is therefore difficult to see how any of §1983's policies would be undermined if Shaw's action were to abate. The goal of compensating those injured by a deprivation of rights provides no basis for requiring compensation of one who is merely suing as the executor of the deceased's estate. And, given that most Louisiana actions survive the plaintiff's death, the fact that a particular action might abate surely would not adversely affect §1983's role in preventing official illegality, at least in situations in which there is no claim that the illegality caused the plaintiff's death. A state official contemplating illegal activity must always be prepared to face the prospect of a §1983 action being filed against him. In light of this prospect, even an official aware of the intricacies of Louisiana survivorship law would hardly be influenced in his behavior by its provisions.

It is true that §1983 provides "a uniquely federal remedy against incursions under the claimed authority of state law upon rights secured by the Constitution and laws of the Nation." That a federal remedy should be available, however, does not mean that a §1983 plaintiff (or his representative) must be allowed to continue an action in disregard of the state law to which §1988 refers us. A state statute cannot be considered "inconsistent" with federal law merely because the statute causes the plaintiff to lose the litigation. If success of the §1983 action were the only benchmark, there would be no reason at all to look to state law, for the appropriate rule would then always be the one favoring the plaintiff, and its source would be essentially irrelevant. But §1988 quite clearly instructs us to refer to state statutes; it does not say that state law is to be accepted or rejected based solely on which side is advantaged thereby. Under the circumstances presented here, the fact that Shaw was not survived by one of several close relatives should not itself be sufficient to cause the Louisiana survivorship provisions to be deemed "inconsistent with the Constitution and laws of the United States."

Our holding today is a narrow one, limited to situations in which no claim is made that state law generally is inhospitable to survival of §1983 actions and in which the particular application of state survivorship law, while it may cause abatement of the action, has no independent adverse effect on the policies underlying §1983. A different situation might well be presented, as the District Court noted, if state law "did not provide for survival of any tort actions," or if it significantly restricted the types of actions that survive.

Here it is agreed that Shaw's death was not caused by the deprivation of rights for which he sued under §1983, and Louisiana law provides for the survival of most tort actions. Respondent's only complaint about Louisiana law is that it would cause Shaw's action to abate. We conclude that the mere fact of abatement of a particular lawsuit is not sufficient ground to declare state law "inconsistent" with federal law.

Justice BLACKMUN, with whom Justice BRENNAN and Justice WHITE join, dissenting.

It is disturbing to see the Court, in this decision, although almost apologetically self-described as "a narrow one," cut back on what is acknowledged, to be the "broad sweep" of 42 U.S.C. §1983. Accordingly, I dissent.

I do not read the emphasis of §1988, as the Court does, to the effect that the Federal District Court "was required to adopt" the Louisiana statute and was free to look to federal common law only as a secondary matter. It seems to me that this places the cart before the horse. Section 1988 requires the utilization of federal law ("shall be exercised and enforced in conformity with the laws of the United States"). It authorizes resort to the state statute only if the federal laws "are not adapted to the object" of "protection of all persons in the United States in their civil rights, and for their vindication" or are "deficient in the provisions necessary to furnish suitable remedies and punish offenses against law." Even then, state statutes are an alternative source of law only if "not inconsistent with the Constitution and laws of the United States." Surely, federal law is the rule and not the exception.

To be sure, survivorship of a civil rights action under §1983 upon the death of either party is not specifically covered by the federal statute. But that does not mean that "the laws of the United States" are not "suitable" or are "not adapted to the object" or are "deficient in the provisions necessary." The federal law and the underlying federal policy stand bright and clear. And in the light of that brightness and of that clarity, I see no need to resort to the myriad of state rules governing the survival of state actions.

Just as the Rules of Decision Act cases disregard state law where there is conflict with federal *policy*, even though no explicit conflict with the terms of a federal statute, so, too, state remedial and procedural law must be disregarded under §1988 where that law fails to give adequate expression to important federal concerns. The opponents of the 1866 Act were distinctly aware that the legislation that became §1988 would give the federal courts power to shape federal common-law rules.

It is unfortunate that the Court restricts the reach of §1983 by today's decision construing §1988. Congress now must act again if the gap in remedy is to be filled.

* * *

2. Express Versus Implied Private Rights of Action Under Federal Statutes

Congressional intent also is the lodestar when determining whether a litigant may bring a suit under a federal statute. In many areas of the federal law, when Congress establishes a right, it also provides that private parties may bring suit to seek redress for violation of the right by creating a cause of action — legal entitlement to relief in court based upon proof of specific facts. The substantive right is thus accompanied by an express right of action. Countless federal laws create causes of action. Consider several examples. *Tafflin*, the case we covered in Chapter 2, involves the RICO statute. In addition to federal criminal penalties the statute creates an express civil cause of action for treble damages for "any person injured in his business or property" by reason of prohibited racketeering activity.

A major federal civil rights statute is 42 U.S.C. §1983, which is discussed in detail in Chapter 7, section B. Section 1983 creates a cause of action against any person who, acting under color of state law, abridges rights created by the Constitution and laws of the United States. It authorizes suits for money damages or injunctive relief. Specifically, the text of this important statute provides:

> Every person who, under color of any statute, ordinance, regulation, custom, or usage of any State or Territory or the District of Columbia, subjects, or causes to be subjected, any citizen of the United States or other person within the jurisdiction thereof to the deprivation of any rights, privileges, or immunities secured by the Constitution and laws, shall be liable to the party injured in an action at law, suit in equity, or other proper proceeding for redress, except that in any action brought against a judicial officer for an act or omission taken in such officer's judicial capacity, injunctive relief shall not be granted unless a declaratory decree was violated or declaratory relief was unavailable. For the purposes of this section, any Act of Congress applicable exclusively to the District of Columbia shall be considered to be a statute of the District of Columbia.

Virtually every claim against a local government or state or local official for violating the Constitution is brought pursuant to Section 1983. (As explained in Chapter 6, state governments cannot be named as defendants in §1983 actions.) Claims for negligence against federal officers are expressly authorized by the Federal Tort Claims Act for harm arising from conduct within the scope of their federal duties. Unlike §1983, which applies to local governments and state and local officers directly, but not the state itself (state sovereign immunity is discussed in Chapter 6), in an action against a federal officer under the FTCA, the United States government is substituted as the party defendant (thereby waiving federal sovereign immunity), there are express limits on the kinds of recovery that can be had, and state tort law provides the rule of decision.

Another example of a federal statute creating a cause of action is the Religious Freedom Restoration Act. In 1990, in *Employment Division v. Smith* (1990), the Court narrowly interpreted the protections of the Free Exercise Clause of the First Amendment. The Religious Freedom Restoration Act of 1993 was adopted to negate the *Smith* test and require strict scrutiny for free exercise clause claims. The Act declares that its purpose is "to restore the compelling interest test . . . and to guarantee its application in all cases where free exercise of religion is substantially burdened; and to provide a claim or defense to persons whose religious exercise is substantially burdened by government." The key provision of the Act states: "Government shall not substantially burden a person's exercise of religion even if the burden results from a rule of general applicability, except . . . [g]overnment may substantially burden a person's exercise of religion only if it demonstrates that application of the burden to the person (1) is in furtherance of a compelling governmental interest; (2) is the least restrictive means of furthering that compelling government interest." The Act authorizes suits for "any appropriate relief." (But it should be noted that the Court, in *City of Boerne v. Flores* (1997), declared the Act unconstitutional as applied to state and local governments as exceeding the scope of Congress's powers.)

There are also federal laws that authorize federal courts to grant injunctive and declaratory relief. The Administrative Procedures Act, in 5 U.S.C. §702, specifically allows suits for injunctive relief to be brought against the United States. It provides:

> An action in a court of the United States seeking relief other than money damages and stating a claim that an agency or an officer or employee thereof acted or failed to act in an official capacity or under color of legal authority shall not be dismissed nor relief therein be denied on the ground that it is against the United States or that the United States is an indispensable party. The United States may be named as a defendant in any such action, and a judgment or decree may be entered against the United States

Section 702 does not provide for suits for monetary relief.

Also, the federal Declaratory Judgment Act of 1934 authorizes a federal court to issue a declaratory judgment in a "case or actual controversy within its jurisdiction." In *Aetna Life Insurance Co. v. Haworth* (1937), the Supreme Court upheld the constitutionality of the act. The Court concluded that "[w]here there is such a concrete case admitting of an immediate and definitive determination of the legal rights of the parties in an adversary proceeding upon the facts alleged, the judicial function may be appropriately exercised although the adjudication of the rights of the litigants may not require the award of process or the payment of damages." In other words, federal courts can issue declaratory judgments if there is an actual dispute between adverse litigants and if there is a substantial likelihood that the favorable federal court decision will bring about some change. Whether requests for declaratory judgments present justiciable disputes under Article III, or impermissible advisory opinions, is discussed in Chapter 3, section C, which explains that the Court treats such requests as justiciable as long as the requirements for ripeness and standing are met.

In other statutes, Congress creates substantive rights but is silent on whether there shall be a private right of action. This raises the question whether the Court may imply a private right of action. As described in the case that follows, the law of implied statutory causes of action shifted considerably over the course of the twentieth century. For much of that time, the Court maintained that "it is the duty of the courts to be alert to provide such remedies as are necessary to make effective the congressional purpose" expressed by a statute. *J.I. Case Co. v. Borak* (1964). The *Borak* rule was central to the development of private enforcement of federal regulatory standards during and after the New Deal. Rather than rely exclusively on agencies whose enforcement efforts are limited by funding constraints, and whose enforcement discretion can be warped by agency capture, individuals closest to the harm flowing from regulated entities' violation of federal law could seek judicial relief. Implied rights of action were recognized by the Court in many federal statutes, ranging from securities laws to environmental laws. In the background of many of these cases was recognition of the fact that regulators are often last to learn about violations of the laws they are charged with enforcing. The mid-century Court was correspondingly less preoccupied with the risks of over-enforcement and conflict with agency enforcement priorities.

By the mid-1970s, however, the Supreme Court began to scrutinize congressional intent more closely. The following case reflects the Burger Court's increased skepticism about implied causes of action. Note that it relies principally on textual evidence from a federal statute, not Congress' remedial purposes, to determine that Congress did not intend to create a cause of action.[25]

Touche Ross & Co. v. Redington

442 U.S. 560 (1979)

Justice REHNQUIST delivered the opinion of the Court.

Once again, we are called upon to decide whether a private remedy is implicit in a statute not expressly providing one. Here we decide whether customers of securities brokerage firms that are required to file certain financial reports with regulatory authorities by §17(a) of the Securities Exchange Act of 1934 (1934 Act), have an implied cause of action for damages under §17(a) against accountants who audit such reports, based on misstatements contained in the reports.

I

Petitioner Touche Ross & Co. is a firm of certified public accountants. Weis Securities, Inc. (Weis), a securities brokerage firm registered as a broker-dealer with the Securities and Exchange Commission (Commission) and a member of the New York Stock Exchange (Exchange), retained Touche Ross to serve as Weis' independent certified public accountant from 1969 to 1973. In this capacity, Touche Ross conducted audits of Weis' books and records and prepared for filing with the Commission the annual reports of financial condition required by §17(a) of the 1934 Act, and the rules and regulations adopted thereunder. Touche Ross also prepared for Weis responses to financial questionnaires required by the Exchange of its member firms.

This case arises out of the insolvency and liquidation of Weis. In 1973, the Commission and the Exchange learned of Weis' precarious financial condition and of possible violations of the 1934 Act by Weis and its officers. In May 1973, the Commission sought and was granted an injunction barring Weis and five of its officers from conducting business in violation of the 1934 Act. At the same time, the Securities Investor Protection Corporation (SIPC), pursuant to statutory authority, applied in the United States District Court for the Southern District of New York for a decree adjudging that Weis' customers were in need of the protection afforded by the Securities Investor Protection Act of 1970 (SIPA). The District Court granted the requested decree and appointed respondent Redington (Trustee) to act as trustee in the liquidation of the Weis business under SIPA.

---

25. There is a separate body of doctrine on implied rights of action to enforce *constitutional* rights against *federal officers*. The arc of these cases—from recognizing implied constitutional rights of action to strictly limiting them—parallels the cases on implied statutory private rights of action we present below. This is discussed in Chapter 7, section B. By contrast, §1983, as we have just seen and examine in detail in Chapter 7, section A, creates an express federal cause of action against *state* actors who violate constitutional rights.

During the liquidation, Weis' cash and securities on hand appeared to be insufficient to make whole those customers who had left assets or deposits with Weis. Accordingly, pursuant to SIPA, SIPC advanced the Trustee $14 million to satisfy, up to specified statutory limits, the claims of the approximately 34,000 Weis customers and certain other creditors of Weis. Despite the advance of $14 million by SIPC, there apparently remain several million dollars of unsatisfied customer claims.

In 1976, SIPC and the Trustee filed this action for damages against Touche Ross in the District Court for the Southern District of New York. The "common allegations" of the complaint, which at this stage of the case we must accept as true, aver that certain of Weis' officers conspired to conceal substantial operating losses during its 1972 fiscal year by falsifying financial reports required to be filed with regulatory authorities pursuant to §17(a) of the 1934 Act. SIPC and the Trustee seek to impose liability upon Touche Ross by reason of its allegedly improper audit and certification of the 1972 Weis financial statements and preparation of answers to the Exchange financial questionnaire. The federal claims are based on §17(a) of the 1934 Act; the complaint also alleges several state common-law causes of action based on accountants' negligence, breach of contract, and breach of warranty.

II

The question of the existence of a statutory cause of action is, of course, one of statutory construction. [O]ur task is limited solely to determining whether Congress intended to create the private right of action asserted by SIPC and the Trustee. And as with any case involving the interpretation of a statute, our analysis must begin with the language of the statute itself.

At the time pertinent to the case before us, §17(a) read, in relevant part, as follows:

> Every national securities exchange, every member thereof, . . . and every broker or dealer registered pursuant to . . . this title, shall make, keep, and preserve for such periods, such accounts, correspondence, . . . and other records, and make such reports, as the Commission by its rules and regulations may prescribe as necessary or appropriate in the public interest or for the protection of investors.

In terms, §17(a) simply requires broker-dealers and others to keep such records and file such reports as the Commission may prescribe. It does not, by its terms, purport to create a private cause of action in favor of anyone. It is true that in the past our cases have held that in certain circumstances a private right of action may be implied in a statute not expressly providing one. *J.I. Case Co. v. Borak* (1964). But in those cases finding such implied private remedies, the statute in question at least prohibited certain conduct or created federal rights in favor of private parties. By contrast, §17(a) neither confers rights on private parties nor proscribes any conduct as unlawful.

The intent of §17(a) is evident from its face. Section 17(a) is like provisions in countless other statutes that simply require certain regulated businesses to keep records and file periodic reports to enable the relevant governmental authorities to perform their regulatory functions. The reports and records provide the regulatory authorities with the necessary information to oversee compliance with and enforce the various statutes and regulations with which they are concerned. But §17(a) does not by any stretch of its language purport to confer private damages rights or, indeed, any remedy in the event the regulatory authorities are unsuccessful in achieving their objectives and the broker becomes insolvent before corrective steps can be taken.

As the Court of Appeals recognized, the legislative history of the 1934 Act is entirely silent on the question whether a private right of action for damages should or should not be available under §17(a) in the circumstances of this case. SIPC and the Trustee nevertheless argue that because Congress did not express an intent to deny a private cause of action under §17(a), this Court should infer one. But implying a private right of action on the basis of congressional silence is a hazardous enterprise, at best. *See Santa Clara Pueblo v. Martinez* (1978). And where, as here, the plain language of the provision weighs against implication of a private remedy, the fact that there is no suggestion whatsoever in the legislative history that §17(a) may give rise to suits for damages reinforces our decision not to find such a right of action implicit within the section.

Further justification for our decision not to imply the private remedy that SIPC and the Trustee seek to establish may be found in the statutory scheme of which §17(a) is a part. First, §17(a) is flanked by provisions of the 1934 Act that explicitly grant private causes of action. Section 9(e) of the 1934 Act also expressly provides a private right of action. Obviously, then, when Congress wished to provide a private damages remedy, it knew how to do so and did so expressly.

Second, §18(a) creates a private cause of action against persons, such as accountants, who "make or cause to be made" materially misleading statements in any reports or other documents filed with the Commission, although the cause of action is limited to persons who, in reliance on the statements, purchased or sold a security whose price was affected by the statements. Since SIPC and the Trustee do not allege that the Weis customers purchased or sold securities in reliance on the §17(a) reports at issue, they cannot sue Touche Ross under §18(a).

[W]e need not decide whether Congress expressly intended §18(a) to provide the exclusive remedy for misstatements contained in §17(a) reports. For where the principal express civil remedy for misstatements in reports created by Congress contemporaneously with the passage of §17(a) is by its terms limited to purchasers and sellers of securities, we are extremely reluctant to imply a cause of action in §17(a) that is significantly broader than the remedy that Congress chose to provide.

SIPC and the Trustee urge, and the Court of Appeals agreed, that the analysis should not stop here. Relying on the factors set forth in *Cort v. Ash* (1975), they assert that we also must consider whether an implied private remedy is necessary to "effectuate the purpose of the section" and whether the cause of action is one traditionally relegated to state law. We need not reach the merits of the arguments concerning the "necessity" of implying a private remedy and the proper forum for enforcement of the rights asserted by SIPC and the Trustee, for we believe such inquiries have little relevance to the decision of this case. It is true that in *Cort v. Ash*, the Court set forth four factors that it considered "relevant" in determining whether a private remedy is implicit in a statute not expressly providing one. But the Court did not decide that each of these factors is entitled to equal weight. The central inquiry remains whether Congress intended to create, either expressly or by implication, a private cause of action. Indeed, the first three factors discussed in *Cort*—the language and focus of the statute, its legislative history, and its purpose—are ones traditionally relied upon in determining legislative intent. The question whether Congress, either expressly or by implication, intended to create a private right of action, has been definitely answered in the negative.

III

SIPC and the Trustee contend that the result we reach sanctions injustice. But even if that were the case, the argument is made in the wrong forum, for we are not at liberty to legislate. If there is to be a federal damages remedy under these circumstances, Congress must provide it.

Justice MARSHALL, dissenting.

In determining whether to imply a private cause of action for damages under a statute that does not expressly authorize such a remedy, this Court has considered four factors:

> First, is the plaintiff "one of the class for whose especial benefit the statute was enacted,"—that is, does the statute create a federal right in favor of the plaintiff? Second, is there any indication of legislative intent, explicit or implicit, either to create such a remedy or to deny one? Third, is it consistent with the underlying purposes of the legislative scheme to imply such a remedy for the plaintiff? And finally, is the cause of action one traditionally relegated to state law, in an area basically the concern of the States, so that it would be inappropriate to infer a cause of action based solely on federal law? *Cort v. Ash* (1975).

[First, i]t is clear that brokerage firm customers are the "favored wards" of §17, and that the initial test of *Cort v. Ash* is satisfied here.

With respect to the second *Cort* factor, the legislative history does not explicitly address the availability of a damages remedy under §17. The majority, however, discerns an intent to deny private remedies from two aspects of the statutory scheme. Because unrelated sections in the 1934 Act expressly grant private rights of action for violation of their terms, the Court suggests that Congress would have made such provision under §17 had it wished to do so. But as we noted recently in *Cannon v. University of Chicago* (1979), "that other provisions of a complex statutory scheme create express remedies has not been accepted as a sufficient reason for refusing to imply an otherwise appropriate remedy under a separate section." The Court finds a further indication of congressional intent in the interaction between §§17 and 18 of the 1934 Act. However, §18 pertains to investors who are injured in the course of securities transactions, while §17 is concerned exclusively with brokerage firm customers who may be injured by a broker's insolvency. Given this divergence in focus, §18 does not reflect an intent to restrict the remedies available under §17.

A cause of action for damages here is also consistent with the underlying purposes of the legislative scheme. Because the SEC lacks the resources to audit all the documents that brokers file, it must rely on certification by accountants. Implying a private right of action would both facilitate the SEC's enforcement efforts and provide an incentive for accountants to perform their certification functions properly.

Finally, enforcement of the 1934 Act's reporting provisions is plainly not a matter of traditional state concern, but rather relates solely to the effectiveness of federal statutory requirements. And, as the Court of Appeals held, since the problems caused by broker insolvencies are national in scope, so too must be the standards governing financial disclosure.

In sum, straightforward application of the four *Cort* factors compels affirmance of the judgment below. Because the Court misapplies this precedent and disregards the evident purpose of §17, I respectfully dissent.

* * *

By the turn of the century, skepticism about the practice of implying private rights of action increased and since then the Court has refused to create any new private rights of action by implication. The sources of the shift included a turn to strict textualism and revived concern with the prerogatives of a federal agency to control enforcement of its organic statute. Private rights of action, which allow any individual who can meet the requirements of standing to seek redress, may not be consistent with the enforcement priorities of the relevant federal agencies. *Alexander v. Sandoval* (2001), the case that crystalized these two principles, arose out of litigation concerning English-only language restrictions in Alabama. English-only language restrictions bar state and local officials from translating government documents into other languages, bar bilingual education in public schools, and limit resources for translation in the provision of government services to people for whom English is a second language.

A 2014 study showed that 31 states in addition to many local governments have imposed these restrictions by declaring English as their "official" language. In many jurisdictions, the adoption of these restrictions were politicized reactions to increases in immigration; in others, events that spark nationalist sentiment have been responsible, as in the anti-German sentiment that fueled Nebraska's 1919 ban on teaching foreign languages in primary schools. Nationwide, in the twenty-first century, 20 percent of the American population (61 million people) speak a language other than English at home, up from 17 percent at the turn of the century. In some states, laws declaring English the official language are unenforced and public resources are provided for translation despite these laws, while in others there are statutory mandates for important government documents and health and safety communication (including the information on prescription bottles sold in the state) to be translated into other languages.[26]

Before adopting English as its official language in 1990, Alabama offered its drivers' license test in 14 languages. Lawyers for Martha Sandoval, a permanent resident who challenged the state's law in drivers tests as a form of national origin discrimination, argued that English-only drivers tests have a significant impact because people for whom English is a second language cannot, in that setting, simply ask a friend of family member to translate for them and the tests required a tenth-grade level of English proficiency.

---

26. Jake Grovum, *A Growing Divide Over Official-English Laws*, PEW TRUSTS STATELINE (AUG. 8, 2014), https://www.pewtrusts.org/en/research-and-analysis/blogs/stateline/2014/08/08/the-growing-divide-over-official-english-laws

Alexander v. Sandoval

532 U.S. 275 (2001)

Justice SCALIA delivered the opinion of the Court.

This case presents the question whether private individuals may sue to enforce disparate-impact regulations promulgated under Title VI of the Civil Rights Act of 1964.

I

Section 601 of that Title provides that no person shall, "on the ground of race, color, or national origin, be excluded from participation in, be denied the benefits of, or be subjected to discrimination under any program or activity" covered by Title VI. 42 U.S.C. §2000d. Section 602 authorizes federal agencies "to effectuate the provisions of [§601] . . . by issuing rules, regulations, or orders of general applicability," 42 U.S.C. §2000d-1, and the DOJ in an exercise of this authority promulgated a regulation forbidding funding recipients to "utilize criteria or methods of administration which have the effect of subjecting individuals to discrimination because of their race, color, or national origin. . . ." 28 CFR §42.104(b)(2) (2000).

The State of Alabama amended its Constitution in 1990 to declare English "the official language of the state of Alabama." Pursuant to this provision and, petitioners have argued, to advance public safety, the Department decided to administer state driver's license examinations only in English. Alexander Sandoval, as representative of a class, brought suit in the United States District Court for the Middle District of Alabama to enjoin the English-only policy, arguing that it violated the DOJ regulation because it had the effect of subjecting non-English speakers to discrimination based on their national origin. The District Court agreed. It enjoined the policy and ordered the Department to accommodate non-English speakers. Petitioners appealed to the Court of Appeals for the Eleventh Circuit, which affirmed. Both courts rejected petitioners' argument that Title VI did not provide respondents a cause of action to enforce the regulation.

II

For purposes of the present case, three aspects of Title VI must be taken as given. First, private individuals may sue to enforce §601 of Title VI and obtain both injunctive relief and damages. *Cannon v. University of Chicago* (1979). Second, it is similarly beyond dispute — and no party disagrees — that §601 prohibits only intentional discrimination. *See Alexander v. Choate* (1985). Third, we must assume for purposes of deciding this case that regulations promulgated under §602 of Title VI may validly proscribe activities that have a disparate impact on racial groups, even though such activities are permissible under §601. We assume for the purposes of deciding this case that the DOJ and DOT regulations proscribing activities that have a disparate impact on the basis of race are valid.

Like substantive federal law itself, private rights of action to enforce federal law must be created by Congress. *Touche Ross & Co. v. Redington* (1979). Statutory intent on this latter point is determinative. Without it, a cause of action does not exist and courts may not create one, no matter how desirable that might be as a policy matter, or how compatible with the statute. "Raising up causes of action where a statute has not created them may be a proper function for common-law courts, but not for federal tribunals." *Lampf, Pleva, Lipkind, Prupis & Petigrow v. Gilbertson* (1991) (SCALIA, J., concurring in part and concurring in judgment).

Respondents would have us revert in this case to the understanding of private causes of action that held sway 40 years ago when Title VI was enacted. That understanding is captured by the Court's statement in *J.I. Case Co. v. Borak* (1964), that "it is the duty of the courts to be alert to provide such remedies as are necessary to make effective the congressional purpose" expressed by a statute. We abandoned that understanding in *Cort v. Ash* (1975) —which itself interpreted a statute enacted under the *ancien regime*—and have not returned to it since. Having sworn off the habit of venturing beyond Congress's intent, we will not accept respondents' invitation to have one last drink. . . . Nor do we agree with the Government that our cases interpreting statutes enacted prior to *Cort v. Ash* have given "dispositive weight" to the "expectations" that the enacting Congress had formed "in light of the 'contemporary legal context.'" . . . We have never accorded dispositive weight to context shorn of text. In determining whether statutes create private rights of action, as in interpreting statutes generally, legal context matters only to the extent it clarifies text.

We therefore begin (and find that we can end) our search for Congress's intent with the text and structure of Title VI.7 Section 602 authorizes federal agencies "to effectuate the provisions of [§601] . . . by issuing rules, regulations, or orders of general applicability." 42 U.S.C. §2000d-1. It is immediately clear that the "rights-creating" language so critical to the Court's analysis in [cases governing §601] is completely absent from §602. Whereas §601 decrees that "[n]o person . . . shall . . . be subjected to discrimination," 42 U.S.C. §2000d, the text of §602 provides that "[e]ach Federal department and agency . . . is authorized and directed to effectuate the provisions of [§601]," 42 U.S.C. §2000d-1. Far from displaying congressional intent to create new rights, §602 limits agencies to "effectuat[ing]" rights already created by §601. And the focus of §602 is twice removed from the individuals who will ultimately benefit from Title VI's protection. Statutes that focus on the person regulated rather than the individuals protected create "no implication of an intent to confer rights on a particular class of persons." *California v. Sierra Club* (1981). Section 602 is yet a step further removed: It focuses neither on the individuals protected nor even on the funding recipients being regulated, but on the agencies that will do the regulating. . . . Section 602 is "phrased as a directive to federal agencies engaged in the distribution of public funds," *University Research Ass'n v. Coutu* (1981). When this is true, "[t]here [is] far less reason to infer a private remedy in favor of individual persons," *Cannon v. Univ. of Chicago* (1979). . . .

Nor do the methods that §602 goes on to provide for enforcing its authorized regulations manifest an intent to create a private remedy; if anything, they suggest the opposite. Section 602 empowers agencies to enforce their regulations either by terminating funding to the "particular program, or part thereof," that has violated the regulation or "by any other means authorized by law," 42 U.S.C. §2000d-1. No enforcement action may be taken, however, "until the department or agency concerned has advised the appropriate person or persons of the failure to comply with the requirement and has determined that compliance cannot be secured by voluntary means." And every agency enforcement action is subject to judicial review. §2000d-2. If an agency attempts to terminate program funding, still more restrictions apply. The agency head must "file with the committees of the House and Senate having legislative jurisdiction over the program or activity involved a full written report" [and] the termination of funding does not "become effective until thirty days have elapsed after the filing of such report." Whatever these elaborate restrictions on agency enforcement may imply for the private enforcement of rights created *outside* of §602, they tend to contradict a congressional intent to create privately enforceable rights through §602 itself. . . . The question whether §602's remedial scheme can overbear other evidence of congressional intent is simply not presented, since we have found no evidence anywhere in the text to suggest that Congress intended to create a private right to enforce regulations promulgated under §602.

Both the Government and respondents argue that the regulations contain rights-creating language and so must be privately enforceable, but that argument skips an analytical step. Language in a regulation may invoke a private right of action that Congress through statutory text created, but it may not create a right that Congress has not. Thus, when a statute has provided a general authorization for private enforcement of regulations, it may perhaps be correct that the intent displayed in each regulation can determine whether or not it is privately enforceable. But it is most certainly incorrect to say that language in a regulation can conjure up a private cause of action that has not been authorized by Congress. Agencies may play the sorcerer's apprentice but not the sorcerer himself. . . .

Justice STEVENS, with whom Justice SOUTER, Justice GINSBURG, and Justice BREYER join, dissenting.

In 1964, as part of a groundbreaking and comprehensive civil rights Act, Congress prohibited recipients of federal funds from discriminating on the basis of race, ethnicity, or national origin. Title VI of the Civil Rights Act of 1964, 42 U.S.C. §§2000d to 2000d-7. Pursuant to powers *expressly delegated by that Act, the federal agencies and departments responsible for awarding and administering federal contracts immediately adopted regulations prohibiting federal contractees from adopting policies that have the "effect" of discriminating on those bases. At the time of the promulgation of these regulations, prevailing principles of statutory construction assumed that Congress intended a private right of action whenever such a cause of action was necessary to protect individual rights granted by valid federal law. Relying both on this presumption and on independent analysis of Title VI, this Court has repeatedly and consistently affirmed the right of private individuals to bring civil suits to enforce rights guaranteed by Title VI. A fair reading of those cases, and coherent implementation of the statutory scheme, requires the same result under Title VI's implementing regulations.

In separate lawsuits spanning several decades, we have endorsed an action identical in substance to the one brought in this case; demonstrated that Congress intended a private right of action to protect the rights guaranteed by Title VI, *see Cannon v. University of Chicago* (1979); and concluded that private individuals may seek declaratory and injunctive relief against state officials for violations of regulations promulgated pursuant to Title VI. Giving fair import to our language and our holdings, every Court of Appeals to address the question has concluded that a private right of action exists to enforce the rights guaranteed both by the text of Title

VI and by any regulations validly promulgated pursuant to that Title, and Congress has adopted several statutes that appear to ratify the status quo.

Today, in a decision unfounded in our precedent and hostile to decades of settled expectations, a majority of this Court carves out an important exception to the right of private action long recognized under Title VI. In so doing, the Court makes three distinct, albeit interrelated, errors. First, the Court provides a muddled account of both the reasoning and the breadth of our prior decisions endorsing a private right of action under Title VI, thereby obscuring the conflict between those opinions and today's decision. Second, the Court offers a flawed and unconvincing analysis of the relationship between §§601 and 602 of the Civil Rights Act of 1964, ignoring more plausible and persuasive explanations detailed in our prior opinions. Finally, the Court badly misconstrues the theoretical linchpin of our decision in *Cannon v. University of Chicago* (1979), mistaking that decision's careful contextual analysis for judicial fiat.

* * *

Sandoval emphasizes that, unlike common-law courts, federal courts cannot raise up new causes of action just because Congress creates new rights and regulatory systems. A key premise is that certain federal rights do not necessarily travel with remedies for their violation. If Congress wants those injured to be able to sue, it has to say so. The mid-twentieth century *Borak* regime of assuming Congress intended remedies to travel with rights is over—an *ancien regime*. Nor will the Court engage in balancing the interests in providing a remedy against the risk of interference with agency prerogatives and state law as it did in *Cort* and *Touche-Ross*.

Sandoval does not overturn the prior cases in which, interpreting other provisions of the 1964 Civil Rights Act or other statutes, the Court had already implied a private right of action. It resolves only the claim that §602 implied a private right of action. But *Sandoval* casts some doubt on the rationale for declining to revisit these cases. One of the primary reasons these implied rights of action have survived is that, at least for statutes written during the *Borak* regime, Congress would not have believed it needed to create express rights of action—the Court at the time was open about its willingness to do so. Taking a textualist approach to these statutes and scrutinizing them for authority on the part of private parties to sue would flatly disregard the context in which they were written. In the period between *Cort* and *Sandoval*, the Court recognized this. *See, e.g., Cannon v. Univ. of Chicago* (1979) (upholding private right of action under Title IX despite fact that text included a "quite different" spending clause remedy in part because, "evaluation of congressional action in 1972 must take into account its contemporary legal context"); *Merrill Lynch v. Curran* (1982) (inferring private right of action under Commodity Exchange Act and subsequent amendments because Congress would not have thought it needed to be explicit given the contemporary legal context). Note, however, that in *Sandoval* the Court says it has never given "dispositive weight" to context shorn of text. Thus the "contemporary legal context" in which a statute was written may not be enough to save other implied rights of action, though, to date, the Court has not revisited cases in which it had upheld a private right of action.

Can the holding in *Sandoval* be reconciled with *Marbury*'s recognition, drawn from Blackstone, the writ system and centuries of English doctrine, that remedies generally travel with rights? The underlying principle is *"ubi jus, ibi remedium"*—meaning where there is a right, there is a remedy.[27] On this view, Congress gives the federal courts all the authority they need when it creates new rights. If Congress wants to prevent overenforcement or limit interference with agency enforcement priorities and discretionary judgment, it can of course specify that certain remedies and enforcement authorities shall be exclusive when it creates the substantive right. But when Congress elects not to do this, is there anything in the constitution that prevents federal courts from exercising their traditional authority to provide remedies for violations of properly legislated rights? Is it relevant that in the early period after the founding Congress recognized this judicial power to create rights of action and remedies?[28]

What about federal statutes that confer jurisdiction on the federal courts to adjudicate in an area without creating a private right of action? What could the jurisdictional grant mean if there were no judicial power to entertain causes of action falling within it? An example which has engendered a great deal of litigation over whether jurisdictional language also permits federal courts to entertain common law causes of action, and, if so, their scope, is the Alien Tort Statute (ATS). Originally adopted in 1789, the ATS gives the federal courts jurisdiction to hear lawsuits filed by non-U.S. citizens for torts committed in violation of international law. The statute, 28 U.S.C. §1350, grants jurisdiction to federal district courts "of all causes where an alien sues for a tort only, committed in violation of the law of nations or of a treaty of the United States."

The statute is important in creating jurisdiction in the federal courts to sue those responsible for international human rights violations, though it raises questions about whether courts distant from wrongs that take place overseas are best situated to see justice done. Modern transnational human rights litigation under the ATS began in the late 1970s when the Center for Constitutional Rights brought a landmark case, *Filártiga v. Peña-Irala* (1980). The Second Circuit Court of Appeals held that the basis for an ATS suit was "the law of nations, which has always been part of the federal common law." Many scholars and human rights advocates praised the decision as crucial for the enforcement and progressive development of human rights law.

Critics of ATS litigation questioned judicial incorporation of international human rights law into U.S. law. They argued that ATS suits could undermine the foreign policy of the United States and the Executive Branch's authority in foreign affairs. These suits, critics contended, created friction between foreign governments and the United States. Many high-profile ATS suits involved allegations that foreign governments and transnational mining and energy corporations had violated norms against extrajudicial killing, forced labor, racial discrimination, and environmental harms. As ATS plaintiffs increasingly brought claims against these transnational corporate defendants for human rights violations abroad, corporations simultaneously argued that they could not be sued for such violations and

---

27. Linda Sheryl Greene, *Judicial Implication of Remedies for Federal Statutory Violations: The Separation of Powers Concerns*, 53 TEMPLE L.Q. 469 (1980).

28. *See* Anthony J. Bellia, Jr. & Bradford R. Clark, *The Original Source of the Cause of Action in Federal Courts: The Example of the Alien Tort Statute*, 101 VA. L. REV. 777 (2015).

pledged to adopt self-regulatory policies, drawing upon a discourse of corporate social responsibility that traces back to the 1950s.

Beginning with *Sosa v. Alvarez-Machain* (2004), the Supreme Court has recognized the ATS as creating federal jurisdiction, but it has narrowly construed the authority of federal courts to entertain causes of action associated with the jurisdictional grant and thus limited its scope as a tool of transnational human rights litigation. The Court treats these causes of action as part of the "ambient law of the era" while insisting that the statute itself created no express right of action and therefore no common law power to expand upon the three historically recognized forms of action. Note as well, the Court's treatment of the other express cause of action in the case under the FTCA for the federal officer defendants.

Sosa v. Alvarez-Machain

542 U.S. 692 (2004)

Justice SOUTER announced the opinion of the Court.

The two issues are whether respondent Alvarez–Machain's allegation that the Drug Enforcement Administration instigated his abduction from Mexico for criminal trial in the United States supports a claim against the Government under the Federal Tort Claims Act (FTCA or Act), and whether he may recover under the Alien Tort Statute (ATS). We hold that he is not entitled to a remedy under either statute.

I

In 1985, an agent of the Drug Enforcement Administration (DEA), Enrique Camarena-Salazar, was captured on assignment in Mexico and taken to a house in Guadalajara, where he was tortured over the course of a 2-day interrogation, then murdered. Based in part on eyewitness testimony, DEA officials in the United States came to believe that respondent Humberto Alvarez-Machain (Alvarez), a Mexican physician, was present at the house and acted to prolong the agent's life in order to extend the interrogation and torture.

In 1990, a federal grand jury indicted Alvarez for the torture and murder of Camarena-Salazar, and the United States District Court for the Central District of California issued a warrant for his arrest. The DEA asked the Mexican Government for help in getting Alvarez into the United States, but when the requests and negotiations proved fruitless, the DEA approved a plan to hire Mexican nationals to seize Alvarez and bring him to the United States for trial. As so planned, a group of Mexicans, including petitioner Jose Francisco Sosa, abducted Alvarez from his house, held him overnight in a motel, and brought him by private plane to El Paso, Texas, where he was arrested by federal officers.

Once in American custody, Alvarez moved to dismiss the indictment on the ground that his seizure was "outrageous governmental conduct," and violated the extradition treaty between the United States and Mexico. The District Court agreed, the Ninth Circuit affirmed, and we reversed, holding that the fact of Alvarez's forcible seizure did not affect the jurisdiction of a federal court. The case was tried in 1992, and ended at the close of the Government's case, when the District Court granted Alvarez's motion for a judgment of acquittal.

In 1993, after returning to Mexico, Alvarez began the civil action before us here. He sued Sosa, Mexican citizen and DEA operative Antonio Garate-Bustamante, five unnamed Mexican civilians, the United States, and four DEA agents. So far as it matters here, Alvarez sought damages from the United States under the FTCA, alleging false arrest, and from Sosa under the ATS, for a violation of the law of nations. The former statute authorizes suit "for . . . personal injury . . . caused by the negligent or wrongful act or omission of any employee of the Government while acting within the scope of his office or employment." The latter provides in its entirety that "[t]he district courts shall have original jurisdiction of any civil action by an alien for a tort only, committed in violation of the law of nations or a treaty of the United States."

II

The Government seeks reversal of the judgment of liability under the FTCA on two principal grounds. It argues that the arrest could not have been tortious, because it was authorized by 21 U.S.C. §87, setting out the arrest authority of the DEA, and it says that in any event the liability asserted here falls within the FTCA exception to waiver of sovereign immunity for claims "arising in a foreign country." We think the exception applies and decide on that ground.

The FTCA "was designed primarily to remove the sovereign immunity of the United States from suits in tort and, with certain specific exceptions, to render the Government liable in tort as a private individual would be under like circumstances." The Act accordingly gives federal district courts jurisdiction over claims against the United States for injury "caused by the negligent or wrongful act or omission of any employee of the Government while acting within the scope of his office or employment, under circumstances where the United States, if a private person, would be liable to the claimant in accordance with the law of the place where the act or omission occurred." But the Act also limits its waiver of sovereign immunity in a number of ways.

Here the significant limitation on the waiver of immunity is the Act's exception for "[a]ny claim arising in a foreign country," a provision that on its face seems plainly applicable to the facts of this action. Alvarez's arrest, however, was said to be "false," and thus tortious, only because, and only to the extent that, it took place and endured in Mexico. The actions in Mexico are thus most naturally understood as the kernel of a "claim arising in a foreign country," and barred from suit under the exception to the waiver of immunity.

III

Alvarez has also brought an action under the ATS against petitioner Sosa, who argues (as does the United States supporting him) that there is no relief under the ATS because the statute does no more than vest federal courts with jurisdiction, neither creating nor authorizing the courts to recognize any particular right of action without further congressional action. Although we agree the statute is in terms only jurisdictional, we think that at the time of enactment the jurisdiction enabled federal courts to hear claims in a very limited category defined by the law of nations and recognized at common law. We do not believe, however, that the limited, implicit sanction to entertain the handful of international law *cum* common law claims understood in 1789 should be taken as authority to recognize the right of action asserted by Alvarez here.

Judge Friendly called the ATS a "legal Lohengrin . . . [because] no one seems to know whence it came," and for over 170 years after its enactment it provided jurisdiction in only one case. The first Congress passed it as part of the Judiciary Act of 1789, in providing that the new federal district courts "shall also have cognizance, concurrent with the courts of the several States, or the circuit courts, as the case may be, of all causes where an alien sues for a tort only in violation of the law of nations or a treaty of the United States."

The parties and *amici* here advance radically different historical interpretations of this terse provision. Alvarez says that the ATS was intended not simply as a jurisdictional grant, but as authority for the creation of a new cause of action for torts in violation of international law. We think that reading is implausible. As enacted in 1789, the ATS gave the district courts "cognizance" of certain causes of action, and the term bespoke a grant of jurisdiction, not power to mold substantive law. The fact that the ATS was placed in §9 of the Judiciary Act, a statute otherwise exclusively concerned with federal-court jurisdiction, is itself support for its strictly jurisdictional nature. Nor would the distinction between jurisdiction and cause of action have been elided by the drafters of the Act or those who voted on it. In sum, we think the statute was intended as jurisdictional in the sense of addressing the power of the courts to entertain cases concerned with a certain subject.

But holding the ATS jurisdictional raises a new question, this one about the interaction between the ATS at the time of its enactment and the ambient law of the era. Sosa would have it that the ATS was stillborn because there could be no claim for relief without a further statute expressly authorizing adoption of causes of action. *Amici* professors of federal jurisdiction and legal history take a different tack, that federal courts could entertain claims once the jurisdictional grant was on the books, because torts in violation of the law of nations would have been recognized within the common law of the time. We think history and practice give the edge to this latter position.

"When the *United States* declared their independence, they were bound to receive the law of nations, in its modern state of purity and refinement." In the years of the early Republic, this law of nations comprised two principal elements, the first covering the general norms governing the behavior of national states with each other: "*the science which teaches the rights subsisting between nations or states, and the obligations correspondent to those rights,*" or "that code of public instruction which defines the rights and prescribes the duties of nations, in their intercourse with each other." This aspect of the law of nations thus occupied the executive and legislative domains, not the judicial.

The law of nations included a second, more pedestrian element, however, that did fall within the judicial sphere, as a body of judge-made law regulating the conduct of individuals situated outside domestic boundaries and consequently carrying an international savor. To Blackstone, the law of nations in this sense was implicated "in mercantile questions, such as bills of exchange and the like; in all marine causes, relating to freight, average, demurrage, insurances, bottomry . . . ; [and] in all disputes relating to prizes, to shipwrecks, to hostages, and ransom bills." The law merchant emerged from the customary practices of international traders and admiralty required its own transnational regulation. And it was the law of nations in this sense that our precursors spoke about when the Court explained the status of coast fishing vessels in wartime grew from "ancient usage among civilized nations, beginning centuries ago, and gradually ripening into a rule of international law. . . ."

There was, finally, a sphere in which these rules binding individuals for the benefit of other individuals overlapped with the norms of state relationships. Blackstone referred to it when he mentioned three specific offenses against the law of nations addressed by the criminal law of England: violation of safe conducts, infringement of the rights of ambassadors, and piracy. An assault against an ambassador, for example, impinged upon the sovereignty of the foreign nation and if not adequately redressed could rise to an issue of war. It was this narrow set of violations of the law of nations, admitting of a judicial remedy and at the same time threatening serious consequences in international affairs, that was probably on minds of the men who drafted the ATS with its reference to tort.

There is no record of congressional discussion about private actions that might be subject to the jurisdictional provision, or about any need for further legislation to create private remedies; there is no record even of debate on the section. Given the poverty of drafting history, modern commentators have necessarily concentrated on the text, remarking on the innovative use of the word "tort," The historical scholarship has also placed the ATS within the competition between federalist and antifederalist forces over the national role in foreign relations. But despite considerable scholarly attention, it is fair to say that a consensus understanding of what Congress intended has proven elusive.

Still, the history does tend to support two propositions. First, there is every reason to suppose that the First Congress did not pass the ATS as a jurisdictional convenience to be placed on the shelf for use by a future Congress or state legislature that might, someday, authorize the creation of causes of action or itself decide to make some element of the law of nations actionable for the benefit of foreigners. The anxieties of the preconstitutional period cannot be ignored easily enough to think that the statute was not meant to have a practical effect. Consider that the principal draftsman of the ATS was apparently Oliver Ellsworth, previously a member of the Continental Congress that had passed the 1781 resolution and a member of the Connecticut Legislature that made good on that congressional request. Consider, too, that the First Congress was attentive enough to the law of nations to recognize certain offenses expressly as criminal, including the three mentioned by Blackstone. It would have been passing strange for Ellsworth and this very Congress to vest federal courts expressly with jurisdiction to entertain civil causes brought by aliens alleging violations of the law of nations, but to no effect whatever until the Congress should take further action. There is too much in the historical record to believe that Congress would have enacted the ATS only to leave it lying fallow indefinitely.

The second inference to be drawn from the history is that Congress intended the ATS to furnish jurisdiction for a relatively modest set of actions alleging violations of the law of nations. Uppermost in the legislative mind appears to have been offenses against ambassadors, violations of safe conduct were probably understood to be actionable, and individual actions arising out of prize captures and piracy may well have also been contemplated. But the common law appears to have understood only those three of the hybrid variety as definite and actionable, or at any rate, to have assumed only a very limited set of claims. As Blackstone had put it, "offences against this law [of nations] are principally incident to whole states or nations," and not individuals seeking relief in court.

The sparse contemporaneous cases and legal materials referring to the ATS tend to confirm both inferences, that some, but few, torts in violation of the law of nations were understood to be within the common law.

IV

We think it is correct, then, to assume that the First Congress understood that the district courts would recognize private causes of action for certain torts in violation of the law of nations, though we have found no basis to suspect Congress had any examples in mind beyond those torts corresponding to Blackstone's three primary offenses: violation of safe conducts, infringement of the rights of ambassadors, and piracy. We assume, too, that no development in the two centuries from the enactment of §1350 to the birth of the modern line of cases has categorically precluded federal courts from recognizing a claim under the law of nations as an element of common law; Congress has not in any relevant way amended §1350 or limited civil common law power by another statute. Still, there are good reasons for a restrained conception of the discretion a federal court should exercise in considering a new cause of action of this kind. Accordingly, we think courts should require any claim based on the present-day law of nations to rest on a norm of international character accepted by the civilized world and defined with a specificity comparable to the features of the 18th-century paradigms we have recognized. This requirement is fatal to Alvarez's claim.

We must still, however, derive a standard or set of standards for assessing the particular claim Alvarez raises, and for this action it suffices to look to the historical antecedents. Whatever the ultimate criteria for accepting a cause of action subject to jurisdiction under §1350, we are persuaded that federal courts should not recognize private claims under federal common law for violations of any international law norm with less definite content and acceptance among civilized nations than the historical paradigms familiar when §1350 was enacted. And the determination whether a norm is sufficiently definite to support a cause of action should (and, indeed, inevitably must) involve an element of judgment about the practical consequences of making that cause available to litigants in the federal courts.

Thus, Alvarez's detention claim must be gauged against the current state of international law, looking to those sources we have long, albeit cautiously, recognized. Whatever may be said for the broad principle Alvarez advances, in the present, imperfect world, it expresses an aspiration that exceeds any binding customary rule having the specificity we require. Creating a private cause of action to further that aspiration would go beyond any residual common law discretion we think it appropriate to exercise. It is enough to hold that a single illegal detention of less than a day, followed by the transfer of custody to lawful authorities and a prompt arraignment, violates no norm of customary international law so well defined as to support the creation of a federal remedy.

Justice SCALIA, with whom THE CHIEF JUSTICE and Justice THOMAS join, concurring in part and concurring in the judgment.

There is not much that I would add to the Court's detailed opinion, and only one thing that I would subtract: its reservation of a discretionary power in the Federal Judiciary to create causes of action for the enforcement of international-law-based norms. Accordingly, I join Parts I, II, and III of the Court's opinion in these consolidated cases. Although I agree with much in Part IV, I cannot join it because the judicial lawmaking role it invites would commit the Federal Judiciary to a task it is neither authorized nor suited to perform.

The Court's detailed exegesis of the ATS conclusively establishes that it is "a jurisdictional statute creating no new causes of action." None of the exceptions to the general rule against finding substantive lawmaking power in a jurisdictional grant apply.

The analysis in the Court's opinion departs from my own in this respect: After concluding in Part III that "the ATS is a jurisdictional statute creating no new causes of action," the Court addresses at length in Part IV the "good reasons for a restrained conception of the *discretion* a federal court should exercise in considering a new cause of action" under the ATS. By framing the issue as one of "discretion," the Court skips over the antecedent question of authority. This neglects the "lesson of *Erie*," that "grants of jurisdiction alone" (which the Court has acknowledged the ATS to be) "are not themselves grants of lawmaking authority." Meltzer, Customary International Law, Foreign Affairs Law, and Federal Common Law, 42 Va. J. Int'l L. (2002). On this point, the Court observes only that no development between the enactment of the ATS (in 1789) and the birth of modern international human rights litigation under that statute (in 1980) "has categorically *precluded* federal courts from recognizing a claim under the law of nations as an element of common law." This turns our jurisprudence regarding federal common law on its head. The question is not what case or congressional action *prevents* federal courts from applying the law of nations as part of the general common law; it is what *authorizes* that peculiar exception from *Erie's* fundamental holding that a general common law *does not exist*.

The Court would apparently find authorization in the understanding of the Congress that enacted the ATS, that "district courts would recognize private causes of action for certain torts in violation of the law of nations." But as discussed above, that understanding rested upon a notion of general common law that has been repudiated by *Erie*.

Although I fundamentally disagree with the discretion-based framework employed by the Court, we seem to be in accord that creating a new federal common law of international human rights is a questionable enterprise.

Though it is not necessary to resolution of the present action, one further consideration deserves mention: Despite the avulsive change of *Erie*, the Framers who included reference to "the Law of Nations" in Article I, §8, cl. 10, of the Constitution would be entirely content with the post-*Erie* system I have described, and quite terrified by the "discretion" endorsed by the Court. That portion of the general common law known as the law of nations was understood to refer to the accepted practices of nations in their dealings with one another (treatment of ambassadors, immunity of foreign sovereigns from suit, etc.) and with actors on the high seas hostile to all nations and beyond all their territorial jurisdictions (pirates). Those accepted practices have for the most part, if not in their entirety, been enacted into United States statutory law, so that insofar as they are concerned the demise of the general common law is inconsequential. The notion that a law of nations, redefined to mean the consensus of states on *any* subject, can be used by a private citizen to control a sovereign's treatment of *its own citizens* within *its own territory* is a 20th-century invention of internationalist law professors and human rights advocates. The Framers would, I am confident, be appalled by the proposition that, for example, the American peoples' democratic adoption of the death penalty, could be judicially nullified because of the disapproving views of foreigners.

We Americans have a method for making the laws that are over us. We elect representatives to two Houses of Congress, each of which must enact the new law and present it for the approval of a President, whom we also elect. For over two decades now, unelected federal judges have been usurping this lawmaking power by converting what they regard as norms of international law into American law. Today's opinion approves that process in principle, though urging the lower courts to be more restrained.

This Court seems incapable of admitting that some matters — *any* matters — are none of its business. In today's latest victory for its Never Say Never Jurisprudence, the Court ignores its own conclusion that the ATS provides only jurisdiction, wags a finger at the lower courts for going too far, and then — repeating the same formula the ambitious lower courts *themselves* have used — invites them to try again.

It would be bad enough if there were some assurance that future conversions of perceived international norms into American law would be approved by this Court itself. (Though we know ourselves to be eminently reasonable, self-awareness of eminent reasonableness is not really a substitute for democratic election.) But in this illegitimate lawmaking endeavor, the lower federal courts will be the principal actors; we review but a tiny fraction of their decisions. And no one thinks that all of them are eminently reasonable.

American law — the law made by the people's democratically elected representatives — does not recognize a category of activity that is so universally disapproved by other nations that it is automatically unlawful here, and automatically gives rise to a private action for money damages in federal court. That simple principle is what today's decision should have announced.

* * *

In subsequent cases, the Court further narrowed the reach of the Alien Tort Statute, holding that it generally cannot be used for international human rights violations that occur outside of the United States injuring foreign nationals.

Kiobel v. Royal Dutch Petroleum

569 U.S. 208 (2013)

Chief Justice ROBERTS announced the opinion of the Court.

Petitioners, a group of Nigerian nationals residing in the United States, filed suit in federal court against certain Dutch, British, and Nigerian corporations.

Petitioners sued under the Alien Tort Statute, 28 U.S.C. §1350, alleging that the corporations aided and abetted the Nigerian Government in committing violations of the law of nations in Nigeria. The question presented is whether and under what circumstances courts may recognize a cause of action under the Alien Tort Statute, for violations of the law of nations occurring within the territory of a sovereign other than the United States.

I

Petitioners were residents of Ogoniland, an area of 250 square miles located in the Niger delta area of Nigeria and populated by roughly half a million people. When the complaint was filed, respondents Royal Dutch Petroleum Company and Shell Transport and Trading Company, p.l.c., were holding companies incorporated in the Netherlands and England, respectively. Their joint subsidiary, respondent Shell Petroleum Development Company of Nigeria, Ltd. (SPDC), was incorporated in Nigeria, and engaged in oil exploration and production in Ogoniland. According to the complaint, after concerned residents of Ogoniland began protesting the environmental effects of SPDC's practices, respondents enlisted the Nigerian Government to violently suppress the burgeoning demonstrations. Throughout the early 1990's, the complaint alleges, Nigerian military and police forces attacked Ogoni villages, beating, raping, killing, and arresting residents and destroying or looting property. Petitioners further allege that respondents aided and abetted these atrocities by, among other things, providing the Nigerian forces with food, transportation, and compensation, as well as by allowing the Nigerian military to use respondents' property as a staging ground for attacks.

Following the alleged atrocities, petitioners moved to the United States where they have been granted political asylum and now reside as legal residents. They filed suit in the United States District Court for the Southern District of New York, alleging jurisdiction under the Alien Tort Statute and requesting relief under customary international law. The ATS provides, in full, that "[t]he district courts shall have original jurisdiction of any civil action by an alien for a tort only, committed in violation of the law of nations or a treaty of the United States." According to petitioners, respondents violated the law of nations by aiding and abetting the Nigerian Government in committing (1) extrajudicial killings; (2) crimes against humanity; (3) torture and cruel treatment; (4) arbitrary arrest and detention; (5) violations of the rights to life, liberty, security, and association; (6) forced exile; and (7) property destruction.

II

Passed as part of the Judiciary Act of 1789, the ATS was invoked twice in the late 18th century, but then only once more over the next 167 years. The statute provides district courts with jurisdiction to hear certain claims, but does not expressly provide any causes of action. We held in *Sosa v. Alvarez-Machain* (2004), however, that the First Congress did not intend the provision to be "stillborn." The grant of jurisdiction is instead "best read as having been enacted on the understanding that the common law would provide a cause of action for [a] modest number of international law violations." We thus held that federal courts may "recognize private claims [for such violations] under federal common law." The Court in *Sosa* rejected the plaintiff's claim in that case for "arbitrary arrest and detention," on the ground that it failed to state a violation of the law of nations with the requisite "definite content and acceptance among civilized nations."

The question here is not whether petitioners have stated a proper claim under the ATS, but whether a claim may reach conduct occurring in the territory of a foreign sovereign. Respondents contend that claims under the ATS do not, relying primarily on a canon of statutory interpretation known as the presumption against extraterritorial application. That canon provides that "[w]hen a statute gives no clear indication of an extraterritorial application, it has none," and reflects the "presumption that United States law governs domestically but does not rule the world."

This presumption "serves to protect against unintended clashes between our laws and those of other nations which could result in international discord." We typically apply the presumption to discern whether an Act of Congress regulating conduct applies abroad. The ATS, on the other hand, is "strictly jurisdictional." It does not directly regulate conduct or afford relief. It instead allows federal courts to recognize certain causes of action based on sufficiently definite norms of international law. But we think the principles underlying the canon of interpretation similarly constrain courts considering causes of action that may be brought under the ATS.

Indeed, the danger of unwarranted judicial interference in the conduct of foreign policy is magnified in the context of the ATS, because the question is not what Congress has done but instead what courts may do. This Court in *Sosa* repeatedly stressed the need for judicial caution in considering which claims could be brought under the ATS, in light of foreign policy concerns. As the Court explained, "the potential [foreign policy] implications . . . of recognizing. . . . causes [under the ATS] should make courts particularly wary of impinging on the discretion of the Legislative and Executive Branches in managing foreign affairs." These concerns, which are implicated in any case arising under the ATS, are all the more pressing when the question is whether a cause of action under the ATS reaches conduct within the territory of another sovereign.

These concerns are not diminished by the fact that *Sosa* limited federal courts to recognizing causes of action only for alleged violations of international law norms that are "specific, universal, and obligatory." The principles underlying the presumption against extraterritoriality thus constrain courts exercising their power under the ATS.

III

Petitioners contend that even if the presumption applies, the text, history, and purposes of the ATS rebut it for causes of action brought under that statute. It is true that Congress, even in a jurisdictional provision, can indicate that it intends federal law to apply to conduct occurring abroad. But to rebut the presumption, the ATS would need to evince a "clear indication of extraterritoriality." It does not.

To begin, nothing in the text of the statute suggests that Congress intended causes of action recognized under it to have extraterritorial reach. The ATS covers actions by aliens for violations of the law of nations, but that does not imply extra-territorial reach—such violations affecting aliens can occur either within or outside the United States. Nor does the fact that the text reaches "*any* civil action" suggest application to torts committed abroad; it is well established that generic terms like "any" or "every" do not rebut the presumption against extraterritoriality.

Finally, there is no indication that the ATS was passed to make the United States a uniquely hospitable forum for the enforcement of international norms. As Justice Story put it, "No nation has ever yet pretended to be the custos morum of the whole world. . . ." *United States v. The La Jeune Eugenie* (1822). It is implausible to suppose that the First Congress wanted their fledgling Republic—struggling to receive international recognition—to be the first. Indeed, the parties offer no evidence that any nation, meek or mighty, presumed to do such a thing.

Moreover, accepting petitioners' view would imply that other nations, also applying the law of nations, could hale our citizens into their courts for alleged violations of the law of nations occurring in the United States, or anywhere else in the world. The presumption against extraterritoriality guards against our courts triggering such serious foreign policy consequences, and instead defers such decisions, quite appropriately, to the political branches.

We therefore conclude that the presumption against extraterritoriality applies to claims under the ATS, and that nothing in the statute rebuts that presumption. "[T]here is no clear indication of extraterritoriality here," *Morrison v. National Australia Bank Ltd.* (2010), and petitioners' case seeking relief for violations of the law of nations occurring outside the United States is barred.

IV

On these facts, all the relevant conduct took place outside the United States. And even where the claims touch and concern the territory of the United States, they must do so with sufficient force to displace the presumption against extraterritorial application. Corporations are often present in many countries, and it would reach too far to say that mere corporate presence suffices. If Congress were to determine otherwise, a statute more specific than the ATS would be required.

Justice BREYER with whom Justice GINSBURG, Justice SOTOMAYOR and Justice KAGAN join, concurring in the judgment.

I agree with the Court's conclusion but not with its reasoning. The Court sets forth four key propositions of law: First, the "presumption against extraterritoriality applies to claims under" the Alien Tort Statute. Second, "nothing in the statute rebuts that presumption." Third, there "is no clear indication of extraterritoria[l application] here," where "all the relevant conduct took place outside the United States" and "where the claims" do not "touch and concern the territory of the United States . . . with sufficient force to displace the presumption." Fourth, that is in part because "[c]orporations are often present in many countries, and it would reach too far to say that mere corporate presence suffices."

Unlike the Court, I would not invoke the presumption against extraterritoriality. Rather, guided in part by principles and practices of foreign relations law, I would find jurisdiction under this statute where (1) the alleged tort occurs on American soil, (2) the defendant is an American national, or (3) the defendant's conduct substantially and adversely affects an important American national interest, and that includes a distinct interest in preventing the United States from becoming a safe harbor (free of civil as well as criminal liability) for a torturer or other common enemy of mankind. In this case, however, the parties and relevant conduct lack sufficient ties to the United States for the ATS to provide jurisdiction.

In my view the majority's effort to answer the question by referring to the "presumption against extraterritoriality" does not work well. That presumption "rests on the perception that Congress ordinarily legislates with respect to domestic, not foreign matters." *Morrison*. The ATS, however, was enacted with "foreign matters" in mind. The statute's text refers explicitly to "alien[s]," "treat[ies]," and "the law of nations." The statute's purpose was to address "violations of the law of nations, admitting of a judicial remedy and at the same time threatening serious consequences in international affairs." And at least one of the three kinds of activities that we found to fall within the statute's scope, namely piracy, normally takes place abroad.

In any event, as the Court uses its "presumption against extraterritorial application," it offers only limited help in deciding the question presented, namely "'under what circumstances the Alien Tort Statute . . . allows courts to recognize a cause of action for violations of the law of nations occurring within the territory of a sovereign other than the United States.'" It leaves for another day the determination of just when the presumption against extraterritoriality might be "overcome."

In applying the ATS to acts "occurring within the territory of a[nother] sovereign," I would assume that Congress intended the statute's jurisdictional reach to match the statute's underlying substantive grasp. That grasp, defined by the statute's purposes set forth in *Sosa*, includes compensation for those injured by piracy and its modern-day equivalents, at least where allowing such compensation avoids "serious" negative international "consequences" for the United States. And just as we have looked to established international substantive norms to help determine the statute's substantive reach, so we should look to international jurisdictional norms to help determine the statute's jurisdictional scope.

Considering these jurisdictional norms in light of both the ATS's basic purpose (to provide compensation for those injured by today's pirates) and *Sosa*'s basic caution (to avoid international friction), I believe that the statute provides jurisdiction where (1) the alleged tort occurs on American soil, (2) the defendant is an American national, or (3) the defendant's conduct substantially and adversely affects an important American national interest, and that includes a distinct interest in preventing the United States from becoming a safe harbor (free of civil as well as criminal liability) for a torturer or other common enemy of mankind.

I would interpret the statute as providing jurisdiction only where distinct American interests are at issue. That restriction also should help to minimize international friction. Further limiting principles such as exhaustion, *forum non conveniens*, and comity would do the same. So would a practice of courts giving weight to the views of the Executive Branch. As I have indicated, we should treat this Nation's interest in not becoming a safe harbor for violators of the most fundamental international norms as an important jurisdiction-related interest justifying application of the ATS in light of the statute's basic purposes—in particular that of compensating those who have suffered harm at the hands of, *e.g.*, torturers or other modern pirates. Nothing in the statute or its history suggests that our courts should turn a blind eye to the plight of victims in that "handful of heinous actions."

Application of the statute in the way I have suggested is consistent with international law and foreign practice. Nations have long been obliged not to provide safe harbors for their own nationals who commit such serious crimes abroad. Many countries permit foreign plaintiffs to bring suits against their own nationals based on unlawful conduct that took place abroad.

Applying these jurisdictional principles to this case, however, I agree with the Court that jurisdiction does not lie. The defendants are two foreign corporations. Their shares, like those of many foreign corporations, are traded on the New York Stock Exchange. Their only presence in the United States consists of an office in New York City (actually owned by a separate but affiliated company) that helps to explain their business to potential investors. The plaintiffs are not United States nationals but nationals of other nations. The conduct at issue took place abroad. And the plaintiffs allege, not that the defendants directly engaged in acts of torture, genocide, or the equivalent, but that they helped others (who are not American nationals) to do so.

Under these circumstances, even if the New York office were a sufficient basis for asserting general jurisdiction, it would be farfetched to believe, based solely upon the defendants' minimal and indirect American presence, that this legal action helps to vindicate a distinct American interest, such as in not providing a safe harbor for an "enemy of all mankind." Thus I agree with the Court that here it would "reach too far to say" that such "mere corporate presence suffices."

* * *

In *Nestle USA, Inc. v. Doe* (2021), the Court held that an American company could not be sued under the Alien Tort Statute for conduct that allegedly occurred in Africa. The plaintiffs were six individuals from Mali who alleged that they were trafficked into the Ivory Coast as child slaves to produce cocoa. They sued Nestlé USA and Cargill, U.S.-based companies, that purchased, processed, and sold cocoa. They did not own or operate farms in the Ivory Coast. But they did buy cocoa from farms located there. They also provided those farms with technical and financial resources—such as training, fertilizer, tools, and cash—in exchange for the exclusive right to purchase cocoa. Plaintiffs sued, alleging that they were enslaved on some of those farms and contending that this arrangement aided and abetted child slavery. Respondents argued that petitioners "knew or should have known" that the farms were exploiting enslaved children yet continued to provide those farms with resources.

The Supreme Court held that the case should be dismissed. Justice Thomas, writing for the Court, said:

> Our decisions since *Sosa*, as well as congressional activity, compel the conclusion that federal courts should not recognize private rights of action for violations of international law beyond the three historical torts identified in *Sosa*. . . . Under existing precedent, then, courts in some circumstances might still apply *Sosa* to recognize causes of action for the three historical torts likely on the mind of the First Congress. But as to other torts, our

precedents already make clear that there always is a sound reason to defer
to Congress, so courts may not create a cause of action for those torts.
Whether and to what extent defendants should be liable under the ATS
for torts beyond the three historical torts identified in *Sosa* lies within the
province of the Legislative Branch.

Justice Sotomayor concurred in the judgment, joined by Justices Breyer and
Kagan. She wrote:

> Because respondents have failed to allege a domestic application of the
> Alien Tort Statute (ATS), their complaint must be dismissed. I do not,
> however, join Justice Thomas' alternative path to that disposition, which
> would overrule *Sosa v. Alvarez-Machain* (2004), in all but name. The First
> Congress enacted the ATS to ensure that federal courts are available to
> foreign citizens who suffer international law violations for which other
> nations may expect the United States to provide a forum for redress. Jus-
> tice Thomas would limit the ATS' reach to only the three international
> law torts that were recognized in 1789. That reading contravenes both this
> Court's express holding in *Sosa* and the text and history of the ATS.

3.   *Implied Rights of Action to Enforce Preemption?*

This Section concludes by considering a third problem closely related to the
doctrine on statutory implied rights of action that we have just covered: whether a
federal statute that contains no express private right of action can, in concert with
the Supremacy Clause, support an implied private right of action to prevent the
enforcement of state law that conflicts with the federal statute.

Recall first from your work in constitutional law that there are two types of
preemption — express and implied. Express preemption is where a federal statute explicitly says that federal law is exclusive and therefore state and local governments cannot regulate. Implied preemption arises when the federal statute is
silent about preemption, but the Court finds preemption based on: (a) a conflict
between federal and state law, (b) state law interfering with the achievement of a
federal objective, or (c) a clear desire by Congress to wholly "occupy" the field. For
all of these types of preemption, express and implied, the courts have to decide
what Congress intended, often where Congress was completely silent about preemption. For example, where courts find preemption based on state interference
with a federal objective, one could characterize this result as flowing from statutory
interpretation or as a doctrine of federal common law, under which judges seek to
identify and fill "gaps" in statutory schemes.[29]

Pliva, Inc. v. Mensing (2011) is an example of the complexities of preemption
analysis. The case involved state tort claims that drug manufacturers failed to provide adequate warning labels. The plaintiffs in *Mensing* were prescribed a drug with
a label that failed to include warnings regarding a well-known side effect (loss of
control of facial movements) which they developed. Defendant drug manufacturers

---

29. Caleb Nelson, *Preemption*, 86 VA. L. REV. 225, 278 (2000).

argued that the state tort drug label claims were preempted by specific federal regulatory standards regarding generic drugs and that the defendants could not comply with both the federal and the safer state standards.

The Court found that it would have been impossible for the defendants to comply with both state and federal law:

> If the Manufacturers had independently changed their labels to satisfy their state-law duty, they would have violated federal law. Taking [plaintiffs'] allegations as true, state law imposed on the Manufacturers a duty to attach a safer label to their generic metoclopramide. Federal law, however, demanded that generic drug labels be the same at all times as the corresponding brand-name drug labels. Thus, it was impossible for the Manufacturers to comply with both their state-law duty to change the label and their federal-law duty to keep the label the same.

The twist in the case was that federal law also provided an avenue for the FDA to modify the label requirements for generic drugs. Plaintiffs therefore claimed that "when a private party's ability to comply with state law depends on approval and assistance from the FDA, proving pre-emption requires that party to demonstrate that the FDA would not have allowed compliance with state law." Here, the defendants did not even attempt to initiate a process leading to FDA revision of the federal label standards. The Court rejected this as evidence that defendants could not comply with both state and federal law:

> We can often imagine that a third party or the Federal Government might do something that makes it lawful for a private party to accomplish under federal law what state law requires of it. In these cases, it is certainly possible that, had the Manufacturers asked the FDA for help, they might have eventually been able to strengthen their warning label. Of course, it is also possible that the Manufacturers could have convinced the FDA to reinterpret its regulations. . . . Following [plaintiffs'] argument to its logical conclusion, it is also possible that, by asking, the Manufacturers could have persuaded the FDA to rewrite its generic drug regulations entirely or talked Congress into amending the Hatch-Waxman Amendments.
>
>   If these conjectures suffice to prevent federal and state law from conflicting for Supremacy Clause purposes, it is unclear when, outside of express pre-emption, the Supremacy Clause would have any force. We do not read the Supremacy Clause to permit an approach to pre-emption that renders conflict pre-emption all but meaningless. The Supremacy Clause, on its face, makes federal law "the supreme Law of the Land" even absent an express statement by Congress. U.S. Const., Art. VI, cl. 2. Moreover, the text of the Clause — that federal law shall be supreme, "any Thing in the Constitution or Laws of any State to the Contrary notwithstanding" — plainly contemplates conflict pre-emption by describing federal law as effectively repealing contrary state law. The phrase "any [state law] to the Contrary notwithstanding" is a non obstante provision. Eighteenth-century legislatures used non obstante provisions to specify the degree to which a new statute was meant to repeal older, potentially conflicting statutes in the same field. A non obstante provision "in [a]

new statute acknowledged that the statute might contradict prior law and instructed courts not to apply the general presumption against implied repeals." The non obstante provision in the Supremacy Clause therefore suggests that federal law should be understood to impliedly repeal conflicting state law.

Further, the provision suggests that courts should not strain to find ways to reconcile federal law with seemingly conflicting state law. Traditionally, courts went to great lengths attempting to harmonize conflicting statutes, in order to avoid implied repeals. A non obstante provision thus was a useful way for legislatures to specify that they did not want courts distorting the new law to accommodate the old. The non obstante provision of the Supremacy Clause indicates that a court need look no further than "the ordinary meanin[g]" of federal law, and should not distort federal law to accommodate conflicting state law. . . .

Wyeth v. Levine (2009) is not to the contrary. In that case, as here, the plaintiff contended that a drug manufacturer had breached a state tort-law duty to provide an adequate warning label. The Court held that the lawsuit was not pre-empted because it was possible for Wyeth, a brandname drug manufacturer, to comply with both state and federal law. Specifically, the CBE regulation, 21 CFR §314.70(c)(6)(iii), permitted a brand-name drug manufacturer like Wyeth "to unilaterally strengthen its warning" without prior FDA approval. Thus, the federal regulations applicable to Wyeth allowed the company, of its own volition, to strengthen its label in compliance with its state tort duty.

Four Justices dissented on the ground that, "[u]ntil today, the mere possibility of impossibility had not been enough to establish preemption. The Court strains to reach the opposite conclusion. It invents new principles of pre-emption law out of thin air to justify its dilution of the impossibility standard. . . . And a plurality of the Court tosses aside our repeated admonition that courts should hesitate to conclude that Congress intended to pre-empt state laws governing health and safety." Given that 75 percent of all prescription drugs are generics, the Court's new preemption rule would, the dissent emphasized, preempt state tort law for the vast majority of mislabeling claims. "Our respect for the States as 'independent sovereigns in our federal system' leads us to assume that 'Congress does not cavalierly pre-empt state-law causes of action.' *Wyeth.* This presumption *against* preemption has particular force when the Federal Government has afforded defendants a mechanism for complying with state law, even when that mechanism requires federal agency action." The new approach adopted by the Court "threatens to infringe the States' authority over traditional matters of state interest — such as the failure-to-warn claims here — when Congress expressed no intent to preempt state law."

Field preemption is exemplified by federal immigration laws and *Arizona v. United States* (2012). When Arizona attempted to supplement federal law by making failure to comply with federal registration requirements for immigrants a state misdemeanor, the Supreme Court held that Congress clearly intended to occupy the field:

> In 1940, as international conflict spread, Congress added to federal immigration law a "complete system for alien registration." The new federal law

struck a careful balance. It punished an alien's willful failure to register but did not require aliens to carry identification cards. There were also limits on the sharing of registration records and fingerprints. . . . Congress intended the federal plan for registration to be a "single integrated and all-embracing system." Because this "complete scheme . . . for the registration of aliens" touched on foreign relations, it did not allow the States to "curtail or complement" federal law or to "enforce additional or auxiliary regulations." As a consequence, the Court ruled [in *Hines v. Davidovitz* [1941]] that Pennsylvania could not enforce its own alien-registration program.

The framework enacted by Congress leads to the conclusion here, as it did in *Hines*, that the Federal Government has occupied the field of alien registration. The federal statutory directives provide a full set of standards governing alien registration, including the punishment for noncompliance. It was designed as a "'harmonious whole.'" *Hines*. Where Congress occupies an entire field, as it has in the field of alien registration, even complementary state regulation is impermissible. Field pre-emption reflects a congressional decision to foreclose any state regulation in the area, even if it is parallel to federal standards.

Federal law makes a single sovereign responsible for maintaining a comprehensive and unified system to keep track of aliens within the Nation's borders. If §3 of the Arizona statute were valid, every State could give itself independent authority to prosecute federal registration violations, "diminish[ing] the [Federal Government]'s control over enforcement" and "detract[ing] from the 'integrated scheme of regulation' created by Congress." *Wis. Dept. of Indus. v. Gould, Inc.* (1986). Even if a State may make violation of federal law a crime in some instances, it cannot do so in a field (like the field of alien registration) that has been occupied by federal law.

The Court struck down other provisions of the Arizona statute (making it a state misdemeanor for an immigrant to apply for work and empowering state police to make warrantless arrests of immigrants possibly subject to removal under federal law). With regard to these provisions, the Court relied not on field preemption, but rather on the interference that they would cause with federal objectives, including the "careful balance" Congress struck on the "unauthorized employment of aliens" and the discretion Congress conferred on federal immigration officials to decide removability.

Keeping this brief summary of preemption doctrine in mind, note that in *Mensing*, federal preemption arises as an affirmative defense to state tort claims. In *Arizona v. United States*, the federal government sued to enjoin enforcement of the state law and protect its own authority under federal immigration legislation. What if a *private party* who is bound by state law wishes to prevent enforcement by arguing that the law is preempted by a federal statute? Must she wait to be named as a defendant in an enforcement proceeding brought under the state law and assert preemption as a defense? If the federal law provides no private right of action, might one be implied from the Supremacy Clause itself?

These questions implicate doctrines we will cover in the next two Chapters on sovereign immunity (when might a government officer be sued in equity to prevent enforcement of an invalid law, discussed in the context of *Ex parte Young* in Chapter 6) and implied rights of action that are derived *from the Constitution* rather than from a federal statute (discussed in the context of *Bivens* suits for damages against federal officers in Chapter 7).

In *Armstrong v. Exceptional Child Center, Inc.* (2015), the Court held that there is no private right of action provided by the Supremacy Clause to prevent enforcement of a state law that is arguably preempted by a federal statute. The case arises in the context of Medicaid reimbursements for health care provided to people who otherwise would go without treatment due to low income. Because Medicaid is the largest public health insurance provider in the country, its reimbursement rates have enormous implications for the health care of people with low incomes. And because Medicaid beneficiaries are disproportionately people of color, this means reduced levels of care for these communities. In 2020, for example, hospitals received less than 90 cents for every dollar spent caring for Medicaid patients — a $24.8 billion dollar aggregate shortfall that affects both access and the scope of health care provided to Medicaid beneficiaries.[30] Closing the gap between what Medicaid reimburses and what private insurance reimburses (for the treatment of patients who can afford such insurance) would, one study found, eliminate entirely the disparity in low income childrens' access to health care and reduce more than two-thirds of disparities in access among adults.[31] Thus, as a practical matter, the issue in *Armstrong* concerned who had the power to enforce the reimbursement rate standards set out in the Medicaid Act for a particularly expensive form of "in-home" health care. The Court held that providers who are not adequately reimbursed do not have a private right of action under the Supremacy Clause. The Medicaid provision could, however, be enforced by the Secretary of Health and Human Services, which had the power to withhold funding to states that do not properly reimburse health care providers.

The Court, in an opinion by Justice Scalia, reasoned that while the Supremacy Clause displaces conflicting state law, it does not create a right of action. The Court explained,

> It is apparent that [the Supremacy] Clause creates a rule of decision: Courts "shall" regard the "Constitution," and all laws "made in Pursuance thereof," as "the supreme Law of the Land." They must not give effect to state laws that conflict with federal laws. It is equally apparent that the Supremacy Clause is not the "'source of any federal rights,'" *Golden State Transit Corp. v. Los Angeles* (1989), and certainly does not create a cause of action. It instructs courts what to do when state and federal law clash, but is silent regarding who may enforce federal laws in court, and in what circumstances they may do so.

---

30. Tiffany N. Ford & Jamila Michener, *Medicaid Reimbursement Rates Are a Racial Justice Issue*, THE COMMONWEALTH FUND BLOG, June 16, 2022, at https://www.commonwealthfund.org/blog/2022/medicaid-reimbursement-rates-are-racial-justice-issue.

31. Diane Alexander & Molly Schnell, Nat'l Bureau of Econ. Res., The Impacts of Physician Payments on Patient Access, Use, and Health (Aug. 2020), at https://www.nber.org/papers/w26095.

If the Supremacy Clause does not provide a right to sue for injunctive relief against state officials, then what is the source of this well-recognized right? The Court went on:

> It is true enough that we have long held that federal courts may in some circumstances grant injunctive relief against state officers who are violating, or planning to violate, federal law. *See, e.g., Osborn v. Bank of United States* (1824); *Ex parte Young* (1908). But that has been true not only with respect to violations of federal law by state officials, but also with respect to violations of federal law by federal officials. *See Am. Sch. of Magnetic Healing* v. *McAnnulty* (1902); *see generally* L. Jaffe, Judicial Control of Administrative Action 152-196 (1965). Thus, the Supremacy Clause need not be (and in light of our textual analysis above, cannot be) the explanation. What our cases demonstrate is that, "in a proper case, relief may be given in a court of equity . . . to prevent an injurious act by a public officer." *Carroll* v. *Safford* (1845).
>
> The ability to sue to enjoin unconstitutional actions by state and federal officers is the creation of courts of equity, and reflects a long history of judicial review of illegal executive action, tracing back to England. *See* Jaffe & Henderson, *Judicial Review and the Rule of Law: Historical Origins,* 72 L.Q. REV. 345 (1956). It is a judge-made remedy, and we have never held or even suggested that, in its application to state officers, it rests upon an implied right of action contained in the Supremacy Clause.

In theory, then, equity might have supplied a right to injunctive relief against state officials for violating the Medicaid reimbursement provision at issue in *Armstrong,* The Court concluded, however, that Congress had implicitly foreclosed equitable relief when it enacted that provision. It gave two reasons for this conclusion. First, quoting *Alexander v. Sandoval* (2001), the *Armstrong* Court reasoned that expressly providing one enforcement mechanism — withholding of funding by a federal agency — "'suggests that Congress intended to preclude others.'" While this alone "might not, by itself, preclude the availability of equitable relief," the Court pointed to a second reason for concluding that Congress intended to deny a right to an equitable remedy: the reimbursement provision was a broad, "judgment-laden standard." The statute mandated that "state plans provide for payments that are 'consistent with efficiency, economy, and quality of care,' all the while 'safeguard[ing] against unnecessary utilization of . . . care and services.'" According to the Court, "[t]he sheer complexity associated with enforcing §30(A), coupled with the express provision of an administrative remedy, §1396c, shows that the Medicaid Act precludes private enforcement of §30(A) in the courts."

Justice Sotomayor, along with Justices Kennedy, Ginsburg, and Kagan, dissented from the Court's opinion. Justice Sotomayor's dissent emphasized the "long" history of "suits in which a party seeks prospective equitable protection from an injurious and preempted state law without regard to whether the federal statute at issue itself provided a right to bring an action." Agreeing with the Court that it is "somewhat misleading" to find an implied right to such relief in the Supremacy Clause, the dissent went on to conclude that Congress had not implicitly precluded an "equitable preemption action[]" to enforce the reimbursement provision at issue in *Armstrong*. Justice Sotomayor reasoned that an equitable action "would be to an anticipated and possibly necessary supplement to [the] limited agency-enforcement mechanism" that Congress expressly created.

Note that the majority and the dissent in *Armstrong* both recognized the availability in other settings of a suit in equity against state officers to prevent enforcement where such a suit is consistent with the remedial scheme Congress has established under the relevant federal statute. This is the *Ex parte Young* suit we will examine in Chapter 6 and is a longstanding form of equity practice.

Some of the issues raised in *Armstrong* must await treatment of *Ex parte Young* and the doctrine on implied rights of action to enforce constitutional rights. For now, note that the parallels between the majority holding here and in *Sandoval* regarding statutory implied rights of action are quite strong.

Are there reasons to think that the analysis of whether an implied right of action is authorized should differ based on the statutory or constitutional status of the right asserted? Are you persuaded by the majority's argument that Congress did not want private suits to enforce the federal Medicaid reimbursement standards — that Congress wanted withholding of funds to be the exclusive remedy? Is withholding of Medicaid funding the only remedy now?

CHAPTER 6

SUITS AGAINST STATE AND LOCAL GOVERNMENTS, NATIVE NATIONS, FOREIGN GOVERNMENTS, AND THEIR OFFICERS

In this Chapter, we examine a range of ways in which governments and their officers (other than the federal government) may be held to account in court. Although our focus will be on whether and on what terms suit may be brought in the federal courts, the availability of other systems of accountability, both judicial and extrajudicial, looms large in this analysis. We begin in Section A with suits against state governments and their officers, paying close attention to the doctrine of state sovereign immunity linked to the Eleventh Amendment and to exceptions to that doctrine. In Section B, we turn to suits against officers of the state, officers of local governments, and suits against local government entities, paying close attention to common law officer immunity doctrines and their expansion by the modern Supreme Court. In Section C, we turn to suits against Native nations and consider their sovereign immunity. And in Section D, we briefly survey the narrow pathways for suing a foreign sovereign made available under the Foreign Sovereign Immunities Act.

One fundamental question underlies all of these inquiries: whether and to what extent governments and the officers who serve them may be held to account in court in order to ensure their compliance with law.

A. SUITS AGAINST STATE GOVERNMENTS: THE ELEVENTH AMENDMENT AND SOVEREIGN IMMUNITY

Congress has enacted broad waivers of sovereign immunity to permit adjudication of claims that the *federal* government has acted illegally. These are discussed in the next Chapter. In this Chapter, we will see that sovereign immunity doctrines concerning state governments, Native nations, and local governments have developed on quite different trajectories. We begin with suits against state governments. Although the plaintiff is often an individual, some of the most significant modern state sovereign immunity cases involve litigation *between* states and either Native nations or foreign governments, so we will confront immunity doctrine that applies in suits between sovereigns as well.

1.   *The History and Ratification of the Eleventh Amendment: Competing Interpretations*

The Constitution is said to have "split the atom of sovereignty" at the Founding by dividing authority to govern between the federal government and the states. *U.S. Term Limits, Inc. v. Thornton* (1995). The atom was in fact split into more than two. The American Revolution replaced a centralized, theocratic form of sovereignty in which the Crown derived authority from God with a principle of *popular* sovereignty. The Preamble to the Constitution states that it is "ordained and established" by "We the People." State governments, which began either as colonies on the Eastern seaboard subject to British control or as territories subject to federal control entering later on an "equal footing," 1 Stat. 491 (1796) (admission of Tennessee), also derive their authority from the people.

Just how much sovereignty the states surrendered upon entering the Union remains a subject of intense debate. This debate over the constitutional status of state sovereignty has to take account of the Union victory in the Civil War, given that it was fought over theories of state sovereignty hotly contested throughout the antebellum period. "State sovereignty" was used to defend the institution of chattel slavery, which by the 1860s enslaved four million Black people, as well as the right of secession and state nullification of federal law. The Reconstruction Amendments, ratified after Union victory on the battlefield and emancipation, included substantial new authority for Congress to legislate in areas traditionally reserved to the states. *See* Thirteenth Amendment, section 2; Fourteenth Amendment, section 5; and Fifteenth Amendment, section 2. The Amendments thus directly limited and reimagined the sovereignty of states under the Constitution.

The scope of the state governments' *immunity from suit* presents questions about the principle of state sovereignty in a more distilled though no less contested form. The conventional narrative, elements of which you will see in the cases that follow, begins from the premise that silence about state sovereign immunity doctrine in the Constitution reflects consensus at the founding that states would enjoy broad immunity from suit absent their consent. Statements by prominent Federalists are often marshalled as evidence of this background consensus. Federalist proponents of the Constitution believed it would aid ratification to dispel concerns that Article III opened the prospect of litigation by individuals against states in federal court.

That consensus was tested in 1793 when the Supreme Court held 4-1 that the diversity jurisdiction provision of Article III, section 2, and the First Judiciary Act authorized an original action in assumpsit in the Supreme Court by a citizen of the state of South Carolina against the state of Georgia. *Chisholm v. Georgia* (1793). Alexander Chisolm sued in his capacity as the executor of one Robert Farquhar to recover payments due Farquhar's estate for goods he had supplied to troops stationed in Savannah, Georgia during the American Revolution.

In separate opinions, the Court rejected Georgia's claim that the state was immune from suit by a citizen of another state. Chief Justice Jay's opinion insisted that sovereign immunity was a "feudal" doctrine anathema to a constitutional democracy founded on the principle of popular sovereignty.

> That system considers the Prince as the sovereign, and the people as his subjects; it regards his person as the object of allegiance, and excludes the idea of his being on an equal footing with a subject, either in a court of justice or elsewhere. [I]t is easy to perceive that such a sovereign could not be amenable to a court of justice, or subjected to judicial controul and actual constraint. It was of necessity that suability became incompatible with such sovereignty. . . . *No such ideas obtain here, at the Revolution the sovereignty devolved on the people, and they are truly the sovereigns of the country.*

Only Justice Iredell dissented, arguing that the First Judiciary Act incorporated the common law doctrine of sovereign immunity. As there could be no action in assumpsit under English common law absent the sovereign's consent, he reasoned, there was no statutory jurisdiction under the First Judiciary Act for a federal court to entertain the case against the state of Georgia. In dicta, Justice Iredell gestured at the larger constitutional question that loomed over his reading of the First Judiciary Act. In his view, the Constitution should not be read "under any circumstances" to permit "a compulsive suit against a State for the recovery of money . . . [and] nothing but express words, or an insurmountable implication (neither of which I think can be found in this case) would authorize the deduction of so high a power."

The Eleventh Amendment was ratified in 1798 to reverse *Chisholm v. Georgia.* In the conventional narrative, *Chisholm* was greeted with such "a shock of surprise" that the amendment sailed through ratification. *Hans v. Louisiana* (1890). Whether disagreement with *Chisholm* was as uniform and vigorous as the dictum from *Hans* suggests, there is no question that concern about the liability of states in court for debts incurred during and after the Revolution was widespread. State "bills of credit" and "requisition certificates" were used to fund approximately 14 percent of the costs of the Revolutionary War. But the country fell into a protracted recession after the war and this limited states' ability to pay interest and principal on their war debts.[1] States therefore would have been keen to limit exposure in court for these debts. Then there was the property of British loyalists. State governments sought to confiscate the property of British loyalists even though the federal government was pledged to protect it by the Treaty of 1783. As we will see in cases like *Hans,* reported below, the problem of state solvency and judicial interference with the budgetary functions of the political branches of state governments looms over interpretation of the Eleventh Amendment.

The Eleventh Amendment provides:

> The judicial power of the United States shall not be construed to extend to any suit in law or equity, commenced or prosecuted against one of the Unites States by citizens of another state, or by citizens or subjects of any foreign state.

---

1. EDWIN J. PERKINS, AMERICAN PUBLIC FINANCE AND FINANCIAL SERVICES, 1700-1815 (1994).

Setting it alongside Article III you can see that it is carefully phrased to disable a very specific reading of federal judicial power—the reading that the diversity jurisdiction clauses of Article III, section 2, establish subject matter jurisdiction in federal court for a state to be sued by a citizen of another state or a foreign state.

The narrowness of this language is drawn into relief by considering the parties, sources of law, forms of action, remedies, and forums in which a state is potentially subject to suit. Absent the defense of sovereign immunity, a claim against a state might be brought in state, federal, or tribal court. With respect to remedies, a complaint could seek equitable relief, such as an injunction, or a traditional common law remedy such as money damages that would have to be paid out of the state treasury. The claim could arise under federal law or the common law of any state. And the range of possible plaintiffs in nothing short of kaleidoscopic.

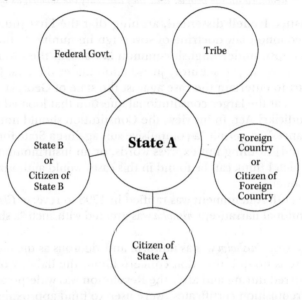

Doctrinal controversy about the scope of state sovereign immunity centers on whether the language of the Eleventh Amendment merely disables diversity jurisdiction suits against states in federal court by "citizens of another state, or by citizens or subjects of any foreign state," or whether it instead marks a more sweeping constitutional commitment to sovereign immunity along the lines drawn by Justice Iredell's closing dictum in *Chisholm.*

2.   *Applications of the Eleventh Amendment and State Sovereign Immunity*

As we turn to the cases, note that the basic rule that a state is not amenable to suit absent its consent is subject to important exceptions. Some are required by the text and structure of the Constitution itself—necessary conditions of states entering the Union. For instance, Article III expressly provides original jurisdiction in the Supreme Court for *suits between states*, so sovereign immunity cannot bar such litigation. *See, e.g., Montana v. Wyoming* (2011) (resolving water rights dispute over Yellowstone River). It is fundamental to the constitutional system that a national forum exist to resolve disputes between states. The same is true of *suits by the federal government against a state* to ensure compliance with federal law. Article III, section 2, provides that "judicial power shall extend . . . to controversies to which the United States shall be a party." *See, e.g., United States v. California* (E.D. Cal. 2020) (dismissing suit by federal government against state of California challenging state's cap-and-trade emissions program on ground that agreement with Quebec to "work jointly" toward cap-and-trade goals violates powers of federal government under treaty and compact clauses of constitution); *Arizona v. United States* (2012) (adjudicating merits of suit against state filed by the U.S. Department of Justice challenging constitutionality of state law as usurping plenary federal authority to set immigration policy and enforce immigration laws); *Veasey v. Abbott* (5th Cir. 2016) (remanding suit by U.S. Department of Justice and other plaintiffs challenging Texas voter identification statute on theory that it violated section 2 of the Voting Rights Act because it unduly burdened rights of Latino and African American voters).

Other important exceptions are discussed in detail in Section A.3 below. These include: (1) the power of Congress to legislatively set aside or "*abrogate*" state sovereign immunity under the enforcement clauses of the Reconstruction Amendments, (2) the use of *officer suits for prospective relief*—as opposed to retrospective monetary awards—to ensure a state's compliance with federal law under *Ex parte Young* (1908), and (3) circumstances in which a state may be deemed to have *waived* the defense of sovereign immunity.

We begin with the first case expanding state sovereign immunity beyond the text of the Eleventh Amendment. As in *Chisholm*, the Court was confronted with the implications of holding a state to answer in federal court for its debts. Unlike *Chisholm*, however, the plaintiff was a citizen of the state named as a defendant, Louisiana. There was thus no diversity of citizenship. And the cause of action was founded on the federal Constitution—a claim that the state of Louisiana had unconstitutionally impaired a contractual obligation—though state law regarding the bonds was certainly relevant to adjudication of the federal claim.

Hans v. Louisiana

134 U.S. 1 (1890)

Bradley, J.

This is an action brought in the circuit court of the United States, in December, 1884, against the state of Louisiana, by Hans, a citizen of that state, to recover the amount of certain coupons annexed to bonds of the state, issued under the provisions of an act of the legislature approved January 24, 1874 [and approved by an amendment to the state constitution authorizing state taxes to be used to pay both interest and principal on the bonds].

[N]otwithstanding said solemn compact with the holders of said bonds, said state hath refused and still refuses to pay said coupons held by petitioner, and by its constitution, adopted in 1879, ordained "[t]hat the coupons of said consolidated bonds falling due the 1st of January, 1880, be, and the same is hereby, remitted, and any interest taxes collected to meet said coupons are hereby transferred to defray the expenses of the state government;' and by article 257 of said constitution also prescribed that 'the constitution of this state, adopted in 1868, and all amendments thereto, is declared to be superseded by this constitution. . . ."

Petitioner also avers that taxes for the payment of the interest upon said bonds due January 1, 1880, were levied, assessed, and collected, but said state unlawfully and wrongfully diverted the money so collected, and appropriated the same to payment of the general expenses of the state [in an unconstitutional impairment of contract] in violation of article 1, section 10, of the constitution of the United States. Wherefore petitioner prays that the state of Louisiana be cited to answer this demand, and that after due proceedings she be condemned to pay your petitioner said sum of ($87,500) eighty-seven thousand five hundred dollars, with legal interest from January 1, 1880, until paid, and all costs of suit.

[The state attorney general moved to dismiss on the ground that the lower federal court was without jurisdiction. The lower court granted the motion.]

The ground taken is that under the constitution, as well as under the act of congress passed to carry it into effect, a case is within the jurisdiction of the federal courts, without regard to the character of the parties, if it arises under the constitution or laws of the United States, or, which is the same thing, if it necessarily involves a question under said constitution or laws. The language relied on is that clause of the third article of the constitution and the corresponding clause of the act conferring jurisdiction upon the circuit court, which, as found in the act of March 3, 1875, [28 U.S.C. §1331].

That a state cannot be sued by a citizen of another state, or of a foreign state, on the mere ground that the case is one arising under the constitution or laws of the United States, is clearly established by the decisions of this court in several recent cases. *Louisiana v. Jumel* (1882). Those were cases arising under the constitution of the United States, upon laws complained of as impairing the obligation of contracts, one of which was the constitutional amendment of Louisiana, complained of in the present case. Relief was sought against state officers who professed to act in obedience to those laws. This court held that the suits were virtually against the states themselves, and were consequently violative of the eleventh amendment of the constitution, and could not be maintained.

In the present case the plaintiff in error contends that he, being a citizen of Louisiana, is not embarrassed by the obstacle of the eleventh amendment, inasmuch as that amendment only prohibits suits against a state which are brought by the citizens of another state, or by citizens or subjects of a foreign state. It is true the amendment does so read, and, if there were no other reason or ground for abating his suit, it might be maintainable; and then we should have this anomalous result, that, in cases arising under the constitution or laws of the United States, a state may be sued in the federal courts by its own citizens, though it cannot be sued for a like cause of action by the citizens of other states, or of a foreign state; and may be thus sued in the federal courts, although not allowing itself to be sued in its own courts. If this is the necessary consequence of the language of the constitution and the law, the result is no less startling and unexpected than was the original decision of this court, that, under the language of the constitution and of the judiciary act of 1789, a state was liable to be sued by a citizen of another state or of a foreign country. That decision was made in the case of *Chisholm v. Georgia* (1793), and created such a shock of surprise throughout the country that, at the first meeting of congress thereafter, the eleventh amendment to the constitution was almost unanimously proposed, and was in due course adopted by the legislatures of the states. This amendment, expressing the will of the ultimate sovereignty of the whole country, superior to all legislatures and all courts, actually reversed the decision of the supreme court. It did not in terms prohibit suits by individuals against the states, but declared that the constitution should not be construed to import any power to authorize the bringing of such suits. The language of the amendment is that "the judicial power of the United States shall not be construed to extend to any suit, in law or equity, commenced or prosecuted against one of the United States by citizens of another state, or by citizens or subjects of any foreign state."

[The majority in *Chisholm v. Georgia* was] swayed by a close observance of the letter of the constitution, without regard to former experience and usage; and because the letter said that the judicial power shall extend to controversies "between a state and citizens of another state;" and "between a state and foreign states, citizens or subjects," they felt constrained to see in this language a power to enable the individual citizens of one state, or of a foreign state, to sue another state of the Union in the federal courts. Justice Iredell, on the contrary, contended that it was not the intention to create new and unheard of remedies, by subjecting sovereign states to actions at the suit of individuals, (which he conclusively showed was never done before,) but only, by proper legislation, to invest the federal courts with jurisdiction to hear and determine controversies and cases, between the parties designated, that were properly susceptible of litigation in courts. Looking back from our present stand-point at the decision in *Chisholm v. Georgia*, we do not greatly wonder at the effect which it had upon the country. Any such power as that of authorizing the federal judiciary to entertain suits by individuals against the states had been expressly disclaimed, and even resented, by the great defenders of the constitution while it was on its trial before the American people.

The eighty-first number of the Federalist, written by Hamilton, has the following profound remarks:

> It has been suggested that an assignment of the public securities of one state to the citizens of another would enable them to prosecute that state in the federal courts for the amount of those securities, a suggestion which the following considerations prove to be without foundation: it is inherent in the nature of sovereignty not to be amenable to the suit of an individual without its consent. This is the general sense and the general practice of mankind; and the exemption, as one of the attributes of sovereignty, is now enjoyed by the government of every state in the Union. Unless, therefore, there is a surrender of this immunity in the plan of the convention, it will remain with the states, and the danger intimated must be merely ideal. [T]here is no color to pretend that the state governments would be divested of the privilege of paying their own debts in their own way, free from every constraint but that which flows from the obligations of good faith. The contracts between a nation and individuals are only binding on the conscience of the sovereign, and have no pretension to a compulsive force. They confer no right of action independent of the sovereign will. To what purpose would it be to authorize suits against states for the debts they owe? How could recoveries be enforced? It is evident that it could not be done without waging war against the contracting state.

It was argued by the opponents of the constitution that [Article III's diversity jurisdiction clauses] would authorize jurisdiction to be given to the federal courts to entertain suits against a state brought by the citizens of another state or of a foreign state. Adhering to the mere letter, it might be so, and so, in fact, the supreme court held in *Chisholm v. Georgia*; but looking at the subject as Hamilton did, and as Mr. Justice Iredell did, in the light of history and experience and the established order of things, the views of the latter were clearly right, as the people of the United States in their sovereign capacity subsequently decided.

But Hamilton was not alone in protesting against the construction put upon the constitution by its opponents. In the Virginia convention the same objections were raised by George Mason and Patrick Henry, and were met by Madison and Marshall as follows. Madison said:

> Its jurisdiction [the federal jurisdiction] in controversies between a state and citizens of another state is much objected to, and perhaps without reason. It is not in the power of individuals to call any state into court. The only operation it can have is that, if a state should wish to bring a suit against a citizen, it must be brought before the federal court. This will give satisfaction to individuals, as it will prevent citizens on whom a state may have a claim being dissatisfied with the state courts.

3 Elliott, Debates. Marshall, in answer to the same objection, said:

> With respect to disputes between a state and the citizens of another state, its jurisdiction has been decried with unusual vehemence. I hope that no gentleman will think that a state will be called at the bar of the federal court. It is not rational to suppose that the sovereign power should be dragged before a court. The intent is to enable states to recover claims of individuals residing in other states. But, say they, there will be partiality in it if a state cannot be a defendant; if an individual cannot proceed to obtain judgment against a state, though he may be sued by a state. It is necessary to be so, and cannot be avoided. I see a difficulty in making a state defendant which does not prevent its being plaintiff.

It seems to us that these views of those great advocates and defenders of the constitution were most sensible and just, and they apply equally to the present case as to that then under discussion. The letter is appealed to now, as it was then, as a ground for sustaining a suit brought by an individual against a state. The reason against it is as strong in this case as it was in that. It is an attempt to strain the constitution and the law to a construction never imagined or dreamed of. Can we suppose that, when the eleventh amendment was adopted, it was understood to be left open for citizens of a state to sue their own state in the federal courts, while the idea of suits by citizens of other states, or of foreign states, was indignantly repelled? Suppose that congress, when proposing the eleventh amendment, had appended to it a proviso that nothing therein contained should prevent a state from being sued by its own citizens in cases arising under the constitution or laws of the United States, can we imagine that it would have been adopted by the states? The supposition that it would is almost an absurdity on its face.

The truth is that the cognizance of suits and actions unknown to the law, and forbidden by the law, was not contemplated by the constitution when establishing the judicial power of the United States. Some things, undoubtedly, were made justifiable which were not known as such at the common law; such, for example, as controversies between states as to boundary lines, and other questions admitting of judicial solution. And yet the case of *Penn v. Lord Baltimore* (Ves Sen 1750), shows that some of these unusual subjects of litigation were not unknown to the courts even in colonial times; and several cases of the same general character arose under the articles of confederation, and were brought before the tribunal provided for that purpose in those articles. The establishment of this new branch of jurisdiction seemed to be necessary from the extinguishment of diplomatic relations between the states.

The suability of a state, without its consent, was a thing unknown to the law. This has been so often laid down and acknowledged by courts and jurists that it is hardly necessary to be formally asserted. It was fully shown by an exhaustive examination of the old law by Mr. Justice Iredell in his opinion in *Chisholm v. Georgia*; and it has been conceded in every case since, where the question has, in any way, been presented, even in the cases which have gone furthest in sustaining suits against the officers or agents of states. *Osborn v. Bank* (1824); *Davis v. Gray* (1872); *Board v. McComb* (1875); *United States v. Lee* (1882); *Poindexter v. Greenhow* (1885); *Virginia Coupon Cases* (1884). In all these cases the effort was to show, and the court held, that the suits were not against the state or the United States, but against the individuals; conceding that, if they had been against either the state or the United States, they could not be maintained.

Undoubtedly a state may be sued by its own consent, as was the case in *Curran v. Arkansas* (1853), and in *Clark v. Barnard* (1883). The suit in the former case was prosecuted by virtue of a state law which the legislature passed in conformity to the constitution of that state. But this court decided, in *Beers v. Arkansas* (1858), that the state could repeal that law at any time; that it was not a contract within the terms of the constitution prohibiting the passage of state laws impairing the obligation of a contract. In that case the law allowing the state to be sued was modified pending certain suits against the state on its bonds, so as to require the bonds to be filed in court, which was objected to as an unconstitutional change of the law. Chief Justice Taney, delivering the opinion of the court, said:

> It is an established principle of jurisprudence in all civilized nations that the sovereign cannot be sued in its own courts, or in any other, without its consent and permission. . . . And, as this permission is altogether voluntary on the part of the sovereignty, it follows that it may prescribe the terms and conditions on which it consents to be sued, and the manner in which the suit shall be conducted, and may withdraw its consent whenever it may suppose that justice to the public requires it. . . . The prior law was not a contract. It was an ordinary act of legislation, prescribing the conditions upon which the state consented to waive the privilege of sovereignty . . . and no such contract can be implied from the law, nor can this court inquire whether the law operated hardly or unjustly upon the parties whose suits were then pending. That was a question for the consideration of the legislature.

The same doctrine was held in *Railroad Co. v. Tennessee* (1880); *Railroad Co. v. Alabama* (1879); and *In re Ayers* (1887).

But besides the presumption that no anomalous and unheard-of proceedings or suits were intended to be raised up by the constitution,—anomalous and unheard of when the constitution was adopted,—an additional reason why the jurisdiction claimed for the circuit court does not exist is the language of the act of congress by which its jurisdiction is conferred. The words are these: "The circuit courts of the United States shall have original cognizance, concurrent with the courts of the several states, of all suits of a civil nature, at common law or in equity, . . . arising under the constitution or laws of the United States, or treaties," etc. "Concurrent with the courts of the several states." The state courts have no power to entertain suits by individuals against a state without its consent. Then how does the circuit court, having only concurrent jurisdiction, acquire any such power? It is true that the same qualification existed in the judiciary act of 1789, which was before the court in *Chisholm v. Georgia,* and the majority of the court did not think that it was sufficient to limit the jurisdiction of the circuit court. Justice Iredell thought differently. In view of the manner in which that decision was received by the country, the adoption of the eleventh amendment, the light of history, and the reason of the thing, we think we are at liberty to prefer Justice Iredell's views in this regard.

Some reliance is placed by the plaintiff upon the observations of Chief Justice Marshall in *Cohens v. Virginia* (1821). The chief justice was there considering the power of review exercisable by this court over the judgments of a state court, wherein it might be necessary to make the state itself a defendant in error. He showed that this power was absolutely necessary in order to enable the judiciary of the United States to take cognizance of all cases arising under the constitution and laws of the United States. "Where," said the chief justice,

> a state obtains a judgment against an individual, and the court rendering such judgment overrules a defense set up under the constitution or laws of the United States, the transfer of this record into the supreme court, for the sole purpose of inquiring whether the judgment violates the constitution or laws of the United States, can, with no propriety, we think, be denominated a suit commenced or prosecuted against the state whose judgment is so far re-examined. [W]rits of error, accompanied with citations, have uniformly issued for the removal of judgments in favor of the United States into a superior court. It has never been suggested that such writ of error was a suit against the United States, and therefore not within the jurisdiction of the appellate court.

To avoid misapprehension, it may be proper to add that, although the obligations of a state rest for their performance upon its honor and good faith, and cannot be made the subjects of judicial cognizance unless the state consents to be sued or comes itself into court, yet, where property or rights are enjoyed under a grant or contract made by a state, they cannot wantonly be invaded. While the state cannot be compelled by suit to perform its contracts, any attempt on its part to violate property or rights acquired under its contracts may be judicially resisted, and any law impairing the obligation of contracts under which such property or rights are held is void and powerless to affect their enjoyment. It is not necessary that we should enter upon an examination of the reason or expediency of the rule which exempts a sovereign state from prosecution in a court of justice at the suit of individuals. This is fully discussed by writers on public law. It is enough for us to declare its existence. The legislative department of a state represents its polity and its will, and is called upon by the highest demands of natural and political law to preserve justice and judgment, and to hold inviolate the public obligations. Any departure from this rule, except for reasons most cogent, (of which the legislature, and not the courts, is the judge,) never fails in the end to incur the odium of the world, and to bring lasting injury upon the state itself. But to deprive the legislature of the power of judging what the honor and safety of the state may require, even at the expense of a temporary failure to discharge the public debts, would be attended with greater evils than such failure can cause. The judgment of the circuit court is affirmed.

HARLAN, J.

I concur with the court in holding that a suit directly against a state by one of its own citizens is not one to which the judicial power of the United States extends, unless the state itself consents to be sued. Upon this ground alone I assent to the judgment. But I cannot give my assent to many things said in the opinion. The comments made upon the decision in *Chisholm v. Georgia* do not meet my approval. They are not necessary to the determination of the present case. Besides, I am of opinion that the decision in that case was based upon a sound interpretation of the constitution as that instrument then was.

* * *

Among the most striking facts about *Hans* is the Court's studied silence about the Civil War and Reconstruction even though the bonds at issue were Reconstruction period bonds and the Union victory squarely repudiated at least the most muscular antebellum theories of state sovereignty. Remarkably, the Court's discussion of state sovereignty was presented as if there had been no protracted, bloody struggle over the principle at all. The *Hans* Court rendered an interpretation of the Eleventh Amendment based upon Founding-era theories of state sovereignty and the terms of the amendment's ratification.

The date of the case is significant in this regard. The retreat from Reconstruction, which began at least as early as the Hayes-Tilden Compromise over the contested presidential election of 1876, was in full swing by 1890. *See* WILLIAM GILLETTE, RETREAT FROM RECONSTRUCTION, 1869-1879 (1982). Jim Crow segregation had taken hold in the South. *See* C. VANN WOODWARD, THE STRANGE CAREER OF JIM CROW (1955). *Plessy v. Fergusson* would not be decided until 1896, but the Supreme Court took a leading role in the retreat decades earlier by reviving antebellum federalism principles to circumscribe federal power conferred by the Reconstruction Amendments over the states. *See Slaughterhouse Cases* (1873); *Civil Rights Cases* (1883). This jurisprudence of selective memory dovetailed with northern Whites' desire for sectional reconciliation after the war, *see* NINA SILBER, THE ROMANCE OF REUNION: NORTHERNERS AND THE SOUTH 1865-1900 (1997), as well as a flagging federal commitment to address violent resistance to Reconstruction and increasing indifference to the terrorization of Black people. *See* ALLEN TRELEASE, WHITE TERROR: THE KU KLUX KLAN CONSPIRACY AND SOUTHERN RECONSTRUCTION (1979).

In *Hans*, the federalism revival the Court first endorsed in the 1870s in cases dealing directly with civil rights enforcement was extended to constrain federal judicial power over the states, canonizing a theory of state sovereign immunity that extended beyond the wording of the Eleventh Amendment. The text of the amendment plainly does not cover a suit between a state and one of its own citizens. The *Hans* Court read the amendment as a kind of synecdoche—one part of a larger principle of state sovereign immunity taken to represent the whole in spite of its narrow textual scope.

The modern Supreme Court has followed a similar interpretive approach, expanding the extra-textual treatment of state sovereign immunity. In the next two cases, the sovereignty of Native nations and the doctrine of state sovereign immunity converge. As you read these cases, concentrate on the justifications the Court offered for its expansion of state sovereign immunity. Consider the implications not only for federal legislative, executive and judicial power, but also for tribal sovereignty. A central question is whether modern state sovereign immunity doctrine eliminates or merely diminishes remedies designed to ensure that state governments meet their obligations under federal law.

Blatchford v. Native Village of Noatak and Circle Village

501 U.S. 775 (1991)

Justice SCALIA delivered the opinion of the Court.

I

In 1980, Alaska enacted a revenue-sharing statute that provided annual payments of $25,000 to each "Native village government" located in a community without a state-chartered municipal corporation. Alaska Stat. Ann. §29.89.050. The State's attorney general believed the statute to be unconstitutional. In his view, Native village governments were "racially exclusive groups" or "racially exclusive organizations" whose status turned exclusively on the racial ancestry of their members; therefore, the attorney general believed, funding these groups would violate the equal protection clause of Alaska's Constitution. Acting on the attorney general's advice, the Commissioner of Alaska's Department of Community and Regional Affairs (petitioner here), enlarged the program to include all unincorporated communities, whether administered by Native governments or not. Shortly thereafter, the legislature increased funding under the program to match its increased scope. Funding, however, never reached the full $25,000 initially allocated to each unincorporated Native community.

The legislature repealed the revenue-sharing statute in 1985 and replaced it with one that matched the program as expanded by the commissioner. In the same year, respondents filed this suit, challenging the commissioner's action on federal equal protection grounds, and seeking an order requiring the commissioner to pay them the money that they would have received had the commissioner not enlarged the program. The District Court initially granted an injunction to preserve sufficient funds for the 1986 fiscal year, but then dismissed the suit as violating the Eleventh Amendment.

The Court of Appeals for the Ninth Circuit reversed, first on the ground that 28 U.S.C. §1362 constituted a congressional abrogation of Eleventh Amendment immunity, and then, upon reconsideration, on the ground that Alaska had no immunity against suits by Indian tribes.

II

The Eleventh Amendment provides as follows:

The Judicial power of the United States shall not be construed to extend to any suit in law or equity, commenced or prosecuted against one of the United States by Citizens of another State, or by Citizens or Subjects of any Foreign State.

Despite the narrowness of its terms, since *Hans v. Louisiana* (1890), we have understood the Eleventh Amendment to stand not so much for what it says, but for the presupposition of our constitutional structure which it confirms: that the States entered the federal system with their sovereignty intact; that the judicial authority in Article III is limited by this sovereignty, and that a State will therefore not be subject to suit in federal court unless it has consented to suit, either expressly or in the "plan of the convention."

Respondents do not ask us to revisit *Hans;* instead they argue that the traditional principles of immunity presumed by *Hans* do not apply to suits by sovereigns like Indian tribes. And even if they did, respondents contend, the States have consented to suits by tribes in the "plan of the convention." We consider these points in turn.

In arguing that sovereign immunity does not restrict suit by Indian tribes, respondents submit, first, that sovereign immunity only restricts suits by *individuals* against sovereigns, not by *sovereigns* against sovereigns, and as we have recognized, *Oklahoma Tax Comm'n v. Citizen Band of Potawatomi Tribe of Okla.* (1991), Indian tribes are sovereigns. Respondents' conception of the nature of sovereign immunity finds some support both in the apparent understanding of the Founders and in dicta of our own opinions.[1] But whatever the reach or meaning of these early statements, the notion that traditional principles of sovereign immunity only restrict suits by individuals was rejected in *Principality of Monaco v. Mississippi* (1934). It is with that opinion, and the conception of sovereignty that it embraces, that we must begin.

In *Monaco*, the Principality had come into possession of Mississippi state bonds, and had sued Mississippi in federal court to recover amounts due under those bonds. Mississippi defended on grounds of the Eleventh Amendment, among others. Had respondents' understanding of sovereign immunity been the Court's, the Eleventh Amendment would not have limited the otherwise clear grant of jurisdiction in Article III to hear controversies "between a State . . . and foreign States." But we held that it did.

> Manifestly, we cannot rest with a mere literal application of the words of §2 of Article III, or assume that the letter of the Eleventh Amendment exhausts the restrictions upon suits against non-consenting States. Behind the words of the constitutional provisions are postulates which limit and control. There is . . . the postulate that States of the Union, still possessing attributes of sovereignty, shall be immune from suits, without their consent, save where there has been a "surrender of this immunity in the plan of the convention." The Federalist, No. 81.

---

1. As Alexander Hamilton said: "It is inherent in the nature of sovereignty, not to be amenable to the suit of an *individual* without its consent." The Federalist No. 81. James Madison expressed a similar understanding at the Virginia Convention ("It is not in the power of *individuals* to call any state into court"), as did Chief Justice Marshall ("[A]n *individual* cannot proceed to obtain judgment against a state, though he may be sued by a state"). In *United States v. Texas* (1892), we adverted to respondents' distinction explicitly, describing *Hans v. Louisiana*, as having "proceeded upon the broad ground that 'it is inherent in the nature of sovereignty not to be amenable to the suit of an *individual* without its consent,'" and concluding that "the suability of one government by another government . . . does no violence to the inherent nature of sovereignty."

Our clear assumption in *Monaco* was that sovereign immunity extends against both individuals and sovereigns, so that there must be found inherent in the plan of the convention a surrender by the States of immunity as to either. Because we perceived in the plan "no ground upon which it can be said that any waiver or consent by a State of the Union has run in favor of a foreign State," we concluded that foreign states were still subject to the immunity of the States.

We pursue the same inquiry in the present case, and thus confront respondents' second contention: that the States waived their immunity against Indian tribes when they adopted the Constitution. Just as in *Monaco* with regard to foreign sovereigns, so also here with regard to Indian tribes, there is no compelling evidence that the Founders thought such a surrender inherent in the constitutional compact.[2] We have hitherto found a surrender of immunity against particular litigants in only two contexts: suits by sister States, *South Dakota v. North Carolina* (1904), and suits by the United States, *United States v. Texas* (1892). We have not found a surrender by the United States to suit by the States, *Kansas v. United States* (1907); nor, again, a surrender by the States to suit by foreign sovereigns, *Monaco*.

Respondents argue that Indian tribes are more like States than foreign sovereigns. That is true in some respects: They are, for example, domestic. The relevant difference between States and foreign sovereigns, however, is not domesticity, but the role of each in the convention within which the surrender of immunity was for the former, but not for the latter, implicit. What makes the States' surrender of immunity from suit by sister States plausible is the mutuality of that concession. There is no such mutuality with either foreign sovereigns or Indian tribes. We have repeatedly held that Indian tribes enjoy immunity against suits by States, *Potawatomi Tribe*, as it would be absurd to suggest that the tribes surrendered immunity in a convention to which they were not even parties. But if the convention could not surrender *the tribes'* immunity for the benefit of the *States*, we do not believe that it surrendered the States' immunity for the benefit of the tribes.

III

Respondents argue that, if the Eleventh Amendment operates to bar suits by Indian tribes against States without their consent, 28 U.S.C. §1362 operates to void that bar. They press two very different arguments, which we consider in turn.

A

In *United States v. Minnesota* (1926), we held that the United States had standing to sue on behalf of Indian tribes as guardians of the tribes' rights, and that, since

---

2. The only evidence alluded to by respondents is a statement by President Washington to Chief Cornplanter of the Seneca Nation:

> Here, then, is the security for the remainder of your lands. No State, nor person, can purchase your lands, unless at some public treaty, held under the authority of the United States.
>
> ...
>
> If . . . you have any just cause of complaint against [a purchaser], and can make satisfactory proof thereof, the federal courts will be open to you for redress, as to all other persons."
>
> But of course, denying Indian tribes the right to sue States in federal court does not disadvantage them in relation to "all other persons." Respondents are asking for access more favorable than that which others enjoy.

"the immunity of the State is subject to the constitutional qualification that she may be sued in this Court by the United States," no Eleventh Amendment bar would limit the United States' access to federal courts for that purpose. Relying upon our decision in *Moe v. Confederated Salish and Kootenai Tribes* (1976), respondents argue that we have read §1362 to embody a general delegation of the authority to sue on the tribes' behalf from the Federal Government back to tribes themselves. Hence, respondents suggest, because the United States would face no sovereign immunity limitation, in no case brought under §1362 can sovereign immunity be a bar.

Section 1362 provides as follows:

> The district courts shall have original jurisdiction of all civil actions, brought by any Indian tribe or band with a governing body duly recognized by the Secretary of the Interior, wherein the matter in controversy arises under the Constitution, laws, or treaties of the United States.

What is striking about this most unremarkable statute is its similarity to any number of other grants of jurisdiction to district courts to hear federal-question claims. Compare it, for example, with §1331(a) as it existed at the time §1362 was enacted:

> The district courts shall have original jurisdiction of all civil actions wherein the matter in controversy exceeds the sum or value of $10,000 exclusive of interest and costs, and arises under the Constitution, laws, or treaties of the United States.

28 U.S.C. §1331(a).

Considering the text of §1362 in the context of its enactment, one might well conclude that its *sole* purpose was to eliminate any jurisdictional minimum for "arising under" claims brought by Indian tribes. Tribes already had access to federal courts for "arising under" claims under §1331, where the amount in controversy was greater than $10,000; for all that appears from its text, §1362 merely extends that jurisdiction to claims below that minimum. Such a reading, moreover, finds support in the very title of the Act that adopted §1362: "To amend the Judicial Code to permit Indian tribes to maintain civil actions in Federal district courts without regard to the $10,000 limitation, and for other purposes." 80 Stat. 880.

Moe, however, found something more in the title's "other purposes" — an implication that "a tribe's access to federal court to litigate [federal-question cases] would be *at least in some respects* as broad as that of the United States suing as the tribe's trustee." The "respect" at issue in *Moe* was access to federal court for the purpose of obtaining injunctive relief from state taxation. The Tax Injunction Act, 28 U.S.C. §1341, denied such access to persons other than the United States; we held that §1362 revoked that denial as to Indian tribes. *Moe* did not purport to be saying that §1362 equated tribal access with the United States' access *generally*, but only "at least in some respects," or "in certain respects." Respondents now urge us, in effect, to eliminate this limitation utterly — for it is impossible to imagine any more extreme replication of the United States' ability to sue than replication even to the point of allowing unconsented suit against state sovereigns. This is a vast expansion upon *Moe*. The obstacle to suit in the present case, by contrast, is a creation not of Congress but of the Constitution. A willingness to eliminate the former in no way bespeaks a willingness to eliminate the latter, especially when limitation to "certain respects" has explicitly been announced.

Moreover, as we shall discuss in Part III-B, our cases require Congress' exercise of the power to abrogate state sovereign immunity, where it exists, to be exercised with unmistakable clarity. To avoid that difficulty, respondents assert that §1362 represents not an abrogation of the States' sovereign immunity, but rather a *delegation* to tribes of the Federal Government's exemption from state sovereign immunity. We doubt, to begin with, that that sovereign exemption *can* be delegated — even if one limits the permissibility of delegation (as respondents propose) to persons on whose behalf the United States itself might sue. The consent, "inherent in the convention," to suit by the United States — at the instance and under the control of responsible federal officers — is not consent to suit by anyone whom the United States might select; and even consent to suit by the United States for a particular person's benefit is not consent to suit by that person himself.

But in any event, assuming that delegation of exemption from state sovereign immunity is theoretically possible, there is no reason to believe that Congress ever contemplated such a strange notion. The delegation theory is entirely a creature of respondents' own invention.

B

Finally, respondents ask us to recognize §1362 as a congressional abrogation of Eleventh Amendment immunity. We have repeatedly said that this power to abrogate can only be exercised by a clear legislative statement. We agree with petitioner that §1362 does not reflect an "unmistakably clear" intent to abrogate immunity, made plain "in the language of the statute." As we have already noted, the text is no more specific than §1331, the grant of general federal question jurisdiction to district courts, and no one contends that §1331 suffices to abrogate immunity for all federal questions.[4]

IV

Finally, respondents argue that even if the Eleventh Amendment bars their claims for damages, they still seek injunctive relief, which the Eleventh Amendment would not bar. The Court of Appeals, of course, did not address this point, and we leave it for that court's initial consideration on remand.

---

4. In asserting that §1362's grant of jurisdiction to "all civil actions" suffices to abrogate a State's defense of immunity the dissent has just repeated the mistake of the Court in *Chisholm v. Georgia* (1793), the case that occasioned the Eleventh Amendment itself. The fact that Congress grants *jurisdiction* to hear a claim does not suffice to show Congress has abrogated all *defenses* to that claim. The issues are wholly distinct. A State may waive its Eleventh Amendment immunity, and if it does, §1362 certainly would grant a district court jurisdiction to hear the claim. The dissent's view returns us, like Sisyphus, to the beginning of this 200-year struggle.

The judgment of the Court of Appeals is reversed, and the case is remanded for further proceedings consistent with this opinion.

Justice BLACKMUN, with whom Justice MARSHALL and Justice STEVENS join, dissenting.

I

As some of us previously have stated, *see Atascadero State Hospital v. Scanlon* (1985) (dissenting opinion), I do not believe the Eleventh Amendment is implicated by a suit such as this one, in which litigants seek to vindicate federal rights against a State. In my view, the Amendment has no application outside the context of State/citizen and State/alien diversity suits.

The substantial historical analysis that supports this view already has been exhaustively detailed, and I shall not repeat it here.

II

Even assuming that the State at one time may have possessed immunity against tribal suits, that immunity was abrogated by Congress when, in 1966, it enacted 28 U.S.C. §1362. The majority rejects this argument, holding that §1362 cannot authorize respondents' suit because the statute's language does not reflect an "unmistakably clear" intent to abrogate the States' sovereign immunity. I have never accepted the validity of that so-called "clear-statement rule" and I remain of the view, expressed by Justice Brennan for four of us in *Atascadero*, that such "special rules of statutory drafting are not justified (nor are they justifiable) as efforts to determine the genuine intent of Congress. . . . [T]he special rules are designed as hurdles to keep the disfavored suits out of the federal courts."

Even if I were to accept the proposition that the clear-statement rule at times might serve as a mechanism for discerning congressional intent, I surely would reject its application here.

[I]t cannot extend to matters concerning federal regulation of Native American affairs; in that sphere of governmental operations, the "balance of power" always has weighed heavily against the States and in favor of the Federal Government. Indeed, "[t]he plenary power of Congress to deal with the special problems of Indians is drawn both explicitly and implicitly from the Constitution itself." *Morton v. Mancari* (1974).

Illustrative of this principle are our cases holding that the law of the State is generally inapplicable to Native American affairs, absent the consent of Congress. *See, e.g., Worcester v. Georgia* (1832). Chief Justice Marshall explained for the Court in *Worcester* that a federally recognized tribe

> is a distinct community, occupying its own territory, with boundaries accurately described, in which the laws of [the State] can have no force, and which the citizens of [the State] have no right to enter, but with the assent of the [tribes] themselves, or in conformity with treaties, and with the acts of Congress. The whole intercourse between the United States and this nation, is, by our Constitution and laws, vested in the government of the United States.

Despite the States' undeniable interest in regulating activities within its borders, and despite traditional principles of federalism, the States' authority has been largely displaced in matters pertaining to Native Americans. *See The Kansas Indians* (1867) (finding state taxes inapplicable to tribal lands despite partial assimilation of tribe into white society); *United States v. Kagama* (1886) (sustaining validity of a prosecution of Native Americans in federal court under the Indian Major Crimes Act). Moreover, federal displacement of state authority regarding Native American affairs has not been limited to the geographic boundaries of "Indian country," *see Antoine v. Washington* (1975) (holding that Congress may constitutionally inhibit a State's exercise of its police power over non-Indian land through federal legislation ratifying an agreement with a tribe), nor to state regulations that directly infringe upon tribal self-government. *See McClanahan v. Arizona State Tax Comm'n* (1973).

Thus, in this area, the pertinent "balance of power" is between the Federal Government and the tribes, with the States playing only a subsidiary role. Because spheres of activity otherwise susceptible to state regulation are, "according to the settled principles of our Constitution, . . . committed exclusively to the government of the Union," *Worcester v. Georgia*, where Native American affairs are concerned, the presumptions underlying the clear-statement rule, and thus the rule itself, have no place in interpreting statutes pertaining to the tribes.

Employing the traditional tools of statutory interpretation, I conclude that Congress intended, through §1362, to authorize constitutional claims for damages by tribes against the States. As the preceding discussion makes clear . . . this is an area in which "a page of history is worth a volume of logic." *New York Trust Co. v. Eisner* (1921). . . .

Prior to 1966, the Indian tribes were largely dependent upon the United States Government to enforce their rights against state encroachment. This arrangement derived from the historic trust relationship between the tribes and the United States. *See* F. Cohen, Handbook of Federal Indian Law. In seeking judicial protection of tribal interests, the Federal Government, of course, was unrestrained by the doctrine of state sovereign immunity. *United States v. Minnesota* (1926).

In 1966, Congress enacted 28 U.S.C. §1362 as part of a larger national policy of "self-determination" for the Native American peoples. *See* M. Price & R. Clinton, Law and the American Indian (1983). Consistent with that policy, "Congress contemplated that §1362 would be used particularly in situations in which the United States suffered from a conflict of interest or was otherwise unable or unwilling to bring suit as trustee for the Indians." *Arizona v. San Carlos Apache Tribe* (1983). In other words, Congress sought to eliminate the tribes' dependence upon the United States for the vindication of federal rights in the federal courts. . . .

I agree with respondents that the litigation authority bestowed on the tribes through §1362 also includes the right to bring federal claims against the States for damages. The legislative history of the statute reveals Congress' intention that the tribes bring litigation "involving issues identical to those" that would have been raised by the United States acting as trustee for the tribes. H.R. Rep. No. 2040, 89th

Cong. (1966) (House Report). There is no reason to believe that this authority would be limited to prospective relief in the broad range of suits brought against the States.

. . . Section 1362 represents a frank acknowledgment by the Government that it often lacks the resources or the political will adequately to fulfill this responsibility. Given this admission, we should not lightly restrict the authority granted the tribes to defend their own interests. Rather, the most reasoned interpretation of §1362 is as a congressional authorization to bring those suits that are necessary to vindicate fully the federal rights of the tribes. It hardly requires explication that monetary remedies are often necessary to afford such relief.

"'[S]tatutes passed for the benefit of dependent Indian tribes . . . are to be liberally construed, doubtful expressions being resolved in favor of the Indians.' [*Alaska Pacific Fisheries v. United States* (1918)]." *Bryan v. Itasca County* (1976). Unlike the ill-conceived interpretive rule adopted so recently in *Atascadero*, this canon of construction dates back to the earliest years of our Nation's history. Indeed, it is rooted in the unique trust relationship between the tribes and the Federal Government that is inherent in the constitutional plan. *See* U.S. Const., Art. I, §8, cl. 3; Art. I, §2, cl. 3. . . .

* * *

The enactment of Section 1362, discussed in *Blatchford*, took place during the same period in which Alaska Native tribes were working to protect their sovereignty over their traditional territories following the admission of Alaska as the 49th state. There are 228 federally recognized Native nations in Alaska, each having a government-to-government relationship with the United States. This legal and political relationship recognizes the sovereignty of Alaska Native tribes, which preexisted the United States' 1867 purchase of Alaska from Russia. Though Russia claimed ownership over the region, Alaska Natives did not cede their sovereignty through a treaty with Russia. To the contrary, "[t]here was no real colonization of Alaska by the Russians," given that Russian settlement at its height involved fewer than 900 settlers.[2] Alaska Natives therefore disputed Russia's right to sell their territory to the United States. The United States, moreover, ended its practice of treatymaking with Native nations in 1871 and did not enter into treaties with Alaska Native tribes. The dispute over ownership persisted into the twentieth century up until (and beyond) the admission of Alaska as a state. In 1959, the United States Court of Claims recognized that Alaska Natives had aboriginal title—that is, property rights—to southeast Alaska. *Tlingit and Haida Indians v. United States* (Ct. Cl. 1959). The Act admitting Alaska to statehood required it to "disclaim all right and title" to Native property, while at the same time affording the state the

---

2. ROBERT T. ANDERSON ET AL., AMERICAN INDIAN LAW: CASES AND COMMENTARY 833 (3d ed. 2015).

right to claim over 100 million acres of "vacant, unappropriated and unreserved" land. Alaska Native peoples protested the state's claims, citing their aboriginal title. These arguments "set the stage of the enactment of the Alaska Native Claims Settlement Act . . . of 1971," which extinguished claims of aboriginal title in exchange for a system through which Alaska Native Village corporations could obtain property rights to public lands and Alaska Natives could enroll and obtain stock in regional corporations supported by funding from congressional appropriations and royalties on mineral leases.[3] All told, roughly 45 million acres of land remained in Alaska Native ownership as a result of the settlement.[4] At the same time, Alaska Native nations retained their sovereign governments. It was against this backdrop of the persistence of Alaska Native sovereignty that the dispute in *Blatchford* arose.

Relying on *Principality of Monaco,* Justice Scalia's opinion for the Court treated Alaska Native tribal sovereignty as indistinguishable from the sovereignty of foreign governments for purposes of state sovereign immunity doctrine. This is the core holding of the case. Just as a foreign government cannot sue a state without its consent, no tribe may do so.

Are you persuaded by the analogy to foreign governments for purposes of determining whether states are immune from suits brought by Native nations? For suits brought by Alaska Native tribes against the state of Alaska? Is the alternative of analogizing Native nations to states superior? A third option the Court appears not to have entertained is that the sovereignty of Native nations is genuinely distinctive, both because tribes are not in the first instance Western legal entities and because of the unique government-to-government relationship of tribes to the federal government under the Constitution. Would this third approach address Justice Scalia's concern about mutuality—the fact that Native nations are generally immune from suit by states? The unique legal status of Native nations, especially their federal recognition as preconstitutional sovereigns, might justify non-mutuality.

A second core holding of the case is that 28 U.S.C. §1362 does not abrogate sovereign immunity. We cover congressional power to abrogate state sovereign immunity in detail in Section A.3.c. What bears emphasis here is that the modern Court's theory of state sovereign immunity not only reaches beyond the text of the Eleventh Amendment—the Eleventh Amendment says absolutely *nothing* about the capacity of tribes to sue states—it also entails certain standards of statutory construction. Justice Scalia applies a rule of strict construction to conclude that §1362 cannot be read to displace the doctrine of sovereign immunity even though it had already been read to do so in the context of suits by tribes to obtain injunctive relief in federal court against state taxation. *Moe* might have been distinguished on the narrower ground that, unlike *Hans, Principality of Monaco* and *Blatchford,* the remedy sought was prospective and thus laid no claim on the state treasury. See Section A.3.c, infra on *Ex parte Young.*

Reading *Hans* and *Blatchford* it is clear that the Supreme Court has not limited the principle of sovereign immunity to the text of the Eleventh Amendment. It has

---

3. David S. Case & David A. Voluck, Alaska Natives and American Laws xi (3d ed. 2012).

4. Anderson et al., *supra* note 2, at 837.

instead treated the Eleventh Amendment as reflecting far broader principles of state sovereign immunity. The modern Court has embraced this approach. As we will see, even when Congress has authorized a private right of action to recover for the violation of federal law, the Court has precluded such litigation in both federal *and state* court where the state is named as a defendant and money damages are sought. The principal case precluding suit against a state for money damages even in the courts of that state is *Alden v. Maine* (1999). We present *Alden* in Section A, *infra*, with other cases and materials on the limits to congressional power to abrogate state sovereign immunity when it legislates under Article I powers.

What if an individual sues a state in the courts of *another* state? Initially, in *Nevada v. Hall* (1979), an employee of the University of Nevada driving a university vehicle was involved in an accident on a California highway. Injured California residents sued the university and the state of Nevada for damages in California state court. Nevada moved to quash the service, but the California Supreme Court held that Nevada was amenable to suit in California courts and remanded the case for trial. At trial, Nevada sought to limit damages to $25,000—the cap provided under Nevada's statute waiving sovereign immunity for tort claims against the state. Nevada's motion relied on the Full Faith and Credit Clause of the U.S. Constitution. The California trial court denied the motion and the jury entered a verdict of $1.15 million. The state court of appeal affirmed and the California Supreme Court denied review.

On certiorari to the U.S. Supreme Court a 6-3 majority affirmed, holding that California was free to take jurisdiction of the case and, having done so, to apply its damage rules rather than Nevada's. Drawing on principles of sovereign immunity in international law, the Court distinguished a sovereign's immunity from suit absent consent *in its own courts*, from its immunity *in the courts of a co-equal sovereign*. The latter circumstance "necessarily implicates the power and authority of a second sovereign; its source must be found either in an agreement, express or implied, between the two sovereigns, or in the voluntary decision of the second to respect the dignity of the first as a matter of comity." Here, there is no agreement and California clearly refused to "extend[] immunity to Nevada as a matter of comity." The Court also rejected Nevada's argument that states of the Union owe distinctive respect for "the sovereignty of one another" because the U.S. Constitution explicitly limits state sovereignty in prohibiting discriminatory state taxes on goods of other states, restrictions on entry barring citizens of other states, deprivation of the privileges and immunities of citizens of the several states, and denial of extradition of fugitive slaves "when a proper demand is made by the executive of another State." The majority acknowledged that these provisions "demonstrate that ours is not a union of 50 wholly independent sovereigns." But "the existence of express limitation on state sovereignty [implies] that caution should be exercised before concluding that unstated limitations on state power were intended by the Framers."

The remaining question was whether the U.S. Constitution implicitly "requires all of the States to adhere to the sovereign immunity principle." The founding era debates about states' amenability to suit in federal court "do not answer the question whether the Constitution places any limit on the exercise of one State's power to authorize its courts to assert jurisdiction over another state. Nor does anything in Article III . . . or in the Eleventh Amendment." The Full Faith and Credit Clause requires that states give effect to judgments of the courts of other states, but the Court had previously held that the clause does not require a state to apply the law of another state "in violation of its own legitimate public policy." Here, California's interest is the "substantial one of providing full protection to those who are injured on its highways through the negligence of both residents and nonresidents. . . . In further implementation of that policy, California has unequivocally waived its own immunity from liability for the torts committed by its own agents and authorized full recovery even against the sovereign."

Justice Blackmun, joined by Chief Justice Burger and Justice Rehnquist, dissented, warning that, despite a footnote in the majority opinion suggesting its holding was limited to the facts of the case, "the Court has opened the door to avenues of liability and interstate retaliation that will prove unsettling and upsetting for our federal system."

The dissent's view now has been adopted. In *Franchise Tax Board v. Hyatt* (2019), the Court expressly overruled *Nevada v. Hall.* Gilbert Hyatt sued California's Franchise Tax Board in the courts of the state of Nevada. Hyatt sold his California house in 1991 and rented an apartment in Nevada. He registered to vote in Nevada that year and also opened a Nevada bank account. The move saved Hyatt millions in California taxes because Nevada has no income tax. Employees of the California Franchise Tax Board believed that Hyatt had not really moved; that it was a sham to evade California's taxes. Employees of the Franchise Tax Board broke into his Nevada home, and the investigation included "rifling through his private mail, combing through his garbage, and examining private activities at his place of worship." One agency investigator referred to Hyatt in antisemitic terms and took "trophy-like pictures" in front of Hyatt's home after the audit. A trial was held and the jury ruled in favor of Hyatt and awarded him $385 million. With interest, the Judgment was worth almost $500 million.

The litigation was lengthy and involved multiple trips to the Supreme Court. By the time the case got there for the last time the judgment had been reduced to $100,000.

Justice Thomas, writing for a 5-4 majority, overruled *Nevada v. Hall,* holding that it is "contrary to our constitutional design and the understanding of sovereign immunity shared by the States." As in *Blatchford, Seminole Tribe,* and *Alden,* the majority used history and structural inference to conclude that even though the Constitution nowhere addresses states' immunity from citizen suits in the courts of another state, such litigation is forbidden — an incursion on the "inviolable sovereignty . . . established and widely accepted at the founding." Immunity from "private suit" is "[a]n integral component of the State's sovereignty." Contrary to the analysis of *Hall,* the "Constitution does not merely allow States to afford each other immunity as a matter of comity; it embeds interstate sovereign immunity within the constitutional design."

Unlike foreign sovereigns, the states are stripped by the Constitution of "traditional diplomatic and military tools," the power to "lay imposts or duties on imports and exports," the Full Faith and Credit Clause "demand[s] that state-court judgments be accorded full effect . . . and preclude[s] States from adopting any policy of hostility to the public Acts of other States," and no state can unilaterally "apply its own law to interstate disputes over borders, water rights, or the interpretation of interstate compacts." Justice Thomas reasoned that "[i]nterstate sovereign immunity is similarly integral to the structure of the Constitution . . . [which] implicitly strips States of any power they once had to refuse each other sovereign immunity." It is therefore, "an essential component of federalism." To look to the text alone for confirmation of this is to engage in "precisely the type of 'ahistorical literalism' that we have rejected when interpreting the scope of the States' sovereign immunity since the discredited decision in *Chisholm*."

Justice Breyer, joined by Justices Ginsburg, Sotomayor and Kagan, dissented. He argued that the majority simply misread the historical record. Although there is ample evidence that states accorded each other sovereign immunity before ratification of the Constitution, just "like foreign nations" this was done by virtue of comity — "as a matter of consent rather than absolute right." Nor are general statements regarding the importance of sovereign immunity from the founding era relevant as they concerned federal court jurisdiction over suits against states. "That issue was a matter of importance in the early days of independence, for it concerned the ability of holders of Revolutionary War debt owed by States to collect that debt in a federal forum." Agreeing that the Constitution contains both "implicit guarantees as well as explicit ones," Justice Breyer admonished that "concepts like 'constitutional design' and 'plan of the Convention'" relied on so heavily by the majority "are highly abstract, making them difficult to apply . . . invit[ing] differing interpretations." Here, he concluded, there is "nothing in the 'plan of the Convention' or elsewhere to suggest that the Constitution converted what had been the customary practice of extending immunity by consent into an absolute federal requirement that no State withdraw. . . . Where the Constitution alters the authority of States *vis-à-vis* other States, it tends to do so explicitly."

Hyatt confirms the modern Court's commitment to the extra-textual theory of state sovereign immunity. Note the majority's inversion of the structural inference in *Hall*. In *Hall*, Justice Stevens wrote that "the existence of express limitation on state sovereignty [implies] that caution should be exercised before concluding that unstated limitations on state power were intended by the Framers." The "power" at issue is the traditional power of the courts of one sovereign either to take jurisdiction of a suit against another state or to forbear on principles of comity. In *Hyatt*, Justice Thomas argued just the opposite, inferring from the textual limits on state sovereignty in the Constitution that there is an equally important limit on this power: "Interstate sovereign immunity is similarly integral to the structure of the Constitution . . . [which] implicitly strips States of any power they once had to refuse each other sovereign immunity." State sovereign immunity was so fundamental, so taken for granted, that no one thought it necessary to make it explicit.

Which is the more natural inference from constitutional silence? One might begin answering that question by asking which is the greater incursion on state sovereignty: Is it more offensive to state sovereignty for California to have to defend its tax collection practices in the state of Nevada, or for the Nevada courts to refuse jurisdiction of a case involving a citizen of the state of Nevada merely because the defendant is another state? State sovereignty is implicated in either case. The question is what balance was struck by the Constitution to resolve these conflicts. The ordinary inference is that, as a document establishing limited national powers and duties, constitutional silence preserves the status quo ante. This would support the inference drawn by Justice Stevens in *Hall*, that the states retained the right to exercise jurisdiction subject to considerations of comity. On the facts of *Hyatt*, is there an obviously superior court system to handle the case? If Hyatt can only file in California, and that state provides complete immunity to its agencies, is it consistent with state sovereignty that the California Franchise Tax Board's tortious investigation of a Nevada citizen may not be litigated anywhere?

Are there other constitutional limits on litigation against a state in the courts of another state? One you may recall from your work in civil procedure is that no court can enter an enforceable judgment, and no litigant can use the Full Faith and Credit Clause to seek enforcement, in the absence of valid personal jurisdiction over the defendant. This is, as you know from *Pennoyer v. Neff* (1878) and *International Shoe Co. v. Washington* (1945), a requirement of the Due Process Clause of the Fourteenth Amendment. As a practical matter, docket pressures may also limit the enthusiasm of state courts to take up cases involving other states and foreign governments or parties, at least where the connection to the state in which the suit is filed are attenuated. There are procedural doctrines such as forum non conveniens that enable courts to focus their energies on higher priority cases. *See Provincial Gov't of Marinduque v. Placer Dome, Inc.* (Nev. 2015).

3. Suits Against State Officers for Prospective Relief, Waiver, and Abrogation of State Sovereign Immunity

a. Suits Against State Officers for Prospective Relief

The most important exception to state sovereign immunity is that a suit *against an officer* of the state seeking prospective relief (such as an injunction in a court's exercise of equity jurisdiction) for violations of federal constitutional rights is not treated as a suit against the state itself. The underlying principle, which can be traced to English law, is that while the sovereign enjoys immunity from retrospective liability in court, the government can be required to follow the law going forward through a suit against its officers. Recall the cause of action in *Marbury v. Madison* (1803), discussed in Chapter 1. Although the federal government was immune from suit for money damages arising from the failure of the Secretary of State to deliver Marbury's commission, the writ of mandamus named the Secretary of State, the officer responsible, and sought to compel delivery of the commission.

In Section B, we discuss officer suits in greater detail, including the availability of retrospective compensatory relief against officers and officer immunity doctrines (absolute and qualified immunity) that apply to these claims. Here our focus is on jurisdiction to compel compliance with law through an officer suit seeking *prospective* relief.

The modern officer suit exception to sovereign immunity derives from a famous case decided early in the twentieth century when railroads were among the nation's largest and most powerful corporations, controlling the flow of goods, services, and information throughout the nation. Setting fair rates for freight and passengers to control monopoly rent seeking was a major object of state and federal regulation at the time. Although the Fourteenth Amendment had been rendered virtually dead letter for Blacks with the rise of Jim Crow segregation and the Court's decision in *Plessy*, the *Lochner* era Court jealously guarded the rights of corporations under that amendment, especially against state regulation. In *Ex parte*

Young (1908), the state of Minnesota formed a railroad commission which, in 1906, made an order setting the rates that railroads operating in the state could charge for carrying merchandise between stations in the state. Subsequent legislation set new rates for passengers traveling in the state as well. As you will read below, these regulations were accompanied by strict criminal penalties. Railroads reduced their rates accordingly, but their shareholders simultaneously filed suit in federal court seeking an injunction against enforcement of the rates on the ground that they confiscated railroad (and therefore shareholder) property without due process of law and denied them equal protection of the laws.

In a suit filed by shareholders of the Northern Pacific Railroad Company seeking to enjoin enforcement of the rate regulations, Attorney General Young was held in contempt. The complaint alleged that the shareholders had demanded that the president and managing directors of the railroad cease complying with the rate regulations. The company's officers allegedly complied "not because they considered the rates a fair and just return upon the capital invested, or that they would not be confiscatory, but because of the severity of the penalties provided for the violation of such acts an orders."

Attorney General Young moved to dismiss on the ground that the court was without jurisdiction over him, insisting that the state of Minnesota had not consented to the suit, "which suit was in truth and effect against the said state of Minnesota, contrary to the 11th Amendment of the Constitution of the United States." The motion to dismiss was denied and a preliminary injunction was granted against the Attorney General preventing him from "taking any steps against the railroads to enforce the remedies or penalties" of the rate regulations.

The day after the injunction issued, the Attorney General filed a petition for a writ of mandamus in state court directing the Northern Pacific Railway Company to "immediately . . . adopt and furnish and keep for public inspection, as provided by law . . . rates and charges that do not exceed those declared to be just and reasonable . . . by the terms and provisions" of the recently enacted rate regulations. On a motion to show cause and hearing, the Attorney General was held in contempt by the federal court for initiating the state proceeding in violation of the federal injunction.

Ex parte Young

209 U.S. 123 (1908)

Justice PECKHAM delivered the opinion of the court.

We conclude that the circuit court had jurisdiction in the case before it, because it involved the decision of Federal questions arising under the Constitution of the United States.

[R]egarding the alleged invalidity of these acts, we take up the contention that they are invalid on their face on account of the penalties. For disobedience to the freight act the officers, directors, agents, and employees of the company are made guilty of a misdemeanor, and upon conviction each may be punished by imprisonment in the county jail for a period not exceeding ninety days. Each violation would be a separate offense, and, therefore, might result in imprisonment of the various agents of the company who would dare disobey for a term of ninety days each for each offense. Disobedience to the passenger-rate act renders the party guilty of a felony and subject to a fine not exceeding $5,000 or imprisonment in the state prison for a period not exceeding five years, or both fine and imprisonment. The sale of each ticket above the price permitted by the act would be a violation thereof.

It would be difficult, if not impossible, for the company to obtain officers, agents, or employees willing to carry on its affairs except in obedience to the act and orders in question. The company itself would also, in case of disobedience, be liable to the immense fines provided for in violating orders of the commission. The company, in order to test the validity of the acts, must find some agent or employee to disobey them at the risk stated. The necessary effect and result of such legislation must be to preclude a resort to the courts (either state or Federal) for the purpose of testing its validity. The officers and employees could not be expected to disobey any of the provisions of the acts or orders at the risk of such fines and penalties being imposed upon them, in case the court should decide that the law was valid. The result would be a denial of any hearing to the company. The observations upon a similar question, made by Mr. Justice Brewer in *Cotting v. Kansas City Stock Yards Co.* (1901):

> It is doubtless true that the state may impose penalties such as will tend to compel obedience to its mandates by all, individuals or corporations, and if extreme and cumulative penalties are imposed only after there has been a final determination of the validity of the statute, the question would be very different from that here presented. But when the legislature, in an effort to prevent any inquiry of the validity of a particular statute, so burdens any challenge thereof in the courts that the party affected is necessarily constrained to submit rather than take the chances of the penalties imposed, then it becomes a serious question whether the party is not deprived of the equal protection of the laws.

The question was not decided in that case, as it went off on another ground. We have the same question now before us, only the penalties are more severe in the way of fines, to which is added, in the case of officers, agents, or employees of the company, the risk of imprisonment for years as a common felon. In *McGahey v. Virginia* (1890), it was held that when the remedy is so onerous and impracticable as to substantially give none at all, the law is invalid, although what is termed a remedy is in fact given. If the law be such as to make the decision of the legislature or of a commission conclusive as to the sufficiency of the rates, this court has held such a law to be unconstitutional. *Chicago, M. & St. P. Ry. Co. v. Minnesota* (1890). A law which indirectly accomplishes a like result by imposing such conditions upon the right to appeal for judicial relief as work an abandonment of the right rather than face the conditions upon which it is offered or may be obtained is also unconstitutional. It may therefore be said that when the penalties for disobedience are by fines so enormous and imprisonment so severe as to intimidate the company and its officers from resorting to the courts to test the validity of the legislation, the result is the same as if the law in terms prohibited the company from seeking judicial construction of laws which deeply affect its rights.

It is urged that there is no principle upon which to base the claim that a person is entitled to disobey a statute at least once, for the purpose of testing its validity, without subjecting himself to the penalties for disobedience provided by the statute in case it is valid. This is not an accurate statement of the case. Ordinarily a law creating offenses in the nature of misdemeanors or felonies relates to a subject over which the jurisdiction of the legislature is complete in any event. In the case, however, of the establishment of certain rates without any hearing, the validity of such rates necessarily depends upon whether they are high enough to permit at least some return upon the investment (how much it is not now necessary to state), and an inquiry as to that fact is a proper subject of judicial investigation. If it turns out that the rates are too low for that purpose, then they are illegal. Now, to impose upon a party interested the burden of obtaining a judicial decision of such a question (no prior hearing having ever been given) only upon the condition that, if unsuccessful, he must suffer imprisonment and pay fines, as provided in these acts, is, in effect, to close up all approaches to the courts, and thus prevent any hearing upon the question whether the rates as provided by the acts are not too low, and therefore invalid. The distinction is obvious between a case where the validity of the act depends upon the existence of a fact which can be determined only after investigation of a very complicated and technical character, and the ordinary case of a statute upon a subject requiring no such investigation, and over which the jurisdiction of the legislature is complete in any event.

We hold, therefore, that the provisions of the acts relating to the enforcement of the rates, either for freight or passengers, by imposing such enormous fines and possible imprisonment as a result of an unsuccessful effort to test the validity of the laws themselves, are unconstitutional on their face, without regard to the question of the insufficiency of those rates. We also hold that the circuit court had jurisdiction under the cases already cited (and it was therefore its duty) to inquire whether the rates permitted by these acts or orders were too low and therefore confiscatory, and, if so held, that the court then had jurisdiction to permanently enjoin the railroad company from putting them in force, and that it also had power, while the inquiry was pending, to grant a temporary injunction to the same effect.

The question that arises is whether there is a remedy that the parties interested may resort to, by going into a Federal court of equity, in a case involving a violation of the Federal Constitution, and obtaining a judicial investigation of the problem, and, pending its solution, obtain freedom from suits, civil or criminal, by a temporary injunction, and, if the question be finally decided favorably to the contention of the company, a permanent injunction restraining all such actions or proceedings.

This inquiry necessitates an examination of the most material and important objection made to the jurisdiction of the circuit court, — the objection being that the suit is, in effect, one against the state of Minnesota, and that the injunction issued against the attorney general illegally prohibits state action, either criminal or civil, to enforce obedience to the statutes of the state. This objection is to be considered with reference to the 11th and 14th Amendments to the Federal Constitution. . . .

The case before the circuit court proceeded upon the theory that the orders and acts heretofore mentioned would, if enforced, violate rights of the complainants protected by the latter amendment. We think that whatever the rights of complainants may be, they are largely founded upon that Amendment, but a decision of this case does not require an examination or decision of the question whether its adoption in any way altered or limited the effect of the earlier Amendment. We may assume that each exists in full force, and that we must give to the 11th Amendment all the effect it naturally would have, without cutting it down or rendering its meaning any more narrow than the language, fairly interpreted, would warrant. It applies to a suit brought against a state by one of its own citizens, as well as to a suit brought by a citizen of another state. *Hans v. Louisiana* (1890). It was adopted after the decision of this court in *Chisholm v. Georgia* (1792), where it was held that a state might be sued by a citizen of another state. Since that time there have been many cases decided in this court involving the 11th Amendment, among them being *Osborn v. Bank of United States* (1824), which held that the Amendment applied only to those suits in which the state was a party on the record. In the subsequent case of *Sundry African Slaves v. Madrazo* (1828), that holding was somewhat enlarged, and Chief Justice Marshall, delivering the opinion of the court, while citing *Osborn v. Bank of United States* said that where the claim was made, as in the case then before the court, against the governor of Georgia as governor, and the demand was made upon him, not personally, but officially (for moneys in the treasury of the state and for slaves in possession of the state government), the state might be considered as the party on the record, and therefore the suit could not be maintained.

Davis v. Gray (1872) reiterates the rule of *Osborn v. Bank of United States,* so far as concerns the right to enjoin a state officer from executing a state law in conflict with the Constitution or a statute of the United States, when such execution will violate the rights of the complainant.

In *Poindexter v. Greenhow* (1885), it was adjudged that a suit against a tax collector who had refused coupons in payment of taxes, and, under color of a void law, was about to seize and sell the property of a taxpayer for nonpayment of his taxes, was a suit against him personally, as a wrongdoer, and not against the state.

Hagood v. Southern (1886) decided that the bill was, in substance, a bill for the specific performance of a contract between the complainants and the state of South Carolina; and, although the state was not in name made a party defendant, yet, being the actual party to the alleged contract the performance of which was sought, and the only party by whom it could be performed, the state was, in effect, a party to the suit, and it could not be maintained for that reason. The things required to be done by the actual defendants were the very things which, when done, would constitute a performance of the alleged contract by the state.

The cases upon the subject were reviewed, and it was held in *In re Ayers* (1887) that a bill in equity brought against officers of a state, who, as individuals, have no personal interest in the subject-matter of the suit, and defend only as representing the state, where the relief prayed for, if done, would constitute a performance by the state of the alleged contract of the state, was a suit against the state, following in this respect *Hagood v. Southern.*

A suit of such a nature was simply an attempt to make the state itself, through its officers, perform its alleged contract, by directing those officers to do acts which constituted such performance. The state alone had any interest in the question, and a decree in favor of plaintiff would affect the treasury of the state.

On the other hand, *United States v. Lee* (1882), determined that an individual in possession of real estate under the government of the United States, which claimed to be its owner, was, nevertheless, properly sued by the plaintiff, as owner, to recover possession, and such suit was not one against the United States, although the individual in possession justified such possession under its authority.

In *Pennoyer v. McConnaughy* (1891), a suit against land commissioners of the state was said not to be against the state, although the complainants sought to restrain the defendants, officials of the state, from violating, under an unconstitutional act, the complainants' contract with the state, and thereby working irreparable damage to the property rights of the complainants. *Osborn v. Bank of United States* was cited, and it was stated: "But the general doctrine of *Osborn v. Bank of United States*, that the circuit courts of the United States will restrain a state officer from executing an unconstitutional statute of the state, when to execute it would violate rights and privileges of the complainant which had been guaranteed by the Constitution, and would work irreparable damage and injury to him, has never been departed from." The same principle is decided in *Scott v. Donald* (1897).

The cases above cited do not include one exactly like this under discussion. They serve to illustrate the principles upon which many cases have been decided. We have not cited all the cases, as we have not thought it necessary. But the injunction asked for in the Ayers Case was to restrain the state officers from commencing suits under the act of May 12, 1887 (alleged to be unconstitutional), in the name of the state and brought to *recover taxes for its use*, on the ground that, if such suits were commenced, they would be a breach of a contract with the state. The injunction was declared illegal because the suit itself could not be entertained, as it was one against the state, to enforce its alleged contract. . . .

Whether the commencement of a suit could ever be regarded as an actionable injury to another, equivalent, in some cases, to a trespass such as is set forth in some of the foregoing cases, has received attention of the rate cases, so called. *Reagan v. Farmers' Loan & T. Co.* (1894) (a rate case), was a suit against the members of a railroad commission (created under an act of the state of Texas) and the attorney general, all of whom were held suable, and that such suit was not one against the state. The commission was enjoined from enforcing the rates it had established under the act, and the attorney general was enjoined from instituting suits to recover penalties for failing to conform to the rates fixed by the commission under such act. It is true the statute in that case creating the board provided that suit might be maintained by any dissatisfied railroad company, or other party in interest, in a court of competent jurisdiction in Travis county, Texas, against the commission as defendant. This court held that such language permitted a suit in the United States circuit court for the western district of Texas, which embraced Travis county, but it also held that, irrespective of that consent, the suit was not in effect a suit against the state (although the attorney general was enjoined), and therefore not prohibited under the Amendment.

In *Smyth v. Ames* (1898) (another rate case), it was again held that a suit against individuals, for the purpose of preventing them, as officers of the state, from enforcing, by the commencement of suits or by indictment, an unconstitutional enactment, to the injury of the rights of the plaintiff, was not a suit against a state, within the meaning of the Amendment. In answer to the objection that the suit was really against the state, it was said: "It is the settled doctrine of this court that a suit against individuals, for the purpose of preventing them, as officers of a state, from enforcing an unconstitutional enactment, to the injury of the rights of the plaintiff, is not a suit against the state within the meaning of that Amendment." The suit was to enjoin the enforcement of a statute of Nebraska because it was alleged to be unconstitutional, on account of the rates being too low to afford some compensation to the company, and contrary, therefore, to the 14th Amendment . . .

This decision was reaffirmed in *Prout v. Starr* (1903). The doctrine of *Smyth v. Ames* is also referred to and reiterated in *Gunter v. Atlantic Coast Line R. Co.* (1906).

The various authorities we have referred to furnish ample justification for the assertion that individuals who, as officers of the state, are clothed with some duty in regard to the enforcement of the laws of the state, and who threaten and are about to commence proceedings, either of a civil or criminal nature, to enforce against parties affected an unconstitutional act, violating the Federal Constitution, may be enjoined by a Federal court of equity from such action.

It is also objected that as the statute does not specifically make it the duty of the attorney general (assuming he has that general right) to enforce it, he has, under such circumstances, a full general discretion whether to attempt its enforcement or not, and the court cannot interfere to control him as attorney general in the exercise of his discretion. In our view there is no interference with his discretion under the facts herein. An injunction to prevent him from doing that which he has no legal right to do is not an interference with the discretion of an officer.

It is also argued that the only proceeding which the attorney general could take to enforce the statute, so far as his office is concerned, was one by mandamus, which would be commenced by the state, in its sovereign and governmental character, and that the right to bring such action is a necessary attribute of a sovereign government.

The answer to all this is the same as made in every case where an official claims to be acting under the authority of the state. The act to be enforced is alleged to be unconstitutional; and if it be so, the use of the name of the state to enforce an unconstitutional act to the injury of complainants is a proceeding without the authority of, and one which does not affect, the state in its sovereign or governmental capacity. It is simply an illegal act upon the part of a state official in attempting, by the use of the name of the state, to enforce a legislative enactment which is void because unconstitutional. If the act which the state attorney general seeks to enforce be a violation of the Federal Constitution, the officer, in proceeding under such enactment, comes into conflict with the superior authority of that Constitution, and he is in that case stripped of his official or representative character and is subjected in his person to the consequences of his individual conduct. The state has no power to impart to him any immunity from responsibility to the supreme authority of the United States. *See In re Ayers.* It would be an injury to complainant to harass it with a multiplicity of suits or litigation generally in an endeavor to enforce penalties under an unconstitutional enactment, and to prevent it ought to be within the jurisdiction of a court of equity. If the question of unconstitutionality, with reference, at least, to the Federal Constitution, be first raised in a Federal court, that court, as we think is shown by the authorities cited hereafter, has the right to decide it, to the exclusion of all other courts.

It is further objected (and the objection really forms part of the contention that the state cannot be sued) that a court of equity has no jurisdiction to enjoin criminal proceedings, by indictment or otherwise, under the state law. This, as a general rule, is true. But there are exceptions. When such indictment or proceeding is brought to enforce an alleged unconstitutional statute, which is the subject-matter of inquiry in a suit already pending in a Federal court, the latter court, having first obtained jurisdiction over the subject-matter, has the right, in both civil and criminal cases, to hold and maintain such jurisdiction, to the exclusion of all other courts, until its duty is fully performed. But the Federal court cannot, of course, interfere in a case where the proceedings were already pending in a state court. [A] court of equity is not always precluded from granting an injunction to stay proceedings in criminal cases, and we have no doubt the principle applies in a case such as the present. *In re Sawyer* (1888) is not to the contrary. That case holds that, in general, a court of equity has no jurisdiction of a bill to stay criminal proceedings, but it expressly states an exception, "unless they are instituted by a party to the suit already pending before it, and to try the same right that is in issue there." Various authorities are cited to sustain the exception. The criminal proceedings here that could be commenced by the state authorities would be under the statutes relating to passenger or freight rates, and their validity is the very question involved in the suit in the United States Circuit Court. The right to restrain proceedings by mandamus is based upon the same foundation, and governed by the same principles.

It is proper to add that the right to enjoin an individual, even though a state official, from commencing suits under circumstances already stated does not include the power to restrain a court from acting in any case brought before it, either of a civil or criminal nature, nor does it include power to prevent any investigation or action by a grand jury. The latter body is part of the machinery of a criminal court, and an injunction against a State court would be a violation of the whole scheme of our government. If an injunction against an individual is disobeyed, and he commences proceedings before a grand jury or in a court, such disobedience is personal only, and the court or jury can proceed without incurring any penalty on that account.

It is further objected that there is a plain and adequate remedy at law open to the complainants, and that a court of equity, therefore, has no jurisdiction in such case. It has been suggested that the proper way to test the constitutionality of the act is to disobey it, at least once, after which the company might obey the act pending subsequent proceedings to test its validity. But in the event of a single violation the prosecutor might not avail himself of the opportunity to make the test, as obedience to the law was thereafter continued, and he might think it unnecessary to start an inquiry. If, however, he should do so while the company was thereafter obeying the law, several years might elapse before there was a final determination of the question, and, if it should be determined that the law was invalid, the property of the company would have been taken during that time without due process of law, and there would be no possibility of its recovery.

Another obstacle to making the test on the part of the company might be to find an agent or employee who would disobey the law, with a possible fine and imprisonment staring him in the face if the act should be held valid. Take the passenger-rate act, for instance: A sale of a single ticket above the price mentioned in that act might subject the ticket agent to a charge of felony, and, upon conviction, to a fine of $5,000 and imprisonment for five years. It is true the company might pay the fine, but the imprisonment the agent would have to suffer personally. It would not be wonderful if, under such circumstances, there would not be a crowd of agents offering to disobey the law. The wonder would be that a single agent should be found ready to take the risk.

To await proceedings against the company in a state court, grounded upon a disobedience of the act, and then, if necessary, obtain a review in this court by writ of error to the highest state court, would place the company in peril of large loss and its agents in great risk of fines and imprisonment if it should be finally determined that the act was valid. This risk the company ought not to be required to take. Over eleven thousand millions of dollars, it is estimated, are invested in railroad property, owned by many thousands of people, who are scattered over the whole country, from ocean to ocean, and they are entitled to equal protection from the laws and from the courts, with the owners of all other kinds of property, — no more, no less.

Finally, it is objected that the necessary result of upholding this suit in the circuit court will be to draw to the lower Federal courts a great flood of litigation of this character, where one Federal judge would have it in his power to enjoin proceedings by state officials to enforce the legislative acts of the state, either by criminal or civil actions. To this it may be answered, in the first place, that no injunction ought to be granted unless in a case reasonably free from doubt. We think such rule is, and will be, followed by all the judges of the Federal courts.

And, again, it must be remembered that jurisdiction of this general character has, in fact, been exercised by Federal courts from the time of *Osborn v. Bank of United States* up to the present.

It is somewhat difficult to appreciate the distinction which, while admitting that the taking of a person from the custody of the state by virtue of service of the writ [of habeas corpus] on the state officer in whose custody he is found is not a suit against the state, and yet service of a writ on the attorney general, to prevent his enforcing an unconstitutional enactment of a state legislature, is a suit against the state.

There is nothing in the case before us that ought properly to breed hostility to the customary operation of Federal courts of justice in cases of this character.

The rule to show cause is discharged and the petition for writs of habeas corpus and certiorari is dismissed.

So ordered.

Justice HARLAN, dissenting:

Let it be observed that the suit instituted . . . was, as to the defendant Young, one against him *as, and only because he was,* attorney general of Minnesota. No relief was sought against him individually, but only in his capacity *as* attorney general. And the manifest, indeed the avowed and admitted, object of seeking such relief, was *to tie the hands* of the *state* so that it could not in any manner or by any mode of proceeding, *in its own courts,* test the validity of the statutes and orders in question. It would therefore seem clear that within the true meaning of the 11th Amendment the suit brought in the Federal court was one, in legal effect, against the state, — as much so as if the state had been formally named on the record as a party, — and therefore it was a suit to which, under the Amendment, so far as the state or its attorney general was concerned, the judicial power of the United States did not and could not extend.

When, therefore, the Federal court forbade the defendant Young, as attorney general of Minnesota, from taking any action, suit, step, or proceeding whatever looking to the enforcement of the statutes in question, it said in effect to the state of Minnesota:

> It is true that the powers not delegated to the United States by the Constitution, nor prohibited by it to the states, are reserved to the states respectively or to its people, and it is true that, under the Constitution, the judicial power of the United States does not extend to any suit brought against a state by a citizen of another state or by a citizen or subject of a foreign state, yet the Federal court adjudges that you, the state, although a sovereign for many important governmental purposes, shall not appear in your own courts, by your law officer, with the view of enforcing, or even for determining the validity of, the state enactments which the Federal court has, upon a preliminary hearing, declared to be in violation of the Constitution of the United States.

This principle, if firmly established, would work a radical change in our governmental system. It would inaugurate a new era in the American judicial system and in the relations of the national and state governments. It would enable the subordinate Federal courts to supervise and control the official action of the states as if they were "dependencies" or provinces. It would place the states of the Union in a condition of inferiority never dreamed of when the Constitution was adopted or when the 11th Amendment was made a part of the supreme law of the land. I cannot suppose that the great men who framed the Constitution ever thought the time would come when a subordinate Federal court, having no power to compel a state, in its corporate capacity, to appear before it as a litigant, would yet assume to deprive a state of the right to be represented in its own courts by its regular law officer. Too little consequence has been attached to the fact that the courts of the states are under an obligation equally strong with that resting upon the courts of the Union to respect and enforce the provisions of the Federal Constitution as the supreme law of the land, and to guard rights secured or guaranteed by that instrument. We must assume—a decent respect for the states requires us to assume—that the state courts will enforce every right secured by the Constitution. If they fail to do so, the party complaining has a clear remedy for the protection of his rights; for he can come by writ of error, in an orderly, judicial way, from the highest court of the state to this tribunal for redress in respect of every right granted or secured by that instrument and denied by the state court.

In my opinion the 11th Amendment has not been modified in the slightest degree as to its scope or meaning by the 14th Amendment, and a suit which, in its essence, is one against the state, remains one of that character and is forbidden even when brought to strike down a state statute alleged to be in violation of that clause of the 14th Amendment, forbidding the deprivation by a state of life, liberty, or property without due process of law. The preservation of the dignity and sovereignty of the states, within the limits of their constitutional powers, is of the last importance, and vital to the preservation of our system of government.

It is said that the *Ayers Case* is not applicable here, because the orders made by the Federal circuit court had for their object to compel Virginia to perform its contract with bondholders, which is not this case. But that difference between the *Ayers Case* and this case cannot affect the principle involved. The proceeding against the attorney general of Virginia had for its object to compel, by indirection, the performance of the contract which that commonwealth was alleged to have made with bondholders. The relief sought in [*Ayers* and this] case was to control the state *by controlling the conduct of its law officer, against its will.*

I dissent from the opinion and judgment.

* * *

The core holding of *Ex parte Young*—that officers of a state may be sued for prospective relief in federal court to ensure that they do not violate federal constitutional rights—remains good law today. Indeed, the same principle applies to litigation against federal government officers for prospective relief. *See Am. Sch. of Magnetic Healing v. McAnnulty* (1902).

Notice that the scope of a defendant's duties can affect the scope of the relief. By suing the state attorney general, the plaintiffs in *Ex parte Young* prevent enforcement of the rate regulations *statewide*. This is part of what concerned Justice Harlan— the prospect that, as a practical matter, the state's hands are tied by a single federal court. At the national level, if the appropriate federal official is named, a single suit in federal district court can result in injunctive relief that hamstrings the entire federal government in the implementation of a policy if the officer sued is sufficiently high ranking. These so-called "national" or "universal" injunctions have attracted attention as opponents of a range of federal policies (both liberal and conservative) have turned to federal courts to prevent their implementation. These suits typically do not rest on an *Ex parte Young* exception to sovereign immunity for officer suits in equity because the federal government has broadly consented to suit for injunctive relief through the Administrative Procedures Act as discussed in Chapter 7.

Notably, the universal injunction against federal law

> "did not emerg[e] for the first time in the 1960s," as many critics have claimed. The Court itself issued a universal injunction in 1913, in the months preceding its opinion in *Lewis Publishing Co. v. Morgan*, when it temporarily enjoined a federal statute from being enforced not just against the plaintiffs but also against "other newspaper publishers." In the following decade, the Court issued two other preliminary injunctions that barred a federal law's enforcement beyond the plaintiffs within a single judicial district, and in one of those cases it specified that similarly broad final relief should issue. Moreover, at least as far back as 1916, three-judge courts issued injunctions against the enforcement of laws that reached beyond the plaintiffs in those suits. The laws thereby enjoined were *state* laws, not federal laws, but the injunctions possessed the characteristic that matters most to the Article III debate over injunctive power: those injunctions gave sweeping protection to nonplaintiffs who would otherwise have been vulnerable to the law's enforcement.[5]

---

5. Mila Sohoni, *The Lost History of the "Universal Injunction,"* 133 HARV. L. REV. 920, 924-25 (2020).

Does the "exception" to sovereign immunity in suits seeking injunctive relief against government officers swallow the rule? On the one hand, Justice Harlan is correct that a suit against an officer regarding official acts operates in every practical sense as a restraint upon the state. On the other hand, the rule of law in any society committed to principles of limited government depends on state officers following the law. The officer suit exception helps ensure that officers comply with law. One might say that the doctrine of sovereign immunity is only justifiable in a democratic society when accompanied by this exception. As Chief Justice Marshall explained in *Osborn v. Bank of United States* (1824), if

> the person who is the real principal—the person who is the true source of the mischief, by whose power and for whose advantage it is done—be himself above the law, be exempt from all judicial process, it would be subversive of the best-established principles to say that the laws could not afford the same remedies against the agent employed in doing the wrong which they would afford against him could this principle be joined in the suit.

Osborn v. Bank of United States enjoined the collection of a state tax by officers of the state of Ohio against the Bank of the United States on the ground that the state had no constitutional power to tax the bank. The exception to sovereign immunity recognized by *Ex parte Young* thus "give[s] life to the Supremacy Clause." *Green v. Mansour* (1985) ("Remedies designed to end a continuing violation of federal law are necessary to vindicate the federal interest in assuring the supremacy of that law.").

NOTES ON THE RIGHT OF ACTION

Ex parte Young ensures the supremacy of federal law by permitting litigation against state officers to bring the state into compliance with federal law. Traditionally, as the majority suggests in its first sentence, it was sufficient to establish federal jurisdiction that an *Ex parte Young* suit arises under federal law within the meaning of 28 U.S.C. §1331, and, for purposes of avoiding state sovereign immunity, that the suit laid in equity and named an officer rather than the state. As the modern Court has become more circumspect about "implied rights of action" (see the discussion of *Alexander v. Sandoval* and *Bivens* in Chapters 5 and 7, respectively) it has used the equitable foundation of *Ex parte Young* to limit enforcement suits against officers. As the Court held in *Armstrong v. Exceptional Child Center, Inc.* (2015), "[t]he ability to sue to enjoin unconstitutional actions by state and federal officers is the creation of courts of equity, and reflects a long history of judicial review of illegal executive action, tracing back to England. It is a judge-made remedy, and we have never held or even suggested that, in its application to state officers, it rests upon an implied right of action contained in the Supremacy Clause. . . . [I]t does not." And because an *Ex parte Young* suit lies in equity, the Court insisted, the remedy at law must be inadequate for a cause of action to lie against a state officer. This entails considering the relationship between a suit under *Ex parte Young* for equitable relief and other remedies Congress has provided for the enforcement of federal law. The district court must also inquire into other traditional limits on equity jurisdiction.

Armstrong involved residential service providers who challenged an Idaho agency official's failure to adjust federal Medicaid reimbursement rates for

Medicaid-eligible individuals housed by plaintiffs. The Court, with Justice Scalia writing for a 5-4 majority, found that the statute's remedial scheme "implicitly precludes private enforcement" through an action seeking equitable relief for two reasons. First, "the sole remedy Congress provided for a State's failure to comply with Medicaid's requirements. . . . is the withholding of Medicaid funds by the Secretary of Health and Human Services (HH&S)" and "the express provision of one method of enforcing a substantive rule suggests that Congress intended to preclude others." Second, the broad, "judgment-laden standard" set out in the statute is "judicially unadministrable"—demonstrating Congress' intent to leave decisions to the expertise and discretion of the Secretary of HH&S. Justice Scalia conceded that, given the broad discretion conferred on the Secretary by the statute, it "may be difficult for respondents to prevail on an APA claim unless it stems from an agency's particularly egregious failure to act," but he brushed this concern aside, emphasizing that the lax enforcement regime was selected by Congress and should not be "circumvent[ed]" by the courts.

Armstrong reflects an approach that appears to be ascendant in the Roberts Court. But it conflicts with earlier decisions holding that equitable relief to enjoin state action subject to federal preemption is appropriate even if Congress has not expressly created a cause of action for this purpose. These earlier cases, the dissent emphasized in *Armstrong*, rest on the assumption that "Congress is undoubtedly aware of the federal courts' long-established practice of enjoining preempted state action," so Congress "should generally be presumed to contemplate such enforcement unless it affirmatively manifests a contrary intent." Justice Sotomayor, joined by Justices Kennedy, Ginsburg, and Kagan, emphasized that the Court has

> long entertained suits in which a party seeks prospective equitable protection from an injurious and preempted state law without regard to whether the federal statute at issue itself provided a right to bring an action. *See, e.g., Foster v. Love* (1997) (state election law that permitted the winner of a state primary to be deemed the winner of election to Congress held preempted by federal statute setting date of congressional elections); *Shaw v. Delta Air Lines, Inc.* (1983) (state law preempted in part by the federal Employee Retirement Income Security Act of 1974); *Railroad Transfer Service, Inc. v. Chicago* (1967) (city ordinance imposing licensing requirements on motor carrier transporting railroad passengers held preempted by federal Interstate Commerce Act); *Campbell v. Hussey* (1961) (state law requiring labeling of certain strains of tobacco held preempted by the federal Tobacco Inspection Act); *Railway Co. v. McShane* (1875) (state taxation of land possessed by railroad company held invalid under federal Act of July 2, 1864). Indeed, for this reason, we have characterized "the availability of prospective relief of the sort awarded in *Ex parte Young* " as giving "life to the Supremacy Clause." *Green v. Mansour* (1985).

In these cases, the Court was explicit that district courts have jurisdiction to grant equitable relief on preemption grounds under 28 U.S.C. §1331.

NOTES ON THE LEGAL RIGHT VIOLATED

Ex parte Young asserts a violation of federal constitutional law. The Court has also upheld suits for injunctive relief against state officers for violations of federal statutory law and associated federal regulations. *Verizon Md. Inc. v. Pub. Servs. Comm'n* (2002) (suit by Verizon against state public utility commissioners challenging their award of compensation to phone service provider under regulatory system established by federal Telecommunications Act and an FCC ruling). What a plaintiff cannot do is sue state officers for violation of state law. In *Pennhurst State Sch. v. Halderman* (1984), a resident of a state school established to care for people with severe mental disabilities challenged conditions at the facility under the federal Eighth and Fourteenth Amendments, federal statutes, and the Pennsylvania Mental Health and Mental Retardation Act of 1966. At trial, the district court found evidence of physical abuse by staff, drugging by staff and "deterioration in physical, intellectual and emotional skills of some residents," in violation of federal and state law. It ordered a range of reforms. After an initial appeal in which the Supreme Court reversed the judgment insofar as it rested on one specific federal statute, the Third Circuit reaffirmed the reforms in the district court's original injunction on the ground that the Pennsylvania statute standing alone "fully supported its prior judgment."

The Supreme Court reversed. Writing for a 5-4 majority, Justice Powell, emphasized that:

> *Ex parte Young* was the culmination of efforts by this Court to harmonize the principles of the Eleventh Amendment with the effective supremacy of rights and powers secured elsewhere in the Constitution. . . . This need to reconcile competing interests is wholly absent, however, when a plaintiff alleges that a state official has violated state law. In such a case, the entire basis for the doctrine of *Young* . . . disappears. A federal court's grant of relief against state officials on the basis of state law, whether prospective of retroactive, does not vindicate the supreme authority of federal law. On the contrary, it is difficult to think of a greater intrusion on state sovereignty. Such a result conflicts directly with the principles of federalism that underlie the Eleventh Amendment.

The Court remanded for reconsideration of whether the remedies ordered by the district court could stand under federal constitutional law.

In dissent, Justice Stevens, joined by Justices Brennan, Marshall, and Blackmun argued that the majority had misread *Ex parte Young*. While the case supports federal supremacy, the "foundation of the rule of *Young*" is that "unlawful acts of an officer should not be attributed to the sovereign," a principle "that has deep roots in the history of sovereign immunity. . . . This rule plainly applies to conduct of state officers in violation of state law. . . . [P]etitioners were acting *ultra vires* because they were acting in a way that the sovereign, by statute, had forbidden." Justice Stevens also objected to the majority's disregard for the rule of constitutional avoidance — the state law ground of decision, which the state can correct by legislation, disposes of the case without reaching constitutional questions that can only be corrected through amendment. In a separate dissent, Justice Brennan again insisted that the Eleventh Amendment has no application where plaintiffs are citizens of the state they sue.

After *Pennhurst,* plaintiffs with both state and federal claims against state officers are put to difficult choices since there can be no federal court jurisdiction over any state law claims. Can you see what they are? One option is to file both state and federal claims in state court. What are the relative costs and benefits of doing so? Alternatively, the plaintiff can split the causes of action, but claim and issue preclusion doctrines can affect this choice.

Why isn't the doctrine of abstention, which rests on federalism principles just like the Eleventh Amendment, adequate to protect the interests of the state and its officers when suit is brought in federal court?

NOTES ON THE IDENTITY OF THE DEFENDANT

The majority in *Ex parte Young* reconciled officer equity suits with principles of state sovereign immunity by insisting that an individual officer who acts in violation of federal law is "stripped of his official or representative character and is subjected in his person to the consequences of his individual conduct. The state has no power to impart to him any immunity from responsibility to the supreme authority of the United States." In *Poindexter v. Greenhow* (1885), cited by the majority, the Court similarly held that a state officer who acts unconstitutionally in collecting a tax, "had no authority of law thereafter to attempt to enforce other payment by seizing [plaintiff's property]. In so doing he ceased to be an officer of the law and became a private wrongdoer." *See also Osborn v. Bank of United States* (1824) ("It may, we think, be laid down as a general rule which admits of no exception, that, in all cases where jurisdiction depends on the party, it is the party named in the record. Consequently, the 11th Amendment, which restrains the jurisdiction granted by the Constitution over suits against States, is, of necessity, limited to those suits in which a State is a party on the record.").

The rule that the officer must be named, rather than the state itself or the state agency for whom the officer works, remains an essential feature of the exception to sovereign immunity. *See Verizon Md. Inc. v. Pub. Servs. Comm'n* (2002) (holding unanimously that Eleventh Amendment does not bar suit for declaratory and injunctive relief against individual state agency commissioners for ordering plaintiff to pay compensation to a competitor under federal Telecommunications Act and associated federal regulations, noting that "*Ex parte Young* itself was a suit against state officials including state utility commissioners, though only the state attorney general appealed"; commission itself was a state agency and could not be sued); *P.R. Aqueduct and Sewer Auth. v. Metcalf & Eddy, Inc.* (1993) (noting that *Ex parte Young* "has no application in suits against the States and their agencies, which are barred regardless of the relief sought"); *Alabama v. Pugh* (1978) (reversing injunction granted against State of Alabama, Alabama Board of Corrections, and various prison officials on ground that "suit against the State and its Board of Corrections is barred by the Eleventh Amendment"; remanding for dismissal of these two parties).

Justice Harlan insisted that the state should be immune for official acts even when its officers are named and that this would not undermine the supremacy of federal law. The supremacy of federal law is ensured, in his view, not by officer suits in federal court, but rather by Supreme Court review of state enforcement decisions when and as they are brought in the state courts. *See also Cohens v. Virginia* (1821) (rejecting Virginia's claim that appeal to Supreme Court by state criminal defendants, convicted of violations of Virginia law regarding sale of lottery tickets, was without Virginia's consent and thus barred by Eleventh Amendment; reasoning that defendants were citizens of the state of Virginia and that a defensive appeal is not barred by state sovereign immunity). What are the costs and benefits of relying on the Supreme Court's appellate jurisdiction to ensure state compliance with federal law?

A case study in the limitations of relying on the Court's appellate jurisdiction is *Whole Woman's Health v. Jackson* (2021), where the Court considered a challenge to an unusual anti-abortion statute passed by the state of Texas, Texas Senate Bill 8 (2021). The statute, enacted before *Dobbs v. Jackson Women's Health Org.* (2022) struck down *Roe v. Wade* (1973), prohibits physicians from performing or inducing an abortion if the physician detects a fetal heartbeat. The statute plainly violated *Roe* by penalizing first trimester abortions. However, by creating private rights of action against physicians, rather than criminal or civil enforcement by executive branch officers of the state of Texas, the statute was designed to avoid suspension in federal court under *Ex parte Young.* The rights of women in Texas who already had plans to terminate their pregnancies or would need to before *Dobbs* were thus directly infringed.

Abortion providers sued a range of state officials in federal court. Defendants included a state court judge, a state court clerk, the Texas attorney general, the executive directors of the state medical board, the state nursing board, the state board of pharmacy, and the state health and human services commission. On appeal from the lower federal courts, a unanimous Court held that state sovereign immunity precluded suit against the state judge and a 5-4 majority reached the same conclusion regarding the state court clerk. *Ex parte Young* itself emphasized that a suit seeking "an injunction against a state court" or "its machinery . . . would be a violation of the whole scheme of our Government." The proper recourse for a state court's violation of constitutional law, the Court held, is certiorari to the Supreme Court for review of private enforcement suits filed against Texas doctors in state court. The Court also noted that there was already litigation challenging the statute pending in state court. The Court added that state courts and clerks are not proper "adverse litigants" under Article III for purposes of standing.

As to the remaining defendants, a 5-4 majority of the Court held that the state attorney general has no enforcement authority against physicians, only against the state medical board, and there was no rule of the medical board subject to that enforcement authority. But eight Justices of the Court voted to uphold the right of plaintiffs to bring officer suits for injunctive relief against the other executive branch officials because the relevant state agencies they lead have enforcement authority over doctors practicing in the state who perform abortions in violation of S.B. 8's fetal heartbeat rule.

Against the charge of the dissent that the Court was "shrinking from the task of the defending the supremacy of the Federal Constitution over state law" by leaving the fate of *Roe* to state judges and the Court's later review on certiorari, Justice Gorsuch, writing for the majority, emphasized that, *Ex parte Young* notwithstanding,

> [the] Court has never recognized an unqualified right to pre-enforcement review of constitutional claims in federal court. In fact, general federal

question jurisdiction did not even exist for much of the nation's history. And pre-enforcement review under the statutory scheme the petitioners invoke, was not prominent until the mid-20th century. To this day, many federal constitutional rights are as a practical matter asserted typically as defenses to state-law claims, not in federal pre-enforcement claims like this one.

How might the nature of the constitutional right violated by S.B. 8 and the irreversible consequences of bringing a pregnancy to term bear on the petitioners' interest in *pre-enforcement* equitable relief to protect the rights of the women they serve? Should the nature of the substantive constitutional right be relevant to the remedy and federal jurisdiction? Research conducted prior to *Dobbs* shows that the rate of abortions fell by only 10 percent as a result of S.B. 8, because women who could afford to do so obtained abortions in nearby states or obtained abortion pills online, rather than undergo a procedure supervised by a Texas physician. An average of 1,400 women every month traveled out of state to obtain abortions and an average of 1,100 ordered pills online each month from Aid Access, an international organization that provides abortion pills outside the U.S. legal and regulatory framework through doctors located in Europe and India. The study found that those "who were unable to get abortions are most likely to be poor" because of the costs of travel. Post-*Dobbs* those costs will increase in states like Texas where many surrounding states have adopted or expanded abortion bans. "Research on past abortion laws has shown that longer distances tend to reduce abortions, as the challenges of travel mount," the resources of support groups dwindle in the face of increased demands, and clinics in remaining states that permit abortion struggle to keep up.[6] Delays in obtaining abortion also increase health risks to women who seek them later in their pregnancies. All of these effects are compounded for women of color who, in the state of Texas were 74 percent of women who received legal abortions in 2020.[7]

NOTES ON THE REMEDY REQUESTED

The remedy sought in *Ex parte Young* is as central to the officer suit exception as the naming of an officer as the party defendant. The majority was careful to distinguish cases in which *prospective* relief, such as an injunction, is granted to bring the state into compliance by preventing state officers from acting in violation of federal law (*Osborn, Davis, Poindexter,* and *McConnaughy*), from cases in which *retrospective* monetary relief is sought against the state treasury (most prominently *Madrazo*). *Osborn* clearly demonstrates the former principle. The Supreme Court upheld a lower court injunction barring state officials from collecting an unconstitutional state tax against the Bank of the United States.

---

6. Margot Sanger-Katz, Claire Cain Miller, & Quoctrung Bui, *Most Women Denied Abortions by Texas Law Got Them Another Way*, N.Y. TIMES, March 6, 2022.

7. *Reported Legal Abortions by Race of Women Who Obtained Abortion by the State of Occurrence*, KFF, https://www.kff.org/womens-health-policy/state-indicator/abortions-by-race/?currentTimeframe=0&sortModel=%7B%22colId%22:%22Location%22,%22sort%22:%22asc%22%7D.

Declaratory relief is also generally allowed in an *Ex parte Young* action as long as it is tied to ensuring future compliance with law and will not, by virtue of res judicata, definitively establish a right to money damages against the state for past liabilities. *Compare Verizon Md.* (even though it "seeks a declaration of the past, as well as the future, ineffectiveness of the Commission's action, so that the past financial liability of private parties may be affected . . . no past liability of the State, or of any of its commissioners, is at issue. . . . Insofar as the exposure of the State is concerned, the prayer for declaratory relief adds nothing to the prayer for injunction."), *with Green v. Mansour* (1985) (where there is "no claimed continuing violation of federal law" on methods of determining eligibility for Aid to Families With Dependent Children "the award of a declaratory judgment in this situation would be useful in resolving the dispute over the past lawfulness of respondent's action only if it might be offered in state-court proceedings as res judicata on the issue of liability, leaving to the state courts only a form of accounting proceeding whereby damages or restitution would be computed;" concluding that suit for declaratory relief is prohibited by the Eleventh Amendment under these circumstances).

With respect to claims for retrospective monetary relief, Eleventh Amendment dismissals were exceedingly rare before *Hans*. Indeed, *Madrazo* is the "only Supreme Court opinion prior to the Civil War that actually dismissed a suit on eleventh amendment grounds."[8] As in many areas of antebellum federalism doctrine, in *Madrazo*, state interests collided with federal court jurisdiction on the question of slavery. The *Madrazo* case involved the illegal importation of enslaved persons. As you read the facts of the case below, note the terms on which the lower federal courts and then the Supreme Court are drawn into the dispute about ending the slave trade. The enforcement regime Congress erects and its intersection with existing remedies are of central importance.

We begin with the enforcement regime. Article I, Section 9, of the Constitution protected the slave trade until 1808. As that date approached, Congress prohibited the importation of enslaved Black people ("any negro, mulatto, or person of colour [brought into the United States] as a slave") by eliminating any property right of importers and those taking title through importers. The statute imposed large fines ($10,000) and jail terms up to ten years for participating in the trade. Those who purchased illegally imported enslaved persons not only would lose title but faced an $800 fine for each enslaved person purchased.

Initially, Congress did not provide adequate funding for federal enforcement of these provisions. President Jefferson was also "deeply hostile to the presence of free blacks in the United States" and therefore had "no interest in freeing Africans who were illegally imported into the nation" nor in "spending any money on returning [them] to their homeland[s]."[9] More than a decade later, between 1818 and 1820, Congress strengthened both the penalties for importation and the incentives for interdiction of slave ships as northern anti-slavery sentiment increased, making participation on the high seas punishable by death and creating bounties for informing on complicit captains and crews. Importation thus fell from 40,000

---

8. John J. Gibbons, *The Eleventh Amendment and State Sovereign Immunity: A Reinterpretation*, 83 COLUM. L. REV. 1889 (1983).

9. Paul Finkelman, *The American Suppression of the African Slave Trade*, 42 AKRON L. REV. 431 (2009).

enslaved people between 1800 and 1807 to 10,000 between 1808 and 1820, to fewer than 2,500 after 1820 as the "internal slave trade" replaced importation.[10]

With respect to the disposition of enslaved Black people seized from importers, the central issue in *Madrazo*, the 1807 statute relied on cooperative federalism, expressly delegating regulatory authority to the states in which they were seized. It provided that illegally imported enslaved Black people would be subject to "any regulation" by the states. As a practical matter, this meant that notwithstanding federal abolition of the slave trade, illegally imported enslaved Black people "would become slaves in some southern state."[11] Thus, for those who were confiscated under the federal statute, prohibition of the Atlantic slave trade did not end their enslavement. And even as federal enforcement gradually suppressed the overall Atlantic slave trade in the early 1800s, the structure of the statute made any continued importation profitable for slave states.

In 1816 a ship belonging to Juan Madrazo, a Spanish slave trader, was caught by an American privateer off the Atlantic coast. The Africans he held were seized and sold in a pirate prize court on a Spanish island off the coast of Florida to an American named Bowen. When Bowen attempted to import 95 of the Africans to Georgia through lands held by the Creek Nation, they were seized again, this time by a U.S. Customs officer who delivered them to the governor without any legal proceedings. Acting pursuant to the authority conferred by the federal anti-slave trade statute Georgia's legislature empowered the governor either to deliver confiscated persons to the recently founded American Colonization Society to promote resettling free Blacks in Africa, or to sell them on the open market. Georgia then advertised the seized Africans for sale. It sold some of them and deposited the proceeds in the state treasury, and the governor arrested further sales when the American Colonization society expressed interest in returning the remainder to Africa.

Two federal suits were subsequently filed, one by the governor, seeking a declaration that the enslaved persons were forfeited by Bowen under the federal statute, and therefore legitimately sold by the state and/or delivered to the American Colonization Society. In the second, Madrazo brought an action in admiralty contested by both the governor and Bowen. The district court heard the cases together and ruled in favor of the governor against both Bowen and Madrazo. The circuit court upheld the dismissal of Bowen's claims but reversed as to Madrazo, holding that the remaining enslaved persons and proceeds of the sale of all others should be restored to him.

Before we turn to the Supreme Court's disposition of the cases, it is worth taking note of the party structure, jurisdictional grounds, and the stakes. One case rested on a federal question (whether the federal statute banning importation applied to the enslaved persons Bowen attempted to bring into Georgia) with a party structure of a state government plaintiff (the governor on behalf of the state of Georgia) aligned against a citizen of the state of Georgia (Bowen). The other rested on the admiralty jurisdiction of the federal courts and was brought by a foreign plaintiff (Madrazo) against a state government (Georgia) and a citizen of the state of Georgia (Bowen). Notice too that any remedy for either Bowen or Madrazo would run directly against the state of Georgia because the proceeds of the sale of

---

10. *Id.* at 462.

11. *Id.*

the enslaved persons were held by the state treasury and the enslaved persons who had not been sold were in the possession of the state.

In terms of the stakes, by the late 1820s pro-slavery sentiment had surged. The state had settled the dispute with Bowen by agreeing to turn both the remaining enslaved persons and the proceeds of the sale of the others to him in open defiance of the federal statute depriving him of title as an importer. The state now saw the American Colonization Society "as a cloak for abolitionism" and refused to pursue its interests.[12] Thus, on appeal to the Supreme Court, the state for the first time raised the Eleventh Amendment as a ground to reverse the circuit court's judgment in favor of Madrazo. Indeed, there was every indication that if the state lost, it would resist enforcement of the judgment. Chief Justice Marshall held that neither the state nor Bowen, from whom the state received the enslaved persons, had good title given the prohibitions of the 1807 Act. Reversing the circuit court, however, the Court held that Madrazo's admiralty claim should also be dismissed because there was no statutory jurisdiction in admiralty without the lower courts formally taking custody of the enslaved persons. For the moment, this avoided both the Eleventh Amendment objection of the state and the possibility that the state would refuse to comply with a federal court order requiring it to make Madrazo whole.

Hoping to avoid the jurisdictional flaw in his first suit, Madrazo refiled—this time an original suit in the Supreme Court under Section 13 of the Judiciary Act authorizing original jurisdiction for litigation between a foreigner and a state. The remedies he requested included the proceeds of the sale of the enslaved persons, return of those not sold, and "just and reasonable compensation" for the taking of his property by the state. The Court again dismissed, this time relying squarely on the Eleventh Amendment. The case, the Court tersely concluded, is "not a case where the property is in custody of a court of admiralty [and] is not, therefore, for the exercise of that jurisdiction. It is a mere personal suit against a state, to recover proceeds in its possession, and in such a case, no private person has a right to commence an original suit in this court against a state." *Ex parte Madrazo* (1833).

In 1837, Madrazo lost a petition to the Committee of Claims of the House of Representatives for compensation. 24th Congress, 1st Session, Rept. No. 629, May 6, 1836; 24th Cong., 2d Session, Rept. No. 250, Feb. 22, 1837 ("The United States had an undoubted right to prohibit the slave trade, and to pass such laws as would most effectively accomplish that object. . . . Wherever the slaves were landed in the United States, the owner's right ceased; he cannot, therefore, take any exception to the proceedings of Georgia, nor of the United States.").

NOTES ON EXPENDITURES ANCILLARY TO PROSPECTIVE RELIEF

Taken together, *Madrazo* and *Ex parte Young* reveal opposite ends of the spectrum of permissible relief under the Eleventh Amendment. On the one hand, retrospective relief requiring monetary payment from the state treasury is unavailable against a state as the Court held in *Madrazo*. On the other hand, forward looking relief against a state officer designed to ensure a state's compliance with federal law is available under *Ex parte Young*.

The line between these two forms of relief is of course not always crystal clear. Recall that Madrazo sought the return of any Africans seized from his ship which

---

12. Gibbons, *supra* note 8.

the state of Georgia had not already sold. This tracks the common law cause of action in forcing the return of goods (retrospective compensation for the wrongful seizure of the goods and the money value of the goods are available only if the goods are not returned). So, the fact that a remedy is styled as a common law remedy does not necessarily mean it entails retrospective monetary relief against the state.

On the other hand, the fact that a party seeks equitable relief does not mean that it will be costless to the state. Consider specific performance. It forces a party to comply with a contract and is therefore prospective, but where the withheld performance is payment on a contract, the effect is to force payment. Thus, in its decision in *Ex parte Young*, the Court took care to distinguish both *Hagood v. Southern* (1886) (upholding Eleventh Amendment immunity where a claimant seeks specific performance of a contract with the state to redeem treasury certificates; according to the relief granted by the lower federal court the state officer defendants "'must use the public money in the treasury and under their official control in one way, when [state] law has directed them to use it in another,'" intruding upon a function that "belongs to the state in its political capacity"), and *In re Ayers* (1887) ("For a breach of its contract by the state it is conceded there is no remedy by suit against the state itself. . . . This immunity includes not only direct actions for damages for the breach of the contract brough against the state by name, but all other actions and suits against it, whether at law or in equity. A bill in equity for the specific performance of the contract against the state by name . . . could not be brought [and the] converse of that proposition must equally be true . . . a bill the object of which is by injunction indirectly to compel the specific performance of the contract by forbidding all those acts and doings which constitute breaches of contract must also necessarily be a suit against the state.").

In the following case, the Court considered whether the Eleventh Amendment barred a cause of action for equitable restitution that would require the state to disgorge welfare benefits withheld in violation of federal law.

Edelman v. Jordan

415 U.S. 651 (1974)

Mr. Chief Justice REHNQUIST delivered the opinion of the Court.

Respondent John Jordan filed a complaint in the United States District Court for the Northern District of Illinois, individually and as a representative of a class, seeking declaratory and injunctive relief against two former directors of the Illinois Department of Public Aid, the director of the Cook County Department of Public Aid, and the comptroller of Cook County. Respondent alleged that these state officials were administering the federal-state programs of Aid to the Aged, Blind, or Disabled (AABD) in a manner inconsistent with various federal regulations and with the Fourteenth Amendment to the Constitution.

AABD is one of the categorical aid programs administered by the Illinois Department of Public Aid pursuant to the Illinois Public Aid Code, c. 23, §§3-1 through 3-12 (1973). Under the Social Security Act, the program is funded by the State and the Federal Governments. 42 U.S.C. §§1381-1385.2. The Department of Health, Education, and Welfare (HEW), which administers these payments for the Federal Government, issued regulations prescribing maximum permissible time standards within which States participating in the program had to process AABD applications. Those regulations, originally issued in 1968, required, at the time of the institution of this suit, that eligibility determinations must be made by the States within 30 days of receipt of applications for aid to the aged and blind, and within 45 days of receipt of applications for aid to the disabled. For those persons found eligible, the assistance check was required to be received by them within the applicable time period. 45 CFR §206.10(a)(3).

Respondent's complaint charged that the Illinois defendants, operating under [Illinois Assistance Manual] regulations, were improperly authorizing grants to commence only with the month in which an application was approved and not including prior eligibility months for which an applicant was entitled to aid under federal law. The complaint also alleged that the Illinois defendants were not processing the applications within the applicable time requirements of the federal regulations; specifically, respondent alleged that his own application for disability benefits was not acted on by the Illinois Department of Public Aid for almost four months. Such actions of the Illinois officials were alleged to violate federal law and deny the equal protection of the laws. Respondent's prayer requested declaratory and injunctive relief, and specifically requested "a permanent injunction enjoining the defendants to award to the entire class of plaintiffs all AABD benefits wrongfully withheld."

In its judgment of March 15, 1972, the District Court declared §4004 of the Illinois Manual to be invalid insofar as it was inconsistent with the federal regulations found in 45 CFR §206.10(a)(3), and granted a permanent injunction requiring compliance with the federal time limits for processing and paying AABD applicants. The District Court, in paragraph 5 of its judgment, also ordered the state officials to "release and remit AABD benefits wrongfully withheld to all applicants for AABD in the State of Illinois who applied between July 1, 1968 (the date of the federal regulations) and April 16, 1971 (the date of the preliminary injunction issued by the District Court) and were determined eligible. . . ."

On appeal to the United States Court of Appeals for the Seventh Circuit, the Illinois officials contended, *inter alia*, that the Eleventh Amendment barred the award of retroactive benefits, that the judgment of inconsistency between the federal regulations and the provisions of the Illinois Categorical Assistance Manual could be given prospective effect only, and that the federal regulations in question were inconsistent with the Social Security Act itself. The Court of Appeals rejected these contentions and affirmed the judgment of the District Court.

Because of an apparent conflict on the Eleventh Amendment issue with the decision of the Court of Appeals for the Second Circuit we granted the petition for certiorari filed by petitioner Joel Edelman, who is the present Director of the Illinois Department of Public Aid.

While the Amendment by its terms does not bar suits against a State by its own citizens, this Court has consistently held that an unconsenting State is immune from suits brought in federal courts by her own citizens as well as by citizens of another State. *Hans v. Louisiana* (1890). It is also well established that even though a State is not named a party to the action, the suit may nonetheless be barred by the Eleventh Amendment. In *Ford Motor Co. v. Dep't of Treasury* (1945), the Court said:

> (W)hen the action is in essence one for the recovery of money from the state, the state is the real, substantial party in interest and is entitled to invoke its sovereign immunity from suit even though individual officials are nominal defendants.

Thus the rule has evolved that a suit by private parties seeking to impose a liability which must be paid from public funds in the state treasury is barred by the Eleventh Amendment.

The Court of Appeals held that the above-cited cases, when read in light of this Court's landmark decision in *Ex parte Young* (1908), do not preclude the grant of such a monetary award in the nature of equitable restitution.

Ex parte Young was a watershed case in which this Court held that the Eleventh Amendment did not bar an action in the federal courts seeking to enjoin the Attorney General of Minnesota from enforcing a statute claimed to violate the Fourteenth Amendment of the United States Constitution. This holding has permitted the Civil War Amendments to the Constitution to serve as a sword, rather than merely as a shield, for those whom they were designed to protect. But the relief awarded in *Ex parte Young* was prospective only; the Attorney General of Minnesota was enjoined to conform his future conduct of that office to the requirement of the Fourteenth Amendment. Such relief is analogous to that awarded by the District Court in the prospective portion of its order under review in this case.

But the retroactive position of the District Court's order here, which requires the payment of a very substantial amount of money which that court held should have been paid, but was not, stands on quite a different footing.

These funds will obviously not be paid out of the pocket of petitioner Edelman. The funds to satisfy the award in this case must inevitably come from the general revenues of the State of Illinois, and thus the award resembles far more closely the monetary award against the State itself than it does the prospective injunctive relief awarded in *Ex parte Young*.

The Court of Appeals, in upholding the award in this case, held that it was permissible because it was in the form of 'equitable restitution' instead of damages, and therefore capable of being tailored in such a way as to minimize disruptions of the state program of categorical assistance. But we must judge the award actually made in this case, and not one which might have been differently tailored in a different case, and we must judge it in the context of the important constitutional principle embodied in the Eleventh Amendment.[11]

---

11. It may be true, as stated by our Brother Douglas in dissent, that "(m)ost welfare decisions by federal courts have a financial impact on the States." But we cannot agree that such a financial impact is the same where a federal court applies *Ex parte Young* to grant prospective declaratory and injunctive relief, as opposed to an order of retroactive payments as was made in the instant case. It is not necessarily true that "(w)hether the decree is prospective only or requires payments for the weeks or months wrongfully skipped over by the state officials, the nature of the impact on the state treasury is precisely the same." This argument neglects the fact that where the State has a definable allocation to be used in the payment of public aid benefits, and pursues a certain course of action such as the processing of applications within certain time periods as did Illinois here, the subsequent ordering by a federal court of retroactive payments to correct delays in such processing will invariably mean there is less money available for payments for the continuing obligations of the public aid system.

As stated by Judge McGowan in *Rothstein v. Wyman* (2d Cir. 1972):

> The second federal policy which might arguably be furthered by retroactive payments is the fundamental goal of congressional welfare legislation — the satisfaction of the ascertained needs of impoverished persons. Federal standards are designed to ensure that those needs are equitably met; and there may perhaps be cases in which the prompt payment of funds wrongfully withheld will serve that end. As time goes by, however, retroactive payments become compensatory rather than remedial; the coincidence between previously ascertained and existing needs becomes less clear.

We do not read *Ex parte Young* or subsequent holdings of this Court to indicate that any form of relief may be awarded against a state officer, no matter how closely it may in practice resemble a money judgment payable out of the state treasury, so long as the relief may be labeled "equitable" in nature. The Court's opinion in *Ex parte Young* hewed to no such line. Its citation of *Hagood v. Southern* (1886), and *In re Ayers* (1887), which were both actions against state officers for specific performance of a contract to which the State was a party, demonstrate that equitable relief may be barred by the Eleventh Amendment.

As in most areas of the law, the difference between the type of relief barred by the Eleventh Amendment and that permitted under *Ex parte Young* will not in many instances be that between day and night. The injunction issued in *Ex parte Young* was not totally without effect on the State's revenues, since the state law which the Attorney General was enjoined from enforcing provided substantial monetary penalties against railroads which did not conform to its provisions. Later cases from this Court have authorized equitable relief which has probably had greater impact on state treasuries than did that awarded in *Ex parte Young*. In *Graham v. Richardson* (1971), Arizona and Pennsylvania welfare officials were prohibited from denying welfare benefits to otherwise qualified recipients who were aliens. In *Goldberg v. Kelly* (1970), New York City welfare officials were enjoined from following New York State procedures which authorized the termination of benefits paid to welfare recipients without prior hearing.[12] But the fiscal consequences to state treasuries in these cases were the necessary result of compliance with decrees which by their terms were prospective in nature. State officials, in order to shape their official conduct to the mandate of the Court's decrees, would more likely have to spend money from the state treasury than if they had been left free to pursue their previous course of conduct. Such an ancillary effect on the state treasury is a permissible and often an inevitable consequence of the principle announced in *Ex parte Young*.

But that portion of the District Court's decree which petitioner challenges on Eleventh Amendment grounds goes much further than any of the cases cited. It requires payment of state funds, not as a necessary consequence of compliance in the future with a substantive federal-question determination, but as a form of compensation to those whose applications were processed on the slower time schedule at a time when petitioner was under no court-imposed obligation to conform to a different standard. While the Court of Appeals described this retroactive award of monetary relief as a form of "equitable restitution," it is in practical effect indistinguishable in many aspects from an award of damages against the State. It will to a

---

12. The Court of Appeals considered the Court's decision in *Griffin v. School Board* (1964), to be of like import. But as may be seen from *Griffin*'s citation of *Lincoln County v. Luning* (1890), a county does not occupy the same position as a State for purposes of the Eleventh Amendment. The fact that the county policies executed by the county officials in *Griffin* were subject to the commands of the Fourteenth Amendment, but the county was not able to invoke the protection of the Eleventh Amendment, is no more than a recognition of the long-established rule that while county action is generally state action for purposes of the Fourteenth Amendment, a county defendant is not necessarily a state defendant for purposes of the Eleventh Amendment.

virtual certainty be paid from state funds, and not from the pockets of the individual state officials who were the defendants in the action. It is measured in terms of a monetary loss resulting from a past breach of a legal duty on the part of the defendant state officials.

Were we to uphold this portion of the District Court's decree, we would be obligated to overrule the Court's holding in *Ford Motor Co. v. Department of Treasury.* There a taxpayer, who had, under protest, paid taxes to the State of Indiana, sought a refund of those taxes from the Indiana state officials who were charged with their collection. The taxpayer claimed that the tax had been imposed in violation of the United States Constitution. The term 'equitable restitution' would seem even more applicable to the relief sought in that case, since the taxpayer had at one time had the money, and paid it over to the State pursuant to an allegedly unconstitutional tax exaction. Yet this Court had no hesitation in holding that the taxpayer's action was a suit against the State, and barred by the Eleventh Amendment. We reach a similar conclusion with respect to the retroactive portion of the relief awarded by the District Court in this case.

The Court of Appeals held in the alternative that even if the Eleventh Amendment be deemed a bar to the retroactive relief awarded respondent in this case, the State of Illinois had waived its Eleventh Amendment immunity and consented to the bringing of such a suit by participating in the federal AABD program. But in this case the threshold fact of congressional authorization to sue a class of defendants which literally includes States is wholly absent.

The Court of Appeals held that as a matter of federal law Illinois had "constructively consented" to this suit by participating in the federal AABD program and agreeing to administer federal and state funds in compliance with federal law. Constructive consent is not a doctrine commonly associated with the surrender of constitutional rights, and we see no place for it here. In deciding whether a State has waived its constitutional protection under the Eleventh Amendment, we will find waiver only where stated "by the most express language or by such overwhelming implications from the text as (will) leave no room for any other reasonable construction." *Murray v. Wilson Distilling Co.* (1909). We see no reason to retreat from the Court's statement in *Great Northern Life Insurance Co. v. Read* (1944):

> (W)hen we are dealing with the sovereign exemption from judicial interference in the vital field of financial administration a clear declaration of the state's intention to submit its fiscal problems to other courts than those of its own creation must be found.

The mere fact that a State participates in a program through which the Federal Government provides assistance for the operation by the State of a system of public aid is not sufficient to establish consent on the part of the State to be sued in the federal courts. . . .

Our Brother Marshall argues in dissent, and the Court of Appeals held, that although the Social Security Act itself does not create a private cause of action, the cause of action created by 42 U.S.C. §1983, coupled with the enactment of the AABD program, and the issuance by HEW or regulations which require the States to make corrective payments after successful "fair hearings" and provide for federal matching funds to satisfy federal court orders of retroactive payments, indicate that Congress intended a cause of action for public aid recipients such as respondent. Though a §1983 action may be instituted by public aid recipients such as respondent, a federal court's remedial power, consistent with the Eleventh Amendment, is necessarily limited to prospective injunctive relief, *Ex parte Young*, and may not include a retroactive award which requires the payment of funds from the state treasury.

For the foregoing reasons we decide that the Court of Appeals was wrong in holding that the Eleventh Amendment did not constitute a bar to that portion of the District Court decree which ordered retroactive payment of benefits found to have been wrongfully withheld. The judgment of the Court of Appeals is therefore reversed and the cause remanded for further proceedings consistent with this opinion.

[The dissenting opinion of Justice DOUGLAS is omitted]

Justice BRENNAN, dissenting.

This suit is brought by Illinois citizens against Illinois officials. In that circumstance, Illinois may not invoke the Eleventh Amendment, since that Amendment bars only federal court suits against States by citizens of other States. Rather, the question is whether Illinois may avail itself of the nonconstitutional but ancient [common law] doctrine of sovereign immunity as a bar to respondent's claim for retroactive AABD payments. In my view Illinois may not assert sovereign immunity [because] the States surrendered that immunity in Hamilton's words, "in the plan of the Convention," that formed the Union, at least insofar as the States granted Congress specifically enumerated powers. Congressional authority to enact the Social Security Act, of which AABD is a part, is to be found in Art. I, §8, cl. 1, one of the enumerated powers granted Congress by the States in the Constitution.

Justice MARSHALL, joined by Justice BLACKMUN, dissenting.

In its contacts with the Social Security Act's assistance programs in recent years, the Court has frequently described the Act as a "scheme of cooperative federalism." While this phrase captures a number of the unique characteristics of these programs, for present purposes it serves to emphasize that the States' decision to participate in the programs is a voluntary one. In deciding to participate, however, the States necessarily give up their freedom to operate assistance programs for the needy as they see fit, and bind themselves to conform their programs to the requirements of the federal statute and regulations. . . .

In agreeing to comply with the requirements of the Social Security Act and HEW regulations, I believe that Illinois has also agreed to subject itself to suit in the federal courts to enforce these obligations. I recognize, of course, that the Social Security Act does not itself provide for a cause of action to enforce its obligations. As the Court points out, the only sanction expressly provided in the Act for a participating State's failure to comply with federal requirements is the cutoff of federal funding by the Secretary of HEW.

But a cause of action is clearly provided by 42 U.S.C. §1983, which in terms authorizes suits to redress deprivations of rights secured by the "laws" of the United States. And we have already rejected the argument that Congress intended the funding cutoff to be the sole remedy for noncompliance with federal requirements. In *Rosado v. Wyman* (1970), we held that suits in federal court under §1983 were proper to enforce the provisions of the Social Security Act against participating States. Mr. Justice Harlan, writing for the Court, examined the legislative history and found "not the slightest indication" that Congress intended to prohibit suits in federal court to enforce compliance with federal standards.

I believe that Congress also intended the full panoply of traditional judicial remedies to be available to the federal courts in these §1983 suits. There is surely no indication of any congressional intent to restrict the courts' equitable jurisdiction.

Equally important, the courts' power to order retroactive payments is an essential remedy to insure future state compliance with federal requirements. No other remedy can effectively deter States from the strong temptation to cut welfare budgets by circumventing the stringent requirements of federal law. The funding cutoff is a drastic sanction, one which HEW has proved unwilling or unable to employ to compel strict compliance with the Act and regulations. Moreover, the cutoff operates only prospectively; it in no way deters the States from even a flagrant violation of the Act's requirements for as long as HEW does not discover the violation and threaten to take such action.

Absent any remedy which may act with retroactive effect, state welfare officials have everything to gain and nothing to lose by failing to comply with the congressional mandate that assistance be paid with reasonable promptness to all eligible individuals. This is not idle speculation without basis in practical experience. In this very case, for example, Illinois officials have knowingly violated since 1968 federal regulations on the strength of an argument as to its invalidity which even the majority deems unworthy of discussion. Without a retroactive-payment remedy, we are indeed faced with "the spectre of a state, perhaps calculatingly, defying federal law and thereby depriving welfare recipients of the financial assistance Congress thought it was giving them." *Jordan v. Weaver* (7th Cir. 1972). Like the Court of Appeals, I cannot believe that Congress could possibly have intended any such result.

Illinois chose to participate in the AABD program with its eyes wide open. Drawn by the lure of federal funds, it voluntarily obligated itself to comply with the Social Security Act and HEW regulations, with full knowledge that Congress had authorized assistance recipients to go into federal court to enforce these obligations and to recover benefits wrongfully denied.

I have no quarrel with the Court's view that waiver of constitutional rights should not lightly be inferred. But I simply cannot believe that the State could have entered into this essentially contractual agreement with the Federal Government without recognizing that it was subjecting itself to the full scope of the §1983 remedy provided by Congress to enforce the terms of the agreement. . . .

Congress undoubtedly has the power to insist upon a waiver of sovereign immunity as a condition of its consent to such a federal-state agreement. Since I am satisfied that Congress has in fact done so here, at least to the extent that the federal courts may do "complete rather than truncated justice," *Porter v. Warner*

Holding Co. (1946), in §1983 actions authorized by Congress against state welfare authorities, I respectfully dissent.

* * *

Edelman makes clear that suits for retrospective monetary relief are barred by the Eleventh Amendment. What about the costs of complying with a truly prospective-only injunction? The Court in *Edelman* stated that these costs are mere "ancillary effects" of compliance incident to the equity power upheld in *Ex parte Young*. Thus, the part of the lower court's injunction requiring that new AABD benefits be allocated in a timely manner as provided by federal regulations was upheld even though that would likely require expenditures to alter the state's administrative structure for making benefits determinations and accelerating payments.

The Court affirmed the ancillary effects doctrine in *Milliken v. Bradley* (1977). In that case, the Supreme Court had previously overturned an injunction requiring busing between school districts in Detroit and other school districts in surrounding suburbs in order to achieve meaningful desegregation. On remand the lower federal court entered a new injunction providing for alternative remedies, including new training for teachers, additional counselors, and other steps to reduce performance gaps among students. The state of Michigan was a defendant in the suit, not just local school districts, because the plaintiffs established that that the state was partly responsible for segregation in public schooling. The injunction required the state to pay 50 percent of the costs of the new programs. In a unanimous opinion, the Supreme Court held that:

> [the] decree to share the future costs of educational components in this case fits squarely withing the prospective compliance exception reaffirmed by *Edelman*. That exception, which had its genesis in *Ex parte Young*, permits federal courts to enjoin state officials to conform their conduct to the requirement of federal law, notwithstanding direct and substantial impact on the state treasury. The order challenged here does no more than that. The decree requires state officials, held responsible for unconstitutional conduct, in findings which are not challenged, to eliminate a de jure segregated school system. [Educational disadvantages] will require time, patience, and the skills of specially trained teachers. That the programs are also "compensatory" in nature does not change the fact that they are part of a plan that operates prospectively to bring about the delayed benefits of a unitary school system. We therefore hold that such prospective relief is not barred by the Eleventh Amendment.

What if the defendant defies a prospective decree? Here, the Court has not hesitated to uphold remedies that directly affect the state treasury. In *Osborn v. Bank of United States* (1824), decided well before *Ex parte Young*, the Court upheld an order requiring state officers, who were already subject to an injunction against collecting the state tax, to disgorge $100,000 they had illegally seized from the U.S. Bank. In *Hutto v. Finney* (1978), the district court found that conditions in the

Arkansas penal system constituted cruel and unusual punishment—"routine conditions that the ordinary Arkansas convict had to endure were characterized by the District Court as 'a dark and evil world completely alien to the free world.'" Inmates were "lashed with a wooden-handled leather strap five feet long and four inches wide . . . for minor offenses until their skin was bloody and bruised"; "[t]he 'Tucker Telephone,' a hand cranked device, was used to administer electrical shocks to various sensitive parts of inmate's body"; "[m]ost of the guards were simply inmates who had been issued guns"; "inmates could obtain access to medical treatment only if they bribed the [armed inmate] in charge of sick call"; "it was within the power of [an armed inmate] to murder another inmate with practical impunity"; and prisoners in punitive isolation were crowded 4-11 at a time into 8 foot by 10 foot cells with no furniture, grouped with prisoners with serious infectious diseases, and received fewer than 1,000 calories a day.

After twice inviting the administrators of the Department of Corrections to design and implement their own plans to rectify the Eighth Amendment violations, the district court finally entered "a series of detailed remedial orders." Although there were initial improvements, within two years the court found "serious deterioration" of conditions at a subsequent hearing and entered revised remedial orders. It also concluded that the defendants had "acted in bad faith" and ordered that plaintiffs' counsel be awarded attorneys' fees in the amount of $20,000 for the costs of litigating defendant's failure to comply with the original decree.

The Supreme Court rejected the state attorney general's Eleventh Amendment objection to the award:

> The line between retroactive and prospective relief cannot be so rigid that it defeats the effective enforcement of prospective relief. The present case requires application of that principle. In exercising their prospective powers under *Ex parte Young* and *Edelman v. Jordan,* federal courts are not reduced to issuing injunctions against state officers and hoping for compliance. Once issued, an injunction may be enforced. Many of the court's most effective enforcement weapons involve financial penalties. A criminal contempt prosecution for "resistance to [the court's] lawful . . . order" may result in a jail term or a fine. 18 U.S.C. §401. Civil contempt proceedings may yield a conditional jail term or fine. *United States v. Mine Workers* (1947). Civil contempt may also be punished by a remedial fine, which compensates the party who won the injunction for the effects of his opponent's noncompliance. If a state agency refuses to adhere to a court order, a financial penalty may be the most effective means of ensuring compliance. The principles of federalism that inform Eleventh Amendment doctrine surely do not require federal courts to enforce their decrees only by sending state officials to jail. The less intrusive power to impose a fine is properly treated as ancillary to the federal court's power to impose injunctive relief.
>
> In this case, the award of attorney's fees for bad faith served the same purpose as a remedial fine imposed for civil contempt. It vindicated the District Court's authority over a recalcitrant litigant. Compensation was not the sole motive for the award; in setting the amount of the fee, the

court said that it would "make no effort to adequately compensate counsel for the work that they have done or for the time that they have spent on the case." The court did allow a "substantial" fee, however, because "the allowance thereof may incline the Department to act in such a manner that further protracted litigation about the prisons will not be necessary. We see no reason to distinguish this award from any other penalty imposed to enforce a prospective injunction. Hence the substantive provisions of the Eleventh Amendment do not prevent an award of attorney's fees against the Department's officers in their official capacities."

b. Waiver

A state can always waive the affirmative defense of sovereign immunity and consent to suit in federal court. Sovereign immunity is "a personal privilege which [the state] may waive at its pleasure." *Clark v. Barnard* (1883). There are two ways in which this can occur. First, a state may make a "clear declaration that it intends to submit itself" to federal court jurisdiction. *Coll. Sav. Bank v. Fla. Prepaid Postsecondary Ed. Expense Bd.* (1999). This is a "stringent" clear statement rule. It is not met merely because a state enacts legislation consenting to suit in "the courts of its own creation," providing that the state has the general power "to sue and be sued," or even legislation authorizing suits against it in "any court of competent jurisdiction." Nor may a state "constructively" or "impliedly" waive immunity by, for instance, engaging in interstate commerce or otherwise having a presence in an area regulated by federal law. *Id.* (overruling constructive waiver doctrine of *Parden v. Terminal Ry. Co.* (1964); "there is little reason to assume actual consent based upon the state's mere presence in a field subject to congressional regulation").

What if a state accepts federal funds under a Spending Clause program? Could waiver of sovereign immunity be an express condition of acceptance? Recall the Court's rejection of this in *Edelman*, emphasizing that waiver can only be a consequence of receiving federal funds if Congress uses "the most express language" or inference from text that "leave[s] no room for any other reasonable construction." *See also National Fed'n of Indep. Bus. v. Sebilius* (2012) ("The legitimacy of Congress' exercise of the spending power . . . rests on whether the State voluntarily and knowingly accepts the terms of the 'contract'"; Affordable Care Act provisions conditioning acceptance of new health care program on threat to remove existing federal funding equal to 20 percent of state's total budget, "with federal funds covering 50 to 83 percent of" state Medicaid costs, is unconstitutionally coercive).

Second, if the state voluntarily initiates federal litigation, it waives sovereign immunity. As the Court held in *Gardner v. New Jersey* (1947), "[W]hen the State becomes the actor and files a claim . . . it waives any immunity which it might otherwise have had respecting the adjudication of the claim." *Id.* (state filed proof of claim for unpaid state taxes in bankruptcy proceeding, trustee sought adjudication of amount of state taxes owed, interest calculated, and existence of lien on debtor's personal property; state attorney general objected on sovereign immunity grounds; Court held that "exercise of that power was not a suit against the State"). Here is the principal modern case.

Lapides v. Board of Regents of University System of Georgia

535 U.S. 613 (2002)

Justice BREYER delivered the opinion of the Court.

The Eleventh Amendment grants a State immunity from suit in federal court by citizens of other States, U.S. Const., Amdt. XI, and by its own citizens as well, *Hans v. Louisiana* (1890). The question before us is whether the State's act of removing a lawsuit from state court to federal court waives this immunity. We hold that it does.

I

Paul Lapides, a professor employed by the Georgia state university system, brought this lawsuit in a Georgia state court. He sued respondents, the Board of Regents of the University System of Georgia (hereinafter Georgia or State) and university officials acting in both their personal capacities and as agents of the State. Lapides' lawsuit alleged that university officials placed allegations of sexual harassment in his personnel files. And Lapides claimed that their doing so violated both Georgia law, *see* Georgia Tort Claims Act, Ga. Code Ann. §50-21-23 (1994), and federal law, *see* Civil Rights Act of 1871, §1979, 42 U.S.C. §1983.

All defendants joined in removing the case to Federal District Court, 28 U.S.C. §1441, where they sought dismissal. The State, while conceding that a state statute had waived sovereign immunity from state-law suits in state court, argued that, by virtue of the Eleventh Amendment, it remained immune from suit in federal court. But the District Court did not agree. Rather, in its view, by removing the case from state to federal court, the State had waived its Eleventh Amendment immunity. . . . [T]he Court of Appeals for the Eleventh Circuit reversed.

It has become clear that we must limit our answer to the context of state-law claims, in respect to which the State has explicitly waived immunity from state-court proceedings. That is because Lapides' only federal claim against the State arises under 42 U.S.C. §1983, that claim seeks only monetary damages, and we have held that a State is not a "person" against whom a §1983 claim for money damages might be asserted. *Will v. Mich. Dep't of State Police* (1989). Hence this case does not present a valid federal claim against the State. Nor need we address the scope of waiver by removal in a situation where the State's underlying sovereign immunity from suit has not been waived or abrogated in state court.

II

It would seem anomalous or inconsistent for a State both (1) to invoke federal jurisdiction, thereby contending that the "Judicial power of the United States" extends to the case at hand, and (2) to claim Eleventh Amendment immunity, thereby denying that the "Judicial power of the United States" extends to the case at hand. And a Constitution that permitted States to follow their litigation interests by freely asserting both claims in the same case could generate seriously unfair results. Thus, it is not surprising that more than a century ago this Court indicated that a State's voluntary appearance in federal court amounted to a waiver of its Eleventh Amendment immunity. *Clark v. Barnard* (1883) (State's "voluntary appearance" in federal court as an intervenor avoids Eleventh Amendment inquiry). The Court subsequently held, in the context of a bankruptcy claim, that a State "waives any immunity . . . respecting the adjudication of" a "claim" that it voluntarily files in federal court. *Gardner v. New Jersey* (1947). And the Court has made clear in general that "where a State *voluntarily* becomes a party to a cause and submits its rights for judicial determination, it will be bound thereby and cannot escape the result of its own voluntary act by invoking the prohibitions of the Eleventh Amendment." *Gunter v. Atlantic Coast Line R. Co.* (1906). The Court has long accepted this statement of the law as valid, often citing with approval the cases embodying that principle.

In this case, the State was brought involuntarily into the case as a defendant in the original state-court proceedings. But the State then voluntarily agreed to remove the case to federal court. *See* 28 U.S.C. §1446(a); *Chicago, R.I. & P.R. Co. v. Martin* (1900) (removal requires the consent of all defendants). In doing so, it voluntarily invoked the federal court's jurisdiction. And unless we are to abandon the general principle just stated, or unless there is something special about removal or about this case, the general legal principle requiring waiver ought to apply.

We see no reason to abandon the general principle. Georgia points out that the cases that stand for the principle, *Gunter, Gardner,* and *Clark,* did not involve suits for money damages against the State — the heart of the Eleventh Amendment's concern. But the principle enunciated in those cases did not turn upon the nature of the relief sought. And that principle remains sound as applied to suits for money damages.

Georgia adds that this Court decided *Gunter, Gardner,* and *Clark* before it decided more recent cases, which have required a "clear" indication of the State's intent to waive its immunity. *Coll. Sav. Bank v. Fla. Prepaid Postsecondary Ed. Expense Bd.* (1999). But *College Savings Bank* distinguished the kind of constructive waivers repudiated there from waivers effected by litigation conduct. And this makes sense because an interpretation of the Eleventh Amendment that finds waiver in the litigation context rests upon the Amendment's presumed recognition of the judicial need to avoid inconsistency, anomaly, and unfairness, and not upon a State's actual preference or desire, which might, after all, favor selective use of "immunity" to achieve litigation advantages. The relevant "clarity" here must focus on the litigation act the State takes that creates the waiver. And that act—removal—is clear.

Georgia argues that state law, while authorizing its attorney general "[t]o represent the state in all civil actions tried in any court," Ga. Code Ann. §45-15-3(6); *see* Ga. Const., Art. 5, §3, ¶4, does not authorize the attorney general to waive the State's Eleventh Amendment immunity, Art. 1, §2, ¶¶9(e), (f). Georgia adds that in *Ford Motor Co. v. Dep't of Treasury* (1945), this Court unanimously interpreted roughly similar state laws similarly, that the Court held that "no properly authorized executive or administrative officer of the state has waived the state's immunity," and that it sustained an Eleventh Amendment defense raised for the first time after a State had litigated a claim brought against it in federal court.

The State makes several other arguments, none of which we find convincing. It points to cases in which this Court has permitted *the United States* to enter into a case voluntarily without giving up immunity or to assert immunity despite a previous effort to waive. Those cases, however, do not involve the Eleventh Amendment—a specific text with a history that focuses upon the State's sovereignty *vis-á-vis* the Federal Government. And each case involves special circumstances not at issue here, for example, an effort by a sovereign (*i.e.*, the United States) to seek the protection of its own courts (*i.e.*, the federal courts), or an effort to protect an Indian tribe.

* * *

c.   Abrogation of Immunity by Congress

As we have seen, state sovereign immunity does not apply to officer suits for prospective relief. And it can be waived by actions of the state. A third way around state sovereign immunity is abrogation — congressional legislation that includes express, unequivocal language subjecting states to suit in federal court pursuant to a clause of the Constitution that authorizes Congress to do so. We saw discussion of this possibility in *Edelman* where the Court found there was no congressional abrogation of state sovereign immunity because the Social Security Act did not contain any explicit authorization to sue.

In the following case the Court held that Congress has authority to abrogate state sovereign immunity when it legislates pursuant to the enforcement clause of the Fourteenth Amendment.

Fitzpatrick v. Bitzer

427 U.S. 445 (1976)

Mr. Justice REHNQUIST delivered the opinion of the Court.

In the 1972 Amendments to Title VII of the Civil Rights Act of 1964, Congress, acting under §5 of the Fourteenth Amendment, authorized federal courts to award money damages in favor of a private individual against a state government found to have subjected that person to employment discrimination on the basis of "race, color, religion, sex, or national origin." The principal question presented by these cases is whether, as against the shield of sovereign immunity afforded the State by the Eleventh Amendment, Congress has the power to authorize Federal courts to enter such an award against the State as a means of enforcing the substantive guarantees of the Fourteenth Amendment.

I

Petitioners sued in the United States District Court for the District of Connecticut on behalf of all present and retired male employees of the State of Connecticut. Their amended complaint asserted, inter alia, that certain provisions in the State's statutory retirement benefit plan discriminated against them because of their sex, and therefore contravened Title VII of the 1964 Act. Title VII, which originally did not include state and local governments, had in the interim been amended to bring the States within its purview.

The District Court held that the Connecticut State Employees Retirement Act violated Title VII's prohibition against sex-based employment discrimination. It entered prospective injunctive relief in petitioners' favor against respondent state officials. Petitioners also sought an award of retroactive retirement benefits as compensation for losses caused by the State's discrimination, as well as "a reasonable attorney's fee as part of the costs." But the District Court held that both would constitute recovery of money damages from the State's treasury, and were therefore precluded by the Eleventh Amendment and by this Court's decision in *Edelman v. Jordan* (1974).

On petitioners' appeal, the Court of Appeals affirmed in part and reversed in part. It agreed that under *Edelman* a "private federal action for retroactive damages" is not a "constitutionally permissible method of enforcing Fourteenth Amendment rights." It reversed the District Court and remanded as to attorneys' fees, however, reasoning that such an award would have only an "ancillary effect" on the state treasury of the kind permitted under *Edelman*.

II

All parties in the instant litigation agree with the Court of Appeals that the suit for retroactive benefits by the petitioners is in fact indistinguishable from that sought to be maintained in Edelman, since what is sought here is a damages award payable to a private party from the state treasury.

Our analysis begins where *Edelman* ended, for in this Title VII case the "threshold fact of congressional authorization" to sue the State as employer is clearly present. This is, of course, the prerequisite found present in *Parden v. Terminal R. Co.* (1964), and wanting in Employees. We are aware of the factual differences between the type of state activity involved in *Parden* and that involved in the present case, but we do not think that difference is material for our purposes. The congressional authorization involved in *Parden* was based on the power of Congress under the Commerce Clause; here, however, the Eleventh Amendment defense is asserted in the context of legislation passed pursuant to Congress' authority under §5 of the Fourteenth Amendment.

As ratified by the States after the Civil War, that Amendment quite clearly contemplates limitations on their authority. In relevant part, it provides:

> Section 1. . . . No State shall make or enforce any law which shall abridge the privileges or immunities of citizens of the United States; nor shall any State deprive any person of life, liberty, or property, without due process of law; nor deny to any person within its jurisdiction the equal protection of the laws.
>
> Section 5. The Congress shall have power to enforce by appropriate legislation, the provisions of this article.

The substantive provisions are by express terms directed at the States. Impressed upon them by those provisions are duties with respect to their treatment of private individuals. Standing behind the imperatives is Congress' power to "enforce" them "by appropriate legislation."

The impact of the Fourteenth Amendment upon the relationship between the Federal Government and the States, and the reach of congressional power under

§5, were examined at length by this Court in *Ex parte State of Virginia* (1880). A state judge had been arrested and indicted under a federal criminal statute prohibiting the exclusion on the basis of race of any citizen from service as a juror in a state court. The judge claimed that the statute was beyond Congress' power to enact under either the Thirteenth or the Fourteenth Amendment. The Court first observed that these Amendments "were intended to be, what they really are, limitations of the power of the States and enlargements of the power of Congress." It then addressed the relationship between the language of §5 and the substantive provisions of the Fourteenth Amendment:

> The prohibitions of the Fourteenth Amendment are directed to the States, and they are to a degree restrictions of State power. It is these which Congress is empowered to enforce, and to enforce against State action, however put forth, whether that action be executive, legislative, or judicial. Such enforcement is no invasion of State sovereignty. No law can be, which the people of the States have, by the Constitution of the United States, empowered Congress to enact. . . . It is said the selection of jurors for her courts and the administration of her laws belong to each State; that they are her rights. This is true in the general. But in exercising her rights, a State cannot disregard the limitations which the Federal Constitution has applied to her power. Her rights do not reach to that extent. Nor can she deny to the general government the right to exercise all its granted powers, though they may interfere with the full enjoyment of rights she would have if those powers had not been thus granted. Indeed, every addition of power to the general government involves a corresponding diminution of the governmental powers of the States. It is carved out of them.
>
> The argument in support of the petition for a Habeas corpus ignores entirely the power conferred upon Congress by the Fourteenth Amendment. Were it not for the fifth section of that amendment, there might be room for argument that the first section is only declaratory of the moral duty of the State. . . . But the Constitution now expressly gives authority for congressional interference and compulsion in the cases embraced within the Fourteenth Amendment. It is but a limited authority, true, extending only to a single class of cases; but within its limits it is complete.

Ex parte State of Virginia's early recognition of this shift in the federal-state balance has been carried forward by more recent decisions of this Court. *See, e.g., South Carolina v. Katzenbach* (1966).

There can be no doubt that this line of cases has sanctioned intrusions by Congress, acting under the Civil War Amendments, into the judicial, executive, and legislative spheres of autonomy previously reserved to the States. The legislation considered in each case was grounded on the expansion of Congress' powers with the corresponding diminution of state sovereignty found to be intended by the Framers and made part of the Constitution upon the States' ratification of those Amendments, a phenomenon aptly described as a "carv(ing) out" in *Ex parte State of Virginia.*

It is true that none of these previous cases presented the question of the relationship between the Eleventh Amendment and the enforcement power granted to

Congress under §5 of the Fourteenth Amendment. But we think that the Eleventh Amendment, and the principle of state sovereignty which it embodies, *see Hans v. Louisiana* (1890), are necessarily limited by the enforcement provisions of §5 of the Fourteenth Amendment. In that section Congress is expressly granted authority to enforce "by appropriate legislation" the substantive provisions of the Fourteenth Amendment, which themselves embody significant limitations on state authority. When Congress acts pursuant to §5, not only is it exercising legislative authority that is plenary within the terms of the constitutional grant, it is exercising that authority under one section of a constitutional Amendment whose other sections by their own terms embody limitations on state authority. We think that Congress may, in determining what is "appropriate legislation" for the purpose of enforcing the provisions of the Fourteenth Amendment, provide for private suits against States or state officials which are constitutionally impermissible in other contexts.

III

In No. 75-283, the state officials contest the Court of Appeals' conclusion that an award of attorneys' fees in this case would under *Edelman* have only an "ancillary effect" on the state treasury and could therefore be permitted as falling outside the Eleventh Amendment under the doctrine of *Ex parte Young* (1908). We need not address this question, since, given the express congressional authority for such an award in a case brought under Title VII, it follows necessarily from our holding in No. 75-251 that Congress' exercise of power in this respect is also not barred by the Eleventh Amendment. We therefore affirm the Court of Appeals' judgment in No. 75-283 on this basis.

[Justice BRENNAN concurred on the ground that Connecticut could not invoke the Eleventh Amendment "since that Amendment bars only federal-court suits against States by citizens of other States," and the states surrendered their "nonconstitutional" common law immunity "in the plan of the Convention that formed the Union, at least insofar as the States granted Congress specifically enumerated powers."]

[Justice STEVENS' concurring opinion is omitted.]

* * *

Fitzpatrick confirms that Congress may subject the states to suit when it legislates under the enforcement clauses of the Reconstruction Amendments.

For a brief period after its decision in *Fitzpatrick* the Supreme Court entertained the possibility that Congress could broadly abrogate state sovereign immunity under legislative powers conferred by Article I. In *Pennsylvania v. Union Gas* (1989), the Court dealt with the first federally designated "Superfund" site in the nation—thousands of gallons of liquid coal tar that were seeping into a creek adjacent to a coal gasification plant run by Union Gas for 50 years. Under the Comprehensive Environmental Response, Compensation, and Liability Act of 1980 (CERCLA), the federal government paid for cleanup costs and then sued Union Gas to recoup its expenses. Union Gas, in turn, filed a third-party complaint against

Pennsylvania, contending that the state was liable under the statute for cleanup costs as an owner and operator of the site because it took part in flood control efforts along the creek for decades and eventually purchased easements to the property adjacent the creek. Pennsylvania moved to dismiss on Eleventh Amendment grounds. In a sharply divided decision, the Supreme Court held that CERCLA validly abrogates state sovereign immunity. Justice Brennan's plurality opinion emphasized that CERCLA expressly makes states subject to suit and that the Commerce Clause provides "plenary authority to regulate interstate commerce." Just as with section 5 of the Fourteenth Amendment, "the Commerce Clause with one hand gives power to Congress while, with the other, it takes power away from the States." Justice White wrote separately, agreeing with Justice Brennan that Congress has authority to abrogate state sovereign immunity under the Commerce Clause. Justice Scalia, joined by Chief Justice Rehnquist, Justice O'Connor and Justice Kennedy, argued that "the position adopted by the Court contradicts the rationale of *Hans.*"

The fragile majority in *Union Gas* was short-lived. The Court returned to congressional power to abrogate under Article I in the next case. As you read, note the unusual nature of the remedy Congress created. It was neither traditional money damages against the state treasury (indeed, the state of Florida may *gain* revenue from a compact on gaming with the Seminole Tribe) nor a traditional form of equitable relief. Congress had instead legislated a unique role for the federal courts to mediate state-tribal conflicts over gaming. Consider how the nature of this remedy intersects with the analysis of congressional power to abrogate and the *Ex parte Young* exception.

Seminole Tribe of Florida v. Florida

517 U.S. 44 (1996)

Chief Justice REHNQUIST delivered the opinion of the Court.

The Indian Gaming Regulatory Act provides that an Indian tribe may conduct certain gaming activities only in conformance with a valid compact between the tribe and the State in which the gaming activities are located. 25 U.S.C. §2710(d)(1)(C). The Act, passed by Congress under the Indian Commerce Clause, U.S. Const., Art. I, §8, cl. 3, imposes upon the States a duty to negotiate in good faith with an Indian tribe toward the formation of a compact, §2710(d)(3)(A), and authorizes a tribe to bring suit in federal court against a State in order to compel performance of that duty, §2710(d)(7). We hold that notwithstanding Congress' clear intent to abrogate the States' sovereign immunity, the Indian Commerce Clause does not grant Congress that power, and therefore §2710(d)(7) cannot grant jurisdiction over a State that does not consent to be sued. We further hold that the doctrine of *Ex parte Young* (1908), may not be used to enforce §2710(d)(3) against a state official.

I

Congress passed the Indian Gaming Regulatory Act in 1988 in order to provide a statutory basis for the operation and regulation of gaming by Indian tribes. *See* 25 U.S.C. §2702. The Act divides gaming on Indian lands into three classes—I,

II, and III — and provides a different regulatory scheme for each class. Class III gaming — the type with which we are here concerned — is defined as "all forms of gaming that are not class I gaming or class II gaming," §2703(8), and includes such things as slot machines, casino games, banking card games, dog racing, and lotteries.[1] It is the most heavily regulated of the three classes. The Act provides that class III gaming is lawful only where it is: (1) authorized by an ordinance or resolution that (a) is adopted by the governing body of the Indian tribe, (b) satisfies certain statutorily prescribed requirements, and (c) is approved by the National Indian Gaming Commission; (2) located in a State that permits such gaming for any purpose by any person, organization, or entity; and (3) "conducted in conformance with a Tribal-State compact entered into by the Indian tribe and the State under paragraph (3) that is in effect." §2710(d)(1).

§2710(d)(3) describes the process by which a State and an Indian tribe begin negotiations toward a Tribal–State compact. [It authorizes tribes to enter negotiations with a state and requires that the state "negotiate with the Indian tribe in good faith to enter such a compact."]. The State's obligation to "negotiate with the Indian tribe in good faith" is made judicially enforceable by §§2710(d)(7)(A)(i) and (B)(i):

> **(A)** The United States district courts shall have jurisdiction over—
> **(i)** any cause of action initiated by an Indian tribe arising from the failure of a State to enter into negotiations with the Indian tribe for the purpose of entering into a Tribal-State compact under paragraph (3) or to conduct such negotiations in good faith. . . .
> **(B)(i)** An Indian tribe may initiate a cause of action described in subparagraph (A)(i) only after the close of the 180-day period beginning on the date on which the Indian tribe requested the State to enter into negotiations under paragraph (3)(A).

Sections 2710(d)(7)(B)(ii)-(vii) describe an elaborate remedial scheme designed to ensure the formation of a Tribal-State compact. A tribe that brings an action under §2710(d)(7)(A)(i) must show that no Tribal-State compact has been entered and that the State failed to respond in good faith to the tribe's request to negotiate; at that point, the burden then shifts to the State to prove that it did in fact negotiate in good faith. §2710(d)(7)(B)(ii). If the district court concludes that the State has failed to negotiate in good faith toward the formation of a Tribal-State compact, then it "shall order the State and Indian Tribe to conclude such

---

1. Class I gaming "means social games solely for prizes of minimal value or traditional forms of Indian gaming engaged in by individuals as a part of, or in connection with, tribal ceremonies or celebrations," 25 U.S.C. §2703(6), and is left by the Act to "the exclusive jurisdiction of the Indian tribes," §2710(a)(1).

Class II gaming is more extensively defined to include bingo, games similar to bingo, non-banking card games not illegal under the laws of the State, and card games actually operated in particular States prior to the passage of the Act. *See* §2703(7). . . . The Act allows class II gaming where the State "permits such gaming for any purpose by any person, organization or entity," and the "governing body of the Indian tribe adopts an ordinance or resolution which is approved by the Chairman" of the National Indian Gaming Commission. §2710(b)(1). . . .

a compact within a 60-day period." §2710(d)(7)(B)(iii). If no compact has been concluded 60 days after the court's order, then "the Indian tribe and the State shall each submit to a mediator appointed by the court a proposed compact that represents their last best offer for a compact." §2710(d)(7)(B)(iv). The mediator chooses from between the two proposed compacts the one "which best comports with the terms of [the Act] and any other applicable Federal law and with the findings and order of the court," and submits it to the State and the Indian tribe, §2710(d)(7)(B)(v). If the State consents to the proposed compact within 60 days of its submission by the mediator, then the proposed compact is "treated as a Tribal-State compact entered into under paragraph (3)." §2710(d)(7)(B)(vi). If, however, the State does not consent within that 60-day period, then the Act provides that the mediator "shall notify the Secretary [of the Interior]" and that the Secretary "shall prescribe . . . procedures . . . under which class III gaming may be conducted on the Indian lands over which the Indian tribe has jurisdiction." §2710(d)(7)(B)(vii).

In September 1991, the Seminole Tribe of Florida, petitioner, sued the State of Florida and its Governor, Lawton Chiles, respondents. Invoking jurisdiction under 25 U.S.C. §2710(d)(7)(A), as well as 28 U.S.C. §§1331 and 1362, petitioner alleged that respondents had "refused to enter into any negotiation for inclusion of [certain gaming activities] in a tribal-state compact," thereby violating the "requirement of good faith negotiation" contained in §2710(d)(3). Respondents moved to dismiss the complaint, arguing that the suit violated the State's sovereign immunity from suit in federal court. The District Court denied respondents' motion, and respondents took an interlocutory appeal of that decision.

The Court of Appeals for the Eleventh Circuit reversed the decision of the District Court, holding that the Eleventh Amendment barred petitioner's suit against respondents.

Petitioner sought our review of the Eleventh Circuit's decision, and we granted certiorari in order to consider two questions: (1) Does the Eleventh Amendment prevent Congress from authorizing suits by Indian tribes against States for prospective injunctive relief to enforce legislation enacted pursuant to the Indian Commerce Clause?; and (2) Does the doctrine of *Ex parte Young* permit suits against a State's Governor for prospective injunctive relief to enforce the good-faith bargaining requirement of the Act? We answer the first question in the affirmative, the second in the negative, and we therefore affirm the Eleventh Circuit's dismissal of petitioner's suit.

Although the text of the Amendment would appear to restrict only the Article III diversity jurisdiction of the federal courts, "we have understood the Eleventh Amendment to stand not so much for what it says, but for the presupposition . . . which it confirms." *Blatchford v. Native Vill. of Noatak* (1991). For over a century we have reaffirmed that federal jurisdiction over suits against unconsenting States "was not contemplated by the Constitution when establishing the judicial power of the United States." *Hans v. Louisiana* (1890).

Here, petitioner has sued the State of Florida and it is undisputed that Florida has not consented to the suit. *See Blatchford* (States by entering into the Constitution did not consent to suit by Indian tribes). Petitioner nevertheless contends that its suit is not barred by state sovereign immunity. First, it argues that Congress through the Act abrogated the States' sovereign immunity. Alternatively, petitioner maintains that its suit against the Governor may go forward under *Ex parte Young.* We consider each of those arguments in turn.

II

In order to determine whether Congress has abrogated the States' sovereign immunity, we ask two questions: first, whether Congress has "unequivocally expresse[d] its intent to abrogate the immunity," *Green v. Mansour* (1985); and second, whether Congress has acted "pursuant to a valid exercise of power."

A

Congress' intent to abrogate the States' immunity from suit must be obvious from "a clear legislative statement." *Blatchford.* In *Atascadero State Hospital v. Scanlon* (1985), we held that "[a] general authorization for suit in federal court is not the kind of unequivocal statutory language sufficient to abrogate the Eleventh Amendment." . . .

Congress has in §2710(d)(7) provided an "unmistakably clear" statement of its intent to abrogate. Section 2710(d)(7)(A)(i) vests jurisdiction in "[t]he United States district courts . . . over any cause of action . . . arising from the failure of a State to enter into negotiations . . . or to conduct such negotiations in good faith." Any conceivable doubt as to the identity of the defendant in an action under §2710(d)(7)(A)(i) is dispelled when one looks to the various provisions of §2710(d)(7)(B), which describe the remedial scheme available to a tribe that files suit under §2710(d)(7)(A)(i) [explicitly setting out burden of proof for the "State" and power of court to order the "State" to mediation].

B

Having concluded that Congress clearly intended to abrogate the States' sovereign immunity through §2710(d)(7), we turn now to consider whether the Act was passed "pursuant to a valid exercise of power." *Green v. Mansour.* Before we address that question here, however, we think it necessary first to define the scope of our inquiry.

Petitioner suggests that one consideration weighing in favor of finding the power to abrogate here is that the Act authorizes only prospective injunctive relief rather than retroactive monetary relief. . . . The Eleventh Amendment does not exist solely in order to "preven[t] federal-court judgments that must be paid out of a State's treasury," *Hess v. Port Auth. Trans-Hudson Corp.* (1994); it also serves to avoid "the indignity of subjecting a State to the coercive process of judicial tribunals at the instance of private parties," *P.R. Aqueduct & Sewer Auth. v. Metcalf* (1993).

Thus our inquiry into whether Congress has the power to abrogate unilaterally the States' immunity from suit is narrowly focused on one question: Was the Act in question passed pursuant to a constitutional provision granting Congress the power to abrogate? *See, e.g., Fitzpatrick v. Bitzer* (1976). Previously, in conducting that inquiry, we have found authority to abrogate under only two provisions of the Constitution. In *Fitzpatrick,* we recognized that the Fourteenth Amendment, by expanding federal power at the expense of state autonomy, had fundamentally altered the balance of state and federal power struck by the Constitution.

In only one other case has congressional abrogation of the States' Eleventh Amendment immunity been upheld. In *Pennsylvania v. Union Gas Co.* (1989), a plurality of the Court found that the Interstate Commerce Clause, Art. I, §8, cl. 3, granted Congress the power to abrogate state sovereign immunity, stating that the power to regulate interstate commerce would be "incomplete without the authority to render States liable in damages." Justice White added the fifth vote necessary to the result in that case, but wrote separately in order to express that he "[did] not agree with much of [the plurality's] reasoning." *Id.* (opinion concurring in judgment in part and dissenting in part).

[The *Union Gas*] plurality's rationale . . . deviated sharply from our established federalism jurisprudence and essentially eviscerated our decision in *Hans.*

Never before the decision in *Union Gas* had we suggested that the bounds of Article III could be expanded by Congress operating pursuant to any constitutional provision other than the Fourteenth Amendment. Indeed, it had seemed fundamental that Congress could not expand the jurisdiction of the federal courts beyond the bounds of Article III. *Marbury v. Madison* (1803). The plurality's citation of prior decisions for support was based upon what we believe to be a misreading of precedent.

Reconsidering the decision in *Union Gas*, we conclude that none of the policies underlying *stare decisis* require our continuing adherence to its holding. We feel bound to conclude that *Union Gas* was wrongly decided and that it should be, and now is, overruled.

In *Principality of Monaco v. Mississippi* (1934), the Court held that the Eleventh Amendment barred a suit brought against a State by a foreign state. Chief Justice Hughes wrote for a unanimous Court:

> Manifestly, we cannot rest with a mere literal application of the words of §2 of Article III, or assume that the letter of the Eleventh Amendment exhausts the restrictions upon suits against non-consenting States. Behind the words of the constitutional provisions are postulates which limit and control. There is the essential postulate that the controversies, as contemplated, shall be found to be of a justiciable character. There is also the postulate that States of the Union, still possessing attributes of sovereignty, shall be immune from suits, without their consent, save where there has been a "surrender of this immunity in the plan of the convention."

The dissent, to the contrary, disregards our case law in favor of a theory cobbled together from law review articles and its own version of historical events. The dissent cites not a single decision since *Hans* (other than *Union Gas*) that supports its view of state sovereign immunity, instead relying upon the now-discredited decision in *Chisholm v. Georgia* (1793).

The dissent mischaracterizes the *Hans* opinion. That decision found its roots not solely in the common law of England, but in the much more fundamental "'jurisprudence in all civilized nations.'" *Hans; see also* The Federalist No. 81 (A. Hamilton) (sovereign immunity "is the general sense and the general practice of mankind"). The dissent's proposition that the common law of England, where adopted by the States, was open to change by the Legislature is wholly unexceptionable and largely beside the point: that common law provided the substantive rules of law rather than jurisdiction. *Cf. Monaco* (state sovereign immunity, like the requirement that there be a "justiciable" controversy, is a constitutionally grounded limit on federal jurisdiction). It also is noteworthy that the principle of state sovereign immunity stands distinct from other principles of the common law in that only the former prompted a specific constitutional amendment.

The dissent's lengthy analysis of the text of the Eleventh Amendment is directed at a straw man — we long have recognized that blind reliance upon the text of the Eleventh Amendment is "'to strain the Constitution and the law to a construction never imagined or dreamed of.'" *Monaco* (quoting *Hans*). The text dealt in terms only with the problem presented by the decision in *Chisholm;* in light of the fact that the federal courts did not have federal question jurisdiction at the time the Amendment was passed (and would not have it until 1875), it seems unlikely that much thought was given to the prospect of federal-question jurisdiction over the States.

In putting forward a new theory of state sovereign immunity, the dissent develops its own vision of the political system created by the Framers, concluding with the statement that "[t]he Framers' principal objectives in rejecting English theories of unitary sovereignty . . . would have been impeded if a new concept of sovereign immunity had taken its place in federal-question cases, and would have been substantially thwarted if that new immunity had been held untouchable by any congressional effort to abrogate it."[14] This sweeping statement ignores the fact that the Nation survived for nearly two centuries without the question of the existence of such power ever being presented to this Court. And Congress itself waited nearly a century before even conferring federal-question jurisdiction on the lower federal courts.

In overruling *Union Gas* today, we reconfirm that the background principle of state sovereign immunity embodied in the Eleventh Amendment is not so ephemeral as to dissipate when the subject of the suit is an area, like the regulation of Indian commerce, that is under the exclusive control of the Federal Government. Even when the Constitution vests in Congress complete lawmaking authority over a particular area, the Eleventh Amendment prevents congressional authorization of suits by private parties against unconsenting States. The Eleventh Amendment restricts the judicial power under Article III, and Article I cannot be used to circumvent the constitutional limitations placed upon federal jurisdiction. Petitioner's suit against the State of Florida must be dismissed for a lack of jurisdiction.

---

14. This argument wholly disregards other methods of ensuring the States' compliance with federal law: The Federal Government can bring suit in federal court against a State, *see, e.g., United States v. Texas* (1892) (finding such power necessary to the "permanence of the Union"); an individual can bring suit against a state officer in order to ensure that the officer's conduct is in compliance with federal law, *see, e.g., Ex parte Young* (1908); and this Court is empowered to review a question of federal law arising from a state-court decision where a State has consented to suit, *see, e.g., Cohens v. Virginia* (1821).

III

Petitioner argues that we may exercise jurisdiction over its suit to enforce §2710(d)(3) against the Governor notwithstanding the jurisdictional bar of the Eleventh Amendment. Petitioner notes that since our decision in *Ex parte Young* (1908), we often have found federal jurisdiction over a suit against a state official when that suit seeks only prospective injunctive relief in order to "end a continuing violation of federal law." *Green v. Mansour.* The situation presented here, however, is sufficiently different from that giving rise to the traditional *Ex parte Young* action so as to preclude the availability of that doctrine.

Here, the "continuing violation of federal law" alleged by petitioner is the Governor's failure to bring the State into compliance with §2710(d)(3). But the duty to negotiate imposed upon the State by that statutory provision does not stand alone. Rather, as we have seen, Congress passed §2710(d)(3) in conjunction with the carefully crafted and intricate remedial scheme set forth in §2710(d)(7).

Where Congress has created a remedial scheme for the enforcement of a particular federal right, we have, in suits against federal officers, refused to supplement that scheme with one created by the judiciary. *Schweiker v. Chilicky* (1988) ("When the design of a Government program suggests that Congress has provided what it considers adequate remedial mechanisms for constitutional violations that may occur in the course of its administration, we have not created additional . . . remedies"). Here, of course, the question is not whether a remedy should be created, but instead is whether the Eleventh Amendment bar should be lifted, as it was in *Ex parte Young*, in order to allow a suit against a state officer. Nevertheless, we think that the same general principle applies: Therefore, where Congress has prescribed a detailed remedial scheme for the enforcement against a State of a statutorily created right, a court should hesitate before casting aside those limitations and permitting an action against a state officer based upon *Ex parte Young*.

Here, Congress intended §2710(d)(3) to be enforced against the State in an action brought under §2710(d)(7); the intricate procedures set forth in that provision show that Congress intended therein not only to define, but also to limit significantly, the duty imposed by §2710(d)(3). For example, where the court finds that the State has failed to negotiate in good faith, the only remedy prescribed is an order directing the State and the Indian tribe to conclude a compact within 60 days. And if the parties disregard the court's order and fail to conclude a compact within the 60-day period, the only sanction is that each party then must submit a proposed compact to a mediator who selects the one which best embodies the terms of the Act. Finally, if the State fails to accept the compact selected by the mediator, the only sanction against it is that the mediator shall notify the Secretary of the Interior who then must prescribe regulations governing class III gaming on the tribal lands at issue. By contrast with this quite modest set of sanctions, an action brought against a state official under *Ex parte Young* would expose that official to the full remedial powers of a federal court, including, presumably, contempt sanctions. If §2710(d)(3) could be enforced in a suit under *Ex parte Young*, §2710(d)(7) would have been superfluous; it is difficult to see why an Indian tribe would suffer through the intricate scheme of §2710(d)(7) when more complete and more immediate relief would be available under *Ex parte Young.*[17]

Here, of course, we have found that Congress does not have authority under the Constitution to make the State suable in federal court under §2710(d)(7). Nevertheless, the fact that Congress chose to impose upon the State a liability that is significantly more limited than would be the liability imposed upon the state officer under *Ex parte Young* strongly indicates that Congress had no wish to create the latter under §2710(d)(3). Nor are we free to rewrite the statutory scheme in order to approximate what we think Congress might have wanted had it known that §2710(d)(7) was beyond its authority. If that effort is to be made, it should be made by Congress, and not by the federal courts. We hold that *Ex parte Young* is inapplicable to petitioner's suit against the Governor of Florida, and therefore that suit is barred by the Eleventh Amendment and must be dismissed for a lack of jurisdiction.

IV

The Eleventh Circuit's dismissal of petitioner's suit is hereby affirmed.
It is so ordered.

Justice STEVENS, dissenting.

The importance of the majority's decision to overrule the Court's holding in *Pennsylvania v. Union Gas Co.* cannot be overstated. The majority's opinion . . . prevents Congress from providing a federal forum for a broad range of actions against States, from those sounding in copyright and patent law, to those concerning bankruptcy, environmental law, and the regulation of our vast national economy.

[T]he shocking character of the majority's affront to a coequal branch of our Government merits additional comment.

I

For the purpose of deciding this case, I can readily assume that Justice Iredell's dissent in *Chisholm v. Georgia* (1793), and the Court's opinion in *Hans v. Louisiana* (1890), correctly stated the law that should govern our decision today. As I shall explain, both of those opinions relied on an interpretation of an Act of Congress rather than a want of congressional power to authorize a suit against the State.

---

17. Contrary to the claims of the dissent, we do not hold that Congress *cannot* authorize federal jurisdiction under *Ex parte Young* over a cause of action with a limited remedial scheme. We find only that Congress did not intend that result in the Indian Gaming Regulatory Act. Although one might argue that the text of §2710(d)(7)(A)(i), taken alone, is broad enough to encompass both a suit against a State (under an abrogation theory) and a suit against a state official (under an *Ex parte Young* theory), subsection (A)(i) of §2710(d)(7) cannot be read in isolation from subsections (B)(ii)-(vii), which repeatedly refer exclusively to "the State." . . .

In concluding that the federal courts could not entertain Chisholm's action against the State of Georgia, Justice Iredell relied on the text of the Judiciary Act of 1789, not the State's assertion that Article III did not extend the judicial power to suits against unconsenting States. Justice Iredell argued that, under Article III, federal courts possessed only such jurisdiction as Congress had provided, and that the Judiciary Act expressly limited federal-court jurisdiction to that which could be exercised in accordance with "'the principles and usages of law.'" *Chisholm v. Georgia* (quoting §14 of the Judiciary Act of 1789). He reasoned that the inclusion of this phrase constituted a command to the federal courts to construe their jurisdiction in light of the prevailing common law, a background legal regime that he believed incorporated the doctrine of sovereign immunity. *Chisholm v. Georgia* (dissenting opinion).[2]

Because Justice Iredell believed that the expansive text of Article III did not prevent Congress from imposing this common-law limitation on federal-court jurisdiction, he concluded that judges had no authority to entertain a suit against an unconsenting State.[3] At the same time, although he acknowledged that the Constitution might allow Congress to extend federal-court jurisdiction to such an action, he concluded that the terms of the Judiciary Act of 1789 plainly had not done so.

> [Congress'] direction, I apprehend, we cannot supersede, because it may appear to us not sufficiently extensive. *If it be not, we must wait till other remedies are provided by the same authority.* From this it is plain that the Legislature did not choose to leave to our own discretion the path to justice, but has prescribed one of its own. . . .

For Justice Iredell then, it was enough to assume that Article III *permitted* Congress to impose sovereign immunity as a jurisdictional limitation; he did not proceed to resolve the further question whether the Constitution went so far as to *prevent* Congress from withdrawing a State's immunity.[4] Thus, it would be ironic to construe the *Chisholm* dissent as precedent for the conclusion that Article III limits Congress' power to determine the scope of a State's sovereign immunity in federal court.

---

2. Because Justice Iredell read the Judiciary Act of 1789 to have incorporated the common law, he did not even conclude that Congress would have to make a clear statement in order to override the common law's recognition of sovereign immunity.

3. Actually, he limited his conclusion to the narrower question whether an action of assumpsit would lie against a State, which he distinguished from the more general question whether a State can ever be sued. *Chisholm v. Georgia.* He did so because he recognized "that in *England*, certain judicial proceedings not inconsistent with the sovereignty, may take place against the Crown, but that an action of *assumpsit* will not lie," and because he had "often found a great deal of confusion to arise from taking too large a view at once."

4. In two sentences at the end of his lengthy opinion, Justice Iredell stated that his then-present view was that the Constitution would not permit a "compulsive suit against a State for the recovery of money." In light of Justice Iredell's express statement that the only question before the Court was the propriety of an individual's action for assumpsit against a State, an action which, of course, results in a money judgment this dicta should not be understood to state the general view that the Constitution bars *all* suits against unconsenting States. Moreover, even as to the limited question whether the Constitution permits actions for money judgments, Justice Iredell took pains to reserve ultimate judgment. *Chisholm v. Georgia.* Thus, nothing in Justice Iredell's two sentences of dicta provides a basis for concluding that Congress lacks the power to authorize the suit for the nonmonetary relief at issue here.

Whatever the precise dimensions of the [Eleventh] Amendment, its express terms plainly do *not* apply to all suits brought against unconsenting States. The question thus becomes whether the relatively modest jurisdictional bar that the Eleventh Amendment imposes should be understood to reveal that a more general jurisdictional bar implicitly inheres in Article III.

The language of Article III certainly gives no indication that such an implicit bar exists. That provision's text specifically provides for federal-court jurisdiction over *all* cases arising under federal law. In sum, little more than speculation justifies the conclusion that the Eleventh Amendment's express but partial limitation on the scope of Article III reveals that an implicit but more general one was already in place.

II

Hans . . . reflects, at the most, this Court's conclusion that, as a matter of federal common law, federal courts should decline to entertain suits against unconsenting States. Because *Hans* did not announce a constitutionally mandated jurisdictional bar, one need not overrule *Hans*, or even question its reasoning, in order to conclude that Congress may direct the federal courts to reject sovereign immunity in those suits not mentioned by the Eleventh Amendment. Instead, one need only follow it.

Justice Bradley's somewhat cryptic opinion for the Court in *Hans* relied expressly on the reasoning of Justice Iredell's dissent in *Chisholm*, which, of course, was premised on the view that the doctrine of state sovereign immunity was a common-law rule that Congress had directed federal courts to respect, not a constitutional immunity that Congress was powerless to displace.

No one has ever suggested that Congress would be powerless to displace the other common-law immunity doctrines that this Court has recognized as appropriate defenses to certain federal claims such as the judicially fashioned remedy in *Bivens v. Six Unknown Fed. Narcotics Agents* (1971). *See Mitchell v. Forsyth* (1985); *Harlow v. Fitzgerald* (1982). Similarly, our cases recognizing qualified officer immunity in 42 U.S.C. §1983 actions rest on the conclusion that, in passing that statute, Congress did not intend to displace the common-law immunity that officers would have retained under suits premised solely on the general jurisdictional statute. For that reason, the federal common law of officer immunity that Congress meant to incorporate, not a contrary state immunity, applies in §1983 cases. *See Martinez v. California* (1980). There is no reason why Congress' undoubted power to displace those common-law immunities should be either greater or lesser than its power to displace the common-law sovereign immunity defense.

Some of our precedents do state that the sovereign immunity doctrine rests on fundamental constitutional "postulates" and partakes of jurisdictional aspects rooted in Article III. Most notably, that reasoning underlies this Court's holding in *Principality of Monaco v. Mississippi* (1934).

Monaco is a most inapt precedent for the majority's holding today. That case barred a foreign sovereign from suing a State in an equitable state-law action to recover payments due on state bonds. It did not, however, involve a claim based on federal law. Instead, the case concerned a purely state-law question to which the

State had interposed a federal defense. *Monaco.* Thus, *Monaco* reveals little about the power of Congress to create a private federal cause of action to remedy a State's violation of federal law.

Moreover, although *Monaco* attributes a quasi-constitutional status to sovereign immunity, even in cases not covered by the Eleventh Amendment's plain text, that characterization does not constitute precedent for the proposition that Congress is powerless to displace a State's immunity. Our abstention doctrines have roots in both the Tenth Amendment and Article III, and thus may be said to rest on constitutional "postulates" or to partake of jurisdictional aspects. Yet it has not been thought that the Constitution would prohibit Congress from barring federal courts from abstaining. The majority offers no reason for making the federal common-law rule of sovereign immunity less susceptible to congressional displacement than any other quasi-jurisdictional common-law rule.

Our clear-statement cases would have been all but unintelligible if *Hans* and *Monaco* had already established that Congress lacked the constitutional power to make States suable in federal court by individuals no matter how clear its intention to do so.

Finally, the particular nature of the federal question involved in *Hans* renders the majority's reliance upon its rule even less defensible. *Hans* deduced its rebuttable presumption in favor of sovereign immunity largely on the basis of its extensive analysis of cases holding that the sovereign could not be forced to make good on its debts via a private suit.

In *Hans*, the plaintiff asserted a Contracts Clause claim against his State and thus asserted a federal right. To show that Louisiana had impaired its federal obligation, however, Hans first had to demonstrate that the State had entered into an enforceable contract as a matter of state law. That Hans chose to bring his claim in federal court as a Contract Clause action could not change the fact that he was, at bottom, seeking to enforce a contract with the State. *See* Burnham, Taming the Eleventh Amendment Without Overruling *Hans v. Louisiana.*

Because Hans' claimed federal right did not arise independently of state law, sovereign immunity was relevant to the threshold state-law question of whether a valid contract existed.[14] *Hans* expressly pointed out, however, that an individual who could show that he had an *enforceable* contract under state law would not be barred from bringing suit in federal court to prevent the State from impairing it. . . . That conclusion casts doubt on the absolutist view that *Hans* definitively establishes that Article III prohibits federal courts from entertaining federal-question suits brought against States by their own citizens. At the very least, *Hans* suggests that such suits may be brought to enjoin States from impairing existing contractual obligations.

. . .

---

14. Significantly, many of the cases decided after *Hans* in which this Court has recognized state sovereign immunity involved claims premised on the breach of rights that were rooted in state law. In such cases, the Court's application of the state-law immunity appears simply to foreshadow (or follow) the rule of *Erie R.R. Co. v. Tompkins* (1938), not to demark the limits of Article III.

Here, of course, no question of a State's contractual obligations is presented. The Seminole Tribe's only claim is that the State of Florida has failed to fulfill a duty to negotiate that federal statutory law alone imposes.

IV

Except insofar as it has been incorporated into the text of the Eleventh Amendment, the doctrine is entirely the product of judge-made law. Three features of its English ancestry make it particularly unsuitable for incorporation into the law of this democratic Nation.

First, the assumption that it could be supported by a belief that "the King can do no wrong" has always been absurd; the bloody path trod by English monarchs both before and after they reached the throne demonstrated the fictional character of any such assumption. Even if the fiction had been acceptable in Britain, the recitation in the Declaration of Independence of the wrongs committed by George III made that proposition unacceptable on this side of the Atlantic.

Second, centuries ago the belief that the monarch served by divine right made it appropriate to assume that redress for wrongs committed by the sovereign should be the exclusive province of still higher authority. While such a justification for a rule that immunized the sovereign from suit in a secular tribunal might have been acceptable in a jurisdiction where a particular faith is endorsed by the government, it should give rise to skepticism concerning the legitimacy of comparable rules in a society where a constitutional wall separates the State from the Church.

Third, in a society where noble birth can justify preferential treatment, it might have been unseemly to allow a commoner to hale the monarch into court. Justice Wilson explained how foreign such a justification is to this Nation's principles. *See Chisholm v. Georgia.* Moreover, Chief Justice Marshall early on laid to rest the view that the purpose of the Eleventh Amendment was to protect a State's dignity. *Cohens v. Virginia* (1821). Its purpose, he explained, was far more practical.

> That its motive was not to maintain the sovereignty of a State from the degradation supposed to attend a compulsory appearance before the tribunal of the nation, may be inferred from the terms of the amendment. . . . We must ascribe the amendment, then, to some other cause than the dignity of a State. . . .

Nevertheless, this Court later put forth the interest in preventing "indignity" as the "very object and purpose of the [Eleventh] Amendment." *In re Ayers* (1887) That, of course, is an "embarrassingly insufficient" rationale for the rule.

Moreover, I find unsatisfying Justice Holmes' explanation that "[a] sovereign is exempt from suit, not because of any formal conception or obsolete theory, but on the logical and practical ground that there can be no legal right as against the authority that makes the law on which the right depends." *Kawananakoa v. Polyblank* (1907).

In this country the sovereignty of the individual States is subordinate both to the citizenry of each State and to the supreme law of the federal sovereign. For that reason, Justice Holmes' explanation for a rule that allows a State to avoid suit in its own courts does not even speak to the question whether Congress should be able to authorize a federal court to provide a private remedy for a State's violation of federal law. In my view, neither the majority's opinion today, nor any earlier opinion by any Member of the Court, has identified any acceptable reason for concluding that the absence of a State's consent to be sued in federal court should affect the power of Congress to authorize federal courts to remedy violations of federal law by States or their officials in actions not covered by the Eleventh Amendment's explicit text.

I recognize that federalism concerns—and even the interest in protecting the solvency of the States that was at work in *Chisholm* and *Hans*—may well justify a grant of immunity from federal litigation in certain classes of cases. Such a grant, however, should be the product of a reasoned decision by the policymaking branch of our Government. . . .

Justice SOUTER, with whom Justice GINSBURG and Justice BREYER join, dissenting.

. . . [As Justice Stevens has shown,] we have two Eleventh Amendments, the one ratified in 1795, the other (so-called) invented by the Court nearly a century later in *Hans v. Louisiana* (1890). The fault I find with the majority today is not in its decision to reexamine *Union Gas*, for the Court in that case produced no majority for a single rationale supporting congressional authority. Instead, I part company from the Court because I am convinced that its decision is fundamentally mistaken.

I

It is useful to separate three questions: (1) whether the States enjoyed sovereign immunity if sued in their own courts in the period prior to ratification of the National Constitution; (2) if so, whether after ratification the States were entitled to claim some such immunity when sued in a federal court exercising jurisdiction either because the suit was between a State and a nonstate litigant who was not its citizen, or because the issue in the case raised a federal question; and (3) whether any state sovereign immunity recognized in federal court may be abrogated by Congress.

A

Whatever the scope of sovereign immunity might have been in the Colonies . . . or during the period of Confederation, the proposal to establish a National Government under the Constitution drafted in 1787 presented a prospect unknown to the common law prior to the American experience: the States would become parts of a system in which sovereignty over even domestic matters would be divided or parcelled out between the States and the Nation, the latter to be invested with its own judicial power and the right to prevail against the States whenever their respective substantive laws might be in conflict.

[But with regard to how to adjust the doctrine of sovereign immunity to these new conditions] there was no consensus on the issue. *See Atascadero State Hosp. v. Scanlon*, (1985) (Brennan, J., dissenting); *Nevada v. Hall* (1979); Jacobs, *The Eleventh Amendment and Sovereign Immunity* ("[T]he legislative history of the Constitution hardly warrants the conclusion drawn by some that there was a general understanding, at the time of ratification, that the states would retain their sovereign immunity"). There was, on the contrary, a clear disagreement, which was left to fester during the ratification period, to be resolved only thereafter. One other point, however, was also clear: the debate addressed only the question whether ratification of the Constitution would, in diversity cases and without more, abrogate the state sovereign immunity or allow it to have some application. We have no record that anyone argued . . . that the Constitution would affirmatively guarantee state sovereign immunity against any congressional action to the contrary. Nor would there have been any apparent justification for any such argument, since no clause in the proposed (and ratified) Constitution even so much as suggested such a position. It may have been reasonable to contend (as we will see that Madison, Marshall, and Hamilton did) that Article III would not alter States' pre-existing common-law immunity despite its unqualified grant of jurisdiction over diversity suits against States. But then, as now, there was no textual support for contending that Article III or any other provision would "constitutionalize" state sovereign immunity, and no one uttered any such contention.

C

In precisely tracking the language in Article III providing for citizen-state diversity jurisdiction, the text of the Amendment does, after all, suggest to common sense that only the Diversity Clauses are being addressed. If the Framers had meant the Amendment to bar federal-question suits as well, they could not only have made their intentions clearer very easily, but could simply have adopted the first post-*Chisholm* proposal, introduced in the House of Representatives by Theodore Sedgwick of Massachusetts on instructions from the Legislature of that Commonwealth. Its provisions would have had exactly that expansive effect:

> [N]o state shall be liable to be made a party defendant, in any of the judicial courts, established, or which shall be established under the authority of the United States, at the suit of any person or persons, whether a citizen or citizens, or a foreigner or foreigners, or of any body politic or corporate, whether within or without the United States.

With its references to suits by citizens as well as non-citizens, the Sedgwick amendment would necessarily have been applied beyond the Diversity Clauses, and for a reason that would have been wholly obvious to the people of the time. Sedgwick sought such a broad amendment because many of the States, including his own, owed debts subject to collection under the Treaty of Paris. Suits to collect such debts would "arise under" that Treaty and thus be subject to federal-question jurisdiction under Article III. Such a suit, indeed, was then already pending against. Massachusetts, having been brought in this Court by Christopher Vassall, an erstwhile Bostonian whose move to England on the eve of revolutionary hostilities had presented his former neighbors with the irresistible temptation to confiscate his vacant mansion. Documentary History of the Supreme Court of the United States, 1789-1800.

Congress took no action on Sedgwick's proposal, however, and the Amendment as ultimately adopted two years later could hardly have been meant to limit federal-question jurisdiction, or it would never have left the States open to federal-question suits by their own citizens. To be sure, the majority of state creditors were not citizens, but nothing in the Treaty would have prevented foreign creditors from selling their debt instruments (thereby assigning their claims) to citizens of the debtor State. If the Framers of the Eleventh Amendment had meant it to immunize States from federal-question suits like those that might be brought to enforce the Treaty of Paris, they would surely have drafted the Amendment differently. *See* Fletcher, *The Diversity Explanation of the Eleventh Amendment: A Reply to Critics.*

It should accordingly come as no surprise that the weightiest commentary following the Amendment's adoption described it simply as constricting the scope of the Citizen–State Diversity Clauses.

III

Three critical errors in *Hans* weigh against constitutionalizing its holding as the majority does today. The first we have already seen: the *Hans* Court misread the Eleventh Amendment. It also misunderstood the conditions under which common-law doctrines were received or rejected at the time of the founding, and it fundamentally mistook the very nature of sovereignty in the young Republic that was supposed to entail a State's immunity to federal-question jurisdiction in a federal court.

A

There is and could be no dispute that the doctrine of sovereign immunity that *Hans* purported to apply had its origins in the "familiar doctrine of the common law," *The Siren* (1869), "derived from the laws and practices of our English ancestors," *United States v. Lee* (1882). Here, as in the mother country, it remained a common-law rule. *See generally* Jaffe, *Suits Against Governments and Officers.*

This fact of the doctrine's common-law status in the period covering the founding and the later adoption of the Eleventh Amendment should have raised a warning flag to the *Hans* Court and it should do the same for the Court today. For although the Court has persistently assumed that the common law's presence in the minds of the early Framers must have functioned as a limitation on their understanding of the new Nation's constitutional powers . . . the adoption of English common law in America was not taken for granted, and . . . the exact manner and extent of the common law's reception were subject to careful consideration by courts and legislatures in each of the new States.

B

Given the refusal to entertain any wholesale reception of common law, given the failure of the new Constitution to make any provision for adoption of common law as such, and given the protests already quoted that no general reception had occurred, the *Hans* Court and the Court today cannot reasonably argue that something like the old immunity doctrine somehow slipped in as a tacit but enforceable background principle. The evidence is even more specific, however, that there was no pervasive understanding that sovereign immunity had limited federal-question jurisdiction.

1

The majority sees. . . . in Hamilton's discussion of sovereign immunity in The Federalist No. 81, an unequivocal mandate "which would preclude all federal jurisdiction over an unconsenting State." But there is no such mandate to be found.

[But] Hamilton is plainly talking about a suit subject to a federal court's jurisdiction under the Citizen–State Diversity Clauses of Article III. No general theory of federal-question immunity can be inferred from Hamilton's discussion of immunity in contract suits.

2

We said in *Blatchford v. Native Village of Noatak* (1991) that "the States entered the federal system with their sovereignty intact," but we surely did not mean that they entered that system with the sovereignty they would have claimed if each State had assumed independent existence in the community of nations, for even the Articles of Confederation allowed for less than that. *See* Articles of Confederation, Art. VI, §1 ("No State without the consent of the United States in Congress assembled, shall send any embassy to, or receive any embassy from, or enter into any conference, agreement, alliance or treaty with any king, prince or state . . .").

In the end, is it plausible to contend that the plan of the convention was meant to leave the National Government without any way to render individuals capable of enforcing their federal rights directly against an intransigent State? . . .

Because neither text, precedent, nor history supports the majority's abdication of our responsibility to exercise the jurisdiction entrusted to us in Article III, I would reverse the judgment of the Court of Appeals.

* * *

The Seminole Tribe was one of the first federally recognized tribes to launch gaming operations in 1979. Such gaming operations have been important components of economic development policies for some Native nations. For tribes with successful gaming operations, studies have shown that gaming has "had a far-reaching and transformative effect on American Indian reservations and their economies [including] marked improvements in several important dimensions of reservation life."[13] The United States government's policies, including the nineteenth and early-twentieth century allotment policies that led to Native nations losing over two-thirds of their lands and resources, "inhibited tribal economic development" for much of U.S. history.[14] During the modern era, Native nations have taken back control of their self-government and economies, with a demonstrable "turnaround

---

13. Randall K.Q. Akee, Katherine A. Spilde, & Jonathan B. Taylor, *The Indian Gaming Regulatory Act and Its Effects on American Indian Economic Development*, 29 J. Econ. Persp. 185 (2015).

14. Cohen's Handbook of Federal Indian Law §21.01 (Nell Newton et al. eds., 2012).

in economic and social conditions in Indian country," including changes in real on-reservation per capita income, educational attainment, public health measures, and infrastructure.[15]

Prior to the enactment of the Indian Gaming Regulatory Act (IGRA), the Supreme Court held in *California v. Cabazon Band of Mission Indians* (1987), that "[s]tate regulation of [gaming on tribal reservations] would impermissibly infringe on tribal government." This landmark case thus denied states regulatory authority over tribal gaming operations on tribal reservations. In *Cabazon Band*, the Court recognized the vital role that gaming could play for Native nations; in that case, for example, the "[t]ribal games . . . provide[d] the sole source of revenue for the operation of tribal governments and the provision of tribal services," and were also "the major sources of employment" on the Cabazon and Morongo reservations. In light of tribal sovereignty, and the federal policy of supporting tribal self-determination, the Court held that states could not regulate tribal economic development in the form of tribal gaming.

Following *Cabazon*, states lobbied for federal legislation on the regulation of tribal gaming. Congress authorized state participation through the compact process established in IGRA. In Florida and other states, the principal concern with Indian gaming was financial—Indian gaming competed with lotteries run directly by states and private casinos from which the state derived tax revenue. IGRA and its compact process would, in theory, promote negotiation to minimize competition by designating which classes of gaming were exempt from the compact process altogether and focusing negotiation on the classes of gaming that are legal under state law. Most compacts result in revenue-sharing arrangements in which the tribes receive exclusive rights to conduct gaming but share some of the profits with states. For example, after years of negotiation, the DOI approved a compact between the Seminole Tribe and Florida in 2010, resulting in hundreds of millions of dollars a year in revenue-sharing payments to the state on over $2 billion in revenue earned by the tribe. In subsequent years, Florida has demanded additional revenue guarantees.

Seminole Tribe represents the apotheosis of the extra-textual expansion of state sovereign immunity. Not only does the doctrine apply well beyond the diversity of citizenship formulation of the Eleventh Amendment to bar in-state citizens (*Hans*), foreign governments (*Principality of Monaco*), and Native nations (*Blatchford*) from suing a state in federal court, it also strictly constrains the authority of Congress to set aside sovereign immunity in areas the Constitution reserves to nearly exclusive federal control like the Indian Commerce Clause. And it does so even with respect to a cause of action that poses no threat to a state legislature's control over the state treasury—the central federalism concern in *Chisholm, Hans, Principality of Monaco,* and *Blatchford*.

On the other hand, is the oversight role that IGRA assigns to federal courts consistent with Article III's requirement that federal courts exercise "judicial power"? What do you make of the fact that at the end of the road the statute vests the power to resolve failed compact negotiations in the hands of the Secretary of the Interior?

The Court closed the door to a tribal suit to enforce of a state's failure to negotiate in good faith under the IGRA. But under the Supremacy Clause, the state of

---

15. Stephen Cornell & Joseph P. Kalt, *American Indian Self-Determination: The Political Economy of a Policy That Works,* HKS Faculty Research Working Paper Series RWP10-043, at 9 & fig.5 (2010), http://nrs.harvard.edu/urn-3:HUL.InstRepos:4553307.

Florida is still bound by the mandates of IGRA. What other avenues remain open to ensure that Florida and other states meet their federal legal obligations? Who can pursue these avenues? As long as other routes are available to enforce IGRA, is there any constitutional objection to prohibiting tribes from suing under the statute? One alternative the majority takes off the table is an *Ex parte Young* suit. As in *Armstrong*, discussed in the notes after *Ex parte Young*, the Court inquired into the presence of adequate alternatives to an officer suit in equity. It would of course be strange to conclude that a statutory alternative that the Court *has struck down* is remedially adequate. So, the inference the Court relied on instead is that Congress created the compact process because it did not want Native nations to rely on *Ex parte Young*.

The dissent offers a counter-history to the Court's recitation of the conventional narrative regarding the ratification of the Eleventh Amendment. What in your view is the most persuasive evidence presented by each side?

The Court returned to state sovereign immunity when a group of probation officers employed by the state of Maine sued the state for failing to pay overtime wages required under the federal Fair Labor Standards Act of 1938. As you read the Court's decision that a state is not answerable even *in its own courts* to a citizen of the state who asserts that the state is violating federal law, consider the tension between this holding and the line of cases we read in Chapter 4.C, concluding that state courts have a constitutional duty under the Supremacy Clause to adjudicate cases that arise under federal law.

Alden v. Maine

527 U.S. 706 (1999)

Justice KENNEDY delivered the opinion of the Court.

In 1992, petitioners, a group of probation officers, filed suit against their employer, the State of Maine, in the United States District Court for the District of Maine. The officers alleged the State had violated the overtime provisions of the Fair Labor Standards Act of 1938 (FLSA), 29 U.S.C. §201, and sought compensation and liquidated damages. While the suit was pending, this Court decided *Seminole Tribe of Fla. v. Florida* (1996), which made it clear that Congress lacks power under Article I to abrogate the States' sovereign immunity from suits commenced or prosecuted in the federal courts. Upon consideration of *Seminole Tribe*, the District Court dismissed petitioners' action, and the Court of Appeals affirmed. Petitioners then filed the same action in state court. The state trial court dismissed the suit on the basis of sovereign immunity, and the Maine Supreme Judicial Court affirmed.

We hold that the powers delegated to Congress under Article I of the United States Constitution do not include the power to subject nonconsenting States to private suits for damages in state courts. We decide as well that the State of Maine has not consented to suits for overtime pay and liquidated damages under the FLSA. On these premises we affirm the judgment sustaining dismissal of the suit.

I

We have sometimes referred to the States' immunity from suit as "Eleventh Amendment immunity." The phrase is convenient shorthand but something of a misnomer, for the sovereign immunity of the States neither derives from, nor is limited by, the terms of the Eleventh Amendment. Rather, as the Constitution's structure, its history, and the authoritative interpretations by this Court make clear, the States' immunity from suit is a fundamental aspect of the sovereignty which the States enjoyed before the ratification of the Constitution, and which they retain today (either literally or by virtue of their admission into the Union upon an equal footing with the other States) except as altered by the plan of the Convention or certain constitutional Amendments.

A

Although the Constitution establishes a National Government with broad, often plenary authority over matters within its recognized competence, the founding document "specifically recognizes the States as sovereign entities." *Seminole Tribe,* accord *Blatchford v. Native Vill. of Noatak* (1991) ("[T]he States entered the federal system with their sovereignty intact"). Any doubt regarding the constitutional role of the States as sovereign entities is removed by the Tenth Amendment, which, like the other provisions of the Bill of Rights, was enacted to allay lingering concerns about the extent of the national power.

[E]ven as to matters within the competence of the National Government, the constitutional design secures the founding generation's rejection of "the concept of a central government that would act upon and through the States" in favor of "a system in which the State and Federal Governments would exercise concurrent authority over the people—who were, in Hamilton's words, 'the only proper objects of government.'" *Printz v. United States* (1997) (quoting The Federalist No. 15); *accord New York v. United States* (1992) ("The Framers explicitly chose a Constitution that confers upon Congress the power to regulate individuals, not States"),

The States thus retain "a residuary and inviolable sovereignty." The Federalist No. 39. They are not relegated to the role of mere provinces or political corporations, but retain the dignity, though not the full authority, of sovereignty.

B

The generation that designed and adopted our federal system considered immunity from private suits central to sovereign dignity. In reciting the prerogatives of the Crown, Blackstone—whose works constituted the preeminent authority on English law for the founding generation—underscored the close and necessary relationship understood to exist between sovereignty and immunity from suit:

> And, first, the law ascribes to the king the attribute of sovereignty, or pre-eminence. . . . Hence it is, that no suit or action can be brought against the king, even in civil matters, because no court can have jurisdiction over him. For all jurisdiction implies superiority of power.

Although the American people had rejected other aspects of English political theory, the doctrine that a sovereign could not be sued without its consent was universal in the States when the Constitution was drafted and ratified.

Although the dissent attempts to rewrite history to reflect a different original understanding, its evidence is unpersuasive. The handful of state statutory and constitutional provisions authorizing suits or petitions of right against States only confirms the prevalence of the traditional understanding that a State could not be sued in the absence of an express waiver, for if the understanding were otherwise, the provisions would have been unnecessary.

II

A

Petitioners contend the text of the Constitution and our recent sovereign immunity decisions establish that the States were required to relinquish this portion of their sovereignty. We turn first to these sources.

1

The Constitution, by delegating to Congress the power to establish the supreme law of the land when acting within its enumerated powers, does not foreclose a State from asserting immunity to claims arising under federal law merely because that law derives not from the State itself but from the national power. A contrary view could not be reconciled with *Hans*, which sustained Louisiana's immunity in a private suit arising under the Constitution itself; with *Employees of Dept. of Public Health and Welfare of Mo. v. Department of Public Health and Welfare of Mo.* (1973), which recognized that the FLSA was binding upon Missouri but nevertheless upheld the State's immunity to a private suit to recover under that Act; or with numerous other decisions to the same effect. We reject any contention that substantive federal law by its own force necessarily overrides the sovereign immunity of the States. When a State asserts its immunity to suit, the question is not the primacy of federal law but the implementation of the law in a manner consistent with the constitutional sovereignty of the States.

Nor can we conclude that the specific Article I powers delegated to Congress necessarily include, by virtue of the Necessary and Proper Clause or otherwise, the incidental authority to subject the States to private suits as a means of achieving objectives otherwise within the scope of the enumerated powers. As we have recognized in an analogous context:

> When a "La[w]. . . for carrying into Execution" the Commerce Clause violates the principle of state sovereignty reflected in the various constitutional provisions. . . it is not a "La[w] . . . *proper* for carrying into Execution the Commerce Clause," and is thus, in the words of The Federalist, "merely [an] ac[t] of usurpation" which "deserve[s] to be treated as such."

Printz.

The cases we have cited, of course, came at last to the conclusion that neither the Supremacy Clause nor the enumerated powers of Congress confer authority to abrogate the States' immunity from suit in federal court. The logic of the decisions, however, does not turn on the forum in which the suits were prosecuted but extends to state-court suits as well. . . .

Although the sovereign immunity of the States derives at least in part from the common-law tradition, the structure and history of the Constitution make clear that the immunity exists today by constitutional design.

2

There are isolated statements in some of our cases suggesting that the Eleventh Amendment is inapplicable in state courts. This, of course, is a truism as to the literal terms of the Eleventh Amendment. As we have explained, however, the bare text of the Amendment is not an exhaustive description of the States' constitutional immunity from suit. *Hilton v. So. Car. Pub. R. Comm'n* (1991). The cases, furthermore, do not decide the question presented here—whether the States retain immunity from private suits in their own courts notwithstanding an attempted abrogation by the Congress.

Petitioners seek support in two additional decisions. In *Reich v. Collins* (1994), we held that, despite its immunity from suit in federal court, a State which holds out what plainly appears to be "a clear and certain" post-deprivation remedy for taxes collected in violation of federal law may not declare, after disputed taxes have been paid in reliance on this remedy, that the remedy does not in fact exist. This case arose in the context of tax-refund litigation, where a State may deprive a taxpayer of all other means of challenging the validity of its tax laws by holding out what appears to be a "clear and certain" postdeprivation remedy. In this context, due process requires the State to provide the remedy it has promised. The obligation arises from the Constitution itself; *Reich* does not speak to the power of Congress to subject States to suits in their own courts.

In *Howlett v. Rose* (1990), we held that a state court could not refuse to hear a §1983 suit against a school board on the basis of sovereign immunity. The school board was not an arm of the State, however, so it could not assert any constitutional defense of sovereign immunity to which the State would have been entitled. In *Howlett*, then, the only question was "whether a state-law defense of 'sovereign immunity' is available to a school board otherwise subject to suit in a Florida court even though such a defense would not be available if the action had been brought in a federal forum." The decision did not address the question of Congress' power to compel a state court to entertain an action against a nonconsenting State.

B

Whether Congress has authority under Article I to abrogate a State's immunity from suit in its own courts is, then, a question of first impression.

1

We look first to evidence of the original understanding of the Constitution. Petitioners contend that because the ratification debates and the events surrounding the adoption of the Eleventh Amendment focused on the States' immunity from suit in federal courts, the historical record gives no instruction as to the founding generation's intent to preserve the States' immunity from suit in their own courts.

We believe, however, that the Founders' silence is best explained by the simple fact that no one, not even the Constitution's most ardent opponents, suggested the document might strip the States of the immunity. In light of the overriding concern regarding the States' war-time debts, together with the well-known creativity, foresight, and vivid imagination of the Constitution's opponents, the silence is most instructive. It suggests the sovereign's right to assert immunity from suit in its own courts was a principle so well established that no one conceived it would be altered by the new Constitution.

The arguments raised against the Constitution confirm this strong inference. In England, the rule was well established that "no lord could be sued by a vassal in his own court, but each petty lord was subject to suit in the courts of a higher lord." *Nevada v. Hall* (1979). It was argued that, by analogy, the States could be sued without consent in federal court. The point of the argument was that federal jurisdiction under Article III would circumvent the States' immunity from suit in their own courts. The argument would have made little sense if the States were understood to have relinquished the immunity in all events.

The language of the Eleventh Amendment, furthermore, was directed toward the only provisions of the constitutional text believed to call the States' immunity from private suits into question. Although Article III expressly contemplated jurisdiction over suits between States and individuals, nothing in the Article or in any other part of the Constitution suggested the States could not assert immunity from private suit in their own courts or that Congress had the power to abrogate sovereign immunity there.

Finally, the Congress which endorsed the Eleventh Amendment rejected language limiting the Amendment's scope to cases where the States had made available a remedy in their own courts. Implicit in the proposal, it is evident, was the premise that the States retained their immunity and the concomitant authority to decide whether to allow private suits against the sovereign in their own courts.

2

The "numerousness of . . . statutes [authorizing suit in state court], contrasted with the utter lack of statutes" subjecting States to suit, "suggests an assumed *absence* of such power." *Printz*. It thus appears early Congresses did not believe they had the power to authorize private suits against the States in their own courts. . . .

The first statute we confronted that even arguably purported to subject the States to private actions was the FELA. As we later recognized, however, even this statute did not clearly create a cause of action against the States. The provisions of the FLSA at issue here, which were enacted in the aftermath of *Parden v. Terminal Ry. Co.* (1964), are among the first statutory enactments purporting in express terms to subject nonconsenting States to private suits. Although similar statutes have multiplied in the last generation, "they are of such recent vintage that they are no more probative than the [FLSA] of a constitutional tradition that lends meaning to the text. Their persuasive force is far outweighed by almost two centuries of apparent congressional avoidance of the practice." *Printz*.

Even the recent statutes, moreover, do not provide evidence of an understanding that Congress has a greater power to subject States to suit in their own courts than in federal courts.

3

We have said on many occasions that the States retain their immunity from private suits prosecuted in their own courts. In particular, the exception to our sovereign immunity doctrine recognized in *Ex parte Young* (1908), is based in part on the premise that sovereign immunity bars relief against States and their officers in both state and federal courts, and that certain suits for declaratory or injunctive relief against state officers must therefore be permitted if the Constitution is to remain the supreme law of the land.

4

Petitioners contend that immunity from suit in federal court suffices to preserve the dignity of the States. Private suits against nonconsenting States, however, present "the indignity of subjecting a State to the coercive process of judicial tribunals at the instance of private parties," *In re Ayers* (1887), regardless of the forum. Not only must a State defend or default but also it must face the prospect of being thrust, by federal fiat and against its will, into the disfavored status of a debtor, subject to the power of private citizens to levy on its treasury or perhaps even government buildings or property which the State administers on the public's behalf.

In some ways, of course, a congressional power to authorize private suits against nonconsenting States in their own courts would be even more offensive to state sovereignty than a power to authorize the suits in a federal forum. A power to press a State's own courts into federal service to coerce the other branches of the State, furthermore, is the power first to turn the State against itself and ultimately to commandeer the entire political machinery of the State against its will and at the behest of individuals. Such plenary federal control of state governmental processes denigrates the separate sovereignty of the States.

It is unquestioned that the Federal Government retains its own immunity from suit not only in state tribunals but also in its own courts. In light of our constitutional system recognizing the essential sovereignty of the States, we are reluctant to conclude that the States are not entitled to a reciprocal privilege.

Underlying constitutional form are considerations of great substance. Private suits against nonconsenting States — especially suits for money damages — may threaten the financial integrity of the States. It is indisputable that, at the time of the founding, many of the States could have been forced into insolvency but for their immunity from private suits for money damages. Even today, an unlimited congressional power to authorize suits in state court to levy upon the treasuries of the States for compensatory damages, attorney's fees, and even punitive damages could create staggering burdens, giving Congress a power and a leverage over the States that is not contemplated by our constitutional design. The potential national power would pose a severe and notorious danger to the States and their resources.

When the States' immunity from private suits is disregarded, "the course of their public policy and the administration of their public affairs" may become "subject to and controlled by the mandates of judicial tribunals without their consent, and in favor of individual interests." *In re Ayers.* Today, as at the time of the founding, the allocation of scarce resources among competing needs and interests lies at the heart of the political process. While the judgment creditor of a State may have a legitimate claim for compensation, other important needs and worthwhile ends compete for access to the public fisc. Since all cannot be satisfied in full, it is inevitable that difficult decisions involving the most sensitive and political of judgments must be made. If the principle of representative government is to be preserved to the States, the balance between competing interests must be reached after deliberation by the political process established by the citizens of the State, not by judicial decree mandated by the Federal Government and invoked by the private citizen. "It needs no argument to show that the political power cannot be thus ousted of its jurisdiction and the judiciary set in its place." *Louisiana v. Jumel* (1883).

The Supremacy Clause does impose specific obligations on state judges. There can be no serious contention, however, that the Supremacy Clause imposes greater obligations on state-court judges than on the Judiciary of the United States itself. The text of Article III, §1, which extends federal judicial power to enumerated classes of suits but grants Congress discretion whether to establish inferior federal courts, does give strong support to the inference that state courts may be opened to suits falling within the federal judicial power. The Article in no way suggests, however, that state courts may be required to assume jurisdiction that could not be vested in the federal courts and forms no part of the judicial power of the United States.

In light of history, practice, precedent, and the structure of the Constitution, we hold that the States retain immunity from private suit in their own courts, an immunity beyond the congressional power to abrogate by Article I legislation.

III

The constitutional privilege of a State to assert its sovereign immunity in its own courts does not confer upon the State a concomitant right to disregard the Constitution or valid federal law. The States and their officers are bound by obligations imposed by the Constitution and by federal statutes that comport with the constitutional design. We are unwilling to assume the States will refuse to honor the Constitution or obey the binding laws of the United States. The good faith of the States thus provides an important assurance that "[t]his Constitution, and the Laws of the United States which shall be made in Pursuance thereof . . . shall be the supreme Law of the Land." U.S. Const., Art. VI.

Sovereign immunity, moreover, does not bar all judicial review of state compliance with the Constitution and valid federal law. Rather, certain limits are implicit in the constitutional principle of state sovereign immunity.

The first of these limits is that sovereign immunity bars suits only in the absence of consent. Many States, on their own initiative, have enacted statutes consenting to a wide variety of suits. . . .

The States have consented, moreover, to some suits pursuant to the plan of the Convention or to subsequent constitutional Amendments. In ratifying the Constitution, the States consented to suits brought by other States or by the Federal Government. *Principality of Monaco v. Mississippi* (1934) (collecting cases). A suit which is commenced and prosecuted against a State in the name of the United States by those who are entrusted with the constitutional duty to "take Care that the Laws be faithfully executed," U.S. Const., Art. II, §3, differs in kind from the suit of an individual: While the Constitution contemplates suits among the members of the federal system as an alternative to extralegal measures, the fear of private suits against nonconsenting States was the central reason given by the Founders who chose to preserve the States' sovereign immunity. Suits brought by the United States itself require the exercise of political responsibility for each suit prosecuted against a State, a control which is absent from a broad delegation to private persons to sue nonconsenting States.

We have held also that in adopting the Fourteenth Amendment, the people required the States to surrender a portion of the sovereignty that had been preserved to them by the original Constitution, so that Congress may authorize private suits against nonconsenting States pursuant to its §5 enforcement power. *Fitzpatrick v. Bitzer* (1976).

The second important limit to the principle of sovereign immunity is that it bars suits against States but not lesser entities. The immunity does not extend to suits prosecuted against a municipal corporation or other governmental entity which is not an arm of the State. Nor does sovereign immunity bar all suits against state officers. . . . *Compare Ex parte Young* (1908), and *In re Ayers with Seminole Tribe* and *Edelman v. Jordan* (1974). . . .

That we have, during the first 210 years of our constitutional history, found it unnecessary to decide the question presented here suggests a federal power to subject nonconsenting States to private suits in their own courts is unnecessary to uphold the Constitution and valid federal statutes as the supreme law.

IV

The sole remaining question is whether Maine has waived its immunity. The State of Maine . . . adheres to the general rule that "a specific authority conferred by an enactment of the legislature is requisite if the sovereign is to be taken as having shed the protective mantle of immunity." Petitioners have not attempted to establish a waiver of immunity under this standard. [T]here is no evidence that the State has manipulated its immunity in a systematic fashion to discriminate against federal causes of action.

V

The Solicitor General of the United States has appeared before this Court, however, and asserted that the federal interest in compensating the States' employees for alleged past violations of federal law is so compelling that the sovereign State of Maine must be stripped of its immunity and subjected to suit in its own courts by its own employees. Yet, despite specific statutory authorization, *see* 29 U.S.C. §216(c), the United States apparently found the same interests insufficient to justify sending even a single attorney to Maine to prosecute this litigation. The difference between a suit by the United States on behalf of the employees and a suit by the employees implicates a rule that the National Government must itself deem the case of sufficient importance to take action against the State; and history, precedent, and the structure of the Constitution make clear that, under the plan of the Convention, the States have consented to suits of the first kind but not of the second. The judgment of the Supreme Judicial Court of Maine is

Affirmed.

Justice SOUTER, with whom Justice STEVENS, Justice GINSBURG, and Justice BREYER join, dissenting.

Today's issue arises naturally in the aftermath of the decision in *Seminole Tribe.* The Court holds that the Constitution bars an individual suit against a State to enforce a federal statutory right under the Fair Labor Standards Act of 1938, when brought in the State's courts over its objection. In thus complementing its earlier decision, the Court of course confronts the fact that the state forum renders the Eleventh Amendment beside the point, and it has responded by discerning a simpler and more straightforward theory of state sovereign immunity than it found in *Seminole Tribe:* a State's sovereign immunity from all individual suits is a "fundamental aspect" of state sovereignty "confirm[ed]" by the Tenth Amendment. As a consequence, *Seminole Tribe*'s contorted reliance on the Eleventh Amendment and its background was presumably unnecessary; the Tenth would have done the work with an economy that the majority in *Seminole Tribe* would have welcomed. Indeed, if the Court's current reasoning is correct, the Eleventh Amendment itself was unnecessary. Whatever Article III may originally have said about the federal judicial power, the embarrassment to the State of Georgia occasioned by attempts in federal court to enforce the State's war debt could easily have been avoided if only the Court that decided *Chisholm v. Georgia* (1793), had understood a State's inherent, Tenth Amendment right to be free of any judicial power, whether the court be state or federal, and whether the cause of action arise under state or federal law.

There is no evidence that the Tenth Amendment constitutionalized a concept of sovereign immunity as inherent in the notion of statehood, and no evidence that any concept of inherent sovereign immunity was understood historically to apply when the sovereign sued was not the font of the law.

I

While sovereign immunity entered many new state legal systems as a part of the common law selectively received from England, it was not understood to be indefeasible or to have been given any such status by the new National Constitution, which did not mention it. There is almost no evidence that the generation of the Framers thought sovereign immunity was fundamental in the sense of being unalterable.

A

The American Colonies did not enjoy sovereign immunity, that being a privilege understood in English law to be reserved for the Crown alone; "antecedent to the Declaration of Independence, none of the colonies were, or pretended to be, sovereign states," 1 J. Story, Commentaries on the Constitution §207. Several colonial charters, including those of Massachusetts, Connecticut, Rhode Island, and Georgia, expressly specified that the corporate body established thereunder could sue and be sued. *See* 5 Sources and Documents of United States Constitutions.

B

The story of the subsequent development of conceptions of sovereignty is complex and uneven; here, it is enough to say that by the time independence was declared in 1776, the locus of sovereignty was still an open question, except that almost by definition, advocates of independence denied that sovereignty with respect to the American Colonies remained with the King in Parliament.

As the concept of sovereignty was unsettled, so was that of sovereign immunity. Some States appear to have understood themselves to be without immunity from suit in their own courts upon independence. Connecticut and Rhode Island adopted their pre-existing charters as constitutions, without altering the provisions specifying their suability. *See* Gibbons, *The Eleventh Amendment and State Sovereign Immunity.* Other new States understood themselves to be inheritors of the Crown's common law sovereign immunity and so enacted statutes authorizing legal remedies against the State parallel to those available in England. There, although the Crown was immune from suit, the contemporary practice allowed private litigants to seek legal remedies against the Crown through the petition of right or the *monstrans de droit* in the Chancery or Exchequer. *See* Blackstone. A Virginia statute provided:

> "Where the auditors according to their discretion and judgment shall disallow or abate any article of demand against the commonwealth, and any person shall think himself aggrieved thereby, he shall be at liberty to petition the high court of chancery or the general court, according to the nature of his case, for redress, and such court shall proceed to do right thereon; and a like petition shall be allowed in all other cases to any other person who is entitled to demand against the commonwealth any right in law or equity."

W. Hening, Statutes at Large: Being a Collection of the Laws of Virginia.

This "petition" was clearly reminiscent of the English petition of right. A New York statute similarly authorized petition to the court of chancery by anyone who thought himself aggrieved by the state auditor general's resolution of his account with the State. *See* An Act Directing a Mode for the Recovery of Debts Due to, and the Settlement of Accounts with, this State, March 30, 1781.

Pennsylvania not only adopted a law conferring the authority to settle accounts upon the Comptroller General, *see* Act of Apr. 13, 1782, ch. 959, but in 1785 provided for appeal from such adjudications to the Pennsylvania Supreme Court, where a jury trial could be had. Although in at least one recorded case before the Pennsylvania Supreme Court the Commonwealth, citing Blackstone, pleaded common law sovereign immunity, *see Respublica v. Sparhawk* (Pa. 1788), the Supreme Court of Pennsylvania did not reach this argument, concluding on other grounds that it lacked jurisdiction. Two years after this decision, under the influence of James Wilson, *see* C. Jacobs, The Eleventh Amendment and Sovereign Immunity, Pennsylvania adopted a new constitution, which provided that "[s]uits may be brought against the commonwealth in such manner, in such courts, and in such cases as the legislature may by law direct." Pa. Const., Art. IX, §11 (1790).

Around the time of the Constitutional Convention, then, there existed among the States some diversity of practice with respect to sovereign immunity; but despite a tendency to announce inalienable and natural rights, no State declared that sovereign immunity was one of those rights. To the extent that States were thought to possess immunity, it was perceived as a prerogative of the sovereign under common law.

C

At the Constitutional Convention, the notion of sovereign immunity, whether as natural law or as common law, was not an immediate subject of debate, and the sovereignty of a State in its own courts seems not to have been mentioned. This comes as no surprise, for although the Constitution required state courts to apply federal law, the Framers did not consider the possibility that federal law might bind

States, say, in their relations with their employees. In the subsequent ratification debates, however, the issue of jurisdiction over a State did emerge in the question whether States might be sued on their debts in federal court, and on this point, too, a variety of views emerged and the diversity of sovereign immunity conceptions displayed itself.

The only arguable support for the Court's absolutist view that I have found among the leading participants in the debate surrounding ratification was the one already mentioned, that of Alexander Hamilton in The Federalist No. 81, where he described the sovereign immunity of the States in language suggesting principles associated with natural law:

> It is inherent in the nature of sovereignty, not to be amenable to the suit of an individual *without its consent.* This is the general sense and the general practice of mankind; and the exemption, as one of the attributes of sovereignty, is now enjoyed by the government of every state in the union. Unless therefore, there is a surrender of this immunity in the plan of the convention, it will remain with the states, and the danger intimated [that States might be sued on their debts in federal court] must be merely ideal. . . .

Hamilton chose his words carefully, and he acknowledged the possibility that at the Convention the States might have surrendered sovereign immunity in some circumstances, but the thrust of his argument was that sovereign immunity was "inherent in the nature of sovereignty."

In the Virginia ratifying convention, Madison . . . maintained that "[i]t is not in the power of individuals to call any state into court," and thought that the phrase "in which a State shall be a Party" in Article III, §2, must be interpreted in light of that general principle, so that "[t]he only operation it can have, is that, if a state should wish to bring a suit against a citizen, it must be brought before the federal court." John Marshall argued along the same lines against the possibility of federal jurisdiction over private suits against States, and he invoked the immunity of a State in its own courts in support of his argument:

> I hope that no gentleman will think that a state will be called at the bar of the federal court. Is there no such case at present? Are there not many cases in which the legislature of Virginia is a party, and yet the state is not sued? It is not rational to suppose that the sovereign power should be dragged before a court.

There was no unanimity among the Virginians either on state- or federal-court immunity, however, for Edmund Randolph anticipated the position he would later espouse as plaintiff's counsel in *Chisholm v. Georgia.* He . . . argued that notwithstanding any natural law view of the nonsuability of States, the Constitution permitted suit against a State in federal court: "I think, whatever the law of nations may say, that any doubt respecting the construction that a state may be plaintiff, and not defendant, is taken away by the words *where a state shall be a party.*" Randolph clearly believed that the Constitution both could, and in fact by its language did, trump any inherent immunity enjoyed by the States; his view on sovereign immunity in state court seems to have been that the issue was uncertain ("whatever the law of nations may say").

[For James] Wilson, "[t]he answer [was] plain and easy: the government of each state ought to be subordinate to the government of the United States."[16] Wilson was also pointed in commenting on federal jurisdiction over cases between a State and citizens of another State: "When this power is attended to, it will be found to be a necessary one. Impartiality is the leading feature in this Constitution; it pervades the whole. When a citizen has a controversy with another state, there ought to be a tribunal where both parties may stand on a just and equal footing." Finally, Wilson laid out his view that sovereignty was in fact not located in the States at all: "Upon what principle is it contended that the sovereign power resides in the state governments? The honorable gentleman has said truly, that there can be no subordinate sovereignty. Now, if there cannot, my position is, that the sovereignty resides in the people; they have not parted with it; they have only dispensed such portions of the power as were conceived necessary for the public welfare."[17] While this statement did not specifically address sovereign immunity, it expressed the major premise of what would later become Justice Wilson's position in *Chisholm:* that because the people, and not the States, are sovereign, sovereign immunity has no applicability to the States.

From a canvass of this spectrum of opinion expressed at the ratifying conventions, one thing is certain. No one was espousing an indefeasible, natural law view of sovereign immunity. . . .

D

At the close of the ratification debates . . . [s]everal state ratifying conventions proposed amendments and issued declarations that would have exempted States from subjection to suit in federal court. The New York Convention's statement of ratification included a series of declarations framed as proposed amendments, among which was one stating "That the judicial power of the United States, in cases in which a state may be a party, does not extend to criminal prosecutions, or to authorize any suit by any person against a state." Whether that amendment was meant to alter or to clarify Article III as ratified is uncertain, but regardless of its

---

16. The Court says this statement of Wilson's is "startling even today," but it is hard to see what is so startling, then or now, about the proposition that, since federal law may bind state governments, the state governments are in this sense subordinate to the national. The Court seems to have forgotten that one of the main reasons a Constitutional Convention was necessary at all was that under the Articles of Confederation Congress lacked the effective capacity to bind the States. The Court speaks as if the Supremacy Clause did not exist or *M'Culloch v. Maryland* (1819), had never been decided. . . .

17. Nor was Wilson alone in this theory. At the South Carolina Convention, General Charles Cotesworth Pinckney, who had attended the Philadelphia Convention, took the position that the States never enjoyed individual and unfettered sovereignty, because the Declaration of Independence was an act of the Union, not of the particular States. In his view, the Declaration "sufficiently confutes the . . . doctrine of the individual sovereignty and independence of the several states. . . . The separate independence and individual sovereignty of the several states were never thought of by the enlightened band of patriots who framed this Declaration; the several states are not even mentioned by name in any part of it,—as if it was intended to impress this maxim on America, that our freedom and independence arose from our union, and that without it we could neither be free nor independent."

precise intent, New York's response to the draft proposed by the Convention of 1787 shows that there was no consensus at all on the question of state suability (let alone on the underlying theory of immunity doctrine). There was, rather, an unclear state of affairs which it seemed advisable to stabilize.

The Rhode Island Convention, when it finally ratified on June 16, 1790, called upon its representatives to urge the passage of a list of amendments. This list incorporated language, some of it identical to that proposed by New York, in the following form:

> It is declared by the Convention, that the judicial power of the United States, in cases in which a state may be a party, does not extend to criminal prosecutions, or to authorize any suit by any person against a state; but, to remove all doubts or controversies respecting the same, that it be especially expressed, as a part of the Constitution of the United States, that Congress shall not, directly or indirectly, either by themselves or through the judiciary, interfere with any one of the states. . . in liquidating and discharging the public securities of any one state.

Even more clearly than New York's proposal, this amendment appears to have been intended to clarify Article III as reflecting some theory of sovereign immunity, though without indicating which one.

Unlike the Rhode Island proposal, which hinted at a clarification of Article III, the Virginia and North Carolina ratifying conventions proposed amendments that by their terms would have fundamentally altered the content of Article III. The Virginia Convention's proposal for a new Article III omitted entirely the language conferring federal jurisdiction over a controversy between a State and citizens of another State, and the North Carolina Convention proposed an identical amendment. These proposals for omission suggest that the conventions of Virginia and North Carolina thought they had subjected themselves to citizen suits under Article III as enacted, and that they wished not to have done so. This uncertainty set the stage for the divergent views expressed in *Chisholm.*

II

The . . . Court believes that the federal constitutional structure itself necessitates recognition of some degree of state autonomy broad enough to include sovereign immunity from suit in a State's own courts, regardless of the federal source of the claim asserted against the State. [But] the State of Maine is not sovereign with respect to the national objectives of the FLSA.[3] It is not the authority that promulgated the FLSA, on which the right of action in this case depends. That authority is the United States acting through the Congress, whose legislative power under Article I of the Constitution to extend FLSA coverage to state employees has already been decided, *see Garcia v. San Antonio Metropolitan Transit Authority* (1985), and is not contested here.

---

3. It is therefore sheer circularity for the Court to talk of the "anomaly," that would arise if a State could be sued on federal law in its own courts, when it may not be sued under federal law in federal court, *Seminole Tribe of Fla. v. Florida* (1996). The short and sufficient answer is that the anomaly is the Court's own creation: the Eleventh Amendment was never intended to bar federal-question suits against the States in federal court.

Nor can it be argued that because the State of Maine creates its own court system, it has authority to decide what sorts of claims may be entertained there, and thus in effect to control the right of action in this case. Maine has created state courts of general jurisdiction; once it has done so, the Supremacy Clause of the Constitution, Art. VI, cl. 2, which requires state courts to enforce federal law and state-court judges to be bound by it, requires the Maine courts to entertain this federal cause of action. Maine has advanced no "'valid excuse,'" *Howlett v. Rose* (1990), for its courts' refusal to hear federal-law claims in which Maine is a defendant, and sovereign immunity cannot be that excuse, simply because the State is not sovereign with respect to the subject of the claim against it. The Court's insistence that the federal structure bars Congress from making States susceptible to suit in their own courts is, then, plain mistake.

B

Apparently beguiled by Gilded Era language describing private suits against States as "'neither becoming nor convenient,'" the Court calls "immunity from private suits central to sovereign dignity," and assumes that this "dignity" is a quality easily translated from the person of the King to the participatory abstraction of a republican State. The thoroughly anomalous character of this appeal to dignity is obvious from a reading of Blackstone's description of royal dignity, which he sets out as a premise of his discussion of sovereignty:

> First, then, of the royal dignity. Under every monarchical establishment, it is necessary to distinguish the prince from his subjects. . . . The law therefore ascribes to the king . . . certain attributes of a great and transcendent nature; by which the people are led to consider him in the light of a superior being, and to pay him that awful respect, which may enable him with greater ease to carry on the business of government. This is what I understand by the royal dignity. . . .

Blackstone.

It would be hard to imagine anything more inimical to the republican conception, which rests on the understanding of its citizens precisely that the government is not above them, but of them, its actions being governed by law just like their own. Whatever justification there may be for an American government's immunity from private suit, it is not dignity.

Least of all does the Court persuade by observing that "other important needs" than that of the "judgment creditor" compete for public money. The "judgment creditor" in question is not a dunning bill collector, but a citizen whose federal rights have been violated, and a constitutional structure that stints on enforcing federal rights out of an abundance of delicacy toward the States has substituted politesse in place of respect for the rule of law.[36]

---

36. The Court also claims that subjecting States to suit puts power in the hands of state courts that the State may wish to assign to its legislature, thus assigning the state judiciary a role "foreign to its experience but beyond its competence. . . ." This comes perilously close to legitimizing political defiance of valid federal law.

III

Today . . . in light of *Garcia*, the law is settled that federal legislation enacted under the Commerce Clause may bind the States without having to satisfy a test of undue incursion into state sovereignty. Because the commerce power is no longer thought to be circumscribed, the dearth of prior private federal claims entertained against the States in state courts does not tell us anything, and reflects nothing but an earlier and less expansive application of the commerce power.

Blackstone considered it "a general and indisputable rule, that where there is a legal right, there is also a legal remedy, by suit or action at law, whenever that right is invaded." Blackstone. The generation of the Framers thought the principle so crucial that several States put it into their constitutions.[42] And when Chief Justice Marshall asked about [whether the laws would afford Marbury a remedy if the Court had jurisdiction of the request for mandamus], the answer [was] clear:

> The very essence of civil liberty certainly consists in the right of every individual to claim the protection of the laws, whenever he receives an injury. One of the first duties of government is to afford that protection. In Great Britain the king himself is sued in the respectful form of a petition, and he never fails to comply with the judgment of his court.

Marbury v. Madison (1803).

Yet today the Court has no qualms about saying frankly that the federal right to damages afforded by Congress under the FLSA cannot create a concomitant private remedy.

* * *

Justice Souter's dissent ended with the suggestion that the majority had eliminated the remedy for the overtime right Congress established in the FLSA. There is no question that states remain obliged to pay overtime to their employees under the FLSA. An "employee" is defined to include "any individual employed by a State." §203(e)(2)(C). Public agencies covered by the statute include "the government of a State or political subdivision thereof" and "the agency of . . . a State." §203(x). What *Alden* holds is that a state employee cannot sue under the FLSA in state court to recover overtime pay. And we know that under *Hans* there is no jurisdiction in federal court for such a suit.

If a state cannot be sued by its employees in either state or federal court for violating the FLSA, how can the FLSA be enforced against a state? One answer given by the majority at the end of its opinion is that if the federal government wants the overtime provisions of the FLSA enforced against state governments, then the federal government must dedicate resources to enforce the statute itself. The majority notes that the FLSA expressly authorizes the federal government to bring suit. Is this an adequate alternative to suits by employees denied overtime?

---

42. *See, e.g.*, A Declaration of Rights and Fundamental Rules of the Delaware State §12 (1776), 2 Sources and Documents of United States Constitutions 197, 198 (W. Swindler ed. 1775); Md. Const., Art. XVII (1776); Mass. Const., Art. XI (1780); Ky. Const., Art. XII, cl. 13 (1792) Tenn. Const., Art. XI, §17 (1796).

Note that in the year *Alden* was decided private suits outnumbered suits initiated by the United States "by a ratio of roughly ten to one."[16]

Here, as in *Blatchford* and *Seminole Tribe*, the Court was divided not just over the scope of state sovereign immunity but the historical record. The central question is not so much what was said at the founding, but what inferences can be drawn from how little was said on the subject. The majority inferred that little was said because all reasonable minds assumed that state sovereign immunity was not only not surrendered on entering the Union but was preserved and structurally embedded in the constitution. Hence the argument that the text of the Eleventh Amendment is but one manifestation of the doctrine, not its limit and measure. For the dissent, little was said because the doctrine was unsettled in terms of its constitutional status, leaving only the common law version which both state and federal legislatures were free to modify.

Both the majority and dissent seemed to agree that state sovereign immunity derives from the larger theories of state sovereignty. Notice however that, as we saw in *Hans*, not a single Justice takes up the question what form of state sovereignty survived the Civil War and Reconstruction. Should *Hans* be read to have foreclosed this inquiry?

Alden is of a piece with other cases such as *Lujan*, see Chapter 3, and *Sandoval*, see Chapter 5, in which the modern Supreme Court has limited citizen suits to enforce federal law. What reasons did the Court offer to conclude that Congress is without constitutional authority to enable citizen suits against state governments? One of the most striking is the suggestion that federal legislation requiring state courts to entertain citizen suits against a state without its consent is a form of commandeering. The majority repeatedly draws on its anti-commandeering decisions in *Printz v. United States* (1997) and *New York v. United States* (1992). Can you distinguish the imposition of the citizen suit provisions of the FLSA on state courts from the federal action involved in these two anti-commandeering cases? Notice that the majority has to distinguish the Supremacy Clause cases we covered in Chapter 4.C, holding that state courts have a duty to adjudicate certain federal question cases.

d. Surrender of State Sovereign Immunity in the "Plan of the Convention"

The Court has found one area of Article I power in which national uniformity is so important to the effectiveness of a regulatory scheme that it has retreated from its position in *Seminole Tribe* that Article I contains no power to set aside state sovereign immunity.

Central Virginia Community College v. Katz

546 U.S. 356 (2006)

Justice STEVENS delivered the opinion of the Court.

Article I, §8, cl. 4, of the Constitution provides that Congress shall have the power to establish "uniform Laws on the subject of Bankruptcies throughout the

---

16. Daniel Meltzer, *State Sovereign Immunity: Five Authors in Search of a Theory*, 75 NOTRE DAME L. REV. 1011, 1022 (2000).

United States." In *Tennessee Student Assistance Corporation v. Hood* (2004), we granted certiorari to determine whether this Clause gives Congress the authority to abrogate States' immunity from private suits. Without reaching that question, we upheld the application of the Bankruptcy Code to proceedings initiated by a debtor against a state agency to determine the dischargeability of a student loan debt. In this case we consider whether a proceeding initiated by a bankruptcy trustee to set aside preferential transfers by the debtor to state agencies is barred by sovereign immunity. Relying in part on our reasoning in *Hood*, we reject the sovereign immunity defense advanced by the state agencies.

I

Petitioners are Virginia institutions of higher education that are considered "arm[s] of the State" entitled to sovereign immunity. *See, e.g., Alden v. Maine* (1999) (observing that only arms of the State can assert the State's immunity). Wallace's Bookstores, Inc., did business with petitioners before it filed a petition for relief under chapter 11 of the Bankruptcy Code in the United States Bankruptcy Court for the Eastern District of Kentucky. Respondent, Bernard Katz, is the court-appointed liquidating supervisor of the bankrupt estate. He has commenced proceedings in the Bankruptcy Court pursuant to §§547(b) and 550(a) to avoid and recover alleged preferential transfers to each of the petitioners made by the debtor when it was insolvent.[1] Petitioners' motions to dismiss those proceedings on the basis of sovereign immunity were denied by the Bankruptcy Court.

The denial was affirmed by the District Court and the Court of Appeals for the Sixth Circuit on the authority of the Sixth Circuit's prior determination that Congress has abrogated the States' sovereign immunity in bankruptcy proceedings. *See Hood.* We granted certiorari.

Bankruptcy jurisdiction, at its core, is *in rem. See Gardner v. N.J.* (1947) ("The whole process of proof, allowance, and distribution is, shortly speaking, an adjudication of interests claimed in a *res.*"). As we noted in *Hood*, it does not implicate States' sovereignty to nearly the same degree as other kinds of jurisdiction. That was as true in the 18th century as it is today. Then, as now, the jurisdiction of courts adjudicating rights in the bankrupt estate included the power to issue compulsory orders to facilitate the administration and distribution of the *res.*

It is appropriate to presume that the Framers of the Constitution were familiar with the contemporary legal context when they adopted the Bankruptcy Clause—a provision which, as we explain in Part IV, reflects the States' acquiescence in a grant of congressional power to subordinate to the pressing goal of harmonizing bankruptcy law sovereign immunity defenses that might have been asserted in bankruptcy proceedings. The history of the Bankruptcy Clause, the reasons it was inserted in the Constitution, and the legislation both proposed and enacted under

---

1. A preferential transfer is defined as "any transfer of an interest of the debtor in property (1) to or for the benefit of a creditor; (2) for or on account of an antecedebt debt owed by the debtor before such transfer was made; (3) made while the debtor was insolvent . . . made within 90 days before the filing of the petition [which] enables such creditor to receive more than such creditor would receive [in bankruptcy proceedings]." 11 U.S.C. §547(b).

its auspices immediately following ratification of the Constitution demonstrate that it was intended not just as a grant of legislative authority to Congress, but also to authorize limited subordination of state sovereign immunity in the bankruptcy arena. Foremost on the minds of those who adopted the Clause were the intractable problems, not to mention the injustice, created by one State's imprisoning of debtors who had been discharged (from prison and of their debts) in and by another State. As discussed below, to remedy this problem, the very first Congresses considered, and the Sixth Congress enacted, bankruptcy legislation authorizing federal courts to, among other things, issue writs of habeas corpus directed at state officials ordering the release of debtors from state prisons.

We acknowledge that statements in both the majority and the dissenting opinions in *Seminole Tribe of Fla. v. Florida* (1996), reflected an assumption that the holding in that case would apply to the Bankruptcy Clause. Careful study and reflection have convinced us, however, that that assumption was erroneous. For the reasons stated by Chief Justice Marshall in *Cohens v. Virginia* (1821), we are not bound to follow our dicta in a prior case in which the point now at issue was not fully debated. *See id.* ("It is a maxim not to be disregarded, that general expressions, in every opinion, are to be taken in connection with the case in which those expressions are used. If they go beyond the case, they may be respected, but ought not to control the judgment in a subsequent suit when the very point is presented for decision").

II

Critical features of every bankruptcy proceeding are the exercise of exclusive jurisdiction over all of the debtor's property, the equitable distribution of that property among the debtor's creditors, and the ultimate discharge that gives the debtor a "fresh start" by releasing him, her, or it from further liability for old debts. "Under our longstanding precedent, States, whether or not they choose to participate in the proceeding, are bound by a bankruptcy court's discharge order no less than other creditors." *Hood.* Petitioners here, like the state agencies that were parties in *Hood*, have conceded as much.

The history of discharges in bankruptcy proceedings demonstrates that the state agencies' concessions, and *Hood's* holding, are correct. The term "discharge" historically had a dual meaning; it referred to both release of debts and release of the debtor from prison. Indeed, the earliest English statutes governing bankruptcy and insolvency authorized discharges of persons, not debts. One statute enacted in 1649 was entitled "An Act for discharging Poor Prisoners unable to satisfie their Creditors." Acts and Ordinances of the Interregnum, 1642–1660. The stated purpose of the Act was to "Discharge. . . the person of [the] Debtor" "of and from his or her Imprisonment." Not until 1705 did the English Parliament extend the discharge (and then only for traders and merchants) to include release of debts. *See* 4 Ann., ch. 17, §7, Statutes at Large (providing that upon compliance with the statute, "all and every person and persons so becoming bankrupt. . . shall be discharged from all debts by him, her, or them due and owing at the time that he, she, or they did become bankrupt"); *see also* McCoid, Discharge: The Most Important Development in Bankruptcy History.

Well into the 18th century, imprisonment for debt was still ubiquitous in England and the American Colonies. Bankruptcy and insolvency laws remained as much concerned with ensuring full satisfaction of creditors (and, relatedly, preventing debtors' flight to parts unknown) as with securing new beginnings for debtors. Illustrative of bankruptcy laws' harsh treatment of debtors during this period was that debtors often fared worse than common criminals in prison; unfortunate insolvents, unlike criminals, were forced to provide their own food, fuel, and clothing while behind bars. *See* B. MANN, REPUBLIC OF DEBTORS: BANKRUPTCY IN THE AGE OF AMERICAN INDEPENDENCE.

Common as imprisonment itself was, the American Colonies, and later the several States, had wildly divergent schemes for discharging debtors and their debts. *Id.* ("The only consistency among debt laws in the eighteenth century was that every colony, and later every state, permitted imprisonment for debt — most on *mesne* process, and all on execution of a judgment"). At least four jurisdictions offered relief through private Acts of their legislatures. Those Acts released debtors from prison upon surrender of their property, and many coupled the release from prison with a discharge of debts. Other jurisdictions enacted general laws providing for release from prison and, in a few places, discharge of debt. Others still granted release from prison, but only in exchange for indentured servitude. Some jurisdictions provided no relief at all for the debtor. *See generally* P. Coleman, *Debtors and Creditors in America: Insolvency, Imprisonment for Debt, and Bankruptcy.*[6]

The difficulties posed by this patchwork of insolvency and bankruptcy laws were peculiar to the American experience. In England, where there was only one sovereign, a single discharge could protect the debtor from his jailer and his creditors. . . . [H]owever, the uncoordinated actions of multiple sovereigns, each laying claim to the debtor's body and effects according to different rules, rendered impossible so neat a solution on this side of the Atlantic.

In . . . *Millar v. Hall* (Pa. 1788), which was decided the year after the Philadelphia Convention, Ingersoll found himself arguing against the principle announced in *James v. Allen* (1786) [(holding that release from debt and debtor's prison in New Jersey did not protect debtor from arrest on same debt in other states)]. His client, a debtor named Hall, had been "discharged under an insolvent law of the state of Maryland, which is in the nature of a general bankrupt[cy] law." Prior to his discharge, Hall had incurred a debt to a Pennsylvanian named Millar. Hall neglected to mention that debt in his schedule of creditors presented to the Maryland court, or to personally notify Millar of the looming discharge. Following the Maryland court's order, Hall traveled to Pennsylvania and was promptly arrested for the unpaid debt to Millar.

Responding to Millar's counsel's argument that the holding of *James* controlled, Ingersoll urged adoption of a rule that "the discharge of the Defendant in one state ought to be sufficient to discharge [a debtor] in every state." Absent such a rule, Ingersoll continued, "perpetual imprisonment must be the lot of every man who fails; and all hope of retrieving his losses by honest and industrious pursuits, will be cut off from the unfortunate bankrupt." The court accepted this argument. Allowing a creditor to execute "upon [a debtor's] person out of the state in which

---

6. "At the time of the Revolution, only three of the thirteen colonies . . . had laws discharging insolvents of their debts. No two of these relief systems were alike in anything but spirit. In four of the other ten colonies, insolvency legislation was either never enacted or, if enacted, never went into effect, and in the remaining six colonies, full relief was available only for scattered, brief periods, usually on an *ad hoc* basis to named insolvents." Coleman, *Debtors and Creditors in America.*

he has been discharged," the court explained, "would be giving a superiority to some creditors, and affording them a double satisfaction — to wit, a proportionable dividend of his property there, and the imprisonment of his person here." Indeed, the debtor having already been obliged to surrender all of his effects, "to permit the taking [of] his person here, would be to attempt to compel him to perform an impossibility, that is, to pay a debt after he has been deprived of every means of payment, — an attempt which would, at least, amount to perpetual imprisonment, unless the benevolence of his friends should interfere to discharge [his] account."

The absence of extensive debate over the text of the Bankruptcy Clause or its insertion indicates that there was general agreement on the importance of authorizing a uniform federal response to the problems presented in cases like *James* and *Millar*.[9]

III

. . . In bankruptcy, "the court's jurisdiction is premised on the debtor and his estate, and not on the creditors." *Hood*. As such, its exercise does not, in the usual case, interfere with state sovereignty even when States' interests are affected.

The text of Article I, §8, cl. 4, of the Constitution, however, provides that Congress shall have the power to establish "uniform Laws on the subject of Bankruptcies throughout the United States." Although the interest in avoiding unjust imprisonment for debt and making federal discharges in bankruptcy enforceable in every State was a primary motivation for the adoption of that provision, its coverage encompasses the entire "subject of Bankruptcies." The power granted to Congress by that Clause is a unitary concept rather than an amalgam of discrete segments.

The Framers would have understood that laws "on the subject of Bankruptcies" included laws providing, in certain limited respects, for more than simple adjudications of rights in the res. The first bankruptcy statute, for example, gave bankruptcy commissioners appointed by the district court the power, *inter alia*, to imprison recalcitrant third parties in possession of the estate's assets. *See* Bankruptcy Act of 1800, §14 (repealed 1803). More generally, courts adjudicating disputes concerning bankrupts' estates historically have had the power to issue ancillary orders enforcing their *in rem* adjudications. *See, e.g.*, W. Blackstone, *Commentaries on the Laws of England* (noting that the assignees of the bankrupt's property — the 18th-century counterparts to today's bankruptcy trustees — could "pursue any *legal* method of recovering [the debtor's] property so vested in them," and could pursue methods in equity with the consent of the creditors).

---

9. Of course, the Bankruptcy Clause, located as it is in Article I, is "'intimately connected'" not just with the Full Faith and Credit Clause, which appears in Article IV of the Constitution, but also with the Commerce Clause. *See Railway Labor Executives' Assn. v. Gibbons* (1982). That does not mean, however, that the state sovereign immunity implications of the Bankruptcy Clause necessarily mirror those of the Commerce Clause. Indeed, the Bankruptcy Clause's unique history, combined with the singular nature of bankruptcy courts' jurisdiction, discussed *infra*, have persuaded us that the ratification of the Bankruptcy Clause does represent a surrender by the States of their sovereign immunity in certain federal proceedings. That conclusion is implicit in our holding in *Tennessee Student Assistance Corp. v. Hood* (2004).

Our decision in *Hood* illustrates the point. As the dissenters in that case pointed out, it was at least arguable that the particular procedure that the debtor pursued to establish dischargeability of her student loan could have been characterized as a suit against the State rather than a purely *in rem* proceeding. But because the proceeding was merely ancillary to the Bankruptcy Court's exercise of its *in rem* jurisdiction, we held that it did not implicate state sovereign immunity. The point is also illustrated by Congress' early grant to federal courts of the power to issue *in personam* writs of habeas corpus directing States to release debtors from state prisons, discussed in Part IV. *See Braden v. 30th Jud. Cir. Ct. of Ky.* (1973) ("The writ of habeas corpus does not act upon the prisoner who seeks relief, but upon the person who holds him in what is alleged to be unlawful custody").

The interplay between *in rem* adjudications and orders ancillary thereto is evident in the case before us. Respondent first seeks a determination under 11 U.S.C. §547 that the various transfers made by the debtor to petitioners qualify as voidable preferences. The §547 determination, standing alone, operates as a mere declaration of avoidance. That declaration may be all that the trustee wants; for example, if the State has a claim against the bankrupt estate, the avoidance determination operates to bar that claim until the preference is turned over. *See* §502(d). In some cases, though, the trustee, in order to marshal the entirety of the debtor's estate, will need to recover the subject of the transfer pursuant to §550(a). A court order mandating turnover of the property, although ancillary to and in furtherance of the court's *in rem* jurisdiction, might itself involve *in personam* process.

As we explain in Part IV, it is not necessary to decide whether actions to recover preferential transfers pursuant to §550(a) are themselves properly characterized as *in rem*. Whatever the appropriate appellation, those who crafted the Bankruptcy Clause would have understood it to give Congress the power to authorize courts to avoid preferential transfers and to recover the transferred property. Petitioners do not dispute that that authority has been a core aspect of the administration of bankrupt estates since at least the 18th century. And it, like the authority to issue writs of habeas corpus releasing debtors from state prisons, *see* Part IV, operates free and clear of the State's claim of sovereign immunity.

IV

. . . This grant of habeas power is remarkable not least because it would be another 67 years, after Congress passed the Fourteenth Amendment, before the writ would be made generally available to state prisoners.[11] Moreover, the provision

---

11. The Judiciary Act of 1789 authorized issuance of the writ, but only to release those held in *federal* custody. Also, in the interim between 1800 and 1867, Congress authorized limited issuance of the writ in response to two crises it viewed as sufficiently pressing to warrant a federal response: the South Carolina nullification controversy of 1828–1833 and the imprisonment of a foreign national by New York State a few years later. *See* 4 Stat. 632 (1833); 5 Stat. 539 (1842); *see also* W. Duker, A Constitutional History of Habeas Corpus. The 1833 statute made the writ available to U.S. citizens imprisoned by States for actions authorized by federal law, while the 1842 statute gave federal judges the power to release foreign nationals imprisoned for actions authorized by foreign governments.

of the 1800 Act granting that power was considered and adopted during a period when state sovereign immunity could hardly have been more prominent among the Nation's concerns. *Chisholm v. Ga.* the case that had so "shock[ed]" the country in its lack of regard for state sovereign immunity, *Principality of Monaco v. Miss.* (1934), was decided in 1793. The ensuing five years that culminated in adoption of the Eleventh Amendment were rife with discussion of States' sovereignty and their amenability to suit. Yet there appears to be no record of any objection to the bankruptcy legislation or its grant of habeas power to federal courts based on an infringement of sovereign immunity.

This history strongly supports the view that the Bankruptcy Clause of Article I, the source of Congress' authority to effect this intrusion upon state sovereignty, simply did not contravene the norms this Court has understood the Eleventh Amendment to exemplify. . . . As demonstrated by the First Congress' immediate consideration and the Sixth Congress' enactment of a provision granting federal courts the authority to release debtors from state prisons, the power to enact bankruptcy legislation was understood to carry with it the power to subordinate state sovereignty, albeit within a limited sphere.

The ineluctable conclusion, then, is that States agreed in the plan of the Convention not to assert any sovereign immunity defense they might have had in proceedings brought pursuant to "Laws on the subject of Bankruptcies." *See Blatchford v. Native Vill. of Noatak* (1991) (observing that a State is not "subject to suit in federal court unless it has consented to suit, either expressly or in the 'plan of the convention'"); *Alden v. Me.* (1999) (same). The scope of this consent was limited; the jurisdiction exercised in bankruptcy proceedings was chiefly *in rem*—a narrow jurisdiction that does not implicate state sovereignty to nearly the same degree as other kinds of jurisdiction. But while the principal focus of the bankruptcy proceedings is and was always the res, some exercises of bankruptcy courts' powers — issuance of writs of habeas corpus included — unquestionably involved more than mere adjudication of rights in a res. In ratifying the Bankruptcy Clause, the States acquiesced in a subordination of whatever sovereign immunity they might otherwise have asserted in proceedings necessary to effectuate the *in rem* jurisdiction of the bankruptcy courts.

V

. . . Congress may, at its option, either treat States in the same way as other creditors insofar as concerns "Laws on the subject of Bankruptcies" or exempt them from operation of such laws. Its power to do so arises from the Bankruptcy Clause itself; the relevant "abrogation" is the one effected in the plan of the Convention, not by statute.

The judgment of the Court of Appeals for the Sixth Circuit is affirmed.

It is so ordered.

Justice THOMAS, with whom THE CHIEF JUSTICE, Justice SCALIA, and Justice KENNEDY join, dissenting.

. . . [N]othing in the text of the Bankruptcy Clause suggests an abrogation or limitation of the States' sovereign immunity. . . . In contending that the States waived their immunity from suit by adopting the Bankruptcy Clause, the majority conflates two distinct attributes of sovereignty: the authority of a sovereign to enact legislation regulating its own citizens, and sovereign immunity against suits by private citizens. Nothing in the history of the Bankruptcy Clause suggests that, by including that clause in Article I, the founding generation intended to waiver the latter aspect of sovereignty. These two attributes of sovereignty often do not run together—and for purposes of enacting a uniform law of bankruptcy, they need not run together. . . . Thus we have recognized that "[t]the need for uniformity in the construction of patent law is undoubtedly important." *Fla. Prepaid Postsecondary Educ. Expense Bd. v. Coll. Savings Bank* (1999). Nonetheless, we have refused, in addressing patent law, to give the need for uniformity the weight the majority today assigns it in the context of bankruptcy, instead recognizing that this need "is a factor which belongs to the Article I patent-power calculus, rather than to any determination of whether a state plea of sovereign immunity deprives a patentee of property without due process of law." *Ibid.* . . .

The majority also greatly exaggerates the depth of the Framers' fervor to enact a national bankruptcy regime [and the post-ratification period]. . . . "For over a century after the Constitution . . . the Bankruptcy Clause [authority] remained largely unexercised by Congress. . . . Thus states were free to act in bankruptcy matters for all but 16 of the first 109 years after the Constitution was ratified." Tabb, The History of the Bankruptcy Laws in the United States. And when Congress did act, it did so only in response to a major financial disaster, and it repealed the legislation in each instance shortly thereafter. *Id.* It was not until 1898 . . . that Congress adopted the first permanent national bankruptcy law. . . .

The availability of habeas relief in bankruptcy between 1800 and 1803 does not support respondent's effort to obtain monetary relief in bankruptcy against state agencies today. . . . [A] petition for the writ is against a state official, not a suit against a State, and thus does not offend the Eleventh Amendment. . . .

The majority's . . . observation [that] debtors were unable to obtain discharge orders issued by the court of one state that would be binding in the court of another State . . . implicates nothing more than the application of full faith and credit. Accordingly it has nothing to do with state sovereign immunity from suit. . . .

Finally, the . . . fact that certain aspects of the bankruptcy power may be characterized as *in rem* . . . does not determine whether or not the States enjoy immunity against such *in rem* suits. . . . Two years ago, this Court held that a State is bound by a bankruptcy court's discharge order, notwithstanding the State's invocation of sovereign immunity, because such actions arise out of *in rem* jurisdiction. *See Tennessee Student Assistance Corp. v. Hood* (2004). In doing so, however, the Court explicitly distinguished recovery of preferential transfers, noting that the debt discharge proceedings there were "unlike any adversary proceeding by the bankruptcy trustee seeking to recover property in the hands of the State on the grounds that the transfer was a voidable preference."

The fact that transfer recovery proceedings fall outside any possible *in rem* exception to sovereign immunity is confirmed by *U.S. v. Nordic Vill., Inc.* (1992), which involved similar facts. There, the Bankruptcy Trustee filed a transfer avoidance action against the United States, in order to recover a recent payment the debtor had made to the Internal Revenue Service on a tax debt. After determining that the

United States had not waived its sovereign immunity, the Court rejected the trustee's alternative argument based on *in rem* jurisdiction. As the Court explained, "[r]espondent sought to recover a sum of money, not 'particular dollars,' so there was no *res* to which the court's *in rem* jurisdiction could have attached."

* * *

A second area in which the Court has recognized state consent to suit in the "plan of the Convention" itself is congressional authority over war powers. In *Torres v. Tex. Dept. of Pub. Safety* (2022), the Court held that Congress could abrogate state sovereign immunity and provide a cause of action for damages against state governments that fail to provide "comparable" work to returning veterans who seek to reclaim their prior jobs under the Uniformed Services Employment and Reemployment Rights Act. Le Roy Torres worked as a Texas State Trooper before being called up for service from the Army Reserves and deployed to Iraq in 2007. After being exposed to toxic burn pits in Iraq he returned from service with health conditions that prevented returning to work as a state trooper and, his complaint alleged, the state refused to accommodate his condition by reemploying him in a different position. Relying on *Katz,* and the extension of *Katz* in *PennEast Pipeline Co. v. N.J.* (2021) (holding that Congress can authorize private suits to enforce federally approved condemnations necessary to build interstate pipelines under its Article I eminent domain power), the Court held that where "the federal power at issue is complete in itself, and the States consented to the exercise of that power—in its entirety—in the plan of the Convention," Congress may authorize private suits because "the States implicitly agreed that their sovereignty would yield to that of the Federal Government so far as is necessary to the enjoyment of the powers conferred upon it by the Constitution. . . . Congress' power to build and maintain the Armed Forces fits" the test set out in *Katz* and *PennEast.* The Court found a "complete delegation of authority to the Federal Government to provide for the common defense" in Article I and Article II, and, more than that, express language "divest[ing] the States of like power. States may not 'engage in War, unless actually invaded,' 'enter into any Treaty,' or 'keep Troops, or Ships of War in time of Peace.'" Art. I. §10, cls. 1, 3. "These substantial limitations on state authority, together with the assignment of sweeping power to the Federal Government, provide strong evidence that the structure of the Constitution prevents States from frustrating national objectives in this field." Justice Thomas, joined by Justices Alito, Gorsuch and Barrett, dissented on the ground that *Seminole Tribe* correctly held there is no Article I power to abrogate state sovereign immunity.

The Court sharply distinguished *Katz* in *Allen v. Cooper* (2020), holding that there is no Article I power to abrogate state sovereign immunity from claims for copyright infringement. The state of North Carolina published videos and photographs taken by a photographer working for the salvage company that discovered a shipwreck belonging to the famous eighteenth-century pirate Blackbeard. Allen sued the state for copyright infringement, invoking the Copyright Remedy Clarification Act of 1990, which provided that a state "shall not be immune, under the Eleventh Amendment [or] any other doctrine of sovereign immunity, from suit in Federal court" for copyright infringement. 17 U.S.C. §511(a). The Court concluded there was "no doubt" that Congress intended to abrogate state sovereign immunity. But there is no power under the "Intellectual Property Clause" of Article I to abrogate. Despite the importance of the clause to "ensure uniform, surefire protection of intellectual property," the Court's decision in *Florida Prepaid* that "Article I cannot be used to circumvent the limits sovereign immunity places upon federal jurisdiction" was controlling. The Court also rejected the argument that *Katz* altered its general view of Article I expressed in *Seminole Tribe* and *Florida Prepaid*, emphasizing that "everything in *Katz* is about and limited to the Bankruptcy Clause; the opinion reflects what might be called bankruptcy exceptionalism. . . . Our decision . . . viewed bankruptcy as on a different plane, governed by principles all its own. Nothing in that understanding invites the kind of general, 'clause-by-clause' reexamination of Article I that Allen proposes."

The Court also rejected Allen's argument that Congress had power to abrogate North Carolina's immunity from suit for copyright infringement under Section 5 of the Fourteenth Amendment. Although copyrights "are a form of property" protected against deprivations without due process of law, not all infringements by a state amount to due process violations. "Under our precedent, a merely negligent act does not 'deprive' a person of property. So an infringement must be intentional, or at least reckless, to come within the reach of the Due Process Clause." And even then, the state must "fail[] to offer an adequate remedy for an infringement" for there to be a deprivation of due process of law. Finally, for the power to abrogate under Section 5 to come into play, there must be a record of "a pattern of unconstitutional . . . infringement" supporting congressional legislation providing for suit in federal court. Examining the legislative record, the Court found that "the concrete evidence of States infringing copyrights (even ignoring whether those acts violate due process) is scarcely more impressive than what the *Florida Prepaid* Court saw. Despite undertaking an exhaustive search [the Register of Copyrights charged by Congress to investigate the issue] came up with only a dozen possible examples of state infringement . . . seven court cases brought against the states (with another two dismissed on the merits) and five anecdotes taken from public comments (but not further corroborated)." Congressional sponsors conceded that "there have not been any significant number." "This is not," the Court concluded, "the stuff from which Section 5 legislation ordinarily arises." The statute therefore "must fail our 'congruence and proportionality' test."

That test emerged from an earlier case holding that Section 5 enforcement clause legislation is valid only when there is a legislative record establishing "congruence and proportionality" between the constitutional harm Congress seeks to prevent or redress and the remedy Congress creates to serve those ends. *City of Boerne v. Flores* (1997). The enforcement clauses of the Reconstruction Amendments allow Congress to create remedies for well documented violations of substantive constitutional rights, not, the Court stressed, to expand or contract those rights. *Id.* ("The design of the Amendment and the text of §5 are inconsistent with the suggestion that Congress has the power to decree the substance of the Fourteenth Amendment's restrictions on the States. Legislation which alters the meaning of the Free Exercise Clause cannot be said to be enforcing the Clause.";

striking down Religious Freedom Restoration Act provisions purporting to overrule a Supreme Court decision interpreting the First Amendment).

Beyond *Fitzpatrick,* abrogation under Section 5 has been upheld when the congressional record supporting remedial legislation includes "evidence of a pattern of constitutional violations on the part of the States." *Nevada Dept. of Human Resources v. Hibbs* (2003) (upholding abrogation of state sovereign immunity by Family Medical Leave Act of 1993 grant of private right of action against state employer for equitable and monetary relief for denial of right to twelve weeks unpaid leave to help with family member's health emergencies; record showed history of state laws discriminating against women in employment and evidence that "States continue to rely on invalid gender stereotypes in the employment context, specifically in the administration of leave benefits. . . . [A] 50-state survey also before Congress demonstrated that the proportion and construction of [maternity and paternity] leave policies available to public sector employees differs little from those offered private sector employees."). *See also Tennessee v. Lane* (2004) (upholding abrogation of state sovereign immunity under Title II of the Americans with Disabilities Act for money damage claims for unequal access to state and local courthouses; emphasizing congressional record showing "pervasive unequal treatment" of persons with disabilities in provision of judicial services).

Absent evidence of a pattern of state wrongdoing supporting remedial legislation, the Court has refused to find a valid abrogation of state sovereign immunity under Section 5. *See Coleman v. Ct. of Appeals of Md.* (2012) (no valid §5 abrogation of state sovereign immunity under self-care provisions of Family Medical Leave Act for money damage claim by male employee challenging denial of self-care; "The evidence did not suggest States had facially discriminatory self-care leave policies or that they administered neutral self-care leave policies in a discriminatory way. And there is scant evidence in the legislative history of a purported stereotype harbored by employers that women take self-care leave more often than men."); *Univ. of Ala. v. Garrett* (2001) ("The legislative record of the ADA . . . simply fails to show that Congress did in fact identify a pattern of irrational state discrimination in employment against the disabled"; declining to examine evidence of discrimination at local government level and finding half a dozen incidents that did involve states "taken together fall far short of even suggesting a pattern of unconstitutional discrimination on which §5 legislation must be based"; no valid §5 abrogation in Title I of the ADA); *Kimel v. Fla. Bd. of Regents* (2000) ("Congress never identified any pattern of age discrimination by the States, much less any discrimination whatsoever that rose to the level of constitutional violation"; no valid §5 abrogation under Age Discrimination in Employment Act); *Fla. Prepaid Postsecondary Educ. Expense Bd. v. Coll. Savings Bank* (1999) ("In enacting the Patent Remedy Act . . . Congress identified no pattern of patent infringement by the States, let alone a pattern of constitutional violations. . . . The House Report acknowledged that 'many states comply with patent law' and could provide only two examples of patent infringement suits against the States. The Federal Circuit in its opinion identified only eight patent-infringement suits prosecuted against the States in the 110 years between 1880 and 1990"; no valid §5 abrogation). As Pamela Karlan once described, "a court that used to see the Fourteenth Amendment as a limitation on the Eleventh has come to see the Eleventh as a constraint on the Fourteenth." Pamela S. Karlan, *Disarming the Private Attorney General*, 2003 U. ILL. L. REV. 183, 189 (2003).

The purpose of the congruence and proportionality test is to prevent Congress from redefining substantive constitutional law. The rights of individuals, the autonomy of the states, and the power of the Supreme Court to interpret the Constitution are all at stake. Is the test relevant when Congress authorizes individuals to sue states not for violating federal statutory law, but for violating constitutional rights? In *U.S. v. Georgia* (2006), a disabled prisoner sued the state pro se, alleging that he was confined 23-24 hours a day in a cell so small that: he could not turn his wheelchair around; he could not access a toilet or shower without assistance he was frequently denied; he was forced to sit in his own feces and urine, and he was denied physical therapy, medical treatment, and access to "virtually all prison programs and services on account of his disability." The Eleventh Circuit affirmed the dismissal of his money damage claim against the state under Title II of the ADA on Eleventh Amendment grounds. A unanimous Supreme Court reversed. Writing for the Court, Justice Scalia emphasized that:

> [w]hile the Members of this Court have disagreed regarding the scope of Congress's 'prophylactic' enforcement powers under §5 of the Fourteenth Amendment, no one doubts that §5 grants Congress the power to enforce the provisions of the Amendment by creating private remedies against the States for *actual* violations of those provisions. This enforcement power includes the power to abrogate state sovereign immunity by authorizing private suits for damages against the States. Thus insofar as Title II creates a private cause of action for damages against the States for conduct that actually violates the Fourteenth Amendment, Title II validly abrogates state sovereign immunity.

The Court reversed and remanded for determination whether allegations violated only Title II or both Title II and the Eighth Amendment.

What distinguishes the congressional authorities and national interests involved in *Katz*, *Torres*, and *Penn East* from those involved in the abrogation cases? Are the national interests reflected in the Indian Commerce Clause, for example, categorically different?

B. FEDERAL COURT RELIEF AGAINST LOCAL GOVERNMENTS AND STATE AND LOCAL GOVERNMENT OFFICERS: 42 U.S.C. §1983

Constitutional violations by state officials take many forms. A group of protesters is teargassed for engaging in unpopular speech protected by the First Amendment. Parents of private school students are denied state tuition assistance due to a "nonsectarian" requirement that violates the Free Exercise Clause of the First Amendment. A gun owner is denied a license to carry a handgun in violation of the Second Amendment. An officer kills or injures someone who does not reasonably constitute a threat under the Fourth Amendment. An inmate is subjected to cruel violence or inhumane conditions in violation of the Eighth Amendment. A government employee person is fired because of her identity in violation of the Fourteenth Amendment. A person is deprived of the right to marry her same-sex partner. An individual faces routine arrests or detention in a jurisdiction because of her inability to pay a fine or fee. A public school district voluntarily considers racial diversity when assigning individual students to schools in potential violation of the Fourteenth Amendment.

These examples vary in a range of ways: the constitutional rights at stake; the types of state actors engaging in the violation; and the remedies that are available to the aggrieved. Across this wide range of constitutional violations, however, the most common cause of action is Section 1983. 42 U.S.C. §1983. The statute reads:

> Every person who, under color of any statute, ordinance, regulation, custom, or usage, of any State or Territory or the District of Columbia, subjects, or causes to be subjected, any citizen of the United States or other person within the jurisdiction thereof to the deprivation of any rights, privileges, or immunities secured by the Constitution and laws, shall be liable to the party injured in an action at law, suit in equity, or other proper proceeding for redress, except that in any action brought against a judicial officer for an act or omission taken in such officer's judicial capacity, injunctive relief shall not be granted unless a declaratory decree was violated or declaratory relief was unavailable. For the purposes of this section, any Act of Congress applicable exclusively to the District of Columbia shall be considered to be a statute of the District of Columbia.

This statute was passed during the Reconstruction Era, in the aftermath of the Civil War, as Congress passed legislation designed to ensure that the rights guaranteed in the Thirteenth, Fourteenth, and Fifteenth Amendments were backed by remedial guarantees when Americans experienced invasions of those rights.

Section 1983 was initially passed as Section 1 of the Ku Klux Act of April 20, 1871. 17 Stat. 13. At the time, the Chairman of the Senate Judiciary Committee explained: "The first section is one that I believe nobody objects to, as defining the rights secured by the Constitution of the United States when they are assailed by any State law or under color of any State law, and it is merely carrying out the principles of the civil rights bill, which has since become a part of the Constitution [through] the Fourteenth Amendment." The law was modeled after an earlier Reconstruction Era state — the Civil Rights Act of 1866, §2 — which criminalized willful violations of federal constitutional rights by those acting under the color of state law.

In the following sections, you will encounter some of the key questions that the Supreme Court has answered concerning the scope of §1983. First, in Chapter 6.B.1, you will learn more about the reach of the language restricting §1983 liability to deprivations of federal rights that occur "*under the color of state law.*" The phrase is generally synonymous with the state action doctrine, though it reflects a congressional purpose to impose liability upon those who assume or act under pretense of legal authority, whether or not they possess it in fact. Second, Chapter 6.B.2 will draw some key distinctions between §1983, and another important source of litigation against state officials violating federal rights: federal collateral habeas review of state convictions and sentences. Third, Chapter 6.B.3 turns to litigation against local governments, and the narrow circumstances in which such suits are allowed. Fourth, Chapter 6.B.4 describes circumstances in which government officials are entitled to various forms of absolute immunity, even when their conduct violates federal constitutional rights. Fifth, Chapter 6.B.5 details the doctrine of qualified immunity: the doctrine's scope and proposed legislative reforms to curtail or eliminate the doctrine.

1. "Under the Color of State Law"

While §1983 was enacted in the aftermath of the Civil War, the birth of modern §1983 jurisprudence can be traced to the year 1961. In *Monroe v. Pape* (1961), the Court interpreted the language "under the color of state law" more expansively than any prior Supreme Court case had. In the case itself, officers invaded the home of a Black family in Chicago without a warrant, in violation of federal and state law. The officers were accused of barging into the home at 5:45 A.M. and awakening James Monroe, Jr. and his wife at gunpoint.[17] According to the complaint, the officers cursed Monroe and repeatedly called him racial slurs that included the n-word. As Monroe stood in his home naked and frightened, officers kicked his 4-year-old son, ransacked the house, and ripped furniture open. This search was precipitated by a widow's false allegation that two Black young men had killed her husband, who was White.[18] The evidence eventually showed the murder victim had been killed by the widow and her boyfriend, resulting in Monroe's release.

Relying on §1983, Monroe sued the officers and the city for the warrantless search. By the time the case reached the Court, one of the key legal questions was whether, given that the officers violated state law, their misuse of state power could still be classified as actions under the color of state law. In the opinion that follows, the Court held that the officers were indeed acting under the color of state law. As the Court reasoned later in another context, "[P]ower, once granted does not disappear like a magic gift when it is wrongfully used." *Bivens v. Six Unknown Named Agents of the Fed. Bureau of Narcotics*, 403 U.S. 388, 390 (1971). When an official's power comes from the state such that one can fairly be said to be a "state actor" under the Fourteenth Amendment, that official is acting under the color of state law.

Monroe v. Pape

365 U.S. 167 (1961)

Mr. Justice DOUGLAS delivered the opinion of the Court.

This case presents important questions concerning the construction of R.S. §1979, 42 U.S.C. §1983, which reads as follows:

---

17. Myriam Gilles, *Police, Race and Crime in 1950s Chicago: Monroe v. Pape as Legal Noir*, in CIVIL RIGHTS STORIES (Myriam Gilles & Risa Goluboff eds., 2007).

18. *Id.*

Every person who, under color of any statute, ordinance, regulation, custom or usage, of any State or Territory, subjects, or causes to be subjected, any citizen of the United States or other person within the jurisdiction thereof to the deprivation of any rights, privileges, or immunities secured by the Constitution and laws, shall be liable to the party injured in an action at law, suit in equity, or other proper proceeding for redress.

The complaint alleges that 13 Chicago police officers broke into petitioners' home in the early morning, routed them from bed, made them stand naked in the living room, and ransacked every room, emptying drawers and ripping mattress covers. It further alleges that Mr. Monroe was then taken to the police station and detained on "open" charges for 10 hours, while he was interrogated about a two-day-old murder, that he was not taken before a magistrate, that he was not permitted to call his family or attorney, that he was subsequently released without criminal charges being preferred against him. It is alleged that the officers had no search warrant and no arrest warrant and that they acted "under color of the statutes, ordinances, regulations, customs and usages" of Illinois and of the City of Chicago. Federal jurisdiction was asserted under [§1983], which we have set out above, and 28 U.S.C. §1343, and 28 U.S.C. §1331.

The City of Chicago moved to dismiss the complaint on the ground that it is not liable under the Civil Rights Acts nor for acts committed in performance of its governmental functions. All defendants moved to dismiss, alleging that the complaint alleged no cause of action under those Acts or under the Federal Constitution. The District Court dismissed the complaint. The Court of Appeals affirmed. The case is here on a writ of certiorari which we granted because of a seeming conflict of that ruling with our prior cases.

I

Petitioners claim that the invasion of their home and the subsequent search without a warrant and the arrest and detention of Mr. Monroe without a warrant and without arraignment constituted a deprivation of their 'rights, privileges, or immunities secured by the Constitution' within the meaning of [Section 1983]. It has been said that when 18 U.S.C. §241, made criminal a conspiracy "to injure, oppress, threaten, or intimidate any citizen in the free exercise or enjoyment of any right or privilege secured to him by the Constitution," it embraced only rights that an individual has by reason of his relation to the central government, not to state governments. But the history of the section of the Civil Rights Act presently involved does not permit such a narrow interpretation.

Section [1983] came onto the books as §1 of the Ku Klux Act of April 20, 1871. 17 Stat. 13. It was one of the means whereby Congress exercised the power vested in it by §5 of the Fourteenth Amendment to enforce the provisions of that Amendment. Senator Edmunds, Chairman of the Senate Committee on the Judiciary, said concerning this section:

The first section is one that I believe nobody objects to, as defining the rights secured by the Constitution of the United States when they are assailed by any State law or under color of any State law, and it is merely carrying out the principles of the civil rights bill, which has since become a part of the Constitution, viz., the Fourteenth Amendment.

Its purpose is plain from the title of the legislation, "An Act to enforce the Provisions of the Fourteenth Amendment to the Constitution of the United States, and for other Purposes." 17 Stat. 13. Allegation of facts constituting a deprivation under color of state authority of a right guaranteed by the Fourteenth Amendment satisfies to that extent the requirement of [Section 1983]. So far petitioners are on solid ground. For the guarantee against unreasonable searches and seizures contained in the Fourth Amendment has been made applicable to the States by reason of the Due Process Clause of the Fourteenth Amendment.

II

There can be no doubt at least since *Ex parte Virginia* (1879) that Congress has the power to enforce provisions of the Fourteenth Amendment against those who carry a badge of authority of a State and represent it in some capacity, whether they act in accordance with their authority or misuse it. The question with which we now deal is the narrower one of whether Congress, in enacting Section 1983 meant to give a remedy to parties deprived of constitutional rights, privileges and immunities by an official's abuse of his position. We conclude that it did so intend.

It is argued that "under color of" enumerated state authority excludes acts of an official or policeman who can show no authority under state law, state custom, or state usage to do what he did. In this case it is said that these policemen, in breaking into petitioners' apartment, violated the Constitution and laws of Illinois. It is pointed out that under Illinois law a simple remedy is offered for that violation and that, so far as it appears, the courts of Illinois are available to give petitioners that full redress which the common law affords for violence done to a person; and it is earnestly argued that no 'statute, ordinance, regulation, custom or usage' of Illinois bars that redress.

The legislation—in particular the section with which we are now concerned—had several purposes. There are threads of many thoughts running through the debates. One who reads them in their entirety sees that the present section had three main aims.

First, it might, of course, override certain kinds of state laws. Second, it provided a remedy where state law was inadequate.

But the purposes were much broader. The third aim was to provide a federal remedy where the state remedy, though adequate in theory, was not available in practice. The opposition to the measure complained that "It overrides the reserved powers of the States," just as they argued that the second section of the bill "absorb[ed] the entire jurisdiction of the State over their local and domestic affairs."

The debates were long and extensive. It is abundantly clear that one reason the legislation was passed was to afford a federal right in federal courts because, by reason of prejudice, passion, neglect, intolerance or otherwise, state laws might not be enforced and the claims of citizens to the enjoyment of rights, privileges, and immunities guaranteed by the Fourteenth Amendment might be denied by the state agencies.

Although the legislation was enacted because of the conditions that existed in the South at that time, it is cast in general language and is as applicable to Illinois as it is to the States whose names were mentioned over and again in the debates. It is no answer that the State has a law which if enforced would give relief. The federal remedy is supplementary to the state remedy, and the latter need not be first sought and refused before the federal one is invoked. Hence the fact that Illinois by its constitution and laws outlaws unreasonable searches and seizures is no barrier to the present suit in the federal court.

We had before us in *U.S. v. Classic*, Title 18 U.S.C. §242, which provides a criminal punishment for anyone who "under color of any law, statute, ordinance, regulation, or custom" subjects any inhabitant of a State to the deprivation of "any rights, privileges, or immunities secured or protected by the Constitution or laws of the United States." Section 242 first came into the law as §2 of the Civil Rights Act, Act of April 9, 1866. After passage of the Fourteenth Amendment, this provision was re-enacted and amended by §§17, 18, Act of May 31, 1870. The right involved in the *Classic* case was the right of voters in a primary to have their votes counted. The laws of Louisiana required the defendants "to count the ballots, to record the result of the count, and to certify the result of the election." But according to the indictment they did not perform their duty. In an opinion written by Mr. Justice (later Chief Justice) Stone, in which Mr. Justice Roberts, Mr. Justice Reed, and Mr. Justice Frankfurter joined, the Court ruled, "Misuse of power, possessed by virtue of state law and made possible only because the wrongdoer is clothed with the authority of state law, is action taken 'under color of' state law." That view of the meaning of the words "under color of" state law, 18 U.S.C. §242, was reaffirmed in *Screws v. United States, supra.*

Since *Screws*, Congress has had several pieces of civil rights legislation before it. In 1956 one bill reached the floor of the House. This measure had at least one provision in it penalizing actions taken "under color of law or otherwise." A vigorous minority report was filed attacking, inter alia, the words "or otherwise." But not a word of criticism of the phrase "under color of" state law as previously construed by the Court is to be found in that report. If the results of our construction of "under color of" law were as horrendous as now claimed, if they were as disruptive of our federal scheme as now urged, if they were such an unwarranted invasion of States' rights as pretended, surely the voice of the opposition would have been heard in those Committee reports. Their silence and the new uses to which "under color of" law have recently been given reinforce our conclusion that our prior decisions were correct on this matter of construction.

We conclude that the meaning given "under color of" law in the *Classic* case and in the *Screws* was the correct one; and we adhere to it.

III

The City of Chicago asserts that it is not liable under §1983. We do not stop to explore the whole range of questions tendered us on this issue at oral argument and in the briefs. For we are of the opinion that Congress did not undertake to bring municipal corporations within the ambit of §1983. We hold that the motion to dismiss the complaint against the City of Chicago was properly granted. But since the complaint should not have been dismissed against the officials the judgment must be and is reversed.

Mr. Justice HARLAN, whom Mr. Justice STEWART joins, concurring.

Were this case here as one of first impression, I would find the "under color of any statute" issue very close indeed. However, in *Classic* and *Screws* this Court considered a substantially identical statutory phrase to have a meaning which, unless we now retreat from it, requires that issue to go for the petitioners here.

From my point of view, the policy of stare decisis, as it should be applied in matters of statutory construction and, to a lesser extent, the indications of congressional acceptance of this Court's earlier interpretation, require that it appear beyond doubt from the legislative history of the 1871 statute that *Classic* and *Screws* misapprehended the meaning of the controlling provision, before a departure from what was decided in those cases would be justified. Since I can find no such justifying indication in that legislative history, I join the opinion of the Court. However, what has been written on both sides of the matter makes some additional observations appropriate. . . .

Mr. Justice FRANKFURTER, dissenting except insofar as the Court holds that this action cannot be maintained against the City of Chicago.

Abstractly stated, this case concerns a matter of statutory construction. So stated, the problem before the Court is denuded of illuminating concreteness and thereby of its far-reaching significance for our federal system. Again abstractly stated, this matter of statutory construction is one upon which the Court has already passed. But it has done so under circumstances and in settings that negative those considerations of social policy upon which the doctrine of stare decisis, calling for the controlling application of prior statutory construction, rests.

This case presents the question of the sufficiency of petitioners' complaint in a civil action for damages brought under the Civil Rights Act, 42 U.S.C. §1983. The complaint alleges that on October 29, 1958, at 5:45 a.m., thirteen Chicago police officers, led by Deputy Chief of Detectives Pape, broke through two doors of the Monroe apartment, woke the Monroe couple with flashlights, and forced them at gunpoint to leave their bed and stand naked in the center of the living room; that the officers roused the six Monroe children and herded them into the living room; that Detective Pape struck Mr. Monroe several times with his flashlight, calling him [the n-word] and "black boy;" that another officer pushed Mrs. Monroe; that other officers hit and kicked several of the children and pushed them to the floor; that the police ransacked every room, throwing clothing from closets to the floor, dumping drawers, ripping mattress covers; that Mr. Monroe was then taken to the police station and detained on "open" charges for ten hours, during which time he was interrogated about a murder and exhibited in lineups; that he was not brought before a magistrate, although numerous magistrate's courts were accessible; that he was not advised of his procedural rights; that he was not permitted to call his family or an attorney; that he was subsequently released without criminal charges having been filed against him . . . [and] that the officers were agents of the city, acting in the course of their employment and engaged in the performance of their duties; and that it is the custom of the

Department to arrest and confine individuals for prolonged periods on "open" charges for interrogation, with the purpose of inducing incriminating statements, exhibiting its prisoners for identification, holding them incommunicado while police officers investigate their activities, and punishing them by imprisonment without judicial trial. On the basis of these allegations various members of the Monroe family seek damages against the individual police officers and against the City of Chicago. . . .

II

This case squarely presents the question whether the intrusion of a city policeman for which that policeman can show no such authority at state law as could be successfully interposed in defense to a state-law action against him, is nonetheless to be regarded as 'under color' of state authority within the meaning of [Section 1983]. Respondents, in breaking into the Monroe apartment, violated the laws of the State of Illinois. Illinois law appears to offer a civil remedy for unlawful searches; petitioners do not claim that none is available. Rather they assert that they have been deprived of due process of law and of equal protection of the laws under color of state law, although from all that appears the courts of Illinois are available to give them the fullest redress which the common law affords for the violence done them, nor does any "statute, ordinance, regulation, custom, or usage" of the State of Illinois bar that redress. Did the enactment by Congress of §1 of the Ku Klux Act of 1871 encompass such a situation?

The Ku Klux Act as a whole encountered in the course of its passage strenuous constitutional objections which focused precisely upon an assertedly unauthorized extension of federal judicial power into areas of exclusive state competence.

The unwisdom of extending federal criminal jurisdiction into areas of conduct conventionally punished by state penal law is perhaps more obvious than that of extending federal civil jurisdiction into the traditional realm of state tort law. But the latter, too, presents its problems of policy appropriately left to Congress. Suppose that a state legislature or the highest court of a State should determine that within its territorial limits no damages should be recovered in tort for pain and suffering, or for mental anguish, or that no punitive damages should be recoverable. Since the federal courts went out of the business of making "general law," *Erie R.R. Co. v. Tompkins,* such decisions of local policy have admittedly been the exclusive province of state lawmakers. Should the civil liability for police conduct which can claim no authority under local law, which is actionable as common-law assault or trespass in the local courts, comport different rules? Should an unlawful intrusion by a policeman in Chicago entail different consequences than an unlawful intrusion by a hoodlum? These are matters of policy in its strictly legislative sense, not for determination by this Court.

* * *

The *Monroe* Court's interpretation of when a government agent is acting under the color of law prevails today. If a person is behaving as a "state actor" in the constitutional sense, the person is acting under the color of law within the meaning of §1983. This holding resulted in an exponential increase in cases seeking monetary damages against state officials for constitutional violations. In 1961, there were 296 federal filings under §1983, excluding suits filed by state prisoners.[19] By 1979, that number increased to 13,168. Moreover, "[c]ivil rights petitions by state prisoners increased from 218 cases in 1966, to 11,195 in 1979."[20] In the decades thereafter, §1983 suits have continued to represent one of the most common sources of litigation in federal court.[21]

The other key holding in *Monroe*—that a municipality is not a "person" under §1983—was reversed 17 years later in *Monell v. Dep't of Soc. Services* (1978) discussed in the next Section.

2.   Section 1983 Suits Against Local Governments

In *Monell v. Dep't of Soc. Services* (1978), the Court held that a local government may be held liable for a policy or custom that violates the Constitution. A "policy" is an action or series of actions by a person with final decision-making authority under state law. *City of St. Louis v. Praprotnik* (1988). A "custom" is a well-settled and permanent practice, the source of which is often difficult to identify. *Adickes v. S. H. Kress & Co.* (1970). Cases in the decades following *Monell* clarified that a plaintiff is also permitted to initiate a suit against a municipality for certain policies or customs that *cause* violations of federal law. Additionally, municipalities are not formally protected by sovereign or officer immunities.

Importantly, a plaintiff's demonstration that a city's employee violated the Constitution, without more, is insufficient to bring suit against a municipality. That is, in contrast to many state-law tort regimes, Section 1983 doctrine does not recognize municipal liability under a theory of *respondeat superior* liability. Instead, under *Monell* and its progeny, a victim of a local violation of federal rights may rely on §1983 to sue a municipality under the following circumstances: (1) a city formally enacts an unconstitutional policy, ordinance, or regulation; (2) a local official with final policymaking authority under state law participates in violation of federal rights, authorizes a violation, or commands a violation; or (3) a person with final policymaking authority exhibits deliberate indifference to known or exceptionally probable violations.

a.   Formally Enacted Policy, Ordinance, or Regulation

Jane Monell served as a social worker for adolescents, employed by the New York City Department of Social Services. In 1970, because Monell was pregnant, her

---

19. Christina B. Whitman, *Constitutional Torts,* 79 MICH. L. REV. 5 (1980).

20. *Id.*

21. Theodore Eisenberg, *Four Decades of Federal Civil Rights Litigation,* 12 J. EMPIRICAL LEGAL STUD. 4 (2015).

employer informed her that as a matter of official city policy she needed to take an unpaid leave of absence. When asked why, her supervisor reportedly replied, "You might get injured . . . the girls might be disturbed . . . anyway, it's policy. . . ."[22] At the time, a citywide policy required pregnant employees to take a leave of absence at the end of their fifth month of pregnancy.

Monell and a class of similarly situated female employees filed suit against the city, arguing that the policy violated the Fourteenth Amendment by penalizing their choice to bear children, and by discriminating on the basis of sex. This suit was not unique; other similar suits were brought against comparable policies across the country as women fought for equitable inclusion in the nation's civic, social, and economic life.[23] In 1972, the EEOC officially adopted the position that indiscriminately forcing women to take unpaid leave violated federal anti-discrimination statutes.[24] And by 1974, a lawyer for the ACLU's Women's Rights Project wrote that "the most litigated area of sex discrimination in employment . . . has been in the treatment of pregnancy and pregnancy-related disabilities."[25]

While Monell's case was progressing in federal court, the Supreme Court ruled in another case that requiring pregnant individuals to take unpaid leave before medically necessary was unconstitutional. *Cleveland Bd. of Educ. v. LaFleur* (1974). The Court reasoned: "[T]here is a right to be free from unwarranted governmental intrusion into matters so fundamentally affecting a person as the decision whether to bear or beget a child. By acting to penalize the pregnant teacher for deciding to bear a child, overly restrictive maternity leave regulations can constitute a heavy burden on the exercise of these protected freedoms."

LaFleur did not explicitly answer, however, the scope of municipal liability under §1983. This question was answered four years later by the Court in *Monell v. Dep't of Soc. Services* (1978). As Monell's family later wrote, "Although [the case] grew out of the social conflict of its time and was thought by its participants to be important from the beginning, no one involved in the case would have guessed that its resolution would reshape the contours of federal jurisdiction."[26] *Monell* held that municipalities may be held liable for causing constitutional violations by way of unconstitutional policies, but that they may not be held liable under a theory of *respondeat superior.*

---

22. Jane Monell's spouse and son described the case in a 1999 law review article. Oscar G. Chase & Arlo Monell Chase, *Monell: The Story Behind the Landmark*, 31 URB. LAW. 491 (1999).

23. Holy McCammon & Amanda Brockman, *Feminist Institutional Activists: Venue Shifting, Strategic Adaptation, and Winning the Pregnancy Discrimination Act*, 42 SOCIOLOGICAL FORUM 5 (2019) ("The litigation campaign began in 1971. While no pregnancy discrimination court cases are on record prior to 1971, in that year, six cases were heard in federal courts . . . "). For a historical treatment of this movement, see Deborah Dinner, *Recovering the Lafleur Doctrine*, 22 YALE J.L. & FEMINISM 343, 348 (2010) ("[L]abor feminists used law, including administrative guidelines and court decisions, as tools in organizing for sex equality in the workplace.").

24. 29 C.F.R. §1604.10(b) (1972).

25. McCammon and Brockman, *supra* note 23.

26. Chase & Chase, *supra* note 22.

Monell v. Department of Social Services

436 U.S. 658 (1978)

Justice BRENNAN delivered the opinion of the Court.

Petitioners, a class of female employees of the Department of Social Services and of the Board of Education of the city of New York, commenced this action under 42 U.S.C. §1983 in July 1971. The gravamen of the complaint was that the Board and the Department had as a matter of official policy compelled pregnant employees to take unpaid leaves of absence before such leaves were required for medical reasons. *Cleveland Bd of Educ. v. LaFleur* (1974). The suit sought injunctive relief and backpay for periods of unlawful forced leave. Named as defendants in the action were the Department and its Commissioner, the Board and its Chancellor, and the city of New York and its Mayor. In each case, the individual defendants were sued solely in their official capacities.

We granted certiorari in this case to consider whether local governmental officials and/or local independent school boards are "persons" within the meaning of 42 U.S.C. §1983 when equitable relief in the nature of back pay is sought against them in their official capacities?

Although, after plenary consideration, we have decided the merits of over a score of cases brought under §1983 in which the principal defendant was a school board—and, indeed, in some of which §1983 and its jurisdictional counterpart, 28 U.S.C. §1343, provided the only basis for jurisdiction—we indicated last Term that the question presented here was open and would be decided "another day." That other day has come and we now overrule *Monroe v. Pape, supra,* insofar as it holds that local governments are wholly immune from suit under §1983.

I

In *Monroe v. Pape,* we held that "Congress did not undertake to bring municipal corporations within the ambit of [§1983]." The sole basis for this conclusion was an inference drawn from Congress' rejection of the "Sherman amendment" to the bill which became the Civil Rights Act of 1871, 17 Stat. 13, the precursor of §1983. The Amendment would have held a municipal corporation liable for damage done to the person or property of its inhabitants by *private* persons "riotously and tumultuously assembled." Cong. Globe, 42d Cong., 1st Sess., 749 (1871) (hereinafter Globe). Although the Sherman amendment did not seek to amend §1 of the Act, which is now §1983, and although the nature of the obligation created by that amendment was vastly different from that created by §1, the Court nonetheless concluded in *Monroe* that Congress must have meant to exclude municipal corporations from the coverage of §1 because "'the House [in voting against the Sherman amendment] had solemnly decided that in their judgment Congress had no constitutional power to impose any *obligation* upon county and town organizations, the mere instrumentality for the administration of state law.'"

A fresh analysis of the debate on the Civil Rights Act of 1871, and particularly of the case law which each side mustered in its support, shows, however, that *Monroe* incorrectly equated the "obligation" of which Representative Poland spoke with "civil liability." Nothing said in debate on the Sherman amendment would have prevented holding a municipality liable under §1 of the Civil Rights Act for its own violations of the Fourteenth Amendment. [Additionally,] an examination of the debate on §1 and application of appropriate rules of construction show unequivocally that §1 was intended to cover legal as well as natural persons.

Representative Shellabarger was the first to explain the function of §1:

> [Section 1] not only provides a civil remedy for persons whose former condition may have been that of slaves, but also to all people where, under color of State law, they or any of them may be deprived of rights to which they are entitled under the Constitution by reason and virtue of their national citizenship.

Globe App. 68.

By extending a remedy to all people, including whites, §1 went beyond the mischief to which the remaining sections of the 1871 Act were addressed. Representative Shellabarger also stated without reservation that the constitutionality of §2 of the Civil Rights Act of 1866 controlled the constitutionality of §1 of the 1871 Act, and that the former had been approved by "the supreme courts of at least three States of this Union" and by Mr. Justice Swayne, sitting on circuit, who had concluded: "'We have no doubt of the constitutionality of every provision of this act.'" Globe App. 68. Representative Shellabarger then went on to describe how the courts would and should interpret §1:

> This act is remedial, and in aid of the preservation of human liberty and human rights. All statutes and constitutional provisions authorizing such statutes are liberally and beneficently construed. It would be most strange and, in civilized law, monstrous were this not the rule of interpretation. As has been again and again decided by your own Supreme Court of the United States, and everywhere else where there is wise judicial interpretation, the largest latitude consistent with the words employed is uniformly given in construing such statutes and constitutional provisions as are meant to protect and defend and give remedies for their wrongs to all the people. . . . Chief Justice Jay and also Story say: "Where a power is remedial in its nature there is much reason to contend that it ought to be construed liberally, and it is generally adopted in the interpretation of laws."—1 *Story on Constitution*, sec. 429."

Globe App., at 68.

In addition, by 1871, it was well understood that corporations should be treated as natural persons for virtually all purposes of constitutional and statutory analysis. This had not always been so. When this Court first considered the question of the status of corporations, Mr. Chief Justice Marshall, writing for the Court, denied that corporations "as such" were persons as that term was used in Art. III and the Judiciary Act of 1789. *See Bank of the U.S. v. Deveaux* (1809). By 1844, however, the *Deveaux* doctrine was unhesitatingly abandoned:

> [A] corporation created by and doing business in a particular state, is to be deemed *to all intents and purposes as a person*, although an artificial person, . . . capable of being treated as a citizen of that state, as much as a natural person.

Louisville R.R. Co. v. Letson (1844) (emphasis added), discussed in Globe 752.

And only two years before the debates on the Civil Rights Act, in *Cowles v. Mercer Cnty.* (1869), the *Letson* principle was automatically and without discussion extended to municipal corporations. Under this doctrine, municipal corporations were routinely sued in the federal courts and this fact was well known to Members of Congress.

That the "usual" meaning of the word "person" would extend to municipal corporations is also evidenced by an Act of Congress which had been passed only months before the Civil Rights Act was passed. This Act provided that "in all acts hereafter passed . . . the word 'person' may extend and be applied to bodies politic and corporate . . . unless the context shows that such words were intended to be used in a more limited sense." Act of Feb. 25, 1871, §2, 16 Stat. 431. Municipal corporations in 1871 were included within the phrase "bodies politic and corporate" and, accordingly, the "plain meaning" of §1 is that local government bodies were to be included within the ambit of the persons who could be sued under §1 of the Civil Rights Act. Indeed, a Circuit Judge, writing in 1873 in what is apparently the first reported case under §1, read the Dictionary Act in precisely this way in a case involving a corporate plaintiff and a municipal defendant. *See Northwestern Fertilizing Co. v. Hyde Park* (No. 10,336) (CC N.D. Ill. 1873).

II

Our analysis of the legislative history of the Civil Rights Act of 1871 compels the conclusion that Congress *did* intend municipalities and other local government units to be included among those persons to whom §1983 applies. Local governing bodies, therefore, can be sued directly under §1983 for monetary, declaratory, or injunctive relief where, as here, the action that is alleged to be unconstitutional implements or executes a policy statement, ordinance, regulation, or decision officially adopted and promulgated by that body's officers. Moreover, although the touchstone of the §1983 action against a government body is an allegation that official policy is responsible for a deprivation of rights protected by the Constitution, local governments, like every other §1983 "person," by the very terms of the statute, may be sued for constitutional deprivations visited pursuant to governmental "custom" even though such a custom has not received formal approval through the body's official decisionmaking channels. As Mr. Justice Harlan, writing for the Court, said in *Adickes v. S. H. Kress & Co.* (1970): "Congress included customs and usages [in §1983] because of the persistent and widespread discriminatory practices of state officials. . . . Although not authorized by written law, such practices of state officials could well be so permanent and well settled as to constitute a 'custom or usage' with the force of law."

On the other hand, the language of §1983, read against the background of the same legislative history, compels the conclusion that Congress did not intend municipalities to be held liable unless action pursuant to official municipal policy of some nature caused a constitutional tort. In particular, we conclude that a municipality cannot be held liable *solely* because it employs a tortfeasor — or, in other words, a municipality cannot be held liable under §1983 on a *respondeat superior* theory.

We begin with the language of §1983 as originally passed:

[A]ny person who, under color of any law, statute, ordinance, regulation, custom, or usage of any State, *shall subject, or cause to be subjected*, any person . . . to the deprivation of any rights, privileges, or immunities secured by the Constitution of the United States, shall, any such law, statute, ordinance, regulation, custom, or usage of the State to the contrary notwithstanding, be liable to the party injured in any action at law, suit in equity, or other proper proceeding for redress. . . .

17 Stat. 13. (emphasis added).

The italicized language plainly imposes liability on a government that, under color of some official policy, "causes" an employee to violate another's constitutional rights. At the same time, that language cannot be easily read to impose liability vicariously on governing bodies solely on the basis of the existence of an employer-employee relationship with a tortfeasor. Indeed, the fact that Congress did specifically provide that A's tort became B's liability if B "caused" A to subject another to a tort suggests that Congress did not intend §1983 liability to attach where such causation was absent. *See Rizzo v. Goode* (1976).

Equally important, creation of a federal law of *respondeat superior* would have raised all the constitutional problems associated with the obligation to keep the peace, an obligation Congress chose not to impose because it thought imposition of such an obligation unconstitutional. To this day, there is disagreement about the basis for imposing liability on an employer for the torts of an employee when the sole nexus between the employer and the tort is the fact of the employer-employee relationship. *See* W. PROSSER, LAW OF TORTS §69, p. 459 (4th ed. 1971). Nonetheless, two justifications tend to stand out. First is the common-sense notion that no matter how blameless an employer appears to be in an individual case, accidents might nonetheless be reduced if employers had to bear the cost of accidents. *See, e.g., ibid.;* 2 F. Harper & F. James, Law of Torts, §26.3, pp. 1368-1369 (1956). Second is the argument that the cost of accidents should be spread to the community as a whole on an insurance theory.

The first justification is of the same sort that was offered for statutes like the Sherman amendment. The second justification was similarly put forward as a justification for the Sherman amendment. We conclude, therefore, that a local government may not be sued under §1983 for an injury inflicted solely by its employees or agents. Instead, it is when execution of a government's policy or custom, whether made by its lawmakers or by those whose edicts or acts may fairly be said to represent official policy, inflicts the injury that the government as an entity is responsible under §1983.

Mr. Justice POWELL, concurring.

I join the opinion of the Court, and express these additional views. Few cases in the history of the Court have been cited more frequently than *Monroe v. Pape* 492 (1961), decided less than two decades ago. Focusing new light on 42 U.S.C. §1983, that decision widened access to the federal courts and permitted expansive interpretations of the reach of the 1871 measure. But *Monroe* exempted local governments from liability at the same time it opened wide the courthouse door to

suits against officers and employees of those entities — even when they act pursuant
to express authorization. The oddness of this result, and the weakness of the historical evidence relied on by the *Monroe* Court in support of it, are well demonstrated
by the Court's opinion today. Yet the gravity of overruling a part of so important a
decision prompts me to write.

[Even] if we continued to adhere to a rule of absolute municipal immunity
under §1983, we could not long avoid the question whether we should, by analogy
to our decision in *Bivens v. Six Unknown Fed. Narcotics Agents* (1971), imply a cause of
action directly from the Fourteenth Amendment which would not be subject to the
limitations contained in §1983.

Difficult questions nevertheless remain for another day. There are substantial
line-drawing problems in determining "when execution of a government's policy
or custom" can be said to inflict constitutional injury such that "government as
an entity is responsible under §1983." *Ante,* at 2038. This case, however, involves
formal, written policies of a municipal department and school board; it is the clear
case. The Court also reserves decision on the availability of a qualified municipal
immunity. Initial resolution of the question whether the protection available at
common law for municipal corporations, or other principles support a qualified
municipal immunity in the context of the §1983 damages action, is left to the lower
federal courts.

* * *

The policy at issue in *Monell* applied routinely to any individual who reached
a specified point in a pregnancy. For a regulation or ordinance to be deemed a
policy, however, does not require that that ordinance announce a rule of general
applicability. In *Owen v. City of Independence* (1980) and *City of Newport v. Fact Concerts, Inc.* (1981), cities were found liable under §1983 for ordinances that were
targeted at one person or entity. In *Owen,* a city council censured and terminated a
police chief without a hearing. In *Fact Concerts,* a city council passed an ordinance
cancelling a permit for a concert by a jazz band based on the perceived content of
the band's expected performance. As the Court later observed as to the import of
Owen and *Fact Concerts*: "Neither decision reflected implementation of a generally
applicable rule. But we did not question that each decision, duly promulgated by
city lawmakers, could trigger municipal liability if the decision itself were found to
be unconstitutional." *Brown v. Bryan Cnty.* (1997).

b.   Authorization or Participation by a Final Policymaker

To trigger municipal liability under the *Monell* doctrine, a policy need not be
enacted by a city council or other legislative body. A city may also be liable when
a violation is attributable to a final policymaker. State law determines whether
someone is a final policymaker. *City of St. Louis v. Praprotnik* (1988) (holding that
whether a local government official has "final policymaking authority" is a question
of state and local law, not a fact question for juries; only a showing of officially promulgated policy will establish liability, not improper but independent conduct by
subordinates in making layoffs). In the following case, a final policymaker directed

policy to engage in an unconstitutional search of a business, therefore rending a municipality liable.

Pembaur v. City of Cincinnati

475 U.S. 469 (1986)

Justice BRENNAN delivered the opinion of the Court, except as to Part II-B.

In *Monell v. N.Y. City Dept. of Soc. Services* the Court concluded that municipal liability under 42 U.S.C. §1983 is limited to deprivations of federally protected rights caused by action taken "pursuant to official municipal policy of some nature. . . ." The question presented is whether, and in what circumstances, a decision by municipal policymakers on a single occasion may satisfy this requirement.

I

During [an] investigation [of Dr. Pembaur for fraudulently accepting reimbursements from state agencies for services not actually provided to patients, a] grand jury issued subpoenas for the appearance of two of [Dr. Bertold] Pembaur's employees. When these employees failed to appear as directed, the Prosecutor obtained capias for their arrest and detention from the Court of Common Pleas of Hamilton County.

On May 19, 1977, two Hamilton County Deputy Sheriffs attempted to serve the capiases at Pembaur's clinic. [Pembaur] refused to let them enter, claiming that the police had no legal authority to be there and requesting that they leave. After attempt[s] to persuade Pembaur voluntarily to allow them to enter, the Deputy Sheriffs tried unsuccessfully to force the door. City police officers, who had been advised of the County Prosecutor's instructions to "go in and get" the witnesses, obtained an axe and chopped down the door. The Deputy Sheriffs then entered and searched the clinic. Two individuals who fit descriptions of the witnesses sought were detained, but turned out not to be the right persons.

[On] April 20, 1981, Pembaur filed [this suit]. Pembaur sought damages under 42 U.S.C. §1983, alleging that the county and city police had violated his rights under the Fourth and Fourteenth Amendments.

II
A

Our analysis must begin with the proposition that "Congress did not intend municipalities to be held liable unless action pursuant to official municipal policy of some nature caused a constitutional tort." *Monell v. N.Y. City Dept. of Soc. Services.* As we read its opinion, the Court of Appeals held that a single decision to take particular action, although made by municipal policymakers, cannot establish the kind of "official policy" required by *Monell* as a predicate to municipal liability under §1983.

Monell is a case about responsibility. In the first part of the opinion, we held that local government units could be made liable under §1983 for deprivations of federal rights, overruling a contrary holding in *Monroe v. Pape.* In the second part of the opinion, we recognized a limitation on this liability and concluded that a municipality cannot be made liable by application of the doctrine of *respondeat superior. See Monell.* In part, this conclusion rested upon the language of §1983, which imposes liability only on a person who "subjects, or causes to be subjected," any individual to a deprivation of federal rights; we noted that this language "cannot easily be read to impose liability vicariously on government bodies solely on the basis of the existence of an employer-employee relationship with a tortfeasor." Primarily, however, our conclusion rested upon the legislative history, which disclosed that, while Congress never questioned its power to impose civil liability on municipalities for their own illegal acts, Congress did doubt its constitutional power to impose such liability in order to oblige municipalities to control the conduct of others. We found that, because of these doubts, Congress chose not to create such obligations in §1983. Recognizing that this would be the effect of a federal law of *respondeat superior,* we concluded that §1983 could not be interpreted to incorporate doctrines of vicarious liability.

The conclusion that tortious conduct, to be the basis for municipal liability under §1983, must be pursuant to a municipality's "official policy" is contained in this discussion. The "official policy" requirement was intended to distinguish acts of the municipality from acts of employees of the municipality, and thereby make clear that municipal liability is limited to action for which the municipality is actually responsible. *Monell* reasoned that recovery from a municipality is limited to acts that are, properly speaking, acts "of the municipality"—that is, acts which the municipality has officially sanctioned or ordered.

With this understanding, it is plain that municipal liability may be imposed for a single decision by municipal policymakers under appropriate circumstances. No one has ever doubted, for instance, that a municipality may be liable under §1983 for a single decision by its properly constituted legislative body—whether or not that body had taken similar action in the past or intended to do so in the future—because even a single decision by such a body unquestionably constitutes an act of official government policy. *See, e.g., Owen v. City of Independence* (City Council passed resolution firing plaintiff without a pre-termination hearing); *Newport v. Fact Concerts, Inc.* (City Council canceled license permitting concert because of dispute over content of performance). But the power to establish policy is no more the exclusive province of the legislature at the local level than at the state or national level. *Monell's* language makes clear that it expressly envisioned other officials "whose acts or edicts may fairly be said to represent official policy," *Monell,* and whose decisions therefore may give rise to municipal liability under §1983.

Indeed, any other conclusion would be inconsistent with the principles underlying §1983. To be sure, "official policy" often refers to formal rules or understandings—often but not always committed to writing—that are intended to, and do, establish fixed plans of action to be followed under similar circumstances consistently and over time.

B

Having said this much, we hasten to emphasize that not every decision by municipal officers automatically subjects the municipality to §1983 liability. Municipal liability attaches only where the decisionmaker possesses final authority to establish municipal policy with respect to the action ordered. The fact that a particular official—even a policymaking official—has discretion in the exercise of particular functions does not, without more, give rise to municipal liability based on an exercise of that discretion. *See, e.g., Oklahoma City v. Tuttle.* The official must also be responsible for establishing final government policy respecting such activity before the municipality can be held liable. Authority to make municipal policy may be granted directly by a legislative enactment or may be delegated by an official who possesses such authority, and of course, whether an official had final policymaking authority is a question of state law. However, like other governmental entities, municipalities often spread policymaking authority among various officers and official bodies. As a result, particular officers may have authority to establish binding county policy respecting particular matters and to adjust that policy for the county in changing circumstances. To hold a municipality liable for actions ordered by such officers exercising their policymaking authority is no more an application of the theory of *respondeat superior* than was holding the municipalities liable for the decisions of the City Councils in *Owen* and *Newport.* In each case municipal liability attached to a single decision to take unlawful action made by municipal policymakers. We hold that municipal liability under §1983 attaches where—and only where—a deliberate choice to follow a course of action is made from among various alternatives by the official or officials responsible for establishing final policy with respect to the subject matter in question.

C

Applying this standard to the case before us, we have little difficulty concluding that the Court of Appeals erred in dismissing petitioner's claim against the county. The Deputy Sheriffs who attempted to serve the capiases at petitioner's clinic found themselves in a difficult situation. Unsure of the proper course of action to follow, they sought instructions from their supervisors. The instructions they received were to follow the orders of the County Prosecutor. The Prosecutor made a considered decision based on his understanding of the law and commanded the officers forcibly to enter petitioner's clinic. That decision directly caused the violation of petitioner's Fourth Amendment rights.

Respondent argues that the County Prosecutor lacked authority to establish municipal policy respecting law enforcement practices because only the County Sheriff may establish policy respecting such practices. Respondent suggests that the County Prosecutor was merely rendering "legal advice" when he ordered the Deputy Sheriffs to "go in and get" the witnesses. Consequently, the argument concludes, the action of the individual Deputy Sheriffs in following this advice and forcibly entering petitioner's clinic was not pursuant to a properly established municipal policy.

We might be inclined to agree with respondent if we thought that the Prosecutor had only rendered "legal advice." However, the Court of Appeals concluded, based upon its examination of Ohio law, that both the County Sheriff and the County Prosecutor could establish county policy under appropriate circumstances, a conclusion that we do not question here. Ohio Rev. Code Ann. §309.09(A) (1979) provides that county officers may "require . . . instructions from [the County Prosecutor], in matters connected with their official duties." Pursuant to standard office procedure, the Sheriff's Office referred this matter to the Prosecutor and then followed his instructions.

The decision of the Court of Appeals is reversed, and the case is remanded for further proceedings consistent with this opinion.

Justice POWELL, with whom THE CHIEF JUSTICE and Justice REHNQUIST join, dissenting.

[P]roper resolution of the question whether official policy has been formed should focus on two factors: (i) the nature of the decision reached or the action taken, and (ii) the process by which the decision was reached or the action was taken.

Focusing on the nature of the decision distinguishes between policies and mere ad hoc decisions. Such a focus also reflects the fact that most policies embody a rule of general applicability. That is the tenor of the Court's statement in *Monell* that local government units are liable under §1983 when the action that is alleged to be unconstitutional "implements or executes a policy statement, ordinance, regulation, or decision officially adopted and promulgated by that body's officers." The clear implication is that policy is created when a rule is formed that applies to all similar situations—a "governing principle [or] plan." *Webster's New Twentieth Century Dictionary* 1392 (2d ed. 1979). When a rule of general applicability has been approved, the government has taken a position for which it can be held responsible.

Another factor indicating that policy has been formed is the process by which the decision at issue was reached. Formal procedures that involve, for example, voting by elected officials, prepared reports, extended deliberation, or official records indicate that the resulting decisions taken "may fairly be said to represent official policy," *Monell, supra. Owen v. City of Independence* provides an example. The City Council met in a regularly scheduled meeting. One member of the Council made a motion to release to the press certain reports that cast an employee in a bad light. After deliberation, the Council passed the motion with no dissents and one abstention. Although this official action did not establish a rule of general applicability, it is clear that policy was formed because of the process by which the decision was reached.

Applying these factors to the instant case demonstrates that no official policy was formulated. Certainly, no rule of general applicability was adopted. Similarly, nothing about the way the decision was reached indicates that official policy was formed. The prosecutor, without time for thoughtful consideration or consultation, simply gave an off-the-cuff answer to a single question. There was no process at all. The Court's holding undercuts the basic rationale of *Monell*, and unfairly increases the risk of liability on the level of government least able to bear it. I dissent.

* * *

c. Deliberate Indifference

Under §1983, a municipality is also liable for a final policymaker's deliberate indifference to known or highly probable constitutional violations. This is a high bar. "A showing of simple or even heightened negligence will not suffice." *Bryan Cnty. v. Brown* (1997). In *Bryan County*, for example, a sheriff hired his 21-year-old great-nephew to serve as a deputy, despite his record of battery, assault, and vehicular crimes—none of which were felonies. The deputy, once hired, violated the Fourth Amendment rights of a woman named Jill Brown during a routine traffic stop. Unprovoked, he slammed her to the ground with such force that he severely injured both of her knees. Brown sued the county, given that the sheriff (whose status as a final policymaker was uncontested) had either failed to adequately screen the deputy or hired him despite his record. While the Fifth Circuit found that the county was liable, the Supreme Court reversed. Although the assailant may have been an "extremely poor candidate for reserve deputy," it was not "plainly obvious" based on his record of infractions that he would commit an act of excessive force. "To prevent municipal liability for a hiring decision from collapsing into respondeat superior liability, a court must carefully test the link between the policymaker's inadequate decision and the particular injury alleged."

In the following case, the Court again applied these principles to reject municipal liability.

Connick v. Thompson

563 U.S. 51 (2011)

Justice Thomas delivered the opinion of the Court.

The Orleans Parish District Attorney's Office now concedes that, in prosecuting respondent John Thompson for attempted armed robbery, prosecutors failed to disclose evidence that should have been turned over to the defense under *Brady v. Md.* (1963). After his release from prison, Thompson sued petitioner Harry Connick, in his official capacity as the Orleans Parish District Attorney, for damages under 42 U.S.C. §1983. Thompson alleged that Connick had failed to train his prosecutors adequately about their duty to produce exculpatory evidence and that the lack of training had caused the nondisclosure in Thompson's robbery case. The jury awarded Thompson $14 million, and the Court of Appeals for the Fifth Circuit affirmed by an evenly divided en banc court. We granted certiorari to decide whether a district attorney's office may be held liable under §1983 for failure to train based on a single *Brady* violation. We hold that it cannot.

I

A

In early 1985, John Thompson was charged with the murder of Raymond T. Liuzza, Jr. in New Orleans. Publicity following the murder charge led the victims of an unrelated armed robbery to identify Thompson as their attacker. The district attorney charged Thompson with attempted armed robbery.

As part of the robbery investigation, a crime scene technician took from one of the victims' pants a swatch of fabric stained with the robber's blood. Approximately one week before Thompson's armed robbery trial, the swatch was sent to the crime laboratory. Two days before the trial, assistant district attorney Bruce Whittaker received the crime lab's report, which stated that the perpetrator had blood type B. There is no evidence that the prosecutors ever had Thompson's blood tested or that they knew what his blood type was. Whittaker claimed he placed the report on assistant district attorney James Williams' desk, but Williams denied seeing it. The report was never disclosed to Thompson's counsel.

Williams tried the armed robbery case with assistant district attorney Gerry Deegan. On the first day of trial, Deegan checked all of the physical evidence in the case out of the police property room, including the blood-stained swatch. Deegan then checked all of the evidence but the swatch into the courthouse property room. The prosecutors did not mention the swatch or the crime lab report at trial, and the jury convicted Thompson of attempted armed robbery.

A few weeks later, Williams and special prosecutor Eric Dubelier tried Thompson for the Liuzza murder. Because of the armed robbery conviction, Thompson chose not to testify in his own defense. He was convicted and sentenced to death. In the 14 years following Thompson's murder conviction, state and federal courts reviewed and denied his challenges to the conviction and sentence. The State scheduled Thompson's execution for May 20, 1999.

In late April 1999, Thompson's private investigator discovered the crime lab report from the armed robbery investigation in the files of the New Orleans Police Crime Laboratory. Thompson was tested and found to have blood type O, proving that the blood on the swatch was not his. Thompson's attorneys presented this evidence to the district attorney's office, which, in turn, moved to stay the execution and vacate Thompson's armed robbery conviction. The Louisiana Court of Appeals then reversed Thompson's murder conviction, concluding that the armed robbery conviction unconstitutionally deprived Thompson of his right to testify in his own defense at the murder trial. In 2003, the district attorney's office retried Thompson for Liuzza's murder. The jury found him not guilty.

B

Thompson then brought this action against the district attorney's office, Connick, Williams, and others, alleging that their conduct caused him to be wrongfully convicted, incarcerated for 18 years, and nearly executed. The only claim that proceeded to trial was Thompson's claim under §1983 that the district attorney's office had violated *Brady* by failing to disclose the crime lab report in his armed robbery trial. *See Brady*. Thompson alleged liability under two theories: (1) the *Brady* violation was caused by an unconstitutional policy of the district attorney's office; and (2) the violation was caused by Connick's deliberate indifference to an obvious need to train the prosecutors in his office in order to avoid such constitutional violations.

Although no prosecutor remembered any specific training session regarding *Brady* prior to 1985, it was undisputed at trial that the prosecutors were familiar with the general *Brady* requirement that the State disclose to the defense evidence in its possession that is favorable to the accused. Prosecutors testified that office policy was to turn crime lab reports and other scientific evidence over to the defense. They also testified that, after the discovery of the undisclosed crime lab report in 1999, prosecutors disagreed about whether it had to be disclosed under *Brady* absent knowledge of Thompson's blood type.

The jury rejected Thompson's claim that an unconstitutional office policy caused the *Brady* violation, but found the district attorney's office liable for failing to train the prosecutors. The jury awarded Thompson $14 million in damages, and the District Court added more than $1 million in attorney's fees and costs.

After the verdict, Connick renewed his objection—which he had raised on summary judgment—that he could not have been deliberately indifferent to an obvious need for more or different *Brady* training because there was no evidence that he was aware of a pattern of similar *Brady* violations. The District Court rejected this argument for the reasons that it had given in the summary judgment order. In that order, the court had concluded that a pattern of violations is not necessary to prove deliberate indifference when the need for training is "so obvious." Relying on *Canton v. Harris* (1989), the court had held that Thompson could demonstrate deliberate indifference by proving that "the DA's office knew to a moral certainty that assistan[t] [district attorneys] would acquire *Brady* material, that without training it is not always obvious what *Brady* requires, and that withholding *Brady* material will virtually always lead to a substantial violation of constitutional rights."

A panel of the Court of Appeals for the Fifth Circuit affirmed. The Court of Appeals sitting en banc vacated the panel opinion, granted rehearing, and divided evenly, thereby affirming the District Court. We granted certiorari.

II

The *Brady* violation conceded in this case occurred when one or more of the four prosecutors involved with Thompson's armed robbery prosecution failed to disclose the crime lab report to Thompson's counsel. Under Thompson's failure-to-train theory, he bore the burden of proving both (1) that Connick, the policy-maker for the district attorney's office, was deliberately indifferent to the need to train the prosecutors about their *Brady* disclosure obligation with respect to evidence of this type and (2) that the lack of training actually caused the *Brady* violation in this case. Connick argues that he was entitled to judgment as a matter of law because Thompson did not prove that he was on actual or constructive notice of, and therefore deliberately indifferent to, a need for more or different *Brady* training. We agree.

A

Title 42 U.S.C. §1983 provides in relevant part:

> Every person who, under color of any statute, ordinance, regulation, custom, or usage, of any State . . . subjects, or causes to be subjected, any citizen of the United States or other person within the jurisdiction thereof to the deprivation of any rights, privileges, or immunities secured by the Constitution and laws, shall be liable to the party injured in an action at law, suit in equity, or other proper proceeding for redress. . . .

A municipality or other local government may be liable under this section if the governmental body itself "subjects" a person to a deprivation of rights or "causes" a person "to be subjected" to such deprivation. *See Monell v. N.Y. City Dept. of Soc. Servs.* (1978). But, under §1983, local governments are responsible only for "their *own* illegal acts." *Pembaur v. Cincinnati* (1986). They are not vicariously liable under §1983 for their employees' actions.

Plaintiffs who seek to impose liability on local governments under §1983 must prove that "action pursuant to official municipal policy" caused their injury. *Monell.* Official municipal policy includes the decisions of a government's lawmakers, the acts of its policymaking officials, and practices so persistent and widespread as to practically have the force of law. *Adickes v. S.H. Kress & Co.* (1970). These are "action[s] for which the municipality is actually responsible." *Pembaur, supra.*

In limited circumstances, a local government's decision not to train certain employees about their legal duty to avoid violating citizens' rights may rise to the level of an official government policy for purposes of §1983. A municipality's culpability for a deprivation of rights is at its most tenuous where a claim turns on a failure to train. *See Okla. City v. Tuttle* (1985) (plurality opinion). To satisfy the statute, a municipality's failure to train its employees in a relevant respect must amount to "deliberate indifference to the rights of persons with whom the [untrained employees] come into contact." *Canton.* Only then "can such a short-coming be properly thought of as a city 'policy or custom' that is actionable under §1983."

"'[D]eliberate indifference' is a stringent standard of fault, requiring proof that a municipal actor disregarded a known or obvious consequence of his action." *Bryan Cty.* Thus, when city policymakers are on actual or constructive notice that a particular omission in their training program causes city employees to violate citizens' constitutional rights, the city may be deemed deliberately indifferent if the policymakers choose to retain that program. The city's "policy of inaction" in light of notice that its program will cause constitutional violations "is the functional equivalent of a decision by the city itself to violate the Constitution." *Canton* (O'Connor, J., concurring in part and dissenting in part). A less stringent standard of fault for a failure-to-train claim "would result in *de facto respondeat superior* liability on municipalities. . . ."

B

A pattern of similar constitutional violations by untrained employees is "ordinarily necessary" to demonstrate deliberate indifference for purposes of failure to train. *Bryan Cty.* Policymakers' "continued adherence to an approach that they know or should know has failed to prevent tortious conduct by employees may establish the conscious disregard for the consequences of their action—the 'deliberate indifference'—necessary to trigger municipal liability." Without notice that a course of training is deficient in a particular respect, decisionmakers can hardly be said to have deliberately chosen a training program that will cause violations of constitutional rights.

Although Thompson does not contend that he proved a pattern of similar *Brady* violations, he points out that, during the ten years preceding his armed robbery trial, Louisiana courts had overturned four convictions because of *Brady* violations by prosecutors in Connick's office. Those four reversals could not have put Connick on notice that the office's *Brady* training was inadequate with respect to the sort of *Brady* violation at issue here. None of those cases involved failure to disclose blood evidence, a crime lab report, or physical or scientific evidence of any kind. Because those incidents are not similar to the violation at issue here, they could not have put Connick on notice that specific training was necessary to avoid this constitutional violation.

C

Instead of relying on a pattern of similar *Brady* violations, Thompson relies on the "single-incident" liability that this Court hypothesized in *Canton*. He contends that the *Brady* violation in his case was the "obvious" consequence of failing to provide specific *Brady* training, and that this showing of "obviousness" can substitute for the pattern of violations ordinarily necessary to establish municipal culpability.

In *Canton*, the Court left open the possibility that, "in a narrow range of circumstances," a pattern of similar violations might not be necessary to show deliberate indifference. *Bryan Cty.* The Court posed the hypothetical example of a city that arms its police force with firearms and deploys the armed officers into the public to capture fleeing felons without training the officers in the constitutional limitation on the use of deadly force. *Canton.* Given the known frequency with which police attempt to arrest fleeing felons and the "predictability that an officer lacking specific tools to handle that situation will violate citizens' rights," the Court theorized that a city's decision not to train the officers about constitutional limits on the use of deadly force could reflect the city's deliberate indifference to the "highly predictable consequence," namely, violations of constitutional rights. *Bryan Cty., supra.* The Court sought not to foreclose the possibility, however rare, that the unconstitutional consequences of failing to train could be so patently obvious that a city could be liable under §1983 without proof of a pre-existing pattern of violations.

Failure to train prosecutors in their *Brady* obligations does not fall within the narrow range of *Canton*'s hypothesized single-incident liability. The obvious need for specific legal training that was present in the *Canton* scenario is absent here. Armed police must sometimes make split-second decisions with life-or-death consequences. There is no reason to assume that police academy applicants are familiar with the constitutional constraints on the use of deadly force. And, in the absence of training, there is no way for novice officers to obtain the legal knowledge they require. Under those circumstances there is an obvious need for some form of training. In stark contrast, legal "[t]raining is what differentiates attorneys from average public employees."

Attorneys are trained in the law and equipped with the tools to interpret and apply legal principles, understand constitutional limits, and exercise legal judgment. Before they may enter the profession and receive a law license, all attorneys must graduate from law school or pass a substantive examination; attorneys in the vast majority of jurisdictions must do both. These threshold requirements are designed to ensure that all new attorneys have learned how to find, understand, and apply legal rules.

Nor does professional training end at graduation. Most jurisdictions require attorneys to satisfy continuing-education requirements. Even those few jurisdictions that do not impose mandatory continuing-education requirements mandate that attorneys represent their clients competently and encourage attorneys to engage in continuing study and education. Before Louisiana adopted continuing-education requirements, it imposed similar general competency requirements on its state bar.

Attorneys who practice with other attorneys, such as in district attorney's offices, also train on the job as they learn from more experienced attorneys. For instance, here in the Orleans Parish District Attorney's Office, junior prosecutors were trained by senior prosecutors who supervised them as they worked together to prepare cases for trial, and trial chiefs oversaw the preparation of the cases. Senior attorneys also circulated court decisions and instructional memoranda to keep the prosecutors abreast of relevant legal developments.

In addition, attorneys in all jurisdictions must satisfy character and fitness standards to receive a law license and are personally subject to an ethical regime designed to reinforce the profession's standards. Trial lawyers have a "duty to bring to bear such skill and knowledge as will render the trial a reliable adversarial testing process." *Strickland v. Washington* (1984).

In light of this regime of legal training and professional responsibility, recurring constitutional violations are not the "obvious consequence" of failing to provide prosecutors with formal in-house training about how to obey the law. *Bryan Cty.* Prosecutors are not only equipped but are also ethically bound to know what *Brady* entails and to perform legal research when they are uncertain. A district attorney is entitled to rely on prosecutors' professional training and ethical obligations in the absence of specific reason, such as a pattern of violations, to believe that those tools are insufficient to prevent future constitutional violations in "the usual and recurring situations with which [the prosecutors] must deal." *Canton.* A licensed attorney making legal judgments, in his capacity as a prosecutor, about *Brady* material simply does not present the same "highly predictable" constitutional danger as *Canton*'s untrained officer.

A second significant difference between this case and the example in *Canton* is the nuance of the allegedly necessary training. The *Canton* hypothetical assumes that the armed police officers have no knowledge at all of the constitutional limits on the use of deadly force. But it is undisputed here that the prosecutors in Connick's office were familiar with the general *Brady* rule. Thompson's complaint therefore cannot rely on the utter lack of an ability to cope with constitutional situations that underlies the *Canton* hypothetical, but rather must assert that prosecutors were not trained about particular *Brady* evidence or the specific scenario related to the violation in his case. That sort of nuance simply cannot support an inference of deliberate indifference here. As the Court said in *Canton*, "[i]n virtually every instance where a person has had his or her constitutional rights violated by a city employee, a §1983 plaintiff will be able to point to something the city 'could have done' to prevent the unfortunate incident."

Thompson suggests that the absence of any *formal* training sessions about *Brady* is equivalent to the complete absence of legal training that the Court imagined in *Canton.* But failure-to-train liability is concerned with the substance of the training, not the particular instructional format. The statute does not provide plaintiffs or courts *carte blanche* to micromanage local governments throughout the United States.

We do not assume that prosecutors will always make correct *Brady* decisions or that guidance regarding specific *Brady* questions would not assist prosecutors. But showing merely that additional training would have been helpful in making difficult decisions does not establish municipal liability. "[P]rov[ing] that an injury or accident could have been avoided if an [employee] had had better or more training, sufficient to equip him to avoid the particular injury-causing conduct" will not suffice. *Canton, supra*. The possibility of single-incident liability that the Court left open in *Canton* is not this case.

2

The dissent rejects our holding that *Canton*'s hypothesized single-incident liability does not, as a legal matter, encompass failure to train prosecutors in their *Brady* obligation. It would instead apply the *Canton* hypothetical to this case, and thus devotes almost all of its opinion to explaining why the evidence supports liability under that theory. But the dissent's attempt to address our holding—by pointing out that not all prosecutors will necessarily have enrolled in criminal procedure class—misses the point. The reason why the *Canton* hypothetical is inapplicable is that attorneys, unlike police officers, are equipped with the tools to find, interpret, and apply legal principles.

3

The District Court and the Court of Appeals panel erroneously believed that Thompson had proved deliberate indifference by showing the "obviousness" of a need for additional training. They based this conclusion on Connick's awareness that (1) prosecutors would confront *Brady* issues while at the district attorney's office; (2) inexperienced prosecutors were expected to understand *Brady*'s requirements; (3) *Brady* has gray areas that make for difficult choices; and (4) erroneous decisions regarding *Brady* evidence would result in constitutional violations. This is insufficient.

It does not follow that, because *Brady* has gray areas and some *Brady* decisions are difficult, prosecutors will so obviously make wrong decisions that failing to train them amounts to "a decision by the city itself to violate the Constitution." *Canton* (O'Connor, J., concurring in part and dissenting in part). To prove deliberate indifference, Thompson needed to show that Connick was on notice that, absent additional specified training, it was "highly predictable" that the prosecutors in his office would be confounded by those gray areas and make incorrect *Brady* decisions as a result. In fact, Thompson had to show that it was *so* predictable that failing to train the prosecutors amounted to *conscious disregard* for defendants' *Brady* rights. *See Bryan Ctny*. He did not do so.

III

The role of a prosecutor is to see that justice is done. *Berger v. U.S.* (1935). By their own admission, the prosecutors who tried Thompson's armed robbery case failed to carry out that responsibility. But the only issue before us is whether Connick, as the policymaker for the district attorney's office, was deliberately indifferent to the need to train the attorneys under his authority. We conclude that this case does not fall within the narrow range of "single-incident" liability hypothesized in *Canton* as a possible exception to the pattern of violations necessary to prove deliberate indifference in §1983 actions alleging failure to train.

The judgment of the United States Court of Appeals for the Fifth Circuit is reversed.

Justice GINSBERG, with whom Justice BREYER, Justice SOTOMAYOR, and Justice KAGAN join, dissenting.

In *Brady*, this Court held that due process requires the prosecution to turn over evidence favorable to the accused and material to his guilt or punishment. That obligation, the parties have stipulated, was dishonored in this case; consequently, John Thompson spent 18 years in prison, 14 of them isolated on death row, before the truth came to light: He was innocent of the charge of attempted armed robbery, and his subsequent trial on a murder charge, by prosecutorial design, was fundamentally unfair.

The Court holds that the Orleans Parish District Attorney's Office (District Attorney's Office or Office) cannot be held liable, in a civil rights action under 42 U.S.C. §1983, for the grave injustice Thompson suffered. That is so, the Court tells us, because Thompson has shown only an aberrant *Brady* violation, not a routine practice of giving short shrift to *Brady*'s requirements. The evidence presented to the jury that awarded compensation to Thompson, however, points distinctly away from the Court's assessment. As the trial record in the §1983 action reveals, the conceded, long-concealed prosecutorial transgressions were neither isolated nor atypical.

From the top down, the evidence showed, members of the District Attorney's Office, including the District Attorney himself, misperceived *Brady*'s compass and therefore inadequately attended to their disclosure obligations. Throughout the pretrial and trial proceedings against Thompson, the team of four engaged in prosecuting him for armed robbery and murder hid from the defense and the court exculpatory information Thompson requested and had a constitutional right to receive. The prosecutors did so despite multiple opportunities, spanning nearly two decades, to set the record straight. Based on the prosecutors' conduct relating to Thompson's trials, a fact trier could reasonably conclude that inattention to *Brady* was standard operating procedure at the District Attorney's Office.

What happened here, the Court's opinion obscures, was no momentary oversight, no single incident of a lone officer's misconduct. Instead, the evidence demonstrated that misperception and disregard of *Brady*'s disclosure requirements were pervasive in Orleans Parish. That evidence, I would hold, established persistent, deliberately indifferent conduct for which the District Attorney's Office bears responsibility under §1983.

I dissent from the Court's judgment mindful that *Brady* violations, as this case illustrates, are not easily detected. But for a chance discovery made by a defense team investigator weeks before Thompson's scheduled execution, the evidence that led to his exoneration might have remained under wraps. The prosecutorial concealment Thompson encountered, however, is bound to be repeated unless municipal agencies bear responsibility—made tangible by §1983 liability—for adequately conveying what *Brady* requires and for monitoring staff compliance.

Failure to train, this Court has said, can give rise to municipal liability under §1983 "where the failure . . . amounts to deliberate indifference to the rights of persons with whom the [untrained employees] come into contact." *Canton v. Harris* (1989). That standard is well met in this case.

In *Canton*, this Court spoke of circumstances in which the need for training may be "so obvious," and the lack of training "so likely" to result in constitutional violations, that policymakers who do not provide for the requisite training "can reasonably be said to have been deliberately indifferent to the need" for such training. This case, I am convinced, belongs in the category *Canton* marked out.

Canton offered an often-cited illustration. "[C]ity policymakers know to a moral certainty that their police officers will be required to arrest fleeing felons." *Ibid.*, n.10. Those policymakers, *Canton* observed, equip police officers with firearms to facilitate such arrests. The need to instruct armed officers about "constitutional limitations on the use of deadly force," *Canton* said, is " 'so obvious,' that failure to [train the officers] could properly be characterized as 'deliberate indifference' to constitutional rights."

The District Court, tracking *Canton*'s language, instructed the jury that Thompson could prevail on his "deliberate indifference" claim only if the evidence persuaded the jury on three points. First, Connick "was certain that prosecutors would confront the situation where they would have to decide which evidence was required by the Constitution to be provided to the accused." Second, "the situation involved a difficult choice[,] or one that prosecutors had a history of mishandling, such that additional training, supervision or monitoring was clearly needed." Third, "the wrong choice by a prosecutor in that situation would frequently cause a deprivation of an accused's constitutional rights."

The jury, furthermore, could reasonably find that *Brady* rights may involve choices so difficult that Connick obviously knew or should have known prosecutors needed more than perfunctory training to make the correct choices. Based on the evidence presented, the jury could conclude that *Brady* errors by untrained prosecutors would frequently cause deprivations of defendants' constitutional rights. The jury learned of several *Brady* oversights in Thompson's trials and heard testimony that Connick's Office had one of the worst *Brady* records in the country. Tr. 163.

Unquestionably, a municipality that leaves police officers untrained in constitutional limits on the use of deadly weapons places lives in jeopardy. *Canton.* But as this case so vividly shows, a municipality that empowers prosecutors to press for a death sentence without ensuring that those prosecutors know and honor *Brady* rights may be no less "deliberately indifferent" to the risk to innocent lives.

Brady, this Court has long recognized, is among the most basic safeguards brigading a criminal defendant's fair trial right. Vigilance in superintending prosecutors' attention to *Brady*'s requirement is all the more important for this reason: A *Brady* violation, by its nature, causes suppression of evidence beyond the defendant's capacity to ferret out. Because the absence of the withheld evidence may result in the conviction of an innocent defendant, it is unconscionable not to impose reasonable controls impelling prosecutors to bring the information to light.

The Court nevertheless holds *Canton*'s example inapposite. It maintains that professional obligations, ethics rules, and training — including on-the-job training—set attorneys apart from other municipal employees, including rookie police officers. Connick "had every incentive at trial to attempt to establish" that he could reasonably rely on the professional education and status of his staff. But the jury heard and rejected his argument to that effect.

The Court advances Connick's argument with greater clarity, but with no greater support. On what basis can one be confident that law schools acquaint students with prosecutors' unique obligation under *Brady*? Whittaker told the jury he did not recall covering *Brady* in his criminal procedure class in law school. Dubelier's *alma mater*, like most other law faculties, does not make criminal procedure a required course.

Connick suggested that the bar examination ensures that new attorneys will know what *Brady* demands. Research indicates, however, that from 1980 to the present, *Brady* questions have not accounted for even 10% of the total points in the criminal law and procedure section of any administration of the Louisiana Bar Examination. A person sitting for the Louisiana Bar Examination, moreover, need pass only five of the exam's nine sections. One can qualify for admission to the profession with no showing of even passing knowledge of criminal law and procedure.

The majority's suggestion that lawyers do not need *Brady* training because they "are equipped with the tools to find, interpret, and apply legal principles," "blinks reality" and is belied by the facts of this case. Connick himself recognized that his prosecutors, because of their inexperience, were not so equipped. Indeed, "understanding and complying with *Brady* obligations are not easy tasks, and the appropriate way to resolve *Brady* issues is not always self-evident

The majority further suggests that a prior pattern of similar violations is necessary to show deliberate indifference to defendants' *Brady* rights. The text of §1983 contains no such limitation. Nor is there any reason to imply such a limitation. A district attorney's deliberate indifference might be shown in several ways short of a prior pattern. This case is one such instance. Connick, who himself had been indicted for suppression of evidence, created a tinderbox in Orleans Parish in which *Brady* violations were nigh inevitable. And when they did occur, Connick insisted there was no need to change anything, and opposed efforts to hold prosecutors accountable on the ground that doing so would make his job more difficult.

For the reasons stated, I would affirm the judgment of the U.S. Court of Appeals for the Fifth Circuit. Like that court and, before it, the District Court, I would uphold the jury's verdict awarding damages to Thompson for the gross, deliberately indifferent, and long-continuing violation of his fair trial right.

* * *

4. Section 1983 v. Collateral Habeas Proceedings

Another important civil rights law passed during Reconstruction, the 1867 Habeas Corpus Act (discussed in detail in Chapter 8), permitted individuals in state custody to seek a federal habeas remedy when held in violation of federal right. In the most literal, textual sense, individuals seeking release from state custody could be said to be suing persons who, acting under the color of state law, are violating federal rights. In the next case, the Supreme Court made clear, however, that §1983 remedies and habeas remedies are distinct. Notably, before filing a petition for habeas corpus, a state prisoner must exhaust state remedies. No such exhaustion requirement is required in suits filed pursuant to §1983. *Patsy v. Fla. Bd. of Regents* (1982). More importantly, habeas claims are available more or less exclusively to challenge the *fact or length of one's confinement.* Section 1983 suits may not be used to challenge the fact or duration of one's confinement. Section 1983 is reserved for most other instances in which a plaintiff claims that a state actor has violated of a federal constitutional right.[27] In some cases, where the constitutional right asserted in the §1983 case is tied to a criminal proceeding, the §1983 remedy may be contingent on prevailing in a habeas proceeding.

Heck v. Humphrey

512 U.S. 477 (1994)

Justice SCALIA delivered the opinion of the Court.

This case presents the question whether a state prisoner may challenge the constitutionality of his conviction in a suit for damages under 42 U.S.C. §1983.

I

Petitioner Roy Heck was convicted in Indiana state court of voluntary manslaughter for the killing of Rickie Heck, his wife, and is serving a 15-year sentence in an Indiana prison. While the appeal from his conviction was pending, petitioner, proceeding *pro se*, filed this suit in Federal District Court under 42 U.S.C. §1983, naming as defendants prosecutors and an investigator with the Indiana State Police. The complaint alleged that respondents, acting under color of state law, had engaged in an "unlawful, unreasonable, and arbitrary investigation" leading to petitioner's arrest; "knowingly destroyed" evidence "which was exculpatory in nature and could have proved [petitioner's] innocence"; and caused "an illegal and unlawful voice identification procedure" to be used at petitioner's trial. The complaint sought, among other things, compensatory and punitive monetary damages. It did not ask for injunctive relief, and petitioner has not sought release from custody in this action. Heck's conviction was upheld on appeal and the lower federal courts denied his petitions for writ of habeas corpus. Heck did not contest that his section 1983 suit effectively challenged the legality of his conviction.

---

27. In *Vega v. Tekoh* (2022), the Supreme Court announced an exception to the rule that plaintiffs may generally rely on §1983 to vindicate States' constitutional violations that do not necessarily challenge the fact of their confinement or the duration of their sentence. In *Miranda v. Arizona* (1966), the Court held that under the Fifth Amendment, officers must inform suspects that during an interrogation, they have a right to remain silent and a right to an attorney. In *Vega*, the Court held that a litigant may not rely on §1983 to challenge officers' failure to heed this legal rule.

II

This case lies at the intersection of the two most fertile sources of federal-court prisoner litigation — §1983 and the federal habeas corpus statute. Both of these provide access to a federal forum for claims of unconstitutional treatment at the hands of state officials, but they differ in their scope and operation. In general, exhaustion of state remedies "is *not* a prerequisite to an action under §1983," *Patsy v. Bd. of Regents of Fla.* (1982), even an action by a state prisoner. The federal habeas corpus statute, by contrast, requires that state prisoners first seek redress in a state forum.[3]

Preiser v. Rodriguez (1973) considered the potential overlap between these two provisions, and held that habeas corpus is the exclusive remedy for a state prisoner who challenges the fact or duration of his confinement and seeks immediate or speedier release, even though such a claim may come within the literal terms of §1983. We emphasize that *Preiser* did *not* create an exception to the "no exhaustion" rule of §1983; it merely held that certain claims by state prisoners are not *cognizable* under that provision, and must be brought in habeas corpus proceedings, which do contain an exhaustion requirement.

This case is clearly not covered by the holding of *Preiser*, for petitioner seeks not immediate or speedier release, but monetary damages, as to which he could not "have sought and obtained fully effective relief through federal habeas corpus proceedings." In dictum, however, *Preiser* asserted that since a state prisoner seeking only damages "is attacking something other than the fact or length of . . . confinement, and . . . is seeking something other than immediate or more speedy release[,] . . . a damages action by a state prisoner could be brought under [§1983] in federal court without any requirement of prior exhaustion of state remedies." That statement may not be true, however, when establishing the basis for the damages claim necessarily demonstrates the invalidity of the conviction. In that situation, the claimant *can* be said to be "attacking . . . the fact or length of . . . confinement."

[T]he question posed by §1983 damages claims that do call into question the lawfulness of conviction or confinement remains open. To answer that question correctly, we see no need to abandon our teaching that §1983 contains no exhaustion requirement beyond what Congress has provided. The issue with respect to monetary damages challenging conviction is not, it seems to us, exhaustion; but rather, the same as the issue was with respect to injunctive relief challenging conviction in *Preiser*: whether the claim is cognizable under §1983 at all. We conclude that it is not.

The common-law cause of action for malicious prosecution provides the closest analogy to claims of the type considered here because, unlike the related cause of action for false arrest or imprisonment, it permits damages for confinement

---

3. 28 U.S.C. §2254(b) provides: "An application for a writ of habeas corpus in behalf of a person in custody pursuant to the judgment of a State court shall not be granted unless it appears that the applicant has exhausted the remedies available in the courts of the State, or that there is either an absence of available State corrective process or the existence of circumstances rendering such process ineffective to protect the rights of the prisoner."

imposed pursuant to legal process. "If there is a false arrest claim, damages for that claim cover the time of detention up until issuance of process or arraignment, but not more." W. KEETON, D. DOBBS, R. KEETON, & D. OWEN, PROSSER AND KEETON ON LAW OF TORTS 888 (5th ed. 1984). But a successful malicious prosecution plaintiff may recover, in addition to general damages, "compensation for any arrest or imprisonment, including damages for discomfort or injury to his health, or loss of time and deprivation of the society."

One element that must be alleged and proved in a malicious prosecution action is termination of the prior criminal proceeding in favor of the accused. This requirement "avoids parallel litigation over the issues of probable cause and guilt . . . and it precludes the possibility of the claimant succeeding in the tort action after having been convicted in the underlying criminal prosecution, in contravention of a strong judicial policy against the creation of two conflicting resolutions arising out of the same or identical transaction." Furthermore, "to permit a convicted criminal defendant to proceed with a malicious prosecution claim would permit a collateral attack on the conviction through the vehicle of a civil suit." This Court has long expressed similar concerns for finality and consistency and has generally declined to expand opportunities for collateral attack. We think the hoary principle that civil tort actions are not appropriate vehicles for challenging the validity of outstanding criminal judgments applies to §1983 damages actions that necessarily require the plaintiff to prove the unlawfulness of his conviction or confinement, just as it has always applied to actions for malicious prosecution.

We hold that, in order to recover damages for allegedly unconstitutional conviction or imprisonment, or for other harm caused by actions whose unlawfulness would render a conviction or sentence invalid,[6] a §1983 plaintiff must prove that the conviction or sentence has been reversed on direct appeal, expunged by executive order, declared invalid by a state tribunal authorized to make such determination, or called into question by a federal court's issuance of a writ of habeas corpus, 28 U.S.C. §2254. A claim for damages bearing that relationship to a conviction or sentence that has *not* been so invalidated is not cognizable under §1983. Thus, when a state prisoner seeks damages in a §1983 suit, the district court must consider whether a judgment in favor of the plaintiff would necessarily imply the invalidity of his conviction or sentence; if it would, the complaint must be dismissed unless the plaintiff can demonstrate that the conviction or sentence has already been invalidated. But if the district court determines that the plaintiff's action, even if successful, will *not* demonstrate the invalidity of any outstanding criminal

---

6. An example of this latter category—a §1983 action that does not seek damages directly attributable to conviction or confinement but whose successful prosecution would necessarily imply that the plaintiff's criminal conviction was wrongful—would be the following: A state defendant is convicted of and sentenced for the crime of resisting arrest, defined as intentionally preventing a peace officer from effecting a *lawful* arrest. (This is a common definition of that offense. He then brings a section 1983 action against the arresting officer, seeking damages for violation of his Fourth Amendment right to be free from unreasonable seizures. In order to prevail in this section 1983 action, he would have to negate an element of the offense of which he has been convicted. Regardless of the state law concerning res judicata, the §1983 action will not lie.)

judgment against the plaintiff, the action should be allowed to proceed,[7] in the absence of some other bar to the suit.[8]

Applying these principles to the present action, in which both courts below found that the damages claims challenged the legality of the conviction, we find that the dismissal of the action was correct. The judgment of the Court of Appeals for the Seventh Circuit is [a]ffirmed.

Justice SOUTER, with whom Justice BLACKMUN, Justice STEVENS, and Justice O'CONNOR join, concurring in the judgment.

Common-law tort rules can provide a "starting point for the inquiry under §1983," but we have relied on the common law in §1983 cases only when doing so was thought to be consistent with ordinary rules of statutory construction, as when common-law principles have textual support in other provisions of [§1983] or when those principles were so fundamental and widely understood at the time §1983 was enacted that the 42d Congress could not be presumed to have abrogated them silently. At the same time, we have consistently refused to allow common-law analogies to displace statutory analysis, declining to import even well-settled common-law rules into §1983 "if [the statute's] history or purpose counsel against applying [such rules] in §1983 actions."

Our enquiry in this case may follow the interpretive methodology employed in *Preiser v. Rodriguez* (1973). In *Preiser*, we read the "general" §1983 statute in light of the "specific federal habeas corpus statute," which applies only to "person[s] in custody," and the habeas statute's policy, embodied in its exhaustion requirement, §2254(b), that state courts be given the first opportunity to review constitutional claims bearing upon a state prisoner's release from custody. Though in contrast to *Preiser* the state prisoner here seeks damages, not release from custody, the distinction makes no difference when the damages sought are for unconstitutional conviction or confinement. As the Court explains, nothing in *Preiser* nor in *Wolff v. McDonnell* (1974), is properly read as holding that the relief sought in a §1983 action dictates whether a state prisoner can proceed immediately to federal court. Whether or not a federal-court §1983 damages judgment against state officials in such an action would have preclusive effect in later litigation against the State, mounting damages against the

---

7. For example, a suit for damages attributable to an allegedly unreasonable search may lie even if the challenged search produced evidence that was introduced in a state criminal trial resulting in the section 1983 plaintiff's still-outstanding conviction. Because of doctrines like independent source and inevitable discovery, and especially harmless error, such a section 1983 action, even if successful, would not *necessarily* imply that the plaintiff's conviction was unlawful. In order to recover compensatory damages, however, the §1983 plaintiff must prove not only that the search was unlawful, but that it caused him actual, compensable injury, which, we hold today, does *not* encompass the "injury" of being convicted and imprisoned (until his conviction has been overturned).

8. For example, if a state criminal defendant brings a federal civil-rights lawsuit during the pendency of his criminal trial, appeal, or state habeas action, abstention may be an appropriate response to the parallel state-court proceedings. Moreover, we do not decide whether abstention might be appropriate in cases where a state prisoner brings a §1983 damages suit raising an issue that also could be grounds for relief in a state court challenge to his conviction or sentence.

defendant-officials for unlawful confinement (damages almost certainly to be paid by state indemnification) would, practically, compel the State to release the prisoner. Because allowing a state prisoner to proceed directly with a federal-court §1983 attack on his conviction or sentence "would wholly frustrate explicit congressional intent" as declared in the habeas exhaustion requirement, the statutory scheme must be read as precluding such attacks. This conclusion flows not from a preference about how the habeas and §1983 statutes ought to have been written, but from a recognition that "Congress has determined that habeas corpus is the appropriate remedy for state prisoners attacking the validity of the fact or length of their confinement, [a] specific determination [that] must override the general terms of §1983."

That leaves the question of how to implement what statutory analysis requires. It is at this point that the malicious-prosecution tort's favorable-termination requirement becomes helpful, not in dictating the elements of a §1983 cause of action, but in suggesting a relatively simple way to avoid collisions at the intersection of habeas and §1983. A state prisoner may seek federal-court §1983 damages for unconstitutional conviction or confinement, but only if he has previously established the unlawfulness of his conviction or confinement, as on appeal or on habeas. This has the effect of requiring a state prisoner challenging the lawfulness of his confinement to follow habeas's rules before seeking §1983 damages for unlawful confinement in federal court, and it is ultimately the Court's holding today. It neatly resolves a problem that has bedeviled lower courts, legal commentators, and law students. The favorable-termination requirement avoids the knotty statute-of-limitations problem that arises if federal courts dismiss §1983 suits filed before an inmate pursues federal habeas, and (because the statute-of-limitations clock does not start ticking until an inmate's conviction is set aside) it does so without requiring federal courts to stay, and therefore to retain on their dockets, prematurely filed §1983 suits.[4]

That would be a sensible way to read the opinion, in part because the alternative would needlessly place at risk the rights of those outside the intersection of §1983 and the habeas statute, individuals not "in custody" for habeas purposes.

_____

4. The requirement that a state prisoner seeking section 1983 damages for unlawful conviction or confinement be successful in state court or on federal habeas strikes me as soundly rooted in the statutory scheme. Because "Congress has determined that habeas corpus is the appropriate remedy for state prisoners attacking the validity of the fact or length of their confinement, [a] specific determination [that] override[s] the general terms of section 1983," a state prisoner whose constitutional attacks on his confinement have been rejected by state courts cannot be said to be unlawfully confined unless a federal habeas court declares his "custody [to be] in violation of the Constitution or laws or treaties of the United States." An unsuccessful federal habeas petitioner cannot, therefore, consistently with the habeas statute, receive section 1983 damages for unlawful confinement. That is not to say, however, that a state prisoner whose request for release has been (or would be) rejected by state courts or by a federal habeas court is necessarily barred from seeking any section 1983 damages for violations of his constitutional rights. If a section 1983 judgment in his favor would not demonstrate the invalidity of his confinement he is outside the habeas statute and may seek damages for a constitutional violation even without showing "favorable termination." A state prisoner may, for example, seek damages for an unreasonable search that produced evidence lawfully or harmlessly admitted at trial, or even nominal damages for, say, a violation of his right to procedural due process.

If these individuals (people who were merely fined, for example, or who have completed short terms of imprisonment, probation, or parole, or who discover (through no fault of their own) a constitutional violation after full expiration of their sentences), like state prisoners, were required to show the prior invalidation of their convictions or sentences in order to obtain §1983 damages for unconstitutional conviction or imprisonment, the result would be to deny any federal forum for claiming a deprivation of federal rights to those who cannot first obtain a favorable state ruling. The reason, of course, is that individuals not "in custody" cannot invoke federal habeas jurisdiction, the only statutory mechanism besides §1983 by which individuals may sue state officials in federal court for violating federal rights. That would be an untoward result.

It is one thing to adopt a rule that forces prison inmates to follow the federal habeas route with claims that fall within the plain language of §1983 when that is necessary to prevent a requirement of the habeas statute from being undermined. It would be an entirely different matter, however, to shut off federal courts altogether to claims that fall within the plain language of §1983.

Nor do I see any policy reflected in a congressional enactment that would justify denying to an individual today federal damages (a significantly less disruptive remedy than an order compelling release from custody) merely because he was unconstitutionally fined by a State, or to a person who discovers after his release from prison that, for example, state officials deliberately withheld exculpatory material. And absent such a statutory policy, surely the common law can give us no authority to narrow the "broad language" of §1983, which speaks of deprivations of "any" constitutional rights, privileges, or immunities, by "[e]very" person acting under color of state law, and to which "we have given full effect [by] recognizing that §1983 'provide[s] a remedy, to be broadly construed, against all forms of official violation of federally protected rights.'"

In sum, while the malicious-prosecution analogy provides a useful mechanism for implementing what statutory analysis requires, congressional policy as reflected in enacted statutes must ultimately be the guide. I would thus be clear that the proper resolution of this case (involving, of course, a state prisoner) is to construe §1983 in light of the habeas statute and its explicit policy of exhaustion. I would not cast doubt on the ability of an individual unaffected by the habeas statute to take advantage of the broad reach of §1983.

* * *

In the years after *Heck v. Humphrey* (1994), federal courts have continued to clarify the boundary between §1983 and habeas in three important contexts. First, inmates on death row have relied on §1983 to challenge their method of execution under the Eighth Amendment as cruel and unusual punishment. To establish such a claim, the litigant (1) needs to show that the State's method of execution presents a "substantial risk of serious harm—severe pain over and above death itself;" and (2) "must identify an alternative method that is feasible, readily implemented, and in fact significantly reduces the risk of harm involved." *Nance v. Ward* (2022). While States have sometimes argued that habeas is the proper avenue for such challenges, the Supreme Court has consistently held that §1983 claims are generally the correct means. *See, e.g., Nelson v. Campbell* (2004); *Hill v. McDonough* (2006); *Nance v. Ward* (2022). In *Nelson,* the Court has reasoned that a claim should go to habeas if granting the prisoner relief "would *necessarily* prevent [the State] from carrying out its execution." Most recently, in *Nance,* the Court held that even when a litigant seeks an alternative method of execution that is unauthorized by State law, §1983 remains the correct avenue for such claims.

Second, lower courts have wrestled with whether challenges to the conditions of probation or parole should be routed through habeas or §1983. *Compare Williams v. Wisc.* (7th Cir. 2003) (reasoning that challenges to conditions of probation should be litigated as habeas claims, because habeas is "the appropriate remedy for a defendant seeking release from custody or expansion of the perimeters of his confinement") *with Thornton v. Brown* (9th Cir. 2013) (holding that "a state parolee may challenge a condition of parole under §1983 if his or her claim, if successful, would neither result in speedier release from parole nor imply, either directly or indirectly, the invalidity of the criminal judgments underlying that parole term").

Third, in recent years, *Heck* has emerged in cases in which litigants have challenged criminal legal systems that impose fines and fees on indigent individuals, with no regard to their ability to pay. Jailing indigent individuals due to their inability to pay a fine or fee violates the Fourteenth Amendment's Equal Protection Clause. *Bearden v. Georgia* (1983). To date, lower courts are divided as to whether these recent legal challenges, which tend to seek additional procedural protections, are barred by *Heck. Compare Carter v. City of Montgomery* (M.D. Ala. 2020) (rejecting *Heck* because litigant challenged "the procedures used to impose probation and jail him" without necessarily implying the sentences were invalid); *Fant v. City of Ferguson* (E.D. Mo. 2015) (same) *with Graff v. Aberdeen Enterprizes, II, Inc.* (N.D. Okla. 2021) (applying *Heck*).

5. *Absolute Immunity*

When an officer is named in a suit, one of the most common affirmative defenses is officer immunity. There are two kinds of officer immunity: absolute and qualified. Both are distinct from sovereign immunity, which attaches to the state itself and its agencies. Further, the Court has derived sovereign immunity from the Constitution, whereas officer immunity doctrines are common law creations. Before we engage the details of these doctrines, note a technical feature of pleading practice. Officer immunity doctrines apply when the officer is named in a *personal* or *individual capacity*—such that, if the plaintiff prevails, the judgment is enforceable against the officer and her assets. If an officer is named in an official capacity, then the "office" itself is being sued and this is treated as a suit against the government as to which sovereign immunity doctrine often applies. The formality of naming the officer in her individual capacity may seem superficial, but it is important in the affirmative defenses it triggers. *Hafer v. Melo,* 502 U.S. 21 (1991) ("[T]he real party in interest in an official-capacity suit is the governmental entity and not the named official . . . Personal-capacity suits, on the other hand, seek to impose individual liability upon a government officer for actions taken under color of state law"). Pleading errors of this kind can be cured by a Rule 15 amendment.

We begin this section with absolute immunity doctrine and then turn to qualified immunity.

Five categories of governmental actors are entitled to absolute immunity when sued in their individual capacities. First, when judges are acting in their judicial capacity, they are immune from claims seeking money damages and, in most instances, injunctive relief. Second, prosecutors are immune from actions taken pursuant to their adversarial, prosecutorial roles. Third, legislators are immune from claims for damages and prospective relief when they are sued for actions taken in their legislative capacities. Fourth, witnesses are generally entitled to immunity from suit for their testimony.[28] Fifth, as described in Chapter 7, presidential actions are absolutely immunized from suit. The first three categories are discussed in more detail below. Qualified immunity is more broadly available to those officers who are not eligible for absolute immunity.

a. Judicial

Stump v. Sparkman

435 U.S. 349 (1978)

Mr. Justice WHITE delivered the opinion of the Court

This case requires us to consider the scope of a judge's immunity from damages liability when sued under 42 U.S.C. §1983.

I

The relevant facts underlying respondents' suit are not in dispute. On July 9, 1971, Ora Spitler McFarlin, the mother of respondent Linda Kay Spitler Sparkman, presented to Judge Harold D. Stump of the Circuit Court of DeKalb County, Ind., a document captioned "Petition To Have Tubal Ligation Performed On Minor and Indemnity Agreement." The document had been drafted by her attorney, a petitioner here. In this petition Mrs. McFarlin stated under oath that her daughter was 15 years of age and was "somewhat retarded," although she attended public school and had been promoted each year with her class. The petition further stated that Linda had been associating with "older youth or young men" and had stayed out overnight with them on several occasions. As a result of this behavior and Linda's mental capabilities, it was stated that it would be in the daughter's best interest if she underwent a tubal ligation in order "to prevent unfortunate circumstances. . . ." In the same document Mrs. McFarlin also undertook to indemnify and hold harmless Dr. John Hines, who was to perform the operation, and the DeKalb Memorial Hospital, where the operation was to take place, against all causes of action that might arise as a result of the performance of the tubal ligation.

The petition was approved by Judge Stump on the same day. He affixed his signature as "Judge, DeKalb Circuit Court," to the statement that he did "hereby approve the above Petition by affidavit form on behalf of Ora Spitler McFarlin, to have Tubal Ligation performed upon her minor daughter, Linda Spitler, subject

---

28. *Briscoe v. LaHue*, 460 U.S. 325 (1983).

to said Ora Spitler McFarlin covenanting and agreeing to indemnify and keep indemnified Dr. John Hines and the DeKalb Memorial Hospital from any matters or causes of action arising therefrom."

On July 15, 1971, Linda Spitler entered the DeKalb Memorial Hospital, having been told that she was to have her appendix removed. The following day a tubal ligation was performed upon her. She was released several days later, unaware of the true nature of her surgery.

Approximately two years after the operation, Linda Spitler was married to respondent Leo Sparkman. Her inability to become pregnant led her to discover that she had been sterilized during the 1971 operation. As a result of this revelation, the Sparkmans filed suit in the United States District Court for the Northern District of Indiana against Mrs. McFarlin, her attorney, Judge Stump, the doctors who had performed and assisted in the tubal ligation, and the DeKalb Memorial Hospital. Respondents sought damages for the alleged violation of Linda Sparkman's constitutional rights; also asserted were pendent state claims for assault and battery, medical malpractice, and loss of potential fatherhood.

II

The governing principle of law is well established and is not questioned by the parties. As early as 1872, the Court recognized that it was "a general principle of the highest importance to the proper administration of justice that a judicial officer, in exercising the authority vested in him, [should] be free to act upon his own convictions, without apprehension of personal consequences to himself." *Bradley v. Fisher* (1871). For that reason the Court held that "judges of courts of superior or general jurisdiction are not liable to civil actions for their judicial acts, even when such acts are in excess of their jurisdiction, and are alleged to have been done maliciously or corruptly." Later we held that this doctrine of judicial immunity was applicable in suits under §1 of the Civil Rights Act of 1871, 42 U.S.C. §1983, for the legislative record gave no indication that Congress intended to abolish this long-established principle. *Pierson v. Ray* (1967).

The Court of Appeals correctly recognized that the necessary inquiry in determining whether a defendant judge is immune from suit is whether at the time he took the challenged action he had jurisdiction over the subject matter before him. Because "some of the most difficult and embarrassing questions which a judicial officer is called upon to consider and determine relate to his jurisdiction . . . ," *Bradley*, the scope of the judge's jurisdiction must be construed broadly where the issue is the immunity of the judge. A judge will not be deprived of immunity because the action he took was in error, was done maliciously, or was in excess of his authority; rather, he will be subject to liability only when he has acted in the "clear absence of all jurisdiction."

We cannot agree that there was a "clear absence of all jurisdiction" in the DeKalb County Circuit Court to consider the petition presented by Mrs. McFarlin. As an Indiana Circuit Court Judge, Judge Stump had "original exclusive jurisdiction in all cases at law and in equity whatsoever . . ."; jurisdiction over the settlement of estates and over guardianships, appellate jurisdiction as conferred by law, and jurisdiction over "all other causes, matters and proceedings where exclusive jurisdiction thereof is not conferred by law upon some other court, board or officer." Ind.

Code §33-4-4-3 (1975). This is indeed a broad jurisdictional grant; yet the Court of Appeals concluded that Judge Stump did not have jurisdiction over the petition authorizing Linda Sparkman's sterilization.

In so doing, the Court of Appeals noted that the Indiana statutes provided for the sterilization of institutionalized persons under certain circumstances, but otherwise contained no express authority for judicial approval of tubal ligations. It is true that the statutory grant of general jurisdiction to the Indiana circuit courts does not itemize types of cases those courts may hear and hence does not expressly mention sterilization petitions presented by the parents of a minor. But in our view, it is more significant that there was no Indiana statute and no case law in 1971 prohibiting a circuit court, a court of general jurisdiction, from considering a petition of the type presented to Judge Stump. The statutory authority for the sterilization of institutionalized persons in the custody of the State does not warrant the inference that a court of general jurisdiction has no power to act on a petition for sterilization of a minor in the custody of her parents, particularly where the parents have authority under the Indiana statutes to "consent to and contract for medical or hospital care or treatment of [the minor] including surgery." The District Court concluded that Judge Stump had jurisdiction under §33-4-4-3 to entertain and act upon Mrs. McFarlin's petition. We agree with the District Court, it appearing that neither by statute nor by case law has the broad jurisdiction granted to the circuit courts of Indiana been circumscribed to foreclose consideration of a petition for authorization of a minor's sterilization.

We conclude that the Court of Appeals, employing an unduly restrictive view of the scope of Judge Stump's jurisdiction, erred in holding that he was not entitled to judicial immunity. Because the court over which Judge Stump presides is one of general jurisdiction, neither the procedural errors he may have committed nor the lack of a specific statute authorizing his approval of the petition in question rendered him liable in damages for the consequences of his actions.

The respondents argue that even if Judge Stump had jurisdiction to consider the petition presented to him by Mrs. McFarlin, he is still not entitled to judicial immunity because his approval of the petition did not constitute a "judicial" act. It is only for acts performed in his "judicial" capacity that a judge is absolutely immune, they say. We do not disagree with this statement of the law, but we cannot characterize the approval of the petition as a nonjudicial act.

Respondents themselves stated in their pleadings before the District Court that Judge Stump was "clothed with the authority of the state" at the time that he approved the petition and that "he was acting as a county circuit court judge." They nevertheless now argue that Judge Stump's approval of the petition was not a judicial act because the petition was not given a docket number, was not placed on file with the clerk's office, and was approved in an *ex parte* proceeding without notice to the minor, without a hearing, and without the appointment of a guardian ad litem.

This Court has not had occasion to consider, for purposes of the judicial immunity doctrine, the necessary attributes of a judicial act; but it has previously rejected the argument, somewhat similar to the one raised here, that the lack of formality involved in the Illinois Supreme Court's consideration of a petitioner's application for admission to the state bar prevented it from being a "judicial proceeding" and from presenting a case or controversy that could be reviewed by this

Court. *In re Summers* (1945). Of particular significance to the present case, the Court in *Summers* noted the following: "The record does not show that any process issued or that any appearance was made. . . . While no entry was placed by the Clerk in the file, on a docket, or in a judgment roll, the Court took cognizance of the petition and passed an order which is validated by the signature of the presiding officer." Because the Illinois court took cognizance of the petition for admission and acted upon it, the Court held that a case or controversy was presented.

The relevant cases demonstrate that the factors determining whether an act by a judge is a "judicial" one relate to the nature of the act itself, i.e., whether it is a function normally performed by a judge, and to the expectations of the parties, i.e., whether they dealt with the judge in his judicial capacity. Here, both factors indicate that Judge Stump's approval of the sterilization petition was a judicial act. The Indiana law vested in Judge Stump the power to entertain and act upon the petition for sterilization. He is, therefore, under the controlling cases, immune from damages liability even if his approval of the petition was in error.

Mr. Justice STEWART, with whom Mr. Justice MARSHALL and Mr. Justice POWELL join, dissenting.

It is established federal law that judges of general jurisdiction are absolutely immune from monetary liability "for their judicial acts, even when such acts are in excess of their jurisdiction, and are alleged to have been done maliciously or corruptly." *Bradley v. Fisher.* It is also established that this immunity is in no way diminished in a proceeding under 42 U.S.C. §1983. But the scope of judicial immunity is limited to liability for "judicial acts" and I think that what Judge Stump did on July 9, 1971, was beyond the pale of anything that could sensibly be called a judicial act.

Neither in *Bradley v. Fisher* nor in *Pierson v. Ray* was there any claim that the conduct in question was not a judicial act, and the Court thus had no occasion in either case to discuss the meaning of that term. Yet the proposition that judicial immunity extends only to liability for "judicial acts" was emphasized no less than seven times in Mr. Justice Field's opinion for the Court in the *Bradley* case. Cf. *Imbler v. Pachtman* (1976). And if the limitations inherent in that concept have any realistic meaning at all, then I cannot believe that the action of Judge Stump in approving Mrs. McFarlin's petition is protected by judicial immunity.

The Court finds two reasons for holding that Judge Stump's approval of the sterilization petition was a judicial act. First, the Court says, it was "a function normally performed by a judge." Second, the Court says, the act was performed in Judge Stump's "judicial capacity." With all respect, I think that the first of these grounds is factually untrue and that the second is legally unsound.

In sum, what Judge Stump did on July 9, 1971, was in no way an act "normally performed by a judge." Indeed, there is no reason to believe that such an act has ever been performed by any other Indiana judge, either before or since.

It seems to me, rather, that the concept of what is a judicial act must take its content from a consideration of the factors that support immunity from liability for the performance of such an act. Those factors were accurately summarized by the Court in *Pierson v. Ray*:

> [I]t "is . . . for the benefit of the public, whose interest it is that the judges should be at liberty to exercise their functions with independence and without fear of consequences." . . . It is a judge's duty to decide all cases

within his jurisdiction that are brought before him, including contro-versial cases that arouse the most intense feelings in the litigants. His errors may be corrected on appeal, but he should not have to fear that unsatisfied litigants may hound him with litigation charging malice or corruption. Imposing such a burden on judges would contribute not to principled and fearless decision-making but to intimidation.

Not one of the considerations thus summarized in the *Pierson* opinion was present here. There was no "case," controversial or otherwise. There were no lit-igants. There was and could be no appeal. And there was not even the pretext of principled decisionmaking. The total absence of any of these normal attributes of a judicial proceeding convinces me that the conduct complained of in this case was not a judicial act.

* * *

One question left unanswered in *Stump* is whether plaintiffs could rely on §1983 to sue judges for prospective relief. In *Pulliam v. Allen* (1984), the Supreme Court allowed prospective relief against a magistrate who was allegedly imposing money bail on individuals who were arrested for non-jailable offenses, and then incarcerating individuals who could not make bail. A federal district court enjoined these practices, and the Fourth Circuit did as well. The Supreme Court affirmed, relying in part on the availability of mandamus against judges at the common law. The Court also identified legislative history suggesting that courts and judges were among the actors §1983 intended to reach. As the Court concluded in *Mitchum v. Foster*, the very purpose of §1983 was to interpose the federal courts between the states and the people, as guardians of the people's federal rights — to protect the people from unconstitutional action under color of state law, "whether that action be executive, legislative, or judicial."

Congress limited the practical reach of *Pulliam*, however, by way of §309 of the Federal Courts Improvement Act of 1996. That provision amended §1983. The statute now expressly prohibits injunctive relief against a judge unless declaratory relief is unavailable, or unless a judge has violated a declaratory decree. For that reason, judicial immunity is the only form of immunity that has an express textual basis on the face of §1983.

b. Prosecutorial

Prosecutors are immune from damages under §1983 when they are sued in their individual capacities. The lead case for this proposition is *Imbler v. Pachtman* (1976). The Court explained:

The common-law immunity of a prosecutor is based upon the same con-siderations that underlie the common-law immunities of judges and grand jurors acting within the scope of their duties. These include concern that harassment by unfounded litigation would cause a deflection of the pros-ecutor's energies from his public duties, and the possibility that he would shade his decisions instead of exercising the independence of judgment required by his public trust.

. . .

A prosecutor is duty bound to exercise his best judgment both in deciding which suits to bring and in conducting them in court. The public trust of the prosecutor's office would suffer if he were constrained in making every decision by the consequences in terms of his own potential liability in a suit for damages. Such suits could be expected with some frequency, for a defendant often will transform his resentment at being prosecuted into the ascription of improper and malicious actions to the State's advocate. *Cf. Bradley v. Fisher* (1871).

Absolute prosecutorial immunity is reserved for traditional prosecutorial activities. The Court has emphasized that this form of immunity does not apply to instances in which prosecutors are serving non-prosecutorial functions, such as investigative functions. In *Burns v. Reed* (1991), a prosecutor authorized officers to subject a suspect to hypnosis; the prosecutor then obtained an arrest warrant based on statements the suspect made while hypnotized. The Court found that while the prosecutor was entitled to absolute immunity for in-court actions to obtain the warrant, the prosecutor was entitled to only to a qualified immunity defense for authorizing the hypnosis. Likewise, in *Buckley v. Fitzsimmons* (1993), the Court denied absolute immunity to a prosecutor who fabricated evidence during an unsolved investigation and made false statements to the press. The plaintiff who was arrested for the crimes was detained for nearly three years. The Court found no historical evidence that "a prosecutor's fabrication of false evidence during the preliminary investigation of an unsolved crime was immune from liability at common law."

Making these distinctions is nuanced and highly fact-intensive, as illustrated by *Kalina v. Fletcher* (1997). In that case, to obtain an arrest warrant, a prosecutor filed an unsworn motion for an arrest warrant, an unsworn information charging the arrestee with burglary, and a sworn declaration in which the prosecutor summarized the evidence. The sworn declaration contained significant factual inaccuracies. The Court found that while the unsworn information and motion were traditional prosecutorial functions protected by absolute immunity, the false, sworn declaration was not. As such, the prosecutor was only entitled to a qualified immunity defense for the sworn declaration. She had not been required by law to personally attest to the factual accuracy of her declaration, and did so nonetheless. In doing so, she "performed the function of a complaining witness," rather than "the traditional functions of an advocate."

It is important to remember that governmental immunities do not operate in a vacuum. Sometimes, multiple doctrines are simultaneously at play and they block different conceivable roads to relief.[29] Some of the practical implications of this limitation are illustrated by *Connick v. Thompson* (2011), which is discussed above in Section B.2(c). In that case, John Thompson was falsely convicted because of a prosecutor's unconstitutional failure to turn over exculpatory evidence. He was not allowed to sue the New Orleans Parrish in light of the strict limits on municipal liability. That result is compounded by absolute immunity, which barred Thompson

---

29. Leah Litman, *Remedial Convergence and Collapse*, 106 CAL. L. REV. 1477, 1528 (2018).

from successfully suing the District Attorney in his individual capacity, or the prosecutors who engaged in the violation most directly. *See Van de Kamp v. Goldstein* (2009) (holding that failing to create policies to ensure compliance with *Brady v. Maryland* (1963) was prosecutorial in nature).

c. Legislative

An additional set of actors who receive absolute immunity are legislators acting in their legislative capacities. These actors are immune from damages and prospective relief. In *Tenney v. Brandhove* (1951), the Supreme Court first considered whether individuals could rely on §1983 to sue state legislators for their legislative acts. The case involved the California Senate's Fact-Finding Committee on Un-American Activities. The Committee was an influential one. In the early 1940s, the Committee played a significant role in stoking fear against Japanese Americans leading up to the infamous forced relocation to internment camps during World War II.[30] The Committee continued investigations after World War II, holding hearings and issuing reports on individuals deemed to be engaged in conduct adverse to American interests.

The underlying suit in *Tenney v. Brandhove* was brought by William Brandhove, a vocal critic of the committee. Brandhove contended that the Committee had made false allegations that politicians, including the Mayor of San Francisco, were "Red" (or Communist). During the escalation of the Cold War, being called a Communist was a loaded and potentially damaging charge.[31] Brandhove circulated a petition, actively urging the state legislature to discontinue funding for the Committee. In apparent response, the Committee called Brandhove as a witness, and charged him with contempt of court when he invoked his right to remain silent. Brandhove sued the head of the Committee, Senator John Tenney, in federal court, contending the actions against him by the Committee were taken not to legislate, but to intimidate and to chill speech.

Tenney v. Brandhove

341 U.S. 367 (1951)

Mr. Justice FRANKFURTER delivered the opinion of the Court.

William Brandhove brought this action in the United States District Court for the Northern District of California, alleging that he had been deprived of rights guaranteed by the Federal Constitution. The defendants are Jack B. Tenney and other members of a committee of the California Legislature, the Senate Fact-Finding Committee on Un-American Activities, colloquially known as the Tenney

---

30. JOHN E. SCHMITZ, ENEMIES AMONG US: THE RELOCATION, INTERNMENT, AND REPATRIATION OF GERMAN, ITALIAN, AND JAPANESE AMERICANS DURING THE SECOND WORLD WAR (2021).

31. Sheldon Nahmod, *Section 1983 Is Born: The Interlocking Supreme Court Stories of Tenney and Monroe*, 17 LEWIS & CLARK L. REV. 1019 (2013).

Committee. Also named as defendants are the Committee and Elmer E. Robinson, Mayor of San Francisco.

The action is based on §§43 and 47(3) of Title 8 of the United States Code. These sections derive from one of the statutes, passed in 1871, aimed at enforcing the Fourteenth Amendment. Section 43 provides:

> Every person who, under color of any statute, ordinance, regulation, custom, or usage, of any State or Territory, subjects, or causes to be subjected, any citizen of the United States or other person within the jurisdiction thereof to the deprivation of any rights, privileges, or immunities secured by the Constitution and laws, shall be liable to the party injured in an action at law, suit in equity, or other proper proceeding for redress.

Section 47(3) provides a civil remedy against "two or more persons" who may conspire to deprive another of constitutional rights, as therein defined.

Reduced to its legal essentials, the complaint shows these facts. The Tenney Committee was constituted by a resolution of the California Senate on June 20, 1947. On January 28, 1949, Brandhove circulated a petition among members of the State Legislature. He alleges that it was circulated in order to persuade the Legislature not to appropriate further funds for the Committee. The petition charged that the Committee had used Brandhove as a tool in order "to smear Congressman Franck R. Havenner as a 'Red' when he was a candidate for Mayor of San Francisco in 1947; and that the Republican machine in San Francisco and the campaign management of Elmer E. Robinson, Franck Havenner's opponent, conspired with the Tenney Committee to this end." In view of the conflict between this petition and evidence previously given by Brandhove, the Committee asked local prosecuting officials to institute criminal proceedings against him. The Committee also summoned Brandhove to appear before them at a hearing held on January 29. Testimony was there taken from the Mayor of San Francisco, allegedly a member of the conspiracy. The plaintiff appeared with counsel, but refused to give testimony. For this, he was prosecuted for contempt in the State courts. Upon the jury's failure to return a verdict this prosecution was dropped. After Brandhove refused to testify, the Chairman quoted testimony given by Brandhove at prior hearings. The Chairman also read into the record a statement concerning an alleged criminal record of Brandhove, a newspaper article denying the truth of his charges, and a denial by the Committee's counsel—who was absent—that Brandhove's charges were true.

Brandhove alleges that the January 29 hearing "was not held for a legislative purpose," but was designed "to intimidate and silence plaintiff and deter and prevent him from effectively exercising his constitutional rights of free speech and to petition the Legislature for redress of grievances, and also to deprive him of the equal protection of the laws, due process of law, and of the enjoyment of equal privileges and immunities as a citizen of the United States under the law, and so did intimidate, silence, deter, and prevent and deprive plaintiff." Damages of $10,000 were asked "for legal counsel, traveling, hotel accommodations, and other matters pertaining and necessary to his defense" in the contempt proceeding arising out of the Committee hearings. The plaintiff also asked for punitive damages.

The action was dismissed without opinion by the District Judge. The Court of Appeals for the Ninth Circuit held, however, that the complaint stated a cause of action against the Committee and its members. We brought the case here because important issues are raised concerning the rights of individuals and the power of State legislatures.

We are again faced with the Reconstruction legislation which caused the Court such concern in *Screws v. United States* and in the *Williams* cases decided this term. But this time we do not have to wrestle with far-reaching questions of constitutionality or even of construction. We think it is clear that the legislation on which this action is founded does not impose liability on the facts before us, once they are related to the presuppositions of our political history.

The privilege of legislators to be free from arrest or civil process for what they do or say in legislative proceedings has taproots in the Parliamentary struggles of the Sixteenth and Seventeenth Centuries. As Parliament achieved increasing independence from the Crown, its statement of the privilege grew stronger. In 1523, Sir Thomas More could make only a tentative claim. In 1668, after a long and bitter struggle, Parliament finally laid the ghost of Charles I, who had prosecuted Sir John Elliot and others for "seditious" speeches in Parliament. In 1689, the Bill of Rights declared in unequivocal language: "That the Freedom of Speech, and Debates or Proceedings in Parliament, ought not to be impeached or questioned in any Court or Place out of Parliament."

Freedom of speech and action in the legislature was taken as a matter of course by those who severed the Colonies from the Crown and founded our Nation. It was deemed so essential for representatives of the people that it was written into the Articles of Confederation and later into the Constitution. Article V of the Articles of Confederation is quite close to the English Bill of Rights: "Freedom of speech and debate in Congress shall not be impeached or questioned in any court or place out of Congress. . . ." Article I, §6, of the Constitution provides: ". . . for any Speech or Debate in either House, [the Senators and Representatives] shall not be questioned in any other Place."

The reason for the privilege is clear. It was well summarized by James Wilson, an influential member of the Committee of Detail which was responsible for the provision in the Federal Constitution. "In order to enable and encourage a representative of the public to discharge his public trust with firmness and success, it is indispensably necessary, that he should enjoy the fullest liberty of speech, and that he should be protected from the resentment of every one, however powerful, to whom the exercise of that liberty may occasion offence."

The provision in the United States Constitution was a reflection of political principles already firmly established in the States. Three State Constitutions adopted before the Federal Constitution specifically protected the privilege. The Maryland Declaration of Rights, Nov. 3, 1776, provided: "That freedom of speech, and debates or proceedings, in the legislature, ought not to be impeached in any other court or judicature." Art. VIII. The Massachusetts Constitution of 1780 provided: "The freedom of deliberation, speech and debate, in either house of the legislature, is so essential to the rights of the people, that it cannot be the foundation of any accusation or prosecution, action, or complaint, in any other court or place whatsoever." The New Hampshire Constitution of 1784 provided: "The freedom of deliberation, speech, and debate, in either house of the legislature, is so essential to the rights of the people, that it cannot be the foundation of any action, complaint, or prosecution, in any other court or place whatsoever."

As other States joined the Union or revised their Constitutions, they took great care to preserve the principle that the legislature must be free to speak and act without fear of criminal and civil liability. Forty-one of the forty-eight States now have specific provisions in their Constitutions protecting the privilege.

Did Congress by the general language of its 1871 statute mean to overturn the tradition of legislative freedom achieved in England by Civil War and carefully preserved in the formation of State and National Governments here? Did it mean to subject legislators to civil liability for acts done within the sphere of legislative activity? Let us assume, merely for the moment, that Congress has constitutional power to limit the freedom of State legislators acting within their traditional sphere. That would be a big assumption. But we would have to make an even rasher assumption to find that Congress thought it had exercised the power. These are difficulties we cannot hurdle. The limits of §§1 and 2 of the 1871 statute—now §§43 and 47(3) of Title 8—were not spelled out in debate. We cannot believe that Congress—itself a staunch advocate of legislative freedom—would impinge on a tradition so well grounded in history and reason by covert inclusion in the general language before us.

The judgment of the Court of Appeals is reversed and that of the District Court *affirmed*.

Mr. Justice Douglas, dissenting.

I agree with the opinion of the Court as a statement of general principles governing the liability of legislative committees and members of the legislatures. But I do not agree that all abuses of legislative committees are solely for the legislative body to police.

We are dealing here with a right protected by the Constitution—the right of free speech. The charge seems strained and difficult to sustain; but it is that a legislative committee brought the weight of its authority down on respondent for exercising his right of free speech. Reprisal for speaking is as much an abridgment as a prior restraint. If a committee departs so far from its domain to deprive a citizen of a right protected by the Constitution, I can think of no reason why it should be immune. Yet that is the extent of the liability sought to be imposed on petitioners under 8 U.S.C. §43.

It is speech and debate in the legislative department which our constitutional scheme makes privileged. Included, of course, are the actions of legislative committees that are authorized to conduct hearings or make investigations so as to lay the foundation for legislative action. But we are apparently holding today that the actions of those committees have no limits in the eyes of the law. May they depart with impunity from their legislative functions, sit as kangaroo courts, and try men for their loyalty and their political beliefs? May they substitute trial before committees for trial before juries? May they sit as a board of censors over industry, prepare their blacklists of citizens, and issue pronouncements as devastating as any bill of attainder?

Even a policeman who exacts a confession by force and violence can be held criminally liable under the Civil Rights Act, as we ruled only the other day in *Williams v. United States* (1951). Yet now we hold that no matter the extremes to which a legislative committee may go it is not answerable to an injured party under the civil rights legislation. I see no reason why any officer of government should be higher than the Constitution from which all rights and privileges of an office obtain.

* * *

In determining whether the doctrine of legislative immunity applies, federal courts focus on the nature of the act the plaintiff is challenging, rather than the office the defendant holds. Not every action a legislator takes is "legislative." Legislative immunity does not prevent a legislator from being sued, for example, for illegal employment discrimination, because employment decisions are not generally considered to be the types of legislative acts traditionally protected by the federal Constitution's Speech and Debate Clause. *See, e.g., Kukla v. Vill. of Antioch,* 647 F. Supp. 799, 814 (N.D. Ill. 1986) ("A legislator making an employment decision functions not as a legislator but essentially as any other employer would. He or she therefore has no absolute immunity from a damage award for an unconstitutional employment decision."); *see also Davis v. Passman,* 442 U.S. 228 (1979) (recognizing a cause of action against a Congressman for sex discrimination under the Fifth Amendment.).

Conversely, not every "legislative" act is performed by a legislator; executive officials may be entitled to absolute immunity when they engage in legislative acts. In *Bogan v. Scott-Harris,* 523 U.S. 44 (1998), a jury found that the City of Fall River, Massachusetts and two of its officials illegally voted to eliminate a local position as a means of retaliation against an employee's protected speech. Among those city officials was the mayor who introduced and signed the legislation that eliminated the position. The Court found that a mayor was entitled to absolute immunity for "introduc[ing] . . . a budget and signing into law an ordinance." These actions, the Court explained, "were formally legislative, even though he was an executive official." *See also Supreme Ct. of Va. v. Consumers Union of U.S., Inc.,* 446 U.S. 719, 731 (1980) (finding that rulemaking by the judicial branch is a legislative act, protected by absolute legislative immunity).

Beyond its holding that executive officials are sometimes entitled to absolute legislative immunity, *Bogan v. Scott-Harris* is also an important case for another reason. The case extended the doctrine of absolute legislative immunity to *local* actors. Before *Bogan,* the Court had only held that Congresspersons, *Kilbourn v. Thompson* (1880); state officials, *Tenney, supra;* and regional actors, *Lake Country Ests., Inc. v. Tahoe Reg'l Plan. Agency* (1979), could invoke this defense. In extending the doctrine to local actors, the *Bogan* Court reasoned:

> Regardless of the level of government, the exercise of legislative discretion should not be inhibited by judicial interference or distorted by the fear of personal liability. Furthermore, the time and energy required to defend against a lawsuit are of particular concern at the local level, where the part-time citizen-legislator remains commonplace. And the threat of liability may significantly deter service in local government, where prestige and pecuniary rewards may pale in comparison to the threat of civil liability. Moreover, certain deterrents to legislative abuse may be greater at the local level than at other levels of government, including the availability of municipal liability for constitutional violations, and the ultimate check on legislative abuse, the electoral process.

In assessing this reasoning, consider whether there are sufficient alternative avenues for constitutional accountability when legislators violate the Constitution. The Court suggests that municipalities can be held liable for constitutional violations. But, as described in greater detail earlier in this Chapter, municipal governments may not be sued under a theory of *respondeat superior* liability. Indeed, in the *Bogan* case itself, the First Circuit had reversed the jury's verdict against the city, finding that only a few government officials had the illegal motive. *See Scott-Harris v. City of Fall River* (1st Cir. 1997). This demonstrates that sometimes, governments and their agents invoke multiple defenses that, collectively, mean that no one is held legally accountable for unconstitutional acts. "[T]hese doctrines interact to expand the rights-remedies gap."[32]

6.   *Qualified Immunity*

Government officials who are not being sued for their judicial, prosecutorial, or legislative acts are generally not entitled to an absolute immunity defense. Instead, when they are sued in their individual capacities for damages, such officials are entitled to raise a defense of qualified immunity. This was not always the case. During the founding and the nineteenth century, executive branch officers were generally personally liable for their actions. Federal officers sued for damages could seek a special bill of indemnification from Congress after being held liable in federal court, but there was no immunity defense available to end the litigation. *See* James E. Pfander & Jonathan L. Hunt, *Public Wrongs and Private Bills: Indemnification and Government Accountability in the Early Republic*, 85 N.Y.U. L. Rev. 1862, 1865-70 (2010). In *Little v. Barreme* (1804), for example, a navy captain captured and seized a Danish vessel sailing *from* a French port under direct orders from the President but in violation of an act of Congress limiting seizures to ships sailing *to* French ports. The Court held that "the instructions [of the President] cannot change the nature of the transaction or legalize an act which without those instructions would have been a plain trespass. . . . Captain Little, then, must be answerable in damages to the owner of this neutral vessel. . . ." The Court affirmed an award of $8,504 for the capture and detention of the vessel.

Even after the defense of qualified immunity emerged, it was not until the end of the twentieth century that the Court expanded the doctrine in ways that now regularly lead to dismissal of suits against state and federal officers, making it one of the most salient doctrines in debates about constitutional accountability. Deaths at the hands of local law enforcement officials have sparked national conversations on the nation's comparatively aberrant levels of state violence and the ways that Black people experience a disproportionate share of that violence.[33] In the context of federal courts, the Court's expansion of qualified immunity has

---

32. Fred O. Smith, Jr., *Local Sovereign Immunity*, 116 Colum. L. Rev. 409, 430-38 (2016) (calling the *Bogan* Court's reliance on the availability of municipal liability, in a case where that theory had already been rejected, "striking, concerning, and revealing").

33. *See* Devon Carbado, *Blue-on-Black Violence: A Provisional Model of Some of the Causes*, 104 Geo. L.J. 1479 (2016).

featured prominently in those conversations.[34] The sections that follow will first provide an overview of the doctrine of qualified immunity and a description of key proposed reforms offered by jurists, legislators, and scholars. We begin with the case that began the modern expansion of the doctrine by eliminating the element of subjective good faith of the officer and the need to wait until trial to adjudicate the defense.

a. What Is Qualified Immunity

Harlow v. Fitzgerald

457 U.S. 800 (1982)

Justice POWELL delivered the opinion of the Court.

The issue in this case is the scope of the immunity available to the senior aides and advisers of the President of the United States in a suit for damages based upon their official acts.

I

In this suit for civil damages petitioners Bryce Harlow and Alexander Butterfield are alleged to have participated in a conspiracy to violate the constitutional and statutory rights of the respondent A. Ernest Fitzgerald [by seeking his discharge from public office in retaliation for his plan to expose "shady" government "purchasing practices"]. Respondent avers that petitioners entered the conspiracy in their capacities as senior White House aides to former President Richard M. Nixon. . . . Harlow asserts he had no reason to believe that a conspiracy existed. He contends that he took all his actions in good faith. . . .

II

[O]ur decisions consistently have held that government officials are entitled to some form of immunity from suits for damages. As recognized at common law, public officers require this protection to shield them from undue interference with their duties and from potentially disabling threats of liability.

Our decisions have recognized immunity defenses of two kinds. For officials whose special functions or constitutional status requires complete protection from suit, we have recognized the defense of "absolute immunity." The absolute immunity of legislators, in their legislative functions, and of judges, in their judicial functions, now is well settled. Our decisions also have extended absolute immunity to certain officials of the Executive Branch. These include prosecutors and similar officials, *see Butz v. Economou* (1978), executive officers engaged in adjudicative functions, and the President of the United States, *see Nixon v. Fitzgerald* (1982).

For executive officials in general, however, our cases make plain that qualified immunity represents the norm. In *Scheuer v. Rhodes* (1974), we acknowledged that high officials require greater protection than those with less complex discretionary

---

34. Katherine Mims Crocker, *Qualified Immunity, Sovereign Immunity, and Systemic Reform,* 71 DUKE L.J. 1701 (2022) (describing qualified immunity's prominence and summarizing debate).

responsibilities. Nonetheless, we held that a governor and his aides could receive the requisite protection from qualified or good-faith immunity. In *Butz v. Economou*, we extended the approach of *Scheuer* to high federal officials of the Executive Branch. Discussing in detail the considerations that also had underlain our decision in *Scheuer*, we explained that the recognition of a qualified immunity defense for high executives reflected an attempt to balance competing values: not only the importance of a damages remedy to protect the rights of citizens, but also "the need to protect officials who are required to exercise their discretion and the related public interest in encouraging the vigorous exercise of official authority." Without discounting the adverse consequences of denying high officials an absolute immunity from private lawsuits alleging constitutional violations—consequences found sufficient in *Spalding v. Vilas* (1896), and *Barr v. Matteo* (1959), to warrant extension to such officials of absolute immunity from suits at common law—we emphasized our expectation that insubstantial suits need not proceed to trial:

> Insubstantial lawsuits can be quickly terminated by federal courts alert to the possibilities of artful pleading. Unless the complaint states a compensable claim for relief . . . , it should not survive a motion to dismiss. Moreover, the Court recognized in *Scheuer* that damages suits concerning constitutional violations need not proceed to trial, but can be terminated on a properly supported motion for summary judgment based on the defense of immunity. . . . In responding to such a motion, plaintiffs may not play dog in the manger; and firm application of the Federal Rules of Civil Procedure will ensure that federal officials are not harassed by frivolous lawsuits.

Butz continued to acknowledge that the special functions of some officials might require absolute immunity. But the Court held that "federal officials who seek absolute exemption from personal liability for unconstitutional conduct must bear the burden of showing that public policy requires an exemption of that scope." This we reaffirmed today in *Nixon v. Fitzgerald*.

III

Petitioners argue that they are entitled to a blanket protection of absolute immunity as an incident of their offices as Presidential aides.

In deciding this claim we do not write on an empty page. In *Butz v. Economou*, the Secretary of Agriculture—a Cabinet official directly accountable to the President—asserted a defense of absolute official immunity from suit for civil damages. We rejected his claim. In so doing we did not question the power or the importance of the Secretary's office. Nor did we doubt the importance to the President of loyal and efficient subordinates in executing his duties of office. Yet we found these factors, alone, to be insufficient to justify absolute immunity. "[The] greater power of [high] officials," we reasoned, "affords a greater potential for a regime of lawless conduct." Damages actions against high officials were therefore "an important means of vindicating constitutional guarantees." Moreover, we concluded that it would be "untenable to draw a distinction for purposes of immunity law between suits brought against state officials under [42 U.S.C.] §1983 and suits brought directly under the Constitution against federal officials."

Having decided in *Butz* that Members of the Cabinet ordinarily enjoy only qualified immunity from suit, we conclude today that it would be equally untenable to hold absolute immunity an incident of the office of every Presidential subordinate based in the White House. . . .

IV

Even if they cannot establish that their official functions require absolute immunity, petitioners assert that public policy at least mandates an application of the qualified immunity standard that would permit the defeat of insubstantial claims without resort to trial. We agree.

A

The resolution of immunity questions inherently requires a balance between the evils inevitable in any available alternative. In situations of abuse of office, an action for damages may offer the only realistic avenue for vindication of constitutional guarantees. It is this recognition that has required the denial of absolute immunity to most public officers. At the same time, however, it cannot be disputed seriously that claims frequently run against the innocent as well as the guilty—at a cost not only to the defendant officials, but to society as a whole. These social costs include the expenses of litigation, the diversion of official energy from pressing public issues, and the deterrence of able citizens from acceptance of public office. Finally, there is the danger that fear of being sued will "dampen the ardor of all but the most resolute, or the most irresponsible [public officials], in the unflinching discharge of their duties." *Gregoire v. Biddle* (CA2 1949).

In identifying qualified immunity as the best attainable accommodation of competing values, in *Butz*, as in *Scheuer*, we relied on the assumption that this standard would permit "[insubstantial] lawsuits [to] be quickly terminated." Yet petitioners advance persuasive arguments that the dismissal of insubstantial lawsuits without trial—a factor presupposed in the balance of competing interests struck by our prior cases—requires an adjustment of the "good faith" standard established by our decisions.

B

Qualified or "good faith" immunity is an affirmative defense that must be pleaded by a defendant official. Decisions of this Court have established that the "good faith" defense has both an "objective" and a "subjective" aspect. The objective element involves a presumptive knowledge of and respect for "basic, unquestioned constitutional rights." *Wood v. Strickland* (1975). The subjective component refers to "permissible intentions." Characteristically, the Court has defined these elements by identifying the circumstances in which qualified immunity would not be available. Referring both to the objective and subjective elements, we have held that qualified immunity would be defeated if an official "knew or reasonably should have known that the action he took within his sphere of official responsibility would violate the constitutional rights of the [plaintiff], or if he took the action with the malicious intention to cause a deprivation of constitutional rights or other injury. . . ."

The subjective element of the good-faith defense frequently has proved incompatible with our admonition in *Butz* that insubstantial claims should not proceed to trial. Rule 56 of the Federal Rules of Civil Procedure provides that disputed questions of fact ordinarily may not be decided on motions for summary judgment. And an official's subjective good faith has been considered to be a question of fact that some courts have regarded as inherently requiring resolution by a jury.

In the context of *Butz*'s attempted balancing of competing values, it now is clear that substantial costs attend the litigation of the subjective good faith of government officials. Not only are there the general costs of subjecting officials to the risks of trial—distraction of officials from their governmental duties, inhibition of discretionary action, and deterrence of able people from public service. There are special costs to "subjective" inquiries of this kind. Immunity generally is available only to officials performing discretionary functions. In contrast with the thought processes accompanying "ministerial" tasks, the judgments surrounding discretionary action almost inevitably are influenced by the decisionmaker's experiences, values, and emotions. These variables explain in part why questions of subjective intent so rarely can be decided by summary judgment. Yet they also frame a background in which there often is no clear end to the relevant evidence. Judicial inquiry into subjective motivation therefore may entail broad-ranging discovery and the deposing of numerous persons, including an official's professional colleagues. Inquiries of this kind can be peculiarly disruptive of effective government.

Consistently with the balance at which we aimed in *Butz*, we conclude today that bare allegations of malice should not suffice to subject government officials either to the costs of trial or to the burdens of broad-reaching discovery. We therefore hold that government officials performing discretionary functions, generally are shielded from liability for civil damages insofar as their conduct does not violate clearly established statutory or constitutional rights of which a reasonable person would have known.[30]

Reliance on the objective reasonableness of an official's conduct, as measured by reference to clearly established law, should avoid excessive disruption of government and permit the resolution of many insubstantial claims on summary judgment. On summary judgment, the judge appropriately may determine, not only the currently applicable law, but whether that law was clearly established at the time an action occurred. If the law at that time was not clearly established, an official could not reasonably be expected to anticipate subsequent legal developments, nor could he fairly be said to "know" that the law forbade conduct not previously identified as unlawful. Until this threshold immunity question is resolved, discovery should not be allowed. If the law was clearly established, the immunity defense ordinarily should fail, since a reasonably competent public official should know the law governing his conduct. Nevertheless, if the official pleading the defense claims extraordinary circumstances and can prove that he neither knew nor should have known of the relevant legal standard, the defense should be sustained. But again, the defense would turn primarily on objective factors.

By defining the limits of qualified immunity essentially in objective terms, we provide no license to lawless conduct. The public interest in deterrence of unlawful conduct and in compensation of victims remains protected by a test that focuses on the objective legal reasonableness of an official's acts. Where an official could

---

30. This case involves no issue concerning the elements of the immunity applicable to state officials sued for constitutional violations under 42 U.S.C. section 1983. We have found previously, however, that it would be "untenable to draw a distinction for purposes of immunity law between suits brought against state officials under section 1983 and suits brought directly under the constitution against federal officials."

be expected to know that certain conduct would violate statutory or constitutional rights, he should be made to hesitate; and a person who suffers injury caused by such conduct may have a cause of action. But where an official's duties legitimately require action in which clearly established rights are not implicated, the public interest may be better served by action taken "with independence and without fear of consequences." *Pierson v. Ray* (1967).[34]

V

The judgment of the Court of Appeals is vacated, and the case is remanded for further action consistent with this opinion.

* * *

b. What Is a "Clearly Established" Right?

Harlow announces an objective standard in which officers may be held liable in damages only for actions that violate clearly established law that a reasonable person would have known at the time of the violation. Federal rights can become clearly established in at least three ways. First, in rare circumstances, the language of the Constitution is sufficient to confer sufficient notice that conduct is illegal. Second, law can be clearly established by way of a prior case from the Supreme Court or the relevant appellate court that applied the right to materially similar facts. Third, when a government official acts in a manner that "obviously" violates a legal rule, this can also lead a court to conclude that the official violated a clearly established right.

(1) Plain Text

Groh v. Ramirez

540 U.S. 551 (2004)

Justice STEVENS delivered the opinion of the Court.

Petitioner conducted a search of respondents' home pursuant to a warrant that failed to describe the "persons or things to be seized." U.S. Const., Amdt. 4. The questions presented are (1) whether the search violated the Fourth Amendment, and (2) if so, whether petitioner nevertheless is entitled to qualified immunity, given that a Magistrate Judge (Magistrate), relying on an affidavit that particularly described the items in question, found probable cause to conduct the search.

I

Respondents, Joseph Ramirez and members of his family, live on a large ranch in Butte-Silver Bow County, Montana. Petitioner, Jeff Groh, has been a Special Agent for the Bureau of Alcohol, Tobacco and Firearms (ATF) since 1989. In

---

34. [O]ur decision applies only to suits for civil damages [and we] express no opinion as to the conditions in which injunctive or declaratory relief might be available.

February 1997, a concerned citizen informed petitioner that on a number of visits to respondents' ranch the visitor had seen a large stock of weaponry, including an automatic rifle, grenades, a grenade launcher, and a rocket launcher. Based on that information, petitioner prepared and signed an application for a warrant to search the ranch. The application stated that the search was for "any automatic firearms or parts to automatic weapons, destructive devices to include but not limited to grenades, grenade launchers, rocket launchers, and any and all receipts pertaining to the purchase or manufacture of automatic weapons or explosive devices or launchers." Petitioner supported the application with a detailed affidavit, which he also prepared and executed, that set forth the basis for his belief that the listed items were concealed on the ranch. Petitioner then presented these documents to a Magistrate, along with a warrant form that petitioner also had completed. The Magistrate signed the warrant form.

Although the application particularly described the place to be searched and the contraband petitioner expected to find, the warrant itself was less specific; it failed to identify any of the items that petitioner intended to seize. In the portion of the form that called for a description of the "person or property" to be seized, petitioner typed a description of respondents' two-story blue house rather than the alleged stockpile of firearms. The warrant did not incorporate by reference the itemized list contained in the application. It did, however, recite that the Magistrate was satisfied the affidavit established probable cause to believe that contraband was concealed on the premises, and that sufficient grounds existed for the warrant's issuance.

The day after the Magistrate issued the warrant, petitioner led a team of law enforcement officers, including both federal agents and members of the local sheriff's department, in the search of respondents' premises. Although respondent Joseph Ramirez was not home, his wife and children were. Petitioner states that he orally described the objects of the search to Mrs. Ramirez in person and to Mr. Ramirez by telephone. According to Mrs. Ramirez, however, petitioner explained only that he was searching for "'an explosive device in a box.'" At any rate, the officers' search uncovered no illegal weapons or explosives. When the officers left, petitioner gave Mrs. Ramirez a copy of the search warrant, but not a copy of the application, which had been sealed. The following day, in response to a request from respondents' attorney, petitioner faxed the attorney a copy of the page of the application that listed the items to be seized. No charges were filed against the Ramirezes.

Respondents sued petitioner and the other officers under raising eight claims, including violation of the Fourth Amendment. . . .

II

The warrant was plainly invalid. The Fourth Amendment states unambiguously that "no Warrants shall issue, but upon probable cause, supported by Oath or affirmation, and *particularly describing* the place to be searched, and the persons or things to be seized." (Emphasis added.) The warrant in this case complied with the first three of these requirements: It was based on probable cause and supported by a sworn affidavit, and it described particularly the place of the search. On the fourth requirement, however, the warrant failed altogether. Indeed, petitioner concedes that "the warrant . . . was deficient in particularity because it provided no description of the type of evidence sought. . . ." The mere fact that the magistrate issued a warrant does not necessarily establish that he agreed that the search should be as broad as [requested].[4]

III

Having concluded that a constitutional violation occurred, we turn to the question whether petitioner is entitled to qualified immunity despite that violation. *See Wilson v. Layne* (1999). The answer depends on whether the right that was transgressed was "'clearly established'"—that is, "whether it would be clear to a reasonable officer that his conduct was unlawful in the situation he confronted." *Saucier v. Katz* (2001).

Given that the particularity requirement is set forth in the text of the Constitution, no reasonable officer could believe that a warrant that plainly did not comply with that requirement was valid. *See Harlow v. Fitzgerald* (1982). Moreover, because petitioner himself prepared the invalid warrant, he may not argue that he reasonably relied on the Magistrate's assurance that the warrant contained an adequate description of the things to be seized and was therefore valid. Even a cursory reading of the warrant in this case—perhaps just a simple glance—would have revealed a glaring deficiency that any reasonable police officer would have known was constitutionally fatal. No reasonable officer could claim to be unaware of the basic rule, well established by our cases, that, absent consent or exigency, a warrantless search of the home is presumptively unconstitutional.

Accordingly, the judgment of the Court of Appeals is affirmed.

* * *

(2) Materially Similar Facts

A legal right can also become "clearly established" if there is a prior case—from the Supreme Court or from the relevant federal circuit's Court of Appeals—applying the legal rule to materially similar facts. With some frequency, the Supreme Court has reversed decisions by lower courts that deny qualified immunity to government officials in the absence of binding authority with materially similar facts. As one commentator notes, in recent years, this category of cases has been given "pride of place on the Court's docket," as the Court often "reverse[d] lower courts at an unusual pace"[35] to grant officials qualified immunity. In *Plumhoff v. Rickard*, 572 U.S. 765

---

4. Although we have previously held that a search is not unreasonable when police reasonably rely on a judge's assurance that a warrant "authorized the search they had requested," *Mass. v. Sheppard* (1984), in this case, petitioner did not alert the Magistrate to the defect in the warrant petitioner had drafted . . . [n]or would it have been reasonable for petitioner to rely on a warrant that was so patently defective, even if the Magistrate was aware of the deficiency. *See U.S. v. Leon* (1984).

35. William Baude, *Is Qualified Immunity Unlawful?*, 106 Calif. L. Rev. 45, 48 (2018) (noting that the Court "has begun to strengthen qualified immunity's protection . . . by giving qualified immunity cases pride of place on the Court's docket. It exercises jurisdiction in cases that would not otherwise satisfy the certiorari criteria and reaches out to summarily reverse lower courts at an unusual pace.").

(2014), for example, the Supreme Court granted qualified immunity to officers who fired into a vehicle during a high-speed chase; the Court found that prior cases finding excessive force under the Fourth Amendment were "materially distinguishable." In the context of the Fourth Amendment, the Court has expressly warned that this means of identifying clearly established rights is particularly demanding.

Lower courts have heeded the Supreme Court's warning. One striking example is *West v. City of Caldwell* (9th Cir. 2019), in which the Ninth Circuit granted qualified immunity to officers who fired tear-gas cannisters into a woman's home, damaging the property to such an extent that she and her children could not live there for three months. In her view, the officers' actions violated the Fourth Amendment's bar against unreasonable searches. While she had granted the officers permission to enter her home to search for a suspect and given them a key, she believed that firing tear-gas cannisters into the home was unnecessary, excessive, and therefore, unreasonable. She identified a prior case from the Ninth Circuit that denied qualified immunity to officers who were "unnecessarily destructive" during a search by "[breaking] down two doors that already were unlocked, and . . . kicking the open patio door while declaring: 'I like to destroy these kind of materials, it's cool.'" The Ninth Circuit found, however, that this prior case was distinguishable because: "Plaintiff does not claim, and the record does not suggest, that Defendants damaged her house because they thought that doing so was 'cool.'"

The following two cases are also illustrative of cases granting qualified immunity to officers in the absence of precedents at the time of the alleged violation with materially similar facts.

Mullenix v. Luna

577 U.S. 7 (2015)

PER CURIAM.

On the night of March 23, 2010, Sergeant Randy Baker of the Tulia, Texas Police Department followed Israel Leija, Jr., to a drive-in restaurant, with a warrant for his arrest. When Baker approached Leija's car and informed him that he was under arrest, Leija sped off, headed for Interstate 27. Baker gave chase and was quickly joined by Trooper Gabriel Rodriguez of the Texas Department of Public Safety (DPS).

Leija entered the interstate and led the officers on an 18-minute chase at speeds between 85 and 110 miles per hour. Twice during the chase, Leija called the Tulia Police dispatcher, claiming to have a gun and threatening to shoot at police officers if they did not abandon their pursuit. The dispatcher relayed Leija's threats, together with a report that Leija might be intoxicated, to all concerned officers.

As Baker and Rodriguez maintained their pursuit, other law enforcement officers set up tire spikes at three locations. Officer Troy Ducheneaux of the Canyon Police Department manned the spike strip at the first location Leija was expected to reach, beneath the overpass at Cemetery Road. Ducheneaux and the other officers had received training on the deployment of spike strips, including on how to take a defensive position so as to minimize the risk posed by the passing driver.

DPS Trooper Chadrin Mullenix also responded. He drove to the Cemetery Road overpass, initially intending to set up a spike strip there. Upon learning of the other spike strip positions, however, Mullenix began to consider another tactic: shooting at Leija's car in order to disable it. Mullenix had not received training in this tactic and had not attempted it before, but he radioed the idea to Rodriguez. Rodriguez responded "10-4," gave Mullenix his position, and said that Leija had slowed to 85 miles per hour. Mullenix then asked the DPS dispatcher to inform his supervisor, Sergeant Byrd, of his plan and ask if Byrd thought it was "worth doing." Before receiving Byrd's response, Mullenix exited his vehicle and, armed with his service rifle, took a shooting position on the overpass, 20 feet above I-27. Respondents allege that from this position, Mullenix still could hear Byrd's response to "stand by" and "see if the spikes work first."

As Mullenix waited for Leija to arrive, he and another officer, Randall County Sheriff's Deputy Tom Shipman, discussed whether Mullenix's plan would work and how and where to shoot the vehicle to best carry it out. Shipman also informed Mullenix that another officer was located beneath the overpass.

Approximately three minutes after Mullenix took up his shooting position, he spotted Leija's vehicle, with Rodriguez in pursuit. As Leija approached the overpass, Mullenix fired six shots. Leija's car continued forward beneath the overpass, where it engaged the spike strip, hit the median, and rolled two and a half times. It was later determined that Leija had been killed by Mullenix's shots, four of which struck his upper body. There was no evidence that any of Mullenix's shots hit the car's radiator, hood, or engine block.

Respondents sued Mullenix under 42 U.S.C. §1983, alleging that he had violated the Fourth Amendment by using excessive force against Leija. Mullenix moved for summary judgment on the ground of qualified immunity, but the District Court denied his motion. Mullenix appealed, and the Court of Appeals for the Fifth Circuit affirmed. We address only the qualified immunity question, not whether there was a Fourth Amendment violation in the first place, and now reverse.

The doctrine of qualified immunity shields officials from civil liability so long as their conduct "'does not violate clearly established statutory or constitutional rights of which a reasonable person would have known.'" *Pearson v. Callahan* (2009) (quoting *Harlow v. Fitzgerald* (1982)). A clearly established right is one that is "sufficiently clear that every reasonable official would have understood that what he is doing violates that right." *Reichle v. Howards* (2012). "We do not require a case directly on point, but existing precedent must have placed the statutory or constitutional question beyond debate." *Ashcroft v. al-Kidd* (2011). Put simply, qualified immunity protects "all but the plainly incompetent or those who knowingly violate the law." *Malley v. Briggs* (1986).

"We have repeatedly told courts . . . not to define clearly established law at a high level of generality." *al-Kidd*. The dispositive question is "whether the violative nature of particular conduct is clearly established." *Ibid.* This inquiry "'must be undertaken in light of the specific context of the case, not as a broad general proposition.'" *Brosseau v. Haugen* (2004) (per curiam). Such specificity is especially important in the Fourth Amendment context, where the Court has recognized that "[i]t is sometimes difficult for an officer to determine how the relevant legal doctrine, here excessive force, will apply to the factual situation the officer confronts."

In this case, the Fifth Circuit held that Mullenix violated the clearly established rule that a police officer may not "'use deadly force against a fleeing felon who does not pose a sufficient threat of harm to the officer or others.'" Yet this Court has previously considered—and rejected—almost that exact formulation of the qualified immunity question in the Fourth Amendment context. In *Brosseau*, which also involved the shooting of a suspect fleeing by car, the Ninth Circuit denied qualified immunity on the ground that the officer had violated the clearly established rule, set forth in *Tennessee v. Garner* (1985), that "deadly force is only permissible where the officer has probable cause to believe that the suspect poses a threat of serious physical harm, either to the officer or to others." This Court summarily reversed, holding that use of Garner's "general" test for excessive force was "mistaken." The correct inquiry, the Court explained, was whether it was clearly established that the Fourth Amendment prohibited the officer's conduct in the "'situation [she] confronted': whether to shoot a disturbed felon, set on avoiding capture through vehicular flight, when persons in the immediate area are at risk from that flight." The Court considered three court of appeals cases discussed by the parties, noted that "this area is one in which the result depends very much on the facts of each case," and concluded that the officer was entitled to qualified immunity because "[n]one of [the cases] squarely governs the case here."

In this case, Mullenix confronted a reportedly intoxicated fugitive, set on avoiding capture through high-speed vehicular flight, who twice during his flight had threatened to shoot police officers, and who was moments away from encountering an officer at Cemetery Road. The relevant inquiry is whether existing precedent placed the conclusion that Mullenix acted unreasonably in these circumstances "beyond debate." *al-Kidd.* The general principle that deadly force requires a sufficient threat hardly settles this matter.

Far from clarifying the issue, excessive force cases involving car chases reveal the hazy legal backdrop against which Mullenix acted. In *Brosseau* itself, the Court held that an officer did not violate clearly established law when she shot a fleeing suspect out of fear that he endangered "other officers on foot who [she] believed were in the immediate area," "the occupied vehicles in [his] path," and "any other citizens who might be in the area." The threat Leija posed was at least as immediate as that presented by a suspect who had just begun to drive off and was headed only in the general direction of officers and bystanders. By the time Mullenix fired, Leija had led police on a 25-mile chase at extremely high speeds, was reportedly intoxicated, had twice threatened to shoot officers, and was racing towards an officer's location.

This Court has considered excessive force claims in connection with high-speed chases on only two occasions since *Brosseau*. In *Scott v. Harris*, the Court held that an officer did not violate the Fourth Amendment by ramming the car of a fugitive whose reckless driving "posed an actual and imminent threat to the lives of any pedestrians who might have been present, to other civilian motorists, and to the officers involved in the chase." [T]he Court reaffirmed Scott by holding that an officer acted reasonably when he fatally shot a fugitive who was "intent on resuming" a chase that "pose[d] a deadly threat for others on the road." The Court has thus never found the use of deadly force in connection with a dangerous car chase to violate the Fourth Amendment, let alone to be a basis for denying qualified immunity. Leija in his flight did not pass as many cars as the drivers in *Scott* or *Plumhoff*; traffic was light on I-27. At the same time, the fleeing fugitives in *Scott* and *Plumhoff* had not verbally threatened to kill any officers in their path, nor were they about to come upon such officers. In any event, none of our precedents "squarely governs" the facts here. Given Leija's conduct, we cannot say that only someone "plainly incompetent" or who "knowingly violate[s] the law" would have perceived a sufficient threat and acted as Mullenix did.

The dissent focuses on the availability of spike strips as an alternative means of terminating the chase. It argues that even if Leija posed a threat sufficient to justify deadly force in some circumstances, Mullenix nevertheless contravened clearly established law because he did not wait to see if the spike strips would work before taking action. Spike strips, however, present dangers of their own, not only to drivers who encounter them at speeds between 85 and 110 miles per hour, but also to officers manning them. The dissent can cite no case from this Court denying qualified immunity because officers entitled to terminate a high-speed chase selected one dangerous alternative over another.

More fundamentally, the dissent repeats the Fifth Circuit's error. It defines the qualified immunity inquiry at a high level of generality—whether any governmental interest justified choosing one tactic over another—and then fails to consider that question in "the specific context of the case." *Brosseau.*

Cases cited by the Fifth Circuit and respondents are simply too factually distinct to speak clearly to the specific circumstances here. Several involve suspects who may have done little more than flee at relatively low speeds. These cases shed little light on whether the far greater danger of a speeding fugitive threatening to kill police officers waiting in his path could warrant deadly force. The court below noted that "no weapon was ever seen," but surely in these circumstances the police were justified in taking Leija at his word when he twice told the dispatcher he had a gun and was prepared to use it.

Because the constitutional rule applied by the Fifth Circuit was not "'beyond debate,'" *Stanton v. Sims* (2013) (per curiam), we grant Mullenix's petition for certiorari and reverse the Fifth Circuit's determination that Mullenix is not entitled to qualified immunity.

Justice SOTOMAYOR, dissenting.

Chadrin Mullenix fired six rounds in the dark at a car traveling 85 miles per hour. He did so without any training in that tactic, against the wait order of his superior officer, and less than a second before the car hit spike strips deployed to stop it. Mullenix's rogue conduct killed the driver, Israel Leija, Jr. Because it was clearly established under the Fourth Amendment that an officer in Mullenix's position should not have fired the shots, I respectfully dissent from the grant of summary reversal.

I

Resolving all factual disputes in favor of plaintiffs, as the Court must on a motion for summary judgment, Mullenix knew the following facts before he shot at Leija's engine block: Leija had led police officers on an 18-minute car chase, at speeds ranging from 85 to 110 miles per hour. Leija had twice called the police dispatcher threatening to shoot at officers if they did not cease the pursuit. Police officers were deploying three sets of spike strips in order to stop Leija's flight. The officers were trained to stop a car using spike strips. This training included how to take a defensive position to minimize the risk of danger from the target car.

Mullenix knew that spike strips were being set up directly beneath the overpass where he was stationed. There is no evidence below that any of the officers with whom Mullenix was in communication—including Officer Troy Ducheneaux, whom Mullenix believed to be below the overpass—had expressed any concern for their safety.

Mullenix had no training in shooting to disable a moving vehicle and had never seen the tactic done before. He also lacked permission to take the shots: When Mullenix relayed his plan to his superior officer, Robert Byrd, Byrd responded "stand by" and "see if the spikes work first." Three minutes after arriving at the overpass, Mullenix fired six rounds at Leija's car. None hit the car's engine block; at least four struck Leija in the upper body, killing Leija.

II

This Court has rejected the idea that "an official action is protected by qualified immunity unless the very action in question has previously been held unlawful." Instead, the crux of the qualified immunity test is whether officers have "fair notice" that they are acting unconstitutionally. *Hope v. Pelzer* (2002).

Respondents here allege that Mullenix violated the Fourth Amendment's prohibition on unreasonable seizures by using deadly force to apprehend Leija. This Court's precedents clearly establish that the Fourth Amendment is violated unless the "'governmental interests'" in effectuating a particular kind of seizure outweigh the "'nature and quality of the intrusion on the individual's Fourth Amendment interests.'" *Scott v. Harris* (2007). There must be a "governmental interes[t]" not only in effectuating a seizure, but also in "how [the seizure] is carried out." *Tenn. v. Garner* (1985).

Balancing a particular governmental interest in the use of deadly force against the intrusion occasioned by the use of that force is inherently a fact-specific inquiry, not susceptible to bright lines. But it is clearly established that the government must have some interest in using deadly force over other kinds of force.

Here, then, the clearly established legal question—the question a reasonable officer would have asked—is whether, under all the circumstances as known to Mullenix, there was a governmental interest in shooting at the car rather than waiting for it to run over spike strips. The majority does not point to any such interest here. It claims that Mullenix's goal was not merely to stop the car, but to stop the car "in a manner that avoided the risks" of relying on spike strips. But there is no evidence in the record that shooting at Leija's engine block would stop the car in such a manner.

Nor was there any evidence that shooting at the car was more reliable than the spike strips. The majority notes that spike strips are fallible. But Mullenix had no information to suggest that shooting to disable a car had a higher success rate, much less that doing so with no training and at night was more likely to succeed. Moreover, not only did officers have training in setting up the spike strips, but they had also placed two backup strips further north along the highway in case the first set failed. A reasonable officer could not have thought that shooting would stop the car with less danger or greater certainty than waiting. . . .

III

The majority largely evades this key legal question by focusing primarily on the governmental interest in whether the car should be stopped rather than the dispositive question of how the car should be stopped. But even assuming that Leija posed a "sufficient," or " immediate," threat, Mullenix did not face a "choice between two evils" of shooting at a suspect's car or letting him go. Instead, Mullenix chose to employ a potentially lethal tactic (shooting at Leija's engine block) in addition to a tactic specifically designed to accomplish the same result (spike strips). By granting Mullenix qualified immunity, this Court goes a step further than our previous cases and does so without full briefing or argument.

Thus framed, it is apparent that the majority's exhortation that the right at stake not be defined at "a high level of generality," is a red herring. The majority adduces various facts that the Fifth Circuit supposedly ignored in its qualified immunity analysis, including that Leija was "a reportedly intoxicated fugitive, set on avoiding capture through high-speed vehicular flight, who twice during his flight had threatened to shoot police officers, and who was moments away from encountering an officer at Cemetery Road." But not one of those facts goes to the governmental interest in shooting over awaiting the spike strips.

Instead of dealing with the question whether Mullenix could constitutionally fire on Leija's car rather than waiting for the spike strips, the majority dwells on the imminence of the threat posed by Leija. The majority recharacterizes Mullenix's decision to shoot at Leija's engine block as a split-second, heat-of-the-moment choice, made when the suspect was "moments away." Indeed, reading the majority opinion, one would scarcely believe that Mullenix arrived at the overpass several minutes before he took his shot, or that the rural road where the car chase occurred had few cars and no bystanders or businesses. The majority also glosses over the facts that Mullenix had time to ask Byrd for permission to fire upon Leija and that Byrd—Mullenix's superior officer—told Mullenix to "stand by." There was no reason to believe that Byrd did not have all the same information Mullenix did, including the knowledge that an officer was stationed beneath the overpass. Even after receiving Byrd's response, Mullenix spent minutes in shooting position discussing his next step with a fellow officer, minutes during which he received no information that would have made his plan more suitable or his superior's orders less so.

. . .

When Mullenix confronted his superior officer after the shooting, his first words were, "How's that for proactive?" (Mullenix was apparently referencing an earlier counseling session in which Byrd suggested that he was not enterprising enough.) The glib comment does not impact our legal analysis; an officer's actual intentions are irrelevant to the Fourth Amendment's "objectively reasonable" inquiry. *See Graham v. Connor* (1989). But the comment seems to me revealing of the culture this Court's decision supports when it calls it reasonable—or even reasonably reasonable—to use deadly force for no discernible gain and over a supervisor's express order to "stand by." By sanctioning a "shoot first, think later" approach to policing, the Court renders the protections of the Fourth Amendment hollow.

For the reasons discussed, I would deny Mullenix's petition for a writ of certiorari. I thus respectfully dissent.

* * *

Jessop v. City of Fresno

936 F.3d 937 (9th Cir. 2019)

M. SMITH, Circuit Judge:

Micah Jessop and Brittan Ashjian appeal an order granting a motion for summary judgment on a defense of qualified immunity. City of Fresno and Fresno police officers Derik Kumagai, Curt Chastain, and Tomas Cantu filed the motion in an action alleging that the City Officers violated the Fourth and Fourteenth Amendments when they stole Appellants' property during the execution of a search and seizure pursuant to a warrant.

At the time of the incident, there was no clearly established law holding that officers violate the Fourth or Fourteenth Amendment when they steal property seized pursuant to a warrant. For that reason, the City Officers are entitled to qualified immunity.

As part of an investigation into illegal gambling machines in the Fresno, California area, the City Officers executed a search warrant at three of Appellants' properties. The warrant authorized "the seizure [of] all monies, negotiable instruments, securities, or things of value furnished or intended to be furnished by any person in connection to illegal gambling or money laundering that may be found on the premises . . . [and] [m]onies and records of said monies derived from the sale and or control of said machines."

If the City Officers found the property listed, they were "to retain it in [their] custody, subject to the order of the court as provided by law."

Following the search, the City Officers gave Appellants an inventory sheet stating that they seized approximately $50,000 from the properties. Appellants allege, however, that the officers actually seized $151,380 in cash and another $125,000 in rare coins. Appellants claim that the City Officers stole the difference between the amount listed on the inventory sheet and the amount actually seized from the properties.

Appellants brought suit in the Eastern District of California alleging, among other things, claims against the City Officers pursuant to 42 U.S.C. §1983 for Fourth and Fourteenth Amendment violations. The City Officers moved for summary judgment based on qualified immunity. The district court granted the motion and dismissed all of Appellants' claims. We have jurisdiction pursuant to 28 U.S.C. §1291. We review summary judgment determinations, and officers' entitlement to qualified immunity, de novo.

"The doctrine of qualified immunity protects government officials 'from liability for civil damages insofar as their conduct does not violate clearly established statutory or constitutional rights of which a reasonable person would have known.'" *Pearson v. Callahan* (2009). "In determining whether an officer is entitled to qualified immunity, we consider (1) whether there has been a violation of a constitutional right; and (2) whether that right was clearly established at the time of the officer's alleged misconduct."

I. Fourth Amendment

The parties dispute whether the City Officers' actions violated the Fourth Amendment. The City Officers insist that because they seized Appellants' assets pursuant to a valid warrant, they did not violate the Fourth Amendment. Appellants, by contrast, argue that the City Officers' alleged theft was an unreasonable seizure under the Fourth Amendment.

Although courts were formerly required to determine whether plaintiffs had been deprived of a constitutional right before proceeding to consider whether that right was clearly established when the alleged violation occurred, *see Saucier v. Katz* (2001), the Supreme Court has since instructed that courts may determine which prong of qualified immunity they should analyze first. *Pearson v. Callahan* (2011). Addressing the second prong before the first is especially appropriate where "a court will rather quickly and easily decide that there was no violation of clearly established law." This is one of those cases.

A defendant violates an individual's clearly established rights only when "'the state of the law' at the time of an incident provided 'fair warning'" to the defendant that his or her conduct was unconstitutional. *Tolan v. Cotton* (2014). "We do not require a case directly on point, but existing precedent must have placed the statutory or constitutional question beyond debate." *Ashcroft v. al-Kidd* (2011). Thus, "[t]he contours of the right must be sufficiently clear that a reasonable official would understand that what he is doing violates that right." *Anderson v. Creighton* (1987). We may look at unpublished decisions and the law of other circuits, in addition to Ninth Circuit precedent.

We have never addressed whether the theft of property covered by the terms of a search warrant, and seized pursuant to that warrant, violates the Fourth Amendment. The only circuit that has addressed that question—the Fourth Circuit—concluded in an unpublished decision that it does. *See Mom's Inc. v. Willman* (4th Cir. 2004).

Although we have not addressed this precise question, our decision in *Brewster v. Beck* (9th Cir. 2017) is instructive. There, officers impounded the plaintiff's vehicle pursuant to a statute that authorized the seizure of vehicles when the driver had a suspended license. *Id.* at 1195. When the plaintiff later "appeared at a hearing . . . with proof that she was the registered owner of the vehicle and her valid California driver's license," however, the government refused to release the vehicle to her. We reasoned that the Fourth Amendment was implicated by the government's actions because "[t]he Fourth Amendment doesn't become irrelevant once an initial seizure has run its course." Because "[t]he exigency that justified the seizure [of the plaintiff's vehicle] vanished once the vehicle arrived in impound and [the plaintiff] showed up with proof of ownership and a valid driver's license," we held that the government's impoundment of the vehicle "constituted a seizure that required compliance with the Fourth Amendment."

Brewster's reasoning suggests that the City Officers' alleged theft of Appellants' property could also implicate the Fourth Amendment. Although the City Officers seized Appellants' money and coins pursuant to a lawful warrant, their continued retention—and alleged theft—of the property might have been a Fourth Amendment seizure because "[t]he Fourth Amendment doesn't become irrelevant once an initial seizure has run its course."

Brewster's facts, however, vary in legally significant ways from those in this case. Whereas Brewster concerned the government's impoundment of a vehicle, Appellants argue that the City Officers stole their property. And while Brewster involved the seizure of property pursuant to an exception to the warrant requirement, the

City Officers seized Appellants' property pursuant to a warrant that authorized the seizure of the items allegedly stolen.

Even if the facts and reasoning of Brewster would dictate the outcome of this case, however, it was not clearly established law when the City Officers executed the search warrant. The City Officers seized Appellants' property in 2013, but Brewster was not decided until 2017. For that reason, we need not decide whether the City Officers violated the Fourth Amendment. The lack of "any cases of controlling authority" or a "consensus of cases of persuasive authority" on the constitutional question compels the conclusion that the law was not clearly established at the time of the incident. *Wilson v. Layne* (1999). Although the City Officers ought to have recognized that the alleged theft of Appellants' money and rare coins was morally wrong, they did not have clear notice that it violated the Fourth Amendment — which, as noted, is a different question. The Fourth Circuit's unpublished decision in *Mom's* — the only case law at the time of the incident holding that the theft of property seized pursuant to a warrant violates the Fourth Amendment — did not put the "constitutional question beyond debate."

Nor is this "one of those rare cases in which the constitutional right at issue is defined by a standard that is so 'obvious' that we must conclude . . . that qualified immunity is inapplicable, even without a case directly on point." *A.D. v. Cal. Highway Patrol* (9th Cir. 2013). We recognize that the allegation of any theft by police officers — most certainly the theft of over $225,000 — is deeply disturbing. Whether that conduct violates the Fourth Amendment's prohibition on unreasonable searches and seizures, however, would not be clear to a reasonable officer. *See Brosseau v. Haugen* (2004) (per curiam).

Appellants have failed to show that it was clearly established that the City Officers' alleged conduct violated the Fourth Amendment. Accordingly, we hold that the City Officers are protected by qualified immunity against Appellants' Fourth Amendment claim.

II. Fourteenth Amendment

Appellants' Fourteenth Amendment claim suffers the same fate. Appellants argue that the City Officers' theft of their property violated their substantive due process rights under the Fourteenth Amendment. Assuming that to be true, however, the City Officers are entitled to qualified immunity because that right was not clearly established. We have not held that officers violate the substantive due process clause of the Fourteenth Amendment when they steal property seized pursuant to a warrant.

Conclusion

We sympathize with Appellants. They allege the theft of their personal property by police officers sworn to uphold the law. If the City Officers committed the acts alleged, their actions were morally reprehensible. Not all conduct that is improper or morally wrong, however, violates the Constitution. Because Appellants did not have a clearly established Fourth or Fourteenth Amendment right to be free from the theft of property seized pursuant to a warrant, the City Officers are entitled to qualified immunity.

* * *

(3) "Obvious" Violations

In the Ninth Circuit's opinion in *Jessop*, the court stated that there are "rare cases in which the constitutional right at issue is defined by a standard that is so 'obvious' that we must conclude that qualified immunity is inapplicable, even without a case directly on point." The following case is the origin of that legal rule. Before *Hope v. Pelzer*, some lower courts had held that rights could generally *only* be clearly established by way of prior cases with materially similar facts. The *Hope* case clarified that a violation can be so flagrant that the governing legal rule should have placed the offender on notice as to the illegality of the conduct.

Hope v. Pelzer

536 U.S. 730 (2002)

STEVENS, J., delivered the opinion of the Court.

Larry Hope, a former prison inmate at the Limestone Prison in Alabama, was subjected to cruel and unusual punishment when prison guards twice handcuffed him to a hitching post to sanction him for disruptive conduct. Because that conclusion [by the Eleventh Circuit Court of Appeals] was not supported by earlier cases with "materially similar" facts, the court held that the respondents were entitled to qualified immunity, and therefore affirmed summary judgment in their favor. We granted certiorari to determine whether the Court of Appeals' qualified immunity holding comports with our decision in *U.S. v. Lanier* (1997).

I

In 1995, Alabama was the only State that followed the practice of chaining inmates to one another in work squads. It was also the only State that handcuffed prisoners to "hitching posts" if they either refused to work or otherwise disrupted work squads. Hope was handcuffed to a hitching post on two occasions. On May 11, 1995, while Hope was working in a chain gang near an interstate highway, he got into an argument with another inmate. Both men were taken back to the Limestone prison and handcuffed to a hitching post. Hope was released two hours later, after the guard captain determined that the altercation had been caused by the other inmate. During his two hours on the post, Hope was offered drinking water and a bathroom break every 15 minutes, and his responses to these offers were recorded on an activity log. Because he was only slightly taller than the hitching post, his arms were above shoulder height and grew tired from being handcuffed so high. Whenever he tried moving his arms to improve his circulation, the handcuffs cut into his wrists, causing pain and discomfort.

On June 7, 1995, Hope was punished more severely. He took a nap during the morning bus ride to the chain gang's worksite, and when it arrived he was less than prompt in responding to an order to get off the bus. An exchange of vulgar remarks led to a wrestling match with a guard. Four other guards intervened, subdued Hope, handcuffed him, placed him in leg irons and transported him back to the prison where he was put on the hitching post. The guards made him take off his shirt, and he remained shirtless all day while the sun burned his skin. He remained attached to the post for approximately seven hours. During this 7-hour period, he was given water only once or twice and was given no bathroom breaks. At one point, a guard taunted Hope about his thirst. According to Hope's affidavit: "[The guard] first gave water to some dogs, then brought the water cooler closer to me, removed its lid, and kicked the cooler over, spilling the water onto the ground."

Hope filed suit under 42 U.S.C. §1983, in the United States District Court for the Northern District of Alabama against three guards involved in the May incident, one of whom also handcuffed him to the hitching post in June. The case was referred to a Magistrate Judge who treated the responsive affidavits filed by the defendants as a motion for summary judgment. Without deciding whether "the very act of placing him on a restraining bar for a period of hours as a form of punishment" had violated the Eighth Amendment, the Magistrate concluded that the guards were entitled to qualified immunity. The District Court agreed, and entered judgment for respondents.

The United States Court of Appeals for the Eleventh Circuit affirmed. Before reaching the qualified immunity issue, however, it answered the constitutional question that the District Court had bypassed. The court found that the use of the hitching post for punitive purposes violated the Eighth Amendment. Nevertheless, applying Circuit precedent concerning qualified immunity, the court stated that "'the federal law by which the government official's conduct should be evaluated must be preexisting, obvious and mandatory,'" and established, not by "'abstractions,'" but by cases that are "'materially similar' to the facts in the case in front of us." The court then concluded that the facts in the two precedents on which Hope primarily relied— *Ort v. White* (CA11 1987), and *Gates v. Collier* (CA5 1974) — "though analogous," were not "'materially similar' to Hope's situation.'" We granted certiorari to review the Eleventh Circuit's qualified immunity holding.

II

The threshold inquiry a court must undertake in a qualified immunity analysis is whether plaintiff's allegations, if true, establish a constitutional violation. The Court of Appeals held that "the policy and practice of cuffing an inmate to a hitching post or similar stationary object for a period of time that surpasses that necessary to quell a threat or restore order is a violation of the Eighth Amendment." The court rejected respondents' submission that Hope could have ended his shackling by offering to return to work, finding instead that the purpose of the practice was punitive, and that the circumstances of his confinement created a substantial risk of harm of which the officers were aware. Moreover, the court relied on Circuit precedent condemning similar practices and the results of a United States Department of Justice (DOJ) report that found Alabama's systematic use of the hitching post to be improper corporal punishment. We agree with the Court of Appeals that the attachment of Hope to the hitching post under the circumstances alleged in this case violated the Eighth Amendment.

As the facts are alleged by Hope, the Eighth Amendment violation is obvious. Any safety concerns had long since abated by the time petitioner was handcuffed to the hitching post because Hope had already been subdued, handcuffed, placed in leg irons, and transported back to the prison. He was separated from his work squad and not given the opportunity to return to work. Despite the clear lack of an emergency situation, the respondents knowingly subjected him to a substantial risk of physical harm, to unnecessary pain caused by the handcuffs and the restricted position of confinement for a 7-hour period, to unnecessary exposure to the heat of the sun, to prolonged thirst and taunting, and to a deprivation of bathroom breaks that created a risk of particular discomfort and humiliation. The use of the hitching post under these circumstances violated the "basic concept underlying the Eighth Amendment [which] is nothing less than the dignity of man." This punitive treatment amounts to gratuitous infliction of "wanton and unnecessary" pain that our precedent clearly prohibits.

Despite their participation in this constitutionally impermissible conduct, the respondents may nevertheless be shielded from liability for civil damages if their actions did not violate "clearly established statutory or constitutional rights of which a reasonable person would have known." In assessing whether the Eighth Amendment violation here met the *Harlow* test, the Court of Appeals required that the facts of previous cases be "'materially similar' to Hope's situation." This rigid gloss on the qualified immunity standard, though supported by Circuit precedent, is not consistent with our cases.

As we have explained, qualified immunity operates "to ensure that before they are subjected to suit, officers are on notice their conduct is unlawful." For a constitutional right to be clearly established, its contours "must be sufficiently clear that a reasonable official would understand that what he is doing violates that right. This is not to say that an official action is protected by qualified immunity unless the very action in question has previously been held unlawful, but it is to say that in the light of pre-existing law the unlawfulness must be apparent." *Anderson v. Creighton* (1987).

Officers sued in a civil action for damages under 42 U.S.C. §1983 have the same right to fair notice as do defendants charged with the criminal offense defined in 18 U.S.C. §242. Section 242 makes it a crime for a state official to act "willfully" and under color of law to deprive a person of rights protected by the Constitution. In *U.S. v. Lanier*, we held that the defendant was entitled to "fair warning" that his conduct deprived his victim of a constitutional right, and that the standard for determining the adequacy of that warning was the same as the standard for determining whether a constitutional right was "clearly established" in civil litigation under §1983.[56]

We explained:

> This is not to say, of course, that the single warning standard points to a single level of specificity sufficient in every instance. In some circumstances, as when an earlier case expressly leaves open whether a general rule applies to the particular type of conduct at issue, a very high degree

---

56. "The object of the 'clearly established' immunity standard is not different from that of 'fair warning' as it relates to law 'made specific' for the purpose of validly applying §242. The fact that one has a civil and the other a criminal law role is of no significance; both serve the same objective, and in effect the qualified immunity test is simply the adaptation of the fair warning standard to give officials (and, ultimately, governments) the same protection from civil liability and its consequences that individuals have traditionally possessed in the face of vague criminal statutes. To require something clearer than 'clearly established' would, then, call for something beyond 'fair warning.'"

of prior factual particularity may be necessary. But general statements of the law are not inherently incapable of giving fair and clear warning, and in other instances a general constitutional rule already identified in the decisional law may apply with obvious clarity to the specific conduct in question, even though "the very action in question has [not] previously been held unlawful."

Our opinion in *Lanier* thus makes clear that officials can still be on notice that their conduct violates established law even in novel factual circumstances. Indeed, in *Lanier*, we expressly rejected a requirement that previous cases be "fundamentally similar." Although earlier cases involving "fundamentally similar" facts can provide especially strong support for a conclusion that the law is clearly established, they are not necessary to such a finding. The same is true of cases with "materially similar" facts. Accordingly, pursuant to *Lanier*, the salient question that the Court of Appeals ought to have asked is whether the state of the law in 1995 gave respondents fair warning that their alleged treatment of Hope was unconstitutional. It is to this question that we now turn.

IV

The use of the hitching post as alleged by Hope "unnecessarily and wantonly inflicted pain," and thus was a clear violation of the Eighth Amendment. Arguably, the violation was so obvious that our own Eighth Amendment cases gave the respondents fair warning that their conduct violated the Constitution. Regardless, in light of binding Eleventh Circuit precedent, an Alabama Department of Corrections (ADOC) regulation, and a DOJ report informing the ADOC of the constitutional infirmity in its use of the hitching post, we readily conclude that the respondents' conduct violated "clearly established statutory or constitutional rights of which a reasonable person would have known." *Harlow*.

Cases decided by the Court of Appeals for the Fifth Circuit before 1981 are binding precedent in the Eleventh Circuit today. In one of those cases, decided in 1974, the Court of Appeals reviewed a District Court decision finding a number of constitutional violations in the administration of Mississippi's prisons. *Gates v. Collier*. That opinion squarely held that several of those "forms of corporal punishment run afoul of the Eighth Amendment [and] offend contemporary concepts of decency, human dignity, and precepts of civilization which we profess to possess." Among those forms of punishment were "handcuffing inmates to the fence and to cells for long periods of time, . . . and forcing inmates to stand, sit or lie on crates, stumps, or otherwise maintain awkward positions for prolonged periods." The fact that *Gates* found several forms of punishment impermissible does not, as respondents suggest, lessen the force of its holding with respect to handcuffing inmates to cells or fences for long periods of time. Nor, for the purpose of providing fair notice to reasonable officers administering punishment for past misconduct, is there any reason to draw a constitutional distinction between a practice of handcuffing an inmate to a fence for prolonged periods and handcuffing him to a hitching post for seven hours. The Court of Appeals' conclusion to the contrary exposes the danger of a rigid, overreliance on factual similarity. As the Government submits in its brief *amicus curiae*: "No reasonable officer could have concluded that the constitutional holding of *Gates* turned on the fact that inmates were handcuffed to fences or the bars of cells, rather than a specially designed metal bar designated for shackling. If anything, the use of a designated hitching post highlights the constitutional problem." In light of *Gates*, the unlawfulness of the alleged conduct should have been apparent to the respondents.

The reasoning, though not the holding, in a case decided by the Eleventh Circuit in 1987 sent the same message to reasonable officers in that Circuit. In *Ort v. White*, the Court of Appeals held that an officer's temporary denials of drinking water to an inmate who repeatedly refused to do his share of the work assigned to a farm squad "should not be viewed as punishment in the strict sense, but instead as necessary coercive measures undertaken to obtain compliance with a reasonable prison rule, *i.e.*, the requirement that all inmates perform their assigned farm squad duties." "The officer's clear motive was to encourage Ort to comply with the rules and to do the work required of him, after which he would receive the water like everyone else."

The respondents violated clearly established law. Our conclusion that "a reasonable person would have known" of the violation is buttressed by the fact that the DOJ specifically advised the ADOC of the unconstitutionality of its practices before the incidents in this case took place. The DOJ had conducted a study in 1994 of Alabama's use of the hitching post. Among other findings, the DOJ report noted that ADOC's officers consistently failed to comply with the policy of immediately releasing any inmate from the hitching post who agrees to return to work.

The obvious cruelty inherent in this practice should have provided respondents with some notice that their alleged conduct violated Hope's constitutional protection against cruel and unusual punishment. Hope was treated in a way antithetical to human dignity—he was hitched to a post for an extended period of time in a position that was painful, and under circumstances that were both degrading and dangerous. This wanton treatment was not done of necessity, but as punishment for prior conduct. Even if there might once have been a question regarding the constitutionality of this practice, the Eleventh Circuit precedent of *Gates* and *Ort*, as well as the DOJ report condemning the practice, put a reasonable officer on notice that the use of the hitching post under the circumstances alleged by Hope was unlawful. The "fair and clear warning," that these cases provided was sufficient to preclude the defense of qualified immunity at the summary judgment stage.

V

. . .

[I]n applying the objective immunity test of what a reasonable officer would understand, the significance of federal judicial precedent is a function in part of the Judiciary's structure. The unreported District Court opinions cited by the officers are distinguishable on their own terms. But regardless, they would be no match for the Circuit precedents in *Gates v. Collier*, which held that "handcuffing inmates to the fence and to cells for long periods of time," was unconstitutional, and *Ort v. White*, which suggested that it would be unconstitutional to inflict gratuitous pain on an inmate (by refusing him water), when punishment was unnecessary to enforce on-the-spot discipline. The vitality of *Gates* and *Ort* could not seriously be questioned in light of our own decisions holding that gratuitous infliction of punishment is unconstitutional, even in the prison context.

Justice THOMAS, with whom THE CHIEF JUSTICE and Justice SCALIA join, dissenting.

[T]he relevant question is whether it should have been clear to McClaran, Pelzer, and Gates in 1995 that attaching petitioner to a restraining bar violated the Eighth Amendment. As the Court notes, at that time Alabama was the only State that used this particular disciplinary method when prisoners refused to work or disrupted work squads. Previous litigation over Alabama's use of the restraining bar, however, did nothing to warn reasonable Alabama prison guards that attaching a prisoner to a restraining bar was unlawful, let alone that the illegality of such conduct was clearly established. In fact, the outcome of those cases effectively forecloses petitioner's claim that it should have been clear to respondents in 1995 that handcuffing petitioner to a restraining bar violated the Eighth Amendment.

For example, a year before the conduct at issue in this case took place, the United States District Court for the Northern District of Alabama rejected the Eighth Amendment claim of an Alabama prisoner who was attached to a restraining bar for five hours after he refused to work and scuffled with guards. *See Lane v. Findley* (N.D. Ala. 1994). The District Court reasoned that attaching the prisoner to a restraining bar "was a measured response to a potentially volatile situation and a clear warning to other inmates that refusal to work would result in immediate discipline subjecting the offending inmate to similar conditions experienced by work detail inmates rather than a return to inside the institution." The District Court therefore concluded that there was a "substantial penological justification" for attaching the plaintiff to the restraining bar.

Federal District Courts in five other Alabama cases decided before 1995 similarly rejected claims that handcuffing a prisoner to a restraining bar or other stationary object violated the Eighth Amendment. By contrast, petitioner is unable to point to any Alabama decision issued before respondents affixed him to the restraining bar holding that a prison guard engaging in such conduct violated the Eighth Amendment.

In the face of these decisions, and the absence of contrary authority, I find it impossible to conclude that respondents either were "plainly incompetent" or "knowingly violating the law" when they affixed petitioner to the restraining bar. A reasonably competent prison guard attempting to obey the law is not only entitled to look at how courts have recently evaluated his colleagues' prior conduct, such judicial decisions are often the only place that a guard can look for guidance, especially in a situation where a State stands alone in adopting a particular policy.

In concluding that respondents are not entitled to qualified immunity, the Court is understandably unwilling to hold that our Eighth Amendment jurisprudence clearly established in 1995 that attaching petitioner to a restraining bar violated the Eighth Amendment. It is far from "obvious," that respondents, by attaching petitioner to a restraining bar, acted with "deliberate indifference" to his health and safety.

Moreover, if the application of this Court's general Eighth Amendment jurisprudence to the use of a restraining bar was as "obvious" as the Court claims, one wonders how Federal District Courts in Alabama could have repeatedly arrived at the opposite conclusion, and how respondents, in turn, were to realize that these courts had failed to grasp the "obvious."

Unable to base its holding that respondents' conduct violated "'clearly established . . . rights of which a reasonable person would have known,'" on this Court's precedents, the Court instead relies upon "binding Eleventh Circuit precedent, an Alabama Department of Corrections (ADOC) regulation, and a [Department of Justice] report informing the ADOC of the constitutional infirmity in its use of the hitching post." I will address these sources in reverse order.

The Department of Justice report referenced by the Court does nothing to demonstrate that it should have been clear to respondents that attaching petitioner to a restraining bar violated his Eighth Amendment rights. To begin with, the Court concedes that there is no indication the Justice Department's recommendation that the ADOC stop using the restraining bar was ever communicated to respondents, prison guards in the small town of Capshaw, Alabama. In any event, an extraordinarily well-informed prison guard in 1995, who had read both the Justice Department's report and Federal District Court decisions addressing the use of the restraining bar, could have concluded only that there was a dispute as to whether handcuffing a prisoner to a restraining bar constituted an Eighth Amendment violation, not that such a practice was clearly unconstitutional.

Finally, the "binding Eleventh Circuit precedent" relied upon by the Court, was plainly insufficient to give respondents fair warning that their alleged conduct ran afoul of petitioner's Eighth Amendment rights. The Court of Appeals held in *Ort v. White*, that a prison guard did not violate an inmate's Eighth Amendment rights by denying him water when he refused to work, and the Court admits that this holding provides no support for petitioner. Instead, it claims that the "reasoning" in *Ort* "gave fair warning to the respondents that their conduct crossed the line of what is constitutionally permissible." But *Ort* provides at least as much support to respondents as it does to petitioner. For instance, *Ort* makes it abundantly clear that prison guards "have the authority to use that amount of force or those coercive measures reasonably necessary to enforce an inmate's compliance with valid prison rules" so long as such measures are not undertaken "maliciously or sadistically."

Admittedly, the other case upon which the Court relies, *Gates v. Collier*, is more on point. Nevertheless, *Gates* is also inadequate to establish clearly the unlawfulness of respondents' alleged conduct. In *Gates*, the Court of Appeals listed "handcuffing inmates to [a] fence and to cells for long periods of time" as one of many unacceptable forms of "physical brutality and abuse" present at a Mississippi prison. Others included administering milk of magnesia as a form of punishment, depriving inmates of mattresses, hygienic materials, and adequate food, and shooting at and around inmates to keep them standing or moving. The Court of Appeals had "no difficulty in reaching the conclusion that these forms of corporal punishment run afoul of the Eighth Amendment."

It is not reasonable, however, to read *Gates* as establishing a bright-line rule forbidding the attachment of prisoners to a restraining bar. For example, in referring to the fact that prisoners were handcuffed to a fence and cells "for long periods of time," the Court of Appeals did not indicate whether it considered a "long period of time" to be 1 hour, 5 hours, or 25 hours. The Court of Appeals also provided no explanation of the circumstances surrounding these incidents. The opinion does not indicate whether the handcuffed prisoners were given water and suitable restroom breaks or whether they were handcuffed in a bid to induce them to comply with prison rules.

It is most unfortunate that the Court holds that Officer McClaran, Sergeant Pelzer, and Lieutenant Gates are not entitled to qualified immunity. It was not at all clear in 1995 that respondents' conduct violated the Eighth Amendment, and they certainly could not have anticipated that this Court or any other would rule against them on the basis of nonexistent allegations or allegations involving the behavior of other prison guards. For the foregoing reasons, I would affirm the judgment of the Court of Appeals. I respectfully dissent.

* * *

Taylor v. Riojas

141 S. Ct. 52 (2020)

PER CURIAM.

Petitioner Trent Taylor is an inmate in the custody of the Texas Department of Criminal Justice. Taylor alleges that, for six full days in September 2013, correctional officers confined him in a pair of shockingly unsanitary cells. The first cell was covered, nearly floor to ceiling, in "'massive amounts' of feces": all over the floor, the ceiling, the window, the walls, and even "'packed inside the water faucet.'" *Taylor v. Stevens* (CA5 2019). Fearing that his food and water would be contaminated, Taylor did not eat or drink for nearly four days. Correctional officers then moved Taylor to a second, frigidly cold cell, which was equipped with only a clogged drain in the floor to dispose of bodily wastes. Taylor held his bladder for over 24 hours, but he eventually (and involuntarily) relieved himself, causing the drain to overflow and raw sewage to spill across the floor. Because the cell lacked a bunk, and because Taylor was confined without clothing, he was left to sleep naked in sewage.

The Court of Appeals for the Fifth Circuit properly held that such conditions of confinement violate the Eighth Amendment's prohibition on cruel and unusual punishment. But, based on its assessment that "[t]he law wasn't clearly established" that "prisoners couldn't be housed in cells teeming with human waste" "for only six days," the court concluded that the prison officials responsible for Taylor's confinement did not have "'fair warning' that their specific acts were unconstitutional."

The Fifth Circuit erred in granting the officers qualified immunity on this basis. "Qualified immunity shields an officer from suit when she makes a decision that, even if constitutionally deficient, reasonably misapprehends the law governing the circumstances she confronted." *Brosseau v. Haugen* (2004) (per curiam). But no reasonable correctional officer could have concluded that, under the extreme circumstances of this case, it was constitutionally permissible to house Taylor in such deplorably unsanitary conditions for such an extended period of time. *See Hope.* The Fifth Circuit identified no evidence that the conditions of Taylor's confinement were compelled by necessity or exigency. Nor does the summary-judgment record reveal any reason to suspect that the conditions of Taylor's confinement could not have been mitigated, either in degree or duration. And although an officer-by-officer analysis will be necessary on remand, the record suggests that at least some officers involved in Taylor's ordeal were deliberately indifferent to the conditions of his cells.

Confronted with the particularly egregious facts of this case, any reasonable officer should have realized that Taylor's conditions of confinement offended the

Constitution. We therefore grant Taylor's petition for a writ of certiorari, vacate the judgment of the Court of Appeals for the Fifth Circuit, and remand the case for further proceedings consistent with this opinion.

It is so ordered.

* * *

c. Sources of Clearly Established Law

What decisions do courts look to in order to determine what constitutes clearly established law? Across the circuits, precedent may furnish the basis for "clearly established" law if that precedent is from the U.S. Supreme Court or the federal court of appeals with authority over the territory where the violation took place. Federal courts offer divergent approaches as to whether or when they will consider precedent from *other* circuits as a basis for a conclusion that, by way of national consensus, a right was clearly established.[36] In *Ashcroft v. al-Kidd* (2011), the Supreme Court seemed to endorse the view that "a robust consensus of cases of persuasive authority" can clearly establish a right in the absence of controlling authority.

Complexities also arise when a federal government official makes decisions that have nationwide implications across multiple circuits. In the years following the September 11th attacks, high-ranking officials in Washington, D.C. made a range of highly-litigated decisions that gave rise to injuries that were not geographically isolated. Allegations that high-ranking officials in D.C. authorized the seizure and detention of individuals based on their nationalities and Muslim faith, for example, gave rise to Free Exercise and Equal Protection claims in New York. *See Ashcroft v. Iqbal* (2009). Allegations that officials authorized the torture of individuals suspected of being enemy combatants resulted in substantive due process claims in California. *Padilla v. Yoo* (9th Cir. 2012). Under these circumstances, what law controls?

Justice Kennedy articulated this complexity in a concurrence in *Ashcroft v. al-Kidd* (2011). In that case, a Kansas college basketball star named Abdullah al-Kidd was detained by federal authorities who had obtained a material witness warrant. He was detained for 16 days, during which time he alleged that he was strip searched and denied access to an attorney. Al-Kidd then remained on supervised release for 14 months. In a federal lawsuit against Attorney General John Ashcoft, he argued that the detention was based on generalized suspicion that he was a terrorist in violation of the Fourth Amendment, rather than any reasonable belief that he was a material witness in a case. The Court granted qualified immunity

---

36. Tyler Finn, Note, *Qualified Immunity Formalism: "Clearly Established Law" and the Right to Record Police Activity*, 119 Colum. L. Rev. 445, 452 (2019) ("Circuit courts differ as to which bodies of law are relevant to the clearly established analysis. As a general rule, courts look first to binding case law from the Supreme Court or their own circuit. When controlling authority is not dispositive, the circuit courts diverge in their approaches."); *see also* Michael S. Catlett, Note, *Clearly Not Established: Decisional Law and the Qualified Immunity Doctrine*, 47 Ariz. L. Rev. 1031, 1044-50 (2005) (detailing circuit court standards regarding germane circuit authority in qualified immunity analysis).

to the Attorney General, observing in part that only a single district court opinion would have provided sufficient notice of the possibility that the federal government's actions violated the Fourth Amendment. In his concurring opinion, Justice Kennedy wrote:

> A national officeholder intent on retaining qualified immunity need not abide by the most stringent standard adopted anywhere in the United States. And the national officeholder need not guess at when a relatively small set of appellate precedents have established a binding legal rule. If national officeholders were subject to personal liability whenever they confronted disagreement among appellate courts, those officers would be deterred from full use of their legal authority. The consequences of that deterrence must counsel caution by the Judicial Branch, particularly in the area of national security. *See Ashcroft v. Iqbal* (2009). Furthermore, too expansive a view of "clearly established law" would risk giving local judicial determinations the effect of rules with de facto national significance, contrary to the normal process of ordered appellate review.

d.   Procedural Issues

There are two important procedural features of qualified immunity cases. First, as discussed in Chapter 2.B, governmental defendants may immediately appeal denials of qualified immunity at the motion to dismiss or summary judgment stage. *Mitchell v. Forsyth* (1985). Such documents are collateral orders, in that they protect important interests that would be forever lost if the losing party waited until a final judgment for an appeal. If governmental immunities are designed, in part, to protect government officials from undue trials burdens, then a key goal of qualified immunity would be lost if governmental defendants were forced to wait until after a judgment to appeal.

Second, when federal courts encounter motions to dismiss and summary judgment motions that invoke qualified immunity, courts generally adjudge those motions using the same procedural standards that they use to resolve other dispositive motions. At the motion to dismiss stage, allegations in the complaint are accepted as true. *Ashcroft v. Iqbal* (2009); *cf. Wood v. Moss* (2014) (holding that the plaintiff must plead the clarity of the law at the time the officer violated plaintiff's rights even though qualified immunity is an affirmative defense). And at the summary judgment stage, "[t]he evidence of the nonmovant is to be believed, and all justifiable inferences are to be drawn in his favor." *Anderson v. Liberty Lobby, Inc.* (1986). The following case illustrates that latter principle.

Tolan v. Cotton

134 S. Ct. 1861 (2014)

PER CURIAM.

During the early morning hours of New Year's Eve, 2008, police sergeant Jeffrey Cotton fired three bullets at Robert Tolan; one of those bullets hit its target and punctured Tolan's right lung. At the time of the shooting, Tolan was unarmed on his parents' front porch about 15 to 20 feet away from Cotton. Tolan sued, alleging that Cotton had exercised excessive force in violation of the Fourth Amendment. The District Court granted summary judgment to Cotton, and the Fifth Circuit affirmed, reasoning that regardless of whether Cotton used excessive force, he was entitled to qualified immunity because he did not violate any clearly established right. In articulating the factual context of the case, the Fifth Circuit failed to adhere to the axiom that in ruling on a motion for summary judgment, "[t]he evidence of the nonmovant is to be believed, and all justifiable inferences are to be drawn in his favor." *Anderson v. Liberty Lobby, Inc.* (1986). For that reason, we vacate its decision and remand the case for further proceedings consistent with this opinion.

I

A

The following facts, which we view in the light most favorable to Tolan, are taken from the record evidence and the opinions below. At around 2:00 on the morning of December 31, 2008, John Edwards, a police officer, was on patrol in Bellaire, Texas, when he noticed a black Nissan sport utility vehicle turning quickly onto a residential street. The officer watched the vehicle park on the side of the street in front of a house. Two men exited: Tolan and his cousin, Anthony Cooper.

Edwards attempted to enter the license plate number of the vehicle into a computer in his squad car. But he keyed an incorrect character; instead of entering plate number 696BGK, he entered 695BGK. That incorrect number matched a stolen vehicle of the same color and make. This match caused the squad car's computer to send an automatic message to other police units, informing them that Edwards had found a stolen vehicle.

Edwards exited his cruiser, drew his service pistol and ordered Tolan and Cooper to the ground. He accused Tolan and Cooper of having stolen the car. Cooper responded, "That's not true." And Tolan explained, "That's my car." Tolan then complied with the officer's demand to lie face-down on the home's front porch.

As it turned out, Tolan and Cooper were at the home where Tolan lived with his parents. Hearing the commotion, Tolan's parents exited the front door in their pajamas. In an attempt to keep the misunderstanding from escalating into something more, Tolan's father instructed Cooper to lie down, and instructed Tolan and Cooper to say nothing. Tolan and Cooper then remained facedown.

Edwards told Tolan's parents that he believed Tolan and Cooper had stolen the vehicle. In response, Tolan's father identified Tolan as his son, and Tolan's mother explained that the vehicle belonged to the family and that no crime had been committed. Tolan's father explained, with his hands in the air, "[T]his is my nephew. This is my son. We live here. This is my house." Tolan's mother similarly offered, "[S]ir this is a big mistake. This car is not stolen. . . . That's our car."

While Tolan and Cooper continued to lie on the ground in silence, Edwards radioed for assistance. Shortly thereafter, Sergeant Jeffrey Cotton arrived on the scene and drew his pistol. Edwards told Cotton that Cooper and Tolan had exited a stolen vehicle. Tolan's mother reiterated that she and her husband owned both the car Tolan had been driving and the home where these events were unfolding.

Cotton then ordered her to stand against the family's garage door. In response to Cotton's order, Tolan's mother asked, "[A]re you kidding me? We've lived her[e] 15 years. We've never had anything like this happen before."

The parties disagree as to what happened next. Tolan's mother and Cooper testified during Cotton's criminal trial that Cotton grabbed her arm and slammed her against the garage door with such force that she fell to the ground. Tolan similarly testified that Cotton pushed his mother against the garage door. In addition, Tolan offered testimony from his mother and photographic evidence to demonstrate that Cotton used enough force to leave bruises on her arms and back that lasted for days. By contrast, Cotton testified in his deposition that when he was escorting the mother to the garage, she flipped her arm up and told him to get his hands off her. He also testified that he did not know whether he left bruises but believed that he had not.

The parties also dispute the manner in which Tolan responded. Tolan testified in his deposition and during the criminal trial that upon seeing his mother being pushed, he rose to his knees. Edwards and Cotton testified that Tolan rose to his feet.

Both parties agree that Tolan then exclaimed, from roughly 15 to 20 feet away, "[G]et your fucking hands off my mom." The parties also agree that Cotton then drew his pistol and fired three shots at Tolan. Tolan and his mother testified that these shots came with no verbal warning. One of the bullets entered Tolan's chest, collapsing his right lung and piercing his liver. While Tolan survived, he suffered a life-altering injury that disrupted his budding professional baseball career and causes him to experience pain on a daily basis.

B

In May 2009, Cooper, Tolan, and Tolan's parents filed this suit in the Southern District of Texas, alleging claims under Rev. Stat. §1979, 42 U.S.C. §1983. Tolan claimed, among other things, that Cotton had used excessive force against him in violation of the Fourth Amendment. After discovery, Cotton moved for summary judgment, arguing that the doctrine of qualified immunity barred the suit. That doctrine immunizes government officials from damages suits unless their conduct has violated a clearly established right.

The District Court granted summary judgment to Cotton. It reasoned that Cotton's use of force was not unreasonable and therefore did not violate the Fourth Amendment. The Fifth Circuit affirmed, but on a different basis. It declined to decide whether Cotton's actions violated the Fourth Amendment. Instead, it held that even if Cotton's conduct did violate the Fourth Amendment, Cotton was entitled to qualified immunity because he did not violate a clearly established right.

In reaching this conclusion, the Fifth Circuit began by noting that at the time Cotton shot Tolan, "it was . . . clearly established that an officer had the right to use deadly force if that officer harbored an objective and reasonable belief that a suspect presented an 'immediate threat to [his] safety.'" The Court of Appeals reasoned that Tolan failed to overcome the qualified-immunity bar because "an objectively-reasonable officer in Sergeant Cotton's position could have . . . believed" that Tolan "presented an 'immediate threat to the safety of the officers.'" In support of this conclusion, the court relied on the following facts: the front porch had been "dimly-lit"; Tolan's mother had "refus[ed] orders to remain quiet and calm": and Tolan's words had amounted to a "verba[l] threa[t]." Most critically, the court also relied on the purported fact that Tolan was "moving to intervene in" Cotton's handling of his mother, and that Cotton therefore could reasonably have feared for his life. Accordingly, the court held, Cotton did not violate clearly established law in shooting Tolan.

II

A

In resolving questions of qualified immunity at summary judgment, courts engage in a two-pronged inquiry. The first asks whether the facts, "[t]aken in the light most favorable to the party asserting the injury, . . . show the officer's conduct violated a [federal] right[.]" *Saucier v. Katz* (2001). When a plaintiff alleges excessive force during an investigation or arrest, the federal right at issue is the Fourth Amendment right against unreasonable seizures. *Graham v. Connor* (1989). The inquiry into whether this right was violated requires a balancing of "'the nature and quality of the intrusion on the individual's Fourth Amendment interests against the importance of the governmental interests alleged to justify the intrusion.'" *Tennessee v. Garner* (1985).

The second prong of the qualified-immunity analysis asks whether the right in question was "clearly established" at the time of the violation. *Hope v. Pelzer* (2002). Governmental actors are "shielded from liability for civil damages if their actions did not violate 'clearly established statutory or constitutional rights of which a reasonable person would have known.'" "[T]he salient question . . . is whether the state of the law" at the time of an incident provided "fair warning" to the defendants "that their alleged [conduct] was unconstitutional."

Courts have discretion to decide the order in which to engage these two prongs. *Pearson v. Callahan* (2009). But under either prong, courts may not resolve genuine disputes of fact in favor of the party seeking summary judgment. This is not a rule specific to qualified immunity; it is simply an application of the more general rule that a "judge's function" at summary judgment is not "to weigh the evidence and determine the truth of the matter but to determine whether there is a genuine issue for trial." *Anderson, supra.* Summary judgment is appropriate only if "the movant shows that there is no genuine issue as to any material fact and the movant is entitled to judgment as a matter of law." Fed. Rule Civ. Proc. 56(a). In making that determination, a court must view the evidence "in the light most favorable to the opposing party." *Adickes v. S.H. Kress & Co.* (1970)

Our qualified-immunity cases illustrate the importance of drawing inferences in favor of the nonmovant, even when, as here, a court decides only the clearly-established prong of the standard. In cases alleging unreasonable searches or seizures, we have instructed that courts should define the "clearly established" right at issue on the basis of the "specific context of the case." *Saucier, supra.* Accordingly, courts must take care not to define a case's "context" in a manner that imports genuinely disputed factual propositions.

B

In holding that Cotton's actions did not violate clearly established law, the Fifth Circuit failed to view the evidence at summary judgment in the light most favorable to Tolan with respect to the central facts of this case. By failing to credit evidence that contradicted some of its key factual conclusions, the court improperly weighed the evidence and resolved disputed issues in favor of the moving party.

First, the court relied on its view that at the time of the shooting, the Tolans' front porch was "dimly-lit." The court appears to have drawn this assessment from Cotton's statements in a deposition that when he fired at Tolan, the porch was " 'fairly dark,' " and lit by a gas lamp that was " 'decorative.' " In his own deposition, however, Tolan's father was asked whether the gas lamp was in fact "more decorative than illuminating." He said that it was not. Moreover, Tolan stated in his deposition that two floodlights shone on the driveway during the incident, and Cotton acknowledged that there were two motion-activated lights in front of the house. And Tolan confirmed that at the time of the shooting, he was "not in darkness."

Second, the Fifth Circuit stated that Tolan's mother "refus[ed] orders to remain quiet and calm," thereby "compound[ing]" Cotton's belief that Tolan "presented an immediate threat to the safety of the officers." But here, too, the court did not credit directly contradictory evidence. Although the parties agree that Tolan's mother repeatedly informed officers that Tolan was her son, that she lived in the home in front of which he had parked, and that the vehicle he had been driving belonged to her and her husband, there is a dispute as to how calmly she provided this information. Cotton stated during his deposition that Tolan's mother was "very agitated" when she spoke to the officers. By contrast, Tolan's mother testified at Cotton's criminal trial that she was neither "aggravated" nor "agitated."

Third, the Court concluded that Tolan was "shouting" and "verbally threatening" the officer, in the moments before the shooting. The court noted, and the parties agree, that while Cotton was grabbing the arm of his mother, Tolan told Cotton, "[G]et your fucking hands off my mom." But Tolan testified that he "was not screaming." And a jury could reasonably infer that his words, in context, did not amount to a statement of intent to inflict harm. Tolan's mother testified in Cotton's criminal trial that he slammed her against a garage door with enough force to cause bruising that lasted for days. A jury could well have concluded that a reasonable officer would have heard Tolan's words not as a threat, but as a son's plea not to continue any assault of his mother.

Fourth, the Fifth Circuit inferred that at the time of the shooting, Tolan was "moving to intervene in Sergeant Cotton's" interaction with his mother. The court appears to have credited Edwards' account that at the time of the shooting, Tolan was on both feet "[i]n a crouch" or a "charging position" looking as if he was going to move forward. Tolan testified at trial, however, that he was on his knees when Cotton shot him, a fact corroborated by his mother. Tolan also testified in his deposition that he "wasn't going anywhere," and emphasized that he did not "jump up."

Considered together, these facts lead to the inescapable conclusion that the court below credited the evidence of the party seeking summary judgment and failed properly to acknowledge key evidence offered by the party opposing that motion. And while this Court is not equipped to correct every perceived error coming from the lower federal courts, we intervene here because the opinion below reflects a clear misapprehension of summary judgment standards in light of our precedents.

The witnesses on both sides come to this case with their own perceptions, recollections, and even potential biases. It is in part for that reason that genuine disputes are generally resolved by juries in our adversarial system. By weighing the evidence and reaching factual inferences contrary to Tolan's competent evidence, the court below neglected to adhere to the fundamental principle that at the summary judgment stage, reasonable inferences should be drawn in favor of the non-moving party.

Applying that principle here, the court should have acknowledged and credited Tolan's evidence with regard to the lighting, his mother's demeanor, whether he shouted words that were an overt threat, and his positioning during the shooting. We instead vacate the Fifth Circuit's judgment so that the court can determine whether, when Tolan's evidence is properly credited and factual inferences are reasonably drawn in his favor, Cotton's actions violated clearly established law.

* * *

e.   The Future of Qualified Immunity

Critiques of qualified immunity have proliferated in recent years, with jurists and commentators charging that the doctrine is untextual,[37] ahistorical,[38] and an unjustifiable impediment to accountability.[39] Critics sometimes contend that the doctrine is based on empirically false assumptions. For example, the doctrine focuses on the impact that damages suits can have on government officials who make incorrect legal judgments on issues governed by unclear law. Yet all but a bare fraction of judgments are paid out by government employers by way of indemnification.[40] The fact that the officer almost never pays undermines the central deterrent function of liability in damages.

Qualified immunity, in turn, also has defenders. Some have emphasized the existence of good-faith defenses at the common law.[41] Commentators have also defended the doctrine as a matter of policy. Defenders have raised questions, for example, about whether it is fair to hold an official accountable for violating a legal standard that was not clearly established when the officer acted, and whether government agents can be expected to fulfill their lawful duties with the specter

---

37. Ziglar v. Abbasi, 137 S. Ct. 1843 (2017).

38. Baude, *supra* note 35, at 45.

39. Jamison v. McClendon, 476 F. Supp. 3d 386 (S.D. Miss. 2020).

40. Joanna C. Schwartz, *Police Indemnification*, 89 N.Y.U. L. Rev. 885 (2014).

41. Scott A. Keller, *Qualified and Absolute Immunity at Common Law*, 73 Stan. L. Rev. 1337, 1338 (2021).

of sweeping liability hanging over their every decision.[42] Moreover, given that governments ultimately pay for officer suits through indemnification, the eradication of qualified immunity would result in increased strain on the public fisc, either directly or perhaps through insurance premiums.[43] Other commentators have relied on stare decisis to defend the doctrine.[44]

The following subpart contextualizes prominent policy discussions about qualified immunity within America's broader contemporary conversations about race and policing. The cases in this subpart help show how lower courts have reconciled the doctrine of qualified immunity with broader debates about racial justice.[45] The subsequent subpart enumerates a non-exhaustive list of proposals for reform that have appeared in judicial opinions and legislative efforts.

(1)   Qualified Immunity and The Reckoning

Estate of Jones by Jones v. City of Martinsburg

961 F.3d 661 (4th Cir. 2020)

In 2013, Wayne Jones, a black man experiencing homelessness, was stopped by law enforcement in Martinsburg, West Virginia for walking alongside, rather than on, the sidewalk. By the end of this encounter, Jones would be dead. Armed only with a knife tucked into his sleeve, he was tased four times, hit in the brachial plexus, kicked, and placed in a choke hold. In his final moments, he lay on the ground between a stone wall and a wall of five police officers, who collectively fired 22 bullets. Jones's Estate sued under 42 U.S.C. §1983, bringing a Fourth Amendment claim against the officers. The district court granted summary judgment to the defendants on both claims, holding that the officers are protected by qualified immunity. We reverse the grant of summary judgment to the officers on qualified immunity grounds, as a reasonable jury could find that Jones was both secured and incapacitated in the final moments before his death.

I

Around 11:30 p.m. on March 13, 2013, Officer Paul Lehman of the Martinsburg Police Department (MPD) was on patrol when he spotted Jones walking in the road, instead of on the sidewalk, near downtown Martinsburg, West Virginia. A state law and a city ordinance both require that pedestrians use sidewalks when available. Jones was a 50-year-old black man and weighed 162 pounds. He was experiencing homelessness and had been diagnosed with schizophrenia.

---

42. Nathan Chapman, *Fair Notice, the Rule of Law, and Reforming Qualified Immunity*, 75 FLA L. REV. 1 (2023).

43. *Cf.* Ernest A. Young, *Its Hour Come Round at Last? State Sovereign Immunity and the Great State Debt Crisis of the Early Twenty-First Century*, 35 HARV. J.L. & PUB. POL'Y 593, 593-96 (2012) (describing state sovereign immunity as means of protecting states during times of economic crisis including, presciently and presently, the Great Recession).

44. Aaron L. Nielson & Christopher J. Walker, *A Qualified Defense of Qualified Immunity*, 93 NOTRE DAME L. REV. 1853 (2018).

45. *See* Brandon Hasbrouck, *Movement Judges*, 97 N.Y.U. L. REV. 631, 685 (2022).

Lehman followed Jones in his marked police car for one minute. Lehman then parked his car near Jones, exited the vehicle, and asked Jones why he was walking in the street. Lehman asked Jones for identification; Jones replied that he did not have any identification. Lehman then asked to search him for weapons. Jones first asked, "What's a weapon?" When Lehman explained that this meant "anything—guns, knives, clubs," Jones acknowledged that he did have "something."

The encounter quickly escalated. Lehman called the MPD for backup and began to demand that Jones put his hands on the police car. Jones did not comply and instead tried to move away from Lehman. Lehman began to repeatedly shout, "Put your hands on the car." Jones responded, "What are you trying to do?"; "What do you want?"; and "What did I do to you?" Lehman never answered Jones's questions. Lehman then pulled out his taser and discharged it on Jones. Officer Daniel North reached the scene at approximately the same time that Lehman was discharging his taser. North tased Jones as well. The officers reported that the tasers appeared to have no effect on Jones. According to Lehman, Jones then "hit" Lehman in the face in such a way that his toboggan was pulled over his eyes.

Jones broke away and ran down the street. North pursued him on foot and was the first officer to catch up with him. According to North, Jones's hands were "about to go up," and he "took that as [Jones] may try to assault him." Unless he was clairvoyant, North could not have known that Jones's hands were "about" to be raised. North then "struck [Jones] in the brachial."

Officer William Staub arrived at the scene and ran toward Jones and North. Jones had "cornered himself" in "a stoop entranceway to a bookstore, up a couple steps." North stated that he told Jones to "just get on the ground, just listen to what we're saying," to which Jones replied: "I didn't do anything wrong." Staub said that "North had his taser out but he wasn't doing nothing" when Staub approached. Jones then moved his hands up. The night of the incident, Staub said that "the guy kind of put his hands up like 'alright' [resigned tone], so me and North both kind of grabbed his hands." Staub and North grabbed Jones, and the three tumbled down the stairs such that North was thrown away from Staub and Jones. Staub "chipped" a bone in his thumb during the fall. Staub wrestled Jones to the ground and put him in "a choke hold, just to kind of stop him from resisting." A loud choking or gurgling sound, which seems to be coming from Jones, is audible on Staub's audio recorder at this time.

Lehman rejoined the group, and Officers Eric Neely and Erik Herb arrived, bringing the number of MPD officers on the scene to five. Jones was on the ground with his feet facing down, moving in a swimmer's kick-like motion. One officer can be heard loudly calling Jones a "motherf**ker." At least one officer can be seen kicking Jones as he lay on the ground. Officer Neely tased Jones for a third time, and North then applied "a drive stun without any probes." The officers reported that these efforts to stun Jones had no visible effect.

Staub was on his knees on the ground and still had Jones in a choke hold when he felt "like a scratch on my hand," which he initially "didn't think much of" because they "were rolling around on the concrete." Then, "a second or two later," at approximately the same time that Officer Neely tased Jones, Staub felt "a sharp poke in [his] side," which "alarmed" him. Staub reported that he then "saw the subject's right hand with a fixed blade knife in his hand" and shouted, "He's got a knife! He's got a knife!" Neely also reportedly saw "a weapon in [Jones's] right hand." At least one officer called to "Get back, get back!"

Having learned of the knife, the officers simultaneously drew back approximately five feet. As they moved back, Jones's left arm dropped lifelessly. Jones was motionless on the ground, laying "with his right side on the ground" and his "right elbow . . . on the ground." All five officers drew their firearms and formed a semi-circle around the recumbent Jones, who was between the officers and the bookstore wall. The officers ordered Jones to drop the weapon. Jones remained motionless and did not verbally respond. Lehman reported that Jones "did not make any overt acts with the knife towards the officers." On the night of the incident, Staub similarly reported that as the officers stepped back, Jones "still had the f**king knife in his hand and he wasn't f**king doing nothing." Seconds later, the five officers fired a total of 22 rounds at Jones, causing wounds, and killing him where he lay on the sidewalk. Neely fired the first shot, but the next rounds immediately followed. Most of the bullets entered Jones's back and buttocks. Jones died shortly before midnight.

In the immediate aftermath on the scene, one or two of the shooting officers called for emergency medical services, but none of them rendered aid themselves. When searching Jones's lifeless body, officers found a small fixed blade knife tucked into his right sleeve. After being told that state police were coming to investigate, officers can be heard saying that the incident would be a "cluster" and that they were going to "have to gather some f**king story."

At the time of the shooting, MPD's aggression response policy was to "meet your aggression with the suspect's aggression." Under that policy, incidents of physical force must be necessary, objectively reasonable, and proportionate. MPD did not have any program or policy pertaining to interactions with people with mental illness. According to the deposition testimony of Chief of Police Kevin Miller, he decided to conduct such a training after the shooting.

One month after Jones's death, his Estate sued the City of Martinsburg and then-unknown police officers in federal court. The amended complaint alleged three §1983 claims that the five named officers used excessive force in violation of the Fourth Amendment.

II

We consider whether the five officers who shot and killed Jones as he lay on the ground are protected by qualified immunity. Awarding the officers summary judgment on qualified immunity grounds is only appropriate if they demonstrate "that there is no genuine dispute as to any material fact and [that they are] entitled to judgment as a matter of law." Fed. R. Civ. P. 56(a). We view the evidence in the light most favorable to the Estate and draw any reasonable inferences in its favor.

Qualified immunity shields police officers who commit constitutional violations from liability when, based on "clearly established law," they "could reasonably believe that their actions were lawful." To determine whether qualified immunity applies, we conduct a two-step inquiry, in either order: (1) whether a constitutional violation occurred; and (2) whether the right was clearly established at the time of the violation (here, on March 13, 2013).

To determine whether this right was clearly established, we must first define the right at the "appropriate level of specificity." Although *Tennessee v. Garner* (1985), and *Graham v. Connor* (1989), guide our analysis of whether deadly force is unconstitutionally excessive, those cases define the right generally and "do not by themselves create clearly established law outside 'an obvious case.'" *White v. Pauly* (2017) (citation omitted); *see also Graham* (holding that among the factors to be considered under the Fourth Amendment's "objective reasonableness" standard are "the severity of the crime at issue, whether the suspect poses an immediate threat to the safety of the officers or others, and whether he is actively resisting arrest or attempting to evade arrest by flight"). In the context of an ongoing police encounter such as this one, we "focus on the moment that the force is employed."

Here, there are two distinct facts that separately define Jones's right to be free from excessive force at an appropriate level of specificity: (1) Jones, although armed, had been secured by the officers immediately before he was released and shot; and (2) Jones, although armed, was incapacitated at the time he was shot. Because it was clearly established that officers may not shoot a secured or incapacitated person, the officers are not entitled to qualified immunity.

A

First, the officers are not protected by qualified immunity because, viewing the evidence in the light most favorable to the Estate, Jones was secured before he was shot. A reasonable jury viewing the videos could find that Jones was secured when he was pinned to the ground by five officers. . . . [I]n 2013, it was already clearly established that suspects can be secured without handcuffs when they are pinned to the ground, and that such suspects cannot be subjected to further force. Indeed, as early as 1993, this Court held that a reasonable officer would know that once he had pinned a 100-pound woman to the ground, he should not further shove her into the pavement, cracking her teeth. *Kane v. Hargis* (4th Cir. 1993). Like Jones, Kane was not handcuffed. Just as one officer pinning a 100-pound suspect secured her, so too could five officers pinning 162-pound Jones secure him.

Moreover, before Jones's death, this Court held that a police officer used excessive force when he continued to tase a domestic violence suspect after that suspect had dropped his weapon and fallen to the ground. *Meyers v. Baltimore Cty.* (4th Cir. 2013).

Given the relatively inaccessible location of the knife, and the physical inability to wield it given his position on the ground, the number of officers on Jones, and Jones's physical state by this time, it would be particularly reasonable to find that Jones was secured while still armed. A jury could reasonably find that Jones was secured before the officers backed away, and that the officers could have disarmed Jones and handcuffed him, rather than simultaneously release him.

If Jones was secured, then police officers could not constitutionally release him, back away, and shoot him. To do so violated Jones's constitutional right to be free from deadly force under clearly established law.

B

Second, and even were it to find that Jones was not secured, a jury could still reasonably find that he was incapacitated by the time of the shooting. Jones had been tased four times, hit in the brachial plexus, kicked, and placed in a choke hold, at which point gurgling can be heard in the video. A jury could reasonably infer that Jones was struggling to breathe. He lay on his side and stomach on the concrete with five officers on him. And when the officers got up and backed away, viewing the evidence in the light most favorable to the Estate, the officers saw his left arm fall limply to his body.

Unsurprisingly, it was clearly established in 2013 that officers may not use force against an incapacitated suspect. In 2011, this Court held that "a reasonable officer would have recognized that deadly force was no longer needed after [a suspect] was injured and helpless with his back on the ground." By shooting an incapacitated, injured person who was not moving, and who was laying on his knife, the police officers crossed a "bright line" and can be held liable. "Indeed, it is just common sense that [shooting] someone who is already incapacitated is not justified under these circumstances." . . .

[IV]

Wayne Jones was killed just over one year before the Ferguson, Missouri shooting of Michael Brown would once again draw national scrutiny to police shootings of black people in the United States. Seven years later, we are asked to decide whether it was clearly established that five officers could not shoot a man 22 times as he lay motionless on the ground. Although we recognize that our police officers are often asked to make split-second decisions, we expect them to do so with respect for the dignity and worth of black lives. Before the ink dried on this opinion, the FBI opened an investigation into yet another death of a black man at the hands of police, this time George Floyd in Minneapolis. This has to stop. To award qualified immunity at the summary judgment stage in this case would signal absolute immunity for fear-based use of deadly force, which we cannot accept. The district court's grant of summary judgment on qualified immunity grounds is reversed, and the dismissal of that claim is hereby vacated.

* * *

Jamison v. McClendon

476 F. Supp. 3d 386 (S.D. Miss. 2020)

CARLTON W. REEVES, United States District Judge.
Clarence Jamison wasn't jaywalking.[1]
He wasn't outside playing with a toy gun.[2]
He didn't look like a "suspicious person."[3]
He wasn't suspected of "selling loose, untaxed cigarettes."[4]

---

1. That was Michael Brown. *See* Max Ehrenfreund, *The Risks of Walking While Black in Ferguson*, WASH. POST (Mar. 4, 2015).

2. That was 12-year-old Tamir Rice. *See* Zola Ray, *This Is the Toy Gun That Got Tamir Rice Killed 3 Years Ago Today*, NEWSWEEK (Nov. 22, 2017).

3. That was Elijah McClain. *See* Claire Lampen, *What We Know About the Killing of Elijah McClain*, THE CUT (July 5, 2020).

4. That was Eric Garner. *See* Assoc. Press, *From Eric Garner's Death to Firing of NYPD Officer: A Timeline of Key Events*, USA TODAY (Aug. 20, 2019).

He wasn't suspected of passing a counterfeit $20 bill.[5]

He didn't look like anyone suspected of a crime.[6]

He wasn't mentally ill and in need of help.[7]

He wasn't assisting an autistic patient who had wandered away from a group home.[8]

He wasn't walking home from an after-school job.[9]

He wasn't walking back from a restaurant.[10]

He wasn't hanging out on a college campus.[11]

He wasn't standing outside of his apartment.[12]

He wasn't inside his apartment eating ice cream.[13]

He wasn't sleeping in his bed.[14]

He wasn't sleeping in his car.[15]

He didn't make an "improper lane change."[16]

He didn't have a broken tail light.[17]

---

5. That was George Floyd. *See* Jemima McEvoy, *New Transcripts Reveal How Suspicion Over Counterfeit Money Escalated into the Death of George Floyd*, FORBES (July 8, 2020).

6. That was Philando Castile and Tony McDade. *See* Andy Mannix, *Police audio: Officer stopped Philando Castile on robbery suspicion*, STAR TRIB. (July 12, 2016); Meredith Deliso, *LGBTQ Community Calls for Justice after Tony McDade, a Black Trans Man, Shot and Killed by Police*, ABC NEWS (June 2, 2020).

7. That was Jason Harrison. *See* Byron Pitts et al., *The Deadly Consequences When Police Lack Proper Training to Handle Mental Illness Calls*, ABC NEWS (Sept. 30, 2015).

8. That was Charles Kinsey. *See Florida Policeman Shoots Autistic Man's Unarmed Black Therapist*, BBC (July 21, 2016).

9. That was 17-year-old James Earl Green. *See* Robert Luckett, *In 50 Years from Gibbs-Green Deaths to Ahmaud Arbery Killing, White Supremacy Still Lives*, JACKSON FREE PRESS (May 8, 2020); *see also* Robert Luckett, *50 Years Ago, Police Fired on Students at a Historically Black College*, N.Y. TIMES (May 14, 2020); Rachel James-Terry & L.A. Warren, *"All Hell Broke Loose": Memories Still Vivid of Jackson State Shooting 50 Years Ago*, CLARION LEDGER (May 15, 2020).

10. That was Ben Brown. *See* Notice to Close File, U.S. Dep't of Justice, Civil Rights Div. (Mar. 24, 2017), *available at* https://www.justice.gov/crt/case-document/benjamin-brown-notice-close-file; *see also* Jackson State Univ., Center for University-Based Development, *The Life of Benjamin Brown, 50 Years Later*, W. JACKSON (May 11, 2017).

11. That was Phillip Gibbs. *See* James-Terry & Warren, *supra*.

12. That was Amadou Diallo. *See Police Fired 41 Shots When They Killed Amadou Diallo. His Mom Hopes Today's Protests Will Bring Change*, CBS NEWS (June 9, 2020).

13. That was Botham Jean. *See* Bill Hutchinson, *Death of an Innocent Man: Timeline of Wrong-Apartment Murder Trial of Amber Guyger*, ABC NEWS (Oct. 2, 2019).

14. That was Breonna Taylor. *See* Amina Elahi, *"Sleeping While Black": Louisville Police Kill Unarmed Black Woman*, NPR (May 13, 2020).

15. That was Rayshard Brooks. *See* Jacob Sullum, *Was the Shooting of Rayshard Brooks "Lawful but Awful"?*, REASON (June 15, 2020).

16. That was Sandra Bland. *See* Ben Mathis-Lilley & Elliott Hannon, *A Black Woman Named Sandra Bland Got Pulled Over in Texas and Died in Jail Three Days Later. Why?*, SLATE (July 16, 2015).

17. That was Walter Scott. *See* Michael E. Miller et al., *How a Cellphone Video Led to Murder Charges Against a Cop in North Charleston, S.C.*, WASH. POST (Apr. 8, 2015).

He wasn't driving over the speed limit.[18]

He wasn't driving under the speed limit.[19]

No, Clarence Jamison was a Black man driving a Mercedes convertible. As he made his way home to South Carolina from a vacation in Arizona, Jamison was pulled over and subjected to one hundred and ten minutes of an armed police officer badgering him, pressuring him, lying to him, and then searching his car top-to-bottom for drugs.

Nothing was found. Jamison isn't a drug courier. He's a welder.

Unsatisfied, the officer then brought out a canine to sniff the car. The dog found nothing. So nearly two hours after it started, the officer left Jamison by the side of the road to put his car back together.

Thankfully, Jamison left the stop with his life. Too many others have not.

The Constitution says everyone is entitled to equal protection of the law—even at the hands of law enforcement. Over the decades, however, judges have invented a legal doctrine to protect law enforcement officers from having to face any consequences for wrongdoing. The doctrine is called "qualified immunity." In real life it operates like absolute immunity.

In a recent qualified immunity case, the Fourth Circuit wrote: "Although we recognize that our police officers are often asked to make split-second decisions, we expect them to do so with respect for the dignity and worth of black lives." *Estate of Jones v. City of Martinsburg, W. Va.* (4th Cir. 2020), as amended (June 10, 2020).

This Court agrees. Tragically, thousands have died at the hands of law enforcement over the years, and the death toll continues to rise. Countless more have suffered from other forms of abuse and misconduct by police. Qualified immunity has served as a shield for these officers, protecting them from accountability.

This Court is required to apply the law as stated by the Supreme Court. Under that law, the officer who transformed a short traffic stop into an almost two-hour, life-altering ordeal is entitled to qualified immunity. The officer's motion seeking as much is therefore granted.

But let us not be fooled by legal jargon. Immunity is not exoneration. And the harm in this case to one man sheds light on the harm done to the nation by this manufactured doctrine.

As the Fourth Circuit concluded, "This has to stop."

I. Factual and Procedural Background

On July 29, 2013, Clarence Jamison was on his way home to Neeses, South Carolina after vacationing in Phoenix, Arizona. Jamison was driving on Interstate 20 in a 2001 Mercedes-Benz CLK-Class convertible. He had purchased the vehicle 13 days before from a car dealer in Pennsylvania.

---

18. That was Hannah Fizer. *See* Luke Nozicka, *"Where's the gun?": Family of Sedalia Woman Killed by Deputy Skeptical of Narrative*, KANSAS CITY STAR (June 15, 2020).

19. That was Ace Perry. *See* Jodi Leese Glusco, *Run-In with Sampson Deputy Leaves Driver Feeling Unsafe*, WRAL (Feb. 14, 2020).

As Jamison drove through Pelahatchie, Mississippi, he passed Officer Nick McClendon, a white officer with the Richland Police Department, who was parked in a patrol car on the right shoulder. Officer McClendon says he decided to stop Jamison because the temporary tag on his car was "folded over to where [he] couldn't see it." Officer McClendon pulled behind Jamison and flashed his blue lights. Jamison immediately pulled over to the right shoulder.

As Officer McClendon approached the passenger side of Jamison's car, Jamison rolled down the passenger side window. Officer McClendon began to speak with Jamison when he reached the window.

[McClendon requested to search Jamison's car four times, to which Jamison responded in the negative. McClendon made a fifth request.] The conversation became "heated." Jamison became frustrated and gave up. [Officer McClendon searched the car and brought a drug sniffing dog to inspect as well.] Officer McClendon admitted in his deposition that he did not find "anything suspicious whatsoever." In total, the stop lasted one hour and 50 minutes.

Jamison subsequently filed this lawsuit against Officer McClendon and the City of Pelahatchie, Mississippi. He raised three claims.

In "Claim 1," Jamison alleged that the defendants violated his Fourth Amendment rights by "falsely stopping him, searching his car, and detaining him." Jamison's second claim, brought under the Fourteenth Amendment, stated that the defendants should be held liable for using "race [as] a motivating factor in the decision to stop him, search his car, and detain him." Jamison's third claim alleged a violation of the Fourth Amendment by Officer McClendon for "recklessly and deliberately causing significant damage to Mr. Jamison's car by conducting an unlawful search of the car in an objectively unreasonable manner amounting to an unlawful seizure of his property."

The defendants filed a motion for summary judgment.

[II.] Historical Context

In accordance with Supreme Court precedent, we begin with a look at the "origins" of the relevant law.

A. Section 1983: A New Hope

Jamison brings his claims under 42 U.S.C. §1983, a statute that has its origins in the Civil War and "Reconstruction," the brief era that followed the bloodshed. If the Civil War was the only war in our nation's history dedicated to the proposition that Black lives matter, Reconstruction was dedicated to the proposition that Black futures matter, too. [Among the] successful legislative effort[s] was the passage of the Thirteenth, Fourteenth, and Fifteenth Amendments, also known as the "Reconstruction Amendments."

For the first time in its history, the United States saw a Black man selected to serve in the United States Senate (two from Mississippi, in fact—Hiram Revels and Blanche K. Bruce), the establishment of public school systems across the South, and increased efforts to pass local anti-discrimination laws. It was a glimpse of a different America.

These "emancipationist" efforts existed alongside white supremacist backlash, terror, and violence.

The terrorism in Mississippi was unparalleled. During the first three months of 1870, 63 Black Mississippians "were murdered . . . and nobody served a day for these crimes."[67] In 1872, the U.S. Attorney for Mississippi wrote that Klan violence was ubiquitous and that "only the presence of the army kept the Klan from overrunning north Mississippi completely."[68]

Many of the perpetrators of racial terror were members of law enforcement. It was a twisted law enforcement, though, as it prevented the laws of the era from being enforced.

"Congress sought to respond to 'the reign of terror imposed by the Klan upon black citizens and their white sympathizers in the Southern States.' "[75] It passed The Ku Klux Act of 1871, which "targeted the racial violence in the South undertaken by the Klan, and the failure of the states to cope with that violence."[76]

The Act's mandate was expansive. Section 2 of the Act provided for civil and criminal sanctions against those who conspired to deprive people of the "equal protection of the laws." Section 1 of the Ku Klux Act, now codified as 42 U.S.C. §1983, uniquely targeted state officials The Act reflected Congress's recognition that – to borrow the words of today's abolitionists — "the whole damn system [was] guilty as hell."[83]

Some parts of the Act were fairly successful. Led by federal prosecutors at the Department of Justice, "federal grand juries, many interracial, brought 3,384 indictments against the KKK, resulting in 1,143 convictions."[84] One of Mississippi's U.S. Senators reported that the Klan largely "suspended their operations" in most of the State.[85] Frederick Douglass proclaimed that "peace has come to many places," and the "slaughter of our people [has] so far ceased."[86]

Douglass had spoken too soon. "By 1873, many white Southerners were calling for 'Redemption' — the return of white supremacy and the removal of rights for blacks — instead of Reconstruction."[87] The federal system largely abandoned the emancipationist efforts of the Reconstruction Era.[88] And the violence returned. . . . Federal courts joined the retreat and decided to place their hand on the scale for white supremacy. As Katherine A. Macfarlane writes:

> In several decisions, beginning with 1873's Slaughter-House Cases, the Supreme Court limited the reach of the Fourteenth Amendment and the

---

67. Ron Chernow, Grant 703 (2017).

68. Stephen Cresswell, *Enforcing the Enforcement Acts: The Department of Justice in Northern Mississippi 1870-1890*, 53 J. S. Hist. 421, 421 (Aug. 1987).

75. Baxter v. Bracey, 140 S. Ct. (2020) (Thomas, J., dissenting from the denial of certiorari) (quoting Briscoe v. LaHue (1983)).

76. Katherine A. Macfarlane, *Accelerated Civil Rights Settlements in the Shadow of Section 1983*, 2018 Utah L. Rev. 639, 661 (2018) (citation omitted).

83. Zach Lass, *Lowe v. Raemisch: Lowering the Bar of the Qualified Immunity Defense*, 96 Denv. L. Rev. 177, 180 (2018) (citation omitted).

84. Chernow, *supra* at 708.

85. *Id.* at 710.

86. *Id.* at 709.

87. *Reconstruction vs. Redemption*, Nat'l Endowment Human. (Feb. 11, 2014).

88. David W. Blight, Race and Reunion: The Civil War in American Memory 137 (2001).

statutes passed pursuant to the power it granted Congress. By 1882, the Court had voided the Ku Klux Act's criminal conspiracy section, a provision "aimed at lynchings and other mob actions of an individual or private nature."

As a result of the Court's narrowed construction of both the Fourteenth Amendment and the civil rights statutes enacted pursuant to it, the Ku Klux Act's "scope and effectiveness" shrunk. The Court never directly addressed Section 1 of the Act, but those sections of the Act [were] left "largely forgotten."[92]

For almost a century, Redemption prevailed. "Lynchings, race riots and other forms of unequal treatment were permitted to abound in the South and elsewhere without power in the federal government to intercede." Jim Crow ruled, and Jim Crow meant that "[a]ny breach of the system could mean one's life." While Reconstruction "saw the basic rights of blacks to citizenship established in law," our country failed "to ensure their political and economic rights."[93] Our courts' "involvement in that downfall and its consequences could not have been greater."[96]

Though civil rights protection was largely abandoned at the federal level, activists continued to fight to realize the broken promise of Reconstruction. The Afro-American League, the Niagara Movement, the National Negro Conference (later renamed the NAACP) and other civil rights groups formed to challenge lynching and the many oppressive laws and practices of discrimination. One group's efforts — the Citizens' Committee — led to a lawsuit designed to create an Equal Protection Clause challenge to Louisiana's segregationist laws on railroad cars. Unfortunately, the ensuing case, *Plessy v. Ferguson* (1896), resulted in the Supreme Court's decision to affirm the racist system of "separate but equal" accommodations. Despite this setback, civil rights activism continued, intensifying after the Supreme Court's *Brown v. Board* decision and resulting in many of the civil rights laws we have today.[99]

It was against this backdrop that the Supreme Court attempted to resuscitate Section 1983.[100] In 1961, the Court decided *Monroe v. Pape*, a case where "13 Chicago police officers broke into [a Black family's] home in the early morning, routed them from bed, made them stand naked in the living room, and ransacked every room, emptying drawers and ripping mattress covers." The Justices held that Section 1983 provides a remedy for people deprived of their constitutional rights by state officials. Accordingly, the Court found that the Monroe family could pursue their lawsuit against the officers.

Section 1983's purpose was finally realized, namely " 'to interpose the federal courts between the States and the people, as guardians of the people's federal rights.' " The statute has since become a powerful "vehicle used by private parties to vindicate their constitutional rights against state and local government officials."

Section 1983 provides, in relevant part:

Every person who, under color of any statute, ordinance, regulation, custom, or usage, of any State or Territory or the District of Columbia,

---

92. Macfarlane, *supra* at 661–62 (citations omitted).

93. Derrick A. Bell, Jr., RACE, RACISM, AND AMERICAN LAW 48 (6th ed. 2008).

96. *Id.* at 49.

99. Macfarlane, *supra* at 665.

100. Sheldon Nahmad, *Section 1983 Discourse: The Move from Constitution to Tort*, 77 GEO. L.J. 1719, 1722 (1989).

subjects, or causes to be subjected, any citizen of the United States or other person within the jurisdiction thereof to the deprivation of any rights, privileges, or immunities secured by the Constitution and laws, shall be liable to the party injured in an action at law, suit in equity, or other proper proceeding for redress. . . .

Invoking this statute, Jamison contends that Officer McClendon violated his Fourth Amendment right to be free from unreasonable searches and seizures.

B.   Qualified Immunity: The Empire Strikes Back

Just as the 19th century Supreme Court neutered the Reconstruction-era civil rights laws, the 20th century Court limited the scope and effectiveness of Section 1983 after *Monroe v. Pape*. The doctrine of qualified immunity is perhaps the most important limitation.

[T]he doctrine of qualified immunity was born, with roots right here in Mississippi. In *Pierson v. Ray* (1967), "15 white and Negro Episcopal clergymen . . . attempted to use segregated facilities at an interstate bus terminal in Jackson, Mississippi, in 1961." The clergymen were arrested and charged with violation of a Mississippi statute—later held unconstitutional—that made it a misdemeanor "to congregate[ ] with others in a public place under circumstances such that a breach of the peace" may occur and to "refuse[ ] to move on when ordered to do so by a police officer." The clergymen sued under Section 1983. In their defense, the officers argued that "they should not be liable if they acted in good faith and with probable cause in making an arrest under a statute that they believed to be valid."

The Supreme Court agreed. It held that officers should be shielded from liability when acting in good faith—at least in the context of constitutional violations that mirrored the common law tort of false arrest and imprisonment.

Subsequent decisions "expanded the policy goals animating qualified immunity."[115] The Supreme Court eventually characterized the doctrine as an "attempt to balance competing values: not only the importance of a damages remedy to protect the rights of citizens, but also the need to protect officials who are required to exercise discretion and the related public interest in encouraging the vigorous exercise of official authority."[116]

A review of our qualified immunity precedent makes clear that the Court has dispensed with any pretense of balancing competing values. Our courts have shielded a police officer who shot a child while the officer was attempting to shoot the family dog;[117] prison guards who forced a prisoner to sleep in cells "covered in feces" for days;[118] police officers who stole over $225,000 worth of property;[119] a deputy who body-slammed a woman after she simply "ignored [the deputy's] command and walked away;"[120] an officer who seriously burned a woman after detonating

---

115. Joanna C. Schwartz, *How Qualified Immunity Fails*, 127 YALE L.J. 2, 14 (2017) (citations omitted).

116.   Harlow v. Fitzgerald (1982).

117.   Corbitt v. Vickers, 929 F.3d 1304, 1323 (11th Cir. 2019), *cert. denied*, No. 19-679, (2020).

118.   Taylor v. Stevens (5th Cir. 2019).

119.   Jessop v. City of Fresno (9th Cir. 2019), *cert. denied*, No. 19-1021 (2020).

120.   Kelsay v. Ernst, 933 F.3d 975, 980 (8th Cir. 2019), *cert. denied*, No. 19-682 (2020).

a "flashbang" device in the bedroom where she was sleeping;[121] an officer who deployed a dog against a suspect who "claim[ed] that he surrendered by raising his hands in the air";[122] and an officer who shot an unarmed woman eight times after she threw a knife and glass at a police dog that was attacking her brother.[123]

If Section 1983 was created to make the courts "'guardians of the people's federal rights,'" what kind of guardians have the courts become? One only has to look at the evolution of the doctrine to answer that question.

Once, qualified immunity protected officers who acted in good faith. The doctrine now protects all officers, no matter how egregious their conduct, if the law they broke was not "clearly established." This "clearly established" requirement is not in the Constitution or a federal statute. The Supreme Court came up with it in 1982. In 1986, the Court then "evolved" the qualified immunity defense to spread its blessings "to all but the plainly incompetent or those who knowingly violate the law." *Malley v. Briggs* (1986). It further ratcheted up the standard in 2011, when it added the words "beyond debate." *Ashcroft v. al-Kidd* (2011). In other words, "for the law to be clearly established, it must have been 'beyond debate' that [the officer] broke the law."

Each step the Court has taken toward absolute immunity heralded a retreat from its earlier pronouncements. Although the Court held in 2002 that qualified immunity could be denied "in novel factual circumstances,"[137] the Court's track record in the intervening two decades renders naïve any judges who believe that pronouncement.

Federal judges now spend an inordinate amount of time trying to discern whether the law was clearly established "beyond debate" at the time an officer broke it. But it is a fool's errand to ask people who love to debate whether something is debatable.

Consider *McCoy v. Alamu*, a 2020 case in which a correctional officer violated a prisoner's Constitutional rights when he sprayed a chemical agent in the prisoner's face, without provocation. The Fifth Circuit then asked if the illegality of the use of force was clearly established beyond debate. The prison didn't think the use of force was debatable: it found the spraying unnecessary and against its rules. It put the officer on three months' probation. Yet the appellate court disregarded the warden's judgment and held for the officer. The case involved only a "single use of pepper spray," after all, and the officer hadn't used "the full can." Based on these factual distinctions, the court concluded that "the spraying crossed that line. But it was not beyond debate that it did, so the law wasn't clearly established."

These kinds of decisions are increasingly common.

Fifth Circuit Judge Don Willett has succinctly explained the problem with the clearly established analysis:

> Section 1983 meets Catch-22. Plaintiffs must produce precedent even as fewer courts are producing precedent. Important constitutional questions

---

121. Dukes v. Deaton (11th Cir. 2017).

122. Baxter v. Bracey (6th Cir. 2018), *cert. denied* (2020).

123. Willingham v. Loughnan (11th Cir. 2001), *cert. granted,* judgment vacated, 537 U.S. 801, 123 S. Ct. 68, 154 L.Ed.2d 2 (2002).

137. Hope v. Pelzer (2002).

go unanswered precisely because no one's answered them before. Courts then rely on that judicial silence to conclude there's no equivalent case on the books. No precedent = no clearly established law = no liability. An Escherian Stairwell. Heads government wins, tails plaintiff loses.[158]

To be clear, it is unnecessary to ascribe malice to the appellate judges deciding these terrible cases. No one wants to be reversed by the Supreme Court, and the Supreme Court's summary reversals of qualified immunity cases are ever-more biting. . . .

There are numerous critiques of qualified immunity by lawyers,[164] judges,[165] and academics.[166] Yet qualified immunity is the law of the land and the undersigned is bound to follow its terms absent a change in practice by the Supreme Court.

[*After a lengthy analysis, the district court granted qualified immunity to the officer.*]

III

I do not envy the task before the Supreme Court. Overturning qualified immunity will undoubtedly impact our society. Yet, the status quo is extraordinary and unsustainable. Just as the Supreme Court swept away the mistaken doctrine of "separate but equal," so too should it eliminate the doctrine of qualified immunity.

Earlier this year, the Court explained something true about wearing the robe:

> Every judge must learn to live with the fact he or she will make some mistakes; it comes with the territory. But it is something else entirely to perpetuate something we all know to be wrong only because we fear the consequences of being right.[288]

Let us waste no time in righting this wrong.

* * *

---

158. Zadeh v. Robinson (5th Cir. 2019) (Willett, J., concurring in part and dissenting in part).

164. *See, e.g.*, Brief of Cross-Ideological Groups Dedicated to Ensuring Official Accountability, Restoring the Public's Trust in Law Enforcement, and Promoting the Rule of Law as Amici Curiae in Support of Petitioner, Baxter v. Bracey (2020) (No. 18-1287).

165. *See, e.g.*, Horvath v. City of Leander (5th Cir. 2020) (Ho, J., concurring in part and dissenting in part); *Zadeh* (Willett, J., concurring in part and dissenting in part); Manzanares v. Roosevelt Cty. Adult Det. Ctr. (D.N.M. 2018); Est. of Smart v. City of Wichita (D. Kan. Aug. 7, 2018); Thompson v. Clark (E.D.N.Y. June 26, 2018); Baldwin v. City of Estherville (Iowa 2018) (Appel, J., dissenting); James A. Wynn, Jr., *As a judge, I have to follow the Supreme Court. It Should Fix This Mistake*, WASH. POST (June 12, 2020).

166. *See, e.g.*, Joanna C. Schwartz, *The Case Against Qualified Immunity*, 93 NOTRE DAME L. REV. 1797 (2018); William Baude, *Is Qualified Immunity Unlawful?*, 106 CALIF. L. REV. 45 (2018); Fred O. Smith, Jr., *Abstention in the Time of Ferguson*, 131 HARV. L. REV. 2283, 2305 (2018); John C. Jeffries, *What's Wrong with Qualified Immunity*, 62 FLA. L. REV. 851, 856 (2010); Christina Brooks Whitman, *Emphasizing the Constitutional in Constitutional Torts*, 72 CHI.-KENT L. REV. 661, 678 (1997).

288. Ramos v. La. (2020).

(2) Proposals for Reform

The following four proposals are among those that have been offered in recent years to reform qualified immunity. Not listed here are proposals to reform state law barriers to constitutional accountability for violations of state constitutions. *See generally* Alexander Reinert et al., *New Federalism and Civil Rights Enforcement*, 116 Nw. U. L. REV. 737, 742-43 (2021) (describing and proposing state-level reforms). In reading these proposals, consider whether suits against individuals should be the sole focus of federal doctrinal or legislative reforms or whether reformers should expand suits against the entities that employ, deploy, and train those individuals.

1. *Revisiting qualified immunity for calculated choices.* Justice Clarence Thomas has, in a series of opinions, raised concerns about the absence of a textual or historical basis for qualified immunity.[46] In a recent opinion dissenting from the denial of certiorari, he observed, "Aside from these problems, the one-size-fits-all doctrine is also an odd fit for many cases because the same test applies to officers who exercise a wide range of responsibilities and functions . . . But why should [government officials], who have time to make calculated choices about enacting or enforcing unconstitutional policies, receive the same protection as a police officer who makes a split-second decision to use force in a dangerous setting?" Implicit in this critique is the potentiality of constructing a doctrine that retains qualified immunity for split-second decisions, but rejects it for calculated decisions.

2. *Elimination of qualified immunity for law enforcement.* The George Floyd Justice in Policing Act—which passed in the House of Representatives twice and stalled in United States Senate—would have eliminated qualified immunity for state and local law enforcement officials.[47]

3. *Ending qualified immunity.* The Ending Qualified Immunity Act, first introduced in June 2020, would have wholly "remove[d] the defense of qualified immunity" in federal constitutional suits against officials acting under the color of state law.[48]

4. *Qualified immunity as affirmative defense.* The proposed Reforming Qualified Immunity Act would prohibit courts from inoculating a state or local official from suit unless defendants could affirmatively show, with some particularity, that the conduct at issue was authorized by law.[49]

---

46. Ziglar v. Abbasi (2017) (opinion concurring in part and concurring in judgment); Baxter v. Bracey (2020) (opinion dissenting from denial of certiorari); Hoggard v. Rhodes (2021) (opinion dissenting from denial of certiorari).

47. *See* H.R. 7120-116th Congress, George Floyd Justice in Policing Act of 2020 (2019-2020).

48. H.R. 7085 -116th Congress, Ending Qualified Immunity Act (2019-2020).

49. S.4036 -116th Congress, Reforming Qualified Immunity Act (2019-2020). Specifically, the proposal would seek to remove the existing doctrine of qualified immunity and instead provide that an individual defendant "shall not be liable" if the defendant reasonably believed that his or her conduct was lawful and either (1) the conduct at issue was "specifically authorized or required" by federal or state law, or (2) a federal or state court had issued a final decision holding that "the specific conduct alleged to be unlawful was consistent with the Constitution of the United States and Federal laws."

C.   FEDERAL COURT RELIEF AGAINST TRIBAL GOVERNMENTS AND TRIBAL GOVERNMENT OFFICERS

Federal lawsuits against the governments and officials of American Indian Tribal Nations present some of the same questions as suits against state governments and officials. As the cases below show, federal courts have considered whether there are implied rights of action to enforce federal statutes against Indian tribes, as well as tribal sovereign immunity and the relevance of *Ex parte Young* to suits against tribal officials.

At the same time, the unique status of tribal governments raises unique questions about the propriety of federal judicial intervention. Under settled U.S. Supreme Court precedent, Indian tribes are pre-constitutional sovereigns whose authority does not depend upon the U.S. Constitution. As such, tribes are not bound by the Constitution, including the Bill of Rights. Tribal governments are, however, bound by tribal law, including tribal civil rights laws enforceable in tribal courts. In 1968, moreover, Congress enacted the Indian Civil Rights Act (ICRA) to impose many of the protections of the Bill of Rights upon tribal governments. ICRA is but one example of a federal statute that imposes duties upon tribal governments. As you read the following cases, pay close attention to similarities and differences between tribal governments and other sovereigns when it comes to federal courts law.

1.   Causes of Action

As we have seen, the Reconstruction Era Congress enacted statutes, including §1983, that today are the basis for litigation challenging state action. We need not look far to see the unique history of Indian tribal governments and their relationships with the federal government. Section 2 of the Fourteenth Amendment explicitly referred to Indians when it provided that "[r]epresentatives shall be apportioned among the several States according to their respective numbers, counting the whole number of persons in each State, *excluding Indians not taxed.*" This constitutional provision echoed Section 2 of Article I, which similarly excluded "Indians not taxed" for apportionment purposes in the same sentence that included the Three-Fifths Clause. Together with the Indian Commerce Clause, which authorized Congress to regulate "commerce with the Indian tribes," the Indians Not Taxed Clauses explicitly recognize the existence of Indians as separate peoples. *Worcester v. Ga.* (1832), which is discussed in Chapter 1, in turn recognized that Indian tribal nations have inherent sovereign authority over tribal territories and analogized tribes to foreign states and nations.

Tribes have constituted governments in an exercise of their inherent sovereignty. Hundreds of Indian tribes, for example, have courts that adjudicate both civil and criminal matters. Individual litigants may—and do—bring claims against tribal governments under tribal law in tribal courts.

The question naturally arises: What is the basis, if any, for federal courts to entertain federal causes of action against tribal governments and tribal government officers? One possibility is that federal judicial review of tribal government action is based upon an exercise of raw power by the federal government, something akin to conquest by judicial action. Federal Indian law and policy has not been consistent since the Founding. During certain periods, including the last decades of the nineteenth century following Reconstruction, the U.S. government pursued a policy of forced assimilation of Indian peoples. To accomplish this goal, Congress enacted statutes such as the Major Crimes Act, extending some federal criminal jurisdiction into Indian Country, and the General Allotment Act, designed to allot (that is, to break up) tribal land ownership. In this period, the Supreme Court held in cases such as *U.S. v. Kagama* (1887), and *Lone Wolf v. Hitchcock* (1903), that Congress had plenary authority to legislate in Indian affairs stemming from the United States's territorial sovereignty and its relationship with Indian peoples. Even as Congress acted to assimilate Indian peoples, the Court did not abandon precedent, such as *Worcester*, that held that Indian tribes had inherent sovereign authority. In *Talton v. Mayes* (1896), the Court held that the Fifth Amendment did not apply to tribal governments, while at the same time suggesting that Congress could legislate otherwise.

In the modern era, the Court has sought to refine its account of the source of Congress's authority to legislate in Indian affairs. More recent cases have attributed this authority variously to the Indian Commerce Clause or to a combination of that Clause and other enumerated powers, such as the federal government's authority to enter into treaties. Under contemporary doctrine, Congress may legislate to limit the authority of tribal governments under federal law, including by enacting statutes that create individual rights against tribal action.

The Indian Civil Rights Act of 1968 (ICRA) is one of these statutes. Congress enacted ICRA during a moment of transition during two periods of federal Indian law and policy. From the 1950s until the late 1960s, Congress adopted a policy of terminating federal recognition of tribal governments and subjecting tribal territories to state jurisdiction. This policy included Public Law 280, a federal statute that authorized some (but by no means all) states to assume criminal jurisdiction and a limited civil jurisdiction in Indian Country. Public Law 280 thus upended the principle, recognized in *Worcester*, that states do not have jurisdiction over tribal territories. By the late 1960s, however, federal policy was starting to shift towards supporting tribal self-determination. Much of the shift was due to the work of tribal advocates and social movement activists who pressed for major reforms to federal Indian law. ICRA's enactment straddled these two periods—the "Termination Era" and the "Self-Determination Era."

ICRA was and remains controversial within Indian Country. Testimony during the congressional hearings on ICRA included evidence of some civil rights violations by tribal governments. But many witnesses, including tribal representatives, testified to systemic violations of Indian civil rights by state governments and the federal government. ICRA did not, however, address their concerns.[50] The Act, which is described in the case below, applied many (though not all) of the

---

50. For discussion of the history of ICRA and *Santa Clara Pueblo v. Martinez* (1978), as well as academic responses to them, see Angela R. Riley, *(Tribal) Sovereignty and Illiberalism*, 95 CALIF. L. REV. 800, 809-20 (2007).

provisions of the Bill of Rights to tribal governments. Crucially, however, Congress did not explicitly authorize a federal cause of action to enforce ICRA through civil relief. Rather, Congress enacted a limited habeas provision.

Federal courts soon addressed the question whether to imply a federal cause of action to enforce ICRA against tribal governments or tribal government officials. Lower federal courts took jurisdiction of suits to enforce ICRA, concluding that it implied a federal cause of action. The Supreme Court confronted this question in 1978 with *Santa Clara Pueblo v. Martinez*. As Judith Resnik has noted, "*Santa Clara Pueblo* is a major case in federal Indian law," one that illustrates "how the United States government conceives of its citizens as holding simultaneous membership in two political entities."[51] It is also a major case in federal courts law, which illustrates its themes of separation of powers and federalism — in this case, however, it is not a question of state vs. federal authority, but rather the allocation of authority between Native nations and the federal government.[52]

When *Santa Clara Pueblo* was decided, federal courts law was more favorable to the implication of causes of action than it is today. There did not need to be clear evidence of congressional intent to imply a cause of action. Moreover, there arguably was an apparent need for a federal forum to adjudicate federal civil rights claims arising under ICRA, which Congress modeled on federal constitutional law. On the other hand, the Indian canon of construction in federal Indian law called for courts to construe ambiguous statutes in favor of Indian tribes. In the face of congressional silence, the Indian canon might have called for federal courts to refrain from implying a federal cause of action. As you read *Santa Clara Pueblo*, pay close attention to how the Court analyzed the questions of inherent tribal sovereignty and the availability of federal remedies for federal rights.

The case arose from a dispute about tribal membership in Santa Clara Pueblo. As the original occupants of part of what is now New Mexico, the Santa Clara Pueblo had faced first Spanish and then U.S. colonialism, including the loss of lands to non-Indians. In 1935, Santa Clara Pueblo adopted an Indian Reorganization Act Constitution based upon a model provided by the federal Bureau of Indian Affairs. Four years later, the Pueblo adopted a membership ordinance that several decades later gave rise to a federal lawsuit alleging gender discrimination in violation of ICRA.

Santa Clara Pueblo v. Martinez

436 U.S. 49 (1978)

Justice MARSHALL delivered the opinion of the Court.

This case requires us to decide whether a federal court may pass on the validity of an Indian tribe's ordinance denying membership to the children of certain female tribal members.

---

51. Judith Resnik, *Dependent Sovereigns: Indian Tribes, States, and Federal Courts*, 56 U. CHI. L. REV. 671, 674 (1989).

52. *Id.* at 675-76.

Petitioner Santa Clara Pueblo is an Indian tribe that has been in existence for over 600 years. Respondents, a female member of the tribe and her daughter, brought suit in federal court against the tribe and its Governor, petitioner Lucario Padilla, seeking declaratory and injunctive relief against enforcement of a tribal ordinance denying membership in the tribe to children of female members who marry outside the tribe, while extending membership to children of male members who marry outside the tribe. Respondents claimed that this rule discriminates on the basis of both sex and ancestry in violation of Title I of the Indian Civil Rights Act of 1968 (ICRA), 25 U.S.C. §§1301-1303, which provides in relevant part that "[n]o Indian tribe in exercising powers of self-government shall . . . deny to any person within its jurisdiction the equal protection of its laws." §1302(8).

Title I of the ICRA does not expressly authorize the bringing of civil actions for declaratory or injunctive relief to enforce its substantive provisions. The threshold issue in this case is thus whether the Act may be interpreted to impliedly authorize such actions, against a tribe or its officers, in the federal courts. For the reasons set forth below, we hold that the Act cannot be so read.

I

Respondent Julia Martinez is a full-blooded member of the Santa Clara Pueblo, and resides on the Santa Clara Reservation in Northern New Mexico. In 1941 she married a Navajo Indian with whom she has since had several children, including respondent Audrey Martinez. Two years before this marriage, the Pueblo passed the membership ordinance here at issue, which bars admission of the Martinez children to the tribe because their father is not a Santa Claran.[2] Although the children were raised on the reservation and continue to reside there now that they are adults, as a result of their exclusion from membership they may not vote in tribal elections or hold secular office in the tribe; moreover, they have no right to remain on the reservation in the event of their mother's death, or to inherit their mother's home or her possessory interests in the communal lands.

After unsuccessful efforts to persuade the tribe to change the membership rule, respondents filed this lawsuit in the United States District Court for the District

---

2. The ordinance, enacted by the Santa Clara Pueblo Council pursuant to its legislative authority under the Constitution of the Pueblo, establishes the following membership rules:

1. All children born of marriages between members of the Santa Clara Pueblo shall be members of the Santa Clara Pueblo.
2. . . . [C]hildren born of marriages between male members of the Santa Clara Pueblo and non-members shall be members of the Santa Clara Pueblo.
3. Children born of marriages between female members of the Santa Clara Pueblo and non-members shall not be members of the Santa Clara Pueblo.
4. Persons shall not be naturalized as members of the Santa Clara Pueblo under any circumstances.

Respondents challenged only subparagraphs 2 and 3. By virtue of subparagraph 4, Julia Martinez's husband is precluded from joining the Pueblo and thereby assuring the children's membership pursuant to subparagraph 1.

of New Mexico, on behalf of themselves and others similarly situated. Petitioners moved to dismiss the complaint on the ground that the court lacked jurisdiction to decide intratribal controversies affecting matters of tribal self-government and sovereignty. The District Court rejected petitioners' contention.

Following a full trial, the District Court found for petitioners on the merits. While acknowledging the relatively recent origin of the disputed rule, the District Court nevertheless found it to reflect traditional values of patriarchy still significant in tribal life. The court recognized the vital importance of respondents' interests, but also determined that membership rules were "no more or less than a mechanism of social . . . self-definition," and as such were basic to the tribe's survival as a cultural and economic entity. In sustaining the ordinance's validity under the "equal protection clause" of the ICRA, 25 U.S.C. §1302(8), the District Court concluded that the balance to be struck between these competing interests was better left to the judgment of the Pueblo.

On respondents' appeal, the Court of Appeals disagreed with the District Court's ruling on the merits. While recognizing that standards of analysis developed under the Fourteenth Amendment's Equal Protection Clause were not necessarily controlling in the interpretation of this statute, the Court of Appeals apparently concluded that because the classification was one based upon sex it was presumptively invidious and could be sustained only if justified by a compelling tribal interest. Because of the ordinance's recent vintage, and because in the court's view the rule did not rationally identify those persons who were emotionally and culturally Santa Clarans, the court held that the tribe's interest in the ordinance was not substantial enough to justify its discriminatory effect.

II

Indian tribes are "distinct, independent political communities, retaining their original natural rights" in matters of local self-government. *Worcester v. Ga.* (1832). Although no longer "possessed of the full attributes of sovereignty," they remain a "separate people, with the power of regulating their internal and social relations." *U.S. v. Kagama* (1886). They have power to make their own substantive law in internal matters, and to enforce that law in their own forums.

As separate sovereigns pre-existing the Constitution, tribes have historically been regarded as unconstrained by those constitutional provisions framed specifically as limitations on federal or state authority. Thus, in *Talton v. Mayes* (1896), this Court held that the Fifth Amendment did not "operat[e] upon" "the powers of local self-government enjoyed" by the tribes. In ensuing years the lower federal courts have extended the holding of *Talton* to other provisions of the Bill of Rights, as well as to the Fourteenth Amendment.

As the Court in *Talton* recognized, however, Congress has plenary authority to limit, modify or eliminate the powers of local self-government which the tribes otherwise possess. *See, e.g., U.S. v. Kagama* (1886). Title I of the ICRA represents an exercise of that authority. In 25 U.S.C. §1302, Congress acted to modify the effect of *Talton* and its progeny by imposing certain restrictions upon tribal governments similar, but not identical, to those contained in the Bill of Rights and the

Fourteenth Amendment.[8] In 25 U.S.C. §1303, the only remedial provision expressly supplied by Congress, the "privilege of the writ of habeas corpus" is made "available to any person, in a court of the United States, to test the legality of his detention by order of an Indian tribe."

Petitioners concede that §1302 modifies the substantive law applicable to the tribe; they urge, however, that Congress did not intend to authorize federal courts to review violations of its provisions except as they might arise on habeas corpus. They argue, further, that Congress did not waive the tribe's sovereign immunity from suit. Respondents, on the other hand, contend that §1302 not only modifies the substantive law applicable to the exercise of sovereign tribal powers, but also authorizes civil suits for equitable relief against the tribe and its officers in federal courts. We consider these contentions first with respect to the tribe.

III

Indian tribes have long been recognized as possessing the common-law immunity from suit traditionally enjoyed by sovereign powers. This aspect of tribal sovereignty, like all others, is subject to the superior and plenary control of Congress. But "without congressional authorization," the "Indian Nations are exempt from suit." *U.S. v. U.S. Fidelity & Guaranty Co.* (1940).

It is settled that a waiver of sovereign immunity "'cannot be implied but must be unequivocally expressed.'" *U.S. v. Testan* (1976). Nothing on the face of Title I of the ICRA purports to subject tribes to the jurisdiction of the federal courts in civil

---

8. Section 1302 in its entirety provides that:

No Indian tribe in exercising powers of self-government shall—

(1) make or enforce any law prohibiting the free exercise of religion, or abridging the freedom of speech, or of the press, or the right of the people peaceably to assemble and to petition for a redress of grievances;

(2) violate the right of the people to be secure in their persons, houses, papers, and effects against unreasonable search and seizures, nor issue warrants, but upon probable cause, supported by oath or affirmation, and particularly describing the place to be searched and the person or thing to be seized;

(3) subject any person for the same offense to be twice put in jeopardy;

(4) compel any person in any criminal case to be a witness against himself;

(5) take any private property for a public use without just compensation;

(6) deny to any person in a criminal proceeding the right to a speedy and public trial, to be informed of the nature and cause of the accusation, to be confronted with the witnesses against him, to have compulsory process for obtaining witnesses in his favor, and at his own expense to have the assistance of counsel for his defense;

(7) require excessive bail, impose excessive fines, inflict cruel and unusual punishments, and in no event impose for conviction of any one offense any penalty or punishment greater than imprisonment for a term of six months or a fine of $500, or both;

(8) deny to any person within its jurisdiction the equal protection of its laws or deprive any person of liberty or property without due process of law;

(9) pass any bill of attainder or ex post facto law; or

(10) deny to any person accused of an offense punishable by imprisonment the right, upon request, to a trial by jury of not less than six persons.

actions for injunctive or declaratory relief. In the absence here of any unequivocal expression of contrary legislative intent, we conclude that suits against the tribe under the ICRA are barred by its sovereign immunity from suit.

IV

As an officer of the Pueblo, petitioner Lucario Padilla is not protected by the tribe's immunity from suit. *Cf. Ex parte Young* (1908). We must therefore determine whether the cause of action for declaratory and injunctive relief asserted here by respondents, though not expressly authorized by the statute, is nonetheless implicit in its terms.

In addressing this inquiry, we must bear in mind that providing a federal forum for issues arising under §1302 constitutes an interference with tribal auton-omy and self-government beyond that created by the change in substantive law itself. Even in matters involving commercial and domestic relations, we have rec-ognized that "subject[ing] a dispute arising on the reservation among reservation Indians to a forum other than the one they have established for themselves," *Fisher v. Dist. Ct.* (1976), may "undermine the authority of the tribal cour[t] . . . and hence . . . infringe on the right of the Indians to govern themselves." *Williams v. Lee* (1959). *A fortiori*, resolution in a foreign forum of intratribal disputes of a more "public" character, such as the one in this case, cannot help but unsettle a tribal government's ability to maintain authority. Although Congress clearly has power to authorize civil actions against tribal officers, and has done so with respect to habeas corpus relief in §1303, a proper respect both for tribal sovereignty itself and for the plenary authority of Congress in this area cautions that we tread lightly in the absence of clear indications of legislative intent.

With these considerations of "Indian sovereignty . . . [as] a backdrop against which the applicable . . . federal statut[e] must be read," *McClanahan v. Ariz. State Tax Comm'n* (1973), we turn now to those factors of more general relevance in determining whether a cause of action is implicit in a statute not expressly provid-ing one. We note at the outset that a central purpose of the ICRA and in particular of Title I was to "secur[e] for the American Indian the broad constitutional rights afforded to other Americans," and thereby to "protect individual Indians from arbi-trary and unjust actions of tribal governments." S. Rep. No. 841, 90th Cong., 1st Sess., 5-6 (1967). There is thus no doubt that respondents, American Indians living on the Santa Clara Reservation, are among the class for whose especial benefit this legislation was enacted. Moreover, we have frequently recognized the propriety of inferring a federal cause of action for the enforcement of civil rights, even when Congress has spoken in purely declarative terms. These precedents, however, are simply not dispositive here. Not only are we unpersuaded that a judicially sanc-tioned intrusion into tribal sovereignty is required to fulfill the purposes of the ICRA, but to the contrary, the structure of the statutory scheme and the legisla-tive history of Title I suggest that Congress' failure to provide remedies other than habeas corpus was a deliberate one.

Two distinct and competing purposes are manifest in the provisions of the ICRA: In addition to its objective of strengthening the position of individual tribal members vis-à-vis the tribe, Congress also intended to promote the well-established federal "policy of furthering Indian self-government." *Morton v. Mancari* (1974).

This commitment to the goal of tribal self-determination is demonstrated by the provisions of Title I itself. Section 1302, rather than providing in wholesale fashion for the extension of constitutional requirements to tribal governments, as had been initially proposed, selectively incorporated and in some instances modified the safeguards of the Bill of Rights to fit the unique political, cultural, and economic needs of tribal governments. Thus, for example, the statute does not prohibit the establishment of religion, nor does it require jury trials in civil cases, or appointment of counsel for indigents in criminal cases.

Where Congress seeks to promote dual objectives in a single statute, courts must be more than usually hesitant to infer from its silence a cause of action that, while serving one legislative purpose, will disserve the other. Creation of a federal cause of action for the enforcement of rights created in Title I, however useful it might be in securing compliance with §1302, plainly would be at odds with the congressional goal of protecting tribal self-government. Not only would it undermine the authority of tribal forums, but it would also impose serious financial burdens on already "financially disadvantaged" tribes.

Moreover, contrary to the reasoning of the court below, implication of a federal remedy in addition to habeas corpus is not plainly required to give effect to Congress' objective of extending constitutional norms to tribal self-government. Tribal forums are available to vindicate rights created by the ICRA, and §1302 has the substantial and intended effect of changing the law which these forums are obliged to apply. Tribal courts have repeatedly been recognized as appropriate forums for the exclusive adjudication of disputes affecting important personal and property interests of both Indians and non-Indians. Nonjudicial tribal institutions have also been recognized as competent law-applying bodies. Under these circumstances, we are reluctant to disturb the balance between the dual statutory objectives which Congress apparently struck in providing only for habeas corpus relief.

Our reluctance is strongly reinforced by the specific legislative history underlying 25 U.S.C. §1303. This history, extending over more than three years, indicates that Congress' provision for habeas corpus relief, and nothing more, reflected a considered accommodation of the competing goals of "preventing injustices perpetrated by tribal governments, on the one hand, and, on the other, avoiding undue or precipitous interference in the affairs of the Indian people."

Congress considered and rejected proposals for federal review of alleged violations of the Act arising in a civil context. As initially introduced, the Act would have required the Attorney General to "receive and investigate" complaints relating to deprivations of an Indian's statutory or constitutional rights, and to bring "such criminal or other action as he deems appropriate to vindicate and secure such right to such Indian." Notwithstanding the screening effect this proposal would have had on frivolous or vexatious lawsuits, it was bitterly opposed by several tribes. The Crow Tribe representative stated:

> This [bill] would in effect subject the tribal sovereignty of self-government to the Federal government. . . . [B]y its broad terms [it] would allow the Attorney General to bring any kind of action as he deems appropriate. By this bill, any time a member of the tribe would not be satisfied with an action by the [tribal] council, it would allow them [*sic*] to file a complaint with the Attorney General and subject the tribe to a multitude of investigations and threat of court action.

In a similar vein, the Mescalero Apache Tribal Council argued that "[i]f the perpetually dissatisfied individual Indian were to be armed with legislation such as proposed in [this bill] he could disrupt the whole of a tribal government." In response, this provision for suit by the Attorney General was completely eliminated from the ICRA. At the same time, Congress rejected a substitute proposed by the Interior Department that would have authorized the Department to adjudicate civil complaints concerning tribal actions, with review in the district courts available from final decisions of the agency.

Given this history, it is highly unlikely that Congress would have intended a private cause of action for injunctive and declaratory relief to be available in the federal courts to secure enforcement of §1302. . . .

V

Although Congress explored the extent to which tribes were adhering to constitutional norms in both civil and criminal contexts, its legislative investigation revealed that the most serious abuses of tribal power had occurred in the administration of criminal justice. In light of this finding, and given Congress' desire not to intrude needlessly on tribal self-government, it is not surprising that Congress chose at this stage to provide for federal review only in habeas corpus proceedings.

By not exposing tribal officials to the full array of federal remedies available to redress actions of federal and state officials, Congress may also have considered that resolution of statutory issues under §1302, and particularly those issues likely to arise in a civil context, will frequently depend on questions of tribal tradition and custom which tribal forums may be in a better position to evaluate than federal courts. Our relations with the Indian tribes have "always been . . . anomalous . . . and of a complex character." *U.S. v. Kagama* (1887). Although we early rejected the notion that Indian tribes are "foreign states" for jurisdictional purposes under Art. III, *Cherokee Nation v. Ga.* (1831), we have also recognized that the tribes remain quasi-sovereign nations which, by government structure, culture, and source of sovereignty are in many ways foreign to the constitutional institutions of the Federal and State Governments. As is suggested by the District Court's opinion in this case, efforts by the federal judiciary to apply the statutory prohibitions of §1302 in a civil context may substantially interfere with a tribe's ability to maintain itself as a culturally and politically distinct entity.

As we have repeatedly emphasized, Congress' authority over Indian matters is extraordinarily broad, and the role of courts in adjusting relations between and among tribes and their members correspondingly restrained. Congress retains authority expressly to authorize civil actions for injunctive or other relief to redress violations of §1302, in the event that the tribes themselves prove deficient in applying and enforcing its substantive provisions. But unless and until Congress makes clear its intention to permit the additional intrusion on tribal sovereignty that adjudication of such actions in a federal forum would represent, we are constrained to find that §1302 does not impliedly authorize actions for declaratory or injunctive relief against either the tribe or its officers.

Justice WHITE, dissenting.

The Court noted in *Bell v. Hood* (1946) that "where federally protected rights have been invaded, it has been the rule from the beginning that courts will be alert to adjust their remedies so as to grant the necessary relief." The fact that a statute is merely declarative and does not expressly provide for a cause of action to enforce its terms "does not, of course, prevent a federal court from fashioning an effective equitable remedy," *Jones v. Alfred H. Mayer Co.* (1968), for "[t]he existence of a statutory right implies the existence of all necessary and appropriate remedies." *Sullivan v. Little Hunting Park, Inc.* (1969).

The ICRA itself gives no indication that the constitutional rights it extends to American Indians are to be enforced only by means of federal habeas corpus actions. On the contrary, since several of the specified rights are most frequently invoked in noncustodial situations, the natural assumption is that some remedy other than habeas corpus must be contemplated.

The most important consideration, of course, is whether a private cause of action would be consistent with the underlying purposes of the Act. [T]he Senate Report states that the purpose of the ICRA "is to insure that the American Indian is afforded the broad constitutional rights secured to other Americans." Not only is a private cause of action consistent with that purpose, it is necessary for its achievement. The legislative history indicates that Congress was concerned, not only about the Indian's lack of substantive rights, but also about the lack of remedies to enforce whatever rights the Indian might have.

Although the Senate Report's statement of the purpose of the ICRA refers only to the granting of constitutional rights to the Indians, I agree with the majority that the legislative history demonstrates that Congress was also concerned with furthering Indian self-government. I do not agree, however, that this concern on the part of Congress precludes our recognition of a federal cause of action to enforce the terms of the Act. The major intrusion upon the tribe's right to govern itself occurred when Congress enacted the ICRA and mandated that the tribe "in exercising powers of self-government" observe the rights enumerated in §1302. The extension of constitutional rights to individual citizens is *intended* to intrude upon the authority of government. And once it has been decided that an individual does possess certain rights vis-à-vis his government, it necessarily follows that he has some way to enforce those rights. Although creating a federal cause of action may "constitut[e] an interference with tribal autonomy and self-government beyond that created by the change in substantive law itself," in my mind it is a further step that must be taken; otherwise, the change in the law may be meaningless.

* * *

In *Santa Clara Pueblo*, the Court held that trusting tribal courts to adjudicate ICRA claims was consistent with Congress' intent to respect tribal self-determination. ICRA does not abrogate the sovereign immunity of Indian tribes. Individual litigants do not have a federal cause of action for civil relief under ICRA. Defenders of the Court's decision have argued that it is consistent with Congress' self-determination policy and the principle, stretching back to the Founding, of inherent tribal sovereignty. Understood thus, *Santa Clara Pueblo* is a forum-selection decision favoring tribal resolution of civil rights violations by tribal governments. Rina Swentzell, a member of Santa Clara Pueblo, has written of the decision:

I am a woman from Santa Clara Pueblo. I was born there. I lived with my great-grandmother on the main plaza next to the Winter kiva until she died when I was thirteen years old. My formal education began there where I went to the Bureau of Indian Affairs school at the Pueblo through the sixth grade. I was 39 years old when the Supreme Court ruled on the *Santa Clara v. Martinez* case. Even then, I wanted the courts to rule in favor of the tribe — to rule for tribal sovereignty. My desire was not because I was not concerned about my children who would not be considered members of the Pueblo, because I am a woman married to a non-Santa Clara person. It was not because I did not know that my cousin would have his children considered members because he is a man, though he was not born in the Pueblo, did not grow up there, and was married to a non-Santa Clara person. Of course, I also knew that it did not make sense; that it was not just or fair. I knew that what was happening in the community was blatant gender discrimination. . . .

[A]s our myths, stories, and songs tell us, there are tensions and struggles in life. Our traditional beliefs tell us that we are all relations, that we are all children of the community, which is part of the universe, which daily harmonizes opposites. It also tells us that it is an inclusive, not exclusive world that we share and cooperation, not competition, is ideal behavior. That world also knows that "things come around" — that things will change.[53]

In 2012, the members of Santa Clara Pueblo voted to change the membership rules to address the gender discrimination at issue in *Santa Clara Pueblo v. Martinez*.[54]

Scholars have described the issue in *Santa Clara Pueblo* as one involving a conflict between individual rights and tribal sovereignty. As Resnik has put it, Julia and Audrey Martinez's equal protection claim had an "obvious problem" insofar as it implicated "the tension arising from being a member of two governments, the Santa Clara Pueblo and the United States."[55] Writing critically of the case's outcome, feminist scholar Catharine MacKinnon stated that "I find *Martinez* a difficult case on a lot of levels, and I don't usually find cases difficult," and argued that the membership ordinance required female members of the Pueblo to "choose between [their] equality" and their "cultural identity."[56]

In response to MacKinnon's critique, legal scholar Gloria Valencia-Weber pointed out that "[t]he voices of American Indian feminists have generally not been invoked in analyzing *Martinez*."[57] Valencia-Weber identified various presumptions

---

53. Rina Swentzell, *Testimony of a Santa Clara Woman*, 14 Kan. J.L. & Pub. Pol'y 97 (2004).

54. Tom Sharpe, *Santa Clara Pueblo Vote on Member Rules Leaves Loose Ends*, The Santa Fe New Mexican (May 1, 2012).

55. Resnik, *supra* note 51, at 674.

56. Catharine A. MacKinnon, *Whose Culture? A Case Note on* Martinez v. Santa Clara Pueblo, *in* Feminism Unmodified 63, 67 (1987).

57. Gloria Valencia-Weber, *Racial Equality: Old and New Strains and American Indians*, 80 Notre Dame L. Rev. 333, 366 (2004).

about the case that do not stand up to scrutiny, including the presumption that all Native nations "have similar laws," and argued for a nuanced understanding of the history of Santa Clara Pueblo and its ordinance, including the "history of struggle" over use and possession of Pueblo lands.[58] Similarly, feminist and critical race theorist Angela Harris argued that the aspiration of women to equality "must depend upon the social historical circumstances," asking, "[w]hat was the meaning of the ordinance within Pueblo discourse, as opposed to a transhistorical and transcultural feminist discourse?"[59]

2. Tribal Sovereign Immunity

Like other sovereigns, federally recognized Native nations enjoy sovereign immunity under federal law. Native nations may waive their immunity and often do so. Many tribes, for example, have waived their immunity to suit in tribal courts, while retaining immunity from suit in federal or state courts. In addition, Congress may abrogate tribal sovereign immunity in an exercise of its authority to legislate in the field of Indian affairs. In *Santa Clara Pueblo v. Martinez* (1978), the Supreme Court applied a settled rule of construction that Congress must speak clearly when it intends to abrogate tribal sovereign immunity.

Tribal sovereign immunity, like other instances of sovereign immunity, has been controversial. Much of the recent controversy concerns cases in which Native nations are engaged in projects of economic development. Over the past several decades, tribal economic development has brought material improvements to the lives of Native peoples.[60] At the same time, it has generated legal disputes, including contractual disputes between tribes and their business partners, as well as disputes between tribes and consumers.

The Supreme Court discussed the basis for tribal sovereign immunity and its scope in *Kiowa Tribe v. Mfg. Tech.* (1998) and *Mich. v. Bay Mills* (2014). As you read these cases, consider the justifications for tribal sovereign immunity and the role that separation of powers plays in committing the question of abrogation to Congress.

Kiowa Tribe v. Mfg. Techs.

523 U.S. 75 (1998)

Justice KENNEDY, delivered the opinion of the Court.

In this commercial suit against an Indian Tribe, the Oklahoma Court of Civil Appeals rejected the Tribe's claim of sovereign immunity. Our case law to date often recites the rule of tribal immunity from suit. While these precedents rest on

---

58. *Id.* at 371-72.

59. Angela P. Harris, *Race and Essentialism in Feminist Legal Theory*, 42 STAN. L. REV. 581, 594 (1990).

60. *See supra* notes 13-15 and accompanying text (discussing *Seminole Tribe* in context of Tribal self-determination and economic development).

early cases that assumed immunity without extensive reasoning, we adhere to these decisions and reverse the judgment.

I

Petitioner Kiowa Tribe is an Indian Tribe recognized by the Federal Government. The Tribe owns land in Oklahoma, and, in addition, the United States holds land in that State in trust for the Tribe. Though the record is vague about some key details, the facts appear to be as follows: In 1990, a tribal entity called the Kiowa Industrial Development Commission agreed to buy from respondent Manufacturing Technologies, Inc., certain stock issued by Clinton-Sherman Aviation, Inc. On April 3, 1990, the then-chairman of the Tribe's business committee signed a promissory note in the name of the Tribe. By its note, the Tribe agreed to pay Manufacturing Technologies $285,000 plus interest. The face of the note recites it was signed at Carnegie, Oklahoma, where the Tribe has a complex on land held in trust for the Tribe. According to respondent, however, the Tribe executed and delivered the note to Manufacturing Technologies in Oklahoma City, beyond the Tribe's lands, and the note obligated the Tribe to make its payments in Oklahoma City. The note does not specify a governing law. In a paragraph entitled "Waivers and Governing Law," it does provide: "Nothing in this Note subjects or limits the sovereign rights of the Kiowa Tribe of Oklahoma."

The Tribe defaulted; respondent sued on the note in state court; and the Tribe moved to dismiss for lack of jurisdiction, relying in part on its sovereign immunity from suit.

II

As a matter of federal law, an Indian tribe is subject to suit only where Congress has authorized the suit or the tribe has waived its immunity. To date, our cases have sustained tribal immunity from suit without drawing a distinction based on where the tribal activities occurred. Nor have we yet drawn a distinction between governmental and commercial activities of a tribe. Though respondent asks us to confine immunity from suit to transactions on reservations and to governmental activities, our precedents have not drawn these distinctions.

We have often noted that the immunity possessed by Indian tribes is not coextensive with that of the States. *See, e.g., Blatchford v. Native Vill. of Noatak* (1991). In *Blatchford,* we distinguished state sovereign immunity from tribal sovereign immunity, as tribes were not at the Constitutional Convention. They were thus not parties to the "mutuality of . . . concession" that "makes the States' surrender of immunity from suit by sister States plausible." So tribal immunity is a matter of federal law and is not subject to diminution by the States.

Though the doctrine of tribal immunity is settled law and controls this case, we note that it developed almost by accident. The doctrine is said by some of our own opinions to rest on the Court's opinion in *Turner v. U.S.* (1919). *Turner's* passing reference to immunity, however, did become an explicit holding that tribes had immunity from suit. We so held in *U.S. v. U.S. Fidelity & Guaranty Co.* (1940), saying: "These Indian Nations are exempt from suit without Congressional authorization." As sovereigns or quasi sovereigns, the Indian Nations enjoyed immunity "from judicial attack" absent consent to be sued. Later cases, albeit with little analysis, reiterated the doctrine.

There are reasons to doubt the wisdom of perpetuating the doctrine. At one time, the doctrine of tribal immunity from suit might have been thought necessary to protect nascent tribal governments from encroachments by States. In our interdependent and mobile society, however, tribal immunity extends beyond what is needed to safeguard tribal self-governance. This is evident when tribes take part in the Nation's commerce. Tribal enterprises now include ski resorts, gambling, and sales of cigarettes to non-Indians. In this economic context, immunity can harm those who are unaware that they are dealing with a tribe, who do not know of tribal immunity, or who have no choice in the matter, as in the case of tort victims.

These considerations might suggest a need to abrogate tribal immunity, at least as an overarching rule. Respondent does not ask us to repudiate the principle outright, but suggests instead that we confine it to reservations or to noncommercial activities. We decline to draw this distinction in this case, as we defer to the role Congress may wish to exercise in this important judgment.

Congress has acted against the background of our decisions. It has restricted tribal immunity from suit in limited circumstances. And in other statutes it has declared an intention not to alter it.

In considering Congress' role in reforming tribal immunity, we find instructive the problems of sovereign immunity for foreign countries. As with tribal immunity, foreign sovereign immunity began as a judicial doctrine. Chief Justice Marshall held that United States courts had no jurisdiction over an armed ship of a foreign state, even while in an American port. *Schooner Exch. v. McFaddon* (1812). While the holding was narrow, "that opinion came to be regarded as extending virtually absolute immunity to foreign sovereigns." *Verlinden B.V. v. Cent. Bank of Nigeria* (1983). In 1952, the State Department issued what came to be known as the Tate Letter, announcing the policy of denying immunity for the commercial acts of a foreign nation. Difficulties in implementing the principle led Congress in 1976 to enact the Foreign Sovereign Immunities Act, resulting in more predictable and precise rules.

Like foreign sovereign immunity, tribal immunity is a matter of federal law. Although the Court has taken the lead in drawing the bounds of tribal immunity, Congress, subject to constitutional limitations, can alter its limits through explicit legislation.

In both fields, Congress is in a position to weigh and accommodate the competing policy concerns and reliance interests. The capacity of the Legislative Branch to address the issue by comprehensive legislation counsels some caution by us in this area. Congress "has occasionally authorized limited classes of suits against Indian tribes" and "has always been at liberty to dispense with such tribal immunity or to limit it." It has not yet done so.

Justice STEVENS, with whom Justice THOMAS and Justice GINSBURG join, dissenting.

There is no federal statute or treaty that provides petitioner, the Kiowa Tribe of Oklahoma, any immunity from the application of Oklahoma law to its off-reservation commercial activities. Nor, in my opinion, should this Court extend the judge-made doctrine of sovereign immunity to pre-empt the authority of the state courts to decide for themselves whether to accord such immunity to Indian tribes as a matter of comity.

Three compelling reasons favor the exercise of judicial restraint.

First, the Court is not deferring to Congress or exercising "caution,"—rather, it is creating law. The Court fails to identify federal interests supporting its extension of sovereign immunity—indeed, it all but concedes that the present doctrine lacks such justification,—and completely ignores the State's interests.

Second, the rule is strikingly anomalous. Why should an Indian tribe enjoy broader immunity than the States, the Federal Government, and foreign nations? As a matter of national policy, the United States has waived its immunity from tort liability and from liability arising out of its commercial activities. Congress has also decided in the Foreign Sovereign Immunities Act of 1976 that foreign states may be sued in the federal and state courts for claims based upon commercial activities carried on in the United States, or such activities elsewhere that have a "direct effect in the United States." §1605(a)(2). And a State may be sued in the courts of another State. *Nevada v. Hall* (1979).[82] The fact that the States surrendered aspects of their sovereignty when they joined the Union does not even arguably present a legitimate basis for concluding that the Indian tribes retained—or, indeed, ever had—any sovereign immunity for off-reservation commercial conduct.

Third, the rule is unjust. This is especially so with respect to tort victims who have no opportunity to negotiate for a waiver of sovereign immunity; yet nothing in the Court's reasoning limits the rule to lawsuits arising out of voluntary contractual relationships. Governments, like individuals, should pay their debts and should be held accountable for their unlawful, injurious conduct.

* * *

Michigan v. Bay Mills Indian Cmty.

572 U.S. 782 (2014)

Justice KAGAN delivered the opinion of the Court.

The question in this case is whether tribal sovereign immunity bars Michigan's suit against the Bay Mills Indian Community for opening a casino outside Indian lands. We hold that immunity protects Bay Mills from this legal action. Congress has not abrogated tribal sovereign immunity from a State's suit to enjoin gaming off a reservation or other Indian lands. And we decline to revisit our prior decisions holding that, absent such an abrogation (or a waiver), Indian tribes have immunity even when a suit arises from off-reservation commercial activity. Michigan must therefore resort to other mechanisms, including legal actions against the responsible individuals, to resolve this dispute.

I

The Indian Gaming Regulatory Act (IGRA or Act), creates a framework for regulating gaming activity on Indian lands. The Act divides gaming into three classes. Class III gaming, the most closely regulated and the kind involved here, includes casino games, slot machines, and horse racing. A tribe may conduct such

---

82. [Editors' Note: In 2019, the Supreme Court overruled *Nev. v. Hall* in *Franchise Tax Bd. of Cal. v. Hyatt*.]

gaming on Indian lands only pursuant to, and in compliance with, a compact it has negotiated with the surrounding State. A compact typically prescribes rules for operating gaming, allocates law enforcement authority between the tribe and State, and provides remedies for breach of the agreement's terms. Notable here, IGRA itself authorizes a State to bring suit against a tribe for certain conduct violating a compact: Specifically, §2710(d)(7)(A)(ii) allows a State to sue in federal court to "enjoin a class III gaming activity located on Indian lands and conducted in violation of any Tribal-State compact . . . that is in effect."

Pursuant to the Act, Michigan and Bay Mills, a federally recognized Indian Tribe, entered into a compact in 1993. The compact empowers Bay Mills to conduct class III gaming on "Indian lands;" conversely, it prohibits the Tribe from doing so outside that territory. The compact also contains a dispute resolution mechanism, which sends to arbitration any contractual differences the parties cannot settle on their own. A provision within that arbitration section states that "[n]othing in this Compact shall be deemed a waiver" of either the Tribe's or the State's sovereign immunity. Since entering into the compact, Bay Mills has operated class III gaming, as authorized, on its reservation in Michigan's Upper Peninsula.

In 2010, Bay Mills opened another class III gaming facility in Vanderbilt, a small village in Michigan's Lower Peninsula about 125 miles from the Tribe's reservation. Bay Mills had bought the Vanderbilt property with accrued interest from a federal appropriation, which Congress had made to compensate the Tribe for 19th-century takings of its ancestral lands. Congress had directed that a portion of the appropriated funds go into a "Land Trust" whose earnings the Tribe was to use to improve or purchase property. According to the legislation, any land so acquired "shall be held as Indian lands are held." Citing that provision, Bay Mills contended that the Vanderbilt property was "Indian land" under IGRA and the compact; and the Tribe thus claimed authority to operate a casino there.

Michigan disagreed: The State sued Bay Mills in federal court to enjoin operation of the new casino, alleging that the facility violated IGRA and the compact because it was located outside Indian lands.

We granted certiorari to consider whether tribal sovereign immunity bars Michigan's suit against Bay Mills.

II

Indian tribes are "'domestic dependent nations'" that exercise "inherent sovereign authority." *Okla. Tax Comm'n v. Citizen Band Potawatomi Tribe of Okla.* (1991) (Potawatomi) (quoting *Cherokee Nation v. Ga.* (1831)). As dependents, the tribes are subject to plenary control by Congress. And yet they remain "separate sovereigns pre-existing the Constitution." *Santa Clara Pueblo v. Martinez* (1978). Thus, unless and "until Congress acts, the tribes retain" their historic sovereign authority. *U.S. v. Wheeler* (1978).

Among the core aspects of sovereignty that tribes possess — subject, again, to congressional action — is the "common-law immunity from suit traditionally enjoyed by sovereign powers." *Santa Clara Pueblo v. Martinez* (1978). That immunity, we have explained, is "a necessary corollary to Indian sovereignty and self-governance." *Three Affiliated Tribes of Fort Berthold Rsrv. v. Wold Eng., P.C.* (1986). Thus, we have time and again treated the "doctrine of tribal immunity [as] settled law" and dismissed any suit against a tribe absent congressional authorization (or a waiver). *Kiowa Tribe of Okla. v. Mfg. Techs. Inc.*, 523 U.S. 751, 756 (1998).

In doing so, we have held that tribal immunity applies no less to suits brought by States (including in their own courts) than to those by individuals. While each State at the Constitutional Convention surrendered its immunity from suit by sister States, "it would be absurd to suggest that the tribes"—at a conference "to which they were not even parties"—similarly ceded their immunity against state-initiated suits. *Blatchford v. Native Vill. of Noatak* (1991).

Equally important here, we declined in Kiowa to make any exception for suits arising from a tribe's commercial activities, even when they take place off Indian lands. Rather, we opted to "defer" to Congress about whether to abrogate tribal immunity for off-reservation commercial conduct.

Our decisions establish as well that such a congressional decision must be clear. The baseline position, we have often held, is tribal immunity; and "[t]o abrogate [such] immunity, Congress must 'unequivocally' express that purpose." *C & L Enterprises, Inc. v. Citizen Band Potawatomi Tribe of Okla.* (2001) (quoting *Santa Clara Pueblo*). That rule of construction reflects an enduring principle of Indian law: Although Congress has plenary authority over tribes, courts will not lightly assume that Congress in fact intends to undermine Indian self-government.

III

IGRA partially abrogates tribal sovereign immunity in §2710(d)(7)(A)(ii)—but this case, viewed most naturally, falls outside that term's ambit. The provision authorizes a State to sue a tribe to "enjoin a class III gaming activity located on Indian lands and conducted in violation of any Tribal-State compact." A key phrase in that abrogation is "on Indian lands"—three words reflecting IGRA's overall scope (and repeated some two dozen times in the statute). A State's suit to enjoin gaming activity on Indian lands (assuming other requirements are met) falls within §2710(d)(7)(A)(ii); a similar suit to stop gaming activity off Indian lands does not. And that creates a fundamental problem for Michigan. After all, the very premise of this suit—the reason Michigan thinks Bay Mills is acting unlawfully—is that the Vanderbilt casino is outside Indian lands. By dint of that theory, a suit to enjoin gaming in Vanderbilt is correspondingly outside §2710(d)(7)(A)(ii)'s abrogation of immunity.

Michigan first attempts to fit this suit within §2710(d)(7)(A)(ii) by relocating the "class III gaming activity" to which it is objecting. True enough, Michigan states, the Vanderbilt casino lies outside Indian lands. But Bay Mills "authorized, licensed, and operated" that casino from within its own reservation. According to the State, that necessary administrative action—no less than, say, dealing craps—is "class III gaming activity," and because it occurred on Indian land, this suit to enjoin it can go forward.

But that argument comes up snake eyes, because numerous provisions of IGRA show that "class III gaming activity" means just what it sounds like—the stuff involved in playing class III games. For example, §2710(d)(3)(C)(i) refers to "the licensing and regulation of [a class III gaming] activity" and §2710(d)(9) concerns the "operation of a class III gaming activity." Those phrases make perfect sense if "class III gaming activity" is what goes on in a casino—each roll of the dice and spin of the wheel. But they lose all meaning if, as Michigan argues, "class III gaming activity" refers equally to the off-site licensing or operation of the games. (Just plug in those words and see what happens.)

Stymied under §2710(d)(7)(A)(ii), Michigan next urges us to adopt a "holistic method" of interpreting IGRA that would allow a State to sue a tribe for illegal gaming off, no less than on, Indian lands. Michigan asks here that we consider "IGRA's text and structure as a whole." Michigan highlights a (purported) anomaly of the statute as written: that it enables a State to sue a tribe for illegal gaming inside, but not outside, Indian country. "[W]hy," Michigan queries, "would Congress authorize a state to obtain a federal injunction against illegal tribal gaming on Indian lands, but not on lands subject to the state's own sovereign jurisdiction?"

But this Court does not revise legislation, as Michigan proposes, just because the text as written creates an apparent anomaly as to some subject it does not address. Truth be told, such anomalies often arise from statutes, if for no other reason than that Congress typically legislates by parts—addressing one thing without examining all others that might merit comparable treatment. Rejecting a similar argument that a statutory anomaly (between property and non-property taxes) made "not a whit of sense," we explained in one recent case that "Congress wrote the statute it wrote"—meaning, a statute going so far and no further. *CSX Transp., Inc. v. Ala. Dept. of Revenue* (2011). The same could be said of IGRA's abrogation of tribal immunity for gaming "on Indian lands." This Court has no roving license, in even ordinary cases of statutory interpretation, to disregard clear language simply on the view that (in Michigan's words) Congress "must have intended" something broader.

In any event, IGRA's history and design provide a more than intelligible answer to the question Michigan poses about why Congress would have confined a State's authority to sue a tribe as §2710(d)(7)(A)(ii) does. Congress adopted IGRA in response to this Court's decision in *Cal. v. Cabazon Band of Mission Indians* (1987), which held that States lacked any regulatory authority over gaming on Indian lands. Cabazon left fully intact a State's regulatory power over tribal gaming outside Indian territory—which, as we will soon show, is capacious. So the problem Congress set out to address in IGRA (Cabazon's ouster of state authority) arose in Indian lands alone. And the solution Congress devised, naturally enough, reflected that fact. Everything—literally everything—in IGRA affords tools (for either state or federal officials) to regulate gaming on Indian lands, and nowhere else. Small surprise that IGRA's abrogation of tribal immunity does that as well.

And the resulting world, when considered functionally, is not nearly so "enigma[tic]" as Michigan suggests. True enough, a State lacks the ability to sue a tribe for illegal gaming when that activity occurs off the reservation. But a State, on its own lands, has many other powers over tribal gaming that it does not possess (absent consent) in Indian territory. Unless federal law provides differently, "Indians going beyond reservation boundaries" are subject to any generally applicable state law. So, for example, Michigan could, in the first instance, deny a license to Bay Mills for an off-reservation casino. And if Bay Mills went ahead anyway, Michigan could bring suit against tribal officials or employees (rather than the Tribe itself) seeking an injunction for, say, gambling without a license. As this Court has stated before, analogizing to *Ex parte Young* (1908), tribal immunity does not bar such a suit for injunctive relief against individuals, including tribal officers, responsible for unlawful conduct. And to the extent civil remedies proved inadequate, Michigan could resort to its criminal law, prosecuting anyone who maintains—or even frequents—an unlawful gambling establishment. In short, the panoply of tools Michigan can use to enforce its law on its own lands—no less than the suit it could bring on Indian lands under §2710(d)(7)(A)(ii)—can shutter, quickly and permanently, an illegal casino.

Finally, if a State really wants to sue a tribe for gaming outside Indian lands, the State need only bargain for a waiver of immunity. Under IGRA, a State and tribe negotiating a compact "may include . . . remedies for breach of contract"—including a provision allowing the State to bring an action against the tribe in the circumstances presented here. States have more than enough leverage to obtain such terms because a tribe cannot conduct class III gaming on its lands without a compact, *see* §2710(d)(1)(C), and cannot sue to enforce a State's duty to negotiate a compact in good faith. So as Michigan forthrightly acknowledges, "a party dealing with a tribe in contract negotiations has the power to protect itself by refusing to deal absent the tribe's waiver of sovereign immunity from suit." And many States have taken that path. To be sure, Michigan did not: As noted earlier, the compact at issue here, instead of authorizing judicial remedies, sends disputes to arbitration and expressly retains each party's sovereign immunity. But Michigan—like any State—could have insisted on a different deal (and indeed may do so now for the future, because the current compact has expired and remains in effect only until the parties negotiate a new one). And in that event, the limitation Congress placed on IGRA's abrogation of tribal immunity—whether or not anomalous as an abstract matter—would have made no earthly difference.

IV

[I]t is fundamentally Congress's job, not ours, to determine whether or how to limit tribal immunity. The special brand of sovereignty the tribes retain—both its nature and its extent—rests in the hands of Congress. Congress, we said [in *Kiowa*]—drawing an analogy to its role in shaping foreign sovereign immunity—has the greater capacity "to weigh and accommodate the competing policy concerns and reliance interests" involved in the issue. Congress should make the call whether to curtail a tribe's immunity for off-reservation commercial conduct—and the Court should accept Congress's judgment.

All that we said in *Kiowa* applies today, with yet one more thing: Congress has now reflected on Kiowa and made an initial (though of course not irrevocable) decision to retain that form of tribal immunity. Following *Kiowa*, Congress considered several bills to substantially modify tribal immunity in the commercial context. Two in particular—drafted by the chair of the Senate Appropriations Subcommittee on the Interior—expressly referred to *Kiowa* and broadly abrogated tribal immunity for most torts and breaches of contract. But instead of adopting those reversals of Kiowa, Congress chose to enact a far more modest alternative requiring tribes either to disclose or to waive their immunity in contracts needing the Secretary of the Interior's approval. Since then, Congress has continued to exercise its plenary authority over tribal immunity, specifically preserving immunity in some contexts and abrogating it in others, but never adopting the change Michigan wants. So rather than confronting, as we did in *Kiowa*, a legislative vacuum as to the precise issue presented, we act today against the backdrop of a congressional choice: to retain tribal immunity (at least for now) in a case like this one.

As *Kiowa* recognized, a fundamental commitment of Indian law is judicial respect for Congress's primary role in defining the contours of tribal sovereignty. Having held in *Kiowa* that this issue is up to Congress, we cannot reverse ourselves because some may think its conclusion wrong. Congress of course may always change its mind—and we would readily defer to that new decision. But it is for Congress, now more than ever, to say whether to create an exception to tribal immunity for off-reservation commercial activity. As in *Kiowa*—except still more so—"we decline to revisit our case law[,] and choose" instead "to defer to Congress."

Justice SOTOMAYOR, concurring.

The doctrine of tribal immunity has been a part of American jurisprudence for well over a century. Despite this history, the principal dissent chides the Court for failing to offer a sufficient basis for the doctrine of tribal immunity, and reasons that we should at least limit the doctrine of tribal sovereign immunity in ways that resemble restrictions on foreign sovereign immunity.

I write separately to further detail why both history and comity counsel against limiting Tribes' sovereign immunity in the manner the principal dissent advances.

Principles of comity strongly counsel in favor of continued recognition of tribal sovereign immunity, including for off-reservation commercial conduct.

Comity—"that is, 'a proper respect for [a sovereign's] functions,'" *Sprint Communications, Inc. v. Jacobs* (2013)—fosters "respectful, harmonious relations" between governments, *Wood v. Milyard* (2012). For two reasons, these goals are best served by recognizing sovereign immunity for Indian Tribes, including immunity for off-reservation conduct, except where Congress has expressly abrogated it. First, a legal rule that permitted States to sue Tribes, absent their consent, for commercial conduct would be anomalous in light of the existing prohibitions against Tribes' suing States in like circumstances. Such disparate treatment of these two classes of domestic sovereigns would hardly signal the Federal Government's respect for tribal sovereignty. Second, Tribes face a number of barriers to raising revenue in traditional ways. If Tribes are ever to become more self-sufficient, and fund a more substantial portion of their own governmental functions, commercial enterprises will likely be a central means of achieving that goal.

The principal dissent contends that Tribes have emerged as particularly "substantial and successful" commercial actors. The dissent expresses concern that, although tribal leaders can be sued for prospective relief, Tribes' purportedly growing coffers remain unexposed to broad damages liability. These observations suffer from two flaws.

First, not all Tribes are engaged in highly lucrative commercial activity. Nearly half of federally recognized Tribes in the United States do not operate gaming facilities at all. And even among the Tribes that do, gaming revenue is far from uniform. As of 2009, fewer than 20% of Indian gaming facilities accounted for roughly 70% of the revenues from such facilities. One must therefore temper any impression that Tribes across the country have suddenly and uniformly found their treasuries filled with gaming revenue.

Second, even if all Tribes were equally successful in generating commercial revenues, that would not justify the commercial-activity exception urged by the principal dissent. For tribal gaming operations cannot be understood as mere profit-making ventures that are wholly separate from the Tribes' core governmental functions. A key goal of the Federal Government is to render Tribes more self-sufficient, and better positioned to fund their own sovereign functions, rather than relying on federal funding. And tribal business operations are critical to the goals of tribal self-sufficiency because such enterprises in some cases "may be the only means by which a tribe can raise revenues," Struve, 36 ARIZ. ST. L.J., at 169. This is due in large part to the insuperable (and often state-imposed) barriers Tribes face in raising revenue through more traditional means.

For example, States have the power to tax certain individuals and companies based on Indian reservations, making it difficult for Tribes to raise revenue from those sources. States may also tax reservation land that Congress has authorized individuals to hold in fee, regardless of whether it is held by Indians or non-Indians.

As commentators have observed, if Tribes were to impose their own taxes on these same sources, the resulting double taxation would discourage economic growth.

If non-Indians controlled only a small amount of property on Indian reservations, and if only a negligible amount of land was held in fee, the double-taxation concern might be less severe. But for many Tribes, that is not the case. History explains why this is so: Federal policies enacted in the late 19th and early 20th centuries rendered a devastating blow to tribal ownership. In 1887, Congress enacted the Dawes Act. That Act had two major components relevant here. First, it converted the property that belonged to Indian Tribes into fee property, and allotted the land to individual Indians. Much of this land passed quickly to non-Indian owners. Indeed, by 1934, the amount of land that passed from Indian Tribes to non-Indians totaled 90 million acres. *See* COHEN'S HANDBOOK OF FEDERAL INDIAN LAW 74 (2012). Other property passed to non-Indians when destitute Indians found themselves unable to pay state taxes, resulting in sheriff's sales.

A second component of the Dawes Act opened "surplus" land on Indian reservations to settlement by non-Indians. Selling surplus lands to non-Indians was part of a more general policy of forced assimilation. Sixty million acres of land passed to non-Indian hands as a result of surplus programs.

These policies have left a devastating legacy, as the cases that have come before this Court demonstrate. We noted in *Mont. v. U.S.* (1981), for example, that due in large part to the Dawes Act, 28% of the Crow Tribe's reservation in Montana was held in fee by non-Indians. Similarly, Justice White observed in *Brendale v. Confederated Tribes and Bands of Yakima Nation* (1989) (plurality opinion), that 20% of the Yakima Nation's reservation was owned in fee. For reservations like those, it is particularly impactful that States and local governments may tax property held by non-Indians and land held in fee as a result of the Dawes Act.

Moreover, Tribes are largely unable to obtain substantial revenue by taxing tribal members who reside on non-fee land that was not allotted under the Dawes Act. As one scholar recently observed, even if Tribes imposed high taxes on Indian residents, "there is very little income, property, or sales they could tax." The poverty and unemployment rates on Indian reservations are significantly greater than the national average. As a result, "there is no stable tax base on most reservations."

To be sure, poverty has decreased over the past few decades on reservations that have gaming activity. One recent study found that between 1990 and 2000, the presence of a tribal casino increased average per capita income by 7.4% and reduced the family poverty rate by 4.9 percentage points. But even reservations that have gaming continue to experience significant poverty, especially relative to the national average. The same is true of Indian reservations more generally.

Justice THOMAS, with whom Justice SCALIA, Justice GINSBURG, and Justice ALITO join, dissenting.

In *Kiowa Tribe of Okla. v. Mfg. Techs. Inc.* (1998), this Court extended the judge-made doctrine of tribal sovereign immunity to bar suits arising out of an Indian tribe's commercial activities conducted outside its territory. That was error. Such an expansion of tribal immunity is unsupported by any rationale for that doctrine, inconsistent with the limits on tribal sovereignty, and an affront to state sovereignty.

That decision, wrong to begin with, has only worsened with the passage of time. In the 16 years since *Kiowa*, tribal commerce has proliferated and the inequities engendered by unwarranted tribal immunity have multiplied. Nevertheless, the Court turns down a chance to rectify its error. Still lacking a substantive justification for *Kiowa*'s rule, the majority relies on notions of deference to Congress and stare decisis. Because those considerations do not support (and cannot sustain) *Kiowa*'s unjustifiable rule and its mounting consequences, I respectfully dissent.

There is no substantive basis for *Kiowa*'s extension of tribal immunity to off-reservation commercial acts. As this Court explained in *Kiowa*, the common-law doctrine of tribal sovereign immunity arose "almost by accident." In fact, far from defending the doctrine of tribal sovereign immunity, the *Kiowa* majority "doubt[ed] the wisdom of perpetuating the doctrine." The majority here suggests just one post hoc justification: that tribes automatically receive immunity as an incident to their historic sovereignty. But that explanation fails to account for the fact that immunity does not apply of its own force in the courts of another sovereign. And none of the other colorable rationales for the doctrine—i.e., considerations of comity, and protection of tribal self-sufficiency and self-government—supports extending immunity to suits arising out of a tribe's commercial activities conducted beyond its territory.

As the commercial activity of tribes has proliferated, the conflict and inequities brought on by blanket tribal immunity have also increased. Tribal immunity significantly limits, and often extinguishes, the States' ability to protect their citizens and enforce the law against tribal businesses. This case is but one example: No one can seriously dispute that Bay Mills' operation of a casino outside its reservation (and thus within Michigan territory) would violate both state law and the Tribe's compact with Michigan. Yet, immunity poses a substantial impediment to Michigan's efforts to halt the casino's operation permanently. The problem repeats itself every time a tribe fails to pay state taxes, harms a tort victim, breaches a contract, or otherwise violates state laws, and tribal immunity bars the only feasible legal remedy.

* * *

D.   FEDERAL COURT RELIEF AGAINST FOREIGN GOVERNMENTS

In *Kiowa Tribe v. Mfg. Techs.* (1998), the Supreme Court compared the sovereign immunity of Indian Tribes to the sovereign immunity of foreign governments. Questions of the separation of powers arise in both cases, as Congress has the authority to legislate with respect to the scope of both instances of sovereign immunity. And as in the case of tribal sovereign immunity, foreign sovereign immunity raises difficult questions as courts have tried to distinguish between uniquely "sovereign" actions and typically "private" actions that a government may engage in.

Traditionally, U.S. courts held that foreign sovereigns were immune from suit in U.S. courts. The foundational precedent was *The Schooner Exchange v. M'Faddon* (1812), which held that foreign sovereign immunity was a matter of comity extended by the U.S. to foreign sovereigns. The U.S. Constitution did not require it. For much of U.S. history, the federal Executive Branch would request that U.S. courts extend immunity, at least to friendly foreign states.

In 1952, the U.S. State Department adopted a more nuanced position, one that distinguished between the "absolute" and "restrictive" theories of foreign sovereign immunity. The absolute theory, as its name suggests, does not distinguish between a state's "sovereign" and its "private" acts. Regardless of the capacity in which the foreign state acted, it is immune from suit in a foreign court. By contrast, the restrictive theory distinguishes between cases in which a state acts as a sovereign and those in which the state acts in ways that a private entity also could act. A foreign state may, for example, run a business. Under the restrictive theory, a foreign state is not immune from suit for its private or commercial acts.

In 1976, Congress enacted the Foreign Sovereign Immunities Act (FSIA) as comprehensive legislation addressing judicial relief against foreign governments. The Act presumptively shields foreign states from suit in a U.S. court. It goes on, however, to enumerate various exceptions to foreign sovereign immunity:

> (a) A foreign state shall not be immune from the jurisdiction of courts of the United States or of the States in any case —
>
> (1) in which the foreign state has waived its immunity either explicitly or by implication . . .
>
> (2) in which the action is based upon a commercial activity carried on in the United States by the foreign state; or upon an act performed in the United States in connection with a commercial activity of the foreign state elsewhere; or upon an act outside the territory of the United States in connection with a commercial activity of the foreign state elsewhere and that act causes a direct effect in the United States;
>
> (3) in which rights in property taken in violation of international law are in issue and that property or any property exchanged for such property is present in the United States in connection with a commercial activity carried on in the United States by the foreign state; or that property or any property exchanged for such property is owned or operated by an agency

or instrumentality of the foreign state and that agency or instrumentality is engaged in a commercial activity in the United States;

(4) in which rights in property in the United States acquired by succession or gift or rights in immovable property situated in the United States are in issue;

(5) not otherwise encompassed in paragraph (2) above, in which money damages are sought against a foreign state for personal injury or death, or damage to or loss of property, occurring in the United States and caused by the tortious act or omission of that foreign state or of any official or employee of that foreign state while acting within the scope of his office or employment; except this paragraph shall not apply to—

(A) any claim based upon the exercise or performance or the failure to exercise or perform a discretionary function regardless of whether the discretion be abused, or

(B) any claim arising out of malicious prosecution, abuse of process, libel, slander, misrepresentation, deceit, or interference with contract rights; or

(6) in which the action is brought, either to enforce an agreement made by the foreign state with or for the benefit of a private party to submit to arbitration all or any differences which have arisen or which may arise between the parties . . . concerning a subject matter capable of settlement by arbitration . . .

(b) A foreign state shall not be immune from the jurisdiction of the courts of the United States in any case in which a suit in admiralty is brought to enforce a maritime lien against a vessel or cargo of the foreign state, which maritime lien is based upon a commercial activity of the foreign state . . .

(c) [setting out notice requirements for exception (b)]

(d) A foreign state shall not be immune from the jurisdiction of the courts of the United States in any action brought to foreclose a preferred mortgage . . . in accordance with the principles of law and rules of practice of suits in rem, whenever it appears that had the vessel been privately owned and possessed a suit in rem might have been maintained.

28 U.S.C. §1605.

As the next case indicates, the Supreme Court has narrowly construed these exceptions. Notice that the Court's analysis dovetails with the presumption against judicial determination of Alien Tort Statute claims arising under the law of nations and occurring "within the territory of a sovereign other than the United States." *See Kiobel v. Royal Dutch Petroleum* (2013), discussed in Chapter 5.

Federal Republic of Germany v. Philipp

141 S.Ct. 703 (2021)

Chief Justice ROBERTS delivered the opinion for a unanimous Court.

I

This case concerns several dozen medieval relics and devotional objects known as the Welfenschatz. The treasure ("schatz") of the German Welf dynasty, the pieces date back to the early days of the Holy Roman Empire and occupy a unique position in German history and culture. The collection was assembled within Germany's Brunswick Cathedral over the course of several centuries, before being moved to a Hanoverian chapel in 1671 and later to Switzerland for safekeeping in the wake of World War I. During the waning years of the Weimar Republic, a consortium of three art firms owned by Jewish residents of Frankfurt purchased the Welfenschatz from the Duke of Brunswick. By 1931, the consortium had sold about half of the collection's pieces to museums and individuals in Europe and the United States, including many to the Cleveland Museum of Art, where they reside today.

Conditions facing the consortium changed dramatically after the collapse of the German economy and the rise of the Nazi government. After ascending to power, Hermann Goering—Adolf Hitler's deputy and the Prime Minister of Prussia—became interested in the remainder of the Welfenschatz. The complaint alleges that he employed a combination of political persecution and physical threats to coerce the consortium into selling the remaining pieces to Prussia in 1935 for approximately one-third of their value. Two of the consortium members fled the country following the sale, and the third died in Germany shortly thereafter.

The United States took possession of the Welfenschatz in the course of the occupation of Nazi Germany at the end of the war, eventually turning the collection over to the Federal Republic of Germany. For nearly 60 years, the treasure has been maintained by Stiftung Preussischer Kulturbesitz (SPK)—the Prussian Cultural Heritage Foundation—and it is now displayed at a museum in Berlin. SPK is an instrumentality of the Federal Republic.

Respondents are two United States citizens and a citizen of the United Kingdom who trace their lineages back to the three members of the consortium. The heirs first approached SPK claiming that the sale of the Welfenschatz to the Prussian Government was unlawful. SPK conducted its own investigation of the sale and determined that the transaction occurred at a fair market price without coercion. In 2014, the parties agreed to submit the claim to the German Advisory Commission for the Return of Cultural Property Seized as a Result of Nazi Persecution, Especially Jewish Property, which likewise concluded that the sale had occurred at a fair price without duress.

Disappointed by the proceedings in Germany, the heirs filed suit in Federal District Court in Washington, D. C. They brought several common law property claims against Germany and SPK, seeking $250 million in compensation. Petitioners moved to dismiss the case. Germany argued that it was immune from suit because the heirs' claims did not fall within the FSIA's exception to immunity for "property taken in violation of international law." *See* 28 U.S.C. §1605(a)(3). Germany reasoned that the purchase of the Welfenschatz could not have violated international law because a sovereign's taking of its own nationals' property is not unlawful under the international law of expropriation. The District Court denied Germany's motion, and the D. C. Circuit affirmed [relying on its earlier decision in *Simon v. Republic of Hungary*, (D.C. Cir. 2016)]. The panel agreed with the heirs that the exception for property taken in violation of international law was satisfied because "genocide perpetrated by a state even against its own nationals is a violation of international law."

II

Enacted in 1976, the Foreign Sovereign Immunities Act supplies the ground rules for "obtaining jurisdiction over a foreign state in the courts of this country." *Argentine Republic v. Amerada Hess Shipping Corp.* (1989). The Act creates a baseline presumption of immunity from suit. "[U]nless a specified exception applies, a federal court lacks subject-matter jurisdiction over a claim against a foreign state." *Saudi Arabia v. Nelson* (1993).

The heirs contend that their claims fall within the exception for "property taken in violation of international law," §1605(a)(3), because the coerced sale of the Welfenschatz, their property, constituted an act of genocide, and genocide is a violation of international human rights law. Germany argues that the exception is inapplicable because the relevant international law is the international law of property—not the law of genocide—and under the international law of property a foreign sovereign's taking of its own nationals' property remains a domestic affair. This "domestic takings rule" assumes that what a country does to property belonging to its own citizens within its own borders is not the subject of international law. *See Bolivarian Republic of Venezuela v. Helmerich & Payne Int'l Drilling Co.* (2017) (citing Restatement (Third) of Foreign Relations Law of the United States §712 (1986) (Restatement (Third))).

A

Known at the founding as the "law of nations," what we now refer to as international law customarily concerns relations among sovereign states, not relations between states and individuals. *See Banco Nacional de Cuba v. Sabbatino* (1964) ("The traditional view of international law is that it establishes substantive principles for determining whether one country has wronged another.").

The domestic takings rule invoked by Germany derives from this premise. Historically, a sovereign's taking of a *foreigner's* property, like any injury of a foreign national, implicated the international legal system because it "constituted an injury to the state of the alien's nationality." Bradley & Goldsmith, Customary International Law as Federal Common Law: A Critique of the Modern Position, 110 Harv. L. Rev. 815, 831, n. 106 (1997); *see* S. Friedman, Expropriation in International Law 5, 139 (1953). Such mistreatment was an affront to the sovereign, and "therefore the alien's state alone, and not the individual, could invoke the remedies of international law." Bradley. A *domestic taking* by contrast did not interfere with relations among states. *See* E. de Vattel, 3 The Law of Nations §81, p. 138 (C. Fenwick transl. 1916) ("Even the property of individuals, taken as a whole, is to be regarded as the property of the Nation with respect to other Nations."); *see also United States v. Belmont* (1937) ("What another country has done in the way of taking over property of its nationals . . . is not a matter for judicial consideration here.").

The domestic takings rule has deep roots not only in international law but also in United States foreign policy. Secretary of State Cordell Hull most famously expressed the principle in a 1938 letter to the Mexican Ambassador following that country's nationalization of American oil fields. The Secretary conceded "the right of a foreign government to treat its own nationals in this fashion if it so desires. This is a matter of domestic concern." Letter from C. Hull to C. Nájera (July 21, 1938). The United States, however, could not "accept the idea" that "these plans can be carried forward at the expense of our citizens."

The domestic takings rule endured even as international law increasingly came to be seen as constraining how states interacted not just with other states but also with individuals, including their own citizens. The United Nations Universal Declaration of Human Rights and Convention on the Prevention of Genocide became part of a growing body of human rights law that made "how a state treats individual human beings . . . a matter of international concern." Bradley, *supra*. These human rights documents were silent, however, on the subject of property rights. *See* Friedman, *supra*. International tribunals therefore continued to maintain that international law governed "confiscation of the property of foreigners," but "measures taken by a State with respect to the property of its own nationals are not subject to these principles." *Gudmundsson v. Iceland* (decision of the European Commission on Human Rights).

Some criticized the treatment of property rights under international law, but they did so on the ground that *all* sovereign takings were outside the scope of international law, not just domestic takings. In the 1950s and 1960s, [for example,] a growing chorus of newly independent states, particularly in Latin America, resisted any foreign restraint on their ability to nationalize property.

We confronted this dispute over the existence of international law constraints on sovereign takings in *Sabbatino*, where we were asked to decide claims arising out of Cuba's nationalization of American sugar interests in 1960. This Court observed that there were "few if any issues in international law today on which opinion seems to be so divided as the limitations on a state's power to expropriate the property *of aliens*." Hesitant to delve into this controversy, we instead invoked the act of state doctrine, which prevents United States courts from determining the validity of the public acts of a foreign sovereign.

Congress did not applaud the Court's reticence. Within months of *Sabbatino*, it passed the Second Hickenlooper Amendment to the Foreign Assistance Act of 1964. The Amendment prohibits United States courts from applying the act of state doctrine where a "right[ ] to property is asserted" based upon a "taking . . . by an act of that state in violation of the principles of international law." 22 U.S.C. §2370(e)(2). Courts and commentators understood the Amendment to permit adjudication of claims the *Sabbatino* decision had avoided — claims against foreign nations for expropriation of American-owned property. But nothing in the Amendment purported to alter any rule of international law, including the domestic takings rule.

Congress used language nearly identical to that of the Second Hickenlooper Amendment 12 years later in crafting the FSIA's expropriation exception. Based on this historical and legal background, courts arrived at a "consensus" that the expropriation exception's "reference to 'violation of international law' does not cover expropriations of property belonging to a country's own nationals." *Republic of Austria v. Altmann* (2004) (Breyer, J., concurring).

B

The heirs urge us to change course. They read "rights in property taken in violation of international law" not as an invocation of the international law governing property rights, but as a broad incorporation of any international norm. Focusing on human rights law, the heirs rely on the United Nations Convention on Genocide, which defines genocide as "deliberately inflicting on [a] group conditions of life calculated to bring about its physical destruction in whole or in part." Convention on the Prevention and Punishment of the Crime of Genocide, Art. II, Dec. 9, 1948. According to the heirs, the forced sale of their ancestors' art constituted an act of genocide because the confiscation of property was one of the conditions the Third Reich inflicted on the Jewish population to bring about their destruction.

We need not decide whether the sale of the consortium's property was an act of genocide, because the expropriation exception is best read as referencing the international law of expropriation rather than of human rights. We do not look to the law of genocide to determine if we have jurisdiction over the heirs' common law property claims. We look to the law of property.

And in 1976, the state of that body of law was clear: A "taking of property" could be "wrongful under international law" only where a state deprived "an alien" of property. Restatement (Second) §185; *see also Permanent Mission of India to United Nations v. City of New York* (2007) (noting our consistent practice of interpreting the FSIA in keeping with "international law at the time of the FSIA's enactment" and looking to the contemporary Restatement for guidance).

The heirs concede that at the time of the FSIA's enactment the international law of expropriation retained the domestic takings rule. But they argue that Congress captured all of international law in the exception—not just the international law of expropriation—and that other areas of international law do not shield a sovereign's actions against its own nationals. In support of that assertion, they note that the exception concerns "property *taken* in violation of international law"—not "property *takings* in violation of international law."

We would not place so much weight on a gerund. The text of the expropriation exception as a whole supports Germany's reading. The exception places repeated emphasis on property and property-related rights, while injuries and acts we might associate with genocide are notably lacking. That would be remarkable if the provision were intended to provide relief for atrocities such as the Holocaust. What is more, the heirs' interpretation of the phrase "taken in violation of international law" is not limited to violations of the law of genocide but extends to any human rights abuse. Their construction would arguably force courts themselves to violate international law, not only ignoring the domestic takings rule but also derogating international law's preservation of sovereign immunity for violations of human rights law.

Germany's interpretation of the exception is also more consistent with the FSIA's express goal of codifying the restrictive theory of sovereign immunity. §1602. Under the absolute or classical theory of sovereign immunity, foreign sovereigns are categorically immune from suit. Under the restrictive view, by contrast, immunity extends to a sovereign's public but not its private acts. Most of the FSIA's exceptions, such as the exception for "commercial activity carried on in the

United States," comport with the overarching framework of the restrictive theory. §1605(a)(2).

It is true that the expropriation exception, because it permits the exercise of jurisdiction over some public acts of expropriation, goes beyond even the restrictive view. In this way, the exception is unique; no other country has adopted a comparable limitation on sovereign immunity. History and context explain this nonconformity. As events such as Secretary Hull's letter and the Second Hickenlooper Amendment demonstrate, the United States has long sought to protect the property of its citizens abroad as part of a defense of America's free enterprise system. *Sabbatino*. Given that the FSIA "largely codifies" the restrictive theory, however, we take seriously the Act's general effort to preserve a dichotomy between private and public acts. *Nelson*. It would destroy that distinction were we to subject all manner of sovereign public acts to judicial scrutiny under the FSIA by transforming the expropriation exception into an all-purpose jurisdictional hook for adjudicating human rights violations.

C

Other provisions of the FSIA confirm Germany's position. The heirs' approach, for example, would circumvent the reticulated boundaries Congress placed in the FSIA with regard to human rights violations. Where Congress did target injuries associated with such acts, including torture or death, it did so explicitly and with precision. The noncommercial tort exception provides jurisdiction over claims only where the [tortious] conduct "occurr[ed] in the United States." §1605(a)(5). Similarly, the terrorism exception eliminates sovereign immunity for state sponsors of terrorism but only for certain human rights claims, brought by certain victims, against certain defendants. §§1605A(a), (h).

These restrictions would be of little consequence if human rights abuses could be packaged as violations of property rights and thereby brought within the expropriation exception to sovereign immunity. We have previously rejected efforts to insert modern human rights law into FSIA exceptions ill suited to the task. *Nelson* (commercial activity exception does not encompass claims that foreign state illegally detained and tortured United States citizen, "however monstrous such abuse undoubtedly may be"). We do so again today.

We have recognized that "United States law governs domestically but does not rule the world." *Kiobel v. Royal Dutch Petroleum Co.* (2013). We interpret the FSIA as we do other statutes affecting international relations: to avoid, where possible, "producing friction in our relations with [other] nations and leading some to reciprocate by granting their courts permission to embroil the United States in expensive and difficult litigation." *Helmerich*.

III

The heirs [also] rely on the 2016 Foreign Cultural Exchange Jurisdictional Immunity Clarification Act. The Act amends the FSIA to explain that participation in specified "art exhibition activities" does not qualify as "commercial activity" within the meaning of the expropriation exception. 28 U.S.C. §1605(h). . . .

According to the heirs, this clarification of the expropriation exception shows that Congress anticipated Nazi-era claims could be adjudicated by way of that exception.

We agree with the heirs, but only to a limited extent. Claims concerning Nazi-era art takings could be brought under the expropriation exception where the claims involve the taking of a *foreign* national's property. *See, e.g., Altmann* (claim concerning Austrian taking of Czechoslovakian national's art brought under the expropriation exception). The Clarification Act did not purport to amend the critical phrase here — "taken in violation of international law" — and we will not construe it to do so. The heirs also rely on other statutes aimed at promoting restitution to the victims of the Holocaust. The Acts include the Holocaust Victims Redress Act of 1998; the Holocaust Expropriated Art Recovery Act of 2016 (HEAR Act; and the Justice for Uncompensated Survivors Today (JUST) Act of 2017. These laws, the heirs suggest, demonstrate Congress's desire for American courts to hear disputes about Holocaust-era property claims.

The statutes do promote restitution for the victims of the Holocaust, but they generally encourage redressing those injuries outside of public court systems. The HEAR Act, for example, states that "the use of alternative dispute resolution" mechanisms will "yield just and fair resolutions in a more efficient and predictable manner" than litigation in court. §2(8). Germany has adopted just such an alternative mechanism, the Advisory Commission, and the heirs availed themselves of that opportunity to resolve their claims.

These laws do not speak to sovereign immunity. That is the province of the FSIA.

IV

We hold that the phrase "rights in property taken in violation of international law," as used in the FSIA's expropriation exception, refers to violations of the international law of expropriation and thereby incorporates the domestic takings rule.

The judgment of the Court of Appeals for the D. C. Circuit is vacated. . . .

* * *

The question what forum human rights violations "belong" in is both exceedingly important and hotly contested. Notice the range of alternatives:

- International tribunals such as the International Criminal Court, which investigates and prosecutes individuals charged with four main crimes: genocide, crimes against humanity (crimes committed in the context of attacks against civilian populations), war crimes (breaches of the Geneva conventions in the context of armed conflict), and the crime of aggression (illegal armed attacks by a state against the sovereignty, integrity, or independence of another State).[61]
- Alternative dispute resolution systems such as the HEAR Act supporting advisory commissions described in *Philipp.*

---

61. Carsten Stahn, A Critical Introduction to International Criminal Law (2019).

- Litigation or reparations legislation *in situ* (in the courts of the country where the violation occurred).
- Restorative and transitional justice policies and practices.[62]
- Litigation in the courts of a foreign country as the plaintiffs in *Philipp* sought.[63]
- Traditional human rights commission investigations and public reporting.

The question is relevant not only to mass atrocities of the twentieth century and other historical injustices, but also to twenty-first century crises, including, for example, where disputes over the damage caused by climate change should be litigated. Climate experts predict that "places with the least level of economic development are . . . in line to feel the impacts with the greatest degree" in part because they are more dependent on natural resources,[64] whereas more developed regions are responsible for the releases of greenhouse gases that drive climate change.[65] What is the right forum for legal claims related to the effects of climate change?[66]

---

62. Theo Gavrielides, Routledge International Handbook of Restorative Justice (2018); Olivera Simic, An Introduction to Transitional Justice (2016).

63. *See also* Turkiye Halk Bankasi A.S. v. United States (No. 21-1450) (certiorari to review power of U.S. district courts to exercise subject matter jurisdiction over criminal prosecution of instrumentality of foreign sovereign under FSIA).

64. Tara Law, *The Climate Crisis is Global, But These 6 Places Face the Most Severe Consequences*, Time, Sept. 30, 2019.

65. Nadia Popovich and Brad Plumer, *Who Has the Most Historical Reponsibility for Climate Change*, New York Times, Nov. 12, 2021 (reporting that wealthy countries, "including the United States, Canada, Japan, and much of western Europe, account for just 12 percent of the global population today but are responsible for 50 percent of all the planet-warming greenhouse gases released from fossil fuels and industry over the past 170 years").

66. Joana Setzer & Catherine Higham, *Global Trends in Climate Change Litigation: 2021 Snapshot* (July 2021) (noting that while there were just 800 climate change cases between 1986 and 2014, over 1,100 were filed between 2014 and 2020; most cases are filed in courts of the Global North; strategic cases both to improve climate change policy and to weaken or undermine mitigation are rising and those "unfavorable" to mitigating climate change compose one third of all decided cases; the vast majority of cases (93 percent) seeking to improve action on climate change name governments rather than corporations).

CHAPTER 7

FEDERAL COURT RELIEF AGAINST THE FEDERAL GOVERNMENT AND FEDERAL OFFICERS

This chapter addresses suits against the federal government and its officers. It focuses on causes of action that aggrieved persons may invoke to redress wrongs committed by the federal government and its officials, as well as limits to those suits, including the doctrine of federal sovereign immunity.

The Supreme Court has recognized the importance of federal court relief to enforce federal rights against the federal government. Accordingly, the federal courts have provided injunctive relief to enforce federal rights in the absence of express causes of action. And in *Bivens v. Six Unknown Named Agents* (1971), the Court held that injured parties may sue federal officials in their individual capacity for money damages when those officials violate federal constitutional rights even if Congress has not expressly authorized the suit. The *Bivens* doctrine, as it came to be known, was based upon the principle that "where federally protected rights have been invaded, . . . courts will be alert to adjust their remedies so as to grant the necessary relief." *Bell v. Hood* (1946). Injured parties have sought to bring *Bivens* claims to challenge a variety of unconstitutional acts by federal officials, including abusive prison conditions, free speech violations, and cross-border shootings. The Court has, however, steadily shrunk the scope of the *Bivens* doctrine to limit the availability of federal court relief in these cases.

In limiting federal court relief against the federal government and its officers, the Court has cited several constitutional concerns, including the separation of powers. As we shall see, respecting the role of Congress in creating rights of action is one reason the Court has given for significantly limiting (though not overruling) *Bivens*. Protecting congressional authority is also one reason cited for the persistence of federal sovereign immunity, a doctrine whose history includes a common law tradition of shielding the English sovereign (that is, the king or queen) from suit in English courts. Executive power is also central to the story of executive privilege and the absolute immunity of the President from civil liability for executive acts. The limits of this principle have been tested in the modern era.

Thus, this Chapter's exploration of federal court relief against the federal government and its officials continues our exploration of the role of the federal courts and the practical stakes of federal court relief in particular social and historical contexts.

A. SUITS AGAINST THE FEDERAL GOVERNMENT

1. Federal Sovereign Immunity

Under the doctrine of sovereign immunity, individuals generally may not sue the federal government directly without its consent. The Court asserted over 70 years ago in *Federal Crop Ins. Corp. v. Merrill* (1947), that "[i]t is too late in the day to urge that the Government is just another private litigant, for purposes of charging it with liability." The Constitution does not expressly refer to the "sovereign immunity" of the United States. But courts and commentators have identified a multitude of potential bases for the doctrine. In an oft-cited article, Professor Vicki Jackson identified at least three reasons the court has historically given for the doctrine of federal sovereign immunity.[1] First, the doctrine is traceable to an English common law tradition in which sovereign governments were entitled to some degree of immunity from suit. Second, under the Appropriations Clause of Article I, it is for Congress to tell the federal government how it must spend funds and, by negative implication, not the role of courts.[2] Third, "Congress's control over the jurisdiction of the federal courts gives it considerable powers simply to refuse to authorize suits against the government."[3]

What follows is one of the leading cases on the subject. It arose from the conduct of a government owned insurance company that was created in 1938 during The Great Depression.[4] As you read the Court's opinion, as well as that of the dissenting Justices, consider which justification for federal sovereign immunity, if any, should apply when the government engages in a business enterprise.

Federal Crop Ins. Corp. v. Merrill

332 U.S. 380 (1947)

Mr. Justice FRANKFURTER delivered the opinion of the Court.

This case involves a question of importance in the administration of the Federal Crop Insurance Act. The Corporation is a wholly Government-owned

---

1. Vicki C. Jackson, *Suing the Federal Government: Sovereignty, Immunity, and Judicial Independence*, 35 GEO. WASH. INT'L L. REV. 521, 542 (2003). For a general primer on the subject of federal sovereign immunity, see Gregory C. Sisk, *A Primer on the Doctrine of Federal Sovereign Immunity*, 58 OKLA. L. REV. 439 (2005).

2. Jackson, *supra* note 1, at 543. *See also* Kate Stith, *Congress' Power of the Purse*, 97 YALE L.J. 1343, 1344 (1988).

3. Jackson, *supra* note 1, at 546.

4. Randall A. Kramer, *Federal Crop Insurance 1938-1982*, 57 AGRIC. HIST. 181 (1982).

enterprise, created by the Federal Crop Insurance Act, as an "agency of and within the Department of Agriculture." To carry out the purposes of the Act, the Corporation, "Commencing with the wheat * * * crops planted for harvest in 1945" is empowered "to insure, upon such terms and conditions not inconsistent with the provisions of this title as it may determine, producers of wheat * * * against loss in yields due to unavoidable causes, including drought * * *." In pursuance of its authority, the Corporation promulgated its Wheat Crop Insurance Regulations.

Respondents applied locally for insurance under the Federal Crop Insurance Act to cover wheat farming operations in Bonneville County, Idaho. Respondents informed the Bonneville County Agricultural Conservation Committee, acting as agent for the Corporation, that they were planting 460 acres of spring wheat and that on 400 of these acres they were reseeding on winter wheat acreage. The Committee advised respondents that the entire crop was insurable, and recommended to the Corporation's Denver Branch Office acceptance of the application. On May 28, 1945, the Corporation accepted the application.

In July, 1945, most of the respondents' crop was destroyed by drought. Upon being notified, the Corporation, after discovering that the destroyed acreage had been reseeded, refused to pay the loss, and this litigation was appropriately begun in one of the lower courts of Idaho. Respondents [contended] they had in fact been misled by petitioner's agent into believing that spring wheat reseeded on winter wheat acreage was insurable by the Corporation. The jury returned a verdict for the loss on all the 460 acres and the Supreme Court of Idaho affirmed the resulting judgment.

The case no doubt presents phases of hardship. We take for granted that, on the basis of what they were told by the Corporation's local agent, the respondents reasonably believed that their entire crop was covered by petitioner's insurance. But the Corporation is not a private insurance company. It is too late in the day to urge that the Government is just another private litigant, for purposes of charging it with liability, whenever it takes over a business theretofore conducted by private enterprise or engages in competition with private ventures. Government is not partly public or partly private, depending upon the governmental pedigree of the type of a particular activity or the manner in which the Government conducts it. The Government may carry on its operations through conventional executive agencies or through corporate forms especially created for defined ends. Whatever the form in which the Government functions, anyone entering into an arrangement with the Government takes the risk of having accurately ascertained that he who purports to act for the Government stays within the bounds of his authority.

The oft-quoted observation in *Rock Island, Arkansas & Louisiana R.R. Co. v. United States* (1920), that "Men must turn square corners when they deal with the Government," does not reflect a callous outlook. It merely expresses the duty of all courts to observe the conditions defined by Congress for charging the public treasury. The "terms and conditions" defined by the Corporation, under authority of Congress, for creating liability on the part of the Government preclude recovery for the loss of the reseeded wheat no matter with what good reason the respondents thought they had obtained insurance from the Government.

Mr. Justice BLACK, RUTLEDGE, JACKSON, and DOUGLAS dissent.

I would affirm the decision of the court below. If crop insurance contracts made by agencies of the United States Government are to be judged by the law of the State in which they are written, I find no error in the court below. If, however, we are to hold them subject only to federal law and to declare what that law is. I can see no reason why we should not adopt a rule which recognizes the practicalities of the business.

It was early discovered that fair dealing in the insurance business required that the entire contract between the policyholder and the insurance company be embodied in the writings which passed between the parties, namely, the written application, if any, and the policy issued. It may be well enough to make some types of contracts with the Government subject to long and involved regulations published in the Federal Register. To my mind, it is an absurdity to hold that every farmer who insures his crops knows what the Federal Register contains or even knows that there is such a publication. If he were to peruse this voluminous and dull publication as it is issued from time to time in order to make sure whether anything has been promulgated that affects his rights, he would never need crop insurance, for he would never get time to plant any crops. Nor am I convinced that a reading of technically-worded regulations would enlighten him much in any event.

In this case, the Government entered a field which required the issuance of large numbers of insurance policies to people engaged in agriculture. It could not expect them to be lawyers, except in rare instances, and one should not be expected to have to employ a lawyer to see whether his own Government is issuing him a policy which in case of loss would turn out to be no policy at all. There was no fraud or concealment, and those who represented the Government in taking on the risk apparently no more suspected the existence of a hidden regulation that would render the contract void than did the policyholder. It is very well to say that those who deal with the Government should turn square corners. But there is no reason why the square corners should constitute a one-way street.

The Government asks us to lift its policies out of the control of the States and to find or fashion a federal rule to govern them. I should respond to that request by laying down a federal rule that would hold these agencies to the same fundamental principles of fair dealing that have been found essential in progressive states to prevent insurance from being an investment in disappointment.

* * *

2.   *Injunctive Relief Against the United States*

You may be familiar with instances in which individuals and organizations bring suits for injunctive relief against the federal government, either by naming a federal agency as a party or suing a federal official in the defendant's official capacity. In *Lujan v. Defenders of Wildlife* (1992) (Chapter 3), for example, an organization sued the Secretary of Interior for issuing an environmental rule that allegedly outpaced the Department's statutory authority. In recent years, courts have entertained suits challenging the legality of many significant federal policies, including federal health care legislation; protections against deportation of individuals who were brought to the United States as children; and executive orders threatening to end federal funding to cities that do not cooperate with federal immigration officials. These suits either named government officials (including the President) or named the United States as a party.

How does sovereign immunity interact with this category of suits? At least two exceptions to sovereign immunity pave the way for this kind of litigation against federal governmental action. First, federal courts have long entertained suits against officers who allegedly have exceeded their legal authority or enforced an unconstitutional statute.[5] In some of the instances discussed above, plaintiffs were seeking injunctive relief for alleged violations of the federal constitution.

Second, Congress has waived its sovereign immunity for suits brought against the United States seeking injunctive relief, even outside of the constitutional context. As amended in 1976, the Administrative Procedure Act reads:

> An action in a court of the United States seeking relief other than money damages and stating a claim that an agency or an officer or employee thereof acted or failed to act in an official capacity or under color of legal authority shall not be dismissed nor relief therein be denied on the ground that it is against the United States or that the United States is an indispensable party. The United States may be named as a defendant in any such action, and a judgment or decree may be entered against the United States.[6]

This language is an unambiguous waiver of federal sovereign immunity in suits not requesting monetary relief.

3. Other Congressional Waivers of Federal Sovereign Immunity

Congress has also enacted statutes that, under specified circumstances, allow injured parties to obtain money damages against the federal government. The most significant examples are the Federal Torts Claims Act, which creates liability when federal officials commit state-law torts, and the Tucker Act, which creates liability for contractual violations, takings, and claims seeking the return of property.

a. The Federal Torts Claims Act

For much of the nation's history, individuals could not recover damages when federal officials engaged in tortious conduct against them. This changed in 1946, when Congress adopted the Federal Tort Claims Act (FTCA). The most important provision of the Act provides that the "United States shall be liable . . . to tort claims in the same manner and to the same extent as a private individual under like circumstances."[7] When a federal official, acting on behalf of the government, violates

---

5. Erwin Chemerinsky, Federal Jurisdiction §9.2.2 (8th ed. 2021). *See also* Schneider v. Smith, 390 U.S. 17 (1968); Philadelphia Co. v. Stimson, 223 U.S. 605 (1912).

6. 5 U.S.C. §702.

7. 28 U.S.C. §2674.

a state-law tort provision, this Act creates liability against the United States government. The Act does not call on courts to create a unique, federal body of tort law; state tort law controls.

The FTCA is supplemented by the Westfall Act,[8] which makes the FTCA the sole means of recovering against a federal official who violates a state tort while acting within the scope of employment. As long as the Attorney General or her designee certifies that the employee was acting within the scope of employment "at the time of the incident out of which the claim arose," the United States is to be substituted as the defendant, and the individual employee is immunized from state tort liability.

There are statutory and common law exceptions to the FTCA.

Foreign-country exception. One important statutory exception is a bar against recovery for "[a]ny claim arising in a foreign country."[9] Under *Sosa v. Alvarez-Machain* (2004), "the FTCA's foreign country exception bars all claims based on any injury suffered in a foreign country, regardless of where the tortious act or omission occurred." In that case, the Supreme Court accordingly denied recovery to a doctor who was illegally kidnapped in Mexico, even though the kidnapping happened at the direction of federal officials who were in the United States.

Intentional tort exception. A second important exception applies to "[a]ny claim arising out of assault, battery, false imprisonment, false arrest, malicious prosecution, abuse of process, libel, slander, misrepresentation, deceit, or interference with contract rights."[10] The net result is that most intentional torts are excluded from the reach of the FTCA unless the suit is for trespass or conversion. Additionally, under a 1974 amendment, plaintiffs may recover for assaults, batteries, false imprisonments, false arrests, abuses of process, and malicious prosecutions committed by federal investigative or law enforcement officials.[11]

Discretionary function exception. A third exception is for discretionary functions. Under this exception, a plaintiff may not maintain an FTCA claim "based upon the exercise or performance or the failure to exercise or perform a discretionary function or duty on the part of a federal agency or an employee of the Government, whether or not the discretion involved be abused."[12]

There is a two-part test to determine whether this exception is applicable. First, for the exception to apply, the governmental action must involve judgment or choice. The judgment-or-choice dimension of the discretionary-function exception is exemplified by *Berkovitz v. United States* (1988). In that case, the Supreme Court unanimously declined to apply the exception where plaintiffs alleged that, in violation of federal and state law, a governmental agency failed to properly inspect a batch of polio vaccine for safety before approving it. The Court emphasized that "conduct cannot be discretionary unless it involves an element of judgment or choice." The conduct alleged fell short of that mark. Given that the federal agents

---

8. 28 U.S.C. §2679.
9. 28 U.S.C. §2680(k).
10. 28 U.S.C. §2680(h).
11. *Id.*
12. 28 U.S.C. §2680(a).

were alleged to have violated the agencies adopted policy, a policy which "allegedly [left] no room for implementing officials to exercise independent policy judgment," the challenged actions involved no policy discretion.

Second, for the discretionary function exception to apply, the judgment or choice involved must be based on considerations of public policy. This is illustrated by *United States v. Gaubert* (1991). In that case, a shareholder of insolvent savings and loan association sued the United States on the ground that federal regulators had engaged in negligent supervision of the association's directors and officers. The Court held that the exception applied because the federal regulators' supervision involved discretionary choices "in furtherance of public policy goals."

Other statutory exceptions. There are other statutory exceptions that require less in the way of description. FTCA may not be used to enforce strict-liability legal regimes. *See Dalehite v. United States* (1953). Moreover, government officials are exempt from this kind of liability if they exercise "due care in the execution of a statute or regulation, whether or not that statute or regulation" is valid.[13] Other statutory exceptions include: negligence by the postal service in the delivery of mail or for claims arising from the collection of taxes or duties;[14] admiralty matters;[15] claims arising from the Trading with the Economy Act of 1917;[16] for the imposition of a quarantine;[17] and claims against the Tennessee Value Authority of the Panama Canal Company.[18]

Military service exception. In addition to the above statutory exceptions, there is also a common law exception for injuries to members of the military arising from their military service. The lead case is *Feres v. United States* (1950). *Feres* involved three consolidated cases. Two were about negligent medical treatment of medical personnel. The third involved a service member who died in a barracks fire, allegedly as a result of the government's negligence. The Supreme Court dismissed all three suits. The court reasoned:

> We conclude that the Government is not liable under the Federal Tort Claims Act for injuries to servicemen where the injuries arise out of or are in the course of activity incident to service. Without exception, the relationship of military personnel to the Government has been governed exclusively by federal law. We do not think that Congress, in drafting this Act, created a new cause of action dependent on local law for service-connected injuries or death due to negligence. We cannot impute to Congress such a radical departure from established law in the absence of express congressional command.

---

13. *See* 28 U.S.C. §2680(a).
14. 28 U.S.C. §2680(b)-(c).
15. 28 U.S.C. §2680(d).
16. 28 U.S.C. §2680(f)
17. 28 U.S.C. §2680(f)
18. 28 U.S.C. §2680(l)-(m).

The *Feres* doctrine is controversial, because it blocks access to justice for members of the military who are illegally harmed.[19] One commentator recently observed, for example, ways that the *Feres* doctrine complicates efforts to achieve access to justice for negligently handled sexual assault allegations in the military.[20]

One federal case that helps illustrate the *Feres* doctrine's wide reach is *United States v. Stanley* (1987).[21] In that case, James Stanley, a member of the U.S. Army was secretly administered LSD as a part of an Army plan to test how drugs affect humans. He had volunteered for participation in a chemical warfare testing program, but believed that the LSD was administered negligently; that the failure to brief him post-experiment about his experiences was also negligent; and that he did not give informed consent to receive psychoactive drugs.[22] He contended that the lack of briefing about the imposition of this drug caused him mental harm and negatively impacted his family life. Moreover, he argued that *Feres* should not apply because he was a volunteer in the chemical warfare program and had been released from his regular duties to participate. The federal courts found that the servicemember's FTCA suit had to be dismissed under *Feres*, because the injuries arose incident to military service.[23]

b.   The Tucker Act

In 1855, Congress created the Court of Claims, giving that judicial body authority to hear cases based upon any act of Congress or regulation of any executive department, "or for any contract, express or implied, with the government of the United States."[24] Initially, the court was only able issue advisory recommendations; Congress could choose whether to adopt them. Then in 1887, Congress amended the Tucker Act to allow the Court of Claims to make binding judgments. That act also expanded the jurisdiction over the Court of Claims to include breaches of contracts.

Congress enacted one of the most recent amendments to the Tucker Act by way of the 1982 Federal Courts Improvement Act. That Act abolished the Court of Claims and created a U.S. Claims Court and the U.S. Court of Appeals for the Federal Circuit. In 1992, Congress changed the name of the U.S. Claims Court to its current name: The U.S. Court of Federal Claims.[25] The Court of Federal Claims has trial jurisdiction, and its decisions are reviewable in the Federal Circuit. It may award money damages against the U.S. government.[26]

---

19. *See, e.g.,* Andrew F. Popper, *Rethinking* Feres: *Granting Access to Justice for Service Members,* 60 B.C. L. REV. 1491 (2019); Christopher G. Froelich, *Closing the Equitable Loophole: Assessing the Supreme Court's Next Move Regarding the Availability of Equitable Relief for Military Plaintiffs,* 35 SETON HALL L. REV. 699 (2005); Nicole Melvani, Comment, *The Fourteenth Exception: How the* Feres *Doctrine Improperly Bars Medical Malpractice Claims of Military Service Members,* 46 CAL. W. L. REV. 395 (2010).

20. Francine Banner, *Immoral Waiver: Judicial Review of Intra-Military Sexual Assault Claims,* 17 LEWIS & CLARK L. REV. 723 (2013).

21. 483 U.S. 669 (1987).

22. Stanley v. Cent. Intel. Agency, 639 F.2d 1146, 1149 (5th Cir. 1981).

23. *Id.*

24. Pub. L. No. 97-164, 96 Stat. 25.

25. Pub. L. 102–572, title IX, §§902(a)(1), 910(b), Oct. 29, 1992, 106 Stat. 4516, 4520.

26. 28 U.S.C. §1491(a)(1).

Federal district courts and the Court of Federal Claims have concurrent jurisdiction over suits against the United States for the recovery of taxes alleged to have been erroneously or illegally assessed or collected.[27] Additionally, the district courts have concurrent jurisdiction for claims less than $10,000, a provision that is often called the Little Tucker Act.[28] The Court of Federal Claims generally has exclusive jurisdiction over claims greater than that amount.[29]

The Tucker Act is a clear waiver of sovereign immunity for money damages claims against the United States, so long as those damages do not arise from torts. The Court has warned, however, that the Tucker Act does not waive sovereign immunity for violations of statutory rights that have their own accompanying regulatory scheme. The following case illustrates these principles.

United States v. Bormes

568 U.S. 6 (2012)

Justice SCALIA delivered the opinion of the Court.

The Little Tucker Act, 28 U.S.C. §1346(a)(2), provides that "[t]he district courts shall have original jurisdiction, concurrent with the United States Court of Federal Claims, of . . . [a]ny . . . civil action or claim against the United States, not exceeding $10,000 in amount, founded . . . upon . . . any Act of Congress." We consider whether the Little Tucker Act waives the sovereign immunity of the United States with respect to damages actions for violations of the Fair Credit Reporting Act (FCRA).

I

The Fair Credit Reporting Act has as one of its purposes to "protect consumer privacy." To that end, FCRA provides, among other things, that "no person that accepts credit cards or debit cards for the transaction of business shall print more than the last 5 digits of the card number or the expiration date upon any receipt provided to the cardholder at the point of the sale or transaction." The Act defines "person" as "any individual, partnership, corporation, trust, estate, cooperative, association, government or governmental subdivision or agency, or other entity."

FCRA imposes civil liability for willful or negligent noncompliance with its requirements: "Any person who willfully fails to comply" with the Act "with respect to any consumer," "is liable to that consumer" for actual damages or damages "of not less than $100 and not more than $1,000," as well as punitive damages, attorney's fees, and costs. The Act includes a jurisdictional provision, which provides that "[a]n action to enforce any liability created under this subchapter may be brought in any appropriate United States district court, without regard to the

---

27. 28 U.S.C. §1346(a)(1).

28. 28 U.S.C. §1346(a)(2). *See, e.g.,* United States v. Bormes, 568 U.S. 6 (2012) (holding that the Little Tucker Act did not waive sovereign immunity for statutory violations of the Federal Credit Reporting Act).

29. *Id.*

amount in controversy, or in any other court of competent jurisdiction" within the earlier of "2 years after the date of discovery by the plaintiff of the violation that is the basis for such liability" or "5 years after the date on which the violation that is the basis for such liability occurs."

James X. Bormes is an attorney who filed a putative class action against the United States in the United States District Court for the Northern District of Illinois seeking damages under FCRA. Bormes alleged that he paid a $350 federal-court filing fee for a client using his own credit card on Pay.gov, an Internet-based system used by federal courts and dozens of federal agencies to process online payment transactions. According to Bormes, his electronic receipt included the last four digits of his credit card, in addition to its expiration date, in willful violation of [the FCRA]. He claimed that he and thousands of similarly situated persons were entitled to recover damages, and asserted jurisdiction FCRA, as well as under the Little Tucker Act, 28 U.S.C. §1346(a)(2).

The Federal Circuit held that the Little Tucker Act provided the Government's consent to suit for violation of FCRA. We granted certiorari.

II

Sovereign immunity shields the United States from suit absent a consent to be sued that is unequivocally expressed. The Little Tucker Act is one statute that unequivocally provides the Federal Government's consent to suit for certain money-damages claims. *United States v. Mitchell* (1983). Subject to exceptions not relevant here, the Little Tucker Act provides that " district courts shall have original jurisdiction, concurrent with the United States Court of Federal Claims," of a "civil action or claim against the United States, not exceeding $10,000 in amount, founded either upon the Constitution, or any Act of Congress, or any regulation of an executive department, or upon any express or implied contract with the United States, or for liquidated or unliquidated damages in cases not sounding in tort." 28 U.S.C. §1346(a)(2). The Little Tucker Act and its companion statute, the Tucker Act, §1491(a)(1), do not themselves "creat[e] substantive rights," but "are simply jurisdictional provisions that operate to waive sovereign immunity for claims premised on other sources of law." *United States v. Navajo Nation* (2009).

Bormes argues that whether or not FCRA itself unambiguously waives sovereign immunity, the Little Tucker Act authorizes his FCRA damages claim against the United States. The question, then, is whether a damages claim under FCRA falls within the terms of the Tucker Act, so that "the United States has presumptively consented to suit." It does not. Where, as in FCRA, a statute contains its own self-executing remedial scheme, we look only to that statute to determine whether Congress intended to subject the United States to damages liability.

A

The Court of Claims was established, and the Tucker Act enacted, to open a judicial avenue for certain monetary claims against the United States. Before the creation of the Court of Claims in 1855, it was not uncommon for statutes to impose monetary obligations on the United States without specifying a means of judicial enforcement. As a result, claimants routinely petitioned Congress for private bills to recover money owed by the Federal Government. As this individualized legislative process became increasingly burdensome for Congress, the Court of Claims was created to relieve the pressure on Congress caused by the volume of private bills. The 1855 Act authorized the Court of Claims to hear claims against the United States "founded upon any law of Congress," §1, 10 Stat. 612, and thus allowed claimants to sue the Federal Government for monetary relief premised on other sources of law.

Enacted in 1887, the Tucker Act was the successor statute to the 1855 and 1863 Acts and replaced most of their provisions. Like the 1855 Act before it, the Tucker Act provided the Federal Government's consent to suit in the Court of Claims for claims "founded upon . . . any law of Congress." Section 2 of the 1887 Act created concurrent jurisdiction in the district courts for claims of up to $1,000. The Tucker Act's jurisdictional grant, and accompanying immunity waiver, supplied the missing ingredient for an action against the United States for the breach of monetary obligations not otherwise judicially enforceable.

B

The Tucker Act is displaced, however, when a law assertedly imposing monetary liability on the United States contains its own judicial remedies. In that event, the specific remedial scheme establishes the exclusive framework for the liability Congress created under the statute. Because a precisely drawn, detailed statute preempts more general remedies, FCRA's self-executing remedial scheme supersedes the gap-filling role of the Tucker Act.

We have long recognized that an additional remedy in the Court of Claims is foreclosed when it contradicts the limits of a precise remedial scheme. In *Nichols v. United States* (1869), the issue was whether the 1855 Act authorized suit in the Court of Claims for improper assessment of duties on imported liquor that had already been paid without protest. The Court held that it did not. The revenue laws already provided a remedy: An aggrieved merchant could sue to recover the tax, but only after paying the duty under protest. The Court rejected the supposition that "Congress, after having carefully constructed a revenue system, with ample provisions to redress wrong, intended to give to the taxpayer and importer a further and different remedy."

Our more recent cases have consistently held that statutory schemes with their own remedial framework exclude alternative relief under the general terms of the Tucker Act. Where a specific statutory scheme provides the accoutrements of a judicial action, the metes and bounds of the liability Congress intended to create can only be divined from the text of the statute itself.

FCRA creates a detailed remedial scheme. Its provisions set out a carefully circumscribed, time-limited, plaintiff-specific cause of action, and also precisely define the appropriate forum. It authorizes aggrieved consumers to hold "any person" who "willfully" or "negligent[ly]" fails to comply with the Act's requirements liable for specified damages. Claims to enforce liability must be brought within a specified limitations period, and jurisdiction will lie "in any appropriate United States district court, without regard to the amount in controversy, or in any other court of competent jurisdiction." Without resort to the Tucker Act, FCRA enables claimants to pursue in court the monetary relief contemplated by the statute.

Plaintiffs cannot, therefore, mix and match FCRA's provisions with the Little Tucker Act's immunity waiver to create an action against the United States. Since

FCRA is a detailed remedial scheme, only its own text can determine whether the damages liability Congress crafted extends to the Federal Government. To hold otherwise—to permit plaintiffs to remedy the absence of a waiver of sovereign immunity in specific, detailed statutes by pleading general Tucker Act jurisdiction—would transform the sovereign-immunity landscape.

The Tucker Act cannot be superimposed on an existing remedial scheme.

* * *

B.   SUITS AGAINST FEDERAL OFFICERS

1.   Causes of Action

Since the earliest days of the republic, federal courts have been asked to consider the proper scope of damages claims against individual federal officials. In 1804, in *Little v. Barreme,* the United States Supreme Court famously awarded damages against a U.S. naval officer. The officer interceded a vessel that was coming from a French port, an act that went beyond his statutory authority. Because the unlawful act went beyond his legal authority, the Supreme Court upheld the damages claim against him. This case is cited by many scholars as one of the earliest and most important examples of the Supreme Court recognizing a money-damages suit against a federal official in his individual capacity.[30]

2.   Implied Causes of Action

a.   For Constitutional Claims[*]

No federal statute authorizes federal courts to hear suits or give relief against federal officers who violate the Constitution of the United States. Although 42 U.S.C. §1983 authorizes suits against state and local officers, it has no application to the federal government or its officers. Nor is there any analogous statute pertaining to violations of federal law by federal officials.

---

30. *See, e.g.,* William Baude, *Is Qualified Immunity Unlawful?,* 106 Calif. L. Rev. 45, 88 (2018) ("As many scholars of official liability have pointed out, lawsuits against officials for constitutional violations did not generally permit a good-faith defense during the early years of the Republic. A paradigmatic example is Chief Justice Marshall's 1804 opinion in *Little v. Barreme*"); James E. Pfander & Jonathan L. Hunt, *Public Wrongs and Private Bills: Indemnification and Government Accountability in the Early Republic,* 85 N.Y.U. L. Rev. 1862, 1863 (2010) ("No case better illustrates the standards to which federal government officers were held than *Little v. Barreme*.").

* The ability of federal courts to infer causes of action from federal statutes, which is quite limited, is discussed in Chapter 5, Section B.

In the landmark decision of *Bivens v. Six Unknown Named Agents of Federal Bureau of Narcotics* (1971), the Supreme Court said that it would infer a cause of action for damages directly from constitutional provisions. But since 1980, the Supreme Court has continually ruled against *Bivens* claims and greatly restricted their availability.

Bivens v. Six Unknown Named Agents of the Fed. Bureau of Narcotics

403 U.S. 388 (1971)

Justice BRENNAN delivered the opinion of the Court.

This case has its origin in an arrest and search carried out on the morning of November 26, 1965. Petitioner's complaint alleged that on that day respondents, agents of the Federal Bureau of Narcotics acting under claim of federal authority, entered his apartment and arrested him for alleged narcotics violations. The agents manacled petitioner in front of his wife and children, and threatened to arrest the entire family. They searched the apartment from stem to stern. Thereafter, petitioner was taken to the federal courthouse in Brooklyn, where he was interrogated, booked, and subjected to a visual strip search.

On July 7, 1967, petitioner brought suit in Federal District Court. In addition to the allegations above, his complaint asserted that the arrest and search were effected without a warrant, and that unreasonable force was employed in making the arrest; fairly read, it alleges as well that the arrest was made without probable cause. Petitioner claimed to have suffered great humiliation, embarrassment, and mental suffering as a result of the agents' unlawful conduct, and sought $15,000 damages from each of them. The District Court, on respondents' motion, dismissed the complaint on the ground, inter alia, that it failed to state a cause of action. The Court of Appeals affirmed on that basis. We reverse.

Respondents do not argue that petitioner should be entirely without remedy for an unconstitutional invasion of his rights by federal agents. In respondents' view, however, the rights that petitioner asserts—primarily rights of privacy—are creations of state and not of federal law. Accordingly, they argue, petitioner may obtain money damages to redress invasion of these rights only by an action in tort, under state law, in the state courts. In this scheme the Fourth Amendment would serve merely to limit the extent to which the agents could defend the state law tort suit by asserting that their actions were a valid exercise of federal power: if the agents were shown to have violated the Fourth Amendment, such a defense would be lost to them and they would stand before the state law merely as private individuals. Candidly admitting that it is the policy of the Department of Justice to remove all such suits from the state to the federal courts for decision, respondents nevertheless urge that we uphold dismissal of petitioner's complaint in federal court, and remit him to filing an action in the state courts in order that the case may properly be removed to the federal court for decision on the basis of state law.

We think that respondents' thesis rests upon an unduly restrictive view of the Fourth Amendment's protection against unreasonable searches and seizures by federal agents, a view that has consistently been rejected by this Court. Respondents seek to treat the relationship between a citizen and a federal agent unconstitutionally exercising his authority as no different from the relationship between two private citizens. In so doing, they ignore the fact that power, once granted, does not disappear like a magic gift when it is wrongfully used. An agent acting—albeit unconstitutionally—in the name of the United States possesses a far greater capacity for harm than an individual trespasser exercising no authority other than his own. Accordingly, as our cases make clear, the Fourth Amendment operates as a limitation upon the exercise of federal power regardless of whether the State in whose jurisdiction that power is exercised would prohibit or penalize the identical act if engaged in by a private citizen. It guarantees to citizens of the United States the absolute right to be free from unreasonable searches and seizures carried out by virtue of federal authority. And "where federally protected rights have been invaded, it has been the rule from the beginning that courts will be alert to adjust their remedies so as to grant the necessary relief." *Bell v. Hood* (1946).

The interests protected by state laws regulating trespass and the invasion of privacy, and those protected by the Fourth Amendment's guarantee against unreasonable searches and seizures, may be inconsistent or even hostile. Thus, we may bar the door against an unwelcome private intruder, or call the police if he persists in seeking entrance. The availability of such alternative means for the protection of privacy may lead the State to restrict imposition of liability for any consequent trespass. A private citizen, asserting no authority other than his own, will not normally be liable in trespass if he demands, and is granted, admission to another's house. But one who demands admission under a claim of federal authority stands in a far different position. The mere invocation of federal power by a federal law enforcement official will normally render futile any attempt to resist an unlawful entry or arrest by resort to the local police; and a claim of authority to enter is likely to unlock the door as well.

Nor is it adequate to answer that state law may take into account the different status of one clothed with the authority of the Federal Government. For just as state law may not authorize federal agents to violate the Fourth Amendment, neither may state law undertake to limit the extent to which federal authority can be exercised. The inevitable consequence of this dual limitation on state power is that the federal question becomes not merely a possible defense to the state law action, but an independent claim both necessary and sufficient to make out the plaintiff's cause of action.

That damages may be obtained for injuries consequent upon a violation of the Fourth Amendment by federal officials should hardly seem a surprising proposition. Historically, damages have been regarded as the ordinary remedy for an invasion of personal interests in liberty. Of course, the Fourth Amendment does not in so many words provide for its enforcement by an award of money damages for the consequences of its violation. But "it is well settled that where legal rights have been invaded, and a federal statute provides for a general right to sue for such invasion, federal courts may use any available remedy to make good the wrong done." *Bell v. Hood.*

The present case involves no special factors counseling hesitation in the absence of affirmative action by Congress. We are not dealing with a question of federal fiscal policy. Nor are we asked in this case to impose liability upon a congressional employee for actions contrary to no constitutional prohibition, but merely said to be in excess of the authority delegated to him by the Congress.

Finally, we cannot accept respondents' formulation of the question as whether the availability of money damages is necessary to enforce the Fourth Amendment. For we have here no explicit congressional declaration that persons injured by a federal officer's violation of the Fourth Amendment may not recover money damages from the agents, but must instead be remitted to another remedy, equally effective in the view of Congress.

The question is merely whether petitioner, if he can demonstrate an injury consequent upon the violation by federal agents of his Fourth Amendment rights, is entitled to redress his injury through a particular remedial mechanism normally available in the federal courts. "The very essence of civil liberty certainly consists in the right of every individual to claim the protection of the laws, whenever he receives an injury." *Marbury v. Madison* (1803). Having concluded that petitioner's complaint states a cause of action under the Fourth Amendment, we hold that petitioner is entitled to recover money damages for any injuries he has suffered as a result of the agents' violation of the Amendment.

Justice HARLAN, concurring in the judgment.

My initial view of this case was that the Court of Appeals was correct in dismissing the complaint, but for reasons stated in this opinion I am now persuaded to the contrary. Accordingly, I join in the judgment of reversal. For the reasons set forth below, I am of the opinion that federal courts do have the power to award damages for violation of 'constitutionally protected interests' and I agree with the Court that a traditional judicial remedy such as damages is appropriate to the vindication of the personal interests protected by the Fourth Amendment.

I

I turn first to the contention that the constitutional power of federal courts to accord Bivens damages for his claim depends on the passage of a statute creating a "federal cause of action." Although the point is not entirely free of ambiguity, I do not understand either the Government or my dissenting Brothers to maintain that Bivens' contention that he is entitled to be free from the type of official conduct prohibited by the Fourth Amendment depends on a decision by the State in which he resides to accord him a remedy. Such a position would be incompatible with the presumed availability of federal equitable relief, if a proper showing can be made in terms of the ordinary principles governing equitable remedies.

Thus the interest which Bivens claims—to be free from official conduct in contravention of the Fourth Amendment—is a federally protected interest. Therefore, the question of judicial power to grant Bivens damages is not a problem of the "source" of the "right"; instead, the question is whether the power to authorize damages as a judicial remedy for the vindication of a federal constitutional right is placed by the Constitution itself exclusively in Congress' hands.

II

The contention that the federal courts are powerless to accord a litigant damage for a claimed invasion of his federal constitutional rights until Congress explicitly authorizes the remedy cannot rest on the notion that the decision to grant compensatory relief involves a resolution of policy considerations not susceptible of judicial discernment. Thus, in suits for damages based on violations of federal statutes lacking any express authorization of a damage remedy, this Court has authorized such relief where, in its view, damages are necessary to effectuate the congressional policy underpinning the substantive provisions of the statute. If it is not the nature of the remedy which is thought to render a judgment as to the appropriateness of damages inherently "legislative," then it must be the nature of the legal interest offered as an occasion for invoking otherwise appropriate judicial relief. But I do not think that the fact that the interest is protected by the Constitution rather than statute or common law justifies the assertion that federal courts are powerless to grant damages in the absence of explicit congressional action authorizing the remedy.

More importantly, the presumed availability of federal equitable relief against threatened invasions of constitutional interests appears entirely to negate the contention that the status of an interest as constitutionally protected divests federal courts of the power to grant damages absent express congressional authorization. And this Court's decisions make clear that, at least absent congressional restrictions, the scope of equitable remedial discretion is to be determined according to the distinctive historical traditions of equity as an institution.

If explicit congressional authorization is an absolute prerequisite to the power of a federal court to accord compensatory relief regardless of the necessity or appropriateness of damages as a remedy simply because of the status of a legal interest as constitutionally protected, then it seems to me that explicit congressional authorization is similarly prerequisite to the exercise of equitable remedial discretion in favor of constitutionally protected interests. Conversely, if a general grant of jurisdiction to the federal courts by Congress is thought adequate to empower a federal court to grant equitable relief for all areas of subject-matter jurisdiction enumerated therein, then it seems to me that the same statute is sufficient to empower a federal court to grant a traditional remedy at law.

III

The major thrust of the Government's position is that, where Congress has not expressly authorized a particular remedy, a federal court should exercise its power to accord a traditional form of judicial relief at the behest of a litigant, who claims a constitutionally protected interest has been invaded, only where the remedy is "essential," or "indispensable for vindicating constitutional rights."

These arguments for a more stringent test to govern the grant of damages in constitutional cases seem to be adequately answered by the point that the judiciary has a particular responsibility to assure the vindication of constitutional interests such as those embraced by the Fourth Amendment. To be sure, "it must be remembered that legislatures are ultimate guardians of the liberties and welfare of the people in quite as great a degree as the courts." But it must also be recognized that the Bill of Rights is particularly intended to vindicate the interests of the individual in the face of the popular will as expressed in legislative majorities; at the very least, it strikes me as no more appropriate to await express congressional authorization of traditional judicial relief with regard to these legal interests than with respect to interests protected by federal statutes.

The question then, is, as I see it, whether compensatory relief is "necessary" or "appropriate" to the vindication of the interest asserted. In resolving that question, it seems to me that the range of policy considerations we may take into account is at least as broad as the range of a legislature would consider with respect to an express statutory authorization of a traditional remedy. In this regard I agree with the Court that the appropriateness of according Bivens compensatory relief does not turn simply on the deterrent effect liability will have on federal official conduct. Damages as a traditional form of compensation for invasion of a legally protected interest may be entirely appropriate even if no substantial deterrent effects on future official lawlessness might be thought to result. Bivens, after all, has invoked judicial processes claiming entitlement to compensation for injuries resulting from allegedly lawless official behavior, if those injuries are properly compensable in money damages. I do not think a court of law—vested with the power to accord a remedy—should deny him his relief simply because he cannot show that future lawless conduct will thereby be deterred.

[margin note: Not just about deterrence]

And I think it is clear that Bivens advances a claim of the sort that, if proved, would be properly compensable in damages. The personal interests protected by the Fourth Amendment are those we attempt to capture by the notion of "privacy"; while the Court today properly points out that the type of harm which officials can inflict when they invade protected zones of an individual's life are different from the types of harm private citizens inflict on one another, the experience of judges in dealing with private trespass and false imprisonment claims supports the conclusion that courts of law are capable of making the types of judgment concerning causation and magnitude of injury necessary to accord meaningful compensation for invasion of Fourth Amendment rights.

Putting aside the desirability of leaving the problem of federal official liability to the vagaries of common-law actions, it is apparent that some form of damages is the only possible remedy for someone in Bivens' alleged position. It will be a rare case indeed in which an individual in Bivens' position will be able to obviate the harm by securing injunctive relief from any court. However desirable a direct remedy against the Government might be as a substitute for individual official liability, the sovereign still remains immune to suit. Finally, assuming Bivens' innocence of the crime charged, the "exclusionary rule" is simply irrelevant. For people in Bivens' shoes, it is damages or nothing.

[margin note: No adequate alternative]

The only substantial policy consideration advanced against recognition of a federal cause of action for violation of Fourth Amendment rights by federal officials is the incremental expenditure of judicial resources that will be necessitated by this class of litigation. There is, however, something ultimately self-defeating about this argument. For if, as the Government contends, damages will rarely be realized by plaintiffs in these cases because of jury hostility, the limited resources of the official concerned, etc., then I am not ready to assume that there will be a significant increase in the expenditure of judicial resources on these claims. Few responsible lawyers and plaintiffs are likely to choose the course of litigation if the statistical chances of success are truly de minimis. And I simply cannot agree with my Brother Black that the possibility of "frivolous" claims—if defined simply as claims with no legal merit—warrants closing the courthouse doors to people in Bivens' situation. There are other ways, short of that, of coping with frivolous lawsuits.

[margin note: Overindexing on efficiency]

On the other hand, if—as I believe is the case with respect, at least, to the most flagrant abuses of official power—damages to some degree will be available when the option of litigation is chosen, then the question appears to be how Fourth Amendment interests rank on a scale of social values compared with, for example, the interests of stockholders defrauded by misleading proxies. Judicial resources, I am well aware, are increasingly scarce these days. Nonetheless, when we automatically close the courthouse door solely on this basis, we implicitly express a value judgment on the comparative importance of classes of legally protected interests. And current limitations upon the effective functioning of the courts arising from budgetary inadequacies should not be permitted to stand in the way of the recognition of otherwise sound constitutional principles.

Chief Justice BURGER, dissenting.

I dissent from today's holding which judicially creates a damage remedy not provided for by the Constitution and not enacted by Congress. We would more surely preserve the important values of the doctrine of separation of powers—and perhaps get a better result—by recommending a solution to the Congress as the branch of government in which the Constitution has vested the legislative power. Legislation is the business of the Congress, and it has the facilities and competence for that task—as we do not.

Justice BLACK, dissenting.

There can be no doubt that Congress could create a federal cause of action for damages for an unreasonable search in violation of the Fourth Amendment. Although Congress has created such a federal cause of action against state officials acting under color of state law, it has never created such a cause of action against federal officials. If it wanted to do so, Congress could, of course, create a remedy against federal officials who violate the Fourth Amendment in the performance of their duties. But the point of this case and the fatal weakness in the Court's judgment is that neither Congress nor the State of New York has enacted legislation creating such a right of action. For us to do so is, in my judgment, an exercise of power that the Constitution does not give us.

Even if we had the legislative power to create a remedy, there are many reasons why we should decline to create a cause of action where none has existed since the formation of our Government. The courts of the United States as well as those of the States are choked with lawsuits. The number of cases on the docket of this Court have reached an unprecedented volume in recent years. A majority of these cases are brought by citizens with substantial complaints—persons who are physically or economically injured by torts or frauds or governmental infringement of their rights; persons who have been unjustly deprived of their liberty or their property; and persons who have not yet received the equal opportunity in education, employment, and pursuit of happiness that was the dream of our forefathers. Unfortunately, there have also been a growing number of frivolous lawsuits, particularly actions for damages against law enforcement officers whose conduct has been judicially sanctioned by state trial and appellate courts and in many instances even by this Court. My fellow Justices on this Court and our brethren throughout the federal judiciary know only too well the time-consuming task of conscientiously poring over hundreds of thousands of pages of factual allegations of misconduct by police, judicial, and corrections officials. Of course, there are instances of legitimate grievances, but legislators might well desire to devote judicial resources to other problems of a more serious nature.

We sit at the top of a judicial system accused by some of nearing the point of collapse. Many criminal defendants do not receive speedy trials and neither society nor the accused are assured of justice when inordinate delays occur. Citizens must wait years to litigate their private civil suits. Substantial changes in correctional and parole systems demand the attention of the lawmakers and the judiciary. If I were a legislator I might well find these and other needs so pressing as to make me believe that the resources of lawyers and judges should be devoted to them rather than to civil damage actions against officers who generally strive to perform within constitutional bounds. There is also a real danger that such suits might deter officials from the proper and honest performance of their duties.

All of these considerations make imperative careful study and weighing of the arguments both for and against the creation of such a remedy under the Fourth Amendment. I would have great difficulty for myself in resolving the competing policies, goals, and priorities in the use of resources, if I thought it were my job to resolve those questions. But that is not my task. The task of evaluating the pros and cons of creating judicial remedies for particular wrongs is a matter for Congress and the legislatures of the States. Congress has not provided that any federal court can entertain a suit against a federal officer for violations of Fourth Amendment rights occurring in the performance of his duties. A strong inference can be drawn from creation of such actions against state officials that Congress does not desire to permit such suits against federal officials. Should the time come when Congress desires such lawsuits, it has before it a model of valid legislation, 42 U.S.C. §1983, to create a damage remedy against federal officers. Cases could be cited to support the legal proposition which I assert, but it seems to me to be a matter of common understanding that the business of the judiciary is to interpret the laws and not to make them.

Justice BLACKMUN, dissenting.

I, too, dissent. I also feel that the judicial legislation, which the Court by its opinion today concededly is effectuating, opens the door for another avalanche of new federal cases. Whenever a suspect imagines, or chooses to assert, that a Fourth Amendment right has been violated, he will now immediately sue the federal officer in federal court. This will tend to stultify proper law enforcement and to make the day's labor for the honest and conscientious officer even more onerous and more critical. Why the Court moves in this direction at this time of our history, I do not know. The Fourth Amendment was adopted in 1791, and in all the intervening years neither the Congress nor the Court has seen fit to take this step. I had thought that for the truly aggrieved person other quite adequate remedies have always been available. If not, it is the Congress and not this Court that should act.

* * *

(1)   The Expansion of *Bivens*

In the decade following the *Bivens* decision, the Court applied it to allow suits for money damages under the Fifth and Eighth Amendments.

In *Davis v. Passman* (1979), the Court considered whether a female aide could sue a congressman for gender discrimination based on a cause of action inferred directly from the Fifth Amendment. Congressman Otto Passman fired his administrative assistant, Shirley Davis, because he wanted a male to fill the position. The Court held that generally federal officers could be sued for money damages for violations of the Fifth Amendment. In allowing the suit against the congressman, the Court emphasized the judiciary's role in ensuring effective protection of constitutional rights. The Court stated:

> [W]e presume that justiciable constitutional rights are to be enforced through the courts. And, unless such rights are to become merely precatory, the class of those litigants who allege that their own constitutional rights have been violated, and who at the same time have no effective means other than the judiciary to enforce these rights, must be able to invoke the existing jurisdiction of the courts for the protection of their justiciable constitutional rights.

A crucial issue was whether Congress's exemption of its own members from federal employment discrimination legislation constituted a preclusion of all such suits against senators and representatives. When Congress amended Title VII of the Civil Rights Act of 1964 to protect federal employees from employment discrimination it specifically exempted congressional employees. The defendant alleged that this was a congressional determination that representatives and senators should not be subject to such suits.

The Court, however, rejected this argument, concluding that Congress did not mean to foreclose other remedies not included in Title VII. In other words, the Court narrowly construed the exemption of congressional employees as solely removing them from liability under Title VII and not precluding all suits for employment discrimination. As such, in *Davis v. Passman*, the plaintiff had a cause of action for money damages against the former congressman for gender discrimination in violation of the Fifth Amendment.

In *Carlson v. Green* (1980), the Supreme Court for the first time considered *Bivens* relief in an instance where an alternative federal law remedy existed. A mother sued federal prison officials on behalf of her deceased son, claiming that he was the victim of gross inadequacies of medical facilities and staff, which caused his death and constituted cruel and unusual punishment. A remedy was available under the Federal Tort Claims Act; thus, the issue before the Court was whether a *Bivens* suit should be allowed in light of this alternative.

The Court concluded that *Bivens* suits were a "counterpart" to the Federal Tort Claims Act because the Act creates liability for the federal government and a *Bivens* cause of action permits recovery from the officers. The Court found no indication that Congress intended for the Act to preempt *Bivens* suits. Although some portions of the Federal Tort Claims Act specified it to be the exclusive remedy, no such provision was applicable in *Carlson v. Green*.

The Court also concluded that the remedies available under the Federal Tort Claims Act were not as effective as a *Bivens* suit. For instance, punitive damages and jury trials are available in *Bivens* litigation, but not under the act. Also, the Court emphasized that damages against individual officers would serve as a more effective deterrent to constitutional violations. Finally, the Court noted that under the Federal Tort Claims Act a cause of action exists only if liability arises under the state's law where the wrong occurred. In the absence of congressional direction, the Court felt that the protection of federal rights should not depend on state law. Justice Rehnquist vehemently dissented, disagreeing with every aspect of the majority's decision and arguing against the very existence of judicially created causes of action for constitutional violations.

(2)   The Narrowing of *Bivens* Suits

Since 1980, the Supreme Court never again has ruled in favor of allowing a *Bivens* suit and has continually narrowed the ability to sue under a constitutional provision for money damages. The Court has done this in many ways.

First, it repeatedly has said that the existence of a federal statute precludes a *Bivens* suit, even if the statute does not provide the remedy that a *Bivens* suit would offer. For the first time, in *Bush v. Lucas* (1983), the Court found that the existence of an alternative remedy foreclosed a *Bivens* suit. In *Bush*, an aerospace engineer employed at the Marshall Space Flight Center operated by the National Aeronautics and Space Administration claimed that he was demoted because of his public statements, which were highly critical of the agency. Bush appealed his demotion to the Federal Employee Appeals Authority, which ruled against him. The authority held that Bush's statements were misleading and that they exceeded the protections of the First Amendment. Two years later, Bush asked the Civil Service Commission Appeals Review Board to reopen the case. The commission did so, found in Bush's favor on First Amendment grounds, and recommended reinstatement with back pay. The recommendation was accepted.

During the pendency of the administrative appeals, Bush filed suit in state court against his superiors, seeking damages for defamation and for violation of his First Amendment rights. The defendants removed the case to federal court. The district court found that a *Bivens* suit did not exist because of the existence of alternative remedies under the Civil Service Commission regulations. The Supreme Court agreed. The Court stated at the outset that it assumed that Bush's First Amendment rights were violated, that the civil service remedies were not as effective as a damages remedy, and that Congress had not explicitly precluded the creation of a *Bivens* suit. Nonetheless, the Court found that the existence of comprehensive civil service remedies prevented Bush from bringing a cause of action directly under the First Amendment.

Previously, the Court had said that to preclude *Bivens* suits Congress must expressly declare that it had provided an alternative remedy that it deemed to be an equally effective substitute for *Bivens* suits. In *Bush*, however, the Court said that Congress could "indicate its intent [to prevent judicial remedies] by statutory language, by clear legislative history, or perhaps even by the statutory remedy itself." The Court said that the question of whether a cause of action should be allowed "cannot be answered simply by noting that existing remedies do not provide complete relief for the plaintiff." Rather, the Court said that Congress was in the best position to make policy judgments about what remedies should be available for federal employees. The Court found that these policy considerations were "special factors counselling hesitation"; therefore, the Court refused to allow *Bivens* suits.

Similarly, in *Schweiker v. Chilicky* (1988), the Supreme Court again found congressionally created remedies to be a special factor counseling hesitation and precluding a *Bivens* cause of action. *Chilicky* arose from the Reagan administration's illegal policy of disqualifying large numbers of Social Security disability recipients. Pursuant to a congressionally created program of Continuing Disability Review, the Social Security Administration wrongfully discontinued benefits to almost 200,000 individuals. Congress concluded that the Social Security Administration was abusing the review process and adopted emergency legislation to stop the disqualifications. However, many individuals—such as James Chilicky—experienced many months of financial hardship and the loss of medical benefits before the benefits were restored.

Chilicky filed suit claiming a violation of his due process rights by one state and two federal officers. The issue before the Supreme Court was whether there is a cause of action for money damages against government officers who allegedly violated the due process clause as the result of improper denial of Social Security benefits.

The Supreme Court concluded that the existence of a congressionally created remedial scheme was a special factor counseling hesitation and precluding a *Bivens* suit. The Court stated, "When the design of a government program suggests that Congress has provided what it considers adequate remedial mechanisms for constitutional violations that may occur in the course of administration, we have not created additional *Bivens* remedies." After reviewing the administrative and judicial procedures that exist to correct wrongful denials of Social Security disability benefits, the Court declared, "The case before us cannot reasonably be distinguished from *Bush v. Lucas*."

Justices Brennan, Marshall, and Blackmun filed a strong dissenting opinion. They argued that "it is inconceivable that Congress meant by such mere silence to bar all redress for such injuries." The dissent described the inadequacies of the existing procedures to remedy the injuries suffered and emphasized the absence of any indication that Congress meant to deny recovery for constitutional violations.

Hui v. Castaneda (2010) also found a *Bivens* suit to be precluded because of the existence of a federal statute. Francisco Castaneda was detained by U.S. Immigration and Customs Enforcement authorities. He repeatedly sought treatment for a lesion on his penis that was growing, frequently bleeding, and emitting a discharge. It became increasingly painful, and a lump developed in his groin. A Public Health Service physician assistant and three outside specialists said that he needed to have a biopsy to determine whether he had cancer. However, he was told that the procedure was "elective," and he was denied the biopsy, treated with ibuprofen, and given an additional ration of boxer shorts.

Almost a year after Castaneda complained of the lesion, a biopsy was performed. It disclosed that he had penile cancer. His penis was amputated, and he was treated with chemotherapy, but he died a year later. Before Castaneda died, he brought a *Bivens* suit against the Public Health Service officials who denied him a biopsy and medical treatment.

The Supreme Court unanimously ruled that a *Bivens* suit was not available because of a federal statute that made the Federal Tort Claims Act the *only* remedy against Public Health Service officers. Justice Sotomayor, writing for the Court, stated:

> Our inquiry in this case begins and ends with the text of §233(a). The statute provides in pertinent part that [t]he remedy *against the United States* provided by sections 1346(b) and 2672 of title 28 . . . for damage for personal injury, including death, resulting from the performance of medical, surgical, dental, or related functions, including the conduct of clinical studies or investigation, by any commissioned officer or employee of the Public Health Service while acting within the scope of his office or employment, *shall be exclusive of any other civil action or proceeding by reason of the same subject-matter against the officer or employee* (or his estate) whose act or omission gave rise to the claim.

The Court held that since the statute creates immunity for Public Health Service officers except under the FTCA, there could be no *Bivens* claims against them. The Court concluded its opinion by declaring that the suit had to be dismissed because "§233(a) plainly precludes a *Bivens* action against petitioners for the harms alleged in this case." *Carlson v. Green* (1980), another case that involved a claim against prison officials, was distinguished on the ground that it did not involve a statute creating immunity.

Second, the Supreme Court has held that *Bivens* suits cannot be brought against government entities, private entities, or employees of private entities. In *F.D.I.C. v. Meyer* (1994), the Court unanimously ruled that a federal agency is not subject to liability for damages under *Bivens*. A discharged employee of a failed savings and loan institution sued the Federal Savings and Loan Insurance Corporation, claiming that due process was violated when it had ordered his firing. The Court held that *Bivens* actions may not be asserted against federal agencies. The Court explained that *Bivens* recognized suits against officers because of the absence of any other remedy, whereas the Federal Tort Claims Act provides a cause of action directly against the federal government. The Court concluded that "[a]n extension of *Bivens* to agencies of the Federal Government is not supported by the logic of *Bivens* itself" and that it is up to Congress to decide the available remedies against the United States.

The Court followed and extended *F.D.I.C. v. Meyer* in *Correctional Services Corp. v. Malesko* (2001), in which it held that a private entity that operates a prison cannot be sued in a *Bivens* action. The issue was whether a *Bivens* suit could be brought against a private company operating a halfway house under a contract with the Federal Bureau of Prisons. John Malesko, an inmate in the halfway house, suffered a heart attack as a result of the facility's refusal to allow him to use an elevator despite a serious heart condition. He brought a *Bivens* claim against the halfway house.

The Supreme Court, in a 5-4 decision, held that private entities may not be sued under *Bivens*. Chief Justice Rehnquist's majority opinion stressed that *Bivens* suits are available against individual federal officers, not against government or private entities. The Court stated: "Respondent instead seeks a marked extension of

This is not the purpose of Bivens!

Bivens, to contexts that would not advance *Bivens'* core purpose of deterring individual officers from engaging in constitutional wrongdoing. The caution toward extending *Bivens* remedies into any new context, a caution consistently and repeatedly recognized for three decades, forecloses such an extension here." The Court noted the availability of remedies under state tort law and Bureau of Prisons' procedures. As discussed above, the decision strongly indicates that there is a majority of the current Court unwilling to extend *Bivens*.

In *Minneci v. Pollard* (2012), the Court considered whether prison guards at a private prison could be sued in a *Bivens* action. Pollard was a prisoner at a private prison that operated under a contract with the federal government. He broke his arm while in prison and claimed that the prison guards did not provide the needed recommended follow-up treatment and it caused him great pain. He sued them in a *Bivens* action under the Eighth Amendment, claiming deliberate indifference to his medical needs.

The Court, in an 8-1 decision, held that no *Bivens* action was available. Justice Breyer, writing for the majority, concluded that no *Bivens* suit was allowed here because state tort law provided an adequate remedy to Pollard. The Court explained:

> [W]e conclude that Pollard cannot assert a *Bivens* claim . . . primarily because Pollard's Eighth Amendment claim focuses upon a kind of conduct that typically falls within the scope of traditional state tort law. And in the case of a privately employed defendant, state tort law provides an "alternative, existing process" capable of protecting the constitutional interests at stake. The existence of that alternative here constitutes a "convincing reason for the Judicial Branch to refrain from providing a new and freestanding remedy in damages."

The Court thus held that no *Bivens* suit can be brought against private defendants, at least if there is state tort liability. The Court concluded that "where, as here, a federal prisoner seeks damages from privately employed personnel working at a privately operated federal prison, where the conduct allegedly amounts to a violation of the Eighth Amendment, and where that conduct is of a kind that typically falls within the scope of traditional state tort law (such as the conduct involving improper medical care at issue here), the prisoner must seek a remedy under state tort law. We cannot imply a *Bivens* remedy in such a case."

Third, in *Wilkie v. Robbins* (2007), the Court held that *Bivens* suits are allowed only if they are, on balance, deemed appropriate. Robbins was a Wyoming landowner who claimed that Wilkie and other employees of the Federal Bureau of Land Management (BLM) had unconstitutionally harassed and persecuted him for refusing to give the government an easement on his land. As Justice Ginsburg expressed in her dissent, when Robbins refused to grant the requested easement, "the BLM officials mounted a seven-year campaign of relentless harassment and intimidation to force Robbins to give in. They refused to maintain the road providing access to the ranch, trespassed on Robbins's property, brought unfounded criminal charges against him, canceled his special recreational use permit and grazing privileges, interfered with his business operations, and invaded the privacy of his ranch guests on cattle drives."

No alt remedies!

The Court, however, said that a *Bivens* suit was not available *even if there were not alternative remedies,* because it, on balance, was not desirable to allow such a claim. Justice Souter, writing for the Court, explained:

[T]he decision whether to recognize a *Bivens* remedy may require two steps. In the first place, there is the question whether any alternative, existing process for protecting the interest amounts to a convincing reason for the Judicial Branch to refrain from providing a new and freestanding remedy in damages. But even in the absence of an alternative, a *Bivens* remedy is a subject of judgment: the federal courts must make the kind of remedial determination that is appropriate for a common-law tribunal, paying particular heed, however, to any special factors counselling hesitation before authorizing a new kind of federal litigation.

The Court said that it was uncertain whether Robbins had an alternative remedy. The Court therefore said, "This, then, is a case for *Bivens* step two, for weighing reasons for and against the creation of a new cause of action, the way common law judges have always done." The Court concluded that it would be undesirable to allow a *Bivens* cause of action because permitting a damages claim could lead to a flood of litigation and because of the difficulty of proving whether government officers were acting out of a retaliatory motive. The Court stated: "The point here is not to deny that Government employees sometimes overreach, for of course they do, and they may have done so here if all the allegations are true. The point is the reasonable fear that a general *Bivens* cure would be worse than the disease."

Only Justice Ginsburg dissented, and she would not bar a *Bivens* suit on the grounds that state tort remedies existed. A tort remedy almost always exists. Wesley Bivens could have sued the agents of the Federal Bureau of Narcotics under state tort law. The Supreme Court's goal was to make sure that there is a federal cause of action for violations of constitutional rights by federal officers. *[Ginsburg dissent]*

Fourth, the Court has not allowed *Bivens* suits in claims arising from military service. In *Chappell v. Wallace* (1983), the Court addressed an allegation of discriminatory practices by superior officers directed at minority enlisted personnel of the U.S. Navy. The Court, in an opinion by Chief Justice Burger, concluded that the special nature of the military was a factor counseling hesitation. The Court reasoned: *[Military, special factors]*

[C]enturies of experience have developed a hierarchical structure of discipline and obedience to command, unique in its application to the military establishment and wholly different from civilian patterns. Civilian courts must, at the very least, hesitate long before entertaining a suit which asks the court to tamper with the established relationship between enlisted military personnel and their superior officers; that relationship is at the heart of the necessarily unique structure of the Military Establishment.

After *Chappell,* there was uncertainty among the lower courts as to whether the Court had barred all *Bivens* suits arising out of military service or whether instances may arise in which competing factors militate in favor of allowing such a suit. The Supreme Court resolved this uncertainty in 1987 in *United States v. Stanley* (1987). See Chapter 7(A)(3)(a).

In *Stanley,* a former serviceman sued because of severe injuries he allegedly sustained as a result of having been given LSD, without his knowledge or consent, in an army experiment in 1958. The Supreme Court held that the U.S. government was immune from suit under the Federal Tort Claims Act because of the *Feres* doctrine, which prohibits suits against the government arising from military service. Moreover, the Court concluded that *Bivens* suits also were not possible against the government officers who subjected Stanley to the medical experimentation without his permission. In an opinion by Justice Scalia, the Court flatly declared "that no *Bivens* remedy is available for injuries that 'arise out of or are in the course of activity incident to service.'" The Court concluded that under *Chappell v. Wallace*, all *Bivens* suits arising from military service were precluded by the need to preserve the military hierarchy.

Several justices wrote scathing dissents to this part of the Court's opinion. Justice O'Connor said that, while she agrees with *Chappell*, "conduct of the type alleged in this case is so far beyond the bounds of human decency that as a matter of law it simply cannot be considered a part of the military mission." Justice O'Connor contended that the defendants did not need insulation from liability resulting from the deliberate exposure of healthy individuals to medical tests without their consent. Likewise, Justice Brennan drew parallels to the Nazis' medical experimentations and argued that victims such as Stanley must have a remedy for violations of their constitutional rights.

The law is now settled that *Bivens* suits are never permitted for constitutional violations arising from military service, no matter how severe the injury or how egregious the rights infringement. *See, e.g., Klay v. Panetta* (D.C. Cir. 2014) (denying a *Bivens* suit to women in the military who were raped and subjected to sexual harassment).

(3)   The Current Test with Regard to *Bivens* Suits

In its most recent cases concerning *Bivens*, the Supreme Court has continued to narrow its availability and has articulated a test for determining whether to allow such a suit. It is clear that although *Bivens* has not been overruled, the Court also is not supportive of *Bivens* actions and is continuing to limit them.

As you read the following trio of recent *Bivens* decisions from the Supreme Court, think carefully about the contexts in which they arose. As you will see, the Court's approach to *Bivens* specifically makes context relevant. The Court asks whether the *Bivens* claim is arising in a "new context." In the following cases, the Court considered—and rejected—*Bivens* claims in contexts involving detention of immigrants following the September 11th terrorist attacks, a cross-border shooting in which a U.S. Border Patrol agent killed a Mexican child, and a claim of First and Fourth Amendment violations arising at the U.S./Canada border. Each in their own way raises questions about borders: between one country and another and between citizens and non-citizens. Together, they raise questions about the extent to which the Court's *Bivens* doctrine has been shaped by substantive and politically controversial debates about executive accountability, national security, and federal policy in the borderlands of the United States.

The first case, *Ziglar v. Abbasi* (2017), is one of a series of cases challenging a dragnet immigration detention policy developed in response to the 9/11 attacks. The first *Bivens* suit that reached the Supreme Court was brought by Javid Iqbal, a Pakistani cable repair technician who was married to an American woman and in the process of seeking a green card when the September 11 attacks took place. Iqbal was placed in the same special housing unit at the Metropolitan Detention Center in Brooklyn, New York, as the plaintiffs in *Ziglar*, and was subjected to the same physical abuse and national origin and religious discrimination.[31] Roundups of this kind were but one of a number of sweeping changes to immigration law and policy after the September 11th attacks. In 2002 Congress abolished the INS and created a cabinet level department (the Department of Homeland Security) charged with immigration enforcement. The government also established a new system for monitoring students and visitors entering and leaving the United States, for gathering information on people from certain countries, for extending immigration detention beyond 48 hours in "exceptional circumstances," for placing people on "no fly" lists, for eavesdropping on Americans' overseas calls without court-approved warrants, and for initiating FBI investigations of Muslim Americans without a "factual predicate."[32]

As you may recall from your work in Civil Procedure, the Supreme Court held in *Iqbal*: (a) that its new plausibility pleading standard applied to *all* civil suits filed in federal court, and (b) that a federal officer with supervisory authority is liable *only* when the supervisor's "own individual actions" violate the plaintiff's constitutional rights. Emphasizing that "supervisory liability" is, in this context, "a misnomer," the majority rejected the government's position that supervisors should be held liable when they have actual knowledge of constitutional violations by subordinates and are "deliberately indifferent" to their constitutional rights. Note that because *Bivens* suits are regarded as federal analogues to §1983, the same rule now applies in §1983 suits asserting supervisory liability. *Respondeat superior* is unavailable.

Other similarly situated plaintiffs continued the litigation. *See Turkmen v. Hasty* (2d Cir. 2015) (en banc). Their fourth amended complaint drew on information learned in discovery in parallel litigation against the lower level officers who worked at the Brooklyn federal detention center. It also incorporated details of two reports issued by the Office of the Inspector General of the U.S. Department of Justice.[33] The Second Circuit, relying heavily on the incorporation of the Inspector General's reports, reversed the district court's dismissal for failure to state a plausible claim. The circuit court emphasized that Attorney General Ashcroft and Director of FBI Muller:

> were aware that illegal aliens were being detained in punitive conditions
> of confinement in New York and further knew that there was no sugges-
> tion that those detainees were tied to terrorism except for the fact that

---

31. Other details about Iqbal, including the fact that he was in Manhattan on the day of the 9/11 attacks only to renew his work authorization card with immigration officials, and the mistreatment of his family when he was removed to Pakistan (where it was assumed he was a CIA spy), can be found in Shirin Sinnar, *The Lost Story of Iqbal*, 105 Geo. L.J. 379 (2017).

32. *See* Symposium, *The 9/11 Effect and its Legacy on U.S. Immigration Laws*, Penn State Law (2011); Emily Berman, Domestic Intelligence: New Powers, New Risks (2011).

33. *See* U.S. Dep't of Justice, Office of the Inspector General, The September 11 Detainees: A Review of the Treatment of Aliens Held on Immigration Charges in Connection with the Investigation of the September 11 Attacks (2003); U.S. Dep't of Justice Office of the Inspector General, Supplemental Report on September 11 Detainees' Allegations of Abuse at the Metropolitan Detention Center in Brooklyn, New York (2003).

they were, or were perceived to be, Arab or Muslim. The MDC Plaintiffs further allege that while knowing these facts, the DOJ Defendants were responsible for a decision to merge the New York List with the national INS List, which contained the names of detainees whose detention was dependent not only on their illegal immigrant status and their perceived Arab or Muslim affiliation, but also a suspicion that they were connected to terrorist activities. The merger ensured that the MDC Plaintiffs would continue to be confined in punitive conditions. This is sufficient to plead a Fifth Amendment substantive due process violation. Given the lack of individualized suspicion, the decision to merge the lists was not "reasonably related to a legitimate goal." *See Bell v. Wolfish* (1979). The only reason why the MDC Plaintiffs were held as if they were suspected of terrorism was because they were, or appeared to be, Arab or Muslim.

Id. After the amended complaint was upheld by the Second Circuit, the Supreme Court granted certiorari. The Court's focus turned from whether the allegations of constitutional violations were plausibly pled to whether high level national security officers named in the complaint were entitled to the defense of qualified immunity and, more fundamentally, whether a *Bivens* cause of action should exist for plaintiffs suing such officers. Ahmer Abbasi is one of the named plaintiffs in *Turkmen.*

Ziglar v. Abbasi

137 S. Ct. 1843 (2017)

Justice KENNEDY announced the decision of the Court.*

After the September 11 terrorist attacks in this country, and in response to the deaths, destruction, and dangers they caused, the United States Government ordered hundreds of illegal aliens to be taken into custody and held. Pending a determination whether a particular detainee had connections to terrorism, the custody, under harsh conditions to be described, continued. In many instances custody lasted for days and weeks, then stretching into months. Later, some of the aliens who had been detained filed suit, leading to the cases now before the Court.

The complaint named as defendants three high executive officers in the Department of Justice and two of the wardens at the facility where the detainees had been held. Most of the claims, alleging various constitutional violations, sought damages under the implied cause of action theory adopted by this Court in *Bivens v. Six Unknown Fed. Narcotics Agents* (1971).

I

Given the present procedural posture of the suit, the Court accepts as true the facts alleged in the complaint. In the weeks following the September 11, 2001,

---

* The decision was 4-2. Justice Kennedy wrote the opinion, joined by Chief Justice Roberts and Justices Thomas, and Alito. Justice Breyer wrote a dissent joined by Justice Ginsburg. Justices Sotomayor and Kagan were recused and Justice Gorsuch was confirmed after the oral arguments in the case and did not participate in the decision.

terrorist attacks—the worst in American history—the Federal Bureau of Investigation (FBI) received more than 96,000 tips from members of the public. Some tips were based on well-grounded suspicion of terrorist activity, but many others may have been based on fear of Arabs and Muslims. FBI agents "questioned more than 1,000 people with suspected links to the [September 11] attacks in particular or to terrorism in general."

While investigating the tips—including the less substantiated ones—the FBI encountered many aliens who were present in this country without legal authorization. As a result, more than 700 individuals were arrested and detained on immigration charges. If the FBI designated an alien as not being "of interest" to the investigation, then he or she was processed according to normal procedures. In other words, the alien was treated just as if, for example, he or she had been arrested at the border after an illegal entry. If, however, the FBI designated an alien as "of interest" to the investigation, or if it had doubts about the proper designation in a particular case, the alien was detained subject to a "hold-until-cleared policy." The aliens were held without bail.

Respondents were among some 84 aliens who were subject to the hold-until-cleared policy and detained at the Metropolitan Detention Center (MDC) in Brooklyn, New York. They were held in the Administrative Maximum Special Housing Unit (or Unit) of the MDC. The complaint includes these allegations: Conditions in the Unit were harsh. Pursuant to official Bureau of Prisons policy, detainees were held in "'tiny cells for over 23 hours a day.'" Lights in the cells were left on 24 hours. Detainees had little opportunity for exercise or recreation. They were forbidden to keep anything in their cells, even basic hygiene products such as soap or a toothbrush. When removed from the cells for any reason, they were shackled and escorted by four guards. They were denied access to most forms of communication with the outside world. And they were strip searched often—any time they were moved, as well as at random in their cells.

Some of the harsh conditions in the Unit were not imposed pursuant to official policy. According to the complaint, prison guards engaged in a pattern of "physical and verbal abuse." Guards allegedly slammed detainees into walls; twisted their arms, wrists, and fingers; broke their bones; referred to them as terrorists; threatened them with violence; subjected them to humiliating sexual comments; and insulted their religion. *[handwritten margin note: violent treatment]*

Respondents are six men of Arab or South Asian descent. Five are Muslims. Each was illegally in this country, arrested during the course of the September 11 investigation, and detained in the Administrative Maximum Special Housing Unit for periods ranging from three to eight months. After being released respondents were removed from the United States.

Respondents then sued on their own behalf, and on behalf of a putative class, seeking compensatory and punitive damages, attorney's fees, and costs. Respondents, it seems fair to conclude from the arguments presented, acknowledge that in the ordinary course aliens who are present in the United States without legal authorization can be detained for some period of time. But here the challenge is to the conditions of their confinement and the reasons or motives for imposing those conditions. The gravamen of their claims was that the Government had no reason to suspect them of any connection to terrorism, and thus had no legitimate reason to hold them for so long in these harsh conditions.

As relevant here, respondents sued two groups of federal officials in their official capacities. The first group consisted of former Attorney General John Ashcroft, former FBI Director Robert Mueller, and former Immigration and Naturalization Service Commissioner James Ziglar. This opinion refers to these three petitioners as the "Executive Officials." The other petitioners named in the complaint were the MDC's warden, Dennis Hasty, and associate warden, James Sherman. This opinion refers to these two petitioners as the "Wardens."

Seeking to invoke the Court's decision in *Bivens*, respondents brought four claims under the Constitution itself. First, respondents alleged that petitioners detained them in harsh pretrial conditions for a punitive purpose, in violation of the substantive due process component of the Fifth Amendment. Second, respondents alleged that petitioners detained them in harsh conditions because of their actual or apparent race, religion, or national origin, in violation of the equal protection component of the Fifth Amendment. Third, respondents alleged that the Wardens subjected them to punitive strip searches unrelated to any legitimate penological interest, in violation of the Fourth Amendment and the substantive due process component of the Fifth Amendment. Fourth, respondents alleged that the Wardens knowingly allowed the guards to abuse respondents, in violation of the substantive due process component of the Fifth Amendment.

II

The first question to be discussed is whether petitioners can be sued for damages under *Bivens* and the ensuing cases in this Court defining the reach and the limits of that precedent.

In 1871, Congress passed a statute that was later codified at 42 U.S.C. §1983. It entitles an injured person to money damages if a state official violates his or her constitutional rights. Congress did not create an analogous statute for federal officials. Indeed, in the 100 years leading up to *Bivens*, Congress did not provide a specific damages remedy for plaintiffs whose constitutional rights were violated by agents of the Federal Government.

In 1971, and against this background, this Court decided *Bivens*. The Court held that, even absent statutory authorization, it would enforce a damages remedy to compensate persons injured by federal officers who violated the prohibition against unreasonable search and seizures.

[I]t is a significant step under separation-of-powers principles for a court to determine that it has the authority, under the judicial power, to create and enforce a cause of action for damages against federal officials in order to remedy a constitutional violation. When determining whether traditional equitable powers suffice to give necessary constitutional protection—or whether, in addition, a damages remedy is necessary—there are a number of economic and governmental concerns to consider. Claims against federal officials often create substantial costs, in the form of defense and indemnification. Congress, then, has a substantial responsibility to determine whether, and the extent to which, monetary and other liabilities should be imposed upon individual officers and employees of the Federal Government. In addition, the time and administrative costs attendant upon intrusions resulting from the discovery and trial process are significant factors to be considered.

For these and other reasons, the Court's expressed caution as to implied causes of actions under congressional statutes led to similar caution with respect to actions in the *Bivens* context, where the action is implied to enforce the Constitution itself. Indeed, in light of the changes to the Court's general approach to recognizing implied damages remedies, it is possible that the analysis in the Court's three *Bivens* cases might have been different if they were decided today. To be sure, no congressional enactment has disapproved of these decisions. And it must be understood that this opinion is not intended to cast doubt on the continued force, or even the necessity, of *Bivens* in the search-and-seizure context in which it arose. *Bivens* does vindicate the Constitution by allowing some redress for injuries, and it provides instruction and guidance to federal law enforcement officers going forward. The settled law of *Bivens* in this common and recurrent sphere of law enforcement, and the undoubted reliance upon it as a fixed principle in the law, are powerful reasons to retain it in that sphere.

Given the notable change in the Court's approach to recognizing implied causes of action, however, the Court has made clear that expanding the *Bivens* remedy is now a "disfavored" judicial activity. This is in accord with the Court's observation that it has "consistently refused to extend *Bivens* to any new context or new category of defendants." *Correctional Servs. Corp. v. Malesko* (2001). Indeed, the Court has refused to do so for the past 30 years.

When a party seeks to assert an implied cause of action under the Constitution itself, just as when a party seeks to assert an implied cause of action under a federal statute, separation-of-powers principles are or should be central to the analysis. The question is "who should decide" whether to provide for a damages remedy, Congress or the courts? *Bush v. Lucas* (1983).

The answer most often will be Congress. When an issue "'involves a host of considerations that must be weighed and appraised,'" it should be committed to "'those who write the laws'" rather than "'those who interpret them.'" *Ibid.* In most instances, the Court's precedents now instruct, the Legislature is in the better position to consider if "'the public interest would be served'" by imposing a "'new substantive legal liability.'" *Schweiker v. Chilicky* (1988). As a result, the Court has urged "caution" before "extending *Bivens* remedies into any new context." The Court's precedents now make clear that a *Bivens* remedy will not be available if there are "'special factors counselling hesitation in the absence of affirmative action by Congress.'" *Carlson v. Green* (1980).

This Court has not defined the phrase "special factors counselling hesitation." The necessary inference, though, is that the inquiry must concentrate on whether the Judiciary is well suited, absent congressional action or instruction, to consider and weigh the costs and benefits of allowing a damages action to proceed. Thus, to be a "special factor counselling hesitation," a factor must cause a court to hesitate before answering that question in the affirmative.

It is not necessarily a judicial function to establish whole categories of cases in which federal officers must defend against personal liability claims in the complex sphere of litigation, with all of its burdens on some and benefits to others. It is true that, if equitable remedies prove insufficient, a damages remedy might be necessary to redress past harm and deter future violations. Yet the decision to recognize a damages remedy requires an assessment of its impact on governmental operations systemwide. Those matters include the burdens on Government employees who are sued personally, as well as the projected costs and consequences to the Government itself when the tort and monetary liability mechanisms of the legal system are used to bring about the proper formulation and implementation of public policies. These and other considerations may make it less probable that Congress would want the Judiciary to entertain a damages suit in a given case.

Sometimes there will be doubt because the case arises in a context in which Congress has designed its regulatory authority in a guarded way, making it less likely that Congress would want the Judiciary to interfere. And sometimes there will be doubt because some other feature of a case — difficult to predict in advance — causes a court to pause before acting without express congressional authorization. In sum, if there are sound reasons to think Congress might doubt the efficacy or necessity of a damages remedy as part of the system for enforcing the law and correcting a wrong, the courts must refrain from creating the remedy in order to respect the role of Congress in determining the nature and extent of federal-court jurisdiction under Article III.

In a related way, if there is an alternative remedial structure present in a certain case, that alone may limit the power of the Judiciary to infer a new *Bivens* cause of action. For if Congress has created "any alternative, existing process for protecting the [injured party's] interest" that itself may "amoun[t] to a convincing reason for the Judicial Branch to refrain from providing a new and freestanding remedy in damages." *Wilkie v. Robbins* (2007).

III

It is appropriate now to turn first to the *Bivens* claims challenging the conditions of confinement imposed on respondents pursuant to the formal policy adopted by the Executive Officials in the wake of the September 11 attacks. The Court will refer to these claims as the "detention policy claims." The detention policy claims allege that petitioners violated respondents' due process and equal protection rights by holding them in restrictive conditions of confinement; the claims further allege that the Wardens violated the Fourth and Fifth Amendments by subjecting respondents to frequent strip searches. The term "detention policy claims" does not include respondents' claim alleging that Warden Hasty allowed guards to abuse the detainees. That claim will be considered separately, and further, below. At this point, the question is whether, having considered the relevant special factors in the whole context of the detention policy claims, the Court should extend a *Bivens*-type remedy to those claims.

The proper test for determining whether a case presents a new *Bivens* context is as follows. If the case is different in a meaningful way from previous *Bivens* cases decided by this Court, then the context is new. Without endeavoring to create an exhaustive list of differences that are meaningful enough to make a given context a new one, some examples might prove instructive. A case might differ in a meaningful way because of the rank of the officers involved; the constitutional right at issue; the generality or specificity of the official action; the extent of judicial guidance as to how an officer should respond to the problem or emergency to be confronted; the statutory or other legal mandate under which the officer was operating; the risk of disruptive intrusion by the Judiciary into the functioning of other branches; or the presence of potential special factors that previous *Bivens* cases did not consider.

In the present suit, respondents' detention policy claims challenge the confinement conditions imposed on illegal aliens pursuant to a high-level executive policy created in the wake of a major terrorist attack on American soil. Those claims bear little resemblance to the three *Bivens* claims the Court has approved in the past: a claim against FBI agents for handcuffing a man in his own home without a warrant; a claim against a Congressman for firing his female secretary; and a claim against prison officials for failure to treat an inmate's asthma. *See Bivens; Davis v. Passman* (1979); *Chappell v. Wallace* (1983).

After considering the special factors necessarily implicated by the detention policy claims, the Court now holds that those factors show that whether a damages action should be allowed is a decision for the Congress to make, not the courts.

With respect to the claims against the Executive Officials, it must be noted that a *Bivens* action is not "a proper vehicle for altering an entity's policy." *Correctional Servs. Corp. v. Malesko* (2001). Furthermore, a *Bivens* claim is brought against the individual official for his or her own acts, not the acts of others. "The purpose of *Bivens* is to deter the officer." *F.D.I.C v. Meyer* (1994). *Bivens* is not designed to hold officers responsible for acts of their subordinates.

Even if the action is confined to the conduct of a particular Executive Officer in a discrete instance, these claims would call into question the formulation and implementation of a general policy. This, in turn, would necessarily require inquiry and discovery into the whole course of the discussions and deliberations that led to the policies and governmental acts being challenged. These consequences counsel against allowing a *Bivens* action against the Executive Officials, <u>for the burden and demand of litigation might well prevent them—or, to be more precise, future officials like them—from devoting the time and effort required for the proper discharge of their duties.</u>

A closely related problem, as just noted, is that the discovery and litigation process would either border upon or directly implicate the discussion and deliberations that led to the formation of the policy in question. Allowing a damages suit in this context, or in a like context in other circumstances, would <u>require courts to interfere in an intrusive way with sensitive functions of the Executive Branch.</u> These considerations also counsel against allowing a damages claim to proceed against the Executive Officials.

In addition to this special factor, which applies to the claims against the Executive Officials, there are three other special factors that apply as well to the detention policy claims against all of the petitioners. First, respondents' detention policy claims challenge more than standard "law enforcement operations." *United States v. Verdugo-Urquidez* (1990). They challenge as well major elements of the Government's whole response to the September 11 attacks, thus of necessity requiring an inquiry into sensitive issues of national security. Were this inquiry to be allowed in a private suit for damages, the *Bivens* action would assume dimensions far greater than those present in *Bivens* itself, or in either of its two follow-on cases, or indeed in any putative *Bivens* case yet to come before the Court.

National-security policy is the prerogative of the Congress and President. Judicial inquiry into the national-security realm raises "concerns for the separation of powers in trenching on matters committed to the other branches." *Christopher v. Harbury* (2002). These concerns are even more pronounced when the judicial inquiry comes in the context of a claim seeking money damages rather than a claim seeking injunctive or other equitable relief. The risk of personal damages liability is more likely to cause an official to second-guess difficult but necessary decisions concerning national-security policy.

For these and other reasons, courts have shown deference to what the Executive Branch "has determined . . . is 'essential to national security.'" *Winter v. Natural Resource Defense Council, Inc.* (2008). Indeed, "courts traditionally have been reluctant to intrude upon the authority of the Executive in military and national security affairs" unless "Congress specifically has provided otherwise." Congress has not provided otherwise here. *Dep't of Navy v. Egan* (1988).

Furthermore, in any inquiry respecting the likely or probable intent of Congress, the silence of Congress is relevant; and here that silence is telling. In the almost 16 years since September 11, the Federal Government's responses to that terrorist attack have been well documented. Congressional interest has been "frequent and intense," and some of that interest has been directed to the conditions of confinement at issue here. *Schweiker*. This silence is notable because it is likely that high-level policies will attract the attention of Congress. Thus, when Congress fails to provide a damages remedy in circumstances like these, it is much more difficult to believe that "congressional inaction" was "inadvertent." *Schweiker*.

It is of central importance, too, that this is not a case like *Bivens* or *Davis* in which "it is damages or nothing." *Bivens* (Harlan, J., concurring in judgment). Unlike the plaintiffs in those cases, respondents do not challenge individual instances of discrimination or law enforcement overreach, which due to their very nature are difficult to address except by way of damages actions after the fact. Respondents instead challenge large-scale policy decisions concerning the conditions of confinement imposed on hundreds of prisoners. To address those kinds of decisions, detainees may seek injunctive relief. And in addition to that, we have left open the question whether they might be able to challenge their confinement conditions via a petition for a writ of habeas corpus.

There is a persisting concern, of course, that absent a *Bivens* remedy there will be insufficient deterrence to prevent officers from violating the Constitution. In circumstances like those presented here, however, the stakes on both sides of the argument are far higher than in past cases the Court has considered. If *Bivens* liability were to be imposed, high officers who face personal liability for damages might refrain from taking urgent and lawful action in a time of crisis. And, as already noted, the costs and difficulties of later litigation might intrude upon and interfere with the proper exercise of their office.

On the other side of the balance, the very fact that some executive actions have the sweeping potential to affect the liberty of so many is a reason to consider proper means to impose restraint and to provide some redress from injury. There is therefore a balance to be struck, in situations like this one, between deterring constitutional violations and freeing high officials to make the lawful decisions necessary to protect the Nation in times of great peril. The proper balance is one for the Congress, not the Judiciary, to undertake. For all of these reasons, the Court of Appeals erred by allowing respondents' detention policy claims to proceed under *Bivens*.

IV

One of respondents' claims under *Bivens* requires a different analysis: the prisoner abuse claim against the MDC's warden, Dennis Hasty. The allegation is that Warden Hasty violated the Fifth Amendment by allowing prison guards to abuse respondents. The complaint alleges that guards routinely abused respondents; that the warden encouraged the abuse by referring to respondents as "terrorists"; that he prevented respondents from using normal grievance procedures; that he stayed away from the Unit to avoid seeing the abuse; that he was made aware of the abuse via "inmate complaints, staff complaints, hunger strikes, and suicide attempts"; that he ignored other "direct evidence of [the] abuse, including logs and other official [records]"; that he took no action "to rectify or address the situation"; and that the abuse resulted in the injuries described above.

These allegations — assumed here to be true, subject to proof at a later stage — plausibly show the warden's deliberate indifference to the abuse. Consistent with the opinion of every judge in this case to have considered the question, including the dissenters in the Court of Appeals, the Court concludes that the prisoner abuse allegations against Warden Hasty state a plausible ground to find a constitutional violation if a *Bivens* remedy is to be implied.

Warden Hasty argues, however, that *Bivens* ought not to be extended to this instance of alleged prisoner abuse. As noted above, the first question a court must ask in a case like this one is whether the claim arises in a new *Bivens* context, *i.e.*, whether "the case is different in a meaningful way from previous *Bivens* cases decided by this Court."

It is true that this case has significant parallels to one of the Court's previous *Bivens* cases, *Carlson v. Green* (1980). Yet even a modest extension is still an extension. And this case does seek to extend *Carlson* to a new context. As noted above, a case can present a new context for *Bivens* purposes if it implicates a different constitutional right; if judicial precedents provide a less meaningful guide for official conduct; or if there are potential special factors that were not considered in previous *Bivens* cases.

The constitutional right is different here, since *Carlson* was predicated on the Eighth Amendment and this claim is predicated on the Fifth. And the judicial guidance available to this warden, with respect to his supervisory duties, was less developed. Furthermore, legislative action suggesting that Congress does not want a damages remedy is itself a factor counseling hesitation. Some 15 years after *Carlson* was decided, Congress passed the Prison Litigation Reform Act of 1995, which made comprehensive changes to the way prisoner abuse claims must be brought in federal court. So it seems clear that Congress had specific occasion to consider the matter of prisoner abuse and to consider the proper way to remedy those wrongs. But the Act itself does not provide for a standalone damages remedy against federal jailers.

The differences between this claim and the one in *Carlson* are perhaps small, at least in practical terms. Given this Court's expressed caution about extending the *Bivens* remedy, however, the new-context inquiry is easily satisfied. Some differences, of course, will be so trivial that they will not suffice to create a new *Bivens* context. But here the differences identified above are at the very least meaningful ones. Thus, before allowing this claim to proceed under *Bivens*, the Court of

Appeals should have performed a special factors analysis. It should have analyzed whether there were alternative remedies available or other "sound reasons to think Congress might doubt the efficacy or necessity of a damages remedy" in a suit like this one.

Although the Court could perform that analysis in the first instance, the briefs have concentrated almost all of their efforts elsewhere. Given the absence of a comprehensive presentation by the parties, and the fact that the Court of Appeals did not conduct the analysis, the Court declines to perform the special factors analysis itself. The better course is to vacate the judgment below, allowing the Court of Appeals or the District Court to do so on remand.

If the facts alleged in the complaint are true, then what happened to respondents in the days following September 11 was tragic. Nothing in this opinion should be read to condone the treatment to which they contend they were subjected. The question before the Court, however, is not whether petitioners' alleged conduct was proper, nor whether it gave decent respect to respondents' dignity and well-being, nor whether it was in keeping with the idea of the rule of law that must inspire us even in times of crisis.

Instead, the question with respect to the *Bivens* claims is whether to allow an action for money damages in the absence of congressional authorization. For the reasons given above, the Court answers that question in the negative as to the detention policy claims. As to the prisoner abuse claim, because the briefs have not concentrated on that issue, the Court remands to allow the Court of Appeals to consider the claim in light of the *Bivens* analysis set forth above.

Justice BREYER, with whom Justice GINSBURG joins, dissenting.

It is by now well established that federal law provides damages actions at least in similar contexts, where claims of constitutional violation arise. Congress has ratified *Bivens* actions, plaintiffs frequently bring them, courts accept them, and scholars defend their importance. Moreover, the courts, in order to avoid deterring federal officials from properly performing their work, have developed safeguards for defendants, including the requirement that plaintiffs plead "plausible" claims, *Ashcroft v. Iqbal* (2009), as well as the defense of "qualified immunity," which frees federal officials from both threat of liability and involvement in the lawsuit, unless the plaintiffs establish that officials have violated "'clearly established . . . constitutional rights.'" "[This] Court has been reluctant to extend *Bivens* liability 'to any new context or new category of defendants.'" *Id.* But the Court has made clear that it would not narrow *Bivens'* existing scope.

The plaintiffs before us today seek dmages for unconstitutional conditions of confinement. They alleged that federal officials slammed them against walls, shackled them, exposed them to nonstop lighting, lack of hygiene, and the like, all based upon invidious discrimination and without penological justification. In my view, these claims are well-pleaded, state violations of clearly established law, and fall within the scope of longstanding *Bivens* law. For those reasons, I would affirm the judgment of the Court of Appeals. The Court, in my view, is wrong to hold that permitting a constitutional tort action here would "extend" *Bivens*, applying it in a new context. To the contrary, I fear that the Court's holding would significantly shrink the existing *Bivens* contexts, diminishing the compensatory remedy constitutional tort law now offers to harmed individuals.

I recognize, and write separately about, the strongest of the Court's arguments, namely, the fact that plaintiffs' claims concern detention that took place soon after a serious attack on the United States and some of them concern actions of high-level Government officials. While these facts may affect the substantive constitutional questions (*e.g.*, were any of the conditions "legitimate"?) or the scope of the qualified-immunity defense, they do not extinguish the *Bivens* action itself. If I may paraphrase Justice Harlan, concurring in *Bivens*: In wartime as well as in peacetime, "it is important, in a civilized society, that the judicial branch of the Nation's government stand ready to afford a remedy" "for the most flagrant and patently unjustified," unconstitutional "abuses of official power."

Thus the Court, as the majority opinion says, repeatedly wrote that it was not "expanding" the scope of the *Bivens* remedy. But the Court nowhere suggested that it would narrow *Bivens* existing scope. In fact, to diminish any ambiguity about its holdings, the Court set out a framework for determining whether a claim of constitutional violation calls for a *Bivens* remedy. At Step One, the court must determine whether the case before it arises in a "new context," that is, whether it involves a "new category of defendants," *Malesko*, or (presumably) a significantly different kind of constitutional harm, such as a purely procedural harm, a harm to speech, or a harm caused to physical property. *If the context is new, then* the court proceeds to Step Two and asks "whether any alternative, existing process for protecting the interest amounts to a convincing reason for the Judicial Branch to refrain from providing a new and freestanding remedy in damages." *Wilkie. If there is none, then* the court proceeds to Step Three and asks whether there are "'any special factors counselling hesitation before authorizing a new kind of federal litigation.'" *Ibid.*

I

Precedent makes this framework applicable here. I would apply it. And, doing so, I cannot get past Step One. This suit, it seems to me, arises in a context similar to those in which this Court has previously permitted *Bivens* actions.

The context here is not "new," *Wilkie*, or "fundamentally different" than our previous *Bivens* cases, *Malesko*. First, the plaintiffs are civilians, not members of the military. They are not citizens, but the Constitution protects noncitizens against serious mistreatment, as it protects citizens. Some or all of the plaintiffs here may have been illegally present in the United States. But that fact cannot justify physical mistreatment. Nor does anyone claim that that fact deprives them of a *Bivens* right available to other persons, citizens and noncitizens alike.

Second, the defendants are Government officials. They are not members of the military or private persons. Two are prison wardens. Three others are high-ranking Department of Justice officials. Prison wardens have been defendants in *Bivens* actions, as have other high-level Government officials. One of the defendants in *Carlson* was the Director of the Bureau of Prisons; the defendant in *Davis* was a Member of Congress. We have also held that the Attorney General of the United States is not entitled to absolute immunity in a damages suit arising out of his actions related to national security.

Third, from a *Bivens* perspective, the injuries that the plaintiffs claim they suffered are familiar ones. They focus upon the conditions of confinement. The plaintiffs say that they were unnecessarily shackled, confined in small unhygienic cells, subjected to continuous lighting (presumably preventing sleep), unnecessarily and frequently strip searched, slammed against walls, injured physically, and subject to verbal abuse. They allege that they suffered these harms because of their race or religion, the defendants having either turned a blind eye to what was happening or themselves introduced policies that they knew would lead to these harms even though the defendants knew the plaintiffs had no connections to terrorism.

These claimed harms are similar to, or even worse than, the harms the plaintiffs suffered in *Bivens* (unreasonable search and seizure in violation of the Fourth Amendment), *Davis* (unlawful discrimination in violation of the Fifth Amendment), and *Carlson* (deliberate indifference to medical need in violation of the Eighth Amendment). Indeed, we have said that, "[i]f a federal prisoner in a [Bureau of Prisons] facility alleges a constitutional deprivation, he may bring a *Bivens* claim against the offending individual officer, subject to the defense of qualified immunity." *Malesko.*

It is true that the plaintiffs bring their "deliberate indifference" claim against Warden Hasty under the Fifth Amendment's Due Process Clause, not the Eighth Amendment's Cruel and Unusual Punishment Clause, as in *Carlson.* But that is because the latter applies to convicted criminals while the former applies to pretrial and immigration detainees. Where the harm is the same, where this Court has held that both the Fifth and Eighth Amendments give rise to *Bivens'* remedies, and where the only difference in constitutional scope consists of a circumstance (the absence of a conviction) that makes the violation here worse, it cannot be maintained that the difference between the use of the two Amendments is "fundamental." If an arrestee can bring a claim of excessive force (*Bivens* itself), and a convicted prisoner can bring a claim for denying medical care (*Carlson*), someone who has neither been charged nor convicted with a crime should also be able to challenge abuse that causes him to need medical care.

Nor has Congress suggested that it wants to withdraw a damages remedy in circumstances like these. By its express terms, the Prison Litigation Reform Act of 1995 (PLRA) does not apply to immigration detainees. And, in fact, there is strong evidence that Congress assumed that *Bivens* remedies would be available to prisoners when it enacted the PLRA — *e.g.*, Congress continued to permit prisoners to recover for physical injuries, the typical kinds of *Bivens* injuries.

Because the context here is not new, I would allow the plaintiffs' constitutional claims to proceed. The plaintiffs have adequately alleged that the defendants were personally involved in imposing the conditions of confinement and did so with knowledge that the plaintiffs bore no ties to terrorism, thus satisfying *Iqbal's* pleading standard. And because it is clearly established that it is unconstitutional to subject detainees to punitive conditions of confinement and to target them based solely on their race, religion, or national origin, the defendants are not entitled to qualified immunity on the constitutional claims.

Even were I wrong and were the context here "fundamentally different," *Malesko,* the plaintiffs' claims would nonetheless survive Step Two and Step Three of the Court's framework for determining whether *Bivens* applies, Step Two consists of asking whether "any alternative, existing process for protecting the interest amounts to a convincing reason for the Judicial Branch to refrain from providing a new and freestanding remedy in damages." *Wilkie*. I can find no such "alternative, existing process" here.

There being no "alternative, existing process" that provides a "convincing reason" for not applying *Bivens*, we must proceed to Step Three. Doing so, I can find no "special factors [that] counse[l] hesitation before authorizing" this *Bivens* action. I turn to this matter next.

II

The Court describes two general considerations that it believes argue against an "extension" of *Bivens*. First, the majority opinion points out that the Court is now far less likely than at the time it decided *Bivens* to imply a cause of action for damages from a statute that does not explicitly provide for a damages claim. Second, it finds the "silence" of Congress "notable" in that Congress, though likely aware of the "high-level policies" involved in this suit, did not "choose to extend to any person the kind of remedies" that the plaintiffs here "seek." I doubt the strength of these two general considerations.

The first consideration, in my view, is not relevant. I concede that the majority and concurring opinions in *Bivens* looked in part for support to the fact that the Court had implied damages remedies from *statutes* silent on the subject. But that was not the main argument favoring the Court's conclusion. Rather, the Court drew far stronger support from the need for such a remedy when measured against a common-law and constitutional history of allowing traditional legal remedies where necessary. The Court believed such a remedy was necessary to make effective the Constitution's protection of certain basic individual rights. Similarly, as the Court later explained, a damages remedy against federal officials prevented the serious legal anomaly I previously mentioned. Its existence made basic constitutional protections of the individual against *Federal* Government abuse (the Bill of Rights' pre-Civil War objective) as effective as protections against abuse by *state* officials (the post-Civil War, post selective-incorporation objective).

Nor is the second circumstance — congressional silence — relevant in the manner that the majority opinion describes. The Court initially saw that silence as indicating an absence of congressional hostility to the Court's exercise of its traditional remedy-inferring powers. Congress' subsequent silence contains strong signs that it accepted *Bivens* actions as part of the law. After all, Congress rejected a proposal that would have eliminated *Bivens* by substituting the U.S. Government as a defendant in suits against federal officers that raised constitutional claims. Later, Congress expressly immunized federal employees acting in the course of their official duties from tort claims *except* those premised on violations of the Constitution. We stated that it is consequently "crystal clear that Congress views [the Federal Tort Claims Act] and *Bivens* as [providing] parallel, complementary causes of action." *Carlson*. Congress has even assumed the existence of a *Bivens* remedy in suits brought by noncitizen detainees suspected of terrorism.

In my view, the Court's strongest argument is that *Bivens* should not apply to policy-related actions taken in times of national-security need, for example, during war or national-security emergency. As the Court correctly points out, the Constitution grants primary power to protect the Nation's security to the Executive and Legislative Branches, not to the Judiciary. But the Constitution also delegates to the Judiciary the duty to protect an individual's fundamental constitutional rights.

Hence when protection of those rights and a determination of security needs conflict, the Court has a role to play. The Court most recently made this clear in cases arising out of the detention of enemy combatants at Guantanamo Bay. Justice O'Connor wrote that "a state of war is not a blank check." *Hamdi v. Rumsfeld* (2004) (plurality opinion).

We have not, however, answered the specific question the Court places at issue here: Should *Bivens* actions continue to exist in respect to policy-related actions taken in time of war or national emergency? In my view, they should.

For one thing, a *Bivens* action comes accompanied by many legal safeguards designed to prevent the courts from interfering with Executive and Legislative Branch activity reasonably believed to be necessary to protect national security. In Justice Jackson's well-known words, the Constitution is not "a suicide pact." *Terminello v. Chicago* (1949). The Constitution itself takes account of public necessity. Thus, for example, the Fourth Amendment does not forbid *all* Government searches and seizures; it forbids only those that are "unreasonable." Ordinarily, it requires that a police officer obtain a search warrant before entering an apartment, but should the officer observe a woman being dragged against her will into that apartment, he should, and will, act at once. The Fourth Amendment makes allowances for such "exigent circumstances." *Brigham City v. Stuart* (2006).

Moreover, *Bivens* comes accompanied with a qualified-immunity defense. Federal officials will face suit only if they have violated a constitutional right that was "clearly established" at the time they acted.

Further, in order to prevent the very presence of a *Bivens* lawsuit from interfering with the work of a Government official, this Court has held that a complaint must state a claim for relief that is "plausible." *Iqbal.* "[C]onclusory" statements and "[t]hreadbare" allegations will not suffice. And the Court has protected high-level officials in particular by requiring that plaintiffs plead that an official was personally involved in the unconstitutional conduct; an official cannot be vicariously liable for another's misdeeds.

Given these safeguards against undue interference by the Judiciary in times of war or national-security emergency, the Court's abolition, or limitation of, *Bivens* actions goes too far. If you are cold, put on a sweater, perhaps an overcoat, perhaps also turn up the heat, but do not set fire to the house.

At the same time, there may well be a particular need for *Bivens* remedies when security-related Government actions are at issue. History tells us of far too many instances where the Executive or Legislative Branch took actions during time of war that, on later examination, turned out unnecessarily and unreasonably to have deprived American citizens of basic constitutional rights. We have read about the Alien and Sedition Acts, the thousands of civilians imprisoned during the Civil War, and the suppression of civil liberties during World War I. The pages of the U.S. Reports themselves recite this Court's refusal to set aside the Government's World War II action removing more than 70,000 American citizens of Japanese origin from their west coast homes and interning them in camps.

Can we, in respect to actions taken during those periods, rely exclusively, as the Court seems to suggest, upon injunctive remedies or writs of habeas corpus, their retail equivalent? Complaints seeking that kind of relief typically come during the emergency itself, when emotions are strong, when courts may have too little or inaccurate information, and when courts may well prove particularly reluctant to interfere with even the least well-founded Executive Branch activity. That reluctance may itself set an unfortunate precedent, which, as Justice Jackson pointed out, can "li[e] about like a loaded weapon" awaiting discharge in another case. *Korematsu v. United States* (1944).

A damages action, however, is typically brought after the emergency is over, after emotions have cooled, and at a time when more factual information is available. In such circumstances, courts have more time to exercise such judicial virtues as calm reflection and dispassionate application of the law to the facts. We have applied the Constitution to actions taken during periods of war and national-security emergency. I should think that the wisdom of permitting courts to consider *Bivens* actions, later granting monetary compensation to those wronged at the time, would follow *a fortiori*.

As is well known, Lord Atkins, a British judge, wrote in the midst of World War II that "amid the clash of arms, the laws are not silent. They may be changed, but they speak the same language in war as in peace." The Court, in my view, should say the same of this *Bivens* action.

* * *

In the next case, *Hernández v. Mesa* (2020), the Court built upon its decision in *Ziglar v. Abbasi* (2017) in narrowly construing the *Bivens* doctrine as applied to a cross-border shooting claim. The facts of *Hernández* are emblematic of the historical context of these claims.

The U.S. Border Patrol (USBP) is the federal law enforcement agency tasked with patrolling the U.S. borders with Canada and Mexico. After its creation in 1924, the USBP's agents were paid a salary and supplied with "a badge and revolver," as well as "oats and hay for [their] horses."[34] Since then, the USBP has dramatically expanded to over 20,000 agents as the U.S. border, particularly its border with Mexico, has become militarized. In the USBP's own words, it responded to a "tremendous increase" in undocumented migrants during the 1980s and 1990s "with increases in manpower and the implementation of modern technology," including the use of "[i]nfrared night-vision scopes, seismic sensors, and a modern computer processing system."[35] Today, the USBP is part of U.S. Customs and Border Protection, an agency within the Department of Homeland Security, which was established in response to the September 11th attacks.

While much has changed since the USBP's founding in 1924, much has stayed the same in the "constant struggle involved with the Border Patrol's enforcement of immigration restrictions," especially along the U.S./Mexico border.[36] There, border enforcement "is widely recognized as a site of racial inequity"[37] and violence.[38]

---

34. *Border Patrol History*, U.S. CUSTOMS & BORDER PROTECTION (July 21, 2020), https://www.cbp.gov/border-security/along-us-borders/history.

35. *Id.*

36. KELLY LYTLE HERNÁNDEZ, MIGRA!: A HISTORY OF THE U.S. BORDER PATROL 4 (2010).

37. *Id.* at 10.

38. *Id.* at 5.

Hernández v. Mesa must be understood against this backdrop. The suit was brought by a Mexican family whose son was shot and killed by a USBP agent who fired across the border between El Paso, Texas, and Ciudad Juarez, Mexico. According to the complaint, Sergio Adrián Hernández Güereca and his friends were playing a game of darting across the border to touch the U.S. border fence. The USBP agent who was sued claimed instead that the children were throwing rocks at him. This is a familiar story.[39] Indeed, a 2022 study found that shootings in response to alleged rock throwing is "one of the most common uses of force by the Border Patrol."[40] USBP policy permits agents to use lethal force against rock throwers at least in some cases, though as of 2022 not one agent had ever been killed by rock throwers in the 98-year history of the agency.[41] Nor has any agent ever been convicted of a crime in a rock-throwing case, despite the "dubious details" of some uses of lethal force.[42] The question in *Hernández v. Mesa* was whether the *Bivens* doctrine would provide a remedy for this all too-typical cross-border shooting.

Hernández v. Mesa

140 S. Ct. 735 (2020)

Justice ALITO announced the decision of the Court.

We are asked in this case to extend *Bivens v. Six Unknown Fed. Narcotics Agents* (1971), and create a damages remedy for a cross-border shooting. As we have made clear in many prior cases, however, the Constitution's separation of powers requires us to exercise caution before extending *Bivens* to a new "context," and a claim based on a cross-border shooting arises in a context that is markedly new. Unlike any previously recognized *Bivens* claim, a cross-border shooting claim has foreign

---

39. *See* Irene I. Vega, *"Reasonable" Force at the U.S.-Mexico Border*, 69 SOC. PROBS. 1154, 1163 (2022) ("Agents have killed at least a dozen people in rocking incidents since 2010 and have shot their weapons at dozens more"); Brian Bennett, *Border Patrol's Use of Deadly Force Criticized in Report*, L.A. TIMES (Feb. 27, 2014) ("Border Patrol agents have deliberately stepped in the path of cars apparently to justify shooting at the drivers and have fired in frustration at people throwing rocks from the Mexican side of the border, according to an independent review of 67 cases that resulted in 19 deaths.").

40. Vega, *supra* note 39, at 1155.

41. A 2010 database of the National Law Enforcement Officers Memorial notes that "rocks were responsible for three of 18,983 fatalities" of police officers in the U.S. from 1792 onward. Brian Palmer, *Getting Stoned: How Many Police Officers Have Been Killed by Rocks?*, SLATE (June 09, 2010), https://slate.com/news-and-politics/2010/06/police-are-shooting-rock-throwers-along-the-u-s-mexico-border-how-many-officers-have-been-killed-by-rocks.html. At the same time, "officers have been badly injured" by thrown rocks. *Id.*

42. Vega, *supra* note 39, at 1163. In 2014, the USBP "tried to prevent [a] scathing 21-page report from coming to light"; this report, which the USBP itself commissioned, found that the USBP had not diligently investigated incidents of the use of lethal force. Bennett, *supra* note 47 (discussing POLICE EXECUTIVE RESEARCH FORUM, U.S. CUSTOMS AND BORDER PROTECTION, USE OF FORCE REVIEW: CASES AND POLICIES 6, 9 (Feb. 2013) (finding that "[t]oo many cases do not appear to meet the test of objective reasonableness with regard to use of deadly force" and that in some cases "frustration is a factor motivating agents to shoot at rock throwers")).

relations and national security implications. In addition, Congress has been notably hesitant to create claims based on allegedly tortious conduct abroad. Because of the distinctive characteristics of cross-border shooting claims, we refuse to extend *Bivens* into this new field.

I

Sergio Adrián Hernández Güereca, a 15-year-old Mexican national, was with a group of friends in a concrete culvert that separates El Paso, Texas, from Ciudad Juarez, Mexico. The border runs through the center of the culvert, which was designed to hold the waters of the Rio Grande River but is now largely dry. Border Patrol Agent Jesus Mesa, Jr., detained one of Hernández's friends who had run onto the United States' side of the culvert. After Hernández, who was also on the United States' side, ran back across the culvert onto Mexican soil, Agent Mesa fired two shots at Hernández; one struck and killed him on the other side of the border.

Petitioners and Agent Mesa disagree about what Hernández and his friends were doing at the time of shooting. According to petitioners, they were simply playing a game, running across the culvert, touching the fence on the U.S. side, and then running back across the border. According to Agent Mesa, Hernández and his friends were involved in an illegal border crossing attempt, and they pelted him with rocks.

The shooting quickly became an international incident, with the United States and Mexico disagreeing about how the matter should be handled. On the United States' side, the Department of Justice conducted an investigation. When it finished, the Department, while expressing regret over Hernández's death, concluded that Agent Mesa had not violated Customs and Border Patrol policy or training, and it declined to bring charges or take other action against him. Mexico was not and is not satisfied with the U.S. investigation. It requested that Agent Mesa be extradited to face criminal charges in a Mexican court, a request that the United States has denied.

Petitioners, Hernández's parents, were also dissatisfied and therefore brought suit for damages in the United States District Court for the Western District of Texas. Among other claims, they sought recovery of damages under *Bivens*, alleging that Mesa violated Hernández's Fourth and Fifth Amendment rights.

II

In *Bivens*, the Court broke new ground by holding that a person claiming to be the victim of an unlawful arrest and search could bring a Fourth Amendment claim for damages against the responsible agents even though no federal statute authorized such a claim. In later years, we came to appreciate more fully the tension between this practice and the Constitution's separation of legislative and judicial power. The Constitution grants legislative power to Congress; this Court and the lower federal courts, by contrast, have only "judicial Power." But when a court recognizes an implied claim for damages on the ground that doing so furthers the "purpose" of the law, the court risks arrogating legislative power. No law "'pursues its purposes at all costs.'" *American Express Co. v. Italian Colors Restaurant* (2013). Instead, lawmaking involves balancing interests and often demands compromise.

Thus, a lawmaking body that enacts a provision that creates a right or prohibits specified conduct may not wish to pursue the provision's purpose to the extent of authorizing private suits for damages. For this reason, finding that a damages remedy is implied by a provision that makes no reference to that remedy may upset the careful balance of interests struck by the lawmakers.

In constitutional cases, we have been at least equally reluctant to create new causes of action. We have recognized that Congress is best positioned to evaluate "whether, and the extent to which, monetary and other liabilities should be imposed upon individual officers and employees of the Federal Government" based on constitutional torts. *Ziglar v. Abbasi* (2017). We have stated that expansion of *Bivens* is "a 'disfavored' judicial activity," and have gone so far as to observe that if "the Court's three *Bivens* cases [had] been . . . decided today," it is doubtful that we would have reached the same result. And for almost 40 years, we have consistently rebuffed requests to add to the claims allowed under *Bivens*.

When asked to extend *Bivens*, we engage in a two-step inquiry. We first inquire whether the request involves a claim that arises in a "new context" or involves a "new category of defendants." And our understanding of a "new context" is broad. We regard a context as "new" if it is "different in a meaningful way from previous *Bivens* cases decided by this Court." *Abbasi*.

When we find that a claim arises in a new context, we proceed to the second step and ask whether there are any "special factors [that] counse[l] hesitation" about granting the extension. *Id.* If there are — that is, if we have reason to pause before applying *Bivens* in a new context or to a new class of defendants — we reject the request.

We have not attempted to "create an exhaustive list" of factors that may provide a reason not to extend *Bivens*, but we have explained that "central to [this] analysis" are "separation-of-powers principles." *Id.* We thus consider the risk of interfering with the authority of the other branches, and we ask whether "there are sound reasons to think Congress might doubt the efficacy or necessity of a damages remedy," and "whether the Judiciary is well suited, absent congressional action or instruction, to consider and weigh the costs and benefits of allowing a damages action to proceed." *Id.*

III

The *Bivens* claims in this case assuredly arise in a new context. Petitioners contend that their Fourth and Fifth Amendment claims do not involve a new context because *Bivens* and *Davis* involved claims under those same two amendments, but that argument rests on a basic misunderstanding of what our cases mean by a new context. A claim may arise in a new context even if it is based on the same constitutional provision as a claim in a case in which a damages remedy was previously recognized. And once we look beyond the constitutional provisions invoked in *Bivens*, *Davis*, and the present case, it is glaringly obvious that petitioners' claims involve a new context, *i.e.*, one that is meaningfully different. *Bivens* concerned an allegedly unconstitutional arrest and search carried out in New York City. *Davis* concerned alleged sex discrimination on Capitol Hill. There is a world of difference between those claims and petitioners' cross-border shooting claims, where "the risk of disruptive intrusion by the Judiciary into the functioning of other branches" is significant. *Abbasi*.

Because petitioners assert claims that arise in a new context, we must proceed to the next step and ask whether there are factors that counsel hesitation. As we will explain, there are multiple, related factors that raise warning flags.

The first is the potential effect on foreign relations. "The political branches, not the Judiciary, have the responsibility and institutional capacity to weigh foreign-policy concerns." *Jesner v. Arab Bank, PLC* (2018). Indeed, we have said that "matters relating 'to the conduct of foreign relations . . . are so exclusively entrusted to the political branches of government as to be largely immune from judicial inquiry or interference.'" *Haig v. Agee* (1981). "Thus, unless Congress specifically has provided otherwise, courts traditionally have been reluctant to intrude upon the authority of the Executive in [these matters]." *Dep't of Navy v. Egan* (1988). We must therefore be especially wary before allowing a *Bivens* remedy that impinges on this arena.

A cross-border shooting is by definition an international incident; it involves an event that occurs simultaneously in two countries and affects both countries' interests. Such an incident may lead to a disagreement between those countries, as happened in this case. The United States, through the Executive Branch, which has "the lead role in foreign policy," *Medellín v. Texas* (2008), has taken the position that this incident should be handled in a particular way—namely, that Agent Mesa should not face charges in the United States nor be extradited to stand trial in Mexico. As noted, the Executive decided not to take action against Agent Mesa because it found that he "did not act inconsistently with [Border Patrol] policy or training regarding use of force." We presume that Border Patrol policy and training incorporate both the Executive's understanding of the Fourth Amendment's prohibition of unreasonable seizures and the Executive's assessment of circumstances at the border. Thus, the Executive judged Agent Mesa's conduct by what it regards as reasonable conduct by an agent under the circumstances that Mesa faced at the time of the shooting, and based on the application of those standards, it declined to prosecute.

The Executive does not want a Mexican criminal court to judge Agent Mesa's conduct by whatever standards would be applicable under Mexican law; nor does it want a jury in a *Bivens* action to apply its own understanding of what constituted reasonable conduct by a Border Patrol agent under the circumstances of this case. Such a jury determination, the Executive claims, would risk the "embarrassment of our government abroad" through "multifarious pronouncements by various departments on one question." For these reasons, petitioners' assertion that their claims have "nothing to do with the substance or conduct of U.S. foreign . . . policy."

Petitioners are similarly incorrect in deprecating the Fifth Circuit's conclusion that the issue here implicates an element of national security. One of the ways in which the Executive protects this country is by attempting to control the movement of people and goods across the border, and that is a daunting task. The United States' border with Mexico extends for 1,900 miles, and every day thousands of persons and a large volume of goods enter this country at ports of entry on the southern border. The lawful passage of people and goods in both directions across the border is beneficial to both countries.

Unfortunately, there is also a large volume of illegal cross-border traffic. During the last fiscal year, approximately 850,000 persons were apprehended attempting to enter the United States illegally from Mexico, and large quantities of drugs were smuggled across the border. In addition, powerful criminal organizations operating on both sides of the border present a serious law enforcement problem for both countries.

On the United States' side, the responsibility for attempting to prevent the illegal entry of dangerous persons and goods rests primarily with the U.S. Customs and Border Protection Agency, and one of its main responsibilities is to "detect, respond to, and interdict terrorists, drug smugglers and traffickers, human smugglers and traffickers, and other persons who may undermine the security of the United States." While Border Patrol agents often work miles from the border, some, like Agent Mesa, are stationed right at the border and have the responsibility of attempting to prevent illegal entry. For these reasons, the conduct of agents positioned at the border has a clear and strong connection to national security, as the Fifth Circuit understood.

Petitioners protest that "shooting people who are just walking down a street in Mexico" does not involve national security, but that misses the point. The question is not whether national security requires such conduct — of course, it does not — but whether the Judiciary should alter the framework established by the political branches for addressing cases in which it is alleged that lethal force was unlawfully employed by an agent at the border.

We have declined to extend *Bivens* where doing so would interfere with the system of military discipline created by statute and regulation, and a similar consideration is applicable here. Since regulating the conduct of agents at the border unquestionably has national security implications, the risk of undermining border security provides reason to hesitate before extending *Bivens* into this field.

Our reluctance to take that step is reinforced by our survey of what Congress has done in statutes addressing related matters. We frequently "loo[k] to analogous statutes for guidance on the appropriate boundaries of judge-made causes of action." *Jesner.* A leading example is 42 U.S.C. §1983, which permits the recovery of damages for constitutional violations by officers acting under color of *state* law. We have described *Bivens* as a "more limited" "federal analog" to §1983. *Hartman v. Moore* (2006). Thus, the limited scope of §1983 weighs against recognition of the *Bivens* claim at issue here. Section 1983's express limitation to the claims brought by citizens and persons subject to United States jurisdiction is especially significant, but even if this explicit limitation were lacking, we would presume that §1983 did not apply abroad.

When Congress has enacted statutes creating a damages remedy for persons injured by United States Government officers, it has taken care to preclude claims for injuries that occurred abroad.

In sum, this case features multiple factors that counsel hesitation about extending *Bivens*, but they can all be condensed to one concern — respect for the separation of powers. "Foreign policy and national security decisions are 'delicate, complex, and involve large elements of prophecy' for which 'the Judiciary has neither aptitude, facilities[,] nor responsibility.'" *Jesner.* To avoid upsetting the delicate web of international relations, we typically presume that even congressionally crafted causes of action do not apply outside our borders. These concerns are only heightened when judges are asked to fashion constitutional remedies. Congress, which has authority in the field of foreign affairs, has chosen not to create liability in similar statutes, leaving the resolution of extraterritorial claims brought by foreign nationals to executive officials and the diplomatic process.

Congress's decision not to provide a judicial remedy does not compel us to step into its shoes. "The absence of statutory relief for a constitutional violation . . . does not by any means necessarily imply that courts should award money damages against the officers responsible for the violation." *Schweiker.*

When evaluating whether to extend *Bivens,* the most important question "is 'who should decide' whether to provide for a damages remedy, Congress or the courts?" The correct "answer most often will be Congress." *Abbasi.* That is undoubtedly the answer here.

Justice THOMAS, with whom Justice GORSUCH joins, concurring.

The Court correctly applies our precedents to conclude that the implied cause of action created in *Bivens v. Six Unknown Fed. Narcotics Agents,* should not be extended to cross-border shootings. I therefore join its opinion.

I write separately because, in my view, the time has come to consider discarding the *Bivens* doctrine altogether. The foundation for *Bivens*—the practice of creating implied causes of action in the statutory context—has already been abandoned. And the Court has consistently refused to extend the *Bivens* doctrine for nearly 40 years, even going so far as to suggest that *Bivens* and its progeny were wrongly decided. *Stare decisis* provides no "veneer of respectability to our continued application of [these] demonstrably incorrect precedents." *Gamble v. United Sates* (2019) (Thomas, J. concurring). To ensure that we are not "perpetuat[ing] a usurpation of the legislative power," *id.,* we should reevaluate our continued recognition of even a limited form of the *Bivens* doctrine.

This usurpation of legislative power is all the more troubling because Congress has demonstrated that it knows how to create a cause of action to recover damages for constitutional violations when it wishes to do so. In 42 U.S.C. §1983, Congress provided a cause of action that allows persons to recover damages for certain deprivations of constitutional rights by *state officers.* Congress has chosen not to provide such a cause of action against *federal officers.* In fact, it has pre-empted the state tort suits that traditionally served as the mechanism by which damages were recovered from federal officers.

The analysis underlying *Bivens* cannot be defended. We have cabined the doctrine's scope, undermined its foundation, and limited its precedential value. It is time to correct this Court's error and abandon the doctrine altogether.

Justice GINSBURG, with whom Justice BREYER, Justice SOTOMAYOR, and Justice KAGAN join, dissenting.

Because this case was resolved on a motion to dismiss, I accept the complaint's allegations, next set out, as true. In 2010, Sergio Adrián Hernández Güereca, a 15-year-old citizen of Mexico, was playing with his friends in the dry culvert that divides El Paso, Texas, from Ciudad Juarez, Mexico. The international boundary line runs down the center of the culvert, but the only visible border-related features are fences and border-crossing posts that sit atop each side. The game Hernández and his friends were playing involved running up the embankment on the United States side, touching the barbed-wire fence, and running back down to the Mexican side. While the game was ongoing, Border Patrol Agent Jesus Mesa, Jr., appeared on his bicycle and detained one of Hernández's friends as he was running down the embankment on the U.S. side. Hernández, who was unarmed, retreated into Mexican territory. Mesa pointed his weapon across the border, "seemingly taking careful aim," and fired at least two shots. At least one of the shots struck Hernández in the face, killing him. Hernández's parents brought suit under *Bivens*, asserting, that Mesa had violated their son's Fourth and Fifth Amendment rights.

Plaintiffs' *Bivens* action arises in a setting kin to *Bivens* itself: Mesa, plaintiffs allege, acted in disregard of instructions governing his conduct and of Hernández's constitutional rights. *Abbasi* acknowledged the "fixed principle" that plaintiffs may bring *Bivens* suits against federal law enforcement officers for "seizure[s]" that violate the Fourth Amendment. Using lethal force against a person who "poses no immediate threat to the officer and no threat to others" surely qualifies as an unreasonable seizure. *Tennessee v. Garner* (1985). The complaint states that Mesa engaged in that very conduct; it alleged, specifically, that Hernández was unarmed and posed no threat to Mesa or others. For these reasons, as Mesa acknowledged at oral argument, Hernández's parents could have maintained a *Bivens* action had the bullet hit Hernández while he was running up or down the United States side of the embankment.

The only salient difference here: the fortuity that the bullet happened to strike Hernández on the Mexican side of the embankment. But Hernández's location at the precise moment the bullet landed should not matter one whit. After all, "[t]he purpose of *Bivens* is to deter the *officer*." *Abbasi*. And primary conduct constrained by the Fourth Amendment is an *officer's* unjustified resort to excessive force. Mesa's allegedly unwarranted deployment of deadly force occurred on United States soil. It scarcely makes sense for a remedy trained on deterring rogue officer conduct to turn upon a happenstance subsequent to the conduct—a bullet landing in one half of a culvert, not the other.

Nor would it make sense to deem some culvert locations "new settings" for *Bivens* purposes, but others (those inside the United States), familiar territory. [T]he culvert "does not itself contain any physical features of a border"; it consists of wide swaths of "concrete-lined empty space" with fencing on each side. It is not asserted that Mesa "knew on which side of the boundary line [his] bullet would land."

Finally, although the bullet happened to land on the Mexican side of the culvert, the United States, as in *Bivens*, unquestionably has jurisdiction to prescribe law governing a Border Patrol agent's conduct. That prescriptive jurisdiction reaches "conduct that . . . takes place within [United States] territory." Restatement (Third) of Foreign Relations law of the United States. The place of a rogue officer's conduct "has peculiar significance" to choice of the applicable law where, as here, "the primary purpose of the tort rule involved is to deter or punish misconduct." Restatement (Second) Conflict of Laws.

Even accepting, *arguendo*, that the setting in this case could be characterized as "new," there is still no good reason why Hernández's parents should face a closed courtroom door. As in *Bivens*, plaintiffs lack recourse to alternative remedies. And not one of the "special factors" the Court identifies weigh any differently based on where a bullet happens to land.

The special factors featured by the Court relate, in the main, to foreign policy and national security. But, as suggested earlier, no policies or policymakers are

[Handwritten note at top: "Majority seems to suggest any relation to national security is enough"]

challenged in this case. Plaintiffs target the rogue actions of a rank-and-file law enforcement officer acting in violation of rules controlling his office.

The Court nevertheless asserts that the instant suit has a "potential effect on foreign relations" because it invites courts "to arbitrate between" the United States and Mexico. Plaintiffs, however, have brought a civil damages action, no different from one a federal court would entertain had the fatal shot hit Hernández before he reached the Mexican side of the border. True, cross-border shootings spark bilateral discussion, but so too does a range of smuggling and other border-related issues that courts routinely address "concurrently with whatever diplomacy may also be addressing them." *Rodriguez v. Swartz* (9th Cir. 2018).

Moreover, the Court, in this case, cannot escape a "potential effect on foreign relations," by declining to recognize a *Bivens* action. As the Mexican Government alerted the Court: "[R]efus[al] to consider [Hernández's] parents' claim on the merits . . . is what has the potential to negatively affect international relations." Notably, recognizing a *Bivens* suit here honors our Nation's international commitments.

Regrettably, the death of Hernández is not an isolated incident. One report reviewed over 800 complaints of alleged physical, verbal, or sexual abuse lodged against Border Patrol agents between 2009 and 2012; in 97% of the complaints resulting in formal decisions, no action was taken. According to *amici* former Customs and Border Protection officials, "the United States has not extradited a Border Patrol agent to stand trial in Mexico, and to [*amici's*] knowledge has itself prosecuted only one agent in a cross-border shooting." These *amici* warn that, "[w]ithout the possibility of civil liability, the unlikely prospect of discipline or criminal prosecution will not provide a meaningful deterrent to abuse at the border." In short, it is all too apparent that to redress injuries like the one suffered here, it is *Bivens* or nothing. *[Handwritten note: "Note the shift towards deterrence"]*

I resist the conclusion that "nothing" is the answer required in this case. I would reverse the Fifth Circuit's judgment and hold that plaintiffs can sue Mesa in federal court for violating their son's Fourth and Fifth Amendment rights.

* * *

The final case, *Egbert v. Boule* (2022), also arose from the borderlands of the United States, though not from the U.S./Mexico border. The lower court had distinguished *Hernández v. Mesa* (2020), but the Supreme Court extended it to hold that no *Bivens* remedy was available. In so doing, the Court did not overrule *Bivens*, but its reasoning may have left little room for *Bivens* to provide remedies beyond its specific facts.

Egbert v. Boule

142 S. Ct. 1793 (2022)

Justice THOMAS announced the decision of the Court.

In *Bivens v. Six Unknown Fed. Narcotics Agents* (1971), this Court authorized a damages action against federal officials for alleged violations of the Fourth

Amendment. Over the past 42 years, however, we have declined 11 times to imply a similar cause of action for other alleged constitutional violations. Nevertheless, the Court of Appeals permitted not one, but two constitutional damages actions to proceed against a U.S. Border Patrol agent: a Fourth Amendment excessive-force claim and a First Amendment retaliation claim. Because our cases have made clear that, in all but the most unusual circumstances, prescribing a cause of action is a job for Congress, not the courts, we reverse.

I

Blaine, Washington, is the last town in the United States along U.S. Interstate Highway 5 before reaching the Canadian border. Respondent Robert Boule is a longtime Blaine resident. The rear of his property abuts the Canadian border at "0 Avenue," a Canadian street. Boule's property line actually extends five feet into Canada. Several years ago, Boule placed a line of small stones on his property to mark the international boundary. [A]ny person could easily enter the United States or Canada through or near Boule's property.

Boule markets his home as a bed-and-breakfast aptly named "Smuggler's Inn." The area surrounding the Inn "is a hotspot for cross-border smuggling of people, drugs, illicit money, and items of significance to criminal organizations." "On numerous occasions," U.S. Border Patrol agents "have observed persons come south across the border and walk into Smuggler's Inn through the back door." Federal agents also have seized from the Inn shipments of cocaine, methamphetamine, ecstasy, and other narcotics. For a time, Boule served as a confidential informant who would help federal agents identify and apprehend persons engaged in unlawful cross-border activity on or near his property. Boule claims that the Government has paid him upwards of $60,000 for his services.

Ever the entrepreneur, Boule saw his relationship with Border Patrol as a business opportunity. Boule would host persons who unlawfully entered the United States as "guests" at the Inn and offer to drive them to Seattle or elsewhere. He also would pick up Canada-bound guests throughout the State and drive them north to his property along the border. Either way, Boule would charge $100–$150 per hour for his shuttle service and require guests to pay for a night of lodging even if they never intended to stay at the Inn. Meanwhile, Boule would inform federal law enforcement if he was scheduled to lodge or transport persons of interest. In short order, Border Patrol agents would arrive to arrest the guests, often within a few blocks of the Inn. Boule would decline to offer his erstwhile customers a refund. In his view, this practice was "nothing any different than [the] normal policies of any hotel/motel."

In light of Boule's business model, local Border Patrol agents, including petitioner Erik Egbert, were well acquainted with Smuggler's Inn and the criminal activity that attended it. On March 20, 2014, Boule informed Agent Egbert that a Turkish national, arriving in Seattle by way of New York, had scheduled transportation to Smuggler's Inn later that day. Agent Egbert grew suspicious, as he could think of "no legitimate reason a person would travel from Turkey to stay at a run-down bed-and-breakfast on the border in Blaine."

Later that afternoon, Agent Egbert observed one of Boule's vehicles—a black SUV with the license plate "SMUGLER"—returning to the Inn. Agent Egbert suspected that Boule's Turkish guest was a passenger and followed the SUV into the driveway so he could check the guest's immigration status. On Boule's account, the situation escalated from there. Boule instructed Agent Egbert to leave his property, but Agent Egbert declined. Instead, Boule claims, Agent Egbert lifted him off the ground and threw him against the SUV. After Boule collected himself, Agent Egbert allegedly threw him to the ground. Agent Egbert then checked the guest's immigration paperwork, concluded that everything was in order, and left. Later that evening, Boule's Turkish guest unlawfully entered Canada from Smuggler's Inn.

Boule lodged a grievance with Agent Egbert's supervisors, alleging that Agent Egbert had used excessive force and caused him physical injury. Boule also filed an administrative claim with Border Patrol pursuant to the Federal Tort Claims Act (FTCA). According to Boule, Agent Egbert retaliated against him while those claims were pending by reporting Boule's "SMUGLER" license plate to the Washington Department of Licensing for referencing illegal conduct, and by contacting the Internal Revenue Service and prompting an audit of Boule's tax returns. Ultimately, Boule's FTCA claim was denied and, after a year-long investigation, Border Patrol took no action against Agent Egbert for his alleged use of force or acts of retaliation. Thereafter, Agent Egbert continued to serve as an active-duty Border Patrol agent.

In January 2017, Boule sued Agent Egbert in his individual capacity in Federal District Court, alleging a Fourth Amendment violation for excessive use of force and a First Amendment violation for unlawful retaliation. Boule invoked *Bivens* and asked the District Court to recognize a damages action for each alleged constitutional violation.

II

Now long past "the heady days in which this Court assumed common-law powers to create causes of action," *Correctional Services Corp. v. Malesko* (2001) (Scalia, J., concurring), we have come "to appreciate more fully the tension between" judicially created causes of action and "the Constitution's separation of legislative and judicial power," *Hernández v. Mesa* (2020).

Nonetheless, rather than dispense with *Bivens* altogether, we have emphasized that recognizing a cause of action under *Bivens* is "a disfavored judicial activity." *Ziglar v. Abbasi* (2017). When asked to imply a Bivens action, "our watchword is caution." *Hernández.* "[I]f there are sound reasons to think Congress might doubt the efficacy or necessity of a damages remedy[,] the courts must refrain from creating [it]." *Ziglar.* Put another way, "the most important question is who should decide whether to provide for a damages remedy, Congress or the courts?" *Hernández.* If there is a rational reason to think that the answer is "Congress"—as it will be in most every case—no *Bivens* action may lie.

To inform a court's analysis of a proposed *Bivens* claim, our cases have framed the inquiry as proceeding in two steps. First, we ask whether the case presents "a new *Bivens* context"—i.e., is it "meaningful[ly]" different from the three cases in which the Court has implied a damages action. *Ziglar.* Second, if a claim arises in a new context, a *Bivens* remedy is unavailable if there are "special factors" indicating that the Judiciary is at least arguably less equipped than Congress to "weigh the costs and benefits of allowing a damages action to proceed." *Id.* If there is even a single "reason to pause before applying *Bivens* in a new context," a court may not recognize a *Bivens* remedy. *Hernández.*

While our cases describe two steps, those steps often resolve to a single question: whether there is any reason to think that Congress might be better equipped to create a damages remedy. For example, we have explained that a new context arises when there are "potential special factors that previous *Bivens* cases did not consider." *Ziglar.* And we have identified several examples of new contexts — *e.g.*, a case that involves a "new category of defendants," *Malesko* — largely because they represent situations in which a court is not undoubtedly better positioned than Congress to create a damages action. We have never offered an "exhaustive" accounting of such scenarios, however, because no court could forecast every factor that might "counse[l] hesitation." *Ziglar.* Even in a particular case, a court likely cannot predict the "systemwide" consequences of recognizing a cause of action under *Bivens. Ziglar.* That uncertainty alone is a special factor that forecloses relief.

Finally, our cases hold that a court may not fashion a *Bivens* remedy if Congress already has provided, or has authorized the Executive to provide, "an alternative remedial structure." *Ziglar.*

III

Applying the foregoing principles, the Court of Appeals plainly erred when it created causes of action for Boule's Fourth Amendment excessive-force claim and First Amendment retaliation claim.

A

The Court of Appeals conceded that Boule's Fourth Amendment claim presented a new context for *Bivens* purposes, yet it concluded there was no reason to hesitate before recognizing a cause of action against Agent Egbert. That conclusion was incorrect for two independent reasons: Congress is better positioned to create remedies in the border-security context, and the Government already has provided alternative remedies that protect plaintiffs like Boule.

The *Bivens* inquiry does not invite federal courts to independently assess the costs and benefits of implying a cause of action. A court faces only one question: whether there is any rational reason (even one) to think that Congress is better suited to "weigh the costs and benefits of allowing a damages action to proceed." *Ziglar.*

The Court of Appeals' analysis betrays the pitfalls of applying the special-factors analysis at too granular a level. The court rested on three irrelevant distinctions from *Hernández.* First, Agent Egbert was several feet from (rather than straddling) the border, but cross-border security is obviously implicated in either event. Second, Boule's guest arrived in Seattle from New York rather than abroad, but an alien's port of entry does not make him less likely to be a national-security threat. And third, Agent Egbert investigated immigration violations on our side of the border, not Canada's, but immigration investigations in this country are perhaps more likely to impact the national security of the United States. In short, the Court of Appeals offered no plausible basis to permit a Fourth Amendment *Bivens* claim against Agent Egbert to proceed.

Second, Congress has provided alternative remedies for aggrieved parties in Boule's position that independently foreclose a *Bivens* action here. The U.S. Border

Patrol is statutorily obligated to "control, direc[t], and supervis[e] . . . all employees." And, by regulation, Border Patrol must investigate "[a]lleged violations of the standards for enforcement activities" and accept grievances from "[a]ny persons wishing to lodge a complaint." As noted, Boule took advantage of this grievance procedure, prompting a year-long internal investigation into Agent Egbert's conduct.

Boule nonetheless contends that Border Patrol's grievance process is inadequate because he is not entitled to participate and has no right to judicial review of an adverse determination. But we have never held that a *Bivens* alternative must afford rights to participation or appeal. That is so because *Bivens* "is concerned solely with deterring the unconstitutional acts of individual officers"—*i.e.*, the focus is whether the Government has put in place safeguards to "preven[t]" constitutional violations "from recurring." *Malesko.* And, again, the question whether a given remedy is adequate is a legislative determination that must be left to Congress, not the federal courts. So long as Congress or the Executive has created a remedial process that it finds sufficient to secure an adequate level of deterrence, the courts cannot second-guess that calibration by superimposing a *Bivens* remedy. That is true even if a court independently concludes that the Government's procedures are "not as effective as an individual damages remedy." *Bush v. Lucas* (1983). Thus here, as in *Hernández*, we have no warrant to doubt that the consideration of Boule's grievance against Agent Egbert secured adequate deterrence and afforded Boule an alternative remedy.

B

Now presented with the question whether to extend *Bivens* to this context, we hold that there is no *Bivens* action for First Amendment retaliation. There are many reasons to think that Congress, not the courts, is better suited to authorize such a damages remedy.

Recognizing any new *Bivens* action "entail[s] substantial social costs, including the risk that fear of personal monetary liability and harassing litigation will unduly inhibit officials in the discharge of their duties." *Anderson v. Creighton* (1987). Extending *Bivens* to alleged First Amendment violations would pose an acute risk of increasing such costs. A plaintiff can turn practically any adverse action into grounds for a retaliation claim. And, "[b]ecause an official's state of mind is easy to allege and hard to disprove, insubstantial claims that turn on [retaliatory] intent may be less amenable to summary disposition." *Crawford-El v. Britton* (1998). Even a frivolous retaliation claim "threaten[s] to set off broad-ranging discovery in which there is often no clear end to the relevant evidence." *Nieves v. Bartlett* (2019).

"[U]ndoubtedly," then, the "prospect of personal liability" under the First Amendment would lead "to new difficulties and expense." *Schweiker v. Chilicky* (1988). Federal employees "face[d with] the added risk of personal liability for decisions that they believe to be a correct response to improper [activity] would be deterred from" carrying out their duties. *Bush.* We are therefore "convinced" that, in light of these costs, "Congress is in a better position to decide whether or not the public interest would be served" by imposing a damages action. *Id.*

Justice GORSUCH, concurring in the judgment.

Our Constitution's separation of powers prohibits federal courts from assuming legislative authority. As the Court today acknowledges, *Bivens v. Six Unknown Fed. Narcotics Agents* (1971), crossed that line by "impl[ying]" a new set of private rights and liabilities Congress never ordained.

Today, the Court . . . recognizes that our two-step inquiry really boils down to a "single question": Is there "any reason to think Congress might be better equipped" than a court to "'weigh the costs and benefits of allowing a damages action to proceed'"? But, respectfully, resolving that much only serves to highlight the larger remaining question: When might a court ever be "better equipped" than the people's elected representatives to weigh the "costs and benefits" of creating a cause of action?

It seems to me that to ask the question is to answer it. To create a new cause of action is to assign new private rights and liabilities—a power that is in every meaningful sense an act of legislation.

If the costs and benefits do not justify a new *Bivens* action on facts so analogous to *Bivens* itself, it's hard to see how they ever could. And if the only question is whether a court is "better equipped" than Congress to weigh the value of a new cause of action, surely the right answer will always be no. Doubtless, these are the lessons the Court seeks to convey. I would only take the next step and acknowledge explicitly what the Court leaves barely implicit.

Justice SOTOMAYOR, with whom Justice BREYER and Justice KAGAN join, concurring in the judgment in part and dissenting in part.

Respondent Robert Boule alleges that petitioner Erik Egbert, a U.S. Customs and Border Patrol agent, violated the Fourth Amendment by entering Boule's property without a warrant and assaulting him. Existing precedent permits Boule to seek compensation for his injuries in federal court. The Court goes to extraordinary lengths to avoid this result: It rewrites a legal standard it established just five years ago, stretches national-security concerns beyond recognition, and discerns an alternative remedial structure where none exists. The Court's innovations, taken together, enable it to close the door to Boule's claim and, presumably, to others that fall squarely within *Bivens'* ambit.

Today's decision does not overrule *Bivens*. It nevertheless contravenes precedent and will strip many more individuals who suffer injuries at the hands of other federal officers, and whose circumstances are materially indistinguishable from those in *Bivens*, of an important remedy. I therefore dissent from the Court's disposition of Boule's Fourth Amendment claim. I concur in the Court's judgment that Boule's First Amendment retaliation claim may not proceed under *Bivens*, but for reasons grounded in precedent rather than this Court's newly announced test.

* * *

b.   The Availability of Injunctive Relief to Enforce Federal Law

Despite the absence of a statute creating a cause of action against federal officers for constitutional transgressions, the Supreme Court long has held that federal officers may be sued for injunctive relief to prevent future infringements of federal laws.[43] In *Free Enterprise Fund v. Public Company Accountability Oversight Board* (2010), the Court stressed the importance of the availability of injunctive relief. Note the Court's reliance on *Ex parte Young* (1908), discussed in detail in Chapter 6.

---

43. *See, e.g.*, Larson v. Domestic & Foreign Commerce Corp., 337 U.S. 682 (1949) (federal officers may be enjoined).

Free Enterprise Fund v. PCAOB

562 U.S. 477 (2010)

Chief Justice ROBERTS delivered the opinion of the Court

Our Constitution divided the "powers of the new Federal Government into three defined categories, Legislative, Executive, and Judicial." *INS v. Chadha* (1983). Article II vests "[t]he executive Power . . . in a President of the United States of America," who must "take Care that the Laws be faithfully executed."

Since 1789, the Constitution has been understood to empower the President to keep these officers accountable — by removing them from office, if necessary. This Court has determined, however, that this authority is not without limit.

We are asked, however, to consider a new situation not yet encountered by the Court. The question is whether these separate layers of protection may be combined. May the President be restricted in his ability to remove a principal officer, who is in turn restricted in his ability to remove an inferior officer, even though that inferior officer determines the policy and enforces the laws of the United States?

We hold that such multilevel protection from removal is contrary to Article II's vesting of the executive power in the President. The President cannot "take Care that the Laws be faithfully executed" if he cannot oversee the faithfulness of the officers who execute them. Here the President cannot remove an officer who enjoys more than one level of good-cause protection, even if the President determines that the officer is neglecting his duties or discharging them improperly. That judgment is instead committed to another officer, who may or may not agree with the President's determination, and whom the President cannot remove simply because that officer disagrees with him. This contravenes the President's "constitutional obligation to ensure the faithful execution of the laws." *Morrison v. Olson* (1988).

After a series of celebrated accounting debacles, Congress enacted the Sarbanes-Oxley Act of 2002. Among other measures, the Act introduced tighter regulation of the accounting industry under a new Public Company Accounting Oversight Board. The Board is composed of five members, appointed to staggered 5-year terms by the Securities and Exchange Commission. It was modeled on private self-regulatory organizations in the securities industry — such as the New York Stock Exchange — that investigate and discipline their own members subject to Commission oversight. Congress created the Board as a private "nonprofit corporation," and Board members and employees are not considered Government "officer[s] or employee[s]" for statutory purposes. The Board can thus recruit its members and employees from the private sector by paying salaries far above the standard Government pay scale.

Unlike the self-regulatory organizations, however, the Board is a Government-created, Government-appointed entity, with expansive powers to govern an entire industry. Every accounting firm — both foreign and domestic — that participates in auditing public companies under the securities laws must register with the Board, pay it an annual fee, and comply with its rules and oversight. The Board is charged with enforcing the Sarbanes–Oxley Act, the securities laws, the Commission's rules, its own rules, and professional accounting standards.

The Act places the Board under the SEC's oversight, particularly with respect to the issuance of rules or the imposition of sanctions (both of which are subject to Commission approval and alteration). But the individual members of the Board—like the officers and directors of the self-regulatory organizations—are substantially insulated from the Commission's control. The Commission cannot remove Board members at will, but only "for good cause shown," "in accordance with" certain procedures.

Those procedures require a Commission finding, "on the record" and "after notice and opportunity for a hearing," that the Board member:

> (A) has willfully violated any provision of th[e] Act, the rules of the Board, or the securities laws;
> (B) has willfully abused the authority of that member; or
> (C) without reasonable justification or excuse, has failed to enforce compliance with any such provision or rule, or any professional standard by any registered public accounting firm or any associated person thereof.

Removal of a Board member requires a formal Commission order and is subject to judicial review. Similar procedures govern the Commission's removal of officers and directors of the private self-regulatory organizations.

We first consider whether the District Court had jurisdiction. We agree with both courts below that the statutes providing for judicial review of Commission action did not prevent the District Court from considering petitioners' claims. The Sarbanes-Oxley Act empowers the Commission to review any Board rule or sanction. Once the Commission has acted, aggrieved parties may challenge "a final order of the Commission" or "a rule of the Commission" in a court of appeals, and "[n]o objection . . . may be considered by the court unless it was urged before the Commission or there was reasonable ground for failure to do so."

The Government reads [the statute] as an exclusive route to review. But the text does not expressly limit the jurisdiction that other statutes confer on district courts. Nor does it do so implicitly. Provisions for agency review do not restrict judicial review unless the "statutory scheme" displays a "fairly discernible" intent to limit jurisdiction, and the claims at issue "are of the type Congress intended to be reviewed within th[e] statutory structure." *Thunder Basin Coal Co. v. Reich* (1994). Generally, when Congress creates procedures "designed to permit agency expertise to be brought to bear on particular problems," those procedures "are to be exclusive." *Whitney Nat'l Bank in Jefferson Parish v. Bank of New Orleans & Trust Co.* (1965). But we presume that Congress does not intend to limit jurisdiction if "a finding of preclusion could foreclose all meaningful judicial review;" if the suit is "wholly collateral to a statute's review provisions"; and if the claims are "outside the agency's expertise." These considerations point against any limitation on review here.

We do not see how petitioners could meaningfully pursue their constitutional claims under the Government's theory. Section 78y provides only for judicial review of *Commission* action, and not every Board action is encapsulated in a final Commission order or rule.

The Government suggests that petitioners could first have sought Commission review of the Board's "auditing standards, registration requirements, or other rules." But petitioners object to the Board's existence, not to any of its auditing standards. Petitioners' general challenge to the Board is "collateral" to any Commission orders or rules from which review might be sought. Requiring petitioners to select and challenge a Board rule at random is an odd procedure for Congress to choose, especially because only *new* rules, and not existing ones, are subject to challenge.

Alternatively, the Government advises petitioners to raise their claims by appealing a Board sanction. But the investigation [may produce] no sanction, and an uncomplimentary inspection report is not subject to judicial review. So the Government proposes that Beckstead and Watts *incur* a sanction (such as a sizable fine) by ignoring Board requests for documents and testimony. If the Commission then affirms, the firm will win access to a court of appeals—and severe punishment should its challenge fail. We normally do not require plaintiffs to "bet the farm . . . by taking the violative action" before "testing the validity of the law," *Med-Immune, Inc. v. Genentech, Inc.* (2007) [upholding standing of a patent licensee to seek declaratory relief on validity of a patent while currently paying royalties to patent holder because breach of the license could result in treble damages equal to 80 percent of licensee's sales revenue]; *Ex parte Young* (1908), and we do not consider this a "meaningful" avenue of relief, *Thunder Basin.*

Petitioners' constitutional claims are also outside the Commission's competence and expertise. In *Thunder Basin,* the petitioner's primary claims were statutory; "at root they arose under the *Mine Act* and fell squarely within the agency's expertise. No similar expertise is required here, and the statutory questions involved do not require technical considerations of agency policy.[2]

[The Court went to "hold that the dual for-cause limitations on the removal of Board members contravene the Constitution's separation of powers."]

* * *

The power of the federal courts to issue injunctive relief is not unlimited. In *Armstrong v. Exceptional Child Center, Inc.* (2015), summarized in Chapter 5, the Court held that federal courts do not have the authority to hear claims for injunctive relief based on the Supremacy Clause of Article VI of the Constitution. The Supremacy Clause provides that "[t]his Constitution, and the Laws of the United States which shall be made in Pursuance thereof; and all Treaties made, or which shall be made, under the Authority of the United States, shall be the supreme Law of the Land; and the Judges in every State shall be bound thereby, any Thing in the Constitution or Laws of any State to the Contrary notwithstanding." In *Armstrong,* the Court reasoned that "this Clause creates a rule of decision" directing courts not to "give effect to state laws that conflict with federal laws." The Clause does not, however, "create a cause of action." It is not, therefore, a source of federal judicial power to issue injunctive relief against state or local agencies or officials that violate federal law. Rather, the Court concluded that "[t]he ability to sue to enjoin unconstitutional actions by state and federal officers is the creation of courts of equity, and reflects a long history of judicial review of illegal executive action, tracing back to England. It is a judge-made remedy[.]" The *Armstrong* Court's conclusion, and the question of implied causes of action to enforce federal law, is discussed further at in Chapter 5.

---

2. The government asserts that petitioners have not pointed to any case in which this Court has recognized an implied right of action directly under the Constitution [regarding the Appointments Clause. But the Court has long recognized] such a right to relief as a general matter. *See, e.g., Correctional Servs. Corp. v. Malesko* (2001) (equitable relief "has long been recognized as the proper means for preventing entities from acting unconstitutionally"); *Bell v. Hood* (1946); *Ex parte Young* (1908).

3.   *Immunity from Monetary Liability and Executive Privilege*

To successfully bring causes of action against federal officials for money damages, plaintiffs must overcome a number of immunity rules. These immunities largely mirror the immunities that state and local officials receive—immunities that are documented in greater detail in Chapter 6.B. As the Court once explained, "without congressional directions to the contrary, we deem it untenable to draw a distinction for purposes of immunity law between suits brought against state officials under §1983 and suits brought directly under the Constitution against federal officials."[44] Accordingly, those acting in their prosecutorial, legislative, and judicial capacities are absolutely immune from liability for those actions. Other federal officials— including the high-ranking cabinet officials[45] and presidential aides[46]—are protected by qualified immunity. That is, they are protected from individual damages suits unless they violated clearly established rights that a reasonable person would have known at the time of the violation.[47]

Moreover, the President is entitled to absolute immunity from civil damage claims for official presidential acts—acts, that is, within the "outer perimeter" of official duties.[48] The Court explained in *Nixon v. Fitzgerald* that "[b]ecause of the singular importance of the President's duties, diversion of his energies by concern with private lawsuits would raise unique risks to the effective functioning of government." Further, "[a]s is the case with prosecutors and judges—for whom absolute immunity now is established—a President must concern himself with matters likely to "arouse the most intense feeling."[49] The Court emphasized, however, that a President is not categorically immune from all legal process and "above the law." *See also* United States v. Nixon (1974) (holding unanimously that President may be subpoenaed to produce evidence for a federal criminal case; "neither the doctrine of separation of powers, nor the need for confidentiality of high-level communications can sustain an absolute, unqualified Presidential privilege of immunity from judicial process under all circumstances").

Nixon v. Fitzgerald

457 U.S. 731 (1982)

Justice POWELL delivered the opinion of the Court.

The plaintiff in this lawsuit seeks relief in civil damages from a former President of the United States. The claim rests on actions allegedly taken in the former President's official capacity during his tenure in office. The issue before us is the scope of the immunity possessed by the President of the United States.

---

44. Butz v. Economou, 438 U.S. 478, 504 (1978).
45. *Id.*
46. Harlow v. Fitzgerald, 457 U.S. 800 (1982).
47. *Id.*
48. Nixon v. Fitzgerald, 457 U.S. 731 (1982).
49. *Id.* at 751–52.

I

   In January 1970 the respondent A. Ernest Fitzgerald lost his job as a management analyst with the Department of the Air Force. Fitzgerald's dismissal occurred in the context of a departmental reorganization and reduction in force, in which his job was eliminated. In announcing the reorganization, the Air Force characterized the action as taken to promote economy and efficiency in the Armed Forces.

   Respondent's discharge attracted unusual attention in Congress and in the press. Fitzgerald had attained national prominence approximately one year earlier, during the waning months of the Presidency of Lyndon B. Johnson. On November 13, 1968, Fitzgerald appeared before the Subcommittee on Economy in Government of the Joint Economic Committee of the United States Congress. To the evident embarrassment of his superiors in the Department of Defense, Fitzgerald testified that cost-overruns on the C–5A transport plane could approximate $2 billion. He also revealed that unexpected technical difficulties had arisen during the development of the aircraft.

   Concerned that Fitzgerald might have suffered retaliation for his congressional testimony, the Subcommittee on Economy in Government convened public hearings on Fitzgerald's dismissal. The press reported those hearings prominently, as it had the earlier announcement that his job was being eliminated by the Department of Defense. At a news conference on December 8, 1969, President Richard Nixon was queried about Fitzgerald's impending separation from Government service. The President responded by promising to look into the matter. Shortly after the news conference the petitioner asked White House Chief of Staff H.R. Haldeman to arrange for Fitzgerald's assignment to another job within the administration. It also appears that the President suggested to Budget Director Robert Mayo that Fitzgerald might be offered a position in the Bureau of the Budget.

   Fitzgerald's proposed reassignment encountered resistance within the administration. In an internal memorandum of January 20, 1970, White House aide Alexander Butterfield reported to Haldeman that "'Fitzgerald is no doubt a top-notch cost expert, but he must be given very low marks in loyalty; and after all, loyalty is the name of the game.'" Butterfield therefore recommended that "'[W]e should let him bleed, for a while at least.'" There is no evidence of White House efforts to reemploy Fitzgerald subsequent to the Butterfield memorandum.

   Absent any offer of alternative federal employment, Fitzgerald complained to the Civil Service Commission. In a letter of January 20, 1970, he alleged that his separation represented unlawful retaliation for his truthful testimony before a congressional Committee. The Commission convened a closed hearing on Fitzgerald's allegations on May 4, 1971. Fitzgerald, however, preferred to present his grievances in public. After he had brought suit and won an injunction, *Fitzgerald v. Hampton* (1972), public hearings commenced on January 26, 1973. The hearings again generated publicity, much of it devoted to the testimony of Air Force Secretary Robert Seamans. Although he denied that Fitzgerald had lost his position in retaliation for congressional testimony, Seamans testified that he had received "some advice" from the White House before Fitzgerald's job was abolished.11 But the Secretary declined to be more specific. He responded to several questions by invoking "executive privilege."

At a news conference on January 31, 1973, the President was asked about Mr. Seamans' testimony. Mr. Nixon took the opportunity to assume personal responsibility for Fitzgerald's dismissal:

I was totally aware that Mr. Fitzgerald would be fired or discharged or asked to resign. I approved it and Mr. Seamans must have been talking to someone who had discussed the matter with me. No, this was not a case of some person down the line deciding he should go. It was a decision that was submitted to me. I made it and I stick by it.

A day later, however, the White House press office issued a retraction of the President's statement. According to a press spokesman, the President had confused Fitzgerald with another former executive employee. On behalf of the President, the spokesman asserted that Mr. Nixon had not had "put before him the decision regarding Mr. Fitzgerald."

After hearing over 4,000 pages of testimony, the Chief Examiner for the Civil Service Commission issued his decision in the Fitzgerald case on September 18, 1973. The Examiner held that Fitzgerald's dismissal had offended applicable civil service regulations. The Examiner, however, explicitly distinguished this narrow conclusion from a suggested finding that Fitzgerald had suffered retaliation for his testimony to Congress.

Following the Commission's decision, Fitzgerald filed a suit for damages in the United States District Court. In it he raised essentially the same claims presented to the Civil Service Commission.

Fitzgerald [later] filed a second amended complaint in the District Court. It was in this amended complaint—more than eight years after he had complained of his discharge to the Civil Service Commission—that Fitzgerald first named the petitioner Nixon as a party defendant. Also included as defendants were White House aide Bryce Harlow and other officials of the Nixon administration. Denying a motion for summary judgment, the District Court ruled that the action must proceed to trial. The court ruled that petitioner was not entitled to claim absolute Presidential immunity.

As this Court has not ruled on the scope of immunity available to a President of the United States, we granted certiorari to decide this important issue.

[III]

A

This Court consistently has recognized that government officials are entitled to some form of immunity from suits for civil damages. In *Spalding v. Vilas* (1896), the Court considered the immunity available to the Postmaster General in a suit for damages based upon his official acts. Drawing upon principles of immunity developed in English cases at common law, the Court concluded that "[t]he interests of the people" required a grant of absolute immunity to public officers. In the absence of immunity, the Court reasoned, executive officials would hesitate to exercise their discretion in a way "injuriously affect[ing] the claims of particular individuals" even when the public interest required bold and unhesitating action. Considerations of "public policy and convenience" therefore compelled a judicial recognition of immunity from suits arising from official acts. "In exercising the functions of his office, the head of an Executive Department, keeping within the limits of his authority, should not be under an apprehension that the motives that control his official conduct may, at any time, become the subject of inquiry in a civil suit for damages. It would seriously cripple the proper and effective administration of public affairs as entrusted to the executive branch of the government, if he were subjected to any such restraint." *Id.*

Decisions subsequent to Spalding have extended the defense of immunity to actions besides those at common law. In *Tenney v. Brandhove* (1951), the Court considered whether the passage of 42 U.S.C. §1983, which made no express provision for immunity for any official, had abrogated the privilege accorded to state legislators at common law. *Tenney* held that it had not. Similarly, the decision in *Pierson v. Ray* (1967), involving a §1983 suit against a state judge, recognized the continued validity of the absolute immunity of judges for acts within the judicial role. This was a doctrine "'not for the protection or benefit of a malicious or corrupt judge, but for the benefit of the public, whose interest it is that the judges should be at liberty to exercise their functions with independence and without fear of consequences.'" *Id. See Bradley v. Fisher* (1872).

In *Scheuer v. Rhodes* (1974), the Court considered the immunity available to state executive officials in a §1983 suit alleging the violation of constitutional rights. In that case we rejected the officials' claim to absolute immunity, finding instead that state executive officials possessed a "good faith" immunity from §1983 suits alleging constitutional violations. Balancing the purposes of §1983 against the imperatives of public policy, the Court held that "in varying scope, a qualified immunity is available to officers of the executive branch of government, the variation being dependent upon the scope of discretion and responsibilities of the office and all the circumstances as they reasonably appeared at the time of the action on which liability is sought to be based."

In *Butz v. Economou* (1978), when we considered for the first time the kind of immunity possessed by federal executive officials who are sued for constitutional violations. In *Butz* the Court rejected an argument, based on decisions involving federal officials charged with common-law torts, that all high federal officials have a right to absolute immunity from constitutional damages actions. Concluding that a blanket recognition of absolute immunity would be anomalous in light of the qualified immunity standard applied to state executive officials, we held that federal officials generally have the same qualified immunity possessed by state officials in cases under §1983. In so doing we reaffirmed our holdings that some officials, notably judges and prosecutors, "because of the special nature of their responsibilities," *id.*, at, "require a full exemption from liability." In *Butz* itself we upheld a claim of absolute immunity for administrative officials engaged in functions analogous to those of judges and prosecutors. *Ibid.* We also left open the question whether other federal officials could show that "public policy requires an exemption of that scope."

B

Because the Presidency did not exist through most of the development of common law, any historical analysis must draw its evidence primarily from our constitutional heritage and structure. Historical inquiry thus merges almost at its inception with the kind of "public policy" analysis appropriately undertaken by a federal court. This inquiry involves policies and principles that may be considered implicit in the nature of the President's office in a system structured to achieve effective government under a constitutionally mandated separation of powers.

[IV]

Applying the principles of our cases to claims of this kind, we hold that petitioner, as a former President of the United States, is entitled to absolute immunity from damages liability predicated on his official acts. We consider this immunity a functionally mandated incident of the President's unique office, rooted in the constitutional tradition of the separation of powers and supported by our history. Justice Story's analysis remains persuasive:

> There are . . . incidental powers, belonging to the executive department, which are necessarily implied from the nature of the functions, which are confided to it. Among these, must necessarily be included the power to perform them . . . . The president cannot, therefore, be liable to arrest, imprisonment, or detention, while he is in the discharge of the duties of his office; and for this purpose his person must be deemed, in civil cases at least, to possess an official inviolability.

3 J. Story, Commentaries on the Constitution of the United States (1st ed. 1833).

A

The President occupies a unique position in the constitutional scheme. Article II, §1, of the Constitution provides that "[t]he executive Power shall be vested in a President of the United States. . . ." This grant of authority establishes the President as the chief constitutional officer of the Executive Branch, entrusted with supervisory and policy responsibilities of utmost discretion and sensitivity. These include the enforcement of federal law—it is the President who is charged constitutionally to "take Care that the Laws be faithfully executed"; the conduct of foreign affairs—a realm in which the Court has recognized that "[i]t would be intolerable that courts, without the relevant information, should review and perhaps nullify actions of the Executive taken on information properly held secret;" and management of the Executive Branch—a task for which "imperative reasons requir[e] an unrestricted power [in the President] to remove the most important of his subordinates in their most important duties."

In arguing that the President is entitled only to qualified immunity, the respondent relies on cases in which we have recognized immunity of this scope for governors and cabinet officers. E.g., *Butz v. Economou* (1978); *Scheuer v. Rhodes* (1974). We find these cases to be inapposite. The President's unique status under the Constitution distinguishes him from other executive officials.

Because of the singular importance of the President's duties, diversion of his energies by concern with private lawsuits would raise unique risks to the effective functioning of government. As is the case with prosecutors and judges—for whom absolute immunity now is established — a President must concern himself with matters likely to arouse the most intense feelings. Yet, as our decisions have recognized, it is in precisely such cases that there exists the greatest public interest in providing an official "the maximum ability to deal fearlessly and impartially with" the duties of his office. *Ferri v. Ackerman* (1979). This concern is compelling where the officeholder must make the most sensitive and far-reaching decisions entrusted to any official under our constitutional system. Nor can the sheer prominence of the President's office be ignored. In view of the visibility of his office and the effect of his actions on countless people, the President would be an easily identifiable target for suits for civil damages. Cognizance of this personal vulnerability frequently could distract a President from his public duties, to the detriment of not only the President and his office but also the Nation that the Presidency was designed to serve.

B

Courts traditionally have recognized the President's constitutional responsibilities and status as factors counseling judicial deference and restraint. For example, while courts generally have looked to the common law to determine the scope of an official's evidentiary privilege, we have recognized that the Presidential privilege is "rooted in the separation of powers under the Constitution." *United States v. Nixon* (1974). It is settled law that the separation-of-powers doctrine does not bar every exercise of jurisdiction over the President of the United States. *See, e.g., United States v. Nixon.* But our cases also have established that a court, before exercising jurisdiction, must balance the constitutional weight of the interest to be served against the dangers of intrusion on the authority and functions of the Executive Branch. When judicial action is needed to serve broad public interests — as when the Court acts, not in derogation of the separation of powers, but to maintain their proper balance, or to vindicate the public interest in an ongoing criminal prosecution, *see United States v. Nixon* — the exercise of jurisdiction has been held warranted. In the case of this merely private suit for damages based on a President's official acts, we hold it is not.

C

In defining the scope of an official's absolute privilege, this Court has recognized that the sphere of protected action must be related closely to the immunity's justifying purposes. In view of the special nature of the President's constitutional office and functions, we think it appropriate to recognize absolute Presidential immunity from damages liability for acts within the "outer perimeter" of his official responsibility.

Under the Constitution and laws of the United States the President has discretionary responsibilities in a broad variety of areas, many of them highly sensitive. In many cases it would be difficult to determine which of the President's innumerable "functions" encompassed a particular action. In this case, for example, respondent argues that he was dismissed in retaliation for his testimony to Congress. The Air Force, however, has claimed that the underlying reorganization was undertaken to promote efficiency. Assuming that petitioner Nixon ordered the reorganization in which respondent lost his job, an inquiry into the President's motives could not be avoided under the kind of "functional" theory asserted both by respondent and the dissent. Inquiries of this kind could be highly intrusive.

[V]

A rule of absolute immunity for the President will not leave the Nation without sufficient protection against misconduct on the part of the Chief Executive. There remains the constitutional remedy of impeachment. In addition, there are formal and informal checks on Presidential action that do not apply with equal force to other executive officials. The President is subjected to constant scrutiny by the press. Vigilant oversight by Congress also may serve to deter Presidential abuses of office, as well as to make credible the threat of impeachment. Other incentives to avoid misconduct may include a desire to earn reelection, the need to maintain prestige as an element of Presidential influence, and a President's traditional concern for his historical stature.

The existence of alternative remedies and deterrents establishes that absolute immunity will not place the President "above the law." For the President, as for judges and prosecutors, absolute immunity merely precludes a particular private remedy for alleged misconduct in order to advance compelling public ends.

Chief Justice BURGER, concurring.

I join the Court's opinion, but I write separately to underscore that the Presidential immunity derives from and is mandated by the constitutional doctrine of separation of powers. Indeed, it has been taken for granted for nearly two centuries. In reaching this conclusion we do well to bear in mind that the focus must not be simply on the matter of judging individual conduct in a fact-bound setting; rather, in those familiar terms of John Marshall, it is a Constitution we are expounding. Constitutional adjudication often bears unpalatable fruit. But the needs of a system of government sometimes must outweigh the right of individuals to collect damages.

It strains the meaning of the words used to say this places a President "above the law." *United States v. Nixon* (1974). The dissents are wide of the mark to the extent that they imply that the Court today recognizes sweeping immunity for a President for all acts. The Court does no such thing. The immunity is limited to civil damages claims. Moreover, a President, like Members of Congress, judges, prosecutors, or congressional aides — all having absolute immunity — are not immune for acts outside official duties.

The Judiciary always must be hesitant to probe into the elements of Presidential decision-making, just as other branches should be hesitant to probe into judicial decision-making. Such judicial intervention is not to be tolerated absent imperative constitutional necessity. The Court's opinion correctly observes that judicial intrusion through private damages actions improperly impinges on and hence interferes with the independence that is imperative to the functioning of the office of a President.

Exposing a President to civil damages actions for official acts within the scope of the Executive authority would inevitably subject Presidential actions to undue judicial scrutiny as well as subject the President to harassment. The enormous range and impact of Presidential decisions—far beyond that of any one Member of Congress—inescapably means that many persons will consider themselves aggrieved by such acts. Absent absolute immunity, every person who feels aggrieved would be free to bring a suit for damages, and each suit—especially those that proceed on the merits—would involve some judicial questioning of Presidential acts, including the reasons for the decision, how it was arrived at, the information on which it was based, and who supplied the information.

Far from placing a President above the law, the Court's holding places a President on essentially the same footing with judges and other officials whose absolute immunity we have recognized.

Justice WHITE, with whom Justice BRENNAN, Justice MARSHALL, and Justice BLACKMUN join, dissenting.

The Court intimates that its decision is grounded in the Constitution. If that is the case, Congress cannot provide a remedy against Presidential misconduct and the criminal laws of the United States are wholly inapplicable to the President. I find this approach completely unacceptable. I do not agree that if the Office of President is to operate effectively, the holder of that Office must be permitted, without fear of liability and regardless of the function he is performing, deliberately to inflict injury on others by conduct that he knows violates the law.

We have not taken such a scatter-gun approach in other cases. *Butz* held that absolute immunity did not attach to the office held by a member of the President's Cabinet but only to those specific functions performed by that officer for which absolute immunity is clearly essential. In *Marbury v. Madison*, (1803), the Court, speaking through The Chief Justice, observed that while there were "important political powers" committed to the President for the performance of which neither he nor his appointees were accountable in court, "the question, whether the legality of an act of the head of a department be examinable in a court of justice or not, must always depend on the nature of that act." The Court nevertheless refuses to follow this course with respect to the President. It makes no effort to distinguish categories of Presidential conduct that should be absolutely immune from other categories of conduct that should not qualify for that level of immunity. The Court instead concludes that whatever the President does and however contrary to law he knows his conduct to be, he may, without fear of liability, injure federal employees or any other person within or without the Government.

Attaching absolute immunity to the Office of the President, rather than to particular activities that the President might perform, places the President above the law. It is a reversion to the old notion that the King can do no wrong. Until now, this concept had survived in this country only in the form of sovereign immunity. That doctrine forecloses suit against the Government itself and against Government officials, but only when the suit against the latter actually seeks relief against the sovereign. Suit against an officer, however, may be maintained where it seeks specific relief against him for conduct contrary to his statutory authority or to the

Constitution. Now, however, the Court clothes the Office of the President with sovereign immunity, placing it beyond the law.

In *Marbury v. Madison*, The Chief Justice, speaking for the Court, observed: "The government of the United States has been emphatically termed a government of laws, and not of men. It will certainly cease to deserve this high appellation, if the laws furnish no remedy for the violation of a vested legal right." Until now, the Court has consistently adhered to this proposition.

We have previously stated that "the law of privilege as a defense to damages actions against officers of Government has 'in large part been of judicial making.'" *Butz v. Economou*. But this does not mean that the Court has simply "enacted" its own view of the best public policy. No doubt judicial convictions about public policy—whether and what kind of immunity is necessary or wise—have played a part, but the courts have been guided and constrained by common-law tradition, the relevant statutory background, and our constitutional structure and history. Our cases dealing with the immunity of Members of Congress are constructions of the Speech or Debate Clause and are guided by the history of such privileges at common law. The decisions dealing with the immunity of state officers involve the question of whether and to what extent Congress intended to abolish the common-law privileges by providing a remedy in the predecessor of 42 U.S.C. §1983 for constitutional violations by state officials. Our decisions respecting immunity for federal officials—including absolute immunity for judges, prosecutors, and those officials doing similar work—also in large part reflect common-law views, as well as judicial conclusions as to what privileges are necessary if particular functions are to be performed in the public interest.

Unfortunately, there is little of this approach in the Court's decision today. The Court casually, but candidly, abandons the functional approach to immunity that has run through all of our decisions. Indeed, the majority turns this rule on its head by declaring that because the functions of the President's office are so varied and diverse and some of them so profoundly important, the office is unique and must be clothed with officewide, absolute immunity. This is policy, not law, and in my view, very poor policy.

No bright line can be drawn between arguments for absolute immunity based on the constitutional principle of separation of powers and arguments based on what the Court refers to as "public policy." This necessarily follows from the Court's functional interpretation of the separation-of-powers doctrine: "[I]n determining whether the Act disrupts the proper balance between the coordinate branches, the proper inquiry focuses on the extent to which it prevents the Executive Branch from accomplishing its constitutionally assigned functions." *Nixon v. Administrator of General Services* (1977).

Petitioner argues that public policy favors absolute immunity because absent such immunity the President's ability to execute his constitutionally mandated obligations will be impaired. The convergence of these two lines of argument is superficially apparent from the very fact that in both instances the approach of the Court has been characterized as a "functional" analysis. The difference is only one of degree. While absolute immunity might maximize executive efficiency and therefore be a worthwhile policy, lack of such immunity may not so disrupt the functioning of the Presidency as to violate the separation-of-powers doctrine. Insofar as liability in this case is of congressional origin, petitioner must demonstrate that subjecting the President to a private damages action will prevent him from "accomplishing [his] constitutionally assigned functions." Insofar as liability is based on a *Bivens* action, perhaps a lower standard of functional disruption is appropriate. Petitioner has surely not met the former burden; I do not believe that he has met the latter standard either.

Taken at face value, the Court's position that as a matter of constitutional law the President is absolutely immune should mean that he is immune not only from damages actions but also from suits for injunctive relief, criminal prosecutions and, indeed, from any kind of judicial process. But there is no contention that the President is immune from criminal prosecution in the courts under the criminal laws enacted by Congress or by the States for that matter. Nor would such a claim be credible. The Constitution itself provides that impeachment shall not bar "Indictment, Trial, Judgment and Punishment, according to Law." Art. I, §3, cl. 7. Similarly, our cases indicate that immunity from damages actions carries no protection from criminal prosecution.

Neither can there be a serious claim that the separation-of-powers doctrine insulates Presidential action from judicial review or insulates the President from judicial process. No argument is made here that the President, whatever his liability for money damages, is not subject to the courts' injunctive powers. Indeed, it is the rule, not the exception, that executive actions—including those taken at the immediate direction of the President—are subject to judicial review.

Nor can private damages actions be distinguished on the ground that such claims would involve the President personally in the litigation in a way not necessitated by suits seeking declaratory or injunctive relief against certain Presidential actions. The President has been held to be subject to judicial process at least since 1807. *United States v. Burr* (1807) (Marshall, C.J., sitting as Circuit Justice). *Burr* squarely ruled that a subpoena may be directed to the President. Chief Justice Marshall flatly rejected any suggestion that all judicial process, in and of itself, constitutes an unwarranted interference in the Presidency: "The guard, furnished to this high officer, to protect him from being harassed by vexatious and unnecessary subpoenas, is to be looked for in the conduct of a court after those subpoenas have issued; not in any circumstance which is to precede their being issued." This position was recently rearticulated by the Court in *United States v. Nixon*: "[N]either the doctrine of separation of powers, nor the need for confidentiality . . . without more, can sustain an absolute, unqualified Presidential privilege of immunity from judicial process under all circumstances."

These two lines of cases establish, then, that neither subjecting Presidential actions to a judicial determination of their constitutionality, nor subjecting the President to judicial process violates the separation-of-powers doctrine. Similarly, neither has been held to be sufficiently intrusive to justify a judicially declared rule of immunity. With respect to intrusion by the judicial process itself on executive functions, subjecting the President to private claims for money damages involves no more than this. If there is a separation-of-powers problem here, it must be found in the nature of the remedy and not in the process involved.

We said in *Butz v. Economou* (1978), that "it is not unfair to hold liable the official who knows or should know he is acting outside the law, and . . . insisting on an awareness of clearly established constitutional limits will not unduly interfere with the exercise of official judgment." Today's decision in *Harlow v. Fitzgerald*, makes clear that the President, were he subject to civil liability, could be held liable only for an action that he knew, or as an objective matter should have known, was illegal and a clear abuse of his authority and power. In such circumstances, the question that must be answered is who should bear the cost of the resulting injury—the wrongdoer or the victim.

The principle that should guide the Court in deciding this question was stated long ago by Chief Justice Marshall: "The very essence of civil liberty certainly consists in the right of every individual to claim the protection of the laws, whenever he receives an injury." *Marbury v. Madison.* Much more recently, the Court considered the role of a damages remedy in the performance of the courts' traditional function of enforcing federally guaranteed rights: "Historically, damages have been regarded as the ordinary remedy for an invasion of personal interests in liberty." *Bivens v. Six Unknown Fed. Narcotics Agents.* To the extent that the Court denies an otherwise appropriate remedy, it denies the victim the right to be made whole and, therefore, denies him "the protection of the laws."

* * *

NOTES ON EXECUTIVE POWER AND EXECUTIVE PRIVILEGE

The Court has reasoned that executive privilege, in the form of absolute immunity, protects executive power within the separation-of-powers. An open question after *Nixon v. Fitzgerald* was whether a sitting President is immune from civil suits for conduct engaged in before taking office, that is, before they were in a position to exercise the power of the federal Executive. The Court addressed this issue in *Clinton v. Jones* (1997). In that case, an Arkansas woman named Paula Jones alleged that when President Bill Clinton was Governor, he sexually harassed her, resulting in her termination from a state job when his advances were rejected. The Court held that the President was not immune from this suit:

> It is settled law that the separation-of-powers doctrine does not bar every exercise of jurisdiction over the President of the United States." *Fitzgerald.* If the Judiciary may severely burden the Executive Branch by reviewing the legality of the President's official conduct, and if it may direct appropriate process to the President himself, it must follow that the federal courts have power to determine the legality of his unofficial conduct. The burden on the President's time and energy that is a mere byproduct of such review surely cannot be considered as onerous as the direct burden imposed by judicial review and the occasional invalidation of his official actions. We therefore hold that the doctrine of separation of powers does not require federal courts to stay all private actions against the President until he leaves office.

Throughout the opinion in *Nixon v. Fitzgerald*, the Court references *United States v. Nixon* (1974), an earlier case concerning the limits of judicial process against a sitting President. In that case, a grand jury issued indictments against seven aides of

President Richard Nixon due to their actions related the burglary of the Democratic National Committee Headquarters at the Watergate office complex during President Nixon's re-election campaign. During the investigation, a special prosecutor issued a subpoena for audio tapes of conversations that Nixon recorded. In turn, President Nixon asserted that the tapes were protected by "executive privilege."

In that case, the Court ruled against Nixon. It balanced the President's "broad, undifferentiated claim of public interest in the confidentiality of such conversations" against "the primary constitutional duty of the Judicial Branch to do justice in criminal prosecutions." In its view,

> the allowance of the privilege to withhold evidence that is demonstrably relevant in a criminal trial would cut deeply into the guarantee of due process of law and gravely impair the basic function of the court. . . . The President's broad interest in confidentiality of communications will not be vitiated by disclosure of a limited number of conversations preliminarily shown to have some bearing on the pending criminal cases.

Accordingly, the Court concluded

> that when the ground for asserting privilege as to subpoenaed materials sought for use in a criminal trial is based only on the generalized interest in confidentiality, it cannot prevail over the fundamental demands of due process of law in the fair administration of criminal justice. The generalized assertion of privilege must yield to the demonstrated, specific need for evidence in a pending criminal trial.

On the other hand, federal courts have been more solicitous of claims of executive privilege in civil suits. The case of *Cheney v. United States District Court* (2004), is instructive. Shortly after taking office in 2001, President George W. Bush assembled an advisory committee—led by Vice President Dick Cheney—to make recommendations on energy policy. When the committee issued its recommendations, a non-profit government watchdog group and an environmentalist organization filed suit, contending that the committee's lack of transparency violated the Federal Advisory Committee Act (FACA). In response, Vice President Cheney claimed that suit and its attendant discovery orders violated separation of powers by seeking documents protected by executive privilege. Cheney sought a writ of mandamus against the District of D.C., aiming to limit discovery. When the issue reached the Supreme Court, it distinguished *United States v. Nixon* in part on the ground that it was a criminal, rather than a civil, case:

> The Court of Appeals dismissed these separation-of-powers concerns. Relying on *United States v. Nixon*, it held that even though respondents' discovery requests are overbroad and "go well beyond FACA's requirements," the Vice President and his former colleagues on the NEPDG "shall bear the burden" of invoking privilege with narrow specificity and objecting to the discovery requests with "detailed precision." In its view, this result was required by Nixon's rejection of an "absolute, unqualified Presidential privilege of immunity from judicial process under all circumstances." If *Nixon* refused to recognize broad claims of confidentiality where the President had asserted executive privilege, the majority reasoned, *Nixon*

must have rejected, a fortiori, petitioners' claim of discovery immunity where the privilege has not even been invoked. According to the majority, because the Executive Branch can invoke executive privilege to maintain the separation of powers, mandamus relief is premature.

This analysis, however, overlooks fundamental differences in the two cases. Nixon cannot bear the weight the Court of Appeals puts upon it. First, unlike this case, which concerns respondents' requests for information for use in a civil suit, *Nixon* involves the proper balance between the Executive's interest in the confidentiality of its communications and the "constitutional need for production of relevant evidence in a criminal proceeding." The Court's decision was explicit that it was "not . . . concerned with the balance between the President's generalized interest in confidentiality and the need for relevant evidence in civil litigation. . . . We address only the conflict between the President's assertion of a generalized privilege of confidentiality and the constitutional need for relevant evidence in criminal trials."

The distinction *Nixon* drew between criminal and civil proceedings is not just a matter of formalism. As the Court explained, the need for information in the criminal context is much weightier because "our historic[al] commitment to the rule of law . . . is nowhere more profoundly manifest than in our view that 'the twofold aim [of criminal justice] is that guilt shall not escape or innocence suffer.'" In light of the "fundamental" and "comprehensive" need for "every man's evidence" in the criminal justice system, not only must the Executive Branch first assert privilege to resist disclosure, but privilege claims that shield information from a grand jury proceeding or a criminal trial are not to be "expansively construed, for they are in derogation of the search for truth." The need for information for use in civil cases, while far from negligible, does not share the urgency or significance of the criminal subpoena requests in *Nixon*. As *Nixon* recognized, the right to production of relevant evidence in civil proceedings does not have the same "constitutional dimensions."

The Court also observed in *Nixon* that a "primary constitutional duty of the Judicial Branch [is] to do justice in criminal prosecutions." Withholding materials from a tribunal in an ongoing criminal case when the information is necessary to the court in carrying out its tasks "conflict[s] with the function of the courts under Art. III." Such an impairment of the "essential functions of [another] branch," is impermissible. Withholding the information in this case, however, does not hamper another branch's ability to perform its "essential functions" in quite the same way. The District Court ordered discovery here, not to remedy known statutory violations, but to ascertain whether FACA's disclosure requirements even apply in the first place. Even if FACA embodies important congressional objectives, the only consequence from respondents' inability to obtain the discovery they seek is that it would be more difficult for private complainants to vindicate Congress' policy objectives under FACA. And even if, for argument's sake, the reasoning in Judge Randolph's dissenting opinion in the end is rejected and FACA's statutory objectives would be to some extent frustrated, it does not follow that a court's Article III authority or Congress' central Article I powers would be impaired. The situation here cannot, in fairness, be compared to *Nixon*, where a court's ability to fulfill its constitutional responsibility to resolve cases and controversies within its jurisdiction hinges on the availability of certain indispensable information.

A party's need for information is only one facet of the problem. An important factor weighing in the opposite direction is the burden imposed by the discovery orders. This is not a routine discovery dispute. The discovery requests are directed to the Vice President and other senior Government officials who served on the [advisory committee] to give advice and make recommendations to the President. The Executive Branch, at its highest level, is seeking the aid of the courts to protect its constitutional prerogatives. As we have already noted, special considerations control when the Executive Branch's interests in maintaining the autonomy of its office and safeguarding the confidentiality of its communications are implicated. This Court has held, on more than one occasion, that "[t]he high respect that is owed to the office of the Chief Executive . . . is a matter that should inform the conduct of the entire proceeding, including the timing and scope of discovery," *Clinton v. Jones* (1997), and that the Executive's "constitutional responsibilities and status [are] factors counseling judicial deference and restraint" in the conduct of litigation against it, *Nixon v. Fitzgerald* (1982).

Even when compared against *United States v. Nixon*'s criminal subpoenas, which did involve the President, the civil discovery here militates against respondents' position. The observation in *Nixon* that production of confidential information would not disrupt the functioning of the Executive Branch cannot be applied in a mechanistic fashion to civil litigation. In the criminal justice system, there are various constraints, albeit imperfect, to filter out insubstantial legal claims. The decision to prosecute a criminal case, for example, is made by a publicly accountable prosecutor subject to budgetary considerations and under an ethical obligation, not only to win and zealously to advocate for his client but also to serve the cause of justice. The rigors of the penal system are also mitigated by the responsible exercise of prosecutorial discretion. In contrast, there are no analogous checks in the civil discovery process here. Although under Federal Rule of Civil Procedure 11, sanctions are available, and private attorneys also owe an obligation of candor to the judicial tribunal, these safeguards have proved insufficient to discourage the filing of meritless claims against the Executive Branch. "In view of the visibility of" the Offices of the President and the Vice President and "the effect of their actions on countless people," they are "easily identifiable target[s] for suits for civil damages." *Nixon v. Fitzgerald*.

Finally, the narrow subpoena orders in *United States v. Nixon* stand on an altogether different footing from the overly broad discovery requests approved by the District Court in this case. The very specificity of the subpoena requests serves as an important safeguard against unnecessary intrusion into the operation of the Office of the President. In contrast to *Nixon*'s subpoena orders, the discovery requests here ask for everything under the sky.

CHAPTER 8

THE WRIT OF HABEAS CORPUS: RELIEF AGAINST A STATE OR FEDERAL OFFICER RESPONSIBLE FOR UNLAWFUL DETENTION

A. INTRODUCTION TO THE WRIT OF HABEAS CORPUS

1. A Brief History of the Writ

In Anglo-American constitutional history, the writ of *habeas corpus ad subjiciendum* has been venerated as "the Great Writ," the "bulwark," even the very "*palladium*" of liberty.[1] It has earned these titles by serving for centuries as the principal means by which liberty against unlawful detention at the hands of the state has been secured. The writ tests the validity of detention by requiring the government officer holding the petitioner to state in court the reasons justifying the restraint on physical liberty. If the reasons given are not satisfactory, the judge who issued the writ may order the petitioner released.

In the U.S. Constitution, the writ is one of the only fundamental personal rights embedded in the original instrument and the "only common law process mentioned."[2] The Suspension Clause provides that

> The Privilege of the Writ of Habeas Corpus shall not be suspended, unless when in Cases of Rebellion or Invasion the public Safety may require it.

---

1. AMANDA TYLER, HABEAS CORPUS IN WARTIME: FROM THE TOWER OF LONDON TO GUANTANAMO BAY 106 (2017); Paul D. Halliday & G. Edward White, *The Suspension Clause: English Text, Imperial Contexts, and American Implications*, 94 VA. L. REV. 575, 579, 623 (2008).

2. MARK E. NEELY, JR., THE FATE OF LIBERTY: ABRAHAM LINCOLN AND CIVIL LIBERTIES xiv (1991).

Art. I, Section 9, cl. 2. The privilege of the writ of habeas corpus and strict limits on its suspension were believed too essential to civil liberty to be left to the contingencies of the amendment process and the Bill of Rights. The close relationship between habeas corpus and civil liberty derived from at least three sources we survey below: the English history of royal and parliamentary detention of dissidents without trial, American experience of the Crown's suspension of the writ in the colonies, and use of the writ by and against African Americans who escaped slavery.

The English history of the writ is intricate but important to consider because modern cases draw extensively upon it in interpreting the Suspension Clause and the contours of the writ. The writ of habeas corpus first emerged as an expression of the power of the Crown to require subordinate officers to justify their decision to detain a subject—a form of sovereign "mercy beyond law's warrant."[3] However, common law judges gradually "capture[d]" this "royal prerogative," using the writ to force officers of the Crown to justify detention according to standards defined by law rather the will of the Crown.[4] The seventeenth century was the pivotal period for this development. During the English Civil War, 1642-1651, King Charles I dissolved Parliament, arrested supposedly disloyal members of Parliament, and attempted to rule by fiat. As the King and Parliament struggled for control, there was "a dramatic rise in the frequency of both executive and parliamentary imprisonment of political enemies without process of any kind. . . . [T]hose in power also increasingly employed the practice of sending prisoners to 'legal islands' (whether true islands or the Tower of London) to escape the reach of writs of habeas corpus."[5] In some cases, judges arbitrarily refused to entertain, denied, or delayed adjudicating writs filed by political prisoners. The most unfortunate languished in detention for years without trial as a result.[6] In other instances, however, "judges stood up to the imprisonment orders made by many of the new officers or agencies" created by Parliament as the King and Parliament wrestled over sovereignty.[7]

In this way, a power originally *of the sovereign* (to require that officers of the state act according to its will) was transformed into a check *against the sovereign* (the Crown, Parliament, and sometimes both) in order to ensure compliance with law. Parliament gradually recognized this common law judicial authority and sought to control it through legislation, most famously in the Habeas Corpus Act of 1679. The statute:

- required the jailer to file a "return" explaining the grounds of detention and to appear in court *with the petitioner* within three days;
- formalized procedures for hearing petitions even when the court was not in session;

---

3. Halliday & White, *supra* note 1, at 607.

4. *Id.* at 670.

5. TYLER, *supra* note 1, at 22.

6. *Id.* at 23 (noting that in "Feimer's Case" the petitioner "had already spent five years in the Tower based solely on a councilor order," and that the King's bench denied his petition on the ground that "[l]ikely he is a dangerous person. . . . We must use a justifiable prudence and not strain the strict rules of law to enlarge those persons which will use their liberties to get the kingdom in a flame").

7. Halliday & White, *supra* note 1, at 621 n.130.

- gave the petitioner a right to recover damages if the jailer failed to file the return and produce the prisoner in court;
- set limitations on moving prisoners to escape a court's habeas jurisdiction;
- clarified that the writ ran to the geographic limits of the kingdom, overturning contrary judicial precedent;
- and set financial penalties against judges who failed to comply with the terms of the statute.[8]

Blackstone referred to the statute as a "second *Magna Carta*."[9] As England had no written constitution, the reference to *Magna Carta* is significant. Legal principles in England achieved constitutional status not through amendment to a single document, but rather through an "organic" process that included Parliamentary recognition (incorporation in the country's "ancient and noble statutes"), elaboration in caselaw, and perhaps most importantly, durability over time.[10] To call Parliament's protection of the writ in 1679 a "second *Magna Carta*" was thus to suggest that access to the writ was a common law rule of constitutional stature. "*Magna carta*," Blackstone emphasized, "declared that no man shall be imprisoned contrary to law: the *habeas corpus* act points him out effectual means . . . to release himself."[11]

Notwithstanding the guarantees of the 1679 statute, Parliament legislated controversial temporary "suspensions" of the writ to protect the "*salus populi*"—the health, welfare, and safety of the people—during periods of perceived unrest.[12] When this occurred in the American colonies, it provoked "outrage" that the writ—"the most important thing that the king's subjects, anywhere on the globe, carried with them"—could be so easily undermined.[13] "None other than General Washington, in his manifesto of September 1777, noted among other wrongs against North Americans that 'arbitrary imprisonment has received the sanction of British laws by the suspension of the Habeas Corpus Act [of 1679].'"[14] The framers of the American Constitution were thus acutely aware of the dangers of an unchecked power of suspension.

In the 1780s, after the American Revolution, courts of the newly formed states entertained petitions for writs of habeas corpus filed by African Americans who had escaped and sought relief from capture and return to slavery. These cases demonstrate an important feature of the early history of the writ: "that the use of the writ was not confined to native-born British-American citizens of European ancestry, and that American usage was paralleling that in England" in the sense that the privilege of the writ extended to subjects of a government's authority "regardless of other social or legal status."[15] But this was by no means a uniform practice. Southern states routinely denied enslaved persons the privilege of the writ:

---

8. Tyler, *supra* note 1, at 28-29.
9. Halliday & White, *supra* note 1, at 611.
10. Ian Ward, The English Constitution: Myths and Realities 1, 4 (2004).
11. Tyler, *supra* note 1, at 25. *Cf.* Halliday & White, *supra* note 1, at 611.
12. Halliday & White, *supra* note 1, at 623.
13. *Id.* at 649.
14. *Id.*
15. *Id.* at 675.

Southern courts ruled that a jury trial was necessary to deprive a master of his slave; a judge could not do so by issuing a simple writ. Thus, a Florida court . . . took the view widely held in the South that the "writ of habeas corpus is not the proper method of trying the right of a negro to Freedom. The doctrine of the court is, that the person claiming him cannot be deprived of his *property* without jury trial."[16]

Even in the North, the writ "became a two-edged sword. Antislavery forces employed writs to free black people claimed by Southerners in free states, but a New York law of 1828, for example, also allowed claimants to request the issuance of writs that would cause the sheriff to bring in an alleged runaway. The lawmakers drew on an analogy with child custody cases, in which writs of habeas corpus were similarly employed."[17] The infamous Fugitive Slave Act of 1850 profoundly disrupted the use of the writ as an antislavery device, allowing "special federal commissioners the power to issue certificates to persons seeking their runaway slaves. And these certificates, the law held, 'shall prevent all . . . molestation of said . . . persons by any process issued by any court, judge, magistrate, or other person whomsoever.'"[18]

As this brief historical survey suggests, at least three features of the writ's early history remain doctrinally important: (1) the longstanding constitutional and common law power of the judiciary to use the writ to check unlawful executive detention, (2) the perceived need for suspension of the writ in times of emergency and the potential for political abuse of that power, and (3) enduring controversy over whether the status of the person detained is relevant to access to the writ.

2.   *Federal Habeas Jurisdiction in the New Republic: The First Judiciary Act of 1789 and the Habeas Corpus Act of 1867*

The Suspension Clause of the U.S. Constitution is most directly addressed to the second feature. Delegates to the constitutional convention "first voted unanimously" to prohibit any form of suspension in order to protect the writ.[19] The language eventually adopted in the Suspension Clause, which permits suspension when narrow conditions are met, was drawn from the Massachusetts Constitution and passed by a vote of seven to three.[20] The modern Court has also read the Suspension Clause as constitutionalizing the first feature — *guaranteeing* access to the writ in the absence of a valid suspension. The third feature has proved the most vexing. To this day, as we will see in the materials that follow, there are questions about the relationship between the site of detention, the status of the person detained — e.g., citizen/noncitizen seeking entry at the border, enemy combatant/civilian, convicted prisoner/person detained without trial, etc. — and access to the writ.

The First Judiciary Act of 1789 recognized the common law power of federal judges to entertain writs of habeas corpus but limited that jurisdiction to cases

---

16. NEELY, *supra* note 2, at xiv.
17. *Id.* at xv.
18. *Id.*
19. *Id.* at xiv.
20. *Id.*

involving "custody, under or by colour of the authority of the United States." Judiciary Act of 1789, c.20, §14; codified at 28 U.S.C. §2241. Thus, federal courts could exercise habeas jurisdiction only in cases where detention was at the hands of *federal* officers. State courts handled petitions involving detention at the hands of state officers. But this reciprocal federal/state division of labor was not exact in the antebellum period. Most prominently, as we studied in Chapter 4, before the Civil War and the Court's decisions in *Ableman v. Booth* (1859) and *Tarble's Case* (1871), *state courts* "routinely granted habeas relief for *federal* extrajudicial detainees . . . individuals being held by federal officials without judicial process."[21] Remarkably, in view of the Court's silence on these cases in *Tarble's Case*, even "when dealing with habeas petitioners in military custody, it was 'settled' that the state and federal courts had concurrent jurisdiction."[22] However common the practice was, as the state court decisions in *Ableman* reveal, abolitionist opposition to the Federal Fugitive Slave Act produced increasingly sharp clashes between Northern state courts, on the one hand, and federal officers and the Supreme Court, on the other, before the Civil War.

The restrictions imposed by the First Judiciary Act on federal court habeas jurisdiction over persons held in state custody persisted, with narrow exceptions,[23] until the Habeas Corpus Act of 1867. Passed during Reconstruction, the 1867 Act was the first enduring grant of *federal court* habeas jurisdiction over persons held in *state custody*. It provided that:

> [the]several courts of the United States . . . within their respective jurisdictions, in addition to the authority already conferred by law, shall have power to grant writs of habeas corpus in all cases where any person maybe restrained of his or her liberty in violation of the Constitution, or of any treaty or law of the United States.

Extending federal habeas jurisdiction over state custody opened lower federal court review of "*state* laws impeding reconstruction and subordinating federal rights,"[24] especially state laws that undermined emancipation by — for example, subjecting African Americans to "indenture of apprenticeship" to their former masters.[25] As the Court emphasized shortly after its passage, the 1867 Habeas Corpus Act, "brings

---

21. Todd E. Pettys, *State Habeas Relief for Federal Extrajudicial Detainees*, 92 MINN. L. REV. 265, 268-69 (2007).

22. *Id.* at 275.

23. An 1833 statute provided that federal officers held in state custody for acts pursuant to federal law could file habeas petitions in federal court. The statute responded to South Carolina's effort to nullify federal tariffs affecting agriculture. An 1843 statute provided for federal habeas jurisdiction over aliens held in custody by a state for acts committed under the "commission, or order, or sanction, of any foreign State or Sovereignty, the validity and effect whereof depend upon the law of nations."

24. William W. Van Alstyne, *A Critical History of* Ex parte McCardle, 15 ARIZ. L. REV. 229, 238 (1973).

25. *See* In re Turner (C.C.D. Md. 1867) (No. 14297) (describing Maryland statute and granting petition of 11-year-old subject to indenture, noting that "many of the freed people in Talbot Count were collected together under some local authority . . . and the younger persons were bound as apprentices, usually, if not always, to their late masters").

within the *Habeas Corpus* jurisdiction . . . every possible case of privation of liberty contrary to the National Constitution, treaties, or laws. It is impossible to widen this jurisdiction" beyond what the statute confers.[26] Expansion of federal habeas jurisdiction was a direct response to state court resistance to federal rights—"interpos[ing] the *federal* judiciary between the individual and the state, largely because of the failure of the state courts adequately to protect the individual."[27] Notably, federal habeas jurisdiction over state custody in violation of federal law preceded by eight years the first extension of general federal question jurisdiction to the federal courts in civil cases under 28 U.S.C. §1331.

With the nation's retreat from Reconstruction and the rise of Jim Crow segregation in the late 1800s, federal judicial review of state custody under the 1867 Act—especially federal constitutional challenges to state criminal convictions—was circumscribed by the Court's assumption that post-conviction habeas review was limited to defects in the subject matter jurisdiction of the court of conviction.[28] That assumption was tied to federalism and an 1830 case involving *federal custody* in which Chief Justice Marshall suggested that imprisonment following a conviction in the Circuit Court for the District of Columbia, which the Court had no power to review on a writ of error, "cannot be unlawful, unless that judgment be an absolute nullity; and it is not a nullity if the court has general jurisdiction of the subject" even if, on the merits, the court's decision is legally "erroneous. The law trusts that court with the whole subject, and has not confided to this court the power of revising its decisions. This court cannot usurp that power by the instrumentality of a writ of habeas corpus." *Ex parte Watkins* (1830).

More searching review of the constitutionality of state court criminal convictions under the 1867 Act occurred in early twentieth century cases. In a landmark case, *Moore v. Dempsey* (1923), the Court granted relief after finding grave constitutional violations a state capital prosecution of twelve Black sharecrop farmers in Arkansas. The Black farmers had assembled in the fall of 1919 in a church with other members of the Black community and the Progressive Farmers and Household Union to discuss retaining a lawyer and other steps to protect them from extortion by local white landowners. On the day of the meeting whites seeking to disrupt labor organizing by the farmers attacked and fired upon the church. During the attack one of the white assailants was killed. News reports of the death of the white man prompted widespread, murderous reprisals and torture of Black residents, known as the Elaine Massacre.[29]

Petitioners were indicted by a grand jury composed of whites responsible for the reprisals. Their trial took place before a jury from which Black people were "systematically excluded" and the court was continuously surrounded by "an adverse crowd that threatened the most dangerous consequences to anyone interfering

---

26. *Id.* (quoting *Ex parte McCardle*).

27. Martin H. Redish, *Abstention, Separation of Powers, and the Limits of Judicial Function*, 94 YALE. L.J. 71, 111 (1984).

28. Henry M. Hart, *The Supreme Court 1958 Term, Forward: The Time Chart of the Justices*, 73 HARV. L. REV. 84, 103-104 (1959); Max Rosen, *The Great Writ – A Reflection of Social Change*, 44 OHIO ST. L.J. 337, 344 (1983). But see new historical research showing this assumption to be erroneous, discussed *infra* note 71, section B.2.

29. *See* IDA B. WELLS, THE ARKANSAS RACE RIOT (1920).

with the desired result." Defense counsel had no consultation with petitioners and called no witnesses for the defense during a 'trial' that lasted "about three quarters of an hour" and produced a jury verdict of guilt for first degree murder and a death sentence "in less than five minutes." The habeas petition established that "no juryman could have voted for an acquittal and continued to live in Phillips County." *Moore v. Dempsey* (1923). The Supreme Court held that although federal habeas jurisdiction is not a writ of error for state criminal convictions, if

> the whole proceeding is mask—that counsel, jury and judge were swept to the fatal end by an irresistible wave of public passion, and that the State Courts failed to correct the wrong; neither perfection in the machinery for correction [by state appellate courts] nor the possibility that the trial court and counsel saw no other way of avoiding an immediate outbreak of the mob can prevent this Court from securing to the petitioners their constitutional rights.
>
> We shall say no more concerning the corrective process afforded to the petitioners [at the state level] than that it does not seem to us sufficient to allow a Judge of the United States to escape the duty of examining the facts for himself when, if true as alleged, they make the trial absolutely void. . . . [I]t appears to us unavoidable that the District Judge should find whether the facts alleged are true and whether they can be explained so far as to leave the state proceedings undisturbed.

Moore v. Dempsey (1923).[30] The principle recognized in *Moore*—that federal habeas jurisdiction is not restricted exclusively to jurisdictional defects under the 1867 Act—was not embraced as a general standard of review of state court convictions until the middle of the twentieth century in another case involving racial discrimination in jury selection. *Brown v. Allen* (1953). We present *Brown v. Allen* in the section on post-conviction habeas, Section B.2. For now, note that the 1867 statute remains the principal jurisdictional grant for review of state court criminal convictions by federal courts.

In the pages that follow we will examine the Suspension Clause, Section 14 of the First Judiciary Act, the 1867 Act, and modern legislation limiting federal habeas jurisdiction, including substantial modifications to review of state convictions imposed by the Anti-terrorism and Effective Death Penalty Act of 1996 (AEDPA), as well as early twentieth century efforts to limit habeas review of federal detention at the navy facility in Guantanamo Bay. The material will be divided into two major categories of modern habeas litigation:

---

30. *Moore* relied in part on *Frank v. Mangum* (1915) (federal habeas petition alleging mob domination and corruption of trial denied on ground that state appellate courts had determined the allegations were largely unfounded, and that "it is open to the courts of the United States, upon application for a writ of habeas corpus, to look beyond forms and inquire into the very substance of the matter, to the extent of deciding whether the prisoner has been deprived of his liberty without due process of law [and] that an investigation . . . must take into consideration the entire course of proceedings in the courts of the state").

1. cases involving executive *detention without trial* and ordinary criminal process (principally in the areas of immigration and national security enforcement); and

2. cases involving petitions for relief from imprisonment *following criminal conviction* by trial and ordinary criminal process (especially federal habeas review of state criminal convictions).

Inquiry into the legal basis for detention at the hands of the government unifies these two areas of habeas litigation, but in other respects—the procedures for filing, the substantive standards of review, and the power of Congress to control these rules of decision and regulate jurisdiction to entertain habeas petitions—they are quite different.

Note, before we begin, that a 2007 analysis a decade after the AEDPA passed showed that just one in every 257 federal petitions (0.0039%) filed by state prisoners in a non-capital case succeeded.[31] The Supreme Court also rarely grants relief under Section 14 of the First Judiciary Act. And as we will see, the Court's executive detention jurisprudence is grounded in deference to executive power. To study habeas doctrine is thus to confront something of a paradox—a constitutionally guaranteed remedy, asserted for centuries to be *vital* to the preservation of liberty, is almost never granted. The reasons, both contextual and doctrinal, for this state of affairs warrant close scrutiny.

3. *Executive Detention*

a. Habeas Corpus and National Security Enforcement: The First Suspension

We begin with executive detention. On April 19, 1861, just days after the firing on Fort Sumpter started the Civil War, a mob in Maryland obstructed Union troops traveling by railroad from Massachusetts to Washington to protect the nation's capital. Later that night, state and local officials sympathetic to the mob burned key railroad bridges on the pretense of seeking to prevent more Union troops arriving and taking "revenge for the riot."[32] Maryland remained a slave state until the legislature enacted a statue abolishing it in November 1864, and great fortunes had been built for the state's elite in agriculture, ship caulking, and iron works using enslaved labor. So, when the war broke out, the state sought to preserve the institution of slavery while remaining in the Union. But many Maryland Democrats favored secession, sympathized with the south, and were willing to resort to violence to obstruct the mobilization of Union troops.

President Lincoln, unwilling to risk further interference and the security of the capitol, authorized General Winfield Scott to suspend the writ of habeas corpus "at any point on or in the vicinity of the military line, which is now being used

---

31. NANCY KING ET AL., FINAL TECHNICAL REPORT: HABEAS LITIGATION IN THE U.S. DISTRICT COURTS: AN EMPIRICAL STUDY OF HABEAS CORPUS CASES FILES BY STATE PRISONERS UNDER THE ANTITERRORISM AND EFFECTIVE DEATH PENALTY ACT OF 1996 (2007).

32. NEELY, *supra* note 2, at 5.

between the City of Philadelphia and the City of Washington."[33] The order emphasized that the General was "engaged in repressing an insurrection against the laws of the United States" and provided that if he found "resistance which renders it necessary to suspend the writ of habeas corpus for the public safety, you personally or through the officer in command at the point where resistance occurs are authorized to suspend the writ." Later in the summer of 1861 Lincoln went even farther, authorizing the arrest of several Maryland legislators on suspicion that a "disunion majority" in the state house would "pass an ordinance to secede."[34]

These orders were the first of several suspensions of the writ of habeas corpus during the Civil War in the North. Congress retroactively approved them, but in the meantime Chief Justice Taney entertained a petition for writ of habeas corpus filed by John Merryman, a planter who had been arrested by federal troops in May 1861. Merryman was believed to be an officer in an armed secessionist group and was held in federal military custody at Fort McHenry in Baltimore without a warrant. Taney held the officer detaining Merryman in contempt for defying the court's process, but subordinates at the Fort refused to permit service of the contempt order upon their superior. Taney's published opinion granting Merryman's petition held that *only* Congress, not the President, could enact a lawful suspension of the writ (in part because the Suspension Clause is located in Article I of the Constitution); that the ostensible grounds for Merryman's detention were "lose and vague"; and that in the absence of any "obstruction or resistance to the action of the civil authorities" and criminal process in civilian courts, there was no reason or authority "for the interposition of the military." *Ex parte Merryman* (1861). Taney warned that:

> if the authority which the Constitution has confided to Judiciary Department, and judicial offices may thus upon any pretext and under any circumstances, be usurped by the military power at its discretion, the people of the United States are no longer living under a Government of laws, but every citizen holds life, liberty and property at the will and pleasure of the army officer in whose military district he may happen to be found.

Lincoln disregarded the grant of Merryman's petition. In his July 4, 1861, address to Congress he publicly defended his decision to suspend the writ in Maryland and famously asked if "all the laws but one [are to] go unexecuted and the government itself go to pieces lest that one be violated." He continued:

> It was decided that we have a case of rebellion and that the public safety does require the qualified suspension of the privilege of the writ. . . . Now it is insisted that Congress, and not the Executive, is vested with this power; but the Constitution itself is silent as to which or who is to exercise the power; and as the provision was plainly made for a dangerous emergency, it cannot be believed the framers of the instrument intended that in every case the danger should run its course until Congress could be called together, the very assembling of which might be prevented, as was intended in this case, by the rebellion.

---

33. *Id.* at 8.
34. *Id.* at 15.

In this first presidential suspension of the writ, many of the lines of contestation that define the modern cases we turn to presently can be seen: assertions of exigent national security threats, suspensions that permit extended executive detention without ordinary criminal process, and efforts to ensure that the suspension of the writ does not work a wholesale suspension of the rule of law and civil liberties. The major doctrinal issues concern the standards of review that apply to petitions challenging executive detention, who is entitled to the privilege of the writ, in what court, and how and on what terms the privilege of the writ can be suspended.

The modern doctrine on suspension and executive detention has developed primarily in response to the terrorist attacks of September 11, 2001. Under the auspices of the Authorization for Use of Military Force passed by Congress in the fall of 2001, the federal government aggressively pursued and detained for interrogation counter-terrorism suspects in the United States and abroad. The first major case to reach the Supreme Court dealt with a habeas petition by a U.S. citizen seized in Afghanistan and detained as a suspected enemy combatant at a naval brig in Norfolk, Virginia.

Hamdi v. Rumsfeld

542 U.S. 507 (2004)

Justice O'CONNOR announced the judgment of the court and delivered an opinion, in which Chief Justice REHNQUIST, Justice KENNEDY, and Justice BREYER join.

At this difficult time in our Nation's history, we are called upon to consider the legality of the Government's detention of a United States citizen on United States soil as an "enemy combatant" and to address the process that is constitutionally owed to one who seeks to challenge his classification as such. The United States Court of Appeals for the Fourth Circuit held that petitioner's detention was legally authorized and that he was entitled to no further opportunity to challenge his enemy-combatant label. We now vacate and remand. We hold that although Congress authorized the detention of combatants in the narrow circumstances alleged here, due process demands that a citizen held in the United States as an enemy combatant be given a meaningful opportunity to contest the factual basis for that detention before a neutral decision maker.

I

On September 11, 2001, the al Qaeda terrorist network used hijacked commercial airliners to attack prominent targets in the United States. Approximately 3,000 people were killed in those attacks. One week later, in response to these "acts of treacherous violence," Congress passed a resolution authorizing the President to "use all necessary and appropriate force against those nations, organizations, or persons he determines planned, authorized, committed, or aided the terrorist attacks" or "harbored such organizations or persons, in order to prevent any future acts of international terrorism against the United States by such nations, organizations or persons." Authorization for Use of Military Force ("the AUMF"), 115 Stat.

224. Soon thereafter, the President ordered United States Armed Forces to Afghanistan, with a mission to subdue al Qaeda and quell the Taliban regime that was known to support it.

This case arises out of the detention of a man whom the Government alleges took up arms with the Taliban during this conflict. His name is Yaser Esam Hamdi. Born an American citizen in Louisiana in 1980, Hamdi moved with his family to Saudi Arabia as a child. By 2001, the parties agree, he resided in Afghanistan. At some point that year, he was seized by members of the Northern Alliance, a coalition of military groups opposed to the Taliban government, and eventually was turned over to the United States military. The Government asserts that it initially detained and interrogated Hamdi in Afghanistan before transferring him to the United States Naval Base in Guantanamo Bay in January 2002. In April 2002, upon learning that Hamdi is an American citizen, authorities transferred him to a naval brig in Norfolk, Virginia, where he remained until a recent transfer to a brig in Charleston, South Carolina. The Government contends that Hamdi is an "enemy combatant," and that this status justifies holding him in the United States indefinitely — without formal charges or proceedings — unless and until it makes the determination that access to counsel or further process is warranted.

In June 2002, Hamdi's father, Esam Fouad Hamdi, filed the present petition for a writ of habeas corpus under 28 U.S.C. §2241 in the Eastern District of Virginia. The elder Hamdi alleges in the petition that he has had no contact with his son since the Government took custody of him in 2001, and that the Government has held his son "without access to legal counsel or notice of any charges pending against him." The petition contends that Hamdi's detention was not legally authorized. It argues that, "[a]s an American citizen, . . . Hamdi enjoys the full protections of the Constitution," and that Hamdi's detention in the United States without charges, access to an impartial tribunal, or assistance of counsel "violated and continue[s] to violate the Fifth and Fourteenth Amendments to the United States Constitution." The habeas petition asks that the court, among other things, (1) appoint counsel for Hamdi; (2) order respondents to cease interrogating him; (3) declare that he is being held in violation of the Fifth and Fourteenth Amendments; (4) "[t]o the extent Respondents contest any material factual allegations in this Petition, schedule an evidentiary hearing, at which Petitioners may adduce proof in support of their allegations", and (5) order that Hamdi be released from his "unlawful custody." Although his habeas petition provides no details with regard to the factual circumstances surrounding his son's capture and detention, Hamdi's father has asserted in documents found elsewhere in the record that his son went to Afghanistan to do "relief work," and that he had been in that country less than two months before September 11, 2001, and could not have received military training. The 20-year-old was traveling on his own for the first time, his father says, and "[b]ecause of his lack of experience, he was trapped in Afghanistan once that military campaign began." The District Court found that Hamdi's father was a proper next friend, appointed the federal public defender as counsel for the petitioners, and ordered that counsel be given access to Hamdi.

[T]he Government filed a response and a motion to dismiss the petition. It attached to its response a declaration from one Michael Mobbs (hereinafter "Mobbs Declaration"), who identified himself as Special Advisor to the Under Secretary of Defense for Policy. Mobbs indicated that in this position, he has been "substantially involved with matters related to the detention of enemy combatants in the current war against the al Qaeda terrorists and those who support and harbor them (including the Taliban)." He expressed his "familiar[ity]" with Department of Defense and United States military policies and procedures applicable to the detention, control, and transfer of al Qaeda and Taliban personnel, and declared that "[b]ased upon my review of relevant records and reports, I am also familiar with the facts and circumstances related to the capture of . . . Hamdi and his detention by U.S. military forces."

Mobbs then set forth what remains the sole evidentiary support that the Government has provided to the courts for Hamdi's detention. The declaration states that Hamdi "traveled to Afghanistan" in July or August 2001, and that he thereafter "affiliated with a Taliban military unit and received weapons training." It asserts that Hamdi "remained with his Taliban unit following the attacks of September 11" and that, during the time when Northern Alliance forces were "engaged in battle with the Taliban," "Hamdi's Taliban unit surrendered" to those forces, after which he "surrender[ed] his Kalishnikov assault rifle" to them. The Mobbs Declaration also states that, because al Qaeda and the Taliban "were and are hostile forces engaged in armed conflict with the armed forces of the United States," "individuals associated with" those groups "were and continue to be enemy combatants." Mobbs states that Hamdi was labeled an enemy combatant "[b]ased upon his interviews and in light of his association with the Taliban." According to the declaration, a series of "U.S. military screening team[s]" determined that Hamdi met "the criteria for enemy combatants," and "a subsequent interview of Hamdi has confirmed that he surrendered and gave his firearm to Northern Alliance forces, which supports his classification as an enemy combatant."

The District Court found that the Mobbs Declaration fell "far short" of supporting Hamdi's detention. It criticized the generic and hearsay nature of the affidavit, calling it "little more than the government's 'say-so.'" It ordered the Government to turn over numerous materials for *in camera* review, including copies of all of Hamdi's statements and the notes taken from interviews with him that related to his reasons for going to Afghanistan and his activities therein; a list of all interrogators who had questioned Hamdi and their names and addresses; statements by members of the Northern Alliance regarding Hamdi's surrender and capture; a list of the dates and locations of his capture and subsequent detentions; and the names and titles of the United States Government officials who made the determinations that Hamdi was an enemy combatant and that he should be moved to a naval brig. The court indicated that all of these materials were necessary for "meaningful judicial review" of whether Hamdi's detention was legally authorized and whether Hamdi had received sufficient process to satisfy the Due Process Clause of the Constitution and relevant treaties or military regulations.

The Fourth Circuit reversed . . . stress[ing] that, because it was "undisputed that Hamdi was captured in a zone of active combat in a foreign theater of conflict," no factual inquiry or evidentiary hearing allowing Hamdi to be heard or to rebut the Government's assertions was necessary or proper.

On the more global question of whether legal authorization exists for the detention of citizen enemy combatants at all, the Fourth Circuit . . . expressed doubt as to Hamdi's argument that 18 U.S.C. §4001(a), which provides that "[n]o citizen shall be imprisoned or otherwise detained by the United States except pursuant to an Act of Congress,"* required express congressional authorization of detentions of this sort. But it held that, in any event, such authorization was found in the post-September 11 Authorization for Use of Military Force.

"The privilege of citizenship," the court held, "entitles Hamdi to a limited judicial inquiry into his detention, but only to determine its legality under the war powers of the political branches. . . ."

We now vacate the judgment below and remand.

II

[On the threshold question whether the President has the authority to detain citizens who qualify as "enemy combatants," Justice O'Connor wrote:]

The AUMF authorizes the President to use "all necessary and appropriate force" against "nations, organizations, or persons" associated with the September 11, 2001, terrorist attacks. There can be no doubt that individuals who fought against the United States in Afghanistan as part of the Taliban, an organization known to have supported the al Qaeda terrorist network responsible for those attacks, are individuals Congress sought to target in passing the AUMF. We conclude that detention of individuals falling into the limited category we are considering, for the duration of the particular conflict in which they were captured, is so fundamental and accepted an incident to war as to be an exercise of the "necessary and appropriate force" Congress has authorized the President to use.

III

[Justice O'Connor then turned to the due process issue:] Even in cases in which the detention of enemy combatants is legally authorized, there remains the question of what process is constitutionally due to a citizen who disputes his enemy-combatant status. Hamdi argues that he is owed a meaningful and timely hearing and that "extra-judicial detention [that] begins and ends with the submission of an affidavit based on third-hand hearsay" does not comport with the Fifth and Fourteenth Amendments. The Government counters that any more process than was provided below would be both unworkable and "constitutionally intolerable."

A

. . . All agree that, absent suspension, the writ of habeas corpus remains available to every individual detained within the United States. U.S. Const., Art. I, §9, cl. 2 ("The Privilege of the Writ of Habeas Corpus shall not be suspended, unless when in Cases of Rebellion or Invasion the public Safety may require it"). Only in the rarest of circumstances has Congress seen fit to suspend the writ. See, e.g., Act of Mar. 3, 1863, ch. 81, §1; Act of April 20, 1871, ch. 22, §4. At all other times, it has remained a critical check on the Executive, ensuring that it does not detain individuals except in accordance with law. See INS v. St. Cyr (2001). All agree suspension of the writ has not occurred here. [Emphasis added.] Thus, it is undisputed that Hamdi

---

* 18 U.S.C. §4001 is the Non-Detention Act, passed by Congress in response to the illegal detention of nearly 120,000 Americans of Japanese ancestry during World War II. — EDS.

was properly before an Article III court to challenge his detention under 28 U.S.C. §2241.

C

The Government . . . [argues] that . . . factual exploration is unwarranted and inappropriate in light of the extraordinary constitutional interests at stake. Under the Government's most extreme rendition of this argument, "[r]espect for separation of powers and the limited institutional capabilities of courts in matters of military decision-making in connection with an ongoing conflict" ought to eliminate entirely any individual process, restricting the courts to investigating only whether legal authorization exists for the broader detention scheme. At most, the Government argues, courts should review its determination that a citizen is an enemy combatant under a very deferential "some evidence" standard. Under this review, a court would assume the accuracy of the Government's articulated basis for Hamdi's detention, as set forth in the Mobbs Declaration, and assess only whether that articulated basis was a legitimate one.

In response, Hamdi emphasizes that this Court consistently has recognized that an individual challenging his detention may not be held at the will of the Executive without recourse to some proceeding before a neutral tribunal to determine whether the Executive's asserted justifications for that detention have basis in fact and warrant in law.

The ordinary mechanism that we use for balancing such serious competing interests, and for determining the procedures that are necessary to ensure that a citizen is not "deprived of life, liberty, or property, without due process of law," U.S. CONST. amend. V, is the test that we articulated in *Mathews v. Eldridge* (1976). *Mathews* dictates that the process due in any given instance is determined by weighing "the private interest that will be affected by the official action" against the Government's asserted interest, "including the function involved" and the burdens the Government would face in providing greater process. The *Mathews* calculus then contemplates a judicious balancing of these concerns, through an analysis of "the risk of an erroneous deprivation" of the private interest if the process were reduced and the "probable value, if any, of additional or substitute safeguards." We take each of these steps in turn.

1

It is beyond question that substantial interests lie on both sides of the scale in this case. Hamdi's "private interest . . . affected by the official action," *id.*, is the most elemental of liberty interests—the interest in being free from physical detention by one's own government. *Foucha v. Louisiana* (1992) ("Freedom from bodily restraint has always been at the core of the liberty protected by the Due Process Clause from arbitrary governmental action"). "In our society liberty is the norm," and detention without trial "is the carefully limited exception." *Salerno.* "We have always been careful not to 'minimize the importance and fundamental nature' of the individual's right to liberty," *Foucha,* and we will not do so today.

Nor is the weight on this side of the *Mathews* scale offset by the circumstances of war or the accusation of treasonous behavior, for "[i]t is clear that commitment for *any* purpose constitutes a significant deprivation of liberty that requires due process protection," *Jones v. United States* (1983), and at this stage in the *Mathews* calculus, we consider the interest of the *erroneously* detained individual. *Carey v. Piphus* (1978) ("Procedural due process rules are meant to protect persons not from the deprivation, but from the mistaken or unjustified deprivation of life, liberty, or property"). . . . Moreover, as critical as the Government's interest may be in detaining those who actually pose an immediate threat to the national security of the United States during ongoing international conflict, history and common sense teach us that an unchecked system of detention carries the potential to become a means for oppression and abuse of others who do not present that sort of threat. *See Ex parte Milligan* (1866) ("[The Founders] knew—the history of the world told them—the nation they were founding, be its existence short or long, would be involved in war; how often or how long continued, human foresight could not tell; and that unlimited power, wherever lodged at such a time, was especially hazardous to freemen").

2

On the other side of the scale are the weighty and sensitive governmental interests in ensuring that those who have in fact fought with the enemy during a war do not return to battle against the United States. As discussed above, the law of war and the realities of combat may render such detentions both necessary and appropriate, and our due process analysis need not blink at those realities. Without doubt, our Constitution recognizes that core strategic matters of warmaking belong in the hands of those who are best positioned and most politically accountable for making them. *Dep't of Navy v. Egan* (1988) (noting the reluctance of the courts "to intrude upon the authority of the Executive in military and national security affairs").

The Government also argues at some length that its interests in reducing the process available to alleged enemy combatants are heightened by the practical difficulties that would accompany a system of trial-like process. In its view, military officers who are engaged in the serious work of waging battle would be unnecessarily and dangerously distracted by litigation half a world away, and discovery into military operations would both intrude on the sensitive secrets of national defense and result in a futile search for evidence buried under the rubble of war.

3

It is during our most challenging and uncertain moments that our Nation's commitment to due process is most severely tested; and it is in those times that we must preserve our commitment at home to the principles for which we fight abroad.

With due recognition of these competing concerns, we believe that neither the process proposed by the Government nor the process apparently envisioned by the District Court below strikes the proper constitutional balance when a United

States citizen is detained in the United States as an enemy combatant. That is, "the risk of erroneous deprivation" of a detainee's liberty interest is unacceptably high under the Government's proposed rule, while some of the "additional or substitute procedural safeguards" suggested by the District Court are unwarranted in light of their limited "probable value" and the burdens they may impose on the military in such cases. *Mathews.*

We therefore hold that a citizen-detainee seeking to challenge his classification as an enemy combatant must receive notice of the factual basis for his classification, and a fair opportunity to rebut the Government's factual assertions before a neutral decisionmaker. *See Cleveland Bd. of Ed. v. Loudermill* (1985) ("An essential principle of due process is that a deprivation of life, liberty, or property 'be preceded by notice and opportunity for hearing appropriate to the nature of the case'" (quoting *Mullane v. Central Hanover Bank & Trust Co.* (1950)). . . . It is equally fundamental that the right to notice and an opportunity to be heard 'must be granted at a meaningful time and in a meaningful manner.'" *Fuentes v. Shevin* (1972). These essential constitutional promises may not be eroded.

At the same time, the exigencies of the circumstances may demand that, aside from these core elements, enemy combatant proceedings may be tailored to alleviate their uncommon potential to burden the Executive at a time of ongoing military conflict. Hearsay, for example, may need to be accepted as the most reliable available evidence from the Government in such a proceeding. Likewise, the Constitution would not be offended by a presumption in favor of the Government's evidence, so long as that presumption remained a rebuttable one and fair opportunity for rebuttal were provided. Thus, once the Government puts forth credible evidence that the habeas petitioner meets the enemy-combatant criteria, the onus could shift to the petitioner to rebut that evidence with more persuasive evidence that he falls outside the criteria. A burden shifting scheme of this sort would meet the goal of ensuring that the errant tourist, embedded journalist, or local aid worker has a chance to prove military error while giving due regard to the Executive once it has put forth meaningful support for its conclusion that the detainee is in fact an enemy combatant. In the words of *Mathews*, process of this sort would sufficiently address the "risk of erroneous deprivation" of a detainee's liberty interest while eliminating certain procedures that have questionable additional value in light of the burden on the Government.

We think it unlikely that this basic process will have the dire impact on the central functions of warmaking that the Government forecasts.

D

In so holding, we necessarily reject the Government's assertion that separation of powers principles mandate a heavily circumscribed role for the courts in such circumstances. . . . We have long since made clear that a state of war is not a blank check for the President when it comes to the rights of the Nation's citizens. *Youngstown Sheet & Tube* (1952). Whatever power the United States Constitution envisions for the Executive in its exchanges with other nations or with enemy organizations in times of conflict, it most assuredly envisions a role for all three branches when individual liberties are at stake. *Home Building & Loan Ass'n v. Blaisdell* (1934) (The war power "is a power to wage war successfully, and thus it permits the harnessing of the entire energies of the people in a supreme cooperative effort to preserve the nation. But even the war power does not remove constitutional limitations safeguarding essential liberties").

Because we conclude that due process demands some system for a citizen detainee to refute his classification, the proposed "some evidence" standard is inadequate. Any process in which the Executive's factual assertions go wholly unchallenged or are simply presumed correct without any opportunity for the alleged combatant to demonstrate otherwise falls constitutionally short.

. . . . Aside from unspecified "screening" processes, and military interrogations in which the Government suggests Hamdi could have contested his classification, Hamdi has received no process. An interrogation by one's captor, however effective an intelligence-gathering tool, hardly constitutes a constitutionally adequate fact-finding before a neutral decision maker.

IV

Hamdi asks us to hold that the Fourth Circuit also erred by denying him immediate access to counsel upon his detention and by disposing of the case without permitting him to meet with an attorney. Since our grant of certiorari in this case, Hamdi has been appointed counsel, with whom he has met for consultation purposes on several occasions, and with whom he is now being granted unmonitored meetings. He unquestionably has the right to access to counsel in connection with the proceedings on remand. No further consideration of this issue is necessary at this stage of the case.

[The opinion of Justice Souter, with whom Justice Ginsburg joins, concurring in part, dissenting in part, and concurring in the judgment, is omitted. Justice Souter's view is that the case should have been resolved without reaching the due process issue. Hamdi's detention is illegal, Justice Souter concludes, because neither the 2001 Authorization for Use of Military Force, nor any other law, overrides the Non-Detention Act.]

Justice SCALIA, with whom Justice STEVENS joins, dissenting.

This case brings into conflict the competing demands of national security and our citizens' constitutional right to personal liberty. Although I share the Court's evident unease as it seeks to reconcile the two, I do not agree with its resolution.

Where the Government accuses a citizen of waging war against it, our constitutional tradition has been to prosecute him in federal court for treason or some other crime. Where the exigencies of war prevent that, the Constitution's Suspension Clause, Art. I, §9, cl. 2, allows Congress to relax the usual protections temporarily. Absent suspension, however, the Executive's assertion of military exigency has not been thought sufficient to permit detention without charge. No one contends that the congressional Authorization for Use of Military Force, on which the Government relies to justify its actions here, is an implementation of the Suspension Clause. Accordingly, I would reverse the decision below.

I

. . . The gist of the Due Process Clause, as understood at the founding and since, was to force the Government to follow those common-law procedures traditionally deemed necessary before depriving a person of life, liberty, or property. When a citizen was deprived of liberty because of alleged criminal conduct, those procedures typically required committal by a magistrate followed by indictment and trial. . . .

These due process rights have historically been vindicated by the writ of habeas corpus. In England before the founding, the writ developed into a tool for challenging executive confinement.

The writ of habeas corpus was preserved in the Constitution—the only common-law writ to be explicitly mentioned. *See* Art. I, §9, cl. 2. Hamilton lauded "the establishment of the writ of *habeas corpus*" in his Federalist defense as a means to protect against "the practice of arbitrary imprisonments . . . in all ages, [one of] the favourite and most formidable instruments of tyranny." The Federalist No. 84. Indeed, availability of the writ under the new Constitution (along with the requirement of trial by jury in criminal cases, *see* Art. III, §2, cl. 3) was his basis for arguing that additional, explicit procedural protections were unnecessary. *See* The Federalist No. 83.

II

A

Justice O'Connor, writing for a plurality of this Court, asserts that captured enemy combatants (other than those suspected of war crimes) have traditionally been detained until the cessation of hostilities and then released. That is probably an accurate description of wartime practice with respect to enemy *aliens.* The tradition with respect to American citizens, however, has been quite different. Citizens aiding the enemy have been treated as traitors subject to the criminal process.

B

There are times when military exigency renders resort to the traditional criminal process impracticable. English law accommodated such exigencies by allowing legislative suspension of the writ of habeas corpus for brief periods. . . . Where the Executive has not pursued the usual course of charge, committal, and conviction, it has historically secured the Legislature's explicit approval of a suspension. In England, Parliament on numerous occasions passed temporary suspensions in times of threatened invasion or rebellion.

Our Federal Constitution contains a provision explicitly permitting suspension, but limiting the situations in which it may be invoked: "The privilege of the Writ of Habeas Corpus shall not be suspended, unless when in Cases of Rebellion or Invasion the public Safety may require it." Art. I, §9, cl. 2. Although this provision does not state that suspension must be effected by, or authorized by, a legislative act, it has been so understood, consistent with English practice and the Clause's placement in Article I. *See Ex parte Bollman* (1807); *Ex parte Merryman*

(C.D. Md. 1861) (Taney, C.J., rejecting Lincoln's unauthorized suspension); 3 Story §1336.

III

Writings from the founding generation also suggest that, without exception, the only constitutional alternatives are to charge the crime or suspend the writ.

In the Founders' view, the "blessings of liberty" were threatened by "those military establishments which must gradually poison its very fountain." The Federalist No. 45 (J. Madison). No fewer than 10 issues of the Federalist were devoted in whole or part to allaying fears of oppression from the proposed Constitution's authorization of standing armies in peacetime. . . . A view of the Constitution that gives the Executive authority to use military force rather than the force of law against citizens on American soil flies in the face of the mistrust that engendered these provisions.

V

Hamdi is entitled to a habeas decree requiring his release unless (1) criminal proceedings are promptly brought, or (2) Congress has suspended the writ of habeas corpus. A suspension of the writ could, of course, lay down conditions for continued detention, similar to those that today's opinion prescribes under the Due Process Clause. *Cf.* Act of Mar. 3, 1863. But there is a world of difference between the people's representatives' determining the need for that suspension (and prescribing the conditions for it), and this Court's doing so.

Having found a congressional authorization for detention of citizens where none clearly exists; and having discarded the categorical procedural protection of the Suspension Clause; the plurality then proceeds, under the guise of the Due Process Clause, to prescribe what procedural protections *it* thinks appropriate. . . . It claims authority to engage in this sort of "judicious balancing" from *Mathews v. Eldridge* (1976), a case involving . . . *the withdrawal of disability benefits*! Whatever the merits of this technique when newly recognized property rights are at issue (and even there they are questionable), it has no place where the Constitution and the common law already supply an answer.

There is a certain harmony of approach in the plurality's making up for Congress's failure to invoke the Suspension Clause and its making up for the Executive's failure to apply what it says are needed procedures—an approach that reflects what might be called a Mr. Fix-it Mentality. The plurality seems to view it as its mission to Make Everything Come Out Right, rather than merely to decree the consequences, as far as individual rights are concerned, of the other two branches' actions and omissions. Has the Legislature failed to suspend the writ in the current dire emergency? Well, we will remedy that failure by prescribing the reasonable conditions that a suspension should have included. And has the Executive failed to live up to those reasonable conditions? Well, we will ourselves make that failure good, so that this dangerous fellow (if he is dangerous) need not be set free. The problem with this approach is not only that it steps out of the courts' modest and limited role in a democratic society; but that by repeatedly doing what it thinks the political branches ought to do it encourages their lassitude and saps the vitality of government by the people.

VI

The Founders well understood the difficult tradeoff between safety and freedom. "Safety from external danger," Hamilton declared,

> is the most powerful director of national conduct. Even the ardent love of liberty will, after a time, give way to its dictates. The violent destruction of life and property incident to war; the continual effort and alarm attendant on a state of continual danger, will compel nations the most attached to liberty, to resort for repose and security to institutions which have a tendency to destroy their civil and political rights. To be more safe, they, at length, become willing to run the risk of being less free. The Federalist No. 8, p. 33.

The Founders warned us about the risk, and equipped us with a Constitution designed to deal with it.

Justice THOMAS, dissenting.

I

The plurality agrees that Hamdi's detention is lawful if he is an enemy combatant. But the question whether Hamdi is actually an enemy combatant is "of a kind for which the Judiciary has neither aptitude, facilities nor responsibility and which has long been held to belong in the domain of political power not subject to judicial intrusion or inquiry." *Chicago & Southern Air Lines, Inc. v. Waterman S.S. Corp.* (1948).

IV

Although I do not agree with the plurality that the balancing approach of *Mathews* is the appropriate analytical tool with which to analyze this case, I cannot help but explain that the plurality misapplies its chosen framework. The plurality devotes two paragraphs to its discussion of the Government's interest, though much of those two paragraphs explain why the Government's concerns are misplaced. But: "It is 'obvious and unarguable' that no governmental interest is more compelling than the security of the Nation." *Haig v. Agee* (1981).

Additional process, the Government explains, will destroy the intelligence gathering function. It also does seem quite likely that, under the process envisioned by the plurality, various military officials will have to take time to litigate this matter. And though the plurality does not say so, a meaningful ability to challenge the Government's factual allegations will probably require the Government to divulge highly classified information to the purported enemy combatant, who might then upon release return to the fight armed with our most closely held secrets.

Undeniably, Hamdi has been deprived of a serious interest, one actually protected by the Due Process Clause. Against this, however, is the Government's overriding interest in protecting the Nation.

I would affirm the judgment of the Court of Appeals.

* * *

Hamdi was released from custody in a settlement reached nearly three years after he was initially seized by the government. The terms of his release required that he give up U.S. citizenship, accept deportation to Saudi Arabia and never travel to certain countries, including the United States. He also waived the right to civil damages against the United States for harm caused by his detention.

Notice that his status as a U.S. citizen at the time he was detained affected his case in a number of important respects. First, the Non-Detention Act prohibits detention of U.S. citizens without express congressional authorization. Secondly, his status as a U.S. citizen is very likely what prompted the government to move him from Guantanamo to a Norfolk, Virginia facility within the jurisdiction of a federal court under 28 U.S.C. §2241. This statute is the modern codification of Section 14 of the First Judiciary Act. It provides that federal courts have power to entertain habeas petitions brought "within their respective jurisdictions," [28 U.S.C. 2241(a),] meaning petitions concerning people detained within the geographic boundaries of the court's jurisdiction. The statute further provides that:

> The writ of habeas corpus shall not extend to a prisoner unless—
>
> (1) He is in custody under or by color of the authority of the United States or is committed for trial before some court thereof; or
>
> (2) He is in custody for an act done or omitted in pursuance of an Act of Congress, or an order, process, judgment or decree of a court or judge of the United States; or
>
> (3) He is in custody in violation of the Constitution or laws or treaties of the United States; or
>
> (4) He, being a citizen of a foreign state and domiciled therein is in custody for an act done or omitted under any alleged right, title, authority, privilege, protection, or exemption claimed under the commission, order or sanction of any foreign state, or under color thereof, the validity and effect of which depend upon the law of nations; or
>
> (5) It is necessary to bring him into court to testify or for trial.

28 U.S.C. §2241(c). Hamdi's status as a U.S. citizen also figures prominently in O'Connor's due process analysis and in Justice Scalia's dissenting opinion arguing that, irrespective of the Non-Detention Act, the only constitutional option for a U.S. citizen believed to be an enemy combatant is indictment and trial in the ordinary civilian courts or release (absent a proper legislative suspension of the writ).

Because of his status as a citizen, the case did not resolve whether a *foreign national* detained as a suspected enemy combatant would be entitled to the same protections if the site of detention was outside the jurisdiction of any federal court under §2241. (Recall from Chapter 4 that no state court has power under *Tarble's Case* to entertain a petition regarding detention at the hands of a federal officer.)

Detentions of suspected enemy combatants at Guantanamo Bay Naval Base began in 2002, four months after the September 11 attacks. Approximately 780 people have been held at the facility, citizens predominantly of Afghanistan, Saudia Arabia, Yemen, and Pakistan. Eight have been convicted in trial by military commission, six of those through plea deals. Nearly two dozen of the detainees were minors, including some as young as 13. Nine detainees have died in custody, seven of them by apparent suicide. By 2022, the population was reduced to 37 by transferring detainees to countries willing to receive them, all of whom had been held there for more than a decade. Ten of those who remain are awaiting trial by military commission.

The government's position early on was that the Constitution had no application whatsoever to foreign nationals detained there. On the same day *Hamdi* was decided, the Supreme Court held that 28 U.S.C. §2241 extends to foreign nationals' detention at Guantanamo. *Rasul v. Bush* (2004). The Court emphasized the petitioners' allegation that they were held in violation of the laws of the United States under §2241(c)(3) and that the U.S. District Court for the District of Columbia plainly had jurisdiction over the federal officers located in D.C. who were responsible for Guantanamo detention decisions. The Court concluded in *Rasul* that "Section 2241, by its terms, requires nothing more." Notice that this means §2241 jurisdiction turns on the habeas court's power *over the custodian*, not the detainee.

The Court squarely rejected the government's argument that the case was controlled by *Johnson v. Eisentrager* (1950) (denying right of access to habeas to 21 German citizens captured by U.S. forces in China, tried and convicted of war crimes by an American military commission headquartered in Nanking, and incarcerated in a U.S. military base in occupied Germany). The *Rasul* Court noted important factual distinctions: Unlike the Germans in *Eisentrager*, the *Rasul* petitioners had received no access "to any tribunal, much less charged with and convicted of wrongdoing;" and "for more than two years they have been imprisoned in territory over which the United States exercises exclusive jurisdiction and control." The Court also noted that *Eisentrager* did not directly address the right to habeas under §2241 because it incorrectly assumed that §2241 required that the habeas court have jurisdiction *over the detainee*. Cases decided since *Eisentrager*, the Court emphasized, had made clear that "the writ of habeas corpus does not act upon the prisoner who seeks relief, but upon the person who holds hum in what is alleged to be unlawful custody." Thus, there is jurisdiction under §2241 so long as "the custodian can be reached by service of process" of the district court in which the petition is filed. *Braden v. 30th Judicial Circuit Ct. Ky.* (1973).

In the wake of *Hamdi* and *Rasul*, the government took two important steps. First, the Department of Defense used the plurality decision in *Hamdi* as a framework to establish Combatant Status Review Tribunals (CSRT) to determine whether existing and new Guantanamo detainees were enemy combatants subject to continued detention. The CSRT Order directed that tribunals were to be composed of three commissioned officers of the U.S. Armed Forces with appropriate security clearances who were not involved in the apprehension or interrogation of the detainee. The Order directed that CSRT's were not bound by ordinary rules of evidence. They could consider any information deemed relevant, including hearsay, decisions about a detainee's status only had to meet a preponderance of the evidence standard of proof, and the government was given a rebuttable presumption in favor of its evidence. Finally, the Order directed that detainees should have the right to testify, to submit documentary evidence, and the assistance of a "personal representative" (a military officer, not a lawyer). The record of CSRT's would not include the deliberations of the tribunal, just their determination of the status of the detainee.

The second step was taken by Congress. In the Detainee Treatment Act of 2005, it stripped §2241 jurisdiction for Guantanamo detainees. The statute further provided that the only avenue for challenging detention would be direct appeal to the U.S. Court of Appeals for the District of Columbia. The "scope of review" limited the D.C. Circuit to determining whether the CSRT had followed the standards and procedures set by the Department of Defense, and, to the extent the Constitution and other U.S. laws apply, whether the DOD standards and procedures are "consistent" with those laws. In *Hamdan v. Rumsfeld* (2006), the Court held that the jurisdiction stripping language of the DTA was not sufficiently clear to deprive the federal courts of habeas jurisdiction in cases *already pending.* Congress responded with the Military Commissions Act of 2006, stripping habeas jurisdiction retroactively for *all* non-citizen detainees held *anywhere* outside the United States.

The following case addressed the constitutionality of these measures. In April 2007, the Court denied certiorari on the ground that the petitioners had failed to exhaust the CSRT process. Justices Breyer, Souter, and Ginsburg dissented from the denial of certiorari. Writing in support of the denial of certiorari, Justices Stevens and Kennedy noted the rule that "the exhaustion of available remedies [is] a precondition to accepting jurisdiction over applications for the writ of habeas corpus," but signaled an openness to rehearing the petition for certiorari by emphasizing that the rule "does not require exhaustion of inadequate remedies." Petitioners filed for rehearing in June 2007, relying on the declaration of Lieutenant Colonel Stephen Abraham to establish that exhaustion was not required due to fundamental flaws in the CSRT process. Abraham had worked as an intelligence officer who both prepared reports for CSRTs and then served on a panel. He stated that he was required to certify that intelligence portfolios on detainees did not contain exculpatory information without being permitted to review the full portfolios, that unclassified summaries were prepared without review for the accuracy of the underlying information, that what "purported to be specific statements of fact lacked even the most fundamental earmarks of objectively credible evidence," and that when a tribunal concluded the detainee was not an enemy combatant, superiors "immediately questioned the validity" of the findings and ordered the tribunal "to reopen the hearing." After again concluding the evidence didn't support detention, Abraham "was not assigned to another CSRT panel." Abraham also stated that this was consistent with other cases — whenever a CSRT found a detainee was not an enemy combatant, the "focus" of follow-up inquiry was on "'what went wrong.'" *Odah v. United States*, Reply to Opposition to Petition for Rehearing, Appendix (June 15, 2007). The court granted certiorari within days of receiving the Abraham Declaration.

Boumediene v. Bush

542 U.S. 466 (2008)

Justice KENNEDY delivered the opinion of the Court.

Petitioners are aliens designated as enemy combatants and detained at the United States Naval Station at Guantanamo Bay, Cuba.

Petitioners present a question not resolved by our earlier cases relating to the detention of aliens at Guantanamo: whether they have the constitutional privilege of habeas corpus, a privilege not to be withdrawn except in conformance with the Suspension Clause, Art. I, §9, cl. 2. We hold these petitioners do have the habeas corpus privilege. Congress has enacted a statute, the Detainee Treatment Act of 2005 (DTA) that provides certain procedures for review of the detainees' status. We hold that those procedures are not an adequate and effective substitute for habeas corpus. Therefore §7 of the Military Commissions Act of 2006 (MCA) operates as an unconstitutional suspension of the writ.

I

Under the Authorization for Use of Military Force (AUMF), §2(a), the President is authorized "to use all necessary and appropriate force against those nations, organizations, or persons he determines planned, authorized, committed, or aided the terrorist attacks that occurred on September 11, 2001, or harbored such organizations or persons, in order to prevent any future acts of international terrorism against the United States by such nations, organizations or persons."

After *Hamdi*, the Deputy Secretary of Defense established Combatant Status Review Tribunals (CSRTs) to determine whether individuals detained at Guantanamo were "enemy combatants," as the Department defines that term. The Government maintains these procedures were designed to comply with the due process requirements identified by the plurality in *Hamdi*.

Interpreting the AUMF, the Department of Defense ordered the detention of these petitioners, and they were transferred to Guantanamo. Some of these individuals were apprehended on the battlefield in Afghanistan, others in places as far away from there as Bosnia and Gambia. All are foreign nationals, but none is a citizen of a nation now at war with the United States. Each denies he is a member of the al Qaeda terrorist network that carried out the September 11 attacks or of the Taliban regime that provided sanctuary for al Qaeda. Each petitioner appeared before a separate CSRT; was determined to be an enemy combatant; and has sought a writ of habeas corpus in the United States District Court for the District of Columbia.

After *Rasul*, petitioners' cases were consolidated and entertained in two separate proceedings.

While appeals were pending from the District Court decisions, Congress passed the DTA. Subsection (e) of §1005 of the DTA amended 28 U.S.C. §2241 to provide that "no court, justice, or judge shall have jurisdiction to hear or consider . . . an application for a writ of habeas corpus filed by or on behalf of an alien detained by the Department of Defense at Guantanamo Bay, Cuba." Section 1005 further provides that the Court of Appeals for the District of Columbia Circuit shall have "exclusive" jurisdiction to review decisions of the CSRTs.

In *Hamdan v. Rumsfeld* (2006), the Court held this provision did not apply to cases (like petitioners') pending when the DTA was enacted. Congress responded by passing the MCA, which again amended §2241. The text of the statutory amendment is discussed below.

Petitioners' cases were consolidated on appeal, and the parties filed supplemental briefs in light of our decision in *Hamdan*. The Court of Appeals' ruling, is the subject of our present review and today's decision.

The Court of Appeals concluded that MCA §7 must be read to strip from it, and all federal courts, jurisdiction to consider petitioners' habeas corpus applications; that petitioners are not entitled to the privilege of the writ or the protections of the Suspension Clause; and, as a result, that it was unnecessary to consider whether Congress provided an adequate and effective substitute for habeas corpus in the DTA.

II

As a threshold matter, we must decide whether MCA §7 denies the federal courts jurisdiction to hear habeas corpus actions pending at the time of its enactment. We hold the statute does deny that jurisdiction, so that, if the statute is valid, petitioners' cases must be dismissed.

As amended by the terms of the MCA, 28 U.S.C.A. §2241(e) now provides:

(1) No court, justice, or judge shall have jurisdiction to hear or consider an application for a writ of habeas corpus filed by or on behalf of an alien detained by the United States who has been determined by the United States to have been properly detained as an enemy combatant or is awaiting such determination.

(2) Except as provided in [§§1005(e)(2) and (e)(3) of the DTA] no court, justice, or judge shall have jurisdiction to hear or consider any other action against the United States or its agents relating to any aspect of the detention, transfer, treatment, trial, or conditions of confinement of an alien who is or was detained by the United States and has been determined by the United States to have been properly detained as an enemy combatant or is awaiting such determination.

Section 7(b) of the MCA provides the effective date for the amendment of §2241(e). It states:

The amendment made by [MCA §7(a)] shall take effect on the date of the enactment of this Act, and shall apply to all cases, without exception, pending on or after the date of the enactment of this Act which relate to any aspect of the detention, transfer, treatment, trial, or conditions of detention of an alien detained by the United States since September 11, 2001.

120 Stat. 2636.

There is little doubt that the effective date provision applies to habeas corpus actions. Those actions, by definition, are cases "which relate to . . . detention."

In *Hamdan* the Court found it unnecessary to address the petitioner's Suspension Clause arguments but noted the relevance of the clear statement rule in deciding whether Congress intended to reach pending habeas corpus cases. This interpretive rule facilitates a dialogue between Congress and the Court. If the Court invokes a clear statement rule to advise that certain statutory interpretations are favored in order to avoid constitutional difficulties, Congress can make an informed legislative choice either to amend the statute or to retain its existing text. If Congress amends, its intent must be respected even if a difficult constitutional question is presented.

If this ongoing dialogue between and among the branches of Government is to be respected, we cannot ignore that the MCA was a direct response to *Hamdan*'s holding that the DTA's jurisdiction-stripping provision had no application to pending cases. The Court of Appeals was correct . . . that the MCA deprives the federal courts of jurisdiction to entertain the habeas corpus actions now before us.

III

In deciding the constitutional questions now presented we must determine whether petitioners are barred from seeking the writ or invoking the protections of the Suspension Clause either because of their status, *i.e.*, petitioners' designation by the Executive Branch as enemy combatants, or their physical location, *i.e.*, their presence at Guantanamo Bay. The Government contends that noncitizens designated as enemy combatants and detained in territory located outside our Nation's borders have no constitutional rights and no privilege of habeas corpus. Petitioners contend they do have cognizable constitutional rights and that Congress, in seeking to eliminate recourse to habeas corpus as a means to assert those rights, acted in violation of the Suspension Clause.

We begin with a brief account of the history and origins of the writ. Our account proceeds from two propositions. First, protection for the privilege of habeas corpus was one of the few safeguards of liberty specified in a Constitution that, at the outset, had no Bill of Rights. In the system conceived by the Framers the writ had a centrality that must inform proper interpretation of the Suspension Clause. Second, to the extent there were settled precedents or legal commentaries in 1789 regarding the extraterritorial scope of the writ or its application to enemy aliens, those authorities can be instructive for the present cases.

A

The Framers viewed freedom from unlawful restraint as a fundamental precept of liberty, and they understood the writ of habeas corpus as a vital instrument to secure that freedom. Experience taught, however, that the common-law writ all too often had been insufficient to guard against the abuse of monarchical power. That history counseled the necessity for specific language in the Constitution to secure the writ and ensure its place in our legal system.

Magna Carta decreed that no man would be imprisoned contrary to the law of the land. ("No free man shall be taken or imprisoned or dispossessed, or outlawed, or banished, or in any way destroyed, nor will we go upon him, nor send upon him, except by the legal judgment of his peers or by the law of the land.") Important as the principle was, the Barons at Runnymede prescribed no specific legal process to enforce it. Holdsworth tells us, however, that gradually the writ of habeas corpus became the means by which the promise of Magna Carta was fulfilled. 9 W. Holdsworth, A History of English Law 112 (1926) (hereinafter Holdsworth).

The development was painstaking, even by the centuries-long measures of English constitutional history. . . . Over time it became clear that by issuing the writ of habeas corpus common-law courts sought to enforce the King's prerogative to inquire into the authority of a jailer to hold a prisoner. *See* M. Hale, Prerogatives of the King 229 (D. Yale ed. 1976); 2 J. Story, Commentaries on the Constitution of the United States §1341, p. 237 (3d ed. 1858) (noting that the writ ran "into all parts of the king's dominions; for it is said, that the king is entitled, at all times, to have an account, why the liberty of any of his subjects is restrained").

Even so, from an early date it was understood that the King, too, was subject to the law. As the writers said of Magna Carta, "it means this, that the king is and shall be below the law." 1 F. Pollock & F. Maitland, History of English Law 173 (2d ed. 1909); *see also* 2 Bracton On the Laws and Customs of England 33 (S. Thorne transl. 1968) ("The king must not be under man but under God and under the law, because law makes the king"). And, by the 1600's, the writ was deemed less an instrument of the King's power and more a restraint upon it.

Still, the writ proved to be an imperfect check. Even when the importance of the writ was well understood in England, habeas relief often was denied by the courts or suspended by Parliament. Denial or suspension occurred in times of political unrest, to the anguish of the imprisoned and the outrage of those in sympathy with them.

A notable example from this period was *Darnel's Case* (K.B. 1627). The events giving rise to the case began when, in a display of the Stuart penchant for authoritarian excess, Charles I demanded that Darnel and at least four others lend him money. Upon their refusal, they were imprisoned. The prisoners sought a writ of habeas corpus; and the King filed a return in the form of a warrant signed by the Attorney General. The court held this was a sufficient answer and justified the subjects' continued imprisonment.

There was an immediate outcry of protest. The House of Commons promptly passed the Petition of Right (1627), which condemned executive "imprison[ment] without any cause" shown, and declared that "no freeman in any such manner as is before mencioned [shall] be imprisoned or deteined." Yet a full legislative response was long delayed. The King soon began to abuse his authority again, and Parliament was dissolved. When Parliament reconvened in 1640, it sought to secure access to the writ by statute. The Act of 1640 expressly authorized use of the writ to test the legality of commitment by command or warrant of the King or the Privy Council. Civil strife and the Interregnum soon followed, and not until 1679 did Parliament try once more to secure the writ, this time through the Habeas Corpus Act of 1679. The Act, which later would be described by Blackstone as the "stable bulwark of our liberties," established procedures for issuing the writ; and it was the model upon which the habeas statutes of the 13 American Colonies were based.

This history was known to the Framers. It no doubt confirmed their view that pendular swings to and away from individual liberty were endemic to undivided, uncontrolled power. The Framers' inherent distrust of governmental power was the driving force behind the constitutional plan that allocated powers among three independent branches. This design serves not only to make Government accountable but also to secure individual liberty.

That the Framers considered the writ a vital instrument for the protection of individual liberty is evident from the care taken to specify the limited grounds for its suspension: "The Privilege of the Writ of Habeas Corpus shall not be suspended, unless when in Cases of Rebellion or Invasion the public Safety may require it." Art. I, §9, cl. 2.

Surviving accounts of the ratification debates provide additional evidence that the Framers deemed the writ to be an essential mechanism in the separation-of-powers scheme. In a critical exchange with Patrick Henry at the Virginia ratifying convention Edmund Randolph referred to the Suspension Clause as an "exception" to the "power given to Congress to regulate courts." *See* 3 Debates in the Several State Conventions on the Adoption of the Federal Constitution 460-464 (J. Elliot 2d ed. 1876). A resolution passed by the New York ratifying convention made clear its understanding that the Clause not only protects against arbitrary suspensions of the writ but also guarantees an affirmative right to judicial inquiry into the causes of detention. *See* Resolution of the New York Ratifying Convention (July 26, 1788), *in* 1 Elliot's Debates 328 (noting the convention's understanding "[t]hat every person restrained of his liberty is entitled to an inquiry into the lawfulness of such restraint, and to a removal thereof if unlawful; and that such inquiry or removal ought not to be denied or delayed, except when, on account of public danger, the Congress shall suspend the privilege of the writ of *habeas corpus*"). Alexander Hamilton likewise explained that by providing the detainee a judicial forum to challenge detention, the writ preserves limited government. As he explained in The Federalist No. 84:

> [T]he practice of arbitrary imprisonments, have been, in all ages, the favorite and most formidable instruments of tyranny. The observations of the judicious Blackstone . . . are well worthy of recital: "To bereave a man of life . . . or by violence to confiscate his estate, without accusation or trial, would be so gross and notorious an act of despotism as must at once convey the alarm of tyranny throughout the whole nation; but confinement of the person, by secretly hurrying him to jail, where his sufferings are unknown or forgotten, is a less public, a less striking, and therefore a *more dangerous engine* of arbitrary government." And as a remedy for this fatal evil he is everywhere peculiarly emphatical in his encomiums on the *habeas corpus* act, which in one place he calls "the BULWARK of the British Constitution."

In our own system the Suspension Clause is designed to protect against these cyclical abuses. The Clause protects the rights of the detained by a means consistent with the essential design of the Constitution. It ensures that, except during periods of formal suspension, the Judiciary will have a time-tested device, the writ, to maintain the "delicate balance of governance" that is itself the surest safeguard of liberty. The Clause protects the rights of the detained by affirming the duty and authority of the Judiciary to call the jailer to account. The separation-of-powers doctrine, and the history that influenced its design, therefore must inform the reach and purpose of the Suspension Clause.

B

The broad historical narrative of the writ and its function is central to our analysis, but we seek guidance as well from founding-era authorities addressing the specific question before us: whether foreign nationals, apprehended and detained in distant countries during a time of serious threats to our Nation's security, may assert the privilege of the writ and seek its protection. The Court has been careful not to foreclose the possibility that the protections of the Suspension Clause have expanded along with post-1789 developments that define the present scope of the writ. But the analysis may begin with precedents as of 1789, for the Court has said that "at the absolute minimum" the Clause protects the writ as it existed when the Constitution was drafted and ratified.

To support their arguments, the parties in these cases have examined historical sources to construct a view of the common-law writ as it existed in 1789 — as have *amici* whose expertise in legal history the Court has relied upon in the past. The Government argues the common-law writ ran only to those territories over which the Crown was sovereign. Petitioners argue that jurisdiction followed the King's officers. Diligent search by all parties reveals no certain conclusions. In none of the cases cited do we find that a common-law court would or would not have granted, or refused to hear for lack of jurisdiction, a petition for a writ of habeas corpus brought by a prisoner deemed an enemy combatant, under a standard like the one the Department of Defense has used in these cases, and when held in a territory, like Guantanamo, over which the Government has total military and civil control.

We know that at common law a petitioner's status as an alien was not a categorical bar to habeas corpus relief. *See, e.g., Sommersett's Case* (1772) (ordering an African slave freed upon finding the custodian's return insufficient); *see generally Khera v. Secretary of State for the Home Dep't* (1984) ("Habeas corpus protection is often expressed as limited to 'British subjects.' Is it really limited to British nationals? Suffice it to say that the case law has given an emphatic 'no' to the question"). We know as well that common-law courts entertained habeas petitions brought by enemy aliens detained in England.

To the extent these authorities suggest the common-law courts abstained altogether from matters involving prisoners of war, there was greater justification for doing so in the context of declared wars with other nation states. Judicial intervention might have complicated the military's ability to negotiate exchange of prisoners with the enemy, a wartime practice well known to the Framers.

We find the evidence as to the geographic scope of the writ at common law informative, but, again, not dispositive. Petitioners argue the site of their detention is analogous to two territories outside of England to which the writ did run: the so-called "exempt jurisdictions," like the Channel Islands; and (in former times) India. There are critical differences between these places and Guantanamo, however.

Because the United States does not maintain formal sovereignty over Guantanamo Bay, *see* Part IV, the naval station there and the exempt jurisdictions discussed in the English authorities are not similarly situated.

Petitioners and their *amici* further rely on cases in which British courts in India granted writs of habeas corpus to noncitizens detained in territory over which the Moghul Emperor retained formal sovereignty and control. The analogy to the present cases breaks down, however, because of the geographic location of the courts in the Indian example. The Supreme Court of Judicature (the British Court) sat in Calcutta; but no federal court sits at Guantanamo. The Supreme Court of Judicature was, moreover, a special court set up by Parliament to monitor certain conduct during the British Raj. That it had the power to issue the writ in nonsovereign territory does not prove that common-law courts sitting in England had the same power.

The Government argues, in turn, that Guantanamo is more closely analogous to Scotland and Hanover, territories that were not part of England but nonetheless controlled by the English monarch (in his separate capacities as King of Scotland and Elector of Hanover). Lord Mansfield can be cited for the proposition that, at the time of the founding, English courts lacked the "power" to issue the writ to Scotland and Hanover, territories Lord Mansfield referred to as "foreign." But what matters for our purposes is why common-law courts lacked this power. Given the English Crown's delicate and complicated relationships with Scotland and Hanover in the 1700's, we cannot disregard the possibility that the common-law courts' refusal to issue the writ to these places was motivated not by formal legal constructs but by what we would think of as prudential concerns. This appears to have been the case with regard to other British territories where the writ did not run.

Even after the Act of Union, Scotland (like Hanover) continued to maintain its own laws and court system. Under these circumstances prudential considerations would have weighed heavily when courts sitting in England received habeas petitions from Scotland or the Electorate. Common-law decisions withholding the writ from prisoners detained in these places easily could be explained as efforts to avoid either or both of two embarrassments: conflict with the judgments of another court of competent jurisdiction; or the practical inability, by reason of distance, of the English courts to enforce their judgments outside their territorial jurisdiction.

The prudential barriers that may have prevented the English courts from issuing the writ to Scotland and Hanover are not relevant here. We have no reason to believe an order from a federal court would be disobeyed at Guantanamo. No Cuban court has jurisdiction to hear these petitioners' claims, and no law other than the laws of the United States applies at the naval station. The modern-day relations between the United States and Guantanamo thus differ in important respects from the 18th-century relations between England and the kingdoms of Scotland and Hanover. This is reason enough for us to discount the relevance of the Government's analogy.

Recent scholarship points to the inherent shortcomings in the historical record. And given the unique status of Guantanamo Bay and the particular dangers of terrorism in the modern age, the common-law courts simply may not have confronted cases with close parallels to this one. We decline, therefore, to infer too much, one way or the other, from the lack of historical evidence on point.

IV

Drawing from its position that at common law the writ ran only to territories over which the Crown was sovereign, the Government says the Suspension Clause affords petitioners no rights because the United States does not claim sovereignty over the place of detention [and sovereignty is a political question].

Guantanamo Bay is not formally part of the United States. And under the terms of the lease between the United States and Cuba, Cuba retains "ultimate sovereignty" over the territory while the United States exercises "complete jurisdiction and control." Under the terms of the 1934 Treaty, however, Cuba effectively has no rights as a sovereign until the parties agree to modification of the 1903 Lease Agreement or the United States abandons the base.

The United States contends, nevertheless, that Guantanamo is not within its sovereign control.

We therefore do not question the Government's position that Cuba, not the United States, maintains sovereignty, in the legal and technical sense of the term, over Guantanamo Bay. But this does not end the analysis. Our cases do not hold it is improper for us to inquire into the objective degree of control the Nation asserts over foreign territory. As commentators have noted, "'[s]overeignty' is a term used in many senses and is much abused." Indeed, it is not altogether uncommon for a territory to be under the *de jure* sovereignty of one nation, while under the plenary control, or practical sovereignty, of another. This condition can occur when the territory is seized during war, as Guantanamo was during the Spanish-American War. *See, e.g., Fleming v. Page* (1850) (noting that the port of Tampico, conquered by the United States during the war with Mexico, was "undoubtedly . . . subject to the sovereignty and dominion of the United States," but that it "does not follow that it was a part of the United States, or that it ceased to be a foreign country"); *King v. Earl of Crewe ex parte Sekgome* (1910) (opinion of Williams, L.J.) (arguing that the Bechuanaland Protectorate in South Africa was "under His Majesty's dominion in the sense of power and jurisdiction, but is not under his dominion in the sense of territorial dominion"). Accordingly, for purposes of our analysis, we accept the Government's position that Cuba, and not the United States, retains *de jure* sovereignty over Guantanamo Bay. As we did in *Rasul*, however, we take notice of the obvious and uncontested fact that the United States, by virtue of its complete jurisdiction and control over the base, maintains *de facto* sovereignty over this territory.

A

The Court has discussed the issue of the Constitution's extraterritorial application on many occasions. These decisions undermine the Government's argument that, at least as applied to noncitizens, the Constitution necessarily stops where *de jure* sovereignty ends.

The Framers foresaw that the United States would expand and acquire new territories. In particular, there was no need to test the limits of the Suspension Clause because, as early as 1789, Congress extended the writ to the Territories. *See* Act of Aug. 7, 1789, 1 Stat. 52 (reaffirming Art. II of Northwest Ordinance of 1787, which provided that "[t]he inhabitants of the said territory, shall always be entitled to the benefits of the writ of habeas corpus").

Fundamental questions regarding the Constitution's geographic scope first arose at the dawn of the 20th century when the Nation acquired noncontiguous Territories: Puerto Rico, Guam, and the Philippines—ceded to the United States by Spain at the conclusion of the Spanish-American War—and Hawaii—annexed by the United States in 1898. At this point Congress chose to discontinue its previous practice of extending constitutional rights to the territories by statute.

In a series of opinions later known as the Insular Cases, the Court addressed whether the Constitution, by its own force, applies in any territory that is not a State. The Court held that the Constitution has independent force in these territories, a force not contingent upon acts of legislative grace. Yet it took note of the difficulties inherent in that position.

Prior to their cession to the United States, the former Spanish colonies operated under a civil-law system, without experience in the various aspects of the Anglo-American legal tradition, for instance the use of grand and petit juries. At least with regard to the Philippines, a complete transformation of the prevailing legal culture would have been not only disruptive but also unnecessary, as the United States intended to grant independence to that Territory. The Court thus was reluctant to risk the uncertainty and instability that could result from a rule that displaced altogether the existing legal systems in these newly acquired Territories.

These considerations resulted in the doctrine of territorial incorporation, under which the Constitution applies in full in incorporated Territories surely destined for statehood but only in part in unincorporated Territories. But, as early as *Balzac* in 1922, the Court took for granted that even in unincorporated Territories the Government of the United States was bound to provide to noncitizen inhabitants "guaranties of certain fundamental personal rights declared in the Constitution." This century-old doctrine informs our analysis in the present matter.

Practical considerations likewise influenced the Court's analysis a half-century later in *Reid v. Covert* (1957). The petitioners there, spouses of American servicemen, lived on American military bases in England and Japan. They were charged with crimes committed in those countries and tried before military courts, consistent with executive agreements the United States had entered into with the British and Japanese governments. Because the petitioners were not themselves military personnel, they argued they were entitled to trial by jury.

That the petitioners in *Reid* were American citizens was a key factor in the case and was central to the plurality's conclusion that the Fifth and Sixth Amendments apply to American civilians tried outside the United States. But practical considerations, related not to the petitioners' citizenship but to the place of their confinement and trial, were relevant to each Member of the *Reid* majority. And to Justices Harlan and Frankfurter (whose votes were necessary to the Court's disposition) these considerations were the decisive factors in the case.

Indeed the majority splintered on this very point. The key disagreement between the plurality and the concurring Justices in *Reid* was over the continued precedential value of the Court's previous opinion in *In re Ross* (1891), which the *Reid* Court understood as holding that under some circumstances Americans abroad have no right to indictment and trial by jury. The petitioner in *Ross* was a sailor serving on an American merchant vessel in Japanese waters who was tried before an American consular tribunal for the murder of a fellow crewman. The *Ross* Court held that the petitioner, who was a British subject, had no rights under the Fifth and Sixth Amendments. The petitioner's citizenship played no role in the disposition of the case, however. The Court assumed (consistent with the maritime custom of the time) that Ross had all the rights of a similarly situated American citizen.

The *Reid* concurring Justices distinguished *Ross* from the cases before them, not on the basis of the citizenship of the petitioners, but on practical considerations that made jury trial a more feasible option for them than it was for the petitioner in *Ross*. If citizenship had been the only relevant factor in the case, it would have been necessary for the Court to overturn *Ross*, something Justices Harlan and Frankfurter were unwilling to do.

Practical considerations weighed heavily as well in *Johnson v. Eisentrager* (1950), where the Court addressed whether habeas corpus jurisdiction extended to enemy aliens who had been convicted of violating the laws of war. The prisoners were detained at Landsberg Prison in Germany during the Allied Powers' postwar occupation. The Court stressed the difficulties of ordering the Government to produce the prisoners in a habeas corpus proceeding.

True, the Court in *Eisentrager* denied access to the writ, and it noted the prisoners "at no relevant time were within any territory over which the United States is sovereign, and [that] the scenes of their offense, their capture, their trial and their punishment were all beyond the territorial jurisdiction of any court of the United States." The Government seizes upon this language as proof positive that the *Eisentrager* Court adopted a formalistic, sovereignty-based test for determining the reach of the Suspension Clause. We reject this reading for three reasons.

First practical considerations were integral to Part II of its opinion.

Second, [e]ven if we assume the *Eisentrager* Court considered the United States' lack of formal legal sovereignty over Landsberg Prison as the decisive factor in that case, its holding is not inconsistent with a functional approach to questions of extraterritoriality. The formal legal status of a given territory affects, at least to some extent, the political branches' control over that territory. *De jure* sovereignty is a factor that bears upon which constitutional guarantees apply there.

Third, if the Government's reading of *Eisentrager* were correct, the opinion would have marked not only a change in, but a complete repudiation of, the *Insular Cases'* (and later *Reid's*) functional approach to questions of extraterritoriality. We cannot accept the Government's view. Our cases need not be read to conflict in this manner. A constricted reading of *Eisentrager* overlooks what we see as a common thread uniting the *Insular Cases, Eisentrager,* and *Reid*: the idea that questions of extraterritoriality turn on objective factors and practical concerns, not formalism.

B

The Government's formal sovereignty-based test raises troubling separation-of-powers concerns as well. The political history of Guantanamo illustrates the

deficiencies of this approach. The United States has maintained complete and unin-
terrupted control of the bay for over 100 years. At the close of the Spanish-American
War, Spain ceded control over the entire island of Cuba to the United States and
specifically "relinquishe[d] all claim[s] of sovereignty . . . and title." . . . The necessary implication of the argument is that by surrendering formal sovereignty over
any unincorporated territory to a third party, while at the same time entering into a
lease that grants total control over the territory back to the United States, it would
be possible for the political branches to govern without legal constraint.

Our basic charter cannot be contracted away like this. The Constitution grants
Congress and the President the power to acquire, dispose of, and govern territory,
not the power to decide when and where its terms apply. Even when the United
States acts outside its borders, its powers are not "absolute and unlimited" but
are subject "to such restrictions as are expressed in the Constitution." *Murphy v.
Ramsey* (1885). Abstaining from questions involving formal sovereignty and territorial governance is one thing. To hold the political branches have the power
to switch the Constitution on or off at will is quite another. The former position
reflects this Court's recognition that certain matters requiring political judgments
are best left to the political branches. The latter would permit a striking anomaly in
our tripartite system of government, leading to a regime in which Congress and the
President, not this Court, say "what the law is." *Marbury v. Madison* (1803).

These concerns have particular bearing upon the Suspension Clause question
in the cases now before us, for the writ of habeas corpus is itself an indispensable
mechanism for monitoring the separation of powers. The test for determining the
scope of this provision must not be subject to manipulation by those whose power
it is designed to restrain.

C

[T]he outlines of a framework for determining the reach of the Suspension
Clause are suggested by the factors the Court relied upon in *Eisentrager*. In addition
to the practical concerns discussed above, the *Eisentrager* Court found relevant that
each petitioner:

> (a) is an enemy alien; (b) has never been or resided in the United States;
> (c) was captured outside of our territory and there held in military cus-
> tody as a prisoner of war; (d) was tried and convicted by a Military Com-
> mission sitting outside the United States; (e) for offenses against laws of
> war committed outside the United States; (f) and is at all times impris-
> oned outside the United States.

Based on this language from *Eisentrager*, and the reasoning in our other extraterritoriality opinions, we conclude that at least three factors are relevant in determining the reach of the Suspension Clause: (1) the citizenship and status of the
detainee and the adequacy of the process through which that status determination
was made; (2) the nature of the sites where apprehension and then detention took
place; and (3) the practical obstacles inherent in resolving the prisoner's entitlement to the writ.

Applying this framework, we note at the onset that the status of these detainees
is a matter of dispute. The petitioners, like those in *Eisentrager*, are not American

citizens. But the petitioners in *Eisentrager* did not contest, it seems, the Court's assertion that they were "enemy alien[s]." *Ibid.* In the instant cases, by contrast, the detainees deny they are enemy combatants. They have been afforded some process in CSRT proceedings to determine their status; but, unlike in *Eisentrager*, there has been no trial by military commission for violations of the laws of war. The difference is not trivial. The records from the *Eisentrager* trials suggest that, well before the petitioners brought their case to this Court, there had been a rigorous adversarial process to test the legality of their detention. The *Eisentrager* petitioners were charged by a bill of particulars that made detailed factual allegations against them. To rebut the accusations, they were entitled to representation by counsel, allowed to introduce evidence on their own behalf, and permitted to cross-examine the prosecution's witnesses.

In comparison the procedural protections afforded to the detainees in the CSRT hearings are far more limited, and, we conclude, fall well short of the procedures and adversarial mechanisms that would eliminate the need for habeas corpus review. Although the detainee is assigned a "Personal Representative" to assist him during CSRT proceedings, the Secretary of the Navy's memorandum makes clear that person is not the detainee's lawyer or even his "advocate." The Government's evidence is accorded a presumption of validity. The detainee is allowed to present "reasonably available" evidence, but his ability to rebut the Government's evidence against him is limited by the circumstances of his confinement and his lack of counsel at this stage. And although the detainee can seek review of his status determination in the Court of Appeals, that review process cannot cure all defects in the earlier proceedings.

As to the second factor relevant to this analysis, the detainees here are similarly situated to the *Eisentrager* petitioners in that the sites of their apprehension and detention are technically outside the sovereign territory of the United States. As noted earlier, this is a factor that weighs against finding they have rights under the Suspension Clause. But there are critical differences between Landsberg Prison, circa 1950, and the United States Naval Station at Guantanamo Bay in 2008. Unlike its present control over the naval station, the United States' control over the prison in Germany was neither absolute nor indefinite. Like all parts of occupied Germany, the prison was under the jurisdiction of the combined Allied Forces. The United States was therefore answerable to its Allies for all activities occurring there. *Cf. Hirota v. MacArthur* (1948) *(per curiam)* (military tribunal set up by Gen. Douglas MacArthur, acting as "the agent of the Allied Powers," was not a "tribunal of the United States"). The Allies had not planned a long-term occupation of Germany, nor did they intend to displace all German institutions even during the period of occupation. . . . Guantanamo Bay, on the other hand, is no transient possession. In every practical sense Guantanamo is not abroad; it is within the constant jurisdiction of the United States.

As to the third factor, we recognize, as the Court did in *Eisentrager*, that there are costs to holding the Suspension Clause applicable in a case of military detention abroad. Habeas corpus proceedings may require expenditure of funds by the Government and may divert the attention of military personnel from other pressing tasks. While we are sensitive to these concerns, we do not find them dispositive. Compliance with any judicial process requires some incremental expenditure of resources. Yet civilian courts and the Armed Forces have functioned along side each other at various points in our history. The Government presents no credible arguments that the military mission at Guantanamo would be compromised if habeas corpus courts had jurisdiction to hear the detainees' claims. And in light of the plenary control the United States asserts over the base, none are apparent to us.

The situation in *Eisentrager* was far different, given the historical context and nature of the military's mission in post-War Germany. When hostilities in the European Theater came to an end, the United States became responsible for an occupation zone encompassing over 57,000 square miles with a population of 18 million. . . . In retrospect the post-War occupation may seem uneventful. But at the time *Eisentrager* was decided, the Court was right to be concerned about judicial interference with the military's efforts to contain "enemy elements, guerilla fighters, and 'were-wolves.'"

Similar threats are not apparent here; nor does the Government argue that they are. The United States Naval Station at Guantanamo Bay consists of 45 square miles of land and water. The base has been used, at various points, to house migrants and refugees temporarily. At present, however, other than the detainees themselves, the only long-term residents are American military personnel, their families, and a small number of workers.

It is true that before today the Court has never held that noncitizens detained by our Government in territory over which another country maintains *de jure* sovereignty have any rights under our Constitution. But the cases before us lack any precise historical parallel.

We hold that Art. I, §9, cl. 2, of the Constitution has full effect at Guantanamo Bay. If the privilege of habeas corpus is to be denied to the detainees now before us, Congress must act in accordance with the requirements of the Suspension Clause. This Court may not impose a *de facto* suspension by abstaining from these controversies. The MCA does not purport to be a formal suspension of the writ; and the Government, in its submissions to us, has not argued that it is. Petitioners, therefore, are entitled to the privilege of habeas corpus to challenge the legality of their detention.

V

In light of this holding the question becomes whether the statute stripping jurisdiction to issue the writ avoids the Suspension Clause mandate because Congress has provided adequate substitute procedures for habeas corpus. The Government submits there has been compliance with the Suspension Clause because the DTA review process in the Court of Appeals, *see* DTA §1005(e), provides an adequate substitute. Congress has granted that court jurisdiction to consider

> (i) whether the status determination of the [CSRT] . . . was consistent with the standards and procedures specified by the Secretary of Defense . . . and (ii) to the extent the Constitution and laws of the United States are applicable, whether the use of such standards and procedures to make the determination is consistent with the Constitution and laws of the United States.

§1005(e)(2)(C).

A

The two leading cases addressing habeas substitutes, *Swain v. Pressley* (1977), and *United States v. Hayman* (1952), likewise provide little guidance here. The statutes at issue were attempts to streamline habeas corpus relief, not to cut it back.

The statute discussed in *Hayman* was 28 U.S.C. §2255. It replaced traditional habeas corpus for federal prisoners (at least in the first instance) with a process that allowed the prisoner to file a motion with the sentencing court [rather than the court with jurisdiction over the prisoner].

The statute in *Swain* applied to prisoners in custody under sentence of the Superior Court of the District of Columbia. . . . The Act, which was patterned on §2255, substituted a new collateral process in the Superior Court for the pre-existing habeas corpus procedure in the District Court. But, again, the purpose and effect of the statute was to expedite consideration of the prisoner's claims, not to delay or frustrate it.

In both cases the statute at issue had a saving clause, providing that a writ of habeas corpus would be available if the alternative process proved inadequate or ineffective. The Court placed explicit reliance upon these provisions in upholding the statutes against constitutional challenges.

Unlike in *Hayman* and *Swain*, here we confront statutes, the DTA and the MCA, that were intended to circumscribe habeas review.

The differences between the DTA and the habeas statute that would govern in MCA §7's absence are likewise telling. In §2241 (2000 ed.) Congress confirmed the authority of "any justice" or "circuit judge" to issue the writ. That statute accommodates the necessity for factfinding that will arise in some cases by allowing the appellate judge or Justice to transfer the case to a district court of competent jurisdiction, whose institutional capacity for factfinding is superior to his or her own. *See* 28 U.S.C. §2241(b). By granting the Court of Appeals "exclusive" jurisdiction over petitioners' cases, *see* DTA §1005(e)(2)(A), Congress has foreclosed that option. This choice indicates Congress intended the Court of Appeals to have a more limited role in enemy combatant status determinations than a district court has in habeas corpus proceedings.

B

We do not endeavor to offer a comprehensive summary of the requisites for an adequate substitute for habeas corpus. We do consider it uncontroversial, however, that the privilege of habeas corpus entitles the prisoner to a meaningful opportunity to demonstrate that he is being held pursuant to "the erroneous application or interpretation" of relevant law. *St. Cyr.* And the habeas court must have the power to order the conditional release of an individual unlawfully detained — though release need not be the exclusive remedy and is not the appropriate one in every case in which the writ is granted. *See Ex parte Bollman* (1807) (where imprisonment is unlawful, the court "can only direct [the prisoner] to be discharged"). . . . These are the easily identified attributes of any constitutionally adequate habeas corpus proceeding. But, depending on the circumstances, more may be required.

Indeed, common-law habeas corpus was, above all, an adaptable remedy. Its precise application and scope changed depending upon the circumstances.

See 3 Blackstone *131 (describing habeas as "the great and efficacious writ, in all manner of illegal confinement"); *see also Schlup v. Delo* (1995) (Habeas "is, at its core, an equitable remedy"); *Jones v. Cunningham* (1963) (Habeas is not "a static, narrow, formalistic remedy; its scope has grown to achieve its grand purpose"). It appears the common-law habeas court's role was most extensive in cases of pretrial and noncriminal detention, where there had been little or no previous judicial review of the cause for detention. Notably, the black-letter rule that prisoners could not controvert facts in the jailer's return was not followed (or at least not with consistency) in such cases.

There is evidence from 19th-century American sources indicating that, even in States that accorded strong res judicata effect to prior adjudications, habeas courts in this country routinely allowed prisoners to introduce exculpatory evidence that was either unknown or previously unavailable to the prisoner. Justice McLean, on Circuit in 1855, expressed his view that a habeas court should consider a prior judgment conclusive "where there was clearly jurisdiction and a full and fair hearing; but that it might not be so considered when any of these requisites were wanting." To illustrate the circumstances in which the prior adjudication did not bind the habeas court, he gave the example of a case in which "[s]everal unimpeached witnesses" provided new evidence to exculpate the prisoner.

The idea that the necessary scope of habeas review in part depends upon the rigor of any earlier proceedings accords with our test for procedural adequacy in the due process context. *See Mathews v. Eldridge* (1976) (noting that the Due Process Clause requires an assessment of, *inter alia*, "the risk of an erroneous deprivation of [a liberty interest;] and the probable value, if any, of additional or substitute procedural safeguards"). This principle has an established foundation in habeas corpus jurisprudence as well, as Chief Justice Marshall's opinion in *Ex parte Watkins* (1830), demonstrates. Like the petitioner in *Swain*, Watkins sought a writ of habeas corpus after being imprisoned pursuant to a judgment of a District of Columbia court. In holding that the judgment stood on "high ground," the Chief Justice emphasized the character of the court that rendered the original judgment, noting it was a "court of record, having general jurisdiction over criminal cases." In contrast to "inferior" tribunals of limited jurisdiction, courts of record had broad remedial powers, which gave the habeas court greater confidence in the judgment's validity.

Accordingly, where relief is sought from a sentence that resulted from the judgment of a court of record, as was the case in *Watkins* and indeed in most federal habeas cases, considerable deference is owed to the court that ordered confinement. *See Brown v. Allen* (1953) (opinion of Frankfurter, J.) (noting that a federal habeas court should accept a state court's factual findings unless "a vital flaw be found in the process of ascertaining such facts in the State court"). . . . The present cases fall outside these categories, however; for here the detention is by executive order.

In this context the need for habeas corpus is more urgent. The intended duration of the detention and the reasons for it bear upon the precise scope of the inquiry. Habeas corpus proceedings need not resemble a criminal trial, even when the detention is by executive order. But the writ must be effective. The habeas court must have sufficient authority to conduct a meaningful review of both the cause for detention and the Executive's power to detain.

To determine the necessary scope of habeas corpus review, therefore, we must assess the CSRT process, the mechanism through which petitioners' designation as enemy combatants became final.

Petitioners identify what they see as myriad deficiencies in the CSRTs. The most relevant for our purposes are the constraints upon the detainee's ability to rebut the factual basis for the Government's assertion that he is an enemy combatant. As already noted, at the CSRT stage the detainee has limited means to find or present evidence to challenge the Government's case against him. He does not have the assistance of counsel and may not be aware of the most critical allegations that the Government relied upon to order his detention. But given that there are in effect no limits on the admission of hearsay evidence — the only requirement is that the tribunal deem the evidence "relevant and helpful," the detainee's opportunity to question witnesses is likely to be more theoretical than real.

The Government defends the CSRT process, arguing that it was designed to conform to the procedures suggested by the plurality in *Hamdi.* Setting aside the fact that the relevant language in *Hamdi* did not garner a majority of the Court, it does not control the matter at hand. None of the parties in *Hamdi* argued there had been a suspension of the writ. Nor could they. The §2241 habeas corpus process remained in place. Accordingly, the plurality concentrated on whether the Executive had the authority to detain and, if so, what rights the detainee had under the Due Process Clause. True, there are places in the *Hamdi* plurality opinion where it is difficult to tell where its extrapolation of §2241 ends and its analysis of the petitioner's Due Process rights begins. But the Court had no occasion to define the necessary scope of habeas review, for Suspension Clause purposes, in the context of enemy combatant detentions.

Even if we were to assume that the CSRTs satisfy due process standards, it would not end our inquiry. Habeas corpus is a collateral process that exists, in Justice Holmes' words, to "cu[t] through all forms and g[o] to the very tissue of the structure. It comes in from the outside, not in subordination to the proceedings, and although every form may have been preserved opens the inquiry whether they have been more than an empty shell." *Frank v. Mangum* (1915) (dissenting opinion). Even when the procedures authorizing detention are structurally sound, the Suspension Clause remains applicable and the writ relevant. *See* 2 Chambers, Course of Lectures on English Law 1767-1773 ("Liberty may be violated either by arbitrary *imprisonment* without law or the appearance of law, or by a lawful magistrate for an unlawful reason"). This is so, as *Hayman* and *Swain* make clear, even where the prisoner is detained after a criminal trial conducted in full accordance with the protections of the Bill of Rights. Were this not the case, there would have been no reason for the Court to inquire into the adequacy of substitute habeas procedures in *Hayman* and *Swain.*

Although we make no judgment as to whether the CSRTs, as currently constituted, satisfy due process standards, we agree with petitioners that, even when all the parties involved in this process act with diligence and in good faith, there is considerable risk of error in the tribunal's findings of fact. This is a risk inherent in any process that, in the words of the former Chief Judge of the Court of Appeals, is "closed and accusatorial." And given that the consequence of error may be detention of persons for the duration of hostilities that may last a generation or more, this is a risk too significant to ignore.

For the writ of habeas corpus, or its substitute, to function as an effective and proper remedy in this context, the court that conducts the habeas proceeding must have the means to correct errors that occurred during the CSRT proceedings. This includes some authority to assess the sufficiency of the Government's evidence against the detainee. It also must have the authority to admit and consider relevant exculpatory evidence that was not introduced during the earlier proceeding. Federal habeas petitioners long have had the means to supplement the record on review, even in the postconviction habeas setting. Here that opportunity is constitutionally required.

Consistent with the historic function and province of the writ, habeas corpus review may be more circumscribed if the underlying detention proceedings are more thorough than they were here. In two habeas cases involving enemy aliens tried for war crimes, *In re Yamashita* (1946), and *Ex parte Quirin* (1942), for example, this Court limited its review to determining whether the Executive had legal authority to try the petitioners by military commission.

The extent of the showing required of the Government in these cases is a matter to be determined. We need not explore it further at this stage. We do hold that when the judicial power to issue habeas corpus properly is invoked the judicial officer must have adequate authority to make a determination in light of the relevant law and facts and to formulate and issue appropriate orders for relief, including, if necessary, an order directing the prisoner's release.

C

We now consider whether the DTA allows the Court of Appeals to conduct a proceeding meeting these standards.

The DTA does not explicitly empower the Court of Appeals to order the applicant in a DTA review proceeding released should the court find that the standards and procedures used at his CSRT hearing were insufficient to justify detention. This is troubling. Yet, for present purposes, we can assume congressional silence permits a constitutionally required remedy. In that case it would be possible to hold that a remedy of release is impliedly provided for. The DTA might be read, furthermore, to allow the petitioners to assert most, if not all, of the legal claims they seek to advance, including their most basic claim: that the President has no authority under the AUMF to detain them indefinitely. (Whether the President has such authority turns on whether the AUMF authorizes—and the Constitution permits—the indefinite detention of "enemy combatants" as the Department of Defense defines that term. Thus a challenge to the President's authority to detain is, in essence, a challenge to the Department's definition of enemy combatant, a "standard" used by the CSRTs in petitioners' cases.)

The absence of a release remedy and specific language allowing AUMF challenges are not the only constitutional infirmities from which the statute potentially suffers, however. The more difficult question is whether the DTA permits the Court of Appeals to make requisite findings of fact.

Assuming the DTA can be construed to allow the Court of Appeals to review or correct the CSRT's factual determinations, as opposed to merely certifying that the tribunal applied the correct standard of proof, we see no way to construe the statute to allow what is also constitutionally required in this context: an opportunity for the detainee to present relevant exculpatory evidence that was not made part of the record in the earlier proceedings.

On its face the statute allows the Court of Appeals to consider no evidence outside the CSRT record. . . . For present purposes, however, we can assume that the Court of Appeals was correct that the DTA allows introduction and consideration of relevant exculpatory evidence that was "reasonably available" to the Government at the time of the CSRT but not made part of the record. Even so, the DTA review proceeding falls short of being a constitutionally adequate substitute, for the detainee still would have no opportunity to present evidence discovered after the CSRT proceedings concluded.

This evidence, however, may be critical to the detainee's argument that he is not an enemy combatant and there is no cause to detain him.

This is not a remote hypothetical. One of the petitioners, Mohamed Nechla, requested at his CSRT hearing that the Government contact his employer. The petitioner claimed the employer would corroborate Nechla's contention he had no affiliation with al Qaeda. Although the CSRT determined this testimony would be relevant, it also found the witness was not reasonably available to testify at the time of the hearing. Petitioner's counsel, however, now represents the witness is available to be heard. If a detainee can present reasonably available evidence demonstrating there is no basis for his continued detention, he must have the opportunity to present this evidence to a habeas corpus court. Even under the Court of Appeals' generous construction of the DTA, however, the evidence identified by Nechla would be inadmissible in a DTA review proceeding. The role of an Article III court in the exercise of its habeas corpus function cannot be circumscribed in this manner.

By foreclosing consideration of evidence not presented or reasonably available to the detainee at the CSRT proceedings, the DTA disadvantages the detainee by limiting the scope of collateral review to a record that may not be accurate or complete. In other contexts, *e.g.*, in post-trial habeas cases where the prisoner already has had a full and fair opportunity to develop the factual predicate of his claims, similar limitations on the scope of habeas review may be appropriate. *See Williams v. Taylor* (2000) (noting that §2254 "does not equate prisoners who exercise diligence in pursuing their claims with those who do not"). In this context, however, where the underlying detention proceedings lack the necessary adversarial character, the detainee cannot be held responsible for all deficiencies in the record.

The Government does not make the alternative argument that the DTA allows for the introduction of previously unavailable exculpatory evidence on appeal. It does point out, however, that if a detainee obtains such evidence, he can request that the Deputy Secretary of Defense convene a new CSRT. Whatever the merits of this procedure, it is an insufficient replacement for the factual review these detainees are entitled to receive through habeas corpus. The Deputy Secretary's determination whether to initiate new proceedings is wholly a discretionary one. And we see no way to construe the DTA to allow a detainee to challenge the Deputy Secretary's decision not to open a new CSRT pursuant to Instruction 5421.1. . . . DTA §1005(e)(2)(A), further narrows the Court of Appeals' jurisdiction to reviewing "any final decision of a Combatant Status Review Tribunal that an alien is properly detained as an enemy combatant." The Deputy Secretary's determination whether to convene a new CSRT is not a "status determination of the Combatant Status Review Tribunal," much less a "final decision" of that body.

To hold that the detainees at Guantanamo may, under the DTA, challenge the President's legal authority to detain them, contest the CSRT's findings of fact, supplement the record on review with exculpatory evidence, and request an order of release would come close to reinstating the §2241 habeas corpus process Congress sought to deny them. The language of the statute, read in light of Congress' reasons for enacting it, cannot bear this interpretation. Petitioners have met their burden of establishing that the DTA review process is, on its face, an inadequate substitute for habeas corpus.

Although we do not hold that an adequate substitute must duplicate §2241 in all respects, it suffices that the Government has not established that the detainees' access to the statutory review provisions at issue is an adequate substitute for the writ of habeas corpus. MCA §7 thus effects an unconstitutional suspension of the writ. In view of our holding we need not discuss the reach of the writ with respect to claims of unlawful conditions of treatment or confinement. . . .

That is a matter yet to be determined. We hold that petitioners may invoke the fundamental procedural protections of habeas corpus. The laws and Constitution are designed to survive, and remain in force, in extraordinary times. Liberty and security can be reconciled; and in our system they are reconciled within the framework of the law. The Framers decided that habeas corpus, a right of first importance, must be a part of that framework, a part of that law.

[Chief Justice ROBERTS, joined by Justices SCALIA, THOMAS and ALITO dissented, lamenting that:

> [t]he Court today strikes down as inadequate the most generous set of procedural protection ever afforded aliens detained by this country as enemy combatants . . . without bothering to say what due process rights the detainees possess. . . . . And to what effect? The majority merely replaces a review system defined by the people's representatives [following the plurality's guidance in *Hamdi*] with a set of shapeless procedures to be defined by federal courts at some future date. . . . [All without] wait[ing] to see whether [the DTA process of D.C. Circuit Court review] will prove sufficient to protect petitioners' rights.

Regarding the limitations on evidence in CSRT's, Roberts emphasized the national security implications of allowing unfettered access to intelligence gathered to support enemy combatant determinations.

> What alternative does the Court propose? Allow free access to classified information and ignore the risk the prisoner may eventually convey what he learns to parties hostile to this country, with deadly consequences for those who helped apprehend the detainee? If the Court can design a better system . . . without fatally compromising national security interests and sources, the majority should come forward with it. Instead, the majority fobs that vexing question off on district courts to answer down the road.

And the Chief Justice challenged the majority's conclusion that new, exculpatory evidence could not be considered, noting that the Court of Appeals could "remand the case to the tribunal to allow that body to consider the evidence in the first instance. The Court of Appeals could later review any new or reinstated decision in light of the supplemental record.

DOD regulations, he noted, also provide for annual review of the status of each prisoner.]

[Justice SCALIA, joined by The CHIEF JUSTICE and Justices THOMAS and ALITO, dissented on the ground that the writ "does not, and never has, run in favor of aliens abroad; the Suspension Clause thus has no application, and the Court's intervention in this military matter is entirely ultra vires." He stressed that:

[a]t least 30 of those prisoners hitherto released from Guantanamo Bay have returned to the battlefield" and some have "succeeded in carrying on their atrocities against innocent civilians. In one case, a detainee released from Guantanamo Bay masterminded the kidnapping of two Chinese dam workers, one of whom was later shot to death when used as a human shield against Pakistani commandoes. Another former detainee promptly resumed his post as a senior Taliban commander and murdered a United Nations engineer and three Afghan soldiers. Still another murdered an Afghan judge. It was reported only last month that a released detainee carried out a suicide bombing against Iraqi soldiers in Mosul, Iraq. These, mind you, were detainees whom the military concluded were not enemy combatants. Their return to the kill illustrates the incredible difficulty of assessing who is and who is not an enemy combatant in a foreign theater of operations where the environment does not lend itself to rigorous evidence collection. Astoundingly, the Court today raises the bar.

With respect to the Suspension Clause, Justice Scalia insisted that ambiguity about the geographic scope of the writ at common law "when that Clause was written" required denial of relief here because "the Constitution could not possibly extend farther than the common law provided" at the founding.]

[Justice SOUTER concurred in the majority opinion, writing separately to emphasize, *contra* the dissents, that the Court's holding was not *sui generis* in light of *Rasul*, which emphasized "the historical reach of the writ" in interpreting §2241.]

* * *

Studies of conditions of detention and interrogation in Afghanistan prior to transfer to Guantanamo have identified evidence of "beatings, stress positions, prolonged hanging by the arms, sleep deprivation, intimidation, and being terrorized with dogs" in addition to violation of "fundamental cultural and religious taboos" and "interference with religious practice" in "contravention of international guidelines for the humane treatment of detainees. In Guantanamo camp procedures were designed to support the work of interrogators" and included "short-shackling, stress positions, prolonged isolation, and exposure to extreme temperatures for extended periods—often simultaneously . . . [and] in conjunction with sensory bombardment," and other physical abuse rising to the level of "torture, and cruel and inhuman treatment."[35] A 2014 Senate Intelligence Committee that reviewed classified files concluded that the use of "enhanced interrogation techniques was not an effective means

---

35. LAUREL E. FLETCHER ET AL., GUANTANAMO AND ITS AFTERMATH: U.S. DETENTION AND INTERROGATION PRACTICES AND THEIR IMPACT ON FORMER DETAINEES 1, 9, 76-77 (2008).

of obtaining accurate information or gaining detainee cooperation," often resulting in information being "fabricated."[36]

Justice Scalia is correct that some detainees released from Guantanamo returned to the battlefield. A Report of the Office of the Director of National Intelligence found that this was true of about 18 percent of released detainees (135 of 730; 121 released by the Bush administration; 14 under the Obama administration).[37] A little fewer than half of these people were subsequently either recaptured or killed. An additional 13 percent are suspected of returning to the battlefield.

The effect of *Boumediene* was to displace the CSRT/D.C. Circuit appeal process with habeas litigation under §2241 in the first instance in the U.S. District Court for the District of Columbia. A 2012 study found that the grant rate in the D.C. district court for the first two years after *Boumediene* was 59 percent.[38] That changed when the D.C. Circuit Court decided *Al-Adahi v. Obama* (D.C. Cir. 2010). In *Al-Adahi* the D.C. Circuit reversed the district court's grant of a habeas petition for failing to take into account the "conditional probability" that any one potentially inculpating fact increases the probability of guilt by a preponderance of the evidence when weighed in relation to other potentially inculpating facts. Thus, according to the D.C. Circuit, "if a particular fact does not itself prove the ultimate proposition (e.g., whether a detainee was part of al-Qaida), the fact [may not] be tossed aside and the next fact . . . evaluated as if the first did not exist." Attendance at an al-Qaida training camp or guesthouse, the court emphasized, "would seem to overwhelmingly, if not definitively, justify detention." The court also assumed without deciding that the government need only meet a preponderance of the evidence standard, emphasizing that a lower threshold of "some evidence" is the standard in immigration deportation and other settings. *See also Al-Bihani v. Obama* (D.C. Cir. 2010) (allowing hearsay evidence).

After *Al-Adahi*, the grant rate in the D.C. district courts fell to 8 percent. In the earlier cases, prior to *Al-Adahi*, "courts rejected the government's allegations 40% of the time. In the [later cases] however, the courts rejected only 14% of these allegations. The effect . . . [is that] careful judicial fact-finding was replaced by judicial deference to the government's allegations."[39] As one D.C. Circuit judge stated plainly in a concurring opinion in another case:

> I doubt any of my colleagues will vote to grant a petition if he or she believes that it is somewhat likely that the petitioner is an al-Qaeda adherent or an active supporter. . . . Of course, if it turns out that regardless of our decisions the executive branch does not release winning petitioners because no other country will accept them and they will not be released into the United States, then the whole process leads to virtual advisory opinions. It becomes a charade prompted by the Supreme Court's defiant – if only theoretical — assertion of judicial supremacy . . . providing litigation exercise for the detainee bar.

Esmail v. Obama (2011) (Silberman, J., concurring).

---

36. Report of the Senate Select Committee on Intelligence, S. Rep. 113-288, at 2 (2014).

37. DIRECTOR OF NATIONAL INTELLIGENCE HAINES, SUMMARY OF THE REENGAGEMENT OF DETAINEES FORMERLY HELD AT GUANTANAMO BAY, CUBA (2022).

38. MARK DENBEAUX ET AL., NO HEARING HABEAS: D.C. CIRCUIT RESTRICTS MEANINGFUL REVIEW (2012).

39. *Id.*

Any lingering doubt about how much deference the D.C. district court's should give the government was resolved in *Latif v. Obama* (D.C. Cir. 2012), which reversed the grant of a habeas petition on the ground that the district court failed to accord official intelligence documents "a presumption of regularity." Drawn from administrative law, the presumption of regularity requires courts, in the absence of clear and convincing evidence to the contrary, to "presume that [public officers responsible for government-produced documents such as tax receipts] have properly discharged their official duties." The court held that district courts adjudicating habeas petitions from Guantanamo must therefore "presume[] the government official accurately identified the [intelligence] source and accurately summarized his statement." The presumption does not require the court to assume "the truth of the underlying non-government source's statement." The dissent in *Latif* asserted that while clear error applies to review of district court determinations that the government's evidence is reliable, transplanting a presumption of regularity into the work of national security agencies "moves the goal posts" when the district court has grounds to find the government's primary evidence "unreliable." On the facts of this case, the dissent continued, the presumption of regularity authorized a "wholesale revision of the district court's careful fact findings" by the majority, finding that errors in the key government document the district court found "serious" to be "minor," and deeming Latif's account, "which the district court found plausible and corroborated by documentary evidence . . . 'hard to swallow.'" The Supreme Court denied certiorari in both *Al-Adahi* and *Latif* and as of this printing has denied certiorari in all post-*Boumediene* Guantanamo cases involving the merits of status determinations justifying continued detention there.

Habeas petitions in the D.C. district courts have raised other issues beyond whether a detainee has properly been deemed an enemy combatant. *See Kiyamba v. Obama* (D.C. Cir. 2009) (detainees who were determined not to be enemy combatants but could not be returned to their home country under the U.N. Convention Against Torture, which prohibits sending someone to a country where they are likely to face torture, do not have a right to be released in the United States because transfer of a non-citizen detainee into the United States is outside the power of a habeas court; the political branches have plenary power over the entry of foreign nationals to the United States); *Al Hela v. Biden* (D.C. Cir. 2020) (holding there is no substantive due process right to challenge detention for nearly two decades, and no procedural due process right to challenge reliance on ex parte secret evidence, hearsay, a presumption of regularity of the government's evidence, and the preponderance of the evidence standard relied upon in the D.C. Circuit), reh'g *en banc* granted (2021); *Al Maqaleh v. Gates* (D.C. Cir. 2010) (holding that, under the factors established in *Boumediene*, the writ does not run to the Bagram military facility in Afghanistan because it is in an active theatre).

Challenges to trials by military commission at Guantanamo have also occurred through habeas petitions. Most significantly, in *Hamdan v. Rumsfeld* (2006), the Supreme Court considered a petition contending that conspiracy is not an offense triable by military commission because it is not a violation of the law of war, and the trial procedures violated both military and international law. The Court held that habeas jurisdiction was not stripped by the DTA because the statute's jurisdiction stripping language applied only to new cases, not cases such as Hamdan's, which were pending when the DTA was passed. The Court also refused to abstain from the case on the ground that the military commission trial was not yet complete, rejecting the government's reliance on abstention doctrine in pending courts-martial proceedings against service members as inapposite given the Court's duty in peace and war, to preserve constitutional liberty, and the fact that proceedings at Guantanamo were not part of the "integrated system of military courts" for service members to which deference was due from Article III courts. On the merits, the Court found no congressional authorization for trial by military commission in the DTA or the AUMF and no inherent presidential war power triggered by the AUMF authorized trial by military commission according to procedures that deviated from the Uniform Code of Military Justice. The Guantanamo procedures violated the UCMJ (and the Geneva Conventions Common Article 3) by excluding the accused and his lawyer from learning evidence presented during the trial when the presiding officer elects to close the proceeding, and by permitting the admission of any evidence the presiding officer deems to have probative value regardless of concerns about its reliability.

The Military Commissions Act of 2006 responded to *Hamdan* by authorizing trial by military commission according to revised procedures. In the trials at Guantanamo, including trials against five men accused of plotting the 9/11 attacks, substantial delays have occurred because of continuing litigation over the evidence withheld from defense lawyers and the applicability of substantive laws supporting the charges. *See* Carol Rosenberg, *The 9/11 Trial: Why Is It Taking So Long*, N.Y. TIMES Apr. 17, 2020.

b. Habeas Corpus and Immigration Detention

Section 2241 is an important tool for challenging executive detention in settings other than national security enforcement. In the area of immigration, the setting of the *Thuraissigiam* case reported below, note that a range of statutes authorize detention of immigrants by federal officers. *See, e.g.,* 8 U.S.C. §1225(b)(1)(A)(b)(iii)(IV) (requiring detention of immigrants arriving at a port of entry of the United States and claiming asylum pending determination whether the applicant has a credible fear of persecution, and continued detention until removal if the applicant is deemed ineligible for asylum); 8 U.S.C. §1226(a) (authorizing discretionary arrest and detention on warrant issued by the Attorney General "pending a decision on whether the alien is to be removed from the United States"); 8 U.S.C. §1226(c) (requiring immigration officials to take into custody "any alien who is inadmissible by reason of having committed" certain crimes); 8 U.S.C. §1231(a)(2) (requiring detention of immigrants who have been ordered removed). Under these and other provisions, 43,826 people were held in immigration detention by Immigration and Customs Enforcement in 2019.[40] The average period of detention is a month and a half, but for immigrants who assert a legal right to remain, the average time rises to well over a year, and in some cases can last several years. This is in no small part due to delays in immigration courts, which in 2022 had over 1.7 million pending cases, and the fact that only 20 percent of immigrants were represented by counsel.[41] In asylum

---

40. AMERICAN IMMIGRATION COUNCIL, IMMIGRATION DETENTION IN THE UNITED STATES BY AGENCY 3 (2020).

41. *Quick Facts*, TRAC IMMIGRATION, https://trac.syr.edu/immigration/quickfacts/?category=eoir.

cases, for example, the wait time for a hearing averaged 1,612 days in 2022, or nearly four and a half years.[42] As this chart reflects, pressure on the system has increased with shifts in enforcement policy priorities for removal from different presidents and increases in asylum claims in response to a global refugee crisis.

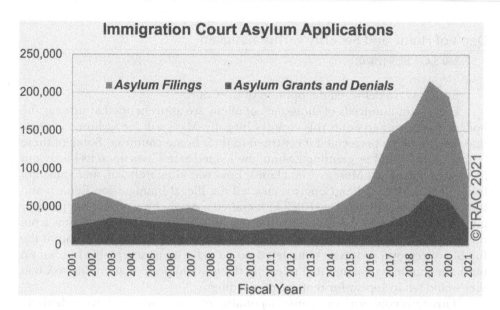

The vast majority of people held in immigration detention have no criminal record (72%) and of those who do, the majority involve minor infractions such as traffic violations. One in ten has a conviction for what ICE considers serious enough that the person presents a threat to public safety.[43] Conditions in immigration detention are generally poor. Office of Inspector General reports have found "unsafe and unhealthy" conditions, including overcrowding, overly restrictive segregation, "significant" food safety issues, "delays calling 911, denial of treatment for serious medical conditions, and inadequate mental health care."[44] More than two-thirds of the detention facilities are run by private contractors and about 30 percent are jails run by local governments. The remoteness of many detention centers can make it difficult to retain and communicate with counsel.

Traditionally, §2241 has provided a means for ensuring judicial review of the legality of immigration detention. In the following case, the Court addressed the

---

42. *A Mounting Asylum Backlog and Growing Waiting Times*, TRAC IMMI-GRATION, https://trac.syr.edu/immigration/reports/672/#:~:text=Current%20wait%20times%20for%20cases,See%20Table%201.&text=*%20This%20includes%20666%2C218%20asylum%20application,additional%20~1%2C000%20cases%20filed%20previously.

43. *Id.*

44. *Id.*

question whether Congress can eliminate the privilege of the writ for immigrants asserting the right to asylum in expedited removal proceedings. As in the context of national security detention at Guantanamo, the status of the detainees, the site of detention, and theories of sovereignty loom large in the Court's analysis.

Dep't of Homeland Security v. Thuraissigiam

140 S.C.t 1959 (2020)

Justice ALITO delivered the opinion of the Court.

Every year, hundreds of thousands of aliens are apprehended at or near the border attempting to enter this country illegally. Many ask for asylum, claiming that they would be persecuted if returned to their home countries. Some of these claims are valid, and by granting asylum, the United States lives up to its ideals and its treaty obligations. Most asylum claims, however, ultimately fail, and some are fraudulent. In 1996, when Congress enacted the Illegal Immigration Reform and Immigrant Responsibility Act (IIRIRA) it crafted a system for weeding out patently meritless claims and expeditiously removing the aliens making such claims from the country. It was Congress's judgment that detaining all asylum seekers until the full-blown removal process is completed would place an unacceptable burden on our immigration system and that releasing them would present an undue risk that they would fail to appear for removal proceedings.

This case concerns the constitutionality of the system Congress devised. Among other things, IIRIRA placed restrictions on the ability of asylum seekers to obtain review under the federal habeas statute, but the United States Court of Appeals for the Ninth Circuit held that these restrictions are unconstitutional. . . . We now review that decision and reverse.

Respondent's Suspension Clause argument fails because it would extend the writ of habeas corpus far beyond its scope "when the Constitution was drafted and ratified." *Boumediene v. Bush* (2008). Indeed, respondent's use of the writ would have been unrecognizable at that time. Habeas has traditionally been a means to secure *release* from unlawful detention, but respondent invokes the writ to achieve an entirely different end, namely, to obtain additional administrative review of his asylum claim and ultimately to obtain authorization to stay in this country.

Respondent's due process argument fares no better. While aliens who have established connections in this country have due process rights in deportation proceedings, the Court long ago held that Congress is entitled to set the conditions for an alien's lawful entry into this country and that, as a result, an alien at the threshold of initial entry cannot claim any greater rights under the Due Process Clause. *See Nishimura Ekiu v. United States* (1892). Respondent attempted to enter the country illegally and was apprehended just 25 yards from the border. He therefore has no entitlement to procedural rights other than those afforded by statute.

I

A

An alien who arrives at a "port of entry," *i.e.*, a place where an alien may lawfully enter, must apply for admission. An alien like respondent who is caught trying to enter at some other spot is treated the same way.

If an alien is inadmissible, the alien may be removed. The usual removal process involves an evidentiary hearing before an immigration judge, and at that hearing an alien may attempt to show that he or she should not be removed. Among other things, an alien may apply for asylum on the ground that he or she would be persecuted if returned to his or her home country. If that claim is rejected and the alien is ordered removed, the alien can appeal the removal order to the Board of Immigration Appeals and, if that appeal is unsuccessful, the alien is generally entitled to review in a federal court of appeals. As of the first quarter of this fiscal year, there were 1,066,563 pending removal proceedings. The average civil appeal takes approximately one year. During the time when removal is being litigated, the alien will either be detained, at considerable expense, or allowed to reside in this country, with the attendant risk that he or she may not later be found.

Congress addressed these problems by providing more expedited procedures for certain "applicants for admission." For these purposes, "[a]n alien present in the United States who has not been admitted or who arrives in the United States (whether or not at a designated port of arrival . . .)" is deemed "an applicant for admission." §1225(a)(1).[2] An applicant is subject to expedited removal if, as relevant here, the applicant (1) is inadmissible because he or she lacks a valid entry document; (2) has not "been physically present in the United States continuously for the 2-year period immediately prior to the date of the determination of inadmissibility"; and (3) is among those whom the Secretary of Homeland Security has designated for expedited removal. §§1225(b)(1)(A)(i), (iii)(I)–(II). Once "an immigration officer determines" that a designated applicant "is inadmissible," "the officer [must] order the alien removed from the United States without further hearing or review." §1225(b)(1)(A)(i).

Applicants can avoid expedited removal by claiming asylum. If an applicant "indicates either an intention to apply for asylum" or "a fear of persecution," the immigration officer "shall refer the alien for an interview by an asylum officer." §§1225(b)(1)(A)(i)-(ii). The point of this screening interview is to determine whether the applicant has a "credible fear of persecution." §1225(b)(1)(B)(v). The applicant need not show that he or she *is in fact eligible* for asylum—a "credible fear" equates to only a "significant possibility" that the alien would be eligible. *Ibid.* Thus, while eligibility ultimately requires a "well-founded fear of persecution on account of," among other things, "race" or "political opinion," all that an alien must show to avoid expedited removal is a "credible fear."

If the asylum officer finds an applicant's asserted fear to be credible,[5] the applicant will receive "full consideration" of his asylum claim in a standard removal

---

2. When respondent entered the country, aliens were treated as applicants for admission if they were "encountered within 14 days of entry without inspection and within 100 air miles of any U.S. international land border."

5. The asylum officer also considers an alien's potential eligibility for withholding of removal under §1231(b)(3) or relief under the Convention Against Torture and Other Cruel, Inhuman or Degrading Treatment or Punishment (CAT). Respondent's habeas petition alleges that "he can show a significan[t] possibility that he could establish eligibility for asylum, withholding of removal, and CAT claims." But he . . . discusses the criteria only for asylum. And [before this Court he] alleges that he was improperly "denied asylum." Moreover, the gravamen of his petition is that he faces persecution in Sri Lanka "because of " his Tamil ethnicity and political opinions. To obtain withholding or CAT relief on that basis, he would need to show "a greater likelihood of persecution or torture at home than is necessary for asylum." *Moncrieffe v. Holder* (2013). And he would not avoid removal, only removal to Sri Lanka. We therefore read his petition as it is plainly intended: to seek another opportunity to apply for asylum.

hearing. If the asylum officer finds that the applicant does not have a credible fear, a supervisor will review the asylum officer's determination. If the supervisor agrees with it, the applicant may appeal to an immigration judge, who can take further evidence and "shall make a de novo determination."

An alien subject to expedited removal thus has an opportunity at three levels to obtain an asylum hearing, and the applicant will obtain one unless the asylum officer, a supervisor, and an immigration judge all find that the applicant has not asserted a credible fear.

Over the last five years, nearly 77% of screenings have resulted in a finding of credible fear. And nearly half the remainder (11% of the total number of screenings) were closed for administrative reasons, including the alien's withdrawal of the claim. As a practical matter, then, the great majority of asylum seekers who fall within the category subject to expedited removal do not receive expedited removal and are instead afforded the same procedural rights as other aliens.

Whether an applicant who raises an asylum claim receives full or only expedited review, the applicant is not entitled to immediate release. Applicants "shall be detained pending a final determination of credible fear of persecution and, if found not to have such a fear, until removed." §1225(b)(1)(B)(iii)(IV). Applicants who are found to have a credible fear may also be detained pending further consideration of their asylum applications.[8]

B

The IIRIRA provision at issue in this case, §1252(e)(2), limits the review that an alien in expedited removal may obtain via a petition for a writ of habeas corpus. That provision allows habeas review of three matters: first, "whether the petitioner is an alien"; second, "whether the petitioner was ordered removed"; and third, whether the petitioner has already been granted entry as a lawful permanent resident, refugee, or asylee. §§1252(e)(2)(A)–(C). If the petitioner has such a status, or if a removal order has not "in fact" been "issued," §1252(e)(5), the court may order a removal hearing, §1252(e)(4)(B).

A major objective of IIRIRA was to "protec[t] the Executive's discretion" from undue interference by the courts; indeed, "that can fairly be said to be the theme of the legislation." *Reno v. American-Arab Anti-Discrimination Comm.* (1999) (*AAADC*). In accordance with that aim, §1252(e)(5) provides that "[t]here shall be no review of whether the alien is actually inadmissible or entitled to any relief from removal." And "[n]otwithstanding" any other "habeas corpus provision"—including 28 U.S.C. §2241—"no court shall have jurisdiction to review" any other "individual determination" or "claim arising from or relating to the implementation or operation of an order of [expedited] removal." §1252(a)(2)(A)(i). In particular, courts may not review "the determination" that an alien lacks a credible fear of persecution. §1252(a)(2)(A)(iii).

Even without the added step of judicial review, the credible-fear process and abuses of it can increase the burdens currently "overwhelming our immigration

---

8. The Department may grant temporary parole "for urgent humanitarian reasons or significant public benefit." 8 U.S.C. §1182(d)(5)(A).

system." 84 Fed. Reg. 33841 (2019).[9] The past decade has seen a 1,883% increase in credible-fear claims, and in 2018 alone, there were 99,035 claims. *See id.*, at 33838 (data for fiscal years 2008 to 2018). The majority have proved to be meritless. Many applicants found to have a credible fear—about 50% over the same 10-year period—did not pursue asylum. . . . In 2019, a grant of asylum followed a finding of credible fear just 15% of the time. Fraudulent asylum claims can also be difficult to detect,[10] especially in a screening process that is designed to be expedited and that is currently handling almost 100,000 claims per year.

The question presented thus has significant consequences for the immigration system.

C

Respondent Vijayakumar Thuraissigiam, a Sri Lankan national, crossed the southern border without inspection or an entry document at around 11 p.m. one night in January 2017. A Border Patrol agent stopped him within 25 yards of the border, and the Department detained him for expedited removal. He claimed a fear of returning to Sri Lanka because a group of men had once abducted and severely beaten him, but he said that he did not know who the men were, why they had assaulted him, or whether Sri Lankan authorities would protect him in the future. He also affirmed that he did not fear persecution based on his race, political opinions, or other protected characteristics.

The asylum officer credited respondent's account of the assault but determined that he lacked a "credible" fear of persecution. . . . The supervising officer agreed and signed the removal order. After hearing further testimony from respondent, an Immigration Judge affirmed on *de novo* review and returned the case to the Department for removal.

Respondent then filed a federal habeas petition. Asserting for the first time a fear of persecution based on his Tamil ethnicity and political views, he argued that . . . the immigration officials deprived him of "a meaningful opportunity to establish his claims" and violated credible-fear procedures by failing to probe past

---

9. References to the factual material in this regulation are not endorsements of the regulation itself. And like the immigration officials in this case, we do not question the basis for respondent's asserted fear. But we note the Department's view that credible-fear claims can be asserted "in the hope of a lengthy asylum process that will enable [the claimants] to remain in the United States for years . . . despite their statutory ineligibility for relief" and that an influx of meritless claims can delay the adjudication of meritorious ones; strain detention capacity and degrade detention conditions; cause the release of many inadmissible aliens into States and localities that must shoulder the resulting costs; divert Department resources from protecting the border; and aggravate "the humanitarian crisis created by human smugglers." 84 Fed. Reg. 33831.

10. *See, e.g.,* GAO Fraud Report 32-33 (discussing Operation Fiction Writer, a criminal investigation of attorneys and application preparers who counseled asylum seekers to lie about religious persecution and forced abortions); Asylum Fraud: Abusing America's Compassion? Hearing before the Subcommittee on Immigration and Border Security of the House Committee on the Judiciary, 113th Cong., 2d Sess. (2014) (testimony of Louis D. Crocetti, Jr.) (describing study in which 58% of randomly selected asylum applications exhibited indicators of possible fraud and 12% were determined to be fraudulent).

his denial of the facts necessary for asylum. Allegedly they also failed to apply the "correct standard" to his claims—the "significant possibility" standard—despite its repeated appearance in the records of their decisions. Respondent requested "a writ of habeas corpus, an injunction, or a writ of mandamus directing [the Department] to provide [him] a new opportunity to apply for asylum and other applicable forms of relief." His petition made no mention of release from custody.

The District Court dismissed the petition. The Ninth Circuit reversed. It found that our Suspension Clause precedent demands "reference to the writ as it stood in 1789." But without citing any pre-1789 case about the scope of the writ, the court held that §1252(e)(2) violates the Suspension Clause. . . . Although the decision applied only to respondent, petitioners across the Circuit have used it to obtain review outside the scope of §1252(e)(2), and petitioners elsewhere have attempted to follow suit.

We granted certiorari.

II

A

The Suspension Clause provides that "[t]he Privilege of the Writ of Habeas Corpus shall not be suspended, unless when in Cases of Rebellion or Invasion the public Safety may require it." In *INS v. St. Cyr* (2001), we wrote that the Clause, at a minimum, "protects the writ as it existed in 1789," when the Constitution was adopted. And in this case, respondent agrees that "there is no reason" to consider whether the Clause extends any further. We therefore proceed on that basis.[12]

B

This principle dooms respondent's Suspension Clause argument, because neither respondent nor his *amici* have shown that the writ of habeas corpus was understood at the time of the adoption of the Constitution to permit a petitioner to claim the right to enter or remain in a country or to obtain administrative review potentially leading to that result. The writ simply provided a means of contesting the lawfulness of restraint and securing release. . . .

Blackstone wrote that habeas was a means to "remov[e] the injury of unjust and illegal confinement." 3 W. Blackstone, Commentaries on the Laws of England 137. Justice Story described the "common law" writ the same way. *See* 3 Commentaries on the Constitution of the United States §1333, p. 206 (1833). Habeas, he explained, "is the appropriate remedy to ascertain whether any person is rightfully in confinement or not."

---

12. The original meaning of the Suspension Clause is the subject of controversy. In *INS v. St. Cyr* (2001), the majority and dissent debated whether the Clause independently guarantees the availability of the writ or simply restricts the temporary withholding of its operation. *See also Ex parte Bollman* (1807). We do not revisit that question. Nor do we consider whether the scope of the writ as it existed in 1789 defines the boundary of the constitutional protection to which the *St. Cyr* Court referred, since the writ has never encompassed respondent's claims. We also do not reconsider whether the common law allowed the issuance of a writ on behalf of an alien who lacked any allegiance to the country. *Compare Boumediene v. Bush*, 553 U.S. 723, 746-747 (2008) (forming "no certain conclusions"), *with* Brief for Criminal Justice Legal Foundation.

We have often made the same point. *See, e.g., Preiser* v. *Rodriguez* (1973) ("It is clear . . . from the common-law history of the writ . . . that the essence of habeas corpus is an attack by a person in custody upon the legality of that custody, and that the traditional function of the writ is to secure release from illegal custody").

In this case, however, respondent did not ask to be released. Instead, he sought entirely different relief: vacatur of his "removal order" and "an order directing [the Department] to provide him with a new . . . opportunity to apply for asylum and other relief from removal." Such relief might fit an injunction or writ of mandamus— which tellingly, his petition also requested—but that relief falls outside the scope of the common-law habeas writ.

Not only did respondent fail to seek release, he does not dispute that confinement during the pendency of expedited asylum review, and even during the additional proceedings he seeks, is lawful. Nor could he. It is not disputed that he was apprehended in the very act of attempting to enter this country; that he is inadmissible because he lacks an entry document, and that, under these circumstances, his case qualifies for the expedited review process, including "[m]andatory detention" during his credible-fear review, §§1225(b)(1)(B)(ii), (iii)(IV). Moreover, simply releasing him would not provide the right to stay in the country that his petition ultimately seeks. Without a change in status, he would remain subject to arrest, detention, and removal.

While respondent does not claim an entitlement to release, the Government is happy to release him—provided the release occurs in the cabin of a plane bound for Sri Lanka. That would be the equivalent of the habeas relief Justice Story ordered in a case while riding circuit. He issued a writ requiring the release of a foreign sailor who jumped ship in Boston, but he provided for the sailor to be released into the custody of the master of his ship. *Ex parte D'Olivera* (CC Mass. 1813).

Respondent does not want anything like that. His claim is more reminiscent of the one we rejected in *Munaf*. In that case, American citizens held in U. S. custody in Iraq filed habeas petitions in an effort to block their transfer to Iraqi authorities for criminal prosecution. Rejecting this use of habeas, we noted that "[h]abeas is at its core a remedy for unlawful executive detention" and that what these individuals wanted was not "simple release" but an order requiring them to be brought to this country. Claims so far outside the "core" of habeas may not be pursued through habeas.

III

Disputing this conclusion, respondent argues that the Suspension Clause guarantees a broader habeas right. To substantiate this claim, he points to three bodies of case law: British and American cases decided prior to or around the time of the adoption of the Constitution, decisions of this Court during the so-called "finality era" (running from the late 19th century to the mid-20th century), and two of our more recent cases. None of these sources support his argument.

A

Because respondent seeks to use habeas to obtain something far different from simple release, his cause is not aided by the many release cases that he and his *amici* have found. Thus, for present purposes, it is immaterial that habeas was used to seek release from confinement that was imposed for, among other things, contempt of court, debt, medical malpractice, failing to pay an assessment for sewers, failure to lend the King money, carrying an authorized "dagg," *i.e.*, handgun, "impressment" into military service or involuntary servitude, or refusing to pay a colonial tax. Nor does it matter that common-law courts sometimes ordered or considered ordering release in circumstances that would be beyond the reach of any habeas statute ever enacted by Congress, such as release from private custody. *See, e.g., Rex v. Delaval* (K.B. 1763) (release of young woman from "indentures of apprenticeship"); *Rex v. Clarkson* (K.B. 1722) (release from boarding school); *Lister's Case* (K.B. 1721) (release of wife from estranged husband's restraint). What matters is that all these cases are about release from restraint.

Respondent and his *amici* note that habeas petitioners were sometimes released on the condition that they conform to certain requirements. For example, they cite a case in which a man was released on condition that he treat his wife well and support her, and another in which a man was released on condition that he issue an apology. But what respondent sought in this case is nothing like that. Respondent does not seek an order releasing him on the condition that he do or refrain from doing something. What he wants—further review of his asylum claim—is not a condition with which he must comply. Equally irrelevant is the practice, discussed in the dissent, of allowing the executive to justify or cure a defect in detention before requiring release. Respondent does not seek this sort of conditional release either, because the legality of his detention is not in question. . . .

Somerset v. Stewart (K.B. 1772), is celebrated but does not aid respondent. James Somerset was a slave who was "detain[ed]" on a ship bound for Jamaica, and Lord Mansfield famously ordered his release on the ground that his detention as a slave was unlawful in England. This relief, release from custody, fell within the historic core of habeas, and Lord Mansfield did not order anything else.

It may well be that a collateral consequence of Somerset's release was that he was allowed to remain in England, but if that is so, it was due not to the writ issued by Lord Mansfield, but to English law regarding entitlement to reside in the country. At the time, England had nothing like modern immigration restrictions. As late as 1816, the word "deportation" apparently "was not to be found in any English dictionary." The Use of the Crown's Power of Deportation Under the Aliens Act, 1793-1826, in J. Dinwiddy, Radicalism and Reform in Britain, 1780–1850, p. 150, n. 4 (1992); *see also, e.g.,* Craies, The Right of Aliens To Enter British Territory, 6 L. Q. Rev. 27, 35 (1890) ("England was a complete asylum to the foreigner who did not offend against its laws.").

For a similar reason, respondent cannot find support in early 19th-century American cases in which deserting foreign sailors used habeas to obtain their release from the custody of American officials. In none of the cases involving deserters that have been called to our attention did the court order anything more than simple release from custody. As noted, Justice Story ordered a sailor's release into the custody of his ship's master. Other decisions, while ordering the release of detained foreign deserters because no statute authorized detention, chafed at having to order even release. . . . These cases thus do not contemplate the quite different relief that respondent asks us to sanction here.

In these cases, as in *Somerset,* it may be that the released petitioners were able to remain in the United States as a collateral consequence of release, but if so, that was due not to the writs ordering their release, but to U.S. immigration law or the lack thereof. These decisions came at a time when an "open door to the immigrant was the . . . federal policy." *Harisiades v. Shaughnessy,* (1952); *see also St. Cyr,* 533 U.S., at 305 (first immigration regulation enacted in 1875). So release may have had the side effect of enabling these individuals to remain in this country, but that is beside the point.

The relief that a habeas court may order and the collateral consequences of that relief are two entirely different things. Ordering an individual's release from custody may have the side effect of enabling that person to pursue all sorts of opportunities that the law allows. For example, release may enable a qualified surgeon to operate on a patient; a licensed architect may have the opportunity to design a bridge; and a qualified pilot may be able to fly a passenger jet. But a writ of habeas could not be used to compel an applicant to be afforded those opportunities or as a means to obtain a license as a surgeon, architect, or pilot. Similarly, while the release of an alien may give the alien the opportunity to remain in the country if the immigration laws permit, we have no evidence that the writ as it was known in 1789 could be used to require that aliens be permitted to remain in a country other than their own, or as a means to seek that permission.

Respondent's final examples involve international extradition, but these cases are no more pertinent than those already discussed. For one thing, they post-date the founding era. . . . In these cases, as in all the others noted above, habeas was used "simply" to seek release from allegedly unlawful detention.[20]

Despite pages of rhetoric, the dissent is unable to cite a single pre-1789 habeas case in which a court ordered relief that was anything like what respondent seeks here. . . . The dissent reveals the true nature of its argument by suggesting that there are "inherent difficulties [in] a strict originalist approach in the habeas context because of, among other things, the dearth of reasoned habeas decisions at the founding." But respondent does not ask us to hold that the Suspension Clause guarantees the writ as it might have evolved since the adoption of the Constitution. On the contrary, as noted at the outset of this discussion, he rests his argument on "the writ as it existed in 1789." . . .

B

We now proceed to consider the second body of case law on which respondent relies, decisions of this Court during the "finality era," which takes its name from a feature of the Immigration Act of 1891 making certain immigration decisions "final." Although respondent claims that his argument is supported by "the writ as it existed in 1789," his argument focuses mainly on this body of case law, which

---

20. *Amici* supporting respondent make an additional argument. They contend that "[i]n eighteenth century practice, the authority of English judges to review habeas petitions was not constrained by past decisions" and that these judges felt free to innovate in order to ensure that justice was done. But the role of federal courts under our Constitution is very different from that of those English judges. The English judges "were considered agents of the Crown, designed to assist the King in the exercise of his power.". . . In our federal courts, by contrast, the scope of habeas has been tightly regulated by statute, from the Judiciary Act of 1789 to the present day, and precedent is as binding in a habeas case as in any other.

began a century later. These cases, he claims, held that "the Suspension Clause mandates a minimum level of judicial review to ensure that the Executive complies with the law in effectuating removal." The Ninth Circuit also relied heavily on these cases and interpreted them to "suggest that the Suspension Clause requires review of legal and mixed questions of law and fact related to removal orders."

This interpretation of the "finality era" cases is badly mistaken. Those decisions were based not on the Suspension Clause but on the habeas statute and the immigration laws then in force. The habeas statute in effect during this time was broad in scope. It authorized the federal courts to review whether a person was being held in custody in violation of any federal law, including immigration laws. Thus, when aliens claimed that they were detained in violation of immigration statutes, the federal courts considered whether immigration authorities had complied with those laws. . . . But the Court exercised that review because it was authorized to do so by statute. The decisions did not hold that this review was required by the Suspension Clause.

In this country, the habeas authority of federal courts has been addressed by statute from the very beginning. The Judiciary Act of 1789, §14, gave the federal courts the power to issue writs of habeas corpus under specified circumstances, but after the Civil War, Congress enacted a much broader statute. That law, the Habeas Corpus Act of 1867, provided that "the several courts of the United States . . . shall have power to grant writs of habeas corpus in all cases where any person may be restrained of his or her liberty in violation of the constitution, or of any treaty or law of the United States." Judiciary Act of Feb. 5, 1867, §1. The Act was "of the most comprehensive character," bringing "within the *habeas corpus* jurisdiction of every court and of every judge every possible case of privation of liberty contrary" to federal law. *Ex parte McCardle* (1868). This jurisdiction was "impossible to widen." The 1867 statute, unlike the current federal habeas statute, was not subject to restrictions on the issuance of writs in immigration matters, and in *United States v. Jung Ah Lung* (1888), the Court held that an alien in immigration custody could seek a writ under that statute. This provided the statutory basis for the writs sought in the finality era cases.

The Immigration Act of 1891, enacted during one of the country's great waves of immigration, required the exclusion of certain categories of aliens and established procedures for determining whether aliens fell within one of those categories. The Act required the exclusion of "idiots, insane persons, paupers or persons likely to become a public charge," persons with infectious diseases, persons with convictions for certain crimes, some individuals whose passage had been paid for by a third party, and certain laborers. Act of Mar. 3, 1891. Inspection officers were authorized to board arriving vessels and inspect any aliens on board. And, in the provision of central importance here, the Act provided that "[a]ll decisions made by the inspection officers or their assistants touching the right of any alien to land, when adverse to such right, shall be final unless appeal be taken to the superintendent of immigration, whose action shall be subject to review by the Secretary of the Treasury." Later immigration Acts, which remained in effect until 1952, contained similar provisions.

The first of the finality era cases, *Nishimura Ekiu v. United States* (1892), required the Court to address the effect of the 1891 Act's finality provision in a habeas case. *Nishimura Ekiu* is the cornerstone of respondent's argument regarding the finality era cases, so the opinion in that case demands close attention.

The case involved an alien who was detained upon arrival based on the immigration inspector's finding that she was liable to become a public charge. Seeking to be released, the alien applied to the Circuit Court for a writ of habeas corpus and argued that the 1891 Act, if construed to give immigration authorities the "exclusive authority to determine" her right to enter, would violate her constitutional right to the writ of habeas corpus and her right to due process. . . .

This Court upheld the denial of the writ. The Court interpreted the 1891 Act to preclude judicial review only with respect to questions of fact. And after interpreting the 1891 Act in this way, the Court found that "the act of 1891 is constitutional."

The Court's narrow interpretation of the 1891 Act's finality provision meant that the federal courts otherwise retained the full authority granted by the Habeas Corpus Act of 1867 to determine whether an alien was detained in violation of federal law. Turning to that question, the Court held that the only procedural rights of an alien seeking to enter the country are those conferred by statute. "As to such persons," the Court explained, "the decisions of executive or administrative officers, acting within powers expressly conferred by Congress, are due process of law." The Court therefore considered whether the procedures set out in the 1891 Act had been followed, and finding no violation, affirmed the denial of the writ. What is critical for present purposes is that the Court did not hold that the Suspension Clause imposed any limitations on the authority of Congress to restrict the issuance of writs of habeas corpus in immigration matters.

Respondent interprets *Nishimura Ekiu* differently. As he reads the decision, the Court interpreted the 1891 Act to preclude review of *all questions* related to an alien's entitlement to enter the country. Any other interpretation, he contends, would fly in the face of the statutory terms. But, he maintains, the Court held that this limitation violated the Suspension Clause except with respect to questions of fact, and it was for this reason that the Court considered whether the procedures specified by the 1891 Act were followed. . . .

This interpretation is wrong. . . . What *Nishimura Ekiu* meant, *Gegiow* [later] explained, was that the immigration authorities' factual findings were conclusive (as *Gegiow* put it, "[t]he conclusiveness of the decisions of immigration officers . . . is conclusiveness upon matters of fact") and therefore, the Court was "not forbidden by the statute to consider" in a habeas proceeding "whether the reasons" for removing an alien "agree with the requirements of the act." In light of this interpretation, the *Nishimura Ekiu* Court had no occasion to decide whether the Suspension Clause would have tolerated a broader limitation, and there is not so much as a hint in the opinion that the Court considered this question. Indeed, the opinion never even mentions the Suspension Clause, and it is utterly implausible that the Court would hold *sub silentio* that Congress had violated that provision.

Holding that an Act of Congress unconstitutionally suspends the writ of habeas corpus is momentous. *See Boumediene* (noting "the care Congress has taken throughout our Nation's history" to avoid suspension). The Justices on the Court at the beginning of the finality era had seen historic occasions when the writ was suspended—during the Civil War by President Lincoln and then by Congress, and later during Reconstruction by President Grant. The suspension of habeas during this era played a prominent role in our constitutional history. *See Ex parte Merryman* (CC Md. 1861) (Taney, C.J.); *Ex parte Milligan* (1866). (Two of the Justices at the beginning of the finality era were on the Court when *Ex parte Milligan* was decided.) The Justices knew a suspension of the writ when they saw one, and it is impossible to believe that the *Nishimura Ekiu* Court identified another occasion when Congress had suspended the writ and based its decision on the Suspension Clause without even mentioning that provision. . . .

According to the dissent, *Nishimura Ekiu* interpreted the 1891 Act as it did based on the doctrine of constitutional avoidance. . . . But even if there were some basis for this interpretation, it would not benefit respondent, and that is undoubtedly why he has not made the argument. IIRIRA unequivocally bars habeas review of respondent's claims and he does not argue that it can be read any other way. The avoidance doctrine "has no application in the absence of ambiguity." *Warger v. Shauers* (2014).

When we look to later finality era cases, any suggestion of a Suspension Clause foundation becomes even less plausible. None of those decisions mention the Suspension Clause or even hint that they are based on that provision, and these omissions are telling. . . .

C

We come, finally, to the more recent cases on which respondent relies. The most recent, *Boumediene*, is not about immigration at all. It held that suspected foreign terrorists could challenge their detention at the naval base in Guantanamo Bay, Cuba. They had been "apprehended on the battlefield in Afghanistan" and elsewhere, not while crossing the border. They sought only to be released from Guantanamo, not to enter this country. And nothing in the Court's discussion of the Suspension Clause suggested that they could have used habeas as a means of gaining entry. Rather, the Court reaffirmed that release is the habeas remedy though not the "exclusive" result of every writ, given that it is often "appropriate" to allow the executive to cure defects in a detention.

Respondent's other recent case is *St. Cyr*, in which the Court's pertinent holding . . . enlisted a quartet of interpretive canons: "the strong presumption in favor of judicial review of administrative action," "the longstanding rule requiring a clear statement of congressional intent to repeal habeas jurisdiction," the rule that a "clear indication" of congressional intent is expected when a proposed interpretation would push "the outer limits of Congress' power," and the canon of constitutional avoidance. In connection with this final canon, the Court observed: "Because of [the Suspension] Clause, some 'judicial intervention in deportation cases' is unquestionably 'required by the Constitution.'"

Respondent pounces on this statement, but . . . it does nothing for him. The writ of habeas corpus as it existed at common law provided a vehicle to challenge all manner of detention by government officials, and the Court had held long before that the writ could be invoked by aliens already in the country who were held in custody pending deportation. *St. Cyr* reaffirmed these propositions, and this statement in *St. Cyr* does not signify approval of respondent's very different attempted use of the writ, which the Court did not consider.

IV

In addition to his Suspension Clause argument, respondent contends that IIRIRA violates his right to due process by precluding judicial review of his allegedly flawed credible-fear proceeding. The Ninth Circuit agreed, holding that respondent "had a constitutional right to expedited removal proceedings that conformed to the dictates of due process."

That holding is contrary to more than a century of precedent. In 1892, the Court wrote that as to "foreigners who have never been naturalized, nor acquired any domicil or residence within the United States, nor even been admitted into the country pursuant to law," "the decisions of executive or administrative officers, acting within powers expressly conferred by Congress, are due process of law." *Nishimura Ekiu.* Since then, the Court has often reiterated this important rule. *See, e.g., Knauff* ("Whatever the procedure authorized by Congress is, it is due process as far as an alien denied entry is concerned."); *Mezei* (same); *Landon v. Plasencia* (1982) ("This Court has long held that an alien seeking initial admission to the United States requests a privilege and has no constitutional rights regarding his application, for the power to admit or exclude aliens is a sovereign prerogative.").

Respondent argues that this rule does not apply to him because he was not taken into custody the instant he attempted to enter the country (as would have been the case had he arrived at a lawful port of entry). Because he succeeded in making it 25 yards into U.S. territory before he was caught, he claims the right to be treated more favorably. The Ninth Circuit agreed with this argument.

We reject it. It disregards the reason for our century-old rule regarding the due process rights of an alien seeking initial entry. That rule rests on fundamental propositions: "[T]he power to admit or exclude aliens is a sovereign prerogative," the Constitution gives "the political department of the government" plenary authority to decide which aliens to admit, *Nishimura Ekiu*; and a concomitant of that power is the power to set the procedures to be followed in determining whether an alien should be admitted.

This rule would be meaningless if it became inoperative as soon as an arriving alien set foot on U.S. soil. When an alien arrives at a port of entry—for example, an international airport—the alien is on U.S. soil, but the alien is not considered to have entered the country for the purposes of this rule. On the contrary, aliens who arrive at ports of entry—even those paroled elsewhere in the country for years pending removal—are "treated" for due process purposes "as if stopped at the border." *Mezei.*

The same must be true of an alien like respondent. . . . The rule advocated by respondent and adopted by the Ninth Circuit would undermine the "sovereign prerogative" of governing admission to this country and create a perverse incentive to enter at an unlawful rather than a lawful location. *Plasencia.*

For these reasons, an alien in respondent's position has only those rights regarding admission that Congress has provided by statute. In respondent's case, Congress provided the right to a "determin[ation]" whether he had "a significant possibility" of "establish[ing] eligibility for asylum," and he was given that right. Because the Due Process Clause provides nothing more, it does not require review of that determination or how it was made. As applied here, therefore, §1252(e)(2) does not violate due process.

* * *

Because the Ninth Circuit erred in holding that §1252(e)(2) violates the Suspension Clause and the Due Process Clause, we reverse the judgment and remand the case with directions that the application for habeas corpus be dismissed.

[Justice BREYER, with whom Justice GINSBURG joins, concurred in the judgment on the ground that enforcing the statute's limitations on the privilege of the writ in an as-applied challenge "*in this particular case* does not violate the Suspension Clause.

Respondent has never lived in, or been lawfully admitted to, the United States. To my mind, those are among the "circumstances" that inform the "scope" of any habeas review that the Suspension Clause might guarantee respondent. *Boumediene.* He is thus in a materially different position for Suspension Clause purposes than the noncitizens in, for example, *Rowoldt v. Perfetto* (1957), *United States ex rel. Accardi v. Shaughnessy* (1954), *Bridges v. Wixon* (1945), and *Hansen v. Haff* (1934). They had all lived in this country for years. The scope of whatever habeas review the Suspension Clause assures respondent need not be as extensive as it might for someone in that position. . . .

[R]espondent concedes [moreover,] that Congress may eliminate habeas review of factual questions in cases like this one. *See, e.g., Nishimura Ekiu.* . . . Respondent, to be sure, casts the brunt of his challenge to this adverse credible-fear determination as two claims of legal error. But it is the factual findings underlying that determination that respondent, armed with strong new *factual* evidence, now disputes. . . . At the heart of both purportedly legal contentions, however, lies a disagreement with immigration officials' findings about the two brute facts underlying their credible-fear determination — again, the identity of respondent's attackers and their motive for attacking him. . . . Mindful that the "Constitution deals with substance, not shadows," *Salazar v. Buono* (2010) (Roberts, C. J., concurring), I accordingly view both claims as factual in nature, notwithstanding respondent's contrary characterization. For that reason, Congress may foreclose habeas review of these claims without running afoul of the Suspension Clause.]

[Justice THOMAS concurred, arguing that the "original meaning" of the Suspension Clause restricts its application to statutes that grant "the executive power to detain without bail or trial based on mere suspicion of a crime or dangerousness." On this view, immigration detention incident to expedited removal with partial, but not universal, access to habeas "is not likely a suspension."]

Justice SOTOMAYOR, joined by Justice KAGAN, dissenting.
[The majority] flouts over a century of this Court's practice [in which] we have heard claims indistinguishable from those respondent raises here, which fall within the heartland of habeas jurisdiction going directly to the origins of the Great Writ. The Court thus purges an entire class of legal challenges to executive detention from habeas review. . . . Making matters worse, the Court deprives [this class] of any means to ensure the integrity of an expedited removal order" under the Due Process Clause. . . .

[R]espondent contended that the inadequate procedures afforded to him in his removal proceedings violated constitutional due process. Among other things, he asserted that the removal proceedings by design did not provide him a meaningful opportunity to establish his claims, that the translator and asylum officer misunderstood him, and that he was not given a "reasoned explanation" for the decision. Again, however, the Court falls short of capturing the procedural relief actually requested. The Court vaguely suggests that respondent merely wanted more cracks at obtaining review of his asylum claims, not that he wanted to challenge the existing expedited removal framework or the process actually rendered in his case as constitutionally inadequate. That misconstrues respondent's procedural challenges to the expedited removal proceedings, which matters crucially; a constitutional challenge to executive detention is just the sort of claim the common law has long recognized as cognizable in habeas. . . .

The Court [also] asserts that respondent did not specifically seek "release" from custody in what the Court styles as the "traditional" sense of the term as understood in habeas jurisprudence. Instead, the Court seems to argue that respondent seeks only a peculiar form of release: admission into the United States or additional asylum procedures that would allow for admission into the United States. Such a request, the Court implies, is more akin to mandamus and injunctive relief.

But it is the Court's directionality requirement that bucks tradition. Respondent asks merely to be freed from wrongful executive custody. He asserts that he has a credible fear of persecution, and asylum statutes authorize him to remain in the country if he does. That request is indistinguishable from, and no less "traditional" than, those long made by noncitizens challenging restraints that prevented them from otherwise entering or remaining in a country not their own. . . .

To start, the Court recognizes the pitfalls of relying on pre-1789 cases to establish principles relevant to immigration and asylum: "At the time, England had nothing like modern immigration restrictions." It notes, too, that our cases have repeatedly observed the relative novelty of immigration laws in the early days of this country. *See also Demore v. Kim,* 538 U.S. 510, 539 (2003) (O'Connor, J., concurring in part and concurring in judgment) ("Because colonial America imposed few restrictions on immigration, there is little case law prior to that time about the availability of habeas review to challenge temporary detention pending exclusion or deportation").

The Court nevertheless seems to require respondent to engage in an exercise in futility. It demands that respondent unearth cases predating comprehensive federal immigration regulation showing that noncitizens obtained release from federal custody onto national soil. But no federal statutes at that time spoke to the permissibility of their entry in the first instance; the United States lacked a comprehensive asylum regime until the latter half of the 20th century. Despite the limitations inherent in this exercise, the Court appears to insist on a wealth of cases mirroring the precise relief requested at a granular level; nothing short of that, in the Court's view, would demonstrate that a noncitizen in respondent's position is entitled to the writ. *See* Neuman, *Habeas Corpus, Executive Detention, and the Removal of Aliens,* 98 COLUM. L. REV. 961 (1998) (noting the inherent difficulties of a strict originalist approach in the habeas context because of, among other things, the dearth of reasoned habeas decisions at the founding).

But this Court has never rigidly demanded a one-to-one match between a habeas petition and a common-law habeas analog. In *St. Cyr,* for example, the Court considered whether a noncitizen with a controlled substance conviction could challenge on habeas the denial of a discretionary waiver of his deportation order. In doing so, the Court did not search high and low for founding-era parallels to waivers of deportation for criminal noncitizens. It simply asked, at a far more general level, whether habeas jurisdiction was historically "invoked on behalf of noncitizens . . . in the immigration context" to "challenge Executive . . . detention in civil cases." That included determining whether "[h]abeas courts . . . answered questions of law that arose in the context of discretionary relief " (including questions regarding the allegedly "erroneous application or interpretation of statutes").

Boumediene is even clearer that the Suspension Clause inquiry does not require a close (much less precise) factual match with historical habeas precedent. There, the Court concluded that the writ applied to noncitizen detainees held in Guantanamo, despite frankly admitting that a "[d]iligent search by all parties reveal[ed] no certain conclusions" about the relevant scope of the common-law writ in 1789. Indeed, the Court reasoned that none of the cited cases illustrated whether a "common-law court would or would not have granted . . . a petition for a writ of habeas corpus" like that brought by the noncitizen-detainee petitioners, and candidly acknowledged that "the common-law courts simply may not have confronted cases with close parallels." But crucially, the Court declined to "infer too much, one way or the other, from the lack of historical evidence on point." Instead, it sought to find comparable common-law habeas cases by "analogy."

There is no squaring the Court's methodology today with *St. Cyr* or *Boumediene. . . .*

Applying the correct (and commonsense) approach to defining the Great Writ's historic scope reveals that respondent's claims have long been recognized in habeas.

Respondent cites *Somerset v. Stewart* (K.B. 1772), as an example on point. There, Lord Mansfield issued a writ ordering release of a slave bound for Jamaica, holding that there was no basis in English law for "sending . . . him over" to another country. Thus, the writ issued even though it "did not free [the] slave so much as it protected him from deportation." P. Halliday, *Habeas Corpus: From England to Empire* 175 (2010). *Somerset* establishes the longstanding availability of the writ to challenge the legality of removal and to secure release into a country in which a petitioner sought shelter. . . .

The Court acknowledges that the petitioner in *Somerset* may have been allowed to remain in England because of his release on habeas, yet declares that this was "due not to the wri[t] ordering [his] release" but rather to the existing state of the law. But the writ clearly did more than permit the petitioner to disembark from a vessel; it prevented him from being "sen[t] . . . over" to Jamaica. What England's immigration laws might have prescribed after the writ's issuance did not bear on the availability of the writ as a means to remain in the country in the first instance.

Colonial governments presumed habeas was available to noncitizens to secure their residence in a territory. For example, in 1755, British authorities sought to deport French Acadian settlers from Nova Scotia, then under the control of Great Britain, to the American Colonies. The Governor and Assembly of South Carolina resisted the migrants' arrival and detained them in ships off the coast of Charleston. They recognized, however, that the exclusion could not persist because the migrants would be entitled to avail themselves of habeas corpus. Ultimately, the Governor released most of the Acadian migrants for resettlement throughout the Colony.

Founding era courts accepted this view of the writ's scope. Rather than credit these decisions, the Court marches through an assorted selection of cases and throws up its hands, contending that the case law merely reflects a wide range of circumstances for which individuals were deprived of their liberty. Thus, the Court concludes, the common law simply did not speak to whether individuals could seek "release" that would allow them to enter a country (as opposed to being expelled from it). . . .

At least two other classes of cases demonstrate that the writ was available from around the founding onward to noncitizens who were detained, and wanted to remain, including those who were prevented from entering the United States at all.

First, common-law courts historically granted the writ to discharge deserting foreign sailors found and imprisoned in the United States. In *Commonwealth v. Holloway* (1815), the Pennsylvania Supreme Court granted a writ of habeas corpus to a Danish sailor who had deserted his vessel in violation of both an employment contract and Danish law. The court explained that the desertion did not violate any domestic law or treaty, and thus imprisonment was inappropriate. By ordering an unconditional discharge and declining to return the noncitizen sailor to the custody of any foreign power, the court used the writ to order a release that authorized a noncitizen to remain in the United States, a country "other than his own." The same was true in similar cases that even the Court cites.

Curiously, the Court does not contest that the writs in these cases were used to secure the liberty of foreign sailors, and consequently their right to enter the country. Rather, it remarks that judges at the time "chafed at having to order even release," which some saw as inconsistent with principles of comity. But reluctance is not inability. That those judges followed the law's dictates despite their distaste for the result should give today's Court pause.

Next, courts routinely granted the writ to release wrongfully detained noncitizens into Territories other than the detainees' "own." Many involved the release of fugitive or former slaves outside their home State. In these cases, courts decided legal questions as to the status of these petitioners. In *Arabas v. Ivers* (Conn. Super. Ct. 1784), for example, a Connecticut court determined that a former slave from New York held in local jail on his alleged master's instructions had, in fact, been freed through his service in the Continental Army. The court ordered him discharged "upon the ground that he was a freeman, absolutely manumitted from his master by enlisting and serving in the army." *See also In re Belt* (1848) (granting habeas to discharge an imprisoned fugitive slave whose owner did not timely apply for his return to Maryland); *In re Ralph* (Iowa 1839) (discharging person from custody on the grounds that he was not a fugitive slave subject to return to Missouri when he had been allowed to travel to the Iowa Territory by his former master); *Commonwealth v. Holloway* (Pa. 1816) (holding on habeas corpus that a child born in a free State to a slave was free); *In re Richardson's Case* (No. 11,778) (CC DC 1837) (ordering prisoner to be discharged in the District of Columbia because warrant was insufficient to establish that he was a runaway slave from Maryland); *Commonwealth v. Griffith* (1823) (contemplating that the status of a freeman seized in

Massachusetts as an alleged fugitive from Virginia could be determined on habeas corpus).

The weight of historical evidence demonstrates that common-law courts at and near the founding granted habeas to noncitizen detainees to enter Territories not considered their own, and thus ordered the kind of release that the Court claims falls outside the purview of the common-law writ.

The Court argues that none of this evidence is persuasive because the writ could not be used to compel authorization to enter the United States. But that analogy is inapt. Perhaps if respondent here sought to use the writ to grant naturalization, the comparison would be closer. But respondent sought only the proper interpretation and application of asylum law (which statutorily permits him to remain if he shows a credible fear of persecution), or in the alternative, release pursuant to the writ (despite being cognizant that he could be denied asylum or rearrested upon release if he were found within the country without legal authorization). But that consequence does not deprive respondent of the ability to invoke the writ in the first instance. *See, e.g., Lewis v. Fullerton* (1821) (affirming that a judgment on habeas corpus in favor of a slave was not conclusive of her rights but merely permitted release from custody on the record before the court and did not prohibit recapture by a master); *Ralph* (noting that an adjudication that petitioner was not a fugitive only exempted him from fugitive-slave laws but did not prohibit master from entering Territory to reclaim him on his own accord). . . .

The Court also appears to contend that respondent sought merely additional procedures in his habeas adjudication and that this kind of relief does not fall within the traditional scope of the writ. That reflects a misunderstanding of the writ. Habeas courts regularly afforded the state additional opportunities to show that a detention was lawful before ordering what the Court now considers a release outright.

The common-law writ of *habeas corpus ad subjiciendum* evolved into what we know and hail as the "Great Writ." *See* 3 W. Blackstone, Commentaries on the Laws of England 131 (1768). That writ, at bottom, allowed a court to elicit the cause for an individual's imprisonment and to ensure that he be released, granted bail, or promptly tried. *See* Oaks, *Habeas Corpus in the States — 1776–1865,* 32 U. Chi. L. Rev. 243, 244 (1965). From its origins, the writ did not require immediate release, but contained procedures that would allow the state to proceed against a detainee. Under the English Habeas Corpus Act of 1679, jailers were ordered to make a "return" to a writ within a designated time period and certify the true causes of imprisonment. Justices of the King's Bench obtained returns that provided full legal accounts justifying detention. They also examined and were guided by depositions upon which a detention was founded to determine whether to admit a petitioner to bail. Indeed, the King's Bench routinely considered facts not asserted in the return to assist scrutiny of detentions.

Moreover, early practice showed that common-law habeas courts routinely held proceedings to determine whether detainees should be discharged immediately or whether the state could subject them to further proceedings, including trial in compliance with proper procedures. *See Ex parte Bollman* (1807) (taking testimony in conjunction with an "inquiry" to determine whether "the accused shall be discharged or held to trial"). In *Ex parte Kaine* (CC SDNY 1853), for example, a federal court analyzed whether a petitioner, who had been found guilty of an offense by a commissioner, was subject to extradition. The court passed on questions of law concerning whether the commissioner had the power to adjudicate petitioner's criminality. Ultimately, the court found that petitioner was "entitled to be discharged from imprisonment" due to defects in the proceedings before the commissioner, but entertained further evidence on whether he could nevertheless be extradited. Only after finding no additional evidence that would permit extradition did the court order release.

Similarly, in *Coleman v. Tennessee* (1879), the petitioner had been convicted of a capital offense by a state court, even though he had committed the offense while a soldier in the United States Army. This Court granted habeas on the grounds that the state-court judgment was void but, because the petitioner had also been found guilty of murder by a military court, nevertheless turned the prisoner over to the custody of the military for appropriate punishment. Not surprisingly, then, the Court has found that habeas courts may discharge detainees in a manner that would allow defects in a proceeding below to be corrected. *In re Bonner* (1894).

These examples confirm that . . . common-law courts understood that relief short of release, such as ordering officials to comply with the law and to correct underlying errors, . . . fell within the scope of a request for habeas corpus.

3

[With respect to the Court's conclusion that Thurassigiam has no due process rights other than those provided by statute, Justice Sotomayor wrote:]

The Court deems that respondent possesses only the rights of noncitizens on the "threshold of initial entry." But that relies on a legal fiction. Respondent, of course, was actually within the territorial limits of the United States.

More broadly, by drawing the line for due process at legal admission rather than physical entry, the Court tethers constitutional protections to a noncitizen's legal status as determined under contemporary asylum and immigration law. But the Fifth Amendment, which of course long predated any admissions program, does not contain limits based on immigration status or duration in the country: It applies to "persons" without qualification. *Yick Wo* (1886). The Court has repeatedly affirmed as much long after Congress began regulating entry to the country. The Court lacks any textual basis to craft an exception to this rule, let alone one hinging on dynamic immigration laws that may be amended at any time, to redefine when an "entry" occurs. Fundamentally, it is out of step with how this Court has conceived the scope of the Due Process Clause for over a century: Congressional policy in the immigration context does not dictate the scope of the Constitution.

Perhaps recognizing the tension between its opinion today and those cases, the Court cabins its holding to individuals who are "in respondent's position." Presumably the rule applies to—and only to—individuals found within 25 feet of the border who have entered within the past 24 hours of their apprehension. Where its logic must stop, however, is hard to say. Taken to its extreme, a rule conditioning due process rights on lawful entry would permit Congress to constitutionally eliminate all procedural protections for any noncitizen the Government deems unlawfully admitted and summarily deport them no matter how many decades they have

1008 Chapter 8. The Writ of Habeas Corpus

lived here, how settled and integrated they are in their communities, or how many members of their family are U.S. citizens or residents.

This judicially fashioned line-drawing is not administrable, threatens to create arbitrary divisions between noncitizens in this country subject to removal proceedings, and, most important, lacks any basis in the Constitution.

* * *

The methodology the Court uses in *Boumediene* to determine whether the writ runs to foreign nationals detained at Guantanamo is explicitly functionalist. Finding ambiguity in the historical record the Court weighs three functional considerations: (1) the citizenship and status of the detainee and the adequacy of the process through which that status determination was made; (2) the nature of the sites where apprehension and then detention took place; and (3) the practical obstacles inherent in resolving the prisoner's entitlement to the writ. The purpose of this approach is to ensure that the writ protects both liberty and separation of powers even in a setting where the executive branch is entitled to deference. In *Thuraissigiam*, by contrast, the approach is decidedly formalist—indeterminacy in the historical record is weighed against the petitioner, the Court treats release from custody as the remedial essence of the writ, and it stresses the unilateral authority of Congress to control the border by, if it wishes, eliminating judicial review altogether for certain people seeking entry.

The first *Boumediene* factor—"adequacy of the process through which" an enemy combatant "status determination is made"—might be thought to have a parallel in Thuraissigiam's assertion that the process for considering his asylum claim was flawed and fundamentally unfair. Procedural defects in executive branch decisions leading to detention are commonly raised in habeas petitions. *See Scaggs v. Larsen* (1969) (petitioner alleged denial of notice and a meaningful opportunity to be heard on violation of the terms of his enlistment contract before being taken into military custody and restored to active duty). Indeed, if one begins with the *Boumediene* framework, Thuraissigiam, an asylum seeker, arguably has a stronger claim to the privilege of the writ than a foreign national suspected of being an enemy combatant. Recall that in *Hamdi* the Court emphasized its obligation to assess the government's procedures with the potentially innocent right-holder in mind, not one who is guilty or poses a threat, for the obvious reason that almost no test will weigh in favor of additional procedural protections for the latter class. *Thuraissigiam* thus raises the question whether *Boumediene*'s methodology is now a derelict in the Court's habeas jurisprudence.

Because Thuraissigiam raised an "as applied" challenge to the jurisdiction stripping provisions of the expedited removal statute, many other questions remain open about how the Court will (1) handle cases in which a habeas petitioner already resides in the United States or can otherwise show deeper connections than someone apprehended in the act of entry 25 yards from the border, and (2) how it will apply its holding that due process of law can be defined by Congress at the border.

Although we have concentrated on §2241 as it has been applied to detention of foreign nationals detained overseas and immigration detention at the border, the statute is trans-substantive and therefore permits review of other forms of unlawful detention. For example, "while the writ may not be used to correct mere errors or irregularities, however flagrant," in a finding of contempt of court, "it is an appropriate writ to obtain the discharge of one imprisoned [for contempt] under the order of a court of the United States which does not possess jurisdiction of the person or of the subject matter." *In re Terry* (1888). A habeas petition may also be filed by a person held in custody pre-trial in violation of the Sixth Amendment right to a speedy trial, *see United States v. Tootle* (4th Cir. 1995), and a person held in military custody who seeks to challenge an order directing return to active duty beyond the term of the enlistment contract. *See Scaggs v. Larsen* (1969); *see also Parisi v. Davidson* (1972) (conscientious objector who had exhausted administrative procedures for relief entitled to pursue habeas to avoid compulsory service; permitting district court to stay pending court martial where conscientious objector status was an available defense).

Lastly, note that while §2254 covers habeas petitions filed by state prisoners whose state criminal convictions have become final, §2241(c)(2) permits challenges to other forms of state detention, including federal officers arrested while performing functions of their office by state officials. *See Clifton v. Cox* (9th Cir. 1977) (federal drug enforcement officer arrested and charged by state prosecutors with second degree murder and involuntary manslaughter after firing weapon in attempting to execute warrants against suspects believed to be armed and dangerous was "in custody for an act done . . . in pursuance of [federal law]" and therefore entitled to habeas to seek release from state custody).

B. COLLATERAL ATTACK ON STATE CRIMINAL CONVICTIONS

The second major area of federal habeas practice involves the review of criminal convictions that have become final on direct appeal. In this context, habeas functions as a form of collateral attack—federal court review of a criminal judgment follows and is collateral to the ordinary process of trial or plea, conviction, sentencing, and direct appeal. Federal courts have statutory authority to review collateral attacks on both state and federal criminal convictions under 28 U.S.C. §§2254 and 2255, respectively. In this Section we will concentrate on the review of state convictions under §2254, which codified the 1867 Act's extension of federal habeas jurisdiction to cases involving detention by state officers.

We do so for a number of reasons. First, there are many such cases in modern practice—about one out of every fourteen civil cases filed in the U.S. district courts every year is a non-capital habeas petition challenging a state conviction.[45] In some districts, the caseload is far higher. The Eastern District of California covers 19 of the state's 33 prisons and houses 60 percent of the state's prison population. In

---

45. *See generally,* James Duff, Judicial Business of the United States Courts (2007).

2007, nearly half (47%) of the court's civil docket was habeas petitions filed by state prisoners:

> Each of the six judges had 420 prisoner petitions during the year. . . . The demands of prisoner petitions, often handwritten by inmates with limited education and no legal training, falls heavily on the remaining caseload. . . . When cases were weighted for complexity, the Eastern District had 869 cases per judgeship, the second-highest rate in the United States. Only the Eastern District of Louisiana had more, after the surge of cases following Hurricane Katrina.[46]

Nationally, filings gradually increased alongside a dramatic increase in the population of American prisons beginning in the 1970s and the Warren Court's expansion of habeas jurisdiction under the 1867 Act.

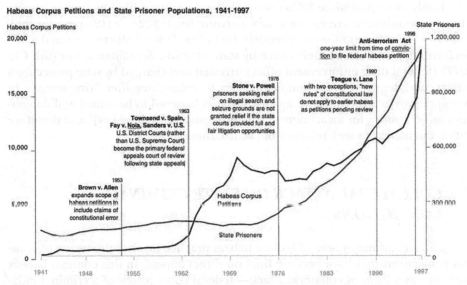

Fred Cheesman et al., Nat'l Ctr. for State Courts, *Prisoner Litigation in Relation to Prisoner Population*, 4 CASELOAD HIGHLIGHTS No. 2, at 2 (Sept. 1998).

Second, the implications of federal habeas review for the administration of criminal justice in state courts are substantial, injecting lower federal courts into the supervision of state criminal enforcement. Collateral review by the lower federal courts is also an important mechanism for enforcing federal constitutional guarantees incorporated against the states—all the more so since, as we will see in Chapter 9, the modern Supreme Court rarely grants certiorari to review state cases on direct appeal. As one major treatise on habeas summarizes, federal habeas jurisdiction over state convictions has been "the most controversial and friction producing issue in the relation between federal and state courts," leaving federal

---

46. Pamela A. MacLean, *Inmate Petitions Swamp Judges*, NAT'L L.J. (Aug. 4, 2008).

judges "unhappy" and state courts "resent[ful]."[47] Controversy and friction is produced not just by the potential intrusiveness of federal habeas review, but by some state courts' "[f]lamboyant gestures of defiance" and "subtler forms of resistance" to basic federal constitutional guarantees.[48] In part to address concerns of federalism and comity, and in part responding to the persistent, tendentious characterization of federal habeas as "a form of occupational therapy" on which state prisoners "thrive,"[49] Congress enacted significant restrictions on federal habeas review of state convictions in the Antiterrorism and Effective Death Penalty Act of 1996. The statute built in some areas on restrictions developed by the modern Supreme Court to curb Warren Court precedents. In other areas, however, the statute surpassed restrictive doctrines developed by the Court and fundamentally altered habeas jurisdiction under the 1867 Act just as the late twentieth century forces contributing to mass incarceration reached their peak.

The most basic question in post-conviction habeas is why cases should be reopened after a defendant has been convicted or pled guilty and had an opportunity to raise any errors on direct appeal. The standard of review determines how far a case may be reopened on habeas. The standard of review is thus one of the most important and contested aspects of this exercise of jurisdiction and the changes made by Congress in 1996. We will study these changes in the standard of review closely. Notice that, unlike executive detention, where there has been *no* judicial process associated with the decision to deprive someone of physical liberty, in post-conviction habeas there has always been, *by definition*, some form of judicial process. Even the entry of a plea bargain must be supervised by a judge who is supposed to ensure that the plea is a knowing, voluntary, and intelligent waiver of the right to trial.

If the central purpose of habeas is to provide for judicial review of the legality of detention, what justifies the extension of habeas jurisdiction to the post-conviction setting? Interposing additional layers of judicial review is very different from ensuring that no one is detained without *any* judicial review at all. Is it enough to justify post-conviction collateral attack to say that Congress has authorized it since the 1867 Act? That state courts, like executive officers, are capable of defying the constitution? That underfunding of state courts and crowded dockets can produce constitutional error among even the most conscientious state judges and well-designed standards for judicial process? That the retreat from Reconstruction and the rise of Jim Crow segregation produced distortions in the states' administration of criminal justice? That these distortions linger?

Especially if you favor searching federal court review of state court convictions, notice that matters are further complicated by assessing state court convictions according to constitutional law that evolves *after* a conviction becomes final. It is no small thing to displace a state court judgment that was constitutionally sound

---

47. 17 A Wright, Miller & Cooper, Federal Practice and Procedure §4261 (2d ed. 1988).

48. Robert G. McCloskey, *Reflections on the Warren Court*, 51 Va. L. Rev. 1229, 1260 (1965). *See also* Del Dickson, *State Court Defiance and the Limits of Supreme Court Authority: Williams v. Georgia Revisited*, 103 Yale L.J. 1423 (1994).

49. *Id.*

when it was made using rules of decision that the state judges who decided the case could not have anticipated. And given that some claims of constitutional error in the adjudication of a criminal case are not tied to actual innocence, habeas jurisdiction under the 1867 Act presents the specter of a federal court superseding the judgment of state judges and jurors and ordering the release of people who are factually guilty. Notice too that protracted litigation over a criminal conviction not only consumes valuable judicial resources and undermines the state's (and victim's) interest in finality, it can interfere with the socially and personally important work of rehabilitation when factually guilty prisoners focus their time in prison on trial errors unconnected to substantive culpability or trial events that are susceptible to collateral attack only through decisions issued long after the trial ended.

On the other hand, bias and constitutional error remain present in state criminal process, and when a state chooses long-term incarceration as a remedy its interest in finality is arguably lower than if the punishment entails no continuing infringement on the liberty of the defendant. We also now know that decades of mass incarceration at the turn of the century resulted in the conviction of people who were innocent, overcharging of people guilty of lesser offenses, and plea bargains obtained by coercion. One study found that "over 2,000 individuals who have been exonerated in the United States in just the past 20 years."[50] Another found 340 DNA-based exonerations, 20 of which involved people who had been sentenced to death. Studies of exonerations suggest that the number of people who have pled guilty to a crime they did not commit since 1989 is between 11 and 20 percent of all exonerations.[51] Judge Learned Hand's conjecture in 1923 that "the ghost of the innocent man convicted" arrives only in an "unreal dream" is plainly counterfactual.[52]

Exonerations have revealed numerous flaws in the way evidence is gathered to support a prosecution, including: unreliable eyewitness testimony that identifies innocent people as perpetrators (because, e.g., the officer administering a lineup knows who the suspect is and subtly biases the lineup, the confidence of the person making the identification is not determined, and failure to videorecord the procedure limits effective assessment cross examination of eyewitnesses identifications at trial), multiple forms of forensic analysis that are known to be scientifically unreliable (e.g., undisclosed lab errors and notorious problems with the methods of hair, fiber, and bite mark analysis) and introduced through flawed expert testimony, and false confessions, especially from young suspects and suspects with disabilities.[53] Another "study found that 37% of the DNA exoneration cases involved the suppression of exculpatory evidence, 25% involved the knowing use of false testimony, and 11% involved the undisclosed use of coerced witness testimony."[54]

---

50. Brandon L. Garrett, *Actual Innocence and Wrongful Convictions*, in 3 A REPORT ON SCHOLARSHIP AND CRIMINAL JUSTICE REFORM 193, 193-194 (Erik Luna ed. 2017).

51. Samuel R. Gross et al., *Exonerations in the United States 1989 Through 2003*, 95 J. CRIM. L. & CRIMINOL. 523, 524 (2005); https://www.nbcnews.com/think/opinion/prisons-are-packed-because-prosecutors-are-coercing-plea-deals-yes-ncna1034201.

52. *United States v. Garsson*, 291 F. 646, 649 (S.D.N.Y. 1923).

53. Brandon L. Garrett, *Wrongful Convictions*, 3 ANNU. REV. CRIMINOL. 245, 250 (2020).

54. *Id.* at 254.

The record of anti-black racial bias in the administration of criminal justice is long and disturbing. "When the Supreme Court struck down Georgia's capital punishment statute [in 1972] it observed that of the 455 persons sentenced to death for rape in this country since the Justice Department started keeping statistics in 1930, 405 were black."[55] By the end of the twentieth century, death row populations and executions across the country, north and south, remained disproportionately black (71% of people executed in Georgia after the Court revived the death penalty in 1976; 75% of those executed in Mississippi; 70% of those executed in Alabama; 79% of death row inmates in Maryland; 61% of Illinois's).[56] In 1990, the U.S. General Accounting Office concluded that studies of capital punishment showed significant bias "in favor of the death penalty in white victim cases."[57]

More recent studies are in accord and reveal that racial bias pervades the administration of criminal justice. Black people are disproportionately likely to be subject to a traffic stop—a study of traffic stop data from 20 states between 2011-2015 "confirms that . . . police officers stopped Black drivers more often than White drivers relative to their appearance in the population of citizens who were old enough to drive."[58] In North Carolina, "the odds of a Black driver in the population appearing in NC traffic stop data were 60-70% higher than the odds of a Black [person driving] in the population in which the traffic stop occurred."[59] Research shows that racial disparities persist in:

- street stops and searches (in New York, Black and Latino men are more likely to be stopped and frisked even though contraband or a weapon was more likely to be found on a White person);
- use of both lethal and non-lethal force ("even after controlling for variables like the rate of crime in the precinct, suspect demeanor, and the presence of a weapon; . . . the odds of an unarmed Black person being shot by police were 3.5 times greater than the odds for a White person");
- arrest rates (especially those tied to law enforcement policies such as which controlled substances to focus on in drug enforcement, outdoor versus indoor sales of illegal drugs, and enhanced enforcement regarding juvenile offenders);
- charging (prosecutors are "more likely to charge Black defendants than White defendants with crimes that carry mandatory minimum sentences");
- pretrial detention ("Blacks and Hispanics were more likely than Whites to be denied bail . . . less likely to make bail . . . [and] the bail amounts offered to Whites were lower than those offered to Blacks and Hispanics even after controlling for relevant legal characteristics, including those associated with risk of dangerousness or flight");

---

55. Bryan A. Stevenson & Ruth E. Friedman, *Deliberate Indifference: Judicial Tolerance of Racial Bias in Criminal Justice*, 51 WASH. & LEE L. REV. 509, 511 (1994) (citing Justice Marshall's opinion in *Furman v. Georgia*, 408 U.S. 280, 305 (1972)).

56. *Id.*

57. *Id.* at 512.

58. Margaret Bull Kovera, *Racial Disparities in the Criminal Justice System: Prevalence, Causes, and a Search for Solutions*, 75 J. Soc. Issues 1139, 1141 (2019).

59. *Id.*

- the value of plea offers (white defendants were "more likely than Black defendants to be offered pleas that involve community service, a fine or time served," and whites were more likely to be offered reduced charges);
- the severity of sentences ("Blacks and Hispanics received harsher sentences than did Whites even after controlling for legally relevant factors that should influence sentencing decisions," including a higher likelihood of sentences involving incarceration, and longer sentences for both first-time and repeat offenders of color); and
- wrongful convictions for certain offenses ("[i]nnocent Black people are 3.5 times more likely than innocent White people to be convicted of sexual assault, 7 times more likely to be convicted of murder, and 12 times more likely to be convicted of drug crimes [in part because] White witnesses are more likely to misidentify Black and Hispanic perpetrators than White perpetrators").[60]

Combined with "tough on crime" policies adopted since the 1970s emphasizing incapacitation through incarceration, the net effect is that the "United States now imprisons a greater proportion of its population than any other country in the world," including non-democratic, authoritarian regimes.[61] And although black people constitute just "13% of those imprisoned, they represent over 30% of those imprisoned, with one in four Black men incarcerated at some point in their lives."[62] Historians have drawn a direct link to Jim Crow segregation and its reliance on criminal law both to justify and enforce the color line through "the stigmatization of crime as 'black'"—treating criminality as an attribute of the group itself—"and the masking of crime among whites as individual failure."[63]

The 1867 Act's extension of federal court jurisdiction over state convictions thus requires coming to terms not only with the terrible suffering and trauma caused by crime, but also the pathologies of racism and constitutional failure in the enforcement of criminal law, and the strengths and limitations of the remedial power of the writ. In the cases and materials that follow, all of these aspects of habeas jurisdiction are visible, alongside questions of federalism and the supremacy of federal law we have investigated in every Chapter.

1. Procedural Prerequisites to Collateral Attack on State Court Judgments

Before turning to the standard of review, notice that there are important, outcome-determinative procedural prerequisites to filing a habeas petition seeking federal court review of a state court conviction. These include requirements that the petitioner:

---

60. *Id.* at 1140-47.

61. *Id.* at 1144.

62. *Id.*

63. KHALIL MUHAMMED, THE CONDEMNATION OF BLACKNESS: RACE, CRIME, AND THE MAKING OF MODERN URBAN AMERICA 3 (2010).

- be "in custody,"
- "exhaust" available state remedies first,
- avoid "procedural default" in state court,
- file within the statute of limitations,
- meet narrow standards set for "second or successive" petitions, and
- meet narrow standards to obtain an evidentiary hearing.

These doctrines are famously intricate, and although not intended to create "hurdle[s] on the path to federal habeas court,"[64] the practical effect is just that, especially in non-capital cases where 93 percent of petitioners appear *pro se*.[65] There is no federal constitutional right to counsel in a habeas proceeding. *Gideon v. Wainwright* (1963) provides a right to counsel at trial in felony cases. The Court extended the right to counsel to misdemeanors involving incarceration in *Argersinger v. Hamlin* (1972), and to direct appeal on equal protection grounds in *Douglas v. California* (1963), but *not* collateral attack. *See Johnson v. Avery* (1969); *Pennsylvania v. Finley* (1987) ("We have never held that prisoners have a constitutional right to counsel when mounting collateral attacks upon their convictions and we decline to so hold today."). Congress has, however, provided a right to counsel by statute in federal habeas proceedings in capital cases since the 1980s. In non-capital cases, counsel may be appointed by a district judge who "determines that the interests of justice so require . . . for any financially eligible person who . . . is seeking relief under section 2241, 2244, or 2254 of title 28." 18 U.S.C. §3006A(a)(2). The Rules Governing Section 2254 cases state that if a petitioner is financially eligible under §3006A, the judge "must appoint an attorney" if an evidentiary hearing "is warranted" or if counsel is "necessary for effective discovery." Rules 6(a) & 8(c). But since district courts grant evidentiary hearings in just 1 of every 243 non-capital cases for reasons we will explore below, there is rarely occasion to appoint counsel on these grounds.

a. Custody

A petitioner must be "in custody pursuant to the judgment of a State court." 28 U.S.C. §2254(a). The state court judgment is most commonly a criminal conviction. Note, however, that the language of the statute is not limited to state criminal convictions. This means that other forms of state custody may be challenged. As the Supreme Court stated in *Duncan v. Walker* (2001):

> Incarceration pursuant to a state criminal conviction may be by far the most common and most familiar basis for satisfaction of the "in custody" requirement in §2254 cases. But there are other types of state court judgments pursuant to which a person may be held in custody within the meaning of the federal habeas statute. For example, federal habeas corpus

---

64. O'Sullivan v. Boerckel, 526 U.S. 838, 845 (1999).

65. Nancy J. King et al., Final Technical Report: Habeas Litigation in U.S. District Courts 8 (August 2007).

review may be available to challenge the legality of a state court order of civil commitment or a state court order of civil contempt. These types of state court judgments neither constitute nor require criminal convictions.

"Custody" under §2254(a) is not strictly limited to immediate physical restraints on liberty either. The Court has held, for instance, that a parolee remains "in custody" for purpose of habeas jurisdiction where the conditions of parole involve "significant" restraints on the petitioner's liberty. *Jones v. Cunningham* (1963) (petitioner could not leave a specified town, move homes, or lose his job; he had to report to a parole officer and remained subject to the supervision of the parole board which could revoke his parole and return him to incarceration). *See also Peyton v. Rowe* (1968) (petitioner serving first of two consecutive sentences was in custody for purposes of challenging the second); *Hensley v. Municipal Court* (1973) (petitioner released while granted a stay of his of sentence prior to serving any time was in custody for purposes of challenging sentence after exhausting available state procedures).

Generally, release from custody moots a habeas petition. *Spencer v. Kemna* (1998). However, when a conviction carries with it significant collateral consequences that endure after release from incarceration, a habeas petition filed while the petitioner is in custody is not mooted by release. *Carafas v. LaVallee* (1960) (collateral consequences such as a bar on service as a labor union officer, voting, and jury service, which "survive the satisfaction of the sentence imposed" gave petitioner a continued stake in challenging the conviction); *cf. Maleng v. Cook* (1989) (petitioner is not "in custody" for purposes of challenging prior conviction, already fully served, but may challenge the use of an allegedly unconstitutional prior conviction as a sentencing enhancement of a new conviction); *Lackawanna Dist. Att'y v. Coss* (2001) (even if custody requirement is met, petitioner serving a sentence that was enhanced due to a prior conviction generally may not obtain federal habeas relief unless denied the right to challenge the prior sentence when it was imposed).

A significant effect of the custody requirement is that habeas is generally unavailable for misdemeanors and other offenses for which the term of imprisonment is brief and therefore expires before one could pursue habeas, or for which the sentence involves financial penalties rather than incarceration. In one study, 60% of state felony defendants did not receive a prison sentence at all, and for those who did, the sentence was less than five years, with only about two-thirds of the sentence actually served.[66] Lesser offenses such as suspension of a driver's license and imposition of a fine—penalties that can have grave consequences for low-income people who depend on a car to get to work and whose job is the only means of paying off even modest fines—do not constitute the kinds of restraints on liberty amounting to "custody" for purposes of §2254(a). *See Lillios v. New Hampshire* (1st Cir. 1986); *Westberry v. Keith* (5th Cir. 1970).

---

66. MATTHEW R. DUROSE & PATRICK A. LANGAN, FELONY SENTENCES IN STATE COURTS, 2004, BUREAU OF JUSTICE STATISTICS BULLETIN 1-2 (July 2007).

b.   Exhaustion

A §2254 petition may not be entertained unless the petitioner has first exhausted available state court remedies. 28 U.S.C. §2254(b) and (c). Exhaustion is required in order to "give the state courts one full opportunity to resolve any constitutional issues by invoking one complete round of the State's established appellate review process." *O'Sullivan v. Boerckel* (1999). The Court has emphasized that giving the state courts an opportunity to address claims of constitutional error first sounds in comity and federalism:

> The exhaustion doctrine existed long before its codification by Congress in 1948. In *Ex parte Royall* (1886), this Court wrote that, as a matter of comity, federal courts should not consider a claim in a habeas corpus petition until after the state courts have had an opportunity to act:
>
>> The injunction to hear the case summarily, and thereupon to dispose of the party as law and justice require does not deprive the court of discretion as to the time and mode in which it will exert the powers conferred upon it. That discretion should be exercised in the light of the relations existing, under our system of government, between the judicial tribunals of the Union and of the States, and in recognition of the fact that the public good requires that those relations be not disturbed by unnecessary conflict between courts equally bound to guard and protect rights secured by the Constitution.
>>
>> Subsequent cases refined the principle that state remedies must be exhausted except in unusual circumstances. *See, e.g., United States ex rel. Kennedy v. Tyler* (1925) (holding that the lower court should have dismissed the petition because none of the questions had been raised in the state courts. "In the regular and ordinary course of procedure, the power of the highest state court in respect of such questions should first be exhausted"). In *Ex parte Hawk* (1944), this Court reiterated that comity was the basis for the exhaustion doctrine:
>>
>>> It is a principle controlling all habeas corpus petitions to the federal courts that those courts will interfere with the administration of justice in the state courts only in rare cases where exceptional circumstances of peculiar urgency are shown to exist.

Granberry v. Greer (1987). The Court has held that exceptional circumstances exist "only if there is no opportunity to obtain redress in state court or if the [state's] corrective process is so clearly deficient as to render futile any effort to obtain relief." *Duckworth v. Serrano* (1981) (reversing circuit court's decision to entertain ineffective assistance of counsel claim based on a conflict of interest of defense counsel so clear as to constitute a per se violation of the Sixth Amendment; "the exhaustion requirement . . . serves to minimize friction between our federal state systems by allowing the State an initial opportunity to pass upon and correct alleged violations of prisoner's federal rights . . . and here neither the Court of Appeals nor the respondent contends that Indiana's postconviction procedures are inadequate to adjudicate the ineffective-assistance claim"). This high threshold has been met only when the state process is a mere sham, *see Ashe v. United States ex rel. Valotta* (1926) (failure to exhaust excused because state court process was "under the domination of a mob" and provided "only the form of a court" and judicial process), or where requiring exhaustion would compromise overriding federal interests such as interference with federal officers performing their duties, *Ohio v. Thomas* (1899) (habeas petition challenging arrest of federal officer providing services at federal disabled veterans facility), state process impedes the administration of justice in a federal tribunal, *In re Loney* (1890) (petitioner was needed for testimony in a federal tribunal), or continued state detention would undermine foreign relations, *see Wildenhus's Case* (1887) (exhaustion not required where foreign national asserted held in state custody in violation of treaty rights).

Generally, in order to meet the exhaustion requirement, a petitioner must have raised any federal claims against the judgment of conviction in the state's ordinary process of direct appeal before pursuing a §2254 petition. *See Brown v. Allen* (1953) (it is not necessary for a petitioner "to ask the state for collateral relief based upon the same evidence and issues already decided by direct review"); *cf. Wade v. Mayo* (1948) (state collateral review is necessary for issues not presented on direct review). Since a state's direct appeal process can take years, exhaustion operates in concert with the custody requirement to diminish the significance of habeas where convictions involve short sentences of incarceration. *See Markuson v. Boucher* (1899) (fact that one-year sentence would be complete before exhaustion of state process is not grounds for relief from exhaustion requirement); *Johnson v. Bauman* (6th Cir. 2022) ("inordinate delay" in state process might excuse exhaustion requirement, but only if the delay is caused by the state and extends beyond a few years).

c. Procedural Default

In the process of seeking to exhaust a federal constitutional claim in state court, a prisoner may violate a rule of state procedure such as a time of filing rule for an appeal. That violation may prompt the state court to decline to address the merits of the federal constitutional claim. Alternatively, a prisoner may fail to present a claim to the state courts before filing a federal petition under circumstances in which returning to state court for exhaustion is not possible due to state procedural law. Procedural default doctrine bars the prisoner from pursuing these claims in federal court.

The Warren Court's approach to procedural default was accommodating. A defendant was free to raise an issue not presented to the state courts unless it could be shown that there was a "deliberate bypass" of state procedures and forfeiture of state remedies; mere "inadvertence or neglect" to pursue state remedies did not bar a federal petition. *Fay v. Noia* (1963) (defendants convicted of murder during a robbery sentenced to life imprisonment permitted to raise coerced confessions in federal habeas petition despite failing to pursue state appeals because "a forfeiture of [state] remedies does not legitimize the unconstitutional conduct by which his conviction was procured"; adequate and independent state ground doctrine forecloses appellate jurisdiction of the Supreme Court's direct review of judgments that rest on state procedural law, but lower federal court habeas jurisdiction extends not to judgments "but detention simpliciter. . . . Indeed, [the federal court] cannot revise the state court judgment; it can only act on the body of the petitioner."). The Burger Court rejected this accommodating approach to procedural default in the following case.

Wainwright v. Sykes

433 U.S. 72 (1977)

Justice REHNQUIST delivered the opinion of the Court.

We granted certiorari to consider the availability of federal habeas corpus to review a state convict's claim that testimony was admitted at his trial in violation of his rights under *Miranda v. Arizona* (1966), a claim which the Florida courts have previously refused to consider on the merits because of noncompliance with a state contemporaneous-objection rule. Petitioner Wainwright, on behalf of the State of Florida, here challenges a decision of the Court of Appeals for the Fifth Circuit ordering a hearing in state court on the merits of respondent's contention.

Respondent Sykes was convicted of third-degree murder after a jury trial in the Circuit Court of DeSoto County. He testified at trial that, on the evening of January 8, 1972, he told his wife to summon the police because he had just shot Willie Gilbert. Other evidence indicated that, when the police arrived at respondent's trailer home, they found Gilbert dead of a shotgun wound, lying a few feet from the front porch. Shortly after their arrival, respondent came from across the road and volunteered that he had shot Gilbert, and a few minutes later respondent's wife approached the police and told them the same thing. Sykes was immediately arrested and taken to the police station.

Once there, it is conceded that he was read his *Miranda* rights, and that he declined to seek the aid of counsel and indicated a desire to talk. He then made a statement, which was admitted into evidence at trial through the testimony of the two officers who heard it, to the effect that he had shot Gilbert from the front porch of his trailer home; there were several references during the trial to respondent's consumption of alcohol during the preceding day and to his apparent state of intoxication, facts which were acknowledged by the officers who arrived at the scene. At no time during the trial, however, was the admissibility of any of respondent's statements challenged by his counsel on the ground that respondent had not understood the *Miranda* warnings. Nor did the trial judge question their admissibility on his own motion or hold a factfinding hearing bearing on that issue.

Respondent appealed his conviction, but apparently did not challenge the admissibility of the inculpatory statements. He later filed in the trial court a motion to vacate the conviction and, in the State District Court of Appeals and Supreme Court, petitions for habeas corpus. These filings, apparently for the first time, challenged the statements made to police on grounds of involuntariness. In all of these efforts, respondent was unsuccessful.

Having failed in the Florida courts, respondent initiated the present action under 28 U.S.C. §2254, asserting the inadmissibility of his statements by reason of his lack of understanding of the *Miranda* warnings.[4] The United States District Court for the Middle District of Florida ruled that *Jackson v. Denno* (1964) requires a hearing in a state criminal trial prior to the admission of an inculpatory out-of-court statement by the defendant. . . .

---

4. Respondent expressly waived "any contention or allegation as regards ineffective assistance of his counsel" at trial. . . .

Petitioner warden appealed this decision to the United States Court of Appeals for the Fifth Circuit. That court first considered the nature of the right to exclusion of statements made without a knowing waiver of the right to counsel and the right not to incriminate oneself. It noted that *Jackson v. Denno, supra,* guarantees a right to a hearing on whether a defendant has knowingly waived his rights as described to him in the *Miranda* warnings, and stated that, under Florida law "[t]he burden is on the State to secure [a] *prima facie* determination of voluntariness, not upon the defendant to demand it."

The court then directed its attention to the effect on respondent's right [to move to suppress under Florida law] which it described as "a contemporaneous objection rule" applying to motions to suppress a defendant's inculpatory statements. It focused on this Court's decisions in *Henry v. Mississippi* (1965), *Davis v. United States* (1973), and *Fay v. Noia* (1963), and concluded that the failure to comply with the rule requiring objection at the trial would only bar review of the suppression claim where the right to object was deliberately bypassed for reasons relating to trial tactics. The Court of Appeals distinguished our decision in *Davis, supra,* (where failure to comply with a rule requiring pretrial objection to the indictment was found to bar habeas review of the underlying constitutional claim absent showing of cause for the failure and prejudice resulting), for the reason that "[a] major tenet of the *Davis* decision was that no prejudice was shown" to have resulted from the failure to object. It found that prejudice is "inherent" in any situation, like the present one, where the admissibility of an incriminating statement is concerned. Concluding that "[t]he failure to object in this case cannot be dismissed as a trial tactic, and thus a deliberate by-pass," the court affirmed the District Court order that the State hold a hearing on whether respondent knowingly waived his *Miranda* rights at the time he made the statements.

The simple legal question before the Court calls for a construction of the language of 28 U.S.C. §2254(a), which provides that the federal courts shall entertain an application for a writ of habeas corpus

> in behalf of a person in custody pursuant to the judgment of a state court only on the ground that he is in custody in violation of the Constitution or laws or treaties of the United States. . . .

In 1867, Congress expanded the statutory language so as to make the writ available to one held in state, as well as federal, custody. For more than a century since the 1867 amendment, this Court has grappled with the relationship between the classical common law writ of habeas corpus and the remedy provided in 28 U.S.C. §2254. Sharp division within the Court has been manifested on more than one aspect of the perplexing problems which have been litigated in this connection. Where the habeas petitioner challenges a final judgment of conviction rendered by a state court, this Court has been called upon to decide no fewer than four different questions, all to a degree interrelated with one another: (1) What types of federal claims may a federal habeas court properly consider? (2) Where a federal claim is cognizable by a federal habeas court, to what extent must that court defer to a resolution of the claim in prior state proceedings? (3) To what extent must the petitioner who seeks federal habeas exhaust state remedies before resorting to the federal court? (4) In what instances will an adequate and independent state ground bar consideration of otherwise cognizable federal issues on federal habeas review?

Each of these four issues has spawned its share of litigation. With respect to the first, the rule laid down in *Ex parte Watkins* (1830), was gradually changed by judicial decisions expanding the availability of habeas relief beyond attacks focused narrowly on the jurisdiction of the sentencing court. *See Ex parte Wells* (1856); *Ex parte Lange* (1874). *Ex parte Siebold* (1880) authorized use of the writ to challenge a conviction under a federal statute where the statute was claimed to violate the United States Constitution. *Frank v. Mangum* (1915) and *Moore v. Dempsey* (1923), though in large part inconsistent with one another, together broadened the concept of jurisdiction to allow review of a claim of "mob domination" of what was in all other respects a trial in a court of competent jurisdiction.

In *Johnson v. Zerbst* (1938), an indigent federal prisoner's claim that he was denied the right to counsel at his trial was held to state a contention going to the "power and authority" of the trial court, which might be reviewed on habeas. Finally, in *Waley v. Johnston* (1942), the Court openly discarded the concept of jurisdiction — by then more a fiction than anything else — as a touchstone of the availability of federal habeas review, and acknowledged that such review is available for claims of "disregard of the constitutional rights of the accused, and where the writ is the only effective means of preserving his rights." In *Brown v. Allen* (1953), it was made explicit that a state prisoner's challenge to the trial court's resolution of dispositive federal issues is always fair game on federal habeas. Only last Term, in *Stone v. Powell* (1976), the Court removed from the purview of a federal habeas court challenges resting on the Fourth Amendment, where there has been a full and fair opportunity to raise them in the state court.

The "exhaustion of state remedies" requirement was first articulated by this Court in the case of *Ex parte Royall* (1886). There, a state defendant sought habeas in advance of trial on a claim that he had been indicted under an unconstitutional statute. The writ was dismissed by the District Court, and this Court affirmed, stating that, while there was power in the federal courts to entertain such petitions, as a matter of comity, they should usually stay their hand pending consideration of the issue in the normal course of the state trial.

There is no need to consider here in greater detail these first three areas of controversy attendant to federal habeas review of state convictions. Only the fourth area — the adequacy of state grounds to bar federal habeas review — is presented in this case. The foregoing discussion of the other three is pertinent here only as it illustrates this Court's historic willingness to overturn or modify its earlier views of the scope of the writ, even where the statutory language authorizing judicial action has remained unchanged.

As to the role of adequate and independent state grounds, it is a well established principle of federalism that a state decision resting on an adequate foundation of state substantive law is immune from review in the federal courts. *Fox Film Corp. v. Muller* (1935); *Murdock v. Memphis* (1875). The application of this principle in the context of a federal habeas proceeding has therefore excluded from consideration any questions of state substantive law, and thus effectively barred federal habeas review where questions of that sort are either the only ones raised by a petitioner or are, in themselves, dispositive of his case. The area of controversy which has developed has concerned the reviewability of federal claims which the state court has declined to pass on because not presented in the manner prescribed by its procedural rules. The adequacy of such an independent state procedural ground to prevent federal habeas review of the underlying federal issue has been treated very differently than where the state law ground is substantive. The pertinent decisions marking the Court's somewhat tortuous efforts to deal with this problem are: *Ex parte Spencer* (1913); *Brown v. Allen* (1953); *Fay v. Noia* (1963); *Davis v. United States* (1973); and *Francis v. Henderson* (1976).

In *Brown*, petitioner Daniels' lawyer had failed to mail the appeal papers to the State Supreme Court on the last day provided by law for filing, and hand delivered them one day after that date. Citing the state rule requiring timely filing, the Supreme Court of North Carolina refused to hear the appeal. This Court, relying in part on its earlier decision in *Ex parte Spencer*, held that federal habeas was not available to review a constitutional claim which could not have been reviewed on direct appeal here because it rested on an independent and adequate state procedural ground.

In *Fay v. Noia*, respondent Noia sought federal habeas to review a claim that his state court conviction had resulted from the introduction of a coerced confession in violation of the Fifth Amendment to the United States Constitution. While the convictions of his two codefendants were reversed on that ground in collateral proceedings following their appeals, Noia did not appeal, and the New York courts ruled that his subsequent *coram nobis* action was barred on account of that failure. This Court held that petitioner was nonetheless entitled to raise the claim in federal habeas, and thereby overruled its decision 10 years earlier in *Brown v. Allen*.

> [T]he doctrine under which state procedural defaults are held to constitute an adequate and independent state law ground barring direct Supreme Court review is not to be extended to limit the power granted the federal courts under the federal habeas statute.

As a matter of comity, but not of federal power, the Court acknowledged

> a limited discretion in the federal judge to deny relief . . . to an applicant who had deliberately by-passed the orderly procedure of the state courts, and, in so doing, has forfeited his state court remedies.

In so stating, the Court made clear that the waiver must be knowing and actual — "an intentional relinquishment or abandonment of a known right or privilege." Noting petitioner's "grisly choice" between acceptance of his life sentence and pursuit of an appeal which might culminate in a sentence of death, the Court concluded that there had been no deliberate bypass of the right to have the federal issues reviewed through a state appeal.

A decade later, we decided *Davis v. United States*, in which a federal prisoner's application under 28 U.S.C. §2255 sought for the first time to challenge the makeup of the grand jury which indicted him. The Government contended that he was barred by the requirement of Fed. Rule Crim. Proc. 12(b)(2) providing that such challenges must be raised "by motion before trial." The Rule further provides that failure to so object constitutes a waiver of the objection, but that "the court for cause shown may grant relief from the waiver." We noted that the Rule

> promulgated by this Court and, pursuant to 18 U.S.C. §3771, "adopted" by Congress, governs by its terms the manner in which the claims of defects in the institution of criminal proceedings may be waived,

and held that this standard contained in the Rule, rather than the *Fay v. Noia* concept of waiver, should pertain in federal habeas as on direct review. Referring to previous constructions of Rule 12(b)(2), we concluded that review of the claim should be barred on habeas, as on direct appeal, absent a showing of cause for the noncompliance and some showing of actual prejudice resulting from the alleged constitutional violation.

Last Term, in *Francis v. Henderson* the rule of *Davis* was applied to the parallel case of a state procedural requirement that challenges to grand jury composition be raised before trial. The Court noted that there was power in the federal courts to entertain an application in such a case, but rested its holding on "considerations of comity and concerns for the orderly administration of criminal justice. . . ." While there was no counterpart provision of the state rule which allowed an exception upon some showing of cause, the Court concluded that the standard derived from the Federal Rule should nonetheless be applied in that context, since

> [t]here is no reason to . . . give greater preclusive effect to procedural defaults by federal defendants than to similar defaults by state defendants.

As applied to the federal petitions of state convicts, the *Davis* "cause and prejudice" standard was thus incorporated directly into the body of law governing the availability of federal habeas corpus review. . . .

Respondent first contends that any discussion as to the effect that noncompliance with a state procedural rule should have on the availability of federal habeas is quite unnecessary, because, in his view, Florida did not actually have a contemporaneous-objection rule. . . . [But] since all of the Florida appellate courts refused to review petitioner's federal claim on the merits after his trial, and since their action in so doing is quite consistent with a line of Florida authorities interpreting the rule in question as requiring a contemporaneous objection, we accept the State's position on this point.

Respondent also urges that a defendant has a right under *Jackson v. Denno* (1964), to a hearing as to the voluntariness of a confession, even though the defendant does not object to its admission. But we do not read *Jackson* as creating any such requirement. . . . Language in subsequent decisions of this Court has reaffirmed the view that the Constitution does not require a voluntariness hearing absent some contemporaneous challenge to the use of the confession.

We therefore conclude that Florida procedure did, consistently with the United States Constitution, require that respondent's confession be challenged at trial or not at all, and thus his failure to timely object to its admission amounted to an independent and adequate state procedural ground which would have prevented direct review here. We thus come to the crux of this case. Shall the rule of *Francis v. Henderson*, barring federal habeas review absent a showing of "cause" and "prejudice" attendant to a state procedural waiver, be applied to a waived objection to the admission of a confession at trial? We answer that question in the affirmative.

We leave open for resolution in future decisions the precise definition of the "cause" and "prejudice" standard, and note here only that it is narrower than the standard set forth in dicta in *Fay v. Noia*, which would make federal habeas review generally available to state convicts absent a knowing and deliberate waiver of the federal constitutional contention. It is the sweeping language of *Fay v. Noia*, going far beyond the facts of the case eliciting it, which we today reject.[12]

The reasons for our rejection of it are several. The contemporaneous-objection rule itself is by no means peculiar to Florida, and deserves greater respect than *Fay* gives it, both for the fact that it is employed by a coordinate jurisdiction within the federal system and for the many interests which it serves in its own right. A contemporaneous objection enables the record to be made with respect to the constitutional claim when the recollections of witnesses are freshest, not years later in a federal habeas proceeding. It enables the judge who observed the demeanor of those witnesses to make the factual determinations necessary for properly deciding the federal constitutional question.

A contemporaneous-objection rule may lead to the exclusion of the evidence objected to, thereby making a major contribution to finality in criminal litigation. Without the evidence claimed to be vulnerable on federal constitutional grounds, the jury may acquit the defendant, and that will be the end of the case; or it may nonetheless convict the defendant, and he will have one less federal constitutional claim to assert in his federal habeas petition. If the state trial judge admits the evidence in question after a full hearing, the federal habeas court . . . will gain significant guidance from the state ruling in this regard. Subtler considerations as well militate in favor of honoring a state contemporaneous-objection rule. An objection on the spot may force the prosecution to take a hard look at its hole card, and, even if the prosecutor thinks that the state trial judge will admit the evidence, he must contemplate the possibility of reversal by the state appellate courts or the ultimate issuance of a federal writ of habeas corpus based on the impropriety of the state court's rejection of the federal constitutional claim.

We think that the rule of *Fay v. Noia*, broadly stated, may encourage "sandbagging" on the part of defense lawyers, who may take their chances on a verdict of not guilty in a state trial court with the intent to raise their constitutional claims in a federal habeas court if their initial gamble does not pay off. The refusal of federal habeas courts to honor contemporaneous-objection rules may also make state courts themselves less stringent in their enforcement. Under the rule of *Fay v. Noia*, state appellate courts know that a federal constitutional issue raised for the first

---

12. We have no occasion today to consider the *Fay* rule as applied to the facts there confronting the Court. Whether the *Francis* rule should preclude federal habeas review of claims not made in accordance with state procedure where the criminal defendant has surrendered, other than for reasons of tactical advantage, the right to have all of his claims of trial error considered by a state appellate court, we leave for another day.

The Court in *Fay* stated its "knowing and deliberate waiver" rule in language which applied not only to the waiver of the right to appeal, but to failures to raise individual substantive objections in the state trial. Then, with a single sentence in a footnote, the Court swept aside all decisions of this Court

to the extent that [they] may be read to suggest a standard of discretion in federal habeas corpus proceedings different from what we lay down today. . . .

We do not choose to paint with a similarly broad brush here.

time in the proceeding before them may well be decided in any event by a federal habeas tribunal. Thus, their choice is between addressing the issue notwithstanding the petitioner's failure to timely object, or else face the prospect that the federal habeas court will decide the question without the benefit of their views.

The failure of the federal habeas courts generally to require compliance with a contemporaneous-objection rule tends to detract from the perception of the trial of a criminal case in state court as a decisive and portentous event. A defendant has been accused of a serious crime, and this is the time and place set for him to be tried by a jury of his peers and found either guilty or not guilty by that jury. To the greatest extent possible, all issues which bear on this charge should be determined in this proceeding: the accused is in the courtroom, the jury is in the box, the judge is on the bench, and the witnesses, having been subpoenaed and duly sworn, await their turn to testify. Society's resources have been concentrated at that time and place in order to decide, within the limits of human fallibility, the question of guilt or innocence of one of its citizens. Any procedural rule which encourages the result that those proceedings be as free of error as possible is thoroughly desirable, and the contemporaneous-objection rule surely falls within this classification.

We believe the adoption of the *Francis* rule in this situation will have the salutary effect of making the state trial on the merits the "main event," so to speak, rather than a "tryout on the road" for what will later be the determinative federal habeas hearing. . . .

The "cause" and "prejudice" exception of the *Francis* rule will afford an adequate guarantee, we think, that the rule will not prevent a federal habeas court from adjudicating for the first time the federal constitutional claim of a defendant who, in the absence of such an adjudication, will be the victim of a miscarriage of justice. Whatever precise content may be given those terms by later cases, we feel confident in holding without further elaboration that they do not exist here. Respondent has advanced no explanation whatever for his failure to object at trial,[14] and, as the proceeding unfolded, the trial judge is certainly not to be faulted for failing to question the admission of the confession himself. The other evidence of guilt presented at trial, moreover, was substantial to a degree that would negate any possibility of actual prejudice resulting to the respondent from the admission of his inculpatory statement.

We accordingly conclude that the judgment of the Court of Appeals for the Fifth Circuit must be reversed, and the cause remanded . . . with instructions to dismiss respondent's petition for a writ of habeas corpus.

Mr. Chief Justice BURGER, concurring.

I concur fully in the judgment and in the Court's opinion. I write separately to emphasize one point which, to me, seems of critical importance to this case. In

---

14. In *Henry v. Mississippi*, the Court noted that decisions of counsel relating to trial strategy, even when made without the consultation of the defendant, would bar direct federal review of claims thereby forgone, except where "the circumstances are exceptional." Last Term, in *Estelle v. Williams*, the Court reiterated the burden on a defendant to be bound by the trial judgments of his lawyer. "Under our adversary system, once a defendant has the assistance of counsel the vast array of trial decisions, strategic and tactical, which must be made before and during trial rests with the accused and his attorney."

my view, the "deliberate bypass" standard enunciated in *Fay*, was never designed for, and is inapplicable to, errors—even of constitutional dimension—alleged to have been committed during trial.

In *Fay* the Court applied the "deliberate bypass" standard to a case where the critical procedural decision—whether to take a criminal appeal—was entrusted to a convicted defendant. Although Noia, the habeas petitioner, was represented by counsel, he himself had to make the decision whether to appeal or not; the role of the attorney was limited to giving advice and counsel. In giving content to the new deliberate bypass standard, *Fay* looked to the Court's decision in *Johnson v. Zerbst* (1938), a case where the defendant had been called upon to make the decision whether to request representation by counsel in his federal criminal trial. Because, in both *Fay* and *Zerbst*, important rights hung in the balance of the *defendant's own decision*, the Court required that a waiver impairing such rights be a knowing and intelligent decision by the defendant himself. As *Fay* put it:

> If a habeas applicant, after consultation with competent counsel or otherwise, understandingly and knowingly forewent the privilege of seeking to vindicate his federal claims in the state courts . . . , then it is open to the federal court on habeas to deny him all relief. . . .

The touchstone of *Fay* and *Zerbst*, then, is the exercise of volition by the defendant himself with respect to his own federal constitutional rights. In contrast, the claim in the case before us relates to events during the trial itself. Typically, habeas petitioners claim that unlawfully secured evidence was admitted, *but see Stone v. Powell* (1976), or that improper testimony was adduced, or that an improper jury charge was given, or that a particular line of examination or argument by the prosecutor was improper or prejudicial. But unlike *Fay* and *Zerbst*, preservation of this type of claim under state procedural rules does not generally involve an assertion by the defendant himself; rather, the decision to assert or not to assert constitutional rights or constitutionally based objections at trial is necessarily entrusted to the defendant's attorney, who must make on-the-spot decisions at virtually all stages of a criminal trial. As a practical matter, a criminal defendant is rarely, if ever, in a position to decide, for example, whether certain testimony is hearsay and, if so, whether it implicates interests protected by the Confrontation Clause; indeed, it is because "[e]ven the intelligent and educated layman has small and sometimes no skill in the science of law" that we held it constitutionally required that every defendant who faces the possibility of incarceration be afforded counsel. *Argersinger v. Hamlin* (1972); *Gideon v. Wainwright* (1963).

Once counsel is appointed, the day-to-day conduct of the defense rests with the attorney. He, not the client, has the immediate—and ultimate—responsibility of deciding if and when to object, which witnesses, if any, to call, and what defenses to develop. Not only do these decisions rest with the attorney, but such decisions must, as a practical matter, be made without consulting the client.[1] The trial process simply does not permit the type of frequent and protracted interruptions

---

1. Only such basic decisions as whether to plead guilty, waive a jury, or testify in one's own behalf are ultimately for the accused to make.

which would be necessary if it were required that clients give knowing and intelligent approval to each of the myriad tactical decisions as a trial proceeds.

Since trial decisions are of necessity entrusted to the accused's attorney, the *Fay-Zerbst* standard of "knowing and intelligent waiver" is simply inapplicable. The dissent in this case, written by the author of *Fay v. Noia*, implicitly recognizes as much. . . . What had always been thought the standard governing the *accused's* waiver of his own constitutional rights the dissent would change, in the trial setting, into a standard of conduct imposed upon the defendant's *attorney*. This vague "standard" would be unmanageable to the point of impossibility. . . . I would leave the core holding of *Fay* where it began, and reject this illogical uprooting of an otherwise defensible doctrine.

Mr. Justice STEVENS, concurring.

Although the Court's decision today may be read as a significant departure from the "deliberate bypass" standard announced in *Fay*, I am persuaded that the holding is consistent with the way other federal courts have actually been applying *Fay*.[67] The notion that a client must always consent to a tactical decision not to assert a constitutional objection to a proffer of evidence has always seemed unrealistic to me. Conversely, if the constitutional issue is sufficiently grave, even an express waiver by the defendant himself may sometimes be excused. Matters such as the competence of counsel, the procedural context in which the asserted waiver occurred, the character of the constitutional right at stake, and the overall fairness of the entire proceeding, may be more significant than the language of the test the Court purports to apply. I therefore believe the Court has wisely refrained from attempting to give precise content to its "cause" and "prejudice" exception to the rule of *Francis v. Henderson*.[4]

In this case, I agree with the Court's holding that collateral attack on the state court judgment should not be allowed. The record persuades me that competent trial counsel could well have made a deliberate decision not to object to the admission of the respondent's in-custody statement. That statement was consistent, in

---

67. The suggestion in *Fay* that the decision must be made personally by the defendant has not fared well, *see United States ex rel. Cruz v. LaVallee* (CA2 1971); *United States ex rel. Green v. Rundle* (CA3 1971), although a decision by counsel may not be binding if made over the objection of the defendant, *Paine v. McCarthy* (CA9 1975). Courts have generally found a "deliberate bypass" where counsel could reasonably have decided not to object, *United States ex rel. Terry v. Henderson* (CA2 1972); *Whitney v. United States* (CA8 1974); *United States ex rel. Broaddus v. Rundle* (CA3 1970), but they have not found a bypass when they consider the right "deeply embedded" in the Constitution, *Frazier v. Roberts* (CA8 1971), or when the procedural default was not substantial, *Minor v. Black* (CA6 1975); *Black v. Beto* (CA5 1967). Sometimes, even a deliberate choice by trial counsel has been held not to be a "deliberate bypass" when the result would be unjust, *Moreno v. Beto* (CA5 1969). In short, the actual disposition of these cases seems to rest on the court's perception of the totality of the circumstances, rather than on mechanical application of the "deliberate bypass" test.

4. As *Fay* makes clear, we are concerned here with a matter of equitable discretion, rather than a question of statutory authority, and equity has always been characterized by its flexibility and regard for the necessities of each case, *cf. Swann v. Charlotte-Mecklenburg Board of Education*.

many respects, with the respondent's trial testimony. It even had some positive value, since it portrayed the respondent as having acted in response to provocation, which might have influenced the jury to return a verdict on a lesser charge.[5] To the extent that it was damaging, the primary harm would have resulted from its effect in impeaching the trial testimony, but it would have been admissible for impeachment in any event. Counsel may well have preferred to have the statement admitted without objection when it was first offered, rather than making an objection which, at best,[6] could have been only temporarily successful.

Moreover, since the police fully complied with *Miranda*, the deterrent purpose of the *Miranda* rule is inapplicable to this case. . . . Accordingly, no matter how the rule is phrased, this case is plainly not one in which a collateral attack should be allowed. I therefore join the opinion of the Court.

[Justice WHITE concurred on the ground that any error was harmless and that, in light of the harmless error test, which requires that an error be harmless beyond a reasonable doubt, there is no need to require both cause *and* prejudice. With respect to cause, Justice White argued that Fay's deliberate bypass rule is sufficient and that the petition should be denied because Sykes had no explanation for the failure to make a contemporaneous objection.]

Justice BRENNAN, with whom Justice MARSHALL joins, dissenting.

I begin with the threshold question: what is the meaning and import of a procedural default? If it could be assumed that a procedural default, more often than not, is the product of a defendant's conscious refusal to abide by the duly constituted, legitimate processes of the state courts, then I might agree that a regime of collateral review weighted in favor of a State's procedural rules would be warranted. *Fay*, however, recognized that such rarely is the case, and therein lies *Fay*'s basic unwillingness to embrace a view of habeas jurisdiction that results in "an airtight system of [procedural] forfeitures."

This, of course, is not to deny that there are times when the failure to heed a state procedural requirement stems from an intentional decision to avoid the presentation of constitutional claims to the state forum. *Fay* was not insensitive to this possibility. Indeed, the very purpose of its bypass test is to detect and enforce such intentional procedural forfeitures of outstanding constitutionally based claims. . . .

---

5. According to the statement the respondent made to the police, the victim came into his trailer, picked up his shotgun, and played with it; they quarreled and the victim cut the respondent's hand with a knife; then the victim left the trailer and made an insulting gesture, at which time the respondent shot him. Other evidence established that respondent was quite drunk at the time. The primary difference between this and the respondent's trial testimony was that, at trial, the respondent testified that the victim had threatened him before leaving the trailer, and had turned and started toward the respondent just before the shooting.

6. The objection was weak, since the police officers gave the respondent the appropriate warnings. His claim that he was too intoxicated to understand the warnings is not only implausible, but also somewhat inconsistent with any attempt to give credibility to his trial testimony, which necessarily required recollection of the circumstances surrounding the shooting.

[A]ny realistic system of federal habeas corpus jurisdiction must be premised on the reality that the ordinary procedural default is born of the inadvertence, negligence, inexperience, or incompetence of trial counsel. The case under consideration today is typical. The Court makes no effort to identify a tactical motive for the failure of Sykes' attorney to challenge the admissibility or reliability of a highly inculpatory statement. While my Brother Stevens finds a possible tactical advantage, I agree with the Court of Appeals that this reading is most implausible. Indeed, there is no basis for inferring that Sykes or his state trial lawyer was even aware of the existence of his claim under the Fifth Amendment; for this is not a case where the trial judge expressly drew the attention of the defense to a possible constitutional contention or procedural requirement, or where the defense signals its knowledge of a constitutional claim by abandoning a challenge previously raised. Rather, any realistic reading of the record demonstrates that we are faced here with a lawyer's simple error.

Fay's answer thus is plain: the bypass test simply refuses to credit what is essentially a lawyer's mistake as a forfeiture of constitutional rights. I persist in the belief that the interests of Sykes and the State of Florida are best rationalized by adherence to this test, and by declining to react to inadvertent defaults through the creation of an "airtight system of forfeitures."

II

. . . With respect to federal habeas corpus jurisdiction, Congress explicitly chose to effectuate the federal court's primary responsibility for preserving federal rights and privileges by authorizing the litigation of constitutional claims and defenses in a district court after the State vindicates its own interest through trial of the substantive criminal offense in the state courts. This, of course, was not the only course that Congress might have followed: as an alternative, it might well have decided entirely to circumvent all state procedure through the expansion of existing federal removal statutes such as 28 U.S.C. §§1442(a)(1) and 1443, thereby authorizing the pretrial transfer of all state criminal cases to the federal courts whenever federal defenses or claims are in issue. But liberal post-trial federal review is the redress that Congress ultimately chose to allow and the consequences of a state procedural default should be evaluated in conformance with this policy choice. Certainly we can all agree that, once a state court has assumed jurisdiction of a criminal case, the integrity of its own process is a matter of legitimate concern. The *Fay* bypass test, by seeking to discover intentional abuses of the rules of the state forum, is, I believe, compatible with this state institutional interest. But whether *Fay* was correct in penalizing a litigant solely for his intentional forfeitures properly must be read in light of Congress' desired norm of widened post-trial access to the federal courts. If the standard adopted today is later construed to require that the simple mistakes of attorneys are to be treated as binding forfeitures, it would serve to subordinate the fundamental rights contained in our constitutional charter to inadvertent defaults of rules promulgated by state agencies, and would essentially leave it to the States, through the enactment of procedure and the certification of the competence of local attorneys, to determine whether a habeas applicant will be permitted the access to the federal forum that is guaranteed him by Congress.

Thus, I remain concerned that undue deference to local procedure can only serve to undermine the ready access to a federal court to which a state defendant otherwise is entitled. But federal review is not the full measure of Sykes' interest, for there is another of even greater immediacy: assuring that his constitutional claims can be addressed to some court. For the obvious consequence of barring Sykes from the federal courthouse is to insulate Florida's alleged constitutional violation from any and all judicial review because of a lawyer's mistake. From the standpoint of the habeas petitioner, it is a harsh rule indeed that denies him "any review at all where the state has granted none," *Brown v. Allen* (Black, J., dissenting) — particularly when he would have enjoyed both state and federal consideration had his attorney not erred.

That the State legitimately desires to preserve an orderly and efficient judicial process is undeniable. But similar interests of efficiency and the like also can be identified with respect to other state institutions, such as its law enforcement agencies. Yet, as was only recently reconfirmed, we would not permit and have not permitted the state police to enhance the orderliness and efficiency of their law enforcement activities by embarking on a campaign of acquiring inadvertent waivers of important constitutional rights, *Brewer v. Williams.*

A procedural default should be treated accordingly. . . .

III

Florida's courts remain entirely free to enforce their own rules as they choose, and to deny any and all state rights and remedies to a defendant who fails to comply with applicable state procedure. The relevant inquiry is whether more is required — specifically, whether the fulfillment of important interests of the State necessitates that federal courts be called upon to impose additional sanctions for inadvertent noncompliance with state procedural requirements such as the contemporaneous objection rule involved here.

Punishing a lawyer's unintentional errors by closing the federal courthouse door to his client is both a senseless and misdirected method of deterring the slighting of state rules. It is senseless because unplanned and unintentional action of any kind generally is not subject to deterrence; and, to the extent that it is hoped that a threatened sanction addressed to the defense will induce greater care and caution on the part of trial lawyers, thereby forestalling negligent conduct or error, the potential loss of all valuable state remedies would be sufficient to this end. And it is a misdirected sanction because, even if the penalization of incompetence or carelessness will encourage more thorough legal training and trial preparation, the habeas applicant, as opposed to his lawyer, hardly is the proper recipient of such a penalty. Especially with fundamental constitutional rights at stake, no fictional relationship of principal-agent or the like can justify holding the criminal defendant accountable for the naked errors of his attorney. This is especially true when so many indigent defendants are without any realistic choice in selecting who ultimately represents them at trial. Indeed, if responsibility for error must be apportioned between the parties, it is the State, through its attorney's admissions and certification policies, that is more fairly held to blame for the fact that practicing lawyers too often are ill-prepared or ill-equipped to act carefully and knowledgeably when faced with decisions governed by state procedural requirements.

IV

Perhaps the primary virtue of *Fay* is that the bypass test at least yields a coherent yardstick for federal district courts in rationalizing their power of collateral review. In contrast, although some four years have passed since its introduction in *Davis v. United States* (1973), the only thing clear about the Court's "cause" and "prejudice" standard is that it exhibits the notable tendency of keeping prisoners in jail without addressing their constitutional complaints. Hence, as of today, all we know of the "cause" standard is its requirement that habeas applicants bear an undefined burden of explanation for the failure to obey the state rule. Left unresolved is whether a habeas petitioner like Sykes can adequately discharge this burden by offering the commonplace and truthful explanation for his default: attorney ignorance or error beyond the client's control. The "prejudice" inquiry, meanwhile, appears to bear a strong resemblance to harmless error doctrine. *Compare Chapman v. California* (1967). I disagree with the Court's appraisal of the harmlessness of the admission of respondent's confession, but if this is what is meant by prejudice, respondent's constitutional contentions could be as quickly and easily disposed of in this regard by permitting federal courts to reach the merits of his complaint. . . .

One final consideration deserves mention. If the scope of habeas jurisdiction previously governed by *Fay v. Noia* is to be redefined so as to enforce the errors and neglect of lawyers with unnecessary and unjust rigor, the time may come when conscientious and fair-minded federal and state courts, in adhering to the teaching of *Johnson v. Zerbst*, will have to reconsider whether they can continue to indulge the comfortable fiction that all lawyers are skilled or even competent craftsmen in representing the fundamental rights of their clients. . . .

* * *

The Court has more recently described the connection between the *Sykes* procedural default test and adequate and independent state ground doctrine in the following way:

> A federal habeas court will not review a claim rejected by a state court "if the decision of [the state] court rests on a state law ground that is independent of the federal question and adequate to support the judgment." *Kindler* (quoting *Coleman v. Thompson* (1991)). The state-law ground may be a substantive rule dispositive of the case, or a procedural barrier to adjudication of the claim on the merits. *See Sykes*.
>
> Ordinarily, a state prisoner seeking federal habeas relief must first "exhaus[t] the remedies available in the courts of the State," 28 U.S.C. §2254(b)(1)(A), thereby affording those courts "the first opportunity to address and correct alleged violations of [the] prisoner's federal rights," *Coleman*. The adequate and independent state ground doctrine furthers that objective, for without it, "habeas petitioners would be able to avoid the exhaustion requirement by defaulting their federal claims in state court." *Id.* Accordingly, absent showings of "cause" and "prejudice," *see Sykes*, federal habeas relief will be unavailable when (1) "a state court [has] declined to address a prisoner's federal claims because the prisoner

had failed to meet a state procedural requirement," and (2) "the state judgment rests on independent and adequate state procedural grounds." *Coleman.*

Walker v. Martin (2011) (discretionary state time of filing rule is not inadequate merely because "outcomes under the rule vary from case to case" as long as the variation is explained by "case-specific considerations" and the understandable impulse to "avoid the harsh results that sometimes attend consistent application of an unyielding rule," rather than "unfair," "novel," or "surprising" exercises of discretion). In *Coleman v. Thompson,* the prisoner missed a time of filing deadline for his direct appeal and the Virginia Supreme Court dismissed on that procedural ground. In affirming the denial of federal habeas on grounds of procedural default, the Court emphasized the federalism interests in honoring state procedural rules:

> The basis for application of the independent and adequate state ground doctrine in federal habeas is somewhat different than on direct review by this Court. When this Court reviews a state court decision on direct review pursuant to 28 U.S.C. §1257, it is reviewing the *judgment;* if resolution of a federal question cannot affect the judgment, there is nothing for the Court to do. This is not the case in habeas. When a federal district court reviews a state prisoner's habeas corpus petition pursuant to 28 U.S.C. §2254, it must decide whether the petitioner is "in custody in violation of the Constitution or laws or treaties of the United States." The court does not review a judgment, but the lawfulness of the petitioner's custody *simpliciter.*
>
> Nonetheless, a state prisoner is in custody *pursuant* to a judgment. When a federal habeas court releases a prisoner held pursuant to a state court judgment that rests on an independent and adequate state ground, it renders ineffective the state rule just as completely as if this Court had reversed the state judgment on direct review. In such a case, the habeas court ignores the State's legitimate reasons for holding the prisoner.
>
> In the habeas context, the application of the independent and adequate state ground doctrine is grounded in concerns of comity and federalism. Without the rule, a federal district court would be able to do in habeas what this Court could not do on direct review; habeas would offer state prisoners whose custody was supported by independent and adequate state grounds an end run around the limits of this Court's jurisdiction and a means to undermine the State's interest in enforcing its laws.

Coleman. The Court also drew a connection to exhaustion, noting that petitioners could make an end run around exhaustion if there were no procedural default rule because "defaulted . . . federal claims in state court meet the technical requirements for exhaustion"—when a claim is defaulted "there are no state remedies any longer 'available'" under 28 U.S.C. §2254(b).

What if the state court's decision is ambiguous? In *Coleman* the Court held that the *Long* clear statement rule applies in habeas, not just direct review: "In habeas, if the decision of the last state court to which the petitioner presented his federal claims fairly appeared to rest primarily on resolution of those claims, or to be interwoven with those claims, and did not clearly and expressly rely on an independent and adequate state ground, a federal court may address the petition." *Id.* (extending the rule from *Harris v. Reed* (1989), and emphasizing that it applies only if the state decision is in fact ambiguous; the rule is not triggered merely because there is no clear statement).

Cause and prejudice have proved difficult to establish. Although constitutionally incompetent performance by a defendant's lawyer is cause, and although ineffective assistance of counsel is the most common claim in federal habeas proceedings challenging state convictions, it is very difficult under *Strickland v. Washington* (1978), to show that a lawyer's performance violates the Sixth Amendment. *Strickland* requires evidence that the lawyer's performance was objectively deficient and that the error affected the outcome of the case. The defendant must overcome a "strong presumption" that the lawyer's decisions fall within the bounds of professional norms to establish objectively deficient performance. This means most attorney errors (e.g., ordinary neglect, malpractice, and errors in judgment), and tactical or otherwise intentional decisions are not Sixth Amendment violations and therefore do not establish "cause" to excuse procedural default. *Murray v. Carrier* (1986) ("the mere fact that counsel failed to recognize the factual or legal basis for a claim, or failed to raise the claim despite recognizing it, does not constitute cause for a procedural default. . . . So long as a defendant is represented by counsel whose performance is not constitutionally ineffective . . . we discern no inequity in requiring him to bear the risk of attorney error that results in procedural default"; no cause where attorney failed on direct appeal to raise trial judge's denial of motion for access to victim statements). Whether the standard for procedural default should bar petitioners from raising claims that were defaulted because of attorney error falling short of a Sixth Amendment violation is clearly part of what animates the disagreement between the majority and the dissent in *Sykes*.

Cause has been found in cases where the "some objective factor external to the defense impeded counsel's efforts to comply with the State procedural rule." *Murray v. Carrier* (1986). Thus, cause exists where prosecutor and jury commissioners developed a secret scheme "to underrepresent black people and women on the master jury list from which all grand and . . . [petit] juries were drawn." *Amadeo v. Zant* (1988). The scheme was revealed in a separate civil case and raised on direct appeal after conviction and sentencing, but the Georgia state courts deemed the challenge to the composition of the defendant's jury untimely. On federal habeas, the district court determined that the scheme had been "concealed by county officials" and the Supreme Court held that this kind of "interference by officials" was cause. Cause also exists when the petitioner could not have raised a constitutional claim because the ground was "reasonably unknown" to counsel at the time. *See Reed v. Ross* (1984) (cause shown where "a constitutional claim is so novel that its legal basis [was] not reasonably available to counsel" during state proceedings and the constitutional claim applies retroactively to convictions that have already become final); *cf. Engle v. Isaac* (1982) (no cause where Court found that at least some lawyers had raised the claim before it was upheld by the Supreme Court).

Cause has also been found where the lawyer abandons the client without informing her. In these circumstances, the client cannot be bound to the actions of her agent because the agency relationship has ended but the client doesn't know she is proceeding pro se. Thus, in *Maples v. Thomas* (2012), the Court found cause where lawyers who agreed to represent the petitioner in state post-conviction litigation filed a petition but then left the law firm and failed to inform the client of their inability to continue the representation. Neither attorney sought leave to withdraw from the court, so they remained attorneys of record and notices in the case were sent to their prior firm and returned to the court unopened. By the time the client discovered the problem, the time for appeal of the trial court's denial of relief had passed. The Supreme Court distinguished claims of "attorney error, however egregious, and a claim that an attorney had essentially abandoned his client," noting that "[c]ommon sense dictates that a litigant cannot be held constructively responsible for the conduct of an attorney who is not operating as his agent in any meaningful sense of that word. . . . Nor can a client be faulted for failing to act on his own behalf when he lacks reason to believe his attorneys of record, in fact are not representing him." The Court remanded for determination of prejudice.

Lastly, the Court has simply set aside the cause and prejudice requirement where there is reliable evidence of actual innocence:

> In an effort to "balance the societal interests in finality, comity, and conservation of scarce judicial resources with the individual interest in justice that arises in the extraordinary case," *Schlup v. Delo* (1995), the Court has recognized a miscarriage-of-justice exception. "[I]n appropriate cases," the Court has said, "the principles of comity and finality that inform the concepts of cause and prejudice must yield to the imperative of correcting a fundamentally unjust incarceration," *Carrier*.
>
> In *Schlup*, the Court adopted a specific rule to implement this general principle [where the petitioner claimed ineffective assistance of counsel and the withholding of exculpatory evidence by the prosecution]. It held that prisoners asserting innocence as a gateway to defaulted claims must establish that, in light of new evidence, "it is more likely than not that no reasonable juror would have found petitioner guilty beyond a reasonable doubt." This formulation, *Schlup* explains, "ensures that petitioner's case is truly 'extraordinary,' while still providing petitioner a meaningful avenue by which to avoid a manifest injustice." In the usual case the presumed guilt of a prisoner convicted in state court counsels against federal review of defaulted claims. Yet a petition supported by a convincing *Schlup* gateway showing "raise[s] sufficient doubt about [the petitioner's] guilt to undermine confidence in the result of the trial without the assurance that that trial was untainted by constitutional error"; hence, "a review of the merits of the constitutional claims" is justified.

d.   The Statute of Limitations

In addition to custody, exhaustion and the absence of procedural default, Congress enacted a strict one-year statute of limitations on §2254 petitions in AEDPA. The statute of limitations runs "from the latest of :

> (A) the date on which the judgment became final by conclusion of direct review or the expiration of the time for seeking such review;
> (B) the date on which the impediment to filing an application created by State action in violation of the Constitution or laws of the United States is removed, if the applicant was prevented from filing by such State action;

(C) the date on which the constitutional right asserted was initially recognized by the Supreme Court, if the right has been newly recognized by the Supreme Court and made retroactively applicable to cases on collateral review; or

(D) the date on which the factual predicate of the claim or claims presented could have been discovered through the exercise of due diligence. . . .

(2) The time during which a properly filed application for State post-conviction or other collateral review with respect to the pertinent judgment or claim is pending shall not be counted toward any period of limitation under this subsection.

28 U.S.C. §2244(d). Prior to AEDPA, there was "no statute of limitations governing federal habeas, and the only laches recognized [was] that which affects the State's ability to defend against the claims raised on habeas." *Brecht v. Abrahamson* (1993). The presumption was that the passage of time cannot cure fundamental constitutional defects in a conviction. *See Penn. ex Rel. Herman v. Claudy* (1956) ("Nor was petitioner barred from presenting his challenge to the conviction because 8 years had passed before this action was commenced. [In another case we] held that a prisoner could challenge the validity of his conviction 18 years after he had been convicted. The sound premise upon which these holdings rested is that men incarcerated in flagrant violation of their constitutional rights have a remedy.").

In the next case, the Court addressed the question whether equitable tolling applies to the new shortened timeframe or whether the factors set out for timely petitions in §2244(d) are exclusive.

Holland v. Florida

560 U.S. 631 (2010)

Justice BREYER delivered the opinion of the Court.

We here decide that the timeliness provision in the federal habeas corpus statute is subject to equitable tolling. *See* Antiterrorism and Effective Death Penalty Act of 1996 (AEDPA), 28 U.S.C. §2244(d). We also consider its application in this case. In the Court of Appeals' view, when a petitioner seeks to excuse a late filing on the basis of his attorney's unprofessional conduct, that conduct, even if it is "negligent" or "grossly negligent," cannot "rise to the level of egregious attorney misconduct" that would warrant equitable tolling unless the petitioner offers "proof of bad faith, dishonesty, divided loyalty, mental impairment or so forth." In our view, this standard is too rigid. We therefore reverse the judgment of the Court of Appeals and remand for further proceedings.

I

A

In 1997, Holland was convicted of first-degree murder and sentenced to death. The Florida Supreme Court affirmed that judgment. On *October 1, 2001*, this Court denied Holland's petition for certiorari. And on that date—the date that our denial of the petition ended further direct review of Holland's conviction—the 1-year AEDPA limitations clock began to run. *See* 28 U.S.C. §2244(d)(1)(A).

Thirty-seven days later, on *November 7, 2001*, Florida appointed attorney Bradley Collins to represent Holland in all state and federal postconviction proceedings. By *September 19, 2002*—316 days after his appointment and 12 days before the 1-year AEDPA limitations period expired—Collins, acting on Holland's behalf, filed a motion for postconviction relief in the state trial court. That filing automatically stopped the running of the AEDPA limitations period, §2244(d)(2), with, as we have said, 12 days left on the clock.

For the next three years, Holland's petition remained pending in the state courts. During that time, Holland wrote Collins letters asking him to make certain that all of his claims would be preserved for any subsequent federal habeas corpus review. Collins wrote back, stating, "I would like to reassure you that we are aware of state time-limitations and federal exhaustion requirements." He also said that he would "presen[t] . . . to the . . . federal courts" any of Holland's claims that the state courts denied. In a second letter Collins added, "should your Motion for Post-Conviction Relief be denied" by the state courts, "your state habeas corpus claims will then be ripe for presentation in a petition for writ of habeas corpus in federal court."

In mid-May 2003, the state trial court denied Holland relief, and Collins appealed that denial to the Florida Supreme Court. Almost two years later, in February 2005, the Florida Supreme Court heard oral argument in the case. But during that 2-year period, relations between Collins and Holland began to break down. Indeed, between April 2003 and January 2006, Collins communicated with Holland only three times—each time by letter.

Holland, unhappy with this lack of communication, twice wrote to the Florida Supreme Court, asking it to remove Collins from his case. In the second letter, filed on June 17, 2004, he said that he and Collins had experienced "a complete breakdown in communication." Holland informed the court that Collins had "not kept [him] updated on the status of [his] capital case" and that Holland had "not seen or spoken to" Collins "since April 2003." He wrote, "Mr. Collins has abandoned [me]" and said, "[I have] no idea what is going on with [my] capital case on appeal." He added that "Collins has never made any reasonable effort to establish any relationship of trust or confidence with [me]," and stated that he "does not trust" or have "any confidence in Mr. Collin's ability to represent [him]." Holland concluded by asking that Collins be "dismissed (removed) off his capital case" or that he be given a hearing in order to demonstrate Collins' deficiencies. The State responded that Holland could not file any *pro se* papers with the court while he was represented by counsel, including papers seeking new counsel. The Florida Supreme Court agreed and denied Holland's requests.

During this same period Holland wrote various letters to the Clerk of the Florida Supreme Court. In the last of these he wrote, "[I]f I had a competent, conflict-free, postconviction, appellate attorney representing me, I would not have to write you this letter. I'm not trying to get on your nerves. I just would like to know *exactly* what is happening with my case on appeal to the Supreme Court of Florida." During that same time period, Holland also filed a complaint against Collins with the Florida Bar Association, but the complaint was denied.

Collins argued Holland's appeal before the Florida Supreme Court on February 10, 2005. Shortly thereafter, Holland wrote to Collins emphasizing the importance of filing a timely petition for habeas corpus in federal court once the Florida Supreme Court issued its ruling. Specifically, on March 3, 2005, Holland wrote:

> Dear Mr. Collins, P. A.:
> How are you? Fine I hope.
> I write this letter to ask that you please write me back, as soon as possible to let me know what the status of my case is on appeal to the Supreme Court of Florida.
> If the Florida Supreme Court denies my [postconviction] and State Habeas Corpus appeals, *please file my 28 U.S.C. §2254 writ of Habeas Corpus petition, before my deadline to file it runs out (expires).*
> Thank you very much.
> Please have a nice day." (emphasis added).

Collins did not answer this letter.
On June 15, 2005, Holland wrote again:

> Dear Mr. Collins:
> How are you? Fine I hope.
> On March 3, 2005 I wrote you a letter, asking that you let me know the status of my case on appeal to the Supreme Court of Florida.
> Also, *have you begun preparing my 28 U.S.C. §2254 writ of Habeas Corpus petition? Please let me know, as soon as possible.*
> *Thank you.* (emphasis added).

But again, Collins did not reply.
Five months later, in November 2005, the Florida Supreme Court affirmed the lower court decision denying Holland relief. Three weeks after that, on *December 1, 2005*, the court issued its mandate, making its decision final. At that point, the AEDPA federal habeas clock again began to tick—with 12 days left on the 1-year meter. Twelve days later, on *December 13, 2005*, Holland's AEDPA time limit expired.

B

Four weeks after the AEDPA time limit expired, on January 9, 2006, Holland, still unaware of the Florida Supreme Court ruling issued in his case two months earlier, wrote Collins a third letter:

> Dear Mr. Bradley M. Collins:
> How are you? Fine I hope.
> I write this letter to ask that you please let me know the status of my appeals before the Supreme Court of Florida. Have my appeals been decided yet?
> Please send me the [necessary information]. . . so that I can determine when the deadline will be to file my 28 U.S.C. Rule 2254 Federal Habeas Corpus Petition, in accordance with all United States Supreme Court and Eleventh Circuit case law and applicable "Antiterrorism and Effective Death Penalty Act," if my appeals before the Supreme Court of Florida are denied.

Please be advised that I want to preserve my privilege to federal review of all of my state convictions and sentences.

Mr. Collins, would you please also inform me as to which United States District Court my 28 U.S.C. Rule 2254 Federal Habeas Corpus Petition will have to be timely filed in and that court's address?

Thank you very much.

Collins did not answer.

Nine days later, on January 18, 2006, Holland, working in the prison library, learned for the first time that the Florida Supreme Court had issued a final determination in his case and that its mandate had issued—five weeks prior. He immediately wrote out his own *pro se* federal habeas petition and mailed it to the Federal District Court for the Southern District of Florida the next day. . . . The same day that he mailed that petition, Holland received a letter from Collins telling him that Collins intended to file a petition for certiorari in this Court from the State Supreme Court's most recent ruling. Holland answered immediately:

Dear Mr. Bradley M. Collins:
* * * * * *

Since recently, the Supreme Court of Florida has denied my [post-conviction] and state writ of Habeas Corpus Petition. I am left to understand that you are planning to seek certiorari on these matters.

It's my understanding that the AEDPA time limitations is not tolled during discretionary appellate reviews, such as certiorari applications resulting from denial of state post-conviction proceedings.

Therefore, I advise you *not* to file certiorari if doing so affects or jeopardizes my one year *grace* period as prescribed by the AEDPA.

Thank you very much.

Holland was right about the law. *See* Coates (AEDPA not tolled during pendency of petition for certiorari from judgment denying state postconviction review).

On January 26, 2006, Holland tried to call Collins from prison. But he called collect and Collins' office would not accept the call. Five days later, Collins wrote to Holland and told him for the very first time that, as Collins understood AEDPA law, the limitations period applicable to Holland's federal habeas application had in fact expired in 2000—*before* Collins had begun to represent Holland. Specifically, Collins wrote:

Dear Mr. Holland:

I am in receipt of your letter dated January 20, 2006 concerning operation of AEDPA time limitations. One hurdle in our upcoming efforts at obtaining federal habeas corpus relief will be that the one-year statutory time frame for filing such a petition began to run after the case was affirmed on October 5, 2000 [when your] Judgment and Sentence . . . were affirmed by the Florida Supreme Court. However, it was not until November 7, 2001, that I received the Order appointing me to the case. As you can see, *I was appointed about a year after your case became final.* . . . "[T]he AEDPA time-period [thus] had run before my appointment and therefore before your [postconviction] motion was filed."

Collins was wrong about the law. As we have said, Holland's 1-year limitations period did not begin to run until *this* Court denied Holland's petition for certiorari from the state courts' denial of relief on direct review, which occurred on October 1, 2001. *See* 28 U.S.C. §2244(d)(1)(A). And when Collins was appointed (on November 7, 2001) the AEDPA clock therefore had 328 days left to go.

Holland immediately wrote back to Collins, pointing this out.

Dear Mr. Collins:

I received your letter dated January 31, 2006. You are incorrect in stating that "the one-year statutory time frame for filing my 2254 petition began to run after my case was affirmed on October 5, 2000, by the Florida Supreme Court." As stated on page three of [the recently filed] Petition for a writ of certiorari, October 1, 2001 is when the United States Supreme Court denied my initial petition for writ of certiorari and that is when my case became final. That meant that the time would be tolled once I filed my [postconviction] motion in the trial court.

Also, Mr. Collins you never told me that my time ran out (expired). I told you to timely file my 28 U.S.C. 2254 Habeas Corpus Petition before the deadline, so that I would not be time-barred.

You never informed me of oral arguments or of the Supreme Court of Florida's November 10, 2005 decision denying my postconviction appeals. You never kept me informed about the status of my case, although you told me that you would immediately inform me of the court's decision as soon as you heard anything.

Mr. Collins, I filed a motion on January 19, 2006 [in federal court] to preserve my rights, because I did not want to be time-barred. Have you heard anything about the aforesaid motion? Do you know what the status of aforesaid motion is?

Mr. Collins, please file my 2254 Habeas Petition immediately. Please do not wait any longer, even though it will be untimely filed at least it will be filed without wasting anymore time. (valuable time).

Again, please file my 2254 Petition at once.

Your letter is the first time that you have ever mentioned anything to me about my time had run out, before you were appointed to represent me, and that my one-year started to run on October 5, 2000.

Please find out the status of my motion that I filed on January 19, 2006 and let me know.

Thank you very much.

Collins did not answer this letter. Nor did he file a federal habeas petition as Holland requested.

On March 1, 2006, Holland filed another complaint against Collins with the Florida Bar Association. This time the bar asked Collins to respond, which he did, through his own attorney, on March 21. And the very next day, over three months after Holland's AEDPA statute of limitations had expired, Collins mailed a proposed federal habeas petition to Holland, asking him to review it.

But by that point Holland had already filed a *pro se* motion in the District Court asking that Collins be dismissed as his attorney. The State responded to that request by arguing once again that Holland could not file a *pro se* motion seeking to have Collins removed while he was represented by counsel, *i.e.*, represented by Collins. But this time the court considered Holland's motion, permitted Collins to withdraw from the case, and appointed a new lawyer for Holland. And it also received briefing on whether the circumstances of the case justified the equitable tolling of the AEDPA limitations period for a sufficient period of time (approximately five weeks) to make Holland's petition timely.

C

After considering the briefs, the Federal District Court held that the facts did not warrant equitable tolling and that consequently Holland's petition was untimely. . . .

The Court of Appeals first agreed with Holland that "'[e]quitable tolling can be applied to . . . AEDPA's statutory deadline.'" But it also held that equitable tolling could not be applied in a case, like Holland's, that involves no more than "[p]ure professional negligence" on the part of a petitioner's attorney because such behavior can never constitute an "extraordinary circumstance." . . . Holland made "no allegation" that Collins had made a "knowing or reckless factual misrepresentation," or that he exhibited "dishonesty," "divided loyalty," or "mental impairment." Hence, the court held, equitable tolling was *per se* inapplicable to Holland's habeas petition. . . .

II

We have not decided whether AEDPA's statutory limitations period may be tolled for equitable reasons. Now, like all 11 Courts of Appeals that have considered the question, we hold that §2244(d) is subject to equitable tolling in appropriate cases.

We base our conclusion on the following considerations. First, the AEDPA "statute of limitations defense . . . is not 'jurisdictional.'" *Day v. McDonough* (2006). It does not set forth "an inflexible rule requiring dismissal whenever" its "clock has run."

We have previously made clear that a nonjurisdictional federal statute of limitations is normally subject to a "rebuttable presumption" in *favor* "of equitable tolling." *Irwin v. Dep't of Veterans Affs.* (1990); *see also Young v. United States* (2002) ("It is hornbook law that limitations periods are 'customarily subject to "equitable tolling."'").

In the case of AEDPA, the presumption's strength is reinforced by the fact that "'equitable principles'" have traditionally "'governed'" the substantive law of habeas corpus, *Munaf v. Geren* (2008), for we will "not construe a statute to displace courts' traditional equitable authority absent the 'clearest command,'" *Miller v. French* (2000). The presumption's strength is yet further reinforced by the fact that Congress enacted AEDPA after this Court decided *Irwin* and therefore was likely aware that courts, when interpreting AEDPA's timing provisions, would apply the presumption.

Second, the statute here differs significantly from the statutes at issue in *United States v. Brockamp* (1997), and *United States v. Beggerly* (1998), two cases in which we held that *Irwin*'s presumption had been overcome. In *Brockamp*, we interpreted a statute of limitations that was silent on the question of equitable tolling as foreclosing application of that doctrine. But in doing so we emphasized that the statute at issue (1) "se[t] forth its time limitations in unusually emphatic form"; (2) used "highly detailed" and "technical" language "that, linguistically speaking, cannot easily be read as containing implicit exceptions"; (3) "reiterate[d] its limitations several times in several different ways"; (4) related to an "underlying subject matter," nationwide tax collection, with respect to which the practical consequences of permitting tolling would have been substantial; and (5) would, if tolled, "require tolling, not only procedural limitations, but also substantive limitations on the amount of recovery—a kind of tolling for which we . . . found no direct precedent." And in *Beggerly* we held that *Irwin's* presumption was overcome where (1) the 12-year statute of limitations at issue was "unusually generous" and (2) the underlying claim "deal[t] with ownership of land" and thereby implicated landowners' need to "know with certainty what their rights are, and the period during which those rights may be subject to challenge."

By way of contrast, AEDPA's statute of limitations, unlike the statute at issue in *Brockamp*, does not contain language that is "unusually emphatic," nor does it "reiterat[e]" its time limitation. Neither would application of equitable tolling here affect the "substance" of a petitioner's claim. Moreover, in contrast to the 12-year limitations period at issue in *Beggerly*, AEDPA's limitations period is not particularly long. And unlike the subject matters at issue in both *Brockamp* and *Beggerly*—tax collection and land claims—AEDPA's subject matter, habeas corpus, pertains to an area of the law where equity finds a comfortable home. In short, AEDPA's 1-year limit reads like an ordinary, run-of-the-mill statute of limitations.

Respondent, citing *Brockamp*, argues that AEDPA should be interpreted to foreclose equitable tolling because the statute sets forth "explicit exceptions to its basic time limits" that do "not include 'equitable tolling.'" The statute does contain multiple provisions relating to the events that *trigger* its running. And we concede that it is silent as to equitable tolling while containing one provision that expressly refers to a different kind of tolling. *See* §2244(d)(2) (stating that "[t]he time during which" a petitioner has a pending request for state postconviction relief "shall not be counted toward" his "period of limitation" under AEDPA). But the fact that Congress *expressly* referred to tolling during state collateral review proceedings is easily explained without rebutting the presumption in favor of equitable tolling. A petitioner cannot bring a federal habeas claim without first exhausting state remedies—a process that frequently takes longer than one year. Hence, Congress had to explain how the limitations statute accounts for the time during which such state proceedings are pending. This special need for an express provision undermines any temptation to invoke the interpretive maxim *inclusio unius est exclusio alterius* (to include one item (*i.e.*, suspension during state-court collateral review) is to exclude other similar items (*i.e.*, equitable tolling)). *See Young* (rejecting claim that an "express tolling provision, appearing in the same subsection as the [limitations] period, demonstrates a statutory intent *not* to toll the [limitations] period").

Third, and finally, we disagree with respondent that equitable tolling undermines AEDPA's basic purposes. We recognize that AEDPA seeks to eliminate delays in the federal habeas review process. But AEDPA seeks to do so without undermining basic habeas corpus principles and while seeking to harmonize the new statute with prior law, under which a petition's timeliness was always determined under equitable principles. *See Slack v. McDaniel* (2000) ("AEDPA's present provisions . . . incorporate earlier habeas corpus principles"). When Congress codified new rules governing this previously judicially managed area of law, it did so without losing sight of the fact that the "writ of habeas corpus plays a vital role in protecting constitutional rights." *Slack*. The importance of the Great Writ, the only writ explicitly protected by the Constitution, Art. I, §9, cl. 2, along with congressional efforts to harmonize the new statute with prior law, counsels hesitancy before interpreting AEDPA's statutory silence as indicating a congressional intent to close courthouse doors that a strong equitable claim would ordinarily keep open.

III

We have previously made clear that a "petitioner" is "entitled to equitable tolling" only if he shows "(1) that he has been pursuing his rights diligently, and (2) that some extraordinary circumstance stood in his way" and prevented timely filing. *Pace*. In this case, the "extraordinary circumstances" at issue involve an attorney's failure to satisfy professional standards of care. The Court of Appeals held that, where that is so, even attorney conduct that is "grossly negligent" can never warrant tolling absent "bad faith, dishonesty, divided loyalty, mental impairment or so forth on the lawyer's part." But in our view, the Court of Appeals' standard is too rigid.

We have said that courts of equity "must be governed by rules and precedents no less than the courts of law." *Lonchar v. Thomas* (1996). But we have also made clear that often the "exercise of a court's equity powers . . . must be made on a case-by-case basis." *Baggett v. Bullitt* (1964). In emphasizing the need for "flexibility," for avoiding "mechanical rules," *Holmberg v. Armbrecht* (1946), we have followed a tradition in which courts of equity have sought to "relieve hardships which, from time to time, arise from a hard and fast adherence" to more absolute legal rules, which, if strictly applied, threaten the "evils of archaic rigidity," *Hazel-Atlas Glass Co. v. Hartford-Empire Co.* (1944). The "flexibility" inherent in "equitable procedure" enables courts "to meet new situations [that] demand equitable intervention, and to accord all the relief necessary to correct . . . particular injustices." *Ibid.* (permitting post deadline filing of bill of review). . . .

We recognize that, in the context of procedural default, we have previously stated, without qualification, that a petitioner "must 'bear the risk of attorney error.'" *Coleman v. Thompson* (1991). But *Coleman* was "a case about federalism," in that it asked whether *federal* courts may excuse a petitioner's failure to comply with a *state court's* procedural rules, notwithstanding the state court's determination that its own rules had been violated. Equitable tolling, by contrast, asks whether federal courts may excuse a petitioner's failure to comply with *federal* timing rules, an inquiry that does not implicate a state court's interpretation of state law. Holland does not argue that his attorney's misconduct provides a substantive ground for relief, *cf.* §2254(i), nor is this a case that asks whether AEDPA's statute of limitations should be recognized at all. Rather, this case asks how equity should be applied once the statute is recognized. And given equity's resistance to rigid rules, we cannot read Coleman as requiring a per se approach in this context.

In short, no pre-existing rule of law or precedent demands a rule like the one set forth by the Eleventh Circuit in this case. That rule is difficult to reconcile with more general equitable principles in that it fails to recognize that, at least sometimes, professional misconduct that fails to meet the Eleventh Circuit's standard could nonetheless amount to egregious behavior and create an extraordinary circumstance that warrants equitable tolling. And, given the long history of judicial application of equitable tolling, courts can easily find precedents that can guide their judgments. Several lower courts have specifically held that unprofessional attorney conduct may, in certain circumstances, prove "egregious" and can be "extraordinary" even though the conduct in question may not satisfy the Eleventh Circuit's rule. *See, e.g., Nara v. Frank* (CA3 2001) (ordering hearing as to whether client who was "effectively abandoned" by lawyer merited tolling); *Calderon* (allowing tolling where client was prejudiced by a last minute change in representation that was beyond his control); *Baldayaque* (finding that where an attorney failed to perform an essential service, to communicate with the client, and to do basic legal research, tolling could, under the circumstances, be warranted); *Spitsyn* (finding that "extraordinary circumstances" may warrant tolling where lawyer denied client access to files, failed to prepare a petition, and did not respond to his client's communications); *United States v. Martin* (C.A.8 2005) (client entitled to equitable tolling where his attorney retained files, made misleading statements, and engaged in similar conduct).

We have previously held that "a garden variety claim of excusable neglect," *Irwin*, as a simple "miscalculation" that leads a lawyer to miss a filing deadline, *Lawrence*, does not warrant equitable tolling. But the case before us does not involve, and we are not considering, a "garden variety claim" of attorney negligence. Rather, the facts of this case present far more serious instances of attorney misconduct. And, as we have said, although the circumstances of a case must be "extraordinary" before equitable tolling can be applied, we hold that such circumstances are not limited to those that satisfy the test that the Court of Appeals used in this case.

IV

The record facts that we have set forth in Part I of this opinion suggest that this case may well be an "extraordinary" instance in which petitioner's attorney's conduct constituted far more than "garden variety" or "excusable neglect." To be sure, Collins failed to file Holland's petition on time and appears to have been unaware of the date on which the limitations period expired — two facts that, alone, might suggest simple negligence. But, in these circumstances, the record facts we have elucidated suggest that the failure amounted to more: Here, Collins failed to file Holland's federal petition on time despite Holland's many letters that repeatedly emphasized the importance of his doing so. Collins apparently did not do the research necessary to find out the proper filing date, despite Holland's letters that went so far as to identify the applicable legal rules. Collins failed to inform Holland in a timely manner about the crucial fact that the Florida Supreme Court had decided his case, again despite Holland's many pleas for that information. And Collins failed to communicate with his client over a period of years, despite various pleas from Holland that Collins respond to his letters.

A group of teachers of legal ethics tells us that these various failures violated fundamental canons of professional responsibility, which require attorneys to perform reasonably competent legal work, to communicate with their clients, to implement clients' reasonable requests, to keep their clients informed of key developments in their cases, and never to abandon a client. And in this case, the failures seriously prejudiced a client who thereby lost what was likely his single opportunity for federal habeas review of the lawfulness of his imprisonment and of his death sentence.

We do not state our conclusion in absolute form, however, because more proceedings may be necessary. The District Court rested its ruling not on a lack of extraordinary circumstances, but rather on a lack of diligence—a ruling that respondent does not defend. We think that the District Court's conclusion was incorrect. The diligence required for equitable tolling purposes is "'reasonable diligence,'" see, e.g., Lonchar, not "maximum feasible diligence," Starns v. Andrews (C.A.5 2008). Here, Holland not only wrote his attorney numerous letters seeking crucial information and providing direction; he also repeatedly contacted the state courts, their clerks, and the Florida State Bar Association in an effort to have Collins—the central impediment to the pursuit of his legal remedy—removed from his case. And, the *very day* that Holland discovered that his AEDPA clock had expired due to Collins' failings, Holland prepared his own habeas petition *pro se* and promptly filed it with the District Court.

Thus, because we conclude that the District Court's determination must be set aside, we leave it to the Court of Appeals to determine whether the facts in this record entitle Holland to equitable tolling, or whether further proceedings, including an evidentiary hearing, might indicate that respondent should prevail.

[Justice Alito concurred, emphasizing that while "it is not practical to attempt to provide an exhaustive compilation of the kinds of situations in which attorney misconduct may provide a basis for equitable tolling . . . our cases make it abundantly clear that attorney negligence is not an extraordinary circumstance warranting equitable tolling . . . [including] counsel's mistake in miscalculating the limitations period [because] mistakes of counsel are constructively attributable to the client, at least in the postconviction context [and] there is no constitutional right to an attorney in state postconviction proceedings. [The same] rationale fully applies to other forms of attorney negligence. [Moreover,] allowing equitable tolling in cases involving gross rather than ordinary attorney negligence . . . would . . . be impractical in the extreme [because the line between the two is] highly artificial." Justice Alito distinguished attorney misconduct so extraordinary "that it is not constructively attributable to the petitioner."]

Justice SCALIA, with whom Justice THOMAS joins, dissenting.

The question . . . is not whether §2244(d)'s time bar is subject to tolling, but whether it is consistent with §2244(d) for federal courts to toll the time bar for *additional* reasons beyond those Congress included.

In my view it is not. It is fair enough to infer, when a statute of limitations says nothing about equitable tolling, that Congress did not displace the default rule. But when Congress has *codified* that default rule and specified the instances where it applies, we have no warrant to extend it to other cases. See United States v. Beggerly (1998). Unless the Court believes §2244(d) contains an implicit, across-the-board exception that subsumes (and thus renders unnecessary) §2244(d)(1)(B)-(D) and (d)(2), it must rely on the untenable assumption that when Congress enumerated the events that toll the limitations period—with no indication the list is merely illustrative—it implicitly authorized courts to add others as they see fit. We should assume the opposite: that by specifying situations in which an equitable principle applies to a specific requirement, Congress has displaced courts' discretion to develop ad hoc exceptions. . . .

Even if §2244(d) left room for equitable tolling in some situations, tolling surely should not excuse the delay here. Where equitable tolling is available, we have held that a litigant is entitled to it only if he has diligently pursued his rights and—the requirement relevant here—if "'some extraordinary circumstance stood in his way.'" *Lawrence v. Florida* (2007). Because the attorney is the litigant's agent, the attorney's acts (or failures to act) within the scope of the representation are treated as those of his client, and thus such acts (or failures to act) are necessarily not extraordinary circumstances.

To be sure, the rule that an attorney's acts and oversights are attributable to the client is relaxed where the client has a constitutional right to effective assistance of counsel. Where a State is constitutionally obliged to provide an attorney but fails to provide an effective one, the attorney's failures that fall below the standard set forth in *Strickland v. Washington* (1984), are chargeable to the State, not to the prisoner. *See Murray v. Carrier* (1986). But where the client has no right to counsel—which in habeas proceedings he does not—the rule holding him responsible for his attorney's acts applies with full force. *See Coleman v. Thompson* (1991). Thus, when a state habeas petitioner's appeal is filed too late because of attorney error, the petitioner is out of luck—no less than if he had proceeded *pro se* and neglected to file the appeal himself.

Congress could, of course, have included errors by state-appointed habeas counsel as a basis for delaying the limitations period, but it did not. Nor was that an oversight: Section 2244(d)(1)(B) expressly allows tolling for state-created impediments that prevent a prisoner from filing his application, but *only if* the impediment violates the Constitution or federal law. . . .

Why Collins did not notify Holland or file a timely federal application for him is unclear, but none of the plausible explanations would support equitable tolling. By far the most likely explanation is that Collins made exactly the same mistake as the attorney in *Lawrence*—*i.e.*, he assumed incorrectly that the pendency of a petition for certiorari in this Court seeking review of the denial of Holland's state habeas petition would toll AEDPA's time bar under §2244(d)(2). In December 2002, Collins had explained to Holland by letter that if his state habeas petition was denied *and* this Court denied certiorari in that proceeding, Holland's claims "*will then be ripe* for presentation in a petition for writ of habeas corpus in federal court." Holland himself interprets that statement as proof that, at that time, "Collins was under the belief that [Holland's] time to file his federal habeas petition would continue to be tolled until this Court denied certiorari" in his state postconviction proceeding. That misunderstanding would entirely account for Collins's conduct—filing a certiorari petition instead of a habeas application, and waiting nearly three months to do so. But it would also be insufficient, as *Lawrence* held it was, to warrant tolling.

Such an oversight is unfortunate, but it amounts to "garden variety" negligence, not a basis for equitable tolling. *Irwin.* Surely it is no more extraordinary than the attorney's error in *Lawrence*, which rudimentary research and arithmetic would have avoided.

The Court's impulse to intervene when a litigant's lawyer has made mistakes is understandable; the temptation to tinker with technical rules to achieve what appears a just result is often strong, especially when the client faces a capital sentence. But the Constitution does not empower federal courts to rewrite, in the name of equity, rules that Congress has made.

* * *

Prior to *Holland,* as many as 22 percent of federal habeas petitions were dismissed as time-barred under AEDPA's statute of limitations and "in less than 2% of capital and non-capital cases did judges explicitly reject the limitations defense."[68] Here, as with procedural default, the competence of defense counsel looms large over a prisoner's right of access to federal habeas. *Holland* permits equitable tolling where a lawyer's misconduct is so extraordinary that the agency relationship between attorney and client is destroyed. But this is far less common than ordinary attorney negligence or gross negligence.

Recall that in *Schlup* the Court applied a "miscarriage of justice" exception to the ordinary cause and prejudice standard for procedural default where the petitioner claimed actual innocence. Following *Schlup* and the *Holland* principle that the Court "will not construe a statute to displace courts' traditional equitable authority absent the clearest command," the Court has extended the "miscarriage of justice" exception for convincing claims of actual innocence to AEDPA's statute of limitations. *See McQuiggin v. Perkins* (2013) (first federal habeas petition not time-barred under §2244(d)(1) where petitioner waited six years to present exculpatory affidavits in his possession indicating another person committed the murder).

Quite apart from actual innocence, the statute of limitations interacts in complex ways with other procedural prerequisites. For example, both AEDPA and pre-AEDPA precedent require "total exhaustion" of federal claims in state courts. *Rose v. Lundy* (1982). But a one-year statute of limitations under AEDPA means that the statute can easily run out for federal petitions dismissed for failure to exhaust and refiled in state court. Matters are even more complicated if the petition is "mixed"—containing both exhausted and unexhausted claims. If the entire petition is dismissed then the statute can run even as to the already exhausted claims properly before a federal district court. The Court addressed this problem in *Rhines v. Weber* (2005), holding that district courts have discretion to issue a stay the petition and hold it in abeyance while colorable unexhausted claims are brought to the state courts if the petitioner "had good cause for . . . fail[ing] to exhaust his claims" in state court before filing the federal petition:

> Even where stay and abeyance is appropriate, the district court's discretion in structuring the stay is limited by the timeliness concerns reflected in AEDPA. A mixed petition should not be stayed indefinitely. Though, generally, a prisoner's "principal interest . . . is in obtaining speedy federal relief on his claims," *Lundy,* not all petitioners have an incentive to obtain federal relief as quickly as possible. In particular, capital petitioners might deliberately engage in dilatory tactics to prolong their incarceration and avoid execution of the sentence of death. Without time limits, petitioners could frustrate AEDPA's goal of finality by dragging out indefinitely their federal habeas review. Thus, district courts should place reasonable time limits on a petitioner's trip to state court and back. And if a petitioner engages in abusive litigation tactics or intentional delay, the district court should not grant him a stay at all.

---

68. NANCY J. KING ET AL., FINAL TECHNICAL REPORT: HABEAS LITIGATION IN THE U.S. DISTRICT COURTS: AN EMPIRICAL STUDY OF HABEAS CORPUS CASES FILED BY STATE PRISONERS UNDER THE AEDPA OF 1996, (2007).

On the other hand, it likely would be an abuse of discretion for a district court to deny a stay and to dismiss a mixed petition if the petitioner had good cause for his failure to exhaust, his unexhausted claims are potentially meritorious, and there is no indication that the petitioner engaged in intentionally dilatory litigation tactics. In such circumstances, the district court should stay, rather than dismiss, the mixed petition.

e. Successive Petitions

A range of rules limit the filing of "second or successive" federal habeas petitions. Claims made in a second or successive §2254 petition that were presented in a prior federal petition "shall be dismissed." 28 U.S.C. §2244(b)(1). If the claim was not presented in a prior federal petition, it may be considered only if it rests on genuinely new law or a claim of factual innocence that was not previously known. The claim "shall be dismissed unless":

(A) the applicant shows that the claim relies on a new rule of constitutional law, made retroactive to cases on collateral review by the Supreme Court, that was previously unavailable; or

(B) (i) the factual predicate for the claim could not have been discovered previously through the exercise of due diligence; and (ii) the facts underlying the claim, if proven and viewed in light of the evidence as a whole, would be sufficient to establish by clear and convincing evidence that, but for constitutional error, no reasonable factfinder would have found the applicant guilty of the underlying offense.

A "claim" for purposes of second or successive petitions is "an asserted federal basis for relief from a state court's judgment of conviction." *Gonzalez v. Crosby* (2005). For this reason, new evidence for a previously filed claim does not make the same legal ground a new claim. *See In re Hill* (11th Cir. 2013) (new expert testimony and different argument about the burden of proof on same Eighth Amendment claim challenging capital sentence on grounds of mental incapacity raised in first petition are barred by §2244(b)(1); even if considered new, claim is barred by §2244(b)(2) because petitioner does not rely on a new rule of constitutional law and mental capacity goes to sentence, not guilt).

Before any second or successive petition is filed, the petitioner must move the court of appeals for to authorize the district court to consider the application. 28 U.S.C. §2244(b)(3). Authority exists "only if it determines that the application makes a prima facie showing that the application satisfies the" new rule or actual innocence requirements. 28 U.S.C. §2244(b)(3)(C). The statute requires the court of appeals to rule within 30 days of the filing of the motion, and it provides that the "grant or denial of an authorization . . . shall not be appealable and shall not be the subject of a petition for rehearing or for a writ of certiorari." In the next case, the Court considered whether this "gatekeeping" rule requiring permission of the court of appeals to file a second or successive petition and foreclosing appeal also foreclosed original petitions under §14 of the First Judiciary Act.

Felker v. Turpin, Warden

518 U.S. 651 (1996)

Chief Justice REHNQUIST delivered the opinion of the Court.

Title I of the Antiterrorism and Effective Death Penalty Act of 1996 (Act) works substantial changes to [federal habeas statutes]. We hold that the Act does not preclude this Court from entertaining an application for habeas corpus relief, although it does affect the standards governing the granting of such relief. We also conclude that the availability of such relief in this Court obviates any claim by petitioner under the Exceptions Clause of Article III, §2, of the Constitution, and that the operative provisions of the Act do not violate the Suspension Clause of the Constitution, Art. I, §9.

I

[In 1976] petitioner was . . . convicted of aggravated sodomy [for sexually assaulting Jane W.] and sentenced to 12 years' imprisonment.

Petitioner was paroled four years later. On November 23, 1981, he met Joy Ludlam, a cocktail waitress, at the lounge where she worked. She was interested in changing jobs, and petitioner used a series of deceptions . . . to induce her to visit him the next day. The last time Joy was seen alive was the evening of the next day. Her dead body was discovered two weeks later in a creek. Forensic analysis established that she had been beaten, raped, and sodomized, and that she had been strangled to death before being left in the creek. Investigators discovered hair resembling petitioner's on Joy's body and clothes, hair resembling Joy's in petitioner's bedroom, and clothing fibers like those in Joy's coat in the hatchback of petitioner's car. One of petitioner's neighbors reported seeing Joy's car at petitioner's house the day she disappeared.

A jury convicted petitioner of murder, rape, aggravated sodomy, and false imprisonment. Petitioner was sentenced to death on the murder charge. The Georgia Supreme Court affirmed petitioner's conviction and death sentence, and we denied certiorari. A state trial court denied collateral relief, the Georgia Supreme Court declined to issue a certificate of probable cause to appeal the denial, and we again denied certiorari.

Petitioner then filed a petition for a writ of habeas corpus in the United States District Court for the Middle District of Georgia, alleging that (1) the State's evidence was insufficient to convict him; (2) the State withheld exculpatory evidence, in violation of *Brady v. Maryland* (1963); (3) petitioner's counsel rendered ineffective assistance at sentencing; (4) the State improperly used hypnosis to refresh a witness' memory; and (5) the State violated double jeopardy and collateral estoppel principles by using petitioner's crime against Jane W. as evidence at petitioner's trial for crimes against Joy Ludlam. The District Court denied the petition. The United States Court of Appeals for the Eleventh Circuit affirmed and we denied certiorari.

The State scheduled petitioner's execution for the period May 2-9, 1996. On April 29, 1996, petitioner filed a second petition for state collateral relief. The state trial court denied this petition on May 1, and the Georgia Supreme Court denied certiorari on May 2.

On April 24, 1996, the President signed the Act into law. Title I of this Act contained a series of amendments to existing federal habeas corpus law. The provisions of the Act pertinent to this case concern second or successive habeas corpus applications by state prisoners. . . . The prospective applicant must file in the court of appeals a motion for leave to file a second or successive habeas application in the district court. §2244(b)(3)(A). A three-judge panel has 30 days to determine whether "the application makes a prima facie showing that the application satisfies the requirements of" §2244(b). §2244(b)(3)(C). Section 2244(b)(3)(E) specifies that "[t]he grant or denial of an authorization by a court of appeals to file a second or successive application shall not be appealable and shall not be the subject of a petition for rehearing or for a writ of certiorari."

On May 2, 1996, petitioner filed in the United States Court of Appeals for the Eleventh Circuit a motion for stay of execution and a motion for leave to file a second or successive federal habeas corpus petition under §2254. Petitioner sought to raise two claims in his second petition, the first being that the state trial court violated due process by equating guilt "beyond a reasonable doubt" with "moral certainty" of guilt in *voir dire* and jury instructions. *See Cage v. Louisiana* (1990). He also alleged that qualified experts, reviewing the forensic evidence after his conviction, had established that Joy must have died during a period when petitioner was under police surveillance for Joy's disappearance and thus had a valid alibi. He claimed that the testimony of the State's forensic expert at trial was suspect because he is not a licensed physician, and that the new expert testimony so discredited the State's testimony at trial that petitioner had a colorable claim of factual innocence.

The Court of Appeals denied both motions the day they were filed, concluding that petitioner's claims had not been presented in his first habeas petition, that they did not meet the standards of §2244(b)(2), and that they would not have satisfied pre-Act standards for obtaining review on the merits of second or successive claims. Petitioner filed in this Court a pleading styled a "Petition for Writ of Habeas Corpus, for Appellate or Certiorari Review of the Decision of the United States Circuit Court for the Eleventh Circuit, and for Stay of Execution." On May 3, we granted petitioner's stay application and petition for certiorari. We ordered briefing on the extent to which the provisions of Title I of the Act apply to a petition for habeas corpus filed in this Court, whether application of the Act suspended the writ of habeas corpus in this case, and whether Title I of the Act, especially the provision to be codified at §2244(b)(3)(E), constitutes an unconstitutional restriction on the jurisdiction of this Court.

II

A

[As described in Chapter 4, the Court held that §2244(b)(3)(E) validly stripped jurisdiction to review denials of leave to file a successive petition by appeal or writ of certiorari.]

Turning to the present case, we conclude that Title I of the Act has not repealed our authority to entertain original habeas petitions [under 28 U.S.C. §2241], for reasons similar to those stated in *Yerger.* No provision of Title I mentions our authority to entertain original habeas petitions. As we declined to find a repeal of §14 of the Judiciary Act of 1789 as applied to this Court by implication then, we decline to find a similar repeal of §2241 of Title 28—its descendant— by implication now.

[S]ince it does not repeal our authority to entertain a petition for habeas corpus, there can be no plausible argument that the Act has deprived this Court of appellate jurisdiction in violation of Article III, §2.

III

Next, we consider whether the Act suspends the writ of habeas corpus in violation of Article I, §9, clause 2, of the Constitution. This Clause provides that "[t]he Privilege of the Writ of Habeas Corpus shall not be suspended, unless when in Cases of Rebellion or Invasion the public Safety may require it."

It was not until 1867 that Congress made the writ generally available in "all cases where any person may be restrained of his or her liberty in violation of the constitution, or of any treaty or law of the United States." And it was not until well into this century that this Court interpreted that provision to allow a final judgment of conviction in a state court to be collaterally attacked on habeas. *See, e.g., Waley v. Johnston* (1942) (per curiam); *Brown v. Allen* (1953). But we assume, for purposes of decision here, that the Suspension Clause of the Constitution refers to the writ as it exists today, rather than as it existed in 1789.

The new restrictions on successive petitions constitute a modified res judicata rule, a restraint on what is called in habeas corpus practice "abuse of the writ." In *McCleskey v. Zant* (1991), we said that "the doctrine of abuse of the writ refers to a complex and evolving body of equitable principles informed and controlled by historical usage, statutory developments, and judicial decisions." The added restrictions which the Act places on second habeas petitions are well within the compass of this evolutionary process, and we hold that they do not amount to a "suspension" of the writ contrary to Article I, §9.

IV

We have answered the questions presented by the petition for certiorari in this case, and we now dispose of the petition for an original writ of habeas corpus. Our Rule 20.4(a) delineates the standards under which we grant such writs:

> A petition seeking the issuance of a writ of habeas corpus shall comply with the requirements of 28 U.S.C. §§2241 and 2242, and in particular with the provision in the last paragraph of §2242 requiring a statement of the "reasons for not making application to the district court of the district in which the applicant is held." If the relief sought is from the judgment of a state court, the petition shall set forth specifically how and wherein the petitioner has exhausted available remedies in the state courts or otherwise comes within the provisions of 28 U.S.C. §2254(b). To justify the granting of a writ of habeas corpus, the petitioner must show exceptional circumstances warranting the exercise of the Court's discretionary powers and must show that adequate relief cannot be obtained in any other form or from any other court. These writs are rarely granted.

Reviewing petitioner's claims here, they do not materially differ from numerous other claims made by successive habeas petitioners which we have had occasion to review on stay applications to this Court. Neither of them satisfies the requirements of the relevant provisions of the Act, let alone the requirement that there be "exceptional circumstances" justifying the issuance of the writ.

The petition for writ of certiorari is dismissed for want of jurisdiction. The petition for an original writ of habeas corpus is denied.

[The concurring opinions of Justices STEVENS and SOUTER, both joined by Justice BREYER, are omitted.]

* * *

f. Fact Finding

AEDPA imposed strict rules of fact deference on federal habeas courts reviewing state court judgments. Findings of fact by the state courts "shall be presumed to be correct" and the presumption may be overcome only by clear and convincing evidence. 18 U.S.C. §2254(e)(1). A federal court is also powerless to conduct "an evidentiary hearing on the claim" where the petitioner "has failed to develop the factual basis of a claim in State court proceedings" unless:

(A) the claim relies on—

(i) a new rule of constitutional law, made retroactive to cases on collateral review by the Supreme Court, that was previously unavailable; or

(ii) a factual predicate that could not have been previously discovered through the exercise of due diligence; and

(B) the facts underlying the claim would be sufficient to establish by clear and convincing evidence that but for constitutional error, no reasonable factfinder would have found the applicant guilty of the underlying offense.

28 U.S.C. §2254(e)(2). These restrictions "apply *a fortiori* when a prisoner seeks relief based on new evidence without an evidentiary hearing." *Holland v. Jackson* (2004) (holding that seven-year delay attributable to attorney negligence does not excuse failure to present evidence to state courts because attorney's negligence "is chargeable to the client and precludes relief unless the conditions of §2254(e)(2) are met"); *see also Cullen v. Pinholster* (2011) (holding that in federal petitions governed by the standard of review in §2254(d), the federal court is restricted to reviewing the record considered by the state court). Given that almost all federal petitions are governed by §2254(d)'s standard of review (*see Harrington v. Richter* (2011), *infra*, Section II.C.), *Pinholster* eliminates the right to an evidentiary hearing in most federal petitions.

Securing an evidentiary hearing has profound effects on the grant rate in §2254 cases—an increase of 21 to 32 percent in the likelihood of relief being granted. The effect of §2254(e) has been to significantly reduce the chance of securing an evidentiary hearing. Prior to AEDPA, evidentiary hearings were conducted in 19 percent of capital cases; after AEDPA they occur in just 9.5 percent. For non-capital cases, evidentiary hearings occur in 0.41 percent of cases post-AEDPA, falling from 1.1 percent of cases prior to AEDPA.[69]

---

69. KING ET AL., FINAL TECHNICAL REPORT: HABEAS LITIGATION IN THE U.S., *supra* note 68, at 5.

The Court has held that §2254(e)'s restrictions "apply *a fortiori* when a prisoner seeks relief based on new evidence without an evidentiary hearing." *Holland v. Jackson* (2004) (holding that seven-year delay attributable to attorney negligence does not excuse failure to present evidence to state courts because attorney's negligence "is chargeable to the client and precludes relief unless the conditions of §2254(e)(2) are met"). It has also held that in federal petitions governed by the standard of review in §2254(d), the federal court is restricted to reviewing the record considered by the state court. *Cullen v. Pinholster* (2011). Given that almost all federal petitions are governed by §2254(d)'s standard of review (*see Harrington v. Richter, infra*, Section II.C.), *Pinholster* effectively forecloses the right to an evidentiary hearing in most federal petitions; *Holland* has similar consequences for introducing new evidence in a federal proceeding by means other than an evidentiary hearing.

State post-conviction procedures for discovery and evidentiary hearings are often dispositive. At least in cases involving claims of innocence, it is notable that over the last three decades "*all legislatures in the United States* have enacted statutes to permit broader post-conviction access to new evidence of innocence, and many have improved procedures concerning interrogations, lineups, and other types of evidence."[70] As late as 1993, by contrast, "seventeen states had limitations periods of less than 60 days, and eighteen had limitations periods between one and three years" for introducing new evidence of innocence.

In *Shinn v. Martinez-Ramirez* (2022), the strict statutory limitation on factfinding, the doctrine of procedural default, and a state rule precluding ineffective assistance of counsel claims on direct review collided. Arizona does not allow prisoners to raise ineffective assistance of counsel on direct appeal. They can only do so via postconviction petitions in state court. There is, however, no federal constitutional right to counsel after direct appeal. In an earlier case, the Supreme Court held that in light of Arizona's rule, procedural default could be excused in the narrow circumstance where post-conviction counsel fails to present a *Strickland* claim regarding trial counsel to the state courts in Arizona's postconviction process. *See Martinez v. Ryan* (2012). The difficulty is that even if procedural default is excused and the federal petition can proceed on the constitutional claim that was not first presented to the state courts, §2254(e)(2) does not permit new evidence to be taken by the federal district court on that constitutional claim if the claim is unrelated to actual innocence. This raises the paradox of a claim that is properly before the district court without any power to take evidence to establish the claim. In *Shinn v. Martinez Ramirez* (2022), the Court held that the restrictions on evidentiary hearings in AEDPA were passed to replace the older "cause and prejudice" approach "with even more stringent requirements." The statute's reference to "fail[ure]" to develop the factual record before the state courts means that "the prisoner must be 'at fault' for the undeveloped record in the state court." Emphasizing the intrusion federal habeas review causes on the state's sovereign function of administering criminal justice, the Court squarely rejected the argument that a prisoner is not "at fault" if the failure is due to attorney negligence. The attorney's negligence "is attributed to the prisoner." The Court also stressed the burden imposed by conducting an evidentiary hearing:

---

70. GARRETT, ACTUAL INNOCENCE, *supra* note 50, at 2 (emphasis added).

The cases under review demonstrate the improper burden imposed on the States when *Martinez* applies beyond its narrow scope. The sprawling evidentiary hearing [the district court conducted] is particularly poignant. Ostensibly to assess cause and prejudice under *Martinez*, the District Court ordered a 7-day hearing that included testimony from no fewer than 10 witnesses, including defense trial counsel, defense postconviction counsel, the lead investigating detective, three forensic pathologists, an emergency medicine and trauma specialist, a biomechanics and functional human anatomy expert, and a crime scene and bloodstain pattern analyst. Of these witnesses, only one of the forensic pathologists and the lead detective testified at the original trial. The remainder testified on virtually every disputed issue in the case, including the timing of Rachel Gray's injuries and her cause of death. This wholesale relitigation of . . . guilt is plainly not what *Martinez* envisioned. . . .

Respondents all but concede that their argument amounts to the same kind of evasion of §2254(e)(2) that we rejected in *Holland.* They nonetheless object that Holland renders many Martinez hearings a nullity, because there is no point in developing a record for cause and prejudice if a federal court cannot later consider that evidence on the merits. While we agree that any such *Martinez* hearing would serve no purpose, that is a reason to dispense with *Martinez* hearings altogether, not to set §2254(e)(2) aside. Thus, if that provision applies and the prisoner cannot satisfy its "stringent requirements," [*Williams v. Taylor* (2000)], a federal court may not hold an evidentiary hearing—or otherwise consider new evidence—to assess cause and prejudice under *Martinez.*

And because a federal habeas court may never "needlessly prolong" a habeas case, *ibid.*, particularly given the "essential" need to promote the finality of state convictions, Calderon, a *Martinez* hearing is improper if the newly developed evidence never would "entitle [the prisoner] to federal habeas relief," *Schriro.* Ultimately, respondents' proposed expansion of factfinding in federal court, whether by *Martinez* or other means, conflicts with any appropriately limited federal habeas review. In our dual-sovereign system, federal courts must afford unwavering respect to the centrality "of the trial of a criminal case in state court." . . . Such intervention is also an affront to the State and its citizens who returned a verdict of guilt after considering the evidence before them. Federal courts, years later, lack the competence and authority to relitigate a State's criminal case.

Justices Sotomayor, Breyer, and Kagan dissented, arguing that the decision

will leave many people who were convicted in violation of the Sixth Amendment to face incarceration or even execution without any meaningful chance to vindicate their right to counsel. . . . It makes no sense to excuse a habeas petitioner's counsel's failure to raise a claim altogether because of ineffective assistance in postconviction proceedings, as *Martinez* . . . did, but to fault the same petitioner for that postconviction counsel's failure to develop evidence in support of the trial-ineffectiveness claim. In so doing, the Court guts *Martinez.* . . .

2. *The Standard of Review*

As we have seen, the procedural prerequisites to a federal habeas petition challenging a state conviction are daunting. Procedural constraints imposed by Congress and the Court overlap with substantial growth in the number of state prisoners and a corresponding increase in the number of federal petitions in the late twentieth century. Procedural constraints are also a response to the Warren Court's revolution in constitutional criminal procedure — the expansion of constitutional rights under the Fourth, Fifth, Sixth, and Eighth Amendments designed to improve the accuracy and fairness of criminal trials. None of these mid-century developments in constitutional law would have mattered much to habeas litigation without the Court's decision in *Brown v. Allen* (1953), and its repudiation of the idea that federal habeas review is limited to jurisdictional errors in state criminal convictions. *Brown* was not an outlier. It built on earlier decisions in *Frank v. Magnum* (1915) and *Moore v. Dempsey* (1923), in which federal habeas petitions challenged state trials corrupted by the influence of violent mobs on due process grounds.

The "jurisdictional error only" interpretation of the 1867 Act (and the equally cramped view of earlier cases limiting review of federal convictions under the First Judiciary Act to jurisdictional error) rest on a sharply contested understanding of the historical breadth of the habeas remedy. Important revisionist historical work has shown that, going back *centuries*, English courts entertained habeas petitions challenging the validity of criminal convictions, not just executive detention without trial and jurisdictional defects in post conviction cases. As one commentator summarizes the early history:

> The common law writ was subject to no such limitation. . . . Although habeas took center stage during the mid seventeenth century conflict between King's Bench and the Crown, in an earlier stage it was used against local Justices of the Peace, to cure overzealous use of the summary conviction process and to void associated orders to jail inmates. King's Bench used habeas to review numerous facets of post-conviction imprisonment, both by Justices of the Peace and by other courts, including: the factual accuracy of the return; the authority of a convicting court; technicalities of a sentence; the findings pertaining to mental health; the severity of noncapital sentences; and the presence of extenuating circumstances. Judges even used habeas to attach conditions to sentences and paroles. Habeas was particularly central to review one type of conviction: murder. . . . The more questionable the process that produced judgments of conviction, the more intense the habeas scrutiny conducted by King's Bench.[71]

On this account, Chief Justice Marshall's influential conclusion in *Ex parte Watkins* that the English history of the writ precluded substantive challenges to convictions on habeas is "one of the most pervasive falsehoods in the habeas literature."[72]

---

71. Lee Kovarsky, *A Constitutional Theory of Habeas Power*, 99 Va. L. Rev. 753, 769-70 (2013) (citing and relying upon Paul D. Halliday, Habeas Corpus: From England to Empire (2010), which examined original King's Bench files and rolls every fourth year from 1592 to 1708).

72. *Id.*

In reality, the traditional common law standard of review was adaptive, and in particular, responsive to the degree of procedural integrity in the judicial process under review. As we have seen in *Sykes* and *Felker*, and as you will see in the cases that follow, modern courts, without knowing this history, have instead addressed the standard of review by taking for granted the backdrop not only of *Watkins'* narrower frame, but also the finality, federalism, and comity interests supporting state convictions. *Brown v. Allen* affirmed the discretion of lower federal courts to grant relief where there were substantive constitutional defects in the state process, not just jurisdictional defects. But, as we will see, this standard of review did not endure. By the 1980s, the Court had retreated under the banner of retroactivity doctrine, limiting the ability of prisoners whose convictions had become final to assert in a habeas proceeding new constitutional law announced by the Court. The principal case is *Teague v. Lane* (1989). Congress, in addition to building on procedural constraints developed by the Court, decisively rejected the standard of review of *Brown v. Allen* in AEDPA.

We cover each of these developments in the pages that follow, beginning with *Brown v. Allen* and ending with the cases interpreting AEDPA's new standard of review in 28 U.S.C. §2254(d).

a. The Warren Court Approach

Brown v. Allen involved certiorari to review three separate cases out of the Fourth Circuit: *Brown v. Allen, Speller v. Allen,* and *Daniels v. Allen.* All three cases involved death sentences imposed upon black men for the rape or murder of white victims. On habeas, the petitioners alleged racial discrimination against black people in the selection of juries by jury commissioners in North Carolina. In *Brown,* for example, the petition alleged that relying on property and poll tax rolls to select jury pools meant that "no more than one or two Negroes at a time have ever served on a Forsyth County grand jury, and that no more than five Negroes have ever previously served on a petit jury panel in the county" even though one-third of the county population was black. Brown, a minor, was convicted and sentenced to death for the beating and rape of a white high-school student by an all-white jury. He was "held without charges for five days, during which time he confessed; he was not given a preliminary hearing until eighteen days after his arrest; and he was not formally appointed counsel until three days after that."[73] Both Brown and Daniels alleged their confessions were coerced. Speller was convicted three times for the rape of a white woman and sentenced to death. The first two convictions were thrown out because of racial discrimination in the jury selection and the failure to permit the defendant to investigate possible racial bias in the jury selection system. The third conviction was affirmed by the state courts after a full evidentiary hearing on his racial discrimination challenge to jury selection.

The Court did not reach the merits in *Daniels,* finding that petitioners missed a state filing deadline by one day and that this procedural default was an adequate and independent state ground. In *Speller* and *Brown,* by contrast, there was full litigation

---

73. Eric M. Freedman, Brown v. Allen: *The Habeas Corpus Revolution* 51 ALA. L. REV. 1541, 1558 (2000).

of the federal constitutional issues in the state courts and the Supreme Court denied certiorari petitions in the direct appeal process. The district court in *Speller* also held an evidentiary hearing. In both *Speller* and *Brown*, the district court doubted that, absent "unusual" circumstances, it could grant the writ where the state courts had fully addressed the claims and the Supreme Court had denied certiorari on direct appeal. As the cases came to the Supreme Court when the habeas petitions were denied by the district court and the Fourth Circuit, the central issue appeared to be whether habeas was ever appropriate when the Court had already denied certiorari on direct appeal. But because an evidentiary hearing was held by the district court in *Speller*, and because some Justices in conference appeared inclined to limit habeas review, Justice Frankfurter pressed the Court bluntly in an internal memo not to diminish the writ.

> Callous and even cruel though it may seem, the fate of the . . . petitioners is to me a matter of little importance. What this Court may say regarding the writ of habeas corpus I deem of the profoundest importance. . . . [I]t makes all the difference in the world whether we treat habeas corpus as just another legal remedy in the procedural arsenal of our law, or regard it as basic to the development of Anglo-American civilization and unlike other legal remedies, which are more or less strictly defined. . . . If such a conception is not merely to be rhetoric and is to be an ever-living process to be enforced, certain consequences follow which cannot be imprisoned within any such rubrics as 'jurisdiction,' or 'habeas corpus is not a substitute for appeal," etc., etc. . . . I am profoundly concerned that in these days, when we boast at international conferences and otherwise through our political leaders, of habeas corpus as one of the great agencies of the Anglo-American world in safeguarding and promoting democracy, this Court should not disregard the historic record, reflecting deep considerations of justice, and treat habeas corpus in a devitalizing manner as though it were construing merely one of the Rules of Civil Procedure. . . . I pray that this Court do not shrivel [the statutory grants of authority] because of fear of potential abuse, or even an occasional abuse which can easily be curbed without damage to the Great Writ.

Frankfurter had reason to be concerned. A law clerk to Justice Jackson (a young William Rehnquist) had written a memo arguing that "[t]o think that state courts would deliberately or in ignorance refuse to follow Supreme Court precedents is to suggest a malady in the body politic which no additional hearing before a federal judge would cure." The proper course is for "federal district judges to observe the ordinary principles of res judicata in passing on habeas corpus petitions from those confined under state sentence," with a possible exception for cases where denial of the right to counsel destroyed any meaningful opportunity to raise constitutional errors on direct appeal in the state courts.

There would ultimately be eight opinions in *Brown v. Allen*. Justice Reed's opinion, technically the opinion of the Court, affirmed the denial of relief in *Speller* and *Brown*. But it is Justice Frankfurter's and Justice Jackson's that have endured: the former as the most lucid statement of the views of the Justices whose separate opinions made up a majority of the Court regarding the standard of review for §2254 petitions; the latter as a statement of reservations about the course set by the majority. As you read Justice Frankfurter's opinion consider the similarities and differences to the model for Article III review of questions of law, of fact, and mixed questions in agency adjudications we studied in *Crowell* and its progeny in Chapter 4. Note as well, the more relaxed approach to procedural prerequisites relative to modern practice under AEDPA.

Brown v. Allen, Warden

344 U.S. 443 (1953)

Justice FRANKFURTER.

This opinion is restricted to the two general questions which must be considered before the Court can pass on the specific situations presented by these cases. The two general problems are these:

    I. The legal significance of a denial of certiorari, in a case required to be presented here under the doctrine of *Darr v. Burford* (1950) when an application for a writ of habeas corpus thereafter comes before a district court.

   II. The bearing that the proceedings in the state courts should have on the disposition of such an application in a district court.

I

. . . If district judges were authorized to deny an application for habeas corpus merely because the issues may have been considered by this Court in denying a petition for certiorari, the duty, which has been entrusted to the Federal Courts since the enlargement of the scope of habeas corpus jurisdiction by the Act of 1867, to deal judicially with applications for writs of habeas corpus by State convicts would be left to the unbounded, because undefined, discretion of the District Judges throughout the land. Judges dealing with the writ of habeas corpus, as with temporary injunctions, must be left some discretion—room for assessing fact and balancing conflicting considerations of public interest—if law is not to be a Procrustes bed. But discretion must be judicial discretion. It must be subject to rational criteria, by which particular situations may be adjudged. To allow applications for habeas corpus to be denied merely because it is deemed, on no reasonable or, at best, on the most fragile, foundations, that the matter has already been adjudicated here is to afford no criterion, but merely a shelter, for district judges to respond according to the individual will.

We must not invite the exercise of judicial impressionism. Discretion there may be, but "methodized by analogy, disciplined by system." Cardozo, *The Nature of the Judicial Process* 139, 141 (1921). Discretion without a criterion for its exercise is authorization of arbitrariness. . . .

The reasons why our denial of certiorari in the ordinary run of cases can be any number of things other than a decision on the merits are only multiplied by the circumstances of this class of petitions. And so we conclude that in habeas corpus cases, as in others, denial of certiorari cannot be interpreted as an "expression of opinion on the merits."

II

This opinion is designed to make explicit and detailed matters that are also the concern of Mr. Justice Reed's opinion. The uncommon circumstances in which a district court should entertain an application ought to be defined with greater particularity, as should be the criteria for determining when a hearing is proper.

. . . Experience may be summoned to support the belief that most claims in these attempts to obtain review of State convictions are without merit. Presumably they are adequately dealt with in the State courts.

Again, no one can feel more strongly than I do that a casual, unrestricted opening of the doors of the federal courts to these claims not only would cast an undue burden upon those courts, but would also disregard our duty to support and not weaken the sturdy enforcement of their criminal laws by the States. That whole-sale opening of State prison doors by federal courts is, however, not at all the real issue before us is best indicated by a survey recently prepared in the Administrative Office of the United States Courts for the Conference of Chief Justices: of all fed-eral question applications for habeas corpus, some not even relating to State con-victions, only 67 out of 3,702 applications were granted in the last seven years. And "only a small number" of these 67 applications resulted in release from prison: "a more detailed study over the last four years shows that, out of 29 petitions granted, there were only 5 petitioners who were released from state penitentiaries. The mer-itorious claims are few, but our procedures must ensure that those few claims are not stifled by undiscriminating generalities. The complexities of our federalism and the workings of a scheme of government involving the interplay of two govern-ments, one of which is subject to limitations enforceable by the other, are not to be escaped by simple, rigid rules which, by avoiding some abuses, generate others.

For surely it is an abuse to deal too casually and too lightly with rights guaran-teed by the Federal Constitution, even though they involve limitations upon State power and may be invoked by those morally unworthy. Under the guise of fashion-ing a procedural rule, we are not justified in wiping out the practical efficacy of a jurisdiction conferred by Congress on the District Courts. Rules which, in effect, treat all these cases indiscriminately as frivolous do not fall far short of abolishing this head of jurisdiction.

Congress could have left the enforcement of federal constitutional rights gov-erning the administration of criminal justice in the States exclusively to the State courts. These tribunals are under the same duty as the federal courts to respect rights under the United States Constitution. *See* The Federalist, No. 82; *Claflin v. Houseman*, (1876) *Testa v. Katt* (1947). Indeed, the jurisdiction given to the federal courts to issue writs of habeas corpus by the First Judiciary Act, §14, extended only to prisoners in custody under authority of the United States. It was not until the Act of 1867 that the power to issue the writ was extended to an applicant under sen-tence of a State court. It is not for us to determine whether this power should have been vested in the federal courts. As Mr. Justice Bradley, with his usual acuteness, commented not long after the passage of that Act,

> although it may appear unseemly that a prisoner, after conviction in a
> state court, should be set at liberty by a single judge on habeas corpus,
> there seems to be no escape from the law.

Ex parte Bridges (1875). His feeling has been recently echoed in a proposal of the Judicial Conference of Senior Circuit Judges that these cases be heard by three-judge courts. But the wisdom of such a modification in the law is for Congress to consider, particularly in view of the effect of the expanding concept of due process upon enforcement by the States of their criminal laws. It is for this Court to give fair effect to the habeas corpus jurisdiction as enacted by Congress. By giving the federal courts that jurisdiction, Congress has imbedded into federal legislation the historic function of habeas corpus adapted to reaching an enlarged area of claims.

In exercising the power thus bestowed, the District Judge must take due account of the proceedings that are challenged by the application for a writ. All that has gone before is not to be ignored as irrelevant. But the prior State determination of a claim under the United States Constitution cannot foreclose consideration of such a claim, else the State court would have the final say which the Congress, by the Act of 1867, provided it should not have. *Cf. Ex parte Royall* (1886). A State determination may help to define the claim urged in the application for the writ and may bear on the seriousness of the claim. That most claims are frivolous has an important bearing upon the procedure to be followed by a district judge. The prior State determination may guide his discretion in deciding upon the appropriate course to be followed in disposing of the application before him. The State record may serve to indicate the necessity of further pleadings or of a quick hearing to clear up an ambiguity, or the State record may show the claim to be frivolous or not within the competence of a federal court because solely dependent on State law.

It may be a matter of phrasing whether we say that the District Judge summarily denies an application for a writ by accepting the ruling of the State court or by making an independent judgment, though he does so on the basis of what the State record reveals. But since phrasing mirrors thought, it is important that the phrasing not obscure the true issue before a federal court. Our problem arises because Congress has told the District Judge to act on those occasions, however rare, when there are meritorious causes in which habeas corpus is the ultimate and only relief and designed to be such. Vague, undefined directions permitting the District Court to give "consideration" to a prior State determination fall short of appropriate guidance for bringing to the surface the meritorious case. . . .

[I]t is important, in order to preclude individualized enforcement of the Constitution in different parts of the Nation, to lay down as specifically as the nature of the problem permits the standards or directions that should govern the District Judges in the disposition of applications for habeas corpus by prisoners under sentence of State courts.

First. Just as in all other litigation, a *prima facie* case must be made out by the petitioner. The application should be dismissed when it fails to state a federal question, or fails to set forth facts which, if accepted at face value, would entitle the applicant to relief.

Care will naturally be taken that the frequent lack of technical competence of prisoners should not strangle consideration of a valid constitutional claim that is bunglingly presented. District judges have resorted to various procedures to that end. Thus, a lawyer may be appointed, in the exercise of the inherent authority of the District Court, either as an *amicus* or as counsel for the petitioner, to examine the claim and to report, or the judge may dismiss the petition without prejudice.

Second. Failure to exhaust an available State remedy is an obvious ground for denying the application. An attempt must have been made in the State court to present the claim now asserted in the District Court, in compliance with §2254 of the Judicial Code. . . .

Of course, nothing we have said suggests that the federal habeas corpus juris-diction can displace a State's procedural rule requiring that certain errors be raised on appeal. Normally rights under the Federal Constitution may be waived at the trial, *Adams v. United States ex rel. McCann* (1992), and may likewise be waived by failure to assert such errors on appeal. However, this does not touch one of those extraordinary cases in which a substantial claim goes to the very foundation of a proceeding, as in *Moore v. Dempsey* (1923).

Third. If the record of the State proceedings is not filed, the judge is required to decide, with due regard to efficiency in judicial administration, whether it is more desirable to call for the record or to hold a hearing. Ordinarily, where the issues are complex, it will be simpler to call for the record, certainly in the first instance. If the issues are simple, or if the record is called for and is found inade-quate to show how the State court decided the relevant historical facts, the District Court shall use appropriate procedures, including a hearing if necessary, to decide the issues.

If the claim is frivolous, the judge should deny the application without more. If the question is one on which he must exercise his legal judgment under the habeas corpus statute, it may be sufficient to have information, perhaps presented by the pleadings of the applicant or of the State, as to the disposition of any dis-puted questions of fact. It seems unduly rigid to require the District Judge to call for the State record in every case.

Moreover, the kinds of State adjudications differ. In some cases, the State court has held a hearing and rendered a decision based on specific findings of fact; there may have been review by a higher State court which had before it the plead-ings, the testimony, opinions and briefs on appeal. It certainly would make only for burdensome and useless repetition of effort if the federal courts were to rehear the facts in such cases. At the other pole is the perfunctory memorandum order deny-ing a badly drawn petition and stating simply that the petitioner is not entitled to relief. The District Judge cannot give the same weight to this sort of adjudication as he does to the first; he has no basis for exercising the judgment the statute requires him to exercise.

These criteria for determining when it is proper to hold a hearing seem to me appropriate in relating the habeas corpus provisions to the realities of these cases. . . . The proviso that no writ or order need be issued if the application shows that the applicant is not entitled thereto certainly permits "entertaining" and nev-ertheless summarily dismissing for failure to state a claim, failure to exhaust State remedies, or proof from the papers themselves, including the record of the State proceedings, if filed, that there is no claim. At the same time, the command that the writ or an order be issued in some cases hardly requires a hearing in every such case. As in any litigation, the pleadings may show, either separately or taken together, that there is no claim.

Fourth. When the record of the State court proceedings is before the court, it may appear that the issue turns on basic facts, and that the facts (in the sense of a recital of external events and the credibility of their narrators) have been tried and adjudicated against the applicant. Unless a vital flaw be found in the process of ascertaining such facts in the State court, the District Judge may accept their deter-mination in the State proceeding and deny the application. On the other hand, State adjudication of questions of law cannot, under the habeas corpus statute, be accepted as binding. It is precisely these questions that the federal judge is commanded to decide.

A State determination of the historical facts, the external events that occurred, may have been made after hearing witnesses perhaps no longer available or whose recollection later may have been affected by the passage of time or by the fact that one judicial determination has already been made. To be sure, these considerations argue equally against hearing the claims at all long after the facts took place. But Congress, by making habeas corpus available, has determined that other considerations prevail. We are left to devise appropriate rules, and the congressional determination does not preclude rules recognizing the soundness of giving great weight to testimony earlier heard, just as it does not undermine the principle that the burden of proving facts inconsistent with judicial records in all proceedings of this kind is heavy.

Fifth. Where the ascertainment of the historical facts does not dispose of the claim, but calls for interpretation of the legal significance of such facts, the District Judge must exercise his own judgment on this blend of facts and their legal values. Thus, so-called mixed questions or the application of constitutional principles to the facts as found leave the duty of adjudication with the federal judge.

For instance, the question whether established primary facts underlying a confession prove that the confession was coerced or voluntary cannot rest on the State decision. Although there is no need for the federal judge, if he could, to shut his eyes to the State consideration of such issues, no binding weight is to be attached to the State determination. The congressional requirement is greater. The State court cannot have the last say when it, though on fair consideration and what procedurally may be deemed fairness, may have misconceived a federal constitutional right.

Sixth. A federal district judge may, under §2244, take into consideration a prior denial of relief by a federal court, and, in that sense, §2244 is, of course, applicable to State prisoners. Section 2244 merely gave statutory form to the practice established by *Salinger v. Loisel* (1924).

These standards, addressed as they are to the practical situation facing the District Judge, recognize the discretion of judges to give weight to whatever may be relevant in the State proceedings, and yet preserve the full implication of the requirement of Congress that the District Judge decide constitutional questions presented by a State prisoner even after his claims have been carefully considered by the State courts. Congress has the power to distribute among the courts of the States and of the United States jurisdiction to determine federal claims. It has seen fit to give this Court power to review errors of federal law in State determinations, and in addition to give to the lower federal courts power to inquire into federal claims, by way of habeas corpus. Such power is in the spirit of our inherited law. It accords with, and is thoroughly regardful of, "the liberty of the subject," from which flows the right in England to go from judge to judge, any one of whose decisions to discharge the prisoner is final.

The reliable figures of the Administrative Office of the United States Courts, showing that, during the last four years, five State prisoners, all told, were discharged by federal district courts, prove beyond peradventure that it is a baseless fear, a bogey man, to worry lest State convictions be upset by allowing district courts to entertain applications for habeas corpus on behalf of prisoners under State sentence. Insofar as this jurisdiction enables federal district courts to entertain claims that State Supreme Courts have denied rights guaranteed by the United States Constitution, it is not a case of a lower court sitting in judgment on a higher court. It is merely one aspect of respecting the Supremacy Clause of the Constitution whereby federal law is higher than State law. It is for the Congress to designate the member in the hierarchy of the federal judiciary to express the higher law. The fact that Congress has authorized district courts to be the organ of the higher law, rather than a Court of Appeals, or exclusively this Court, does not mean that it allows a lower court to overrule a higher court. It merely expresses the choice of Congress how the superior authority of federal law should be asserted.

I yield to no member of this Court in awareness of the enormity of the difficulties of dealing with crime that is the concomitant of our industrialized society. And I am deeply mindful of the fact that the responsibility for this task largely rests with the States. I would not for a moment hamper them in the effective discharge of this responsibility. Equally am I aware that misuse of legal procedures, whereby the administration of criminal justice is too often rendered leaden-footed, is one of the disturbing features about American criminal justice. On the other hand, it must not be lost sight of that there are also abuses by the law-enforcing agencies. It does not lessen the mischief that it is due more often to lack of professional competence and want of an austere employment of the awful processes of criminal justice than to wilful misconduct. In this connection, it is relevant to quote the observations of one of the most esteemed of Attorneys General of the United States, William D. Mitchell:

> Detection and punishment of crime must be effected by strictly lawful methods. Nothing has a greater tendency to beget lawlessness than lawless methods of law enforcement. The greater the difficulties of detecting and punishing crime, the greater the temptation to place a strained construction on statutes to supply what may be thought to be more efficient means of enforcing law. The statutory and constitutional rights of all persons must be regarded, and their violation, inadvertent or otherwise, is to be avoided.

(Department of Justice release, for April 8, 1929.)

Unfortunately, instances are not wanting in which even the highest State courts have failed to recognize violations of these precepts that offend the limitations which the Constitution of the United States places upon enforcement by the States of their criminal law. *See, e.g., De Meerleer v. Michigan* (1947), and *Marino v. Ragen* (1947).

The uniqueness of habeas corpus in the procedural armory of our law cannot be too often emphasized. It differs from all other remedies in that it is available to bring into question the legality of a person's restraint and to require justification for such detention. Of course, this does not mean that prison doors may readily be opened. It does mean that explanation may be exacted why they should remain closed. It is not the boasting of empty rhetoric that has treated the writ of habeas corpus as the basic safeguard of freedom in the Anglo-American world. "The great writ of habeas corpus has been for centuries esteemed the best and only sufficient defense of personal freedom." Chief Justice Chase, writing for the Court in *Ex parte Yerger*. Its history and function in our legal system and the unavailability of the writ in totalitarian societies are naturally enough regarded as one of the decisively differentiating factors between our democracy and totalitarian governments.

But the writ has potentialities for evil, as well as for good. Abuse of the writ may undermine the orderly administration of justice, and therefore weaken the forces of authority that are essential for civilization.

The circumstances and conditions for bringing into action a legal remedy having such potentialities obviously cannot be defined with a particularity appropriate to legal remedies of much more limited scope. To attempt rigid rules would either give spuriously concrete form to wide-ranging purposes or betray the purposes by strangulating rigidities. Equally unmindful, however, of the purposes of the writ— its history and its functions — would it be to advise the Federal district courts as to their duty in regard to habeas corpus in terms so ambiguous as in effect to leave their individual judgment unguided. This would leave them free to misuse the writ by being either too lax or too rigid in its employment. . . .

Justice JACKSON, concurring in the result.

Controversy as to the undiscriminating use of the writ of habeas corpus by federal judges to set aside state court convictions is traceable to three principal causes: (1) this Court's use of the generality of the Fourteenth Amendment to subject state courts to increasing federal control, especially in the criminal law field; (2) *ad hoc* determination of due process of law issues by personal notions of justice, instead of by known rules of law; and (3) the breakdown of procedural safeguards against abuse of the writ.

1. In 1867, Congress authorized federal courts to issue writs of habeas corpus to prisoners "in custody in violation of the Constitution or laws or treaties of the United States." At that time, the writ was not available here nor in England to challenge any sentence imposed by a court of competent jurisdiction.[2] The historic purpose of the writ has been to relieve detention by executive authorities without judicial trial.[3] It might have been expected that, if Congress intended a reversal of this traditional concept of habeas corpus, it would have said so. However, this one sentence in the Act eventually was construed as authority for federal judges to entertain collateral attacks on state court criminal judgments.[4] Whatever its justification, it created potentialities for conflict certain to lead to the antagonisms we have now, unless the power given to federal judges were responsibly used according to lawyerly procedures and with genuine respect for state court fact finding.

---

2. . . . *Ex parte Watkins.*

3. For this purpose, the writ has not been conspicuously successful in the United States. I have reviewed its failures, especially in wartimes, in Wartime Security and Liberty under Law, 1 Buff. L.R. 103.

4. See the equivocal discussion of the question in *Frank v. Magnum* (1935), and the more explicit assumption of the dissent. An earlier case, *Ex parte Royall* (1886), contained a dictum to the effect that . . . the validity of the statute under which conviction was had in the state court [] could be challenged on habeas corpus in the federal courts. While this represents a certain expansion of traditional notions of jurisdiction in the judicial sense, it by no means supports the broad reach given to federal habeas corpus by recent cases.

But, once established, this jurisdiction obviously would grow with each expansion of the substantive grounds for habeas corpus. The generalities of the Fourteenth Amendment are so indeterminate as to what state actions are forbidden that this Court has found it a ready instrument, in one field or another, to magnify federal, and incidentally its own, authority over the states. The expansion now has reached a point where any state court conviction, disapproved by a majority of this Court, thereby becomes unconstitutional and subject to nullification by habeas corpus.

This might not be so demoralizing if state judges could anticipate, and so comply with, this Court's due process requirements or ascertain any standards to which this Court will adhere in prescribing them. But they cannot. Of course, considerable uncertainty is inherent in decisional law which, in changing times, purports to interpret implications of constitutional provisions so cryptic and vagrant. How much obscurity is inevitable will be a matter of opinion. However, in considering a remedy for habeas corpus problems, it is prudent to assume that the scope and reach of the Fourteenth Amendment will continue to be unknown and unknowable, that what seems established by one decision is apt to be unsettled by another, and that its interpretation will be more or less swayed by contemporary intellectual fashions and political currents.

We may look upon this unstable prospect complacently, but state judges cannot. They are not only being gradually subordinated to the federal judiciary but federal courts have declared that state judicial and other officers are personally liable to federal prosecution and to civil suit by convicts if they fail to carry out this Court's constitutional doctrines.[6]

2. Rightly or wrongly, the belief is widely held by the practicing profession that this Court no longer respects impersonal rules of law, but is guided in these matters by personal impressions which from time to time may be shared by a majority of Justices. Whatever has been intended, this Court also has generated an impression in much of the judiciary that regard for precedents and authorities is obsolete, that words no longer mean what they have always meant to the profession, that the law knows no fixed principles.

A manifestation of this is seen in the diminishing respect shown for state court adjudications of fact. Of course, this Court never has considered itself foreclosed by a state court's decision as to the facts when that determination results in alleged denial of a federal right. But captious use of this power was restrained by observance of a rule, elementary in all appellate procedure, that the findings of fact on a trial are to be accepted by an appellate court in absence of clear showing of error. The trial court, seeing the demeanor of witnesses, hearing the parties, giving to each case far more time than an appellate court can give, is in a better position to

---

6. This Court's decision in *Screws v. United States* (1945), as the dissenters anticipated, has led a Federal Court of Appeals to hold that federal law enforced in federal courts imposes personal liability upon state judicial officers, though that court admits that "The result is of fateful portent to the judiciary of the several states." Contrast to this the absolute immunity from suit enjoyed by federal officials, even in administrative capacities. While the *Screws* decision held out promise of protection for state officials by requiring that any denial of constitutional right must be proved to be wilful in the sense of knowing and intentional, that protection has since been withdrawn.

unravel disputes of fact than is an appellate court on a printed transcript. Recent decisions avow no candid alteration of these rules, but revision of state fact finding has grown by emphasis, and respect for it has withered by disregard.

3. The fact that the substantive law of due process is and probably must remain so vague and unsettled as to invite farfetched or borderline petitions makes it important to adhere to procedures which enable courts readily to distinguish a probable constitutional grievance from a convict's mere gamble on persuading some indulgent judge to let him out of jail. Instead, this Court has sanctioned progressive trivialization of the writ until floods of stale, frivolous and repetitious petitions inundate the docket of the lower courts and swell our own.[8] Judged by our own disposition of habeas corpus matters, they have, as a class, become peculiarly undeserving. It must prejudice the occasional meritorious application to be buried in a flood of worthless ones. He who must search a haystack for a needle is likely to end up with the attitude that the needle is not worth the search. Nor is it any answer to say that few of these petitions in any court really result in the discharge of the petitioner. That is the condemnation of the procedure which has encouraged frivolous cases. In this multiplicity of worthless cases, states are compelled to default or to defend the integrity of their judges and their official records, sometimes concerning trials or pleas that were closed many years ago. State Attorneys General recently have come habitually to ignore these proceedings, responding only when specially requested and sometimes not then. Some state courts have wearied of our repeated demands upon them, and have declined to further elucidate grounds for their decisions. The assembled Chief Justices of the highest courts of the states have taken the unusual step of condemning the present practice by resolution.[13]

Once upon a time, the writ could not be substituted for appeal or other reviewing process, but challenged only the legal competence or jurisdiction of the committing court.

Conflict with state courts is the inevitable result of giving the convict a virtual new trial before a federal court sitting without a jury. Whenever decisions of one court are reviewed by another, a percentage of them are reversed. That reflects a difference in outlook normally found between personnel comprising different courts. However, reversal by a higher court is not proof that justice is thereby better done. There is no doubt that, if there were a super-Supreme Court, a substantial proportion of our reversals of state courts would also be reversed. We are not final because we are infallible, but we are infallible only because we are final.

It is sometimes said that *res judicata* has no application whatever in habeas corpus cases, and surely it does not apply with all of its conventional severity. Habeas corpus differs from the ordinary judgment in that, although an adjudication has become final, the application is renewable, at least if new evidence and material is

---

8. There were filed in federal district courts during 1941 one hundred twenty-seven petitions for habeas corpus challenging state convictions; in 1943 there were two hundred sixty-nine; in 1948 five hundred forty-three; in 1952 five hundred forty-one. . . .

13. "Now therefore be it resolved that it is the considered view of the Chief Justices of the States of the Union, in conference duly assembled, that orderly Federal procedure under our dual system of government should require that a final judgment of a State's highest court be subject to review or reversal only by the Supreme Court of the United States."

discovered or if, perhaps as the result of a new decision, a new law becomes applicable to the case. This is quite proper so long as its issues relate to jurisdiction. But call it *res judicata* or what one will, courts ought not to be obliged to allow a convict to litigate again and again exactly the same question on the same evidence. Nor is there any good reason why an identical contention rejected by a higher court should be reviewed on the same facts in a lower one.

The chief objection to giving this limited finality to our denial of certiorari is that we pass upon these writs of habeas corpus so casually or upon grounds so unrelated to their merits that our decision should not have the weight of finality. . . . The fact is that superficial consideration of these cases is the inevitable result of depreciation of the writ. The writ has no enemies so deadly as those who sanction the abuse of it, whatever their intent.

My conclusion is that whether or not this Court has denied certiorari from a state court's judgment in a habeas corpus proceeding, no lower federal court should entertain a petition except on the following conditions: (1) that the petition raises a jurisdictional question involving federal law on which the state law allowed no access to its courts, either by habeas corpus or appeal from the conviction and that he therefore has no state remedy; or (2) that the petition shows that, although the law allows a remedy, he was actually improperly obstructed from making a record upon which the question could be presented, so that his remedy by way of ultimate application to this Court for certiorari has been frustrated. There may be circumstances so extraordinary that I do not now think of them which would justify a departure from this rule, but the run-of-the-mill case certainly does not.

* * *

Brown v. Allen is conventionally read as expanding the standard of review for federal habeas jurisdiction by permitting district court judges to: (a) go beyond the state record and conduct evidentiary hearings, (b) set aside state record facts if they are based on a "vital flaw," and (c) review for federal constitutional error *de novo* (determinations of federal law, Justice Frankfurter wrote, "cannot be accepted as binding" and the state court "cannot have the last say"). It is apparent, however, from the conference memos and Justice Jackson's opinion that the Court was just as concerned with preventing the evisceration of the writ by members of the Court who saw the cases as an opportunity to restrict the jurisdiction of lower federal courts, at least where the Supreme Court had already denied certiorari on direct review.[74] Jackson's concerns were grounded not just in federalism, but the practical significance of finality—a due process value in its own right. Repeated re-litigation was not, in his view, guaranteed to increase accuracy.

The Cold War context of the decision is equally significant. Just as Jim Crow segregation reduced the nation's credibility in defending democracy abroad, Justice Frankfurter emphasized that meaningful access to the writ of habeas corpus

---

74. Eric M. Freedman, Brown v. Allen: *The Habeas Corpus Revolution That Wasn't*, 51 ALA. L. REV. 1541 (2000); Bernard Schwartz, *Chief Justice Rehnquist, Justice Jackson, and the* Brown *Case*, 1988 S. CT. REV. 245.

distinguished the nation from regimes where inadequate trials (indeed, "show trials" in some countries) and imprisonment subject only to the whim of an autocrat occurred. Form without substance in a standard of review and too narrow a standard of review would betray the exceptional status of the writ and its remedial power.

In *Stone v. Powell* (1976), the Supreme Court held that at least with respect to Fourth Amendment claims that evidence obtained via an unconstitutional search and seizure was admitted in violation of the exclusionary rule, there can be no federal review on habeas as long as there was a full and fair opportunity to litigate the federal claim in the state courts. The Court reasoned that a Fourth Amendment claim does not concern the conduct of the trial or the court but instead the executive branch law enforcement officers responsible for the search and seizure. The exclusionary rule, moreover, is not a personal constitutional right, but rather a remedy designed to deter police invasions of privacy. The Court has declined to extend *Stone* to other constitutional rights. *See Rose v. Mitchell* (1979) (federal habeas is a proper remedy for claim of racial discrimination in the selection of grand jury that indicts petitioner; the selection and supervision of grand juries is a judicial function directly regulated by the Equal Protection Clause); *Jackson v. Virginia* (1979) (*Stone* does not apply to due process claim of insufficient evidence to support a conviction which is central to the "basic question of guilt or innocence"); *Winthrow v. Williams* (1993) (*Stone* doctrine is prudential, not jurisdictional, and does not apply to Fifth Amendment challenges to compulsory interrogations in violation of *Miranda* and the privilege against self-incrimination; *Miranda* "safeguards a fundamental trial right," the violation of which directly undermines the reliability of evidence introduced at trial used to establish guilt and eliminating review of *Miranda* claims would not "significantly benefit the federal courts in their exercise of habeas jurisdiction, or advance the cause of federalism in any substantial way" because barred *Miranda* claims will simply be refiled as due process claims that the conviction rests on an involuntary confession).

Notice, lastly, the paradox that in *Brown v. Allen* Justice Frankfurter is comfortable with a robust standard of review only on the assurance that relief is rarely, if ever, granted — that it is the rare state case in which constitutional error will warrant a remedy. Review can be searching only because in most cases he is confident nothing will be found. In the modern cases, this assumption is inverted — the standard of review is narrow because only truly egregious error warrants relief. Indeed, the modern Court has drifted toward Justice Jackson's position, reviving the tendentious claim that *Brown v. Allen* was an unprecedented innovation in habeas jurisdiction inconsistent with principles of federalism and finality. In *Brown v. Davenport* (2022), five Justices signed an opinion by Justice Gorsuch drawing *Brown v. Allen* into doubt:

> When English monarchs jailed their subjects summarily and indefinitely, common-law courts employed the writ as a way to compel the crown to explain its actions — and, if necessary, ensure adequate process, such as a trial, before allowing any further detention. *See* Petition of Right, 3 Car. (1628). The Great Writ was, in this way, no less than "the instrument by which due process could be insisted upon." *Hamdi v. Rumsfeld* (2004) (Scalia, J., dissenting).

At the same time, even this writ had its limits. Usually, a prisoner could not use it to challenge a final judgment of conviction issued by a court of competent jurisdiction. If the point of the writ was to ensure due process attended an individual's confinement, a trial was generally considered proof he had received just that.). This traditional understanding extended from England to this country and persisted through much of our history. Asked to apply the Nation's first habeas statute to a duly convicted prisoner, Chief Justice Marshall invoked the common-law rule that a judgment of conviction after trial was "conclusive on all the world." *Ex parte Watkins* (1830). Acknowledging that Congress had authorized the Court to "inquire into the sufficiency of" the cause of the petitioner's detention, Marshall asked rhetorically, "is not that judgment in itself sufficient cause?" If the answer was nearly always yes, an important exception existed in both English and American law: A habeas court could grant relief if the court of conviction lacked jurisdiction over the defendant or his offense. A perceived "error in the judgment or proceedings, under and by virtue of which the party is imprisoned, constitute[d] no ground for" relief. *Ex parte Siebold* (1880). Instead, a habeas court could "examin[e] only the power and authority of the court to act, not the correctness of its conclusions." *Harlan v. McGourin* (1910). To be sure, the line between mere errors and jurisdictional defects was not always a "luminous beacon" and it evolved over time. But this Court generally sought to police the doctrine's boundaries in cases involving federal and state prisoners alike.

By 1953, however, federal habeas practice began to take on a very different shape. That year in *Brown v. Allen* this Court held that a state-court judgment "is not res judicata" in federal habeas proceedings with respect to a petitioner's federal constitutional claims. . . . The traditional distinction between jurisdictional defects and mere errors in adjudication no longer restrained federal habeas courts. Full-blown constitutional error correction became the order of the day. . . . Exercising its equitable discretion, and informed by these concerns, the Court began to develop doctrines "aimed at returning the Great Writ closer to its historic office." *Edwards v. Vannoy* (Gorsuch, J., concurring).

Justice Kagan, suspecting the majority of laying foundation for a broader attack on *Brown v. Allen*, insisted in her dissenting opinion that the case was no innovation in relation to earlier precedent:

Because the majority begins with some law-chambers history, I do too—though fair warning: My discussion is no more relevant than the majority's to the issue before us. Not surprisingly, neither of the parties to this small and legally mundane case thought it a suitable occasion for a from-Blackstone-onward theory of habeas practice. Yet the majority, unprompted, embarks on that project, perhaps hoping that the seeds it sows now will yield more succulent fruit in cases to come. In the majority's story, post-conviction habeas relief was all but unavailable until the mid-20th century—when in an instant the Court in *Brown v. Allen* (1953), upended the rules. That account repeats the views expressed in a recent concurrence, authored by the same Justice as today delivers the majority opinion. *See Edwards v. Vannoy* (2021) (Gorsuch, J., concurring) (Habeas historically "provided no recourse for a prisoner confined pursuant to a final judgment of conviction"). But the theory, in its fundamentals, is wrong. Federal courts long before *Brown* extended habeas relief to prisoners held in violation of the Constitution—even after a final conviction.

This Court started reviewing post-conviction constitutional claims under Congress's first grant of habeas authority, included in the Judiciary Act of 1789. That provision, applying only to federal prisoners, did not specifically provide for collateral review of constitutional claims. *See* Act of Sept. 24, 1789, §14 (enabling federal courts to grant habeas writs to "inquir[e] into the cause of [a federal prisoner's] commitment"). But even without explicit permission, the Court in the mid-19th century invoked the habeas law to adjudicate those claims—including some from petitioners already convicted and sentenced. *See* 1 R. Hertz & J. Liebman, *Federal Habeas Corpus Practice and Procedure* §2.4[d][i], p. 51 (7th ed. 2020). In *Ex parte Wells* (1856), for example, only the dissent thought that the fact of a conviction and sentence precluded granting habeas relief (as today's opinion says was the firm rule). *See id.* (Curtis, J., dissenting) (asserting that habeas could not aid a person "imprisoned under a [circuit court's] criminal sentence"). The majority, ignoring that objection, scrutinized the merits of the claim in detail before deciding that no constitutional violation had occurred and the applicant should remain in prison. *Id.* And in *Ex parte Lange* (1874), the Court (again acting under the original habeas law) went further: It granted relief to a convicted prisoner after finding a violation of the Double Jeopardy Clause. The Court explained that it was carrying out a "sacred duty" in declaring that the prisoner was being held "without authority, and [that] he should therefore be discharged." *Id.*

When Congress amended the Judiciary Act after the Civil War, the scope of federal habeas review—including over post-conviction claims—grew far larger. The text of the amendment (similar to current law) gave federal courts expansive power: "to grant writs of habeas corpus in all cases where any person may be restrained of his or her liberty" in violation of the Federal Constitution. Act of Feb. 5, 1867; *see* 28 U.S.C. §§2241(a), (c)(3). And "any person" in "all cases" meant just that: State prisoners, not just federal ones, could now apply for habeas relief. Those state cases of course involved separate sovereigns, acting under their own laws. But even in that sphere, the Court soon decided that the federal judiciary's authority extended to hearing constitutional challenges to final convictions. Under the new statute, the Court explained, "a single [federal] judge on habeas corpus" could free "a prisoner, after conviction in a State court," upon finding him unconstitutionally restrained. *Ex parte Royall* (1886). Or as held in another decision, a "party [was] entitled to a [writ of] habeas corpus," even after his case "had gone to conviction and sentence," when the state court "ha[d] no constitutional authority or power to condemn" him. *In re Nielsen* (1889). A leading treatise of the time summarized the state of the law: A federal court "may, on habeas corpus, release one who is restrained of his liberty in violation of the constitution of the United States, though held under the criminal process of a state court, and either before or after judgment." W. Church, *Writ of Habeas Corpus* §84, p. 117 (2d ed. 1893).

In line with that view, this Court granted habeas relief, on an assortment of constitutional grounds, to both federal and state prisoners challenging their convictions or sentences. The Court granted post-conviction relief to protect habeas applicants' rights to a grand jury indictment, to a jury trial, to assistance of counsel, and against self-incrimination. *See, e.g., Ex parte Wilson* (1885); *Callan v. Wilson* (1888); *Counselman v. Hitchcock* (1892); *Johnson v. Zerbst* (1938). The Court granted post-conviction relief for violations of the Equal Protection Clause, the Double Jeopardy Clause, and the Ex Post Facto Clause. *See, e.g., Yick Wo v. Hopkins* (1886); *Nielsen; In re Medley* (1890). And as due process rights expanded in the first half of the 20th century, the Court held post-conviction habeas relief proper for those claims too. *See, e.g., Moore v. Dempsey* (1923); *Waley v. Johnston* (1942) (per curiam); *Wade v. Mayo* (1948). The modern Court has repeatedly acknowledged that history. "[O]ver the years," the Court explained (referencing most of the cases cited above), "the writ of habeas corpus evolved as a remedy available to effect discharge from any confinement contrary to the Constitution or fundamental law." *Preiser v. Rodriguez* (1973). . . . The majority tries to cram the many habeas decisions belying its position into a narrow jurisdictional "exception," but its effort does no more than reveal the peril of looking at history through a 21st-century lens. In the majority's view, a habeas court could grant relief only "if the court of conviction lacked jurisdiction," not if it committed "errors in adjudication." But some of the decisions the majority must contend with made no mention at all of the convicting (or sentencing) court's jurisdiction. And those that did so often used the word to mean something different from what it does today. The concept of "jurisdictional defects" could at that time include — rather than contrast with — constitutional errors of the kind described above. . . . The jurisdictional inquiry was then (though of course not now) often "merits based." A. Woolhandler, *Demodeling Habeas*, 45 Stan. L. Rev. 575, 630 (1993). . . . From the mid-1800s on, federal courts granted habeas writs to prisoners, federal and state alike, who on the way to conviction or sentence had suffered serious constitutional harms. Contrary to the majority, then, our decision in *Brown* built on decades and decades of history.

The innovation in *Brown*, she concluded, was simply that it "made explicit" what the Court had always done.

b. Non-Retroactivity of "New" Rules

After *Brown v. Allen*, one of the most basic problems was how new rules of constitutional law should apply to habeas petitions filed years after the petitioner's conviction became final. Should every state prisoner, no matter how old their conviction was, have their case reopened on habeas when the Court developed new doctrine? Although the problem was acute during the Warren Court's expansion of constitutional criminal procedural law, it remains relevant today whenever the Court considers a case that would require announcing a new rule. The Court has

developed two responses to this problem beyond the expansion of elaborate procedural prerequisites discussed above.

First, as we saw in the notes after *Brown v. Allen*, the Court has simply deemed
habeas an inappropriate remedy and barred assertion of the right through §2254.
This is true of the Fourth Amendment. In *Stone v. Powell* (1976), the Court held that
where a state has provided a full and fair opportunity to litigate a Fourth Amendment claim that evidence was admitted following an unconstitutional search and
seizure in violation of the exclusionary rule, a state prisoner cannot raise that claim
in a federal habeas petition. Powell was convicted for the murder of the wife of a
shop manager following an altercation in the store. The murder weapon was found
when Powell was searched in a separate arrest for vagrancy. Powell contended
that there was no probable cause for that search and attempted, unsuccessfully, to
exclude the murder weapon on that ground in the murder trial. Powell then raised
the same Fourth Amendment claim in his federal habeas petition. The Court
rejected the claim, and all such Fourth Amendment claims raised on habeas, on
the ground that the purpose of exclusion of evidence unconstitutionally obtained is
deterrence of illegal searches and seizures and that deterrent effect is not advanced
by the granting relief on habeas:

> The primary justification for the exclusionary rule . . . is the deter-
> rence of police conduct that violates Fourth Amendment rights. Post-*Mapp*
> decisions have established that the rule is not a personal constitutional
> right. It is not calculated to redress the injury to the privacy of the victim
> of the search or seizure, for any "[r]eparation comes too late." *Linkletter v.
> Walker* (1965). Instead,
>
>> the rule is a judicially created remedy designed to safeguard Fourth Amend-
>> ment rights generally through its deterrent effect. . . .

United States v. Calandra (1974).

> *Mapp* involved the enforcement of the exclusionary rule at state trials
> and on direct review. . . . But despite the broad deterrent purpose of the
> exclusionary rule, it has never been interpreted to proscribe the introduc-
> tion of illegally seized evidence in all proceedings or against all persons.
> As in the case of any remedial device, "the application of the rule has been
> restricted to those areas where its remedial objectives are thought most
> efficaciously served." *United States v. Calandra*. Thus, our refusal to extend
> the exclusionary rule to grand jury proceedings was based on a balancing
> of the potential injury to the historic role and function of the grand jury
> by such extension against the potential contribution to the effectuation of
> the Fourth Amendment through deterrence of police misconduct:
>
>> Any incremental deterrent effect which might be achieved by extending the
>> rule to grand jury proceedings is uncertain, at best. Whatever deterrence of
>> police misconduct may result from the exclusion of illegally seized evidence
>> from criminal trials, it is unrealistic to assume that application of the rule to
>> grand jury proceedings would significantly further that goal. Such an exten-
>> sion would deter only police investigation consciously directed toward the dis-
>> covery of evidence solely for use in a grand jury investigation. . . . We therefore
>> decline to embrace a view that would achieve a speculative and undoubtedly

minimal advance in the deterrence of police misconduct at the expense of substantially impeding the role of the grand jury.

The same pragmatic analysis of the exclusionary rule's usefulness in a particular context was evident earlier in *Walder v. United States* (1959), where the Court permitted the Government to use unlawfully seized evidence to impeach the credibility of a defendant who had testified broadly in his own defense. The Court held, in effect, that the interests safeguarded by the exclusionary rule in that context were outweighed by the need to prevent perjury and to assure the integrity of the trial process. The judgment in *Walder* revealed most clearly that the policies behind the exclusionary rule are not absolute. . . .

The balancing process at work in these cases also finds expression in the standing requirement. Standing to invoke the exclusionary rule has been found to exist only when the Government attempts to use illegally obtained evidence to incriminate the victim of the illegal search. The standing requirement is premised on the view that the "additional benefits of extending the . . . rule" to defendants other than the victim of the search or seizure are outweighed by the "further encroachment upon the public interest in prosecuting those accused of crime and having them acquitted or convicted on the basis of all the evidence which exposes the truth." *Alderman v. United States* (1968).

Evidence obtained by police officers in violation of the Fourth Amendment is excluded at trial in the hope that the frequency of future violations will decrease. Despite the absence of supportive empirical evidence, we have assumed that the immediate effect of exclusion will be to discourage law enforcement officials from violating the Fourth Amendment by removing the incentive to disregard it. More importantly, over the long-term, this demonstration that our society attaches serious consequences to violation of constitutional rights is thought to encourage those who formulate law enforcement policies, and the officers who implement them, to incorporate Fourth Amendment ideals into their value system.

We adhere to the view that these considerations support the implementation of the exclusionary rule at trial and its enforcement on direct appeal of state court convictions. But the additional contribution, if any, of the consideration of search and seizure claims of state prisoners on collateral review is small in relation to the costs. . . . The view that the deterrence of Fourth Amendment violations would be furthered rests on the dubious assumption that law enforcement authorities would fear that federal habeas review might reveal flaws in a search or seizure that went undetected at trial and on appeal. Even if one rationally could assume that some additional incremental deterrent effect would be present in isolated cases, the resulting advance of the legitimate goal of furthering Fourth Amendment rights would be outweighed by the acknowledged costs to other values vital to a rational system of criminal justice.

The second response has been to develop retroactivity rules that bar petitioners whose convictions have become final from asserting constitutional claims grounded in Supreme Court decisions issued after the direct appeal has ended. Retroactivity is unavoidable. Anytime the Court develops constitutional rules of decision, there is a question of who benefits from the rule—certainly the litigant in that case, but who else? The possible options are: (a) defendants in any future criminal prosecutions (a rule of complete non-retroactivity), (b) defendants in currently pending criminal prosecutions, (c) defendants whose convictions are not yet final because their cases are pending on direct appeal, and (d) defendants whose convictions have become final but may seek collateral relief by filing habeas petitions (a rule of complete retroactivity). Notice that, depending on the nature of the constitutional right, the complete retroactivity approach could result in the release of prisoners whose convictions became final decades before the right was recognized. The complete non-retroactivity approach would deny relief to petitioners whose cases are virtually indistinguishable from the one in which the right is recognized. Does due process or any other constitutional principle require one or another approach?

The Warren Court's retroactivity rule was flexible and prudential:

> [W]e believe that the Constitution neither prohibits nor requires retrospective effect. As Justice Cardozo said, "We think the Federal Constitution has no voice upon the subject."
>
> Once the premise is accepted that we are neither required to apply, nor prohibited from applying, a decision retrospectively, we must then weigh the merits and demerits in each case by looking to the prior history of the rule in question, its purpose and effect, and whether retrospective operation will further or retard its operation.

Linkletter v. Walker (1965) (declining to apply the exclusionary rule of *Mapp v. Ohio* for Fourth Amendment Violations retroactively because its primary purpose is to "deter the lawless action of the police" and that purpose would not be advanced if applied to police misconduct that "has already occurred and will not be corrected by releasing the prisoners involved"). Justices Black and Douglas dissented, conceding that "there might be circumstances in which applying a new interpretation of the law to past events might lead to unjust consequences which, as we said in *Chicot*, 'cannot justly be ignored,'" but insisting that "[n]o such unjust consequences . . . can possibly result here by giving [Linkletter] and others like him the benefit of a changed constitutional interpretation where he is languishing in jail on the basis of evidence concededly used unconstitutionally to convict him. [The] State of Louisiana has [no] 'vested interest' that we should recognize in these circumstances in order to keep Linkletter in jail."

As a practical matter, this meant that the Supreme Court could recognize a new constitutional right either on direct appeal or in a habeas case and then, in a subsequent case, decide whether or not other habeas petitioners, whose convictions became final before the date of the case recognizing the new right, should get the benefit of this 'new' constitutional rule of decision. In *Griffin v. California* (1965), for example, the Supreme Court held that a prosecutor violates the defendant's privilege against self-incrimination under the Fifth Amendment by commenting to the jury on the defendant's refusal to testify, referring to many "things [the defendant] has not seen fit to take the stand and deny or explain. [The victim] is dead; she can't tell you her side of the story. The defendant won't." The defendant was sentenced to death. The Court reversed the conviction. Then in *Tehan v. Shott* (1966), the Court addressed the retroactivity issue. The defendant was tried and convicted in Ohio state court in 1961. As permitted by Ohio law at the time, the prosecutor commented "extensively" on his failure to testify. His conviction became final in 1963, two years before *Griffin*. "By 'final,'" the Court has held, "we mean a case in which a judgment of conviction has been rendered, the availability of an appeal exhausted, and the time for a certiorari petition elapsed or a petition for certiorari denied." *Griffin*. The federal habeas petition in *Tehan* invoked *Griffin* and the Court decided that retroactive application was not warranted because the right not to testify is not connected to the search for truth in a criminal trial, the states had relied for decades on the understanding of the Fifth Amendment privilege *Griffin* reversed, and almost every state conviction based on a jury trial would be affected in states that allowed comment on a defendant's failure to testify because the practice was so common:

> As in *Mapp* . . . we deal here with a doctrine which rests on considerations of quite a different order from those underlying other recent constitutional decisions which have been applied retroactively. The basic purpose of a trial is the determination of truth, and it is self-evident that to deny a lawyer's help through the technical intricacies of a criminal trial or to deny a full opportunity to appeal a conviction because the accused is poor is to impede that purpose, and to infect a criminal proceeding with the clear danger of convicting the innocent. *See Gideon v. Wainwright* (1963). The same can surely be said of the wrongful use of a coerced confession. *See Jackson v. Denno* (1964). By contrast, the Fifth Amendment's privilege against self-incrimination is not an adjunct to the ascertainment of truth. That privilege, like the guarantees of the Fourth Amendment, stands as a protection of quite different constitutional values — values reflecting the concern of our society for the right of each individual to be let alone.

> There can be no doubt of the States' reliance upon the rule for more than half a century [that comment on a defendant's failure to testify was permissible], nor can it be doubted that they relied upon that constitutional doctrine in the utmost good faith. Two States amended their constitutions so as expressly to permit comment upon a defendant's failure to testify, Ohio in 1912, and California in 1934.

> A retrospective application of *Griffin v. California* would create stresses upon the administration of justice more concentrated, but fully as great, as would have been created by a retrospective application of *Mapp*. A retrospective application of *Mapp* would have had an impact only in those States which had not themselves adopted the exclusionary rule, apparently some 24 in number. A retrospective application of *Griffin* would have an impact only upon those States which have not themselves adopted the no-comment rule, apparently six in number. But, upon those six States, the impact would be very grave indeed. It is not in every criminal trial that tangible evidence of a kind that might raise *Mapp* issues is offered. But it may fairly be assumed that there has been comment in every single trial in the courts of California, Connecticut, Iowa, New Jersey, New Mexico, and

Ohio, in which the defendant did not take the witness stand—in accordance with state law and with the United States Constitution as explicitly interpreted by this Court for 57 years.

The Rehnquist Court jettisoned this approach in favor of a strict presumption of non-retroactivity for habeas petitions. Cases on direct appeal when a new Supreme Court decision is announced benefit from the new rule, but absent exceptional circumstances, the rule does not apply to collateral attacks on state convictions. The Rehnquist Court's non-retroactivity rule also requires that the question of retroactivity be addressed *first* in any habeas petition, before addressing whether a constitutional right of the petitioner has been violated. And if the right the petitioner asserts is "new," the petition will be dismissed unless one of the narrow exceptions to the presumption of non-retroactivity is met. Generally, this means that new constitutional rights can only be developed on direct appeal.

The following case initiated the Court's shift to this stricter approach.

Teague v. Lane

489 U.S. 288 (1989)

Justice O'CONNOR announced the judgment of the Court and delivered the opinion of the Court with respect to Parts I, II, and III, and an opinion with respect to Parts IV and V, in which THE CHIEF JUSTICE, Justice SCALIA, and Justice KENNEDY join.

In *Taylor v. Louisiana* (1975), this Court held that the Sixth Amendment required that the jury venire be drawn from a fair cross-section of the community. The Court stated, however, that,

> in holding that petit juries must be drawn from a source fairly representative of the community, we impose no requirement that petit juries actually chosen must mirror the community and reflect the various distinctive groups in the population. Defendants are not entitled to a jury of any particular composition.

The principal question presented in this case is whether the Sixth Amendment's fair cross-section requirement should now be extended to the petit jury. Because we adopt Justice Harlan's approach to retroactivity for cases on collateral review, we leave the resolution of that question for another day.

I

Petitioner, a black man, was convicted by an all-white Illinois jury of three counts of attempted murder, two counts of armed robbery, and one count of aggravated battery. During jury selection for petitioner's trial, the prosecutor used all 10 of his peremptory challenges to exclude blacks. Petitioner's counsel used one of his 10 peremptory challenges to exclude a black woman who was married to a police officer. After the prosecutor had struck six blacks, petitioner's counsel moved for a mistrial. The trial court denied the motion. When the prosecutor struck four more blacks, petitioner's counsel again moved for a mistrial, arguing that petitioner was "entitled to a jury of his peers." The prosecutor defended the challenges by stating that he was trying to achieve a balance of men and women on the jury. The trial court denied the motion, reasoning that the jury "appear[ed] to be a fair [one]."

On appeal, petitioner argued that the prosecutor's use of peremptory challenges denied him the right to be tried by a jury that was representative of the community. The Illinois Appellate Court rejected petitioner's fair cross-section claim. The Illinois Supreme Court denied leave to appeal, and we denied certiorari.

Petitioner then filed a petition for a writ of habeas corpus in the United States District Court for the Northern District of Illinois. Petitioner repeated his fair cross-section claim, and argued that the opinions of several Justices concurring in and dissenting from the denial of certiorari in *McCray v. New York* (1983), had invited a reexamination of *Swain v. Alabama* (1965), which prohibited States from purposefully and systematically denying blacks the opportunity to serve on juries. He also argued, for the first time, that, under *Swain*, a prosecutor could be questioned about his use of peremptory challenges once he volunteered an explanation. The District Court, though sympathetic to petitioner's arguments, held that it was bound by *Swain* and Circuit precedent.

On appeal, petitioner repeated his fair cross-section claim and his McCray argument. A panel of the Court of Appeals agreed with petitioner that the Sixth Amendment's fair cross-section requirement applied to the petit jury, and held that petitioner had made out a *prima facie* case of discrimination. A majority of the judges on the Court of Appeals voted to rehear the case en banc, and the panel opinion was vacated. Rehearing was postponed until after our decision in *Batson v. Kentucky* (1986), which overruled a portion of *Swain*. After *Batson* was decided, the Court of Appeals held that petitioner could not benefit from the rule in that case because *Allen v. Hardy* (1986) (*per curiam*), had held that *Batson* would not be applied retroactively to cases on collateral review. The Court of Appeals also held that petitioner's *Swain* claim was procedurally barred and, in any event, meritless. The Court of Appeals rejected petitioner's fair cross-section claim, holding that the fair cross-section requirement was limited to the jury venire.

II

Petitioner's first contention is that he should receive the benefit of our decision in *Batson* even though his conviction became final before *Batson* was decided. . . .

In *Batson*, the Court overruled that portion of *Swain* setting forth the evidentiary showing necessary to make out a *prima facie* case of racial discrimination under the Equal Protection Clause. The Court held that a defendant can establish a *prima facie* case by showing that he is a "member of a cognizable racial group," that the prosecutor exercised "peremptory challenges to remove from the venire members of the defendant's race," and that those

> facts and any other relevant circumstances raise an inference that the prosecutor used that practice to exclude the veniremen from the petit jury on account of their race.

Once the defendant makes out a *prima facie* case of discrimination, the burden shifts to the prosecutor "to come forward with a neutral explanation for challenging black jurors."

In *Allen v. Hardy* (1986), the Court held that *Batson* constituted an "explicit and substantial break with prior precedent" because it overruled a portion of *Swain*. Employing the retroactivity standard of *Linkletter v. Walker* (1965), the Court concluded that the rule announced in *Batson* should not be applied retroactively on collateral review of convictions that became final before *Batson* was announced. The Court defined final to mean a case

> "where the judgment of conviction was rendered, the availability of appeal exhausted, and the time for petition for certiorari had elapsed before our decision in" *Batson*. . . .

Hardy.

Petitioner's conviction became final 2½ years prior to Batson, thus depriving petitioner of any benefit from the rule announced in that case. Petitioner argues, however, that *Batson* should be applied retroactively to all cases pending on direct review at the time certiorari was denied in *McCray* because the opinions filed in *McCray* destroyed the precedential effect of *Swain*. The issue in *McCray* and its companion cases was whether the Constitution prohibited the use of peremptory challenges to exclude members of a particular group from the jury, based on the prosecutor's assumption that they would be biased in favor of other members of that same group. JUSTICES MARSHALL and BRENNAN dissented from the denial of certiorari, expressing the views that *Swain* should be reexamined, and that the conduct complained of violated a defendant's Sixth Amendment right to be tried by an impartial jury drawn from a fair cross-section of the community. JUSTICES STEVENS, BLACKMUN, and POWELL concurred in the denial of certiorari. They agreed that the issue was an important one, but stated that it was a

> sound exercise of discretion for the Court to allow the various States to serve as laboratories in which the issue receives further study before it is addressed.

We reject the basic premise of petitioner's argument. As we have often stated, the "denial of a writ of certiorari imports no expression of opinion upon the merits of the case." *United States v. Carver* (1923) (Holmes, J.). We find that *Allen v. Hardy* is dispositive, and that petitioner cannot benefit from the rule announced in *Batson*.

III

Petitioner's second contention is that he has established a violation of the Equal Protection Clause under *Swain*. Recognizing that he has not shown any systematic exclusion of blacks from petit juries in case after case, petitioner contends that, when the prosecutor volunteers an explanation for the use of his peremptory challenges, *Swain* does not preclude an examination of the stated reasons to determine the legitimacy of the prosecutor's motive.

Petitioner candidly admits that he did not raise the *Swain* claim at trial or on direct appeal. Because of this failure, petitioner has forfeited review of the claim in the Illinois courts [which apply res judicata to "all issues actually raised, and those that could have been presented but ere not" absent "fundamental unfairness," a narrow exception under Illinois law.]

Under *Wainwright v. Sykes* (1977), petitioner is barred from raising the *Swain* claim in a federal habeas corpus proceeding unless he can show cause for the default and prejudice resulting therefrom. [Concluding that petitioner defaulted his *Swain* claim by failing to raise it before the state courts.]

IV

Petitioner's third and final contention is that the Sixth Amendment's fair cross-section requirement applies to the petit jury. As we noted at the outset, *Taylor* expressly stated that the fair cross-section requirement does not apply to the petit jury. Petitioner nevertheless contends that the *ratio decidendi* of *Taylor* cannot be limited to the jury venire, and he urges adoption of a new rule. Because we hold that the rule urged by petitioner should not be applied retroactively to cases on collateral review, we decline to address petitioner's contention.

A

In the past, the Court has, without discussion, often applied a new constitutional rule of criminal procedure to the defendant in the case announcing the new rule, and has confronted the question of retroactivity later, when a different defendant sought the benefit of that rule. In several cases, however, the Court has addressed the retroactivity question in the very case announcing the new rule. These two lines of cases do not have a unifying theme, and we think it is time to clarify how the question of retroactivity should be resolved for cases on collateral review.

The question of retroactivity with regard to petitioner's fair cross-section claim has been raised only in an *amicus* brief. Nevertheless, that question is not foreign to the parties, who have addressed retroactivity with respect to petitioner's *Batson* claim. Moreover, our *sua sponte* consideration of retroactivity is far from novel. In *Allen v. Hardy,* we addressed the retroactivity of *Batson* even though that question had not been presented by the petition for certiorari or addressed by the lower courts.

In our view, the question "whether a decision [announcing a new rule should] be given prospective or retroactive effect should be faced at the time of [that] decision." Mishkin, *Foreword: the High Court, the Great Writ, and the Due Process of Time and Law,* 79 HARV. L. REV. 56, 64 (1965). *Cf. Bowen v. United States* (1975) (when "issues of both retroactivity and application of constitutional doctrine are raised," the retroactivity issue should be decided first). Retroactivity is properly treated as a threshold question, for, once a new rule is applied to the defendant in the case announcing the rule, evenhanded justice requires that it be applied retroactively to all who are similarly situated. Thus, before deciding whether the fair cross-section requirement should be extended to the petit jury, we should ask whether such a rule would be applied retroactively to the case at issue. This retroactivity determination would normally entail application of the *Linkletter* standard, but we believe that our approach to retroactivity for cases on collateral review requires modification.

It is admittedly often difficult to determine when a case announces a new rule, and we do not attempt to define the spectrum of what may or may not constitute a new rule for retroactivity purposes. In general, however, a case announces a new rule when it breaks new ground or imposes a new obligation on the States or the Federal Government. *See, e.g., Rock v. Arkansas* (1987) (*per se* rule excluding all hypnotically refreshed testimony infringes impermissibly on a criminal defendant's right to testify on his behalf); *Ford v. Wainwright* (1986) (Eighth Amendment prohibits the execution of prisoners who are insane). To put it differently, a case announces a new rule if the result was not *dictated* by precedent existing at the time the defendant's conviction became final. Given the strong language in *Taylor* and our statement in *Akins v. Texas* (1945), that "[f]airness in [jury] selection has never been held to require proportional representation of races upon a jury," application of the fair cross-section requirement to the petit jury would be a new rule.[1] . . .

The *Linkletter* retroactivity standard has not led to consistent results. Instead, it has been used to limit application of certain new rules to cases on direct review, other new rules only to the defendants in the cases announcing such rules, and still other new rules to cases in which trials have not yet commenced. Not surprisingly, commentators have "had a veritable field day" with the *Linkletter* standard, with much of the discussion being "more than mildly negative." Beytagh, *Ten Years of Non-Retroactivity: A Critique and a Proposal*, 61 VA. L. REV. 1557, 1558, and n.3 (1975) (citing sources).

Application of the *Linkletter* standard led to the disparate treatment of similarly situated defendants on direct review. For example, in *Miranda v. Arizona* (1966), the Court held that, absent other effective measures to protect the Fifth Amendment privilege against self-incrimination, a person in custody must be warned prior to interrogation that he has certain rights, including the right to remain silent. The Court applied that new rule to the defendants in *Miranda* and its companion cases, and held that their convictions could not stand because they had been interrogated without the proper warnings. In *Johnson v. New Jersey* (1966), the Court held, under the *Linkletter* standard, that *Miranda* would only be applied to trials commencing after that decision had been announced. Because the defendant in *Johnson*, like the defendants in *Miranda*, was on direct review of his conviction, the Court's refusal to give *Miranda* retroactive effect resulted in unequal treatment of those who were similarly situated. This inequity also generated vehement criticism.

Dissatisfied with the *Linkletter* standard, Justice Harlan advocated a different approach to retroactivity. He argued that new rules should always be applied retroactively to cases on direct review, but that generally they should not be applied retroactively to criminal cases on collateral review. *See Mackey v. United States* (1971) (opinion concurring in judgments in part and dissenting in part); *Desist v. United States* (1969) (dissenting opinion).

In *Griffith v. Kentucky* (1987), we rejected as unprincipled and inequitable the *Linkletter* standard for cases pending on direct review at the time a new rule is announced, and adopted the first part of the retroactivity approach advocated by Justice Harlan. We agreed with Justice Harlan that "failure to apply a newly declared

---

1. . . . Petitioner recognizes this, as he compares the percentage of blacks in his petit jury to the percentage of blacks in the population of Cook County, Illinois, from which the petit jury was drawn. *See* Brief for Petitioner 17-18 (arguing that blacks were underrepresented on petitioner's petit jury by 25.62%). In short, the very standard that petitioner urges us to adopt includes, and indeed requires, the sort of proportional analysis we declined to endorse in *Akins v. Texas* (1945), and *Taylor v. Louisiana* (1975).

constitutional rule to criminal cases pending on direct review violates basic norms of constitutional adjudication." We gave two reasons for our decision. First, because we can only promulgate new rules in specific cases, and cannot possibly decide all cases in which review is sought, "the integrity of judicial review" requires the application of the new rule to "all similar cases pending on direct review." We quoted approvingly from Justice Harlan's separate opinion in *Mackey*:

> If we do not resolve all cases before us on direct review in light of our best understanding of governing constitutional principles, it is difficult to see why we should so adjudicate any case at all. . . . In truth, the Court's assertion of power to disregard current law in adjudicating cases before us that have not already run the full course of appellate review is quite simply an assertion that our constitutional function is not one of adjudication, but in effect of legislation.

Second, because "selective application of new rules violates the principle of treating similarly situated defendants the same," we refused to continue to tolerate the inequity that resulted from not applying new rules retroactively to defendants whose cases had not yet become final. Although new rules that constituted clear breaks with the past generally were not given retroactive effect under the *Linkletter* standard, we held that

> a new rule for the conduct of criminal prosecutions is to be applied retroactively to all cases, state or federal, pending on direct review or not yet final, with no exception for cases in which the new rule constitutes a "clear break" with the past.

The *Linkletter* standard also led to unfortunate disparity in the treatment of similarly situated defendants on collateral review. An example will best illustrate the point. In *Edwards v. Arizona* (1981), the Court held that, once a person invokes his right to have counsel present during custodial interrogation, a valid waiver of that right cannot be inferred from the fact that the person responded to police-initiated questioning. It was not until *Solem v. Stumes* (1984), that the Court held, under the *Linkletter* standard, that *Edwards* was not to be applied retroactively to cases on collateral review. In the interim, several lower federal courts had come to the opposite conclusion, and had applied *Edwards* to cases that had become final before that decision was announced. Thus, some defendants on collateral review whose *Edwards* claims were adjudicated prior to *Stumes* received the benefit of *Edwards*, while those whose *Edwards* claims had not been addressed prior to *Stumes* did not. This disparity in treatment was a product of two factors: our failure to treat retroactivity as a threshold question and the *Linkletter* standard's inability to account for the nature and function of collateral review. Having decided to rectify the first of those inadequacies, we now turn to the second.

B

Justice Harlan believed that new rules generally should not be applied retroactively to cases on collateral review. He argued that retroactivity for cases on collateral review could be responsibly [determined] only by focusing, in the first instance, on the nature, function, and scope of the adjudicatory process in which such cases arise. The relevant frame of reference, in other words, is not the purpose of the new rule whose benefit the [defendant] seeks, but instead the purposes for which the writ of habeas corpus is made available.

Mackey. With regard to the nature of habeas corpus, Justice Harlan wrote:

Habeas corpus always has been a collateral remedy, providing an avenue for upsetting judgments that have become otherwise final. It is not designed as a substitute for direct review. The interest in leaving concluded litigation in a state of repose, that is, reducing the controversy to a final judgment not subject to further judicial revision, may quite legitimately be found by those responsible for defining the scope of the writ to outweigh in some, many, or most instances the competing interest in readjudicating convictions according to all legal standards in effect when a habeas petition is filed.

Given the "broad scope of constitutional issues cognizable on habeas," Justice Harlan argued that it is "sounder, in adjudicating habeas petitions, generally to apply the law prevailing at the time a conviction became final than it is to seek to dispose of [habeas] cases on the basis of intervening changes in constitutional interpretation."

As he had explained in *Desist*, "the threat of habeas serves as a necessary additional incentive for trial and appellate courts throughout the land to conduct their proceedings in a manner consistent with established constitutional standards. In order to perform this deterrence function, . . . the habeas court need only apply the constitutional standards that prevailed at the time the original proceedings took place." *See also Stumes* (Powell, J., concurring in judgment) ("Review on habeas to determine that the conviction rests upon correct application of the law in effect at the time of the conviction is all that is required to forc[e] trial and appellate courts . . . to toe the constitutional mark").

Justice Harlan identified only two exceptions to his general rule of nonretroactivity for cases on collateral review. First, a new rule should be applied retroactively if it places "certain kinds of primary, private individual conduct beyond the power of the criminal law-making authority to proscribe." *Mackey.* Second, a new rule should be applied retroactively if it requires the observance of "those procedures that . . . are *implicit in the concept of ordered liberty.*'" (quoting *Palko v. Connecticut* (1937) (Cardozo, J.)). . . .

We agree with Justice Harlan's description of the function of habeas corpus. "[T]he Court never has defined the scope of the writ simply by reference to a perceived need to assure that an individual accused of crime is afforded a trial free of constitutional error." *Kuhlmann v. Wilson* (1986) (plurality opinion). Rather, we have recognized that interests of comity and finality must also be considered in determining the proper scope of habeas review. Thus, if a defendant fails to comply with state procedural rules and is barred from litigating a particular constitutional claim in state court, the claim can be considered on federal habeas only if the defendant shows cause for the default and actual prejudice resulting therefrom.

See Wainwright v. Sykes. We have declined to make the application of the procedural default rule dependent on the magnitude of the constitutional claim at issue, or on the State's interest in the enforcement of its procedural rule.

This Court has not "always followed an unwavering line in its conclusions as to the availability of the Great Writ. Our development of the law of federal habeas corpus has been attended, seemingly, with some backing and filling." *Fay v. Noia* (1963). *See also Stone v. Powell* (1976). Nevertheless, it has long been established that a final civil judgment entered under a given rule of law may withstand subsequent judicial change in that rule. In *Chicot County Drainage District v. Baxter State Bank* (1940), the Court held that a judgment based on a jurisdictional statute later found to be unconstitutional could have *res judicata* effect. The Court based its decision in large part on finality concerns. "The actual existence of a statute, prior to such a determination [of unconstitutionality], is an operative fact, and may have consequences which cannot justly be ignored. The past cannot always be erased by a new judicial declaration. . . . Questions of . . . prior determinations deemed to have finality and acted upon accordingly . . . demand examination." *Accord, Rooker v. Fidelity Trust Co.* (1923) ("Unless and until . . . reversed or modified" on appeal, an erroneous constitutional decision is "an effective and conclusive adjudication"); *Thompson v. Tolmie* (1829) (errors or mistakes of court with competent jurisdiction "cannot be corrected or examined when brought up collaterally").

These underlying considerations of finality find significant and compelling parallels in the criminal context. Application of constitutional rules not in existence at the time a conviction became final seriously undermines the principle of finality which is essential to the operation of our criminal justice system. Without finality, the criminal law is deprived of much of its deterrent effect. The fact that life and liberty are at stake in criminal prosecutions "shows only that 'conventional notions of finality' should not have as much place in criminal as in civil litigation, not that they should have none." Friendly, *Is Innocence Irrelevant? Collateral Attacks on Criminal Judgments*, 38 U. Chi. L. Rev. 142, 150 (1970). "[I]f a criminal judgment is ever to be final, the notion of legality must at some point include the assignment of final competence to determine legality." Bator, *Finality in Criminal Law and Federal Habeas Corpus for State Prisoners*, 76 Harv. L. Rev. 441, 450-451 (1963). *See also Mackey* (Harlan, J., concurring in judgments in part and dissenting in part) ("No one, not criminal defendants, not the judicial system, not society as a whole is benefited by a judgment providing a man shall tentatively go to jail today, but tomorrow and every day thereafter his continued incarceration shall be subject to fresh litigation"). . . .

In many ways, the application of new rules to cases on collateral review may be more intrusive than the enjoining of criminal prosecutions, *cf. Younger v. Harris* (1971), for it *continually* forces the States to marshal resources in order to keep in prison defendants whose trials and appeals conformed to then-existing constitutional standards. Furthermore, as we recognized in *Engle v. Isaac*, "[s]tate courts are understandably frustrated when they faithfully apply existing constitutional law only to have a federal court discover, during a [habeas] proceeding, new constitutional commands." *See also Brown v. Allen* (Jackson, J., concurring in result) (state courts cannot "anticipate, and so comply with, this Court's due process requirements or ascertain any standards to which this Court will adhere in prescribing them").

We find these criticisms to be persuasive, and we now adopt Justice Harlan's view of retroactivity for cases on collateral review. Unless they fall within an exception to the general rule, new constitutional rules of criminal procedure will not be applicable to those cases which have become final before the new rules are announced.

V

Petitioner's conviction became final in 1983. As a result, the rule petitioner urges would not be applicable to this case, which is on collateral review, unless it would fall within an exception.

The first exception suggested by Justice Harlan — that a new rule should be applied retroactively if it places "certain kinds of primary, private individual conduct beyond the power of the criminal lawmaking authority to proscribe," *Mackey* — is not relevant here. Application of the fair cross-section requirement to the petit jury would not accord constitutional protection to any primary activity whatsoever.

The second exception suggested by Justice Harlan — that a new rule should be applied retroactively if it requires the observance of "those procedures that . . . are implicit in the concept of ordered liberty,'" — we apply with a modification. The language used by Justice Harlan in *Mackey* leaves no doubt that he meant the second exception to be reserved for watershed rules of criminal procedure:

> Typically, it should be the case that any conviction free from federal constitutional error at the time it became final will be found, upon reflection, to have been fundamentally fair and conducted under those procedures essential to the substance of a full hearing. However, in some situations it might be that time and growth in social capacity, as well as judicial perceptions of what we can rightly demand of the adjudicatory process, will properly alter our understanding of the *bedrock procedural elements* that must be found to vitiate the fairness of a particular conviction. For example, such, in my view, is the case with the right to counsel at trial now held a necessary condition precedent to any conviction for a serious crime.

Id. (emphasis added).

In *Desist*, Justice Harlan had reasoned that one of the two principal functions of habeas corpus was "to assure that no man has been incarcerated under a procedure which creates an impermissibly large risk that the innocent will be convicted," and concluded "from this that all 'new' constitutional rules which significantly improve the preexisting factfinding procedures are to be retroactively applied on habeas." . . . [W]e believe that Justice Harlan's concerns about the difficulty in identifying both the existence and the value of accuracy-enhancing procedural rules can be addressed by limiting the scope of the second exception to those new procedures without which the likelihood of an accurate conviction is seriously diminished.

Because we operate from the premise that such procedures would be so central to an accurate determination of innocence or guilt, we believe it unlikely that many such components of basic due process have yet to emerge. We are also of the view that such rules are "best illustrated by recalling the classic grounds for the issuance of a writ of habeas corpus—that the proceeding was dominated by mob violence; that the prosecutor knowingly made use of perjured testimony; or that the conviction was based on a confession extorted from the defendant by brutal methods." *Rose v. Lundy* (1982) (Stevens, J., dissenting).

An examination of our decision in *Taylor* applying the fair cross-section requirement to the jury venire leads inexorably to the conclusion that adoption of the rule petitioner urges would be a far cry from the kind of absolute prerequisite to fundamental fairness that is "implicit in the concept of ordered liberty." The requirement that the jury venire be composed of a fair cross-section of the community is based on the role of the jury in our system. Because the purpose of the jury is to guard against arbitrary abuses of power by interposing the common sense judgment of the community between the State and the defendant, the jury venire cannot be composed only of special segments of the population.

"Community participation in the administration of the criminal law . . . is not only consistent with our democratic heritage, but is also critical to public confidence in the fairness of the criminal justice system." *Taylor*. But as we stated in *Daniel v. Louisiana* (1975), which held that *Taylor* was not to be given retroactive effect, the fair cross-section requirement "[does] not rest on the premise that every criminal trial, or any particular trial, [is] necessarily unfair because it [is] not conducted in accordance with what we determined to be the requirements of the Sixth Amendment."

Because the absence of a fair cross-section on the jury venire does not undermine the fundamental fairness that must underlie a conviction or seriously diminish the likelihood of obtaining an accurate conviction, we conclude that a rule requiring that petit juries be composed of a fair cross-section of the community would not be a "bedrock procedural element" that would be retroactively applied under the second exception we have articulated.

Were we to recognize the new rule urged by petitioner in this case, we would have to give petitioner the benefit of that new rule even though it would not be applied retroactively to others similarly situated. In the words of Justice Brennan, such an inequitable result would be "an unavoidable consequence of the necessity that constitutional adjudications not stand as mere dictum." *Stovall v. Denno* (1967). But the harm caused by the failure to treat similarly situated defendants alike cannot be exaggerated: such inequitable treatment "hardly comports with the ideal of administration of justice with an even hand." *Hankerson v. North Carolina* (Powell, J., concurring in judgment).

We therefore hold that, implicit in the retroactivity approach we adopt today, is the principle that habeas corpus cannot be used as a vehicle to create new constitutional rules of criminal procedure unless those rules would be applied retroactively to all defendants on collateral review through one of the two exceptions we have articulated. Because a decision extending the fair cross-section requirement to the petit jury would not be applied retroactively to cases on collateral review under the approach we adopt today, we do not address petitioner's claim.

[Justice WHITE joined Parts I, II, and III of Justice O'CONNOR's opinion and concurred in the judgment.]

[Justice STEVENS, joined by Justice BLACKMUN, joined Part I and concurred in the judgment. Although agreeing with Justice Harlan's view of retroactivity, Justice STEVENS disagreed with prioritizing that analysis over whether there was a violation of the petitioner's constitutional rights:

> When a criminal defendant claims that a procedural error tainted his conviction, an appellate court often decides whether error occurred before deciding whether that error requires reversal or should be classified as harmless. I would follow a parallel approach in cases raising novel questions of constitutional law on collateral review, first determining whether the trial process violated any of the petitioner's constitutional rights and then deciding whether the petitioner is entitled to relief. If error occurred, factors relating to retroactivity—most importantly, the magnitude of unfairness—should be examined before granting the petitioner relief. Proceeding in reverse, a plurality of the Court today declares that a new rule should not apply retroactively without ever deciding whether there is such a rule.

Justice STEVENS also dissented from the Justice O'CONNOR's narrowing of the procedural integrity exception:

> The plurality wrongly resuscitates Justice Harlan's early view, indicating that the only procedural errors deserving correction on collateral review are those that undermine "an accurate determination of innocence or guilt. . . ." I cannot agree that it is "unnecessarily anachronistic," to issue a writ of habeas corpus to a petitioner convicted in a manner that violates fundamental principles of liberty. Furthermore, a touchstone of factual innocence would provide little guidance in certain important types of cases, such as those challenging the constitutionality of capital sentencing hearings.]

[Justice BRENNAN, joined by Justice MARSHALL, dissented on the ground that "[o]ur precedents . . . supply no support for the plurality's curtailment of habeas relief:]

> Although the plurality declines to "define the spectrum of what may or may not constitute a new rule for retroactivity purposes," it does say that, generally, "a case announces a new rule when it breaks new ground or imposes a new obligation on the States or the Federal Government." Otherwise phrased, "a case announces a new rule if the result was not *dictated* by precedent existing at the time the defendant's conviction became final." This account is extremely broad. Few decisions on appeal or collateral review are "*dictated*" by what came before. Most such cases involve a question of law that is at least debatable, permitting a rational judge to resolve the case in more than one way. Virtually no case that prompts a dissent on the relevant legal point, for example, could be said to be "*dictated*" by prior decisions. By the plurality's test, therefore, a great many cases could only be heard on habeas if the rule urged by the petitioner fell within one of the two exceptions the plurality has sketched. Those exceptions, however, are narrow. . . . The plurality's approach today can thus be expected to contract substantially the Great Writ's sweep.

Its impact is perhaps best illustrated by noting the abundance and variety of habeas cases we have decided in recent years that could never have been adjudicated had the plurality's new rule been in effect. [There are] numerous right-to-counsel and representation claims we have decided where the wrong alleged by the habeas petitioner was unlikely to have produced an erroneous conviction. . . . Likewise, because "the Fifth Amendment's privilege against self-incrimination is not an adjunct to the ascertainment of truth," *Tehan v. Shott* (1966), claims that a petitioner's right to remain silent was violated would, if not dictated by earlier decisions, ordinarily fail to qualify under the plurality's second exception. . . . Habeas claims under the Double Jeopardy Clause will also be barred under the plurality's approach if the rules they seek to establish would "brea[k] new ground or impos[e] a new obligation on the States or the Federal Government," because they bear no relation to the petitioner's guilt or innocence. . . . And of course, cases closely related to Teague's, such as *Lockhart v. McCree* (1986), where we held that the removal for cause of so-called "*Witherspoon*-excludables" does not violate the Sixth Amendment's fair cross-section requirement, would be beyond the purview of this Court when they arrived on habeas.

These are massive changes, unsupported by precedent. . . .

Other things being equal, our concern for fairness and finality ought to therefore lead us to render our decision in a case that comes to us on direct review.

Other things are not always equal, however. Sometimes a claim which, if successful, would create a new rule not appropriate for retroactive application on collateral review is better presented by a habeas case than by one on direct review. In fact, sometimes the claim is *only* presented on collateral review. In that case, while we could forgo deciding the issue in the hope that it would eventually be presented squarely on direct review, that hope might be misplaced, and even if it were in time fulfilled, the opportunity to check constitutional violations and to further the evolution of our thinking in some area of the law would in the meanwhile have been lost.

The plurality appears oblivious to these advantages of our settled approach to collateral review. Instead, it would deny itself these benefits because adherence to precedent would occasionally result in one habeas petitioner's obtaining redress while another petitioner with an identical claim could not qualify for relief. In my view, the uniform treatment of habeas petitioners is not worth the price the plurality is willing to pay. Permitting the federal courts to decide novel habeas claims not substantially related to guilt or innocence has profited our society immensely. Congress has not seen fit to withdraw those benefits by amending the statute that provides for them. And although a favorable decision for a petitioner might not extend to another prisoner whose identical claim has become final, it is at least arguably better that the wrong done to one person be righted than that none of the injuries inflicted on those whose convictions have become final be redressed, despite the resulting inequality in treatment.

* * *

The same year *Teague* was decided, Justice O'Connor's plurality opinion was endorsed as the correct approach to retroactivity by a majority of the Court. *See Penry v. Lynaugh* (1989); *Butler v. McKellar* (1990). The Court has consistently followed it since then. This is the conventional formulation the Court uses to summarize what *Teague* requires:

> [A] case announces a new rule if the result was not *dictated* by precedent existing at the time the defendant's conviction became final." *Teague v. Lane.* In determining whether a state prisoner is entitled to habeas relief, a federal court should apply *Teague* by proceeding in three steps. First, the court must ascertain the date on which the defendant's conviction and sentence became final for *Teague* purposes. Second, the court must "[s]urve[y] the legal landscape as it then existed," *Graham v. Collins*, and "determine whether a state court considering [the defendant's] claim at the time his conviction became final would have felt compelled by existing precedent to conclude that the rule [he] seeks was required by the Constitution," *Saffle v. Parks* (1990). Finally, even if the court determines that the defendant seeks the benefit of a new rule, the court must decide whether that rule falls within one of the two narrow exceptions to the nonretroactivity principle.
>
> A state conviction and sentence become final for purposes of retroactivity analysis when the availability of direct appeal to the state courts has been exhausted and the time for filing a petition for a writ of certiorari has elapsed or a timely filed petition has been finally denied.

Caspari v. Bohlen (1994).

Justice Brennan's prediction that most cases would be treated as calling for a "new rule" if claims not "dictated" by precedent must be treated as "new" has proved prescient. The Court has insisted that state court's "good faith interpretations of existing precedents" should be upheld even if they are "contrary to" later Supreme Court decisions. And petitions that challenge a state court's failure to apply or extend a well-established principle to new circumstances are treated as calling for a "new rule" even if the circumstance is an a fortiori case in relation to the old rule. *See, e.g., Saffle v. Parks* (1990) ("The 'new rule' principle . . . validates reasonable, good-faith interpretations of existing precedents made by state courts even though they are shown to be contrary to later decisions. Under this functional view of what constitutes a new rule, our task is to determine whether a state court considering Parks' claim at the time his conviction became final *would have felt compelled by existing precedent* to conclude that the rule Parks seeks was required by the Constitution.") (emphasis added); *id.* (holding petitioner seeks a new rule because cases decided before petitioner's conviction became final holding that it violates the Eighth Amendment to bar mitigating evidence do not "compel" or "dictate" the outcome of petitioner's claim that the Eight Amendment is violated by "antisympathy" jury instruction; decisions that "inform, or even control or govern, the analysis of his claim" do not "dictate" or "compel" under *Teague*); *see also O'Dell v. Netherland* (1997) (holding petitioner's claim rested on "new law" by distinguishing the specific type of evidence regarding future dangerousness the exclusion of which from the sentencing jury in capital cases the Court held unconstitutional under the Eighth Amendment; in the prior cases the evidence concerned information about the defendant's character and record whereas petitioner challenged exclusion of the fact that the petitioner could not be released on parole and therefore posed no danger to society if the jury decided against imposing the death penalty). *Compare Penry* (petition challenging state's clear failure to follow settled rule regarding introduction and jury instruction of mitigating evidence of mental incapacity and child abuse does not call for creation of a "new rule").

The claim that a rule is "old" will be rejected if surveying the landscape at the time the conviction became final discloses ambiguity. In *Caspari*, for example, the defendant challenged the introduction of prior convictions at a resentencing hearing on the ground that this violated double jeopardy principles. In rejecting the argument this claim was grounded in old law, the Court looked not only to its own precedent, but how it was interpreted by lower courts at the time:

> While our cases may not have foreclosed the application of the Double Jeopardy Clause to noncapital sentencing, neither did any of them apply the Clause in that context. On the contrary, *Goldhammer* and *Strickland* strongly suggested that *Bullington* was limited to capital sentencing. We therefore conclude that a reasonable jurist reviewing our precedents at the time respondent's conviction and sentence became final would not have considered the application of the Double Jeopardy Clause to a noncapital sentencing proceeding to be dictated by our precedents.
>
> This analysis is confirmed by the experience of the lower courts. Prior to the time respondent's conviction and sentence became final, one Federal Court of Appeals and two state courts of last resort had held that the Double Jeopardy Clause did not bar the introduction of evidence of prior convictions at resentencing in noncapital cases, while another Federal Court of Appeals and two other state courts of last resort had held to the contrary. Moreover, the Missouri Court of Appeals had previously rejected precisely the same claim raised by respondent.

Caspari v. Bohlen (1994).

(i)   Exceptions to *Teague*'s Non-Retroactivity Principle

The first exception to *Teague* allows a habeas petitioner to benefit from retroactive application of a new rule where "the rule places a class of private conduct beyond the power of the State to proscribe, *see Teague,* or addresses a substantive categorical guarante[e] accorded by the Constitution, such as a rule "prohibiting a certain category of punishment for a class of defendants because of their status or offense." *Saffle v. Parks* (1990). Only rules that "decriminalize a class of conduct" or "prohibit the imposition of . . . punishment" such as capital punishment "on a particular class of persons" meet this exception. Thus, if the Court has overturned or narrowed a criminal statute or otherwise placed "particular conduct or persons beyond the state's power to punish" these rules "alter[] the range of conduct or the class of persons that the law punishes;" they "apply retroactively because they carry a significant risk that a defendant stands convicted of an act that the law does not make criminal or faces a punishment that the law [can no longer] impose upon him." *Schriro v. Summerlin* (2004). The first exception, in this sense, deals with rules "more accurately characterized as substantive rules not subject to *Teague*'s bar." The

Court has narrowly construed the exception. *See Caspari* ("Imposing a double jeopardy bar in this case would have no . . . effect" on the state's power to punish petitioner since he can be imprisoned for the conduct underlying "each of his three convictions, regardless of whether he is sentenced as a persistent offender.").

The second exception is procedural. The Court emphasized in *Teague* that it believed most "watershed" rules designed to ensure the procedural integrity of state criminal prosecutions had already been announced. Indeed, in no case has the Court recognized a new "watershed" rule worthy of retroactive application. In the following case, the Court concluded that there are no such cases—eliminating the second exception altogether.

Edwards v. Vannoy

593 U.S. _ (2021)

Justice KAVANAUGH delivered the opinion of the Court.

Last Term in *Ramos v. Louisiana* (2020), this Court held that a state jury must be unanimous to convict a criminal defendant of a serious offense. *Ramos* repudiated this Court's 1972 decision in *Apodaca v. Oregon* (1972), which had allowed non-unanimous juries in state criminal trials. The question in this case is whether the new rule of criminal procedure announced in *Ramos* applies retroactively to overturn final convictions on federal collateral review. Under this Court's retroactivity precedents, the answer is no.

This Court has repeatedly stated that a decision announcing a new rule of criminal procedure ordinarily does not apply retroactively on federal collateral review. Indeed, in the 32 years since *Teague* underscored that principle, this Court has announced many important new rules of criminal procedure. But the Court has not applied *any* of those new rules retroactively on federal collateral review. *See, e.g., Whorton v. Bockting* (2007) (Confrontation Clause rule recognized in *Crawford v. Washington* (2004), does not apply retroactively). And for decades before *Teague,* the Court also regularly declined to apply new rules retroactively, including on federal collateral review.

In light of the Court's well-settled retroactivity doctrine, we conclude that the *Ramos* jury-unanimity rule likewise does not apply retroactively on federal collateral review. We therefore affirm the judgment of the U.S. Court of Appeals for the Fifth Circuit.

I

Edwards was indicted in Louisiana state court for armed robbery, kidnapping, and rape. Edwards pled not guilty and went to trial. Before trial, Edwards moved to suppress [his] videotaped confession on the ground that the confession was involuntary. The trial court denied the suppression motion.

At trial, the jury heard Edwards's confession and other evidence against him, including the testimony of eyewitnesses. The jury convicted Edwards of five counts of armed robbery, two counts of kidnapping, and one count of rape. At the time, Louisiana law permitted guilty verdicts if at least 10 of the 12 jurors found the defendant guilty. The jury convicted Edwards by an 11-to-1 vote on one of the armed robbery counts, the two kidnapping counts, and the rape count. The jury convicted Edwards by a 10-to-2 vote on the four remaining armed robbery counts.

At sentencing, the trial judge stated: "I can say without hesitation that this is the most egregious case that I've had before me." The judge sentenced Edwards to life imprisonment without parole. The Louisiana First Circuit Court of Appeal affirmed the conviction and sentence. In March 2011, Edwards's conviction became final on direct review.

After his conviction became final, Edwards applied for state post-conviction relief in the Louisiana courts. The Louisiana courts denied relief.

In 2015, Edwards filed a petition for a writ of habeas corpus in the U.S. District Court for the Middle District of Louisiana. He argued that the non-unanimous jury verdict violated his constitutional right to a unanimous jury. The District Court rejected that claim as foreclosed by this Court's 1972 decision in *Apodaca v. Oregon*.

In *Apodaca*, this Court ruled that the Constitution does not require unanimous jury verdicts in state criminal trials. The *Apodaca* majority consisted of a plurality opinion by four Justices and an opinion concurring in the judgment by Justice Powell. In his opinion, Justice Powell acknowledged that the Sixth Amendment requires a unanimous jury in *federal* criminal trials. *Johnson v. Louisiana* (1972). But in his view, the Fourteenth Amendment did not incorporate that right against the States, meaning that a unanimous jury was not constitutionally required in *state* criminal trials. In subsequent years, many federal and state courts viewed Justice Powell's opinion as the controlling opinion from *Apodaca*.

In Edwards's case, the District Court likewise followed Justice Powell's opinion from *Apodaca* and concluded that a unanimous jury is not constitutionally required in state criminal trials. The U.S. Court of Appeals for the Fifth Circuit denied a certificate of appealability.* Edwards then petitioned for a writ of certiorari in this Court, arguing that the Constitution requires a unanimous jury in state criminal trials.

II

A

In stating that new procedural rules ordinarily do not apply retroactively on federal collateral review, *Teague* reinforced what had already been the Court's regular practice for several decades. [E]ven under *Linkletter*, "new rules that constituted clear breaks with the past generally were not given retroactive effect," including on federal collateral review. *Teague*.

As the Court has explained, applying "constitutional rules not in existence at the time a conviction became final seriously undermines the principle of finality which is essential to the operation of our criminal justice system." Here, for

---

* [Rule 11 for §2254 cases requires district courts to "issue or deny a certificate of appealability when it enters a final order adverse to the applicant. If the certificate is denied, the petitioner "may not appeal the denial but may seek a certificate from the court of appeals" under FRAP 22.—Eds.].

example, applying *Ramos* retroactively would potentially overturn decades of convictions obtained in reliance on *Apodaca.* Moreover, conducting scores of retrials years after the crimes occurred would require significant state resources. And a State may not be able to retry some defendants at all because of "lost evidence, faulty memory, and missing witnesses." *Allen v. Hardy* (1986). When previously convicted perpetrators of violent crimes go free merely because the evidence needed to conduct a retrial has become stale or is no longer available, the public suffers, as do the victims. Even when the evidence can be reassembled, conducting retrials years later inflicts substantial pain on crime victims who must testify again and endure new trials. In this case, the victims of the robberies, kidnappings, and rapes would have to relive their trauma and testify again, 15 years after the crimes occurred.

Put simply, the "costs imposed upon the States by retroactive application of new rules of constitutional law on habeas corpus thus generally far outweigh the benefits of this application." *Sawyer v. Smith* (1990). For that reason, the Court has repeatedly stated that new rules of criminal procedure ordinarily do not apply retroactively on federal collateral review.

B

To determine whether *Ramos* applies retroactively on federal collateral review, we must answer two questions.

First, did *Ramos* announce a new rule of criminal procedure, as opposed to applying a settled rule? A new rule ordinarily does not apply retroactively on federal collateral review.

Second, if *Ramos* announced a new rule, does it fall within an exception for watershed rules of criminal procedure that apply retroactively on federal collateral review?

1

Ramos held that a state jury must be unanimous to convict a defendant of a serious offense. In so holding, *Ramos* announced a new rule. . . . The starkest example of a decision announcing a new rule is a decision that overrules an earlier case. The jury-unanimity requirement announced in *Ramos* was not dictated by precedent or apparent to all reasonable jurists when Edwards's conviction became final in 2011. On the contrary, before *Ramos,* many courts interpreted *Apodaca* to allow for non-unanimous jury verdicts in state criminal trials. In addition, in *Ramos* itself the Court indicated that the decision was not dictated by precedent or apparent to all reasonable jurists.

Edwards responds that the Court's decision in *Ramos* must have applied a settled rule, not a new rule, because the decision adhered to the original meaning of the Sixth Amendment's right to a jury trial and the Fourteenth Amendment's incorporation of that right (and others) against the States. That argument conflates the merits question presented in *Ramos* with the retroactivity question presented here. On the merits question, the critical point, as the Court thoroughly explained in *Ramos,* is that the Constitution's text and history require a unanimous jury in state criminal trials. On the retroactivity question, the critical point is that reasonable jurists who considered the question before *Ramos* interpreted *Apodaca* to allow non-unanimous jury verdicts in state criminal trials.

By renouncing *Apodaca* and expressly requiring unanimous jury verdicts in state criminal trials, *Ramos* plainly announced a new rule for purposes of this Court's retroactivity doctrine.

2

Having determined that *Ramos* announced a new rule requiring jury unanimity, we must consider whether that new rule falls within an exception for watershed rules of criminal procedure that apply retroactively on federal collateral review.

This Court has stated that the watershed exception is "extremely narrow" and applies only when, among other things, the new rule alters "our understanding of the bedrock procedural elements essential to the fairness of a proceeding." *Whorton.*

In the abstract, those various adjectives — watershed, narrow, bedrock, essential — do not tell us much about whether a particular decision of this Court qualifies for the watershed exception. In practice, the exception has been theoretical, not real. The Court has identified only one pre-*Teague* procedural rule as watershed: the right to counsel recognized in the Court's landmark decision in *Gideon v. Wainwright* (1963). The Court has never identified any other pre-*Teague* or post-*Teague* rule as watershed. None.

Moreover, the Court has flatly proclaimed on multiple occasions that the watershed exception is unlikely to cover any more new rules. Even 32 years ago in *Teague* itself, the Court stated that it was "unlikely" that additional watershed rules would "emerge." And since *Teague*, the Court has often reiterated that "it is unlikely that any such rules have yet to emerge." *Whorton.*

Consistent with those many emphatic pronouncements, the Court since *Teague* has rejected *every* claim that a new procedural rule qualifies as a watershed rule. For example, in *Beard v. Banks* (2006), the Court declined to retroactively apply the rule announced in *Mills v. Maryland* (1988), that capital juries may not be required to disregard certain mitigating factors. In *O'Dell v. Netherland* (1997), the Court refused to retroactively apply the rule announced in *Simmons v. South Carolina* (1994), that a capital defendant must be able, in certain circumstances, to inform the sentencing jury that he is parole ineligible. In *Lambrix v. Singletary*, the Court declined to retroactively apply the rule announced in *Espinosa v. Florida* (1992) (*per curiam*), that sentencers may not weigh invalid aggravating circumstances before recommending or imposing the death penalty. In *Sawyer v. Smith*, the Court refused to retroactively apply the rule announced in *Caldwell v. Mississippi* (1985), which prohibited a death sentence by a jury led to the false belief that responsibility for the sentence rested elsewhere.

The list of cases declining to retroactively apply a new rule of criminal procedure extends back long before *Teague* to some of this Court's most historic criminal procedure decisions. For example, in *Johnson v. New Jersey* (1966), the Court declined to retroactively apply *Miranda v. Arizona* (1966), which required that police inform individuals in custody of certain constitutional rights before questioning them. And in *Linkletter v. Walker*, the Court refused to retroactively apply *Mapp v. Ohio* (1961), which incorporated the Fourth Amendment exclusionary rule against the States.

Edwards seeks to distinguish *Ramos* from the long line of cases where the Court has declined to retroactively apply new procedural rules. Edwards emphasizes three aspects of *Ramos*: (i) the significance of the jury-unanimity right; (ii) *Ramos*'s reliance on the original meaning of the Constitution; and (iii) the effect of *Ramos* in preventing racial discrimination in the jury process.

But Edwards's attempts to distinguish *Ramos* are unavailing because the Court has already considered and rejected those kinds of arguments in prior retroactivity cases.

First, Edwards emphasizes the significance of the jury-unanimity right for criminal defendants. But that argument for retroactivity cannot be squared with the Court's decisions in *Duncan v. Louisiana* (1968), and *DeStefano v. Woods* (1968). In *Duncan*, the Court repudiated several precedents and ruled that a defendant has a constitutional right to a jury trial in a state criminal case. Notwithstanding the extraordinary significance of *Duncan* in guaranteeing a jury trial and expanding the rights of criminal defendants, the Court in *DeStefano* declined to retroactively apply the jury right. *See also Summerlin* (relying on *DeStefano* and rejecting retroactivity of jury right recognized in *Ring v. Arizona* (2002)). We cannot discern a principled basis for retroactively applying the subsidiary *Ramos* jury-unanimity right when the Court in *DeStefano* declined to retroactively apply the broader jury right itself.

Second, Edwards stresses that *Ramos* relied on the original meaning of the Sixth Amendment. But that argument for retroactivity is inconsistent with *Crawford v. Washington* (2004), and *Whorton v. Bockting* (2007). In *Crawford*, the Court relied on the original meaning of the Sixth Amendment's Confrontation Clause to overrule precedent and restrict the use of hearsay evidence against criminal defendants. Notwithstanding *Crawford*'s reliance on the original meaning of the Sixth Amendment, the Court in *Whorton* declined to retroactively apply *Crawford*.

Third, Edwards says that *Ramos* prevents racial discrimination by ensuring that the votes of all jurors, regardless of race, matter in the jury room. But that argument for retroactivity cannot prevail in light of *Batson v. Kentucky* (1986), and *Allen v. Hardy* (1986). In *Batson*, the Court overruled precedent and revolutionized day-to-day jury selection by holding that state prosecutors may not discriminate on the basis of race when exercising individual peremptory challenges. Nonetheless, the Court in *Allen* declined to retroactively apply *Batson*.

The Court's decisions in *Duncan*, *Crawford*, and *Batson* were momentous and consequential. All three decisions fundamentally reshaped criminal procedure throughout the United States and significantly expanded the constitutional rights of criminal defendants. One involved the jury-trial right, one involved the original meaning of the Sixth Amendment's Confrontation Clause, and one involved racial discrimination in jury selection. Yet the Court did not apply any of those decisions retroactively on federal collateral review. *Ramos* is likewise momentous and consequential. But we see no good rationale for treating *Ramos* differently from *Duncan*, *Crawford*, and *Batson*. Consistent with the Court's long line of retroactivity precedents, we hold that the *Ramos* jury-unanimity rule does not apply retroactively on federal collateral review.[6]

---

6. The *Ramos* rule does not apply retroactively on *federal* collateral review. States remain free, if they choose, to retroactively apply the jury-unanimity rule as a matter of state law in state post-conviction proceedings. *See Danforth v. Minnesota* (2008).

In so concluding, we recognize that the Court's many retroactivity precedents taken together raise a legitimate question: If landmark and historic criminal procedure decisions—including *Mapp, Miranda, Duncan, Crawford, Batson,* and now *Ramos*—do not apply retroactively on federal collateral review, how can any additional new rules of criminal procedure apply retroactively on federal collateral review? At this point, some 32 years after *Teague,* we think the only candid answer is that none can—that is, no new rules of criminal procedure can satisfy the watershed exception. We cannot responsibly continue to suggest otherwise to litigants and courts.

Continuing to articulate a theoretical exception that never actually applies in practice offers false hope to defendants, distorts the law, misleads judges, and wastes the resources of defense counsel, prosecutors, and courts. Moreover, no one can reasonably rely on an exception that is non-existent in practice, so no reliance interests can be affected by forthrightly acknowledging reality. It is time—probably long past time—to make explicit what has become increasingly apparent to bench and bar over the last 32 years: New procedural rules do not apply retroactively on federal collateral review. The watershed exception is moribund. It must "be regarded as retaining no vitality." *Herrera v. Wyoming* (2019).

Ramos announced a new rule of criminal procedure. It does not apply retroactively on federal collateral review. We affirm the judgment of the U.S. Court of Appeals for the Fifth Circuit.

It is so ordered.

[Justice THOMAS, joined by Justice GORSUCH, concurred separately, emphasizing that the Court could have resolved the case under §2254(d), which states that a state decision cannot be overturned on federal habeas unless the state court's decision "was contrary to, or involved an unreasonable application of, clearly established Federal law, as determined by the Supreme Court." Since *Apodaca* was the governing rule when petitioner's conviction became final, it is irrelevant that the Court later decided *Ramos.*]

[Justice GORSUCH's concurring opinion, joined by Justice THOMAS, is omitted.]

Justice KAGAN, with whom Justice BREYER and Justice SOTOMAYOR join, dissenting.

"A verdict, taken from eleven, [i]s no verdict at all," this Court proclaimed just last Term. *Ramos v. Louisiana* (2020). Citing centuries of history, the Court in *Ramos* termed the Sixth Amendment right to a unanimous jury "vital," "essential," "indispensable," and "fundamental" to the American legal system. The Court therefore saw fit to disregard *stare decisis* and overturn a 50-year-old precedent enabling States to convict criminal defendants based on non-unanimous verdicts. And in taking that weighty step, the Court also vindicated core principles of racial justice. For in the Court's view, the state laws countenancing non-unanimous verdicts originated in white supremacism and continued in our own time to have racially discriminatory effects. Put all that together, and it is easy to see why the opinions in *Ramos* read as historic. Rarely does this Court make such a fundamental change in the rules thought necessary to ensure fair criminal process. If you were scanning a thesaurus for a single word to describe the decision, you would stop when you came to "watershed."

Yet the Court insists that *Ramos*'s holding does not count as a "watershed" procedural rule under *Teague*. The result of today's ruling is easily stated. *Ramos* will not apply retroactively, meaning that a prisoner whose appeals ran out before the decision can receive no aid from the change in law it made. So Thedrick Edwards, unlike Evangelisto Ramos, will serve the rest of his life in prison based on a 10-to-2 jury verdict. Only the reasoning of today's holding resists explanation. The majority cannot (and indeed does not) deny, given all *Ramos* said, that the jury unanimity requirement fits to a tee *Teague*'s description of a watershed procedural rule. Nor can the majority explain its result by relying on precedent. Although flaunting decisions since *Teague* that held rules non-retroactive, the majority comes up with none comparable to this case. Search high and low the settled law of retroactivity, and the majority still has no reason to deny *Ramos* watershed status.

So everything rests on the majority's last move — the overturning of *Teague*'s watershed exception. If there can never be *any* watershed rules — as the majority here asserts out of the blue — then, yes, jury unanimity cannot be one. The result follows trippingly from the premise. But adopting the premise requires departing from judicial practice and principle. In overruling a critical aspect of *Teague*, the majority follows none of the usual rules of *stare decisis*. It discards precedent without a party requesting that action. And it does so with barely a reason given, much less the "special justification" our law demands. *Halliburton Co. v. Erica P. John Fund, Inc.* (2014). The majority in that way compounds its initial error: Not content to misapply *Teague*'s watershed provision here, the majority forecloses any future application. It prevents any procedural rule ever — no matter how integral to adjudicative fairness — from benefiting a defendant on habeas review. Thus does a settled principle of retroactivity law die, in an effort to support an insupportable ruling.

If, as today's majority says, *Teague* is full of "adjectives," so too is *Ramos*—and mostly the same ones. Jury unanimity, the Court pronounced, is an "essential element[]" of the jury trial right, and thus is "fundamental to the American scheme of justice." The Court discussed the rule's "ancient" history—"400 years of English and American cases requiring unanimity" leading up to the Sixth Amendment. As early as the 14th century, English common law recognized jury unanimity as a "vital right." Adopting that view, the early American States likewise treated unanimity as an "essential feature of the jury trial." So by the time the Framers drafted the Sixth Amendment, "the right to a jury trial *meant* a trial in which the jury renders a unanimous verdict." Because that was so, no jury verdict could stand (or in some metaphysical sense, even exist) absent full agreement: "A verdict, taken from eleven, was no verdict at all." Unanimity served as a critical safeguard, needed to protect against wrongful deprivations of citizens' "hard-won liberty." Or as Justice Story summarized the law a few decades after the Founding: To obtain a conviction, "unanimity in the verdict of the jury is indispensable."

If a rule so understood isn't a watershed one, then nothing is. (And that is, of course, what the majority eventually says.) No wonder today's majority declares a new-found aversion to "adjectives." The unanimity rule, as *Ramos* described it, is as "bedrock" as bedrock comes. *Teague*. It is as grounded in the Nation's constitutional traditions—with centuries-old practice becoming part of the Sixth Amendment's original meaning. And it is as central to the Nation's idea of a fair and reliable guilty verdict. When can the State punish a defendant for committing a crime? Return again to *Ramos*, this time going back to Blackstone: Only when "the truth of [an] accusation" is "confirmed by the unanimous suffrage" of a jury "of his equals and neighbours." *Ramos* (quoting 4 Commentaries on the Laws of England 343 (1769)). For only then is the jury's finding of guilt certain enough—secure enough, mistake-proof enough—to take away the person's freedom.

Twice before, this Court retroactively applied rules that are similarly integral to jury verdicts. First, in *Ivan V. v. City of New York* (1972), we gave "complete retroactive effect" to the rule of *In re Winship* (1970), that a jury must find guilt "beyond a reasonable doubt." Like *Ramos*, *Winship* rested on an "ancient" legal tradition incorporated into the Constitution. As in *Ramos*, that tradition served to "safeguard men" from "unjust convictions, with resulting forfeitures" of freedom. *Winship*. And as in *Ramos*, that protection plays a "vital" part in "the American scheme of criminal procedure." With all that established, the *Ivan V.* Court needed just two pages to hold *Winship* retroactive, highlighting the reasonable-doubt standard's "indispensable" role in "reducing the risk" of wrongful convictions. Second, in *Brown v. Louisiana* (1980), we retroactively applied the rule of *Burch v. Louisiana* (1979), that a six-person guilty verdict must be unanimous. Think about that for a moment: We held retroactive a unanimity requirement, no different from the one here save that it applied to a smaller jury. The reasoning should by now sound familiar. Allowing conviction by a non-unanimous jury "impair[s]" the "purpose and functioning of the jury," undermining the Sixth Amendment's very "essence." *Brown*. It "raises serious doubts about the fairness of [a] trial." And it fails to "assure the reliability of [a guilty] verdict." So when a jury has divided, as when it has failed to apply the reasonable-doubt standard, "there has been no jury verdict within the meaning of the Sixth Amendment." *Sullivan v. Louisiana* (1993).[4]

And something still more supports retroactivity here, for the opinions in *Ramos* (unlike in *Winship* or *Burch*) relied on a strong claim about racial injustice. The Court detailed the origins of Louisiana's and Oregon's non-unanimity rules, locating them (respectively) in a convention to "establish the supremacy of the white race" and "the rise of the Ku Klux Klan." Those rules, the Court explained, were meant

---

4. The majority argues that *Ivan V.* and *Brown* applied these new rules only to cases on direct appeal. But that isn't right. Although *Ivan V.* itself involved a direct appeal, the Court has made clear that the "complete retroactive effect" *Ivan V.* gave *Winship* included cases in habeas. *See, e.g., United States v. Johnson*, (1982). And similarly, lower courts uniformly understood *Brown* to govern habeas cases, even though a concurring opinion (which supplied the ruling's fifth and sixth votes) addressed only cases on direct appeal. Those applications to habeas cases make sense because the Court of that time did not often distinguish in its retroactivity rulings between direct and collateral review. For that reason, the majority must fall back on the argument that "*Brown* and *Ivan V.* were pre-*Teague* decisions" and "*Teague* tightened the previous standard" for retroactivity. That is true enough, but irrelevant here given *Brown* and *Ivan V*'s reasoning. As just noted, each of those decisions said everything a court would say today in designating a new rule "watershed"—in essence, that the rule is central to the process of fairly deciding on a defendant's guilt.

"to dilute the influence [on juries] of racial, ethnic, and religious minorities" — and particularly, "to ensure that African-American juror service would be meaningless." Two concurring opinions linked that history to current practice. "In light of the[ir] racist origins," Justice Kavanaugh stated, "it is no surprise that non-unanimous juries can make a difference" — that "[t]hen and now" they can "negate the votes of black jurors, especially in cases with black defendants." But that statement precludes today's result. If the old rule functioned "as an engine of discrimination against black defendants," *id.* (Kavanaugh, J.), its replacement must "implicat[e]" (as watershed rules do) "the fundamental fairness and accuracy of the criminal proceeding," *Beard.* Or as Justice Kavanaugh put the point more concretely, the unanimity rule then helps prevent "racial prejudice" from resulting in wrongful convictions. The rule should therefore apply not just forward but back, to all convictions rendered absent its protection.

The majority argues in reply that the jury unanimity rule is not so fundamental because. . . . Well, no, scratch that. Actually, the majority doesn't contest anything I've said about the foundations and functions of the unanimity requirement. Nor could the majority reasonably do so. For everything I've said about the unanimity rule comes straight out of *Ramos*'s majority and concurring opinions. Just check the citations: I've added barely a word to what those opinions (often with soaring rhetoric) proclaim. Start with history. The ancient foundations of the unanimous jury rule? Check. The inclusion of that rule in the Sixth Amendment's original meaning? Check. Now go to function. The fundamental (or bedrock or central) role of the unanimous jury in the American system of criminal justice? Check. The way unanimity figures in ensuring fairness in criminal trials and protecting against wrongful guilty verdicts? Check. The link between those purposes and safeguarding the jury system from (past and present) racial prejudice? Check. In sum: As to every feature of the unanimity rule conceivably relevant to watershed status, *Ramos* has already given the answer — check, check, check — and today's majority can say nothing to the contrary.

Instead, the majority relies on decisions holding non-retroactive various other — even though dissimilar — procedural rules. In making that argument from past practice, the majority adopts two discrete tactics. Call the first "throw everything against the wall." Call the second "slice and dice." Neither can avail to render the jury unanimity rule anything less than what *Ramos* thought it — as the majority concedes, "momentous."

As its first move, the majority lists as many decisions holding rules non-retroactive as it can muster. The premise here is that sheer volume matters: The majority presents the catalog as if every rule is as important as every other and as if comparing any to the unanimity requirement is beside the point. But that idea founders on this Court's constant refrain that watershed rules are only a small subset of procedural rules.

Enter the majority's second stratagem, which tries to conquer by dividing. Here, the majority picks out "three aspects of *Ramos*" pointing toward watershed status, and names one prior decision to match each of the three. So in addressing the unanimity rule's "significance," the majority notes that the Court once held the jury-trial right non-retroactive. [*DeStephano* and *Duncan*]. In tackling *Ramos*'s return to "original meaning," the majority points to our decision that an originalist rule about hearsay evidence should not apply backward [in *Whorton* and *Crawford*]. And in discussing *Ramos*'s role in "prevent[ing] racial discrimination," the majority invokes our denial of retroactivity to a rule making it easier to prove race-based peremptory strikes. [*Allen* and *Batson*].

What the majority doesn't find—or even pretend to—is any decision corresponding to *Ramos* on all of those dimensions. . . .

I would not discard *Teague*'s watershed exception and so keep those unfairly convicted people from getting new trials. Instead, I would accept the consequences of last Term's holding in *Ramos*. A decision like that comes with a promise, or at any rate should. If the right to a unanimous jury is so fundamental—if a verdict rendered by a divided jury is "no verdict at all"—then Thedrick Edwards should not spend his life behind bars over two jurors' opposition. I respectfully dissent.

* * *

The evidence in *Ramos* was overwhelming that both Louisiana's and Oregon's non-unanimity rule was motivated by White supremacy and designed to nullify the voices of non-White jurors. The majority opinion recounted direct evidence of discriminatory motive:

> Louisiana first endorsed nonunanimous verdicts for serious crimes at a constitutional convention in 1898. According to one committee chairman, the avowed purpose of that convention was to "establish the supremacy of the white race," and the resulting document included many of the trappings of the Jim Crow era: a poll tax, a combined literacy and property ownership test, and a grandfather clause that in practice exempted white residents from the most onerous of these requirements. Nor was it only the prospect of African-Americans voting that concerned the delegates. Just a week before the convention, the U.S. Senate passed a resolution calling for an investigation into whether Louisiana was systemically excluding African-Americans from juries. Seeking to avoid unwanted national attention, and aware that this Court would strike down any policy of overt discrimination against African-American jurors as a violation of the Fourteenth Amendment, the delegates sought to undermine African-American participation on juries in another way. With a careful eye on racial demographics, the convention delegates sculpted a "facially race-neutral" rule permitting 10-to-2 verdicts in order "to ensure that African-American juror service would be meaningless." Adopted in the 1930s, Oregon's rule permitting nonunanimous verdicts can be similarly traced to the rise of the Ku Klux Klan and efforts to dilute "the influence of racial, ethnic, and religious minorities on Oregon juries."

Ramos. One of the sharpest clashes between the majority and the dissent in *Edwards* is over how this evidence, which both concede, bears on the retroactivity of *Ramos*. The majority relies on the non-retroactivity of *Batson*, a case that also involved a procedural rule (for jury selection) subject to racially discriminatory use; the dissent contends that it is unconscionable not to give retroactive application to a rule that corrects for possible racial bias in state convictions.

A second clash is over how the grounding of a new rule in history bears on retroactivity analysis. For the majority, the historical pedigree of the unanimity rule is not relevant to retroactivity. For the dissent, the stronger the historical pedigree, the more likely a new rule meets the threshold for treatment as a "watershed" rule.

Whatever one makes of these debates, if *Edwards* is correct that there are no new "watershed" rules, the second exception to *Teague* is gone. That means the only potentially retroactive new rules are those which meet the first exception.

(ii)   Retroactivity Rules for State Courts

A final question is how *Teague* bears upon state retroactivity doctrine. In *Danforth v. Minnesota* (2008), the Court held that *Teague*'s general principle of non-retroactivity interprets §2254 and therefore does not bind state courts when they make their own decisions in state habeas litigation about whether to give retroactive application to a new constitutional rule. The Minnesota courts followed a standard of retroactivity *more generous* than *Teague*'s and the Supreme Court upheld their discretion to do so. That left open the question whether a state court could exercise its discretion to adopt a non-retroactivity principle *even more strict* than *Teague*'s and deny relief to a petitioner who would be entitled to a *Teague* exception — especially *Teague*'s first exception which deprives the state of the power to punish. A related question was whether the Supreme Court, or any federal court, would have jurisdiction over a case challenging a state's non-retroactivity doctrine. If *Teague* is not constitutionally required, as most assumed after *Danforth*, then state's were presumably free to reject *Teague*'s exceptions.

The Court took up these questions in the context of a series of cases involving harsh sentences for juvenile offenders. In the late twentieth century, "[a]t least 45 states passed laws making it easier for youth to be tried and sentenced as adults, including sentences of life without parole. The emphasis on deterrence, incapacitation, and punishment" over rehabilitation and alternative programing "resulted in the confinement of more youth in adult jails and prisons. From 1990 to 1999, there was a 10-fold increase in the number of juvenile life without parole sentences. . . . In the context of evolving standards of decency and neuroscience research" showing among other things that children's frontal lobes do not fully develop until they reach mid-twenties, "the Court concluded that "'children are different' and deserve special protection under the Eighth Amendment."[75] *Roper v. Simmons* (2005) held that it violates the Eighth Amendment prohibition on cruel and unusual punishment to impose the death penalty on defendants whose crimes were committed as juveniles. *Graham v. Florida* (2010) held that sentences of life without parole for juveniles who committed crimes other than murder also violated the Eighth Amendment. *Miller v. Alabama* (2012) further extended the principles of *Roper* and held that a mandatory sentence of life without parole violates the Eighth Amendment for

---

75. Peter J. Benekos & Alida V. Merlo, *A Decade of Change: Roper v. Simmons, Defending Childhood, and Juvenile Justice Policy*, 30 Crim. J. Pol'y. Rev. 102, 103-04 (2016).

juveniles convicted of homicide. The retroactivity of *Miller* came before the Court in the next case.

Montgomery v. Louisiana

577 U.S. _ (2016)

Justice KENNEDY delivered the opinion of the Court.

In the wake of *Miller* [*v. Alabama* (2012) (holding that a juvenile convicted of a homicide offense cannot be sentenced to life without parole absent consideration of whether the crime reflects the "transient immaturity of youth")], the question has arisen whether its holding is retroactive to juvenile offenders whose convictions and sentences were final when *Miller* was decided. Certiorari was granted in this case to resolve the question.

I

Petitioner is Henry Montgomery. In 1963, Montgomery killed Charles Hurt, a deputy sheriff in East Baton Rouge, Louisiana. Montgomery was 17 years old at the time of the crime. He was convicted of murder and sentenced to death, but the Louisiana Supreme Court reversed his conviction after finding that public prejudice had prevented a fair trial.

Montgomery was retried. The jury returned a verdict of "guilty without capital punishment." Under Louisiana law, this verdict required the trial court to impose a sentence of life without parole. The sentence was automatic upon the jury's verdict, so Montgomery had no opportunity to present mitigation evidence to justify a less severe sentence. That evidence might have included Montgomery's young age at the time of the crime; expert testimony regarding his limited capacity for foresight, self-discipline, and judgment; and his potential for rehabilitation. Montgomery, now 69 years old, has spent almost his entire life in prison. Almost 50 years after Montgomery was first taken into custody, this Court decided [in] *Miller v. Alabama* . . . that . . . "[b]y making youth (and all that accompanies it) irrelevant to imposition of that harshest prison sentence," mandatory life without parole "poses too great a risk of disproportionate punishment." *Miller* required that sentencing courts consider a child's "diminished culpability and heightened capacity for change" before condemning him or her to die in prison. Although *Miller* did not foreclose a sentencer's ability to impose life without parole on a juvenile, the Court explained that a lifetime in prison is a disproportionate sentence for all but the rarest of children, those whose crimes reflect "'irreparable corruption.'" *Ibid.* (quoting *Roper v. Simmons* (2005)).

After this Court issued its decision in *Miller*, Montgomery sought collateral review of his mandatory life-without-parole sentence. As a general matter, it appears that prisoners must raise Eighth Amendment sentencing challenges on direct review.

Louisiana's collateral review courts will, however, consider a motion to correct an illegal sentence based on a decision of this Court holding that the Eighth Amendment to the Federal Constitution prohibits a punishment for a type of crime or a class of offenders. When, for example, this Court held in *Graham v. Florida*

(2010), that the Eighth Amendment bars life-without-parole sentences for juvenile nonhomicide offenders, Louisiana courts heard *Graham* claims brought by prisoners whose sentences had long been final. Montgomery's motion argued that *Miller* rendered his mandatory life-without-parole sentence illegal.

The trial court denied Montgomery's motion on the ground that *Miller* is not retroactive on collateral review. Montgomery then filed an application for a supervisory writ. The Louisiana Supreme Court denied the application. The court relied on its earlier decision . . . which held that Miller does not have retroactive effect in cases on state collateral review.

This Court granted Montgomery's petition for certiorari. The petition presented the question "whether *Miller* adopts a new substantive rule that applies retroactively on collateral review to people condemned as juveniles to die in prison." In addition, the Court directed the parties to address the following question: "Do we have jurisdiction to decide whether the Supreme Court of Louisiana correctly refused to give retroactive effect in this case to our decision in *Miller*?"

II

The parties agree that the Court has jurisdiction to decide this case. . . . *Amicus* [appointed to brief the jurisdictional question] argues that a State is under no obligation to give a new rule of constitutional law retroactive effect in its own collateral review proceedings. As those proceedings are created by state law and under the State's plenary control, *amicus* contends, it is for state courts to define applicable principles of retroactivity. Under this view, the Louisiana Supreme Court's decision does not implicate a federal right; it only determines the scope of relief available in a particular type of state proceeding—a question of state law beyond this Court's power to review.

If, however, the Constitution establishes a rule and requires that the rule have retroactive application, then a state court's refusal to give the rule retroactive effect is reviewable by this Court. *Cf. Griffith v. Kentucky* (holding that on direct review, a new constitutional rule must be applied retroactively "to all cases, state or federal"). States may not disregard a controlling, constitutional command in their own courts. *See Martin v. Hunter's Lessee* (1816); *see also Yates v. Aiken* (1988) (when a State has not "placed any limit on the issues that it will entertain in collateral proceedings . . . it has a duty to grant the relief that federal law requires"). *Amicus'* argument therefore hinges on the premise that this Court's retroactivity precedents are not a constitutional mandate.

Justice O'Connor's plurality opinion in *Teague v. Lane* (1989), set forth a framework for retroactivity in cases on federal collateral review. Under *Teague*, a new constitutional rule of criminal procedure does not apply, as a general matter, to convictions that were final when the new rule was announced. *Teague* recognized, however, two categories of rules that are not subject to its general retroactivity bar [substantive rules and 'watershed' procedural rules].

It is undisputed, then, that *Teague* requires the retroactive application of new substantive and watershed procedural rules in federal habeas proceedings. . . . Neither *Teague* nor *Danforth* [*v. Minnessota* (2008) in which a majority of the Court held that *Teague* does not preclude state courts from giving retroactive effect to a *broader* set of new constitutional rules than *Teague* itself required] had reason to address whether States are required as a constitutional matter to give retroactive effect to new substantive or watershed procedural rules. *Teague* originated in a federal, not state, habeas proceeding; so it had no particular reason to discuss whether any part of its holding was required by the Constitution in addition to the federal habeas statute. And *Danforth* held only that *Teague's* general rule of nonretroactivity was an interpretation of the federal habeas statute and does not prevent States from providing *greater* relief in their own collateral review courts. The *Danforth* majority limited its analysis to *Teague's* general retroactivity bar, leaving open the question whether *Teague's* two exceptions are binding on the States as a matter of constitutional law. *Id.* ("[T]he case before us now does not involve either of the '*Teague* exceptions'").

In this case, the Court must address part of the question left open in *Danforth*. The Court now holds that when a new substantive rule of constitutional law controls the outcome of a case, the Constitution requires state collateral review courts to give retroactive effect to that rule. *Teague's* conclusion establishing the retroactivity of new substantive rules is best understood as resting upon constitutional premises. That constitutional command is, like all federal law, binding on state courts. This holding is limited to *Teague's* first exception for substantive rules; the constitutional status of *Teague's* exception for watershed rules of procedure need not be addressed here.

This Court's precedents addressing the nature of substantive rules, their differences from procedural rules, and their history of retroactive application establish that the Constitution requires substantive rules to have retroactive effect regardless of when a conviction became final.

The category of substantive rules discussed in *Teague* originated in Justice Harlan's approach to retroactivity. *Teague* adopted that reasoning. Justice Harlan defined substantive constitutional rules as "those that place, as a matter of constitutional interpretation, certain kinds of primary, private individual conduct beyond the power of the criminal law-making authority to proscribe." *Mackey v. United States* (1971). In *Penry v. Lynaugh* (1989), decided four months after *Teague*, the Court recognized that "the first exception set forth in *Teague* should be understood to cover not only rules forbidding criminal punishment of certain primary conduct but also rules prohibiting a certain category of punishment for a class of defendants because of their status or offense." *Penry* explained that Justice Harlan's first exception spoke "in terms of substantive categorical guarantees accorded by the Constitution, regardless of the procedures followed." Whether a new rule bars States from proscribing certain conduct or from inflicting a certain punishment, "[i]n both cases, the Constitution itself deprives the State of the power to impose a certain penalty."

Substantive rules, then, set forth categorical constitutional guarantees that place certain criminal laws and punishments altogether beyond the State's power to impose. It follows that when a State enforces a proscription or penalty barred by the Constitution, the resulting conviction or sentence is, by definition, unlawful. Procedural rules, in contrast, are designed to enhance the accuracy of a conviction or sentence by regulating "the *manner of determining* the defendant's culpability." *Schriro v. Summerlin* (2004). Those rules "merely raise the possibility that someone convicted with use of the invalidated procedure might have been acquitted otherwise." Even where procedural error has infected a trial, the resulting conviction or sentence may still be accurate; and, by extension, the defendant's continued confinement may still be lawful. For this reason, a trial conducted under a procedure found to be unconstitutional in a later case does not, as a general matter, have the automatic consequence of invalidating a defendant's conviction or sentence.

The same possibility of a valid result does not exist where a substantive rule has eliminated a State's power to proscribe the defendant's conduct or impose a given punishment. "[E]ven the use of impeccable factfinding procedures could not legitimate a verdict" where "the conduct being penalized is constitutionally immune from punishment." *United States v. United States Coin & Currency* (1971). Nor could the use of flawless sentencing procedures legitimate a punishment where the Constitution immunizes the defendant from the sentence imposed. "No circumstances call more for the invocation of a rule of complete retroactivity."

By holding that new substantive rules are, indeed, retroactive, *Teague* continued a long tradition of giving retroactive effect to constitutional rights that go beyond procedural guarantees. *See Mackey* (opinion of Harlan, J.) ("[T]he writ has historically been available for attacking convictions on [substantive] grounds"). Even in the pre-1953 era of restricted federal habeas . . . an exception was made "when the habeas petitioner attacked the constitutionality of the state statute under which he had been convicted. Since, in this situation, the State had no power to proscribe the conduct for which the petitioner was imprisoned, it could not constitutionally insist that he remain in jail." *Desist v. United States* (1969) (Harlan, J., dissenting).

In *Ex parte Siebold* (1880), the Court addressed why substantive rules must have retroactive effect regardless of when the defendant's conviction became final. At the time of that decision, "[m]ere error in the judgment or proceedings, under and by virtue of which a party is imprisoned, constitute[d] no ground for the issue of the writ." Before *Siebold*, the law might have been thought to establish that so long as the conviction and sentence were imposed by a court of competent jurisdiction, no habeas relief could issue. In *Siebold*, however, the petitioners attacked the judgments on the ground that they had been convicted under unconstitutional statutes. The Court explained that if "this position is well taken, it affects the foundation of the whole proceedings." A conviction under an unconstitutional law

> is not merely erroneous, but is illegal and void, and cannot be a legal cause of imprisonment. It is true, if no writ of error lies, the judgment may be final, in the sense that there may be no means of reversing it. But . . . if the laws are unconstitutional and void, the Circuit Court acquired no jurisdiction of the causes.

It follows, as a general principle, that a court has no authority to leave in place a conviction or sentence that violates a substantive rule, regardless of whether the conviction or sentence became final before the rule was announced.

Siebold and the other cases discussed in this opinion, of course, do not directly control the question the Court now answers for the first time. These precedents did not involve a state court's postconviction review of a conviction or sentence and so did not address whether the Constitution requires new substantive rules to have retroactive effect in cases on state collateral review. These decisions, however, have important bearing on the analysis necessary in this case.

In support of its holding that a conviction obtained under an unconstitutional law warrants habeas relief, the *Siebold* Court explained that "[a]n unconstitutional law is void, and is as no law." A penalty imposed pursuant to an unconstitutional law is no less void because the prisoner's sentence became final before the law was held unconstitutional. There is no grandfather clause that permits States to enforce punishments the Constitution forbids. To conclude otherwise would undercut the Constitution's substantive guarantees. Writing for the Court in *United States Coin & Currency*, Justice Harlan made this point when he declared that "[n]o circumstances call more for the invocation of a rule of complete retroactivity" than when "the conduct being penalized is constitutionally immune from punishment." *United States Coin & Currency* involved a case on direct review; yet, for the reasons explained in this opinion, the same principle should govern the application of substantive rules on collateral review. As Justice Harlan explained, where a State lacked the power to proscribe the habeas petitioner's conduct, "it could not constitutionally insist that he remain in jail." *Desist.*

If a State may not constitutionally insist that a prisoner remain in jail on federal habeas review, it may not constitutionally insist on the same result in its own postconviction proceedings. Under the Supremacy Clause of the Constitution, state collateral review courts have no greater power than federal habeas courts to mandate that a prisoner continue to suffer punishment barred by the Constitution. If a state collateral proceeding is open to a claim controlled by federal law, the state court "has a duty to grant the relief that federal law requires." *Yates.* Where state collateral review proceedings permit prisoners to challenge the lawfulness of their confinement, States cannot refuse to give retroactive effect to a substantive constitutional right that determines the outcome of that challenge.

As a final point, it must be noted that the retroactive application of substantive rules does not implicate a State's weighty interests in ensuring the finality of convictions and sentences. *Teague* warned against the intrusiveness of "*continually* forc[ing] the States to marshal resources in order to keep in prison defendants whose trials and appeals conformed to then-existing constitutional standards." This concern has no application in the realm of substantive rules, for no resources marshaled by a State could preserve a conviction or sentence that the Constitution deprives the State of power to impose. *See Mackey* (opinion of Harlan, J.) ("There is little societal interest in permitting the criminal process to rest at a point where it ought properly never to repose").

Montgomery alleges that *Miller* announced a substantive constitutional rule and that the Louisiana Supreme Court erred by failing to recognize its retroactive effect. This Court has jurisdiction to review that determination.

III

This leads to the question whether *Miller*'s prohibition on mandatory life without parole for juvenile offenders indeed did announce a new substantive rule that, under the Constitution, must be retroactive.

The "foundation stone" for *Miller*'s analysis was this Court's line of precedent holding certain punishments disproportionate when applied to juveniles. Those cases include *Graham v. Florida*, which held that the Eighth Amendment bars life without parole for juvenile nonhomicide offenders, and *Roper v. Simmons*, which held that the Eighth Amendment prohibits capital punishment for those under the age of 18 at the time of their crimes. Protection against disproportionate punishment is the central substantive guarantee of the Eighth Amendment and goes far beyond the manner of determining a defendant's sentence. *See Graham* ("The concept of proportionality is central to the Eighth Amendment").

Miller took as its starting premise the principle established in *Roper* and *Graham* that "children are constitutionally different from adults for purposes of sentencing." These differences result from children's "diminished culpability and greater prospects for reform," and are apparent in three primary ways:

> First, children have a "lack of maturity and an underdeveloped sense of responsibility," leading to recklessness, impulsivity, and heedless risk-taking. Second, children "are more vulnerable to negative influences and outside pressures," including from their family and peers; they have limited "control over their own environment" and lack the ability to extricate themselves from horrific, crime-producing settings. And third, a child's character is not as "well formed" as an adult's; his traits are "less fixed" and his actions less likely to be "evidence of irretrievable depravity."

As a corollary to a child's lesser culpability, *Miller* recognized that "the distinctive attributes of youth diminish the penological justifications" for imposing life without parole on juvenile offenders. Because retribution "relates to an offender's blameworthiness, the case for retribution is not as strong with a minor as with an adult." The deterrence rationale likewise does not suffice, since "the same characteristics that render juveniles less culpable than adults—their immaturity, recklessness, and impetuosity—make them less likely to consider potential punishment." The need for incapacitation is lessened, too, because ordinary adolescent development diminishes the likelihood that a juvenile offender "'forever will be a danger to society.'" Rehabilitation is not a satisfactory rationale, either. Rehabilitation cannot justify the sentence, as life without parole "forswears altogether the rehabilitative ideal."

These considerations underlay the Court's holding in *Miller* that mandatory life-without-parole sentences for children "pos[e] too great a risk of disproportionate punishment." *Miller* requires that before sentencing a juvenile to life without parole, the sentencing judge take into account "how children are different, and how those differences counsel against irrevocably sentencing them to a lifetime in prison." The Court recognized that a sentencer might encounter the rare juvenile offender who exhibits such irretrievable depravity that rehabilitation is impossible and life without parole is justified. But in light of "children's diminished culpability and heightened capacity for change," *Miller* made clear that "appropriate occasions for sentencing juveniles to this harshest possible penalty will be uncommon."

Miller, then, did more than require a sentencer to consider a juvenile offender's youth before imposing life without parole; it established that the penological justifications for life without parole collapse in light of "the distinctive attributes of youth." Even if a court considers a child's age before sentencing him or her to a lifetime in prison, that sentence still violates the Eighth Amendment for a child whose crime reflects "unfortunate yet transient immaturity." Because *Miller* determined that sentencing a child to life without parole is excessive for all but "'the rare juvenile offender whose crime reflects irreparable corruption,'" it rendered life without parole an unconstitutional penalty for "a class of defendants because of their status"—that is, juvenile offenders whose crimes reflect the transient immaturity of youth. *Penry*. As a result, *Miller* announced a substantive rule of constitutional law. Like other substantive rules, *Miller* is retroactive because it "necessarily carr[ies] a significant risk that a defendan"—here, the vast majority of juvenile offenders—"faces a punishment that the law cannot impose upon him." *Schriro*.

Louisiana nonetheless argues that *Miller* is procedural because it did not place any punishment beyond the State's power to impose; it instead required sentencing courts to take children's age into account before condemning them to die in prison. In support of this argument, Louisiana points to *Miller*'s statement that the decision "does not categorically bar a penalty for a class of offenders or type of crime—as, for example, we did in *Roper* or *Graham*. Instead, it mandates only that a sentencer follow a certain process—considering an offender's youth and attendant characteristics—before imposing a particular penalty." *Miller*, it is true, did not bar a punishment for all juvenile offenders, as the Court did in *Roper* or *Graham*. *Miller* did bar life without parole, however, for all but the rarest of juvenile offenders, those whose crimes reflect permanent incorrigibility. For that reason, *Miller* is no less substantive than are *Roper* and *Graham*. Before *Miller*, every juvenile convicted of a homicide offense could be sentenced to life without parole. After *Miller*, it will be the rare juvenile offender who can receive that same sentence. The only difference between *Roper* and *Graham*, on the one hand, and *Miller*, on the other hand, is that *Miller* drew a line between children whose crimes reflect transient immaturity and those rare children whose crimes reflect irreparable corruption. The fact that life without parole could be a proportionate sentence for the latter kind of juvenile offender does not mean that all other children imprisoned under a disproportionate sentence have not suffered the deprivation of a substantive right.

To be sure, *Miller*'s holding has a procedural component. *Miller* requires a sentencer to consider a juvenile offender's youth and attendant characteristics before determining that life without parole is a proportionate sentence. Louisiana contends that because *Miller* requires this process, it must have set forth a procedural rule. This argument, however, conflates a procedural requirement necessary to implement a substantive guarantee with a rule that "regulate[s] only the manner of determining the defendant's culpability." *Schriro*.

The conclusion that *Miller* states a substantive rule comports with the principles that informed *Teague*. *Teague* sought to balance the important goals of finality and comity with the liberty interests of those imprisoned pursuant to rules later deemed unconstitutional. *Miller*'s conclusion that the sentence of life without parole is disproportionate for the vast majority of juvenile offenders raises a grave risk that many are being held in violation of the Constitution.

Giving *Miller* retroactive effect, moreover, does not require States to relitigate sentences, let alone convictions, in every case where a juvenile offender received mandatory life without parole. A State may remedy a *Miller* violation by permitting juvenile homicide offenders to be considered for parole, rather than by resentencing them. . . .

Petitioner has discussed in his submissions to this Court his evolution from a troubled, misguided youth to a model member of the prison community. . . .

These claims have not been tested or even addressed by the State, so the Court does not confirm their accuracy. The petitioner's submissions are relevant, however, as an example of one kind of evidence that prisoners might use to demonstrate rehabilitation.

Henry Montgomery has spent each day of the past 46 years knowing he was condemned to die in prison. Perhaps it can be established that, due to exceptional circumstances, this fate was a just and proportionate punishment for the crime he committed as a 17-year-old boy. In light of what this Court has said in *Roper, Graham,* and *Miller* about how children are constitutionally different from adults in their level of culpability, however, prisoners like Montgomery must be given the opportunity to show their crime did not reflect irreparable corruption; and, if it did not, their hope for some years of life outside prison walls must be restored.

Justice SCALIA, with whom Justice THOMAS and Justice ALITO join, dissenting.

The Court has no jurisdiction to decide this case, and the decision it arrives at is wrong. I respectfully dissent.

I. Jurisdiction

Louisiana postconviction courts willingly entertain Eighth Amendment claims but, with limited exceptions, apply the law as it existed when the state prisoner was convicted and sentenced. Shortly after this Court announced *Teague v. Lane,* the Louisiana Supreme Court adopted *Teague's* framework to govern the provision of postconviction remedies available to *state* prisoners in its *state* courts as a matter of *state* law. In doing so, the court stated that it was "not bound" to adopt that federal framework. One would think, then, that it is none of our business that a 69-year-old Louisiana prisoner's state-law motion to be resentenced according to *Miller v. Alabama,* a case announced almost half a century after his sentence was final, was met with a firm rejection on state-law grounds by the Louisiana Supreme Court. But a majority of this Court, eager to reach the merits of this case, resolves the question of our jurisdiction by deciding that the Constitution *requires* state postconviction courts to adopt *Teague's* exception for so-called "substantive" new rules and to provide state-law remedies for the violations of those rules to prisoners whose sentences long ago became final. This conscription into federal service of state postconviction courts is nothing short of astonishing.

A

Neither *Teague* nor its exceptions are constitutionally compelled. Unlike today's majority, the *Teague*-era Court understood that cases on collateral review are fundamentally different from those pending on direct review because of "considerations of finality in the judicial process." *Shea v. Louisiana* (1985). That line of finality demarcating the constitutionally required rule in *Griffith* from the habeas rule in *Teague* supplies the answer to the not-so-difficult question whether a state postconviction court must remedy the violation of a new substantive rule: No. A state court need only apply the law as it existed at the time a defendant's conviction and sentence became final. . . . Any relief a prisoner might receive in a state court after finality is a matter of grace, not constitutional prescription.

B

The majority can marshal no case support for its contrary position. It creates a constitutional rule where none had been before.

Because of the Supremacy Clause, says the majority. But the Supremacy Clause cannot possibly answer the question before us here. It only elicits another question: What federal law is supreme? Old or new? The majority's champion, Justice Harlan, said the old rules apply for federal habeas review of a state-court conviction: "[T]he habeas court need only apply the constitutional standards that prevailed at the time the original proceedings took place," *Desist*, for a state court cannot "toe the constitutional mark" that does not yet exist, *Mackey* (opinion of Harlan, J.). Following his analysis, we have clarified time and again — recently in *Greene v. Fisher* (2011) — that *federal* habeas courts are to review state-court decisions against the law and factual record that existed at the time the decisions were made." Section 2254(d)(1) refers, in the past tense, to a state-court adjudication that "resulted in" a decision that was contrary to, or "involved" an unreasonable application of, established law. This backward-looking language requires an examination of the state-court decision at the time it was made." *Cullen v. Pinholster* (2011). How can it possibly be, then, that the Constitution requires a *state* court's review of its own convictions to be governed by "new rules" rather than (what suffices when federal courts review state courts) "old rules"?

The majority also misappropriates *Yates v. Aiken* (1988), which reviewed a state habeas petitioner's Fourteenth Amendment claim that the jury instructions at his trial lessened the State's burden to prove every element of his offense beyond a reasonable doubt. That case at least did involve a conviction that was final. But the majority is oblivious to the critical fact that Yates's claim depended upon an old rule, settled at the time of his trial.

The other sleight of hand performed by the majority is its emphasis on *Ex parte Siebold* (1880). That case considered a petition for a federal writ of habeas corpus following a federal conviction, and the initial issue it confronted was its jurisdiction. A federal court has no inherent habeas corpus power, *Ex parte Bollman* (1807), but only that which is conferred (and limited) by statute, *see, e.g., Felker v. Turpin* (1996). *Siebold* is thus a decision that expands the limits of this Court's power to issue a federal habeas writ for a federal prisoner.

No "general principle" can rationally be derived from *Siebold* about constitutionally required remedies in state courts; indeed, the opinion does not even speak to constitutionally required remedies in *federal* courts. It is a decision about this Court's statutory power to grant the Original Writ, not about its constitutional obligation to do so.

Until today, no federal court was constitutionally obliged to grant relief for the past violation of a newly announced substantive rule. Until today, it was Congress's prerogative to do away with *Teague*'s exceptions altogether. Indeed, we had left unresolved the question whether Congress had already done that when it amended a section of the habeas corpus statute to add backward-looking language governing the review of state-court decisions. *See* Antiterrorism and Effective Death Penalty Act of 1996, *codified at* 28 U.S.C. §2254(d)(1); *Greene v. Fischer* (2011). A maxim shown to be more relevant to this case, by the analysis that the majority omitted, is this: The Supremacy Clause does not impose upon state courts a constitutional obligation it fails to impose upon federal courts.

C

All that remains to support the majority's conclusion is that all-purpose Latin canon: *ipse dixit.* The majority opines that because a substantive rule eliminates a State's power to proscribe certain conduct or impose a certain punishment, it has "the automatic consequence of invalidating a defendant's conviction or sentence." What provision of the Constitution could conceivably produce such a result? The Due Process Clause? It surely cannot be a denial of due process for a court to pronounce a final judgment which, though fully in accord with federal constitutional law at the time, fails to anticipate a change to be made by this Court half a century into the future. The Equal Protection Clause? . . . No principle of equal protection requires the criminal law of all ages to be the same.

The majority grandly asserts that "[t]here is no grandfather clause that permits States to *enforce punishments the Constitution forbids.*" (emphasis added). Of course the italicized phrase begs the question. There most certainly is a grandfather clause—one we have called *finality*—which says that the Constitution does not require States to revise punishments that were lawful when they were imposed. . . . And the States are unquestionably entitled to take that view of things.

The majority's imposition of *Teague*'s first exception upon the States is all the worse because it . . . endorses the exception as expanded by *Penry*, to include "rules prohibiting a certain category of punishment for a class of defendants because of their status or offense." That expansion empowered and obligated federal (and after today state) habeas courts to invoke this Court's Eighth Amendment "evolving standards of decency" jurisprudence to upset punishments that were constitutional when imposed but are "cruel and unusual," U.S. Const., Amdt. 8, in our newly enlightened society. . . . [F]or the five decades Montgomery has spent in prison, not one of this Court's precedents called into question the legality of his sentence—until the People's "standards of decency," as perceived by five Justices, "evolved" yet again in *Miller.* . . .

Our ever-evolving Constitution changes the rules of "cruel and unusual punishments" every few years. . . . Today's holding not only forecloses Congress from eliminating this expansion of *Teague* in federal courts, but also foists this distortion upon the States.

II. The Retroactivity of *Miller*

Having created jurisdiction by ripping *Teague*'s first exception from its moorings, converting an equitable rule governing federal habeas relief to a constitutional command governing state courts as well, the majority proceeds to the merits. And here it confronts a second obstacle to its desired outcome. *Miller,* the opinion it wishes to impose upon state postconviction courts, simply does not decree what the first part of the majority's opinion says *Teague*'s first exception requires to be given retroactive effect: a rule "set[ting] forth *categorical* constitutional guarantees that place certain criminal laws and punishments *altogether* beyond the State's power to impose." No problem. Having distorted *Teague*, the majority simply proceeds to rewrite *Miller*.

The majority asserts that *Miller* "rendered life without parole an unconstitutional penalty for 'a class of defendants because of their status'—that is, juvenile offenders whose crimes reflect the transient immaturity of youth." . . . "For that reason, *Miller* is no less substantive than are *Roper* and *Graham*." The problem is that *Miller* stated, quite clearly, precisely the opposite: "Our decision does not categorically bar a penalty for a class of offenders or type of crime—as, for example, we did in *Roper* or *Graham*. Instead, it mandates only that a sentencer *follow a certain process*—considering an offender's youth and attendant characteristics—before imposing a particular penalty." (emphasis added).

It is plain as day that the majority is not applying *Miller*, but rewriting it. . . . How wonderful. Federal and (like it or not) state judges are henceforth to resolve the knotty "legal" question: whether a 17-year-old who murdered an innocent sheriff's deputy half a century ago was at the time of his trial "incorrigible."

But have no fear. The majority does not seriously expect state and federal collateral-review tribunals to engage in this silliness, probing the evidence of "incorrigibility" that existed decades ago when defendants were sentenced. What the majority expects (and intends) to happen is set forth in the following not-so-subtle invitation: "A State may remedy a *Miller* violation by permitting juvenile homicide offenders to be considered for parole, rather than by resentencing them." Of course. This whole exercise, this whole distortion of *Miller*, is just a devious way of eliminating life without parole for juvenile offenders. The Court might have done that expressly (as we know, the Court can decree *anything*), but that would have been something of an embarrassment. After all, one of the justifications the Court gave for decreeing an end to the death penalty for murders (no matter how many) committed by a juvenile was that life without parole was a severe enough punishment. *See Roper.* How could the majority—in an opinion written by the very author of *Roper*—now say *that* punishment is *also* unconstitutional? The Court expressly refused to say so in *Miller*. So the Court refuses again today, but merely makes imposition of that severe sanction a practical impossibility. And then, in Godfather fashion, the majority makes state legislatures an offer they can't refuse: Avoid all the utterly impossible nonsense we have prescribed by simply "permitting juvenile homicide offenders to be considered for parole." Mission accomplished.

Justice THOMAS, dissenting.

No provision of the Constitution supports the Court's [jurisdictional] holding. The Court invokes only the Supremacy Clause, asserting that the Clause deprives state and federal postconviction courts alike of power to leave an unconstitutional sentence in place. But that leaves the question of what provision of the Constitution supplies that underlying prohibition.

The Supremacy Clause does not do so. That Clause merely supplies a rule of decision: *If* a federal constitutional right exists, that right supersedes any contrary provisions of state law. *See* Art. VI, cl. 2 ("This Constitution, and the Laws of the United States which shall be made in Pursuance thereof . . . shall be the supreme Law of the Land; and the Judges in every State shall be bound thereby, any Thing in the Constitution or Laws of any State to the Contrary notwithstanding.")

Accordingly, as we reaffirmed just last Term, the Supremacy Clause is no independent font of substantive rights. *Armstrong v. Exceptional Child Center, Inc.* (2015).

The Court's new constitutional right also finds no basis in the history of state and federal postconviction proceedings. Throughout our history, postconviction relief for alleged constitutional defects in a conviction or sentence was available as a matter of legislative grace, not constitutional command.

There is one silver lining to today's ruling: States still have a way to mitigate its impact on their court systems. As the Court explains, States must enforce a constitutional right to remedies on collateral review only if such proceedings are "open to a claim controlled by federal law." State courts, on collateral review, thus must provide remedies for claims under *Miller v. Alabama* (2012), only if those courts are open to "claims that a decision of this Court has rendered certain sentences illegal . . . under the Eighth Amendment."

* * *

The majority's conclusion that the state must give retroactive effect to *Miller* in state habeas proceedings is grounded in the Supremacy Clause and is reminiscent of *Testa* and *Haywood* even though the Court makes no reference to these cases. Note that Montgomery sought certiorari in the Supreme Court from the Louisiana courts' denial of his state habeas petition. Could Montgomery have filed a §2254 petition in the lower federal courts instead? The answer turns on whether §2254 incorporates *Teague*'s exceptions. On its face, nothing in the statute's standard of review provisions in §2254(d) indicates that federal courts have power to give retroactive effect to a substantive rule or a "watershed" procedural rule. The Court has not addressed the question directly, but as Justice Scalia indicates in his dissenting opinion, it has denied that AEDPA codified *Teague* and assumed Congress meant what it said when it required federal petitions to be adjudicated on the basis of the law as it stood when the conviction became final. Justice Scalia's dissenting opinion cites *Greene v. Fisher* (2011), which stated emphatically that:

> AEDPA did not codify *Teague*, and that "the AEDPA and *Teague* inquiries are distinct." *Horn v. Banks* (2002) (per curiam). The retroactivity rules that govern federal habeas review on the merits—which include *Teague*—are quite separate from the relitigation bar imposed by AEDPA; neither abrogates or qualifies the other. If §2254(d)(1) was, indeed, pegged to *Teague*, it would authorize relief when a state-court merits adjudication "resulted in a decision that *became* contrary to, or an unreasonable application of, clearly established Federal law, *before the conviction became final*." The statute says no such thing, and we see no reason why *Teague* should alter AEDPA's plain meaning.

The *Montgomery* majority appears to assume that *Teague*'s exceptions are not available in a §2254 petition as well. This background assumption supports the argument that state courts must give retroactive effect to a new substantive rule. If they don't, and AEDPA precludes retroactive application of new rules, then there would be no forum in which the absence of state power to punish a defendant (under the new rule) could be raised. This is the foundation of Justice Scalia's objection that the majority has imposed a mandate on state courts which does not exist in a federal habeas proceeding.

Lastly, note that the Court has assumed that *Teague* applies to collateral review of *federal* convictions. *See Chaidez v. U.S.* (2013); *U.S. v. Hopkins* (10th Cir. 2019) (*"Teague* provides guidance on (1) whether a Supreme Court decision recognized a new right and (2) whether the right is retroactively applicable on collateral review. We follow this guidance when evaluating timeliness under §2255(f)(3).").

c.   Congress Intervenes: AEDPA §2254(d)

Although the Court had already imposed a powerful limitation on federal habeas review of state convictions by making retroactivity analysis a "threshold" question that had to be addressed before the merits of a federal petitioner's claim and broadly defining "new law" in *Teague*, Congress further circumscribed federal habeas by amendments to the 1867 Act in AEDPA in 1996. We have already studied the procedural prerequisites Congress either tightened or added to existing court-developed rules such as exhaustion; a one-year statute of limitations; restrictions on second and successive petitions; and procedural default. But the most sweeping change was the adoption of a strict new standard of review that displaced the centuries old, adaptive common law standard we saw elaborated in *Brown v. Allen.* Section 2254(d) provides:

> An application for a writ of habeas corpus on behalf of a person in custody pursuant to the judgment of a State court shall not be granted with respect to any claim that was adjudicated on the merits in State court proceedings unless the adjudication of the claim—
>
> (1) resulted in a decision that was contrary to, or involved an unreasonable application of, clearly established Federal law, as determined by the Supreme Court of the United States; or
>
> (2) resulted in a decision that was based on an unreasonable determination of the facts in light of the evidence presented in the State court proceeding.

Notice that the language assumes the petitioner has properly exhausted federal claims before the state courts and has not procedurally defaulted—the standard of review applies *only* to claims "adjudicated on the merits in State court proceedings."

This language does not mean, however, that a federal petitioner can avoid the strict standard of review set out in §2254(d) by arguing that the state court, appropriately presented with the petitioner's federal claims, issued an opinion that gives scant, passing, or even no attention to those claims in the course of denying relief. The Court has held that even a so-called "post-card" denial (a one line post card opinion denying relief) shall be treated as an "adjudication on the merits" by the state court. In *Harrington v. Richter* (2011), a California prisoner convicted of murder and sentenced to life without parole challenged the conviction by filing a habeas petition directly in the California Supreme Court, arguing that his lawyer provided ineffective assistance of counsel by failing to present expert testimony on blood evidence. The court denied relief in a one sentence summary order that contained no statement of reasons.

In his federal petition, Richter argued that §2254(d)'s standard of review did not apply because the summary order failed to disclose an "adjudication on the merits" of his properly presented federal claims. The Supreme Court categorically rejected this argument, emphasizing that "[t]here is no text in the statute requiring a statement of reasons," and there are many reasons a state court might decline to state reasons, including a desire to "concentrate its resources on the cases where opinions are most needed," especially in a state like California where the highest court disposes of "more than 3,400 original habeas petitions" each year. Thus, "[w]hen a federal claim has been presented to a state court and the state court has denied relief, it may be presumed that the state court adjudicated the claim on the merits in the absence of any indication or state-law procedural principles to the contrary."

In *Richter*, there was only one state court decision. The Court has since held that when a state's final decision does not provide reasons for the denial of relief, the federal court should "'look through' the unexplained decision to the last related state-court decision that does provide a relevant rationale [and] presume that the unexplained decision adopted the same reasoning." *Wilson v. Sellers* (2018). The earlier decision then becomes the "adjudication on the merits" for purposes of §2254(d). *See also Johnson v. Williams* (2013) (*Richter* presumption applies to state decision that addresses some but not all of petitioners' federal claims because state courts do not "always separately address[] every single claim that is mentioned in a defendant's papers"; petitioners' reference to federal law may be disregarded by the state court as merely "fleeting" or "too insubstantial to merit discussion"; noting that the *Richter* presumption is not irrebuttable and that, for example, rejection of a federal claim "as a result of sheer inadvertence" is not an adjudication "on the merits"); *id.* (state court's attention to state claim is "so similar" to the federal Sixth Amendment claim that it is "unlikely [the state court] decided one while overlooking the other").

The net effect of *Richter* and subsequent precedents is that almost everything a state court says, including saying nothing at all, counts as an adjudication on the merits triggering §2254(d)'s strict standard of review. Together with more exacting procedural prerequisites the standard of review has stemmed the increase in habeas filings that began after *Brown v. Allen*. It also reduced the grant rate. In non-capital cases, the grant rate fell from 1 in every 100 cases prior to AEDPA, to 1 in every 284. The denial rate nearly tripled. In capital cases, the grant rate fell from 40 percent to 12.4 percent.[76]

Lurking behind the data on grant rates and inferences one might be inclined to draw about the merits of federal habeas petitions is the fact that most petitions challenging state convictions, in both capital and non-capital cases, rest on a claim of ineffective assistance of counsel.[77] The absence of competent trial counsel is compounded by lack of access to counsel in post-conviction proceedings in non-capital

---

76. NANCY J. KING ET AL., FINAL TECHNICAL REPORT: HABEAS LITIGATION IN UNITED STATES DISTRICT COURTS at 9-10.

77. *Id.* at 7 (81 percent of capital petitioners and over 50 percent of non-capital petitioners assert ineffective assistance of counsel claims).

cases and the absence of a right to competent post-conviction counsel even when a lawyer is provided. Recall as well that 93 percent of non-capital petitioners file *pro se*. As we turn to how the new standard of review has been interpreted and applied by the Court, the presence or absence of competent counsel before and after conviction is important to bear in mind.

Most litigation on the standard of review has concentrated on §2254(d)(1), which precludes relief unless the state adjudication "resulted in a decision that was contrary to, or involved an unreasonable application of, clearly established Federal law, as determined by the Supreme Court of the United States." There is no question that this standard of review is more exacting than the *de novo* standard for legal questions the Court endorsed in *Brown v. Allen*. It also plainly directs federal courts to focus on whether the state court's decision was consistent with clearly established law at the time the state court acted. The most difficult questions have been (a) what it means for a decision to be "contrary to" or an "unreasonable application of clearly established law, and (b) how clearly established the law must have been when the state court acted. The following case takes up these questions in the context of a challenge to the conduct of trial counsel in a capital case.

Terry Williams v. Taylor

529 U.S. 362 (2000)

Justice STEVENS announced the judgment of the Court and delivered the opinion of the Court with respect to Parts I, III, and IV [joined by Justices SOUTER, GINSBURG, BREYER, O'CONNOR, and KENNEDY], and a [plurality joined only by Justices SOUTER, GINSBURG, and BREYER] with respect to Parts II and V.

The questions presented are whether Terry Williams' constitutional right to the effective assistance of counsel as defined in *Strickland v. Washington* (1984), was violated, and whether the judgment of the Virginia Supreme Court refusing to set aside his death sentence "was contrary to, or involved an unreasonable application of, clearly established Federal law, as determined by the Supreme Court of the United States," within the meaning of 28 U.S.C. §2254(d)(1). We answer both questions affirmatively.

I

On November 3, 1985, Harris Stone was found dead in his residence on Henry Street in Danville, Virginia. Finding no indication of a struggle, local officials determined that the cause of death was blood alcohol poisoning, and the case was considered closed. Six months after Stone's death, Terry Williams, who was then incarcerated in the "I" unit of the city jail for an unrelated offense, wrote a letter to the police stating that he had killed "'that man down on Henry Street'" and also stating that he "'did it'" to that "'lady down on West Green Street'" and was "'very sorry.'" The letter was unsigned, but it closed with a reference to "I cell." The police readily identified Williams as its author, and, on April 25, 1986, they obtained several statements from him. In one Williams admitted that, after Stone refused to lend him "'a couple of dollars,'" he had killed Stone with a mattock and taken the money from his wallet. In September 1986, Williams was convicted of robbery and capital murder.

At Williams' sentencing hearing, the prosecution proved that Williams had been convicted of armed robbery in 1976 and burglary and grand larceny in 1982. The prosecution also introduced the written confessions that Williams had made in April. The prosecution described two auto thefts and two separate violent assaults on elderly victims perpetrated after the Stone murder. On December 4, 1985, Williams had started a fire outside one victim's residence before attacking and robbing him. On March 5, 1986, Williams had brutally assaulted an elderly woman on West Green Street, an incident he had mentioned in his letter to the police. That confession was particularly damaging because other evidence established that the woman was in a "vegetative state" and not expected to recover. Williams had also been convicted of arson for setting a fire in the jail while awaiting trial in this case. Two expert witnesses employed by the State testified that there was a "high probability" that Williams would pose a serious continuing threat to society.

The evidence offered by Williams' trial counsel at the sentencing hearing consisted of the testimony of Williams' mother, two neighbors, and a taped excerpt from a statement by a psychiatrist. One of the neighbors had not been previously interviewed by defense counsel, but was noticed by counsel in the audience during the proceedings and asked to testify on the spot. The three witnesses briefly described Williams as a "nice boy" and not a violent person. The recorded psychiatrist's testimony did little more than relate Williams' statement during an examination that in the course of one of his earlier robberies, he had removed the bullets from a gun so as not to injure anyone.

In his cross-examination of the prosecution witnesses, Williams' counsel repeatedly emphasized the fact that Williams had initiated the contact with the police that enabled them to solve the murder and to identify him as the perpetrator of the recent assaults, as well as the car thefts. In closing argument, Williams' counsel characterized Williams' confessional statements as "dumb," but asked the jury to give weight to the fact that he had "turned himself in, not on one crime but on four . . . that the [police otherwise] would not have solved." The weight of defense counsel's closing, however, was devoted to explaining that it was difficult to find a reason why the jury should spare Williams' life.[2]

The jury found a probability of future dangerousness and unanimously fixed Williams' punishment at death. The trial judge . . . imposed the death sentence. The Virginia Supreme Court affirmed the conviction and sentence [in 1987]. It rejected

---

2. In defense counsel's words: "I will admit too that it is very difficult to ask you to show mercy to a man who maybe has not shown much mercy himself. I doubt very seriously that he thought much about mercy when he was in Mr. Stone's bedroom that night with him. I doubt very seriously that he had mercy very highly on his mind when he was walking along West Green and the incident with Alberta Stroud. I doubt very seriously that he had mercy on his mind when he took two cars that didn't belong to him. Admittedly it is very difficult to get us and ask that you give this man mercy when he has shown so little of it himself. But I would ask that you would."

Williams' argument that when the trial judge imposed sentence, he failed to give mitigating weight to the fact that Williams had turned himself in.

State Habeas Corpus Proceedings

In 1988 Williams filed for state collateral relief in the Danville Circuit Court. The petition was subsequently amended, and the Circuit Court (the same judge who had presided over Williams' trial and sentencing) held an evidentiary hearing on Williams' claim that trial counsel had been ineffective. Based on the evidence adduced after two days of hearings, Judge Ingram found that Williams' conviction was valid, but that his trial attorneys had been ineffective during sentencing. Among the evidence reviewed that had not been presented at trial were documents prepared in connection with Williams' commitment when he was 11 years old that dramatically described mistreatment, abuse, and neglect during his early childhood, as well as testimony that he was "borderline mentally [disabled]," had suffered repeated head injuries, and might have mental impairments organic in origin. The habeas hearing also revealed that the same experts who had testified on the State's behalf at trial believed that Williams, if kept in a "structured environment," would not pose a future danger to society.

Counsel's performance thus "did not measure up to the standard required under the holding of *Strickland v. Washington,* and [if it had,] there is a reasonable probability that the result of the sentencing phase would have been different." Judge Ingram therefore recommended that Williams be granted a rehearing on the sentencing phase of his trial.

The Virginia Supreme Court disagreed with the trial judge's conclusion that Williams had suffered sufficient prejudice to warrant relief. . . . First, relying on our decision in *Lockhart v. Fretwell* (1993), the court held that it was wrong for the trial judge to rely "'on mere outcome determination'" when assessing prejudice. Second, it construed the trial judge's opinion as having "adopted a *per se* approach" that would establish prejudice whenever any mitigating evidence was omitted.

The court then . . . found that the excluded mitigating evidence which it characterized as merely indicating "that numerous people, mostly relatives, thought that defendant was nonviolent and could cope very well in a structured environment . . . barely would have altered the profile of this defendant that was presented to the jury." On this basis, the court concluded that there was no reasonable possibility that the omitted evidence would have affected the jury's sentencing recommendation, and that Williams had failed to demonstrate that his sentencing proceeding was fundamentally unfair.

Federal Habeas Corpus Proceedings

Having exhausted his state remedies, Williams sought a federal writ of habeas corpus. . . . [T]he federal trial judge agreed with the Virginia trial judge: The death sentence was constitutionally infirm. . . . He identified five categories of mitigating evidence that counsel had failed to introduce,"[4] and he rejected the argument that counsel's failure to conduct an adequate investigation had been a strategic decision to rely almost entirely on the fact that Williams had voluntarily confessed.

Turning to the prejudice issue, the judge determined that there was "'a reasonable probability that, but for counsel's unprofessional errors, the result of the proceeding would have been different.'" *Strickland.* He found that the Virginia Supreme Court had erroneously assumed that *Lockhart* had modified the *Strickland* standard for determining prejudice, and that it had made an important error of fact in discussing its finding of no prejudice. . . .

The Federal Court of Appeals reversed. It construed §2254(d)(1) as prohibiting the grant of habeas corpus relief unless the state court "'decided the question by interpreting or applying the relevant precedent in a manner that reasonable jurists would all agree is unreasonable.'" Applying that standard, it could not say that the Virginia Supreme Court's decision on the prejudice issue was an unreasonable application of the tests developed in either *Strickland* or *Lockhart.* It explained that the evidence that Williams presented a future danger to society was "simply overwhelming," it endorsed the Virginia Supreme Court's interpretation of *Lockhart,* and it characterized the state court's understanding of the facts in this case as "reasonable."

We granted certiorari and now reverse.

II*

In 1867, Congress enacted a statute providing that federal courts "shall have power to grant writs of habeas corpus in all cases where any person may be restrained of his or her liberty in violation of the constitution, or of any treaty or law of the United States. . . ." Over the years, the federal habeas corpus statute has been repeatedly amended, but the scope of that jurisdictional grant remains the same. It is, of course, well settled that . . . errors that undermine confidence in the fundamental fairness of the state adjudication certainly justify the issuance of the federal writ. The deprivation of the right to the effective assistance of counsel recognized in *Strickland* is such an error.

The warden here contends that federal habeas corpus relief is prohibited by the amendment to 28 U.S.C. §2254, enacted as a part of the Antiterrorism and Effective Death Penalty Act of 1996 (AEDPA).

---

4. "(i) Counsel did not introduce evidence of the Petitioner's background. . . . (ii) Counsel did not introduce evidence that Petitioner was abused by his father. (iii) Counsel did not introduce testimony from correctional officers who were willing to testify that defendant would not pose a danger while incarcerated. Nor did counsel offer prison commendations awarded to Williams for his help in breaking up a prison drug ring and for returning a guard's missing wallet. (iv) Several character witnesses were not called to testify. . . . [T]he testimony of Elliott, a respected CPA in the community, could have been quite important to the jury. . . . (v) Finally, counsel did not introduce evidence that Petitioner was borderline mentally [disabled], though he was found competent to stand trial."

* [Note that Section II of Stevens' opinion is not the opinion of the Court. Justice O'Connor's opinion is the opinion of the Court on the interpretation of §2254(d).]

We are convinced that [the Circuit Court's] interpretation of the amendment is incorrect. It would . . . wrongly require the federal courts, including this Court, to defer to state judges' interpretations of federal law. . . .

When federal judges exercise their federal question jurisdiction under the "judicial Power" of Article III of the Constitution, it is "emphatically the province and duty" of those judges to "say what the law is." *Marbury v. Madison* (1803). At the core of this power is the federal courts' independent responsibility—independent from its coequal branches in the Federal Government, and independent from the separate authority of the several States—to interpret federal law. A construction of AEDPA that would require the federal courts to cede this authority to the courts of the States would be inconsistent with the practice that federal judges have traditionally followed in discharging their duties under Article III of the Constitution. If Congress had intended to require such an important change in the exercise of our jurisdiction, we believe it would have spoken with much greater clarity than is found in the text of AEDPA.

In *Teague v. Lane* (1989), we held that the petitioner was not entitled to federal habeas relief because he was relying on a rule of federal law that had not been announced until after his state conviction became final. The antiretroactivity rule recognized in *Teague*, which prohibits reliance on "new rules," is the functional equivalent of a statutory provision commanding exclusive reliance on "clearly established law." Because there is no reason to believe that Congress intended to require federal courts to ask both whether a rule sought on habeas is "new" under *Teague* which remains the law-and also whether it is "clearly established" under AEDPA, it seems safe to assume that Congress had congruent concepts in mind. It is perfectly clear that AEDPA codifies *Teague* to the extent that *Teague* requires federal habeas courts to deny relief that is contingent upon a rule of law not clearly established at the time the state conviction became final.[12]

Teague's core principles are therefore relevant to our construction of this requirement. . . . To this, AEDPA has added, immediately following the "clearly established law" requirement, a clause limiting the area of relevant law to that "determined by the Supreme Court of the United States." 28 U.S.C. §2254(d)(1). If this Court has not broken sufficient legal ground to establish an asked-for constitutional principle, the lower federal courts cannot themselves establish such a principle with clarity sufficient to satisfy the AEDPA bar.

---

12. We are not persuaded by the argument that because Congress used the words "clearly established law" and not "new rule," it meant in this section to codify an aspect of the doctrine of executive qualified immunity rather than *Teague*'s antiretroactivity bar. The warden refers us specifically to §2244(b)(2)(A) and 28 U.S.C. §2254(e)(2), in which the statute does in so many words employ the "new rule" language familiar to *Teague* and its progeny. Congress thus knew precisely the words to use if it had wished to codify *Teague per se*. We think, quite the contrary, that the verbatim adoption of the *Teague* language in these other sections bolsters our impression that Congress had *Teague*—and not any unrelated area of our jurisprudence specifically in mind in amending the habeas statute. These provisions, seen together, make it impossible to conclude that Congress was not fully aware of, and interested in codifying into law, that aspect of this Court's habeas doctrine. We will not assume that in a single subsection of an amendment entirely devoted to the law of habeas corpus, Congress made the anomalous choice of reaching into the doctrinally distinct law of qualified immunity for a single phrase that just so happens to be the conceptual twin of a dominant principle in habeas law of which Congress was fully aware.

In the context of this case, we also note that, as our precedent interpreting *Teague* has demonstrated, rules of law may be sufficiently clear for habeas purposes even when they are expressed in terms of a generalized standard rather than as a bright-line rule.

The message that Congress intended to convey by using the phrases "contrary to" and "unreasonable application of" is not entirely clear. The prevailing view in the Circuits is that the former phrase requires *de novo* review of "pure" questions of law and the latter requires some sort of "reasonability" review of so-called mixed questions of law and fact.

We are not persuaded that the phrases define two mutually exclusive categories of questions. Most constitutional questions that arise in habeas corpus proceedings—and therefore most "decisions" to be made—require the federal judge to apply a rule of law to a set of facts, some of which may be disputed and some undisputed. For example, an erroneous conclusion that particular circumstances established the voluntariness of a confession, or that there exists a conflict of interest when one attorney represents multiple defendants, may well be described either as "contrary to" or as an "unreasonable application of" the governing rule of law.

The statutory text likewise does not obviously prescribe a specific, recognizable standard of review for dealing with either phrase. Significantly, it does not use any term, such as *"de novo"* or "plain error," that would easily identify a familiar standard of review. . . . We thus anticipate that there will be a variety of cases, like this one, in which both phrases may be implicated.

Even though we cannot conclude that the phrases establish "a body of rigid rules," they do express a "mood" that the Federal Judiciary must respect. *Universal Camera Corp. v. NLRB* (1951). In this respect, it seems clear that Congress intended federal judges to attend with the utmost care to state-court decisions, including all of the reasons supporting their decisions, before concluding that those proceedings were infected by constitutional error sufficiently serious to warrant the issuance of the writ. . . . AEDPA plainly sought to ensure a level of "deference to the determinations of state courts," provided those determinations did not conflict with federal law or apply federal law in an unreasonable way. H.R. Conf. Rep. No. 104-518, p. 111 (1996). Congress wished to curb delays, to prevent "retrials" on federal habeas, and to give effect to state convictions to the extent possible under law. . . .

On the other hand . . . [w]hatever "deference" Congress had in mind with respect to both phrases, it surely is not a requirement that federal courts actually defer to a state-court application of the federal law that is, in the independent judgment of the federal court, in error. As Judge Easterbrook noted with respect to the phrase "contrary to":

> "Section 2254(d) requires us to give state courts' opinions a respectful reading, and to listen carefully to their conclusions, but when the state court addresses a legal question, it is the law 'as determined by the Supreme Court of the United States' that prevails." *Lindh v. Murphy* (7th Cir. 1996).[14]

---

14 [W]hile we certainly agree [with Justice O'Connor] that AEDPA wrought substantial changes in habeas law, *see, e. g.,* 28 U.S.C. §2244(b) (strictly limiting second or successive petitions); §2244(d) (1-year statute of limitations for habeas petitions); §2254(e)(2) (limiting availability of evidentiary hearings on habeas); §§2263, 2266 (strict deadlines for habeas court rulings), there is an obvious fallacy in the assumption that because the statute changed pre-existing law in some respects, it must have rendered this specific change here.

We all agree that state court judgments must be upheld unless, after the closest examination, a federal court is firmly convinced that a federal constitutional right has been violated. Our difference is as to the cases in which, at first blush, a state-court judgment seems entirely reasonable, but thorough analysis by a federal court produces a firm conviction that that judgment is infected by constitutional error. In our view, such an erroneous judgment is "unreasonable" within the meaning of the Act even though that conclusion was not immediately apparent.

In sum, the statute directs federal courts to attend to every state-court judgment with utmost care, but it does not require them to defer to the opinion of every reasonable state-court judge on the content of federal law. If, after carefully weighing all the reasons for accepting a state court's judgment, a federal court is convinced that a prisoner's custody—or, as in this case, his sentence of death—violates the Constitution, that independent judgment should prevail. Otherwise, the federal "law as determined by the Supreme Court of the United States" might be applied by the federal courts one way in Virginia and another way in California. In light of the well-recognized interest in ensuring that federal courts interpret federal law in a uniform way, we are convinced that Congress did not intend the statute to produce such a result.

III

In this case, Williams contends that he was denied his constitutionally guaranteed right to the effective assistance of counsel when his trial lawyers failed to investigate and to present substantial mitigating evidence to the sentencing jury.

We explained in *Strickland* that a violation of the right on which Williams relies has two components:

> First, the defendant must show that counsel's performance was deficient. This requires showing that counsel made errors so serious that counsel was not functioning as the 'counsel' guaranteed the defendant by the Sixth Amendment. Second, the defendant must show that the deficient performance prejudiced the defense. This requires showing that counsel's errors were so serious as to deprive the defendant of a fair trial, a trial whose result is reliable.

To establish ineffectiveness, a "defendant must show that counsel's representation fell below an objective standard of reasonableness." *Id.* To establish prejudice he "must show that there is a reasonable probability that, but for counsel's unprofessional errors, the result of the proceeding would have been different. A reasonable probability is a probability sufficient to undermine confidence in the outcome."

It is past question that the rule set forth in *Strickland* qualifies as "clearly established Federal law, as determined by the Supreme Court of the United States." That the *Strickland* test "of necessity requires a case-by-case examination of the evidence," *Wright v. West* (1992) (Kennedy, J., concurring in judgment), obviates neither the clarity of the rule nor the extent to which the rule must be seen as "established" by this Court.

IV

The Virginia Supreme Court erred in holding that our decision in *Lockhart v. Fretwell* (1993), modified or in some way supplanted the rule set down in *Strickland.* It is true that while the *Strickland* test provides sufficient guidance for resolving virtually all ineffective-assistance-of counsel claims, there are situations in which the overriding focus on fundamental fairness may affect the analysis. Thus, on the one hand, as *Strickland* itself explained, there are a few situations in which prejudice may be presumed. And, on the other hand, there are also situations in which it would be unjust to characterize the likelihood of a different outcome as legitimate "prejudice." Even if a defendant's false testimony might have persuaded the jury to acquit him, it is not fundamentally unfair to conclude that he was not prejudiced by counsel's interference with his intended perjury. *Nix v. Whiteside* (1986).

Similarly, in *Lockhart*, we concluded that, given the overriding interest in fundamental fairness, the likelihood of a different outcome attributable to a [lawyer's failure to assert what turned out to be an] incorrect interpretation of the law should be regarded as a potential "windfall" to the defendant rather than the legitimate "prejudice" contemplated by our opinion in *Strickland.*

Cases such as *Nix v. Whiteside* (1986), and *Lockhart v. Fretwell* (1993), do not justify a departure from a straightforward application of *Strickland* when the ineffectiveness of counsel *does* deprive the defendant of a substantive or procedural right to which the law entitles him. In the instant case, it is undisputed that Williams had a right—indeed, a constitutionally protected right—to provide the jury with the mitigating evidence that his trial counsel either failed to discover or failed to offer.

Nevertheless, the Virginia Supreme Court read our decision in *Lockhart* to require a separate inquiry into fundamental fairness even when Williams is able to show that his lawyer was ineffective and that his ineffectiveness probably affected the outcome of the proceeding.

The trial judge analyzed the ineffective-assistance claim under the correct standard; the Virginia Supreme Court did not.

We are likewise persuaded that the Virginia trial judge correctly applied both components of that standard to Williams' ineffectiveness claim. Although he concluded that counsel competently handled the guilt phase of the trial, he found that their representation during the sentencing phase fell short of professional standards. . . . The record establishes that counsel did not begin to prepare for that phase of the proceeding until a week before the trial. They failed to conduct an investigation that would have uncovered extensive records graphically describing Williams' nightmarish childhood, not because of any strategic calculation but because they incorrectly thought that state law barred access to such records. Had they done so, the jury would have learned that Williams' parents had been imprisoned for the criminal neglect of Williams and his siblings, that Williams had been severely and repeatedly beaten by his father, that he had been committed to the custody of the social services bureau for two years during his parents' incarceration (including one stint in an abusive foster home), and then, after his parents were released from prison, had been returned to his parents' custody.

Counsel failed to introduce available evidence that Williams was "borderline mentally [disabled]" and did not advance beyond sixth grade in school. They failed to seek prison records recording Williams' commendations for helping to crack a prison drug ring and for returning a guard's missing wallet, or the testimony of prison officials who described Williams as among the inmates "least likely to act in a violent, dangerous or provocative way." Counsel failed even to return the phone call of a certified public accountant who had offered to testify that he had visited Williams frequently when Williams was incarcerated as part of a prison ministry program, that Williams "seemed to thrive in a more regimented and structured environment," and that Williams was proud of the carpentry degree he earned while in prison.

Of course, not all of the additional evidence was favorable to Williams. The juvenile records revealed that he had been thrice committed to the juvenile system — for aiding and abetting larceny when he was 11 years old, for pulling a false fire alarm when he was 12, and for breaking and entering when he was 15. But as the Federal District Court correctly observed, the failure to introduce the comparatively voluminous amount of evidence that did speak in Williams' favor was not justified by a tactical decision to focus on Williams' voluntary confession.

We are also persuaded, unlike the Virginia Supreme Court, that counsel's unprofessional service prejudiced Williams within the meaning of *Strickland*. After hearing the additional evidence developed in the postconviction proceedings, the very judge who presided at Williams' trial, and who once determined that the death penalty was "just" and "appropriate," concluded that there existed "a reasonable probability that the result of the sentencing phase would have been different" if the jury had heard that evidence.

The Virginia Supreme Court's own analysis of prejudice reaching the contrary conclusion was thus unreasonable in at least two respects. First, as we have already explained, the State Supreme Court mischaracterized at best the appropriate rule.

Second, the State Supreme Court's prejudice determination was unreasonable insofar as it failed to evaluate the totality of the available mitigation evidence — both that adduced at trial, and the evidence adduced in the habeas proceeding — in reweighing it against the evidence in aggravation. . . . Mitigating evidence unrelated to dangerousness may alter the jury's selection of penalty, even if it does not undermine or rebut the prosecution's death-eligibility case. The Virginia Supreme Court did not entertain that possibility. It thus failed to accord appropriate weight to the body of mitigation evidence available to trial counsel.

V

It follows that the Virginia Supreme Court rendered a "decision that was contrary to, or involved an unreasonable application of, clearly established Federal law." Williams' constitutional right to the effective assistance of counsel as defined in *Strickland v. Washington* was violated.

Justice O'CONNOR [joined by Justices KENNEDY, THOMAS, SCALIA, and THE CHIEF JUSTICE], delivered the opinion of the Court with respect to Part II, concurred in part, and concurred in the judgment.

. . . The Court holds today that the Virginia Supreme Court's adjudication of Terry Williams' application for state habeas corpus relief resulted in just such a decision. I agree with that determination and join Parts I, III, and IV of the Court's opinion. Because I disagree, however, with the interpretation of §2254(d)(1) set forth in Part II of Justice Stevens' opinion, I write separately to explain my views.

I

Before 1996, this Court held that a federal court entertaining a state prisoner's application for habeas relief . . . owed no deference to a state court's resolution of such questions of law or mixed questions. In 1991, in the case of *Wright v. West* we revisited our prior holdings. [I wrote in *Wright* that although] *Teague* did hold that state prisoners could not receive "the retroactive benefit of new rules of law," it "did *not* create any deferential standard of review with regard to old rules." . . . I [also] stated my disagreement with [the view] that *de novo* review is incompatible with the maxim that federal habeas courts should "give great weight to the considered conclusions of a coequal state judiciary," *Miller.* Our statement in *Miller* signified only that a state-court decision is due the same respect as any other "persuasive, well-reasoned authority." *Wright.* "But this does not mean that we have held in the past that federal courts must presume the correctness of a state court's legal conclusions on habeas, or that a state court's incorrect legal determination has ever been allowed to stand because it was reasonable. We have always held that federal courts, even on habeas, have an independent obligation to say what the law is." *Id.* Under the federal habeas statute as it stood in 1992, then, our precedents dictated that a federal court should grant a state prisoner's petition for habeas relief if that court were to conclude in its independent judgment that the relevant state court had erred on a question of constitutional law or on a mixed constitutional question.

If today's case were governed by the federal habeas statute prior to Congress' enactment of AEDPA in 1996, I would agree with Justice Stevens that Williams' petition for habeas relief must be granted if we, in our independent judgment, were to conclude that his Sixth Amendment right to effective assistance of counsel was violated.

II
A

Williams' case is *not* governed by the pre-1996 version of the habeas statute. . . . Accordingly, for Williams to obtain federal habeas relief, he must first demonstrate that his case satisfies the condition set by §2254(d)(1). That provision modifies the role of federal habeas courts in reviewing petitions filed by state prisoners.

Justice Stevens' opinion in Part II essentially contends that §2254(d)(1) does not alter the previously settled rule of independent review. Indeed, the opinion concludes its statutory inquiry with the somewhat empty finding that §2254(d)(1) does no more than express a "'mood' that the Federal Judiciary must respect."

One need look no further than our decision in *Miller* to see that Justice Stevens' interpretation of §2254(d)(1) gives the 1996 amendment no effect whatsoever. The command that federal courts should now use the "utmost care" by "carefully weighing" the reasons supporting a state court's judgment echoes our pre-AEDPA statement in *Miller* that federal habeas courts "should, of course, give great weight to the considered conclusions of a coequal state judiciary." Similarly, the requirement that the independent judgment of a federal court must in the end prevail essentially repeats the conclusion we reached in the very next sentence in *Miller.*

Justice Stevens arrives at his erroneous interpretation by means of one critical misstep. He fails to give independent meaning to both the "contrary to" and "unreasonable application" clauses of the statute. . . . It is, however, a cardinal principle of statutory construction that we must "give effect, if possible, to every clause and word of a statute." *United States v. Menasche* (1955).

The word "contrary" is commonly understood to mean "diametrically different," "opposite in character or nature," or "mutually opposed." Webster's Third New International Dictionary 495 (1976). The text of §2254(d)(1) therefore suggests that the state court's decision must be substantially different from the relevant precedent of this Court. . . . A state-court decision will certainly be contrary to our clearly established precedent if the state court applies a rule that contradicts the governing law set forth in our cases. Take, for example, our decision in *Strickland v. Washington* (1984). If a state court were to reject a prisoner's claim of ineffective assistance of counsel on the grounds that the prisoner had not established by a preponderance of the evidence that the result of his criminal proceeding would have been different, that decision would be "diametrically different," "opposite in character or nature," and "mutually opposed" to our clearly established precedent because we held in *Strickland* that the prisoner need only demonstrate a "reasonable probability that . . . the result of the proceeding would have been different." A state-court decision will also be contrary to this Court's clearly established precedent if the state court confronts a set of facts that are materially indistinguishable from a decision of this Court and nevertheless arrives at a result different from our precedent.

On the other hand, a run-of-the-mill state-court decision applying the correct legal rule from our cases to the facts of a prisoner's case would not fit comfortably within §2254(d)(1)'s "contrary to" clause. Assume, for example, that a state-court decision on a prisoner's ineffective assistance claim correctly identifies *Strickland* as the controlling legal authority and, applying that framework, rejects the prisoner's claim. Quite clearly, the state-court decision would be in accord with our decision in *Strickland* as to the legal prerequisites for establishing an ineffective assistance claim, even assuming the federal court considering the prisoner's habeas application might reach a different result applying the *Strickland* framework itself. It is difficult, however, to describe such a run-of-the-mill state-court decision as "diametrically different" from, "opposite in character or nature" from, or "mutually opposed" to *Strickland,* our clearly established precedent. Although the state-court decision may be contrary to the federal court's conception of how *Strickland* ought to be applied in that particular case, the decision is not "mutually opposed" to *Strickland* itself.

Justice Stevens would instead construe §2254(d)(1)'s "contrary to" clause to encompass such a routine state-court decision. That construction, however, saps the "unreasonable application" clause of any meaning. If a federal habeas court can, under the "contrary to" clause, issue the writ whenever it concludes that the state court's *application* of clearly established federal law was incorrect, the "unreasonable application" clause becomes a nullity.

[With respect to the latter prong of §2254(d), a] state-court decision that correctly identifies the governing legal rule but applies it unreasonably to the facts of a particular prisoner's case certainly would qualify as a decision "involv[ing] an unreasonable application of . . . clearly established Federal law." Indeed, we used the almost identical phrase "application of law" to describe a state court's application of law to fact in the certiorari question we posed to the parties in *Wright*.

B

There remains the task of defining what exactly qualifies as an "unreasonable application" of law under §2254(d)(1). The Fourth Circuit held in *Green* that a state-court decision involves an "unreasonable application of . . . clearly established Federal law" only if the state court has applied federal law "in a manner that reasonable jurists would all agree is unreasonable." The placement of this additional overlay on the "unreasonable application" clause was erroneous. It is difficult to fault the Fourth Circuit for using this language given the fact that we have employed nearly identical terminology to describe the related inquiry undertaken by federal courts in applying the nonretroactivity rule of *Teague*. For example, in *Lambrix v. Singletary* (1997), we stated that a new rule is not dictated by precedent unless it would be "apparent to *all reasonable jurists*." In *Graham v. Collins* (1993), another nonretroactivity case, we employed similar language, stating that we could not say "that *all reasonable jurists* would have deemed themselves compelled to accept Graham's claim in 1984."

Defining an "unreasonable application" by reference to a "reasonable jurist," however, is of little assistance to the courts that must apply §2254(d)(1) and, in fact, may be misleading. Stated simply, a federal habeas court making the "unreasonable application" inquiry should ask whether the state court's application of clearly established federal law was objectively unreasonable. The federal habeas court should not transform the inquiry into a subjective one by resting its determination instead on the simple fact that at least one of the Nation's jurists has applied the relevant federal law in the same manner the state court did in the habeas petitioner's case. The "all reasonable jurists" standard would tend to mislead federal habeas courts by focusing their attention on a subjective inquiry rather than on an objective one.

The term "unreasonable" is no doubt difficult to define. That said, it is a common term in the legal world and, accordingly, federal judges are familiar with its meaning. For purposes of today's opinion, the most important point is that an *unreasonable* application of federal law is different from an *incorrect* application of federal law. . . . In my separate opinion in *Wright*, I made the same distinction, maintaining that "a state court's *incorrect* legal determination has [never] been allowed to stand because it was *reasonable*. We have always held that federal courts, even on habeas, have an independent obligation to say what the law is." In §2254(d)(1), Congress specifically used the word "unreasonable," and not a term like "erroneous" or "incorrect." Under §2254(d)(1)'s "unreasonable application" clause, then, a federal habeas court may not issue the writ simply because that court concludes in its independent judgment that the relevant state-court decision applied clearly established federal law erroneously or incorrectly. Rather, that application must also be unreasonable.

Throughout this discussion the meaning of the phrase "clearly established Federal law, as determined by the Supreme Court of the United States" has been put to the side. That statutory phrase refers to the holdings, as opposed to the dicta, of this Court's decisions as of the time of the relevant state-court decision. In this respect, the "clearly established Federal law" phrase bears only a slight connection to our *Teague* jurisprudence. With one caveat, whatever would qualify as an old rule under our *Teague* jurisprudence will constitute "clearly established Federal law, as determined by the Supreme Court of the United States" under §2254(d)(1). The one caveat, as the statutory language makes clear, is that §2254(d)(1) restricts the source of clearly established law to this Court's jurisprudence.

In sum, §2254(d)(1) places a new constraint on the power of a federal habeas court to grant a state prisoner's application for a writ of habeas corpus with respect to claims adjudicated on the merits in state court. . . . Under the "contrary to" clause, a federal habeas court may grant the writ if the state court arrives at a conclusion opposite to that reached by this Court on a question of law or if the state court decides a case differently than this Court has on a set of materially indistinguishable facts. Under the "unreasonable application" clause, a federal habeas court may grant the writ if the state court identifies the correct governing legal principle from this Court's decisions but unreasonably applies that principle to the facts of the prisoner's case.

III

Although I disagree with Justice Stevens concerning the standard we must apply under §2254(d)(1) in evaluating Terry Williams' claims on habeas, . . . I believe that the Court's discussion in Parts III and IV is correct and that it demonstrates the reasons that the Virginia Supreme Court's decision in Williams' case, even under the interpretation of §2254(d)(1) I have set forth above, was both contrary to and involved an unreasonable application of our precedent.

Chief Justice REHNQUIST, with whom Justice SCALIA and Justice THOMAS join, concurring in part and dissenting in part.

I agree with the Court's interpretation of 28 U.S.C. §2254(d)(1) [set out in Justice O'Connor's opinion], but disagree with its decision to grant habeas relief in this case.

Petitioner argues, and the Court agrees, that the Virginia Supreme Court improperly held that *Lockhart v. Fretwell* "modified or in some way supplanted" the rule set down in *Strickland*. I agree that such a holding would be improper. But the Virginia Supreme Court did not so hold as it did not rely on *Lockhart* to reach its decision.

Before delving into the evidence presented at the sentencing proceeding, the Virginia Supreme Court [made an] initial allusion to *Lockhart* [but thereafter] the Virginia Supreme Court's analysis explicitly proceeds under *Strickland* alone. Because the Virginia Supreme Court did not rely on *Lockhart* to make its decision, and, instead, appropriately relied on *Strickland*, that court's adjudication was not "contrary to" this Court's clearly established precedent.

* * *

It is fairly unusual for a state court to fail to identify a controlling Supreme Court precedent or fail to recognize that the case before it is "materially indistinguishable" from a Supreme Court case. That means it is rare for a federal habeas petition to turn on the "contrary to" provision of §2254(d). Instead, most cases turn on whether the state court's application of clearly established law to fact was "objectively unreasonable"—the interpretation adopted in *Williams*—and whether the law was clearly established at the time of the state court's decision.

In the *Williams* case, the Court rejected the Fourth Circuit's "all reasonable jurists" rule as too subjective. Relief cannot be granted unless the state court's application of law to fact is "objectively unreasonable," more than one the federal habeas court believes to be "incorrect" in its independent judgment. In *Lockyer v. Andrade* (2003), the Court held that even *clearly erroneous* state court applications of law to fact are not "objectively unreasonable" under §2554(d). Andrade was convicted of petty theft of $150 worth of video tapes but since this was his third offense, he received a sentence of two consecutive 25-years-to-life terms under California's three-strikes law. Andrade challenged the sentence in state court as grossly disproportionate to the gravity of his offense and therefore cruel and unusual punishment under the Eighth Amendment. On the merits of that claim, the state court compared Andrade's sentence to *Solem v. Helm* (1983) (striking down as unconstitutionally disproportionate a sentence of life without parole for petty fraud under South Dakota's recidivist statute), and *Rummel v. Estelle* (1980) (upholding sentence of life with possibility of parole for petty theft under Texas' recidivist statute; not grossly disproportionate given possibility of parole). It found *Rummel* (1980) persuasive in light of a later case in which members of the Supreme Court voiced doubts about *Solem* and denied Andrade's Eighth Amendment claim.

The federal district court denied Andrade's federal petition under §2254(d). The Ninth Circuit reversed on the ground that an unreasonable application of law to fact is a "clearly erroneous" application of law to fact—the most deferential standard of review in ordinary appellate review of fact determinations. The Supreme Court reversed, holding that clear error did not reflect the level of deference to state court judgments Congress intended in adopting the "unreasonable application" prong of §2254(d):

> The Ninth Circuit made an initial error in its "unreasonable application" analysis [by defining] "objectively unreasonable" to mean "clear error." These two standards, however, are not the same. The gloss of clear error fails to give proper deference to state courts by conflating error (even clear error) with unreasonableness.
>
> It is not enough that a federal habeas court, in its "independent review of the legal question," is left with a "firm conviction" that the state court was "erroneous." *Andrade* (9th Cir.). We have held precisely the opposite: "Under §2254(d)(1)'s 'unreasonable application' clause, then, a federal

habeas court may not issue the writ simply because that "court concludes in its independent judgment that the relevant state-court decision applied clearly established federal law erroneously or incorrectly." *Williams v. Taylor.* Rather, that application must be objectively unreasonable.

Section 2254(d)(1) permits a federal court to grant habeas relief based on the application of a governing legal principle to a set of facts different from those of the case in which the principle was announced. *See, e.g., Williams v. Taylor* (noting that it is "an unreasonable application of this Court's precedent if the state court identifies the correct governing legal rule from this Court's cases but unreasonably applies it to the facts of the particular state prisoner's case"). Here, however, the governing legal principle gives legislatures broad discretion to fashion a sentence that fits within the scope of the proportionality principle—the "precise contours" of which "are unclear." *Harmelin v. Michigan* (1991) (Kennedy, J., concurring in part and concurring in judgment). And it was not objectively unreasonable for the California Court of Appeal to conclude that these "contours" permitted an affirmance of Andrade's sentence.

The gross disproportionality principle reserves a constitutional violation for only the extraordinary case. In applying this principle for §2254(d)(1) purposes, it was not an unreasonable application of our clearly established law for the California Court of Appeal to affirm Andrade's sentence of two consecutive terms of 25 years to life in prison.

One implication of *Andrade* is that when a governing constitutional principle involves the exercise of discretion (as with the Eighth Amendment's gross disproportionality standard), it is more difficult to challenge a state court's exercise of such discretion as "objectively unreasonable." Indeed, one might say that the more discretion a constitutional principle involves, the less likely a state judge's exercise of it will be objectively unreasonable. As the Court put it in another case, "the more general the [federal] rule . . . the more leeway [state] courts have in reaching outcomes in case-by-case determinations" under §2254(d). *Renico v. Lett* (2010). Notice, however, that this reading of the statute places federal court judges in the peculiar position of being obliged by statute to deny relief from state convictions that rest on clear *constitutional* error.

Andrade also reveals the connection between the Court's "unreasonable application" analysis and its determination of whether the law was clearly established at the time of the state court's decision. The Court found that only a broad principle of gross disproportionality was clearly established at the time the California courts considered Andrade's Eighth Amendment challenge:

As a threshold matter here, we first decide what constitutes "clearly established Federal law, as determined by the Supreme Court of the United States." §2254(d)(1). Andrade relies upon a series of precedents from this Court—*Rummel v. Estelle* (1980), *Solem v. Helm* (1983), and *Harmelin v. Michigan* (1991)—that he claims clearly establish a principle that his sentence is so grossly disproportionate that it violates the Eighth Amendment. Section 2254(d)(1)'s "clearly established" phrase "refers to the holdings, as opposed to the dicta, of this Court's decisions as of the time of the relevant state-court decision." *Williams v. Taylor* (2000). In other words, "clearly established Federal law" under §2254(d)(1) is the governing legal principle or principles set forth by the Supreme Court *at the time the state court renders its decision.* In most situations, the task of determining what we have clearly established will be straightforward. The difficulty with Andrade's position, however, is that our precedents in this area have not been a model of clarity. Indeed, in determining whether a particular sentence for a term of years can violate the Eighth Amendment, we have not established a clear or consistent path for courts to follow.

Through this thicket of Eighth Amendment jurisprudence, one governing legal principle emerges as "clearly established" under §2254(d)(1): A gross disproportionality principle is applicable to sentences for terms of years.

Our cases exhibit a lack of clarity regarding what factors may indicate gross disproportionality. In *Solem* (the case upon which Andrade relies most heavily), we stated: "It is clear that a 25-year sentence generally is more severe than a 15-year sentence, but in most cases it would be difficult to decide that the former violates the Eighth Amendment while the latter does not." And in *Harmelin*, both Justice Kennedy and Justice Scalia repeatedly emphasized this lack of clarity: that *"Solem* was scarcely the expression of clear . . . constitutional law" (opinion of Scalia, J.), that in "adher[ing] to the narrow proportionality principle . . . our proportionality decisions have not been clear or consistent in all respects" (Kennedy, J., concurring in part and concurring in judgment), that "we lack clear objective standards to distinguish between sentences for different terms of years" (Kennedy, J., concurring in part and concurring in judgment), and that the "precise contours" of the proportionality principle "are unclear" (Kennedy, J., concurring in part and concurring in judgment).

Thus, in this case, the only relevant clearly established law amenable to the "contrary to" or "unreasonable application of" framework is the gross disproportionality principle, the precise contours of which are unclear, applicable only in the "exceedingly rare" and "extreme" case. *Id.*

In explaining why Andrade did not present a claim that was contrary to clearly established law in light of *Solem v. Helm*, the Court said that *Solem v. Helm* was not on point for purposes of §2254(d) because the defendant there received life without parole, while Andrade would be eligible for parole after 50 years in prison, in the year 2046 when he would be 87 years old. Even if the only clearly established law was the general standard of gross disproportionality, it is revealing of the deference the Court reads Congress to have required that the Supreme Court denied relief in the face of a sentence as long as Andrade's. Justice Souter's dissenting opinion, joined by Justices Stevens, Breyer, and Ginsburg, emphasized this:

> *Solem* . . . is controlling here because it established a benchmark in applying the general principle. We specifically held that a sentence of life imprisonment without parole for uttering a $100 "no account" check was disproportionate to the crime, even though the defendant had committed six prior nonviolent felonies. In explaining our proportionality review,

we contrasted the result with *Rummel*'s on the ground that the life sentence there had included parole eligibility after 12 years, *Solem.*

The facts here are on all fours with those of *Solem* and point to the same result. Andrade, like the defendant in *Solem,* was a repeat offender who committed theft of fairly trifling value, some $150, and their criminal records are comparable, including burglary (though Andrade's were residential), with no violent crimes or crimes against the person. The respective sentences, too, are strikingly alike.

The only ways to reach a different conclusion are to reject the practical equivalence of a life sentence without parole and one with parole eligibility at 87 ([The majority emphasizes that] "Andrade retains the possibility of parole"), or to discount the continuing authority of *Solem*'s example, as the California court did. The former is unrealistic; an 87-year-old man released after 50 years behind bars will have no real life left, if he survives to be released at all. And the latter, disparaging *Solem* as a point of reference on Eighth Amendment analysis, is wrong as a matter of law.

Perhaps even more tellingly, no one could seriously argue that the second theft of videotapes provided any basis to think that Andrade would be so dangerous after 25 years, the date on which the consecutive sentence would begin to run, as to require at least 25 years more. I know of no jurisdiction that would add 25 years of imprisonment simply to reflect the fact that the two temporally related thefts took place on two separate occasions, and I am not surprised that California has found no such case, not even under its three-strikes law.

In cases decided since *Williams v. Taylor* and *Andrade,* the Court has continued to insist that §2254(d) requires a high level of deference to state court adjudications of federal constitutional law. The Court has been particularly vigilant regarding ineffective assistance of counsel claims, the federal constitutional right most commonly presented in federal habeas petitions. Lower federal courts are not, for instance, allowed to first ask whether the right to effective assistance of counsel under *Strickland* was violated at trial, and then decide whether the state appellate or state habeas court's denial of that claim was "unreasonable" under §2254(d). In *Harrington v. Richter* (2011), the Court held that this approach involves a form of "de novo" review of the constitutional claim which §2254(d) forbids.

> AEDPA demands more. Under §2254(d), *a habeas court must determine what arguments or theories supported or, as here, could have supported, the state court's decision; and then it must ask whether it is possible fairminded jurists could disagree that those arguments or theories are inconsistent with the holding in a prior decision of this Court.* The opinion of the Court of Appeals all but ignored "the only question that matters under §2254(d)(1)." *Lockyer v. Andrade* (2003).
>
> The Court of Appeals appears to have treated the unreasonableness question as a test of its confidence in the result it would reach under *de novo* review: Because the Court of Appeals had little doubt that Richter's *Strickland* claim had merit, the Court of Appeals concluded the state court must have been unreasonable in rejecting it. This analysis overlooks

arguments that would otherwise justify the state court's result and ignores further limitations of §2254(d), including its requirement that the state court's decision be evaluated according to the precedents of this Court. It bears repeating that even a strong case for relief does not mean the state court's contrary conclusion was unreasonable. *See Lockyer.*

If this standard is difficult to meet, that is because it was meant to be. As amended by AEDPA, §2254(d) stops short of imposing a complete bar on federal court relitigation of claims already rejected in state proceedings. *Cf. Felker v. Turpin* (1996) (discussing AEDPA's "modified res judicata rule" under §2244). . . . Section 2254(d) reflects the view that habeas corpus is a guard against extreme malfunctions in the state criminal justice systems, not a substitute for ordinary error correction through appeal. As a condition for obtaining habeas corpus from a federal court, a state prisoner must show that the state court's ruling on the claim being presented in federal court was so lacking in justification that there was an error well understood and comprehended in existing law beyond any possibility for fairminded disagreement.

The reasons for this approach are familiar. "Federal habeas review of state convictions frustrates both the States' sovereign power to punish offenders and their good-faith attempts to honor constitutional rights." *Calderon v. Thompson* (1998). It "disturbs the State's significant interest in repose for concluded litigation, denies society the right to punish some admitted offenders, and intrudes on state sovereignty to a degree matched by few exercises of federal judicial authority." *Reed* (Kennedy, J., dissenting). . . .

"Surmounting *Strickland*'s high bar is never an easy task." *Padilla v. Kentucky* (2010). An ineffective-assistance claim can function as a way to escape rules of waiver and forfeiture and raise issues not presented at trial, and so the *Strickland* standard must be applied with scrupulous care, lest "intrusive post-trial inquiry" threaten the integrity of the very adversary process the right to counsel is meant to serve. *Strickland.* Even under *de novo* review, the standard for judging counsel's representation is a most deferential one.

Establishing that a state court's application of *Strickland* was unreasonable under §2254(d) is all the more difficult. The standards created by *Strickland* and §2254(d) are both "highly deferential," and when the two apply in tandem, review is "doubly" so, *Knowles.* The *Strickland* standard is a general one, so the range of reasonable applications is substantial. Federal habeas courts must guard against the danger of equating unreasonableness under *Strickland* with unreasonableness under §2254(d). When §2254(d) applies, the question is not whether counsel's actions were reasonable. The question is whether there is any reasonable argument that counsel satisfied *Strickland*'s deferential standard.

The Court went on to conclude that the state court reasonably found the defense lawyer's failure to consult or prepare testimony of blood evidence experts was an understandable strategic choice at the time. It appeared unreasonable to the Ninth Circuit only with hindsight triggered by recently discovered forensic evidence regarding the blood pool at the scene of the crime. But "[r]eliance on 'the harsh light of hindsight' to cast doubt on a trial that took place now more than 15 years ago is precisely what *Strickland* and AEDPA seek to prevent. Even if it had been apparent that expert blood testimony could support Richter's defense, it would be reasonable to conclude that a competent attorney might elect not to use it," and thus it provides no foundation to challenge the reasonableness of the state court's denial of the *Strickland* claim. *Harrington.*

Finally, note the Court's language in *Andrade* that the law must have been clearly established "*at the time the state court renders its decision.*" In *Williams*, the Court analogized this element to the *Teague* retroactivity analysis, but the Court has since stated that §2254(d):

> [does]not codify *Teague*, and that "the AEDPA and *Teague* inquiries are distinct." *Horn v. Banks* (2002) (per curiam). The retroactivity rules that govern federal habeas review on the merits—which include *Teague*—are quite separate from the relitigation bar imposed by AEDPA; neither abrogates or qualifies the other. If §2254(d)(1) was, indeed, pegged to *Teague*, it would authorize relief when a state-court merits adjudication "resulted in a decision *that became* contrary to, or an unreasonable application of, clearly established Federal law, *before the conviction became final.*" The statute says no such thing, and we see no reason why *Teague* should alter AEDPA's plain meaning.

Greene v. Fisher (2011) (holding that clearly established law is the law as it stood "at the time the state court renders its decision" on the federal questions; Supreme Court decision rendered after lower state court adjudicated Confrontation Clause claim, but before state supreme court declined to entertain an appeal; was not clearly established law). *Greene* relied directly on the analysis in *Cullen v. Pinholster* (2011) (restricting §2254(d) review to the state court record) for the proposition that §2254(d)'s "backward-looking language requires an examination of the state-court decision at the time it was made").

(i)   *Teague*'s Non-Retroactivity Principle and §2254(d)

Even if the standard of review in AEDPA did not "codify *Teague*," did §2254(d) simply displace *Teague?* The short answer is no. Although it would be unusual, one could imagine a case in which the state courts make no adjudication "on the merits" for purposes of §2254(d) of federal claims that the petitioner nevertheless properly presented to the state courts. In such a case, the exhaustion requirement would be met, and the petitioner would not have procedurally defaulted. As long as a federal petition is timely filed within the statute of limitations, the federal court has jurisdiction, but §2254(d) "falls away" and would not apply. *Brown v. Davenport* (2022). In such a case, *Teague* presumably controls.

More importantly, note that the Court has relied on *Teague* in other cases where §2254(d) unquestionably controls—asking as a threshold matter whether the federal petitioner's claim requires retroactive application of a "new rule," and, if it does, denying relief on those grounds; or using *Teague*'s "threshold inquiry" as a basis for taking jurisdiction. *Edwards v. Vannoy, supra,* Section B.2.b.i., is an example of the former—the Court addressed the watershed procedural exception to *Teague* when, as Justice Thomas pointed out in dissent, it simply could have denied relief under §2254(d) by holding that Arizona's non-unanimity rule was not contrary to or an unreasonable application of clearly established law at the time it was applied to Edwards's case. The majority's approach dovetails with the Court's most direct statement of how *Teague* and §2254(d) relate to each other in cases where either rule could support denial of the petition and the state invokes *Teague*'s non-retroactivity principle:

> While it is of course a necessary prerequisite to federal habeas relief that a prisoner satisfy the AEDPA standard of review set forth in 28 U.S.C. §2254(d) ("[a]n application . . . shall not be granted . . . *unless*" the AEDPA standard of review is satisfied (emphasis added)), none of our post-AEDPA cases have suggested that a writ of habeas corpus should automatically issue if a prisoner satisfies the AEDPA standard, or that AEDPA relieves courts from the responsibility of addressing properly raised *Teague* arguments. To the contrary, if our post-AEDPA cases suggest anything about AEDPA's relationship to *Teague*, it is that the AEDPA and *Teague* inquiries are distinct. Thus, in addition to performing any analysis required by AEDPA, a federal court considering a habeas petition must conduct a threshold *Teague* analysis when the issue is properly raised by the state.

Horn v. Banks (2002) (reversing Third Circuit for failing to conduct *Teague*'s threshold retroactivity analysis after finding that petitioner met §2254(d)'s standard). In *Horn*, the Third Circuit concluded §2254(d) was violated by the state court's treatment of *Mills v. Maryland* (1988), a case decided after petitioner's conviction became final but during his state habeas litigation and considered by the state supreme court when it denied relief. *Mills* was thus "clearly established law" under §2254(d) at the time of the challenged state court decision, but a "new" rule unavailable on federal habear under *Teague*.

Montgomery v. Louisiana, supra, Section B.2.b.ii., is an example of the use of retroactivity principles to support jurisdiction. As Justice Scalia points out in dissent, the power of Congress over Article III jurisdiction traditionally included the power to modify common law rules of decision developed by the courts in the exercise of any such jurisdiction. *Teague*, he argued, was precisely such a common law rule, subject to congressional modification or elimination. If §2254(d) does not incorporate *Teague*'s exceptions, then the proper course was to deny the petition without taking up the question of whether *Miller* was retroactive, let alone whether a *state* court must give retroactive effect to *Miller*.

(ii)   Harmless Error and §2254(d)

The same questions about how court-developed retroactivity rules interact with the §2254(d) standard of review have arisen with harmless error doctrine. The traditional harmless error doctrine applied on direct review of a criminal conviction requires *the government* to establish that any error was "harmless beyond a reasonable doubt." *Chapman v. California* (1967) (rejecting claim that constitutional error can never be harmless). In *Brecht v. Abrahamson* (1993), the Court held that because a federal habeas petition challenging a state conviction is an "extraordinary remedy" warranted only for "extreme malfunctions in the state criminal justice system," federal courts must follow a harmless error rule more deferential to the government: *the petitioner* must show "substantial and injurious effect or influence" of the error on the verdict. To upset a state conviction on mere "speculation that the defendant was prejudiced by trial error," the Court has emphasized, fails to give due regard to the state's "sovereign interest" in the finality of its criminal enforcement. *Calderon v. Coleman* (1998).

And *Brecht's* harmless error test remains in force after AEDPA. Congress, the Court has held, "left intact the equitable discretion traditionally invested in federal courts by preexisting habeas statutes":

> So even a petitioner who prevails under AEDPA must still today persuade a federal habeas court that "law and justice require" relief. And whatever else those inquiries involve, they continue to require federal habeas courts to apply this Court's precedents governing the appropriate exercise of equitable discretion—including *Brecht.* Today, then, a federal court must deny relief to a state habeas petitioner who fails to satisfy either this Court's equitable precedents or AEDPA. But to grant relief, a court must find that the petitioner has cleared both tests. . . . [T]he two tests impose analytically distinct preconditions to relief.

Brown v. Davenport (2022) (reversing Sixth Circuit decision that granted relief after finding that the state court's constitutional error, permitting defendant to be shackled during trial, was not harmless under *Brecht* without considering whether §2254(d) was met). Under §2254(d), the Court held, there was no ground to conclude that the state court's finding of harmlessness was contrary to or an unreasonable application of federal law. *Id.* (noting that, under *Greene,* the Court would look to the harmlessness ruling of the state courts because that was the last state court adjudication of the merits of the federal claim). Although the shackling of the defendant at trial may have been unconstitutional, the Court concluded, the state court made a reasonable application of law to fact when it found that error harmless in view of the "'overwhelming evidence against'" the petitioner, and juror statements that the shackling did not affect their verdict.

(iii)   Actual Innocence in Capital Cases

Lastly, consider a federal petitioner who has newly discovered evidence of factual innocence, but can point to no state decision that is contrary to or an unreasonable application of clearly established federal law. Recall that the Court has occasionally exercised its equitable discretion to recognize a "miscarriage of justice" exception to the procedural prerequisites of a federal petition such as the bar on second or successive petitions and procedural default. The exception is most salient where the petitioner presents evidence of actual innocence. However, the Court has declined to extend this equitable exception to claims of innocence that are unconnected to procedural flaws that prevented the petitioner from raising constitutional claims. In the case declining to extend the equitable exception, *Herrera v. Collins* (1993), the Court assumed without deciding that, at least in a capital case, some form of relief must be available on a sufficiently strong showing of actual innocence.

> The fundamental miscarriage of justice exception is available "only where the prisoner *supplements* his constitutional claim with a colorable showing

of factual innocence." *Kuhlmann* (emphasis added). We have never held that it extends to freestanding claims of actual innocence. Therefore, the exception is inapplicable here.

Petitioner asserts that this case is different because he has been sentenced to death. But we have "refused to hold that the fact that a death sentence has been imposed requires a different standard of review on federal habeas corpus." *Murray v. Giarratano* (1989) (plurality opinion). We have, of course, held that the Eighth Amendment requires increased reliability of the process by which capital punishment may be imposed. But petitioner's claim does not fit well into the doctrine of these cases, since, as we have pointed out, it is far from clear that a second trial 10 years after the first trial would produce a more reliable result.

We may assume, for the sake of argument in deciding this case, that in a capital case a truly persuasive demonstration of "actual innocence" made after trial would render the execution of a defendant unconstitutional, and warrant federal habeas relief if there were no state avenue open to process such a claim. But because of the very disruptive effect that entertaining claims of actual innocence would have on the need for finality in capital cases, and the enormous burden that having to retry cases based on often stale evidence would place on the States, the threshold showing for such an assumed right would necessarily be extraordinarily high. The showing made by petitioner in this case falls far short of any such threshold.

Herrera v. Collins. Justice O'Connor concurred separately to emphasize that "the execution of a legally and factually innocent person would be a constitutionally intolerable event. Dispositive to this case, however, is an equally fundamental fact: Petitioner is not innocent, in any sense of the word." A year later, the risk of wrongful conviction in capital cases prompted Justice Blackmun to write:

> From this day forward, I shall no longer tinker with the machinery of death. . . . The problem is that the inevitability of factual, legal, and moral error gives us a system that we know must wrongly kill some defendants, a system that fails to deliver the fair, consistent, and reliable sentences of death required by the Constitution. . . . Even under the most sophisticated death penalty statutes, race continues to play a major role in determining who shall live and who shall die.

Callins v. Collins (1994) (dissenting from the denial of certiorari in capital habeas petition).

Justice Scalia, concurring in the denial of certiorari in *Callins*, stressed that, whatever Justice Blackmun's moral objections, capital punishment is contemplated by the text of the Fifth Amendment, which speaks of the deprivation of "life" in guaranteeing due process of law and "establishes beyond doubt that the death penalty is not one of the 'cruel and unusual punishments' prohibited by the Eighth Amendment." Justice Scalia concurred in *Herrera* as well, noting that he would have reached the question the majority avoided regarding claims of actual innocence:

> There is no basis in text, tradition, or even in contemporary practice (if that were enough) for finding in the Constitution a right to demand judicial consideration of newly discovered evidence of innocence brought

forward after conviction. . . . If the system that has been in place for 200 years (and remains widely approved) "shock[s]" the dissenters' consciences, perhaps they should doubt the calibration of their consciences, or, better still, the usefulness of "conscience shocking" as a legal test.

I nonetheless join the entirety of the Court's opinion . . . because there is no legal error in deciding a case by assuming, *arguendo*, that an asserted constitutional right exists, and because I can understand, or at least am accustomed to, the reluctance of the present Court to admit publicly that Our Perfect Constitution lets stand any injustice, much less the execution of an innocent man who has received, though to no avail, all the process that our society has traditionally deemed adequate. With any luck, we shall avoid ever having to face this embarrassing question again, since it is improbable that evidence of innocence as convincing as today's opinion requires would fail to produce an executive pardon.

Post-AEDPA, the Court has retained the miscarriage of justice exception as an equitable exception for failure to comply with procedural prerequisites to a federal petition. But *Herrera*'s dictum notwithstanding, the Court has not granted a habeas petition on a claim of actual innocence unmoored from some other claim of constitutional error in the state conviction.

It is clear from our study of §2254(d) that relief will be granted in only the most extraordinary of circumstances, and, given the rule in *Herrera*, even some claims of actual innocence will not warrant relief. A more exacting standard of review than §2254(d) is difficult to imagine. This returns us to Justice Frankfurter's opinion in *Brown v. Allen*, and his conclusion that federal review of state convictions can be justified by the fact that relief will rarely be granted, albeit with the twist that §2254(d) is far narrower than the standard of review Justice Frankfurter supported in 1953. He also emphasized that Congress could of course limit jurisdiction under the 1867 Act, and that has come to pass, with the full endorsement of the modern Court. How states use the latitude afforded them by §2254(d) and the Court is one of the most important questions for the integrity of the administration of criminal justice in the twenty-first century.

CHAPTER 9

SUPREME COURT REVIEW

INTRODUCTION: THE SUPREME COURT'S FUNCTIONS

There is relatively little disagreement about the institutional functions of the Supreme Court in the American system of government, although there obviously is a great divergence of views about how the Court should carry out its tasks. Specifically, the Court serves a number of important functions. First, it serves as an authoritative voice as to the meaning of the U.S. Constitution. Long ago, Chief Justice John Marshall declared that "it is emphatically the province and duty of the judicial department to say what the law is."[1] Thus, jurisdictional rules should facilitate the ability of the Supreme Court to decide important constitutional questions through its review of state court and lower federal court rulings.

A second and related function of the Supreme Court is to ensure the supremacy of federal law. In *Cooper v. Aaron* (see Chapter 1), the Court rejected a state's attempt to disregard Supreme Court precedent, concluding that *Marbury v. Madison* established "the basic principle that the federal judiciary is supreme in the exposition of the law of the Constitution, and that principle has ever since been respected by this Court and the Country as a permanent and indispensable feature of our constitutional system."[2] Without Supreme Court review of state court decisions, states would be free to disregard federal statutes and even the Constitution. Because state court decisions generally are not reviewable in the lower federal courts, only the Supreme Court can ensure the supremacy of federal law.

Third, the Supreme Court resolves conflicting interpretations of federal law among the various state and federal courts. The Court thus serves to ensure the uniformity of federal law. Although differences in local law are an advantage of a federalist system of government, it is widely believed that federal law should mean the same thing in all parts of the country.

Fourth, the Supreme Court is the final voice in interpreting federal statutes. There are obvious advantages to having a final resolution of difficult questions of statutory construction.

This brief description of the Supreme Court's functions reveals several things. The Court may decide only questions of federal law. The Court has no authority

---

1. 5 U.S. (1 Cranch) 137, 177 (1803).
2. Cooper v. Aaron, 358 U.S. 1, 19 (1958).

to decide matters of state law in reviewing the decisions of state courts. The state courts are the ultimate interpreters of state law, absent the presence of a federal issue.[3] In fact, it is firmly established that the Court will grant review only if there is a substantial federal question.[4]

Article III, section 2, authorizes Supreme Court jurisdiction and provides, "In all cases affecting ambassadors, other public ministers and consuls, and those in which a state shall be party, the Supreme Court shall have original jurisdiction. In all the other cases before mentioned, the Supreme Court shall have appellate jurisdiction, both as to law and fact, with such exceptions, and under such regulations as the Congress shall make."

Article III allows the Supreme Court to exercise "original jurisdiction"—that is, to be the Court where a matter is initially filed—in limited circumstances. A federal statute, 28 U.S.C. §1251, provides:

> (a) The Supreme Court shall have original and exclusive jurisdiction of all controversies between two or more States.
>
> (b) The Supreme Court shall have original but not exclusive jurisdiction of:
>> (1) All actions or proceedings to which ambassadors, other public ministers, consuls, or vice consuls of foreign states are parties;
>> (2) All controversies between the United States and a State;
>> (3) All actions or proceedings by a State against the citizens of another State or against aliens.

In other words, only the Supreme Court can hear cases between state governments, but other federal courts may hear the other type of cases where original jurisdiction is allowed by Article III. In reality, the Court only exercises original jurisdiction for suits between state governments. In *Marbury v. Madison* (1803), the Supreme Court held that the categories of original jurisdiction enumerated in Article III are exhaustive; it is unconstitutional for Congress to expand the Supreme Court's original jurisdiction beyond the Constitution's text.

Additionally, federal statutes authorize the exercise of the Supreme Court's appellate jurisdiction. For example, 28 U.S.C. §1257, provides for Supreme Court review of state court decisions. It states:

> Final judgments or decrees rendered by the highest court of a State in which a decision could be had, may be reviewed by the Supreme Court by writ of certiorari where the validity of a treaty or statute of the United States is drawn in question or where the validity of a statute of any State is drawn in question on the ground of its being repugnant to the Constitution, treaties, or laws of the United States, or where any title, right, privilege, or immunity is specially set up or claimed under the Constitution or the treaties or statutes of, or any commission held or authority exercised under, the United States.

---

3. *See* Murdock v. City of Memphis, 87 U.S. (20 Wall.) 590 (1875), discussed in Chapter 9.C.3, *infra*.

4. *See, e.g.*, Zucht v. King, 260 U.S. 174 (1922); see discussion in Chapter 9.C, *infra*.

And 28 U.S.C. §1254 provides for Supreme Court review of decisions of the United States Courts of Appeals:

> Cases in the courts of appeals may be reviewed by the Supreme Court by the following methods:
>
> (1) By writ of certiorari granted upon the petition of any party to any civil or criminal case, before or after rendition of judgment or decree;
>
> (2) By certification at any time by a court of appeals of any question of law in any civil or criminal case as to which instructions are desired, and upon such certification the Supreme Court may give binding instructions or require the entire record to be sent up for decision of the entire matter in controversy.

These statutes defining the Supreme Court's jurisdiction draw a distinction between "appeal" and "certiorari" as vehicles for appellate review of the decisions of state and lower federal courts. Where the statute provides for "appeal" to the Supreme Court, the Court is obligated to take and decide the case when appellate review is requested. Where the state provides for review by "writ of certiorari," the Court has complete discretion whether to hear the matter; the Court takes the case if there are four votes to grant certiorari. Effective September 25, 1988, the distinction between appeal and certiorari as a vehicle for Supreme Court review was virtually eliminated. Now almost all cases come to the Supreme Court by writ of certiorari.

The distinction has its origins in the late nineteenth and early twentieth centuries. Under the Judiciary Act of 1789, review was available in the Supreme Court by writ of error and the Court was obligated to hear all such cases. In 1891, the Court's jurisdiction was modified when the U.S. Circuit Courts of Appeals were created. The Supreme Court was given authority to review decisions from these courts in diversity, admiralty, patent, and revenue cases by writ of certiorari. Unlike the writ of error, where jurisdiction was mandatory, the writ of certiorari was completely discretionary with the Court. In 1914, the Supreme Court was given authority for the first time to review state court decisions upholding a federal statute or invalidating a state statute. Review in such cases also was discretionary with the Court and was by writ of certiorari.

In 1925, an act known as the "Judges' Bill" was adopted in order to reduce the workload of the Supreme Court. It articulated the distinction between appeal and certiorari and made most of the Court's jurisdiction pursuant to certiorari. Until 1988, there were only minor changes. In general, final judgments from a state court came by appeal only if the state court invalidated a federal statute or upheld a state statute. Final judgments of a federal court of appeals came by appeal only if the court invalidated a state statute or declared a federal law unconstitutional in a civil action to which the U.S. government is a party. All other cases came to the U.S. Supreme Court by certiorari.

A law enacted in 1988 eliminated appeals in these cases; now almost all cases from courts of appeals or state highest courts come to the Supreme Court by writ of certiorari. Review by appeals remains in the limited circumstances where three-judge federal district courts make decisions and where specific statutes authorize appeals to the Supreme Court. There are a relatively small number of federal laws that prescribe that cases under them be heard in a three-judge federal district court. For example, the Voting Rights Act of 1965 provides that challenges to election districts be heard in a three-judge federal district court.

If there is a three-judge federal district court and appellate review is requested, the case skips the U.S. Court of Appeals and goes directly to the Supreme Court. Review is by appeal. This is provided for in 28 U.S.C. §1253:

> Except as otherwise provided by law, any party may appeal to the Supreme Court from an order granting or denying, after notice and hearing, an interlocutory or permanent injunction in any civil action, suit or proceeding required by any Act of Congress to be heard and determined by a district court of three judges.

Many issues have arisen in terms of Supreme Court review of state court judgments and proceedings. That is the focus of this Chapter. We turn first, however, to original jurisdiction.

A.   ORIGINAL JURISDICTION

The Supreme Court's original jurisdiction extends to "all cases affecting ambassadors, other public ministers and consuls, and in those in which a state shall be a party." Article III, Section 2, ¶ 3. Notice that each of these heads of jurisdiction concerns disputes that are arguably national in character: the resolution of disputes involving representatives of foreign sovereigns and the resolution of disputes involving states as parties. The grant, one observer bluntly concludes, "was predicated on distrust of state courts."[5] Even under the Articles of Confederation, disputes between states were to be resolved nationally, albeit by Congress as "the last resort on appeal in all disputes and differences . . . between two or more states concerning boundary, jurisdiction, or any other cause whatever." *Articles of Confederation*, Art. IX. When the Constitution was ratified, there were no fewer than 11 pending state boundary disputes. *See United States v. Texas* (1862). Water rights disputes between states remain one of the principal categories of cases reaching the Court in its exercise of original jurisdiction. *See Montana v. Wyoming and North Dakota* (2011) (holding that Wyoming did not breach the Yellowstone River Compact in adopting new irrigation systems that returned less wastewater to the river for use in downstream states). The need for a forum other than the "home" court of one party seems obvious in such cases.

Recall that *Marbury v. Madison* is an original jurisdiction case. The Court held that Congress has no power to *enlarge* the Court's original jurisdiction. As a practical matter, enlarging the Court's original jurisdiction would impose delays in the resolution of disputes involving parties which the jurisdiction was designed to protect (states and officers who represent foreign sovereigns). The Court has also suggested that Congress is without power to *limit* its original jurisdiction. *See California*

---

5. James Pfander, *Rethinking the Supreme Court's Original Jurisdiction in State-Party Cases*, 82 Calif. L. Rev. 555, 620 (1994).

v. Arizona (1979) (refusing, in a suit by California against Arizona and the federal government, to read a federal statute vesting "exclusive" jurisdiction over certain quiet title actions in federal district courts, as precluding original jurisdiction in the Supreme Court; noting that "a grave constitutional question would immediately arise . . . whether Congress can deprive this Court of original jurisdiction conferred upon it by the Constitution."); *see also California v. Southern Pacific Co.* (1895). Diminishing the Court's original jurisdiction would leave foreign sovereigns to the contingencies of war and diplomacy to resolve their disputes, and states to less suitable forums and the political process.

Notwithstanding these rejections of congressional interference with the Court's original jurisdiction, other forms of control over the Court's original jurisdiction have been asserted by Congress. For example, under 28 U.S.C. §1251(a), only disputes between states are exclusively within the Court's original jurisdiction, whereas §1251(b) provides for concurrent jurisdiction of all other disputes within the Court's original jurisdiction. Emphasizing that concurrent jurisdiction has been the rule since the First Judiciary Act, the Court has upheld the power of Congress to create this rule, explaining that:

> [i]n view of the practical construction put on this provision of the Constitution by Congress at the very moment of the organization of the government, and of the significant fact that from 1789 until now, no court of the United States has ever in its actual adjudications determined to the contrary, we are unable to say that it is not within the power of Congress to grant to the inferior courts of the United States jurisdiction in cases where the Supreme Court has been vested by the Constitution with original jurisdiction. It rests with the legislative department of the government to say to what extent such grants shall be made, and it may safely be assumed that nothing will ever be done to encroach upon the high privileges of those for whose protection the constitutional provision was intended. At any rate, we are unwilling to say that the power to make the grant does not exist.

Ames v. Kansas (1884).

Parties have also regularly contended that legislation setting rules of procedure and remedial powers of other federal courts apply to the Supreme Court in its exercise of original jurisdiction. In response, the Court has exercised discretion to follow or deviate from these rules. *Compare Kansas v. Colorado* (2009) (following federal statute setting expert witness attendance fees for a proceeding "in any court of the United States" without deciding whether Article III "permit[s] Congress to impose such a restriction"), *with South Carolina v. Regan* (1984) (refusing, in litigation by South Carolina against the Secretary of the Treasury, to apply the Anti-Injunction Act barring suits seeking to restrain collection of taxes on ground that, whereas the statute contemplated ex post refund litigation, there was no alternative legal forum open to the state to challenge the validity of a tax).

These cases reflect concerns about congressional control of the contours of original jurisdiction once it is invoked. A more fundamental question is whether the Court itself can, of its own accord, decline to hear a case within its original jurisdiction.

Ohio v. Wyandotte Chemicals Corp.

401 U.S. 493 (1971)

Justice HARLAN delivered the opinion of the Court.

By motion for leave to file a bill of complaint, Ohio seeks to invoke this Court's original jurisdiction. For reasons that follow, we deny the motion for leave to file.

The action, for abatement of a nuisance, is brought on behalf of the State and its citizens, and names as defendants Wyandotte Chemicals Corp. (Wyandotte), Dow Chemical Co. (Dow America), and Dow Chemical Company of Canada, Ltd. (Dow Canada). Wyandotte is incorporated in Michigan and maintains its principal office and place of business there. Dow America is incorporated in Delaware, has its principal office and place of business in Michigan, and owns all the stock of Dow Canada. Dow Canada is incorporated, and does business, in Ontario. A majority of Dow Canada's directors are residents of the United States.

The complaint alleges that Dow Canada and Wyandotte have each dumped mercury into streams whose courses ultimately reach Lake Erie, thus contaminating and polluting that lake's waters, vegetation, fish, and wildlife, and that Dow America is jointly responsible for the acts of its foreign subsidiary. Assuming the State's ability to prove these assertions, Ohio seeks a decree: (1) declaring the introduction of mercury into Lake Erie's tributaries a public nuisance; (2) perpetually enjoining these defendants from introducing mercury into Lake Erie or its tributaries; (3) requiring defendants either to remove the mercury from Lake Erie or to pay the costs of its removal into a fund to be administered by Ohio and used only for that purpose; (4) directing defendants to pay Ohio monetary damages for the harm done to Lake Erie, its fish, wildlife, and vegetation, and the citizens and inhabitants of Ohio.

Original jurisdiction is said to be conferred on this Court by Art. III of the Federal Constitution. 28 U.S.C. §1251(b) provides:

> The Supreme Court shall have original but not exclusive jurisdiction of . . . (3) All actions or proceedings by a State against the citizens of another State or against aliens.

While we consider that Ohio's complaint does state a cause of action that falls within the compass of our original jurisdiction, we have concluded that this Court should nevertheless decline to exercise that jurisdiction.

I

That we have jurisdiction seems clear enough. Beyond doubt, the complaint, on its face, reveals the existence of a genuine "case or controversy" between one State and citizens of another, as well as a foreign subject. Diversity of citizenship is absolute. While we have refused to entertain, for example, original actions designed to exact compliance with a State's penal laws, *Wisconsin v. Pelican Ins. Co.* (1888), or that seek to embroil this tribunal in "political questions," *Mississippi v. Johnson* (1867), this Court has often adjudicated controversies between States and between a State and citizens of another State seeking to abate a nuisance that exists in one State yet produces noxious consequences in another.

Ordinarily, the foregoing would suffice to settle the issue presently under consideration: whether Ohio should be granted leave to file its complaint. For it is a time-honored maxim of the Anglo-American common law tradition that a court possessed of jurisdiction generally must exercise it. *Cohens v. Virginia* (1821). Nevertheless, although it may initially have been contemplated that this Court would always exercise its original jurisdiction when properly called upon to do so, it seems evident to us that changes in the American legal system and the development of American society have rendered untenable, as a practical matter, the view that this Court must stand willing to adjudicate all or most legal disputes that may arise between one State and a citizen or citizens of another.

As our social system has grown more complex, the States have increasingly become enmeshed in a multitude of disputes with persons living outside their borders. Consider, for example, the frequency with which States and nonresidents clash over the application of state laws concerning taxes, motor vehicles, decedents' estates, business torts, government contracts, and so forth. It would indeed be anomalous were this Court to be held out as a potential principal forum for settling such controversies. The simultaneous development of "long-arm jurisdiction" means, in most instances, that no necessity impels us to perform such a role. And the evolution of this Court's responsibilities in the American legal system has brought matters to a point where much would be sacrificed, and little gained, by our exercising original jurisdiction over issues bottomed on local law. This Court's paramount responsibilities to the national system lie almost without exception in the domain of federal law. As the impact on the social structure of federal common, statutory, and constitutional law has expanded, our attention has necessarily been drawn more and more to such matters. We have no claim to special competence in dealing with the numerous conflicts between States and nonresident individuals that raise no serious issues of federal law.

This Court is, moreover, structured to perform as an appellate tribunal, ill-equipped for the task of factfinding, and so forced, in original cases, awkwardly to play the role of factfinder without actually presiding over the introduction of evidence. "Thus, we think it apparent that we must recognize the need [for] the exercise of a sound discretion in order to protect this Court from an abuse of the opportunity to resort to its original jurisdiction in the enforcement by States of claims against citizens of other States."

In our opinion, we may properly exercise such discretion, not simply to shield this Court from noisome, vexatious, or unfamiliar tasks, but also, and we believe principally, as a technique for promoting and furthering the assumptions and value choices that underlie the current role of this Court in the federal system. Thus, at this stage, we go no further than to hold that, as a general matter, we may decline to entertain a complaint brought by a State against the citizens of another State or country only where we can say with assurance that (1) declination of jurisdiction would not disserve any of the principal policies underlying the Article III jurisdictional grant, and (2) the reasons of practical wisdom that persuade us that this Court is an inappropriate forum are consistent with the proposition that our discretion is legitimated by its use to keep this aspect of the Court's functions attuned to its other responsibilities.

II

In applying this analysis to the facts here presented, we believe that the wiser course is to deny Ohio's motion for leave to file its complaint.

A

Two principles seem primarily to have underlain conferring upon this Court original jurisdiction over cases and controversies between a State and citizens of another State or country. The first was the belief that no State should be compelled to resort to the tribunals of other States for redress, since parochial factors might often lead to the appearance, if not the reality, of partiality to one's own. *Chisholm v. Georgia* (1793). The second was that a State, needing an alternative forum, of necessity had to resort to this Court in order to obtain a tribunal competent to exercise jurisdiction over the acts of nonresidents of the aggrieved State.

Neither of these policies is, we think, implicated in this lawsuit. The courts of Ohio, under modern principles of the scope of subject matter and *in personam* jurisdiction, have a claim as compelling as any that can be made out for this Court to exercise jurisdiction to adjudicate the instant controversy, and they would decide it under the same common law of nuisance upon which our determination would have to rest. In essence, the State has charged Dow Canada and Wyandotte with the commission of acts, albeit beyond Ohio's territorial boundaries, that have produced and, it is said, continue to produce, disastrous effects within Ohio's own domain. While this Court, and doubtless Canadian courts, if called upon to assess the validity of any decree rendered against either Dow Canada or Wyandotte, would be alert to ascertain whether the judgment rested upon an even-handed application of justice, it is unlikely that we would totally deny Ohio's competence to act if the allegations made here are proved true.

B

Our reasons for thinking that, as a practical matter, it would be inappropriate for this Court to attempt to adjudicate the issues Ohio seeks to present are several. History reveals that the course of this Court's prior efforts to settle disputes regarding interstate air and water pollution has been anything but smooth. In *Missouri v. Illinois* (1906), Justice Holmes was at pains to underscore the great difficulty that the Court faced in attempting to pronounce a suitable general rule of law to govern such controversies. Justice Clarke's closing plea in *New York v. New Jersey* (1921), strikingly illustrates the sense of futility that has accompanied this Court's attempts to treat with the complex technical and political matters that inhere in all disputes of the kind at hand:

> We cannot withhold the suggestion, inspired by the consideration of this case, that the grave problem of sewage disposal presented by the large and growing populations living on the shores of New York Bay is one more likely to be wisely solved by cooperative study and by conference and mutual concession on the part of representatives of the States so vitally interested in it than by proceedings in any court however constituted.

The difficulties that ordinarily beset such cases are severely compounded by the particular setting in which this controversy has reached us. For example, the parties have informed us, without contradiction, that a number of official bodies are already actively involved in regulating the conduct complained of here. A Michigan circuit court has enjoined Wyandotte from operating its mercury cell process without judicial authorization. The company is, moreover, currently utilizing a recycling process specifically approved by the Michigan Water Resources Commission, and remains subject to the continued scrutiny of that agency. Dow Canada reports monthly to the Ontario Water Resources Commission on its compliance with the commission's order prohibiting the company from passing any mercury into the environment.

Additionally, Ohio and Michigan are both participants in the Lake Erie Enforcement Conference, convened a year ago by the Secretary of the Interior pursuant to the Federal Water Pollution Control Act, 62 Stat. 1155, as amended. The Conference is studying all forms and sources of pollution, including mercury, infecting Lake Erie. The purpose of this Conference is to provide a basis for concerted remedial action by the States or, if progress in that regard is not rapidly made, for corrective proceedings initiated by the Federal Government. 33 U.S.C. §466g. And the International Joint Commission, established by the Boundary Waters Treaty of 1909 between the United States and Canada issued on January 14, 1971, a comprehensive report, the culmination of a six-year study carried out at the request of the contracting parties, concerning the contamination of Lake Erie. That document makes specific recommendations for joint programs to abate these environmental hazards and recommends that the IJC be given authority to supervise and coordinate this effort.

In view of all this, granting Ohio's motion for leave to file would, in effect, commit this Court's resources to the task of trying to settle a small piece of a much larger problem that many competent adjudicatory and conciliatory bodies are actively grappling with on a more practical basis.

The nature of the case Ohio brings here is equally disconcerting. It can fairly be said that what is in dispute is not so much the law as the facts. And the factfinding process we are asked to undertake is, to say the least, formidable. We already know, just from what has been placed before us on this motion, that Lake Erie suffers from several sources of pollution other than mercury; that the scientific conclusion that mercury is a serious water pollutant is a novel one; that whether and to what extent the existence of mercury in natural waters can safely or reasonably be tolerated is a question for which there is presently no firm answer; and that virtually no published research is available describing how one might extract mercury that is in fact contaminating water. Indeed, Ohio is raising factual questions that are essentially ones of first impression to the scientists. The notion that appellate judges, even with the assistance of a most competent Special Master, might appropriately undertake at this time to unravel these complexities is, to say the least, unrealistic. Other factual complexities abound. For example, the Department of the Interior has stated that eight American companies are discharging, or have discharged, mercury into Lake Erie or its tributaries. We would, then, need to assess the business practices and relative culpability of each to frame appropriate relief as to the one now before us.

Finally, in what has been said, it is vitally important to stress that we are not called upon by this lawsuit to resolve difficult or important problems of federal law.

III

What has been said here cannot, of course, be taken as denigrating in the slightest the public importance of the underlying problem Ohio would have us tackle. Reversing the increasing contamination of our environment is manifestly a matter of fundamental import and utmost urgency.

Ohio's motion for leave to file its complaint is denied without prejudice to its right to commence other appropriate judicial proceedings.

Justice DOUGLAS, dissenting.

The complaint in this case presents basically a classic type of case congenial to our original jurisdiction. It is to abate a public nuisance. Such was the claim of Georgia against a Tennessee company which was discharging noxious gas across the border into Georgia. *Georgia v. Tennessee Copper Co.* (1907). The Court said:

> It is a fair and reasonable demand on the part of a sovereign that the air over its territory should not be polluted on a great scale by sulphurous acid gas, that the forests on its mountains, be they better or worse, and whatever domestic destruction they have suffered, should not be further destroyed or threatened by the act of persons beyond its control, that the crops and orchards on its hills should not be endangered from the same source.

Dumping of sewage in an interstate stream, *Missouri v. Illinois* (1906) or towing garbage to sea only to have the tides carry it to a State's beaches, *New Jersey v. New York City* (1931) have presented analogous situations which the Court has entertained in suits invoking our original jurisdiction. The pollution of Lake Erie or its tributaries by the discharge of mercury or compounds thereof, if proved, certainly creates a public nuisance of a seriousness and magnitude which a State, by our historic standards, may prosecute or pursue as *parens patriae.*

The suit is not precluded by the Boundary Waters Treaty of 1909 [because] it does not evince a purpose on the part of the national governments of the United States and Canada to exclude their States and Provinces from seeking other remedies for water pollution.

This litigation, as it unfolds, will, of course, implicate much federal law. The case will deal with an important portion of the federal domain — the navigable streams and the navigable inland waters which are under the sovereignty of the Federal Government.

Congress has enacted numerous laws reaching that domain. [Justice Douglas discussed the Rivers and Harbors Act of 1899, "fish and wildlife legislation . . . enacted [in the 1930s] granting the Secretary of the Interior various heads of jurisdiction over the effects on fish and wildlife of 'domestic sewage, mine, petroleum, and industrial wastes, erosion silt, and other polluting substances,'" the Federal Water Pollution Control Act, "[which] gives broad powers to the Secretary to take action respecting water pollution on complaints of States, and other procedures to secure federal abatement of the pollution," and the National Environmental Policy Act of 1969, "[which] gives elaborate ecological directions to federal agencies and supplies procedures for their enforcement."]

Yet the federal scheme is not preemptive of state action. Section 1(b) of the Water Pollution Control Act declares that the policy of Congress is "to recognize, preserve, and protect the primary responsibilities and rights of the States in preventing and controlling water pollution." Section 10 provides that, except where the Attorney General has actually obtained a court order of pollution abatement on behalf of the United States, "State and interstate action to abate pollution of . . . navigable waters . . . shall not . . . be displaced by Federal enforcement action."

There is much complaint that, in spite of the arsenal of federal power, little is being done. That, of course, is not our problem. But it is our concern that state action is not preempted by federal law. In light of the history of water pollution control efforts in this country, it cannot be denied that a vast residual authority rests in the States. And there is no better established remedy in state law than authority to abate a nuisance.

Much is made of the burdens and perplexities of these original actions. Some are complex, notably those involving water rights. The apportionment of the waters of the North Platte River among Colorado, Wyoming, and Nebraska came to us in an original action in which we named as Special Master Hon. Michael J. Doherty. We entered a complicated decree which dissenters viewed with alarm, *Nebraska v. Wyoming* (1945) but which has not demanded even an hour of the Court's time during the 26 years since it was entered.

[T]he practice has been to appoint a Special Master, which we certainly would do in this case. We could also appoint—or authorize the Special Master to retain—a panel of scientific advisers. The problems in this case are simple compared with those in the water cases discussed above. It is now known that metallic mercury deposited in water is often transformed into a dangerous chemical. This lawsuit would determine primarily the extent, if any, to which the defendants are contributing to that contamination at the present time. It would determine, secondarily, the remedies within reach—the importance of mercury in the particular manufacturing processes, the alternative processes available, the need for a remedy against a specified polluter as contrasted to a basin-wide regulation, and the like.

The problem, though clothed in chemical secrecies, can be exposed by the experts. It would indeed be one of the simplest problems yet posed in the category of cases under the head of our original jurisdiction.

I can think of no case of more transcending public importance than this one.

* * *

Whatever one makes of the discretion to decline to exercise original jurisdiction where there are plainly other forums in which the parties can resolve their dispute, the stakes of declining jurisdiction are particularly high in litigation between states because only the Supreme Court has authority to hear these cases under 28 U.S.C. §1251(a). As you read the next case, consider whether Justice Thomas is correct to give weight to Congress' policy judgments regarding the creation of exclusive jurisdiction in §1251(a) given the Court's reluctance to accept limitations imposed by Congress on its original jurisdiction.

Nebraska v. Colorado

136 S. Ct. 1034 (2016)

The motion for leave to file a bill of complaint is denied.

Justice THOMAS, with whom Justice ALITO joins, dissenting from the denial of motion for leave to file complaint.

Federal law does not, on its face, give this Court discretion to decline to decide cases within its original jurisdiction. Yet the Court has long exercised such discretion, and does so again today in denying, without explanation, Nebraska and Oklahoma's motion for leave to file a complaint against Colorado. I would not dispose of the complaint so hastily. Because our discretionary approach to exercising our original jurisdiction is questionable, and because the plaintiff States have made a reasonable case that this dispute falls within our original and exclusive jurisdiction, I would grant the plaintiff States leave to file their complaint.

I

The Constitution provides that "[i]n all Cases . . . in which a State shall be [a] Party, the supreme Court shall have original Jurisdiction." Art. III, §2, cl. 2. In accordance with Article III, Congress has long provided by statute that this Court "shall have original and exclusive jurisdiction of all controversies between two or more States." 28 U.S.C. §1251(a).

Federal law is unambiguous: If there is a controversy between two States, this Court—and only this Court—has jurisdiction over it. Nothing in §1251(a) suggests that the Court can opt to decline jurisdiction over such a controversy. Context confirms that §1251(a) confers no such discretion. When Congress has chosen to give this Court discretion over its merits docket, it has done so clearly. Compare §1251(a) (the Court "shall have" jurisdiction over controversies between States) with §1254(1) (cases in the courts of appeals "may be reviewed" by this Court by writ of certiorari) and §1257(a) (final judgments of state courts "may be reviewed" by this Court by writ of certiorari).

The Court's lack of discretion is confirmed by the fact that, unlike other matters within our original jurisdiction, our jurisdiction over controversies between States is exclusive. Compare §1251(a) with §1251(b) (the Court "shall have original but not exclusive jurisdiction" of other cases over which Article III gives this Court original jurisdiction). If this Court does not exercise jurisdiction over a controversy between two States, then the complaining State has no judicial forum in which to seek relief. When presented with such a controversy, "[w]e have no more right to decline the exercise of jurisdiction which is given, than to usurp that which is not given." *Cohens v. Virginia* (1821) (Marshall, C.J.).

Nonetheless, the Court has exercised discretion and declined to hear cases that fall within the terms of its original jurisdiction. *See, e.g., United States v. Nevada* (1973) (controversy between United States and individual States); *Ohio v. Wyandotte Chemicals Corp.* (1971) (action by a State against citizens of other States). The Court has even exercised this discretion to decline cases where, as here, the dispute is between two States and thus falls within our *exclusive* jurisdiction. *See, e.g., Arizona v. New Mexico* (1976). The Court has concluded that its original jurisdiction is "obligatory only in appropriate cases" and has favored a "sparing use" of that jurisdiction. *Illinois v. Milwaukee* (1972). The Court's reasons for transforming its mandatory, original jurisdiction into discretionary jurisdiction have been rooted in policy considerations. The Court has, for example, cited its purported lack of "special competence in dealing with" many interstate disputes and emphasized its modern role "as an appellate tribunal." *Wyandotte Chemicals Corp.*

Because our discretionary approach appears to be at odds with the statutory text, it bears reconsideration. Moreover, the "reasons" we have given to support the discretionary approach are policy judgments that are in conflict with the policy choices that Congress made in the statutory text specifying the Court's original jurisdiction.

II

This case involves a suit brought by two States against another State, and thus presents an opportunity for us to reevaluate our discretionary approach to our original jurisdiction.

Federal law generally prohibits the manufacture, distribution, dispensing, and possession of marijuana. *See* Controlled Substances Act (CSA). Emphasizing the breadth of the CSA, this Court has stated that the statute establishes "a comprehensive regime to combat the international and interstate traffic in illicit drugs." *Gonzales v. Raich* (2005). Despite the CSA's broad prohibitions, in 2012 the State of Colorado adopted Amendment 64, which amends the State Constitution to legalize, regulate, and facilitate the recreational use of marijuana. *See* Colo. Const., Art. XVIII, §16. Amendment 64 exempts from Colorado's criminal prohibitions certain uses of marijuana. Amendment 64 directs the Colorado Department of Revenue to promulgate licensing procedures for marijuana establishments. And the amendment requires the Colorado General Assembly to enact an excise tax for sales of marijuana from cultivation facilities to manufacturing facilities and retail stores.

In December 2014, Nebraska and Oklahoma filed in this Court a motion seeking leave to file a complaint against Colorado. The plaintiff States—which share borders with Colorado—allege that Amendment 64 affirmatively facilitates the violation and frustration of federal drug laws. They claim that Amendment 64 has "increased trafficking and transportation of Colorado-sourced marijuana" into their territories, requiring them to expend significant "law enforcement, judicial system, and penal system resources" to combat the increased trafficking and transportation of marijuana. The plaintiff States seek a declaratory judgment that the CSA pre-empts certain of Amendment 64's licensing, regulation, and taxation provisions and an injunction barring their implementation.

The complaint, on its face, presents a "controvers[y] between two or more States" that this Court alone has authority to adjudicate. 28 U.S.C. §1251(a). The plaintiff States have alleged significant harms to their sovereign interests caused by another State. Whatever the merit of the plaintiff States' claims, we should let this complaint proceed further rather than denying leave without so much as a word of explanation.

I respectfully dissent from the denial of the motion for leave to file a complaint.

* * *

Justices Alito and Thomas again dissented from the denial of the motion for leave to file a complaint in *Texas v. Pennsylvania* (2020), a suit brought by the state of Texas seeking to prevent Georgia, Michigan, Pennsylvania, and Wisconsin from certifying their 2020 election results on the basis of unfounded "irregularities." Pennsylvania's attorney general opposed the motion as a "seditious abuse of the judicial process" and the motion was denied on the ground that Texas had no "judicially cognizable interest in the manner in which another state conducts its elections." While expressing "no view on any other issue in the case," Justice Alito, joined by Justice Thomas, stated that "[i]n my view, we do not have discretion to deny the filing of a bill of complaint in a case that falls within our original jurisdiction."

B.   APPELLATE JURISDICTION OVER FEDERAL COURTS

The Supreme Court's appellate jurisdiction is not constitutionally mandatory or self-executing. Instead, Article III provides that in all cases other than those subject to the Court's original jurisdiction, "the Supreme Court shall have appellate Jurisdiction, both as to Law and Fact, *with such Exceptions, and under such Regulations as the Congress shall make.*" Art. III, Section 2, ¶ 3 (emphasis added). We examine the constitutional limits on congressional control of the appellate jurisdiction of the Court in considerable detail in Chapter 4. Here we focus on the basic statutory grants of appellate jurisdiction to review the decisions of the federal courts of appeal, the decisions of three-judge district courts, and the decisions of the state's highest courts.

One unmistakable trend worth noting before we begin is the general reduction of the Supreme Court's appellate docket. "During the 1940s, the Supreme Court decided roughly 177 appeals per Term," and the number remained in the low to mid 100s until the 1990s.[6] "By the 2000 Term, the Court decided only 87 appeals" and by 2017, "the Court decided 68 appeals, which represent[ed] the fewest number of merits decisions at any point since the mid-twentieth century."[7] In 2020, the number had fallen to just 60 appeals—a figure that is consistent with the size of the Court's appellate docket in the antebellum period of the nineteenth century.[8]

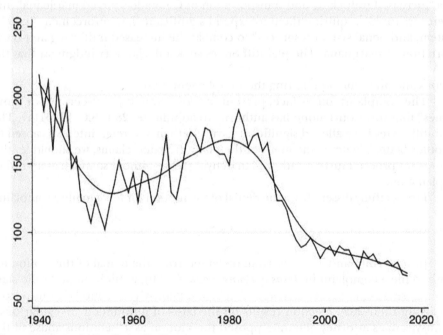

Source : Heise et al., *Does Docket Size Matter.*

---

6. Michael Heise et al., *Does Docket Size Matter? Revisiting Empirical Accounts of the Supreme Court's Incredibly Shrinking Docket*, 95 NOTRE DAME L. REV. 1565, 1567 (2020).

7. *Id.*

8. *The Statistics*, 134 HARV. L. REV. 610, 618 (2020) (summarizing data for 2019 Term); Heise et al., *supra* note 6 at 1569.

The reasons for the trend are complex and hotly debated. They include a 1988 statute that eliminated appeals as of right, leaving all appeals to the Court discretionary under the writ of certiorari, development of a cert pool of law clerks who screen certiorari petitions, and ideological changes in the composition of the Court.[9]

Diminished merits decision of appeals has overlapped with a significant expansion of the Court's orders and summary disposition of cases on expedited review without grant of certiorari, full merits briefing, public oral argument, or signed, reasoned, published opinions. We take up the Court's so-called "shadow docket" in the final part of this section.

1. *Review of Federal Courts of Appeals*

Hohn v. United States

524 U.S. 236 (1998)

Justice KENNEDY delivered the opinion of the Court.

We granted certiorari to determine whether the Court has jurisdiction to review decisions of the courts of appeals denying applications for certificates of appealability. The Court, we hold, does have jurisdiction.

I

In 1992, petitioner Arnold Hohn was charged with a number of drug-related offenses, including the use or carrying of a firearm during and in relation to a drug trafficking offense, 18 U.S.C. §924(c)(1). Over defense counsel's objection, the District Court instructed the jury that "use" of a firearm meant having the firearm "available to aid in the commission of" the offense. The jury convicted Hohn on all counts. Hohn did not challenge the instruction in his direct appeal, and the Court of Appeals affirmed.

Two years after Hohn's conviction became final, we held the term "use" in §924(c)(1) required active employment of the firearm. Proximity and accessibility alone were not sufficient. *Bailey v. United States* (1995). Hohn filed a *pro se* motion under 28 U.S.C. §2255 to vacate his 18 U.S.C. §924(c)(1) conviction in light of *Bailey* on the grounds the evidence presented at his trial was insufficient to prove use of a firearm. Although the Government conceded the jury instruction given at Hohn's trial did not comply with *Bailey*, the District Court denied relief because, in its view, Hohn had waived the claim by failing to challenge the instruction on direct appeal.

While Hohn's motion was pending before the District Court, Congress enacted the Antiterrorism and Effective Death Penalty Act of 1996 (AEDPA). Section 102 of AEDPA amends the statutory provision which had required state prisoners to

---

9. Heise et al., *supra* note 6 at 1570-73.

obtain a certificate of probable cause before appealing the denial of a habeas petition. The amended provision provides:

> Unless a circuit justice or judge issues a certificate of appealability, an appeal may not be taken to the court of appeals from—
> (A) the final order in a habeas corpus proceeding in which the detention complained of arises out of process issued by a State court; or
> (B) the final order in a proceeding under section 2255.

28 U.S.C. §2253(c)(1).

Certificates of appealability may issue "only if the applicant has made a substantial showing of the denial of a constitutional right." §2253(c)(2).

Hohn filed a notice of appeal on July 29, 1996, three months after AEDPA's enactment. The Court of Appeals treated the notice of appeal as an application for a certificate of appealability and referred it to a three-judge panel. The panel decided Hohn's application did not meet the standard for a §2253(c) certificate. In the panel's view, "*Bailey* did no more than interpret a statute, and an incorrect application of a statute by a district court, or any other court, does not violate the Constitution." Given this determination, the panel declined to issue a certificate of appealability.

Judge McMillian dissented. In his view, *Bailey* cast doubt on whether Hohn's conduct in fact violated 18 U.S.C. §924(c)(1). The Due Process Clause, he reasoned, does not "tolerat[e] convictions for conduct that was never criminal," so Hohn had made a sufficient showing of a constitutional deprivation. . . .

Hohn petitioned this Court for a writ of certiorari to review the denial of the certificate, seeking to invoke our jurisdiction under 28 U.S.C. §1254(1). The Government now found itself in agreement with Hohn, saying his claim was, in fact, constitutional in nature. It asked us to vacate the judgment and remand so the Court of Appeals could reconsider in light of this concession. We may not vacate and remand, of course, unless we first have jurisdiction over the case; and since Hohn and the Government both argue in favor of our jurisdiction, we appointed an *amicus curiae* to argue the contrary position.

II

Title 28 U.S.C. §1254 is the statute most often invoked for jurisdiction in this Court. It provides in relevant part:

> Cases in the courts of appeals may be reviewed by the Supreme Court by the following methods:
> (1) By writ of certiorari granted upon the petition of any party to any civil or criminal case, before or after rendition of judgment or decree.

The first phrase of the quoted statute confines our jurisdiction to "[c]ases in" the courts of appeals. *Nixon v. Fitzgerald* (1982). The question is whether an application for a certificate meets the description.

There can be little doubt that Hohn's application for a certificate of appealability constitutes a case under §1254(1). As we have noted, "[t]he words 'case' and 'cause' are constantly used as synonyms in statutes . . . , each meaning a proceeding in court, a suit, or action." *Blyew v. United States* (1871). The dispute over Hohn's entitlement to a certificate falls within this definition. It is a proceeding seeking relief for an immediate and redressable injury, *i.e.*, wrongful detention in violation of the Constitution. There is adversity as well as the other requisite qualities of a "case" as the term is used in both Article III of the Constitution and the statute here under consideration. This is significant, we think, for cases are addressed in the ordinary course of the judicial process, and, as a general rule, when the district court has denied relief and applicable requirements of finality have been satisfied, the next step is review in the court of appeals. That the statute permits the certificate to be issued by a "circuit justice or judge" does not mean the action of the circuit judge in denying the certificate is his or her own action, rather than the action of the court of appeals to whom the judge is appointed.

The course of events here illustrates the point. The application moved through the Eighth Circuit in the same manner as cases in general do. The matter was entered on the docket of the Court of Appeals, submitted to a panel, and decided in a published opinion, including a dissent. The court entered judgment on it, issued a mandate, and entertained a petition for rehearing and suggestion for rehearing en banc. The Eighth Circuit has since acknowledged its rejection of Hohn's application made Circuit law. *United States v. Apker* (8th Cir. 1996). One judge specifically indicated he was bound by the decision even though he believed it was wrongly decided. These factors suggest Hohn's certificate application was as much a case in the Court of Appeals as are the other matters decided by it.

We also draw guidance from the fact that every Court of Appeals except the Court of Appeals for the District of Columbia Circuit has adopted Rules to govern the disposition of certificate applications. We also note the Internal Operating Procedures for the Court of Appeals for the Eighth Circuit require certificate applications to be heard as a general matter by three-judge administrative panels. These directives would be meaningless if applications for certificates of appealability were not matters subject to the control and disposition of the courts of appeals.

In this instance, as in all other cases of which we are aware, the order denying the certificate was issued in the name of the court and under its seal. That is as it should be, for the order was judicial in character and had consequences with respect to the finality of the order of the District Court and the continuing jurisdiction of the Court of Appeals.

The Federal Rules of Appellate Procedure make specific provision for consideration of applications for certificates of appealability by the entire court. Rule 22(b) states:

> In a habeas corpus proceeding in which the detention complained of arises out of process issued by a State court, an appeal by the applicant for the writ may not proceed unless a district or a circuit judge issues a certificate of appealability pursuant to section 2253(c) of title 28, United States Code. . . . If the district judge has denied the certificate, the applicant for the writ may then request issuance of the certificate by a circuit judge. If such a request is addressed to the court of appeals, it shall be deemed addressed to the judges thereof and shall be considered by a circuit judge or judges as the court deems appropriate. If no express request for a certificate is filed, the notice of appeal shall be deemed to constitute a request addressed to the judges of the court of appeals.

On its face, the Rule applies only to state, and not federal, prisoners. It is nonetheless instructive on the proper construction of §2253(c).

Rule 22(b) by no means prohibits application to an individual judge, nor could it, given the language of the statute. There would be incongruity, nevertheless, were the same ruling deemed in one instance the order of a judge acting *ex curia* and in a second the action of the court, depending upon the caption of the application or the style of the order.

Some early cases from this Court acknowledged a distinction between acting in an administrative and a judicial capacity. When judges perform administrative functions, their decisions are not subject to our review. *United States v. Ferreira* (1851) *see also Gordon v. United States* (1864). Those opinions were careful to say it was the nonjudicial character of the judges' actions which deprived this Court of jurisdiction. *Ferreira* (tribunal not judicial when the proceedings were *ex parte* and did not involve the issuance of process, summoning of witnesses, or entry of a judgment); *Gordon* (tribunal not judicial when it lacks power to enter and enforce judgments). Decisions regarding applications for certificates of appealability, in contrast, are judicial in nature. It is typical for both parties to enter appearances and to submit briefs at appropriate times and for the court of appeals to enter a judgment and to issue a mandate at the end of the proceedings, as happened here. Construing the issuance of a certificate of appealability as an administrative function, moreover, would suggest an entity not wielding judicial power might review the decision of an Article III court. In light of the constitutional questions which would surround such an arrangement, *see Gordon; Hayburn's Case* (1792), we should avoid any such implication.

We further disagree with the contention, advanced by the dissent and by Court-appointed *amicus*, that a request to proceed before a court of appeals should be regarded as a threshold inquiry separate from the merits which, if denied, prevents the case from ever being in the court of appeals. Precedent forecloses this argument. In *Ex parte Quirin* (1942), we confronted the analogous question whether a request for leave to file a petition for a writ of habeas corpus was a case in a district court for the purposes of the then-extant statute governing court of appeals review of district court decisions. *See* 28 U.S.C. §225(a) (courts of appeals had jurisdiction to review final decisions "[i]n the district courts, in all cases save where a direct review of the decision may be had in the Supreme Court"). We held the request for leave constituted a case in the district court over which the court of appeals could assert jurisdiction, even though the district court had denied the request. We reasoned, "[p]resentation of the petition for judicial action is the institution of a suit. Hence the denial by the district court of leave to file the petitions in these causes was the judicial determination of a case or controversy, reviewable on appeal to the Court of Appeals."

We reached a similar conclusion in *Nixon v. Fitzgerald*. There President Nixon sought to appeal an interlocutory District Court order rejecting his claim of absolute immunity. The Court of Appeals summarily dismissed the appeal because, in its view, the order failed to present a "serious and unsettled question" of law sufficient to bring the case within the collateral order doctrine announced in *Cohen v. Beneficial Industrial Loan Corp.* (1949). Because the Court of Appeals had dismissed for failure to satisfy this threshold jurisdictional requirement, respondent Fitzgerald argued, "the District Court's order was not an appealable 'case' properly 'in' the Court of Appeals within the meaning of §1254." *Nixon v. Fitzgerald* (1983). Turning aside this argument, we ruled "petitioner did present a 'serious and unsettled' and therefore appealable question to the Court of Appeals. It follow[ed] that the case was 'in' the Court of Appeals under §1254 and properly within our certiorari jurisdiction." We elaborated: "There can be no serious doubt concerning our power to review a court of appeals' decision to dismiss for lack of jurisdiction. . . . If we lacked authority to do so, decisions to dismiss for want of jurisdiction would be insulated entirely from review by this Court." *Id.*; *see also United States v. Nixon* (1974) (holding appeal of District Court's denial of motion to quash *subpoena duces tecum* was in the Court of Appeals for purposes of §1254(1)).

We have shown no doubts about our jurisdiction to review dismissals by the Courts of Appeals for failure to file a timely notice of appeal under §1254(1). The filing of a proper notice of appeal is mandatory and jurisdictional. *Torres v. Oakland Scavenger Co.* (1988). The failure to satisfy this jurisdictional prerequisite has not kept the case from entering the Court of Appeals, however. We have reviewed these dismissals often and without insisting the petitioner satisfy the requirements for an extraordinary writ and without suggesting our lack of jurisdiction to do so.

We have also held that §1254(1) permits us to review denials of motions for leave to intervene in the Court of Appeals in proceedings to review the decision of an administrative agency. *Automobile Workers v. Scofield* (1965). Together these decisions foreclose the proposition that the failure to satisfy a threshold prerequisite for court of appeals jurisdiction, such as the issuance of a certificate of appealability, prevents a case from being in the court of appeals for purposes of §1254(1).

It would have made no difference had the Government declined to oppose Hohn's application for a certificate of appealability. In *Scofield*, we held that §1254(1) gave us jurisdiction to review the Court of Appeals' denial of a motion for leave to intervene despite the fact that neither the agency nor any of the other parties opposed intervention. In the same manner, petitions for certiorari to this Court are often met with silence or even acquiescence; yet no one would suggest this deprives the petitions of the adversity needed to constitute a case. Assuming, of course, the underlying action satisfies the other requisites of a case, including injury in fact, the circumstance that the question before the court is a preliminary issue, such as the denial of a certificate of appealability or venue, does not oust appellate courts of the jurisdiction to review a ruling on the matter. For instance, a case does not lack adversity simply because the remedy sought from a particular court is dismissal for improper venue rather than resolution of the merits. Federal Rule of Civil Procedure 12(b)(3) specifically permits a party to move to dismiss for improper venue before joining issue on any substantive point through the filing of a responsive pleading, and we have long treated appeals of dismissals for improper venue as cases in the courts of appeals. It is true we have held appellate jurisdiction improper when district courts have denied, rather than granted, motions to dismiss for improper venue. The jurisdictional problem in those cases, however, was the interlocutory nature of the appeal, not the absence of a proper case.

The argument that this Court lacks jurisdiction under §1254(1) to review threshold jurisdictional inquiries is further refuted by the recent amendment to 28 U.S.C. §2244(b)(3). The statute requires state prisoners filing second or successive habeas applications under §2254 to first "move in the appropriate court of appeals for an order authorizing the district court to consider the application." 28 U.S.C.

§2244(b)(3)(A). The statute further provides "[t]he grant or denial of an authorization by a court of appeals to file a second or successive application shall not be appealable and shall not be the subject of a petition for rehearing or for a writ of certiorari." §2244(b)(3)(E). It would have been unnecessary to include a provision barring certiorari review if a motion to file a second or successive application would not otherwise have constituted a case in the court of appeals for purposes of 28 U.S.C. §1254(1). We are reluctant to adopt a construction making another statutory provision superfluous. . . .

The clear limit on this Court's jurisdiction to review denials of motions to file second or successive petitions by writ of certiorari contrasts with the absence of an analogous limitation to certiorari review of denials of applications for certificates of appealability. . . . [W]e think a Congress concerned enough to bar our jurisdiction in one instance would have been just as explicit in denying it in the other, were that its intention. *See, e.g., Bates v. United States* (1997) ("'[W]here Congress includes particular language in one section of a statute but omits it in another section of the same Act, it is generally presumed that Congress acts intentionally and purposely in the disparate inclusion or exclusion'").

Today's holding conforms our commonsense practice to the statutory scheme, making it unnecessary to invoke our extraordinary jurisdiction in routine cases, which present important and meritorious claims. . . .

Our decision, we must acknowledge, is in direct conflict with the portion of our decision in *House v. Mayo* (1945), holding that we lack statutory certiorari jurisdiction to review refusals to issue certificates of probable cause. . . . Its conclusion was erroneous, and it should not be followed.

We hold this Court has jurisdiction under §1254(1) to review denials of applications for certificates of appealability by a circuit judge or a panel of a court of appeals. The portion of *House v. Mayo* holding this Court lacks statutory certiorari jurisdiction over denials of certificates of probable cause is overruled. In light of the position asserted by the Solicitor General in the brief for the United States filed August 18, 1997, the judgment of the Court of Appeals is vacated, and the case is remanded for further consideration consistent with this opinion.

[The concurring opinion of Justice SOUTER is omitted.]

Justice SCALIA, with whom THE CHIEF JUSTICE, Justice O'CONNOR, and Justice THOMAS join, dissenting.

This Court's jurisdiction under 28 U.S.C. §1254(1) is limited to "[c]ases in the courts of appeals." Section 102 of AEDPA provides that "[u]nless a circuit justice or judge issues a certificate of appealability, an appeal may not be taken to the court of appeals from . . . the final order in a habeas corpus proceeding under section 2255," that is, a district court habeas proceeding challenging federal custody. Petitioner, who is challenging federal custody under 28 U.S.C. §2255, did not obtain a certificate of appealability (COA). By the plain language of AEDPA, his appeal "from" the district court's "final order" "may not be taken to the court of appeals." Because it could not be taken *to* the Court of Appeals, it quite obviously was never *in* the Court of Appeals; and because it was never in the Court of Appeals, we lack jurisdiction under §1254(1) to entertain it.

An application for a COA, standing alone, does not have the requisite qualities of a legal "case" under any known definition. It does not assert a grievance against anyone, does not seek remedy or redress for any legal injury, and does not even require a "party" on the other side. It is nothing more than a request for permission to seek review. Petitioner's grievance is with respondent for unlawful custody, and the remedy he seeks is release from that custody pursuant to §2255. The request for a COA is not some separate "case" that can subsist apart from that underlying suit; it is merely a procedural requirement that must be fulfilled before petitioner's §2255 action—his "case" or "cause"—can advance to the appellate court. . . .

The purpose of AEDPA is not obscure. It was to eliminate the interminable delays in the execution of state and federal criminal sentences, and the shameful overloading of our federal criminal justice system, produced by various aspects of this Court's habeas corpus jurisprudence. And the purpose of the specific provision of AEDPA at issue here is also not obscure: It was designed . . . to end §2255 litigation in the district court unless a court of appeals judge or the circuit justice finds reasonable basis to appeal. By giving literally unprecedented meaning to the words in two relevant statutes, and overruling the premise of Congress's enactment, the Court adds new, Byzantine detail to a habeas corpus scheme Congress meant to streamline and simplify. I respectfully dissent.

* * *

The Class Action Fairness Act gives the courts of appeal discretion to review an interlocutory decision of a district court either granting or denying a motion to remand a class action. *See* 28 U.S.C. §1453(c)(1) ("a court of appeals *may accept* an appeal from an order of a district court granting or denying a motion to remand a class action to the State court from which it was removed if application is made to the court of appeals not more than 10 days after entry of the order.") (emphasis added). This is not unlike the certificate of appealability in habeas proceedings—the court of appeals is granted discretion by Congress to decide whether to take up the appeal. If a court of appeals denies a party permission to appeal a district court decision about remand in the class action removal context, is that denial subject to review by certiorari in the Supreme Court under 28 U.S.C. §1254(1)?

In *Dark Cherokee Basin Operating Co., LLC v. Owens* (2014), the Court confronted this question. The Tenth Circuit denied permission to appeal a remand order by the district court that rested on the incorrect assumption that the party seeking removal to federal court had to submit evidence establishing the amount in controversy in the initial removal. Under 28 U.S.C. §1446(a) only a short, plain statement is necessary, and these allegations are to be "accepted if made in good faith." If the amount in controversy is formally contested, then proof may be required. The district court erroneously held that proof was required in the notice of removal. The defendant sought permission from the Tenth Circuit to appeal under §1453, but the Tenth Circuit denied permission, stating it had "done so [u]pon careful consideration of the parties' submissions, as well as the applicable law." The defendant then sought certiorari in the Supreme Court under §1254(1).

An amicus brief contended the Supreme Court had no jurisdiction because the merits of the district court's remand order were not before it, only the circuit court's discretionary decision to deny an appeal. The Court upheld its jurisdiction, relying on *Hohn* and emphasizing that reviewing the Tenth Circuit's exercise of discretion implicated the merits of the district court's remand order:

> The case was "in" the Court of Appeals because of Dart's leave-to-appeal application, and we have jurisdiction to review what the Court of Appeals did with that application. *See* 28 U.S.C. §1254; *Hohn v. United States* (1998). . . .
>
> Discretion to review a remand order is not rudderless. *See Highmark Inc. v. Allcare Health Management System, Inc.* (2014) ("matters of discretion are reviewable for abuse of discretion"). A court "would necessarily abuse its discretion if it based its ruling on an erroneous view of the law." *Cooter & Gell v. Hartmarx Corp.* (1990).

The Court also pointed to the practical problem that would arise were it to deny certiorari: future litigants in the Tenth Circuit will assume they have to prove the amount in controversy to avoid remand, and having marshalled that proof, they will not be in a position to assert their right to make a short and plain statement.

> In practical effect, the Court of Appeals' denial of review established the law not simply for this case, but for future CAFA removals sought by defendants in the Tenth Circuit. The likelihood is slim that a later case will arise in which the Tenth Circuit will face a plea to retract the rule that both Owens and the District Court ascribed to decisions of the Court of Appeals: Defendants seeking to remove under CAFA must be sent back to state court unless they submit with the notice of removal evidence proving the alleged amount in controversy. On this point, Judge Hartz's observation, dissenting from the Tenth Circuit's denial of rehearing en banc, bears recounting in full:
>
>> After today's decision any diligent attorney (and one can assume that an attorney representing a defendant in a case involving at least $5 million—the threshold for removal under CAFA—would have substantial incentive to be diligent) would submit to the evidentiary burden rather than take a chance on remand to state court.
>
> With no responsible attorney likely to renew the fray, Judge Hartz anticipated, "the issue will not arise again." Consequently, the law applied by the District Court—demanding that the notice of removal contain evidence documenting the amount in controversy—will be frozen in place for all venues within the Tenth Circuit.

Justice Scalia, joined by Justices Kennedy, Justice Kagan and Justice Thomas, dissented, arguing that the majority's analysis rested on the unwarranted assumption that the Tenth Circuit denied permission to appeal because it agreed with the district court's amount in controversy analysis. This "allows the Court to pretend to review the appellate court's exercise of discretion while actually reviewing the trial court's legal analysis." The proper course, he insisted, was to dismiss the writ as improvidently granted.

Justice Thomas dissented separately to emphasize that, just as Justice Scalia had argued in his dissent in *Hohn*, there is no jurisdiction because a decision to deny permission to appeal is not a "case" under §1254(1): "*Hohn* was wrongly decided, and the majority's uncritical extension of its holding only compounds the error. . . . The application here is nothing more than a request for discretionary permission to seek review. The Tenth Circuit having denied that permission, no 'case' ever arrived 'in the court of appeals.' I would dismiss for lack of jurisdiction."

2. *Review of Three-Judge District Courts*

Where federal law provides for the unusual procedure of a three-judge federal district court, appellate review is directly in the Supreme Court and the Court is obligated to hear the case. Three-judge district courts were first created by Congress in 1910. After the Supreme Court's decision in *Ex parte Young*, striking down progressive state legislation regulating railroad regulations, Congress created the three-judge district court system to avoid the problem of a single federal judge chosen by the plaintiff having the power to invalidate state law on federal constitutional grounds. In 1937 the New Deal Congress, concerned about individual district court judges undermining New Deal legislation, expanded the jurisdiction of three-judge district courts to handle constitutional challenges to federal laws. In 1976, Congress abolished three-judge district courts in all but a few specialized areas. These include redistricting, campaign finance, and some forms of prison conditions litigation. Significantly, 28 U.S.C. §1253 permits a losing party to appeal decisions of a three-judge district court panel directly to the Supreme Court, skipping the courts of appeal where the remedy is injunctive. In the mid-twentieth century, these direct appeals represented a substantial percentage of the Supreme Court's docket, sometimes as much as one in three cases before the Court.[10] Between 2000 and 2015, one study found that "nearly half of the Court's sixty election law cases came on mandatory review from three judge district courts."[11] Advantages of the process include faster resolution, deeper deliberation at the trial level, and diminishing forum shopping for a single favorably disposed district court judge. In the next case, however, we see some of the downsides, including the confusion created regarding the constitutionality (and therefore enforceability) of a state criminal statute.

Gunn v. University Committee

399 U.S. 383 (1970)

Justice STEWART delivered the opinion of the Court.

On December 12, 1967, President Lyndon Johnson made a speech in Bell County, Texas, to a crowd of some 25,000 people, including many servicemen from

---

10. Michael E. Solimine, *The Fall and Rise of Specialized Federal Constitutional Courts*, 17 U. PA. CONST. L. 115 (2014).

11. Joshua A. Douglas & Michael E. Solimine, *Precedent, Three-Judge District Courts and the Legitimacy of Democracy*, 107 GEO. L.J. 413, 422-23 (2019) (gathering sources).

nearby Fort Hood. The individual appellees [members and sympathizers of the University Committee to End the War in Vietnam] arrived at the edge of the crowd with placards signifying their strong opposition to our country's military presence in Vietnam. Almost immediately after their arrival, they were set upon by members of the crowd, subjected to some physical abuse, promptly removed from the scene by military police, turned over to Bell County officers, and taken to jail. Soon afterwards, they were brought before a justice of the peace on a complaint signed by a deputy sheriff, charging them with "Dist the Peace." They pleaded not guilty, were returned briefly to jail, and were soon released on $500 bond.

Nine days later, they brought this action in a federal district court against Bell County officials, asking that a three-judge court be convened, that enforcement of the state disturbing the peace statute be temporarily and permanently enjoined, and that the statute be declared unconstitutional on its face, "and/or as applied to the conduct of the Plaintiffs herein." The statute in question is Article 474 of the Texas Penal Code, which then provided as follows:

> Whoever shall go into or near any public place, or into or near any private house, and shall use loud and vociferous, or obscene, vulgar or indecent language or swear or curse, or yell or shriek or expose his or her person to another person of the age of sixteen (16) years or over, or rudely display any pistol or deadly weapon, in a manner calculated to disturb the person or persons present at such place or house, shall be punished by a fine not exceeding Two Hundred Dollars ($200).

A few days after institution of the federal proceedings, the state charges were dismissed upon motion of the county attorney because the appellees' conduct had taken place within a military enclave over which Texas did not have jurisdiction. After dismissal of the state charges, the defendants in the federal court filed a motion to dismiss the complaint on the ground that "no useful purpose could now be served by the granting of an injunction to prevent the prosecution of these suits, because same no longer exists."

The appellees filed a memorandum in opposition to this motion, conceding that there was no remaining controversy with respect to the prosecution of the state charges, but asking the federal court nonetheless to retain jurisdiction and to grant injunctive and declaratory relief against the enforcement of Article 474 upon the ground of its unconstitutionality. A stipulation of facts was submitted by the parties, along with memoranda, affidavits, and other documentary material.

With the case in that posture, the three-judge District Court a few weeks later rendered a per curiam opinion, expressing the view that Article 474 is constitutionally invalid. The opinion ended with the following final paragraph:

> We reach the conclusion that Article 474 is impermissibly and unconstitutionally broad. The Plaintiffs herein are entitled to their declaratory judgment to that effect, and to injunctive relief against the enforcement of Article 474 as now worded, insofar as it may affect rights guaranteed under the First Amendment. However, it is the Order of this Court that the mandate shall be stayed, and this Court shall retain jurisdiction of the cause pending the next session, special or general, of the Texas legislature, at

which time the State of Texas may, if it so desires, enact such disturbing the peace statute as will meet constitutional requirements.

The defendants took a direct appeal to this Court, relying upon 28 U.S.C. §1253, and we noted probable jurisdiction. . . . We now dismiss the appeal for want of jurisdiction.

The jurisdictional statute upon which the parties rely, 28 U.S.C. §1253, provides as follows:

> Except as otherwise provided by law, any party may appeal to the Supreme Court from an order granting or denying, after notice and hearing, an interlocutory or permanent injunction in any civil action, suit or proceeding required by any Act of Congress to be heard and determined by a district court of three judges.

The statute is thus explicit in authorizing a direct appeal to this Court only from an order of a three-judge district court "granting or denying . . . an interlocutory or permanent injunction." Earlier this Term, we had occasion to review the history and construe the meaning of this statute in *Goldstein v. Cox* (1970). In that case, a divided Court held that the only *interlocutory* orders that this Court has power to review under §1253 are those granting or denying preliminary injunctions. The present case, however, involves no such refined a question as did *Goldstein*. For here there was no order of any kind either granting or denying an injunction — interlocutory or permanent. All that the District Court did was to write a rather discursive per curiam opinion, ending with the paragraph quoted above. Although the Texas Legislature, at its next session, took no action with respect to Article 474, the District Court entered no further order of any kind. And even though the question of this Court's jurisdiction under §1253 was fully exposed at the original oral argument of this case, the District Court still entered no order and no injunction during the 15-month period that elapsed before the case was argued again.

What we deal with here is no mere technicality. In *Goldstein v. Cox*, we pointed out that:

> This Court has more than once stated that its jurisdiction under the Three-Judge Court Act is to be narrowly construed, since any loose construction of the requirements of [the Act] would defeat the purposes of Congress . . . to keep within narrow confines our appellate docket.

But there are underlying policy considerations in this case more fundamental than mere economy of judicial resources.

One of the basic reasons for the limit in 28 U.S.C. §1253 upon our power of review is that, until a district court issues an injunction, or enters an order denying one, it is simply not possible to know with any certainty what the court has decided — a state of affairs that is conspicuously evident here. The complaint in this case asked for an injunction

> [r]estraining the appropriate Defendants, their agents, servants, employees and attorneys and all others acting in concert with them from the enforcement, operation or execution of Article 474.

Is that the "injunctive relief" to which the District Court thought the appellees were "entitled"? If not, what less was to be enjoined, or what more? And against whom was the injunction to run? Did the District Court intend to enjoin enforcement of all the provisions of the statute? Or did the court intend to hold the statute unconstitutional only as applied to speech, including so-called symbolic speech? Or was the court confining its attention to that part of the statute that prohibits the use, in certain places and under certain conditions, of "loud and vociferous . . . language"? The answers to these questions imply cannot be divined with any degree of assurance from the per curiam opinion.

Rule 65(d) of the Federal Rules of Civil Procedure provides that any order granting an injunction "shall be specific in terms," and "shall describe in reasonable detail . . . the act or acts sought to be restrained."

As we pointed out in *International Longshoremen's Assn. v. Philadelphia Marine Trade Assn.* (1967), the "Rule . . . was designed to prevent precisely the sort of confusion with which this District Court clouded its command." An injunctive order is an extraordinary writ, enforceable by the power of contempt.

> The judicial contempt power is a potent weapon. When it is founded upon a decree too vague to be understood, it can be a deadly one. Congress responded to that danger by requiring that a federal court frame its orders so that those who must obey them will know what the court intends to require and what it means to forbid.

That requirement is essential in cases where private conduct is sought to be enjoined, as we held in the *Longshoremen's* case. It is absolutely vital in a case where a federal court is asked to nullify a law duly enacted by a sovereign State.[12]

The absence of an injunctive order in this case has, in fact, been fully recognized by the parties. In their motion for a new trial, the appellants pointed out to the District Court that it had given no more than "an advisory opinion." And the appellees, in their brief in this Court, emphasized that "[n]o final relief—of any kind—has been ordered below." Accordingly, they said, "no question is now properly raised as to the precise form of federal remedy which may be granted." They asserted that "the issuance of declaratory and injunctive relief will . . . be appropriate at an appropriate time, to-wit, on remand to the court below." But it is precisely because the District Court has issued neither an injunction nor an order granting or denying one that we have no power under §1253 either to "remand to the court below" or deal with the merits of this case in any way at all.

The restraint and tact that evidently motivated the District Court in refraining from the entry of an injunctive order in this case are understandable. But when a three-judge district court issues an opinion expressing the view that a state statute should

---

12. This is not to suggest that lack of specificity in an injunctive order would alone deprive the Court of jurisdiction under §1253. But the absence of any semblance of effort by the District Court to comply with Rule 65(d) makes clear that the court did not think that its per curiam opinion itself constituted an order granting an injunction.

be enjoined as unconstitutional—and then fails to follow up with an injunction—the result is unfortunate, at best. For when confronted with such an opinion by a federal court, state officials would no doubt hesitate long before disregarding it. Yet, in the absence of an injunctive order, they are unable to know precisely what the three-judge court intended to enjoin, and unable as well to appeal to this Court.

It need hardly be added that any such result in the present case was doubtless unintended or inadvertent. We make the point only for the guidance of future three-judge courts when they are asked to enjoin the enforcement of state laws as unconstitutional.

The appeal is dismissed for want of jurisdiction.

Justice WHITE, with whom Justice BRENNAN joins, concurring.

I join the opinion of the Court but deem it appropriate to express my view that the opinion of the District Court should be viewed as having the operative effect of a declaratory judgment invalidating the Texas statute at issue in this case. The appellants were thus entitled to have this phase of the case reviewed in the Court of Appeals, but could not come directly here, since our §1253 jurisdiction is limited to appeals from injunctive orders. I agree with the Court that the opinion of the District Court cannot be construed as an order granting an injunction, and that, if it amounts to an order denying an injunction, it is not appealable to this Court by the appellants.

* * *

C. APPELLATE REVIEW OF STATE COURTS

1. Origins of Supreme Court Review of State Courts

Section 25 of the First Judiciary Act granted the Supreme Court appellate jurisdiction over state court judgments *invalidating* federal law "upon a writ of error." Review upon writ of error was mandatory, but limited to correcting legal error on the record. Discretionary review upon writ of certiorari, and the power to review decisions of state courts *upholding* federal law, were not granted by Congress until 1914. In 1988 Congress eliminated mandatory review entirely, making all appeals discretionary through the writ of certiorari. A marked decline in Supreme Court review of state court judgments has ensued, with the Court deciding fewer than a dozen cases each term out of the state courts. In 1989, the year after Congress eliminated the Court's mandatory jurisdiction, the Court issued full opinions in 41 cases from the state courts, representing 30 percent of its total merits cases.[13] Indeed, "[i]n the 1990s both the absolute and proportional number of cases from state courts reviewed on the merits by the Supreme Court . . . declined."[14] By 2019,

---

13. Michael E. Solimine, *Supreme Court Monitoring of State Courts in the Twenty-First Century*, 35 IND. L. REV. 335, 353 (2002).

14. *Id.*

the court issued full opinions in just 11 cases from the state courts, as compared to 48 cases from the lower federal courts. This is consistent with the Roberts Court in general, in which state cases have ranged from 7 to at most 20 percent of the Court's docket.

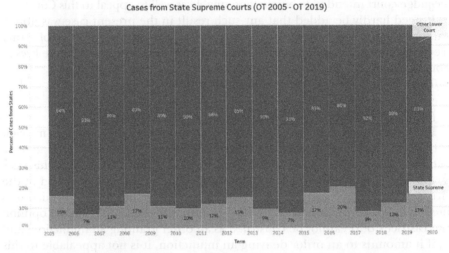

Adam Feldman, Empirical Scotus: The Importance of State Cases Before the Supreme Court, ScotusBlog.com, Sept 4, 2020.

It must be remembered that because of the *Rooker-Feldman* doctrine, direct review in the Supreme Court is usually the only way to have a federal court review a state court decision, other than habeas corpus to review state court criminal convictions. The *Rooker-Feldman* doctrine expressly bars federal district courts from reviewing state court judgments. The doctrine takes its name from two Supreme Court cases, *Rooker v. Fidelity Trust Co.* (1923), and *District of Columbia Court of Appeals v. Feldman* (1983). In *Rooker*, a federal court plaintiff sought to have a state court judgment declared "null and void" and the Supreme Court held that federal courts do not have jurisdiction to "entertain a proceeding to reverse or modify" a state court judgment. In *Feldman*, the Court again concluded that a federal district court has "no authority to review the final judgments of a state court in judicial proceedings."

Thus, the *Rooker-Feldman* doctrine provides that "a party losing in state court is barred from seeking what in substance would be appellate review of the state judgment in a United States District Court based on the losing party's claim that the state judgment itself violates the loser's federal rights." *Johnson v. De Grandy* (1994). The Supreme Court has stressed that the *Rooker-Feldman* doctrine is limited to preventing federal courts from reviewing completed state court proceedings. In *Exxon Mobil Corp. v. Saudi Basic Industries Corp.* (2005), the Supreme Court held that the doctrine is "confined to cases of the kind from which [it] derived its name: cases brought by state-court losers complaining of injuries caused by state-court judgments rendered before the district court proceedings commenced and inviting district court review and rejection of these judgments."

Habeas corpus, discussed in Chapter 8, is the primary exception to this, allowing a person who has been convicted in state court to seek review in federal court on the ground that the conviction violates the Constitution, laws, or treaties of the United States. Otherwise, Supreme Court review is the only avenue for federal court review of state court decisions.

Historically, as the next case suggests, the Supreme Court's exercise of appellate jurisdiction over the decisions of state courts has been greeted with hostility. *Martin v. Hunter's Lessee* concerned an extensive piece of land spanning hundreds of thousands of acres in the Northern Neck of Virginia, whose owner was Lord Fairfax. Upon his death in 1871, his will devised his interest in vacant lands in the estate as well as his vast manors to his nephew Denny Martin. As a British subject, Martin was ineligible to hold lands in the commonwealth under state law. In a process called "escheat," the state sought to revert title back to the state.[15] This began with legislation during the Revolution in 1779, and again in 1785, purporting to confiscate the property.

The case that reached the Supreme Court began in 1791 as an action in ejectment in state court by David Hunter, a land speculator who purchased portions of the property from the state after it took title. He sued on behalf of his lessees against Martin and those to whom he had conveyed title. Martin defended on the ground that the formal prerequisites under Virginia state law for escheat had not been followed to revert title back to the state. Crucially, he argued, there had been no "inquest of office" by the state (a procedure for inquiry into the sovereign's right to property by reason of escheat, treason, or other ground of forfeiture) or other legally equivalent confiscation before the Treaty of Peace, ratified in 1783. The Treaty of Peace explicitly protected the property rights of British subjects against confiscation "'for or by reason of the part which he or they may have taken in the present war.'"[16] The Jay Treaty of 1794 also protected the rights of British subjects to "continue to enjoy their estates and to dispose of them in the same manner as American citizens."[17] Hunter contended that the 1779 and 1785 statutes had vested title in the state, that the Treaty of Peace did not apply to the state's escheat,

---

15. Charles F. Hobson, *John Marshall and the Fairfax Litigation: The Background of* Martin v. Hunter's Lessee, 2 J. SUP. CT. HIST. 36 (1996).

16. *Id.* at 38.

17. *Id.* at 47.

that even if it did, "title had vested in the commonwealth before the treaty's ratification," and, as the case developed, that a state Act of Compromise in 1796 conclusively settled title in favor of Hunter.[18]

The central federal question thus concerned the Treaty of Peace which, under the Supremacy Clause, required the state and its courts to protect the property rights of British subjects such as Martin, state escheat law and confiscation statutes notwithstanding.

The Virginia Court of Appeals upheld Hunter's claim on the ground that the Treaty of Peace had no bearing on escheats resulting simply from British alienage rather than the loyalty of a British subject to England during the war, and even if the treaty did apply, the state had perfected title before its ratification. Moreover, the Act of Compromise "settled the matter in Hunter's favor."[19] On appeal, the Supreme Court reversed, relying principally on the Jay Treaty of 1794 and the conclusion that neither the 1779 nor the 1785 statutes met the requirements for a proper inquest of office to complete escheat and "vest[] title in the commonwealth."[20] The Court then entered a mandate directing the Virginia Court of Appeals to execute judgment in favor of Martin.

After taking "elaborate, able, and profound" argument on the Supreme Court mandate, the Virginia Court of Appeals refused to obey the mandate, concluding that there was no constitutional power to authorize appellate jurisdiction over the decisions of state courts. The reports of the Virginia Court of Appeals state that the following paragraph was entered the courts' judgment:

> The court is unanimously of opinion, that the appellate power of the Supreme Court of the United States, does not extend to this court, under a sound construction of the constitution of the United States; — that so much of the 25th section of the act of congress, to establish the judicial courts of the United States, as extends the appellate jurisdiction of the Supreme Court to this court, is not in pursuance of the constitution of the United States; that the writ of error in this case was improvidently allowed under the authority of that act; that the proceedings thereon in the Supreme Court were corum non judice in relation to this court; and that obedience to its mandate be declined by this court.

Judge Roane's opinion emphasized that there is no power in Congress to provide for appellate review of state court judgments:

> We come now to enquire, whether the twenty-fifth section of the judicial act, so far as it relates to the case before us, is justified by the constitution? . . .
>
> In order to understand that question correctly, it is proper to recollect, that the . . . governments of the several states, in all their parts, remain in full force, except as they are impaired, by grants of power, to the general government.

---

18. *Id.* at 39, 45.
19. *Id.* at 46.
20. *Id.* at 47.

. . . [S]everal sovereign states, may unite themselves together, by a perpetual confederacy, without each, in particular, ceasing to be a perfect state—that they will then form a federal republic, and that each state will remain independent, but will continue liable to fulfil the engagements into which it has entered. As to our own particular government, this position . . . has grown into a maxim. It has run through the general government, in all its modifications and changes [from the Articles of Confederation through the Twelfth Amendment.]

It is next to be observed, that, naturally the jurisdiction granted to a government, is confined to the courts of that government. It does not, naturally, run into and affect the courts of another and distinct government; whether that government operates upon the same, or another tract of country. . . .

[The Supremacy Clause] merely declares the supremacy of the constitution, laws and treaties of the United States, over those of the several states, but evinces no distrust of the state Judges. . . . But if such distrust was any how deducible from this clause of the constitution, the antidote is, also, provided therein: it exists in the oath imposed on them . . . to support the constitution of the United States.

It is not for Congress to distrust those in whom the constitution has confided; to distrust them in the exercise of an ancient and ordinary jurisdiction, and which has not been taken away, or impaired by any specific grant in the constitution.

Judge Cabell was even more emphatic about the absence of constitutional authority to provide for appellate review of state court judgments:

The present government of the United States, grew out of the weakness and inefficacy of the confederation, and was intended to remedy its evils. . . . It must have been foreseen that controversies would sometimes arise as to the boundaries of the two jurisdictions. Yet the constitution has provided no umpire, has erected no tribunal by which they shall be settled. The omission proceeded, probably, from the belief, that such a tribunal would produce evils greater than those of the occasional collisions which it would be designed to remedy. Be this as it may, to give to the general government or any of its departments, a direct and controlling operation upon the state departments, as such, would be to change at once, the whole character of our system. The independence of the state authorities would be extinguished, and a superiority, unknown to the constitution, would be created, which would, sooner or later terminate in an entire consolidation of the states into one complete national sovereignty.

We are required, as State Judges to enter up a judgment, not our own, but dictated and prescribed to us by another Court. This as to us would be either a judicial or a ministerial act—If it be the latter, I presume it will not be contended that the Federal Court has a right to make the Judges of this Court its ministerial agents—Let it then be a judicial act. But, before one Court can dictate to another, the judgment it shall pronounce, it must bear, to that other, the relation of an appellate Court. The term appellate, however, necessarily includes the idea of superiority. But one Court cannot be correctly said to be superior to another, unless both of them belong to the same sovereignty. . . . The Courts of the United States, therefore, belonging to one sovereignty, cannot be appellate Courts in relation to the State Courts, which belong to a different sovereignty—and of course, their commands or instructions impose no obligation. . . .

The term supreme must be understood in reference to the Inferior Courts [Congress may create]; and it must be in relation to them, and not to the State Courts, that the Supreme Court is to exercise appellate jurisdiction.

This produced a second appeal to the Supreme Court drawn up by none other than Chief Justice Marshall. Marshall had been involved in the case for years because Martin sold a large portion of the estate to him and his brother. More than that, Marshall worked as Martin's lawyer on litigation involving the Fairfax estate "on the one hand, challenging the sale of the confiscated land, and, on the other hand, defending the claim of the Fairfax family to the land being escheated which the Marshall syndicate wished to purchase" and eventually did.[21] "Although Marshall saw the appeal as an opportunity to obtain a Supreme Court decision on all the questions relating to the Fairfax title . . . [i]n no sense was the appeal contrived to be a test case for determining the extent of the Supreme Court's appellate jurisdiction over the state judiciaries. That it became a landmark case . . . was, so far as Marshall was concerned, an unforeseen and unintended consequence. His primary aim was to secure his brother's title to valuable acreage. . . ."[22] In light of the conflict of interest, Marshall did not participate in the decision of the case as Chief Justice. He recused himself. But he "personally" forwarded "the record in the hopes of having the [first] appeal argued at the ensuing term," and when the Virginia Court of Appeals denied the Supreme Court's appellate jurisdiction in refusing to enforce its mandate, Marshall took it upon himself to draft the second writ of error (the writ was unsigned, "but in his hand").[23] He also apparently "drafted the argument . . . for the use of [Martin's] counsel."[24]

In this remarkable way, the table was now set for the Supreme Court to answer the assertion that the Constitution did not contemplate the exercise of appellate jurisdiction over state court judgments. Was it enough to simply recuse himself from the case given that the central issue was the legitimacy of the Supreme Court's appellate jurisdiction? It's easy to read the Virginia Court of Appeals decisions as raising questions about the fidelity of the judges on that court to federal law—the treaties and Section 25 of the First Judiciary Act. But if the Chief Justice of the

---

21. F. Thorton Miller, *John Marshall in Spencer Roane's Virginia*, 33 JOHN MARSHALL L. REV. 1131, 1134 (2000) (as a member of the Virginia General Assembly he also supported the Act of Compromise of 1796, providing the "Marshall syndicate . . . some of the choicest land in northern Virginia").

22. Hobson, *supra* note 15, at 47.

23. *Id.* at 48.

24. *Id.*

Supreme Court was known to have been pursuing his own interest in a case before the newly established Court, that surely undermined the appearance of impartiality and integrity of the Court to which deference was supposedly owed on questions of federal law.[25]

Justice Story's opinion for the Court is intricate. Notice, as you read, both the tone of the opinion (the manner in which the rhetorical fire of Judge Cabell's dual sovereignty analysis is met) and the manner in which Story draws on the text of Article III to support inferences about the nature and scope of the Court's appellate jurisdiction.

Martin v. Hunter's Lessee

14 U.S. 304 (1816)

Justice STORY delivered the opinion of the court.

This is a writ of error from the court of appeals of Virginia, founded upon the refusal of that court to obey the mandate of this court, requiring the judgment rendered in this very cause, at February term, 1813, to be carried into due execution. ....

The questions involved in this judgment are of great importance and delicacy. Perhaps it is not too much to affirm, that, upon their right decision, rest some of the most solid principles which have hitherto been supposed to sustain and protect the constitution itself. The great respectability, too, of the court whose decisions we are called upon to review, and the entire deference which we entertain for the learning and ability of that court, add much to the difficulty of the task which has so unwelcomely fallen upon us.

The constitution of the United States was ordained and established, not by the states in their sovereign capacities, but emphatically, as the preamble of the constitution declares, by "the people of the United States." There can be no doubt that it was competent to the people to invest the general government with all the powers which they might deem proper and necessary; to extend or restrain these powers according to their own good pleasure, and to give them a paramount and supreme authority. As little doubt can there be, that the people had a right to prohibit to the states the exercise of any powers which were, in their judgment, incompatible with the objects of the general compact; to make the powers of the state governments, in given cases, subordinate to those of the nation, or to reserve to themselves those sovereign authorities which they might not choose to delegate to either.

The constitution was not, therefore, necessarily carved out of existing state sovereignties, nor a surrender of powers already existing in state institutions, for

_____

25. *Cf. id.* at 49 (arguing that there was "nothing improper about Chief Justice Marshall's personal involvement in the appeal" because the "main portion" of Marshall's "huge investment" did not hinge on the outcome of the case in light of the Compromise of 1796; but conceding that "a definitive ruling by the Court on the peace treaty could serve a limited purpose by placing the Marshalls' rights to the additional lands purchased in 1797 on a more secure foundation").

the powers of the states depend upon their own constitutions; and the people of every state had the right to modify and restrain them, according to their own views of the policy or principle. On the other hand, it is perfectly clear that the sovereign powers vested in the state governments, by their respective constitutions, remained unaltered and unimpaired, except so far as they were granted to the government of the United States.

The third article of the constitution is that which must principally attract our attention.

The language of the article throughout is manifestly designed to be mandatory upon the legislature. Its obligatory force is so imperative, that congress could not, without a violation of its duty, have refused to carry it into operation. The judicial power of the United States shall be vested (not may be vested) in one supreme court, and in such inferior courts as congress may, from time to time, ordain and establish. Could congress have lawfully refused to create a supreme court, or to vest in it the constitutional jurisdiction? "The judges, both of the supreme and inferior courts, shall hold their offices during good behaviour, and shall, at stated times, receive, for their services, a compensation which shall not be diminished during their continuance in office." Could congress create or limit any other tenure of the judicial office? Could they refuse to pay, at stated times, the stipulated salary, or diminish it during the continuance in office? But one answer can be given to these questions: it must be in the negative.

The object of the constitution was to establish three great departments of government; the legislative, the executive, and the judicial departments. The first was to pass laws, the second to approve and execute them, and the third to expound and enforce them. Without the latter, it would be impossible to carry into effect some of the express provisions of the constitution. How, otherwise, could crimes against the United States be tried and punished? How could causes between two states be heard and determined?

If, then, it is a duty of congress to vest the judicial power of the United States, it is a duty to vest the whole judicial power. The language, if imperative as to one part, is imperative as to all. If it were otherwise, this anomaly would exist, that congress might successively refuse to vest the jurisdiction in any one class of cases enumerated in the constitution, and thereby defeat the jurisdiction as to all; for the constitution has not singled out any class on which congress are bound to act in preference to others.

The next consideration is as to the courts in which the judicial power shall be vested. It is manifest that a supreme court must be established; but whether it be equally obligatory to establish inferior courts, is a question of some difficulty. If congress may lawfully omit to establish inferior courts, it might follow, that in some of the enumerated cases the judicial power could nowhere exist. The supreme court can have original jurisdiction in two classes of cases only, viz. in cases affecting ambassadors, other public ministers and consuls, and in cases in which a state is a party. Congress cannot vest any portion of the judicial power of the United States, except in courts ordained and established by itself; and if in any of the cases enumerated in the constitution, the state courts did not then possess jurisdiction, the appellate jurisdiction of the supreme court (admitting that it could act on state courts) could not reach those cases, and, consequently, the injunction of the constitution, that the judicial power "shall be vested," would be disobeyed. It would seem, therefore, to follow, that congress are bound to create some inferior courts, in which to vest all that jurisdiction which, under the constitution, is exclusively vested in the United States, and of which the supreme court cannot take original cognizance. They might establish one or more inferior courts; they might parcel out the jurisdiction among such courts, from time to time, at their own pleasure. But the whole judicial power of the United States should be, at all times, vested either in an original or appellate form, in some courts created under its authority.

This construction will be fortified by an attentive examination of the second section of the third article. The words are "the judicial power shall extend," &c. Much minute and elaborate criticism has been employed upon these words. It has been argued that they are equivalent to the words "may extend," and that "extend" means to widen to new cases not before within the scope of the power. For the reason which have been already stated, we are of opinion that the words are used in an imperative sense. They import an absolute grant of judicial power. They cannot have a relative signification applicable to powers already granted; for the American people had not made any previous grant. The constitution was for a new government, organized with new substantive powers, and not a mere supplementary charter to a government already existing. The confederation was a compact between states; and its structure and powers were wholly unlike those of the national government. The constitution was an act of the people of the United States to supercede the confederation, and not to be ingrafted on it, as a stock through which it was to receive life and nourishment.

It is declared that . . . "in all the other cases before mentioned the supreme court shall have appellate jurisdiction, both as to law and fact, with such exceptions, and under such regulations, as the congress shall make." The very exception here shows that the framers of the constitution used the words in an imperative sense. What necessity could there exist for this exception if the preceding words were not used in that sense? Without such exception, congress would, by the preceding words, have possessed a complete power to regulate the appellate jurisdiction, if the language were only equivalent to the words "may have" appellate jurisdiction. It is apparent, then, that the exception was intended as a limitation upon the preceding words, to enable congress to regulate and restrain the appellate power, as the public interests might, from time to time, require.

It being, then, established that the language ["the judicial power shall extend"] is imperative, the next question is as to the cases to which it shall apply. The answer is found in the constitution itself. The judicial power shall extend to all the cases enumerated in the constitution. As the mode is not limited, it may extend to all such cases, in any form, in which judicial power may be exercised. It may, therefore, extend to them in the shape of original or appellate jurisdiction, or both; for there is nothing in the nature of the cases which binds to the exercise of the one in preference to the other.

In what cases (if any) is this judicial power exclusive, or exclusive at the election of congress? It will be observed that there are two classes of cases enumerated in the constitution, between which a distinction seems to be drawn. The first class includes cases arising under the constitution, laws, and treaties of the United States; cases affecting ambassadors, other public ministers and consuls, and cases of admiralty and maritime jurisdiction. In this class the expression is, and that the judicial power shall extend to all cases; but in the subsequent part of the clause which embraces all the other cases of national cognizance, and forms the second class, the word 'all' is dropped seemingly ex industria. Here the judicial authority is to extend to controversies (not to all controversies) to which the United States shall be a party, &c. From this difference of phraseology, perhaps, a difference of constitutional intention may, with propriety, be inferred. It is hardly to be presumed that the variation in the language could have been accidental. It must have been the result of some determinate reason; and it is not very difficult to find a reason sufficient to support the apparent change of intention. In respect to the first class, it may well have been the intention of the framers of the constitution imperatively to extend the judicial power either in an original or appellate form to all cases; and in the latter class to leave it to congress to qualify the jurisdiction, original or appellate, in such manner as public policy might dictate.

The vital importance of all the cases enumerated in the first class to the national sovereignty, might warrant such a distinction. In the first place, as to cases arriving under the constitution, laws, and treaties of the United States. Here the state courts could not ordinarily possess a direct jurisdiction. The jurisdiction over such cases could not exist in the state courts previous to the adoption of the constitution, and it could not afterwards be directly conferred on them; for the constitution expressly requires the judicial power to be vested in courts ordained and established by the United States. This class of cases would embrace civil as well as criminal jurisdiction, and affect not only our internal policy, but our foreign relations. It would, therefore, be perilous to restrain it in any manner whatsoever, inasmuch as it might hazard the national safety. The same remarks may be urged as to cases affecting ambassadors, other public ministers, and consuls, who are emphatically placed under the guardianship of the law of nations; and as to cases of admiralty and maritime jurisdiction, the admiralty jurisdiction embraces all questions of prize and salvage, in the correct adjudication of which foreign nations are deeply interested; it embraces also maritime torts, contracts, and offences, in which the principles of the law and comity of nations often form an essential inquiry. All these cases, then, enter into the national policy, affect the national rights, and may compromise the national sovereignty. The original or appellate jurisdiction ought not, therefore, to be restrained, but should be commensurate with the mischiefs intended to be remedied, and, of course, should extend to all cases whatsoever.

At all events, whether the one construction or the other prevail, it is manifest that the judicial power of the United States is unavoidably, in some cases, exclusive of all state authority, and in all others, may be made so at the election of congress. No part of the criminal jurisdiction of the United States can, consistently with the constitution, be delegated to state tribunals. The admiralty and maritime jurisdiction is of the same exclusive cognizance; and it can only be in those cases where, previous to the constitution, state tribunals possessed jurisdiction independent of national authority, that they can now constitutionally exercise a concurrent jurisdiction. . . .

This leads us to the consideration of the great question as to the nature and extent of the appellate jurisdiction of the United States.

If the constitution meant to limit the appellate jurisdiction to cases pending in the courts of the United States, it would necessarily follow that the jurisdiction of these courts would, in all the cases enumerated in the constitution, be exclusive of state tribunals. How otherwise could the jurisdiction extend to all cases arising under the constitution, laws, and treaties of the United States, or to all cases of admiralty and maritime jurisdiction? If some of these cases might be entertained by state tribunals, and no appellate jurisdiction as to them should exist, then the appellate power would not extend to all, but to some, cases.

It must, therefore, be conceded that the constitution not only contemplated, but meant to provide for cases within the scope of the judicial power of the United States, which might yet depend before state tribunals. It was foreseen that in the exercise of their ordinary jurisdiction, state courts would incidentally take cognizance of cases arising under the constitution, the laws, and treaties of the United States. Yet to all these cases the judicial power, by the very terms of the constitution, is to extend. It cannot extend by original jurisdiction if that was already rightfully and exclusively attached in the state courts, which (as has been already shown) may occur; it must, therefore, extend by appellate jurisdiction, or not at all. It would seem to follow that the appellate power of the United States must, in such cases, extend to state tribunals; and if in such cases, there is no reason why it should not equally attach upon all others within the purview of the constitution.

It has been argued that such an appellate jurisdiction over state courts is inconsistent with the genius of our governments, and the spirit of the constitution. That the latter was never designed to act upon state sovereignties, but only upon the people, and that if the power exists, it will materially impair the sovereignty of the states, and the independence of their courts. We cannot yield to the force of this reasoning.

It is a mistake that the constitution was not designed to operate upon states, in their corporate capacities. It is crowded with provisions which restrain or annul the sovereignty of the states in some of the highest branches of their prerogatives. The tenth section of the first article contains a long list of disabilities and prohibitions imposed upon the states. Surely, when such essential portions of state sovereignty are taken away, or prohibited to be exercised, it cannot be correctly asserted that the constitution does not act upon the states. The language of the constitution is also imperative upon the states as to the performance of many duties. It is imperative upon the state legislatures to make laws prescribing the time, places, and manner of holding elections for senators and representatives, and for electors of president and vice-president. And in these, as well as some other cases, congress have a right to revise, amend, or supersede the laws which may be passed by state legislatures. When, therefore, the states are stripped of some of the highest attributes of sovereignty, and the same are given to the United States; when the legislatures of the states are, in some respects, under the control of congress, and in every case are, under the constitution, bound by the paramount authority of the United States; it is certainly difficult to support the argument that the appellate power over the decisions of state courts is contrary to the genius of our institutions. The courts of the United States can, without question, revise the proceedings of the executive and legislative authorities of the states, and if they are found to be contrary to the constitution, may declare them to be of no legal validity. Surely the exercise of the same right over judicial tribunals is not a higher or more dangerous act of sovereign power.

Nor can such a right be deemed to impair the independence of state judges. It is assuming the very ground in controversy to assert that they possess an absolute independence of the United States. In respect to the powers granted to the United States, they are not independent; they are expressly bound to obedience by the letter of the constitution; and if they should unintentionally transcend their authority, or misconstrue the constitution, there is no more reason for giving their judgments an absolute and irresistible force, than for giving it to the acts of the other co-ordinate departments of state sovereignty.

It is further argued that no great public mischief can result from a construction which shall limit the appellate power of the United States to cases in their own Courts, first because State judges are bound by an oath to support the Constitution of the United States, and must be presumed to be men of learning and integrity, and secondly because Congress must have an unquestionable right to remove all cases within the scope of the judicial power from the State courts to the courts of the United States at any time before final judgment, though not after final judgment. As to the first reason—admitting that the judges of the State courts are, and always will be, of as much learning, integrity, and wisdom as those of the courts of the United States (which we very cheerfully admit), it does not aid the argument. It is manifest that the Constitution has proceeded upon a theory of its own, and given or withheld powers according to the judgment of the American people, by whom it was adopted. We can only construe its powers, and cannot inquire into the policy or principles which induced the grant of them. The Constitution has presumed (whether rightly or wrongly we do not inquire) that State attachments, State prejudices, State jealousies, and State interests might sometimes obstruct or control, or be supposed to obstruct or control, the regular administration of justice. Hence, in controversies between States, between citizens of different States, between citizens claiming grants under different States, between a State and its citizens, or foreigners, and between citizens and foreigners, it enables the parties, under the authority of Congress, to have the controversies heard, tried, and determined before the national tribunals. No other reason than that which has been stated can be assigned why some, at least, of those cases should not have been left to the cognizance of the State courts. In respect to the other enumerated cases—the cases arising under the Constitution, laws, and treaties of the United States, cases affecting ambassadors and other public ministers, and cases of admiralty and maritime jurisdiction—reasons of a higher and more extensive nature, touching the safety, peace, and sovereignty of the nation, might well justify a grant of exclusive jurisdiction.

This is not all. A motive of another kind, perfectly compatible with the most sincere respect for State tribunals, might induce the grant of appellate power over their decisions. That motive is the importance, and even necessity, of uniformity of decisions throughout the whole United States upon all subjects within the purview of the Constitution. Judges of equal learning and integrity in different States might differently interpret a statute or a treaty of the United States, or even the Constitution itself; if there were no revising authority to control these jarring and discordant judgments and harmonize them into uniformity, the laws, the treaties, and the Constitution of the United States would be different in different States, and might perhaps never have precisely the same construction, obligation, or efficacy in any two States. The public mischiefs that would attend such a State of things would be truly deplorable, and it cannot be believed that they could have escaped the enlightened convention which formed the Constitution. What, indeed, might then have been only prophecy has now become fact, and the appellate jurisdiction must continue to be the only adequate remedy for such evils.

We are referred to the power which it is admitted Congress possess to remove suits from State courts to the national Courts, and this forms the second ground upon which the argument we are considering has been attempted to be sustained.

If the right of removal from State courts exist before judgment, because it is included in the appellate power, it must for the same reason exist after judgment. And if the appellate power by the Constitution does not include cases pending in State courts, the right of removal, which is but a mode of exercising that power, cannot be applied to them. Precisely the same objections therefore exist as to the right of removal before judgment as after, and both must stand or fall together. Nor, indeed, would the force of the arguments on either side materially vary if the right of removal were an exercise of original jurisdiction. It would equally trench upon the jurisdiction and independence of State tribunals.

The remedy, too, of removal of suits would be utterly inadequate to the purposes of the Constitution if it could act only on the parties, and not upon the State courts. In respect to criminal prosecutions, the difficulty seems admitted to be insurmountable; and in respect to civil suits, there would, in many cases, be rights without corresponding remedies. If State courts should deny the constitutionality of the authority to remove suits from their cognizance, in what manner could they be compelled to relinquish the jurisdiction? In respect to criminal cases, there would at once be an end of all control, and the state decisions would be paramount to the Constitution; and though, in civil suits, the courts of the United States might act upon the parties, yet the State courts might act in the same way, and this conflict of jurisdictions would not only jeopardise private rights, but bring into imminent peril the public interests.

On the whole, the Court are of opinion that the appellate power of the United States does extend to cases pending in the State courts, and that the 25th section of the judiciary act, which authorizes the exercise of this jurisdiction in the specified cases by a writ of error, is supported by the letter and spirit of the Constitution. . . . It is an historical fact that this exposition of the Constitution, extending its appellate power to State courts, was, previous to its adoption, uniformly and publicly avowed by its friends and admitted by its enemies as the basis of their respective reasonings, both in and out of the State conventions.

The next question which has been argued is whether the case at bar be within the purview of the 25th section of the Judiciary Act, so that this Court may rightfully sustain the present writ of error.

That the present writ of error is founded upon a judgment of the Court below which drew in question and denied the validity of a statute of the United States is incontrovertible, for it is apparent upon the face of the record. The case . . . is a final judgment in a suit in a State court denying the validity of a statute of the United States, and unless a distinction can be made between proceedings under a mandate and proceedings in an original suit, a writ of error is the proper remedy to revise that judgment. In our opinion, no legal distinction exists between the cases.

The error now assigned is not in the former proceedings, but in the judgment rendered upon the mandate issued after the former judgment. The question now litigated is not upon the construction of a treaty, but upon the constitutionality of a statute of the United States, which is clearly within our jurisdiction.

How, indeed, can it be possible to decide whether a title be within the protection of a treaty until it is ascertained what that title is, and whether it have a legal validity? From the very necessity of the case, there must be a preliminary inquiry into the existence and structure of the title before the Court can construe the treaty in reference to that title. If the Court below should decide, that the title was bad, and therefore not protected by the treaty, must not this Court have a power to decide the title to be good, and therefore protected by the treaty? Is not the treaty, in both instances, equally construed, and the title of the party, in reference to the treaty, equally ascertained and decided? Nor does the clause relied on in the objection impugn this construction. It requires that the error upon which the Appellate Court is to decide shall appear on the face of the record, and immediately respect the questions before mentioned in the section. One of the questions is as to the construction of a treaty upon a title specially set up by a party, and every error that immediately respects that question must, of course, be within the cognizance, of the Court. The title set up in this case is apparent upon the face of the record, and immediately respects the decision of that question; any error therefore in respect to that title must be reexaminable, or the case could never be presented to the Court.

We are therefore satisfied that, upon principle, the case was rightfully before us.

It is the opinion of the whole Court that the judgment of the Court of Appeals of Virginia, rendered on the mandate in this cause, be reversed, and the judgment of the District Court, held at Winchester, be, and the same is hereby, *affirmed.*

JOHNSON, J.

The only point necessary to be decided in the case then before [the Virginia Court of Appeals] was "whether they were bound to obey the mandate emanating from this Court?" But, in the judgment entered on their minutes, they have affirmed that the case was, in this Court, *coram non judice*, or, in other words, that this Court had not jurisdiction over it.

This is assuming a truly alarming latitude of judicial power. Where is it to end? Are, then, the judgments of this Court to be reviewed in every court of the Union? and is every recovery of money, every change of property, that has taken place under our process to be considered as null, void, and tortious?

In the case before us, the collision has been, on our part, wholly unsolicited. The exercise of this appellate jurisdiction over the State decisions has long been acquiesced in, and when the writ of error in this case was allowed by the President of the Court of Appeals of Virginia, we were sanctioned in supposing that we were to meet with the same acquiescence there. . . .

* * *

The structure of Justice Story's argument for the constitutionality of appellate jurisdiction over state court judgements is worth lingering over. He does not begin with a Supremacy Clause argument that uniformity of federal law requires

appellate jurisdiction to resolve conflicts between state courts over the meaning of the treaties at issue in the case. That argument, which resonates with Hamilton's famous statement in the *Federalist Papers*,[26] is compelling, but is left to the end of his analysis.

Instead, Justice Story begins by arguing that federal judicial power is constitutionally mandatory under Article III. The Constitution sets up "three great departments," not two. Article III courts must therefore be created or the federal government cannot function as designed. The text of Article III directly commands the creation of the Supreme Court. The lower federal courts present a more "difficult" question, he allows, but because Article III says that the "judicial Power of the United States *shall be vested*," that requires *all* the judicial power of the United States, not part of it, to be vested somewhere: "the whole judicial power of the United States should be, at all times, vested either in an original or appellate form, in some courts created under its authority." If Congress could pick and choose one element of federal judicial power to withhold, then it could do so as to any, with the result that the whole judicial power would not be vested. But "the language, if imperative as to one part, is imperative as to all."

With respect to the courts in which federal judicial power shall be vested, he continues, the Supreme Court has only narrowly limited original jurisdiction and appellate jurisdiction. Since the states courts cannot exercise concurrent jurisdiction over all federal questions (at a minimum federal crimes, admiralty and maritime, he indicates, cannot be adjudicated in state courts), the only way for the *whole* judicial power of the United States to be vested is for Congress to create lower federal courts. Moreover, Article III provides that the judicial power shall extend to "all cases" arising under federal law, so some federal forum, appellate or original must be available for these cases.

This sets up Story's main argument about appellate jurisdiction over the state courts. If Section 25 of the First Judiciary Act is unconstitutional because appellate jurisdiction is limited to decisions only of the lower federal courts, as the Virginia Court of Appeals concluded, and if, on the other hand, it is clear that Article III requires a federal judicial forum, appellate or original for *all* federal questions, then the lower federal courts would have to have exclusive jurisdiction of all federal questions, including federal issues that arise "incidentally in cases pending in the state courts" and involving mainly state law questions. Otherwise, he reasons, state courts could decide federal questions and there would be no federal judicial review of them whatsoever. "If some of these cases might be entertained by state tribunals, and no appellate jurisdiction as to them should exist, then the appellate power would not extend to all, but to some, cases." But such sweeping exclusive federal question jurisdiction, "would abridge the jurisdiction of [state] courts far more than has ever been contemplated in any act of congress."

This leaves the more plausible conclusion, Story reasons, that appellate jurisdiction must exist over state court decisions of federal law. This works no intrusion on the sovereignty of the states, he insists, given all the other concessions to

---

26. "The mere necessity of uniformity in the interpretation of the national laws, decides the question. Thirteen independent courts of final jurisdiction over the same causes, arising upon the same laws, is a hydra in government, from which nothing but contradiction and confusion can proceed." FEDERALIST PAPERS, No. 80.

national sovereignty the Constitution demands from the states—including disabilities, prohibitions, and duties imposed on the states. Story then rejects the argument that removal jurisdiction would cure the problem on the ground that if, as the Virginia Court of Appeals believed, there is no appellate jurisdiction, there certainly can be no removal. Indeed, unlike appellate jurisdiction, removal is not even mentioned in Article III and therefore cannot be privileged above appellate jurisdiction. Lastly, if state courts do not recognize the constitutionality of removal, they may continue to litigate the same case removed to federal court ("in what manner could [state] courts be compelled to relinquish the jurisdiction," Story queries), whereas appellate jurisdiction takes up the judgments of the state courts.

Story's argument is not watertight. Most prominently, the Supreme Court has generally assumed that the existence of the lower federal courts is contingent on the will of Congress and it has read the Exceptions Clause of Article III to give Congress sweeping authority over the Supreme Court's appellate jurisdiction, not just to make narrow exceptions. Recall that until 1914, Congress deprived the Supreme Court of appellate jurisdiction over state court decisions upholding federal law. The point worth stressing is that Congress has *never* vested all of the judicial power of the United States in Article III courts.

Once it is conceded that the scope of any constitutionally mandatory jurisdiction is narrower than Justice Story believes, what arguments support the constitutionality of appellate jurisdiction over the state courts? The point of the question is twofold. First, it invites you to consider, as Justice Story's opinion does at length, when and under what circumstances there must be access to a federal judicial forum, which is one of the most important questions in the field. Second, even if it seems obvious to you that there must be appellate jurisdiction over state court judgments, it is important to recognize how hotly contested the question was in the antebellum period. As the next case involving appeal of a state criminal conviction shows, the Commonwealth of Virginia continued to resist the authority of the Supreme Court.

Cohens v. Virginia

19 U.S. 264 (1821)

Chief Justice MARSHALL delivered the opinion of the Court.

This is a writ of error to a judgment rendered in the Court of Hustings for the borough of Norfolk, on an information for selling lottery tickets, contrary to an act of the Legislature of Virginia [criminally punishing sale of out-of-state lottery tickets]. In the State court, the defendant claimed the protection of an act of Congress [authorizing the sale of federal lottery tickets to raise funds for the District of Columbia].

Judgment was rendered against the defendants; and the Court in which it was rendered being the highest Court of the State in which the cause was cognizable, the record has been brought into this Court by writ of error.

The defendant in error moves to dismiss this writ, for want of jurisdiction [on the ground that a state party is not subject to the appellate jurisdiction of the Supreme Court].

The questions presented . . . are of great magnitude, and may be truly said vitally to affect the Union. [Counsel for the Commonwealth of Virginia raised arguments similar to those of the Court of Appeals in *Martin* that:] the nation does not possess a department capable of restraining peaceably, and by authority of law, any attempts which may be made, by a part, against the legitimate powers of the whole, and that the government is reduced to the alternative of submitting to such attempts or of resisting them by force. They maintain that the Constitution of the United States has provided no tribunal for the final construction of itself, or of the laws or treaties of the nation, but that this power may be exercised in the last resort by the Courts of every State in the Union. That the Constitution, laws, and treaties may receive as many constructions as there are States; and that this is not a mischief, or, if a mischief, is irremediable. . . .

1st. The first question to be considered is whether the jurisdiction of this Court is excluded by the character of the parties, one of them being a State, and the other a citizen of that State?

The second section of the third article of the Constitution defines the extent of the judicial power of the United States. Jurisdiction is given to the Courts of the Union in two classes of cases. In the first, their jurisdiction depends on the character of the cause, whoever may be the parties. This class comprehends

> all cases in law and equity arising under this Constitution, the laws of the United States, and treaties made, or which shall be made, under their authority.

This clause extends the jurisdiction of the Court to all the cases described, without making in its terms any exception whatever, and without any regard to the condition of the party. If there by any exception, it is to be implied against the express words of the article.

In the second class, the jurisdiction depends entirely on the character of the parties. In this are comprehended "controversies between two or more States, between a State and citizens of another State," "and between a State and foreign States, citizens or subjects." If these be the parties, it is entirely unimportant what may be the subject of controversy. Be it what it may, these parties have a constitutional right to come into the Courts of the Union.

The counsel for the defendant in error have stated that the cases which arise under the Constitution must grow out of those provisions which are capable of self-execution . . . [or] a right given by some act which becomes necessary to execute the powers given in the Constitution, of which the law of naturalization is mentioned as an example. . . .

[In either case] we think the construction too narrow. A case in law or equity consists of the right of the one party, as well as of the other, and may truly be said to arise under the Constitution or a law of the United States whenever its correct decision depends on the construction of either. . . .

The counsel for the defendant in error . . . have laid down the general proposition that a sovereign independent State is not suable except by its own consent.

This general proposition will not be controverted. But its consent is not requisite in each particular case. It may be given in a general law. And if a State has surrendered any portion of its sovereignty, the question whether a liability to suit be a part of this portion depends on the instrument by which the surrender is made. If, upon a just construction of that instrument, it shall appear that the State has submitted to be sued, then it has parted with this sovereign right of judging in every case on the justice of its own pretensions, and has entrusted that power to a tribunal in whose impartiality it confides.

The American States, as well as the American people, have believed a close and firm Union to be essential to their liberty and to their happiness. They have been taught by experience that this Union cannot exist without a government for the whole, and they have been taught by the same experience that this government would be a mere shadow, that must disappoint all their hopes, unless invested with large portions of that sovereignty which belongs to independent States. . . .

The general government, though limited as to its objects, is supreme with respect to those objects. This principle is a part of the Constitution, and if there be any who deny its necessity, none can deny its authority. . . .

With the ample powers confided to this supreme government, for these interesting purposes are connected many express and important limitations on the sovereignty of the States which are made for the same purposes. The powers of the Union, on the great subjects of war, peace, and commerce, and on many others, are in themselves limitations of the sovereignty of the States; but, in addition to these, the sovereignty of the States is surrendered in many instances where the surrender can only operate to the benefit of the people, and where, perhaps, no other power is conferred on Congress than a conservative power to maintain the principles established in the Constitution. The maintenance of these principles in their purity is certainly among the great duties of the government. One of the instruments by which this duty may be peaceably performed is the judicial department. It is authorized to decide all cases of every description arising under the Constitution or laws of the United States. From this general grant of jurisdiction, no exception is made of those cases in which a State may be a party. When we consider the situation of the government of the Union and of a State in relation to each other; the nature of our Constitution; the subordination of the State governments to that Constitution; the great purpose for which jurisdiction over all cases arising under the Constitution and laws of the United States is confided to the judicial department; are we at liberty to insert in this general grant an exception of those cases in which a State may be a party? Will the spirit of the Constitution justify this attempt to control its words? We think it will not. We think a case arising under the Constitution or laws of the United States is cognizable in the Courts of the Union whoever may be the parties to that case.

Had any doubt existed with respect to the just construction of this part of the section, that doubt would have been removed by the enumeration of those cases to which the jurisdiction of the federal Courts is extended in consequence of the character of the parties. In that enumeration, we find "controversies between two or more States, between a State and citizens of another State," "and between a State and foreign States, citizens, or subjects."

One of the express objects, then, for which the judicial department was established is the decision of controversies between States, and between a State and individuals. The mere circumstance that a State is a party gives jurisdiction to the Court. How, then, can it be contended that the very same instrument, in the very same section, should be so construed as that this same circumstance should with-draw a case from the jurisdiction of the Court where the Constitution or laws of the United States are supposed to have been violated? . . .

The mischievous consequences of the construction contended for on the part of Virginia are also entitled to great consideration. It would prostrate, it has been said, the government and its laws at the feet of every State in the Union. And would not this be its effect? What power of the government could be executed by its own means in any State disposed to resist its execution by a course of legislation? The laws must be executed by individuals acting within the several States. If these indi-viduals may be exposed to penalties, and if the Courts of the Union cannot correct the judgments by which these penalties may be enforced, the course of the govern-ment may be at any time arrested by the will of one of its members. Each member will possess a veto on the will of the whole.

The answer which has been given to this argument does not deny its truth, but insists that confidence is reposed, and may be safely reposed, in the State insti-tutions, and that, if they shall ever become so insane or so wicked as to seek the destruction of the government, they may accomplish their object by refusing to perform the functions assigned to them.

Different States may entertain different opinions on the true construction of the constitutional powers of Congress. We know that, at one time, the assumption of the debts contracted by the several States during the war of our revolution was deemed unconstitutional by some of them. We know, too, that, at other times, cer-tain taxes imposed by Congress have been pronounced unconstitutional. Other laws have been questioned partially, while they were supported by the great major-ity of the American people. We have no assurance that we shall be less divided than we have been. States may legislate in conformity to their opinions, and may enforce those opinions by penalties. It would be hazarding too much to assert that the judicatures of the States will be exempt from the prejudices by which the legis-latures and people are influenced, and will constitute perfectly impartial tribunals. In many States, the judges are dependent for office and for salary on the will of the legislature.

There is certainly nothing in the circumstances under which our Constitution was formed, nothing in the history of the times, which would justify the opinion that the confidence reposed in the States was so implicit as to leave in them and their tribunals the power of resisting or defeating, in the form of law, the legitimate measures of the Union.

The counsel for Virginia endeavor to obviate the force of these arguments by saying that the dangers they suggest, if not imaginary, are inevitable; that the Constitution can make no provision against them; and that, therefore, in constru-ing that instrument, they ought to be excluded from our consideration. This state of things, they say, cannot arise until there shall be a disposition so hostile to the present political system as to produce a determination to destroy it; and, when that determination shall be produced, its effects will not be restrained by parchment stipulations. The fate of the Constitution will not then depend on judicial decisions.

It is very true that, whenever hostility to the existing system shall become uni-versal, it will be also irresistible. The people made the Constitution, and the people can unmake it. It is the creature of their will, and lives only by their will. But this supreme and irresistible power to make or to unmake resides only in the whole body of the people, not in any subdivision of them. The attempt of any of the parts to exercise it is usurpation, and ought to be repelled by those to whom the people have delegated their power of repelling it.

The acknowledged inability of the government, then, to sustain itself against the public will and, by force or otherwise, to control the whole nation, is no sound argument in support of its constitutional inability to preserve itself against a section of the nation acting in opposition to the general will.

Suppose a State to institute proceedings against an individual which depended on the validity of an act emitting bills of credit; suppose a State to prosecute one of its citizens for refusing paper money, who should plead the Constitution in bar of such prosecution. If his plea should be overruled, and judgment rendered against him, his case would resemble this; and, unless the jurisdiction of this Court might be exercised over it, the Constitution would be violated, and the injured party be unable to bring his case before that tribunal to which the people of the United States have assigned all such cases.

It is most true that this Court will not take jurisdiction if it should not; but it is equally true that it must take jurisdiction if it should. . . . We have no more right to decline the exercise of jurisdiction which is given than to usurp that which is not given. The one or the other would be treason to the Constitution. Questions may occur which we would gladly avoid, but we cannot avoid them. . . .

We think, then that, as the Constitution originally stood, the appellate jurisdiction of this Court, in all cases arising under the Constitution, laws, or treaties of the United States, was not arrested by the circumstance that a State was a party.

This leads to a consideration of the Eleventh Amendment.

It is in these words:

> The judicial power of the United States shall not be construed to extend to any suit in law or equity commenced or prosecuted against one of the United States, by citizens of another State, or by citizens or subjects of any foreign State.

It is a part of our history that, at the adoption of the Constitution, all the States were greatly indebted, and the apprehension that these debts might be prosecuted in the federal Courts formed a very serious objection to that instrument. Suits were instituted, and the Court maintained its jurisdiction. The alarm was general, and, to quiet the apprehensions that were so extensively entertained, this amendment was proposed in Congress and adopted by the State legislatures. That its motive was not to maintain the sovereignty of a State from the degradation supposed to attend a compulsory appearance before the tribunal of the nation may be inferred from the terms of the amendment. It does not comprehend controversies between two or more States, or between a State and a foreign State. The jurisdiction of the Court still extends to these cases, and in these a State may still be sued. We must ascribe the amendment, then, to some other cause than the dignity of a State. There is no difficulty in finding this cause. Those who were inhibited from commencing a suit against a State, or from prosecuting one which might be commenced before the adoption of the amendment, were persons who might probably be its creditors. There was not much reason to fear that foreign or sister States would be creditors to any considerable amount, and there was reason to retain the jurisdiction of the

Court in those cases, because it might be essential to the preservation of peace. The amendment, therefore, extended to suits commenced or prosecuted by individuals, but not to those brought by States. . . .

If a suit, brought in one Court and carried by legal process to a supervising Court, be a continuation of the same suit, then this suit is not commenced nor prosecuted against a State. It is clearly in its commencement the suit of a State against an individual, which suit is transferred to this Court not for the purpose of asserting any claim against the State, but for the purpose of asserting a constitutional defence against a claim made by a State. . . .

Under the Judiciary Act, the effect of a writ of error is simply to bring the record into Court, and submit the judgment of the inferior tribunal to reexamination. It does not in any manner act upon the parties; it acts only on the record. It removes the record into the supervising tribunal. Where, then, a State obtains a judgment against an individual, and the Court, rendering such judgment, overrules a defence set up under the Constitution or laws of the United States, the transfer of this record into the Supreme Court, for the sole purpose of inquiring whether the judgment violates the Constitution or laws of the United States, can, with no propriety, we think, be denominated a suit commenced or prosecuted against the State whose judgment is so far reexamined. . . .

But should we in this be mistaken, the error does not affect the case now before the Court. If this writ of error be a suit in the sense of the Eleventh Amendment, it is not a suit commenced or prosecuted "by a citizen of another State, or by a citizen or subject of any foreign State." It is not then within the Amendment, but is governed entirely by the Constitution as originally framed, and we have already seen that, in its origin, the judicial power was extended to all cases arising under the Constitution or laws of the United States, without respect to parties. . . .

[T]he Court is unanimously of opinion that the objections to its jurisdiction are not sustained, and that the motion ought to be overruled.

Motion denied.

[On the merits, the Court upheld the convictions, finding that the federal statute did not authorize sales outside the District of Columbia.]

* * *

The position of the Virginia Court of Appeals in *Cohens* and *Martin* is no outlier. "[D]efiance of the authority of the [federal] government on the part of antebellum American states" was neither isolated to the commonwealth of Virginia, nor to the issue of the impact of federal treaties on local property disputes.[27] As one review of the data indicates, defiance of federal authority, especially federal judicial authority, was remarkably common.

> In an American union that began as thirteen states and numbered thirty-three by 1860, a total of nineteen different states participated in these incidents, several of them as repeat players. While prior to 1860 most American states at any given point did recognize the legitimacy

---

27. Leslie Friedman Goldstein, Constituting Federal Sovereignty: The European Union in Comparative Context 19 (2001).

of the U.S. Supreme Court's power to take appeals from state supreme courts on questions of federal law, individual state resistance to the federal judicial authority began immediately and continued until the Civil War (1861-1865), which confirmed federal authority by force.

The story summarized numerically in Table 1 is essentially as follows: American states, intermittently but in a steady and not regionally concentrated stream, resisted federal authority when feelings in particular states on particular issues ran high. Indeed, that a particular state at one time explicitly endorsed federal judicial authority was no guarantee that some issue in the future would not arouse passions strong enough to evoke resistance by that state to federal authority. The range of issues that provoked such resistance was wide and variegated. Tax laws, debtor laws, controversies over land ownership, embargo laws, laws concerning Native Americans, laws concerning judicial procedures, laws regulating speech and press, fugitive slave laws—all at one time or another provoked state denial of federal judicial authority.[28]

Table 1.   Incidents of State Governmental Defiance of Central Authority in the United States, 1790-1859[29]

Type	Number
a. Defiance of specified federal court interpretation of law	32
b. Rejection of authority of federal courts to interpret federal law	22
c. Defiance of the evident meaning of federal law	32
d. Formal acts of nullification of federal law	21
e. Defiance of a federal court order	20
f. Authorization of forceful resistance to federal enforcement	7
g. Openly permitting violent resistance to federal authority	2
h. Threats to secede from the union	2

What do you make of this evidence of state defiance of federal legal and judicial authority? Certainly it shows that the inclusion of Article III and the Supremacy Clause did not, of their own force, resolve the question. Nor did ratification in the states of the Constitution. Notice the temptation—from the historical perspective formed after a Civil War in which national sovereignty was reaffirmed in the repudiation of slavery, secession, and the aggressive state's rights doctrine that supported them—to minimize the significance of this evidence. There is a temptation, that is, to dismiss the evidence of state defiance of federal authority either as merely situational—limited to strong "feelings" in "particular states" on "particular issues." The precedents the Supreme Court established in the period are canonical despite the fact that contests over federal legal and judicial authority not only contributed

---

28. *Id.* at 19-20.
29. *Id.*

to the Civil War, but were instrumental in resistance to Reconstruction, and resurfaced repeatedly during and after Jim Crow segregation in the twentieth century.

On the first point, it may well have been "particular issues" that provoked state defiance, but respect for judicial authority arguably matters more in cases where sentiment runs high, less so in cases where the stakes are trivial. After all, when compliance is costless, it's easy to offer, and reveals little about the actual authority of the court to which it is offered. On the second point, consider the efforts of the state of Alabama during the 1950s and 1960s to prevent the NAACP from operating in the state and to force the disclosure of its state membership list—an act that would have increased the vulnerability of its members to racist coercion. The ostensible legal foundation for the legal proceedings initiated by the state was state corporation law on out-of-state corporations. Over the course of a decade comprising the most intense periods of the civil rights movement (between the Court's decision in *Brown* and the passage of the 1964 Civil Rights Act), Alabama's courts refused to comply with Supreme Court orders upholding the free association rights of the NAACP under the First Amendment. The Court's *fourth* intervention in the case gave the following account of the state court's resistance.

NAACP v. Alabama ex rel. Flowers

377 U.S. 288 (1964)

This case, involving the right of the petitioner, the NAACP, to carry on activities in Alabama, reaches the Court for the fourth time. In 1956, the Attorney General of Alabama brought a suit in equity to oust the association, a New York "membership" corporation, from the State. The basis of the proceeding was the NAACP's alleged failure to comply with Alabama statutes requiring foreign corporations to register with the Alabama Secretary of State and perform other acts in order to qualify to do business in the State.

On the day the complaint was filed, the Attorney General obtained an *ex parte* restraining order barring the Association, *pendente lite*, from conducting any business within the State and from taking any steps to qualify to do business under state law. Before the case was heard on the merits, the Association was adjudged in contempt for failing to comply with a court order directing it to produce various records, including membership lists. The Supreme Court of Alabama dismissed a petition for certiorari to review the final judgment of contempt on procedural grounds, which this Court, on review, found inadequate to bar consideration of the Association's constitutional claims. *NAACP v. Alabama ex rel. Patterson* (1958). Upholding those claims, we reversed the judgment of contempt without reaching the question of the validity of the underlying restraining order. [Our holding on the First Amendment issue was:

> that the immunity from state scrutiny of membership lists which the Association claims on behalf of its members is here so related to the right of the members to pursue their lawful private interests privately and to associate freely with others in so doing as to come within the protection of the Fourteenth Amendment. And we conclude that Alabama has fallen

short of showing a controlling justification for the deterrent effect on the free enjoyment of the right to associate which disclosure of membership lists is likely to have. Accordingly, the judgment of civil contempt and the $100,000 fine which resulted from petitioner's refusal to comply with the production order in this respect must fall.

In the second round of these proceedings, the Supreme Court of Alabama, on remand "for proceedings not inconsistent" with this Court's opinion, again affirmed the judgment of contempt which this Court had overturned. This decision was grounded on belief that this Court's judgment had rested on a "mistaken premise." Observing that the premise of our prior decision had been one which the State had "plainly accepted" throughout the prior proceedings here, this Court ruled that the State could not, for the first time on remand, change its stance. We noted that the Supreme Court of Alabama "evidently was not acquainted with the detailed basis of the proceedings here" when it reaffirmed the judgment of contempt, and again remanded without considering the validity of the restraining order. In so doing, the Court said:

> "We assume that the State Supreme Court . . . will not fail to proceed promptly with the disposition of the matters left open under our mandate for further proceedings. . . ." rendered in the prior case.

Our second decision was announced on June 8, 1959. Unable to obtain a hearing on the merits in the Alabama courts, the Association, in June, 1960, commenced proceedings in the United States District Court to obtain a hearing there. Alleging that the restraining order and the failure of the Alabama courts to afford it a hearing on the validity of the order were depriving it of constitutional rights, the Association sought to enjoin enforcement of the order. Without passing on the merits, the District Court dismissed the action, because it would not assume that the executive and judicial officers of Alabama involved in the litigation would fail to protect "the constitutional rights of all citizens." *NAACP v. Gallion* (M.D. Ala. 1960). The Court of Appeals agreed that the matter "should be litigated initially in the courts of the State." It, however, vacated the judgment below and remanded the case to the District Court with instructions "to permit the issues presented to be determined with expedition in the State courts," but to retain jurisdiction and take steps necessary to protect the Association's right to be heard on its constitutional claims.

The jurisdiction of this Court was invoked a third time. On October 23, 1961, we entered an order as follows:

> . . . The judgment below is vacated, and the case is remanded to the Court of Appeals with instructions to direct the District Court to proceed with the trial of the issues in this action unless within a reasonable time, no later than January 2, 1962, the State of Alabama shall have accorded to petitioner an opportunity to be heard on its motion to dissolve the state restraining order of June 1, 1956, and upon the merits of the action in which such order was issued. Pending the final determination of all proceedings in the state action, the District Court is authorized to retain

jurisdiction over the federal action and to take such steps as may appear necessary and appropriate to assure a prompt disposition of all issues involved in, or connected with, the state action. . . .

In December, 1961, more than five years after it was "temporarily" ousted from Alabama, the Association obtained a hearing on the merits in the Circuit Court of Montgomery County, the court which had issued the restraining order in 1956. On December 29, 1961, the Circuit Court entered a final decree in which the court found that the Association had continued to do business in Alabama "in violation of the Constitution and laws of the State relating to foreign corporations," and that the Association's activities in the State were

in violation of other laws of the State of Alabama and are and have been a usurpation and abuse of its corporate functions and detrimental to the State of Alabama. . . .

The decree permanently enjoined the Association and those affiliated with it from doing "any further business of any description or kind" in Alabama and from attempting to qualify to do business there. The Association appealed to the Supreme Court of Alabama, which, on February 28, 1963, affirmed the judgment below without considering the merits. The Supreme Court relied wholly on procedural grounds, detailed more fully below. This Court again granted certiorari.

I

We consider first the nonfederal basis of the decision of the Alabama Supreme Court, which is asserted by the State as a barrier to consideration of the constitutionality of the Association's ouster from Alabama.

The Supreme Court of Alabama based its decision entirely on the asserted failure of the Association's brief to conform to rules of the court. Although it referred to Rule 9 of its Rules, which concerns the form of an appellant's brief, the Supreme Court gave no indication of any respect in which the Association's brief fell short of the requirements of that Rule, and appears to have placed no reliance on it at all. The basis of the decision below was, rather,

"a rule of long standing and frequent application that, where unrelated assignments of error are argued together and one is without merit, the others will not be considered."

Proceeding to apply that rule to the Association's brief, the Supreme Court held that at least one of the assignments of error contained in each of the five numbered subdivisions of the "Argument" section of the brief was without merit, and that it would therefore not consider the merit of any of the other assignments. The Attorney General of Alabama argues that this is a nonfederal ground of decision adequate to bar review in this Court of the serious constitutional claims which the Association presents. We find this position wholly unacceptable.

Paying full respect to the state court's opinion, it seems to us crystal clear that the rule invoked by it cannot reasonably be deemed applicable to this case. In its brief, the Association referred to each of its assignments of error separately, and specified the argument pertaining thereto. A separate paragraph was devoted to each of the assignments of error except, as noted above, for two related assignments included in one paragraph and four other related assignments included in another paragraph.

These six assignments, like all the others, were specified and explicitly tied to the argument relating to each. We are at a loss to understand how it could be concluded that the structure of the brief did not fully meet the requirement that unrelated assignments of error not be "argued together." The consideration of asserted constitutional rights may not be thwarted by simple recitation that there has not been observance of a procedural rule with which there has been compliance in both substance and form, in every real sense. *Davis v. Wechsler* (1923); *Staub v. City of Baxley* (1958). To the same effect, see this Court's discussion of a similar aspect of prior proceedings in this case, [Patterson].

The Alabama courts have not heretofore applied their rules respecting the preparation of briefs with the pointless severity shown here. In the early case of *Bell v. Fulgham* (1958), the court said:

> "The brief filed by appellant is characterized by a degree of informality and an apparent lack of attention to Rule 10 . . . (predecessor to the present Rule 9); but the rule is directory, and, from the time of its adoption, the court has exercised its discretion in the consideration of briefs which fairly and helpfully make the points upon which appellant relies. Agreeably with the practice thus established, the brief for appellant has been considered."

The cases cited in the Alabama Supreme Court's opinion and in the brief of the State Attorney General in this Court quite evidently do not support the State's position. None of these cases even approaches a ruling that when, as here, assignments of error are individually specified in connection with the argument relevant to each, they are to be regarded as "argued in bulk" because, forsooth, the argument as a whole is divided on the pages of the brief into numbered subdivisions.

In sum, we think that what we said when this litigation was first here, with respect to the procedural point there asserted as a state ground of decision adequate to bar review on the merits, also fits the present situation:

> "Novelty in procedural requirements cannot be permitted to thwart review in this Court applied for by those who, in justified reliance upon prior decisions, seek vindication in state courts of their federal constitutional rights."

[*Patterson.*]

The State has urged that if the nonfederal ground relied on below be found inadequate, as we find it to be, the case be remanded to the Supreme Court of Alabama for decision on the merits. While this might be well enough in other circumstances, in view of what has gone before, we reject that contention and proceed to the merits.

[On the merits, the court held that "the complete suppression of the Association's activities in Alabama accomplished by the order below is [a] serious abridgment" of the First Amendment right of free association. Reversing, remanding and advising "prompt entry of a decree, in accordance with state procedures, vacating in all respects the permanent injunction order . . . and permitting the Association to take all steps necessary to qualify it to do business in Alabama. Should we be unhappily mistaken in our belief that the Supreme Court of Alabama to apply to this Court for further appropriate relief."]

* * *

Williams v. Georgia similarly involved state court rejection of the authority of the Supreme Court during the civil rights movement. Aubry Williams, a black man, was tried, convicted, and sentenced to death for the murder of a white woman by a jury that was selected according to a state procedure in which the trial judge drew cards with the names of jurors on them, but the cards of white jurors were white while the cards of black jurors were yellow. Williams raised this in an emergency appeal, pointing to a United States Supreme Court case decided two months after his conviction that had concluded the procedure was unconstitutional under the Equal Protection Clause. *See Avery v. Georgia* (1953). The Georgia Supreme Court refused to grant a new trial. Although it acknowledged that the jury selection process was unconstitutional under *Avery,* and although its own decision prior to certiorari in the *Avery* case explicitly disapproved of the use of color-coded juror tickets, it concluded that Williams' claim was waived because his lawyers failed to raise the problem when the jury was selected.

The Supreme Court granted certiorari and reversed. *Williams v. Georgia* (1955). Before reaching the merits, the Court had to deal with the jurisdictional objection that the state court's decision rested on state procedural law—if so, then under adequate and independent state ground doctrine, see Section A.3 *infra,* the Supreme Court could not review the federal constitutional issue in the case. "A state procedural rule which forbids the raising of federal questions at late stages in the case, or by any other than the prescribed method," Justice Frankfurter's opinion for the Court acknowledged, "has been recognized as a valid exercise of state power" and, in most cases therefore "presents an adequate nonfederal ground, so that this Court is without jurisdiction. . . ." Here, however, the state's procedural rule was discretionary, and the rule "allows questions of this sort to be raised at a late stage . . . we are not concluded from assuming jurisdiction and deciding whether the state court action in the particular circumstances is, in effect, an avoidance of the federal right. A state court may not, in the exercise of its discretion, decline to entertain a constitutional claim while passing upon kindred issues in the same manner." Pointing to a series of other cases in which the Georgia Supreme Court had granted relief in challenges to jury selection, the Court reasoned that "the discretionary decision to deny the motion does not deprive this Court of jurisdiction to find that the substantive issue is properly before us" given that it rests on a federal constitutional claim. "The facts of this case are extraordinary, particularly in view of the use of yellow and white tickets by a judge . . . almost a year after the State's own Supreme Court had condemned the practice in the *Avery* case. That life is at stake is, of course, another important factor in creating the extraordinary situation."

On remand, the Georgia Supreme Court nevertheless refused to grant Williams a new trial. Instead, it reaffirmed its earlier decision on the ground that it owed no fidelity to the Supreme Court's decision.

> The powers not delegated to the United States by the Constitution, nor prohibited by it to the States, are reserved served to the States respectively, or to the people." Constitution of the United States, 10th Amendment. Even though executives and legislators, not being constitutional lawyers, might often overstep the foregoing unambiguous constitutional prohibition of Federal invasion of State jurisdiction, there can never be an acceptable excuse for judicial failure to strictly observe it.
>
> This court bows to the Supreme Court on all Federal questions of law, but we will not supinely surrender sovereign powers of this State. . . .
>
> The Supreme Court undertakes to remand the case for further consideration, and in its opinion has pointed to Georgia law vesting in the trial judge discretion in ruling upon an extraordinary motion for new trial, and apparently concluded therefrom that this court should reverse the trial court because that discretion was not exercised in the way the Supreme Court would have exercised it. We know and respect the universally recognized rule that the exercise of discretion never authorizes a violation or defiance of law. In this case, as pointed out by us, that law is that the question sought to be raised must be raised before trial and not otherwise.
>
> Not in recognition of any jurisdiction of the Supreme Court to influence or in any manner to interfere with the functioning of this court on strictly State questions . . . we state that our opinion in *Williams v. State* (Ga. 1054) is supported by sound and unchallenged law, conforms with the State and Federal Constitutions, and stands as the judgment of all seven of the Justices of this Court.
>
> Judgment of affirmance rendered May 10, 1954, adhered to. All the Justices concur.

Williams v. State (Ga. 1955).

* * *

The Supreme Court denied certiorari when Williams again appealed. He was executed by the state of Georgia on March 30, 1956. Justice Frankfurter thought that certiorari should be granted if only to answer the challenge presented to the Court's appellate jurisdiction and demonstrate "by appropriately impressive language that the Fourteenth Amendment . . . is a qualification of the Tenth and not the other way around. . . . Reliance on the Tenth Amendment . . . is a recurring manifestation of obfuscation by members of the profession . . . who ought to know better."[30] But he would not support revisiting the merits, and the other Justices read

---

30. Del Dickson, *State Court Defiance and the Limits of Supreme Court Authority:* Williams v. Georgia *Revisited,* 103 YALE L.J. 1423, 1464 (1994).

the state court's opinion as clarifying that state law in fact provided no discretion for an exception to the rule that Williams' objection had to be made during jury selection, removing away the jurisdictional hook the first decision rested upon. After discussion, "all nine Justices voted to deny certiorari" and Williams was executed by the state of Georgia on March 30, 1956.[31]

After surveying a range of sources one observer concludes that the case "demonstrated [to Southern government officials and lawyers] that it was possible for the South to stand up to the Warren Court on issues of race and get away with it."[32]

2. The Final Judgment Rule

Under 28 U.S.C. Section 1257, Supreme Court review of state court decisions requires that there be a final judgment in the highest court where review can be obtained. The Court has articulated a simple definition of "final judgment": a decision is final if it "ends the litigation on the merits and leaves nothing for the court to do but execute the judgment." *Catlin v. United States* (1945). For example, in criminal cases, there is not a final judgment prior to the rendering of a verdict or the imposition of a sentence. *See, e.g., Flynt v. Ohio* (1981) (no final judgment because there was not a conviction or a sentence).

In *Jefferson v. City of Tarrant, Alabama* (1997), the Court said that for a state court judgment to be final it must be (a) subject to no further review or correction in any other state tribunal; and (b) it also must be final as an effective determination of the litigation and not of merely interlocutory or intermediate steps within it. *Jefferson* involved a claim by an estate following the death of a Black woman in a fire. The estate claimed that the death occurred because the fire department inadequately provided services to the minority community and as a result failed to rescue her promptly after arriving at the scene.

The trial court found that federal common law, rather than the Alabama Wrongful Death Act, governed the survivability of the decedent's cause of action, and the city sought interlocutory review. The Alabama Supreme Court held that the Alabama Wrongful Death Act's allowance of only punitive damages governed recovery on federal civil rights claims and remanded the case for further proceedings on the remaining state law claims. The U.S. Supreme Court held that the Alabama decision was not a final judgment and was therefore not proper for review.

The Supreme Court said that the Alabama Supreme Court decision was not final, but only an interlocutory ruling. Instead of terminating the litigation, the state court had answered a single certified question that addressed only two of the four counts in the plaintiff's complaint. The case was remanded for further proceedings, and absent settlement or dispositive motions, there would be a trial on the merits. Thus, there was no final judgment, and Supreme Court review was not available.

---

31. *Id.* at 1464-65.
32. *Id.* at 1469.

The complexity surrounding the final judgment rule arises because the Supreme Court has recognized four situations in which it will grant review even though additional state proceedings remain. *Cox Broadcasting Corp. v. Cohn* is the key Supreme Court decision articulating these exceptions.

Cox Broadcasting Corp. v. Cohn

420 U.S. 469 (1975)

Justice WHITE delivered the opinion of the Court.

The issue before us in this case is whether, consistently with the First and Fourteenth Amendments, a State may extend a cause of action for damages for invasion of privacy caused by the publication of the name of a deceased rape victim which was publicly revealed in connection with the prosecution of the crime.

I

In August 1971, appellee's 17-year-old daughter was the victim of a rape and did not survive the incident. Six youths were soon indicted for murder and rape. Although there was substantial press coverage of the crime and of subsequent developments, the identity of the victim was not disclosed pending trial, perhaps because of sec. 26-9901 which makes it a misdemeanor to publish or broadcast the name or identity of a rape victim. In April 1972, some eight months later, the six defendants appeared in court. Five pleaded guilty to rape or attempted rape, the charge of murder having been dropped. The guilty pleas were accepted by the court, and the trial of the defendant pleading not guilty was set for a later date.

In the course of the proceedings that day, appellant Wassell, a reporter covering the incident for his employer, learned the name of the victim from an examination of the indictments which were made available for his inspection in the courtroom. That the name of the victim appears in the indictments and that the indictments were public records available for inspection are not disputed. Later that day, Wassell broadcast over the facilities of station WSB-TV, a television station owned by appellant Cox Broadcasting Corp., a news report concerning the court proceedings. The report named the victim of the crime and was repeated the following day.

In May 1972, appellee brought an action for money damages against appellants claiming that his right to privacy had been invaded by the television broadcasts giving the name of his deceased daughter. Appellants admitted the broadcasts but claimed that they were privileged under both state law and the First and Fourteenth Amendments. The trial court, rejecting appellants' constitutional claims and holding that the Georgia statute gave a civil remedy to those injured by its violation, granted summary judgment to appellee as to liability, with the determination of damages to await trial by jury.

On appeal, the Georgia Supreme Court, in its initial opinion, held that the trial court had erred in construing sec. 26-9901 to extend a civil cause of action for invasion of privacy and thus found it unnecessary to consider the constitutionality of the statute. The court went on to rule, however, that the complaint stated a cause of action "for the invasion of the appellee's right of privacy, or for the tort of public disclosure" — a "common law tort exist(ing) in this jurisdiction without the help of the statute that the trial judge in this case relied on." Although the privacy invaded was not that of the deceased victim, the father was held to have stated a claim for invasion of his own privacy by reason of the publication of his daughter's name. The court explained, however, that liability did not follow as a matter of law and that summary judgment was improper; whether the public disclosure of the name actually invaded appellee's "zone of privacy," and if so, to what extent, were issues to be determined by the trier of fact.

Upon motion for rehearing the Georgia court countered the argument that the victim's name was a matter of public interest and could be published with impunity by relying on sec. 26-9901 as an authoritative declaration of state policy that the name of a rape victim was not a matter of public concern. This time the court felt compelled to determine the constitutionality of the statute and sustained it as a "legitimate limitation on the right of freedom of expression contained in the First Amendment." The court could discern "no public interest or general concern about the identity of the victim of such a crime as will make the right to disclose the identity of the victim rise to the level of First Amendment protection."

We conclude that the Court has jurisdiction, and reverse the judgment of the Georgia Supreme Court.

II

Two questions concerning our jurisdiction must be resolved: (1) whether the constitutional validity of sec. 26-9901 was "drawn in question," with the Georgia Supreme Court upholding its validity, and (2) whether the decision from which this appeal has been taken is a "(f)inal judgment or decree."

Appellants clearly raised the issue of the constitutionality of sec. 26-9901 in their motion for rehearing in the Georgia Supreme Court. In denying that motion that court held: "A majority of this court does not consider this statute to be in conflict with the First Amendment." Since the court relied upon the statute as a declaration of the public policy of Georgia that the disclosure of a rape victim's name was not to be protected expression, the statute was drawn in question in a manner directly bearing upon the merits of the action, and the decision in favor of its constitutional validity invokes this Court's appellate jurisdiction.

Since 1789, Congress has granted this Court appellate jurisdiction with respect to state litigation only after the highest state court in which judgment could be had has rendered a "(f)inal judgment or decree." Title 28 U.S.C. sec. 1257 retains this limitation on our power to review cases coming from state courts. The Court has noted that "(c)onsiderations of English usage as well as those of judicial policy" would justify an interpretation of the final-judgment rule to preclude review "where anything further remains to be determined by a State court, no matter how dissociated from the only federal issue that has finally been adjudicated by the highest court of the State." But the Court there observed that the rule had not been administered in such a mechanical fashion and that there were circumstances in which there has been "a departure from this requirement of finality for federal appellate jurisdiction."

These circumstances were said to be "very few," but as the cases have unfolded, the Court has recurringly encountered situations in which the highest court of a State has finally determined the federal issue present in a particular case, but in which there are further proceedings in the lower state courts to come. There are now at least four categories of such cases in which the Court has treated the decision on the federal issue as a final judgment for the purposes of 28 U.S.C. sec. 1257 and has taken jurisdiction without awaiting the completion of the additional proceedings anticipated in the lower state courts. In most, if not all, of the cases in these categories, these additional proceedings would not require the decision of other federal questions that might also require review by the Court at a later date, and immediate rather than delayed review would be the best way to avoid "the mischief of economic waste and of delayed justice," as well as precipitate interference with state litigation. In the cases in the first two categories considered below, the federal issue would not be mooted or otherwise affected by the proceedings yet to be had because those proceedings have little substance, their outcome is certain, or they are wholly unrelated to the federal question. In the other two categories, however, the federal issue would be mooted if the petitioner or appellant seeking to bring the action here prevailed on the merits in the later state-court proceedings, but there is nevertheless sufficient justification for immediate review of the federal question finally determined in the state courts.

In the first category are those cases in which there are further proceedings—even entire trials—yet to occur in the state courts but where for one reason or another the federal issue is conclusive or the outcome of further proceedings preordained. In these circumstances, because the case is for all practical purposes concluded, the judgment of the state court on the federal issue is deemed final. In *Mills v. Alabama* (1966), for example, a demurrer to a criminal complaint was sustained on federal constitutional grounds by a state trial court. The State Supreme Court reversed, remanding for jury trial. This Court took jurisdiction on the reasoning that the appellant had no defense other than his federal claim and could not prevail at trial on the facts or any nonfederal ground. To dismiss the appeal "would not only be an inexcusable delay of the benefits Congress intended to grant by providing for appeal to this Court, but it would also result in a completely unnecessary waste of time and energy in judicial systems already troubled by delays due to congested dockets."

Second, there are cases such as *Radio Station WOW v. Johnson* (1945), and *Brady v. Maryland* (1963), in which the federal issue, finally decided by the highest court in the State, will survive and require decision regardless of the outcome of future state-court proceedings. In *Radio Station WOW*, the Nebraska Supreme Court directed the transfer of the properties of a federally licensed radio station and ordered an accounting, rejecting the claim that the transfer order would interfere with the federal license. The federal issue was held reviewable here despite the pending accounting on the "presupposition . . . that the federal questions that could come here have been adjudicated by the State court, and that the accounting which remains to be taken could not remotely give rise to a federal question . . . that may later come here. . . ." The judgment rejecting the federal claim and directing the transfer was deemed "dissociated from a provision for an accounting even though that is decreed in the same order." Nothing that could happen in the course of the accounting, short of settlement of the case, would foreclose or make unnecessary decision on the federal question.

In the third category are those situations where the federal claim has been finally decided, with further proceedings on the merits in the state courts to come, but in which later review of the federal issue cannot be had, whatever the ultimate outcome of the case. Thus, in these cases, if the party seeking interim review ultimately prevails on the merits, the federal issue will be mooted; if he were to lose on the merits, however, the governing state law would not permit him again to present his federal claims for review. The Court has taken jurisdiction in these circumstances prior to completion of the case in the state courts. *California v. Stewart* (1966) (decided with *Miranda v. Arizona*), epitomizes this category. There the state court reversed a conviction on federal constitutional grounds and remanded for a new trial. Although the State might have prevailed at trial, we granted its petition for certiorari and affirmed, explaining that the state judgment was "final" since an acquittal of the defendant at trial would preclude, under state law, an appeal by the State.

A recent decision in this category is *North Dakota State Board of Pharmacy v. Snyder's Drug Stores, Inc.* (1973), in which the Pharmacy Board rejected an application for a pharmacy operating permit relying on a state statute specifying ownership requirements which the applicant did not meet. The State Supreme Court held the statute unconstitutional and remanded the matter to the Board for further consideration of the application, freed from the constraints of the ownership statute. The Board brought the case here, claiming that the statute was constitutionally acceptable under modern cases. After reviewing the various circumstances under which the finality requirement has been deemed satisfied despite the fact that litigation had not terminated in the state courts, we entertained the case over claims that we had no jurisdiction. The federal issue would not survive the remand, whatever the result of the state administrative proceedings. The Board might deny the license on state-law grounds, thus foreclosing the federal issue, and the Court also ascertained that under state law the Board could not bring the federal issue here in the event the applicant satisfied the requirements of state law except for the invalidated ownership statute. Under these circumstances, the issue was ripe for review.

Lastly, there are those situations where the federal issue has been finally decided in the state courts with further proceedings pending in which the party seeking review here might prevail on the merits on nonfederal grounds, thus rendering unnecessary review of the federal issue by this Court, and where reversal of the state court on the federal issue would be preclusive of any further litigation on the relevant cause of action rather than merely controlling the nature and character of, or determining the admissibility of evidence in, the state proceedings still to come. In these circumstances, if a refusal immediately to review the state court decision might seriously erode federal policy, the Court has entertained and decided the federal issue, which itself has been finally determined by the state courts for purposes of the state litigation.

Miami Herald Publishing Co. v. Tornillo (1974) is the latest case in this category. There a candidate for public office sued a newspaper for refusing, allegedly contrary to a state statute, to carry his reply to the paper's editorial critical of his qualifications. The trial court held the act unconstitutional, denying both injunctive relief and damages. The State Supreme Court reversed, sustaining the statute against the challenge based upon the First and Fourteenth Amendments and remanding the case for a trial and appropriate relief, including damages. The newspaper brought the case here. We sustained our jurisdiction, relying on the principles elaborated in the *North Dakota* case and observing: "Whichever way we were to decide on the merits, it would be intolerable to leave unanswered, under these circumstances, an important question of freedom of the press under the First Amendment; an uneasy and unsettled constitutional posture of sec. 104.38 could only further harm the operation of a free press."

In light of the prior cases, we conclude that we have jurisdiction to review the judgment of the Georgia Supreme Court rejecting the challenge under the First and Fourteenth Amendments to the state law authorizing damage suits against the press for publishing the name of a rape victim whose identity is revealed in the course of a public prosecution. The Georgia Supreme Court's judgment is plainly final on the federal issue and is not subject to further review in the state courts. Appellants will be liable for damages if the elements of the state cause of action are proved. They may prevail at trial on nonfederal grounds, it is true, but if the Georgia court erroneously upheld the statute, there should be no trial at all. Moreover, even if appellants prevailed at trial and made unnecessary further consideration of the constitutional question, there would remain in effect the unreviewed decision of the State Supreme Court that a civil action for publishing the name of a rape victim disclosed in a public judicial proceeding may go forward despite the First and Fourteenth Amendments. Delaying final decision of the First Amendment claim until after trial will "leave unanswered . . . an important question of freedom of the press under the First Amendment," "an uneasy and unsettled constitutional posture (that) could only further harm the operation of a free press."

On the other hand, if we now hold that the First and Fourteenth Amendments bar civil liability for broadcasting the victim's name, this litigation ends. Given these factors—that the litigation could be terminated by our decision on the merits and that a failure to decide the question now will leave the press in Georgia operating in the shadow of the civil and criminal sanctions of a rule of law and a statute the constitutionality of which is in serious doubt—we find that reaching the merits is consistent with the pragmatic approach that we have followed in the past in determining finality.

[The Supreme Court then went on to declare the press could not be held liable because it truthfully reported documents lawfully gained from public, court records. It concluded:]

Appellant Wassell based his televised report upon notes taken during the court proceedings and obtained the name of the victim from the indictments handed to him at his request during a recess in the hearing. Appellee has not contended that the name was obtained in an improper fashion or that it was not on an official court document open to public inspection. Under these circumstances, the protection of freedom of the press provided by the First and Fourteenth Amendments bars the State of Georgia from making appellants' broadcast the basis of civil liability.

Justice REHNQUIST, dissenting.

Because I am of the opinion that the decision which is the subject of this appeal is not a "final" judgment or decree, as that term is used in 28 U.S.C. §1257, I would dismiss this appeal for want of jurisdiction.

Radio Station WOW, Inc. v. Johnson (1945) established that in a "very few" circumstances review of state-court decisions could be had in this Court even though something "further remain(ed) to be determined by a State court." Over the years, however, and despite vigorous protest by Mr. Justice Harlan, this Court has steadily discovered new exceptions to the finality requirement, such that they can hardly any longer be described as "very few." Whatever may be the unexpressed reasons for this process of expansion, it has frequently been the subject of no more formal an express explanation than cursory citations to preceding cases in the line. Although the Court's opinion today does accord detailed consideration to this problem, I do not believe that the reasons it expresses can support its result.

The Court has taken what it terms a "pragmatic" approach to the finality problem presented in this case. In so doing, [the Court stresses that] the finality requirement is imposed as a matter of minimizing "the inconvenience and costs of piecemeal review." This proposition is undoubtedly sound so long as one is considering the administration of the federal court system. Were judicial efficiency the only interest at stake there would be less inclination to challenge the Court's resolution in this case, although, as discussed below, I have serious reservations that the standards the Court has formulated are effective for achieving even this single goal. The case before us, however, is an appeal from a state court, and this fact introduces additional interests which must be accommodated in fashioning any exception to the literal application of the finality requirement. I consider sec. 1257 finality to be but one of a number of congressional provisions reflecting concern that uncontrolled federal judicial interference with state administrative and judicial functions would have untoward consequences for our federal system. That comity and federalism are significant elements of sec. 1257 finality has been recognized by other members of the Court as well, perhaps most notably by Mr. Justice Harlan.

But quite apart from the considerations of federalism which counsel against an expansive reading of our jurisdiction under sec. 1257, the Court's holding today enunciates a virtually formless exception to the finality requirement, one which differs in kind from those previously carved out.

While the totality of these exceptions certainly indicates that the Court has been willing to impart to the language "final judgment or decree" a great deal of flexibility, each of them is arguably consistent with the intent of Congress in enacting sec. 1257, if not with the language it used, and each of them is relatively workable in practice.

To those established exceptions is now added one so formless that it cannot be paraphrased, but instead must be quoted: "Given these factors—that the litigation could be terminated by our decision on the merits and that a failure to decide the question now will leave the press in Georgia operating in the shadow of the civil and criminal sanctions of a rule of law and a statute the constitutionality of which is in serious doubt—we find that reaching the merits is consistent with the pragmatic approach that we have followed in the past in determining finality."

There are a number of difficulties with this test. One of them is the Court's willingness to look to the merits. It is not clear from the Court's opinion, however, exactly now great a look at the merits we are to take. On the one hand, the Court emphasizes that if we reverse the Supreme Court of Georgia the litigation will end, and it refers to cases in which the federal issue has been decided "arguably wrongly." On the other hand, it claims to look to the merits "only to the extent of determining that the issue is substantial." If the latter is all the Court means, then the inquiry is no more extensive than is involved when we determine whether a case is appropriate for plenary consideration; but if no more is meant, our decision is just as likely to be a costly intermediate step in the litigation as it is to be the concluding event. If, on the other hand, the Court really intends its doctrine to reach only so far as cases in which our decision in all probability will terminate the litigation, then the Court is reversing the traditional sequence of judicial decisionmaking. Heretofore, it has generally been thought that a court first assumed jurisdiction of a case, and then went on to decide the merits of the questions it presented. But henceforth in determining our own jurisdiction we may be obliged to determine whether or not we agree with the merits of the decision of the highest court of a State.

Yet another difficulty with the Court's formulation is the problem of transposing to any other case the requirement that "failure to decide the question now will leave the press in Georgia operating in the shadow of the civil and criminal sanctions of a rule of law and a statute the constitutionality of which is in serious doubt." Assuming that we are to make this determination of "serious doubt" at the time we note probable jurisdiction of such an appeal, is it enough that the highest court of the State has ruled against any federal constitutional claim? If that is the case, then because sec. 1257 by other language imposes that requirement, we will have completely read out of the statute the limitation of our jurisdiction to a "final judgment or decree." Perhaps the Court's new standard for finality is limited to cases in which a First Amendment freedom is at issue. The language used by Congress, however, certainly provides no basis for preferring the First Amendment, as incorporated by the Fourteenth Amendment, to the various other Amendments which are likewise "incorporated," or indeed for preferring any of the "incorporated" Amendments over the due process and equal protection provisions which are embodied literally in the Fourteenth Amendment.

Another problem is that in applying the second prong of its test, the Court has not engaged in any independent inquiry as to the consequences of permitting the decision of the Supreme Court of Georgia to remain undisturbed pending final state-court resolution of the case. This suggests that in order to invoke the benefit of today's rule, the "shadow" in which an appellant must stand need be neither deep nor wide. In this case nothing more is at issue than the right to report the name of the victim of a rape. No hindrance of any sort has been imposed on reporting the fact of a rape or the circumstances surrounding it.

But the greatest difficulty with the test enunciated today is that it totally abandons the principle that constitutional issues are too important to be decided save when absolutely necessary, and are to be avoided if there are grounds for decision of lesser dimension. The long line of cases which established this rule makes clear that it is a principle primarily designed, not to benefit the lower courts, or state-federal relations, but rather to safeguard this Court's own process of constitutional adjudication. I would dismiss for want of jurisdiction.

* * *

3. The Independent and Adequate State Ground Doctrine

a. Origins of the Doctrine

An important and complex limitation on Supreme Court review of state court decisions is the independent and adequate state grounds doctrine. Simply stated, the Supreme Court will not hear a case if the decision of the state's highest court is supported by a state law rationale that is independent of federal law and adequate to sustain the result. Phrased slightly differently, the Court must decline to hear the case if its reversal of the state court's federal law ruling will not change the outcome of the case because the result is independently supported by the state court's decision on state law grounds.

The independent and adequate state grounds doctrine has its basis, analytically if not historically, in the Supreme Court decision in *Murdock v. City of Memphis,* which held that the Court may not review state court decisions on state law matters.

The First Judiciary Act provided that a state court decision invalidating federal law

> may be reexamined and reversed or affirmed in the Supreme Court of the United States upon a writ of error. . . . *But no other error shall be assigned or regarded as a ground of reversal in any such case as aforesaid than such as appears on the face of the record and immediately respects the before-mentioned questions of validity or construction of the said Constitution, treaties, statutes, commissions, or authorities in dispute.*

The most important 1867 Amendment deleted the entire italicized sentence, leaving the impression that Congress intended the Supreme Court to have the power to adjudicate not only the federal issues in a state case, but all aspects of the case, including questions of state law.

The Court took up the significance of this amendment in the context of a case involving rights to land in the City of Memphis and the question whether a federal statute affected those rights. The Court gave the following statement of facts:

> The suit was a bill in chancery [in Tennessee state court] brought by Murdock and others against the City of Memphis to have a decree establishing their right in certain real estate near that city. The United States having determined to build a navy yard at Memphis, about the year 1844 . . . the City of Memphis . . . conveyed to the United States the land in controversy by an ordinary deed of general warranty, expressing on its face the consideration of $20,000 paid, and designating no purpose for which the land

was conveyed. After retaining possession of the land for about ten years without building a navy yard, the United States abandoned that purpose, and by an Act approved August 5, 1854, ceded the property to the City of Memphis by its corporate name for the use and benefit of said city.

The plaintiffs in error, by their bill, allege that the title was originally conveyed to the City of Memphis, in trust, for [the purpose] of having a navy yard built on it by the United States; that when the title reverted to the city by reason of the abandonment of the place as a navy yard by the United States [in 1854 by] the Act of Congress . . . the city received the title in trust for the original grantors, who are the plaintiffs. . . . A demurrer to the bill was filed. Also an answer denying the trust and pleading the statute of limitations. On the hearing, the bill was dismissed, and this decree was affirmed by the supreme court of the state. The complainants, in their bill and throughout the case insisted that the effect of the Act of 1854 was to vest the title in the mayor or aldermen of the city in trust for them.

It may be very true that it is not easy to see anything in the deed by which the United States received the title from the city, or the act by which they ceded it back, which raises such a trust, but the complainants claimed a right under this act of the United States, which was decided against them by the Supreme Court of Tennessee. . . .

Murdock v. City of Memphis

87 U.S. 590 (1874)

Justice MILLER delivered the opinion of the Court.

In the year 1867, Congress passed an Act, approved February 5th, entitled an act to amend "An act to establish the judicial courts of the United States, approved September the 24th, 1789." This act consisted of two sections, the first of which conferred upon the federal courts and upon the judges of those courts additional power in regard to writs of habeas corpus, and regulated appeals and other proceedings in that class of cases. The second section was a reproduction, with some changes, of the twenty-fifth section of the Act of 1789, to which, by its title, the Act of 1867 was an amendment, and it related to the appellate jurisdiction of this Court over judgments and decrees of state courts.

The proposition [raised in this case] is that by a fair construction of the act of 1867 this Court must, when it obtains jurisdiction of a case decided in a state court, by reason of one of the questions stated in the act, proceed to decide every other question which the case presents which may be found necessary to a final judgment on the whole merits. . . .

1. The act of 1867 has no repealing clause nor any express words of repeal. If there is any repeal, therefore, it is one of implication. . . . It is the words that are wholly omitted in the new statute which constitute the important feature. . . .

A careful comparison of these two sections can leave no doubt that . . . the twenty-fifth section of the act of 1789 is technically repealed, and that the second section of the act of 1867 has taken its place. . . .

2. The . . . last sentence of the twenty-fifth section of the Act of 1789 . . . in express terms limited the power of the Supreme Court in reversing the judgment of a state court, to errors apparent on the face of the record and which respected questions, that for the sake of brevity, though not with strict verbal accuracy, we shall call federal questions, namely those in regard to the validity of construction of the Constitution, treaties, statutes, commissions, or authority of the federal government.

The [question before us is whether] by reenacting the statute in the same terms as to the removal of cases from the state courts, without the restrictive clause, Congress is to be understood as conferring the power which that clause prohibited. . . .

No doubt there were those who, believing that the Constitution gave no right to the federal judiciary to go beyond the line marked by the omitted clause, thought its presence or absence immaterial, and in a revision of the statute it was wise to leave it out, because its presence implied that such a power was within the competency of Congress to bestow. There were also, no doubt, those who believed that the section standing without that clause did not confer the power which it pro-hibited, and that it was therefore better omitted. It may also have been within the thought of a few that all that is now claimed would follow the repeal of the clause. But if Congress, or the framers of the bill, had a clear purpose to enact affirmatively that the court *should consider* the class of errors which that clause forbid, nothing hindered that they should say so in positive terms, and in reversing the policy of the government from its foundation in one of the most important subjects on which that body could act, it is reasonably to be expected that Congress would use plain, unmistakable language in giving expression to such intention.

There is therefore no sufficient reason for holding that Congress, by repealing or omitting this restrictive clause, intended to enact affirmatively the thing which that clause had prohibited. . . .

It is strenuously maintained that as the office of a writ of error at the common law, and as it is used in relation to the inferior courts of the United States when issued from this Court, is to remove the whole case to this Court for revision upon its merits, or at least upon all the errors found in the record of the case so removed, and as this statute enacts that these cases shall be reexamined in the same manner, and under the same regulations, and the writ shall have the same effect as in those cases, therefore *all* the errors found in a record so removed from a *state* court must be reviewed so far as they are essential to a correct final judgment on the whole case.

The proposition as thus stated has great force, and is entitled to our most careful consideration. . . .

[The] most important part of the statute . . . declares that it is only upon the existence of certain questions in the case that this Court can entertain juris-diction at all. Nor is the mere existence of such a question in the case sufficient to give jurisdiction — the question must have been *decided* in the state court. Nor is it sufficient that such a question was raised and was decided. It must have been decided in a certain way, that is, against the right set up under the Constitution, laws, treaties, or authority of the United States. The federal question may have been erroneously decided. It may be quite apparent to this Court that a wrong construction has been given to the federal law, but if the right claimed under it by plaintiff in error has been conceded to him, this Court cannot entertain jurisdiction of the case, so very careful is the statute, both of 1789 and of 1867, to narrow, to limit, and define the jurisdiction which this Court exercises over the judgments of the state courts. Is it consistent with this extreme caution to suppose that Congress intended, when those cases came here, that this Court should not only examine *those questions*, but all others found in the record? — questions of common law, of state statutes, of controverted facts, and conflicting evidence. Or is it the more reasonable inference that Congress intended that the cases should be brought here that those questions might be decided and *finally* decided by the court established by the Constitution of the Union, and the court which has always been supposed to be not only the most appropriate but the only proper tribunal for their final decision? No such reason nor any necessity exists for the decision by this Court of other questions in those cases. The jurisdiction has been exercised for nearly a century without serious inconvenience to the due administration of justice. The state courts are the appropriate tribunals, as this Court has repeatedly held, for the decision of questions arising under their local law, whether statutory or otherwise. And it is not lightly to be presumed that Congress acted upon a principle which implies a distrust of their integrity or of their ability to construe those laws correctly.

Let us look for a moment into the effect of the proposition contended for upon the cases as they come up for consideration in the conference room. If it is found that no such question is raised or decided in the court below, then all will concede that it must be dismissed for want of jurisdiction. But if it is found that the federal question was raised and was decided against the plaintiff in error, then the first duty of the court obviously is to determine whether it was correctly decided by the state court. Let us suppose that we find that the court below was right in its decision on that question. What, then, are we to do? Was it the intention of Congress to say that while you can only bring the case here on account of this question, yet, when it is here, though it may turn out that the plaintiff in error was wrong on that question, and the judgment of the court below was right, though he has wrongfully dragged the defendant into this Court by the allegation of an error which did not exist, and without which the case could not rightfully be here, he can still insist on an inquiry into all the other matters which were litigated in the case? This is neither reasonable nor just.

In such case both the nature of the jurisdiction conferred and the nature and fitness of things demand that, no error being found in the matter which authorized the reexamination, the judgment of the state court should be affirmed, and the case remitted to that court for its further enforcement.

The whole argument we are combating, however, goes upon the assumption that when it is found that the record shows that one of the questions mentioned has been decided against the claim of the plaintiff in error, this Court has jurisdiction, and that jurisdiction extends to the whole case. If it extends to the whole case then the court must reexamine the whole case, and if it reexamines it must decide the whole case. It is difficult to escape the logic of the argument if the first premise be conceded. But it is here the error lies. We are of opinion that upon a fair construction of the whole language of the section the jurisdiction conferred is limited to the decision of the questions mentioned in the statute, and, as a necessary consequence of this, to the exercise of such powers as may be necessary to cause the judgment in that decision to be respected.

We will now advert to one or two considerations apart from the mere language of the statute, which seem to us to give additional force to this conclusion. . . .

[I]f when we once get jurisdiction, everything in the case is open to reexamination, it follows that every case tried in any state court, from that of a justice of the peace to the highest court of the state, may be brought to this Court for final decision on all the points involved in it.

Suppose a party is sued before a justice of the peace for assault and battery. He pleads that he was a deputy marshal of the United States, and in severing a warrant of arrest on plaintiff he gently laid his hands on him and used no more force than was necessary. He also pleads the general issue. We will suppose that to the special plea some response is made which finally leads to a decision against the defendant on that plea. And judgment is rendered against him on the general issue also. He never was a deputy marshal. He never had a writ from a United States court; but he insists on that plea through all the courts up to this, and when he gets here the record shows a federal question decided against him, and this Court must reexamine the whole case, though there was not a particle of truth in his plea, and it was a mere device to get the case into this Court. Very many cases are brought here now of that character. Also, cases where the moment the federal question is stated by counsel we all know that there is nothing in it. . . . [I]t follows that there is no conceivable case so insignificant in amount or unimportant in principle that a perverse and obstinate man may not bring it to this Court by the aid of a sagacious lawyer raising a federal question in the record—a point which he may be wholly unable to support by the facts, or which he may well know will be decided against him the moment it is stated. But he obtains his object, if this Court, when the case is once open to reexamination on account of that question, must decide all the others that are to be found in the record.

It is impossible to believe that Congress intended this result, and equally impossible that they did not see that it would follow if they intended to open the cases that are brought here under this section to reexamination on all the points involved in them and necessary to a final judgment on the merits. . . .

It requires a very bold reach of thought, and a readiness to impute to Congress a radical and hazardous change of a policy vital in its essential nature to the independence of the state courts, to believe that that body contemplated, or intended, what is claimed, by the mere omission of a clause in the substituted statute, which may well be held to have been superfluous, or nearly so, in the old one. . . .

It was no doubt the purpose of Congress to secure to every litigant whose rights depended on any question of federal law that that question should be decided for him by the highest federal tribunal if he desired it, when the decisions of the state courts were against him on that question. That rights of this character, guaranteed to him by the Constitution and laws of the Union, should not be left to the exclusive and final control of the state courts.

There may be some plausibility in the argument that these rights cannot be protected in all cases unless the Supreme Court has final control of the whole case. But the experience of eighty-five years of the administration of the law under the opposite theory would seem to be a satisfactory answer to the argument. It is not to be presumed that the state courts, where the rule is clearly laid down to them on the federal question, and its influence on the case fully seen, will disregard or overlook it, and this is all that the rights of the party claiming under it require. Besides, by the very terms of this statute, when the Supreme Court is of opinion that the question of federal law is of such relative importance to the whole case that it should control the final judgment, that court is authorized to render such judgment and enforce it by its own process. It cannot, therefore, be maintained that it is in any case necessary for the security of the rights claimed under the Constitution, laws, or treaties of the United States that the Supreme Court should examine and decide other questions not of a federal character.

And we are of opinion that the Act of 1867 does not confer such a jurisdiction.

This renders unnecessary a decision of the question whether, if Congress had conferred such authority, the act would have been constitutional. . . .

What shall be done by this Court when the question has been found to exist in the record, and to have been decided against the plaintiff in error, and rightfully decided, we have already seen, and it presents no difficulties.

But when it appears that the federal question was decided erroneously against the plaintiff in error, we must then reverse the case undoubtedly, if there are no other issues decided in it than that. It often has occurred, however, and will occur again, that there are other points in the case than those of federal cognizance, on which the judgment of the court below may stand; those points being of themselves sufficient to control the case.

Or it may be, that there are other issues in the case, but they are not of such controlling influence on the whole case that they are alone sufficient to support the judgment.

It may also be found that notwithstanding there are many other questions in the record of the case, the issue raised by the federal question is such that its decision must dispose of the whole case. In the two latter instances there can be no doubt that the judgment of the state court must be reversed, and under the new act this Court can either render the final judgment or decree here, or remand the case to the state court for that purpose.

But in the other cases supposed, why should a judgment be reversed for an error in deciding the federal question, if the same judgment must be rendered on the other points in the case? And why should this Court reverse a judgment which is right on the whole record presented to us; or where the same judgment will be rendered by the court below, after they have corrected the error in the federal question?

We have already laid down the rule that we are not authorized to examine these other questions for the purpose of deciding whether the state court ruled correctly on them or not. We are of opinion that on these subjects not embraced in the class of questions stated in the statute, we must receive the decision of the state courts as conclusive.

But when we find that the state court had decided the federal question erroneously, then to prevent a useless and profitless reversal, which can do the plaintiff in error no good, and can only embarrass and delay the defendant, we must so far look into the remainder of the record as to see whether the decision of the federal question alone is sufficient to dispose of the case, or to require its reversal; or on the other hand, whether there exist other matters in the record actually decided by the state court which are sufficient to maintain the judgment of that court, not-withstanding the error in deciding the federal question. In the latter case, the court would not be justified in reversing the judgment of the state court.

But this examination into the points in the record other than the federal question is not for the purpose of determining whether they were correctly or erroneously decided, but to ascertain if any such have been decided, and their sufficiency to maintain the final judgment, as decided by the state court.

Beyond this we are not at liberty to go, and we can only go this far to prevent the injustice of reversing a judgment which must in the end be reaffirmed, even in this Court, if brought here again from the state court after it has corrected its error in the matter of federal law.

Finally, we hold the following propositions on this subject as flowing from the statute as it now stands:

1. That it is essential to the jurisdiction of this Court over the judgment of a state court, that it shall appear that one of the questions mentioned in the act must have been raised, and presented to the state court.

2. That it must have been decided by the state court, or that its decision was necessary to the judgment or decree, rendered in the case.

3. That the decision must have been against the right claimed or asserted by plaintiff in error under the Constitution, treaties, laws, or authority of the United States.

4. These things appearing, this Court has jurisdiction and must examine the judgment so far as to enable it to decide whether this claim of right was correctly adjudicated by the state court.

5. If it finds that it was rightly decided, the judgment must be affirmed.

6. If it was erroneously decided against plaintiff in error, then this Court must further inquire, whether there is any other matter or issue adjudged by the state court, which is sufficiently broad to maintain the judgment of that court, notwithstanding the error in deciding the issue raised by the federal question. If this is found to be the case, the judgment must be affirmed without inquiring into the soundness of the decision on such other matter or issue.

7. But if it be found that the issue raised by the question of federal law is of such controlling character that its correct decision is necessary to any final judgment in the case, or that there has been no decision by the state court of any other matter or issue which is sufficient to maintain the judgment of that court without regard to the federal question, then this Court will reverse the judgment of the state court, and will either render such judgment here as the state court should have rendered, or remand the case to that court, as the circumstances of the case may require.

Applying the principles here laid down to the case now before the Court, we are of opinion that this Court has jurisdiction, and that the judgment of the Supreme Court of Tennessee must be affirmed. . . .

[W]e need not consume many words to prove that neither by the deed of the city to the United States, which is an ordinary deed of bargain and sale for a valuable consideration, nor from anything found in the act of 1854, is there any . . . trust to be inferred. The act, so far from recognizing or implying any such trust, cedes the property to the mayor and aldermen *for the use of the city*. We are therefore of opinion that this, the only federal question in the case, was rightly decided by the Supreme Court of Tennessee.

But conceding this to be true, the plaintiffs in error have argued that the court having jurisdiction of the case must now examine it upon all the questions which affect its merits; and they insist that the conveyance by which the City of Memphis received the title [in 1844] previous to the deed from the city to the government, and the circumstances attending the making of the former deed are such, that when the title reverted to the city, a trust was raised for the benefit of plaintiffs.

After what has been said in the previous part of this opinion, we need discuss this matter no further. The claim of right here set up is one to be determined by the general principles of equity jurisprudence, and is unaffected by anything found in the Constitution, laws, or treaties of the United States. Whether decided well or otherwise by the state court, we have no authority to inquire. According to the principles we have laid down as applicable to this class of cases, the judgment of the Supreme Court of Tennessee must be *Affirmed*.

Justice CLIFFORD, with whom concurred Justice SWAYNE, dissenting:

I dissent from so much of the opinion of the Court as denies the jurisdiction of this Court to determine the whole case, where it appears that the record presents a federal question and that the federal question was erroneously decided to the prejudice of the plaintiff in error, as in that state of the record it is, in my judgment, the duty of this Court, under the recent act of Congress, to decide the whole merits of the controversy, and to affirm or reverse the judgment of the state court. . . .

Justice BRADLEY, dissenting:

I deem it very doubtful whether the court has any jurisdiction at all over this particular case. The complainants claim the property in question under the terms, and what they regard as the true construction, of the trust deed of July, 1844, whereby the property was conveyed to the City of Memphis "for the location of the naval depot," and to Wheatley, trustee for the grantors, "in case the same shall not be appropriated by the United States for that purpose." This deed was acknowledged on the 19th of September, 1844, and (probably at the same time) a deed dated 14th of September, 1844, was executed by the city to the United States, conveying the land in fee without any conditions or uses expressed. Operations for erecting and establishing a navy yard on the premises were commenced and were continued for several years, but were finally abandoned, and on the 5th of August, 1854, Congress, by an act, ceded the property to the City of Memphis for the use and benefit of the city. The defendants, the City of Memphis, claim both legal and beneficial title to the property under this act of Congress, and the Supreme Court of Tennessee sustained the claim—or at least did not sustain the adverse claim of the complainants. The claim of the complainants was not based on this act of Congress, but on the original deed of 1844, which limited the estate in the lands to their trustee "in case the same shall not be appropriated by the United States for that purpose," *i.e.*, the purpose of a navy yard. They claim that by the true construction of this clause a right to the land accrued to them, as well by an abandonment of the project of a navy yard as by its never being adopted. The conduct of the government in relation to the land, it is true, is claimed by them to be such as calls into operative effect the clause of the deed on which they rely. They construe that conduct as an abandonment of the enterprise. The act of cession by Congress to the City of Memphis is only one fact in a long chain of circumstances which they educe to show such abandonment.

It seems to me, therefore, that their claim is based entirely on the deed of 1844; and that the subsequent action of the government, so far as it has any effect in the case, is merely matter of evidence on the question of fact of abandonment, and that the failure of the government, from the beginning, to take any steps for establishing a navy yard on the land would have been no more a mere fact *in pais* to be proved in order to support the claim of the complainants, than were all the acts of the government which did in fact take place. Proving that the government did not appropriate the land for a navy yard is a very different thing from setting up a claim to the land under an act of Congress.

I think, therefore, that in this case there was no title or right claimed by the appellants under any statute of, or authority exercised under, the United States, and consequently that there was no decision against any such title, and therefore that this Court has no jurisdiction.

But supposing, as the majority of the court holds, that it has jurisdiction, I cannot concur in the conclusion that we can only decide the federal question raised by the record. If we have jurisdiction at all, in my judgment we have jurisdiction of the *case*, and not merely of a *question* in it. . . . This act derives its authority and is intended to carry into effect, at least in part, that clause of the Constitution which declares that the judicial power shall extend to all *cases*, in law and equity, arising under this Constitution, the laws of the United States, and treaties made under their authority – not to all *questions*, but to all *cases*. This word "cases," in the residue of the section, has frequently been held to mean suits, actions, embracing the whole cases, not mere questions in them; and that is undoubtedly the true construction. The Constitution, therefore, would have authorized a revision by the judiciary of the United States of all *cases* decided in state courts in which questions of United States law or federal rights are necessarily involved. Congress in carrying out that clause could have so ordained [in the First Judiciary Act].

Now, Congress, in the Act of 1867 . . . omitted the clause above referred to, which restricted the court to a consideration of the federal questions. This omission cannot be regarded as having no meaning. . . .

In my judgment, therefore, if the court had jurisdiction of the case, it was bound to consider not only the federal question raised by the record, but the whole case.

* * *

While *Murdock* stands for the narrow proposition that the Supreme Court may not ordinarily review state courts' final interpretations of state law, it contains elements of the rule that has come to be known as the "independent and adequate state grounds" doctrine. The basic rule is that where a state court decision rests on two grounds, one of which is federal law and the other is state law, the Supreme Court will not review the case if the state law ground is independent of the federal law ground and is adequate by itself to support the result. *See Fox Film Corp. v. Muller* (1935) ("[W]here the judgment of a state court rests upon two grounds, one of which is federal and the other nonfederal in character, our jurisdiction fails if the nonfederal ground is independent of the federal ground and adequate to support the judgment.").

Murdock rejects the proposition that Congress intended to expand appellate jurisdiction to the "whole case" in part on the ground that state courts can be trusted not to "disregard or overlook" federal questions, but is silent on the state's defiance of federal law during Reconstruction. Note that within a year of *Murdock* Congress creates arising under jurisdiction for federal district courts in 28 U.S.C. §1331. If Section 25 appellate jurisdiction is limited to "questions mentioned in the statute"—that is, to federal questions—why do you think the Court in *Martin* opined on the validity of Virginia's escheat process?

b. Justifications and Criticisms of the Independent and Adequate State Grounds Doctrine

There are many justifications for this rule. The Court often has observed that the prohibition against advisory opinions prevents it from hearing cases when there is an independent and adequate state law ground for the decision. For example, in *Herb v. Pitcairn* (1945), the Court stated, "We are not permitted to render an advisory opinion, and if the same judgment would be rendered by the state court after we corrected its views of federal laws, our review would amount to nothing more than an advisory opinion."

Also, the independent and adequate grounds doctrine allows the Court to avoid unnecessary constitutional rulings. The Court frequently stresses the desirability of avoiding constitutional questions wherever possible. *See, e.g., Ashwander v. TVA* (1936) (Brandeis, J., concurring). When the state court rules on both federal constitutional grounds and on state law grounds, the Court avoids the former when the state law is independent and adequate to support the result in the case.

The doctrine also promotes harmony between the federal and state systems by minimizing Supreme Court review of state court decisions. The argument is that any federal court reversal of a state court ruling is a possible source of friction. By confining review to instances where the Supreme Court decision might make a difference, the Court avoids unnecessary tension between federal and state courts.

Does it strike the correct balance between federalism and the Supremacy Clause to permit inconsistent and incorrect interpretations of federal law to remain unreviewed? A state court decision wrongly interpreting federal law that remains on the books potentially influences other courts around the country. And any inconsistent state interpretations of federal law will not be resolved if they are accompanied by state law grounds. Accuracy and uniformity in the application of federal law are sacrificed. The importance of Supreme Court review of state decisions in such instances is reflected in an exception the Court created to the final judgment rule. In *Cohn*, the Court said that review is permitted in the absence of a final judgment from the state's highest court when the Court otherwise would not have the chance to correct a state court's errors regarding federal law.

Also, the independent and adequate state grounds doctrine invites state courts to try to immunize their decisions from Supreme Court review by manufacturing a state basis for the decision. In many civil rights cases during the 1960s, the state courts tried to prevent Supreme Court review of their anti–civil rights rulings by invoking a state law ground of decision. One of the exceptions to the doctrine is when the state law ground was created or imposed for the purpose of frustrating Supreme Court review. *See NAACP v. Flowers* (1964), *supra,* and discussion below.

Despite the criticisms of the doctrine, it is well entrenched in current law and the Supreme Court has given no indication that it is about to abandon it. The precise legal basis for the doctrine is uncertain, but most commentators regard it not as constitutionally required but instead as a prudential rule of judicial self-restraint.

c. When Is There an "Independent" and "Adequate" State Ground?

A state court's decision on a state law issue is deemed adequate to support its result if the Supreme Court's reversal of the state court's federal law ruling will not alter the outcome of the case. An adequate state law ground exists where the state law basis for the decision is sufficient by itself to support the judgment, regardless of whether the federal law issue is affirmed or reversed.

State law obviously is not adequate to support the result when there is a claim that the state law itself violates the U.S. Constitution. An unconstitutional state law cannot support the state court's holding. For example, in *Staub v. City of Baxley* (1958), a city ordinance made it an offense to solicit membership in any organization without a permit. Appellant was convicted of violating the ordinance notwithstanding her claims that the law violated the First Amendment. The state court of appeals affirmed, refusing to decide the merits of the case because it concluded that, under state law, the failure to request a permit deprived the appellant of standing to present constitutional issues on appeal. The Court held that the state law was not adequate to support the judgment because it was unconstitutional. The Court observed that "[t]he decisions of this Court have uniformly held that the failure to apply for a license under an ordinance which on its face violated the Constitution does not preclude review in this Court of a judgment of conviction under such an ordinance."

Among the most common controversies in determining the adequacy of state grounds is failure to comply with state *procedural* requirements. A simple example is illustrative. Imagine that a state's highest court ruled against an appellant presenting a constitutional claim because the appellant failed to file a notice of appeal within the required 90 days. The state court did not reach the merits, but instead based its decision entirely on the state law procedural requirement. Is the procedural ruling, then, an adequate ground for the decision precluding Supreme Court review of the federal constitutional question?

The general answer is that decisions on fair state procedural grounds are deemed "adequate" and are sufficient to prevent the Supreme Court from reviewing substantive constitutional issues. The Supreme Court observed that "[f]ailure to present a federal question in conformance with state procedure constitutes an adequate and independent state ground of decision barring review in this Court, so long as the State has a legitimate interest in enforcing its procedural rules." *Michigan v. Tyler* (1978).

First, and most obviously, state procedural rules are not adequate if they deny due process of law. This is simply a restatement of the rule described above: a state law cannot be adequate if it is unconstitutional. For example, in *Reece v. Ga.* (1955), the state court refused to allow a defendant to challenge the racial composition of a grand jury because of a state law requiring such challenges to be made prior to the issuance of an indictment. The Court, however, found that this rule denied due process because the state refused to provide counsel until after an indictment was made.

The second situation in which state procedural rules do not constitute adequate grounds supporting the state court's decision is where the rules fail to promote a sufficiently important state interest and prevent the vindication of federal rights. That is, the Supreme Court will grant review even though state procedures were not followed if the state's rules "heavily burden the assertion of federal rights without significantly advancing any important state policy."

The most important case holding that state procedural rules preclude Supreme Court review only if they serve an important state purpose is *Henry v. Miss.* (1965). Aaron Henry, a civil rights activist, was arrested by the Mississippi police for having made "indecent proposals" to and having had "offensive contact" with an 18-year-old hitchhiker whom he had allegedly given a ride. Henry's conviction was based in large part on the testimony by a police officer concerning what was observed during a search of Henry's car, which was done pursuant to the consent of Henry's wife. Henry's attorney did not object to the evidence at the time it was admitted during the trial but did object later in a motion for a directed verdict at the conclusion of the state's case.

The Mississippi Supreme Court reversed Henry's conviction, holding that the wife's consent did not waive Henry's constitutional rights. The court reversed the conviction despite a state rule requiring a contemporaneous objection to evidence at the time of its admission. The court concluded that the fact that Henry was not represented by local counsel justified the deviation from the procedural rule. Subsequently, the Mississippi Supreme Court learned that Henry actually was represented by local counsel. The court then withdrew its earlier opinion and issued a new one affirming the conviction.

The U.S. Supreme Court vacated the conviction and remanded the case for a determination of whether Henry knowingly waived his federal claim when no objection was made at the time the evidence was offered. The Court emphasized the need to distinguish between state substantive and procedural law in determining whether there is an independent and adequate state ground of decision. Whereas a state substantive ground always is deemed adequate if reversal of the federal law holding would not alter the outcome of the case, a procedural ground should be deemed adequate only if it serves a "legitimate state interest." The Court explained that the "question of when and how defaults in compliance with state procedural rules can preclude our consideration of a federal question is itself a federal question." As such, in every case, it is the Supreme Court's rule to "inquire whether the enforcement of a procedural forfeiture serves such a [legitimate] state interest."

The Court recognized that state courts have an important interest in requiring litigants to make contemporaneous objections to the introduction of evidence. However, the Court observed that the state's interests might have been served equally well by the objection made in the course of the motion for the directed verdict. The Court said that "[i]f this is so, and enforcement of the rule here would serve no substantial state interest, then settled principles would preclude treating the state ground as adequate; giving effect to the contemporaneous-objection rule for its own sake 'would be to force resort to an arid ritual of meaningless form.'"

Under the law of waiver in effect at the time of the *Henry* decision, a waiver required demonstrating that the defendant deliberately bypassed the available procedures — that is, showing that the defendant made a strategic decision to not make a contemporaneous objection. The Court remanded the case to the state court for a determination of whether a waiver occurred under this standard.

The crucial question after *Henry* is what constitutes a legitimate state interest in a procedural rule as opposed to an "arid ritual of meaningless form." The Supreme Court has not articulated any clear criteria for this determination, instead proceeding on a case-by-case basis.

For instance, in *Douglas v. Ala.* (1965), a defendant's attorney objected to the reading of a codefendant's confession. However, the objection was not repeated at the time the confession was actually put into evidence and the Alabama Supreme Court deemed this a procedural forfeiture that prevented it from hearing the defendant's constitutional claim. The Supreme Court reversed. The Court explained that the defense counsel already had objected three times to the introduction of the confession and that "[n]o legitimate state interest would have been served by requiring repetition of a patently futile objection, already thrice rejected, in a situation in which repeated objection might well affront the court or prejudice the jury beyond repair."

In contrast, in *Parker v. N.C.* (1970), the state defendant was convicted of burglary pursuant to his guilty plea. Subsequently, the defendant attempted to have the conviction reversed on the grounds that Blacks had been excluded from the grand jury that indicted him. The state court refused to hear this constitutional argument because of a state procedural rule requiring that such a contention must be raised in a motion to quash the indictment before the entry of a guilty plea. The Supreme Court declined to review the constitutional claim because it concluded that the state had a legitimate interest in ensuring timely objections to grand jury composition.

In considering what state procedural rules are sufficiently important to prevent Supreme Court review, it should be noted that the Court now is far more deferential to such rules — especially those requiring contemporaneous objections — than was the situation at the time *Henry* was decided.

The third major situation in which a state procedural rule does not constitute an adequate state law ground for the decision is when the Court concludes that the state court tried to prevent review of a federal constitutional claim by creating a new procedural hurdle or by applying a rule that is not consistently followed. The Court obviously is concerned that state courts might try to insulate their rulings from Supreme Court review by manufacturing or manipulating procedural doctrines in an effort to create independent and adequate state grounds of decision. Thus, the Court long has recognized that a procedural rule will not prevent Supreme Court review, even if it serves a legitimate state interest or if it "is an obvious subterfuge to evade consideration of a federal issue." *Radio Station WOW, Inc. v. Johnson* (1945).

For example, the Court has held that there is not an independent and adequate state ground of decision when the state court creates a new procedural rule that would foreclose Supreme Court review. As we saw in Section C.1, in *NAACP v. Ala. ex rel. Patterson* (1958), the state of Alabama sued the NAACP to halt its activities in the state in the midst of the organization's advocacy supporting the civil rights movement and desegregation. The organization was held in contempt of court because of its failure to comply with an order requiring it to produce its membership lists. Production of the lists would have interfered with the free association rights of the members and exposed them to racist violence. The Alabama Supreme Court refused to hear the NAACP's appeal because it said that the organization did not comply with the procedural rule that writs of mandamus were the only basis for challenging contempt orders. The U.S. Supreme Court refused to allow this procedure to constitute an independent and adequate state ground of decision because there was "nothing in the prior [state] cases which suggests that mandamus is the exclusive remedy for reviewing state court orders after disobedience of them has led to contempt judgments."

After the Supreme Court reversed, the state court reinstated its contempt judgment, and the Supreme Court reversed again, all without reaching the merits of the contempt order. The NAACP then sued in federal court alleging the failure of the state courts to provide a hearing on the merits. The Supreme Court ordered such a hearing. The Alabama trial court then ruled against the NAACP on the merits and permanently enjoined it from operating in the state. The Alabama Supreme Court affirmed, refusing to consider the NAACP's federal constitutional claims, solely on the basis of a procedural rule regarding the NAACP's brief. The Alabama Supreme Court said that when unrelated issues are argued together and one is without merit, the others will not be considered.

The U.S. Supreme Court reversed and remanded, ordering prompt entry of a decree vacating the injunction and permitting the NAACP to operate in Alabama. *NAACP v. Ala. ex rel. Flowers* (1964). The Court refused to allow the Alabama procedural rule to bar Supreme Court review because it previously never had been applied in that manner. The Court explained, "Novelty in procedural requirements cannot be permitted to thwart review in this Court applied for by those who, in justified reliance upon prior decisions, seek vindication in state courts of their federal constitutional rights."

Also, the Court has held that it will not deem a state procedural rule to be an adequate ground for the decision if the rule is inconsistently followed by the state courts. The Court has observed that "state procedural requirements which are not strictly or regularly followed cannot deprive us of the right to review." *Barr v. City of Columbia* (1964).

James v. Kentucky (1984) is instructive. The defendant requested an "admonition" to the jury that no inference could be drawn from his failure to testify at the trial. The trial court denied the request and the Kentucky Supreme Court affirmed, holding that Kentucky law draws a distinction between instructions and admonitions. The Supreme Court, however, refused to allow the Kentucky procedural rule to bar review. The Court explained that "Kentucky's distinction between admonitions and instructions is not the sort of firmly established and regularly followed state practice that can prevent implementation of federal constitutional rights." Furthermore, the Court explained that to insist on the defense counsel's use of a particular label would "force resort to an arid ritual of meaningless form and would further no perceivable state interest."

Indeed, the Supreme Court has held that a state procedural rule cannot constitute an adequate state ground for decision if the rule is discretionary rather than mandatory. In other words, if the state court is not required to follow a particular rule, then that rule will not foreclose Supreme Court review. The Court's obvious concern is that state courts might use such discretionary rules to prevent review of federal claims.

Sullivan v. Little Hunting Park, Inc. (1969), is one of the most famous cases in which the Supreme Court held that a state court's application of discretionary procedural requirements does not preclude federal review. In *Sullivan*, a recreational association expelled a member for renting a home in the community to a Black man in violation of an agreement. The trial court ruled in favor of the recreational association, concluding that it was a private club and therefore did not need to comply with the Constitution or federal civil rights laws. The Virginia court of appeals denied review based on a procedural rationale that the plaintiffs did not give the recreation association's attorneys sufficient time to examine and correct the trial transcripts.

The Supreme Court held that this procedural rule did not bar review. Although it was not a novel requirement created for the first time in this case, it also was not a rule that was uniformly followed by the Virginia court of appeals. The Court concluded that "[s]uch a rule, more properly deemed discretionary than jurisdictional, does not bar review."

Another application of this principle that discretionary rules do not bar Supreme Court review is *Hathorn v. Lovorn* (1982). In *Hathorn*, the Mississippi Supreme Court reversed the trial court's conclusion that a county had violated the Voting Rights Act. The Mississippi Supreme Court concluded that the trial court's decision was inconsistent with "the law of the case" — that is, the trial court erred by relying on federal law because prior rulings in the litigation had focused on state law issues. The Supreme Court reversed and concisely explained the requirement that a state procedural rule must be regularly followed to constitute an independent and adequate state ground of decision. The Court stated: "[A] state procedural ground is not 'adequate' unless the procedural rule is 'strictly or regularly followed.' State courts may not avoid deciding federal issues by invoking procedural rules that they do not apply evenhandedly to all similar claims."

It also is important that the state ground of decision must be "independent" of federal law. The Supreme Court is precluded from reviewing a state court's judgment only if the state grounds of decision are both adequate to support the judgment and independent of federal law. A state ground is deemed independent if it is based entirely on state law and is not tied to federal law. For example, a state highest court decision that relies solely on federal law is reviewable by the Supreme Court because there are no independent state law grounds for the ruling.

It should be noted that to constitute an independent state ground of decision, the state's highest court must have explicitly relied on it as a basis for its ruling. The Court has explained that the "mere existence of a basis for a state procedural bar does not deprive this Court of jurisdiction; the state court must actually have relied on the procedural bar as an independent basis for its disposition of the case." *Caldwell v. Miss.* (1985).

The Court has held that there is not an independent state ground of decision if the state law incorporates federal law. In *Del. v. Prouse* (1979), the Delaware
Supreme Court ruled that a search by police officers violated both the Fourth
Amendment and the Delaware Constitution. Although there was a state law ground
of decision, the U.S. Supreme Court nonetheless granted review because it was convinced that the sole basis for the Delaware court's decision was its interpretation of
federal law. The Court stated: "This is one of those cases where 'at the very least,
the [state] court felt compelled by what it understood to be federal constitutional
considerations to construe . . . its own law in the manner it did.' . . . If the state
court misapprehended federal law, '[i]t should be freed to decide . . . these suits
according to its own local law.'"

d. How to Proceed When the State Court's Decision Is Unclear?

A crucial problem that has received a great deal of recent attention is how the
Supreme Court should proceed when it is unclear whether the state law ground
was meant to incorporate federal law or whether it was intended to be an independent basis for the decision. Prior to the Supreme Court's decision in 1983 in
Mich. v. Long, the Supreme Court had used several inconsistent approaches.[33] In
some cases, the Court appeared to create a presumption that the discussion of state
law constituted an independent ground of decision precluding Supreme Court
review.[34] At minimum, the Court would carefully examine the state court's opinion
to decide whether it was likely that the state court intended to rely on independent
state law grounds.

In other cases, the Court refused to hear the matter until the state court clarified whether its decision was meant to rest on an independent state law basis.
For example, in some instances the Court vacated the state court judgment and
remanded the matter to the state court for a clarification of whether the ruling was
based on state law.[35] In other instances, the Court retained the case on its docket
while the matter was sent back to state court for a clarification as to whether there
was an independent state law ground.[36]

In yet other cases, the Court presumed that there was no independent state
basis for the decision unless the state court expressly stated that it had relied on
state law.[37] In other words, under this approach, unless the state court explicitly
invoked state law, the Court assumed that the decision was based on federal law and
heard the case.

The Court resolved this issue of what to do when it is unclear whether a state
court was relying on an independent and adequate state ground in *Mich. v. Long*.

---

33. For a discussion of the alternative approaches to how the Court should proceed
when it is unclear whether there is an independent state ground of decision, see Ann Althouse, *How to Build a Separate Sphere: Federal Courts and State Power*, 100 HARV. L. REV. 1485,
1500-07 (1987).

34. *Memphis Natural Gas Co. v. Beeler* (1942).

35. *See, e.g., Paschall v. Christie-Stewart* (1973); *Minnesota v. Nat. Tea Co.* (1940).

36. *See, e.g., Herb v. Pitcairn* (1945).

37. *See, e.g., Zacchini v. Scripps-Howard Broadcasting Co.* (1977); *Stembridge v. Georgia*
(1952).

The case grows out of several intersecting events. The first is litigation percolating in the states on the constitutional limits surrounding so-called "*Terry* stops" — referring to the 1968 case in which the Supreme Court upheld the power of police to "stop and frisk" a person for weapons without a warrant or probable cause on the basis of "specific reasonable inferences" from the facts that the officer's "safety or the safety of others [is] in danger." *Terry v. Ohio* (1968). The case was significant because it rejected both earlier precedent indicating that government restraints on physical liberty and searches require probable cause, and the argument that the Fourth Amendment was irrelevant to ostensibly minor detentions and intrusions on privacy. Instead, the Court chose a middle path, holding that the Fourth Amendment governs police interactions short of arrest, but that these encounters are justified if the officer has reasonable suspicion that the person is armed and dangerous.

A bewildering array of fact scenarios arose on what counts as reasonable suspicion and the Court was repeatedly asked to accept appellate jurisdiction of litigation testing the discretionary decisions of police officers. As the Burger Court became more interested in limiting the Fourth Amendment, it became more open to taking jurisdiction of cases where a motion to suppress evidence had been granted and upheld in the state courts.

The volume of *Terry* cases also rose with the "war on drugs" in the 1970s and early 1980s and the dramatic expansion in investigation, prosecution, and imposition of severe criminal sentences for petty possession and possession with intent to distribute. Recent empirical studies show that the contextual and discretionary factors used to justify *Terry* stops are often unconnected to the probability someone presents a safety risk and that these low-yield stops have been imposed disproportionately on Black people and Latinos.[38]

Long was decided as all of these trends converged — a high volume of litigation on motions to suppress evidence gathered in or after arrests following *Terry* stops, expansive use of *Terry* stops for drug interdiction, and the efforts of some state courts to check abuse of the practice. State courts would often rely on federal cases interpreting *Terry* even when the court was adjudicating *state constitutional* analogues to the federal Fourth Amendment. This practice created ambiguity, as we will see, over whether the state ground of decision was independent of the federal ground.

Michigan v. Long

463 U.S. 1032 (1983)

Justice O'CONNOR delivered the opinion of the Court.

In *Terry v. Ohio* (1968), we upheld the validity of a protective search for weapons in the absence of probable cause to arrest because it is unreasonable to deny

---

38. Sharad Goel et al., *Precinct of Prejudice? Understanding Racial Disparities in New York City's Stop-and-Frisk Policy*, 10 ANNALS OF APPLIED STAT. 365, 383 (2016) (describing factors empirically known to have only a one percent chance of finding a weapon disproportionately used to justify *Terry* stops of people of color); *see also* Devon Carbado, *Blue-on-Black Violence: A Provisional Model of Some of the Causes*, 104 GEO. L.J. 1479 (2016).

a police officer the right "to neutralize the threat of physical harm," when he possesses an articulable suspicion that an individual is armed and dangerous. We did not, however, expressly address whether such a protective search for weapons could extend to an area beyond the person in the absence of probable cause to arrest.

In the present case, respondent David Long was convicted for possession of marijuana found by police in the passenger compartment and trunk of the automobile that he was driving. The police searched the passenger compartment because they had reason to believe that the vehicle contained weapons potentially dangerous to the officers. We hold that the protective search of the passenger compartment was reasonable under the principles articulated in *Terry* and other decisions of this Court. We also examine Long's argument that the decision below rests upon an adequate and independent state ground, and we decide in favor of our jurisdiction.

I

Deputies Howell and Lewis were on patrol in a rural area one evening when, shortly after midnight, they observed a car traveling erratically and at excessive speed. The officers observed the car turning down a side road, where it swerved off into a shallow ditch. The officers stopped to investigate. Long, the only occupant of the automobile, met the deputies at the rear of the car, which was protruding from the ditch onto the road. The door on the driver's side of the vehicle was left open.

Deputy Howell requested Long to produce his operator's license, but he did not respond. After the request was repeated, Long produced his license. Long again failed to respond when Howell requested him to produce the vehicle registration. After another repeated request, Long, whom Howell thought "appeared to be under the influence of something," turned from the officers and began walking toward the open door of the vehicle. The officers followed Long and both observed a large hunting knife on the floorboard of the driver's side of the car. The officers then stopped Long's progress and subjected him to a *Terry* protective pat-down, which revealed no weapons.

Long and Deputy Lewis then stood by the rear of the vehicle while Deputy Howell shined his flashlight into the interior of the vehicle, but did not actually enter it. The purpose of Howell's action was "to search for other weapons." The officer noticed that something was protruding from under the armrest on the front seat. He knelt in the vehicle and lifted the armrest. He saw an open pouch on the front seat, and upon flashing his light on the pouch, determined that it contained what appeared to be marijuana. After Deputy Howell showed the pouch and its contents to Deputy Lewis, Long was arrested for possession of marijuana. A further search of the interior of the vehicle, including the glovebox, revealed neither more contraband nor the vehicle registration. The officers decided to impound the vehicle. Deputy Howell opened the trunk, which did not have a lock, and discovered inside it approximately 75 pounds of marijuana.

The Barry County Circuit Court denied Long's motion to suppress the marijuana taken from both the interior of the car and its trunk. He was subsequently convicted of possession of marijuana. The Michigan Court of Appeals affirmed Long's conviction, holding that the search of the passenger compartment was valid as a protective search under *Terry, supra*, and that the search of the trunk was valid as an inventory search.

The Michigan Supreme Court reversed. The court held that "the sole justification of the *Terry* search, protection of the police officers and others nearby, cannot justify the search in this case." The marijuana found in Long's trunk was considered by the court below to be the "fruit" of the illegal search of the interior, and was also suppressed.

We granted certiorari in this case to consider the important question of the authority of a police officer to protect himself by conducting a *Terry*-type search of the passenger compartment of a motor vehicle during the lawful investigatory stop of the occupant of the vehicle.

II

Before reaching the merits, we must consider Long's argument that we are without jurisdiction to decide this case because the decision below rests on an adequate and independent state ground. The court below referred twice to the state constitution in its opinion, but otherwise relied exclusively on federal law. Long argues that the Michigan courts have provided greater protection from searches and seizures under the state constitution than is afforded under the Fourth Amendment, and the references to the state constitution therefore establish an adequate and independent ground for the decision below.

It is, of course, "incumbent upon this Court . . . to ascertain for itself . . . whether the asserted non-federal ground independently and adequately supports the judgment." Although we have announced a number of principles in order to help us determine whether various forms of references to state law constitute adequate and independent state grounds,[4] we openly admit that we have thus far not developed a satisfying and consistent approach for resolving this vexing issue. In some instances, we have taken the strict view that if the ground of decision was at all unclear, we would dismiss the case. In other instances, we have vacated, or continued a case, in order to obtain clarification about the nature of a state court decision. In more recent cases, we have ourselves examined state law to determine whether state courts have used

---

4. For example, we have long recognized that, "where the judgment of a state court rests upon two grounds, one of which is federal and the other nonfederal in character, our jurisdiction fails if the nonfederal ground is independent of the federal ground and adequate to support the judgment." *Fox Film Corp. v. Muller* (1935). We may review a state case decided on a federal ground even if it is clear that there was an available state ground for decision on which the state court could properly have relied. *Beecher v. Alabama* (1967) [state supreme court could have, but did not, decline to review federal constitutional objection to admission of an involuntary confession on state procedural ground that new trial motion was improper method of raising it]. Also, if, in our view, the state court "felt compelled by what it understood to be federal constitutional considerations to construe . . . its own law in the manner it did," then we will not treat a normally adequate state ground as independent, and there will be no question about our jurisdiction. *Delaware v. Prouse* (1979). Finally, "where the nonfederal ground is so interwoven with the [federal ground] as not to be an independent matter, or is not of sufficient breadth to sustain the judgment without any decision of the other, our jurisdiction is plain." *Enterprise Irrigation District v. Farmers Mutual Canal Co.* (1917).

federal law to guide their application of state law or to provide the actual basis for the decision that was reached.

This *ad hoc* method of dealing with cases that involve possible adequate and independent state grounds is antithetical to the doctrinal consistency that is required when sensitive issues of federal-state relations are involved. Moreover, none of the various methods of disposition that we have employed thus far recommends itself as the preferred method that we should apply to the exclusion of others, and we therefore determine that it is appropriate to reexamine our treatment of this jurisdictional issue in order to achieve the consistency that is necessary.

The process of examining state law is unsatisfactory because it requires us to interpret state laws with which we are generally unfamiliar, and which often, as in this case, have not been discussed at length by the parties. Vacation and continuance for clarification have also been unsatisfactory both because of the delay and decrease in efficiency of judicial administration, and, more important, because these methods of disposition place significant burdens on state courts to demonstrate the presence or absence of our jurisdiction. Finally, outright dismissal of cases is clearly not a panacea because it cannot be doubted that there is an important need for uniformity in federal law, and that this need goes unsatisfied when we fail to review an opinion that rests primarily upon federal grounds and where the *independence* of an alleged state ground is not apparent from the four corners of the opinion. We have long recognized that dismissal is inappropriate "where there is strong indication . . . that the federal constitution as judicially construed controlled the decision below."

Respect for the independence of state courts, as well as avoidance of rendering advisory opinions, have been the cornerstones of this Court's refusal to decide cases where there is an adequate and independent state ground. It is precisely because of this respect for state courts, and this desire to avoid advisory opinions, that we do not wish to continue to decide issues of state law that go beyond the opinion that we review, or to require state courts to reconsider cases to clarify the grounds of their decisions. Accordingly, when, as in this case, a state court decision fairly appears to rest primarily on federal law, or to be interwoven with the federal law, and when the adequacy and independence of any possible state law ground is not clear from the face of the opinion, we will accept as the most reasonable explanation that the state court decided the case the way it did because it believed that federal law required it to do so. If a state court chooses merely to rely on federal precedents as it would on the precedents of all other jurisdictions, then it need only make clear by a plain statement in its judgment or opinion that the federal cases are being used only for the purpose of guidance, and do not themselves compel the result that the court has reached. In this way, both justice and judicial administration will be greatly improved. If the state court decision indicates clearly and expressly that it is alternatively based on bona fide separate, adequate, and independent grounds, we, of course, will not undertake to review the decision.

This approach obviates in most instances the need to examine state law in order to decide the nature of the state court decision, and will at the same time avoid the danger of our rendering advisory opinions. It also avoids the unsatisfactory and intrusive practice of requiring state courts to clarify their decisions to the satisfaction of this Court. We believe that such an approach will provide state judges with a clearer opportunity to develop state jurisprudence unimpeded by federal interference, and yet will preserve the integrity of federal law. "It is fundamental that state courts be left free and unfettered by us in interpreting their state constitutions. But it is equally important that ambiguous or obscure adjudications by state courts do not stand as barriers to a determination by this Court of the validity under the federal constitution of state action."

The principle that we will not review judgments of state courts that rest on adequate and independent state grounds is based, in part, on "the limitations of our own jurisdiction." The jurisdictional concern is that we not "render an advisory opinion, and if the same judgment would be rendered by the state court after we corrected its views of federal laws, our review could amount to nothing more than an advisory opinion." Our requirement of a "plain statement" that a decision rests upon adequate and independent state grounds does not in any way authorize the rendering of advisory opinions. Rather, in determining, as we must, whether we have jurisdiction to review a case that is alleged to rest on adequate and independent state grounds, we merely assume that there are no such grounds when it is not clear from the opinion itself that the state court relied upon an adequate and independent state ground and when it fairly appears that the state court rested its decision primarily on federal law.

Our review of the decision below under this framework leaves us unconvinced that it rests upon an independent state ground. Apart from its two citations to the state constitution, the court below relied *exclusively* on its understanding of *Terry* and other federal cases. Not a single state case was cited to support the state court's holding that the search of the passenger compartment was unconstitutional. Indeed, the court declared that the search in this case was unconstitutional because "[t]he Court of Appeals erroneously applied the principles of *Terry v. Ohio* . . . to the search of the interior of the vehicle in this case." The references to the state constitution in no way indicate that the decision below rested on grounds in any way *independent* from the state court's interpretation of federal law. Even if we accept that the Michigan constitution has been interpreted to provide independent protection for certain rights also secured under the Fourth Amendment, it fairly appears in this case that the Michigan Supreme Court rested its decision primarily on federal law.

Rather than dismissing the case, or requiring that the state court reconsider its decision on our behalf solely because of a mere possibility that an adequate and independent ground supports the judgment, we find that we have jurisdiction in the absence of a plain statement that the decision below rested on an adequate and independent state ground. It appears to us that the state court "felt compelled by what it understood to be federal constitutional considerations to construe . . . its own law in the manner it did."

[On the merits, the Court reversed, finding the search was constitutional.]

Justice BLACKMUN, concurring in part and concurring in the judgment.

While I am satisfied that the Court has jurisdiction in this particular case, I do not join the Court, in Part II of its opinion, in fashioning a new presumption of jurisdiction over cases coming here from state courts. Although I agree with the Court that uniformity in federal criminal law is desirable, I see little efficiency and an increased danger of advisory opinions in the Court's new approach.

Justice BRENNAN, with whom Justice MARSHALL joins, dissenting.

The Court today holds that "the protective search of the passenger compartment" of the automobile involved in this case "was reasonable under the principles articulated in *Terry* and other decisions of this Court." I disagree. *Terry v. Ohio* (1968) does not support the Court's conclusion and the reliance on "other decisions" is patently misplaced. Plainly, the Court is simply continuing the process of distorting *Terry* beyond recognition and forcing it into service as an unlikely weapon against the Fourth Amendment's fundamental requirement that searches and seizures be based on probable cause. . . .

Justice STEVENS, dissenting.

The jurisprudential questions presented in this case are far more important than the question whether the Michigan police officer's search of respondent's car violated the Fourth Amendment. The case raises profoundly significant questions concerning the relationship between two sovereigns — the State of Michigan and the United States of America.

The Supreme Court of the State of Michigan expressly held "that the deputies' search of the vehicle was proscribed by the Fourth Amendment of the United States Constitution and *art. 1, §11 of the Michigan Constitution.*"

The state law ground is clearly adequate to support the judgment, but the question whether it is independent of the Michigan Supreme Court's understanding of federal law is more difficult. Four possible ways of resolving that question present themselves: (1) asking the Michigan Supreme Court directly, (2) attempting to infer from all possible sources of state law what the Michigan Supreme Court meant, (3) presuming that adequate state grounds are independent unless it clearly appears otherwise, or (4) presuming that adequate state grounds are *not* independent unless it clearly appears otherwise. This Court has, on different occasions, employed each of the first three approaches; never until today has it even hinted at the fourth. In order to "achieve the consistency that is necessary," the Court today undertakes a reexamination of all the possibilities. It rejects the first approach as inefficient and unduly burdensome for state courts, and rejects the second approach as an inappropriate expenditure of our resources. Although I find both of those decisions defensible in themselves, I cannot accept the Court's decision to choose the fourth approach over the third — to presume that adequate state grounds are intended to be dependent on federal law unless the record plainly shows otherwise. I must therefore dissent.

If we reject the intermediate approaches, we are left with a choice between two presumptions: one in favor of our taking jurisdiction, and one against it. Historically, the latter presumption has always prevailed. The Court today points out that in several cases we have weakened the traditional presumption by using the other two intermediate approaches identified above. Since those two approaches are now to be rejected, however, I would think that *stare decisis* would call for a return to historical principle. Instead, the Court seems to conclude that because some precedents are to be rejected, we must overrule them all.

Even if I agreed with the Court that we are free to consider as a fresh proposition whether we may take presumptive jurisdiction over the decisions of sovereign states, I could not agree that an expansive attitude makes good sense. It appears to be common ground that any rule we adopt should show "respect for state courts, and [a] desire to avoid advisory opinions." And I am confident that all members of this Court agree that there is a vital interest in the sound management of scarce federal judicial resources. All of those policies counsel against the exercise of federal jurisdiction. They are fortified by my belief that a policy of judicial restraint—one that allows other decisional bodies to have the last word in legal interpretation until it is truly necessary for this Court to intervene—enables this Court to make its most effective contribution to our federal system of government.

The nature of the case before us hardly compels a departure from tradition. These are not cases in which an American citizen has been deprived of a right secured by the United States Constitution or a federal statute. Rather, they are cases in which a state court has upheld a citizen's assertion of a right, finding the citizen to be protected under both federal and state law. The complaining party is an officer of the state itself, who asks us to rule that the state court interpreted federal rights too broadly and "overprotected" the citizen.

Such cases should not be of inherent concern to this Court. The reason may be illuminated by assuming that the events underlying this case had arisen in another country, perhaps the Republic of Finland. If the Finnish police had arrested a Finnish citizen for possession of marijuana, and the Finnish courts had turned him loose, no American would have standing to object. If instead they had arrested an American citizen and acquitted him, we might have been concerned about the arrest but we surely could not have complained about the acquittal, even if the Finnish Court had based its decision on its understanding of the United States Constitution. That would be true even if we had a treaty with Finland requiring it to respect the rights of American citizens under the United States Constitution. We would only be motivated to intervene if an American citizen were unfairly arrested, tried, and convicted by the foreign tribunal.

In this case the State of Michigan has arrested one of its citizens and the Michigan Supreme Court has decided to turn him loose. The respondent is a United States citizen as well as a Michigan citizen, but since there is no claim that he has been mistreated by the State of Michigan, the final outcome of the state processes offended no federal interest whatever. Michigan simply provided greater protection to one of its citizens than some other State might provide or, indeed, than this Court might require throughout the country.

I believe that in reviewing the decisions of state courts, the primary role of this Court is to make sure that persons who seek to *vindicate* federal rights have been fairly heard. Until recently we had virtually no interest in cases of this type. Some time during the past decade, our priorities shifted. The result is a docket swollen with requests by states to reverse judgments that their courts have rendered in favor of their citizens. I am confident that a future Court will recognize the error of this allocation of resources. When that day comes, I think it likely that the Court will also reconsider the propriety of today's expansion of our jurisdiction.

The Court offers only one reason for asserting authority over cases such as the one presented today: "an important need for uniformity in federal law [that] goes unsatisfied when we fail to review an opinion that rests primarily upon federal grounds and where the independence of an alleged state ground is not apparent from the four corners of the opinion." Of course, the supposed need to "review an opinion" clashes directly with our oft-repeated reminder that "our power is to correct wrong judgments, not to revise opinions." The clash is not merely one of form: the "need for uniformity in federal law" is truly an ungovernable engine. That same need is no less present when it is perfectly clear that a state ground is both independent and adequate. In fact, it is equally present if a state prosecutor announces that he believes a certain policy of nonenforcement is commanded by federal law. Yet we have never claimed jurisdiction to correct such errors, no matter how egregious they may be, and no matter how much they may thwart the desires of the state electorate. We do not sit to expound our understanding of the Constitution to interested listeners in the legal community; we sit to resolve disputes. If it is not apparent that our views would affect the outcome of a particular case, we cannot presume to interfere.

Finally, I am thoroughly baffled by the Court's suggestion that it must stretch its jurisdiction and reverse the judgment of the Michigan Supreme Court in order to show "[r]espect for the independence of state courts." Would we show respect for the Republic of Finland by convening a special sitting for the sole purpose of declaring that its decision to release an American citizen was based upon a misunderstanding of American law?

* * *

What do you make of Justice Stevens' suggestion that the Court should not dedicate its limited docket to cases where the state court might have overprotected the federal right?

Why has the Court adopted a rule for dealing with ambiguous grounds of decision that is the *least* deferential to the states and their courts of all the alternatives discussed in the majority opinion? Is there a Supremacy Clause problem when a state may have given an interpretation of a federal right that is *broader* than the Court's? Since *Michigan v. Long* was decided, relatively few state courts make the clear statement *Long* invites. Are there reasons a state's highest court may prefer ambiguity regarding the ground of decision?

D. *EXPEDITED APPELLATE REVIEW*

Section 1254 provides that the Supreme Court may exercise appellate jurisdiction over cases in the courts of appeal on petition for writ of certiorari by "any party to any civil or criminal case, before or after rendition of judgment or decree." And the All Writs Act gives the Court and its individual Justices power to "issue all writs necessary or appropriate in aid of their respective jurisdictions and agreeable to the usages and principles of law." 28 U.S.C. §1651(a). Thus, the Court not only has authority to issue a stay for a lower court's injunction, and lift a lower court's stay, but also to issue an injunction itself where the lower court has failed to act.[39]

---

39. *See* STEPHEN M. SHAPIOR ET AL., SUPREME COURT PRACTICE (10th ed. 2013); Stephen I. Vladeck, *The Supreme Court, 2018 Term Essay: The Solicitor General and the Shadow Docket*, 133 HARV. L. REV. 123 (2019).

Emergency intervention is also authorized to preserve the status quo "for a reasonable time to enable the aggrieved party to obtain a writ of certiorari from the Supreme Court." 28 U.S.C. §2101(f).

Although there is ample authority for emergency relief, the Court's own rules make clear that only "exceptional circumstances warrant the exercise of the Court's discretionary powers," and it must be clear that "adequate relief cannot be obtained in any other form." Supreme Court Rule 20.1. In general, the modern Supreme Court has been exceedingly reluctant to exercise these discretionary powers: "the last extraordinary writ of habeas corpus was in 1925, and the last writ of mandamus was granted in 1962."[40]

The dramatic expansion in the Court's emergency relief docket has come instead in response to the many requests it receives to stay or enter other relief from the decision of a lower court or the state courts. One commentator has referred to this as the Court's "shadow docket."[41] Professor William Baude gives the following illustration of the Court's use of stays in litigation following the Court's decision in *U.S. v. Windsor*, striking down provisions of the federal Defense of Marriage Act that defined "marriage" and "spouse" as excluding same-sex partners for purposes of federal law, including federal tax exemption for surviving spouses. After *Windsor*, federal courts of appeal began applying the Court's Fourteenth Amendment analysis to nullify state laws banning same sex marriage.

> In *Herbert v. Kitchen*, the Supreme Court stayed a federal ruling in Utah while it was on appeal. A stay was granted in another Utah case in late June. Those orders were controversial but important. In an insightful opinion in one case pending in the Ninth Circuit, Judge Andrew Hurwitz wrote that while his own view of the procedural requirements would not have justified a stay, the Supreme Court's order in *Kitchen* "virtually instructed courts of appeals to grant stays in the circumstances before us today." He concluded:
>
> > Although the Supreme Court's terse two-sentence order did not offer a statement of reasons . . . and although the Supreme Court's order in *Herbert* is not in the strictest sense precedential, it provides a clear message—the Court (without noted dissent) decided that district court injunctions against the application of laws forbidding same sex unions should be stayed at the request of state authorities pending court of appeals review.
>
> But other courts refused to stay their orders until the Supreme Court stepped in once again. None of the Court's orders contained any explanation. The lack of explanation was compounded when the Court then denied certiorari in all of these cases at the end of the summer. The Court almost never provides explanation for the denial of certiorari, but one would have guessed that the stays were premised on the probability that the Court would take up the issue.[42]

---

40. Vladeck, *supra* note 39, at 130.

41. William Baude, *Foreward: The Supreme Court's Shadow Docket*, 9 N.Y.U. J.L. LIB. 1 (2015).

42. *Id.* at 8-9.

The Court decided *Obergefell v. Hodges* the following term, holding that the right to marry extends to same-sex marriage. But in the interim, confusion reigned in the lower courts and in states where same-sex marriage was contested. The Court's stays may have been intended to avoid other confusion and harm (marriages that may have been only temporarily valid), but without a reasoned opinion, lower courts were left to attempt to "follow the Supreme Court's lead without an explanation of where they are being led."[43] A precedent without reasoning is exceedingly difficult to follow. There has been increasing criticism of the Court's use of the shadow docket to rule on important issues without the benefits of briefing and oral argument.

On the other hand, there is no avoiding the problem that some appeals are time-sensitive. Voting rights cases have featured prominently in the Court's emergency orders in part because of the need to resolve disputes arising from last minute legislative modifications of voting procedures before voting begins. In 2014, for example, "the Court issued a divided 5-4 stay authorizing the state of Ohio to reduce the days available for early voting."[44] The plaintiffs, including voting rights advocacy groups, prevailed in the district court and won a preliminary injunction restoring the early voting rules, set to begin on September 30. The state defendants sought expedited review and a stay in the Sixth Circuit. The Sixth Circuit set up an expedited briefing and argument calendar but denied the stay. On September 24, just six days before early voting was set to begin, the Sixth Circuit upheld the district court's decision restoring the early voting procedures. The state both requested en banc review and filed an emergency appeal to the Supreme Court. The Court took briefing over the next two days and on September 29, 2014, entered a stay of the district court's order on terms that prompted the Sixth Circuit to vacate all the lower court orders in the case, ending the relevance of the case to the election that year. *See NAACP v. Husted* (6th Cir. 2014).

Emergency requests in death penalty cases to stay pending executions and requests to intervene in cases involving public health restrictions during the Covid pandemic and other emergencies also present exigent circumstances.

Requests for emergency relief by the United States Solicitor General appear to have increased significantly as well. "In contrast to the eight applications for emergency relief filed by the Justice Department between January 2001 and January 2017, [there were] 41 applications for relief over [the following] four years. . . . [T]he Justices granted 24 of the . . . applications in full and four in part. Even among the eight applications that were denied in full, only a few were denied with prejudice"[45] (noting that "less than half of the DOJ requests for injunctive relief involved nationwide injunctions").

In the following two cases, two Justices, sitting "in chambers" respectively as the "Circuit Justice" designated to handle emergency requests, describe and apply

---

43. *Id.* at 18.

44. *Id.* at 12.

45. Stephen Vladeck, Testimony at the Hearing Before the Subcommittee on Courts, Intellectual Property and the Internet of the House Committee on the Judiciary: The Supreme Court's Shadow Docket 5 (Feb. 18, 2021).

the high standard that is required for a stay. Notice the similarity to the traditional standards for granting equitable relief.

Conkright v. Frommert

556 U.S. 1401 (2009)

Opinion in Chambers
on application for stay
[April 30, 2009]

Justice GINSBURG, Circuit Justice.

Sally L. Conkright, Administrator of the Xerox Corporation Pension Plan, et al., have reapplied for a stay of the mandate of the United States Court of Appeals for the Second Circuit. In their initial application, filed October 16, 2008, the applicants sought a stay pending the filing and disposition of their petition for certiorari. The Second Circuit's decision in their case, they asserted, was erroneous, created a Circuit conflict, and would cause irreparable harm if given effect. Without a stay, the applicants explained, they would be required to make additional payments to dozens of pension plan beneficiaries—money that could prove difficult to recoup if this Court were to grant certiorari and rule in their favor.

Acting in my capacity as Circuit Justice, I denied the stay application on October 20, 2008. Denial of such in-chambers stay applications is the norm; relief is granted only in "extraordinary cases." *Rostker v. Goldberg* (1980) (Brennan, J., in chambers). Specifically, the applicant must demonstrate (1) "a 'reasonable probability' that four Justices will consider the issue sufficiently meritorious to grant certiorari or to note probable jurisdiction"; (2) "a fair prospect that a majority of the Court will conclude that the decision below was erroneous"; and (3) a likelihood that "irreparable harm [will] result from the denial of a stay." *Ibid.* In addition, "in a close case it may be appropriate to 'balance the equities'—to explore the relative harms to applicant and respondent, as well as the interests of the public at large." I earlier determined, taking account of the Second Circuit's evaluation, that this case did not meet the above-stated criteria.

The applicants seek reconsideration based on a change in circumstances. Specifically, after I denied their initial application, the applicants filed their petition for certiorari, and, on March 2, 2009, the Court called for the views of the Solicitor General (CVSG). The Solicitor General has yet to respond. According to the applicants, a stay is now in order because the Court's invitation to the Solicitor General—a step taken in only a small fraction of cases—establishes a "reasonable probability" that certiorari will be granted.

Our request for the Solicitor General's view, although relevant to the "reasonable probability" analysis, is hardly dispositive of an application to block implementation of a Court of Appeals' judgment. CVSG'd petitions, it is true, are granted at a far higher rate than other petitions. But it is also true that the Court denies certiorari in such cases more often than not. Consideration of the guiding criteria in the context of the particular case remains appropriate.

A "reasonable probability" of a grant is only one of the hurdles an applicant must clear. Relief is not warranted unless the other factors also counsel in favor of a stay. The Court's invitation to the Solicitor General does not lead me to depart from my previous assessment of those factors. With respect to irreparable harm, the applicants urge that, should they prevail in this Court, they may have trouble recouping any funds they disburse to beneficiaries. But they do not establish that recoupment will be impossible; nor do they suggest that the outlays at issue will place the plan itself in jeopardy. *Cf. Sampson v. Murray* (1974) ("Mere injuries, however substantial, in terms of money, time and energy necessarily expended in the absence of a stay, are not enough. The possibility that adequate compensatory or other corrective relief will be available at a later date, in the ordinary course of litigation, weighs heavily against a claim of irreparable harm.").

Accordingly, the request for a stay is denied.

* * *

Maryland v. King

567 U.S. 1301 (2012)

Opinion in Chambers
On application for Stay
July 30, 2012

Chief Justice ROBERTS, Circuit Justice.

Maryland's DNA Collection Act authorizes law enforcement officials to collect DNA samples from individuals charged with but not yet convicted of certain crimes, mainly violent crimes and first-degree burglary. In 2009, police arrested Alonzo Jay King, Jr., for first-degree assault. When personnel at the booking facility collected his DNA, they found it matched DNA evidence from a rape committed in 2003. Relying on the match, the State charged and successfully convicted King of, among other things, first degree rape. A divided Maryland Court of Appeals overturned King's conviction, holding the collection of his DNA violated the Fourth Amendment because his expectation of privacy outweighed the State's interests. Maryland now applies for a stay of that judgment pending this Court's disposition of its petition for a writ of certiorari.

To warrant that relief, Maryland must demonstrate (1) "a reasonable probability" that this Court will grant certiorari, (2) "a fair prospect" that the Court will then reverse the decision below, and (3) "a likelihood that irreparable harm [will] result from the denial of a stay." *Conkright v. Frommert* (Ginsburg, J., in chambers).

To begin, there is a reasonable probability this Court will grant certiorari. Maryland's decision conflicts with decisions of the U.S. Courts of Appeals for the Third and Ninth Circuits as well as the Virginia Supreme Court, which have upheld statutes similar to Maryland's DNA Collection Act. *See also Mario W. v. Kaipio* (Ariz. 2012) (holding that seizure of a juvenile's buccal cells does not violate the Fourth Amendment but that extracting a DNA profile before the juvenile is convicted does).

The split implicates an important feature of day-to-day law enforcement practice in approximately half the States and the Federal Government. *[S]ee* 42 U.S.C. §14135a(a)(1)(A) (authorizing the Attorney General to "collect DNA samples from individuals who are arrested, facing charges, or convicted"). Indeed, the decision below has direct effects beyond Maryland: Because the DNA samples Maryland collects may otherwise be eligible for the FBI's national DNA database, the decision renders the database less effective for other States and the Federal Government. These factors make it reasonably probable that the Court will grant certiorari to resolve the split on the question presented. In addition, given the considered analysis of courts on the other side of the split, there is a fair prospect that this Court will reverse the decision below.

Finally, the decision below subjects Maryland to ongoing irreparable harm. "[A]ny time a State is enjoined by a court from effectuating statutes enacted by representatives of its people, it suffers a form of irreparable injury." *New Motor Vehicle Bd. of Cal. v. Orrin W. Fox Co.* (1977) (Rehnquist, J., in chambers). Here there is, in addition, an ongoing and concrete harm to Maryland's law enforcement and public safety interests. According to Maryland, from 2009 — the year Maryland began collecting samples from arrestees — to 2011, "matches from arrestee swabs [from Maryland] have resulted in 58 criminal prosecutions." Collecting DNA from individuals arrested for violent felonies provides a valuable tool for investigating unsolved crimes and thereby helping to remove violent offenders from the general population. Crimes for which DNA evidence is implicated tend to be serious, and serious crimes cause serious injuries. That Maryland may not employ a duly enacted statute to help prevent these injuries constitutes irreparable harm.

King responds that Maryland's eight-week delay in applying for a stay undermines its allegation of irreparable harm. In addition, he points out that of the 10,666 samples Maryland seized last year, only 4,327 of them were eligible for entry into the federal database and only 19 led to an arrest (of which fewer than half led to a conviction). These are sound points. Nonetheless, in the absence of a stay, Maryland would be disabled from employing a valuable law enforcement tool for several months — a tool used widely throughout the country and one that has been upheld by two Courts of Appeals and another state high court.

Accordingly, the judgment and mandate below are hereby stayed pending the disposition of the petition for a writ of certiorari. Should the petition for a writ of certiorari be denied, this stay shall terminate automatically. In the event the petition for a writ of certiorari is granted, the stay shall terminate upon the issuance of the mandate of this Court.

* * *

What are the other factors that might be relevant to a decision to grant a stay? Is it relevant that the granting of a stay may effectively decide the merits?

A stay carries with it the power to hold in contempt a party who defies it. *See* 18 U.S.C. §401. One of the most notorious twentieth century examples of defiance of a stay issued by the Supreme Court is the lynching of a 19-year-old Black man, Ed Johnson, while a federal habeas petition challenging his conviction for sexual assault of a White woman was pending before the Supreme Court. Johnson had maintained his factual innocence, providing the names of a dozen alibi witnesses against the single White man who claimed he saw Johnson near the scene of the crime. His habeas petition, filed by two prominent Black lawyers in Chattanooga, Noah Parden and Styles Hutchins, who agreed to assist after he was convicted, asserted numerous constitutional errors in the state court trial. Their petition claimed that "Johnson's original lawyers were denied the right to file pretrial motions, that the trial was unfairly influenced by the threat of mob violence, that only White people were summoned to jury service, that Johnson's lawyers abandoned their client by advising him to waive his rights to appeal, and that there were numerous irregularities during the trial, including the fact that a juror tried to attack the defendant in the middle of the trial."

The day after the Court issued a stay of the petitioner's execution to consider the merits of the petition, County Sheriff Shipp having custody of Johnson "fail[ed] to make the slightest preparation to resist" the lynch mob that had formed to storm the jail. *U.S. v. Shipp* (1909). Among other things, only a 72-year-old guard was left there for the evening even though the sheriff and his deputies knew the mob was coming and the sheriff made no effort to protect Johnson upon arriving at the jail while Johnson was being removed by the mob—"this in utter disregard of [the Supreme Court's] mandate, and in defiance of this Court's orders. . . . Only one conclusion can be drawn from these facts, all of which are clearly established by the evidence—Shipp not only made the work of the mob easy, but in effect aided and abetted it."

A week after the lynching, the state judge responsible for Johnson's criminal trial and Sheriff Shipp were "re-elected in landslides." When the Justice Department launched an investigation a few months later, Shipp gave an interview for a newspaper insisting that "the Supreme Court was responsible for this lynching. I must be frank in saying that I did not attempt to hurt any of the mob and would not have made such an attempt if I could."[46]

In proceedings initiated by the Supreme Court for contempt, Shipp and his deputies argued that the federal courts were without jurisdiction over the habeas petition, and therefore without power to punish contempt to orders issued to preserve the status quo while the petition was before the Supreme Court. Justice Holmes, writing for a unanimous Court, rejected this argument:

> It has been held, it is true, that orders made by a court having no jurisdiction to make them may be disregarded without liability to process for contempt. *In re Sawyer* (1888). But even if the circuit court had no jurisdiction to entertain Johnson's petition, and if this Court had no jurisdiction of the appeal, this Court, and this Court alone, could decide that such was the law. It and it alone necessarily had jurisdiction to decide whether the case was properly before it. On that question, at least, it was its duty to permit argument, and to take the time required for such consideration as it might need. Until its judgment declining jurisdiction should be announced, it had authority, from the necessity of the case, to make orders to preserve the existing conditions and the subject of the petition, just as the state court was bound to refrain from further proceedings until the same time. Rev. Stat. §766. The fact that the petitioner was entitled to

---

46. Mark Curriden, *A Supreme Case of Contempt*, ABA J. (June 2, 2009).

argue his case shows what needs no proof, that the law contemplates the possibility of a decision either way, and therefore must provide for it. Of course, the provision of Rev. Stat. §766, that, until final judgment on the appeal, further proceedings in the state court against the prisoner shall be deemed void, applies to every case. There is no implied exception if the final judgment shall happen to be that the writ should not have issued or that the appeal should be dismissed.

It is proper that we should add that we are unable to agree with the premises upon which the conclusion just denied is based. We cannot regard the grounds upon which the petition for habeas corpus was presented as frivolous, or a mere pretense. The murder of the petitioner has made it impossible to decide that case, and what we have said makes it unnecessary to pass upon it as a preliminary to deciding the question before us. Therefore we shall say no more than that it does not appear to us clear that the subject matter of the petition was beyond the jurisdiction of the circuit court, and that, in our opinion, the facts that might have been found would have required the gravest and most anxious consideration before the petition could have been denied.

U.S. v. Shipp (1906).

After conducting a trial on the contempt charges, the Supreme Court held Shipp and some of his deputies in contempt. *U.S. v. Shipp* (1909). Shipp and two others were sentenced to 90 days in prison; 3 others to 60 days. All were "released early" without serving the full sentences and upon "[r]eturning to Chattanooga . . . greeted with a hero's welcome by more than 10,000 cheering supporters." A monument was erected in Shipp's honor by the city. "Fearing for their lives, Noah Parden and Stles Hutchins never returned to Chattanooga," moving out of state to start new lives.

Although this was "the first and only criminal trial in [the Court's] history," the sentences imposed obviously do not match the consequences of Shipp's contempt of court.

CHAPTER 10

THE RELATIONSHIP BETWEEN FEDERAL DISTRICT COURTS AND THE STATE COURTS

This Chapter focuses upon statutory and judge-made doctrines that shape the relationship between federal district courts and state courts. This relationship raises questions about not only federalism but also the separation of powers. These questions are at the heart of the federal courts course and must be understood in light of the historical contexts within which they arise.

The first part of this Chapter focuses upon Congress' statutory control of the relationship between federal and state courts. As you read the statutes and cases in this part, consider what policy concerns motivated Congress to shape that relationship in particular ways at particular times in U.S. history. In construing these statutes, federal courts have grappled with the history and purposes behind them. The cases show not only that the Supreme Court Justices have disagreed about the proper approach to construing these statutes, but also about the fundamental roles and relationships of the federal courts and the state courts.

The second part of this Chapter addresses judge-made doctrines of abstention. These abstention doctrines direct federal courts to abstain from adjudicating cases even when they have Article III jurisdiction and Congress has allowed the suit. Here too, you will see the Supreme Court Justices grappling with questions of history and disagreeing about the relationship between federal and state courts.

Together, the two parts of this Chapter raise several themes. First, they raise questions of judicial federalism, comity, and parity. These questions include whether federal courts should defer to state courts and assume that they will provide adequate remedies for federal rights. The idea of parity—that is, that state courts and federal courts are equally open to protecting federal rights—is central to the debates over the relationship between federal district courts and state courts. Second, they raise questions of the separation of powers, including whether it is appropriate for federal courts to abstain when Congress has enacted statutes permitting them to adjudicate a case. Third, and finally, this Chapter raises questions about the contexts in which federal courts' law is made. To the extent that the statutes and doctrines in this Chapter are subject-matter specific, they raise the question whether the relationship between federal district courts and state courts is inevitably shaped by underlying political judgments and disagreements about substantive doctrines.

Two important aspects of the relationship between federal courts and state courts are addressed elsewhere in this book. Chapter 8 explores habeas corpus, a consequential and complex area of law. Also important to the relationship between federal courts and state courts is the *Rooker-Feldman* doctrine, which is addressed in Chapter 9.

A.   STATUTORY CONTROL

Congress has used its broad power over federal jurisdiction to shape the relationship between federal courts and state courts. This Section explores four examples, focusing first upon three federal statutes that limit federal court intervention in state proceedings: the Anti-Injunction Act, the Tax Injunction Act, and the Johnson Act. It then turns to the Civil Rights Removal Act, which is an example of congressional authorization of federal judicial intervention into state proceedings. These four examples are by no means exhaustive of the federal statutes that shape federal court review of state courts. They represent two choices that Congress might make — that is, to require federal judicial deference to state courts on the one hand or to authorize federal intervention on the other. Studying these statutes in their historical contexts reveals the concerns that might lead Congress to make one choice or the other. It also shows how federal courts have approached the interpretation of statutes defining their relationships with state courts in light of those historical contexts.

1.   The Anti-Injunction Act

The Anti-Injunction Act is a federal law that bars federal courts from enjoining pending state court proceedings.[1] This bar is not absolute, however. The Act, codified in 22 U.S.C. §2283, contains three exceptions that permit federal courts to enjoin state proceedings:

> A court of the United States may not grant an injunction to stay proceedings in a State court except as expressly authorized by Act of Congress,

---

1. This Anti-Injunction Act should not be confused with another federal statute, also known as the Anti-Injunction Act, which denies federal jurisdiction to enjoin "the assessment or collection" of *federal* taxes. 26 U.S.C. §7421(a). In *National Federation of Independent Business v. Sebelius* (2012), the Supreme Court held that this Anti-Injunction Act did not bar a challenge to the individual mandate of the Patient Protection and Affordable Care Act. The individual mandate required individuals to buy health insurance or pay a penalty to the Internal Revenue Service. The Court reasoned that the mandate, which was labeled a "penalty," was not "a tax for purposes of the Anti-Injunction Act."

or where necessary in aid of its jurisdiction, or to protect or effectuate its judgments.

Federal courts have interpreted the Act in light of the Act's purpose and history. The purpose of the modern Anti-Injunction Act is to foster harmony between federal and state courts by limiting direct conflicts between federal injunctions and state proceedings. If federal courts freely enjoined pending state proceedings, state judges might come to resent their federal counterparts. Worse still, state judges might refuse to comply with federal orders.

For much of its history, however, the statutory prohibition on federal injunctions was all but toothless. That history begins in 1793, when Congress enacted a predecessor to the Anti-Injunction Act. It stated that no "writ of injunction [shall] be granted to stay proceedings in any court of a state" and apparently was aimed at limiting individual Supreme Court justices from granting such stays.[2] With the exception of one opinion in 1871, which mentioned this provision,[3] the Supreme Court had nothing to say about the Act in the eighteenth or nineteenth centuries. In 1874, the provision was codified and modified with Section 720 of the Revised Statutes: "The writ of injunction shall not be granted by any court of the United States to stay proceedings in any court of a State, except in cases where such injunction may be authorized by any law relating to proceedings in bankruptcy." Thus, the Act was expanded to apply to all federal courts, not just to individual Supreme Court Justices. The practical impact of this change was limited, however, over the next six decades by Supreme Court opinions that recognized various exceptions to the bar on federal injunctions against state court proceedings.

The turning point in the Act's history was *Toucey v. New York Life Insurance Co.* (1941). In an opinion by Justice Frankfurter, the Court held that a federal court could not issue an injunction to halt state court proceedings that were clearly aimed to create a conflict with already-decided federal court proceedings. The dispute concerned a claim for disability insurance payments. The plaintiff sued the insurance company in state court, which removed the case to federal court under diversity jurisdiction. The federal court held for the defendant. But the plaintiff was not done. He assigned his rights to someone else, who then sued in state court. The defendant obtained a federal injunction against that state proceeding. The Supreme Court held, however, the Anti-Injunction Act barred the federal injunction. Federal courts should, Justice Frankfurter reasoned, "scrupulous[ly]" construe the statutory "limits" that Congress has placed upon them. Prior decisions recognizing various exceptions to the Act's limits were dismissed as "ill-considered."

In 1948, Congress responded with an amendment that overruled *Toucey* and codified three exceptions to the Act's prohibition on federal injunctive relief. Today's Act prohibits federal courts from enjoining state courts themselves or enjoining parties from litigating in state court. The first exception to this prohibition is for injunctions that are expressly authorized by statute. The second is for injunctions in aid of federal jurisdiction. And the third is for injunctions to promote or effectuate a federal court's judgments.

---

2. William T. Mayton, *Ersatz Federalism Under the Anti-Injunction Statute*, 78 COLUM. L. REV. 330, 346 (1978).

3. Watson v. Jones, 80 U.S. (13 Wall.) 679 (1871).

The following opinions illustrate the Court's approach to construing the Act and its exceptions. The first opinion, *Atlantic Coast Line R.R. Co. v. Brotherhood of Locomotive Engineers* (1970), involved the second and third exceptions in the context of a labor dispute. *Atlantic Coast Line* is presented first because the Court's opinion held that the three exceptions to the Act's prohibition are exclusive and "should not be enlarged by loose statutory construction." The second opinion, *Mitchum v. Foster* (1972), addresses the first exception for statutorily authorized injunctions in the context of a civil rights dispute litigated under 42 U.S.C. §1983. It raises a question about the relationship between Congress' statutory control of federal court review of state courts and judge-made doctrines of abstention, the subject of Part B of this Chapter.

Like several canonical federal jurisdiction cases, including *In re Debs* (see ch. 3), *Atlantic Coast Line* involved a dispute between a railroad and a labor union. A state court enjoined union picketing of the railroad even though a federal court had already refused to do so. After the state judge refused to dissolve the injunction, concluding that intervening Supreme Court precedent was not controlling, the union sought a federal injunction against enforcement of the state injunction. From the union's perspective, *Atlantic Coast Line* raised a perennial issue in federal jurisdiction — namely, to what extent state courts and federal courts are equally open to protecting federal rights. The union argued that it had a federal right to picket and that the state courts were negating that right. It further argued that the federal injunction was proper under the second and third exceptions to the Anti-Injunction Act. As you read the case, pay close attention to the Supreme Court's reasons for rejecting those arguments as well as the Court's account of the purpose and history of the Anti-Injunction Act.

Atlantic Coast Line R.R. Co. v. Brotherhood of Locomotive Engineers

398 U.S. 281 (1970)

Mr. Justice BLACK delivered the opinion of the Court.

Congress in 1793, shortly after the American Colonies became one united Nation, provided that in federal courts "a writ of injunction [shall not] be granted to stay proceedings in any court of a state." Although certain exceptions to this general prohibition have been added, that statute, directing that the state courts shall remain free from interference by federal courts, has remained in effect until this time. Today that amended statute provides:

"A court of the United States may not grant an injunction to stay proceedings in a State court except as expressly authorized by Act of Congress, or where necessary in aid of its jurisdiction, or to protect or effectuate its judgments." 28 U.S.C. §2283.

Despite the existence of this longstanding prohibition, in this case a federal court did enjoin the petitioner, Atlantic Coast Line Railroad Co. (ACL), from invoking an injunction issued by a Florida state court which prohibited certain picketing by respondent Brotherhood of Locomotive Engineers (BLE). The case arose in the following way.

In 1967 BLE began picketing the Moncrief Yard, a switching yard located near Jacksonville, Florida, and wholly owned and operated by ACL. As soon as this picketing began ACL went into federal court seeking an injunction. When the federal judge denied the request, ACL immediately went into state court and there succeeded in obtaining an injunction. No further legal action was taken in this dispute until two years later in 1969, after this Court's decision in *Brotherhood of Railroad Trainmen v. Jacksonville Terminal Co.* In that case the Court considered the validity of a state injunction against picketing by the BLE and other unions at the Jacksonville Terminal, located immediately next to Moncrief Yard. The Court reviewed the factual situation surrounding the Jacksonville Terminal picketing and concluded that the unions had a federally protected right to picket under the Railway Labor Act, and that that right could not be interfered with by state court injunctions. Immediately after a petition for rehearing was denied in that case, the respondent BLE filed a motion in state court to dissolve the Moncrief Yard injunction, arguing that under the Jacksonville Terminal decision the injunction was improper. The state judge refused to dissolve the injunction, holding that this Court's Jacksonville Terminal decision was not controlling. The union did not elect to appeal that decision directly, but instead went back into the federal court and requested an injunction against the enforcement of the state court injunction. The District Judge granted the injunction and upon application a stay of that injunction, pending the filing and disposition of a petition for certiorari, was granted. The Court of Appeals summarily affirmed on the parties' stipulation, and we granted a petition for certiorari to consider the validity of the federal court's injunction against the state court.

In this Court the union contends that the federal injunction was proper either "to protect or effectuate" the District Court's denial of an injunction in 1967, or as "necessary in aid of" the District Court's jurisdiction. Although the questions are by no means simple and clear, and the decision is difficult, we conclude that the injunction against the state court was not justified under either of these two exceptions to the anti-injunction statute. We therefore hold that the federal injunction in this case was improper.

I

Before analyzing the specific legal arguments advanced in this case, we think it would be helpful to discuss the background and policy that led Congress to pass the anti-injunction statute in 1793. While all the reasons that led Congress to adopt this restriction on federal courts are not wholly clear, it is certainly likely that one reason stemmed from the essentially federal nature of our national government. When this Nation was established by the Constitution, each State surrendered only a part of its sovereign power to the national government. But those powers that were not surrendered were retained by the States and unless a State was restrained by "the supreme Law of the Land" as expressed in the Constitution, laws, or treaties of the United States, it was free to exercise those retained powers as it saw fit. One of the reserved powers was the maintenance of state judicial systems for the decision of legal controversies. Many of the Framers of the Constitution felt that separate federal courts were unnecessary and that the state courts could be entrusted to protect both state and federal rights. Others felt that a complete system of federal courts to take care of federal legal problems should be provided for in the Constitution itself. This dispute resulted in compromise. One "supreme Court" was created by the Constitution, and Congress was given the power to create other federal courts. In the first Congress this power was exercised and a system of federal trial and appellate courts with limited jurisdiction was created by the Judiciary Act of 1789.

While the lower federal courts were given certain powers in the 1789 Act, they were not given any power to review directly cases from state courts, and they have not been given such powers since that time. Only the Supreme Court was authorized to review on direct appeal the decisions of state courts. Thus from the beginning we have had in this country two essentially separate legal systems. Each system proceeds independently of the other with ultimate review in this Court of the federal questions raised in either system. Understandably this dual court system was bound to lead to conflicts and frictions. Litigants who foresaw the possibility of more favorable treatment in one or the other system would predictably hasten to invoke the powers of whichever court it was believed would present the best chance of success. Obviously this dual system could not function if state and federal courts were free to fight each other for control of a particular case. Thus, in order to make the dual system work and "to prevent needless friction between state and federal courts," *Oklahoma Packing Co. v. Gas Co.* (1940), it was necessary to work out lines of demarcation between the two systems. Some of these limits were spelled out in the 1789 Act. Others have been added by later statutes as well as judicial decisions. The 1793 Anti-Injunction Act was at least in part a response to these pressures.

On its face the present Act is an absolute prohibition against enjoining state court proceedings, unless the injunction falls within one of three specifically defined exceptions. The respondents here have intimated that the Act only establishes a "principle of comity," not a binding rule on the power of the federal courts. The argument implies that in certain circumstances a federal court may enjoin state court proceedings even if that action cannot be justified by any of the three exceptions.

We cannot accept any such contention. In 1955, when this Court interpreted this statute, it stated: "This is not a statute conveying a broad general policy for appropriate ad hoc application. Legislative policy is here expressed in a clear-cut prohibition qualified only by specifically defined exceptions." *Amalgamated Clothing Workers v. Richman Bros.* (1955). Since that time Congress has not seen fit to amend the statute and we therefore adhere to that position and hold that any injunction against state court proceedings otherwise proper under general equitable principles must be based on one of the specific statutory exceptions to §2283 if it is to be upheld. Moreover since the statutory prohibition against such injunctions in part rests on the fundamental constitutional independence of the States and their courts, the exceptions should not be enlarged by loose statutory construction. Proceedings in state courts should normally be allowed to continue unimpaired by intervention of the lower federal courts, with relief from error, if any, through the state appellate courts and ultimately this Court.

II

Neither party argues that there is any express congressional authorization for injunctions in this situation and we agree with that conclusion. The respondent union does contend that the injunction was proper either as a means to protect or effectuate the District Court's 1967 order, or in aid of that court's jurisdiction. We do not think that either alleged basis can be supported.

A

The argument based on protecting the 1967 order is not clearly expressed, but in essence it appears to run as follows: In 1967 the railroad sought a temporary restraining order which the union opposed. In the course of deciding that request, the United States District Court determined that the union had a federally protected right to picket Moncrief Yard and that this right could not be interfered with by state courts. When the Florida Circuit Court enjoined the picketing, the United States District Court could, in order to protect and effectuate its prior determination, enjoin enforcement of the state court injunction. Although the record on this point is not unambiguously clear, we conclude that no such interpretation of the 1967 order can be supported.

In this Court the union asserts that the [District Court's] determination that it was "free to engage in self-help" was a determination that it had a federally protected right to picket and that state law could not be invoked to negate that right. The railroad, on the other hand, argues that the order merely determined that the federal court could not enjoin the picketing, in large part because of the general prohibition in the Norris-LaGuardia Act, against issuance by federal courts of injunctions in labor disputes. Based solely on the state of the record when the order was entered, we are inclined to believe that the District Court did not determine whether federal law precluded an injunction based on state law. Not only was that point never argued to the court, but there is no language in the order that necessarily implies any decision on that question. In short we feel that the District Court in 1967 determined that federal law could not be invoked to enjoin the picketing at Moncrief Yard, and that the union did have a right "to engage in self-help" as far as the federal courts were concerned. But that decision is entirely different from a decision that the Railway Labor Act precludes state regulation of the picketing as well, and this latter decision is an essential prerequisite for upholding the 1969 injunction as necessary "to protect or effectuate" the 1967 order. Finally we think it highly unlikely that the brief statements in the order conceal a determination of a disputed legal point that later was to divide this Court in a 4-to-3 vote in *Jacksonville Terminal*, in opinions totaling 28 pages. While judicial writing may sometimes be thought cryptic and tightly packed, the union's contention here stretches the content of the words well beyond the limits of reasonableness.

[The] record, we think, conclusively shows that neither the parties themselves nor the District Court construed the 1967 order as the union now contends it should be construed. Rather we are convinced that the union in effect tried to get the Federal District Court to decide that the state court judge was wrong in distinguishing the *Jacksonville Terminal* decision. Such an attempt to seek appellate review of a state decision in the Federal District Court cannot be justified as necessary "to protect or effectuate" the 1967 order.

B

This brings us to the second prong of the union's argument in which it is suggested that even if the 1967 order did not determine the union's right to picket free from state interference, once the decision in *Jacksonville Terminal* was announced, the District Court was then free to enjoin the state court on the theory that such action was "necessary in aid of [the District Court's] jurisdiction." Again the argument is somewhat unclear, but it appears to go in this way: The District Court had acquired jurisdiction over the labor controversy in 1967 when the railroad filed its complaint, and it determined at that time that it did have jurisdiction. The dispute involved the legality of picketing by the union and the *Jacksonville Terminal* decision clearly indicated that such activity was not only legal, but was protected from state court interference. The state court had interfered with that right, and thus a federal injunction was "necessary in aid of its jurisdiction." For several reasons we cannot accept the contention.

First, a federal court does not have inherent power to ignore the limitations of §2283 and to enjoin state court proceedings merely because those proceedings interfere with a protected federal right or invade an area preempted by federal law, even when the interference is unmistakably clear. This rule applies regardless of whether the federal court itself has jurisdiction over the controversy, or whether it is ousted from jurisdiction for the same reason that the state court is. This conclusion is required because Congress itself set forth the only exceptions to the statute, and those exceptions do not include this situation. Second, if the District Court does have jurisdiction, it is not enough that the requested injunction is related to that jurisdiction, but it must be "necessary in aid of" that jurisdiction. While this language is admittedly broad, we conclude that it implies something similar to the concept of injunctions to "protect or effectuate" judgments. Both exceptions to the general prohibition of §2283 imply that some federal injunctive relief may be necessary to prevent a state court from so interfering with a federal court's consideration or disposition of a case as to seriously impair the federal court's flexibility and authority to decide that case. Third, no such situation is presented here. Although the federal court did have jurisdiction of the railroad's complaint based on federal law, the state court also had jurisdiction over the complaint based on state law and the union's asserted federal defense as well. In short, the state and federal courts had concurrent jurisdiction in this case, and neither court was free to prevent either party from simultaneously pursuing claims in both courts. Therefore the state court's assumption of jurisdiction over the state law claims and the federal preclusion issue did not hinder the federal court's jurisdiction so as to make an injunction necessary to aid that jurisdiction. Nor was an injunction necessary because the state court may have taken action which the federal court was certain was improper under the *Jacksonville Terminal* decision. Again, lower federal courts possess no power whatever to sit in direct review of state court decisions. If the union was adversely affected by the state court's decision, it was free to seek vindication of its federal right in the Florida appellate courts and ultimately, if necessary, in this Court. Similarly if, because of the Florida Circuit Court's action, the union faced the threat of immediate irreparable injury sufficient to justify an injunction under usual equitable principles, it was undoubtedly free to seek such relief from the Florida appellate courts, and might possibly in certain emergency circumstances seek such relief from this Court as well. Unlike the Federal District Court, this Court does have potential appellate jurisdiction over federal questions raised in state court proceedings, and that broader jurisdiction allows this Court correspondingly broader authority to issue injunctions "necessary in aid of its jurisdiction."

III

This case is by no means an easy one. The arguments in support of the union's contentions are not insubstantial. But whatever doubts we may have are strongly affected by the general prohibition of §2283. Any doubts as to the propriety of a federal injunction against state court proceedings should be resolved in favor of permitting the state courts to proceed in an orderly fashion to finally determine the controversy. The explicit wording of §2283 itself implies as much, and the fundamental principle of a dual system of courts leads inevitably to that conclusion.

Mr. Justice MARSHALL took no part in the consideration or decision of this case.

The concurring opinion of Justice HARLAN is omitted.

Mr. Justice BRENNAN, with whom Mr. Justice WHITE joins, dissenting.

My disagreement with the Court in this case is a relatively narrow one. I do not disagree with much that is said concerning the history and policies underlying 28 U.S.C. §2283. Nor do I dispute the Court's holding on the basis of *Amalgamated Clothing Workers v. Richman Bros.* (1955), that federal courts do not have authority to enjoin state proceedings merely because it is asserted that the state court is improperly asserting jurisdiction in an area pre-empted by federal law or federal procedures. Nevertheless, in my view the District Court had discretion to enjoin the state proceedings in the present case because it acted pursuant to an explicit exception to the prohibition of §2283, that is, "to protect or effectuate [the District Court's] judgments."

In my view, what the District Court decided in 1967 was that BLE had a federally protected right to picket at the Moncrief Yard and, by necessary implication, that this right could not be subverted by resort to state proceedings. I find it difficult indeed to ascribe to the District Judge the views that the Court now says he held, namely, that ACL, merely by marching across the street to the state court, could render wholly nugatory the District Judge's declaration that BLE had a federally protected right to strike at the Moncrief Yard.

Unquestionably §2283 manifests a general design on the part of Congress that federal courts not precipitately interfere with the orderly determination of controversies in state proceedings. However, this policy of nonintervention is by no means absolute, as the explicit exceptions in §2283 make entirely clear. Thus, §2283 itself evinces a congressional intent that resort to state proceedings not be permitted to undermine a prior judgment of a federal court. But that is exactly what has occurred in the present case. Indeed, the federal determination that BLE may picket at the Moncrief Yard has been rendered wholly ineffective by the state injunction. The crippling restrictions that the Court today places upon the power of the District Court to effectuate and protect its orders are totally inconsistent with both the plain language of §2283 and the policies underlying that statutory provision.

* * *

The first exception to the Anti-Injunction Act is for injunctions "expressly authorized by Act of Congress." Some federal statutes specifically authorize federal courts to enjoin state proceedings. The Interpleader Act, for example, authorizes a federal court in an interpleader action to enjoin the "instituting or prosecuting [of] any proceeding in any State or United States court." Interpleader actions arise when there are multiple claims to the same assets. The policy is to ensure that all claims to a limited fund will be decided by one court in a single adjudication. The federal bankruptcy statute also authorizes bankruptcy courts to stay litigation by or against the person or entity filing for bankruptcy.

Where a federal statute does not specifically authorize an injunction against a state "proceeding," the federal courts have had to determine how express Congress must be to "expressly authorize[]" federal injunctions within the meaning of the Anti-Injunction Act's first exception. The next case, *Mitchum v. Foster* (1972), addressed that question. The Court held that a statute may authorize a federal injunction, and thus fall within the Act's first exception, if the purposes of the statute would be frustrated by denial of federal jurisdiction to enjoin state proceedings. Applying this test, the Court held that 42 U.S.C. §1983 was an express authorization of injunctions of state proceedings.

Mitchum also raised a question that is at the heart of this Chapter—namely, what is the relationship between Congress' statutory control of federal court review and judge-made doctrines of abstention? You should connect the *Mitchum* decision with Court's abstention decision in *Younger v. Harris* (1971), decided the year before *Mitchum*. *See infra* Chapter 10(B)(5)(a). In *Younger*, a plaintiff filed a federal complaint challenging state criminal proceedings based upon §1983 and the First Amendment. The Court held that a federal injunction would be improper based upon principles of comity and respect for state courts. *Mitchum* should stand out against the backdrop of *Younger*. Read together, the cases hold that (1) §1983 is an exception to the Anti-Injunction Act, but (2) federal courts should nevertheless abstain from enjoining state criminal proceedings under §1983. This result seems odd from a separation of powers perspective. In the Anti-Injunction Act, Congress specifically defined when injunctions of state proceedings are allowed and when they are not. It is not clear that the federal courts have the authority to abstain when Congress has allowed federal injunctive relief.

Mitchum v. Foster

407 U.S. 225 (1972)

Mr. Justice STEWART delivered the opinion of the Court.

The federal anti-injunction statute provides that a federal court "may not grant an injunction to stay proceedings in a State court except as expressly authorized by Act of Congress, or where necessary in aid of its jurisdiction, or to protect or effectuate its judgments." An Act of Congress, 42 U.S.C. §1983, expressly authorizes a "suit in equity" to redress "the deprivation," under color of state law, "of any rights, privileges, or immunities secured by the Constitution. . . ." The question before us is whether this "Act of Congress" comes within the "expressly authorized" exception of the anti-injunction statute so as to permit a federal court in a §1983 suit to grant an injunction to stay a proceeding pending in a state court. This question, which has divided the federal courts, has lurked in the background of many of our recent cases, but we have not until today explicitly decided it.

I

The prosecuting attorney of Bay County, Florida, brought a proceeding in a Florida court to close down the appellant's bookstore as a public nuisance under the claimed authority of Florida law. The state court entered a preliminary order prohibiting continued operation of the bookstore. After further inconclusive proceedings in the state courts, the appellant filed a complaint in the United States District Court for the Northern District of Florida, alleging that the actions of the state judicial and law enforcement officials were depriving him of rights protected by the First and Fourteenth Amendments. Relying upon 42 U.S.C. §1983, he asked for injunctive and declaratory relief against the state court proceedings, on the ground that Florida laws were being unconstitutionally applied by the state court so as to cause him great and irreparable harm. A single federal district judge issued temporary restraining orders, and a three-judge court was convened pursuant to 28 U.S.C. §§2281 and 2284. After a hearing, the three-judge court dissolved the temporary restraining orders and refused to enjoin the state court proceeding. An appeal was brought directly here under 28 U.S.C. §1253, and we noted probable jurisdiction.

II

In denying injunctive relief, the District Court relied on this Court's decision in *Atlantic Coast Line R. Co. v. Brotherhood of Locomotive Engineers* (1970). The *Atlantic Coast Line* case did not deal with the "expressly authorized" exception of the anti-injunction statute, but the Court's opinion in that case does bring into sharp focus the critical importance of the question now before us. For in that case we expressly rejected the view that the anti-injunction statute merely states a flexible doctrine of comity, and made clear that the statute imposes an absolute ban upon the issuance of a federal injunction against a pending state court proceeding, in the absence of one of the recognized exceptions.

It follows, in the present context, that if 42 U.S.C. §1983 is not within the "expressly authorized" exception of the anti-injunction statute, then a federal equity court is wholly without power to grant any relief in a §1983 suit seeking to stay a state court proceeding. In short, if a §1983 action is not an "expressly authorized" statutory exception, the anti-injunction law absolutely prohibits in such an action all federal equitable intervention in a pending state court proceeding, whether civil or criminal, and regardless of how extraordinary the particular circumstances may be.

Last Term, in *Younger v. Harris* (1971), and its companion cases, the Court dealt at length with the subject of federal judicial intervention in pending state criminal prosecutions. In *Younger*, a three-judge federal district court in a §1983 action had enjoined a criminal prosecution pending in a California court. In asking us to reverse that judgment, the appellant argued that the injunction was in violation of the federal anti-injunction statute. But the Court carefully eschewed any reliance on the statute in reversing the judgment, basing its decision instead upon what the Court called "Our Federalism"—upon "the national policy forbidding federal courts to stay or enjoin pending state court proceedings except under special circumstances."

In *Younger*, this Court emphatically reaffirmed "the fundamental policy against federal interference with state criminal prosecutions." It made clear that even "the possible unconstitutionality of a statute 'on its face' does not in itself justify an injunction against good-faith attempts to enforce it." At the same time, however, the Court clearly left room for federal injunctive intervention in a pending state court prosecution in certain exceptional circumstances—where irreparable injury is "both great and immediate," where the state law is "'flagrantly and patently violative of express constitutional prohibitions,'" or where there is a showing of "bad faith, harassment, or . . . other unusual circumstances that would call for equitable relief."

While the Court in *Younger* and its companion cases expressly disavowed deciding the question now before us—whether §1983 comes within the "expressly authorized" exception of the anti-injunction statute—it is evident that our decisions in those cases cannot be disregarded in deciding this question. In the first place, if §1983 is not within the statutory exception, then the anti-injunction statute would have absolutely barred the injunction issued in *Younger*, as the appellant in that case argued, and there would have been no occasion whatever for the Court to decide that case upon the "policy" ground of "Our Federalism." Secondly, if §1983 is not within the "expressly authorized" exception of the anti-injunction statute, then we must overrule *Younger* and its companion cases insofar as they recognized the permissibility of injunctive relief against pending criminal prosecutions in certain limited and exceptional circumstances. For, under the doctrine of *Atlantic Coast Line*, the anti-injunction statute would, in a §1983 case, then be an "absolute prohibition" against federal equity intervention in a pending state criminal or civil proceeding—under any circumstances whatever.

The *Atlantic Coast Line* and *Younger* cases thus serve to delineate both the importance and the finality of the question now before us. And it is in the shadow of those cases that the question must be decided.

III

The anti-injunction statute goes back almost to the beginnings of our history as a Nation. In 1793, Congress enacted a law providing that no "writ of injunction be granted [by any federal court] to stay proceedings in any court of a state. . . ." The precise origins of the legislation are shrouded in obscurity, but the consistent understanding has been that its basic purpose is to prevent "needless friction between state and federal courts." *Oklahoma Packing Co. v. Gas Co.* (1939). The law remained unchanged until 1874, when it was amended to permit a federal court to stay state court proceedings that interfered with the administration of a federal bankruptcy proceeding. The present wording of the legislation was adopted with the enactment of Title 28 of the United States Code in 1948.

Despite the seemingly uncompromising language of the anti-injunction statute prior to 1948, the Court soon recognized that exceptions must be made to its blanket prohibition if the import and purpose of other Acts of Congress were to be given their intended scope. So it was that, in addition to the bankruptcy law exception that Congress explicitly recognized in 1874, the Court through the years found that federal courts were empowered to enjoin state court proceedings, despite the anti-injunction statute, in carrying out the will of Congress under at least six other federal laws. These covered a broad spectrum of congressional action: (1) legislation providing for removal of litigation from state to federal courts, (2) legislation limiting the liability of shipowners, (3) legislation providing for federal interpleader actions, (4) legislation conferring federal jurisdiction over farm mortgages, (5) legislation governing federal habeas corpus proceedings, and (6) legislation providing for control of prices.

In addition to the exceptions to the anti-injunction statute found to be embodied in these various Acts of Congress, the Court recognized other "implied" exceptions to the blanket prohibition of the anti-injunction statute. One was an "in rem" exception, allowing a federal court to enjoin a state court proceeding in order to protect its jurisdiction of a res over which it had first acquired jurisdiction. Another was a "relitigation" exception, permitting a federal court to enjoin relitigation in a state court of issues already decided in federal litigation. Still a third exception, more recently developed, permits a federal injunction of state court proceedings when the plaintiff in the federal court is the United States itself, or a federal agency asserting "superior federal interests."

In *Toucey v. New York Life Ins. Co.*, the Court in 1941 issued an opinion casting considerable doubt upon the approach to the anti-injunction statute reflected in its previous decisions. The Court's opinion expressly disavowed the "relitigation" exception to the statute, and emphasized generally the importance of recognizing the statute's basic directive "of 'hands off' by the federal courts in the use of the injunction to stay litigation in a state court." The congressional response to *Toucey* was the enactment in 1948 of the anti-injunction statute in its present form in 28 U.S.C. §2283, which, as the Reviser's Note makes evident, served not only to overrule the specific holding of *Toucey*, but to restore "the basic law as generally understood and interpreted prior to the *Toucey* decision."

We proceed, then, upon the understanding that in determining whether §1983 comes within the "expressly authorized" exception of the anti-injunction statute, the criteria to be applied are those reflected in the Court's decisions prior to *Toucey*. A review of those decisions makes reasonably clear what the relevant criteria are. In the first place, it is evident that, in order to qualify under the "expressly authorized" exception of the anti-injunction statute, a federal law need not contain an express reference to that statute. As the Court has said, "no prescribed formula is required; an authorization need not expressly refer to §2283." *Amalgamated Clothing Workers v. Richman Bros. Co.* (1955). Indeed, none of the previously recognized statutory exceptions contains any such reference. Secondly, a federal law need not expressly authorize an injunction of a state court proceeding in order to qualify as an exception. Three of the six previously recognized statutory exceptions contain no such authorization. Thirdly, it is clear that, in order to qualify as an "expressly authorized" exception to the anti-injunction statute, an Act of Congress must have created a specific and uniquely federal right or remedy, enforceable in a federal court of equity, that could be frustrated if the federal court were not empowered to enjoin a state court proceeding. This is not to say that in order to come within the exception an Act of Congress must, on its face and in every one of its provisions, be totally incompatible with the prohibition of the anti-injunction statute. The test, rather, is whether an Act of Congress, clearly creating a federal right or remedy enforceable in a federal court of equity, could be given its intended scope only by the stay of a state court proceeding.

With these criteria in view, we turn to consideration of 42 U.S.C. §1983.

IV

Section 1983 was originally §1 of the Civil Rights Act of 1871. It was "modeled" on §2 of the Civil Rights Act of 1866, and was enacted for the express purpose of "enforc[ing] the Provisions of the Fourteenth Amendment." The predecessor of §1983 was thus an important part of the basic alteration in our federal system wrought in the Reconstruction era through federal legislation and constitutional amendment. As a result of the new structure of law that emerged in the post-Civil War era—and especially of the Fourteenth Amendment, which was its centerpiece—the role of the Federal Government as a guarantor of basic federal rights against state power was clearly established. Section 1983 opened the federal courts to private citizens, offering a uniquely federal remedy against incursions under the claimed authority of state law upon rights secured by the Constitution and laws of the Nation.

It is clear from the legislative debates surrounding passage of §1983's predecessor that the Act was intended to enforce the provisions of the Fourteenth Amendment "against State action, . . . whether that action be executive, legislative, or judicial." *Ex parte Virginia* (1880). Proponents of the legislation noted that state courts were being used to harass and injure individuals, either because the state courts were powerless to stop deprivations or were in league with those who were bent upon abrogation of federally protected rights.

Those who opposed the Act of 1871 clearly recognized that the proponents were extending federal power in an attempt to remedy the state courts' failure to secure federal rights. The debate was not about whether the predecessor of §1983 extended to actions of state courts, but whether this innovation was necessary or desirable.

This legislative history makes evident that Congress clearly conceived that it was altering the relationship between the States and the Nation with respect to the protection of federally created rights; it was concerned that state instrumentalities could not protect those rights; it realized that state officers might, in fact, be antipathetic to the vindication of those rights; and it believed that these failings extended to the state courts.

V

Section 1983 was thus a product of a vast transformation from the concepts of federalism that had prevailed in the late 18th century when the anti-injunction statute was enacted. The very purpose of §1983 was to interpose the federal courts between the States and the people, as guardians of the people's federal rights—to protect the people from unconstitutional action under color of state law, "whether that action be executive, legislative, or judicial." *Ex parte Virginia* (1880). In carrying out that purpose, Congress plainly authorized the federal courts to issue injunctions in §1983 actions, by expressly authorizing a "suit in equity" as one of the means of redress. And this Court long ago recognized that federal injunctive relief against a state court proceeding can in some circumstances be essential to prevent great, immediate, and irreparable loss of a person's constitutional rights. *Ex parte Young* (1908). For these reasons we conclude that, under the criteria established in our previous decisions construing the anti-injunction statute, §1983 is an Act of Congress that falls within the "expressly authorized" exception of that law.

In so concluding, we do not question or qualify in any way the principles of equity, comity, and federalism that must restrain a federal court when asked to enjoin a state court proceeding. These principles, in the context of state criminal prosecutions, were canvassed at length last Term in *Younger v. Harris*, and its companion cases. They are principles that have been emphasized by this Court many times in the past. Today we decide only that the District Court in this case was in error in holding that, because of the anti-injunction statute, it was absolutely without power in this §1983 action to enjoin a proceeding pending in a state court under any circumstances whatsoever.

Mr. Justice POWELL and Mr. Justice REHNQUIST took no part in the consideration or decision of this case.

Mr. Chief Justice BURGER, with whom Mr. Justice WHITE and Mr. Justice BLACKMUN join, concurring.

I concur in the opinion of the Court and add a few words to emphasize what the Court is and is not deciding today as I read the opinion. [O]n remand in this case, it seems to me the District Court, before reaching a decision on the merits of appellant's claim, should properly consider whether general notions of equity or principles of federalism, similar to those invoked in *Younger*, prevent the issuance of an injunction against the state "nuisance abatement" proceedings in the circumstances of this case.

* * *

2. *The Tax Injunction Act*

The Tax Injunction Act limits federal injunctions against the collection of state taxes. The Court has held that the Act imposes a subject-matter limitation on federal jurisdiction. Codified at 28 U.S.C. §1341, it states:

> [The] District Courts shall not enjoin, suspend or restrain the assessment, levy or collection of any tax under State law where a plain, speedy and efficient remedy may be had in the courts of such State.

Taxation is, of course, crucial to funding the operation of any government. Recognizing as much, the Supreme Court has reasoned that the Tax Injunction Act stays federal intervention in light of "the imperative need of a State to administer its own fiscal operations." *Tully v. Griffin* (1976).

Federalism concerns are reflected in the federal courts' approach to interpreting the Act. Federal courts have construed "any tax" to apply broadly to all types of state and local taxes. The test is whether an obligation to pay money was for revenue raising purposes, in which case it is a tax, or instead for regulatory or punitive purposes, in which case it is not a tax. This distinction arguably makes little sense because taxes may be "regulatory" in the sense that they aim to (and in fact do) change behavior while, conversely, a regulation may involve a "tax" in the sense that it imposes penalties that raise revenue. In applying the test, the federal courts have been guided by the understanding that Congress meant to respect state control of fiscal administration and an intuitive sense of the primary purposes of particular state and local obligations

To get a sense of the Act's breadth, consider *Wright v. McClain* (6th Cir. 1987), in which a federal court of appeals held that the Act barred a parolee from seeking a federal injunction against the obligation to make monthly payments to a supervision fund and a victim compensation fund. The parolee argued that these obligations were fees, not taxes. The court of appeals explained that "[t]he Tax Injunction Act is an expression of congressional purpose to promote comity and to afford states the broadest independence, consistent with the federal constitution, in the administration of their affairs, particularly revenue raising." The court reasoned that the parolee's obligations were taxes because they defrayed "the cost to the general public of monitoring and supervising the behavior of convicted offenders and . . . compensate[d], in some measure, victims of criminal misconduct." Because those "purposes relate[d] directly to the general welfare of the citizens of Tennessee," they were "general revenue raising levies." The Tax Injunction Act therefore barred the suit.

In the next case, *Hibbs v. Winn* (2004), the Court held that the Act does not bar a federal injunction against a state tax credit. The question arose in the context of an Establishment Clause challenge to tax credits for contributions to organizations that disburse money to parochial schools. As you read the opinions in *Hibbs*, consider the relationship between the jurisdictional question and the merits. The Justices seemed to disagree about how important it is for federal courts to be open to enforcing the Establishment Clause, with the dissenters accusing the members of the majority with unjustified skepticism of state courts.

Hibbs v. Winn

542 U.S. 88 (2004)

Justice GINSBURG delivered the opinion of the Court, in which Justices STEVENS, O'CONNOR, SOUTER, and BREYER joined.

Arizona law authorizes income-tax credits for payments to organizations that award educational scholarships and tuition grants to children attending private schools. Plaintiffs below, respondents here, brought an action in federal court challenging [the Arizona law], and seeking to enjoin its operation, on Establishment Clause grounds. The question presented is whether the Tax Injunction Act (TIA or Act), which prohibits a lower federal court from restraining "the assessment, levy or collection of any tax under State law," bars the suit. Plaintiffs-respondents do not contest their own tax liability. Nor do they seek to impede Arizona's receipt of tax revenues. Their suit, we hold, is not the kind [that the TIA] proscribes.

In decisions spanning a near half century, courts in the federal system, including this Court, have entertained challenges to tax credits authorized by state law, without conceiving of [the TIA] as a jurisdictional barrier. On this first occasion squarely to confront the issue, we confirm the authority federal courts exercised in those cases.

It is hardly ancient history that States, once bent on maintaining racial segregation in public schools, and allocating resources disproportionately to benefit white students to the detriment of black students, fastened on tuition grants and tax credits as a promising means to circumvent *Brown v. Board of Education* (1954). The federal courts, this Court among them, adjudicated the ensuing challenges, instituted under 42 U.S.C. §1983, and upheld the Constitution's equal protection requirement.

In the instant case, petitioner Hibbs, Director of Arizona's Department of Revenue, argues, in effect, that we and other federal courts were wrong in those civil-rights cases. The TIA, petitioner maintains, trumps §1983; the Act, according to petitioner, bars all lower federal-court interference with state tax systems, even when the challengers are not endeavoring to avoid a tax imposed on them, and no matter whether the State's revenues would be raised or lowered should the plaintiffs prevail. The alleged jurisdictional bar, which petitioner asserts has existed since the TIA's enactment in 1937, was not even imagined by the jurists in the pathmarking civil-rights cases just cited, or by the defendants in those cases, litigants with every interest in defeating federal-court adjudicatory authority. Our prior decisions command no respect, petitioner urges, because they constitute mere "sub silentio holdings." We reject that assessment.

We examine in this opinion both the scope of the term "assessment" as used in the TIA, and the question whether the Act was intended to insulate state tax laws from constitutional challenge in lower federal courts even when the suit would have no negative impact on tax collection. Concluding that this suit implicates neither [the TIA's] conception of assessment nor any of the statute's underlying purposes, we affirm the judgment of the Court of Appeals.

I

Plaintiffs-respondents, Arizona taxpayers, filed suit in the United States District Court for the District of Arizona, challenging Ariz. Rev. Stat. Ann. §43-1089 as incompatible with the Establishment Clause. Section 43-1089 provides a credit to taxpayers who contribute money to "school tuition organizations" (STOs). An STO is a nonprofit organization that directs moneys, in the form of scholarship grants, to students enrolled in private elementary or secondary schools. STOs must disburse as scholarship grants at least 90 percent of contributions received, may allow donors to direct scholarships to individual students, may not allow donors to name their own dependents, must designate at least two schools whose students will receive funds, and must not designate schools that "discriminate on the basis of race, color, handicap, familial status or national origin." STOs are not precluded by Arizona's statute from designating schools that provide religious instruction or that give admissions preference on the basis of religion or religious affiliation. When taxpayers donate money to a qualified STO, §43-1089 allows them, in calculating their Arizona tax liability, to credit up to $500 of their donation (or $625 for a married couple filing jointly).

In effect, §43-1089 gives Arizona taxpayers an election. They may direct $500 (or, for joint-return filers, $625) to an STO, or to the Arizona Department of Revenue. As long as donors do not give STOs more than their total tax liability, their $500 or $625 contributions are costless.

Respondents' federal-court complaint against the Director of Arizona's Department of Revenue (Director) alleged that §43-1089 "authorizes the formation of agencies that have as their sole purpose the distribution of State funds to children of a particular religious denomination or to children attending schools of a particular religious denomination." Respondents sought injunctive and declaratory relief, and an order requiring STOs to pay funds still in their possession "into the state general fund."

The Director moved to dismiss the action, relying on the TIA. . . . Agreeing with the Director, the District Court held that the TIA required dismissal of the suit.

The Court of Appeals for the Ninth Circuit reversed, holding that "a federal action challenging the granting of a state tax credit is not prohibited by the [TIA]." We now affirm the judgment of the Ninth Circuit.

II

[The Court held that the Director's petition for certiorari was timely.]

III

To determine whether this litigation falls within the TIA's prohibition, it is appropriate, first, to identify the relief sought. Respondents seek prospective relief only. Specifically, their complaint requests "injunctive relief prohibiting [the Director] from allowing taxpayers to utilize the tax credit authorized by A.R.S. §43-1089 for payments made to STOs that make tuition grants to children attending religious schools, to children attending schools of only one religious denomination, or to children selected on the basis of their religion." Respondents further ask for a "declaration that A.R.S. §43-1089, on its face and as applied," violates the Establishment Clause "by affirmatively authorizing STOs to use State income-tax revenues to pay tuition for students attending religious schools or schools that discriminate on the basis of religion." Finally, respondents seek "[a]n order that [the Director] inform all [such] STOs that . . . all funds in their possession as of the date of this Court's order must be paid into the state general fund." Taking account of the prospective nature of the relief requested, does respondents' suit, in 28 U.S.C. §1341's words, seek to "enjoin, suspend or restrain the assessment, levy or collection of any tax under State law"? The answer to that question turns on the meaning of the term "assessment" as employed in the TIA.

As used in the Internal Revenue Code (IRC), the term "assessment" involves a "recording" of the amount the taxpayer owes the Government. Section 6201(a) of the IRC authorizes the Secretary of the Treasury "to make . . . assessments of all taxes . . . imposed by this title." An assessment is made "by recording the liability of the taxpayer in the office of the Secretary in accordance with rules or regulations prescribed by the Secretary." §6203.

We do not focus on the word "assessment" in isolation, however. Instead, we follow "the cardinal rule that statutory language must be read in context [since] a phrase gathers meaning from the words around it." *General Dynamics Land Systems, Inc. v. Cline* (2004). In §1341 and tax law generally, an assessment is closely tied to the collection of a tax, *i.e.*, the assessment is the official recording of liability that triggers levy and collection efforts.

The rule against superfluities complements the principle that courts are to interpret the words of a statute in context. If, as the Director asserts, the term "assessment," by itself, signified "[t]he entire plan or scheme fixed upon for charging or taxing," the TIA would not need the words "levy" or "collection"; the term "assessment," alone, would do all the necessary work.

Earlier this Term, in *United States v. Galletti* (2004), the Government identified "two important consequences" that follow from the IRS's timely tax assessment: "[T]he IRS may employ administrative enforcement methods such as tax liens and levies to collect the outstanding tax;" and "the time within which the IRS may collect the tax either administratively or by a 'proceeding in court' is extended [from 3 years] to 10 years after the date of assessment." The Government thus made clear in briefing Galletti that, under the IRC definition, the tax "assessment" serves as the trigger for levy and collection efforts. The Government did not describe the term as synonymous with the entire plan of taxation. Nor did it disassociate the word "assessment" from the company ("levy or collection") that word keeps.[4] Instead, and in accord with our understanding, the Government related "assessment" to the term's collection-propelling function.

IV

In composing the TIA's text, Congress drew particularly on an 1867 measure, sometimes called the Anti-Injunction Act (AIA), which bars "any court" from entertaining a suit brought "for the purpose of restraining the assessment or collection of any [federal] tax." While [this provision] "apparently has no recorded legislative history," *Bob Jones Univ. v. Simon* (1974), the Court has recognized, from the AIA's text, that the measure serves twin purposes: It responds to "the Government's need to assess and collect taxes as expeditiously as possible with a minimum of preenforcement judicial interference"; and it "'require[s] that the legal right to the disputed sums be determined in a suit for refund.'" Lower federal courts have similarly comprehended §7421(a).

Just as the AIA shields federal tax collections from federal-court injunctions, so the TIA shields state tax collections from federal-court restraints. In both [Acts], Congress directed taxpayers to pursue refund suits instead of attempting to restrain collections. Third-party suits not seeking to stop the collection (or contest the validity) of a tax imposed on plaintiffs, were outside Congress' purview. The TIA's legislative history is not silent in this regard. The Act was designed expressly to restrict

---

4. The dissent is of two minds in this regard. On the one hand, it twice suggests that a proper definition of the term "assessment," for §1341 purposes, is "the entire plan or scheme fixed upon for charging or taxing." *Post*, at 117. On the other hand, the dissent would disconnect the word from the enforcement process ("levy or collection") that "assessment" sets in motion. *See post*, at 117-119.

"the jurisdiction of the district courts of the United States over suits relating to the collection of State taxes."

In short, in enacting the TIA, Congress trained its attention on taxpayers who sought to avoid paying their tax bill by pursuing a challenge route other than the one specified by the taxing authority. Nowhere does the legislative history announce a sweeping congressional direction to prevent "federal-court interference with all aspects of state tax administration." Brief for Petitioner 20.

[T]his Court has interpreted and applied the TIA only in cases Congress wrote the Act to address, *i.e.*, cases in which state taxpayers seek federal-court orders enabling them to avoid paying state taxes. We have read harmoniously the §1341 instruction conditioning the jurisdictional bar on the availability of "a plain, speedy and efficient remedy" in state court. The remedy inspected in our decisions was not one designed for the universe of plaintiffs who sue the State. Rather, it was a remedy tailor-made for taxpayers.

. . .

In a procession of cases not rationally distinguishable from this one, no Justice or member of the bar of this Court ever raised a [TIA] objection that, according to the petitioner in this case, should have caused us to order dismissal of the action for want of jurisdiction. Consistent with the decades-long understanding prevailing on this issue, respondents' suit may proceed without any TIA impediment.

[The concurring opinion of Justice STEVENS is omitted.]

Justice KENNEDY, with whom THE CHIEF JUSTICE, JUSTICE SCALIA, and JUSTICE THOMAS join, dissenting.

In this case, the Court shows great skepticism for the state courts' ability to vindicate constitutional wrongs. Two points make clear that the Court treats States as diminished and disfavored powers, rather than merely applies statutory text. First, the Court's analysis of the Tax Injunction Act (TIA or Act), contrasts with a literal reading of its terms. Second, the Court's assertion that legislative histories support the conclusion that "[t]hird-party suits not seeking to stop the collection (or contest the validity) of a tax imposed on plaintiffs . . . were outside Congress' purview" in enacting the TIA and the anti-injunction provision on which the TIA was modeled, is not borne out by those sources. In light of these points, today's holding should probably be attributed to the concern the Court candidly shows animates it. The concern, it seems, is that state courts are second rate constitutional arbiters, unequal to their federal counterparts. State courts are due more respect than this. Dismissive treatment of state courts is particularly unjustified since the TIA, by express terms, provides a federal safeguard: The Act lifts its bar on federal-court intervention when state courts fail to provide "a plain, speedy, and efficient remedy."

In view of the TIA's text, the congressional judgment that state courts are qualified constitutional arbiters, and the respect state courts deserve, I disagree with the majority's superseding the balance the Act strikes between federal- and state-court adjudication.

I

Today is the first time the Court has considered whether the TIA bars federal district courts from granting injunctive relief that would prevent States from giving citizens statutorily mandated state tax credits. There are cases, some dating back almost 50 years, which proceeded as if the jurisdictional bar did not apply to tax credit challenges; but some more recent decisions have said the bar is applicable. While unexamined custom favors the first position, the statutory text favors the latter. In these circumstances a careful explanation for the conclusion is necessary; but in the end the scope and purpose of the Act should be understood from its terms alone.

Guided first by the Internal Revenue Code, an assessment under §1341, at a minimum, is the recording of taxpayers' liability on the State's tax rolls. The TIA, though a federal statute that must be interpreted as a matter of federal law, operates in a state-law context. In this respect, the Act must be interpreted so as to apply evenly to the 50 various state-law regimes and to the various recording schemes States employ. It is therefore irrelevant whether state officials record taxpayer liabilities with their own pen in a specified location, by collecting and maintaining taxpayers' self-reported filing forms, or in some other manner. The recordkeeping that equates to the determination of taxpayer liability on the State's tax rolls is the assessment, whatever the method. The Court seems to agree with this.

The dictionary definition of assessment provides further relevant information. Contemporaneous dictionaries from the time of the TIA's enactment define assessment in expansive terms. They would broaden any understanding of the term, and so the Act's bar. The Court need not decide the full scope of the term assessment in the TIA, however. For present purposes, a narrow definition of the term suffices. Applying the narrowest definition, the TIA's literal text bars district courts from enjoining, suspending, or restraining a State's recording of taxpayer liability on its tax rolls, whether the recordings are made by self-reported taxpayer filing forms or by a State's calculation of taxpayer liability.

Respondents argue the TIA does not bar the injunction they seek because even after the credit is enjoined, the Director will be able to record and enforce taxpayers' liabilities. In fact, respondents say, with the credit out of the way the Director will be able to record and enforce a higher level of liability and so profit the State. The argument, however, ignores an important part of the Act: "under State law." 28 U.S.C. §1341 ("The district courts shall not enjoin, suspend or restrain the assessment . . . of any tax under State law."). The Act not only bars district courts from enjoining, suspending, or restraining a State's recording of taxpayer liabilities altogether; but it also bars them from enjoining, suspending, or restraining a State from recording the taxpayer liability that state law mandates.

Arizona Rev. Stat. Ann. §43-1089 is state law. It is an integral part of the State's tax statute; it is reflected on state tax forms; and the State Supreme Court has held that it is part of the calculus necessary to determine tax liability. A recording of a taxpayer's liability under state law must be made in accordance with §43-1089. The same can be said with respect to each and every provision of the State's tax law. To order the Director not to record on the State's tax rolls taxpayer liability that reflects the operation of §43-1089 (or any other state tax law provision for that matter) would be to bar the Director from recording the correct taxpayer liability. The TIA's language bars this relief and so bars this suit.

The Court tries to avoid this conclusion by saying that the recordings that constitute assessments under §1341 must have a "collection-propelling function," and that the recordings at issue here do not have such a function. That is wrong. A recording of taxpayer liability on the State's tax rolls of course propels collection. In most cases the taxpayer's payment will accompany his filing, and thus will accompany the assessment so that no literal collection of moneys is necessary. As anyone who has paid taxes must know, however, if owed payment were not included with the tax filing, the State's recording of one's liability on the State's rolls would certainly cause subsequent collection efforts, for the filing's recording (*i.e.*, the assessment) would propel collection by establishing the State's legal right to the taxpayer's moneys.

II

The majority offers prior judicial interpretations of the Code's similarly worded anti-injunction provision to support its contrary conclusions about the statutory text. *See ante*, at 102-103. That this Court and other federal courts have allowed nontaxpayer suits challenging tax credits to proceed in the face of the anti-injunction provision is not at all controlling. Those cases are quite distinguishable. Had the plaintiffs in those cases been barred from suit, there would have been no available forum at all for their claims. The Court ratified those decisions only insofar as they relied on this limited rationale as the basis for an exception to the statutory bar on adjudication. *See South Carolina v. Regan* (1984).

In contrast to the anti-injunction provision, the TIA on its own terms ensures an adequate forum for claims it bars. The TIA specially exempts actions that could not be heard in state courts by providing an exception for instances "where a plain, speedy, and efficient remedy may [not] be had in the courts of [the] State."

The TIA's text thus already incorporates the check that *Regan* concluded could be read into the anti-injunction provision even though "[t]he [anti-injunction provision]'s language 'could scarcely be more explicit' in prohibiting nontaxpayer suits like this one." *South Carolina v. Regan* (O'Connor, J., concurring in judgment) (quoting *Bob Jones Univ. v. Simon*, 416 U.S. 725, 736 (1974)). The practical effect is that a literal reading of the TIA provides for federal district courts to stand at the ready where litigants encounter legal or practical obstacles to challenging state tax credits in state courts. And this Court, of course, stands at the ready to review decisions by state courts on these matters.

The Court does not discuss this codified exception, yet the clause is crucial. It represents a congressional judgment about the balance that should exist between the respect due to the States (for both their administration of tax schemes and their courts' interpretation of tax laws) and the need for constitutional vindication. To ignore the provision is to ignore that Congress has already balanced these interests.

Respondents admit they would be heard in state court. Indeed a quite similar action previously was heard there. As a result, the TIA's exception (akin to that recognized by *Regan*) does not apply. To proceed as if it does is to replace Congress' balancing of the noted interests with the Court's.

III

The Act is designed to respect not only the administration of state tax systems but also state-court authority to say what state law means. This too establishes that the TIA's purpose is not solely to ensure that the State's fisc is not decreased. There would be only a diminished interest in allowing state courts to say what the State's tax statutes mean if the Act protected just the state fisc. The TIA protects the responsibility of the States and their courts to administer their own tax systems and to be accountable to the citizens of the State for their policies and decisions. The litigation in large part turns on what state law requires and whether the product of those requirements violates the Constitution. More to the point, however, even if there were no controversy about the statutory framework the Arizona tax provision creates, the majority's ruling has implications far beyond this case and will most certainly result in federal courts in other States and in other cases being required to interpret state tax law in order to complete their review of challenges to state tax statutes.

Our heretofore consistent interpretation of the Act's legislative history to prohibit interference with state tax systems and their administration accords with the direct, broad, and unqualified language of the statute. The Act bars all orders that enjoin, suspend, or restrain the assessment of any tax under state law. In effecting congressional intent we should give full force to simple and broad proscriptions in the statutory language.

IV

The final basis on which both the majority and respondents rest is that years of unexamined habit by litigants and the courts alike have resulted in federal courts' entertaining challenges to state tax credits. While we should not reverse the course of our unexamined practice lightly, our obligation is to give a correct interpretation of the statute. We are not obliged to maintain the status quo when the status quo is unfounded. The exercise of federal jurisdiction does not and cannot establish jurisdiction.

* * *

In *Hibbs*, the Court rejected the state's argument that the Tax Injunction Act was "a sweeping congressional directive to prevent 'federal court interference with all aspects of state tax administration.'" Justice Kennedy, by contrast, would have read the Act broadly "to prohibit interference with state tax systems and their administration." At one level, the disagreement between the majority and the dissenters concerned interpretation of the Act and its history. At another level, however, the Justices apparently disagreed about the role and importance of federal jurisdiction when state courts are also available to enforce federal rights.

This type of disagreement is reflected in the federal courts' assessment of what constitutes a "plain, speedy and efficient remedy in State court" under the Act. *Hibbs* is only a recent entry in a long line of cases interpreting the Act. Tracing these cases shows how the judicial approach to the adequacy of state remedies is changing over time. The Supreme Court's earliest cases interpreting the Act held that mere "uncertainty" about the "adequacy" of the state remedy was enough for a court to conclude that the Act did not bar federal relief. *Spector Motor Service, Inc. v. McLaughlin* (1944). In the 1970s, at roughly the same time that it expanded judge-made abstention in cases such as *Younger v. Harris* (1971), the Court began to adopt a strong presumption that state remedies are adequate.

In *Tully v. Griffin* (1976), the Court concluded that state remedies were adequate even where state law made it financially impossible for some individuals to obtain relief. The state law in that case required that an individual challenging a state tax either prepay or post a bond as a prerequisite to seeking relief. The district court found that the plaintiff "lacked the means" to pay and held that the state remedy was inadequate. The Supreme Court reversed, referring to a federal courts' "equitable duty to refrain from interfering with a State's collection of its revenue," which, it reasoned, was "reflected and confirmed in the congressional command" of the Tax Injunction Act.

In a subsequent case, *Rosewell v. LaSalle National Bank* (1981), the Court went further to hold that the substance of a state remedy is irrelevant to its adequacy under the Act. If the state's remedy is procedurally adequate, then it is "plain, speedy and efficient" within the meaning of the Act. Therefore, the Court held, a state's failure to pay interest on a tax refund did not make the state remedy inadequate. The dissenting Justices pointed out the artificiality of the procedure/substance distinction. Under the Court majority's holding, the dissent noted, "a state remedy which could not possibly afford any relief or which had the potential for only nominal relief would defeat federal jurisdiction."

Tully and *Rosewell* do not preclude federal jurisdiction where a state withdraws a remedy that it had promised to make available. This was the case in *Reich v. Collins* (1994). A state statute provided for a refund of "any and all taxes or fees which are determined to have been illegally assessed and collected." When a taxpayer filed for relief under this statute, the state supreme court denied it because the taxpayer had not used a predeprivation remedy that was also available under state law. The U.S. Supreme Court held that a state may not, consistent with due process, "hold out what plainly appears to be a 'clear and certain' postdeprivation remedy and then declare, only after the disputed taxes have been paid, that no such remedy exists." Thus, a federal court could exercise jurisdiction over the taxpayer's suit notwithstanding the Tax Injunction Act.

The Tax Injunction Act also presents other interpretive questions, including the types of relief that are barred by it. The Act provides that federal courts "shall not enjoin, suspend or restrain the assessment, levy or collection of any tax under State law," which plainly refers to injunctive relief. The Supreme Court has held the Act also bars declaratory judgments that would have the effect of barring the collection of state taxes. *California v. Grace Brethren Church* (1982).

The Tax Injunction Act sets a floor, not a ceiling, for federal judicial restraint in matters of state tax administration. The Court has held the judge-made doctrine of comity may require a federal court challenge even where the Tax Injunction Act does not. In *Levin v. Commerce Energy, Inc.* (2010), for instance, the Court stated that "[m]ore embracive than the Tax Injunction Act, the comity doctrine applicable in state taxation cases restrains federal courts from claims for relief that risk disrupting state tax administration." The Court has extended this principle of comity to constitutional challenges to state tax systems, even where the plaintiff seeks damages, not an injunction or declaratory relief. *Fair Assessment in Real Estate Ass'n v. McNary* (1981).

At the same time, the Court has created some exceptions to the Tax Injunction Act that are not suggested by its text. For example, it has held that the Act does not bar a suit by the United States or its departments, agencies, and instrumentalities. *See Department of Employment v. United States* (1997).

3. The Johnson Act

The Johnson Act sets a subject-matter specific limitation on federal injunctive relief in matters involving utility rates. There are extensive federal regulatory schemes for utilities, including the interstate transmission of electricity, natural gas and oil, with Congress delegating authority to agencies such as the Federal Energy Regulatory Commission (FERC). At the same time, states and their subdivisions have authority to address various questions involving energy policy, including utility rates.

The Act balances the need for some federal regulation of utility rates with concerns about state and local autonomy:

> The District Courts shall not enjoin, suspend or restrain the operation of, or compliance with, any order affecting rates chargeable by a public utility and made by a state administrative agency or rate-making body of a State political subdivision, where:
>
> (1) Jurisdiction is based solely on diversity of citizenship or repugnance of the order to the Federal Constitution; and
>
> (2) The order does not interfere with interstate commerce; and
>
> (3) The order has been made after reasonable notice and hearing; and
>
> (4) A plain, speedy and efficient remedy may be had in the courts of such State.

This provision generally directs challenges to state and local rate regulation into state courts. It does not, however, bar federal jurisdiction over every type of challenge to utility regulation. Indeed, some challenges to state and local rate regulations may proceed under the Act, which does not preclude a district court from enjoining a state order that is preempted by federal law. Nor does it bar relief when a state interferes with interstate commerce, although this exception has been narrowly construed. In addition, where the state remedies are not "plain, speedy and efficient," a federal court may intervene. And, as with the Anti-Injunction Act and the Tax Injunction Act, the Court has held that the Johnson Act does not bar a suit by the United States. *Public Utils. Comm'n of Cal. v. United States* (1958).

4. The Civil Rights Removal Act

The Anti-Injunction Act, the Tax Injunction Act and the Johnson Act, each discussed above, limit federal court intervention into state proceedings. The Civil Rights Removal Act is different. Enacted as part of the first major civil rights law after the Civil War, this Act aimed to protect Blacks from harassment and biased prosecutions and civil suits in state courts. Congress provided for the removal of criminal and civil proceedings from state to federal courts, on the theory that federal courts would be less biased than state courts against Black Americans and their allies in the South.

The Civil Rights Removal Act states:

> Any of the following civil actions or criminal prosecutions, commenced in a State court may be removed by the defendant to the district court of the United States for the district and division embracing the place where it is pending:
>
> (1) Against any person who is denied or cannot enforce in the courts of such State a right under any law providing for the equal civil rights of citizens of the United States, or of all persons within the jurisdiction thereof;
>
> (2) For any act under color of authority derived from any law providing for equal rights, or for refusing to do any act on the ground that it would be inconsistent with such law.

Thus, there are two scenarios in which removal of a pending case may be proper. First, a defendant may remove a case if the state courts will deny federal civil rights. Second, a defendant may remove a case if their defense is that federal civil rights laws required their challenged action or prohibited their challenged inaction.

The Supreme Court has narrowly construed the Act and thus limited its practical impact. Under the Court's interpretation, evidence of state court bias and discrimination is not enough to remove a case. Instead, the first ground for removal is limited to cases in which a person will be deprived of a right under federal law dealing with racial equality, and the deprivation will occur pursuant to a specific state statute or state constitutional provision. And the second ground for removal is limited to cases in which the defendant is a government officer, or someone assisting a government officer in the performance of official duties, and the state proceedings will violate a federal law dealing with racial equality.

The Court's narrow interpretation of the Act is a window into some of the central themes of federal courts law and history. In the Reconstruction Era, Congress envisioned the federal courts as playing a central role in protecting civil rights against hostile state courts. The Civil Rights Removal Act was part of that vision. In narrowly interpreting the Act and limiting federal court review of state courts, the Court has shown respect for the state courts. But the Act was premised upon congressional recognition of the problem of state court discrimination. The following case illustrates the debate about Congress's intent and the Court's narrow interpretation of the Act. The case arose during the height of the Civil Rights Movement in the 1960s, a movement that responded to the U.S.'s nearly-century-long failure to realize the full promise of Reconstruction.

City of Greenwood v. Peacock (1966), as the Court noted, was a "sequel[] to *Georgia v. Rachel*," decided the same year. In *Rachel*, the State of Georgia prosecuted 20 individuals for trespass when they sought service at a restaurant in Atlanta. They obtained removal to federal court under the Civil Rights Removal Act. The Court held that removal was appropriate under subparagraph (1) of the Act. First, the defendants could point to a specific federal statute, Title II of the Civil Rights Act of 1964, that prohibited racial discrimination by public accommodations, including restaurants. Thus, their request for removal rested upon a the "a limited category of rights, specifically defined in terms of racial equality," that Congress "intended to protect" when it enacted the Civil Rights Removal Act. Second, although the defendants could not point to a specific state law mandating discrimination against them, they had shown that "*any* proceedings in the courts of the State [would] constitute a denial of the rights conferred by the Civil Rights Act of 1964." Thus, under *Rachel,* state courts may be found to deny federal civil rights not only when there is a specific state law that is facially discriminatory, but also when the state proceeding itself is inherently unconstitutional.

In *Peacock,* the next case, the Court distinguished *Rachel* and held that removal was inappropriate. *Peacock* underscores the narrowness of the Court's interpretation of the Civil Rights Removal Act. As you read the Court's opinion, consider how it construes the Act in light of its history. The Court's majority was motivated by a concern that federal judges should not "put their brethren of the state judiciary on trial." The dissenting Justices, by contrast, read the Civil Rights Removal Act to reflect congressional distrust of state courts in federal civil rights cases.

City of Greenwood v. Peacock

384 U.S. 808 (1966)

Mr. Justice STEWART delivered the opinion of the Court.

These consolidated cases, sequels to *Georgia v. Rachel,* involve prosecutions on various state criminal charges against 29 people who were allegedly engaged in the spring and summer of 1964 in civil rights activity in Leflore County, Mississippi. In the first case, 14 individuals were charged with obstructing the public streets of the City of Greenwood in violation of Mississippi law. They filed petitions to remove their cases to the United States District Court for the Northern District of Mississippi under 28 U.S.C. §1443. Alleging that they were members of a civil rights group engaged in a drive to encourage Negro voter registration in Leflore County, their petitions stated that they were denied or could not enforce in the courts of the State rights under laws providing for the equal civil rights of citizens of the United States, and that they were being prosecuted for acts done under color of authority of the Constitution of the United States and 42 U.S.C. §1971 *et seq.* Additionally, their removal petitions alleged that the statute under which they were charged was unconstitutionally vague on its face, that it was unconstitutionally applied to their conduct, and that its application was a part of a policy of racial discrimination fostered by the State of Mississippi and the City of Greenwood. The District Court sustained the motion of the City of Greenwood to remand the cases to the city police court for trial. The Court of Appeals for the Fifth Circuit reversed, . . . [and] remanded to the District Court for a hearing on the truth of the defendants' allegations.

In the second case, 15 people allegedly affiliated with a civil rights group were arrested at different times in July and August of 1964 and charged with various offenses against the laws of Mississippi or ordinances of the City of Greenwood. These defendants filed essentially identical petitions for removal in the District Court, denying that they had engaged in any conduct prohibited by valid laws and stating that their arrests and prosecutions were for the "sole purpose and effect of harassing Petitioners and of punishing them for and deterring them from the exercise of their constitutionally protected right to protest the conditions of racial discrimination and segregation" in Mississippi. The District Court held that the cases had been improperly removed and remanded them to the police court of the City of Greenwood. In a per curiam opinion finding the issues "identical with" those determined in the *Peacock* case, the Court of Appeals for the Fifth Circuit reversed and remanded the cases to the District Court for a hearing on the truth of the defendants' allegations.

I

The individual petitioners contend that, quite apart from 28 U.S.C. §1443(1), they are entitled to remove their cases to the District Court under 28 U.S.C. §1443(2), which authorizes the removal of a civil action or criminal prosecution for "any act under color of authority derived from any law providing for equal rights. . . ." The core of their contention is that the various federal constitutional and statutory provisions invoked in their removal petitions conferred "color of authority" upon them to perform the acts for which they are being prosecuted by the State. We reject this argument, because we have concluded that the history of §1443(2) demonstrates convincingly that this subsection of the removal statute is available only to federal officers and to persons assisting such officers in the performance of their official duties.

II

We come, then, to the issues which this case raises as to the scope of 28 U.S.C. §1443(1). In *Georgia v. Rachel*, decided today, we have held that removal of a state court trespass prosecution can be had under §1443(1) upon a petition alleging that the prosecution stems exclusively from the petitioners' peaceful exercise of their right to equal accommodation in establishments covered by the Civil Rights Act of 1964. Since that Act itself, as construed by this *Court in Hamm v. City of Rock Hill* (1964), specifically and uniquely guarantees that the conduct alleged in the removal petition in *Rachel* may "not be the subject of trespass prosecutions," the defendants inevitably are "denied or cannot enforce in the courts of [the] State a right under any law providing for . . . equal civil rights," by merely being brought before a state court to defend such a prosecution. The present case, however, is far different.

In the first place, the federal rights invoked by the individual petitioners include some that clearly cannot qualify under the statutory definition as rights under laws providing for "equal civil rights." The First Amendment rights of free expression, for example, so heavily relied upon in the removal petitions, are not rights arising under a law providing for "equal civil rights" within the meaning of §1443(1). The First Amendment is a great charter of American freedom, and the precious rights of personal liberty it protects are undoubtedly comprehended in the concept of "civil rights." But the reference in §1443(1) is to "equal civil rights." That phrase does not include the broad constitutional guarantees of the First Amendment. A precise definition of the limitations of the phrase "any law providing for . . . equal civil rights" in §1443(1) is not a matter we need pursue to a conclusion, however, because we may proceed here on the premise that at least the two federal statutes specifically referred to in the removal petitions, 42 U.S.C. §1971 and 42 U.S.C. §1981, do qualify under the statutory definition.[5]

The fundamental claim in this case, then, is that a case for removal is made under §1443(1) upon a petition alleging: (1) that the defendants were arrested by state officers and charged with various offenses under state law because they were Negroes or because they were engaged in helping Negroes assert their rights under federal equal civil rights laws, and that they are completely innocent of the charges against them, or (2) that the defendants will be unable to obtain a fair trial in the state court. The basic difference between this case and *Rachel* is thus immediately apparent. In *Rachel* the defendants relied on the specific provisions of a pre-emptive federal civil rights law—§§201(a) and 203(c) of the Civil Rights Act of 1964, 42 U.S.C. §§2000a (a) and 2000a-2 (c) (1964 ed.), as construed in *Hamm v. City of Rock Hill*—that, under the conditions alleged, gave them: (1) the federal statutory right to remain on the property of a restaurant proprietor after being ordered to leave, despite a state law making it a criminal offense not to leave, and (2) the further federal statutory right that no State should even attempt to prosecute them for their conduct. The Civil Rights Act of 1964 as construed in *Hamm* thus specifically and uniquely conferred upon the defendants an absolute right to "violate" the explicit terms of the state criminal trespass law with impunity under the conditions alleged in the *Rachel* removal petition, and any attempt by the State to make them answer in a court for this conceded "violation" would directly deny their federal right "in the courts of [the] State." The present case differs from *Rachel* in two significant respects. First, no federal law confers an absolute right on private citizens—on civil rights advocates, on Negroes, or on anybody else—to obstruct a public street, to contribute to the delinquency of a minor, to drive an automobile without a license, or to bite a policeman. Second, no federal law confers immunity from state prosecution on such charges.

To sustain removal of these prosecutions to a federal court upon the allegations of the petitions in this case would therefore mark a complete departure from the terms of the removal statute, which allow removal only when a person is "denied or cannot enforce" a specified federal right "in the courts of [the] State," and a complete departure as well from the consistent line of this Court's decisions. Those cases all stand for at least one basic proposition: It is not enough to support removal under §1443(1) to allege or show that the defendant's federal equal civil rights have been illegally and corruptly denied by state administrative officials in advance of trial, that the charges against the defendant are false, or that the

---

5. [Authors' note: 42 U.S.C. §1971 provided, "No person, whether acting under color of law or otherwise, shall intimidate, threaten, coerce, or attempt to intimidate, threaten or coerce any other person for the purpose of interfering with the right of such other person to vote or to vote as he may choose." 42 U.S.C. §1981 provided, "All persons within the jurisdiction of the United States shall have the same right in every State and Territory to make and enforce contracts, to sue, be parties, give evidence, and to the full and equal benefit of all laws and proceedings for the security of persons and property as is enjoyed by white citizens, and shall be subject to like punishment, pains, penalties, taxes, licenses, and exactions of every kind, and to no other."]

defendant is unable to obtain a fair trial in a particular state court. The motives of the officers bringing the charges may be corrupt, but that does not show that the state trial court will find the defendant guilty if he is innocent, or that in any other manner the defendant will be "denied or cannot enforce in the courts" of the State any right under a federal law providing for equal civil rights. The civil rights removal statute does not require and does not permit the judges of the federal courts to put their brethren of the state judiciary on trial. Under §1443(1), the vindication of the defendant's federal rights is left to the state courts except in the rare situations where it can be clearly predicted by reason of the operation of a pervasive and explicit state or federal law that those rights will inevitably be denied by the very act of bringing the defendant to trial in the state court.

What we have said is not for one moment to suggest that the individual petitioners in this case have not alleged a denial of rights guaranteed to them under federal law. If, as they allege, they are being prosecuted on baseless charges solely because of their race, then there has been an outrageous denial of their federal rights, and the federal courts are far from powerless to redress the wrongs done to them. The most obvious remedy is . . . vindication of their federal claims on direct review by this Court, if those claims have not been vindicated by the trial or reviewing courts of the State.

But there are many other remedies available in the federal courts to redress the wrongs claimed by the individual petitioners in the extraordinary circumstances they allege in their removal petitions. If the state prosecution or trial on the charge of obstructing a public street or on any other charge would itself clearly deny their rights protected by the First Amendment, they may under some circumstances obtain an injunction in the federal court. If they go to trial and there is a complete absence of evidence against them, their convictions will be set aside because of a denial of due process of law. If at their trial they are in fact denied any federal constitutional rights, and these denials go uncorrected by other courts of the State, the remedy of federal habeas corpus is freely available to them. If their federal claims at trial have been denied through an unfair or deficient fact-finding process, that, too, can be corrected by a federal court.

Other sanctions, civil and criminal, are available in the federal courts against officers of a State who violate the petitioners' federal constitutional and statutory rights. Under 42 U.S.C. §1983 the officers may be made to respond in damages not only for violations of rights conferred by federal equal civil rights laws, but for violations of other federal constitutional and statutory rights as well. And only this Term we have held that the provisions of 18 U.S.C. §241, a criminal law that imposes punishment of up to 10 years in prison, may be invoked against those who conspire to deprive any citizen of the "free exercise or enjoyment of any right or privilege secured to him by the Constitution or laws of the United States" by "causing the arrest of Negroes by means of false reports that such Negroes had committed criminal acts." *United States v. Guest* (1966).

But the question before us now is not whether state officials in Mississippi have engaged in conduct for which they may be civilly or criminally liable under federal law. The question, precisely, is whether the individual petitioners are entitled to remove these state prosecutions to a federal court under the provisions of 28 U.S.C. §1443(1). Unless the words of this removal statute are to be disregarded and the previous consistent decisions of this Court completely repudiated, the answer must clearly be that no removal is authorized in this case.

It is worth contemplating what the result would be if the strained interpretation of §1443(1) urged by the individual petitioners were to prevail. In the fiscal year 1963 there were 14 criminal removal cases of all kinds in the entire Nation; in fiscal 1964 there were 43. The present case was decided by the Court of Appeals for the Fifth Circuit on June 22, 1965, just before the end of the fiscal year. In that year, fiscal 1965, there were 1,079 criminal removal cases in the Fifth Circuit alone. But this phenomenal increase is no more than a drop in the bucket of what could reasonably be expected in the future. For if the individual petitioners should prevail in their interpretation of §1443(1), then every criminal case in every court of every State—on any charge from a five-dollar misdemeanor to first-degree murder—would be removable to a federal court upon a petition alleging (1) that the defendant was being prosecuted because of his race and that he was completely innocent of the charge brought against him, or (2) that he would be unable to obtain a fair trial in the state court. On motion to remand, the federal court would be required in every case to hold a hearing, which would amount to at least a preliminary trial of the motivations of the state officers who arrested and charged the defendant, of the quality of the state court or judge before whom the charges were filed, and of the defendant's innocence or guilt. And the federal court might, of course, be located hundreds of miles away from the place where the charge was brought. This hearing could be followed either by a full trial in the federal court, or by a remand order. Every remand order would be appealable as of right to a United States Court of Appeals and, if affirmed there, would then be reviewable by petition for a writ of certiorari in this Court. If the remand order were eventually affirmed, there might, if the witnesses were still available, finally be a trial in the state court, months or years after the original charge was brought. If the remand order were eventually reversed, there might finally be a trial in the federal court, also months or years after the original charge was brought.

We have no doubt that Congress, if it chose, could provide for exactly such a system. We may assume that Congress has constitutional power to provide that all federal issues be tried in the federal courts, that all be tried in the courts of the States, or that jurisdiction of such issues be shared. And in the exercise of that power, we may assume that Congress is constitutionally fully free to establish the conditions under which civil or criminal proceedings involving federal issues may be removed from one court to another.

We need not attempt to catalog the issues of policy that Congress might feel called upon to consider before making such an extreme change in the removal statute. But prominent among those issues, obviously, would be at least two fundamental questions: Has the historic practice of holding state criminal trials in state courts—with power of ultimate review of any federal questions in this Court—been such a failure that the relationship of the state and federal courts should now be revolutionized? Will increased responsibility of the state courts in the area of federal civil rights be promoted and encouraged by denying those courts any power at all to exercise that responsibility?

We postulate these grave questions of practice and policy only to point out that if changes are to be made in the long-settled interpretation of the provisions of this century-old removal statute, it is for Congress and not for this Court to make them. Fully aware of the established meaning the removal statute had been given by a consistent series of decisions in this Court, Congress in 1964 declined to act on proposals to amend the law. All that Congress did was to make remand orders appealable, and thus invite a contemporary judicial consideration of the meaning of the unchanged provisions of 28 U.S.C. §1443. We have accepted that invitation and have fully considered the language and history of those provisions. Having done so, we find that §1443 does not justify removal of these state criminal prosecutions to a federal court.

Mr. Justice DOUGLAS, with whom THE CHIEF JUSTICE, Mr. Justice BRENNAN and Mr. Justice FORTAS concur, dissenting.

These state court defendants who seek the protection of the federal court were civil rights workers in Mississippi. Some were affiliated with the Student Non-Violent Coordinating Committee engaged in getting Negroes registered as voters. They were charged in the state courts with obstructing the public streets. Other defendants were civil rights workers affiliated with the Council of Federated Organizations which aims to achieve full and complete integration of Negroes into the political and economic life of Mississippi. Some alleged that, while peacefully picketing, they were arrested and charged with assault and battery or interfering with an officer. Others were charged with illegal operation of motor vehicles, or for contributing to the delinquency of a minor or parading without a permit. Some were charged with disturbing the peace or inciting a riot.

All sought removal, some alleging in their motions that the state prosecution was part and parcel of Mississippi's policy of racial segregation. Others alleged that they were wholly innocent, the state prosecutions being for the sole purpose of harassing them and of punishing them for exercising their constitutional rights to protest the conditions of racial discrimination and segregation.

As I will show, the federal regime was designed from the beginning to afford some protection against local passions and prejudices by the important pretrial federal remedy of removal; and the civil rights legislation with which we deal supports the mandates of the Court of Appeals.

I

The Federal District Courts were created by the First Congress which designated a few heads of jurisdiction for the District Courts and for the Circuit Courts—some being concurrent with those of the state courts, others being exclusive. These categories of jurisdiction—later enlarged—were largely for the benefit of plaintiffs. There was concern that the rivalries, jealousies, and animosities among the States made necessary and appropriate the creation of a dual system of courts.

Lack of trust in some of the state courts for execution of federal laws was reflected in the First Congress that established the dual system. Thus Madison said:

> . . . a review of the constitution of the courts in many States will satisfy us that they cannot be trusted with the execution of the Federal laws. In some of the States, it is true, they might, and would be safe and proper organs of such a jurisdiction; but in others they are so dependent on State

Legislatures, that to make the Federal laws dependent on them, would throw us back into all the embarrassments which characterized our former situation. In Connecticut the Judges are appointed annually by the Legislature, and the Legislature is itself the last resort in civil cases.

Though federal question jurisdiction was originally limited to a few classes of cases, the creation of diversity jurisdiction was a significant manifestation of this same feeling. As Chief Justice Marshall said in *Bank of United States v. Deveaux* (1809):

The judicial department was introduced into the American constitution under impressions, and with views, which are too apparent not to be perceived by all. However true the fact may be, that the tribunals of the states will administer justice as impartially as those of the nation, to parties of every description, it is not less true that the constitution itself either entertains apprehensions on this subject, or views with such indulgence the possible fears and apprehensions of suitors, that it has established national tribunals for the decision of controversies between aliens and a citizen, or between citizens of different states.

The alternative — the one India took — was to let the state courts be the arbiters of federal as well as state rights with ultimate review in the Federal Supreme Court. But the federal court system was the choice we made and those courts have functioned throughout our history. In the years since 1789, the jurisdiction of the federal courts where federal rights are in issue has been steadily expanded, particularly with the creation of a general "federal question" jurisdiction in 1875.

While the federal courts were for the most part custodians of rights asserted by plaintiffs, from the very beginning they were also the haven of a restricted group of defendants as well. I refer to §12 of the Judiciary Act of 1789, which permitted removal of cases from a state court to a federal court on the ground of diversity of citizenship. Thus from the very start we have had a removal jurisdiction for the protection of defendants on a partial parity with federal jurisdiction for protection of plaintiffs.

With the coming of the Civil War it became plain that some state courts might be instruments for the destruction through harassment of guaranteed federal civil rights. We have seen this demonstrated in the flow of cases coming this way.

The removal laws passed from time to time have responded to two main concerns: First, a federal factfinding forum is often indispensable to the effective enforcement of those guarantees against local action. The federal guarantee turns ordinarily upon contested issues of fact. Those rights, therefore, will be of only academic value in many areas of the country unless the facts are objectively found. Secondly, swift enforcement of the federal right is imperative if the guarantees are to survive and not be slowly strangled by long, drawn-out, costly, cumbersome proceedings which the Congress feared might result in some state courts. The delays of state criminal process, the perilous vicissitudes of litigation in the state courts, the onerous burdens on the poor and the indigent who usually espouse unpopular causes — these threaten to engulf the federal guarantees. It is in that light that 28 U.S.C. §1443(1) should be read and construed.

II

The critical words, so far as the present cases are concerned, are "denied or cannot enforce in the courts or judicial tribunals" of the State or locality where they may be those rights which, in the most recent version of the removal statute, are characterized as those secured by "any law providing for the equal civil rights of citizens of the United States, or of all persons within the jurisdiction thereof."

A

A defendant "is denied" his federal right when "disorderly conduct" statutes, "breach of the peace" ordinances, and the like are used as the instrument to suppress his promotion of civil rights. We know that such laws are sometimes used as a club against civil rights workers.

There are two ways which §1443(1) may be read, either of which leads to the conclusion that these cases are covered by the "is denied" clause. As Judge Sobeloff said, dissenting in *Baines v. City of Danville* (4th Cir. 1966), the clause in question may be paraphrased in either of the following ways:

> (A) Removal is permissible by:
>   (i) any person who is denied[,] or cannot enforce[,] in the courts of such State a right under any law . . .
>   or
>   (ii) any person who is denied[,] or cannot enforce in the courts of such State[,] a right under any law. . . .

If the latter construction is taken, a right "is denied" by state action at any time — before, as well as during, a trial. I agree with Judge Sobeloff that this reading of the provisions is more in keeping with the spirit of 1866, for the remedies given were broad and sweeping: "If a Negro's rights were denied by the actions of such state officer, the aggrieved party was permitted to have vindication in the federal court; either by filing an original claim or, if a prosecution had already been commenced against him, by removing the case to the federal forum." *Id.*, at 781.

Yet even if the "is denied" clause is read more restrictively, the present cases constitute denials of federal civil rights "in the courts" of the offending State within the meaning of §1443(1), for the local judicial machinery is implicated even prior to actual trial by issuance of a warrant or summons, by commitment of the prisoner, or by accepting and filing the information or indictment. Initiation of an unwarranted judicial proceeding to suppress or punish the assertion of federal civil rights makes out a case of civil rights "denied" within the meaning of §1443(1). Prosecution for a federally protected act is punishment for that act. The cost of proceeding court by court until the federal right is vindicated is great. Restraint of liberty may be present; the need to post bonds may be present; the hire of a lawyer may be considerable; the gantlet of state court proceedings may entail destruction of a federal right through unsympathetic and adverse fact-findings that are in effect unreviewable. The presence of an unresolved criminal charge may hang over the head of a defendant for years.

In early 1964, for example, the Supreme Court of Mississippi affirmed convictions in harassment prosecutions arising out of the May 1961 Freedom Rides.

More than another year was to pass before this Court reached and reversed those convictions.

Continuance of an illegal local prosecution, like the initiation of a new one, can have a chilling effect on a federal guarantee of civil rights. We said in *NAACP v. Button* (1963), respecting some of these federal rights, that "[t]he threat of sanctions may deter their exercise almost as potently as the actual application of sanctions."

For reasons not clear, a baseless prosecution, designed to punish and deter the exercise of such federally protected rights as voting, is not seen by the majority to constitute a denial of equal civil rights. This seems to me to overlook two very important federal statutes. The first, 42 U.S.C. §1981, provides:

> All persons within the jurisdiction of the United States shall have the same right in every State . . . to the full and equal benefit of all laws and proceedings for the security of persons and property as is enjoyed by white citizens, and shall be subject to like punishment, pains, penalties, taxes, licenses, and exactions of every kind, and to no other.

The other, §11(b) of the Voting Rights Act of 1965, provides:

> No person, whether acting under color of law or otherwise, shall intimidate, threaten, or coerce, or attempt to intimidate, threaten, or coerce any person for voting or attempting to vote, or . . . urging or aiding any person to vote or attempt to vote. . . .

Those sections make clear beyond debate that, if the defendants' allegations are true, these state prosecutions themselves constitute a denial of "a right under any law providing for the equal civil rights of citizens."

B

Defendants also allege that they "cannot enforce" in the courts of Greenwood, the locality in which their cases are to be tried, their equal civil rights. This, unlike a claim of present denial of rights, rests on prediction of the future performance of the state courts. . . .

I think that the words "cannot enforce" should be construed in the spirit of 1866. Senator Lane speaking for the first Civil Rights Act said:

> The State courts already have jurisdiction of every single question that we propose to give to the courts of the United States. Why then the necessity of passing the law? Simply because we fear the execution of these laws if left to the State courts. That is the necessity for this provision.

Senator Trumbull, who was the Chairman of the Judiciary Committee and who managed the bill on the floor, many times reflected the same view. He stated that the person discriminated against "should have authority to go into the Federal courts in all cases where a custom prevails in a State, or where there is a statute-law of the State discriminating against him."

It was not the existence of a statute, he said, any more than the existence of a custom discriminating against the person that would authorize removal, but whether, in either case, it was probable that the state court would fail adequately to enforce the federal guarantees.

The Black Codes were not the only target of this law. Vagrancy laws were another—laws fair on their face which were enforced so as to reduce free men to slaves "in punishment of crimes of the slightest magnitude," laws which declare men "vagrants because they have no homes and because they have no employment" in order "to retain them still in a state of real servitude."

In my view, §1443(1) requires the federal court to decide whether the defendant's allegation (that the state court will not fairly enforce his equal rights) is true.

If the defendant is unable to demonstrate this inability to enforce his rights, the case is remanded to the state court. But if the federal court is persuaded that the state court indeed will not make a good-faith effort to apply the paramount federal law pertaining to "equal civil rights," then the federal court must accept the removal and try the case on the merits.

Such removal under the "cannot enforce" clause would occur only in the unusual case. The courts of the States generally try conscientiously to apply the law of the land. To be sure, state court judges have on occasion taken a different view of the law than that which this Court ultimately announced. But these honest differences of opinion are not the sort of recalcitrance which the "cannot enforce" clause contemplates. What Congress feared was the exceptional situation. It realized that considerable damage could be done by even a single court which harbored such hostility toward federally protected civil rights as to render it unable to meet its responsibilities. The "cannot enforce" clause is directed to that rare case.

Execution of the legislative mandate calls for particular sensitivity on the part of federal district judges; but the delicacy of the task surely does not warrant a refusal to attempt it. I am confident that the federal district judges would exercise care and good judgment in passing on "cannot enforce" claims. A district judge could not lightly assume that the state court would shirk its responsibilities, and should remand the case to the state court unless it appeared by clear and convincing evidence that the allegations of an inability to enforce equal civil rights were true. A requirement that defendants seeking removal demonstrate a basis for "firm prediction" of inability to enforce equal civil rights in the state court is the only necessary consequence of the revision of 1874 which silently deleted the provision for post-trial removal from the statute. In this way, the legitimate interests of federalism . . . would be respected without emasculating this statute.

* * *

B.   ABSTENTION

The express language of Article III does not address whether or when federal judges can refrain from hearing or deciding cases to which their judicial power extends. Relying on norms of federalism, however, the Supreme Court has created doctrines that restrain federal courts from entertaining cases. Federal courts have adopted abstention doctrines in two primary circumstances: to avoid deciding unclear questions of state law that are better suited for a state forum, and to avoid interfering with contemporaneous proceedings in a state forum. These abstention doctrines take two primary forms. First, federal courts stay (or pause) federal proceedings until contemporaneous state proceedings have ended. Second, federal courts rely on abstention doctrines to dismiss claims for equitable relief.

The Supreme Court has often cautioned that abstention should be the exception to the general rule that federal courts exercise jurisdiction when it is properly invoked. Two centuries ago, writing for a unanimous court, Chief Justice Marshall remarked that federal courts "have no more right to decline the exercise of jurisdiction which is given, than to usurp that which is not given." *Cohens v. Virginia*, 19 U.S. (6 Wheat.) 264, 404 (1821). Rather, "[w]ith whatever doubts, with whatever difficulties, a case may be attended, we must decide it if it be brought before us"—even if it raises questions that judges "would gladly avoid." More recently, the Supreme Court has unanimously affirmed that "[i]n the main, federal courts" have a "virtually unflagging" obligation "to decide cases within the scope of federal jurisdiction." *Sprint Commc'ns, Inc. v. Jacobs*, 571 U.S. 69, 72, 77 (2013) (quoting *Colo. River Water Conservation Dist. v. United States*, 424 U.S. 800, 817 (1976)).

This section begins by describing the limited abstention doctrines that have arisen alongside federal courts' virtually unflagging obligation. First, you will encounter doctrines designed to channel a narrow set of unclear questions of state law into state courts. Under the doctrine of *Pullman* abstention—and a related set of procedures—a federal court may decline to decide a federal constitutional question if it must first necessarily decide a threshold, unclear question of state law. Additionally, the doctrine of *Thibodaux* abstention encourages federal courts to stay their hand in diversity jurisdiction cases when asked to decide unclear questions of state law that fundamentally implicate state sovereignty. The highly related doctrine *Burford* abstention prevents federal courts from hearing unclear questions of state law that implicate complex ongoing administrative proceedings.

Second, you will encounter the doctrines that discourage federal courts from interfering with state proceedings. Under *Colorado River* abstention, federal courts should be cautious about entertaining civil cases when there is parallel litigation in state court. Finally, the doctrine of *Younger* abstention discourages interfering with state criminal cases, civil cases that are akin to criminal cases, and cases fundamentally implicating the judicial enforcement, when there is an adequate opportunity to raise federal constitutional objections in the state proceedings.

This list of abstention doctrines is not exhaustive. This Chapter will not discuss, for example, what has been called "international comity" abstention, in which lower courts sometimes abstain from deciding issues that implicate sensitive areas of foreign affairs.[6] Also not covered here is the "tribal exhaustion" requirement, under which federal courts will defer to tribal juridical remedies on matters within their jurisdiction. *See Nat'l Farmers Union Ins. Cos. v. Crow Tribe of Indians* (1985); *Iowa Mut. Ins. Co. v. LaPlante* (1987). This Chapter focuses instead on abstention doctrines that implicate the federal-state relationship.

---

6. William S. Dodge, *International Comity in American Law*, 115 Colum. L. Rev. 2071 (2015); Maggie Gardner, *Abstention at the Border*, 105 Va. L. Rev. 63 (2019).

1.   Unclear State Law and Federal Constitutional Avoidance

Under the doctrine of *Pullman* abstention, federal courts avoid deciding federal constitutional questions if there is an unclear question of state law that, if resolved, would make it unnecessary to decide the federal constitutional question. *See R.R. Comm'n of Tex. v. Pullman Co.* (1941). This doctrine emerged in the early 1940s, as the Court increasingly confronted challenges to Jim Crow Era laws that fortified racial segregation. The case was also decided during an era in which the Court articulated other doctrines expressly designed to avoid unnecessary opinions about the federal constitution's reach.[7] In *Pullman* itself, the Supreme Court was asked to decide whether the State of Texas violated the federal Constitution by effectively banning Black individuals from operating sleeping railcars in the State. At the time, under the dominant custom, only Whites could hold the title "conductor" when operating sleeping railcars. Black individuals who engaged in that vocation held the title "porter." Under the order, issued in 1939, only conductors could operate sleeping railcars in the state. (At the urging of conductors, similar orders were enacted in Florida, Kentucky, and South Carolina during the same period.)[8] The Texas Railroad Commissioner's reasons for issuing the order were filled with racist stereotypes. For example, the commission found that it would be "impossible for a colored porter to maintain proper order and decorum" on the train because "every Texan . . . resents any interference or instructions from a negro man or from a negro porter."[9]

A railroad company challenged the order in federal district court, contending that the restriction violated the federal Equal Protection Clause. A group of porters intervened in the suit, pressing the same legal theory. As historians have documented, porters were a highly organized group who, across contexts far beyond this lawsuit, "pressed the claim that they had the right, as Americans, to live and work on equal basis with white Americans."[10] A three-judge district court panel ruled for the rail company and the porters, finding that "the fact that they are negros and are called porters-in-charge does not disqualify them or render them incompetent."[11]

---

7. *See, e.g,* Ashwander v. Tenn. Valley Auth., 297 U.S. 288, 346 (1936) (Brandeis, J., concurring) ("The Court developed, for its own governance in the cases confessedly within its jurisdiction, a series of rules under which it has avoided passing upon a large part of all the constitutional questions pressed upon it for decision."). Brandeis's list included the idea that "[t]he Court will not pass upon the constitutionality of legislation in a friendly, nonadversary, proceeding, declining because to decide such questions 'is legitimate only in the last resort, and as a necessity in the determination of real, earnest, and vital controversy between individuals. . . .'"

8. Lauren Robel, *Riding the Color Line: The Story of* Railroad Commission of Texas v. Pullman, *in* FEDERAL COURTS STORIES 168 (Vicki Jackson and Judith Resnik eds., 2010).

9. *Id.* at 169, *citing* Railroad Commission of Texas, Order, Nov. 4, 1939, at 44-47, Transcript of Record, Supreme Court of the United States, No. 283, R.R. Comm'n of Texas v. Pullman Co.

10. Beth Tompkins Bates, PULLMAN PORTERS AND THE RISE OF PROTEST POLITICS IN BLACK AMERICA, 1925-1945 (2003), 5.

11. Transcript of Record, Supreme Court of the United States, No. 283, R.R. Comm'n of Texas v. Pullman Co, 367 as quoted in Robel, *supra* note 8, at 178.

On appeal, however, the Supreme Court avoided the constitutional question, concluding that state courts were best positioned to determine whether, as an initial matter, the agency that imposed the segregation order had the authority to do so under state law. The Court also articulated its view that the case implicated a "sensitive area of social policy upon which the federal courts ought not to enter unless no alternative to its adjudication is open."

Railroad Comm'n of Texas v. Pullman Co.

312 U.S. 496 (1941)

Mr. Justice FRANKFURTER delivered the opinion of the Court.

In those sections of Texas where the local passenger traffic is slight, trains carry but one sleeping car. These trains, unlike trains having two or more sleepers, are without a Pullman conductor; the sleeper is in charge of a porter who is subject to the train conductor's control. As is well known, porters on Pullmans are colored and conductors are white. Addressing itself to this situation, the Texas Railroad Commission after due hearing ordered that "no sleeping car shall be operated on any line of railroad in the State of Texas * * * unless such cars are continuously in the charge of an employee * * * having the rank and position of Pullman conductor." Thereupon, the Pullman Company and the railroads affected brought this action in a federal district court to enjoin the Commission's order. Pullman porters were permitted to intervene as complainants, and Pullman conductors entered the litigation in support of the order. Three judges having been convened, the court enjoined enforcement of the order. From this decree, the case came here directly.

The Pullman Company and the railroads assailed the order as unauthorized by Texas law as well as violative of the Equal Protection, the Due Process and the Commerce Clauses of the Constitution. The intervening porters adopted these objections but mainly objected to the order as a discrimination against Negroes in violation of the Fourteenth Amendment.

The complaint of the Pullman porters undoubtedly tendered a substantial constitutional issue. It is more than substantial. It touches a sensitive area of social policy upon which the federal courts ought not to enter unless no alternative to its adjudication is open. Such constitutional adjudication plainly can be avoided if a definitive ruling on the state issue would terminate the controversy. It is therefore our duty to turn to a consideration of questions under Texas law.

The Commission found justification for its order in a Texas statute. It is common ground that if the order is within the Commission's authority its subject matter must be included in the Commission's power to prevent "unjust discrimination and to prevent any and all other abuses" in the conduct of railroads. Whether arrangements pertaining to the staffs of Pullman cars are covered by the Texas concept of "discrimination" is far from clear. What practices of the railroads may be deemed to be "abuses" subject to the Commission's correction is equally doubtful. Reading the Texas statutes and the Texas decisions as outsiders without special competence in Texas law, we would have little confidence in our independent judgment regarding the application of that law to the present situation.

The lower court did deny that the Texas statutes sustained the Commission's assertion of power. And this represents the view of an able and experienced circuit judge of the circuit which includes Texas and of two capable district judges trained in Texas law. Had we or they no choice in the matter but to decide what is the law of the state, we should hesitate long before rejecting their forecast of Texas law. But no matter how seasoned the judgment of the district court may be, it cannot escape being a forecast rather than a determination. The last word on the meaning of Article 6445 of the Texas Civil Statutes, and therefore the last word on the statutory authority of the Railroad Commission in this case, belongs neither to us nor to the district court but to the supreme court of Texas. In this situation a federal court of equity is asked to decide an issue by making a tentative answer which may be displaced tomorrow by a state adjudication. The reign of law is hardly promoted if an unnecessary ruling of a federal court is thus supplanted by a controlling decision of a state court. The resources of equity are equal to an adjustment that will avoid the waste of a tentative decision as well as the friction of a premature constitutional adjudication.

An appeal to the chancellor, as we had occasion to recall only the other day, is an appeal to the "exercise of the sound discretion, which guides the determination of courts of equity." *Beal v. Missouri Pacific R.R.* (1941). The history of equity jurisdiction is the history of regard for public consequences in employing the extraordinary remedy of the injunction. There have been as many and as variegated applications of this supple principle as the situations that have brought it into play. Few public interests have a higher claim upon the discretion of a federal chancellor than the avoidance of needless friction with state policies. [A] doctrine of abstention appropriate to our federal system whereby the federal courts, "exercising a wise discretion," restrain their authority because of "scrupulous regard for the rightful independence of the state governments" and for the smooth working of the federal judiciary. This use of equitable powers is a contribution of the courts in furthering the harmonious relation between state and federal authority without the need of rigorous congressional restriction of those powers.

Regard for these important considerations of policy in the administration of federal equity jurisdiction is decisive here. If there was no warrant in state law for the Commission's assumption of authority there is an end of the litigation; the constitutional issue does not arise. The law of Texas appears to furnish easy and ample means for determining the Commission's authority. Article 6453 of the Texas Civil Statutes gives a review of such an order in the state courts. Or, if there are difficulties in the way of this procedure of which we have not been apprised, the issue of state law may be settled by appropriate action on the part of the State to enforce obedience to the order. In the absence of any showing that these obvious methods for securing a definitive ruling in the state courts cannot be pursued with full protection of the constitutional claim, the district court should exercise its wise discretion by staying its hands.

We therefore remand the cause to the district court, with directions to retain the bill pending a determination of proceedings, to be brought with reasonable promptness, in the state court in conformity with this opinion.

* * *

It would take another 13 years for the Court to hold, for the first time, that state-sanctioned racial segregation violated the Equal Protection Clause. *Brown v. Board of Education* (1954); *see also Browder v. Gayle* (1956) (upholding an order desegregating the bus system in Montgomery, Alabama). And even then, legal historians have contended that the Court relied on other methods of avoidance to delay ruling on the constitutionality of another building block of racial apartheid—bans on interracial marriage. *Naim v. Naim* (1956) (dismissing case as "devoid of a properly presented federal question"); Gregory Michael Dorr, *Principled Expediency: Eugenics, Naim v. Naim, and the Supreme Court*, 42 Am. J. Legal Hist. 119, 145-55 (1998) (presenting evidence of the Justices' calculated decision to avoid the merits of "miscegenation" bans in the heated aftermath of *Brown*). In an ultimately unpublished draft dissent in *Naim*, Chief Justice Earl Warren wrote:

> Since I regard the order of dismissal as completely impermissible in view of this Court's obligatory jurisdiction and its deeply rooted rules of decision, I am constrained to express my dissent. . . . Wordsworth accurately called Duty the Stern Daughter of the voice of God. Here, sternness cannot make us shrink from her call. Congress has obliged this Court to decide the substantial constitutional questions which are properly and adequately presented in this appeal.[12]

a. Exceptions

There are two exceptions to the doctrine of *Pullman* abstention. First, when a plaintiff alleges that a state law is void for vagueness, federal courts should not dismiss that claim on *Pullman* abstention grounds. The very essence of such a claim, after all, is that state law is unclear. Therefore, if federal courts are meaningfully to entertain this category of suits, applying *Pullman* abstention would be unduly obstructive. Second, federal courts should not abstain solely because a plaintiff includes a claim that a state law not only violates a federal constitutional provision, but also violates an unclear, parallel state constitutional provision. Federal constitutional rights often have similar counterparts in state constitutions. The Supreme Court has concluded that under such circumstances, it would be unfair to force plaintiffs to litigate state constitutional claims in state court before asking federal courts to protect federal rights. *Wisconsin v. Constantineau* (1971). Indeed, if abstention were required in such circumstances, rarely could federal courts decide constitutional claims because there almost always are parallel state constitutional provisions.

b. *England* Reservation

When a federal district court does abstain under *Pullman,* and thereby requires the plaintiff to file a state suit to resolve the unclear issue of state law, the plaintiff faces a choice. The litigant may choose to raise the state law issue *and* the federal law issue in state court. If the plaintiff uses this option, a ruling from the state court on the federal law matter is binding, entitled to preclusive effect. *See Propper*

---

12. Dorr, n.170.

v. Clark, 337 U.S. 472, 491 (1949). Alternatively, the litigant may choose to raise only the state law claim, and make clear that she is not asking the state court to litigate the federal claim. While litigants are to inform the state court about the existence of their federal claims, the Supreme Court explained in *England v. Louisiana State Bd. of Med. Examiners*, 375 U.S. 411, 421-22 (1964), that *Pullman* abstention "does not require that federal claims be actually litigated in the state courts."

If the plaintiff chooses the second option, the Supreme Court has encouraged litigants to expressly reserve their federal law claims by asking the state court not to reach them. To preserve one's ability to raise the federal law claims, the plaintiff "may inform the state courts that . . . he intends, should the state courts hold against him on the question of state law, to return to the [federal] District Court for disposition of his federal contentions." This kind of express reservation of federal claims protects the plaintiff's ability to raise those claims later in federal court, assuming that the ruling on the state law matter does not resolve the dispute. The *England* court also explained that while this kind of express reservation decidedly protects the federal claims, "in no event" should a plaintiff be denied the ability to litigate the federal claims in federal court "unless it clearly appears that he voluntarily . . . fully litigated his federal claims in the state courts."

c.   Certification

Today, in the vast majority of states, federal courts are permitted to ask state courts of last resort to clarify unclear questions of state law that arise during the course of federal litigation.[13] State courts, though, are not required to accept the certification and decide the questions that have been certified to them by the federal court. The second half of the twentieth century ushered in the exponential growth in the number of such statutes, as the Supreme Court shined positive light on the practice. Writing for the Court, Justice Frankfurter—the architect of *Pullman* abstention—praised certification as an alternative to the traditional approach of dismissing or staying cases while plaintiffs filed cases anew in state trial courts. *Clay v. Sun Ins. Office Ltd.* (1960). And in 1974, the Court again lauded certification, reasoning that it "save[s] time, energy, and resources and helps build a cooperative judicial federalism." *Lehman Bros. v. Schein* (1974).

By 1977, America's leading academic voice on *Pullman* abstention also endorsed the view that certification represented a worthy, improved successor to

---

13. North Carolina does not provide for certification. *See* Vikram David Amar & Jason Mazzone, *The Value of Certification of State Law Questions by the U.S. Supreme Court to the North Carolina Supreme Court in the Pending North Carolina Berger Case: Part One in a Series*, VERDICT, May 9, 2022, at https://verdict.justia.com/2022/05/09/the-value-of-certification-of-state-law-questions-by-the-u-s-supreme-court-to-the-north-carolina-supreme-court-in-the-pending-north-carolina-berger-case. Missouri has a statute providing for certification, but the state supreme court has held it to be unconstitutional under state law. *See* Grantham v. Missouri Dep't of Corrections, 1990 WL 602159 (Mo. 1990); 17 Mo. Prac., Civil Rules Practice §81.01:3 (2021 ed.) ("Thus, although V.A.M.S. §477.004 authorizes the court to answer questions of law certified to it by federal courts, the court has held that statute unconstitutional.").

the traditional practice.[14] The following excerpt from *Arizonans for Off. Eng. v. Arizona*, 520 U.S. 43, 75-77 (1997), outlines the relative permits of traditional *Pullman* abstention and certification:

> Certification today covers territory once dominated by a deferral device called "*Pullman* abstention," after the generative case, *Railroad Comm'n of Tex. v. Pullman Co.*, 312 U.S. 496 (1941). Designed to avoid federal-court error in deciding state-law questions antecedent to federal constitutional issues, the *Pullman* mechanism remitted parties to the state courts for adjudication of the unsettled state-law issues. If settlement of the state-law question did not prove dispositive of the case, the parties could return to the federal court for decision of the federal issues. Attractive in theory because it placed state-law questions in courts equipped to rule authoritatively on them, *Pullman* abstention proved protracted and expensive in practice, for it entailed a full round of litigation in the state court system before any resumption of proceedings in federal court. *See generally* 17A C. Wright, A. Miller, & E. Cooper, Federal Practice and Procedure §§4242, 4243 (2d ed. 1988 and Supp. 1996).
>
> Certification procedure, in contrast, allows a federal court faced with a novel state-law question to put the question directly to the State's highest court, reducing the delay, cutting the cost, and increasing the assurance of gaining an authoritative response. *See* Note, *Federal Courts — Certification Before Facial Invalidation: A Return to Federalism*, 12 W. NEW ENG. L. REV. 217 (1990). Most States have adopted certification procedures. *See generally* 17A Wright, Miller, & Cooper, *supra*, §4248. Through certification of novel or unsettled questions of state law for authoritative answers by a State's highest court, a federal court may save "time, energy, and resources and hel[p] build a cooperative judicial federalism." *Lehman Brothers v. Schein* (1974).

The following recent case — in which a police officer sued a leader in the Black Lives Matters movement for injuries the officer sustained during a protest — is illustrative of this certification procedure.

Mckesson v. Doe

141 S. Ct. 48 (2020)

PER CURIAM.

Petitioner DeRay Mckesson organized a demonstration in Baton Rouge, Louisiana, to protest a shooting by a local police officer. The protesters, allegedly at Mckesson's direction, occupied the highway in front of the police headquarters. As officers began making arrests to clear the highway, an unknown individual threw a "piece of concrete or a similar rock-like object," striking respondent Officer Doe in the face. Officer Doe suffered devastating injuries in the line of duty, including loss of teeth and brain trauma.

---

14. Martha A. Field, *The Abstention Doctrine Today*, 125 U. PA. L. REV. 590, 592 (1977).

Though the culprit remains unidentified, Officer Doe sought to recover damages from Mckesson on the theory that he negligently staged the protest in a manner that caused the assault. The District Court dismissed the negligence claim as barred by the First Amendment. A divided panel of the Court of Appeals for the Fifth Circuit reversed. As the Fifth Circuit recognized at the outset, Louisiana law generally imposes no "duty to protect others from the criminal activities of third persons." But the panel majority held that a jury could plausibly find that Mckesson breached his "duty not to negligently precipitate the crime of a third party" because "a violent confrontation with a police officer was a foreseeable effect of negligently directing a protest" onto the highway. The dissent would have demanded something more—a "special relationship" between Mckesson and Officer Doe—before recognizing such a duty under Louisiana law. The dissent likewise doubted that an intentional assault is the "particular risk" for which Officer Doe could recover for a breach of "Louisiana's prohibitions on highway-blocking," which "have as their focus the protection of other motorists."

The panel majority also rejected Mckesson's argument that *NAACP v. Claiborne Hardware Co.* (1982), forbids liability for speech-related activity that negligently causes a violent act unless the defendant specifically intended that the violent act would result. According to the Fifth Circuit, the First Amendment imposes no barrier to tort liability so long as the rock-throwing incident was "one of the 'consequences' of 'tortious activity,' which itself was 'authorized, directed, or ratified' by Mckesson in violation of his duty of care." Because Mckesson allegedly directed an unlawful obstruction of a highway, *see* La. Rev. Stat. Ann. §14:97 (West 2018), the Fifth Circuit held that the First Amendment did not shield him from liability for the downstream consequences. Again, the dissent disagreed, deeming the "novel 'negligent protest' theory of liability" to be "incompatible with the First Amendment and foreclosed—squarely—by" *Claiborne Hardware.*

The question presented for our review is whether the theory of personal liability adopted by the Fifth Circuit violates the First Amendment. Mckesson contends that his role in leading the protest onto the highway, even if negligent and punishable as a misdemeanor, cannot make him personally liable for the violent act of an individual whose only association with him was attendance at the protest. We think that the Fifth Circuit's interpretation of state law is too uncertain a premise on which to address the question presented. The constitutional issue, though undeniably important, is implicated only if Louisiana law permits recovery under these circumstances in the first place. The dispute thus could be "greatly simplifie[d]" by guidance from the Louisiana Supreme Court on the meaning of Louisiana law.

Fortunately, the Rules of the Louisiana Supreme Court, like the rules of 47 other States, provide an opportunity to obtain such guidance. In the absence of "clear controlling precedents in the decisions of the" Louisiana Supreme Court, those Rules specify that the federal courts of appeals may certify dispositive questions of Louisiana law on their own accord or on motion of a party. La. Sup. Ct. Rule 12, §§1-2 (2019).

Certification is by no means "obligatory" merely because state law is unsettled; the choice instead rests in the sound discretion of the federal court. Our system of "cooperative judicial federalism" presumes federal and state courts alike are competent to apply federal and state law. In exceptional instances, however, certification is advisable before addressing a constitutional issue.

Two aspects of this case, taken together, persuade us that the Court of Appeals should have certified to the Louisiana Supreme Court the questions (1) whether Mckesson could have breached a duty of care in organizing and leading the protest and (2) whether Officer Doe has alleged a particular risk within the scope of protection afforded by the duty, provided one exists. First, the dispute presents novel issues of state law peculiarly calling for the exercise of judgment by the state courts. To impose a duty under Louisiana law, courts must consider various moral, social, and economic factors, among them the fairness of imposing liability, the historical development of precedent, and the direction in which society and its institutions are evolving. Speculation by a federal court about how a state court would weigh, for instance, the moral value of protest against the economic consequences of withholding liability "is particularly gratuitous when the state courts stand willing to address questions of state law on certification." *Arizonans for Official English v. Arizona* (1997)

Second, certification would ensure that any conflict in this case between state law and the First Amendment is not purely hypothetical. The novelty of the claim at issue here only underscores that "[w]arnings against premature adjudication of constitutional questions bear heightened attention when a federal court is asked to invalidate a State's law."

We therefore grant the petition for writ of certiorari, vacate the judgment of the United States Court of Appeals for the Fifth Circuit, and remand the case to that court for further proceedings consistent with this opinion.

* * *

2. Unclear State Law and Diversity Jurisdiction

Because federal courts apply state law in diversity jurisdiction suits, they sometimes encounter state law questions that are unresolved or unclear. Should federal courts refrain from hearing those cases, leaving unresolved questions to state courts? In *Meredith v. Winter Haven* (1943), the Supreme Court rejected the position that federal courts should abstain from hearing a case merely because state law was unclear. In that case, bondholders filed suit in federal court against a city, arguing that under state law, the city had illegally failed to pay them interest. Although Florida law was unclear as to whether the city owed the bondholders, the Court ruled that abstention would be inappropriate. The Court reasoned, "Congress having adopted the policy of opening the federal courts to suitors in all diversity cases involving the jurisdictional amount, we can discern in its action no recognition of a policy which would exclude cases from the jurisdiction merely because they involve state law or because the law is uncertain or difficult to determine."

In the case that follows, *Louisiana Power & Light Company v. City of Thibodaux* (1959), the Court nonetheless held that federal courts should abstain from addressing unclear questions of state law that implicate a state's sovereign prerogatives.

Louisiana Power & Light Co. v. City of Thibodaux

360 U.S. 25 (1959)

Mr. Justice FRANKFURTER delivered the opinion of the Court.

The City of Thibodaux, Louisiana, filed a petition for expropriation in one of the Louisiana District Courts, asserting a taking of the land, buildings, and equipment of petitioner Power and Light Company. Petitioner, a Florida corporation, removed the case to the United States District Court for the Eastern District of Louisiana on the basis of diversity of citizenship. After a pre-trial conference in which various aspects of the case were discussed, the district judge, on his own motion, ordered that "[f]urther proceedings herein, therefore, will be stayed until the Supreme Court of Louisiana has been afforded an opportunity to interpret Act 111 of 1900 (LSA—R.S. 19:101 et seq.)," the authority on which the city's expropriation order was based. The Court of Appeals for the Fifth Circuit reversed, holding that the procedure adopted by the district judge was not available in an expropriation proceeding, and that in any event no exceptional circumstances were present to justify the procedure even if available. We granted certiorari because of the importance of the question in the judicial enforcement of the power of eminent domain under diversity jurisdiction.

In connection with the first decision in which a closely divided Court considered and upheld jurisdiction over an eminent domain proceeding removed to the federal courts on the basis of diversity of citizenship, *Madisonville Traction Co. v. St. Bernard Mining Co.* (1905), Mr. Justice Holmes made the following observation: "The fundamental fact is that eminent domain is a prerogative of the state, which on the one hand, may be exercised in any way that the state thinks fit, and, on the other, may not be exercised except by an authority which the state confers."

While this was said in the dissenting opinion, the distinction between expropriation proceedings and ordinary diversity cases, though found insufficient to restrict diversity jurisdiction, remains a relevant and important consideration in the appropriate judicial administration of such actions in the federal courts. We have increasingly recognized the wisdom of staying actions in the federal courts pending determination by a state court of decisive issues of state law. *Railroad Commission of Texas v. Pullman Co.* (1941). On the other hand, we have held that the mere difficulty of state law does not justify a federal court's relinquishment of jurisdiction in favor of state court action. *Meredith v. City of Winter City of Chicago v. Fieldcrest Dairies* (1943).

These prior cases have been cases in equity, but they did not apply a technical rule of equity procedure. They reflect a deeper policy derived from our federalism. We have drawn upon the judicial discretion of the chancellor to decline jurisdiction over a part or all of a case brought before him. Although an eminent domain proceeding is deemed for certain purposes of legal classification a "suit at common law," it is of a special and peculiar nature. It is intimately involved with sovereign prerogative. And when, as here, a city's power to condemn is challenged, a further aspect of sovereignty is introduced. A determination of the nature and extent of delegation of the power of eminent domain concerns the apportionment of governmental powers between City and State. The issues normally turn on legislation with much local variation interpreted in local settings.

The special nature of eminent domain justifies a district judge, when his familiarity with the problems of local law so counsels him, to ascertain the meaning of a disputed state statute from the only tribunal empowered to speak definitively—the courts of the State under whose statute eminent domain is sought to be exercised—rather than himself make a dubious and tentative forecast. This course does not constitute abnegation of judicial duty. On the contrary, it is a wise and productive discharge of it. There is only postponement of decision for its best fruition. Eventually the District Court will award compensation if the taking is sustained. If for some reason a declaratory judgment is not promptly sought from the state courts and obtained within a reasonable time, the District Court, having retained complete control of the litigation, will doubtless assert it to decide also the question of the meaning of the state statute. The justification for this power, to be exercised within the indicated limits, lies in regard for the respective competence of the state and federal court systems and for the maintenance of harmonious federal-state relations in a matter close to the political interests of a State.

It would imply an unworthy conception of the federal judiciary to give weight to the suggestion that acknowledgment of this power will tempt some otiose or timid judge to shuffle off responsibility. Such apprehension implies a lack of discipline and of disinterestedness on the part of the lower courts, hardly a worthy or wise basis for fashioning rules of procedure. Procedures for effective judicial administration presuppose a federal judiciary composed of judges well-equipped and of sturdy character in whom may safely be vested, as is already, a wide range of judicial discretion, subject to appropriate review on appeal.

In light of these considerations, the immediate situation quickly falls into place. In providing on his own motion for a stay in this case, an experienced district judge was responding in a sensible way to a quandary about the power of the City of Thibodaux into which he was placed by an opinion of the Attorney General of Louisiana in which it was concluded that in a strikingly similar case a Louisiana city did not have the power here claimed by the City. A Louisiana statute apparently seems to grant such a power. But that statute has never been interpreted, in respect to a situation like that before the judge, by the Louisiana courts and it would not be the first time that the authoritative tribunal has found in a statute less than meets the outsider's eye. Informed local courts may find meaning not discernible to the outsider. The consequence of allowing this to come to pass would be that this case would be the only case in which the Louisiana statute is construed as we would construe it, whereas the rights of all other litigants would be thereafter governed by a decision of the Supreme Court of Louisiana quite different from ours.

Caught between the language of an old but uninterpreted statute and the pronouncement of the Attorney General of Louisiana, the district judge determined to solve his conscientious perplexity by directing utilization of the legal resources of Louisiana for a prompt ascertainment of meaning through the only tribunal whose interpretation could be controlling—the Supreme Court of Louisiana. The District Court was thus exercising a fair and well-considered judicial discretion in staying proceedings pending the institution of a declaratory judgment action and subsequent decision by the Supreme Court of Louisiana.

Mr. Justice BRENNAN, with whom THE CHIEF JUSTICE and Mr. Justice DOUGLAS join, dissenting.

Until today, the standards for testing this order of the District Court sending the parties to this diversity action to a state court for decision of a state law question might have been said to have been reasonably consistent with the imperative duty of a District Court, imposed by Congress under 28 U.S.C. §1332, 28 U.S.C. §1441, and 28 U.S.C. §1332, to render prompt justice in cases between citizens of different States. To order these suitors out of the federal court and into a state court in the circumstances of this case passes beyond disrespect for the diversity jurisdiction to plain disregard of this imperative duty. The doctrine of abstention, in proper perspective, is an extraordinary and narrow exception to this duty, and abdication of the obligation to decide cases can be justified under this doctrine only in the exceptional circumstances where the order to the parties to repair to the state court would clearly serve one of two important countervailing interests: either the avoidance of a premature and perhaps unnecessary decision of a serious federal constitutional question, or the avoidance of the hazard of unsettling some delicate balance in the area of federal-state relationships.

These exceptional circumstances provided until now a very narrow corridor through which a District Court could escape from its obligation to decide state law questions when federal jurisdiction was properly invoked. The doctrine of abstention originated in the area of the federal courts' duty to avoid, if possible, decision of a federal constitutional question. This was *Railroad Commission of Texas v. Pullman Co.* (1941). There this Court held that the District Court should have stayed its hand while state issues were resolved in a state court when an injunction was sought to restrain the enforcement of the order of a state administrative body on the ground that the order was not authorized by the state law and was violative of the Federal Constitution. The Court reasoned that if the state courts held that the order was not authorized under state law there could be avoided "the friction of a premature constitutional adjudication." Abstention has also been sanctioned on grounds of comity with the States—to avoid a result in "needless friction with state policies." *Pullman.* Thus, this Court has upheld an abstention when the exercise by the federal court of jurisdiction would disrupt a state administrative process, *Burford v. Sun Oil Co.* (1943).

But neither of the two recognized situations justifying abstention is present in the case before us. The Court therefore turns the holding on the purported existence of the other situation justifying abstention, stating the bald conclusion that: "The considerations that prevailed in conventional equity suits for avoiding the hazards of serious disruption by federal courts of state government or needless friction between state and federal authorities are similarly appropriate in a state eminent domain proceeding brought in, or removed to, a federal court." But the fact of the matter is that this case does not involve the slightest hazard of friction with a State, the indispensable ingredient for upholding abstention on grounds of comity, and one which has been present in all of the prior cases in which abstention has been approved by this Court on that ground. First of all, the District Court has not been asked to grant injunctive relief which would prohibit state officials from acting. Secondly, this case does not involve the potential friction that results when a federal court applies paramount federal law to strike down state action. Far from disrupting state policy, the District Court would be applying state policy, as embodied in the state statute, to the facts of this case. There is no more possibility of conflict with the State in this situation than there is in the ordinary negligence or contract case in which a District Court applies state law under its diversity jurisdiction. A decision by the District Court in this case would not interfere with Louisiana administrative processes, prohibit the collection of state taxes, or otherwise frustrate the execution of state domestic policies. Quite the reverse, this action is part of the process which the City must follow in order to carry out the State's policy of expropriating private property for public uses. Finally, in this case the State of Louisiana, represented by its constituent organ the City of Thibodaux, urges the District Court to adjudicate the state law issue. How, conceivably, can the Court justify the abdication of responsibility to exercise jurisdiction on the ground of avoiding interference and conflict with the State when the State itself desires the federal court's adjudication? It is obvious that the abstention in this case was for the convenience of the District Court, not for the State. The Court forgets, in upholding this abstention, that "The diversity jurisdiction was not conferred for the benefit of the federal courts or to serve their convenience." *Meredith v. City of Winter Haven* (1943).

The Court of Appeals, in my view, correctly considered, in reversing the action of the District Court, that there is not shown a semblance of a countervailing interest which meets the standards permitting abstention.

[T]he interpretation of Act 111, presents a difficult question of state law. It is true that there are no Louisiana decisions interpreting Act 111, and that there is a confusing opinion of the State's Attorney General on the question. But mere difficulty of construing the state statute is not justification for running away from the task. "Questions may occur which we would gladly avoid; but we cannot avoid them. All we can do is, to exercise our best judgment, and conscientiously to perform our duty." *Cohens v. Commonwealth of Virginia* (1821). When exceptional circumstances are not present, denial of that opportunity by the federal courts merely because the answers to the questions of state law are difficult or uncertain or have not yet been given by the highest court of the state, would thwart the purpose of the jurisdictional act.

The possible reason explaining the Court's holding is that it reflects is distaste for the diversity jurisdiction. But distaste for diversity jurisdiction certainly cannot be reason to license district judges to retreat from their responsibility. The roots of that jurisdiction are inextricably intertwined with the roots of our federal system. They stem from Art. III, sec. 2 of the Constitution and the first Judiciary Act, the Act of 1789, 1 Stat. 73, 78.5 I concede the liveliness of the controversy over the utility or desirability of diversity jurisdiction, but it has stubbornly outlasted the many and persistent attacks against it and the attempts in the Congress to curtail or eliminate it. Until Congress speaks otherwise, the federal judiciary has no choice but conscientiously to render justice for litigants from different States entitled to have their controversies adjudicated in the federal courts.

One must regret that this Court's departure from the long-settled criteria governing abstention should so richly fertilize the Power and Light Company's strategy of delay which now has succeeded, I dare say, past the fondest expectation of counsel who conceived it. It is especially unfortunate in that departure from these criteria fashions an opening wedge for District Courts to refer hard cases of state law to state courts in even the routine diversity negligence and contract actions.

* * *

The same day that the Court decided *Thibodaux*, it also decided *County of Allegheny v. Frank Mashuda Company* (1959). The case bears factual resemblance to *Thibodaux*. The County of Allegheny, Pennsylvania filed action in state court, seeking to condemn land to build an airport. While that proceeding was ongoing, landowners sued in federal district court, arguing that the taking violated state law because it was being taken for private use. The district court dismissed the suit on the ground that it interfered with state sovereignty. Notably, the Supreme Court disagreed, finding that dismissal was not warranted in this circumstance. Unlike in *Thibodaux*, the state law at issue in *Mashuda* was not unclear.

3.   Unclear State Law and Complex Regulatory Schemes

Under the doctrine of *Burford* abstention, when timely and adequate state-court review is available, a federal court sitting in equity must abstain from interfering with "the proceedings or orders of state administrative agencies: (1) when there are difficult questions of state law bearing on policy problems of substantial public import whose importance transcends the result in the case then at bar; or (2) where the exercise of federal review of the question in a case and in similar cases would be disruptive of state efforts to establish a coherent policy with respect to a matter of substantial public concern." *New Orleans Pub. Serv., Inc. v. Council of City of New Orleans* (1989) (*NOPSI*). See *Burford v. Sun Oil Co.*, 319 U.S. 315 (1943).

In *Burford*, a federal district court considered a Fourteenth Amendment equitable challenge to the Texas Railroad Commission's grant of an oil drilling permit. The State of Texas had constructed a system of judicial review of commission orders in state court. The Supreme Court found the state courts' review of the Commission's decisions was "expeditious and adequate." Moreover, federal courts' subject-matter expertise was no match for state courts, which had required specialized knowledge regarding the adequacy of oil drilling permits. Federal-court review had repeatedly prompted "[d]elay, misunderstanding of local law, and needless federal conflict with the state policy." The Court therefore concluded that "a sound respect for the independence of state action requir[ed] the federal equity court to stay its hand."

The following case offers an important description of *Burford* abstention, and it limits, reaffirming that abstention should represent a narrow, carefully circumscribed exception the rule that federal courts must exercise jurisdiction that the Constitution and Congress has conferred.

New Orleans Pub. Serv., Inc. v. Council of City of New Orleans

491 U.S. 350 (1989)

Justice SCALIA delivered the opinion of the Court.

In *Nantahala Power & Light Co. v. Thornburg* (1986), we held that for purposes of setting intrastate retail rates a State may not differ from the Federal Energy Regulatory Commission's allocations of wholesale power by imposing its own judgment of what would be just and reasonable. Last Term, in *Mississippi Power & Light Co. v. Mississippi ex rel. Moore* (1988), we held that FERC's allocation of the $3 billion-plus cost of the Grand Gulf 1 nuclear reactor among the operating companies that jointly agreed to finance its construction and operation pre-empted Mississippi's inquiry into the prudence of a utility retailer's decision to participate in the joint venture. Today we confront once again a legal issue arising from the question of who must pay for Grand Gulf 1. Here the state ratemaking authority deferred to FERC's implicit finding that New Orleans Public Service, Inc.'s decision to participate in the Grand Gulf venture was reasonable, but determined that the costs incurred thereby should not be completely reimbursed because, it asserted, the utility's management was negligent in failing later to diversify its supply portfolio by selling a portion of its Grand Gulf power. [Today], we address the threshold question whether the District Court, which the utility petitioned for declaratory and injunctive relief from the state ratemaking authority's order, properly abstained from exercising jurisdiction in deference to the state review process.

I

Because the abstention questions at stake here have little to do with the intricacies of the factual and procedural history underlying the controversy, we may sketch the background of this case in brief. Petitioner New Orleans Public Service, Inc. (NOPSI), [is] a producer, wholesaler, and retailer of electricity that provides retail electrical service to the city of New Orleans. In 1974, NOPSI and its fellow operating companies entered a contract to finance construction and operation of two nuclear reactors, Grand Gulf 1 and 2, in return for the right to the reactors' electrical output.

During the late 1970's, consumer demand turned out to be far lower than expected, and regulatory delays, enhanced construction requirements, and high inflation led to spiraling costs. Acting pursuant to its exclusive regulatory authority over interstate wholesale power transactions, FERC conducted extensive proceedings to determine "just and reasonable" rates for Grand Gulf 1 power and to prescribe a "just, reasonable, and nondiscriminatory" allocation of Grand Gulf's costs and output. In June 1985, the Commission issued a final order [outlining this allocation].

When NOPSI sought from the New Orleans City Council (Council) — the local ratemaking body with final authority over the utility's retail rates, a rate increase to cover the increase in wholesale rates resulting from FERC's allocation of Grand Gulf costs, the Council denied an immediate rate adjustment, explaining that a public hearing was necessary. NOPSI responded by filing an action for injunctive and declaratory relief in the United States District Court for the Eastern District of Louisiana, asserting that federal law required the Council to allow it to recover, through an increase in retail rates, its FERC-allocated share of the Grand Gulf expenses.

The District Court granted the Council's motion to dismiss, holding that it had no jurisdiction to entertain the action, and that even if it had jurisdiction it would be compelled by *Burford v. Sun Oil Co* (1943) to abstain. On appeal, the Fifth Circuit held that abstention was proper both under *Burford* and under *Younger v. Harris* (1971).

II

From *Burford v. Sun Oil Co.*, we have distilled the principle now commonly referred to as the "*Burford* doctrine." Where timely and adequate state-court review is available, a federal court sitting in equity must decline to interfere with the proceedings or orders of state administrative agencies: (1) when there are "difficult questions of state law bearing on policy problems of substantial public import whose importance transcends the result in the case then at bar"; or (2) where the "exercise of federal review of the question in a case and in similar cases would be disruptive of state efforts to establish a coherent policy with respect to a matter of substantial public concern." *Colorado River Water Conservation Dist. v. United States* (1976).

The present case does not involve a state-law claim, nor even an assertion that the federal claims are "in any way entangled in a skein of state-law that must be untangled before the federal case can proceed," *McNeese v. Board of Education Community Unit School Dist. 187, Cahokia* (1963). The Fifth Circuit acknowledged as much in NOPSI I, but found "the absence of a state law claim . . . not fatal" because, it thought, "[t]he motivating force behind *Burford* abstention is . . . a reluctance to intrude into state proceedings where there exists a complex state regulatory system." Finding that this case involved a complex regulatory scheme of "paramount local concern and a matter which demands local administrative expertise," it held that the District Court appropriately applied *Burford*.

While *Burford* is concerned with protecting complex state administrative processes from undue federal interference, it does not require abstention whenever there exists such a process, or even in all cases where there is a "potential for conflict" with state regulatory law or policy. *Colorado River Water Conservation Dist.* (1976). Here, NOPSI's primary claim is that the Council is prohibited by federal law from refusing to provide reimbursement for FERC-allocated wholesale costs. Unlike a claim that a state agency has misapplied its lawful authority or has failed to take into consideration or properly weigh relevant state-law factors, federal adjudication of this sort of pre-emption claim would not disrupt the State's attempt to ensure uniformity in the treatment of an "essentially local problem."

In the case at bar, no inquiry beyond the four corners of the Council's retail rate order is needed to determine whether it is facially pre-empted by FERC's allocative decree and relevant provisions of the Federal Power Act. Such an inquiry would not unduly intrude into the processes of state government or undermine the State's ability to maintain desired uniformity. It may, of course, result in an injunction against enforcement of the rate order, but "there is . . . no doctrine requiring abstention merely because resolution of a federal question may result in the overturning of a state policy." *Zablocki v. Redhail* (1978).

The principles underlying Burford are therefore not implicated.

* * *

4.   *Parallel Civil Proceedings*

There are many ways in which the same matter might come to be simultaneously litigated in both state and federal court. For example, a defendant sued in state court who cannot remove the case might choose to file his or her own action in federal court against the state court plaintiff when there is diversity of citizenship. Or a plaintiff might to gain a strategic advantage file the same action against the same defendant in a federal and a state court when the latter cannot be removed to federal court. These are just two of many examples of how the same matter can come to be litigated in both state and federal courts at the same time, something that occurs more frequently than it might seem.

When duplicate litigation emerges in federal and state court, should federal courts abstain? As a general rule, the mere fact that a case is pending in one jurisdiction does not defeat jurisdiction in federal court. There are exceptions to this general rule, however. One exception is real property; the court that first exercises jurisdiction over a matter concerning real property has exclusive jurisdiction. *Donovan v. City of Dallas* (1964). Additionally, in the case that follows, *Colorado River Water Conservation District v. United States* (1976), the Court describes other "exceptional" circumstances in which abstention is appropriate to avoid duplicative litigation, despite "the virtually unflagging obligation of the federal courts to exercise the jurisdiction given them."

Contextually, the *Colorado River* case is a dispute about water rights and access. Because fresh water is a scare resource in parts of the western United States, legal and political disputes have erupted as to how that water is to be allocated.[15] Western states traditionally have followed a prior appropriation doctrine under which the first party who removes water from a stream for beneficial use gets a senior right that gives its holder priority over junior rights holders when water is scarce and insufficient to fulfill the claims of all users. And water in the West is scarce, increasingly so today. Thus, the legal and political controversies over water rights are often particularly pronounced in the West, including with respect to water rights linked to land reserved for Native nations.[16] In *Colorado River*, due to disputes about water allocation in Colorado, the United States commenced two suits: one in state court to litigate some federal water rights and a second in federal court as trustee for multiple Native nations. Among the legal issues was whether the federal court should abstain in light of the ongoing state litigation.

One might think that water rights disputes are governed solely by state law. To the contrary, federal law plays an important role. The *Colorado River* case arose at the intersection of several doctrines of federal law. First, under the reserved rights doctrine of *Winters v. United States* (1908) and subsequent cases, the reservation of land for particular purposes, such as the creation of a reservation for a Native nation, implies the reservation of rights to an amount of water to accomplish the purposes of the reservation. As the Court asked rhetorically in *Winters*, "The Indians had command of the lands and the waters—command of all their beneficial use, whether kept for hunting, 'and grazing roving herds of stock,' or turned to agriculture and the arts of civilization. Did they give up all this?" The *Winters* doctrine

---

15. John Shurts, INDIAN RESERVED WATER RIGHTS: THE WINTERS DOCTRINE IN ITS SOCIAL AND LEGAL CONTEXT (2000).

16. *See also* Margaret Redsteer, et al., *Unique Challenges Facing Southwestern Tribes, in* ASSESSMENT OF CLIMATE CHANGE IN THE SOUTHWEST UNITED STATES (Greg Garfin et al. eds., 2013) ("Tribal water resources on arid reservations are typically marginal and highly susceptible to frequent water shortages.").

has been applied liberally to reserve water rights to meet the present and future needs of Native nations. Because they are secured under preemptive federal law, *Winters* rights take precedence over contrary state law. Thus, the creation of a reservation entails the reservation of federally-protected water rights for Native nations that may trump water rights claims by non-Natives under state law. Second, as in *Winters* itself, the United States government may sue to protect reserved rights as a trustee for Native nations. The U.S.'s trustee status stems from the unique government-to-government relationship between Native nations and the federal government.[17] More generally, federal law has largely excluded the states from matters of Indian affairs, especially when it comes to the regulation of Native nations. Third, in the McCarran Amendment of 1952, Congress authorized state courts to hear water disputes that involve federal water rights. That amendment also waived federal sovereign immunity for certain water disputes. Consider the Supreme Court's analysis of federal abstention in *Colorado River* against this backdrop of *Winters* rights and the unique relationship between Native nations and the United States, which the dissenting opinion highlights.

Colorado River Water Conservation Dist. v. United States

424 U.S. 800 (1976)

Justice BRENNAN delivered the opinion of the Court.

[I]

It is probable that no problem of the Southwest section of the Nation is more critical than that of scarcity of water. As southwestern populations have grown, conflicting claims to this scarce resource have increased. To meet these claims, several Southwestern States have established elaborate procedures for allocation of water and adjudication of conflicting claims to that resource. In 1969, Colorado enacted its Water Rights Determination and Administration Act in an effort to revamp its legal procedures for determining claims to water within the State.

Under the Colorado Act, the State is divided into seven Water Divisions, each Division encompassing one or more entire drainage basins for the larger rivers in Colorado. Adjudication of water claims within each Division occurs on a continuous basis. Each month, Water Referees in each Division rule on applications for water rights filed within the preceding five months or refer those applications to the Water Judge of their Division. Every six months, the Water Judge passes on referred applications and contested decisions by Referees. A State Engineer and engineers for each Division are responsible for the administration and distribution of the waters of the State according to the determinations in each Division.

Colorado applies the doctrine of prior appropriation in establishing rights to the use of water. Under that doctrine, one acquires a right to water by diverting it

---

17. COHEN'S HANDBOOK OF FEDERAL INDIAN LAW §19.03; Barbara Cosens & Judith V. Royster, eds., THE FUTURE OF INDIAN AND FEDERAL RESERVED WATER RIGHTS, THE *WINTERS* CENTENNIAL (2012).

from its natural source and applying it to some beneficial use. Continued beneficial use of the water is required in order to maintain the right. In periods of shortage, priority among confirmed rights is determined according to the date of initial diversion.

The reserved rights of the United States extend to Indian reservations, *Winters v. United States* (1908), and other federal lands, such as national parks and forests. The reserved rights claimed by the United States in this case affect waters within Colorado Water Division No. 7. On November 14, 1972, the Government instituted this suit in the United States District Court for the District of Colorado. The District Court is located in Denver, some 300 miles from Division 7. The suit, against some 1,000 water users, sought declaration of the Government's rights to waters in certain rivers and their tributaries located in Division 7. In the suit, the Government asserted reserved rights on its own behalf and on behalf of certain Indian tribes, as well as rights based on state law. It sought appointment of a water master to administer any waters decreed to the United States.

Shortly after the federal suit was commenced, one of the defendants in that suit filed an application in the state court for Division 7, seeking an order directing service of process on the United States in order to make it a party to proceedings in Division 7 for the purpose of adjudicating all of the Government's claims, both state and federal. On January 3, 1973, the United States was served.

[The district court dismissed the case], stating that the doctrine of abstention required deference to the [state court] proceedings. On appeal, the Court of Appeals for the Tenth Circuit reversed, holding that abstention was inappropriate.

[II]

We consider whether the District Court's dismissal was appropriate under the doctrine of abstention. We hold that the dismissal cannot be supported under that doctrine in any of its forms.

Abstention from the exercise of federal jurisdiction is the exception, not the rule. "The doctrine of abstention, under which a District Court may decline to exercise or postpone the exercise of its jurisdiction, is an extraordinary and narrow exception to the duty of a District Court to adjudicate a controversy properly before it. Abdication of the obligation to decide cases can be justified under this doctrine only in the exceptional circumstances where the order to the parties to repair to the state court would clearly serve an important countervailing interest." *County of Allegheny v. Frank Mashuda Co.* (1959). It was never a doctrine of equity that a federal court should exercise its judicial discretion to dismiss a suit merely because a State court could entertain it. Our decisions have confined the circumstances appropriate for abstention to three general categories.

(a) Abstention is appropriate in cases presenting a federal constitutional issue which might be mooted or presented in a different posture by a state court determination of pertinent state law. *See, e. g., Railroad Comm'n of Texas v. Pullman Co.* (1941). This case, however, presents no federal constitutional issue for decision.

(b) Abstention is also appropriate where there have been presented difficult questions of state law bearing on policy problems of substantial public import whose importance transcends the result in the case then at bar. *Louisiana Power & Light Co. v. City of Thibodaux* (1959), for example, involved such a question. In particular, the concern there was with the scope of the eminent domain power of municipalities under state law. In some cases, however, the state question itself need not be determinative of state policy. It is enough that exercise of federal review of the question in a case and in similar cases would be disruptive of state efforts to establish a coherent policy with respect to a matter of substantial public concern. *Burford v. Sun Oil Co.* (1943).

The present case clearly does not fall within this second category of abstention. While state claims are involved in the case, the state law to be applied appears to be settled. No questions bearing on state policy are presented for decision. Nor will decision of the state claims impair efforts to implement state policy as in Burford. To be sure, the federal claims that are involved in the case go to the establishment of water rights which may conflict with similar rights based on state law. But the mere potential for conflict in the results of adjudications, does not, without more, warrant staying exercise of federal jurisdiction. *See Meredith v. Winter Haven* (1943). The potential conflict here, involving state claims and federal claims, would not be such as to impair impermissibly the State's effort to effect its policy respecting the allocation of state waters. Nor would exercise of federal jurisdiction here interrupt any such efforts by restraining the exercise of authority vested in state officers.

(c) Finally, abstention is appropriate where, absent bad faith, harassment, or a patently invalid state statute, federal jurisdiction has been invoked for the purpose of restraining state criminal proceedings, *Younger v. Harris* (1971). Like the previous two categories, this category also does not include this case.

[III]

Although this case falls within none of the abstention categories, there are principles unrelated to considerations of proper constitutional adjudication and regard for federal-state relations which govern in situations involving the contemporaneous exercise of concurrent jurisdictions, either by federal courts or by state and federal courts. These principles rest on considerations of wise judicial administration, giving regard to conservation of judicial resources and comprehensive disposition of litigation. Generally, as between state and federal courts, the rule is that "the pendency of an action in the state court is no bar to proceedings concerning the same matter in the Federal court having jurisdiction. As between federal district courts, however, though no precise rule has evolved, the general principle is to avoid duplicative litigation. *See Kerotest Mfg. Co. v. C-O-Two Fire Equipment Co.* (1952). This difference in general approach between state-federal concurrent jurisdiction and wholly federal concurrent jurisdiction stems from the virtually unflagging obligation of the federal courts to exercise the jurisdiction given them. *Cohens v. Virginia* (1821) (dictum). Given this obligation, and the absence of weightier considerations of constitutional adjudication and state-federal relations, the circumstances permitting the dismissal of a federal suit due to the presence of a concurrent state proceeding for reasons of wise judicial administration are considerably more limited than the circumstances appropriate for abstention. The former circumstances, though exceptional, do nevertheless exist.

It has been held, for example, that the court first assuming jurisdiction over property may exercise that jurisdiction to the exclusion of other courts. *See, e.g., Princess Lida v. Thompson* (1939). In assessing the appropriateness of dismissal in the event of an exercise of concurrent jurisdiction, a federal court may also consider such factors as the inconvenience of the federal forum; the desirability of avoiding piecemeal litigation; and the order in which jurisdiction was obtained by the concurrent forums. No one factor is necessarily determinative; a carefully considered judgment taking into account both the obligation to exercise jurisdiction and the combination of factors counselling against that exercise is required. Only the clearest of justifications will warrant dismissal.

Turning to the present case, a number of factors clearly counsel against concurrent federal proceedings. The most important of these is the McCarran Amendment. [The McCarran Amendment, 43 U.S.C. §666, provides that "consent is hereby given to join the United States as a defendant in any suit (1) for the adjudication of rights to the use of water of a river system or other source, or (2) for the administration of such rights, where it appears that the United States is the owner of or is in the process of acquiring water rights by appropriation under State law, by purchase, by exchange, or otherwise, and the United States is a necessary party to such suit."]. The clear federal policy evinced by that legislation is the avoidance of piecemeal adjudication of water rights in a river system. This policy is akin to that underlying the rule requiring that jurisdiction be yielded to the court first acquiring control of property, for the concern in such instances is with avoiding the generation of additional litigation through permitting inconsistent dispositions of property. This concern is heightened with respect to water rights, the relationships among which are highly interdependent. Indeed, we have recognized that actions seeking the allocation of water essentially involve the disposition of property and are best conducted in unified proceedings. The consent to jurisdiction given by the McCarran Amendment bespeaks a policy that recognizes the availability of comprehensive state systems for adjudication of water rights as the means for achieving these goals.

As has already been observed, the Colorado Water Rights Determination and Administration Act established such a system for the adjudication and management of rights to the use of the State's waters. As the Government concedes, the Act established a single continuous proceeding for water rights adjudication which antedated the suit in District Court. That proceeding "reaches all claims, perhaps month by month but inclusively in the totality." *Ibid.* Additionally, the responsibility of managing the State's waters, to the end that they be allocated in accordance with adjudicated water rights, is given to the State Engineer.

Beyond the congressional policy expressed by the McCarran Amendment and consistent with furtherance of that policy, we also find significant (a) the apparent absence of any proceedings in the District Court, other than the filing of the complaint, prior to the motion to dismiss, (b) the extensive involvement of state water rights occasioned by this suit naming 1,000 defendants, (c) the 300-mile distance between the District Court in Denver and the court in Division 7, and (d) the existing participation by the Government in [similar suits in Colorado state courts].

We emphasize, however, that we do not overlook the heavy obligation to exercise jurisdiction. We need not decide, for example, whether, despite the McCarran Amendment, dismissal would be warranted if more extensive proceedings had occurred in the District Court prior to dismissal, if the involvement of state water rights were less extensive than it is here, or if the state proceeding were in some respect inadequate to resolve the federal claims. But the opposing factors here, particularly the policy underlying the McCarran Amendment, justify the District Court's dismissal in this particular case.

Mr. Justice STEWARD, with whom Mr. Justice BLACKMUN and Mr. Justice STEVENS concur, dissenting.

The Court says that the United States District Court for the District of Colorado clearly had jurisdiction over this lawsuit. I agree. The Court further says that the McCarran Amendment "in no way diminished" the District Court's jurisdiction. I agree. The Court also says that federal courts have a "virtually unflagging obligation . . . to exercise the jurisdiction given them." I agree. And finally, the Court says that nothing in the abstention doctrine "in any of its forms" justified the District Court's dismissal of the Government's complaint. I agree. These views would seem to lead ineluctably to the conclusion that the District Court was wrong in dismissing the complaint. Yet the Court holds that the order of dismissal was "appropriate." With that conclusion I must respectfully disagree.

In holding that the United States shall not be allowed to proceed with its lawsuit, the Court relies principally on cases reflecting the rule that where "control of the property which is the subject of the suit (is necessary) in order to proceed with the cause and to grant the relief sought, the jurisdiction of one court must of necessity yield to that of the other." But this rule applies only when exclusive control over the subject matter is necessary to effectuate a court's judgment. Here the federal court did not need to obtain In rem or Quasi in rem jurisdiction in order to decide the issues before it. The court was asked simply to determine as a matter of federal law whether federal reservations of water rights had occurred, and, if so, the date and scope of the reservations. The District Court could make such a determination without having control of the river.

The rule invoked by the Court thus does not support the conclusion that it reaches. In the *Princess Lida* case, for example, the reason for the surrender of federal jurisdiction over the administration of a trust was the fact that a state court had already assumed jurisdiction over the trust estate. But the Court in that case recognized that this rationale "ha(d) no application to a case in a federal court . . . wherein the plaintiff seeks merely an adjudication of his right or his interest as a basis of a claim against a fund in the possession of a state court."

The precedents cited by the Court thus not only fail to support the Court's decision in this case, but expressly point in the opposite direction. The present suit, in short, is not analogous to the administration of a trust, but rather to a claim of a "right to participate," since the United States in this litigation does not ask the court to control the administration of the river, but only to determine its specific rights in the flow of water in the river. This is an almost exact analogue to a suit seeking a determination of rights in the flow of income from a trust.

As the Court says, it is the virtual "unflagging obligation" of a federal court to exercise the jurisdiction that has been conferred upon it. Obedience to that obligation is particularly "appropriate" in this case, for at least two reasons.

First, the issues involved are issues of federal law. A federal court is more likely than a state court to be familiar with federal water law and to have had experience in interpreting the relevant federal statutes, regulations, and Indian treaties.

Moreover, if tried in a federal court, these issues of federal law will be reviewable in a federal appellate court, whereas federal judicial review of the state courts' resolution of issues of federal law will be possible only on review by this Court in the exercise of its certiorari jurisdiction.

Second, some of the federal claims in this lawsuit relate to water reserved for Indian reservations. It is not necessary to determine that there is no state-court jurisdiction of these claims to support the proposition that a federal court is a more appropriate forum than a state court for determination of questions of life-and-death importance to Indians. This Court has long recognized that "(t)he policy of leaving Indians free from state jurisdiction and control is deeply rooted in the Nation's history." *McClanahan v. Arizona State Tax Comm'n* (1973).

The Court says that "(o)nly the clearest of justifications will warrant dismissal" of a lawsuit within the jurisdiction of a federal court. In my opinion there was no justification at all for the District Court's order of dismissal in this case.

* * *

From *Colorado River*, we can extract four factors that guide federal courts in determining whether to avoid duplicative litigation. Courts are to consider whether two courts are exercising jurisdiction over the same res; the relative inconvenience of the federal forum; a policy against piecemeal litigation; and the order in which the cases were filed. But abstention is the exception, not the rule. Indeed, the Court later reaffirmed the "exceptional" nature of this form of abstention in *Moses H. Cone Memorial Hospital v. Mercury Construction Co.* (1983). In that case, the Fourth Circuit reversed a district court's decision to stay a federal lawsuit arising from a contractual dispute. The Supreme Court affirmed the decision to reverse the stay, emphasizing that its "task in cases such as this is not to find some substantial reason for the exercise of federal jurisdiction by the district court; rather, the task is to ascertain whether there exist 'exceptional' circumstances, the 'clearest of justifications,' that can suffice under *Colorado River* to justify the surrender of that jurisdiction." The Court found no such exceptional circumstances. The Court balanced the same factors it articulated in *Colorado River*, while also encouraging federal courts to consider whether a federal question is present; which forum's substantive law would govern the litigation; and the adequacy of the state forum. It noted that "the presence of federal-law issues must always be a major consideration weighing against surrender."

Notably, the Court has been more forgiving of district courts' abstention orders under *Colorado River* when federal suits are based on the Declaratory Judgment Act. In *Wilton v. Seven Falls Co.* (1995), the Court affirmed a lower court's decision to stay a federal declaratory judgment action while parallel litigation proceeded in state court. The Court reasoned that the Declaratory Judgment Act is "an enabling Act, which confers a discretion on courts rather than an absolute right upon the litigant." *See also Brillhart v. Excess Ins. Co. of America* (1942) ("Ordinarily it would be uneconomical as well as vexatious for a federal court to proceed in a declaratory judgment suit where another suit is pending in a state court presenting the same issues, not governed by federal law, between the same parties.").

Consistent with *Wilton*, lower courts in the Fourth, Sixth, and Eleventh Circuits have adopted principles or "guideposts" to determine when federal courts should abstain from deciding a declaratory judgment action when duplicative litigation is proceeding in state court.[18] The Eleventh Circuit has articulated the following list:

> (1) the strength of the state's interest in having the issues raised in the federal declaratory action decided in the state courts;
>
> (2) whether the judgment in the federal declaratory action would settle the controversy;
>
> (3) whether the federal declaratory action would serve a useful purpose in clarifying the legal relations at issue;
>
> (4) whether the declaratory remedy is being used merely for the purpose of "procedural fencing"—that is, to provide an arena for a race for res judicata or to achieve a federal hearing in a case otherwise not removable;
>
> (5) whether the use of a declaratory action would increase the friction between our federal and state courts and improperly encroach on state jurisdiction;
>
> (6) whether there is an alternative remedy that is better or more effective;
>
> (7) whether the underlying factual issues are important to an informed resolution of the case;
>
> (8) whether the state trial court is in a better position to evaluate those factual issues than is the federal court; and
>
> (9) whether there is a close nexus between the underlying factual and legal issues and state law and/or public policy, or whether federal common or statutory law dictates a resolution of the declaratory judgment action.

In articulating these guideposts, the Eleventh Circuit simultaneously cautioned that this "list is neither absolute nor is any one factor controlling, these are merely guideposts in furtherance of the Supreme Court's admonitions in *Brillhart* and *Wilton*."

5. Ongoing State Coercive Proceedings

a. Equitable Restraint and "Our Federalism"

In the following case of *Younger v. Harris* (1971), the Court works to reconcile two traditions. The first tradition—articulated most starkly by Chief Justice Marshall 200 years ago—is that federal courts "have no more right to decline the exercise of jurisdiction which is given, than to usurp that which is not given." *Cohens v. Virginia*, 19 U.S. (6 Wheat.) 264, 404 (1821). Chief Justice Marshall added that "[w]ith whatever doubts, with whatever difficulties, a case may be attended, we must decide it if it be brought before us"—even if it raises questions that judges "would gladly avoid." *Id.* To do otherwise "would be treason to the constitution,"

---

18. Centennial Life Ins. v. Poston, 88 F.3d 255, 257 (4th Cir. 1996); Scottsdale Ins. Co. v. Roumph, 211 F.3d 964, 968 (6th Cir. 2000); Ameritas Variable Life Ins. Co. v. Roach, 411 F.3d 1328, 1330-31 (11th Cir. 2005).

even when the question is whether a state law or action is "repugnant to the constitution and laws of the United States" and thus "absolutely void."

The case of *Ex parte Young* (1908), is a canonical example of the Supreme Court extending this tradition into the realm federal cases implicating state criminal legal systems. There, the Court held that federal jurisdiction exists over lawsuits against state officers seeking to enjoin official actions that violate federal law, even if the Eleventh Amendment protects the state itself from suit (and even if the state officer might soon bring a criminal prosecution against the plaintiff). *Ex parte Young* (1908). *See* Chapter 6. Over the next 35 years following the *Ex parte Young* decision, the Court decided about 90 cases involving injunctions against the enforcement of state statutes; injunctions issued in 33 of those cases.[19] Between 1943 and 1965, the Court "ordered or affirmed at least 56 district court injunctions or declaratory judgments preventing enforcement" of state laws.[20]

The second tradition is that federal courts have acted with caution when issuing injunctions against state court proceedings, especially in the realm of states' criminal systems. Under the Anti-Injunction Act, federal courts may not enjoin state court proceedings "except as expressly authorized by Act of Congress, or where necessary in aid of its jurisdiction, or to protect or effectuate its judgments," a rule that dates back to the Judiciary Act of 1789. While the Supreme Court ruled in *Mitchum v. Foster*, 407 U.S. 225 (1972), that Section 1983 expressly authorizes such injunctions, the Act nonetheless stands as evidence of a tradition of restraint for that particular remedy. Moreover, even as the Supreme Court enjoined state criminal proceedings throughout the twentieth century, the court simultaneously expressed that for reasons of comity, such injunctions should be reserved for instances in which "great and immediate" or "irreparable" harm would arise absent a federal judicial remedy. *Dombrowski v. Pfister* (1965).

These two traditions sometimes meet at important crossroads. In the case that follows, for example, John Harris filed federal suit because the state was wielding a potentially unconstitutional law to prosecute him. Harris was arrested for the crime of "criminal syndicalism" while passing out Progressive Party leaflets about local police brutality and racial discrimination.[21] Harris believed that the law invoked to arrest him violated the First Amendment. Harris's case is but one example of the types of federal cases litigants file to correct illegalities in states' criminal systems. In other cases, for example, litigants challenge procedural issues instead of substantive criminal law— *i.e.* systemic denial of counsel; lack of access to prompt post-arrest hearings; or routine detention for failure to pay debts or bail without procedural safeguard to determine detainees' ability to pay.[22] When litigants bring these important categories of litigation aimed at protecting civil liberties and civil rights, federal courts must contend with their general obligation to hear cases on the one hand, and federalism-based concepts like comity and state autonomy on the other.

---

19. Douglas Laycock, *Federal Interference with State Prosecutions: The Cases* Dombrowski *Forgot*, 46 U. CHI. L. REV. 636, 642 & n.48 (1979) (collecting cases).

20. *Id.*

21. PAUL FINKELMAN, ENCYCLOPEDIA OF AMERICAN CIVIL LIBERTIES 1809 (2013).

22. *See* Fred O. Smith, Jr., *Abstention in the Time of Ferguson*, 131 HARV. L. REV. 2283, 2285 (2018).

Younger v. Harris

401 U.S. 37 (1971)

Mr. Justice BLACK delivered the opinion of the Court.

Appellee, John Harris, Jr., was indicted in a California state court, charged with violation of the California Penal Code §§11400 and 11401, known as the California Criminal Syndicalism Act. He then filed a complaint in the Federal District Court, asking that court to enjoin the appellant, Younger, the District Attorney of Los Angeles County, from prosecuting him, and alleging that the prosecution and even the presence of the Act inhibited him in the exercise of his rights of free speech and press, rights guaranteed him by the First and Fourteenth Amendments. [He and other intervening plaintiffs] claimed that unless the United States court restrained the state prosecution of Harris each would suffer immediate and irreparable injury. A three-judge Federal District Court, held that it had jurisdiction and power to restrain the District Attorney from prosecuting, held that the State's Criminal Syndicalism Act was void for vagueness and overbreadth in violation of the First and Fourteenth Amendments, and accordingly restrained the District Attorney from "further prosecution of the currently pending action against plaintiff Harris for alleged violation of the Act."

The case is before us on appeal by the State's District Attorney Younger, pursuant to 28 U.S.C. sec. 1253. In this Court the brief for the State of California, filed at our request, also argues that only Harris, who was indicted, has standing to challenge the State's law, and that issuance of the injunction was a violation of a longstanding judicial policy. Without regard to the questions raised about the constitutionality of the state law, we have concluded that the judgment of the District Court, enjoining appellant Younger from prosecuting under these California statutes, must be reversed as a violation of the national policy forbidding federal courts to stay or enjoin pending state court proceedings except under special circumstances.

I

Appellee Harris has been indicted, and was actually being prosecuted by California for a violation of its Criminal Syndicalism Act at the time this suit was filed. He thus has an acute, live controversy with the State and its prosecutor. But none of the other parties plaintiffs in the District Court, Dan, Hirsch, or Broslawsky, has such a controversy. None has been indicted, arrested, or even threatened by the prosecutor. Since Harris is actually being prosecuted under the challenged laws, however, we proceed with him as a proper party.

II

Since the beginning of this country's history Congress has, subject to few exceptions, manifested a desire to permit state courts to try state cases free from interference by federal courts. In 1793 an Act unconditionally provided: "(N)or shall a writ of injunction be granted to stay proceedings in any court of a state * * *." 1 Stat. 335, c. 22, sec. 5. A comparison of the 1793 Act with 28 U.S.C. sec.

2283, its present-day successor, graphically illustrates how few and minor have been the exceptions granted from the flat, prohibitory language of the old Act. During all this lapse of years from 1793 to 1970 the statutory exceptions to the 1793 congressional enactment have been only three: (1) "except as expressly authorized by Act of Congress"; (2) "where necessary in aid of its jurisdiction"; and (3) "to protect or effectuate its judgments." In addition, a judicial exception to the longstanding policy evidenced by the statute has been made where a person about to be prosecuted in a state court can show that he will, if the proceeding in the state court is not enjoined, suffer irreparable damages. *See Ex parte Young* (1908).

The precise reasons for this longstanding public policy against federal court interference with state court proceedings have never been specifically identified but the primary sources of the policy are plain. One is the basic doctrine of equity jurisprudence that courts of equity should not act, and particularly should not act to restrain a criminal prosecution, when the moving party has an adequate remedy at law and will not suffer irreparable injury if denied equitable relief. The doctrine may originally have grown out of circumstances peculiar to the English judicial system and not applicable in this country, but its fundamental purpose of restraining equity jurisdiction within narrow limits is equally important under our Constitution, in order to prevent erosion of the role of the jury and avoid a duplication of legal proceedings and legal sanctions where a single suit would be adequate to protect the rights asserted. This underlying reason for restraining courts of equity from interfering with criminal prosecutions is reinforced by an even more vital consideration, the notion of "comity," that is, a proper respect for state functions, a recognition of the fact that the entire country is made up of a Union of separate state governments, and a continuance of the belief that the National Government will fare best if the States and their institutions are left free to perform their separate functions in their separate ways.

This, perhaps for lack of a better and clearer way to describe it, is referred to by many as "Our Federalism," and one familiar with the profound debates that ushered our Federal Constitution into existence is bound to respect those who remain loyal to the ideals and dreams of "Our Federalism." The concept does not mean blind deference to "States' Rights" any more than it means centralization of control over every important issue in our National Government and its courts. The Framers rejected both these courses. What the concept does represent is a system in which there is sensitivity to the legitimate interests of both State and National Governments, and in which the National Government, anxious though it may be to vindicate and protect federal rights and federal interests, always endeavors to do so in ways that will not unduly interfere with the legitimate activities of the States. It should never be forgotten that this slogan, "Our Federalism," born in the early struggling days of our Union of States, occupies a highly important place in our Nation's history and its future.

This brief discussion should be enough to suggest some of the reasons why it has been perfectly natural for our cases to repeat time and time again that the normal thing to do when federal courts are asked to enjoin pending proceedings in state courts is not to issue such injunctions. In *Fenner v. Boykin* (1926), suit had been brought in the Federal District Court seeking to enjoin state prosecutions under a recently enacted state law that allegedly interfered with the free flow of interstate commerce. The Court, in a unanimous opinion made clear that such a suit, even with respect to state criminal proceedings not yet formally instituted, could be proper only under very special circumstances:

> *Ex parte Young* and following cases have established the doctrine that, when absolutely necessary for protection of constitutional rights, courts of the United States have power to enjoin state officers from instituting criminal actions. But this may not be done, except under extraordinary circumstances, where the danger of irreparable loss is both great and immediate.

These principles, made clear in the *Fenner* case, have been repeatedly followed and reaffirmed in other cases involving threatened prosecutions. In all of these cases the Court stressed the importance of showing irreparable injury, the traditional prerequisite to obtaining an injunction. In addition, however, the Court also made clear that in view of the fundamental policy against federal interference with state criminal prosecutions, even irreparable injury is insufficient unless it is "both great and immediate." Certain types of injury, in particular, the cost, anxiety, and inconvenience of having to defend against a single criminal prosecution, could not by themselves be considered "irreparable" in the special legal sense of that term. Instead, the threat to the plaintiff's federally protected rights must be one that cannot be eliminated by his defense against a single criminal prosecution. *See, e.g., Ex parte Young.*

This is where the law stood when the Court decided *Dombrowski v. Pfister* (1965), and held that an injunction against the enforcement of certain state criminal statutes could properly issue under the circumstances presented in that case. In Dombrowski, unlike many of the earlier cases denying injunctions, the complaint made substantial allegations that:

> the threats to enforce the statutes against appellants are not made with any expectation of securing valid convictions, but rather are part of a plan to employ arrests, seizures, and threats of prosecution under color of the statutes to harass appellants and discourage them and their supporters from asserting and attempting to vindicate the constitutional rights of Negro citizens of Louisiana.

The appellants in *Dombrowski* had offered to prove that their offices had been raided and all their files and records seized pursuant to search and arrest warrants that were later summarily vacated by a state judge for lack of probable cause. They also offered to prove that despite the state court order quashing the warrants and suppressing the evidence seized, the prosecutor was continuing to threaten to initiate new prosecutions of appellants under the same statutes, was holding public hearings at which photostatic copies of the illegally seized documents were being used, and was threatening to use other copies of the illegally seized documents to obtain grand jury indictments against the appellants on charges of violating the same statutes. These circumstances, as viewed by the Court sufficiently establish the kind of irreparable injury, above and beyond that associated with the defense of a single prosecution brought in good faith, that had always been considered sufficient to justify federal intervention.

It is against the background of these principles that we must judge the propriety of an injunction under the circumstances of the present case. Here a proceeding was already pending in the state court, affording Harris an opportunity to raise his constitutional claims. There is no suggestion that this single prosecution against Harris is brought in bad faith or is only one of a series of repeated prosecutions to which he will be subjected. In other words, the injury that Harris faces is solely "that incidental to every criminal proceeding brought lawfully and in good faith," and therefore under the settled doctrine we have already described he is not entitled to equitable relief "even if such statutes are unconstitutional."

For these reasons, fundamental not only to our federal system but also to the basic functions of the Judicial Branch of the National Government under our Constitution, we hold that the *Dombrowski* decision should not be regarded as having upset the settled doctrines that have always confined very narrowly the availability of injunctive relief against state criminal prosecutions. We do not think that opinion stands for the proposition that a federal court can properly enjoin enforcement of a statute solely on the basis of a showing that the statute "on its face" abridges First Amendment rights. There may, of course, be extraordinary circumstances in which the necessary irreparable injury can be shown even in the absence of the usual prerequisites of bad faith and harassment. For example, as long ago as the *Buck* case, supra, we indicated:

> It is of course conceivable that a statute might be flagrantly and patently violative of express constitutional prohibitions in every clause, sentence and paragraph, and in whatever manner and against whomever an effort might be made to apply it.

Other unusual situations calling for federal intervention might also arise, but there is no point in our attempting now to specify what they might be. It is sufficient for purposes of the present case to hold, as we do, that the possible unconstitutionality of a statute 'on its face' does not in itself justify an injunction against good-faith attempts to enforce it, and that appellee Harris has failed to make any showing of bad faith, harassment, or any other unusual circumstance that would call for equitable relief.

The judgment of the District Court is reversed, and the case is remanded for further proceedings not inconsistent with this opinion.

Reversed.

Mr. Justice BRENNAN with whom Mr. Justice WHITE and Mr. Justice MARSHALL join, concurring in the result.

I agree that the judgment of the District Court should be reversed. Appellee Harris had been indicted for violations of the California Criminal Syndicalism Act before he sued in federal court. He has not alleged that the prosecution was brought in bad faith to harass him. His constitutional contentions may be adequately adjudicated in the state criminal proceeding, and federal intervention at his instance was therefore improper.

* * *

In *Younger*, the Court famously extolled "Our Federalism." One scholar recently observed that this phrase "'Our Federalism' had no clear referent as a 'slogan.' Indeed, Black's initial draft did not capitalize the phrase or set it off in quotation marks."[23] Regardless of its etymology, it is worth reflecting on what is meant by it. The Court emphasizes "comity" and the importance of ensuring that "the States and their institutions are left free to perform their separate functions in their separate ways." However, the Court also espouses the importance of ensuring access to a federal remedy for federal constitutional violations that provoke "great," "irreparable" harm. As you learn about *Younger*'s reach, and its exceptions, consider whether the doctrine balances those dual (and dueling) considerations.[24] Some scholars have asked, for example, whether the conception of state sovereignty at the heart of *Younger* is sufficiently attentive to the history and goals of the Reconstruction Amendments.[25]

b.   What Is an "Ongoing" Proceeding

In the decade following *Younger*, the Court continued to clarify the circumstances in which federal courts could correct unconstitutional harm in state criminal proceedings. One important question was what constituted an "ongoing" proceeding. In *Younger* itself, John Harris faced an active prosecution; he had been convicted, and the appellate process had not yet concluded. One can easily envision other temporal scenarios, however, that implicate similar principles. Suppose a plaintiff maintains a suit while state criminal charges are merely threatened, but are not formally pending? Or, suppose a plaintiff filed a federal case in the absence of any state proceedings, but then was charged with a crime later that day? At the other end of the temporal spectrum, suppose a plaintiff files a case after one's conviction, but before exhausting one's direct appeals? Does *Younger* apply under these circumstances? The Court issued guidance for these timing questions in the *Steffel v. Thompson* (1974), *Hicks v. Miranda* (1975), and *Huffman v. Pursue, Ltd.* (1975).

In *Steffel v. Thompson*, the Court held that a federal court may entertain a case challenging the constitutionality of a state criminal law when no prosecution is pending, even if prosecution has been threatened. Nonetheless, in *Hicks v. Miranda*, the Court held that a federal claim for injunctive relief should be dismissed even where criminal charges are brought after a case has been filed, so long as the charges are filed "before any proceedings of substance on the merits have taken place in the federal court."

> We hold that, where state criminal proceedings are begun against the federal plaintiffs after the federal complaint is filed but before any proceedings of substance on the merits have taken place in the federal court, the principles of *Younger v. Harris* should apply in full force. Here, appellees

---

23. Kellen Funk, *Equity's Federalism*, 97 NOTRE DAME L. REV. 2057, 2094 n.149 (2022).

24. Fred O. Smith, Jr., *Abstaining Equitably*, 97 NOTRE DAME L. REV. 2095 (2022) (arguing that Supreme Court doctrine strikes a reasonable balance, but that lower courts sometimes superimpose other requirements that upset this balance).

25. *See, e.g.*, Aviam Soifer & H.C. Macgill, *The* Younger *Doctrine: Reconstructing Reconstruction*, 55 TEX. L. REV. 1141, 1141-43 (1977); John Gibbons, *Our Federalism*, 12 SUFFOLK U. L. REV. 1087 (1978)

were charged on prior to answering the federal case and prior to any proceedings whatsoever before the three-judge court. Unless we are to trivialize the principles of *Younger v. Harris*, the federal complaint should have been dismissed on the appellants' motion absent satisfactory proof of those extraordinary circumstances calling into play one of the limited exceptions to the rule of *Younger v. Harris* and related cases.

In *Huffman v. Pursue, Ltd.*, the Court held that *Younger* abstention also applies when a person has not exhausted direct appeals, given that trials and direct appeals are constitutive of the same "unitary system."

Virtually all of the evils at which *Younger* is directed would inhere in federal intervention prior to completion of state appellate proceedings, just as surely as they would if such intervention occurred at or before trial. Intervention at the later stage is, if anything, more highly duplicative, since an entire trial has already taken place, and it is also a direct aspersion on the capabilities and good faith of state appellate courts. Nor, in these state-initiated nuisance proceedings, is federal intervention at the appellate stage any the less a disruption of the State's efforts to protect interests which it deems important.

The Court reaffirmed these principles, in dictum, in *New Orleans Pub. Serv., Inc. v. Council of City of New Orleans* (1989). A plaintiff must pursue appellate remedies that form the same "unitary system":

When, in a proceeding to which *Younger* applies, a state trial court has entered judgment, the losing party cannot, of course, pursue equitable remedies in federal district court while concurrently challenging the trial court's judgment on appeal. For *Younger* purposes, the State's trial-and-appeals process is treated as a unitary system, and for a federal court to disrupt its integrity by intervening in mid-process would demonstrate a lack of respect for the State as sovereign. For the same reason, a party may not procure federal intervention by terminating the state judicial process prematurely—forgoing the state appeal to attack the trial court's judgment in federal court.

c. What Type of State Proceedings?

The doctrine of *Younger* abstention is not limited to criminal proceedings. It also applies to civil proceedings that are akin to criminal prosecutions, as well as proceedings like contempt-of-court hearings that are uniquely important to enforcing state courts judgments. The civil proceedings to which *Younger* has applied have involved state-initiated enforcement actions. In *Huffman v. Pursue, Ltd.* (1975), the Court applied *Younger* abstention to avoid interference with state-initiated civil nuisance proceeding against an adult movie theatre for allegedly exhibiting obscene films in violation of state law. In *Trainor v. Hernandez* (1977), the Court similarly applied *Younger* to a state-initiated civil fraud proceeding to recover welfare benefits from a couple that concealed assets. The Court noted, "the State was a party to the suit in its role of administering its public assistance programs." Likewise, in *Moore v. Sims* (1979), the Court abstained from interfering with a state proceeding to remove children from their parents' home.

In the following case, the Court emphasizes the narrowness of those rulings. As a way of ensuring that abstention does not morph into abdication or abnegation, the following case instructs lower courts not to apply the doctrine to civil proceedings that are not akin to criminal prosecutions.

Sprint Communications, Inc. v. Jacobs

134 S. Ct. 584 (2013)

Justice GINSBURG delivered the opinion of the Court.

This case involves two proceedings, one pending in state court, the other in federal court. Each seeks review of an Iowa Utilities Board (IUB or Board) order. And each presents the question whether Windstream Iowa Communications, Inc. (Windstream), a local telecommunications carrier, may impose on Sprint Communications, Inc. (Sprint), intrastate access charges for telephone calls transported via the Internet. Invoking *Younger v. Harris* (1971), the federal district court abstained from adjudicating Sprint's complaint in deference to the parallel state-court proceeding, and the Court of Appeals for the Eighth Circuit affirmed.

We reverse. In the main, federal courts are obliged to decide cases within the scope of federal jurisdiction. Abstention is not in order simply because a pending state-court proceeding involves the same subject matter. *New Orleans Public Service, Inc. v. Council of City of New Orleans* (1989) (*NOPSI*). This Court has recognized, however, certain instances in which the prospect of undue interference with state proceedings counsels against federal relief.

Younger exemplifies one class of cases in which federal-court abstention is required. When there is a parallel, pending state criminal proceeding, federal courts must refrain from enjoining the state prosecution. This Court has extended *Younger* abstention to particular state civil proceedings that are akin to criminal prosecutions, *see Huffman v. Pursue, Ltd.* (1975), or that implicate a State's interest in enforcing the orders and judgments of its courts, *see Pennzoil Co. v. Texaco Inc.* (1987). We have cautioned, however, that federal courts ordinarily should entertain and resolve on the merits an action within the scope of a jurisdictional grant, and should not "refus[e] to decide a case in deference to the States." *NOPSI*.

Circumstances fitting within the *Younger* doctrine, we have stressed, are "exceptional"; they include "state criminal prosecutions," "civil enforcement proceedings," and "civil proceedings involving certain orders that are uniquely in furtherance of the state courts' ability to perform their judicial functions." Because this case presents none of the circumstances the Court has ranked as "exceptional," the general rule governs: "[T]he pendency of an action in [a] state court is no bar to proceedings concerning the same matter in the Federal court having jurisdiction." *Colorado River Water Conservation Dist. v. United States* (1976).

I

Sprint, a national telecommunications service provider, has long paid intercarrier access fees to the Iowa communications company Windstream (formerly Iowa Telecom) for certain long distance calls placed by Sprint customers to

Windstream's in-state customers. In 2009, however, Sprint decided to withhold payment for a subset of those calls, classified as Voice over Internet Protocol (VoIP), after concluding that the Telecommunications Act of 1996 preempted intrastate regulation of VoIP traffic. In response, Windstream threatened to block all calls to and from Sprint customers.

Sprint filed a complaint against Windstream with the IUB asking the Board to enjoin Windstream from discontinuing service to Sprint. In Sprint's view, Iowa law entitled it to withhold payment while it contested the access charges and prohibited Windstream from carrying out its disconnection threat. In answer to Sprint's complaint, Windstream retracted its threat to discontinue serving Sprint, and Sprint moved, successfully, to withdraw its complaint. Because the conflict between Sprint and Windstream over VoIP calls was "likely to recur," however, the IUB decided to continue the proceedings to resolve the underlying legal question, *i.e.*, whether VoIP calls are subject to intrastate regulation. The question retained by the IUB, Sprint argued, was governed by federal law, and was not within the IUB's adjudicative jurisdiction. The IUB disagreed, ruling that the intrastate fees applied to VoIP calls.

Seeking to overturn the Board's ruling, Sprint commenced two lawsuits. First, Sprint sued the members of the IUB (respondents here) in their official capacities in the United States District Court for the Southern District of Iowa. In its federal-court complaint, Sprint sought a declaration that the Telecommunications Act of 1996 preempted the IUB's decision; as relief, Sprint requested an injunction against enforcement of the IUB's order. Second, Sprint petitioned for review of the IUB's order in Iowa state court. The state petition reiterated the preemption argument Sprint made in its federal-court complaint; in addition, Sprint asserted state law and procedural due process claims. Because Eighth Circuit precedent effectively required a plaintiff to exhaust state remedies before proceeding to federal court, *see Alleghany Corp. v. McCartney* (8th Cir. 1990), Sprint urges that it filed the state suit as a protective measure. Failing to do so, Sprint explains, risked losing the opportunity to obtain any review, federal or state, should the federal court decide to abstain after the expiration of the Iowa statute of limitations.

As Sprint anticipated, the IUB filed a motion asking the Federal District Court to abstain in light of the state suit, citing *Younger v. Harris* (1971). The District Court granted the IUB's motion and dismissed the suit. The IUB's decision, and the pending state-court review of it, the District Court said, composed one "uninterruptible process" implicating important state interests. On that ground, the court ruled, *Younger* abstention was in order.

For the most part, the Eighth Circuit agreed with the District Court's judgment. The Court of Appeals rejected the argument, accepted by several of its sister courts, that *Younger* abstention is appropriate only when the parallel state proceedings are "coercive," rather than "remedial," in nature. Instead, the Eighth Circuit read this Court's precedent to require *Younger* abstention whenever "an ongoing state judicial proceeding . . . implicates important state interests, and . . . the state proceedings provide adequate opportunity to raise [federal] challenges." *See Middlesex County Ethics Comm. v. Garden State Bar Assn.* (1982). Those criteria were satisfied here, the appeals court held, because the ongoing state-court review of the

IUB's decision concerned Iowa's "important state interest in regulating and enforcing its intrastate utility rates." Recognizing the "possibility that the parties [might] return to federal court," however, the Court of Appeals vacated the judgment dismissing Sprint's complaint. In lieu of dismissal, the Eighth Circuit remanded the case, instructing the District Court to enter a stay during the pendency of the state-court action.

We granted certiorari to decide whether, consistent with our delineation of cases encompassed by the *Younger* doctrine, abstention was appropriate here.

II

A

Federal courts, it was early and famously said, have "no more right to decline the exercise of jurisdiction which is given, than to usurp that which is not given." *Cohens v. Virginia* (1821). Jurisdiction existing, this Court has cautioned, a federal court's "obligation" to hear and decide a case is "virtually unflagging." *Colorado River Water Conservation Dist. v. United States* (1976). Parallel state-court proceedings do not detract from that obligation.

In *Younger*, we recognized a "far-from-novel" exception to this general rule. *New Orleans Public Service, Inc. v. Council of City of New Orleans* (1989) (*NOPSI*). Requesting an injunction against the Act's enforcement, the federal-court plaintiff was at the time the defendant in a pending state criminal prosecution under the Act. In those circumstances, we said, the federal court should decline to enjoin the prosecution, absent bad faith, harassment, or a patently invalid state statute. Abstention was in order, we explained, under "the basic doctrine of equity jurisprudence that courts of equity should not act . . . to restrain a criminal prosecution, when the moving party has an adequate remedy at law and will not suffer irreparably injury if denied equitable relief."

We have since applied *Younger* to bar federal relief in certain civil actions. *Huffman v. Pursue, Ltd.*(1975) is the pathmarking decision. There, Ohio officials brought a civil action in state court to abate the showing of obscene movies. Because the State was a party and the proceeding was "in aid of and closely related to [the State's] criminal statutes," the Court held *Younger* abstention appropriate.

More recently, in *NOPSI*, the Court had occasion to review and restate our *Younger* jurisprudence. *NOPSI* addressed and rejected an argument that a federal court should refuse to exercise jurisdiction to review a state council's ratemaking decision. "[O]nly exceptional circumstances," we reaffirmed, "justify a federal court's refusal to decide a case in deference to the States." Those "exceptional circumstances" exist, the Court determined after surveying prior decisions, in three types of proceedings. First, *Younger* precluded federal intrusion into ongoing state criminal prosecutions. Second, certain "civil enforcement proceedings" warranted abstention. Finally, federal courts refrained from interfering with pending "civil proceedings involving certain orders . . . uniquely in furtherance of the state courts' ability to perform their judicial functions." We have not applied *Younger* outside these three "exceptional" categories, and today hold, in accord with *NOPSI*, that they define *Younger*'s scope.

B

The IUB does not assert that the Iowa state court's review of the Board decision, considered alone, implicates *Younger*. Rather, the initial administrative proceeding justifies staying any action in federal court, the IUB contends, until the state review process has concluded. The same argument was advanced in *NOPSI*. We will assume without deciding, as the Court did in *NOPSI*, that an administrative adjudication and the subsequent state court's review of it count as a "unitary process" for *Younger* purposes. The question remains, however, whether the initial IUB proceeding is of the "sort . . . entitled to *Younger* treatment."

The IUB proceeding, we conclude, does not fall within any of the three exceptional categories described in *NOPSI* and therefore does not trigger *Younger* abstention. The first and third categories plainly do not accommodate the IUB's proceeding. That proceeding was civil, not criminal in character, and it did not touch on a state court's ability to perform its judicial function.

Nor does the IUB's order rank as an act of civil enforcement of the kind to which *Younger* has been extended. Our decisions applying *Younger* to instances of civil enforcement have generally concerned state proceedings "akin to a criminal prosecution" in "important respects." Such enforcement actions are characteristically initiated to sanction the federal plaintiff, *i.e.*, the party challenging the state action, for some wrongful act. In cases of this genre, a state actor is routinely a party to the state proceeding and often initiates the action. Investigations are commonly involved, often culminating in the filing of a formal complaint or charges.

The IUB proceeding does not resemble the state enforcement actions this Court has found appropriate for *Younger* abstention. It is not "akin to a criminal prosecution." Nor was it initiated by the State in its sovereign capacity. A private corporation, Sprint, initiated the action. No state authority conducted an investigation into Sprint's activities, and no state actor lodged a formal complaint against Sprint. The IUB's adjudicative authority was invoked to settle a civil dispute between two private parties, not to sanction Sprint for commission of a wrongful act. Nothing here suggests that the IUB proceeding was more akin to a criminal prosecution than are most civil cases.

In holding that abstention was the proper course, the Eighth Circuit relied heavily on this Court's decision in *Middlesex*. *Younger* abstention was warranted, the Court of Appeals read *Middlesex* to say, whenever three conditions are met: There is (1) "an ongoing state judicial proceeding, which (2) implicates important state interests, and (3) . . . provide[s] an adequate opportunity to raise [federal] challenges." The Court of Appeals and the IUB attribute to this Court's decision in *Middlesex* extraordinary breadth. We invoked *Younger* in *Middlesex* to bar a federal court from entertaining a lawyer's challenge to a New Jersey state ethics committee's pending investigation of the lawyer. Unlike the IUB proceeding here, the state ethics committee's hearing'In *Middlesex* was indeed "akin to a criminal proceeding." As we noted, an investigation and formal complaint preceded the hearing, an agency of the Stat's Supreme Court initiated the hearing, and the purpose of the hearing was to determine whether the lawyer should be disciplined for his failure to meet the Stat's standards of professional conduct. The three *Middlesex* conditions recited above were not dispositive; they were, instead, *additional* factors appropriately considered by the federal court before invoking *Younger*.

Divorced from their quasi-criminal context, the three *Middlesex* conditions would extend *Younger* to virtually all parallel state and federal proceedings, at least where a party could identify a plausibly important state interest. That result is irreconcilable with our dominant instruction that, even in the presence of parallel state proceedings, abstention from the exercise of federal jurisdiction is the exception, not the rule. In short, to guide other federal courts, we today clarify and affirm that *Younger* extends to the three "exceptional circumstances" identified in *NOPSI*, but no further.

* * *

d.   What Type of Federal Relief Implicates *Younger*?

Younger is a doctrine of equitable restraint, and therefore undoubtedly has force when a plaintiff is seeking an equitable remedy such as an injunction. The more difficult question is whether, or how, *Younger* should apply to claims other than injunctive relief. The Court has never directly answered the question whether *Younger* abstention should apply to suits at law for money damages. On the same day *Younger* was decided, however, the Court made clear that the doctrine can halt suits for declaratory relief.

Samuels v. Mackell

401 U.S. 66 (1971)

Mr. Justice BLACK delivered the opinion of the Court.

The appellants in these two cases were all indicted in a New York state court on charges of criminal anarchy, in violation New York law. They later filed these actions in federal district court, alleging (1) that the anarchy statute was void for vagueness in violation of due process, and an abridgment of free speech, press, and assembly, in violation of the First and Fourteenth Amendments; (2) that the anarchy statute had been pre-empted by federal law; and (3) that the New York laws under which the grand jury had been drawn violated the Due Process and Equal Protection Clauses of the Fourteenth Amendment because they disqualified from jury service any member of the community who did not own real or personal property of the value of at least $250, and because the laws furnished no definite standards for determining how jurors were to be selected. Appellants charged that trial of these indictments in state courts would harass them, and cause them to suffer irreparable damages, and they therefore prayed that the state courts should be enjoined from further proceedings. In the alternative, appellants asked the District Court to enter a declaratory judgment to the effect that the challenged state laws were unconstitutional and void on the same grounds. The three-judge [district] court held that the New York criminal anarchy law was constitutional as it had been construed by the New York courts and held that the complaints should therefore be dismissed.

In *Younger v. Harris* (1971), we today decided on facts very similar to the facts in these cases that a United States District Court could not issue an injunction to stay proceedings pending in a state criminal court at the time the federal suit was begun. This was because it did not appear from the record that the plaintiffs would suffer immediate irreparable injury. Since in the present case there is likewise no sufficient showing in the record that the plaintiffs have suffered or would suffer irreparable injury, our decision in the *Younger* case is dispositive of the prayers for injunctions here. The plaintiffs in the present cases also included in their complaints an alternative prayer for a declaratory judgment, but for the reasons indicated below, we hold that this alternative prayer does not require a different result, and that under the circumstances of these cases, the plaintiffs were not entitled to federal relief, declaratory or injunctive. Accordingly we affirm the judgment of the District Court, although not for the reasons given in that court's opinion.

In our opinion in the *Younger* case, we set out in detail the historical and practical basis for the settled doctrine of equity that a federal court should not enjoin a state criminal prosecution begun prior to the institution of the federal suit except in very unusual situations, where necessary to prevent immediate irreparable injury. The question presented here is whether under ordinary circumstances the same considerations that require the withholding of injunctive relief will make declaratory relief equally inappropriate. The question is not, however, a novel one. It was presented and fully considered by this Court in *Great Lakes Dredge & Dock Co. v. Huffman* (1943). We find the reasoning of this Court in the *Great Lakes* case fully persuasive and think that its holding is controlling here.

In the *Great Lakes* case several employers had brought suit against a Louisiana state official, seeking a declaratory judgment that the State's unemployment compensation law, which required the employers to make contributions to a state compensation fund, was unconstitutional. The lower courts had dismissed the complaint on the ground that the challenged law was constitutional. This Court affirmed the dismissal, "but solely on the ground that, in the appropriate exercise of the court's discretion, relief by way of a declaratory judgment should have been denied without consideration of the merits." The Court noted first that under long-settled principles of equity, the federal courts could not have enjoined the Louisiana official from collecting the state tax at issue there unless, as was not true in that case, there was no adequate remedy available in the courts of the State. This judicial doctrine had been approved by Congress in the then recent Tax Injunction Act of 1937, 50 Stat. 738, now 28 U.S.C. §1341. Although the declaratory judgment sought by the plaintiffs was a statutory remedy rather than a traditional form of equitable relief, the Court made clear that a suit for declaratory judgment was nevertheless "essentially an equitable cause of action," and was "analogous to the equity jurisdiction in suits *quia timet* or for a decree quieting title." In addition, the legislative history of the Federal Declaratory Judgment Act of 1934, 28 U.S.C. §2201, showed that Congress had explicitly contemplated that the courts would decide to grant or withhold declaratory relief on the basis of traditional equitable principles. Accordingly, the Court held that in an action for a declaratory judgment, "the district court was as free as in any other suit in equity to grant or withhold the relief prayed, upon equitable grounds."

Although we have found no case in this Court dealing with the application of this doctrine to cases in which the relief sought affects state criminal prosecutions rather than state tax collections, we can perceive no relevant difference between the two situations with respect to the limited question whether, in cases where the criminal proceeding was begun prior to the federal civil suit, the propriety of declaratory and injunctive relief should be judged by essentially the same standards. In both situations deeply rooted and long-settled principles of equity have narrowly restricted the scope for federal intervention, and ordinarily a declaratory judgment will result in precisely the same interference with and disruption of state proceedings that the longstanding policy limiting injunctions was designed to avoid. Even if the declaratory judgment is not used as a basis for actually issuing an injunction, the declaratory relief alone has virtually the same practical impact as a formal injunction would.

We therefore hold that, in cases where the state criminal prosecution was begun prior to the federal suit, the same equitable principles relevant to the propriety of an injunction must be taken into consideration by federal district courts in determining whether to issue a declaratory judgment, and that where an injunction would be impermissible under these principles, declaratory relief should ordinarily be denied as well.

We do not mean to suggest that a declaratory judgment should never be issued in cases of this type if it has been concluded that injunctive relief would be improper. There may be unusual circumstances in which an injunction might be withheld because, despite a plaintiff's strong claim for relief under the established standards, the injunctive remedy seemed particularly intrusive or offensive; in such a situation, a declaratory judgment might be appropriate and might not be contrary to the basic equitable doctrines governing the availability of relief. Ordinarily, however, the practical effect of the two forms of relief will be virtually identical, and the basic policy against federal interference with pending state criminal prosecutions will be frustrated as much by a declaratory judgment as it would be by an injunction.

* * *

e.   Exceptions

i.   Bad Faith

In *Dombrowski v. Pfister* (1965), plaintiffs were members of the Southern Conference Educational Fund, Inc. (SCEF), an organization that fostered civil rights for Black Americans in Louisiana and other states of the South. Those plaintiffs had been charged with violations of the Louisiana Subversive Activities and Communist Control Law and the Communist Propaganda Control Law. Detailing the pattern of bad-faith harassment plaintiffs had experienced, and the important First Amendment rights at stake, the Court found that the civil rights advocates would face irreparable harm in the absence of federal judicial intervention.

> In *Ex parte Young* (1908), the fountainhead of federal injunctions against state prosecutions, the Court characterized the power and its proper exercise in broad terms: it would be justified where state officers "threaten and are about to commence proceedings, either of a civil or criminal nature, to enforce against parties affected an unconstitutional act, violating the Federal Constitution." Since that decision, however, considerations of federalism have tempered the exercise of equitable power, for the Court has recognized that federal interference with a State's good-faith administration of its criminal laws is peculiarly inconsistent with our federal framework. It is generally to be assumed that state courts and prosecutors will observe constitutional limitations as expounded by this Court, and that

the mere possibility of erroneous initial application of constitutional standards will usually not amount to the irreparable injury necessary to justify a disruption of orderly state proceedings.

But the allegations in this complaint depict a situation in which defense of the State's criminal prosecution will not assure adequate vindication of constitutional rights. They suggest that a substantial loss or impairment of freedoms of expression will occur if appellants must await the state court's disposition and ultimate review in this Court of any adverse determination. These allegations, if true, clearly show irreparable injury.

Appellants' allegations and offers of proof outline the chilling effect on free expression of prosecutions initiated and threatened in this case. Early in October 1963 appellant Dombrowski and intervenors Smith and Waltzer were arrested by Louisiana state and local police and charged with violations of the two statutes. Their offices were raided and their files and records seized. Later in October a state judge quashed the arrest warrants as not based on probable cause, and discharged the appellants. Subsequently, the court granted a motion to suppress the seized evidence on the ground that the raid was illegal. Louisiana officials continued, however, to threaten prosecution of the appellants, who thereupon filed this action in November. Shortly after the three-judge court was convened, a grand jury was summoned in the Parish of Orleans to hear evidence looking to indictments of the individual appellants. On appellants' application Judge Wisdom issued a temporary restraining order against prosecutions pending hearing and decision of the case in the District Court. Following a hearing the District Court, over Judge Wisdom's dissent, dissolved the temporary restraining order and, at the same time, handed down an order dismissing the complaint. Thereafter the grand jury returned indictments under the Subversive Activities and Communist Control Law against the individual appellants.

Appellants have attacked the good faith of the appellees in enforcing the statutes, claiming that they have invoked, and threaten to continue to invoke, criminal process without any hope of ultimate success, but only to discourage appellants' civil rights activities. If these allegations state a claim under the Civil Rights Act, 42 U.S.C. §1983, as we believe they do, the interpretation ultimately put on the statutes by the state courts is irrelevant. For an interpretation rendering the statute inapplicable to SCEF would merely mean that appellants might ultimately prevail in the state courts. It would not alter the impropriety of appellees' invoking the statute in bad faith to impose continuing harassment in order to discourage appellants' activities, as appellees allegedly are doing and plan to continue to do.

ii. Bias

Gibson v. Berryhill
411 U.S. 564 (1973)

Justice WHITE delivered the opinion of the Court.

Prior to 1965, the laws of Alabama relating to the practice of optometry permitted any person, including a business firm or corporation, to maintain a department in which "eyes are examined or glasses fitted," provided that such department was in the charge of a duly licensed optometrist. The permission was expressly conferred by §210 of Title 46 of the Alabama Code of 940, and also inferentially by §211 of the Code which regulates the advertising practices of optometrists, and which, until 1965, appeared to contemplate the existence of commercial stores with optical departments. In 1965, §210 was repealed in its entirety by the Alabama Legislature, and §211 was amended so as to eliminate any direct reference to optical departments maintained by corporations or other business establishments under the direction of employee optometrists.

Soon after these statutory changes, the Alabama Optometric Association, a professional organization whose membership is limited to independent practitioners of optometry not employed by others, filed charges against various named optometrists, all of whom were duly licensed under Alabama law but were the salaried employees of Lee Optical Co. The charges were filed with the Alabama Board of Optometry, the statutory body with authority to issue, suspend, and revoke licenses for the practice of optometry. The gravamen of these charges was that the named optometrists, by accepting employment from Lee Optical, a corporation, had engaged in 'unprofessional conduct' within the meaning of the Alabama optometry statute and hence were practicing their profession unlawfully. More particularly, the Association charged the named individuals with, among other things, aiding and abetting a corporation in the illegal practice of optometry; practicing optometry under a false name, that is, Lee Optical Co.; unlawfully soliciting the sale of glasses; lending their licenses to Lee Optical Co.; and splitting or dividing fees with Lee Optical. It was apparently the Association's position that, following the repeal of §210 and the amendment of §211, the practice of optometry by individuals as employees of business corporations was no longer permissible in Alabama, and that, by accepting such employment the named optometrists had violated the ethics of their profession. It was prayed that the Board revoke the licenses of the individuals charged following due notice and a proper hearing.

Two days after these charges were filed by the Association in October 1965, the Board filed a suit of its own in state court against Lee Optical, seeking to enjoin the company from engaging in the "unlawful practice of optometry." The Board's complaint also named 13 optometrists employed by Lee Optical as parties defendant, charging them with aiding and abetting the company in its illegal activities, as well as with other improper conduct very similar to that charged by the Association in its complaint to the Board.

Proceedings on the Association's charges were held in abeyance by the Board while its own state court suit progressed. The individual defendants in that suit were dismissed on grounds that do not adequately appear in the record before us; and, eventually, on March 17, 1971, the state trial court rendered judgment for the Board, and enjoined Lee Optical both from practicing optometry without a license and from employing licensed optometrists. The company appealed this judgment.

Meanwhile, following its victory in the trial court, the Board reactivated the proceedings pending before it since 1965 against the individual optometrists employed by Lee, noticing them for hearings to be held on May 26 and 27, 1971. Those individuals countered on May 14, 1971, by filing a complaint in the United

States District Court naming as defendants the Board of Optometry and its individual members, as well as the Alabama Optometric Association and other individuals. The suit, brought under the Civil Rights Act of 1871, 42 U.S.C. §1983, sought an injunction against the scheduled hearings on the grounds that the statutory scheme regulating the practice of optometry in Alabama6 was unconstitutional insofar as it permitted the Board to hear the pending charges against the individual plaintiffs in the federal suit. The thrust of the complaint was that the Board was biased and could not provide the plaintiffs with a fair and impartial hearing in conformity with due process of law.

A three-judge court was convened in August 1971, and shortly thereafter entered judgment for plaintiffs, enjoining members of the State Board and their successors "from conducting a hearing on the charges heretofore preferred against the Plaintiffs" and from revoking their licenses to practice optometry in the State of Alabama.

In its supporting opinion, the District Court first considered whether it should stay its hand and defer to the then-pending state proceedings — that is, whether the situation presented was one which would permit of immediate federal intervention to restrain the actions of a state administrative body. That question was answered in the affirmative, the court holding that 28 U.S.C. §2283, the federal anti-injunction statute, was not applicable to state administrative proceedings even where those proceedings were adjudicatory in character. Moreover, the District Court also held that neither *Younger v. Harris* (1971), nor the doctrine normally requiring exhaustion of administrative remedies forbade a federal injunction where, as the court found to be true here, the administrative process was so defective and inadequate as to deprive the plaintiffs of due process of law.

This conclusion with respect to the deficiencies in the pending proceedings against plaintiffs, although an amalgam of several elements, amounted basically to a sustaining of the plaintiffs' allegation of bias. For the District Court, the inquiry was not whether the Board members were "actually biased but whether, in the natural course of events, there is an indication of a possible temptation to an average man sitting as a judge to try the case with bias for or against any issue presented to him." Such a possibility of bias was found to arise in the present case from a number of factors. First, the Board, which acts as both prosecutor and judge in delicensing proceedings, had previously brought suit against the plaintiffs on virtually identical charges in the state courts. This the District Court took to indicate that members of the Board might have "preconceived opinions" with regard to the cases pending before them. Second, the court found as a fact that Lee Optical Co. did a large business in Alabama, and that if it were forced to suspend operations the individual members of the Board, along with other private practitioners of optometry, would fall heir to this business. Thus, a serious question of a personal financial stake in the matter in controversy was raised. Finally, the District Court appeared to regard the Board as a suspect adjudicative body in the cases then pending before it, because only members of the Alabama Optometric Association could be members of the Board, and because the Association excluded from membership optometrists such as the plaintiffs who were employed by other persons or entities. The result was that 92 of the 192 practicing optometrists in Alabama were denied participation in the governance of their own profession.

The court's ultimate conclusion was "that to require the Plaintiffs to resort to the protection offered by state law in these cases would effectively deprive them of their property, that is, their right to practice their professions, without due process of law and that irreparable injury would follow in the normal course of events."

Appeal was taken to this Court. Meanwhile, the Supreme Court of Alabama reversed the judgment of the state trial court in the Lee Optical Co. case, holding that nothing in the Alabama statutes pertaining to optometry evidenced "a legislative policy that an optometrist duly qualified and licensed under the laws of this state, may not be employed by another to examine eyes for the purpose of prescribing eyeglasses."

I

We agree with the District Court that neither statute nor case law precluded it from adjudicating the issues before it and from issuing the injunction if its decision on the merits was correct.

Title 28 U.S.C. §2283, the anti-injunction statute, prohibits federal courts from enjoining state court proceedings, but the statute excepts from its prohibition injunctions which are "expressly authorized" by another Act of Congress. Last Term, after the District Court's decision here, this Court determined that actions brought under the Civil Rights Act of 1871, 42 U.S.C. §1983, were within the "expressly authorized" exception to the ban on federal injunctions. *Mitchum v. Foster* (1972).

Our decision in *Mitchum*, however, held only that a district court was not absolutely barred by statute from enjoining a state court proceeding when called upon to do so in a §1983 suit. As we expressly stated in *Mitchum*, nothing in that decision purported to call into question the established principles of equity, comity, and federalism which must, under appropriate circumstances, restrain a federal court from issuing such injunctions. These principles have been emphasized by this Court many times in the past, albeit under a variety of different rubrics.

II

This brings us to the question of whether *Younger v. Harris* (1971), *Samuels v. Mackell* (1971), or the principles of equity, comity, and federalism for which those cases stand, precluded the District Court from acting, in view of the fact that proceedings against appellees were pending before the Alabama Board of Optometry. Those cases and principles would, under ordinary circumstances, forbid either a declaratory judgment or injunction with respect to the validity or enforcement of a state statute when a criminal proceeding under the statute has been commenced. Whether a like rule obtains where state civil proceedings are pending was left open in *Younger* and its companion cases.

Such a course naturally presupposes the opportunity to raise and have timely decided by a competent state tribunal the federal issues involved. Here the predicate for a *Younger v. Harris* dismissal was lacking, for the appellees alleged, and the District Court concluded, that the State Board of Optometry was incompetent by reason of bias to adjudicate the issues pending before it. If the District Court's conclusion was correct in this regard, it was also correct that it need not defer to the Board. Nor, in these circumstances, would a different result be required simply because judicial review, de novo or otherwise, would be forthcoming at the conclusion of the administrative proceedings.

III

We do think that considerations of equity, comity, and federalism warrant vacating the judgment of the District.

* * *

iii. Timeliness

For *Younger* to apply, the state tribunal must provide a timely opportunity to avoid constitutional harm. In *Gibson v. Berryhill* (1973), *supra*, the Court rejected the view that the availability of an eventual appeal meant that abstention was warranted, despite the bias of the initial adjudicator. As the Court explained, *Younger* abstention "naturally presupposes the opportunity to raise and have timely decided by a competent state tribunal the federal issues involved." *Younger* abstention is not "required simply because judicial review, de novo or otherwise, would be forthcoming at the conclusion of the administrative proceedings." Were the rule otherwise, a person could experience unjustified, irreparable harm while waiting to raise one's claim in an uninfected forum.

This timeliness requirement was reaffirmed in *Gerstein v. Pugh* (1975), an important case that set limits on how long someone could be held after an arrest without seeing a judge for a preliminary hearing. Arguing that these detentions violated due process, a group of detained individuals filed a federal class action. The Fifth Circuit declined to impose abstention, observing that if the plaintiffs were not allowed to raise their claims in federal court while detained, it was far from apparent when they would get to raise the claims later. The Fifth Circuit panel asked: "If these plaintiffs were barred by *Younger* from this forum, what relief might they obtain in their state court trials? Since their pre-trial incarceration would have ended as of the time of trial, no remedy would exist. Their claims to pre-trial preliminary hearings would be mooted by conviction or exoneration." The Supreme Court affirmed that conclusion, finding that the lower court correctly resolved the issue. The Court added that the requested injunction "was not directed at the state prosecutions as such, but only at the legality of pretrial detention without a judicial hearing, an issue that could not be raised in defense of the criminal prosecution."

iv. Patently Unconstitutional

Finally, another ostensible exception to *Younger* abstention is that it does not apply to "patently unconstitutional laws." In *Younger*, the Court stated that federal intervention would conceivably be warranted if a statute was "flagrantly and patently violative of express constitutional prohibitions in every clause, sentence and paragraph, and in whatever manner and against whomever an effort might be made to apply it." *Younger v. Harris,* 401 U.S. 37, 53 (1971). The Supreme Court has never concluded that the exception is applicable.[26]

* * *

In this Chapter, we encountered legislative and judicial doctrines that aim to reconcile federalism's tensions. The aim of comity has clashed with accountability and access. Constitutional guarantees of personal autonomy have clashed with states' autonomy to run their own affairs. Two dimensions of the nation's constitutional design principally inform efforts to resolve these battles in our federalism. First, states entered as sovereigns and retained the residual capacity for democratic self-governance. Second, the Reconstruction amendments reshaped the relationship between the national government and the states, bolstering the role of national government in the enforcement of equality and rights. In addition to this constitutional design (or redesign), the shape of our federalism—its institutions, its narratives, its importance—has also been defined and refined though past policies, movements, struggles, and ideologies. This history is still being written, and it is still being made. As future guardians of the law and justice, the republic will depend on you to help define our federalism's shape.

---

26. Erwin Chemerinsky, Federal Jurisdiction §13.5, at 909 (7th ed. 2016).

Principal cases appear in italics.

ABA Standing Comm. On Ethics and Professional Responsibility, Formal Opinion 490, Ethical Obligations of Judges in Collecting Legal Financial Obligations and Other Debts (2020), 9

Gregory Ablavsky, *The Savage Constitution*, 63 Duke L.J. 999 (2014), 28

Randall K.Q. Akee, Katherine A. Spilde, & Jonathan B. Taylor, *The Indian Gaming Regulatory Act and Its Effects on American Indian Economic Development*, 29 J. Econ. Persp. 185 (2015), 719

Ann Althouse, *How to Build a Separate Sphere: Federal Courts and State Power*, 100 Harv. L. Rev. 1485 (1987), 1214

Akhil Reed Amar, *Parity as a Constitutional Question*, 71 B.U. L. Rev. 645 (1991), 9

Vikram David Amar & Jason Mazzone, *The Value of Certification of State Law Questions by the U.S. Supreme Court to the North Carolina Supreme Court in the Pending North Carolina Berger Case: Part One in a Series*, Verdict, May 9, 2022, 1272

American Immigration Council, Immigration Detention in the United States by Agency (2020), 988

David Ames et al., *Due Process and Mass Adjudication: Crisis and Reform*, 72 Stan. L. Rev. 1 (2020), 472

Robert T. Anderson et al., American Indian Law: Cases and Commentary 833 (3d ed. 2015), 663-64

Association of American Law Schools & The Law School Admission Council, 1973-74 Prewlaw Handbook — Official Law School Guide (1973), 333

Anthony Aust, *Advisory Opinions*, 1 J. Intl. Disp. Settlement 123 (2010), 167

Lynn A. Baker, Note, *Unnecessary and Improper: The Judicial Councils Reform and Judicial Conduct and Disability Act of 1980*, 94 Yale L.J. 1117 (1985), 49

Aditya Bamzai & Samuel L. Bray, Debs *and the Federal Equity Jurisdiction*, 98 Notre Dame L. Rev. 699, 701 (2022), 266

Francine Banner, *Immoral Waiver: Judicial Review of Intra-Military Sexual Assault Claims*, 17 Lewis & Clark L. Rev. 723 (2013), 878

Stuart Banner, How the Indians Lost Their Land: Law and Power on the Frontier (2005), 34

Beth Tompkins Bates, Pullman Porters and the Rise of Protest Politics in Black America, 1925-1945 (2003), 1268

Paul M. Bator, *Finality in Criminal Law and Federal Habeas Corpus for State Prisoners*, 76 Harv. L. Rev. 441 (1963), 11

William Baude, *Foreword: The Supreme Court's Shadow Docket*, 9 N.Y.U. J.L. Lib. 1 (2015), 1223-24

William Baude, *Is Qualified Immunity Unlawful?*, 106 Calif. L. Rev. 45 (2018), 801, 825, 882

Melba Pattillo Beals, Warriors Don't Cry (1994), 63

Charles & Mary Beard, *The Second American Revolution, in* The Rise of American Civilization (1927), 41

Monica C. Bell, *Police Reform and the Dismantling of Legal Estrangement*, 126 Yale L.J. 2054 (2017), 324